NCAA

FOOTBALL

THE OFFICIAL 1998 FOOTBALL RECORDS BOOK

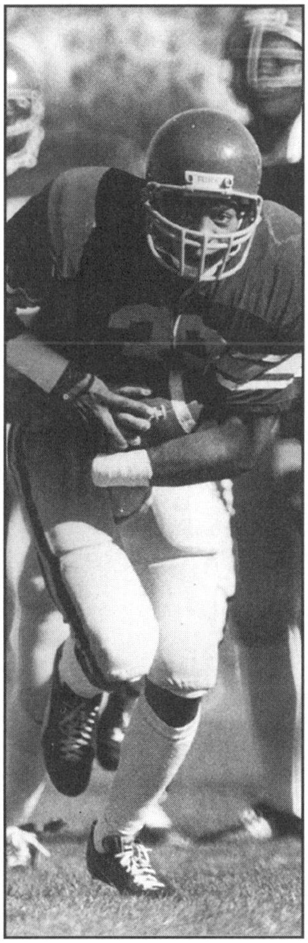

NCAA®

THE NATIONAL COLLEGIATE ATHLETIC ASSOCIATION

THE NATIONAL COLLEGIATE ATHLETIC ASSOCIATION
6201 College Boulevard, Overland Park, Kansas 66211-2422
913/339-1906
http://www.ncaa.org

August 1998

Compiled By:
Richard M. Campbell, *Statistics Coordinator.*
John D. Painter, *Statistics Coordinator.*
Sean W. Straziscar, *Statistics Coordinator.*

Edited By:
Ted Breidenthal, *Publications Editor.*

Typesetting/Production By:
Cindy A. Wissman, *Graphic Technician.*
Teresa S. Wolfgang, *Senior Graphic Artist.*

Cover Design By:
Vic Royal, *Director of Graphics.*

Distributed to sports information directors and conference publicity directors.

ISSN 0735-5475
NCAA 12609-8/98

Contents

Division I-A Records

Individual Records

Under a three-division reorganization plan adopted by the special NCAA Convention of August 1973, teams classified major-college in football on August 1, 1973, were placed in Division I. College-division teams were divided into Division II and Division III. At the NCAA Convention of January 1978, Division I was divided into Division I-A and Division I-AA for football only.

From 1937, when official national statistics rankings began, through 1969, individual rankings were by totals. Beginning in 1970, most season individual rankings were by per-game averages. In total offense, rushing and scoring, it is yards or points per game; in receiving, catches per game and yards per game; in interceptions, catches per game; and in punt and kickoff returns, yards per return. Punting always has been by average, and all team rankings have been per game. Beginning in 1979, passers were rated in all divisions on "efficiency rating points," which are derived from a formula that compares passers to the national averages for 14 seasons of two-platoon Division I football starting with the 1965 season. One hundred points equals the 14-year averages for all players in Division I. Those averages break down to 6.29 yards per attempt, 47.14 percent completions, 3.97 percent touchdown passes and 6.54 percent interceptions. The formula assumes that touchdowns are as good as interceptions are bad; therefore, these two figures offset each other for the average player. To determine efficiency rating points, multiply a passer's yards per attempt by 8.4, add his completion percentage, add his touchdown percentage times 3.3, then subtract his interception percentage times two.

Passers must have a minimum of 15 attempts per game to determine rating points because fewer attempts could allow a player to win the championship with fewer than 100 attempts in a season. A passer must play in at least 75 percent of his team's games to qualify for the rankings (e.g., a player on a team with a nine-game season could qualify by playing in seven games); thus, a passer with 105 attempts could qualify for the national rankings.

A pass efficiency rating comparison for each year since 1979 has been added to the passing section of all-time leaders.

All individual and team records and rankings include regular-season games only. Career records of players include only those years in which they competed in Division I-A.

Statistics in some team categories were not tabulated until the advent of the computerized statistics program in 1966. The records listed in those categories begin with the 1966 season and are so indicated.

In 1954, the regular-season schedule was limited to a maximum of 10 games, and in 1970, to a limit of 11 games, excluding postseason competition.

A player whose career includes statistics for parts of five seasons (or an active player who will play in five seasons) because he was granted an additional season of competition for reasons of hardship or a freshman redshirt are denoted by "$."

COLLEGIATE RECORDS

Individual collegiate records are determined by comparing the best records in all four divisions (I-A, I-AA, II and III) in comparable categories. Included are career records of players who played parts of their careers in different divisions (such as Dennis Shaw of San Diego State, Howard Stevens of Randolph-Macon and Louisville, and Doug Williams of Grambling). For individual collegiate career leaders, see page 205.

Total Offense

(Rushing Plus Passing)

MOST PLAYS

Quarter
36—Rusty LaRue, Wake Forest vs. Duke, Oct. 28, 1995 (4th; 35 passes, 1 rush)

Half
57—Rusty LaRue, Wake Forest vs. Duke, Oct. 28, 1995 (2nd; 56 passes, 1 rush)

Game
94—Matt Vogler, Texas Christian vs. Houston, Nov. 3, 1990 (696 yards)

Season
704—David Klingler, Houston, 1990 (5,221 yards)

2 Yrs
1,293—David Klingler, Houston, 1990-91 (8,447 yards)

3 Yrs
1,610—Ty Detmer, Brigham Young, 1989-91 (13,456 yards)

Career
(4 yrs.) 1,795—Ty Detmer, Brigham Young, 1988-91 (14,665 yards)

MOST PLAYS PER GAME

Season
64.0—David Klingler, Houston, 1990 (704 in 11)

2 Yrs
61.6—David Klingler, Houston, 1990-91 (1,293 in 21)

Career
48.5—Doug Gaynor, Long Beach St., 1984-85 (1,067 in 22)

MOST PLAYS BY A FRESHMAN

Game
76—Sandy Schwab, Northwestern vs. Michigan, Oct. 23, 1982 (431 yards)

Season
594—Jon Denton, UNLV, 1996 (3,629 yards)
Also holds per-game record at 49.5 (594 in 12)

MOST YARDS GAINED

Quarter
347—Jason Davis, UNLV vs. Idaho, Sept. 17, 1994 (4th)

Half
510—Andre Ware, Houston vs. Southern Methodist, Oct. 21, 1989 (1st)

Game
732—David Klingler, Houston vs. Arizona St., Dec. 2, 1990 (16 rushing, 716 passing)

Season
5,221—David Klingler, Houston, 1990 (81 rushing, 5,140 passing)

2 Yrs
9,455—Ty Detmer, Brigham Young, 1989-90 (-293 rushing, 9,748 passing)

3 Yrs
13,456—Ty Detmer, Brigham Young, 1989-91 (-323 rushing, 13,779 passing)

Career
(4 yrs.) 14,665—Ty Detmer, Brigham Young, 1988-91 (-366 rushing, 15,031 passing)

MOST YARDS GAINED PER GAME

Season
474.6—David Klingler, Houston, 1990 (5,221 in 11)

2 Yrs
402.2—David Klingler, Houston, 1990-91 (8,447 in 21)

Career
320.9—Chris Vargas, Nevada, 1992-93 (6,417 in 20)

MOST YARDS GAINED, FIRST TWO SEASONS
6,710—Doug Gaynor, Long Beach St., 1984-85
Also holds per-game record at 305.0

MOST SEASONS GAINING 4,000 YARDS OR MORE
3—Ty Detmer, Brigham Young, 1989-91

MOST SEASONS GAINING 3,000 YARDS OR MORE
3—Ty Detmer, Brigham Young, 1989-91

MOST SEASONS GAINING 2,500 YARDS OR MORE
3—Peyton Manning, Tennessee, 1995-97; Stoney Case, New Mexico, 1992-94; Shane Matthews, Florida, 1990-92; Ty Detmer, Brigham Young, 1989-91; Shawn Moore, Virginia, 1988-90; Erik Wilhelm, Oregon St., 1986-88; Brian McClure, Bowling Green, 1983-85; Randall Cunningham, UNLV, 1982-84; Doug Flutie, Boston College, 1982-84; John Elway, Stanford, 1980-82

MOST YARDS GAINED BY A FRESHMAN

Game
513—Jon Denton, UNLV vs. San Diego St., Nov. 16, 1996 (59 plays)

Season
3,629—Jon Denton, UNLV, 1996 (594 plays)
Also holds per-game record at 302.4

MOST YARDS GAINED BY A SOPHOMORE

Game
625—Scott Mitchell, Utah vs. Air Force, Oct. 15, 1988 (-6 rushing, 631 passing)

Season
4,433—Ty Detmer, Brigham Young, 1989 (12 games, 497 plays)
Per-game record—390.8, Scott Mitchell, Utah, 1988

MOST YARDS GAINED IN FIRST GAME OF CAREER
483—Billy Stevens, UTEP vs. North Texas, Sept. 18, 1965

MOST YARDS GAINED IN TWO, THREE AND FOUR CONSECUTIVE GAMES

2 Games
1,310—David Klingler, Houston, 1990 (578 vs. Eastern Wash., Nov. 17; 732 vs. Arizona St., Dec. 2)

3 Games
1,651—David Klingler, Houston, 1990 (341 vs. Texas, Nov. 10; 578 vs. Eastern Wash., Nov. 17; 732 vs. Arizona St., Dec. 2)

4 Games
2,276—David Klingler, Houston, 1990 (625 vs. Texas Christian, Nov. 3; 341 vs. Texas, Nov. 10; 578 vs. Eastern Wash., Nov. 17; 732 vs. Arizona St., Dec. 2)

MOST GAMES GAINING 300 YARDS OR MORE

Season
12—Ty Detmer, Brigham Young, 1990

Career
33—Ty Detmer, Brigham Young, 1988-91

MOST CONSECUTIVE GAMES GAINING 300 YARDS OR MORE

Season
12—Ty Detmer, Brigham Young, 1990

Career
19—Ty Detmer, Brigham Young, 1989-90

MOST GAMES GAINING 400 YARDS OR MORE

Season
9—David Klingler, Houston, 1990

Career
13—Ty Detmer, Brigham Young, 1988-91

MOST CONSECUTIVE GAMES GAINING 400 YARDS OR MORE

Season
5—Ty Detmer, Brigham Young, 1990
Also holds career record at 5

MOST YARDS GAINED AGAINST ONE OPPONENT

Career
1,483—Ty Detmer, Brigham Young vs. San Diego St., 1988-91

MOST YARDS GAINED PER GAME AGAINST ONE OPPONENT
Career
(Min. 3 games) 399.0—Cody Ledbetter, New Mexico St. vs. UNLV, 1993-95 (1,197 yards)
(Min. 4 games) 370.8—Ty Detmer, Brigham Young vs. San Diego St., 1988-91 (1,483 yards)

MOST YARDS GAINED BY TWO OPPOSING PLAYERS
Game
1,321—Matt Vogler, Texas Christian (696) & David Klingler, Houston (625), Nov. 3, 1990

GAINING 1,000 YARDS RUSHING AND 1,000 YARDS PASSING
Season
Scott Frost (QB), Nebraska, 1997 (1,095 rushing, 1,237 passing); Chris McCoy (QB), Navy, 1997 (1,370 rushing, 1,203 passing); Beau Morgan (QB), Air Force, 1996 (1,494 rushing, 1,210 passing); Beau Morgan (QB), Air Force, 1995 (1,285 rushing, 1,165 passing); Michael Carter (QB), Hawaii, 1991 (1,092 rushing, 1,172 passing); Brian Mitchell (QB), Southwestern La., 1989 (1,311 rushing, 1,966 passing); Dee Dowis (QB), Air Force, 1989 (1,286 rushing, 1,285 passing); Darian Hagan (QB), Colorado, 1989 (1,004 rushing, 1,002 passing); Bart Weiss (QB), Air Force, 1985 (1,032 rushing, 1,449 passing); Reggie Collier (QB), Southern Miss., 1981 (1,005 rushing, 1,004 passing); Johnny Bright (HB), Drake, 1950 (1,232 rushing, 1,168 passing)

A QUARTERBACK GAINING 2,000 YARDS RUSHING AND 4,000 YARDS PASSING
Career
Major Harris, West Va., 1987-89 (2,030 rushing, 4,834 passing); Brian Mitchell, Southwestern La., 1986-89 (3,335 rushing, 5,447 passing); Rickey Foggie, Minnesota, 1984-87 (2,038 rushing, 4,903 passing); John Bond, Mississippi St., 1980-83 (2,280 rushing, 4,621 passing); Prince McJunkins, Wichita St., 1979-82 (2,047 rushing, 4,544 passing)

A QUARTERBACK GAINING 3,000 YARDS RUSHING AND 3,000 YARDS PASSING
Career
Beau Morgan, Air Force, 1994-96 (3,379 rushing, 3,248 passing); Brian Mitchell, Southwestern La., 1986-89 (3,335 rushing, 5,447 passing)

A QUARTERBACK GAINING 300 YARDS PASSING AND 100 YARDS RUSHING
Game
Donald Douglas, Houston vs. Southern Methodist, Oct. 19, 1991 (103 rushing, 319 passing); Randy Welniak, Wyoming vs. Air Force, Sept. 24, 1988 (108 rushing, 359 passing); Ned James, New Mexico vs. Wyoming, Nov. 1, 1986 (118 rushing, 406 passing)

A QUARTERBACK GAINING 200 YARDS RUSHING AND 200 YARDS PASSING
Game
Brian Mitchell, Southwestern La. vs. Colorado St., Nov. 21, 1987 (271 rushing, 205 passing); Steve Gage, Tulsa vs. New Mexico, Nov. 8, 1986 (212 rushing, 209 passing); Reds Bagnell, Pennsylvania vs. Dartmouth, Oct. 14, 1950 (214 rushing, 276 passing)

TEAMS HAVING A 3,000-YARD PASSER, 1,000-YARD RUSHER AND 1,000-YARD RECEIVER IN THE SAME YEAR
13 teams. Most recent: Nevada, 1997 (John Dutton [3,526 passer], Chris Lemon [1,055 rusher], and Geoff Noisy [1,184 receiver] and Trevor Insley [1,151 receiver]; Tennessee, 1997 (Peyton Manning [3,819 passer], Jamal Lewis [1,364 rusher] and Marcus Nash [1,170 receiver]); Nevada, 1995 (Mike Maxwell [3,611 passer], Alex Van Dyke [1,854 receiver] and Kim Minor [1,052 rusher]); New Mexico St., 1995 (Cody Ledbetter [3,501 passer], Denvis Manns [1,120 rusher] and Lucious Davis [1,018 receiver]); Ohio St., 1995 (Bobby Hoying [3,023 passer], Eddie George [1,826 rusher] and Terry Glenn [1,316 receiver]); San Diego St., 1995 (Billy Blanton [3,300 passer], George Jones [1,842 rusher], Will Blackwell [1,207 receiver] and Az Hakim [1,022 receiver])

(Note: Nevada, 1997 and San Diego St., 1995, are the only teams to have two 1,000-yard receivers.)

TEAMS HAVING A 2,000-YARD RUSHER AND 2,000-YARD PASSER IN THE SAME YEAR
2—Colorado, 1994 (Rashaan Salaam [2,055 rusher] and Kordell Stewart [2,071 passer]); Oklahoma St., 1988 (Barry Sanders [2,628 rusher] and Mike Gundy [2,163 passer])

HIGHEST AVERAGE GAIN PER PLAY
Game
(Min. 37-62 plays) 14.3—Jason Martin, Louisiana Tech vs. Toledo, Oct. 19, 1996 (37 for 529)
(Min. 63 plays) 9.9—David Klingler, Houston vs. Texas Christian, Nov. 3, 1990 (63 for 625)
Season
(Min. 3,000 yards) 8.9—Ty Detmer, Brigham Young, 1989 (497 for 4,433)
Career
(Min. 7,500 yards) 8.2—Ty Detmer, Brigham Young, 1988-91 (1,795 for 14,665)

MOST TOUCHDOWNS RESPONSIBLE FOR (TDs Scored and Passed For)
Game
11—David Klingler, Houston vs. Eastern Wash., Nov. 17, 1990 (passed for 11)
Season
55—David Klingler, Houston, 1990 (scored 1, passed for 54)
2 Yrs
85—David Klingler, Houston, 1990-91 (scored 2, passed for 83)
3 Yrs
122—Ty Detmer, Brigham Young, 1989-91 (scored 14, passed for 108)
Career
135—Ty Detmer, Brigham Young, 1988-91 (scored 14, passed for 121)

MOST TOUCHDOWNS RESPONSIBLE FOR PER GAME
Season
5.0—David Klingler, Houston, 1990 (55 in 11)
2 Yrs
4.0—David Klingler, Houston, 1990-91 (85 in 21)
3 Yrs
3.4—Ty Detmer, Brigham Young, 1989-91 (122 in 36)
Career
2.9—Ty Detmer, Brigham Young, 1988-91 (135 in 46)
Collegiate record—3.6, Dennis Shaw, San Diego St., 1968-69 (72 in 20)

MOST POINTS RESPONSIBLE FOR (Points Scored and Passed For)
Game
66—David Klingler, Houston vs. Eastern Wash., Nov. 17, 1990 (passed for 11 TDs)
Season
334—David Klingler, Houston, 1990 (scored 1 TD, passed for 54 TDs, accounted for 2 two-point conversions)
2 Yrs
514—David Klingler, Houston, 1990-91 (scored 2 TDs, passed for 83 TDs, accounted for 2 two-point conversions)
3 Yrs
582—Ty Detmer, Brigham Young, 1988-90 (scored 10 TDs, passed for 86 TDs, accounted for 3 two-point conversions)
Career
820—Ty Detmer, Brigham Young, 1988-91 (scored 14 TDs, passed for 121 TDs, accounted for 5 two-point conversions)

MOST POINTS RESPONSIBLE FOR PER GAME
Season
30.4—David Klingler, Houston, 1990 (334 in 11)
2 Yrs
22.8—Jim McMahon, Brigham Young, 1980-81 (502 in 22)
3 Yrs
17.1—Ty Detmer, Brigham Young, 1988-90 (582 in 34)
Career
17.8—Ty Detmer, Brigham Young, 1988-91 (820 in 46)
Collegiate record—21.6, Dennis Shaw, San Diego St., 1968-69 (432 in 20)

SCORING 200 POINTS AND PASSING FOR 200 POINTS
Career
Rick Leach, Michigan, 1975-78 (scored 204, passed for 270)

Rushing

MOST RUSHES
Quarter
22—Alex Smith, Indiana vs. Michigan St., Nov. 11, 1995 (1st, 114 yards)
Half
34—Tony Sands, Kansas vs. Missouri, Nov. 23, 1991 (2nd, 240 yards)
Game
58—Tony Sands, Kansas vs. Missouri, Nov. 23, 1991 (396 yards)
Season
403—Marcus Allen, Southern Cal, 1981 (2,342 yards)
2 Yrs
757—Marcus Allen, Southern Cal, 1980-81 (3,905 yards)
Career
(3 yrs.) 994—Herschel Walker, Georgia, 1980-82 (5,259 yards)
(4 yrs.) 1,215—Steve Bartalo, Colorado St., 1983-86 (4,813 yards)

MOST RUSHES PER GAME
Season
39.6—Ed Marinaro, Cornell, 1971 (356 in 9)
2 Yrs
36.0—Marcus Allen, Southern Cal, 1980-81 (757 in 21)
Career
34.0—Ed Marinaro, Cornell, 1969-71 (918 in 27)

MOST RUSHES BY A FRESHMAN
Game
50—Ron Dayne, Wisconsin vs. Minnesota, Nov. 9, 1996 (297 yards)
Season
295—Ron Dayne, Wisconsin, 1996 (1,863 yards)

MOST RUSHES PER GAME BY A FRESHMAN
Season
29.2—Steve Bartalo, Colorado St., 1983 (292 in 10)

MOST CONSECUTIVE RUSHES BY SAME PLAYER
Game
16—William Howard, Tennessee vs. Mississippi, Nov. 15, 1986 (during two possessions)

MOST RUSHES IN TWO CONSECUTIVE GAMES
Season
102—Lorenzo White, Michigan St., 1985 (53 vs. Purdue, Oct. 26; 49 vs. Minnesota, Nov. 2)

MOST YARDS GAINED
Quarter
222—Corey Dillon, Washington vs. San Jose St., Nov. 16, 1996 (1st, 16 rushes)
Half
287—Stacey Robinson, Northern Ill. vs. Fresno St., Oct. 6, 1990 (1st; 114 in first quarter, 173 in second quarter; 20 rushes)
Game
396—Tony Sands, Kansas vs. Missouri, Nov. 23, 1991 (58 rushes) (240 yards on 34 carries, second half)
Season
2,628—Barry Sanders, Oklahoma St., 1988 (344 rushes, 11 games)
2 Yrs
4,195—Troy Davis, Iowa St., 1995-96 (747 rushes)
Career
(3 yrs.) 5,259—Herschel Walker, Georgia, 1980-82 (994 rushes)
(4 yrs.) 6,082—Tony Dorsett, Pittsburgh, 1973-76 (1,074 rushes)

MOST YARDS GAINED PER GAME
Season
238.9—Barry Sanders, Oklahoma St., 1988 (2,628 in 11)
2 Yrs
190.7—Troy Davis, Iowa St., 1995-96 (4,195 in 22)
Career
174.6—Ed Marinaro, Cornell, 1969-71 (4,715 in 27)

MOST YARDS GAINED BY A FRESHMAN
Game
386—Marshall Faulk, San Diego St. vs. Pacific (Cal.), Sept. 14, 1991 (37 rushes)
Season
1,863—Ron Dayne, Wisconsin, 1996 (295 rushes)
Per-game record—158.8, Marshall Faulk, San Diego St., 1991 (1,429 in 9)

MOST YARDS GAINED BY A SOPHOMORE
Game
351—Scott Harley, East Caro. vs. North Caro. St., Nov. 30, 1996 (42 rushes)
Season
2,010—Troy Davis, Iowa St., 1995 (345 rushes)
Also holds per-game record at 182.7 (2,010 in 11)

FRESHMEN GAINING 1,000 YARDS OR MORE
Season
By 45 players (see chart after Annual Rushing Champions). Most recent: Jamal Lewis, Tennessee, 1997; Robert Sanford, Western Mich., 1997; Ron Dayne, Wisconsin, 1996 (1,863); Demond Parker, Oklahoma, 1996 (1,184); Sedrick Irvin, Michigan St., 1996 (1,036)

TWO FRESHMEN, SAME TEAM, GAINING 1,000 YARDS OR MORE
Season
Mike Smith (1,062) & Gwain Durden (1,049), Tenn.-Chatt., 1977

EARLIEST GAME A FRESHMAN REACHED 1,000 YARDS
Season
7—Marshall Faulk, San Diego St., 1991 (1,157 vs. Colorado St., Nov. 9); Emmitt Smith, Florida, 1987 (1,011 vs. Temple, Oct. 17)

FIRST PLAYER TO GAIN 1,000 YARDS OR MORE
Season
Byron "Whizzer" White, Colorado, 1937 (1,121)
(Note: Before NCAA records began in 1937, Morley Drury of Southern Cal gained 1,163 yards in 1927)

EARLIEST GAME GAINING 1,000 YARDS OR MORE
Season
5—Marcus Allen, Southern Cal, 1981 (1,136); Byron Hanspard, Texas Tech, 1996 (1,112); Troy Davis, Iowa St., 1996 (1,047); Ernest Anderson, Oklahoma St., 1982 (1,042); Ed Marinaro, Cornell, 1971 (1,026); Ricky Bell, Southern Cal, 1976 (1,008); Barry Sanders, Oklahoma St., 1988 (1,002)

MOST YARDS GAINED BY A QUARTERBACK
Game
308—Stacey Robinson, Northern Ill. vs. Fresno St., Oct. 6, 1990 (22 rushes)
Season
1,494—Beau Morgan, Air Force, 1996 (225 rushes)
Also holds per-game record at 135.8 (1,494 in 11)
Career
3,612—Dee Dowis, Air Force, 1986-89 (543 rushes)
Per-game record—109.1, Stacey Robinson, Northern Ill., 1988-90 (2,727 in 25)

LONGEST GAIN BY A QUARTERBACK
Game
98—Mark Malone, Arizona St. vs. Utah St., Oct. 27, 1979 (TD)

MOST GAMES GAINING 100 YARDS OR MORE
Season
11—By 14 players. Most recent: Ahman Green, Nebraska, 1997; Troy Davis, Iowa St., 1996; Wasean Tait, Toledo, 1995; Darnell Autry, Northwestern, 1995
Career
33—Tony Dorsett, Pittsburgh, 1973-76 (43 games); Archie Griffin, Ohio St., 1972-75 (42 games)

MOST GAMES GAINING 100 YARDS OR MORE BY A FRESHMAN
Season
9—Tony Dorsett, Pittsburgh, 1973; Ron "Po" James, New Mexico St., 1968
James holds consecutive record at 8

MOST CONSECUTIVE GAMES GAINING 100 YARDS OR MORE
Career
31—Archie Griffin, Ohio St., Began Sept. 15, 1973 (vs. Minnesota), ended Nov. 22, 1975 (vs. Michigan)

MOST GAMES GAINING 200 YARDS OR MORE
Season
8—Marcus Allen, Southern Cal, 1981
Career
11—Marcus Allen, Southern Cal, 1978-81 (in 21 games during 1980-81)

MOST GAMES GAINING 200 YARDS OR MORE BY A FRESHMAN
Season
4—Ron Dayne, Wisconsin, 1996; Herschel Walker, Georgia, 1980

MOST CONSECUTIVE GAMES GAINING 200 YARDS OR MORE
Season
5—Barry Sanders, Oklahoma St., 1988 (320 vs. Kansas St., Oct. 29; 215 vs. Oklahoma, Nov. 5; 312 vs. Kansas, Nov. 12; 293 vs. Iowa St., Nov. 19; 332 vs. Texas Tech, Dec. 3); Marcus Allen, Southern Cal, 1981 (210 vs. Tennessee, Sept. 12; 274 vs. Indiana, Sept. 19; 208 vs. Oklahoma, Sept. 26; 233 vs. Oregon St., Oct. 3; 211 vs. Arizona, Oct. 10)

MOST GAMES GAINING 300 YARDS OR MORE
Season
4—Barry Sanders, Oklahoma St., 1988
Also holds career record at 4

MOST YARDS GAINED IN TWO, THREE, FOUR AND FIVE CONSECUTIVE GAMES
2 Games
628—Ron Dayne, Wisconsin, 1996 (289 vs. Illinois, Nov. 23; 339 vs. Hawaii, Nov. 30)
3 Games
937—Barry Sanders, Oklahoma St., 1988 (312 vs. Kansas, Nov. 12; 293 vs. Iowa St., Nov. 19; 332 vs. Texas Tech, Dec. 3)
4 Games
1,152—Barry Sanders, Oklahoma St., 1988 (215 vs. Oklahoma, Nov. 5; 312 vs. Kansas, Nov. 12; 293 vs. Iowa St., Nov. 19; 332 vs. Texas Tech, Dec. 3)
5 Games
1,472—Barry Sanders, Oklahoma St., 1988 (320 vs. Kansas St., Oct. 29; 215 vs. Oklahoma, Nov. 5; 312 vs. Kansas, Nov. 12; 293 vs. Iowa St., Nov. 19; 332 vs. Texas Tech, Dec. 3)

MOST SEASONS GAINING 1,500 YARDS OR MORE
Career
3—Herschel Walker, Georgia, 1980-82; Tony Dorsett, Pittsburgh, 1973, 1975-76

MOST SEASONS GAINING 1,000 YARDS OR MORE
Career
4—Amos Lawrence, North Caro., 1977-80; Tony Dorsett, Pittsburgh, 1973-76
Collegiate record tied by Howard Stevens, Randolph-Macon, 1968-69, Louisville, 1971-72

TWO PLAYERS, SAME TEAM, EACH GAINING 1,000 YARDS OR MORE
Season
25 times. Most recent: Nebraska, 1997—Ahman Green (1,698) & Scott Frost (1,016); Ohio, 1996—Steve Hookfin (1,125) & Kareem Wilson (1,072); Colorado St. 1996—Calvin Branch (1,279) & Damon Washington (1,075)

TWO PLAYERS, SAME TEAM, EACH GAINING 200 YARDS OR MORE
Game
Sedrick Irvin, 238 (28 rushes) & Marc Renaud, 203 (21 rushes), Michigan St. vs. Penn St., Nov. 29, 1997; Gordon Brown, 214 (23 rushes) & Steve Gage (QB), 206 (26 rushes), Tulsa vs. Wichita St., Nov. 2, 1985

TWO OPPOSING I-A PLAYERS EACH GAINING 200 YARDS OR MORE
Game
De'Mond Parker, Oklahoma (291) & Ricky Williams, Texas (223), Oct. 11, 1997; Ricky Williams, Texas (249) & Michael Perry, Rice (211), Sept. 27, 1997; Barry Sanders, Oklahoma St. (215) & Mike Gaddis, Oklahoma (213), Nov. 5, 1988; George Swarn, Miami (Ohio) (239) & Otis Cheathem, Western Mich. (219), Sept. 8, 1984

MOST YARDS GAINED BY TWO OPPOSING PLAYERS
Game
553—Marshall Faulk, San Diego St. (386) & Ryan Benjamin, Pacific (Cal.) (167), Sept. 14, 1991

MOST YARDS GAINED BY TWO PLAYERS, SAME TEAM
Game
476—Tony Sands (396) & Chip Hilleary (80), Kansas vs. Missouri, Nov. 23, 1991
Season
2,997—Barry Sanders (2,628) & Gerald Hudson (Sanders' backup, 369), Oklahoma St., 1988
Also hold per-game record at 272.5
Career
8,193—Eric Dickerson (4,450) & Craig James (3,743), Southern Methodist, 1979-82 (alternated at the same position during the last 36 games)

MOST YARDS GAINED IN FIRST GAME OF CAREER
273—Chris McCoy (Soph.), Navy vs. Southern Methodist, Sept. 9, 1995

MOST YARDS GAINED BY A FRESHMAN IN FIRST GAME OF CAREER
212—Greg Hill, Texas A&M vs. LSU, Sept. 14, 1991 (30 carries)

LONGEST RUSH BY A FRESHMAN IN FIRST GAME OF CAREER
98—Jerald Sowell, Tulane vs. Alabama, Sept. 4, 1993

MOST YARDS GAINED IN OPENING GAME OF SEASON
343—Tony Jeffery, Texas Christian vs. Tulane, Sept. 13, 1986 (16 rushes)

MOST YARDS GAINED AGAINST ONE OPPONENT
Career
(3 yrs.) 690—Mike Gaddis, Oklahoma vs. Oklahoma St., 1988-89, 1991 (82 rushes)
(4 yrs.) 754—Tony Dorsett, Pittsburgh vs. Notre Dame, 1973-76 (96 rushes)

MOST YARDS GAINED PER GAME AGAINST ONE OPPONENT
Career
(Min. 2 games) 292.0—Anthony Thompson, Indiana vs. Wisconsin, 1986, 89 (584 yards, 91 rushes)
(Min. 3 games) 230.0—Mike Gaddis, Oklahoma vs. Oklahoma St., 1988-89, 1991 (690 yards, 82 rushes)

HIGHEST AVERAGE GAIN PER RUSH
Game
(Min. 8-14 rushes) 30.2—Kevin Lowe, Wyoming vs. South Dak. St., Nov. 10, 1984 (10 for 302)
(Min. 15-25 rushes) 21.4—Tony Jeffery, Texas Christian vs. Tulane, Sept. 13, 1986 (16 for 343)
(Min. 26 rushes) 13.7—Eddie Lee Ivery, Georgia Tech vs. Air Force, Nov. 11, 1978 (26 for 356)
Season
(Min. 75-100 rushes) 11.5—Glenn Davis, Army, 1945 (82 for 944)
(Min. 101-213 rushes) 9.6—Chuck Weatherspoon, Houston, 1989 (119 for 1,146)
(Min. 214-281 rushes) 7.8—Mike Rozier, Nebraska, 1983 (275 for 2,148)
(Min. 282 rushes) 7.6—Barry Sanders, Oklahoma St., 1988 (344 for 2,628)
Career
(Min. 300-413 rushes) 8.3—Glenn Davis, Army, 1943-46 (358 for 2,957)
(Min. 414-780 rushes) 7.2—Mike Rozier, Nebraska, 1981-83 (668 for 4,780)
(Min. 781 rushes) 6.1—Archie Griffin, Ohio St., 1972-75 (845 for 5,177)

MOST TOUCHDOWNS SCORED BY RUSHING
Game
8—Howard Griffith, Illinois vs. Southern Ill., Sept. 22,

1990 (5, 51, 7, 41, 5, 18, 5, 3 yards; Griffith scored three touchdowns [51, 7, 41] on consecutive carries and scored four touchdowns in the third quarter)

Season
37—Barry Sanders, Oklahoma St., 1988 (11 games)
Also holds per-game record at 3.4 (37 in 11)

Career
64—Anthony Thompson, Indiana, 1986-89

MOST GAMES SCORING TWO OR MORE TOUCHDOWNS BY RUSHING
Season
11—Barry Sanders, Oklahoma St., 1988

MOST CONSECUTIVE GAMES SCORING TWO OR MORE TOUCHDOWNS BY RUSHING
Career
12—Barry Sanders, Oklahoma St. (last game of 1987, all 11 in 1988)

MOST TOUCHDOWNS SCORED BY RUSHING BY A FRESHMAN
Game
7—Marshall Faulk, San Diego St. vs. Pacific (Cal.), Sept. 14, 1991

Season
21—Marshall Faulk, San Diego St., 1991
Also holds per-game record at 2.3 (21 in 9)

MOST RUSHING TOUCHDOWNS SCORED BY A QUARTERBACK
Game
6—Dee Dowis, Air Force vs. San Diego St., Sept. 1, 1989 (55, 28, 12, 16, 60, 17 yards; 249 yards rushing on 13 carries)

Season
20—Chris McCoy, Navy, 1997

Career
47—Brian Mitchell, Southwestern La., 1986-89 (in 43 games)

MOST TOUCHDOWNS SCORED IN ONE QUARTER
4—Frank Moreau, Louisville vs. East Caro., Nov. 1, 1997 (all rushing, 2nd quarter); Howard Griffith, Illinois vs. Southern Ill., Sept. 22, 1990 (all rushing, 3rd quarter); Dick Felt, Brigham Young vs. San Jose St., Nov. 8, 1952 (all rushing, 4th quarter)

MOST CONSECUTIVE RUSHES FOR A TOUCHDOWN IN A GAME
3—Chris McCoy, Navy vs. Rutgers, Sept. 13, 1997 (TDs of 2, 9 and 2 yards); Tiki Barber, Virginia vs. Texas, Sept. 28, 1996 (TDs of 16, 26 and 12 yards)

MOST RUSHING TOUCHDOWNS SCORED BY A QUARTERBACK IN TWO CONSECUTIVE SEASONS
38—Stacey Robinson, Northern Ill., 1989-90 (19 and 19)

MOST YARDS GAINED BY TWO BROTHERS
Season
3,690—Barry Sanders, Oklahoma St. (2,628) & Byron Sanders, Northwestern (1,062), 1988

Passing

HIGHEST PASSING EFFICIENCY RATING POINTS
Game
(Min. 12-24 atts.) 403.4—Tim Clifford, Indiana vs. Colorado, Sept. 26, 1980 (14 attempts, 11 completions, 0 interceptions, 345 yards, 5 TD passes)
(Min. 25-49 atts.) 277.6—Jason Martin, Louisiana Tech vs. Toledo, Oct. 19, 1996 (36 attempts, 28 completions, 0 interceptions, 542 yards, 8 TD passes)
(Min. 50 atts.) 197.8—David Klingler, Houston vs. Eastern Wash., Nov. 17, 1990 (58 attempts, 41 completions, 2 interceptions, 572 yards, 11 TD passes)

Season
(Min. 15 atts. per game) 178.4—Danny Wuerffel, Florida, 1995 (325 attempts, 210 completions, 10 interceptions, 3,266 yards, 35 TD passes)

Career
(Min. 200 comps.) 163.6—Danny Wuerffel, Florida, 1993-96 (1,170 attempts, 708 completions, 42 interceptions, 10,875 yards, 114 TD passes)

HIGHEST PASSING EFFICIENCY RATING POINTS BY A FRESHMAN
Season
(Min. 15 atts. per game) 162.3—Donovan McNabb, Syracuse, 1995 (207 attempts, 128 completions, 6 interceptions, 1,991 yards, 16 TD passes)

MOST PASSES ATTEMPTED
Quarter
41—Jason Davis, UNLV vs. Idaho, Sept. 17, 1994 (4th, completed 28)

Half
56—Rusty LaRue, Wake Forest vs. Duke, Oct. 28, 1995 (2nd, completed 41)

Game
79—Matt Vogler, Texas Christian vs. Houston, Nov. 3, 1990 (completed 44)

Season
643—David Klingler, Houston, 1990 (11 games, completed 374)

2 Yrs
1,140—David Klingler, Houston, 1990-91 (completed 652)

3 Yrs
1,377—Ty Detmer, Brigham Young, 1989-91 (completed 875)

Career
(4 yrs.) 1,530—Ty Detmer, Brigham Young, 1988-91 (completed 958)

MOST PASSES ATTEMPTED PER GAME
Season
58.5—David Klingler, Houston, 1990 (643 in 11)

Career
39.6—Mike Perez, San Jose St., 1986-87 (792 in 20)

MOST PASSES ATTEMPTED BY A FRESHMAN
Game
71—Sandy Schwab, Northwestern vs. Michigan, Oct. 23, 1982 (completed 45)

Season
506—Jon Denton, UNLV, 1996 (completed 277)

MOST PASSES COMPLETED
Quarter
28—Jason Davis, UNLV vs. Idaho, Sept. 17, 1994 (4th, attempted 41)

Half
41—Rusty LaRue, Wake Forest vs. Duke, Oct. 28, 1995 (2nd, attempted 56)

Game
55—Rusty LaRue, Wake Forest vs. Duke, Oct. 28, 1995 (attempted 78)

Season
374—David Klingler, Houston, 1990 (11 games, attempted 643)

2 Yrs
652—David Klingler, Houston, 1990-91 (attempted 1,140)
Also holds per-game record at 31.0 (652 in 21)

3 Yrs
875—Ty Detmer, Brigham Young, 1989-91 (attempted 1,377)
Per-game record—24.8, David Klingler, Houston, 1989-91 (720 in 29)

Career
(4 yrs.) 958—Ty Detmer, Brigham Young, 1988-91 (attempted 1,530)

MOST PASSES COMPLETED PER GAME
Season
34.0—David Klingler, Houston, 1990 (374 in 11)

Career
25.9—Doug Gaynor, Long Beach St., 1984-85 (569 in 22)

MOST PASSES COMPLETED BY A FRESHMAN
Game
45—Sandy Schwab, Northwestern vs. Michigan, Oct. 23, 1982 (attempted 71)

Season
282—Mike Romo, Southern Methodist, 1989 (attempted 503)
Also holds per-game record at 25.6 (282 in 11)

MOST CONSECUTIVE PASSES COMPLETED
Game
22—Chuck Long, Iowa vs. Indiana, Oct. 27, 1984

Season
23—Rob Johnson, Southern Cal, 1994 (completed last 15 attempts vs. Arizona, Nov. 12, and first 8 vs. UCLA, Nov. 19); Scott Milanovich, Maryland, 1994 (completed last 4 attempts vs. Tulane, Oct. 29, and first 19 vs. North Caro. St., Nov. 5)

MOST PASSES COMPLETED IN TWO, THREE AND FOUR CONSECUTIVE GAMES
2 Games
96—Rusty LaRue, Wake Forest, 1995 (55 vs. Duke, Oct. 28; 41 vs. Georgia Tech, Nov. 4)

3 Games
146—Rusty LaRue, Wake Forest, 1995 (55 vs. Duke, Oct. 28; 41 vs. Georgia Tech, Nov. 4; 50 vs. North Caro. St., Nov. 18)

4 Games
157—Rusty LaRue, Wake Forest, 1995 (11 vs. North Caro., Oct. 21; 55 vs. Duke, Oct. 28; 41 vs. Georgia Tech, Nov. 4; 50 vs. North Caro. St., Nov. 18)

HIGHEST PERCENTAGE OF PASSES COMPLETED
Game
(Min. 20-29 comps.) 92.6%—Rick Neuheisel, UCLA vs. Washington, Oct. 29, 1983 (25 of 27)
(Min. 30-39 comps.) 91.2%—Steve Sarkisian, Brigham Young vs. Fresno St., Nov. 25, 1995 (31 of 34)
(Min. 40 comps.) 81.1%—Rich Campbell, California vs. Florida, Sept. 13, 1980 (43 of 53)

Season
(Min. 150 atts.) 71.3%—Steve Young, Brigham Young, 1983 (306 of 429)

Career
(Min. 875-999 atts.) 66.2%—Scott Milanovich, Maryland, 1992-95 (650 of 982)
(Min. 1,000-1,099 atts.) 64.6%—$Chuck Long, Iowa, 1981-85 (692 of 1,072)
(Min. 1,100 atts.) 63.9%—Jack Trudeau, Illinois, 1981, 1983-85 (736 of 1,151)

$ *See page 6 for explanation.*

HIGHEST PERCENTAGE OF PASSES COMPLETED BY A FRESHMAN
Season
(Min. 200 atts.) 66.2%—Grady Benton, Arizona St., 1992 (149 of 225)

MOST PASSES HAD INTERCEPTED
Game
9—John Reaves, Florida vs. Auburn, Nov. 1, 1969 (attempted 66)

Season
34—John Eckman, Wichita St., 1966 (attempted 458)
Also holds per-game record at 3.4 (34 in 10)

Career
(3 yrs.) 68—Zeke Bratkowski, Georgia, 1951-53 (attempted 734)
(4 yrs.) 73—Mark Herrmann, Purdue, 1977-80 (attempted 1,218)
Per-game record—2.3, Steve Ramsey, North Texas, 1967-69 (67 in 29)

Photo from Brigham Young sports information

Brigham Young's Ty Detmer owns the four-year career pass completion record with 958 completions.

LOWEST PERCENTAGE OF PASSES HAD INTERCEPTED

Season

(Min. 150-349 atts.) 0.0%—Matt Blundin, Virginia, 1991 (0 of 224)

(Min. 350 atts.) 1.1%—Peyton Manning, Tennessee, 1995 (4 of 380); Charlie Ward, Florida St., 1993 (4 of 380)

Career

(Min. 600-799 atts.) 1.7%—Damon Allen, Cal St. Fullerton, 1981-84 (11 of 629)

(Min. 800-1,049 atts.) 2.3%—Anthony Calvillo, Utah St., 1992-93 (19 of 829)

(Min. 1,050 atts.) 2.6%—Eric Zeier, Georgia, 1991-94 (37 of 1,402)

MOST PASSES ATTEMPTED WITHOUT AN INTERCEPTION

Game

68—David Klingler, Houston vs. Baylor, Oct. 6, 1990 (completed 35)

Entire Season

224—Matt Blundin, Virginia, 1991 (completed 135)

MOST CONSECUTIVE PASSES ATTEMPTED WITHOUT AN INTERCEPTION

Season

271—Trent Dilfer, Fresno St., 1993

Also holds career record at 271

MOST CONSECUTIVE PASSES ATTEMPTED WITH JUST ONE INTERCEPTION

Career

329—Damon Allen, Cal St. Fullerton, 1983-84 (during 16 games; began Oct. 8, 1983, vs. Nevada, ended Nov. 3, 1984, vs. Fresno St. Interception occurred vs. Idaho, Sept. 15, 1984)

MOST CONSECUTIVE PASSES ATTEMPTED WITHOUT AN INTERCEPTION AT THE START OF A CAREER BY A FRESHMAN

138—Mike Gundy, Oklahoma St., 1986 (during 8 games)

MOST CONSECUTIVE PASSES ATTEMPTED WITHOUT AN INTERCEPTION AT THE START OF A DIVISION I-A CAREER

202—Brad Otton, Southern Cal, 1994-95 (played 1993 at I-AA Weber St.)

MOST YARDS GAINED

Quarter

347—Jason Davis, UNLV vs. Idaho, Sept. 17, 1994 (4th)

Half

517—Andre Ware, Houston vs. Southern Methodist, Oct. 21, 1989 (1st, completed 25 of 41)

Game

716—David Klingler, Houston vs. Arizona St., Dec. 2, 1990 (completed 41 of 70)

Season

(11 games) 5,140—David Klingler, Houston, 1990 (completed 374 of 643)

(12 games) 5,188—Ty Detmer, Brigham Young, 1990 (completed 361 of 562)

2 Yrs

9,748—Ty Detmer, Brigham Young, 1989-90 (completed 626 of 974)

3 Yrs

13,779—Ty Detmer, Brigham Young, 1989-91 (completed 875 of 1,377)

Career

(4 yrs.) 15,031—Ty Detmer, Brigham Young, 1988-91 (completed 958 of 1,530)

MOST YARDS GAINED PER GAME

Season

467.3—David Klingler, Houston, 1990 (5,140 in 11)

2 Yrs

406.2—Ty Detmer, Brigham Young, 1989-90 (9,748 in 24)

3 Yrs

382.8—Ty Detmer, Brigham Young, 1989-91 (13,779 in 36)

Career

326.8—Ty Detmer, Brigham Young, 1988-91 (15,031 in 46)

MOST YARDS GAINED BY A FRESHMAN

Game

503—Jon Denton, UNLV vs. San Diego St., Nov. 16, 1996

Season

3,591—Jon Denton, UNLV, 1996

Also holds per-game record at 299.3 (3,591 in 12)

MOST YARDS GAINED BY A SOPHOMORE

Game

631—Scott Mitchell, Utah vs. Air Force, Oct. 15, 1988

Season

4,560—Ty Detmer, Brigham Young, 1989

Per-game record—392.9, Scott Mitchell, Utah, 1988 (4,322 in 11)

MOST SEASONS GAINING 2,000 YARDS OR MORE

Career

4—Glenn Foley, Boston College, 1990-93 (2,189—2,225—2,231—3,397); Alex Van Pelt, Pittsburgh, 1989-92 (2,527—2,427—2,796—3,163); T. J. Rubley, Tulsa, 1987-89, 1991 (2,058—2,497—2,292—2,054); Tom Hodson, LSU, 1986-89 (2,261—2,125—2,074—2,655); Todd Santos, San Diego St., 1984-87 (2,063—2,877—2,553—3,932); Kevin Sweeney, Fresno St., 1983-86 (2,359—3,259—2,604—2,363)

MOST YARDS GAINED IN TWO, THREE AND FOUR CONSECUTIVE GAMES

2 Games

1,288—David Klingler, Houston, 1990 (572 vs. Eastern Wash., Nov. 17; 716 vs. Arizona St., Dec. 2)

3 Games

1,798—David Klingler, Houston, 1990-91 (572 vs. Eastern Wash., Nov. 17, 1990; 716 vs. Arizona St., Dec. 2, 1990; 510 vs. Louisiana Tech, Aug. 31, 1991)

4 Games

2,150—David Klingler, Houston, 1990 (563 vs. Texas Christian, Nov. 3; 299 vs. Texas, Nov. 10; 572 vs. Eastern Wash., Nov. 17; 716 vs. Arizona St., Dec. 2)

MOST GAMES GAINING 200 YARDS OR MORE

Season

12—Ty Detmer, Brigham Young, 1990, 1989; Robbie Bosco, Brigham Young, 1985, 1984

Career

38—Ty Detmer, Brigham Young, 1988-91

MOST CONSECUTIVE GAMES GAINING 200 YARDS OR MORE

Season

12—Ty Detmer, Brigham Young, 1990, 1989; Robbie Bosco, Brigham Young, 1984

Career

27—Ty Detmer, Brigham Young (from Sept. 2, 1989, to Sept. 21, 1991)

MOST GAMES GAINING 300 YARDS OR MORE

Season

12—Ty Detmer, Brigham Young, 1990, 1989

Career

33—Ty Detmer, Brigham Young, 1988-91

MOST CONSECUTIVE GAMES GAINING 300 YARDS OR MORE

Season

12—Ty Detmer, Brigham Young, 1990, 1989

Career

24—Ty Detmer, Brigham Young (from Sept. 2, 1989, to Dec. 1, 1990)

MOST GAMES GAINING 400 YARDS OR MORE

Season

9—David Klingler, Houston, 1990

Career

12—Ty Detmer, Brigham Young, 1988-91

MOST YARDS GAINED BY TWO OPPOSING PLAYERS

Game

1,253—Matt Vogler, Texas Christian (690) & David Klingler, Houston (563), Nov. 3, 1990

TWO PLAYERS, SAME TEAM, EACH PASSING FOR 250 YARDS OR MORE

Game

Jason Davis (381) & Jared Brown (254), UNLV vs. Idaho, Sept. 17, 1994; Andre Ware (517) & David Klingler (254), Houston vs. Southern Methodist, Oct. 21, 1989; Steve Cottrell (311) & John Elway (270), Stanford vs. Arizona St., Oct. 24, 1981

MOST YARDS GAINED IN OPENING GAME OF SEASON

536—Steve Sarkisian, Brigham Young vs. Texas A&M, August 24, 1996

MOST YARDS GAINED AGAINST ONE OPPONENT

Career

1,495—Ty Detmer, Brigham Young vs. New Mexico, 1988-91

MOST YARDS GAINED PER GAME AGAINST ONE OPPONENT

Career

(Min. 3 games) 410.7—Gary Schofield, Wake Forest vs. Maryland, 1981-83 (1,232 yards)

(Min. 4 games) 373.8—Ty Detmer, Brigham Young vs. New Mexico, 1988-91 (1,495 yards)

MOST YARDS GAINED PER ATTEMPT

Game

(Min. 25-39 atts.) 15.8—Koy Detmer, Colorado vs. Northeast La., Sept. 16, 1995 (27 for 426)

(Min. 40-59 atts.) 14.1—John Walsh, Brigham Young vs. Utah St., Oct. 30, 1993 (44 for 619)

(Min. 60 atts.) 10.5—Scott Mitchell, Utah vs. Air Force, Oct. 15, 1988 (60 for 631)

Season

(Min. 412 atts.) 11.1—Ty Detmer, Brigham Young, 1989 (412 for 4,560)

Career

(Min. 1,000 atts.) 9.8—Ty Detmer, Brigham Young, 1988-91 (1,530 for 15,031)

MOST YARDS GAINED PER COMPLETION

Game

(Min. 22-41 comps.) 22.9—John Walsh, Brigham Young vs. Utah St., Oct. 30, 1993 (27 for 619)

(Min. 42 comps.) 15.7—Matt Vogler, Texas Christian vs. Houston, Nov. 3, 1990 (44 for 690)

Season

(Min. 109-204 comps.) 18.2—Doug Williams, Grambling, 1977 (181 for 3,286)

(Min. 205 comps.) 17.5—Danny Wuerffel, Florida, 1996 (207 for 3,625)

Career

(Min. 275-399 comps.) 17.3—J. J. Joe, Baylor, 1990-93 (347 for 5,995)

(Min. 400 comps.) 15.7—Shawn Moore, Virginia, 1987-90 (421 for 6,629)

MOST TOUCHDOWN PASSES

Quarter

6—David Klingler, Houston vs. Louisiana Tech, Aug. 31, 1991 (2nd)

Half

7—Doug Johnson, Florida vs. Central Mich., Sept. 6, 1997 (1st); Terry Dean, Florida vs. New Mexico St., Sept. 3, 1994 (1st); Dennis Shaw, San Diego St. vs. New Mexico St., Nov. 15, 1969 (1st)

Game

11—David Klingler, Houston vs. Eastern Wash., Nov. 17, 1990

Season

54—David Klingler, Houston, 1990 (11 games)

2 Yrs

83—David Klingler, Houston, 1990-91

Also holds per-game record at 4.0 (83 in 21)

3 Yrs

108—Ty Detmer, Brigham Young, 1989-91

Career

121—Ty Detmer, Brigham Young, 1988-91

MOST TOUCHDOWN PASSES PER GAME

Season

4.9—David Klingler, Houston, 1990 (54 in 11)

Career

2.8—David Klingler, Houston, 1988-91 (91 in 32)

Collegiate record—2.9, Dennis Shaw, San Diego St., 1968-69 (58 in 20)

HIGHEST PERCENTAGE OF PASSES FOR TOUCHDOWNS

Season

(Min. 175-374 atts.) 11.6%—Dennis Shaw, San Diego St., 1969 (39 of 335)

(Min. 375 atts.) 10.6%—Jim McMahon, Brigham Young, 1980 (47 of 445)

Career

(Min. 400-499 atts.) 9.7%—Rick Leach, Michigan, 1975-78 (45 of 462)

(Min. 500 atts.) 9.7%—Danny Wuerffel, Florida, 1993-96 (114 of 1,170)

MOST CONSECUTIVE GAMES THROWING A TOUCHDOWN PASS

Career

35—Ty Detmer, Brigham Young (from Sept. 7, 1989, to Nov. 23, 1991)

MOST CONSECUTIVE PASSES COMPLETED FOR TOUCHDOWNS
Game
6—Brooks Dawson, UTEP vs. New Mexico, Oct. 28, 1967 (first six completions of the game)

MOST TOUCHDOWN PASSES IN FIRST GAME OF CAREER
5—John Reaves, Florida vs. Houston, Sept. 20, 1969

MOST TOUCHDOWN PASSES BY A FRESHMAN
Game
6—Bob Hoernschemeyer, Indiana vs. Nebraska, Oct. 9, 1943
Season
25—Jon Denton, UNLV, 1996

MOST TOUCHDOWN PASSES IN FRESHMAN AND SOPHOMORE SEASONS
45—Ty Detmer, Brigham Young, 1988 (13) & 1989 (32)

MOST TOUCHDOWN PASSES BY A SOPHOMORE
39—Chad Pennington, Marshall, 1997

MOST TOUCHDOWN PASSES AT CONCLUSION OF JUNIOR YEAR
86—Ty Detmer, Brigham Young, 1988 (13), 1989 (32) & 1990 (41)

MOST TOUCHDOWN PASSES, SAME PASSER AND RECEIVER
Season
24—Chad Pennington to Randy Moss, Marshall, 1997
Career
33—Troy Kopp to Aaron Turner, Pacific (Cal.), 1989-92

MOST PASSES ATTEMPTED WITHOUT A TOUCHDOWN PASS
Season
266—Stu Rayburn, Kent, 1984 (completed 125)

FEWEST TIMES SACKED ATTEMPTING TO PASS
Season
(Min. 300 atts.) 4—Steve Walsh, Miami (Fla.), 1988, in 390 attempts. Last 4 games of the season: Tulsa, 1 for -8 yards; LSU, 1 for -2; Arkansas, 1 for -12; Brigham Young, 1 for-9.

Receiving

MOST PASSES CAUGHT
Game
23—Randy Gatewood, UNLV vs. Idaho, Sept. 17, 1994 (363 yards)
Season
142—Manny Hazard, Houston, 1989 (1,689 yards)
Career
(2 yrs.) 227—Alex Van Dyke, Nevada, 1994-95 (3,100 yards)
(3 yrs.) 261—Howard Twilley, Tulsa, 1963-65 (3,343 yards)
(4 yrs.) 266—Aaron Turner, Pacific (Cal.), 1989-92 (4,345 yards)

MOST PASSES CAUGHT PER GAME
Season
13.4—Howard Twilley, Tulsa, 1965 (134 in 10)
Career
10.5—Manny Hazard, Houston, 1989-90 (220 in 21)

MOST PASSES CAUGHT BY TWO PLAYERS, SAME TEAM
Season
212—Damond Wilkins (114) & Geoffery Noisy (98), Nevada, 1996 (2,556 yards, 13 TDs); Howard Twilley (134) & Neal Sweeney (78), Tulsa, 1965 (2,662 yards, 24 TDs)
Career
453—Mark Templeton (262) & Charles Lockett (191), Long Beach St., 1983-86 (4,871 yards, 30 TDs)

MOST PASSES CAUGHT IN CONSECUTIVE GAMES
38—Manny Hazard, Houston, 1989 (19 vs. Texas Christian, Nov. 4; 19 vs. Texas, Nov. 11)

MOST CONSECUTIVE GAMES CATCHING A PASS
Career
46—Carl Winston, New Mexico, 1990-93 (every game)

MOST PASSES CAUGHT BY A TIGHT END
Game
17—Jon Harvey, Northwestern vs. Michigan, Oct. 23, 1982 (208 yards); Emilio Vallez, New Mexico vs. UTEP, Oct. 27, 1967 (257 yards)
Season
73—Dennis Smith, Utah, 1989 (1,089 yards)
Career
190—Pete Mitchell, Boston College, 1991-94 (2,389 yards)

MOST PASSES CAUGHT PER GAME BY A TIGHT END
Season
6.4—Jamie Asher, Louisville, 1994 (70 in 11); Mark Dowdell, Bowling Green, 1983 (70 in 11); Chuck Scott, Vanderbilt, 1983 (70 in 11)
Career
5.4—Gordon Hudson, Brigham Young, 1980-83 (178 in 33)

MOST PASSES CAUGHT BY A RUNNING BACK
Game
18—Mark Templeton, Long Beach St. vs. Utah St., Nov. 1, 1986 (173 yards)
Season
99—Mark Templeton, Long Beach St., 1986 (688 yards)
Career
262—Mark Templeton, Long Beach St., 1983-86 (1,969 yards)

MOST PASSES CAUGHT BY A FRESHMAN
Game
18—Richard Woodley (WR), Texas Christian vs. Texas Tech, Nov. 10, 1990 (180 yards)
Season
75—Brandon Stokley, Southwestern La., 1995 (1,121 yards)
Also holds per-game record at 6.8

CATCHING AT LEAST 50 PASSES AND GAINING AT LEAST 1,000 YARDS RUSHING
Season
By 10 players. Most recent: Ryan Benjamin, Pacific (Cal.), 1991 (51 catches and 1,581 yards rushing)
Darrin Nelson, Stanford, holds record for most seasons at 3 (1977-78, 1981)

CATCHING AT LEAST 60 PASSES AND GAINING AT LEAST 1,000 YARDS RUSHING
Johnny Johnson, San Jose St., 1988 (61 catches and 1,219 yards rushing); Brad Muster, Stanford, 1986 (61 catches and 1,053 yards rushing); Darrin Nelson, Stanford, 1981 (67 catches and 1,014 yards rushing)

MOST YARDS GAINED
Game
363—Randy Gatewood, UNLV vs. Idaho, Sept. 17, 1994 (caught 23)
Season
1,854—Alex Van Dyke, Nevada, 1995 (caught 129)
Career
4,518—Marcus Harris, Wyoming, 1993-96 (caught 259)

MOST YARDS GAINED PER GAME
Season
177.9—Howard Twilley, Tulsa, 1965 (1,779 in 10)
Career
140.9—Alex Van Dyke, Nevada, 1994-95 (3,100 in 22)

MOST YARDS GAINED BY A TIGHT END
Game
259—Gordon Hudson, Brigham Young vs. Utah, Nov. 21, 1981 (caught 13)
Season
1,156—Chris Smith, Brigham Young, 1990 (caught 68)
Career
2,484—Gordon Hudson, Brigham Young, 1980-83 (caught 178)

MOST YARDS GAINED PER GAME BY A TIGHT END
Season
102.0—Mike Moore, Grambling, 1977 (1,122 in 11)
Career
75.3—Gordon Hudson, Brigham Young, 1980-83 (2,484 in 33)

MOST YARDS GAINED BY A FRESHMAN
Game
263—Corey Alston, Western Mich. vs. Eastern Mich., Nov. 1, 1997 (caught 9)
Season
1,121—Brandon Stokley, Southwestern La., 1995 (caught 75)
Also holds per-game record at 101.9

MOST GAMES GAINING 100 YARDS OR MORE
Season
11—Aaron Turner, Pacific (Cal.), 1991
Also holds consecutive record at 11
Career
24—Marcus Harris, Wyoming, 1993-96 (in 46 games played)
Consecutive record: 11, Keyshawn Johnson, Southern Cal, 1994-95 (over two seasons), and Aaron Turner, Pacific (Cal.), 1991 (all one season)

MOST GAMES GAINING 200 YARDS OR MORE
Season
5—Howard Twilley, Tulsa, 1965
Also holds consecutive record at 3

MOST YARDS GAINED BY TWO PLAYERS, SAME TEAM
Game
640—Rick Eber (322) & Harry Wood (318), Tulsa vs. Idaho St., Oct. 7, 1967 (caught 33, 6 TDs)
Season
2,732—Alex Van Dyke (1,854) & Steve McHenry (878), Nevada, 1995

TWO PLAYERS, SAME TEAM, EACH GAINING 1,000 YARDS
10 times. Geoff Noisy (1,184; 86 catches) & Trevor Insley (1,151; 59 catches), Nevada, 1997; Geof Noisy (1,435; 98 catches) & Damond Wilkins (1,121; 114 catches), Nevada, 1996; Chris Doering (1,045; 70 catches) & Ike Hilliard (1,008; 57 catches), Florida, 1995; E. G. Green (1,007; 60 catches) & Andre Cooper (1,002; 71 catches), Florida St., 1995; Will Blackwell (1,207; 86 catches) & Az Hakim (1,022; 57 catches), San Diego St., 1995; Bryan Reeves (1,362; 91 catches) & Michael Stephens (1,062; 80 catches), Nevada, 1993; Charles Johnson (1,149; 57 catches) & Michael Westbrook (1,060; 76 catches), Colorado, 1992; Andy Boyce (1,241; 79 catches) & Chris Smith (1,156; 68 catches), Brigham Young, 1990; Patrick Rowe (1,392; 71 catches) & Dennis Arey (1,118; 68 catches), San Diego St., 1990; Jason Phillips (1,444; 108 catches) & James Dixon (1,103; 102 catches), Houston, 1988

TWO PLAYERS, SAME TEAM, RANKED NO. 1 & NO. 2 IN FINAL RECEIVING RANKINGS
Season
Jason Phillips (No. 1, 9.8 catches per game) & James Dixon (No. 2, 9.3 catches per game), Houston, 1988

THREE PLAYERS, SAME TEAM, EACH CATCHING 60 PASSES OR MORE
Patrick Rowe (71), Dennis Arey (68) & Jimmy Raye (62), San Diego St., 1990

MOST 1,000-YARD RECEIVING SEASONS
3—Marcus Harris, Wyoming, 1993-96 (1,431 in 1994; 1,423 in 1995; 1,650 in 1996); Ryan Yarborough, Wyoming, 1991-93 (1,081 in 1991; 1,351 in 1992; 1,512 in 1993); Aaron Turner, Pacific (Cal.), 1990-92 (1,264 in 1990; 1,604 in 1991; 1,171 in 1992); Clarkston Hines, Duke, 1987-89 (1,084 in 1987; 1,067 in 1988; 1,149 in 1989); Marc Zeno, Tulane, 1985-87 (1,137 in 1985; 1,033 in 1986; 1,206 in 1987)

MOST RECEIVING SEASONS OVER 1,400 YARDS
3—Marcus Harris, Wyoming, 1993-96 (1,431 in 1994; 1,423 in 1995; 1,650 in 1996)

HIGHEST AVERAGE GAIN PER RECEPTION
Game
(Min. 3-4 receps.) 72.7—Terry Gallaher, East Caro. vs. Appalachian St., Sept. 13, 1975 (3 for 218; 82, 77, 59 yards)
(Min. 5-9 receps.) 52.6—Alexander Wright, Auburn vs. Pacific (Cal.), Sept. 9, 1989 (5 for 263; 78, 60, 41, 73, 11 yards)
(Min. 10 receps.) 34.9—Chuck Hughes, UTEP vs. North Texas, Sept. 18, 1965 (10 for 349)
Season
(Min. 30-49 receps.) 27.9—Elmo Wright, Houston, 1968 (43 for 1,198)
(Min. 50 receps.) 24.4—Henry Ellard, Fresno St., 1982 (62 for 1,510)

Career

(Min. 75-104 receps.) 25.7—Wesley Walker, California, 1973-76 (86 for 2,206)

(Min. 105 receps.) 22.0—Herman Moore, Virginia, 1988-90 (114 for 2,504)

HIGHEST AVERAGE GAIN PER RECEPTION BY A TIGHT END

Season

(Min. 30 receps.) 22.6—Jay Novacek, Wyoming, 1984 (33 for 745)

Career

(Min. 75 receps.) 19.2—Clay Brown, Brigham Young, 1978-80 (88 for 1,691)

MOST TOUCHDOWN PASSES CAUGHT

Game

6—Tim Delaney, San Diego St. vs. New Mexico St., Nov. 15, 1969 (16 receptions)

Season

25—Randy Moss, Marshall, 1997 (90 receptions)

Per-game record—2.3, Tom Reynolds, San Diego St., 1969 (18 in 8)

Career

43—Aaron Turner, Pacific (Cal.), 1989-92 (266 receptions)

MOST GAMES CATCHING A TOUCHDOWN PASS

Season

12—Randy Moss, Marshall, 1997

Career

27—Ryan Yarborough, Wyoming, 1990-93 (caught a total of 42 in 46 games)

MOST CONSECUTIVE GAMES CATCHING A TOUCHDOWN PASS

Season

12—Randy Moss, Marshall, 1997

Career

12—Randy Moss, Marshall, 1997 (all in 1997); Desmond Howard, Michigan (last two games of 1990 and first 10 games of 1991); Aaron Turner, Pacific (Cal.) (last three games of 1990 and first nine games of 1991)

MOST TOUCHDOWN PASSES CAUGHT BY A TIGHT END

Season

18—Dennis Smith, Utah, 1989 (73 receptions)

Career

24—Dennis Smith, Utah, 1987-89 (156 receptions); Dave Young, Purdue, 1977-80 (172 receptions)

HIGHEST PERCENTAGE OF PASSES CAUGHT FOR TOUCHDOWNS

Season

(Min. 10 TDs) 58.8%—Kevin Williams, Southern Cal, 1978 (10 of 17)

Career

(Min. 20 TDs) 35.3%—Kevin Williams, Southern Cal, 1977-80 (24 of 68)

HIGHEST AVERAGE YARDS PER TOUCHDOWN PASS

Season

(Min. 10) 56.1—Elmo Wright, Houston, 1968 (11 for 617 yards; 87, 50, 75, 2, 80, 79, 13, 67, 61, 43, 60 yards)

Career

(Min. 15) 46.5—Charles Johnson, Colorado, 1990-93 (15 for 697 yards)

MOST TOUCHDOWN PASSES CAUGHT, 50 YARDS OR MORE

Season

8—Henry Ellard, Fresno St., 1982 (68, 51, 80, 61, 67, 72, 80, 72 yards); Elmo Wright, Houston, 1968 (87, 50, 75, 80, 79, 67, 61, 60 yards)

MOST CONSECUTIVE PASSES CAUGHT FOR TOUCHDOWNS

6—Gerald Armstrong, Nebraska, 1992 (1 vs. Utah, Sept. 5; 1 vs. Arizona St., Sept. 26; 1 vs. Oklahoma St., Oct. 10; 1 vs. Colorado, Oct. 31; 2 vs. Kansas, Nov. 7); Carlos Carson, LSU, 1977 (5 vs. Rice, Sept. 24; 1 vs. Florida, Oct. 1; first receptions of his career)

MOST TOUCHDOWN PASSES CAUGHT BY A FRESHMAN

Season

10—Dwight Collins, Pittsburgh, 1980

Punting

MOST PUNTS

Game

36—Charlie Calhoun, Texas Tech vs. Centenary (La.), Nov. 11, 1939 (1,318 yards; 20 were returned, 8 went out of bounds, 6 were downed, 1 was blocked [blocked kicks counted against the punter until 1955] and 1 went into the end zone for a touchback. Thirty-three of the punts occurred on first down during a heavy downpour in the game played at Shreveport, Louisiana)

Season

101—Jim Bailey, Va. Military, 1969 (3,507 yards)

Career

(3 yrs.) 276—Jim Bailey, Va. Military, 1969-71 (10,127 yards)

(4 yrs.) 320—Cameron Young, Texas Christian, 1976-79 (12,947 yards)

HIGHEST AVERAGE PER PUNT

Game

(Min. 5-9 punts) 60.4—Lee Johnson, Brigham Young vs. Wyoming, Oct. 8, 1983 (5 for 302; 53, 44, 63, 62, 80 yards)

(Min. 10 punts) 53.6—Jim Benien, Oklahoma St. vs. Colorado, Nov. 13, 1971 (10 for 536)

Season

(Min. 36-39 punts) 50.3—Chad Kessler, LSU, 1997 (39 for 1,961)

(Min. 40-49 punts) 49.8—Reggie Roby, Iowa, 1981 (44 for 2,193)

(Min. 50-74 punts) 48.4—Todd Sauerbrun, West Va., 1994 (72 for 3,486)

(Min. 75 punts) 46.6—Bill Marinangel, Vanderbilt, 1996 (77 for 3,586)

Career

(Min. 150-199 punts) 46.3—Todd Sauerbrun, West Va., 1991-94 (167 for 7,733)

(Min. 200-249 punts) 44.7—Ray Guy, Southern Miss., 1970-72 (200 for 8,934)

(Min. 250 punts) 44.3—Bill Smith, Mississippi, 1983-86 (254 for 11,260)

HIGHEST AVERAGE PER PUNT BY A FRESHMAN

Season

(Min. 40 punts) 47.0—Tom Tupa, Ohio St., 1984 (41 for 1,927)

MOST YARDS ON PUNTS

Game

1,318—Charlie Calhoun, Texas Tech vs. Centenary (La.), Nov. 11, 1939 (36 punts)

Season

4,138—Johnny Pingel, Michigan St., 1938 (99 punts)

Career

12,947—Cameron Young, Texas Christian, 1976-79 (320 punts)

MOST GAMES WITH A 40-YARD AVERAGE OR MORE

Career

(Min. 4 punts) 36—Bill Smith, Mississippi, 1983-86 (punted in 44 games)

MOST PUNTS, 50 YARDS OR MORE

Season

32—Todd Sauerbrun, West Va., 1994 (72 punts)

Career

(2 yrs.) 51—Marv Bateman, Utah, 1970-71 (133 punts)

(3 yrs.) 61—Russ Henderson, Virginia, 1976-78 (226 punts)

(4 yrs.) 88—Bill Smith, Mississippi, 1983-86 (254 punts)

MOST CONSECUTIVE GAMES WITH AT LEAST ONE PUNT OF 50 YARDS OR MORE

Career

32—Bill Smith, Mississippi, 1983-86

MOST PUNTS IN A CAREER WITHOUT HAVING ONE BLOCKED

300—Tony DeLeone, Kent, 1981-84

Also holds consecutive record at 300

LONGEST PUNT

99—Pat Brady, Nevada vs. Loyola Marymount, Oct. 28, 1950

RANKING IN TOP 12 IN BOTH PUNTING AND FIELD GOALS

Daron Alcorn, Akron, 1992 (No. 11 in punting, 43.6-yard average and tied for No. 9 in field goals, 1.64 per game); Dan Eichloff, Kansas, 1991 (No. 12 in punting, 42.3-yard average and No. 3 in field goals, 1.64 per game); Chris Gardocki, Clemson, 1990 (No. 4 in punting, 44.3-yard average and No. 4 in field goals, 1.73 per game), 1989 (No. 10 in punting, 42.7-yard average and No. 6 in field goals, 1.82 per game); Rob Keen, California, 1988 (No. 11 in punting, 42.6-yard average and No. 3 in field goals, 1.91 per game); Steve Little, Arkansas, 1977 (No. 4 in punting, 44.3-yard average and No. 2 in field goals, 1.73 per game)

Interceptions

MOST PASSES INTERCEPTED

Game

5—Dan Rebsch, Miami (Ohio) vs. Western Mich., Nov. 4, 1972 (88 yards); Byron Beaver, Houston vs. Baylor, Sept. 22, 1962 (18 yards); Walt Pastuszak, Brown vs. Rhode Island, Oct. 8, 1949 (47 yards); Lee Cook, Oklahoma St. vs. Detroit, Nov. 28, 1942 (15 yards). Special note: Prior to NCAA College-division records, Dick Miller of Akron intercepted six passes vs. Baldwin-Wallace on Oct. 23, 1937.

Season

14—Al Worley, Washington, 1968 (130 yards)

Career

29—Al Brosky, Illinois, 1950-52 (356 yards)

MOST PASSES INTERCEPTED PER GAME

Season

1.4—Al Worley, Washington, 1968 (14 in 10)

Career

1.1—Al Brosky, Illinois, 1950-52 (29 in 27)

MOST PASSES INTERCEPTED BY A LINEBACKER

Game

3—Nate Kvamme, Colorado St. vs. San Jose St., Oct. 11, 1997 (17, 57 & 26 yards, two TDs)

Season

9—Bill Sibley, Texas A&M, 1941 (57 yards)

MOST PASSES INTERCEPTED BY A FRESHMAN

Game

3—Lamont Thompson, Washington St. vs. Washington, Nov. 22, 1997 (12 yards); Dre' Bly, North Caro. vs. Georgia Tech, Sept. 21, 1996 (52 yards); Torey Hunter, Washington St. vs. Arizona St., Oct. 19, 1991 (22 yards); Keith McMeans, Virginia vs. North Caro. St., Nov. 21, 1987 (0 yards); Shawn Simms, Bowling Green vs. Toledo, Oct. 24, 1981 (46 yards)

Season

13—George Shaw, Oregon, 1951 (136 yards)

Also holds per-game record at 1.3 (13 in 10)

MOST YARDS ON INTERCEPTION RETURNS

Game

182—Ashley Lee, Virginia Tech vs. Vanderbilt, Nov. 12, 1983 (2 interceptions)

Season

302—Charles Phillips, Southern Cal, 1974 (7 interceptions)

Career

501—Terrell Buckley, Florida St., 1989-91 (21 interceptions)

MOST TOUCHDOWNS SCORED ON INTERCEPTION RETURNS

Game

3—Johnny Jackson, Houston vs. Texas, Nov. 7, 1987 (31, 53, 97 yards)

Season

3—By many players. Most recent: Reggie Tongue, Oregon St., 1994 (5 interceptions)

Career

5—Ken Thomas, San Jose St., 1979-82 (14 interceptions); Jackie Walker, Tennessee, 1969-71 (11 interceptions)

MOST TOUCHDOWNS SCORED ON INTERCEPTION RETURNS BY A LINEBACKER

Game

2—Nate Kvamme, Colorado St. vs. San Jose St., Oct. 11, 1997 (15 & 57 yards); Patrick Brown, Kansas vs. UAB, Aug. 28, 1997 (51 & 23 yards); Randy Neal, Virginia vs. Virginia Tech, Nov. 21, 1992 (37, 30 yards); Tom Fisher, New Mexico St. vs. Lamar, Nov. 14, 1970 (52, 28 yards in one quarter.)

Season

2—Mike Rose, Purdue, 1997; Randy Neal, Virginia, 1994, 1992; Jerry Robinson, UCLA, 1976; Tom Fisher, New Mexico St., 1970

Career

4—Randy Neal, Virginia, 1991-94 (37, 30, 77, 28 yards)

HIGHEST AVERAGE GAIN PER INTERCEPTION

Game

(Min. 2 ints.) 91.0—Ashley Lee, Virginia Tech vs. Vanderbilt, Nov. 12, 1983 (2 for 182)

Season

(Min. 5 ints.) 50.6—Norm Thompson, Utah, 1969 (5 for 253)

Career

(Min. 15 ints.) 26.5—Tom Pridemore, West Va., 1975-77 (15 for 398)

MOST CONSECUTIVE GAMES INTERCEPTING A PASS

15—Al Brosky, Illinois, began Nov. 11, 1950 (vs. Iowa), ended Oct. 18, 1952 (vs. Minnesota)

Punt Returns

MOST PUNT RETURNS

Game

20—Milton Hill, Texas Tech vs. Centenary (La.), Nov. 11, 1939 (110 yards)

Season

55—Dick Adams, Miami (Ohio), 1970 (578 yards)
Also holds per-game record at 5.5

Career

153—Vai Sikahema, Brigham Young, 1980-81, 1984-85 (1,312 yards)

MOST YARDS ON PUNT RETURNS

Game

225—Chris McCranie, Georgia vs. South Caro., Sept. 2, 1995 (5 returns)

Season

791—Lee Nalley, Vanderbilt, 1948 (43 returns)
Also holds per-game record at 79.1

Career

1,695—Lee Nalley, Vanderbilt, 1947-49 (109 returns)

HIGHEST AVERAGE GAIN PER RETURN

Game

(Min. 3-4 rets.) 59.7—Chip Hough, Air Force vs. Southern Methodist, Oct. 9, 1971 (3 for 179)

(Min. 5 rets.) 45.0—Chris McCranie, Georgia vs. South Caro., Sept. 2, 1995 (5 for 225)

Season

(Min. 1.2 rets. per game) 25.9—Bill Blackstock, Tennessee, 1951 (12 for 311)

(Min. 1.5 rets. per game) 25.0—George Sims, Baylor, 1948 (15 for 375)

Career

(Min. 1.2 rets. per game) 23.6—Jack Mitchell, Oklahoma, 1946-48 (39 for 922)

(Min. 1.5 rets. per game) 20.5—Gene Gibson, Cincinnati, 1949-50 (37 for 760)

MOST TOUCHDOWNS SCORED ON PUNT RETURNS

Game

2—By many players. Most recent: Tinker Keck, Cincinnati vs. Louisville, Nov. 8, 1997 (44 & 78 yards)

Season

4—Quinton Spotwood, Syracuse, 1997; Tinker Keck, Cincinnati, 1997; James Henry, Southern Miss., 1987; Golden Richards, Brigham Young, 1971; Cliff Branch, Colorado, 1971

Career

7—Johnny Rodgers, Nebraska, 1970-72 (2 in 1970, 3 in 1971, 2 in 1972); Jack Mitchell, Oklahoma, 1946-48 (3 in 1946, 1 in 1947, 3 in 1948)

Kickoff Returns

MOST KICKOFF RETURNS

Game

11—Reidel Anthony, Florida vs. Tennessee, Sept. 16, 1995 (123 yards); Trevor Cobb, Rice vs. Houston, Dec. 2, 1989 (166 yards)

Season

46—Cedric Johnson, UTEP, 1995 (1,039 yards)

Career

123—Jeff Liggon, Tulane, 1993-96 (2,922 yards)

MOST RETURNS PER GAME

Season

4.6—Dwayne Owens, Oregon St., 1990 (41 in 9)

Career

3.0—Steve Odom, Utah, 1971-73 (99 in 33)

MOST YARDS ON KICKOFF RETURNS

Game

248—Tyrone Watley, Iowa St. vs. Nebraska, Nov. 15, 1997 (10 returns)

Season

1,065—Tijan Redmon, Duke, 1995 (45 returns)

Career

2,922—Jeff Liggon, Tulane, 1993-96 (123 returns)

MOST YARDS RETURNED PER GAME

Season

112.7—Dwayne Owens, Oregon St., 1990 (1,014 in 9)

Career

78.2—Steve Odom, Utah, 1971-73 (2,582 in 33)

HIGHEST AVERAGE GAIN PER RETURN

Game

(Min. 3 rets.) 72.7—Anthony Davis, Southern Cal vs. Notre Dame, Dec. 2, 1972 (3 for 218)

Season

(Min. 1.2 rets. per game) 40.1—Paul Allen, Brigham Young, 1961 (12 for 481)

(Min. 1.5 rets. per game) 38.2—Forrest Hall, San Francisco, 1946 (15 for 573)

Career

(Min. 1.2 rets. per game) 36.2—Forrest Hall, San Francisco, 1946-47 (22 for 796)

(Min. 1.5 rets. per game) 31.0—Overton Curtis, Utah St., 1957-58 (32 for 991)

MOST TOUCHDOWNS SCORED ON KICKOFF RETURNS

Game

2—Tutu Atwell, Minnesota vs. Iowa St., Sept. 13, 1997 (89 & 93 yards); Leeland McElroy, Texas A&M vs. Rice, Oct. 23, 1993 (93 & 88 yards); Stacey Corley, Brigham Young vs. Air Force, Nov. 11, 1989 (99 & 85 yards); *Raghib Ismail, Notre Dame vs. Michigan, Sept. 16, 1989 (88 & 92 yards); Raghib Ismail, Notre Dame vs. Rice, Nov. 5, 1988 (87 & 83 yards); Anthony Davis, Southern Cal vs. Notre Dame, Dec. 2, 1972 (97 & 96 yards); Ollie Matson, San Francisco vs. Fordham, Oct. 20, 1951 (94 & 90 yards); Ron Horwath, Detroit vs. Hillsdale, Sept. 22, 1950 (96 & 96 yards); Paul Copoulos, Marquette vs. Iowa Pre-Flight, Nov. 6, 1943 (85 & 82 yards)

Season

3—Leeland McElroy, Texas A&M, 1993; Terance Mathis, New Mexico, 1989; Willie Gault, Tennessee, 1980; Anthony Davis, Southern Cal, 1974; Stan Brown, Purdue, 1970; Forrest Hall, San Francisco, 1946

Career

6—Anthony Davis, Southern Cal, 1972-74

**Ismail is the only player in history to score twice in two games.*

SCORING A TOUCHDOWN ON TEAM'S OPENING KICKOFF OF TWO SEASONS

Season

Barry Sanders, Oklahoma St., 1988 (100 yards vs. Miami, Ohio, Sept. 10) & 1987 (100 yards vs. Tulsa, Sept. 5)

Total Kick Returns

(Combined Punt and Kickoff Returns)

MOST KICK RETURNS

Game

20—Milton Hill, Texas Tech vs. Centenary, Nov. 11, 1939 (20 punts, 110 yards)

Season

70—Keith Stephens, Louisville, 1986 (28 punts, 42 kickoffs, 1,162 yards); Dick Adams, Miami (Ohio), 1970 (55 punts, 15 kickoffs, 944 yards)

Career

199—Thomas Bailey, Auburn, 1991-94 (125 punts, 74 kickoffs, 2,690 yards); Tony James, Mississippi St., 1989-92 (121 punts, 78 kickoffs, 3,194 yards)

MOST YARDS ON KICK RETURNS

Game

248—Tyrone Watley, Iowa St. vs. Nebraska, Nov. 15, 1997 (10 returns)

Season

1,228—Steve Odom, Utah, 1972

Per-game record—116.2, Dion Johnson, East Caro., 1990 (1,046 yards, with 167 on punt returns and 879 on kickoff returns in 9 games)

Career

3,194—Tony James, Mississippi St., 1989-92 (1,332 on punts, 1,862 on kickoffs)

GAINING 1,000 YARDS ON PUNT RETURNS AND 1,000 YARDS ON KICKOFF RETURNS

Career

Tim Dwight, Iowa, 1994-97 (1,051 & 1,133); Thomas Bailey, Auburn, 1991-94 (1,170 & 1,520); Tony James, Mississippi St., 1989-92 (1,332 & 1,862); Willie Drewrey, West Va., 1981-84 (1,072 & 1,302); Anthony Carter, Michigan, 1979-82 (1,095 & 1,504); Devon Ford, Appalachian St., 1973-76 (1,197 & 1,761); Troy Slade, Duke, 1973-75 (1,021 & 1,757)

HIGHEST AVERAGE PER KICK RETURN (Min. 1.2 Punt Returns and 1.2 Kickoff Returns Per Game)

Season

27.2—Erroll Tucker, Utah, 1985 (40 for 1,087; 16 for 389 on punt returns, 24 for 698 on kickoff returns)

HIGHEST AVERAGE PER KICK RETURN (Min. 1.2 Punt Returns and 1.2 Kickoff Returns Per Game)

Career

22.0—Erroll Tucker, Utah, 1984-85 (79 for 1,741; 38 for 650 on punt returns, 41 for 1,091 on kickoff returns)

AVERAGING 20 YARDS EACH ON PUNT RETURNS AND KICKOFF RETURNS (Min. 1.2 Returns Per Game Each)

Season

By 7 players. Most recent: Lee Gissendaner, Northwestern, 1992 (21.8 on punt returns, 15 for 327; 22.4 on kickoff returns, 17 for 381)

MOST TOUCHDOWNS SCORED ON KICK RETURNS (Must Have at Least One Punt Return and One Kickoff Return)

Game

2—By 6 players. Most recent: Joe Rowe, Virginia vs. Central Mich., Sept. 7, 1996 (1 punt, 1 kickoff)

Season

5—Robert Woods, Grambling, 1977 (3 punts, 2 kickoffs); Pinky Rohm, LSU, 1937 (3 punts, 2 kickoffs)

Career

8—Johnny Rodgers, Nebraska, 1970-72 (7 punts, 1 kickoff); Cliff Branch, Colorado, 1970-71 (6 punts, 2 kickoffs)

WINNING BOTH PUNT RETURN AND KICKOFF RETURN CHAMPIONSHIPS

Season

Erroll Tucker, Utah, 1985

Career

Erroll Tucker, Utah, 1985; Ira Matthews, Wisconsin, kickoff returns (1976) and punt returns (1978)

All Runbacks

(Combined Interceptions, Punt Returns and Kickoff Returns)

SCORING MORE THAN ONE TOUCHDOWN IN EACH CATEGORY

Season

Erroll Tucker, Utah, 1985 (3 interceptions, 2 punt returns, 2 kickoff returns)

SCORING ONE TOUCHDOWN IN EACH CATEGORY

Season

Joe Crocker, Virginia, 1994; Scott Thomas, Air Force, 1985; Mark Haynes, Arizona St., 1974; Dick Harris, South Caro., 1970

HIGHEST AVERAGE PER RUNBACK
Season
(Min. 40 rets.) 28.3—Erroll Tucker, Utah, 1985 (6 for 216 on interceptions, 16 for 389 on punt returns, 24 for 698 on kickoff returns; total 46 for 1,303)

HIGHEST AVERAGE PER RUNBACK (At Least 7 Interceptions and Min. 1.3 Punt Returns and 1.3 Kickoff Returns Per Game)
Career
22.6—Erroll Tucker, Utah, 1984-85 (8 for 224 on interceptions, 38 for 650 on punt returns, 41 for 1,091 on kickoff returns; total 87 for 1,965)

MOST TOUCHDOWNS ON INTERCEPTIONS, PUNT RETURNS AND KICKOFF RETURNS (Must Have at Least One Touchdown in Each Category)
Season
7—Erroll Tucker, Utah, 1985 (3 interceptions, 2 punt returns, 2 kickoff returns)
Career
9—Allen Rossum, Notre Dame, 1994-97 (3 interceptions, 3 punt returns, 3 kickoff returns)

Opponent's Kicks Blocked

MOST OPPONENT'S PUNTS BLOCKED BY
Game
4—Ken Irvin, Memphis vs. Arkansas, Sept. 26, 1992 (4 punts)
Season
8—James Francis (LB), Baylor, 1989 (11 games); Jimmy Lisko, Arkansas St., 1975 (11 games)

MOST OPPONENT'S PAT KICKS BLOCKED BY
Season
5—Ray Farmer, Duke, 1993
Career
8—Ray Farmer, Duke, 1992-95

MOST OPPONENT'S TOTAL KICKS BLOCKED BY (Includes Punts, PAT Attempts, FG Attempts)
Game
4—Ken Irvin, Memphis vs. Arkansas, Sept. 26, 1992 (4 punts)
Career
19—James Ferebee, New Mexico St., 1978-81 (8 FG attempts, 6 PAT attempts, 5 punts)

MOST TOUCHDOWNS SCORED ON BLOCKED PUNTS
Game
2—Frank Staine-Pyne, Air Force vs. Hawaii, Nov. 1, 1997 (first half)
Season
3—Joe Wessel, Florida St., 1984

MOST FIELD GOAL ATTEMPTS BLOCKED BY
Quarter
2—Pat Larson, Wyoming vs. Fresno St., Nov. 18, 1995 (2nd quarter); Jerald Henry, Southern Cal vs. California, Oct. 22, 1994 (1st quarter, returned first one 60 yards for touchdown);
Game
2—Pat Larson, Wyoming vs. Fresno St., Nov. 18, 1995; Jerald Henry, Southern Cal vs. California, Oct. 22, 1994

All-Purpose Yards

(Yardage Gained From Rushing, Receiving and All Runbacks)

MOST PLAYS
Game
58—Tony Sands, Kansas vs. Missouri, Nov. 23, 1991 (58 rushes)
Season
432—Marcus Allen, Southern Cal, 1981 (403 rushes, 29 receptions)
Career
(3 yrs.) 1,034—Herschel Walker, Georgia, 1980-82 (994 rushes, 26 receptions, 14 kickoff returns)
(4 yrs.) 1,347—Steve Bartalo, Colorado St., 1983-86 (1,215 rushes, 132 receptions)

MOST YARDS GAINED
Quarter
305—Corey Dillon, Washington vs. San Jose St., Nov. 16, 1996 (1st Qtr., 222 rushing, 83 receiving)
Game
435—Brian Pruitt, Central Mich. vs. Toledo, Nov. 5, 1994 (356 rushing, 79 kickoff returns)
Season
3,250—Barry Sanders, Oklahoma St., 1988 (2,628 rushing, 106 receiving, 95 punt returns, 421 kickoff returns; 11 games)
Career
(3 yrs.) 5,749—Herschel Walker, Georgia, 1980-82 (5,259 rushing, 243 receiving, 247 kickoff returns; 1,034 plays)
(4 yrs.) 7,172—$Napoleon McCallum, Navy, 1981-85 (4,179 rushing, 796 receiving, 858 punt returns, 1,339 kickoff returns; 1,138 plays)

$ See page 6 for explanation.

MOST YARDS GAINED PER GAME
Season
295.5—Barry Sanders, Oklahoma St., 1988 (3,250 in 11 games)
Career
237.8—Ryan Benjamin, Pacific (Cal.), 1990-92 (5,706 in 24 games; 3,119 rushing, 1,063 receiving, 100 punt returns, 1,424 kickoff returns)

MOST YARDS GAINED BY A FRESHMAN
Game
422—Marshall Faulk, San Diego St. vs. Pacific (Cal.), Sept. 14, 1991 (386 rushing, 11 receiving, 25 kickoff returns)
Season
2,026—Terrell Willis, Rutgers, 1993 (1,261 rushing, 61 receiving, 704 kickoff returns; 234 plays)
Per-game record—184.8, Marshall Faulk, San Diego St., 1991 (1,663 in 9)

MOST SEASONS WITH 2,000 OR MORE YARDS
2—Troy Davis, Iowa St., 1995 (2,466) & 1996 (2,364); Ryan Benjamin, Pacific (Cal.), 1991 (2,995) & 1992 (2,597); Glyn Milburn, Stanford, 1990 (2,222) & 1992 (2,121); Sheldon Canley, San Jose St., 1989 (2,513) & 1990 (2,213); Chuck Weatherspoon, Houston, 1989 (2,391) & 1990 (2,038); Napoleon McCallum, Navy, 1983 (2,385) & 1985 (2,330); Howard Stevens, Randolph-Macon, 1968 (2,115) & Louisville, 1972 (2,132)

GAINED 1,000 YARDS RUSHING AND 1,000 YARDS RECEIVING
Career
By nine players. Most recent: Hines Ward, Georgia, 1994-97 (1,063 rushing & 1,965 receiving)

HIGHEST AVERAGE GAIN PER PLAY
Game
(Min. 300 yards, 25 plays) 16.8—Randy Gatewood, UNLV vs. Idaho, Sept. 17, 1994 (419 on 25)
Season
(Min. 1,500 yards, 100-124 plays) 18.5—Henry Bailey, UNLV, 1992 (1,883 on 102)
(Min. 1,500 yards, 125 plays) 16.5—Troy Edwards, Louisiana Tech, 1997 (2,144 on 130)
Career
(Min. 5,000 yards, 275-374 plays) 17.4—Anthony Carter, Michigan, 1979-82 (5,197 on 298)
(Min. 5,000 yards, 375 plays) 14.6—Terance Mathis, New Mexico, 1985-87, 1989 (6,691 on 457)

MOST YARDS GAINED BY TWO PLAYERS, SAME TEAM
Career
10,253—Marshall Faulk (5,595) & Darnay Scott (4,658), San Diego St., 1991-93

Scoring

MOST POINTS SCORED (By Non-Kickers)
Game
48—Howard Griffith, Illinois vs. Southern Ill., Sept. 22, 1990 (8 TDs on runs of 5, 51, 7, 41, 5, 18, 5, 3 yards)
Game vs. Major-College Opponent
44—Marshall Faulk, San Diego St. vs. Pacific (Cal.), Sept. 14, 1991 (7 TDs, 1 two-point conversion)
Season
234—Barry Sanders, Oklahoma St., 1988 (39 TDs in 11 games)
2 Yrs
312—Barry Sanders, Oklahoma St., 1987-88 (52 TDs in 22 games)
Career
(3 yrs.) 376—Marshall Faulk, San Diego St., 1991-93 (62 TDs, 2 two-point conversions)
(4 yrs.) 394—Anthony Thompson, Indiana, 1986-89 (65 TDs, 4 PATs)

MOST POINTS SCORED PER GAME
Season
21.3—Barry Sanders, Oklahoma St., 1988 (234 in 11)
2 Yrs
14.2—Barry Sanders, Oklahoma St., 1987-88 (312 in 22)
Career
12.1—Marshall Faulk, San Diego St., 1991-93 (376 in 31)

MOST POINTS SCORED BY A FRESHMAN
Game
44—Marshall Faulk, San Diego St. vs. Pacific (Cal.), Sept. 14, 1991 (7 TDs, 1 two-point conversion)
Season
140—Marshall Faulk, San Diego St., 1991 (23 TDs, 1 two-point conversion)
Also holds per-game record at 15.6 (140 in 9)

MOST TOUCHDOWNS SCORED
Quarter
4—Frank Moreau, Louisville vs. East Caro., Nov. 1, 1997 (all rushing, 2nd quarter); Corey Dillon, Washington vs. San Jose St., Nov. 16, 1996 (3 rushing, 1 receiving, 1st quarter); Howard Griffith, Illinois vs. Southern Ill., Sept. 22, 1990 (all rushing, 3rd quarter); Dick Felt, Brigham Young vs. San Jose St., Nov. 8, 1952 (all rushing, 4th quarter)
Game
8—Howard Griffith, Illinois vs. Southern Ill., Sept. 22, 1990 (all 8 by rushing on runs of 5, 51, 7, 41, 5, 18, 5, 3 yards)
Game vs. Major-College Opponent
7—Marshall Faulk, San Diego St. vs. Pacific (Cal.), Sept. 14, 1991; Arnold "Showboat" Boykin, Mississippi vs. Mississippi St., Dec. 1, 1951
Season
39—Barry Sanders, Oklahoma St., 1988 (11 games)
Also holds per-game record at 3.5 (39 in 11)
2 Yrs
52—Barry Sanders, Oklahoma St., 1987-88 (22 games)
Also holds per-game record at 2.4 (52 in 22)
Career
(3 yrs.) 62—Marshall Faulk, San Diego St., 1991-93 (57 rushing, 5 pass receptions)
Also holds per-game record at 2.0 (62 in 31)
(4 yrs.) 65—Anthony Thompson, Indiana, 1986-89 (64 rushing, 1 pass reception)

MOST TOUCHDOWNS SCORED IN TWO AND THREE CONSECUTIVE GAMES
2 Games
11—Kelvin Bryant, North Caro., 1981 (6 vs. East Caro., Sept. 12; 5 vs. Miami, Ohio, Sept. 19)
3 Games
15—Kelvin Bryant, North Caro., 1981 (6 vs. East Caro., Sept. 12; 5 vs. Miami, Ohio, Sept. 19; 4 vs. Boston College, Sept. 26)

MOST TOUCHDOWNS SCORED BY A FRESHMAN
Game
7—Marshall Faulk, San Diego St. vs. Pacific (Cal.), Sept. 14, 1991 (all by rushing)
Season
23—Marshall Faulk, San Diego St., 1991 (21 rushing, 2 pass receptions)
Also holds per-game record at 2.6 (23 in 9)

MOST CONSECUTIVE GAMES SCORING A TOUCHDOWN
Career
23—Bill Burnett, Arkansas (from Oct. 5, 1968, through Oct. 31, 1970; 47 touchdowns)

MOST GAMES SCORING A TOUCHDOWN
Season
12—Randy Moss, Marshall, 1997
Career
31—Ted Brown, North Caro. St., 1975-78; Tony Dorsett, Pittsburgh, 1973-76; Glenn Davis, Army, 1943-46

MOST GAMES SCORING TWO OR MORE TOUCHDOWNS
Season
11—Barry Sanders, Oklahoma St., 1988
Career
20—Anthony Thompson, Indiana, 1986-89

MOST CONSECUTIVE GAMES SCORING TWO OR MORE TOUCHDOWNS
Season
11—Barry Sanders, Oklahoma St., 1988
Career
13—Barry Sanders, Oklahoma St. (from Nov. 14, 1987, through 1988)

MOST GAMES SCORING THREE OR MORE TOUCHDOWNS
Season
9—Barry Sanders, Oklahoma St., 1988

MOST CONSECUTIVE GAMES SCORING THREE OR MORE TOUCHDOWNS
Season
5—Barry Sanders, Oklahoma St., 1988 (from Sept. 10 through Oct. 15); Paul Hewitt, San Diego St., 1987 (from Oct. 10 through Nov. 7)

MOST TOUCHDOWNS AND POINTS SCORED BY TWO PLAYERS, SAME TEAM
Season
54 and 324—Barry Sanders (39-234) & Hart Lee Dykes (15-90), Oklahoma St., 1988
Career
97 and 585—Glenn Davis (59-354) & Doc Blanchard (38-231), Army, 1943-46

PASSING FOR A TOUCHDOWN AND SCORING TOUCHDOWNS BY RUSHING AND RECEIVING
Game
By many players. Most recent: Jacquez Green, Florida vs. Auburn, Oct. 18, 1997

PASSING FOR A TOUCHDOWN AND SCORING ON A PASS RECEPTION AND PUNT RETURN
Game
By many players. Most recent: Tim Dwight, Iowa vs. Indiana, Oct. 25, 1997

PLAYER RETURNING A BLOCKED PUNT, FUMBLE RECOVERY AND INTERCEPTION RETURN FOR A TOUCHDOWN
Season
By many players. Most recent: Tim Curry, Air Force, 1997.

MOST EXTRA POINTS ATTEMPTED BY KICKING
Game
14—Terry Leiweke, Houston vs. Tulsa, Nov. 23, 1968 (13 made)
Season
71—Scott Bentley, Florida St., 1995 (67 made); Bart Edmiston, Florida, 1995 (71 made); Kurt Gunther, Brigham Young, 1980 (64 made)
Career
222—Derek Mahoney, Fresno St., 1990-93 (216 made)

MOST EXTRA POINTS MADE BY KICKING
Game
13—Derek Mahoney, Fresno St. vs. New Mexico, Oct. 5, 1991 (13 attempts); Terry Leiweke, Houston vs. Tulsa, Nov. 23, 1968 (14 attempts)
Season
71—Bart Edmiston, Florida, 1995 (71 attempts)
Per-game record—6.1, Scott Bentley, Florida St., 1995, and Cary Blanchard, Oklahoma St., 1988 (67 in 11)
Career
216—Derek Mahoney, Fresno St., 1990-93 (222 attempts)
Per-game record—5.3, Bart Edmiston, Florida, 1993-96 (137 in 26)

BEST PERFECT RECORD OF EXTRA POINTS MADE
Season
71 of 71—Bart Edmiston, Florida, 1995

HIGHEST PERCENTAGE OF EXTRA POINTS MADE
Career
(Min. 100 atts.) 100%—John Becksvoort, Tennessee, 1991-94 (161 of 161); David Browndyke, LSU, 1986-89 (109 of 109); Pete Stoyanovich, Indiana, 1985-88 (101 of 101); Van Tiffin, Alabama, 1983-86 (135 of 135)

MOST CONSECUTIVE EXTRA POINTS MADE
Game
13—Derek Mahoney, Fresno St. vs. New Mexico, Oct. 5, 1991 (13 attempts)
Season
71—Bart Edmiston, Florida, 1995 (71 attempts)
Career
161—John Becksvoort, Tennessee, 1991-94

MOST POINTS SCORED BY KICKING
Game
24—Mike Prindle, Western Mich. vs. Marshall, Sept. 29, 1984 (7 FGs, 3 PATs)
Season
131—Roman Anderson, Houston, 1989 (22 FGs, 65 PATs)
Also holds per-game record at 11.9 (131 in 11)
Career
423—Roman Anderson, Houston, 1988-91 (70 FGs, 213 PATs)
Also holds per-game record at 9.6 (423 in 44)

HIGHEST PERCENTAGE OF EXTRA POINTS AND FIELD GOALS MADE
Season
(Min. 30 PATs and 15 FGs made) 98.3%—Chuck Nelson, Washington, 1982 (34 of 34 PATs, 25 of 26 FGs)
(Min. 40 PATs and 20 FGs made) 97.3%—Chris Jacke, UTEP, 1988 (48 of 48 PATs, 25 of 27 FGs)
Career
(Min. 100 PATs and 50 FGs made) 93.3%—John Lee, UCLA, 1982-85 (116 of 117 PATs, 79 of 92 FGs)

MOST TWO-POINT ATTEMPTS MADE
Game
6—Jim Pilot, New Mexico St. vs. Hardin-Simmons, Nov. 25, 1961 (all by running, attempted 7)
Season
6—Howard Twilley, Tulsa, 1964 (all on pass receptions); Jim Pilot, New Mexico St., 1961 (all by running); Pat McCarthy, Holy Cross, 1960 (all by running)
Career
13—Pat McCarthy, Holy Cross, 1960-62 (all by running)

MOST SUCCESSFUL TWO-POINT PASSES
Season
12—John Hangartner, Arizona St., 1958 (attempted 21)
Career
19—Pat McCarthy, Holy Cross, 1960-62 (attempted 33)

Defensive Extra Points

MOST DEFENSIVE EXTRA POINTS RETURNED
Game
2—Corey Ivy, Oklahoma vs. California, Sept. 20, 1997

MOST DEFENSIVE EXTRA POINTS SCORED
Game
1—By many players
Season
1—By many players

LONGEST RETURN OF A DEFENSIVE EXTRA-POINT ATTEMPT
Game
100—Laymar Grant, Duke vs. Maryland, Oct. 26, 1996 (returned conversion pass attempt); Joe Crocker (CB), Virginia vs. North Caro. St., Nov. 25, 1994 (intercepted pass five yards deep in North Caro. St. end zone); William Price (CB), Kansas St. vs. Indiana St., Sept. 7, 1991 (intercepted pass three yards deep in Indiana St. end zone); Curt Newton (LB), Washington St. vs. Oregon St., Oct. 20, 1990 (returned conversion pass attempt from Washington St. goal line); Quintin Parker (DB), Illinois vs. Wisconsin, Oct. 28, 1989 (returned kick from Illinois goal line); Lee Ozmint (SS), Alabama vs. LSU, Nov. 11, 1989 (intercepted pass at Alabama goal line)

FIRST DEFENSIVE EXTRA-POINT ATTEMPT
Season
Thomas King (S), Southwestern La. vs. Cal St. Fullerton, Sept. 3, 1988 (returned blocked kick 6 yards)

MOST DEFENSIVE EXTRA-POINT KICKS BLOCKED
Game
2—Nigel Codrington (DB), Rice vs. Notre Dame, Nov. 5, 1988 (1 resulted in a score)
Also holds season record at 2

Fumble Returns

(Since 1992)

LONGEST FUMBLE RETURN FOR A TOUCHDOWN
100—Paul Rivers, Rutgers vs. Pittsburgh, Oct. 28, 1995

MOST FUMBLE RETURNS
Game
2—By many players.

MOST FUMBLE RETURNS RETURNED FOR TOUCHDOWNS
Game
2—Tyrone Carter, Minnesota vs. Syracuse, Sept. 21, 1996 (63 & 20 yards)

Field Goals

MOST FIELD GOALS ATTEMPTED
Game
9—Mike Prindle, Western Mich. vs. Marshall, Sept. 29, 1984 (7 made)
Season
38—Jerry DePoyster, Wyoming, 1966 (13 made)
Also holds per-game record at 3.8
Career
(3 yrs.) 93—Jerry DePoyster, Wyoming, 1965-67 (36 made)
Also holds per-game record at 3.1 (93 in 30)
(4 yrs.) 105—Philip Doyle, Alabama, 1987-90 (78 made); Luis Zendejas, Arizona St., 1981-84 (78 made)
Doyle holds per-game record at 2.4 (105 in 43)

MOST FIELD GOALS MADE
Quarter
4—By 4 players. Most recent: David Hardy, Texas A&M vs. Texas-Arlington, Sept. 18, 1982 (2nd)
Half
5—Dat Ly, New Mexico St. vs. Kansas, Oct. 1, 1988 (1st); Dale Klein, Nebraska vs. Missouri, Oct. 19, 1985 (1st)

Photo from Minnesota sports information

Minnesota's Tyrone Carter set a Division I-A record when he returned two fumble recoveries for touchdowns in a 1996 game vs. Syracuse.

Game
7—Dale Klein, Nebraska vs. Missouri, Oct. 19, 1985 (32, 22, 43, 44, 29, 43, 43 yards), 7 attempts; Mike Prindle, Western Mich. vs. Marshall, Sept. 29, 1984 (32, 44, 42, 23, 48, 41, 27 yards), 9 attempts
Season
29—John Lee, UCLA, 1984 (33 attempts)
2 Yrs
50—John Lee, UCLA, 1984-85 (57 attempts)
Career
80—Jeff Jaeger, Washington, 1983-86 (99 attempts)

MOST FIELD GOALS MADE PER GAME
Season
2.6—John Lee, UCLA, 1984 (29 in 11)
Career
1.8—John Lee, UCLA, 1982-85 (79 in 43)

BEST PERFECT RECORD OF FIELD GOALS MADE
Game
7 of 7—Dale Klein, Nebraska vs. Missouri, Oct. 19, 1985
Season
20 of 20—Marc Primanti, North Caro. St., 1996

MOST FIELD GOALS MADE BY A FRESHMAN
Game
6—*Mickey Thomas, Virginia Tech vs. Vanderbilt, Nov. 4, 1989 (6 attempts)
Season
23—Collin Mackie, South Caro., 1987 (30 attempts)
**Conventional-style kicker.*

HIGHEST PERCENTAGE OF FIELD GOALS MADE
Season
(Min. 15 atts.) 100.0%—Marc Primanti, North Caro. St., 1996 (20 of 20)
Career
(Min. 45-54 atts.) 87.8%—Bobby Raymond, Florida, 1983-84 (43 of 49)
(Min. 55 atts.) 85.9%—John Lee, UCLA, 1982-85 (79 of 92)

MOST CONSECUTIVE FIELD GOALS MADE
Season
25—Chuck Nelson, Washington, 1982 (first 25, missed last attempt of season vs. Washington St., Nov. 20)
Career
30—Chuck Nelson, Washington, 1981-82 (last 5 in 1981, from Southern Cal, Nov. 14, and first 25 in 1982, ending with last attempt vs. Washington St., Nov. 20)

MOST GAMES KICKING A FIELD GOAL
Career
40—Gary Gussman, Miami (Ohio), 1984-87 (in 44 games played)

MOST CONSECUTIVE GAMES KICKING A FIELD GOAL
19—Gary Gussman, Miami (Ohio), 1986-87; Larry Roach, Oklahoma St., 1983-84

MOST FIELD GOALS MADE, 60 YARDS OR MORE
Game
2—Tony Franklin, Texas A&M vs. Baylor, Oct. 16, 1976 (65 & 64 yards)
Season
3—Russell Erxleben, Texas, 1977 (67 vs. Rice, Oct. 1; 64 vs. Baylor, Oct. 16; 60 vs. Texas Tech, Oct. 29) (4 attempts)
Career
3—Russell Erxleben, Texas, 1975-78 (see Season Record above)

MOST FIELD GOALS ATTEMPTED, 60 YARDS OR MORE
Season
5—Tony Franklin, Texas A&M, 1976 (2 made)
Career
11—Tony Franklin, Texas A&M, 1975-78 (2 made)

MOST FIELD GOALS MADE, 50 YARDS OR MORE
Game
3—Sergio Lopez-Chavero, Wichita St. vs. Drake, Oct. 27, 1984 (54, 54, 51 yards); Jerry DePoyster, Wyoming vs. Utah, Oct. 8, 1966 (54, 54, 52 yards)
Season
8—Fuad Reveiz, Tennessee, 1982 (10 attempts)
Career
20—Jason Hanson, Washington St., 1988-91 (35 attempts)

MOST FIELD GOALS ATTEMPTED, 50 YARDS OR MORE
Season
17—Jerry DePoyster, Wyoming, 1966 (5 made)
Career
38—Tony Franklin, Texas A&M, 1975-78 (16 made)

HIGHEST PERCENTAGE OF FIELD GOALS MADE, 50 YARDS OR MORE
Season
(Min. 10 atts.) 80.0%—Fuad Reveiz, Tennessee, 1982 (8 of 10)
Career
(Min. 15 atts.) 60.9%—Max Zendejas, Arizona, 1982-85 (14 of 23)

MOST FIELD GOALS MADE, 40 YARDS OR MORE
Game
5—Alan Smith, Texas A&M vs. Arkansas St., Sept. 17, 1983 (44, 45, 42, 59, 57 yards)
Season
14—Chris Jacke, UTEP, 1988 (16 attempts)
Career
39—Jason Hanson, Washington St., 1988-91 (66 attempts) (19 of 31, 40-49 yards; 20 of 35, 50 or more yards)

MOST FIELD GOALS ATTEMPTED, 40 YARDS OR MORE
Season
25—Jerry DePoyster, Wyoming, 1966 (6 made)
Career
66—Jason Hanson, Washington St., 1988-91 (39 made)

HIGHEST PERCENTAGE OF FIELD GOALS MADE, 40 YARDS OR MORE
Season
(Min. 10 made) 90.9%—John Carney, Notre Dame, 1984 (10 of 11)
Career
(Min. 20 made) 69.4%—John Lee, UCLA, 1982-85 (25 of 36)

HIGHEST PERCENTAGE OF FIELD GOALS MADE, 40-49 YARDS
Season
(Min. 10 made) 100%—John Carney, Notre Dame, 1984 (10 of 10)
Career
(Min. 15 made) 82.6%—Jeff Jaeger, Washington, 1983-86 (19 of 23)

MOST CONSECUTIVE FIELD GOALS MADE, 40-49 YARDS
Career
12—John Carney, Notre Dame, 1984-85

HIGHEST PERCENTAGE OF FIELD GOALS MADE, UNDER 40 YARDS
Season
(Min. 16 made) 100%—Philip Doyle, Alabama, 1989 (19 of 19); Scott Slater, Texas A&M, 1986 (16 of 16); Bobby Raymond, Florida, 1984 (18 of 18); John Lee, UCLA, 1984 (16 of 16); Randy Pratt, California, 1983 (16 of 16); Paul Woodside, West Va., 1982 (23 of 23)
Career
(Min. 30-39 made) 97.0%—Bobby Raymond, Florida, 1983-84 (32 of 33)
(Min. 40 made) 96.4%—John Lee, UCLA, 1982-85 (54 of 56)

LONGEST AVERAGE DISTANCE FIELD GOALS MADE
Game
(Min. 4 made) 49.5—Jeff Heath, East Caro. vs. Texas-Arlington, Nov. 6, 1982 (58, 53, 42, 45 yards)
Season
(Min. 10 made) 50.9—Jason Hanson, Washington St., 1991 (10 made)
Career
(Min. 25 made) 42.4—Russell Erxleben, Texas, 1975-78 (49 made)

LONGEST AVERAGE DISTANCE FIELD GOALS ATTEMPTED
Season
(Min. 20 atts.) 51.2—Jason Hanson, Washington St., 1991 (22 attempts)
Career
(Min. 40 atts.) 44.7—Russell Erxleben, Texas, 1975-78 (78 attempts)

MOST TIMES KICKING TWO OR MORE FIELD GOALS IN A GAME
Season
10—Paul Woodside, West Va., 1982
Career
27—Kevin Butler, Georgia, 1981-84

MOST TIMES KICKING THREE OR MORE FIELD GOALS IN A GAME
Season
6—Joe Allison, Memphis, 1992; Luis Zendejas, Arizona St., 1983
Career
13—Luis Zendejas, Arizona St., 1981-84

MOST TIMES KICKING FOUR FIELD GOALS IN A GAME
Season
4—Matt Bahr, Penn St., 1978
Career
6—John Lee, UCLA, 1982-85
Also holds career record for most times kicking four or more field goals in a game at 8

LONGEST FIELD GOAL MADE
67—Joe Williams, Wichita St. vs. Southern Ill., Oct. 21, 1978; Steve Little, Arkansas vs. Texas, Oct. 15, 1977; Russell Erxleben, Texas vs. Rice, Oct. 1, 1977

LONGEST INDOOR FIELD GOAL MADE
62—Chip Lohmiller, Minnesota vs. Iowa, Nov. 22, 1986 (in Minnesota's Metrodome)

LONGEST FIELD GOAL MADE WITHOUT USE OF A KICKING TEE
62—Jason Hanson, Washington St. vs. UNLV, Sept. 28, 1991

LONGEST FIELD GOAL MADE BY A FRESHMAN
61—Kyle Bryant, Texas A&M vs. Southern Miss., Sept. 24, 1994

LONGEST FIELD GOAL MADE ON FIRST ATTEMPT OF CAREER
61—Ralf Mojsiejenko, Michigan St. vs. Illinois, Sept. 11, 1982

MOST FIELD GOALS MADE IN FIRST GAME OF CAREER
5—Jose Oceguera, Long Beach St. vs. Kansas St., Sept. 3, 1983 (5 attempts); Nathan Ritter, North Caro. St. vs. East Caro., Sept. 9, 1978 (6 attempts); Joe Liljenquist, Brigham Young vs. Colorado St., Sept. 20, 1969 (6 attempts)

MOST GAMES IN WHICH FIELD GOAL(S) PROVIDED THE WINNING MARGIN
Season
6—Henrik Mike-Mayer, Drake, 1981
Career
10—Jeff Ward, Texas, 1983-86; John Lee, UCLA, 1982-85; Dan Miller, Miami (Fla.), 1978-81

Team Records

SINGLE GAME—Offense

Total Offense

MOST PLAYS
112—Montana vs. Montana St., Nov. 1, 1952 (475 yards)

MOST PLAYS, BOTH TEAMS
196—San Diego St. (99) & North Texas (97), Dec. 4, 1971 (851 yards)

FEWEST PLAYS
12—Texas Tech vs. Centenary (La.), Nov. 11, 1939 (10 rushes, 2 passes, -1 yard)

FEWEST PLAYS, BOTH TEAMS
33—Texas Tech (12) & Centenary (La.) (21), Nov. 11, 1939 (28 rushes, 5 passes, 30 yards)

MOST YARDS GAINED
1,021—Houston vs. Southern Methodist, Oct. 21, 1989 (250 rushing, 771 passing, 86 plays)

MOST YARDS GAINED, BOTH TEAMS
1,563—Houston (827) & Texas Christian (736), Nov. 3, 1990 (187 plays)

FEWEST YARDS GAINED
Minus 47—Syracuse vs. Penn St., Oct. 18, 1947 (-107 rushing, gained 60 passing, 49 plays)

FEWEST YARDS GAINED, BOTH TEAMS
30—Texas Tech (-1) & Centenary (La.) (31), Nov. 11, 1939 (33 plays)

MOST YARDS GAINED BY A LOSING TEAM
736—Texas Christian vs. Houston, Nov. 3, 1990 (lost 56-35)

BOTH TEAMS GAINING 600 YARDS OR MORE
In 17 games. Most recent: Tennessee (695) & Kentucky (634), Nov. 22, 1997; Kent (615) & Central Fla. (612), Oct. 4, 1997 (154 plays); San Diego St. (670) & UNLV (627), Nov. 16, 1996; Nevada (727) & Louisiana Tech (607), Oct. 21, 1995 (180 plays); Idaho (707) & UNLV (614), Sept. 17, 1994 (181 plays); Houston (684) & Texas Tech (636), Nov. 30, 1991 (182 plays); Brigham Young (767) & San Diego St. (695), Nov. 16, 1991 (168 plays); San Jose St. (616) & Pacific (Cal.) (603), Oct. 19, 1991 (157 plays)

FEWEST YARDS GAINED BY A WINNING TEAM
10—North Caro. St. vs. Virginia, Sept. 30, 1944 (won 13-0)

HIGHEST AVERAGE GAIN PER PLAY (Min. 75 Plays)
11.9—Houston vs. Southern Methodist, Oct. 21, 1989 (86 for 1,021)

MOST TOUCHDOWNS SCORED BY RUSHING AND PASSING
15—Wyoming vs. Northern Colo., Nov. 5, 1949 (9 rushing, 6 passing)

Rushing

MOST RUSHES
99—Missouri vs. Colorado, Oct. 12, 1968 (421 yards)

MOST RUSHES, BOTH TEAMS
141—Colgate (82) & Bucknell (59), Nov. 6, 1971 (440 yards)

FEWEST RUSHES
5—Houston vs. Texas Tech, Nov. 25, 1989 (36 yards)

FEWEST RUSHES, BOTH TEAMS
28—Texas Tech (10) & Centenary (La.) (18), Nov. 11, 1939 (23 yards)

MOST YARDS GAINED
768—Oklahoma vs. Kansas St., Oct. 15, 1988 (72 rushes)

MOST YARDS GAINED, BOTH TEAMS
1,039—Lenoir-Rhyne (837) & Davidson (202), Oct. 11, 1975 (111 rushes)

MOST YARDS GAINED, BOTH TEAMS, MAJOR-COLLEGE OPPONENTS
956—Oklahoma (711) & Kansas St. (245), Oct. 23, 1971 (111 rushes)

FEWEST YARDS GAINED
Minus 109—Northern Ill. vs. Toledo, Nov. 11, 1967 (33 rushes)

FEWEST YARDS GAINED, BOTH TEAMS
Minus 24—San Jose St. (-102) & UTEP (78), Oct. 22, 1966 (75 rushes)

MOST YARDS GAINED WITHOUT LOSS
677—Nebraska vs. New Mexico St., Sept. 18, 1982 (78 rushes)

MOST YARDS GAINED BY A LOSING TEAM
525—Air Force vs. New Mexico, Nov. 2, 1991 (70 rushes, lost 34-32)

HIGHEST AVERAGE GAIN PER RUSH (Min. 50 Rushes)
11.9—Alabama vs. Virginia Tech, Oct. 27, 1973 (63 for 748)

MOST PLAYERS ON ONE TEAM EACH GAINING 100 YARDS OR MORE
4—Army vs. Montana, Nov. 17, 1984 (Doug Black 183, Nate Sassaman 155, Clarence Jones 130, Jarvis Hollingsworth 124); Alabama vs. Virginia Tech, Oct. 27, 1973 (Jimmy Taylor 142, Wilbur Jackson 138, Calvin Culliver 127, Richard Todd 102); Texas vs. Southern Methodist, Nov. 1, 1969 (Jim Bertelsen 137, Steve Worster 137, James Street 121, Ted Koy 111); Arizona St. vs. Arizona, Nov. 10, 1951 (Bob Tarwater 140, Harley Cooper 123, Duane Morrison 118, Buzz Walker 113)

MOST TOUCHDOWNS SCORED BY RUSHING
12—UTEP vs. New Mexico St., Nov. 25, 1948

Passing

MOST PASSES ATTEMPTED
81—Houston vs. Southern Methodist, Oct. 20, 1990 (completed 53)

MOST PASSES ATTEMPTED, BOTH TEAMS
135—Texas Christian (79) & Houston (56), Nov. 3, 1990 (completed 81)

FEWEST PASSES ATTEMPTED
0—By many teams. Most recent: Ohio vs. Akron, Oct. 25, 1997 (61 rushes; won 21-17)

FEWEST PASSES ATTEMPTED, BOTH TEAMS
1—Michigan St. (0) & Maryland (1), Oct. 20, 1944 (not completed)

MOST PASSES ATTEMPTED WITHOUT COMPLETION
18—West Va. vs. Temple, Oct. 18, 1946

MOST PASSES ATTEMPTED WITHOUT INTERCEPTION
72—Houston vs. Texas Christian, Nov. 4, 1989 (completed 47)

MOST PASSES ATTEMPTED WITHOUT INTERCEPTION, BOTH TEAMS
114—Illinois (67) & Purdue (47), Oct. 12, 1985 (completed 67)

MOST CONSECUTIVE PASSES ATTEMPTED WITHOUT A RUSHING PLAY
32—North Caro. St. vs. Duke, Nov. 11, 1989 (3rd & 4th quarters, completed 16)

MOST PASSES COMPLETED
55—Wake Forest vs. Duke, Oct. 28, 1995 (attempted 78)

MOST PASSES COMPLETED, BOTH TEAMS
81—Texas Christian (44) & Houston (37), Nov. 3, 1990 (attempted 135)

BEST PERFECT GAME (1.000 Pct.)
11 of 11—North Caro. vs. William & Mary, Oct. 5, 1991; Air Force vs. Northwestern, Sept. 17, 1988; Oregon St. vs. UCLA, Oct. 2, 1971; Southern Cal vs. Washington, Oct. 9, 1965

HIGHEST PERCENTAGE OF PASSES COMPLETED
(Min. 15-24 comps.) 95.0%—Mississippi vs. Tulane, Nov. 6, 1982 (19 of 20)
(Min. 25-34 comps.) 92.6%—UCLA vs. Washington, Oct. 29, 1983 (25 of 27)
(Min. 35 comps.) 87.0%—South Caro. vs. Mississippi St., Oct. 14, 1995 (40 of 46)

HIGHEST PERCENTAGE OF PASSES COMPLETED, BOTH TEAMS (Min. 40 Completions)
84.6%—UCLA & Washington, Oct. 29, 1983 (44 of 52)

MOST PASSES HAD INTERCEPTED
10—California vs. UCLA, Oct. 21, 1978 (52 attempts); Detroit vs. Oklahoma St., Nov. 28, 1942

MOST YARDS GAINED
771—Houston vs. Southern Methodist, Oct. 21, 1989 (completed 40 of 61)

MOST YARDS GAINED, BOTH TEAMS
1,253—Texas Christian (690) & Houston (563), Nov. 3, 1990 (135 attempts)

FEWEST YARDS GAINED, BOTH TEAMS
Minus 13—North Caro. (-7 on 1 of 3 attempts) & Pennsylvania (-6 on 2 of 12 attempts), Nov. 13, 1943

MOST YARDS GAINED PER ATTEMPT
(Min. 30-39 atts.) 15.5—Mississippi St. vs. Tulane, Oct. 22, 1994 (30 for 466)
(Min. 40 atts.) 15.9—UTEP vs. North Texas, Sept. 18, 1965 (40 for 634)

MOST YARDS GAINED PER COMPLETION
(Min. 15-24 comps.) 31.9—UTEP vs. New Mexico, Oct. 28, 1967 (16 for 510)
(Min. 25 comps.) 25.4—UTEP vs. North Texas, Sept. 18, 1965 (25 for 634)

MOST TOUCHDOWN PASSES
11—Houston vs. Eastern Wash., Nov. 17, 1990

MOST TOUCHDOWN PASSES, MAJOR-COLLEGE OPPONENTS
10—Houston vs. Southern Methodist, Oct. 21, 1989; San Diego St. vs. New Mexico St., Nov. 15, 1969

MOST TOUCHDOWN PASSES, BOTH TEAMS
14—Houston (11) & Eastern Wash. (3), Nov. 17, 1990

MOST TOUCHDOWN PASSES, BOTH TEAMS, MAJOR-COLLEGE OPPONENTS
13—San Diego St. (10) & New Mexico St. (3), Nov. 15, 1969

Punting

MOST PUNTS
39—Texas Tech vs. Centenary (La.), Nov. 11, 1939 (1,377 yards)
38—Centenary (La.) vs. Texas Tech, Nov. 11, 1939 (1,248 yards)

MOST PUNTS, BOTH TEAMS
77—Texas Tech (39) & Centenary (La.) (38), Nov. 11, 1939 (2,625 yards) (The game was played in a heavy downpour in Shreveport, Louisiana. Forty-two punts were returned, 19 went out of bounds, 10 were downed, 1 went into the end zone for a touchback, 4 were blocked and 1 was fair caught. Sixty-seven punts [34 by Texas Tech and 33 by Centenary] occurred on first-down plays, including 22 consecutively in the third and fourth quarters. The game was a scoreless tie.)

FEWEST PUNTS
0—By many teams. Most recent: Nebraska vs. Akron, Aug. 30, 1997 (won 59-14)

FEWEST PUNTS BY A LOSING TEAM
0—By many teams. Most recent: Idaho vs. Southwest Tex. St., Sept. 28, 1996 (lost 27-21)

HIGHEST AVERAGE PER PUNT
(Min. 5-9 punts) 60.4—Brigham Young vs. Wyoming, Oct. 8, 1983 (5 for 302)
(Min. 10 punts) 53.6—Oklahoma St. vs. Colorado, Nov. 13, 1971 (10 for 536)

HIGHEST AVERAGE PER PUNT, BOTH TEAMS (Min. 10 Punts)
55.3—Brigham Young & Wyoming, Oct. 8, 1983 (11 for 608)

Punt Returns

MOST PUNT RETURNS
22—Texas Tech vs. Centenary (La.), Nov. 11, 1939 (112 yards)

MOST PUNT RETURNS, BOTH TEAMS
42—Texas Tech (22) & Centenary (La.) (20), Nov. 11, 1939 (233 yards)

MOST YARDS ON PUNT RETURNS
319—Texas A&M vs. North Texas, Sept. 21, 1946 (10 returns)

HIGHEST AVERAGE GAIN PER RETURN (Min. 5 Returns)
45.0—Georgia vs. South Caro., Sept. 2, 1995 (5 for 225)

MOST TOUCHDOWNS SCORED ON PUNT RETURNS
3—Notre Dame vs. Pittsburgh, Nov. 16, 1996; Arizona St. vs. Pacific (Cal.), Nov. 15, 1975; Holy Cross vs. Brown, Sept. 21, 1974; LSU vs. Mississippi, Dec. 5, 1970; Wichita St. vs. Northern St., Oct. 22, 1949; Wisconsin vs. Iowa, Nov. 8, 1947

Kickoff Returns

MOST KICKOFF RETURNS
14—Arizona St. vs. Nevada, Oct. 12, 1946 (290 yards)

MOST YARDS ON KICKOFF RETURNS
295—Cincinnati vs. Memphis, Oct. 30, 1971 (8 returns)

HIGHEST AVERAGE GAIN PER RETURN (Min. 6 Returns)
46.2—Southern Cal vs. Washington St., Nov. 7, 1970 (6 for 277)

MOST TOUCHDOWNS SCORED ON KICKOFF RETURNS
2—By many teams. Most recent: Texas A&M vs. Rice, Oct. 23, 1993; Brigham Young vs. Air Force, Nov. 11, 1989; Notre Dame vs. Michigan, Sept. 16, 1989; New Mexico St. vs. Drake, Oct. 15, 1983 (consecutive returns)

TOUCHDOWNS SCORED ON BACK-TO-BACK KICKOFF RETURNS, BOTH TEAMS
2—By many teams. Most recent: Wisconsin & Northern Ill., Sept. 14, 1985

Total Kick Returns

(Combined Punt and Kickoff Returns)

MOST YARDS ON KICK RETURNS
376—Florida St. vs. Virginia Tech, Nov. 16, 1974 (9 returns)

HIGHEST AVERAGE GAIN PER RETURN (Min. 7 Returns)
41.8—Florida St. vs. Virginia Tech, Nov. 16, 1974 (9 for 376)

Scoring

MOST POINTS SCORED
103—Wyoming vs. Northern Colo. (0), Nov. 5, 1949 (15 TDs, 13 PATs)

MOST POINTS SCORED AGAINST A MAJOR-COLLEGE OPPONENT
100—Houston vs. Tulsa (6), Nov. 23, 1968 (14 TDs, 13 PATs, 1 FG)

MOST POINTS SCORED, BOTH TEAMS
124—Oklahoma (82) & Colorado (42), Oct. 4, 1980

MOST POINTS SCORED BY A LOSING TEAM
56—Purdue vs. Minnesota (59), Oct. 9, 1993

MOST POINTS, BOTH TEAMS IN A TIE GAME
104—Brigham Young (52) & San Diego St. (52), Nov. 16, 1991

MOST POINTS SCORED IN ONE QUARTER
49—Fresno St. vs. New Mexico, Oct. 5, 1991 (2nd quarter); Davidson vs. Furman, Sept. 27, 1969 (2nd quarter); Houston vs. Tulsa, Nov. 23, 1968 (4th quarter)

MOST POINTS SCORED IN ONE HALF
76—Houston vs. Tulsa, Nov. 23, 1968 (2nd half)

MOST TOUCHDOWNS SCORED
15—Wyoming vs. Northern Colo., Nov. 5, 1949 (9 rushing, 6 passing)

MOST TOUCHDOWNS SCORED, BOTH TEAMS
18—Oklahoma (12) & Colorado (6), Oct. 4, 1980

MOST EXTRA POINTS MADE BY KICKING
13—Fresno St. vs. New Mexico, Oct. 5, 1991 (attempted 13); Houston vs. Tulsa, Nov. 23, 1968 (attempted 14); Wyoming vs. Northern Colo., Nov. 5, 1949 (attempted 15)

MOST TWO-POINT ATTEMPTS SCORED
7—Pacific (Cal.) vs. San Diego St., Nov. 22, 1958 (attempted 9)

MOST DEFENSIVE EXTRA-POINT ATTEMPTS
2—Oklahoma vs. California, Sept. 20, 1997 (2 kick returns; 1 scored); Northern Ill. vs. Akron, Nov. 3, 1990 (2 interception returns); Rice vs. Notre Dame, Nov. 5, 1988 (2 kick returns; 1 scored)

MOST DEFENSIVE EXTRA POINTS SCORED
1—By many teams

MOST FIELD GOALS MADE
7—Nebraska vs. Missouri, Oct. 19, 1985 (attempted 7); Western Mich. vs. Marshall, Sept. 29, 1984 (attempted 9)

MOST FIELD GOALS MADE, BOTH TEAMS
9—Southwestern La. (5) & Central Mich. (4), Sept. 9, 1989 (attempted 11)

MOST FIELD GOALS ATTEMPTED
9—Western Mich. vs. Marshall, Sept. 29, 1984 (made 7)

MOST FIELD GOALS ATTEMPTED, BOTH TEAMS
12—Clemson (6) & Georgia (6), Sept. 17, 1983 (made 6)

MOST FIELD GOALS MISSED
7—LSU vs. Florida, Nov. 25, 1972 (attempted 8)

First Downs

MOST FIRST DOWNS
44—Nebraska vs. Utah St., Sept. 7, 1991 (33 rush, 10 pass, 1 penalty)

MOST FIRST DOWNS, BOTH TEAMS
72—New Mexico (37) & San Diego St. (35), Sept. 27, 1986

FEWEST FIRST DOWNS BY A WINNING TEAM
0—Michigan vs. Ohio St., Nov. 25, 1950 (won 9-3); North Caro. St. vs. Virginia, Sept. 30, 1944 (won 13-0)

MOST FIRST DOWNS BY RUSHING
36—Nebraska vs. New Mexico St., Sept. 18, 1982

MOST FIRST DOWNS BY PASSING
30—Brigham Young vs. Colorado St., Nov. 7, 1981; Tulsa vs. Idaho St., Oct. 7, 1967

Fumbles

MOST FUMBLES
17—Wichita St. vs. Florida St., Sept. 20, 1969 (lost 10)

MOST FUMBLES, BOTH TEAMS
27—Wichita St. (17) & Florida St. (10), Sept. 20, 1969 (lost 17)

MOST FUMBLES LOST
10—Wichita St. vs. Florida St., Sept. 20, 1969 (17 fumbles)

MOST FUMBLES LOST, BOTH TEAMS
17—Wichita St. (10) & Florida St. (7), Sept. 20, 1969 (27 fumbles)

MOST FUMBLES LOST IN A QUARTER
5—San Diego St. vs. California, Sept. 18, 1982 (1st quarter); East Caro. vs. Southwestern La., Sept. 13, 1980 (3rd quarter on 5 consecutive possessions)

Penalties

MOST PENALTIES AGAINST
24—San Jose St. vs. Fresno St., Oct. 4, 1986 (199 yards)

MOST PENALTIES, BOTH TEAMS
36—San Jose St. (24) & Fresno St. (12), Oct. 4, 1986 (317 yards)

FEWEST PENALTIES, BOTH TEAMS
0—By many teams. Most recent: Army & Navy, Dec. 6, 1986

MOST YARDS PENALIZED
238—Arizona St. vs. UTEP, Nov. 11, 1961 (13 penalties)

MOST YARDS PENALIZED, BOTH TEAMS
421—Grambling (16 for 216 yards) & Texas Southern (17 for 205 yards), Oct. 29, 1977

Turnovers

(Number of Times Losing the Ball on Interceptions and Fumbles)

MOST TURNOVERS LOST
13—Georgia vs. Georgia Tech, Dec. 1, 1951 (8 interceptions, 5 fumbles)

MOST TURNOVERS, BOTH TEAMS
20—Wichita St. (12) & Florida St. (8), Sept. 20, 1969 (17 fumbles, 3 interceptions)

MOST TOTAL PLAYS WITHOUT A TURNOVER (Rushes, Passes, All Runbacks)
110—Baylor vs. Rice, Nov. 13, 1976; California vs. San Jose St., Oct. 5, 1968 (also did not fumble)

MOST TOTAL PLAYS WITHOUT A TURNOVER, BOTH TEAMS
184—Arkansas (93) & Texas A&M (91), Nov. 2, 1968

MOST TOTAL PLAYS WITHOUT A TURNOVER OR A FUMBLE, BOTH TEAMS
158—Stanford (88) & Oregon (70), Nov. 2, 1957

MOST TURNOVERS BY A WINNING TEAM
11—Purdue vs. Illinois, Oct. 2, 1943 (9 fumbles, 2 interceptions; won 40-21)

MOST PASSES HAD INTERCEPTED BY A WINNING TEAM
7—Florida vs. Kentucky, Sept. 11, 1993 (52 attempts; won 24-20); Pittsburgh vs. Army, Nov. 15, 1980 (54 attempts; won 45-7)

MOST FUMBLES LOST BY A WINNING TEAM
9—Arizona St. vs. Utah, Oct. 14, 1972 (10 fumbles; won 59-48); Purdue vs. Illinois, Oct. 2, 1943 (10 fumbles; won 40-21)

Overtimes

MOST OVERTIME PERIODS
4—North Ala. (Div. II) (48) vs. Southwestern La. (42), Oct. 11, 1997; Georgia (56) vs. Auburn (49), Nov. 16, 1996; California (56) vs. Arizona (55), Nov. 2, 1996

MOST POINTS SCORED IN OVERTIME PERIODS
28—Georgia (56) vs. Auburn (49), Nov. 16, 1996 (4 overtime periods)

MOST POINTS SCORED IN OVERTIME PERIODS, BOTH TEAMS
49—Georgia (28) vs. Auburn (21), Nov. 16, 1996 (4 overtime periods; Georgia won, 56-49

LARGEST WINNING MARGIN IN OVERTIME
13—Arizona St. (48) vs. Southern Cal (35), Oct. 19, 1996 (2 overtime periods)

CONSECUTIVE OVERTIME GAMES (SEASON)
2—Cincinnati (38) vs. Houston (41), Oct. 18, 1997 & Cincinnati (34) vs. Miami (Ohio) (31), Oct. 25, 1997; Oklahoma St. (50) vs. Missouri (51), Oct. 25, 1997 & Oklahoma St. (25) vs. Texas A&M (28), Nov. 1, 1997; Southern Cal (41) vs. UCLA (48), Nov. 23, 1996 & Southern Cal (27) vs. Notre Dame (20), Nov. 30, 1996

CONSECUTIVE OVERTIME GAMES WITH SAME OPPONENT
2—Cincinnati (34) vs. Miami (Ohio) (31), Oct. 25, 1997 & Cincinnati (30) vs. Miami (Ohio) (23), Sept. 28, 1996; Oregon (43) vs. Fresno St. (40), Sept. 20, 1997 & Oregon (30) vs. Fresno St. (27), Aug. 31, 1996; Missouri (51) vs. Oklahoma St. (50), Oct. 25, 1997 & Missouri (35) vs. Oklahoma St. (28), Oct. 26, 1996; Arizona (41) vs. California (38), Nov. 15, 1997 & Arizona (55) vs. California (56), Nov. 2, 1996

SINGLE GAME—Defense

Total Defense

FEWEST PLAYS ALLOWED
12—Centenary (La.) vs. Texas Tech, Nov. 11, 1939 (10 rushes, 2 passes; -1 yard)

FEWEST YARDS ALLOWED
Minus 47—Penn St. vs. Syracuse, Oct. 18, 1947 (-107 rushing, 60 passing; 49 plays)

MOST YARDS ALLOWED
1,021—Southern Methodist vs. Houston, Oct. 21, 1989 (250 rushing, 771 passing)

Rushing Defense

FEWEST RUSHES ALLOWED
5—Texas Tech vs. Houston, Nov. 25, 1989 (36 yards)

FEWEST RUSHING YARDS ALLOWED
Minus 109—Toledo vs. Northern Ill., Nov. 11, 1967 (33 rushes)

Pass Defense

FEWEST ATTEMPTS ALLOWED
0—By many teams. Most recent: Colorado vs. Oklahoma, Nov. 15, 1986

FEWEST COMPLETIONS ALLOWED
0—By many teams. Most recent: Brigham Young vs. Rice, Nov. 9, 1996 (5 attempts)

LOWEST COMPLETION PERCENTAGE ALLOWED (Min. 10 Attempts)
.000—San Jose St. vs. Cal St. Fullerton, Oct. 10, 1992 (0 of 11 attempts); Temple vs. West Va., Oct. 18, 1946 (0 of 18 attempts); North Caro. vs. Penn St., Oct. 2, 1943 (0 of 12 attempts)

FEWEST YARDS ALLOWED
Minus 16—Va. Military vs. Richmond, Oct. 5, 1957 (2 completions)

MOST PASSES INTERCEPTED BY
11—Brown vs. Rhode Island, Oct. 8, 1949 (136 yards)

MOST PASSES INTERCEPTED BY AGAINST A MAJOR-COLLEGE OPPONENT
10—UCLA vs. California, Oct. 21, 1978; Oklahoma St. vs. Detroit, Nov. 28, 1942

MOST PASSES INTERCEPTED BY A LOSING TEAM
7—Kentucky vs. Florida, Sept. 11, 1993 (52 attempts)

MOST YARDS ON INTERCEPTION RETURNS
240—Kentucky vs. Mississippi, Oct. 1, 1949 (6 returns)

MOST TOUCHDOWNS ON INTERCEPTION RETURNS
4—Houston vs. Texas, Nov. 7, 1987 (198 yards; 3 TDs in the fourth quarter)

First Downs

FEWEST FIRST DOWNS ALLOWED
0—By many teams. Most recent: North Caro. St. vs. Western Caro., Sept. 1, 1990

Opponent's Kicks Blocked

MOST OPPONENT'S PUNTS BLOCKED
4—Memphis vs. Arkansas, Sept. 26, 1992 (10 attempts); Michigan vs. Ohio St., Nov. 25, 1950; Southern Methodist vs. Texas-Arlington, Sept. 30, 1944

MOST OPPONENT'S PUNTS BLOCKED, ONE QUARTER
3—Purdue vs. Northwestern, Nov. 11, 1989 (4 attempts)

BLOCKED OPPONENTS' FIELD GOAL, PUNT AND EXTRA-POINT KICK
Oregon St. blocked each type of kick against Southern Cal, Sept. 14, 1996.

MOST OPPONENT'S FIELD GOALS BLOCKED, ONE QUARTER
2—Southern Cal vs. California, Oct. 22, 1994

Turnovers Gained

(Number of Times Gaining the Ball on Interceptions and Fumbles)

MOST TURNOVERS GAINED
13—Georgia Tech vs. Georgia, Dec. 1, 1951 (8 interceptions, 5 fumbles)

MOST CONSECUTIVE OPPONENT'S SERIES RESULTING IN TURNOVERS
7—Florida vs. Florida St., Oct. 7, 1972 (3 interceptions, 4 fumbles lost; first seven series of the game)

Fumble Returns

(Since 1992)

MOST TOUCHDOWNS ON FUMBLE RETURNS
2—Arizona St. vs. Washington St., Nov. 1, 1997; Florida vs. Southwestern La., Aug. 31, 1996; Minnesota vs. Syracuse, Sept. 21, 1996; Iowa vs. Minnesota, Nov. 19, 1994; Duke vs. Wake Forest, Oct. 22, 1994 (Both occurred in first quarter); Arizona vs. Illinois, Sept. 18, 1993; Toledo vs. Arkansas St., Sept. 5, 1992

LONGEST RETURN OF A FUMBLE
100—Rutgers vs. Pittsburgh, Oct. 28, 1995

Defensive Extra Points

MOST DEFENSIVE EXTRA POINTS SCORED AGAINST
1—By many teams. Most recent: Nevada vs. Utah St., Nov. 4, 1995 (interception return)

MOST DEFENSIVE EXTRA-POINT ATTEMPTS AGAINST
2—California vs. Oklahoma, Sept. 20, 1997 (2 kick returns; 1 scored); Akron vs. Northern Ill., Nov. 3, 1990 (2 interception returns); Notre Dame vs. Rice, Nov. 5, 1988 (2 blocked kick returns, 1 scored)

Safeties

MOST SAFETIES BY A DEFENSE
3—Arizona St. vs. Nebraska, Sept. 21, 1996

SEASON—Offense

Total Offense

MOST YARDS GAINED PER GAME
624.9—Houston, 1989 (6,874 in 11)

MOST YARDS GAINED
6,874—Houston, 1989 (11 games)

HIGHEST AVERAGE GAIN PER PLAY
7.9—Army, 1945 (526 for 4,164)

GAINING 300 YARDS OR MORE PER GAME RUSHING AND 200 YARDS OR MORE PER GAME PASSING
Arizona St., 1973 (310.2 rushing, 255.3 passing); Houston, 1968 (361.7 rushing, 200.3 passing)

MOST PLAYS PER GAME
92.4—Notre Dame, 1970 (924 in 10)

MOST TOUCHDOWNS RUSHING AND PASSING
84—Nebraska, 1983
Also holds per-game record at 7.0

Rushing

MOST YARDS GAINED PER GAME
472.4—Oklahoma, 1971 (5,196 in 11)

HIGHEST AVERAGE GAIN PER RUSH
7.6—Army, 1945 (424 for 3,238)

HIGHEST AVERAGE GAIN PER RUSH (Min. 500 Rushes)
7.0—Nebraska, 1995 (627 for 4,398)

MOST RUSHES PER GAME
73.9—Oklahoma, 1974 (813 in 11)

MOST TOUCHDOWNS RUSHING PER GAME
5.5—Nebraska, 1997 (66 in 12)

Passing

MOST YARDS GAINED PER GAME
511.3—Houston, 1989 (5,624 in 11)

MOST YARDS GAINED
5,624—Houston, 1989 (11 games)

HIGHEST AVERAGE GAIN PER ATTEMPT (Min. 350 Attempts)
10.9—Brigham Young, 1989 (433 for 4,732)

HIGHEST AVERAGE GAIN PER COMPLETION
(Min. 100-174 comps.) 19.1—Houston, 1968 (105 for 2,003)
(Min. 175-224 comps.) 18.0—Grambling, 1977 (187 for 3,360)
(Min. 225 comps.) 17.1—Florida, 1996 (234 for 4,007)

MOST PASSES ATTEMPTED PER GAME
63.1—Houston, 1989 (694 in 11)

MOST PASSES COMPLETED PER GAME
39.4—Houston, 1989 (434 in 11)

HIGHEST PERCENTAGE COMPLETED (Min. 150 Attempts)
70.8%—Long Beach St., 1985 (323 of 456)

LOWEST PERCENTAGE HAD INTERCEPTED
(Min. 300-399 atts.) 1.0%—Tennessee, 1995 (4 of 391)
(Min. 400 atts.) 1.2%—Southern Cal, 1993 (5 of 432)

MOST TOUCHDOWN PASSES PER GAME
5.0—Houston, 1989 (55 in 11)

MOST TOUCHDOWN PASSES
55—Houston, 1989 (11 games)

FEWEST TOUCHDOWN PASSES
0—By 6 teams since 1975. Most recent: Vanderbilt, 1993 (11 games, 157 attempts)

HIGHEST PASSING EFFICIENCY RATING POINTS (Min. 150 Attempts)
174.5—Brigham Young, 1989 (433 attempts, 279 completions, 15 interceptions, 4,732 yards, 33 TD passes)

A TEAM WITH A 3,000-YARD PASSER, 1,000-YARD RECEIVER AND 1,000-YARD RUSHER
13 teams. Most recent: Nevada, 1997 (John Dutton [3,526 passer], Chris Lemon [1,055 rusher] and Geoff Noisy [1,184 receiver] and Trevor Insley [1,151 receiver]); Tennessee, 1997 (Peyton Manning [3,819 passer], Jamal Lewis [1,364 rusher] and Marcus Nash [1,170 receiver]); Nevada, 1995 (Mike Maxwell [3,611 passer], Alex Van Dyke [1,854 receiver] and Kim Minor [1,052 rusher]); New Mexico St., 1995 (Cody Ledbetter [3,501 passer], Lucious Davis [1,018 receiver] and Denvis Manns [1,120 rusher]); Ohio St., 1995 (Bobby Hoying [3,023 passer], Terry Glenn [1,316 receiver] and Eddie George [1,826 rusher]); San Diego St., 1995 (Billy Blanton [3,300 passer], Will Blackwell [1,207 receiver], Az Hakim [1,022 receiver] and George Jones [1,842 rusher])

(Note: Nevada, 1997 and San Diego St., 1995, are the only teams to have two 1,000-yard receivers.)

A TEAM WITH TWO 1,000-YARD RECEIVERS
Nevada, 1997 (Geoff Noisy 1,184 & Trevor Insley 1,151); Nevada, 1996 (Geoff Noisy 1,435 & Damond Wilkins 1,121); Florida, 1995 (Chris Doering 1,045 & Ike Hilliard 1,008); Florida St., 1995 (E. G. Green 1,007 & Andre Cooper 1,002); San Diego St., 1995 (Will Blackwell 1,207 & Az Hakim 1,022); Nevada, 1993 (Bryan Reeves 1,362 & Michael Stephens 1,062); Colorado, 1992 (Charles Johnson 1,149 & Michael Westbrook

1,060); San Diego St., 1990 (Patrick Rowe 1,392 & Dennis Arey 1,118); Brigham Young, 1990 (Andy Boyce 1,241 & Chris Smith 1,156); Houston, 1988 (Jason Phillips 1,444 & James Dixon 1,103)

A TEAM WITH THE NO. 1 & NO. 2 RECEIVERS
Houston, 1988 (Jason Phillips, No. 1, 9.82 catches per game & James Dixon, No. 2, 9.27 catches per game)

MOST 100-YARD RECEIVING GAMES IN A SEASON, ONE TEAM
19—San Diego St., 1990 (Patrick Rowe 9, Dennis Arey 8 & Jimmy Raye 2)

Punting

MOST PUNTS PER GAME
13.9—Tennessee, 1937 (139 in 10)

FEWEST PUNTS PER GAME
2.0—Nevada, 1948 (18 in 9)

HIGHEST PUNTING AVERAGE
50.6—Brigham Young, 1983 (24 for 1,215 yards)

HIGHEST PUNTING AVERAGE (Min. 40 Punts)
47.6—Vanderbilt, 1984 (59 for 2,810)

HIGHEST NET PUNTING AVERAGE
45.0—Brigham Young, 1983 (24 for 1,215 yards, 134 yards in punts returned)

HIGHEST NET PUNTING AVERAGE (Min. 40 Punts)
44.9—San Diego St., 1996 (48 for 2,234, 77 in punts returned)

Punt Returns

MOST PUNT RETURNS PER GAME
6.9—Texas A&M, 1943 (69 in 10)

FEWEST PUNT RETURNS PER GAME
0.5—Iowa St., 1996 (5 in 11)

MOST PUNT-RETURN YARDS PER GAME
114.5—Colgate, 1941 (916 in 8)

HIGHEST AVERAGE GAIN PER RETURN
(Min. 15-29 rets.) 25.2—Arizona St., 1952 (18 for 454 yards)
(Min. 30 rets.) 22.4—Oklahoma, 1948 (43 for 963)

MOST TOUCHDOWNS SCORED ON PUNT RETURNS (Since 1966)
7—Southern Miss., 1987 (on 46 returns)

Kickoff Returns

MOST KICKOFF RETURNS PER GAME
7.3—Cal St. Fullerton, 1990 (80 in 11)

FEWEST KICKOFF RETURNS PER GAME
0.7—Boston College, 1939 (7 in 10)

MOST KICKOFF-RETURN YARDS
1,588—Pittsburgh, 1996 (66 returns)

MOST KICKOFF-RETURN YARDS PER GAME
144.4—Pittsburgh, 1996 (1,588 in 11)

HIGHEST AVERAGE GAIN PER RETURN
(Min. 25-34 rets.) 30.3—Florida St., 1992 (27 for 819)
(Min. 35 rets.) 27.5—Rice, 1973 (39 for 1,074)

MOST TOUCHDOWNS SCORED ON KICKOFF RETURNS (Since 1966)
4—Dayton, 1974 (on 44 returns)

Scoring

MOST POINTS PER GAME
56.0—Army, 1944 (504 in 9)

MOST POINTS SCORED
624—Nebraska, 1983 (12 games)

HIGHEST SCORING MARGIN
52.1—Army, 1944 (scored 504 points for 56.0 average and allowed 35 points for 3.9 average in 9 games)

MOST POINTS SCORED, TWO CONSECUTIVE GAMES
177—Houston, 1968 (77-3 vs. Idaho, Nov. 16, and 100-6 vs. Tulsa, Nov. 23)

MOST TOUCHDOWNS PER GAME
8.2—Army, 1944 (74 in 9)

MOST TOUCHDOWNS
89—Nebraska, 1983 (12 games)

MOST EXTRA POINTS MADE BY KICKING
77—Nebraska, 1983 (77 in 12, attempted 85)
Also holds per-game record at 6.4

MOST CONSECUTIVE EXTRA POINTS MADE BY KICKING
71—Nebraska, 1997 (attempted 71); Florida, 1995 (attempted 71)

MOST TWO-POINT ATTEMPTS MADE PER GAME
2.2—Rutgers, 1958 (20 in 9, attempted 31)

MOST DEFENSIVE EXTRA-POINT ATTEMPTS
3—Rice, 1988 (1 vs. Southwestern La., Sept. 24, blocked kick return; 2 vs. Notre Dame, Nov. 5, 2 blocked kick returns, 1 scored)

MOST DEFENSIVE EXTRA POINTS SCORED
1—By many teams

MOST FIELD GOALS PER GAME
2.6—UCLA, 1984 (29 in 11)

First Downs

MOST FIRST DOWNS PER GAME
30.9—Brigham Young, 1983 (340 in 11)

MOST RUSHING FIRST DOWNS PER GAME
21.4—Oklahoma, 1974 (235 in 11)

MOST PASSING FIRST DOWNS PER GAME
19.8—Nevada, 1995 (218 in 11)

Fumbles

MOST FUMBLES
73—Cal St. Fullerton, 1992 (lost 41)

MOST FUMBLES LOST
41—Cal St. Fullerton, 1992 (fumbled 73 times)

FEWEST OWN FUMBLES LOST
1—Bowling Green, 1996

MOST CONSECUTIVE FUMBLES LOST
14—Oklahoma, 1983 (during 5 games, Oct. 8-Nov. 5)

Penalties

MOST PENALTIES PER GAME
12.9—Grambling, 1977 (142 in 11, 1,476 yards)

MOST YARDS PENALIZED PER GAME
134.2—Grambling, 1977 (1,476 in 11, 142 penalties)

Turnovers (Giveaways)

(Passes Had Intercepted and Fumbles Lost)

FEWEST TURNOVERS
8—Miami (Ohio), 1966 (4 interceptions, 4 fumbles lost); Clemson, 1940 (6 interceptions, 2 fumbles lost)

FEWEST TURNOVERS PER GAME
0.8—Miami (Ohio), 1966 (8 in 10 games)

MOST TURNOVERS
61—Tulsa, 1976 (24 interceptions, 37 fumbles lost); North Texas, 1971 (33 interceptions, 28 fumbles lost)

MOST TURNOVERS PER GAME
6.1—Mississippi St., 1949 (55 in 9 games; 25 interceptions, 30 fumbles lost)

SEASON—Defense

Total Defense

FEWEST YARDS ALLOWED PER GAME
69.9—Santa Clara, 1937 (559 in 8)

FEWEST RUSHING AND PASSING TOUCHDOWNS ALLOWED PER GAME
0.0—Tennessee, 1939; Duke, 1938

LOWEST AVERAGE YARDS ALLOWED PER PLAY
1.7—Texas A&M, 1939 (447 for 763)

LOWEST AVERAGE YARDS ALLOWED PER PLAY
(Min. 600-699 plays) 2.5—Nebraska, 1967 (627 for 1,576)
(Min. 700 plays) 2.7—Toledo, 1971 (734 for 1,795)

MOST YARDS ALLOWED PER GAME
553.0—Maryland, 1993 (6,083 in 11)

Rushing Defense

FEWEST YARDS ALLOWED PER GAME
17.0—Penn St., 1947 (153 in 9)

MOST YARDS LOST BY OPPONENTS PER GAME
70.1—Wyoming, 1968 (701 in 10, 458 rushes)

LOWEST AVERAGE YARDS ALLOWED PER RUSH
(Min. 240-399 rushes) 0.6—Penn St., 1947 (240 for 153)
(Min. 400-499 rushes) 1.3—North Texas, 1966 (408 for 513)
(Min. 500 rushes) 2.1—Nebraska, 1971 (500 for 1,031)

Pass Defense

FEWEST YARDS ALLOWED PER GAME
13.1—Penn St., 1938 (105 in 8)

FEWEST YARDS ALLOWED PER ATTEMPT
(Min. 200-299 atts.) 3.4—Toledo, 1970 (251 for 856)
(Min. 300 atts.) 3.8—Notre Dame, 1967 (306 for 1,158)

FEWEST YARDS ALLOWED PER COMPLETION
(Min. 100-149 comps.) 8.8—Michigan, 1997 (145 for 1,275)
(Min. 150 comps.) 9.5—Notre Dame, 1993 (263 for 2,502)

LOWEST COMPLETION PERCENTAGE ALLOWED
(Min. 150-199 atts.) 31.1%—Virginia, 1952 (50 of 161)
(Min. 200 atts.) 33.3%—Notre Dame, 1967 (102 of 306)

FEWEST TOUCHDOWNS ALLOWED BY PASSING
0—By many teams. Most recent: LSU, 1959; North Texas, 1959

LOWEST PASS EFFICIENCY DEFENSIVE RATING (Since 1990)
75.0—Texas A&M, 1993 (292 attempts, 116 completions, 13 interceptions, 1,339 yards, 5 TDs)

MOST PASSES INTERCEPTED BY PER GAME
4.1—Pennsylvania, 1940 (33 in 8)

HIGHEST PERCENTAGE INTERCEPTED BY (Min. 200 Attempts)
17.9%—Army, 1944 (36 of 201)

MOST YARDS GAINED ON INTERCEPTION RETURNS
782—Tennessee, 1971 (25 interceptions)

MOST INTERCEPTION YARDS PER GAME
72.5—Texas, 1943 (580 in 8)

HIGHEST AVERAGE PER INTERCEPTION RETURN
(Min. 10-14 ints.) 36.3—Oregon St., 1959 (12 for 436)
(Min. 15 ints.) 31.3—Tennessee, 1971 (25 for 782)

MOST TOUCHDOWNS ON INTERCEPTION RETURNS
7—Tennessee, 1971 (25 interceptions; 287 pass attempts against)

Punting

MOST OPPONENT'S PUNTS BLOCKED BY
11—Arkansas St., 1975 (11 games, 95 punts against)

Punt Returns

FEWEST RETURNS ALLOWED
5—Nebraska, 1995 (12 yards); Notre Dame, 1968 (52 yards)

FEWEST YARDS ALLOWED
2—Miami (Fla.), 1989 (12 returns)

LOWEST AVERAGE YARDS ALLOWED PER PUNT RETURN
0.2—Miami (Fla.), 1989 (12 for 2 yards)

Kickoff Returns

LOWEST AVERAGE YARDS ALLOWED PER KICKOFF RETURN
8.3—Richmond, 1951 (23 for 192 yards)

Opponent's Kicks Blocked

MOST PAT KICKS BLOCKED
Season
6—Duke, 1993

Scoring

FEWEST POINTS ALLOWED PER GAME
0.0—Tennessee, 1939 (10 games); Duke, 1938 (9 games)

MOST POINTS ALLOWED
553—Southwestern La., 1997 (11 games)

MOST POINTS ALLOWED PER GAME
50.3 Southwestern La., 1997 (553 in 11)

Fumbles

MOST OPPONENT'S FUMBLES RECOVERED
36—Brigham Young, 1977; North Texas, 1972

MOST TOUCHDOWNS SCORED ON FUMBLE RETURNS
4—Florida, 1996; Alabama, 1994; Duke, 1994

Turnovers (Takeaways)

(Opponent's Passes Intercepted and Fumbles Recovered)

MOST OPPONENT'S TURNOVERS
57—Tennessee, 1970 (36 interceptions, 21 fumbles recovered)

MOST OPPONENT'S TURNOVERS PER GAME
5.4—UCLA, 1954 (49 in 9); UCLA, 1952 (49 in 9); Pennsylvania, 1950 (49 in 9); Wyoming, 1950 (49 in 9)

HIGHEST MARGIN OF TURNOVERS PER GAME OVER OPPONENTS
4.0—UCLA, 1952 (36 in 9; 13 giveaways vs. 49 takeaways)
Also holds total-margin record at 36

HIGHEST MARGIN OF TURNOVERS PER GAME BY OPPONENTS
3.1—Southern Miss., 1969 (31 in 10; 45 giveaways vs. 14 takeaways)

Defensive Extra Points

MOST DEFENSIVE EXTRA-POINT ATTEMPTS AGAINST
2—Oklahoma, 1997 (2 kick returns, 1 scored); Oklahoma, 1992 (2 kick returns, 2 scored); Akron, 1990 (2 interception returns, none scored); Notre Dame, 1988 (2 kick returns, 1 scored); Southwestern La., 1988 (2 kick returns, none scored)

MOST DEFENSIVE EXTRA POINTS SCORED AGAINST
2—Oklahoma, 1992 (vs. Texas Tech, Sept. 3, and vs. Oklahoma St., Nov. 14)

Safeties

MOST SAFETIES BY A DEFENSE
4—Wisconsin, 1951

Consecutive Records

MOST CONSECUTIVE VICTORIES
47—Oklahoma, 1953-57

MOST CONSECUTIVE GAMES WITHOUT DEFEAT
48—Oklahoma, 1953-57 (1 tie)

MOST CONSECUTIVE LOSSES
34—Northwestern, from Sept. 22, 1979, vs. Syracuse through Sept. 18, 1982, vs. Miami (Ohio) (ended with 31-6 victory over Northern Ill., Sept. 25, 1982)

MOST CONSECUTIVE GAMES WITHOUT A VICTORY ON THE ROAD
46—Northwestern (including one tie), from Nov. 23, 1974, through Oct. 30, 1982

MOST CONSECUTIVE GAMES WITHOUT A TIE (Includes Bowl Games)
345—Miami (Fla.), from Nov. 11, 1968, through 1995 season (after 1995 tiebreaker used in Division I-A)

MOST CONSECUTIVE GAMES WITHOUT BEING SHUT OUT
286—Brigham Young (current), from Oct. 3, 1975

MOST CONSECUTIVE SHUTOUTS
(Regular Season)
17—Tennessee, from Nov. 5, 1938, through Oct. 12, 1940

MOST CONSECUTIVE QUARTERS OPPONENTS HELD SCORELESS
(Regular Season)
71—Tennessee, from 2nd quarter vs. LSU, Oct. 29, 1938, to 2nd quarter vs. Alabama, Oct. 19, 1940

MOST CONSECUTIVE VICTORIES AT HOME
58—Miami (Fla.) (Orange Bowl), from Oct. 12, 1985, to Sept. 24, 1994 (lost to Washington, 38-20)

MOST CONSECUTIVE WINNING SEASONS
(All-Time)
42—Notre Dame, 1889-1932 (no teams in 1890 & 1891) (see list on page 79)

MOST CONSECUTIVE WINNING SEASONS
(Current)
36—Nebraska, from 1962

MOST CONSECUTIVE NON-LOSING SEASONS
49—Penn St., 1939-1987

MOST CONSECUTIVE NON-WINNING SEASONS
28—Rice, 1964-91

MOST CONSECUTIVE SEASONS WINNING NINE OR MORE GAMES
29—Nebraska (current), from 1969

MOST CONSECUTIVE SEASONS PLAYING IN A BOWL GAME
29—Nebraska (current), from 1969

MOST CONSECUTIVE GAMES SCORING ON A PASS
62—Florida, from Oct. 1, 1992, to Oct. 4, 1997

MOST CONSECUTIVE GAMES PASSING FOR 200 YARDS OR MORE
64—Brigham Young, from Sept. 13, 1980, through Oct. 19, 1985

MOST CONSECUTIVE GAMES INTERCEPTING A PASS
(Includes Bowl Games)
39—Virginia, from Nov. 6, 1993, through Nov. 29, 1996

MOST CONSECUTIVE GAMES WITHOUT POSTING A SHUTOUT
245—New Mexico St. (current), from Sept. 21, 1974

MOST CONSECUTIVE EXTRA POINTS MADE
262—Syracuse, from Nov. 18, 1978, to Sept. 9, 1989. (By the following kickers: Dave Jacobs, last PAT of 1978; Gary Anderson, 72 from 1979 through 1981; Russ Carpentieri, 17 in 1982; Don McAulay, 62 from 1983 through 1985; Tim Vesling, 71 in 1986 and 1987; Kevin Greene, 37 in 1988; John Biskup, 2 in 1989.)

MOST CONSECUTIVE STADIUM SELLOUTS
220—Nebraska (current), from 1962

Additional Records

HIGHEST-SCORING TIE GAME
52-52—Brigham Young & San Diego St., Nov. 16, 1991

MOST TIE GAMES IN A SEASON
4—Central Mich., 1991 (11 games); UCLA, 1939 (10 games); Temple, 1937 (9 games)

MOST SCORELESS TIE GAMES IN A SEASON
4—Temple, 1937 (9 games)

MOST CONSECUTIVE SCORELESS TIE GAMES
2—Alabama, 1954, vs. Georgia, Oct. 30 & vs. Tulane, Nov. 6; Georgia Tech, 1938, vs. Florida, Nov. 19 & vs. Georgia, Nov. 26

LAST SCORELESS TIE GAME
Nov. 19, 1983—Oregon & Oregon St.

MOST POINTS OVERCOME TO WIN A GAME (Between Division I-A Teams)
31—Ohio St. (41) vs. Minnesota (37), Oct. 28, 1989 (trailed 31-0 with 4:29 remaining in 2nd quarter); Maryland (42) vs. Miami (Fla.) (40), Nov. 10, 1984 (trailed 31-0 with 12:35 remaining in 3rd quarter)
30—California (42) vs. Oregon (41), Oct. 2, 1993 (trailed 30-0 in 2nd quarter)

MOST POINTS SCORED IN FOURTH QUARTER TO WIN OR TIE A GAME
28—Florida St. (31) vs. Florida (31), Nov. 26, 1994 (trailed 31-3 beginning fourth quarter); Washington St. (49) vs. Stanford (42), Oct. 20, 1984 (trailed 42-14 with 5:38 remaining in third quarter and scored 35 consecutive points); Utah (28) vs. Arizona (27), Nov. 4, 1972 (trailed 27-0 beginning fourth quarter)

MOST POINTS SCORED IN A BRIEF PERIOD OF TIME BY ONE TEAM
41 in 2:55 of possession time during six drives—Nebraska vs. Colorado, Oct. 15, 1983 (6 TDs, 5 PATs in 3rd quarter. Drives occurred during 9:10 of total playing time in the period)
21 in 1:24 of total playing time—San Jose St. (42) vs. Fresno St. (7), Nov. 17, 1990 (3 TDs, 3 PATs in second quarter; 1:17 of possession time on two drives and one intercepted pass returned for a TD)
15 in :10 of total playing time—Utah (22) vs. Air Force (21), Oct. 21, 1995 (2 TDs, 2-point conversion, 1 PAT. Drives occurred during :41of final quarter)

MOST IMPROVED WON-LOST RECORD
8 games—Purdue, 1943 (9-0) from 1942 (1-8); Stanford, 1940 (10-0, including a bowl win) from 1939 (1-7-1)

MOST IMPROVED WON-LOST RECORD AFTER WINLESS SEASON
7 games—Florida, 1980 (8-4-0, including a bowl win) from 1979 (0-10-1)

Photo from Tennessee sports information

Tennessee's Peyton Manning averaged 250.5 yards per game in total offense during his career and was responsible for 101 touchdowns.

Annual Champions, All-Time Leaders

Total Offense

CAREER YARDS PER GAME
(Minimum 5,500 yards)

Player, Team	Years	G	Plays	Yards	TDR‡	Yd. PG
Chris Vargas, Nevada	1992-93	20	872	6,417	48	*320.9
Ty Detmer, Brigham Young	1988-91	46	*1,795	*14,665	*135	318.8
Mike Perez, San Jose St.	1986-87	20	875	6,182	37	309.1
Josh Wallwork, Wyoming	1995-96	22	845	6,753	60	307.0
Doug Gaynor, Long Beach St.	1984-85	22	1,067	6,710	45	305.0
Tony Eason, Illinois	1981-82	22	1,016	6,589	43	299.5
David Klingler, Houston	1988-91	32	1,439	9,363	93	292.6
Steve Sarkisian, Brigham Young	1995-96	25	953	7,253	56	290.1
Steve Young, Brigham Young	1981-83	31	1,177	8,817	74	284.4
Doug Flutie, Boston College	1981-84	42	1,558	11,317	74	269.5
Brent Snyder, Utah St.	1987-88	22	1,040	5,916	43	268.9
Scott Mitchell, Utah	1987-89	33	1,306	8,836	71	267.8
Mike Maxwell, Nevada	1993-95	27	946	7,226	66	267.6
Anthony Calvillo, Utah St.	1992-93	22	983	5,838	43	265.4
Shane Matthews, Florida	1989-92	35	1,397	9,241	82	264.0
Joe Hughes, Wyoming	1992-93	23	911	6,007	49	261.2
Larry Egger, Utah	1985-86	22	903	5,651	42	256.9
Jim Plunkett, Stanford	1968-70	31	1,174	7,887	62	254.4
Stoney Case, New Mexico	1991-94	42	1,673	10,651	98	253.6
Troy Kopp, Pacific (Cal.)	1989-92	40	1,595	10,037	90	250.9
Peyton Manning, Tennessee	1994-97	44	1,534	11,020	101	250.5
Randall Cunningham, UNLV	1982-84	33	1,330	8,224	67	249.2
Eric Zeier, Georgia	1991-94	44	1,560	10,841	71	246.4
Erik Wilhelm, Oregon St.	1985-88	37	1,689	9,062	55	244.9
Todd Dillon, Long Beach St.	1982-83	23	1,031	5,588	38	243.0
Bernie Kosar, Miami (Fla.)	1983-84	23	847	5,585	48	242.8
Charlie Batch, Eastern Mich.	1994-97	32	1,179	7,715	58	241.1
Alex Van Pelt, Pittsburgh	1989-92	45	1,570	10,814	58	240.3
Steve Stenstrom, Stanford	1991-94	41	1,550	9,825	75	239.6
Jack Trudeau, Illinois	1981, 83-85	34	1,318	8,096	56	238.1
Chuck Hixson, Southern Methodist	1968-70	29	1,358	6,884	50	237.4
Robbie Bosco, Brigham Young	1983-85	35	1,159	8,299	72	237.1
Dan McGwire, Iowa/San Diego St.	1986-87, 89-90	32	1,067	7,557	50	236.2
Johnny Bright, Drake	1949-51	25	825	5,903	64	236.1
Kordell Stewart, Colorado	1991-94	33	1,087	7,770	48	235.5
Jeff Garcia, San Jose St.	1991-93	31	1,146	7,274	63	234.6
Cody Ledbetter, New Mexico St.	1991, 93-95	35	1,362	8,207	68	234.5
Brian McClure, Bowling Green	1982-85	42	1,630	9,774	67	232.7
Marc Wilson, Brigham Young	1977-79	33	1,183	7,602	68	230.4
Todd Santos, San Diego St.	1984-87	46	1,722	10,513	71	228.5
Danny Wuerffel, Florida	1993-96	46	1,355	10,500	122	228.3
Pat Sullivan, Auburn	1969-71	30	970	6,844	71	228.1
John Reaves, Florida	1969-71	32	1,258	7,283	58	227.6

**Record. ‡Touchdowns-responsible-for are player's TDs scored and passed for.*

SEASON YARDS PER GAME

Player, Team	Year	G	Plays	Yards	TDR‡	Yd. PG
David Klingler, Houston	†1990	11	*704	*5,221	*55	*474.6
Andre Ware, Houston	†1989	11	628	4,661	49	423.7
Ty Detmer, Brigham Young	1990	12	635	5,022	45	418.5
Mike Maxwell, Nevada	†1995	9	443	3,623	34	402.6
Steve Young, Brigham Young	†1983	11	531	4,346	41	395.1
Chris Vargas, Nevada	†1993	11	535	4,332	35	393.8
Scott Mitchell, Utah	†1988	11	589	4,299	29	390.8
Jim McMahon, Brigham Young	†1980	12	540	4,627	53	385.6
Ty Detmer, Brigham Young	1989	12	497	4,433	38	369.4
Troy Kopp, Pacific (Cal.)	1990	9	485	3,276	32	364.0
Tim Rattay, Louisiana Tech	†1997	11	541	3,968	35	360.7
Josh Wallwork, Wyoming	†1996	12	525	4,209	35	350.8
Jim McMahon, Brigham Young	†1981	10	487	3,458	30	345.8
Jimmy Klingler, Houston	†1992	11	544	3,768	34	342.5
Tim Couch, Kentucky	1997	11	613	3,759	40	341.7
Cody Ledbetter, New Mexico St.	1995	11	543	3,724	32	338.6
Anthony Dilweg, Duke	1988	11	539	3,713	26	337.6
Bill Anderson, Tulsa	†1965	10	580	3,343	35	334.3
Ty Detmer, Brigham Young	†1991	12	478	4,001	39	333.4
Dan McGwire, San Diego St.	1990	11	484	3,664	28	333.1
Mike McCoy, Utah	1993	12	529	3,969	21	330.8
Mike Perez, San Jose St.	†1986	9	425	2,969	14	329.9
Robbie Bosco, Brigham Young	†1984	12	543	3,932	35	327.7
Doug Flutie, Boston College	1984	11	448	3,603	30	327.5
Ryan Fien, Idaho	1996	11	514	3,597	29	327.0
Jim Everett, Purdue	†1985	11	518	3,589	24	326.3
Todd Dillon, Long Beach St.	†1982	11	585	3,587	23	326.1
Ryan Leaf, Washington St.	1997	11	447	3,583	39	325.7
Marc Wilson, Brigham Young	†1979	11	488	3,580	32	325.5

**Record. †National champion. ‡Touchdowns-responsible-for are player's TDs scored and passed for.*

Photo from Pacific (Cal.) sports information

Troy Kopp compiled 10,037 yards in total offense from 1989-92 as Pacific (California) quarterback to rank 10th in career yards.

CAREER YARDS

Player, Team	Years	Plays	Yards Rush	Pass	Total	Avg.
Ty Detmer, Brigham Young	1988-91	*1,795	-366	*15,031	*14,665	#8.17
Doug Flutie, Boston College	1981-84	1,558	738	10,579	11,317	7.26
Peyton Manning, Tennessee	1994-97	1,534	-181	11,201	11,020	7.18
Eric Zeier, Georgia	1991-94	1,560	-312	11,153	10,841	6.95
Alex Van Pelt, Pittsburgh	1989-92	1,570	-99	10,913	10,814	6.89
Stoney Case, New Mexico	1991-94	1,673	1,191	9,460	10,651	6.37
Todd Santos, San Diego St.	1984-87	1,722	-912	11,425	10,513	6.11
Danny Wuerffel, Florida	1993-96	1,355	-375	10,875	10,500	7.75
Kevin Sweeney, Fresno St.	$1982-86	1,700	-371	10,623	10,252	6.03
Troy Kopp, Pacific (Cal.)	1989-92	1,595	-221	10,258	10,037	6.29
Steve Stenstrom, Stanford	1991-94	1,550	-706	10,531	9,825	6.34
Brian McClure, Bowling Green	1982-85	1,630	-506	10,280	9,774	6.00
Jim McMahon, Brigham Young	1977-78, 80-81	1,325	187	9,536	9,723	7.34
Glenn Foley, Boston College	1990-93	1,440	-340	10,042	9,702	6.74
Terrence Jones, Tulane	1985-88	1,620	1,761	7,684	9,445	5.83
David Klingler, Houston	1988-91	1,439	-103	9,466	9,363	6.51
Shawn Jones, Georgia Tech	1989-92	1,609	855	8,441	9,296	5.78
Shane Matthews, Florida	1989-92	1,397	-46	9,287	9,241	6.61
Spence Fischer, Duke	1992-95	1,612	89	9,021	9,110	5.65
T. J. Rubley, Tulsa	1987-89, 91	1,541	-244	9,324	9,080	5.89
Brad Tayles, Western Mich.	1989-92	1,675	354	8,717	9,071	5.42
John Elway, Stanford	1979-82	1,505	-279	9,349	9,070	6.03
Erik Wilhelm, Oregon St.	1985-88	1,689	-331	9,393	9,062	5.37
Ben Bennett, Duke	1980-83	1,582	-553	9,614	9,061	5.73
Chuck Long, Iowa	$1981-85	1,410	-176	9,210	9,034	6.41
Todd Ellis, South Caro.	1986-89	1,517	-497	9,519	9,022	5.95
Jason Martin, Louisiana Tech	1993-96	1,439	-127	9,066	8,939	6.21
Tom Hodson, LSU	1986-89	1,307	-177	9,115	8,938	6.84
Jake Delhomme, Southwestern La.	1993-96	1,476	-340	9,216	8,876	6.01
Scott Mitchell, Utah	1987-89	1,306	-145	8,981	8,836	6.77
Steve Young, Brigham Young	1981-83	1,177	1,084	7,733	8,817	7.49
Brian Mitchell, Southwestern La.	1986-89	1,521	3,335	5,447	8,782	5.77
Marvin Graves, Syracuse	1990-93	1,373	286	8,466	8,752	6.37
Jeremy Leach, New Mexico	1988-91	1,695	-762	9,382	8,620	5.09
Jake Plummer, Arizona St.	1993-96	1,375	-107	8,626	8,519	6.20
Robert Hall, Texas Tech	1990-93	1,341	581	7,908	8,489	6.33
Mark Herrmann, Purdue	1977-80	1,354	-744	9,188	8,444	6.24
Mike McCoy, Long Beach St./Utah	1991, 92-94	1,315	97	8,342	8,439	6.42
Robbie Bosco, Brigham Young	1983-85	1,158	-101	8,400	8,299	7.17
Cody Ledbetter, New Mexico St.	1991, 93-95	1,362	727	7,480	8,207	6.03
Troy Taylor, California	1986-89	1,490	110	8,126	8,236	5.53
Randall Cunningham, UNLV	1982-84	1,330	204	8,020	8,224	6.18
Steve Taneyhill, South Caro.	1992-95	1,423	-392	8,555	8,163	5.74
Ryan Huzjak, Toledo	1993-96	1,478	1,480	6,672	8,152	5.52
Steve Slayden, Duke	1984-87	1,546	125	8,004	8,129	5.26
Jack Trudeau, Illinois	1981, 83-85	1,318	-50	8,146	8,096	6.14
Mark Barsotti, Fresno St.	1988-91	1,192	768	7,321	8,089	6.79
Gene Swick, Toledo	1972-75	1,579	807	7,267	8,074	5.11
Andre Ware, Houston	1987-89	1,194	-144	8,202	8,058	6.75
James Brown, Texas	1994-97	1,196	411	7,638	8,049	6.73

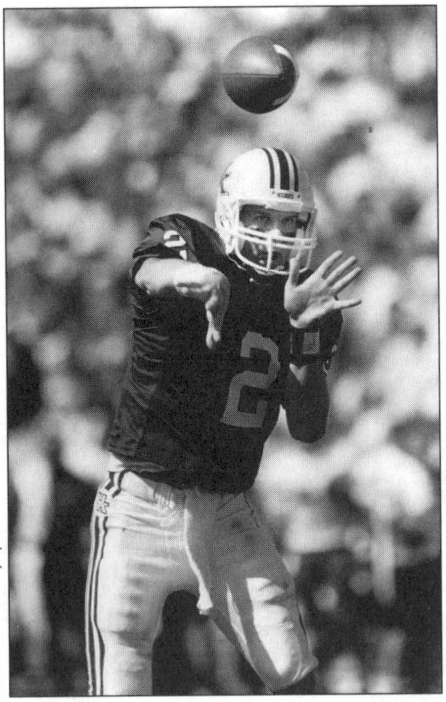

Photo from Kentucky sports information

Kentucky quarterback Tim Couch had 3,759 yards in total offense last season to rank 18th among all-time leaders.

			Yards			
Player, Team	**Years**	**Plays**	**Rush**	**Pass**	**Total**	**Avg.**
Len Williams, Northwestern	1990-93	1,614	542	7,486	8,028	4.97
Billy Blanton, San Diego St.	1993-96	1,108	-151	8,165	8,014	7.23
Joe Adams, Tennessee St.	1977-80	1,256	-677	8,649	7,972	6.35
Rodney Peete, Southern Cal	1985-88	1,226	309	7,640	7,949	6.48
Stan White, Auburn	1990-93	1,481	-96	8,016	7,920	5.35
Shawn Moore, Virginia	1987-90	1,177	1,268	6,629	7,897	6.71
Jim Plunkett, Stanford	1968-70	1,174	343	7,544	7,887	6.72
Art Schlichter, Ohio St.	1978-81	1,316	1,285	6,584	7,869	5.98
Mike Gundy, Oklahoma St.	1986-89	1,275	-248	8,072	7,824	6.14
John Holman, Northeast La.	1979-82	1,376	-25	7,827	7,802	5.67
Kordell Stewart, Colorado	1991-94	1,087	1,289	6,481	7,770	7.15
Gino Torretta, Miami (Fla.)	1989-92	1,101	32	7,690	7,722	7.01
John Walsh, Brigham Young	1991-94	1,152	-654	8,375	7,721	6.70

**Record. $See page 6 for explanation. #Record for minimum of 7,500 yards. (Note: Chris Vargas of Nevada competed two years in Division I-A and two years in Division I-AA. Four-year total: 8,184 yards.)*

CAREER YARDS RECORD PROGRESSION

(Record Yards—Player, Team, Seasons Played)

3,481—Davey O'Brien, Texas Christian, 1936-38; **3,882**—Paul Christman, Missouri, 1938-40; **4,602**—Frank Sinkwich, Georgia, 1940-42; **4,627**—Bob Fenimore, Oklahoma St., 1943-46; **4,871**—Charlie Justice, North Caro., 1946-49; **5,903**—Johnny Bright, Drake, 1949-51; **6,354**—Virgil Carter, Brigham Young, 1964-66; **6,568**—Steve Ramsey, North Texas, 1967-69; **7,887**—Jim Plunkett, Stanford, 1968-70; **8,074**—Gene Swick, Toledo, 1972-75; **8,444**—Mark Herrmann, Purdue, 1977-80; **9,723**—Jim McMahon, Brigham Young, 1977-78, 1980-81; **11,317**—Doug Flutie, Boston College, 1981-84; **14,665**—Ty Detmer, Brigham Young, 1988-91.

SEASON YARDS

				Yards			
Player, Team	**Year**	**G**	**Plays**	**Rush**	**Pass**	**Total**	**Avg.**
David Klingler, Houston	†1990	11	*704	81	5,140	*5,221	7.42
Ty Detmer, Brigham Young	1990	12	635	-106	*5,188	5,022	7.91
Andre Ware, Houston	†1989	11	628	-38	4,699	4,661	7.42
Jim McMahon, Brigham Young	†1980	12	540	56	4,571	4,627	8.57
Ty Detmer, Brigham Young	1989	12	497	-127	4,560	4,433	@8.92
Steve Young, Brigham Young	†1983	11	531	444	3,902	4,346	8.18
Chris Vargas, Nevada	†1993	11	535	67	4,265	4,332	8.10
Scott Mitchell, Utah	†1988	11	589	-23	4,322	4,299	7.30
Josh Wallwork, Wyoming	†1996	12	525	119	4,090	4,209	8.02
Robbie Bosco, Brigham Young	1985	13	578	-132	4,273	4,141	7.16
Ty Detmer, Brigham Young	†1991	12	478	-30	4,031	4,001	8.37
Steve Sarkisian, Brigham Young	1996	14	486	-44	4,027	3,983	8.20
Mike McCoy, Utah	1993	12	529	109	3,860	3,969	7.50
Tim Rattay, Louisiana Tech	†1997	11	541	87	3,881	3,968	7.33
Robbie Bosco, Brigham Young	†1984	12	543	57	3,875	3,932	7.24
Peyton Manning, Tennessee	1997	12	526	-30	3,819	3,789	7.20
Jimmy Klingler, Houston	†1992	11	544	-50	3,818	3,768	6.93
Tim Couch, Kentucky	1997	11	613	-125	3,884	3,759	6.13
Cody Ledbetter, New Mexico St.	1995	11	543	223	3,501	3,724	6.86
Anthony Dilweg, Duke	1988	11	539	-111	3,824	3,713	6.89
Todd Santos, San Diego St.	†1987	12	562	-244	3,932	3,688	6.56
Troy Kopp, Pacific (Cal.)	1991	12	496	-81	3,767	3,686	7.43
Dan McGwire, San Diego St.	1990	11	484	-169	3,833	3,664	7.57
Stoney Case, New Mexico	1994	12	549	532	3,117	3,649	6.65
Jon Denton, UNLV	1996	12	594	38	3,591	3,629	6.11
Mike Maxwell, Nevada	†1995	9	443	12	3,611	3,623	8.18
Doug Flutie, Boston College	1984	11	448	149	3,454	3,603	8.04
Ryan Fien, Idaho	1996	11	514	-65	3,662	3,597	7.00
Jim Everett, Purdue	†1985	11	518	-62	3,651	3,589	6.93
Todd Dillon, Long Beach St.	†1982	11	585	70	3,517	3,587	6.13
Ryan Leaf, Washington St.	1997	11	447	-54	3,637	3,583	8.02
Marc Wilson, Brigham Young	†1979	11	488	-140	3,720	3,580	7.34
Sam King, UNLV	1981	12	507	-216	3,778	3,562	7.03
Matt Kofler, San Diego St.	1981	11	594	191	3,337	3,528	5.94
Danny Wuerffel, Florida	1996	12	423	-100	3,625	3,525	8.33
Daunte Culpepper, Central Fla.	1997	11	517	438	3,086	3,524	6.82
John Dutton, Nevada	1997	11	411	-4	3,526	3,522	8.57
Steve Young, Brigham Young	1982	11	481	407	3,100	3,507	7.29
Mike Maxwell, Nevada	†1994	11	477	-39	3,537	3,498	7.33
Eric Zeier, Georgia	1993	11	484	-43	3,525	3,482	7.19
John Walsh, Brigham Young	1994	12	540	-239	3,712	3,473	6.43
John Kaleo, Maryland	1992	11	588	80	3,392	3,472	5.90
Doug Gaynor, Long Beach St.	1985	12	589	-96	3,563	3,467	5.89
Jim McMahon, Brigham Young	1981	10	487	-97	3,555	3,458	7.10

**Record. †National champion. @ Record for minimum of 3,000 yards.*

SINGLE-GAME YARDS

Yds.	**Rush**	**Pass**	**Player, Team (Opponent)**	**Date**
732	16	716	David Klingler, Houston (Arizona St.)	Dec. 2, 1990
696	6	690	Matt Vogler, Texas Christian (Houston)	Nov. 3, 1990
625	62	563	David Klingler, Houston (Texas Christian)	Nov. 3, 1990
625	-6	631	Scott Mitchell, Utah (Air Force)	Oct. 15, 1988
612	-1	613	Jimmy Klingler, Houston (Rice)	Nov. 28, 1992
603	4	599	Ty Detmer, Brigham Young (San Diego St.)	Nov. 16, 1991
601	37	564	Troy Kopp, Pacific, Cal. (New Mexico St.)	Oct. 20, 1990
599	86	513	Virgil Carter, Brigham Young (UTEP)	Nov. 5, 1966
597	-22	619	John Walsh, Brigham Young (Utah St.)	Oct. 30, 1993
594	-28	622	Jeremy Leach, New Mexico (Utah)	Nov. 11, 1989

Yds.	Rush	Pass	Player, Team (Opponent)	Date
585	-36	621	Dave Wilson, Illinois (Ohio St.)	Nov. 8, 1980
582	11	571	Marc Wilson, Brigham Young (Utah)	Nov. 5, 1977
578	6	572	David Klingler, Houston (Eastern Wash.)	Nov. 17, 1990
568	11	557	John Dutton, Nevada (Boise St.)	Nov. 8, 1997
562	25	537	Ty Detmer, Brigham Young (Washington St.)	Sept. 7, 1989
559	13	546	Cody Ledbetter, New Mexico St. (UNLV)	Nov. 18, 1995
554	9	545	Rusty LaRue, Wake Forest (North Caro. St.)	Nov. 18, 1995
552	-13	565	Jim McMahon, Brigham Young (Utah)	Nov. 21, 1981
548	12	536	Dave Telford, Fresno St. (Pacific [Cal.])	Oct. 24, 1987
543	-9	552	Mike Maxwell, Nevada (UNLV)	Oct. 28, 1995
541	6	535	Mike Maxwell, Nevada (Louisiana Tech)	Oct. 21, 1995
540	-45	585	Robbie Bosco, Brigham Young (New Mexico)	Oct. 19, 1985
540	104	436	Archie Manning, Mississippi (Alabama)	Oct. 4, 1969
539	1	538	Jim McMahon, Brigham Young (Colorado St.)	Nov. 7, 1981
537	65	472	Anthony Calvillo, Utah St. (Brigham Young)	Oct. 30, 1993
537	-1	538	Chris Vargas, Nevada (UNLV)	Oct. 2, 1993
537	2	535	Shane Montgomery, North Caro. St. (Duke)	Nov. 11, 1989
537	-24	561	Tony Adams, Utah St. (Utah)	Nov. 11, 1972
536	58	478	Tim Schade, Minnesota (Penn St.)	Sept. 4, 1993
536	28	508	Mike Perez, San Jose St. (Pacific [Cal.])	Oct. 25, 1986
534	-17	551	Jose Davis, Kent (Central Fla.)	Oct. 4, 1997
532	0	532	Jeff Van Raaphorst, Arizona St. (Florida St.)	Nov. 3, 1984
531	-11	542	Ryan Fien, Idaho (Wyoming)	Aug. 31, 1996
531	13	518	Jeff Graham, Long Beach St. (Hawaii)	Oct. 29, 1988
529	-13	542	Jason Martin, Louisiana Tech (Toledo)	Oct. 19, 1996
528	-40	568	David Lowery, San Diego St. (Brigham Young)	Nov. 16, 1991
528	-2	530	Dan McGwire, San Diego St. (New Mexico)	Nov. 17, 1990
527	-17	544	Eric Zeier, Georgia (Southern Miss.)	Oct. 9, 1993
527	17	510	David Klingler, Houston (Louisiana Tech)	Aug. 31, 1991
525	-29	554	Greg Cook, Cincinnati (Ohio)	Nov. 16, 1968
524	118	406	Ned James, New Mexico (Wyoming)	Nov. 1, 1986
521	-39	560	Ty Detmer, Brigham Young (Utah St.)	Nov. 24, 1990
521	57	464	Whit Taylor, Vanderbilt (Tennessee)	Nov. 28, 1981

ANNUAL CHAMPIONS

				Yards		
Year	**Player, Team**	**Class**	**Plays**	**Rush**	**Pass**	**Total**
1937	Byron "Whizzer" White, Colorado	Sr.	224	1,121	475	1,596
1938	Davey O'Brien, Texas Christian	Sr.	291	390	1,457	1,847
1939	Kenny Washington, UCLA	Sr.	259	811	559	1,370
1940	Johnny Knolla, Creighton	Sr.	298	813	607	1,420
1941	Bud Schwenk, Washington (Mo.)	Sr.	354	471	1,457	1,9282
1942	Frank Sinkwich, Georgia	Sr.	341	795	1,392	2,187
1943	Bob Hoernschemeyer, Indiana	Fr.	355	515	1,133	1,648
1944	Bob Fenimore, Oklahoma St.	So.	241	897	861	1,758
1945	Bob Fenimore, Oklahoma St.	Jr.	203	1,048	593	1,641
1946	Travis Tidwell, Auburn	Fr.	339	772	943	1,715
1947	Fred Enke, Arizona	So.	329	535	1,406	1,941
1948	Stan Heath, Nevada	Sr.	233	-13	2,005	1,992
1949	Johnny Bright, Drake	So.	275	975	975	1,950
1950	Johnny Bright, Drake	Jr.	320	1,232	1,168	2,400
1951	Dick Kazmaier, Princeton	Sr.	272	861	966	1,827
1952	Ted Marchibroda, Detroit	Sr.	305	176	1,637	1,813
1953	Paul Larson, California	Jr.	262	141	1,431	1,572
1954	George Shaw, Oregon	Sr.	276	178	1,358	1,536
1955	George Welsh, Navy	Sr.	203	29	1,319	1,348
1956	John Brodie, Stanford	Sr.	295	9	1,633	1,642
1957	Bob Newman, Washington St.	Jr.	263	53	1,391	1,444
1958	Dick Bass, Pacific (Cal.)	Jr.	218	1,361	79	1,440
1959	Dick Norman, Stanford	Jr.	319	55	1,963	2,018
1960	Bill Kilmer, UCLA	Sr.	292	803	1,086	1,889
1961	Dave Hoppmann, Iowa St.	Jr.	320	920	718	1,638
1962	Terry Baker, Oregon St.	Sr.	318	538	1,738	2,276
1963	George Mira, Miami (Fla.)	Sr.	394	163	2,155	2,318
1964	Jerry Rhome, Tulsa	Sr.	470	258	2,870	3,128
1965	Bill Anderson, Tulsa	Sr.	580	-121	3,464	3,343
1966	Virgil Carter, Brigham Young	Sr.	388	363	2,182	2,545
1967	Sal Olivas, New Mexico St.	Sr.	368	-41	2,225	2,184
1968	Greg Cook, Cincinnati	Sr.	507	-62	3,272	3,210
1969	Dennis Shaw, San Diego St.	Sr.	388	12	3,185	3,197

Beginning in 1970, ranked on per-game (instead of total) yards

					Yards			
Year	**Player, Team**	**Class**	**G**	**Plays**	**Rush**	**Pass**	**Total**	**Avg.**
1970	Pat Sullivan, Auburn	Jr.	10	333	270	2,586	2,856	285.6
1971	Gary Huff, Florida St.	Jr.	11	386	-83	2,736	2,653	241.2
1972	Don Strock, Virginia Tech	Sr.	11	480	-73	3,243	3,170	288.2
1973	Jesse Freitas, San Diego St.	Sr.	11	410	-92	2,993	2,901	263.7
1974	Steve Joachim, Temple	Sr.	10	331	277	1,950	2,227	222.7
1975	Gene Swick, Toledo	Sr.	11	490	219	2,487	2,706	246.0
1976	Tommy Kramer, Rice	Sr.	11	562	-45	3,317	3,272	297.5
1977	Doug Williams, Grambling	Sr.	11	377	-57	3,286	3,229	293.5
1978	Mike Ford, Southern Methodist	So.	11	459	-50	3,007	2,957	268.8
1979	Marc Wilson, Brigham Young	Sr.	11	488	-140	3,720	3,580	325.5
1980	Jim McMahon, Brigham Young	Jr.	12	540	56	4,571	4,627	385.6
1981	Jim McMahon, Brigham Young	Sr.	10	487	-97	3,555	3,458	345.8
1982	Todd Dillon, Long Beach St.	Jr.	11	585	70	3,517	3,587	326.1
1983	Steve Young, Brigham Young	Sr.	11	531	444	3,902	4,346	395.1
1984	Robbie Bosco, Brigham Young	Jr.	12	543	57	3,875	3,932	327.7

Year	Player, Team	Class	G	Plays	Rush	Pass	Total	Avg.
1985	Jim Everett, Purdue	Sr.	11	518	-62	3,651	3,589	326.3
1986	Mike Perez, San Jose St.	Jr.	9	425	35	2,934	2,969	329.9
1987	Todd Santos, San Diego St.	Sr.	12	562	-244	3,932	3,688	307.3
1988	Scott Mitchell, Utah	So.	11	589	-23	4,322	4,299	390.8
1989	Andre Ware, Houston	Jr.	11	628	-38	4,699	4,661	423.7
1990	David Klingler, Houston	Jr.	11	*704	81	5,140	*5,221	*474.6
1991	Ty Detmer, Brigham Young	Sr.	12	478	-30	4,031	4,001	333.4
1992	Jimmy Klingler, Houston	So.	11	544	-50	3,818	3,768	342.5
1993	Chris Vargas, Nevada	Sr.	11	535	67	4,265	4,332	393.8
1994	Mike Maxwell, Nevada	Jr.	11	477	-39	3,537	3,498	318.0
1995	Mike Maxwell, Nevada	Sr.	9	443	12	3,611	3,623	402.6
1996	Josh Wallwork, Wyoming	Sr.	12	525	119	4,090	4,209	350.8
1997	Tim Rattay, Louisiana Tech	So.	11	541	87	3,881	3,968	360.7

**Record.*

Rushing

CAREER YARDS PER GAME
(Minimum 2,500 yards)

Player, Team	Years	G	Plays	Yards	TD	Yd. PG
Ed Marinaro, Cornell	1969-71	27	918	4,715	50	*174.6
O. J. Simpson, Southern Cal	1967-68	19	621	3,124	33	164.4
Herschel Walker, Georgia	1980-82	33	994	5,259	49	159.4
LeShon Johnson, Northern Ill.	1992-93	22	592	3,314	18	150.6
Marshall Faulk, San Diego St.	1991-93	31	766	4,589	57	148.0
George Jones, San Diego St.	1995-96	19	486	2,810	34	147.9
Tony Dorsett, Pittsburgh	1973-76	43	1,074	*6,082	55	141.4
Troy Davis, Iowa St.	1994-96	31	782	4,382	36	141.4
Mike Rozier, Nebraska	1981-83	35	668	4,780	50	136.6
Howard Stevens, Louisville	1971-72	20	509	2,723	25	136.2
Jerome Persell, Western Mich.	1976-78	31	842	4,190	39	135.2
Rudy Mobley, Hardin-Simmons	1942,46	19	414	2,543	32	133.8
Alex Smith, Indiana	1994-96	27	723	3,492	21	129.3
Vaughn Dunbar, Indiana	1990-91	22	565	2,842	24	129.2
Steve Owens, Oklahoma	1967-69	30	905	3,867	56	128.9
Byron Hanspard, Texas Tech	1994-96	33	760	4,219	29	127.8
Charles White, Southern Cal	1976-79	44	1,023	5,598	46	127.2
Johnny Bright, Drake	1949-51	25	513	3,134	39	125.4
Woody Green, Arizona St.	1971-73	30	601	3,754	33	125.1
Archie Griffin, Ohio St.	1972-75	42	845	5,177	25	123.3
Anthony Thompson, Indiana	1986-89	41	1,089	4,965	*64	121.1
Mark Kellar, Northern Ill.	1971-73	31	743	3,745	32	120.8
Paul Gipson, Houston	1966-68	23	447	2,769	25	120.4
John Cappelletti, Penn St.	‡1972-73	22	519	2,639	29	120.0
Brian Pruitt, Central Mich.	1992-94	31	671	3,693	31	119.1
Ahman Green, Nebraska	1995-97	33	574	3,880	42	117.6
Steve Bartalo, Colorado St.	1983-86	41	*1,215	4,813	46	117.4
Louie Giammona, Utah St.	1973-75	30	756	3,499	21	116.6
Paul Palmer, Temple	1983-86	42	948	4,895	39	116.5
Bill Marek, Wisconsin	1972-75	32	719	3,709	44	115.9
Toraino Singleton, UTEP	1994-95	23	560	2,635	19	114.6
Darren Lewis, Texas A&M	1987-90	44	909	5,012	44	113.9
Dick Jauron, Yale	1970-72	26	515	2,947	27	113.3
Bo Jackson, Auburn	1982-85	38	650	4,303	43	113.2
Rashaan Salaam, Colorado	1992-94	27	486	3,057	33	113.2
Joe Morris, Syracuse	1978-81	38	813	4,299	25	113.1
Darnell Autry, Northwestern	1994-96	32	738	3,617	30	113.0
Eugene "Mercury" Morris, West Tex. A&M	1966-68	30	541	3,388	34	112.9

**Record. ‡Defensive back in 1971.*

SEASON YARDS PER GAME

Player, Team	Year	G	Plays	Yards	TD	Yd. PG
Barry Sanders, Oklahoma St.	†1988	11	344	*2,628	*37	*238.9
Marcus Allen, Southern Cal	†1981	11	*403	2,342	22	212.9
Ed Marinaro, Cornell	†1971	9	356	1,881	24	209.0
Troy Davis, Iowa St.	†1996	11	402	2,185	21	198.6
Byron Hanspard, Texas Tech	1996	11	339	2,084	13	189.5
Rashaan Salaam, Colorado	†1994	11	298	2,055	24	186.8
Troy Davis, Iowa St.	†1995	11	345	2,010	15	182.7
Charles White, Southern Cal	†1979	10	293	1,803	18	180.3
LeShon Johnson, Northern Ill.	†1993	11	327	1,976	12	179.6
Mike Rozier, Nebraska	†1983	12	275	2,148	29	179.0
Tony Dorsett, Pittsburgh	†1976	11	338	1,948	21	177.1
Ollie Matson, San Francisco	†1951	9	245	1,566	20	174.0
Lorenzo White, Michigan St.	†1985	11	386	1,908	17	173.5
Wasean Tait, Toledo	1995	11	357	1,905	20	173.2
Ricky Williams, Texas	†1997	11	279	1,893	25	172.1
Herschel Walker, Georgia	1981	11	385	1,891	18	171.9
Brian Pruitt, Central Mich.	1994	11	292	1,890	20	171.8
O. J. Simpson, Southern Cal	†1968	10	355	1,709	22	170.9
Ernest Anderson, Oklahoma St.	†1982	11	353	1,877	8	170.6
Ricky Bell, Southern Cal	†1975	11	357	1,875	13	170.5

**Record. †National champion.*

CAREER YARDS

Player, Team	Years	Plays	Yards	Avg.	Long
Tony Dorsett, Pittsburgh	1973-76	1,074	*6,082	5.66	73
Charles White, Southern Cal	1976-79	1,023	5,598	5.47	79
Herschel Walker, Georgia	1980-82	994	5,259	5.29	76
Archie Griffin, Ohio St.	1972-75	845	5,177	††6.13	75
Darren Lewis, Texas A&M	1987-90	909	5,012	5.51	84
Anthony Thompson, Indiana	1986-89	1,089	4,965	4.56	52
George Rogers, South Caro.	1977-80	902	4,958	5.50	80
Trevor Cobb, Rice	1989-92	1,091	4,948	4.54	79
Paul Palmer, Temple	1983-86	948	4,895	5.16	78
Steve Bartalo, Colorado St.	1983-86	*1,215	4,813	3.96	39
Mike Rozier, Nebraska	1981-83	668	4,780	#7.16	93
Ed Marinaro, Cornell	1969-71	918	4,715	5.14	79
Marcus Allen, Southern Cal	1978-81	893	4,682	5.24	45
Ted Brown, North Caro. St.	1975-78	860	4,602	5.35	95
Thurman Thomas, Oklahoma St.	1984-87	898	4,595	5.12	66
Marshall Faulk, San Diego St.	1991-93	766	4,589	5.99	71
Terry Miller, Oklahoma St.	1974-77	847	4,582	5.41	81
Darrell Thompson, Minnesota	1986-89	911	4,518	4.96	98
Lorenzo White, Michigan St.	1984-87	991	4,513	4.55	73
Eric Dickerson, Southern Methodist	1979-82	790	4,450	5.63	80
Earl Campbell, Texas	1974-77	765	4,443	5.81	‡‡83
Amos Lawrence, North Caro.	1977-80	881	4,391	4.98	62
Troy Davis, Iowa St.	1994-96	782	4,382	5.60	80
Deland McCullough, Miami (Ohio)	1992-95	949	4,368	4.60	51
David Thompson, Oklahoma St.	1993-96	846	4,318	5.10	91
Bo Jackson, Auburn	1982-85	650	4,303	6.62	80
Joe Morris, Syracuse	1978-81	813	4,299	5.29	75
Reggie Taylor, Cincinnati	1983-86	876	4,242	4.48	‡‡68
Byron Hanspard, Texas Tech	1994-96	760	4,219	5.55	72
Mike Mayweather, Army	1987-90	832	4,212	5.06	52
Jerome Persell, Western Mich.	1976-78	842	4,190	4.98	86
Napoleon McCallum, Navy	$1981-85	908	4,179	4.60	60
Tico Duckett, Michigan St.	1989-92	824	4,176	5.07	88
George Swarn, Miami (Ohio)	1983-86	881	4,172	4.74	98
Errict Rhett, Florida	$1989-93	873	4,163	4.77	49
Curtis Adams, Central Mich.	1981-84	761	4,162	5.47	87
¢Ricky Williams, Texas	1995-97	650	4,155	6.39	87
Allen Pinkett, Notre Dame	1982-85	889	4,131	4.65	76
Robert Holcombe, Illinois	1994-97	943	4,105	4.35	67
James Gray, Texas Tech	1986-89	742	4,066	5.48	72
Robert Lavette, Georgia Tech	1981-84	914	4,066	4.45	83
Stump Mitchell, Citadel	1977-80	756	4,062	5.37	77
Dalton Hilliard, LSU	1982-85	882	4,050	4.59	66
Napoleon Kaufman, Washington	1991-94	710	4,041	5.69	91
Charles Alexander, LSU	1975-78	855	4,035	4.72	64
Darrin Nelson, Stanford	1977-78, 80-81	703	4,033	5.74	80
Joe Washington, Oklahoma	1972-75	656	3,995	6.09	71
Astron Whatley, Kent	1994-97	878	3,989	4.54	91
Mike Voight, North Caro.	1973-76	826	3,971	4.81	84
Warrick Dunn, Florida St.	1993-96	575	3,958	6.88	63
Jamie Morris, Michigan	1984-87	742	3,944	5.32	74
Eric Bieniemy, Colorado	1987-90	699	3,940	5.64	69
Abu Wilson, Utah St.	1992, 94-96	792	3,931	4.96	59
Emmitt Smith, Florida	1987-89	700	3,928	5.61	96
Sedrick Shaw, Iowa	1993-96	792	3,894	4.92	80
Ron "Po" James, New Mexico St.	1968-71	818	3,884	4.75	69
Ahman Green, Nebraska	1995-97	574	3,880	6.76	70
Steve Owens, Oklahoma	1967-69	905	3,867	4.27	‡‡49
Mike Williams, New Mexico	1975-78	857	3,862	4.51	36
June Henley, Kansas	1993-96	823	3,841	4.67	77
Sonny Collins, Kentucky	1972-75	777	3,835	4.94	66
Eric Wilkerson, Kent	1985-88	735	3,830	5.21	74
Billy Sims, Oklahoma	$1975-79	538	3,813	7.09	‡‡71
James McDougald, Wake Forest	1976-79	880	3,811	4.33	62
Tony Sands, Kansas	1988-91	778	3,788	4.87	66

**Record. $See page 6 for explanation. ‡‡Did not score. ††Record for minimum 781 carries. #Record for minimum 414 carries. ¢Active player.*

CAREER YARDS RECORD PROGRESSION
(Record Yards—Player, Team, Seasons Played)

1,961—Marshall Goldberg, Pittsburgh, 1936-38; **2,105**—Tom Harmon, Michigan, 1938-40; **2,271**—Frank Sinkwich, Georgia, 1940-42; **2,301**—Bill Daley, Minnesota, 1940-42, Michigan, 1943; **2,957**—Glenn Davis, Army, 1943-46; **3,095**—Eddie Price, Tulane, 1946-49; **3,238**—John Papit, Virginia, 1947-50; **3,381**—Art Luppino, Arizona, 1953-56; **3,388**—Eugene "Mercury" Morris, West Tex. A&M, 1966-68; **3,867**—Steve Owens, Oklahoma, 1967-69; **4,715**—Ed Marinaro, Cornell, 1969-71; **5,177**—Archie Griffin, Ohio St., 1972-75; **6,082**—Tony Dorsett, Pittsburgh, 1973-76.

CAREER RUSHING TOUCHDOWNS

Player, Team	Years	G	TDs
Anthony Thompson, Indiana	1986-89	41	*64
Marshall Faulk, San Diego St.	1991-93	31	57
Steve Owens, Oklahoma	1967-69	30	56
Tony Dorsett, Pittsburgh	1973-76	43	55
Pete Johnson, Ohio St.	1973-76	41	51
Mike Rozier, Nebraska	1982-83	35	50
Billy Sims, Oklahoma	1975, 77-79	42	50
Ed Marinaro, Cornell	1969-71	27	50
Allen Pinkett, Notre Dame	1982-85	44	49
Herschel Walker, Georgia	1980-82	33	49
Ted Brown, North Caro. St.	1975-78	43	49
Skip Hicks, UCLA	$1993-97	40	48
Brian Mitchell, Southwestern La.	1986-89	43	47
Barry Sanders, Oklahoma St.	1986-88	30	47
Eric Dickerson, Southern Methodist	1979-82	42	47
Steve Bartalo, Colorado St.	1983-86	41	46
Charles White, Southern Cal	1976-79	44	46
¢Ricky Williams	1995-97	35	45
James Gray, Texas Tech	1986-89	44	45
Keith Byars, Ohio St.	1982-85	33	45
Robert Lavette, Georgia Tech	1981-84	43	45
Marcus Allen, Southern Cal	1978-81	44	45
Terry Miller, Oklahoma St.	1974-77	41	45

**Record. (Note: Howard Stevens of Louisville played two years at college division Randolph-Macon, 1968-69, with 33 touchdowns and two years at Louisville, 1971-72, with 25 touchdowns, scoring a total of 58 touchdowns in four years.) ¢Active player. $ See page 6 for explanation.*

SEASON YARDS

Player, Team	Year	G	Plays	Yards	Avg.
Barry Sanders, Oklahoma St.	†1988	11	344	*2,628	‡7.64
Marcus Allen, Southern Cal	†1981	11	*403	2,342	5.81
Troy Davis, Iowa St.	†1996	11	402	2,185	5.44
Mike Rozier, Nebraska	†1983	12	275	2,148	#7.81
Byron Hanspard, Texas Tech	1996	11	339	2,084	6.15
Rashaan Salaam, Colorado	†1994	11	298	2,055	6.90
Troy Davis, Iowa St.	†1995	11	345	2,010	5.83
LeShon Johnson, Northern Ill.	†1993	11	327	1,976	6.04
Tony Dorsett, Pittsburgh	†1976	11	338	1,948	5.76
Lorenzo White, Michigan St.	†1985	11	386	1,908	4.94
Wasean Tait, Toledo	1995	11	357	1,905	5.34
Ricky Williams, Texas	†1997	11	279	1,893	6.78
Herschel Walker, Georgia	1981	11	385	1,891	4.91
Brian Pruitt, Central Mich.	1994	11	292	1,890	6.47
Ed Marinaro, Cornell	†1971	9	356	1,881	5.28
Ahman Green, Nebraska	1997	12	278	1,877	6.75
Ernest Anderson, Oklahoma St.	†1982	11	353	1,877	5.32
Ricky Bell, Southern Cal	†1975	11	357	1,875	5.25
Paul Palmer, Temple	†1986	11	346	1,866	5.39
Ron Dayne, Wisconsin	1996	12	295	1,863	6.32
George Jones, San Diego St.	1995	12	305	1,842	6.04
Eddie George, Ohio St.	1995	12	303	1,826	6.03
Charles White, Southern Cal	†1979	10	293	1,803	6.15
Anthony Thompson, Indiana	†1989	11	358	1,793	5.01
Obie Graves, Cal St. Fullerton	1978	12	275	1,789	6.51
Bo Jackson, Auburn	1985	11	278	1,786	6.42
George Rogers, South Caro.	†1980	11	297	1,781	6.00
Billy Sims, Oklahoma	†1978	11	231	1,762	7.63
Charles White, Southern Cal	1978	12	342	1,760	5.15
Robert Newhouse, Houston	1971	11	277	1,757	6.34
Byron Morris, Texas Tech	1993	11	298	1,752	5.88
Herschel Walker, Georgia	1982	11	335	1,752	5.23
Scott Harley, East Caro.	1996	11	307	1,745	5.68
Earl Campbell, Texas	†1977	11	267	1,744	6.53
Mike Pringle, Cal St. Fullerton	1989	11	296	1,727	5.83
Tim Biakabutuka, Michigan	1995	12	279	1,724	6.18
Lawrence Phillips, Nebraska	1994	12	286	1,722	6.02
Don McCauley, North Caro.	1970	11	324	1,720	5.31

**Record. †National champion. ‡Record for minimum 282 carries. #Record for minimum 214 carries.*

SINGLE-GAME YARDS

Yds.	Player, Team (Opponent)	Date
396	Tony Sands, Kansas (Missouri)	Nov. 23, 1991
386	Marshall Faulk, San Diego St. (Pacific [Cal.])	Sept. 14, 1991
378	Troy Davis, Iowa St. (Missouri)	Sept. 28, 1996
377	Anthony Thompson, Indiana (Wisconsin)	Nov. 11, 1989
373	Astron Whatley, Kent (Eastern Mich.)	Sept. 20, 1997
357	Mike Pringle, Cal St. Fullerton (New Mexico St.)	Nov. 4, 1989
357	Rueben Mayes, Washington St. (Oregon)	Oct. 27, 1984
356	Brian Pruitt, Central Mich. (Toledo)	Nov. 5, 1994
356	Eddie Lee Ivery, Georgia Tech (Air Force)	Nov. 11, 1978
351	Scott Harley, East Caro. (North Caro. St.)	Nov. 30, 1996
350	Eric Allen, Michigan St. (Purdue)	Oct. 30, 1971
349	Paul Palmer, Temple (East Caro.)	Oct. 11, 1986
347	Ricky Bell, Southern Cal (Washington St.)	Oct. 9, 1976
347	Ron Johnson, Michigan (Wisconsin)	Nov. 16, 1968
343	Tony Jeffery, Texas Christian (Tulane)	Sept. 13, 1986
342	Roosevelt Leaks, Texas (Southern Methodist)	Nov. 3, 1973
342	Charlie Davis, Colorado (Oklahoma St.)	Nov. 13, 1971
340	Eugene "Mercury" Morris, West Tex. A&M (Montana St.)	Oct. 5, 1968
339	Ron Dayne, Wisconsin, (Hawaii)	Nov. 30, 1996
332	Barry Sanders, Oklahoma St. (Texas Tech)	Dec. 3, 1988
329	John Leach, Wake Forest (Maryland)	Nov. 20, 1993
328	Derrick Fenner, North Caro. (Virginia)	Nov. 15, 1986
326	George Swarn, Miami, Ohio (Eastern Mich.)	Nov. 16, 1985
326	Fred Wendt, UTEP (New Mexico St.)	Nov. 25, 1948
325	Andre Davis, Texas Christian (New Mexico)	Sept. 10, 1994
322	LeShon Johnson, Northern Ill. (Southern Ill.)	Oct. 2, 1993
322	Greg Allen, Florida St. (Western Caro.)	Oct. 31, 1981
321	David Thompson, Oklahoma St. (Baylor)	Nov. 23, 1996
321	Frank Mordica, Vanderbilt (Air Force)	Nov. 18, 1978
320	Barry Sanders, Oklahoma St. (Kansas St.)	Oct. 29, 1988
319	Andre Herrera, Southern Ill. (Northern Ill.)	Oct. 23, 1976
319	Jim Pilot, New Mexico St. (Hardin-Simmons)	Nov. 25, 1961
317	Rashaan Salaam, Colorado (Texas)	Oct. 1, 1994
316	Emmitt Smith, Florida (New Mexico)	Oct. 21, 1989
316	Mike Adamle, Northwestern (Wisconsin)	Oct. 18, 1969
315	Robert Holcombe, Illinois (Minnesota)	Nov. 16, 1996
314	Eddie George, Ohio St. (Illinois)	Nov. 11, 1995
314	Tavian Banks, Iowa (Tulsa)	Sept. 13, 1997
313	Tim Biakabutuka, Michigan (Ohio St.)	Nov. 25, 1995
312	Mark Brus, Tulsa (New Mexico St.)	Oct. 27, 1990
312	Barry Sanders, Oklahoma St. (Kansas)	Nov. 12, 1988
310	Tony Alford, Colorado St. (Utah)	Oct. 28, 1989
310	Mitchell True, Pacific, Cal. (UC Davis)	Nov. 18, 1972
308	Stacey Robinson (QB), Northern Ill. (Fresno St.)	Oct. 6, 1990
307	Curtis Kuykendall, Auburn (Miami [Fla.])	Nov. 24, 1944
306	LeShon Johnson, Northern Ill. (Iowa)	Nov. 6, 1993
304	Casey McBeth, Toledo (Akron)	Oct. 22, 1994
304	Barry Sanders, Oklahoma St. (Tulsa)	Oct. 1, 1988
304	Sam Dejarnette, Southern Miss. (Florida St.)	Sept. 25, 1982
304	Bill Marek, Wisconsin (Minnesota)	Nov. 23, 1974
303	Tony Dorsett, Pittsburgh (Notre Dame)	Nov. 15, 1975
302	Troy Davis, Iowa St. (UNLV)	Sept. 23, 1995
302	Jason Davis, Louisiana Tech (Southwestern La.)	Sept. 29, 1990
302	Kevin Lowe, Wyoming (South Dak. St.)	Nov. 10, 1984
300	Marshall Faulk, San Diego St. (Hawaii)	Nov. 14, 1992

ANNUAL CHAMPIONS

Year	Player, Team	Class	Plays	Yards
1937	Byron "Whizzer" White, Colorado	Sr.	181	1,121
1938	Len Eshmont, Fordham	So.	132	831
1939	John Polanski, Wake Forest	So.	137	882
1940	Al Ghesquiere, Detroit	Sr.	146	957
1941	Frank Sinkwich, Georgia	Jr.	209	1,103
1942	Rudy Mobley, Hardin-Simmons	So.	187	1,281
1943	Creighton Miller, Notre Dame	Sr.	151	911
1944	Wayne "Red" Williams, Minnesota	Jr.	136	911
1945	Bob Fenimore, Oklahoma St.	Jr.	142	1,048
1946	Rudy Mobley, Hardin-Simmons	Sr.	227	1,262
1947	Wilton Davis, Hardin-Simmons	So.	193	1,173
1948	Fred Wendt, UTEP	Sr.	184	1,570
1949	John Dottley, Mississippi	Jr.	208	1,312
1950	Wilford White, Arizona St.	Sr.	199	1,502
1951	Ollie Matson, San Francisco	Sr.	245	1,566
1952	Howie Waugh, Tulsa	Sr.	164	1,372
1953	J. C. Caroline, Illinois	So.	194	1,256
1954	Art Luppino, Arizona	So.	179	1,359
1955	Art Luppino, Arizona	Jr.	209	1,313
1956	Jim Crawford, Wyoming	Sr.	200	1,104
1957	Leon Burton, Arizona St.	Sr.	117	1,126
1958	Dick Bass, Pacific (Cal.)	Jr.	205	1,361
1959	Pervis Atkins, New Mexico St.	Jr.	130	971
1960	Bob Gaiters, New Mexico St.	Sr.	197	1,338
1961	Jim Pilot, New Mexico St.	So.	191	1,278

Year	Player, Team	Class	Plays	Yards
1962	Jim Pilot, New Mexico St.	Jr.	208	1,247
1963	Dave Casinelli, Memphis	Sr.	219	1,016
1964	Brian Piccolo, Wake Forest	Sr.	252	1,044
1965	Mike Garrett, Southern Cal	Sr.	267	1,440
1966	Ray McDonald, Idaho	Sr.	259	1,329
1967	O. J. Simpson, Southern Cal	Jr.	266	1,415
1968	O. J. Simpson, Southern Cal	Sr.	355	1,709
1969	Steve Owens, Oklahoma	Sr.	358	1,523

Beginning in 1970, ranked on per-game (instead of total) yards

Year	Player, Team	Class	G	Plays	Yards	Avg.
1970	Ed Marinaro, Cornell	Jr.	9	285	1,425	158.3
1971	Ed Marinaro, Cornell	Sr.	9	356	1,881	209.0
1972	Pete VanValkenburg, Brigham Young	Sr.	10	232	1,386	138.6
1973	Mark Kellar, Northern Ill.	Sr.	11	291	1,719	156.3
1974	Louie Giammona, Utah St.	Jr.	10	329	1,534	153.4
1975	Ricky Bell, Southern Cal	Jr.	11	357	1,875	170.5
1976	Tony Dorsett, Pittsburgh	Sr.	11	338	1,948	177.1
1977	Earl Campbell, Texas	Sr.	11	267	1,744	158.5
1978	Billy Sims, Oklahoma	Jr.	11	231	1,762	160.2
1979	Charles White, Southern Cal	Sr.	10	293	1,803	180.3
1980	George Rogers, South Caro.	Sr.	11	297	1,781	161.9
1981	Marcus Allen, Southern Cal	Sr.	11	*403	2,342	212.9
1982	Ernest Anderson, Oklahoma St.	Jr.	11	353	1,877	170.6
1983	Mike Rozier, Nebraska	Sr.	12	275	2,148	179.0
1984	Keith Byars, Ohio St.	Jr.	11	313	1,655	150.5
1985	Lorenzo White, Michigan St.	So.	11	386	1,908	173.5
1986	Paul Palmer, Temple	Sr.	11	346	1,866	169.6
1987	Elbert "Ickey" Woods, UNLV	Sr.	11	259	1,658	150.7
1988	Barry Sanders, Oklahoma St.	Jr.	11	344	*2,628	*238.9
1989	Anthony Thompson, Indiana	Sr.	11	358	1,793	163.0
1990	Gerald Hudson, Oklahoma St.	Sr.	11	279	1,642	149.3
1991	Marshall Faulk, San Diego St.	Fr.	9	201	1,429	158.8
1992	Marshall Faulk, San Diego St.	So.	10	265	1,630	163.0
1993	LeShon Johnson, Northern Ill.	Sr.	11	327	1,976	179.6
1994	Rashaan Salaam, Colorado	Jr.	11	298	2,055	186.8
1995	Troy Davis, Iowa St.	So.	11	345	2,010	182.7
1996	Troy Davis, Iowa St.	Jr.	11	402	2,185	198.6
1997	Ricky Williams, Texas	Jr.	11	279	1,893	172.1

**Record.*

FRESHMAN 1,000-YARD RUSHERS

Player, Team	Year	Yards
Ron "Po" James, New Mexico St.	1968	1,291
Tony Dorsett, Pittsburgh	1973	1,586
James McDougald, Wake Forest	1976	1,018
Mike Harkrader, Indiana	1976	1,003
Amos Lawrence, North Caro.	1977	1,211
Darrin Nelson, Stanford	1977	1,069
Mike Smith, Chattanooga	1977	1,062
Gwain Durden, Chattanooga	1977	1,049
Allen Ross, Northern Ill.	1977	1,043
Allen Harvin, Cincinnati	1978	1,238
Joe Morris, Syracuse	1978	1,001
Ron Lear, Marshall	1979	1,162
Herschel Walker, Georgia	1980	1,616
Kerwin Bell, Kansas	1980	1,114
Joe McIntosh, North Caro. St.	1981	1,190
Steve Bartalo, Colorado St.	1983	1,113
Spencer Tillman, Oklahoma	1983	1,047
D. J. Dozier, Penn St.	1983	1,002
Eddie Johnson, Utah	1984	1,021
Darrell Thompson, Minnesota	1986	1,240
Emmitt Smith, Florida	1987	1,341
Reggie Cobb, Tennessee	1987	1,197
Bernie Parmalee, Ball St.	1987	1,064
Curvin Richards, Pittsburgh	1988	1,228
Chuck Webb, Tennessee	1989	1,236
Robert Smith, Ohio St.	1990	1,064
Marshall Faulk, San Diego St.	1991	1,429
Greg Hill, Texas A&M	1991	1,216
David Small, Cincinnati	1991	1,004
Winslow Oliver, New Mexico	1992	1,063
Deland McCullough, Miami (Ohio)	1992	1,026
Terrell Willis, Rutgers	1993	1,261
June Henley, Kansas	1993	1,127
Marquis Williams, Arkansas St.	1993	1,060
Leon Johnson, North Caro.	1993	1,012
Alex Smith, Indiana	1994	1,475
Astron Whatley, Kent	1994	1,003
Denvis Manns, New Mexico St.	1995	1,120
Silas Massey, Central Mich.	1995	1,089
Ahman Green, Nebraska	1995	1,086
Ron Dayne, Wisconsin	1996	*1,863
Demond Parker, Oklahoma	1996	1,184
Sedrick Irvin, Michigan St.	1996	1,036
Jamal Lewis, Tennessee	1997	1,364
Robert Sanford, Western Mich.	1997	1,033

**Record for freshman.*

Quarterback Rushing

SEASON YARDS

Player, Team	Year	G	Plays	Yards	TD	Avg.
Beau Morgan, Air Force	1996	11	225	*1,494	18	6.64
Stacey Robinson, Northern Ill.	1989	11	223	1,443	19	6.47
Chris McCoy, Navy	1997	11	246	1,370	*20	5.57
Dee Dowis, Air Force	1987	12	194	1,315	10	6.78
Brian Mitchell, Southwestern La.	1989	11	237	1,311	19	5.53
Fred Solomon, Tampa	1974	11	193	1,300	19	6.74
Dee Dowis, Air Force	1989	12	172	1,286	18	*7.48
Beau Morgan, Air Force	1995	12	229	1,285	19	5.61
Stacey Robinson, Northern Ill.	1990	11	193	1,238	19	6.41
Chris McCoy, Navy	1996	11	268	1,228	16	4.58
Rob Perez, Air Force	1991	12	233	1,157	10	4.97
Jack Mildren, Oklahoma	1971	11	193	1,140	17	5.91
Nolan Cromwell, Kansas	1975	11	218	1,124	9	5.16
Scott Frost, Nebraska	1997	12	176	1,095	19	6.22
Michael Carter, Hawaii	1991	12	221	1,092	16	4.94
Tory Crawford, Army	1986	11	*244	1,075	15	4.41
Kareem Wilson, Ohio	1996	12	275	1,072	14	3.90
Bart Weiss, Air Force	1985	12	180	1,032	12	5.73
Jimmy Sidle, Auburn	1963	10	185	1,006	10	5.44
Reggie Collier, Southern Miss.	1981	11	153	1,005	12	6.57
Darian Hagan, Colorado	1989	11	186	1,004	17	5.40

**Record.*

CAREER YARDS

Player, Team	Year	G	Plays	Yards	TD	Avg.
Dee Dowis, Air Force	1986-89	47	543	*3,612	41	76.9
Chris McCoy, Navy	1995-97	32	682	3,401	43	106.3
Beau Morgan, Air Force	1994-96	35	594	3,379	42	96.5
Brian Mitchell, Southwestern La.	1986-89	43	678	3,335	*47	77.6
Fred Solomon, Tampa	1971-74	43	557	3,299	39	76.7
Stacey Robinson, Northern Ill.	1988-90	25	429	2,727	38	*109.1
Jamelle Holieway, Oklahoma	1985-88	38	505	2,699	30	71.0
Bill Hurley, Syracuse	1975-79	46	*685	2,551	19	55.5
Michael Carter, Hawaii	1990-93	46	574	2,534	39	55.1
Chad Nelson, Rice	1994-97	40	466	2,415	24	60.4
Bill Deery, William & Mary	1972-74	33	443	2,401	19	72.8
Reggie Collier, Southern Miss.	1979-82	39	446	2,304	26	59.1
John Bond, Mississippi St.	1980-83	44	572	2,280	24	51.8
Tory Crawford, Army	1984-87	31	495	2,255	34	72.7
Tom Parr, Colgate	1971-73	30	435	2,221	31	74.0
Alton Grizzard, Navy	1987-90	38	599	2,174	15	57.2
Gary Wood, Cornell	1961-63	27	433	2,156	19	79.9
Roy DeWalt, Texas-Arlington	1975, 77-79	38	468	2,136	27	56.2
Steve Taylor, Nebraska	1985-88	37	431	2,125	32	57.4
Bucky Richardson, Texas A&M	1987-88, 90-91	41	370	2,095	30	51.1
Rocky Long, New Mexico	1969-71	31	469	2,071	21	66.8
Steve Davis, Oklahoma	1973-75	33	515	2,069	33	62.7
Rick Leach, Michigan	1975-78	43	440	2,053	34	47.7
Prince McJunkins, Wichita St.	1979-82	44	613	2,047	27	46.5
Rickey Foggie, Minnesota	1984-87	42	517	2,038	24	48.5
Chris McCoy, Navy	1995-96	21	436	2,031	23	96.7
Major Harris, West Va.	1987-89	33	386	2,030	18	51.5
Steve Gage, Tulsa	1983-84, 86	33	522	2,029	30	61.5
Harry Gilmer, Alabama	1944-47	40	390	2,025	19	50.6
Darian Hagan, Colorado	1988-91	41	489	2,007	27	49.0

**Record.*

Passing

SAMPLE COMPILATION OF NCAA PASSING EFFICIENCY RATING

Player	G	Att.	Cmp.	Yds.	TD	Int.
Danny Wuerffel, Florida	46	1,170	708	10,875	114	42

Completion Percentage:	60.51
Yards Per Attempted Pass:	9.29
Percent of Passes for TDs:	9.74
Percent of Passes Intercepted:	3.59

ADD the first three factors:

		Rating Points
Completion Percentage:	60.51	60.51
Yards Per Attempted Pass:	9.295 times 8.4	78.08
Percent of Passes for TDs:	9.74 times 3.3	32.14
		170.73

SUBTRACT the last factor:

Percent of Passes Intercepted:	3.59 times 2	-7.18
	Round off to:	**163.6**

DIVISION I-A PASSING EFFICIENCY RATING COMPARISON
1979-97

Passing statistics in Division I-A have increased dramatically since 1979, the first year that the NCAA official national statistics used the passing efficiency formula to rank passers in all divisions. Because passers have become more proficient every year, the average passing efficiency rating (based on final regular-season trends) also has risen at a similar rate. For historical purposes, the average passing efficiency rating for the division by year is presented below to show how any individual or team might rank in a particular season.

Year	Pass Effic. Rating	Year	Pass Effic. Rating
1979	104.49	1989	118.35
1980	106.63	1990	117.39
1981	107.00	1991	117.94
1982	110.77	1992	114.50
1983	113.56	1993	122.43
1984	113.02	1994	120.59
1985	114.58	1995	120.17
1986	115.00	1996	120.24
1987	112.67	1997	122.86
1988	114.32		

Photo from Stanford sports information

Stanford's John Elway ranks 20th in all-time career passing efficiency among quarterbacks with a minimum of 500 completions.

CAREER PASSING EFFICIENCY
(Minimum 500 Completions)

Player, Team	Years	Att.	Cmp.	Int.	Pct.	Yds.	TD	Pts.
Danny Wuerffel, Florida	1993-96	1,170	708	42	.605	10,875	114	*163.6
Ty Detmer, Brigham Young	1988-91	*1,530	*958	65	.626	*15,031	*121	162.7
Steve Sarkisian, Brigham Young	1995-96	789	528	26	.669	7,464	53	162.0
Billy Blanton, San Diego St.	1993-96	920	588	25	.639	8,165	67	157.1
Jim McMahon, Brigham Young	1977-78, 80-81	1,060	653	34	.616	9,536	84	156.9
Steve Young, Brigham Young	1981-83	908	592	33	.652	7,733	56	149.8
Robbie Bosco, Brigham Young	1983-85	997	638	36	.640	8,400	66	149.4
Mike Maxwell, Nevada	1993-95	881	560	33	.636	7,256	62	148.5
Chuck Long, Iowa	$1981-85	1,072	692	46	‡.646	9,210	64	147.8
John Walsh, Brigham Young	1991-94	973	587	35	.603	8,375	66	147.8
Peyton Manning, Tennessee	1994-97	1,381	863	33	.625	11,201	89	147.1
Rob Johnson, Southern Cal	1991-94	963	623	24	.647	7,743	52	145.1
Andre Ware, Houston	1987-89	1,074	660	28	.615	8,202	75	143.3
Steve Stenstrom, Stanford	1991-94	1,320	833	36	.631	10,531	72	142.7
Marvin Graves, Syracuse	1990-93	943	563	45	.597	8,466	48	142.4
Doug Gaynor, Long Beach St.	1984-85	837	569	35	.680	6,793	35	141.6
Danny Kanell, Florida St.	1992-95	851	529	26	.622	6,372	57	141.1
Dan McGwire, Iowa/San Diego St.	1986-87, 89-90	973	575	30	.591	8,164	49	140.0
Chris Vargas, Nevada	1992-93	806	502	34	.623	6,359	47	139.4
John Elway, Stanford	1979-82	1,246	774	39	.621	9,349	77	139.3
Mike McCoy, Long Beach St./Utah	1991, 92-94	1,069	650	26	.608	8,342	56	138.8
David Klingler, Houston	1988-91	1,268	732	38	.577	9,466	91	138.1
Scott Milanovich, Maryland	1992-95	982	650	35	**.662	7,301	49	138.0
Scott Mitchell, Utah	1987-89	1,165	669	38	.574	8,981	68	137.7
Shane Matthews, Florida	1989-92	1,202	722	46	.601	9,287	74	137.6
Marc Wilson, Brigham Young	1977-79	937	535	46	.571	7,637	61	137.2
Eric Zeier, Georgia	1991-94	1,402	838	37	.598	11,153	67	137.1
Randall Cunningham, UNLV	1982-84	1,029	597	29	.580	8,020	59	136.8
Kerwin Bell, Florida	1984-87	953	549	35	.576	7,585	56	136.5
Tom Hodson, LSU	1986-89	1,163	674	41	.580	9,115	69	136.3
Rodney Peete, Southern Cal	1985-88	972	571	32	.587	7,640	52	135.8
Ron Powlus, Notre Dame	1994-97	969	558	27	.576	7,602	52	135.6
Darrell Bevell, Wisconsin	1992-95	1,012	625	37	.618	7,429	58	135.0
Pat Barnes, California	1993-96	912	522	26	.572	7,047	51	134.9
Troy Kopp, Pacific (Cal.)	1989-92	1,374	798	47	.581	10,258	87	134.9
Joe Adams, Tennessee St.	1977-80	1,100	604	60	.549	8,649	81	134.4
Mike Gundy, Oklahoma St.	1986-89	1,037	606	37	.584	8,072	54	133.9
Todd Santos, San Diego St.	1984-87	1,484	910	57	.613	11,425	70	133.9
Tony Eason, Illinois	1981-82	856	526	29	.615	6,608	37	133.8
Jake Plummer, Arizona St.	1993-96	1,107	613	34	.554	8,626	64	133.8

Player, Team	Years	Att.	Cmp.	Int.	Pct.	Yds.	TD	Pts.
Danny McCoin, Cincinnati	1984-87	899	544	26	.605	6,801	39	132.6
Rich Campbell, California	1977-80	891	574	42	.644	6,933	33	132.6
Jim Everett, Purdue	$1981-85	923	550	30	.596	7,158	40	132.5
Matt Rodgers, Iowa	1988-91	844	516	30	.611	6,308	40	132.5
Doug Flutie, Boston College	1981-84	1,270	677	54	.533	10,579	67	132.2
Gino Torretta, Miami (Fla.)	1989-92	991	555	24	.560	7,690	47	132.0
Robert Hall, Texas Tech	1990-93	997	548	28	.550	7,908	48	131.9
Jack Trudeau, Illinois	1981, 83-85	1,151	736	38	†.639	8,146	51	131.4
Kevin Sweeney, Fresno St.	$1982-86	1,336	731	48	.547	10,623	66	130.6
Bill Musgrave, Oregon	1987-90	1,018	582	38	.572	7,631	55	130.6
Stoney Case, New Mexico	1991-94	1,237	677	39	.547	9,460	67	130.5
Glenn Foley, Boston College	1990-93	1,275	703	60	.551	10,042	72	130.5
Gene Swick, Toledo	1972-75	938	556	45	.593	7,267	44	130.3
Steve Taneyhill, South Caro.	1992-95	1,209	727	37	.601	8,555	61	130.1
Jason Verduzco, Illinois	1989-92	986	622	29	.631	6,974	40	130.0
Brian McClure, Bowling Green	1982-85	1,427	900	58	.631	10,280	63	130.0

(400-499 Completions)

Player, Team	Years	Att.	Cmp.	Int.	Pct.	Yds.	TD	Pts.
Vinny Testaverde, Miami (Fla.)	1982, 84-86	674	413	25	.613	6,058	48	152.9
Josh Wallwork, Wyoming	1995-96	729	449	28	.616	6,453	54	152.7
Trent Dilfer, Fresno St.	1991-93	774	461	21	.596	6,944	51	151.2
Troy Aikman, Oklahoma/UCLA	1984-85, 87-88	637	401	18	.630	5,436	40	149.7
Chuck Hartlieb, Iowa	1985-88	716	461	17	.643	6,269	34	148.9
Elvis Grbac, Michigan	1989-92	754	477	29	.633	5,859	64	148.9
Bobby Hoying, Ohio St.	1992-95	782	463	33	.592	6,751	54	146.1
Gifford Nielsen, Brigham Young	1975-77	708	415	29	.586	5,833	55	145.3
Tom Ramsey, UCLA	1979-82	691	411	33	.595	5,844	48	143.9
Shawn Moore, Virginia	1987-90	762	421	32	.552	6,629	55	143.8
Moses Moreno, Colorado St.	1994-97	787	457	28	.581	6,689	49	142.9
Jerry Rhome, Southern Methodist/Tulsa	1961, 63-64	713	448	23	.628	5,472	47	142.6
Thad Busby, Florida St.	1994-97	715	420	27	.587	5,916	46	141.9
Charlie Ward, Florida St.	1989, 91-93	759	474	21	.625	5,747	49	141.8
Ryan Leaf, Washington St.	1995-97	845	456	23	.540	7,102	58	141.8
Bernie Kosar, Miami (Fla.)	1983-84	743	463	29	.623	5,971	40	139.8
Craig Erickson, Miami (Fla.)	1987-90	752	420	22	.559	6,056	46	137.8
Mike Bobo, Georgia	1994-97	766	445	26	.581	6,334	38	137.1
Dave Yarema, Michigan St.	$1982-86	727	447	29	.615	5,569	41	136.5
Ryan Clement, Miami (Fla.)	1994-97	720	427	27	.593	5,730	35	134.7
Gary Huff, Florida St.	1970-72	796	436	42	.548	6,378	52	133.1
Joe Hughes, Wyoming	1992-93	744	424	25	.570	5,841	38	133.1
Jeff Francis, Tennessee	1985-88	768	476	26	.620	5,867	31	132.7
Mike Perez, San Jose St.	1986-87	792	471	30	.595	6,194	36	132.6
Cale Gundy, Oklahoma	1990-93	751	420	31	.559	6,142	36	132.2

(325-399 Completions)

Player, Team	Years	Att.	Cmp.	Int.	Pct.	Yds.	TD	Pts.
Jim Harbaugh, Michigan	1983-86	582	368	19	.632	5,215	31	149.6
Koy Detmer, Colorado	1992, 94-96	594	350	25	.589	5,390	40	148.9
Danny White, Arizona St.	1971-73	649	345	36	.532	5,932	59	148.9
Tim Gutierrez, San Diego St.	1992-94	580	357	19	.616	4,740	36	144.1
Jim Karsatos, Ohio St.	1983-86	573	330	19	.576	4,698	36	140.6
Mike Fouts, Utah	1995-96	625	356	19	.570	5,107	39	140.1
Jerry Tagge, Nebraska	1969-71	581	348	19	.599	4,704	33	140.1
Garrett Gabriel, Hawaii	1987-90	661	356	31	.539	5,631	47	139.5
Rick Mirer, Notre Dame	1989-92	698	377	23	.540	5,996	41	139.0
Gary Sheide, Brigham Young	1973-74	594	358	31	.603	4,524	45	138.8
Dan Speltz, Cal St. Fullerton	1988-89	583	350	19	.600	4,595	33	138.4
Don McPherson, Syracuse	$1983-87	687	367	29	.534	5,812	46	138.1
Joe Youngblood, Central Mich.	1990-93	572	331	28	.579	4,718	35	137.6
Kerry Collins, Penn St.	1991-94	657	370	21	.563	5,304	39	137.3
Sam King, UNLV	1979-81	625	360	29	.576	5,393	30	136.6
J. J. Joe, Baylor	1990-93	665	347	28	.522	5,995	31	134.9
Jesse Freitas, Stanford/San Diego St.	1970, 72-73	547	338	33	.618	4,408	28	134.3
Jeff Blake, East Caro.	1988-91	667	360	20	.540	5,133	43	133.9

**Record. $See page 6 for explanation. **Record for minimum 875 attempts. ‡Record for minimum 1,000 attempts. †Record for minimum 1,100 attempts.*

SEASON PASSING EFFICIENCY

(Minimum 15 Attempts Per Game)

Player, Team	Year	G	Att.	Cmp.	Int.	Pct.	Yds.	TD	Pts.
Danny Wuerffel, Florida	†1995	11	325	210	10	.646	3,266	35	*178.4
Jim McMahon, Brigham Young	#†1980	12	445	284	18	.638	4,571	47	176.9
Ty Detmer, Brigham Young	†1989	12	412	265	15	.643	4,560	32	175.6
Steve Sarkisian, Brigham Young	†1996	14	404	278	12	.688	4,027	33	173.6
Trent Dilfer, Fresno St.	†1993	11	333	217	4	.652	3,276	28	173.1
Kerry Collins, Penn St.	†1994	11	264	176	7	.667	2,679	21	172.9
Jerry Rhome, Tulsa	#†1964	10	326	224	4	.687	2,870	32	172.6
Danny Wuerffel, Florida	1996	12	360	207	13	.575	3,625	39	170.6
Bobby Hoying, Ohio St.	1995	12	303	192	11	.634	3,023	28	170.4
Billy Blanton, San Diego St.	1996	11	344	227	5	.660	3,221	29	169.6
Elvis Grbac, Michigan	†1991	11	228	152	5	.667	1,955	24	169.0
Cade McNown, UCLA	†1997	11	283	173	5	.611	2,877	22	168.6
Ty Detmer, Brigham Young	#1991	12	403	249	12	.618	4,031	35	168.5
Steve Young, Brigham Young	#†1983	11	429	306	10	*.713	3,902	33	168.5
Vinny Testaverde, Miami (Fla.)	†1986	10	276	175	9	.634	2,557	26	165.8

Player, Team	Year	G	Att.	Cmp.	Int.	Pct.	Yds.	TD	Pts.
Brian Dowling, Yale	1968	9	160	92	10	.575	1,554	19	165.8
Dave Barr, California	1993	11	275	187	12	.680	2,619	21	164.5
Don McPherson, Syracuse	†1987	11	229	129	11	.563	2,341	22	164.3
Dave Wilson, Ball St.	1977	11	177	115	7	.650	1,589	17	164.2
Bob Berry, Oregon	1963	10	171	101	7	.591	1,675	16	164.0
Jim Harbaugh, Michigan	†1985	11	212	139	6	.656	1,913	18	163.7
Troy Aikman, UCLA	1987	11	243	159	6	.654	2,354	16	163.6
Turk Schonert, Stanford	†1979	11	221	148	6	.670	1,922	19	163.0
Donovan McNabb, Syracuse	1995	11	207	128	6	.618	1,991	16	162.3
Brian Broomell, Temple	1979	11	214	120	11	.561	2,103	22	162.3
Dennis Shaw, San Diego St.	†1969	10	335	199	26	.594	3,185	39	162.2
Timm Rosenbach, Washington St.	†1988	11	302	199	10	.659	2,791	23	162.0
Davey O'Brien, Texas Christian	¢#†1938	10	167	93	4	.557	1,457	19	161.7
Chuck Hartlieb, Iowa	1987	12	299	196	8	.656	2,855	19	161.4
Ryan Leaf, Washington St.	1997	11	375	210	10	.560	3,637	33	161.2
Darrell Bevell, Wisconsin	1993	11	256	177	10	.691	2,294	19	161.1
David Brown, Duke	1989	9	163	104	6	.638	1,479	14	161.0
Shawn Moore, Virginia	†1990	10	241	144	8	.598	2,262	21	160.7
Joe Germaine, Ohio St.	1997	12	184	119	7	.647	1,674	15	160.4
Chuck Long, Iowa	1983	10	236	144	8	.610	2,434	14	160.4
Mike Maxwell, Nevada	#1995	9	409	277	17	.677	3,611	33	160.2
Jeff Garcia, San Jose St.	1991	9	160	99	5	.619	1,519	12	160.1
Matt Blundin, Virginia	1991	9	224	135	0	.603	1,902	19	159.6
Kerwin Bell, Florida	1985	11	288	180	8	.625	2,687	21	159.4
Mike Gundy, Oklahoma St.	1988	11	236	153	12	.648	2,163	19	158.2
Charlie Ward, Florida St.	1993	11	380	264	4	.695	3,032	27	157.8
Maurice DeShazo, Virginia Tech	1993	11	230	129	7	.561	2,080	22	157.5
Danny White, Arizona St.	1973	11	265	146	12	.551	2,609	23	157.4
Matt Miller, Kansas St.	1995	11	240	154	11	.642	2,059	22	157.3
Heath Shuler, Tennessee	1993	11	285	184	8	.646	2,354	25	157.3
Stan Heath, Nevada	#†1948	9	222	126	9	.568	2,005	22	157.2
Glenn Foley, Boston College	1993	11	363	222	10	.612	3,397	25	157.0
Jim Harbaugh, Michigan	1986	11	254	167	8	.658	2,557	10	157.0
John Dutton, Nevada	1997	11	367	225	6	.613	3,526	20	156.7
Brock Huard, Washington	1997	10	244	146	10	.598	2,140	23	156.4
Chris Vargas, Nevada	#1993	11	490	331	18	.676	4,265	34	156.2
Shawn Moore, Virginia	1989	11	221	125	7	.566	2,078	18	156.1
Dan Speltz, Cal St. Fullerton	1989	11	309	214	11	.693	2,671	20	156.1
John Walsh, Brigham Young	1993	11	397	244	15	.615	3,727	28	156.0
Ty Detmer, Brigham Young	1990	12	562	361	28	.642	*5,188	41	155.9
Mike Bobo, Georgia	1997	11	306	199	8	.650	2,751	19	155.8
Terry Dean, Florida	1994	10	180	109	10	.606	1,492	20	155.7
Rob Johnson, Southern Cal	1993	12	405	278	5	.686	3,285	26	155.5
Doug Williams, Grambling	#1977	11	352	181	18	.514	3,286	38	155.2
John Huarte, Notre Dame	1964	10	205	114	11	.556	2,062	16	155.1
Jim McMahon, Brigham Young	#†1981	10	423	272	7	.643	3,555	30	155.0

**Record. †National pass-efficiency champion. #National total-offense champion. ¢Available records before 1946 do not include TD passes except for O'Brien and relatively few other passers; thus, passing efficiency points cannot be compiled for those players without TD passes.*

ANNUAL PASSING EFFICIENCY LEADERS

(% Minimum 11 Attempts Per Game)

1946—Bill Mackrides, Nevada, 176.9; **1947**—Bobby Layne, Texas, 138.9; **1948**—Stan Heath, Nevada, 157.2 (#); **1949**—Bob Williams, Notre Dame, 159.1; **1950**—Claude Arnold, Oklahoma, 157.3; **1951**—Dick Kazmaier, Princeton, 155.3 (#); **1952**—Ron Morris, Tulsa, 177.4; **1953**—Bob Garrett, Stanford, 142.2; **1954**—Pete Vann, Army, 166.5; **1955**—George Welsh, Navy, 146.1 (#); **1956**—Tom Flores, Pacific (Cal.), 147.5; **1957**—Lee Grosscup, Utah, 175.5; **1958**—John Hangartner, Arizona St., 150.1; **1959**—Charley Johnson, New Mexico St., 135.7; **1960**—Eddie Wilson, Arizona, 140.8; **1961**—Ron DiGravio, Purdue, 140.1; **1962**—John Jacobs, Arizona St., 153.9; **1963**—Bob Berry, Oregon, 164.0; **1964**—Jerry Rhome, Tulsa, 172.6 (#).

(Minimum 15 Attempts Per Game)

1946—Ben Raimondi, Indiana, 117.0; **1947**—Charley Conerly, Mississippi, 125.8; **1948**—Stan Heath, Nevada, 157.2 (#); **1949**—Dick Doheny, Fordham, 153.3; **1950**—Dick Doheny, Fordham, 149.5; **1951**—Babe Parilli, Kentucky, 130.8; **1952**—Gene Rossi, Cincinnati, 149.7; **1953**—Bob Garrett, Stanford, 142.2; **1954**—Len Dawson, Purdue, 145.8; **1955**—George Welsh, Navy, 146.1 (#); **1956**—Bob Reinhart, San Jose St., 121.3; **1957**—Bob Newman, Washington St., 126.5 (#); **1958**—Randy Duncan, Iowa, 135.1; **1959**—Charley Johnson, New Mexico St., 135.7; **1960**—Charley Johnson, New Mexico St., 134.1; **1961**—Eddie Wilson, Arizona, 134.2; **1962**—Terry Baker, Oregon St., 146.5 (#); **1963**—Bob Berry, Oregon, 164.0; **1964**—Jerry Rhome, Tulsa, 172.6 (#).

(Minimum 15 Attempts Per Game)

Year	Player, Team	G	Att.	Cmp.	Int.	Pct.	Yds.	TD	Pts.
1965	Steve Sloan, Alabama	10	160	97	3	.606	1,453	10	153.8
1966	Dewey Warren, Tennessee	10	229	136	7	.594	1,716	18	142.2
1967	Bill Andrejko, Villanova	10	187	114	6	.610	1,405	13	140.6
1968	Brian Dowling, Yale	9	160	92	10	.575	1,554	19	165.8
1969	#Dennis Shaw, San Diego St.	10	335	199	26	.594	3,185	39	162.2
1970	Jerry Tagge, Nebraska	11	165	104	7	.630	1,383	12	149.0
1971	Jerry Tagge, Nebraska	12	239	143	4	.598	2,019	17	150.9
1972	John Hufnagel, Penn St.	11	216	115	8	.532	2,039	15	148.0
1973	Danny White, Arizona St.	11	265	146	12	.551	2,609	23	157.4
1974	#Steve Joachim, Temple	10	221	128	13	.579	1,950	20	150.1
1975	James Kubacki, Harvard	8	137	77	9	.562	1,273	11	147.6
1976	Steve Haynes, Louisiana Tech	10	216	120	11	.556	1,981	16	146.9
1977	Dave Wilson, Ball St.	11	177	115	7	.650	1,589	17	164.2
1978	Paul McDonald, Southern Cal	11	194	111	7	.572	1,667	18	152.8

Photo from Pittsburgh sports information

Pittsburgh quarterback Alex Van Pelt threw for 10,913 yards during his career to rank fifth among all-time leaders in passing yardage.

(See page 37 for annual leaders beginning in 1979)

#National total-offense champion. %In many seasons during 1946-64, only a few passers threw as many as 15 passes per game; thus, a lower minimum was used.

CAREER YARDS

Player, Team	Years	Att.	Cmp.	Int.	Pct.	Yds.	TD	Long
Ty Detmer, Brigham Young	1988-91	*1,530	*958	65	.626	*15,031	*121	76
Todd Santos, San Diego St.	1984-87	1,484	910	57	.613	11,425	70	84
Peyton Manning, Tennessee	1994-97	1,381	863	33	.625	11,201	89	80
Eric Zeier, Georgia	1991-94	1,402	838	37	.598	11,153	67	80
Alex Van Pelt, Pittsburgh	1989-92	1,463	845	59	.578	10,913	64	91
Danny Wuerffel, Florida	1993-96	1,170	708	42	.605	10,875	114	85
Kevin Sweeney, Fresno St.	$1982-86	1,336	731	48	.547	10,623	66	95
Doug Flutie, Boston College	1981-84	1,270	677	54	.533	10,579	67	80
Steve Stenstrom, Stanford	1991-94	1,320	833	36	.631	10,531	72	92
Brian McClure, Bowling Green	1982-85	1,427	900	58	.631	10,280	63	90
Troy Kopp, Pacific (Cal.)	1989-92	1,374	798	47	.581	10,258	87	80
Glenn Foley, Boston College	1990-93	1,275	703	60	.551	10,042	72	78
Ben Bennett, Duke	1980-83	1,375	820	57	.596	9,614	55	88
Jim McMahon, Brigham Young	1977-78, 80-81	1,060	653	34	.616	9,536	84	80
Todd Ellis, South Caro.	1986-89	1,266	704	66	.556	9,519	49	97
David Klingler, Houston	1988-91	1,268	732	38	.577	9,466	91	95
Stoney Case, New Mexico	1991-94	1,237	677	39	.547	9,460	67	79
Erik Wilhelm, Oregon St.	1985-88	1,480	870	61	.588	9,393	52	‡74
Jeremy Leach, New Mexico	1988-91	1,432	735	62	.513	9,382	50	82
John Elway, Stanford	1979-82	1,246	774	39	.621	9,349	77	70
T. J. Rubley, Tulsa	1987-89, 91	1,336	682	54	.510	9,324	73	75
Shane Matthews, Florida	1989-92	1,202	722	46	.601	9,287	74	70
Jake Delhomme, Southwestern La.	1993-96	1,246	655	57	.526	9,216	64	79
Chuck Long, Iowa	$1981-85	1,072	692	46	‡‡.646	9,210	64	89
Mark Herrmann, Purdue	1977-80	1,218	717	*73	.589	9,188	62	75
Tom Hodson, LSU	1986-89	1,163	674	41	.580	9,115	69	80
Spence Fischer, Duke	1992-95	1,369	786	46	.574	9,021	48	80
Jason Martin, Louisiana Tech	1993-96	1,320	705	55	.534	9,066	64	80
Scott Mitchell, Utah	1987-89	1,165	669	38	.574	8,981	68	72
Brad Tayles, Western Mich.	1989-92	1,370	663	67	.484	8,717	49	84
Joe Adams, Tennessee St.	1977-80	1,100	604	60	.549	8,649	81	71
Jake Plummer, Arizona St.	1993-96	1,107	613	34	.554	8,626	64	83
Steve Taneyhill, South Caro.	1992-95	1,209	727	37	.601	8,555	61	93
Marvin Graves, Syracuse	1990-93	943	563	45	.597	8,466	48	84
Shawn Jones, Georgia Tech	1989-92	1,217	652	50	.536	8,441	51	82
Robbie Bosco, Brigham Young	1983-85	997	638	36	.640	8,400	66	‡89
John Walsh, Brigham Young	1991-94	973	587	35	.603	8,375	66	93
Mike McCoy, Long Beach St./Utah	1991, 92-94	1,069	650	26	.608	8,342	56	87
Andre Ware, Houston	1987-89	1,074	660	28	.615	8,202	75	87
Billy Blanton, San Diego St.	1993-96	920	588	25	.639	8,165	67	85
Dan McGwire, Iowa/San Diego St.	1986-87, 89-90	973	575	30	.591	8,164	49	71
Jack Trudeau, Illinois	1981, 83-85	1,151	736	38	†.639	8,146	51	83
Troy Taylor, California	1986-89	1,162	683	46	.588	8,126	51	79
Mike Gundy, Oklahoma St.	1986-89	1,037	606	37	.584	8,072	54	‡84
Jeff Graham, Long Beach St.	1985-88	1,175	664	42	.565	8,063	42	85
Randall Cunningham, UNLV	1982-84	1,029	597	29	.580	8,020	59	69
Stan White, Auburn	1990-93	1,231	659	52	.535	8,016	40	78
Steve Slayden, Duke	1984-87	1,204	699	53	.581	8,004	48	73
Robert Hall, Texas Tech	1990-93	997	548	28	.550	7,908	48	95
Dan Marino, Pittsburgh	1979-82	1,084	626	64	.577	7,905	74	65
John Holman, Northeast La.	1979-82	1,201	593	54	.494	7,827	51	85
Jack Thompson, Washington St.	1975-78	1,086	601	49	.553	7,818	53	80
Bobby Fuller, Appalachian St./South Caro.	1987-88, 90-91	1,061	596	32	.562	7,746	52	79
Rob Johnson, Southern Cal	1991-94	963	623	24	.647	7,743	52	72
Steve Young, Brigham Young	1981-83	908	592	33	.652	7,733	56	63
Brett Favre, Southern Miss.	1987-90	1,169	613	34	.524	7,695	52	80
Gino Torretta, Miami (Fla.)	1989-92	991	555	24	.560	7,690	47	99
Terrence Jones, Tulane	1985-88	1,042	570	41	.547	7,684	46	76
John Paye, Stanford	1983-86	1,198	715	44	.597	7,669	38	80
Rodney Peete, Southern Cal	1985-88	972	571	32	.587	7,640	52	‡68

**Record. $See page 6 for explanation. ‡Did not score. †Record for minimum 1,100 attempts. ‡‡Record for minimum 1,000 attempts.*

CAREER YARDS RECORD PROGRESSION

(Record Yards—Player, Team, Seasons Played)

3,075—Billy Patterson, Baylor, 1936-38; **3,777**—Bud Schwenk, Washington (Mo.), 1939-41; **4,004**—Johnny Rauch, Georgia, 1945-48; **4,736**—John Ford, Hardin-Simmons, 1947-50; **4,863**—Zeke Bratkowski, Georgia, 1951-53; **5,472**—Jerry Rhome, Southern Methodist, 1961, Tulsa, 1963-64; **6,495**—Billy Stevens, UTEP, 1965-67; **7,076**—Steve Ramsey, North Texas, 1967-69; **7,544**—Jim Plunkett, Stanford, 1968-70; **7,549**—John Reaves, Florida, 1969-71; **7,818**—Jack Thompson, Washington St., 1975-78; **9,188**—Mark Herrmann, Purdue, 1977-80; **9,536**—Jim McMahon, BrighamYoung, 1977-78, 1980-81; **9,614**—Ben Bennett, Duke, 1980-83; **10,579**—Doug Flutie, Boston College, 1981-84; **10,623**—Kevin Sweeney, Fresno St., $1982-86; **11,425**—Todd Santos, San Diego St., 1984-87; **15,031**—Ty Detmer, Brigham Young, 1988-91.

$See page 6 for explanation.

CAREER YARDS PER GAME

(Minimum 5,000 yards)

Player, Team	Years	G	Att.	Cmp.	Int.	Pct.	Yds.	TD	Yd.PG
Ty Detmer, Brigham Young	1988-91	46	*1,530	*958	65	.626	*15,031	*121	*326.8
Chris Vargas, Nevada	1992-93	20	806	502	34	.623	6,359	47	318.0

Player, Team	Years	G	Att.	Cmp.	Int.	Pct.	Yds.	TD	Yd.PG
Mike Perez, San Jose St.	1986-87	20	792	471	30	.595	6,194	36	309.7
Doug Gaynor, Long Beach St.	1984-85	22	837	569	35	.680	6,793	35	308.8
Tony Eason, Illinois	1981-82	22	856	526	29	.614	6,608	37	300.4
Steve Sarkisian, Brigham Young	1995-96	25	789	528	26	.669	7,464	53	298.6
David Klingler, Houston	1988-91	32	1,268	732	38	.577	9,466	91	295.8
Josh Wallwork, Wyoming	1995-96	22	729	449	28	.616	6,453	54	293.3
Brent Snyder, Utah St.	1987-88	22	875	472	36	.539	6,105	39	277.5
Mike Maxwell, Nevada	1993-95	27	881	560	33	.636	7,256	62	268.7
Shane Matthews, Florida	1989-92	35	1,202	722	46	.601	9,287	74	265.3
Larry Egger, Utah	1985-86	22	799	470	31	.588	5,749	39	261.3
Bernie Kosar, Miami (Fla.)	1983-84	23	743	463	29	.623	5,971	40	259.6

**Record.*

Photo from Washington State sports information

Washington State quarterback Ryan Leaf completed 210 of 375 passes for 3,637 yards and 33 touchdowns last season.

CAREER TOUCHDOWN PASSES

Player, Team	Years	G	TD Passes
Ty Detmer, Brigham Young	1988-91	46	*121
Danny Wuerffel, Florida	1993-96	46	114
David Klingler, Houston	1988-91	32	91
Peyton Manning, Tennessee	1994-97	44	89
Troy Kopp, Pacific (Cal.)	1989-92	40	87
Jim McMahon, Brigham Young	1977-78, 80-81	44	84
Joe Adams, Tennessee St.	1977-80	41	81
John Elway, Stanford	1979-82	43	77
Andre Ware, Houston	1987-89	29	75
Shane Matthews, Florida	1989-92	35	74
Dan Marino, Pittsburgh	1979-82	40	74
T. J. Rubley, Tulsa	1987-89, 91	47	73
Steve Stenstrom, Stanford	1991-94	41	72
Glenn Foley, Boston College	1990-93	44	72
Todd Santos, San Diego St.	1984-87	46	70
Tom Hodson, LSU	1986-89	44	69
Steve Ramsey, North Texas	1967-69	29	69
Scott Mitchell, Utah	1987-89	33	68
Billy Blanton, San Diego St.	1993-96	38	67
Stoney Case, New Mexico	1991-94	42	67
Eric Zeier, Georgia	1991-94	44	67
Doug Flutie, Boston College	1981-84	42	67
John Walsh, Brigham Young	1991-94	35	66
Kevin Sweeney, Fresno St.	1983-86	47	66
Robbie Bosco, Brigham Young	1983-85	35	66
Jake Delhomme, Southwestern La.	1993-96	44	64
Jason Martin, Louisiana Tech	1993-96	41	64
Jake Plummer, Arizona St.	1993-96	42	64
Elvis Grbac, Michigan	1989-92	41	64
Alex Van Pelt, Pittsburgh	1989-92	45	64
Chuck Long, Iowa	$1981-85	45	64

**Record. $See page 6 for explanation.*

SEASON YARDS

Player, Team	Year	G	Att.	Cmp.	Int.	Pct.	Yards	TD	Yds. Per Att.
Ty Detmer, Brigham Young	1990	12	562	361	28	.642	*5,188	41	9.23
David Klingler, Houston	1990	11	*643	*374	20	.582	5,140	*54	7.99
Andre Ware, Houston	1989	11	578	365	15	.631	4,699	46	8.13
Jim McMahon, Brigham Young	†1980	12	445	284	18	.638	4,571	47	10.27
Ty Detmer, Brigham Young	†1989	12	412	265	15	.643	4,560	32	11.07
Scott Mitchell, Utah	1988	11	533	323	15	.606	4,322	29	8.11
Robbie Bosco, Brigham Young	1985	13	511	338	24	.661	4,273	30	8.36
Chris Vargas, Nevada	1993	11	490	331	18	.676	4,265	34	8.70
Josh Wallwork, Wyoming	1996	12	458	286	15	.625	4,090	33	8.93
Ty Detmer, Brigham Young	1991	12	403	249	12	.618	4,031	35	10.00
Steve Sarkisian, Brigham Young	†1996	14	404	278	12	.688	4,027	33	9.97
Todd Santos, San Diego St.	1987	12	492	306	15	.622	3,932	26	7.99
Steve Young, Brigham Young	†1983	11	429	306	10	*.713	3,902	33	9.10
Tim Couch, Kentucky	1997	11	547	363	19	.664	3,884	37	7.10
Tim Rattay, Louisiana Tech	†1997	11	477	293	10	.614	3,881	34	8.14
Robbie Bosco, Brigham Young	1984	12	458	283	11	.618	3,875	33	8.46
Mike McCoy, Utah	1993	12	430	276	10	.642	3,860	21	8.98
Dan McGwire, San Diego St.	1990	11	449	270	7	.601	3,833	27	8.54
Anthony Dilweg, Duke	1988	11	484	287	18	.593	3,824	24	7.90
Peyton Manning, Tennessee	1997	12	477	287	11	.602	3,819	36	8.01
Jimmy Klingler, Houston	1992	11	504	303	18	.601	3,818	32	7.58
Sam King, UNLV	1981	12	433	255	19	.589	3,778	18	8.73
Troy Kopp, Pacific (Cal.)	1991	12	449	275	16	.612	3,767	37	8.39
John Walsh, Brigham Young	1993	11	397	244	15	.615	3,727	28	9.39
Marc Wilson, Brigham Young	1979	12	427	250	15	.585	3,720	29	8.71
John Walsh, Brigham Young	1994	12	463	284	14	.613	3,712	29	8.02
Ryan Fien, Idaho	1996	11	455	267	12	.587	3,662	27	8.05
Dan McGwire, San Diego St.	1989	12	440	258	19	.586	3,651	16	8.30
Jim Everett, Purdue	1985	11	450	285	11	.633	3,651	23	8.11
Bernie Kosar, Miami (Fla.)	1984	12	416	262	16	.630	3,642	25	8.75
Ryan Leaf, Washington St.	1997	11	375	210	10	.560	3,637	33	9.70
Steve Stenstrom, Stanford	1993	11	455	300	14	.659	3,627	27	7.97
Danny Wuerffel, Florida	1996	12	360	207	13	.575	3,625	39	10.07
Mike Maxwell, Nevada	1995	9	409	277	17	.677	3,611	33	8.83

**Record. †National pass-efficiency champion.*

SEASON YARDS PER GAME

Player, Team	Year	G	Att.	Cmp.	Int.	Pct.	Yards	TD	Yd.PG
David Klingler, Houston	1990	11	*643	*374	20	.582	5,140	*54	*467.3
Ty Detmer, Brigham Young	1990	12	562	361	28	.642	*5,188	41	432.3
Andre Ware, Houston	1989	11	578	365	15	.631	4,699	46	427.2
Mike Maxwell, Nevada	1995	9	409	277	17	.677	3,611	33	401.2
Scott Mitchell, Utah	1988	11	533	323	15	.606	4,322	29	392.9
Chris Vargas, Nevada	1993	11	490	331	18	.676	4,265	34	387.7
Jim McMahon, Brigham Young	†1980	12	445	284	18	.638	4,571	47	380.9
Ty Detmer, Brigham Young	†1989	12	412	265	15	.643	4,560	32	380.0
Troy Kopp, Pacific (Cal.)	1990	9	428	243	14	.568	3,311	31	367.9
Jim McMahon, Brigham Young	†1981	10	423	272	7	.643	3,555	30	355.5
Steve Young, Brigham Young	†1983	11	429	306	10	*.713	3,902	33	354.7
Tim Couch, Kentucky	1997	11	547	363	19	.664	3,884	37	353.1
Tim Rattay, Louisiana Tech	†1997	11	477	293	10	.614	3,881	34	352.8
Dan McGwire, San Diego St.	1990	11	449	270	7	.601	3,833	27	348.5
Anthony Dilweg, Duke	1988	11	484	287	18	.593	3,824	24	347.6
Jimmy Klingler, Houston	1992	11	504	303	18	.601	3,818	32	347.1
Bill Anderson, Tulsa	†1965	10	509	296	14	.582	3,464	30	346.4
Josh Wallwork, Wyoming	1996	12	458	286	15	.625	4,090	33	340.8
David Klingler, Houston	1991	10	497	278	17	.559	3,388	29	338.8
Marc Wilson, Brigham Young	1979	12	427	250	15	.585	3,720	29	338.2

**Record. †National pass-efficiency champion.*

SEASON TOUCHDOWN PASSES

Player, Team	Year	G	TD Passes
David Klingler, Houston	1990	11	*54
Jim McMahon, Brigham Young	1980	12	47
Andre Ware, Houston	1989	11	46
Ty Detmer, Brigham Young	1990	12	41
Chad Pennington, Marshall	1997	12	39
Danny Wuerffel, Florida	1996	12	39
Dennis Shaw, San Diego St.	1969	10	39
Doug Williams, Grambling	1977	11	38
Tim Couch, Kentucky	1997	11	37
Troy Kopp, Pacific (Cal.)	1991	12	37
Peyton Manning, Tennessee	1997	12	36
Danny Wuerffel, Florida	1995	11	35
Ty Detmer, Brigham Young	1991	12	35
Tim Rattay, Louisiana Tech	1997	11	34
Chris Vargas, Nevada	1993	11	34
Dan Marino, Pittsburgh	1981	11	34
Ryan Leaf, Washington St.	1997	11	33
Steve Sarkisian, Brigham Young	1996	14	33
Josh Wallwork, Wyoming	1996	12	33
Mike Maxwell, Nevada	1995	9	33
Robbie Bosco, Brigham Young	1984	12	33
Steve Young, Brigham Young	1983	11	33
Jose Davis, Kent	1997	10	32
Jason Martin, Louisiana Tech	1996	11	32
Danny Kanell, Florida St.	1995	11	32
Jimmy Klingler, Houston	1992	11	32
Ty Detmer, Brigham Young	1989	12	32
Jerry Rhome, Tulsa	1964	10	32
Pat Barnes, California	1996	11	31
Troy Kopp, Pacific (Cal.)	1990	9	31

**Record.*

CAREER YARDS PER ATTEMPT
(Minimum 900 Attempts)

Player, Team	Years	Att.	Cmp.	Pct.	Yards	Yards Per Cmp.	Yards Per Att.
Ty Detmer, Brigham Young	1988-91	*1,530	*958	.626	*15,031	*15.69	*9.82
Danny Wuerffel, Florida	1993-96	1,170	708	.605	10,875	15.36	9.29
Jim McMahon, Brigham Young	1977-78, 80-81	1,060	653	.616	9,536	14.60	9.00
Marvin Graves, Syracuse	1990-93	943	563	.597	8,466	15.04	8.98
Billy Blanton, San Diego St.	1993-96	920	588	.639	8,165	13.89	8.88
John Walsh, Brigham Young	1991-94	973	587	.603	8,375	14.27	8.61
Chuck Long, Iowa	$1981-85	1,072	692	#.646	9,210	13.31	8.59
Steve Young, Brigham Young	1981-83	908	592	.652	7,733	13.06	8.52
Robbie Bosco, Brigham Young	1983-85	997	638	.640	8,400	13.17	8.43
Dan McGwire, Iowa/San Diego St.	1986-87, 89-90	973	575	.591	8,164	14.20	8.39
Doug Flutie, Boston College	1981-84	1,270	677	.533	10,579	15.63	8.33
Marc Wilson, Brigham Young	1977-79	937	535	.571	7,637	14.27	8.15
Peyton Manning, Tennessee	1994-97	1,381	863	.625	11,201	12.98	8.11
Rob Johnson, Southern Cal	1991-94	963	623	.647	7,743	12.43	8.04
Steve Stenstrom, Stanford	1991-94	1,320	833	.631	10,531	12.64	7.98
Kerwin Bell, Florida	1984-87	953	549	.576	7,585	13.82	7.96
Eric Zeier, Georgia	1991-94	1,402	838	.598	11,153	13.31	7.96
Kevin Sweeney, Fresno St.	$1982-86	1,336	731	.547	10,623	14.53	7.95
Robert Hall, Texas Tech	1990-93	997	548	.550	7,908	14.43	7.93
Glenn Foley, Boston College	1990-93	1,275	703	.551	10,042	14.28	7.88
Joe Adams, Tennessee St.	1977-80	1,100	604	.549	8,649	14.32	7.86
Rodney Peete, Southern Cal	1985-88	972	571	.587	7,640	13.38	7.86
Ron Powlus, Notre Dame	1994-97	969	558	.576	7,602	13.62	7.85

Player, Team	Years	Att.	Cmp.	Pct.	Yards	Yards Per Cmp.	Yards Per Att.
Tom Hodson, LSU	1986-89	1,163	674	.580	9,115	13.52	7.84
Jim Plunkett, Stanford	1968-70	962	530	.551	7,544	14.23	7.84

**Record. $See page 6 for explanation. #Record for minimum 1,000 attempts.*

SINGLE-GAME YARDS

Yds.	Player, Team (Opponent)	Date
716	David Klingler, Houston (Arizona St.)	Dec. 2, 1990
690	Matt Vogler, Texas Christian (Houston)	Nov. 3, 1990
631	Scott Mitchell, Utah (Air Force)	Oct. 15, 1988
622	Jeremy Leach, New Mexico (Utah)	Nov. 11, 1989
621	Dave Wilson, Illinois (Ohio St.)	Nov. 8, 1980
619	John Walsh, Brigham Young (Utah St.)	Oct. 30, 1993
613	Jimmy Klingler, Houston (Rice)	Nov. 28, 1992
599	Ty Detmer, Brigham Young (San Diego St.)	Nov. 16, 1991
585	Robbie Bosco, Brigham Young (New Mexico)	Oct. 19, 1985
572	David Klingler, Houston (Eastern Wash.)	Nov. 17, 1990
571	Marc Wilson, Brigham Young (Utah)	Nov. 5, 1977
568	David Lowery, San Diego St. (Brigham Young)	Nov. 16, 1991
565	Jim McMahon, Brigham Young (Utah)	Nov. 21, 1981
564	Troy Kopp, Pacific, Cal. (New Mexico St.)	Oct. 20, 1990
563	David Klingler, Houston (Texas Christian)	Nov. 3, 1990
561	Tony Adams, Utah St. (Utah)	Nov. 11, 1972
560	Ty Detmer, Brigham Young (Utah St.)	Nov. 24, 1990
558	Chuck Hartlieb, Iowa (Indiana)	Oct. 29, 1988
557	John Dutton, Nevada (Boise St.)	Nov. 8, 1997
554	Greg Cook, Cincinnati (Ohio)	Nov. 16, 1968
552	Mike Maxwell, Nevada (UNLV)	Oct. 28, 1995
546	Cody Ledbetter, New Mexico St. (UNLV)	Nov. 18, 1995
551	Jose Davis, Kent (Central Fla.)	Oct. 4, 1997
545	Rusty LaRue, Wake Forest (North Caro. St.)	Nov. 18, 1995
544	Eric Zeier, Georgia (Southern Miss.)	Oct. 9, 1993
542	Jason Martin, Louisiana Tech (Toledo)	Oct. 19, 1996
542	Ryan Fien, Idaho (Wyoming)	Aug. 31, 1996
538	Chris Vargas, Nevada (UNLV)	Oct. 2, 1993
538	Jim McMahon, Brigham Young (Colorado St.)	Nov. 7, 1981
537	Ty Detmer, Brigham Young (Washington St.)	Sept. 7, 1989
536	Steve Sarkisian, Brigham Young (Texas A&M)	Aug. 24, 1996
536	Dave Telford, Fresno St. (Pacific [Cal.])	Oct. 24, 1987
536	Todd Santos, San Diego St. (Stanford)	Oct. 17, 1987
536	David Spriggs, New Mexico St. (Southern Ill.)	Sept. 30, 1978
535	Mike Maxwell, Nevada (Louisiana Tech)	Oct. 21, 1995
535	Shane Montgomery, North Caro. St. (Duke)	Nov. 11, 1989
534	Paul Justin, Arizona St. (Washington St.)	Oct. 28, 1989
533	David Klingler, Houston (Texas Tech)	Nov. 30, 1991
532	Jeff Van Raaphorst, Arizona St. (Florida St.)	Nov. 3, 1984

SINGLE-GAME ATTEMPTS

No.	Player, Team (Opponent)	Date
79	Matt Vogler, Texas Christian (Houston)	Nov. 3, 1990
78	Rusty LaRue, Wake Forest (Duke)	Oct. 28, 1995
76	David Klingler, Houston (Southern Methodist)	Oct. 20, 1990
75	Chris Vargas, Nevada (McNeese St.)	Sept. 19, 1992
73	Jeff Handy, Missouri (Oklahoma St.)	Oct. 17, 1992
73	Troy Kopp, Pacific, Cal. (Hawaii)	Oct. 27, 1990
73	Shane Montgomery, North Caro. St. (Duke)	Nov. 11, 1989
72	Matt Vogler, Texas Christian (Texas Tech)	Nov. 10, 1990
71	Jimmy Klingler, Houston (Rice)	Nov. 28, 1992
71	Sandy Schwab, Northwestern (Michigan)	Oct. 23, 1982
70	David Klingler, Houston (Texas Tech)	Nov. 30, 1991
70	David Klingler, Houston (Arizona St.)	Dec. 2, 1990
70	Dave Telford, Fresno St. (Utah St.)	Nov. 14, 1987
69	Dave Wilson, Illinois (Ohio St.)	Nov. 8, 1980
69	Chuck Hixson, Southern Methodist (Ohio St.)	Sept. 28, 1968
68	David Klingler, Houston (Baylor)	Oct. 6, 1990
68	Jeremy Leach, New Mexico (Utah)	Nov. 11, 1989
68	Steve Smith, Stanford (Notre Dame)	Oct. 7, 1989
68	Andre Ware, Houston (Arizona St.)	Sept. 23, 1989
67	Rusty LaRue, Wake Forest (North Caro. St.)	Nov. 18, 1995
67	Danny Kanell, Florida St. (Virginia)	Nov. 2, 1995
67	Mike Hohensee, Minnesota (Ohio St.)	Nov. 7, 1981
66	Tim Couch, Kentucky (LSU)	Nov. 1, 1997
66	Chuck Clements, Houston (Cincinnati)	Nov. 13, 1993
66	Tim Schade, Minnesota (Penn St.)	Sept. 4, 1993
66	Drew Bledsoe, Washington St. (Montana)	Sept. 5, 1992
66	Jack Trudeau, Illinois (Purdue)	Oct. 12, 1985
66	John Reaves, Florida (Auburn)	Nov. 1, 1969
65	Peyton Manning, Tennessee (Florida)	Sept. 21, 1996
65	Rusty LaRue, Wake Forest (Georgia Tech)	Nov. 4, 1995
65	Jason Martin, Louisiana Tech (Nevada)	Oct. 21, 1995
65	Eric Zeier, Georgia (Florida)	Oct. 30, 1993
65	Jimmy Klingler, Houston (Texas Christian)	Oct. 31, 1992
65	Scott Mitchell, Utah (UTEP)	Oct. 1, 1988
65	Mike Bates, Miami, Ohio (Toledo)	Oct. 24, 1987

No.	Player, Team (Opponent)	Date
65	Craig Burnett, Wyoming (San Diego St.)	Nov. 15, 1986
65	Gary Schofield, Wake Forest (Maryland)	Oct. 16, 1982
65	Jim McMahon, Brigham Young (Colorado St.)	Nov. 7, 1981
65	Brooks Dawson, UTEP (UC Santa Barb.)	Sept. 14, 1968
65	Bill Anderson, Tulsa (Southern Ill.)	Oct. 30, 1965
65	Bill Anderson, Tulsa (Memphis)	Oct. 9, 1965

SINGLE-GAME COMPLETIONS

No.	Player, Team (Opponent)	Date
55	Rusty LaRue, Wake Forest (Duke)	Oct. 28, 1995
50	Rusty LaRue, Wake Forest (North Caro. St.)	Nov. 18, 1995
48	David Klingler, Houston (Southern Methodist)	Oct. 20, 1990
46	Scott Milanovich, Maryland (Florida St.)	Nov. 18, 1995
46	Jimmy Klingler, Houston (Rice)	Nov. 28, 1992
45	Sandy Schwab, Northwestern (Michigan)	Oct. 23, 1982
44	Matt Vogler, Texas Christian (Houston)	Nov. 3, 1990
44	Chuck Hartlieb, Iowa (Indiana)	Oct. 29, 1988
44	Jim McMahon, Brigham Young (Colorado St.)	Nov. 7, 1981
43	Jeff Handy, Missouri (Oklahoma St.)	Oct. 17, 1992
43	Chris Vargas, Nevada (McNeese St.)	Sept. 19, 1992
43	Gary Schofield, Wake Forest (Maryland)	Oct. 17, 1981
43	Dave Wilson, Illinois (Ohio St.)	Nov. 8, 1980
43	Rich Campbell, California (Florida)	Sept. 13, 1980
42	Jimmy Klingler, Houston (Texas Christian)	Oct. 31, 1992
42	Troy Kopp, Pacific, Cal. (Hawaii)	Oct. 27, 1990
42	Andre Ware, Houston (Texas Christian)	Nov. 4, 1989
42	Dan Speltz, Cal St. Fullerton (Utah St.)	Oct. 7, 1989
42	Robbie Bosco, Brigham Young (New Mexico)	Oct. 19, 1985
42	Bill Anderson, Tulsa (Southern Ill.)	Oct. 30, 1965
41	Tim Couch, Kentucky (Georgia)	Oct. 25, 1997
41	Tim Couch, Kentucky (LSU)	Nov. 1, 1997
41	Rusty LaRue, Wake Forest (Georgia Tech)	Nov. 4, 1995
41	Mike Maxwell, Nevada (UNLV)	Oct. 28, 1995
41	Danny Kanell, Florida St. (Georgia Tech)	Oct. 21, 1995
41	David Klingler, Houston (Texas Tech)	Nov. 30, 1991
41	David Klingler, Houston (Arizona St.)	Dec. 2, 1990
41	David Klingler, Houston (Eastern Wash.)	Nov. 17, 1990
41	Jeremy Leach, New Mexico (Utah)	Nov. 11, 1989
41	Scott Mitchell, Utah (UTEP)	Oct. 1, 1988
41	Doug Gaynor, Long Beach St. (Utah St.)	Sept. 7, 1985
40	Danny Kanell, Florida St. (Florida)	Nov. 26, 1994
40	Mike Romo, Southern Methodist (Rice)	Nov. 10, 1990
40	Andre Ware, Houston (Arizona St.)	Sept. 23, 1989
40	Dave Telford, Fresno St. (Utah St.)	Nov. 14, 1987
40	Todd Santos, San Diego St. (Stanford)	Oct. 17, 1987
40	Larry Egger, Utah (UTEP)	Nov. 29, 1986
40	John Paye, Stanford (San Diego St.)	Oct. 5, 1985
40	Gary Schofield, Wake Forest (Maryland)	Oct. 16, 1982
40	Jim McMahon, Brigham Young (North Texas)	Nov. 8, 1980

ANNUAL CHAMPIONS

Year	Player, Team	Class	Att.	Cmp.	Int.	Pct.	Yds.	TD
1937	Davey O'Brien, Texas Christian	Jr.	234	94	18	.402	969	—
1938	Davey O'Brien, Texas Christian	Sr.	167	93	4	.557	1,457	—
1939	Kay Eakin, Arkansas	Sr.	193	78	18	.404	962	—
1940	Billy Sewell, Washington St.	Sr.	174	86	17	.494	1,023	—
1941	Bud Schwenk, Washington (Mo.)	Sr.	234	114	19	.487	1,457	—
1942	Ray Evans, Kansas	Jr.	200	101	9	.505	1,117	—
1943	Johnny Cook, Georgia	Fr.	157	73	20	.465	1,007	—
1944	Paul Rickards, Pittsburgh	So.	178	84	20	.472	997	—
1945	Al Dekdebrun, Cornell	Sr.	194	90	15	.464	1,227	—
1946	Travis Tidwell, Auburn	Fr.	158	79	10	.500	943	5
1947	Charlie Conerly, Mississippi	Sr.	233	133	7	.571	1,367	18
1948	Stan Heath, Nevada	Sr.	222	126	9	.568	2,005	22
1949	Adrian Burk, Baylor	Sr.	191	110	6	.576	1,428	14
1950	Don Heinrich, Washington	Jr.	221	134	9	.606	1,846	14
1951	Don Klosterman, Loyola Marymount	Sr.	315	159	21	.505	1,843	9
1952	Don Heinrich, Washington	Sr.	270	137	17	.507	1,647	13
1953	Bob Garrett, Stanford	Sr.	205	118	10	.576	1,637	17
1954	Paul Larson, California	Sr.	195	125	8	.641	1,537	10
1955	George Welsh, Navy	Sr.	150	94	6	.627	1,319	8
1956	John Brodie, Stanford	Sr.	240	139	14	.579	1,633	12
1957	Ken Ford, Hardin-Simmons	Sr.	205	115	11	.561	1,254	14
1958	Buddy Humphrey, Baylor	Sr.	195	112	8	.574	1,316	7
1959	Dick Norman, Stanford	Jr.	263	152	12	.578	1,963	11
1960	Harold Stephens, Hardin-Simmons	Sr.	256	145	14	.566	1,254	3
1961	Chon Gallegos, San Jose St.	Sr.	197	117	13	.594	1,480	14
1962	Don Trull, Baylor	Jr.	229	125	12	.546	1,627	11
1963	Don Trull, Baylor	Sr.	308	174	12	.565	2,157	12
1964	Jerry Rhome, Tulsa	Sr.	326	224	4	.687	2,870	32
1965	Bill Anderson, Tulsa	Sr.	509	296	14	.582	3,464	30
1966	John Eckman, Wichita St.	Jr.	458	195	*34	.426	2,339	7
1967	Terry Stone, New Mexico	Jr.	336	160	19	.476	1,946	9
1968	Chuck Hixson, Southern Methodist	So.	468	265	23	.566	3,103	21
1969	John Reaves, Florida	So.	396	222	19	.561	2,896	24

Beginning in 1970, ranked on per-game (instead of total) completions

Year	Player, Team	Class	G	Att.	Cmp.	Avg.	Int.	Pct.	Yds.	TD
1970	Sonny Sixkiller, Washington	So.	10	362	186	18.6	22	.514	2,303	15
1971	Brian Sipe, San Diego St.	Sr.	11	369	196	17.8	21	.531	2,532	17
1972	Don Strock, Virginia Tech	Sr.	11	427	228	20.7	27	.534	3,243	16
1973	Jesse Freitas, San Diego St.	Sr.	11	347	227	20.6	17	.654	2,993	21
1974	Steve Bartkowski, California	Sr.	11	325	182	16.5	7	.560	2,580	12
1975	Craig Penrose, San Diego St.	Sr.	11	349	198	18.0	24	.567	2,660	15
1976	Tommy Kramer, Rice	Sr.	11	501	269	24.5	19	.537	3,317	21
1977	Guy Benjamin, Stanford	Sr.	10	330	208	20.8	15	.630	2,521	19
1978	Steve Dils, Stanford	Sr.	11	391	247	22.5	15	.632	2,943	22

Beginning in 1979, ranked on passing efficiency rating points (instead of per-game completions)

Year	Player, Team	Class	G	Att.	Cmp.	Int.	Pct.	Yds.	TD	Pts.
1979	Turk Schonert, Stanford	Sr.	11	221	148	6	.670	1,922	19	163.0
1980	Jim McMahon, Brigham Young	Jr.	12	445	284	18	.638	4,571	47	176.9
1981	Jim McMahon, Brigham Young	Sr.	10	423	272	7	.643	3,555	30	155.0
1982	Tom Ramsey, UCLA	Sr.	11	311	191	10	.614	2,824	21	153.5
1983	Steve Young, Brigham Young	Sr.	11	429	306	10	*.713	3,902	33	168.5
1984	Doug Flutie, Boston College	Sr.	11	386	233	11	.604	3,454	27	152.9
1985	Jim Harbaugh, Michigan	Jr.	11	212	139	6	.656	1,913	18	163.7
1986	Vinny Testaverde, Miami (Fla.)	Sr.	10	276	175	9	.634	2,557	26	165.8
1987	Don McPherson, Syracuse	Sr.	11	229	129	11	.563	2,341	22	164.3
1988	Timm Rosenbach, Washington St.	Jr.	11	302	199	10	.659	2,791	23	162.0
1989	Ty Detmer, Brigham Young	So.	12	412	265	15	.643	4,560	32	175.6
1990	Shawn Moore, Virginia	Sr.	10	241	144	8	.598	2,262	21	160.7
1991	Elvis Grbac, Michigan	Jr.	11	228	152	5	.667	1,955	24	169.0
1992	Elvis Grbac, Michigan	Sr.	9	169	112	12	.663	1,465	15	154.2
1993	Trent Dilfer, Fresno St.	Jr.	11	333	217	4	.652	3,276	28	173.1
1994	Kerry Collins, Penn St.	Sr.	11	264	176	7	.667	2,679	21	172.9
1995	Danny Wuerffel, Florida	Jr.	11	325	210	10	.646	3,266	35	*178.4
1996	Steve Sarkisian, Brigham Young	Sr.	14	404	278	12	.688	4,027	33	173.6
1997	Cade McNown, UCLA	Jr.	11	283	173	5	.611	2,877	22	168.6

*Record.

Photo from Utah State sports information

Utah State's Nakia Jenkins averaged seven catches a game and had 2,483 receiving yards over the last two seasons.

Receiving

CAREER RECEPTIONS PER GAME
(Minimum 125 Receptions)

Player, Team	Years	G	Rec.	Yards	TD	Rec.PG
Manny Hazard, Houston	1989-90	21	220	2,635	31	*10.5
Alex Van Dyke, Nevada	1994-95	22	227	3,100	26	10.3
Howard Twilley, Tulsa	1963-65	26	261	3,343	32	10.0
Jason Phillips, Houston	1987-88	22	207	2,319	18	9.4
Bryan Reeves, Nevada	1992-93	21	172	2,476	27	8.2
David Williams, Illinois	1983-85	33	245	3,195	22	7.4
James Dixon, Houston	1987-88	22	161	1,762	14	7.3
John Love, North Texas	1965-66	20	144	2,124	17	7.2
Fred Gilbert, UCLA/Houston	1989, 91-92	22	158	1,672	14	7.2
Ron Sellers, Florida St.	1966-68	30	212	3,598	23	7.1
Keyshawn Johnson, Southern Cal	1994-95	21	148	2,358	12	7.1
Nakia Jenkins, Utah St.	1996-97	22	155	2,483	14	7.0
Barry Moore, North Texas	1968-69	20	140	2,183	12	7.0
Mike Kelly, Davidson	1967-69	23	156	2,114	17	6.8
Guy Liggins, San Jose St.	1986-87	22	149	2,191	16	6.8
Dave Petzke, Northern Ill.	1977-78	22	148	1,960	16	6.7
Loren Richey, Utah	1985-86	21	140	1,746	13	6.7
Antonio Wilson, Idaho	1996-97	22	142	2,113	17	6.5
Chris Penn, Tulsa	1991, 93	22	142	2,370	17	6.5
Tim Delaney, San Diego St.	1968-70	29	180	2,535	22	6.2
Larry Willis, Fresno St.	1983-84	23	142	2,260	14	6.2
Phil Odle, Brigham Young	1965-67	30	183	2,548	25	6.1
Randy Gatewood, UNLV	1993-94	21	128	1,832	13	6.1
Aaron Turner, Pacific (Cal.)	1989-92	44	*266	4,345	*43	6.0
Mike Mikolayunas, Davidson	1968-70	29	175	1,768	14	6.0
Chad Mackey, Louisiana Tech	1993-96	44	264	3,789	22	6.0
Terance Mathis, New Mexico	1985-87, 89	44	263	4,254	36	6.0
Michael Stephens, Nevada	1992-93	21	125	1,712	15	6.0

*Record.

SEASON RECEPTIONS PER GAME

Player, Team	Year	G	Rec.	Yards	TD	Rec.PG
Howard Twilley, Tulsa	†1965	10	134	1,779	16	*13.4
Manny Hazard, Houston	†1989	11	*142	1,689	22	12.9
Alex Van Dyke, Nevada	†1995	11	129	*1,854	16	11.7
Damond Wilkins, Nevada	†1996	11	114	1,121	4	10.4
Jason Phillips, Houston	†1988	11	108	1,444	15	9.8
Fred Gilbert, Houston	†1991	11	106	957	7	9.6
Chris Penn, Tulsa	†1993	11	105	1,578	12	9.5
Jerry Hendren, Idaho	†1969	10	95	1,452	12	9.5
Howard Twilley, Tulsa	†1964	10	95	1,178	13	9.5
Eugene Baker, Kent	†1997	11	103	1,549	18	9.4
Sherman Smith, Houston	†1992	11	103	923	6	9.4
Troy Edwards, Louisiana Tech	1997	11	102	1,707	13	9.3
James Dixon, Houston	1988	11	102	1,103	11	9.3
David Williams, Illinois	†1984	11	101	1,278	8	9.2
Bryan Reeves, Nevada	1993	10	91	1,362	17	9.1
Glenn Meltzer, Wichita St.	†1966	10	91	1,115	4	9.1
Jay Miller, Brigham Young	†1973	11	100	1,181	8	9.1
Marcus Harris, Wyoming	1996	12	109	1,650	13	9.1

*Record. †National champion.

CAREER RECEPTIONS

Player, Team	Years	Rec.	Yards	Avg.	TD
Aaron Turner, Pacific (Cal.)	1989-92	*266	4,345	16.3	*43
Chad Mackey, Louisiana Tech	1993-96	264	3,789	14.4	22
Terance Mathis, New Mexico	1985-87, 89	263	4,254	16.2	36
Mark Templeton, Long Beach St. (RB)	1983-86	262	1,969	7.5	11
Howard Twilley, Tulsa	1963-65	261	3,343	12.8	32
Marcus Harris, Wyoming	1993-96	259	*4,518	17.4	38
David Williams, Illinois	1983-85	245	3,195	13.0	22
Marc Zeno, Tulane	1984-87	236	3,725	15.8	25
Jason Wolf, Southern Methodist	1989-92	235	2,232	9.5	17
Ryan Yarborough, Wyoming	1990-93	229	4,357	‡19.0	42
Alex Van Dyke, Nevada	1994-95	227	3,100	13.7	26
Manny Hazard, Houston	1989-90	220	2,635	12.0	31
Kevin Lockett, Kansas St.	1993-96	217	3,032	14.0	26
Darrin Nelson, Stanford (RB)	1977-78, 80-81	214	2,368	11.1	16
Ron Sellers, Florida St.	1966-68	212	3,598	17.0	23
Jason Phillips, Houston	1987-88	207	2,319	11.2	18
Hart Lee Dykes, Oklahoma St.	1985-88	203	3,171	15.6	29
Carl Winston, New Mexico	1990-93	202	2,972	14.7	14
Keith Edwards, Vanderbilt	1980, 82-84	200	1,757	8.8	3
Bobby Slaughter, Louisiana Tech	1987-90	198	2,544	12.9	14
Richard Buchanan, Northwestern	1987-90	197	2,474	12.6	22
Gerald Harp, Western Caro.	1977-80	197	3,305	16.8	26
Matt Bellini, Brigham Young (RB)	1987-90	196	2,544	13.0	13
Brad Muster, Stanford (FB)	1984-87	196	1,669	8.5	6
Jermaine Lewis, Maryland	1992-95	193	2,932	15.2	21
Greg Primus, Colorado St.	1989-92	192	3,200	16.7	16
Charles Lockett, Long Beach St.	1983-86	191	2,902	15.1	19
Pete Mitchell, Boston College (TE)	1991-94	190	2,389	12.6	20
Kez McCorvey, Florida St.	1991-94	189	2,660	14.1	16
Lloyd Hill, Texas Tech	1990-93	189	3,059	16.2	20
Clarkston Hines, Duke	1986-89	189	3,318	17.6	38
Brian Roberson, Fresno St.	1993-96	188	2,956	15.7	15
Wil Ursin, Tulane	1990-93	188	2,466	13.1	17
Ricky Proehl, Wake Forest	1986-89	188	2,949	15.7	25
Boo Mitchell, Vanderbilt	1985-88	188	2,964	15.8	9
Monty Gilbreath, San Diego St.	1986-89	187	2,241	12.0	8
Mick Rossley, Southern Methodist	1991-94	186	1,911	10.3	10
Eric Henley, Rice	1988-91	186	2,200	11.8	16
Geroy Simon, Maryland	1993-96	185	2,059	11.1	10
Johnnie Morton, Southern Cal	1990-93	185	2,957	16.0	21
Jeff Champine, Colorado St.	1980-83	184	2,811	15.3	21

Player, Team	Years	Rec.	Yards	Avg.	TD
Joey Kent, Tennessee	1993-96	183	2,814	15.4	25
Wendell Davis, LSU	1984-85	183	2,708	14.8	19
Phil Odle, Brigham Young	1965-67	183	2,548	13.9	25
Brice Hunter, Georgia	1992-95	182	2,373	13.0	19
Mark Szlachcic, Bowling Green	1989-92	182	2,507	13.8	18
Duane Gregory, New Mexico St.	1994-97	181	2,641	14.6	14
Charlie Jones, Fresno St.	1992-95	181	3,260	18.0	25
Kelly Blackwell, Texas Christian (TE)	1988-91	181	2,155	11.9	13
Eugene Baker, Kent	¢1995-97	180	2,828	15.7	31
Tim Delaney, San Diego St.	1968-70	180	2,535	14.1	22
Michael Smith, Kansas St.	1988-91	179	2,457	13.7	11
Darnay Scott, San Diego St.	1991-93	178	3,139	17.6	25
Walter Murray, Hawaii	1982-85	178	2,865	16.1	20
Gordon Hudson, Brigham Young (TE)	1980-83	178	2,484	14.0	22
Rick Beasley, Appalachian St.	1978-80	178	3,124	17.6	23
Bobby Shaw, California	1994-97	177	2,693	15.2	25
Marcus Nash, Tennessee	1994-97	177	2,447	13.8	20
Mike Adams, Texas	1992-93, 95-96	177	3,032	17.1	16
Bryan Rowley, Utah	$1989-93	177	3,143	17.8	25

**Record. $See page 6 for explanation. ‡Record for minimum of 200 catches. ¢Active player.*

SEASON RECEPTIONS

Player, Team	Year	G	Rec.	Yards	TD
Manny Hazard, Houston	†1989	11	*142	1,689	22
Howard Twilley, Tulsa	†1965	10	134	1,779	16
Alex Van Dyke, Nevada	†1995	11	129	*1,854	16
Damond Wilkins, Nevada	†1996	11	114	1,121	4
Marcus Harris, Wyoming	1996	12	109	1,650	13
Jason Phillips, Houston	†1988	11	108	1,444	15
Fred Gilbert, Houston	†1991	11	106	957	7
Chris Penn, Tulsa	†1993	11	105	1,578	12
Eugene Baker, Kent	†1997	11	103	1,549	18
Sherman Smith, Houston	†1992	11	103	923	6
Troy Edwards, Louisiana Tech	1997	11	102	1,707	13
James Dixon, Houston	1988	11	102	1,103	11
David Williams, Illinois	†1984	11	101	1,278	8
Jay Miller, Brigham Young	†1973	11	100	1,181	8
Jason Phillips, Houston	†1987	11	99	875	3
Mark Templeton, Long Beach St. (RB)	†1986	11	99	688	2
Geoffery Noisy, Nevada	1996	11	98	1,435	9
Alex Van Dyke, Nevada	†1994	11	98	1,246	10
Rodney Carter, Purdue	†1985	11	98	1,099	4
Keith Edwards, Vanderbilt	†1983	11	97	909	0
Jerry Hendren, Idaho	†1969	10	95	1,452	12
Howard Twilley, Tulsa	†1964	10	95	1,178	136
Richard Buchanan, Northwestern	1989	11	94	1,115	9
Kevin Alexander, Utah St.	1995	11	92	1,400	6
Aaron Turner, Pacific (Cal.)	1991	11	92	1,604	18
Bryan Reeves, Nevada	1993	10	91	1,362	17
Dave Petzke, Northern Ill.	†1978	11	91	1,217	11
Glenn Meltzer, Wichita St.	†1966	10	91	1,115	4

**Record. †National champion.*

SEASON TOUCHDOWN RECEPTIONS

Player, Team	Year	G	TD
Randy Moss, Marshall	1997	12	*25
Manny Hazard, Houston	1989	11	22
Desmond Howard, Michigan	1991	11	19
Eugene Baker, Kent	1997	11	18
Reidel Anthony, Florida	1996	12	18
Aaron Turner, Pacific (Cal.)	1991	11	18
Dennis Smith, Utah	1989	12	18
Tom Reynolds, San Diego St.	1971	10	18
Terry Glenn, Ohio St.	1995	11	17
Chris Doering, Florida	1995	12	17
Bryan Reeves, Nevada	1993	10	17
J. J. Stokes, UCLA	1993	11	17
Mario Bailey, Washington	1991	11	17
Clarkston Hines, Duke	1989	11	17
Torry Holt, North Caro. St.	1997	11	16
Alex Van Dyke, Nevada	1995	11	16
Ryan Yarborough, Wyoming	1993	11	16
Dan Bitson, Tulsa	1989	11	16
Howard Twilley, Tulsa	1965	10	16
Andre Cooper, Florida St.	1995	11	15
Ike Hilliard, Florida	1995	11	15
Jack Jackson, Florida	1994	12	15
Jason Phillips, Houston	1988	11	15
Henry Ellard, Fresno St.	1982	11	15

**Record.*

SINGLE-GAME RECEPTIONS

Rec.	Player, Team (Opponent)	Date
23	Randy Gatewood, UNLV (Idaho)	Sept. 17, 1994
22	Jay Miller, Brigham Young (New Mexico)	Nov. 3, 1973
20	Rick Eber, Tulsa (Idaho St.)	Oct. 7, 1967
19	Manny Hazard, Houston (Texas)	Nov. 11, 1989
19	Manny Hazard, Houston (Texas Christian)	Nov. 4, 1989
19	Ron Fair, Arizona St. (Washington St.)	Oct. 28, 1989
19	Howard Twilley, Tulsa (Colorado St.)	Nov. 27, 1965
18	Geoff Noisy, Nevada (Oregon)	Sept. 13, 1997
18	Geoff Noisy, Nevada (Arkansas St.)	Nov. 16, 1996
18	Albert Connell, Texas A&M (Colorado)	Sept. 28, 1996
18	Alex Van Dyke, Nevada (UNLV)	Oct. 28, 1995
18	Alex Van Dyke, Nevada (Toledo)	Sept. 23, 1995
18	Richard Woodley, Texas Christian (Texas Tech)	Nov. 10, 1990
18	Mark Templeton (RB), Long Beach St. (Utah St.)	Nov. 1, 1986
18	Howard Twilley, Tulsa (Southern Ill.)	Oct. 30, 1965
17	Willie Gosha, Auburn (Arkansas)	Oct. 28, 1995
17	Chad Mackey, Louisiana Tech (Nevada)	Oct. 21, 1995
17	Curtis Shearer, San Diego St. (Air Force)	Oct. 1, 1994
17	Loren Richey, Utah (UTEP)	Nov. 29, 1986
17	Keith Edwards, Vanderbilt (Georgia)	Oct. 15, 1983
17	Jon Harvey, Northwestern (Michigan)	Oct. 23, 1982
17	Don Roberts, San Diego St. (California)	Sept. 18, 1982
17	Tom Reynolds, San Diego St. (Utah St.)	Oct. 22, 1971
17	Mike Mikolayunas, Davidson (Richmond)	Oct. 11, 1969
17	Jerry Hendren, Idaho (Southern Miss.)	Oct. 4, 1969
17	Emilio Vallez, New Mexico (New Mexico St.)	Oct. 27, 1967
17	Chuck Hughes, UTEP (Arizona St.)	Oct. 30, 1965

CAREER YARDS

Player, Team	Years	Rec.	Yards	Avg.	TD
Marcus Harris, Wyoming	1993-96	259	*4,518	17.4	38
Ryan Yarborough, Wyoming	1990-93	229	4,357	#19.0	42
Aaron Turner, Pacific (Cal.)	1989-92	*266	4,345	16.3	*43
Chad Mackey, Louisiana Tech	1993-96	264	3,789	14.4	22
Terance Mathis, New Mexico	1985-87, 89	263	4,254	16.2	36
Marc Zeno, Tulane	1984-87	236	3,725	15.8	25
Ron Sellers, Florida St.	1966-68	212	3,598	17.0	23
Elmo Wright, Houston	1968-70	153	3,347	21.9	34
Howard Twilley, Tulsa	1963-65	261	3,343	12.8	32
Clarkston Hines, Duke	1986-89	189	3,318	17.6	38
Gerald Harp, Western Caro.	1977-80	197	3,305	16.8	26
Dan Bitson, Tulsa	1987-89, 91	163	3,300	20.2	29
Charlie Jones, Fresno St.	1992-95	181	3,260	18.0	25
Greg Primus, Colorado St.	1989-92	192	3,200	16.7	16
David Williams, Illinois	1983-85	245	3,195	13.0	22
Hart Lee Dykes, Oklahoma St.	1985-88	203	3,171	15.6	29
Bryan Rowley, Utah	$1989-93	177	3,143	17.8	25
Darnay Scott, San Diego St.	1991-93	178	3,139	17.6	25
Rick Beasley, Appalachian St.	1978-80	178	3,124	17.6	23
Alex Van Dyke, Nevada	1994-95	227	3,100	13.7	26
Eric Drage, Brigham Young	1990-93	162	3,065	18.9	29
Lloyd Hill, Texas Tech	1990-93	189	3,059	16.2	20
Mike Adams, Texas	1992-93, 95-96	177	3,032	17.1	16
Kevin Lockett, Kansas St.	1993-96	217	3,032	14.0	26
Bobby Engram, Penn St.	1991, 93-95	167	3,026	18.1	31
Carl Winston, New Mexico	1990-93	202	2,972	14.7	14
Brian Alford, Purdue	1994-97	160	2,968	18.6	30
Boo Mitchell, Vanderbilt	1985-88	188	2,964	15.8	9
Johnnie Morton, Southern Cal	1990-93	185	2,957	16.0	21
Brian Roberson, Fresno St.	1993-96	188	2,956	15.7	15
Ricky Proehl, Wake Forest	1986-89	188	2,949	15.7	25
Henry Ellard, Fresno St.	1979-82	138	2,947	21.4	25
Kendal Smith, Utah St.	1985-88	169	2,943	17.4	25
Jermaine Lewis, Maryland	1992-95	193	2,932	15.2	21
E. G. Green, Florida St.	1994-97	166	2,920	17.6	29
Charles Lockett, Long Beach St.	1983-86	191	2,902	15.1	19
Chuck Hughes, UTEP	1964-66	162	2,882	17.8	19
Walter Murray, Hawaii	1982-85	178	2,865	16.1	20

**Record. $See page 6 for explanation. #Record for minimum 200 catches.*

CAREER YARDS PER GAME

(Minimum 2,200 Yards)

Player, Team	Years	G	Yards	Yd.PG
Alex Van Dyke, Nevada	1994-95	22	3,100	*140.9
Manny Hazard, Houston	1989-90	21	2,635	125.5
Ron Sellers, Florida St.	1966-68	30	3,598	119.9
Bryan Reeves, Nevada	1992-93	21	2,476	117.9
Nakia Jenkins, Utah St.	1996-97	22	2,483	112.9
Keyshawn Johnson, Southern Cal	1994-95	21	2,358	112.3
Elmo Wright, Houston	1968-70	30	3,347	111.6
Howard Twilley, Tulsa	1963-65	30	3,343	111.4
Chris Penn, Tulsa	1991, 93	22	2,370	107.7

Player, Team	Years	G	Yards	Yd.PG
Jason Phillips, Houston	1987-88	22	2,319	105.4
Aaron Turner, Pacific (Cal.)	1989-92	44	4,345	98.8
Marcus Harris, Wyoming	1993-96	46	4,518	98.2
Rick Beasley, Appalachian St.	†1977-80	32	3,124	97.6
David Williams, Illinois	1982-85	33	3,195	96.8
Terance Mathis, New Mexico	1985-87, 89	44	4,254	96.7
Ryan Yarborough, Wyoming	1990-93	46	*4,357	94.7
Darnay Scott, San Diego St.	1991-93	34	3,139	92.3
Lloyd Hill, Texas Tech	1990-93	34	3,059	90.0
Chad Mackey, Louisiana Tech	1993-96	44	3,789	86.1
Marc Zeno, Tulane	1984-87	44	3,725	84.7
Tim Delaney, San Diego St.	1968-70	30	2,535	84.5

*Record. †Played defensive back in 1977.

CAREER TOUCHDOWN RECEPTIONS

Player, Team	Years	G	TD
Aaron Turner, Pacific (Cal.)	1989-92	44	*43
Ryan Yarborough, Wyoming	1990-93	46	42
Marcus Harris, Wyoming	1993-96	46	38
Clarkston Hines, Duke	1986-89	44	38
Terance Mathis, New Mexico	1985-87, 89	44	36
Elmo Wright, Houston	1968-70	30	34
Steve Largent, Tulsa	1973-75	30	32
Howard Twilley, Tulsa	1963-65	30	32
Eugene Baker, Kent	¢1995-97	33	31
Chris Doering, Florida	1992-95	40	31
Lucious Davis, New Mexico St.	1992-95	42	31
Bobby Engram, Penn St.	1991, 93-95	42	31
Manny Hazard, Houston	1989-90	21	31
Brian Alford, Purdue	1994-97	38	30
Sean Dawkins, California	1990-92	33	30
Desmond Howard, Michigan	1989-91	33	30
Jade Butcher, Indiana	1967-69	30	30
E. G. Green, Florida St.	1994-97	44	29
Ike Hilliard, Florida	1994-96	32	29
Jack Jackson, Florida	1992-94	34	29
Eric Drage, Brigham Young	1990-93	46	29
Dan Bitson, Tulsa	1987-89, 91	44	29
Hart Lee Dykes, Oklahoma St.	1985-88	41	29

*Record.

SEASON YARDS

Player, Team	Year	Rec.	Yards	Avg.	TD
Alex Van Dyke, Nevada	†1995	129	*1,854	14.4	16
Howard Twilley, Tulsa	1965	134	1,779	13.3	16
Troy Edwards, Louisiana Tech	†1997	102	1,707	16.7	13
Manny Hazard, Houston	1989	*142	1,689	11.9	22
Marcus Harris, Wyoming	†1996	109	1,650	15.1	13
Randy Moss, Marshall	1997	90	1,647	18.3	*25
Aaron Turner, Pacific (Cal.)	†1991	92	1,604	17.4	18
Chris Penn, Tulsa	†1993	105	1,578	15.0	12
Eugene Baker, Kent	1997	103	1,549	15.0	18
Chuck Hughes, UTEP	1965	80	1,519	19.0	12
Ryan Yarborough, Wyoming	1993	67	1,512	22.6	16
Henry Ellard, Fresno St.	1982	62	1,510	††24.4	15
Ron Sellers, Florida St.	1968	86	1,496	17.4	12
Chad Mackey, Louisiana Tech	1996	85	1,466	17.3	10
Jerry Hendren, Idaho	1969	95	1,452	15.3	12
Jason Phillips, Houston	1988	108	1,444	13.4	15

*Record. †National champion. ††Record for minimum 50 catches.

SINGLE-GAME YARDS

Yds.	Player, Team (Opponent)	Date
363	Randy Gatewood, UNLV (Idaho)	Sept. 17, 1994
349	Chuck Hughes, UTEP (North Texas)	Sept. 18, 1965
322	Rick Eber, Tulsa (Idaho St.)	Oct. 7, 1967
318	Harry Wood, Tulsa (Idaho St.)	Oct. 7, 1967
316	Jeff Evans, New Mexico St. (Southern Ill.)	Sept. 30, 1978
314	Alex Van Dyke, Nevada (San Jose St.)	Nov. 18, 1995
310	Chad Mackey, Louisiana Tech (Toledo)	Oct. 19, 1996
297	Brian Oliver, Ball St. (Toledo)	Oct. 9, 1993
296	Geoffery Noisy, Nevada (Utah St.)	Nov. 9 1996
290	Tom Reynolds, San Diego St. (Utah St.)	Oct. 22, 1971
289	Wesley Walker, California (San Jose St.)	Oct. 2, 1976
288	Mike Siani, Villanova (Xavier [Ohio])	Oct. 30, 1971
285	Thomas Lewis, Indiana (Penn St.)	Nov. 6, 1993
284	Lennie Johnson, Arkansas St. (Southwest Mo. St.)	Nov. 8, 1997
284	Don Clune, Pennsylvania (Harvard)	Oct. 30, 1971
283	Jeremy McDaniel, Arizona (California)	Nov. 2, 1996
283	Chris Castor, Duke (Wake Forest)	Nov. 6, 1982
282	Larry Willis, Fresno St. (Montana St.)	Nov. 17, 1984
280	Will Blackwell, San Diego St. (California)	Sept. 14, 1996
278	Derek Graham, Princeton (Yale)	Nov. 14, 1981

ANNUAL CHAMPIONS

Year	Player, Team	Class	Rec.	Yards	TD
1937	Jim Benton, Arkansas	Sr.	48	814	7
1938	Sam Boyd, Baylor	Sr.	32	537	—
1939	Ken Kavanaugh, LSU	Sr.	30	467	—
1940	Eddie Bryant, Virginia	So.	30	222	2
1941	Hank Stanton, Arizona	Sr.	50	820	—
1942	Bill Rogers, Texas A&M	Sr.	39	432	—
1943	Neil Armstrong, Oklahoma St.	Fr.	39	317	—
1944	Reid Moseley, Georgia	So.	32	506	—
1945	Reid Moseley, Georgia	Jr.	31	662	—
1946	Neil Armstrong, Oklahoma St.	Sr.	32	479	1
1947	Barney Poole, Mississippi	Jr.	52	513	8
1948	Johnny "Red" O'Quinn, Wake Forest	Jr.	39	605	7
1949	Art Weiner, North Caro.	Sr.	52	762	7
1950	Gordon Cooper, Denver	Jr.	46	569	8
1951	Dewey McConnell, Wyoming	Sr.	47	725	9
1952	Ed Brown, Fordham	Sr.	57	774	6
1953	John Carson, Georgia	Sr.	45	663	4
1954	Jim Hanifan, California	Sr.	44	569	7
1955	Hank Burnine, Missouri	Sr.	44	594	2
1956	Art Powell, San Jose St.	So.	40	583	5
1957	Stuart Vaughan, Utah	Sr.	53	756	5
1958	Dave Hibbert, Arizona	Jr.	61	606	4
1959	Chris Burford, Stanford	Sr.	61	756	6
1960	Hugh Campbell, Washington St.	So.	66	881	10
1961	Hugh Campbell, Washington St.	Jr.	53	723	5
1962	Vern Burke, Oregon St.	Jr.	69	1,007	10
1963	Lawrence Elkins, Baylor	Jr.	70	873	8
1964	Howard Twilley, Tulsa	Jr.	95	1,178	13
1965	Howard Twilley, Tulsa	Sr.	134	1,779	16
1966	Glenn Meltzer, Wichita St.	So.	91	1,115	4
1967	Bob Goodridge, Vanderbilt	Sr.	79	1,114	6
1968	Ron Sellers, Florida St.	Sr.	86	1,496	12
1969	Jerry Hendren, Idaho	Sr.	95	1,452	12

Beginning in 1970, ranked on per-game (instead of total) catches

Year	Player, Team	Class	G	Rec.	Avg.	Yards	TD
1970	Mike Mikolayunas, Davidson	Sr.	10	87	8.7	1,128	8
1971	Tom Reynolds, San Diego St.	Sr.	10	67	6.7	1,070	7
1972	Tom Forzani, Utah St.	Sr.	11	85	7.7	1,169	8
1973	Jay Miller, Brigham Young	So.	11	100	9.1	1,181	8
1974	Dwight McDonald, San Diego St.	Sr.	11	86	7.8	1,157	7
1975	Bob Farnham, Brown	Jr.	9	56	6.2	701	2
1976	Billy Ryckman, Louisiana Tech	Sr.	11	77	7.0	1,382	10
1977	Wayne Tolleson, Western Caro.	Sr.	11	73	6.6	1,101	7
1978	Dave Petzke, Northern Ill.	Sr.	11	91	8.3	1,217	11
1979	Rick Beasley, Appalachian St.	Jr.	11	74	6.7	1,205	12
1980	Dave Young, Purdue	Sr.	11	67	6.1	917	8
1981	Pete Harvey, North Texas	Sr.	9	57	6.3	743	3
1982	Vincent White, Stanford	Sr.	10	68	6.8	677	8
1983	Keith Edwards, Vanderbilt	Jr.	11	97	8.8	909	8
1984	David Williams, Illinois	Jr.	11	101	9.2	1,278	8
1985	Rodney Carter, Purdue	Sr.	11	98	8.9	1,099	4
1986	Mark Templeton, Long Beach St. (RB)	Sr.	11	99	9.0	688	2
1987	Jason Phillips, Houston	Jr.	11	99	9.0	875	3
1988	Jason Phillips, Houston	Sr.	11	108	9.8	1,444	15
1989	Manny Hazard, Houston	Jr.	11	*142	12.9	1,689	*22

Beginning in 1990, ranked on both per-game catches and yards per game

PER-GAME CATCHES

Year	Player, Team	Class	G	Rec.	Avg.	Yards	TD
1990	Manny Hazard, Houston	Sr.	10	78	7.8	946	9
1991	Fred Gilbert, Houston	Jr.	11	106	9.6	957	7
1992	Sherman Smith, Houston	Jr.	11	103	9.4	923	6
1993	Chris Penn, Tulsa	Sr.	11	105	9.6	1,578	12
1994	Alex Van Dyke, Nevada	Jr.	11	98	8.9	1,246	10
1995	Alex Van Dyke, Nevada	Sr.	11	129	11.7	*1,854	16
1996	Damond Wilkins, Nevada	Sr.	11	114	10.4	1,121	4
1997	Eugene Baker, Kent	Jr.	11	103	9.4	1,549	18

YARDS PER GAME

Year	Player, Team	Class	G	Rec.	Yards	Avg.	TD
1990	Patrick Rowe, San Diego St.	Jr.	11	71	1,392	126.6	8
1991	Aaron Turner, Pacific (Cal.)	Jr.	11	92	1,604	145.8	18
1992	Lloyd Hill, Texas Tech	Jr.	11	76	1,261	114.6	12
1993	Chris Penn, Tulsa	Sr.	11	105	1,578	143.5	12
1994	Marcus Harris, Wyoming	So.	12	71	1,431	119.3	11
1995	Alex Van Dyke, Nevada	Sr.	11	129	*1,854	168.6	16
1996	Marcus Harris, Wyoming	Sr.	12	109	1,650	137.5	13
1997	Troy Edwards, Louisiana Tech	Jr.	11	102	1,707	155.2	13

*Record.

Scoring

CAREER POINTS PER GAME

(Minimum 225 Points)

Player, Team	Years	G	TD	XPt.	FG	Pts.	Pt.PG
Marshall Faulk, San Diego St.	1991-93	31	‡62	4	0	‡376	*12.1
Ed Marinaro, Cornell	1969-71	27	52	6	0	318	11.8
Bill Burnett, Arkansas	1968-70	26	49	0	0	294	11.3
Steve Owens, Oklahoma	1967-69	30	56	0	0	336	11.2
Eddie Talboom, Wyoming	1948-50	28	34	99	0	303	10.8
Howard Twilley, Tulsa	1963-65	26	32	67	0	259	10.0
Player, Team	**Years**	**G**	**TD**	**XPt.**	**FG**	**Pts.**	**Pt.PG**
Tom Harmon, Michigan	1938-40	24	33	33	2	237	9.9
Roman Anderson, Houston	1988-91	44	0	213	70	*423	9.6
Anthony Thompson, Indiana	1986-89	41	*65	4	0	394	9.6
Johnny Bright, Drake	1949-51	25	40	0	0	240	9.6
Glenn Davis, Army	1943-46	37	59	0	0	354	9.6
Stacey Robinson, Northern Ill. (QB)	1988-90	25	38	6	0	234	9.4
Floyd Little, Syracuse	1964-66	30	46	2	0	278	9.3
Felix "Doc" Blanchard, Army	1944-46	25	38	3	0	231	9.2
Anthony Davis, Southern Cal	1972-74	33	50	2	0	302	9.2

**Record. ‡Three-year totals record.*

SEASON POINTS PER GAME

Player, Team	Year	G	TD	XPt.	FG	Pts.	Pt.PG
Barry Sanders, Oklahoma St.	†1988	11	*39	0	0	*234	*21.3
Bobby Reynolds, Nebraska	†1950	9	22	25	0	157	17.4
Art Luppino, Arizona	†1954	10	24	22	0	166	16.6
Ed Marinaro, Cornell	†1971	9	24	4	0	148	16.4
Lydell Mitchell, Penn St.	1971	11	29	0	0	174	15.8
Marshall Faulk, San Diego St.	†1991	9	23	2	0	140	15.6
Byron "Whizzer" White, Colorado	†1937	8	16	23	1	122	15.3

**Record. †National champion.*

CAREER POINTS

(Non-Kickers)

Player, Team	Years	TD	XPt.	FG	Pts.
Anthony Thompson, Indiana	1986-89	*65	4	0	*394
Marshall Faulk, San Diego St.	1991-93	‡62	4	0	‡376
Tony Dorsett, Pittsburgh	1973-76	59	2	0	356
Glenn Davis, Army	1943-46	59	0	0	354
Art Luppino, Arizona	1953-56	48	49	0	337
Steve Owens, Oklahoma	1967-69	56	0	0	336
Wilford White, Arizona St.	1947-50	48	27	4	327
Skip Hicks, UCLA	$1993-97	54	0	0	324
Barry Sanders, Oklahoma St.	1986-88	54	0	0	324
Allen Pinkett, Notre Dame	1982-85	53	2	0	320
Pete Johnson, Ohio St.	1973-76	53	0	0	318
Ed Marinaro, Cornell	1969-71	52	6	0	318
Herschel Walker, Georgia	1980-82	52	2	0	314
James Gray, Texas Tech	1986-89	52	0	0	312
Mike Rozier, Nebraska	1981-83	52	0	0	312
Ted Brown, North Caro. St.	1975-78	51	6	0	312
Leon Johnson, North Caro.	1993-96	50	3	0	306
John Harvey, UTEP	1985-88	51	0	0	306
Eddie Talboom, Wyoming	1948-50	34	99	0	303
Anthony Davis, Southern Cal	1972-74	50	2	0	302
Dalton Hilliard, LSU	1982-85	50	0	0	300
Billy Sims, Oklahoma	$1975-79	50	0	0	300
Charles White, Southern Cal	1976-79	49	2	0	296
Nolan Jones, Arizona St.	1958-61	30	77	13	296
Warrick Dunn, Florida St.	1993-96	49	0	0	294
Steve Bartalo, Colorado St.	1983-86	49	0	0	294
Bill Burnett, Arkansas	1968-70	49	0	0	294
Brian Mitchell, Southwestern La.	1986-89	47	4	0	286
Rick Badanjek, Maryland	1982-85	46	10	0	286
Keith Byars, Ohio St.	1982-85	48	0	0	286

**Record. $See page 6 for explanation. ‡Three-year totals record.*

CAREER POINTS

(Kickers)

Player, Team	Years	PAT	PAT Att.	FG	FG Att.	Pts.
Roman Anderson, Houston	1988-91	213	217	70	101	*423
Carlos Huerta, Miami (Fla.)	1988-91	178	181	73	91	397
Jason Elam, Hawaii	$1988-92	158	161	79	100	395
Derek Schmidt, Florida St.	1984-87	174	178	73	102	393
Luis Zendejas, Arizona St.	1981-84	134	135	78	*105	368
Jeff Jaeger, Washington	1983-86	118	123	*80	99	358
John Lee, UCLA	1982-85	116	117	79	92	353
Max Zendejas, Arizona	1982-85	122	124	77	104	353
Kevin Butler, Georgia	1981-84	122	125	77	98	353
Derek Mahoney, Fresno St.	1990-93	*216	*222	45	63	351
Philip Doyle, Alabama	1987-90	105	108	78	*105	†345
Phil Dawson, Texas	1994-97	162	170	59	79	339
Andy Trakas, San Diego St.	1989-92	170	178	56	82	338
Scott Bentley, Florida St.	1993-96	200	215	42	61	326
Michael Proctor, Alabama	1992-95	131	132	65	91	326
Barry Belli, Fresno St.	1984-87	116	123	70	99	326
Kyle Bryant, Texas A&M	1994-97	145	152	60	85	325
Jason Hanson, Washington St.	1988-91	136	141	62	95	322
R. D. Lashar, Oklahoma	1987-90	194	200	42	60	320
Collin Mackie, South Caro.	1987-90	112	113	69	95	319
John Becksvoort, Tennessee	1991-94	161	161	52	75	317
Cary Blanchard, Oklahoma St.	1987-90	150	151	54	73	#314
Fuad Reveiz, Tennessee	1981-84	101	103	71	95	314
Sean Fleming, Wyoming	1988-91	150	155	54	92	312
Van Tiffin, Alabama	1983-86	135	135	59	87	312
Jess Atkinson, Maryland	1981-84	128	131	60	82	308
Gary Gussman, Miami (Ohio)	1984-87	102	104	68	94	306
Greg Cox, Miami (Fla.)	1984-87	162	169	47	64	303
Peter Holt, San Diego St.	1993-96	158	169	48	72	302
Dan Eichloff, Kansas	1990-93	116	119	62	87	302
Cory Wedel, Wyoming	1994-97	139	140	54	73	301

**Record. $See page 6 for explanation. †Includes one TD reception. #Includes one two-point conversion.*

SEASON POINTS

Player, Team	Year	TD	XPt.	FG	Pts.
Barry Sanders, Oklahoma St.	†1988	*39	0	0	*234
Mike Rozier, Nebraska	†1983	29	0	0	174
Lydell Mitchell, Penn St.	1971	29	0	0	174
Art Luppino, Arizona	†1954	24	22	0	166
Bobby Reynolds, Nebraska	†1950	22	25	0	157
Anthony Thompson, Indiana	†1989	25	4	0	154
Ricky Williams, Texas	†1997	25	2	0	152
Randy Moss, Marshall	1997	25	2	0	152
Fred Wendt, UTEP	†1948	20	32	0	152
Skip Hicks, UCLA	1997	25	0	0	150
Travis Prentice, Miami (Ohio)	1997	25	0	0	150
Pete Johnson, Ohio St.	†1975	25	0	0	150

**Record. †National champion.*

SINGLE-GAME POINTS

No.	Player, Team (Opponent)	Date
48	Howard Griffith, Illinois (Southern Ill.)	Sept. 22, 1990
44	Marshall Faulk, San Diego St. (Pacific [Cal.])	Sept. 14, 1991
43	Jim Brown, Syracuse (Colgate)	Nov. 17, 1956
42	Arnold "Showboat" Boykin, Mississippi (Mississippi St.)	Dec. 1, 1951
42	Fred Wendt, UTEP (New Mexico St.)	Nov. 25, 1948
38	Dick Bass, Pacific, Cal. (San Diego St.)	Nov. 22, 1958
37	Jimmy Nutter, Wichita St. (Northern St.)	Oct. 22, 1949
36	Scott Harley, East Caro. (Ohio)	Nov. 16, 1996
36	Antowain Smith, Houston (Southern Miss.)	Nov. 9, 1996
36	Madre Hill, Arkansas (South Caro.)	Sept. 9, 1995
36	Calvin Jones, Nebraska (Kansas)	Nov. 9, 1991
36	Blake Ezor, Michigan St. (Northwestern)	Nov. 18, 1989
36	Dee Dowis, Air Force (San Diego St.)	Sept. 2, 1989
36	Kelvin Bryant, North Caro. (East Caro.)	Sept. 12, 1981
36	Andre Herrera, Southern Ill. (Northern Ill.)	Oct. 23, 1976
36	Anthony Davis, Southern Cal (Notre Dame)	Dec. 2, 1972
36	Tim Delaney, San Diego St. (New Mexico St.)	Nov. 15, 1969
36	Tom Francisco, Virginia Tech (VMI)	Nov. 24, 1966
36	Howard Twilley, Tulsa (Louisville)	Nov. 6, 1965
36	Pete Pedro, West Tex. A&M (UTEP)	Sept. 30, 1961
36	Tom Powers, Duke (Richmond)	Oct. 21, 1950

ANNUAL CHAMPIONS

Year	Player, Team	Class	TD	XPt.	FG	Pts.
1937	Byron "Whizzer" White, Colorado	Sr.	16	23	1	122
1938	Parker Hall, Mississippi	Sr.	11	7	0	73
1939	Tom Harmon, Michigan	Jr.	14	15	1	102
1940	Tom Harmon, Michigan	Sr.	16	18	1	117
1941	Bill Dudley, Virginia	Sr.	18	23	1	134
1942	Bob Steuber, Missouri	Sr.	18	13	0	121
1943	Steve Van Buren, LSU	Sr.	14	14	0	98
1944	Glenn Davis, Army	So.	20	0	0	120
1945	Felix "Doc" Blanchard, Army	Jr.	19	1	0	115
1946	Gene Roberts, Chattanooga	Sr.	18	9	0	117
1947	Lou Gambino, Maryland	Jr.	16	0	0	96
1948	Fred Wendt, UTEP	Sr.	20	32	0	152
1949	George Thomas, Oklahoma	Sr.	19	3	0	117
1950	Bobby Reynolds, Nebraska	So.	22	25	0	157
1951	Ollie Matson, San Francisco	Sr.	21	0	0	126

Year	Player, Team	Class	TD	XPt.	FG	Pts.
1952	Jackie Parker, Mississippi St.	Jr.	16	24	0	120
1953	Earl Lindley, Utah St.	Sr.	13	3	0	81
1954	Art Luppino, Arizona	So.	24	22	0	166
1955	Jim Swink, Texas Christian	Jr.	20	5	0	125
1956	Clendon Thomas, Oklahoma	Jr.	18	0	0	108
1957	Leon Burton, Arizona St.	Jr.	16	0	0	96
1958	Dick Bass, Pacific (Cal.)	Jr.	18	8	0	116
1959	Pervis Atkins, New Mexico St.	Jr.	17	5	0	107
1960	Bob Gaiters, New Mexico St.	Sr.	23	7	0	145
1961	Jim Pilot, New Mexico St.	So.	21	12	0	138
1962	Jerry Logan, West Tex. A&M	Sr.	13	32	0	110
1963	Cosmo Iacavazzi, Princeton	Jr.	14	0	0	84
	Dave Casinelli, Memphis	Sr.	14	0	0	84
1964	Brian Piccolo, Wake Forest	Sr.	17	9	0	111
1965	Howard Twilley, Tulsa	Sr.	16	31	0	127
1966	Ken Hebert, Houston	Jr.	11	41	2	113
1967	Leroy Keyes, Purdue	Jr.	19	0	0	114
1968	Jim O'Brien, Cincinnati	Jr.	12	31	13	142
1969	Steve Owens, Oklahoma	Sr.	23	0	0	138

Beginning in 1970, ranked on per-game (instead of total) points

Year	Player, Team	Class	G	TD	XPt.	FG	Pts.	Avg.
1970	Brian Bream, Air Force	Jr.	10	20	0	0	120	12.0
	Gary Kosins, Dayton	Jr.	9	18	0	0	108	12.0
1971	Ed Marinaro, Cornell	Sr.	9	24	4	0	148	16.4
1972	Harold Henson, Ohio St.	So.	10	20	0	0	120	12.0
1973	Jim Jennings, Rutgers	Sr.	11	21	2	0	128	11.6
1974	Bill Marek, Wisconsin	Jr.	9	19	0	0	114	12.7
1975	Pete Johnson, Ohio St.	Jr.	11	25	0	0	150	13.6
1976	Tony Dorsett, Pittsburgh	Sr.	11	22	2	0	134	12.2
1977	Earl Campbell, Texas	Sr.	11	19	0	0	114	10.4
1978	Billy Sims, Oklahoma	Jr.	11	20	0	0	120	10.9
1979	Billy Sims, Oklahoma	Sr.	11	22	0	0	132	12.0
1980	Sammy Winder, Southern Miss.	Jr.	11	20	0	0	120	10.9
1981	Marcus Allen, Southern Cal	Sr.	11	23	0	0	138	12.5
1982	Greg Allen, Florida St.	So.	11	21	0	0	126	11.5
1983	Mike Rozier, Nebraska	Sr.	12	29	0	0	174	14.5
1984	Keith Byars, Ohio St.	Jr.	11	24	0	0	144	13.1
1985	Bernard White, Bowling Green	Sr.	11	19	0	0	114	10.4
1986	Steve Bartalo, Colorado St.	Sr.	11	19	0	0	114	10.4
1987	Paul Hewitt, San Diego St.	Jr.	12	24	0	0	144	12.0
1988	Barry Sanders, Oklahoma St.	Jr.	11	*39	0	0	*234	*21.3
1989	Anthony Thompson, Indiana	Sr.	11	25	4	0	154	14.0
1990	Stacey Robinson, Northern Ill. (QB)	Sr.	11	19	6	0	120	10.9
1991	Marshall Faulk, San Diego St.	Fr.	9	23	2	0	140	15.6
1992	Garrison Hearst, Georgia	Jr.	11	21	0	0	126	11.5
1993	Byron Morris, Texas Tech	Jr.	11	22	2	0	134	12.2
1994	Rashaan Salaam, Colorado	Jr.	11	24	0	0	144	13.1
1995	Eddie George, Ohio St.	Sr.	12	24	0	0	144	12.0
1996	Corey Dillon, Washington	Jr.	11	23	0	0	138	12.6
1997	Ricky Williams, Texas	Jr.	11	25	2	0	152	13.8

**Record.*

Interceptions

CAREER INTERCEPTIONS

Player, Team	Years	No.	Yards	Avg.
Al Brosky, Illinois	1950-52	*29	356	12.3
Martin Bayless, Bowling Green	1980-83	27	266	9.9
John Provost, Holy Cross	1972-74	27	470	17.4
Tracy Saul, Texas Tech	1989-92	25	425	17.0
Tony Thurman, Boston College	1981-84	25	221	8.8
Tom Curtis, Michigan	1967-69	25	440	17.6
Jeff Nixon, Richmond	1975-78	23	377	16.4
Bennie Blades, Miami (Fla.)	1984-87	22	355	16.1
Jim Bolding, East Caro.	1973-76	22	143	6.5
Terrell Buckley, Florida St.	1989-91	21	*501	23.9
Chuck Cecil, Arizona	1984-87	21	241	11.5
Barry Hill, Iowa St.	1972-74	21	202	9.6
Mike Sensibaugh, Ohio St.	1968-70	21	226	10.8
Kevin Smith, Texas A&M	1988-91	20	289	14.5
Mark Collins, Cal St. Fullerton	1982-85	20	193	9.7
Anthony Young, Temple	1981-84	20	230	11.5
Chris Williams, LSU	1977-80	20	91	4.6
Charles Jefferson, McNeese St.	1975-78	20	95	4.8
Artimus Parker, Southern Cal	1971-73	20	268	13.4
Dave Atkinson, Brigham Young	1971-73	20	222	11.1
Jackie Wallace, Arizona	1970-72	20	250	12.5
Tom Wilson, Colgate	1964-66	20	215	10.8
Lynn Chandnois, Michigan St.	1946-49	20	410	20.5
Bobby Wilson, Mississippi	1946-49	20	369	18.5

**Record.*

SEASON INTERCEPTIONS

Player, Team	Year	No.	Yards
Al Worley, Washington	†1968	*14	130
George Shaw, Oregon	†1951	13	136
Terrell Buckley, Florida St.	†1991	12	238
Cornelius Price, Houston	†1989	12	187
Bob Navarro, Eastern Mich.	†1989	12	73
Tony Thurman, Boston College	†1984	12	99
Terry Hoage, Georgia	†1982	12	51
Frank Polito, Villanova	†1971	12	261
Bill Albrecht, Washington	1951	12	140
Hank Rich, Arizona St.	†1950	12	135

**Record. †National champion.*

ANNUAL CHAMPIONS

Year	Player, Team	Class	No.	Yards
1938	Elmer Tarbox, Texas Tech	Sr.	11	89
1939	Harold Van Every, Minnesota	Sr.	8	59
1940	Dick Morgan, Tulsa	Jr.	7	210
1941	Bobby Robertson, Southern Cal	Sr.	9	126
1942	Ray Evans, Kansas	Jr.	10	76
1943	Jay Stoves, Washington	Sr.	7	139
1944	Jim Hardy, Southern Cal	Sr.	8	73
1945	Jake Leicht, Oregon	So.	9	195
1946	Larry Hatch, Washington	So.	8	114
1947	John Bruce, William & Mary	Jr.	9	78
1948	Jay Van Noy, Utah St.	Jr.	8	228
1949	Bobby Wilson, Mississippi	Sr.	10	70
1950	Hank Rich, Arizona St.	Sr.	12	135
1951	George Shaw, Oregon	Fr.	13	136
1952	Cecil Ingram, Alabama	Jr.	10	163
1953	Bob Garrett, Stanford	Sr.	9	80
1954	Gary Glick, Colorado St.	Jr.	8	168
1955	Sam Wesley, Oregon St.	Jr.	7	61
1956	Jack Hill, Utah St.	Sr.	7	132
1957	Ray Toole, North Texas	Sr.	7	133
1958	Jim Norton, Idaho	Jr.	9	222
1959	Bud Whitehead, Florida St.	Jr.	6	111
1960	Bob O'Billovich, Montana	Jr.	7	71
1961	Joe Zuger, Arizona St.	Sr.	10	121
1962	Byron Beaver, Houston	Sr.	10	56
1963	Dick Kern, William & Mary	Sr.	8	116
1964	Tony Carey, Notre Dame	Jr.	8	121
1965	Bob Sullivan, Maryland	Sr.	10	61
1966	Henry King, Utah St.	Sr.	11	180
1967	Steve Haterius, West Tex. A&M	Sr.	11	90
1968	Al Worley, Washington	Sr.	*14	130
1969	Seth Miller, Arizona St .	Sr.	11	63

Beginning in 1970, ranked on per-game (instead of total) number

Year	Player, Team	Class	G	No.	Avg.	Yards
1970	Mike Sensibaugh, Ohio St.	Sr.	8	8	1.00	40
1971	Frank Polito, Villanova	So.	10	12	1.20	261
1972	Mike Townsend, Notre Dame	Jr.	10	10	1.00	39
1973	Mike Gow, Illinois	Jr.	11	10	0.91	142
1974	Mike Haynes, Arizona St.	Jr.	11	10	0.91	115
1975	Jim Bolding, East Caro.	Jr.	10	10	1.00	51
1976	Anthony Francis, Houston	Jr.	11	10	0.91	118
1977	Paul Lawler, Colgate	Sr.	9	7	0.78	53
1978	Pete Harris, Penn St.	Jr.	11	10	0.91	155
1979	Joe Callan, Ohio	Sr.	9	9	1.00	110
1980	Ronnie Lott, Southern Cal	Sr.	11	8	0.73	166
	Steve McNamee, William & Mary	Sr.	11	8	0.73	125
	Greg Benton, Drake	Sr.	11	8	0.73	119
	Jeff Hipp, Georgia	Sr.	11	8	0.73	104
	Mike Richardson, Arizona St.	So.	11	8	0.73	89
	Vann McElroy, Baylor	Jr.	11	8	0.73	73
1981	Sam Shaffer, Temple	Sr.	10	9	0.90	76
1982	Terry Hoage, Georgia	Jr.	10	12	1.20	51
1983	Martin Bayless, Bowling Green	Sr.	11	10	0.91	64
1984	Tony Thurman, Boston College	Sr.	11	12	1.09	99
1985	Chris White, Tennessee	Sr.	11	9	0.82	168
	Kevin Walker, East Caro.	Sr.	11	9	0.82	155
1986	Bennie Blades, Miami (Fla.)	Jr.	11	10	0.91	128
1987	Keith McMeans, Virginia	Fr.	10	9	0.90	35
1988	Kurt Larson, Michigan St. (LB)	Sr.	11	8	0.73	78
	Andy Logan, Kent	Sr.	11	8	0.73	54
1989	Cornelius Price, Houston	Jr.	11	12	1.09	187
	Bob Navarro, Eastern Mich.	Jr.	11	12	1.09	73
1990	Jerry Parks, Houston	Jr.	11	8	0.73	124
1991	Terrell Buckley, Florida St.	Jr.	12	12	1.00	238
1992	Carlton McDonald, Air Force	Sr.	11	8	0.73	109
1993	Orlanda Thomas, Southwestern La.	Jr.	11	9	0.82	84
1994	Aaron Beasley, West Va.	Jr.	12	10	0.83	133
1995	Willie Smith, Louisiana Tech	Jr.	10	8	0.80	65

Year	Player, Team	Class	G	No.	Avg.	Yards
1996	Dre' Bly, North Caro.	Fr.	11	11	1.00	141
1997	Brian Lee, Wyoming	Sr.	11	8	0.73	103

*Record.

Punting

CAREER AVERAGE

(Minimum 250 Punts)

Player, Team	Years	No.	Yards	Avg.	Long
Bill Smith, Mississippi	1983-86	254	11,260	*44.3	92
Jim Arnold, Vanderbilt	1979-82	277	12,171	43.9	79
Ralf Mojsiejenko, Michigan St.	1981-84	275	11,997	43.6	72
Jim Miller, Mississippi	1976-79	266	11,549	43.4	82
Russ Henderson, Virginia	1975-78	276	11,957	43.3	74
Maury Buford, Texas Tech	1978-81	293	12,670	43.2	75
Nate Cochran, Pittsburgh	1993-96	252	10,851	43.1	80
Chris Becker, Texas Christian	1985-88	265	11,407	43.0	77
Ron Keller, New Mexico	1983-86	252	10,737	42.6	77
James Gargus, Texas Christian	1981-84	255	10,862	42.6	74

(Minimum 150-249 Punts)

Player, Team	Years	No.	Yards	Avg.	Long
Todd Sauerbrun, West Va.	1991-94	167	7,733	*46.3	90
Reggie Roby, Iowa	1979-82	172	7,849	45.6	69
Greg Montgomery, Michigan St.	1985-87	170	7,721	45.4	86
Tom Tupa, Ohio St.	1984-87	196	8,854	45.2	75
Barry Helton, Colorado	1984-87	153	6,873	44.9	68
Ray Guy, Southern Miss.	1970-72	200	8,934	44.7	93
Bucky Scribner, Kansas	1980-82	217	9,670	44.6	70
Terry Daniel, Auburn	1992-94	169	7,522	44.5	71
Greg Horne, Arkansas	1983-86	180	8,002	44.5	72
Ray Criswell, Florida	1982-85	161	7,153	44.4	73
Mark Simon, Air Force	1984-86	164	7,283	44.4	64
Russell Erxleben, Texas	1975-78	214	9,467	44.2	80
Brad Maynard, Ball St.	1993-96	242	10,702	44.2	76
Mark Simon, Air Force	1984-86	156	6,898	44.2	64
Johnny Evans, North Caro. St.	1974-77	185	8,143	44.0	81
Chuck Ramsey, Wake Forest	1971-73	205	9,010	44.0	70
Jimmy Colquitt, Tennessee	1981-84	201	8,816	43.9	70
John Teltschik, Texas	1982-85	217	9,496	43.8	81

*Record.

SEASON AVERAGE

(Qualifiers for Championship)

Player, Team	Year	No.	Yards	Avg.
Chad Kessler, LSU	†1997	39	1,961	*50.3
Reggie Roby, Iowa	†1981	44	2,193	49.8
Kirk Wilson, UCLA	†1956	30	1,479	49.3
Todd Sauerbrun, West Va.	†1994	72	3,486	‡48.4
Zack Jordan, Colorado	†1950	38	1,830	48.2
Ricky Anderson, Vanderbilt	†1984	58	2,793	48.2
Reggie Roby, Iowa	†1982	52	2,501	48.1
Marv Bateman, Utah	†1971	68	3,269	48.1
Owen Price, UTEP	†1940	30	1,440	48.0
Jack Jacobs, Oklahoma	1940	31	1,483	47.8
Bill Smith, Mississippi	1984	44	2,099	47.7
Ed Bunn, UTEP	†1992	41	1,955	47.7

*Record. †National champion. ‡Record for minimum 50 punts.

ANNUAL CHAMPIONS

Year	Player, Team	Class	No.	Yards	Avg.
1937	Johnny Pingel, Michigan St.	Jr.	49	2,101	42.9
1938	Jerry Dowd, St. Mary's (Cal.)	Sr.	62	2,711	43.7
1939	Harry Dunkle, North Caro.	So.	37	1,725	46.6
1940	Owen Price, UTEP	Jr.	30	1,440	48.0
1941	Owen Price, UTEP	Sr.	40	1,813	45.3
1942	Bobby Cifers, Tennessee	Jr.	37	1,586	42.9
1943	Harold Cox, Arkansas	Fr.	37	1,518	41.0
1944	Bob Waterfield, UCLA	Sr.	60	2,575	42.9
1945	Howard Maley, Southern Methodist	Sr.	59	2,458	41.7
1946	Johnny Galvin, Purdue	Sr.	30	1,286	42.9
1947	Leslie Palmer, North Caro. St.	Sr.	65	2,816	43.3
1948	Charlie Justice, North Caro.	Jr.	62	2,728	44.0
1949	Paul Stombaugh, Furman	Sr.	57	2,550	44.7
1950	Zack Jordan, Colorado	So.	38	1,830	48.2
1951	Chuck Spaulding, Wyoming	Jr.	37	1,610	43.5
1952	Des Koch, Southern Cal	Jr.	47	2,043	43.5
1953	Zeke Bratkowski, Georgia (QB)	Sr.	50	2,132	42.6
1954	A. L. Terpening, New Mexico	Sr.	41	1,869	45.6
1955	Don Chandler, Florida	Sr.	22	975	44.3
1956	Kirk Wilson, UCLA	So.	30	1,479	49.3
1957	Dave Sherer, Southern Methodist	Jr.	36	1,620	45.0
1958	Bobby Walden, Georgia	So.	44	1,991	45.3
1959	John Hadl, Kansas	So.	43	1,960	45.6
1960	Dick Fitzsimmons, Denver	So.	25	1,106	44.2
1961	Joe Zuger, Arizona St.	Sr.	31	1,305	42.1
1962	Joe Don Looney, Oklahoma	Jr.	34	1,474	43.4
1963	Danny Thomas, Southern Methodist	Jr.	48	2,110	44.0
1964	Frank Lambert, Mississippi	Sr.	50	2,205	44.1
1965	Dave Lewis, Stanford	Jr.	29	1,302	44.9
1966	Ron Widby, Tennessee	Sr.	48	2,104	43.8
1967	Zenon Andrusyshyn, UCLA	So.	34	1,502	44.2
1968	Dany Pitcock, Wichita St.	Sr.	71	3,068	43.2
1969	Ed Marsh, Baylor	Jr.	68	2,965	43.6
1970	Marv Bateman, Utah	Jr.	65	2,968	45.7
1971	Marv Bateman, Utah	Sr.	68	3,269	48.1
1972	Ray Guy, Southern Miss.	Sr.	58	2,680	46.2
1973	Chuck Ramsey, Wake Forest	Sr.	87	3,896	44.8
1974	Joe Parker, Appalachian St.	So.	63	2,788	44.3
1975	Tom Skladany, Ohio St.	Jr.	36	1,682	46.7
1976	Russell Erxleben, Texas	So.	61	2,842	46.6
1977	Jim Miller, Mississippi	So.	66	3,029	45.9
1978	Maury Buford, Texas Tech	Fr.	71	3,131	44.1
1979	Clay Brown, Brigham Young	Jr.	43	1,950	45.3

Beginning in 1980, ranked on minimum 3.6 punts per game

Year	Player, Team	Class	No.	Yards	Long	Avg.
1980	Steve Cox, Arkansas	Sr.	47	2,186	86	46.5
1981	Reggie Roby, Iowa	Jr.	44	2,193	68	49.8
1982	Reggie Roby, Iowa	Sr.	52	2,501	66	48.1
1983	Jack Weil, Wyoming	Sr.	52	2,369	86	45.6
1984	Ricky Anderson, Vanderbilt	Sr.	58	2,793	82	48.2
1985	Mark Simon, Air Force	Jr.	53	2,506	71	47.3
1986	Greg Horne, Arkansas	Sr.	49	2,313	65	47.2
1987	Tom Tupa, Ohio St. (QB)	Sr.	63	2,963	72	47.0
1988	Keith English, Colorado	Sr.	51	2,297	77	45.0
1989	Tom Rouen, Colorado	So.	36	1,651	63	45.8
1990	Cris Shale, Bowling Green	Sr.	66	3,087	81	46.8
1991	Mark Bounds, Texas Tech	Sr.	53	2,481	78	46.8
1992	Ed Bunn, UTEP	Sr.	41	1,955	73	47.7
1993	Chris MacInnis, Air Force	Sr.	49	2,303	74	47.0
1994	Todd Sauerbrun West Va.	Sr.	72	3,486	90	‡48.4
1995	Brad Maynard, Ball St.	Jr.	66	3,071	67	46.5
1996	Bill Marinangel, Vanderbilt	Sr.	77	3,586	79	46.6
1997	Chad Kessler, LSU	Sr.	39	1,961	66	*50.3

*Record. ‡Record for minimum of 50 punts.

Punt Returns

CAREER AVERAGE

(Minimum 1.2 Returns Per Game; Minimum 30 Returns)

Player, Team	Years	No.	Yards	TD	Long	Avg.
Jack Mitchell, Oklahoma	1946-48	39	922	**7	70	*23.6
Gene Gibson, Cincinnati	1949-50	37	760	4	75	‡20.5
Eddie Macon, Pacific (Cal.)	1949-51	48	907	4	**100	18.9
Jackie Robinson, UCLA	1939-40	37	694	2	89	18.8
Mike Fuller, Auburn	1972-74	50	883	3	63	17.7
Bobby Dillon, Texas	1949-51	47	830	1	84	17.7
James Dye, Brigham Young/Utah St.	1992-93, 95-96	61	1,046	5	90	17.2
Erroll Tucker, Utah	1984-85	38	650	3	89	17.1
George Hoey, Michigan	1966-68	31	529	1	60	17.1
Jack Christiansen, Colorado St.	1948-50	37	626	2	89	16.9
Henry Pryor, Rutgers	1948-49	37	625	1	85	16.9
Adolph Bellizeare, Pennsylvania	1972-74	33	557	3	73	16.9
Ken Hatfield, Arkansas	1962-64	70	1,135	5	95	16.2
Gene Rossides, Columbia	1945-48	53	851	3	70	16.1
Bill Hillenbrand, Indiana	1941-42	65	1,042	2	88	16.0

*Record. **Record tied. ‡Record for minimum 1.5 returns per game.

SEASON AVERAGE

(Minimum 1.2 Returns Per Game)

Player, Team	Year	No.	Yards	Avg.
Bill Blackstock, Tennessee	1951	12	311	*25.9
George Sims, Baylor	1948	15	375	25.0
Gene Derricotte, Michigan	1947	14	347	24.8
Erroll Tucker, Utah	†1985	16	389	24.3
George Hoey, Michigan	1967	12	291	24.3
Floyd Little, Syracuse	1965	18	423	23.5

*Record. †National champion. ‡Ranked for minimum 1.5 returns per game.

ANNUAL CHAMPIONS

(Ranked on Total Yards Until 1970)

Year	Player, Team	Class	No.	Yards	Avg.
1939	Bosh Pritchard, VMI	So.	42	583	13.9
1940	Junie Hovious, Mississippi	Sr.	33	498	15.1
1941	Bill Geyer, Colgate	Sr.	33	616	18.7
1942	Bill Hillenbrand, Indiana	Jr.	23	481	20.9
1943	Marion Flanagan, Texas A&M	Jr.	49	475	9.7
1944	Joe Stuart, California	Jr.	39	372	9.5
1945	Jake Leicht, Oregon	So.	28	395	14.1
1946	Harry Gilmer, Alabama	Jr.	37	436	11.8
1947	Lindy Berry, Texas Christian	So.	42	493	11.7
1948	Lee Nalley, Vanderbilt	Jr.	43	*791	18.4
1949	Lee Nalley, Vanderbilt	Sr.	35	498	14.2
1950	Dave Waters, Wash. & Lee	Jr.	30	445	14.8
1951	Tom Murphy, Holy Cross	So.	25	533	21.3
1952	Horton Nesrsta, Rice	Jr.	44	536	12.2
1953	Paul Giel, Minnesota	Sr.	17	288	16.9
1954	Dicky Maegle, Rice	Sr.	15	293	19.5
1955	Mike Sommer, Geo. Washington	So.	24	330	13.8
1956	Bill Stacy, Mississippi St.	Jr.	24	290	12.1
1957	Bobby Mulgado, Arizona St.	Sr.	14	267	19.1
1958	Howard Cook, Colorado	Sr.	24	242	10.1
1959	Pervis Atkins, New Mexico St.	Jr.	16	241	15.1
1960	Lance Alworth, Arkansas	Jr.	18	307	17.1
1961	Lance Alworth, Arkansas	Sr.	28	336	12.0
1962	Darrell Roberts, Utah St.	Sr.	16	333	20.8
1963	Ken Hatfield, Arkansas	Jr.	21	350	16.7
1964	Ken Hatfield, Arkansas	Sr.	31	518	16.7
1965	Nick Rassas, Notre Dame	Sr.	24	459	19.1
1966	Vic Washington, Wyoming	Jr.	34	443	13.0
1967	Mike Battle, Southern Cal	Jr.	47	570	12.1
1968	Roger Wehrli, Missouri	Sr.	41	478	11.7
1969	Chris Farasopoulous, Brigham Young	Jr.	35	527	15.1

Beginning in 1970, ranked on average per return (instead of total yards)‡

Year	Player, Team	Class	No.	Yards	TD	Long	Avg.
1970	Steve Holden, Arizona St.	So.	17	327	2	94	19.2
1971	Golden Richards, Brigham Young	Jr.	33	624	**4	87	18.9
1972	Randy Rhino, Georgia Tech	So.	25	441	1	96	17.6
1973	Gary Hayman, Penn St.	Sr.	23	442	1	83	19.2
1974	John Provost, Holy Cross	Sr.	13	238	2	85	18.3
1975	Donnie Ross, New Mexico St.	Sr.	21	338	1	#81	16.1
1976	Henry Jenkins, Rutgers	Sr.	30	449	0	#40	15.0
1977	Robert Woods, Grambling	Sr.	††11	279	3	72	25.4
1978	Ira Matthews, Wisconsin	Sr.	16	270	3	78	16.9
1979	Jeffrey Shockley, Tennessee St.	Sr.	27	456	1	79	16.9
1980	Scott Woerner, Georgia	Sr.	31	488	1	67	15.7
1981	Glen Young, Mississippi St.	Jr.	19	307	2	87	16.2
1982	Lionel James, Auburn	Jr.	25	394	0	#63	15.8
1983	Jim Sandusky, San Diego St.	Sr.	20	381	1	90	19.0
1984	Ricky Nattiel, Florida	So.	22	346	1	67	15.7
1985	Erroll Tucker, Utah	Sr.	16	389	2	89	24.3
1986	Rod Smith, Nebraska	Jr.	‡‡12	227	1	63	18.9
1987	Alan Grant, Stanford	Jr.	27	446	2	77	16.5
1988	Deion Sanders, Florida St.	Sr.	33	503	1	76	15.2
1989	Larry Hargrove, Ohio	Sr.	17	309	2	83	18.2
1990	Dave McCloughan, Colorado	Sr.	32	524	2	90	16.4
1991	Bo Campbell, Virginia Tech	Jr.	15	273	0	45	18.2
1992	Lee Gissendaner, Northwestern	Jr.	15	327	1	72	21.8
1993	Aaron Glenn, Texas A&M	Sr.	17	339	2	76	19.9
1994	Steve Clay, Eastern Mich.	Jr.	14	278	1	65	19.9
1995	James Dye, Brigham Young	Jr.	20	438	2	90	21.9
1996	Allen Rossum, Notre Dame	Jr.	15	344	3	83	22.9
1997	Tim Dwight, Iowa	Sr.	19	367	3	—	19.3

**Record. **Record tied. #Did not score. ‡Ranked on minimum 1.5 returns per game, 1970-73; 1.2 from 1974. ††Declared champion; with three more returns (making 1.3 per game) for zero yards still would have highest average. ‡‡Declared champion; with two more returns (making 1.2 per game) for zero yards still would have highest average.*

ANNUAL PUNT RETURN LEADERS (1939-69) BASED ON AVERAGE PER RETURN

(Minimum 1.2 Returns Per Game)

1939—Jackie Robinson, UCLA, 20.0; **1940**—Jackie Robinson, UCLA, 21.0; **1941**—Walt Slater, Tennessee, 20.4; **1942**—Billy Hillenbrand, Indiana, 20.9; **1943**—Otto Graham, Northwestern, 19.7; **1944**—Glenn Davis, Army, 18.4; **1945**—Jake Leicht, Oregon, 14.8; **1946**—Harold Griffin, Florida, 20.1; **1947**—Gene Derricotte, Michigan, 24.8; **1948**—George Sims, Baylor, ‡25.0; **1949**—Gene Evans, Wisconsin, 21.8; **1950**—Lindy Hanson, Boston U., 22.5; **1951**—Bill Blackstock, Tennessee, *25.9; **1952**—Gil Reich, Kansas, 17.2; **1953**—Bobby Lee, New Mexico, 19.4; **1954**—Dicky Maegle, Rice, 19.5; **1955**—Ron Lind, Drake, 21.1; **1956**—Ron Lind, Drake, 19.1; **1957**—Bobby Mulgado, Arizona St., 19.1; **1958**—Herb Hallas, Yale, 23.4; **1959**—Jacque MacKinnon, Colgate, 17.5; **1960**—Pat Fischer, Nebraska, 21.2; **1961**—Tom Larscheid, Utah St., 23.4; **1962**—Darrell Roberts, Utah St., 20.8; **1963**—Rickie Harris, Arizona, 17.4; **1964**—Ken Hatfield, Arkansas, 16.7; **1965**—Floyd Little, Syracuse, 23.5; **1966**—Don Bean, Houston, 20.2; **1967**—George Hoey, Michigan, 24.3; **1968**—Rob Bordley, Princeton, 20.5; **1969**—George Hannen, Davidson, 22.4.

**Record. ‡Record for minimum 1.5 returns per game.*

Kickoff Returns

CAREER AVERAGE

(Minimum 1.2 Returns Per Game; Minimum 30 Returns)

Player, Team	Years	No.	Yards	Avg.
Anthony Davis, Southern Cal	1972-74	37	1,299	*35.1
Eric Booth, Southern Miss.	1994-97	35	1,135	32.4
Overton Curtis, Utah St.	1957-58	32	991	‡31.0
Fred Montgomery, New Mexico St.	1991-92	39	1,191	30.5
Altie Taylor, Utah St.	1966-68	40	1,170	29.3
Stan Brown, Purdue	1968-70	49	1,412	28.8
Henry White, Colgate	1974-77	41	1,180	28.8
Pat Johnson, Oregon	1994-97	36	1,023	28.4
Paul Loughran, Temple	1970-72	40	1,123	28.1
Jim Krieg, Washington	1970-71	31	860	27.7

**Record. ‡Record for minimum 1.5 returns per game.*

SEASON AVERAGE

(Minimum 1.2 Returns Per Game)

Player, Team	Year	No.	Yards	Avg.
Paul Allen, Brigham Young	1961	12	481	*40.1
Tremain Mack, Miami (Fla.)	†1996	13	514	39.5
Leeland McElroy, Texas A&M	†1993	15	590	39.3
Forrest Hall, San Francisco	†1946	15	573	‡38.2
Tony Ball, Chattanooga	†1977	13	473	36.4
George Marinkov, North Caro. St.	1954	13	465	35.8
Bob Baker, Cornell	1964	11	386	35.1

**Record. †National champion. ‡Record for minimum 1.5 returns per game.*

ANNUAL CHAMPIONS

(Ranked on Total Yards Until 1970)

Year	Player, Team	Class	No.	Yards	Avg.
1939	Nile Kinnick, Iowa	Sr.	15	377	25.1
1940	Jack Emigh, Montana	Sr.	18	395	21.9
1941	Earl Ray, Wyoming	So.	23	496	21.6
1942	Frank Porto, California	Sr.	17	483	28.4
1943	Paul Copoulos, Marquette	So.	11	384	34.9
1944	Paul Copoulos, Marquette	Jr.	14	337	24.1
1945	Al Dekdebrun, Cornell	Sr.	14	321	22.9
1946	Forrest Hall, San Francisco	Jr.	15	573	**38.2
1947	Doak Walker, Southern Methodist	So.	10	387	38.7
1948	Bill Gregus, Wake Forest	Jr.	19	503	26.5
1949	Johnny Subda, Nevada	Sr.	18	444	24.7
1950	Chuck Hill, New Mexico	Jr.	27	729	27.0
1951	Chuck Hill, New Mexico	Sr.	17	504	29.6
1952	Curly Powell, VMI	Sr.	27	517	19.1
1953	Max McGee, Tulane	Sr.	17	371	21.8
1954	Art Luppino, Arizona	So.	20	632	31.6
1955	Sam Woolwine, VMI	Jr.	22	471	21.4
1956	Sam Woolwine, VMI	Sr.	18	503	27.9
1957	Overton Curtis, Utah St.	Jr.	23	695	30.2
1958	Sonny Randle, Virginia	Sr.	21	506	24.1
1959	Don Perkins, New Mexico	Sr.	15	520	34.7
1960	Bruce Samples, Brigham Young	Sr.	23	577	25.1
1961	Dick Mooney, Idaho	Sr.	23	494	21.5
1962	Donnie Frederick, Wake Forest	Sr.	29	660	22.8
1963	Gary Wood, Cornell	Sr.	19	618	32.5
1964	Dan Bland, Mississippi St.	Jr.	20	558	27.9
1965	Eric Crabtree, Pittsburgh	Sr.	25	636	25.4
1966	Marcus Rhoden, Mississippi St.	Sr.	26	572	22.0
1967	Joe Casas, New Mexico	Sr.	23	602	26.2
1968	Mike Adamle, Northwestern	So.	34	732	21.5
1969	Stan Brown, Purdue	Jr.	26	698	26.8

Beginning in 1970, ranked on average per return (instead of total yards)‡

Year	Player, Team	Class	No.	Yards	Avg.
1970	Stan Brown, Purdue	Sr.	19	638	33.6
1971	Paul Loughran, Temple	Jr.	15	502	33.5
1972	Larry Williams, Texas Tech	So.	16	493	30.8
1973	Steve Odom, Utah	Sr.	21	618	29.4
1974	Anthony Davis, Southern Cal	Sr.	††11	467	42.5
1975	John Schultz, Maryland	Sr.	13	403	31.0
1976	Ira Matthews, Wisconsin	So.	14	415	29.6
1977	Tony Ball, Chattanooga	Fr.	13	473	36.4
1978	Drew Hill, Georgia Tech	Sr.	19	570	30.0
1979	Stevie Nelson, Ball St.	Fr.	18	565	31.4
1980	Mike Fox, San Diego St.	So.	†11	361	32.8

Year	Player, Team	Class	No.	Yards	Avg.
1981	Frank Minnifield, Louisville	Jr.	11	334	30.4
1982	Carl Monroe, Utah	Sr.	14	421	30.1
1983	Henry Williams, East Caro.	Jr.	19	591	31.1
1984	Keith Henderson, Texas Tech	Fr.	13	376	28.9
1985	Erroll Tucker, Utah	Sr.	24	698	29.1
1986	Terrance Roulhac, Clemson	Sr.	17	561	33.0
1987	Barry Sanders, Oklahoma St.	So.	14	442	31.6
1988	Raghib Ismail, Notre Dame	Fr.	#12	433	36.1
1989	Tony Smith, Southern Miss.	So.	14	455	32.5
1990	Dale Carter, Tennessee	Jr.	17	507	29.8
1991	Fred Montgomery, New Mexico St.	Jr.	25	734	29.4
1992	Fred Montgomery, New Mexico St.	Sr.	14	457	32.6
1993	Leeland McElroy, Texas A&M	Fr.	15	590	39.3
1994	Eric Moulds, Mississippi St.	Jr.	†13	426	32.8
1995	Robert Tate, Cincinnati	Jr.	15	515	34.3
1996	Tremain Mack, Miami (Fla.)	Jr.	13	514	39.5
1997	Eric Booth, Southern Miss.	Sr.	22	766	34.8

***Record for minimum 1.5 returns per game. #Declared champion; with two more returns (making 1.3 per game) for zero yards still would have highest average. †Declared champion; with one more return (making 1.2 per game) for zero yards still would have highest average. ††Declared champion; with three more returns (making 1.3 per game) for zero yards still would have highest average. ‡Ranked on minimum 1.5 returns per game, 1970-73; 1.2 from 1974.*

ANNUAL KICKOFF RETURN LEADERS (1939-69) BASED ON AVERAGE PER RETURN

(Minimum 1.2 Returns Per Game)

1939—Nile Kinnick, Iowa, 25.1; **1940**—Bill Geyer, Colgate, 27.0; **1941**—Vern Lockard, Colorado, 24.4; **1942-45**—Not compiled; **1946**—Forrest Hall, San Francisco, ‡38.2; **1947**—Skippy Minisi, Pennsylvania, 28.8; **1948**—Jerry Williams, Washington St., 29.9; **1949**—Billy Conn, Georgetown, 31.1; **1950**—Johnny Turco, Holy Cross, 27.4; **1951**—Bob Mischak, Army, 31.3; **1952**—Carroll Hardy, Colorado, 32.2; **1953**—Carl Bolt, Wash. & Lee, 27.1; **1954**—George Marinkov, North Caro. St., 35.8; **1955**—Jim Brown, Syracuse, 32.0; **1956**—Paul Hornung, Notre Dame, 31.0; **1957**—Overton Curtis, Utah St., 30.2; **1958**—Marshall Starks, Illinois, 26.3; **1959**—Don Perkins, New Mexico, 34.7; **1960**—Tom Hennessey, Holy Cross, 33.4; **1961**—Paul Allen, Brigham Young, *40.1; **1962**—Larry Coyer, Marshall, 30.2; **1963**—Gary Wood, Cornell, 32.5; **1964**—Bob Baker, Cornell, 35.1; **1965**—Tom Barrington, Ohio St., 34.3; **1966**—Frank Moore, Louisville, 27.9; **1967**—Altie Taylor, Utah St., 31.9; **1968**—Kerry Reardon, Iowa, 32.1; **1969**—Chris Farasopoulous, Brigham Young, 32.2.

**Record. ‡Record for minimum 1.5 returns per game.*

Photo from Southern Cal sports information

Marcus Allen compiled 2,559 all-purpose yards in 1981 and averaged more than 230 yards a game to rank seventh among all-time leaders in season yards per game.

All-Purpose Yards

CAREER YARDS PER GAME

(Minimum 3,500 Yards)

Player, Team	Years	Rush	Rcv.	Int.	PR	KOR	Yds.	Yd.PG
Ryan Benjamin, Pacific (Cal.)	1990-92	3,119	1,063	0	100	1,424	5,706	*237.8
Sheldon Canley, San Jose St.	1988-90	2,513	828	0	5	1,800	5,146	205.8
Howard Stevens, Louisville	1971-72	2,723	389	0	401	360	3,873	193.7
O. J. Simpson, Southern Cal	1967-68	3,124	235	0	0	307	3,666	192.9
Alex Van Dyke, Nevada	1994-95	7	3,100	0	5	1,034	4,146	188.5
Ed Marinaro, Cornell	1969-71	4,715	225	0	0	0	4,940	183.0
Marshall Faulk, San Diego St.	1991-93	4,589	973	0	0	33	5,595	180.5
Herschel Walker, Georgia	1980-82	5,259	243	0	0	247	5,749	174.2
Louie Giammona, Utah St.	1973-75	3,499	171	0	188	1,345	5,203	173.4

**Record.*

SEASON YARDS PER GAME

Player, Team	Years	Rush	Rcv.	Int.	PR	KOR	Yds.	Yd.PG
Barry Sanders, Oklahoma St.	†1988	*2,628	106	0	95	421	*3,250	*295.5
Ryan Benjamin, Pacific (Cal.)	†1991	1,581	612	0	4	798	2,995	249.6
Byron "Whizzer" White, Colorado	†1937	1,121	0	103	587	159	1,970	246.3
Mike Pringle, Cal St. Fullerton	†1989	1,727	249	0	0	714	2,690	244.6
Paul Palmer, Temple	†1986	1,866	110	0	0	657	2,633	239.4
Ryan Benjamin, Pacific (Cal.)	†1992	1,441	434	0	96	626	2,597	236.1
Marcus Allen, Southern Cal	†1981	2,342	217	0	0	0	2,559	232.6
Sheldon Canley, San Jose St.	1989	1,201	353	0	0	959	2,513	228.5
Ollie Matson, San Francisco	†1951	1,566	58	18	115	280	2,037	226.3
Troy Davis, Iowa St.	†1995	2,010	159	0	0	297	2,466	224.2
Alex Van Dyke, Nevada	1995	6	*1,854	0	0	583	2,443	222.1
Art Luppino, Arizona	†1954	1,359	50	84	68	632	2,193	219.3
Chuck Weatherspoon, Houston	1989	1,146	735	0	715	95	2,391	217.4
Anthony Thompson, Indiana	1989	1,793	201	0	0	394	2,388	217.1
Napoleon McCallum, Navy	†1983	1,587	166	0	272	360	2,385	216.8
Troy Davis, Iowa St.	†1996	2,185	61	0	0	118	2,364	214.9
Ed Marinaro, Cornell	†1971	1,881	51	0	0	0	1,932	214.7
Rashaan Salaam, Colorado	†1994	2,055	294	0	0	0	2,349	213.6
Howard Stevens, Louisville	†1972	1,294	221	0	337	240	2,132	213.2
Napoleon McCallum, Navy	†1985	1,327	358	0	157	488	2,330	211.8
Brian Pruitt, Central Mich.	1994	1,890	69	0	0	330	2,289	208.1
Keith Byars, Ohio St.	†1984	1,655	453	0	0	176	2,284	207.6
Mike Rozier, Nebraska	1983	2,148	106	0	0	232	2,486	207.2

**Record. †National champion.*

CAREER YARDS

Player, Team	Years	Rush	Rcv.	Int.	PR	KOR	Yds.	Yd.PP
Napoleon McCallum, Navy	$1981-85	4,179	796	0	858	1,339	*7,172	6.3
Darrin Nelson, Stanford	1977-78, 80-81	4,033	2,368	0	471	13	6,885	7.1
Terance Mathis, New Mexico	1985-87, 89	329	4,254	0	115	1,993	6,691	**14.6
Tony Dorsett, Pittsburgh	1973-76	*6,082	406	0	0	127	6,615	5.9
Paul Palmer, Temple	1983-86	4,895	705	0	12	997	6,609	6.1
Charles White, Southern Cal	1976-79	5,598	507	0	0	440	6,545	6.0
Trevor Cobb, Rice	1989-92	4,948	892	0	21	651	6,512	5.3
Glyn Milburn, Oklahoma/Stanford	1988, 90-92	2,302	1,495	0	1,145	1,246	6,188	8.1
Anthony Thompson, Indiana	1986-89	4,965	713	0	0	412	6,090	5.1
Archie Griffin, Ohio St.	1972-75	5,177	286	0	0	540	6,003	6.7

Player, Team	Years	Rush	Rcv.	Int.	PR	KOR	Yds.	Yd.PP
Ron "Po" James, New Mexico St.	1968-71	3,884	217	0	8	1,870	5,979	6.5
Eric Wilkerson, Kent	1985-88	3,830	506	0	0	1,638	5,974	7.0
Steve Bartalo, Colorado St.	1983-86	4,813	1,079	0	0	0	5,892	4.4
Wilford White, Arizona St.	1947-50	3,173	892	212	798	791	5,866	9.2
Leon Johnson, North Caro.	1993-96	3,693	1,288	0	390	457	5,828	5.9
Joe Washington, Oklahoma	1972-75	3,995	253	0	807	726	5,781	7.3
Herschel Walker, Georgia	1980-82	5,259	243	0	0	247	‡5,749	5.6
George Swarn, Miami (Ohio)	1983-86	4,172	1,057	0	0	498	5,727	5.6
Chuck Weatherspoon, Houston	1987-90	3,247	1,375	0	611	482	5,715	9.7
Ryan Benjamin, Pacific (Cal.)	1990-92	3,119	1,063	0	100	1,424	‡5,706	8.8
Eric Metcalf, Texas	1985-88	2,661	1,394	0	1,076	574	5,705	6.7
George Rogers, South Caro.	1977-80	4,958	371	0	0	339	5,668	5.9
Napoleon Kaufman, Washington	1991-94	4,041	424	0	368	825	5,658	6.7
Jamie Morris, Michigan	1984-87	3,944	703	0	0	984	5,631	6.4
Joe Morris, Syracuse	1978-81	4,299	278	0	0	1,023	5,600	6.3
James Brooks, Auburn	1977-80	3,523	219	0	128	1,726	5,596	7.6
Marshall Faulk, San Diego St.	1991-93	4,589	973	0	0	33	‡5,595	6.6
Johnny Rodgers, Nebraska	1970-72	745	2,479	0	1,515	847	‡5,586	13.8
Thurman Thomas, Oklahoma St.	1984-87	4,595	551	0	143	237	5,526	5.5
Mike Rozier, Nebraska	1981-83	4,780	216	0	0	449	‡5,445	7.7

*Record. $See page 6 for explanation. ‡Three-year totals. **Record for minimum 375 plays

SEASON YARDS

Player, Team	Year	Rush	Rcv.	Int.	PR	KOR	Yds.	Yd.PP
Barry Sanders, Oklahoma St.	†1988	*2,628	106	0	95	421	*3,250	8.3
Ryan Benjamin, Pacific (Cal.)	†1991	1,581	612	0	4	798	2,995	9.6
Mike Pringle, Cal St. Fullerton	†1989	1,727	249	0	0	714	2,690	7.6
Paul Palmer, Temple	†1986	1,866	110	0	0	657	2,633	6.8
Ryan Benjamin, Pacific (Cal.)	†1992	1,441	434	0	96	626	2,597	8.1
Marcus Allen, Southern Cal	†1981	2,342	217	0	0	0	2,559	5.9
Sheldon Canley, San Jose St.	1989	1,201	353	0	0	959	2,513	7.4
Mike Rozier, Nebraska	1983	2,148	106	0	0	232	2,486	8.4
Troy Davis, Iowa St.	†1995	2,010	159	0	0	297	2,466	6.7
Alex Van Dyke, Nevada	1995	6	*1,854	0	0	583	2,443	15.7
Chuck Weatherspoon, Houston	1989	1,146	735	0	415	95	2,391	10.7
Anthony Thompson, Indiana	1989	1,793	201	0	0	394	2,388	5.8
Napoleon McCallum, Navy	†1983	1,587	166	0	272	360	2,385	6.1
Troy Davis, Iowa St.	†1996	2,185	61	0	0	118	2,364	5.7
Rashaan Salaam, Colorado	†1994	2,055	294	0	0	0	2,349	7.3
Napoleon McCallum, Navy	†1985	1,327	358	0	157	488	2,330	6.3
Brian Pruitt, Central Mich.	1994	1,890	69	0	0	330	2,289	7.3
Keith Byars, Ohio St.	†1984	1,655	453	0	0	176	2,284	6.4
Byron Hanspard, Texas Tech	1996	2,084	192	0	0	0	2,276	6.4
Eddie George, Ohio St.	1995	1,826	399	0	0	0	2,225	6.4
Glyn Milburn, Stanford	†1990	729	632	0	267	594	2,222	8.4
Vaughn Dunbar, Indiana	1991	1,699	252	0	0	262	2,213	5.9
Sheldon Canley, San Jose St.	1990	1,248	386	0	5	574	2,213	6.3
Johnny Johnson, San Jose St.	1988	1,219	668	0	0	315	2,202	7.1
Art Luppino, Arizona	†1954	1,359	50	84	68	632	2,193	10.4
Corey Dillon, Washington	1996	1,555	273	0	0	357	2,185	7.2
Rick Calhoun, Cal St. Fullerton	1986	1,398	125	0	138	522	2,183	7.0
Randy Moss, Marshall	1997	2	1,647	0	266	263	2,178	‡16.9
Marshall Faulk, San Diego St.	1993	1,530	644	0	0	0	2,174	6.3
Troy Edwards, Louisiana Tech	1997	190	1,707	0	6	241	2,144	16.5
Terance Mathis, New Mexico	1989	38	1,315	0	0	785	2,138	15.7
Howard Stevens, Louisville	†1972	1,294	221	0	377	240	2,132	6.4

*Record. †National champion. ‡Record for minimum 125 plays.

ALL-PURPOSE SINGLE-GAME HIGHS

Yds.	Player, Team (Opponent)	Date
435	Brian Pruitt, Central Mich. (Toledo)	Nov. 5, 1994
429	Moe Williams, Kentucky (South Caro.)	Sept. 23, 1995
422	Marshall Faulk, San Diego St. (Pacific [Cal.])	Sept. 14, 1991
419	Randy Gatewood, UNLV (Idaho)	Sept. 17, 1994
417	Paul Palmer, Temple (East Caro.)	Nov. 10, 1986
417	Greg Allen, Florida St. (Western Caro.)	Oct. 31, 1981
416	Anthony Thompson, Indiana (Wisconsin)	Nov. 11, 1989
411	John Leach, Wake Forest (Maryland)	Nov. 20, 1993
402	Ryan Benjamin, Pacific, Cal. (Utah St.)	Nov. 21, 1992
401	Chuck Hughes, UTEP (North Texas)	Sept. 18, 1965
397	Eric Allen, Michigan St. (Purdue)	Oct. 30, 1971
388	Astron Whatley, Kent (Eastern Mich.)	Sept. 20, 1997
388	Ryan Benjamin, Pacific, Cal. (Cal St. Fullerton)	Oct. 5, 1991
387	Kendal Smith, Utah St. (San Jose St.)	Oct. 22, 1988
387	Ron Johnson, Michigan (Wisconsin)	Nov. 16, 1968
386	Barry Sanders, Oklahoma St. (Kansas)	Nov. 12, 1988
379	Glyn Milburn, Stanford (California)	Nov. 17, 1990
376	Kevin Faulk, LSU (Houston)	Sept. 7, 1996
375	Alex Van Dyke, Nevada (Toledo)	Sept. 23, 1995
375	Rueben Mayes, Washington St. (Oregon St.)	Nov. 3, 1984
374	Troy Davis, Iowa St. (Missouri)	Sept. 28, 1996
374	Tony Dorsett, Pittsburgh (Penn St.)	Nov. 22, 1975
373	Barry Sanders, Oklahoma St. (Oklahoma)	Nov. 5, 1988
372	Peter Warrick, Florida St. (Clemson)	Sept. 20, 1997
372	Chuck Weatherspoon, Houston (Eastern Wash.)	Nov. 17, 1990

ANNUAL CHAMPIONS

Year	Player, Team	Class	Rush	Rcv.	Int.	PR	KOR	Yds.	Yd.PG
1937	Byron "Whizzer" White, Colorado	Sr.	1,121	0	103	587	159	1,970	246.3
1938	Parker Hall, Mississippi	Sr.	698	0	128	0	594	1,420	129.1
1939	Tom Harmon, Michigan	Jr.	868	110	98	0	132	1,208	151.0
1940	Tom Harmon, Michigan	Sr.	844	0	20	244	204	1,312	164.0
1941	Bill Dudley, Virginia	Sr.	968	60	76	481	89	1,674	186.0
1942	records not available	—	—	—	—	—	—	—	—
1943	Stan Koslowski, Holy Cross	Fr.	784	63	50	438	76	1,411	176.4
1944	Red Williams, Minnesota	Jr.	911	0	0	242	314	1,467	163.0
1945	Bob Fenimore, Oklahoma St.	Jr.	1,048	12	129	157	231	1,577	197.1
1946	Rudy Mobley, Hardin-Simmons	Sr.	1,262	13	79	273	138	1,765	176.5
1947	Wilton Davis, Hardin-Simmons	So.	1,173	79	0	295	251	1,798	179.8
1948	Lou Kusserow, Columbia	Sr.	766	463	19	130	359	1,737	193.0
1949	Johnny Papit, Virginia	Jr.	1,214	0	0	0	397	1,611	179.0
1950	Wilford White, Arizona St.	Sr.	1,502	225	0	64	274	2,065	206.5
1951	Ollie Matson, San Francisco	Sr.	1,566	58	18	115	280	2,037	226.3
1952	Billy Vessels, Oklahoma	Sr.	1,072	165	10	120	145	1,512	151.2
1953	J. C. Caroline, Illinois	So.	1,256	52	0	129	33	1,470	163.3
1954	Art Luppino, Arizona	So.	1,359	50	84	68	632	2,193	219.3
1955	Jim Swink, Texas Christian	Jr.	1,283	111	46	64	198	1,702	170.2
	Art Luppino, Arizona	Jr.	1,313	74	0	62	253	1,702	170.2
1956	Jack Hill, Utah St.	Sr.	920	215	132	21	403	1,691	169.1
1957	Overton Curtis, Utah St.	Jr.	616	193	60	44	695	1,608	160.8
1958	Dick Bass, Pacific (Cal.)	Jr.	1,361	121	5	164	227	1,878	187.8
1959	Pervis Atkins, New Mexico St.	Jr.	971	301	23	241	264	1,800	180.0
1960	Pervis Atkins, New Mexico St.	Sr.	611	468	23	218	293	1,613	161.3
1961	Jim Pilot, New Mexico St.	So.	1,278	20	0	161	147	1,606	160.6
1962	Gary Wood, Cornell	Jr.	889	7	0	69	430	1,395	155.0
1963	Gary Wood, Cornell	Sr.	818	15	0	57	618	1,508	167.6
1964	Donny Anderson, Texas Tech	Jr.	966	396	0	28	320	1,710	171.0
1965	Floyd Little, Syracuse	Jr.	1,065	248	0	423	254	1,990	199.0
1966	Frank Quayle, Virginia	So.	727	420	0	30	439	1,616	161.6
1967	O. J. Simpson, Southern Cal	Jr.	1,415	109	0	0	176	1,700	188.9
1968	O. J. Simpson, Southern Cal	Sr.	1,709	126	0	0	131	1,966	196.6
1969	Lynn Moore, Army	Sr.	983	44	0	223	545	1,795	179.5
1970	Don McCauley, North Caro.	Sr.	1,720	235	0	0	66	2,021	183.7
1971	Ed Marinaro, Cornell	Sr.	1,881	51	0	0	0	1,932	214.7
1972	Howard Stevens, Louisville	Sr.	1,294	221	0	377	240	2,132	213.2
1973	Willard Harrell, Pacific (Cal.)	Jr.	1,319	18	0	88	352	1,777	177.7
1974	Louie Giammona, Utah St.	Jr.	1,534	79	0	16	355	1,984	198.4
1975	Louie Giammona, Utah St.	Sr.	1,454	33	0	124	434	2,045	185.9
1976	Tony Dorsett, Pittsburgh	Sr.	1,948	73	0	0	0	2,021	183.7
1977	Earl Campbell, Texas	Sr.	1,744	111	0	0	0	1,855	168.6
1978	Charles White, Southern Cal	Jr.	1,760	191	0	0	145	2,096	174.7
1979	Charles White, Southern Cal	Sr.	1,803	138	0	0	0	1,941	194.1
1980	Marcus Allen, Southern Cal	Jr.	1,563	231	0	0	0	1,794	179.4
1981	Marcus Allen, Southern Cal	Sr.	2,342	217	0	0	0	2,559	232.6
1982	Carl Monroe, Utah	Sr.	1,507	108	0	0	421	2,036	185.1
1983	Napoleon McCallum, Navy	Jr.	1,587	166	0	272	360	2,385	216.8
1984	Keith Byars, Ohio St.	Jr.	1,655	453	0	0	176	2,284	207.6
1985	Napoleon McCallum, Navy	Sr.	1,327	358	0	157	488	2,330	211.8
1986	Paul Palmer, Temple	Sr.	1,866	110	0	0	657	2,633	239.4
1987	Eric Wilkerson, Kent	Jr.	1,221	269	0	0	584	2,074	188.6
1988	Barry Sanders, Oklahoma St.	Jr.	*2,628	106	0	95	421	*3,250	*295.5
1989	Mike Pringle, Cal St. Fullerton	Sr.	1,727	249	0	0	714	2,690	244.6
1990	Glyn Milburn, Stanford	So.	729	632	0	267	594	2,222	202.0
1991	Ryan Benjamin, Pacific (Cal.)	Jr.	1,581	612	0	4	798	2,995	249.6
1992	Ryan Benjamin, Pacific (Cal.)	Sr.	1,441	434	0	96	626	2,597	236.1
1993	LeShon Johnson, Northern Ill.	Sr.	1,976	106	0	0	0	2,082	189.3
1994	Rashaan Salaam, Colorado	Jr.	2,055	294	0	0	0	2,349	213.6
1995	Troy Davis, Iowa St.	So.	2,010	159	0	0	297	2,466	224.2
1996	Troy Davis, Iowa St.	Jr.	2,185	61	0	0	118	2,364	214.9
1997	Troy Edwards, Louisiana Tech	Jr.	190	1,707	0	6	241	2,144	194.9

**Record.*

Field Goals

CAREER FIELD GOALS

(One-inch tees were permitted in 1949, two-inch tees were permitted in 1965, and use of tees was eliminated in 1989. The goal posts were widened from 18 feet, 6 inches to 23 feet, 4 inches in 1959 and were narrowed back to 18 feet, 6 inches in 1991. In 1993, the hash marks were moved 6 feet, 8 inches closer to the center of the field, to 60 feet from each sideline.)

Player, Team	Years	Total	Pct.	Under 40 Yds.	40 Plus	Long	‡Won
Jeff Jaeger, Washington (S)	1983-86	*80-99	.808	59-68	21-31	52	5
John Lee, UCLA (S)	1982-85	79-92	@.859	54-56	25-36	52	**10
Jason Elam, Hawaii (S)	$1988-92	79-100	.790	50-55	29-45	56	3
Philip Doyle, Alabama (S)	1987-90	78-*105	.743	57-61	21-44	53	6
Luis Zendejas, Arizona St. (S)	1981-84	78-*105	.743	53-59	25-46	55	1
Kevin Butler, Georgia (S)	1981-84	77-98	.786	50-56	27-42	60	7
Max Zendejas, Arizona (S)	1982-85	77-104	.740	47-53	30-51	57	7
Carlos Huerta, Miami (Fla.) (S)	1988-91	73-91	.802	56-60	17-31	52	3

Player, Team	Years	Total	Pct.	Under 40 Yds.	40 Plus	Long	‡Won
Derek Schmidt, Florida St. (S)	1984-87	73-104	.702	44-55	29-49	54	1
Fuad Reveiz, Tennessee (S)	1981-84	71-95	.747	45-53	26-42	60	7
Barry Belli, Fresno St. (S)	1984-87	70-99	.707	47-53	23-46	55	5
Nelson Welch, Clemson (S)	1991-94	70-100	.700	49-64	21-36	53	7
Roman Anderson, Houston (S)	1988-91	70-101	.693	*61-*72	9-29	53	3
Collin Mackie, South Caro. (S)	1987-90	69-95	.726	48-57	21-38	52	5
Gary Gusman, Miami (Ohio) (S)	1984-87	68-94	.723	50-57	18-37	53	2
Rusty Hanna, Toledo (S)	1989-92	68-99	.687	51-58	17-41	51	3
Larry Roach, Oklahoma St. (S)	1981-84	68-101	.673	46-54	22-47	56	5
Paul Woodside, West Va. (S)	1981-84	65-81	.802	45-49	20-32	55	5
Michael Proctor, Alabama (S)	1992-95	65-91	.714	48-64	17-27	53	5
John Diettrich, Ball St. (S)	1983-86	63-90	.700	42-50	21-40	62	5
Jason Hanson, Washington St. (S)	1988-91	63-96	.656	24-30	*39-*66	62	4
Dan Eichloff, Kansas (S)	1990-93	62-87	.713	40-50	22-37	61	5
Kenny Stucker, Ball St. (S)	1988-91	62-87	.713	45-51	17-36	52	4
David Browndyke, LSU (S)	1986-89	61-75	.813	49-53	12-22	52	3
Todd Gregoire, Wisconsin (S)	1984-87	61-81	.753	48-56	13-25	54	6
Kanon Parkman, Georgia (S)	1991, 93-95	61-85	.718	52-61	9-24	48	1
Todd Wright, Arkansas (S)	1989-92	60-79	.759	41-47	19-32	50	2
Jess Atkinson, Maryland (S)	1981-84	60-82	.732	40-48	20-34	50	5
Kyle Bryant, Texas A&M (S)	1994-97	60-85	.706	38-48	22-37	61	3
Scott Sisson, Georgia Tech (S)	1989-92	60-88	.682	45-53	15-35	51	6
Obed Ariri, Clemson (S)	1977-80	60-92	.652	47-55	13-37	57	5
Chuck Nelson, Washington (S)	1980-82	59-72	.819	47-53	12-19	51	5
Phil Dawson, Texas (S)	1994-97	59-79	.747	33-38	26-41	54	3
Van Tiffin, Alabama (S)	1983-86	59-87	.678	32-38	27-49	57	5
John Hopkins, Stanford (S)	1987-90	59-88	.670	43-50	16-38	54	4
Rafael Garcia, Virginia	1994-96	58-76	.763	42-50	16-26	56	5
Remy Hamilton, Michigan	1993-96	58-76	.763	49-60	9-16	49	3
Jeff Ward, Texas (S)	1983-86	58-78	.744	36-41	22-37	57	**10
Jeff Shudak, Iowa St. (S)	1987-90	58-79	.734	38-45	20-34	55	5

**Record. $See page 6 for explanation. **Record tied. @Record for minimum 55 attempts. ‡Number of games in which his field goal(s) provided the winning margin. (S) Soccer-style kicker.*

SEASON FIELD GOALS

Player, Team	Years	Total	Pct.	Under 40 Yds.	40 Plus	Long	‡Won
John Lee, UCLA (S)	†1984	*29-33	.879	16-16	13-17	51	5
Paul Woodside, West Va. (S)	†1982	28-31	.903	23-23	5-8	45	2
Luis Zendejas, Arizona St. (S)	†1983	28-37	.757	19-22	9-15	52	1
Fuad Reveiz, Tennessee (S)	1982	27-31	.871	14-14	13-17	60	2
Chuck Nelson, Washington (S)	1982	25-26	*.962	22-23	3-3	49	1
Chris Jacke, UTEP (S)	1988	25-27	.926	11-11	*14-16	52	2
John Diettrich, Ball St. (S)	†1985	25-29	.862	16-17	9-12	54	2
Kendall Trainor, Arkansas (S)	†1988	24-27	.889	14-15	10-12	58	4
Carlos Reveiz, Tennessee (S)	1985	24-28	.857	12-14	12-14	52	2
Chris White, Illinois (S)	1984	24-28	.857	16-17	8-11	52	1
Remy Hamilton, Michigan (S)	†1994	24-29	.828	23-27	1-2	42	2
Philip Doyle, Alabama (S)	†1990	24-29	.828	16-17	8-12	47	2
Bruce Kallmeyer, Kansas (S)	1983	24-29	.828	13-14	11-15	57	1
Mike Prindle, Western Mich. (S)	1984	24-30	.800	17-20	7-10	56	1
Michael Reeder, Texas Christian (S)	†1995	23-25	.920	19-19	4-6	47	3
Joe Allison, Memphis (S)	†1992	23-25	.920	13-14	10-11	51	1
Bobby Raymond, Florida (S)	1984	23-26	.885	18-18	5-8	51	1
Mike Bass, Illinois (S)	1982	23-26	.885	12-13	11-13	53	1
Kevin Butler, Georgia (S)	1984	23-28	.821	12-14	11-14	60	2
Steve McLaughlin, Arizona (S)	1994	23-29	.793	11-13	12-16	54	4
Brad Palazzo, Tulane (S)	†1997	23-28	.821	15-15	8-13	52	0
Collin Mackie, South Caro. (S)	†1987	23-30	.767	17-21	6-9	49	0
Obed Ariri, Clemson (S)	†1980	23-30	.767	18-19	5-11	52	3
Derek Schmidt, Florida St. (S)	†1987	23-31	.742	16-21	7-10	53	0

**Record. †National champion. ‡Number of games in which his field goal(s) provided the winning margin. (S) Soccer-style kicker.*

SINGLE-GAME FIELD GOALS

No.	Player, Team (Opponent)	Date
7	Dale Klein, Nebraska (Missouri)	Oct. 19, 1985
7	Mike Prindle, Western Mich. (Marshall)	Sept. 29, 1984
6	Rusty Hanna, Toledo (Northern Ill.)	Nov. 21, 1992
6	Cory Wedel, Wyoming (Idaho)	Aug. 31, 1996
6	Philip Doyle, Alabama (Southwestern La.)	Oct. 6, 1990
6	Sean Fleming, Wyoming (Arkansas St.)	Sept. 15, 1990
6	Bobby Raymond, Florida (Kentucky)	Nov. 17, 1984
6	John Lee, UCLA (San Diego St.)	Sept. 8, 1984
6	Bobby Raymond, Florida (Florida St.)	Dec. 3, 1983
6	Alan Smith, Texas A&M (Arkansas St.)	Sept. 17, 1983
6	Al Del Greco, Auburn (Kentucky)	Oct. 9, 1982
6	Vince Fusco, Duke (Clemson)	Oct. 16, 1976
6	Frank Nester, West Va. (Villanova)	Sept. 9, 1972
6	Charley Gogolak, Princeton (Rutgers)	Sept. 25, 1965

ANNUAL CHAMPIONS

(From 1959-90, goal posts were 23 feet, 4 inches; and from 1991, narrowed to 18 feet, 6 inches)

Year	Player, Team	Total	PG	Pct.	Under 40 Yds.	40 Plus	Long	‡Won
1959	Karl Holzwarth, Wisconsin (C)	7-8	0.8	.875	7-8	0-0	29	4
1960	Ed Dyas, Auburn (C)	13-18	1.3	.722	13-17	0-1	37	2
1961	Greg Mather, Navy (C)	11-15	1.1	.733	9-12	2-3	45	1
1962	Bob Jencks, Miami (Ohio) (C)	8-11	0.8	.727	7-9	1-2	52	3
	Al Woodall, Auburn (C)	8-20	0.8	.400	8-13	0-7	35	0
1963	Billy Lothridge, Georgia Tech (C)	12-16	1.2	.750	10-14	2-2	41	3
1964	Doug Moreau, LSU (C)	13-20	1.3	.650	13-20	0-0	36	0
1965	Charley Gogolak, Princeton (S)	16-23	1.8	.696	7-10	9-13	54	0
1966	Jerry DePoyster, Wyoming (C)	13-*38	1.3	.342	7-13	6-*25	54	1
1967	Gerald Warren, North Caro. St. (C)	17-22	1.7	.773	13-14	4-8	47	1
1968	Bob Jacobs, Wyoming (C)	14-29	1.4	.483	10-15	4-14	51	2
1969	Bob Jacobs, Wyoming (C)	18-27	1.8	.667	13-16	5-11	43	2

Beginning in 1970, ranked on per-game (instead of total) made

Year	Player, Team	Total	PG	Pct.	Under 40 Yds.	40 Plus	Long	‡Won
1970	Kim Braswell, Georgia (C)	13-17	1.3	.765	11-14	2-3	43	0
1971	Nick Mike-Mayer, Temple (S)	12-17	1.3	.706	8-10	4-7	48	1
1972	Nick Mike-Mayer, Temple (S)	13-20	1.4	.650	10-11	3-9	44	3
1973	Rod Garcia, Stanford (S)	18-29	1.6	.621	10-14	8-15	59	2
1974	Dave Lawson, Air Force (C)	19-31	1.7	.613	13-14	6-17	60	1
1975	Don Bitterlich, Temple (S)	21-31	1.9	.677	13-14	8-17	56	0
1976	Tony Franklin, Texas A&M (S)	17-26	1.6	.654	9-12	8-14	65	0
1977	Paul Marchese, Kent (S)	18-27	1.8	.667	13-15	5-12	51	2
1978	Matt Bahr, Penn St. (S)	22-27	2.0	.815	19-20	3-7	50	3
1979	Ish Ordonez, Arkansas (S)	18-22	1.6	.818	12-14	6-8	50	2
1980	Obed Ariri, Clemson (S)	23-30	2.1	.767	18-19	5-11	52	3
1981	Bruce Lahay, Arkansas (S)	19-24	1.7	.792	12-15	7-9	49	4
	Kevin Butler, Georgia (S)	19-26	1.7	.731	11-14	8-12	52	0
	Larry Roach, Oklahoma St. (S)	19-28	1.7	.679	12-14	7-14	56	3
1982	Paul Woodside, West Va. (S)	28-31	2.6	.903	23-23	5-8	45	2
1983	Luis Zendejas, Arizona St. (S)	28-37	2.6	.757	19-22	9-15	52	1
1984	John Lee, UCLA (S)	*29-33	*2.6	.879	16-16	13-17	51	5
1985	John Diettrich, Ball St. (S)	25-29	2.3	.862	16-17	9-12	54	2
1986	Chris Kinzer, Virginia Tech (C)	22-27	2.0	.815	14-17	8-10	50	5
1987	Collin Mackie, South Caro. (S)	23-30	2.1	.767	17-21	6-9	49	0
	Derek Schmidt, Florida St. (S)	23-31	2.1	.742	16-21	7-10	53	0
1988	Kendall Trainor, Arkansas (S)	24-27	2.2	.889	14-15	10-12	58	4
1989	Philip Doyle, Alabama (S)	22-25	2.0	.880	19-19	3-6	44	2
	Gregg McCallum, Oregon (S)	22-29	2.0	.759	15-15	7-14	47	2
	Roman Anderson, Houston (S)	22-34	2.0	.647	17-20	5-14	51	0
1990	Philip Doyle, Alabama (S)	24-29	2.2	.828	16-17	8-12	47	2
1991	Doug Brien, California (S)	19-28	1.7	.679	15-20	4-8	50	2
1992	Joe Allison, Memphis (S)	23-25	2.1	.920	13-14	10-11	51	1
1993	Michael Proctor, Alabama (S)	22-29	1.8	.759	15-20	7-9	53	0
1994	Remy Hamilton, Michigan (S)	24-29	2.2	.828	23-27	1-2	42	2
1995	Michael Reeder, Texas Christian (S)	23-25	2.1	.920	19-19	4-6	47	3
1996	Rafael Garcia, Virginia (S)	21-27	1.9	.778	16-17	5-10	46	1
1997	Brad Palazzo, Tulane (S)	23-28	2.1	.821	15-15	8-15	52	0

**Record. ‡Number of games in which his field goal(s) provided the winning margin. (C) Conventional kicker. (S) Soccer-style kicker.*

All-Time Longest Plays

Since 1941, official maximum length of all plays fixed at 100 yards.

RUSHING

Yds.	Player, Team (Opponent)	Year
99	Eric Vann, Kansas (Oklahoma)	1997
99	Kelsey Finch, Tennessee (Florida)	1977
99	Ralph Thompson, West Tex. A&M (Wichita St.)	1970
99	Max Anderson, Arizona St. (Wyoming)	1967
99	Gale Sayers, Kansas (Nebraska)	1963
98	Jerald Sowell, Tulane (Alabama)	1993
98	Darrell Thompson, Minnesota (Michigan)	1987
98	George Swarn, Miami, Ohio (Western Mich.)	1984
98	Mark Malone, Arizona St. (Utah St.)	1979
98	Stanley Howell, Mississippi St. (Southern Miss.)	1979
98	Steve Atkins, Maryland (Clemson)	1978
98	Granville Amos, VMI (William & Mary)	1964
98	Jim Thacker, Davidson (Geo. Washington)	1952
98	Bill Powell, California (Oregon St.)	1951
98	Al Yannelli, Bucknell (Delaware)	1946
98	Meredith Warner, Iowa St. (Iowa Pre-Flight)	1943

PASSING

Yds.	Passer-Receiver, Team (Opponent)	Year
99	Troy DeGar-Wes Caswell, Tulsa (Oklahoma)	1996
99	John Paci-Thomas Lewis, Indiana (Penn St.)	1993
99	Gino Torretta-Horace Copeland, Miami (Fla.) (Arkansas)	1991
99	Scott Ankrom-James Maness, Texas Christian (Rice)	1984
99	Cris Collinsworth-Derrick Gaffney, Florida (Rice)	1977
99	Terry Peel-Robert Ford, Houston (San Diego St.)	1972
99	Terry Peel-Robert Ford, Houston (Syracuse)	1970
99	Colin Clapton-Eddie Jenkins, Holy Cross (Boston U.)	1970
99	Bo Burris-Warren McVea, Houston (Washington St.)	1966
99	Fred Owens-Jack Ford, Portland (St. Mary's [Cal.])	1947
98	Jose Davis-Eugene Baker, Kent (Central Fla.)	1997
98	Mike Neu-Brian Oliver, Ball St. (Toledo)	1993
98	Tom Dubs-Richard Hill, Ohio (Kent)	1991
98	Paul Oates-Sean Foster, Long Beach St. (San Diego St.)	1989
98	Barry Garrison-Al Owens, New Mexico (Brigham Young)	1987
98	Kelly Donohoe-Willie Vaughn, Kansas (Colorado)	1987
98	Jeff Martin-Mark Flaker, Drake (New Mexico St.)	1976
98	Pete Woods-Joe Stewart, Missouri (Nebraska)	1976
98	Dan Hagemann-Jack Steptoe, Utah (New Mexico)	1976
98	Bruce Shaw-Pat Kenney, North Caro. St. (Penn St.)	1972
98	Jerry Rhome-Jeff Jordan, Tulsa (Wichita St.)	1963
98	Bob Dean-Norman Dawson, Cornell (Navy)	1947

INTERCEPTION RETURNS

Since 1941, 67 players have returned interceptions 100 yards. The most recent:

Yds.	Player, Team (Opponent)	Year
100	Steve Rosga, Colorado (Oklahoma St.)	1996
100	Michael Hicks, UTEP (Brigham Young)	1996
100	Mario Smith, Kansas St. (Missouri)	1996
100	Keion Carpenter, Virginia Tech (Miami [Fla.])	1996

Yds.	Player, Team (Opponent)	Year
100	Reggie Love, North Caro. (Tulane)	1994
100	Harold Lusk, Utah (Colorado St.)	1994
100	Marlon Kerner, Ohio St. (Purdue)	1993
100	Ray Jackson, Colorado St. (UTEP)	1993
100	John Hardy, California (Wisconsin)	1990
100	Ed Givens, Army (Lafayette)	1990

PUNT RETURNS

Yds.	Player, Team (Opponent)	Year
100	Courtney Davis, Bowling Green (Kent)	1996
100	Eddie Kennison, LSU (Mississippi St.)	1994
100‡	Richie Luzzi, Clemson (Georgia)	1968
100‡	Don Guest, California (Washington St.)	1966
100	Jimmy Campagna, Georgia (Vanderbilt)	1952
100	Hugh McElhenny, Washington (Southern Cal)	1951
100	Frank Brady, Navy (Maryland)	1951
100	Bert Rechichar, Tennessee (Wash. & Lee)	1950
100	Eddie Macon, Pacific, Cal. (Boston U.)	1950

‡Return of field goal attempt.

KICKOFF RETURNS

Since 1941, 190 players have returned kickoffs 100 yards. The most recent:

Yds.	Player, Team (Opponent)	Year
100	Eric Vann, Kansas (Oklahoma)	1997
100	Nate Terry, West Va. (East Caro.)	1997
100	Michael Wiley, Ohio St. (Bowling Green)	1997
100	John Avery, Mississippi (Alabama)	1997
100	Boo Williams, South Caro. (Vanderbilt)	1997
100	Kalief Muhammad, Baylor (Oregon St.)	1996
100	Jim Turner, Syracuse (Pittsburgh)	1996
100	Terry Battle, Arizona St. (Oregon St.)	1996
100	John Avery, Mississippi (LSU)	1996
100	Chris McAlister, Arizona (UCLA)	1996
100	Cedric Johnson, UTEP (New Mexico)	1996
100	James Dye, Brigham Young (UTEP)	1996
100	Jason Jacoby, Tulsa (Brigham Young)	1995
100	Aaron Stecker, Wisconsin (Minnesota)	1995

PUNTS

Yds.	Player, Team (Opponent)	Year
99	Pat Brady, Nevada (Loyola Marymount)	1950
96	George O'Brien, Wisconsin (Iowa)	1952
94	John Hadl, Kansas (Oklahoma)	1959
94	Carl Knox, Texas Christian (Oklahoma St.)	1947
94	Preston Johnson, Southern Methodist (Pittsburgh)	1940

FUMBLE RETURNS

(Since 1992)

Yds.	Player, Team (Opponent)	Year
100	Paul Rivers, Rutgers (Pittsburgh)	1995
99	Dennis Gibbs, Idaho (Boise St.)	1997
99	Izell McGill, Mississippi St. (Memphis)	1996
98	Cornelius Pearson, Eastern Mich. (Western Mich.)	1996

Yds.	Player, Team (Opponent)	Year
97	Chris Martin, Northwestern (Air Force)	1994
97	Mike Collins, West Va. (Missouri)	1993
97	Ernie Lewis, East Caro. (West Va.)	1992
96	Jeff Arneson, Illinois (Ohio St.)	1992
95	Ben Hanks, Florida (Arkansas)	1995
94	Dorian Boose, Washington St. (Colorado)	1996
93	Parrish Foster, New Mexico St. (Nevada)	1993
92	Lamont Morgan, Arizona St. (North Texas)	1996
92	Marcus Coleman, Texas Tech (New Mexico)	1995
92	Gerald Nickelberry, Northern Ill. (Arkansas St.)	1993
92	David Thomas, Miami, Ohio (Akron)	1993

FIELD GOALS

Yds.	Player, Team (Opponent)	Year
67	Joe Williams, Wichita St. (Southern Ill.)	1978
67	Steve Little, Arkansas (Texas)	1977
67	Russell Erxleben, Texas (Rice)	1977
65	Tony Franklin, Texas A&M (Baylor)	1976
64	Russell Erxleben, Texas (Oklahoma)	1977
64	Tony Franklin, Texas A&M (Baylor)	1976
63	Morten Andersen, Michigan St. (Ohio St.)	1981
63	Clark Kemble, Colorado St. (Arizona)	1975
62†	Jason Hanson, Washington St. (UNLV)	1991
62	John Diettrich, Ball St. (Ohio)	1986
62#	Chip Lohmiller, Minnesota (Iowa)	1986
62	Tom Whelihan, Missouri (Colorado)	1986
62	Dan Christopulos, Wyoming (Colorado St.)	1977
62	Iseed Khoury, North Texas (Richmond)	1977
62	Dave Lawson, Air Force (Iowa St.)	1975
61$	Kyle Bryant, Texas A&M (Southern Miss.)	1994
61	Dan Eichloff, Kansas (Ball St.)	1992
61	Mark Porter, Kansas St. (Nebraska)	1988
61	Ralf Mojsiejenko, Michigan St. (Illinois)	1982
61	Steve Little, Arkansas (Tulsa)	1976
61	Wayne Latimer, Virginia Tech (Florida St.)	1975
61	Ray Guy, Southern Miss. (Utah St.)	1972
60	Derek Schorejs, Bowling Green (Toledo)	1995
60	John Hall, Wisconsin (Minnesota)	1995
60	Joe Nedney, San Jose St. (Wyoming)	1992
60	Don Shafer, Southern Cal (Notre Dame)	1986
60	Steve DeLine, Colorado St. (Air Force)	1985
60	Kevin Butler, Georgia (Clemson)	1984
60	Chris Perkins, Florida (Tulane)	1984
60	Fuad Reveiz, Tennessee (Georgia Tech)	1982
60	Russell Erxleben, Texas (Texas Tech)	1977
60	Bubba Hicks, Baylor (Rice)	1975
60	Dave Lawson, Air Force (Colorado)	1974
60	Tony Di Rienzo, Oklahoma (Kansas)	1973
60	Bill McClard, Arkansas (Southern Methodist)	1970

†Longest collegiate field goal without use of a kicking tee; all kicks after 1988 season were without the use of a tee. Also longest field goal with narrower (18'6") goal posts. $Longest field goal made by a freshman. #Longest field goal made indoors.

Team Champions

Annual Offense Champions

TOTAL OFFENSE

Year	Team	Avg.
1937	Colorado	375.4
1938	Fordham	341.6
1939	Ohio St.	309.3
1940	Lafayette	368.2
1941	Duke	372.2
1942	Georgia	429.5
1943	Notre Dame	418.0
1944	Tulsa	434.7
1945	Army	462.7
1946	Notre Dame	441.3
1947	Michigan	412.7
1948	Nevada	487.0
1949	Notre Dame	434.8
1950	Arizona St.	470.4
1951	Tulsa	480.1
1952	Tulsa	466.6
1953	Cincinnati	409.5
1954	Army	448.7
1955	Oklahoma	410.7
1956	Oklahoma	481.7
1957	Arizona St.	444.9
1958	Iowa	405.9
1959	Syracuse	451.5
1960	New Mexico St.	419.6
1961	Mississippi	418.7
1962	Arizona St.	384.4
1963	Utah St.	395.3
1964	Tulsa	461.8
1965	Tulsa	427.8
1966	Houston	437.2
1967	Houston	427.9
1968	Houston	562.0
1969	San Diego St.	532.2
1970	Arizona St.	514.5
1971	Oklahoma	566.5
1972	Arizona St.	516.5
1973	Arizona St.	565.5
1974	Oklahoma	507.7
1975	California	458.5
1976	Michigan	448.1
1977	Colgate	486.1
1978	Nebraska	501.4
1979	Brigham Young	521.4
1980	Brigham Young	535.0
1981	Arizona St.	498.7
1982	Nebraska	518.6
1983	Brigham Young	584.2
1984	Brigham Young	486.5
1985	Brigham Young	500.2
1986	San Jose St.	481.4
1987	Oklahoma	499.7
1988	Utah	526.8
1989	Houston	*624.9
1990	Houston	586.8
1991	Fresno St.	541.9
1992	Houston	519.5
1993	Nevada	569.1
1994	Penn St.	520.2
1995	Nevada	569.4
1996	Nevada	527.3
1997	Nebraska	513.7

**Record.*

RUSHING OFFENSE

Year	Team	Avg.
1937	Colorado	310.0
1938	Fordham	297.1
1939	Wake Forest	290.3
1940	Lafayette	306.4
1941	Missouri	307.7
1942	Hardin-Simmons	307.4
1943	Notre Dame	313.7
1944	Army	298.6
1945	Army	359.8
1946	Notre Dame	340.1
1947	Detroit	319.7
1948	UTEP	378.3
1949	UTEP	333.2
1950	Arizona St.	347.0
1951	Arizona St.	334.8
1952	Tulsa	321.5
1953	Oklahoma	306.9
1954	Army	322.0
1955	Oklahoma	328.9
1956	Oklahoma	391.0
1957	Colorado	322.4
1958	Pacific (Cal.)	259.6
1959	Syracuse	313.6
1960	Utah St.	312.0
1961	New Mexico St.	299.1
1962	Ohio St.	278.9
1963	Nebraska	262.6
1964	Syracuse	251.0
1965	Nebraska	290.0
1966	Harvard	269.0
1967	Houston	270.9
1968	Houston	361.7
1969	Texas	363.0
1970	Texas	374.5
1971	Oklahoma	*472.4
1972	Oklahoma	368.8
1973	UCLA	400.3
1974	Oklahoma	438.8
1975	Arkansas St.	340.5
1976	Michigan	362.6
1977	Oklahoma	328.9
1978	Oklahoma	427.5
1979	East Caro.	368.5
1980	Nebraska	378.3
1981	Oklahoma	334.3
1982	Nebraska	394.3
1983	Nebraska	401.7
1984	Army	345.3
1985	Nebraska	374.3
1986	Oklahoma	404.7
1987	Oklahoma	428.8
1988	Nebraska	382.3
1989	Nebraska	375.3
1990	Northern Ill.	344.6
1991	Nebraska	353.2
1992	Nebraska	328.2
1993	Army	298.5
1994	Nebraska	340.0
1995	Nebraska	399.8
1996	Army	346.5
1997	Nebraska	392.6

**Record.*

PASSING OFFENSE

Year	Team	Avg.
1937	Arkansas	185.0
1938	Texas Christian	164.1
1939	Texas Christian	148.5
1940	Cornell	186.3
1941	Arizona	177.7
1942	Tulsa	233.9
1943	Brown	133.1
1944	Tulsa	206.3
1945	St. Mary's (Cal.)	161.3
1946	Nevada	198.1
1947	Michigan	173.9
1948	Nevada	255.0
1949	Fordham	183.4
1950	Southern Methodist	214.6
1951	Loyola Marymount	210.6
1952	Fordham	225.8
1953	Stanford	179.5
1954	Purdue	177.3
1955	Navy	185.1
1956	Washington St.	206.8
1957	Utah	195.2
1958	Army	172.2
1959	Stanford	227.8
1960	Washington St.	185.5
1961	Wisconsin	188.4
1962	Tulsa	199.3
1963	Tulsa	244.8
1964	Tulsa	317.9
1965	Tulsa	346.4
1966	Tulsa	272.0
1967	UTEP	301.1
1968	Cincinnati	335.8
1969	San Diego St.	374.2
1970	Auburn	288.5
1971	San Diego St.	251.4
1972	Virginia Tech	304.4
1973	San Diego St.	305.0
1974	Colorado St.	261.8
1975	San Diego St.	291.3
1976	Brigham Young	307.8
1977	Brigham Young	341.6
1978	Southern Methodist	276.2
1979	Brigham Young	368.3
1980	Brigham Young	409.8
1981	Brigham Young	356.9
1982	Long Beach St.	326.8
1983	Brigham Young	381.2
1984	Brigham Young	346.2
1985	Brigham Young	354.5
1986	San Jose St.	312.5
1987	San Jose St.	338.1
1988	Utah	395.9
1989	Houston	*511.3
1990	Houston	473.9
1991	Houston	372.8
1992	Houston	407.1
1993	Nevada	397.5
1994	Georgia	338.3
1995	Nevada	416.3
1996	Wyoming	359.2
1997	Nevada	370.2

**Record.*

SCORING OFFENSE

Year	Team	Avg.
1937	Colorado	31.0
1938	Dartmouth	28.2
1939	Utah	28.4
1940	Boston College	32.0
1941	Texas	33.8
1942	Tulsa	42.7
1943	Duke	37.2
1944	Army	*56.0
1945	Army	45.8
1946	Georgia	37.2
1947	Michigan	38.3
1948	Nevada	44.4
1949	Army	39.3
1950	Princeton	38.8
1951	Maryland	39.2
1952	Oklahoma	40.7
1953	Texas Tech	38.9
1954	UCLA	40.8
1955	Oklahoma	36.5
1956	Oklahoma	46.6
1957	Arizona St.	39.7
1958	Rutgers	33.4
1959	Syracuse	39.0
1960	New Mexico St.	37.4
1961	Utah St.	38.7
1962	Wisconsin	31.7
1963	Utah St.	31.7
1964	Tulsa	38.4
1965	Arkansas	32.4
1966	Notre Dame	36.2
1967	UTEP	35.9
1968	Houston	42.5
1969	San Diego St.	46.4
1970	Texas	41.2
1971	Oklahoma	44.9
1972	Arizona St.	46.6
1973	Arizona St.	44.6
1974	Oklahoma	43.0
1975	Ohio St.	34.0
1976	Michigan	38.7

Year	Team	Avg.
1977	Grambling	42.0
1978	Oklahoma	40.0
1979	Brigham Young	40.6
1980	Brigham Young	46.7
1981	Brigham Young	38.7
1982	Nebraska	41.1
1983	Nebraska	52.0
1984	Boston College	36.7
1985	Fresno St.	39.1
1986	Oklahoma	42.4
1987	Oklahoma	43.5
1988	Oklahoma St.	47.5
1989	Houston	53.5
1990	Houston	46.5
1991	Fresno St.	44.2
1992	Fresno St.	40.5
1993	Florida St.	43.2
1994	Penn St.	47.8
1995	Nebraska	52.4
1996	Florida	46.6
1997	Nebraska	47.1

**Record.*

Annual Defense Champions

TOTAL DEFENSE

Year	Team	Avg.
1937	Santa Clara	*69.9
1938	Alabama	77.9
1939	Texas A&M	76.3
1940	Navy	96.0
1941	Duquesne	110.6
1942	Texas	117.3
1943	Duke	121.7
1944	Virginia	96.8
1945	Alabama	109.9
1946	Notre Dame	141.7
1947	Penn St.	76.8
1948	Georgia Tech	151.3
1949	Kentucky	153.8
1950	Wake Forest	163.2
1951	Wisconsin	154.8
1952	Tennessee	166.7
1953	Cincinnati	184.3
1954	Mississippi	172.3
1955	Army	160.7
1956	Miami (Fla.)	189.4
1957	Auburn	133.0
1958	Auburn	157.5
1959	Syracuse	96.2
1960	Wyoming	149.6
1961	Alabama	132.6
1962	Mississippi	142.2
1963	Southern Miss.	131.2
1964	Auburn	164.7
1965	Southern Miss.	161.1
1966	Southern Miss.	163.7
1967	Nebraska	157.6
1968	Wyoming	206.8
1969	Toledo	209.1
1970	Toledo	185.8
1971	Toledo	179.5
1972	Louisville	202.5
1973	Miami (Ohio)	177.4
1974	Notre Dame	195.2
1975	Texas A&M	183.8
1976	Rutgers	179.2
1977	Jackson St.	207.0
1978	Penn St.	203.9
1979	Yale	175.4
1980	Pittsburgh	205.5
1981	Pittsburgh	224.8
1982	Arizona St.	228.9
1983	Texas	212.0
1984	Nebraska	203.3
1985	Oklahoma	193.5
1986	Oklahoma	169.6
1987	Oklahoma	208.1
1988	Auburn	218.1
1989	Miami (Fla.)	216.5
1990	Clemson	216.9
1991	Texas A&M	222.4
1992	Alabama	194.2
1993	Mississippi	234.5
1994	Miami (Fla.)	220.9
1995	Kansas St.	250.8
1996	West Va.	217.5
1997	Michigan	206.9

**Record.*

RUSHING DEFENSE

Year	Team	Avg.
1937	Santa Clara	25.3
1938	Oklahoma	43.3
1939	Texas A&M	41.5
1940	Texas A&M	44.3
1941	Duquesne	56.0
1942	Boston College	48.9
1943	Duke	39.4
1944	Navy	53.8
1945	Alabama	33.9
1946	Oklahoma	58.0
1947	Penn St.	*17.0
1948	Georgia Tech	74.9
1949	Oklahoma	55.6
1950	Ohio St.	64.0
1951	San Francisco	51.6
1952	Michigan St.	83.9
1953	Maryland	83.9
1954	UCLA	73.2
1955	Maryland	75.9
1956	Miami (Fla.)	106.9
1957	Auburn	67.4
1958	Auburn	79.6
1959	Syracuse	19.3
1960	Wyoming	82.4
1961	Utah St.	50.8
1962	Minnesota	52.2
1963	Mississippi	77.3
1964	Washington	61.3
1965	Michigan St.	45.6
1966	Wyoming	38.5
1967	Wyoming	42.3
1968	Arizona St.	57.0
1969	LSU	38.9
1970	LSU	52.2
1971	Michigan	63.3
1972	Louisville	82.1
1973	Miami (Ohio)	77.0
1974	Notre Dame	102.8
1975	Texas A&M	80.3
1976	Rutgers	83.9
1977	Jackson St.	67.8
1978	Penn St.	54.5
1979	Yale	75.0
1980	Pittsburgh	65.3
1981	Pittsburgh	62.4
1982	Virginia Tech	49.5
1983	Virginia Tech	69.4
1984	Oklahoma	68.8
1985	UCLA	70.3
1986	Oklahoma	60.7
1987	Michigan St.	61.5
1988	Auburn	63.2
1989	Southern Cal	61.5
1990	Washington	66.8
1991	Clemson	53.4
1992	Alabama	55.0
1993	Arizona	30.1
1994	Virginia	63.6
1995	Virginia Tech	77.4
1996	Florida St.	59.0
1997	Florida St.	51.9

**Record.*

PASSING DEFENSE

Year	Team	Avg.
1937	Harvard	31.0
1938	Penn St.	*13.1
1939	Kansas	34.1
1940	Harvard	33.3
1941	Purdue	27.1
1942	Harvard	45.4
1943	North Caro.	36.5
1944	Michigan St.	26.7
1945	Holy Cross	37.7
1946	Holy Cross	53.7
1947	North Caro. St.	39.3
1948	Northwestern	54.1
1949	Miami (Fla.)	54.7
1950	Tennessee	67.5
1951	Wash. & Lee	67.9
1952	Virginia	50.3
1953	Richmond	40.3
1954	Alabama	45.8
1955	Florida	42.0
1956	Villanova	43.8
1957	Georgia Tech	33.4
1958	Iowa St.	39.0
1959	Alabama	45.7
1960	Iowa St.	30.2
1961	Pennsylvania	56.9
1962	New Mexico	56.8
1963	UTEP	43.8
1964	Kent	53.6
1965	Toledo	69.8
1966	Toledo	70.4
1967	Nebraska	90.1
1968	Kent	107.6
1969	Dayton	90.0
1970	Toledo	77.8
1971	Texas Tech	60.1
1972	Vanderbilt	80.3
1973	Nebraska	39.9
1974	Iowa	65.7
1975	VMI	51.1
1976	Western Mich.	78.5
1977	Tennessee St.	67.9
1978	Boston College	65.1
1979	Western Caro.	77.5
1980	Kansas St.	91.4
1981	Nebraska	100.1
1982	Missouri	123.5
1983	Ohio	115.3
1984	Texas Tech	114.8
1985	Oklahoma	103.6
1986	Oklahoma	108.9
1987	Oklahoma	102.4
1988	Baylor	117.8
1989	Kansas St.	129.3
1990	Alabama	82.5
1991	Texas	77.4
1992	Western Mich.	83.2
1993	Texas A&M	75.0
1994	Miami (Fla.)	81.3
1995	Miami (Ohio)	85.5
1996	Ohio St.	81.3
1997	Michigan	75.8

**Record. $Beginning in 1990, ranked on passing-efficiency defense rating points instead of per-game yardage allowed.*

SCORING DEFENSE

Year	Team	Avg.
1937	Santa Clara	1.1
1938	Duke	**0.0
1939	Tennessee	**0.0
1940	Tennessee	2.6
1941	Duquesne	2.9
1942	Tulsa	3.2
1943	Duke	3.8
1944	Army	3.9
1945	St. Mary's (Cal.)	4.0
1946	Notre Dame	2.7
1947	Penn St.	3.0
1948	Michigan	4.9
1949	Kentucky	4.8
1950	Army	4.4
1951	Wisconsin	5.9
1952	Southern Cal	4.7
1953	Maryland	3.1
1954	UCLA	4.4
1955	Georgia Tech	4.6
1956	Georgia Tech	3.3
1957	Auburn	2.8
1958	Oklahoma	4.9
1959	Mississippi	2.1
1960	LSU	5.0

Year	Team	Avg.
1961	Alabama	2.2
1962	LSU	3.4
1963	Mississippi	3.7
1964	Arkansas	5.7
1965	Michigan St.	6.2
1966	Alabama	3.7
1967	Oklahoma	6.8
1968	Georgia	9.8
1969	Arkansas	7.6
1970	Dartmouth	4.7
1971	Michigan	6.4
1972	Michigan	5.2
1973	Ohio St.	4.3
1974	Michigan	6.8
1975	Alabama	6.0
1976	Michigan	7.4
	Rutgers	7.4
1977	North Caro.	7.4
1978	Ball St.	7.5
1979	Alabama	5.3
1980	Florida St.	7.7
1981	Southern Miss.	8.1
1982	Arkansas	10.5
1983	Virginia Tech	8.3
1984	Nebraska	9.5
1985	Michigan	6.8
1986	Oklahoma	6.6
1987	Oklahoma	7.5
1988	Auburn	7.2
1989	Miami (Fla.)	9.3
1990	Central Mich.	8.9
1991	Miami (Fla.)	9.1
1992	Arizona	8.9
1993	Florida St.	9.4
1994	Miami (Fla.)	10.8
1995	Northwestern	12.7
1996	North Caro.	10.0
1997	Michigan	8.9

***Record tied.*

Other Annual Team Champions

PUNTING

Year	Team	#Avg.
1937	Iowa	43.0
1938	Arkansas	41.6
1939	Auburn	43.3
1940	Auburn	42.3
1941	Clemson	42.3
1942	Tulsa	41.3
1943	Michigan	39.2
1944	UCLA	43.0
1945	Miami (Fla.)	39.9
1946	UTEP	41.2
1947	Duke	41.9
1948	North Caro.	44.0
1949	Furman	44.7
1950	Colorado	45.1
1951	Alabama	41.8
1952	Colorado	43.3
1953	Georgia	41.2
1954	New Mexico	42.6
1955	Michigan St.	41.2
1956	Colorado St.	42.2
1957	Utah St.	40.1
1958	Georgia	41.9
1959	Brigham Young	43.2
1960	Georgia	43.7
1961	Arizona St.	42.1
1962	Wyoming	42.6
1963	Southern Methodist	41.4
1964	Mississippi	44.1
1965	Arizona St.	44.0
1966	Tennessee	43.4
1967	Houston	44.4
1968	Wichita St.	43.2
1969	Georgia	43.5
1970	Utah	45.0
1971	Utah	46.7
1972	Southern Miss.	45.1
1973	Wake Forest	44.1
1974	Ohio St.	44.9
1975	Ohio St.	44.1
1976	Colorado St.	**44.4
1977	Mississippi	43.4
1978	Texas	41.7
1979	Mississippi	42.4
1980	Florida St.	42.6
1981	Michigan	43.1
1982	Vanderbilt	42.1
1983	Brigham Young	*45.0
1984	Ohio St.	44.0
1985	Colorado	43.6
1986	Michigan	43.1
1987	Ohio St.	40.7
1988	Brigham Young	42.9
1989	Colorado	43.8
1990	Pittsburgh	41.2
1991	Texas Tech	40.6
1992	Nebraska	41.7
1993	New Mexico	41.8
1994	Ball St.	42.2
1995	Ball St.	41.3
1996	San Diego St.	44.9
1997	LSU	43.3

*#Beginning in 1975, ranked on net punting average. *Record for net punting average. **Record for net punting average, minimum 40 punts.*

PUNT RETURNS

Year	Team	Avg.
1937	—	—
1938	—	—
1939	UCLA	16.3
1940	UCLA	16.2
1941	Colgate	18.7
1942	—	—
1943	Columbia	20.9
1944	New York U.	22.0
1945	—	—
1946	Columbia	16.8
1947	Florida	19.7
1948	Oklahoma	*22.4
1949	Wichita St.	18.3
1950	Texas A&M	17.6
1951	Holy Cross	18.1
1952	Arizona St.	**25.2
1953	Kansas St.	23.8
1954	Miami (Fla.)	19.7
1955	North Caro.	22.5
1956	Cincinnati	17.7
1957	North Texas	17.5
1958	Notre Dame	17.6
1959	Wyoming	16.6
1960	Arizona	17.7
1961	Memphis	17.4
1962	West Tex. A&M	18.4
1963	Army	18.1
1964	UTEP	16.9
1965	Georgia Tech	23.0
1966	Brown	21.0
1967	Memphis	16.3
1968	Army	17.4
1969	Davidson	21.3
1970	Wichita St.	28.5
1971	Mississippi St.	20.8
1972	Georgia Tech	17.3
1973	Utah	23.4
1974	Auburn	16.6
1975	New Mexico St.	15.3
1976	Wichita St.	15.0
1977	Grambling	16.9
1978	McNeese St.	15.7
1979	Tennessee St.	16.9
1980	Georgia	16.5
1981	North Caro. St.	13.4
1982	Auburn	15.8
1983	San Diego St.	17.0
1984	Florida	13.8
1985	Utah	20.7
1986	Arizona St.	17.9
1987	Stanford	15.4
1988	Florida St.	15.5
1989	Ohio	18.2
1990	Michigan	15.6
1991	Alabama	16.9
1992	Northwestern	21.8
1993	Texas A&M	17.9
1994	Ball St.	19.9
1995	Eastern Mich.	20.8
1996	Kansas	19.5
1997	Iowa	18.2

**Record for minimum 30 punt returns. **Record for minimum 15 punt returns.*

KICKOFF RETURNS

Year	Team	Avg.
1937	—	—
1938	—	—
1939	Wake Forest	32.9
1940	Minnesota	36.4
1941	Tulane	32.1
1942	—	—
1943	Navy	28.8
1944	—	—
1945	—	—
1946	William & Mary	31.7
1947	Southern Methodist	31.4
1948	Wyoming	27.4
1949	Army	34.1
1950	Wyoming	29.3
1951	Marquette	25.0
1952	Wake Forest	25.1
1953	Texas Tech	23.8
1954	Arizona	26.1
1955	Southern Cal	25.8
1956	Georgia Tech	24.6
1957	Notre Dame	27.6
1958	Tulsa	25.8
1959	Auburn	25.8
1960	Yale	26.7
1961	Harvard	25.9
1962	Alabama	28.9
1963	Memphis	27.7
1964	Cornell	27.1
1965	Dartmouth	28.7
1966	Notre Dame	29.6
1967	Air Force	25.3
1968	Louisville	25.7
1969	Brigham Young	28.7
1970	South Caro.	26.5
1971	Miami (Fla.)	24.1
1972	Michigan	26.9
1973	Rice	*27.5
1974	Southern Cal	25.7
1975	Maryland	**29.5
1976	South Caro.	27.0
1977	Miami (Ohio)	24.6
1978	Utah St.	26.7
1979	Brigham Young	26.3
1980	Oklahoma	33.2
1981	Iowa	29.1
1982	Utah	25.5
1983	Tennessee	28.8
1984	Texas Tech	25.2
1985	Air Force	27.0
1986	Clemson	26.1
1987	Oklahoma St.	23.7
1988	Notre Dame	24.2
1989	Colorado	26.1
1990	Nebraska	27.8
1991	New Mexico St.	25.2
1992	Florida St.	30.3
1993	Texas A&M	31.2
1994	Texas A&M	27.8
1995	New Mexico	27.1
1996	Miami (Fla.)	28.9
1997	Southern Miss.	28.2

**Record for minimum 35 kickoff returns. **Record for minimum 25 kickoff returns.*

Toughest-Schedule Annual Leaders

The NCAA's toughest-schedule program (which began in 1977) is based on what all Division I-A opponents did against other Division I-A teams when not playing the team in question. Games against non-I-A teams are deleted, and nine intradivision games are required to qualify. (Bowl games are not included.) The leaders:

		¢Opponents' Record			
Year	Team (†Record)	W	L	T	Pct.
1977	Miami (Fla.) (3-8-0)	66	42	2	.609
	Penn St. (10-1-0)	61	39	2	.608
1978	Notre Dame (8-3-0)	77	31	2	.709
	Southern Cal (11-1-0)	79	40	1	.663
1979	UCLA (5-6-0)	71	37	2	.655
	South Caro. (8-3-0)	69	38	2	.642
1980	Florida St. (10-1-0)	70	34	0	.673
	Miami (Fla.) (8-3-0)	64	33	1	.658
1981	Penn St. (9-2-0)	71	33	2	.679
	Temple (5-5-0)	71	33	2	.669
1982	Penn St. (10-1-0)	63	34	2	.646
	Kentucky (0-10-1)	63	34	5	.642
1983	Auburn (10-1-0)	70	31	3	.688
	UCLA (6-4-1)	68	37	5	.641
1984	Penn St. (6-5-0)	58	36	3	.613
	Georgia (7-4-0)	60	39	4	.602
1985	Notre Dame (5-6-0)	72	29	3	.707
	Alabama (8-2-1)	65	32	5	.662
1986	Florida (6-5-0)	64	29	3	.682
	LSU (9-2-0)	67	36	2	.648
1987	Notre Dame (8-3-0)	71	34	2	.673
	Florida St. (10-1-0)	60	29	4	.667
1988	Virginia Tech (3-8-0)	74	36	0	.673
	Arizona (7-4-0)	70	37	3	.650
1989	Notre Dame (11-1-0)	74	38	4	.655
	LSU (4-7-0)	67	41	1	.619
1990	Colorado (10-1-1)	72	42	3	.628
	Stanford (5-6-0)	67	39	4	.627
1991	South Caro. (3-6-2)	57	31	2	.644
	Florida (10-2-0)	66	37	1	.639
1992	Southern Cal. (6-5-1)	68	38	4	.636
	Stanford (10-3-0)	73	43	4	.625

†Not including bowl games. ¢When not playing the team listed.

Top 10 Toughest-Schedule Leaders for 1993-97

1993

	Team	¢Opp. Record	Pct.
1.	LSU	67-38-5	.632
2.	Purdue	66-38-3	.631
3.	Miami (Fla.)	62-36-2	.630
4.	Maryland	68-40-0	.630
5.	Florida	72-42-5	.626
6.	Pittsburgh	65-39-3	.621
7.	Southern Cal	73-46-1	.613
8.	Northwestern	65-41-2	.611
9.	UCLA	67-43-0	.609
10.	Florida St.	71-46-0	.607

1994

	Team	¢Opp. Record	Pct.
1.	Michigan	67-38-6	.631
2.	Oklahoma	66-39-4	.624
3.	Florida St.	64-40-1	.614
4.	Southern Cal	67-42-1	.614
5.	Southern Miss.	58-38-2	.602
6.	Michigan St.	61-42-7	.586
7.	Tennessee	64-45-2	.586
8.	Florida	66-49-2	.573
9.	Alabama	60-45-3	.569
10.	Miami (Fla.)	56-42-3	.569

1995

	Team	¢Opp. Record	Pct.
1.	Notre Dame	67-37-5	.638
2.	Illinois	69-40-2	.631
3.	Minnesota	64-38-5	.621
4.	Cincinnati	66-40-2	.620
5.	Vanderbilt	68-42-1	.617
6.	Indiana	66-41-3	.614
7.	Washington	64-40-2	.613
8.	Purdue	67-42-2	.613
9.	Houston	66-42-3	.608
	Northwestern	65-41-5	.608

1996

	Team	¢Opp. Record	Pct.
1.	Florida	70-41	.631
2.	UCLA	66-41	.617
3.	Purdue	68-44	.607
4.	Washington	68-46	.596
5.	Arkansas	62-42	.596
6.	Tulane	63-43	.594
7.	Minnesota	63-44	.589
8.	Nebraska	70-49	.588
9.	Rutgers	57-40	.588
10.	Iowa St.	59-42	.584

1997

	Team	¢Opp. Record	Pct.
1.	Colorado	76-37-0	.673
2.	Auburn	80-39-0	.672
3.	Florida	72-40-0	.643
4.	Arkansas	71-40-0	.640
5.	Tennessee	77-44-0	.636
6.	Washington	70-42-0	.625
7.	Mississippi	68-43-0	.613
8.	Bowling Green	67-43-0	.609
9.	South Caro.	66-44-0	.600
10.	Alabama	67-45-0	.598

†Not including bowl games. ¢When not playing the team listed.

Annual Most-Improved Teams

Year	Team	$Games Improved	From		To		Coach
1937	California	4½	1936	6-5-0	1937	*10-0-1	Stub Allison
	Syracuse	4½	1936	1-7-0	1937	5-2-1	#Ossie Solem
1938	Texas Christian	5½	1937	4-4-2	1938	*11-0-0	Dutch Meyer
1939	Texas A&M	5½	1938	4-4-1	1939	*11-0-0	Homer Norton
1940	Stanford	8	1939	1-7-1	1940	*10-0-0	#Clark Shaughnessy
1941	Vanderbilt	4½	1940	3-6-1	1941	8-2-0	Red Sanders
1942	Utah St.	5½	1941	0-8-0	1942	6-3-1	Dick Romney
1943	Purdue	8	1942	1-8-0	1943	9-0-0	Elmer Burnham
1944	Ohio St.	6	1943	3-6-0	1944	9-0-0	#Carroll Widdoes
1945	Miami (Fla.)	7	1944	1-7-1	1945	*9-1-1	Jack Harding
1946	Illinois	5	1945	2-6-1	1946	*8-2-0	Ray Eliot
	Kentucky	5	1945	2-8-0	1946	7-3-0	#Paul "Bear" Bryant
1947	California	6½	1946	2-7-0	1947	9-1-0	#Lynn "Pappy" Waldorf
1948	Clemson	6	1947	4-5-0	1948	*11-0-0	Frank Howard
1949	Tulsa	5	1948	0-9-1	1949	5-4-1	J. O. Brothers
1950	Brigham Young	5	1949	0-11-0	1950	4-5-1	Chick Atkinson
	Texas A&M	5	1949	1-8-1	1950	*7-4-0	Harry Stiteler
1951	Georgia Tech	6	1950	5-6-0	1951	*11-0-1	Bobby Dodd
1952	Alabama	4½	1951	5-6-0	1952	*10-2-0	Harold "Red" Drew
1953	Texas Tech	7	1952	3-7-1	1953	*11-1-0	DeWitt Weaver
1954	Denver	5	1953	3-5-2	1954	9-1-0	Bob Blackman
1955	Texas A&M	6½	1954	1-9-0	1955	7-2-1	Paul "Bear" Bryant
1956	Iowa	5	1955	3-5-1	1956	*9-1-0	Forest Evashevski
1957	Notre Dame	5	1956	2-8-0	1957	7-3-0	Terry Brennan
	Texas	5	1956	1-9-0	1957	†6-4-1	#Darrell Royal
1958	Air Force	6	1957	3-6-1	1958	‡9-0-1	#Ben Martin
1959	Washington	6½	1958	3-7-0	1959	*10-1-0	Jim Owens
1960	Minnesota	5½	1959	2-7-0	1960	†8-2-0	Murray Warmath
	North Caro. St.	5½	1959	1-9-0	1960	6-3-1	Earle Edwards
1961	Villanova	6	1960	2-8-0	1961	*8-2-0	Alex Bell
1962	Southern Cal	6	1961	4-5-1	1962	*11-0-0	John McKay
1963	Illinois	6	1962	2-7-0	1963	*8-1-1	Pete Elliott
1964	Notre Dame	6½	1963	2-7-0	1964	9-1-0	#Ara Parseghian
1965	UTEP	6½	1964	0-8-2	1965	*8-3-0	#Bobby Dobbs
1966	Dayton	6½	1965	1-8-1	1966	8-2-0	John McVay
1967	Indiana	7	1966	1-8-1	1967	†9-2-0	John Pont
1968	Arkansas	5	1967	4-5-1	1968	*10-1-0	Frank Broyles
1969	UCLA	5½	1968	3-7-0	1969	8-1-1	Tommy Prothro
1970	Tulsa	5	1969	1-9-0	1970	6-4-0	#Claude Gibson
1971	Army	5	1970	1-9-1	1971	6-4-0	Tom Cahill
	Georgia	5	1970	5-5-0	1971	*11-1-0	Vince Dooley
1972	Pacific (Cal.)	5	1971	3-8-0	1972	8-3-0	Chester Caddas
	Southern Cal	5	1971	6-4-1	1972	*12-0-0	John McKay
	UCLA	5	1971	2-7-1	1972	8-3-0	Pepper Rodgers
1973	Pittsburgh	5	1972	1-10-0	1973	†6-5-1	#Johnny Majors
1974	Baylor	5½	1973	2-9-0	1974	†8-4-0	Grant Teaff
1975	Arizona St.	5	1974	7-5-0	1975	*12-0-0	Frank Kush
1976	Houston	7	1975	2-8-0	1976	*10-2-0	Bill Yeoman
1977	Miami (Ohio)	7	1976	3-8-0	1977	10-1-0	Dick Crum
1978	Tulsa	6	1977	3-8-0	1978	9-2-0	John Cooper
1979	Wake Forest	6½	1978	1-10-0	1979	†8-4-0	John Mackovic
1980	Florida	7	1979	0-10-1	1980	*8-4-0	Charley Pell
1981	Clemson	5½	1980	6-5-0	1981	*12-0-0	Danny Ford
1982	New Mexico	6	1981	4-7-1	1982	10-1-0	Joe Morrison
	Southwestern La.	6	1981	1-9-1	1982	7-3-1	Sam Robertson
1983	Kentucky	5½	1982	0-10-1	1983	†6-5-1	Jerry Claiborne
	Memphis	5½	1982	1-10-0	1983	6-4-1	Rex Dockery
1984	Army	6	1983	2-9-0	1984	*8-3-1	Jim Young
1985	Colorado	5½	1984	1-10-0	1985	†7-5-0	Bill McCartney
	Fresno St.	5½	1984	6-6-0	1985	*11-0-1	Jim Sweeney
1986	San Jose St.	7	1985	2-8-1	1986	*10-2-0	Claude Gilbert
1987	Syracuse	6	1986	5-6-0	1987	‡11-0-1	Dick MacPherson
1988	West Va.	5	1987	6-6-0	1988	†11-1-0	Don Nehlen
	Washington St.	5	1987	3-7-1	1988	*9-3-0	Dennis Erickson
1989	Tennessee	5½	1988	5-6-0	1989	*11-1-0	Johnny Majors
1990	Temple	6	1989	1-10-0	1990	7-4-0	Jerry Berndt
1991	Tulsa	6½	1990	3-8-0	1991	*10-2-0	Dave Rader
1992	Hawaii	6	1991	4-7-1	1992	*11-2-0	Bob Wagner
1993	Southwestern La.	6	1992	2-9-0	1993	8-3-0	Nelson Stokley
	Virginia Tech	6	1992	2-8-1	1993	*9-3-0	Frank Beamer
1994	Colorado St.	4½	1993	5-6-0	1994	†10-2-0	Sonny Lubick
	Duke	4½	1993	3-8-0	1994	†8-4-0	#Fred Goldsmith
	East Caro.	4½	1993	2-9-0	1994	†7-5-0	Steve Logan
1995	Northwestern	6	1994	3-7-1	1995	†10-2-0	Gary Barnett
1996	Brigham Young	5	1995	7-4-0	1996	*14-1-0	LaVell Edwards
1997	Western Mich.	6	1996	2-9-0	1997	8-3-0	Gary Darnell

$To determine games improved, add the difference in victories between the two seasons to the difference in losses, then divide by two; ties not counted. Bowl victory (*), loss (†), tie (‡) included in record. #First year as head coach at that college.

Photo from Western Michigan sports information

Coach Gary Darnell led Western Michigan to the 1997 most-improved team honor with an 8-3 record, a six-game improvement in victories from 1996.

All-Time Most-Improved Teams

Games	Team (Year)	Games	Team (Year)
8	Purdue (1943)	6½	Tulsa (1991)
8	Stanford (1940)	6½	Wake Forest (1979)
7	San Jose St. (1986)	6½	Toledo (1967)
7	Florida (1980)	6½	Dayton (1966)
7	Miami (Ohio) (1977)	6½	UTEP (1965)
7	Houston (1976)	6½	Notre Dame (1964)
7	Indiana (1967)	6½	Washington (1959)
7	Texas Tech (1953)	6½	Texas A&M (1955)
7	Miami (Fla.) (1945)	6½	California (1947)

1997 Most-Improved Teams

College (Coach)	1997	1996	$Games Improved
Western Mich. (Gary Darnell)	8-3-0	2-9-0	+6
Purdue (Joe Tiller)	9-3-0	3-8-0	+5 ½
Tulane (Tommy Bowden)	7-4-0	2-9-0	+5
Georgia (Jim Donnan)	10-2-0	5-6-0	+4 ½
UCLA (Bob Toledo)	10-2-0	5-6-0	+4 ½
Washington St. (Mike Price)	10-2-0	5-6-0	+4 ½
Michigan (Lloyd Carr)	12-0-0	8-4-0	+4
Colorado St. (Sonny Lubick)	11-2-0	7-5-0	+3 ½
Louisiana Tech (Gary Crowton)	9-2-0	6-5-0	+3
Air Force (Fisher DeBerry)	10-3-0	6-5-0	+3
North Caro. St. (Mike O'Cain)	6-5-0	3-8-0	+3
Ohio (Jim Grobe)	8-3-0	6-6-0	+2 ½
Texas A&M (R. C. Slocum)	9-4-0	6-6-0	+2 ½
Mississippi (Tommy Turberville)	8-4-0	5-6-0	+2 ½
Oklahoma St. (Bob Simmons)	8-4-0	5-6-0	+2 ½
Boise St. (Houston Nutt)	4-7-0	2-10-0	+2 ½
UNLV (Jeff Horton)	3-8-0	1-11-0	+2 ½

$To determine games improved, add the difference in victories between the two seasons to the difference in losses, then divide by two, ties not counted. Includes bowl games.

All-Time Team Won-Lost Records

PERCENTAGE (TOP 47)

Terms listed with years in parentheses have been reclassified within the past 10 years. The year in parentheses is the first year of Division I-A membership. Won-lost-tied record.

Team	Yrs.	Won	Lost	Tied	Pct.+	Total Games
Notre Dame#	109	753	228	42	.757	1,023
Michigan	118	776	254	36	.745	1,066
Alabama@	103	717	260	43	.724	1,020
Ohio St.	108	700	275	53	.707	1,028
Oklahoma	103	677	267	53	.706	997
Texas	105	717	291	33	.705	1,041
Nebraska$	108	722	292	40	.704	1,054
Southern Cal	105	659	270	54	.698	983
Penn St.	111	715	299	41	.697	1,055
Tennessee@	101	677	285	52	.693	1,014
Florida St.@	51	358	181	17	.659	556
Boise St. (1996)	30	225	119	2	.653	346
Washington@	108	593	325	50	.638	968
Central Mich.	97	500	280	36	.635	816
Miami (Ohio)@	109	574	322	44	.634	940
LSU	104	603	341	47	.632	991
Arizona St.	85	473	272	24	.631	769
Army	108	611	348	51	.630	1,010
Georgia	104	616	351	54	.630	1,021
Auburn@	105	593	347	47	.625	987
Colorado	108	593	359	36	.618	988
Miami (Fla.)	71	443	274	19	.615	736
Florida	91	535	338	40	.608	913
Texas A&M	103	583	374	48	.604	1,005
Syracuse	108	617	397	49	.603	1,063
UCLA	79	464	299	37	.603	800
Bowling Green	79	410	265	52	.600	727
Michigan St.@	101	540	355	44	.599	939
Arkansas@	104	571	386	40	.593	997
Southern Miss.@	81	446	303	26	.592	775
Fresno St.	76	451	307	29	.591	787
Clemson	102	553	376	45	.591	974
West Va.	105	584	400	45	.589	1,029
Arizona	93	485	333	33	.589	851
Georgia Tech	105	574	395	43	.588	1,012
Minnesota	114	568	391	43	.588	1,002
San Diego St.	75	425	294	32	.587	751
North Caro.	107	584	407	54	.585	1,045
Stanford	91	502	351	49	.584	902
Louisiana Tech (1989)@	94	477	335	37	.584	849
Pittsburgh	108	582	414	42	.581	1,038
UAB (1996)	7	42	30	3	.580	75
Tulsa	93	487	350	27	.579	864
Virginia Tech	104	548	393	46	.579	987
Boston College	99	517	377	36	.575	930
Mississippi@	103	537	401	35	.570	973
California	102	546	408	51	.569	1,005

ALPHABETICAL LISTING

Team	Yrs.	Won	Lost	Tied	Pct.+	Total Games
Air Force	42	242	214	13	.530	469
Akron	97	423	395	36	.516	854
Alabama@	103	717	260	43	.724	1,020
UAB (1996)	7	42	30	3	.580	75
Arizona	93	485	333	33	.589	851
Arizona St.	85	473	272	24	.631	769
Arkansas@	104	571	386	40	.593	997
Arkansas St. (1992)	83	360	354	37	.504	751
Army	108	611	348	51	.630	1,010
Auburn@	105	593	347	47	.625	987
Ball St.	73	349	277	32	.555	658
Baylor	95	488	427	43	.532	958
Boise St. (1996)	30	225	119	2	.653	346
Boston College	99	517	377	36	.575	930
Bowling Green	79	410	265	52	.600	727
Brigham Young	73	407	321	26	.557	754
California	102	546	408	51	.569	1,005
Central Fla. (1996)	19	105	98	1	.517	204
Central Mich.	97	500	280	36	.635	816
Cincinnati	110	467	478	52	.494	997
Clemson	102	553	376	45	.591	974
Colorado	108	593	359	36	.618	988
Colorado St.	99	393	447	33	.469	873
Duke	85	427	353	31	.546	811
East Caro.	62	311	286	12	.521	609
Eastern Mich.	105	386	405	46	.489	837
Florida	91	535	338	40	.608	913
Florida St.@	51	358	181	17	.659	556
Fresno St.	76	451	307	29	.591	787
Georgia	104	616	351	54	.630	1,021
Georgia Tech	105	574	395	43	.588	1,012
Hawaii	82	426	322	26	.567	774
Houston	52	295	250	15	.540	560
Idaho (1996)	100	386	446	25	.465	857
Illinois	107	510	437	50	.537	997
Indiana@	110	396	518	44	.436	958
Iowa	109	494	449	39	.523	982
Iowa St.	106	427	497	46	.464	970
Kansas	108	502	473	58	.514	1,033
Kansas St.@	102	365	546	42	.405	953
Kent	75	265	394	28	.406	687
Kentucky@	107	504	475	44	.514	1,023
LSU@	104	603	341	47	.632	991
Louisiana Tech (1989)@	94	477	335	37	.584	849
Louisville@	79	344	374	17	.480	735
Marshall (1997)	94	424	442	44	.490	.910
Maryland	105	522	465	42	.528	1,029
Memphis@	82	372	374	32	.499	778
Miami (Fla.)	71	443	274	19	.615	736
Miami (Ohio)@	109	574	322	44	.634	940
Michigan	118	776	254	36	.745	1,066
Michigan St.@	101	540	355	44	.599	939
Minnesota	114	568	391	43	.588	1,002
Mississippi@	103	537	401	35	.570	973
Mississippi St.@	98	430	450	39	.489	919
Missouri	107	525	452	52	.535	1,029
Navy	117	570	446	57	.558	1,073
Nebraska$	108	722	292	40	.704	1,054
UNLV	30	175	155	4	.530	334
Nevada (1992)	87	420	347	32	.546	799
New Mexico	99	385	442	31	.467	858
New Mexico St.	102	373	462	32	.449	867
North Caro.	107	584	407	54	.585	1,045
North Caro. St.	106	455	457	55	.499	967

Team	Yrs.	Won	Lost	Tied	Pct.+	Total Games
North Texas (1995)	82	420	347	33	.546	800
Northeast La. (1994)	47	220	263	8	.456	491
Northern Ill.	96	426	389	51	.521	866
Northwestern@	110	399	541	43	.428	983
Notre Dame#	109	753	228	42	.757	1,023
Ohio	102	437	435	48	.501	920
Ohio St.	108	700	275	53	.707	1,028
Oklahoma	103	677	267	53	.706	997
Oklahoma St.	96	430	452	48	.488	930
Oregon	102	464	422	46	.523	932
Oregon St.	101	402	475	50	.461	927
Penn St.	111	715	299	41	.697	1,055
Pittsburgh	108	582	414	42	.581	1,038
Purdue@	110	492	428	48	.533	968
Rice@	86	372	464	32	.447	868
Rutgers	128	541	515	42	.512	1,098
San Diego St.	75	425	294	32	.587	751
San Jose St.	79	392	347	38	.529	777
South Caro.@	104	467	457	44	.505	968
Southern Cal	105	659	270	54	.698	983
Southern Methodist&	81	404	384	54	.512	842
Southern Miss.@	81	446	303	26	.592	775
Southwestern La.	90	424	412	32	.507	868
Stanford	91	502	351	49	.584	902
Syracuse	108	617	397	49	.603	1,063
Temple	99	374	428	52	.468	854
Tennessee@	101	677	285	52	.693	1,014
Texas	105	717	291	33	.705	1,041
Texas A&M	103	583	374	48	.604	1,005
Texas Christian	101	458	473	56	.492	987
UTEP	80	302	432	30	.415	764
Texas Tech	73	413	340	32	.546	785
Toledo	77	378	333	24	.531	735
Tulane@	104	431	489	38	.470	958
Tulsa	93	487	350	27	.579	864
UCLA	79	464	299	37	.603	800
Utah	104	504	379	31	.568	914
Utah St.	00	436	391	31	.526	858
Vanderbilt@	108	515	459	50	.527	1,024
Virginia	108	533	475	48	.527	1,056
Virginia Tech	104	548	393	46	.579	987
Wake Forest	96	338	520	23	.397	881
Washington@	108	593	325	50	.638	968
Washington St.	101	427	418	45	.505	890
West Va.	105	584	400	45	.589	1,029
Western Mich.	92	437	329	24	.568	790
Wisconsin@	108	506	419	53	.544	978
Wyoming	101	427	427	28	.500	882

BY VICTORIES

Team	Wins
Michigan	776
Notre Dame#	753
Nebraska	722
Alabama@	717
Texas	717
Penn St.	715
Ohio St.	700
Oklahoma	677
Tennessee@	677
Southern Cal	659
Syracuse	617
Georgia	616
Army	611
LSU@	603
Auburn@	593
Colorado	593
Washington@	593
North Caro.	584
West Va.	584
Texas A&M	583
Pittsburgh	582
Georgia Tech	574
Miami (Ohio)	574
Arkansas@	571
Navy	570
Minnesota	568
Clemson	553
Virginia Tech	548
California	546
Rutgers	541
Michigan St.@	540
Mississippi@	537
Florida	535
Virginia	533
Missouri	525
Maryland	522
Boston College	517
Vanderbilt@	515
Illinois	510
Wisconsin@	506
Kentucky@	504
Utah	504
Kansas	502
Stanford	502
Central Mich.	500
Iowa	494
Purdue@	492
Baylor	488
Tulsa	487
Arizona	485
Louisiana Tech (1989)	477
Arizona	473
Cincinnati	467
South Caro.@	467
Oregon	464
UCLA	464
Texas Christian	458
North Caro. St.	455
Fresno St.	451
Southern Miss.@	446
Miami (Fla.)	443
Ohio	437
Western Mich.	437
Utah St.	436
Tulane@	431
Mississippi St.@	430
Oklahoma St.	430
Duke	427
Iowa St.	427
Washington St.	427
Wyoming	427
Hawaii	426
Northern Ill.	426
San Diego St.	425
Marshall (1997)	424
Southwestern La.	424
Akron	423
Nevada (1992)	420
North Texas (1995)	420
Texas Tech	413
Bowling Green	410
Brigham Young	407
Southern Methodist	404
Oregon St.	402
Northwestern@	399
Indiana@	396
Colorado St.	393
San Jose St.	392
Eastern Mich.	386
Idaho (1996)	386
New Mexico	385
Toledo	378
Temple	374
New Mexico St.	373
Memphis@	372
Rice@	372
Kansas St.@	365
Arkansas St. (1992)	360
Florida St.@	358
Ball St.	349
Louisville@	344
Wake Forest	338
East Caro.	311
UTEP	302
Houston	295
Kent	265
Air Force	242
Boise St. (1996)	225
Northeast La. (1994)	220
UNLV	175
Central Fla. (1996)	105
UAB (1996)	42

*Ties computed as half won and half lost. *Record in a major bowl game only (i.e., a team's opponent was classified as a major-college team that season or it was classified as a major-college team at the time). #Leader since 1948. Notre Dame displaced all-time leader Yale .8082 to .8081, after the 1947 season. $Record adjusted in 1989 (8 less victories, 1 less defeat). &Football program suspended 1987-88. @ Includes games forfeited or changed by action of the NCAA Council and/or Committee on Infractions.*

Records in the 1990s

(1990-91-92-93-94-95-96-97, Including Bowls and Playoffs; Tiebreaker Began 1996)

PERCENTAGE

Team	W-L-T	*Pct.
Nebraska	87-11-1	.884
Florida St.	86-11-1	.883
Florida	83-16-1	.835
Penn St.	78-20-0	.796
Tennessee	77-19-2	.796
Marshall++	89-24-0	.788
Miami (Fla.)	74-20-0	.787
Texas A&M	75-21-2	.776
Colorado	72-20-4	.771
Michigan	73-21-3	.768
Ohio St.	74-22-3	.763
Washington	69-24-1	.739
Nevada++	71-26-0	.732
Notre Dame	70-25-2	.732
North Caro.	68-26-1	.721
Syracuse	67-26-3	.714
Auburn	64-26-3	.704
Kansas St.	65-27-1	.704
Brigham Young	69-30-2	.693
Alabama	66-32-0	.673
Toledo	59-28-3	.672
Virginia	62-32-1	.658
Clemson	60-33-1	.644
Idaho	61-34-0	.642
Iowa	58-35-2	.621
Virginia Tech	57-35-1	.618
Air Force	60-38-0	.612
Texas	56-36-2	.606
Colorado St.	58-38-0	.604
Georgia	55-36-1	.603
UCLA	55-37-0	.598
Bowling Green	51-34-4	.596
Central Fla.++	54-37-0	.593
Western Mich.	51-35-2	.591
Utah	55-39-0	.585
Fresno St.	55-39-2	.583
Southern Cal	54-38-4	.583
UAB++	42-30-2	.581
West Va.	53-38-2	.581
Wyoming	55-40-1	.578
Ball St.	51-37-2	.578
Arizona	53-39-1	.575
Miami (Ohio)	48-35-5	.574
Southern Miss.	51-38-1	.572
East Caro.	52-39-0	.571
Mississippi	52-39-0	.571
North Caro. St.	53-40-1	.569
Arizona St.	51-39-0	.567
Oregon	53-41-0	.564
Oklahoma	49-40-3	.549
San Diego St.	50-41-2	.548
Louisiana Tech	47-39-3	.545
Stanford	49-42-2	.538
Texas Tech	49-43-0	.533
Wisconsin	48-42-4	.532
Boise St.++	51-45-0	.531
Georgia Tech	48-43-1	.527
Kansas	47-43-1	.522
LSU	47-43-1	.522
Northeast La.++	48-44-1	.522
Central Mich.	44-41-5	.517
Mississippi St.	46-43-2	.516
Washington St.	47-440	.516
Baylor	46-441	.511
Louisville	45-441	.506
Michigan St.	46-45-2	.505
Army	44-44-1	.500
California	46-46-1	.500
Boston College	45-46-2	.495
Rice	42-45-1	.483
South Caro.	41-45-3	.478
Utah St.	41-48-1	.461
Indiana	39-50-2	.440
Memphis	38-49-1	.438
Illinois	39-51-2	.435
Cincinnati	38-50-1	.433
Arkansas	38-51-2	.429
Hawaii	40-55-2	.423
San Jose St.	37-51-2	.422
Northwestern	37-53-1	.412
Texas Christian	36-52-1	.410
New Mexico	38-55-0	.409
North Texas++	35-52-2	.404
Southwestern La.	35-52-1	.403
Navy	35-54-0	.393
Tulsa	34-54-1	.388
Houston	32-56-1	.365
Purdue	31-55-3	.365
Missouri	31-56-3	.361
Oklahoma St.	31-56-3	.361
Rutgers	31-56-1	.358
Kentucky	31-58-0	.348
Maryland	30-58-1	.343
Akron	29-57-2	.341
Pittsburgh	30-59-1	.339
UNLV	30-60-0	.333
Eastern Mich.	28-59-1	.324
Wake Forest	28-61-0	.315

Team	W-L-T	*Pct.	Team	W-L-T	*Pct.
Vanderbilt	27-61-0	.307	Tulane	23-66-0	.258
Minnesota	27-62-0	.303	Iowa St.	20-65-3	.244
Duke	26-62-1	.298	Arkansas St.	20-65-2	.241
Ohio	24-62-3	.287	UTEP	20-69-2	.231
Northern Ill.	25-63-0	.284	Temple	18-70-0	.205
New Mex. St.	24-64-0	.273	Oregon St.	17-70-1	.199
SMU	22-63-3	.267	Kent	13-74-1	.153

BY VICTORIES

Team	Wins	Team	Wins
Marshall++	89	Colorado St.	58
Nebraska	87	Iowa	58
Florida St.	86	Virginia Tech	57
Florida	83	Texas	56
Penn St.	78	Fresno St.	55
Tennessee#	77	Georgia	55
Texas A&M	75	UCLA	55
Miami (Fla.)	74	Utah	55
Ohio St.	74	Wyoming	55
Michigan	73	Central Fla.	54
Colorado	72	Southern Cal	54
Nevada++	71	Arizona	53
Notre Dame	70	North Caro. St.	53
Brigham Young	69	Oregon	53
Washington	69	West Va.	53
North Caro.	68	East Caro.	52
Syracuse	67	Mississippi	52
Alabama@	66	Arizona St.	51
Kansas St.	65	Ball St.	51
Auburn	64	Boise St.	51
Virginia	62	Bowling Green	51
Idaho	61	Southern Miss.	51
Air Force	60	Western Mich.	51
Clemson	60	San Diego St.	50
Toledo	59		

(Minimum 50 Victories)

**Ties counted as half won and half lost. @Alabama forfeited eight victories and one tie from 1993 by order of NCAA Committee on Infractions. #Includes forfeit win over Alabama in 1993 by order of NCAA Committee on Infractions. ++Joined I-A during the decade as follows: Nevada (1992), Northeast La. (1994), North Texas (1995), UAB (1996), Boise St. (1996), Central Fla. (1996) and Marshall (1997).*

Winningest Teams by Decade

(By Percentage; Bowls and Playoffs Included, Unless Noted)

1980-89

Rank	Team	W-L-T	Pct.†	Rank	Team	W-L-T	Pct.†
1.	Nebraska	103-20-0	.837	11.	Alabama	85-32-2	.723
2.	Miami (Fla.)	98-20-0	.831		Arkansas	85-32-2	.723
3.	Brigham Young	102-26-0	.797	13.	UCLA	81-30-6	.718
4.	Oklahoma	91-25-2	.780	14.	Washington	83-33-1	.714
5.	Clemson	86-25-4	.765	15.	Fresno St.	80-34-1	.700
6.	Penn St.	89-27-2	.763	16.	Ohio St.	82-35-2	.697
7.	Georgia	88-27-4	.756	17.	Southern Meth.	63-28-1	.690
8.	Florida St.	87-28-3	.750	18.	Southern Cal	78-35-3	.685
	Michigan	89-29-2	.750	19.	Florida	76-37-3	.668
10.	Auburn	86-31-1	.733	20.	Arizona St.	73-36-4	.664

1970-79

Rank	Team	W-L-T	Pct.†	Rank	Team	W-L-T	Pct.†
1.	Oklahoma	102-13-3	.877	11.	Arizona St.	90-28-0	.763
2.	Alabama	103-16-1	.863	12.	Yale@	67-21-2	.756
3.	Michigan	96-16-3	.848	13.	San Diego St.	82-26-2	.755
4.	Tennessee St.*	85-17-2	.827	14.	Miami (Ohio)	80-26-2	.750
5.	Nebraska	98-20-4	.820	15.	Central Mich.#	80-27-3	.741
6.	Penn St.	96-22-0	.814	16.	Arkansas	79-31-5	.709
7.	Ohio St.	91-20-3	.811	17.	Houston	80-33-2	.704
8.	Notre Dame	91-22-0	.805	18.	Louisiana Tech#	77-34-2	.690
9.	Southern Cal	93-21-5	.803	19.	McNeese St.#	75-33-4	.688
10.	Texas	88-26-1	.770	20.	Dartmouth@	60-27-3	.683

1960-69

(By Percentage; Bowls and Playoffs Not Included)

Rank	Team	W-L-T	Pct.†	Rank	Team	W-L-T	Pct.†
1.	Alabama	85-12-3	.865	11.	Memphis	70-25-1	.734
2.	Texas	80-18-2	.810	12.	Arizona St.	72-26-1	.732
3.	Arkansas	80-19-1	.805	13.	LSU	70-25-5	.725
4.	Mississippi	72-20-6	.765		Nebraska	72-27-1	.725
5.	Bowling Green	71-22-2	.758	15.	Wyoming	69-26-4	.717
6.	Dartmouth@	68-22-0	.756	16.	Princeton@	64-26-0	.711
	Ohio St.	67-21-2	.756	17.	Utah St.	68-29-3	.695
8.	Missouri	72-22-6	.750	18.	Purdue	64-28-3	.689
	Southern Cal	73-23-4	.750	19.	Syracuse	68-31-0	.687
10.	Penn St.	73-26-0	.737	20.	Florida	66-30-4	.680
					Miami (Ohio)	66-30-4	.680
					Tennessee	65-29-6	.680

1950-59

Rank	Team	W-L-T	Pct.†	Rank	Team	W-L-T	Pct.†
1.	Oklahoma	93-10-2	.895	11.	Syracuse	62-29-2	.677
2.	Mississippi	80-21-5	.778	12.	Army	58-27-5	.672
3.	Michigan St.	70-21-1	.766	13.	Cincinnati	64-30-7	.668
4.	Princeton@	67-22-1	.750	14.	Notre Dame	64-31-4	.667
5.	Georgia Tech	79-26-6	.739	15.	Clemson	64-32-5	.658
6.	UCLA	68-26-3	.716	16.	Wisconsin	57-28-7	.658
7.	Ohio St.	63-24-5	.712	17.	Colorado	62-33-6	.644
8.	Tennessee	71-31-4	.692	18.	Duke	62-33-7	.642
9.	Penn St.	62-28-4	.681	19.	Navy	55-30-8	.634
10.	Maryland	67-31-3	.678	20.	Yale@	54-30-6	.633

†Ties computed as half won and half lost. *In I-A less than 8 years, now a member of I-AA. @Now a member of I-AA. #A member of I-A less than 8 years.

Winningest Teams of Last Five Years

(By Percentage and Wins; Bowls included)

PERCENTAGE

Team	W-L-T	*Pct.	Team	W-L-T	*Pct.
Nebraska	60-3-0	.952	Notre Dame	41-18-1	.692
Florida St.	54-6-1	.893	Syracuse	40-18-1	.686
Florida	55-8-1	.867	Nevada	39-18-0	.684
Penn St.	51-10-0	.836	Colorado St.	41-19-0	.683
Marshall	60-12-0	.833	Toledo	37-18-2	.667
Tennessee	50-11-0	.820	Washington	38-19-1	.664
Ohio St.	51-11-1	.817	Virginia	39-21-0	.650
Kansas St.	48-11-1	.808	Utah	38-21-0	.644
Auburn	46-12-1	.788	Wisconsin	37-20-4	.639
Colorado	44-14-1	.754	Southern Cal	37-21-2	.633
North Caro.	46-15-0	.754	West Va.	38-22-0	.633
Texas A&M	44-15-1	.742	Idaho	37-22-0	.627
Michigan	45-16-0	.738	Arizona	36-22-0	.621
Virginia Tech	44-16-0	.733	Wyoming	37-23-0	.617
Miami (Fla.)	41-17-0	.707	Arizona St.	35-22-0	.614
Brigham Young	43-19-0	.694	LSU	35-22-1	.612

BY VICTORIES

Team	Wins	Team	Wins
Nebraska	60	Notre Dame	41
Marshall	60	Syracuse	40
Florida	55	Nevada	39
Florida St.	54	Virginia	39
Ohio St.	51	Utah	38
Penn St.	51	Washington	38
Tennessee	50	West Va.	38
Kansas St.	48	Idaho	37
Auburn	46	Southern Cal	37
North Caro.	46	Toledo	37
Michigan	45	Wisconsin	37
Colorado	44	Wyoming	37
Texas A&M	44	Air Force	36
Virginia Tech	44	Arizona	36
Brigham Young	43	Clemson	36
Colorado St.	41	Oregon	36
Miami (Fla.)	41		

National Poll Rankings

National Champion Major Selectors (1869 to Present)

Selector	Selection Format	Active Seasons First	Last	Total	Predated Seasons	Total Rankings
Frank Dickinson	Math	1926	1940	15	1924-25	17
Deke Houlgate	Math	1927	1958	32	1885-1926	72
Dick Dunkel	Math	1929	1997	69		69
William Boand	Math	1930	1960	31	1919-29	42
Paul Williamson	Math	1932	1963	32		32
Parke Davis	Research	1933	1933	1	1869-1932	65
Edward Litkenhous	Math	1934	1984	51		51
Richard Poling	Math	1935	1984	50	1924-34	61
Associated Press	Poll	1936	1997	62		62
Helms Athletic Foundation	Poll	1941	1982	42	1883-1940	100
Harry DeVold	Math	1945	1997	53	1939-44	59
United Press International	Poll	1950	1995	44		44
International News Service	Poll	1952	1957	6		6
Football Writers Association	Poll	1954	1997	44		44
Football News	Poll	1958	1997	40		40
National Football Foundation	Poll	1959	1997	35		35
Billingsley	Math	1970	1997	28	1869-70, 1872-1969	128
Herman Matthews	Math	1966	1996	30		30
FACT	Math	1968	1997	30		30
Sporting News	Poll	1975	1997	23		23
Sagarin	Math	1978	1997	20	1938, 56-77	43
New York Times	Math	1979	1997	19		19
National Championship Foundation	Poll	1980	1997	18	1869-70, 1872-1979	128
College Football Researchers Association	Poll	1982	1992	11	1919-81	74
USA Today/CNN	Poll	1982	1996	15		15
Berryman	Math	1990	1997	8	1940-89	58
UPI/National Football Foundation	Poll	1991	1992	2		2
USA Today/National Football Foundation	Poll	1993	1994	2		2
Alderson	Math	1994	1997	4		4
USA Today/ESPN	Poll	1997	1997	1		1

POLL SYSTEMS HISTORY

Alderson System (1994-present), a mathematical rating system based strictly on a point value system reflecting competition as well as won-lost record. Developed by Bob Alderson of Muldrow, Oklahoma.

Associated Press (1936-present), the first major nationwide poll for ranking college football teams was voted on by sportswriters and broadcasters. It continues to this day and is probably the most well-known and widely circulated among all of history's polls. The Associated Press annual national champions were awarded the Williams Trophy and the Reverend J. Hugh O'Donnell Trophy. In 1947, Notre Dame retired the Williams Trophy (named after Henry L. Williams, Minnesota coach, and sponsored by the M Club of Minnesota). In 1956, Oklahoma retired the O'Donnell Trophy (named for Notre Dame's president and sponsored by Notre Dame alumni). Beginning with the 1957 season, the award was known as the AP Trophy, and since 1983 the award has been known as the Paul "Bear" Bryant Trophy.

Berryman (QPRS) (1990-present), a mathematical rating system based on a quality point rating formula developed by Clyde P. Berryman of Washington, D.C. Predated national champions from 1940-1989.

Billingsley Report (1970-present), a mathematically based power rating system developed by Richard Billingsley of Nashville, Tennessee. His work is published annually as the Billingsley Report through his own company, the College Football Research Center. In 1996, he finished his three-year research project ranking the national champions from 1869-95. The research is located on the World Wide Web at www.CFRC.com. Predated national champions from 1869-1970.

Boand System (1930-60), known as the Azzi Ratem System developed by William Boand of Tucson, Arizona. He moved to Chicago in 1932. Appeared in many newspapers as well as Illustrated Football Annual (1932-42) and weekly in Football News (1942-44, 1951-60). Predated national champions from 1919-29.

College Football Researchers Association (1982-92), founded by Anthony Cusher of Reeder, North Dakota, and Robert Kirlin of Spokane, Washington. Announced its champion in its monthly bulletin and No. 1 team determined by top-10 vote of membership on a point system. Predated national champions from 1919-81, conducted on a poll by Harry Carson Frye.

DeVold System (1945-present), a mathematical rating system developed by Harry DeVold from Minneapolis, Minnesota, a former football player at Cornell. He eventually settled in the Detroit, Michigan, area and worked in the real estate business. The ratings have appeared in The Football News since 1962. Predated national champions from 1939-44.

Dickinson System (1926-40), a mathematical point system devised by Frank Dickinson, a professor of economics at Illinois. The annual Dickinson ratings were emblematic of the national championship and the basis for awarding the Rissman National Trophy and the Knute K. Rockne Intercollegiate Memorial Trophy. Notre Dame gained permanent possession of the Rissman Trophy (named for Jack F. Rissman, a Chicago clothing manufacturer) after its third victory in 1930. Minnesota retired the Rockne Trophy (named in honor of the famous Notre Dame coach) after winning it for a third time in 1940.

Dunkel System (1929-present), a power index system devised by Dick Dunkel Sr. (1929-71); from 1972 by Dick Dunkel Jr. of the Daytona (Fla.) Beach News-Journal.

FACT (1968-present), a computerized mathematical ranking system developed by David Rothman of Hawthorne, California. FACT is the Foundation for the Analysis of Competitions and Tournaments, which began selecting a national champion in 1968. Rothman is a semiretired defense and aerospace statistician and was cochair of the Committee on Statistics in Sports and Competition of the American Statistical Association in the 1970s.

Football News (1958-present), weekly poll of its staff writers has named a national champion since 1958.

Football Writers Association of America (1954-present), the No. 1 team of the year is determined by a five-person panel representing the nation's football writers. The national championship team named receives the Grantland Rice Award.

Helms Athletic Foundation (1941-82), originally known by this name from 1936-69 and established by the founding sponsor, Paul H. Helms, Los Angeles sportsman and philanthropist. After Helms' death in 1957, United Savings & Loan Association became its benefactor during 1970-72. A merger of United Savings and Citizen Savings was completed in 1973, and the Athletic Foundation became known as Citizens Savings Athletic Foundation. In 1982, First Interstate Bank assumed sponsorship for its final rankings. In 1941, Bill Schroeder, managing director of the Helms Athletic Foundation, retroactively selected the national football champions for the period beginning in 1883 (the first year of a scoring system) through 1940. Thereafter, Schroeder, who died in 1988, then chose, with the assistance of a Hall Board, the annual national champion after the bowl games.

Houlgate System (1927-58), a mathematical rating system developed by Deke Houlgate of Los Angeles, California. His ratings were syndicated in newspapers and published in Illustrated Football and the Football Thesaurus (1946-58).

International News Service (1952-57), a poll conducted for six years by members of the International News Service (INS) before merger with United Press in 1958.

Litkenhous (1934-84), a difference-by-score formula developed by Edward E. Litkenhous, a professor of chemical engineering at Vanderbilt, and his brother, Frank.

Matthews Grid Ratings (1966-96), a mathematical rating system developed by college mathematics professor Herman Matthews of Middlesboro, Kentucky. Has appeared in newspapers and The Football News.

National Championship Foundation (1980-present), established by Mike Riter of Germantown, New York. Issues annual report. Predated national champions from 1869-1979.

National Football Foundation (1959-present), the National Football Foundation and Hall of Fame named its first national champion in 1959. Headquartered in Larchmont, New York, the present National Football Foundation was established in 1947 to promote amateur athletics in America. The national champion was awarded the MacArthur Bowl from 1959-90. In 1991 and 1992, the NFF/HOF joined with UPI to award the MacArthur Bowl, and in 1993 the NFF/HOF joined with USA Today to award the MacArthur Bowl.

New York Times (1979-present), a mathematical rating system introduced by this major newspaper.

Parke Davis (1933), a noted college football historian and former Princeton lineman, Parke H. Davis went back and named the championship teams from 1869 through the 1932 season. He also named a national champion at the conclusion of the 1933 season. Interestingly, the years 1869-75 were identified by Davis as the Pioneer Period; the years 1876-93 were called the Period of the American Intercollegiate Football Association, and the years 1894-1933 were referred to as the Period of Rules Committees and Conferences. He also coached at Wisconsin, Amherst and Lafayette.

Poling System (1935-84), a mathematical rating system for college football teams developed by Richard Poling from Mansfield, Ohio, a former football player at Ohio Wesleyan. Poling's football ratings were published annually in the Football Review Supplement and in various newspapers. Predated national champions from 1924-34.

Sagarin Ratings (1978-present), a mathematical rating system developed by Jeff Sagarin of Bloomington, Indiana, a 1970 MIT mathematics graduate. Runs annually in USA Today newspaper. Predated national champions from 1938 and 1956-1977.

Sporting News (1975-present), voted on annually by the staff of this St. Louis-based nationally circulated sports publication.

United Press International (1950-90, 1993-95), in 1950, the United Press news service began its poll of football coaches (replaced as coaches' poll after 1990 season). When the United Press merged with the International News Service in 1958, it became known as United Press International. The weekly UPI rankings were featured in newspapers and on radio and television nationwide. UPI and the National Football Foundation formed a coalition for 1991 and 1992 to name the MacArthur Bowl national champion. Returned to single poll in 1994-95.

USA Today/Cable News Network and ESPN (1982-1996;1997), introduced a weekly poll of sportswriters in 1982 and ranked the top 25 teams in the nation with a point system. The poll results were featured in USA Today, a national newspaper, and on the Cable News Network, a national cable television network. Took over as the coaches' poll in 1991. USA Today also formed a coalition with the National Football Foundation in 1993 to name the MacArthur Bowl national champion. Combined with ESPN in 1997 to distribute the coaches' poll nationally.

Williamson System (1932-63), a power rating system chosen by Paul Williamson of New Orleans, Louisiana, a geologist and member of the Sugar Bowl committee.

Thanks from the NCAA Statistics Service to Robert A. Rosiek of Dearborn, Michigan, who researched much of the former polls' history, and to Tex Noel of Bedford, Indiana, who provided information about Parke H. Davis.

National Poll Champions

Over the last 128 years, there have been nearly 30 selectors of national champions using polls, historical research and mathematical rating systems. Beginning in 1936, The Associated Press began the best-known and most widely circulated poll of sportswriters and broadcasters. Before 1936, national champions were determined by historical research and retroactive ratings and polls.

*Note: * indicates selectors that chose multiple schools. The national champion was selected before bowl games as follows: AP (1936-64 and 1966-67); UP-UPI (1950-73); FWAA (1954); NFF-HOF (1959-70). In all other latter-day polls, champions were selected after bowl games.*

1869
Princeton: Billingsley, National Championship Foundation, Parke Davis*
Rutgers: Parke Davis*

1870
Princeton: Billingsley, National Championship Foundation, Parke Davis

1871
No national champions selected.

1872
Princeton: Billingsley, National Championship Foundation, Parke Davis*
Yale: Parke Davis*

1873
Princeton: Billingsley, National Championship Foundation, Parke Davis

1874
Harvard: Parke Davis*
Princeton: Billingsley, Parke Davis*
Yale: National Championship Foundation, Parke Davis*

1875
Colgate: Parke Davis*
Harvard: National Championship Foundation, Parke Davis*
Princeton: Billingsley, Parke Davis*

1876
Yale: Billingsley, National Championship Foundation, Parke Davis

1877
Princeton: Parke Davis*
Yale: Billingsley, National Championship Foundation, Parke Davis*

1878
Princeton: Billingsley, National Championship Foundation, Parke Davis

1879
Princeton: Billingsley, National Championship Foundation, Parke Davis*
Yale: Parke Davis*

1880
Princeton: National Championship Foundation*, Parke Davis*
Yale: Billingsley, National Championship Foundation*, Parke Davis*

1881
Princeton: Billingsley, Parke Davis*
Yale: National Championship Foundation, Parke Davis*

1882
Yale: Billingsley, National Championship Foundation, Parke Davis

1883
Yale: Billingsley, Helms, National Championship Foundation, Parke Davis

1884
Princeton: Parke Davis*
Yale: Billingsley, Helms, National Championship Foundation, Parke Davis*

1885
Princeton: Billingsley, Helms, Houlgate, National Championship Foundation, Parke Davis

1886
Princeton: Parke Davis*
Yale: Billingsley, Helms, National Championship Foundation, Parke Davis*

1887
Yale: Billingsley, Helms, Houlgate, National Championship Foundation, Parke Davis

1888
Yale: Billingsley, Helms, Houlgate, National Championship Foundation, Parke Davis

1889
Princeton: Billingsley, Helms, Houlgate, National Championship Foundation, Parke Davis

1890
Harvard: Billingsley, Helms, Houlgate, National Championship Foundation, Parke Davis

1891
Yale: Billingsley, Helms, Houlgate, National Championship Foundation, Parke Davis

1892
Yale: Billingsley, Helms, Houlgate, National Championship Foundation, Parke Davis

1893
Princeton: Billingsley, Helms, Houlgate, National Championship Foundation
Yale: Parke Davis

1894
Pennsylvania: Parke Davis*
Princeton: Houlgate
Yale: Billingsley, Helms, National Championship Foundation, Parke Davis*

1895
Pennsylvania: Billingsley, Helms, Houlgate, National Championship Foundation, Parke Davis*
Yale: Parke Davis*

1896
Lafayette: National Championship Foundation*, Parke Davis*
Princeton: Billingsley, Helms, Houlgate, National Championship Foundation*, Parke Davis*

1897
Pennsylvania: Billingsley, Helms, Houlgate, National Championship Foundation, Parke Davis*
Yale: Parke Davis*

1898
Harvard: Billingsley, Helms, Houlgate, National Championship Foundation
Princeton: Parke Davis

1899
Harvard: Billingsley, Helms, Houlgate, National Championship Foundation
Princeton: Parke Davis

1900
Yale: Billingsley, Helms, Houlgate, National Championship Foundation, Parke Davis

1901
Michigan: Billingsley, Helms, Houlgate, National Championship Foundation
Yale: Parke Davis

1902
Michigan: Billingsley, Helms, Houlgate, National Championship Foundation, Parke Davis*
Yale: Parke Davis*

1903
Michigan: Billingsley, National Championship Foundation*
Princeton: Helms, Houlgate, National Championship Foundation*, Parke Davis

1904
Michigan: Billingsley, National Championship Foundation*
Pennsylvania: Helms, Houlgate, National Championship Foundation*, Parke Davis

1905
Chicago: Billingsley, Helms, Houlgate, National Championship Foundation
Yale: Parke Davis

1906
Princeton: Helms, National Championship Foundation
Vanderbilt: Billingsley
Yale: Parke Davis

1907
Pennsylvania: Billingsley
Yale: Helms, Houlgate, National Championship Foundation, Parke Davis

1908
LSU: National Championship Foundation*
Pennsylvania: Billingsley, Helms, Houlgate, National Championship Foundation*, Parke Davis

1909
Yale: Billingsley, Helms, Houlgate, National Championship Foundation, Parke Davis

1910
Auburn: Billingsley
Harvard: Helms, Houlgate, National Championship Foundation*
Pittsburgh: National Championship Foundation*

1911
Penn St.: National Championship Foundation*
Princeton: Helms, Houlgate, National Championship Foundation*, Parke Davis
Vanderbilt: Billingsley

1912
Harvard: Helms, Houlgate, National Championship Foundation*, Parke Davis
Penn St.: National Championship Foundation*
Wisconsin: Billingsley

1913
Chicago: Billingsley, Parke Davis*
Harvard: Helms, Houlgate, National Championship Foundation, Parke Davis*

1914
Army: Helms, Houlgate, National Championship Foundation, Parke Davis*
Illinois: Billingsley, Parke Davis*

1915
Cornell: Helms, Houlgate, National Championship Foundation, Parke Davis*
Nebraska: Billingsley
Pittsburgh: Parke Davis*

1916
Army: Parke Davis*
Pittsburgh: Billingsley, Helms, Houlgate, National Championship Foundation, Parke Davis*

1917
Georgia Tech: Billingsley, Helms, Houlgate, National Championship Foundation

1918
Michigan: Billingsley, National Championship Foundation*
Pittsburgh: Helms, Houlgate, National Championship Foundation*

1919
Harvard: Football Research*, Helms, Houlgate, National Championship Foundation*, Parke Davis*
Illinois: Billingsley, Boand, Football Research*, Parke Davis*
Notre Dame: National Championship Foundation*, Parke Davis*
Texas A&M: National Championship Foundation*

1920
California: Billingsley, Football Research, Helms, Houlgate, National Championship Foundation
Harvard: Boand*
Notre Dame: Parke Davis*
Princeton: Boand*, Parke Davis*

1921
California: Boand*, Football Research
Cornell: Helms, Houlgate, National Championship Foundation, Parke Davis*
Iowa: Billingsley, Parke Davis*
Lafayette: Boand*, Parke Davis*
Wash. & Jeff.: Boand*

1922
California: Houlgate, National Championship Foundation*
Cornell: Helms, Parke Davis*
Iowa: Billingsley
Princeton: Boand, Football Research, National Championship Foundation*, Parke Davis*

1923
California: Houlgate
Illinois: Boand, Football Research, Helms, National Championship Foundation*, Parke Davis
Michigan: Billingsley, National Championship Foundation*

1924
Notre Dame: Billingsley, Boand, Dickinson, Football Research, Helms, Houlgate, National Championship Foundation, Poling
Pennsylvania: Parke Davis

1925
Alabama: Billingsley, Boand, Football Research, Helms, Houlgate, National Championship Foundation, Poling
Dartmouth: Dickinson, Parke Davis

1926
Alabama: Billingsley, Football Research, Helms*, National Championship Foundation*, Poling
Lafayette: Parke Davis
Navy: Boand, Houlgate
Stanford: Dickinson, Helms*, National Championship Foundation*

1927
Georgia: Boand, Poling
Illinois: Billingsley, Dickinson, Helms, National Championship Foundation, Parke Davis
Notre Dame: Houlgate
Yale: Football Research

1928
Detroit: Parke Davis*
Georgia Tech: Billingsley, Boand, Football Research, Helms, Houlgate, National Championship Foundation, Parke Davis*, Poling
Southern Cal: Dickinson

1929
Notre Dame: Billingsley, Boand, Dickinson, Dunkel, Football Research, Helms, National Championship Foundation, Poling
Pittsburgh: Parke Davis
Southern Cal: Houlgate

1930
Alabama: Football Research, Parke Davis*
Notre Dame: Billingsley, Boand, Dickinson, Dunkel, Helms, Houlgate, National Championship Foundation, Parke Davis*, Poling

1931
Pittsburgh: Parke Davis*
Purdue: Parke Davis*
Southern Cal: Billingsley, Boand, Dickinson, Dunkel, Helms, Houlgate, Football Research, National Championship Foundation, Poling, Williamson

1932
Colgate: Parke Davis*
Michigan: Dickinson, Parke Davis*
Southern Cal: Billingsley, Boand, Dunkel, Football Research, Helms, Houlgate, National Championship Foundation, Parke Davis*, Poling, Williamson

1933
Michigan: Billingsley, Boand, Dickinson, Helms, Houlgate, Football Research, National Championship Foundation, Parke Davis*, Poling
Ohio St.: Dunkel
Princeton: Parke Davis*
Southern Cal: Williamson

1934
Alabama: Billingsley, Dunkel, Houlgate, Poling, Williamson
Minnesota: Boand, Dickinson, Football Research, Helms, Litkenhous, National Championship Foundation

1935
LSU: Williamson*
Minnesota: Billingsley, Boand, Football Research, Helms, Litkenhous, National Championship Foundation, Poling
Princeton: Dunkel
Southern Methodist: Dickinson, Houlgate
Texas Christian: Williamson*

1936
LSU: Williamson
Minnesota: AP, Billingsley, Dickinson, Dunkel, Helms, Litkenhous, National Championship Foundation, Poling
Pittsburgh: Boand, Football Research, Houlgate

1937
California: Dunkel, Helms
Pittsburgh: AP, Billingsley, Boand, Dickinson, Football Research, Houlgate, Litkenhous, National Championship Foundation, Poling, Williamson

1938
Notre Dame: Dickinson
Tennessee: Billingsley, Boand, Dunkel, Football Research, Houlgate, Litkenhous, Poling, Sagarin
Texas Christian: AP, Helms, National Championship Foundation, Williamson

1939
Cornell: Litkenhous
Southern Cal: Dickinson
Texas A&M: AP, Billingsley, Boand, DeVold, Dunkel, Football Research, Helms, Houlgate, National Championship Foundation, Poling, Williamson

1940
Minnesota: AP, Berryman, Billingsley, Boand, DeVold, Dickinson, Football Research, Houlgate, Litkenhous, National Championship Foundation
Stanford: Helms, Poling
Tennessee: Dunkel, Williamson

1941
Alabama: Houlgate
Minnesota: AP, Billingsley, Boand, DeVold, Dunkel, Football Research, Helms, Litkenhous, National Championship Foundation, Poling
Texas: Berryman, Williamson

1942
Georgia: Berryman, DeVold, Houlgate, Litkenhous, Poling, Williamson
Ohio St.: AP, Billingsley, Boand, Dunkel, Football Research, National Championship Foundation
Wisconsin: Helms

1943
Notre Dame: AP, Berryman, Billingsley, Boand, DeVold, Dunkel, Football Research, Helms, Houlgate, Litkenhous, National Championship Foundation, Poling, Williamson

1944
Army: AP, Berryman, Billingsley, Boand, DeVold, Dunkel, Football Research, Helms, Houlgate, Litkenhous, National Championship Foundation*, Poling, Williamson
Ohio St.: National Championship Foundation*

1945
Alabama: National Championship Foundation*
Army: AP, Berryman, Billingsley, Boand, DeVold, Dunkel, Football Research, Helms, Houlgate, Litkenhous, National Championship Foundation*, Poling, Williamson

1946
Army: Boand*, Football Research, Helms*, Houlgate, Poling*
Georgia: Williamson
Notre Dame: AP, Berryman, Billingsley, Boand*, DeVold, Dunkel, Helms*, Litkenhous, National Championship Foundation, Poling*

1947
Michigan: Berryman, Billingsley, Boand, DeVold, Dunkel, Football Research, Helms*, Houlgate, Litkenhous, National Championship Foundation, Poling
Notre Dame: AP, Helms*, Williamson

1948
Michigan: AP, Berryman, Billingsley, Boand, DeVold, Dunkel, Football Research, Helms, Houlgate, Litkenhous, National Championship Foundation, Poling, Williamson

1949
Notre Dame: AP, Berryman, Boand, DeVold, Dunkel, Helms, Houlgate, Litkenhous, National Championship Foundation, Poling, Williamson
Oklahoma: Billingsley, Football Research

1950
Oklahoma: AP, Berryman, Helms, Litkenhous, UPI, Williamson
Princeton: Boand, Poling
Tennessee: Billingsley, DeVold, Dunkel, Football Research, National Championship Foundation

1951
Georgia Tech: Berryman, Boand*
Illinois: Boand*
Maryland: Billingsley, DeVold, Dunkel, Football Research, National Championship Foundation
Michigan St.: Helms, Poling
Tennessee: AP, Litkenhous, UPI, Williamson

1952
Georgia Tech: Berryman, INS, Poling
Michigan St.: AP, Billingsley, Boand, DeVold, Dunkel, Football Research, Helms, Litkenhous, National Championship Foundation, UPI, Williamson

1953
Maryland: AP, INS, UPI
Notre Dame: Billingsley, Boand, DeVold, Dunkel, Helms, Litkenhous, National Championship Foundation, Poling, Williamson
Oklahoma: Berryman, Football Research

1954
Ohio St.: AP, Berryman, Boand, DeVold, Football Research*, Helms*, INS, National Championship Foundation*, Poling, Williamson
UCLA: Billingsley, Dunkel, Football Research*, FW, Helms*, Litkenhous, National Championship Foundation*, UPI

1955
Michigan St.: Boand
Oklahoma: AP, Berryman, Billingsley, DeVold, Dunkel, Football Research, FW, Helms, INS, Litkenhous, National Championship Foundation, Poling, UPI, Williamson

1956
Georgia Tech: Berryman
Iowa: Football Research
Oklahoma: AP, Billingsley, Boand, DeVold, Dunkel, FW, Helms, INS, Litkenhous, National Championship Foundation, Sagarin, UPI, Williamson

1957
Auburn: AP, Football Research, Helms, National Championship Foundation, Poling, Williamson
Michigan St.: Billingsley, Dunkel, Sagarin
Ohio St.: Boand, DeVold, FW, INS, Litkenhous, UPI
Oklahoma: Berryman

1958
Iowa: FW, Sagarin
LSU: AP, Berryman, Billingsley, Boand, DeVold, Dunkel, FB News, Football Research, Helms, Litkenhous, National Championship Foundation, Poling, UPI, Williamson

1959
Mississippi: Berryman, Billingsley, Dunkel, Sagarin
Syracuse: AP, Boand, DeVold, FB News, Football Research, FW, Helms, Litkenhous, National Championship Foundation, NFF, Poling, UPI, Williamson

1960
Iowa: Berryman, Billingsley, Boand, Litkenhous, Sagarin
Minnesota: AP, FB News, NFF, UPI
Mississippi: DeVold, Dunkel, Football Research, FW, National Championship Foundation, Williamson
Missouri: Poling
Washington: Helms

1961
Alabama: AP, Berryman, Billingsley, DeVold, Dunkel, FB News, Football Research, Helms, Litkenhous, National Championship Foundation, NFF, UPI, Williamson
Ohio St.: FW, Poling
Texas: Sagarin

1962
Alabama: Billingsley, Sagarin
LSU: Berryman*
Southern Cal: AP, Berryman*, DeVold, Dunkel, FB News, Football Research, FW, Helms, National Championship Foundation, NFF, Poling, UPI, Williamson
Mississippi: Litkenhous

1963
Texas: AP, Berryman, Billingsley, DeVold, Dunkel, FB News, Football Research, FW, Helms, Litkenhous, National Championship Foundation, NFF, Poling, Sagarin, UPI, Williamson

1964
Alabama: AP, Berryman, Litkenhous, UPI
Arkansas: Billingsley, Football Research, FW, Helms, National Championship Foundation, Poling
Michigan: Dunkel
Notre Dame: DeVold, FB News, NFF, Sagarin

1965
Alabama: AP, Billingsley, Football Research, FW*, National Championship Foundation
Michigan St.: Berryman, DeVold, Dunkel, FB News, FW*, Helms, Litkenhous, NFF, Poling, Sagarin, UPI

1966
Alabama: Berryman
Michigan St.: Football Research, Helms*, NFF*, Poling*
Notre Dame: AP, Billingsley, DeVold, Dunkel, FB News, FW, Helms*, Litkenhous, Matthews, National Championship Foundation, NFF*, Poling*, Sagarin, UPI

1967
Notre Dame: Dunkel
Oklahoma: Poling
Southern Cal: AP, Berryman, Billingsley, DeVold, FB News, Football Research, FW, Helms, Matthews, National Championship Foundation, NFF, Sagarin, UPI
Tennessee: Litkenhous

1968
Georgia: Litkenhous
Ohio St.: AP, Berryman, Billingsley, Dunkel, FACT, FB News, Football Research, FW, Helms, National Championship Foundation, NFF, Poling, UPI
Texas: DeVold, Matthews, Sagarin

1969
Ohio St.: Matthews
Penn St.: FACT*
Texas: AP, Berryman, Billingsley, DeVold, Dunkel, FACT*, FB News, Football Research, FW, Helms, Litkenhous, National Championship Foundation, NFF, Poling, Sagarin, UPI

1970
Arizona St.: Poling
Nebraska: AP, Billingsley, DeVold, Dunkel, FACT*, FB News, Football Research, FW, Helms, National Championship Foundation
Notre Dame: FACT*, Matthews, Sagarin
Ohio St.: NFF*
Texas: Berryman, FACT*, Litkenhous, NFF*, UPI

1971
Nebraska: AP, Berryman, Billingsley, DeVold, Dunkel, FACT, FB News, Football Research, FW, Helms, Litkenhous, Matthews, National Championship Foundation, NFF, Poling, Sagarin, UPI

1972
Southern Cal: AP, Berryman, Billingsley, DeVold, Dunkel, FACT, FB News, Football Research, FW, Helms, Litkenhous, Matthews, National Championship Foundation, NFF, Poling, Sagarin, UPI

1973
Alabama: Berryman, UPI
Michigan: National Championship Foundation*, Poling*
Notre Dame: AP, FB News, FW, Helms, National Championship Foundation*, NFF
Ohio St.: FACT, National Championship Foundation*, Poling*, Sagarin
Oklahoma: Billingsley, DeVold, Dunkel, Football Research

1974
Ohio St.: Matthews
Oklahoma: AP, Berryman, Billingsley, DeVold, Dunkel, FACT, FB News, Football Research, Helms*, Litkenhous, National Championship Foundation*, Poling, Sagarin
Southern Cal: FW, Helms*, National Championship Foundation*, NFF, UPI

1975
Alabama: Matthews*
Arizona St.: National Championship Foundation*, Sporting News
Ohio St.: Berryman, FACT*, Helms*, Matthews*, Poling
Oklahoma: AP, Billingsley, DeVold, Dunkel, FACT*, FB News, Football Research, FW, Helms*, National Championship Foundation*, NFF, Sagarin, UPI

1976
Pittsburgh: AP, FACT, FB News, FW, Helms, National Championship Foundation, NFF, Poling, Sagarin, Sporting News, UPI
Southern Cal: Berryman, Billingsley, DeVold, Dunkel, Football Research, Matthews

1977
Alabama: Football Research*
Arkansas: FACT*
Notre Dame: AP, Billingsley, DeVold, Dunkel, FACT*, FB News, Football Research*, FW, Helms, Matthews, National Championship Foundation, NFF, Poling, Sagarin, Sporting News, UPI
Texas: Berryman, FACT*

1978
Alabama: AP, FACT*, Football Research, FW, Helms*, National Championship Foundation*, NFF
Oklahoma: Billingsley, DeVold, Dunkel, FACT*, Helms*, Litkenhous, Matthews, Poling, Sagarin
Southern Cal: Berryman, FACT*, FB News, Helms*, National Championship Foundation*, Sporting News, UPI

1979
Alabama: AP, Berryman, Billingsley, DeVold, Dunkel, FACT, FB News, FW, Helms, Matthews, National Championship Foundation, NFF, NY Times, Poling, Sagarin, Sporting News, UPI
Southern Cal: Football Research

1980
Florida St.: FACT*
Georgia: AP, Berryman, FACT*, FB News, FW, Helms, National Championship Foundation, NFF, Poling, Sporting News, UPI
Nebraska: FACT*, Sagarin
Oklahoma: Billingsley, Dunkel, Matthews
Pittsburgh: DeVold, FACT*, Football Research, NY Times

1981
Clemson: AP, Berryman, Billingsley, DeVold, FACT, FB News, Football Research, FW, Helms, Litkenhous, Matthews, National Championship Foundation*, NFF, NY Times, Poling, Sporting News, UPI
Nebraska: National Championship Foundation*
Penn St.: Dunkel, Sagarin
Pittsburgh: National Championship Foundation*
Texas: National Championship Foundation*
Southern Methodist: National Championship Foundation*

1982
Nebraska: Berryman
Penn St.: AP, Billingsley, DeVold, Dunkel, FACT, FB News, Football Research, FW, Helms*, Litkenhous, Matthews, National Championship Foundation, NFF, NY Times, Poling, Sagarin, Sporting News, UPI, USA/CNN
Southern Methodist: Helms*

1983
Auburn: FACT*, Football Research, NY Times
Miami (Fla.): AP, Billingsley, Dunkel, FB News, FW, National Championship Foundation, NFF, Sporting News, UPI, USA/CNN
Nebraska: Berryman, DeVold, FACT*, Litkenhous, Matthews, Poling, Sagarin

1984
Brigham Young: AP, Football Research, FW, National Championship Foundation*, NFF, Poling, UPI, USA/CNN
Florida: Billingsley, DeVold, Dunkel, FACT, Matthews, NY Times, Sagarin, Sporting News
Nebraska: Litkenhous
Washington: Berryman, FB News, National Championship Foundation*

1985
Michigan: Matthews, Sagarin
Oklahoma: AP, Berryman, Billingsley, DeVold, Dunkel, FACT, FB News, Football Research, FW, National Championship Foundation, NFF, NY Times, Sporting News, UPI, USA/CNN

1986
Miami (Fla.): FACT*
Oklahoma: Berryman, Billingsley, DeVold, Dunkel, Football Research, NY Times, Sagarin
Penn St.: AP, FACT*, FB News, FW, Matthews, National Championship Foundation, NFF, Sporting News, UPI, USA/CNN

1987
Florida St.: Berryman, Sagarin
Miami (Fla.): AP, Billingsley, DeVold, Dunkel, FACT, FB News, Football Research, FW, Matthews, National Championship Foundation, NFF, NY Times, Sporting News, UPI, USA/CNN

1988
Miami (Fla.): Berryman, Sagarin
Notre Dame: AP, Billingsley, DeVold, Dunkel, FACT, FB News, Football Research, FW, Matthews, National Championship Foundation, NFF, NY Times, Sporting News, UPI, USA/CNN

1989
Florida St.: Billingsley
Miami (Fla.): AP, DeVold, Dunkel, FACT*, FB News, Football Research, FW, Matthews, National Championship Foundation, NFF, NY Times, Sporting News, UPI, USA/CNN
Notre Dame: Berryman, FACT*, Sagarin

1990
Colorado: AP, Berryman, DeVold, FACT*, FB News, Football Research, FW, Matthews, National Championship Foundation*, NFF, Sporting News, USA/CNN
Georgia Tech: Dunkel, FACT*, National Championship Foundation*, UPI
Miami (Fla.): Billingsley, FACT*, NY Times, Sagarin
Washington: FACT*

1991
Miami (Fla.): AP, Football Research, National Championship Foundation*, NY Times, Sporting News
Washington: Berryman, Billingsley, DeVold, Dunkel, FACT, FB News, FW, Matthews, National Championship Foundation*, Sagarin, UPI/NFF, USA/CNN

1992
Alabama: AP, Berryman, Billingsley, DeVold, Dunkel, FACT, FB News, Football Research, FW, Matthews, National Championship Foundation, NY Times, Sporting News, UPI/NFF, USA/CNN
Florida St.: Sagarin

1993
Auburn: National Championship Foundation*
Florida St.: AP, Berryman, Billingsley, DeVold, Dunkel, FACT, FB News, FW, National Championship Foundation*, NY Times, Sagarin, Sporting News, UPI, USA/CNN, USA/NFF
Nebraska: National Championship Foundation*
Notre Dame: Matthews, National Championship Foundation*

1994

Florida St.: Dunkel

Nebraska: Alderson, AP, Berryman, FACT*, FB News, FW, National Championship Foundation*, Sporting News, UPI, USA/CNN, USA/NFF

Penn St.: Billingsley, DeVold, FACT*, Matthews, National Championship Foundation*, NY Times, Sagarin

1995

Nebraska: Alderson, AP, Berryman, Billingsley, DeVold, Dunkel, FACT, FB News, FW, Matthews, National Championship Foundation, NFF, NY Times, Sagarin, Sporting News, UPI, USA/CNN

1996

Florida: AP, Berryman, Billingsley, FACT, FB News, FW, NFF, Sagarin, Sporting News, USA/CNN, NY Times, National Championship Foundation, Dunkel, Matthews, DeVold

Florida St.: Alderson

1997

Michigan: AP, FB News, FW, National Championship Foundation*, NFF, Sporting News

Nebraska: Alderson, Berryman, Billingsley, DeVold, Dunkel, FACT, National Championship Foundation*, NY Times, Sagarin, USA/ESPN

(**Legend of Present Major Selectors:** Associated Press (AP) from 1936-present; Football Writers Association of America (FW) from 1954-present; National Football Foundation and Hall of Fame (NFF) from 1959-90 and 1995 to present; USA Today/Cable News Network (USA/CNN) from 1982-96; USA Today/ESPN (USA/ESPN) from 1997-present; USA Today/National Football Foundation and Hall of Fame (USA/NFF) from 1993-94 to present. The Associated Press has been the designated media poll since 1936. United Press International served as the coaches' poll from 1950 to 1991 when it was taken over by USA Today/Cable News Network and in 1997 became USA Today/ESPN. In 1991-92, the No. 1 team in the final UPI/NFF ratings received the MacArthur Bowl as the national champion by the NFF. In 1993-94 and again in 1996, the No. 1 team in the USA Today/NFF final poll received the MacArthur Bowl.)

Major Selectors Since 1936

Year	ASSOCIATED PRESS Team	Record	NATIONAL FOOTBALL FOUNDATION AND COLLEGE FOOTBALL HALL OF FAME(MacArthur Bowl) Team	Record	UNITED PRESS Team	Record	FOOTBALL WRITERS' Team	Record	USA TODAY/ESPN Team	Record
1936	Minnesota	7-1-0								
1937	Pittsburgh	9-0-1								
1938	Texas Christian	11-0-0								
1939	Texas A&M	11-0-0								
1940	Minnesota	8-0-0								
1941	Minnesota	8-0-0								
1942	Ohio St.	9-1-0								
1943	Notre Dame	9-1-0								
1944	Army	9-0-0								
1945	Army	9-0-0								
1946	Notre Dame	8-0-1								
1947	Notre Dame	9-0-0								
1948	Michigan	9-0-0								
1949	Notre Dame	10-0-0								
1950	Oklahoma	10-1-0			Oklahoma	10-1-0				
1951	Tennessee	10-0-0			Tennessee	10-0-0				
1952	Michigan St.	9-0-0			Michigan St.	9-0-0				
1953	Maryland	10-1-0			Maryland	10-1-0				
1954	Ohio St.	10-0-0			UCLA	9-0-0	UCLA	9-0-0		
1955	Oklahoma	11-0-0			Oklahoma	11-0-0	Oklahoma	11-0-0		
1956	Oklahoma	10-0-0			Oklahoma	10-0-0	Oklahoma	10-0-0		
1957	Auburn	10-0-0			Ohio St.	9-1-0	Ohio St.	9-1-0		
1958	LSU	11-0-0			LSU	11-0-0	Iowa	8-1-1		
1959	Syracuse	11-0-0	Syracuse	11-0-0	Syracuse	11-0-0	Syracuse	11-0-0		
1960	Minnesota	8-2-0	Minnesota	8-2-0	Minnesota	8-2-0	Mississippi	10-0-1		
1961	Alabama	11-0-0	Alabama	11-0-0	Alabama	11-0-0	Ohio St.	8-0-1		
1962	Southern Cal	11-0-0	Southern Cal	11-0-0	Southern Cal	11-0-0	Southern Cal	11-0-0		
1963	Texas	11-0-0	Texas	11-0-0	Texas	11-0-0	Texas	11-0-0		
1964	Alabama	10-1-0	Notre Dame	9-1-0	Alabama	10-1-0	Arkansas	11-0-0		
1965	Alabama	9-1-1	Michigan St.	10-1-0	Michigan St.	10-1-0	Alabama Michigan St.	9-1-1 10-1-0		
1966	Notre Dame	9-0-1	Michigan St. 9-0-1/Notre Dame 9-0-1		Notre Dame	9-0-1	Notre Dame	9-0-1		
1967	Southern Cal	10-1-0	Southern Cal	10-1-0	Southern Cal	10-1-0	Southern Cal	10-1-0		
1968	Ohio St.	10-0-0	Ohio St.	10-0-0	Ohio St.	10-0-0	Ohio St.	10-0-0		
1969	Texas	11-0-0	Texas	11-0-0	Texas	11-0-0	Texas	11-0-0		
1970	Nebraska	11-0-1	Ohio St. 10-1-0/Texas	10-1-0	Texas	10-1-0	Nebraska	11-0-1		
1971	Nebraska	13-0-0	Nebraska	13-0-0	Nebraska	13-0-0	Nebraska	13-0-0		
1972	Southern Cal	12-0-0	Southern Cal	12-0-0	Southern Cal	12-0-0	Southern Cal	12-0-0		
1973	Notre Dame	11-0-0	Notre Dame	11-0-0	Alabama	11-1-0	Notre Dame	11-0-0		
1974	Oklahoma	11-0-0	Southern Cal	10-1-1	Southern Cal	10-1-1	Southern Cal	10-1-1		
1975	Oklahoma	11-1-0	Oklahoma	11-1-0	Oklahoma	11-1-0	Oklahoma	11-1-0		
1976	Pittsburgh	12-0-0	Pittsburgh	12-0-0	Pittsburgh	12-0-0	Pittsburgh	12-0-0		
1977	Notre Dame	11-1-0	Notre Dame	11-1-0	Notre Dame	11-1-0	Notre Dame	11-1-0		
1978	Alabama	12-1-0	Alabama	11-1-0	Southern Cal	12-1-0	Alabama	11-1-0		
1979	Alabama	12-0-0	Alabama	12-0-0	Alabama	12-0-0	Alabama	12-0-0		
1980	Georgia	12-0-0	Georgia	12-0-0	Georgia	12-0-0	Georgia	12-0-0		
1981	Clemson	12-0-0	Clemson	12-0-0	Clemson	12-0-0	Clemson	12-0-0		
1982	Penn St.	11-1-0	Penn St.	11-1-0	Penn St.	11-1-0	Penn St.	11-1-0	Penn St.	11-1-0
1983	Miami (Fla.)	11-1-0	Miami (Fla.)	11-1-0	Miami (Fla.)	11-1-0	Miami (Fla.)	11-1-0	Miami (Fla.) (CNN)	11-1-0
1984	Brigham Young	13-0-0	Brigham Young	13-0-0	Brigham Young	13-0-0	Brigham Young	13-0-0	Brigham Young (CNN)	13-0-0
1985	Oklahoma	11-1-0	Oklahoma	11-1-0	Oklahoma	11-1-0	Oklahoma	11-1-0	Oklahoma (CNN)	11-1-0
1986	Penn St.	12-0-0	Penn St.	12-0-0	Penn St.	12-0-0	Penn St.	12-0-0	Penn St. (CNN)	12-0-0
1987	Miami (Fla.)	12-0-0	Miami (Fla.)	12-0-0	Miami (Fla.)	12-0-0	Miami (Fla.)	12-0-0	Miami (Fla.) (CNN)	12-0-0
1988	Notre Dame	12-0-0	Notre Dame	12-0-0	Notre Dame	12-0-0	Notre Dame	12-0-0	Notre Dame (CNN)	12-0-0
1989	Miami (Fla.)	11-1-0	Miami (Fla.)	11-1-0	Miami (Fla.)	11-1-0	Miami (Fla.)	11-1-0	Miami (Fla.) (CNN)	11-1-0
1990	Colorado	11-1-1	Colorado	11-1-1	Georgia Tech	11-0-1	Colorado	11-1-1	Colorado (CNN)	11-1-1
1991	Miami (Fla.)	12-0-0	Wash. (UPI/NFF)	12-0-0	Washington	12-0-0	Washington	12-0-0	Washington (CNN)	12-0-0
1992	Alabama	13-0-0	Alabama (UPI/NFF)	13-0-0	Alabama	13-0-0	Alabama	13-0-0	Alabama (CNN)	13-0-0
1993	Florida St.	12-1-0	Florida St. (USA/NFF)	12-1-0	Florida St.	12-1-0	Florida St.	12-1-0	Florida St. (CNN)	12-1-0
1994	Nebraska	13-0-0	Nebraska (USA/NFF)	13-0-0	Nebraska	13-0-0	Nebraska	13-0-0	Nebraska (CNN)	13-0-0
1995	Nebraska	12-0-0	Nebraska (USA/NFF)	12-0-0	Nebraska	12-0-0	Nebraska	12-0-0	Nebraska (CNN)	12-0-0
1996	Florida	12-1-0	Florida (USA/NFF)	12-1-0			Florida	12-1-0	Florida (CNN)	12-1-0
1997	Michigan	12-0-0	Michigan	12-0-0			Michigan	12-0-0	Nebraska (ESPN)	13-0-0

National Poll Champions in Bowl Games

Year	Team	Coach (Years†)	Record	Bowl (Result)
1900	Yale	Malcolm McBride	12-0-0	None
1901	Michigan	Fielding Yost	11-0-0	Rose (beat Stanford, 49-0)
	Harvard	William Reid	12-0-0	None
1902	Michigan	Fielding Yost	11-0-0	None
	Yale	Joseph Swan	11-0-1	None
1903	Princeton	Art Hillebrand	11-0-0	None
1904	Pennsylvania	Carl Williams	12-0-0	None
1905	Chicago	Amos Alonzo Stagg	11-0-0	None
	Yale	J. E. Owsley	10-0-0	None
1906	Princeton	Bill Roper	9-0-1	None
	Yale	Foster Rockwell	9-0-1	None
1907	Yale	William Knox	9-0-1	None
1908	Pennsylvania	Sol Metzer	11-0-1	None
	Harvard	Percy Haughton	9-0-1	None
1909	Yale	Howard Jones	10-0-0	None
1910	Harvard	Percy Haughton	8-0-1	None
1911	Princeton	Bill Roper	8-0-2	None
1912	Harvard	Percy Haughton	9-0-0	None
1913	Harvard	Percy Haughton	9-0-0	None
1914	Army	Charley Daly	9-0-0	None
	Harvard	Percy Haughton	7-0-2	None
1915	Cornell	Al Sharpe	9-0-0	None
1916	Pittsburgh	Glenn "Pop" Warner	8-0-0	None
1917	Georgia Tech	John Heisman	9-0-0	None
1918	Pittsburgh	Glenn "Pop" Warner	4-1-0	None
1919	Harvard	Robert Fisher	9-0-1	Rose (beat Oregon, 7-6)
	Penn St.	Hugo Bezdek	7-1-0	None
1920	California	Andy Smith	9-0-0	Rose (beat Ohio St., 28-0)
	Princeton	Bill Roper	6-0-1	None
1921	Cornell	Gil Dobie	8-0-0	None
	Penn St.	Hugo Bezdek	8-0-2	None
1922	Cornell	Gil Dobie	8-0-0	None
	Princeton	Bill Roper	8-0-0	None
1923	Illinois	Robert Zuppke	8-0-0	None
1924	Notre Dame	Knute Rockne	10-0-0	Rose (beat Stanford, 27-10)
1925	Alabama	Wallace Wade	10-0-0	Rose (beat Washington, 20-19)
	Dartmouth	Jesse Hawley	8-0-0	None
1926	Alabama	Wallace Wade	9-0-1	Rose (tied Stanford, 7-7)
	Stanford	Glenn "Pop" Warner	10-0-1	Rose (tied Alabama, 7-7)
1927	Illinois	Robert Zuppke	7-0-1	None
1928	Georgia Tech	Bill Alexander	10-0-0	Rose (beat California, 8-7)
	Southern Cal	Howard Jones	9-0-1	None
1929	Notre Dame	Knute Rockne	9-0-0	None
1930	Notre Dame	Knute Rockne	10-0-0	None
1931	Southern Cal	Howard Jones	10-1-0	Rose (beat Tulane, 21-12)
1932	Michigan	Harry Kipke	8-0-0	None
	Southern Cal	Howard Jones	10-0-0	Rose (beat Pittsburgh, 35-0)
1933	Michigan	Harry Kipke	7-0-1	None
1934	Minnesota	Bernie Bierman	8-0-0	None
1935	Minnesota	Bernie Bierman	8-0-0	None
	Southern Methodist	Matty Bell	12-1-0	Rose (lost to Stanford, 7-0)
1936	Minnesota	Bernie Bierman (5-15)	7-1-0	None
1937	Pittsburgh	Jock Sutherland (13-18)	9-0-1	None
1938	Texas Christian	Dutch Meyer (5-5)	11-0-0	Sugar (beat Carnegie Mellon, 15-7)
1939	Texas A&M	Homer Norton (6-16)	11-0-0	Sugar (beat Tulane, 14-13)
1940	Minnesota	Bernie Bierman (9-19)	8-0-0	None
1941	Minnesota	Bernie Bierman (10-20)	8-0-0	None
1942	Ohio St.	Paul Brown (2-2)	9-1-0	None
1943	Notre Dame	Frank Leahy (3-5)	9-1-0	None
1944	Army	Earl "Red" Blaik (4-11)	9-0-0	None
1945	Army	Earl "Red" Blaik (5-12)	9-0-0	None
1946	Notre Dame	Frank Leahy (4-6)	8-0-1	None
1947	Notre Dame	Frank Leahy (5-7)	9-0-0	None
1948	Michigan	Bennie Oosterbaan (1-1)	9-0-0	None
1949	Notre Dame	Frank Leahy (7-9)	10-0-0	None
1950	Oklahoma	Bud Wilkinson (4-4)	10-1-0	Sugar (lost to Kentucky, 13-7)
1951	Tennessee	Robert Neyland (20-20)	10-0-0	Sugar (lost to Maryland, 28-13)
1952	Michigan St.	Clarence "Biggie" Munn (6-9)	9-0-0	None
1953	Maryland	Jim Tatum (7-9)	10-1-0	Orange (lost to Oklahoma, 7-0)
1954	Ohio St.	Woody Hayes (4-9)	10-0-0	Rose (beat Southern Cal, 20-7)
	UCLA	Red Sanders (6-12)	9-0-0	None
1955	Oklahoma	Bud Wilkinson (9-9)	11-0-0	Orange (beat Maryland, 20-6)
1956	Oklahoma	Bud Wilkinson (10-10)	10-0-0	None
1957	Auburn	Ralph "Shug" Jordan (7-7)	10-0-0	None
	Ohio St.	Woody Hayes (7-12)	9-1-0	Rose (beat Oregon, 10-7)
1958	LSU	Paul Dietzel (4-4)	11-0-0	Sugar (beat Clemson, 7-0)
	Iowa	Forest Evashevski (5-8)	8-1-1	Rose (beat California, 38-12)
1959	Syracuse	Ben Schwartzwalder (11-14)	11-0-0	Cotton (beat Texas, 23-14)
1960	Minnesota	Murray Warmath (7-9)	8-2-0	Rose (lost to Washington, 17-7)
	Mississippi	Johnny Vaught (14-14)	10-0-1	Sugar (beat Rice, 14-6)

CONSENSUS NATIONAL CHAMPIONS

SINCE 1950

AP — Associated Press
UPI — United Press International
FWAA — Football Writers Association of America
NFF— National Football Foundation/College Football Hall of Fame
USA/CNN — USA Today/CNN
USA/ESPN — USA Today/ESPN

Year	Champion (Selectors)
1950	Oklahoma (AP, UPI)
1951	Tennessee (AP, UPI)
1952	Michigan St. (AP, UPI)
1953	Maryland (AP, UPI)
1954	UCLA (FWAA, UPI)
	Ohio St. (AP
1955	Oklahoma (AP, FWAA, UPI)
1956	Oklahoma (AP, FWAA, UPI)
1957	Ohio St. (FWAA, UPI)
	Auburn (AP)
1958	LSU (AP, UPI)
	Iowa (FWAA)
1959	Syracuse (AP, FWAA, NFF, UPI)
1960	Minnesota (AP, NFF, UPI)
	Mississippi (FWAA)
1961	Alabama (AP, NFF, UPI)
	Ohio St. (FWAA)
1962	Southern Cal (AP, FWAA, NFF, UPI)
1963	Texas (AP, FWAA, NFF, UPI)
1964	Alabama (AP, UPI)
	Arkansas (FWAA)
	Notre Dame (NFF)
1965	Michigan St. (FWAA, NFF, UPI)
	Alabama (AP, FWAA)
1966	Notre Dame (AP, FWAA, NFF, UPI)
	Michigan St. (NFF)
1967	Southern Cal (AP, FWAA, NFF, UPI)
1968	Ohio St. (AP, FWAA, NFF, UPI)
1969	Texas (AP, FWAA, NFF, UPI)
1970	Nebraska (AP, FWAA)
	Texas (NFF, UPI)
	Ohio St. (NFF)
1971	Nebraska (AP, FWAA, NFF, UPI)
1972	Southern Cal (AP, FWAA, NFF, UPI)
1973	Notre Dame (AP, FWAA, NFF)
	Alabama (UPI)
1974	Southern Cal (FWAA, NFF, UPI)
	Oklahoma (AP)
1975	Oklahoma (AP, FWAA, NFF, UPI)
1976	Pittsburgh (AP, FWAA, NFF, UPI)
1977	Notre Dame (AP, FWAA, NFF, UPI)
1978	Alabama (AP, FWAA, NFF)
	Southern Cal (UPI)
1979	Alabama (AP, FWAA, NFF, UPI)
1980	Georgia (AP, FWAA, NFF, UPI)
1981	Clemson (AP, FWAA, NFF, UPI)
1982	Penn St. (AP, FWAA, NFF, UPI, USA/CNN)
1983	Miami (Fla.) (AP, FWAA, NFF, UPI, USA/CNN)
1984	Brigham Young (AP, FWAA, NFF, UPI, USA/CNN)
1985	Oklahoma (AP, FWAA, NFF, UPI, USA/CNN)
1986	Penn St. (AP, FWAA, NFF, UPI, USA/CNN)
1987	Miami (Fla.) (AP, FWAA, NFF, UPI, USA/CNN)
1988	Notre Dame (AP, FWAA, NFF, UPI, USA/CNN)
1989	Miami (Fla.) (AP, FWAA, NFF, UPI, USA/CNN)
1990	Colorado (AP, FWAA, NFF, USA/CNN)
	Georgia Tech (UPI)
1991	Washington (FWAA, NFF, USA/CNN, UPI)
	Miami (Fla.) (AP)
1992	Alabama (AP, FWAA, NFF, USA/CNN, UPI)
1993	Florida St. (AP, FWAA, NFF, USA/CNN, UPI)
1994	Nebraska (AP, FWAA, NFF, USA/CNN, UPI)
1995	Nebraska (AP, FWAA, NFF, USA/CNN, UPI)
1996	Florida (AP, FWAA, NFF, USA/CNN)
1997	Michigan (AP, FWAA, NFF)
	Nebraska (USA/ESPN)

Photo from Michigan sports information

Heisman Trophy winner Charles Woodson helped lead the Wolverines to a 12-0 record and a share of the No. 1 ranking in the polls.

Year	Team	Coach (Years†)	Record	Bowl (Result)
1961	Alabama	Paul "Bear" Bryant (4-17)	11-0-0	Sugar (beat Arkansas, 10-3)
	Ohio St.	Woody Hayes (11-16)	8-0-1	None
1962	Southern Cal	John McKay (3-3)	11-0-0	Rose (beat Wisconsin, 42-37)
1963	Texas	Darrell Royal (7-10)	11-0-0	Cotton (beat Navy, 28-6)
1964	Alabama	Paul "Bear" Bryant (7-20)	10-1-0	Orange (lost to Texas, 21-17)
	Arkansas	Frank Broyles (3-4)	11-0-0	Cotton (beat Nebraska, 10-7)
	Notre Dame	Ara Parseghian (1-14)	9-1-0	None
1965	Alabama	Paul "Bear" Bryant (8-21)	9-1-1	Orange (beat Nebraska, 39-28)
	Michigan St.	Duffy Daugherty (12-12)	10-1-0	Rose (lost to UCLA, 14-12)
1966	Michigan St.	Duffy Daugherty (13-13)	9-0-1	None
	Notre Dame	Ara Parseghian (3-17)	9-0-1	None
1967	Southern Cal	John McKay (8-8)	10-1-0	Rose (beat Indiana, 14-3)
1968	Ohio St.	Woody Hayes (18-23)	10-0-0	Rose (beat Southern Cal, 27-16)
1969	Texas	Darrell Royal (13-16)	11-0-0	Cotton (beat Notre Dame, 21-17)
1970	Nebraska	Bob Devaney (9-14)	11-0-1	Orange (beat LSU, 17-12)
	Ohio St.	Woody Hayes (20-25)	9-1-0	Rose (lost to Stanford, 27-17)
	Texas	Darrell Royal (14-17)	10-1-0	Cotton (lost to Notre Dame, 24-11)
1971	Nebraska	Bob Devaney (10-15)	13-0-0	Orange (beat Alabama, 38-6)
1972	Southern Cal	John McKay (13-13)	12-0-0	Rose (beat Ohio St., 42-17)
1973	Alabama	Paul "Bear" Bryant (16-29)	11-1-0	Sugar (lost to Notre Dame, 24-23)
	Notre Dame	Ara Parseghian (10-23)	11-0-0	Sugar (beat Alabama, 24-23)
1974	Oklahoma	Barry Switzer (2-2)	11-0-0	None
	Southern Cal	John McKay (15-15)	10-1-1	Rose (beat Ohio St., 18-17)
1975	Oklahoma	Barry Switzer (3-3)	11-1-0	Orange (beat Michigan, 14-6)
1976	Pittsburgh	Johnny Majors (4-9)	12-0-0	Sugar (beat Georgia, 27-3)
1977	Notre Dame	Dan Devine (3-19)	11-1-0	Cotton (beat Texas, 38-10)
1978	Alabama	Paul "Bear" Bryant (21-34)	11-1-0	Sugar (beat Penn St., 14-7)
	Southern Cal	John Robinson (3-3)	12-1-0	Rose (beat Michigan, 17-10)
1979	Alabama	Paul "Bear" Bryant (22-35)	12-0-0	Sugar (beat Arkansas, 24-9)
1980	Georgia	Vince Dooley (17-17)	12-0-0	Sugar (beat Notre Dame, 17-10)
1981	Clemson	Danny Ford (4-4#)	12-0-0	Orange (beat Nebraska, 22-15)
1982	Penn St.	Joe Paterno (17-17)	11-1-0	Sugar (beat Georgia, 27-23)
1983	Miami (Fla.)	Howard Schnellenberger (5-5)	11-1-0	Orange (beat Nebraska, 31-30)
1984	Brigham Young	LaVell Edwards (13-13)	13-0-0	Holiday (beat Michigan, 24-17)
1985	Oklahoma	Barry Switzer (13-13)	11-1-0	Orange (beat Penn St., 25-10)
1986	Penn St.	Joe Paterno (21-21)	12-0-0	Fiesta (beat Miami, Fla., 14-10)
1987	Miami (Fla.)	Jimmy Johnson (3-9)	12-0-0	Orange (beat Oklahoma, 20-14)
1988	Notre Dame	Lou Holtz (3-19)	12-0-0	Fiesta (beat West Va., 34-21)
1989	Miami (Fla.)	Dennis Erickson (1-8)	11-1-0	Sugar (beat Alabama, 33-25)
1990	Colorado	Bill McCartney (9-9)	11-1-1	Orange (beat Notre Dame, 10-9)
	Georgia Tech	Bobby Ross (4-14)	11-0-1	Fla. Citrus (beat Nebraska, 45-21)
1991	Miami (Fla.)	Dennis Erickson (3-10)	12-0-0	Orange (beat Nebraska, 22-0)
	Washington	Don James (17-21)	12-0-0	Rose (beat Michigan, 34-14)
1992	Alabama	Gene Stallings (3-10)	13-0-0	Sugar (beat Miami, Fla., 34-13)
1993	Florida St.	Bobby Bowden (18-28)	12-1-0	Orange (beat Nebraska, 18-16)
1994	Nebraska	Tom Osborne (22-22)	13-0-0	Orange (beat Miami, Fla., 24-17)
1995	Nebraska	Tom Osborne (23-23)	12-0-0	Fiesta (beat Florida, 62-24)
1996	Florida	Steve Spurrier (7-10)	12-1-0	Sugar (beat Florida St., 52-20)
1997	Michigan	Lloyd Carr (3-3)	12-0-0	Rose (beat Washington St., 21-16)
	Nebraska	Tom Osborne (25-25)	13-0-0	Orange (beat Tennessee, 42-17)

†Years head coach at that college and total years at four-year colleges. #Includes last game of 1978 season.

Associated Press Weekly Poll Leaders

The weekly dates are for Monday or Tuesday, the most frequent release dates of the poll, except when the final poll was taken after January 1-2 bowl games. A team's record includes its last game before the weekly poll. A new weekly leader's rank the previous week is indicated in parentheses after its record. Final poll leaders (annual champions) are in bold face. (Note: Only 10 teams were ranked in the weekly polls during 1962, 1963, 1964, 1965, 1966 and 1967; 20 were ranked in all other seasons until 1989, when 25 were ranked.)

1936

10-20	Minnesota	(3-0-0)
10-27	Minnesota	(4-0-0)
11-3	Northwestern	(5-0-0) (3)
11-10	Northwestern	(6-0-0)
11-17	Northwestern	(7-0-0)
11-24	Minnesota	(7-1-0) (2)
12-1	**Minnesota**	**(7-1-0)**

1937

10-20	California	(5-0-0)
10-27	California	(6-0-0)
11-2	California	(7-0-0)
11-9	Pittsburgh	(6-0-1) (3)
11-16	Pittsburgh	(7-0-1)
11-23	Pittsburgh	(8-0-1)
11-30	**Pittsburgh**	**(9-0-1)**

1938

10-18	Pittsburgh	(4-0-0)
10-25	Pittsburgh	(5-0-0)
11-1	Pittsburgh	(6-0-0)
11-8	Texas Christian	(7-0-0) (2)
11-15	Notre Dame	(7-0-0) (2)
11-22	Notre Dame	(8-0-0)
11-29	Notre Dame	(8-0-0)
12-6	**Texas Christian**	**(10-0-0) (2)**

1939

10-17	Pittsburgh	(3-0-0)
10-24	Tennessee	(4-0-0) (5)
10-31	Tennessee	(5-0-0)
11-7	Tennessee	(6-0-0)
11-14	Tennessee	(7-0-0)
11-21	Texas A&M	(9-0-0) (2)
11-28	(tie) Texas A&M	(9-0-0)
	(tie) Southern Cal	(6-0-1) (4)
12-5	Texas A&M	(10-0-0)
12-12	**Texas A&M**	**(10-0-0)**

1940

10-15	Cornell	(2-0-0)
10-22	Cornell	(3-0-0)
10-29	Cornell	(4-0-0)
11-5	Cornell	(5-0-0)
11-12	Minnesota	(6-0-0) (2)
11-19	Minnesota	(7-0-0)
11-26	Minnesota	(8-0-0)
12-3	**Minnesota**	**(8-0-0)**

1941

10-14	Minnesota	(2-0-0)
10-21	Minnesota	(3-0-0)
10-28	(tie) Minnesota	(4-0-0)
	(tie) Texas	(5-0-0) (2)
11-4	Texas	(6-0-0)
11-11	Minnesota	(6-0-0) (2)
11-18	Minnesota	(7-0-0)
11-25	Minnesota	(8-0-0)
12-2	**Minnesota**	**(8-0-0)**

1942

10-13	Ohio St.	(3-0-0)
10-20	Ohio St.	(4-0-0)
10-27	Ohio St.	(5-0-0)
11-3	Georgia	(7-0-0) (2)
11-10	Georgia	(8-0-0)
11-17	Georgia	(9-0-0)
11-24	Boston College	(8-0-0) (3)
12-1	**Ohio St.**	**(9-1-0) (3)**

1943

10-5	Notre Dame	(2-0-0)
10-12	Notre Dame	(3-0-0)
10-19	Notre Dame	(4-0-0)
10-26	Notre Dame	(5-0-0)
11-2	Notre Dame	(6-0-0)
11-9	Notre Dame	(7-0-0)
11-16	Notre Dame	(8-0-0)
11-23	Notre Dame	(9-0-0)
11-30	**Notre Dame**	**(9-1-0)**

1944

10-10	Notre Dame	(2-0-0)
10-17	Notre Dame	(3-0-0)
10-24	Notre Dame	(4-0-0)

10-31	Army	(5-0-0) (2)
11-7	Army	(6-0-0)
11-14	Army	(7-0-0)
11-21	Army	(8-0-0)
11-28	Army	(8-0-0)
12-5	**Army**	**(9-0-0)**

1945

10-9	Army	(2-0-0)
10-16	Army	(3-0-0)
10-23	Army	(4-0-0)
10-30	Army	(5-0-0)
11-6	Army	(6-0-0)
11-13	Army	(7-0-0)
11-20	Army	(8-0-0)
11-27	Army	(8-0-0)
12-4	**Army**	**(9-0-0)**

1946

10-8	Texas	(3-0-0)
10-15	Army	(4-0-0) (2)
10-22	Army	(5-0-0)
10-29	Army	(6-0-0)
11-5	Army	(7-0-0)
11-12	Army	(7-0-1)
11-19	Army	(8-0-1)
11-26	Army	(8-0-1)
12-3	**Notre Dame**	**(8-0-1) (2)**

1947*

10-7	Notre Dame	(1-0-0)
10-14	Michigan	(3-0-0) (2)
10-21	Michigan	(4-0-0)
10-28	Notre Dame	(4-0-0) (2)
11-4	Notre Dame	(5-0-0)
11-11	Notre Dame	(6-0-0)
11-18	Michigan	(8-0-0) (2)
11-25	Notre Dame	(8-0-0) (2)
12-2	Notre Dame	(8-0-0)
12-9	**Notre Dame**	**(9-0-0)**

1948

10-5	Notre Dame	(2-0-0)
10-12	North Caro.	(3-0-0) (2)
10-19	Michigan	(4-0-0) (4)
10-26	Michigan	(5-0-0)
11-2	Notre Dame	(6-0-0) (2)
11-9	Michigan	(7-0-0) (2)
11-16	Michigan	(8-0-0)
11-23	Michigan	(9-0-0)
11-30	**Michigan**	**(9-0-0)**

1949

10-4	Michigan	(2-0-0)
10-11	Notre Dame	(3-0-0) (2)
10-18	Notre Dame	(4-0-0)
10-25	Notre Dame	(4-0-0)
11-1	Notre Dame	(5-0-0)
11-8	Notre Dame	(6-0-0)
11-15	Notre Dame	(7-0-0)
11-22	Notre Dame	(8-0-0)
11-29	**Notre Dame**	**(9-0-0)**

1950

10-3	Notre Dame	(1-0-0)
10-10	Army	(2-0-0) (4)
10-17	Army	(3-0-0)
10-24	Southern Methodist	(5-0-0) (3)
10-31	Southern Methodist	(5-0-0)
11-7	Army	(6-0-0) (2)
11-14	Ohio St.	(6-1-0) (2)
11-21	Oklahoma	(8-0-0) (2)
11-28	**Oklahoma**	**(9-0-0)**

1951

10-2	Michigan St.	(2-0-0)
10-9	Michigan St.	(3-0-0)
10-16	California	(4-0-0) (2)
10-23	Tennessee	(4-0-0) (2)
10-30	Tennessee	(5-0-0)
11-6	Tennessee	(6-0-0)
11-13	Michigan St.	(7-0-0)(5)
11-20	Tennessee	(8-0-0) (2)
11-27	Tennessee	(9-0-0)
12-4	**Tennessee**	**(10-0-0)**

1952

9-30	Michigan St.	(1-0-0)
10-7	Wisconsin	(2-0-0) (8)
10-14	Michigan St.	(3-0-0)(2)
10-21	Michigan St.	(4-0-0)
10-28	Michigan St.	(5-0-0)
11-4	Michigan St.	(6-0-0)
11-11	Michigan St.	(7-0-0)
11-18	Michigan St.	(8-0-0)
11-25	Michigan St.	(9-0-0)
12-1	**Michigan St.**	**(9-0-0)**

1953

9-29	Notre Dame	(1-0-0)
10-6	Notre Dame	(2-0-0)
10-13	Notre Dame	(2-0-0)
10-20	Notre Dame	(3-0-0)
10-27	Notre Dame	(4-0-0)
11-3	Notre Dame	(5-0-0)
11-10	Notre Dame	(6-0-0)
11-17	Notre Dame	(7-0-0)
11-24	Maryland	(10-0-0) (2)
12-1	**Maryland**	**(10-0-0)**

1954

9-21	Oklahoma	(1-0-0)
9-28	Notre Dame	(1-0-0) (2)
10-5	Oklahoma	(2-0-0) (2)
10-12	Oklahoma	(3-0-0)
10-19	Oklahoma	(4-0-0)
10-26	Ohio St.	(5-0-0) (4)
11-2	UCLA	(7-0-0) (3)
11-9	UCLA	(8-0-0)
11-16	Ohio St.	(8-0-0) (2)
11-23	Ohio St.	(9-0-0)
11-30	**Ohio St.**	**(9-0-0)**

1955

9-20	UCLA	(1-0-0)
9-27	Maryland	(2-0-0) (5)
10-4	Maryland	(3-0-0)
10-11	Michigan	(3-0-0) (2)
10-18	Michigan	(4-0-0)
10-25	Maryland	(6-0-0) (2)
11-1	Maryland	(7-0-0)
11-8	Oklahoma	(7-0-0) (2)
11-15	Oklahoma	(8-0-0)
11-22	Oklahoma	(9-0-0)
11-29	**Oklahoma**	**(10-0-0)**

1956

9-25	Oklahoma	(0-0-0)
10-2	Oklahoma	(1-0-0)
10-9	Oklahoma	(2-0-0)
10-16	Oklahoma	(3-0-0)
10-23	Michigan St.	(4-0-0) (2)
10-30	Oklahoma	(5-0-0) (2)
11-6	Oklahoma	(6-0-0)
11-13	Tennessee	(7-0-0) (3)
11-20	Oklahoma	(8-0-0) (2)
11-27	Oklahoma	(9-0-0)
12-4	**Oklahoma**	**(10-0-0)**

1957

9-24	Oklahoma	(1-0-0)
10-1	Oklahoma	(1-0-0)
10-8	Oklahoma	(2-0-0)
10-15	Michigan St.	(3-0-0) (2)
10-22	Oklahoma	(4-0-0) (2)
10-29	Texas A&M	(6-0-0) (2)
11-5	Texas A&M	(7-0-0)
11-12	Texas A&M	(8-0-0)
11-19	Michigan St.	(7-1-0)(4)
11-26	Auburn	(9-0-0) (2)
12-3	**Auburn**	**(10-0-0)**

1958

9-23	Ohio St.	(0-0-0)
9-30	Oklahoma	(1-0-0) (2)
10-7	Auburn	(2-0-0) (2)
10-14	Army	(3-0-0) (3)
10-21	Army	(4-0-0)
10-28	LSU	(6-0-0) (3)
11-4	LSU	(7-0-0)
11-11	LSU	(8-0-0)
11-18	LSU	(9-0-0)
11-25	LSU	(10-0-0)
12-2	**LSU**	**(10-0-0)**

1959

9-22	LSU	(1-0-0)
9-29	LSU	(2-0-0)
10-6	LSU	(3-0-0)
10-13	LSU	(4-0-0)
10-20	LSU	(5-0-0)
10-27	LSU	(6-0-0)
11-3	LSU	(7-0-0)
11-10	Syracuse	(7-0-0) (4)
11-17	Syracuse	(8-0-0)
11-24	Syracuse	(9-0-0)
12-1	Syracuse	(9-0-0)
12-8	**Syracuse**	**(10-0-0)**

1960

9-20	Mississippi	(1-0-0)
9-27	Mississippi	(2-0-0)
10-4	Syracuse	(2-0-0) (2)
10-11	Mississippi	(4-0-0) (2)
10-18	Iowa	(4-0-0) (2)
10-25	Iowa	(5-0-0)
11-1	Iowa	(6-0-0)
11-8	Minnesota	(7-0-0) (3)
11-15	Missouri	(9-0-0) (2)
11-22	Minnesota	(8-1-0) (4)
11-29	**Minnesota**	**(8-1-0)**

1961

9-26	Iowa	(0-0-0)
10-3	Iowa	(1-0-0)
10-10	Mississippi	(3-0-0) (2)
10-17	Michigan St.	(3-0-0) (5)
10-24	Michigan St.	(4-0-0)
10-31	Michigan St.	(5-0-0)
11-7	Texas	(7-0-0) (3)
11-14	Texas	(8-0-0)
11-21	Alabama	(9-0-0) (2)
11-28	Alabama	(9-0-0)
12-5	**Alabama**	**(10-0-0)**

1962

9-25	Alabama	(1-0-0)
10-2	Ohio St.	(1-0-0) (2)
10-9	Alabama	(3-0-0) (2)
10-16	Texas	(4-0-0) (2)
10-23	Texas	(5-0-0)
10-30	Northwestern	(5-0-0) (3)
11-6	Northwestern	(6-0-0)
11-13	Alabama	(8-0-0) (3)
11-20	Southern Cal	(8-0-0) (2)
11-27	Southern Cal	(9-0-0)
12-4	**Southern Cal**	**(10-0-0)**

1963

9-24	Southern Cal	(1-0-0)
10-1	Oklahoma	(1-0-0) (3)
10-8	Oklahoma	(2-0-0)
10-15	Texas	(4-0-0) (3)
10-22	Texas	(5-0-0)
10-29	Texas	(6-0-0)
11-5	Texas	(7-0-0)
11-12	Texas	(8-0-0)
11-19	Texas	(9-0-0)
11-26	Texas	(9-0-0)
12-3	Texas	(10-0-0)
12-10	**Texas**	**(10-0-0)**

1964

9-29	Texas	(2-0-0)
10-6	Texas	(3-0-0)
10-13	Texas	(4-0-0)
10-20	Ohio St.	(4-0-0)(2)
10-27	Ohio St.	(5-0-0)
11-3	Notre Dame	(6-0-0)(2)
11-10	Notre Dame	(7-0-0)
11-17	Notre Dame	(8-0-0)
11-24	Notre Dame	(9-0-0)
12-1	**Alabama**	**(10-0-0) (2)**

1965

9-21	Notre Dame	(1-0-0)
9-28	Texas	(2-0-0) (3)
10-5	Texas	(3-0-0)
10-12	Texas	(4-0-0)
10-19	Arkansas	(5-0-0) (3)
10-26	Michigan St.	(6-0-0) (2)
11-2	Michigan St.	(7-0-0)
11-9	Michigan St.	(8-0-0)
11-16	Michigan St.	(9-0-0)
11-23	Michigan St.	(10-0-0)
11-30	Michigan St.	(10-0-0)
1-4	**Alabama**	**(9-1-1) (4)**

1966

9-20	Michigan St.	(1-0-0)

9-27	Michigan St.	(2-0-0)
10-4	Michigan St.	(3-0-0)
10-11	Michigan St.	(4-0-0)
10-18	Notre Dame	(4-0-0) (2)
10-25	Notre Dame	(5-0-0)
11-1	Notre Dame	(6-0-0)
11-8	Notre Dame	(7-0-0)
11-15	Notre Dame	(8-0-0)
11-22	Notre Dame	(8-0-1)
11-29	Notre Dame	(9-0-1)
12-5	**Notre Dame**	**(9-0-1)**

1967

9-19	Notre Dame	(0-0-0)
9-26	Notre Dame	(1-0-0)
10-3	Southern Cal	(3-0-0) (2)
10-10	Southern Cal	(4-0-0)
10-17	Southern Cal	(5-0-0)
10-24	Southern Cal	(6-0-0)
10-31	Southern Cal	(7-0-0)
11-7	Southern Cal	(8-0-0)
11-14	UCLA	(7-0-1) (2)
11-21	Southern Cal	(9-1-0) (4)
11-28	**Southern Cal**	**(9-1-0)**

1968

9-17	Purdue	(0-0-0)
9-24	Purdue	(1-0-0)
10-1	Purdue	(2-0-0)
10-8	Purdue	(3-0-0)
10-15	Southern Cal	(4-0-0) (2)
10-22	Southern Cal	(5-0-0)
10-29	Southern Cal	(5-0-0)
11-5	Southern Cal	(6-0-0)
11-12	Southern Cal	(7-0-0)
11-19	Southern Cal	(8-0-0)
11-26	Ohio St.	(9-0-0) (2)
12-2	Ohio St.	(9-0-0)
12-9	**Ohio St.**	**(10-0-0)**

1969

9-23	Ohio St.	(0-0-0)
9-30	Ohio St.	(1-0-0)
10-7	Ohio St.	(2-0-0)
10-14	Ohio St.	(3-0-0)
10-21	Ohio St.	(4-0-0)
10-28	Ohio St.	(5-0-0)
11-4	Ohio St.	(6-0-0)
11-11	Ohio St.	(7-0-0)
11-18	Ohio St.	(8-0-0)
11-25	Texas	(8-0-0) (2)
12-2	Texas	(9-0-0)
12-9	Texas	(10-0-0)
1-4	**Texas**	**(11-0-0)**

1970

9-15	Ohio St.	(0-0-0)
9-22	Ohio St.	(0-0-0)
9-29	Ohio St.	(1-0-0)
10-6	Ohio St.	(2-0-0)
10-13	Ohio St.	(3-0-0)
10-20	Ohio St.	(4-0-0)
10-27	Texas	(5-0-0) (2)
11-3	Texas	(6-0-0)
11-10	Texas	(7-0-0)
11-17	Texas	(8-0-0)
11-24	Texas	(8-0-0)
12-1	Texas	(9-0-0)
12-8	Texas	(10-0-0)
1-6	**Nebraska**	**(11-0-1) (3)**

1971

9-14	Nebraska	(1-0-0)
9-21	Nebraska	(2-0-0)
9-28	Nebraska	(3-0-0)
10-5	Nebraska	(4-0-0)
10-12	Nebraska	(5-0-0)
10-19	Nebraska	(6-0-0)
10-26	Nebraska	(7-0-0)
11-2	Nebraska	(8-0-0)
11-9	Nebraska	(9-0-0)
11-16	Nebraska	(10-0-0)
11-23	Nebraska	(10-0-0)
11-30	Nebraska	(11-0-0)
12-7	Nebraska	(12-0-0)
1-4	**Nebraska**	**(13-0-0)**

1972

9-12	Southern Cal	(1-0-0)
9-19	Southern Cal	(2-0-0)
9-26	Southern Cal	(3-0-0)
10-3	Southern Cal	(4-0-0)
10-10	Southern Cal	(5-0-0)
10-17	Southern Cal	(6-0-0)
10-24	Southern Cal	(7-0-0)
10-31	Southern Cal	(8-0-0)
11-7	Southern Cal	(9-0-0)
11-14	Southern Cal	(9-0-0)
11-21	Southern Cal	(10-0-0)
11-28	Southern Cal	(10-0-0)
12-5	Southern Cal	(11-0-0)
1-3	**Southern Cal**	**(12-0-0)**

1973

9-11	Southern Cal	(0-0-0)
9-18	Southern Cal	(1-0-0)
9-25	Southern Cal	(2-0-0)
10-2	Ohio St.	(2-0-0) (3)
10-9	Ohio St.	(3-0-0)
10-16	Ohio St.	(4-0-0)
10-23	Ohio St.	(5-0-0)
10-30	Ohio St.	(6-0-0)
11-6	Ohio St.	(7-0-0)
11-13	Ohio St.	(8-0-0)
11-20	Ohio St.	(9-0-0)
11-27	Alabama	(10-0-0) (2)
12-4	Alabama	(11-0-0)
1-3	**Notre Dame**	**(11-0-0) (3)**

1974

9-10	Oklahoma	(0-0-0)
9-17	Notre Dame	(1-0-0) (2)
9-24	Ohio St.	(2-0-0) (2)
10-1	Ohio St.	(3-0-0)
10-8	Ohio St.	(4-0-0)
10-15	Ohio St.	(5-0-0)
10-22	Ohio St.	(6-0-0)
10-29	Ohio St.	(7-0-0)
11-5	Ohio St.	(8-0-0)
11-12	Oklahoma	(8-0-0) (2)
11-19	Oklahoma	(9-0-0)
11-26	Oklahoma	(10-0-0)
12-3	Oklahoma	(11-0-0)
1-3	**Oklahoma**	**(11-0-0)**

1975

9-9	Oklahoma	(0-0-0)
9-16	Oklahoma	(1-0-0)
9-23	Oklahoma	(2-0-0)
9-30	Oklahoma	(3-0-0)
10-7	Ohio St.	(4-0-0) (2)
10-14	Ohio St.	(5-0-0)
10-21	Ohio St.	(6-0-0)
10-28	Ohio St.	(7-0-0)
11-4	Ohio St.	(8-0-0)
11-11	Ohio St.	(9-0-0)
11-18	Ohio St.	(10-0-0)
11-25	Ohio St.	(11-0-0)
12-2	Ohio St.	(11-0-0)
1-3	**Oklahoma**	**(11-1-0) (3)**

1976

9-14	Michigan	(1-0-0)
9-21	Michigan	(2-0-0)
9-28	Michigan	(3-0-0)
10-5	Michigan	(4-0-0)
10-12	Michigan	(5-0-0)
10-19	Michigan	(6-0-0)
10-26	Michigan	(7-0-0)
11-2	Michigan	(8-0-0)
11-9	Pittsburgh	(9-0-0) (2)
11-16	Pittsburgh	(10-0-0)
11-23	Pittsburgh	(10-0-0)
11-30	Pittsburgh	(11-0-0)
1-5	**Pittsburgh**	**(12-0-0)**

1977

9-13	Michigan	(1-0-0)
9-20	Michigan	(2-0-0)
9-27	Oklahoma	(3-0-0) (3)
10-4	Southern Cal	(4-0-0) (2)
10-11	Michigan	(5-0-0) (3)
10-18	Michigan	(6-0-0)
10-25	Texas	(6-0-0) (2)
11-1	Texas	(7-0-0)
11-8	Texas	(8-0-0)
11-15	Texas	(9-0-0)
11-22	Texas	(10-0-0)
11-29	Texas	(11-0-0)
1-4	**Notre Dame**	**(11-1-0) (5)**

1978

9-12	Alabama	(1-0-0)
9-19	Alabama	(2-0-0)
9-26	Oklahoma	(3-0-0) (tie 3)
10-3	Oklahoma	(4-0-0)
10-10	Oklahoma	(5-0-0)
10-17	Oklahoma	(6-0-0)
10-24	Oklahoma	(7-0-0)
10-31	Oklahoma	(8-0-0)
11-7	Oklahoma	(9-0-0)
11-14	Penn St.	(10-0-0) (2)
11-21	Penn St.	(10-0-0)
11-28	Penn St.	(11-0-0)
12-5	Penn St.	(11-0-0)
1-4	**Alabama**	**(11-1-0) (2)**

1979

9-11	Southern Cal	(1-0-0)
9-18	Southern Cal	(2-0-0)
9-25	Southern Cal	(3-0-0)
10-2	Southern Cal	(4-0-0)
10-9	Southern Cal	(5-0-0)
10-16	Alabama	(5-0-0) (2)
10-23	Alabama	(6-0-0)
10-30	Alabama	(7-0-0)
11-6	Alabama	(8-0-0)
11-13	Alabama	(9-0-0)
11-20	Alabama	(10-0-0)
11-27	Alabama	(10-0-0)
12-4	Ohio St.	(11-0-0) (3)
1-3	**Alabama**	**(12-0-0) (2)**

1980

9-9	Ohio St.	(0-0-0)
9-16	Alabama	(1-0-0) (2)
9-23	Alabama	(2-0-0)
9-30	Alabama	(3-0-0)
10-7	Alabama	(4-0-0)
10-14	Alabama	(5-0-0)
10-21	Alabama	(6-0-0)
10-28	Alabama	(7-0-0)
11-4	Notre Dame	(7-0-0) (3)
11-11	Georgia	(9-0-0) (2)
11-18	Georgia	(10-0-0)
11-25	Georgia	(10-0-0)
12-2	Georgia	(11-0-0)
12-9	Georgia	(11-0-0)
1-4	**Georgia**	**(12-0-0)**

1981

9-8	Michigan	(0-0-0)
9-15	Notre Dame	(1-0-0) (4)
9-22	Southern Cal	(2-0-0) (2)
9-29	Southern Cal	(3-0-0)
10-6	Southern Cal	(4-0-0)
10-13	Texas	(4-0-0) (3)
10-20	Penn St.	(5-0-0) (2)
10-27	Penn St.	(6-0-0)
11-3	Pittsburgh	(7-0-0) (2)
11-10	Pittsburgh	(8-0-0)
11-17	Pittsburgh	(9-0-0)
11-24	Pittsburgh	(10-0-0)
12-1	Clemson	(11-0-0) (2)
1-3	**Clemson**	**(12-0-0)**

1982

9-7	Pittsburgh	(0-0-0)
9-14	Washington	(1-0-0) (2)
9-21	Washington	(2-0-0)
9-28	Washington	(3-0-0)
10-5	Washington	(4-0-0)
10-12	Washington	(5-0-0)
10-19	Washington	(6-0-0)
10-26	Pittsburgh	(6-0-0) (2)
11-2	Pittsburgh	(7-0-0)
11-9	Georgia	(9-0-0) (3)
11-16	Georgia	(10-0-0)
11-23	Georgia	(10-0-0)
11-30	Georgia	(11-0-0)
12-7	Georgia	(11-0-0)
1-3	**Penn St.**	**(11-1-0) (2)**

1983

9-6	Nebraska	(1-0-0)
9-13	Nebraska	(2-0-0)
9-20	Nebraska	(3-0-0)
9-27	Nebraska	(4-0-0)
10-4	Nebraska	(5-0-0)
10-11	Nebraska	(6-0-0)
10-18	Nebraska	(7-0-0)

10-25 Nebraska (8-0-0)
11-1 Nebraska (9-0-0)
11-8 Nebraska (10-0-0)
11-15 Nebraska (11-0-0)
11-22 Nebraska (11-0-0)
11-29 Nebraska (12-0-0)
12-6 Nebraska (12-0-0)
1-3 Miami (Fla.) (11-1-0) (5)

1984

9-4 Miami (Fla.) (2-0-0)
9-11 Nebraska (1-0-0) (2)
9-18 Nebraska (2-0-0)
9-25 Nebraska (3-0-0)
10-2 Texas (2-0-0) (2)
10-9 Texas (3-0-0)
10-16 Washington (6-0-0) (2)
10-23 Washington (7-0-0)
10-30 Washington (8-0-0)
11-6 Washington (9-0-0)
11-13 Nebraska (9-1-0) (2)
11-20 Brigham Young (11-0-0) (3)
11-27 Brigham Young (12-0-0)
12-4 Brigham Young (12-0-0)
1-3 Brigham Young (13-0-0)

1985

9-3 Oklahoma (0-0-0)
9-10 Auburn (1-0-0) (2)
9-17 Auburn (2-0-0)
9-24 Auburn (2-0-0)
10-1 Iowa (3-0-0) (3)
10-8 Iowa (4-0-0)
10-15 Iowa (5-0-0)
10-22 Iowa (6-0-0)
10-29 Iowa (7-0-0)
11-5 Florida (7-0-1) (2)
11-12 Penn St. (9-0-0) (2)
11-19 Penn St. (10-0-0)
11-26 Penn St. (11-0-0)
12-3 Penn St. (11-0-0)
1-3 Oklahoma (11-1-0) (4)

1986

9-9 Oklahoma (1-0-0)
9-16 Oklahoma (1-0-0)
9-23 Oklahoma (2-0-0)
9-30 Miami (Fla.) (4-0-0) (2)
10-7 Miami (Fla.) (5-0-0)
10-14 Miami (Fla.) (6-0-0)
10-21 Miami (Fla.) (7-0-0)
10-28 Miami (Fla.) (7-0-0)
11-4 Miami (Fla.) (8-0-0)
11-11 Miami (Fla.) (9-0-0)
11-18 Miami (Fla.) (10-0-0)
11-25 Miami (Fla.) (10-0-0)
12-2 Miami (Fla.) (11-0-0)
1-4 Penn St. (12-0-0) (2)

1987

9-8 Oklahoma (1-0-0)
9-15 Oklahoma (2-0-0)
9-22 Oklahoma (2-0-0)
9-29 Oklahoma (3-0-0)
10-6 Oklahoma (4-0-0)
10-13 Oklahoma (5-0-0)
10-20 Oklahoma (6-0-0)
10-27 Oklahoma (7-0-0)
11-3 Oklahoma (8-0-0)
11-10 Oklahoma (9-0-0)
11-17 Nebraska (9-0-0) (2)
11-24 Oklahoma (11-0-0) (2)
12-1 Oklahoma (11-0-0)
12-8 Oklahoma (11-0-0)
1-3 Miami (Fla.) (12-0-0) (2)

1988

9-6 Miami (Fla.) (1-0-0)
9-13 Miami (Fla.) (1-0-0)
9-20 Miami (Fla.) (2-0-0)
9-27 Miami (Fla.) (3-0-0)
10-4 Miami (Fla.) (4-0-0)
10-11 Miami (Fla.) (4-0-0)
10-18 UCLA (6-0-0) (2)
10-25 UCLA (7-0-0)
11-1 Notre Dame (8-0-0) (2)
11-8 Notre Dame (9-0-0)
11-15 Notre Dame (9-0-0)
11-22 Notre Dame (10-0-0)
11-29 Notre Dame (11-0-0)
12-6 Notre Dame (11-0-0)
1-3 Notre Dame (12-0-0)

1989

9-5 Notre Dame (1-0-0)
9-12 Notre Dame (1-0-0)
9-19 Notre Dame (2-0-0)
9-26 Notre Dame (3-0-0)
10-3 Notre Dame (4-0-0)
10-10 Notre Dame (5-0-0)
10-17 Notre Dame (6-0-0)
10-24 Notre Dame (7-0-0)
10-31 Notre Dame (8-0-0)
11-7 Notre Dame (9-0-0)
11-14 Notre Dame (10-0-0)
11-21 Notre Dame (11-0-0)
11-28 Colorado (11-0-0) (2)
12-5 Colorado (11-0-0)
1-2 Miami (Fla.) (11-1-0) (2)

1990

9-4 Miami (Fla.) (0-0-0)
9-11 Notre Dame (0-0-0) (2)
9-18 Notre Dame (1-0-0)
9-25 Notre Dame (2-0-0)
10-2 Notre Dame (3-0-0)
10-9 Michigan (3-1-0) (3)
10-16 Virginia (6-0-0) (2)
10-23 Virginia (7-0-0)
10-30 Virginia (7-0-0)
11-6 Notre Dame (7-1-0) (2)
11-13 Notre Dame (8-1-0)
11-20 Colorado (10-1-1) (2)
11-27 Colorado (10-1-1)
12-4 Colorado (10-1-1)
1-2 Colorado (11-1-1)

1991

9-3 Florida St. (1-0-0)
9-10 Florida St. (2-0-0)
9-17 Florida St. (3-0-0)
9-23 Florida St. (3-0-0)
9-30 Florida St. (4-0-0)
10-7 Florida St. (5-0-0)
10-14 Florida St. (6-0-0)
10-21 Florida St. (7-0-0)
10-28 Florida St. (8-0-0)
11-4 Florida St. (9-0-0)
11-11 Florida St. (10-0-0)
11-18 Miami (Fla.) (9-0-0) (2)
11-25 Miami (Fla.) (10-0-0)
12-2 Miami (Fla.) (11-0-0)
1-2 Miami (Fla.) (12-0-0)

1992

9-8 Miami (Fla.) (1-0-0)
9-15 Miami (Fla.) (1-0-0)
9-22 Miami (Fla.) (2-0-0)
9-29 Washington (3-0-0) (2)
10-6 Washington (4-0-0)
10-13 Washington (5-0-0)
10-20 Miami (Fla.)† (6-0-0) (2)
10-27 Miami (Fla.) (7-0-0)
11-3 Washington (8-0-0) (2)
11-10 Miami (Fla.) (8-0-0) (2)
11-17 Miami (Fla.) (9-0-0)
11-24 Miami (Fla.) (10-0-0)
12-1 Miami (Fla.) (11-0-0)
12-8 Miami (Fla.) (11-0-0)
1-2 Alabama (13-0-0) (2)

1993

8-31 Florida St. (1-0-0)
9-7 Florida St. (2-0-0)
9-14 Florida St. (3-0-0)
9-21 Florida St. (4-0-0)
9-28 Florida St. (4-0-0)
10-5 Florida St. (5-0-0)
10-12 Florida St. (6-0-0)
10-19 Florida St. (7-0-0)
10-26 Florida St. (7-0-0)
11-2 Florida St. (8-0-0)
11-9 Florida St. (9-0-0)
11-16 Notre Dame (10-0-0) (2)
11-23 Florida St. (10-1-0) (2)
11-30 Florida St. (11-1-0)
12-7 Florida St. (11-1-0)
1-3 Florida St. (12-1-0)

1994

8-31 Florida (0-0-0)
9-6 Nebraska (1-0-0) (2)
9-13 Florida (2-0-0) (2)
9-20 Florida (3-0-0)
9-27 Florida (3-0-0)
10-4 Florida (4-0-0)
10-11 Florida (5-0-0)
10-18 Penn St. (6-0-0) (3)
10-25 Penn St. (6-0-0)
11-1 Nebraska (9-0-0) (3)
11-8 Nebraska (10-0-0)
11-15 Nebraska (11-0-0)
11-22 Nebraska (11-0-0)
11-29 Nebraska (12-0-0)
12-6 Nebraska (12-0-0)
1-3 Nebraska (13-0-0)

1995

8-29 Florida St. (0-0-0)
9-5 Florida St. (1-0-0)
9-12 Florida St. (2-0-0)
9-19 Florida St. (3-0-0)
9-26 Florida St. (4-0-0)
10-3 Florida St. (4-0-0)
10-10 Florida St. (5-0-0)
10-17 Florida St. (6-0-0)
10-24 Florida St. (7-0-0)
10-31 Nebraska (8-0-0) (2)
11-7 Nebraska (9-0-0)
11-14 Nebraska (10-0-0)
11-21 Nebraska (10-0-0)
11-28 Nebraska (11-0-0)
12-5 Nebraska (11-0-0)
1-3 Nebraska (12-0-0)

1996

8-26 Nebraska (0-0-0)
9-2 Nebraska (0-0-0)
9-9 Nebraska (1-0-0)
9-16 Nebraska (1-0-0)
9-23 Florida (3-0-0) (4)
9-30 Florida (4-0-0)
10-7 Florida (5-0-0)
10-14 Florida (6-0-0)
10-21 Florida (7-0-0)
10-28 Florida (7-0-0)
11-4 Florida (8-0-0)
11-11 Florida (9-0-0)
11-18 Florida (10-0-0)
11-25 Florida (10-0-0)
12-2 Florida St. (11-0-0) (2)
12-9 Florida St. (11-0-0)
1-3 Florida (12-1-0)

1997

8-25 Penn St. (0-0-0)
9-2 Penn St. (0-0-0)
9-8 Penn St. (1-0-0)
9-15 Penn St. (2-0-0)
9-22 Florida (3-0-0) (3)
9-29 Florida (4-0-0)
10-6 Florida (5-0-0)
10-13 Penn St. (5-0-0) (2)
10-20 Nebraska (6-0-0) (2)
10-27 Nebraska (7-0-0)
11-3 Nebraska (8-0-0)
11-10 Michigan (9-0-0) (4)
11-17 Michigan (10-0-0)
11-24 Michigan (11-0-0)
12-1 Michigan (11-0-0)
12-8 Michigan (11-0-0)
1-3 Michigan (12-0-0)

**On January 6, 1948, in a special postseason poll after the Rose Bowl, The Associated Press voted Michigan No. 1 and Notre Dame No. 2. However, the postseason poll did not supersede the final regular-season poll of December 9, 1947. †Miami (Fla.) and Washington actually tied for first place in The Associated Press poll for the first time in 51 years, but Miami (Fla.) had one more first-place vote, 31-30, than Washington.*

1997 Associated Press Week-By-Week Polls

Preseason 8/11	A25	S2	S8	S15	S22	S29	O6	O13	O20	O27	N3	N10	N17	N24	D1	D8	J3
1. Penn St.	1	1	1	1	2	2	2	1	2	2	2	6	6	4	12	11	16
2. Florida	2	2	2	3	1	1	1	7	6	6	13	12	10	7	6	6	4
3. Florida St.	3	5	5	5	4	4	4	3	3	3	3	2	2	5	4	4	3
4. Washington	4	4	3	2	10	10	10	10	7	7	6	13	17	21	21	21	18
5. Tennessee	5	3	4	4	9	9	9	9	8	8	8	5	5	3	3	3	7
6. Nebraska	6	6	6	7	3	3	3	2	1	1	1	3	3	2	2	2	2
7. North Caro.	7	7	7	6	5	5	5	4	4	5	5	8	8	8	7	7	6
8. Colorado	8	8	8	15	16	16	24	NR	NR	NR	NR	NR	NR	NR	NR	NR	NR
9. Ohio St.	9	9	9	9	7	7	7	11	9	9	7	4	4	9	9	9	12
10. LSU	10	10	10	10	13	13	14	8	17	16	14	11	20	17	16	15	13
11. Notre Dame	11	11	12	NR	NR	NR	NR	NR	NR	NR	NR	NR	NR	NR	NR	NR	NR
12. Texas	12	12	11	NR	NR	NR	NR	NR	NR	NR	NR	NR	NR	NR	NR	NR	NR
13. Miami (Fla.)	14	13	13	22	NR	NR	NR	NR	NR	NR	NR	NR	NR	NR	NR	NR	NR
14. Michigan	15	14	14	8	6	6	6	5	5	4	4	1	1	1	1	1	1
15. Alabama	16	15	15	11	21	20	NR	NR	NR	NR	NR	NR	NR	NR	NR	NR	NR
16. Auburn	17	16	16	12	8	8	8	6	11	11	17	16	13	13	11	13	11
17. Syracuse	13	NR	NR	NR	NR	NR	NR	NR	NR	NR	22	21	18	16	15	14	21
18. Stanford	18	17	17	21	20	19	16	25	NR	NR	NR	NR	NR	NR	NR	NR	NR
19. Brigham Young	19	19	NR	NR	23	24	21	NR	NR	NR	NR	NR	NR	NR	NR	NR	NR
20. Clemson	20	18	19	16	17	NR	NR	NR	NR	NR	NR	NR	NR	NR	NR	NR	NR
21. Iowa	21	20	18	13	11	11	17	15	18	15	12	22	NR	NR	NR	NR	NR
22. Southern Cal	23	23	23	NR	NR	NR	NR	NR	NR	NR	NR	NR	NR	NR	NR	NR	NR
23. Kansas St.	22	21T	20	20	18	17	22	20	14	13	11	10	9	11	10	10	8
24. Wisconsin	NR	NR	NR	NR	NR	NR	NR	24	NR	NR	NR	23	24	NR	NR	NR	NR
25. Michigan St.	25	25	21	17	12	12	11	12	15	21	NR	NR	NR	NR	25	25	NR
NR Northwestern	24	21T	NR	NR	NR	NR	NR	NR	NR	NR	NR	NR	NR	NR	NR	NR	NR
NR Colorado St.	NR	24	25	23	NR	NR	NR	NR	NR	NR	NR	NR	25	20	20	18	17
NR Virginia Tech	NR	NR	22	18	14	14	23	22	19	23	20	19T	19	NR	NR	NR	NR
NR Arizona St.	NR	NR	24	14	25	25	NR	NR	23	20	15	15	12	12	17	16	14
NR Washington St.	NR	NR	NR	19	15	15	12	13	10	10	16	14	11	10	8	8	9
NR UCLA	NR	NR	NR	24	24	22	18	17	13	12	10	9	7	6	5	5	5
NR Georgia	NR	NR	NR	25	19	18	13	19	16	14	9	7	14	14	13	12	10
NR Texas A&M	NR	NR	NR	NR	22	21	15	14	20	25	21	18	16	15	14	20	20
NR Air Force	NR	NR	NR	NR	NR	23	19	18	NR	NR	NR	NR	NR	24	23	23	NR
NR Oklahoma St.	NR	NR	NR	NR	NR	NR	20	16	12	19	25	24	NR	25	24	24	24
NR Georgia Tech	NR	NR	NR	NR	NR	NR	25	21	NR	NR	NR	NR	NR	NR	NR	NR	25
NR West Va.	NR	NR	NR	NR	NR	NR	NR	23	21	17	NR	NR	22	NR	NR	NR	NR
NR Purdue	NR	NR	NR	NR	NR	NR	NR	NR	22	18	23	19T	23	18	18	17	15
NR Mississippi	NR	NR	NR	NR	NR	NR	NR	NR	25	NR	NR	NR	NR	NR	NR	NR	22
NR Southern Miss.	NR	NR	NR	NR	NR	NR	NR	NR	NR	24	24	NR	NR	23	22	22	19
NR Mississippi St.	NR	NR	NR	NR	NR	NR	NR	NR	NR	NR	19	17	15	22	NR	NR	NR
NR Missouri	NR	NR	NR	NR	NR	NR	NR	NR	NR	NR	NR	25	21	19	19	19	23
NR Toledo	NR	NR	NR	NR	NR	NR	NR	NR	24	22	18	NR	NR	NR	NR	NR	NR

No. 1 vs. No. 2

The No. 1 and No. 2 teams in The Associated Press poll (begun in 1936) have faced each other 31 times (20 in regular-season games and 11 in bowl games). The No. 1 team has won 18, with two games ending in ties.

Date	Score	Stadium (Site)
10-9-43	No. 1 Notre Dame 35, No. 2 Michigan 12	Michigan Stadium (Ann Arbor)
11-20-43	No. 1 Notre Dame 14, No. 2 Iowa Pre-Flight 13	Notre Dame (South Bend)
12-2-44	No. 1 Army 23, No. 2 Navy 7	Municipal (Baltimore)
11-10-45	No. 1 Army 48, No. 2 Notre Dame 0	Yankee (New York)
12-1-45	No. 1 Army 32, No. 2 Navy 13	Municipal (Philadelphia)
11-9-46	No. 1 Army 0, No. 2 Notre Dame 0 (tie)	Yankee (New York)
1-1-63	No. 1 Southern Cal 42, No. 2 Wisconsin 37 (Rose Bowl)	Rose Bowl (Pasadena)
10-12-63	No. 2 Texas 28, No. 1 Oklahoma 7	Cotton Bowl (Dallas)
1-1-64	No. 1 Texas 28, No. 2 Navy 6 (Cotton Bowl)	Cotton Bowl (Dallas)
11-19-66	No. 1 Notre Dame 10, No. 2 Michigan St. 10 (tie)	Spartan (East Lansing)
9-28-68	No. 1 Purdue 37, No. 2 Notre Dame 22	Notre Dame (South Bend)
1-1-69	No. 1 Ohio St. 27, No. 2 Southern Cal 16 (Rose Bowl)	Rose Bowl (Pasadena)
12-6-69	No. 1 Texas 15, No. 2 Arkansas 14	Razorback (Fayetteville)
11-25-71	No. 1 Nebraska 35, No. 2 Oklahoma 31	Owen Field (Norman)
1-1-72	No. 1 Nebraska 38, No. 2 Alabama 6 (Orange Bowl)	Orange Bowl (Miami)
1-1-79	No. 2 Alabama 14, No. 1 Penn St. 7 (Sugar Bowl)	Sugar Bowl (New Orleans)
9-26-81	No. 1 Southern Cal 28, No. 2 Oklahoma 24	Coliseum (Los Angeles)
1-1-83	No. 2 Penn St. 27, No. 1 Georgia 23 (Sugar Bowl)	Sugar Bowl (New Orleans)
10-19-85	No. 1 Iowa 12, No. 2 Michigan 10	Kinnick (Iowa City)
9-27-86	No. 2 Miami (Fla.) 28, No. 1 Oklahoma 16	Orange Bowl (Miami)
1-2-87	No. 2 Penn St. 14, No. 1 Miami (Fla.) 10 (Fiesta Bowl)	Sun Devil (Tempe)
11-21-87	No. 2 Oklahoma 17, No. 1 Nebraska 7	Memorial (Lincoln)
1-1-88	No. 2 Miami (Fla.) 20, No. 1 Oklahoma 14 (Orange Bowl)	Orange Bowl (Miami)
11-26-88	No. 1 Notre Dame 27, No. 2 Southern Cal 10	Coliseum (Los Angeles)
9-16-89	No. 1 Notre Dame 24, No. 2 Michigan 19	Michigan (Ann Arbor)
11-16-91	No. 2 Miami (Fla.) 17, No. 1 Florida St. 16	Doak Campbell (Tallahassee)
1-1-93	No. 2 Alabama 34, No. 1 Miami (Fla.) 13 (Sugar Bowl)	Superdome (New Orleans)
11-13-93	No. 2 Notre Dame 31, No. 1 Florida St. 24	Notre Dame (South Bend)
1-1-94	No. 1 Florida St. 18, No. 2 Nebraska 16 (Orange Bowl)	Orange Bowl (Miami)
1-2-96	No. 1 Nebraska 62, No. 2 Florida 24 (Fiesta Bowl)	Sun Devil (Tempe)
11-30-96	No. 2 Florida St. 24, No. 1 Florida 21	Doak Campbell (Tallahassee)

Games in Which a No. 1-Ranked Team Was Defeated or Tied

Listed here are 111 games in which the No. 1-ranked team in The Associated Press poll was defeated or tied. An asterisk (*) indicates the home team, an (N) a neutral site. In parentheses after the winning or tying team is its rank in the previous week's poll (NR indicates it was not ranked), its won-lost record entering the game and its score. The defeated or tied No. 1-ranked team follows with its score, and in parentheses is its rank in the poll the following week. Before 1965, the polls were final before bowl games. (Note: Only 10 teams were ranked in the weekly polls during 1962, 1963, 1964, 1965, 1966 and 1967; 20 teams all other seasons until 1989, when 25 teams were ranked.)

10-31-36	*Northwestern (3, 4-0-0) 6, Minnesota 0 (2)
11-21-36	*Notre Dame (11, 5-2-0) 26, Northwestern 6 (7)
10-30-37	(Tie) Washington (NR, 3-2-1) 0, *California 0 (2)
10-29-38	Carnegie Mellon (T19, 4-1-0) 20, *Pittsburgh 10 (3)
12-2-38	*Southern Cal (8, 7-2-0) 13, Notre Dame 0 (5)
10-14-39	Duquesne (NR, 3-0-0) 21, *Pittsburgh 13 (18)
11-8-41	(Tie) Baylor (NR, 3-4-0) 7, *Texas 7 (2)
10-31-42	*Wisconsin (6, 5-0-1) 17, Ohio St. 7 (6)
11-21-42	(N) Auburn (NR, 4-4-1) 27, Georgia 13 (5)
11-28-42	Holy Cross (NR, 4-4-1) 55, *Boston College 12 (8)
11-27-43	*Great Lakes NTS (NR, 9-2-0) 19, Notre Dame 14 (1)
11-9-46	(Tie) (N) Notre Dame (2, 5-0-0) 0, Army 0 (1)
10-8-49	Army (7, 2-0-0) 21, *Michigan 7 (7)
10-7-50	Purdue (NR, 0-1-0) 28, *Notre Dame 14 (10)
11-4-50	*Texas (7, 4-1-0) 23, Southern Methodist 20 (7)
11-18-50	*Illinois (10, 6-1-0) 14, Ohio St. 7 (8)
1-1-51	(Sugar Bowl) Kentucky (7, 10-1-0) 13, Oklahoma 7 (1)
10-20-51	Southern Cal (11, 4-1-0) 21, *California 14 (9)
1-1-52	(Sugar Bowl) Maryland (3, 9-0-0) 28, Tennessee 13 (1)
10-11-52	*Ohio St. (NR, 1-1-0) 23, Wisconsin 14 (12)
11-21-53	(Tie) Iowa (20, 5-3-0) 14, *Notre Dame 14 (2)
1-1-54	(Orange Bowl) Oklahoma (4, 8-1-1) 7, Maryland 0 (1)
10-2-54	Purdue (19, 1-0-0) 27, *Notre Dame 14 (8)
9-24-55	*Maryland (5, 1-0-0) 7, UCLA 0 (7)
10-27-56	*Illinois (NR, 1-3-0) 20, Michigan St. 13 (4)
10-19-57	Purdue (NR, 0-3-0) 20, *Michigan St. 13 (8)
11-16-57	*Rice (20, 4-3-0) 7, Texas A&M 6 (4)
10-25-58	(Tie) *Pittsburgh (NR, 4-1-0) 14, Army 14 (3)
11-7-59	*Tennessee (13, 4-1-1) 14, LSU 13 (3)
11-5-60	*Minnesota (3, 6-0-0) 27, Iowa 10 (5)
11-12-60	Purdue (NR, 2-4-1) 23, *Minnesota 14 (4)
11-19-60	Kansas (NR, 6-2-1) 23, *Missouri 7 (5)
1-1-61	(Rose Bowl) Washington (6, 9-1-0) 17, Minnesota 7 (1)
11-4-61	*Minnesota (NR, 4-1-0) 13, Michigan St. 0 (6)
11-18-61	Texas Christian (NR, 2-4-1) 6, *Texas 0 (5)
10-6-62	*UCLA (NR, 0-0-0) 9, Ohio St. 7 (10)
10-27-62	(Tie) *Rice (NR, 0-3-1) 14, Texas 14 (5)
11-10-62	*Wisconsin (8, 5-1-0) 37, Northwestern 6 (9)
11-17-62	*Georgia Tech (NR, 5-2-1) 7, Alabama 6 (6)
9-28-63	Oklahoma (3, 1-0-0) 17, *Southern Cal 12 (8)
10-12-63	(N) Texas (2, 3-0-0) 28, Oklahoma 7 (6)
10-17-64	Arkansas (8, 4-0-0) 14, *Texas 13 (6)
11-28-64	*Southern Cal (NR, 6-3-0) 20, Notre Dame 17 (3)
1-1-65	(Orange Bowl) Texas (5, 9-1-0) 21, Alabama 17 (1)
9-25-65	*Purdue (6, 1-0-0) 25, Notre Dame 21 (8)
10-16-65	*Arkansas (3, 4-0-0) 27, Texas 24 (5)
1-1-66	(Rose Bowl) UCLA (5, 7-2-1) 14, Michigan St. 12 (2)
11-19-66	(Tie) *Michigan St. (2, 9-0-0) 10, Notre Dame 10 (1)
9-30-67	*Purdue (10, 1-0-0) 28, Notre Dame 21 (6)
11-11-67	*Oregon St. (NR, 5-2-1) 3, Southern Cal 0 (4)
11-18-67	*Southern Cal (4, 8-1-0) 21, UCLA 20 (4)
10-12-68	*Ohio St. (4, 2-0-0) 13, Purdue 0 (5)
11-22-69	*Michigan (12, 7-2-0) 24, Ohio St. 12 (4)
1-1-71	(Cotton Bowl) Notre Dame (6, 8-1-1) 24, Texas 11 (3)
9-29-73	(Tie) Oklahoma (8, 1-0-0) 7, *Southern Cal 7 (4)
11-24-73	(Tie) *Michigan (4, 10-0-0) 10, Ohio St. 10 (3)
12-31-73	(Sugar Bowl) Notre Dame (3, 10-0-0) 24, Alabama 23 (4)
11-9-74	*Michigan St. (NR, 4-3-1) 16, Ohio St. 13 (4)
1-1-76	(Rose Bowl) UCLA (11, 8-2-1) 23, Ohio St. 10 (4)
11-6-76	*Purdue (NR, 3-5-0) 16, Michigan 14 (4)
10-8-77	Alabama (T7, 3-1-0) 21, *Southern Cal 20 (6)
10-22-77	*Minnesota (NR, 4-2-0) 16, Michigan 0 (6)
1-2-78	(Cotton Bowl) Notre Dame (5, 10-1-0) 38, Texas 10 (4)
9-23-78	(N) Southern Cal (7, 2-0-0) 24, Alabama 14 (3)
11-11-78	*Nebraska (4, 8-1-0) 17, Oklahoma 14 (4)
1-1-79	(Sugar Bowl) Alabama (2, 10-1-0) 14, Penn St. 7 (4)
10-13-79	(Tie) Stanford (NR, 3-2-0) 21, *Southern Cal 21 (4)
1-1-80	(Rose Bowl) Southern Cal (3, 10-0-1) 17, Ohio St. 16 (4)
11-1-80	(N) Mississippi St. (NR, 6-2-0) 6, Alabama 3 (6)
11-8-80	(Tie) *Georgia Tech (NR, 1-7-0) 3, Notre Dame 3 (6)
9-12-81	*Wisconsin (NR, 0-0-0) 21, Michigan 14 (11)
9-19-81	*Michigan (11, 0-1-0) 25, Notre Dame 7 (13)
10-10-81	Arizona (NR, 2-2-0) 13, *Southern Cal 10 (7)
10-17-81	*Arkansas (NR, 4-1-0) 42, Texas 11 (10)
10-31-81	*Miami (Fla.) (NR, 4-2-0) 17, Penn St. 14 (5)
11-28-81	Penn St. (11, 8-2-0) 48, *Pittsburgh 14 (10)
11-6-82	Notre Dame (NR, 5-1-1) 31, *Pittsburgh 16 (8)
1-1-83	(Sugar Bowl) Penn St. (2, 10-1-0) 27, Georgia 23 (4)
1-2-84	(Orange Bowl) Miami (Fla.) (5, 10-1-0) 31, Nebraska 30 (4)
9-8-84	*Michigan (14, 0-0-0) 22, Miami (Fla.) 14 (5)
9-29-84	*Syracuse (NR, 2-1-0) 17, Nebraska 9 (8)
10-13-84	(N) (Tie) Oklahoma (3, 4-0-0) 15, Texas 15 (3)
11-10-84	*Southern Cal (12, 7-1-0) 16, Washington 7 (5)
11-17-84	Oklahoma (6, 7-1-1) 17, *Nebraska 7 (7)
9-28-85	*Tennessee (NR, 0-0-1) 38, Auburn 20 (14)
11-2-85	*Ohio St. (7, 6-1-0) 22, Iowa 13 (6)
11-9-85	(N) Georgia (17, 6-1-1) 24, Florida 3 (11)
1-1-86	(Orange Bowl) Oklahoma (4, 9-1-0) 25, Penn St. 10 (3)
9-27-86	*Miami (Fla.) (2, 3-0-0) 28, Oklahoma 16 (6)
1-2-87	(Fiesta Bowl) Penn St. (2, 11-0-0) 14, Miami (Fla.) 10 (2)
11-21-87	Oklahoma (2, 11-0-0) 17, *Nebraska 7 (5)
1-1-88	(Orange Bowl) Miami (Fla.) (2, 11-1-0) 20, Oklahoma 14 (3)
10-15-88	*Notre Dame (4, 5-0-0) 31, Miami (Fla.) 30 (4)
10-29-88	Washington St. (NR, 4-3-0) 34, *UCLA 30 (6)
11-25-89	*Miami (Fla.) (7, 9-1-0) 27, Notre Dame 10 (5)
1-1-90	(Orange Bowl) Notre Dame (4, 11-1-0) 21, Colorado 6 (4)
9-8-90	*Brigham Young (16, 1-0-0) 28, Miami (Fla.) 21 (10)
10-6-90	Stanford (NR, 1-3-0) 36, *Notre Dame 31 (8)
10-13-90	Michigan St. (NR, 1-2-1) 28, *Michigan 27 (10)
11-3-90	Georgia Tech (16, 6-0-1) 41, *Virginia 38 (11)
11-17-90	Penn St. (18, 7-2-0) 24, *Notre Dame 21 (7)
11-16-91	Miami (Fla.) (2, 8-0-0) 17, *Florida St. 16 (3)
11-7-92	*Arizona (12, 5-2-1) 16, Washington 3 (6)
1-1-93	(Sugar Bowl) Alabama (2, 12-0) 34, Miami (Fla.) 13 (3)
11-13-93	*Notre Dame (2, 9-0-0) 31, Florida St. 24 (2)
11-20-93	Boston College (17, 7-2-0) 41, *Notre Dame 39 (4)
10-15-94	Auburn (6, 6-0-0) 36, *Florida 33 (5)
9-21-96	*Arizona St. (17, 2-0-0) 19, Nebraska 0 (8)
11-30-96	*Florida St. (2, 10-0-0) 24, Florida 21 (4)
1-2-97	(Sugar Bowl) Florida (3, 11-1-0) 52, Florida St. 20 (3)
10-11-97	LSU (14, 4-1-0) 28, Florida 21 (7)

Associated Press Preseason No. 1 Teams

(The No. 1-ranked team in the annual Associated Press preseason college football poll. The preseason poll started in 1950.)

Year	Team+	Year	Team+	Year	Team+	Year	Team+
1950	Notre Dame	1963	Southern Cal	1977	Oklahoma	1990	Miami (Fla.)
1951	Tennessee+	1964	Mississippi	1978	Alabama+	1991	Florida St.
1952	Michigan St.+	1965	Nebraska	1979	Southern Cal	1992	Miami (Fla.)
1953	Notre Dame	1966	Alabama	1980	Ohio St.	1993	Florida St.+
1954	Notre Dame	1967	Notre Dame	1981	Michigan	1994	Florida
1955	UCLA	1968	Purdue	1982	Pittsburgh	1995	Florida St.
1956	Oklahoma+	1969	Ohio St.	1983	Nebraska	1996	Nebraska
1957	Oklahoma	1970	Ohio St.	1984	Auburn	1997	Penn St.
1958	Ohio St.	1971	Notre Dame	1985	Oklahoma+		
1959	LSU	1972	Nebraska	1986	Oklahoma		
1960	Syracuse	1973	Southern Cal	1987	Oklahoma		
1961	Iowa	1974	Oklahoma+	1988	Florida St.		
1962	Ohio St.	1975	Oklahoma+	1989	Michigan		
		1976	Nebraska				

+Indicated eventual national champion.

Associated Press (Writers and Broadcasters) Final Polls

1936
Team
1. Minnesota
2. LSU
3. Pittsburgh
4. Alabama
5. Washington
6. Santa Clara
7. Northwestern
8. Notre Dame
9. Nebraska
10. Pennsylvania
11. Duke
12. Yale
13. Dartmouth
14. Duquesne
15. Fordham
16. Texas Christian
17. Tennessee
18. Arkansas
    Navy
20. Marquette

1937
Team
1. Pittsburgh
2. California
3. Fordham
4. Alabama
5. Minnesota
6. Villanova
7. Dartmouth
8. LSU
9. Notre Dame
    Santa Clara
11. Nebraska
12. Yale
13. Ohio St.
14. Holy Cross
    Arkansas
16. Texas Christian
17. Colorado
18. Rice
19. North Caro.
20. Duke

1938
Team
1. Texas Christian
2. Tennessee
3. Duke
4. Oklahoma
5. Notre Dame
6. Carnegie Mellon
7. Southern Cal
8. Pittsburgh
9. Holy Cross
10. Minnesota
11. Texas Tech
12. Cornell
13. Alabama
14. California
15. Fordham
16. Michigan
17. Northwestern
18. Villanova
19. Tulane
20. Dartmouth

1939
Team
1. Texas A&M
2. Tennessee
3. Southern Cal
4. Cornell
5. Tulane
6. Missouri
7. UCLA
8. Duke
9. Iowa
10. Duquesne
11. Boston College
12. Clemson
13. Notre Dame
14. Santa Clara
15. Ohio St.
16. Georgia Tech
17. Fordham
18. Nebraska
19. Oklahoma
20. Michigan

1940
Team
1. Minnesota
2. Stanford
3. Michigan
4. Tennessee
5. Boston College
6. Texas A&M
7. Nebraska
8. Northwestern
9. Mississippi St.
10. Washington
11. Santa Clara
12. Fordham
13. Georgetown
14. Pennsylvania
15. Cornell
16. Southern Methodist
17. Hardin-Simmons
18. Duke
19. Lafayette

1941
Team
1. Minnesota
2. Duke
3. Notre Dame
4. Texas
5. Michigan
6. Fordham
7. Missouri
8. Duquesne
9. Texas A&M
10. Navy
11. Northwestern
12. Oregon St.
13. Ohio St.
14. Georgia
15. Pennsylvania
16. Mississippi St.
17. Mississippi
18. Tennessee
19. Washington St.
20. Alabama

1942
Team
1. Ohio St.
2. Georgia
3. Wisconsin
4. Tulsa
5. Georgia Tech
6. Notre Dame
7. Tennessee
8. Boston College
9. Michigan
10. Alabama
11. Texas
12. Stanford
13. UCLA
14. William & Mary
15. Santa Clara
16. Auburn
17. Washington St.
18. Mississippi St.
19. Minnesota
    Holy Cross
    Penn St.

1943
Team
1. Notre Dame
2. Iowa Pre-Flight
3. Michigan
4. Navy
5. Purdue
6. Great Lakes
7. Duke
8. Del Monte P-F
9. Northwestern
10. March Field
11. Army
12. Washington
13. Georgia Tech
14. Texas
15. Tulsa
16. Dartmouth
17. Bainbridge NTS
18. Colorado Col.
19. Pacific (Cal.)
20. Pennsylvania

1944
Team
1. Army
2. Ohio St.
3. Randolph Field
4. Navy
5. Bainbridge NTS
6. Iowa Pre-Flight
7. Southern Cal
8. Michigan
9. Notre Dame
10. March Field
11. Duke
12. Tennessee
13. Georgia Tech
    Norman Pre-Flight
15. Illinois
16. El Toro Marines
17. Great Lakes
18. Fort Pierce
19. St. Mary's Pre-Flight
20. Second Air Force

1945
Team
1. Army
2. Alabama
3. Navy
4. Indiana
5. Oklahoma St.
6. Michigan
7. St. Mary's (Cal.)
8. Pennsylvania
9. Notre Dame
10. Texas
11. Southern Cal
12. Ohio St.
13. Duke
14. Tennessee
15. LSU
16. Holy Cross
17. Tulsa
18. Georgia
19. Wake Forest
20. Columbia

1946
Team
1. Notre Dame
2. Army
3. Georgia
4. UCLA
5. Illinois
6. Michigan
7. Tennessee
8. LSU
9. North Caro.
10. Rice
11. Georgia Tech
12. Yale
13. Pennsylvania
14. Oklahoma
15. Texas
16. Arkansas
17. Tulsa
18. North Caro. St.
19. Delaware
20. Indiana

*1947
Team
1. Notre Dame
2. Michigan
3. Southern Methodist
4. Penn St.
5. Texas
6. Alabama
7. Pennsylvania
8. Southern Cal
9. North Caro.
10. Georgia Tech
11. Army
12. Kansas
13. Mississippi
14. William & Mary
15. California
16. Oklahoma
17. North Caro. St.
18. Rice
19. Duke
20. Columbia

1948
Team
1. Michigan
2. Notre Dame
3. North Caro.
4. California
5. Oklahoma
6. Army
7. Northwestern
8. Georgia
9. Oregon
10. Southern Methodist
11. Clemson
12. Vanderbilt
13. Tulane
14. Michigan St.
15. Mississippi
16. Minnesota
17. William & Mary
18. Penn St.
19. Cornell
20. Wake Forest

1949
Team
1. Notre Dame
2. Oklahoma
3. California
4. Army
5. Rice
6. Ohio St.
7. Michigan
8. Minnesota
9. LSU
10. Pacific (Cal.)
11. Kentucky
12. Cornell
13. Villanova
14. Maryland
15. Santa Clara
16. North Caro.
17. Tennessee
18. Princeton
19. Michigan St.
20. Missouri
    Baylor

1950
Team
1. Oklahoma
2. Army
3. Texas
4. Tennessee
5. California
6. Princeton
7. Kentucky
8. Michigan St.
9. Michigan
10. Clemson
11. Washington
12. Wyoming
13. Illinois
14. Ohio St.
15. Miami (Fla.)
16. Alabama
17. Nebraska
18. Wash. & Lee
19. Tulsa
20. Tulane

1951
Team
1. Tennessee
2. Michigan St.
3. Maryland
4. Illinois
5. Georgia Tech
6. Princeton
7. Stanford
8. Wisconsin
9. Baylor
10. Oklahoma
11. Texas Christian
12. California
13. Virginia
14. San Francisco
15. Kentucky
16. Boston U.
17. UCLA
18. Washington St.
19. Holy Cross
20. Clemson

1952
Team
1. Michigan St.
2. Georgia Tech
3. Notre Dame
4. Oklahoma
5. Southern Cal
6. UCLA
7. Mississippi
8. Tennessee
9. Alabama
10. Texas
11. Wisconsin
12. Tulsa
13. Maryland
14. Syracuse
15. Florida
16. Duke
17. Ohio St.
18. Purdue
19. Princeton
20. Kentucky

1953
Team
1. Maryland
2. Notre Dame
3. Michigan St.
4. Oklahoma
5. UCLA
6. Rice
7. Illinois
8. Georgia Tech
9. Iowa
10. West Va.
11. Texas
12. Texas Tech
13. Alabama
14. Army
15. Wisconsin
16. Kentucky
17. Auburn
18. Duke
19. Stanford
20. Michigan

1954
Team
1. Ohio St.
2. UCLA
3. Oklahoma
4. Notre Dame
5. Navy
6. Mississippi
7. Army
8. Maryland
9. Wisconsin
10. Arkansas
11. Miami (Fla.)
12. West Va.
13. Auburn
14. Duke
15. Michigan
16. Virginia Tech
17. Southern Cal
18. Baylor
19. Rice
20. Penn St.

1955
Team
1. Oklahoma
2. Michigan St.
3. Maryland
4. UCLA
5. Ohio St.
6. Texas Christian
7. Georgia Tech
8. Auburn
9. Notre Dame
10. Mississippi
11. Pittsburgh
12. Michigan
13. Southern Cal
14. Miami (Fla.)
15. Miami (Ohio)
16. Stanford
17. Texas A&M
18. Navy
19. West Va.
20. Army

1956
Team
1. Oklahoma
2. Tennessee
3. Iowa
4. Georgia Tech
5. Texas A&M
6. Miami (Fla.)
7. Michigan
8. Syracuse
9. Michigan St.
10. Oregon St.
11. Baylor
12. Minnesota
13. Pittsburgh
14. Texas Christian
15. Ohio St.
16. Navy
17. Geo. Washington
18. Southern Cal
19. Clemson
20. Colorado

1957
Team
1. Auburn
2. Ohio St.
3. Michigan St.
4. Oklahoma
5. Navy
6. Iowa
7. Mississippi
8. Rice
9. Texas A&M
10. Notre Dame
11. Texas
12. Arizona St.
13. Tennessee
14. Mississippi St.
15. North Caro. St.
16. Duke
17. Florida
18. Army
19. Wisconsin
20. Va. Military

1958
Team
1. LSU
2. Iowa
3. Army
4. Auburn
5. Oklahoma
6. Air Force
7. Wisconsin
8. Ohio St.
9. Syracuse
10. Texas Christian
11. Mississippi
12. Clemson
13. Purdue
14. Florida
15. South Caro.
16. California
17. Notre Dame
18. Southern Methodist
19. Oklahoma St.
20. Rutgers

1959
Team
1. Syracuse
2. Mississippi
3. LSU
4. Texas
5. Georgia
6. Wisconsin
7. Texas Christian
8. Washington
9. Arkansas
10. Alabama
11. Clemson
12. Penn St.
13. Illinois
14. Southern Cal
15. Oklahoma
16. Wyoming
17. Notre Dame
18. Missouri
19. Florida
20. Pittsburgh

1960
Team
1. Minnesota
2. Mississippi
3. Iowa
4. Navy
5. Missouri
6. Washington
7. Arkansas
8. Ohio St.
9. Alabama
10. Duke
11. Kansas
12. Baylor
13. Auburn
14. Yale
15. Michigan St.
16. Penn St.
17. New Mexico St.
18. Florida
19. Syracuse
   Purdue

1961
Team
1. Alabama
2. Ohio St.
3. Texas
4. LSU
5. Mississippi
6. Minnesota
7. Colorado
8. Michigan St.
9. Arkansas
10. Utah St.
11. Missouri
12. Purdue
13. Georgia Tech
14. Syracuse
15. Rutgers
16. UCLA
17. Rice
   Penn St.
   Arizona
20. Duke

1962
Team
1. Southern Cal
2. Wisconsin
3. Mississippi
4. Texas
5. Alabama
6. Arkansas
7. LSU
8. Oklahoma
9. Penn St.
10. Minnesota

Only 10 ranked

1963
Team
1. Texas
2. Navy
3. Illinois
4. Pittsburgh
5. Auburn
6. Nebraska
7. Mississippi
8. Alabama
9. Oklahoma
10. Michigan St.

Only 10 ranked

1964
Team
1. Alabama
2. Arkansas
3. Notre Dame
4. Michigan
5. Texas
6. Nebraska
7. LSU
8. Oregon St.
9. Ohio St.
10. Southern Cal

Only 10 ranked

1965
Team
1. Alabama
2. Michigan St.
3. Arkansas
4. UCLA
5. Nebraska
6. Missouri
7. Tennessee
8. LSU
9. Notre Dame
10. Southern Cal

Only 10 ranked

1966
Team
1. Notre Dame
2. Michigan St.
3. Alabama
4. Georgia
5. UCLA
6. Nebraska
7. Purdue
8. Georgia Tech
9. Miami (Fla.)
10. Southern Methodist

Only 10 ranked

1967
Team
1. Southern Cal
2. Tennessee
3. Oklahoma
4. Indiana
5. Notre Dame
6. Wyoming
7. Oregon St.
8. Alabama
9. Purdue
10. Penn St.

Only 10 ranked

1968
Team
1. Ohio St.
2. Penn St.
3. Texas
4. Southern Cal
5. Notre Dame
6. Arkansas
7. Kansas
8. Georgia
9. Missouri
10. Purdue
11. Oklahoma
12. Michigan
13. Tennessee
14. Southern Methodist
15. Oregon St.
16. Auburn
17. Alabama
18. Houston
19. LSU
20. Ohio

1969
Team
1. Texas
2. Penn St.
3. Southern Cal
4. Ohio St.
5. Notre Dame
6. Missouri
7. Arkansas
8. Mississippi
9. Michigan
10. LSU
11. Nebraska
12. Houston
13. UCLA
14. Florida
15. Tennessee
16. Colorado
17. West Va.
18. Purdue
19. Stanford
20. Auburn

1970
Team
1. Nebraska
2. Notre Dame
3. Texas
4. Tennessee
5. Ohio St.
6. Arizona St.
7. LSU
8. Stanford
9. Michigan
10. Auburn
11. Arkansas
12. Toledo
13. Georgia Tech
14. Dartmouth
15. Southern Cal
16. Air Force
17. Tulane
18. Penn St.
19. Houston
20. Oklahoma
   Mississippi

1971
Team
1. Nebraska
2. Oklahoma
3. Colorado
4. Alabama
5. Penn St.
6. Michigan
7. Georgia
8. Arizona St.
9. Tennessee
10. Stanford
11. LSU
12. Auburn
13. Notre Dame
14. Toledo
15. Mississippi
16. Arkansas
17. Houston
18. Texas
19. Washington
20. Southern Cal

1972
Team
1. Southern Cal
2. Oklahoma
3. Texas
4. Nebraska
5. Auburn
6. Michigan
7. Alabama
8. Tennessee
9. Ohio St.
10. Penn St.
11. LSU
12. North Caro.
13. Arizona St.
14. Notre Dame
15. UCLA
16. Colorado
17. North Caro. St.
18. Louisville
19. Washington St.
20. Georgia Tech

1973
Team
1. Notre Dame
2. Ohio St.
3. Oklahoma
4. Alabama
5. Penn St.
6. Michigan
7. Nebraska
8. Southern Cal
9. Arizona St.
   Houston
11. Texas Tech
12. UCLA
13. LSU
14. Texas
15. Miami (Ohio)
16. North Caro. St.
17. Missouri
18. Kansas
19. Tennessee
20. Maryland
    Tulane

1974
Team
1. Oklahoma
2. Southern Cal
3. Michigan
4. Ohio St.
5. Alabama
6. Notre Dame
7. Penn St.
8. Auburn
9. Nebraska
10. Miami (Ohio)
11. North Caro. St.
12. Michigan St.
13. Maryland
14. Baylor
15. Florida
16. Texas A&M
17. Mississippi St.
    Texas
19. Houston
20. Tennessee

1975
Team
1. Oklahoma
2. Arizona St.
3. Alabama
4. Ohio St.
5. UCLA
6. Texas
7. Arkansas
8. Michigan
9. Nebraska
10. Penn St.
11. Texas A&M
12. Miami (Ohio)
13. Maryland
14. California
15. Pittsburgh
16. Colorado
17. Southern Cal
18. Arizona
19. Georgia
20. West Va.

1976
Team
1. Pittsburgh
2. Southern Cal
3. Michigan
4. Houston
5. Oklahoma
6. Ohio St.
7. Texas A&M
8. Maryland
9. Nebraska
10. Georgia
11. Alabama
12. Notre Dame
13. Texas Tech
14. Oklahoma St.
15. UCLA
16. Colorado
17. Rutgers
18. Kentucky
19. Iowa St.
20. Mississippi St.

1977
Team
1. Notre Dame
2. Alabama
3. Arkansas
4. Texas
5. Penn St.
6. Kentucky
7. Oklahoma
8. Pittsburgh
9. Michigan
10. Washington
11. Ohio St.
12. Nebraska
13. Southern Cal
14. Florida St.
15. Stanford
16. San Diego St.
17. North Caro.
18. Arizona St.
19. Clemson
20. Brigham Young

1978
Team
1. Alabama
2. Southern Cal
3. Oklahoma
4. Penn St.
5. Michigan
6. Clemson
7. Notre Dame
8. Nebraska
9. Texas
10. Houston
11. Arkansas
12. Michigan St.
13. Purdue
14. UCLA
15. Missouri
16. Georgia
17. Stanford
18. North Caro. St.
19. Texas A&M
20. Maryland

1979
Team
1. Alabama
2. Southern Cal
3. Oklahoma
4. Ohio St.
5. Houston
6. Florida St.
7. Pittsburgh
8. Arkansas
9. Nebraska
10. Purdue
11. Washington
12. Texas
13. Brigham Young
14. Baylor
15. North Caro.
16. Auburn
17. Temple
18. Michigan
19. Indiana
20. Penn St.

1980
Team
1. Georgia
2. Pittsburgh
3. Oklahoma
4. Michigan
5. Florida St.
6. Alabama
7. Nebraska
8. Penn St.
9. Notre Dame
10. North Caro.
11. Southern Cal
12. Brigham Young
13. UCLA
14. Baylor
15. Ohio St.
16. Washington
17. Purdue
18. Miami (Fla.)
19. Mississippi St.
20. Southern Methodist

1981
Team
1. Clemson
2. Texas
3. Penn St.
4. Pittsburgh
5. Southern Methodist
6. Georgia
7. Alabama
8. Miami (Fla.)
9. North Caro.
10. Washington
11. Nebraska
12. Michigan
13. Brigham Young
14. Southern Cal
15. Ohio St.
16. Arizona St.
17. West Va.
18. Iowa
19. Missouri
20. Oklahoma

1982
Team
1. Penn St.
2. Southern Methodist
3. Nebraska
4. Georgia
5. UCLA
6. Arizona St.
7. Washington
8. Clemson
9. Arkansas
10. Pittsburgh
11. LSU
12. Ohio St.
13. Florida St.
14. Auburn
15. Southern Cal
16. Oklahoma
17. Texas
18. North Caro.
19. West Va.
20. Maryland

1983
Team
1. Miami (Fla.)
2. Nebraska
3. Auburn
4. Georgia
5. Texas
6. Florida
7. Brigham Young
8. Michigan
9. Ohio St.
10. Illinois
11. Clemson
12. Southern Methodist
13. Air Force
14. Iowa
15. Alabama
16. West Va.
17. UCLA
18. Pittsburgh
19. Boston College
20. East Caro.

1984
Team
1. Brigham Young
2. Washington
3. Florida
4. Nebraska
5. Boston College
6. Oklahoma
7. Oklahoma St.
8. Southern Methodist
9. UCLA
10. Southern Cal
11. South Caro.
12. Maryland
13. Ohio St.
14. Auburn
15. LSU
16. Iowa
17. Florida St.
18. Miami (Fla.)
19. Kentucky
20. Virginia

1985
Team
1. Oklahoma
2. Michigan
3. Penn St.
4. Tennessee
5. Florida
6. Texas A&M
7. UCLA
8. Air Force
9. Miami (Fla.)
10. Iowa
11. Nebraska
12. Arkansas
13. Alabama
14. Ohio St.
15. Florida St.
16. Brigham Young
17. Baylor
18. Maryland
19. Georgia Tech
20. LSU

1986
Team
1. Penn St.
2. Miami (Fla.)
3. Oklahoma
4. Arizona St.
5. Nebraska
6. Auburn
7. Ohio St.
8. Michigan
9. Alabama
10. LSU
11. Arizona
12. Baylor
13. Texas A&M
14. UCLA
15. Arkansas
16. Iowa
17. Clemson
18. Washington
19. Boston College
20. Virginia Tech

1987
Team
1. Miami (Fla.)
2. Florida St.
3. Oklahoma
4. Syracuse
5. LSU
6. Nebraska
7. Auburn
8. Michigan St.
9. UCLA
10. Texas A&M
11. Oklahoma St.
12. Clemson
13. Georgia
14. Tennessee
15. South Caro.
16. Iowa
17. Notre Dame
18. Southern Cal
19. Michigan
20. Arizona St.

1988
Team
1. Notre Dame
2. Miami (Fla.)
3. Florida St.
4. Michigan
5. West Va.
6. UCLA
7. Southern Cal
8. Auburn
9. Clemson
10. Nebraska
11. Oklahoma St.
12. Arkansas
13. Syracuse
14. Oklahoma
15. Georgia
16. Washington St.
17. Alabama
18. Houston
19. LSU
20. Indiana

†1989
Team
1. Miami (Fla.)
2. Notre Dame
3. Florida St.
4. Colorado
5. Tennessee
6. Auburn
7. Michigan
8. Southern Cal
9. Alabama
10. Illinois
11. Nebraska
12. Clemson
13. Arkansas
14. Houston
15. Penn St.
16. Michigan St.
17. Pittsburgh
18. Virginia
19. Texas Tech
20. Texas A&M
21. West Va.
22. Brigham Young
23. Washington
24. Ohio St.
25. Arizona

1990
Team
1. Colorado
2. Georgia Tech
3. Miami (Fla.)
4. Florida St.
5. Washington
6. Notre Dame
7. Michigan
8. Tennessee
9. Clemson
10. Houston
11. Penn St.
12. Texas
13. Florida
14. Louisville
15. Texas A&M
16. Michigan St.
17. Oklahoma
18. Iowa
19. Auburn
20. Southern Cal
21. Mississippi
22. Brigham Young
23. Virginia
24. Nebraska
25. Illinois

1991
Team
1. Miami (Fla.)
2. Washington
3. Penn St.
4. Florida St.
5. Alabama
6. Michigan
7. Florida
8. California
9. East Caro.
10. Iowa
11. Syracuse
12. Texas A&M
13. Notre Dame
14. Tennessee
15. Nebraska
16. Oklahoma
17. Georgia
18. Clemson
19. UCLA
20. Colorado
21. Tulsa
22. Stanford
23. Brigham Young
24. North Caro. St.
25. Air Force

1992
Team
1. Alabama
2. Florida St.
3. Miami (Fla.)
4. Notre Dame
5. Michigan
6. Syracuse
7. Texas A&M
8. Georgia
9. Stanford
10. Florida
11. Washington
12. Tennessee
13. Colorado
14. Nebraska
15. Washington St.
16. Mississippi
17. North Caro. St.
18. Ohio St.
19. North Caro.
20. Hawaii
21. Boston College
22. Kansas
23. Mississippi St.
24. Fresno St.
25. Wake Forest

1993
Team
1. Florida St.
2. Notre Dame
3. Nebraska
4. Auburn
5. Florida
6. Wisconsin
7. West Va.
8. Penn St.
9. Texas A&M
10. Arizona
11. Ohio St.
12. Tennessee
13. Boston College
14. Alabama
15. Miami (Fla.)
16. Colorado
17. Oklahoma
18. UCLA
19. North Caro.
20. Kansas St.
21. Michigan
22. Virginia Tech
23. Clemson
24. Louisville
25. California

1994
Team
1. Nebraska
2. Penn St.
3. Colorado
4. Florida St.
5. Alabama
6. Miami (Fla.)
7. Florida
8. Texas A&M
9. Auburn
10. Utah
11. Oregon
12. Michigan
13. Southern Cal
14. Ohio St.
15. Virginia
16. Colorado St.
17. North Caro. St.
18. Brigham Young
19. Kansas St.
20. Arizona
21. Washington St.
22. Tennessee
23. Boston College
24. Mississippi St.
25. Texas

1995
Team
1. Nebraska
2. Florida
3. Tennessee
4. Florida St.
5. Colorado
6. Ohio St.
7. Kansas St.
8. Northwestern
9. Kansas
10. Virginia Tech
11. Notre Dame
12. Southern Cal
13. Penn St.
14. Texas
15. Texas A&M
16. Virginia
17. Michigan
18. Oregon
19. Syracuse
20. Miami (Fla.)
21. Alabama
22. Auburn
23. Texas Tech
24. Toledo
25. Iowa

1996
Team
1. Florida (12-1)
2. Ohio St. (11-1)
3. Florida St.(11-1)
4. Arizona St. (11-1)
5. Brigham Young (14-1)
6. Nebraska (11-2)
7. Penn St. (11-2)
8. Colorado (10-2)
9. Tennessee (10-2)
10. North Caro.(10-2)
11. Alabama (10-3)
12. LSU (10-2)
13. Virginia Tech (10-2)
14. Miami (Fla.) (9-3)
15. Northwestern (9-3)
16. Washington (9-3)
17. Kansas St. (9-3)
18. Iowa (9-3)
19. Notre Dame (8-3)
20. Michigan (8-4)
21. Syracuse (9-3)
22. Wyoming (10-2)
23. Texas (8-5)
24. Auburn (8-4)
25. Army (10-2)

1997
Team
1. Michigan (12-0)
2. Nebraska (13-0)
3. Florida St. (11-1)
4. Florida (10-2)
5. UCLA (10-2)
6. North Caro. (11-1)
7. Tennessee (11-2)
8. Kansas St. (11-1)
9. Washington St. (10-2)
10. Georgia (10-2)
11. Auburn (10-3)
12. Ohio St. (10-3)
13. LSU (9-3)
14. Arizona St. (9-3)
15. Purdue (9-3)
16. Penn St. (9-3)
17. Colorado St. (11-2)
18. Washington (8-4)
19. Southern Miss. (9-3)
20. Texas A&M (9-4)
21. Syracuse (9-4)
22. Mississippi (8-4)
23. Missouri (7-5)
24. Oklahoma St. (8-4)
25. Georgia Tech (7-5)

**On January 6, 1948, in a special postseason poll after the Rose Bowl, the Associated Press voted Michigan No. 1 and Notre Dame No. 2. However, the postseason poll did not supersede the final regular-season poll of December 6, 1947. †Beginning in 1989 season, AP selected top 25 teams instead of 20.*

United Press International Final Polls

United Press (UP), 1950-57; United Press International (UPI) from 1958-95 after merger with International News Service (INS). Served as the coaches' poll until 1991, when it was taken over by USA Today/Cable News Network (CNN)/ESPN poll.

1950
Team
1. Oklahoma
2. Texas
3. Tennessee
4. California
5. Army
6. Michigan
7. Kentucky
8. Princeton
9. Michigan St.
10. Ohio St.
11. Illinois
12. Clemson
13. Miami (Fla.)
14. Wyoming
15. Washington
    Baylor
17. Alabama
18. Wash. & Lee
19. Navy
20. Nebraska
    Wisconsin
    Cornell

1951
Team
1. Tennessee
2. Michigan St.
3. Illinois
4. Maryland
5. Georgia Tech
6. Princeton
7. Stanford
8. Wisconsin
9. Baylor
10. Texas Christian
11. Oklahoma
12. California
13. Notre Dame
14. San Francisco
    Purdue
    Washington St.
17. Holy Cross
    UCLA
    Kentucky
20. Kansas

1952
Team
1. Michigan St.
2. Georgia Tech
3. Notre Dame
4. Oklahoma
    Southern Cal
6. UCLA
7. Mississippi
8. Tennessee
9. Alabama
10. Wisconsin
11. Texas
12. Purdue
13. Maryland
14. Princeton
15. Ohio St.
    Pittsburgh
17. Navy
18. Duke
19. Houston
    Kentucky

1953
Team
1. Maryland
2. Notre Dame
3. Michigan St.
4. UCLA
5. Oklahoma
6. Rice
7. Illinois
8. Texas
9. Georgia Tech
10. Iowa
11. Alabama
12. Texas Tech
13. West Va.
14. Wisconsin
15. Kentucky
16. Army
17. Stanford
18. Duke
19. Michigan
20. Ohio St.

1954
Team
1. UCLA
2. Ohio St.
3. Oklahoma
4. Notre Dame
5. Navy
6. Mississippi
7. Army
8. Arkansas
9. Miami (Fla.)
10. Wisconsin
11. Southern Cal
    Maryland
    Georgia Tech
14. Duke
15. Michigan
16. Penn St.
17. Southern Methodist
18. Denver
19. Rice
20. Minnesota

1955
Team
1. Oklahoma
2. Michigan St.
3. Maryland
4. UCLA
5. Ohio St.
6. Texas Christian
7. Georgia Tech
8. Auburn
9. Mississippi
10. Notre Dame
11. Pittsburgh
12. Southern Cal
13. Michigan
14. Texas A&M
15. Army
16. Duke
17. West Va.
18. Miami (Fla.)
19. Iowa
20. Navy
    Stanford
    Miami (Ohio)

1956
Team
1. Oklahoma
2. Tennessee
3. Iowa
4. Georgia Tech
5. Texas A&M
6. Miami (Fla.)
7. Michigan
8. Syracuse
9. Minnesota
10. Michigan St.
11. Baylor
12. Pittsburgh
13. Oregon St.
14. Texas Christian
15. Southern Cal
16. Wyoming
17. Yale
18. Colorado
19. Navy
20. Duke

1957
Team
1. Ohio St.
2. Auburn
3. Michigan St.
4. Oklahoma
5. Iowa
6. Navy
7. Rice
8. Mississippi
9. Notre Dame
10. Texas A&M
11. Texas
12. Arizona St.
13. Army
14. Duke
    Wisconsin
16. Tennessee
17. Oregon
18. Clemson
    UCLA
20. North Caro. St.

1958
Team
1. LSU
2. Iowa
3. Army
4. Auburn
5. Oklahoma
6. Wisconsin
7. Ohio St.
8. Air Force
9. Texas Christian
10. Syracuse
11. Purdue
12. Mississippi
13. Clemson
14. Notre Dame
15. Florida
16. California
17. Northwestern
18. Southern Methodist

(Only 18 teams received votes)

1959
Team
1. Syracuse
2. Mississippi
3. LSU
4. Texas
5. Georgia
6. Wisconsin
7. Washington
8. Texas Christian
9. Arkansas
10. Penn St.
11. Clemson
12. Illinois
13. Alabama
    Southern Cal
15. Auburn
16. Michigan St.
17. Oklahoma
18. Notre Dame
19. Pittsburgh
    Missouri
    Florida

1960
Team
1. Minnesota
2. Iowa
3. Mississippi
4. Missouri
5. Wisconsin
6. Navy
7. Arkansas
8. Ohio St.
9. Kansas
10. Alabama
11. Duke
    Baylor
    Michigan St.
14. Auburn
15. Purdue
16. Florida
17. Texas
18. Yale
19. New Mexico St.
    Tennessee

1961
Team
1. Alabama
2. Ohio St.
3. LSU
4. Texas
5. Mississippi
6. Minnesota
7. Colorado
8. Arkansas
9. Michigan St.
10. Utah St.
11. Purdue
    Missouri
13. Georgia Tech
14. Duke
15. Kansas
16. Syracuse
17. Wyoming
18. Wisconsin
19. Miami (Fla.)
    Penn St.

1962
Team
1. Southern Cal
2. Wisconsin
3. Mississippi
4. Texas
5. Alabama
6. Arkansas
7. Oklahoma
8. LSU
9. Penn St.
10. Minnesota
11. Georgia Tech
12. Missouri
13. Ohio St.
14. Duke
    Washington
16. Northwestern
    Oregon St.
18. Arizona St.
    Illinois
    Miami (Fla.)

1963
Team
1. Texas
2. Navy
3. Pittsburgh
4. Illinois
5. Nebraska
6. Auburn
7. Mississippi
8. Oklahoma
9. Alabama
10. Michigan St.
11. Mississippi St.
12. Syracuse
13. Arizona St.
14. Memphis
15. Washington
16. Penn St.
    Southern Cal
    Missouri
19. North Caro.
20. Baylor

1964
Team
1. Alabama
2. Arkansas
3. Notre Dame
4. Michigan
5. Texas
6. Nebraska
7. LSU
8. Oregon St.
9. Ohio St.
10. Southern Cal
11. Florida St.
12. Syracuse
13. Princeton
14. Penn St.
    Utah
16. Illinois
    New Mexico
18. Tulsa
    Missouri
20. Mississippi
    Michigan St.

1965
Team
1. Michigan St.
2. Arkansas
3. Nebraska
4. Alabama
5. UCLA
6. Missouri
7. Tennessee
8. Notre Dame
9. Southern Cal
10. Texas Tech
11. Ohio St.
12. Florida
13. Purdue
14. LSU
15. Georgia
16. Tulsa
17. Mississippi
18. Kentucky
19. Syracuse
20. Colorado

1966
Team
1. Notre Dame
2. Michigan St.
3. Alabama
4. Georgia
5. UCLA
6. Purdue
7. Nebraska
8. Georgia Tech
9. Southern Methodist
10. Miami (Fla.)
11. Florida
12. Mississippi
13. Arkansas
14. Tennessee
15. Wyoming
16. Syracuse
17. Houston
18. Southern Cal
19. Oregon St.
20. Virginia Tech

1967
Team
1. Southern Cal
2. Tennessee
3. Oklahoma
4. Notre Dame
5. Wyoming
6. Indiana
7. Alabama
8. Oregon St.
9. Purdue
10. UCLA
11. Penn St.
12. Syracuse
13. Colorado
14. Minnesota
15. Florida St.
16. Miami (Fla.)
17. North Caro. St.
18. Georgia
19. Houston
20. Arizona St.

1968

Team
1. Ohio St.
2. Southern Cal
3. Penn St.
4. Georgia
5. Texas
6. Kansas
7. Tennessee
8. Notre Dame
9. Arkansas
10. Oklahoma
11. Purdue
12. Alabama
13. Oregon St.
14. Florida St.
15. Michigan
16. Southern Methodist
17. Missouri
18. Ohio
    Minnesota
20. Houston
    Stanford

1969

Team
1. Texas
2. Penn St.
3. Arkansas
4. Southern Cal
5. Ohio St.
6. Missouri
7. LSU
8. Michigan
9. Notre Dame
10. UCLA
11. Tennessee
12. Nebraska
13. Mississippi
14. Stanford
15. Auburn
16. Houston
17. Florida
18. Purdue
    San Diego St.
    West Va.

1970

Team
1. Texas
2. Ohio St.
3. Nebraska
4. Tennessee
5. Notre Dame
6. LSU
7. Michigan
8. Arizona St.
9. Auburn
10. Stanford
11. Air Force
12. Arkansas
13. Houston
    Dartmouth
15. Oklahoma
16. Colorado
17. Georgia Tech
    Toledo
19. Penn St.
    Southern Cal

1971

Team
1. Nebraska
2. Alabama
3. Oklahoma
4. Michigan
5. Auburn
6. Arizona St.
7. Colorado
8. Georgia
9. Tennessee
10. LSU
11. Penn St.
12. Texas
13. Toledo
14. Houston
15. Notre Dame
16. Stanford
17. Iowa St.
18. North Caro.
19. Florida St.
20. Arkansas
    Mississippi

1972

Team
1. Southern Cal
2. Oklahoma
3. Ohio St.
4. Alabama
5. Texas
6. Michigan
7. Auburn
8. Penn St.
9. Nebraska
10. LSU
11. Tennessee
12. Notre Dame
13. Arizona St.
14. Colorado
    North Caro.
16. Louisville
17. UCLA
    Washington St.
19. Utah St.
20. San Diego St.

1973

Team
1. Alabama
2. Oklahoma
3. Ohio St.
4. Notre Dame
5. Penn St.
6. Michigan
7. Southern Cal
8. Texas
9. UCLA
10. Arizona St.
11. Nebraska
    Texas Tech
13. Houston
14. LSU
15. Kansas
    Tulane
17. Miami (Ohio)
18. Maryland
19. San Diego St.
    Florida

*1974

Team
1. Southern Cal
2. Alabama
3. Ohio St.
4. Notre Dame
5. Michigan
6. Auburn
7. Penn St.
8. Nebraska
9. North Caro. St.
10. Miami (Ohio)
11. Houston
12. Florida
13. Maryland
14. Baylor
15. Texas A&M
    Tennessee
17. Mississippi St.
18. Michigan St.
19. Tulsa

1975

Team
1. Oklahoma
2. Arizona St.
3. Alabama
4. Ohio St.
5. UCLA
6. Arkansas
7. Texas
8. Michigan
9. Nebraska
10. Penn St.
11. Maryland
12. Texas A&M
13. Arizona
    Pittsburgh
15. California
16. Miami (Ohio)
17. Notre Dame
    West Va.
19. Georgia
    Southern Cal

1976

Team
1. Pittsburgh
2. Southern Cal
3. Michigan
4. Houston
5. Ohio St.
6. Oklahoma
7. Nebraska
8. Texas A&M
9. Alabama
10. Georgia
11. Maryland
12. Notre Dame
13. Texas Tech
14. Oklahoma St.
15. UCLA
16. Colorado
17. Rutgers
18. Iowa St.
19. Baylor
    Kentucky

1977

Team
1. Notre Dame
2. Alabama
3. Arkansas
4. Penn St.
5. Texas
6. Oklahoma
7. Pittsburgh
8. Michigan
9. Washington
10. Nebraska
11. Florida St.
12. Ohio St.
    Southern Cal
14. North Caro.
15. Stanford
16. North Texas
    Brigham Young
18. Arizona St.
19. San Diego St.
    North Caro. St.

1978

Team
1. Southern Cal
2. Alabama
3. Oklahoma
4. Penn St.
5. Michigan
6. Notre Dame
7. Clemson
8. Nebraska
9. Texas
10. Arkansas
11. Houston
12. UCLA
13. Purdue
14. Missouri
15. Georgia
16. Stanford
17. Navy
18. Texas A&M
19. Arizona St.
    North Caro. St.

1979

Team
1. Alabama
2. Southern Cal
3. Oklahoma
4. Ohio St.
5. Houston
6. Pittsburgh
7. Nebraska
8. Florida St.
9. Arkansas
10. Purdue
11. Washington
12. Brigham Young
13. Texas
14. North Caro.
15. Baylor
16. Indiana
17. Temple
18. Penn St.
19. Michigan
20. Missouri

1980

Team
1. Georgia
2. Pittsburgh
3. Oklahoma
4. Michigan
5. Florida St.
6. Alabama
7. Nebraska
8. Penn St.
9. North Caro.
10. Notre Dame
11. Brigham Young
12. Southern Cal
13. Baylor
14. UCLA
15. Ohio St.
16. Purdue
17. Washington
18. Miami (Fla.)
19. Florida
20. Southern Methodist

1981

Team
1. Clemson
2. Pittsburgh
3. Penn St.
4. Texas
5. Georgia
6. Alabama
7. Washington
8. North Caro.
9. Nebraska
10. Michigan
11. Brigham Young
12. Ohio St.
13. Southern Cal
14. Oklahoma
15. Iowa
16. Arkansas
17. Mississippi St.
18. West Va.
19. Southern Miss.
20. Missouri

1982

Team
1. Penn St.
2. Southern Methodist
3. Nebraska
4. Georgia
5. UCLA
6. Arizona St.
7. Washington
8. Arkansas
9. Pittsburgh
10. Florida St.
11. LSU
12. Ohio St.
13. North Caro.
14. Auburn
15. Michigan
16. Oklahoma
17. Alabama
18. Texas
19. West Va.
20. Maryland

1983

Team
1. Miami (Fla.)
2. Nebraska
3. Auburn
4. Georgia
5. Texas
6. Florida
7. Brigham Young
8. Ohio St.
9. Michigan
10. Illinois
11. Southern Methodist
12. Alabama
13. UCLA
14. Iowa
15. Air Force
16. West Va.
17. Penn St.
18. Oklahoma St.
19. Pittsburgh
20. Boston College

1984

Team
1. Brigham Young
2. Washington
3. Nebraska
4. Boston College
5. Oklahoma St.
6. Oklahoma
7. Florida
8. Southern Methodist
9. Southern Cal
10. UCLA
11. Maryland
12. Ohio St.
13. South Caro.
14. Auburn
15. Iowa
16. LSU
17. Virginia
18. West Va.
19. Kentucky
    Florida St.

1985

Team
1. Oklahoma
2. Michigan
3. Penn St.
4. Tennessee
5. Air Force
6. UCLA
7. Texas A&M
8. Miami (Fla.)
9. Iowa
10. Nebraska
11. Ohio St.
12. Arkansas
13. Florida St.
14. Alabama
15. Baylor
16. Fresno St.
17. Brigham Young
18. Georgia Tech
19. Maryland
20. LSU

1986

Team
1. Penn St.
2. Miami (Fla.)
3. Oklahoma
4. Nebraska
5. Arizona St.
6. Ohio St.
7. Michigan
8. Auburn
9. Alabama
10. Arizona
11. LSU
12. Texas A&M
13. Baylor
14. UCLA
15. Iowa
16. Arkansas
17. Washington
18. Boston College
19. Clemson
20. Florida St.

1987

Team
1. Miami (Fla.)
2. Florida St.
3. Oklahoma
4. Syracuse
5. LSU
6. Nebraska
7. Auburn
8. Michigan St.
9. Texas A&M
10. Clemson
11. UCLA
12. Oklahoma St.
13. Tennessee
14. Georgia
15. South Caro.
16. Iowa
17. Southern Cal
18. Michigan
19. Texas
20. Indiana

1988

Team
1. Notre Dame
2. Miami (Fla.)
3. Florida St.
4. Michigan
5. West Va.
6. UCLA
7. Auburn
8. Clemson
9. Southern Cal
10. Nebraska
11. Oklahoma St.
12. Syracuse
13. Arkansas
14. Oklahoma
15. Georgia
16. Washington St.
17. North Caro. St.
    Alabama
19. Indiana
20. Wyoming

1989

Team
1. Miami (Fla.)
2. Florida St.
3. Notre Dame
4. Colorado
5. Tennessee
6. Auburn
7. Alabama
8. Michigan
9. Southern Cal
10. Illinois
11. Clemson
12. Nebraska
13. Arkansas
14. Penn St.
15. Virginia
16. Texas Tech
    Michigan St.
18. Brigham Young
19. Pittsburgh
20. Washington

#1990

Team
1. Georgia Tech
2. Colorado
3. Miami (Fla.)
4. Florida St.
5. Washington
6. Notre Dame
7. Tennessee
8. Michigan
9. Clemson
10. Penn St.
11. Texas
12. Louisville
13. Texas A&M
14. Michigan St.
15. Virginia
16. Iowa
17. Brigham Young
    Nebraska
19. Auburn
20. San Jose St.
21. Syracuse
22. Southern Cal
23. Mississippi
24. Illinois
25. Virginia Tech

¢1991

Team
1. Washington
2. Miami (Fla.)
3. Penn St.
4. Florida St.
5. Alabama
6. Michigan
7. Florida
8. California
9. East Caro.
10. Iowa
11. Syracuse
12. Notre Dame
13. Texas A&M
14. Tennessee
15. Nebraska
16. Oklahoma
17. Clemson
18. Colorado
19. UCLA
20. Georgia
21. Tulsa
22. Stanford
23. North Caro. St.
24. Brigham Young
25. Ohio St.

1992

Team
1. Alabama
2. Florida St.
3. Miami (Fla.)
4. Notre Dame
5. Michigan
6. Syracuse
7. Texas A&M
8. Georgia
9. Stanford
10. Florida
11. Washington
12. Tennessee
13. Colorado
14. Nebraska
15. Washington St.
16. Mississippi
17. North Caro. St.
18. North Caro.
19. Ohio St.
20. Hawaii
21. Boston College
22. Kansas
23. Fresno St.
24. Penn St.
25. Mississippi St.

1993

Team
1. Florida St.
2. Notre Dame
3. Nebraska
4. Florida
5. Wisconsin
6. Texas A&M
7. Penn St.
8. West Va.
9. Ohio St.
10. Arizona
11. Boston College
12. Tennessee
13. Alabama
14. Miami (Fla.)
15. Oklahoma
16. Colorado
17. UCLA
18. Kansas St.
19. Michigan
20. North Caro.
21. Virginia Tech
22. Louisville
23. Clemson
24. California
25. Southern Cal

1994

Team
1. Nebraska
2. Penn St.
3. Colorado
4. Florida St.
5. Alabama
6. Miami (Fla.)
7. Florida
8. Utah
9. Michigan
10. Ohio St.
11. Oregon
12. Brigham Young
13. Southern Cal
14. Colorado St.
15. Virginia
16. Kansas St.
17. North Caro. St.
18. Tennessee
19. Washington St.
20. Arizona
21. North Caro.
22. Boston College
23. Texas
24. Virginia Tech
25. Mississippi St.

1995

Team
1. Nebraska
2. Florida
3. Tennessee
4. Colorado
5. Florida St.
6. Ohio St.
7. Kansas St.
8. Northwestern
9. Virginia Tech
10. Kansas
11. Southern Cal
12. Penn St.
13. Notre Dame
14. Texas A&M
15. Texas
16. Virginia
17. Syracuse
18. Oregon
19. Michigan
20. Texas Tech
21. Auburn
22. Toledo
23. Iowa
24. East Caro.
25. LSU

**Beginning in 1974, by agreement with the American Football Coaches Association, teams on probation by the NCAA were ineligible for ranking and national championship consideration by the UPI Board of Coaches. #Beginning in 1990 season, UPI selected top 25 teams instead of 20. ¢In 1991-92, the No. 1 team in the final UPI/NFF poll received the MacArthur Bowl, awarded by the NFF since 1959 to recognize its national champion. Beginning in 1993, the No. 1 team in the USA Today/Hall of Fame poll was awarded the MacArthur Bowl. The National Football Foundation and Hall of Fame MacArthur Bowl national champions before 1991 are listed in national polls section.*

USA Today/ESPN (Coaches) Weekly Poll Leaders

1992

9-8	Miami (Fla.)	(1-0-0)
9-15	Miami (Fla.)	(1-0-0)
9-22	Miami (Fla.)	(2-0-0)
9-29	Washington	(3-0-0) (2)
10-6	Washington	(4-0-0)
10-13	Miami (Fla.)	(5-0-0) (2)
10-20	Miami (Fla.)	(6-0-0)
10-27	Miami (Fla.)	(7-0-0)
11-3	Miami (Fla.)	(8-0-0)
11-10	Miami (Fla.)	(8-0-0)
11-17	Miami (Fla.)	(9-0-0)
11-24	Miami (Fla.)	(10-0-0)
12-1	Miami (Fla.)	(11-0-0)
12-8	Miami (Fla.)	(11-0-0)
1-2	**Alabama**	**(13-0-0) (2)**

1993

8-31	Florida St.	(1-0-0)
9-7	Florida St.	(2-0-0)
9-14	Florida St.	(3-0-0)
9-21	Florida St.	(4-0-0)
9-28	Florida St.	(4-0-0)
10-5	Florida St.	(5-0-0)
10-12	Florida St.	(6-0-0)
10-19	Florida St.	(7-0-0)
10-26	Florida St.	(7-0-0)
11-2	Florida St.	(8-0-0)
11-9	Florida St.	(9-0-0)
11-16	Notre Dame	(10-0-0) (2)
11-23	Nebraska	(10-0-0) (2)
11-30	Nebraska	(11-0-0)
12-7	Nebraska	(11-0-0)
1-3	**Florida St.**	**(12-1-0) (3)**

1994

9-6	Nebraska	(1-0-0)
9-13	Nebraska	(2-0-0)
9-20	Nebraska	(3-0-0)
9-27	Nebraska	(4-0-0)
10-4	Florida	(4-0-0) (2)
10-11	Florida	(5-0-0)
10-18	Penn St.	(6-0-0) (3)
10-25	Penn St.	(6-0-0)
11-1	Penn St.	(7-0-0)
11-8	Nebraska	(10-0-0) (2)
11-15	Nebraska	(11-0-0)
11-22	Nebraska	(11-0-0)
11-29	Nebraska	(12-0-0)
12-6	Nebraska	(12-0-0)
1-3	**Nebraska**	**(13-0-0)**

1995

9-5	Florida St.	(1-0-0)
9-12	Florida St.	(2-0-0)
9-19	Florida St.	(3-0-0)
9-26	Florida St.	(4-0-0)
10-3	Florida St.	(4-0-0)
10-10	Florida St.	(5-0-0)
10-17	Florida St.	(6-0-0)
10-24	Florida St.	(7-0-0)
10-31	Nebraska	(8-0-0) (2)
11-7	Nebraska	(9-0-0)
11-14	Nebraska	(10-0-0)
11-21	Nebraska	(10-0-0)
11-28	Nebraska	(11-0-0)
12-5	Nebraska	(11-0-0)
1-3	**Nebraska**	**(12-0-0)**

1996

9-2	Nebraska	(0-0-0)
9-9	Nebraska	(1-0-0)
9-16	Nebraska	(1-0-0)
9-23	Florida	(3-0-0) (4)
9-30	Florida	(4-0-0)
10-7	Florida	(5-0-0)
10-14	Florida	(6-0-0)
10-21	Florida	(7-0-0)
10-28	Florida	(7-0-0)
11-4	Florida	(8-0-0)
11-11	Florida	(9-0-0)
11-18	Florida	(10-0-0)
11-25	Florida	(10-0-0)
12-2	Florida St.	(11-0-0) (2)
12-9	Florida St.	(11-0-0)
1-3	**Florida**	**(12-1-0)**

1997

8-8	Florida	(0-0-0)
9-2	Florida	(1-0-0)
9-8	Florida	(2-0-0)
9-15	Florida	(2-0-0)
9-22	Florida	(3-0-0)
9-29	Florida	(4-0-0)
10-6	Florida	(5-0-0)
10-13	Penn St.	(5-0-0) (2)
10-20	Nebraska	(6-0-0) (2)
10-27	Nebraska	(7-0-0)
11-3	Nebraska	(8-0-0)
11-10	Florida St.	(9-0-0) (2)
11-17	Florida St.	(10-0-0)
11-24	Michigan	(11-0-0) (2)
12-1	Michigan	(11-0-0)
12-8	Michigan	(11-0-0)
1-3	**Nebraska**	**(13-0-0) (2)**

1997 USA Today/ESPN Week-by-Week Polls

Preseason 8/8	S2	S8	S15	S22	S29	O6	O13	O20	O27	N3	N10	N17	N24	D1	D8	J3
1. Florida	1	1	1	1	1	1	6	6	6	13	12	10	8	8	8	6
2. Penn St.	2	2	2	2	2	2	1	2	2	3	6	6	4	12	12	17
3. Washington	4	3	3	11	11	9	8	7	7	6	14	20	22	22	23	18
4. Florida St.	5	6	5	4	4	4	3	3	3	2	1	1	5	4	4	3
5. Tennessee	3	4	4	10	10	10	9	8	8	7	5	5	3	3	3	8
6. Nebraska	6	5	6	3	3	3	2	1	1	1	3	3	2	2	2	1
7. Colorado	7	7	16	16	18	25	NR	NR	NR	NR	NR	NR	NR	NR	NR	NR
8. North Caro.	8	8	7	5	5	5	4	4	5	5	9	8	6	5	5	4
9. Ohio St.	9	9	8	7	7	7	12	9	9	8	4	4	11	10	10	12
10. Texas	10	10	24	NR	NR	NR	NR	NR	NR	NR	NR	NR	NR	NR	NR	NR
11. LSU	11	11	10	15	14	14	10	15	14	12	11	18	17	16	15	13
12. Notre Dame	13	15	NR	NR	NR	NR	NR	NR	NR	NR	NR	NR	NR	NR	NR	NR
13. Michigan	14	13	9	6	6	6	5	5	4	4	2	2	1	1	1	2
14. Miami (Fla.)	12	12	21	NR	NR	NR	NR	NR	NR	NR	NR	NR	NR	NR	NR	NR
15. Alabama	15	14	11	19	20	NR	NR	NR	NR	NR	NR	NR	NR	NR	NR	NR
16. Syracuse	NR	NR	NR	NR	NR	NR	NR	25	24	19	19	17	16	15	14	20
17. Brigham Young	16	NR	NR	24	24	22	NR	NR	25	NR	NR	NR	NR	NR	NR	NR
18. Stanford	17	18	23	22	21	17	23	NR	NR	NR	NR	NR	NR	NR	NR	NR
19. Auburn	18	16	12	8	9	8	7	11	11	17	16	13	13	11	13	11
20. Iowa	19	17	13	9	8	16	15	19	16	14	22	NR	NR	NR	NR	NR
21. Clemson	20	21	15	21	NR	NR	NR	NR	NR	NR	NR	NR	NR	NR	NR	NR
22. Southern Cal	21	22	NR	NR	NR	NR	NR	NR	NR	NR	NR	NR	NR	NR	NR	NR
23. Kansas St.	23	20	19	17	16	23	20	13	12	10	8	7	9	9	9	7
24. Wisconsin	NR	NR	NR	NR	NR	NR	24	NR	NR	NR	24	24	NR	NR	NR	NR
25. Virginia Tech	22	19	14	12	12	20T	19	17	22	18	17	15	21	NR	NR	NR
NR Northwestern	24	NR	NR	NR	NR	NR	NR	NR	NR	NR	NR	NR	NR	NR	NR	NR
NR Colorado St.	25	NR	NR	NR	NR	NR	NR	NR	NR	NR	NR	22	19	18	17	16
NR Michigan St.	NR	23	18	13	13	11	11	14	20	NR	NR	NR	NR	NR	25	NR
NR West Va.	NR	24	NR	NR	NR	24	22	20	17	22	23	21	NR	NR	NR	NR
NR North Caro. St.	NR	25	NR	NR	NR	NR	NR	NR	NR	NR	NR	NR	NR	NR	NR	NR
NR Arizona St.	NR	NR	17	23	22	NR	NR	22	21	16	15	12	12	19	18	14
NR Washington St.	NR	NR	20	14	15	12	13	10	10	15	13	11	10	7	7	9
NR Texas A&M	NR	NR	22	18	17	13	14	21	NR	21	18	16	15	14	19	21
NR Georgia	NR	NR	25	20	19	15	21	18	15	9	7	14	14	13	11	10
NR Air Force	NR	NR	NR	25	23	18	17	24	NR	NR	NR	NR	23	21	21	25
NR UCLA	NR	NR	NR	NR	25	19	18	16	13	11	10	9	7	6	6	5
NR Oklahoma St.	NR	NR	NR	NR	NR	20T	16	12	19	23	21	NR	25	24	24	24
NR Georgia Tech	NR	NR	NR	NR	NR	NR	25	NR	NR	NR	NR	NR	NR	NR	NR	NR
NR Purdue	NR	NR	NR	NR	NR	NR	NR	23	18	24	20	25	18	17	16	15
NR Toledo	NR	NR	NR	NR	NR	NR	NR	NR	23	20	NR	NR	NR	NR	NR	NR
NR Southern Miss.	NR	NR	NR	NR	NR	NR	NR	NR	NR	25	NR	NR	24	23	22	19
NR Mississippi St.	NR	NR	NR	NR	NR	NR	NR	NR	NR	NR	25	19	NR	NR	NR	NR
NR Missouri	NR	NR	NR	NR	NR	NR	NR	NR	NR	NR	NR	23	20	20	20	23
NR New Mexico	NR	NR	NR	NR	NR	NR	NR	NR	NR	NR	NR	NR	NR	25	NR	NR
NR Mississippi	NR	NR	NR	NR	NR	NR	NR	NR	NR	NR	NR	NR	NR	NR	NR	22

USA Today/ESPN Final Polls (Coaches)

Took over as coaches poll in 1991. (Cable News Network, 1982-96; ESPN 1997-)

1982
Team
1. Penn St.
2. Southern Methodist
3. Nebraska
4. Georgia
5. UCLA
6. Arizona St.
7. Pittsburgh
8. Arkansas
9. Clemson
10. Washington
11. LSU
12. Florida St.
13. Ohio St.
14. Southern Cal
15. Oklahoma
16. Auburn
17. West Va.
18. Maryland
19. North Caro.
20. Texas
21. Michigan
22. Alabama
23. Tulsa
24. Iowa
25. Florida

1983
Team
1. Miami (Fla.)
2. Auburn
3. Nebraska
4. Georgia
5. Texas
6. Brigham Young
7. Michigan
8. Ohio St.
9. Florida
10. Clemson
11. Illinois
12. Southern Methodist
13. Alabama
14. Air Force
15. West Va.
16. Iowa
17. Tennessee
18. UCLA
19. Pittsburgh
20. Penn St.
21. Oklahoma
22. Boston College
23. Oklahoma St.
24. Maryland
25. East Caro.

1984
Team
1. Brigham Young
2. Washington
3. Florida
4. Nebraska
5. Oklahoma
6. Boston College
7. Oklahoma St.
8. Southern Methodist
9. Maryland
10. South Caro.
11. Southern Cal
12. UCLA
13. LSU
14. Ohio St.
15. Auburn
16. Miami (Fla.)
17. Florida St.
18. Virginia
19. Kentucky
20. Iowa
21. West Va.
22. Army
23. Georgia
24. Air Force
25. Notre Dame

1985
Team
1. Oklahoma
2. Penn St.
3. Michigan
4. Tennessee
5. Florida
6. Miami (Fla.)
7. Air Force
8. Texas A&M
9. UCLA
10. Iowa
11. Nebraska
12. Alabama
13. Ohio St.
14. Florida St.
15. Arkansas
16. Brigham Young
17. Maryland
18. Georgia Tech
19. Baylor
20. Auburn
21. LSU
22. Army
23. Fresno St.
24. Georgia
25. Oklahoma St.

1986
Team
1. Penn St.
2. Miami (Fla.)
3. Oklahoma
4. Nebraska
5. Arizona St.
6. Ohio St.
7. Auburn
8. Michigan
9. Alabama
10. LSU
11. Arizona
12. Texas A&M
13. UCLA
14. Baylor
15. Boston College
16. Iowa
17. Arkansas
18. Clemson
19. Washington
20. Virginia Tech
21. Florida St.
22. Stanford
23. Georgia
24. North Caro. St.
25. San Diego St.

1987
Team
1. Miami (Fla.)
2. Florida St.
3. Oklahoma
4. Syracuse
5. Nebraska
6. LSU
7. Auburn
8. Michigan St.
9. Texas A&M
10. UCLA
11. Clemson
12. Oklahoma St.
13. Georgia
14. Tennessee
15. Iowa
16. Notre Dame
17. Southern Cal
18. South Caro.
19. Michigan
20. Texas
21. Pittsburgh
22. Indiana
23. Penn St.
24. Ohio St.
25. Alabama

1988
Team
1. Notre Dame
2. Miami (Fla.)
3. Florida St.
4. UCLA
5. Michigan
6. West Va.
7. Southern Cal
8. Nebraska
9. Auburn
10. Clemson
11. Oklahoma St.
12. Syracuse
13. Oklahoma
14. Arkansas
15. Washington St.
16. Georgia
17. Alabama
18. North Caro. St.
19. Houston
20. Indiana
21. Wyoming
22. LSU
23. Colorado
24. Southern Miss.
25. Brigham Young

1989
Team
1. Miami (Fla.)
2. Notre Dame
3. Florida St.
4. Colorado
5. Tennessee
6. Auburn
7. Southern Cal
8. Michigan
9. Alabama
10. Illinois
11. Nebraska
12. Clemson
13. Arkansas
14. Houston
15. Penn St.
16. Virginia
17. Michigan St.
18. Texas Tech
19. Pittsburgh
20. Texas A&M
21. West Va.
22. Brigham Young
23. Syracuse
24. Ohio St.
25. Washington

1990
Team
1. Colorado
2. Georgia Tech
3. Miami (Fla.)
4. Florida St.
5. Washington
6. Notre Dame
7. Tennessee
8. Michigan
9. Clemson
10. Texas
11. Penn St.
12. Houston
13. Florida
14. Louisville
15. Michigan St.
16. Texas A&M
17. Oklahoma
18. Iowa
19. Auburn
20. Brigham Young
21. Mississippi
22. Southern Cal
23. Nebraska
24. Illinois
25. Virginia

1991
Team
1. Washington
2. Miami (Fla.)
3. Penn St.
4. Florida St.
5. Alabama
6. Michigan
7. California
8. Florida
9. East Caro.
10. Iowa
11. Syracuse
12. Notre Dame
13. Texas A&M
14. Oklahoma
15. Tennessee
16. Nebraska
17. Clemson
18. UCLA
19. Georgia
20. Colorado
21. Tulsa
22. Stanford
23. Brigham Young
24. Air Force
25. North Caro. St.

1992
Team
1. Alabama
2. Florida St.
3. Miami (Fla.)
4. Notre Dame
5. Michigan
6. Texas A&M
7. Syracuse
8. Georgia
9. Stanford
10. Washington
11. Florida
12. Tennessee
13. Colorado
14. Nebraska
15. North Caro. St.
16. Mississippi
17. Washington St.
18. North Caro.
19. Ohio St.
20. Hawaii
21. Boston College
22. Fresno St.
23. Kansas
24. Penn St.
25. Wake Forest

1993
Team
1. Florida St.
2. Notre Dame
3. Nebraska
4. Florida
5. Wisconsin
6. West Va.
7. Penn St.
8. Texas A&M
9. Arizona
10. Ohio St.
11. Tennessee
12. Boston College
13. Alabama
14. Oklahoma
15. Miami (Fla.)
16. Colorado
17. UCLA
18. Kansas St.
19. Michigan
20. Virginia Tech
21. North Caro.
22. Clemson
23. Louisville
24. California
25. Southern Cal

1994
Team
1. Nebraska
2. Penn St.
3. Colorado
4. Alabama
5. Florida St.
6. Miami (Fla.)
7. Florida
8. Utah
9. Ohio St.
10. Brigham Young
11. Oregon
12. Michigan
13. Virginia
14. Colorado St.
15. Southern Cal
16. Kansas St.
17. North Caro. St.
18. Tennessee
19. Washington St.
20. Arizona
21. North Caro.
22. Boston College
23. Texas
24. Virginia Tech
25. Mississippi St.

1995
Team
1. Nebraska
2. Tennessee
3. Florida
4. Colorado
5. Florida St.
6. Kansas St.
7. Northwestern
8. Ohio St.
9. Virginia Tech
10. Kansas
11. Southern Cal
12. Penn St.
13. Notre Dame
14. Texas
15. Texas A&M
16. Syracuse
17. Virginia
18. Oregon
19. Michigan
20. Texas Tech
21. Auburn
22. Iowa
23. East Caro.
24. Toledo
25. LSU

1996
Team
1. Florida (12-1)
2. Ohio St. (11-1)
3. Florida St. (11-1)
4. Arizona St. (11-1)
5. Brigham Young (14-1)
6. Nebraska (11-2)
7. Penn St. (11-2)
8. Colorado (10-2)
9. Tennessee (10-2)
10. North Caro. (10-2)
11. Alabama (10-3)
12. Virginia Tech (10-2)
13. LSU (10-2)
14. Miami (Fla.) (9-3)
15. Washington (9-3)
16. Northwestern (9-3)
17. Kansas St. (9-3)
18. Iowa (9-3)
19. Syracuse (9-3)
20. Michigan (8-4)
21. Notre Dame (8-3)
22. Wyoming (10-2)
23. Texas (8-5)
24. Army (10-2)
25. Auburn (8-4)

1997
Team
1. Nebraska (13-0)
2. Michigan (12-0)
3. Florida St. (11-1)
4. North Caro. (11-1)
5. UCLA (10-2)
6. Florida (10-2)
7. Kansas St. (11-1)
8. Tennessee (11-2)
9. Washington St. (10-2)
10. Georgia (10-2)
11. Auburn (10-3)
12. Ohio St. (10-3)
13. LSU (9-3)
14. Arizona St. (9-3)
15. Purdue (9-3)
16. Colorado St. (11-2)
17. Penn St. (9-3)
18. Washington (8-4)
19. Southern Miss. (9-3)
20. Syracuse (9-4)
21. Texas A&M (9-4)
22. Mississippi (8-4)
23. Missouri (7-5)
24. Oklahoma St. (8-4)
25. Air Force (10-3)

College Football Bowl Alliance Final Polls

Combined point totals of the final regular-season Associated Press (media) and USA Today/CNN (coaches) polls to determine bowl matchups. Utilized 1993-95.

1993

Team

1. Nebraska
2. Florida St.
3. West Va.
4. Notre Dame
5. Auburn*
6. Tennessee
7. Texas A&M
8. Florida
9. Wisconsin
10. Miami (Fla.)
11. Ohio St.
12. North Caro.
13. Penn St.
14. UCLA
15. Boston College
16. Arizona
17. Colorado
18. Alabama
19. Oklahoma
20. Kansas St.
21. Indiana
22. Virginia Tech
23. Michigan
24. Clemson
25. Fresno St.

1994

Team

1. Nebraska
2. Penn St.
3. Miami (Fla.)
4. Colorado
5. Florida
6. Alabama
7. Florida St.
8. Texas A&M*
9. Auburn*
10. Kansas St.
11. Oregon
12. Colorado St.
13. Ohio St.
14. Utah
15. Arizona
16. Virginia Tech
17. North Caro.
18. Mississippi St.
19. Virginia
20. Michigan
21. Brigham Young
22. Southern Cal
23. North Caro. St.
24. Duke
25. Washington St.

1995

Team

1. Nebraska
2. Florida
3. Northwestern
4. Tennessee
5. Ohio St.
6. Texas
7. Colorado
8. Notre Dame
9. Florida St.
10. Kansas St.
11. Virginia Tech
12. Oregon
13. Kansas
14. Michigan
15. Penn St.
16. Auburn
17. Southern Cal
18. Texas A&M
19. Virginia
20. Washington
21. Alabama*
22. Miami (Fla.)*
23. Clemson
24. Syracuse
25. Arkansas

**Ineligible for bowl participation because of NCAA sanctions.*

Undefeated, Untied Teams

(Regular-Season Games Only)

Minimum of five games played against opponents above the high-school level. Subsequent bowl win is indicated by (†), loss (‡) and tie ($). Unscored-on teams are indicated by (•).

(*Note:* Following are undefeated, untied teams in regular-season games not included with major colleges at the time—Centre, 1919 & 1921; Lafayette, 1921, 1926 & 1937; Wash. & Jeff., 1921; Marquette, 1923; Louisville, 1925; Centenary (La.), 1927; Memphis, 1938; San Jose St., 1939; Hardin-Simmons, 1940; Arizona, 1945; Pacific [Cal.], 1949; Fresno St., 1961; and San Diego St., 1966.)

Year	College	Wins
1878	Princeton	6
1882	Yale	8
1883	Yale	8
1885	Princeton	9
1887	Yale	9
1888	Yale	•13
1889	Princeton	10
1890	Harvard	11
1891	Yale	•13
1892	Minnesota	5
	Purdue	8
	Yale	•13
1893	Minnesota	6
	Princeton	11
1894	Pennsylvania	12
	Va. Military	5
	Yale	16
1895	Pennsylvania	14
1896	LSU	6
1897	Pennsylvania	15
1898	Harvard	11
	Kentucky	•7
	Michigan	10
	North Caro.	9
1899	Kansas	10
	Sewanee	12
1900	Clemson	6
	Texas	6
	Tulane	•5
	Yale	12
1901	Harvard	12
	Michigan	†•10
	Wisconsin	9
1902	Arizona	•5
	California	8
	Michigan	11
	Nebraska	•9
1903	Nebraska	10
	Princeton	11
1904	Auburn	5
	Michigan	10
	Minnesota	13
	Pennsylvania	12
	Pittsburgh	10
	Vanderbilt	9
1905	Chicago	10
	Stanford	8
	Yale	10
1906	New Mexico St.	5
	Washington St.	•6
	Wisconsin	5
1907	Oregon St.	•6
1908	Kansas	9
	LSU	10
1909	Arkansas	7
	Colorado	•6
	Washington	7
	Yale	•10
1910	Colorado	6
	Illinois	•7
	Pittsburgh	•9
	Washington	6
1911	Colorado	6
	Oklahoma	8
	Utah St.	•5
	Washington	7
1912	Harvard	9
	Notre Dame	7
	Penn St.	8
	Washington	6
	Wisconsin	7
1913	Auburn	8
	Chicago	7
	Harvard	9
	Michigan St.	7
	Nebraska	8
	Notre Dame	7
	Washington	7
1914	Army	9
	Illinois	7
	Tennessee	9
	Texas	8
	Wash. & Lee	9
1915	Colorado St.	7
	Columbia	5
	Cornell	9
	Nebraska	8
	Oklahoma	10
	Pittsburgh	8
	Washington	7
	Washington St.	†6
1916	Army	9
	Ohio St.	7
	Pittsburgh	8
	Tulsa	10
1917	Denver	9
	Georgia Tech	9
	Pittsburgh	9
	Texas A&M	•8
	Washington St.	6
1918	Michigan	5
	Oklahoma	6
	Texas	9
	Virginia Tech	7
	Washington (Mo.)	6
1919	Notre Dame	9
	Texas A&M	•10
1920	Boston College	8
	California	†8
	Notre Dame	9
	Ohio St.	‡7
	Southern Cal	6
	Texas	9
	Va. Military	9
1921	California	$9
	Cornell	8
	Iowa	7
1922	California	9
	Cornell	8
	Drake	7
	Iowa	7
	Princeton	8
	Tulsa	7
1923	Colorado	9
	Cornell	8
	Illinois	8
	Michigan	8
	Southern Methodist	9
	Yale	8
1924	Notre Dame	†9
1925	Alabama	†9
	Dartmouth	8
1926	Alabama	$9
	Stanford	$10
	Utah	7
1927	(None)	
1928	Boston College	9
	Detroit	9
	Georgia Tech	†9
1929	Notre Dame	9
	Pittsburgh	‡9
	Purdue	8
	Tulane	9
	Utah	7
1930	Alabama	†9
	Notre Dame	10
	Utah	8
	Washington St.	‡9
1931	Tulane	‡11
1932	Colgate	•9
	Michigan	8
	Southern Cal	†9
1933	Princeton	9
1934	Alabama	†9
	Minnesota	8
1935	Minnesota	8
	Princeton	9
	Southern Methodist	‡12
1936	(None)	
1937	Alabama	‡9
	Colorado	‡8

Year	College	Wins
	Santa Clara	†8
1938	Duke	‡•9
	Georgetown	8
	Oklahoma	‡10
	Tennessee	†10
	Texas Christian	†10
	Texas Tech	‡10
1939	Cornell	8
	Tennessee	‡•10
	Texas A&M	†10
1940	Boston College	†10
	Lafayette	9
	Minnesota	8
	Stanford	†9
	Tennessee	‡10
1941	Duke	‡9
	Duquesne	8
	Minnesota	8
1942	Tulsa	‡10
1943	Purdue	9
1944	Army	9
	Ohio St.	9
1945	Alabama	†9
	Army	9
	Oklahoma St.	†8
1946	Georgia	†10
	Hardin-Simmons	†10
	UCLA	‡10
1947	Michigan	†9
	Notre Dame	9
	Penn St.	$9
1948	California	‡10
	Clemson	†10
	Michigan	9
1949	Army	9
	California	‡10
	Notre Dame	10
	Oklahoma	†10
1950	Oklahoma	‡10
	Princeton	9
	Wyoming	†9
1951	Maryland	†9
	Michigan St.	9
	Princeton	9
	San Francisco	9
	Tennessee	‡10
1952	Georgia Tech	†11
	Michigan St.	9
1953	Maryland	‡10
1954	Ohio St.	†9
	Oklahoma	10
	UCLA	9
1955	Maryland	‡10
	Oklahoma	†10
1956	Oklahoma	10
	Tennessee	‡10
	Wyoming	10
1957	Arizona St.	10
	Auburn	10
1958	LSU	†10
1959	Syracuse	†10
1960	New Mexico St.	†10
	Yale	9
1961	Alabama	†10
	Rutgers	9
1962	Dartmouth	9
	Mississippi	†9
	Southern Cal	†10
1963	Texas	†10
1964	Alabama	‡10
	Arkansas	†10
	Princeton	9
1965	Arkansas	‡10
	Dartmouth	9
	Michigan St.	‡10
	Nebraska	‡10
1966	Alabama	†10
1967	Wyoming	‡10
1968	Ohio	‡10
	Ohio St.	†9
	Penn St.	†10
1969	Penn St.	†10
	San Diego St.	†10
	Texas	†10
	Toledo	†10
1970	Arizona St.	†10
	Dartmouth	9
	Ohio St.	‡9
	Texas	‡10
	Toledo	†11
1971	Alabama	‡11
	Michigan	‡11
	Nebraska	†12
	Toledo	†11
1972	Southern Cal	†11
1973	Alabama	‡11
	Miami (Ohio)	†10
	Notre Dame	†10
	Penn St.	†11
1974	Alabama	‡11
	Oklahoma	11
1975	Arizona St.	†11
	Arkansas St.	11
	Ohio St.	‡11
1976	Maryland	‡11
	Pittsburgh	†11
	Rutgers	11
1977	Texas	‡11
1978	Penn St.	‡11
1979	Alabama	†11
	Brigham Young	‡11
	Florida St.	‡11
	McNeese St.	‡11
	Ohio St.	‡11
1980	Georgia	†11
1981	Clemson	†11
1982	Georgia	‡11
1983	Nebraska	‡12
	Texas	‡11
1984	Brigham Young	†12
1985	Bowling Green	‡11
	Penn St.	‡11
1986	Miami (Fla.)	‡11
	Penn St.	†11
1987	Miami (Fla.)	†11
	Oklahoma	‡11
	Syracuse	$11
1988	Notre Dame	†11
	West Va.	‡11
1989	Colorado	‡11
1990	(None)	
1991	Miami (Fla.)	†11
	Washington	†11
1992	Alabama	†12
	Miami (Fla.)	‡11
	Texas A&M	‡12
1993	Auburn	11
	Nebraska	‡11
	West Va.	‡11
1994	Nebraska	†12
	Penn St.	†11
1995	Florida	‡12
	Nebraska	†11
1996	Arizona St.	‡11
	Florida St.	‡11
1997	Nebraska	†13
	Michigan	†12

The Spoilers

(From 1937 Season)

Following is a list of the spoilers of major-college teams that lost their perfect (undefeated, untied) record in their **final** game of the season, including a bowl game (in parentheses). Confrontations of two undefeated, untied teams at the time are in bold face. An asterisk (*) indicates the home team in a regular-season game, a dagger (†) indicates a neutral site.

Date	Spoiler	Victim	Score
1-1-38	California	Alabama (Rose)	13-0
1-1-38	Rice	Colorado (Cotton)	28-14
12-3-38	*Southern Cal	Notre Dame	13-0
1-2-39	Southern Cal	Duke (Rose)	7-3
1-2-39	**Tennessee**	**Oklahoma (Orange)**	17-0
1-2-39	St. Mary's (Cal.)	Texas Tech (Cotton)	20-13
12-2-39	*Duquesne	Detroit	tie 10-10
1-1-40	Southern Cal	Tennessee (Rose)	14-0
1-1-41	**Boston College**	**Tennessee (Sugar)**	19-13
1-1-42	Oregon St.	Duke (Rose)	20-16
11-27-43	*Great Lakes	Notre Dame	19-14
1-1-44	Southern Cal	Washington (Rose)	29-0
11-25-44	*Virginia	Yale	tie 6-6
1-1-47	Illinois	UCLA (Rose)	45-14
1-1-48	Southern Methodist	Penn St. (Cotton)	tie 13-13
11-27-48	†Navy	Army	tie 21-21
12-2-48	*Southern Cal	Notre Dame	tie 14-14
1-1-49	Northwestern	California (Rose)	20-14
1-2-50	Ohio St.	California (Rose)	17-14
12-2-50	†Navy	Army	14-2
1-1-51	Kentucky	Oklahoma (Sugar)	13-7
1-1-52	**Maryland**	**Tennessee (Sugar)**	28-13
11-22-52	Southern Cal	*UCLA	14-12
1-1-54	Oklahoma	Maryland (Orange)	7-0
1-2-56	**Oklahoma**	**Maryland (Orange)**	20-6
1-1-57	Baylor	Tennessee (Sugar)	13-7
11-28-64	*Southern Cal	Notre Dame	20-17
1-1-65	Texas	Alabama (Orange)	21-17
11-20-65	**Dartmouth**	***Princeton**	28-14
1-1-66	UCLA	Michigan St. (Rose)	14-12
1-1-66	Alabama	Nebraska (Orange)	39-28
1-1-66	LSU	Arkansas (Cotton)	14-7
11-19-66	**Notre Dame**	***Michigan St.**	tie 10-10
1-1-68	LSU	Wyoming (Sugar)	20-13
11-23-68	***Harvard**	**Yale**	tie 29-29
12-27-68	Richmond	Ohio (Tangerine)	49-42
11-22-69	*Michigan	Ohio St.	24-12
11-22-69	*Princeton	Dartmouth	35-7
11-21-70	***Ohio St.**	**Michigan**	20-9
1-1-71	Stanford	Ohio St. (Rose)	27-17
1-1-71	Notre Dame	Texas (Cotton)	24-11
1-1-72	Stanford	Michigan (Rose)	13-12
1-1-72	**Nebraska**	**Alabama (Orange)**	38-6
11-25-72	*Ohio St.	Michigan	14-11
11-24-73	**Ohio St.**	***Michigan**	tie 10-10
12-31-73	**Notre Dame**	**Alabama (Sugar)**	24-23
11-23-74	*Ohio St.	Michigan	12-10
11-23-74	*Harvard	Yale	21-16
1-1-75	Notre Dame	Alabama (Orange)	13-11
1-1-76	UCLA	Ohio St. (Rose)	23-10
1-1-77	Houston	Maryland (Cotton)	30-21
11-19-77	*Delaware	Colgate	21-3
1-2-78	Notre Dame	Texas (Cotton)	38-10
1-1-79	Alabama	Penn St. (Sugar)	14-7
11-17-79	Harvard	*Yale	22-7
12-15-79	Syracuse	McNeese St. (Independence)	31-7
12-21-79	Indiana	Brigham Young (Holiday)	38-37
1-1-80	Southern Cal	Ohio St. (Rose)	17-16
1-1-80	Oklahoma	Florida St. (Orange)	24-7
1-1-83	Penn St.	Georgia (Sugar)	27-23
1-2-84	Georgia	Texas (Cotton)	10-9
1-2-84	Miami (Fla.)	Nebraska (Orange)	31-30
12-14-85	Fresno St.	Bowling Green (California)	51-7
1-1-86	Oklahoma	Penn St. (Orange)	25-10
1-2-87	**Penn St.**	**Miami (Fla.) (Fiesta)**	14-10
1-1-88	Auburn	Syracuse (Sugar)	tie 16-16
1-1-88	**Miami (Fla.)**	**Oklahoma (Orange)**	20-14
1-2-89	**Notre Dame**	**West Va. (Fiesta)**	34-21
1-1-90	Notre Dame	Colorado (Orange)	21-6
1-1-93	Notre Dame	Texas A&M (Cotton)	28-3
1-1-93	**Alabama**	**Miami (Fla.) (Sugar)**	34-13
1-1-94	Florida St.	Nebraska (Orange)	18-16
1-1-94	Florida	West Va. (Sugar)	41-7
1-2-96	**Nebraska**	**Florida (Fiesta)**	62-24
1-1-97	Ohio St.	Arizona St. (Rose)	20-17
1-2-97	Florida	Florida St. (Sugar)	52-20

Streaks and Rivalries

Longest Winning Streaks

(Includes Bowl Games)

Wins	Team	Years	Ended by	Score
47	Oklahoma	1953-57	Notre Dame	7-0
39	Washington	1908-14	Oregon St.	0-0
37	Yale	1890-93	Princeton	6-0
37	Yale	1887-89	Princeton	10-0
35	Toledo	1969-71	Tampa	21-0
34	Pennsylvania	1894-96	Lafayette	6-4
31	Oklahoma	1948-50	Kentucky	*13-7
31	Pittsburgh	1914-18	Cleveland Naval Reserve	10-9
31	Pennsylvania	1896-98	Harvard	10-0
30	Texas	1968-70	Notre Dame	*24-11
29	Miami (Fla.)	1990-93	Alabama	*34-13
29	Michigan	1901-03	Minnesota	6-6
28	Alabama	1991-93	Tennessee	17-17
28	Alabama	1978-80	Mississippi St.	6-3
28	Oklahoma	1973-75	Kansas	23-3
28	Michigan St.	1950-53	Purdue	6-0
26	Nebraska	1994-96	Arizona St.	19-0
26	Cornell	1921-24	Williams	14-7
26	Michigan	1903-05	Chicago	2-0
25	Brigham Young	1983-85	UCLA	27-24
25	San Diego St.	1965-67	Utah St.	31-25
25	Michigan	1946-49	Army	21-7
25	Army	1944-46	Notre Dame	0-0
25	Southern Cal	1931-33	Oregon St.	0-0
24	Princeton	1949-52	Pennsylvania	13-7
24	Minnesota	1903-05	Wisconsin	16-12
24	Nebraska	1901-04	Colorado	6-0
24	Yale	1894-95	Boston AC	0-0
24	Harvard	1890-91	Yale	10-0
24	Yale	1882-84	Princeton	0-0
23	Alabama	1991-92	#	
23	Notre Dame	1988-89	Miami (Fla.)	27-10
23	Nebraska	1970-71	UCLA	20-17
23	Penn St.	1968-70	Colorado	41-13
23	Tennessee	1937-39	Southern Cal	*14-0
23	Harvard	1901-02	Yale	23-0
22	Washington	1990-92	Arizona	16-3
22	Nebraska	1982-83	Miami (Fla.)	*31-30
22	Ohio St.	1967-69	Michigan	24-12
22	Arkansas	1963-65	LSU	*14-7
22	Harvard	1912-14	Penn St.	13-13
22	Yale	1904-06	Princeton	0-0
21	Arizona St.	1969-71	Oregon St.	24-18
21	San Diego St.	1968-70	Long Beach St.	27-11
21	Notre Dame	1946-48	Southern Cal	14-14
21	Minnesota	1933-36	Northwestern	6-0
21	Colorado	1908-12	Colorado St.	21-0
21	Pennsylvania	1903-05	Lafayette	6-6
21	Yale	1900-01	Army	5-5
21	Harvard	1898-99	Yale	0-0
20	Penn St.	1993-95	Wisconsin	17-9
20	Auburn	1993-94	Georgia	23-23
20	Oklahoma	1986-87	Miami (Fla.)	*20-14
20	Tennessee	1950-51	Maryland	*28-13
20	Texas A&M	1938-40	Texas	7-0
20	Notre Dame	1929-31	Northwestern	0-0
20	Alabama	1924-26	Stanford	*7-7
20	Iowa	1920-23	Illinois	9-6
20	Notre Dame	1919-21	Iowa	10-7

**Streak ended in bowl game. #Eight victories and one tie in 1993 forfeited by action of the NCAA Committee on Infractions.*

Longest Unbeaten Streaks

(Includes Bowl Games; May Include Ties)

No.	Wins	Ties	Team	Years	Ended by	Score
63	59	4	Washington	1907-17	California	27-0
56	55	1	Michigan	1901-05	Chicago	2-0
50	46	4	California	1920-25	Olympic Club	15-0
48	47	1	Oklahoma	1953-57	Notre Dame	7-0
48	47	1	Yale	1885-89	Princeton	10-0
47	42	5	Yale	1879-85	Princeton	6-5
44	42	2	Yale	1894-96	Princeton	24-6
42	39	3	Yale	1904-08	Harvard	4-0
39	37	2	Notre Dame	1946-50	Purdue	28-14
37	37	0	Yale	1890-93	Princeton	6-0
37	36	1	Oklahoma	1972-75	Kansas	23-3
35	35	0	Toledo	1969-71	Tampa	21-0
35	34	1	Minnesota	1903-05	Wisconsin	16-12
34	34	0	Pennsylvania	1894-96	Lafayette	6-4
34	33	1	Nebraska	1912-16	Kansas	7-3
34	32	2	Princeton	1884-87	Harvard	12-0
34	29	5	Princeton	1877-82	Harvard	1-0
33	31	2	Georgia Tech	1914-18	Pittsburgh	32-0
33	30	3	Tennessee	1926-30	Alabama	18-6
33	30	3	Harvard	1911-15	Cornell	10-0
32	31	1	Nebraska	1969-71	UCLA	20-17
32	31	1	Harvard	1898-00	Yale	28-0
32	30	2	Army	1944-47	Columbia	21-20
31	31	0	Oklahoma	1948-50	Kentucky	13-7
31	31	0	Pittsburgh	1914-18	Cleveland Naval	10-9
31	31	0	Pennsylvania	1896-98	Harvard	10-0
31	30	1	Penn St.	1967-70	Colorado	41-13
31	30	1	San Diego St.	1967-70	Long Beach St.	27-11
31	29	2	Georgia Tech	1950-53	Notre Dame	27-14
30	30	0	Texas	1968-70	Notre Dame	24-11
30	28	2	Pennsylvania	1903-06	Swarthmore	4-0
30	25	5	Penn St.	1919-22	Navy	14-0
29	29	0	Miami (Fla.)	1990-93	Alabama	34-13
28	28	0	Alabama	1978-80	Mississippi St.	6-3
28	28	0	Michigan St.	1950-53	Purdue	6-0
28	26	2	Southern Cal	1978-80	Washington	20-10
28	26	2	Army	1947-50	Navy	14-2
28	26	2	Tennessee	1930-33	Duke	10-2
28	24	4	Minnesota	1933-36	Northwestern	6-0
27	26	1	Southern Cal	1931-33	Stanford	13-7
27	24	3	Notre Dame	1910-14	Yale	28-0

Longest Home Winning Streaks

(Includes Bowl Games)

Wins	Team	Years	Ended by	Score
58	Miami (Fla.)	1985-94	Washington	38-20
57	Alabama	1963-82	Southern Miss.	38-29
56	Harvard	1890-95	Boston AA	0-0
50	Michigan	1901-07	Pennsylvania	6-0
42	Texas	1968-76	Houston	30-0
42	Nebraska	1991-97	Current	
40	Notre Dame	1907-18	Great Lakes	7-7
38	Notre Dame	1919-27	Minnesota	7-7
37	Yale	1904-08	Brown	10-10
37	Yale	1900-03	Princeton	11-6
33	Nebraska	1901-06	Iowa St.	14-2
33	Harvard	1900-03	Amherst	5-0
31	Texas A&M	1990-95	Texas	16-6
31	Yale	1890-93	Princeton	6-0
30	Auburn	1952-61	Kentucky	14-12
30	Tennessee	1928-33	Alabama	12-6
29	Yale	1885-89	Princeton	10-0
28	Michigan	1969-73	Ohio St.	0-0
28	Notre Dame	1942-50	Purdue	28-14
27	Vanderbilt	1903-07	Michigan	8-0
26	Utah	1928-34	Oregon	8-7
26	California	1919-23	Nevada	0-0
25	Ohio St.	1972-76	Missouri	22-21
25	Oklahoma	1947-53	Notre Dame	28-21
25	Wisconsin	1900-03	Chicago	15-6
24	Georgia	1980-83	Auburn	13-7
24	Georgia Tech	1916-19	Wash. & Lee	3-0
24	Virginia	1899-04	Navy	5-0
23	Florida	1990-93	Florida St.	33-21
23	Tulane	1929-32	Vanderbilt	6-6
23	Michigan St.	1904-08	Michigan	0-0
23	Michigan	1897-00	Ohio St.	0-0
23	Harvard	1887-89	Princeton	41-15
22	Wyoming	1965-70	Air Force	41-17
22	Navy	1953-64	Syracuse	14-6
22	Minnesota	1933-37	Notre Dame	7-6
22	LSU	1907-12	Mississippi	10-7
22	Notre Dame	1901-05	Wabash	5-0
21	Arizona St.	1969-72	Air Force	39-31
21	Mississippi	1952-60	LSU	6-6
21	Oklahoma	1953-57	Notre Dame	7-0
21	Miami (Ohio)	1942-48	Xavier (Ohio)	27-19
21	North Caro.	1893-00	Virginia Tech	0-0
20	Florida	1994-97	Current	
20	Fresno St.	1987-90	Utah St.	24-24
20	Rutgers	1974-78	Colgate	14-9
20	Mississippi St.	1939-45	Mississippi	7-6
20	Missouri	1938-43	Oklahoma	20-13
20	Southern Cal	1927-29	California	15-7
20	Southern Cal	1919-23	California	13-7
20	Iowa	1918-23	Illinois	9-6
20	Harvard	1912-14	Penn St.	13-13

Longest Losing Streaks

Losses	Team	Years	Ended with	Score
34	Northwestern	1979-82	Northern Ill.	31-6
28	Virginia	1958-61	William & Mary	21-6
28	Kansas St.	1944-48	Arkansas St.	37-6
27	New Mexico St.	1988-90	Cal St. Fullerton	43-9
27	Eastern Mich.	1980-82	Kent	9-7
26	Colorado St.	1960-63	Pacific (Cal.)	20-0
21	Kent	1981-83	Eastern Mich.	37-13
21	New Mexico	1967-69	Kansas	16-7
20	Texas Christian	1974-75	Rice	28-21
20	Florida St.	1972-74	Miami (Fla.)	21-14
18	Northern Ill.	1996-97	Current	
18	Rice	1987-89	Southern Methodist	35-6
18	Wisconsin	1967-69	Iowa	23-17
18	Wake Forest	1962-63	South Caro.	20-19
17	Illinois	1996-97	Current	
17	Kent	1992-94	Akron	32-16
17	Kent	1989-90	Ohio	44-15
17	Memphis	1981-82	Arkansas St.	12-0
17	Tulane	1961-63	South Caro.	20-7
17	Alabama	1954-56	Mississippi St.	13-12
17	Kansas	1953-55	Washington St.	13-0
16	Indiana	1983-85	Louisville	41-28
16	Vanderbilt	1961-62	Tulane	20-0
16	Iowa St.	1929-31	Simpson	6-0

Most Consecutive Winning Seasons

(All-Time and Current) (.500 percentage and above)

No.	School	Years
42	Notre Dame	1889-1932#
38	Alabama	1911-50†
36	Nebraska	1962-97*
29	Oklahoma	1966-94
28	Virginia	1888-1915
27	Michigan	1892-1918
26	Penn St.	1939-64
23	Syracuse	1913-35
21	Ohio St.	1967-87
21	Southern Cal	1962-82
21	Vanderbilt	1915-35
21	Florida St.	1977-97*
21	Wyoming	1949-69
21	Washington	1977-97*
19	Ohio St.	1899-1917
19	Wisconsin	1891-1909
18	Florida	1980-97*
18	Nebraska	1920-37
17	San Diego St.	1961-77
17	Miami (Ohio)	1943-59
17	Miami (Fla.)	1980-96
16	LSU	1958-73
16	Texas A&M	1914-29
15	Texas A&M	1983-97*
15	Miami (Ohio)	1961-75
15	Bowling Green	1955-69
15	Southern Cal	1919-33
15	Georgia Tech	1908-22
14	Marshall	1984-97*
14	Kentucky	1903-16
14	Virginia Tech	1901-14
13	Arkansas	1977-89

No.	School	Years
13	Georgia	1964-76
13	Navy	1889-01
12	Colorado	1985-96
12	Georgia	1978-89
12	Auburn	1953-64
12	Colorado	1950-61
12	Ohio St.	1928-39
12	Tulane	1928-39
12	Texas Christian	1925-36
12	West Va.	1914-26@
11	Notre Dame	1987-97*
11	Syracuse	1987-97*
11	Virginia	1987-97*

**Current streak. #No teams in 1890 and 1891. †No teams in 1918 and 1943. @No team in 1918.*

Most-Played Rivalries

(Ongoing Unless Indicated)

Games	Opponents (Series leader listed first)	Rivalry Record	First Game
107	Minnesota-Wisconsin	57-42-8	1890
106	Missouri-Kansas	49-48-9	1891
104	Nebraska-Kansas	80-21-3	1892
104	Texas-Texas A&M	66-33-5	1894
103	%Baylor-Texas Christian	49-47-7	1899
102	Miami (Ohio)-Cincinnati	54-41-7	1888
102	North Caro.-Virginia	55-43-4	1892
101	Auburn-Georgia	48-45-8	1892
101	Oregon-Oregon St.	51-40-10	1894
100	Purdue-Indiana	60-34-6	1891
100	Stanford-California	50-39-11	1892
98	Army-Navy	47-44-7	1890
95	Utah-Utah St.	62-29-4	1892
95	Clemson-South Caro.	56-35-4	1896
95	Kansas-Kansas St.	61-29-5	1902
95	Oklahoma-Kansas	62-27-6	1903
94	North Caro.-Wake Forest	63-29-2	1888
94	Michigan-Ohio St.	54-34-6	1897
94	Mississippi-Mississippi St.	54-34-6	1901
93	LSU-Tulane	*64-22-7	1893
93	Tennessee-Kentucky	61-23-9	1893
93	Penn St.-Pittsburgh	48-41-4	1893
92	Georgia-Georgia Tech	52-35-5	1893
92	Nebraska-Iowa St.	76-14-2	1896
92	Texas-Oklahoma	53-34-5	1900
92	Oklahoma-Oklahoma St.	72-13-7	1904
91	Illinois-Northwestern	47-39-5	1892
91	Nebraska-Missouri	56-32-3	1892
91	Tennessee-Vanderbilt	60-26-5	1892
91	North Caro. St.-Wake Forest	55-30-6	1895
90	#Auburn-Georgia Tech	47-39-4	1892
90	Pittsburgh-West Va.	56-31-3	1895
90	Michigan-Michigan St.	59-26-5	1898
90	Washington-Washington St.	57-27-6	1900

**Disputed series record: Tulane claims 23-61-7 record; LSU and Tulane have not met since 1994. #Have not met since 1989. %Have not met since 1995.*

"Heartbreak Kids"

Div. I-A Teams With Most Losses on Final Play (Since 1971)

(5 losses)
Stanford

(4 losses)
California, Michigan

(3 losses)
Cincinnati, Louisville, Southwestern La., Virginia, Wisconsin

Additional Records

Longest Uninterrupted Series (Must have played every year)

95 games—Kansas-Oklahoma (from 1903)
92 games—Kansas-Nebraska (from 1906)
91 games—Minnesota-Wisconsin (from 1907)
89 games—Clemson-South Caro. (from 1909)
88 games—Wake Forest-North Caro. St. (from 1910)

87 games—Kansas-Kansas St. (from 1911)
86 games—North Caro.-Virginia (from 1910)*
84 games—Illinois-Ohio St. (from 1914)
80 games—Southern Methodist-Baylor (1916-95)
80 games—Michigan-Ohio St. (from 1918)

79 games—Kansas-Missouri (from 1919)
79 games—Missouri-Iowa St. (from 1919)
77 games—Missouri-Oklahoma (1919-95)
77 games—Tulane-LSU (1919-1994)
78 games—Indiana-Purdue (from 1920)

77 games—Southern Methodist-Texas Christian (from 1921)
76 games—Southern Methodist-Texas A&M (1920-95)
76 games—Missouri-Nebraska (from 1922)
76 games—North Caro.-Duke (from 1922)
74 games—Michigan-Illinois (from 1924)

72 games—Southern Methodist-Texas (1924-95)

**Neither school fielded a team in 1917-18 due to World War I.*

Most Consecutive Wins Over a Major Opponent in an Uninterrupted Series (Must have played in consecutive years)

34—Notre Dame over Navy, 1964-97 (current)
32—Oklahoma over Kansas St., 1937-68
28—Texas over Rice, 1966-93
29—Nebraska over Kansas, 1969-97 (current)
29—Nebraska over Kansas St., 1969-97 (current)

26—Syracuse over Hobart, 1906-31
25—Penn St. over West Va., 1959-83
22—Arkansas over Texas Christian, 1959-80
22—Alabama over Mississippi St., 1958-79
20—Purdue over Iowa, 1961-80

18—UCLA over California, 1972-89
17—New Mexico over UTEP, 1970-86
17—Arizona St. over UTEP, 1957-73
17—LSU over Tulane, 1956-72
16—Michigan over Illinois, 1967-82

16—North Caro. over Wake Forest, 1908-23
15—Southern Methodist over Texas Christian, 1972-86
15—Iowa over Iowa St., 1983-97 (current)

Most Consecutive Wins Over a Major Opponent in a Nonconsecutive Series (Did not play in consecutive years)

29—Clemson over Virginia, 1955-90 (over 36-year period)
24—Southern Cal over Oregon St., 1968-97 (30-year period)
19—Michigan over Northwestern, 1966-92 (27-year period)
19—Vanderbilt over Mississippi, 1894-1938 (45-year period)
17—Tulsa over Drake, 1939-85 (47-year period)

17—Mississippi over Memphis, 1921-62 (42-year period)
17—North Caro. over Wake Forest, 1893-1923 (29-year period)

Most Consecutive Current Wins Over a Major Opponent in a Series (Must have played every year)

34—Notre Dame over Navy, 1964-97 (61-9-1 in rivalry)
29—Nebraska over Kansas, 1969-97 (80-21-3 in rivalry)
29—Nebraska over Kansas St., 1969-97 (70-10-2 in rivalry)
14—Iowa over Iowa St., 1983-96 (32-12-0 in rivalry)
14—Colorado over Iowa St., 1984-97 (40-11-1 in rivalry)

13—San Diego St. over New Mexico, 1984-96 (18-5-0 in rivalry)
13—Virginia over Wake Forest, 1984-96 (27-11-0 in rivalry)

Most Consecutive Games Without a Loss Against a Major Opponent

34—Oklahoma over Kansas St., 1935-68 (1 tie)
34—Notre Dame over Navy, 1964-97 (0 ties)

Cliffhangers

Regular-season Division I-A games won on the final play (since 1971, when first recorded). The extra point is listed when it provided the margin of victory after the winning touchdown on the game's final play. Overtime games are not included but follow Cliffhangers.

Date	Opponents, Score	Game-Winning Play
9-25-71	Marshall 15, Xavier (Ohio) 13	Terry Gardner 13 pass from Reggie Oliver
10-9-71	California 30, Oregon St. 27	Steve Sweeney 7 pass from Jay Cruze
10-23-71	Washington St. 24, Stanford 23	Don Sweet 27 FG
11-6-71	Kentucky 14, Vanderbilt 7	Darryl Bishop 43 interception return
11-4-72	LSU 17, Mississippi 16	Brad Davis 10 pass from Bert Jones (Rusty Jackson kick)
11-18-72	California 24, Stanford 21	Steve Sweeney 7 pass from Vince Ferragamo
9-15-73	Lamar 21, Howard Payne 17	Larry Spears 14 pass from Jabo Leonard
9-22-73	Hawaii 13, Fresno St. 10	Reinhold Stuprich 29 FG

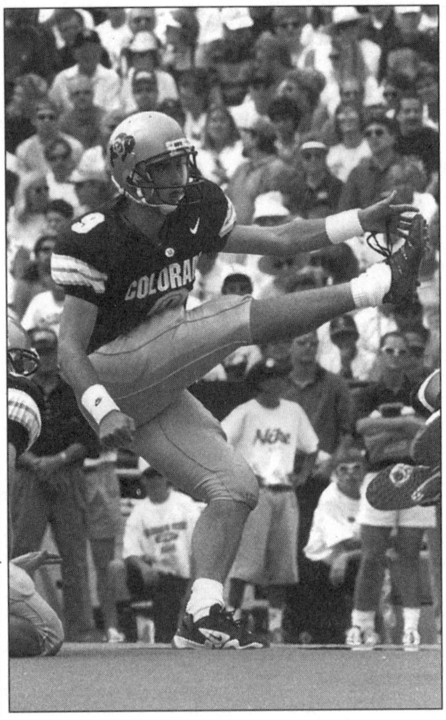

Photo from Colorado sports information

Jeremy Aldrich's 18-yard field goal as time expired gave Colorado a 20-19 victory over Wyoming last season.

Date	Opponents, Score	Game-Winning Play
11-17-73	New Mexico 23, Wyoming 21	Bob Berg 43 FG
11-23-74	Stanford 22, California 20	Mike Langford 50 FG
9-20-75	Indiana St. 23, Southern Ill. 21	Dave Vandercook 50 FG
10-18-75	Cal St. Fullerton 32, UC Riverside 31	John Choukair 52 FG
11-8-75	West Va. 17, Pittsburgh 14	Bill McKenzie 38 FG
11-8-75	Stanford 13, Southern Cal 10	Mike Langford 37 FG
11-15-75	North Caro. 17, Tulane 15	Tom Biddle 40 FG
11-6-76	Eastern Mich. 30, Central Mich. 27	Ken Dudal 38 FG
9-30-78	Virginia Tech 22, William & Mary 19	Ron Zollicoffer 50 pass from David Lamie
10-21-78	Arkansas St. 6, McNeese St. 3	Doug Dobbs 42 FG
11-9-78	San Jose St. 33, Pacific (Cal.) 31	Rick Parma 5 pass from Ed Luther
10-6-79	Stanford 27, UCLA 24	Ken Naber 56 FG
10-20-79	UNLV 43, Utah 41	Todd Peterson 49 FG
10-27-79	Michigan 27, Indiana 21	Anthony Carter 45 pass from John Wangler
11-10-79	Penn St. 9, North Caro. St. 7	Herb Menhardt 54 FG
11-17-79	Air Force 30, Vanderbilt 29	Andy Bark 14 pass from Dave Ziebart
11-24-79	Arizona 27, Arizona St. 24	Brett Weber 27 FG
9-13-80	Southern Cal 20, Tennessee 17	Eric Hipp 47 FG
9-13-80	Illinois 20, Michigan St. 17	Mike Bass 38 FG
9-20-80	Notre Dame 29, Michigan 27	Harry Oliver 51 FG
9-27-80	Tulane 26, Mississippi 24	Vince Manalla 29 FG
10-18-80	Connecticut 18, Holy Cross 17	Ken Miller 4 pass from Ken Sweitzer (Keith Hugger pass from Sweitzer)
10-18-80	Washington 27, Stanford 24	Chuck Nelson 25 FG
11-1-80	Tulane 24, Kentucky 22	Vince Manalla 22 FG
11-15-80	Florida 17, Kentucky 15	Brian Clark 34 FG
10-16-82	Arizona 16, Notre Dame 13	Max Zendejas 48 FG
10-23-82	Illinois 29, Wisconsin 28	Mike Bass 46 FG
11-20-82	California 25, Stanford 20	57 (5 laterals) kickoff return involving, in order: Kevin Moen, Richard Rodgers, Dwight Garner, Rodgers, Mariet Ford and Moen
10-8-83	Iowa St. 38, Kansas 35	Marc Bachrodt 47 FG
10-29-83	Bowling Green 15, Central Mich. 14	Stan Hunter 8 pass from Brian McClure
11-5-83	Baylor 24, Arkansas 21	Marty Jimmerson 24 FG
11-12-83	Pacific (Cal.) 30, San Jose St. 26	Ron Woods 85 pass from Mike Pitz
11-12-83	Miami (Fla.) 17, Florida St. 16	Jeff Davis 19 FG
11-26-83	Arizona 17, Arizona St. 15	Max Zendejas 45 FG
9-8-84	Southwestern La. 17, Louisiana Tech 16	Patrick Broussard 21 FG
9-15-84	Syracuse 13, Northwestern 12	Jim Tait 2 pass from Todd Norley (Don McAulay kick)
10-13-84	UCLA 27, Washington St. 24	John Lee 47 FG
11-17-84	Southwestern La. 18, Tulsa 17	Patrick Broussard 45 FG
11-17-84	Temple 19, West Va. 17	Jim Cooper 36 FG
11-23-84	Boston College 47, Miami (Fla.) 45	Gerard Phelan 48 pass from Doug Flutie
9-14-85	Clemson 20, Virginia Tech 17	David Treadwell 36 FG
9-14-85	Oregon St. 23, California 20	Jim Nielsen 20 FG
9-14-85	Utah 29, Hawaii 27	Andre Guardi 19 FG
9-21-85	New Mexico St. 22, UTEP 20	Andy Weiler 32 FG
10-5-85	Mississippi St. 31, Memphis 28	Artie Cosby 54 FG
10-5-85	Illinois 31, Ohio St. 28	Chris White 38 FG
10-12-85	Tulsa 37, Long Beach St. 35	Jason Staurovsky 46 FG
10-19-85	Northwestern 17, Wisconsin 14	John Duvic 42 FG
10-19-85	Iowa 12, Michigan 10	Rob Houghtlin 29 FG
10-19-85	Utah 39, San Diego St. 37	Andre Guardi 42 FG
11-30-85	Alabama 25, Auburn 23	Van Tiffin 52 FG
9-13-86	Oregon 32, Colorado 30	Matt MacLeod 35 FG
9-13-86	Wyoming 23, Pacific (Cal.) 20	Greg Worker 38 FG
9-20-86	Clemson 31, Georgia 28	David Treadwell 46 FG
9-20-86	Southern Cal 17, Baylor 14	Don Shafer 32 FG
10-18-86	Michigan 20, Iowa 17	Mike Gillette 34 FG
10-25-86	Syracuse 27, Temple 24	Tim Vesling 32 FG
11-1-86	North Caro. St. 23, South Caro. 22	Danny Peebles 33 pass from Erik Kramer
11-1-86	North Caro. 32, Maryland 30	Lee Gliarmis 28 FG
11-8-86	Southern Miss. 23, East Caro. 21	Rex Banks 31 FG
11-15-86	Minnesota 20, Michigan 17	Chip Lohmiller 30 FG
11-29-86	Notre Dame 38, Southern Cal 37	John Carney 19 FG
9-12-87	Youngstown St. 20, Bowling Green 17	John Dowling 36 FG
9-19-87	Utah 31, Wisconsin 28	Scott Lieber 39 FG
10-10-87	Marshall 34, Louisville 31	Keith Baxter 31 pass from Tony Petersen
10-17-87	Texas 16, Arkansas 14	Tony Jones 18 pass from Bret Stafford
11-12-88	New Mexico 24, Colorado St. 23	Tony Jones 28 pass from Jeremy Leach
9-16-89	Southern Methodist 31, Connecticut 30	Mike Bowen 4 pass from Mike Romo
9-30-89	Kansas St. 20, North Texas 17	Frank Hernandez 12 pass from Carl Straw
10-7-89	Florida 16, LSU 13	Arden Czyzewski 41 FG
10-14-89	Southern Miss. 16, Louisville 10	Darryl Tillman 79 pass from Brett Favre
10-28-89	Virginia 16, Louisville 15	Jake McInerney 37 FG
11-4-89	Toledo 19, Western Mich. 18	Romauldo Brown 9 pass from Kevin Meger
11-4-89	Northern Ill. 23, Southwestern La. 20	Stacey Robinson 7 run
9-8-90	Utah 35, Minnesota 29	Lavon Edwards 91 run of blocked FG
9-29-90	North Caro. St. 12, North Caro. 9	Damon Hartman 56 FG
10-6-90	Colorado 33, Missouri 31	Charles S. Johnson 1 run
10-20-90	Alabama 9, Tennessee 6	Philip Doyle 47 FG
11-3-90	Southern Miss. 14, Southwestern La. 13	Michael Welch 11 pass from Brett Favre (Jim Taylor kick)
11-10-90	Ohio St. 27, Iowa 26	Bobby Olive 3 pass from Greg Frey
11-17-90	Stanford 27, California 25	John Hopkins 39 FG
11-24-90	Michigan 16, Ohio St. 13	J. D. Carlson 37 FG
9-7-91	Central Mich. 27, Southwestern La. 24	L. J. Muddy 2 pass from Jeff Bender

Date	Opponents, Score	Game-Winning Play
9-21-91	California 23, Arizona 21	Doug Brien 33 FG
9-21-91	Georgia Tech 24, Virginia 21	Scott Sisson 33 FG
9-21-91	Louisiana Tech 17, Eastern Mich. 14	Chris Bonoil 54 FG
10-12-91	Ball St. 10, Eastern Mich. 8	Kenny Stucker 41 FG
11-2-91	Kentucky 20, Cincinnati 17	Doug Pelphrey 53 FG
11-2-91	Tulsa 13, Southern Miss. 10	Eric Lange 24 FG
9-5-92	Louisiana Tech 10, Baylor 9	Chris Bonoil 30 FG
9-19-92	Miami (Ohio) 17, Cincinnati 14	Chad Seitz 21 FG
9-19-92	Southern Miss. 16, Louisiana Tech 13	Johnny Lomoro 46 FG
10-3-92	Texas A&M 19, Texas Tech 17	Terry Venetoulias 21 FG
10-3-92	Georgia Tech 16, North Caro. St. 13	Scott Sisson 29 FG
10-3-92	San Jose St. 26, Wyoming 24	Joe Nedney 60 FG
10-24-92	Maryland 27, Duke 25	Marcus Badgett 38 pass from John Kaleo
10-31-92	Rutgers 50, Virginia Tech 49	Chris Brantley 15 pass from Bryan Fortay
11-14-92	UCLA 9, Oregon 6	Louis Perez 40 FG
10-2-93	Tulane 27, Navy 25	Bart Baldwin 43 FG
10-9-93	Ball St. 31, Toledo 30	Eric McCray 6 pass from Mike Neu (Matt Swart kick)
10-9-93	North Caro. St. 36, Texas Tech 34	Gary Downs 11 pass from Robert Hinton
10-16-93	Arizona 27, Stanford 24	Steve McLaughlin 27 FG
10-30-93	Missouri 37, Iowa St. 34	Kyle Pooler 40 FG
11-20-93	Maryland 33, Wake Forest 32	Russ Weaver 8 pass from Scott Milanovich (John Milligan kick)
11-20-93	Boston College 41, Notre Dame 39	David Gordon 41 FG
11-20-93	Arkansas St. 23, Nevada 21	Reginald Murphy 30 pass from Johnny Covington
9-10-94	Tulane 15, Rice 13	Bart Baldwin 47 FG
9-10-94	San Diego St. 22, California 20	Peter Holt 32 FG
9-24-94	Colorado 27, Michigan 26	Michael Westbrook 64 pass from Kordell Stewart
10-22-94	Central Mich. 32, Miami (Ohio) 30	Terrance McMillan 19 pass from Erik Timpf
10-22-94	Army 25, Citadel 24	Kurt Heiss 24 FG
11-19-94	Eastern Mich. 40, Toledo 37	Ontario Pryor 16 pass from Charlie Batch
8-26-95	Michigan18, Virginia 17	Mercury Hayes 15 pass from Scott Dreisbach
9-9-95	Kansas St. 23, Cincinnati 21	Kevin Lockett 22 pass from Matt Miller
10-21-95	Texas 17, Virginia 16	Phil Dawson 50 FG
10-28-95	East Caro. 36, Southern Miss. 34	Chad Holcomb 29 FG
8-31-96	Boston College 24, Hawaii 21	John Matich 42 FG
9-7-96	Arizona St. 45, Washington 42	Robert Nycz 38 FG
9-21-96	Notre Dame 27, Texas 24	Jim Sanson 39 FG
9-21-96	Navy 19, Southern Methodist 17	Tom Vanderhorst 38 FG
10-12-96	Louisville 23, Tulane 20	David Akers 39 FG
9-27-97	Colorado 20, Wyoming 19	Jeremy Aldrich 18 FG

"CARDIAC SEASONS"

(From 1937; Won-Lost Record in Parentheses)

Games Decided by Two Points or Less

6—Kansas, 1973 (3-2-1): Tennessee 27-28, Nebraska 9-10, Iowa St. 22-20, Oklahoma St. 10-10, Colorado 17-15, Missouri 14-13 (season record: 7-3-1)

5—Illinois, 1992 (2-2-1): Minnesota 17-18, Ohio St. 18-16, Northwestern 26-27, Wisconsin 13-12, Michigan 22-22 (season record: 6-4-1)

5—Columbia, 1971 (4-1-0): Princeton 22-20, Harvard 19-21, Yale 15-14, Rutgers 17-16, Dartmouth 31-29 (season record: 6-3-0)

5—Missouri, 1957 (2-2-1): Vanderbilt 7-7, Southern Methodist 7-6, Nebraska 14-13, Kansas St. 21-23, Kansas 7-9 (season record: 5-4-1)

Games Decided by Three Points or Less

7—Bowling Green, 1980 (2-5-0): Ohio 20-21, Ball St. 24-21, Western Mich. 17-14, Kentucky 20-21, Long Beach St. 21-23, Eastern Mich. 16-18, Richmond 17-20 (season record: 4-7-0)

7—Columbia, 1971 (4-3-0): Lafayette 0-3, Princeton 22-20, Harvard 19-21, Yale 15-14, Rutgers 17-16, Cornell 21-24, Dartmouth 31-29 (season record: 6-3-0)

6—Illinois, 1992 (3-2-1): Minnesota 17-18, Ohio St. 18-16, Northwestern 26-27, Wisconsin 13-12, Purdue 20-17, Michigan 22-22 (season record: 6-4-1)

6—Central Mich., 1991 (2-0-4): Ohio 17-17, Southwestern La. 27-24, Akron 31-29, Toledo 16-16, Miami (Ohio) 10-10, Eastern Mich. 14-14 (season record: 6-1-4)

6—Kansas, 1973 (3-2-1): Tennessee 27-28, Nebraska 9-10, Iowa St. 22-20, Oklahoma St. 10-10, Colorado 17-15, Missouri 14-13 (season record: 7-3-1)

6—Air Force, 1967 (2-2-2): Oklahoma St. 0-0, California 12-14, North Caro. 10-8, Tulane 13-10, Colorado St. 17-17, Army 7-10 (season record: 2-6-2)

6—Missouri, 1957 (3-2-1): Vanderbilt 7-7, Southern Methodist 7-6, Nebraska 14-13, Colorado 9-6, Kansas St. 21-23, Kansas 7-9 (season record: 5-4-1)

1997 DIVISION I-A OVERTIME FOOTBALL GAMES

Date	Div.	Winner's Conf.	Score (Loser's Conf.)	OT Periods	Reg. Score	Team With Choice	Choice
8-30	I-A	SEC	Mississippi 24, Central Fla. 23 (Indep.)	1	17-17	Central Fla.	Defense
8-30	I-A	ACC	North Caro. St. 32, Syracuse 31 (Big East)	1	24-24	North Caro. St.	Defense
9-20	I-A	Pac-10	Oregon 43, Fresno St. 40 (WAC)	1	37-37	Oregon	Defense
9-27	I-A	WAC	Brigham Young 19, Southern Methodist 16 (WAC)	1	13-13	BYU	Defense
9-27	I-A	WAC	Air Force 24, San Diego St. 18 (WAC)	1	18-18	Air Force	Defense
10-4	I-A	SEC	Kentucky 40, Alabama 34 (SEC)	1	34-34	Kentucky	Defense
10-4	I-A	I-AA	Cal Poly SLO 38, New Mexico St. 35 (Big West)	1	35-35	Cal Poly SLO	Defense
10-11	I-A	Div. II	North Ala. 48, Southwestern La. 42 (Indep.)	4	27-27	SW La.	Defense
10-18	I-A	WAC	San Diego St. 20, UNLV 17 (WAC)	1	17-17	San Diego St.	Defense
10-18	I-A	Big E	Miami (Fla.) 45, Boston College 44 (Big East)	2	31-31	Miami (Fla.)	Defense

Date	Div.	Winner's Conf.	Score (Loser's Conf.)	OT Periods	Reg. Score	Team With Choice	Choice
10-18	I-A	MAC	Ball St. 37, Central Mich. 34 (MAC)	1	34-34	Ball St.	Defense
10-18	I-A	C-USA	Houston 41, Cincinnati 38 (C-USA)	2	31-31	Houston	Defense
10-25	I-A	Big E	Pittsburgh 55, Rutgers 48 (Big East)	2	41-41	Rutgers	Defense
10-25	I-A	Indep.	Northeast La. 28, Southwestern La. 21 (Indep.)	1	21-21	SW La.	Defense
10-25	I-A	C-USA	Cincinnati 34, Miami (Ohio) 31 (MAC)	2	24-24	Miami (Ohio)	Defense
10-25	I-A	Pac-10	Washington St. 35, Arizona 34 (Pac-10)	1	28-28	Arizona	Defense
10-25	I-A	Big 12	Missouri 51, Oklahoma St. 50 (Big 12)	2	37-37	Missouri	Defense
11-1	I-A	Big 12	Texas A&M 28, Oklahoma St. 25 (Big 12)	1	22-22	Texas A&M	Defense
11-8	I-A	ACC	Clemson 29, Duke 20 (ACC)	1	20-20	Duke	Defense
11-8	I-A	Big 12	Nebraska 45, Missouri 38 (Big 12)	1	38-38	Nebraska	Offense
11-15	I-A	Pac-10	Arizona 41, California 38 (Pac-10)	2	31-31	Arizona	Defense
11-22	I-A	WAC	San Jose St. 55, UNLV 48 (WAC)	1	48-48	UNLV	Defense
11-22	I-A	Big W	Boise St. 30, Idaho 23 (Big W)	1	23-23	Idaho	Defense
11-22	I-A	Indep.	Northeast La. 23, Hawaii 20 (WAC)	1	17-17	NE La.	Defense
11-28	I-A	Big E	Pittsburgh 41, West Va. 38 (Big East)	3	35-35	Pittsburgh	Defense

Division I-A Stadiums

STADIUMS LISTED ALPHABETICALLY BY SCHOOL

School	Stadium	Conference	Year Built	Cap.	Surface* (Year)
Air Force	Falcon	Western Ath.-M	1962	52,480	Grass
Akron	^Rubber Bowl	Mid-American-E	1940	35,202	AstroTurf (83)
Alabama	^Legion Field	Southeastern-W	1927	83,091	Grass (S95)
	Bryant-Denny	Southeastern-W	1929	70,123	PAT (S91)
UAB	^Legion Field	Independent	1927	83,091	Grass (S95)
Arizona	Arizona	Pacific-10	1929	57,803	Grass
Arizona St.	Sun Devil	Pacific-10	1959	73,656	Grass
Arkansas	^War Memorial	Southeastern-W	1948	53,727	Grass (S94)
	Razorback	Southeastern-W	1938	50,019	Grass (S95)
Arkansas St.	Indian	Big West	1974	33,410	Grass
Army	Michie	Conference USA	1924	39,929	AstroTurf (92)
Auburn	Jordan-Hare	Southeastern-W	1939	85,214	Grass
Ball St.	Ball St.	Mid-American-W	1967	21,581	Grass
Baylor	Floyd Casey	Big 12-S	1950	50,000	Grass (S98)
Boise St.	Bronco	Big West	1970	30,000	Blue AstroTurf
Boston College	Alumni	Big East	1957	44,500	PolyknitTurf
Bowling Green	Doyt Perry	Mid-American-E	1966	30,599	Grass
Brigham Young	Cougar	Western Ath.-P	1964	65,000	Grass
California	Memorial	Pacific-10	1923	75,662	Grass (S95)
Central Fla.	^Florida Citrus	Independent	1936	70,188	Grass
Central Mich.	Kelly/Shorts	Mid-American-W	1972	20,086	AstroTurf (83)
Cincinnati	Nippert	Conference USA	1916	35,000	AstroTurf-8 (92)
Clemson	Memorial	Atlantic Coast	1942	81,474	Grass
Colorado	Folsom Field	Big 12-N	1924	51,808	AstroTurf-8 (89)
Colorado St.	Hughes	Western Ath.-M	1968	30,000	Grass
Duke	Wallace Wade	Atlantic Coast	1929	33,941	Grass
East Caro.	Dowdy-Ficklen	Conference USA	1963	43,000	Grass
Eastern Mich.	Rynearson	Mid-American-W	1969	30,200	StadiaTurf (91)
Florida	Florida Field	Southeastern-E	1930	83,000	Grass (S90)
Florida St.	Doak Campbell	Atlantic Coast	1950	80,000	PAT (88)
Fresno St.	Bulldog	Western Ath.-P	1980	41,031	Grass
Georgia	Sanford	Southeastern-E	1929	86,117	Grass
Georgia Tech	Dodd/Grant	Atlantic Coast	1913	46,000	Grass (S95)
Hawaii	^Aloha	Western Ath.-P	1975	50,000	AstroTurf (85)
Houston	^Astrodome@	Conference USA	1965	60,000	AstroTurf
	Robertson	Conference USA	1940	22,000	Grass
Idaho	Kibbie Dome@	Big West	1971	16,000	AstroTurf
Illinois	Memorial	Big Ten	1923	70,904	AstroTurf (89)
Indiana	Memorial	Big Ten	1960	52,354	PAT (98)
Iowa	Kinnick	Big Ten	1929	70,397	PAT (S89)
Iowa St.	Cyclone-Jack Trice	Big 12-N	1975	50,000	Grass (S96)
Kansas	Memorial	Big 12-N	1921	50,250	AstroTurf (90)
Kansas St.	KSU	Big 12-N	1968	42,000	AstroTurf-8 (91)
Kent	Dix	Mid-American-E	1969	30,520	Turf (S97)
Kentucky	Commonwealth	Southeastern-E	1973	57,800	Grass
LSU	Tiger	Southeastern-W	1924	79,940	Grass
Louisiana Tech	Joe Aillet	Independent	1968	30,600	Grass
Louisville	Papa John's Cardinal	Conference USA	1998	45,000	SportGrass (98)
Marshall	Marshall University	Mid-American-E	1991	30,000	PolyTurf
Maryland	Byrd	Atlantic Coast	1950	48,055	Grass
Memphis	^Liberty Bowl	Conference USA	1965	62,380	PAT (87)
Miami (Fla.)	^Orange Bowl	Big East	1935	74,476	PAT (S77)
Miami (Ohio)	Fred Yager	Mid-American-E	1983	30,012	Grass
Michigan	Michigan	Big Ten	1927	102,501	PAT (S91)
Michigan St.	Spartan	Big Ten	1957	76,000	AstroTurf (83)
Minnesota	^Metrodome@	Big Ten	1982	63,669	AstroTurf-8
Mississippi	Vaught-Hemingway	Southeastern-W	1941	42,577	Grass
Mississippi St.	Scott Field	Southeastern-W	1915	40,656	PAT (86)
Missouri	Faurot Field	Big 12-N	1926	62,000	Grass (S95)
Navy	Navy-MC	Independent	1959	30,000	Grass

School	Stadium	Conference	Year Built	Cap.	Surface* (Year)
Nebraska	Memorial	Big 12-N	1923	72,700	AstroTurf-8 (92)
UNLV	^Sam Boyd	Western Ath.-M	1971	32,000	MonsantoTurf (85)
Nevada	Mackay	Big West	1965	31,545	Grass
New Mexico	University	Western Ath.-P	1960	31,218	Grass
New Mexico St.	Aggie Memorial	Big West	1978	30,343	Grass
North Caro.	Kenan Memorial	Atlantic Coast	1927	60,000	Grass
North Caro. St.	^Carter-Finley	Atlantic Coast	1966	51,500	Grass
North Texas	Fouts Field	Big West	1952	30,500	All-Pro Turf
Northeast La.	Malone	Independent	1978	30,427	Grass
Northern Ill.	Huskie	Mid-American-W	1965	30,998	AstroTurf (89)
Northwestern	Ryan Field	Big Ten	1926	47,129	Grass (S97)
Notre Dame	Notre Dame	Independent	1930	80,225	Grass
Ohio	Peden	Mid-American-E	1929	20,000	Grass
Ohio St.	Ohio	Big Ten	1922	89,841	PAT (S90)
Oklahoma	Memorial	Big 12-S	1923	72,422	Grass (S94)
Oklahoma St.	Lewis	Big 12-S	1920	50,614	AstroTurf (87)
Oregon	Autzen	Pacific-10	1967	41,678	Omni-Turf (91)
Oregon St.	Parker	Pacific-10	1953	35,362	All-Pro Turf (84)
Penn St.	Beaver	Big Ten	1960	93,967	Grass
Pittsburgh	Pitt	Big East	1925	56,150	AstroTurf (90)
Purdue	Ross-Ade	Big Ten	1924	67,332	PAT (75)
Rice	Rice	Western Ath.-M	1950	70,000	AstroTurf-12 (97)
Rutgers	Rutgers	Big East	1994	42,500	Grass
San Diego St.	^Qualcom	Western Ath.-P	1967	73,000	Grass
San Jose St.	Spartan	Western Ath.-P	1933	31,218	Grass
South Caro.	Williams-Brice	Southeastern-E	1934	80,250	Grass
Southern Cal	^LA Mem. Coliseum	Pacific-10	1923	92,000	Grass
Southern Methodist	Cotton Bowl	Western Ath.-M	1930	68,252	Grass (S93)
Southern Miss.	Roberts	Conference USA	1976	33,000	Grass
Southwestern La.	Cajun Field	Independent	1971	31,000	Grass
Stanford	Stanford	Pacific-10	1921	85,500	Grass
Syracuse	Carrier Dome@	Big East	1980	50,000	AstroTurf
Temple	Veterans	Big East	1971	66,592	AstroTurf-8
Tennessee	Neyland	Southeastern-E	1921	102,544	Grass (S94)
Texas	Memorial	Big 12-S	1924	75,512	PAT (S96)
UTEP	^Sun Bowl	Western Ath.-P	1963	51,270	AstroTurf (83)
Texas A&M	Kyle Field	Big 12-S	1925	70,210	Grass (S96)
Texas Christian	Amon Carter	Western Ath.-M	1929	46,000	Grass (S92)
Texas Tech	Jones	Big 12-S	1947	50,500	AstroTurf-8 (88)
Toledo	Glass Bowl	Mid-American-W	1937	26,248	AstroTurf (90)
Tulane	^Superdome@	Conference USA	1975	69,767	AstroTurf (95)
Tulsa	Skelly	Western Ath.-M	1930	40,385	Stadia Turf (91)
UCLA	^Rose Bowl	Pacific-10	1922	100,089	Grass
Utah	Robert Rice	Western Ath.-P	1927	32,500	SportGrass (S95)
Utah St.	E. L. Romney	Big West	1968	30,257	Grass
Vanderbilt	Vanderbilt	Southeastern-E	1922	41,600	AstroTurf (81)
Virginia	Scott	Atlantic Coast	1931	40,000	PAT (S95)
Virginia Tech	Lane	Big East	1965	50,000	Grass
Wake Forest	Groves	Atlantic Coast	1968	31,500	Grass
Washington	Husky	Pacific-10	1920	72,500	AstroTurf (95)
Washington St.	Martin	Pacific-10	1972	37,600	Omni-Turf (90)
West Va.	Mountaineer	Big East	1980	63,500	Omni-Turf (88)
Western Mich.	Waldo	Mid-American-W	1939	30,200	PAT (92)
Wisconsin	Camp Randall	Big Ten	1917	76,129	AstroTurf (90)
Wyoming	War Memorial	Western Ath.-M	1950	33,500	Grass

STADIUMS LISTED BY CAPACITY (TOP 26)

School	Stadium	Surface* (Year)	Capacity
Tennessee	Neyland	Grass (S94)	102,544
Michigan	Michigan	PAT (S91)	102,501
UCLA	^Rose Bowl	Grass	100,089
Penn St.	Beaver	Grass	93,967
Southern Cal	^LA Mem. Coliseum	Grass	92,000
Ohio St.	Ohio	PAT (S90)	89,841
Georgia	Sanford	Grass	86,117
Stanford	Stanford	Grass	85,500
Auburn	Jordan-Hare	Grass	85,214
Alabama	^Legion Field	Grass (S95)	83,091
UAB	^Legion Field	Grass (S95)	83,091
Florida	Florida Field	Grass (S90)	83,000
Clemson	Memorial	Grass	81,474
South Caro.	Williams-Brice	Grass	80,250
Notre Dame	Notre Dame	Grass	80,225
Florida St.	Doak Campbell	PAT (88)	80,000
LSU	Tiger	Grass	79,940
Wisconsin	Camp Randall	AstroTurf (90)	76,129
Michigan St.	Spartan	AstroTurf (83)	76,000
California	Memorial	Grass (S95)	75,662
Texas	Memorial	PAT (S96)	75,512
Miami (Fla.)	^Orange Bowl	PAT (S77)	74,476
Arizona St.	Sun Devil	Grass	73,656
San Diego St.	^Qualcom	Grass	73,000
Nebraska	Memorial	AstroTurf-8(92)	72,700
Oklahoma	Memorial	Grass (S94)	72,422

^Not located on campus. @ Indoor facility. S=switch to grass or vice-versa and year switched.

Surface Notes: **This column indicates the type of surface (either artificial or natural grass) present this year in the stadium. The brand name of the artificial turf, if known, is listed as well as the year the last installation occurred. The "S" preceding the year indicates that the school has switched either from natural grass to artificial turf or vice-versa. Legend: Turf—Any of several types of artificial turfs (name brands include AstroTurf, All-Pro, Omni-Turf, SuperTurf, etc.); Grass—Natural grass surface; PAT—Prescription Athletic Turf (a "natural-artificial" surface featuring a network of pipes connected to pumps capable of sucking water from the natural turf or watering it. The pipes are located 18 inches from the surface and covered with a mixture of sand and filler. The turf also is lined with heating coils to keep it from freezing in temperatures below 32 degrees). SportGrass—Combines natural grass with a below-the-surface system of synthetic elements.*

Division I-A Stadium Facts: *Houston and Tulsa claim to be the first college football teams to play in an indoor stadium (the Astrodome on September 11, 1965). But actually, Utah and West Virginia met December 19, 1964, in the Liberty Bowl in the Atlantic City Convention Hall. Technically, the Astrodome was the first indoor stadium built specially for football and baseball. The first major-college football game ever played on artificial turf was between Houston and Washington State on September 23, 1966.*

Famous Major-College Dynasties

The following are singled out because of their historical significance, and all represent an outstanding record as well as at least one national championship.

NOTRE DAME (1919-30)

Under Knute Rockne, the Fighting Irish posted an overall record of 101-11-3 (.891 winning percentage) and captured three national titles during this 12-year period. Rockne, who died in an airplane crash in 1931, did not accomplish this by himself, with athletes like George Gipp and the legendary Four Horsemen (Harry Stuhldreher, Elmer Layden, Jim Crowley and Don Miller) around. The longest unbeaten streak was 22 games, which began in 1918 under Gipp, but the South Benders had three other streaks of at least 15 games in the period.

MINNESOTA (1933-41)

Bernie Bierman, known as "The Silver Fox" for his prematurely gray hair, led the Golden Gophers through their best era. In the nine-year span, Minnesota posted a 58-9-5 (.840) record and won five national titles (1934, 1936, 1940 and 1941 outright and 1935 shared). Bierman oversaw five undefeated teams in the span, and the longest unbeaten streak was 28 games. Defense was a trademark of the Gophers, who notched 23 shutouts in the 72 games. The top offensive player was 1941 Heisman Trophy winner Bruce Smith.

NOTRE DAME (1946-53)

Under head coach Frank Leahy, Notre Dame began another streak almost as successful as the Rockne era. Leahy led the Irish to a national title in 1943, and beginning in 1946, Notre Dame set off on a 63-8-6 (.857) journey that yielded three more national championships (1946, 1947 and 1949) in four years. The longest unbeaten streak stretched to 39 games. The top players were Heisman Trophy winners Johnny Lujack (1947), Leon Hart (1949) and John Lattner (1953).

OKLAHOMA (1948-58)

Many felt this particular span featured the greatest accomplishment in modern-day collegiate football—Oklahoma's Bud Wilkinson-led 47-game winning streak from 1953-57. The Sooners posted a 107-8-2 (.923) mark during the 11-year stretch that included three consensus national titles (1950, 1955 and 1956). Halfback Billy Vessels, the 1952 Heisman winner, was the outstanding individual player in the streak, but Wilkinson's teams were typified by overall speed and quickness.

ALABAMA (1959-67)

Paul "Bear" Bryant's return to his alma mater started a chain of events that eventually yielded one of the greatest dynasties in history. During the nine-year span, Bryant's teams fashioned an 83-10-6 (.869) record and captured three national prizes (1961, 1964 and 1965). His players included Joe Namath, Ken Stabler, Pat Trammell, Ray Perkins, Steve Sloan and Lee Roy Jordan, an eclectic group that featured no Heisman winners. All his players knew how to do was win football games, and the 1963-67 teams never lost a home game.

SOUTHERN CAL (1967-79)

Two coaches—John McKay and John Robinson—shared this dynasty, which posted a 122-23-7 (.826) record and four national titles (1967, 1972 and 1974 under McKay and 1978 under Robinson). The longest unbeaten streak was 28 games. Southern Cal had two Heisman winners—O. J. Simpson (1968) and Charles White (1979)—and 18 consensus all-Americans in the 13-year period.

ALABAMA (1971-80)

This was the second great run for the Crimson Tide under Bryant. Alabama reeled off a 28-game unbeaten streak and posted a 107-13-0 (.892) record during the 10-year span, including national championships in 1973, 1978 and 1979. Again, there were no Heisman winners for Bryant, but he had a list of players like John Hannah, Steadman Shealy, Jeff Rutledge, Tony Nathan and Major Ogilvie. Bryant died in 1983 as the winningest college coach.

OKLAHOMA (1971-80)

Barry Switzer led the Sooner dynasty to a 102-14-2 (.873) record that included a 37-game unbeaten string and 10 Big Eight championships. Back-to-back national titles in 1974 and 1975 were the result of enormous talent and Switzer's coaching. Some of the Sooner all-Americans during the 10-year period included Jack Mildren, Greg Pruitt, Lucious Selmon, Rod Shoate, Tinker Owens, Dewey Selmon, Lee Roy Selmon, Joe Washington, Billy Brooks and George Cumby. Heisman Trophy winner Billy Sims (1978) was the biggest name in a Sooner rushing attack that was virtually unstoppable.

MIAMI (FLA.) (1983-92)

The loss to Alabama in the 1993 Sugar Bowl ended a real streak for the Hurricanes, going for a fifth national title since 1983. Few would argue that during the 1980s under three different coaches—Howard Schnellenberger, Jimmy Johnson and Dennis Erickson—the Hurricanes were the most successful team in America. With a 107-13-0 (.892) record that included national titles in 1983, 1987, 1989 and 1991, the Hurricanes served notice that an undefeated season was a possibility every year.

FLORIDA ST. (1987-95)

Under Bobby Bowden, Florida State fashioned one of the most remarkable regular-season and postseason records over this nine-year period. The Seminoles did what no other Division I school ever accomplished—win at least 10 games in all nine seasons. In fact, Florida State posted a 76-13-1 mark during the streak, which also includes an unprecedented 11 straight bowl victories. Bowden led teams that finished in the top five of The Associated Press poll for nine consecutive years. Florida State captured Bowden's first national title in 1993.

NEBRASKA (1988-97)

Some suggest that Nebraska under Tom Osborne was on a 25-year dynasty streak, beginning with the fact that every one of his first 25 teams posted at least nine victories. But that aside, these 10 years were a remarkable run for the Cornhuskers, with an 108-15-1 (.875) record including back-to-back national championships in 1994 and 1995 and a co-championship in 1997. The Huskers' 26-game win streak was the nation's longest through 1996, and the 29-year consecutive bowl string was a collegiate record. Actually, the Huskers were just a last-second field goal away from four national titles in the 1990s, losing to Florida State, 18-16, in the 1994 FedEx Orange Bowl.

FLORIDA (1990-97)

The beginning of Steve Spurrier's career at Florida also marked the start of a terrific dynasty in Gatorland. Not only did the Gators win at least nine games every season in the 1990s, but captured five of seven Southeastern Conference crowns in one streak. Florida's record was 83-16-1 (.835) during the eight-year stretch, The Gators captured the 1996 national championship trophy with a 52-20 victory over state rival Florida State in the Sugar Bowl.

Other College Football Dynasties

(Listed Because of Their Historical Significance)

School (Years)..	W-L-T	Pct.	Duration	Titles*
Yale (1876-1909)	315-14-18	.934	34 years	19
Princeton (1877-1903)	233-21-11	.900	27 years	12
Pennsylvania (1894-1908)	168-21-7	.875	15 years	4
Michigan (1901-09)	75-6-2	.916	9 years	2
Harvard (1908-15)	64-4-5	.911	8 years	5
Pittsburgh (1913-20)	55-5-4	.891	8 years	3
Southern Cal (1919-33)	129-18-3	.870	15 years	2
Tennessee (1938-46)#	72-9-2	.880	9 years	2
Michigan (1940-48)	68-13-2	.831	9 years	2
Army (1943-50)	64-5-5	.899	8 years	3
Michigan St. (1950-66)	117-37-4	.753	17 years	4
Ohio St. (1954-61)	56-14-4	.784	8 years	3
Texas (1961-72)	107-21-2	.831	12 years	3
Nebraska (1969-76)	79-14-4	.835	8 years	2
Penn St. (1980-87)	76-19-1	.797	8 years	2

**Some titles were shared. No team in 1943 due to World War II.*

(Special thanks to Bob Kirlin of Spokane, Wash., for his compilations.)

Major-College Statistics Trends†

(Average Per Game, One Team)

Year	Rushing Plays	Rushing Yds.	Rushing Avg.	Passing Att.	Passing Cmp.	Passing Pct.	Passing Yds.	Passing Av. Att.	Total Offense Plays	Total Offense Yds.	Total Offense Avg.	Scoring TD	Scoring FG	Scoring Pts.
1937	-	133.8	-	13.0	5.0	.381	64.5	4.96	-	198.4	-	-	-	10.1
1938	40.8	140.1	3.43	14.0	5.2	.371	70.1	5.01	54.8	210.2	3.85	1.75	0.06	11.8
1939	40.8	135.9	3.33	13.8	5.2	.374	66.4	4.81	54.6	202.3	3.70	1.66	0.09	11.4
1940	41.9	140.5	3.35	14.8	5.8	.386	77.8	5.26	56.7	218.5	3.85	1.97	0.08	13.3
1941	42.2	141.2	3.35	15.0	5.9	.392	80.7	5.38	57.2	221.8	3.88	2.03	0.06	13.8
1946	42.3	152.4	3.60	15.5	6.1	.389	88.2	5.69	57.8	240.7	4.16	2.39	0.04	16.1
1947	42.3	158.7	3.75	15.3	6.3	.414	90.3	5.91	57.6	248.8	4.32	2.37	0.04	15.9
1948	43.7	162.2	3.71	15.9	6.7	.423	94.6	5.95	59.5	256.5	4.31	2.52	0.05	17.1
1949	47.2	180.6	3.83	17.7	7.6	.431	110.4	6.24	64.9	290.7	4.48	2.86	0.04	19.4
1950	47.0	180.2	3.83	17.5	7.7	.438	108.5	6.19	64.5	288.6	4.47	2.79	0.04	18.9
1951	48.6	182.5	3.76	18.9	8.4	.446	113.7	6.02	67.5	296.1	4.39	2.86	0.05	19.4
1952	48.3	176.4	3.65	18.4	8.1	.441	111.9	6.09	66.7	288.2	4.32	2.68	0.07	18.4
1953	45.1	176.6	3.92	15.2	6.5	.428	91.7	6.03	60.3	268.2	4.45	2.54	0.05	17.1
1954	45.5	184.1	*4.05	14.9	6.5	.437	91.1	6.14	60.3	225.1	4.56	2.59	0.05	17.4
1955	46.1	176.7	3.83	13.6	5.9	.435	84.7	6.24	59.6	261.3	4.38	2.37	0.05	16.1
1956	49.2	193.1	3.93	14.1	6.2	.437	85.9	6.09	63.3	279.0	4.41	2.45	0.05	16.5
1957	49.3	177.5	3.60	14.4	6.4	.444	85.5	5.94	63.6	263.0	4.14	2.31	0.06	15.6
1958	47.1	170.7	3.62	16.1	7.4	.458	97.7	6.06	63.2	268.4	4.24	2.31	0.09	16.0
1959	46.2	166.0	3.59	16.5	7.5	.451	98.5	5.96	62.7	264.5	4.21	2.25	0.17	15.9
1960	45.3	169.9	3.75	15.8	7.2	.454	93.6	5.94	61.1	263.4	4.31	2.19	0.19	15.6
1961	45.6	166.7	3.66	15.9	7.2	.448	94.7	5.95	61.5	261.4	4.25	2.23	0.23	16.0
1962	45.3	164.0	3.63	17.2	8.0	.463	105.0	6.10	62.5	269.0	4.31	2.30	0.21	16.4
1963	44.1	160.0	3.63	17.6	8.1	.461	105.3	5.98	61.7	265.3	4.30	2.19	0.27	15.8
1964	43.7	149.7	3.43	17.9	8.5	.472	110.0	6.14	61.6	259.6	4.21	2.07	0.29	15.1
1965	45.1	149.4	3.31	20.8	9.7	.464	123.2	5.93	65.9	272.5	4.14	2.26	0.42	16.7
1966	44.3	148.7	3.36	22.0	10.3	.470	133.2	6.07	66.2	281.8	4.26	2.35	0.42	17.5
1967	47.3	154.7	3.27	22.9	10.7	.467	139.8	6.10	70.2	294.5	4.19	2.48	0.46	18.4
1968	49.7	170.8	3.44	25.4	12.1	.474	157.7	6.22	*75.1	328.5	4.38	2.89	0.46	21.2
1969	49.5	171.8	3.47	25.5	12.0	.471	157.1	6.17	74.9	328.9	4.39	2.90	0.54	21.6
1970	49.3	175.7	3.57	25.0	11.7	.467	152.7	6.12	74.2	328.3	4.42	2.83	0.57	21.3
1971	49.7	182.2	3.67	21.7	10.1	.463	132.3	6.10	71.3	314.5	4.41	2.69	0.54	20.2
1972	49.8	184.5	3.70	22.0	10.2	.462	136.9	6.24	71.8	321.4	4.48	2.71	0.61	20.6
1973	50.1	192.8	3.85	20.4	9.6	.472	130.9	6.41	70.5	323.6	4.59	2.75	0.65	21.0
1974	51.8	201.8	3.89	18.8	8.9	.474	122.3	6.50	70.7	324.1	4.59	2.64	0.63	20.2
1975	*51.9	*204.5	3.94	18.4	8.7	.473	119.6	6.52	70.3	324.1	4.61	2.57	0.74	20.1
1976	51.4	198.8	3.87	19.1	9.1	.474	123.5	6.49	70.4	322.2	4.58	2.57	0.75	20.0
1977	51.3	194.6	3.80	20.2	9.8	.483	134.5	6.67	71.5	329.1	4.61	2.67	0.73	20.8
1978	50.9	192.6	3.79	21.2	10.3	.486	138.9	6.55	72.1	331.5	4.60	2.64	0.76	20.6
1979	49.1	187.9	3.83	21.6	10.6	.491	139.3	6.47	70.6	327.2	4.63	2.55	0.77	20.0
1980	47.7	178.3	3.74	23.3	11.6	.500	151.9	6.52	71.0	330.2	4.65	2.61	0.81	20.5
1981	46.3	169.4	3.66	25.3	12.7	.502	164.7	6.51	71.6	334.1	4.67	2.57	0.87	20.5
1982	45.1	169.3	3.75	27.6	14.5	.522	182.4	6.61	72.7	351.7	4.84	2.71	1.02	21.9
1983	44.6	169.5	3.80	27.0	14.4	.536	182.8	6.79	71.6	352.3	4.92	2.73	1.06	22.1
1984	44.7	168.1	3.76	26.8	14.1	.527	181.1	6.77	71.5	349.2	4.89	2.66	1.15	22.1
1985	44.6	169.2	3.80	27.3	14.7	.537	186.1	6.82	71.8	355.3	4.95	2.74	1.09	22.4
1986	44.2	167.9	3.80	27.2	14.6	.537	185.1	6.81	71.4	353.0	4.95	2.80	1.07	22.7
1987	44.4	174.2	3.92	27.1	14.2	.526	183.6	6.78	71.5	357.8	5.01	2.83	1.13	23.1
1988	44.0	174.6	3.97	27.1	14.3	.529	185.8	6.87	71.1	360.3	5.07	2.91	*1.16	23.8
1989	42.7	166.4	3.90	28.5	15.4	.540	200.9	7.05	71.2	367.3	5.16	2.97	1.13	24.1
1990	43.1	167.7	3.90	28.3	15.1	.534	197.2	6.96	71.4	364.8	5.11	3.04	1.08	24.4
1991	43.3	169.7	3.91	27.2	14.6	.535	189.6	6.98	70.5	359.4	5.10	2.95	0.89	23.1
1992	42.7	165.6	3.89	28.1	14.9	.530	190.5	6.77	70.8	356.1	5.03	2.84	1.04	22.9
1993	41.8	166.3	3.98	28.7	15.9	*.551	204.9	*7.13	70.5	371.2	5.27	3.09	0.97	24.4
1994	41.8	166.8	3.99	28.5	15.6	.547	198.3	6.96	70.3	365.1	5.19	3.11	0.99	24.6
1995	41.5	167.3	4.03	*29.7	*16.3	.547	*205.5	6.92	71.2	*372.8	5.24	3.21	0.93	25.1
1996	41.5	164.4	3.97	28.9	15.4	.533	202.0	6.99	70.4	366.3	5.21	*3.26	0.94	25.5
1997	40.2	158.7	3.94	29.2	15.8	.543	207.6	7.12	69.4	366.3	*5.28	3.25	0.97	*25.5

**Record. +Records not compiled in 1942-45 except for Scoring Points Per Game: 1942 (15.7); 1943 (15.7); 1944 (16.3); 1945 (16.1).*

Additional Major-College Statistics Trends†

Rules changes and statistics changes affecting trends: PUNTING—Beginning in 1965, 20 yards not deducted from a punt into the end zone for a touchback. INTERCEPTIONS—Interception yards not compiled, 1958-65. KICKOFF RETURNS—During 1937-45, if a kickoff went out of bounds, the receiving team put the ball in play on its 35-yard line instead of a second kickoff; in 1984 (rescinded in 1985), a 30-yard-line touchback for kickoffs crossing the goal line in flight and first touching the ground out of the end zone; in 1986, kickoffs from the 35-yard line. PUNT RETURNS—In 1967, interior linemen restricted from leaving until the ball is kicked.

(Average Per Game, One Team)

Year	Punting No.	Punting Avg.	Punting Net Avg.	Interceptions No.	Interceptions Avg. Ret.	Interceptions Yds.	Punt Returns No.	Punt Returns Avg. Ret.	Punt Returns Yds.	Kickoff Returns No.	Kickoff Returns Avg. Ret.	Kickoff Returns Yds.	Kickoff Returns Pct. Ret'd
1937	9.2	36.3	-	1.68	-	-	-	-	-	-	-	-	-
1938	9.3	37.2	-	1.70	9.19	15.8	-	-	-	-	-	-	-
1939	*9.4	36.7	-	1.67	9.84	16.5	*4.42	9.40	41.6	2.14	19.3	41.3	.764
1940	9.1	36.6	-	1.79	10.05	18.0	4.21	10.58	44.5	2.32	*20.4	47.5	.753
1941	8.9	36.1	-	*1.81	11.28	20.4	4.27	11.10	*47.4	*2.41	20.2	48.6	.768
1946	7.3	35.7	-	1.75	11.79	20.6	3.70	11.32	41.9	3.01	18.9	56.9	.870
1947	6.7	36.4	30.3	1.61	11.93	19.2	3.47	11.73	40.7	3.04	18.9	57.3	.884
1948	6.3	36.3	30.2	1.60	12.59	20.2	3.09	*12.16	37.6	3.17	18.5	58.6	.873
1949	6.3	36.6	30.3	1.69	*13.23	*22.3	3.21	12.13	38.9	3.51	17.9	62.8	.885
1950	6.0	36.3	30.8	1.61	11.99	19.3	3.04	10.72	32.6	3.46	16.6	57.4	.889

(Average Per Game, One Team)	Punting			Interceptions			Punt Returns			Kickoff Returns			
Year	No.	Avg.	Net Avg.	No.	Avg. Ret.	Yds.	No.	Avg. Ret.	Yds.	No.	Avg. Ret.	Yds.	Pct. Ret'd
1951	6.4	35.9	30.7	1.67	12.00	20.1	3.10	10.58	32.8	3.53	17.0	59.9	.884
1952	6.3	36.4	31.6	1.60	11.60	18.5	3.07	9.95	30.5	3.45	17.6	60.7	.908
1953	5.2	34.9	29.7	1.37	12.12	16.6	2.57	10.66	27.4	3.27	17.8	58.2	.903
1954	4.9	34.9	29.4	1.36	12.48	16.9	2.42	11.16	27.0	3.32	18.4	61.0	*.910
1955	4.9	34.9	29.8	1.26	12.96	16.8	2.39	10.54	25.2	3.09	18.5	57.2	.892
1956	5.0	35.1	30.1	1.29	12.86	16.6	2.49	10.07	25.1	3.19	18.0	57.4	.906
1957	5.3	34.8	30.2	1.26	11.95	15.0	2.53	9.57	24.2	3.05	18.7	57.1	.897
1958	5.6	35.4	30.9	1.33	–	–	2.57	9.70	24.9	3.02	18.9	57.0	.880
1959	5.5	35.9	31.5	1.33	–	–	2.67	9.06	24.2	3.09	18.7	57.8	.892
1960	5.1	36.0	31.4	1.24	–	–	2.39	9.73	23.3	3.05	18.8	57.3	.890
1961	5.2	35.5	35.5	1.22	–	–	2.43	9.44	22.9	3.06	18.3	56.1	.873
1962	5.2	35.7	35.7	1.25	–	–	2.36	9.66	22.8	3.10	19.6	60.7	.876
1963	5.2	36.3	32.5	1.19	–	–	2.34	9.71	22.7	3.08	20.1	61.9	.880
1964	5.3	36.4	32.5	1.20	–	–	2.33	8.99	20.9	2.93	19.6	57.3	.862
1965	5.9	38.5	38.5	1.42	–	–	2.73	9.99	27.3	3.15	18.8	59.3	.849
1966	5.9	37.5	33.5	1.50	12.07	18.1	2.63	8.82	23.2	3.24	18.7	60.8	.849
1967	6.5	36.8	31.6	1.52	11.39	17.3	3.42	9.92	33.9	3.31	18.7	61.7	.831
1968	6.7	37.4	33.3	1.61	11.51	18.6	3.01	8.95	26.9	3.64	19.1	69.6	.829
1969	6.6	37.5	33.4	1.70	11.07	18.8	3.00	9.00	27.0	3.67	18.9	69.4	.818
1970	6.3	37.4	37.4	1.66	11.65	19.4	2.89	9.28	26.9	3.69	19.0	70.1	.828
1971	6.2	37.6	33.4	1.49	11.75	17.5	2.89	9.04	26.2	3.57	19.2	68.6	.834
1972	6.1	37.2	33.4	1.54	11.54	17.7	2.72	8.61	23.4	3.50	19.0	66.4	.803
1973	5.8	37.8	34.1	1.36	11.30	15.4	2.52	8.65	21.8	3.54	19.6	69.2	.797
1974	5.6	37.6	34.2	1.23	11.30	13.9	2.40	7.92	19.0	3.38	19.1	64.3	.784
1975	5.4	38.1	35.0	1.21	11.26	13.6	2.39	7.19	17.2	3.20	19.3	61.7	.733
1976	5.7	38.0	35.1	1.23	11.44	14.0	2.42	6.83	16.5	3.14	18.3	57.4	.722
1977	5.8	38.0	35.0	1.26	11.05	13.9	2.45	7.10	17.3	3.16	18.4	58.1	.711
1978	6.0	38.0	34.9	1.34	10.83	14.5	2.51	7.39	18.6	3.18	18.7	59.6	.665
1979	5.8	37.7	34.8	1.31	10.66	14.0	2.38	7.09	16.9	3.02	18.8	56.9	.637
1980	5.8	38.3	35.4	1.37	10.85	14.9	2.44	7.01	17.1	2.91	19.0	55.1	.651
1981	6.0	38.9	35.9	1.38	10.22	14.1	2.45	7.22	17.7	2.86	18.8	53.9	.636
1982	5.9	39.8	*36.5	1.39	10.70	14.9	2.40	8.00	19.2	2.69	19.3	51.9	.561
1983	5.5	39.5	35.9	1.37	10.43	14.3	2.47	7.95	19.7	2.65	19.2	50.8	.549
1984	5.6	39.7	36.3	1.31	10.07	13.2	2.47	7.61	18.8	3.03	18.6	56.2	.621
1985	5.5	39.6	36.1	1.30	10.47	13.6	2.45	7.92	19.4	2.94	19.4	57.0	.603
1986	5.4	39.2	35.4	1.30	10.99	14.3	2.51	8.23	20.7	3.78	19.8	74.6	.770
1987	5.4	38.6	34.7	1.32	10.82	14.3	2.48	8.31	20.6	3.89	19.1	74.5	.780
1988	5.2	38.4	34.7	1.24	11.17	14.0	2.39	7.96	19.1	*3.97	19.4	77.1	.778
1989	5.2	38.5	34.3	1.28	10.75	13.8	2.36	8.46	20.0	3.92	19.7	*77.2	.776
1990	5.3	38.6	34.3	1.23	11.40	14.0	2.45	9.33	22.9	3.79	19.6	74.5	.738
1991	5.3	38.4	34.3	1.18	11.30	13.3	2.50	8.74	21.9	3.43	19.4	66.6	.741
1992	5.6	39.0	34.9	1.20	11.00	13.2	2.63	9.04	23.8	3.30	20.1	66.4	.732
1993	5.2	38.8	35.1	1.14	11.00	12.5	2.28	8.28	18.9	3.43	20.0	68.7	.679
1994	5.3	39.2	35.3	1.10	12.10	13.3	2.38	8.64	20.5	3.50	20.0	69.8	.714
1995	5.3	38.7	34.9	1.12	11.67	13.1	2.23	8.98	20.0	3.57	19.5	69.7	.848
1996	5.5	40.0	35.8	1.04	12.83	13.4	2.39	9.56	22.8	3.34	20.4	68.0	.783
1997	5.4	*40.5	36.2	1.05	12.45	13.0	2.47	9.49	23.4	3.47	20.3	70.5	.816

**Record. †Records not compiled in 1942-45.*

Field Goal Trends (1938-1968)

Year	Made	Year	Made	Year	Made	Atts.	Pct.
1938	47	1951	53	1961	277		
1939	80	1952	83	1962	261		
1940	84	1953	50	1963	314		
1941	59	1954	48	1964	368		
1942-45	*	1955	57	1965	484	1,035	.468
1946	44	1956	53	1966	522	1,125	.464
1947	38	1957	64	1967	555	1,266	.438
1948	53	1958	103	1968	566	1,287	.440
1949	46	1959	†199				
1950	46	1960	224				

**Records not compiled. †Goal posts widened from 18 feet, 6 inches to 23 feet, 4 inches in 1959.*

Field Goal Trends (From 1969)

(Includes Field Goal Attempts by Divisions I-AA, II and III Opponents)

	Totals			Breakdown by Distances								
Year	Made	Atts.	Pct.	16-39	Pct.	16-49	Pct.	40-49	Pct.	50 Plus	Pct.	60 Plus
1969	669	1,402	.477	538-872	.617	654-1,267	.516	116-395	.294	15-135	.111	0-8
1970	754	1,548	.487	614-990	.620	740-1,380	.536	126-390	.323	14-168	.083	1-9
1971	780	1,625	.480	607-1,022	.594	760-1,466	.518	153-444	.345	20-159	.126	0-11
1972	876	1,828	.479	705-1,150	.613	855-1,641	.521	150-491	.305	21-187	.112	1-12
1973	958	1,920	.499	728-1,139	.639	914-1,670	.547	186-531	.350	44-250	.176	1-21
1974	947	1,905	.497	706-1,096	.644	906-1,655	.547	200-559	.358	41-250	.164	1-17
1975	1,164	2,237	.520	849-1,255	.676	1,088-1,896	.574	239-641	.373	76-341	.223	4-32
1976	1,187	2,330	.509	854-1,301	.656	1,131-1,997	.566	277-696	.398	56-333	.168	3-24
1977	1,238	2,514	.492	882-1,315	.671	1,160-2,088	.556	278-773	.360	78-426	.183	6-40
1978	1,229	2,113	.582	938-1,361	.689	1,193-1,982	.602	255-621	.411	36-131	.275	1-4

	Totals			Breakdown by Distances											
Year	Made	Atts.	Pct.	Under 20	Pct.	20-29	Pct.	30-39	Pct.	40-49	Pct.	50-59	Pct.	60 Plus	Pct.
1979	1,241	2,129	.583	34-43	.791	455-601	.757	425-706	.602	286-600	.477	41-173	.237	0-6	.000
1980	1,245	2,128	.585	31-39	.795	408-529	.771	452-696	.649	317-682	.465	37-175	.211	0-7	.000
1981	1,368	2,254	.607	42-48	.875	471-598	.788	461-731	.631	335-698	.480	58-169	.343	1-10	.100
1982	1,224	1,915	.639	31-34	.912	384-475	.808	415-597	.695	319-604	.528	73-190	.384	2-15	.133
1983	1,329	2,025	.656	34-37	.919	417-508	.821	477-636	.750	329-628	.524	72-201	.358	0-15	.000
1984	1,442	2,112	.683	44-49	.898	450-532	.846	503-681	.739	363-630	.576	80-206	.388	2-14	.143
1985	1,360	2,106	.646	40-47	.851	416-511	.814	478-657	.728	341-647	.527	84-227	.370	1-17	.059
1986	1,326	2,034	.652	45-48	.938	445-525	.848	448-641	.699	340-629	.541	44-182	.242	4-9	.444
1987	1,381	2,058	.671	45-48	.938	484-559	.866	469-638	.735	311-604	.515	72-200	.360	0-9	.000
1988	1,421	2,110	.673	33-35	.943	487-573	.850	495-664	.745	337-610	.552	68-217	.313	1-11	.091
1989#	1,389	2,006	*.692	50-53	.943	497-565	.880	471-655	.719	319-573	.557	52-154	.338	0-6	.000
1990	1,348	2,011	.670	39-42	.929	477-546	.874	454-626	.725	319-625	.510	59-167	.353	0-5	.000
1991$	1,092	1,831	.596	31-32	.969	395-519	.761	366-612	.598	254-531	.478	45-132	.341	1-5	.200
1992	1,288	1,986	.649	32-38	.842	464-569	.815	447-673	.664	294-577	.510	49-126	.389	2-3	.667
1993§	1,182	1,832	.645	23-25	.920	490-599	.818	407-617	.660	224-488	.459	38-98	.388	0-5	.000
1994	1,220	1,877	.650	39-40	.975	458-528	.867	419-626	.669	263-547	.481	40-128	.313	1-8	.125
1995	1,150	1,759	.654	32-32	1.000	468-549	.852	373-587	.635	244-489	.499	31-100	.310	2-2	1.000
1996	1,207	1,899	.636	28-29	.966	431-509	.847	422-632	.668	277-581	.477	49-147	.333	0-1	.000
1997	1,255	1,895	.662	47-48	.979	445-524	.849	446-659	.677	272-540	.504	45-122	.369	0-2	.000

**Record. #First year after kicking tee became illegal. $First year after goal-post width narrowed back to 18'6" from 23'4". §First year after hash marks narrowed to 60 feet from each sideline.*

Field Goal Trends by Soccer-Style and Conventional Kickers

(Division I-A Kickers Only)

(Pete Gogolak of Cornell was documented as the first soccer-style kicker in college football history. The Hungarian-born kicker played at Cornell from 1961 through 1963. He set a national major-college record of 44 consecutive extra-point conversions and finished 54 of 55 for his career. His younger brother, Charley, also a soccer-styler, kicked at Princeton from 1963 through 1965.)

SOCCER-STYLE

		Totals			Breakdown by Distances								
Year	†No.	Made	Atts.	Pct.	16-39	Pct.	16-49	Pct.	40-49	Pct.	50 Plus	Pct.	60 Plus
1975	70	528	1,012	.522	370-540	.685	479-816	.587	109-276	.395	49-196	.250	1-17
1976	84	517	1,019	.507	350-517	.677	477-831	.574	127-314	.404	40-188	.213	3-16
1977	96	665	1,317	.505	450-649	.693	615-1,047	.587	165-398	.415	50-270	.185	2-27
1978	98	731	1,244	.588	540-768	.703	703-1,148	.612	163-380	.429	28-96	.292	1-3

		Totals			Breakdown by Distances					
Year	†No.	Made	Atts.	Pct.	Under 20	20-29	30-39	40-49	50-59	60 Plus
1979	116	839	1,413	.594	23-28	288-380	282-455	214-419	32-126	0-5
1980	121	988	1,657	.596	26-32	327-416	342-522	261-540	32-147	0-5
1981	138	1,108	1,787	.620	32-36	377-476	376-576	279-551	43-142	1-6
1982	105	1,026	1,548	.663	26-27	317-375	346-482	273-495	62-156	2-13
1983	110	1,139	1,724	.661	29-31	345-416	403-541	294-543	68-179	0-14
1984	127	1,316	1,898	*.694	43-47	414-480	438-589	341-572	78-197	2-13
1985	133	1,198	1,838	.652	35-41	369-452	415-578	306-560	72-191	1-16
1986	128	1,201	1,829	.657	37-40	398-467	410-575	313-576	39-162	4-9
1987	122	1,275	1,892	.674	40-43	458-523	424-574	290-566	63-177	0-9
1988	140	1,317	1,947	.676	31-33	445-521	468-630	311-562	61-201	1-11
1989	138	1,313	1,897	.692	49-52	462-526	441-612	310-551	51-150	0-6
1990	135	1,282	1,890	.678	36-38	450-515	432-589	308-590	56-154	0-4
1991	132	1,048	1,763	.594	30-31	381-500	349-589	243-512	44-130	1-1
1992	135	1,244	1,926	.646	31-37	447-554	429-647	288-561	47-124	2-3
1993	132	1,153	1,776	.649	23-25	475-578	398-600	219-475	38-93	0-5
1994	138	1,203	1,856	.648	38-39	452-522	410-617	263-543	39-127	1-8
1995	148	1,150	1,759	.654	32-32	468-549	373-587	244-489	31-100	2-2
1996	149	1,207	1,899	.636	28-29	431-509	422-632	277-581	49-147	0-1
1997	146	1,255	1,895	.662	47-48	445-524	446-659	272-540	45-122	0-2

CONVENTIONAL

		Totals			Breakdown by Distances								
Year	†No.	Made	Atts.	Pct.	16-39	Pct.	16-49	Pct.	40-49	Pct.	50 Plus	Pct.	60 Plus
1975	116	564	1,085	.520	427-640	.667	541-959	.564	114-319	.357	23-126	.183	3-13
1976	101	608	1,192	.510	460-720	.639	594-1,065	.558	134-345	.388	14-127	.110	0-7
1977	98	513	1,054	.487	384-586	.655	487-916	.532	103-330	.312	26-138	.188	4-14
1978	86	440	761	.578	352-516	.682	434-729	.595	82-213	.385	6-32	.188	0-0

		Totals			Breakdown by Distances					
Year	†No.	Made	Atts.	Pct.	Under 20	20-29	30-39	40-49	50-59	60 Plus
1979	70	333	585	.569	10-14	140-185	111-198	63-150	9-37	0-1
1980	62	258	471	.548	5-7	81-113	110-174	56-142	6-33	0-2
1981	50	195	367	.531	8-9	70-97	69-126	41-112	7-22	0-1
1982	25	103	195	.528	3-4	36-50	34-62	25-59	5-18	0-2
1983	23	112	181	.619	4-5	40-55	46-58	22-50	0-12	0-1
1984	10	44	76	.579	0-1	17-26	20-33	7-15	0-1	0-0
1985	12	81	138	.587	3-4	22-29	29-40	19-44	8-20	0-1
1986	8	58	89	.652	4-4	21-28	17-27	14-24	2-6	0-0
1987	4	35	50	.700	4-4	10-14	14-16	6-9	1-7	0-0
1988	5	26	40	.650	0-0	17-21	5-7	4-10	0-2	0-0
1989	2	37	47	.787	1-1	19-20	12-16	5-9	0-1	0-0
1990	2	23	38	.605	1-1	8-10	8-9	4-13	2-5	0-0
1991	2	16	24	.667	0-0	5-9	6-7	5-7	0-1	0-0
1992	1	12	18	.667	0-0	5-6	6-8	1-4	0-0	0-0
1993	1	6	11	.545	0-0	4-5	2-3	0-3	0-0	0-0
1994	1	17	21	*.810	1-1	6-6	9-9	0-4	1-1	0-0
1995	0	0	0	.000	0-0	0-0	0-0	0-0	0-0	0-0
1996	0	0	0	.000	0-0	0-0	0-0	0-0	0-0	0-0
1997	0	0	0	.000	0-0	0-0	0-0	0-0	0-0	0-0

**Record. †Number of kickers attempting at least one field goal.*

Average Yardage of Field Goals

(Division I-A Kickers Only)

	Soccer-Style			Conventional			Nation		
Year	Made	Missed	Total	Made	Missed	Total	Made	Missed	Total
1975	35.1	43.2	39.0	33.1	41.3	37.0	34.1	42.2	37.9
1976	35.0	43.1	39.0	33.2	40.7	36.9	34.0	41.8	37.9
1977	34.7	44.3	39.5	33.3	41.9	37.7	34.1	43.2	38.7
1978	34.0	39.9	36.4	31.9	38.3	34.6	33.2	39.3	35.7
1979	33.7	39.9	36.2	31.9	38.0	34.5	33.2	39.3	35.7
1980	34.0	40.7	36.7	33.4	39.6	36.2	33.8	40.4	36.6
1981	33.9	40.1	36.2	33.2	38.6	35.7	33.8	39.8	36.1
1982	34.8	41.8	37.2	34.0	39.8	36.7	34.7	41.5	37.1
1983	34.7	42.1	37.2	32.3	40.5	35.5	34.5	41.9	37.0
1984	34.4	41.8	36.7	32.3	34.9	33.4	34.3	41.5	36.5
1985	34.5	41.3	36.8	35.4	41.7	38.0	34.5	41.3	36.9
1986	33.9	41.6	36.6	32.5	38.6	34.7	33.9	41.4	36.5
1987	33.5	41.8	36.2	32.3	41.4	35.1	33.5	41.8	36.2
1988	33.9	41.7	36.4	30.0	37.6	32.7	32.0	39.3	34.4
1989	33.5	41.2	35.9	30.5	39.6	32.4	33.4	41.2	35.8
1990	33.4	41.3	36.0	33.4	42.0	36.7	33.4	41.3	36.0
1991	33.2	40.7	35.8	28.6	31.9	40.7	35.9	40.4	36.1
1992	34.1	41.2	36.7	30.1	37.8	32.7	37.2	41.3	37.8
1993	32.4	38.9	34.7	26.8	38.0	31.9	32.3	38.9	34.6
1994	32.9	40.6	35.6	31.4	45.5	34.0	32.9	40.7	35.6
1995	32.4	40.1	35.0	—	—	—	32.4	40.1	35.0
1996	33.4	40.5	36.0	—	—	—	33.4	40.5	36.0
1997	33.2	40.1	35.5	—	—	—	33.2	40.1	35.5

Division I-A Extra-Point Trends

(From Start of Two-Point Attempts)

		Percent Total Tries		Kick Attempts			Two-Point Attempts		
Year	Games	Kick	2-Pt.	Atts.	Made	Pct.	Atts.	Made	Pct.
1958	578	#.486	*.514	1,295	889	.686	*1,371	*613	.447
1959	578	.598	.402	1,552	1,170	.754	1,045	421	.403
1960	596	.701	.299	1,849	1,448	.783	790	345	.437
1961	574	.723	.277	1,842	1,473	.800	706	312	.442
1962	602	.724	.276	1,987	1,549	.780	757	341	.450
1963	605	.776	.224	2,057	1,659	.807	595	256	.430
1964	613	.814	.186	2,053	1,704	.830	469	189	.403
1965	619	.881	.119	2,460	2,083	.847	331	134	.405
1966	626	.861	.139	2,530	2,167	.857	410	165	.402
1967	611	.869	.131	2,629	2,252	.857	397	160	.403
1968	615	.871	.129	3,090	2,629	.851	456	181	.397
1969	621	.880	.120	3,168	2,781	.878	432	170	.394
1970	667	.862	.138	3,255	2,875	.883	522	246	*.471
1971	726	.889	.111	3,466	3,081	.889	433	173	.400
1972	720	.872	.128	3,390	3,018	.890	497	219	.441
1973	741	.893	.107	3,637	3,258	.896	435	180	.414
1974	749	.885	.115	3,490	3,146	.901	455	211	.464
1975	785	.891	.109	3,598	3,266	.908	440	171	.389
1976	796	.877	.123	3,579	3,241	.906	502	203	.404
1977	849	.891	.109	*4,041	*3,668	.908	495	209	.422
1978	816	.884	.116	3,808	3,490	.916	498	208	.418
1979	811	.897	.103	3,702	3,418	.923	424	176	.415
1980	810	.895	.105	3,785	3,480	.919	442	170	.384
1981	788	.901	.099	3,655	3,387	.927	403	172	.427
1982	599	.901	.099	2,920	2,761	.946	320	120	.375
1983	631	.896	.104	3,080	2,886	.937	356	151	.424
1984	626	.889	.111	2,962	2,789	.942	370	173	.468
1985	623	.899	.101	3,068	2,911	.949	345	121	.351
1986	619	.905	.095	3,132	2,999	.958	330	131	.397
1987	615	.892	.108	3,094	2,935	.949	375	163	.435
1988	616	.899	.101	3,215	3,074	.956	363	156	.430
1989	614	.888	.112	3,233	3,090	.956	409	179	.438
1990	623	.911	.089	3,429	3,291	*.960	335	138	.412
1991	617	.906	.094	3,279	3,016	.920	342	128	.374
1992	619	.899	.101	3,156	2,967	.940	353	159	.450
1993	613	.912	#.088	3,455	3,251	.941	333	143	.429
1994	617	.897	.103	3,433	3,207	.934	395	163	.413
1995	622	.902	.098	3,594	3,354	.933	389	173	.445
1996	644	*.923	.077	3,862	3,630	.940	322	144	.447
1997	646	.913	.087	3,828	3,572	.933	367	155	.422

**Record high. #Record low.*

Division I-A Extra-Point Kick Attempts (1938-1957)

Year	Pct. Made	Year	Pct. Made	Year	Pct. Made	Year	Pct. Made
1938	.608	1946	.657	1951	.711	1956	.666
1939	.625	1947	.657	1952	.744	1957	.653
1940	.607	1948	.708	1953	.650		
1941	.638	1949	.738	1954	.656		
1942-45	*	1950	.713	1955	.669		

**Not compiled.*

All-Divisions Defensive Extra-Point Trends

In 1988, the NCAA Football Rules Committee adopted a rule that gave defensive teams an opportunity to score two points on point-after-touchdown tries. The two points were awarded for returning an interception or advancing a blocked kick for a touchdown on point-after tries.

DIVISION I-A

Year	Games	Kick Ret./TDs	Int. Ret./TDs	Total Ret./TDs
1988	616	8/2	6/0	14/2
1989	614	12/3	9/2	21/5
1990	623	9/3	5/2	14/5
1991	617	9/3	10/3	19/6
1992	619	8/5	1/0	9/5
1993	613	5/2	6/1	11/3
1994	617	4/0	8/3	12/3
1995	622	12/5	5/3	17/8
1996	644	9/4	7/3	16/7
1997	646	13/3	6/1	19/4

DIVISION I-AA

Year	Games	Kick Ret./TDs	Int. Ret./TDs	Total Ret./TDs
1988	553	4/1	7/1	11/2
1989	554	11/4	4/2	15/6
1990	548	7/3	4/2	11/5
1991	560	12/3	9/2	21/5
1992	553	9/5	8/5	17/10
1993	725	11/5	19/3	30/8
1994	733	4/1	5/1	9/2
1995	736	9/2	9/4	18/6
1996	723	8/3	3/0	11/3
1997	723	11/1	7/5	18/6

DIVISION II

Year	Games	Kick Ret./TDs	Int. Ret./TDs	Total Ret./TDs
1988	580	19/4	9/0	28/4
1989	590	18/8	11/3	29/11
1990	596	9/3	2/2	11/5
1991	575	10/3	8/2	18/5
1992	580	9/4	7/3	16/7
1993	694	16/6	9/5	25/11
1994	663	15/8	6/4	21/12
1995	681	16/3	14/2	30/5
1996	717	11/7	7/4	18/11
1997	679	18/12	6/4	24/16

DIVISION III

Year	Games	Kick Ret./TDs	Int. Ret./TDs	Total Ret./TDs
1988	994	29/8	25/3	54/11
1989	1,012	16/5	13/4	29/9
1990	1,020	25/10	16/6	41/16
1991	1,006	18/7	14/5	32/12
1992	1,028	14/6	17/7	31/13
1993	997	17/5	18/6	35/11
1994	1,002	25/8	17/7	42/15
1995	948	37/12	15/7	52/19
1996	938	14/7	5/2	19/9
1997	939	28/9	11/3	39/12

ALL DIVISIONS—NATIONWIDE

Year	Games	Kick Ret./TDs	Int. Ret./TDs	Total Ret./TDs
1988	2,743	60/15	47/4	107/19
1989	2,770	57/20	37/11	94/31
1990	2,787	50/19	27/12	77/31
1991	2,758	49/16	41/12	90/28
1992	2,780	40/20	33/15	73/35
1993	3,029	49/18	52/15	101/33
1994	3,015	48/17	36/15	84/32
1995	2,987	74/22	43/16	117/38
1996	3,022	42/21	22/9	64/30
1997	2,987	70/25	30/13	100/38

All-Divisions Fumble-Recovery Returns

In 1990, the NCAA Football Rules Committee adopted a rule that gave the defense an opportunity to advance fumbles that occur beyond the neutral zone (or line of scrimmage). In 1992, the rule was changed to allow defenses to advance any fumble regardless of position behind or beyond the line of scrimmage. Here are the number of fumble recoveries by division that were advanced, and the number that resulted in a score.

DIVISION I-A

Year	Games	Fumble Rec./TDs
1990	623	51/17
1991	617	60/16
1992	619	126/34
1993	613	117/24
1994	617	131/43
1995	622	148/49
1996	644	195/86
1997	646	206/76

DIVISION I-AA

Year	Games	Fumble Rec./TDs
1990	548	34/16
1991	560	42/13
1992	553	96/42
1993	725	86/25
1994	733	99/23
1995	736	164/58
1996	723	169/63
1997	723	149/63

DIVISION II

Year	Games	Fumble Rec./TDs
1990	596	46/25
1991	575	43/19
1992	580	77/39
1993	694	110/41
1994	663	92/38
1995	681	108/47
1996	717	164/55
1997	679	217/60

DIVISION III

Year	Games	Fumble Rec./TDs
1990	1,020	55/19
1991	1,006	62/22
1992	1,028	94/47
1993	997	88/33
1994	1,002	108/54
1995	948	117/60
1996	938	177/60
1997	939	212/52

ALL DIVISIONS—NATIONWIDE

Year	Games	Fumble Rec./TDs
1990	2,787	186/77
1991	2,758	207/70
1992	2,780	393/162
1993	3,029	401/123
1994	3,015	430/158
1995	2,987	537/214
1996	3,022	705/264
1997	2,987	784/251

Major-College Tie Games

The record for most tie games in a single week is six—on October 27, 1962; September 28, 1963; and October 9, 1982.

Note: Tiebreaker procedures added for 1996 season.

Year	No.	Games	Pct.	Scoreless
1954	15	551	2.72	2
1955	22	536	4.10	1
1956	28	558	5.02	2
1957	24	570	4.21	4
1958*	19	578	3.29	2
1959	13	578	2.25	4
1960	23	596	3.86	4
1961	11	574	1.92	1
1962	20	602	3.32	2
1963	25	605	4.13	4
1964	19	613	3.10	2
1965	19	619	3.07	4
1966	13	626	2.08	0
1967	14	611	2.29	1
1968	17	615	2.76	1
1969	9	621	1.45	0
1970	7	667	1.05	0
1971	12	726	1.65	1
1972	14	720	1.94	1
1973	18	741	2.43	2
1974	18	749	2.40	0
1975	16	785	2.04	0
1976	13	796	1.63	1
1977	16	849	1.88	1
1978	16	816	1.96	1
1979	17	811	2.10	1
1980	12	810	1.48	0
1981	17	788	2.16	0
1982	14	599	2.34	0
1983	13	631	2.06	†1
1984	15	626	2.40	0
1985	13	623	2.09	0
1986	10	619	1.62	0
1987	13	615	2.11	0
1988	12	616	1.95	0
1989	15	614	2.44	0
1990	15	623	2.41	0
1991	14	617	2.27	0
1992	13	619	2.10	0
1993	11	613	1.79	0
1994	13	617	2.11	0
1995	9	622	1.45	0
1996	0	644	0.00	0
1997	0	646	0.00	0

**First year of two-point conversion rule. †Last scoreless tie game: Nov. 19, 1983, Oregon vs. Oregon St.*

Highest-Scoring Tie Games

(Home Team Listed First; Both Teams Classified Major-College or Division I-A at Time)

Note: Tiebreaker procedures added for 1996 season.

Score	Date	Opponents
52-52	11-16-91	San Diego St.-Brigham Young
48-48	9-8-79	San Jose St.-Utah St.
43-43	11-12-88	Duke-North Caro. St.
41-41	9-10-94	Northwestern-Stanford
41-41	9-23-89	San Diego St.-Cal St. Fullerton
40-40	11-8-75	Idaho-Weber St.
39-39	11-7-82	Texas Tech-Texas Christian
37-37	9-23-67	*Alabama-Florida St.
36-36	9-30-72	Georgia Tech-Rice
35-35	9-23-95	Michigan St.-Purdue
35-35	11-16-91	San Jose St.-Hawaii
35-35	12-9-89	Hawaii-Air Force
35-35	9-23-89	Colorado St.-Eastern Mich.
35-35	10-7-78	Ohio St.-Southern Methodist
35-35	10-19-74	Idaho-Montana
35-35	10-9-71	New Mexico-New Mexico St.
35-35	9-27-69	Minnesota-Ohio
35-35	9-21-68	Washington-Rice
35-35	11-18-67	Navy-Vanderbilt
35-35	12-11-48	†Pacific (Cal.)—Hardin-Simmons
34-34	10-6-90	Iowa St.-Kansas
33-33	10-1-83	California-Arizona
33-33	9-24-49	Texas Christian-Oklahoma St.
33-33	10-31-31	Yale-Dartmouth

**At Birmingham. †Grape Bowl, Lodi, Calif.*

Home-Field Records

(Includes Host Teams at Neutral-Site Games)

Year	Games	Home Team Won	Lost	Tied	Pct.
1966	626	365	248	13	.594
1967	611	333	264	14	.557
1968	615	348	250	17	.580
1969	621	366	246	9	.596
1970	667	399	261	7	.603
1971	726	416	298	12	.581
1972	720	441	265	14	.622
1973	741	439	284	18	.605
1974	749	457	274	18	.622
1975	785	434	335	16	.563
1976	796	463	320	13	.590
1977	849	501	332	16	.600
1978	816	482	318	16	.601
1979	811	460	334	17	.578
1980	809	471	327	12	.589
1981	788	457	314	17	.591
1982	599	368	217	14	.626
1983	631	364	254	13	.587
1984	626	371	240	15	.605
1985	623	371	239	13	.606
1986	619	363	246	10	.595
1987	615	387	215	13	*.640
1988	616	370	234	12	.610
1989	614	365	234	15	.607
1990	623	373	235	15	.611
1991	617	362	241	14	.598
1992	619	388	218	13	.637
1993	613	375	227	11	.621
1994	617	357	247	13	.589
1995	622	354	259	9	.576
1996	644	389	255	0	.604
1997	646	392	254	0	.607

** Record.*

I-A Members Since 1978

The following list shows years of active membership for current and former Division I-A football-playing institutions. The lists are from 1978, the year Division I was divided into I-A and I-AA.

Active Members

Air Force	1978-98
Akron	1987-98
Alabama	1978-98
UAB	1996-98
Arizona	1978-98
Arizona St.	1978-98
Arkansas	1978-98
Arkansas St.	1978-81, 92-98
Army	1978-98
Auburn	1978-98
Ball St.	1978-81, 83-98
Baylor	1978-98
Boise St.	1996-98
Boston College	1978-98
Bowling Green	1978-81, 83-98
Brigham Young	1978-98
California	1978-98
Central Fla.	1996-98
Central Mich.	1978-98
Cincinnati	1978-81, 83-98
Clemson	1978-98
Colorado	1978-98
Colorado St.	1978-98
Duke	1978-98
East Caro.	1978-98
Eastern Mich.	1978-81, 83-98
Florida	1978-98
Florida St.	1978-98
Fresno St.	1978-98
Georgia	1978-98
Georgia Tech	1978-98
Hawaii	1978-98
Houston	1978-98
Idaho	1997-98
Illinois	1978-98
Indiana	1978-98
Iowa	1978-98
Iowa St.	1978-98
Kansas	1978-98
Kansas St.	1978-98
Kent	1978-81, 83-98
Kentucky	1978-98
LSU	1978-98
Louisiana Tech	1978-81, 89-98
Louisville	1978-98
Marshall	1978-81, 98
Maryland	1978-98
Memphis	1978-98
Miami (Fla.)	1978-98
Miami (Ohio)	1978-81, 83-98
Michigan	1978-98
Michigan St.	1978-98
Minnesota	1978-98
Mississippi	1978-98
Mississippi St.	1978-98
Missouri	1978-98
Navy	1978-98
Nebraska	1978-98
UNLV	1978-98
Nevada	1992-98
New Mexico	1978-98
New Mexico St.	1978-98
North Caro.	1978-98
North Caro. St.	1978-98
North Texas	1978-81, 95-98
Northeast La.	1978-81, 94-98
Northern Ill.	1978-81, 83-98
Northwestern	1978-98
Notre Dame	1978-98
Ohio	1978-81, 83-98
Ohio St.	1978-98
Oklahoma	1978-98
Oklahoma St.	1978-98
Oregon	1978-98
Oregon St.	1978-98
Penn St.	1978-98
Pittsburgh	1978-98
Purdue	1978-98
Rice	1978-98
Rutgers	1978-98
San Diego St.	1978-98
San Jose St.	1978-98
South Caro.	1978-98
Southern Cal	1978-98
Southern Meth.	1978-86, 89-98
Southern Miss.	1978-98
SW La.	1978-98
Stanford	1978-98
Syracuse	1978-98
Temple	1978-98
Tennessee	1978-98
Texas	1978-98
Texas A&M	1978-98
Texas Christian	1978-98
UTEP	1978-98
Texas Tech	1978-98
Toledo	1978-98
Tulane	1978-98
Tulsa	1978-98
UCLA	1978-98
Utah	1978-98
Utah St.	1978-98
Vanderbilt	1978-98
Virginia	1978-98
Va. Tech	1978-98
Wake Forest	1978-98
Washington	1978-98
Wash. St.	1978-98
West Va.	1978-98
Western Mich.	1978-81, 83-98
Wisconsin	1978-98
Wyoming	1978-98

Former Members

Appalachian St.	1978-81
Brown	1978-81
Cal St. Fullerton	1978-92
Chattanooga	1978-81
Citadel	1978-81
Colgate	1978-81
Columbia	1978-81
Cornell	1978-81
Dartmouth	1978-81
Drake	1978-80
East Tenn. St.	1978-81
Furman	1978-81
Harvard	1978-81
Holy Cross	1978-81
Illinois St.	1978-81
Indiana St.	1978-81
Lamar	1978-81
Long Beach St.	1978-91
McNeese St.	1978-81
Pacific (Cal.)	1978-95
Pennsylvania	1978-81
Princeton	1978-81
Richmond	1978-81
Southern Ill.	1978-81
Tennessee St.	1978-80
Tex.-Arlington	1978-81
Villanova	1978-80
VMI	1978-81
West Tex. A&M	1978-80
Western Caro.	1978-81
Wichita St.	1978-86
William & Mary	1978-81
Yale	1978-81

College Football Rules Changes

The Ball

1869—Round, rubber Association ball.
1875—Egg-shaped, leather-covered Rugby ball.
1896—Prolate spheroid, without specific measurements.
1912—28-28 1/2 inches around ends, 22 1/2-23 inches around middle, weight 14-15 ounces.
1929—28-28 1/2 inches around ends, 22-22 1/2 inches around middle, weight 14-15 ounces.
1934—28-28 1/2 inches around ends, 21 1/4-21 1/2 inches around middle, weight 14-15 ounces.
1941—For night games, a white ball or other colored ball with two black stripes around the ball may be used at the discretion of the referee.
1952—Ball may be inclined no more than 45 degrees by snapper.
1956—Rubber-covered ball permitted.
1973—Teams allowed to use ball of their choice while in possession.
1978—Ball may not be altered, and new or nearly new balls added.
1982—10 7/8 to 11 7/16 inches long, 20 3/4 to 21 1/4 inches around middle, and 27 3/4 to 28 1/2 inches long-axis circumference.
1993—Rubber or composition ball ruled illegal.

The Field

1869—120 yards by 75 yards; uprights 24 feet apart.
1871—166 2/3 yards by 100 yards.
1872—133 1/3 yards by 83 1/3 yards.
1873—Uprights 25 feet apart.
1876—110 yards by 53 1/3 yards. Uprights 18 1/2 feet apart; crossbar 10 feet high.
1882—Field marked with transverse lines every five yards. This distance to be gained in three downs to retain possession.
1912—Field 120 yards by 53 1/3 yards, including two 10-yard end zones.
1927—Goal posts moved back 10 yards, to end line.
1957—Team area at 35-yard lines.
1959—Uprights widened to 23 feet, 4 inches apart.
1966—Pylons placed in corners of end zone and at goal lines mandatory in 1974.
1991—Uprights moved back to 18 feet, 6 inches apart.
1993—Hash marks moved six feet, eight inches closer to center of field to 60 feet from each sideline (40 feet apart).

Scoring

1869—All goals count 1 each.
1883—Safety 1, touchdown 4, goal after TD 4, goal from field 5.
1884—Safety 2, touchdown 4, goal from field 5.
1897—Touchdown 4, field goal 5, touchdown failing goal 5, safety 2.
1902—Teams change goals after every try at goal following a touchdown, after every goal from the field and also at the beginning of the half.
1904—Goal from field 4.
1909—Goal from field 3.
1912—Touchdown 4.
1921—Ball put in play at 30-yard line after a safety, 20-yard line after a touchback.
1922—Try-for-point by scrimmage play from 5-yard line.
1924—Try-for-point by scrimmage play from 3-yard line.
1927—Goal posts placed on end lines.
1929—Try-for-point by scrimmage play from 2-yard line.
1958—One-point & two-point conversion (from 3-yard line). One-point safety added.
1974—Ball must go between the uprights for a successful field goal, over the uprights previously scored.
1976—Forfeit score changed from 1-0 to score at time of forfeit if the offended team is ahead at time of forfeit.
1984—Try may be eliminated at end of game if both captains agree.
1995—Try at end of game mandatory unless team behind in score leaves field.

Scoring Values

1882—Touchdown 2 points; field goal 5 points; extra points 4 points
1883-87—Touchdown 4 points; field goal 5 points; extra points 4 points
1888-97—Touchdown 4 points; field goal 5 points; extra points 2 points
1898-1903—Touchdown 5 points; field goal 5 points; extra points 1 point
1904-08—Touchdown 5 points; field goal 4 points; extra points 1 point
1909-11—Touchdown 5 points; field goal 3 points; extra points 1 point
1912-57—Touchdown 6 points; field goal 3 points; extra points 1 point
1958-present—Touchdown 6 points; field goal 3 points; extra points 1 point/kick, 2 points/run or pass.
1988-present—Extra points 2 points/defense.

Note: Safety worth 1 point from 1882-1883, 2 points in all seasons since 1884.

Players

1869—Each team consisted of 25 players.
1873—Each team consisted of 20 players.
1876—Each team consisted of 15 players.
1880—Each team consisted of 11 players.
1895—Only one man in motion forward before the snap. No more than three players behind the line. One player permitted in motion toward own goal line.
1910—Seven players required on line.
1911—Illegal to conceal ball beneath a player's clothing.
1947—All players urged to be numbered in a uniform manner. Ends to wear numbers in the 80s; tackles, 70s; guards, 60s; centers, 50s; and backs, 10-49.
1966—Mandatory numbering of five players on the line 50-79.
1970—All players numbered 1-99.

Equipment

1894—No one wearing projecting nails or iron plates on his shoes, or any metal substance upon his person, is allowed to play. No greasy or sticky substance shall be used on the person of players.
1903—If head protectors are worn, there can be no sole leather or other hard or unyielding substances in their construction. Leather cleats on shoes allowed.
1908—First documented jersey numbers used by Washington & Jefferson.
1915—Numbering of players recommended.
1927—Rubber cleats allowed, but under no conditions are cleats to be dangerously sharp.
1930—No player shall wear equipment that endangers players. The committee forbids the use of head protectors or jerseys that are so similar in color to the ball that they give the wearer an unfair and unsportsmanlike advantage over the opponent. Stripes may be used to break up the solid colors.
1933—Head protectors or helmets recommended to be worn by all players.

1937—All players must wear minimum 6-inch Arabic numerals on the front and minimum 8-inch Arabic numerals on the back of jerseys.
1939—All players must wear helmets.
1946—All players must wear minimum 8-inch Arabic numerals on front (changed from 6 inches) and minimum 10-inch Arabic numerals on back of jerseys (changed from 8 inches), of a single color which must be in sharp contrast with the color of the jerseys.
1948—One-inch kicking tees permitted.
1951—Any circular or ring cleat prohibited unless it has rounded edges and a wall at least 3/16-inch thick. Any face mask—unless it is made of non-breakable, molded plastic with rounded edges or of rubber-covered wire—prohibited.
1962—All players recommended to wear properly fitted mouth protectors.
1965—Two-inch kicking tees permitted.
1966—Players prohibited from wearing equipment with electronic, mechanical or other signal devices for the purpose of communicating with any source.
1968—Metal face masks having surfaces with material as resilient as rubber are allowed.
1970—Shoe cleats more than one-half inch in length (changed from three-quarters inch) prohibited.
1972—All players must wear mouth protectors, beginning with 1973 season.
1973—All players shall wear head protectors with a secured chin strap.
1974—All players shall wear shoulder pads.
1976—All players shall wear hip pads and thigh guards.
1979—Beginning in 1981, one team shall wear white jerseys.
1982—Tearaway jersey eliminated by charging a timeout.
1983—Mandatory white jersey for visiting teams.
1986—Therapeutic or preventive knee braces must be worn under the pants.
1989—Kicking tees eliminated for field goals and extra-point attempts.
1991—Rib and back pad covering mandatory.
1994—Standards established to limit glove stickiness. Jerseys that extend below the top of the pants must be tucked into the pants.
1995—Home team may wear white jerseys if both teams agree before the season.
1996—Cleats limited to one-half inch in length (see 1970). Violators disqualified for remainder of game and entire next game. Rule a dead ball when a ball carrier's helmet comes completely off, with the ball belonging to runner's team at that spot. Jerseys must extend to top of pants and must be tucked in if longer.
1997—Require all players on the same team to wear white or team-colored socks of the same design and length. Leg coverings, such as tights, if worn, must be in team colors and of a uniform design for all players on the same team.
1998—All eye shields, if worn, must be clear (transparent) and made from molded and rigid material. NCAA member institutions can, in the case of a death or catastrophic injury or illness, memorialize a player or person with a patch or decal not greater than 1 1/2 inches in diameter that displays the number, name or initials of the individual on the uniform or helmet.

Substitutions

1876—Fifteen players to a team and few if any substitutions.
1882—Replacements for disqualified or injured players.
1897—Substitutions may enter the game any time at discretion of captains.
1922—Players withdrawn during the first half may be returned during the second half. A player withdrawn in the second half may not return.
1941—A player may substitute any time but may not be withdrawn or the outgoing player returned to the game until one play had intervened. Platoon football made possible.
1948—Unlimited substitution on change of team possession.
1953—Two-platoon abolished and players allowed to enter the game only once in each quarter.
1954-64—Changes each year toward more liberalized substitution rule and platoon football.
1965—Platoon football returns. Unlimited substitutions between periods, after a score or try.
1974—Substitutes must be in for one play and replaced players out for one play.
1993—Players who are bleeding or whose uniforms are saturated with blood must come out of the game until their return has been approved by medical personnel.

Passing Game

1906—One forward pass legalized behind the line if made five yards right or left of center. Ball went to opponents if it failed to touch a player of either side before touching the ground. Either team could recover a pass touched by an opponent. One pass each scrimmage down.
1910—Pass interference does not apply 20 yards beyond the line of scrimmage. Passer must be five yards behind the line of scrimmage. One forward pass permitted during each down.
1914—Roughing the passer added.
1923—Handing the ball forward is an illegal forward pass and receivers going out of bounds and returning prohibited.
1934—Three changes encourage use of pass. (1) First forward pass in series of downs can be incomplete in the end zone without loss of ball except on fourth down. (2) Circumference of ball reduced, making it easier to throw. (3) Five-yard penalty for more than one incomplete pass in same series of downs eliminated.
1941—Fourth-down forward pass incomplete in end zone no longer a touchback. Ball goes to opponent at spot where put in play.
1945—Forward pass may be thrown from anywhere behind the line, encouraging use of modern T formation.
1966—Compulsory numbering system makes only players numbered other than 50-79 eligible forward-pass receivers.
1976—Offensive blocking changed to provide half extension of arms to assist pass blocking.
1980—Retreat blocking added with full arm extension to assist pass blocking, and illegal use of hands reduced to five yards.
1982—Pass interference only on a catchable forward pass. Forward pass intentionally grounded to conserve time permitted.
1983—First down added to roughing the passer.
1985—Retreat block deleted and open hands and extended arms permitted anywhere on the field.
1990—Pass thrown immediately to the ground to conserve time legal.
1994—Ball must be catchable for offensive player to be charged with pass interference.
1996—Principle of "reasonable opportunity to catch the pass" applied to intentional grounding situations.
1998—A backward pass can be recovered and advanced by the defense.

General Changes

1876—Holding and carrying the ball permitted.
1880—Eleven players on a side and a scrimmage line established.
1882—Downs and yards to gain enter the rules.
1883—Scoring system established.
1906—Forward passes permitted. Ten yards for first down.
1920—Clipping defined.
1922—Try-for-point introduced. Ball brought out five yards from goal line for scrimmage, allowing try for extra point by place kick, drop kick, run or forward pass.
1925—Kickoff returned to 40-yard line. Clipping made a violation, with penalty of 25 yards.
1927—One-second pause imposed on shift. Thirty seconds allowed for putting ball in play. Huddle limited to 15 seconds. To encourage use of lateral pass, missed backward pass other than from center declared dead ball when it hits the ground and cannot be recovered by opponents.
1929—All fumbles ruled dead at point of recovery.
1932—Most far-reaching changes in nearly a quarter of a century set up safeguards against hazards of game. (1) Ball declared dead when any portion of player in possession, except his hands or feet, touches ground. (2) Use of flying block and flying tackle barred under penalty of five yards. (3) Players on defense forbidden to strike opponents on head, neck or face. (4) Hard and dangerous equipment must be covered with padding.
1941—Legal to hand ball forward behind the neutral zone.
1949—Blockers required to keep hands against their chest.
1951—Fair catch restored.
1952—Penalty for striking with forearm, elbow or locked hands, or for flagrantly rough play or unsportsmanlike conduct, changed from 15 yards to mandatory suspension.
1957—Penalty for grabbing face mask.
1959—Distance penalties limited to one-half distance to offending team's goal line.
1967—Coaching from sideline permitted.
1971—Crack-back block (blocking below waist) illegal.
1972—Freshman eligibility restored.
1977—Clock started on snap after a penalty.
1978—Unsuccessful field goal returned to the previous spot.
1983—Offensive encroachment changed...no offensive player permitted in or beyond the neutral zone after snapper touches ball.
1985—One or both feet on ground required for blocking below waist foul.
1986—Kickoff from the 35-yard line.
1988—Defensive team allowed to score two points on return of blocked extra-point kick attempt or interception of extra-point pass attempt.
1990—Defense allowed to advance fumbles that occur beyond the neutral zone.
1991—Width between goal-post uprights reduced from 23 feet, 4 inches to 18 feet, 6 inches. Kickoffs out of bounds allow receiving team to elect to take ball 30 yards beyond yard line where kickoff occurred.
1992—Defense allowed to advance fumbles regardless of where they occur. Changes ruling of 1990 fumble advancement.
1993—Guard-around or "fumblerooski" play ruled illegal.
1994—Players involved in a fight after half time disqualified for first half of next game; substitutes and coaches who participate in a fight in their team area or leave the team area to join a fight disqualified for entire next game; squad members and coaches involved in a fight during half time disqualified for first half of next game.
1995—Defense penalized five yards for entering neutral zone before snap and causing offensive player to react immediately. Players prohibited from removing helmets on the field. Players disqualified after second unsportsmanlike-conduct foul in one game. Fight suspensions allowed to carry over to next season.
1996—NCAA tiebreaker system to be used in all games tied after four periods.
1997—In overtime tiebreaker system, require a team that scores a touchdown to attempt a two-point conversion in the third overtime period. Approved a rule requiring a game to be declared a tie if it is in overtime but cannot be finished due to weather, darkness or other conditions. Chop block redefined to be penalized if "obviously delayed" and added restrictions to the "crack-back" block to make it illegal up to five yards beyond line of scrimmage regardless of position of the ball. Officials prompted to enforce mouthpiece rule, charging a timeout to offending team if clock is stopped and player does not have mouthpiece in place. To prevent opponents from leveling punt returners with unnecessarily vicious hits, the penalty was increased from five to 15 yards.
1998—For the first time in history, a backward pass can be recovered and advanced by the defense. It is now consistent with the application of the rules similar to how the defense is allowed to advance a fumble.

Division I-AA Records

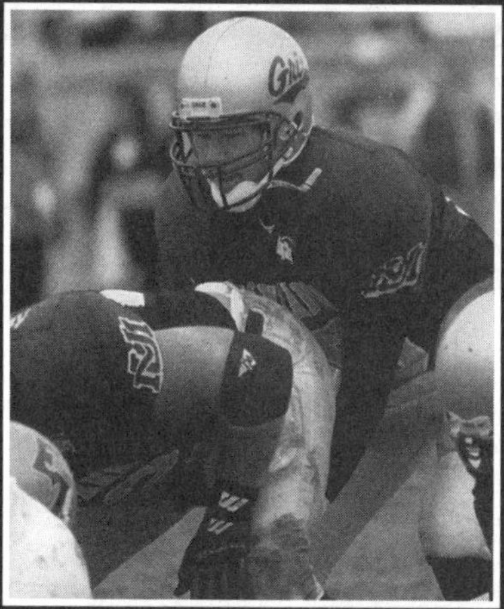

Individual Records

Total Offense

(Rushing Plus Passing)

MOST PLAYS
Quarter
33—Mickey Fein, Maine vs. Connecticut, Oct. 11, 1997 (4th)
Half
48—John Witkowski, Columbia vs. Dartmouth, Nov. 6, 1982 (2nd)
Game
89—Thomas Leonard, Mississippi Val. vs. Texas Southern, Oct. 25, 1986 (440 yards)
Season
649—Steve McNair, Alcorn St., 1994 (5,799 yards)
Career
2,055—Steve McNair, Alcorn St., 1991-94 (16,823 yards)

MOST PLAYS PER GAME
Season
59.0—Steve McNair, Alcorn St., 1994 (649 in 11)
Career
49.5—Tom Proudian, Iona, 1993-95 (1,337 in 27)

MOST PLAYS BY A FRESHMAN
Game
81—Kevin Glenn, Illinois St. vs. Western Ill., Nov. 8, 1997 (470 yards)
Season
462—Greg Wyatt, Northern Ariz., 1986 (2,695 yards)
Per-game record—48.9—James Lopusznick, Fairfield, 1996 (440 in 9)

MOST YARDS GAINED
Quarter
278—Willie Totten, Mississippi Val. vs. Kentucky St., Sept. 1, 1984 (2nd)
Half
404—Todd Hammel, Stephen F. Austin vs. Northeast La., Nov. 11, 1989 (1st)
Game
649—Steve McNair, Alcorn St. vs. Samford, Oct. 29, 1994 (587 passing, 62 rushing)
Season
5,799—Steve McNair, Alcorn St., 1994 (4,863 passing, 936 rushing)
2 Yrs
9,629—Steve McNair, Alcorn St., 1993-94 (8,060 passing, 1,569 rushing)
3 Yrs
13,686—Steve McNair, Alcorn St., 1992-94 (11,601 passing, 2,085 rushing)
Career
(4 yrs.) 16,823—Steve McNair, Alcorn St., 1991-94 (14,496 passing, 2,327 rushing)

MOST YARDS GAINED PER GAME
Season
527.2—Steve McNair, Alcorn St., 1994 (5,799 in 11)
Career
400.5—Steve McNair, Alcorn St., 1991-94 (16,823 in 42)

MOST SEASONS GAINING 3,000 YARDS OR MORE
4—Steve McNair, Alcorn St., 1991-94

MOST YARDS GAINED BY A FRESHMAN
Game
536—Brad Otton, Weber St. vs. Northern Ariz., Nov. 6, 1993 (48 plays)
Season
3,336—Travis Brown, Northern Ariz., 1996
Per-game record—313.7, Steve McNair, Alcorn St., 1991 (3,137 in 10)

MOST YARDS GAINED IN TWO, THREE AND FOUR CONSECUTIVE GAMES
2 Games
1,280—Steve McNair, Alcorn St., 1994 (633 vs. Grambling, Sept. 3; 647 vs. Chattanooga, Sept. 10)
3 Games
1,859—Steve McNair, Alcorn St., 1994 (649 vs. Samford, Oct. 29; 624 vs. Mississippi Val., Nov. 5; 586 vs. Troy St., Nov. 12)
4 Games
2,423—Steve McNair, Alcorn St., 1994 (649 vs. Samford, Oct. 29; 624 vs. Mississippi Val., Nov. 5; 586 vs. Troy St., Nov. 12; 564 vs. Jackson St., Nov. 19)

MOST GAMES GAINING 300 YARDS OR MORE
Season
11—Steve McNair, Alcorn St., 1994
Career
32—Steve McNair, Alcorn St., 1991-94

MOST CONSECUTIVE GAMES GAINING 300 YARDS OR MORE
Season
11—Steve McNair, Alcorn St., 1994
Career
13—Steve McNair, Alcorn St., 1992-93; Willie Totten, Mississippi Val., 1984-85; Neil Lomax, Portland St., 1979-80

MOST GAMES GAINING 400 YARDS OR MORE
Season
9—Steve McNair, Alcorn St., 1994
Career
15—Steve McNair, Alcorn St., 1991-94

MOST CONSECUTIVE GAMES GAINING 400 YARDS OR MORE
Season
5—Steve McNair, Alcorn St., 1994; Willie Totten, Mississippi Val., 1984

MOST GAMES GAINING 500 YARDS OR MORE
Season
6—Steve McNair, Alcorn St., 1994
Career
9—Steve McNair, Alcorn St., 1991-94

MOST YARDS GAINED AGAINST ONE OPPONENT
Career
1,772—Steve McNair, Alcorn St. vs. Jackson St., 1991-94
Also holds per-game record at 443.0 (1,772 in 4)

GAINING 1,000 YARDS RUSHING AND 1,000 YARDS PASSING
Season
Alcede Surtain (QB), Alabama St., 1995 (1,024 rushing, 1,224 passing); Tracy Ham (QB), Ga. Southern, 1986 (1,048 rushing, 1,772 passing)

GAINING 2,000 YARDS RUSHING AND 4,000 YARDS PASSING
Career
Steve McNair (QB), Alcorn St., 1991-94 (2,327 rushing, 14,496 passing); Bill Vergantino (QB), Delaware, 1989-92 (2,287 rushing, 6,177 passing); Tracy Ham (QB), Ga. Southern, 1984-86 (2,506 rushing, 4,871 passing)

HIGHEST AVERAGE GAIN PER PLAY
Game
(Min. 39-49 plays) 12.4—John Whitcomb, UAB vs. Prairie View, Nov. 19, 1994 (43 for 533)
(Min. 50-59 plays) 11.4—Steve McNair, Alcorn St. vs. Chattanooga, Sept. 10, 1994 (57 for 647)
(Min. 60 plays) 9.7—Steve McNair, Alcorn St. vs. Grambling, Sept. 3, 1994 (65 for 633)
Season
(Min. 2,500-3,299 yards) 9.6—Frank Baur, Lafayette, 1988 (285 for 2,727)
(Min. 3,300 yards) 8.9—Steve McNair, Alcorn St., 1994 (649 for 5,799)
Career
(Min. 4,000-4,999 yards) 7.5—Reggie Lewis, Sam Houston St., 1986-87 (653 for 4,929)
(Min. 5,000 yards) 8.2—Steve McNair, Alcorn St., 1991-94 (2,055 for 16,823)

MOST TOUCHDOWNS RESPONSIBLE FOR (TDs Scored and Passed For)
Game
9—Willie Totten, Mississippi Val. vs. Prairie View, Oct. 27, 1984 (passed for 8, scored 1) & vs. Kentucky St., Sept. 1, 1984 (passed for 9); Neil Lomax, Portland St. vs. Delaware St., Nov. 8, 1980 (passed for 8, scored 1)
Season
61—Willie Totten, Mississippi Val., 1984 (passed for 56, scored 5)
Also holds per-game record at 6.1 (61 in 10)
Career
157—Willie Totten, Mississippi Val., 1982-85 (passed for 139, scored 18)
Also holds per-game record at 3.9 (157 in 40)

MOST POINTS RESPONSIBLE FOR (Points Scored and Passed For)
Game
56—Willie Totten, Mississippi Val. vs. Kentucky St., Sept. 1, 1984 (passed for 9 TDs and 1 two-point conversion)
Season
368—Willie Totten, Mississippi Val., 1984 (passed for 56 TDs, scored 5 TDs and passed for 1 two-point conversion)
Also holds per-game record at 36.8 (368 in 10)
Career
946—Willie Totten, Mississippi Val., 1982-85 (passed for 139 TDs, scored 18 TDs and passed for 1 two-point conversion)
Also holds per-game record at 23.7 (946 in 40)

Rushing

MOST RUSHES
Quarter
20—Arnold Mickens, Butler vs. Dayton, Oct. 15, 1994 (4th)
Half
32—Arnold Mickens, Butler vs. Valparaiso, Oct. 8, 1994 (1st); David Clark, Dartmouth vs. Pennsylvania, Nov. 18, 1989 (2nd)
Game
56—Arnold Mickens, Butler vs. Valparaiso, Oct. 8, 1994 (295 yards)
Season
409—Arnold Mickens, Butler, 1994 (2,255 yards)
Career
1,027—Erik Marsh, Lafayette, 1991-94 (4,834 yards)

MOST RUSHES PER GAME
Season
40.9—Arnold Mickens, Butler, 1994 (409 in 10)
Career
38.2—Arnold Mickens, Butler, 1994-95 (763 in 20)

MOST RUSHES IN TWO CONSECUTIVE GAMES
110—Arnold Mickens, Butler, 1994 (56 vs. Valparaiso, Oct. 8; 54 vs. Dayton, Oct. 15)

MOST CONSECUTIVE CARRIES BY SAME PLAYER
Game
26—Arnold Mickens, Butler vs. Valparaiso, Oct. 8, 1994 (during 6 series)

MOST YARDS GAINED
Quarter
194—Otto Kelly, Nevada vs. Idaho, Nov. 12, 1983 (3rd, 8 rushes)
Half
272—Tony Vinson, Towson vs. Morgan St., Nov. 20, 1993 (1st, 26 rushes)
Game
379—Reggie Greene, Siena vs. St. John's (N.Y.), Nov. 2, 1996 (44 rushes)
Season
2,255—Arnold Mickens, Butler, 1994 (409 rushes)
Career
5,415—Reggie Greene, Siena, 1994-97 (890 rushes)

MOST YARDS GAINED PER GAME
Season
225.5—Arnold Mickens, Butler, 1994 (2,255 in 10)
Career
(2 yrs.) 190.7—Arnold Mickens, Butler, 1994-95 (3,813 in 20)
(3 yrs.) 144.3—Thomas Haskins, VMI, 1994-96 (4,761 in 33)
(4 yrs.) 150.4—Reggie Greene, Siena, 1994-97 (5,415 in 36)

MOST YARDS GAINED BY A FRESHMAN
Game
304—Tony Citizen, McNeese St. vs. Prairie View, Sept. 6, 1986 (30 rushes)
Season
1,620—Markus Thomas, Eastern Ky., 1989 (232 rushes)

MOST YARDS GAINED PER GAME BY A FRESHMAN
Season
147.3—Markus Thomas, Eastern Ky., 1989 (1,620 in 11)

MOST YARDS GAINED BY A QUARTERBACK
Game
309—Eddie Thompson, Western Ky. vs. Southern Ill., Oct. 31, 1992 (28 rushes)
Season
1,246—Joe Dupaix, Southern Utah, 1996 (271 rushes)
Per-game record—121.7 by Willie Taggart, Western Ky., 1997 (152 for 1,217)
Career
3,674—Jack Douglas, Citadel, 1989-92 (832 rushes)

MOST GAMES GAINING 100 YARDS OR MORE
Season
11—Rich Lemon, Bucknell, 1994; Frank Hawkins, Nevada, 1980
Career
29—Kenny Gamble, Colgate, 1984-87 (42 games); Frank Hawkins, Nevada, 1977-80 (43 games)

MOST CONSECUTIVE GAMES GAINING 100 YARDS OR MORE
Season
11—Rich Lemon, Bucknell, 1994; Frank Hawkins, Nevada, 1980
Career
20—Frank Hawkins, Nevada, 1979-80

MOST GAMES GAINING 100 YARDS OR MORE BY A FRESHMAN
8—David Wright, Indiana St., 1992; Markus Thomas, Eastern Ky., 1989

MOST GAMES GAINING 200 YARDS OR MORE
Season
8—Arnold Mickens, Butler, 1994
Career
10—Arnold Mickens, Butler, 1994-95

MOST CONSECUTIVE GAMES GAINING 200 YARDS OR MORE
Season
8—Arnold Mickens, Butler, 1994

MOST YARDS GAINED IN TWO, THREE AND FOUR CONSECUTIVE GAMES
2 Games
691—Tony Vinson, Towson, 1993 (364 vs. Bucknell, Nov. 13; 327 vs. Morgan St., Nov. 20)
3 Games
876—Arnold Mickens, Butler, 1994 (288 vs. Wis.-Stevens Point, Sept. 24; 293 vs. Drake, Oct. 1; 295 vs. Valparaiso, Oct. 8)
4 Games
1,109—Arnold Mickens, Butler, 1994 (233 vs. Georgetown, Ky., Sept. 17; 288 vs. Wis.-Stevens Point, Sept. 24; 293 vs. Drake, Oct. 1; 295 vs. Valparaiso, Oct. 8)

MOST SEASONS GAINING 1,000 YARDS OR MORE
Career
3—By 25 players. Most recent: Reggie Greene, Siena, 1995-97; Claude Mathis, Southwest Tex. St., 1995-97; Jermaine Creighton, St. John's (N. Y.), 1994, 96-97

TWO PLAYERS, SAME TEAM, EACH GAINING 1,000 YARDS OR MORE
Southern Utah, 1997—Brook Madsen (1,214) & Matt Cannon (1,024); Cal Poly, 1997—Antonio Warren (1,151) & Craig Young (1,038); Colgate, 1997—Ed Weiss (1,069) & Daymon Smith (1,012); Southern Utah, 1996—Brook Madsen (1,405) & Joe Dupaix (1,246); Massachusetts, 1995—Frank Alessio (1,276) & Rene Ingoglia (1,178); South Caro. St., 1994—Michael Hicks (1,368) & Marvin Marshall (1,201); Eastern Ky., 1993—Mike Penman (1,139) & Leon Brown (1,046); Northeast La., 1992—Greg Robinson (1,011) & Roosevelt Potts (1,004); Yale, 1991—Chris Kouri (1,101) & Nick Crawford (1,024); William & Mary, 1990—Robert Green (1,185) & Tyrone Shelton (1,020); Citadel, 1988—Adrian Johnson (1,091) & Gene Brown (1,006); Eastern Ky., 1986—Elroy Harris (1,152) & James Crawford (1,070); Eastern Ky., 1985—James Crawford (1,282) & Elroy Harris (1,134); Nevada, 1983—Otto Kelly (1,090) & Tony Corley (1,006); Jackson St., 1978—Perry Harrington (1,105) & Jeffrey Moore (1,094)

MOST YARDS GAINED BY TWO PLAYERS, SAME TEAM
Game
471—Eddie Thompson (309) & Dion Bryant (162), Western Ky., vs. Southern Ill., Oct. 29, 1992
Season
2,651—Brook Madsen (1,405) & Joe Dupaix (1,246), Southern Utah, 1996

EARLIEST GAME GAINING 1,000 YARDS OR MORE
Season
5—Arnold Mickens, Butler, 1994 (1,106)

MOST YARDS GAINED IN OPENING GAME OF SEASON
304—Tony Citizen, McNeese St. vs. Prairie View, Sept. 6, 1986 (30 rushes)

MOST YARDS GAINED IN FIRST GAME OF CAREER
304—Tony Citizen, McNeese St. vs. Prairie View, Sept. 6, 1986 (30 rushes)

HIGHEST AVERAGE GAIN PER RUSH
Game
(Min. 15-19 rushes) 19.1—Gene Brown, Citadel vs. VMI, Nov. 12, 1988 (15 for 286)
(Min. 20 rushes) 17.3—Russell Davis, Idaho vs. Portland St., Oct. 3, 1981 (20 for 345)
Season
(Min. 150-199 rushes) 8.7—Tim Hall, Robert Morris, 1994 (154 for 1,336)
(Min. 200 rushes) 7.3—Mike Clark, Akron, 1986 (245 for 1,786)
Career
(Min. 350-599 rushes) 7.4—Tim Hall, Robert Morris, 1994-95 (393 for 2,908)
(Min. 600 rushes) 6.6—Markus Thomas, Eastern Ky., 1989-92 (784 for 5,149)

MOST TOUCHDOWNS SCORED BY RUSHING
Game
7—Archie Amerson, Northern Ariz. vs. Weber St., Oct. 5, 1996
Season
25—Archie Amerson, Northern Ariz., 1996
Career
55—Kenny Gamble, Colgate, 1984-87

MOST TOUCHDOWNS SCORED PER GAME BY RUSHING
Season
2.3—Tony Vinson, Towson, 1993 (23 in 10)
Career
1.7—Archie Amerson, Northern Ariz., 1995-96 (37 in 22)

MOST TOUCHDOWNS SCORED BY RUSHING BY A QUARTERBACK
Season
21—Alcede Surtain, Alabama St., 1995
Career
48—Jack Douglas, Citadel, 1989-92
Also holds per-game record at 1.1 (48 in 44)

LONGEST PLAY
99—Jermaine Creighton, St. John's (N. Y.) vs. Siena, Nov. 2, 1996; Jim Varick, Monmouth (N. J.) vs. Sacred Heart, Oct. 29, 1994; Phillip Collins, Southwest Mo. St. vs. Western Ill., Sept. 16, 1989; Pedro Bacon, Western Ky. vs. West Ala., Sept. 13, 1986 (only rush of the game); Hubert Owens, Mississippi Val. vs. Ark.-Pine Bluff, Sept. 20, 1980

Passing

HIGHEST PASSING EFFICIENCY RATING POINTS
Game
(Min. 15-24 atts.) 368.5—Rich Green, New Hampshire vs. Rhode Island, Nov. 13, 1993 (15 attempts, 12 completions, 0 interceptions, 358 yards, 4 TD passes)
(Min. 25-44 atts.) 287.2—Doug Turner, Morehead St. vs. Miles, Oct. 18, 1997 (26 attempts, 20 completions, 0 interceptions, 415 yards, 6 TD passes)
(Min. 45 atts.) 220.8—Todd Hammel, Stephen F. Austin vs. Northeast La., Nov. 11, 1989 (45 attempts, 31 completions, 3 interceptions, 571 yards, 8 TD passes)
Season
(Min. 15 atts. per game) 204.6—Shawn Knight, William & Mary, 1993 (177 attempts, 125 completions, 4 interceptions, 2,055 yards, 22 TD passes)
Career
(Min. 300-399 comps.) 170.8—Shawn Knight, William & Mary, 1991-94 (558 attempts, 367 completions, 15 interceptions, 5,527 yards, 46 TD passes)
(Min. 400 comps.) 166.3—Dave Dickenson, Montana, 1992-95 (1,208 attempts, 813 completions, 26 interceptions, 11,080 yards, 96 TD passes)

MOST PASSES ATTEMPTED
Quarter
29—Mickey Fein, Maine vs. Connecticut, Oct. 11, 1997 (4th) (completed 19)
Half
42—Doug Pederson, Northeast La. vs. Stephen F. Austin, Nov. 11, 1989 (1st, completed 27); Mike Machurek, Idaho St. vs. Weber St., Sept. 20, 1980 (2nd, completed 18)
Game
77—Neil Lomax, Portland St. vs. Northern Colo., Oct. 20, 1979 (completed 44)
Season
530—Steve McNair, Alcorn St., 1994 (completed 304)
Per-game record—51.8, Willie Totten, Mississippi Val., 1984 (518 in 10)
Career
1,680—Steve McNair, Alcorn St., 1991-94 (completed 927)
Per-game record—42.9, Stan Greene, Boston U., 1989-90 (944 in 22)

MOST PASSES ATTEMPTED BY A FRESHMAN
Game
66—Kevin Glenn, Illinois St. vs. Western Ill., Nov. 8, 1997 (completed 41); Chris Swartz, Morehead St. vs. Tennessee Tech, Oct. 17, 1987 (completed 35)
Season
411—Travis Brown, Northern Ariz., 1996 (completed 223)
Per-game record—37.8, Jason Whitmer, Idaho St., 1987 (340 in 9)

MOST PASSES COMPLETED
Quarter
19—Mickey Fein, Maine vs. Connecticut, Oct. 11, 1997 (4th) (attempted 29)
Half
28—Mickey Fein, Maine vs. Connecticut, Oct. 11, 1997 (2nd) (attempted 40)
Game
48—Clayton Millis, Cal St. Northridge vs. St. Mary's (Cal.), Nov. 11, 1995 (attempted 65)
Season
324—Willie Totten, Mississippi Val., 1984 (attempted 518)
Also holds per-game record at 32.4
Career
934—Jamie Martin, Weber St., 1989-92 (attempted 1,544)
Per-game record—25.1—Aaron Flowers, Cal St. Northridge, 1996-97 (502 in 20)

MOST PASSES COMPLETED BY A FRESHMAN
Game
42—Travis Brown, Northern Ariz. vs. Montana, Oct. 26, 1996 (attempted 65)
Season
250—Greg Wyatt, Northern Ariz., 1986 (attempted 392)
Also holds per-game record at 22.7 (250 in 11)

MOST PASSES COMPLETED IN FRESHMAN AND SOPHOMORE SEASONS
518—Greg Wyatt, Northern Ariz., 1986-87 (attempted 804)

MOST CONSECUTIVE PASSES COMPLETED
Game
19—Kirk Schulz, Villanova vs. Central Conn. St., Oct. 10, 1987

MOST CONSECUTIVE PASS COMPLETIONS TO START GAME
18—Jeff Lewis, Northern Ariz. vs. Cal St. Northridge, Sept. 23, 1995; Scott Auchenbach, Bucknell vs. Colgate, Nov. 11, 1989

MOST CONSECUTIVE PASS COMPLETIONS TO START FIRST GAME AS A FRESHMAN
12—Daunte Culpepper, Central Fla. vs. Eastern Ky., Aug. 31, 1995

HIGHEST PERCENTAGE OF PASSES COMPLETED
Game
(Min. 20-29 comps.) 95.7%—Butch Mosby, Murray St. vs. Tenn.-Martin, Oct. 2, 1993 (22 of 23)
(Min. 30 comps.) 81.6%—Eric Beavers, Nevada vs. Idaho St., Nov. 17, 1984 (31 of 38)
Season
(Min. 200 atts.) 70.6%—Giovanni Carmazzi, Hofstra, 1997 (288 of 408)
Career
(Min. 750 atts.) 67.3%—Dave Dickenson, Montana, 1992-95 (813 of 1,208)

MOST PASSES HAD INTERCEPTED
Game
7—Dan Crowley, Towson vs. Maine, Nov. 16, 1991 (53 attempts); Carlton Jenkins, Mississippi Val. vs. Prairie View, Oct. 31, 1987 (34 attempts); Charles Hebert, Southeastern La. vs. Northwestern St., Nov. 12, 1983 (23 attempts); Mick Spoon, Idaho St. vs. Montana, Oct. 21, 1978 (attempted 35)
Season
29—Willie Totten, Mississippi Val., 1985 (492 attempts)
Also holds per-game record at 2.6 (29 in 11)
Career
75—Willie Totten, Mississippi Val., 1982-85
Per-game record—2.0, John Witkowski, Columbia, 1981-83 (60 in 30)

LOWEST PERCENTAGE OF PASSES HAD INTERCEPTED
Season
(Min. 175-324 atts.) 0.6%—Kharon Brown, Hofstra, 1995 (2 of 320)
(Min. 325 atts.) 1.2%—Bill Lazor, Cornell, 1992 (4 of 328)
Career
(Min. 500-749 atts.) 1.8%—Jason Garrett, Princeton, 1987-88 (10 of 550)
(Min. 750 atts.) 1.8%—Jeff Lewis, Northern Ariz., 1992-95 (24 of 1,315)

MOST PASSES ATTEMPTED WITHOUT INTERCEPTION
Game
68—Tony Petersen, Marshall vs. Western Caro., Nov. 14, 1987 (completed 34)

MOST CONSECUTIVE PASSES ATTEMPTED WITHOUT INTERCEPTION
Season
203—Braniff Bonaventure, Furman, 1996 (in 10 games, from Sept. 7 through Nov. 16)
Career
215—Braniff Bonaventure, Furman, began Nov. 23, 1995, ended Nov. 16, 1996

MOST YARDS GAINED
Quarter
278—Willie Totten, Mississippi Val. vs. Kentucky St., Sept. 1, 1984 (2nd)
Half
383—Michael Payton, Marshall vs. VMI, Nov. 16, 1991 (1st)
Game
624—Jamie Martin, Weber St. vs. Idaho St., Nov. 23, 1991
Season
4,863—Steve McNair, Alcorn St., 1994
Career
14,496—Steve McNair, Alcorn St., 1991-94

MOST YARDS GAINED PER GAME
Season
455.7—Willie Totten, Mississippi Val., 1984 (4,557 in 10)
Career
350.0—Neil Lomax, Portland St., 1978-80 (11,550 in 33)

MOST YARDS GAINED BY A FRESHMAN
Game
540—Brad Otton, Weber St. vs. Northern Ariz., Nov. 6, 1993
Season
3,398—Travis Brown, Northern Ariz., 1996
Also holds per-game record at 308.9 (3,398 in 11)

MOST YARDS GAINED IN FRESHMAN AND SOPHOMORE SEASONS
6,793—Travis Brown, Northern Ariz., 1996-97

MOST YARDS GAINED IN TWO, THREE AND FOUR CONSECUTIVE GAMES
2 Games
1,150—Steve McNair, Alcorn St., 1994 (587 vs. Samford, Oct. 29; 563 vs. Mississippi Val., Nov. 5)
3 Games
1,626—Steve McNair, Alcorn St., 1994 (587 vs. Samford, Oct. 29; 563 vs. Mississippi Val., Nov. 5; 476 vs. Troy St., Nov. 12)
4 Games
2,159—Steve McNair, Alcorn St., 1994 (587 vs. Samford, Oct. 29; 563 vs. Mississippi Val., Nov. 5; 476 vs. Troy St., Nov. 12; 533 vs. Jackson St., Nov. 19)

MOST GAMES GAINING 200 YARDS OR MORE
Season
11—By 13 players. Most recent: Steve McNair, Alcorn St., 1994; Chris Hakel, William & Mary, 1991; Jamie Martin, Weber St., 1991
Career
41—Steve McNair, Alcorn St., 1991-94 (42 games)

MOST CONSECUTIVE GAMES GAINING 200 YARDS OR MORE
Season
11—By 11 players. Most recent: Steve McNair, Alcorn St., 1994; Chris Hakel, William & Mary, 1991; Jamie Martin, Weber St., 1991
Career
28—Steve McNair, Alcorn St., 1991-93; Neil Lomax, Portland St., 1978-80

MOST GAMES GAINING 300 YARDS OR MORE
Season
10—Steve McNair, Alcorn St., 1994; John Friesz, Idaho, 1989; Willie Totten, Mississippi Val., 1984
Career
28—Neil Lomax, Portland St., 1978-80

MOST CONSECUTIVE GAMES GAINING 300 YARDS OR MORE
Season
10—John Friesz, Idaho, 1989; Willie Totten, Mississippi Val., 1984
Career
13—Neil Lomax, Portland St., 1979-80

MOST YARDS GAINED AGAINST ONE OPPONENT
Career
1,675—Willie Totten, Mississippi Val. vs. Prairie View, 1982-85
Also holds per-game record at 418.8 (1,675 in 4)

MOST YARDS PER ATTEMPT
Game
(Min. 30-44 atts.) 16.1—Gilbert Renfroe, Tennessee St. vs. Dist. Columbia, Nov. 5, 1983 (30 for 484)
(Min. 45 atts.) 12.7—Todd Hammel, Stephen F. Austin vs. Northeast La., Nov. 11, 1989 (45 for 571)
Season
(Min. 250-324 atts.) 10.3—Mike Smith, Northern Iowa, 1986 (303 for 3,125)
(Min. 325 atts.) 9.5—John Friesz, Idaho, 1989 (425 for 4,041)
Career
(Min. 500-999 atts.) 9.5—Jay Johnson, Northern Iowa, 1989-92 (744 for 7,049)
(Min. 1,000 atts.) 9.2—Dave Dickenson, Montana, 1992-95 (1,208 for 11,080)

MOST YARDS GAINED PER COMPLETION
Game
(Min. 15-19 comps.) 28.5—Kendrick Nord, Grambling vs. Alcorn St., Sept. 3, 1994 (17 for 485)
(Min. 20 comps.) 22.5—Michael Payton, Marshall vs. VMI, Nov. 16, 1991 (22 for 496)
Season
(Min. 200 comps.) 16.4—Todd Hammel, Stephen F. Austin, 1989 (238 for 3,914)
Career
(Min. 350-399 comps.) 17.8—Jay Johnson, Northern Iowa, 1989-92 (397 for 7,049)
(Min. 400 comps.) 15.6—Steve McNair, Alcorn St., 1991-94 (927 for 14,496)

MOST TOUCHDOWN PASSES
Quarter
7—Neil Lomax, Portland St. vs. Delaware St., Nov. 8, 1980 (1st)
Half
7—Neil Lomax, Portland St. vs. Delaware St., Nov. 8, 1980 (1st)
Game
9—Willie Totten, Mississippi Val. vs. Kentucky St., Sept. 1, 1984
Season
56—Willie Totten, Mississippi Val., 1984
Also holds per-game record at 5.6 (56 in 10)
Career
139—Willie Totten, Mississippi Val., 1982-85
Also holds per-game record at 3.5 (139 in 40)

MOST CONSECUTIVE GAMES THROWING A TOUCHDOWN PASS
Career
36—Steve McNair, Alcorn St., 1991-94

MOST TOUCHDOWN PASSES, SAME PASSER AND RECEIVER
Season
27—Willie Totten to Jerry Rice, Mississippi Val., 1984
Career
47—Willie Totten to Jerry Rice, Mississippi Val., 1982-84

HIGHEST PERCENTAGE OF PASSES FOR TOUCHDOWNS
Season
(Min. 200-299 atts.) 12.5%—Ted White, Howard, 1996 (36 of 289)
(Min. 300 atts.) 10.9%—Doug Nussmeier, Idaho, 1993 (33 of 304)
Career
(Min. 500-749 atts.) 8.5%—Mike Williams, Grambling, 1977-80 (44 of 520)
(Min. 750 atts.) 7.9%—Dave Dickenson, Montana, 1992-95 (96 of 1,208)

Receiving

MOST PASSES CAUGHT
Game
24—Jerry Rice, Mississippi Val. vs. Southern U., Oct. 1, 1983 (219 yards)
Season
115—Brian Forster, Rhode Island, 1985 (1,617 yards)
Career
301—Jerry Rice, Mississippi Val., 1981-84 (4,693 yards)

MOST PASSES CAUGHT PER GAME
Season
11.5—Brian Forster, Rhode Island, 1985 (115 in 10)
Career
7.3—Jerry Rice, Mississippi Val., 1981-84 (301 in 41)

MOST PASSES CAUGHT BY A TIGHT END
Game
18—Brian Forster, Rhode Island vs. Brown, Sept. 28, 1985 (327 yards)
Season
115—Brian Forster, Rhode Island, 1985 (1,617 yards)
Also holds per-game record at 11.5 (115 in 10)
Career
245—Brian Forster, Rhode Island, 1983-85, 1987 (3,410 yards)

MOST PASSES CAUGHT BY A RUNNING BACK
Game
21—David Pandt, Montana St. vs. Eastern Wash., Sept. 21, 1985 (169 yards)
Season
78—Gordie Lockbaum, Holy Cross, 1987 (1,152 yards)
2 Yrs
135—Gordie Lockbaum, Holy Cross, 1986-87 (2,012 yards)
Also holds per-game record at 6.1 (135 in 22)

Career
182—Merril Hoge, Idaho St., 1983-86 (1,734 yards)

MOST PASSES CAUGHT BY A FRESHMAN
Game
15—Emerson Foster, Rhode Island vs. Northeastern, Nov. 9, 1985 (205 yards)
Season
69—Thomas Lopusznick, Fairfield, 1996 (857 yards)

MOST PASSES CAUGHT BY TWO PLAYERS, SAME TEAM
Season
183—Jerry Rice (103 for 1,682 yards and 27 TDs) & Joe Thomas (80 for 1,119 yards and 11 TDs), Mississippi Val., 1984
Career
420—Darrell Colbert (217 for 3,177 yards and 33 TDs) & Donald Narcisse (203 for 2,429 yards and 26 TDs), Texas Southern, 1983-86

MOST YARDS GAINED
Game
370—Michael Lerch, Princeton vs. Brown, Oct. 12, 1991 (caught 9)
Season
1,682—Jerry Rice, Mississippi Val., 1984 (caught 103)
Career
4,693—Jerry Rice, Mississippi Val., 1981-84 (caught 301)

MOST YARDS GAINED PER GAME
Season
168.2—Jerry Rice, Mississippi Val., 1984 (1,682 in 10)
Career
(Min. 2,000-2,999 yds.) 116.9—Derrick Ingram, UAB, 1993-94 (2,572 in 22)
(Min. 3,000 yds.) 114.5—Jerry Rice, Mississippi Val., 1981-84 (4,693 in 41)

MOST YARDS GAINED BY A TIGHT END
Game
327—Brian Forster, Rhode Island vs. Brown, Sept. 28, 1985 (caught 18)
Season
1,617—Brian Forster, Rhode Island, 1985 (caught 115)
Also holds per-game record at 161.7 (1,617 in 10)
Career
3,410—Brian Forster, Rhode Island, 1983-85, 1987 (caught 245)

MOST YARDS GAINED BY A RUNNING BACK
Game
220—Alvin Atkinson, Davidson vs. Furman, Nov. 3, 1979 (caught 9)
Season
1,152—Gordie Lockbaum, Holy Cross, 1987 (caught 78)
Also holds per-game record at 104.7 (1,152 in 11)

MOST YARDS GAINED BY A FRESHMAN
Game
284—Jacquay Nunnally, Florida A&M vs. North Caro. A&T, Oct. 11, 1997 (caught 13)
Season
1,073—Randy Moss, Marshall, 1996 (55 catches)

MOST YARDS GAINED BY TWO PLAYERS, SAME TEAM
Season
2,801—Jerry Rice (1,682, 103 caught and 27 TDs) & Joe Thomas (1,119, 80 caught and 11 TDs), Mississippi Val., 1984
Career
5,806—Roy Banks (3,177, 184 caught and 38 TDs) & Cal Pierce (2,629, 163 caught and 13 TDs), Eastern Ill., 1983-86

HIGHEST AVERAGE GAIN PER RECEPTION
Game
(Min. 5-9 receps.) 44.6—John Taylor, Delaware St. vs. St. Paul's, Sept. 21, 1985 (5 for 223)
(Min. 10 receps.) 29.0—Jason Cristino, Lehigh vs. Lafayette, Nov. 21, 1992 (11 for 319)
Season
(Min. 35-59 receps.) 28.9—Mikhael Ricks, Stephen F. Austin, 1997 (47 for 1,358)
(Min. 60 receps.) 20.7—Golden Tate, Tennessee St., 1983 (63 for 1,307)
Career
(Min. 90-124 receps.) 24.3—John Taylor, Delaware St., 1982-85 (100 for 2,426)
(Min. 125 receps.) 22.0 Dedric Ward, Northern Iowa, 1993-96 (176 for 3,876)

MOST GAMES GAINING 100 YARDS OR MORE
Career
23—Jerry Rice, Mississippi Val., 1981-84 (in 41 games played)

MOST TOUCHDOWN PASSES CAUGHT
Game
5—Rod Marshall, Northern Ariz. vs. Abilene Christian, Sept. 16, 1995 (154 yards); Wayne Chrebet, Hofstra vs. Delaware, Nov. 12, 1994 (245 yards); Rennie Benn, Lehigh vs. Indiana (Pa.), Sept. 14, 1985 (266 yards); Jerry Rice, Mississippi Val. vs. Prairie View, Oct. 27, 1984 & vs. Kentucky St., Sept. 1, 1984
Season
27—Jerry Rice, Mississippi Val., 1984
Career
50—Jerry Rice, Mississippi Val., 1981-84

MOST TOUCHDOWN PASSES CAUGHT BY A FRESHMAN
Season
19—Randy Moss, Marshall, 1996

MOST TOUCHDOWN PASSES CAUGHT PER GAME
Season
2.7—Jerry Rice, Mississippi Val., 1984 (27 in 10)
Career
1.2—Jerry Rice, Mississippi Val., 1981-84 (50 in 41)

MOST GAMES CATCHING A TOUCHDOWN PASS
Season
11—Randy Moss, Marshall, 1996
Also holds consecutive record at 11 (1996)
Career
26—Jerry Rice, Mississippi Val., 1981-84
Also holds consecutive record at 17 (1983-84)

Punting

MOST PUNTS
Game
16—Matt Stover, Louisiana Tech vs. Northeast La., Nov. 18, 1988 (567 yards)
Season
98—Barry Hickingbotham, Louisiana Tech, 1987 (3,821 yards)
Career
301—Barry Bowman, Louisiana Tech, 1983-86 (11,441 yards)

HIGHEST AVERAGE PER PUNT
Game
(Min. 5-9 punts) 55.7—Harold Alexander, Appalachian St. vs. Citadel, Oct. 3, 1992 (6 for 334); Jody Farmer, Montana vs. Nevada, Oct. 1, 1988 (9 for 501)
(Min. 10 punts) 52.2—Stuart Dodds, Montana St. vs. Northern Ariz., Oct. 20, 1979 (10 for 522)
Season
(Min. 60 punts) 47.0—Harold Alexander, Appalachian St., 1991 (64 for 3,009)
Career
(Min. 150 punts) 44.4—Pumpy Tudors, Chattanooga, 1989-91 (181 for 8,041)

LONGEST PUNT
91—Bart Helsley, North Texas vs. Northeast La., Nov. 17, 1990

Interceptions

MOST PASSES INTERCEPTED
Game
5—Mark Cordes, Eastern Wash. vs. Boise St., Sept. 6, 1986 (48 yards); Michael Richardson, Northwestern St. vs. Southeastern La., Nov. 12, 1983 (128 yards); Karl Johnson, Jackson St. vs. Grambling, Oct. 23, 1982 (29 yards)
Season
12—Dean Cain, Princeton, 1987 (98 yards)
Also holds per-game record at 1.2 (12 in 10)
Career
28—Dave Murphy, Holy Cross, 1986-89 (309 yards)
Per-game record—0.73, Dean Cain, Princeton, 1985-87 (22 in 30)

MOST YARDS ON INTERCEPTION RETURNS
Game
216—Keiron Bigby, Brown vs. Yale, Sept. 29, 1984 (3 interceptions) (first career game)
Season
280—William Hampton, Murray St., 1995 (8 interceptions)
Career
488—Darren Sharper, William & Mary, 1993-96 (24 interceptions)

MOST TOUCHDOWNS SCORED ON INTERCEPTION RETURNS
Game
2—By nine players. Most recent: Corey Cobb, Tenn.-Martin vs. Austin Peay, Nov. 15, 1997; Cedric Allen, Western Ky. vs. Ky. Wesleyan, Aug. 29, 1996; William Hampton, Murray St. vs. Tenn.-Martin, Oct. 7, 1995
Season
4—William Hampton, Murray St., 1995 (8 interceptions, 280 yards); Joseph Vaughn, Cal St. Northridge, 1994 (9 interceptions, 265 yards); Robert Turner, Jackson St., 1990 (9 interceptions, 212 yards)
Career
6—William Hampton, Murray St., 1993-96 (20 interceptions)

HIGHEST AVERAGE GAIN PER INTERCEPTION
Game
(Min. 3 ints.) 72.0—Keiron Bigby, Brown vs. Yale, Sept. 29, 1984 (3 for 216)
Season
(Min. 3 ints.) 72.0—Keiron Bigby, Brown, 1984 (3 for 216)
Career
(Min. 12 ints.) 25.8—Zack Bronson, McNeese St., 1993-96 (16 for 413)

Punt Returns

MOST PUNT RETURNS
Game
9—By 15 players. Most recent: Colby Skelton, Harvard vs. Dartmouth, Nov. 1, 1997 (50 yards)
Season
55—Tommy Houk, Murray St., 1980 (442 yards)
Also holds per-game record at 5.0 (55 in 11)
Career
123—Chuck Calhoun, Southwest Mo. St., 1990-93 (978 yards)
Per-game record—3.8, Tommy Houk, Murray St., 1979-80 (84 in 22)

MOST YARDS ON PUNT RETURNS
Game
216—Ricky Pearsall, Northern Ariz. vs. Western N. M., Aug. 29, 1996 (5 returns); Gary Harrell, Howard vs. Morgan St., Nov. 3, 1990 (7 returns); Willie Ware, Mississippi Val. vs. Washburn, Sept. 15, 1984 (7 returns)
Season
563—Dewayne Harper, Tenn.-Martin, 1994 (45 returns)
Per-game record—54.7—Joe Rosato, Duquesne, 1996 (547 in 10)
Career
1,230—David McCrary, Chattanooga, 1982-85 (117 returns)

HIGHEST AVERAGE GAIN PER RETURN
Game
(Min. 5 rets.) 43.2—Ricky Pearsall, Northern Ariz. vs. Western N. M., Aug. 29, 1996 (5 for 216)
Season
(Min. 1.2 rets. per game) 23.0—Tim Egerton, Delaware St., 1988 (16 for 368)
Career
(Min. 1.2 rets. per game) 16.4—Willie Ware, Mississippi Val., 1982-85 (61 for 1,003)

MOST TOUCHDOWNS SCORED ON PUNT RETURNS

Game

3—Aaron Fix, Canisius vs. Siena, Sept. 24, 1994 (5 returns)

Season

4—Aaron Fix, Canisius, 1994 (34 returns); Kenny Shedd, Northern Iowa, 1992 (27 returns); Howard Huckaby, Florida A&M, 1988 (26 returns)

Career

7—Kenny Shedd, Northern Iowa, 1989-92

LONGEST PUNT RETURN

98—Willie Ware, Mississippi Val. vs. Bishop, Sept. 21, 1985; Barney Bussey, South Caro. St. vs. Johnson Smith, Oct. 10, 1981

MOST CONSECUTIVE GAMES RETURNING PUNT FOR TOUCHDOWN

3—Troy Jones, McNeese St., 1989 (vs. Mississippi Col., Sept. 2; vs. Samford, Sept. 9; vs. Northeast La., Sept. 16)

Kickoff Returns

MOST KICKOFF RETURNS

Game

10—Ryan Steen, Cal Poly vs. Eastern Wash., Sept. 10, 1994 (203 yards); Merril Hoge, Idaho St. vs. Weber St., Oct. 25, 1986 (179 yards)

Season

50—David Primus, Samford, 1989 (1,411 yards)

Career

118—Clarence Alexander, Mississippi Val., 1986-89 (2,439 yards)

MOST KICKOFF RETURNS PER GAME

Season

4.5—David Primus, Samford, 1989 (50 in 11)

Career

3.0—Lorenza Rivers, Tennessee Tech, 1985, 1987 (62 in 21)

MOST YARDS ON KICKOFF RETURNS

Game

268—Jay Jones, James Madison vs. Richmond, Oct. 19, 1996 (6 returns)

Season

1,411—David Primus, Samford, 1989 (50 returns)

Career

2,439—Clarence Alexander, Mississippi Val., 1986-89 (118 returns)

MOST YARDS PER GAME ON KICKOFF RETURNS

Season

128.3—David Primus, Samford, 1989 (1,411 in 11)

Career

61.0—Clarence Alexander, Mississippi Val., 1986-89 (2,439 in 40)

HIGHEST AVERAGE GAIN PER RETURN

Game

(Min. 5 rets.) 45.6—Jerome Stelly, Western Ill. vs. Youngstown St., Nov. 7, 1981 (5 for 228)

Season

(Min. 1.2 rets. per game) 37.3—David Fraterrigo, Canisius, 1993 (13 for 485)

Career

(Min. 1.2 Returns Per Game)

(Min. 30-44 rets.) 29.7—Troy Brown, Marshall, 1991-92 (32 for 950)

(Min. 45 rets.) 29.3—Charles Swann, Indiana St., 1989-91 (45 for 1,319)

MOST TOUCHDOWNS SCORED ON KICKOFF RETURNS

Game

2—Joey Stockton, Western Ky. vs. Southern Ill., Nov. 2, 1996; Rory Lee, Western Ill. vs. St. Ambrose, Nov. 13, 1993; Kerry Hayes, Western Caro. vs. VMI, Oct. 10, 1992 (90 & 94 yards); Paul Ashby, Alabama St. vs. Grambling, Nov. 9, 1991 (97 & 94 yards); David Lucas, Florida A&M vs. North Caro. A&T, Oct. 12, 1991 (99 & 93 yards); Jerome Stelly, Western Ill. vs. Youngstown St., Nov. 7, 1981 (99 & 97 yards)

Season

3—Todd Cleveland, Central Fla., 1994; Kerry Hayes, Western Caro., 1993; Troy Brown, Marshall, 1991; David Lucas, Florida A&M, 1991

Career

5—Kerry Hayes, Western Caro., 1991-94

Total Kick Returns

(Combined Punt and Kickoff Returns)

MOST KICK RETURNS

Game

12—Craig Hodge, Tennessee St. vs. Morgan St., Oct. 24, 1987 (8 punts, 4 kickoffs; 319 yards)

Season

64—Joe Markus, Connecticut, 1981 (34 punts, 30 kickoffs; 939 yards)

Career

199—Herman Hunter, Tennessee St., 1981-84 (103 punts, 96 kickoffs; 3,232 yards)

MOST YARDS ON KICK RETURNS

Game

319—Craig Hodge, Tennessee St. vs. Morgan St., Oct. 24, 1987 (12 returns, 206 on punts, 113 on kickoffs)

Season

1,469—David Primus, Samford, 1989 (1,411 on kickoffs, 58 on punts)

Also holds per-game record at 133.5 (1,469 in 11)

Career

3,232—Herman Hunter, Tennessee St., 1981-84 (974 on punts, 2,258 on kickoffs)

Also holds per-game record at 75.2 (3,232 in 43)

GAINING 1,000 YARDS ON PUNT RETURNS AND 1,000 YARDS ON KICKOFF RETURNS

Career

Joe Rosato, Duquesne, 1994-97 (1,036 on punt returns and 1,661 on kickoffs); Kenny Shedd, Northern Iowa, 1989-92 (1,081 on punts and 1,359 on kickoffs); Joe Markus, Connecticut, 1979-82 (1,012 on punts and 1,185 on kickoffs)

HIGHEST AVERAGE PER KICK RETURN

Game

(Min. 6 rets.) 44.7—Jay Jones, James Madison vs. Richmond, Oct. 19, 1996 (6 for 268)

Season

(Min. 40 rets.) 26.7—David Primus, Samford, 1989 (55 for 1,469)

Career

(Min. 60 rets.) 20.9—Bill LaFreniere, Northeastern, 1978-81 (112 for 2,336)

MOST TOUCHDOWNS SCORED ON KICK RETURNS

Game

3—Aaron Fix, Canisius vs. Siena, Sept. 24, 1994 (1 kickoff and 5 punt returns, 3 touchdowns)

Season

4—Andrew McFadden, Liberty, 1995 (2 kickoffs and 2 punts); Aaron Fix, Canisius, 1994 (4 punts); Troy Brown, Marshall, 1991 (3 kickoffs and 1 punt); Howard Huckaby, Florida A&M, 1988 (4 punts); Willie Ware, Mississippi Val., 1985 (2 punts and 2 kickoffs)

Career

7—Joe Rosato, Duquesne, 1994-97 (4 punts and 3 kickoffs); Kerry Hayes, Western Caro., 1991-94 (2 punts and 5 kickoffs); Kenny Shedd, Northern Iowa, 1989-92 (7 punts); Willie Ware, Mississippi Val., 1982-85 (5 punts and 2 kickoffs)

All-Purpose Yards

(Yardage Gained From Rushing, Receiving and All Runbacks; Must Have One Attempt From at Least Two Categories)

MOST PLAYS

Game

54—Ron Darby, Marshall vs. Western Caro., Nov. 12, 1988 (47 rushes, 4 receptions, 3 kickoff returns; 329 yards)

(Note: 56—Arnold Mickens, Butler vs. Valparaiso, Oct. 8, 1994; all rushes)

Season

411—Arnold Mickens, Butler, 1994 (409 rushes, 2 receptions; 2,262 yards)

Career

1,147—Rich Lemon, Bucknell, 1993-96 (994 rushes, 129 receptions, 16 punt returns, 8 kickoff returns; 5,952 yards)

MOST YARDS GAINED

Game

467—Joey Stockton, Western Ky. vs. Austin Peay, Sept. 16, 1995 (29 rushing, 276 receiving, 18 punt returns, 144 kickoff returns; 14 plays)

Season

2,429—Archie Amerson, Northern Ariz., 1996 (2,079 rushing, 262 receiving, 88 kickoff returns; 365 plays)

Career

7,623—Kenny Gamble, Colgate, 1984-87 (5,220 rushing, 53 receiving, 104 punt returns, 1,763 kickoff returns; 1,096 plays)

MOST YARDS GAINED PER GAME

Season

234.0—Reggie Greene, Siena, 1996 (2,106 in 9)

Career

197.4—Arnold Mickens, Butler, 1994-95 (3,947 in 20)

MOST YARDS GAINED BY A FRESHMAN

Season

2,014—David Wright, Indiana St., 1992 (1,313 rushing, 108 receiving, 593 kickoff returns; 254 plays)

HIGHEST AVERAGE GAIN PER PLAY

Game

(Min. 20 plays) 20.6—Herman Hunter, Tennessee St. vs. Mississippi Val., Nov. 13, 1982 (453 on 22)

Season

(Min. 1,000 yards, 100 plays) 19.7—Otis Washington, Western Caro., 1988 (2,086 on 106)

Career

(Min. 4,000 yards, 350 plays) 14.8—Pete Mandley, Northern Ariz., 1979-80, 1982-83 (5,925 on 401)

Scoring

MOST POINTS SCORED

Game

42—Archie Amerson, Northern Ariz. vs. Weber St., Oct. 5, 1996 (7 TDs)

Season

170—Geoff Mitchell, Weber St., 1991 (28 TDs, 2 PATs)

Career

385—Marty Zendejas, Nevada, 1984-87 (72 FGs, 169 PATs)

MOST POINTS SCORED PER GAME

Season

16.2—Jerry Rice, Mississippi Val., 1984 (162 in 10)

Career

(Min. 200-299 pts.) 10.9—Tim Hall, Robert Morris, 1994-95 (208 in 19)

(Min. 300 pts.) 10.7—Keith Elias, Princeton, 1991-93 (320 in 30)

MOST TOUCHDOWNS SCORED

Game

7—Archie Amerson, Northern Ariz. vs. Weber St., Oct. 5, 1996 (7 TDs)

Season

28—Geoff Mitchell, Weber St., 1991

Career

61—Sherriden May, Idaho, 1992-94

MOST TOUCHDOWNS SCORED PER GAME

Season

2.7—Jerry Rice, Mississippi Val., 1984 (27 in 10)

Career

(Min. 18-29 games) 1.8—Tim Hall, Robert Morris, 1994-95 (34 in 19)

(Min. 30 games) 1.7—Keith Elias, Princeton, 1991-93 (52 in 30)

MOST TOUCHDOWNS SCORED BY A FRESHMAN

Season

19—Randy Moss, Marshall, 1996

Per-game record—Charvez Foger, Nevada, 1985 (18 in 10)

PASSING FOR A TOUCHDOWN AND SCORING TOUCHDOWNS BY RUSHING, RECEIVING AND PUNT RETURN

WR Sean Beckton, Central Fla., threw a 33-yard touchdown pass, rushed for an 11-yard touchdown, caught a 17-yard touchdown pass and returned a punt 60 yards for a touchdown vs. Texas Southern, Nov. 17, 1990

MOST EXTRA POINTS ATTEMPTED BY KICKING
Game
15—John Kincheloe, Portland St. vs. Delaware St., Nov. 8, 1980 (15 made)
Season
74—John Kincheloe, Portland St., 1980 (70 made)
Per-game record—7.2, Jonathan Stokes, Mississippi Val., 1984 (72 in 10)
Career
194—Gilad Landau, Grambling, 1991-94 (181 made)

MOST EXTRA POINTS MADE BY KICKING
Game
15—John Kincheloe, Portland St. vs. Delaware St., Nov. 8, 1980 (15 attempts)
Season
70—John Kincheloe, Portland St., 1980 (74 attempts)
Per-game record—6.8, Jonathan Stokes, Mississippi Val., 1984 (68 in 10)
Career
181—Gilad Landau, Grambling, 1991-94 (194 attempts)
Per-game record—4.8, Tim Openlander, Marshall, 1994-96 (159 in 33)

BEST PERFECT RECORD OF EXTRA POINTS MADE
Season
68 of 68—Mike Hollis, Idaho, 1993

HIGHEST PERCENTAGE OF EXTRA POINTS MADE
Season
(Min. 50 atts.) 100.0—Mike Hollis, Idaho, 1993 (68 of 68); Tim Openlander, Marshall, 1996 (58 of 58); Chris Dill, Murray St., 1995 (56 of 56); Jim Hodson, Lafayette, 1988 (51 of 51); Billy Hayes, Sam Houston St., 1987 (50 of 50)
Career
(Min. 100-119 atts.) 100%—Anders Larsson, Montana St., 1985-88 (101 of 101)
(Min. 120 atts.) 99.2%—Brian Mitchell, Marshall/Northern Iowa, 1987, 1989-91 (130 of 131)

MOST CONSECUTIVE EXTRA POINTS MADE
Game
15—John Kincheloe, Portland St. vs. Delaware St., Nov. 8, 1980
Season
68—Mike Hollis, Idaho, 1993
Career
121—Brian Mitchell, Marshall/Northern Iowa, 1987, 1989-91

MOST POINTS SCORED BY KICKING
Game
24—Goran Lingmerth, Northern Ariz. vs. Idaho, Oct. 25, 1986 (8 FGs)
Season
112—Rob Hart, Murray St., 1996 (22 FGs, 46 PATs)
Career
385—Marty Zendejas, Nevada, 1984-87 (72 FGs, 169 PATs)

MOST POINTS SCORED BY KICKING PER GAME
Season
10.1—Rob Hart, Murray St., 1996 (112 in 11)
Career
9.1—Tony Zendejas, Nevada, 1981-83 (300 in 33)

MOST DEFENSIVE EXTRA-POINT RETURNS, ONE GAME, SINGLE PLAYER
2—Joe Lee Johnson, Western Ky. vs. Indiana St., Nov. 10, 1990 (both kick returns, scored on neither)

MOST DEFENSIVE EXTRA POINTS SCORED
Game
1—By many players
Season
2—Jackie Kellogg, Eastern Wash. vs. Weber St., Oct. 6, 1990 (90-yard interception return) & vs. Portland St., Oct. 27, 1990 (94-yard interception return)

LONGEST RETURN OF A DEFENSIVE EXTRA POINT
100—Rich Kinsman (DB), William & Mary vs. Lehigh, Nov. 14, 1992; Morgan Ryan (DB), Montana St. vs. Sam Houston St., Sept. 7, 1991 (interception return)

FIRST DEFENSIVE EXTRA-POINT ATTEMPTS
Mike Rogers (DB), Davidson vs. Lehigh, Sept. 10, 1988 (30-yard interception return); Dave Benna (LB), Towson vs. Northeastern, Sept. 10, 1988 (35-yard interception return)

MOST TWO-POINT ATTEMPTS
Season
11—Jamie Martin, Weber St., 1990; Brent Woods, Princeton, 1982

MOST SUCCESSFUL TWO-POINT PASSES
Game
3—Brent Woods, Princeton vs. Lafayette, Nov. 6, 1982 (attempted 3)
Season
7—Jamie Martin, Weber St., 1992 (attempted 7)
Career
15—Jamie Martin, Weber St., 1989-92 (attempted 28)

Opponent's Kicks Blocked

MOST OPPONENT'S TOTAL KICKS BLOCKED BY (Includes Punts, PAT Attempts, FG Attempts)
Game
3—Adrian Hardy, Northwestern St. vs. Arkansas St., Oct. 3, 1992 (2 PATs, 1 FG)
Season
5—Mario Wilson, Marist, 1994 (3 FGs, 2 punts); Trey Woods, Sam Houston St., 1993 (3 punts, 1 FG, 1 PAT)
Career
12—Trey Woods, Sam Houston St., 1992-95 (8 punts, 2 FGs, 2 PATs)

Field Goals

MOST FIELD GOALS ATTEMPTED
Game
8—Goran Lingmerth, Northern Ariz. vs. Idaho, Oct. 25, 1986 (made 8)
Season
33—David Ettinger, Hofstra, 1995 (made 22); Tony Zendejas, Nevada, 1982 (made 26)
Career
102—Kirk Roach, Western Caro., 1984-87 (made 71)

MOST FIELD GOALS MADE
Quarter
4—Ryan Weeks, Tennessee Tech vs. Chattanooga, Sept. 9, 1989 (3rd); Tony Zendejas, Nevada vs. Northern Ariz., Oct. 16, 1982 (4th)
Half
5—Ryan Weeks, Tennessee Tech vs. Chattanooga, Sept. 9, 1989 (2nd); Tony Zendejas, Nevada vs. Northern Ariz., Oct. 16, 1982 (2nd); Dean Biasucci, Western Caro. vs. Mars Hill, Sept. 18, 1982 (1st)
Game
8—Goran Lingmerth, Northern Ariz. vs. Idaho, Oct. 25, 1986 (39, 18, 20, 33, 46, 27, 22, 35 yards; by quarters—1, 3, 2, 2), 8 attempts
Season
26—Brian Mitchell, Northern Iowa, 1990 (27 attempts); Tony Zendejas, Nevada, 1982 (33 attempts)
Career
72—Marty Zendejas, Nevada, 1984-87 (90 attempts)

MOST FIELD GOALS MADE PER GAME
Season
2.4—Brian Mitchell, Northern Iowa, 1990 (26 in 11); Tony Zendejas, Nevada, 1982 (26 in 11)
Career
2.1—Tony Zendejas, Nevada, 1981-83 (70 in 33)

HIGHEST PERCENTAGE OF FIELD GOALS MADE
Season
(Min. 20 atts.) 96.3%—Brian Mitchell, Northern Iowa, 1990 (26 of 27)
Career
(Min. 50 atts.) 81.4%—Tony Zendejas, Nevada, 1981-83 (70 of 86)

BEST PERFECT RECORD OF FIELD GOALS MADE
Season
100.0%—John Coursey, James Madison, 1995 (14 of 14)

MOST CONSECUTIVE FIELD GOALS MADE
Game
8—Goran Lingmerth, Northern Ariz. vs. Idaho, Oct. 25, 1986
Season
21—Brian Mitchell, Northern Iowa, 1990
Career
26—Brian Mitchell, Northern Iowa, 1990-91

MOST CONSECUTIVE GAMES KICKING A FIELD GOAL
Career
33—Tony Zendejas, Nevada, 1981-83 (at least one in every game played)

MOST FIELD GOALS MADE, 50 YARDS OR MORE
Game
3—Terry Belden, Northern Ariz. vs. Cal St. Northridge, Sept. 18, 1993 (60, 50, 54 yards); Jesse Garcia, Northeast La. vs. McNeese St., Oct. 29, 1983 (52, 56, 53 yards)
Season
7—Kirk Roach, Western Caro., 1987 (12 attempts); Jesse Garcia, Northeast La., 1983 (12 attempts)
Career
11—Kirk Roach, Western Caro., 1984-87 (26 attempts)

HIGHEST PERCENTAGE OF FIELD GOALS MADE, 50 YARDS OR MORE
Season
(Min. 5 atts.) 100.0%—Wayne Boyer, Southwest Mo. St., 1996 (5 of 5)
Career
(Min. 10 atts.) 90.9%—Tim Foley, Ga. Southern, 1984-87 (10 of 11)

MOST FIELD GOALS MADE, 40 YARDS OR MORE
Season
12—Marty Zendejas, Nevada, 1985 (15 attempts)
Career
30—Marty Zendejas, Nevada, 1984-87 (45 attempts)

HIGHEST PERCENTAGE OF FIELD GOALS MADE, 40 YARDS OR MORE
Season
(Min. 8 made) 100.0%—Tim Foley, Ga. Southern, 1985 (8 of 8)
Career
(Min. 15 made) 72.0%—Tim Foley, Ga. Southern, 1984-87 (18 of 25)

HIGHEST PERCENTAGE OF FIELD GOALS MADE, 40-49 YARDS
Season
(Min. 8 made) 90.0%—Marty Zendejas, Nevada, 1985 (9 of 10)

Photo from Sam Houston State sports information

Sam Houston State's Trey Woods recorded eight blocked punts, two field goals and two point-after-touchdown attempts during his career.

DIVISION I-AA

Career
(Min. 12 made) 72.0%—Tony Zendejas, Nevada, 1981-83 (18 of 25)

HIGHEST PERCENTAGE OF FIELD GOALS MADE, UNDER 40 YARDS
Season
(Min. 15 made) 100.0%—Brian Mitchell, Northern Iowa, 1990 (23 of 23); Kirk Roach, Western Caro., 1986 (17 of 17); Matt Stover, Louisiana Tech, 1986 (15 of 15)
Career
(Min. 25 made) 93.3%—Marty Zendejas, Nevada, 1984-87 (42 of 45)

MOST TIMES KICKING TWO OR MORE FIELD GOALS IN A GAME
Season
10—Brian Mitchell, Northern Iowa, 1991
Career
25—Kirk Roach, Western Caro., 1984-87

MOST TIMES KICKING THREE OR MORE FIELD GOALS IN A GAME
Season
7—Brian Mitchell, Northern Iowa, 1991
Career
11—Brian Mitchell, Marshall/Northern Iowa, 1987, 1989-91

MOST CONSECUTIVE QUARTERS KICKING A FIELD GOAL
Season
7—Scott Roper, Arkansas St., 1986 (last 3 vs. McNeese St., Oct. 25; all 4 vs. North Texas, Nov. 1)

LONGEST AVERAGE DISTANCE FIELD GOALS MADE
Game
(Min. 3 made) 54.7—Terry Belden, Northern Ariz. vs. Cal St. Northridge, Sept. 18, 1993 (60, 50, 54 yards)
Season
(Min. 14 made) 45.0—Jesse Garcia, Northeast La., 1983 (15 made)
Career
(Min. 35 made) 37.5—Roger Ruzek, Weber St., 1979-82 (46 made)

LONGEST AVERAGE DISTANCE FIELD GOALS ATTEMPTED
Season
(Min. 20 atts.) 45.9—Jesse Garcia, Northeast La., 1983 (26 attempts)
Career
(Min. 60 atts.) 40.5—Kirk Roach, Western Caro., 1984-87 (102 attempts)

LONGEST FIELD GOAL MADE
63—Scott Roper, Arkansas St. vs. North Texas, Nov. 7, 1987; Tim Foley, Ga. Southern vs. James Madison, Nov. 7, 1987

LONGEST FIELD GOAL MADE BY A FRESHMAN
60—David Cool, Ga. Southern vs. James Madison, Nov. 5, 1988

MOST FIELD GOALS MADE BY A FRESHMAN
Game
5—Chuck Rawlinson, Stephen F. Austin vs. Prairie View, Sept. 10, 1988 (5 attempts); Marty Zendejas, Nevada vs. Idaho St., Nov. 17, 1984 (5 attempts); Mike Powers, Colgate vs. Army, Sept. 10, 1983 (6 attempts)
Season
22—Marty Zendejas, Nevada, 1984 (27 attempts)

MOST FIELD GOALS MADE IN FIRST GAME OF CAREER
5—Mike Powers, Colgate vs. Army, Sept. 10, 1983 (6 attempts)

MOST GAMES IN WHICH FIELD GOAL(S) PROVIDED WINNING MARGIN
Career
11—John Dowling, Youngstown St., 1984-87

LONGEST RETURN OF A MISSED FIELD GOAL
89—Pat Bayers, Western Ill. vs. Youngstown St., Nov. 6, 1982 (TD)

Team Records

SINGLE GAME—Offense

Total Offense

MOST PLAYS
115—Buffalo vs. Connecticut, Oct. 4, 1997 (437 yards)

MOST PLAYS, BOTH TEAMS
196—Villanova (113) & Connecticut (83), Oct. 7, 1989 (904 yards)

MOST YARDS GAINED
876—Weber St. vs. Idaho St., Nov. 23, 1991 (252 rushing, 624 passing)

MOST YARDS GAINED, BOTH TEAMS
1,418—Howard (740) & Bethune-Cookman (678), Sept. 19, 1987 (161 plays)

MOST YARDS GAINED BY A LOSING TEAM
756—Alcorn St. vs. Grambling, Sept. 3, 1994 (lost 62-56)

FEWEST YARDS GAINED BY A WINNING TEAM
31—Middle Tenn. St. vs. Murray St., Oct. 17, 1981 (won 14-9)

HIGHEST AVERAGE GAIN PER PLAY (Min. 55 Plays)
12.7—Marshall vs. VMI, Nov. 16, 1991 (62 for 789)

MOST TOUCHDOWNS SCORED BY RUSHING AND PASSING
14—Portland St. vs. Delaware St., Nov. 8, 1980 (10 passing, 4 rushing)

Rushing

MOST RUSHES
90—VMI vs. East Tenn. St., Nov. 17, 1990 (311 yards)

MOST RUSHES, BOTH TEAMS
125—Austin Peay (81) & Murray St. (44), Nov. 17, 1990 (443 yards); Southwest Mo. St. (71) & Northern Ill. (54), Oct. 17, 1987 (375 yards)

FEWEST RUSHES
11—Western Ill. vs. Northern Iowa, Oct. 24, 1987 (-11 yards); Mississippi Val. vs. Kentucky St., Sept. 1, 1984 (17 yards)

MOST YARDS GAINED
681—Southwest Mo. St. vs. Mo. Southern St., Sept. 10, 1988 (83 rushes)

MOST YARDS GAINED, BOTH TEAMS
762—Arkansas St. (604) & Tex. A&M-Commerce (158), Sept. 26, 1987 (102 rushes)

MOST YARDS GAINED BY A LOSING TEAM
448—Western Ky. vs. Southern Ill., Nov. 4, 1995 (lost 30-28)

HIGHEST AVERAGE GAIN PER RUSH (Min. 45 Rushes)
11.2—Southwest Mo. St. vs. Truman St., Oct. 5, 1985 (45 for 505)

MOST TOUCHDOWNS SCORED BY RUSHING
10—Arkansas St. vs. Tex. A&M-Commerce, Sept. 26, 1987

Passing

MOST PASSES ATTEMPTED
77—Portland St. vs. Northern Colo., Oct. 20, 1979 (completed 44 for 499 yards)

MOST PASSES ATTEMPTED, BOTH TEAMS
122—Idaho (62) & Idaho St. (60), Sept. 24, 1983 (completed 48 for 639 yards)

FEWEST PASSES ATTEMPTED
1—By many teams. Most recent: Northeastern vs. Towson, Sept. 9, 1989 (completed 1)

FEWEST PASSES ATTEMPTED, BOTH TEAMS
11—Citadel (3) & Ga. Southern (8), Nov. 19, 1994 (completed 6); North Caro. A&T (5) & Western Ky. (6), Nov. 19, 1988 (completed 2); Memphis (3) & Arkansas St. (8), Nov. 27, 1982 (completed 6)

MOST PASSES ATTEMPTED WITHOUT INTERCEPTION
72—Marshall vs. Western Caro., Nov. 14, 1987 (completed 35)

MOST PASSES COMPLETED
50—Mississippi Val. vs. Prairie View, Oct. 27, 1984 (attempted 66 for 642 yards); Mississippi Val. vs. Southern U., Sept. 29, 1984 (attempted 70 for 633 yards)

MOST PASSES COMPLETED, BOTH TEAMS I-AA
77—Northeast La. (46) & Stephen F. Austin (31), Nov. 11, 1989 (attempted 116 for 1,190 yards)

MOST PASSES COMPLETED, BOTH TEAMS
80—Hofstra (50) & Fordham (30), Oct. 19, 1991 (attempted 120 for 987 yards)

FEWEST PASSES COMPLETED
0—By many teams. Most recent: Ga. Southern vs. Liberty, Nov. 11, 1995; Citadel vs. East Tenn. St., Sept. 19, 1992

FEWEST PASSES COMPLETED, BOTH TEAMS
2—North Caro. A&T (0) & Western Ky. (2), Nov. 19, 1988 (attempted 11)

HIGHEST PERCENTAGE COMPLETED
(Min. 30-44 atts.) 81.6%—Nevada vs. Idaho St., Nov. 17, 1984 (31 of 38)
(Min. 45 atts.) 79.2%—Montana vs. Weber St., Oct. 7, 1995 (38 of 48)

LOWEST PERCENTAGE COMPLETED (Min. 20 Attempts)
9.5%—Florida A&M vs. Central St., Oct. 11, 1986 (2 of 21)

MOST PASSES HAD INTERCEPTED
10—Boise St. vs. Montana, Oct. 28, 1989 (55 attempts); Mississippi Val. vs. Grambling, Oct. 17, 1987 (47 attempts)

MOST YARDS GAINED
699—Mississippi Val. vs. Kentucky St., Sept. 1, 1984

MOST YARDS GAINED, BOTH TEAMS
1,190—Northeast La. (619) & Stephen F. Austin (571), Nov. 11, 1989

MOST YARDS GAINED PER ATTEMPT (Min. 25 Attempts)
17.4—Marshall vs. VMI, Nov. 16, 1991 (37 for 642)

MOST YARDS GAINED PER COMPLETION
(Min. 10-24 comps.) 33.0—Jackson St. vs. Southern U., Oct. 13, 1990 (14 for 462)
(Min. 25 comps.) 22.9—Marshall vs. VMI, Nov. 16, 1991 (28 for 642)

MOST TOUCHDOWN PASSES
11—Mississippi Val. vs. Kentucky St., Sept. 1, 1984

MOST TOUCHDOWN PASSES, BOTH TEAMS
14—Mississippi Val. (8) & Texas Southern (6), Oct. 26, 1985

Punting

MOST PUNTS
16—Louisiana Tech vs. Northeast La., Nov. 19, 1988 (567 yards)

MOST PUNTS, BOTH TEAMS
26—Hofstra (14) vs. Buffalo (12), Nov. 2, 1996

HIGHEST AVERAGE PER PUNT
(Min. 5-9 punts) 55.7—Appalachian St. vs. Citadel, Oct. 3, 1992 (6 for 334); Montana vs. Nevada, Oct. 1, 1988 (9 for 501)
(Min. 10 punts) 52.2—Montana St. vs. Northern Ariz., Oct. 20, 1979 (10 for 522)

FEWEST PUNTS
0—By many teams. Most recent: Connecticut vs. Central Conn. St., Sept. 16, 1995; Delaware vs. James Madison, Nov. 21, 1995; Central Fla. vs. Buffalo, Nov. 19, 1994; Western Ill. vs. Murray St., Nov. 19, 1994

FEWEST PUNTS, BOTH TEAMS
0—Ga. Southern & James Madison, Nov. 15, 1986

MOST OPPONENT'S PUNTS BLOCKED BY
4—Middle Tenn. St. vs. Mississippi Val., Oct. 8, 1988 (7 punts); Montana vs. Montana St., Oct. 31, 1987 (13 punts)

Punt Returns

MOST PUNT RETURNS
12—Northern Iowa vs. Youngstown St., Oct. 20, 1984 (83 yards)

MOST YARDS ON PUNT RETURNS
322—Northern Ariz. vs. Western N. M., Aug. 29, 1996 (10 returns)

HIGHEST AVERAGE GAIN PER RETURN (Min. 6 Returns)
32.2—Northern Ariz. vs. Western N. M., Aug. 29, 1996 (10 for 322, 2 TDs)

MOST TOUCHDOWNS SCORED ON PUNT RETURNS
3—Northern Ariz. vs. Western N. M., Aug. 29, 1996; Canisius vs. Siena, Sept. 24, 1994

Kickoff Returns

MOST KICKOFF RETURNS
15—Delaware St. vs. Portland St., Nov. 8, 1980 (209 yards)

MOST YARDS ON KICKOFF RETURNS
277—Idaho St. vs. Tex. A&M-Kingsville, Sept. 12, 1987 (10 returns)

HIGHEST AVERAGE GAIN PER RETURN
(Min. 3-5 rets.) 50.5—Eastern Ky. vs. Murray St., Oct. 28, 1978 (4 for 202)
(Min. 6 rets.) 46.3—Western Caro. vs. VMI, Oct. 10, 1992 (6 for 278)

MOST TOUCHDOWNS SCORED ON KICKOFF RETURNS
2—Western Ky. vs. Southern Ill., Oct. 26, 1996; Western Ill. vs. St. Ambrose, Nov. 13, 1993; Western Caro. vs. VMI, Oct. 10, 1992; Western Ill. vs. Youngstown St., Nov. 7, 1981

Total Kick Returns

(Combined Punt and Kickoff Returns)

MOST YARDS ON KICK RETURNS
338—Northern Ariz. vs. Western N. M., Aug. 29, 1996 (11 returns)

HIGHEST AVERAGE GAIN PER RETURN (Min. 6 Returns)
46.8—Connecticut vs. Yale, Sept. 24, 1983 (6 for 281)

Scoring

MOST POINTS SCORED
105—Portland St. vs. Delaware St., Nov. 8, 1980 (15 TDs, 15 PATs)

MOST POINTS SCORED, BOTH TEAMS
122—Weber St. (63) & Eastern Wash. (59), Sept. 28, 1991 (17 TDs, 14 PATs, 2 FGs)

MOST POINTS SCORED BY A LOSING TEAM
59—Eastern Wash. vs. Weber St. (63), Sept. 28, 1991

MOST POINTS SCORED EACH QUARTER
1st: 49—Portland St. vs. Delaware St., Nov. 8, 1980
2nd: 50—Alabama St. vs. Prairie View, Oct. 26, 1991
3rd: 35—Northeast La. vs. Arkansas St., Nov. 6, 1993; Portland St. vs. Delaware St., Nov. 8, 1980
4th: 39—Montana vs. South Dak. St., Sept. 4, 1993

MOST POINTS SCORED EACH HALF
1st: 73—Montana St. vs. Eastern Ore. St., Sept. 14, 1985
2nd: 56—Brown vs. Columbia, Nov. 19, 1994

MOST TOUCHDOWNS SCORED
15—Portland St. vs. Delaware St., Nov. 8, 1980

MOST TOUCHDOWNS SCORED, BOTH TEAMS
17—Grambling (9) & Alcorn St. (8), Sept. 3, 1994; Weber St. (9) & Eastern Wash. (8), Sept. 28, 1991; Furman (9) & Davidson (8), Nov. 3, 1979

MOST EXTRA POINTS MADE BY KICKING
15—Portland St. vs. Delaware St., Nov. 8, 1980 (15 attempts)

MOST TWO-POINT ATTEMPTS MADE
5—Weber St. vs. Eastern Wash., Oct. 6, 1990 (5 passes attempted)

MOST FIELD GOALS MADE
8—Northern Ariz. vs. Idaho, Oct. 25, 1986 (8 attempts)

MOST FIELD GOALS ATTEMPTED
8—Northern Ariz. vs. Idaho, Oct. 25, 1986 (made 8)

MOST FIELD GOALS MADE, BOTH TEAMS
9—Nevada (5) & Weber St. (4), Nov. 6, 1982 (11 attempts, 3 OT); Nevada (5) & Northern Ariz. (4), Oct. 9, 1982 (12 attempts)

MOST SAFETIES SCORED
3—Alabama St. vs. Albany St. (Ga.), Oct. 15, 1988

MOST DEFENSIVE EXTRA POINTS SCORED
2—VMI vs. Davidson, Nov. 4, 1989 (Jeff Barnes, 95-yard interception return, and Wayne Purcell, 90-yard interception return)

MOST DEFENSIVE EXTRA-POINT ATTEMPTS
2—Western Ky. vs. Indiana St., Nov. 10, 1990 (2 interception returns); VMI vs. Davidson, Nov. 4, 1989 (2 interception returns)

First Downs

MOST FIRST DOWNS
46—Weber St. vs. Idaho St., Nov. 23, 1991 (12 rushing, 31 passing, 3 penalty)

MOST FIRST DOWNS, BOTH TEAMS
72—Bethune-Cookman (40) & Howard (32), Sept. 19, 1987

MOST FIRST DOWNS BY RUSHING
29—By six teams. Most recent: Arkansas St. vs. Southern Ill., Nov. 5, 1988; Southwest Mo. St. vs. Mo. Southern St., Sept. 10, 1988

MOST FIRST DOWNS BY PASSING
31—Weber St. vs. Idaho St., Nov. 23, 1991

MOST FIRST DOWNS BY PENALTY
11—Towson vs. Liberty, Oct. 21, 1990

Fumbles

MOST FUMBLES
16—Delaware St. vs. Portland St., Nov. 8, 1980 (lost 6)

MOST FUMBLES, BOTH TEAMS
21—North Caro. A&T (15) & Lane (6), Nov. 11, 1995 (lost 12)

MOST FUMBLES LOST
9—North Caro. A&T vs. Lane, Nov. 11, 1995 (15 fumbles)

MOST FUMBLES LOST, BOTH TEAMS
12—North Caro. A&T (9) & Lane (3), Nov. 11, 1995 (21 fumbles); Austin Peay (8) & Mars Hill (4), Nov. 17, 1979 (18 fumbles); Virginia St. (7) & Howard (5), Oct. 13, 1979 (16 fumbles)

Penalties

MOST PENALTIES AGAINST
23—Idaho vs. Idaho St., Oct. 10, 1992 (204 yards)

MOST PENALTIES, BOTH TEAMS
39—In four games. Most recent: Jackson St. (22) & Grambling (17), Oct. 24, 1987 (370 yards)

MOST YARDS PENALIZED
260—Southern U. vs. Howard, Nov. 4, 1978 (22 penalties)

MOST YARDS PENALIZED, BOTH TEAMS
423—Southern U. (260) & Howard (163), Nov. 4, 1978 (37 penalties)

Turnovers

(Passes Had Intercepted and Fumbles Lost)

MOST TURNOVERS
12—Texas Southern vs. Lamar, Sept. 6, 1980 (4 interceptions, 8 fumbles lost)

MOST TURNOVERS, BOTH TEAMS
15—Stephen F. Austin (8) & Nicholls St. (7), Sept. 22, 1990 (8 interceptions, 7 fumbles lost); Bucknell (8) & Hofstra (7), Sept. 8, 1990 (10 interceptions, 5 fumbles lost)

Overtimes

MOST OVERTIME PERIODS
6—Florida A&M (59) vs. Hampton (58), Oct. 5, 1996; Villanova (41) vs. Connecticut (35), Oct. 7, 1989; Rhode Island (58) vs. Maine (55), Sept. 18, 1982

MOST POINTS SCORED IN OVERTIME PERIODS
39—Florida A&M (59) vs. Hampton (58), Oct. 5, 1996 (6 overtime periods)

MOST POINTS SCORED IN OVERTIME PERIODS, BOTH TEAMS
77—Florida A&M (39) vs. Hampton (38), Oct. 5, 1996 (6 overtime periods; Florida A&M won, 59-58)

LARGEST WINNING MARGIN IN OVERTIME
13—Nicholls St. (49) vs. Southwest Tex. St. (36), Oct. 26, 1996 (5 overtime periods)

MOST CONSECUTIVE OVERTIME GAMES PLAYED
2—Montana, 1991 (Montana 35, Nevada, 2 OT, Nov. 9; and Montana 35, Idaho 34, Nov. 16); Connecticut, 1989 (Villanova 41, Connecticut 35, 6 OT, Oct. 7; and Connecticut 39, Massachusetts 33, Oct. 14); Maine, 1982 (Rhode Island 58, Maine 55, 6 OT, Sept. 18; and Boston U. 48, Maine 45, 4 OT, Sept. 25)

SINGLE GAME—Defense

Total Defense

FEWEST PLAYS ALLOWED
31—Howard vs. Dist. Columbia, Sept. 2, 1989 (32 yards)

FEWEST YARDS ALLOWED
Minus 12—Eastern Ill. vs. Kentucky St., Nov. 13, 1982 (-67 rushing, 55 passing)

Rushing Defense

FEWEST RUSHES ALLOWED
10—Ga. Southern vs. Valdosta St., Sept. 12, 1992 (21 yards)

FEWEST RUSHING YARDS ALLOWED
Minus 88—Austin Peay vs. Morehead St., Oct. 8, 1983 (31 rushes)

Pass Defense

FEWEST ATTEMPTS ALLOWED
1—By five teams. Most recent: Towson vs. Northeastern, Sept. 9, 1989 (1 completed)

FEWEST COMPLETIONS ALLOWED
0—By many teams. Most recent: South Fla. vs. Cumberland, Nov. 8, 1997 (4 attempts); Colgate vs. Army, Nov. 18, 1989 (2 attempts); Illinois St. vs. Arkansas St., Nov. 11, 1989 (3 attempts); Marshall vs. VMI, Oct. 28, 1989 (4 attempts)

LOWEST COMPLETION PERCENTAGE ALLOWED (Min. 30 Attempts)
11.8%—Southern U. vs. Nicholls St., Oct. 11, 1980 (4 of 34)

FEWEST YARDS ALLOWED
Minus 2—Florida A&M vs. Albany St. (Ga.), Oct. 16, 1982

MOST PASSES INTERCEPTED BY
10—Montana vs. Boise St., Oct. 28, 1989 (55 attempts); Grambling vs. Mississippi Val., Oct. 17, 1987 (47 attempts)

MOST TIMES OPPONENT TACKLED FOR LOSS ATTEMPTING TO PASS
13—Austin Peay vs. Morehead St., Oct. 8, 1983 (110 yards)

MOST INTERCEPTIONS RETURNED FOR TOUCHDOWNS
3—Nicholls St. vs. Southwest Tex. St., Oct. 26, 1996 (4 for 166 yards); Canisius vs. Siena, Sept. 16, 1995 (6 for 120 yards); Delaware St. vs. Akron, Oct. 17, 1987 (5 for 124 yards); Montana vs. Eastern Wash., Nov. 12, 1983 (4 for 134 yards); Chattanooga vs. Southwestern La., Sept. 17, 1983 (4 for 122 yards)

Opponent's Kicks Blocked

MOST OPPONENT'S PUNTS BLOCKED
4—Middle Tenn. St. vs. Mississippi Val., Oct. 8, 1988 (7 punts); Montana vs. Montana St., Oct. 31, 1987 (13) punts

MOST OPPONENT'S TOTAL KICKS BLOCKED (Includes punts, field goals, PATs)
4—Middle Tenn. St. vs. Mississippi Val., Oct. 8, 1988 (all punts); Montana vs. Montana St., Oct. 31, 1987 (all punts)

Fumble Returns

(Since 1992)

MOST FUMBLES RETURNED FOR TOUCHDOWNS
2—Idaho vs. Weber St., Nov. 12, 1994; Marshall vs. VMI, Oct. 9, 1993

Safeties

MOST SAFETIES BY A DEFENSE
2—By several teams. Most recent: Georgetown vs. St. John's (N. Y.), Nov. 8, 1996

SEASON—Offense

Total Offense

MOST YARDS GAINED PER GAME
640.1—Mississippi Val., 1984 (6,401 in 10)

HIGHEST AVERAGE GAIN PER PLAY
7.8—Alcorn St., 1994 (848 for 6,577)

MOST PLAYS PER GAME
89.6—Weber St., 1991 (986 in 11)

MOST TOUCHDOWNS BY RUSHING AND PASSING PER GAME
8.4—Mississippi Val., 1984 (84 in 10)

Rushing

MOST YARDS GAINED PER GAME
382.0—Citadel, 1994 (4,202 in 11)

HIGHEST AVERAGE GAIN PER RUSH
6.6—Citadel, 1994 (633 for 4,202)

MOST RUSHES PER GAME
69.8—Northeastern, 1986 (698 in 10)

MOST TOUCHDOWNS BY RUSHING PER GAME
4.5—Howard, 1987 (45 in 10)

Passing

MOST YARDS GAINED PER GAME
496.8—Mississippi Val., 1984 (4,968 in 10)

HIGHEST AVERAGE GAIN PER ATTEMPT
(Min. 250-399 atts.) 10.7—Northern Iowa, 1996 (252 for 2,700)
(Min. 400 atts.) 9.3—Idaho, 1989 (445 for 4,117)

HIGHEST AVERAGE GAIN PER COMPLETION
(Min. 125-199 comps.) 19.3—Jackson St., 1990 (156 for 3,006)
(Min. 200 comps.) 16.6—Stephen F. Austin, 1989 (240 for 3,985)

MOST PASSES ATTEMPTED PER GAME
55.8—Mississippi Val., 1984 (558 in 10)

MOST PASSES COMPLETED PER GAME
35.1—Mississippi Val., 1984 (351 in 10)

HIGHEST PERCENTAGE COMPLETED
(Min. 200-449 atts.) 70.6%—Hofstra, 1997 (293 of 415)
(Min. 450 atts.) 67.2%—Montana, 1995 (336 of 500)

LOWEST PERCENTAGE HAD INTERCEPTED
(Min. 200-399 atts.) 0.85%—Furman, 1996 (2 of 235)
(Min. 400 atts.) 1.2%—Lamar, 1988 (5 of 411)

MOST CONSECUTIVE PASSES ATTEMPTED WITHOUT AN INTERCEPTION
275—Lamar, 1988 (during 8 games, Sept. 3 to Oct. 29)

MOST TOUCHDOWN PASSES PER GAME
6.4—Mississippi Val., 1984 (64 in 10)

HIGHEST PASSING EFFICIENCY RATING POINTS
190.6—William & Mary, 1993 (232 attempts, 161 completions, 4 interceptions, 2,499 yards, 24 TDs)

Punting

MOST PUNTS PER GAME
9.6—Louisiana Tech, 1987 (106 in 11)

FEWEST PUNTS PER GAME
2.2—Alcorn St., 1994 (24 in 11)

HIGHEST PUNTING AVERAGE
47.0—Appalachian St., 1991 (64 for 3,009)

HIGHEST NET PUNTING AVERAGE
44.5—Marshall, 1996 (38 for 1,739; 47 yards returned)

MOST PUNTS HAD BLOCKED
8—Western Ky., 1982

Punt Returns

MOST PUNT RETURNS PER GAME
5.4—Murray St., 1980 (59 in 11)

FEWEST PUNT RETURNS PER GAME
0.6—Southern Ill., 1991 (7 in 11); Prairie View, 1991 (7 in 11); Youngstown St., 1990 (7 in 11)

MOST PUNT-RETURN YARDS PER GAME
64.8—Duquesne, 1996 (648 in 10)

HIGHEST AVERAGE GAIN PER PUNT RETURN
(Min. 20-29 rets.) 19.5—Towson, 1994 (27 for 526)
(Min. 30 rets.) 18.1—Mississippi Val., 1985 (31 for 561)

MOST TOUCHDOWNS SCORED ON PUNT RETURNS
5—Southern Ill., 1985

Kickoff Returns

MOST KICKOFF RETURNS PER GAME
7.7—Morehead St., 1994 (85 in 11; 1,582 yards)

FEWEST KICKOFF RETURNS PER GAME
1.2—McNeese St., 1997 (13 in 11)

MOST KICKOFF-RETURN YARDS PER GAME
143.8—Morehead St., 1994 (1,582 in 11; 85 returns)

HIGHEST AVERAGE GAIN PER KICKOFF RETURN (Min. 20 Returns)
29.5—Eastern Ky., 1986 (34 for 1,022)

Combined Returns

(Interceptions, Punt Returns and Kickoff Returns)

MOST TOUCHDOWNS SCORED
9—Delaware St., 1987 (5 interceptions, 3 punt returns, 1 kickoff return)

Scoring

MOST POINTS PER GAME
60.9—Mississippi Val., 1984 (609 in 10)

MOST TOUCHDOWNS PER GAME
8.7—Mississippi Val., 1984 (87 in 10)

MOST EXTRA POINTS MADE BY KICKING PER GAME
7.7—Mississippi Val., 1984 (77 in 10)

MOST CONSECUTIVE EXTRA POINTS MADE BY KICKING
56—Murray St., 1995

MOST TWO-POINT ATTEMPTS MADE
9—Weber St., 1992 (11 attempts)

MOST DEFENSIVE EXTRA-POINT ATTEMPTS
2—Western Ky., 1990; Eastern Wash., 1990; VMI, 1989

MOST DEFENSIVE EXTRA POINTS SCORED
2—Eastern Wash., 1990 (2 interception returns); VMI, 1989 (2 interception returns)

MOST FIELD GOALS MADE PER GAME
2.4—Northern Iowa, 1990 (26 in 11); Nevada, 1982 (26 in 11)

MOST SAFETIES SCORED
5—Jackson St., 1986

First Downs

MOST FIRST DOWNS PER GAME
31.7—Mississippi Val., 1984 (317 in 10)

MOST RUSHING FIRST DOWNS PER GAME
18.1—Citadel, 1994 (199 in 11)

MOST PASSING FIRST DOWNS PER GAME
21.4—Mississippi Val., 1984 (214 in 10)

MOST FIRST DOWNS BY PENALTY PER GAME
3.7—Texas Southern, 1987 (41 in 11; 134 penalties by opponents); Alabama St., 1984 (41 in 11; 109 penalties by opponents)

Fumbles

MOST FUMBLES PER GAME
5.3—Prairie View, 1984 (58 in 11)

MOST FUMBLES LOST PER GAME
3.1—Delaware St., 1980 (31 in 10); Idaho, 1978 (31 in 10)

FEWEST OWN FUMBLES LOST
2—Brown, 1994 (13 fumbles)

Penalties

MOST PENALTIES PER GAME
13.7—Grambling, 1984 (151 in 11; 1,206 yards)

MOST YARDS PENALIZED PER GAME
125.5—Tennessee St., 1982 (1,255 in 10; 132 penalties)

Turnovers

FEWEST TURNOVERS
9—Hofstra, 1995 (6 fumbles, 3 interceptions)

MOST TURNOVERS
59—Texas Southern, 1980 (27 fumbles, 32 interceptions)

HIGHEST TURNOVER MARGIN PER GAME OVER OPPONENTS
2.5—Appalachian St., 1985; Florida A&M, 1981

SEASON—Defense

Total Defense

FEWEST YARDS ALLOWED PER GAME
149.9—Florida A&M, 1978 (1,649 in 11)

FEWEST RUSHING AND PASSING TOUCHDOWNS ALLOWED PER GAME
0.7—Western Mich., 1982 (8 in 11)

LOWEST AVERAGE YARDS ALLOWED PER PLAY
2.4—South Caro. St., 1978 (719 for 1,736)

Rushing Defense

FEWEST YARDS ALLOWED PER GAME
40.4—Marist, 1997 (404 in 10)

LOWEST AVERAGE YARDS ALLOWED PER RUSH
1.3—Marist, 1997 (319 for 404)

FEWEST RUSHING TOUCHDOWNS ALLOWED PER GAME
0.3—Florida A&M, 1978 (3 in 11)

Pass Defense

FEWEST YARDS ALLOWED PER GAME
59.9—Bethune-Cookman, 1981 (659 in 11)

FEWEST YARDS ALLOWED PER ATTEMPT (Min. 200 Attempts)
4.0—Middle Tenn. St., 1988 (251 for 999)

FEWEST YARDS ALLOWED PER COMPLETION (Min. 100 Completions)
9.1—Middle Tenn. St., 1988 (110 for 999)

LOWEST COMPLETION PERCENTAGE ALLOWED
(Min. 200-299 atts.) 32.3%—Alcorn St., 1979 (76 of 235)
(Min. 300 atts.) 34.2%—Tennessee St., 1986 (107 of 313)

FEWEST TOUCHDOWNS ALLOWED BY PASSING
1—Pennsylvania, 1994; Middle Tenn. St., 1990; Nevada, 1978

LOWEST PASSING EFFICIENCY DEFENSE RATING (Since 1990)
63.1—Pennsylvania, 1994 (235 attempts, 90 completions, 15 interceptions, 1,013 yards, 1 TD)

MOST PASSES INTERCEPTED BY, PER GAME
3.2—Florida A&M, 1981 (35 in 11)

HIGHEST PERCENTAGE INTERCEPTED BY
13.4%—Florida A&M, 1981 (35 of 262)

MOST YARDS GAINED ON INTERCEPTIONS
551—Weber St., 1996 (26 interceptions)

MOST YARDS GAINED PER GAME ON INTERCEPTIONS
51.3—Canisius, 1996 (462 in 9)

HIGHEST AVERAGE PER INTERCEPTION RETURN (Min. 15 Returns)
24.7—Marist, 1997 (16 for 395)

MOST TOUCHDOWNS ON INTERCEPTION RETURNS
7—Northeastern, 1996; Jackson St., 1985

Punting

MOST OPPONENT'S PUNTS BLOCKED BY
9—Middle Tenn. St., 1988 (73 punts)

Punt Returns

LOWEST AVERAGE YARDS ALLOWED PER PUNT RETURN
1.0—Yale, 1988 (24 for 23)

FEWEST RETURNS ALLOWED
7—Cal Poly, 1997 (11 games, 108 yards); Furman, 1984 (11 games, 8 yards)

Kickoff Returns

LOWEST AVERAGE YARDS ALLOWED PER KICKOFF RETURN
10.6—Southern Utah, 1996 (33 for 350)

Scoring

FEWEST POINTS ALLOWED PER GAME
6.5—South Caro. St., 1978 (72 in 11)

Fumbles

MOST OPPONENT'S FUMBLES RECOVERED
29—Western Ky., 1982 (43 fumbles)

Fumble Returns

(Since 1992)

MOST FUMBLES RETURNED FOR TOUCHDOWNS
2—Marshall, 1993 (both vs. VMI, Oct. 9); Citadel, 1992 (vs. Arkansas, Sept. 5 & vs. Western Caro., Oct. 24)

Turnovers

MOST OPPONENT'S TURNOVERS PER GAME
4.9—Canisius, 1996 (44 in 9)

Additional Records

MOST CONSECUTIVE VICTORIES
24—Pennsylvania, from Nov. 14, 1992, through Sept. 30, 1995 (ended Oct. 7, 1995, with 24-14 loss to Columbia)

MOST CONSECUTIVE HOME VICTORIES
38—Ga. Southern, from Oct. 5, 1985, through Sept. 22, 1990 (includes 10 I-AA playoff games)

MOST CONSECUTIVE LOSSES
77—Prairie View, from Nov. 4, 1989 (current)

MOST CONSECUTIVE GAMES WITHOUT A WIN
77—Prairie View, from Nov. 4, 1989 (current)

MOST CONSECUTIVE GAMES WITHOUT BEING SHUT OUT
193—Boise St., from Sept. 21, 1968, through Nov. 10, 1984
(Note: Dayton currently has a 246-game streak without being shut out but has been a I-AA member only since 1993)

MOST SHUTOUTS IN A SEASON
5—South Caro. St., 1978

MOST CONSECUTIVE QUARTERS HOLDING OPPONENTS SCORELESS
15—Robert Morris, 1996

MOST CONSECUTIVE GAMES WITHOUT A TIE
343—Richmond, from Nov. 2, 1963, to Oct. 14, 1995 (ended Oct. 21, 1995, with 3-3 tie with Fordham)

LAST SCORELESS-TIE GAME
Oct. 26, 1985—McNeese St. & North Texas

MOST CONSECUTIVE PASSES ATTEMPTED WITHOUT AN INTERCEPTION
297—Lamar (in 9 games from Nov. 21, 1987, to Oct. 29, 1988)

MOST POINTS OVERCOME IN SECOND HALF TO WIN A GAME
35—Nevada (55) vs. Weber St. (49), Nov. 2, 1991 (trailed 49-14 with 12:16 remaining in 3rd quarter)
32—Morehead St. (36) vs. Wichita St. (35), Sept. 20, 1986 (trailed 35-3 with 9:03 remaining in 3rd quarter)
31—Montana (52) vs. South Dak. St. (48), Sept. 4, 1993 (trailed 38-7 with 8:12 remaining in 3rd quarter)

MOST POINTS OVERCOME IN FOURTH QUARTER TO WIN A GAME
28—Delaware St. (38) vs. Liberty (37), Oct. 6, 1990 (trailed 37-9 with 13:00 remaining in 4th quarter)

MOST POINTS SCORED IN FOURTH QUARTER TO WIN A GAME
39—Montana (52) vs. South Dak. St. (48), Sept. 4, 1993 (trailed 38-13 to begin 4th quarter)
33—Southwest Mo. St. (40) vs. Illinois St. (28), Oct. 9, 1993 (trailed 21-7 with 11:30 remaining in 4th quarter)

MOST CONSECUTIVE EXTRA-POINT KICKS MADE
134—Boise St. (began Oct. 27, 1984; ended Nov. 12, 1988)

MOST CONSECUTIVE WINNING SEASONS
27—Grambling (1960-86)

MOST IMPROVED WON-LOST RECORD
9 1/2 games—Montana St., 1984 (12-2-0, including 3 Division I-AA playoff games) from 1983 (1-10-0)

Annual Champions, All-Time Leaders

Total Offense

CAREER YARDS PER GAME

(Minimum 5,500 Yards)

Player, Team	Years	G	Plays	Yards	TDR‡	Yd. PG
Steve McNair, Alcorn St.	1991-94	42	*2,055	*16,823	152	*400.5
Neil Lomax, Portland St.	1978-80	33	1,680	11,647	100	352.9
Aaron Flowers, Cal St. Northridge	1996-97	20	944	6,754	60	337.7
Dave Dickenson, Montana	1992-95	35	1,539	11,523	116	329.2
Willie Totten, Mississippi Val.	1982-85	40	1,812	13,007	*157	325.2
Tom Ehrhardt, Rhode Island	1984-85	21	1,010	6,492	66	309.1
Doug Nussmeier, Idaho	1990-93	39	1,556	12,054	109	309.1
Oteman Sampson, Florida A&M	1996-97	22	906	6,751	57	306.9
Jamie Martin, Weber St.	1989-92	41	1,838	12,287	93	299.7
Tom Proudian, Iona	1993-95	27	1,337	7,939	61	294.0
Robert Dougherty, Boston U.	1993-94	21	918	6,135	56	292.1
Stan Greene, Boston U.	1989-90	22	1,167	6,408	49	291.3
John Friesz, Idaho	1986-89	35	1,459	10,187	79	291.1
Grady Bennett, Montana	1988-90	31	1,389	8,304	69	267.9
Sean Payton, Eastern Ill.	1983-86	39	1,690	10,298	91	264.1
John Whitcomb, UAB	1993-94	22	800	5,683	43	258.3
John Witkowski, Columbia	1981-83	30	1,330	7,748	58	258.3
Ken Hobart, Idaho	1980-83	44	1,847	11,127	105	252.9
Tony Hilde, Boise St.	1993-95	29	1,175	7,284	64	251.2
Jeff Wiley, Holy Cross	1985-88	40	1,428	9,877	76	246.9
Doug Butler, Princeton	1983-85	29	1,137	7,157	52	246.8
Tom Ciaccio, Holy Cross	1988-91	37	1,283	9,066	87	245.0
Greg Wyatt, Northern Ariz.	1986-89	42	1,753	10,277	75	244.7
Jeff Lewis, Northern Ariz.	1992-95	40	1,654	9,769	82	244.2
Jay Fiedler, Dartmouth	1991-93	30	1,063	7,249	73	241.6
Chris Hakel, William & Mary	1988-91	28	915	6,458	56	239.2
Bob Jean, New Hampshire	1985-88	32	1,287	7,621	59	238.2
Michael Proctor, Murray St.	1986-89	43	1,577	9,886	66	230.0
Fred Gatlin, Nevada	1989-91	32	1,109	7,329	61	229.0
Mike Cawley, James Madison	1993-95	32	1,199	7,249	64	226.5
Frank Baur, Lafayette	1985, 87-89	38	1,312	8,579	72	225.8
Eric Beavers, Nevada	1983-86	40	1,307	9,025	85	225.6

**Record. ‡Touchdowns-responsible-for are player's TDs scored and passed for.*

SEASON YARDS PER GAME

Player, Team	Years	G	Plays	Yards	TDR‡	Yd. PG
Steve McNair, Alcorn St.	†1994	11	*649	*5,799	53	*527.2
Willie Totten, Mississippi Val.	†1984	10	564	4,572	*61	457.2
Steve McNair, Alcorn St.	†1992	10	519	4,057	39	405.7
Jamie Martin, Weber St.	†1991	11	591	4,337	37	394.3
Dave Dickenson, Montana	†1995	11	544	4,209	41	382.6
Neil Lomax, Portland St.	†1980	11	550	4,157	42	377.9
Dave Dickenson, Montana	†1993	11	530	3,978	46	361.6
Neil Lomax, Portland St.	†1979	11	611	3,966	31	360.5
John Friesz, Idaho	†1989	11	464	3,853	31	350.3
Steve McNair, Alcorn St.	1993	11	493	3,830	30	348.2
Aaron Flowers, Cal St. Northridge	†1997	9	456	3,132	26	348.0
Todd Hammel, Stephen F. Austin	1989	11	487	3,822	38	347.5
Tom Ehrhardt, Rhode Island	†1985	10	529	3,460	35	346.0
Ken Hobart, Idaho	†1983	11	578	3,800	37	345.5
Dave Dickenson, Montana	1994	9	431	3,108	27	345.3
Dave Stireman, Weber St.	1985	11	502	3,759	33	341.7
Brian Ah Yat, Montana	†1996	11	501	3,744	45	340.4
Willie Totten, Mississippi Val.	1985	11	561	3,742	43	340.2
Jeff Wiley, Holy Cross	†1987	11	445	3,722	34	338.4
Jamie Martin, Weber St.	†1990	11	508	3,713	25	337.6
Giovanni Carmazzi, Hofstra	1997	11	524	3,707	36	337.0
Sean Payton, Eastern Ill.	1984	11	584	3,661	31	332.8
Tod Mayfield, West Tex. A&M	1985	10	526	3,328	21	332.8
Tom Proudian, Iona	1993	10	521	3,322	30	332.2

**Record. †National champion. ‡Touchdowns-responsible-for are player's TDs scored and passed for.*

CAREER YARDS

Player, Team	Years	Plays	Yards	Avg.
Steve McNair, Alcorn St.	1991-94	*2,055	*16,823	*8.19
Willie Totten, Mississippi Val.	1982-85	1,812	13,007	7.18
Jamie Martin, Weber St.	1989-92	1,838	12,287	6.68
Doug Nussmeier, Idaho	1990-93	1,556	12,054	7.75
Neil Lomax, Portland St.	1978-80	1,680	11,647	6.93
Dave Dickenson, Montana	1992-95	1,539	11,523	7.49
Ken Hobart, Idaho	1980-83	1,847	11,127	6.02
Sean Payton, Eastern Ill.	1983-86	1,690	10,298	6.09
Greg Wyatt, Northern Ariz.	1986-89	1,753	10,277	5.86
John Friesz, Idaho	1986-89	1,459	10,187	6.98
Michael Proctor, Murray St.	1986-89	1,577	9,886	6.27
Jeff Wiley, Holy Cross	1985-88	1,428	9,877	6.92
Jeff Lewis, Northern Ariz.	1992-95	1,654	9,769	5.91
Matt DeGennaro, Connecticut	1987-90	1,619	9,269	5.73
Tom Ciaccio, Holy Cross	1988-91	1,283	9,066	7.07
Eric Beavers, Nevada	1983-86	1,307	9,025	6.91
Marty Horn, Lehigh	1982-85	1,612	8,956	5.56
Kirk Schulz, Villanova	1986-89	1,534	8,900	5.80
Darin Hinshaw, Central Fla.	1991-94	1,266	8,841	6.98
Robbie Justino, Liberty	1989-92	1,469	8,803	5.99
Dan Crowley, Towson	1991-94	1,263	8,797	6.97
Mitch Maher, North Texas	1991-94	1,417	8,735	6.16
Chris Swartz, Morehead St.	1987-90	1,559	8,648	5.55
Frank Baur, Lafayette	1985, 87-89	1,312	8,579	6.54
Steve Calabria, Colgate	1981-84	1,342	8,532	6.36
Mike Buck, Maine	1986-89	1,288	8,457	6.57
Jason Whitmer, Idaho St.	1987-90	1,618	8,449	5.22
Scott Davis, North Texas	1987-90	1,548	8,436	5.45
Grady Bennett, Montana	1988-90	1,389	8,304	5.98
Bill Vergantino, Delaware	1989-92	1,459	8,225	5.64
Stan Yagiello, William & Mary	$1981-85	1,492	8,168	5.47
Mike Smith, Northern Iowa	1984-87	1,163	8,145	7.00
Eric Randall, Southern U.	1992-95	1,383	7,991	5.78
Bob Bleier, Richmond	1983-86	1,313	7,991	6.09
Tom Proudian, Iona	1993-95	1,337	7,939	5.94
Alan Hooker, North Caro. A&T	1984-87	1,476	7,787	5.28
John Witkowski, Columbia	1981-83	1,330	7,748	5.83
Michael Payton, Marshall	1989-92	1,106	7,744	7.00
Kelly Bradley, Montana St.	1983-86	1,547	7,740	5.00
Greg Ryan, East Tenn. St.	1993-96	1,347	7,708	5.72
Jeff Cesarone, Western Ky.	1984-87	1,502	7,694	5.12

**Record. $See page 6 for explanation.*

SEASON YARDS

Player, Team	Year	G	Plays	Yards	Avg.
Steve McNair, Alcorn St.	†1994	11	*649	*5,799	*8.94
Willie Totten, Mississippi Val.	†1984	10	564	4,572	8.11
Jamie Martin, Weber St.	†1991	11	591	4,337	7.34
Dave Dickenson, Montana	†1995	11	544	4,209	7.74
Neil Lomax, Portland St.	†1980	11	550	4,157	7.56
Steve McNair, Alcorn St.	†1992	10	519	4,057	7.82
Dave Dickenson, Montana	†1993	11	530	3,978	7.51
Neil Lomax, Portland St.	†1979	11	611	3,966	6.49
John Friesz, Idaho	†1989	11	464	3,853	8.30
Steve McNair, Alcorn St.	1993	11	493	3,830	7.77
Todd Hammel, Stephen F. Austin	1989	11	487	3,822	7.85
Ken Hobart, Idaho	†1983	11	578	3,800	6.57
Dave Stireman, Weber St.	1985	11	502	3,759	7.49
Brian Ah Yat, Montana	†1996	11	501	3,744	7.47
Willie Totten, Mississippi Val.	1985	11	561	3,742	6.67
Jeff Wiley, Holy Cross	†1987	11	445	3,722	8.36
Jamie Martin, Weber St.	†1990	11	508	3,713	7.31
Giovanni Carmazzi, Hofstra	1997	11	524	3,707	7.07
Sean Payton, Eastern Ill.	1984	11	584	3,661	6.27
Todd Brunner, Lehigh	1989	11	504	3,639	7.22
Oteman Sampson, Florida A&M	1997	11	492	3,625	7.37
Aaron Flowers, Cal St. Northridge	†1996	11	488	3,622	7.42
Scott Semptimphelter, Lehigh	1993	11	515	3,528	6.85
Neil Lomax, Portland St.	†1978	11	519	3,524	6.79
Doug Nussmeier, Idaho	1993	11	400	3,514	8.79
Glenn Kempa, Lehigh	1991	11	513	3,511	6.84
John Friesz, Idaho	1987	11	543	3,489	6.43
Jay Walker, Howard	1993	11	466	3,469	7.44
Doug Nussmeier, Idaho	1991	11	472	3,460	7.33
Tom Ehrhardt, Rhode Island	†1985	10	529	3,460	6.54

**Record. †National champion.*

SINGLE-GAME YARDS

Yds.	Player, Team (Opponent)	Date
649	Steve McNair, Alcorn St. (Southern U.)	Oct. 22, 1994
647	Steve McNair, Alcorn St. (Chattanooga)	Sept. 10, 1994
643	Jamie Martin, Weber St. (Idaho St.)	Nov. 23, 1991
633	Steve McNair, Alcorn St. (Grambling)	Sept. 3, 1994
624	Steve McNair, Alcorn St. (Samford)	Oct. 29, 1994
621	Willie Totten, Mississippi Val. (Prairie View)	Oct. 27, 1984
614	Bryan Martin, Weber St. (Cal Poly SLO)	Sept. 23, 1995
604	Steve McNair, Alcorn St. (Jackson St.)	Nov. 21, 1992
595	Doug Pederson, Northeast La. (Stephen F. Austin)	Nov. 11, 1989
587	Vern Harris, Idaho St. (Montana)	Oct. 12, 1985

Yds.	Player, Team (Opponent)	Date
586	Steve McNair, Alcorn St. (Troy St.)	Nov. 12, 1994
574	Dave Dickenson, Montana (Idaho)	Oct. 21, 1995
570	Steve McNair, Alcorn St. (Texas Southern)	Sept. 11, 1993
566	Brian Ah Yat, Montana (Eastern Wash.)	Oct. 19, 1996
566	Tom Ehrhardt, Rhode Island (Connecticut)	Nov. 16, 1985
564	Steve McNair, Alcorn St. (Jackson St.)	Nov. 19, 1994
562	Todd Hammel, Stephen F. Austin (Northeast La.)	Nov. 11, 1989
561	Willie Totten, Mississippi Val. (Southern U.)	Sept. 29, 1984
549	Brian Ah Yat, Montana (Northern Ariz.)	Oct. 26, 1996
549	Steve McNair, Alcorn St. (Jacksonville St.)	Oct. 31, 1992
547	Tod Mayfield, West Tex. A&M (New Mexico St.)	Nov. 16, 1985
546	Dave Stireman, Weber St. (Montana)	Nov. 2, 1985
543	Ken Hobart, Idaho (Southern Colo.)	Sept. 10, 1983
539	Dave Dickenson, Montana (Idaho)	Nov. 6, 1993
539	Jamie Martin, Weber St. (Montana St.)	Sept. 26, 1992
536	Brad Otten, Weber St. (Northern Ariz.)	Nov. 6, 1993
536	Willie Totten, Mississippi Val. (Kentucky St.)	Sept. 1, 1984
533	John Whitcomb, UAB (Prairie View)	Nov. 19, 1994
527	Willie Totten, Mississippi Val. (Grambling)	Oct. 13, 1984
519	Bernard Hawk, Bethune-Cookman (Ga. Southern)	Oct. 6, 1984

ANNUAL CHAMPIONS

Year	Player, Team	Class	G	Plays	Yards	Avg.
1978	Neil Lomax, Portland St.	So.	11	519	3,524	320.4
1979	Neil Lomax, Portland St.	Jr.	11	611	3,966	360.5
1980	Neil Lomax, Portland St.	Sr.	11	550	4,157	377.9
1981	Mike Machurek, Idaho St.	Sr.	9	363	2,645	293.9
1982	Brent Woods, Princeton	Sr.	10	577	3,079	307.9
1983	Ken Hobart, Idaho	Sr.	11	578	3,800	345.5
1984	Willie Totten, Mississippi Val.	Jr.	10	564	4,572	457.2
1985	Tom Ehrhardt, Rhode Island	Sr.	10	529	3,460	346.0
1986	Brent Pease, Montana	Sr.	10	499	3,094	309.4
1987	Jeff Wiley, Holy Cross	Jr.	11	445	3,722	338.4
1988	John Friesz, Idaho	Jr.	10	424	2,751	275.1
1989	John Friesz, Idaho	Sr.	11	464	3,853	350.3
1990	Jamie Martin, Weber St.	So.	11	508	3,713	337.6
1991	Jamie Martin, Weber St.	Jr.	11	591	4,337	394.3
1992	Steve McNair, Alcorn St.	So.	10	519	4,057	405.7
1993	Dave Dickenson, Montana	So.	11	530	3,978	361.6
1994	Steve McNair, Alcorn St.	Sr.	11	*649	*5,799	*527.2
1995	Dave Dickenson, Montana	Sr.	11	544	4,209	382.6
1996	Brian Ah Yat, Montana	So.	11	501	3,744	340.4
1997	Aaron Flowers, Cal St. Northridge	Sr.	9	456	3,132	348.0

**Record.*

Rushing

CAREER YARDS PER GAME

(Minimum 2,500 Yards)

Player, Team	Years	G	Plays	Yards	TD	Yd. PG
Arnold Mickens, Butler	1994-95	20	763	3,813	29	*190.7
Tim Hall, Robert Morris	1994-95	19	393	2,908	27	153.1
Reggie Greene, Siena	1994-97	36	890	5,415	45	150.4
Archie Amerson, Northern Ariz.	1995-96	22	526	3,196	37	145.3
Keith Elias, Princeton	1991-93	30	736	4,208	49	140.3
Mike Clark, Akron	1984-86	32	804	4,257	24	133.0
Michael Hicks, South Caro. St.	1993-95	32	701	4,093	51	127.9
Rich Erenberg, Colgate	1982-83	21	464	2,618	22	124.7
Kenny Gamble, Colgate	1984-87	42	963	5,220	*55	124.3
Frank Hawkins, Nevada	1977-80	43	945	5,333	39	124.0
Elroy Harris, Eastern Ky.	1985, 87-88	31	648	3,829	47	123.5
Chad Levitt, Cornell	1993-96	38	922	4,657	44	122.6
Thomas Haskins, VMI	1993-96	44	899	*5,355	50	121.7
Gill Fenerty, Holy Cross	1983-85	30	622	3,618	26	120.6
Markus Thomas, Eastern Ky.	1989-92	43	784	5,149	51	119.7
Marquette Smith, Central Fla.	1994-95	22	467	2,569	19	116.8
Erik Marsh, Lafayette	1991-94	42	*1,027	4,834	35	115.1
Sherriden May, Idaho	1992-94	33	689	3,748	50	113.6
Rene Ingoglia, Massachusetts	1992-95	41	905	4,623	54	112.8
Rabih Abdullah, Lehigh	1994-97	33	672	3,696	33	112.0
Willie High, Eastern Ill.	1992-95	38	913	4,231	37	111.3
Rich Lemon, Bucknell	1993-96	43	994	4,742	35	110.3
Derrick Harmon, Cornell	1981-83	28	545	3,074	26	109.8
Paul Lewis, Boston U.	1982-84	37	878	3,995	50	108.0
Eric Gant, Grambling	1990-93	34	617	3,667	32	107.9
Derrick Franklin, Indiana St.	1989-91	30	710	3,231	23	107.7
Charvez Foger, Nevada	1985-88	42	864	4,484	52	106.8
Claude Mathis, Southwest Tex. St.	1994-97	44	882	4,691	45	106.6
James Crawford, Eastern Ky.	1985-87	32	661	3,404	22	106.4
Eion Hu, Harvard	1994-96	29	714	3,073	26	106.0
Bryan Keys, Pennsylvania	1987-89	30	609	3,137	34	104.6
Judd Garrett, Princeton	1987-89	30	687	3,109	32	103.6

**Record.*

SEASON YARDS PER GAME

Player, Team	Year	G	Plays	Yards	TD	Yd. PG
Arnold Mickens, Butler	†1994	10	*409	*2,255	18	*225.5
Tony Vinson, Towson	†1993	10	293	2,016	23	201.6
Reggie Greene, Siena	†1997	9	256	1,778	18	197.6
Reggie Greene, Siena	†1996	9	280	1,719	12	191.0
Archie Amerson, Northern Ariz.	1996	11	333	2,079	*25	189.0
Aaron Stecker, Western Ill.	1997	11	298	1,957	24	177.9
Keith Elias, Princeton	1993	10	305	1,731	19	173.1
Gene Lake, Delaware St.	†1984	10	238	1,722	20	172.2
Rich Erenberg, Colgate	†1983	11	302	1,883	20	171.2
Sean Bennett, Evansville	1997	10	235	1,668	16	166.8
Kenny Gamble, Colgate	†1986	11	307	1,816	21	165.1
Kenny Bynum, South Caro. St.	1996	10	236	1,649	14	164.9
Mike Clark, Akron	1986	11	245	1,786	8	162.4
Reggie Greene, Siena	†1995	9	273	1,461	11	162.3
Derrick Cullors, Murray St.	1995	11	269	1,765	16	160.5
Chad Levitt, Cornell	1996	9	267	1,435	13	159.4
Keith Elias, Princeton	†1992	10	245	1,575	18	157.5
Tim Hall, Robert Morris	1995	10	239	1,572	16	157.2
Frank Hawkins, Nevada	†1980	11	307	1,719	9	156.3
Arnold Mickens, Butler	1995	10	354	1,558	11	155.8
Brad Baxter, Alabama St.	1986	11	302	1,705	13	155.0
Thomas Haskins, VMI	1996	11	287	1,704	15	154.9
Elroy Harris, Eastern Ky.	1988	10	277	1,543	21	154.3
Richard Johnson, Butler	1993	10	322	1,535	10	153.5
Frank Hawkins, Nevada	†1979	11	293	1,683	13	153.0
Carl Smith, Maine	†1989	11	305	1,680	20	152.7
Harvey Reed, Howard	†1987	10	211	1,512	20	151.2
John Settle, Appalachian St.	1986	11	317	1,661	20	151.0
Rex Prescott, Eastern Wash.	1997	10	212	1,494	12	149.4
Tim Hall, Robert Morris	1994	9	154	1,336	11	148.4
Garry Pearson, Massachusetts	†1982	11	312	1,631	13	148.3
Rick Sarille, Wagner	1996	10	279	1,475	11	147.5
Lorenzo Bouier, Maine	1980	11	349	1,622	9	147.5

**Record. †National champion.*

CAREER YARDS

Player, Team	Years	Plays	Yards	Avg.	Long
Reggie Greene, Siena	1994-97	890	*5,415	6.08	82
Thomas Haskins, VMI	1993-96	899	5,355	5.96	80
Frank Hawkins, Nevada	1977-80	945	5,333	5.64	50
Kenny Gamble, Colgate	1984-87	963	5,220	5.42	91
Markus Thomas, Eastern Ky.	1989-92	784	5,149	‡6.57	90
Erik Marsh, Lafayette	1991-94	*1,027	4,834	4.71	62
Rich Lemon, Bucknell	1993-96	994	4,742	4.77	83
Claude Mathis, Southwest Tex. St.	1994-97	882	4,691	5.32	79
Chad Levitt, Cornell	1993-96	922	4,657	5.05	88

Photo from Western Illinois sports information

Western Illinois running back Aaron Stecker averaged 177.9 yards per game last year to rank among the all-time leaders in season yards per game.

Player, Team	Years	Plays	Yards	Avg.	Long
Rene Ingoglia, Massachusetts	1992-95	905	4,623	5.11	84
Chris Parker, Marshall	1992-95	780	4,571	5.86	89
Cedric Minter, Boise St.	1977-80	752	4,475	5.95	77
John Settle, Appalachian St.	1983-86	891	4,409	4.95	88
Jermaine Creighton, St. John's (N.Y.)	1994-97	948	4,271	4.51	99
Mike Clark, Akron	1984-86	804	4,257	5.29	†65
Willie High, Eastern Ill.	1992-95	913	4,231	4.63	55
Keith Elias, Princeton	1991-93	736	4,208	5.72	69
David Wright, Indiana St.	1992-95	784	4,181	5.33	75
Warren Marshall, James Madison	$1982-86	737	4,168	5.66	59
Carl Tremble, Furman	1989-92	696	4,149	5.96	65
Harvey Reed, Howard	1984-87	635	4,142	6.52	85
Michael Hicks, South Caro. St.	1993-95	701	4,093	5.84	82
Paul Lewis, Boston U.	1981-84	878	3,995	4.55	80
Daryl Brown, Delaware	1991-94	678	3,932	5.80	71
Joe Ross, Ga. Southern	1987-90	687	3,876	5.64	75
Garry Pearson, Massachusetts	1979-82	808	3,859	4.78	71
Elroy Harris, Eastern Ky.	1985, 87-88	648	3,829	5.91	64
Lorenzo Bouier, Maine	1979-82	879	3,827	4.35	77
Lewis Tillman, Jackson St.	$1984-88	779	3,824	4.91	39
Joe Campbell, Middle Tenn. St.	1988-91	638	3,823	5.99	81
Carl Smith, Maine	1988-91	759	3,815	5.03	89
Arnold Mickens, Butler	1994-95	763	3,813	5.00	70
Damon Scott, Appalachian St.	1993-96	745	3,800	5.10	49
Sherriden May, Idaho	1992-94	689	3,748	5.44	68
Derek Fitzgerald, William & Mary	1992-95	720	3,744	5.20	66
Brad Baxter, Alabama St.	1985-88	773	3,732	4.83	71
Toby Davis, Illinois St.	1989-92	825	3,702	4.49	34

**Record. †Did not score. $See page 6 for explanation. ‡Record for minimum 600 carries.*

CAREER RUSHING TOUCHDOWNS

Player, Team	Years	G	TDs
Kenny Gamble, Colgate	1984-87	42	*55
Rene Ingoglia, Massachusetts	1992-95	41	54
Charvez Foger, Nevada	1985-88	42	52
Michael Hicks, South Caro. St.	1993-95	32	51
Markus Thomas, Eastern Ky.	1989-92	43	51
Thomas Haskins, VMI	1993-96	44	50
Sherriden May, Idaho	1992-94	33	50
Paul Lewis, Boston U.	1981-84	37	50
Chris Parker, Marshall	1992-95	45	49
Keith Elias, Princeton	1991-93	30	49
Elroy Harris, Eastern Ky.	1985, 87-88	31	47
Harvey Reed, Howard	1984-87	41	47

**Record. (Note: Anthony Russo of St. John's, N.Y., scored 16 TDs in 1993 at I-AA level but had 57 total touchdowns during 1990-94.)*

SEASON YARDS

Player, Team	Year	G	Plays	Yards	Avg.
Arnold Mickens, Butler	†1994	10	*409	*2,255	5.51
Archie Amerson, Northern Ariz.	1996	11	333	2,079	6.24
Tony Vinson, Towson	†1993	10	293	2,016	6.89
Aaron Stecker, Western Ill.	1997	11	298	1,957	6.57
Rich Erenberg, Colgate	†1983	11	302	1,883	6.24
Kenny Gamble, Colgate	†1986	11	307	1,816	5.92
Mike Clark, Akron	1986	11	245	1,786	‡7.29
Reggie Greene, Siena	†1997	9	256	1,778	6.95
Derrick Cullors, Murray St.	1995	11	269	1,765	6.56
Keith Elias, Princeton	1993	10	305	1,731	5.68
Gene Lake, Delaware St.	†1984	10	238	1,722	7.24
Reggie Greene, Siena	†1996	9	280	1,719	6.14
Frank Hawkins, Nevada	†1980	11	307	1,719	5.60
Brad Baxter, Alabama St.	1986	11	302	1,705	5.65
Thomas Haskins, VMI	1996	11	287	1,704	5.94
Frank Hawkins, Nevada	†1979	11	293	1,683	5.74
Carl Smith, Maine	†1989	11	305	1,680	5.51
Sean Bennett, Evansville	1997	10	235	1,668	7.10
John Settle, Appalachian St.	1986	11	317	1,661	5.24
Kenny Bynum, South Caro. St.	1996	10	236	1,649	6.99
Garry Pearson, Massachusetts	†1982	11	312	1,631	5.23
Lorenzo Bouier, Maine	1980	11	349	1,622	4.65
Markus Thomas, Eastern Ky.	1989	11	232	1,620	6.98
Claude Mathis, Southwest Tex. St.	1997	11	311	1,595	5.13
Claude Mathis, Southwest Tex. St.	1996	11	294	1,593	5.42
Keith Elias, Princeton	†1992	10	245	1,575	6.43
Jerry Azumah, New Hampshire	1997	11	269	1,572	5.84
Tim Hall, Robert Morris	1995	10	239	1,572	6.58
Don Wilkerson, Southwest Tex. St.	1994	11	302	1,569	5.20
James Black, Akron	1983	11	351	1,568	4.47
Irving Spikes, Northeast La.	1993	11	246	1,563	6.35
Toby Davis, Illinois St.	1992	11	341	1,561	4.58
Arnold Mickens, Butler	1995	10	354	1,558	4.40
Anthony Russo, St. John's (N.Y.)	1993	11	311	1,558	5.01
Carl Tremble, Furman	1992	11	228	1,555	6.82
Thomas Haskins, VMI	1995	11	248	1,548	6.24
Burton Murchison, Lamar	†1985	11	265	1,547	5.84
Jerome Bledsoe, Massachusetts	†1991	11	264	1,545	5.85

**Record. †National champion. ‡Record for minimum of 200 carries.*

SINGLE-GAME YARDS

Yds.	Player, Team (Opponent)	Date
379	Reggie Greene, Siena (St. John's [N.Y.])	Nov. 2, 1996
364	Tony Vinson, Towson (Bucknell)	Nov. 13, 1993
346	William Arnold, Jackson St. (Texas Southern)	Nov. 6, 1993
345	Russell Davis, Idaho (Portland St.)	Oct. 3, 1981
337	Frank Alessio, Massachusetts (Boston U.)	Nov. 11, 1995
337	Gill Fenerty, Holy Cross (Columbia)	Oct. 29, 1983
336	Gene Lake, Delaware St. (Liberty)	Nov. 10, 1984
327	Tony Vinson, Towson (Morgan St.)	Nov. 20, 1993
324	Robert Vaughn, Alabama St. (Tuskegee)	Nov. 24, 1994
323	Matt Johnson, Harvard (Brown)	Nov. 9, 1991
313	Sean Bennett, Evansville (San Diego)	Oct. 19, 1996
313	Rene Ingoglia, Massachusetts (Rhode Island)	Oct. 1, 1994
312	Surkano Edwards, Samford (Tenn.-Martin)	Nov. 14, 1992
310	Claude Mathis, Southwest Tex. St. (Stephen F. Austin)	Nov. 16, 1996
309	Eddie Thompson, Western Ky. (Southern Ill.)	Oct. 29, 1992
308	Claude Mathis, Southwest Tex. St. (Jacksonville St.)	Nov. 15, 1997
307	Kenny Bynum, South Caro. St. (North Caro. A&T)	Nov. 23, 1996
305	Lawrence Worthington, Liberty (Charleston So.)	Nov. 19, 1994
305	Lucius Floyd, Nevada (Montana St.)	Sept. 27, 1986
304	Tony Citizen, McNeese St. (Prairie View)	Sept. 6, 1986
302	Lorenzo Bouier, Maine (Northeastern)	Nov. 1, 1980
301	Jovan Rhodes, Marist (Siena)	Nov. 12, 1994
300	Jerry Azumah, New Hampshire (Boston U.)	Nov. 15, 1997
300	Markus Thomas, Eastern Ky. (Marshall)	Oct. 21, 1989

ANNUAL CHAMPIONS

Year	Player, Team	Class	G	Plays	Yards	Avg.
1978	Frank Hawkins, Nevada	So.	10	259	1,445	144.5
1979	Frank Hawkins, Nevada	Jr.	11	293	1,683	153.0
1980	Frank Hawkins, Nevada	Sr.	11	307	1,719	156.3
1981	Gregg Drew, Boston U.	Jr.	10	309	1,257	125.7
1982	Garry Pearson, Massachusetts	Sr.	11	312	1,631	148.3
1983	Rich Erenberg, Colgate	Sr.	11	302	1,883	171.2
1984	Gene Lake, Delaware St.	Jr.	10	238	1,722	172.2
1985	Burton Murchison, Lamar	So.	11	265	1,547	140.6
1986	Kenny Gamble, Colgate	Jr.	11	307	1,816	165.1
1987	Harvey Reed, Howard	Sr.	10	211	1,512	151.2
1988	Elroy Harris, Eastern Ky.	Jr.	10	277	1,543	154.3
1989	Carl Smith, Maine	So.	11	305	1,680	152.7
1990	Walter Dean, Grambling	Sr.	11	221	1,401	127.4
1991	Al Rosier, Dartmouth	Sr.	10	258	1,432	143.2
1992	Keith Elias, Princeton	Jr.	10	245	1,575	157.5
1993	Tony Vinson, Towson	Sr.	10	293	2,016	201.6
1994	Arnold Mickens, Butler	Jr.	10	*409	*2,255	*225.5
1995	Reggie Greene, Siena	So.	9	273	1,461	162.3
1996	Reggie Greene, Siena	Jr.	9	280	1,719	191.0
1997	Reggie Greene, Siena	Sr.	9	256	1,778	197.6

**Record.*

Quarterback Rushing

CAREER YARDS

(Since 1978)

Player, Team	Years	G	Plays	Yards	TD	Yd. PG
Jack Douglas, Citadel	1989-92	44	*832	*3,674	*48	83.5
Willie Taggart, Western Ky.	1995-97	30	474	2,644	31	*88.1
Tracy Ham, Ga. Southern	1984-86	33	511	2,506	32	75.9
Tony Scales, VMI	1989-92	44	561	2,475	19	56.3
Eddie Thompson, Western Ky.	1991-93	27	387	2,349	19	87.0
Steve McNair, Alcorn St.	1991-94	42	375	2,327	33	55.4
Eriq Williams, James Madison	1989-92	43	642	2,321	32	54.0
Raymond Gross, Ga. Southern	1987-90	42	695	2,290	20	54.5
Bill Vergantino, Delaware	1989-92	44	656	2,287	34	52.0
Dwane Brown, Arkansas St.	1984-87	42	595	2,192	33	52.2
Roy Johnson, Arkansas St.	1988-91	43	558	2,182	22	50.7
DeAndre Smith, Southwest Mo. St.	1987-90	42	558	2,140	36	50.9
Ken Hobart, Idaho	1980-83	44	628	1,827	26	41.5
Darin Kehler, Yale	1987-90	28	402	1,643	13	58.7

**Record.*

SEASON YARDS

(Since 1978)

Player, Team	Year	G	Plays	Yards	TD	Avg.
Joe Dupaix, Southern Utah	1996	11	*271	*1,246	12	4.60
Willie Taggart, Western Ky.	1997	10	152	1,217	15	*8.01
Marvin Marshall, South Caro. St.	1994	11	160	1,201	10	7.51
Jack Douglas, Citadel	1991	11	266	1,152	13	4.33
Tony Scales, VMI	1991	11	185	1,105	8	5.97
Tracy Ham, Ga. Southern	1986	11	207	1,048	18	5.06
Matt Cannon, Southern Utah	1997	11	137	1,024	10	7.47
Alcede Surtain, Alabama St.	1995	11	178	1,024	*21	5.75
Nick Crawford, Yale	1991	10	210	1,024	8	4.98
Gene Brown, Citadel	1988	9	152	1,006	13	6.62
Willie Taggart, Western Ky.	1996	10	167	997	8	5.97
Kharon Brown, Hofstra	1995	11	151	977	7	6.47
Corey Thomas, Nicholls St.	1994	11	158	962	8	6.09
Steve McNair, Alcorn St.	1994	11	119	936	9	7.87
Jack Douglas, Citadel	1992	11	178	926	13	5.20
Roy Johnson, Arkansas St.	1989	11	193	925	6	4.79
Darin Kehler, Yale	1989	10	210	903	6	4.30
Greg Hill, Ga. Southern	1997	11	160	898	14	5.61
Jim O'Leary, Northeastern	1986	10	195	884	10	4.53
Earl Easley, Arkansas St.	1988	11	196	861	11	4.39
Brad Brown, Northwestern St.	1990	11	192	843	8	4.39
DeAndre Smith, Southwest Mo. St.	1989	11	176	841	12	4.78
Eddie Thompson, Western Ky.	1992	9	113	837	9	7.41
Gilbert Price, Southwest Tex. St.	1991	11	244	837	8	3.43
Jack Douglas, Citadel	1990	11	211	836	13	3.96

**Record.*

Passing

CAREER PASSING EFFICIENCY

(Minimum 300 Completions)

Player, Team	Years	Att.	Cmp.	Int.	Pct.	Yards	TD	Pts.
Shawn Knight, William & Mary	1991-94	558	367	15	.658	5,527	46	*170.8
Dave Dickenson, Montana	1992-95	1,208	813	26	*.673	11,080	96	166.3
Doug Nussmeier, Idaho	1990-93	1,225	746	32	.609	10,824	91	154.4
Mike Simpson, Eastern Ill.	1996-97	493	331	15	.671	3,901	32	148.9
Jay Johnson, Northern Iowa	1989-92	744	397	25	.534	7,049	51	148.9
Michael Payton, Marshall	1989-92	876	542	32	.619	7,530	57	148.2
Bryan Martin, Weber St.	1992-95	606	365	14	.602	5,211	37	148.0
Aaron Flowers, Cal St. Northridge	1996-97	819	502	21	.613	6,766	54	147.3
Willie Totten, Mississippi Val.	1982-85	1,555	907	*75	.583	12,711	*139	146.8
Kenneth Biggles, Tennessee St.	1981-84	701	397	28	.566	5,933	57	146.6
Oteman Sampson, Florida A&M	1996-97	686	387	26	.564	6,104	46	145.7
Steve McNair, Alcorn St.	1991-94	*1,680	927	58	.552	*14,496	119	144.1
Mike Smith, Northern Iowa	1984-87	943	557	43	.591	8,219	58	143.5
Braniff Bonaventure, Furman	1993-96	672	413	17	.615	5,361	39	142.6
Tom Ciaccio, Holy Cross	1988-91	1,073	658	46	.613	8,603	72	142.2
Jim Zaccheo, Nevada	1987-88	554	326	27	.588	4,750	35	142.0
Todd Donnan, Marshall	1991-94	712	425	25	.597	5,566	51	142.0
Mike Cherry, Murray St.	1995-96	526	305	24	.580	4,490	34	141.9
Eric Beavers, Nevada	1983-86	1,094	646	37	.591	8,626	77	141.8
Scott Semptimphelter, Lehigh	1990-93	823	493	27	.599	6,668	50	141.5
John Whitcomb, UAB	1993-94	738	448	28	.607	6,043	43	141.1
Harry Leons, Eastern Wash.	1995-97	523	307	23	.587	4,363	33	140.8
Jason Garrett, Princeton	1987-88	550	368	10	.669	4,274	20	140.6
Neil Lomax, Portland St.	1978-80	1,425	836	50	.587	11,550	88	140.1
Jamie Martin, Weber St.	1989-92	1,544	*934	56	.605	12,207	87	138.2
Darin Hinshaw, Central Fla.	1991-94	1,113	614	52	.552	9,000	82	138.1
Ricky Jones, Alabama St.	1988-91	644	324	30	.503	5,472	49	137.5
Jeff Carlson, Weber St.	1984, 86-88	723	384	33	.531	6,147	47	136.9
Chris Hakel, William & Mary	1988-91	812	489	26	.602	6,447	40	136.7
Jeff Wiley, Holy Cross	1985-88	1,208	723	63	.599	9,698	71	136.3
Robert Dougherty, Boston U.	1993-94	705	405	26	.574	5,608	41	136.1
Eriq Williams, James Madison	1989-92	617	326	35	.528	5,356	40	135.8
Tom Ehrhardt, Rhode Island	1984-85	919	526	35	.572	6,722	66	134.8
Tony Hilde, Boise St.	1993-95	842	459	23	.545	6,634	49	134.4
Jeff Lewis, Northern Ariz.	1992-95	1,316	785	24	.597	9,655	67	134.4
Tom Kirchoff, Lafayette	1989-92	878	510	36	.581	6,721	53	134.1
Dan Sabella, Monmouth	1994-97	868	500	17	.576	6,229	52	133.7
Mike Buck, Maine	1986-89	1,134	637	41	.562	8,721	68	133.4
Frankie DeBusk, Furman	1987-90	634	333	29	.525	5,414	35	133.3
Frank Novak, Lafayette	1981-83	834	478	36	.573	6,378	51	133.1
Robbie Justino, Liberty	1989-92	1,267	769	51	.607	9,548	64	132.6
Rick Worman, Eastern Wash.	1984-85	672	381	23	.567	5,004	41	132.5
Glenn Kempa, Lehigh	1989-91	901	520	27	.577	6,722	49	132.3
Jay Walker, Howard	1991-93	718	377	23	.525	5,671	42	131.8
James Ritchey, Stephen F. Austin	1992-95	613	325	25	.530	4,766	40	131.7
Gilbert Renfroe, Tennessee St.	1982-85	721	370	23	.513	5,556	48	131.6
Tracy Ham, Ga. Southern	1984-86	568	301	31	.530	4,881	29	131.1

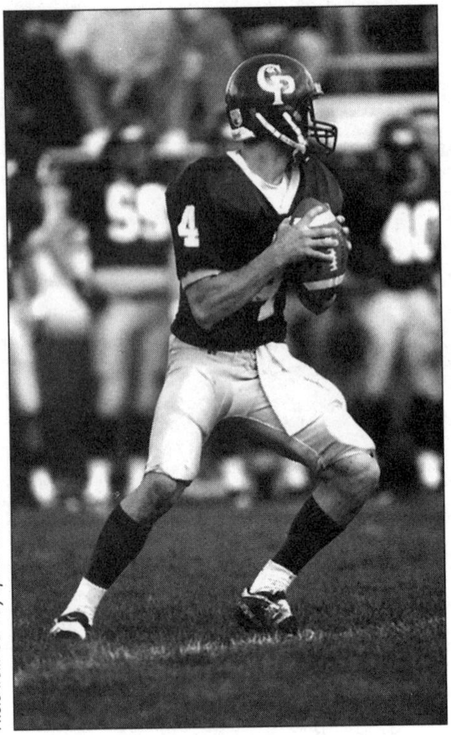

Photo from Cal Poly sports information

Cal Poly quarterback Alli Abrew led Division I-AA in passing efficiency in 1997 by connecting on 130 of 191 pass attempts and throwing only four interceptions.

Player, Team	Years	Att.	Cmp.	Int.	Pct.	Yards	TD	Pts.
Matt DeGennaro, Connecticut	1987-90	1,319	803	49	.609	9,288	73	130.9
Lonnie Galloway, Western Caro.	1990-93	639	355	43	.556	5,545	30	130.5
Dan Crowley, Towson	1991-94	1,170	617	54	.527	8,900	81	130.3
Ken Hobart, Idaho	1980-83	1,219	629	42	.516	9,300	79	130.2

*Record. $See page 6 for explanation.

SEASON PASSING EFFICIENCY

(Minimum 15 Attempts Per Game)

Player, Team	Year	G	Att.	Cmp.	Int.	Pct.	Yards	TD	Pts.
Shawn Knight, William & Mary	†1993	10	177	125	4	.706	2,055	22	*204.6
Michael Payton, Marshall	†1991	9	216	143	5	.622	2,333	19	181.3
Alli Abrew, Cal Poly	†1997	11	191	130	4	.681	1,961	17	179.5
Doug Turner, Morehead St.	1997	10	290	190	6	.655	2,869	29	177.5
Ted White, Howard	†1996	11	289	174	10	.602	2,814	36	176.2
Doug Nussmeier, Idaho	1993	11	304	185	5	.609	2,960	33	175.2
Brian Kadel, Dayton	†1995	11	183	115	6	.628	1,880	18	175.0
Chris Boden, Villanova	1997	11	345	231	4	.670	3,079	36	174.0
Kelvin Simmons, Troy St.	1993	11	224	143	6	.638	2,144	23	172.8
Frank Baur, Lafayette	†1988	10	256	164	11	.641	2,621	23	171.1
Bobby Lamb, Furman	†1985	11	181	106	6	.586	1,856	18	170.9
Harry Leons, Eastern Wash.	1997	10	257	159	5	.619	2,588	21	169.5
Steven Beard, Northern Iowa	1996	11	238	140	9	.588	2,526	21	169.5
Jay Fiedler, Dartmouth	†1992	10	273	175	13	.641	2,748	25	169.4
Dave Dickenson, Montana	1995	11	455	309	9	.679	4,176	38	168.6
Mike Smith, Northern Iowa	†1986	11	303	190	16	.627	3,125	27	168.2
Dave Dickenson, Montana	1993	11	390	262	9	.672	3.640	32	168.0
Simon Fuentes, Eastern Ky.	1997	11	189	116	2	.614	1,932	13	167.8
Willie Totten, Mississippi Val.	†1983	9	279	174	9	.624	2,566	29	167.5
Lonnie Galloway, Western Caro.	1992	11	211	128	12	.607	2,181	20	167.4
Leo Hamlett, Delaware	1995	11	174	95	6	.546	1,849	15	165.4
Eriq Williams, James Madison	1991	11	192	107	7	.557	1,914	19	164.8
Dave Dickenson, Montana	†1994	9	336	229	6	.682	3,053	24	164.5
Willie Totten, Mississippi Val.	†1984	10	518	*324	22	.626	4,557	*56	163.6
Jeff Wiley, Holy Cross	†1987	11	400	265	17	.663	3,677	34	163.0
Todd Hammel, Stephen F. Austin	†1989	11	401	238	13	.594	3,914	34	162.8
Mike Williams, Grambling	†1980	11	239	127	5	.531	2,116	28	162.0
Giovanni Carmazzi, Hofstra	1997	11	408	288	8	.706	3,554	27	161.7
Dan Crowley, Towson	1993	10	217	125	4	.576	1,882	23	161.7
Mike Stadler, San Diego	1997	11	262	152	10	.580	2,287	30	161.5
John Friesz, Idaho	1989	11	425	260	8	.612	4,041	31	161.4
Wendal Lowrey, Northeast La.	1992	11	227	147	9	.648	2,190	16	161.1
Donny Simmons, Western Ill.	1992	11	281	182	11	.648	2,496	25	160.9
Chris Berg, Northern Iowa	1995	10	206	113	6	.549	2,144	15	160.5
Sean Laird, St. Mary's (Cal.)	1996	10	256	161	4	.629	2,199	22	160.3
David Charpia, Furman	1983	9	155	99	4	.635	1,419	12	160.1
Todd Donnan, Marshall	1994	11	288	182	8	.632	2,403	28	159.8
Joe Aliotti, Boise St.	†1979	11	219	144	7	.658	1,870	19	159.7
Gilbert Renfroe, Tennessee St.	1984	11	165	95	5	.576	1,458	17	159.7
Mike Buck, Maine	1989	11	264	170	3	.644	2,315	19	159.5
Bobby Lamb, Furman	1984	11	191	106	7	.555	1,781	19	159.3
Kenneth Biggles, Tennessee St.	1984	11	258	157	7	.609	2,242	24	159.1
Michael Payton, Marshall	1992	11	313	200	11	.639	2,788	26	159.1

*Record. †National champion.

CAREER YARDS

Player, Team	Years	Att.	Cmp.	Int.	Pct.	Yards	TD
Steve McNair, Alcorn St.	1991-94	*1,680	927	58	.552	*14,496	119
Willie Totten, Mississippi Val.	1982-85	1,555	907	*75	.583	12,711	*139
Jamie Martin, Weber St.	1989-92	1,544	*934	56	.605	12,207	87
Neil Lomax, Portland St.	1978-80	1,425	836	50	.587	11,550	88
Dave Dickenson, Montana	1992-95	1,208	813	26	*.673	11,080	96
Doug Nussmeier, Idaho	1990-93	1,225	746	32	.609	10,824	91
John Friesz, Idaho	1986-89	1,350	801	40	.593	10,697	77
Greg Wyatt, Northern Ariz.	1986-89	1,510	926	49	.613	10,697	70
Sean Payton, Eastern Ill.	1983-86	1,408	756	55	.537	10,655	75
Jeff Wiley, Holy Cross	1985-88	1,208	723	63	.599	9,698	71
Jeff Lewis, Northern Ariz.	1992-95	1,316	785	24	.597	9,655	67
Robbie Justino, Liberty	1989-92	1,267	769	51	.607	9,548	64
Kirk Schulz, Villanova	1986-89	1,297	774	70	.597	9,305	70
Ken Hobart, Idaho	1980-83	1,219	629	42	.516	9,300	79
Matt DeGennaro, Connecticut	1987-90	1,319	803	49	.609	9,288	73
Marty Horn, Lehigh	1982-85	1,390	744	64	.535	9,120	62
Jason Whitmer, Idaho St.	1987-90	1,349	721	53	.534	9,081	55
Chris Swartz, Morehead St.	1987-90	1,408	774	47	.550	9,027	56
Darin Hinshaw, Central Fla.	1991-94	1,114	614	52	.551	9,000	82
Dan Crowley, Towson	1991-94	1,170	617	54	.527	8,900	81
Michael Proctor, Murray St.	1986-89	1,148	578	45	.503	8,682	52
Eric Beavers, Nevada	1983-86	1,094	646	37	.590	8,626	77
Tom Ciaccio, Holy Cross	1988-91	1,073	658	46	.613	8,603	72
Steve Calabria, Colgate	1981-84	1,143	626	68	.548	8,555	54
Mike Buck, Maine	1986-89	1,102	619	39	.562	8,491	67
Jeff Cesarone, Western Ky.	1984-87	1,339	714	39	.533	8,404	45
Frank Baur, Lafayette	1985, 87-89	1,103	636	46	.577	8,399	62
Mitch Maher, North Texas	1991-94	1,100	610	47	.555	8,252	66
Stan Yagiello, William & Mary	$1981-85	1,247	737	36	.591	8,249	51
Mike Smith, Northern Iowa	1984-87	943	557	43	.591	8,219	58

Player, Team	Years	Att.	Cmp.	Int.	Pct.	Yards	TD
Kelly Bradley, Montana St.	1983-86	1,238	714	45	.577	8,152	60
Tom Proudian, Iona	1993-95	1,134	656	48	.578	8,088	58
Bob Bleier, Richmond	1983-86	1,169	672	56	.575	8,057	54
Chris Goetz, Towson	1987-90	1,172	648	51	.553	7,882	42
Paul Singer, Western Ill.	1985-88	1,171	646	43	.552	7,850	61
John Witkowski, Columbia	1981-83	1,176	613	60	.521	7,849	56
Greg Ryan, East Tenn. St.	1993-96	1,148	694	49	.605	7,826	56
Grady Bennett, Montana	1987-90	1,097	641	42	.584	7,778	55
Bernard Hawk, Bethune-Cookman	1982-85	1,120	554	51	.495	7,737	56
Bob Jean, New Hampshire	1985-88	1,126	567	49	.504	7,704	51

**Record. $See page 6 for explanation.*

CAREER YARDS PER GAME
(Minimum 5,000 Yards)

Player, Team	Years	G	Att.	Cmp.	Yards	TD	Yd. PG
Neil Lomax, Portland St.	1978-80	33	1,425	836	11,550	88	*350.0
Steve McNair, Alcorn St.	1991-94	42	*1,680	927	*14,496	119	345.1
Aaron Flowers, Cal St. Northridge	1996-97	20	819	502	6,766	54	338.3
Willie Totten, Mississippi Val.	1982-85	40	1,555	907	12,711	*139	317.8
Dave Dickenson, Montana	1992-95	35	1,208	813	11,080	96	316.6
John Friesz, Idaho	1986-89	35	1,350	801	10,697	77	305.6
Tom Proudian, Iona	1993-95	27	1,134	656	8,088	58	299.6
Jamie Martin, Weber St.	1989-92	41	1,544	*934	12,207	87	297.7
Sean Payton, Eastern Ill.	1983-86	37	1,408	756	10,655	75	288.0
Doug Nussmeier, Idaho	1990-93	39	1,225	746	10,824	91	277.5
Oteman Sampson, Florida A&M	1996-97	22	686	387	6,104	46	277.5
Robert Dougherty, Boston U.	1993-94	21	705	405	5,608	41	267.0
Scott Semptimphelter, Lehigh	1990-93	26	823	493	6,668	50	256.5
Greg Wyatt, Northern Ariz.	1986-89	42	1,510	926	10,697	70	254.7

**Record.*

CAREER TOUCHDOWN PASSES

Player, Team	Years	G	TD Passes
Willie Totten, Mississippi Val.	1982-85	40	*139
Steve McNair, Alcorn St.	1991-94	42	119
Dave Dickenson, Montana	1992-95	35	96
Doug Nussmeier, Idaho	1990-93	39	91
Neil Lomax, Portland St.	1978-80	33	88
Jamie Martin, Weber St.	1989-92	41	87
Darin Hinshaw, Central Fla.	1991-94	40	82
Dan Crowley, Towson	1991-94	40	81
Ken Hobart, Idaho	1980-83	44	79
John Friesz, Idaho	1986-89	35	77
Eric Beavers, Nevada	1983-86	40	77
Sean Payton, Eastern Ill.	1983-86	39	75
Matt DeGennaro, Connecticut	1987-90	43	73
Tom Ciaccio, Holy Cross	1988-91	37	72
Jeff Wiley, Holy Cross	1985-88	41	71
Kirk Schulz, Villanova	1986-89	42	70
Greg Wyatt, Northern Ariz.	1986-89	42	70

**Record.*

SEASON YARDS

Player, Team	Year	G	Att.	Cmp.	Int.	Pct.	Yards	TD
Steve McNair, Alcorn St.	1994	11	*530	304	17	.574	*4,863	44
Willie Totten, Mississippi Val.	†1984	10	518	*324	22	.626	4,557	*56
Dave Dickenson, Montana	1995	11	455	309	9	.679	4,176	38
Jamie Martin, Weber St.	1991	11	500	310	17	.620	4,125	35
Neil Lomax, Portland St.	1980	11	473	296	12	.626	4,094	37
John Friesz, Idaho	1989	11	425	260	8	.612	4,041	31
Neil Lomax, Portland St.	1979	11	516	299	16	.579	3,950	26
Todd Hammel, Stephen F. Austin	†1989	11	401	238	13	.594	3,914	34
Sean Payton, Eastern Ill.	1984	11	473	270	15	.571	3,843	28
Jamie Martin, Weber St.	1990	11	428	256	15	.598	3,700	23
Willie Totten, Mississippi Val.	1985	11	492	295	*29	.600	3,698	39
Jeff Wiley, Holy Cross	†1987	11	400	265	17	.663	3,677	34
John Friesz, Idaho	1987	11	502	311	14	.620	3,677	28
Dave Dickenson, Montana	1993	11	390	262	9	.672	3,640	32
Ken Hobart, Idaho	1983	11	477	268	19	.562	3,618	32
Brian Ah Yat, Montana	1996	11	432	265	16	.613	3,615	42
Glenn Kempa, Lehigh	1991	11	474	286	15	.603	3,565	31
Giovanni Carmazzi, Hofstra	1997	11	408	288	8	.706	3,554	27
Tom Ehrhardt, Rhode Island	1985	10	497	283	19	.569	3,542	35
Steve McNair, Alcorn St.	1992	10	427	231	11	.541	3,541	29
Aaron Flowers, Cal St. Northridge	1996	11	415	247	11	.595	3,540	30
Tony Petersen, Marshall	1987	11	466	251	25	.539	3,529	22
Todd Brunner, Lehigh	1989	11	450	273	19	.607	3,516	26
Kelly Bradley, Montana St.	1984	11	499	289	20	.579	3,508	30
Neil Lomax, Portland St.	†1978	11	436	241	22	.553	3,506	25

**Record. †National pass-efficiency champion.*

SEASON YARDS PER GAME

Player, Team	Year	G	Att.	Cmp.	Int.	Pct.	Yards	TD	Yd.PG
Willie Totten, Mississippi Val.	†1984	10	518	*324	22	.626	4,557	*56	*455.7
Steve McNair, Alcorn St.	1994	11	*530	304	17	.574	*4,863	44	442.1

Photo from Cal St. Northridge sports information

Cal State Northridge quarterback Aaron Flowers threw for 3,540 during the 1996 season to rank among the all-time leaders in season yards.

Player, Team	Year	G	Att.	Cmp.	Int.	Pct.	Yards	TD	Yd.PG
Dave Dickenson, Montana	1995	11	455	309	9	.679	4,176	38	379.6
Jamie Martin, Weber St.	1991	11	500	310	17	.620	4,125	35	375.0
Neil Lomax, Portland St.	1980	11	473	296	12	.626	4,094	37	372.2
John Friesz, Idaho	1989	11	425	260	8	.612	4,041	31	367.4
Neil Lomax, Portland St.	1979	11	516	299	16	.579	3,950	26	359.1
Aaron Flowers, Cal St. Northridge	1997	9	404	255	10	.631	3,226	24	358.4
Todd Hammel, Stephen F. Austin	†1989	11	401	238	13	.594	3,914	34	355.8
Tom Ehrhardt, Rhode Island	1985	10	497	283	19	.569	3,542	35	354.2
Steve McNair, Alcorn St.	1992	10	427	231	11	.541	3,541	29	354.1
Sean Payton, Eastern Ill.	1984	11	473	270	15	.571	3,843	28	349.4
Dave Dickenson, Montana	†1994	9	336	229	6	.682	3,053	24	339.2
Tom Proudian, Iona	1993	10	440	262	13	.595	3,368	29	336.8
Jamie Martin, Weber St.	1990	11	428	256	15	.598	3,700	23	336.4
Willie Totten, Mississippi Val.	1985	11	492	295	*29	.600	3,698	39	336.2

**Record. †National pass-efficiency champion.*

SEASON TOUCHDOWN PASSES

Player, Team	Years	G	TD Passes
Willie Totten, Mississippi Val.	1984	10	*56
Steve McNair, Alcorn St.	1994	11	44
Brian Ah Yat, Montana	1996	11	42
Willie Totten, Mississippi Val.	1985	11	39
Dave Dickenson, Montana	1995	11	38
Neil Lomax, Portland St.	1980	11	37
Chris Boden, Villanova	1997	11	36
Ted White, Howard	1996	11	36
Jamie Martin, Weber St.	1991	11	35
Tom Ehrhardt, Rhode Island	1985	10	35
Todd Hammel, Stephen F. Austin	1989	11	34
Jeff Wiley, Holy Cross	1987	11	34
Doug Nussmeier, Idaho	1993	11	33
Dave Dickenson, Montana	1993	11	32
Doug Hudson, Nicholls St.	1986	11	32
Ken Hobart, Idaho	1983	11	32
Glenn Kempa, Lehigh	1991	11	31
John Friesz, Idaho	1989	11	31
Mike Stadler, San Diego	1997	11	30
Aaron Flowers, Cal St. Northridge	1996	11	30
Scott Semptimphelter, Lehigh	1993	11	30
Brent Pease, Montana	1986	11	30
Kelly Bradley, Montana St.	1984	11	30

**Record.*

SINGLE-GAME YARDS

Yds.	Player, Team (Opponent)	Date
624	Jamie Martin, Weber St. (Idaho St.)	Nov. 23, 1991
619	Doug Pederson, Northeast La. (Stephen F. Austin)	Nov. 11, 1989
599	Willie Totten, Mississippi Val. (Prairie View)	Oct. 27, 1984
589	Vern Harris, Idaho St. (Montana)	Oct. 12, 1985
587	Steve McNair, Alcorn St. (Southern U.)	Oct. 22, 1994
571	Todd Hammel, Stephen F. Austin (Northeast La.)	Nov. 11, 1989
566	Tom Ehrhardt, Rhode Island (Connecticut)	Nov. 16, 1985
563	Steve McNair, Alcorn St. (Samford)	Oct. 29, 1994
560	Brian Ah Yat, Montana (Eastern Wash.)	Oct. 19, 1996
558	Dave Dickenson, Montana (Idaho)	Oct. 21, 1995
553	Willie Totten, Mississippi Val. (Southern U.)	Sept. 29, 1984
547	Jamie Martin, Weber St. (Montana St.)	Sept. 26, 1992
545	Willie Totten, Mississippi Val. (Grambling)	Oct. 13, 1984
540	Brad Otten, Weber St. (Northern Ariz.)	Nov. 6, 1993
539	John Whitcomb, UAB (Prairie View)	Nov. 19, 1994
537	Tod Mayfield, West Tex. A&M (New Mexico St.)	Nov. 16, 1985
536	Willie Totten, Mississippi Val. (Kentucky St.)	Sept. 1, 1984
534	Steve McNair, Alcorn St. (Grambling)	Sept. 3, 1994
534	Todd Hammel, Stephen F. Austin (Sam Houston St.)	Nov. 4, 1989
533	Steve McNair, Alcorn St. (Jackson St.)	Nov. 19, 1994
527	Bernard Hawk, Bethune-Cookman (Ga. Southern)	Oct. 6, 1984
527	Ken Hobart, Idaho (Southern Colo.)	Sept. 1, 1983
526	Willie Totten, Mississippi Val. (Jackson St.)	Sept. 22, 1984

SINGLE-GAME ATTEMPTS

No.	Player, Team (Opponent)	Date
77	Neil Lomax, Portland St. (Northern Colo.)	Oct. 20, 1979
74	Paul Peterson, Idaho St. (Nevada)	Oct. 1, 1983
72	Dave Dickenson, Montana (Idaho)	Oct. 21, 1995
71	Doug Pederson, Northeast La. (Stephen F. Austin)	Nov. 11, 1989
70	Greg Farland, Rhode Island (Boston U.)	Oct. 18, 1986
69	Aaron Flowers, Cal St. Northridge (Cal St. Sacramento)	Oct. 25, 1997
69	Steve McNair, Alcorn St. (Jacksonville St.)	Oct. 31, 1992
68	Tony Petersen, Marshall (Western Caro.)	Nov. 14, 1987
67	Tom Proudian, Iona (Siena)	Oct. 1, 1994
67	Michael Payton, Marshall (Western Caro.)	Oct. 31, 1992
67	Vern Harris, Idaho St. (Montana)	Oct. 12, 1985
67	Rick Worman, Eastern Wash. (Nevada)	Oct. 12, 1985
67	Tod Mayfield, West Tex. A&M (Indiana St.)	Oct. 5, 1985
67	Tom Ehrhardt, Rhode Island (Brown)	Sept. 28, 1985
66	Kevin Glenn, Illinois St. (Western Ill.)	Nov. 8, 1997

No.	Player, Team (Opponent)	Date
66	Chris Swartz, Morehead St. (Tennessee Tech)	Oct. 17, 1987
66	Sean Cook, Texas Southern (Tex. A&M-Kingsville)	Sept. 6, 1986
66	Kelly Bradley, Montana St. (Eastern Wash.)	Sept. 21, 1985
66	Bernard Hawk, Bethune-Cookman (Ga. Southern)	Oct. 6, 1984
66	Willie Totten, Mississippi Val. (Southern U.)	Sept. 29, 1984
66	Paul Peterson, Idaho St. (Cal Poly)	Oct. 22, 1983

SINGLE-GAME COMPLETIONS

No.	Player, Team (Opponent)	Date
48	Clayton Millis, Cal St. Northridge (St. Mary's [Cal.])	Nov. 11, 1995
47	Jamie Martin, Weber St. (Idaho St.)	Nov. 23, 1991
46	Doug Pederson, Northeast La. (Stephen F. Austin)	Nov. 11, 1989
46	Willie Totten, Mississippi Val. (Southern U.)	Sept. 29, 1984
45	Willie Totten, Mississippi Val. (Prairie View)	Oct. 27, 1984
44	Neil Lomax, Portland St. (Northern Colo.)	Oct. 20, 1979
43	Aaron Flowers, Cal St. Northridge (Cal St. Sacramento)	Oct. 25, 1997
43	Dave Dickenson, Montana (Idaho)	Oct. 21, 1995
42	Travis Brown, Northern Ariz. (Montana)	Oct. 26, 1996
42	Tod Mayfield, West Tex. A&M (Indiana St.)	Oct. 5, 1985
42	Kelly Bradley, Montana St. (Eastern Wash.)	Sept. 21, 1985
42	Rusty Hill, North Texas (Tulsa)	Nov. 20, 1982

ANNUAL CHAMPIONS

Year	Player, Team	Class	G	Att.	Cmp.	Avg.	Int.	Pct.	Yds.	TD
1978	Neil Lomax, Portland St.	So.	11	436	241	21.9	22	.553	3,506	25

Beginning in 1979, ranked on passing efficiency rating points (instead of per-game completions)

Year	Player, Team	Class	G	Att.	Cmp.	Int.	Pct.	Yds.	TD	Pts.
1979	Joe Aliotti, Boise St.	Jr.	11	219	144	7	.658	1,870	19	159.7
1980	Mike Williams, Grambling	Sr.	11	239	127	5	.531	2,116	28	162.0
1981	Mike Machurek, Idaho St.	Sr.	9	313	188	11	.601	2,752	22	150.1
1982	Frank Novak, Lafayette	Jr.	10	257	154	12	.599	2,257	20	150.0
1983	Willie Totten, Mississippi Val.	So.	9	279	174	9	.624	2,566	29	167.5
1984	Willie Totten, Mississippi Val.	Jr.	10	518	*324	22	.626	4,557	*56	163.6
1985	Bobby Lamb, Furman	Sr.	11	181	106	6	.586	1,856	18	170.9
1986	Mike Smith, Northern Iowa	Jr.	11	303	190	16	.627	3,125	27	168.2
1987	Jeff Wiley, Holy Cross	Jr.	11	400	265	17	.663	3,677	34	163.0
1988	Frank Baur, Lafayette	Jr.	10	256	164	11	.641	2,621	23	171.1
1989	Todd Hammel, Stephen F. Austin	Sr.	11	401	238	13	.594	3,914	34	162.8
1990	Connell Maynor, North Caro. A&T	Jr.	11	191	123	10	.644	1,699	16	156.3
1991	Michael Payton, Marshall	Jr.	9	216	143	5	.662	2,333	19	181.3
1992	Jay Fiedler, Dartmouth	Jr.	10	273	175	13	.641	2,748	25	169.4
1993	Shawn Knight, William & Mary	Jr.	10	177	125	4	.706	2,055	22	*204.6
1994	Dave Dickenson, Montana	Jr.	9	336	229	6	.682	3,053	24	164.5
1995	Brian Kadel, Dayton	Sr.	11	183	115	6	.628	1,880	18	175.0
1996	Ted White, Howard	So.	11	289	174	10	.602	2,814	36	176.2
1997	Alli Abrew, Cal Poly	Sr.	11	191	130	4	.681	1,961	17	179.5

**Record.*

Receiving

CAREER RECEPTIONS PER GAME

(Minimum 125 Receptions)

Player, Team	Years	G	Rec.	Yards	TD	Rec. PG
Jerry Rice, Mississippi Val.	1981-84	41	*301	*4,693	*50	*7.3
Derrick Ingram, UAB	1993-94	22	159	2,572	21	7.2
Jeff Johnson, East Tenn. St.	1993-94	20	142	1,772	19	7.1
Miles Macik, Pennsylvania	1993-95	29	200	2,364	26	6.9
Kevin Guthrie, Princeton	1981-83	28	193	2,645	16	6.9
Eric Yarber, Idaho	1984-85	19	129	1,920	17	6.8
Joe Douglass, Montana	1995-96	22	145	2,301	25	6.6
Brian Forster, Rhode Island (TE)	1983-85, 87	38	245	3,410	31	6.5
Kasey Dunn, Idaho	1988-91	42	268	3,847	25	6.4
Gordie Lockbaum, Holy Cross (RB)	‡1986-87	22	135	2,012	17	6.1
Derek Graham, Princeton	1981, 83-84	29	176	2,819	19	6.1
Stuart Gaussoin, Portland St.	1978-80	23	135	1,909	14	5.9
Don Lewis, Columbia	1981-83	30	176	2,207	11	5.9
Mike Barber, Marshall	1985-88	36	209	3,520	20	5.8
Rennie Benn, Lehigh	1982-85	41	237	3,662	44	5.8
Daren Altieri, Boston U.	1987-90	39	225	2,518	15	5.8
Bill Reggio, Columbia	1981-83	30	170	2,384	26	5.7

**Record. ‡Defensive back in 1984-85.*

SEASON RECEPTIONS PER GAME

Player, Team	Years	G	Rec.	Yards	TD	Rec. PG
Brian Forster, Rhode Island (TE)	†1985	10	*115	1,617	12	*11.5
Jerry Rice, Mississippi Val.	†1984	10	103	*1,682	*27	10.3
Jerry Rice, Mississippi Val.	†1983	10	102	1,450	14	10.2
Stuart Gaussoin, Portland St.	†1979	9	90	1,132	8	10.0
Eric Krawczyk, Cornell	†1997	10	89	1,042	11	8.9
Kevin Guthrie, Princeton	1983	10	88	1,259	9	8.8
David Romines, Cal St. Northridge	†1996	10	87	1,300	12	8.7
Alfred Pupunu, Weber St. (TE)	†1991	11	93	1,204	12	8.5
Derek Graham, Princeton	1983	10	84	1,363	11	8.4
Don Lewis, Columbia	†1982	10	84	1,000	6	8.4
Peter Macon, Weber St.	†1989	11	92	1,047	6	8.4
Marvin Walker, North Texas	1982	11	91	934	11	8.3

**Record. †National champion.*

CAREER RECEPTIONS

Player, Team	Years	Rec.	Yards	Avg.	TD
Jerry Rice, Mississippi Val.	1981-84	*301	*4,693	15.6	*50
Kasey Dunn, Idaho	1988-91	268	3,847	14.4	25
Brian Forster, Rhode Island	1983-85, 87	245	3,410	13.9	31
Mark Didio, Connecticut	1988-91	239	3,535	14.8	21
Rennie Benn, Lehigh	1982-85	237	3,662	15.5	44
Daren Altieri, Boston U.	1987-90	225	2,518	11.2	15
Darrell Colbert, Texas Southern	1983-86	217	3,177	14.6	33
David Rhodes, Central Fla.	1991-94	213	3,618	17.0	29
Robert Wilson, Florida A&M	1993-96	209	2,949	14.1	24
Mike Barber, Marshall	1985-88	209	3,520	16.8	20
Trevor Shaw, Weber St.	1989-90, 92-93	206	2,383	11.6	17
William Brooks, Boston U.	1982-85	204	3,154	15.5	26
Donald Narcisse, Texas Southern	1983-86	203	2,429	12.0	26
Alex Davis, Connecticut	1989-92	202	2,567	12.7	24
Shawn Collins, Northern Ariz.	1985-88	201	2,764	13.8	24
Miles Macik, Pennsylvania	1993-95	200	2,364	11.8	26
Leland Melvin, Richmond	1982-85	198	2,669	13.5	16
Mike Wilson, Boise St.	1990-93	196	3,017	15.4	13
Blake Tuffli, St. Mary's (Cal.)	1993-96	194	2,990	15.4	25
Curtis Olds, New Hampshire	1985-88	193	3,028	15.7	23
Kevin Guthrie, Princeton	1981-83	193	2,645	13.7	16
Matt Wells, Montana	1992-95	189	2,733	14.5	19

Player, Team	Years	Rec.	Yards	Avg.	TD
Sergio Hebra, Maine	1984-87	189	2,612	13.8	17
John Perry, New Hampshire	1989-92	186	2,798	15.0	19
Glenn Antrum, Connecticut	1985-88	186	2,552	13.7	14
Joe Thomas, Mississippi Val.	1982-85	186	2,816	15.1	36
Gary Harrell, Howard	1990-93	184	2,619	14.2	19
Roy Banks, Eastern Ill.	1983-86	184	3,177	17.3	38
Merril Hoge, Idaho St. (RB)	1983-86	182	1,734	9.5	13
George Delaney, Colgate	1988-91	181	2,938	16.2	25
Robert Brady, Villanova	1986-89	180	2,725	15.1	28

**Record.*

SEASON RECEPTIONS

Player, Team	Year	G	Rec.	Yards	TD
Brian Forster, Rhode Island (TE)	†1985	10	*115	1,617	12
Jerry Rice, Mississippi Val.	†1984	10	103	*1,682	*27
Jerry Rice, Mississippi Val.	†1983	10	102	1,450	14
Alfred Pupunu, Weber St. (TE)	†1991	11	93	1,204	12
Peter Macon, Weber St.	†1989	11	92	1,047	6
Marvin Walker, North Texas	1982	11	91	934	11
Stuart Gaussoin, Portland St.	†1979	9	90	1,132	8
Eric Krawczyk, Cornell	†1997	10	89	1,042	11
Dave Cecchini, Lehigh	†1993	11	88	1,318	16
Rameck Wright, Maine	1997	11	88	1,176	7
Mark Didio, Connecticut	1991	11	88	1,354	8
Kasey Dunn, Idaho	†1990	11	88	1,164	7
Donald Narcisse, Texas Southern	†1986	11	88	1,074	15
Kevin Guthrie, Princeton	1983	10	88	1,259	9
David Romines, Cal St. Northridge	†1996	10	87	1,300	12
Kasey Dunn, Idaho	1991	11	85	1,263	6
Derek Graham, Princeton	1983	10	84	1,363	11
Don Lewis, Columbia	†1982	10	84	1,000	6

**Record. †National champion.*

SEASON TOUCHDOWN RECEPTIONS

Player, Team	Year	G	TD
Jerry Rice, Mississippi Val.	1984	10	*27
Randy Moss, Marshall	1996	11	19
Joe Douglass, Montana	1996	11	18
Brian Finneran, Villanova	1997	11	17
Mark Carrier, Nicholls St.	1986	11	17
Dameon Reilly, Rhode Island	1985	11	17
Joe Thomas, Mississippi Val.	1985	11	17
Roy Banks, Eastern Ill.	1984	11	17
Wayne Chrebet, Hofstra	1994	10	16
Dave Cecchini, Lehigh	1993	11	16
Sean Morey, Brown	1997	10	15
Donald Narcisse, Texas Southern	1986	11	15
Rennie Benn, Lehigh	1983	11	15
Macey Brooks, James Madison	1996	11	14
Dedric Ward, Northern Iowa	1996	11	14
Rennie Benn, Lehigh	1985	11	14
Jerry Rice, Mississippi Val.	1983	10	14
Bill Reggio, Columbia	1982	10	14

**Record.*

SINGLE-GAME RECEPTIONS

No.	Player, Team (Opponent)	Date
24	Jerry Rice, Mississippi Val. (Southern U.)	Oct. 1, 1983
22	Marvin Walker, North Texas (Tulsa)	Nov. 20, 1982
21	David Pandt, Montana St. (Eastern Wash.)	Sept. 21, 1985
20	Tim Hilton, Cal St. Northridge (St. Mary's [Cal.])	Nov. 11, 1995
18	David Romines, Cal St. Northridge (UC Davis)	Sept. 14, 1996
18	Jerome Williams, Morehead St. (Eastern Ky.)	Nov. 18, 1989
18	Brian Forster, Rhode Island (Brown)	Sept. 28, 1985
17	Rameek Wright, Maine (Buffalo)	Nov. 16, 1996
17	Elliot Miller, St. Francis [Pa.] (Central Conn. St.)	Oct. 2, 1993
17	Lifford Jackson, Louisiana Tech (Kansas St.)	Oct. 1, 1988
17	Brian Forster, Rhode Island (Lehigh)	Oct. 12, 1985
17	Jerry Rice, Mississippi Val. (Southern U.)	Sept. 29, 1984
17	Jerry Rice, Mississippi Val. (Kentucky St.)	Sept. 1, 1984

CAREER YARDS

Player, Team	Years	Rec.	Yards	Avg.	TD
Jerry Rice, Mississippi Val.	1981-84	*301	*4,693	15.6	*50
Dedric Ward, Northern Iowa	1993-96	176	3,876	*22.0	41
Kasey Dunn, Idaho	1988-91	268	3,847	14.4	25
Rennie Benn, Lehigh	1982-85	237	3,662	15.5	44
David Rhodes, Central Fla.	1991-94	213	3,618	17.0	29
Mark Didio, Connecticut	1988-91	239	3,535	14.8	21
Mike Barber, Marshall	1985-88	209	3,520	16.8	20
Brian Forster, Rhode Island (TE)	1983-85, 87	245	3,410	13.9	31
Tracy Singleton, Howard	1979-82	159	3,187	20.0	16
Courtney Batts, Delaware	1994-97	153	3,181	20.8	26
Roy Banks, Eastern Ill.	1983-86	184	3,177	17.3	38
Darrell Colbert, Texas Southern	1983-86	217	3,177	14.6	33
William Brooks, Boston U.	1982-85	204	3,154	15.5	26

**Record.*

CAREER YARDS PER GAME

(Minimum 2,000 Yards)

Player, Team	Years	G	Yards	Yds. PG
Derrick Ingram, UAB	1993-94	22	2,572	*116.9
Jerry Rice, Mississippi Val.	1981-84	41	*4,693	114.5
Joe Douglass, Montana	1995-96	22	2,301	104.6
Derek Graham, Princeton	1981, 83-84	29	2,819	97.2
Kevin Guthrie, Princeton	1981-83	28	2,645	94.5
Tracy Singleton, Howard	1979-82	34	3,187	93.7
David Rhodes, Central Fla.	1991-94	39	3,618	92.8
Kasey Dunn, Idaho	1988-91	42	3,847	91.6
Gordie Lockbaum, Holy Cross	‡1986-87	22	2,012	91.5
Bryan Calder, Nevada	1984-86	28	2,559	91.4
Mike Barber, Marshall	1985-88	36	3,250	90.3
Dedric Ward, Northern Iowa	1993-96	43	3,876	90.1
Brian Forster, Rhode Island	1983-85, 87	38	3,410	89.7

**Record. ‡Defensive back in 1984-85.*

CAREER TOUCHDOWN RECEPTIONS

Player, Team	Year	G	TD
Jerry Rice, Mississippi Val.	1981-84	41	*50
Rennie Benn, Lehigh	1982-85	41	44
Dedric Ward, Northern Iowa	1993-96	43	41
Roy Banks, Eastern Ill.	1983-86	38	38
Mike Jones, Tennessee St.	1979-82	42	38
Joe Thomas, Mississippi Val.	1982-85	41	36
Dameon Reilly, Rhode Island	1983-85	32	35
Darrell Colbert, Texas Southern	1983-86	43	33
John Taylor, Delaware St.	1982-85	43	33
Trumaine Johnson, Grambling	1979-82	44	32
Brian Forster, Rhode Island	1983-85, 87	38	31
¢Sean Morey, Brown	1995-97	30	29
David Rhodes, Central Fla.	1991-94	39	29
Tom Stenglein, Colgate	1983-85	32	29

**Record. ¢Active player.*

SEASON YARDS

Player, Team	Year	Rec.	Yards	Avg.	TD
Jerry Rice, Mississippi Val.	1984	103	*1,682	16.3	*27
Brian Forster, Rhode Island	1985	*115	1,617	14.1	12
Joe Douglass, Montana	1996	82	1,469	17.9	18
Derrick Ingram, UAB	1994	83	1,457	17.6	13
Jerry Rice, Mississippi Val.	1983	102	1,450	14.2	14
Sean Morey, Brown	†1997	73	1,427	19.6	15
B. J. Adigun, East Tenn. St.	1997	68	1,389	20.4	12
Derek Graham, Princeton	1983	84	1,363	16.2	11
Mikhael Ricks, Stephen F. Austin	1997	47	1,358	28.9	13
Mark Didio, Connecticut	†1991	88	1,354	15.4	8
Dave Cecchini, Lehigh	†1993	88	1,318	15.0	16
Golden Tate, Tennessee St.	1983	63	1,307	20.7	13

**Record. †National champion.*

SINGLE-GAME YARDS

Yds.	Player, Team (Opponent)	Date
370	Michael Lerch, Princeton (Brown)	Oct. 12, 1991
330	Nate Singleton, Grambling (Virginia Union)	Sept. 14, 1991
327	Brian Forster, Rhode Island (Brown)	Sept. 28, 1985
319	Jason Cristino, Lehigh (Lafayette)	Nov. 21, 1992
316	Marcus Hinton, Alcorn St. (Chattanooga)	Sept. 10, 1994
299	Treamelle Taylor, Nevada (Montana)	Oct. 14, 1989
299	Brian Forster, Rhode Island (Lehigh)	Oct. 12, 1985
294	Jerry Rice, Mississippi Val. (Kentucky St.)	Sept. 1, 1984
289	Derrick Ingram, UAB (Prairie View)	Nov. 19, 1994
285	Jerry Rice, Mississippi Val. (Jackson St.)	Sept. 22, 1984
284	Jacquay Nunnally, Florida A&M (North Caro. A&T)	Oct. 11, 1997
280	Rondel Menendez, Eastern Ky. (Eastern Ill.)	Nov. 22, 1997
279	Joe Douglass, Montana (Eastern Wash.)	Oct. 19, 1996
279	Jerry Rice, Mississippi Val. (Southern U.)	Oct. 1, 1983
276	Joey Stockton, Western Ky. (Austin Peay)	Sept. 16, 1995
266	Mark Orlando, Towson (American Int'l)	Oct. 22, 1994
266	Rennie Benn, Lehigh (Indiana [Pa.])	Sept. 14, 1985
264	Jason Anderson, Eastern Wash. (Montana)	Sept. 17, 1994
263	Mark Stock, VMI (East Tenn. St.)	Nov. 22, 1986
262	Andre Motley, Marshall (Chattanooga)	Oct. 20, 1990
262	Kenneth Gilstrap, Tennessee Tech (Morehead St.)	Oct. 17, 1987
261	Joel Pelagio-Williams, Weber St. (Cal Poly)	Sept. 23, 1995
260	Reggie Barlow, Alabama St. (Grambling)	Nov. 5, 1994

Yds.	Player, Team (Opponent)	Date
254	Kamil Loud, Cal Poly (Cal St. Sacramento)	Oct. 21, 1995
253	Chris Johnson, Indiana St. (Illinois St.)	Oct. 18, 1986
252	Jeff Sanders, William & Mary (Miami [Ohio])	Sept. 11, 1982
251	Lifford Jackson, Louisiana Tech (Kansas St.)	Oct. 1, 1988

ANNUAL CHAMPIONS

Year	Player, Team	Class	G	Rec.	Avg.	Yards	TD
1978	Dan Ross, Northeastern	Sr.	11	68	6.2	988	7
1979	Stuart Gaussoin, Portland St.	Jr.	9	90	10.0	1,132	8
1980	Kenny Johnson, Portland St.	So.	11	72	6.5	1,011	11
1981	Ken Harvey, Northern Iowa	Sr.	11	78	7.1	1,161	15
1982	Don Lewis, Columbia	Jr.	10	84	8.4	1,000	6
1983	Jerry Rice, Mississippi Val.	Jr.	10	102	10.2	1,450	14
1984	Jerry Rice, Mississippi Val.	Sr.	10	103	10.3	*1,682	*27
1985	Brian Forster, Rhode Island (TE)	Jr.	10	*115	*11.5	1,617	12
1986	Donald Narcisse, Texas Southern	Sr.	11	88	8.0	1,074	15
1987	Mike Barber, Marshall	Jr.	11	78	7.1	1,237	7
	Gordie Lockbaum, Holy Cross (RB)	Sr.	11	78	7.1	1,152	9
1988	Glenn Antrum, Connecticut	Sr.	11	77	7.0	1,130	7
1989	Peter Macon, Weber St.	Sr.	11	92	8.4	1,047	6

Beginning in 1990, ranked on both per-game catches and yards per game

PER-GAME RECEPTIONS

Year	Player, Team	Class	G	Rec.	Avg.	Yards	TD
1990	Kasey Dunn, Idaho	Jr.	11	88	8.0	1,164	7
1991	Alfred Pupunu, Weber St. (TE)	Sr.	11	93	8.5	1,204	12
1992	Glenn Krupa, Southeast Mo. St.	Sr.	11	77	7.0	773	4
1993	Dave Cecchini, Lehigh	Sr.	11	88	8.0	1,318	16
1994	Jeff Johnson, East Tenn. St.	Sr.	9	73	8.1	857	8
1995	Ed Mantie, Boston U.	Sr.	11	81	7.4	943	1
1996	David Romines, Cal St. Northridge	Sr.	10	87	8.7	1,300	12
1997	Eric Krawczyk, Cornell	Sr.	10	89	8.9	1,042	11

YARDS PER GAME

Year	Player, Team	Class	G	Rec.	Avg.	Yards	TD
1990	Kasey Dunn, Idaho	Jr.	11	88	105.8	1,164	7
1991	Mark Didio, Connecticut	Sr.	11	88	123.1	1,354	8
1992	Jason Cristino, Lehigh	Sr.	11	65	116.5	1,282	9
1993	Dave Cecchini, Lehigh	Sr.	11	88	119.8	1,318	16
1994	Mark Orlando, Towson	Sr.	9	55	135.9	1,223	12
1995	Dedric Ward, Northern Iowa	Jr.	10	44	116.4	1,164	12
1996	Joe Douglass, Montana	Sr.	11	82	133.6	1,469	18
1997	Sean Morey, Brown	Jr.	10	73	142.7	1,427	15

*Record.

Scoring

CAREER POINTS PER GAME

(Minimum 225 Points)

Player, Team	Years	G	TD	XPt.	FG	Pts.	Pt. PG
Keith Elias, Princeton	1991-93	30	52	8	0	320	*10.7
Archie Amerson, Northern Ariz.	1995-96	22	38	0	0	228	10.4
Michael Hicks, South Caro. St.	1993-95	32	52	4	0	316	9.9
Elroy Harris, Eastern Ky.	1985, 87-88	31	47	6	0	288	9.3
Joel Sigel, Portland St.	1978-80	30	46	2	0	278	9.3
Tony Zendejas, Nevada	1981-83	33	0	90	70	300	9.1
Gerald Harris, Ga. Southern	1984-86	31	45	2	0	272	8.8
Marty Zendejas, Nevada	1984-87	44	0	169	*72	*385	8.8
Charvez Foger, Nevada	1985-88	42	60	2	0	362	8.6
Paul Lewis, Boston U.	1981-84	37	51	2	0	308	8.3
Sherriden May, Idaho	1991-94	44	*61	0	0	366	8.3
Judd Garrett, Princeton	1987-89	30	41	1	0	248	8.3
Andre Garron, New Hampshire	1982-85	30	41	0	0	246	8.2
Kenny Gamble, Colgate	1984-87	42	57	0	0	342	8.1
Rene Ingoglia, Massachusetts	1992-95	41	55	2	0	332	8.1
Reggie Greene, Siena	1994-97	36	48	2	0	290	8.1
Barry Bourassa, New Hampshire	1989-92	39	51	0	0	306	7.8
Tim Openlander, Marshall	1994-96	33	0	159	32	255	7.7
Dave Ettinger, Hofstra	1994-97	43	0	140	62	326	7.6
Chad Levitt, Cornell	1993-96	39	48	4	0	292	7.5
Markus Thomas, Eastern Ky.	1989-92	43	53	4	0	322	7.5
Jerry Rice, Mississippi Val.	1981-84	41	50	2	0	302	7.4
Brian Mitchell, Marshall/ Northern Iowa	1987, 89-91	44	0	130	64	322	7.3
David Ettinger, Hofstra	1994-96	32	0	98	45	233	7.3
Stan House, Central Conn. St.	1994-97	40	48	2	0	290	7.3
Harvey Reed, Howard	1984-87	41	48	6	0	294	7.2
Thayne Doyle, Idaho	1988-91	43	0	160	49	307	7.1
Chris Parker, Marshall	1992-95	44	52	2	0	314	7.1

*Record.

SEASON POINTS PER GAME

Player, Team	Year	G	TD	XPt.	FG	Pts.	Pt. PG
Jerry Rice, Mississippi Val.	†1984	10	27	0	0	162	*16.2
Geoff Mitchell, Weber St.	†1991	11	*28	1	0	*170	15.5
Tony Vinson, Towson	†1993	10	24	0	0	144	14.4
Archie Amerson, Northern Ariz.	†1996	11	26	0	0	156	14.2
Aaron Stecker, Western Ill.	†1997	11	25	0	0	150	13.6
Sherriden May, Idaho	†1992	11	25	0	0	150	13.6
Keith Elias, Princeton	1993	10	21	4	0	130	13.0
Elroy Harris, Eastern Ky.	†1988	10	21	2	0	128	12.8
Sean Sanders, Weber St.	†1987	10	21	0	0	126	12.6
Rich Erenberg, Colgate	†1983	11	21	10	0	136	12.4
Reggie Greene, Siena	1997	9	18	2	0	110	12.2
Sean Bennett, Evansville	1997	10	20	2	0	122	12.2
Harvey Reed, Howard	1987	10	20	2	0	122	12.2
Paul Lewis, Boston U.	1983	10	20	2	0	122	12.2
Stan House, Central Conn. St.	1996	10	20	0	0	120	12.0
Alcede Surtain, Alabama St.	†1995	11	21	6	0	132	12.0
Tim Hall, Robert Morris	†1995	10	20	0	0	120	12.0
Michael Hicks, South Caro. St.	†1994	11	22	0	0	132	12.0
Sherriden May, Idaho	1993	11	22	0	0	132	12.0
Gordie Lockbaum, Holy Cross	1987	11	22	0	0	132	12.0
Gordie Lockbaum, Holy Cross	†1986	11	22	0	0	132	12.0
Gene Lake, Delaware St.	1984	10	20	0	0	120	12.0
Sean Bennett, Evansville	1996	10	19	4	0	118	11.8
Ernest Thompson, Ga. Southern	1988	10	19	2	0	116	11.6
Jerry Azumall, New Hampshire	1996	11	21	0	0	126	11.5
Barry Bourassa, New Hampshire	1991	11	21	0	0	126	11.5
Kenny Gamble, Colgate	1986	11	21	0	0	126	11.5
Gerald Harris, Ga. Southern	1984	9	17	0	0	102	11.3
Stan House, Central Conn. St.	1997	10	18	2	0	110	11.0
Richard Howell, Davidson	1993	10	18	2	0	110	11.0
Keith Elias, Princeton	1992	10	18	2	0	110	11.0
Harvey Reed, Howard	1986	10	18	2	0	110	11.0
Derrick Cullors, Murray St.	1995	11	20	0	0	120	10.9
Rupert Grant, Howard	1993	11	20	0	0	120	10.9
Toby Davis, Illinois St.	1992	11	20	0	0	120	10.9
Carl Smith, Maine	†1989	11	20	0	0	120	10.9
Joe Segreti, Holy Cross	1988	11	20	0	0	120	10.9
Luther Turner, Sam Houston St.	1987	11	20	0	0	120	10.9
John Settle, Appalachian St.	1986	11	20	0	0	120	10.9

*Record. †National champion.

CAREER POINTS

(Non-Kickers)

Player, Team	Years	TD	XPt.	Pts.
Sherriden May, Idaho	1991-94	*61	0	366
Charvez Foger, Nevada	1985-88	60	2	362
Kenny Gamble, Colgate	1984-87	57	0	342
Rene Ingoglia, Massachusetts	1992-95	55	2	332
Markus Thomas, Eastern Ky.	1989-92	53	4	322
Keith Elias, Princeton	1991-93	52	8	320
Michael Hicks, South Caro. St.	1993-95	52	4	316
Chris Parker, Marshall	1992-95	52	2	314
Thomas Haskins, VMI	1993-96	50	8	308
Paul Lewis, Boston U.	1981-84	51	2	308
Barry Bourassa, New Hampshire	1989-92	51	0	306
Erick Torain, Lehigh	1987-90	50	6	306
Jerry Rice, Mississippi Val.	1981-84	50	2	302
Claude Mathis, Southwest Tex. St.	1994-97	49	0	294
Harvey Reed, Howard	1984-87	48	6	294
Chad Levitt, Cornell	1993-96	48	4	292
Reggie Greene, Siena	1994-97	48	2	290
Stan House, Central Conn. St.	1994-97	48	2	290
Jack Douglas, Citadel (QB)	1989-92	48	0	288
Elroy Harris, Eastern Ky.	1985, 87-88	47	6	288
Joel Sigel, Portland St.	1978-80	46	2	278
Joe Campbell, Middle Tenn. St.	1988-91	45	2	272
Gerald Harris, Ga. Southern	1984-86	45	2	272
Carl Tremble, Furman	1989-92	45	0	270
Norm Ford, New Hampshire	1986-89	45	0	270
John Settle, Appalachian St.	1983-86	44	4	268
Ernest Thompson, Ga. Southern	1985, 87-89	44	2	266
Rennie Benn, Lehigh	1982-85	44	2	266
Joe Segreti, Holy Cross	1987-90	44	0	264
Gordie Lockbaum, Holy Cross	1984-87	44	0	264
Frank Hawkins, Nevada	1977-80	44	0	264

*Record.

CAREER POINTS

(Kickers)

Player, Team	Years	PAT	PAT Att.	FG	FG Att.	Pts.
Marty Zendejas, Nevada	1984-87	169	175	*72	90	*385
Dave Ettinger, Hofstra	1994-97	140	155	62	93	326
Brian Mitchell, Marshall/ Northern Iowa	1987, 89-91	130	131	64	81	322

Player, Team	Years	PAT	PAT Att.	FG	FG Att.	Pts.
Thayne Doyle, Idaho	1988-91	160	174	49	75	307
Jose Larios, McNeese St.	1992-95	133	136	57	89	304
Kirk Roach, Western Caro.	1984-87	89	91	71	*102	302
Tim Foley, Ga. Southern	1984-87	151	156	50	62	301
Dewey Klein, Marshall	1988-91	156	165	48	66	300
Tony Zendejas, Nevada	1981-83	90	96	70	86	300
Jeff Wilkins, Youngstown St.	1990-93	134	136	50	73	286
Garth Petrilli, Middle Tenn. St.	1991-94	166	170	38	60	280
Steve Christie, William & Mary	1986-89	108	116	57	83	279
Franco Grilla, Central Fla.	1989-92	141	147	45	69	278
Gilad Landau, Grambling	1991-94	*181	*194	32	50	277
Mike Black, Boise St.	1988-91	122	127	51	75	275
Kirk Duce, Montana	1988-91	131	141	47	78	272
Todd Kurz, Illinois St.	1993-96	89	94	59	87	266
Paul Hickert, Murray St.	1984-87	116	121	49	79	263
Dean Biasucci, Western Caro.	1980-83	101	106	54	80	263
Andy Larson, Montana	1993-96	177	188	28	45	261
Kelly Potter, Middle Tenn. St.	1981-84	105	109	52	78	261
Steve Largent, Eastern Ill.	1992-95	122	126	46	73	260
Brian Shallcross, William & Mary	1994-97	117	131	47	73	258
Billy Hayes, Sam Houston St.	1985-88	117	120	47	71	258
Michael O'Neal, Samford	1989-92	142	152	38	60	256
Tim Openlander, Marshall	1994-96	159	162	32	42	255
Jason McLaughlin, Lafayette	1991-94	131	138	41	74	254
Jim Hodson, Lafayette	1987-90	134	140	40	66	254
Dave Parkinson, Delaware St.	1985-88	134	143	40	77	254
Chuck Rawlinson, Stephen F. Austin	1988-91	106	110	49	69	253
Paul Politi, Illinois St.	1983-86	101	103	50	78	251
Wayne Boyer, Southwest Mo. St.	1993-96	100	104	49	71	247
Teddy Garcia, Northeast La.	1984-87	78	81	56	88	246
Paul McFadden, Youngstown St.	1980-83	87	90	52	90	243

*Record.

SEASON POINTS

Player, Team	Year	TD	XPt.	FG	Pts.
Geoff Mitchell, Weber St.	†1991	*28	2	0	*170
Jerry Rice, Mississippi Val.	†1984	27	0	0	162
Archie Amerson, Northern Ariz.	†1996	26	0	0	156
Aaron Stecker, Western Ill.	†1997	25	0	0	150
Sherriden May, Idaho	†1992	25	0	0	150
Tony Vinson, Towson	†1993	24	0	0	144
Rich Erenberg, Colgate	†1983	21	10	0	136
Alcede Surtain, Alabama St.	†1995	21	6	0	132
Michael Hicks, South Caro. St.	†1994	22	0	0	132
Sherriden May, Idaho	1993	22	0	0	132
Gordie Lockbaum, Holy Cross	1987	22	0	0	132
Gordie Lockbaum, Holy Cross	†1986	22	0	0	132
Keith Elias, Princeton	1993	21	4	0	130
Elroy Harris, Eastern Ky.	†1988	21	1	0	128
Jerry Azumah, New Hampshire	1996	21	0	0	126
Barry Bourassa, New Hampshire	1991	21	0	0	126
Sean Sanders, Weber St.	†1987	21	0	0	126
Kenny Gamble, Colgate	1986	21	0	0	126
Sean Bennett, Evansville	1997	20	2	0	122
Harvey Reed, Howard	1987	20	2	0	122
Paul Lewis, Boston U.	1983	20	2	0	122
Stan House, Central Conn. St.	1996	20	0	0	120
Tim Hall, Robert Morris	†1995	20	0	0	120
Derrick Cullors, Murray St.	1995	20	0	0	120
Rupert Grant, Howard	1993	20	0	0	120
Toby Davis, Illinois St.	1992	20	0	0	120
Carl Smith, Maine	†1989	20	0	0	120
Joe Segreti, Holy Cross	1988	20	0	0	120
Luther Turner, Sam Houston St.	1987	20	0	0	120
John Settle, Appalachian St.	1986	20	0	0	120
Gene Lake, Delaware St.	1984	20	0	0	120

*Record. †National champion.

ANNUAL CHAMPIONS

Year	Player, Team	Class	G	TD	XPt.	FG	Pts.	Avg.
1978	Frank Hawkins, Nevada	So.	10	17	0	0	102	10.2
1979	Joel Sigel, Portland St.	Jr.	10	16	0	0	96	9.6
1980	Ken Jenkins, Bucknell	Jr.	10	16	0	0	96	9.6
1981	Paris Wicks, Youngstown St.	Jr.	11	17	2	0	104	9.5
1982	Paul Lewis, Boston U.	So.	10	18	0	0	108	10.8
1983	Rich Erenberg, Colgate	Sr.	11	21	10	0	136	12.4
1984	Jerry Rice, Mississippi Val.	Sr.	10	27	0	0	162	*16.2
1985	Charvez Foger, Nevada	Fr.	10	18	0	0	108	10.8
1986	Gordie Lockbaum, Holy Cross	Jr.	11	22	0	0	132	12.0
1987	Sean Sanders, Weber St.	Sr.	10	21	0	0	126	12.6
1988	Elroy Harris, Eastern Ky.	Jr.	10	21	1	0	128	12.8
1989	Carl Smith, Maine	So.	11	20	0	0	120	10.9
1990	Barry Bourassa, New Hampshire	So.	9	16	0	0	96	10.7
1991	Geoff Mitchell, Weber St.	Sr.	11	*28	1	0	*170	15.5
1992	Sherriden May, Idaho	So.	11	25	0	0	150	13.6
1993	Tony Vinson, Towson	Sr.	10	24	0	0	144	14.4
1994	Michael Hicks, South Caro. St.	Jr.	11	22	0	0	132	12.0
1995	Alcede Surtain, Alabama St.	Sr.	11	21	6	0	132	12.0
	Tim Hall, Robert Morris	Sr.	10	20	0	0	120	12.0
1996	Archie Amerson, Northern Ariz.	Sr.	11	26	0	0	156	14.2
1997	Aaron Stecker, Western Ill.	Jr.	11	25	0	0	150	13.6

*Record.

Interceptions

CAREER INTERCEPTIONS

Player, Team	Years	No.	Yards	Avg.
Dave Murphy, Holy Cross	1986-89	*28	309	11.0
Cedric Walker, Stephen F. Austin	1990-93	25	230	9.2
Darren Sharper, William & Mary	1993-96	24	488	20.3
Issiac Holt, Alcorn St.	1981-84	24	319	13.3
Bill McGovern, Holy Cross	1981-84	24	168	7.0
Adrion Smith, Southwest Mo. St.	1990-93	23	219	9.5
William Carroll, Florida A&M	1989-92	23	328	14.3
Kevin Smith, Rhode Island	1987-90	23	287	12.5
Mike Prior, Illinois St.	1981-84	23	211	9.2
Robert Taylor, Tennessee Tech	1993-96	22	267	12.1
Chris Helon, Boston U.	1991-94	22	110	5.0
Morgan Ryan, Montana St.	1990-93	22	245	11.1
Dave Roberts, Youngstown St.	1989-92	22	131	6.0
Frank Robinson, Boise St.	1988-91	22	203	9.2
Dean Cain, Princeton	1985-87	22	203	9.2
Derek Carter, Maine	1994-97	21	301	14.3
Brian Randall, Delaware St.	1990-93	21	367	17.4
Kevin Dent, Jackson St.	1985-88	21	280	13.3
Mark Seals, Boston U.	1985-88	21	169	8.0
Jeff Smith, Illinois St.	1985-88	21	152	7.2
Chris Demarest, Northeastern	1984-87	21	255	12.1
Greg Greely, Nicholls St.	1981-84	21	218	10.4
George Floyd, Eastern Ky.	1978-81	21	318	15.1
William Hampton, Murray St.	1993-96	20	409	20.5
Rick Harris, East Tenn. St.	1986-88	20	*452	22.6
Mark Kelso, William & Mary	1981-84	20	171	8.6
Leslie Frazier, Alcorn St.	1977-80	20	269	13.5
Bob Jordan, New Hampshire	1990-93	19	96	5.1
Ricky Thomas, South Caro. St.	1988-91	19	374	19.7
Dwayne Harper, South Caro. St.	1984-87	19	163	8.6
Joe Burton, Delaware St.	1983-86	19	248	13.1
Michael Richardson, Northwestern St.	1981-84	19	344	18.1
Mike Genetti, Northeastern	1980-83	19	296	15.6
George Schmitt, Delaware	1980-82	19	280	14.7

*Record.

SEASON INTERCEPTIONS

Player, Team	Year	No.	Yards
Dean Cain, Princeton	†1987	*12	98
Aeneas Williams, Southern U.	‡1990	11	173
Claude Pettaway, Maine	‡1990	11	161
Bill McGovern, Holy Cross	†1984	11	102
Everson Walls, Grambling	†1980	11	145
Anthony Young, Jackson St.	†1978	11	108
Darren Sharper, William & Mary	1996	10	228
Scott Shields, Weber St.	1996	10	101
Chris Helon, Boston U.	†1993	10	42
Cedric Walker, Stephen F. Austin	1990	10	11
Chris Demarest, Northeastern	1987	10	129
Kevin Dent, Jackson St.	‡1986	10	192
Eric Thompson, New Hampshire	‡1986	10	94
Anthony Anderson, Grambling	‡1986	10	37
Mike Armentrout, Southwest Mo. St.	†1983	10	42
George Schmitt, Delaware	†1982	10	186
Mike Genetti, Northeastern	†1981	10	144
Bob Mahr, Lafayette	1981	10	48
Neale Henderson, Southern U.	†1979	10	151

*Record. †National champion. ‡National championship shared.

ANNUAL CHAMPIONS

(Ranked on Per-Game Average)

Year	Player, Team	Class	G	No.	Avg.	Yards
1978	Anthony Young, Jackson St.	Sr.	11	11	1.00	108
1979	Neale Henderson, Southern U.	Sr.	11	10	0.91	151
1980	Everson Walls, Grambling	Sr.	11	11	1.00	145
1981	Mike Genetti, Northeastern	So.	10	10	1.00	144
1982	George Schmitt, Delaware	Sr.	11	10	0.91	186

Year	Player, Team	Class	G	No.	Avg.	Yards
1983	Mike Armentrout, Southwest Mo. St.	Jr.	11	10	0.91	42
1984	Bill McGovern, Holy Cross	Sr.	11	11	1.00	102
1985	Mike Cassidy, Rhode Island	Sr.	10	9	0.90	169
	George Duarte, Northern Ariz.	Jr.	10	9	0.90	150
1986	Kevin Dent, Jackson St.	So.	11	10	0.91	192
	Eric Thompson, New Hampshire	Sr.	11	10	0.91	94
	Anthony Anderson, Grambling	Sr.	11	10	0.91	37
1987	Dean Cain, Princeton	Sr.	10	*12	*1.20	98
1988	Kevin Smith, Rhode Island	So.	10	9	0.90	94
1989	Mike Babb, Weber St.	Sr.	11	9	0.82	90
1990	Aeneas Williams, Southern U.	Sr.	11	11	1.00	173
	Claude Pettaway, Maine	Sr.	11	11	1.00	161
1991	Warren McIntire, Delaware	Jr.	11	9	0.82	208
1992	Dave Roberts, Youngstown St.	Sr.	11	9	0.82	39
1993	Chris Helon, Boston U.	Jr.	11	10	0.91	42
1994	Joseph Vaughn, Cal St. Northridge	Sr.	10	9	0.90	265
	Brian Clark, Hofstra	Jr.	10	9	0.90	56
1995	Picasso Nelson, Jackson St.	Sr.	9	8	0.89	101
1996	Shane Hurd, Canisius	Jr.	7	7	1.00	198
1997	Roderic Parson, Brown	Sr.	8	8	1.00	93

*Record.

Punting

CAREER AVERAGE

(Minimum 150 Punts)

Player, Team	Years	No.	Yards	Long	Avg.
Pumpy Tudors, Chattanooga	1989-91	181	8,041	79	*44.4
Case de Bruijn, Idaho St.	1978-81	256	11,184	76	43.7
Terry Belden, Northern Ariz.	1990-93	225	9,760	76	43.4
George Cimadevilla, East Tenn. St.	1983-86	225	9,676	72	43.0
Harold Alexander, Appalachian St.	1989-92	259	11,100	78	42.9
Brad Costello, Boston U.	1995-97	193	8,206	73	42.5
John Christopher, Morehead St.	1979-82	298	12,633	62	42.4
Colin Godfrey, Tennessee St.	1989-92	213	9,012	69	42.3
Bret Wright, Southeastern La.	1981-83	165	6,963	66	42.2
Jeff Kaiser, Idaho St.	1982-84	156	6,571	88	42.1
Greg Davis, Citadel	1983-86	263	11,076	81	42.1
Mark Royals, Appalachian St.	1983-85	223	9,372	67	42.0

*Record.

SEASON AVERAGE

(Qualifiers for Championship)

Player, Team	Year	No.	Yards	Avg.
Harold Alexander, Appalachian St.	†1991	64	3,009	*47.0
Terry Belden, Northern Ariz.	†1993	59	2,712	46.0
Case de Bruijn, Idaho St.	†1981	42	1,928	45.9
Colin Godfrey, Tennessee St.	†1990	57	2,614	45.9
Barry Cantrell, Fordham	†1997	65	2,980	45.9
Stuart Dodds, Montana St.	†1979	59	2,689	45.6
Pumpy Tudors, Chattanooga	1991	53	2,414	45.5
Mark Gagliano, Southern Ill.	†1996	54	2,432	45.0
Paul Asbury, Southwest Tex. St.	1990	39	1,749	44.9
Tom Sugg, Idaho	1991	53	2,371	44.7
Chad Stanley, Stephen F. Austin	1997	62	2,771	44.7
Mike Rice, Montana	†1985	62	2,771	44.7
Case de Bruijn, Idaho St.	1979	73	3,261	44.7
George Cimadevilla, East Tenn. St.	1985	66	2,948	44.7
Greg Davis, Citadel	†1986	61	2,723	44.6
Pumpy Tudors, Chattanooga	1990	63	2,810	44.6
Pat Velarde, Marshall	†1983	64	2,852	44.6
Bart Bradley, Sam Houston St.	1986	44	1,957	44.5
Harold Alexander, Appalachian St.	†1992	55	2,445	44.5
Curtis Moody, Texas Southern	1985	64	2,844	44.4
Terry Belden, Northern Ariz.	1991	43	1,908	44.4
Brad Costello, Boston U.	1997	73	3,239	44.4
Terry Belden, Northern Ariz.	1992	59	2,614	44.3
Bret Wright, Southeastern La.	1983	66	2,923	44.3
George Cimadevilla, East Tenn. St.	1986	65	2,876	44.2
Ken Hinsley, Western Caro.	1997	46	2,032	44.2
Steve Thorns, Cal St. Sacramento	1997	66	2,907	44.1
Case de Bruijn, Idaho St.	†1980	67	2,945	44.0

*Record. †National champion.

ANNUAL CHAMPIONS

Year	Player, Team	Class	No.	Yards	Avg.
1978	Nick Pavich, Nevada	So.	47	1,939	41.3
1979	Stuart Dodds, Montana St.	Sr.	59	2,689	45.6
1980	Case de Bruijn, Idaho St.	Jr.	67	2,945	44.0
1981	Case de Bruijn, Idaho St.	Sr.	42	1,928	45.9
1982	John Christopher, Morehead St.	Sr.	93	4,084	43.9
1983	Pat Velarde, Marshall	Sr.	64	2,852	44.6
1984	Steve Kornegay, Western Caro.	Jr.	49	2,127	43.4
1985	Mike Rice, Montana	Jr.	62	2,771	44.7
1986	Greg Davis, Citadel	Sr.	61	2,723	44.6
1987	Eric Stein, Eastern Wash.	Sr.	74	3,193	43.2
1988	Mike McCabe, Illinois St.	Sr.	69	3,042	44.1
1989	Pumpy Tudors, Chattanooga	So.	65	2,817	43.3
1990	Colin Godfrey, Tennessee St.	So.	57	2,614	45.9
1991	Harold Alexander, Appalachian St.	Jr.	64	3,009	*47.0
1992	Harold Alexander, Appalachian St.	Sr.	55	2,445	44.5
1993	Terry Belden, Northern Ariz.	Sr.	59	2,712	46.0
1994	Scott Holmes, Samford	Jr.	49	2,099	42.8
1995	Kevin O'Leary, Northern Ariz.	Sr.	44	1,881	42.8
1996	Mark Gagliano, Southern Ill.	Sr.	54	2,432	45.0
1997	Barry Cantrell, Forham	Sr.	65	2,980	45.9

*Record.

Punt Returns

CAREER AVERAGE

(Minimum 1.2 Returns Per Game; Minimum 30 Returns)

Player, Team	Years	No.	Yards	Avg.
Willie Ware, Mississippi Val.	1982-85	61	1,003	*16.4
Buck Phillips, Western Ill.	1994-95	40	656	16.4
Tim Egerton, Delaware St.	1986-89	59	951	16.1
Mark Orlando, Towson	1991-94	41	644	15.7
John Armstrong, Richmond	1984-85	31	449	14.5
Ricky Pearsall, Northern Ariz.	1994-97	39	546	14.0
Undre Williams, Florida A&M	1995-97	31	429	13.8
Kenny Shedd, Northern Iowa	1989-92	79	1,081	13.7
Chris Berry, Morehead St.	1994-97	37	505	13.7
Dione Tyler, Southeast Mo. St.	1994-95	39	523	13.5
Reggie Barlow, Alabama St.	1992-95	49	645	13.2
Joe Fuller, Northern Iowa	1982-85	69	888	12.9
Eric Yarber, Idaho	1984-85	32	406	12.7
Troy Brown, Marshall	1991-92	36	455	12.6
Goree White, Alcorn St.	1993-96	70	902	12.5
Kerry Hayes, Western Caro.	1991-94	70	876	12.5
Trumaine Johnson, Grambling	1979-82	53	662	12.5
Tony Merriwether, North Texas	1982-83	41	507	12.4
Eric Alden, Idaho St.	1992-93	31	383	12.4
Thaylen Armstead, Grambling	1989-91	44	540	12.3
Trevor Bell, Idaho St.	1995-97	38	461	12.3
Barney Bussey, South Caro. St.	1980-83	47	573	12.2
Cornell Johnson, Southern U.	1990-92	40	482	12.1
Ricky Ellis, St. Mary's (Cal.)	1994-96	32	384	12.0
John Taylor, Delaware St.	1982-85	48	576	12.0

*Record.

SEASON AVERAGE

(Minimum 1.2 Returns Per Game and Qualifiers for Championship)

Player, Team	Year	No.	Yards	Avg.
Tim Egerton, Delaware St.	†1988	16	368	*23.0
Ryan Priest, Lafayette	†1982	12	271	22.6
Chris Berry, Morehead St.	†1997	13	273	21.0
Craig Hodge, Tennessee St.	†1987	19	398	21.0
Reggie Barlow, Alabama St.	†1995	12	249	20.8
John Armstrong, Richmond	†1985	19	391	20.6
Mark Orlando, Towson	†1994	19	377	19.8
Willie Ware, Mississippi Val.	†1984	19	374	19.7
Buck Phillips, Western Ill.	1994	24	464	19.3
Mark Hurt, Alabama St.	1988	10	185	18.5
Howard Huckaby, Florida A&M	1988	26	478	18.4
Ashley Ambrose, Mississippi Val.	†1991	28	514	18.4
Quincy Miller, South Caro. St.	†1992	17	311	18.3
Barney Bussey, South Caro. St.	†1981	14	255	18.2
Chris Darrington, Weber St.	†1986	16	290	18.1
Willie Ware, Mississippi Val.	1985	31	*561	18.1
Kerry Lawyer, Boise St.	1992	18	325	18.1
Kenny Shedd, Northern Iowa	1992	27	477	17.7
Claude Mathis, Southwest Tex. St.	1995	20	352	17.6
Clarence Alexander, Mississippi Val.	1986	22	380	17.3
Henry Richard, Northeast La.	†1989	15	258	17.2
Ray Marshall, St. Peter's	†1993	10	171	17.1
Delvin Joyce, James Madison	1997	17	289	17.0
Ricky Pearsall, Northern Ariz.	†1996	29	490	16.9
Carl Williams, Texas Southern	1981	16	269	16.8
Jerome Bledsoe, Massachusetts	1988	17	285	16.8

*Record. †National champion.

ANNUAL CHAMPIONS

Year	Player, Team	Class	No.	Yards	Avg.
1978	Ray Smith, Northern Ariz.	Sr.	13	181	13.9
1979	Joseph Markus, Connecticut	Fr.	17	219	12.9
1980	Trumaine Johnson, Grambling	So.	††13	226	17.4
1981	Barney Bussey, South Caro. St.	So.	14	255	18.2
1982	Ryan Priest, Lafayette	Fr.	12	271	22.6
1983	Joe Fuller, Northern Iowa	So.	22	344	15.6
1984	Willie Ware, Mississippi Val.	Jr.	19	374	19.7
1985	John Armstrong, Richmond	Sr.	19	391	20.6
1986	Chris Darrington, Weber St.	Sr.	16	290	18.1
1987	Craig Hodge, Tennessee St.	Sr.	19	398	21.0
1988	Tim Egerton, Delaware St.	Jr.	16	368	*23.0
1989	Henry Richard, Northeast La.	Jr.	15	258	17.2
1990	Gary Harrell, Howard	Fr.	26	417	16.0
1991	Ashley Ambrose, Mississippi Val.	Sr.	28	514	18.4
1992	Quincy Miller, South Caro. St.	Jr.	17	311	18.3
1993	Ray Marshall, St. Peter's	Jr.	10	171	17.1
1994	Mark Orlando, Towson	Sr.	19	377	19.8
1995	Reggie Barlow, Alabama St.	Sr.	12	249	20.8
1996	Ricky Pearsall, Northern Ariz.	Jr.	29	490	16.9
1997	Chris Berry, Morehead St.	Sr.	13	273	21.0

Record. ††Declared champion; with one more return (making 1.3 per game) for zero yards, still would have highest average.

Kickoff Returns

CAREER AVERAGE

(Minimum 1.2 Returns Per Game; Minimum 30 Returns)

Player, Team	Years	No.	Yards	Avg.
Troy Brown, Marshall	1991-92	32	950	*29.7
Charles Swann, Indiana St.	1989-91	45	1,319	29.3
Craig Richardson, Eastern Wash.	1983-86	71	2,021	28.5
Kenyatta Sparks, Southern U.	1992-95	39	1,100	28.2
Kerry Hayes, Western Caro.	1991-94	73	2,058	28.2
Daryl Holcombe, Eastern Ill.	1986-89	49	1,379	28.1
Dwight Robinson, James Madison	1990-93	51	1,434	28.1
Curtis Chappell, Howard	1984-87	42	1,177	28.0
Leon Brown, Eastern Ky.	1990-93	44	1,230	28.0
Josh Cole, Furman	1993-96	65	1,808	27.8
Joe Rosato, Duquesne	1994-97	60	1,661	27.7
Marcus Durgin, Samford	1990-93	44	1,218	27.7
Cornelius Turner, Mississippi Val.	1992-94	50	1,379	27.6
Anthony Taylor, Northern Iowa	1992-95	30	821	27.4
Jerry Parrish, Eastern Ky.	1978-81	61	1,668	27.3
Tony James, Eastern Ky.	1982-84	57	1,552	27.2
Ricky Ellis, St. Mary's (Cal.)	1994-96	31	836	27.0
Frank Selto, Idaho St.	1986-87	30	803	26.8
Chris Hickman, Northeast La.	1991-92	30	798	26.6
Chris Pollard, Dartmouth	1986-88	52	1,376	26.5
John Jarvis, Howard	1986-88	39	1,031	26.4
Ronald Scott, Southern U.	1982-85	38	1,003	26.4
Rob Tesch, Montana St.	1989-92	50	1,317	26.3
Vernon Williams, Eastern Wash.	1986-88	40	1,052	26.3
Steve Ortman, Pennsylvania	1982-84	31	808	26.1
John Armstrong, Richmond	1984-85	32	826	25.8
Renard Coleman, Montana	1985-88	57	1,465	25.7
Michael Haynes, Northern Ariz.	1986-87	36	925	25.7
Jeb Dougherty, San Diego	1993-96	62	1,589	25.6
Kevin Gainer, Bethune-Cookman	1988-90	42	1,070	25.5
Archie Herring, Youngstown St.	1987-90	79	2,005	25.4
Kenny Shedd, Northern Iowa	1989-92	54	1,359	25.2
Damon Boddie, Montana	1993-94	49	1,232	25.1
Joey Stockton, Western Ky.	1994-97	87	2,175	25.0
Michael High, North Texas	1991-93	47	1,171	24.9
David Smith, Northeastern	1994-97	60	1,484	24.7
Andy Swafford, Troy St.	1995-97	31	764	24.7
Jerome Stelly, Western Ill.	1981-82	42	1,024	24.4
Kino Carson, Northern Ariz.	1996-97	32	778	24.3
Chris Pierce, Rhode Island	1989-92	63	1,521	24.1
Albert Brown, Western Ill.	1985-86	30	723	24.1
Sylvester Stamps, Jackson St.	1980, 82-83	42	1,012	24.1
Sean Hill, Montana St.	1991-93	44	1,060	24.1

Record.

SEASON AVERAGE

(Minimum 1.2 Returns Per Game and Qualifiers for Championship)

Player, Team	Year	No.	Yards	Avg.
David Fraterrigo, Canisius	†1993	13	485	*37.3
Kerry Hayes, Western Caro.	1993	16	584	36.5
Craig Richardson, Eastern Wash.	†1984	21	729	34.7
Randy Moss, Marshall	†1996	14	484	34.6
Errin Hatwood, St. John's (N.Y.)	†1994	12	401	33.4
Marcus Durgin, Samford	†1992	15	499	33.3
Rory Lee, Western Ill.	1993	16	527	32.9
Dave Meggett, Towson	†1988	13	418	32.2
Josh Cole, Furman	†1995	17	546	32.1
Charles Swann, Indiana St.	†1990	20	642	32.1
Tyree Talton, Northern Iowa	1996	22	703	32.0
Archie Herring, Youngstown St.	1990	18	575	31.9
Dwight Robinson, James Madison	1994	16	510	31.9
Davlin Mullen, Western Ky.	†1982	18	574	31.9
Todd Cleveland, Central Fla.	1994	15	476	31.7
Naylon Albritton, South Caro. St.	1993	15	475	31.7
Jermine Sharp, Southern U.	1995	16	504	31.5
Andy Swafford, Troy St.	†1997	14	440	31.4
Ozzie Young, Valparaiso	1994	17	533	31.4
Danny Copeland, Eastern Ky.	†1986	26	812	31.2
Chris Chappell, Howard	1986	17	528	31.1
Thomas Haskins, VMI	1994	15	464	30.9
Dave Loehle, New Hampshire	†1978	15	460	30.7
Paul Ashby, Alabama St.	†1991	17	520	30.6
Juan Jackson, North Caro. A&T	1986	16	487	30.4
Kevin Gainer, Bethune-Cookman	1990	21	635	30.2
Ed Williams, St. Mary's (Cal.)	1996	16	482	30.1
Howard Huckaby, Florida A&M	†1987	20	602	30.1
Tony James, Eastern Ky.	†1983	17	511	30.1

Record. †National champion.

ANNUAL CHAMPIONS

Year	Player, Team	Class	No.	Yards	Avg.
1978	Dave Loehle, New Hampshire	Jr.	15	460	30.7
1979	Garry Pearson, Massachusetts	Fr.	12	348	29.0
1980	Danny Thomas, North Caro. A&T	Fr.	15	381	25.4
1981	Jerry Parrish, Eastern Ky.	Sr.	18	534	29.7
1982	Davlin Mullen, Western Ky.	Sr.	18	574	31.9
1983	Tony James, Eastern Ky.	Jr.	17	511	30.1
1984	Craig Richardson, Eastern Wash.	So.	21	729	34.7
1985	Rodney Payne, Murray St.	Fr.	16	464	29.0
1986	Danny Copeland, Eastern Ky.	Jr.	26	812	31.2
1987	Howard Huckaby, Florida A&M	So.	20	602	30.1
1988	Dave Meggett, Towson	Sr.	13	418	32.2
1989	Scott Thomas, Liberty	Fr.	13	373	28.7
1990	Charles Swann, Indiana St.	Jr.	20	642	32.1
1991	Paul Ashby, Alabama St.	Jr.	17	520	30.6
1992	Marcus Durgin, Samford	Jr.	15	499	33.3
1993	David Fraterrigo, Canisius	Sr.	13	485	*37.3
1994	Errin Hatwood, St. John's (N.Y.)	Sr.	12	401	33.4
1995	Josh Cole, Furman	Jr.	17	546	32.1
1996	Randy Moss, Marshall	Fr.	14	484	34.6
1997	Andy Swafford, Troy St.	Sr.	14	440	31.4

Record.

All-Purpose Yards

CAREER YARDS PER GAME

(Minimum 3,200 Yards)

Player, Team	Years	Rush	Rcv.	Int.	PR	KOR	Yds.	Yd. PG
Arnold Mickens, Butler	1994-95	3,813	47	0	0	87	3,947	*197.4
Tim Hall, Robert Morris	1994-95	2,908	793	0	0	0	3,701	194.8
Reggie Greene, Siena	1994-97	*5,415	274	0	53	1,217	6,959	193.3
Dave Meggett, Towson	1987-88	1,658	788	0	212	745	3,403	189.1
Archie Amerson, Northern Ariz.	1995-96	3,196	484	0	0	382	4,062	184.6
Kenny Gamble, Colgate	1984-87	5,220	536	0	104	1,763	*7,623	181.5
Rich Erenberg, Colgate	1982-83	2,618	423	0	268	315	3,624	172.6
Claude Mathis, Southwest Tex. St.	1994-97	4,691	744	0	635	1,353	7,423	168.7
Thomas Haskins, VMI	1993-96	5,355	179	0	216	1,661	7,411	168.4
Ozzie Young, Valparaiso	1993-95	1,576	1,123	0	418	1,728	4,845	167.1
Fine Unga, Weber St.	1987-88	2,298	391	0	7	967	3,663	166.5
Gill Fenerty, Holy Cross	1983-85	3,618	477	0	1	731	4,827	160.9
Keith Elias, Princeton	1991-93	4,208	508	0	0	25	4,741	158.0
Don Wilkerson, Southwest Tex. St.	1993-94	2,356	255	0	83	757	3,451	156.9
Kito Lockwood, Wagner	1993-95	2,576	891	0	0	420	3,887	155.5
Barry Bourassa, New Hampshire	1989-92	2,960	1,307	0	306	1,370	5,943	152.4
Judd Garrett, Princeton	1987-89	3,109	1,385	0	0	10	4,510	150.3
Treamelle Taylor, Nevada	1987-90	0	1,926	0	662	687	3,275	148.9
Troy Brown, Marshall	1991-92	138	1,716	0	455	950	3,259	148.1
Andre Garron, New Hampshire	1982-85	2,901	809	0	8	651	4,369	145.6
Carl Boyd, Northern Iowa	1983, 85-87	2,735	1,987	0	0	183	4,905	144.3
Merril Hoge, Idaho St.	1983-86	2,713	1,734	0	1	1,005	5,453	139.8
Rich Lemon, Bucknell	1993-96	4,742	961	0	99	150	5,952	138.4
Pete Mandley, Northern Ariz.	1979-80, 82-83	436	2,598	11	901	1,979	5,925	137.8
Erik Marsh, Lafayette	1991-94	4,834	383	0	76	490	5,783	137.7
Joey Stockton, Western Ky.	1994-97	248	1,878	0	627	2,175	4,928	136.9
Kerry Hayes, Western Caro.	1991-94	75	2,594	0	876	2,058	5,603	136.7
Frank Hawkins, Nevada	1977-80	5,333	519	0	0	0	5,852	136.1
Derrick Harmon, Cornell	1981-83	3,074	679	0	5	42	3,800	135.7
Dorron Hunter, Morehead St.	1977-80	1,336	1,320	0	510	1,970	5,136	135.2

*Record.

SEASON YARDS PER GAME

Player, Team	Year	Rush	Rcv.	Int.	PR	KOR	Yds.	Yd. PG
Reggie Greene, Siena	†1996	1,719	50	0	0	337	2,106	*234.0
Arnold Mickens, Butler	†1994	*2,255	7	0	0	0	2,262	226.2
Reggie Greene, Siena	†1997	1,719	50	0	0	158	2,009	223.2
Archie Amerson, Northern Ariz.	1996	2,079	262	0	0	88	*2,429	220.8
Kenny Gamble, Colgate	†1986	1,816	178	0	40	391	2,425	220.5
Reggie Greene, Siena	†1995	1,461	77	0	53	363	1,954	217.1
Michael Clemons, William & Mary	1986	1,065	516	0	330	423	2,334	212.2
Tony Vinson, Towson	†1993	2,016	57	0	0	0	2,073	207.3
Derrick Cullors, Murray St.	1995	1,765	312	0	0	201	2,278	207.1
Clarence Matthews, Northwestern St.	1995	1,384	194	0	145	554	2,277	207.0
Claude Mathis, Southwest Tex. St.	1995	1,286	315	0	352	308	2,261	205.6
Anthony Jordan, Samford	1994	924	400	0	169	767	2,260	205.5
Sean Bennett, Evansville	1997	1,668	260	0	81	34	2,043	204.3
Aaron Stecker, Western Ill.	1997	1,957	288	0	0	0	2,245	204.1
Rich Erenberg, Colgate	†1983	1,883	214	0	126	18	2,241	203.7
Kenny Bynum, South Caro. St.	1996	1,649	118	0	1	255	2,023	202.3
Jerry Azumah, New Hampshire	1997	1,572	297	0	0	351	2,220	201.8
Tim Hall, Robert Morris	1994	1,336	460	0	0	0	1,796	199.6
Joey Stockton, Western Ky.	1995	46	863	0	147	934	1,990	199.0
Dave Meggett, Towson	†1987	814	572	0	78	327	1,791	199.0
Gordie Lockbaum, Holy Cross	1986	827	860	34	0	452	2,173	197.6
Gill Fenerty, Holy Cross	†1985	1,368	187	0	1	414	1,970	197.0
Barry Bourassa, New Hampshire	†1991	1,130	426	0	0	596	2,152	195.6
Sean Bennett, Evansville	1996	1,189	740	0	0	27	1,956	195.6
Thomas Haskins, VMI	1995	1,548	33	0	0	553	2,134	194.0
Keith Elias, Princeton	1993	1,731	193	0	0	15	1,939	193.9
Rick Sarille, Wagner	1996	1,475	36	0	0	427	1,938	193.8
Barry Bourassa, New Hampshire	†1990	957	276	0	133	368	1,734	192.7
Sean Morey, Brown	1997	10	1,427	0	15	465	1,922	192.2
Merril Hoge, Idaho St.	1985	1,041	708	0	0	364	2,113	192.1
Jerry Azumah, New Hampshire	1996	1,308	521	0	0	280	2,109	191.7
Thomas Haskins, VMI	1996	1,704	66	0	216	112	2,098	190.7
Andre Garron, New Hampshire	1983	1,009	539	0	0	359	1,907	190.7
Kenny Gamble, Colgate	1987	1,411	151	0	64	471	2,097	190.6
Tim Hall, Robert Morris	1995	1,572	333	0	0	0	1,905	190.5
Kito Lockwood, Wagner	1995	1,018	187	0	0	127	1,332	190.3
Otis Washington, Western Caro.	†1988	64	907	0	0	1,113	2,086	189.6
Rick Sarille, Wagner	1997	1,285	85	0	0	514	1,884	188.4
Ken Jenkins, Bucknell	†1980	1,270	293	0	65	256	1,884	188.4
Don Wilkerson, Southwest Tex. St.	1994	1,569	131	0	21	327	2,048	186.2
Kenny Gamble, Colgate	1985	1,361	162	0	0	520	2,043	185.7
Gordie Lockbaum, Holy Cross	1987	403	1,152	0	209	277	2,041	185.6
Ozzie Young, Valparaiso	1994	606	426	0	96	533	1,661	184.6
Thomas Haskins, VMI	1994	1,509	50	0	0	464	2,023	183.9

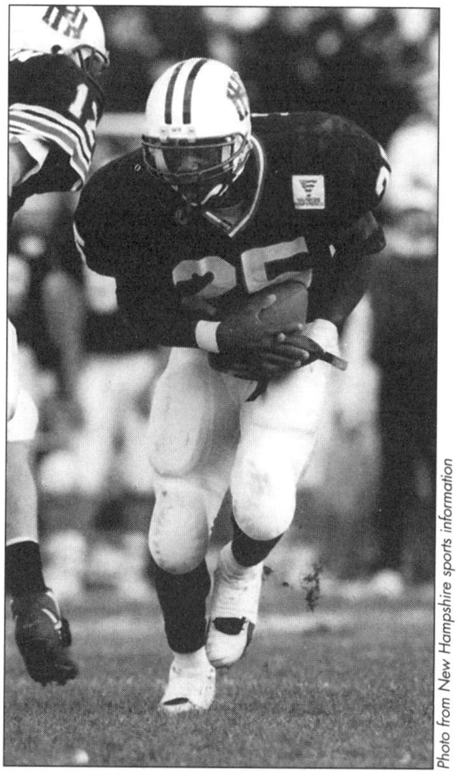

Photo from New Hampshire sports information

New Hampshire running back Jerry Azumah gained 2,109 all-purpose yards in 1996 and followed that up with 2,220 more in 1997.

DIVISION I-AA

Player, Team	Year	Rush	Rcv.	Int.	PR	KOR	Yds.	Yd. PG
Dominic Corr, Eastern Wash.	†1989	796	52	0	0	807	1,655	183.9
Al Rosier, Dartmouth	1991	1,432	113	0	0	290	1,835	183.5
Jerome Bledsoe, Massachusetts	1991	1,545	178	0	0	293	2,016	183.3
David Wright, Indiana St.	†1992	1,313	108	0	0	593	2,014	183.1

**Record. †National champion.*

CAREER YARDS

Player, Team	Years	Rush	Rcv.	Int.	PR	KOR	Yds.	Yd. PP
Kenny Gamble, Colgate	1984-87	5,220	536	0	104	1,763	*7,623	7.0
Claude Mathis, Southwest Tex. St.	1994-97	4,691	744	0	635	1,353	7,423	7.0
Thomas Haskins, VMI	1993-96	5,355	179	0	216	1,661	7,411	7.2
Reggie Greene, Siena	1994-97	*5,415	274	0	53	1,217	6,959	7.1
Rich Lemon, Bucknell	1993-96	4,742	961	0	99	150	5,952	5.2
Barry Bourassa, New Hampshire	1989-92	2,960	1,307	0	306	1,370	5,943	7.5
Pete Mandley, Northern Ariz.	1979-80, 82-83	436	2,598	11	901	1,979	5,925	14.8
Frank Hawkins, Nevada	1977-80	5,333	519	0	0	0	5,852	5.8
Erik Marsh, Lafayette	1991-94	4,834	383	0	76	490	5,783	5.2
Kerry Hayes, Western Caro.	1991-94	5	2,594	0	876	2,058	5,603	*19.1
Jamie Jones, Eastern Ill.	1988-91	3,466	816	0	66	1,235	5,583	6.2
Chris Parker, Marshall	1992-95	4,571	838	0	0	133	5,542	6.5
Sherriden May, Idaho	1991-94	3,748	926	0	153	646	5,473	6.9
Merril Hoge, Idaho St.	1983-86	2,713	1,734	0	1	1,005	5,453	6.6
Herman Hunter, Tennessee St.	1981-84	1,049	1,129	0	974	*2,258	5,410	10.5
David Wright, Indiana St.	1992-95	4,181	255	0	0	904	5,340	6.2
Cedric Minter, Boise St.	1977-80	4,475	525	0	49	267	5,316	6.5
Charvez Foger, Nevada	1985-88	4,484	821	0	0	0	5,305	5.7
Garry Pearson, Massachusetts	1979-82	3,859	466	0	0	952	5,277	5.9
John Settle, Appalachian St.	1983-86	4,409	526	0	0	319	5,254	5.3
Joe Rosato, Duquesne	1994-97	80	2,360	0	1,036	1,661	5,137	15.6
Dorron Hunter, Morehead St.	1977-80	1,336	1,320	0	510	1,970	5,136	9.6

**Record.*

SEASON YARDS

Player, Team	Years	Rush	Rcv.	Int.	PR	KOR	Yds.	Yd. PP
Archie Amerson, Northern Ariz.	1996	2,079	262	0	0	88	*2,429	6.9
Kenny Gamble, Colgate	†1986	1,816	178	0	40	391	2,425	7.1
Michael Clemons, William & Mary	1986	1,065	516	0	330	423	2,334	6.7
Derrick Cullors, Murray St.	1995	1,765	312	0	0	201	2,278	7.6
Clarence Matthews, Northwestern St.	1995	1,384	194	0	145	554	2,277	7.7
Arnold Mickens, Butler	†1994	*2,255	7	0	0	0	2,262	5.5
Claude Mathis, Southwest Tex. St.	1995	1,286	315	0	352	308	2,261	7.3
Anthony Jordan, Samford	1994	924	400	0	169	767	2,260	10.8
Aaron Stecker, Western Ill.	1997	1,957	288	0	0	0	2,245	6.9
Rich Erenberg, Colgate	†1983	1,883	214	0	126	18	2,241	6.7
Jerry Azumah, New Hampshire	1997	1,572	297	0	0	351	2,220	7.2
Gordie Lockbaum, Holy Cross	1986	827	860	34	0	452	2,173	9.7
Barry Bourassa, New Hampshire	†1991	1,130	426	0	0	596	2,152	7.5
Thomas Haskins, VMI	1995	1,548	33	0	0	553	2,134	7.6
Merril Hoge, Idaho St.	1985	1,041	708	0	0	364	2,113	7.4
Jerry Azumah, New Hampshire	1996	1,308	521	0	0	280	2,109	7.0
Reggie Greene, Siena	1996	1,719	50	0	0	337	2,106	6.9
Thomas Haskins, VMI	1996	1,704	66	0	216	112	2,098	6.4
Kenny Gamble, Colgate	1987	1,411	151	0	64	471	2,097	6.5
Otis Washington, Western Caro.	†1988	66	907	0	0	1,113	2,086	*19.7
Tony Vinson, Towson	†1993	2,016	57	0	0	0	2,073	6.8
Don Wilkerson, Southwest Tex. St.	1994	1,569	131	0	21	327	2,048	6.2
Sean Bennett, Evansville	1997	1,668	260	0	81	34	2,043	7.7
Kenny Gamble, Colgate	1985	1,361	162	0	0	520	2,043	7.3
Gordie Lockbaum, Holy Cross	1987	403	1,152	0	209	277	2,041	10.4
Kenny Bynum, South Caro. St.	1996	1,649	118	0	1	255	2,023	7.7
Thomas Haskins, VMI	1994	1,509	50	0	0	464	2,023	7.2
Jerome Bledsoe, Massachusetts	1991	1,545	178	0	0	293	2,016	6.7
David Wright, Indiana St.	†1992	1,313	108	0	0	593	2,014	7.9
Mark Stock, VMI	1988	90	1,161	0	260	500	2,011	14.0
Reggie Greene, Siena	†1997	1,778	73	0	0	158	2,009	7.4
Michael Cosey, Southwest Mo. St.	†1996	1,453	555	0	0	0	2,008	5.9
Jamie Jones, Eastern Ill.	1991	1,403	299	0	0	305	2,007	7.2

**Record. †National champion.*

ALL-PURPOSE SINGLE-GAME HIGHS

Yds.	Player, Team (Opponent)	Date
467	Joey Stockton, Western Ky. (Austin Peay)	Sept. 16, 1995
463	Michael Lerch, Princeton (Brown)	Oct. 12, 1991
453	Herman Hunter, Tennessee St. (Mississippi Val.)	Nov. 13, 1982
420	Reggie Greene, Siena (St. Johns [N.Y.])	Nov. 2, 1996
395	Scott Oliaro, Cornell (Yale)	Nov. 3, 1990
386	Gill Fenerty, Holy Cross (Columbia)	Oct. 29, 1983
378	Joe Delaney, Northwestern St. (Nicholls St.)	Oct. 28, 1978
373	Aaron Stecker, Western Ill. (Southern Ill.)	Nov. 1, 1997
373	William Arnold, Jackson St. (Texas Southern)	Nov. 6, 1993
372	Gary Harrell, Howard (Morgan St.)	Nov. 3, 1990

Yds.	Player, Team (Opponent)	Date
372	Treamelle Taylor, Nevada (Montana)	Oct. 14, 1989
369	Flip Johnson, McNeese St. (Southwestern La.)	Nov. 15, 1986
367	Chris Darrington, Weber St. (Idaho St.)	Oct. 25, 1986
365	Erwin Matthews, Richmond (Delaware)	Sept. 26, 1987
361	Patrick Robinson, Tennessee St. (Jackson St.)	Sept. 12, 1992
358	Claude Mathis, Southwest Tex. St. (Eastern Wash.)	Sept. 7, 1995
357	Tony Vinson, Towson (Bucknell)	Nov. 13, 1993
352	Jason Anderson, Eastern Wash. (Montana)	Sept. 17, 1994
352	Andre Garron, New Hampshire (Lehigh)	Oct. 15, 1983
349	Jerry Azumah, New Hampshire (Lehigh)	Oct. 12, 1996
347	Tony Vinson, Towson (Morgan St.)	Nov. 20, 1993
345	Kenny Bynum, South Caro. St. (North Caro. A&T)	Nov. 23, 1996
345	Russell Davis, Idaho (Weber St.)	Oct. 2, 1982
343	Jason Corle, Towson, (Robert Morris)	Oct. 18, 1997
343	Rick Sarille, Wagner (St. Peter's)	Sept. 29, 1995
342	Chris Berry, Morehead St. (Charleston So.)	Nov. 8, 1997
341	Tyrone Taylor, Cal St. Sacramento (Cal St. Northridge)	Oct. 25, 1997
341	Barry Bourassa, New Hampshire (Delaware)	Oct. 5, 1991
340	Reggie Greene, Siena (St. John's [N.Y.])	Oct. 28, 1995
340	Gene Lake, Delaware St. (Liberty)	Nov. 10, 1984

ANNUAL CHAMPIONS

Year	Player, Team	Class	Rush	Rcv.	Int.	PR	KOR	Yds.	Yd. PG
1978	Frank Hawkins, Nevada	So.	1,445	211	0	0	0	1,656	165.6
1979	Frank Hawkins, Nevada	Jr.	1,683	123	0	0	0	1,806	164.2
1980	Ken Jenkins, Bucknell	Jr.	1,270	293	0	65	256	1,884	188.4
1981	Garry Pearson, Massachusetts	Jr.	1,026	105	0	0	450	1,581	175.7
1982	Pete Mandley, Northern Ariz.	Jr.	36	1,067	0	344	532	1,979	179.9
1983	Rich Erenberg, Colgate	Sr.	1,883	214	0	126	18	2,241	203.7
1984	Gene Lake, Delaware St.	Jr.	1,722	37	0	0	0	1,759	175.9
1985	Gill Fenerty, Holy Cross	Sr.	1,368	187	0	1	414	1,970	197.0
1986	Kenny Gamble, Colgate	Jr.	1,816	178	0	40	391	*2,425	220.5
1987	Dave Meggett, Towson	Jr.	814	572	0	78	327	1,791	199.0
1988	Otis Washington, Western Caro.	Sr.	66	907	0	0	1,113	2,086	189.6
1989	Dominic Corr, Eastern Wash.	Sr.	796	52	0	0	807	1,655	183.9
1990	Barry Bourassa, New Hampshire	So.	957	276	0	133	368	1,734	192.7
1991	Barry Bourassa, New Hampshire	Jr.	1,130	426	0	0	596	2,152	195.6
1992	David Wright, Indiana St.	Fr.	1,313	108	0	0	593	2,014	183.1
1993	Tony Vinson, Towson	Sr.	2,016	57	0	0	0	2,073	207.3
1994	Arnold Mickens, Butler	Jr.	*2,255	7	0	0	0	2,262	226.2
1995	Reggie Greene, Siena	So.	1,461	77	0	53	363	1,954	217.1
1996	Reggie Greene, Siena	Jr.	1,719	50	0	0	337	2,106	*234.0
1997	Reggie Greene, Siena	Sr.	1,778	73	0	0	158	2,009	223.2

**Record.*

Field Goals

CAREER FIELD GOALS

Player, Team	Years	Total	Pct.	Under 40 Yds.	40 Plus	Long
Marty Zendejas, Nevada (S)	1984-87	*72-90	.800	42-45	30-45	54
Kirk Roach, Western Caro. (S)	1984-87	71-*102	.696	45-49	26-53	57
Tony Zendejas, Nevada (S)	1981-83	70-86	*.814	45-49	25-37	58
Brian Mitchell, Marshall/Northern Iowa (S)	1987, 89-91	64-81	.790	48-55	16-26	57
Dave Ettinger, Hofstra (S)	1994-97	62-93	.667	37-48	24-45	54
Todd Kurz, Illinois St. (S)	1993-96	59-87	.678	40-53	19-34	51
Jose Larios, McNeese St. (S)	1992-95	57-89	.640	47-57	10-32	47
Steve Christie, William & Mary (S)	1986-89	57-83	.686	39-49	18-34	53
Teddy Garcia, Northeast La. (S)	1984-87	56-88	.636	35-43	21-45	55
Bjorn Nittmo, Appalachian St. (S)	1985-88	55-74	.743	35-40	20-34	54
Kelly Potter, Middle Tenn. St. (S)	1981-84	52-78	.667	37-49	15-29	57
Paul McFadden, Youngstown St. (S)	1980-83	52-90	.578	28-42	24-48	54
Mike Black, Boise St. (S)	1988-91	51-75	.680	35-43	16-32	48
Jeff Wilkins, Youngstown St. (S)	1990-93	50-73	.685	33-38	17-35	54
Tim Foley, Ga. Southern (S)	1984-87	50-62	.806	32-37	18-25	**63
Paul Politi, Illinois St. (S)	1983-86	50-78	.641	34-48	16-30	50
Wayne Boyer, Southwest Mo. St. (S)	1993-96	49-71	.690	36-45	13-26	57
Chuck Rawlinson, Stephen F. Austin (S)	1988-91	49-69	.710	34-43	15-26	58
Thayne Doyle, Idaho (S)	1988-91	49-75	.653	35-51	14-24	52
Matt Stover, Louisiana Tech (S)	1986-88	49-68	.721	29-34	20-34	57
Scott Roper, Texas-Arlington/Arkansas St. (S)	1985, 86-87	49-75	.653	35-43	14-32	**63
Paul Hickert, Murray St. (S)	1984-87	49-79	.620	34-48	15-31	62
Dewey Klein, Marshall (S)	1988-91	48-66	.727	37-47	11-19	54
John Dowling, Youngstown St. (S)	1984-87	48-76	.632	36-44	12-32	49
Brian Shallcross, William & Mary (S)	1994-97	47-73	.644	41-54	6-19	49
Kirk Duce, Montana (S)	1988-91	47-78	.603	37-51	10-27	51
Billy Hayes, Sam Houston St. (S)	1985-88	47-71	.662	37-55	10-16	54
Steve Largent, Eastern Ill. (S)	1992-95	46-73	.630	30-38	16-35	53
Roger Ruzek, Weber St. (S)	1979-82	46-78	.590	28-37	18-41	51

**Record. **Record tied. (S)Soccer-style kicker.*

SEASON FIELD GOALS

Player, Team	Year	Total	Pct.	Under 40 Yds.	40 Plus	Long
Brian Mitchell, Northern Iowa (S)	†1990	**26-27	*.963	23-23	3-4	45
Tony Zendejas, Nevada (S)	†1982	**26-**33	.788	18-20	8-13	52
Wayne Boyer, Southwest Mo. St. (S)	†1996	25-30	.833	16-18	9-12	57
Kirk Roach, Western Caro. (S)	†1986	24-28	.857	17-17	7-11	52
George Benyola, Louisiana Tech (S)	†1985	24-31	.774	15-18	9-13	53
Goran Lingmerth, Northern Ariz. (S)	1986	23-29	.793	16-19	7-10	55
Tony Zendejas, Nevada (S)	†1983	23-29	.793	14-15	9-14	58
Rob Hart, Murray St. (S)	1996	22-27	.815	18-20	4-7	52
David Ettinger, Hofstra (S)	†1995	22-**33	.667	17-22	5-11	54
Jose Larios, McNeese St. (S)	†1993	22-28	.786	19-21	3-7	47
Mike Dodd, Boise St. (S)	†1992	22-31	.710	16-21	6-10	50
Marty Zendejas, Nevada (S)	†1984	22-27	.815	12-13	10-14	52
Travis Brawner, Southwest Mo. St. (S)	†1997	21-28	.750	15-17	6-11	52
Kevin McKelvie, Nevada (S)	1990	21-24	.875	16-17	5-7	52
Matt Stover, Louisiana Tech (S)	1986	21-25	.840	15-15	6-10	53
Scott Roper, Arkansas St. (S)	1986	21-28	.750	15-17	6-11	50
Tony Zendejas, Nevada (S)	†1981	21-24	.875	13-14	8-10	55
Darren Goodman, Idaho St. (S)	1990	20-28	.714	12-14	8-14	53
Steve Christie, William & Mary (S)	†1989	20-29	.690	16-17	4-12	53
Teddy Garcia, Northeast La. (S)	1987	20-28	.714	10-11	10-17	55

**Record. **Record tied. †National champion. (S) Soccer-style kicker.*

ANNUAL CHAMPIONS

(Ranked on Per-Game Average)

Year	Player, Team	Total	PG	Pct.	Under 40 Yds.	40 Plus	Long
1978	Tom Sarette, Boise St. (S)	12-20	1.2	.600	8-10	4-10	47
1979	Wilfredo Rosales, Alcorn St. (S)	13-20	1.3	.650	10-11	3-9	45
	Sandro Vitiello, Massachusetts (S)	13-22	1.3	.591	10-12	3-10	47
1980	Scott Norwood, James Madison (S)	15-21	1.5	.714	10-11	5-10	48
1981	Tony Zendejas, Nevada (S)	21-24	1.9	.875	13-14	8-10	55
1982	Tony Zendejas, Nevada (S)	**26-**33	**2.4	.788	18-20	8-13	52
1983	Tony Zendejas, Nevada (S)	23-29	2.1	.793	14-15	9-14	58
1984	Marty Zendejas, Nevada (S)	22-27	2.0	.815	12-13	10-14	52
1985	George Benyola, Louisiana Tech (S)	24-31	2.2	.774	15-18	9-13	53
1986	Kirk Roach, Western Caro. (S)	24-28	2.2	.857	17-17	7-11	52
1987	Micky Penaflor, Northern Ariz. (S)	19-27	1.9	.704	12-16	7-11	51
1988	Chris Lutz, Princeton (S)	19-24	1.9	.792	19-21	0-3	39
1989	Steve Christie, William & Mary (S)	20-29	1.8	.690	16-17	4-12	53
1990	Brian Mitchell, Northern Iowa (S)	**26-27	**2.4	*.963	23-23	3-4	45
1991	Brian Mitchell, Northern Iowa (S)	19-24	1.7	.792	15-16	4-8	57
1992	Mike Dodd, Boise St. (S)	22-31	2.0	.710	16-21	6-10	50
1993	Jose Larios, McNeese St. (S)	22-28	2.0	.786	19-21	3-7	47
1994	Andy Glockner, Pennsylvania (S)	14-20	1.6	.700	10-14	4-6	44
1995	David Ettinger, Hofstra (S)	22-**33	2.0	.667	17-22	5-11	54
1996	Wayne Boyer, Southwest Mo. St. (S)	25-30	2.3	.833	16-18	9-12	57
1997	Travis Brawner, Southwest Mo. St. (S)	21-28	1.9	.750	15-17	6-11	52

**Record. **Record tied. (S) Soccer-style kicker.*

All-Time Longest Plays

Since 1941, official maximum length of all plays fixed at 100 yards.

RUSHING

Yds.	Player, Team (Opponent)	Year
99	Jermaine Creighton, St. John's (N. Y.) (Siena)	1996
99	Jim Varick, Monmouth, N. J. (Sacred Heart)	1994
99	Phillip Collins, Southwest Mo. St. (Western Ill.)	1989
99	Pedro Bacon, Western Ky. (West Ala.)	1986
99	Hubert Owens, Mississippi Val. (Ark.-Pine Bluff)	1980
98	Johnny Gordon, Nevada (Montana St.)	1984
97	Pat Williams, Delaware (West Chester)	1995
97	Norman Bradford, Grambling (Prairie View)	1992
97	David Clark, Dartmouth (Harvard)	1989
97	David Clark, Dartmouth (Princeton)	1988
96	Jerry Azumah, New Hampshire (Connecticut)	1996
96	Jim Pizano, Massachusetts (Rhode Island)	1996
96	Kelvin Anderson, Southeast Mo. St. (Murray St.)	1992
96	Andre Lockhart, Chattanooga (East Tenn. St.)	1986
95	Corey Hill, Colgate (Brown)	1996
95	Brett Chappell, Western Caro. (Elon)	1995
95	Tim Hall, Robert Morris (Gannon)	1994
95	Jeff Sawulski, Siena (Iona)	1993
95	Jerry Ellison, Chattanooga (Boise St.)	1992
95	Joe Sparksman, James Madison (William & Mary)	1990
94	Kenny Bynum, South Caro. St. (Delaware St.)	1996
94	Mark Vigil, Idaho (Simon Fraser)	1980

PASSING

Yds.	Passer-Receiver, Team (Opponent)	Year
99	Michael Moore-Otis Covington, Morgan St. (Florida A&M)	1995
99	Todd Bennett-Jason Anderson, Eastern Wash. (Montana)	1994
99	Aaron Garcia-Greg Ochoa, Cal St. Sacramento (Cal Poly)	1993
99	Todd Donnan-Troy Brown, Marshall (East Tenn. St.)	1991
99	Antoine Ezell-Tyrone Davis, Florida A&M (Bethune-Cookman)	1991
99	Jay Johnson-Kenny Shedd, Northern Iowa (Oklahoma St.)	1990
99	John Bonds-Hendricks Johnson, Northern Ariz. (Boise St.)	1990
99	Scott Stoker-Victor Robinson, Northwestern St. (Northeast La.)	1989
98	Ben Anderson-Courtney Freeman, Liberty (Charleston So.)	1996
98	Derek Jensen-Jason Cannon, Southwest Mo. St. (Eastern Ill.)	1995
98	Jonathan Quinn-Dee Mostiller, Middle Tenn. St. (Tennessee Tech)	1995
98	Antoine Ezell-Tim Daniel, Florida A&M (Delaware St.)	1991
98	John Friesz-Lee Allen, Idaho (Northern Ariz.)	1989
98	Fred Gatlin-Treamelle Taylor, Nevada (Montana)	1989
98	Steve Monaco-Emerson Foster, Rhode Island (Holy Cross)	1988
98	Frank Baur-Maurice Caldwell, Lafayette (Columbia)	1988
98	David Gabianelli-Craig Morton, Dartmouth (Columbia)	1986
98	Joe Pizzo-Bryan Calder, Nevada (Eastern Wash.)	1984
98	Bobby Hebert-Randy Liles, Northwestern St. (Southeastern La.)	1980
97	Lester Anderson-Kevin Glenn, Illinois St. (Ball St.)	1993
97	Nate Harrison-Brian Thomas, Southern U. (Dist. Columbia)	1989
97	Jerome Baker-John Taylor, Delaware St. (St. Paul's)	1985
97	John McKenzie-Chris Burkett, Jackson St. (Mississippi Val.)	1983
96	Chris Berg-Dedric Ward, Northern Iowa (Western Ill.)	1995
96	Damon Williams-Ryan Blakely, Alabama St. (Texas Southern)	1994

Yds.	Passer-Receiver, Team (Opponent)	Year
96	Greg Wyatt-Shawn Collins, Northern Ariz. (Montana St.)	1988
96	Rick Fahnestock-Albert Brown, Western Ill. (Northern Iowa)	1986
96	Jeff Cesarone-Keith Paskett, Western Ky. (Akron)	1985
96	Mike Williams-Trumaine Johnson, Grambling (Jackson St.)	1980

INTERCEPTION RETURNS

Yds.	Player, Team (Opponent)	Year
100	Derek Grier, Marshall (East Tenn. St.)	1991
100	Ricky Fields, Samford (Concord [W.Va.])	1990
100	Warren Smith, Stephen F. Austin (Nicholls St.)	1990
100	Rob Pouliot, Montana St. (Boise St.)	1988
100	Rick Harris, East Tenn. St. (Davidson)	1986
100	Bruce Alexander, Stephen F. Austin (Lamar)	1986
100	Guy Carbone, Rhode Island (Lafayette)	1985
100	Moses Aimable, Northern Iowa (Western Ill.)	1985
100	Kervin Fontennette, Southeastern La. (Nicholls St.)	1985
100	Jim Anderson, Princeton (Cornell)	1984
100	Keiron Bigby, Brown (Yale)	1984
100	Vencie Glenn, Indiana St. (Wayne St. [Mich.])	1984
100	George Floyd, Eastern Ky. (Youngstown St.)	1980

PUNT RETURNS

Yds.	Player, Team (Opponent)	Year
98	Willie Ware, Mississippi Val. (Bishop)	1985
98	Barney Bussey, South Caro. St. (Johnson Smith)	1981
96	Carl Williams, Texas Southern (Grambling)	1981
95	Clarence Weathers, Delaware St. (Salisbury St.)	1980
94	Brad Friedman, Towson (St. Francis [Pa.])	1996
93	Andrew McFadden, Liberty (Delaware St.)	1995
93	Patrick Plott, Jacksonville St. (Southwest Mo. St.)	1995
93	Joe Fuller, Northern Iowa (Wis.-Whitewater)	1984

KICKOFF RETURNS

Forty-one players have returned kickoffs 100 yards. The most recent:

Yds.	Player, Team (Opponent)	Year
100	Darriel Ruffin, Tenn.-Martin (Murray St.)	1997
100	Clemente Sainten, Weber St. (Western St.)	1996
100	Robert Davis, Fordham (Brown)	1996
100	Joey Stockton, Western Ky. (Southern Ill.)	1996
100	Goree White, Alcorn St. (Ark.-Pine Bluff)	1995
100	Joe Rosato, Duquesne (Robert Morris)	1995
100	Chris Watson, Eastern Ill. (Northern Iowa)	1995
100	Todd Cleveland, Central Fla. (Bethune-Cookman)	1994
100	Montrel Williams, Idaho (Eastern Wash.)	1994
100	Len Raney, Northern Ariz. (Idaho St.)	1994
100	Jason Anderson, Eastern Wash. (Cal Poly)	1994

PUNTS

Yds.	Player, Team (Opponent)	Year
91	Bart Helsley, North Texas (Northeast La.)	1990
89	Jim Carriere, Connecticut (Maine)	1987
88	Jeff Kaiser, Idaho St. (UTEP)	1983
87	John Starnes, North Texas (Texas-Arlington)	1983
85	Don Alonzo, Nicholls St. (Northwestern St.)	1980
84	Billy Smith, Chattanooga (Appalachian St.)	1988
83	Jason Harkins, Appalachian St. (Citadel)	1986
82	Scott White, Delaware (Maine)	1996
82	Scott Shields, Weber St. (Cal St. Northridge)	1996
82	Tim Healy, Delaware (Boston U.)	1987
82	John Howell, Chattanooga (Vanderbilt)	1982

FIELD GOALS

Yds.	Player, Team (Opponent)	Year
63	Scott Roper, Arkansas St. (North Texas)	1987
63	Tim Foley, Ga. Southern (James Madison)	1987
62	Paul Hickert, Murray St. (Eastern Ky.)	1986
60	Terry Belden, Northern Ariz. (Cal St. Northridge)	1993
58	Rich Emke, Eastern Ill. (Northern Iowa)	1986
58	Tony Zendejas, Nevada (Boise St.)	1983

Team Champions

Annual Offense Champions

TOTAL OFFENSE

Year	Team	Avg.
1978	Portland St.	477.4
1979	Portland St.	460.7
1980	Portland St.	504.3
1981	Idaho	438.8
1982	Drake	444.8
1983	Idaho	479.5
1984	Mississippi Val.	*640.1
1985	Weber St.	516.1
1986	Nevada	492.0
1987	Holy Cross	552.2
1988	Lehigh	485.6
1989	Idaho	495.9
1990	William & Mary	498.7
1991	Weber St.	581.4
1992	Alcorn St.	502.9
1993	Idaho	532.0
1994	Alcorn St.	597.9
1995	Montana	512.5
1996	Northern Ariz.	522.8
1997	Eastern Wash.	505.6

*Record.

RUSHING OFFENSE

Year	Team	Avg.
1978	Jackson St.	314.5
1979	Jackson St.	288.4
1980	North Caro. A&T	322.1
1981	Idaho	266.3
1982	Delaware	258.4
1983	Furman	287.1
1984	Delaware St.	377.3
1985	Southwest Mo. St.	298.7
1986	Northeastern	336.0
1987	Howard	381.6
1988	Eastern Ky.	303.0
1989	Ga. Southern	329.2
1990	Delaware St.	298.7
1991	VMI	316.9
1992	Citadel	345.5
1993	Western Ky.	300.1
1994	Citadel	*382.0
1995	Massachusetts	302.5
1996	Southern Utah	330.8
1997	Western Ky.	366.0

*Record.

PASSING OFFENSE

Year	Team	Avg.
1978	Portland St.	367.1
1979	Portland St.	368.9
1980	Portland St.	434.9
1981	Idaho St.	325.7
1982	West Tex. A&M	313.7
1983	Idaho	336.1
1984	Mississippi Val.	*496.8
1985	Rhode Island	384.3
1986	Eastern Ill.	326.1
1987	Holy Cross	358.4
1988	Lehigh	330.1
1989	Idaho	374.3
1990	Weber St.	342.2
1991	Weber St.	389.1
1992	Alcorn St.	360.5
1993	Montana	359.0
1994	Alcorn St.	442.3
1995	Montana	408.2
1996	Montana	339.6
1997	Cal. St. Northridge	358.1

*Record.

SCORING OFFENSE

Year	Team	Avg.
1978	Nevada	35.6
1979	Portland St.	34.3
1980	Portland St.	49.2
1981	Delaware	34.1
1982	Delaware	34.1
1983	Mississippi Val.	39.2
1984	Mississippi Val.	*60.9
1985	Mississippi Val.	41.5
1986	Nevada	39.4
1987	Holy Cross	46.5
1988	Lafayette	38.2
1989	Grambling	37.1
1990	Jackson St.	38.0
1991	Nevada	45.1
1992	Marshall	42.4
1993	Idaho	47.5
1994	Alcorn St.	45.7
1995	Montana	42.5
1996	Northern Ariz.	43.2
1997	Morehead St.	41.9

*Record.

Annual Defense Champions

TOTAL DEFENSE

Year	Team	Avg.
1978	Florida A&M	*149.9
1979	Alcorn St.	166.3
1980	Massachusetts	193.5
1981	South Caro. St.	204.0
1982	South Caro. St.	191.4
1983	Grambling	206.0
1984	Tennessee St.	187.0

Year	Team	Avg.
1985	Arkansas St.	258.8
1986	Tennessee St.	178.5
1987	Southern U.	202.8
1988	Alcorn St.	215.4
1989	Howard	220.0
1990	Middle Tenn. St.	244.8
1991	South Caro. St.	208.9
1992	South Caro. St.	250.9
1993	McNeese St.	249.5
1994	Pennsylvania	218.9
1995	Georgetown	216.4
1996	Georgetown	218.2
1997	Marist	213.6

**Record.*

RUSHING DEFENSE

Year	Team	Avg.
1978	Florida A&M	48.6
1979	Alcorn St.	56.7
1980	South Caro. St.	61.8
1981	South Caro. St.	60.8
1982	South Caro. St.	59.4
1983	Jackson St.	79.2
1984	Grambling	44.5
1985	Jackson St.	63.0
1986	Eastern Ky.	62.8
1987	Southern U.	64.5
1988	Stephen F. Austin	83.5
1989	Montana	70.2
1990	Delaware St.	77.2
1991	Boise St.	84.4
1992	Villanova	77.8
1993	Wagner	87.0
1994	Idaho	65.3
1995	McNeese St.	60.9
1996	Georgetown	53.2
1997	Marist	*40.4

**Record.*

PASSING DEFENSE

Year	Team	$Avg.
1978	Southern U.	85.6
1979	Mississippi Val.	64.2
1980	Howard	93.8
1981	Bethune-Cookman	*59.9
1982	Northeastern	98.8
1983	Louisiana Tech	111.4
1984	Louisiana Tech	105.5
1985	Dartmouth	110.3
1986	Bethune-Cookman	99.8
1987	Alcorn St.	101.3
1988	Middle Tenn. St.	90.8
1989	Chattanooga	104.4
1990	Middle Tenn. St.	78.83
1991	South Caro. St.	70.01
1992	Middle Tenn. St.	76.93
1993	Georgetown	76.92
1994	Pennsylvania	*63.15
1995	Canisius	69.13
1996	Canisius	71.99
1997	McNeese St.	79.05

**Record. $Beginning in 1990, ranked on passing-efficiency defense rating points instead of per-game yardage allowed.*

SCORING DEFENSE

Year	Team	Avg.
1978	South Caro. St.	*6.5
1979	Lehigh	7.2
1980	Murray St.	9.1
1981	Jackson St.	9.4
1982	Western Mich.	7.1
1983	Grambling	8.6
1984	Northwestern St.	9.0
1985	Appalachian St.	9.9
1986	Tennessee St.	8.3
1987	Holy Cross	10.0
1988	Furman	9.7
1989	Howard	10.5
1990	Middle Tenn. St.	9.2
1991	Villanova	12.0
1992	Citadel	13.0
1993	Marshall	11.2
1994	Pennsylvania	7.6
1995	McNeese St.	8.9
1996	Duquesne	10.1
1997	McNeese St.	10.5

**Record.*

Toughest-Schedule Annual Leaders

The Division I-AA toughest-schedule program, which began in 1982, is based on what all Division I-AA opponents did against other Division I-AA and Division I-A teams when *not* playing the team in question. Games against non-I-AA and I-A teams are deleted. (Playoff or postseason games are not included.) The top two leaders by year:

		¢Opponents' Record			
Year	Team (Record†)	W	L	T	Pct.
1982	Massachusetts (5-6-0)	50	30	1	.623
	Lehigh (4-6-0)	44	31	0	.587
1983	Florida A&M (7-4-0)	42	23	3	.640
	Grambling (8-1-2)	49	31	0	.613
1984	North Texas (2-9-0)	55	35	2	.609
	VMI (1-9-0)	53	37	2	.587
1985	South Caro. St. (5-6-0)	43	20	1	.680
	Lehigh (5-6-0)	47	33	1	.586
1986	James Madison (5-5-1)	46	28	1	.620
	Bucknell (3-7-0)	43	27	0	.614
1987	Ga. Southern (8-3-0)	47	31	0	.603
	Northeastern (6-5-0)	50	37	0	.575
1988	Northwestern St. (9-2-0)	54	36	2	.598
	Ga. Southern (9-2-0)	43	31	1	.580
1989	Liberty (7-3-0)	39	22	2	.635
	Western Caro. (3-7-1)	46	34	2	.573
1990	Ga. Southern (8-3-0)	53	25	1	.677
	Western Ky. (2-8-0)	55	36	1	.603
1991	Bucknell (1-9-0)	53	29	1	.645
	William & Mary (5-6-0)	62	43	0	.590
1992	VMI (3-8-0)	46	36	0	.561
	Harvard (3-7-0)	51	40	0	.560
1993	Samford (5-6-0)	55	26	0	.679
	Delaware St. (6-5-0)	44	30	0	.595
1994	Montana (9-2-0)	46	30	1	.604
	McNeese St. (9-2-0)	44	29	5	.596
1995	Western Ky. (2-8-0)	59	32	0	.648
	Nicholls St. (0-11-0)	61	38	0	.616
1996	Indiana St. (6-5)	50	32	0	.610
	Towson (6-4)	42	29	0	.592
1997	Lehigh (4-7)	65	39	0	.625
	William & Mary (7-4)	65	42	0	.607

†Not including playoff or postseason games. ¢When not playing the team listed.

Top 10 Toughest-Schedule Leaders for 1993-97†

1993

	Team	¢Opp. Record	Pct.
1.	Samford	55-26-0	.679
2.	Delaware St.	44-30-0	.595
3.	Troy St.	47-32-1	.594
4.	Eastern Wash.	46-32-0	.590
5.	James Madison	52-37-0	.584
6.	Illinois St.	58-42-2	.578
7.	Nicholls St.	53-39-0	.576
8.	Alcorn St.	44-32-4	.575
9.	North Texas	53-41-0	.564
10.	Idaho	56-44-0	.560

1994

	Team	¢Opp. Record	Pct.
1.	Montana	46-30-1	.604
2.	McNeese St.	44-29-5	.596
3.	Montana St.	44-30-2	.592
4.	Idaho	55-38-2	.589
5.	Buffalo	50-35-4	.584
6.	Eastern Wash.	50-37-0	.575
7.	Stephen F. Austin	46-35-0	.568
8.	Pennsylvania	46-35-1	.567
9.	Rhode Island	59-45-2	.566
10.	Northeastern	60-47-1	.560

1995

	Team	¢Opp. Record	Pct.
1.	Western Ky.	59-32-0	.648
2.	Nicholls St.	61-38-0	.616
3.	William & Mary	65-43-1	.601
4.	Northwestern St.	48-33-0	.593
5.	Central Fla.	55-38-0	.591
6.	East Tenn. St.	62-43-1	.590
7.	Western Ill.	52-38-0	.578
8.	Columbia	49-37-2	.568
9.	Rhode Island	60-46-0	.566
10.	VMI	58-46-1	.557

1996

	Team	¢Opp. Record	Pct.
1.	Indiana St.	50-32	.610
2.	Towson	42-29	.592
3.	McNeese St.	47-33	.587
4.	Fordham	56-40	.583
5.	Alcorn St.	47-34	.580
6.	Rhode Island	50-38	.568
7.	Jacksonville St.	47-37	.560
8.	Sam Houston St.	45-36	.556
9.	Yale	51-41	.554
10.	Marshall	52-42	.553

1997

	Team	¢Opp. Record	Pct.
1.	Lehigh	65-39-0	.625
2.	William & Mary	65-42-0	.607
3.	Dayton	32-21-0	.604
4.	Florida A&M	59-39-0	.589
5.	Yale	52-37-0	.584
6.	Howard	45-33-0	.577
7.	Tennessee St.	60-45-0	.571
8.	New Hampshire	60-46-0	.566
9.	Holy Cross	57-46-0	.553
10.	Northern Iowa	48-39-0	.552

†Not including playoff or postseason games. ¢When not playing the team listed.

Annual Most-Improved Teams

Year	Team	$Games Improved	From		To		Coach
1978	Western Ky.	6½	1977	1-8-1	1978	8-2-0	Jimmy Feix
1979	Murray St.	5	1978	4-7-0	1979	*9-2-1	Mike Gottfried
1980	Idaho St.	6	1979	0-11-0	1980	6-5-0	#Dave Kragthorpe
1981	Lafayette	5½	1980	3-7-0	1981	9-2-0	#Bill Russo
1982	Pennsylvania	6	1981	1-9-0	1982	7-3-0	Jerry Berndt
1983	North Texas	5½	1982	2-9-0	1983	*8-4-0	Corky Nelson
	Southern Ill.	5½	1982	6-5-0	1983	*13-1-0	Rey Dempsey
1984	Montana St.	9½	1983	1-10-0	1984	*12-2-0	Dave Arnold
1985	Appalachian St.	4	1984	4-7-0	1985	8-3-0	Sparky Woods
	Massachusetts	4	1984	3-8-0	1985	7-4-0	Bob Stull
	West Tex. A&M	4	1984	3-8-0	1985	6-3-1	#Bill Kelly
1986	Morehead St.	6	1985	1-10-0	1986	7-4-0	Bill Baldridge
1987	Weber St.	6	1986	3-8-0	1987	*10-3-0	Mike Price
1988	Stephen F. Austin	5½	1987	3-7-1	1988	*10-3-0	Jim Hess
1989	Yale	4½	1988	3-6-1	1989	8-2-0	Carmen Cozza
1990	Nevada	4	1989	7-4-0	1990	*13-2-0	Chris Ault
	North Caro. A&T	4	1989	5-6-0	1990	9-2-0	Bill Hayes
1991	Alcorn St.	5	1990	2-7-0	1991	7-2-1	#Cardell Jones
	Austin Peay	5	1990	0-11-0	1991	5-6-0	#Roy Gregory
	Princeton	5	1990	3-7-0	1991	8-2-0	Steve Tosches
	Southern Ill.	5	1990	2-9-0	1991	7-4-0	Bob Smith
1992	Howard	5	1991	2-9-0	1992	7-4-0	Steve Wilson
	Pennsylvania	5	1991	2-8-0	1992	7-3-0	#Al Bagnoli
	Richmond	5	1991	2-9-0	1992	7-4-0	Jim Marshall
	Tennessee Tech	5	1991	2-9-0	1992	7-4-0	Jim Ragland
	Western Caro.	5	1991	2-9-0	1992	7-4-0	Steve Hodgin
1993	Boston U.	8	1992	3-8-0	1993	*12-1-0	Dan Allen
1994	Boise St.	8	1993	3-8-0	1994	*13-2-0	Pokey Allen
1995	Murray St.	5½	1994	5-6-0	1995	*11-1-0	Houston Nutt
1996	Nicholls St.	7½	1995	0-11	1996	*8-4-0	Darren Barbier
1997	McNeese St.	8	1996	3-8-0	1997	*13-2-0	Bobby Keasler

*$To determine games improved, add the difference in victories between the two seasons to the difference in losses, then divide by two; ties not counted. *I-AA playoff included. #First year as head coach at that college.*

Photo from McNeese State sports information

McNeese State quarterback Blake Prejean helped the Cowboys rebound from a 3-8 record in 1996 to a 13-2 mark in 1997 and a berth in the Division I-AA playoffs.

DIVISION I-AA

ALL-TIME MOST-IMPROVED TEAMS

Games	Team (Year)
9½	Montana St. (1984)
8	McNeese St. (1997)
8	Boise St. (1994)
8	Boston U. (1993)
7½	Nicholls St. (1996)
6½	Western Ky. (1978)
6	Colgate (1996)
6	Weber St. (1987)
6	Morehead St. (1986)
6	Pennsylvania (1982)
6	Idaho St. (1980)
5½	Fairfield (1997)
5½	Murray St. (1995)
5½	Southern U. (1993)
5½	Stephen F. Austin (1988)
5½	East Tenn. St. (1986)
5½	Holy Cross (1986)
5½	Yale (1984)
5½	North Texas (1983)
5½	Southern Ill. (1983)
5½	Lafayette (1981)

1997 MOST-IMPROVED TEAMS
(Includes Playoff Games)

College (Coach)	1997	1996	$Games Improved
McNeese St. (Bobby Keasler)	13-2-0	3-8-0	8.0
Fairfield (Kevin Kiesel)	7-3-0	1-8-0	5.5
Cal Poly SLO (Larry Welsh)	10-1-0	5-6-0	5.0
Harvard (Tim Murphy)	9-1-0	4-6-0	5.0
Ga. Southern (Paul Johnson)	10-3-0	4-7-0	5.0
Eastern Wash. (Mike Kramer)	12-2-0	6-5-0	4.5
Hampton (Joe Taylor)	10-2-0	5-6-0	4.5
Southern (Pete Richardson)	11-1-0	7-5-0	4.0
Bucknell (Tom Gadd)	10-1-0	6-5-0	4.0
Liberty (Sam Rutigliano)	9-2-0	5-6-0	4.0
South Caro. St. (Willie Jeffries)	9-3-0	4-6-0	4.0
Siena (Ed Zaloom)	6-3-0	2-7-0	4.0
Chattanooga (Buddy Green)	7-4-0	3-8-0	4.0
Richmond (Jim Reid)	6-5-0	2-9-0	4.0

$To determine games improved, add the difference in victories between the two seasons to the difference in losses, then divide by two, ties not counted. Includes playoff games.

All-Time Team Won-Lost Records

PERCENTAGE (TOP 23)

Includes records as senior college only, minimum of 20 seasons of competition. Bowl and playoff games are included, and each tie game is computed as half won and half lost. Note: Tiebreaker rule began with 1996 season.

Team	Yrs.	Won	Lost	Tied	Pct.+	Total Games
Yale	125	785	292	55	.718	1,132
Florida A&M	65	453	182	18	.708	653
Grambling	55	408	165	15	.707	588
Tennessee St.@	70	438	180	30	.699	648
Princeton	128	730	304	50	.696	1,084
Harvard	123	720	343	50	.669	1,113
Jackson St.	52	339	180	13	.649	532
Dartmouth	116	620	334	46	.643	1,000
Fordham	99	682	369	53	.642	1,104
Eastern Ky.	74	451	256	27	.633	734
Southern	76	449	260	25	.629	734
South Caro. St.	70	389	229	27	.624	645
Pennsylvania	121	716	426	42	.622	1,184
Dayton	90	513	311	26	.619	850
Hofstra	57	328	203	11	.615	542
Ga. Southern	29	192	119	7	.615	318
McNeese St.	47	303	189	14	.613	506
Appalachian St.	68	419	261	29	.611	709
Middle Tenn. St.	81	453	296	28	.601	777
Delaware	106	545	358	43	.599	946
Youngstown St.	57	334	224	17	.596	575

+Ties counted as half won and half lost. @Tennessee State's participation in the 1981 and 1982 Division I-AA championships (1-2 record) voided.

ALPHABETICAL LISTING

Team	Yrs.	Won	Lost	Tied	Pct.+	Total Games
Alabama St.	92	373	360	43	.508	776
Alcorn St.	74	364	243	39	.594	646
Appalachian St.	68	419	261	29	.611	709
Austin Peay	61	224	371	16	.380	611
Bethune-Cookman	59	309	224	22	.577	555
Brown	112	500	491	40	.504	1,031
Bucknell	112	504	459	51	.522	1,014
Buffalo	84	300	358	29	.458	687
Butler	108	491	337	35	.589	863
Cal Poly	57	309	232	9	.570	550
Cal St. Northridge	36	163	206	4	.442	373
Cal St. Sacramento	44	192	244	8	.441	444
Canisius	52	221	189	24	.537	434
Central Conn. St.	59	219	259	22	.460	500
Charleston So.	7	12	59	0	.169	71
Chattanooga	90	433	397	33	.521	863
Citadel	90	407	425	32	.490	864
Colgate	107	496	402	50	.550	948
Columbia	107	333	523	43	.394	899
Connecticut	99	396	429	38	.481	863
Cornell	110	570	395	34	.588	999
Dartmouth	116	620	334	46	.643	1,000
Davidson	100	341	493	45	.414	879
Dayton	90	513	311	26	.619	850
Delaware	106	545	358	43	.599	946
Delaware St.	52	231	258	8	.473	497
Drake	104	475	431	29	.524	935
Duquesne	50	222	207	18	.517	447
East Tenn. St.	74	311	361	27	.464	699
Eastern Ill.	97	388	413	44	.485	845
Eastern Ky.	74	451	256	27	.633	734
Eastern Wash.	87	380	318	23	.543	721
Evansville	72	265	369	22	.421	656
Fairfield	2	8	11	0	.421	19
Florida A&M	65	453	182	18	.708	653
Fordham	99	682	369	53	.642	1,104
Furman	84	459	358	37	.559	854
Georgetown	86	415	280	31	.593	726
Ga. Southern	29	192	119	7	.615	318
Grambling	55	408	165	15	.707	588
Hampton	96	430	329	34	.564	793
Harvard	123	720	343	50	.669	1,113
Hofstra	57	328	203	11	.615	542
Holy Cross	102	532	394	55	.570	981
Howard	101	416	326	42	.557	784
Idaho St.	93	396	361	20	.523	777
Illinois St.	98	366	437	65	.459	868
Indiana St.	81	315	354	20	.472	689
Iona	20	81	113	3	.419	197
Jackson St.	52	339	180	13	.649	532
Jacksonville St.	65	341	248	27	.575	616
James Madison	25	150	119	3	.557	272
La Salle	1	1	8	0	.111	9
Lafayette	116	581	475	39	.548	1,095
Lehigh	114	531	521	45	.505	1,097
Liberty	25	128	123	4	.510	255
Maine	106	412	392	38	.512	842
Marist	20	79	102	3	.438	184
Massachusetts	115	447	466	51	.490	964
McNeese St.	47	303	189	14	.613	506
Middle Tenn. St.	81	453	296	28	.601	777
Mississippi Val.	45	186	229	11	.450	426
Monmouth	4	26	12	0	.684	38
Montana	98	394	432	26	.478	852
Montana St.	94	366	380	34	.491	780
Morehead St.	68	236	361	22	.399	619
Morgan St.	77	363	282	30	.560	675
Murray St.	73	385	300	34	.559	719
New Hampshire	101	426	366	54	.535	846
Nicholls St.	26	127	157	4	.448	288
Norfolk St.	37	185	166	7	.527	358
North Caro. A&T	74	366	297	39	.549	702
Northeastern	62	235	283	17	.455	535
Northern Ariz.	73	321	326	22	.496	669
Northern Iowa	99	498	333	47	.594	878
Northwestern St.	89	420	339	33	.551	792
Pennsylvania	121	716	426	42	.622	1,184
Prairie View	71	327	349	31	.484	707
Princeton	128	730	304	50	.696	1,084
Rhode Island	97	332	438	41	.435	811
Richmond	114	404	540	53	.432	997
Robert Morris	4	30	10	1	.744	41
St. Francis (Pa.)	49	150	232	13	.396	395
St. John's (N. Y.)	29	155	111	7	.581	273

Team	Yrs.	Won	Lost	Tied	Pct.†	Total Games
St. Mary's (Cal.)	69	344	241	20	.585	605
St. Peter's	26	53	154	1	.257	208
Sam Houston St.	81	332	331	47	.501	710
Samford	82	370	368	34	.501	772
San Diego	30	141	136	8	.509	285
Siena	10	21	70	0	.231	91
South Caro. St.	70	389	229	27	.624	645
South Fla.	1	5	6	0	.455	11
Southeast Mo. St.	85	362	363	37	.499	762
Southern Ill.	82	322	407	33	.444	762
Southern	76	449	260	25	.629	734
Southern Utah	35	168	169	6	.499	343
Southwest Mo. St.	86	381	365	40	.510	786
Southwest Tex. St.	83	411	316	27	.563	754
Stephen F. Austin%	71	292	388	30	.432	710
Tenn.-Martin	41	180	238	5	.431	423
Tennessee St.@	70	438	180	30	.699	648
Tennessee Tech	76	325	378	31	.464	734
Texas Southern	52	247	266	27	.482	540
Towson	29	164	129	4	.559	297
Troy St.	67	353	276	15	.560	644
Valparaiso	77	307	350	24	.468	681
Villanova	100	470	388	41	.546	899
VMI	107	426	516	43	.454	985
Wagner	67	302	251	17	.545	570
Weber St.	36	187	191	3	.495	381
Western Caro.	64	264	348	23	.434	635
Western Ill.	94	402	348	37	.534	787
Western Ky.	79	427	287	31	.594	745
William & Mary	102	456	453	37	.502	946
Wofford	89	379	413	36	.479	828
Yale	125	785	292	55	.718	1,132
Youngstown St.	57	334	224	17	.596	575

**Also includes any participation in major bowl games. +Ties computed as half won and half lost. @Tennessee State's participation in 1981 and 1982 Division I-AA championships (1-2 record) voided. %Stephen F. Austin's particpation in 1989 Division I-AA championships (3-1 record) voided.*

VICTORIES

Team	Wins
Yale	785
Princeton	730
Harvard	720
Pennsylvania	716
Fordham	682
Dartmouth	620
Lafayette	581
Cornell	570
Delaware	545
Holy Cross	532
Lehigh	531
Dayton	513
Bucknell	504
Brown	500
Northern Iowa	498
Colgate	496
Butler	491
Drake	475
Villanova	470
Furman	459
William & Mary	456
Florida A&M	453
Middle Tenn. St.	453
Eastern Ky.	451
Southern U.	449
Massachusetts	447
Tennessee St.	438
Chattanooga	433
Hampton	430
Western Ky.	427
New Hampshire	426
VMI	426
Northwestern St.	420
Appalachian St.	419
Howard	416
Georgetown	415
Maine	412
Southwest Tex. St.	411
Grambling	408
Citadel	407
Richmond	404
Western Ill.	402
Connecticut	396
Idaho St.	396
Montana	394

Team	Wins
South Caro. St.	389
Eastern Ill.	388
Murray St.	385
Southwest Mo. St.	381
Eastern Wash.	380
Wofford	379
Alabama St.	373
Samford	370
Illinois St.	366
Montana St.	366
North Caro. A&T	366
Alcorn St.	364
Morgan St.	363
Southeast Mo. St.	362
Troy St.	353
St. Mary's (Cal.)	344
Davidson	341
Jacksonville St.	341
Jackson St.	339
Youngstown St.	334
Columbia	333
Rhode Island	332
Sam Houston St.	332
Hofstra	328
Prairie View	327
Tennessee Tech	325
Southern Ill.	322
Northern Ariz.	321
Indiana St.	315
East Tenn. St.	311
Bethune-Cookman	309
Cal Poly	309
Valparaiso	307
McNeese St.	303
Wagner	302
Buffalo	300
Stephen F. Austin	292
Evansville	265
Western Caro.	264
Texas Southern	247
Morehead St.	236
Northeastern	235
Delaware St.	231
Austin Peay	224
Duquesne	222

Team	Wins	Team	Wins
Canisius	221	San Diego	141
Central Conn. St.	219	Liberty	128
Cal St. Sacramento	192	Nicholls St.	127
Ga. Southern	192	Iona	81
Weber St.	187	Marist	79
Mississippi Val.	186	St. Peter's	53
Norfolk St.	185	Robert Morris	30
Tenn.-Martin	180	Monmouth	26
Southern Utah	168	Siena	21
Towson	164	Charleston So.	12
Cal St. Northridge	163	Fairfield	8
St. John's (N. Y.)	155	South Fla.	5
James Madison	150	La Salle	1
St. Francis (Pa.)	150		

Records in the 1990s

(1990-91-92-93-94-95-96-97, including playoffs; tiebreaker began in 1996)

PERCENTAGE

Team	W-L-T	*Pct.	Team	W-L-T	*Pct.
Dayton++	80-9-0	.899	Citadel	48-43-0	.527
Youngstown St.	85-22-2	.789	Bucknell	44-43-0	.506
Montana	76-25-0	.752	Murray St.	45-46-0	.495
Delaware	74-25-1	.745	Sam Houston St.	42-43-3	.494
Robert Morris$	30-10-1	.744	Connecticut	43-44-0	.494
Dartmouth	58-19-3	.744	Tennessee Tech	42-46-0	.477
Eastern Ky.	72-26-0	.735	Lafayette	40-44-3	.477
Northern Iowa	74-27-0	.733	Western Ky.	41-45-0	.477
Troy St.++	68-26-1	.721	Towson	39-43-0	.476
Hofstra++	62-24-2	.716	Morgan St.	17-19-0	.472
William & Mary	65-28-0	.699	Evansville++	37-42-0	.468
Drake++	56-24-2	.695	South Fla.	5-6-0	.455
McNeese St.	69-31-2	.686	Mississippi Val.	36-44-3	.452
Monmouth (N. J.)$	26-12-0	.684	Holy Cross	39-48-1	.449
Hampton++	61-29-1	.676	East Tenn. St.	40-50-0	.444
North Caro. A&T	60-30-0	.667	Cal St. Northridge++	37-47-0	.440
Jackson St.	60-30-1	.665	Southwest Tex. St.	38-49-1	.438
Ga. Southern	65-33-0	.663	Indiana St.	38-50-0	.432
Princeton	51-28-1	.644	Southern Utah++	37-49-2	.432
Middle Tenn. St.	60-33-1	.644	Harvard	34-45-1	.431
Southern U.	59-33-0	.641	Davidson++	33-44-1	.429
Appalachian St.	60-34-0	.638	Iona++	33-45-1	.424
New Hampshire	56-32-2	.633	Fairfield	8-11-0	.421
St. Mary's (Cal.)++	50-29-1	.631	Illinois St.	36-50-2	.420
San Diego++	50-29-1	.631	Montana St.	37-51-0	.420
Florida A&M	58-34-0	.630	Boston U.	38-53-0	.418
Wagner++	51-30-0	.630	Cal St. Sacramento++	34-48-1	.416
St. John's (N. Y.)++	52-31-0	.627	Chattanooga	36-52-0	.409
South Caro. St.	55-33-0	.625	Texas Southern	34-52-1	.397
Samford	56-34-2	.620	Canisius++	30-47-1	.391
Marist++	48-30-2	.613	Western Caro.	34-53-0	.391
Villanova	56-37-0	.602	Colgate	34-54-1	.388
Portland St.	57-38-0	.600	Brown	31-49-0	.388
Cal Poly++	51-34-1	.599	Southeast Mo. St.++	34-54-0	.386
Howard	53-37-0	.589	Tennessee St.	34-54-0	.386
Western Ill.	53-38-1	.582	Richmond	33-54-1	.381
James Madison	54-39-0	.581	Maine	33-55-0	.375
Liberty	51-37-0	.580	Yale	30-50-0	.375
Georgetown++	45-33-0	.577	Northeastern	32-55-1	.369
Furman	52-39-1	.571	Valparaiso++	29-51-1	.364
Alabama St.	48-36-4	.568	Morehead St.	30-55-0	.353
Cornell	45-35-0	.563	Columbia	27-51-2	.350
Weber St.	50-39-0	.562	St. Francis (Pa.)++	27-51-1	.348
Pennsylvania	44-35-0	.557	Idaho St.	30-57-1	.347
Wofford++	49-39-1	.556	Rhode Island	30-57-0	.345
Grambling	50-40-0	.556	Nicholls St.	30-58-1	.343
Lehigh	48-39-1	.551	Tenn.-Martin++	30-58-0	.341
Eastern Ill.	49-40-1	.550	Bethune-Cookman	29-57-0	.337
Southwest Mo. St.	48-40-1	.545	Southern Ill.	29-59-0	.330
Eastern Wash.	49-41-0	.544	Buffalo++	26-59-0	.306
Duquesne++	43-36-1	.544	Central Conn. St.++	23-54-1	.301
Butler++	44-37-1	.543	St. Peter's	20-50-0	.286
Norfolk St.++	44-37-1	.543	VMI	20-68-0	.227
Northern Ariz.	48-41-0	.539	Siena++	16-56-0	.222
Northwestern St.	48-41-0	.539	Fordham	16-67-1	.196
Jacksonville St.	49-42-1	.538	Austin Peay	17-70-0	.195
Massachusetts	46-40-1	.534	Charleston So.++	12-59-0	.169
Stephen F. Austin	47-41-3	.533	La Salle	1-8-0	.111
Alcorn St.	44-39-3	.529	Prairie View@	0-75-0	.000
Delaware St.	46-41-0	.529			

**Ties counted as half won and half lost. ++Joined I-AA in 1990s: Southeast Mo. St. (1991); Tenn.-Martin (1992); Buffalo (1993), Butler (1993), Cal St. Northridge (1993), Cal St. Sacramento (1993), Canisius (1993), Central Conn. St. (1993), Davidson (1993), Dayton (1993), Drake (1993), Duquesne (1993), Evansville (1993), Georgetown (1993), Hofstra (1993), Iona (1993), Marist (1993), Norfolk St. (1997); St. Francis (Pa.) (1993), St. John's (N.Y.) (1993), St. Mary's (Cal.) (1993), St. Peter's (1993), San Diego (1993), Siena (1993), Southern Utah (1993), Troy St. (1993), Valparaiso (1993) and Wagner (1993); Cal Poly (1994); Hampton (1995), Jacksonville St. (1995), Wofford (1995) and Norfolk St. (1997). $Began varsity program in 1994. @Did not play in 1990.*

BY VICTORIES

(Minimum 50 victories)

Team	Wins	Team	Wins
Youngstown St.	85	Portland St.	57
Dayton	80	Drake	56
Montana	76	New Hampshire	56
Delaware	74	Samford	56
Northern Iowa	74	Villanova	56
Eastern Ky.	72	South Caro. St.	55
McNeese St.	69	James Madison	54
Troy St.	68	Howard	53
Ga. Southern	65	Western Ill.	53
William & Mary	65	Furman	52
Hofstra	62	St. John's (N. Y.)	52
Hampton	61	Cal Poly	51
Appalachian St.	60	Liberty	51
Jackson St.	60	Wagner	51
Middle Tenn. St.	60	Princeton	51
North Caro. A&T	60	Grambling	50
Southern U.	59	St. Mary's (Cal.)	50
Dartmouth	58	San Diego	50
Florida A&M	58	Weber St.	50

Records in the 1980s

(Playoffs Included)

PERCENTAGE

Rank	Team	W-L-T	Pct.†	Rank	Team	W-L-T	Pct.†
1	Eastern Ky.	88-24-2	.781	11	Delaware	68-36-0	.654
2	Furman	83-23-4	.773	12	Middle Tenn. St.	65-36-0	.644
3	Ga. Southern	68-22-1	*.753	13	Boise St.	66-38-0	.635
4	Jackson St.	71-25-5	.728	14	Southwest Tex. St.	66-39-0	.629
5	Grambling	68-30-3	.688	15	Murray St.	61-36-2	.626
6	Nevada	71-35-1	.668	16	Northern Iowa	64-38-2	.625
7	Holy Cross	67-33-2	.667	17	Towson	60-36-2	.622
8	Tennessee St.	64-32-4	.660	18	Alcorn St.	56-34-0	.622
9	Eastern Ill.	70-36-1	.659	19	Northeast La.	64-39-0	.621
10	Idaho	69-36-0	.657	20	South Caro. St.	55-34-1	.617

*†Ties counted as half won and half lost. *Includes two nonvarsity seasons and five varsity seasons; varsity record, 55-14-0 for .797.*

National Poll Rankings

Final Poll Leaders

(Released Before Division Championship Playoffs)

Year	Team, Record*	Coach	Record in Championship†
1978	Nevada (10-0-0)	Chris Ault	0-1 Lost in semifinals
1979	Grambling (8-2-0)	Eddie Robinson	Did not compete
1980	Lehigh (9-0-2)	John Whitehead	0-1 Lost in semifinals
1981	Eastern Ky. (9-1-0)	Roy Kidd	2-1 Runner-up
1982	Eastern Ky. (10-0-0)	Roy Kidd	3-0 Champion
1983	Southern Ill. (10-1-0)	Rey Dempsey	3-0 Champion
1984	Alcorn St. (9-0-0)	Marino Casem	0-1 Lost in quarterfinals
1985	Middle Tenn. St. (11-0-0)	James Donnelly	0-1 Lost in quarterfinals
1986	Nevada (11-0-0)	Chris Ault	2-1 Lost in semifinals
1987	Holy Cross (11-0-0)	Mark Duffner	Did not compete
1988	Idaho (9-1-0)	Keith Gilbertson	2-1 Lost in semifinals
1989	Ga. Southern (11-0-0)	Erk Russell	4-0 Champion
1990	Middle Tenn. St. (10-1-0)	James Donnelly	1-1 Lost in quarterfinals
1991	Nevada (11-0-0)	Chris Ault	1-1 Lost in quarterfinals
1992	tie Citadel (10-1-0)	Charlie Taaffe	1-1 Lost in quarterfinals
	Northeast La. (9-2-0)	Dave Roberts	1-1 Lost in quarterfinals
1993	Troy St. (10-0-1)	Larry Blakeney	2-1 Lost in semifinals
1994	Youngstown St. (10-0-1)	Jim Tressel	4-0 Champion
1995	McNeese St. (11-0-0)	Bobby Keasler	2-1 Lost in semifinals
1996	Marshall (11-0-0)	Bob Pruett	4-0 Champion
1997	Villanova (11-0-0)	Andy Talley	1-1 Lost in quarterfinals

**Final poll record; in some cases, a team had one or two games remaining before the championship playoffs. †Number of teams in the championship: 4 (1978-80); 8 (1981); 12 (1982-85); 16 (1986-present).*

Final Regular-Season Polls

1978
(NCAA)

Team
1. Nevada
2. Jackson St.
3. Florida A&M
4. Massachusetts
5. Western Ky.
6. South Caro. St.
7. Northern Ariz.
   Montana St.
   Eastern Ky.
   Lehigh
   Rhode Island

1979
(NCAA)

Team
1. Grambling
2. Murray St.
3. Eastern Ky.
   Lehigh
5. Nevada
6. Alcorn St.
7. Boston U.
8. Jackson St.
9. Montana St.
10. Northern Ariz.
    Southern U.

1980
(NCAA)

Team
1. Lehigh
2. Grambling
3. Eastern Ky.
4. South Caro. St.
5. Western Ky.
6. Delaware
7. Boise St.
8. Northwestern St.
9. Boston U.
10. Connecticut
    Massachusetts
    Murray St.

1981
(NCAA)

Team
1. Eastern Ky.
2. Idaho St.
3. South Caro. St.
4. Jackson St.
5. Boise St.
6. Tennessee St.
7. Delaware
8. Lafayette
9. Murray St.
10. New Hampshire

1982
(NCAA)

Team
1. Eastern Ky.
2. Louisiana Tech
3. Delaware
4. Tennessee St.
5. Eastern Ill.
6. Furman
7. South Caro. St.
8. Jackson St.
9. Colgate
10. Grambling
11. Idaho
12. Northern Ill.
13. Holy Cross
14. Bowling Green
15. Boise St.
16. Western Mich.
17. Chattanooga
18. Northwestern St.
19. Montana
20. Lafayette

1983
(NCAA)

Team
1. Southern Ill.
2. Furman
3. Holy Cross
4. North Texas
5. Indiana St.
6. Eastern Ill.
7. Colgate
8. Eastern Ky.
9. Western Caro.
10. Grambling
11. Nevada
12. Idaho St.
13. Boston U.
    Northeast La.
15. Jackson St.
16. Middle Tenn. St.
17. Tennessee St.
18. South Caro. St.
19. Mississippi Val.
20. New Hampshire

1984
(NCAA)

Team
1. Alcorn St.
2. Montana St.
   Rhode Island
4. Boston U.
5. Indiana St.
6. Middle Tenn. St.
   Mississippi Val.
8. Eastern Ky.
9. Louisiana Tech
10. Arkansas St.
11. New Hampshire
12. Richmond
13. Murray St.
14. Western Caro.
15. Holy Cross
16. Furman
17. Chattanooga
18. Northern Iowa
19. Delaware
20. McNeese St.

1985
(NCAA)

Team
1. Middle Tenn. St.
2. Furman
   Nevada
4. Northern Iowa
5. Idaho
6. Arkansas St.
7. Rhode Island
8. Grambling
9. Ga. Southern
10. Akron
11. Eastern Wash.
12. Appalachian St.
    Delaware St.
14. Louisiana Tech
15. Jackson St.
16. William & Mary
17. Murray St.
18. Richmond
19. Eastern Ky.
20. Alcorn St.

1986
(NCAA)

Team
1. Nevada
2. Arkansas St.
3. Eastern Ill.
4. Ga. Southern
5. Holy Cross
6. Appalachian St.
7. Pennsylvania
8. William & Mary
9. Jackson St.
10. Eastern Ky.
11. Sam Houston St.
12. Nicholls St.
13. Delaware
14. Tennessee St.
15. Furman
16. Idaho
17. Southern Ill.
18. Murray St.
19. Connecticut
20. North Caro. A&T

1987
(NCAA)

Team
1. Holy Cross
2. Appalachian St.
3. Northeast La.
4. Northern Iowa
5. Idaho
6. Ga. Southern
7. Eastern Ky.
8. James Madison
9. Jackson St.
10. Weber St.
11. Western Ky.
12. Arkansas St.
13. Maine
14. Marshall
15. Youngstown St.
16. North Texas
17. Richmond
18. Howard
19. Sam Houston St.
20. Delaware St.

1988
(NCAA)

Team
1. Stephen F. Austin
2. Idaho
3. Ga. Southern
4. Western Ill.
5. Furman
6. Jackson St.
7. Marshall
8. Eastern Ky.
9. Citadel
10. Northwestern St.
11. Massachusetts
12. North Texas
13. Boise St.
14. Florida A&M
    Pennsylvania
16. Western Ky.
17. Connecticut
18. Grambling
19. Montana
20. New Hampshire

1989
(NCAA)

Team
1. Ga. Southern
2. Furman
3. Stephen F. Austin
4. Holy Cross
   Idaho
6. Montana
7. Appalachian St.
8. Maine
9. Southwest Mo. St.
10. Middle Tenn. St.
    William & Mary
12. Eastern Ky.
13. Grambling
14. Youngstown St.
15. Eastern Ill.
16. Villanova
17. Jackson St.
18. Connecticut
19. Nevada
20. Northern Iowa

1990
(NCAA)

Team
1. Middle Tenn. St.
2. Youngstown St.
3. Ga. Southern
4. Nevada
5. Eastern Ky.
6. Southwest Mo. St.
7. William & Mary
8. Holy Cross
9. Massachusetts
10. Boise St.
11. Northern Iowa
12. Furman
13. Idaho
14. Northeast La.
15. Citadel
16. Jackson St.
17. Dartmouth
18. Central Fla.
19. New Hampshire
    North Caro. A&T

1991
(NCAA)

Team
1. Nevada
2. Eastern Ky.
3. Holy Cross
4. Northern Iowa
5. Alabama St.
6. Delaware
7. Villanova
8. Marshall
9. Middle Tenn. St.
10. Samford
11. New Hampshire
12. Sam Houston St.
13. Youngstown St.
14. Western Ill.
15. Weber St.
16. James Madison
17. Appalachian St.
18. Northeast La.
19. McNeese St.
20. Citadel
    Furman

1992
(NCAA)

Team
1. Citadel
   Northeast La.
3. Northern Iowa
4. Middle Tenn. St.
5. Idaho
6. Marshall
7. Youngstown St.
8. Delaware
9. Samford
10. Villanova
11. McNeese St.
12. Eastern Ky.
13. William & Mary
14. Eastern Wash.
15. Florida A&M
16. Appalachian St.
17. North Caro. A&T
18. Alcorn St.
19. Liberty
20. Western Ill.

1993
(Sports Network)

Team
1. Troy St.
2. Ga. Southern
3. Montana
4. Northeast La.
5. McNeese St.
6. Boston U.
7. Youngstown St.
8. Howard
9. Marshall
10. William & Mary
11. Idaho
12. Central Fla.
13. Northern Iowa
14. Stephen F. Austin
15. Southern U.
16. Pennsylvania
17. Eastern Ky.
18. Delaware
19. Western Ky.
20. Eastern Wash.
21. North Caro. A&T
22. Tennessee Tech
23. Alcorn St.
24. Towson
25. Massachusetts

1994
(Sports Network)

Team
1. Youngstown St.
2. Marshall
3. Boise St.
4. Eastern Ky.
5. McNeese St.
6. Idaho
7. Grambling
8. Montana
9. Boston U.
10. Troy St.
11. Northern Iowa
12. New Hampshire
13. James Madison
14. Pennsylvania
15. Alcorn St.
16. Middle Tenn. St.
17. Appalachian St.
18. North Texas
19. William & Mary
20. Central Fla.
21. Stephen F. Austin
22. South Caro. St.
23. Hofstra
24. Western Ill.
25. Northern Ariz.

1995
(Sports Network)

Team
1. McNeese St.
2. Appalachian St.
3. Troy St.
4. Murray St.
5. Stephen F. Austin
6. Marshall
7. Delaware
8. Montana
9. Hofstra
10. Eastern Ky.
11. Southern U.
12. Eastern Ill.
13. James Madison
14. Jackson St.
15. Ga. Southern
16. Florida A&M
17. Idaho
18. Northern Iowa
19. William & Mary
20. Richmond
21. Boise St.
22. Northern Ariz.
23. Connecticut
24. Indiana St.
25. Middle Tenn. St.

1996
(Sports Network)

Team
1. Marshall
2. Montana
3. Northern Iowa
4. Murray St.
5. Troy St.
6. Northern Ariz.
7. William & Mary
8. Jackson St.
(tie) East Tenn. St.
10. Western Ill.
11. Delaware
12. Florida A&M
13. Furman
14. Villanova
15. Youngstown St.
16. Eastern Ill.
17. Dartmouth
18. New Hampshire
19. Nicholls St.
20. Howard
21. Southwest Mo. St.
22. Stephen F. Austin
23. James Madison
24. Dayton
25. Appalachian St.

1997
(Sports Network)

Team
1. Villanova
2. Western Ill.
3. Delaware
4. Eastern Wash.
5. Western Ky.
6. McNeese St.
7. Hampton
8. Ga. Southern
9. Youngstown St.
10. Florida A&M
11. Montana
12. Southern U.
13. Jackson St.
14. Hofstra
15. Eastern Ky.
16. Cal Poly
17. Northwestern St.
18. Stephen F. Austin
19. South Caro. St.
20. Liberty
21. Eastern Ill.
22. Appalachian St.
23. Dayton
24. Northeastern
25. Colgate

1997
(USA Today/ESPN)

Team
1. Youngstown St.
2. McNeese St.
3. Delaware
4. Eastern Wash.
5. Villanova
6. Western Ill.
7. Western Ky.
8. Ga. Southern
9. Montana
10. Hampton
11. Southern U.
12. Florida A&M
13. Jackson St.
14. Northwestern St.
15. Eastern Ky.
16. Hofstra
17. Cal Poly
18. Stephen F. Austin
19. Liberty
20. South Caro. St.
21. Colgate
22. Eastern Ill.
23. Appalachian St.
24. Northeastern
25. Dayton

1997 Week-by-Week Polls by The Sports Network

Preseason 8/25	9-9	9-16	9-23	9-30	10-7	10-14	10-21	10-28	11-4	11-11	11-18	11-25
Montana	1	1	1	1	2	2	6	15	13	11	11	11
Troy St.	2	2	7	7	19	16	25	NR	NR	NR	NR	NR
William & Mary	3	3	9	8	23	18	14	20	NR	NR	NR	NR
Northern Iowa	13	12	23	23	17	24	17	NR	NR	NR	NR	NR
Western Ill.	5	4	8	9	5	5	3	2	2	2	2	2
Delaware	4	11	10	11	6	6	4	3	3	3	3	3
East Tenn. St.	6	14	14	14	8	14	13	12	20	19	24	NR
Appalachian St.	11	9	6	6	14	NR	22	18	17	15	15	22
Northern Ariz.	8	7	5	5	12	11	11	10	16	NR	NR	NR
Youngstown St.	7	5	2	2	1	1	5	4	4	4	4	9
Murray St.	17	NR	NR	NR	20	17	NR	NR	NR	NR	NR	NR
Western Ky.	9	6	3	3	7	7	7	5	5	5	5	5
Furman	10	18	18	18	NR	22	19	NR	NR	NR	NR	NR
Jackson St.	12	8	19	19	15	13	20	17	14	13	14	13
Stephen F. Austin	14	17	17	16	13	12	10	7	7	14	13	18
Florida A&M	16	15	12	12	16	21	21	NR	15	10	10	10
Northwestern St.	24	23	24	21	21	NR	NR	NR	NR	25	21	17
Southern U.	15	13	13	13	9	8	8	6	6	12	12	12
Villanova	18	10	4	4	3	3	1	1	1	1	1	1
Howard	23	NR	NR	NR	NR	NR	NR	NR	NR	NR	NR	NR
Eastern Ky.	22	NR	NR	NR	NR	NR	NR	NR	24	23	19	15
Nicholls St.	25	25	15	24	18	15	NR	25	NR	NR	NR	NR
Ga. Southern	21	20	20	17	11	9	16	14	11	8	8	8
Eastern Ill.	19	19	16	15	10	10	9	8	9	16	16	21
McNeese St.	20	16	11	10	4	4	2	9	10	7	7	6
Eastern Wash.	NR	21	21	20	NR	20	12	11	8	6	6	4
Chattanooga	NR	22	22	NR	NR	NR	NR	23	NR	NR	NR	NR
Weber St.	NR	24	NR	NR	NR	NR	NR	NR	NR	NR	NR	NR
James Madison	NR	NR	25	22	NR	NR	NR	NR	NR	NR	NR	NR
Murray St.	NR	NR	NR	25	24	NR	NR	NR	NR	NR	NR	NR
Southwest Tex. St.	NR	NR	NR	NR	22	25	NR	NR	NR	NR	NR	NR
Hampton	NR	NR	NR	NR	25	19	15	13	12	9	9	7
South Caro. St.	NR	NR	NR	NR	NR	23	18	22	19	17	22	19
Dayton	NR	NR	NR	NR	NR	NR	23	21	18	18	23	23
North Caro. A&T	NR	NR	NR	NR	NR	NR	24	NR	NR	NR	NR	NR
Cal Poly	NR	NR	NR	NR	NR	NR	NR	19	23	22	18	16
Hofstra	NR	NR	NR	NR	NR	NR	NR	24	21	21	17	14
Liberty	NR	NR	NR	NR	NR	NR	NR	NR	22	20	25	20
Northeastern	NR	NR	NR	NR	NR	NR	NR	NR	25	24	20	24
Colgate	NR	NR	NR	NR	NR	NR	NR	NR	NR	NR	NR	25

NR=Not ranked

1997 Week-by-Week Polls by USA Today/ESPN

Preseason 9/2	9-30	10-7	10-14	10-21	10-28	11-4	11-11	11-18	11-25	12-22
Montana	1	2	2	7	13	12	11	10	10	9
William & Mary	7	15	15	13	16	23T	NR	NR	NR	NR
Troy St.	9	18	16	25	NR	NR	NR	NR	NR	NR
Northern Ariz.	4	10	11	12	10	17	NR	NR	NR	NR
Northern Iowa	22	20	24	16	25	NR	NR	NR	NR	NR
Furman	NR	24	19	17	24	23T	NR	NR	NR	NR
Eastern Ill.	18	12	10	9	9	9	14	14	21	22
Western Ill.	8	5	5	3	2	2	2	2	2	6
East Tenn. St.	15	7	14	14	12	18	17	25	25	NR
Youngstown St.	2	1	1	5	5	6	4	4	7	1
Delaware	13	9	7	6	3	3	3	3	3	3
Jackson St.	17	13	13	20	17	14	15	15	15	13
Northwestern St.	21	25	NR	NR	NR	NR	25	21	17	14
Eastern Ky.	NR	NR	NR	NR	NR	25	22	19	13	15
Murray St.	19	NR	20	NR	NR	NR	NR	NR	NR	NR
McNeese St.	6	4	4	2	8	8	6	6	5	2
Appalachian St.	10	14	23	21	19	16	16	16	22	23
Florida A&M	11	16T	21	19	18	15	10	11	11	12
Ga. Southern	16	11	9	15	14	11	8	8	8	8
Villanova	5	3	3	1	1	1	1	1	1	5
Southwest Mo. St.	NR	NR	NR	NR	NR	NR	NR	NR	NR	NR
Nicholls St.	24	21	18	NR	NR	NR	NR	NR	NR	NR
Howard	NR	NR	NR	NR	NR	NR	NR	NR	NR	NR
Stephen F. Austin	20	16T	12	10	7	7	12	12	19	18
Eastern Wash.	14	19	17	11	11	10	7	7	6	4
Western Ky.	3	6	6	4	4	4	5	5	4	7
Southern U.	12	8	8	8	6	5	13	13	12	11
James Madison	23	NR	NR	NR	NR	NR	NR	NR	NR	NR
Richmond	25	22	25	NR	NR	NR	NR	NR	NR	NR
Connecticut	NR	23	NR	NR	NR	NR	NR	NR	NR	NR
Hampton	NR	NR	22	18	15	13	9	9	9	10
South Caro. St.	NR	NR	NR	22	23	20	18	22	20	20
Dayton	NR	NR	NR	23	21	19	20	NR	24	25
Montana St.	NR	NR	NR	24	NR	NR	NR	NR	NR	NR
Cal Poly	NR	NR	NR	NR	20	NR	23	18	16	17
Chattanooga	NR	NR	NR	NR	22	NR	NR	NR	NR	NR
Hofstra	NR	NR	NR	NR	NR	21	21	17	14	16
Liberty	NR	NR	NR	NR	NR	22	19	23	18	19
Northeastern	NR	NR	NR	NR	NR	NR	24	20	23	24
Bucknell	NR	NR	NR	NR	NR	NR	NR	24	NR	NR
Colgate	NR	NR	NR	NR	NR	NR	NR	NR	NR	21

NR=Not ranked

Undefeated, Untied Teams

Regular-season games only, from 1978. Subsequent loss in Division I-AA championship is indicated by (††).

Year	Team	Wins
1978	Nevada	††11
1979	(None)	
1980	(None)	
1981	(None)	
1982	*Eastern Ky.	10
1983	(None)	
1984	Tennessee St.	11
	Alcorn St.	††9
1985	Middle Tenn. St.	††11
1986	Nevada	††11
	Pennsylvania	10
1987	Holy Cross	11
1988	(None)	
1989	*Ga. Southern	11
1990	Youngstown St.	††11
1991	Holy Cross	11
	Nevada	††11
1992	(None)	
1993	Boston U.	††11
	Howard	††11
	Pennsylvania	10
1994	Pennsylvania	9
1995	Appalachian St.	††11
	McNeese St.	††11
	Murray St.	††11
	Troy St.	††11
1996	Dartmouth	10
	Dayton	11
	*Marshall	11
	Montana	††11
1997	Villanova	††11

Won Division I-AA championship.

The Spoilers

(From 1978 Season)

Following is a list of the spoilers of Division I-AA teams that lost their perfect (undefeated, untied) record in their **season-ending** game, including the Division I-AA championship playoffs. An asterisk (*) indicates a championship playoff game and a dagger (†) indicates the home team in a regular-season game.

Date	Spoiler	Victim	Score
12-9-78	*Massachusetts	Nevada	44-21
11-15-80	†Grambling	South Caro. St.	26-3
11-22-80	†Murray St.	Western Ky.	49-0
12-1-84	*Louisiana Tech	Alcorn St.	44-21
12-7-85	*Ga. Southern	Middle Tenn. St.	28-21
11-22-86	Boston College	†Holy Cross	56-26
12-19-86	*Ga. Southern	Nevada	48-38
11-19-88	*Cornell	Pennsylvania	19-6
11-24-90	*Central Fla.	Youngstown St.	20-17
12-7-91	*Youngstown St.	Nevada	30-28
11-27-93	*Marshall	Howard	28-14
12-4-93	*Idaho	Boston U.	21-14
11-25-95	*Ga. Southern	Troy St.	24-21
11-25-95	*Northern Iowa	Murray St.	35-34
12-2-95	*Stephen F. Austin	Appalachian St.	27-17
12-9-95	*Marshall	McNeese St.	25-13
11-23-96	Robert Morris	Duquesne	28-26
12-21-96	*Marshall	Montana	49-29
11-22-97	†Colgate	Bucknell	48-14
12-6-97	*Youngstown St.	Villanova	37-34

Streaks and Rivalries

Because Division I-AA began in 1978, only those streaks from the period (1978-present) are listed. Only schools that have been I-AA members for five years are eligible for inclusion.

Longest Winning Streaks

(From 1978; Includes Playoff Games)

Wins	Team	Years	Ended by	Score
24	Pennsylvania	1992-95	Columbia	14-24
21	Montana	1995-96	Marshall	49-29
20	Dayton	1996-97	Cal Poly	24-44
20	Holy Cross	1990-92	Army	7-17
18	Eastern Ky.	1982-83	Western Ky.	10-10
16	Ga. Southern	1989-90	Middle Tenn. St.	13-16
15	Dartmouth	1996-97	Lehigh	26-46
15	Marshall	1996	Moved to Division I-A	
14	Youngstown St.	1994	Kent	14-17
14	Delaware	1979-80	Lehigh	20-27
13	McNeese St.	1995	Marshall	13-25
13	Holy Cross	1988-89	Army	9-45
13	Nevada	1986	Ga. Southern	38-48
13	Tennessee St.	1983-85	Western Ky.	17-22
13	Eastern Ill.	1978-79	Western Ill.	7-10
12	Bucknell	1996-97	Colgate	14-48
12	Appalachian St.	1995	Stephen F. Austin	17-27
12	Nevada	1989-90	Boise St.	14-30
12	Furman	1989	Stephen F. Austin	19-21
12	Holy Cross	1987-88	Army	3-23
12	Southern Ill.	1982-83	Wichita St.	6-28
12	Florida A&M	1978-79	Tennessee St.	3-20

Longest Unbeaten Streaks

(From 1978; Includes Playoff Games and Ties)

No.	Wins	Ties	Team	Years	Ended by
24	24	0	Pennsylvania	1992-95	Columbia
22	21	1	Dartmouth	1995-97	Lehigh
21	21	0	Montana	1995-96	Marshall
20	20	0	Dayton	1996-97	Cal Poly
20	20	0	Holy Cross	1990-92	Army
20	19	1	Youngstown St.	1993-94	Kent
19	18	1	Eastern Ky.	1982-83	Murray St.
17	16	1	Alabama St.	1990-92	Alcorn St.
17	16	1	Grambling	1977-78	Florida A&M
16	16	0	Ga. Southern	1989-90	Middle Tenn. St.
15	15	0	Marshall	1996	Moved to Division I-A
15	14	1	Delaware	1994-95	Navy
14	14	0	Delaware	1979-80	Lehigh
13	13	0	McNeese St.	1995	Marshall
13	13	0	Holy Cross	1988-89	Army
13	13	0	Nevada	1986	Ga. Southern
13	13	0	Tennessee St.	1983-85	Western Ky.
13	13	0	Eastern Ill.	1978-79	Western Ill.
13	12	1	Mississippi Val.	1983-84	Alcorn St.
13	12	1	Eastern Ill.	1981-82	Tennessee St.
12	12	0	Bucknell	1996-97	Colgate
12	12	0	Appalachian St.	1995	Stephen F. Austin
12	12	0	Nevada	1989-90	Boise St.
12	12	0	Furman	1989	Stephen F. Austin
12	12	0	Holy Cross	1987-88	Army
12	12	0	Southern Ill.	1982-83	Wichita St.
12	12	0	Florida A&M	1978-79	Tennessee St.
12	11	1	Tennessee St.	1985-86	Alabama St.
12	11	1	Tennessee St.	1981-83	Jackson St.
11	11	0	Murray St.	1996	Troy St.
11	11	0	Pennsylvania	1985-87	Cornell
10	9	1	Stephen F. Austin	1989	Ga. Southern
10	9	1	Holy Cross	1983	Boston College
10	9	1	Jackson St.	1980	Grambling

Longest Home Winning Streaks

(From 1978; Includes Playoff Games)

Wins	Team	Years	Ended by
38	Ga. Southern	1985-90	Eastern Ky.
34	Eastern Ky.	1978-83	Western Ky.
31	Middle Tenn. St.	1987-94	Eastern Ky.
30	Montana	1994-97	Eastern Wash.
25	Northern Iowa	1989-92	Youngstown St.
23	Northern Iowa	1983-87	Montana
22	Nevada	1989-91	Youngstown St.
20	Arkansas St.	1984-87	Northwestern St.
16	Pennsylvania	1992-95	Princeton
16	Southwest Tex. St.	1981-83	Central St.
16	Citadel	1980-82	East Tenn. St.
15	Holy Cross	1987-89	Massachusetts
14	Delaware	1994-97	Villanova
14	William & Mary	1991-94	Massachusetts
13	Youngstown St.	1992-93	Stephen F. Austin
13	William & Mary	1988-91	Delaware
13	Idaho	1987-89	Eastern Ill.
13	Sam Houston St.	1986-88	Stephen F. Austin
13	Delaware St.	1983-86	Northeastern
12	Rhode Island	1984-85	Towson
12	Eastern Ill.	1981-83	Indiana St.

Longest Losing Streaks

(From 1978; Can Include Playoff Games)

Losses	Team	Years	Ended by
77	Prairie View	1989-97	Current
44	Columbia	1983-88	Princeton
19	Charleston So.	1993-95	Morehead St.
19	Idaho St.	1978-80	Portland St.
17	Davidson	1985-87	Wofford
16	Colgate	1994-96	Brown
16	Siena	1994-96	Iona
16	Middle Tenn. St.	1978-79	Tennessee Tech
14	Nicholls St.	1994-96	Jacksonville St.
14	Fordham	1993-95	Marist
12	St. Francis (Pa.)	1994-96	Waynesburg
12	Fordham	1991-92	Bucknell
12	Central Fla.	1981-82	Elizabeth City St.

Most-Played Rivalries

(Ongoing Unless Indicated)

Games	Opponents (Series leader listed first)	Rivalry Record	First Game
133	Lafayette-Lehigh	71-66-5	1884
120	Yale-Princeton	64-46-10	1873
114	Yale-Harvard	61-45-8	1875
107	William & Mary-Richmond	55-47-5	1898
104	Pennsylvania-Cornell	59-40-5	1893
102	Yale-Brown	72-25-5	1880
101	Harvard-Dartmouth	53-43-5	1882
99	Western Ill.-Illinois St.	41-35-5	1904
97	Montana-Montana St.	60-32-5	1897
97	Harvard-Brown	69-26-2	1893
90	Princeton-Harvard	49-34-7	1877
89	Princeton-Pennsylvania	60-28-1	1876
87	Connecticut-Rhode Island	46-33-8	1897
86	Illinois St.-Eastern Ill.	41-36-9	1901
85	New Hampshire-Maine	39-38-8	1903
85	Cornell-Columbia	54-28-3	1889
81	Cornell-Colgate	47-31-3	1896

Additional Rivalry Records

LONGEST UNINTERRUPTED SERIES
(Must have played every year; current unless indicated)

108 games—Lafayette-Lehigh (from 1897)$
105 games—Cornell-Pennsylvania (from 1893)
79 games—Cornell-Dartmouth (from 1919)
72 games—Dartmouth-Yale (from 1926)
66 games—Brown-Yale (from 1932)
65 games—Dartmouth-Princeton (from 1933)
56 games—Columbia-Dartmouth (from 1942)
55 games—Columbia-Yale (from 1943)
54 games—Richmond-William & Mary (from 1944)
54 games—VMI-William & Mary (from 1944)
54 games—Dartmouth-Holy Cross (1942-93)
53 games—Brown-Harvard (from 1945)
53 games—Bucknell-Lafayette (from 1945)
53 games—Harvard-Yale (from 1945)
53 games—Princeton-Yale (from 1945)
52 games—Eastern Ky.-Western Ky. (from 1946)
52 games—Harvard-Princeton (from 1946)
52 games—Sam Houston St.-Southwest Tex. St. (from 1946)
52 games—Southwest Tex. St.-Stephen F. Austin (from 1946)
52 games—Montana-Montana St. (from 1946)

$Played twice in 1897-1901 and 1943-44.

MOST CONSECUTIVE WINS OVER AN OPPONENT IN AN UNINTERRUPTED SERIES
(Must have played in consecutive years)

22—Eastern Ky. over Tennessee Tech, 1976-97 (current)
21—Grambling over Prairie View, 1977-97 (current)
20—Eastern Ky. over Austin Peay, 1978-97 (current)
18—Eastern Ky. over Morehead St., 1972-89
18—Southeast Mo. St. over Lincoln (Mo.), 1972-89
17—Princeton over Columbia, 1954-70
16—Harvard over Columbia, 1979-94
16—Middle Tenn. St. over Morehead St., 1951-66
15—Delaware over West Chester, 1968-82
15—Dartmouth over Brown, 1960-74
15—Evansville over Ky. Wesleyan, 1983-97 (current)
14—Yale over Princeton, 1967-80
14—Marshall over VMI, 1983-96
14—Dartmouth over Columbia, 1984-97 (current)
14—Western Ill. over Southern Ill., 1984-97 (current)
13—Duquesne over St. Francis (Pa.), 1977-89
12—Montana over Montana St., 1986-97 (current)
12—Idaho over Boise St., 1982-93
12—Cornell over Columbia, 1977-88
11—Wofford over Newberry, 1960-70
11—Tennessee Tech over Morehead St., 1951-61
11—William & Mary over Richmond, 1944-54

MOST CONSECUTIVE WINS OVER AN OPPONENT IN A SERIES
(Did not have to play in consecutive years)

46—Yale over Wesleyan (Conn.), 1875-1913
30—Harvard over Williams, 1883-1920
23—Harvard over Bates, 1899-1944
23—Brown over Rhode Island, 1909-34
21—Grambling over Mississippi Val., 1957-77
17—Harvard over Columbia, 1979-95
16—Yale over Connecticut, 1948-64
14—Delaware over Massachusetts, 1958-89
12—Yale over Pennsylvania, 1879-92
12—Idaho over Ricks College, 1919-33

MOST CONSECUTIVE CURRENT WINS OVER AN OPPONENT IN AN UNINTERRUPTED SERIES
(Must have played in consecutive years)

22—Eastern Ky. over Tennessee Tech, 1976-97
21—Grambling over Prairie View, 1977-97
15—Evansville over Ky. Wesleyan, 1983-97
14—Dartmouth over Columbia, 1984-97
14—Western Ill. over Southern Ill., 1984-97

Cliffhangers

Regular-season Division I-AA games won on the final play in regulation time. The extra point is listed when it provided the margin of victory after the winning touchdown on the game's final play.

Date	Opponents, Score	Game-Winning Play
10-21-78	Western Ky. 17, Eastern Ky. 16	Kevin McGrath 25 FG
9-8-79	Northern Ariz. 22, Portland St. 21	Ken Fraser 15 pass from Brian Potter (Mike Jenkins pass from Potter)
11-15-80	Morris Brown 19, Bethune-Cookman 18	Ray Mills 1 run (Carlton Johnson kick)
9-26-81	Abilene Christian 41, Northwestern St. 38	David Russell 17 pass from Loyal Proffitt
10-10-81	LIU-C.W. Post 37, James Madison 36	Tom DeBona 10 pass from Tom Ehrhardt
11-13-82	Pennsylvania 23, Harvard 21	Dave Shulman 27 FG
10-1-83	Connecticut 9, New Hampshire 7	Larry Corn 7 run
9-8-84	Southwestern La. 17, Louisiana Tech 16	Patrick Broussard 21 FG
9-15-84	Lehigh 10, Connecticut 7	Dave Melick 45 FG
9-15-84	William & Mary 23, Delaware 21	Jeff Sanders 18 pass from Stan Yagiello
10-13-84	Lafayette 20, Connecticut 13	Ryan Priest 2 run
10-20-84	Central Fla. 28, Illinois St. 24	Jeff Farmer 30 punt return
10-27-84	Western Ky. 33, Morehead St. 31	Arnold Grier 50 pass from Jeff Cesarone
9-7-85	Central Fla. 39, Bethune-Cookman 37	Ed O'Brien 55 FG
10-26-85	VMI 39, William & Mary 38	Al Comer 3 run (James Wright run)
8-30-86	Texas Southern 38, Prairie View 35	Don Espinoza 23 FG
9-20-86	Delaware 33, West Chester 31	Fred Singleton 3 run
10-4-86	Northwestern St. 17, Northeast La. 14	Keith Hodnett 27 FG
10-11-86	Eastern Ill. 31, Northern Iowa 30	Rich Ehmke 58 FG
9-12-87	Youngstown St. 20, Bowling Green 17	John Dowling 36 FG
10-3-87	Northeast La. 33, Northwestern St. 31	Jackie Harris 48 pass from Stan Humphries
10-10-87	Marshall 34, Louisville 31	Keith Baxter 31 pass from Tony Petersen
10-17-87	Princeton 16, Lehigh 15	Rob Goodwin 38 FG
11-12-87	South Caro. St. 15, Grambling 13	William Wrighten 23 FG
9-24-88	Holy Cross 30, Princeton 26	70 kickoff return; Tim Donovan 55 on lateral from Darin Cromwell (15)
10-15-88	Weber St. 37, Nevada 31	Todd Beightol 57 pass from Jeff Carlson
10-29-88	Nicholls St. 13, Southwest Tex. St. 10	Jim Windham 33 FG
9-2-89	Alabama St. 16, Troy St. 13	Reggie Brown 28 pass from Antonius Smith
9-16-89	Western Caro. 26, Chattanooga 20	Terrell Wagner 68 interception return
9-23-89	Northwestern St. 18, McNeese St. 17	Chris Hamler 25 FG

Date	Opponents, Score	Game-Winning Play
10-14-89	East Tenn. St. 24, Chattanooga 23	George Searcy 1 run
9-29-90	Southwest Tex. St. 33, Nicholls St. 30	Robbie Roberson 32 FG
10-6-90	Grambling 27, Alabama A&M 20	Dexter Butcher 28 pass from Shawn Burras
11-2-91	Grambling 30, Texas Southern 27	Gilad Landau 37 FG
9-19-92	Eastern Ky. 26, Northeast La. 21	Sean Little recovered fumble in end zone
10-10-92	Appalachian St. 27, James Madison 21	Craig Styron 44 pass from D. J. Campbell
11-14-92	Towson 33, Northeastern 32	Mark Orlando 10 pass from Dan Crowley
9-4-93	Delaware St. 31, Fayetteville St. 28	Jon Jensen 17 FG
9-11-93	Connecticut 24, New Hampshire 23	Wilbur Gilliard 14 run (Nick Sosik kick)
10-16-93	Howard 44, Towson 41	Germaine Kohn 9 pass from Jay Walker
10-7-95	Valparaiso 44, Butler 42	Cameron Hatten 27 FG
10-14-95	Montana 24, Northern Ariz. 21	Andy Larson 29 FG
10-14-95	Connecticut 31, Maine 30	David DeArmas 38 FG
10-28-95	Northern Iowa 19, Southwest Mo. St. 17	Matt Waller 39 FG
10-28-95	William & Mary 18, Villanova 15	Brian Shallcross 49 FG
9-7-96	Valparaiso 23, Hope 22	Cameron Hatten 37 FG
9-21-96	Charleston So. 17, West Va. St. 14	Clint Kelly 20 FG
11-2-96	Butler 33, Evansville 31	Shawn Wood 32 FG
11-2-96	Wagner 38, Robert Morris 35	Carl Franke 41 FG
11-9-96	Murray St. 17, Eastern Ky. 14	Rob Hart 36 FG
9-6-97	Butler 10, Howard Payne 9	Jeremy Harkin 26 pass from Eli Stoddard (Shawn Wood kick)
9-13-97	Southern U. 36, Ark.-Pine Bluff 33	Chris Diaz 23 FG
9-20-97	Dayton 16, Robert Morris 13	Ryan Hulme 18 FG
10-4-97	Southwest Mo. St. 36, Southern Ill. 35	Travis Brawner 32 FG
11-8-97	Cal Poly 20, Montana St. 19	Alan Beilke 50 FG
11-15-97	James Madison 39, Rhode Island 37	Lindsay Fleshman 3 pass from Greg Maddox
11-22-97	Montana 27, Montana St. 25	Kris Heppner 37 FG

Photo from Montana sports information

Montana's Kris Heppner connected on a game-winning 37-yard field goal to edge Montana State, 27-25, in one of the seven Division I-AA games during the 1997 season that were decided on the last play of regulation.

DIVISION I-AA

Regular-Season Overtime Games Prior to 1996

In 1981, the NCAA Football Rules Committee approved an overtime tiebreaker system to decide a tie game for the purpose of determining a conference champion. The following conferences used the tiebreaker system to decide conference-only tie games. (Beginning in 1996, all college football games used the tiebreaker if the score was tied after four periods.) In an overtime period, one end of the field is used and each team gets an offensive possession beginning at the 25-yard line. Each team shall have possession until it has scored, failed to gain a first down or lost possession. The team scoring the greater number of points after completion of both possessions is declared the winner. The periods continue until a winner is determined.

NUMBER OF DIVISION I-AA OVERTIME GAMES SINCE 1981

1981	2	1986	4	1991	5	*1996	23
1982	4	1987	6	1992	2	*1997	23
1983	0	1988	6	1993	4		
1984	4	1989	2	1994	6		
1985	2	1990	6	1995	8		

**All games tied at end of four periods use tiebreaker system.*

BIG SKY CONFERENCE

Date	Opponents, Score	No. OTs	Score, Reg.
10-31-81	‡Weber St. 24, Northern Ariz. 23	1	17-17
11-21-81	‡Idaho St. 33, Weber St. 30	3	23-23
10-2-82	‡Montana St. 30, Idaho St. 27	3	17-17
11-6-82	Nevada 46, ‡Weber St. 43	3	30-30
10-13-84	‡Montana St. 44, Nevada 41	4	21-21
9-17-88	Boise St. 24, ‡Northern Ariz. 21	2	14-14
10-15-88	‡Montana 33, Northern Ariz. 26	2	26-26
9-15-90	‡Weber St. 45, Idaho St. 38	2	31-31
9-29-90	‡Nevada 31, Idaho 28	1	28-28
11-3-90	Eastern Wash. 33, ‡Idaho St. 26	1	26-26
11-10-90	Montana St. 28, ‡Eastern Wash. 25	1	25-25
10-26-91	Eastern Wash. 34, ‡Idaho 31	2	24-24
11-16-91	Montana 35, ‡Idaho 34	1	28-28
10-29-94	‡Eastern Wash. 34, Montana St. 31	3	31-31

GATEWAY CONFERENCE

Date	Opponents, Score	No. OTs	Score, Reg.
9-24-94	Western Ill. 31, ‡Southwest Mo. St. 24	1	24-24
9-30-95	Illinois St. 20, ‡Southwest Mo. St. 17	1	17-17
10-14-95	‡Southern Ill. 33, Southwest Mo. St. 30	1	30-30

MID-EASTERN ATHLETIC CONFERENCE

Date	Opponents, Score	No. OTs	Score, Reg.
11-1-86	‡North Caro. A&T 30, Bethune-Cookman 24	1	24-24

Date	Opponents, Score	No. OTs	Score, Reg.
10-22-93	Howard 41, ‡North Caro. A&T 35	1	35-35
11-20-93	‡South Caro. St. 58, North Caro. A&T 52	1	52-52

OHIO VALLEY CONFERENCE

Date	Opponents, Score	No. OTs	Score, Reg.
10-13-84	Youngstown St. 17, ‡Austin Peay 13	1	10-10
11-3-84	‡Murray St. 20, Austin Peay 13	2	10-10
10-19-85	‡Middle Tenn. St. 31, Murray St. 24	2	17-17
11-2-85	‡Middle Tenn. St. 28, Youngstown St. 21	2	14-14
10-4-86	‡Austin Peay 7, Middle Tenn. St. 0	1	0-0
10-10-87	‡Austin Peay 20, Morehead St. 13	1	13-13
11-7-87	‡Youngstown St. 20, Murray St. 13	1	13-13
10-1-88	Tennessee Tech 16, ‡Murray St. 13	1	10-10
10-29-88	Eastern Ky. 31, ‡Murray St. 24	1	24-24
11-18-89	Eastern Ky. 38, ‡Morehead St. 31	3	24-24
11-10-90	‡Tennessee Tech 20, Austin Peay 14	1	14-14
11-17-90	Murray St. 31, ‡Austin Peay 24	3	24-24
11-7-92	‡Eastern Ky. 21, Murray St. 18	1	18-18
10-2-93	Murray St. 28, ‡Tenn.-Martin 21	1	21-21
11-20-93	Tenn.-Martin 39, ‡Austin Peay 33	2	26-26

PATRIOT LEAGUE

Date	Opponents, Score	No. OTs	Score, Reg.
11-11-95	Bucknell 21, ‡Colgate 14	1	14-14
11-11-95	‡Lafayette 24, Fordham 21	2	21-21
11-18-95	‡Lehigh 37, Lafayette 30	2	30-30

SOUTHERN CONFERENCE

Date	Opponents, Score	No. OTs	Score, Reg.
10-19-91	Appalachian St. 26, Furman 23	3	20-20
11-2-91	Marshall 27, Western Caro. 24	3	20-20
11-21-92	VMI 37, Chattanooga 34	1	34-34
11-19-94	VMI 26, Appalachian St. 23	1	20-20

YANKEE CONFERENCE

Date	Opponents, Score	No. OTs	Score, Reg.
9-18-82	Rhode Island 58, ‡Maine 55	6	21-21
9-25-82	‡Boston U. 48, Maine 45	4	24-24
10-27-84	Maine 13, ‡Connecticut 10	1	10-10
9-13-86	New Hampshire 28, ‡Delaware 21	1	21-21
11-15-86	‡Connecticut 21, Rhode Island 14	1	14-14
9-19-87	‡Richmond 52, Massachusetts 51	4	28-28
9-19-87	New Hampshire 27, ‡Boston U. 20	3	17-17
10-31-87	Maine 59, ‡Delaware 56	2	49-49
11-21-87	‡Delaware 17, Boston U. 10	1	10-10
9-24-88	Villanova 31, ‡Boston U. 24	1	24-24
10-8-88	‡Richmond 23, New Hampshire 17	1	17-17
10-7-89	‡Villanova 41, Connecticut 35	6	21-21
11-16-91	Boston U. 29, ‡Connecticut 26	2	23-23
9-11-93	‡Connecticut 24, New Hampshire 23	1	17-17
10-16-93	Maine 26, ‡Rhode Island 23	2	17-17
9-17-94	Delaware 38, ‡Villanova 31	1	31-31
11-19-94	Northeastern 9, ‡James Madison 6	1	6-6
9-23-95	James Madison 28, ‡Villanova 27	1	21-21
10-7-95	‡Richmond 26, Northeastern 23	1	23-23
11-4-95	‡Maine 24, Massachusetts 21	1	21-21
11-19-94	New Hampshire 52, ‡Boston U. 51	2	45-45

‡Home team.

1997 DIVISION I-AA OVERTIME FOOTBALL GAMES

Date	Div.	Score (Scoring Play)	OT Periods	Reg. Score	Team With Choice	Choice
9-6	I-AA	Western Ky. 52, Murray St. 50	3OT	37-37	Murray St.	Defense
9-6	I-AA	Valparaiso 35, Hope (Div. III) 34	2OT	21-21	Valparaiso	Defense
9-13	I-AA	Fordham 42, Lehigh 35	1OT	35-35	Lehigh	Defense
9-13	I-AA	Southern U. 36, Ark.-Pine Bluff (NAIA) 33	3OT	30-30	Southern U.	Defense
9-27	I-AA	Colgate 44, Cornell 38	1OT	38-38	Colgate	Defense
10-4	I-AA	Cal Poly 38, New Mexico St. (I-A) 35	1OT	35-35	Cal Poly	Defense
10-4	I-AA	South Caro. St. 34, Morgan St. 27	1OT	27-27	So. Caro. St.	Defense
10-4	I-AA	Jackson St. 55, Texas Southern 49	1OT	49-49	Jackson St.	Defense
10-11	I-AA	Maine 49, Connecticut 47	3OT	34-34	Connecticut	Offense
10-11	I-AA	Citadel 23, East Tenn. St. 20	1OT	20-20	Citadel	Defense
10-11	I-AA	Hampton 33, Liberty 27	1OT	27-27	Hampton	Defense
10-11	I-AA	North Caro. A&T 40, Florida A&M 37	2OT	31-31	Florida A&M	Defense
10-11	I-AA	Troy St. 13, Sam Houston St. 10	1OT	7-7	Troy St.	Defense
10-11	I-AA	Western Ill. 29, Northern Iowa 22	2OT	22-22	No. Iowa	Defense
10-18	I-AA	Cornell 41, Lafayette 34	2OT	27-27	Lafayette	Defense
10-25	I-AA	Hampton 20, South Caro. St. 14	1OT	14-14	Hampton	Defense
10-25	I-AA	Indiana St. 16, Illinois St. 13	2OT	10-10	Illinois St.	Defense
10-25	I-AA	Cal St. Sacramento 45, Cal St. Northridge 38	1OT	38-38	CS North.	Defense
11-1	I-AA	Tennessee Tech 16, Murray St. 13	1OT	13-13	Tenn. Tech	Defense
11-15	I-AA	Bridgewater (Va.)(Div. III) 13, Davidson 10	1OT	10-10	Davidson	Defense
11-15	I-AA	James Madison 39, Rhode Island 37	3OT	21-21	James Mad.	Defense
11-15	I-AA	Northern Iowa 29, Indiana St. 21	3OT	14-14	Indiana St.	Defense
11-22	I-AA	Dartmouth 12, Princeton 9	1OT	9-9	Dartmouth	Defense

Division I-AA Stadiums

STADIUMS LISTED ALPHABETICALLY BY SCHOOL

School	Stadium	Conference	Year Built	Cap.	Surface*
Alabama St.	√Cramton Bowl	SWAC	1922	24,600	Grass
Alcorn St.	Jack Spinks	SWAC	1992	25,000	Grass
Appalachian St.	Kidd Brewer	Southern	1962	16,650	AstroTurf
Ark.-Pine Bluff	Pumphrey	SWAC	NA	6,000	Grass
Austin Peay	Governors	Independent	1946	10,000	Stadia Turf
Bethune-Cookman	Municipal	MEAC	NA	10,000	Grass
Brown	Brown	Ivy	1925	20,000	Grass
Bucknell	Christy Mathewson	Patriot	1924	13,100	Grass
Buffalo	UB Stadium	Independent	1992	16,500	Grass
Butler	Butler Bowl	Pioneer	1928	18,000	Grass
Cal Poly	Mustang	Independent	1935	8,000	Grass
Cal St. Northridge	North Campus	Big Sky	#1944	6,000	Grass
Cal St. Sacramento	Hornet Field	Big Sky	%1969	21,418	Grass
Canisius	Demske	MAAC	1989	1,000	AstroTurf
Central Conn. St.	Arute Field	Northeast	1969	5,000	Grass
Charleston So.	CSU	Independent	1991	3,000	Grass
Chattanooga	√Finley	Southern	1997	20,000	Grass
Citadel	Johnson Hagood	Southern	1948	22,500	Grass
Colgate	Andy Kerr	Patriot	1939	10,221	Grass
Columbia	Lawrence Wien	Ivy	1984	17,000	Grass
Connecticut	Memorial	Atlantic 10	1953	16,200	Grass
Cornell	Schoellkopf Field	Ivy	1915	25,597	All-Pro Turf
Dartmouth	Memorial Field	Ivy	1923	20,416	Grass
Davidson	Richardson	Independent	1924	5,200	Grass
Dayton	Welcome	Pioneer	1949	11,000	AstroTurf
Delaware	Delaware	Atlantic 10	1952	23,000	Grass
Delaware St.	Alumni Field	MEAC	1957	5,000	Grass
Drake	Drake	Pioneer	1925	18,000	Grass
Duquesne	Arthur Rooney Field	MAAC	1993	4,500	AstroTurf
East Tenn. St.	@Memorial	Southern	1977	12,000	AstroTurf
Eastern Ill.	O'Brien	Ohio Valley	1970	10,000	Grass
Eastern Ky.	Roy Kidd	Ohio Valley	1969	20,000	Grass
Eastern Wash.	Woodward	Big Sky	1967	6,000	Grass
Fairfield	Fairfield	MAAC	1980	3,000	Grass
Florida A&M	Bragg Memorial	MEAC	1957	25,500	Grass
Fordham	Jack Coffey Field	Patriot	1930	7,000	Grass
Furman	Paladin	Southern	1981	16,000	Grass
Georgetown	Kehoe Field	MAAC	NA	2,400	AstroTurf
Ga. Southern	Paulson	Southern	1984	18,000	PAT
Grambling	Robinson	SWAC	1983	19,600	Grass
Hampton	Armstrong Field	MEAC	1928	11,000	Grass
Harvard	Harvard	Ivy	1903	37,967	Grass
Hofstra	Hofstra	Independent	1963	15,000	AstroTurf
Holy Cross	Fitton Field	Patriot	1924	23,500	Grass
Howard	William H. Greene	MEAC	1986	12,500	AstroTurf

School	Stadium	Conference	Year Built	Cap.	Surface*
Idaho St.	@Holt Arena	Big Sky	1970	12,000	AstroTurf
Illinois St.	Hancock	Gateway	1967	15,000	AstroTurf
Indiana St.	Memorial	Gateway	!1924	20,500	All-Pro Turf
Iona	Mazzella Field	MAAC	1989	1,200	AstroTurf
Jackson St.	√Miss. Veterans	SWAC	1949	62,512	Grass
Jacksonville	NA	Independent	1998	NA	NA
Jacksonville St.	Paul Snow	Southland	1947	15,000	Grass
James Madison	Bridgeforth	Atlantic 10	1974	12,500	AstroTurf
La Salle	McCarthy	Independent	1936	7,500	Grass
Lafayette	Fisher Field	Patriot	1926	13,750	Grass
Lehigh	Goodman	Patriot	1988	16,000	Grass
Liberty	Williams	Independent	1989	12,000	OmniTurf
Maine	Alumni	Atlantic 10	1942	10,000	Grass
Marist	Leonidoff	MAAC	1965	2,500	Grass
Massachusetts	McGuirk	Atlantic 10	1965	16,000	Grass
McNeese St.	Cowboy	Southland	1965	17,500	Grass
Middle Tenn. St.	Johnny (Red) Floyd	Ohio Valley	!!1933	15,000	AstroTurf
Mississippi Val.	Magnolia	SWAC	1958	10,500	Grass
Monmouth	Kessler Field	Northeast	1993	4,600	Grass
Montana	Wash.-Grizzly	Big Sky	1986	18,845	Grass
Montana St.	Reno Sales	Big Sky	1973	15,197	Grass
Morehead St.	Jayne	Independent	1964	10,000	OmniTurf
Morgan St.	Hughes	MEAC	NA	10,000	Grass
Murray St.	Roy Stewart	Ohio Valley	1973	16,800	AstroTurf
New Hampshire	Cowell	Atlantic 10	1936	9,571	Grass
Nicholls St.	John L. Guidry	Southland	1972	12,800	Grass
Norfolk St.	√Foreman Field	MEAC	1935	26,000	TartanTurf
North Caro. A&T	Aggie	MEAC	1981	17,500	Grass
Northeastern	E. S. Parsons	Atlantic 10	1932	7,000	AstroTurf
Northern Ariz.	@Walkup Skydome	Big Sky	1977	15,300	AstroTurf
Northern Iowa	@UNI-Dome	Gateway	1976	16,324	AstroTurf
Northwestern St.	Turpin	Southland	1976	15,971	AstroTurf
Pennsylvania	Franklin Field	Ivy	1895	60,546	AstroTurf
Portland St.	√Civic	Big Sky	1928	23,150	AstroTurf
Prairie View	Blackshear	SWAC	1960	6,000	Grass
Princeton	Princeton	Ivy	1998	30,000	Grass
Rhode Island	Meade	Atlantic 10	1933	8,000	Grass
Richmond	Richmond	Atlantic 10	1929	22,611	SuperTurf
Robert Morris	Moon	Northeast	1950	7,000	Grass
St. Francis (Pa.)	Pine Bowl	Northeast	1979	1,500	Grass
St. John's (N. Y.)	Redmen Field	MAAC	1961	3,000	OmniTurf
St. Mary's (Cal.)	St. Mary's	Independent	1973	6,700	Grass
St. Peter's	JFK	MAAC	1990	4,000	Turf
Sam Houston St.	Bowers	Southland	1986	14,000	All-Pro Turf
Samford	Siebert	Independent	1958	6,700	Grass
San Diego	USD Torero	Pioneer	1955	4,000	Grass
Siena	Siena Field	MAAC	NA	500	Grass
South Caro. St.	Dawson Bulldog	MEAC	1955	22,000	Grass
South Fla.	√Tampa	Independent	1967	46,500	Grass
Southeast Mo. St.	Houck	Ohio Valley	1930	10,000	Grass
Southern U.	Mumford	SWAC	1928	24,000	Grass
Southern Ill.	McAndrew	Gateway	1975	17,324	OmniTurf
Southern Utah	Coliseum	Independent	1967	6,500	Grass
Southwest Mo. St.	Plaster Field	Gateway	1941	16,300	OmniTurf
Southwest Tex. St.	Bobcat	Southland	1981	14,104	Grass
Stephen F. Austin	Homer Bryce	Southland	1973	14,575	All-Pro Turf
Tenn.-Martin	Pacer	Ohio Valley	1964	7,500	Grass
Tennessee St.	W. J. Hale	Ohio Valley	1953	16,000	Grass
Tennessee Tech	Tucker	Ohio Valley	1966	16,500	Stadia Turf
Texas Southern	√Robertson	SWAC	1965	25,000	Grass
Towson	Minnegan	Patriot	1978	5,000	Grass
Troy St.	Memorial	Southland	1950	12,000	Grass
Valparaiso	Brown Field	Pioneer	1947	5,000	Grass
Villanova	Villanova	Atlantic 10	1927	12,000	AstroTurf-8
VMI	Alumni Field	Southern	1962	10,000	Grass
Wagner	Fischer Memorial	Northeast	1967	5,000	Grass
Weber St.	Elizabeth Dee Shaw Stewart	Big Sky	1966	17,500	Grass
Western Caro.	E. J. Whitmire	Southern	1974	12,000	AstroTurf
Western Ill.	Hanson Field	Gateway	1950	15,000	Grass
Western Ky.	L. T. Smith	Independent	1968	17,500	Grass
William & Mary	Walter Zable	Atlantic 10	1935	15,000	Grass
Wofford	Gibbs	Southern	1996	13,000	Grass
Yale	Yale Bowl	Ivy	1914	60,000	Grass

DIVISION I-AA

STADIUMS LISTED BY CAPACITY (TOP 25)

School	Stadium	Surface	Capacity
Jackson St.	√Miss. Veterans	Grass	62,512
Pennsylvania	Franklin Field	AstroTurf	60,546
Yale	Yale Bowl	Grass	60,000
South Fla.	√Tampa	Grass	46,500
Harvard	Harvard	Grass	37,967
Princeton	Princeton	Grass	30,000
Norfolk St.	√Foreman Field	Tartan Turf	26,000
Cornell	Schoellkopf Field	All-Pro Turf	25,597
Florida A&M	Bragg Memorial	Grass	25,500
Alcorn St.	Jack Spinks	Grass	25,000
Texas Southern	√Robertson	Grass	25,000
Alabama St.	√Cramton Bowl	Grass	24,600
Southern U.	Mumford	Grass	24,000
Holy Cross	Fitton Field	Grass	23,500
Portland St.	√Civic	AstroTurf	23,150
Delaware	Delaware	Grass	23,000
Richmond	Richmond	SuperTurf	22,611
Citadel	Johnson Hagood	Grass	22,500
South Caro. St.	Dawson Bulldog	Grass	22,000
Cal St. Sacramento	Hornet Field	Grass	21,418
Indiana St.	Memorial	All-Pro Turf	20,500
Dartmouth	Memorial Field	Grass	20,416
Brown	Brown	Grass	20,000
Eastern Ky.	Roy Kidd	Grass	20,000
Chattanooga	√Finley	Grass	20,000

*√Not located on campus. @ Indoor facility. *This column indicates the type of surface (either artificial or natural grass) present this year in the stadium. The brand name of the artificial turf, if known, is listed. #Built in 1944 as Devonshire Downs Race Track, refurbished in 1971 for football. %Originally built in 1969 with 6,000 capacity, renovated 1992 and increased to 23,000. $Built in 1971, roof added in 1975. !Built in 1924 as minor league baseball field, acquired by school in 1967 and renovated for football in 1967. !!Built in 1933, remodeled and expanded in 1953 and 1968.*

Division I-AA Statistics Trends

(Average Per Game, One Team)

	Rushing			Passing					Total Offense			Scoring		
Year	Plays	Yds.	Avg.	Att.	Cmp.	Pct.	Yds.	Av. Att.	Plays	Yds.	Avg.	TD	FG	Pts.
1978	*48.4	*171.8	3.55	20.7	9.5	46.2	129.3	6.24	69.1	301.1	4.36	2.60	0.52	19.5
1979	47.1	164.7	3.50	20.5	9.2	45.0	125.2	6.13	67.5	289.9	4.30	2.40	0.62	18.5
1980	45.2	164.8	3.65	22.4	10.4	46.5	144.4	6.45	67.6	309.2	4.58	2.58	0.59	19.6
1981	44.3	155.0	3.50	24.9	11.9	47.7	161.5	6.49	69.1	316.4	4.58	2.71	0.69	20.9
1982	44.4	156.6	3.53	26.1	12.8	48.9	166.0	6.35	70.5	322.6	4.57	2.62	0.80	20.5
1983	43.9	155.2	3.54	26.2	13.0	49.4	167.3	6.38	70.1	322.4	4.60	2.69	0.79	21.1
1984	42.9	152.6	3.56	27.9	14.0	50.0	181.0	6.49	70.7	333.5	4.72	2.80	0.80	21.8
1985	42.4	157.6	3.72	*28.9	*14.6	50.4	187.3	6.49	*71.2	344.9	4.84	2.84	0.81	22.1
1986	42.4	157.9	3.72	28.3	14.1	49.7	186.4	6.60	70.7	344.3	4.87	2.90	0.86	22.7
1987	43.1	158.6	3.68	27.1	13.6	50.1	175.6	6.48	70.2	334.2	4.76	2.78	0.91	22.0
1988	43.2	161.3	3.74	26.5	13.3	50.2	172.7	6.53	69.6	334.0	4.80	2.80	*0.92	22.1
1989	42.5	160.2	3.77	27.7	14.2	51.3	186.0	6.71	70.2	346.2	4.93	2.72	0.75	22.8
1990	42.7	161.5	3.79	27.8	14.1	50.6	187.0	6.73	70.5	348.5	4.95	2.98	0.84	23.2
1991	43.2	170.6	3.95	26.9	14.0	*51.9	184.7	6.87	70.1	*355.3	5.07	3.19	0.67	24.1
1992	43.0	171.4	*3.99	26.0	13.5	51.7	179.4	6.89	69.0	350.8	5.08	3.16	0.68	23.9
1993	42.4	168.3	3.97	27.0	14.0	51.8	186.4	*6.90	69.4	354.7	*5.11	*3.20	0.70	*24.2
1994	41.6	164.1	3.95	27.5	14.3	51.9	*188.1	6.85	69.0	352.1	5.10	3.18	0.70	24.1
1995	42.0	165.1	3.94	27.1	13.9	51.3	177.7	6.57	69.0	342.8	4.97	3.06	0.68	23.2
1996	42.0	162.0	3.86	26.9	13.7	51.1	177.6	6.62	68.8	339.6	4.94	3.05	0.72	23.2
1997	40.2	153.2	3.81	27.8	14.3	51.3	185.2	6.67	68.0	338.4	4.98	3.06	0.72	23.3

**Record.*

Additional Division I-AA Statistics Trends

(Average Per Game, One Team)

	Punting			Interceptions			Punt Returns			Kickoff Returns		
			Net		Avg.			Avg.			Avg.	
Year	No.	Avg.	Avg.	No.	Ret.	Yds.	No.	Ret.	Yds.	No.	Ret.	Yds.
1978	*6.1	36.5	33.6	1.42	11.92	17.0	2.39	7.49	17.9	3.23	18.4	59.2
1979	6.0	36.5	33.4	1.44	11.39	16.4	2.41	7.46	18.0	3.06	18.4	56.2
1980	5.8	37.0	33.7	1.37	10.06	13.8	2.44	7.94	19.4	3.09	17.4	53.7
1981	5.9	37.2	33.9	*1.60	10.63	*17.0	2.50	7.77	19.4	3.27	18.4	60.1
1982	6.0	37.1	34.0	1.50	10.15	15.2	2.44	7.63	18.6	3.08	19.0	58.4
1983	6.0	37.3	34.1	1.52	9.99	15.1	*2.59	7.58	19.6	3.06	18.6	56.9
1984	5.8	37.3	33.9	1.53	10.40	15.9	2.55	7.84	20.0	3.23	18.6	60.0
1985	5.7	37.6	*34.2	1.51	10.56	16.0	2.55	7.52	19.2	3.20	18.1	57.9
1986	5.6	*37.6	34.0	1.51	10.90	16.4	2.55	7.92	20.2	*4.02	19.4	*77.9
1987	5.6	36.8	33.4	1.40	10.57	14.9	2.48	7.51	18.7	3.96	19.0	74.6
1988	5.5	36.3	32.8	1.34	10.61	14.2	2.40	7.96	19.2	3.95	18.8	74.3
1989	5.5	36.1	32.8	1.31	10.40	13.7	2.32	7.93	18.4	3.96	18.9	74.7
1990	5.4	36.7	32.7	1.38	11.94	16.5	2.49	8.46	21.0	4.02	18.9	75.9
1991	5.3	36.6	32.6	1.35	10.81	14.6	2.46	8.57	21.1	3.84	19.1	73.4
1992	5.3	36.6	32.2	1.21	10.24	12.3	2.53	*9.35	*23.6	3.82	19.5	74.4
1993	5.2	36.0	32.3	1.23	10.79	13.2	2.35	8.26	19.5	3.72	19.3	71.7
1994	5.2	36.3	32.1	1.27	10.94	13.8	2.38	9.20	21.9	3.83	*19.9	76.0
1995	5.4	35.8	32.0	1.16	12.20	14.1	2.36	8.57	20.2	3.73	18.6	69.4
1996	5.5	36.6	32.8	1.22	12.25	15.0	2.44	8.54	20.9	3.60	19.0	68.4
1997	5.6	37.3	33.3	1.18	*12.32	14.5	2.53	8.90	22.5	3.60	19.1	68.8

**Record.*

Rules changes and statistics changes affecting trends: PUNTING–Beginning in 1965, 20 yards not deducted from a punt into the end zone for a touchback. INTERCEPTIONS–Interceptions yards not compiled, 1958-65. KICKOFF RETURNS–During 1937-45, if a kickoff went out of bounds, the receiving team put the ball in play on its 35-yard line instead of a second kickoff; in 1984 (rescinded in 1985), a 30-yard-line touchback for kickoffs crossing the goal line in flight and first touching the ground out of the end zone; in 1986, kickoffs from the 35-yard line. PUNT RETURNS–In 1967, interior linemen restricted from leaving until the ball is kicked.

Classification History

SINCE 1978

The following lists show years of active membership for current and former Division I-AA football-playing institutions. The lists are from 1978, the year that Division I was divided into I-A and I-AA. *Provisional members are described below.

ACTIVE MEMBERS (119)

Alabama St.	1982-98
Alcorn St.	1978-98
Appalachian St.	1982-98
Ark.-Pine Bluff	1998
Austin Peay	1978-98
Bethune-Cookman	1980-98
Brown	1982-98
Bucknell	1978-98
Buffalo	1993-98
Butler	1993-98
Cal Poly	1994-98
Cal St. Northridge	1993-98
Cal St. Sacramento	1993-98
Canisius	1993-98
Central Conn. St.	1993-98
Charleston So.	1993-98
Chattanooga	1982-98
Citadel	1982-98
Colgate	1982-98
Columbia	1982-98
Connecticut	1978-98
Cornell	1982-98
Dartmouth	1982-98
Davidson	1978-90, 93-98
Dayton	1993-98
Delaware	1980-98
Delaware St.	1978, 80-98
Drake	1982-85, 93-98
Duquesne	1993-98
East Tenn. St.	1982-98
Eastern Ill.	1981-98
Eastern Ky.	1978-98
Eastern Wash.	1984-98
Fairfield	1997-98
Florida A&M	1979-98
Fordham	1989-98
Furman	1982-98
Georgetown	1993-98
Ga. Southern	1984-98
Grambling	1978-98
Hampton	1997-98
Harvard	1982-98
Hofstra	1993-98
Holy Cross	1982-98
Howard	1978, 80-98
Idaho St.	1978-98
Illinois St.	1982-98
Indiana St.	1982-98
Iona	1993-98
Jackson St.	1978-98
Jacksonville	1998
Jacksonville St.	1997-98
James Madison	1980-98
La Salle	1997-98
Lafayette	1978-98
Lehigh	1978-98
Liberty	1989-98
Maine	1978-98
Marist	1993-98
Massachusetts	1978-98
McNeese St.	1982-98
Middle Tenn. St.	1978-98
Mississippi Val.	1980-98
Monmouth	1994-98
Montana	1978-98
Montana St.	1978-98
Morehead St.	1978-98
Morgan St.	1986-98
Murray St.	1978-98
New Hampshire	1978-98
Nicholls St.	1980-98
Norfolk St.	1997-98
North Caro. A&T	1978, 80-98
Northeastern	1978-98
Northern Ariz.	1978-98
Northern Iowa	1981-98
Northwestern St.	1978-98
Pennsylvania	1982-98
Portland St.	1978-80, 98
Prairie View	1980-89, 92-98
Princeton	1982-98
Rhode Island	1978-98
Richmond	1982-98
Robert Morris	1998
St. Francis (Pa.)	1993-98
St. John's (N. Y.)	1993-98
St. Mary's (Cal.)	1993-98
St. Peter's	1993-98
Samford	1989-98
Sam Houston St.	1986-98
San Diego	1993-98
Siena	1993-98
South Caro. St.	1978, 80-98
South Fla.	1997-98
Southeast Mo. St.	1990-98
Southern Ill.	1982-98
Southern U.	1978-98
Southern Utah	1993-98
Southwest Mo. St.	1982-98
Southwest Tex. St.	1984-98
Stephen F. Austin	1986-98
Tenn.-Martin	1992-98
Tennessee St.	1981-98
Tennessee Tech	1978-98
Texas Southern	1978-98
Towson	1987-98
Troy St.	1993-98
Valparaiso	1993-98
Villanova	1987-98
VMI	1982-98
Wagner	1993-98
Weber St.	1978-98
Western Caro.	1982-98
Western Ill.	1981-98
Western Ky.	1978-98
William & Mary	1982-98
Wofford	1997-98
Yale	1982-98
Youngstown St.	1981-98

MEMBERS CHANGING STATUS (5)

Alabama A&M (Div. II)	1999
Albany (N. Y.) (Div. II)	1999
Elon (Div. II)	1999
Sacred Heart (Div. II)	1999
Stony Brook (Div. II)	1999

FORMER MEMBERS

UAB	1993-95
Akron	1980-86
Arkansas St.	1982-91
Ball St.	1982
Boise St.	1978-98
Boston U.	1978-97
Bowling Green	1982
Central Fla.	1990-95
Eastern Mich.	1982
Evansville	1993-97
Idaho	1978-96
Kent	1982
Lamar	1982-89
Louisiana Tech	1982-88
Marshall	1982-96
Nevada	1978-91
North Texas	1982-94
Northeast La.	1982-93
Northern Ill.	1982
Ohio	1982
Southeastern La.	1980-85
Tex.-Arlington	1982-85
West Tex. A&M	1982-85

*Provisional members are not active members of the Association and, thus are not eligible for NCAA statistics, records and championship play.

Black College National Champions

Sheridan Poll

Selected by the Pittsburgh Courier, 1920-1980, and compiled by Collie Nicholson, former Grambling sports information director; William Nunn Jr., Pittsburgh Courier sports editor; and Eric "Ric" Roberts, Pittsburgh Courier sports writer and noted black college sports historian. Selected from 1981 by the Sheridan Broadcasting Network, 411 Seventh Ave., Suite 1500, Pittsburgh, Pa. 15219-1905. Records include postseason games.

Year	Team	Won	Lost	Tied	Coach
1920	Howard	7	0	0	Edward Morrison
	Talladega	5	0	1	Jubie Bragg
1921	Talladega	6	0	1	Jubie Bragg
	Wiley	7	0	1	Jason Grant
1922	Hampton	6	1	0	Gideon Smith
1923	Virginia Union	6	0	1	Harold Martin
1924	Tuskegee	9	0	1	Cleve Abbott
	Wiley	8	0	1	Fred Long
1925	Tuskegee	8	0	1	Cleve Abbott
	Howard	6	0	2	Louis Watson
1926	Tuskegee	10	0	0	Cleve Abbott
	Howard	7	0	0	Louis Watson
1927	Tuskegee	9	0	1	Cleve Abbott
	Bluefield St.	8	0	1	Harry Jefferson
1928	Bluefield St.	8	0	1	Harry Jefferson
	Wiley	8	0	1	Fred Long
1929	Tuskegee	10	0	0	Cleve Abbott
1930	Tuskegee	11	0	1	Cleve Abbott
1931	Wilberforce	9	0	0	Harry Graves
1932	Wiley	9	0	0	Fred Long
1933	Morgan St.	9	0	0	Edward Hurt
1934	Kentucky St.	9	0	0	Henry Kean
1935	Texas College	9	0	0	Arnett Mumford
1936	West Va. St.	8	0	0	Adolph Hamblin
	Virginia St.	7	0	2	Harry Jefferson
1937	Morgan St.	7	0	0	Edward Hurt
1938	Florida A&M	8	0	0	Bill Bell
1939	Langston	9	0	0	Felton "Zip" Gayles
1940	Morris Brown	9	1	0	Artis Graves
1941	Morris Brown	8	1	0	William Nicks
1942	Florida A&M	9	0	0	Bill Bell
1943	Morgan St.	5	0	0	Edward Hurt
1944	Morgan St.	6	1	0	Edward Hurt
1945	Wiley	10	0	0	Fred Long
1946	Tennessee St.	10	1	0	Henry Kean
	Morgan St.	8	0	0	Edward Hurt
1947	Tennessee St.	10	0	0	Henry Kean
	Shaw	10	0	0	Brutus Wilson
1948	Southern U.	12	0	0	Arnett Mumford
1949	Southern U.	10	0	1	Arnett Mumford
	Morgan St.	8	0	0	Edward Hurt
1950	Southern U.	10	0	1	Arnett Mumford
	Florida A&M	8	1	1	Alonzo "Jake" Gaither
1951	Morris Brown	10	1	0	Edward "Ox" Clemons
1952	Florida A&M	8	2	0	Alonzo "Jake" Gaither
	Texas Southern	10	0	1	Alexander Durley
	Lincoln (Mo.)	8	0	1	Dwight Reed
	Virginia St.	8	1	0	Sylvester "Sal" Hall
1953	Prairie View	12	0	0	William Nicks
1954	Tennessee St.	10	1	0	Henry Kean
	Southern U.	10	1	0	Arnett Mumford
	Florida A&M	8	1	0	Alonzo "Jake" Gaither
	Prairie View	10	1	0	William Nicks
1955	Grambling	10	0	0	Eddie Robinson
1956	Tennessee St.	10	0	0	Howard Gentry
1957	Florida A&M	9	0	0	Alonzo "Jake" Gaither
1958	Prairie View	10	0	1	William Nicks
1959	Florida A&M	10	0	0	Alonzo "Jake" Gaither
1960	Southern U.	9	1	0	Arnett Mumford
1961	Florida A&M	10	0	0	Alonzo "Jake" Gaither
1962	Jackson St.	10	1	0	John Merritt
1963	Prairie View	10	1	0	William Nicks
1964	Prairie View	9	0	0	William Nicks
1965	Tennessee St.	9	0	1	John Merritt
1966	Tennessee St.	10	0	0	John Merritt
1967	Morgan St.	8	0	0	Earl Banks
	Grambling	9	1	0	Eddie Robinson
1968	Alcorn St.	9	1	0	Marino Casem
	North Caro. A&T	8	1	0	Hornsby Howell
1969	Alcorn St.	8	0	1	Marino Casem
1970	Tennessee St.	11	0	0	John Merritt
1971	Tennessee St.	9	1	0	John Merritt
1972	Grambling	11	2	0	Eddie Robinson
1973	Tennessee St.	10	0	0	John Merritt
1974	Grambling	11	1	0	Eddie Robinson
	Alcorn St.	9	2	0	Marino Casem
1975	Grambling	10	2	0	Eddie Robinson
1976	South Caro. St.	10	1	0	Willie Jeffries
1977	South Caro. St.	9	1	1	Willie Jeffries
	Grambling	10	1	0	Eddie Robinson
	Florida A&M	11	0	0	Rudy Hubbard
1978	Florida A&M	12	1	0	Rudy Hubbard
1979	Tennessee St.	8	3	0	John Merritt
1980	Grambling	10	2	0	Eddie Robinson
1981	South Caro. St.	10	3	0	Bill Davis
1982	* Tennessee St.	9	0	1	John Merritt
1983	Grambling	8	1	2	Eddie Robinson
1984	Alcorn St.	9	1	0	Marino Casem
1985	Jackson St.	8	3	0	W. C. Gorden
1986	Central St.	10	1	1	Billy Joe
1987	Central St.	10	1	1	Billy Joe
1988	Central St.	11	2	0	Billy Joe
1989	Central St.	10	2	0	Billy Joe
1990	# Central St.	11	1	0	Billy Joe
1991	Alabama St.	11	0	1	Houston Markham
1992	Grambling	10	2	0	Eddie Robinson
1993	Southern U.	11	1	0	Pete Richardson
1994	Hampton	10	1	0	Joe Taylor
1995	Southern U.	11	1	0	Pete Richardson
1996	Jackson St.	10	2	0	James Carson
1997	Southern U.	11	1	0	Pete Richardson

**Tennessee State's participation in the 1982 Division I-AA championship (1-1 record) voided. #NAIA Division I national champion.*

American Sports Wire

Selected by American Sports Wire and compiled by Dick Simpson, CEO. Selected from 1990 by the American Sports Wire, P.O. Box 802031, Santa Clarita, Calif. 91380-2031. Record includes postseason games.

Year	Team	Won	Lost	Tied	Coach
1990	North Caro. A&T	9	2	0	Bill Hayes
1991	Alabama St.	11	0	1	Houston Markham
1992	Grambling	10	2	0	Eddie Robinson
1993	Southern U.	11	1	0	Pete Richardson
1994	Hampton	10	1	0	Joe Taylor
1995	Southern U.	11	1	0	Pete Richardson
1996	Jackson St.	10	2	0	James Carson
1997	Southern U.	11	1	0	Pete Richardson

Heritage Bowl

The first bowl game matching historically black schools in Division I-AA. The champion of the Southwestern Athletic Conference meets the champion of the Mid-Eastern Athletic Conference.

Date	Score (Attendance)	Site
12-21-91	Alabama St. 36, North Caro. A&T 13 (7,724)	Miami, Fla.
1-2-93	Grambling 45, Florida A&M 15 (11,273)	Tallahassee, Fla.
1-1-94	Southern U. 11, South Caro. St. 0 (36,128)	Atlanta, Ga.
12-30-94	South Caro. St. 31, Grambling 27 (22,179)	Atlanta, Ga.
12-29-95	Southern U. 30, Florida A&M 25 (25,164)	Atlanta, Ga.
12-31-96	Howard 27, Southern U. 24 (18,126)	Atlanta, Ga.
12-27-97	Southern U. 34, South Caro. St. 28 (32,629)	Atlanta, Ga.

All-Time Black College Football Team

(Selected by the Sheridan Broadcasting Network in 1993)

OFFENSE

QB	Doug Williams	Grambling
RB	Walter Payton	Jackson St.
RB	Tank Younger	Grambling
WR	Jerry Rice	Mississippi Val.
WR	John Stallworth	Alabama A&M
WR	Charlie Joiner	Grambling
OL	Art Shell	Md.-East. Shore
OL	Rayfield Wright	Fort Valley St.
OL	Jackie Slater	Jackson St.
OL	Larry Little	Bethune-Cookman
OL	Ernie Barnes	N.C. Central

DEFENSE

DL	Willie Davis	Grambling
DL	Ed "Too Tall" Jones	Tennessee St.
DL	Deacon Jones	South Caro. St.
DL	L. C. Greenwood	Arkansas A&M
LB	Robert Brazile	Jackson St.
LB	Harry Carson	South Caro. St.
LB	Willie Lanier	Morgan St.
DB	Mel Blount	Southern U.
DB	Lem Barney	Jackson St.
DB	Donnie Shell	South Caro. St.
DB	Everson Walls	Grambling

Division II Records

Individual Records

Official national statistics for all nonmajor four-year colleges began in 1946 with a limited post-season survey. In 1948, the service was expanded to include weekly individual and team statistics rankings in all categories except interceptions, field goals, punt returns and kickoff returns; these categories were added to official individual rankings and records in 1970. In 1992, statistics compilations for individual all-purpose yards and team net punting, punt returns, kickoff returns and turnover margin were begun.

From 1946, individual rankings were by totals. Beginning in 1970, most season individual rankings were by per-game averages. In total offense, receiving yards, all-purpose yards, rushing and scoring, yards or points per game determine rankings; in receiving and interceptions, catches per game; in punt and kickoff returns, yards per return; and in field goals, number made per game. Punting always has been by average, and all team rankings have been per game.

Beginning in 1979, passers were ranked in all divisions on efficiency rating points, and team pass defense rankings changed to the same rating system in 1990 (see page 6 for explanation).

Before 1967, rankings and records included all four-year colleges that reported their statistics to the NCAA. Beginning with the 1967 season, rankings and records included only members of the NCAA.

In 1973, College Division teams were divided into Division II and Division III under a three-division reorganization plan adopted by the special NCAA Convention on August 1, 1973. Career records of players include only those years in which they competed in Division II.

Collegiate records for all NCAA divisions can be determined by comparing records for all four divisions.

All individual and team statistics rankings include regular-season games only.

Total Offense

(Rushing Plus Passing)

MOST PLAYS

Game

88—Jarrod DeGeorgia, Wayne St. (Neb.) vs. Drake, Nov. 9, 1996 (594 yards)

Season

594—Chris Hegg, Truman St., 1985 (3,782 yards)
Per-game record—58.3, Dave Walter, Michigan Tech, 1986 (525 in 9)

Career

2,045—Earl Harvey, N.C. Central, 1985-88 (10,667 yards)
Also holds per-game record at 49.9 (2,045 in 41)

MOST PLAYS BY A FRESHMAN

Season

538—Earl Harvey, N.C. Central, 1985 (3,008 yards)
Also holds per-game record at 53.8 (538 in 10)

MOST YARDS GAINED

Game

651—Wilkie Perez, Glenville St. vs. Concord, Oct. 25, 1997 (9 rushing, 642 passing)

Season

4,301—Wilkie Perez, Glenville St., 1997 (112 rushing, 4,189 passing)
Per-game record—411.0, Grady Benton, West Tex. A&M, 1994 (3,699 in 9)

Career

11,227—Vernon Buck, Wingate, 1991-94 (1,343 rushing, 9,884 passing)
Per-game record—323.9, Grady Benton, West Tex. A&M, 1994-95 (5,831 in 18)

MOST SEASONS GAINING 3,000 YARDS OR MORE

2—Lance Funderburk, Valdosta St., 1995 (3,549) & 1996 (3,676); Chris Hatcher, Valdosta St., 1993 (3,532) & 1994 (3,512); Pat Brennan, Franklin, 1983 (3,239) & 1984 (3,248)

MOST SEASONS GAINING 2,500 YARDS OR MORE

3—Bob McLaughlin, Lock Haven, 1993 (2,928), 1994 (2,996) & 1995 (3,092); Thad Trujillo, Fort Lewis, 1992 (3,047), 1993 (2,784) & 1994 (2,535); Jim Lindsey, Abilene Christian, 1968 (2,740), 1969 (2,646) & 1970 (2,654)

GAINING 1,000 YARDS RUSHING AND 1,000 YARDS PASSING

Season

Ed Thompson, Neb.-Omaha, 1997 (1,075 rushing, 1,164 passing)

GAINING 2,000 YARDS RUSHING AND 4,000 YARDS PASSING

Career

Brad Cornelson, Mo. Southern St., 1995-97 (2,134 rushing, 4,186 passing)

GAINING 2,500 YARDS RUSHING AND 3,000 YARDS PASSING

Career

Jeff Bentrim, North Dak. St., 1983-86 (2,946 rushing, 3,453 passing)

MOST YARDS GAINED BY A FRESHMAN

Game

482—Matt Montgomery, Hampton vs. Tuskegee, Oct. 26, 1991

Season

3,008—Earl Harvey, N.C. Central, 1985 (538 plays)
Per-game record—318.1, Shawn Dupris, Southwest St., 1993 (2,863 in 9)

MOST GAMES GAINING 300 YARDS OR MORE

Season

8—Chris Hegg, Truman St., 1985

Career

16—Thad Trujillo, Fort Lewis, 1991-94

HIGHEST AVERAGE GAIN PER PLAY

Season

(Min. 350 plays) 8.8—Brett Salisbury, Wayne St. (Neb.), 1993 (424 for 3,732)

Career

(Min. 950 plays) 7.4—Donald Smith, Langston, 1958-61 (998 for 7,376)

MOST TOUCHDOWNS RESPONSIBLE FOR (TDs Scored and Passed For)

Game

10—Bruce Swanson, North Park vs. North Central, Oct. 12, 1968 (passed for 10)
Also holds Most Points Responsible For record at 60

Season

50—Chris Hatcher, Valdosta St., 1994 (passed for 50)
Also holds Most Points Responsible For record at 300

Career

120—Chris Hatcher, Valdosta St., 1991-94 (scored 4, passed for 116)
Also holds Most Points Responsible For record at 722

Rushing

MOST RUSHES

Game

62—Nelson Edmonds, Northern Mich. vs. Wayne St. (Mich.), Oct. 26, 1991 (291 yards)

Season

385—Joe Gough, Wayne St. (Mich.), 1994 (1,593 yards)
Per-game record—38.6, Mark Perkins, Hobart, 1968 (309 in 8)

Career

1,072—Bernie Peeters, Luther, 1968-71 (4,435 yards)
Also holds per-game record at 29.8 (1,072 in 36)

MOST CONSECUTIVE RUSHES BY SAME PLAYER

Game

21—Roger Graham, New Haven vs. Knoxville, Oct. 29, 1994 (during six possessions)

MOST RUSHES BY A QUARTERBACK

Career

730—Shawn Graves, Wofford, 1989-92

MOST YARDS GAINED

Half

223—Albert Bland, Mo. Southern St. vs. Washburn, Oct. 29, 1994 (21 rushes)

Game

382—Kelly Ellis, Northern Iowa vs. Western Ill., Oct. 13, 1979 (40 rushes)

Season

2,220—Anthony Gray, Western N.M, 1997 (277 rushes)
Also holds per-game record at 222.0 (2,220 in 10)

Career

6,320—Johnny Bailey, Tex. A&M-Kingsville, 1986-89 (885 rushes)
Also holds per-game record at 162.1 (6,320 in 39)

MOST YARDS GAINED BY A FRESHMAN

Game

370—Jim Hissam, Marietta vs. Bethany (W.Va.), Nov. 15, 1958 (22 rushes)

Season

2,011—Johnny Bailey, Tex. A&M-Kingsville, 1986 (271 rushes)
Also holds per-game record at 182.8 (2,011 in 11)

MOST YARDS GAINED IN FIRST GAME OF CAREER

238—Johnny Bailey, Tex. A&M-Kingsville vs. Texas Southern, Sept. 6, 1986

MOST YARDS GAINED BY TWO PLAYERS, SAME TEAM

Game

514—Thelbert Withers (333) & Derrick Ray (181), N.M. Highlands vs. Fort Lewis, Oct. 17, 1992

Season

3,526—Johnny Bailey (2,011) & Heath Sherman (1,515), Tex. A&M-Kingsville, 1986
Also hold per-game record at 320.5 (3,526 in 11)

Career

8,594—Johnny Bailey (5,051) & Heath Sherman (3,543), Tex. A&M-Kingsville, 1986-88 (1,317 rushes)

TWO PLAYERS, SAME TEAM, EACH GAINING 200 YARDS OR MORE

Game

Four times. Most recent: Ed Tillison (272) & Jeremy Wilson (204), Northwest Mo. St. vs. Neb.-Kearney, Nov. 11, 1990

TWO PLAYERS, SAME TEAM, EACH GAINING 1,000 YARDS OR MORE

Season

13 times. Most recent: Clarion, 1996—Ron DeJidas (1,027) & Steve Witte (1,019)

MOST GAMES GAINING 100 YARDS OR MORE

Season

11—Brian Shay, Emporia St., 1996; Ronald Moore, Pittsburg St., 1992; Johnny Bailey, Tex. A&M-Kingsville, 1986
Bailey also holds freshman record at 11

Career

33—Roger Graham, New Haven, 1991-94 (40 games); Johnny Bailey, Tex. A&M-Kingsville, 1986-89 (39 games)

MOST CONSECUTIVE GAMES GAINING 100 YARDS OR MORE

Season

11—Brian Shay, Emporia St., 1996; Ronald Moore, Pittsburg St., 1992; Johnny Bailey, Tex. A&M-Kingsville, 1986
Bailey also holds freshman record at 11

Career
25—Roger Graham, New Haven, 1992-94

MOST GAMES GAINING 200 YARDS OR MORE
Season
5—Five times. Most recent: Anthony Gray, Western N.M., 1997; Phillip Moore, North Dak., 1997; Irv Sigler, Bloomsburg, 1997;
Bailey also holds freshman record at 5
Career
11—Johnny Bailey, Tex. A&M-Kingsville, 1986-89 (39 games)

MOST CONSECUTIVE GAMES GAINING 200 YARDS OR MORE
Season
5—Irv Sigler, Bloomsburg, 1997

MOST GAMES GAINING 300 YARDS OR MORE
Season
4—Anthony Gray, Western N.M., 1997

MOST YARDS GAINED BY A QUARTERBACK
Game
323—Shawn Graves, Wofford vs. Lenoir-Rhyne, Sept. 15, 1990 (23 rushes)
Season
1,483—Shawn Graves, Wofford, 1989 (241 rushes)
Career
5,128—Shawn Graves, Wofford, 1989-92 (730 rushes)

MOST SEASONS GAINING 1,000 YARDS OR MORE
Career
4—Jarrett Anderson, Truman St., 1993-96; Jeremy Monroe, Michigan Tech, 1990-93; Johnny Bailey, Tex. A&M-Kingsville, 1986-89

HIGHEST AVERAGE GAIN PER RUSH
Game
(Min. 20 rushes) 17.5—Don Polkinghorne, Washington (Mo.) vs. Wash. & Lee, Nov. 23, 1957 (21 for 367)
Season
(Min. 140 rushes) 10.5—Billy Johnson, Widener, 1972 (148 for 1,556)
(Min. 200 rushes) 8.6—Roger Graham, New Haven, 1992 (200 for 1,717)
(Min. 250 rushes) 8.0—Anthony Gray, Western N.M., 1997 (277 for 2,220)
Career
(Min. 500 rushes) 8.5—Bill Rhodes, Western St., 1953-56 (506 for 4,294)
(Min. 750 rushes) 7.3—Roger Graham, New Haven, 1991-94 (821 for 5,953)

MOST RUSHING TOUCHDOWNS SCORED
Game
8—Junior Wolf, Okla. Panhandle vs. St. Mary (Kan.), Nov. 8, 1958
Season
29—Brian Shay, Emporia St., 1997
Career
72—Shawn Graves, Wofford, 1989-92
Per-game record—1.8, Jeff Bentrim, North Dak. St., 1983-86 (64 in 35)

MOST RUSHING TOUCHDOWNS SCORED BY A FRESHMAN
Season
24—Shawn Graves, Wofford, 1989
Also holds per-game record at 2.2 (24 in 11)

MOST RUSHING TOUCHDOWNS SCORED BY A QUARTERBACK
Season
24—Shawn Graves, Wofford, 1989
Per-game record—2.3, Jeff Bentrim, North Dak. St., 1986 (23 in 10)
Career
72—Shawn Graves, Wofford, 1989-92
Per-game record—1.8, Jeff Bentrim, North Dak. St., 1983-86 (64 in 35)

MOST RUSHING TOUCHDOWNS SCORED BY TWO PLAYERS, SAME TEAM
Season
41—Roger Graham (22) & A. J. Livingston (19), New Haven, 1992; Heath Sherman (23) & Johnny Bailey (18), Tex. A&M-Kingsville, 1986
Per-game record—4.1, Roger Graham & A. J. Livingston, New Haven, 1992 (41 in 10)
Career
106—Heath Sherman (55) & Johnny Bailey (51), Tex. A&M-Kingsville, 1985-88

LONGEST PLAY
99 yards—20 times. Most recent: Thelbert Withers, N.M. Highlands vs. Fort Lewis, Oct. 17, 1992

Passing

HIGHEST PASSING EFFICIENCY RATING POINTS
Season
(Min. 15 atts. per game) 210.1—Boyd Crawford, Col. of Idaho, 1953 (120 attempts, 72 completions, 6 interceptions, 1,462 yards, 21 TD passes)
(Min. 100 comps.) 189.0—Chuck Green, Wittenberg, 1963 (182 attempts, 114 completions, 8 interceptions, 2,181 yards, 19 TD passes)
(Min. 200 comps.) 179.0—Chris Hatcher, Valdosta St., 1994 (430 attempts, 321 completions, 9 interceptions, 3,591 yards, 50 TD passes)
Career
(Min. 375 comps.) 164.0—Chris Petersen, UC Davis, 1985-86 (553 attempts, 385 completions, 13 interceptions, 4,988 yards, 39 TD passes)
(Min. 750 comps.) 153.1—Chris Hatcher, Valdosta St., 1991-94 (1,451 attempts, 1,001 completions, 38 interceptions, 10,878 yards, 116 TD passes)

MOST PASSES ATTEMPTED
Game
76—Jarrod DeGeorgia, Wayne St. (Neb.) vs. Drake, Nov. 9, 1996 (completed 56)
Season
544—Lance Funderburk, Valdosta St., 1995 (completed 356)
Per-game record—50.5, Marty Washington, West Ala., 1993 (404 in 8)
Career
1,719—Bob McLaughlin, Lock Haven, 1992-95 (completed 910)
Per-game record—46.2, Tim Von Dulm, Portland St., 1969-70 (924 in 20)

MOST PASSES COMPLETED
Game
56—Jarrod DeGeorgia, Wayne St. (Neb.) vs. Drake, Nov. 9, 1996 (attempted 76)
Season
356—Lance Funderburk, Valdosta St., 1995 (attempted 544)
Also holds per-game record at 32.4 (356 in 11)
Career
1,001—Chris Hatcher, Valdosta St., 1991-94 (attempted 1,451)
Also holds per-game record at 25.7 (1,001 in 39)

MOST PASSES COMPLETED BY A FRESHMAN
Game
41—Neil Lomax, Portland St. vs. Montana St., Nov. 19, 1977 (attempted 59)

MOST CONSECUTIVE PASSES COMPLETED
Game
20—Chris Hatcher, Valdosta St. vs. New Haven, Oct. 8, 1994; Rod Bockwoldt, Weber St. vs. South Dak. St., Nov. 6, 1976
Season
23—Mike Ganey, Allegheny, 1967 (completed last 16 attempts vs. Carnegie Mellon, Oct. 9, and first 7 vs. Oberlin, Oct. 16)

HIGHEST PERCENTAGE OF PASSES COMPLETED
Game
(Min. 20 comps.) 90.9%—Rod Bockwoldt, Weber St. vs. South Dak. St., Nov. 6, 1976 (20 of 22)
(Min. 35 comps.) 88.6%—Chris Hatcher, Valdosta St. vs. New Haven, Oct. 8, 1994 (39 of 44)
Season
(Min. 225 atts.) 74.7%—Chris Hatcher, Valdosta St., 1994 (321 of 430)
Career
(Min. 500 atts.) 69.6%—Chris Petersen, UC Davis, 1985-86 (385 of 553)
(Min. 1,000 atts.) 69.0%—Chris Hatcher, Valdosta St., 1991-94 (1,001 of 1,451)

MOST PASSES HAD INTERCEPTED
Game
9—Pat Brennan, Franklin vs. Saginaw Valley, Sept. 24, 1983; Henry Schafer, Johns Hopkins vs. Haverford, Oct. 16, 1965
Season
32—Joe Stetser, Cal St. Chico, 1967 (attempted 464)
Career
88—Bob McLaughlin, Lock Haven, 1992-95 (attempted 1,719)

LOWEST PERCENTAGE OF PASSES HAD INTERCEPTED
Season
(Min. 200 atts.) 0.4%—James Weir, New Haven, 1993 (1 of 266)
(Min. 300 atts.) 1.0%—Jesse Showerda, New Haven, 1996 (3 of 300)
Career
(Min. 500 atts.) 2.4%—Chris Petersen, UC Davis, 1985-86 (13 of 553)
(Min. 1,000 atts.) 2.6%—Chris Hatcher, Valdosta St., 1991-94 (38 of 1,451)

MOST PASSES ATTEMPTED WITHOUT INTERCEPTION
Game
70—Tim Von Dulm, Portland St. vs. Eastern Wash., Nov. 21, 1970
Season
113—Jeff Allen, New Hampshire, 1975

MOST CONSECUTIVE PASSES ATTEMPTED WITHOUT INTERCEPTION
280—Jesse Showerda, New Haven, during 10 games from Sept. 7 to Nov. 16, 1996

MOST YARDS GAINED
Game
642—Wilkie Perez, Glenville St. vs. Concord, Oct. 25, 1997
Season
4,189—Wilkie Perez, Glenville St., 1997
Per-game record—393.4, Grady Benton, West Tex. A&M, 1994 (3,541 in 9)
Career
10,878—Chris Hatcher, Valdosta St., 1991-94
Per-game record—312.1, Grady Benton, West Tex. A&M, 1994-95 (5,618 in 18)

MOST YARDS GAINED BY A FRESHMAN
Game
469—Neil Lomax, Portland St. vs. Montana St., Nov. 19, 1977
Season
3,190—Earl Harvey, N.C. Central, 1985

Photo from Wayne State (Nebraska) sports information

Quarterback Jarrod DeGeorgia of Wayne State (Nebraska) set Division II records for single-game pass attempts (76) and pass completions (56) in a 54-41 loss at Drake November 9, 1996.

MOST GAMES GAINING 200 YARDS OR MORE
Season
11—Five times. Most recent: Lance Funderburk, Valdosta St., 1995
Career
31—Chris Hatcher, Valdosta St., 1991-94

MOST CONSECUTIVE GAMES GAINING 200 YARDS OR MORE
Career
28—Chris Hatcher, Valdosta St., during last six games of 1992, all 11 games of 1993 and all 11 games of 1994

MOST GAMES GAINING 300 YARDS OR MORE
Season
10—Brett Salisbury, Wayne St. (Neb.), 1993
Career
16—Chris Hatcher, Valdosta St., 1991-94

MOST CONSECUTIVE GAMES GAINING 300 YARDS OR MORE
Season
10—Brett Salisbury, Wayne St. (Neb.), 1993

MOST YARDS GAINED PER ATTEMPT
Season
(Min. 300 atts.) 11.3—Jayson Merrill, Western St., 1991 (309 for 3,484)
Career
(Min. 500 atts.) 10.6—John Charles, Portland St., 1991-92 (510 for 5,389)
(Min. 700 atts.) 9.0—Bruce Upstill, Col. of Emporia, 1960-63 (769 for 6,935)

MOST YARDS GAINED PER COMPLETION
Season
(Min. 125 comps.) 18.7—Matt Cook, Mo. Southern St., 1991 (141 for 2,637)
(Min. 175 comps.) 17.9—Damian Poalucci, East Stroudsburg, 1996 (214 for 3,831)
Career
(Min. 300 comps.) 17.8—Jayson Merrill, Western St., 1990-91 (328 for 5,830)
(Min. 600 comps.) 15.4—Earl Harvey, N.C. Central, 1985-88 (690 for 10,621)

MOST TOUCHDOWN PASSES
Quarter
5—Kevin Russell, Calif. (Pa.) vs. Frostburg St., Nov. 5, 1983 (2nd quarter)
Game
10—Bruce Swanson, North Park vs. North Central, Oct. 12, 1968
Season
50—Chris Hatcher, Valdosta St., 1994
Also holds per-game record at 4.5 (50 in 11)
Career
116—Chris Hatcher, Valdosta St., 1991-94
Also holds per-game record at 3.0 (116 in 39)

MOST TOUCHDOWN PASSES BY A FRESHMAN
Game
6—Earl Harvey, N.C. Central vs. Johnson Smith, Nov. 9, 1985
Season
29—Justin Coleman, Neb.-Kearney, 1997

HIGHEST PERCENTAGE OF PASSES FOR TOUCHDOWNS
Season
(Min. 150 atts.) 16.0%—John Ford, Hardin-Simmons, 1949 (26 of 163)
(Min. 300 atts.) 11.6%—Chris Hatcher, Valdosta St., 1994 (50 of 430)
Career
(Min. 500 atts.) 12.2%—Al Niemela, West Chester, 1985-88 (73 of 600)

MOST CONSECUTIVE GAMES THROWING A TOUCHDOWN PASS
Career
24—Matt Cook, Mo. Southern St., 1990-93 (last 2 in 1990, all 11 in 1991, 1 in 1992, all 10 in 1993)

MOST GAMES THROWING A TOUCHDOWN PASS
Career
41—John Craven, Gardner-Webb, 1991-94 (played in 43 games)

LONGEST COMPLETION
99 yards—20 times. Most recent: Justin Coleman to Mike Smith, Neb.-Kearney vs. Wayne St. (Neb.), Oct. 25, 1997

Receiving

MOST PASSES CAUGHT
Game
23—Chris George, Glenville St. vs. West Va. Wesleyan, Oct. 15, 1994 (303 yards); Barry Wagner, Alabama A&M vs. Clark Atlanta, Nov. 4, 1989 (370 yards)
Season
119—Brad Bailey, West Tex. A&M, 1994 (1,552 yards)
Per-game record—11.7, Chris George, Glenville St., 1993 (117 in 10)
Career
262—Carlos Ferralls, Glenville St., 1994-97 (3,835 yards)
Per-game record—11.5, Chris George, Glenville St., 1993-94 (230 in 20)

MOST CONSECUTIVE GAMES CATCHING A PASS
Career
43—Jon Spinosa, Lock Haven, 1992-95 (43 of 43 games played)

MOST PASSES CAUGHT BY A TIGHT END
Game
15—By six players. Most recent: Mark Martin, Cal St. Chico vs. San Fran. St., Oct. 21, 1989 (223 yards)
Season
77—Bob Tucker, Bloomsburg, 1967 (1,325 yards)
Career
199—Barry Naone, Portland St., 1985-88 (2,237 yards)

MOST PASSES CAUGHT BY A RUNNING BACK
Season
94—Billy Joe Masters, Evansville, 1987 (960 yards)
Also holds per-game record at 9.4 (94 in 10)
Career
200—Mark Steinmeyer, Kutztown, 1988-91 (2,118 yards)
Per-game record—5.4, Mark Marana, Northern Mich., 1979-80 (107 in 20)

MOST PASSES CAUGHT BY A FRESHMAN
Season
94—Jarett Vito, Emporia St., 1995 (932 yards)

MOST PASSES CAUGHT BY TWO PLAYERS, SAME TEAM
Career
399—Jon Spinosa (218) & Bryan McGinty (181), Lock Haven, 1993-95 (4,615 yards)

MOST YARDS GAINED
Game
370—Barry Wagner, Alabama A&M vs. Clark Atlanta, Nov. 4, 1989 (caught 23)
Season
1,876—Chris George, Glenville St., 1993 (caught 117)
Also holds per-game record at 187.6 (1,876 in 10)
Career
4,468—James Roe, Norfolk St., 1992-95 (caught 239)
Per-game record—160.8, Chris George, Glenville St., 1993-94 (3,215 in 20)

MOST YARDS GAINED BY A TIGHT END
Game
290—Bob Tucker, Bloomsburg vs. Susquehanna, Oct. 7, 1967 (caught 15)
Season
1,325—Bob Tucker, Bloomsburg, 1967 (caught 77)
Career
2,494—Dan Anderson, Northwest Mo. St., 1982-85 (caught 186)

MOST YARDS GAINED BY A RUNNING BACK
Game
209—Don Lenhard, Bucknell vs. Delaware, Nov. 19, 1966 (caught 11)
Season
1,202—Larry Bales, Emory & Henry, 1968 (caught 62)
Also holds per-game record at 120.2 (1,202 in 10)
Career
2,118—Mark Steinmeyer, Kutztown, 1988-91 (caught 200)

MOST YARDS GAINED BY TWO PLAYERS, SAME TEAM
Career
6,528—Robert Clark (4,231) & Robert Green (2,297), N.C. Central, 1983-86 (caught 363)

HIGHEST AVERAGE GAIN PER RECEPTION
Season
(Min. 30 receps.) 32.5—Tyrone Johnson, Western St., 1991 (32 for 1,039)
(Min. 40 receps.) 27.6—Chris Harkness, Ashland, 1987 (41 for 1,131)
(Min. 55 receps.) 24.0—Rod Smith, Mo. Southern St., 1991 (60 for 1,439)
Career
(Min. 135 receps.) 22.8—Tyrone Johnson, Western St., 1990-93 (163 for 3,717)
(Min. 180 receps.) 20.1—Robert Clark, N.C. Central, 1983-86 (210 for 4,231)

HIGHEST AVERAGE GAIN PER RECEPTION BY A RUNNING BACK
Season
(Min. 40 receps.) 19.4—Larry Bales, Emory & Henry, 1968 (62 for 1,202)
Career
(Min. 80 receps.) 18.1—John Smith, Boise St., 1972-75 (89 for 1,608)

MOST TOUCHDOWN PASSES CAUGHT
Game
8—Paul Zaeske, North Park vs. North Central, Oct. 12, 1968 (11 receptions)
Season
21—Chris Perry, Adams St., 1995 (88 receptions)
Also holds per-game record at 2.1 (21 in 10)
Career
49—Bruce Cerone, Yankton/Emporia St., 1965-66, 1968-69 (241 receptions)
Per-game record—1.6, Ed Bell, Idaho St., 1968-69 (30 in 19)

MOST TOUCHDOWN PASSES CAUGHT BY A TIGHT END
Game
5—Mike Palomino, Portland St. vs. Cal Poly SLO, Nov. 16, 1991; Alex Preuss, Grand Valley St. vs. Winona St., Sept. 17, 1988
Season
13—Bob Tucker, Bloomsburg, 1967

MOST TOUCHDOWN PASSES CAUGHT BY A RUNNING BACK
Season
12—Larry Bales, Emory & Henry, 1968
Career
24—John Smith, Boise St., 1972-75

MOST TOUCHDOWN PASSES CAUGHT BY A FRESHMAN
Season
13—Sean Scott, Millersville, 1997

HIGHEST PERCENTAGE OF PASSES CAUGHT FOR TOUCHDOWNS
Season
(Min. 10 TDs) 68.8%—Jim Callahan, Temple, 1966 (11 of 16)
Career
(Min. 20 TDs) 30.0%—Bob Cherry, Wittenberg, 1960-63 (27 of 90)

MOST CONSECUTIVE PASSES CAUGHT FOR TOUCHDOWNS
Season
10—Jim Callahan, Temple, 1966 (first 5 games of career)

MOST CONSECUTIVE GAMES CATCHING A TOUCHDOWN PASS
Career
20—Brian Penecale, West Chester, from Oct. 30, 1993, through Oct. 7, 1995

MOST GAMES CATCHING A TOUCHDOWN PASS
Career
27—James Roe, Norfolk St., 1992-95 (in 41 games)

LONGEST RECEPTION
99 yards—20 times. Mike Smith from Justin Coleman, Neb.-Kearney vs. Wayne St. (Neb.), Oct. 25, 1997

Punting

MOST PUNTS
Game
32—Jan Jones, Sam Houston St. vs. Tex. A&M-Commerce, Nov. 2, 1946 (1,203 yards)
Season
98—John Tassi, Lincoln (Mo.), 1981 (3,163 yards)
Career
328—Dan Brown, Nicholls St., 1976-79 (12,883 yards)

HIGHEST AVERAGE PER PUNT
Game
(Min. 5 punts) 57.5—Tim Baer, Colorado Mines vs. Fort Lewis, Oct. 25, 1986 (8 for 460)
Season
(Min. 20 punts) 49.1—Steve Ecker, Shippensburg, 1965 (32 for 1,570)
(Min. 40 punts) 46.3—Mark Bounds, West Tex. A&M, 1990 (69 for 3,198)
Career
(Min. 100 punts) 44.3—Tim Baer, Colorado Mines, 1986-89 (235 for 10,406)

LONGEST PUNT
97 yards—Earl Hurst, Emporia St. vs. Central Mo. St., Oct. 3, 1964

Interceptions

(From 1970)

MOST PASSES INTERCEPTED
Quarter
3—Anthony Devine, Millersville vs. Cheyney, Oct. 13, 1990 (3rd quarter; 90 yards); Mike McDonald, Southwestern La. vs. Lamar, Oct. 24, 1970 (4th quarter; 25 yards)
Game
5—By five players. Most recent: Gary Evans, Truman St. vs. Mo.-Rolla, Oct. 18, 1975
Season
14—By five players. Most recent: Luther Howard, Delaware St., 1972 (99 yards); Eugene Hunter, Fort Valley St., 1972 (211 yards)
Per-game record—1.6, Luther Howard, Delaware St., 1972 (14 in 9); Eugene Hunter, Fort Valley St., 1972 (14 in 9); Tom Rezzuti, Northeastern, 1971 (14 in 9)
Career
37—Tom Collins, Indianapolis, 1982-85 (390 yards)

MOST CONSECUTIVE GAMES INTERCEPTING A PASS
Career
8—Darin Nix, Mo.-Rolla, 1993-94

MOST YARDS ON INTERCEPTION RETURNS
Game
152—Desmond Brown, Tuskegee vs. Morris Brown, Sept. 15, 1990 (2 interceptions)
Season
300—Mike Brim, Virginia Union, 1986 (8 interceptions)
Career
504—Anthony Leonard, Virginia Union, 1973-76 (17 interceptions)

HIGHEST AVERAGE GAIN PER INTERCEPTION
Season
(Min. 6 ints.) 44.7—Ray Cannon, Bowie St., 1997 (6 for 268)
Career
(Min. 10 ints.) 37.4—Greg Anderson, Montana, 1974-76 (11 for 411)
(Min. 15 ints.) 29.6—Anthony Leonard, Virginia Union, 1973-76 (17 for 504)

MOST TOUCHDOWNS SCORED ON INTERCEPTIONS
Season
4—Clay Blalack, Tenn.-Martin, 1976 (8 interceptions)

LONGEST INTERCEPTION RETURN
100 yards—Many times. Most recent: Scott Reiland, Bentley vs. Assumption, Nov. 2, 1996

Punt Returns

(From 1970)

MOST PUNT RETURNS
Game
12—David Nelson, Ferris St. vs. Northern Mich., Oct. 2, 1993 (240 yards)
Season
61—Armin Anderson, UC Davis, 1984 (516 yards)
Career
153—Armin Anderson, UC Davis, 1983-85 (1,207 yards)

MOST YARDS ON PUNT RETURNS
Game
265—Billy Johnson, Widener vs. St. John's (N.Y.), Sept. 23, 1972 (4 returns)
Season
604—David Nelson, Ferris St., 1993 (50 returns)
Career
1,228—Brian Pinks, Northern Mich., 1994-97 (111 returns)

HIGHEST AVERAGE GAIN PER RETURN
Game
(Min. 4 rets.) 66.3—Billy Johnson, Widener vs. St. John's (N.Y.), Sept. 23, 1972 (4 for 265)
Season
(Min. 1.2 rets. per game) 34.1—Billy Johnson, Widener, 1972 (15 for 511)
Career
(Min. 1.2 rets. per game) 26.2—Billy Johnson, Widener, 1971-72 (29 for 759)

MOST TOUCHDOWNS SCORED ON PUNT RETURNS
Game
3—Virgil Seay, Troy St. vs. West Ala., Sept. 29, 1979; Billy Johnson, Widener vs. St. John's (N.Y.), Sept. 23, 1972; Bobby Ahu, Hawaii vs. Linfield, Nov. 15, 1969
Season
4—By four players. Most recent: Bootsie Washington, Shepherd, 1997
Career
6—Billy Johnson, Widener, 1971-72

LONGEST PUNT RETURN
100 yards—Many times. Most recent: Randy Ladson, Fayetteville St. vs. St. Paul's, Sept. 19, 1987

Kickoff Returns

(From 1970)

MOST KICKOFF RETURNS
Game
12—Johnny Cox, Fort Lewis vs. Mesa St., Nov. 3, 1990
Season
47—Sean Tarrant, Lincoln (Mo.), 1986 (729 yards)
Career
116—Johnny Cox, Fort Lewis, 1990-93 (2,476 yards)

MOST YARDS ON KICKOFF RETURNS
Game
276—Matt Pericolosi, Central Conn. St. vs. Hofstra, Sept. 14, 1991 (6 returns); Tom Dufresne, Hamline vs. Minn.-Duluth, Sept. 30, 1972 (7 returns)
Season
1,002—Doug Parrish, San Fran. St., 1990 (35 returns)
Career
2,630—Dave Ludy, Winona St., 1991-94 (89 returns)

HIGHEST AVERAGE GAIN PER RETURN
Game
(Min. 3 rets.) 71.7—Clarence Martin, Cal Poly SLO vs. Cal Poly Pomona, Nov. 20, 1982 (3 for 215)
Season
(Min. 1.2 rets. per game) 39.4—LaVon Reis, Western St., 1993 (14 for 552)
Career
(Min. 1.2 rets. per game) 34.0—Glen Printers, Southern Colo., 1973-74 (25 for 851)

MOST TOUCHDOWNS SCORED ON KICKOFF RETURNS
Game
2—By four players. Most recent: Lamart Cooper, Wayne St. (Neb.) vs. Moorhead St., Oct. 29, 1994
Season
3—By seven players. Most recent: Mike Smith, Neb.-Kearney, 1996
Career
8—Dave Ludy, Winona St., 1991-94

LONGEST KICKOFF RETURN
100 yards—Many times. Most recent: Mike Erlandson, Shippensburg vs. Bloomsburg, Oct. 24, 1997

Total Kick Returns

(Combined Punt and Kickoff Returns)

MOST KICK RETURNS
Season
63—Bobby Yates, Central Mo. St., 1990 (31 kickoffs, 32 punts, 840 yards)

MOST KICK-RETURN YARDS
Career
3,219—Sean Smith, Bloomsburg, 1993-96 (171 returns, 1,049 on punt returns, 2,170 on kickoff returns)

MOST TOUCHDOWNS
Career
10—Anthony Leonard, Virginia Union, 1973-76 (6 punt returns, 4 kickoff returns)

MOST CONSECUTIVE TOUCHDOWNS ON KICK RETURNS
Game
3—Bootsie Washington, Shepherd vs. West Va. Tech, Oct. 18, 1997 (89-yard kickoff return, 60-yard punt return, 59-yard punt return)

All Runbacks

(Combined Interceptions, Punt Returns and Kickoff Returns)

MOST TOUCHDOWNS
Season
6—Bootsie Washington, Shepherd, 1997 (1 interception, 4 punt returns, 1 kickoff return); Terry Guess, Gardner-Webb, 1994 (3 punt returns, 3 kickoff returns); Anthony Leonard, Virginia Union, 1974 (2 interceptions, 2 punt returns, 2 kickoff returns)
Career
13—Anthony Leonard, Virginia Union, 1973-76 (3 interceptions, 6 punt returns, 4 kickoff returns)

LONGEST RETURN OF A MISSED FIELD GOAL
100—Kalvin Simmons, Clark Atlanta vs. Morris Brown, Sept. 5, 1987 (actually from 6 yards in end zone)

Opponent's Punts Blocked

Season
6—Tim Bowie, Northern Colo., 1995

All-Purpose Yards

(Yardage Gained From Rushing, Receiving and All Runbacks)

MOST PLAYS
Season
415—Steve Roberts, Butler, 1989 (325 rushes, 49 receptions, 21 punt returns, 20 kickoff returns; 2,669 yards)
Career
1,195—Steve Roberts, Butler, 1986-89 (1,026 rushes, 120 receptions, 21 punt returns, 28 kickoff returns)

MOST YARDS GAINED
Game
525—Andre Johnson, Ferris St. vs. Clarion, Sept. 16, 1989 (19 rushing, 235 receiving, 10 punt returns, 261 kickoff returns; 17 plays)
Season
2,738—Brian Shay, Emporia St., 1996 (2,103 rushing, 247 receiving, 48 punt returns, 340 kickoff returns, 378 plays)
Per-game record—266.9, Steve Roberts, Butler, 1989 (2,669 in 10)
Career
7,803—Johnny Bailey, Tex. A&M-Kingsville, 1986-89

(6,302 rushing, 452 receiving, 20 punt returns, 1,011 kickoff returns)

Per-game record—234.0, Chris George, Glenville St., 1993-94 (4,679 in 20)

MOST YARDS GAINED BY A FRESHMAN
Season
2,425—Johnny Bailey, Tex. A&M-Kingsville, 1986 (2,011 rushing, 54 receiving, 20 punt returns, 340 kickoff returns; 296 plays)
Also holds per-game record at 220.5 (2,425 in 11)

MOST YARDS GAINED BY TWO PLAYERS, SAME TEAM
Season
4,112—Brian Shay (2,738) & Chet Pobolish (1,374), Emporia St., 1996
Also hold per-game record at 373.8 (4,112 in 11)

HIGHEST AVERAGE GAIN PER PLAY
Game
(Min. 15 plays) 30.9—Andre Johnson, Ferris St. vs. Clarion, Sept. 16, 1989 (17 for 525)
Season
(Min. 150 plays, 1,500 yards) 12.9—Billy Johnson, Widener, 1972 (175 for 2,265)
Career
(Min. 300 plays, 4,000 yards) 15.2—Chris George, Glenville St., 1993-94 (307 for 4,679)

Scoring

MOST POINTS SCORED
Game
48—Paul Zaeske, North Park vs. North Central, Oct. 12, 1968 (8 TDs); Junior Wolf, Okla. Panhandle vs. St. Mary (Kan.), Nov. 8, 1958 (8 TDs)
Season
198—Brian Shay, Emporia St., 1997 (32 TDs, 3 PATs)
Per-game record—21.0, Carl Herakovich, Rose-Hulman, 1958 (168 in 8)
Career
464—Walter Payton, Jackson St., 1971-74 (66 TDs, 53 PATs, 5 FGs)
Per-game record—13.4, Ole Gunderson, St. Olaf, 1969-71 (362 in 27)

MOST POINTS SCORED BY A FRESHMAN
Season
144—Shawn Graves, Wofford, 1989
Also holds per-game record at 13.1 (144 in 11)

MOST POINTS SCORED BY A QUARTERBACK
Season
144—Shawn Graves, Wofford, 1989
Per-game record—13.8, Jeff Bentrim, North Dak. St., 1986 (138 in 10)
Career
438—Shawn Graves, Wofford, 1989-92
Per-game record—11.0, Jeff Bentrim, North Dak. St., 1983-86 (386 in 35)

MOST POINTS SCORED BY TWO PLAYERS, SAME TEAM
Season
254—Heath Sherman (138) & Johnny Bailey (116), Tex. A&M-Kingsville, 1986
Career
666—Heath Sherman (336) & Johnny Bailey (330), Tex. A&M-Kingsville, 1986-88

MOST TOUCHDOWNS SCORED
Game
8—Paul Zaeske, North Park vs. North Central, Oct. 12, 1968 (all on pass receptions); Junior Wolf, Okla. Panhandle vs. St. Mary (Kan.), Nov. 8, 1958 (all by rushing)
Season
32—Brian Shay, Emporia St., 1997
Per-game record—3.1, Carl Herakovich, Rose-Hulman, 1958 (25 in 8)
Career
73—Jarrett Anderson, Truman St., 1993-96
Per-game record—2.2, Ole Gunderson, St. Olaf, 1969-71 (60 in 27)

MOST TOUCHDOWNS SCORED BY A FRESHMAN
Season
24—Shawn Graves, Wofford, 1989
Also holds per-game record at 2.2 (24 in 11)

MOST TOUCHDOWNS SCORED BY A QUARTERBACK
Season
24—Shawn Graves, Wofford, 1989
Per-game record—2.3, Jeff Bentrim, North Dak. St., 1986 (23 in 10)
Career
72—Shawn Graves, Wofford, 1989-92
Per-game record—1.8, Jeff Bentrim, North Dak. St., 1983-86 (64 in 35)

MOST TOUCHDOWNS SCORED BY TWO PLAYERS, SAME TEAM
Season
42—Heath Sherman (23) & Johnny Bailey (19), Tex. A&M-Kingsville, 1986
Career
110—Heath Sherman (56) & Johnny Bailey (54), Tex. A&M-Kingsville, 1986-88

MOST CONSECUTIVE GAMES SCORING A TOUCHDOWN
Career
22—Billy Johnson, Widener, 1971-72

MOST EXTRA POINTS MADE BY KICKING
Game
14—Art Anderson, North Park vs. North Central, Oct. 12, 1968 (attempted 15); Matt Johnson, Connecticut vs. Newport Naval Training, Oct. 22, 1949 (attempted 17)
Season
71—John O'Riordan, New Haven, 1993 (attempted 78)
Career
163—Miguel Sagaro, Grand Valley St., 1989-92 (attempted 179)

MOST EXTRA POINTS ATTEMPTED BY KICKING
Game
17—Matt Johnson, Connecticut vs. Newport Naval Training, Oct. 22, 1949 (made 14)
Season
78—John O'Riordan, New Haven, 1993 (made 71)
Career
179—Miguel Sagaro, Grand Valley St., 1989-92 (made 163); James Jenkins, Pittsburg St., 1988-91 (made 156)

HIGHEST PERCENTAGE OF EXTRA POINTS MADE BY KICKING
Season
(Best perfect season) 100.0%—Bryan Thompson, Angelo St., 1989 (51 of 51)
Career
(Min. 90 atts.) 98.9%—Mark DeMoss, Liberty, 1980-83 (92 of 93)
(Min. 130 atts.) 93.7%—Billy Watkins, Tex. A&M-Commerce, 1990-93 (134 of 143)

MOST CONSECUTIVE EXTRA POINTS MADE BY KICKING
Season
51—Bryan Thompson, Angelo St., 1989 (entire season)
Career
82—Mark DeMoss, Liberty (from Sept. 13, 1980, to Oct. 1, 1983; ended with missed PAT vs. Central St., Oct. 1, 1983)

MOST POINTS SCORED BY KICKING
Game
20—Clarence Joseph, Central St. vs. Kentucky St., Oct. 16, 1982 (5 FGs, 5 PATs)
Season
96—Dave Purnell, Northwest Mo. St., 1997 (14 FGs, 54 PATs)
Per Game Record—9.3, Michael Geary, Indiana (Pa.), 1993 (93 in 10)
Career
281—Billy Watkins, Tex. A&M-Commerce, 1990-93 (49 FGs, 134 PATs)
Per-game record *(min. 145 pts.)*—8.3, Dave Austinson, Truman St., 1981-82 (149 in 18)
Per-game record *(min. 200 pts.)*—6.7, Eddie Loretto, UC Davis, 1985-88 (266 in 40)

Defensive Extra Points

MOST DEFENSIVE EXTRA POINTS SCORED
Game and Season
1—Many times

LONGEST DEFENSIVE EXTRA POINT BLOCKED-KICK RETURN
99—Robert Fair (DB), Carson-Newman vs. Mars Hill, Oct. 15, 1994 (scored)

LONGEST DEFENSIVE EXTRA POINT FUMBLE RETURN
87—Rod Beauchamp (DB), Colorado Mines vs. Hastings, Sept. 3, 1988

LONGEST DEFENSIVE EXTRA POINT INTERCEPTION RETURN
100—Jonathan Mitchell (DB), Central Ark. vs. Delta St., Sept. 27, 1997; Brian Muldrow (CB), St. Francis (Ill.) vs. Northwood, Oct. 8, 1994 (scored); Morice Mabry (DB), UC Davis vs. St. Mary's (Cal.), Sept. 28, 1991 (scored)

FIRST DEFENSIVE EXTRA POINT SCORED
Herman Rice (DB), Springfield vs. Worcester Tech, Sept. 9, 1988 (80-yard blocked kick return)

Fumble Returns

LONGEST FUMBLE RETURN
95—Derek Chance, Winona St. vs. Bemidji St., Oct. 11, 1997 (scored); Chris Butler, Morningside vs. North Dak., Sept. 27, 1997 (scored)

Field Goals

MOST FIELD GOALS MADE
Game
6—Steve Huff, Central Mo. St. vs. Southeast Mo. St., Nov. 2, 1985 (37, 45, 37, 24, 32, 27 yards; 6 attempts)
Season
20—Raul De la Flor, Humboldt St., 1993 (26 attempts); Pat Beaty, North Dak., 1988 (26 attempts); Tom Jurich, Northern Ariz., 1977 (29 attempts)
Per-game record—1.9, Dennis Hochman, Sonoma St., 1986 (19 in 10); Jaime Nunez, Weber St., 1971 (19 in 10)
Career
64—Mike Wood, Southeast Mo. St., 1974-77 (109 attempts)
Also holds per-game record at 1.5 (64 in 44)

MOST CONSECUTIVE FIELD GOALS MADE
Career
17—Greg Payne, Catawba (from Oct. 5, 1996, to Sept. 20, 1997; ended with missed FG vs. Charleston So., Sept. 27, 1997)

MOST FIELD GOALS ATTEMPTED
Game
7—Jim Turcotte, Mississippi Col. vs. Troy St., Oct. 3, 1981 (made 2)
Season
35—Mike Wood, Southeast Mo. St., 1977 (made 16)
Per-game record—3.3, Skipper Butler, Texas-Arlington, 1968 (33 in 10)
Career
109—Mike Wood, Southeast Mo. St., 1974-77 (made 64)
Per-game record—2.7, Jaime Nunez, Weber St., 1969-71 (83 in 31)

HIGHEST PERCENTAGE OF FIELD GOALS MADE
Season
(Min. 15 atts.) 88.2%—Howie Guarini, Shippensburg, 1990 (15 of 17); Kurt Seibel, South Dak., 1983 (15 of 17)
(Min. 20 atts.) 86.4%—Dennis Hochman, Sonoma St., 1986 (19 of 22)
Career
(Min. 35 made) 80.0%—Bill May, Clarion, 1977-80 (48 of 60)

LONGEST FIELD GOAL
67 yards—Tom Odle, Fort Hays St. vs. Washburn, Nov. 5, 1988

Team Records

Single Game—Offense

Total Offense

MOST YARDS GAINED
910—Hanover vs. Franklin, Oct. 30, 1948 (426 rushing, 484 passing; 75 plays)

MOST YARDS GAINED, BOTH TEAMS
1,267—North Ala. (752) vs. Arkansas Tech (515), Sept. 27, 1997

MOST PLAYS
117—Tex. A&M-Kingsville vs. Angelo St., Oct. 30, 1982 (96 rushes, 21 passes; 546 yards)

HIGHEST AVERAGE GAIN PER PLAY
12.1—Hanover vs. Franklin, Oct. 30, 1948 (75 for 910)

MOST TOUCHDOWNS SCORED BY RUSHING AND PASSING
15—North Park vs. North Central, Oct. 12, 1968 (4 by rushing, 11 by passing)

MOST TOUCHDOWNS SCORED BY RUSHING AND PASSING, BOTH TEAMS
20—North Park (15) & North Central (5), Oct. 12, 1968

MOST YARDS GAINED BY A LOSING TEAM
736—East Stroudsburg vs. New Haven, Sept. 14, 1996 (lost 59-56)

Rushing

MOST YARDS GAINED
719—Coe vs. Beloit, Oct. 16, 1971 (73 rushes)

MOST RUSHES
97—Hobart vs. Union (N.Y.), Oct. 23, 1971 (444 yards)

HIGHEST AVERAGE GAIN PER RUSH (Min. 50 Rushes)
11.2—Wofford vs. Charleston So., Nov. 12, 1994 (53 for 595)

MOST TOUCHDOWNS SCORED BY RUSHING
12—Coe vs. Beloit, Oct. 16, 1971

MOST PLAYERS, ONE TEAM, EACH GAINING 100 YARDS OR MORE
5—South Dak. vs. St. Cloud St., Nov. 1, 1986 (James Hambrick 125, Darryl Colvin 123, Tony Higgins 118, Dave Elle 109, Joe Longueville [QB] 106; team gained 581)

Passing

MOST PASSES ATTEMPTED
85—West Tex. A&M vs. Eastern N.M., Nov. 5, 1994 (completed 47)

MOST PASSES ATTEMPTED, BOTH TEAMS
121—Franklin (68) & Saginaw Valley (53), Sept. 22, 1984 (completed 63)

MOST PASSES COMPLETED
56—Wayne St. (Neb.) vs. Drake, Nov. 9, 1996 (attempted 76)

MOST PASSES COMPLETED, BOTH TEAMS
72—Western N.M. (39) & West Tex. A&M (33), Oct. 8, 1994 (attempted 111)

MOST PASSES HAD INTERCEPTED
11—Hamline vs. Concordia-M'head, Nov. 5, 1955; Rhode Island vs. Brown, Oct. 8, 1949

MOST PASSES ATTEMPTED WITHOUT INTERCEPTION
63—Hamline vs. St. John's (Minn.), Oct. 8, 1955 (completed 34)

HIGHEST PERCENTAGE OF PASSES COMPLETED (Min. 20 Attempts)
90.0%—Northwestern St. vs. Southwestern La., Nov. 12, 1966 (20 of 22)

MOST YARDS GAINED
678—Portland St. vs. Mont. St.-Billings, Nov. 20, 1976

MOST YARDS GAINED, BOTH TEAMS
1,065—Western N.M. (614) & West Tex. A&M (451), Oct. 8, 1994

MOST TOUCHDOWN PASSES
11—North Park vs. North Central, Oct. 12, 1968

MOST TOUCHDOWN PASSES, BOTH TEAMS
14—North Park (11) & North Central (3), Oct. 12, 1968

Punting

MOST PUNTS
32—Sam Houston St. vs. Tex. A&M-Commerce, Nov. 2, 1946 (1,203 yards)

MOST PUNTS, BOTH TEAMS
63—Sam Houston St. (32) & Tex. A&M-Commerce (31), Nov. 2, 1946

HIGHEST AVERAGE PER PUNT (Min. 5 Punts)
57.5—Colorado Mines vs. Fort Lewis, Oct. 21, 1989 (8 for 460)

Punt Returns

MOST YARDS ON PUNT RETURNS
265—Widener vs. St. John's (N.Y.), Sept. 23, 1972 (4 returns)

MOST TOUCHDOWNS SCORED ON PUNT RETURNS
3—Troy St. vs. West Ala., Sept. 29, 1979; Widener vs. St. John's (N.Y.), Sept. 23, 1972; Hawaii vs. Linfield, Nov. 15, 1969

Scoring

MOST POINTS SCORED
125—Connecticut vs. Newport Naval Training, Oct. 22, 1949

MOST POINTS SCORED AGAINST A COLLEGE OPPONENT
106—Fort Valley St. vs. Knoxville, Oct. 11, 1969 (14 TDs, 2 PATs, 9 two-point conversions, 1 safety)

MOST POINTS SCORED BY A LOSING TEAM
60—New Haven vs. Southern Conn. St. (64), Oct. 25, 1991

MOST POINTS SCORED, BOTH TEAMS
136—North Park (104) & North Central (32), Oct. 12, 1968

MOST POINTS SCORED IN TWO CONSECUTIVE GAMES
172—Tuskegee, 1966 (93-0 vs. Morehouse, Oct. 14; 79-0 vs. Lane, Oct. 22)

MOST POINTS OVERCOME TO WIN A GAME
28—Ferris St. (46) vs. Saginaw Valley (42), Nov. 11, 1995 (trailed 28-0 with 11:17 remaining in 2nd quarter)

MOST POINTS SCORED IN A BRIEF PERIOD OF TIME
21 in 1:20—Winona St. vs. Bemidji St., Oct. 15, 1994 (turned 14-0 game into 35-0 in first quarter)

MOST TOUCHDOWNS SCORED
17—Connecticut vs. Newport Naval Training, Oct. 22, 1949

MOST TOUCHDOWNS SCORED AGAINST A COLLEGE OPPONENT
15—North Park vs. North Central, Oct. 12, 1968; Alcorn St. vs. Paul Quinn, Sept. 9, 1967; Iowa Wesleyan vs. William Penn, Oct. 31, 1953

MOST SAFETIES SCORED
3—Fort Valley St. vs. Miles, Oct. 16, 1993

MOST POINTS AFTER TOUCHDOWN MADE BY KICKING
14—North Park vs. North Central, Oct. 12, 1968 (attempted 15); Connecticut vs. Newport Naval Training, Oct. 22, 1949 (attempted 17)

MOST TWO-POINT ATTEMPTS
11—Fort Valley St. vs. Knoxville, Oct. 11, 1969 (made 9)

MOST TWO-POINT ATTEMPTS MADE
9—Fort Valley St. vs. Knoxville, Oct. 11, 1969 (attempted 11)

MOST FIELD GOALS MADE
6—Central Mo. St. vs. Southeast Mo. St., Nov. 2, 1985 (6 attempts)

MOST DEFENSIVE EXTRA POINTS SCORED
1—By many teams

MOST DEFENSIVE EXTRA-POINT OPPORTUNITIES
2—Mo. Southern St. vs. Central Mo. St., Sept. 28, 1996 (2 interceptions; none scored); North Dak. St. vs. Augustana (S.D.), Sept. 24, 1988 (2 interceptions; none scored)

First Downs

MOST TOTAL FIRST DOWNS
42—Delaware vs. Baldwin-Wallace, Oct. 6, 1973

MOST FIRST DOWNS BY PENALTY
14—La Verne vs. Northern Ariz., Oct. 11, 1958

MOST TOTAL FIRST DOWNS, BOTH TEAMS
66—North Dak. (36) & Tex. A&M-Kingsville (30), Sept. 13, 1986; Ferris St. (33) & Northwood (33), Oct. 26, 1985

Penalties

MOST PENALTIES
28—Northern Ariz. vs. La Verne, Oct. 11, 1958 (155 yards)

MOST PENALTIES, BOTH TEAMS
42—N.C. Central (23) & St. Paul's (19), Sept. 13, 1986 (453 yards)

MOST YARDS PENALIZED
293—Cal Poly SLO vs. Portland St., Oct. 31, 1981 (26 penalties)

MOST YARDS PENALIZED, BOTH TEAMS
453—N.C. Central (256) & St. Paul's (197), Sept. 13, 1986 (42 penalties)

Fumbles

MOST FUMBLES
16—Carthage vs. North Park, Nov. 14, 1970 (lost 7)

SINGLE GAME—Defense

Total Defense

FEWEST TOTAL OFFENSE PLAYS ALLOWED
29—North Park vs. Concordia (Ill.), Sept. 26, 1964

FEWEST TOTAL OFFENSE YARDS ALLOWED
Minus 69—Fort Valley St. vs. Miles, Oct. 16, 1993 (39 plays)

FEWEST RUSHES ALLOWED
7—Indianapolis vs. Valparaiso, Oct. 30, 1982 (-57 yards)

FEWEST RUSHING YARDS ALLOWED
Minus 95—San Diego St. vs. U.S. Int'l, Nov. 27, 1965 (35 plays)

FEWEST PASS COMPLETIONS ALLOWED
0—By many teams. Most recent: Winona St. vs. Wis.-River Falls, Sept. 6, 1997 (attempted 7)

FEWEST PASSING YARDS ALLOWED
Minus 19—Ashland vs. Heidelberg, Sept. 25, 1948 (completed 4)

MOST QUARTERBACK SACKS
19—Southern Conn. St. vs. Albany (N.Y.), Oct. 6, 1984

Punting

MOST OPPONENT'S PUNTS BLOCKED
5—Winston-Salem vs. N.C. Central, Oct. 4, 1986; Southeastern La. vs. Troy St., Oct. 7, 1978 (holds record for most consecutive punts blocked with 4)

MOST TOUCHDOWNS SCORED ON BLOCKED PUNT RETURNS
2—Northern Colo. vs. Western St., Sept. 7, 1996

Interceptions

MOST PASSES INTERCEPTED BY
11—St. Cloud St. vs. Bemidji St., Oct. 31, 1970 (45 attempts); Concordia-M'head vs. Hamline, Nov. 5, 1955 (37 attempts)

MOST TOUCHDOWNS ON INTERCEPTION RETURNS
3—By many teams. Most recent: Fort Valley St. vs. North Ala., Oct. 12, 1991

SEASON—Offense

Total Offense

MOST YARDS GAINED
6,284—West Tex. A&M, 1994 (931 plays, 11 games)
Per-game record—624.1, Hanover, 1948 (4,993 in 8)

HIGHEST AVERAGE GAIN PER PLAY
(Min. 500 plays) 9.2—Hanover, 1948 (543 for 4,993)
(Min. 800 plays) 6.8—Emporia St., 1997 (857 for 5,846)

MOST PLAYS PER GAME
88.7—Cal St. Chico, 1967 (887 in 10)

Rushing

MOST YARDS GAINED
4,347—Tex. A&M-Kingsville, 1986 (689 rushes, 11 games)
Per-game record—404.8, Col. of Emporia, 1954 (3,643 in 9)

HIGHEST AVERAGE GAIN PER RUSH
(Min. 300 rushes) 8.4—Hanover, 1948 (382 for 3,203)
(Min. 600 rushes) 6.3—Tex. A&M-Kingsville, 1986 (689 for 4,347)

MOST RUSHES PER GAME
78.9—Okla. Panhandle, 1963 (789 in 10)

Passing

MOST YARDS GAINED
5,000—West Tex. A&M, 1994 (363 completions, 11 games)
Also holds per-game record at 454.5 (5,000 in 11)

HIGHEST AVERAGE GAIN PER ATTEMPT (Min. 175 Attempts)
10.8—Western St., 1991 (330 for 3,574)

HIGHEST AVERAGE GAIN PER COMPLETION
(Min. 100 comps.) 19.4—Calif. (Pa.), 1966 (116 for 2,255)
(Min. 200 comps.) 18.0—East Stroudsburg, 1996 (224 for 4,041)

MOST PASSES ATTEMPTED
623—Emporia St., 1995 (completed 322)
Also holds per-game record at 56.6 (623 in 11)

MOST PASSES COMPLETED
373—Valdosta St., 1995 (attempted 570)
Also holds per-game record at 33.9 (373 in 11)

FEWEST PASSES COMPLETED PER GAME
0.4—Hobart, 1971 (4 in 9)

HIGHEST PERCENTAGE COMPLETED (Min. 200 Attempts)
70.8%—Valdosta St., 1993 (363 of 513)

LOWEST PERCENTAGE OF PASSES HAD INTERCEPTED (Min. 275 Attempts)
0.7%—New Haven, 1993 (2 of 296)

MOST TOUCHDOWN PASSES PER GAME
4.9—San Fran. St., 1967 (49 in 10)

HIGHEST PASSING EFFICIENCY RATING POINTS
(Min. 200 atts.) 183.8—Wittenberg, 1963 (216 attempts, 138 completions, 10 interceptions, 2,457 yards, 22 TDs)
(Min. 300 atts.) 180.2—Western St., 1991 (330 attempts, 203 completions, 12 interceptions, 3,574 yards, 35 TDs)

Punting

MOST PUNTS PER GAME
10.0—Wash. & Lee, 1968 (90 in 9)

FEWEST PUNTS PER GAME
1.9—Kent, 1954 (17 in 9)

HIGHEST PUNTING AVERAGE
48.0—Adams St., 1966 (36 for 1,728)

Punt Returns

MOST PUNT RETURNS
64—UC Davis, 1984 (557 yards)

MOST TOUCHDOWNS SCORED ON PUNT RETURNS
6—Northern Colo., 1996 (52 returns)

Kickoff Returns

MOST KICKOFF RETURNS
73—Lock Haven, 1995 (1,255 yards); Catawba, 1994 (1,368 yards); Lock Haven, 1993 (1,257 yards)

Scoring

MOST POINTS PER GAME
54.7—New Haven, 1993 (547 in 10)

MOST TOUCHDOWNS PER GAME
7.8—New Haven, 1993 (78 in 10)

MOST CONSECUTIVE EXTRA POINTS MADE BY KICKING
51—Angelo St., 1989 (entire season)

MOST CONSECUTIVE FIELD GOALS MADE
13—UC Davis, 1976

MOST TWO-POINT ATTEMPTS PER GAME
6.8—Florida A&M, 1961 (61 in 9, made 32)

MOST TWO-POINT ATTEMPTS MADE PER GAME
3.6—Florida A&M, 1961 (32 in 9, attempted 61)

MOST FIELD GOALS MADE
20—Humboldt St., 1993 (attempted 26); North Dak., 1988 (attempted 26); Northern Ariz., 1977 (attempted 29)

MOST DEFENSIVE EXTRA POINTS SCORED
2—Wingate, 1997 (2 blocked kick returns); UC Davis, 1991 (1 blocked kick return, 1 interception)

MOST DEFENSIVE EXTRA-POINT OPPORTUNITIES
3—UC Davis, 1991 (2 interceptions, 1 blocked kick return; two scored); Central Okla., 1989 (2 blocked kick returns, 1 interception; one scored); Northern Colo., 1988 (2 blocked kick returns, 1 interception; none scored)

Penalties

MOST PENALTIES AGAINST
146—Portland St., 1994 (1,340 yards); Gardner-Webb, 1992 (1,344 yards)
Per-game record—14.6, Portland St., 1994 (146 in 10)

MOST YARDS PENALIZED
1,356—Hampton, 1977 (124 penalties, 11 games)

Turnovers (Giveaways)

(From 1985)

FEWEST TURNOVERS
8—Lenoir-Rhyne, 1994 (4 interceptions, 4 fumbles lost)
Also holds per-game record at 0.8 (8 in 10)

MOST TURNOVERS
61—Cheyney, 1990 (36 interceptions, 25 fumbles lost)
Per-game record—5.8, Livingstone, 1986 (58 in 10)

FEWEST FUMBLES LOST
2—Michigan Tech, 1995 (9 fumbles)

SEASON—Defense

Total Defense

FEWEST YARDS ALLOWED PER GAME
44.4—John Carroll, 1962 (311 in 7)

LOWEST AVERAGE YARDS ALLOWED PER PLAY
(Min. 300 plays) 1.0—John Carroll, 1962 (310 for 311 yards)
(Min. 600 plays) 1.8—Alcorn St., 1976 (603 for 1,089)

Rushing Defense

FEWEST YARDS ALLOWED PER GAME
Minus 16.7—Tennessee St., 1967 (-150 in 9)

LOWEST AVERAGE YARDS ALLOWED PER RUSH
(Min. 250 rushes) Minus 0.5—Tennessee St., 1967 (296 for -150 yards)
(Min. 400 rushes) 1.3—Luther, 1971 (414 for 518)

Pass Defense

FEWEST YARDS ALLOWED PER GAME
10.1—Ashland, 1948 (91 in 9)

FEWEST YARDS ALLOWED PER ATTEMPT
(Min. 200 atts.) 3.1—Virginia St., 1971 (205 for 630)
(Min. 300 atts.) 3.2—Southwest Mo. St., 1966 (315 for 996)

FEWEST YARDS ALLOWED PER COMPLETION (Min. 100 Completions)
8.8—Long Beach St., 1965 (144 for 1,264)

LOWEST COMPLETION PERCENTAGE ALLOWED (Min. 250 Attempts)
24.1%—Southwest Mo. St., 1966 (76 of 315)

MOST PASSES INTERCEPTED PER GAME
3.9—Whitworth, 1959 (35 in 9); Delaware, 1946 (35 in 9)

FEWEST PASSES INTERCEPTED (Min. 150 Attempts)
1—Gettysburg, 1972 (175 attempts; 0 yards returned)

HIGHEST PERCENTAGE INTERCEPTED
(Min. 150 atts.) 21.7%—Stephen F. Austin, 1949 (35 of 161)
(Min. 275 atts.) 11.8%—Mo.-Rolla, 1978 (35 of 297)

MOST TOUCHDOWNS ON INTERCEPTION RETURNS
7—Gardner-Webb, 1992 (35 interceptions); Fort Valley St., 1991 (15 interceptions); Virginia Union, 1986 (31 interceptions)

LOWEST PASSING EFFICIENCY RATING ALLOWED (Min. 250 Attempts)
41.7—Fort Valley St., 1985 (allowed 283 attempts, 90 completions, 1,039 yards, 2 TDs and intercepted 33)

Blocked Kicks

MOST BLOCKED KICKS
27—Winston-Salem, 1986 (16 punts, 7 field goal attempts, 4 point-after-touchdown kicks)

Scoring

FEWEST POINTS ALLOWED PER GAME
0.0—Albany St. (Ga.), 1960 (0 in 9 games)

MOST POINTS ALLOWED PER GAME
64.5—Rose-Hulman, 1961 (516 in 8)

Turnovers (Takeaways)

(From 1985)

HIGHEST TURNOVER MARGIN PER GAME
2.7—Hillsdale, 1993 (plus 30 in 11; 11 giveaways vs. 41 takeaways)

MOST TAKEAWAYS
56—Gardner-Webb, 1992 (35 interceptions, 21 fumble recoveries)
Also holds per-game record at 5.1 (56 in 11)

Additional Records

MOST CONSECUTIVE VICTORIES
34—Hillsdale (from Oct. 2, 1954, to Nov. 16, 1957; ended with 27-26 loss to Pittsburg St., Dec. 21, 1957)

MOST CONSECUTIVE VICTORIES OVER DIVISION II OPPONENT
40—North Ala. (from Sept. 4, 1993, to Dec. 9, 1995; ended with 17-10 loss to Albany St. [Ga.], Aug. 31, 1996)

MOST CONSECUTIVE HOME VICTORIES
28—North Ala. (from Sept. 4, 1993, to Sept. 14, 1996; ended with 38-35 loss to Arkansas Tech, Sept. 28, 1996); North Dak. St. (from Sept. 12, 1964, to Nov. 1, 1969; ended with 14-14 tie vs. Eastern Mich., Sept. 12, 1970)

MOST CONSECUTIVE GAMES UNBEATEN
54—Morgan St. (from Nov. 5, 1931, to Nov. 18, 1938; ended with 15-0 loss to Virginia St., Nov. 30, 1938)

MOST CONSECUTIVE VICTORIES OVER ONE OPPONENT
40—West Chester vs. Millersville (from Nov. 18, 1922, to Oct. 5, 1974; ended with 17-12 loss Oct. 4, 1975)

MOST CONSECUTIVE VICTORIES OVER ONE OPPONENT IN AN UNINTERRUPTED SERIES (Must have played in consecutive years)
25—UC Davis vs. San Fran. St. (from Sept. 26, 1970, to Nov. 12, 1994; San Fran. St. dropped football program after 1994 season)

MOST CONSECUTIVE GAMES WITHOUT BEING SHUT OUT
178—North Dak. (from Oct. 7, 1967, to Nov. 10, 1984; ended with 41-0 loss to Northern Ariz., Aug. 31, 1985)

MOST CONSECUTIVE WINNING SEASONS
31—West Chester (from 1940-72; ended with 5-5-0 record in 1973)

MOST CONSECUTIVE NON-LOSING SEASONS
33—West Chester (from 1940-74; ended with 4-5-0 record in 1975)

MOST CONSECUTIVE LOSSES
39—St. Paul's (from Oct. 23, 1948, to Oct. 24, 1953; ended with 7-6 win over Delaware St., Oct. 31, 1953)

MOST CONSECUTIVE GAMES WITHOUT A VICTORY
49—Paine (1954-61, includes 1 tie)

MOST CONSECUTIVE GAMES WITHOUT A TIE
329—West Chester (from Oct. 26, 1945, to Oct. 31, 1980; ended with 24-24 tie vs. Cheyney, Nov. 8, 1980)

MOST TIE GAMES IN A SEASON
5—Wofford, 1948 (Sept. 25 to Oct. 23, consecutive)

HIGHEST-SCORING TIE GAME
54-54—Norfolk St. vs. Winston-Salem, Oct. 9, 1993

MOST CONSECUTIVE QUARTERS WITHOUT YIELDING A RUSHING TOUCHDOWN
51—Butler (from Sept. 25, 1982, to Oct. 15, 1983)

MOST CONSECUTIVE POINT-AFTER-TOUCHDOWN KICKS MADE
123—Liberty (from 1976 to Sept. 10, 1983; ended with missed PAT vs. Saginaw Valley, Sept. 10, 1983)

MOST IMPROVED WON-LOST RECORD
11 games—Northern Mich., 1975 (13-1, including three Division II playoff victories, from 0-10 in 1974)

Annual Champions, All-Time Leaders

Total Offense

CAREER YARDS PER GAME

(Minimum 5,000 Yards)

Player, Team	Years	G	Plays	Yards	Yd. PG
Grady Benton, West Tex. A&M	1994-95	18	844	5,831	*323.9
Marty Washington, West Ala.	1992-93	17	773	5,212	306.6
Scott Otis, Glenville St.	1994-95	20	755	5,911	295.6
Jarrod DeGeorgia, Wayne St. (Neb.)	1995-96	18	753	5,145	285.8
Jayson Merrill, Western St.	1990-91	20	641	5,619	281.0
Jermaine Whitaker, N.M. Highlands	1992-94	31	1,374	8,650	279.0
Chris Petersen, UC Davis	1985-86	20	735	5,532	276.6
Tim Von Dulm, Portland St.	1969-70	20	989	5,501	275.1
Vernon Buck, Wingate	1991-94	41	1,761	*11,227	273.8
Chris Hatcher, Valdosta St.	1991-94	39	1,557	10,588	271.5
Chris Hegg, Truman St.	1984-85	20	930	5,418	270.9
Pat Graham, Augustana (S.D.)	1995-96	21	948	5,672	270.1
June Jones, Portland St.	1975-76	21	760	5,590	266.2
Troy Mott, Wayne St. (Neb.)	1991-92	20	943	5,212	260.6
Earl Harvey, N.C. Central	1985-88	41	*2,045	10,667	260.2
Jim Zorn, Cal Poly Pomona	1973-74	21	946	5,364	255.4
Steve Wray, Franklin	1979, 81-82	26	1,178	6,564	252.5
Bob McLaughlin, Lock Haven	1992-95	44	2,007	11,041	250.9
Thad Trujillo, Fort Lewis	1991-94	41	1,787	10,209	249.0
Lance Funderburk, Valdosta St.	1993-96	30	1,126	7,469	249.0
Rob Tomlinson, Cal St. Chico	1988-91	40	1,656	9,921	248.0
Pat Brennan, Franklin	1981-84	30	1,286	7,316	243.9
Carl Wright, Virginia Union	1989-91	31	1,104	7,517	242.5
John Hebgen, Mankato St.	1993-96	41	1,545	9,772	238.3
Dave MacDonald, West Chester	1991-94	36	1,257	8,453	234.8

*Record.

SEASON YARDS PER GAME

Player, Team	Years	G	Plays	Yards	Yd. PG
Grady Benton, West Tex. A&M	†1994	9	505	3,699	*411.0
Perry Klein, LIU-C. W. Post	†1993	10	499	4,052	405.2
Marty Washington, West Ala.	1993	8	453	3,146	393.3
Wilkie Perez, Glenville St.	†1997	11	509	*4,301	391.0
Damian Poalucci, East Stroudsburg	†1996	10	505	3,883	388.3
Brett Salisbury, Wayne St. (Neb.)	1993	10	424	3,732	373.2
Jed Drenning, Glenville St.	1993	10	473	3,593	359.3
Alfred Montez, Western N.M.	1994	6	244	2,130	355.0
Rob Tomlinson, Cal St. Chico	†1989	10	534	3,525	352.5
Chris Hegg, Truman St.	†1985	11	*594	3,782	343.8
Jarrod DeGeorgia, Wayne St. (Neb.)	1996	10	495	3,416	341.6
Rod Smith, Glenville St.	1996	10	472	3,410	341.0
Bob Toledo, San Fran. St.	†1967	10	409	3,407	340.7
Jayson Merrill, Western St.	†1991	10	337	3,400	340.0
John Charles, Portland St.	†1992	8	303	2,708	338.5
Lance Funderburk, Valdosta St.	1996	11	490	3,676	334.2
Aaron Sparrow, Norfolk St.	†1995	10	464	3,300	330.0
George Bork, Northern Ill.	†1963	9	413	2,945	327.2
Richard Strasser, San Fran. St.	1985	10	536	3,259	325.9
Pat Brennan, Franklin	†1984	10	583	3,248	324.8

*Record. †National champion.

CAREER YARDS

Player, Team	Years	Plays	Yards
Vernon Buck, Wingate	1991-94	1,761	*11,227
Bob McLaughlin, Lock Haven	1992-95	2,007	11,041
Earl Harvey, N.C. Central	1985-88	*2,045	10,667
Chris Hatcher, Valdosta St.	1991-94	1,557	10,588
Thad Trujillo, Fort Lewis	1991-94	1,787	10,209
Rob Tomlinson, Cal St. Chico	1988-91	1,656	9,921
John Hebgen, Mankato St.	1993-96	1,545	9,772
Jarrod Fergason, Farimont St.	$1993-97	1,583	9,638
John Craven, Gardner-Webb	1991-94	1,666	9,630
Sam Mannery, Calif. (Pa.)	1987-90	1,669	9,125
Andy Breault, Kutztown	1989-92	1,459	8,975
Jermaine Whitaker, N.M. Highlands	1992-94	1,374	8,650
Damian Poalucci, East Stroudsburg	1994-97	1,365	8,569
Dave MacDonald, West Chester	1991-94	1,257	8,453
Jim Lindsey, Abilene Christian	1967-70	1,510	8,385
Dave Walter, Michigan Tech	1983-86	1,660	8,345
Maurice Heard, Tuskegee	1988-91	1,289	8,321
Aaron Sparrow, Norfolk St.	1992-95	1,345	8,301
Jack Hull, Grand Valley St.	1988-91	1,196	8,221
Dave DenBraber, Ferris St.	1984-87	1,522	8,115
Tracy Kendall, Alabama A&M	1988-91	1,480	8,112
Bill Bair, Mansfield	1989-92	1,352	8,101
Ned Cox, Angelo St.	1983-86	1,831	8,097
Matt Montgomery, Hampton	1991-94	1,220	8,091
Heath Rylance, Augustana (S.D.)	1991-94	1,667	7,883

*Record. $See page 6 for explanation.

SEASON YARDS

Player, Team	Year	G	Plays	Yards
Wilkie Perez, Glenville St.	†1997	11	509	*4,301
Perry Klein, LIU-C. W. Post	†1993	10	499	4,052
Damian Poalucci, East Stroudsburg	†1996	10	505	3,883
Chris Hegg, Truman St.	†1985	11	*594	3,782
Brett Salisbury, Wayne St. (Neb.)	1993	10	424	3,732
Grady Benton, West Tex. A&M	†1994	9	505	3,699
Lance Funderburk, Valdosta St.	1996	11	490	3,676
Jed Drenning, Glenville St.	1993	10	473	3,593
Lance Funderburk, Valdosta St.	1995	11	581	3,549
Jamie Pass, Mankato St.	1993	11	543	3,537
Tod Mayfield, West Tex. A&M	†1986	11	555	3,533
Chris Hatcher, Valdosta St.	1993	11	495	3,532
Rob Tomlinson, Cal St. Chico	†1989	10	534	3,525
Chris Hatcher, Valdosta St.	1994	11	452	3,512
June Jones, Portland St.	†1976	11	465	3,463
Jarrod DeGeorgia, Wayne St. (Neb.)	1996	10	495	3,416
Rod Smith, Glenville St.	1996	10	472	3,410
Bob Toledo, San Fran. St.	†1967	10	409	3,407
Jayson Merrill, Western St.	†1991	10	337	3,400
Gregory Clark, Virginia St.	1993	11	425	3,386

Record. †National champion.

SINGLE-GAME YARDS

Yds.	Player, Team (Opponent)	Date
651	Wilkie Perez, Glenville St. (Concord)	Oct. 25, 1997
623	Perry Klein, LIU-C. W. Post (Salisbury St.)	Nov. 6, 1993
614	Alfred Montez, Western N.M. (West Tex. A&M)	Oct. 8, 1994
597	Damian Poalucci, East Stroudsburg (Mansfield)	Nov. 2, 1996
594	Jarrod DeGeorgia, Wayne St. (Neb.) (Drake)	Nov. 9, 1996
591	Marty Washington, West Ala. (Nicholls St.)	Sept. 11, 1993
584	Tracy Kendall, Alabama A&M (Clark Atlanta)	Nov. 4, 1989
580	Grady Benton, West Tex. A&M (Howard Payne)	Sept. 17, 1994
575	Scott Otis, Glenville St. (West Va. Wesleyan)	Oct. 15, 1994
573	Pat Graham, Augustana (S.D.) (Mankato St.)	Oct. 28, 1995
571	John Charles, Portland St. (Cal Poly SLO)	Nov. 16, 1991
569	Bob McLaughlin, Lock Haven (Calif. [Pa.])	Oct. 29, 1994
562	Bob Toledo, San Fran. St. (Cal St. Hayward)	Oct. 21, 1967
555	A. J. Vaughn, Wayne St. (Mich.) (Wis.-Milwaukee)	Sept. 30, 1967
545	Damian Poalucci, East Stroudsburg (Cheyney)	Oct. 26, 1996

ANNUAL CHAMPIONS

Year	Player, Team	Class	Plays	Yards
1946	Buster Dixon, Abilene Christian	Sr.	170	960
1947	Jim Peterson, Hanover	So.	108	1,449
1948	Jim Peterson, Hanover	Jr.	130	1,589
1949	Connie Callahan, Morningside	Sr.	311	2,006
1950	Bob Heimerdinger, Northern Ill.	Jr.	286	1,782
1951	Bob Heimerdinger, Northern Ill.	Sr.	292	1,775
1952	Don Gottlob, Sam Houston St.	Sr.	303	2,470
1953	Ralph Capitani, Northern Iowa	Jr.	317	1,755
1954	Bill Engelhardt, Neb.-Omaha	So.	243	1,645
1955	Jim Stehlin, Brandeis	Sr.	222	1,455
1956	Dick Jamieson, Bradley	So.	240	1,925
1957	Stan Jackson, Cal Poly Pomona	Jr.	301	2,145
1958	Stan Jackson, Cal Poly Pomona	Sr.	334	2,478
1959	Gary Campbell, Whittier	Sr.	309	2,383
1960	Charles Miller, Austin	Sr.	287	1,966
1961	Denny Spurlock, Whitworth	Sr.	224	1,684
1962	George Bork, Northern Ill.	Jr.	397	2,398
1963	George Bork, Northern Ill.	Sr.	413	2,945
1964	Jerry Bishop, Austin	Jr.	332	2,152
1965	Ron Christian, Northern Ill.	Sr.	377	2,307
1966	Joe Stetser, Cal St. Chico	Jr.	406	2,382
1967	Bob Toledo, San Fran. St.	Sr.	409	3,407
1968	Terry Bradshaw, Louisiana Tech	Jr.	426	2,987
1969	Tim Von Dulm, Portland St.	Jr.	462	2,736

Beginning in 1970, ranked on per-game (instead of total) yards

Year	Player, Team	Class	G	Plays	Yards	Avg.
1970	Jim Lindsey, Abilene Christian	Sr.	9	440	2,654	294.9
1971	Randy Mattingly, Evansville	Jr.	9	402	2,234	248.2
1972	Bob Biggs, UC Davis	Sr.	9	381	2,356	261.8
1973	Jim Zorn, Cal Poly Pomona	Jr.	11	499	3,000	272.7
1974	Jim McMillan, Boise St.	Sr.	10	403	3,101	310.1
1975	Lynn Hieber, Indiana (Pa.)	Sr.	10	402	2,503	250.3
1976	June Jones, Portland St.	Sr.	11	465	3,463	314.8
1977	Steve Mariucci, Northern Mich.	Sr.	8	270	1,780	222.5
1978	Charlie Thompson, Western St.	Jr.	9	304	2,138	237.6
1979	Phil Kessel, Northern Mich.	Jr.	9	368	2,164	240.4
1980	Curt Strasheim, Southwest St.	Jr.	10	501	2,565	256.5
1981	Steve Wray, Franklin	Jr.	10	488	2,726	272.6
1982	Steve Wray, Franklin	Sr.	8	382	2,114	264.3
1983	Pat Brennan, Franklin	Jr.	10	524	3,239	323.9
1984	Pat Brennan, Franklin	Sr.	10	583	3,248	324.8
1985	Chris Hegg, Truman St.	Sr.	11	*594	3,782	343.8
1986	Tod Mayfield, West Tex. A&M	Sr.	11	555	3,533	312.2
1987	Randy Hobson, Evansville	Sr.	10	457	2,964	296.4
1988	Mark Sedinger, Northern Colo.	Sr.	10	413	2,828	282.8
1989	Rob Tomlinson, Cal St. Chico	So.	10	534	3,525	352.5
1990	Andy Breault, Kutztown	Jr.	11	562	3,173	288.5
1991	Jayson Merrill, Western St.	Sr.	10	337	3,400	340.0
1992	John Charles, Portland St.	Sr.	8	303	2,708	338.5
1993	Perry Klein, LIU-C. W. Post	Sr.	10	499	4,052	405.2
1994	Grady Benton, West Tex. A&M	Jr.	9	505	3,699	*411.0
1995	Aaron Sparrow, Norfolk St.	Sr.	10	464	3,300	330.0
1996	Damian Poalucci, East Stroudsburg	Jr.	10	505	3,883	388.3
1997	Wilkie Perez, Glenville St.	Jr.	11	509	*4,301	391.0

Record.

Photo from Truman State sports information

Truman State running back Jarrett Anderson set the Division II record for rushing yards per game when he averaged 194.5 yards in 11 games in 1996. His season total of 2,140 also set the single-season standard.

Rushing

CAREER YARDS PER GAME
(Minimum 2,500 Yards)

Player, Team	Years	G	Plays	Yards	Yd. PG
Johnny Bailey, Tex. A&M-Kingsville	1986-89	39	885	*6,320	*162.1
Fred Lane, Lane	1994-96	29	700	4,433	152.9
Ole Gunderson, St. Olaf	1969-71	27	639	4,060	150.4
Richard Huntley, Winston-Salem	1992-95	42	932	6,286	149.7
Roger Graham, New Haven	1991-94	40	821	5,953	148.8
Brad Hustad, Luther	1957-59	27	655	3,943	146.0
Jarrett Anderson, Truman St.	1993-96	43	979	6,166	143.4
Quincy Tillmon, Emporia St.	1990-92, 94	29	790	4,141	142.8
Joe Iacone, West Chester	1960-62	27	565	3,767	139.5
Leonard Davis, Lenoir-Rhyne	$1990-94	35	839	4,853	138.7
Don Aleksiewicz, Hobart	1969-72	34	819	4,525	133.1
Jim VanWagner, Michigan Tech	1973-76	36	958	4,788	133.0
Steve Roberts, Butler	1986-89	35	1,026	4,623	132.1

Record. $See page 6 for explanation.

SEASON YARDS PER GAME

Player, Team	Year	G	Plays	Yards	TD	Yd. PG
Anthony Gray, Western N.M.	†1997	10	277	*2,220	12	*222.0
Irv Sigler, Bloomsburg	1997	10	299	2,038	20	203.8
Jarrett Anderson, Truman St.	†1996	11	321	2,140	27	194.5
Brian Shay, Emporia St.	1996	11	342	2,103	18	191.2
Richard Huntley, Winston-Salem	†1995	10	273	1,889	16	188.9
Fred Lane, Lane	1995	10	273	1,833	19	183.3

Player, Team	Year	G	Plays	Yards	TD	Yd. PG
Johnny Bailey, Tex. A&M-Kingsville	†1986	11	271	2,011	18	182.8
Bob White, Western N.M.	†1951	9	202	1,643	20	182.6
Kevin Mitchell, Saginaw Valley	†1989	8	236	1,460	6	182.5
Rashaan Dumas, Southern Conn. St.	1996	9	291	1,639	18	182.1
Don Aleksiewicz, Hobart	†1971	9	276	1,616	19	179.6
Jim Holder, Okla. Panhandle	†1963	10	275	1,775	9	177.5
Phillip Moore, North Dak.	1997	10	293	1,771	14	177.1
Wilmont Perry, Livingstone	1997	10	195	1,770	20	177.0
Jim Baier, Wis.-River Falls	†1966	9	240	1,587	17	176.3
James Suber, Indiana (Pa.)	1996	10	300	1,744	17	174.4
Keith Higdon, Cheyney	†1993	10	330	1,742	17	174.2
Brian Shay, Emporia St.	1997	11	269	1,912	*29	173.8
Leonard Davis, Lenoir-Rhyne	†1994	9	216	1,559	19	173.2
Billy Johnson, Widener	†1972	9	148	1,556	23	172.9

**Record. †National champion.*

CAREER YARDS

Player, Team	Years	Plays	Yards	Avg.
Johnny Bailey, Tex. A&M-Kingsville	1986-89	885	*6,320	7.14
Richard Huntley, Winston-Salem	1992-95	932	6,286	6.74
Jarrett Anderson, Truman St.	1993-96	979	6,166	6.30
Roger Graham, New Haven	1991-94	821	5,953	+7.25
Antonio Leroy, Albany St. (Ga.)	1993-96	973	5,152	5.29
Shawn Graves, Wofford	1989-92	730	5,128	7.02
Chris Cobb, Eastern Ill.	1976-79	930	5,042	5.42
Irv Sigler, Bloomsburg	1994-97	820	5,034	6.14
Harry Jackson, St. Cloud St.	1986-89	915	4,890	5.34
Leonard Davis, Lenoir-Rhyne	$1990-94	839	4,853	5.78
Jerry Linton, Okla. Panhandle	1959-62	648	4,839	7.47
Jim VanWagner, Michigan Tech	1973-76	958	4,788	5.00
¢Brian Shay, Emporia St.	1995-97	714	4,693	6.57
Jeremy Monroe, Michigan Tech	1990-93	666	4,661	7.00
Heath Sherman, Tex. A&M-Kingsville	1985-88	804	4,654	5.79
Steve Roberts, Butler	1986-89	1,026	4,623	4.51
Randy Martin, St. Cloud St.	1993-96	814	4,618	5.67
Don Aleksiewicz, Hobart	1969-72	819	4,525	5.53
Dale Mills, Truman St.	1957-60	751	4,502	5.99
Scott Schulte, Hillsdale	1990-93	879	4,495	5.11
Leo Lewis, Lincoln (Mo.)	1951-54	623	4,458	7.16
Bernie Peeters, Luther	1968-71	*1,072	4,435	4.14
Fred Lane, Lane	1994-96	700	4,433	6.33
Larry Schreiber, Tennessee Tech	1966-69	878	4,421	5.04
Brad Rowland, McMurry	1947-50	683	4,347	6.36

**Record. +Record for minimum 750 rushes. $See page 6 for explanation. ¢ Active player.*

SEASON YARDS

Player, Team	Year	G	Plays	Yards	Avg.
Anthony Gray, Western N.M.	†1997	10	277	*2,220	‡8.01
Jarrett Anderson, Truman St.	†1996	11	321	2,140	6.67
Brian Shay, Emporia St.	1996	11	342	2,103	6.15
Irv Sigler, Bloomsburg	1997	10	299	2,038	6.82
Johnny Bailey, Tex. A&M-Kingsville	†1986	11	271	2,011	7.42
Brian Shay, Emporia St.	1997	11	269	1,912	7.11
Richard Huntley, Winston-Salem	†1995	10	273	1,889	6.92
Ronald Moore, Pittsburg St.	1992	11	239	1,864	7.80
Fred Lane, Lane	1995	10	273	1,833	6.71
Zed Robinson, Southern Utah	1991	11	254	1,828	7.20
Richard Huntley, Winston-Salem	1994	11	251	1,815	7.23
Fred Lane, Lane	1994	11	280	1,779	6.35
Jim Holder, Okla. Panhandle	†1963	10	275	1,775	6.45
Phillip Moore, North Dak.	1997	10	293	1,771	6.04
Wilmont Perry, Livingstone	1997	10	195	1,770	9.08
James Suber, Indiana (Pa.)	1996	10	300	1,744	5.81
Keith Higdon, Cheyney	†1993	10	330	1,742	5.28
Mike Thomas, UNLV	†1973	11	274	1,741	6.35
Roger Graham, New Haven	†1992	10	200	1,717	+8.59
Jake Morris, North Dak. St.	1997	11	280	1,710	6.11

**Record. †National champion. ‡Record for minimum 250 rushes. +Record for minimum 200 rushes.*

SINGLE-GAME YARDS

Yds.	Player, Team (Opponent)	Date
382	Kelly Ellis, Northern Iowa (Western Ill.)	Oct. 13, 1979
373	Dallas Garber, Marietta (Wash. & Jeff.)	Nov. 7, 1959
370	Jim Baier, Wis.-River Falls (Wis.-Stevens Point)	Nov. 5, 1966
370	Jim Hissam, Marietta (Bethany [W.Va.])	Nov. 15, 1958
367	Don Polkinghorne, Washington (Mo.) (Wash. & Lee)	Nov. 23, 1957
363	Richie Weaver, Widener (Moravian)	Oct. 17, 1970
361	Brian Shay, Emporia St. (Washburn)	Oct. 5, 1996
361	Richard Huntley, Winston-Salem (Virginia Union)	Nov. 5, 1994
359	Anthony Gray, Western N.M. (Hardin-Simmons)	Oct. 4, 1997
356	Ole Gunderson, St. Olaf (Monmouth [Ill.])	Oct. 11, 1969
350	Ricke Stonewall, Millersville (New Haven)	Nov. 13, 1982
343	Zed Robinson, Southern Utah (Santa Clara)	Oct. 12, 1991
343	Jesse Lakes, Central Mich. (Wis.-Milwaukee)	Sept. 27, 1969
342	Leonard Davis, Lenoir-Rhyne (Gardner-Webb)	Oct. 9, 1993
337	Anthony Gray, Western N.M. (N.M. Highlands)	Nov. 15, 1997
337	Harry Jackson, St. Cloud St. (South Dak.)	Nov. 4, 1989

ANNUAL CHAMPIONS

Year	Player, Team	Class	Plays	Yards
1946	V. T. Smith, Abilene Christian	So.	99	733
1947	John Williams, Jacksonville St.	Jr.	150	931
1948	Hank Treesh, Hanover	Jr.	100	1,383
1949	Odie Posey, Southern U.	Jr.	121	1,399
1950	Meriel Michelson, Eastern Wash.	Sr.	180	1,234
1951	Bob White, Western N.M.	Jr.	202	1,643
1952	Al Conway, William Jewell	Sr.	134	1,325
1953	Elroy Payne, McMurry	So.	183	1,274
1954	Lem Harkey, Col. of Emporia	Sr.	121	1,146
1955	Gene Scott, Centre	Sr.	107	1,138
1956	Bill Rhodes, Western St.	Sr.	130	1,200
1957	Brad Hustad, Luther	So.	219	1,401
1958	Dale Mills, Truman St.	So.	186	1,358
1959	Dale Mills, Truman St.	Jr.	248	1,385
1960	Joe Iacone, West Chester	So.	199	1,438
1961	Bobby Lisa, St. Mary (Kan.)	Jr.	156	1,082
1962	Jerry Linton, Okla. Panhandle	Sr.	272	1,483
1963	Jim Holder, Okla. Panhandle	Sr.	275	1,775
1964	Jim Allison, San Diego St.	Sr.	174	1,186
1965	Allen Smith, Findlay	Jr.	207	1,240
1966	Jim Baier, Wis.-River Falls	Sr.	240	1,587
1967	Dickie Moore, Western Ky.	Jr.	208	1,444
1968	Howard Stevens, Randolph-Macon	Fr.	191	1,468
1969	Leon Burns, Long Beach St.	Jr.	350	1,659

Beginning in 1970, ranked on per-game (instead of total) yards

Year	Player, Team	Class	G	Plays	Yards	Avg.
1970	Dave Kiarsis, Trinity (Conn.)	Sr.	8	201	1,374	171.8
1971	Don Aleksiewicz, Hobart	Jr.	9	276	1,616	179.6
1972	Billy Johnson, Widener	So.	9	148	1,556	172.9
1973	Mike Thomas, UNLV	Jr.	11	274	1,741	158.3
1974	Jim VanWagner, Michigan Tech	So.	9	246	1,453	161.4
1975	Jim VanWagner, Michigan Tech	Jr.	9	289	1,331	147.9
1976	Ted McKnight, Minn.-Duluth	Sr.	10	220	1,482	148.2
1977	Bill Burnham, New Hampshire	Sr.	10	281	1,422	142.2
1978	Mike Harris, Truman St.	Sr.	11	329	1,598	145.3
1979	Chris Cobb, Eastern Ill.	Sr.	11	293	1,609	146.3
1980	Louis Jackson, Cal Poly SLO	Sr.	10	287	1,424	142.4
1981	Rick Porter, Slippery Rock	Sr.	9	208	1,179	131.0
1982	Ricke Stonewall, Millersville	So.	10	191	1,387	138.7
1983	Mark Corbin, Central St.	So.	10	208	1,502	150.2
1984	Charles Sanders, Slippery Rock	Jr.	10	269	1,280	128.0
1985	Dan Sonnek, South Dak. St.	So.	11	303	1,518	138.0
1986	Johnny Bailey, Tex. A&M-Kingsville	Fr.	11	271	2,011	182.8
1987	Johnny Bailey, Tex. A&M-Kingsville	So.	10	217	1,598	159.8
1988	Johnny Bailey, Tex. A&M-Kingsville	Jr.	10	229	1,442	144.2
1989	Kevin Mitchell, Saginaw Valley	Jr.	8	236	1,460	182.5
1990	David Jones, Chadron St.	Sr.	10	225	1,570	157.0
1991	Quincy Tillmon, Emporia St.	So.	9	259	1,544	171.6
1992	Roger Graham, New Haven	So.	10	200	1,717	171.7
1993	Keith Higdon, Cheyney	Sr.	10	330	1,742	174.2
1994	Leonard Davis, Lenoir-Rhyne	Sr.	9	216	1,559	173.2
1995	Richard Huntley, Winston-Salem	Sr.	10	273	1,889	188.9
1996	Jarrett Anderson, Truman St.	Sr.	11	321	2,140	194.5
1997	Anthony Gray, Wetern N.M.	Jr.	10	277	*2,220	*222.0

**Record.*

Passing

CAREER PASSING EFFICIENCY

(Minimum 375 Completions)

Player, Team	Years	Att.	Cmp.	Int.	Pct.	Yards	TD	Pts.
Chris Petersen, UC Davis	1985-86	553	385	13	*.696	4,988	39	*164.0
Chris Hatcher, Valdosta St.	1991-94	1,451	*1,001	38	‡.690	*10,878	*116	+153.1
Jim McMillan, Boise St.	1971-74	640	382	29	.597	5,508	58	152.8
Jack Hull, Grand Valley St.	1988-91	835	485	22	.581	7,120	64	149.7
Scott Otis, Glenville St.	1994-95	693	421	21	.608	5,563	56	148.8
Jesse Showerda, New Haven	1993-96	675	402	15	.596	5,175	57	147.4
Grady Benton, West Tex. A&M	1994-95	686	421	22	.614	5,618	49	147.3
Bruce Upstill, Col. of Emporia	1960-63	769	438	36	.570	6,935	48	144.0
Jarrod DeGeorgia, Wayne St. (Neb.)	1995-96	645	428	18	.664	5,161	31	143.9
Lance Funderburk, Valdosta St.	1993-96	1,054	689	23	.654	7,698	64	142.4
George Bork, Northern Ill.	1960-63	902	577	33	.640	6,782	60	141.8
June Jones, Portland St.	1975-76	658	375	34	.570	5,798	41	141.2
Steve Mariucci, Northern Mich.	1974-77	678	380	33	.561	6,022	41	140.9
Scott Barry, UC Davis	1982-84	588	377	16	.641	4,421	33	140.4
Matt Cook, Mo. Southern St.	$1989-93	816	411	29	.504	6,715	63	137.9
Aaron Sparrow, Norfolk St.	1992-95	1,117	615	38	.551	8,758	79	137.5
Chris Crawford, Portland St.	1985-88	954	588	35	.616	7,543	48	137.3
Trevor Spradley, Southwest Baptist	1990-92	712	441	27	.619	5,881	29	137.2
Dan Miles, Southern Ore.	1964-67	871	577	56	.662	6,531	52	136.1
Damian Poalucci, East Stroudsburg	1994-97	1,067	583	47	.546	8,654	69	135.3
Jarrod Furgason, Fairmont St.	$1993-97	1,392	798	44	.573	9,856	101	134.4
Al Niemela, West Chester	1985-88	1,063	600	36	.564	7,853	73	134.4
Pete Jelovic, Emporia St.	1995-97	776	462	30	.595	5,970	42	134.3
Jody Dickerson, Edinboro	1991-94	845	447	42	.529	6,787	60	133.9
Denny Spurlock, Whitworth	1958-61	723	388	48	.537	5,526	63	133.4

**Record. ‡Record for minimum 1,000 attempts. +Record for minimum 750 completions. $See page 6 for explanation.*

SEASON PASSING EFFICIENCY

(Minimum 15 Attempts Per Game)

Player, Team	Year	G	Att.	Cmp.	Int.	Pct.	Yards	TD	Pts.
Boyd Crawford, Col. of Idaho	†1953	8	120	72	6	.600	1,462	21	*210.1
Chuck Green, Wittenberg	†1963	9	182	114	8	.626	2,181	19	+189.0
Jayson Merrill, Western St.	†1991	10	309	195	11	.631	3,484	35	188.1
Jim Feely, Johns Hopkins	†1967	7	110	69	5	.627	1,264	12	186.2
John Charles, Portland St.	1991	11	247	147	7	.595	2,619	32	185.7
Steve Smith, Western St.	†1992	10	271	180	5	.664	2,719	30	183.5
Jim Peterson, Hanover	†1948	8	125	81	12	.648	1,571	12	182.9
John Wristen, Southern Colo.	†1982	8	121	68	2	.562	1,358	13	182.6
John Charles, Portland St.	1992	8	263	179	7	.681	2,770	24	181.3
Richard Basil, Savannah St.	†1989	9	211	120	7	.569	2,148	29	181.1
Chris Hatcher, Valdosta St.	†1994	11	430	321	9	*.747	3,591	*50	‡179.0
Wilkie Perez, Glenville St.	†1997	11	425	280	12	.658	*4,189	45	178.0
Jim Cahoon, Ripon	†1964	8	127	74	7	.583	1,206	19	176.4
Ken Suhl, New Haven	1992	10	239	148	5	.619	2,336	26	175.7
Tony Aliucci, Indiana (Pa.)	†1990	10	181	111	10	.613	1,801	21	172.2
James Weir, New Haven	†1993	10	266	161	1	.605	2,336	31	172.0
Shawn Behr, Fort Hays St.	†1995	11	318	191	6	.600	3,158	31	171.9
John Costello, Widener	†1956	9	149	74	10	.497	1,702	17	169.8
Kurt Coduti, Michigan Tech	1992	9	155	92	3	.594	1,518	15	169.7
Chris Petersen, UC Davis	†1985	10	242	167	6	.690	2,366	17	169.4

**Record. †National champion. +Record for minimum 100 completions. ‡Record for minimum 200 completions.*

CAREER YARDS PER GAME

(Minimum 4,500 Yards)

Player, Team	Years	G	Att.	Cmp.	Int.	Pct.	Yards	TD	Avg.
Grady Benton, West Tex. A&M	1994-95	18	686	421	22	.614	5,618	49	*312.1
Tim Von Dulm, Portland St.	1969-70	20	924	500	41	.541	5,967	51	298.4
Marty Washington, West Ala.	1992-93	17	690	379	25	.549	5,018	40	295.2
Jayson Merrill, Western St.	1990-91	20	580	328	25	.566	5,830	56	291.5
Jarrod DeGeorgia, Wayne St. (Neb.)	1995-96	18	645	428	18	.664	5,161	31	286.7
John Charles, Portland St.	1991-92	19	510	326	14	.639	5,389	56	283.6
Chris Hatcher, Valdosta St.	1991-94	39	1,451	*1,001	38	‡.690	*10,878	*116	278.9
Scott Otis, Glenville St.	1994-95	20	693	421	21	.608	5,563	56	278.2
June Jones, Portland St.	1975-76	21	658	375	34	.570	5,798	41	276.1
Jermaine Whitaker, N.M. Highlands	1992-94	31	1,150	625	45	.543	8,532	71	275.2
Steve Wray, Franklin	1979, 81-82	26	1,070	511	40	.478	7,019	56	270.0
Pat Graham, Augustana (S.D.)	1995-96	21	820	469	26	.572	5,636	43	268.4
Earl Harvey, N.C. Central	1985-88	40	1,442	690	81	.479	10,621	86	265.5
Chris Hegg, Truman St.	1984-85	20	771	410	32	.532	5,306	44	265.3
Pat Brennan, Franklin	1981-84	30	1,123	535	62	.476	7,717	53	257.2
Jay McLucas, New Haven	1989-90	20	699	370	30	.529	5,139	37	257.0
Lance Funderburk, Valdosta St.	1993-96	30	1,054	689	23	.654	7,698	64	256.6
Troy Mott, Wayne St. (Neb.)	1991-92	20	757	437	37	.577	5,003	25	250.2
Chris Petersen, UC Davis	1985-86	20	553	385	13	*.696	4,988	39	249.4
Rich Ingold, Indiana (Pa.)	1983-85	26	852	499	36	.586	6,454	48	248.2
Jeff Phillips, Central Mo. St.	1986-88	26	892	496	54	.556	6,294	46	242.1
Bob McLaughlin, Lock Haven	1992-95	44	*1,719	910	*88	.529	10,640	60	241.8
Vernon Buck, Wingate	1991-94	41	1,393	728	61	.523	9,884	72	241.1

Player, Team	Years	G	Att.	Cmp.	Int.	Pct.	Yards	TD	Avg.
Thad Trujillo, Fort Lewis	1991-94	41	1,455	760	57	.522	9,873	78	240.8
Joe Stetser, Cal St. Chico	1966-67	20	813	394	48	.485	4,803	40	240.2

**Record. ‡Record for minimum 1,000 attempts.*

SEASON YARDS PER GAME

Player, Team	Year	G	Att.	Cmp.	Int.	Pct.	Yards	TD	Avg.
Grady Benton, West Tex. A&M	1994	9	409	258	13	.631	3,541	30	*393.4
Damian Poalucci, East Stroudsburg	1996	10	393	214	13	.545	3,831	40	383.1
Marty Washington, West Ala.	1993	8	404	221	13	.547	3,062	26	382.8
Wilkie Perez, Glenville St.	†1997	11	425	280	12	.658	*4,189	45	380.8
Perry Klein, LIU-C. W. Post	1993	10	407	248	18	.609	3,757	38	375.7
Brett Salisbury, Wayne St. (Neb.)	1993	10	395	276	14	.699	3,729	29	372.9
Alfred Montez, Western N.M.	1994	6	231	133	7	.576	2,182	18	363.7
Bob Toledo, San Fran. St.	1967	10	396	211	24	.533	3,513	45	351.3
Pat Brennan, Franklin	1983	10	458	226	30	.493	3,491	25	349.1
Jayson Merrill, Western St.	†1991	10	309	195	11	.631	3,484	35	348.4
John Charles, Portland St.	1992	8	263	179	7	.681	2,770	24	346.3
Rod Smith, Glenville St.	1996	10	409	249	14	.609	3,455	29	345.5
Aaron Sparrow, Norfolk St.	1995	10	409	238	14	.581	3,434	32	343.4
George Bork, Northern Ill.	†1963	9	374	244	12	.652	3,077	32	341.9
Chris Hegg, Truman St.	†1985	11	503	284	20	.565	3,741	32	340.1
Lance Funderburk, Valdosta St.	1996	11	459	300	10	.654	3,732	35	339.3
Jed Drenning, Glenville St.	1993	10	390	244	12	.626	3,391	25	339.1
Jarrod DeGeorgia, Wayne St. (Neb.)	1996	10	420	286	12	.681	3,388	19	338.8
Lance Funderburk, Valdosta St.	1995	11	*544	*356	12	.654	3,706	26	336.9
Pat Brennan, Franklin	1984	10	502	238	20	.474	3,340	18	334.0

**Record. †National champion.*

CAREER YARDS

Player, Team	Years	Att.	Cmp.	Int.	Pct.	Yards	TD
Chris Hatcher, Valdosta St.	1991-94	1,451	*1,001	38	‡.690	*10,878	*116
Bob McLaughlin, Lock Haven	1992-95	*1,719	910	*88	.529	10,640	60
Earl Harvey, N.C. Central	1985-88	1,442	690	81	.479	10,621	86
John Craven, Gardner-Webb	1991-94	1,535	828	82	.539	9,934	80
Vernon Buck, Wingate	1991-94	1,393	728	61	.523	9,884	72
Thad Trujillo, Fort Lewis	1991-94	1,455	760	57	.522	9,873	78
Jarrod Furgason, Fairmont St.	$1993-97	1,392	798	44	.573	9,856	101
Rob Tomlinson, Cal St. Chico	1988-91	1,328	748	43	.563	9,434	52
John Hebgen, Mankato St.	1993-96	1,268	727	38	.573	9,410	71
Andy Breault, Kutztown	1989-92	1,259	733	63	.582	9,086	86
Aaron Sparrow, Norfolk St.	1992-95	1,117	615	38	.551	8,758	79
Sam Mannery, Calif. (Pa.)	1987-90	1,283	649	68	.506	8,680	64
Damian Poalucci, East Stroudsburg	1994-97	1,067	583	47	.546	8,654	69
Dave DenBraber, Ferris St.	1984-87	1,254	661	45	.527	8,536	52
Jermaine Whitaker, N.M. Highlands	1992-94	1,150	625	45	.543	8,532	71
Jim Lindsey, Abilene Christian	1967-70	1,237	642	69	.519	8,521	61
Dave MacDonald, West Chester	1991-94	1,123	604	46	.538	8,449	82
Maurice Heard, Tuskegee	1988-91	1,134	556	54	.490	8,434	87
John St. Jacques, Santa Clara	1988-89, 91-92	1,060	543	36	.512	7,968	68
Rex Lamberti, Abilene Christian	1984-86, 93	1,133	595	44	.525	7,934	84
Al Niemela, West Chester	1985-88	1,063	600	36	.564	7,853	73
Ned Cox, Angelo St.	1983-86	1,205	589	58	.489	7,843	56
Matt Montgomery, Hampton	1991-94	1,036	545	34	.526	7,839	63
Loyal Proffitt, Abilene Christian	1981-84	1,157	550	80	.475	7,824	54
Pat Brennan, Franklin	1981-84	1,123	535	62	.476	7,717	53

**Record. ‡Record for minimum 1,000 attempts.*

SEASON YARDS

Player, Team	Year	G	Att.	Cmp.	Int.	Pct.	Yards	TD
Wilkie Perez, Glenville St.	†1997	11	425	280	12	.658	*4,189	45
Damian Poalucci, East Stroudsburg	1996	10	393	214	13	.545	3,831	40
Perry Klein, LIU-C. W. Post	1993	10	407	248	18	.609	3,757	38
Chris Hegg, Truman St.	1985	11	503	284	20	.565	3,741	32
Lance Funderburk, Valdosta St.	1996	11	459	300	10	.654	3,732	35
Brett Salisbury, Wayne St. (Neb.)	1993	10	395	276	14	.699	3,729	29
Lance Funderburk, Valdosta St.	1995	11	*544	*356	12	.654	3,706	26
Tod Mayfield, West Tex. A&M	1986	11	515	317	20	.616	3,664	31
Chris Hatcher, Valdosta St.	1993	11	471	335	11	.711	3,651	37
Chris Hatcher, Valdosta St.	†1994	11	430	321	9	*.747	3,591	*50
Grady Benton, West Tex. A&M	1994	9	409	258	13	.631	3,541	30
June Jones, Portland St.	†1976	11	423	238	24	.563	3,518	25
Bob Toledo, San Fran. St.	1967	10	396	211	24	.533	3,513	45
Pat Brennan, Franklin	1983	10	458	226	30	.493	3,491	25
Jayson Merrill, Western St.	†1991	10	309	195	11	.631	3,484	35
Rod Smith, Glenville St.	1996	10	409	249	14	.609	3,455	29
Gregory Clark, Virginia St.	1993	11	380	227	11	.597	3,437	38
Aaron Sparrow, Norfolk St.	1995	10	409	238	14	.581	3,434	32
Jed Drenning, Glenville St.	1993	10	390	244	12	.626	3,391	25
Jarrod DeGeorgia, Wayne St. (Neb.)	1996	10	420	286	12	.681	3,388	19

**Record. †National champion.*

SINGLE-GAME YARDS

Yds.	Player, Team (Opponent)	Date
642	Wilkie Perez, Glenville St. (Concord)	Oct. 25, 1997
616	Damian Poalucci, East Stroudsburg (Mansfield)	Nov. 2, 1996
614	Alfred Montez, Western N.M. (West Tex. A&M)	Oct. 8, 1994
614	Perry Klein, LIU-C. W. Post (Salisbury St.)	Nov. 6, 1993
599	Jarrod DeGeorgia, Wayne St. (Neb.) (Drake)	Nov. 9, 1996
592	John Charles, Portland St. (Cal Poly SLO)	Nov. 16, 1991
568	Scott Otis, Glenville St. (West Va. Wesleyan)	Oct. 15, 1994
568	Bob Toledo, San Fran. St. (Cal St. Hayward)	Oct. 21, 1967
564	Pat Graham, Augustana (S.D.) (Mankato St.)	Oct. 28, 1995
551	Jamie Sander, N.M. Highlands (Neb.-Kearney)	Nov. 9, 1996
550	Earl Harvey, N.C. Central (Jackson St.)	Aug. 30, 1986
549	Matt LaTour, Northern Mich. (Ashland)	Nov. 5, 1994
541	Arnold Marcha, West Tex. A&M (Okla. Panhandle)	Nov. 12, 1994
539	Maurice Heard, Tuskegee (Alabama A&M)	Nov. 10, 1990
538	Grady Benton, West Tex. A&M (Howard Payne)	Sept. 17, 1994

SINGLE-GAME ATTEMPTS

No.	Player, Team (Opponent)	Date
76	Jarrod DeGeorgia, Wayne St. (Neb.) (Drake)	Nov. 9, 1996
74	Jamie Sander, N.M. Highlands (Neb.-Kearney)	Nov. 9, 1996
74	Jermaine Whitaker, N.M. Highlands (Western St.)	Nov. 5, 1994
72	Kurt Otto, North Dak. (Tex. A&M-Kingsville)	Sept. 13, 1986
72	Kaipo Spencer, Santa Clara (Portland St.)	Oct. 11, 1975
72	Joe Stetser, Cal St. Chico (Oregon Tech)	Sept. 23, 1967
71	Pat Brennan, Franklin (Ashland)	Nov. 3, 1984

SINGLE-GAME COMPLETIONS

No.	Player, Team (Opponent)	Date
56	Jarrod DeGeorgia, Wayne St. (Neb.) (Drake)	Nov. 9, 1996
45	Chris Hatcher, Valdosta St. (Mississippi Col.)	Oct. 23, 1993
45	Chris Hatcher, Valdosta St. (West Ga.)	Oct. 16, 1993
44	Wilkie Perez, Glenville St. (Concord)	Oct. 25, 1997
44	Tom Bonds, Cal Lutheran (St. Mary's [Cal.])	Nov. 22, 1986
43	George Bork, Northern Ill. (Central Mich.)	Nov. 9, 1963
42	Lance Funderburk, Valdosta St. (West Ga.)	Nov. 11, 1995
42	Jermaine Whitaker, N.M. Highlands (Western St.)	Nov. 5, 1994
42	Marty Washington, West Ala. (Jacksonville St.)	Nov. 7, 1992
42	Chris Teal, West Ga. (Valdosta St.)	Oct. 19, 1991
42	Tim Von Dulm, Portland St. (Eastern Wash.)	Nov. 21, 1970
41	Pat Graham, Augustana (S.D.) (Mankato St.)	Oct. 28, 1995
41	Steve Lopez, Cal St. Chico (St. Mary's [Cal.])	Sept. 9, 1995
41	Chris Hatcher, Valdosta St. (West Ga.)	Oct. 15, 1994
41	Grady Benton, West Tex. A&M (Howard Payne)	Sept. 17, 1994
41	Kurt Otto, North Dak. (Tex. A&M-Kingsville)	Sept. 13, 1986
41	Neil Lomax, Portland St. (Montana St.)	Nov. 19, 1977

ANNUAL CHAMPIONS

Year	Player, Team	Class	Att.	Cmp.	Int.	Pct.	Yds.	TD
1946	Hank Caver, Presbyterian	Sr.	128	59	13	.461	790	7
1947	James Batchelor, Tex. A&M-Commerce	Sr.	184	94	10	.511	1,114	9
1948	Sam Gary, Swarthmore	Jr.	153	93	11	.608	1,218	16
1949	Sam McGowan, New Mexico St.	Sr.	219	112	22	.511	1,712	12
1950	Andy MacDonald, Central Mich.	Jr.	200	109	12	.545	1,577	15
1951	Andy MacDonald, Central Mich.	Sr.	183	114	7	.623	1,560	12
1952	Wes Bair, Illinois St.	So.	242	135	18	.558	1,375	14
1953	Pence Dacus, Southwest Tex. St.	Sr.	207	113	10	.546	1,654	11
1954	Tommy Egan, Brandeis	Sr.	144	87	8	.604	1,050	11
1955	Jerry Foley, Hamline	Fr.	167	87	8	.521	1,034	6
1956	James Stehlin, Brandeis	Sr.	206	116	11	.563	1,155	6
1957	Jay Roelen, Pepperdine	Sr.	214	106	16	.495	1,428	13
1958	Stan Jackson, Cal Poly Pomona	Sr.	256	123	14	.480	1,994	16
1959	Gary Campbell, Whittier	Sr.	183	111	4	.607	1,717	12
1960	Denny Spurlock, Whitworth	Jr.	257	135	16	.525	1,892	14
1961	Tom Gryzwinski, Defiance	Jr.	258	127	17	.492	1,684	14
1962	George Bork, Northern Ill.	Jr.	356	232	11	.652	2,506	22
1963	George Bork, Northern Ill.	Sr.	374	244	12	.652	3,077	32
1964	Jerry Bishop, Austin	Jr.	300	182	16	.607	2,246	17
1965	Bob Caress, Bradley	Sr.	393	210	21	.534	2,167	24
1966	Paul Krause, Dubuque	Sr.	318	179	22	.563	2,210	16
1967	Joe Stetser, Cal St. Chico	Sr.	464	220	*32	.474	2,446	14
1968	Jim Lindsey, Abilene Christian	So.	396	204	19	.515	2,717	18
1969	Tim Von Dulm, Portland St.	Jr.	434	241	18	.555	2,926	26

Beginning in 1970, ranked on per-game (instead of total) completions

Year	Player, Team	Class	G	Att.	Cmp.	Avg.	Int.	Pct.	Yds.	TD
1970	Tim Von Dulm, Portland St.	Sr.	10	490	259	25.9	23	.529	3,041	25
1971	Bob Baron, Rensselaer	Sr.	9	302	168	18.7	13	.556	2,105	15
1972	Bob Biggs, UC Davis	Sr.	9	327	186	20.7	16	.569	2,291	15
1973	Kim McQuilken, Lehigh	Sr.	11	326	196	17.8	13	.601	2,603	19
1974	Jim McMillan, Boise St.	Sr.	10	313	192	19.2	15	.613	2,900	13
1975	Dan Hayes, UC Riverside	Sr.	10	316	171	17.1	20	.541	2,215	21
1976	June Jones, Portland St.	Sr.	11	423	238	21.6	24	.563	3,518	25
1977	Ed Schultz, Moorhead St.	Sr.	10	304	187	18.7	16	.615	1,943	21

Year	Player, Team	Class	G	Att.	Cmp.	Avg.	Int.	Pct.	Yds.	TD
1978	Jeff Knapple, Northern Colo.	Sr.	10	349	178	17.8	21	.510	2,191	16

Beginning in 1979, ranked on passing efficiency rating points (instead of per-game completions)

Year	Player, Team	Class	G	Att.	Cmp.	Int.	Pct.	Yds.	TD	Pts.
1979	Dave Alfaro, Santa Clara	Jr.	9	168	110	9	.655	1,721	13	166.3
1980	Willie Tullis, Troy St.	Sr.	10	203	108	8	.532	1,880	15	147.5
1981	Steve Michuta, Grand Valley St.	Sr.	8	173	114	11	.659	1,702	17	168.3
1982	John Wristen, Southern Colo.	Jr.	8	121	68	2	.562	1,358	13	182.6
1983	Kevin Parker, Fort Valley St.	Jr.	9	168	87	8	.518	1,539	18	154.6
Year	**Player, Team**	**Class**	**G**	**Att.**	**Cmp.**	**Int.**	**Pct.**	**Yds.**	**TD**	**Pts.**
1984	Brian Quinn, Northwest Mo. St.	Sr.	10	178	96	2	.539	1,561	14	151.3
1985	Chris Petersen, UC Davis	Jr.	10	242	167	6	.690	2,366	17	169.4
1986	Chris Petersen, UC Davis	Sr.	10	311	218	7	.701	2,622	22	159.7
1987	Dave Biondo, Ashland	Jr.	10	177	95	11	.537	1,828	14	154.1
1988	Al Niemela, West Chester	Sr.	10	217	138	9	.636	1,932	21	162.0
1989	Richard Basil, Savannah St.	Sr.	9	211	120	7	.569	2,148	29	181.1
1990	Tony Aliucci, Indiana (Pa.)	Jr.	10	181	111	10	.613	1,801	21	172.2
1991	Jayson Merrill, Western St.	Sr.	10	309	195	11	.631	3,484	35	188.1
1992	Steve Smith, Western St.	Sr.	10	271	180	5	.664	2,719	30	183.5
1993	James Weir, New Haven	Jr.	10	266	161	1	.605	2,336	31	172.0
1994	Chris Hatcher, Valdosta St.	Sr.	11	430	321	9	*.747	3,591	*50	‡179.0
1995	Shawn Behr, Fort Hays St.	Sr.	11	318	191	6	.600	3,158	31	171.9
1996	Jesse Showerda, New Haven	Sr.	10	300	180	3	.600	2,625	31	165.6
1997	Wilkie Perez, Glenville St.	Jr.	11	425	280	12	.658	*4,189	45	178.0

**Record. ‡Record for minimum 200 completions.*

ANNUAL PASSING EFFICIENCY LEADERS BEFORE 1979

(Minimum 11 Attempts Per Game)

1948—Jim Peterson, Hanover, 182.9; **1949**—John Ford, Hardin-Simmons, 179.6; **1950**—Edward Ludorf, Trinity (Conn.), 167.8; **1951**—Vic Lesch, Western Ill., 182.4; **1952**—Jim Gray, Tex. A&M-Commerce, 205.5; **1953**—Boyd Crawford, Col. of Idaho, *210.1; **1954**—Bill Englehardt, Neb.-Omaha, 170.7; **1955**—Robert Alexander, Trinity (Conn.), 208.7; **1956**—John Costello, Widener, 169.8; **1957**—Doug Maison, Hillsdale, 200.0; **1958**—Kurt Duecker, Ripon, 161.7; **1959**—Fred Whitmire, Humboldt St., 188.7; **1960**—Larry Cline, Otterbein, 195.2.

(Minimum 15 Attempts Per Game)

Year	Player, Team	G	Att.	Cmp.	Int.	Pct.	Yds.	TD	Pts.
1961	Denny Spurlock, Whitworth	10	189	115	16	.608	1,708	26	165.2
1962	Roy Curry, Jackson St.	10	194	104	8	.536	1,862	15	151.5
Year	**Player, Team**	**G**	**Att.**	**Cmp.**	**Int.**	**Pct.**	**Yds.**	**TD**	**Pts.**
1963	Chuck Green, Wittenberg	9	182	114	8	.626	2,181	19	+189.0
1964	Jim Cahoon, Ripon	8	127	74	7	.583	1,206	19	176.4
1965	Ed Buzzell, Ottawa	9	238	118	5	.496	2,170	31	165.0
1966	Jim Alcorn, Clarion	9	199	107	4	.538	1,714	24	161.9
1967	Jim Feely, Johns Hopkins	7	110	69	5	.627	1,264	12	186.2
1968	Larry Green, Doane	9	182	97	7	.533	1,592	22	159.0
1969	George Kaplan, Northern Colo.	9	155	92	5	.594	1,396	16	162.6
1970	Gary Wichard, LIU-C. W. Post	9	186	100	5	.538	1,527	12	138.6
1971	Peter Mackey, Middlebury	8	180	101	4	.561	1,597	19	161.0
1972	David Hamilton, Fort Valley St.	9	180	99	9	.550	1,571	24	162.3
1973	Jim McMillan, Boise St.	11	179	110	5	.615	1,525	17	158.8
1974	Jim McMillan, Boise St.	10	313	192	15	.613	2,900	33	164.4
1975	Joe Sterrett, Lehigh	11	228	135	13	.592	2,114	22	157.5
1976	Mike Makings, Western St.	10	179	90	6	.503	1,617	14	145.3
1977	Mike Rieker, Lehigh	11	230	137	14	.596	2,431	23	169.2
1978	Mike Moroski, UC Davis	10	205	119	9	.580	1,689	17	145.9

**Record. +Record for minimum 100 completions.*

(See page 142 for annual leaders beginning in 1979.

Receiving

CAREER RECEPTIONS PER GAME

(Minimum 125 Receptions)

Player, Team	Years	G	Rec.	Yards	TD	Rec. PG
Chris George, Glenville St.	1993-94	20	230	3,215	30	*11.5
Ed Bell, Idaho St.	1968-69	19	163	2,608	30	8.6
Byron Chamberlain, Wayne St. (Neb.)	1993-94	19	161	1,941	14	8.3
Carlos Ferralls, Glenville St.	1994-97	32	262	3,835	43	8.2
Jerry Hendren, Idaho	1967-69	30	230	3,435	27	7.7
Gary Garrison, San Diego St.	1964-65	20	148	2,188	26	7.4
Brad Bailey, West Tex. A&M	1992-94	30	221	2,677	22	7.4
Chris Myers, Kenyon	1967-70	35	253	3,897	33	7.2

**Record.*

SEASON RECEPTIONS PER GAME

Player, Team	Year	G	Rec.	Yards	TD	Rec. PG
Chris George, Glenville St.	†1993	10	117	*1,876	15	*11.7
Chris George, Glenville St.	†1994	10	113	1,339	15	11.3
Brad Bailey, West Tex. A&M	1994	11	*119	1,552	16	10.8
Carlos Ferralls, Glenville St.	†1996	8	81	965	6	10.1
Bruce Cerone, Emporia St.	1968	9	91	1,479	15	10.1
Mike Healey, Valparaiso	†1985	10	101	1,279	11	10.1
Sean Pender, Valdosta St.	†1995	11	111	983	2	10.1
Barry Wagner, Alabama A&M	†1989	11	106	1,812	17	9.6
Ed Bell, Idaho St.	†1969	10	96	1,522	20	9.6
Jerry Hendren, Idaho	1968	9	86	1,457	14	9.6
Dick Hewins, Drake	†1968	10	95	1,316	13	9.5
Carlos Ferralls, Glenville St.	†1997	10	94	1,566	19	9.4
Jarett Vito, Emporia St.	1995	10	+94	932	7	9.4
Billy Joe Masters, Evansville	†1987	10	‡94	‡960	4	‡9.4
Joe Dittrich, Southwest St.	†1980	9	83	974	7	9.2
Manley Sarnowsky, Drake	†1966	10	92	1,114	7	9.2

**Record. †National champion. +Record for a freshman. ‡Record for a running back.*

CAREER RECEPTIONS

Player, Team	Years	Rec.	Yards	TD
Carlos Ferralls, Glenville St.	1994-97	*262	3,835	43
Jon Spinosa, Lock Haven	1992-95	261	2,710	12
Chris Myers, Kenyon	1967-70	253	3,897	33
Bruce Cerone, Yankton/Emporia St.	1965-66, 68-69	241	4,354	*49
James Roe, Norfolk St.	1992-95	239	*4,468	46
Bryan McGinty, Lock Haven	1993-96	238	3,100	18
"Red" Roberts, Austin Peay	1967-70	232	3,005	31
Chris George, Glenville St.	1993-94	230	3,215	30
Jerry Hendren, Idaho	1967-69	230	3,435	27
Mike Healey, Valparaiso	1982-85	228	3,212	26

Player, Team	Years	Rec.	Yards	TD
William Mackall, Tenn.-Martin	1985-88	224	2,488	16
Brad Bailey, West Tex. A&M	1992-94	221	2,677	22
Johnny Cox, Fort Lewis	1990-93	220	3,611	33
Greg Hopkins, Slippery Rock	1991-94	215	3,382	28
Robert Clark, N.C. Central	1983-86	210	4,231	38
Terry Fredenberg, Wis.-Milwaukee	1965-68	206	2,789	24
Dan Bogar, Valparaiso	1981-84	204	2,816	26
Rich Otte, Truman St.	1980-83	202	2,821	16
Mark Steinmeyer, Kutztown (RB)	1988-91	200	2,118	23
Barry Naone, Portland St. (TE)	1985-88	199	2,237	8
Mike Smith, Neb.-Kearney	1994-97	195	2,975	25
Tony Willis, New Haven	1990-93	194	3,420	38
Jon Braff, St. Mary's (Cal.) (TE)	1985-88	193	2,461	20
Shannon Sharpe, Savannah St.	1986-89	192	3,744	40
Sedrick Robinson, Ky. Wesleyan	1993-96	191	3,328	42

*Record.

SEASON RECEPTIONS

Player, Team	Year	G	Rec.	Yards	TD
Brad Bailey, West Tex. A&M	1994	11	*119	1,552	16
Chris George, Glenville St.	†1993	10	117	*1,876	15
Chris George, Glenville St.	†1994	10	113	1,339	15
Sean Pender, Valdosta St.	†1995	11	111	983	2
Barry Wagner, Alabama A&M	†1989	11	106	1,812	17
Mike Healey, Valparaiso	†1985	10	101	1,279	11
Ed Bell, Idaho St.	†1969	10	96	1,522	20
Dick Hewins, Drake	†1968	10	95	1,316	13
Carlos Ferralls, Glenville St.	†1997	10	94	1,566	19
Jarett Vito, Emporia St.	1995	10	+94	932	7
Billy Joe Masters, Evansville	†1987	10	‡94	‡960	4
Stan Carraway, West Tex. A&M	†1986	11	94	1,175	9
Manley Sarnowsky, Drake	†1966	10	92	1,114	7
Rus Bailey, N.M. Highlands	1993	10	91	1,192	12
Bruce Cerone, Emporia St.	1968	9	91	1,479	15
Rodney Robinson, Gardner-Webb	1992	11	89	1,496	16
Chris Perry, Adams St.	1995	10	88	1,719	*21
Matt Carman, West Ala.	1993	10	88	1,085	14
Harvey Tanner, Murray St.	†1967	10	88	1,019	3

*Record. †National champion. +Record for a freshman. ‡Record for a running back.

SINGLE-GAME RECEPTIONS

No.	Player, Team (Opponent)	Date
23	Chris George, Glenville St. (West Va. Wesleyan)	Oct. 15, 1994
23	Barry Wagner, Alabama A&M (Clark Atlanta)	Nov. 4, 1989
21	Kevin Swayne, Wayne St. (Neb.) (Drake)	Nov. 9, 1996
21	Jarett Vito, Emporia St. (Truman St.)	Nov. 4, 1995
20	Sean Pender, Valdosta St. (Mississippi Col.)	Nov. 4, 1995
20	Keylie Martin, N.M. Highlands (Western St.)	Nov. 5, 1994
20	"Red" Roberts, Austin Peay (Murray St.)	Nov. 8, 1969
19	Preston Cunningham, Southwest St. (Mo. Western St.)	Sept. 3, 1994
19	Matt Carman, West Ala. (Jacksonville St.)	Nov. 7, 1992
19	Aaron Marsh, Eastern Ky. (Northwood)	Oct. 14, 1967
19	Donnie Pruitt, Emory & Henry vs. Carson-Newman	Sept. 23, 1967
19	George LaPorte, Union (N.Y.) (Rensselaer)	Oct. 16, 1965

CAREER YARDS PER GAME

(Minimum 2,200 yards)

Player, Team	Years	G	Rec.	Yards	Avg.
Chris George, Glenville St.	1993-94	20	230	3,215	*160.8
Ed Bell, Idaho St.	1968-69	19	163	2,608	137.3
Bruce Cerone, Yankton/Emporia St.	1965-66, 68-69	36	241	4,354	120.9
Carlos Ferralls, Glenville St.	1994-97	32	*262	3,835	119.8
Jerry Hendren, Idaho	1967-69	30	230	3,435	114.5
Chris Myers, Kenyon	1967-70	35	253	3,897	111.3
James Roe, Norfolk St.	1992-95	41	239	*4,468	109.0

*Record.

SEASON YARDS PER GAME

Player, Team	Years	G	Rec.	Yards	Avg.
Chris George, Glenville St.	†1993	10	117	*1,876	*187.6
Chris Perry, Adams St.	†1995	10	88	1,719	171.9
Barry Wagner, Alabama A&M	†1989	11	106	1,812	164.7
Bruce Cerone, Emporia St.	1968	9	91	1,479	164.3
Jerry Hendren, Idaho	†1969	9	86	1,457	161.9
Carlos Ferralls, Glenville St.	†1997	10	94	1,566	156.6
Ed Bell, Idaho St.	†1969	10	96	1,522	152.2
James Roe, Norfolk St.	†1994	10	77	1,454	145.4
Dan Fulton, Neb.-Omaha	1976	11	67	1,581	143.7
Brad Bailey, West Tex. A&M	1994	11	*119	1,552	141.1

*Record. †National champion.

CAREER YARDS

Player, Team	Years	Rec.	Yards	Avg.	TD
James Roe, Norfolk St.	1992-95	239	*4,468	18.7	46
Bruce Cerone, Yankton/Emporia St.	1965-66, 68-69	241	4,354	18.1	*49
Robert Clark, N.C. Central	1983-86	210	4,231	‡20.1	38
Chris Myers, Kenyon	1967-70	253	3,897	15.4	33
Carlos Ferralls, Glenville St.	1994-97	*262	3,835	14.6	43
Shannon Sharpe, Savannah St.	1986-89	192	3,744	19.5	40
Tyrone Johnson, Western St.	1990-93	163	3,717	*22.8	35
Jeff Tiefenthaler, South Dak. St.	1983-86	173	3,621	20.9	31
Willie Richardson, Jackson St.	1959-62	166	3,616	21.8	36
Johnny Cox, Fort Lewis	1990-93	220	3,611	16.4	33

*Record. ‡Record for minimum 180 catches.

SEASON YARDS

Player, Team	Year	Rec.	Yards	Avg.	TD
Chris George, Glenville St.	†1993	117	*1,876	16.0	15
Barry Wagner, Alabama A&M	1989	106	1,812	17.1	17
Chris Perry, Adams St.	†1995	88	1,719	19.5	*21
Dan Fulton, Neb.-Omaha	1976	67	1,581	23.6	16
Carlos Ferralls, Glenville St.	†1997	94	1,566	16.6	19
Brad Bailey, West Tex. A&M	1994	*119	1,552	13.0	16
Jeff Tiefenthaler, South Dak. St.	1986	73	1,534	21.0	11
Ed Bell, Idaho St.	1969	96	1,522	15.9	20
Rodney Robinson, Gardner-Webb	†1992	89	1,496	16.8	16
Bruce Cerone, Emporia St.	1968	91	1,479	16.3	15
Jerry Hendren, Idaho	1968	86	1,457	16.9	14

*Record. †National champion.

ANNUAL CHAMPIONS

Year	Player, Team	Class	Rec.	Yards	TD
1946	Hugh Taylor, Oklahoma City	Jr.	23	457	8
1947	Bill Klein, Hanover	So.	52	648	12
1948	Bill Klein, Hanover	Jr.	43	812	6
1949	Cliff Coggin, Southern Miss.	Sr.	53	1,087	9
1950	Jack Bighead, Pepperdine	Jr.	38	551	6
1951	Jim Stefoff, Kalamazoo	Jr.	45	680	5
1952	Jim McKinzie, Northern Ill.	Sr.	44	703	6
1953	Dick Beetsch, Northern Iowa	So.	54	837	9
1954	R. C. Owens, Col. of Idaho	Sr.	48	905	7
1955	Dick Donlin, Hamline	Sr.	41	480	2
1956	Tom Rychlec, American Int'l	Sr.	40	353	3
1957	Tom Whitaker, Nevada	Jr.	40	527	4
1958	Bruce Shenk, West Chester	Sr.	39	580	9
1959	Fred Tunnicliffe, UC Santa Barb.	So.	48	1,087	11
1960	Ken Gregory, Whittier	Sr.	74	1,018	4
1961	Marty Baumhower, Defiance	Jr.	57	708	4
1962	Hugh Rohrschneider, Northern Ill.	Jr.	76	795	5
1963	Hugh Rohrschneider, Northern Ill.	Sr.	75	1,036	14
1964	Steve Gilliatt, Parsons	So.	81	984	12
1965	George LaPorte, Union (N.Y.)	Sr.	74	724	5
1966	Manley Sarnowsky, Drake	Sr.	92	1,114	7
1967	Harvey Tanner, Murray St.	Jr.	88	1,019	3
1968	Dick Hewins, Drake	Sr.	95	1,316	13
1969	Ed Bell, Idaho St.	Sr.	96	1,522	20

Beginning in 1970, ranked on per-game (instead of total) catches

Year	Player, Team	Class	G	Rec.	Avg.	Yards	TD
1970	Steve Mahaffey, Wash. & Lee	Sr.	9	74	8.2	897	2
1971	Kalle Kontson, Rensselaer	Sr.	9	69	7.7	1,031	7
1972	Freddie Scott, Amherst	Jr.	8	66	8.3	936	12
1973	Ron Gustafson, North Dak.	Jr.	10	67	6.7	1,210	10
1974	Andy Sanchez, Cal Poly Pomona	Sr.	10	62	6.2	903	0
1975	Butch Johnson, UC Riverside	Sr.	8	67	8.4	1,027	8
1976	Bo Darden, Shaw	So.	9	57	6.3	863	4
1977	Jeff Tesch, Moorhead St.	Sr.	10	67	6.7	760	9
1978	Mike Chrobot, Butler	Sr.	10	55	5.5	628	5
	Tom Ferguson, Cal St. Hayward	Jr.	10	55	5.5	698	6
	Mark McDaniel, Northern Colo.	Sr.	10	55	5.5	761	6
1979	Robbie Ray, Franklin	Sr.	10	63	6.3	987	3
1980	Joe Dittrich, Southwest St.	Sr.	9	83	9.2	974	7
1981	Paul Choudek, Southwest St.	Sr.	10	70	7.0	747	5
1982	Jay Barnett, Evansville	Sr.	10	81	8.1	1,181	12
1983	Perry Kemp, Calif. (Pa.)	Sr.	10	74	7.4	1,101	9
1984	Dan Bogar, Valparaiso	Sr.	10	73	7.3	861	11
1985	Mike Healey, Valparaiso	Sr.	10	101	10.1	1,279	11
1986	Stan Carraway, West Tex. A&M	Sr.	11	94	8.5	1,175	9
1987	Billy Joe Masters, Evansville	Sr.	10	‡94	‡9.4	‡960	4
1988	Todd Smith, Morningside	Sr.	11	86	7.8	1,006	8
1989	Barry Wagner, Alabama A&M	Sr.	11	106	9.6	1,812	17

Beginning in 1990, ranked on both per-game catches and yards per game.

PER-GAME RECEPTIONS

Year	Player, Team	Class	G	Rec.	Avg.	Yards	TD
1990	Mark Steinmeyer, Kutztown	Jr.	11	86	7.8	940	5
1991	Jesse Lopez, Cal St. Hayward	Sr.	10	86	8.6	861	4
1992	Randy Bartosh, Southwest Baptist	Sr.	8	65	8.1	860	2
1993	Chris George, Glenville St.	Jr.	10	117	*11.7	*1,876	15
1994	Chris George, Glenville St.	Sr.	10	113	11.3	1,339	15
1995	Sean Pender, Valdosta St.	Jr.	11	111	10.1	983	2
1996	Carlos Ferralls, Glenville St.	Jr.	8	81	10.1	965	6
1997	Carlos Ferralls, Glenville St.	Sr.	10	94	9.4	1,566	19

YARDS PER GAME

Year	Player, Team	Class	G	Rec.	Yards	Avg.	TD
1990	Ernest Priester, Edinboro	Sr.	8	45	1,060	132.5	14
1991	Rod Smith, Mo. Southern St.	Jr.	11	60	1,439	130.8	15
1992	Rodney Robinson, Gardner-Webb	Sr.	11	89	1,496	136.0	16
1993	Chris George, Glenville St.	Jr.	10	117	*1,876	*187.6	15
1994	James Roe, Norfolk St.	Jr.	10	77	1,454	145.4	17
1995	Chris Perry, Adams St.	Sr.	10	88	1,719	171.9	*21
1996	Ron Lelko, Bloomsburg	Jr.	11	87	1,455	132.3	15
1997	Carlos Ferralls, Glenville St.	Sr.	10	94	1,566	156.6	19

**Record. ‡Record for a running back.*

Scoring

CAREER POINTS PER GAME

(Minimum 225 Points)

Player, Team	Years	G	TD	XPt.	FG	Pts.	Pt. PG
Ole Gunderson, St. Olaf	1969-71	27	60	2	0	362	*13.4
Leon Burns, Long Beach St.	1969-70	22	47	2	0	284	12.9
Billy Johnson, Widener	1971-72	19	39	0	0	234	12.3
Dale Mills, Truman St.	1957-60	36	64	23	0	407	11.3
Walter Payton, Jackson St.	1971-74	42	66	53	5	*464	11.0
Steve Roberts, Butler	1986-89	35	63	4	0	386	11.0
Jeff Bentrim, North Dak. St.	1983-86	35	64	2	0	386	11.0
Shawn Graves, Wofford	1989-92	40	72	3	0	438	11.0
Johnny Bailey, Tex. A&M-Kingsville	1986-89	39	70	3	0	426	10.9
Garney Henley, Huron	1956-59	37	63	16	0	394	10.6
Roger Graham, New Haven	1991-94	40	70	2	0	424	10.6

**Record.*

SEASON POINTS PER GAME

Player, Team	Years	G	TD	XPt.	FG	Pts.	Pt. PG
Carl Herakovich, Rose-Hulman	†1958	8	25	18	0	168	*21.0
Jim Switzer, Col. of Emporia	†1963	9	28	0	0	168	18.7
Brian Shay, Emporia St.	†1997	11	*32	6	0	*198	18.0
Billy Johnson, Widener	†1972	9	27	0	0	162	18.0
Carl Garrett, N.M. Highlands	†1966	9	26	2	0	158	17.6
Ted Scown, Sul Ross St.	†1948	10	28	0	0	168	16.8

**Record. †National champion.*

CAREER POINTS

Player, Team	Years	TD	XPt.	FG	Pts.
Walter Payton, Jackson St.	1971-74	66	53	5	*464
Jarrett Anderson, Truman St.	1993-96	*73	2	0	440
Shawn Graves, Wofford	1989-92	72	3	0	438
Johnny Bailey, Tex. A&M-Kingsville	1986-89	70	3	0	426
Roger Graham, New Haven	1991-94	70	2	0	424
Dale Mills, Truman St.	1957-60	64	23	0	407
Jeremy Monroe, Michigan Tech	1990-93	67	0	0	402
Garney Henley, Huron	1956-59	63	16	0	394
Steve Roberts, Butler	1986-89	63	4	0	386
Jeff Bentrim, North Dak. St.	1983-86	64	2	0	386
Leo Lewis, Lincoln (Mo.)	1951-54	64	0	0	384
Bob Miller, Emory & Henry	1948-51	63	1	0	379
Antonio Leroy, Albany St. (Ga.)	1993-96	62	6	0	378
Heath Sherman, Tex. A&M-Kingsville	1985-88	63	0	0	378
Tank Younger, Grambling	1945-48	60	9	0	369
¢Brian Shay, Emporia St.	1995-97	59	7	0	368
Richard Huntley, Winston-Salem	1992-95	60	8	0	368
Bill Cooper, Muskingum	1957-60	54	37	1	364

**Record. ¢ Active player.*

SEASON POINTS

Player, Team	Year	TD	XPt.	FG	Pts.
Brian Shay, Emporia St.	†1997	*32	6	0	*198
Travis Walch, Winona St.	1997	30	2	0	182
Terry Metcalf, Long Beach St.	1971	29	4	0	178
Jarrett Anderson, Truman St.	†1996	28	0	0	168
Jim Switzer, Col. of Emporia	†1963	28	0	0	168
Carl Herakovich, Rose-Hulman	†1958	25	18	0	168
Ted Scown, Sul Ross St.	†1948	28	0	0	168
Ronald Moore, Pittsburg St.	1992	27	4	0	166
Leon Burns, Long Beach St.	†1969	27	2	0	164
Mike Deutsch, North Dak.	1972	27	0	0	162
Billy Johnson, Widener	†1972	27	0	0	162

**Record. †National champion.*

ANNUAL CHAMPIONS

Year	Player, Team	Class	TD	XPt.	FG	Pts.
1946	Joe Carter, Florida N&I	So.	21	26	0	152
1947	Darwin Horn, Pepperdine	Jr.	19	1	0	115
	Chuck Schoenherr, Wheaton (Ill.)	So.	19	1	0	115
1948	Ted Scown, Sul Ross St.	So.	28	0	0	168
1949	Sylvester Polk, Md.-East. Shore	Jr.	19	15	0	129
1950	Carl Taseff, John Carroll	Sr.	23	0	0	138
1951	Paul Yackey, Heidelberg	Jr.	22	0	0	132
1952	Al Conway, William Jewell	Sr.	22	1	0	133
1953	Leo Lewis, Lincoln (Mo.)	Jr.	22	0	0	132
1954	Jim Podoley, Central Mich.	Jr.	18	1	0	109
	Dick Nyers, Indianapolis	Sr.	16	13	0	109
1955	Nate Clark, Hillsdale	Jr.	24	0	0	144
1956	Larry Houdek, Kan. Wesleyan	Sr.	19	0	0	114
1957	Lenny Lyles, Louisville	Sr.	21	6	0	132
1958	Carl Herakovich, Rose-Hulman	Sr.	25	18	0	168
1959	Garney Henley, Huron	Sr.	22	9	0	141
1960	Bill Cooper, Muskingum	Sr.	23	14	0	152
1961	John Murio, Whitworth	Jr.	15	33	2	129
1962	Mike Goings, Bluffton	So.	22	0	0	132
1963	Jim Switzer, Col. of Emporia	Sr.	28	0	0	168
1964	Henry Dyer, Grambling	Jr.	17	2	0	104
	Dunn Marteen, Cal St. Los Angeles	Sr.	11	38	0	104
1965	Allen Smith, Findlay	Jr.	24	2	0	146
1966	Carl Garrett, N.M. Highlands	So.	26	2	0	158
1967	Bert Nye, West Chester	Jr.	19	13	0	127
1968	Howard Stevens, Randolph-Macon	Fr.	23	4	0	142
1969	Leon Burns, Long Beach St.	Jr.	27	2	0	164

Beginning in 1970, ranked on per-game (instead of total) points

Year	Player, Team	Class	G	TD	XPt.	FG	Pts.	Avg.
1970	Mike DiBlasi, Mount Union	Sr.	9	22	0	0	132	14.7
1971	Larry Ras, Michigan Tech	Sr.	9	24	0	0	144	16.0
1972	Billy Johnson, Widener	Jr.	9	27	0	0	162	18.0
1973	Walter Payton, Jackson St.	Jr.	11	24	13	1	160	14.5
1974	Walter Payton, Jackson St.	Sr.	10	19	6	1	123	12.3
1975	Dale Kasowski, North Dak.	Sr.	7	16	4	0	100	14.3
1976	Ted McKnight, Minn.-Duluth	Sr.	10	24	0	0	144	14.4
1977	Bill Burnham, New Hampshire	Sr.	10	22	0	0	132	13.2
1978	Marschell Brunfield, Youngstown St.	Sr.	9	14	0	0	84	9.3
	Charlie Thompson, Western St.	Sr.	9	14	0	0	84	9.3
1979	Robby Robson, Youngstown St.	Jr.	10	20	0	0	120	12.0
1980	Amory Bodin, Minn.-Duluth	Sr.	10	19	2	0	116	11.6
1981	George Works, Northern Mich.	Jr.	10	21	0	0	126	12.6
1982	George Works, Northern Mich.	Sr.	10	23	0	0	138	13.8
1983	Clarence Johnson, North Ala.	Jr.	10	16	0	0	96	9.6
1984	Jeff Bentrim, North Dak. St.	So.	9	14	0	0	84	9.3
1985	Jeff Bentrim, North Dak. St.	Jr.	8	18	2	0	110	††13.8
1986	Jeff Bentrim, North Dak. St.	Sr.	10	23	0	0	138	13.8
1987	Johnny Bailey, Tex. A&M-Kingsville	So.	10	20	0	0	120	12.0
1988	Steve Roberts, Butler	Jr.	10	23	4	0	142	14.2
1989	Jimmy Allen, St. Joseph's (Ind.)	Jr.	10	23	0	0	138	13.8
1990	Ernest Priester, Edinboro	Sr.	8	16	0	0	96	12.0
1991	Quincy Tillmon, Emporia St.	So.	9	19	0	0	114	12.7
1992	David McCartney, Chadron St.	Jr.	10	25	4	0	154	15.4
1993	Roger Graham, New Haven	Jr.	10	23	0	0	138	13.8
1994	Leonard Davis, Lenoir-Rhyne	Sr.	9	19	0	0	114	12.7
1995	Antonio Leroy, Albany St. (Ga.)	Jr.	11	24	0	0	144	13.1
1996	Jarrett Anderson, Truman St.	Sr.	11	28	0	0	168	15.3
1997	Brian Shay, Emporia St.	Jr.	11	*32	6	0	*198	18.0

††Declared champion; with one more game (to meet 75 percent of games played minimum) for zero points, still would have highest per-game average (12.2).

Interceptions

CAREER INTERCEPTIONS

Player, Team	Years	No.	Yards	Avg.
Tom Collins, Indianapolis	1982-85	*37	390	10.5
Dean Diaz, Humboldt St.	1980-83	31	328	10.6
Bill Grantham, Mo.-Rolla	1977-80	29	263	9.1
Jason Johnson, Shepherd	1991-94	28	321	11.5
Tony Woods, Bloomsburg	1982-85	26	105	4.0
Buster West, Gust. Adolphus	1967-70	26	192	7.4

Player, Team	Years	No.	Yards	Avg.
Nate Gruber, Winona St.	1991-94	25	275	11.0
Gary Rubeling, Towson St.	1980-83	25	122	4.9
Greg Mercier, Ripon	1968-70	25	243	9.7

**Record.*

SEASON INTERCEPTIONS

Player, Team	Year	No.	Yards
Eugene Hunter, Fort Valley St.	†1972	**14	211
Luther Howard, Delaware St.	†1972	**14	99
Tom Rezzuti, Northeastern	†1971	**14	153
Jim Blackwell, Southern U.	†1970	**14	196
Carl Ray Harris, Fresno St.	1970	**14	98

***Record tied. †National champion.*

ANNUAL CHAMPIONS

Year	Player, Team	Class	G	No.	Avg.	Yards
1970	Jim Blackwell, Southern U.	Sr.	11	**14	1.27	196
1971	Tom Rezzuti, Northeastern	Jr.	9	**14	**1.56	153
1972	Eugene Hunter, Fort Valley St.	So.	9	**14	**1.56	211
	Luther Howard, Delaware St.	Sr.	9	**14	**1.56	99
1973	Mike Pierce, Northern Colo.	Sr.	7	7	1.00	158
	James Smith, Shaw	So.	8	8	1.00	94
1974	Terry Rusin, Wayne St. (Mich.)	Fr.	10	10	1.00	62
1975	Jim Poettgen, Cal Poly Pomona	Jr.	11	12	1.09	156
1976	Johnny Tucker, Tennessee Tech	Sr.	11	10	0.91	74
1977	Mike Ellis, Norfolk St.	So.	11	12	1.09	257
	Cornelius Washington, Winston-Salem	Sr.	11	12	1.09	128
1978	Bill Grantham, Mo.-Rolla	So.	11	11	1.00	109
1979	Jeff Huffman, Michigan Tech	Sr.	10	11	1.10	97
1980	Mike Lush, East Stroudsburg	Sr.	10	12	1.20	208
1981	Bobby Futrell, Elizabeth City St.	So.	9	11	1.22	159
1982	Greg Maack, Central Mo. St.	Sr.	10	11	1.10	192
1983	Matt Didio, Wayne St. (Mich.)	Sr.	10	13	1.30	131
1984	Bob Jahelka, LIU-C. W. Post	Sr.	8	9	1.13	83
1985	Duvaal Callaway, Fort Valley St.	Sr.	11	10	0.91	175
	Tony Woods, Bloomsburg	Sr.	11	10	0.91	10
1986	Doug Smart, Winona St.	Jr.	8	10	1.25	56
1987	Mike Petrich, Minn.-Duluth	Jr.	11	9	0.82	151
1988	Pete Jaros, Augustana (S.D.)	Jr.	11	13	1.18	120
1989	Jacque DeMatteo, Clarion	Jr.	8	6	0.75	21

Year	Player, Team	Class	G	No.	Avg.	Yards
1990	Eric Turner, Tex. A&M-Commerce	So.	11	10	0.91	105
1991	Jeff Fickes, Shippensburg	Sr.	11	12	1.09	154
1992	Pat Williams, Tex. A&M-Commerce	Sr.	11	13	1.18	145
1993	Troy Crissman, Ky. Wesleyan	So.	10	9	0.90	39
1994	Keith Hawkins, Humboldt St.	Sr.	10	11	1.10	159
	Elton Rhoades, Central Okla.	Sr.	10	11	1.10	126
1995	Chenelle Jones, Western N.M.	Sr.	8	7	0.88	61
1996	Britt Henderson, Savannah St.	Sr.	11	12	1.09	180
1997	Jamey Hutchinson, Winona St.	Jr.	11	11	1.00	125
	Tim Bednarski, Mercyhurst	Jr.	9	9	1.00	59

***Record tied.*

Punting

CAREER AVERAGE
(Minimum 100 Punts)

Player, Team	Years	No.	Yards	Avg.
Tim Baer, Colorado Mines	1986-89	235	10,406	*44.3
Jeff Guy, Western St.	1983-85	113	4,967	44.0
Russ Pilcher, Carroll (Mont.)	1964-66	124	5,424	43.7
Russell Gonzales, Morris Brown	1976-77	111	4,833	43.5
Gerald Circo, Cal St. Chico	1964-65	103	4,470	43.4
Trent Morgan, Cal St. Northridge	1987-88	128	5,531	43.2
Bryan Wagner, Cal St. Northridge	1981-84	203	8,762	43.2
Tom Kolesar, Nevada	1973-74	140	6,032	43.1
Jimmy Morris, Angelo St.	1991-92	101	4,326	42.8
Don Geist, Northern Colo.	1981-84	263	11,247	42.8
Jan Chapman, San Diego	1958-60	106	4,533	42.8
Warner Robertson, Md.-East. Shore	1968-70	131	5,578	42.6

**Record.*

SEASON AVERAGE
(Qualifiers for Championship)

Player, Team	Year	No.	Yards	Avg.
Steve Ecker, Shippensburg	†1965	32	1,570	*49.1
Don Cockroft, Adams St.	†1966	36	1,728	48.0
Jack Patterson, William Jewell	1965	29	1,377	47.5
Art Calandrelli, Canisius	†1949	25	1,177	47.1
Grover Perkins, Southern U.	†1961	22	1,034	47.0
Erskine Valrie, Alabama A&M	1966	36	1,673	46.5
Mark Bounds, West Tex. A&M	†1990	69	3,198	+46.3
Bruce Swanson, North Park	†1967	53	2,455	46.3
Lyle Johnston, Weber St.	1965	29	1,340	46.2

**Record. †National champion. +Record for minimum 40 punts.*

ANNUAL CHAMPIONS

Year	Player, Team	Class	No.	Yards	Avg.
1948	Arthur Teixeira, Central Mich.	Sr.	42	1,867	44.5
1949	Art Calandrelli, Canisius	Jr.	25	1,177	47.1
1950	Flavian Weidekamp, Butler	Sr.	41	1,762	43.0
1951	Curtiss Harris, Savannah St.	Sr.	42	1,854	44.1
1952	Virgil Stan, Western St.	Sr.	37	1,622	43.8
1953	Bill Bradshaw, Bowling Green	Jr.	50	2,199	44.0
1954	Bill Bradshaw, Bowling Green	Sr.	28	1,228	43.9
1955	Don Baker, North Texas	Sr.	30	1,349	45.0
1956	Marion Zody, Ashland	Jr.	34	1,475	43.4
1957	Lawson Persley, Mississippi Val.	Sr.	36	1,659	46.1
1958	Tom Lewis, Lake Forest	Jr.	24	1,089	45.4
1959	Buck Grover, Salem-Teikyo	Fr.	27	1,203	44.6
1960	Joe Roy, N.M. Highlands	So.	40	1,744	43.6
1961	Grover Perkins, Southern U.	Fr.	22	1,034	47.0
1962	Ron Crouse, Catawba	Jr.	37	1,653	44.7
1963	Steve Bailey, Kentucky St.	Sr.	39	1,747	44.8
1964	Russ Pilcher, Carroll (Mont.)	So.	34	1,545	45.4
1965	Steve Ecker, Shippensburg	Sr.	32	1,570	*49.1
1966	Don Cockroft, Adams St.	Sr.	36	1,728	48.0
1967	Bruce Swanson, North Park	Jr.	53	2,455	46.3
1968	Warner Robertson, Md.-East. Shore	Fr.	61	2,699	44.2
1969	Warner Robertson, Md.-East. Shore	So.	37	1,629	44.0
1970	John Bonner, Tenn.-Chatt.	Sr.	73	3,243	44.4
1971	Ken Gamble, Fayetteville St.	Sr.	47	2,092	44.5
1972	Raymond Key, Jackson St.	Jr.	44	1,883	42.8
1973	Jerry Pope, Louisiana Tech	Fr.	48	2,064	43.0
1974	Mike Shawen, Middle Tenn. St.	Sr.	62	2,720	43.9
1975	Mike Wood, Southeast Mo. St.	Jr.	40	1,729	43.2
1976	Russell Gonzales, Morris Brown	So.	54	2,474	45.8
1977	Jeff Gossett, Eastern Ill.	Jr.	62	2,668	43.0
1978	Bill Moats, South Dak.	Sr.	77	3,377	43.9
1979	Bob Fletcher, Truman St.	Sr.	79	3,409	43.2
1980	Sean Landeta, Towson St.	So.	47	2,038	43.4
1981	Gregg Lowery, Jacksonville St.	Jr.	64	2,787	43.5
1982	Don Geist, Northern Colo.	So.	66	2,966	44.4
1983	Jeff Guy, Western St.	So.	39	1,734	44.5
1984	Jeff Guy, Western St.	Jr.	46	2,012	43.7
1985	Jeff Williams, Slippery Rock	Sr.	46	1,977	43.0
1986	Tim Baer, Colorado Mines	Fr.	62	2,797	45.1
1987	Jeff McComb, Southern Utah	Sr.	42	1,863	44.4
1988	Tim Baer, Colorado Mines	Jr.	65	2,880	43.9
1989	Tim Baer, Colorado Mines	Sr.	55	2,382	43.3
1990	Mark Bounds, West Tex. A&M	Jr.	69	3,198	+46.3
1991	Doug O'Neill, Cal Poly SLO	Sr.	42	1,895	45.1
1992	Jimmy Morris, Angelo St.	So.	45	2,001	44.5
1993	Chris Carter, Henderson St.	Sr.	53	2,305	43.5
1994	Pat Hogelin, Colorado Mines	Sr.	48	2,167	45.1
1995	Jon Mason, West Tex. A&M	Sr.	54	2,459	45.5
1996	Tom O'Brien, South Dak. St.	So.	60	2,671	44.5
1997	Brian Moorman, Pittsburg St.	Jr.	36	1,657	46.0

**Record. +Record for minimum 40 punts.*

Punt Returns

CAREER AVERAGE
(Minimum 1.2 Returns Per Game)

Player, Team	Years	No.	Yards	Avg.
Billy Johnson, Widener	1971-72	29	759	*26.2
Bootsie Washington, Shepherd	1996-97	26	512	19.7
Chuck Goehl, Monmouth (Ill.)	1970-72	48	911	19.0
Robbie Martin, Cal Poly SLO	1978-80	69	1,168	16.9
Roscoe Word, Jackson St.	1970-73	35	554	15.8
Darryl Skinner, Hampton	1983-86	53	835	15.8
Michael Fields, Mississippi Col.	1984-85	50	695	13.9

**Record.*

SEASON AVERAGE
(Minimum 1.2 Returns Per Game)

Player, Team	Year	No.	Yards	Avg.
Billy Johnson, Widener	†1972	15	511	*34.1
William Williams, Livingstone	†1976	16	453	28.3
Terry Egerdahl, Minn.-Duluth	†1975	13	360	27.7
Ennis Thomas, Bishop	†1971	18	450	25.0
Chuck Goehl, Monmouth (Ill.)	1972	17	416	24.5
Doug Grant, Savannah St.	†1992	15	366	24.4

Player, Team	Year	No.	Yards	Avg.
Bootsie Washington, Shepherd	†1997	19	461	24.3

**Record. †National champion.*

ANNUAL CHAMPIONS

Year	Player, Team	Class	No.	Yards	Avg.
1970	Kevin Downs, Benedictine (Ill.)	Jr.	11	255	23.2
1971	Ennis Thomas, Bishop	So.	18	450	25.0
1972	Billy Johnson, Widener	Jr.	15	511	*34.1
1973	Roscoe Word, Jackson St.	Sr.	19	316	16.6
1974	Greg Anderson, Montana	So.	13	263	20.2
1975	Terry Egerdahl, Minn.-Duluth	Sr.	13	360	27.7
1976	William Williams, Livingstone	So.	16	453	28.3
1977	Armando Olivieri, New York Tech	So.	14	270	19.3
1978	Dwight Walker, Nicholls St.	Fr.	16	284	17.8
1979	Ricky Eberhart, Morris Brown	Fr.	18	401	22.3
1980	Ron Bagby, Puget Sound	So.	16	242	15.1
1981	Ron Trammell, Tex. A&M-Commerce	Jr.	29	467	16.1
1982	Darrel Green, Tex. A&M-Kingsville	Sr.	19	392	20.6
1983	Steve Carter, Albany St. (Ga.)	Sr.	27	511	18.9
1984	Michael Fields, Mississippi Col.	Jr.	23	487	21.2
1985	Darryl Skinner, Hampton	Jr.	19	426	22.4
1986	Ben Frazier, Cheyney	So.	14	246	17.6
1987	Ronald Day, Savannah St.	Sr.	12	229	19.1
1988	Donnie Morris, Norfolk St.	Jr.	12	283	23.6
1989	Dennis Mailhot, East Stroudsburg	Jr.	16	284	17.8
1990	Ron West, Pittsburg St.	Jr.	23	388	16.9
1991	Doug Grant, Savannah St.	So.	19	331	17.4
1992	Doug Grant, Savannah St.	Jr.	15	366	24.4
1993	Jerry Garrett, Wayne St. (Neb.)	Jr.	26	498	19.2
1994	Terry Guess, Gardner-Webb	So.	16	312	19.5
1995	Kevin Cannon, Millersville	Sr.	16	277	17.3
1996	Sean Smith, Bloomsburg	Sr.	25	481	19.2
1997	Bootsie Washington, Shepherd	Sr.	19	461	24.3

**Record.*

Kickoff Returns

CAREER AVERAGE
(Minimum 1.2 Returns Per Game)

Player, Team	Years	No.	Yards	Avg.
Glen Printers, Southern Colo.	1973-74	25	851	*34.0
Karl Evans, Mo. Southern St.	1991-92	32	959	30.0
Kevin Cannon, Millersville	1992-95	67	1,999	29.8
Dave Ludy, Winona St.	1991-94	89	*2,630	29.6
Doug Parrish, San Fran. St.	1990	35	1,002	28.6
Clarence Chapman, Eastern Mich.	1973-75	45	1,278	28.4
Greg Wilson, East Tenn. St.	1975-77	34	952	28.0
Bernie Rose, North Ala.	1974-76	62	1,681	27.1
Roscoe Word, Jackson St.	1970-73	74	1,980	26.8

**Record.*

SEASON AVERAGE
(Minimum 1.2 Returns Per Game)

Player, Team	Year	No.	Yards	Avg.
LaVon Reis, Western St.	†1993	14	552	*39.43
Danny Lee, Jacksonville St.	†1992	12	473	39.42
Fran DeFalco, Assumption	1993	12	461	38.4
Kendall James, Carson-Newman	1993	15	549	36.6
Roscoe Word, Jackson St.	†1973	18	650	36.1
Steve Levenseller, Puget Sound	†1978	17	610	35.9
Winston Horshaw, Shippensburg	†1991	15	536	35.7
Boobie Thornton, Midwestern St.	†1997	12	426	35.5
Anthony Rivera, Western St.	1991	18	635	35.3
Dave Ludy, Winona St.	1992	25	881	35.2
Mike Scullin, Baldwin-Wallace	†1970	14	492	35.1
Rufus Smith, Eastern N.M.	†1985	11	386	35.1
Rebert Mack, West Tex. A&M	†1996	14	489	34.9
Norman Miller, Tex. A&M-Kingsville	1995	12	405	33.8
Greg Anderson, Montana	†1974	10	335	33.5
Kevin Cannon, Millersville	1995	14	463	33.1
Kevin McDevitt, Butler	†1975	12	395	32.9

**Record. †National champion.*

ANNUAL CHAMPIONS

Year	Player, Team	Class	No.	Yards	Avg.
1970	Mike Scullin, Baldwin-Wallace	So.	14	492	35.1
1971	Joe Brockmeyer, Western Md.	Jr.	16	500	31.3
1972	Rick Murphy, Indiana St.	Jr.	22	707	32.1
1973	Roscoe Word, Jackson St.	Sr.	18	650	36.1
1974	Greg Anderson, Montana	So.	10	335	33.5
1975	Kevin McDevitt, Butler	Jr.	12	395	32.9
1976	Henry Vereen, UNLV	So.	20	628	31.4
1977	Dickie Johnson, Southern Colo.	Jr.	13	385	29.6
1978	Steve Levenseller, Puget Sound	Sr.	17	610	35.9
1979	Otha Hill, Central St.	Sr.	18	526	29.2
1980	Charlie Taylor, Southeast Mo. St.	Sr.	13	396	30.5
1981	Willie Canady, Fort Valley St.	Jr.	13	415	31.9
1982	Clarence Martin, Cal Poly SLO	So.	11	360	32.7
1983	David Anthony, Southern Ore.	Jr.	14	436	31.1
1984	Larry Winters, St. Paul's	Sr.	20	644	32.2
1985	Rufus Smith, Eastern N.M.	Fr.	11	386	35.1
1986	John Barron, Butler	So.	21	653	31.1
1987	Albert Fann, Cal St. Northridge	Fr.	16	468	29.3
1988	Pierre Fils, New Haven	So.	12	378	31.5
1989	Dennis Mailhot, East Stroudsburg	Jr.	11	359	32.6
1990	Alfred Banks, West Ala.	Sr.	17	529	31.1
1991	Winston Horshaw, Shippensburg	Jr.	15	536	35.7
1992	Danny Lee, Jacksonville St.	Sr.	12	473	39.4
1993	LaVon Reis, Western St.	Sr.	14	552	*39.4
1994	Darell Whitaker, Eastern N.M.	Sr.	20	642	32.1
1995	Melvin German, Southwest St.	Sr.	9	413	††45.9
1996	Rebert Mack, West Tex. A&M	Jr.	14	489	34.9
1997	Boobie Thornton, Midwestern St.	Fr.	12	426	35.5

**Record. ††Declared champion; with two more returns (to make 1.2 per game minimum) for zero yards, still would have highest average (37.5).*

All-Purpose Yards

CAREER YARDS PER GAME
(Minimum 3,500 Yards)

Player, Team	Years	G	Rush	Rcv.	Int.	PR	KOR	Yds.	Yd. PG
Chris George, Glenville St.	1993-94	20	23	3,215	0	391	1,050	4,679	*234.0
Howard Stevens, Randolph-Macon	1968-69	18	2,574	349	0	380	388	3,691	205.1
Johnny Bailey, Tex. A&M-Kingsville	1986-89	39	*6,320	452	0	20	1,011	*7,803	200.1
Steve Roberts, Butler	1986-89	35	4,623	1,201	0	272	578	6,674	190.7
Billy Johnson, Widener	1971-72	19	2,241	242	43	759	251	3,536	186.1

**Record.*

SEASON YARDS PER GAME

Player, Team	Year	G	Rush	Rcv.	Int.	PR	KOR	Yds.	Yd. PG
Steve Roberts, Butler	1989	10	1,450	532	0	272	415	2,669	*266.9
Bobby Felix, Western N.M.	†1994	8	439	853	0	150	667	2,109	263.6
Chris George, Glenville St.	†1993	10	23	*1,876	0	157	562	2,618	261.8
Billy Johnson, Widener	1972	9	1,556	40	43	511	115	2,265	251.7
Brian Shay, Emporia St.	†1996	11	2,103	247	0	48	340	*2,738	248.9
Brian Shay, Emporia St.	†1997	11	1,912	277	0	56	478	2,723	247.5
Roger Graham, New Haven	1993	10	1,687	116	0	0	516	2,319	231.9
Anthony Gray, Western N.M.	1997	10	*2,220	78	0	0	0	2,298	229.8
Larry Jackson, Edinboro	1994	10	1,660	237	0	0	387	2,284	228.4
Johnny Bailey, Tex. A&M-Kingsville	1986	11	2,011	54	0	20	340	2,425	220.5
Johnny Cox, Fort Lewis	†1992	10	95	1,331	0	80	679	2,185	218.5
Steve Papin, Portland St.	†1995	11	1,619	525	0	1	252	2,397	217.9

Emporia State sports information photo by Neal Von Murphy

Emporia State sophomore running back Brian Shay set the Division II record with 2,738 all-purpose yards in 1996. Shay's per-game average of 248.9 ranks fifth on the single-season chart.

Player, Team	Year	G	Rush	Rcv.	Int.	PR	KOR	Yds.	Yd. PG
Ronald Moore, Pittsburg St.	1992	11	1,864	141	0	0	388	2,393	217.6
Karl Evans, Mo. Southern St.	1992	10	1,586	10	0	0	571	2,167	216.7
Roger Graham, New Haven	1994	10	1,607	197	0	0	333	2,137	213.7
Irv Sigler, Bloomsburg	1997	10	2,038	37	0	0	56	2,131	213.1
Jarrett Anderson, Truman St.	1996	11	2,140	167	0	0	0	2,307	209.7
Dave Ludy, Winona St.	1994	11	1,553	153	0	0	568	2,274	206.7
Chris George, Glenville St.	1994	10	0	1,339	0	234	488	2,061	206.1
Sedrick Robinson, Ky. Wesleyan	1996	11	71	1,099	0	286	797	2,253	204.8

**Record. †National champion.*

CAREER YARDS

Player, Team	Years	Rush	Rcv.	Int.	PR	KOR	Yds.
Johnny Bailey, Tex. A&M-Kingsville	1986-89	*6,320	452	0	20	1,011	*7,803
Roger Graham, New Haven	1991-94	5,953	393	0	0	870	7,216
Dave Ludy, Winona St.	1991-94	3,501	906	0	34	*2,630	7,071
Albert Fann, Cal St. Northridge	1987-90	4,090	803	0	0	2,141	7,032
Curtis Delgardo, Portland St.	$1986-90	4,178	1,258	0	318	1,188	6,942
Jarrett Anderson, Truman St.	1993-96	6,166	633	0	0	127	6,926
Johnny Cox, Fort Lewis	1990-93	112	3,611	0	495	2,476	6,694
Steve Roberts, Butler	1986-89	4,623	1,201	0	272	578	6,674
Richard Huntley, Winston-Salem	1992-95	6,286	333	0	0	0	6,619
Mike Smith, Neb.-Kearney	1994-97	348	2,975	0	932	2,255	6,510
¢Brian Shay, Emporia St.	1995-97	4,693	867	0	104	818	6,482
Chris Cobb, Eastern Ill.	1976-79	5,042	520	0	37	478	6,077
Don Aleksiewicz, Hobart	1969-72	4,525	470	0	320	748	6,063

**Record. $See page 6 for explanation. ¢Active player.*

SEASON YARDS

Player, Team	Year	Rush	Rcv.	Int.	PR	KOR	Yds.
Brian Shay, Emporia St.	†1996	2,103	247	0	48	340	*2,738
Brian Shay, Emporia St.	†1997	1,912	277	0	56	478	2,723
Steve Roberts, Butler	1989	1,450	532	0	272	415	2,669
Chris George, Glenville St.	†1993	23	*1,876	0	157	562	2,618
Johnny Bailey, Tex. A&M-Kingsville	1986	2,011	54	0	20	340	2,425
Rick Wegher, South Dak. St.	1984	1,317	264	0	0	824	2,405
Steve Papin, Portland St.	†1995	1,619	525	0	1	252	2,397
Ronald Moore, Pittsburg St.	1992	1,864	141	0	0	388	2,393
Roger Graham, New Haven	1993	1,687	116	0	0	516	2,319
Jarrett Anderson, Truman St.	1996	2,140	167	0	0	0	2,307
Anthony Gray, Western N.M.	1997	*2,220	78	0	0	0	2,298
Larry Jackson, Edinboro	1994	1,660	237	0	0	387	2,284
Dave Ludy, Winona St.	1994	1,553	153	0	0	568	2,274
Billy Johnson, Widener	1972	1,556	40	43	511	115	2,265
Sedrick Robinson, Ky. Wesleyan	1996	71	1,099	0	286	797	2,253
Johnny Cox, Fort Lewis	†1992	95	1,331	0	80	679	2,185
Karl Evans, Mo. Southern St.	1992	1,586	10	0	0	571	2,167
Tom Skoog, Northern St.	1996	1,097	487	0	0	573	2,157
Roger Graham, New Haven	1994	1,607	197	0	0	333	2,137
Irv Sigler, Bloomsburg	1997	2,038	37	0	0	56	2,131

**Record. †National champion.*

ANNUAL CHAMPIONS

Year	Player, Team	Cl.	G	Rush	Rcv.	Int.	PR	KOR	Yds.	Yd. PG
1992	Johnny Cox, Fort Lewis	Jr.	10	95	1,331	0	80	679	2,185	218.5
1993	Chris George, Glenville St.	Jr.	10	23	1,876	0	157	562	2,618	261.8
1994	Bobby Felix, Western N.M.	Jr.	8	439	853	0	150	667	2,109	263.6
1995	Steve Papin, Portland St.	Sr.	11	1,619	525	0	1	252	2,397	217.9
1996	Brian Shay, Emporia St.	So.	11	2,103	247	0	48	340	*2,738	248.9
1997	Brian Shay, Emporia St.	Jr.	11	1,912	277	0	56	478	2,723	247.5

Field Goals

CAREER FIELD GOALS

Player, Team	Years	Made	Atts.	Pct.
Mike Wood, Southeast Mo. St. (S)	1974-77	*64	*109	.587
Pat Beaty, North Dak. (S)	1985-88	52	82	.634
Bob Gilbreath, Eastern N.M. (S)	1986-89	50	77	.649
Ed O'Brien, Central Fla. (S)	1984-87	50	77	.649
Billy Watkins, Tex. A&M-Commerce (S)	1990-93	49	84	.583
Bill May, Clarion (C)	1977-80	48	60	*.800
Ed Detwiler, East Stroudsburg (S)	1989-92	48	87	.552
Steve Huff, Central Mo. St. (C)	1982-85	47	80	.588
Phil Brandt, Central Mo. St. (S)	1987-90	46	66	.697
Scott Doyle, Chadron St. (S)	1992-95	46	69	.667
Eric Myers, West Va. Wesleyan (S)	1993-96	45	67	.672
Howie Guarini, Shippensburg (S)	1988-91	45	62	.726
James Knowles, North Ala. (C)	1982-85	45	77	.584
Ed Hotz, Southeast Mo. St. (S)	1978-81	45	77	.584
Kurt Seibel, South Dak. (C)	1980-83	44	62	.710
Jason Monday, Lenoir-Rhyne (S)	1989-92	44	64	.688
Pat Bolton, Montana St. (C)	1972-75	44	76	.579
Skipper Butler, Texas-Arlington (C)	1966-69	44	101	.436

**Record. (C) Conventional kicker. (S) Soccer-style kicker.*

SEASON FIELD GOALS

Player, Team	Years	Made	Atts.	Pct.
Raul De la Flor, Humboldt St. (S)	†1993	**20	26	.769
Pat Beaty, North Dak. (S)	†1988	**20	26	.769
Tom Jurich, Northern Ariz. (C)	†1977	**20	29	.690
Dennis Hochman, Sonoma St. (S)	†1986	19	22	+.864
Cory Solberg, North Dak. (S)	†1989	19	27	.704
Jaime Nunez, Weber St. (S)	†1971	19	32	.594
Jon Ruff, Indiana (Pa.) (S)	†1995	18	23	.783
Shane Meyer, Central Mo. St. (S)	†1997	18	25	.720
Bernard Henderson, Albany St. (Ga.) (S)	†1985	18	26	.692
Ki Tok Chu, Tenn.-Martin (S)	1988	17	22	.773
Jack McTyre, Valdosta St. (S)	1990	17	23	.739
Dino Beligrinis, Winston-Salem (S)	1988	17	23	.739
David Dell, Tex. A&M-Commerce (S)	1995	17	26	.654
Ed O'Brien, Central Fla. (S)	†1987	17	26	.654
Mike Wood, Southeast Mo. St. (S)	1976	17	33	.515

***Record tied. +Record for minimum 20 attempts. (C) Conventional kicker. (S) Soccer-style kicker.*

ANNUAL CHAMPIONS

Year	Player, Team	Class	Made	Atts.	Pct.	PG
1970	Chris Guerrieri, Alfred (S)	Sr.	11	21	.524	1.38
1971	Jaime Nunez, Weber St. (S)	Sr.	19	32	.594	**1.90
1972	Randy Walker, Northwestern St. (C)	Jr.	13	19	.684	1.30
1973	Reinhold Struprich, Hawaii (S)	Jr.	15	23	.652	1.36
1974	Mike Wood, Southeast Mo. St. (S)	Fr.	16	23	.696	1.45
1975	Wolfgang Taylor, Western St. (S)	Sr.	14	21	.667	1.56
1976	Rolf Benirschke, UC Davis (S)	Sr.	14	19	.737	1.56
1977	Tom Jurich, Northern Ariz. (C)	Sr.	**20	29	.690	1.81
1978	Frank Friedman, Cal St. Northridge (S)	Jr.	15	22	.682	1.50
1979	Bill May, Clarion (C)	Jr.	16	21	.762	1.60
1980	Nelson McMurain, North Ala. (S)	Jr.	14	22	.636	1.40
	Sean Landeta, Towson (S)	So.	14	28	.500	1.40
1981	Russ Meier, South Dak. St. (S)	Fr.	16	21	.762	1.60
1982	Joey Malone, Alabama A&M (C)	Fr.	15	21	.714	1.36
	Rick Ruszkiewicz, Edinboro (S)	Sr.	15	24	.625	1.36
1983	Mike Thomas, Angelo St. (S)	Sr.	16	22	.727	1.45
1984	Terry Godfrey, South Dak. (S)	Jr.	16	26	.615	1.60
1985	Bernard Henderson, Albany St. (Ga.) (S)	Sr.	18	26	.692	1.64
1986	Dennis Hochman, Sonoma St. (S)	Sr.	19	22	+.864	**1.90
1987	Ed O'Brien, Central Fla. (S)	Sr.	17	26	.654	1.70
1988	Pat Beaty, North Dak. (S)	Sr.	**20	26	.769	1.82
1989	Cory Solberg, North Dak. (S)	Jr.	19	27	.704	1.73
1990	Jack McTyre, Valdosta St. (S)	Sr.	17	23	.739	1.70
1991	Billy Watkins, Tex. A&M-Commerce (S)	So.	15	24	.625	1.36
1992	Mike Estrella, St. Mary's (Cal.) (S)	Jr.	15	27	.556	1.67
1993	Raul De la Flor, Humboldt St. (S)	Sr.	**20	26	.769	1.82
1994	Matt Seagreaves, East Stroudsburg (S)	So.	15	26	.577	1.50
1995	Jon Ruff, Indiana (Pa.) (S)	Sr.	18	23	.783	1.64
1996	Juan Gomez-Tagle, North Dak. (S)	Sr.	15	20	.750	1.50
1997	Shane Meyer, Central Mo. St. (S)	Jr.	18	25	.720	1.64

***Record tied. +Record for minimum 20 attempts.* (C) *Conventional kicker.* (S) *Soccer-style kicker.*

All-Time Longest Plays

Since 1941, official maximum length of all plays fixed at 100 yards.

RUSHING

Rushing plays have covered 99 yards 20 times. The most recent:

Yds.	Player, Team (Opponent)	Year
99	Thelbert Withers, N.M. Highlands (Fort Lewis)	1992
99	Lester Frye, Edinboro (Calif. [Pa.])	1991
99	Kelvin Minefee, Southern Utah (Mesa St.)	1988
99	Fred Deutsch, Springfield (Wagner)	1977
99	Sammy Croom, San Diego (Azusa Pacific)	1972
99	John Stenger, Swarthmore (Widener)	1970
99	Jed Knuttila, Hamline (St. Thomas [Minn.])	1968
99	Dave Lanoha, Colorado Col. (Texas Lutheran)	1967
99	Tom Pabst, UC Riverside (Cal Tech)	1965
99	George Phillips, Concord (Davis & Elkins)	1961

PASSING

Pass plays have resulted in 99-yard completions 21 times. The most recent:

Yds.	Passer-Receiver, Team (Opponent)	Year
99	Justin Coleman-Mike Smith, Neb.-Kearney (Wayne St. [Neb.])	1997
99	Antonio Hawkins-Jovelle Tillman, Virgina St. (Fayetteville St.)	1997
99	Matt Morris-Casey Cowan, Tex. A&M-Commerce (Midwestern St.)	1997
99	Rod Smith-Scott Hammond, Glenville St. (Concord)	1996
99	Ken Collums-Jerome Davis, Central Ark. (Delta St.)	1994
99	Greg Younger-Marty Walsh, Hillsdale (St. Francis [Ill.])	1994
99	Ray Morrow-Jeff Williamson, Cal St. Hayward (Redlands)	1993
99	Bob McLaughlin-Eric Muldowney, Lock Haven (Mansfield)	1993
99	Rob Rayl-John Unger, Valparaiso (Hillsdale)	1992
99	Bret Comp-Ken Kopetchny, East Stroudsburg (Mansfield)	1990

PUNTS

Yds.	Player, Team (Opponent)	Year
97	Earl Hurst, Emporia St. (Central Mo. St.)	1964
96	Alex Campbell, Morris Brown (Clark Atlanta)	1994
96	Gary Frens, Hope (Olivet)	1966
96	Jim Jarrett, North Dak. (South Dak.)	1957
93	Elliot Mills, Carleton (Monmouth [Ill.])	1970
93	Kaspar Fitins, Taylor (Georgetown [Ky.])	1966
93	Leeroy Sweeney, Pomona-Pitzer (UC Riverside)	1960

FIELD GOALS

Yds.	Player, Team (Opponent)	Year
67	Tom Odle, Fort Hays St. (Washburn)	1988
63	Joe Duren, Arkansas St. (McNeese St.)	1974
62	Mike Flater, Colorado Mines (Western St.)	1973
61	Duane Christian, Cameron (Southwestern Okla.)	1976
61	Mike Wood, Southeast Mo. St. (Lincoln [Mo.])	1975
61	Bill Shear, Cortland St. (Hobart)	1966
60	Mike Panasuk, Ferris St. (St. Joseph's [Ind.])	1990
60	Ed Beaulac, Sonoma St. (St. Mary's [Cal.])	1989
60	Roger McCoy, Grand Valley St. (Grand Rapids)	1976
60	Skipper Butler, Texas-Arlington (East Tex. St.)	1968

Since 1941, many players have returned interceptions, punts and kickoffs 100 yards. For the 1995 season leaders, see pages 414-415.

Team Champions

Annual Offense Champions

TOTAL OFFENSE

Year	Team	Avg.
1948	Hanover	*624.1
1949	Pacific (Cal.)	505.3
1950	West Tex. A&M	465.3
1951	Western Ill.	473.6
1952	Sam Houston St.	448.2
1953	Col. of Idaho	476.3
1954	Col. of Emporia	469.7
1955	Centre	431.0
1956	Florida A&M	475.0
1957	Denison	430.8
1958	Missouri Valley	449.6
1959	Whittier	461.3
1960	Muskingum	456.4
1961	Florida A&M	413.6
1962	Baker	438.4
1963	Col. of Emporia	517.1
1964	San Diego St.	422.6
1965	Long Beach St.	439.5
1966	Weber St.	460.1
1967	San Fran. St.	490.0
1968	Louisiana Tech	459.1
1969	Delaware	488.9
1970	Grambling	457.7
1971	Delaware	515.6
1972	Hobart	457.3
1973	Boise St.	466.5
1974	Boise St.	516.9
1975	Portland St.	472.4
1976	Portland St.	497.5
1977	Portland St.	506.7
1978	Western St.	487.0
1979	Delaware	450.5
1980	Southwest Tex. St.	423.0
1981	Southwest Tex. St.	482.3
1982	Northern Mich.	450.4
1983	Central St.	491.1
1984	North Dak. St.	455.3
1985	Truman St.	471.4
1986	Tex. A&M-Kingsville	542.6
1987	Tex. A&M-Kingsville	486.4
1988	Cal St. Sacramento	486.0
1989	Grand Valley St.	480.8
1990	Chadron St.	479.6
1991	Western St.	549.8
1992	New Haven	587.7
1993	Wayne St. (Neb.)	581.5
1994	West Tex. A&M	571.3
1995	Portland St.	472.0
1996	East Stroudsburg	509.1
1997	Emporia St.	531.5

**Record.*

RUSHING OFFENSE

Year	Team	Avg.
1948	Hanover	400.4
1949	Southern U.	382.9
1950	St. Lawrence	356.1
1951	Western N.M.	379.2
1952	William Jewell	345.0
1953	McPherson	375.9
1954	Col. of Emporia	*404.8
1955	Centre	373.4
1956	Tufts	359.9
1957	Denison	372.1
1958	Huron	353.3
1959	Bemidji St.	326.6
1960	Muskingum	355.2
1961	Huron	313.1
1962	Northern St.	355.3
1963	Luther	356.0
1964	Cal St. Los Angeles	325.9
1965	Huron	303.3
1966	Neb.-Kearney	370.1
1967	North Dak. St.	299.6
1968	Delaware	315.8
1969	St. Olaf	369.1
1970	Delaware	385.9
1971	Delaware	371.2
1972	Hobart	380.7
1973	Bethune-Cookman	308.8
1974	Central Mich.	324.6
1975	North Dak.	344.4
1976	Montana St.	287.5
1977	South Caro. St.	321.5
1978	Western St.	320.2
1979	Mississippi Col.	314.5
1980	Minn.-Duluth	307.3

Year	Team	Avg.
1981	Millersville	322.9
1982	Mississippi Col.	297.0
1983	Jamestown	297.7
1984	North Dak. St.	334.7
1985	Saginaw Valley	300.4
1986	Tex. A&M-Kingsville	395.2
1987	Tex. A&M-Kingsville	330.5
1988	North Dak. St.	373.1
1989	Wofford	373.7
1990	North Dak. St.	364.2
1991	Wofford	347.9
1992	Pittsburg St.	353.8
1993	North Ala.	371.5
1994	Moorhead St.	375.0
1995	Pittsburg St.	318.8
1996	North Dak. St.	325.9
1997	Saginaw Valley	334.8

**Record.*

PASSING OFFENSE

Year	Team	Avg.
1948	Hanover	223.8
1949	Baldwin-Wallace	196.9
1950	Northern Ill.	187.0
1951	Central Mich.	213.8
1952	Sam Houston St.	263.0
1953	Southern Conn. St.	193.5
1954	Northern Iowa	206.1
1955	Hamline	210.7
1956	Widener	207.7
1957	Cal Poly Pomona	236.0
1958	Cal Poly Pomona	217.6
1959	Whittier	199.3
1960	Whitworth	213.6
1961	Cal Poly Pomona	244.1
1962	Northern Ill.	285.6
1963	Northern Ill.	349.3
1964	Parsons	301.3
1965	Southern Ore. St.	268.9
1966	San Diego St.	268.1
1967	San Fran. St.	387.0
1968	Louisiana Tech	316.4
1969	Portland St.	308.6
1970	Portland St.	313.8
1971	LIU-C. W. Post	262.5
1972	Maryville (Tenn.)	277.8
1973	Lehigh	275.0
1974	Boise St.	334.5
1975	Portland St.	361.7
1976	Portland St.	404.1
1977	Portland St.	378.5
1978	Northern Mich.	242.3
1979	Northern Mich.	284.2
1980	Northern Mich.	269.6
1981	Franklin	306.5
1982	Evansville	313.0
1983	Franklin	358.0
1984	Franklin	334.0
1985	Truman St.	345.1
1986	West Tex. A&M	345.5
1987	Evansville	306.6
1988	Central Fla.	292.2
1989	Cal St. Chico	328.8
1990	New Haven	335.4
1991	Western St.	357.4
1992	Gardner-Webb	367.8
1993	LIU-C. W. Post	409.0
1994	West Tex. A&M	*454.5
1995	Norfolk St.	367.4
1996	East Stroudsburg	404.1
1997	Glenville St.	381.9

**Record.*

SCORING OFFENSE

Year	Team	Avg.
1948	Sul Ross St.	43.1
1949	Pacific (Cal.)	50.0
1950	West Tex. A&M	37.2
1951	Western Ill.	42.1
1952	Tex. A&M-Commerce	49.6
1953	Col. of Idaho	42.4
1954	Col. of Emporia	43.2
1955	Central Mich.	36.3
1956	Florida A&M	45.9
1957	Denison	38.6
1958	West Chester	51.4
1959	Florida A&M	42.6
1960	Florida A&M	52.8
1961	Florida A&M	54.7
1962	Florida A&M	42.0
1963	Col. of Emporia	42.4
1964	San Diego St.	42.3
1965	Ottawa	43.2
1966	N.M. Highlands	48.1
1967	Waynesburg	53.7
1968	Doane	52.9
1969	St. Olaf	45.2
1970	Wittenberg	40.0
1971	Michigan Tech	42.4
1972	Fort Valley St.	45.0
1973	Western Ky.	37.7
1974	Boise St.	44.6
1975	Bethune-Cookman	37.9
1976	Northern Mich.	43.0
1977	South Caro. St.	38.4
1978	Western St.	45.2
1979	Delaware	35.5
1980	Minn.-Duluth	35.4
1981	Southwest Tex. St.	37.5
1982	Truman St.	40.0
1983	Central St.	43.6
1984	North Dak. St.	39.0
1985	UC Davis	37.6
1986	Tex. A&M-Kingsville	43.1
1987	Central Fla.	34.5
	West Chester	34.5
1988	North Dak. St.	39.6
	Tex. A&M-Kingsville	39.6
1989	Grand Valley St.	44.5
1990	Indiana (Pa.)	44.2
1991	Western St.	46.1
1992	New Haven	50.5
1993	New Haven	*54.7
1994	Hampton	46.4
1995	Tex. A&M-Kingsville	40.1
1996	Clarion	43.5
1997	New Haven	43.3

**Record.*

Annual Defense Champions

TOTAL DEFENSE

Year	Team	Avg.
1948	Morgan St.	104.4
1949	Southern Conn. St.	95.6
1950	Southern Conn. St.	93.6
1951	Southern Conn. St.	84.3
1952	West Chester	128.4
1953	Shippensburg	81.9
1954	Geneva	106.3
1955	Col. of Emporia	102.0
1956	Tennessee St.	118.9
1957	West Chester	90.2
1958	Rose-Hulman	95.8
1959	Md.-East. Shore	75.3
1960	Md.-East. Shore	104.8
1961	Florida A&M	85.3
1962	John Carroll	*44.4
1963	West Chester	100.8
1964	Morgan St.	126.4
1965	Morgan St.	91.5
1966	Tennessee St.	85.7
1967	Tennessee St.	61.6
1968	Alcorn St.	103.4
1969	Livingstone	148.5
1970	Delaware St.	103.5
1971	Hampden-Sydney	115.6
1972	Wis.-Whitewater	143.8
1973	Livingstone	114.9
1974	Livingstone	120.5
1975	South Caro. St.	100.6
1976	Alcorn St.	108.9
1977	Virginia Union	160.3
1978	East Stroudsburg	153.8
1979	Virginia Union	138.2
1980	Concordia-M'head	191.7
1981	Fort Valley St.	148.3
1982	Jamestown	187.9
1983	Virginia Union	143.7
1984	Virginia St.	180.6
1985	Fort Valley St.	162.2
1986	Virginia Union	163.5
1987	Alabama A&M	167.1
1988	Alabama A&M	175.8
1989	Winston-Salem	185.7
1990	Sonoma St.	218.5
1991	Ashland	195.5
1992	Ashland	211.5
1993	Bentley	188.3
1994	Bentley	195.5
1995	Kentucky St.	205.1
1996	Stonehill	194.0
1997	Livingstone	171.5

**Record.*

RUSHING DEFENSE

Year	Team	Avg.
1948	Morgan St.	44.8
1949	Hanover	43.5
1950	Lewis & Clark	50.3
1951	Southern Conn. St.	17.1
1952	Tex. A&M-Commerce	48.5
1953	Shippensburg	53.6
1954	Tennessee St.	29.2
1955	Muskingum	52.5
1956	Hillsdale	51.1
1957	West Chester	27.9
1958	Ithaca	48.4
1959	Md.-East. Shore	36.3
1960	West Chester	41.4
1961	Florida A&M	20.1
1962	John Carroll	-1.0
1963	St. John's (Minn.)	12.9
1964	Fort Valley St.	39.7
1965	Morgan St.	15.0
1966	Tennessee St.	13.9
1967	Tennessee St.	*-16.7
1968	Alcorn St.	8.8
1969	Merchant Marine	16.2
1970	Delaware St.	-4.9
1971	Northern Colo.	27.5
1972	Alcorn St.	49.8
1973	Alcorn St.	45.9
1974	Livingstone	53.0
1975	Alcorn St.	15.9
1976	Alcorn St.	32.5
1977	Virginia Union	63.6
1978	East Stroudsburg	52.2
1979	Virginia Union	41.0
1980	Mo.-Rolla	34.6
1981	Fort Valley St.	46.9
1982	Butler	71.1
1983	Butler	38.2
1984	Norfolk St.	53.8
1985	Norfolk St.	50.9
1986	Central St.	44.5
1987	West Chester	67.2
1988	Cal Poly SLO	56.4
1989	Tex. A&M-Kingsville	60.7
1990	Sonoma St.	58.3
1991	Sonoma St.	63.6
1992	Ashland	64.4
1993	Albany St. (Ga.)	59.1
1994	Hampton	66.0
1995	North Ala.	56.8
1996	Livingstone	66.9
1997	Livingstone	52.8

**Record.*

PASSING DEFENSE

Year	Team	$Avg.
1948	Ashland	*10.1
1949	Wilmington (Ohio)	39.8
1950	Vermont	34.4

Year	Team	$Avg.
1951	Alfred	52.0
1952	Cortland St.	45.9
1953	Shippensburg	28.3
1954	St. Augustine's	26.5
1955	Ithaca	15.5
1956	West Va. Tech	29.1
1957	Lake Forest	25.0
1958	Coast Guard	25.4
1959	Huron	21.9
1960	Susquehanna	27.3
1961	Westminster (Utah)	24.8
1962	Principia	27.8
1963	Western Caro.	39.3
1964	Mont. St.-Billings	44.1
1965	Minot St.	44.5
1966	Manchester	54.7
1967	Mount Union	61.4
1968	Bridgeport	47.6
1969	Wabash	72.0
1970	Hampden-Sydney	62.9
1971	Western Ky.	57.7
1972	Howard	48.8
1973	East Stroudsburg	37.6
1974	Tennessee St.	52.6
1975	N.C. Central	60.2
1976	Morris Brown	60.8
1977	Delaware St.	64.3
1978	Concordia-M'head	55.8
1979	Kentucky St.	62.3
1980	Norfolk St.	71.5
1981	Bowie St.	75.7
1982	Elizabeth City St.	49.0
1983	Elizabeth City St.	65.0
1984	Virginia St.	80.4
1985	Fort Valley St.	94.5
1986	Virginia Union	84.7
1987	Alabama A&M	72.5
1988	Alabama A&M	84.3
1989	Mo. Southern St.	93.0
1990	Angelo St.	65.4
1991	Carson-Newman	64.9
1992	Tex. A&M-Commerce	61.8
1993	Alabama A&M	71.5
1994	Bentley	55.6
1995	Savannah St.	72.4
1996	N.C. Central	62.1
1997	Kentucky St.	64.4

**Record. $Beginning in 1990, based on pass efficiency ranking instead of yards per game.*

SCORING DEFENSE

Year	Team	Avg.
1959	Huron	2.1
1960	Albany St. (Ga.)	*0.0
1961	Florida A&M	2.8
1962	John Carroll	2.9
1963	Massachusetts	1.3

Year	Team	$Avg.
1964	Central (Iowa)	4.8
1965	St. John's (Minn.)	2.2
1966	Morgan St.	3.6
1967	Waynesburg	4.3
1968	Central Conn. St.	4.4
1969	Carthage	6.0
1970	Hampden-Sydney	2.8
1971	Hampden-Sydney	3.4
1972	Ashland	5.6
1973	Virginia Union	3.8
1974	Minn.-Duluth	5.5
1975	South Caro. St.	2.9
1976	South Caro. St.	3.4
1977	Minn.-Duluth	7.8
1978	Southwestern La.	7.1
1979	Virginia Union	6.1
1980	Minn.-Duluth	7.6
1981	Moorhead St.	5.0
1982	Jamestown	5.9
1983	Towson St.	5.8
1984	Cal Poly SLO	9.0
1985	Fort Valley St.	6.3
1986	North Dak. St.	6.8
1987	Tuskegee	9.1
1988	Alabama A&M	7.5
1989	Jacksonville St.	7.0
1990	Cal Poly SLO	11.3
1991	Butler	7.1
1992	Ferris St.	10.5
1993	Albany St. (Ga.)	8.7
1994	Bentley	6.0
1995	North Ala.	10.6
1996	Carson-Newman	10.7
1997	Albany St. (Ga.)	7.3

**Record.*

Other Annual Team Champions

NET PUNTING

Year	Team	Avg.
1992	Fort Lewis	37.9
1993	North Ala.	39.5
1994	Colorado Mines	42.9
1995	New Haven	38.7
1996	Adams St.	40.2
1997	North Ala.	39.5

PUNT RETURNS

Year	Team	Avg.
1992	Savannah St.	21.2
1993	Wayne St. (Neb.)	19.1
1994	Adams St.	16.7
1995	Elizabeth City St.	23.1
1996	Angelo St.	14.7

Year	Team	$Avg.
1997	Gardner-Webb	19.8

KICKOFF RETURNS

Year	Team	Avg.
1992	Jacksonville St.	34.0
1993	Adams St.	27.5
1994	Western N.M.	31.8
1995	Millersville	26.0
1996	Northern Colo.	27.5
1997	Carson-Newman	30.4

TURNOVER MARGIN

Year	Team	Avg.
1992	Hillsdale	2.2
1993	Hillsdale	*2.7
1994	Lenoir-Rhyne	2.6
1995	Central Okla.	2.6
1996	Central Okla.	2.3
1997	North Dak. St.	2.0

MOST IMPROVED

Year	Team	From	To	Imp.
1996	St. Joseph's (Ind.)	1-9	9-2	7½
1997	Carson-Newman	2-9	8-3	6

**Record.*

1997 Most-Improved Teams

School (Coach)	1996	1995	$Games Improved
Gardner Webb (Steve Patton)	2-9	8-3	6
West Tex. A&M (Stan McGarvey)	1-9	7-4	5½
Ashland (Gary Keller)	4-7	9-2	5
Winona St. (Tom Sawyer)	4-7	9-2	5
Southern Ark. (Steve Roberts)	4-6	9-2	4½
Indianapolis (Joe Polizzi)	4-7	8-3	4
Virginia Union (Willard Bailey)	2-8	6-5	4
Wingate (Doug Malone)	4-6	8-3	3½
Ky. Wesleyan (John Johnson)	3-8	6-4	3½
Shippensburg (Rocky Rees)	3-8	6-4	3½
Albany (N.Y.) (Robert Ford)	7-3	11-1	3
New Haven (Tony Sparano)	7-3	12-2	3
Slippery Rock (George Mihalik)	7-4	11-2	3
Angelo St. (Jerry Vandergriff)	6-4	10-2	3
Elon (Al Seagraves)	4-7	7-4	3
Neb.-Kearney (Claire Boroff)	4-7	7-4	3
Morris Brown (Joseph Crosby)	3-8	6-5	3
Southwest St. (Brent Jeffers)	2-9	5-6	3
Minn.-Morris (John Parker)	0-10	3-7	3

$To determine games improved, add the difference in victories between the two seasons to the difference in losses, then divide by two; ties not counted. Includes postseason.

DIVISION II

All-Time Team Won-Lost Records

Includes records as a senior college only, minimum 20 seasons of competition since 1937. Postseason games are included, and each tie game is computed as half won and half lost.

PERCENTAGE (TOP 25)

Team	Yrs.	Won	Lost	Tied	Pct.
West Chester	69	443	190	17	.695
Tex. A&M-Kingsville	69	479	208	16	.693
Grand Valley St.	27	178	97	3	.646
Indiana (Pa.)	68	391	210	23	.645
Central Okla.	92	515	280	47	.640
Pittsburg St.	90	525	288	47	.638
Neb.-Kearney	74	415	237	27	.631
Carson-Newman	74	435	252	30	.628
Minn.-Duluth	65	339	204	24	.619
Angelo St.	34	221	136	7	.617
North Dak. St.	101	515	314	34	.616
Truman St.	90	470	288	34	.615
Northern St.	92	454	280	33	.613
Virginia St.	86	439	270	48	.612
Hillsdale	105	515	321	46	.610
Westminster (Pa.)	103	509	316	53	.610
North Ala.	49	301	195	16	.604
Tuskegee	102	500	320	50	.603
East Stroudsburg	70	359	233	19	.603
Arkansas Tech	83	439	283	41	.602
North Dak.	101	491	322	30	.600
Albany (N.Y.)	25	148	99	0	.599
Virginia Union	97	437	291	47	.594
Fort Valley St.	52	284	193	21	.591
LIU-C. W. Post	41	231	160	5	.590

VICTORIES (TOP 25)

Team	Yrs.	Won	Lost	Tied	Pct.
Pittsburg St.	90	525	288	47	.638
Central Okla.	92	515	280	47	.640
North Dak. St.	101	515	314	34	.616
Hillsdale	105	515	321	46	.610
Westminster (Pa.)	103	509	316	53	.610
Tuskegee	102	500	320	50	.603
North Dak.	101	491	322	30	.600
Tex. A&M-Kingsville	69	479	208	16	.693

Team	Yrs.	Won	Lost	Tied	Pct.
Truman St.	90	470	288	34	.615
Northern St.	92	454	280	33	.613
South Dak. St.	100	447	371	38	.544
West Chester	69	443	190	17	.695
Virginia St.	86	439	270	48	.612
Arkansas Tech	83	439	283	41	.602
Virginia Union	97	437	291	47	.594
South Dak.	102	437	407	34	.517
Carson-Newman	74	435	252	30	.628
Central Ark.	86	429	301	42	.583
Washburn	106	429	476	40	.475
Tex. A&M-Commerce	80	421	314	31	.570
Neb.-Kearney	74	415	237	27	.631
Elon	76	406	314	18	.562
Ouachita Baptist	91	406	345	42	.538
Presbyterian	85	402	385	35	.510
Emporia St.	100	396	430	44	.480

ALPHABETICAL LISTING

(No Minimum Seasons of Competition)

Team	Yrs.	Won	Lost	Tied	Pct.
Abilene Christian	76	382	316	32	.545
Adams St.	63	271	257	17	.513
Alabama A&M	60	276	250	26	.524
Albany (N.Y.)	25	148	99	0	.599
Albany St. (Ga.)	52	258	214	21	.545
American Int'l	61	248	261	20	.488
Angelo St.	34	221	136	7	.617
Ark.-Monticello	80	304	369	25	.453
Arkansas Tech	83	439	286	41	.602
Ashland	75	350	287	29	.547
Assumption	10	33	59	1	.360
Augustana (S.D.)	77	299	359	14	.455
Bemidji St.	72	226	349	23	.397
Bentley	10	72	21	1	.771
Bloomsburg	70	287	286	21	.501
Bowie St.	26	84	162	6	.345
UC Davis	79	286	307	33	.554
Calif. (Pa.)	68	247	307	19	.448
Carson-Newman	74	435	252	30	.628
Catawba	78	377	355	26	.515
Central Ark.	86	429	301	42	.583
Central Mo. St.	101	394	441	51	.473
Central Okla.	92	515	280	47	.640
Central Wash.	79	363	253	23	.586
Chadron St.	83	373	299	15	.554
Cheyney	44	82	309	5	.213
Clarion	69	323	249	17	.563
Clark Atlanta	59	191	285	23	.406
Colorado Mines	108	319	464	32	.411
Concord	73	322	307	27	.511
Delta St.	68	309	315	23	.495
East Central	85	389	371	38	.511
East Stroudsburg	70	359	233	19	.603
Eastern N.M.	54	267	259	15	.507
Edinboro	69	261	291	24	.474
Elizabeth City St.	56	242	248	18	.494
Elon	76	406	314	18	.562
Emporia St.	100	396	430	44	.480
Fairmont St.	84	362	301	44	.543
Fayetteville St.	52	173	284	26	.385
Ferris St.	69	262	297	34	.470
Fort Hays St.	76	346	352	49	.496
Fort Lewis	35	117	209	3	.360
Fort Valley St.	52	284	193	21	.591
Gannon	10	54	39	2	.579
Gardner-Webb	28	137	158	2	.465
Glenville St.	85	271	327	37	.456
Grand Valley St.	27	178	97	3	.646
Harding	44	196	212	16	.481
Henderson St.	90	388	340	44	.531
Hillsdale	105	515	321	46	.610
Humboldt St.	70	315	276	20	.532
Indiana (Pa.)	68	391	210	23	.345
Indianapolis	60	251	278	23	.476
Johnson Smith	70	277	319	34	.467
Kentucky St.	69	293	348	26	.459
Ky. Wesleyan	37	114	157	16	.425
Kutztown	67	227	314	21	.423
Lane	74	193	351	26	.361
Lenoir-Rhyne	78	393	329	34	.542
Livingstone	49	199	241	15	.454
Lock Haven	69	252	351	25	.421
LIU-C. W. Post	41	231	160	5	.590
Mankato St.	72	314	291	27	.518
Mansfield	68	212	335	30	.393
Mars Hill	34	154	177	10	.466
Mass.-Lowell	18	78	91	2	.462
Mercyhurst	17	85	66	4	.561
Merrimack	2	8	10	0	.444
Mesa St.	22	126	101	5	.554
Michigan Tech	75	262	266	17	.496
Midwestern St.	21	94	115	6	.451
Miles	28	59	187	7	.247
Millersville	66	300	244	21	.550
Minn.-Duluth	65	339	204	24	.619
Minn.-Morris	36	167	173	10	.491
Mo.-Rolla	92	645	418	36	.454
Mo. Southern St.	30	166	131	7	.558
Mo. Western St.	28	133	152	9	.468
Moorhead St.	80	352	291	31	.545
Morehouse	98	335	357	19	.485
Morningside	96	332	448	37	.429
Morris Brown	72	318	306	37	.509
Neb.-Kearney	74	415	237	27	.631
Neb.-Omaha	81	339	242	30	.498
New Haven	25	146	102	5	.587
N.M. Highlands	71	253	313	27	.449
Newberry	84	313	454	33	.412
North Ala.	49	301	195	16	.604
N.C. Central	67	340	262	24	.562
North Dak.	101	491	322	30	.600
North Dak. St.	101	515	314	34	.616
Northeastern St.	75	364	289	30	.555
Northern Colo.	85	649	335	24	.510
Northern Mich.	84	654	261	26	.573
Northern St.	92	454	280	33	.613
Northwest Mo. St.	80	336	363	32	.482
Northwood	36	139	182	8	.435
Ouachita Baptist	91	406	345	42	.538
Pace	20	75	114	2	.398
Pittsburg St.	90	525	288	47	.638
Presbyterian	85	402	385	35	.510
Quincy	11	49	52	1	.485
Sacred Heart	7	19	47	0	.288
Saginaw Valley	23	125	111	3	.529
St. Cloud St.	70	327	266	21	.550
St. Francis (Ill.)	12	59	66	0	.472
St. Joseph's (Ind.)	78	248	313	24	.444
Savannah St.	45	159	227	15	.415
Shepherd	74	318	277	26	.533
Shippensburg	68	321	277	21	.536
Slippery Rock	70	347	252	28	.576
South Dak.	102	437	407	34	.517
South Dak. St.	100	447	371	38	.544
Southern Ark.	78	345	297	27	.536
Southern Conn. St.	50	265	193	11	.577
Southwest Baptist	15	42	103	2	.293
Southwest St.	30	114	179	5	.391
Southwestern Okla.	88	390	353	37	.524
Stonehill	10	54	31	3	.631
Stony Brook	15	70	68	2	.507
Tarleton St.	37	152	215	3	.415
Tex. A&M-Commerce	80	421	314	31	.570
Tex. A&M-Kingsville	69	479	208	16	.693
Truman St.	90	470	288	34	.615
Tusculum	48	97	201	24	.339
Tuskegee	102	500	320	50	.603
Valdosta St.	16	103	66	3	.608
Virginia St.	86	439	270	48	.612
Virginia Union	97	437	291	47	.594
Washburn	106	429	476	40	.475
Wayne St. (Mich.)	80	280	363	29	.438
Wayne St. (Neb.)	72	308	348	38	.471
West Ala.	56	214	287	15	.429
West Chester	69	443	190	17	.395
West Ga.	19	95	101	0	.485
West Liberty St.	71	343	280	35	.548
West Tex. A&M	86	379	406	22	.483
West Va. St.	74	267	332	40	.449
West Va. Tech	78	264	348	35	.435
West Va. Wesleyan	92	343	398	30	.464
Western N.M.	61	229	285	15	.447
Western St.	75	319	314	14	.504
Western Wash.	81	312	312	32	.500
Westminster (Pa.)	103	509	316	53	.610
Wingate	12	53	68	0	.438
Winona St.	97	280	421	32	.404
Winston-Salem	54	279	223	22	.553

Winningest Teams of the 1990s

ACTIVE TEAMS BY PERCENTAGE

School	Years*	Won	Lost	Tied	Pct.
Pittsburg St.	8	86	13	2	.861
Carson-Newman	7	66	15	1	.811
Indiana (Pa.)	8	75	20	1	.786
North Dak. St.	8	72	21	0	.774
New Haven	8	69	21	1	.764
North Dak.	8	64	22	1	.741
Grand Valley St.	8	66	23	2	.736
Tex. A&M-Kingsville	8	69	25	0	.734
North Ala.	8	64	23	1	.733
Northern Colo.	8	70	27	0	.722
Ferris St.	8	66	25	3	.718
Albany St. (Ga.)	8	63	25	1	.713
Chadron St.	8	61	25	1	.707
Millersville	8	56	23	2	.704
UC Davis	8	61	27	2	.689
Western St.	8	60	27	1	.688
Edinboro	8	58	27	1	.680
Central Ark.	6	42	21	2	.662
Valdosta St.	8	57	30	2	.652
Angelo St.	8	53	28	2	.651
Slippery Rock	8	55	31	1	.638
Truman St.	8	56	32	0	.636
Fort Hays St.	8	55	31	3	.635
Virginia St.	8	52	30	0	.634
Ashland	8	54	31	1	.634

Less than six years in Division II and still active

School	Years*	Won	Lost	Tied	Pct.
Bentley	5	44	8	0	.846
Southern Ark.	1	9	2	0	.818
Glenville St.	5	41	15	0	.732
Stonehill	5	34	16	0	.680
Albany (N.Y.)	3	21	11	0	.656
LIU-C.W. Post	5	34	18	0	.654

ACTIVE TEAMS BY VICTORIES

School	Years*	Won	Lost	Tied	Pct.
Pittsburg St.	8	86	13	2	.861
Indiana (Pa.)	8	57	20	1	.786
North Dak. St.	8	72	21	0	.774
Northern Colo.	8	70	27	0	.722
New Haven	8	69	21	1	.764
Tex. A&M-Kingsville	8	69	25	0	.734
Carson-Newman	7	66	15	1	.811
Grand Valley St.	8	66	23	2	.736
Ferris St.	8	66	25	3	.718
North Dak.	8	64	22	1	.741
North Ala.	8	64	23	1	.733
Albany St. (Ga.)	8	63	25	1	.713
Chadron St.	8	61	25	1	.707
UC Davis	8	61	27	2	.689
Western St.	8	60	27	1	.688
Edinboro	8	58	27	1	.680
Valdosta St.	8	57	30	2	.652
Portland St.	8	57	38	0	.600
Millersville	8	56	23	2	.704
Truman St.	8	56	32	0	.636
Slippery Rock	8	55	31	1	.638
Fort Hays St.	8	55	31	3	.635
Ashland	8	54	31	1	.634
Tex. A&M-Commerce	8	54	37	1	.592
Angelo	8	53	28	2	.651
Saginaw Valley	8	53	32	0	.624

**Years of NCAA Division II active membership.*

National Poll Rankings

Wire Service National Champions

(1958-74)

(For what was then known as College Division teams. Selections by United Press International from 1958 and Associated Press from 1960.)

Year	Team	Coach	Record*
1958	Southern Miss.	Thad "Pie" Vann	9-0-0
1959	Bowling Green	Doyt Perry	9-0-0
1960	Ohio	Bill Hess	10-0-0
1961	Pittsburg St.	Carnie Smith	9-0-0
1962	Southern Miss. (UPI)	Thad "Pie" Vann	9-1-0
	Florida A&M (AP)	Jake Gaither	9-0-0
1963	Delaware (UPI)	Dave Nelson	8-0-0
	Northern Ill. (AP)	Howard Fletcher	9-0-0
1964	Cal St. Los Angeles (UPI)	Homer Beatty	9-0-0
	Wittenberg (AP)	Bill Edwards	8-0-0
1965	North Dak. St.	Darrell Mudra	10-0-0
1966	San Diego St.	Don Coryell	10-0-0
1967	San Diego St.	Don Coryell	9-1-0
1968	San Diego St. (UPI)	Don Coryell	9-0-1
	North Dak. St. (AP)	Ron Erhardt	9-0-0
1969	North Dak. St.	Ron Erhardt	9-0-0
1970	Arkansas St.	Bennie Ellender	10-0-0
1971	Delaware	Harold "Tubby" Raymond	9-1-0
1972	Delaware	Harold "Tubby" Raymond	10-0-0
1973	Tennessee St.	John Merritt	10-0-0
1974	Louisiana Tech (UPI)	Maxie Lambright	10-0-0
	Central Mich. (AP)	Roy Kramer	9-1-0

**Regular season.*

Final Poll Leaders

(Released Before Division Championship Playoffs)

Year	Team (Record*)	Coach	Record in Championship†
1975	North Dak. (9-0)	Jerry Olson	0-1 Lost in first round
1976	Northern Mich. (10-0)	Gil Krueger	1-1 Lost in semifinals
1977	North Dak. St. (8-1-1)	Jim Wacker	1-1 Lost in semifinals
1978	Winston-Salem (10-0)	Bill Hayes	Did not compete
1979	Delaware (9-1)	Harold "Tubby" Raymond	3-0 Champion
1980	Eastern Ill. (8-2)	Darrell Mudra	2-1 Runner-up
1981	Southwest Tex. St. (9-0)	Jim Wacker	3-0 Champion
1982	Southwest Tex. St. (11-0)	Jim Wacker	3-0 Champion
1983	UC Davis (9-0)	Jim Sochor	1-1 Lost in semifinals
1984	North Dak. St. (9-1)	Don Morton	2-1 Runner-up
1985	UC Davis (9-1)	Jim Sochor	0-1 Lost in first round
1986	North Dak. St. (10-0)	Earle Solomonson	3-0 Champion
1987	Tex. A&M-Kingsville (9-1)	Ron Harms	Did not compete
1988	North Dak. St. (10-0)	Rocky Hager	4-0 Champion
1989	Tex. A&M-Kingsville (10-0)	Ron Harms	0-1 Lost in first round
1990	North Dak. St. (10-0)	Rocky Hager	4-0 Champion
1991	Indiana (Pa.) (10-0)	Frank Cignetti	2-1 Lost in semifinals
1992	Pittsburg St. (11-0)	Chuck Broyles	3-1 Runner-up
1993	North Ala. (10-0)	Bobby Wallace	4-0 Champion
1994	North Ala. (8-1)	Bobby Wallace	4-0 Champion
1995	North Ala. (9-0)	Bobby Wallace	4-0 Champion
1996	Tex. A&M-Kingsville (7-2)	Ron Harms	0-1 Lost in first round
1997	Carson-Newman (9-0)	Ken Sparks	2-1 Lost in semifinals

**Final poll record; in some cases, a team had one game remaining before the championship playoffs. †Number of teams in the championship: 8 (1975-87); 16 (1988-present).*

DIVISION II

Weekly Poll Leaders

Poll conducted by the NCAA Division II Football Committee. Information for 1982-96 researched and submitted by Jeff Hodges, SID, University of North Alabama. Information on missing weekly polls should be submitted to NCAA Statistics Service.

1982

9-30..........Southwest Tex. St.
Final..........Southwest Tex. St.

1983

9-26..........Southwest Tex. St.
10-10..........Southwest Tex. St.
10-24..........Mississippi Col.
10-31..........UC Davis
11-7..........UC Davis
Final..........UC Davis

1984

9-17..........Troy St.
9-24..........Central St.
10-8..........Central St.
10-15..........Central St.
10-29..........North Dak. St.
Final..........North Dak. St.

1985

9-23..........South Dak.
9-30..........South Dak.
10-14..........South Dak.
10-21..........Central St.
10-28..........Central St.
11-11..........UC Davis
11-18..........UC Davis
Final..........UC Davis

1986

9-15..........North Dak. St.
9-22..........North Dak. St.
9-29..........North Dak. St.
10-6..........North Dak. St.

10-13 ....North Dak. St.
10-20 ....North Dak. St.
10-27 ....North Dak. St.
11-3 ....North Dak. St.
11-10 ....North Dak. St.
Final ....North Dak. St.

1987
9-15 ....South Dak.
9-29 ....South Dak.
10-5 ....South Dak.
10-19 ....Northern Mich.
10-26 ....Northern Mich.
11-8 ....Tex. A&M-Kingsville
Final ....Tex. A&M-Kingsville

1988
Pre ....Troy St.
9-12 ....Troy St.
9-19 ....North Dak. St.
9-26 ....North Dak. St.
10-3 ....North Dak. St.
10-10 ....North Dak. St.
10-17 ....North Dak. St.
10-24 ....North Dak. St.
10-31 ....North Dak. St.
Final ....North Dak. St.

1989
Pre ....North Dak. St.
9-11 ....North Dak. St.
9-18 ....North Dak. St.
9-25 ....North Dak. St.
10-2 ....North Dak. St.
10-9 ....North Dak. St.
10-16 ....North Dak. St.
10-23 ....Tex. A&M-Kingsville
10-30 ....Tex. A&M-Kingsville
11-6 ....Tex. A&M-Kingsville

1990
9-17 ....North Dak. St.
9-24 ....North Dak. St.
10-1 ....North Dak. St.
10-8 ....North Dak. St.
10-15 ....North Dak. St.
10-22 ....North Dak. St.
10-29 ....North Dak. St.
Final ....North Dak. St.

1991
Pre ....North Dak. St.
9-16 ....Indiana (Pa.)
9-23 ....Indiana (Pa.)
9-30 ....Indiana (Pa.)
10-7 ....Indiana (Pa.)
10-14 ....Indiana (Pa.)
10-21 ....Indiana (Pa.)
10-28 ....Indiana (Pa.)
11-4 ....Indiana (Pa.)
Final ....Indiana (Pa.)

1992
Pre ....Pittsburg St.
9-14 ....Pittsburg St.
9-21 ....Pittsburg St.
9-28 ....Pittsburg St.
10-5 ....Pittsburg St.
10-12 ....Pittsburg St.
10-19 ....Pittsburg St.
10-26 ....Pittsburg St.
11-2 ....Pittsburg St.
Final ....Pittsburg St.

1993
Pre ....North Dak. St.
9-20 ....North Dak. St.
9-27 ....North Dak. St.
10-4 ....North Dak. St.
10-11 ....North Ala.
10-18 ....North Ala.
10-25 ....North Ala.
11-1 ....North Ala.
11-8 ....North Ala.
Final ....North Ala.

1994
Pre ....North Ala.
9-12 ....North Ala.
9-19 ....North Ala.
9-26 ....North Ala.
10-3 ....North Ala.
10-10 ....North Ala.
10-17 ....North Ala.
10-24 ....North Ala.
10-31 ....North Ala.
Final ....North Ala.

1995
Pre ....North Ala.
9-11 ....North Ala.
9-18 ....North Ala.
9-25 ....North Ala.
10-2 ....North Ala.
10-9 ....North Ala.
10-16 ....North Ala.
10-23 ....North Ala.
10-30 ....North Ala.
Final ....North Ala.

1996
Pre ....North Ala.
9-9 ....Ferris St.
9-16 ....Ferris St.
9-23 ....North Dak. St.
9-30 ....Carson-Newman
10-7 ....Indiana (Pa.)
10-14 ....Indiana (Pa.)
10-21 ....Valdosta St.
10-28 ....Valdosta St.
11-4 ....Tex. A&M-Kingsville
Final ....Tex. A&M-Kingsville

1997
9-8 ....Northern Colo.
9-15 ....Carson-Newman
9-22 ....Carson-Newman
9-29 ....Carson-Newman
10-6 ....Carson-Newman
10-13 ....Carson-Newman
10-20 ....Carson-Newman
10-27 ....Carson-Newman
11-3 ....Carson-Newman
11-10 ....Carson-Newman
Final ....Carson-Newman

Undefeated, Untied Teams

(Regular-Season Games Only)

In 1948, official national statistics rankings began to include all nonmajor four-year colleges. Until the 1967 season, rankings and records included all four-year colleges that reported their statistics to the NCAA. Beginning with the 1967 season, statistics (and won-lost records) included only members of the NCAA.

Since 1981, conference playoff games have been included in a team's regular-season statistics and won-lost record (previously, such games were considered postseason contests).

The regular-season list includes games in which a home team served as a predetermined, preseason host of a "bowl game" regardless of its record and games scheduled before the season, thus eliminating postseason designation for the Orange Blossom Classic, annually hosted by Florida A&M, and the Prairie View Bowl, annually hosted by Prairie View, for example.

Figures are regular-season wins only. A subsequent postseason win(s) is indicated by (*), a loss by (†) and a tie by (‡).

Year	College	Wins
1948	Alma	8
	Bloomsburg	9
	Denison	8
	Heidelberg	9
	Michigan Tech	7
	Missouri Valley	†‡9
	Occidental	*8
	Southern U.	*11
	Sul Ross St.	‡10
	Wesleyan (Conn.)	8
1949	Ball St.	8
	Emory & Henry	*†10
	Gannon	8
	Hanover	†8
	Lewis	8
	Md.-East. Shore	8
	Morgan St.	8
	Pacific (Cal.)	11
	St. Ambrose	8
	St. Vincent	*9
	Trinity (Conn.)	8
	Wayne St. (Neb.)	9
	Wofford	11
1950	Abilene Christian	*10
	Canterbury	8
	Florida St.	8
	Frank. & Marsh	9
	Lehigh	9
	Lewis & Clark	*8
	Md.-East. Shore	8
	Mission House	6
	New Hampshire	8
	St. Lawrence	8
	St. Norbert	7
	Thiel	7
	Valparaiso	†9
	West Liberty St.	*8
	Wis.-La Crosse	*9
	Wis.-Whitewater	6
1951	Bloomsburg	8
	Bucknell	9
	Col. of Emporia	8
	Ill. Wesleyan	8
	Lawrence	7
	Northern Ill.	9
	Principia	6
	St. Michael's	6
	South Dak. Tech	8
	Susquehanna	6
	Col. of New Jersey	6
	Valparaiso	9
	Western Md.	8
1952	Beloit	8
	Clarion	*8
	Tex. A&M-Commerce	*10
	Fairmont St.	6
	Idaho St.	8
	Lenoir-Rhyne	†8
	Northeastern St.	†9
	Peru St.	10
	Rochester	8
	St. Norbert	6
	Shippensburg	7
	West Chester	7
1953	Cal Poly SLO	9
	Col. of Emporia	8
	Col. of Idaho	†8
	Defiance	8
	Tex. A&M-Commerce	‡10
	Florida A&M	10
	Indianapolis	8
	Iowa Wesleyan	†9
	Juniata	7
	Northern St.	8
	Martin Luther	6
	Peru St.	8
	Prairie View	10
	St. Olaf	8
	Shippensburg	8
	Westminster (Pa.)	8
	Wis.-La Crosse	‡9
	Wis.-Platteville	6
1954	Ashland	7
	Carleton	8
	Central Conn. St.	6
	Col. of Emporia	†9
	Delta St.	8
	Hastings	*8
	Hobart	8
	Juniata	8
	Luther	9
	Miles	8
	Neb.-Omaha	*9
	Martin Luther	6
	Pomona-Pitzer	8
	Principia	7
	Southeastern La.	9
	Tennessee St.	†10
	Trinity (Conn.)	7
	Trinity (Tex.)	9
	Whitworth	8
	Widener	7
	Worcester Tech	6
1955	Alfred	8
	Centre	8
	Coe	8
	Col. of Emporia	9
	Drexel	8
	Grambling	10
	Heidelberg	9
	Hillsdale	9
	Juniata	‡8
	Md.-East. Shore	9
	Miami (Ohio)	9
	Muskingum	8
	Northern St.	†9
	Parsons	8
	Shepherd	8
	Southeast Mo. St.	9
	Trinity (Conn.)	7

Year	College	Wins
	Whitworth	9
	Wis.-Stevens Point	8
1956	Alfred	7
	Central Mich.	9
	Hillsdale	9
	Lenoir-Rhyne	10
	Milton	6
	Montana St.	‡9
	Neb.-Kearney	9
	Redlands	9
	St. Thomas (Minn.)	8
	Sam Houston St.	*9
	Southern Conn. St.	9
	Tennessee St.	10
	Westminster (Pa.)	8
1957	Elon	6
	Fairmont St.	7
	Florida A&M	9
	Hillsdale	†9
	Hobart	6
	Idaho St.	9
	Jamestown	7
	Juniata	7
	Lock Haven	8
	Middle Tenn. St.	10
	Pittsburg St.	*10
	Ripon	8
	St. Norbert	8
	West Chester	9
1958	Calif. (Pa.)	8
	Chadron St.	8
	Gust. Adolphus	†8
	Missouri Valley	†8
	Neb.-Kearney	9
	Northeastern St.	**9
	Northern Ariz.	*†10
	Rochester	8
	Rose-Hulman	8
	St. Benedict's	†10
	Sewanee	8
	Southern Miss.	9
	Wheaton (Ill.)	8
1959	Bowling Green	9
	Butler	9
	Coe	8
	Fairmont St.	9
	Florida A&M	10
	Hofstra	9
	John Carroll	7
	Lenoir-Rhyne	*†9
	San Fran. St.	10
	Western Ill.	9
1960	Albright	9
	Arkansas Tech	†10
	Humboldt St.	*†10
	Langston	9
	Lenoir-Rhyne	*‡10
	Montclair St.	8
	Muskingum	9
	Northern Iowa	†9
	Ohio	10
	Ottawa	9
	Wagner	9
	West Chester	9
	Whitworth	9
	Willamette	8
1961	Albion	8
	Baldwin-Wallace	9
	Butler	9
	Central Okla.	9
	Florida A&M	10
	Fresno St.	*9
	Linfield	*†10
	Mayville St.	8
	Millikin	8
	Northern St.	9
	Ottawa	9
	Pittsburg St.	**9
	Wash. & Lee	9
	Wheaton (Ill.)	8
	Whittier	†9
1962	Carthage	8
	Central Okla.	**9
	Col. of Emporia	†10
	Earlham	8
	East Stroudsburg	†8
	John Carroll	7
	Kalamazoo	8
	Lenoir-Rhyne	*†10
	Northern St.	†9
	Parsons	9
	St. John's (Minn.)	9
	Susquehanna	9
	Wittenberg	9
1963	Alabama A&M	8
	Central Wash.	9
	Coast Guard	†8
	Col. of Emporia	10
	Delaware	8
	John Carroll	7
	Lewis & Clark	8
	Luther	9
	McNeese St.	8
	Neb.-Kearney	†9
	Northeastern	†8
	Northeastern St.	*10
	Northern Ill.	*9
	Prairie View	*†9
	Ripon	8
	St. John's (Minn.)	**8
	Sewanee	8
	Southwest Mo. St.	†9
	Southwest Tex. St.	10
	Wis.-Eau Claire	7
1964	Albion	8
	Amherst	8
	Cal St. Los Angeles	9
	Concordia-M'head	*‡9
	Frank. & Marsh.	8
	Montclair St.	7
	Prairie View	9
	Wagner	10
	Western St.	†9
	Westminster (Pa.)	8
	Wittenberg	8
1965	Ball St.	‡9
	East Stroudsburg	*9
	Fairmont St.	†8
	Georgetown (Ky.)	9
	Ill. Wesleyan	8
	Ithaca	8
	Middle Tenn. St.	10
	Morgan St.	9
	North Dak. St.	*10
	Northern Ill.	†9
	Ottawa	9
	St. John's (Minn.)	**9
	Springfield	9
	Sul Ross St.	†10
	Tennessee St.	‡9
1966	Central (Iowa)	†9
	Clarion	*9
	Defiance	9
	Morgan St.	*8
	Muskingum	†9
	Northwestern St.	9
	San Diego St.	*10
	Tennessee St.	*9
	Waynesburg	**9
	Wilkes	8
	Wis.-Whitewater	*†9

Beginning in 1967, NCAA members only.

Year	College	Wins
1967	Alma	8
	Central (Iowa)	9
	Doane	‡8
	Lawrence	8
	Morgan St.	8
	North Dak. St.	†9
	Northern Mich.	†9
	Wagner	9
	West Chester	*†9
	Wilkes	8
1968	Alma	8
	Doane	*9
	East Stroudsburg	‡8
	Indiana (Pa.)	†9
	North Dak. St.	*9
	Randolph-Macon	9
1969	Albion	8
	Carthage	9
	Defiance	9
	Doane	8
	Montana	†10
	North Dak. St.	*9
	Northern Colo.	10
	Wesleyan (Conn.)	8
	Wittenberg	*9
1970	Arkansas St.	*10
	Jacksonville St.	10
	Montana	†10
	St. Olaf	9
	Tennessee St.	*10
	Westminster (Pa.)	**8
	Wittenberg#	9
1971	Alfred	8
	Hampden-Sydney	†10
	Westminster (Pa.)	†‡8
1972	Ashland	11
	Bridgeport	*10
	Delaware	10
	Doane	†10
	Frank. & Marsh.	9
	Heidelberg	**9
	Louisiana Tech	*11
	Middlebury	8
	Monmouth (Ill.)	9
1973	Tennessee St.	10
	Western Ky.	**†10
1974	Louisiana Tech	*†10
	Michigan Tech	9
	UNLV	*†11
1975	East Stroudsburg	*9
	North Dak.	†9
1976	East Stroudsburg	‡9
1977	UC Davis	*†10
	Florida A&M	11
	Winston-Salem	†11
1978	Western St.	*†9
	Winston-Salem	*†10
1979	(None)	
1980	Minn.-Duluth	10
	Mo.-Rolla	10
1981	Northern Mich.	*†10
	Shippensburg	*†11
	Virginia Union	†11
1982	UC Davis	**†10
	North Dak. St.	*†11
	Southwest Tex. St.	***11
1983	UC Davis	*†10
	Central St.	**†10
1984	(None)	
1985	Bloomsburg	*†11
1986	UC Davis	†10
	North Dak. St.	***10
	Virginia Union	†11
1987	(None)	
1988	North Dak. St.	****10
	St. Mary's (Cal.)	10
1989	Grand Valley St.	†11
	Jacksonville St.	***†10
	Pittsburg St.	*†11
	Tex. A&M-Kingsville	†10
1990	North Dak. St.	****10
	Pittsburg St.	**†10
1991	Carson-Newman	†10
	Indiana (Pa.)	**†10
	Jacksonville St.	***†9
1992	New Haven	**†10
	Pittsburg St.	***†11
1993	Albany St. (Ga.)	†11
	Bentley	10
	Hampton	*†11
	Indiana (Pa.)	***†10
	New Haven	*†10
	North Ala.	****10
	Quincy	9
1994	Bentley	*10
	Ferris St.	*†10
	Pittsburg St.	†10
1995	Ferris St.	**†10
	North Ala.	****10
1996	(None)	
1997	Albany St. (Ga.)	*†10
	Carson-Newman	**†9
	Livingstone##	10
	Northwest Mo. St.	*†10

#Later forfeited all games. ## Later forfeited two games.

DIVISION II

The Spoilers

Compiled since 1973, when the three-division reorganization plan was adopted by the special NCAA Convention. Following is a list of the spoilers of Division II teams that lost their perfect (undefeated, untied) record in their season-ending game, including the Division II championship playoffs. An asterisk (*) indicates an NCAA championship playoff game, a pound sign (#) indicates an NAIA championship playoff game, a dagger (†) indicates the home team in a regular-season game, and (@) indicates a neutral-site game. A game involving two undefeated, untied teams is in **bold** face.

Date	Spoiler	Victim	Score
12-15-73	* Louisiana Tech	Western Ky.	34-0
11-30-74	* Louisiana Tech	Western Caro.	10-7
11-15-75	† LIU-C. W. Post	American Int'l	21-0
11-15-75	Eastern N.M.	† Northern Colo.	16-14
11-29-75	* West Ala.	North Dak.	34-14
11-20-76	† Shippensburg	East Stroudsburg	tie 14-14
12-3-77	‡ South Caro. St.	Winston-Salem	10-7
12-3-77	* Lehigh	UC Davis	39-30
12-2-78	* Delaware	Winston-Salem	41-0
11-28-81	* Shippensburg	Virginia Union	40-27
12-5-81	* North Dak. St.	Shippensburg	18-6
12-5-81	* Southwest Tex. St.	Northern Mich.	62-0
12-4-82	* UC Davis	North Dak. St.	19-14
12-11-82	*** Southwest Tex. St.**	**UC Davis**	34-9
12-3-83	* North Dak. St.	UC Davis	26-17
12-10-83	* North Dak. St.	Central St.	41-21
12-7-85	* North Ala.	Bloomsburg	34-0
11-15-86	West Chester	† Millersville	7-3
11-29-86	* Troy St.	Virginia Union	31-7
11-29-86	* South Dak.	UC Davis	26-23
12-10-88	# Adams St.	Pittsburg St.	13-10
11-18-89	* Mississippi Col.	Tex. A&M-Kingsville	34-19
11-18-89	* Indiana (Pa.)	Grand Valley St.	34-24
11-25-89	* Angelo St.	Pittsburg St.	24-21
12-9-89	* Mississippi Col.	Jacksonville St.	3-0
12-1-90	*** North Dak. St.**	**Pittsburg St.**	39-29
11-23-91	# Western St.	Carson-Newman	38-21
12-7-91	*** Jacksonville St.**	**Indiana (Pa.)**	27-20
12-14-91	* Pittsburg St.	Jacksonville St.	23-6
11-14-92	@Moorhead St.	Michigan Tech	36-35
12-5-92	* Jacksonville St.	New Haven	46-35
12-12-92	* Jacksonville St.	Pittsburg St.	17-13
11-13-93	@Minn.-Duluth	Wayne St. (Neb.)	29-28
11-20-93	*** Hampton**	**Albany St. (Ga.)**	33-7
11-27-93	*** Indiana (Pa.)**	**New Haven**	38-35
11-27-93	*** North Ala.**	**Hampton**	45-20
12-11-93	*** North Ala.**	**Indiana (Pa.)**	41-34
11-19-94	* North Dak. St.	Pittsburg St.	(3 OT) 18-12
11-26-94	* Indiana (Pa.)	Ferris St.	21-17
12-2-95	*** North Ala.**	**Ferris St.**	45-7
11-29-97	*** Carson-Newman**	**Albany St. (Ga.)**	23-22
11-29-97	* Northern Colo.	Northwest Mo. St.	35-28
12-6-97	* Northern Colo.	Carson-Newman	30-29

‡*Gold Bowl.*

Streaks and Rivalries

Longest Winning Streaks

(From 1931; Includes Postseason Games)

Wins	Team	Years
34	Hillsdale	1954-57
32	Wilkes	1965-69
31	Morgan St.	1965-68
31	Missouri Valley	1946-48
30	Bentley	1993-95
29	Tex. A&M-Commerce	1951-53
27	Truman St.	1931-35
25	Pittsburg St.	1991-92
25	San Diego St.	1965-67
25	Peru St.	1951-54
25	Md.-East. Shore	1948-51
24	North Dak. St.	1964-66
24	Wesleyan (Conn.)	1945-48

Longest Unbeaten Streaks

(From 1931; Includes Postseason Games)

No.	Wins	Ties	Team	Years
54	47	7	Morgan St.	1931-38
38	36	2	Doane	1965-70
37	35	2	Southern U.	1947-51
35	34	1	North Dak. St.	1968-71
34	34	0	Hillsdale	1954-57
32	32	0	Wilkes	1965-69
31	31	0	Morgan St.	1965-68
31	31	0	Missouri Valley	1946-48
31	29	2	St. Ambrose	1935-38
30	30	0	Bentley	1993-95
30	29	1	Wittenberg	1961-65
30	29	1	Tex. A&M-Commerce	1951-53
28	27	1	Wesleyan (Conn.)	†1942-48
28	27	1	Case Reserve	1934-37
27	26	1	Pittsburg St.	1991-92
27	26	1	Juniata	1956-59
27	27	0	Truman St.	1931-35

†*Did not field teams in 1943-44.*

Most-Played Rivalries

Games	Opponents (Series leader listed first)	Series Record	First Game
104	North Dak.-North Dak. St.	57-44-3	1894
98	South Dak.-South Dak. St.	49-42-7	1889
94	Emporia St.-Washburn	46-42-6	1899
88	Colorado Mines-Colorado Col.	46-37-5	1889
88	South Dak.-Morningside	55-28-5	1898
86	Presbyterian-Newberry	50-31-5	1913
86	Tuskegee-Morehouse	53-25-8	1902
84	North Dak. St.-South Dak. St.	44-34-5	1903
83	Virginia Union-Hampton	41-39-3	1906

Trophy Games

Following is a list of the current Division II football trophy games. The games are listed alphabetically by the trophy-object name. The date refers to the season the trophy was first exchanged and is not necessarily the start of competition between the participants. All games involving a Division II team are listed.

Trophy	Date	Colleges
Axe Bowl	1975	Northwood-Saginaw Valley
Backyard Bowl	1987	Cheyney-West Chester
Battle Axe	1948	Bemidji St.-Moorhead St.
Battle of the Ravine	1976	Henderson St.-Ouachita Baptist
Bishop's	1970	Lenoir-Rhyne—Newberry
Bronze Derby	1946	Newberry-Presbyterian
Eagle-Rock	1980	Chadron St.-Black Hills St.
East Meets West	1987	Chadron St.-Peru St.
Elm City	1983	New Haven-Southern Conn. St.
Field Cup	1983	Ky. Wesleyan-Evansville
Governor's	1979	Southern Conn. St.-Central Conn. St.
Heritage Bell	1979	Delta St.-Mississippi Col.
John Wesley	1984	Ky. Wesleyan-Union (Ky.)
Miner's Bowl	1986	Mo. Southern St.-Pittsburg St.
Nickel	1938	North Dak.-North Dak. St.
Old Hickory Stick	1931	Northwest Mo. St.-Truman St.
Old Settler's Musket	1975	Adams St.-Fort Lewis
Sitting Bull	1953	North Dak.-South Dak.
Springfield Mayor's	1941	American Int'l-Springfield
Textile	1960	Clark Atlanta-Fort Valley St.
Top Dog	1971	Indianapolis-Butler
Traveling	1976	Ashland-Hillsdale
Traveling	1997	Harding-Ouachita Baptist
Traveling Training Kit	1978	Mankato St.-St. Cloud St.
Victory Carriage	1960	UC Davis-Cal St. Sacramento
Wagon Wheel	1986	Eastern N.M.-West Tex. A&M
Wooden Shoes	1977	Grand Valley St.-Wayne St. (Mich.)

Cliffhangers

Regular-season games won by Division II teams on the final play of the game (from 1973). The extra point is listed when it provided the margin of victory after the winning touchdown.

Date	Opponents, Score	Game-Winning Play
9-22-73	South Dak. 9, North Dak. St. 7	Kelly Higgins 5 pass from Mark Jenkins
11-23-74	Arkansas St. 22, McNeese St. 20	Joe Duren 56 FG
10-11-75	Indiana (Pa.) 16, Westminster (Pa.) 14	Tom Alper 37 FG
9-25-76	Portland St. 50, Montana 49	Dave Stief 2 pass from June Jones
10-30-76	South Dak. St. 16, Northern Iowa 13	Monte Mosiman 53 pass from Dick Weikert
10-27-77	Albany (N.Y.) 42, Maine 39	Larry Leibowitz 19 FG
10-6-79	Indiana (Pa.) 31, Shippensburg 24	Jeff Heath 4 run
10-20-79	North Dak. 23, South Dak. 22	Tom Biolo 6 run
9-6-80	Ferris St. 20, St. Joseph's (Ind.) 15	Greg Washington 17 pass from (holder) John Gibson (after bad snap on 34 FG attempt)
11-15-80	Morris Brown 19, Bethune-Cookman 18	Ray Mills 1 run (Carlton Jackson kick)
11-15-80	Tuskegee 23, Alabama A&M 21	Korda Joseph 45 FG
9-26-81	Abilene Christian 41, Northwestern St. 38	David Russell 17 pass from Loyal Proffitt
9-26-81	Cal St. Chico 10, Santa Clara 7	Mike Sullivan 46 FG
10-10-81	LIU-C. W. Post 37, James Madison 36	Tom DeBona 10 pass from Tom Ehrhardt (Ehrhardt run)
10-9-82	Grand Valley St. 38, Ferris St. 35	Randy Spangler 20 FG
11-6-82	South Dak. 30, Augustana (S.D.) 28	Kurt Seibel 47 FG
9-17-83	Central Mo. St. 13, Sam Houston St. 10	Steve Huff 27 FG
9-22-84	Clarion 16, Shippensburg 13	Eric Fairbanks 26 FG
9-29-84	Angelo St. 18, Eastern N.M. 17	Ned Cox 3 run
10-13-84	UC Davis 16, Cal St. Chico 13	Ray Sullivan 48 FG
10-13-84	Northwest Mo. St. 35, Central Mo. St. 34	Pat Johnson 20 FG
11-3-84	Bloomsburg 34, West Chester 31	Curtis Still 50 pass from Jay Dedea
11-20-84	Central Fla. 28, Illinois St. 24	Jeff Farmer 30 punt return
9-7-85	Central Fla. 39, Bethune-Cookman 37	Ed O'Brien 55 FG
10-12-85	South Dak. 40, Morningside 38	Scott Jones 2 run
9-13-86	Michigan Tech 34, St. Norbert 30	Jim Wallace 41 pass from Dave Walter
10-18-86	Indianapolis 25, Evansville 24	Ken Bruce 18 FG
10-24-87	Indianapolis 27, Evansville 24	Doug Sabotin 2 pass from Tom Crowell
11-7-87	Central Mo. St. 35, Truman St. 33	Phil Brandt 25 FG
9-3-88	Alabama A&M 17, North Ala. 16	Edmond Allen 30 FG
9-17-88	Michigan Tech 17, Hope 14	Pete Weiss 22 FG
9-17-89	Morehouse 22, Fort Valley St. 21	David Boone 18 pass from Jimmie Davis
11-11-89	East Stroudsburg 22, Central Conn. St. 19	Frank Magolon 4 pass from Tom Taylor
10-13-90	East Stroudsburg 23, Bloomsburg 21	Ken Kopetchny 3 pass from Bret Comp
11-10-90	Southern Conn. St. 12, Central Conn. St. 10	Paul Boulanger 48 FG
9-21-91	West Ala. 22, Albany St. (Ga.) 21	Matt Carman 24 pass from Deon Timmons (Anthony Armstrong kick)
10-26-91	Central Mo. St. 38, Truman St. 37	Chris Pyatt 45 FG
10-26-91	Eastern N.M. 17, Tex. A&M-Commerce 14	Jodie Peterson 35 FG
10-9-93	Delta St. 20, Henderson St. 19	Greg Walker 3 run (Stephen Coker kick)
11-6-93	Henderson St. 46, West Ala. 44	Craig Moses 44 FG
9-24-94	Mo.-Rolla 15, Emporia St. 14	Jason Politte 1 run
9-24-94	St. Cloud St. 18, North Dak. 17	Todd Bouman 1 run
9-16-95	West Va. Wesleyan 16, Kutztown 14	Eric Myers 42 FG
9-30-95	Michigan Tech 37, Saginaw Valley 35	Matt Johnson 46 FG
11-8-97	Harding 31, Ouchita Baptist 28	Jeremy Thompson 34 FG

Stadiums

LISTED ALPHABETICALLY

School	Stadium	Year Built	Capacity	Surface
Abilene Christian	Shotwell	1959	15,000	Grass
Adams St.	Rex Field	1949	2,800	Grass
Alabama A&M	Louis Crews	1996	21,000	Grass
Albany (N.Y.)	University Field	1967	10,000	Grass
Albany St. (Ga.)	Mills Memorial	1957	11,000	Grass
American Int'l	John Homer Miller	1964	5,000	Grass
Angelo St.	San Angelo	1962	17,500	Grass
Ark.-Monticello	Cotton Boll	NA	5,000	Grass
Arkansas Tech	Buerkle	1970	6,000	Grass
Ashland	Community	1963	5,700	Grass
Assumption	Rocheleau Field	1961	1,200	Grass
Augustana (S.D.)	Howard Wood	1957	10,000	Grass
Bemidji St.	Chet Anderson	1937	4,000	Grass
Bentley	Bentley College	1990	3,000	Grass
Bloomsburg	Robert B. Redman	1974	5,000	Grass
Bowie St.	Bulldog	1992	6,000	Grass
UC Davis	Toomey Field	1949	10,111	Grass
Calif. (Pa.)	Adamson	1970	5,000	Grass
Carson-Newman	Burke-Tarr	1966	5,000	Grass
Catawba	Shuford Field	1926	4,000	Grass
Central Ark.	Estes	1939	8,500	Grass
Central Mo. St.	Audrey J. Walton	1995	10,000	Grass
Central Okla.	Wantland	1965	10,000	Grass
Central Wash.	Tomlinson	NA	4,000	Grass
Chadron St.	Elliott Field	1930	2,500	Grass
Cheyney	O'Shield-Stevenson	NA	3,500	Grass
Clarion	Memorial Field	1965	5,000	Grass
Clark Atlanta	Georgia Dome#	1992	71,000	AstroTurf
Colorado Mines	Brooks Field	1922	5,000	Grass
Concord	Callahan	NA	5,000	Grass
Delta St.	Travis Parker Field	1970	8,000	Grass
East Central	Norris Field	NA	5,000	Grass
East Stroudsburg	Eiler-Martin	1969	6,000	Grass
Eastern N.M.	Greyhound	1969	5,200	Grass
Edinboro	Sox-Harrison	1965	5,000	Grass
Elizabeth City St.	Roebuck	NA	6,500	Grass
Elon	Burlington Memorial	1949	10,000	Grass
Emporia St.	Welch	1937	7,000	Grass
Fairmont St.	Rosier Field	1929	6,000	Grass
Fayetteville St.	Jeralds Ath. Complex	1993	6,100	Grass
Ferris St.	Top Taggart Field	1957	9,100	Grass
Fort Hays St.	Lewis Field	1936	5,862	Stadia-Turf
Fort Lewis	Ray Dennison Memorial	1958	4,000	Grass
Fort Valley St.	Wildcat	1957	7,500	Grass
Gannon	Erie Veterans Memorial	1958	10,500	AstroTurf
Gardner-Webb	Spangler	1969	5,000	Grass
Glenville St.	Pioneer	1977	5,000	Grass
Grand Valley St.	Arend D. Lubbers	1979	4,146	PAT
Harding	Alumni Field	1959	4,500	Grass
Henderson St.	Carpenter-Haygood	1968	9,600	Grass
Hillsdale	Frank Waters	1982	8,500	PAT
Humboldt St.	Redwood Bowl	1946	7,000	Grass
Indiana (Pa.)	George P. Miller	1962	6,500	AstroTurf
Indianapolis	Key	1971	5,500	Grass
Johnson Smith	The Bullpit	1990	7,500	Grass
Kentucky St.	Alumni Field	1978	6,000	Grass
Ky. Wesleyan	Apollo	1989	3,000	Grass
Kutztown	University Field	1987	5,600	Grass
Lane	Rothrock	1930	3,500	Grass
Lenoir-Rhyne	Moretz	1923	8,500	Grass
Livingstone	Alumni	NA	5,500	Grass
Lock Haven	Hubert Jack	NA	3,000	Turf
LIU-C. W. Post	Hickox Field	1966	5,000	Grass
Mankato St.	Blakeslee Field	1962	7,500	Grass
Mansfield	Van Norman Field	NA	3,000	Grass
Mars Hill	Meares	1965	5,000	Grass
Mass.-Lowell	LeLacheur Park	NA	4,800	Grass
Mercyhurst	Tullio Field	1996	2,000	Grass
Merrimack	Merrimack	NA	2,000	Grass
Mesa St.	Stocker	1949	8,000	Grass
Michigan Tech	Sherman Field	1954	3,000	Grass
Midwestern St.	Memorial	NA	14,500	Turf
Miles	Alumni	NA	3,400	Grass
Millersville	Biemesderfer	1970	6,500	Grass
Minn.-Duluth	Griggs Field	1966	4,000	SuperTurf II
Minn.-Morris	UMM Field	NA	5,000	Grass
Mo.-Rolla	Jackling Field	1967	8,000	Grass
Mo. Southern St.	Fred G. Hughes	1975	7,000	Turf
Mo. Western St.	Spratt	1979	6,000	Grass
Moorhead St.	Alex Nemzek	1960	5,000	Grass
Morehouse	B. T. Harvey	1983	10,000	Grass
Morningside	Roberts	1939	9,000	Grass
Morris Brown	A. F. Herndon	1996	15,000	Turf
Neb.-Kearney	Foster Field	1929	6,500	Grass
Neb.-Omaha	Al F. Caniglia Field	1949	9,500	AstroTurf
New Haven	Robert B. Dodds	NA	3,500	Grass
N.M. Highlands	Perkins	1941	5,000	Grass
Newberry	Setzler Field	1930	4,000	Grass
North Ala.	Braly Municipal	1940	13,000	PAT
N.C. Central	O'Kelly-Riddick	1975	11,500	Grass
North Dak.	Memorial	1927	10,000	Turf
North Dak. St.	FargoDome#	1992	18,700	AstroTurf
Northeastern St.	Gable Field	NA	12,000	Grass
Northern Colo.	Nottingham Field	1995	7,000	Grass
Northern Mich.	Superior Dome#	1991	8,000	Turf
Northern St.	Swisher	1975	6,000	Grass
Northwest Mo. St.	Rickenbrode	1917	7,500	Grass
Northwood	Louis Juillerat	1964	2,500	Grass
Okla. Panhandle	Carl Wooten	NA	4,000	Grass
Ouachita Baptist	A. U. Williams	NA	5,200	Grass
Pace	Finnerty Field	NA	1,650	Grass
Pittsburg St.	Carnie Smith	1924	5,600	Grass
Presbyterian	Bailey Memorial	NA	5,000	Grass
Quincy	QU	1938	2,500	Grass
Sacred Heart	Campus Field	1993	2,000	Turf
Saginaw Valley	Harvey R. Wickes	1975	4,028	PAT
St. Cloud St.	Selke Field	1937	4,000	Grass
St. Francis (Ill.)	Joliet Memorial	1951	10,000	Grass
St. Joseph's (Ind.)	Alumni Field	1947	4,000	Grass
Savannah St.	Ted Wright	1967	7,500	Grass
Shepherd	Ram	1959	3,000	Grass
Shippensburg	Grove	1972	7,700	Grass
Slippery Rock	N. Kerr Thompson	1974	10,000	Grass
South Dak.	DakotaDome#	1979	10,000	Monsanto
South Dak. St.	Coughlin-Alumni	1962	16,000	Grass
Southeastern Okla.	Paul Laird Field	NA	4,000	Grass
Southern Ark.	Wilkins	1949	6,000	Grass
Southern Conn. St.	Jess Dow Field	1988	6,000	Balsam
Southwest Baptist	Plaster	1986	2,500	Grass
Southwest St.	Mattke Field	1971	5,000	Grass
Southwestern Okla.	Milam	NA	9,000	Grass
Stonehill	Chieftain	1980	2,000	Grass
Stony Brook	Seawolves Field	1978	2,000	Grass
Tarleton St.	Memorial	1976	5,284	Grass
Tex. A&M-Commerce	Memorial	1950	10,000	Grass
Tex. A&M-Kingsville	Javelina	1950	15,000	Grass
Truman St.	Stokes	1962	4,000	Grass
Tusculum	Pioneer Field	1991	2,500	Grass
Tuskegee	Alumni Bowl	1925	10,000	Grass
Valdosta St.	Cleveland Field	1922	11,500	Grass
Virginia St.	Rogers	1950	13,500	Grass
Virginia Union	Hovey Field	NA	10,000	Grass
Washburn	Moore Bowl	1928	7,200	Grass
Wayne St. (Mich.)	Wayne State	1968	6,000	Grass
Wayne St. (Neb.)	Memorial	1931	3,500	Grass
West Ala.	Tiger	1952	7,000	Grass
West Chester	Farrell	1970	7,500	Grass
West Ga.	Grisham	1966	6,500	Grass
West Liberty St.	Russek Field	1960	4,000	Grass
West Tex. A&M	Kimbrough	1959	20,000	Grass
West Va. St.	Lakin Field	1964	5,000	Grass
West Va. Tech	Martin Field	NA	3,000	Turf
West Va. Wesleyan	Cebe Ross Field	1957	3,000	Grass
Western N.M.	Silver Sports Complex	1969	2,000	Grass
Western St.	Mountaineer Bowl	1950	2,400	Grass
Western Wash.	Bellingham Civic	NA	4,500	Grass
Westminster (Pa.)	Memorial Field	NA	4,500	Grass
Wingate	Belk	NA	3,000	Grass
Winona St.	Maxwell Field	NA	3,500	Grass
Winston-Salem	Bowman-Gray	1940	18,000	Grass

LISTED BY CAPACITY (TOP 16)

School	Stadium	Surface	Capacity
Clark Atlanta	Georgia Dome#	AstroTurf	71,000
Alabama A&M	Louis Crews	Grass	21,000
West Tex. A&M	Kimbrough	Grass	20,000
North Dak. St.	FargoDome#	AstroTurf	18,700
Winston-Salem	Bowman-Gray	Grass	18,000
Angelo St.	San Angelo	Grass	17,500
South Dak. St.	Coughlin-Alumni	Grass	16,000
Abilene Christian	Shotwell	Grass	15,000
Morris Brown	A. F. Herndon	Turf	15,000
Tex. A&M-Kingsville	Javelina	Grass	15,000
Midwestern St.	Memorial	Turf	14,500
Virginia St.	Rogers	Grass	13,500
North Ala.	Braly Municipal	PAT	13,000
Northeastern St.	Gable Field	Grass	12,000

#Indoor facility. PAT=Prescription Athletic Turf.

Statistics Trends

For valid comparisons from 1973, when College Division teams were divided into Division II and Division III.

(Average Per Game, Both Teams)

	Rushing			Passing					Total Offense			Scoring		
Year	Plays	Yds.	Avg.	Att.	Cmp.	Pct.	Yds.	Av. Att.	Plays	Yds.	Avg.	TD	FG	Pts.
1973	47.6	169.6	3.57	20.0	8.8	.442	121.5	6.08	67.6	291.1	4.31	2.53	0.42	18.2
1974	47.6	156.3	3.29	19.5	8.7	.445	122.4	6.28	67.1	278.7	4.16	2.55	0.43	19.0
1975	47.3	168.6	3.56	19.5	8.7	.448	120.6	6.21	66.8	289.2	4.33	2.49	0.45	18.6
1976	47.4	165.7	3.50	19.9	9.1	.457	125.9	6.32	67.3	291.6	4.34	2.52	0.47	18.7
1977	*48.4	173.8	3.59	20.3	9.2	.453	126.2	6.21	68.7	300.0	4.37	2.58	0.46	19.1
1978	48.0	169.3	3.52	20.6	9.2	.448	124.3	6.05	68.6	293.6	4.29	2.56	0.49	19.3
1979	45.8	154.7	3.38	21.0	9.5	.450	125.8	6.00	66.8	280.5	4.20	2.37	0.52	17.9
1980	45.3	153.8	3.40	22.4	10.4	.463	137.6	6.16	67.7	291.4	4.31	2.51	0.52	18.9
1981	44.6	146.6	3.29	24.0	11.0	.457	145.9	6.09	68.6	292.5	4.27	2.48	0.54	18.7
1982	43.3	144.1	3.32	26.1	12.3	.469	161.0	6.17	69.4	305.1	4.40	2.63	0.62	19.8
1983	43.2	145.4	3.37	26.1	12.5	.479	164.5	6.31	69.3	309.9	4.48	2.64	0.62	19.6
1984	41.9	142.2	3.39	26.0	12.5	.481	164.8	6.33	67.9	307.0	4.52	2.63	0.62	19.4
1985	41.7	144.0	3.46	27.4	13.2	.483	170.6	6.23	69.1	314.6	4.56	2.73	0.65	20.9
1986	41.8	148.9	3.56	26.9	13.0	.484	168.4	6.27	68.7	317.3	4.62	2.89	0.64	22.0
1987	42.8	151.9	3.55	24.6	11.9	.483	155.5	6.31	67.4	307.4	4.56	2.65	0.64	20.2
1988	43.9	159.4	3.64	24.6	11.9	.484	159.8	6.49	68.5	319.2	4.66	2.92	0.65	22.1
1989	43.7	166.0	3.80	25.1	12.2	.485	161.5	6.45	68.8	327.5	4.77	2.97	0.62	22.6
1990	43.7	168.3	3.86	26.4	12.8	.485	173.3	6.57	70.1	341.6	4.88	3.10	0.65	23.4
1991	43.7	167.8	3.84	26.4	12.8	.484	172.4	6.54	70.1	340.2	4.86	3.05	*0.66	23.2
1992	44.1	167.6	3.80	25.6	12.4	.484	171.4	6.70	69.7	339.0	4.87	3.01	0.65	23.1
1993	42.7	167.3	3.92	*27.4	*13.6	.495	*180.2	6.11	*70.1	347.5	4.96	3.28	0.53	24.0
1994	42.6	*174.5	*4.10	26.3	13.2	.503	178.0	*6.79	68.9	*352.5	*5.13	*3.42	0.54	*25.1
1995	41.6	164.0	3.95	26.8	13.4	.501	176.9	6.61	68.4	340.9	4.99	3.22	0.56	23.7
1996	41.9	161.5	3.86	26.0	12.9	.495	173.1	6.65	67.9	334.6	4.93	3.15	0.58	23.4
1997	42.2	167.6	3.97	25.0	12.2	.489	166.3	6.66	67.2	333.9	4.97	3.24	0.58	24.0

**Record.*

Additional Statistics Trends

(Average Per Game, Both Teams)

			Punting		PAT Kick Attempts		Two-Point Attempts		Field Goals
Year	Teams†	Games	No.	Avg.	Pct. Made	Pct. of Total Tries	Pct. Made	Pct. of Total Tries	Pct. Made
1973	131	1,326	5.8	36.0	.833	.876	.419	.124	.439
1974	136	1,388	5.7	*36.8	.830	.859	.432	.141	.472
1975	126	1,282	5.5	36.3	.837	.874	.464	.126	.476
1976	122	1,244	5.8	36.2	.841	.878	.419	.122	.461
1977	124	1,267	5.9	36.1	.832	.874	.436	.126	.442
1978	91	921	6.0	35.9	.830	.880	.452	.120	.519
1979	99	1,016	6.1	35.2	.854	.861	.459	.139	.543
1980	103	1,040	5.9	35.6	.852	.864	.438	.136	.512
1981	113	1,138	*6.1	35.6	.856	.861	.440	.139	.531
1982	118	1,196	6.1	36.4	.862	.877	.431	.123	.560
1983	115	1,175	6.0	36.1	.866	.847	.428	.153	.564
1984	112	1,150	5.9	36.4	.876	.875	.448	.125	.567
1985	107	1,098	5.8	35.9	*.905	.864	.414	.136	.549
1986	109	1,124	5.6	36.5	.870	.865	.466	.135	.576*
1987	105	1,100	5.7	35.7	.857	.865	.435	.135	.547
1988	111	1,114	5.6	35.6	.886	.868	.399	.132	.555
1989	106	1,084	5.5	36.7	.873	.845	.376	.155	.567
1990	105	1,065	5.7	35.7	.876	*.885	*.474	.115	.568
1991	114	1,150	5.5	36.1	.882	.880	.426	.120	.572
1992	115	1,145	5.5	35.9	.888	.870	.442	.130	.575
1993	136	1,354	5.3	35.2	.839	.853	.438	.147	.528
1994	128	1,325	5.1	36.0	.850	.840	.439	.160	.559
1995	131	1,362	5.3	34.9	.835	.837	.473	*.163	.552
1996	137	1,434	5.5	35.6	.837	.846	.473	.154	.560
1997	129	1,357	5.4	36.2	.841	.879	.425	.121	.561

**Record. †Teams reporting statistics, not the total number of teams in the division.*

Classification History (1973-98)

The following lists show years of active membership for current and former Division II football-playing institutions. Provisional members also are shown, along with the year in which they will become active memvbers.

ACTIVE MEMBERS (150)

Abilene Christian 1981-98
Adams St. 1983, 90-98
Alabama A&M 1973-98
Albany (N.Y.) 1995-98
Albany St. (Ga.) 1976-98
American Int'l 1974-98
Angelo St. 1981-98
Ark.-Monticello 1997-98
Arkansas Tech 1997-98
Ashland 1980-98
Assumption 1993-98
Augustana (S.D.) 1973-98
Bemidji St. 1979-98
Bentley 1993-98
Bloomsburg 1980-98
Bowie St. 1980-98
UC Davis 1973-98
Calif. (Pa.) 1973-98
Carson-Newman 1991-98
Catawba 1991-98
Central Ark. 1992-98
Central Mo. St. 1973-98

DIVISION II

Central Okla.	1976-78, 88-98
Central Wash.	1973-75, 82-83, 98
Chadron St.	1990-98
Cheyney	1980-98
Clarion	1973-98
Clark Atlanta	1980-98
Colorado Mines	1974-98
Concord	1993-98
Delta St.	1973-98
East Central	1998
East Stroudsburg	1973-98
Eastern N.M.	1985-98
Edinboro	1973-98
Elizabeth City St.	1973-98
Elon	1991-98
Emporia St.	1990-98
Fairmont St.	1978-79, 93-98
Fayetteville St.	1973-98
Ferris St.	1977-98
Fort Hays St.	1988-98
Fort Lewis	1973-84, 90-98
Fort Valley St.	1981-98
Gannon	1993-98
Gardner-Webb	1991-98
Glenville St.	1993-98
Grand Valley St.	1976-98
Harding	1997-98
Henderson St.	1992-98
Hillsdale	1976-78, 84-98
Humboldt St.	1973, 80-98
Indiana (Pa.)	1973-98
Indianapolis	1976-98
Johnson Smith	1973-98
Kentucky St.	1973-98
Ky. Wesleyan	1993-98
Kutztown	1980-98
Lane	1993-98
Lenoir-Rhyne	1989-98
Livingstone	1973-98
Lock Haven	1980-98
LIU-C.W. Post	1973, 78-84, 93-98
Mankato St.	1973-76, 78-98
Mansfield	1980-98
Mars Hill	1991-98
Mass.-Lowell	1993-98
Mercyhurst	1993-98
Merrimack	1996-98
Mesa St.	1982-83, 90-98
Michigan Tech	1973-98
Midwestern St.	1997-98
Miles	1988-98
Millersville	1980-98
Minn.-Duluth	1973-98
Minn.-Morris	1993-98
Mo.-Rolla	1973-98
Mo. Southern St.	1988-98
Mo. Western St.	1988-98
Moorhead St.	1973-82, 93-98
Morehouse	1981-98
Morningside	1973-98
Morris Brown	1973-98
Neb.-Kearney	1988-98
Neb.-Omaha	1973-98
New Haven	1975-76, 81-98
N.M. Highlands	1982-84, 91-98
Newberry	1990-98
North Ala.	1973-98
N.C. Central	1973-98
North Dak.	1973-98
North Dak. St.	1973-98
Northeastern St.	1998
Northern Colo.	1973-98
Northern Mich.	1973-98
Northern St.	1980-81, 93-98
Northwest Mo. St.	1973-98
Northwood	1981-87, 92-98
Okla. Panhandle	1998
Ouachita Baptist	1997-98
Pace	1993-98
Pittsburg St.	1988-98
Presbyterian	1991-98
Quincy	1993-94, 96-98
Sacred Heart	1993-98
Saginaw Valley	1981-98
St. Cloud St.	1973-98
St. Francis (Ill.)	1993-98
St. Joseph's (Ind.)	1979-98
Savannah St.	1981-98
Shepherd	1990-98
Shippensburg	1976-98
Slippery Rock	1979-98
South Dak.	1973-98
South Dak. St.	1973-98
Southeastern Okla.	1998
Southern Ark.	1997-98
Southern Conn. St.	1973-98
Southwest Baptist	1986-98
Southwest St.	1978-83, 93-98
Southwestern Okla.	1998
Stonehill	1993-98
Stony Brook	1995-98
Tarleton St.	1994-98
Tex. A&M-Commerce	1981-98
Tex. A&M-Kingsville	1980-98
Truman St.	1973-98
Tusculum	1998
Tuskegee	1973-98
Valdosta St.	1982-98
Virginia St.	1973-98
Virginia Union	1973-98
Washburn	1988-98
Wayne St. (Mich.)	1973-98
Wayne St. (Neb.)	1988-98
West Ala.	1974-98
West Chester	1973-98
West Ga.	1983-98
West Liberty St.	1991-98
West Tex. A&M	1986-90, 92-98
West Va. St.	1997-98
West Va. Tech	1993-98
W.Va. Wesleyan	1973-80, 93-98
Western N.M.	1983, 94-98
Western St.	1973-78, 82-85, 90-98
Western Wash.	1998
Westminster (Pa.)	1998
Wingate	1991-98
Winona St.	1978-98
Winston-Salem	1973-98

PROVISIONAL MEMBERS (1)*

Findlay	1999

FORMER MEMBERS (122)

Akron	1973-79
Alabama St.	1973-81
Alcorn St.	1973-76
Ark.-Pine Bluff	1973-82
Arkansas St.	1973-74
Austin Peay	1973-77
Ball St.	1973-74
Bethune-Cookman	1973-79
Boise St.	1973-77
Boston U.	1973-77
Bucknell	1973-77
Butler	1973-92
UC Riverside	1973-75
UC Santa Barb.	1991
Cal Lutheran	1985-90
Cal Poly Pomona	1973-82
Cal Poly SLO	1973-93
Cal St. Chico	1978-96
Cal St. Fullerton	1973-74
Cal St. Hayward	1973-93
Cal St. Los Angeles	1973-77
Cal St. Northridge	1973-92
Cal St. Sacramento	1973-92
Cameron	1988-92
Central Conn. St.	1973-92
Central Fla.	1982-89
Central Mich.	1973-74
Central St.	1973-87
Chattanooga	1973-76
Connecticut	1973-77
Davidson	1977
Delaware	1973-79
Dist. Columbia	1973-75
East Tenn. St.	1973-77
Eastern Ill.	1973-80
Eastern Ky.	1973-77
Eastern Mich.	1973-75
Eastern Wash.	1978-83
Evansville	1978-88
Florida A&M	1973-77
Franklin	1979-85
Georgetown (Ky.)	1980-82
Grambling	1973-76
Hampton	1973-94
Hardin-Simmons	1993
Howard	1973-77
Howard Payne	1981-86
Idaho St.	1973-77
Illinois St.	1973-75
Indiana St.	1973-75
Jackson St.	1973-76
Jacksonville St.	1973-94
James Madison	1974-76
Jamestown	1982-83
Knoxville	1989
Lafayette	1973-77
Lehigh	1973-77
Liberty	1981-87
Louisiana Tech	1973-74
Maine	1973-77
Md.-East. Shore	1973-79
Massachusetts	1973-77
McNeese St.	1973-74
Merchant Marine	1978-81
Middle Tenn. St.	1973-77
Mississippi Col.	1973-96
Mississippi Val.	1973-79
Montana	1973-77
Montana St.	1973-77
Morehead St.	1973-77
Morgan St.	1973-85
Murray St.	1973-77
Nevada	1973-77
UNLV	1973-77
New Hampshire	1973-77
New York Tech	1974-83
Nicholls St.	1973-79
Norfolk St.	1973-96
North Caro. A&T	1973-77
Northeastern	1973-77
Northeast La.	1973-74
Northern Ariz.	1973-77
Northern Iowa	1973-80
Northwestern St.	1973-75
Portland St.	1973-77, 81-97
Prairie View	1973-79
Puget Sound	1973-88
Rhode Island	1973-77
St. Mary's (Cal.)	1981-92
St. Paul's	1973-87
Sam Houston St.	1981-85
San Fran. St.	1979-94
Santa Clara	1973-92
Sonoma St.	1984-96
South Caro. St.	1973-77
Southeast Mo. St.	1973-90
Southeastern La.	1973-79
Southern U.	1973-76
Southern Ore.	1981-83
Southern Utah	1982-92
Southwest Mo. St.	1973-81
Southwest Tex. St.	1978-83
Springfield	1973-94
Stephen F. Austin	1981-85
Tenn.-Martin	1973-91
Tennessee St.	1973-76
Tennessee Tech	1973-77
Texas Lutheran	1983
Texas Southern	1973-76
Towson	1980-86
Troy St.	1973-92
Valparaiso	1979-92
Vermont	1973-74
Weber St.	1973-77
Western Caro.	1973-76
Western Ill.	1973-80
Western Ky.	1973-77
Wis.-Milwaukee	1973-74
Wis.-La Crosse	1975
Wis.-Oshkosh	1973-74
Wofford	1988-94
Youngstown St.	1973-80

**Provisional members are not active members of the Association and, thus, are not eligible for NCAA statistics, records and championship play. The end of the three-year provisional status and first season of active membership in Division II football is listed to the right of the school name.*

Division III Records

Individual Records

Division III football records are based on the performances of Division III teams since the three-division reorganization plan was adopted by the special NCAA Convention in August 1973.

Total Offense

(Rushing Plus Passing)

MOST PLAYS

Quarter

33—Aaron Keen, Washington (Mo.) vs. Trinity (Tex.), Oct. 3, 1992 (4th)

Half

59—Justin Peery, Westminster (Mo.) vs. Bethel (Tenn.), Nov. 8, 1997 (2nd); Mike Wallace, Ohio Wesleyan vs. Denison, Oct. 3, 1981 (2nd)

Game

91—Jordan Poznick, Principia vs. Blackburn, Oct. 10, 1992 (81 passes, 10 rushes; 538 yards)

Season

614—Tim Peterson, Wis.-Stout, 1989 (3,244 yards)
Per-game record—64.9, Jordan Poznick, Principia, 1992 (519 in 8)

Career

2,007—Kirk Baumgartner, Wis.-Stevens Point, 1986-89 (12,767 yards)
Also holds per-game record at 49.0 (2,007 in 41)

MOST PLAYS BY A FRESHMAN

Season

491—Mark Novara, Lakeland, 1994 (2,572 yards)
Also holds per-game record at 54.6 (491 in 9)

MOST YARDS GAINED

Half

517—Justin Peery, Westminster (Mo.) vs. Bethel (Tenn.), Nov. 8, 1997 (497 passing, 20 rushing)

Game

596—John Love, North Park vs. Elmhurst, Oct. 13, 1990 (533 passing, 63 rushing)

Season

3,981—Terry Peebles, Hanover, 1995 (460 rushing, 3,521 passing)
Also holds per-game record at 398.1 (3,981 in 10)

Career

12,767—Kirk Baumgartner, Wis.-Stevens Point, 1986-89 (-261 rushing, 13,028 passing)
Per-game record—333.6, Terry Peebles, Hanover, 1992-95 (7,672 in 23)

MOST YARDS GAINED BY A FRESHMAN

Season

2,572—Mark Novara, Lakeland, 1994 (491 plays)
Also holds per-game record at 285.8 (2,572 in 9)

MOST GAMES GAINING 300 YARDS OR MORE

Season

8—Kirk Baumgartner, Wis.-Stevens Point, 1989

Career

26—Kirk Baumgartner, Wis.-Stevens Point, 1986-89

MOST CONSECUTIVE GAMES GAINING 300 YARDS OR MORE

Season

6—Kirk Baumgartner, Wis.-Stevens Point, 1987

GAINING 4,000 YARDS RUSHING AND 2,000 YARDS PASSING

Career

Chris Spriggs, Denison, 1983-86 (4,248 rushing & 2,799 passing)
Also holds record for yards gained by a running back at 7,047

GAINING 3,000 YARDS RUSHING AND 3,000 YARDS PASSING

Career

Clay Sampson (TB), Denison, 1977-80 (3,726 rushing & 3,194 passing)

HIGHEST AVERAGE GAIN PER PLAY

Season

(Min. 2,500 yards) 11.0—Lon Erickson, Ill. Wesleyan, 1996 (231 for 2,552)

Career

(Min. 6,000 yards) 8.4—Bill Borchert, Mount Union, 1994-97 (1,274 for 10,639)

MOST TOUCHDOWNS RESPONSIBLE FOR (TDs Scored and Passed For)

Career

147—Bill Borchert, Mount Union, 1994-97 (141 passing 6 rushing) Also holds per-game record at 3.7 (147 in 40)

Rushing

MOST RUSHES

Game

58—Bill Kaiser, Wabash vs. DePauw, Nov. 9, 1985 (211 yards)

Season

380—Mike Birosak, Dickinson, 1989 (1,798 yards)
Also holds per-game record at 38.0 (380 in 10)

Career

1,112—Mike Birosak, Dickinson, 1986-89 (4,662 yards)
Per-game record—32.7, Chris Sizemore, Bridgewater (Va.), 1972-74 (851 in 26)

MOST RUSHES BY A QUARTERBACK

Season

231—Jeff Saueressig, Wis.-River Falls, 1988 (1,095 yards)
Also holds per-game record at 25.7 (231 in 9)

MOST CONSECUTIVE RUSHES BY THE SAME PLAYER

Game

46—Dan Walsh, Montclair St. vs. Ramapo, Sept. 30, 1989 (during 13 possessions)

Season

51—Dan Walsh, Montclair St., 1989 (Sept. 23 to Sept. 30)

MOST YARDS GAINED

Half

310—Leroy Horn, Montclair St. vs. Jersey City St., Nov. 9, 1985 (21 rushes)

Game

441—Dante Brown, Marietta vs. Baldwin-Wallace, Oct. 5, 1996

Season

2,385—Dante Brown, Marietta, 1996 (314 rushes)
Also holds per-game record at 238.5 (2,385 in 10)

Career

6,125—Carey Bender, Coe, 1991-94 (926 rushes)
Per-game record—175.1, Ricky Gales, Simpson, 1988-89 (3,326 in 19)

MOST YARDS GAINED BY A FRESHMAN

Season

1,380—Fredrick Nanhed, Cal Lutheran, 1995 (242 rushes)
Also holds per-game record at 153.3 (1,380 in 9)

MOST RUSHING YARDS GAINED BY A QUARTERBACK

Game

235—Mark Cota, Wis.-River Falls vs. Minn.-Morris, Sept. 13, 1986 (27 rushes)

Season

1,279—Mark Cota, Wis.-River Falls, 1986 (227 rushes)
Also holds per-game record at 127.9 (1,279 in 10)

Career

3,252—Adam Kowles, Wis.-River Falls, 1992-95 (487 rushes)

LONGEST GAIN BY A QUARTERBACK

Game

98 yards—Jon Hinds, Principia vs. Illinois Col., Sept. 20, 1986 (TD)

MOST GAMES GAINING 100 YARDS OR MORE

Career

30—Joe Dudek, Plymouth St., 1982-85 (41 games)

MOST CONSECUTIVE GAMES GAINING 100 YARDS OR MORE

Career

19—Brandon Steinheim, Wesley, Sept. 9, 1995-Nov. 16, 1996

MOST GAMES GAINING 200 YARDS OR MORE

Season

8—Ricky Gales, Simpson, 1989 (consecutive)

Career

11—Rob Marchitello, Maine Maritime, 1993-95; Ricky Gales, Simpson, 1988-89

MOST SEASONS GAINING 1,000 YARDS OR MORE

Career

4—Carey Bender, Coe, 1991-94; Steve Dixon, Beloit, 1990-93; Jim Romagna, Loras, 1989-92; Joe Dudek, Plymouth St., 1982-85; Rich Kowalski, Hobart, 1972-75

TWO PLAYERS, SAME TEAM, EACH GAINING 1,000 YARDS OR MORE

Season

By 10 teams. Most recent: Cornell College, 1996—Tim Hinton (RB) 1,095 & Ben King (RB) 1,000; Luras, 1996—Shane Davis (RB) 1,306 & Kevin Coy (RB) 1,087

MOST YARDS GAINED RUSHING BY TWO PLAYERS, SAME TEAM

Game

519—Carey Bender 417 & Jason Whitaker 102, Coe vs. Grinnell, Oct. 9, 1993

Season

2,738—Dante Brown (RB) 2,385 & Aaron Conte (QB) 353, Marietta, 1996 (10 games)

HIGHEST AVERAGE GAIN PER RUSH

Game

(Min. 15 rushes) 19.1—Billy Johnson, Widener vs. Swarthmore, Nov. 10, 1973 (15 for 286)
(Min. 24 rushes) 15.9—Pete Baranek, Carthage vs. North Central, Oct. 5, 1985 (24 for 382)

Season

(Min. 140 rushes) 8.9—Billy Johnson, Widener, 1973 (168 for 1,494)
(Min. 200 rushes) 7.9—Jamie Lee, MacMurray, 1997 (207 for 1,639)
(Min. 250 rushes) 7.6—Carey Bender, Coe, 1994 (295 for 2,243)

Career

(Min. 500 rushes) 7.1—Joe Dudek, Plymouth St., 1982-85 (785 for 5,570)

MOST TOUCHDOWNS SCORED BY RUSHING

Game

8—Carey Bender, Coe vs. Beloit, Nov. 12, 1994

Season

29—Doug Steiner, Grove City, 1997; Carey Bender, Coe, 1994
Per-game record—3.0, Stanley Drayton, Allegheny, 1991 (27 in 9)

Career

76—Joe Dudek, Plymouth St., 1982-85
Also holds per-game record at 1.9 (76 in 41)

MOST RUSHING TOUCHDOWNS SCORED BY A QUARTERBACK

Season

17—Mark Reed, Monmouth (Ill.), 1987
Also holds per-game record at 1.7 (17 in 10)

Passing

HIGHEST PASSING EFFICIENCY RATING POINTS

Season

(Min. 15 atts. per game) 225.0—Mike Simpson, Eureka, 1994 (158 attempts, 116 completions, 5 interceptions, 1,988 yards, 25 TDs)
(Min. 25 atts. per game) 216.7—Bill Borchert, Mount Union, 1997 (272 attempts, 190 completions, 1 interception, 2,933 yards, 47 TDs)

Career

(Min. 650 comps.) 194.2—Bill Borchert, Mount Union, 1994-97 (1,009 attempts, 671 completions, 17

interceptions, 10,201 yards, 141 TDs)

MOST PASSES ATTEMPTED
Quarter
31—Mike Wallace, Ohio Wesleyan vs. Denison, Oct. 3, 1981 (4th)
Half
57—Justin Peery, Westminster (Mo.) vs. Bethel (Tenn.), Nov. 8, 1997 (2nd); Mike Wallace, Ohio Wesleyan vs. Denison, Oct. 3, 1981 (2nd)
Game
81—Jordan Poznick, Principia vs. Blackburn, Oct. 10, 1992 (completed 48)
Season
527—Kirk Baumgartner, Wis.-Stevens Point, 1988 (completed 276)
Per-game record—56.4, Jordan Poznick, Principia, 1992 (451 in 8)
Career
1,696—Kirk Baumgartner, Wis.-Stevens Point, 1986-89 (completed 883)
Per-game record—42.3, Keith Bishop, Ill. Wesleyan/Wheaton (Ill.), 1981, 1983-85 (1,311 in 31)

MOST PASSES ATTEMPTED BY A FRESHMAN
Season
453—Mark Novara, Lakeland, 1994 (completed 227)
Also holds per-game record at 50.3 (453 in 9)

MOST PASSES COMPLETED
Quarter
21—Rob Bristow, Pomona-Pitzer vs. Whittier, Oct. 19, 1985 (4th)
Half
36—Mike Wallace, Ohio Wesleyan vs. Denison, Oct. 3, 1981 (2nd)
Game
50—Tim Lynch, Hofstra vs. Fordham, Oct. 19, 1991 (attempted 69)
Season
283—Terry Peebles, Hanover, 1995 (attempted 488)
Per-game record—30.1, Jordan Poznick, Principia, 1992 (241 in 8)
Career
883—Kirk Baumgartner, Wis.-Stevens Point, 1986-89 (attempted 1,696)
Per-game record—24.9, Keith Bishop, Ill. Wesleyan/Wheaton (Ill.), 1981, 1983-85 (772 in 31)

MOST PASSES COMPLETED BY A FRESHMAN
Season
227—Mark Novara, Lakeland, 1994 (attempted 453)
Also holds per-game record at 25.2 (227 in 9)

HIGHEST PERCENTAGE OF PASSES COMPLETED
Game
(Min. 20 comps.) 91.3%—Chris Esterley, St. Thomas (Minn.) vs. St. Olaf, Sept. 23, 1995 (21 of 23)
(Min. 35 comps.) 83.3%—Scott Driggers, Colorado Col. vs. Neb. Wesleyan, Sept. 10, 1983 (35 of 42)
Season
(Min. 250 atts.) 72.9%—Jim Ballard, Mount Union, 1993 (229 of 314)
Career
(Min. 750 atts.) 66.5%—Bill Borchert, Mount Union, 1994-97 (671 of 1,009)

MOST CONSECUTIVE PASSES COMPLETED
Game
17—Jim Ballard, Mount Union vs. Ill. Wesleyan, Nov. 28, 1992; William Snyder, Carnegie Mellon vs. Wooster, Oct. 20, 1990
Season
25—Ty Grovesteen, Wis.-Whitwater vs. Wis.-Oshkosh (1), Oct. 11, vs. Wis.-Stout (9), Oct. 18 and Wis.-Platteville (15), Oct. 25, 1997

MOST CONSECUTIVE PASSES COMPLETED BY TWO PLAYERS, SAME TEAM
Game
20—Kevin Keefe (16) & David Skarupa (4), Baldwin-Wallace vs. Moravian, Sept. 10, 1994

MOST PASSES HAD INTERCEPTED
Game
8—Jason Clark, Ohio Northern vs. John Carroll, Nov. 9, 1991; Jim Higgins, Brockport St. vs. Buffalo St., Sept. 29, 1990; Dennis Bogacz, Wis.-Oshkosh vs. Wis.-Stevens Point, Oct. 29, 1988; Kevin Karwath, Canisius vs. Liberty, Nov. 19, 1979
Season
43—Steve Hendry, Wis.-Superior, 1982 (attempted 480)
Also holds per-game record at 3.9 (43 in 11)
Career
117—Steve Hendry, Wis.-Superior, 1980-83 (attempted 1,343)
Per-game record—3.2, Willie Martinez, Oberlin, 1973-74 (58 in 18)

LOWEST PERCENTAGE OF PASSES HAD INTERCEPTED
Season
(Min. 150 atts.) 0.4%—Bill Borchert, Mount Union, 1997 (1 of 272)
Career
(Min. 600 atts.) 1.7%—Bill Borchert, Mount Union 1994-97 (17 of 1,009)

MOST PASSES ATTEMPTED WITHOUT INTERCEPTION
Game
67—Brian Van Deusen, Western Md. vs. Frank. & Marsh., Oct. 23, 1993 (37 completions)
Season
124—Tim Tenhet, Sewanee, 1982

MOST CONSECUTIVE PASSES ATTEMPTED WITHOUT AN INTERCEPTION
Season
221—Bill Borchert, Mount Union, 1997 (during 8 games; began Sept. 27 vs. Otterbein, ended Nov. 15 vs. Hiram)

MOST YARDS GAINED
Half
497—Justin Peery, Westminster (Mo.) vs. Bethel (Tenn.), Nov. 8, 1997 (2nd)
Game
602—Tom Stallings, St. Thomas (Minn.) vs. Bethel (Minn.), Nov. 13, 1993
Season
3,828—Kirk Baumgartner, Wis.-Stevens Point, 1988
Also holds per-game record at 369.2 (3,692 in 10, 1989)
Career
13,028—Kirk Baumgartner, Wis.-Stevens Point, 1986-89
Also holds per-game record at 317.8 (13,028 in 41)

MOST YARDS GAINED BY A FRESHMAN
Season
2,576—Mark Novara, Lakeland, 1994
Also holds per-game record at 286.2 (2,576 in 9)

MOST GAMES PASSING FOR 200 YARDS OR MORE
Season
10—Kirk Baumgartner, Wis.-Stevens Point, 1989, 1988, 1987
Career
32—Kirk Baumgartner, Wis.-Stevens Point, 1986-89

MOST CONSECUTIVE GAMES PASSING FOR 200 YARDS OR MORE
Season
10—Kirk Baumgartner, Wis.-Stevens Point, 1989 (entire season)
Career
27—Keith Bishop, Ill. Wesleyan/Wheaton (Ill.), 1981, 1983-85

MOST GAMES PASSING FOR 300 YARDS OR MORE
Season
9—Kirk Baumgartner, Wis.-Stevens Point, 1989
Career
24—Kirk Baumgartner, Wis.-Stevens Point, 1986-89

MOST CONSECUTIVE GAMES PASSING FOR 300 YARDS OR MORE
Season
9—Kirk Baumgartner, Wis.-Stevens Point, 1989 (began Sept. 9 vs. St. Norbert, through Nov. 4 vs. Wis.-Superior)
Career
13—Kirk Baumgartner, Wis.-Stevens Point, 1988-89 (began Oct. 22, 1988, vs. Wis.-Stout, through Nov. 4, 1989, vs. Wis.-Superior)

MOST YARDS GAINED BY TWO OPPOSING PLAYERS
Game
928—Brion Demski, Wis.-Stevens Point (477) & Steve Hendry, Wis.-Superior (451), Oct. 17, 1981 (completed 70 of 123)

MOST YARDS GAINED PER ATTEMPT
Season
(Min. 175 atts.) 12.9—Willie Seiler, St. John's (Minn.), 1993 (205 for 2,648)
(Min. 275 atts.) 10.5—Jim Ballard, Mount Union, 1993 (314 for 3,304)
Career
(Min. 950 atts.) 10.1—Bill Borchert, Mount Union, 1994-97 (1,009 for 10,201)

MOST YARDS GAINED PER COMPLETION
Season
(Min. 100 comps.) 19.7—David Parker, Bishop, 1981 (114 for 2,242)
(Min. 200 comps.) 16.1—John Furmaniak, Eureka, 1995 (210 for 3,372)
Career
(Min. 300 comps.) 18.3—David Parker, Bishop, 1981-84 (378 for 6,934)
(Min. 425 comps.) 15.2—Bill Borchert, Mount Union, 1994-97 (671 for 10,201)

MOST TOUCHDOWN PASSES
Quarter
5—David Sullivan, Williams vs. Hamilton, Oct. 30, 1993 (2nd)
Game
8—John Koz, Baldwin-Wallace vs. Ohio Northern, Nov. 6, 1993; Steve Austin, Mass.-Boston vs. Framingham St., Nov. 14, 1992; Kirk Baumgartner, Wis.-Stevens Point vs. Wis.-Superior, Nov. 4, 1989
Season
47—Bill Borchert, Mount Union, 1997
Also hold per-game record at 4.7 (47 in 10)
Career
141—Bill Borchert, Mount Union 1994-97
Also holds per-game record at 3.5 (141 in 40)

HIGHEST PERCENTAGE OF PASSES FOR TOUCHDOWNS
Season
(Min. 200 atts.) 17.3—Bill Borchert, Mount Union, 1997 (47 of 272)
(Min. 300 atts.) 11.8%—Jim Ballard, Mount Union, 1993 (37 of 314)
Career
(Min. 800 atts.) 14.0%—Bill Borchert, Mount Union, 1994-97 (141 of 1,009)

MOST TOUCHDOWN PASSES BY A FRESHMAN
Season
26—Bill Borchert, Mount Union, 1994
Also holds per-game record at 2.6 (26 in 10)

MOST CONSECUTIVE GAMES THROWING A TOUCHDOWN PASS
Career
40—Bill Borchert, Mount Union (from Sept. 10, 1994, through Nov. 15, 1997

Receiving

MOST PASSES CAUGHT
Game
23—Sean Munroe, Mass.-Boston vs. Mass. Maritime, Oct. 10, 1992 (332 yards)
Season
112—Jeff Clay (WR), Catholic, 1997 (1,625 yards)
Per-game record—12.3, Matt Newton, Principia, 1992 (98 in 8)
Career
287—Matt Newton, Principia, 1990-93 (3,646 yards)
Also holds per-game record at 8.7 (287 in 33)

MOST PASSES CAUGHT BY A TIGHT END
Game
17—Matt Surette, Worcester Tech vs. Springfield, Oct. 25, 1997
Season
75—Matt Surette, Worcester Tech, 1997 (1,287 yards); Ryan Davis, St. Thomas (Minn.), 1994 (1,164 yards)
Career
185—Hanz Hoag, Evansville, 1991-93 (2,173 yards)

MOST PASSES CAUGHT BY A RUNNING BACK
Game
17—Theo Blanco, Wis.-Stevens Point vs. Wis.-Oshkosh, Oct. 31, 1987 (271 yards); Tim Mowery, Wis.-Superior vs. Wis.-Stevens Point, Oct. 17, 1981 (154 yards)

Season
106—Theo Blanco, Wis.-Stevens Point, 1987 (1,616 yards)
Career
169—Mike Christman, Wis.-Stevens Point, 1983-86 (2,190 yards)

MOST PASSES CAUGHT BY A FRESHMAN
Season
86—Matt Plummer, Dubuque, 1996 (1,237 yards)

MOST PASSES CAUGHT BY TWO PLAYERS, SAME TEAM
Season
158—Theo Blanco (RB) 106 & Aatron Kenney (WR) 52, Wis.-Stevens Point, 1987 (2,713 yards, 24 TDs)

MOST PASSES CAUGHT BY THREE PLAYERS, SAME TEAM
Season
217—Theo Blanco (WR) 80, Don Moehling (TE) 72 & Jim Mares (RB) 65, Wis.-Stevens Point, 1988. Totaled 2,959 yards and 19 TDs (team totals: 285–3,924–26)

MOST CONSECUTIVE GAMES CATCHING A PASS
Career
37—Junior Lord, Guilford, 1994-97; Kendall Griffin, Loras, 1990-93

MOST YARDS GAINED
Game
364—Jeff Clay, Catholic vs. Albright, Nov. 16, 1996 (caught 18)
Season
1,693—Sean Munroe, Mass.-Boston, 1992 (caught 95)
Also holds per-game record at 188.1 (1,693 in 9)
Career
4,311—Kurt Barth, Eureka, 1994-97 (caught 256)
Per-game record—113.9, Jeff Clay, Catholic, 1994-97 (4,101 in 36)

MOST YARDS GAINED BY A TIGHT END
Game
362—Matt Surette, Worcester Tech vs. Springfield, Oct. 25, 1997 (caught 17)
Season
1,290—Don Moehling, Wis.-Stevens Point, 1988 (caught 72)
Career
2,663—Don Moehling, Wis.-Stevens Point, 1986-89 (caught 152)

MOST YARDS GAINED BY A RUNNING BACK
Game
271—Theo Blanco, Wis.-Stevens Point vs. Wis.-Oshkosh, Oct. 31, 1987 (caught 17)

Photo from Catholic sports information

Catholic's Jeff Clay set the Division III record for receiving yards in a game when he caught 18 passes for 364 yards in a November 16, 1996, game against Albright.

Season
1,616—Theo Blanco, Wis.-Stevens Point, 1987 (caught 106)
Career
2,190—Mike Christman, Wis.-Stevens Point, 1983-86 (caught 169)

MOST YARDS GAINED BY TWO PLAYERS, SAME TEAM
Season
2,713—Theo Blanco (RB) 1,616 & Aatron Kenney (WR) 1,097, Wis.-Stevens Point, 1987 (158 receptions, 24 TDs)

HIGHEST AVERAGE GAIN PER RECEPTION
Game
(Min. 3 receps.) 68.3—Paul Jaeckel, Elmhurst vs. Ill. Wesleyan, Oct. 8, 1983 (3 for 205)
(Min. 5 receps.) 56.8—Tom Casperson, Col. of New Jersey vs. Ramapo, Nov. 15, 1980 (5 for 284)
Season
(Min. 35 receps.) 26.9—Marty Redlawsk, Concordia (Ill.), 1985 (38 for 1,022)
(Min. 50 receps.) 23.5—Evan Elkington, Worcester Tech, 1989 (52 for 1,220)
Career
(Min. 125 receps.) 21.7—R. J. Hoppe, Carroll (Wis.), 1993-96 (152 for 3,295)

HIGHEST AVERAGE GAIN PER RECEPTION BY A RUNNING BACK
Season
(Min. 50 receps.) 17.5—Barry Rose, Wis.-Stevens Point, 1989 (67 for 1,171)

MOST TOUCHDOWN PASSES CAUGHT
Game
5—By 12 players. Most recent: Kurt Barth, Eureka vs. Lakeland, Nov. 4, 1995
Season
20—Jeff Clay, Catholic, 1997; John Aromando, Col. of New Jersey, 1983
Also hold per-game record at 2.0 (20 in 10)
Career
55—Chris Bisaillon, Ill. Wesleyan, 1989-92 (223 receptions)
Also holds per-game record at 1.5 (55 in 36)

MOST TOUCHDOWN PASSES CAUGHT BY A FRESHMAN
Season
12—Matt Plummer, Dubuque, 1996; Chris Bisaillon, Ill. Wesleyan, 1989

HIGHEST PERCENTAGE OF PASSES CAUGHT FOR TOUCHDOWNS
Season
(Min. 12 TDs) 54.3%—Keith Gilliam, Randolph-Macon, 1984 (19 of 35)
Career
(Min. 20 TDs) 32.2%—R. J. Hoppe, Carroll (Wis.), 1993-96 (49 of 152)

MOST CONSECUTIVE PASSES CAUGHT FOR TOUCHDOWNS
9—Keith Gilliam, Randolph-Macon, 1984 (during four games)

Punting

MOST PUNTS
Game
17—Jerry Williams, Frostburg St. vs. Salisbury St., Sept. 30, 1978
Season
106—Bob Blake, Wis.-Superior, 1977 (3,404 yards)
Per-game record—11.0, Mark Roedelbronn, FDU-Madison, 1990 (99 in 9)
Career
263—Chris Gardner, Loras, 1987-90 (9,394 yards)

HIGHEST AVERAGE PER PUNT
Season
(Min. 40 punts) 45.5—Justin Shively, Anderson (Ind.), 1997 (55 for 2,502)
Career
(Min. 100 punts) 43.4—Jeff Shea, Cal Lutheran, 1994-97 (183 for 7,939)

Interceptions

MOST PASSES INTERCEPTED
Game
5—By eight players. Most recent: Chris Butts, Worcester St. vs. Fitchburg St., Oct. 10, 1992
Season
15—Mark Dorner, Juniata, 1987 (202 yards)
Also holds per-game record at 1.5 (15 in 10)
Career
29—Ralph Gebhardt, Rochester, 1973-75 (384 yards)

MOST CONSECUTIVE GAMES INTERCEPTING A PASS
Season
9—Brent Sands, Cornell College, 1992
Also holds career record at 9

MOST YARDS ON INTERCEPTION RETURNS
Game
164—Rick Conner, Western Md. vs. Dickinson, Oct. 15, 1983 (89-yard interception and 75-yard lateral after an interception)
Season
358—Rod Pesek, Whittier, 1987 (10 interceptions)
Career
443—Mark Dorner, Juniata, 1984-87 (26 interceptions)

HIGHEST AVERAGE GAIN PER INTERCEPTION
Season
(Min. 7 ints.) 38.4—Randy Ames, Hope, 1996 (7 for 269)
Career
(Min. 20 ints.) 20.4—Todd Schoelzel, Wis.-Oshkosh, 1985-88 (22 for 448)

MOST TOUCHDOWNS SCORED ON INTERCEPTIONS
Game
3—Krumie Mabry, Alfred vs. Denison, Sept. 4, 1993
Season
3—By eight players. Most recent: Krumie Mabry, Alfred, 1993 (7 interceptions)

Punt Returns

MOST PUNT RETURNS
Game
10—Ellis Wangelin, Wis.-River Falls vs. Wis.-Platteville, Oct. 12, 1985 (87 yards)
Season
48—Rick Bealer, Lycoming, 1989 (492 yards)
Career
126—Mike Caterbone, Frank. & Marsh., 1980-83 (1,141 yards)

MOST YARDS ON PUNT RETURNS
Game
212—Melvin Dillard, Ferrum vs. Newport News App., Oct. 13, 1990 (6 returns)
Season
688—Melvin Dillard, Ferrum, 1990 (25 returns)
Career
1,239—Charles Warren, Dickinson, 1993-96 (117 returns)

HIGHEST AVERAGE GAIN PER RETURN
Season
(Min. 1.2 rets. per game) 31.2—Chuck Downey, Stony Brook, 1986 (17 for 530)
Career
(Min. 1.2 rets. per game) 22.9—Keith Winston, Knoxville, 1986-87 (30 for 686)
(Min. 50 rets.) 20.3—Chuck Downey, Stony Brook, 1984-87 (59 for 1,198)

MOST TOUCHDOWNS SCORED ON PUNT RETURNS
Game
2—By nine players. Most recent: LaVant King, Ohio Northern vs. Otterbein, Oct. 7, 1995 (50 & 73 yards)
Season
4—Chris Warren, Ferrum, 1989 (18 returns); Keith Winston, Knoxville, 1986 (14 returns); Chuck Downey, Stony Brook, 1986 (17 returns); Matt Pekarske, Wis.-La Crosse, 1986 (37 returns)
Career
7—Chuck Downey, Stony Brook, 1984-87 (59 returns)

Kickoff Returns

MOST KICKOFF RETURNS
Game
11—Mason Tootell, Swarthmore vs. Johns Hopkins, Sept. 19, 1997 (197 yards)
Season
48—Mason Tootell, Swarthmore, 1997 (944 yards)
Career
104—Simeon Henderson, Elmhurst, 1991-94 (2,063 yards)

MOST YARDS ON KICKOFF RETURNS
Game
279—Chuck Downey, Stony Brook vs. Col. of New Jersey, Oct. 5, 1984 (7 returns)
Season
973—Dirk Blood, Ohio Northern, 1987 (42 returns)
Career
2,075—Ryan Kuttler, Claremont-M-S, 1993-96 (98 returns)

HIGHEST AVERAGE GAIN PER RETURN
Game
(Min. 3 rets.) 68.0—Victor Johnson, Elmhurst vs. Wheaton (Ill.), Sept. 15, 1979 (3 for 204)
Season
(Min. 1.2 rets. per game) 42.2—Brandon Steinheim, Wesley, 1994 (10 for 422)
Career
(Min. 1.2 rets. per game) 29.2—Daryl Brown, Tufts, 1974-76 (38 for 1,111)

MOST TOUCHDOWNS SCORED ON KICKOFF RETURNS
Game
2—By many players. Most recent: Homer Atkins, Muskingum vs. Mount Union, Oct. 26, 1996
Season
4—Byron Womack, Iona, 1989
Career
6—Byron Womack, Iona, 1988-91

Total Kick Returns

(Combined Punt and Kickoff Returns)

MOST YARDS ON KICK RETURNS
Game
354—Chuck Downey, Stony Brook vs. Col. of New Jersey, Oct. 5, 1984 (7 kickoff returns for 279 yards, 1 punt return for 75 yards)

GAINING 1,000 YARDS ON PUNT RETURNS AND 1,000 YARDS ON KICKOFF RETURNS
Career
Charles Warren, Dickinson, 1993-96 (1,239 on punt returns, 1,021 on kickoff returns); LaVant King, Ohio Northern, 1991, 93-95 (1,298 on kickoff returns, 1,074 on punt returns); Chuck Downey, Stony Brook, 1984-87 (1,281 on kickoff returns, 1,198 on punt returns)

MOST TOUCHDOWNS ON KICK RETURNS
Game
3—Chuck Downey, Stony Brook vs. Col. of New Jersey, Oct. 5, 1984 (2 kickoff returns 98 & 95 yards, 1 punt return 75 yards)
Season
5—Charles Jordan, Occidental, 1993 (2 punt returns, 3 kickoff returns); Chris Warren, Ferrum, 1989 (4 punt returns, 1 kickoff return); Chuck Downey, Stony Brook, 1986 (4 punt returns, 1 kickoff return)
Career
10—Chuck Downey, Stony Brook, 1984-87 (7 punt returns, 3 kickoff returns)

HIGHEST AVERAGE PER KICK RETURN (Min. 1.2 Returns Per Game Each)
Career
23.6—Chuck Downey, Stony Brook, 1984-87 (59 for 1,198 on punt returns, 46 for 1,281 on kickoff returns)

AVERAGING 20 YARDS EACH ON PUNT RETURNS AND KICKOFF RETURNS (Min. 1.2 Returns Per Game Each)
Career
Chuck Downey, Stony Brook, 1984-87 (20.3 on punt returns, 59 for 1,198; 27.8 on kickoff returns, 46 for 1,281)

All Runbacks

(Combined Interceptions, Punt Returns and Kickoff Returns)

MOST TOUCHDOWNS ON INTERCEPTIONS, PUNT RETURNS AND KICKOFF RETURNS
Season
6—Chuck Downey, Stony Brook, 1986 (4 punt returns, 1 kickoff return, 1 interception return)
Career
11—Chuck Downey, Stony Brook, 1984-87 (7 punt returns, 3 kickoff returns, 1 interception return)

Punts Blocked By

MOST PUNTS BLOCKED BY
Game
3—Jim Perryman, Millikin vs. Carroll (Wis.), Nov. 1, 1980
Season
9—Jim Perryman, Millikin, 1980
Career
13—Frank Lyle, Millsaps, 1979-82
Note: Daryl Hobson, Benedictine (Ill.) DB, blocked 9 punts during 17 games in 1987-88

All-Purpose Yards

(Yardage Gained From Rushing, Receiving and All Runbacks)

MOST PLAYS
Season
383—Mike Birosak, Dickinson, 1989 (380 rushes, 3 receptions)
Career
1,158—Eric Frees, Western Md., 1988-91 (1,059 rushes, 34 receptions, 58 kickoff returns, 7 punt returns)

MOST YARDS GAINED
Game
509—Carey Bender, Coe vs. Grinnell, Oct. 9, 1993 (417 rushing, 92 receiving)
Season
2,973—Dante Brown, Marietta, 1996 (2,385 rushing, 174 receiving, 46 punt returns, 368 kickoff returns; 338 plays)
Also holds per-game record at 297.3 (2,973 in 10)
Career
7,970—Carey Bender, Coe, 1991-94 (6,125 rushing, 1,751 receiving, 7 punt returns, 87 kickoff returns; 1,046 plays)
Per-game record—210.8, $Kirk Matthieu, Maine Maritime, 1989-93 (6,955 in 33)

$See page 6 for explanation.

HIGHEST AVERAGE GAIN PER PLAY
Season
(Min. 1,500 yards, 125 plays) 12.0—Darnell Morgan, Chapman, 1995 (1,602 in 134)
Career
(Min. 4,000 yards, 300 plays) 16.0—Chris Wiesehan, Wabash, 1990-93 (4,825 yards on 301)

Scoring

MOST POINTS SCORED
Game
48—Carey Bender, Coe vs. Beloit, Nov. 12, 1994
Season
194—Carey Bender, Coe, 1994 (32 TDs & 2 PATs)
Also holds per-game record at 19.4 (194 in 10)
Career
528—Carey Bender, Coe, 1991-94 (86 TDs & 12 PATs)
Per-game record—14.4, Ricky Gales, Simpson, 1988-89 (274 in 19)

TWO PLAYERS, SAME TEAM, EACH SCORING 100 POINTS OR MORE
Season
Andrew Notarfrancesco (130) & Jeff Clay (120), Catholic, 1997; Steve Harris (122) & R. J. Hoppe (106), Carroll (Wis.), 1994; Denis McDermott (126) & Manny Tsantes (102), St. John's (N.Y.), 1989; Theo Blanco (102) & Aatron Kenney (102), Wis.-Stevens Point, 1987

MOST TOUCHDOWNS SCORED
Season
32—Carey Bender, Coe, 1994
Also holds per-game record at 3.2 (32 in 10)
Career
86—Carey Bender, Coe, 1991-94
Also holds per-game record at 2.2 (86 in 39)

MOST GAMES SCORING A TOUCHDOWN
Career
36—Carey Bender, Coe, 1991-94 (39 games)

MOST GAMES SCORING TWO OR MORE TOUCHDOWNS
Career
24—Joe Dudek, Plymouth St., 1982-85 (41 games)

MOST EXTRA POINTS ATTEMPTED BY KICKING
Game
14—Kurt Christenson, Concordia-M'head vs. Macalester, Sept. 24, 1977 (made 13)
Season
70—Bill Andrea, Mount Union, 1997 (made 67); Greg Poulin, St. John's (Minn.), 1993 (made 63)
Career
194—Tim Mercer, Ferrum, 1987-90 (made 183)

MOST EXTRA POINTS MADE BY KICKING
Game
13—Kurt Christenson, Concordia-M'head vs. Macalester, Sept. 24, 1977 (attempted 14)
Season
67—Bill Andrea, Mount Union, 1997 (attempted 70)
Career
183—Tim Mercer, Ferrum, 1987-90 (attempted 194)

HIGHEST PERCENTAGE OF EXTRA POINTS MADE (Best Perfect Season)
100.0%—Mike Duvic, Dayton, 1989 (46 of 46)

HIGHEST PERCENTAGE OF EXTRA POINTS MADE
Career
(Min. 80 atts.) 100.0%—Mike Farrell, Adrian, 1983-85 (84 of 84)
(Min. 100 atts.) 98.5%—Rims Roof, Coe, 1982-85 (135 of 137)

MOST CONSECUTIVE EXTRA POINTS MADE BY KICKING
Game
13—Kurt Christenson, Concordia-M'head vs. Macalester, Sept. 24, 1977
Career
102—Rims Roof, Coe (from Sept. 24, 1983, through Nov. 9, 1985)

MOST POINTS SCORED BY KICKING
Game
20—Jim Hever, Rhodes vs. Millsaps, Sept. 22, 1984 (6 FGs, 2 PATs)
Season
102—Ken Edelman, Mount Union, 1990 (20 FGs, 42 PATs)
Also holds per-game record at 10.2 (102 in 10)
Career
274—Ken Edelman, Mount Union, 1987-90 (52 FGs, 118 PATs)
Also holds per-game record at 6.9 (274 in 40)

MOST SUCCESSFUL TWO-POINT PASS ATTEMPTS
Game
4—Rob Bristow, Pomona-Pitzer vs. Whittier, Oct. 19, 1985 (all in 4th quarter); Dave Geissler, Wis.-Stevens Point vs. Wis.-La Crosse, Sept. 21, 1985 (all in 4th quarter)
Season
10—Justin Peery, Westminster (Mo.), 1997 (14 attempts)
Career
14—Justin Peery, Westminster (Mo.), 1996-present (23 attempts)
Note: Rob Bristow, Pomona-Pitzer, 1983-86, holds record for highest percentage of successful two-point pass attempts (best perfect record) at 9 of 9

MOST TWO-POINT PASSES CAUGHT
Season
8—Scott Pingel, Westminster (Mo.), 1997

Defensive Extra Points

MOST DEFENSIVE EXTRA POINTS SCORED
Game
1—By many players
Season
2—Dan Fichter, Brockport St., 1990 (2 blocked kick returns)

LONGEST DEFENSIVE EXTRA POINT BLOCKED KICK RETURN
97—Keith Mottram (CB), Colorado Col. vs. Austin, Oct. 10, 1992 (scored)

LONGEST DEFENSIVE EXTRA POINT INTERCEPTION
100—By many players. Most recent: Kent Essner (DB), Westminster (Mo.) vs. Concordia-M'head, Sept. 13, 1997 (scored)

FIRST DEFENSIVE EXTRA POINT SCORED
Steve Nieves (DB), St. John's (N.Y.) vs. Iona, Sept. 10, 1988 (83-yard blocked kick return)

Field Goals

MOST FIELD GOALS MADE
Game
6—Jim Hever, Rhodes vs. Millsaps, Sept. 22, 1984 (30, 24, 42, 44, 46, 30 yards; attempted 8)
Season
20—Ken Edelman, Mount Union, 1990 (attempted 27)
Also holds per-game record at 2.0 (20 in 10)
Career
52—Ken Edelman, Mount Union, 1987-90 (attempted 71)
Also holds per-game record *(Min. 30)* at 1.3 (52 in 40)

MOST FIELD GOALS ATTEMPTED
Game
8—Jim Hever, Rhodes vs. Millsaps, Sept. 22, 1984 (made 6)
Season
29—Scott Ryerson, Central Fla., 1981 (made 18)
Career
71—Ken Edelman, Mount Union, 1987-90 (made 52); Doug Hart, Grove City, 1985-88 (made 40)

HIGHEST PERCENTAGE OF FIELD GOALS MADE
Season
(Min. 15 atts.) 93.8%—Steve Graeca, John Carroll, 1988 (15 of 16)
Career
(Min. 50 atts.) *77.6%—Mike Duvic, Dayton, 1986-89 (38 of 49)
**Declared champion; with one more attempt (making 50), failed, still would have highest percentage (76.0).*

LONGEST FIELD GOAL MADE
62—Dom Antonini, Rowan vs. Salisbury St., Sept. 18, 1976

MOST FIELD GOALS ATTEMPTED WITHOUT SUCCESS
Season
11—Scott Perry, Moravian, 1986

Team Records

Single Game—Offense

Total Offense

MOST PLAYS
112—Gust. Adolphus vs. Bethel (Minn.), Nov. 2, 1985 (65 passes, 47 rushes; 493 yards)

MOST PLAYS, BOTH TEAMS
214—Gust. Adolphus (112) & Bethel (Minn.) (102), Nov. 2, 1985 (143 passes, 71 rushes; 930 yards)

MOST YARDS GAINED
788—Simpson vs. William Penn, Sept. 24, 1989

MOST YARDS GAINED, BOTH TEAMS
1,395—Occidental (753) & Claremont-M-S (642), Oct. 30, 1993 (136 plays)

MOST TOUCHDOWNS SCORED BY RUSHING AND PASSING
14—Concordia-M'head vs. Macalester, Sept. 24, 1977 (12 rushing, 2 passing)

Rushing

MOST RUSHES
92—Wis.-River Falls vs. Wis.-Platteville, Oct. 21, 1989 (464 yards)

MOST YARDS GAINED RUSHING
642—Wis.-River Falls vs. Wis.-Superior, Oct. 14, 1989 (88 rushes)

MOST TOUCHDOWNS SCORED BY RUSHING
12—Concordia-M'head vs. Macalester, Sept. 24, 1977

Passing

MOST PASSES ATTEMPTED
81—Principia vs. Blackburn, Oct. 10, 1992 (completed 48)

MOST PASSES ATTEMPTED, BOTH TEAMS
143—Bethel (Minn.) (78) & Gust. Adolphus (65), Nov. 2, 1985 (completed 65)

MOST PASSES ATTEMPTED WITHOUT AN INTERCEPTION
68—Western Md. vs. Frank. & Marsh., Oct. 23, 1994 (completed 38)

MOST PASSES COMPLETED
50—Hofstra vs. Fordham, Oct. 19, 1991 (attempted 69)

MOST PASSES COMPLETED, BOTH TEAMS
72—Wis.-Superior (41) & Wis.-Stevens Point (31), Oct. 17, 1981 (attempted 131)

HIGHEST PERCENTAGE OF PASSES COMPLETED (Min. 35 Attempts)
78.9%—Wheaton (Ill.) vs. North Park, Oct. 8, 1983 (30 of 38)

MOST YARDS GAINED
643—Westminster (Mo.) vs. Bethel (Tenn.), Nov. 8, 1997

MOST YARDS GAINED, BOTH TEAMS
1,100—St. Thomas (Minn.) (602) & Bethel (Minn.) (498), Nov. 13, 1993 (attempted 113, completed 69)

MOST TOUCHDOWN PASSES
8—Mass.-Boston vs. Framingham St., Nov. 14, 1992; Wis.-Stevens Point vs. Wis.-Superior, Nov. 4, 1989

MOST TOUCHDOWN PASSES, BOTH TEAMS
12—St. Thomas (Minn.) (6) & Bethel (Minn.) (6), Nov. 13, 1993

Punt Returns

MOST TOUCHDOWNS SCORED ON PUNT RETURNS
3—Emory & Henry vs. Tenn. Wesleyan, Sept. 27, 1986

Kickoff Returns

MOST YARDS ON KICKOFF RETURNS
283—Oberlin vs. Wittenberg, Oct. 30, 1993

Scoring

MOST POINTS SCORED
97—Concordia-M'head vs. Macalester, Sept. 24, 1977

MOST POINTS SCORED, BOTH TEAMS
113—Grinnell (64) vs. Illinois Col. (49), Nov. 1, 1997

MOST POINTS SCORED BY A LOSING TEAM
54—Carleton vs. St. Thomas (Minn.) (55), Sept. 28, 1996

MOST POINTS OVERCOME TO WIN A GAME
33—Lakeland vs. Concordia (Wis.), Oct. 11, 1997 (trailed 33-0 with 7:53 left in 3rd quarter; won 41-33; Salisbury St. vs. Randolph-Macon, Sept. 15, 1984 (trailed 33-0 with 14:18 left in 2nd quarter; won 34-33); Wis.-Platteville vs. Wis.-Eau Claire, Nov. 8, 1980 (trailed 33-0 with 7:00 left in 2nd quarter; won 52-43)

MOST POINTS SCORED IN A BRIEF PERIOD OF TIME
21 in 33 seconds—Mount Union vs. Defiance, Sept. 14, 1996 (turned 13-3 game into 34-3 in 2nd quarter, won 62-10)
32 in 4:04—Wis.-Stevens Point vs. Wis.-La Crosse, Sept. 21, 1985 (trailed 27-3 and 35-11 in 4th quarter; ended in 35-35 tie)

MOST POINTS SCORED IN FIRST VARSITY GAME
63—Bentley vs. Brooklyn (26), Sept. 24, 1988

MOST TOUCHDOWNS SCORED
14—Concordia-M'head vs. Macalester, Sept. 24, 1977

MOST PLAYERS SCORING TOUCHDOWNS
10—Johns Hopkins vs. Swarthmore, Sept. 19, 1997

MOST EXTRA POINTS MADE BY KICKING
13—Concordia-M'head vs. Macalester, Sept. 24, 1977 (attempted 14)

MOST FIELD GOALS MADE
6—Rhodes vs. Millsaps, Sept. 22, 1984 (attempted 8)

MOST FIELD GOALS ATTEMPTED
8—Rhodes vs. Millsaps, Sept. 22, 1984 (made 6)

MOST DEFENSIVE EXTRA-POINT RETURNS SCORED
1—By many teams

MOST DEFENSIVE EXTRA-POINT OPPORTUNITIES
2—Frank. & Marsh. vs. Johns Hopkins, Nov. 7, 1992 (1 interception & 1 kick return; none scored); Wis.-River Falls vs. Wis.-La Crosse, Nov. 11, 1989 (2 kick returns; 1 scored); Wis.-Platteville vs. Wis.-Oshkosh, Oct. 15, 1988 (2 interceptions; none scored); Buffalo St. vs. Brockport St., Oct. 1, 1988 (1 interception & 1 kick return; none scored)

Turnovers

(Most Times Losing the Ball on Interceptions and Fumbles)

MOST TURNOVERS
13—St. Olaf vs. St. Thomas (Minn.), Oct. 12, 1985 (10 interceptions, 3 fumbles); Mercyhurst vs. Buffalo St., Oct. 23, 1982 (12 fumbles, 1 interception); Albany (N.Y.) vs. Rochester Inst., Oct. 1, 1977

MOST TURNOVERS, BOTH TEAMS
24—Albany (N.Y.) (13) & Rochester Inst. (11), Oct. 1, 1977

First Downs

MOST TOTAL FIRST DOWNS
40—Upper Iowa vs. Loras, Nov. 7, 1992 (19 rushing, 17 passing, 4 by penalty)

Penalties

MOST PENALTIES AGAINST
25—Norwich vs. Coast Guard, Sept. 29, 1985 (192 yards)

SINGLE GAME—Defense

Total Defense

FEWEST YARDS ALLOWED
Minus 52—Worcester St. vs. Maine Maritime, Sept. 28, 1996 (-71 rushing, 19 passing)

Rushing Defense

FEWEST RUSHES ALLOWED
9—Wis.-La Crosse vs. Huron, Sept. 21, 1996 (-63 yards)

FEWEST YARDS ALLOWED
Minus 112—Coast Guard vs. Wesleyan (Conn.), Oct. 7, 1989 (23 plays)

Pass Defense

FEWEST ATTEMPTS ALLOWED
0—By many teams. Most recent: Concordia-M'head vs. Macalester, Oct. 12, 1991

FEWEST COMPLETIONS ALLOWED
0—By many teams. Most recent: Hartwick vs. Rensselaer, Oct. 26, 1996 (8 attempts)

FEWEST YARDS ALLOWED
Minus 6—Central (Iowa) vs. Simpson, Oct. 19, 1985 (1 completion)

MOST PASSES INTERCEPTED BY
10—St. Thomas (Minn.) vs. St. Olaf, Oct. 12, 1985 (91 yards; 50 attempts)

MOST PLAYERS INTERCEPTING A PASS
8—Samford vs. Anderson, Oct. 11, 1986 (8 interceptions in the game)

Punts Blocked By

MOST OPPONENT'S PUNTS BLOCKED BY
4—Benedictine (Ill.) vs. Olivet Nazarene, Oct. 22, & vs. Aurora, Oct. 29, 1988 (consecutive games, resulting in 4 TDs and 1 safety). Blocked 9 punts in three consecutive games, vs. MacMurray, Oct. 15, Olivet Nazarene and Aurora, resulting in 4 TDs and 2 safeties

First Downs

FEWEST FIRST DOWNS ALLOWED
0—Case Reserve vs. Wooster, Sept. 21, 1985

SEASON—Offense

Total Offense

MOST YARDS GAINED PER GAME
549.7—St. John's (Minn.), 1993 (5,497 in 10)

HIGHEST AVERAGE GAIN PER PLAY
8.1—Ferrum, 1990 (534 for 4,350)

MOST PLAYS PER GAME
85.6—Hampden-Sydney, 1978 (856 in 10)

MOST TOUCHDOWNS SCORED PER GAME BY RUSHING AND PASSING
8.4—St. John's (Minn.), 1993 (84 in 10; 44 rushing, 40 passing)

Rushing

MOST YARDS GAINED PER GAME
434.7—Ferrum, 1990 (3,912 in 9)

HIGHEST AVERAGE GAIN PER RUSH
8.3—Ferrum, 1990 (470 for 3,912)

MOST RUSHES PER GAME
71.4—Wis.-River Falls, 1988 (714 in 10)

MOST TOUCHDOWNS SCORED PER GAME BY RUSHING
5.4—Ferrum, 1990 (49 in 9)

Passing

MOST YARDS GAINED PER GAME
403.5—Hofstra, 1991 (4,035 in 10)

FEWEST YARDS GAINED PER GAME
18.4—Wis.-River Falls, 1983 (184 in 10)

HIGHEST AVERAGE GAIN PER ATTEMPT
(Min. 250 atts.) 11.1—St. John's (Minn.), 1993 (299 for 3,308)
(Min. 350 atts.) 8.7—Wheaton (Ill.), 1983 (393 for 3,424)

HIGHEST AVERAGE GAIN PER COMPLETION (Min. 200 Completions)
15.4—Wis.-Stevens Point, 1987 (249 for 3,836)

MOST PASSES ATTEMPTED PER GAME
58.5—Hofstra, 1991 (585 in 10)

FEWEST PASSES ATTEMPTED PER GAME
4.0—Wis.-River Falls, 1988 (40 in 10)

MOST PASSES COMPLETED PER GAME
34.4—Hofstra, 1991 (344 in 10)

FEWEST PASSES COMPLETED PER GAME
1.3—Wis.-River Falls, 1983 (13 in 10)

HIGHEST PERCENTAGE COMPLETED (Min. 200 Attempts)
70.7%—Mount Union, 1993 (244 of 345)

LOWEST PERCENTAGE OF PASSES HAD INTERCEPTED (Min. 150 Attempts)
0.7%—San Diego, 1990 (1 of 153)

MOST TOUCHDOWN PASSES PER GAME
4.8—Mount Union, 1997 (48 in 10)

HIGHEST PASSING EFFICIENCY RATING POINTS
(Min. 15 atts. per game) 211.3—Eureka, 1994 (205 attempts, 142 completions, 8 interceptions, 2,478 yards, 30 TDs)
(Min. 300 atts.) 202.8—Mount Union, 1997 (311 attempts, 212 completions, 3 interceptions, 3,171 yards, 48 TDs)

Punting

MOST PUNTS PER GAME
11.0—FDU-Madison, 1990 (99 in 9)

FEWEST PUNTS PER GAME
2.2—Mount Union, 1997 (22 in 10)

HIGHEST PUNTING AVERAGE
45.0—Anderson (Ind.), 1997 (59 for 2,655)

Scoring

MOST POINTS PER GAME
61.5—St. John's (Minn.), 1993 (615 in 10)

MOST TOUCHDOWNS PER GAME
8.9—St. John's (Minn.), 1993 (89 in 10)

BEST PERFECT RECORD ON EXTRA POINTS MADE BY KICKING
49 of 49—Dayton, 1989

MOST TWO-POINT ATTEMPTS PER GAME
2.8—Martin Luther, 1990 (17 in 6)

MOST FIELD GOALS MADE PER GAME
2.0—Mount Union, 1990 (20 in 10)

HIGHEST SCORING MARGIN
51.8—St. John's (Minn.), 1993 (averaged 61.5 and allowed 9.7 in 10 games)

MOST TOUCHDOWNS ON BLOCKED PUNT RETURNS
5—Widener, 1990

MOST SAFETIES
4—Upper Iowa, 1995; Alfred, 1992; Central (Iowa), 1992; Westfield St., 1992; Wis.-Stevens Point, 1990

MOST DEFENSIVE EXTRA-POINT RETURNS SCORED
2—Eureka, 1991; Brockport St., 1990

MOST DEFENSIVE EXTRA POINT BLOCKED KICK RETURNS
3—Assumption, 1992 (1 scored); Ohio Wesleyan, 1991 (0 scored); Brockport St., 1990 (2 scored)

MOST DEFENSIVE EXTRA POINT INTERCEPTIONS
2—Swarthmore, 1989 (1 scored); Wis.-Platteville, 1988 (none scored)

Penalties

MOST PENALTIES PER GAME
13.3—Kean, 1990 (133 in 10, 1,155 yards)

MOST YARDS PENALIZED PER GAME
121.9—Hofstra, 1991 (1,219 in 10, 124 penalties)

Turnovers (Giveaways)

(Passes Had Intercepted and Fumbles Lost, From 1985)

FEWEST TURNOVERS
6—Mount Union, 1995 (4 interceptions, 2 fumbles lost)
Also holds per-game record at 0.6 (6 in 10)

MOST TURNOVERS
52—William Penn, 1985 (19 interceptions, 33 fumbles lost)
Also holds per-game record at 5.2 (52 in 10)

SEASON—Defense

Total Defense

FEWEST YARDS ALLOWED PER GAME
94.0—Knoxville, 1977 (940 in 10)

LOWEST AVERAGE YARDS ALLOWED PER PLAY
(Min. 500 plays) 1.8—Bowie St., 1978 (576 for 1,011)
(Min. 650 plays) 2.0—Plymouth St., 1987 (733 for 1,488)

FEWEST RUSHING AND PASSING TOUCHDOWNS ALLOWED PER GAME
0.3—Montclair St., 1984 (3 in 10)

Rushing Defense

FEWEST YARDS ALLOWED PER GAME
Minus 2.3—Knoxville, 1977 (-23 in 10 games)

LOWEST AVERAGE YARDS ALLOWED PER RUSH
(Min. 275 rushes) Minus 0.1—Knoxville, 1977 (333 for -23)
(Min. 400 rushes) 1.0—Lycoming, 1976 (400 for 399)

FEWEST TOUCHDOWNS BY RUSHING ALLOWED
0—Union (N.Y.), 1983 (9 games); New Haven, 1978 (9 games)

Pass Defense

FEWEST YARDS ALLOWED PER GAME
48.5—Mass. Maritime, 1976 (388 in 8)

FEWEST YARDS ALLOWED PER ATTEMPT
(Min. 150 atts.) 2.9—Plymouth St., 1982 (170 for 488)
(Min. 225 atts.) 3.3—Plymouth St., 1987 (281 for 919)

FEWEST YARDS ALLOWED PER COMPLETION (Min. 100 Completions)
8.6—Baldwin-Wallace, 1990 (151 for 1,305)

LOWEST COMPLETION PERCENTAGE ALLOWED
(Min. 150 atts.) 24.3%—Doane, 1973 (41 of 169)
(Min. 250 atts.) 33.5%—Plymouth St., 1987 (94 of 281)

HIGHEST PERCENTAGE INTERCEPTED BY (Min. 200 Attempts)
15.2%—Rose-Hulman, 1977 (32 of 210)

MOST PASSES INTERCEPTED BY
35—Plymouth St., 1987 (12 games, 281 attempts against, 348 yards returned)
Per-game record—3.4, Montclair St., 1981 (34 in 10)

FEWEST PASSES INTERCEPTED BY (Min. 125 Attempts)
1—Bates, 1987 (134 attempts against in 8 games, 0 yards returned)

MOST YARDS ON INTERCEPTION RETURNS
576—Emory & Henry, 1987 (31 interceptions)

MOST TOUCHDOWNS SCORED ON INTERCEPTIONS
6—Coe, 1992 (22 interceptions, 272 passes against); Augustana (Ill.), 1987 (23 interceptions, 229 passes against)

FEWEST TOUCHDOWN PASSES ALLOWED
0—By many teams. Most recent: Dayton, 1980 (11 games)

LOWEST PASSING EFFICIENCY RATING POINTS ALLOWED OPPONENTS
(Min. 150 atts.) 27.8—Plymouth St., 1982 (allowed 170 attempts, 53 completions, 488 yards, 1 TD & intercepted 25 passes)
(Min. 275 atts.) 43.1—Plymouth St., 1987 (allowed 281 attempts, 94 completions, 919 yards, 6 TDs & intercepted 35 passes)

Punting

MOST OPPONENT'S PUNTS BLOCKED BY
11—Benedictine (Ill.) 1987 (78 punts against in 10 games). Blocked 17 punts in 18 games during 1987-88, resulting in 5 TDs and 3 safeties

Scoring

FEWEST POINTS ALLOWED PER GAME
3.4—Millsaps, 1980 (31 in 9)

FEWEST TOUCHDOWNS ALLOWED
4—Baldwin-Wallace, 1981 (10 games); Millsaps, 1980 (9 games); Bentley, 1990 (8 games)

MOST SHUTOUTS
6—Cortland St., 1989; Plymouth St., 1982 (consecutive)

MOST CONSECUTIVE SHUTOUTS
6—Plymouth St., 1982

MOST POINTS ALLOWED PER GAME
59.1—Macalester, 1977 (532 in 9; 76 TDs, 64 PATs, 4 FGs)

MOST DEFENSIVE EXTRA-POINT ATTEMPTS BY OPPONENTS
5—Norwich, 1992 (4 blocked kick returns, 1 interception; none scored)

Turnovers (Takeaways)

(Opponent's Passes Intercepted and Fumbles Recovered, From 1985)

HIGHEST MARGIN OF TURNOVERS PER GAME OVER OPPONENTS
2.9—Macalester, 1986 (29 in 10; 29 giveaways vs. 58 takeaways)

MOST TAKEAWAYS
58—Macalester, 1986 (28 interceptions, 30 fumbles gained)
Also holds per-game record at 5.8 (58 in 10)

Additional Records

MOST CONSECUTIVE VICTORIES
37—Augustana (Ill.) (from Sept. 17, 1983, through 1985 Division III playoffs; ended with 0-0 tie vs. Elmhurst, Sept. 13, 1986)

MOST CONSECUTIVE REGULAR-SEASON VICTORIES
49—Augustana (Ill.) (from Oct. 25, 1980, through 1985; ended with 0-0 tie vs. Elmhurst, Sept. 13, 1986)

MOST CONSECUTIVE GAMES WITHOUT DEFEAT
60—Augustana (Ill.), (from Sept. 17, 1983, through Nov. 22, 1987; ended with 38-36 loss to Dayton, Nov. 29, 1987, in Division III playoffs and included one tie)

MOST CONSECUTIVE REGULAR-SEASON GAMES WITHOUT DEFEAT
70—Augustana (Ill.) (from Oct. 25, 1980, through Oct. 1, 1988; ended with 24-21 loss to Carroll [Wis.], Oct. 8, 1988)

MOST CONSECUTIVE WINNING SEASONS
37—Central (Iowa) (from 1961 to present)

MOST CONSECUTIVE GAMES WITHOUT BEING SHUT OUT
224—Carnegie Mellon (from Sept. 30, 1972, through Nov. 4, 1995; ended with 3-0 loss to Case Reserve, Nov. 11, 1995)

MOST CONSECUTIVE LOSSES
50—Macalester (from Oct. 5, 1974, to Nov. 10, 1979; ended with 17-14 win over Mount Senario, Sept. 6, 1980)

MOST CONSECUTIVE GAMES WITHOUT A TIE
371—Widener (from Oct. 29, 1949, to Nov. 11, 1989; ended with 14-14 tie against Gettysburg, Sept. 8, 1990)

HIGHEST-SCORING TIE GAME
50-50—Catholic & Randolph-Macon, Sept. 16, 1995

LAST SCORELESS GAME
Sept. 10, 1988—Wis.-Oshkosh & Valparaiso

MOST CONSECUTIVE QUARTERS WITHOUT YIELDING A TOUCHDOWN BY RUSHING
61—Augustana (Ill.) (in 16 games from Sept. 27, 1986, to Nov. 7, 1987; 77 including four 1986 Division III playoff games); Union (N.Y.) (in 16 games from Oct. 23, 1982, to Sept. 29, 1984)

MOST CONSECUTIVE QUARTERS WITHOUT YIELDING A TOUCHDOWN BY PASSING
44—Swarthmore (from Oct. 31, 1981, to Nov. 13, 1982)

MOST IMPROVED WON-LOST RECORD (Including Postseason Games)
7 games—Catholic, 1994 (8-2-0) from 1993 (1-9-0); Susquehanna, 1986 (11-1-0) from 1985 (3-7-0); Maryville (Tenn.), 1976 (7-2-0) from 1975 (0-9-0)

Annual Champions, All-Time Leaders

Total Offense

CAREER YARDS PER GAME

(Minimum 5,000 Yards)

Player, Team	Years	G	Plays	Yards	Yd. PG
Terry Peebles, Hanover	1992-95	23	1,140	7,672	*333.6
Kirk Baumgartner, Wis.-Stevens Point	1986-89	41	*2,007	*12,767	311.4
Willie Reyna, La Verne	1991-92	17	551	4,996	293.9
Keith Bishop, Ill. Wesleyan/ Wheaton (Ill.)	1981, 83-85	31	1,467	9,052	292.0
Mark Novara, Lakeland	1994-97	38	1,653	10,801	284.2
Jordan Poznick, Principia	1990-93	32	1,757	8,983	280.7
John Rooney, Ill. Wesleyan	1982-84	27	1,260	7,393	273.8
Tim Peterson, Wis.-Stout	1986-89	36	1,558	9,701	269.5
Gregg McDonald, Kalamazoo	1994-96	27	1,155	7,273	269.4
Bill Borchert, Mount Union	1994-97	40	1,274	10,639	266.0
Jim Ballard, Wilmington (Ohio)/ Mount Union	1990, 91-93	40	1,328	10,545	263.6
Kevin Ricca, Catholic	1994-97	38	1,533	9,982	262.7
Robert Farra, Claremont-M-S	1978-79	16	690	4,179	261.2
Chris Ings, Wabash	1992-95	37	1,532	9,608	259.7
Jack Ramirez, Pomona-Pitzer	1994-97	34	1,328	8,721	256.5
Eric Noble, Wilmington (Ohio)	1992-95	38	1,513	9,731	256.0
Brian Van Deusen, Western Md.	1992-95	30	1,415	7,172	239.1
Kurt Ramler, St. John's (Minn.)	1994-96	28	958	6,639	237.1
Lon Erickson, Ill. Wesleyan	1993-96	29	1,001	6,753	232.9
Dennis Bogacz, Wis.-Oshkosh/ Wis.-Whitewater	1988-89, 90-91	38	1,394	8,850	232.9
John Clark, Wis.-Eau Claire	1987-90	38	1,354	8,838	232.6
Ed Smith, Benedictine (Ill.)	1991-93	29	892	6,599	227.6
Tom Stallings, St. Thomas (Minn.)	1990-93	24	819	5,460	227.5
Mark Peterson, Neb. Wesleyan	1982-84	28	1,151	6,367	227.4
Scott Scesney, St. John's (N.Y.)	1986-89	32	1,048	7,196	224.9

*Record.

SEASON YARDS PER GAME

Player, Team	Year	G	Plays	Yards	Yd. PG
Terry Peebles, Hanover	†1995	10	572	*3,981	*398.1
Keith Bishop, Wheaton (Ill.)	†1983	9	421	3,193	354.8
Kirk Baumgartner, Wis.-Stevens Point	†1989	10	530	3,540	354.0
Bill Nietzke, Alma	†1996	9	468	3,185	353.9
John Furmaniak, Eureka	1995	10	414	3,503	350.3
Gregg McDonald, Kalamazoo	1996	9	415	3,101	344.6
Kirk Baumgartner, Wis.-Stevens Point	†1988	11	604	3,790	344.5
Terry Peebles, Hanover	†1994	10	520	3,441	344.1
Jordan Poznick, Principia	†1992	8	519	2,747	343.4
Eric Noble, Wilmington (Ohio)	1994	9	460	3,072	341.3
Jordan Poznick, Principia	†1993	8	488	2,705	338.1
Kirk Baumgartner, Wis.-Stevens Point	1987	11	561	3,712	337.5
Jim Ballard, Mount Union	1993	10	372	3,371	337.1
Steve Austin, Mass.-Boston	1992	9	466	3,003	333.7
Willie Reyna, La Verne	†1991	8	220	2,633	329.1
Keith Bishop, Wheaton (Ill.)	†1985	9	521	2,951	327.9
Mark Novara, Lakeland	1996	10	454	3,250	325.0
Tim Peterson, Wis.-Stout	1989	10	*614	3,244	324.4
Matt Bunyan, Wis.-Stout	†1997	10	422	3,216	321.6
Chris Stormer, Hanover	1997	8	403	2,563	320.4
Kevin Ricca, Catholic	1997	10	392	3,200	320.0
John Shipp, Claremont-M-S	1994	9	442	2,871	319.0
Jon Nielsen, Claremont-M-S	1995	9	405	2,848	316.4
Tom Stallings, St. Thomas (Minn.)	1993	10	438	3,158	315.8
Scott Isphording, Hanover	1992	10	484	3,150	315.0

*Record. †National champion.

CAREER YARDS

Player, Team	Years	Plays	Yards
Kirk Baumgartner, Wis.-Stevens Point	1986-89	*2,007	*12,767
Mark Novara, Lakeland	1994-97	1,653	10,801
Bill Borchert, Mount Union	1994-97	1,274	10,639
Jim Ballard, Wilmington (Ohio)/Mount Union	1990, 91-93	1,328	10,545
Kevin Ricca, Catholic	1994-97	1,533	9,982
Eric Noble, Wilmington (Ohio)	1992-95	1,513	9,731
Tim Peterson, Wis.-Stout	1986-89	1,558	9,701
Chris Ings, Wabash	1992-95	1,532	9,608
Keith Bishop, Ill. Wesleyan/Wheaton (Ill.)	1981, 83-85	1,467	9,052
Dave Geissler, Wis.-Stevens Point	1982-85	1,695	8,990
Jordan Poznick, Principia	1990-93	1,757	8,983
Dennis Bogacz, Wis.-Oshkosh/Wis.-Whitewater	1988-89, 90-91	1,394	8,850
John Clark, Wis.-Eau Claire	1987-90	1,354	8,838
Jack Ramirez, Pomona-Pitzer	1994-97	1,328	8,721
Matt Jozokos, Plymouth St.	1987-90	1,234	8,188
Darryl Kosut, William Penn	1983-86	1,583	7,817
Mark Novara, Lakeland#	1994-96	1,302	7,733
Luke Hanks, Otterbein	1990-93	1,503	7,686
Terry Peebles, Hanover	1992-95	1,140	7,672
Bill Borchert, Mount Union#	1994-96	961	7,590
Chris Esterley, St. Thomas (Minn.)	1993-96	1,182	7,549
Steve Osterberger, Drake	1987-90	1,263	7,520
David Parker, Bishop	1981-84	1,257	7,516
John Koz, Baldwin-Wallace	1990-93	1,171	7,511
Mark Thompson, Earlham	1993-96	1,129	7,474

**Record. #Active player.*

SEASON YARDS

Player, Team	Year	G	Plays	Yards
Terry Peebles, Hanover	†1995	10	572	*3,981
Kirk Baumgartner, Wis.-Stevens Point	†1988	11	604	3,790
Kirk Baumgartner, Wis.-Stevens Point	1987	11	561	3,712
Kirk Baumgartner, Wis.-Stevens Point	†1989	10	530	3,540
John Furmaniak, Eureka	1995	10	414	3,503
Terry Peebles, Hanover	†1994	10	520	3,441
Jim Ballard, Mount Union	1993	10	372	3,371
Mark Novara, Lakeland	†1996	10	454	3,250
Tim Peterson, Wis.-Stout	1989	10	*614	3,244
Matt Bunyan, Wis.-Stout	†1997	10	422	3,216
Kevin Ricca, Catholic	1997	10	392	3,200
Keith Bishop, Wheaton (Ill.)	†1983	9	421	3,193
Bill Nietzke, Alma	1996	9	468	3,185
Tom Stallings, St. Thomas (Minn.)	1993	10	438	3,158
Scott Isphording, Hanover	1992	10	484	3,150
Sidney Chappell, Randolph-Macon	1997	10	463	3,149
Sean Hoolihan, Wis.-Eau Claire	1997	10	369	3,148
Gregg McDonald, Kalamazoo	1996	9	415	3,101
Eric Noble, Wilmington (Ohio)	1994	9	460	3,072
Mark Novara, Lakeland	1997	10	469	3,064
Tim Peterson, Wis.-Stout	1987	11	393	3,052
Bill Borchert, Mount Union	1997	10	313	3,049
Steve Austin, Mass.-Boston	1992	9	466	3,003
Derrin Lamker, Augsburg	1997	10	462	2,976
Keith Bishop, Wheaton (Ill.)	†1985	9	521	2,951

**Record. †National champion.*

SINGLE-GAME YARDS

Yds.	Player, Team (Opponent)	Date
596	John Love, North Park (Elmhurst)	Oct. 13, 1990
590	Tom Stallings, St. Thomas (Minn.) (Bethel [Minn.])	Nov. 13, 1993
577	Eric Noble, Wilmington (Ohio) (Urbana)	Nov. 5, 1994
567	Jim Newland, Heidelberg (Ohio Northern)	Nov. 12, 1994
564	Tim Lynch, Hofstra (Fordham)	Oct. 19, 1991
555	Bill Nietzke, Alma (Hope)	Oct. 26, 1996
545	Terry Peebles, Hanover (Franklin)	Nov. 12, 1994
539	Justin Peery, Westminster (Mo.) (Bethel [Tenn.])	Nov. 8, 1997
538	Jordan Poznick, Principia (Blackburn)	Oct. 10, 1992
534	Cliff Scott, Buffalo (New Haven)	Sept. 12, 1992
528	Scott Burre, Capital (Heidelberg)	Sept. 30, 1995
528	Steve Austin, Mass.-Boston (Mass. Maritime)	Oct. 10, 1992
527	Rob Shippy, Concordia (Ill.) (Concordia [Wis.])	Oct. 5, 1985
525	Chris Stormer, Hanover (Manchester)	Oct. 4, 1997
515	Seamus Crotty, Hamilton (Middlebury)	Oct. 27, 1984
513	Terry Peebles, Hanover (DePauw)	Oct. 7, 1995
512	Bob Monroe, Knox (Cornell College)	Oct. 11, 1986
511	Kirk Baumgartner, Wis.-Stevens Point (Wis.-Superior)	Nov. 4, 1989
511	Kirk Baumgartner, Wis.-Stevens Point (Wis.-Stout)	Oct. 24, 1987
509	Michael Ferraro, LIU-C. W. Post (Alfred)	Nov. 14, 1992
509	Craig Solomon, Rhodes (Rose-Hulman)	Nov. 11, 1978

ANNUAL CHAMPIONS

Year	Player, Team	Class	G	Plays	Yards	Avg.
1973	Bob Dulich, San Diego	Jr.	11	340	2,543	231.2
1974	Larry Cenotto, Pomona-Pitzer	Sr.	9	436	2,127	236.3
1975	Ricky Haygood, Millsaps	Jr.	9	332	2,176	241.8
1976	Rollie Wiebers, Buena Vista	So.	9	353	2,198	244.2
1977	Tom Hamilton, Occidental	Sr.	9	358	2,050	227.8
1978	Robert Farra, Claremont-M-S	Jr.	9	427	2,685	298.3
1979	Clay Sampson, Denison	Jr.	9	412	2,255	250.6
1980	Jeff Beer, Bethany (W.Va.)	Sr.	9	372	2,331	259.0
1981	Brion Demski, Wis.-Stevens Point	Sr.	10	503	2,895	289.5
1982	Dave McCarrell, Wheaton (Ill.)	Sr.	9	387	2,503	278.1
1983	Keith Bishop, Wheaton (Ill.)	So.	9	421	3,193	354.8
1984	Keith Bishop, Wheaton (Ill.)	Jr.	9	479	2,777	308.6
1985	Keith Bishop, Wheaton (Ill.)	Sr.	9	521	2,951	327.9
1986	Larry Barretta, Lycoming	Sr.	10	453	2,875	287.5
1987	Todde Greenough, Willamette	Jr.	9	436	2,567	285.2
1988	Kirk Baumgartner, Wis.-Stevens Point	Jr.	11	604	3,790	344.5
1989	Kirk Baumgartner, Wis.-Stevens Point	Sr.	10	530	3,540	354.0
1990	Rhory Moss, Hofstra	Jr.	9	372	2,775	308.3
1991	Willie Reyna, La Verne	Jr.	8	220	2,633	329.1
1992	Jordan Poznick, Principia	Jr.	8	519	2,747	343.4
1993	Jordan Poznick, Principia	Sr.	8	488	2,705	338.1
1994	Terry Peebles, Hanover	Jr.	10	520	3,441	344.1
1995	Terry Peebles, Hanover	Sr.	10	572	*3,981	*398.1
1996	Bill Nietzke, Alma	Sr.	9	468	3,185	353.9
1997	Matt Bunyan, Wis.-Stout	Jr.	10	422	3,216	321.6

**Record.*

Rushing

CAREER YARDS PER GAME

(Minimum 2,200 Yards)

Player, Team	Years	G	Plays	Yards	Yd. PG
Ricky Gales, Simpson	1988-89	19	530	3,326	*175.1
Rob Marchitello, Maine Maritime	1993-95	26	879	4,300	165.4
Kelvin Gladney, Millsaps	1993-94	19	510	3,085	162.4
Carey Bender, Coe	1991-94	39	926	*6,125	157.1
Brad Olson, Lawrence	1994-97	34	792	5,325	156.6
Kirk Matthieu, Maine Maritime	$1989-93	33	964	5,107	154.8
Terry Underwood, Wagner	1985-88	33	742	5,010	151.8
Anthony Russo, St. John's (N.Y.)	1990-92	30	841	4,276	142.5
Joe Dudek, Plymouth St.	1982-85	41	785	5,570	135.9
Mark Kacmarynski, Central (Iowa)	$1992-96	41	854	5,434	132.5
Rich Kowalski, Hobart	1973-75	27	762	3,574	132.4
Eric Frees, Western Md.	1988-91	40	1,059	5,281	132.0
Rick Etienne, Franklin	1994-96	30	676	3,952	131.7
Tim Barrett, John Carroll	1973-74	19	457	2,469	129.9
Heath Butler, Martin Luther	1990-93	31	767	4,000	129.0
Scott Reppert, Lawrence	1979-82	33	757	4,211	127.6
Dan McGovern, Rensselaer	1994-97	28	665	3,572	127.6
Chris Babirad, Wash. & Jeff.	1989-92	35	683	4,419	126.3
Steve Dixon, Beloit	1990-93	38	986	4,792	126.1

**Record.* *$See page 6 for explanation.*

SEASON YARDS PER GAME

Player, Team	Year	G	Plays	Yards	TD	Yd. PG
Dante Brown, Marietta	†1996	10	314	*2,385	25	*238.5
Carey Bender, Coe	†1994	10	295	2,243	*29	224.3
Jamie Lee, MacMurray	†1997	8	207	1,639	11	204.9
Ricky Gales, Simpson	†1989	10	297	2,035	26	203.5
Terry Underwood, Wagner	†1988	9	245	1,809	21	201.0
Brad Olson, Lawrence	†1995	9	242	1,760	16	195.6
Kirk Matthieu, Maine Maritime	†1992	9	327	1,733	16	192.6
Kelvin Gladney, Millsaps	1994	10	307	1,882	19	188.2
Brandon Steinheim, Wesley	1996	9	319	1,684	20	187.1
Jon Warga, Wittenberg	†1990	10	254	1,836	15	183.6
Anthony Jones, La Verne	1995	8	200	1,453	19	181.6
Hank Wineman, Albion	†1991	9	307	1,629	14	181.0
Eric Grey, Hamilton	1991	8	217	1,439	13	179.9
Mike Birosak, Dickinson	1989	10	*380	1,798	18	179.8
Shane Davis, Loras	1997	10	267	1,774	18	177.4
Rob Marchitello, Maine Maritime	1995	8	292	1,413	19	176.6
Chris Babirad, Wash. & Jeff.	1992	9	243	1,589	22	176.6
Mark Kacmarynski, Central (Iowa)	1994	10	236	1,741	21	174.1
Carey Bender, Coe	†1993	10	261	1,718	15	171.8
Heath Butler, Martin Luther	1993	8	236	1,371	15	171.4
Spencer Johnson, Wis.-Whitewater	1994	10	290	1,697	18	169.7
Brandon Graham, Hope	1996	9	270	1,525	21	169.4
Clay Sampson, Denison	†1979	9	323	1,517	13	168.6
Anthony Russo, St. John's (N.Y.)	1991	10	287	1,685	18	168.5
Brandon Graham	1997	9	275	1,516	20	168.4

**Record. †National champion.*

CAREER YARDS

Player, Team	Years	Plays	Yards	Avg.
Carey Bender, Coe	1991-94	926	*6,125	6.61
Joe Dudek, Plymouth St.	1982-85	785	5,570	‡7.10
Mark Kacmarynski, Central (Iowa)	$1992-96	854	5,434	6.36
Brad Olson, Lawrence	1994-97	792	5,325	6.72
Eric Frees, Western Md.	1988-91	1,059	5,281	4.99
Kirk Matthieu, Maine Maritime	$1989-93	964	5,107	5.30
Terry Underwood, Wagner	1985-88	742	5,010	6.75
Steve Dixon, Beloit	1990-93	986	4,792	4.86
Shane Davis, Loras	1994-97	694	4,738	6.83
Mike Birosak, Dickinson	1986-89	*1,112	4,662	4.19
Dante Brown, Marietta	1994-97	712	4,512	6.34
Jim Romagna, Loras	1989-92	983	4,493	4.57
Chris Babirad, Wash. & Jeff.	1989-92	683	4,419	6.47
Petie Davis, Wesley	1991-94	741	4,414	5.96
Tim Lightfoot, Westfield St.	1992-95	876	4,380	5.00
Willie Beers, John Carroll	1989-92	848	4,332	5.11
Rob Marchitello, Maine Maritime	1993-95	879	4,300	4.89
Bob Beatty, Wartburg	1991-94	875	4,292	4.91
Frank Baker, Chicago	1990-93	855	4,283	5.01
Anthony Russo, St. John's (N.Y.)	1990-92	841	4,276	5.08
Ray Neosh, Coe	#1995-97	608	4,273	7.03
Remon Smith, Randolph-Macon	1984-87	737	4,249	5.77
Chris Spriggs, Denison	1983-86	787	4,248	5.40
Brandon Graham, Hope	1994-97	781	4,226	5.41
Scott Reppert, Lawrence	1979-82	757	4,211	5.56

#Active Player. Record. $See page 6 for explanation. ‡Record for minimum 500 carries.*

SEASON YARDS

Player, Team	Year	G	Plays	Yards	Avg.
Dante Brown, Marietta	†1996	10	314	*2,385	7.60
Carey Bender, Coe	†1994	10	295	2,243	7.60
Ricky Gales, Simpson	†1989	10	297	2,035	6.85
Kelvin Gladney, Millsaps	1994	10	307	1,882	6.13
Jon Warga, Wittenberg	†1990	10	254	1,836	7.23
Terry Underwood, Wagner	†1988	9	245	1,809	6.75
Mike Birosak, Dickinson	1989	10	*380	1,798	4.73
Shane Davis, Loras	1997	10	267	1,774	6.64
Brad Olson, Lawrence	†1995	9	242	1,760	7.27
Mark Kacmarynski, Central (Iowa)	1994	10	236	1,741	7.38
Kirk Matthieu, Maine Maritime	†1992	9	327	1,733	5.30
Sandy Rogers, Emory & Henry	†1986	11	231	1,730	7.49
Carey Bender, Coe	†1993	10	261	1,718	6.58
Spencer Johnson, Wis.-Whitewater	1994	10	290	1,697	5.85
Anthony Russo, St. John's (N.Y.)	†1991	10	287	1,685	5.87
Brandon Steinheim, Wesley	1996	9	319	1,684	5.28
John Bernatavitz, Dickinson	1990	10	266	1,666	6.26
Jamie Lee, MacMurray	†1997	8	207	1,639	‡7.92
Hank Wineman, Albion	1991	9	307	1,629	5.31
Gary Trettel, St. Thomas (Minn.)	1990	10	293	1,620	5.53
Joe Dudek, Plymouth St.	†1985	11	216	1,615	7.48
Ronnie Howard, Bridgewater (Va.)	1993	10	281	1,610	5.73
Frank Baker, Chicago	1993	10	281	1,606	5.72
Mark Kacmarynski, Central (Iowa)	1996	10	288	1,603	5.57
Eric Frees, Western Md.	1990	10	295	1,594	5.40

**Record. †National champion. ‡Record for minimum 195 carries.*

SINGLE-GAME YARDS

Yds.	Player, Team (Opponent)	Date
441	Dante Brown, Marietta (Baldwin-Wallace)	Oct. 5, 1996
436	A. J. Pittorino, Hartwick (Waynesburg)	Nov. 2, 1996
417	Carey Bender, Coe (Grinnell)	Oct. 9, 1993
413	Dante Brown, Marietta (Heidelberg)	Nov. 9, 1996
382	Shane Davis, Loras (Dubuque)	Nov. 8, 1997
382	Pete Baranek, Carthage (North Central)	Oct. 5, 1985
363	Terry Underwood, Wagner (Hofstra)	Oct. 15, 1988
354	Terry Underwood, Wagner (Western Conn. St.)	Oct. 3, 1986
352	Steve Tardif, Maine Maritime (Westfield St.)	Nov. 16, 1996
348	Carey Bender, Coe (Beloit)	Nov. 12, 1994
347	Chuck Wotkowicz, Johns Hopkins (Georgetown)	Oct. 22, 1993
342	Trevor Shannon, Wartburg (Loras)	Oct. 5, 1996
342	Dave Bednarek, Wis.-River Falls (Wis.-Stevens Point)	Oct. 29, 1983
337	Kirk Matthieu, Maine Maritime (Curry)	Oct. 27, 1990
337	Ted Helsel, St. Francis (Pa.) (Gallaudet)	Nov. 3, 1979
334	Oliver Bridges, Stony Brook (Pace)	Nov. 16, 1991
333	Mike Leon, Maine Maritime (Mass.-Boston)	Oct. 21, 1995
331	Brad Olson, Lawrence (Eureka)	Sept. 16, 1995
329	Don Williams, Lowell (Colby)	Oct. 4, 1985
326	Mike Krueger, Tufts (Amherst)	Oct. 25, 1980

ANNUAL CHAMPIONS

Year	Player, Team	Class	G	Plays	Yards	Avg.
1973	Billy Johnson, Widener	Sr.	9	168	1,494	166.0
1974	Tim Barrett, John Carroll	Sr.	9	256	1,409	156.6
1975	Ron Baker, Monmouth (Ill.)	Sr.	8	200	1,116	139.5
1976	Chuck Evans, Ferris St.	Jr.	10	224	1,509	150.9
1977	Don Taylor, Central (Iowa)	Sr.	9	267	1,329	147.7
1978	Dino Hall, Rowan	Sr.	10	239	1,330	133.0
1979	Clay Sampson, Denison	Jr.	9	323	1,517	168.6
1980	Scott Reppert, Lawrence	So.	8	223	1,223	152.9
1981	Scott Reppert, Lawrence	Jr.	9	250	1,410	156.7
1982	Scott Reppert, Lawrence	Sr.	8	254	1,323	165.4
1983	John Franco, Wagner	Sr.	8	175	1,166	145.8
1984	Gary Errico, Mass.-Lowell	Sr.	9	165	1,404	156.0
1985	Bruce Montella, Chicago	Sr.	9	265	1,372	152.4
1986	Sandy Rogers, Emory & Henry	Sr.	11	231	1,730	157.3
1987	Chris Dabrow, Claremont-M-S	Sr.	9	265	1,486	165.1
1988	Terry Underwood, Wagner	Sr.	9	245	1,809	201.0
1989	Ricky Gales, Simpson	Sr.	10	297	2,035	203.5
1990	Jon Warga, Wittenberg	Sr.	10	254	1,836	183.6
1991	Hank Wineman, Albion	Sr.	9	307	1,629	181.0
1992	Kirk Matthieu, Maine Maritime	Jr.	9	327	1,733	192.6
1993	Carey Bender, Coe	Jr.	10	261	1,718	171.8
1994	Carey Bender, Coe	Sr.	10	295	2,243	224.3
1995	Brad Olson, Lawrence	So.	9	242	1,760	195.6
1996	Dante Brown, Marietta	Jr.	10	314	*2,385	*238.5
1997	Jamie Lee, MacMurray	Sr.	8	207	1,639	204.9

**Record.*

MacMurray College photo

MacMurray running back Jamie Lee led Division III last season in rushing with 1,639 yards on 207 carries.

Passing

CAREER PASSING EFFICIENCY

(Minimum 325 Completions)

Player, Team	Years	Att.	Cmp.	Int.	Pct.	Yards	TD	Pts.
Bill Borchert, Mount Union	1994-97	1,009	671	17	‡.665	10,201	*141	*194.2
Kurt Ramler, St. John's (Minn.)	1994-96	722	420	16	.582	6,475	75	163.4
Kyle Adamson, Allegheny	1995-97	608	388	18	.638	5,506	48	160.0
Craig Kusick, Wis.-La Crosse	1993-95	537	327	14	.609	4,767	48	159.8
Jim Ballard, Wilmington (Ohio)/Mount Union	1990, 91-93	1,199	743	41	.620	10,379	115	159.5
Jason Baer, Wash. & Jeff.	1993-96	671	406	24	.605	5,632	66	156.3
Joe Blake, Simpson	1987-90	672	399	15	.594	6,183	43	153.3
Willie Reyna, La Verne	1991-92	542	346	19	.638	4,712	37	152.4
Greg Lister, Rowan	1994-97	773	454	29	.587	6,553	66	150.6
Gary Collier, Emory & Henry	1984-87	738	386	33	.523	6,103	80	148.6
John Koz, Baldwin-Wallace	1990-93	981	609	28	.621	7,724	71	146.4
Greg Heeres, Hope	1981-84	630	347	21	.537	5,120	53	144.4
Jeff Brown, Wheaton (Ill.)	1992-95	767	441	30	.575	6,219	60	143.6
Kevin Ricca, Catholic	1994-97	1,109	713	56	.643	9,469	89	142.0
Lon Erickson, Ill. Wesleyan	1993-96	786	461	24	.587	6,108	58	142.2
Chris Esterley, St. Thomas (Minn.)	1993-96	1,012	615	30	.608	7,709	71	142.0
Ed Hesson, Rowan	1990-93	895	504	26	.563	7,035	67	141.2
Bruce Crosthwaite, Adrian	1984-87	618	368	31	.596	4,959	45	141.0
Jack Ramirez, Pomona-Pitzer	1994-97	959	558	39	.582	7,523	71	140.3
Matt Jozokos, Plymouth St.	1987-90	1,003	527	39	.525	7,658	95	140.2
Brad Jorgensen, Simpson	1994-97	741	450	27	.607	6,068	39	139.6
Joe Coviello, Frank. & Marsh.	1973-76	591	334	36	.565	4,651	52	139.5
Bryan Snyder, Albright	1994-97	1,294	763	49	.590	9,865	92	138.9
Terry Peebles, Hanover	1992-95	969	550	29	.568	6,928	79	137.7
John Clark, Wis.-Eau Claire	1987-90	1,119	645	42	.576	9,196	63	137.7

**Record. ‡Record for minimum 750 attempts. ¢Record for minimum 650 completions.*

SEASON PASSING EFFICIENCY

(Minimum 15 Attempts Per Game)

Player, Team	Year	G	Att.	Cmp.	Int.	Pct.	Yards	TD	Pts.
Mike Simpson, Eureka	†1994	10	158	116	5	.734	1,988	25	*225.0
Willie Seiler, St. John's (Minn.)	†1993	10	205	141	6	.687	2,648	33	224.6
Bill Borchert, Mount Union	†1997	10	272	190	1	.698	2,933	*47	‡216.7
Bill Borchert, Mount Union	†1996	10	240	165	6	.687	2,655	38	208.9
Bill Borchert, Mount Union	†1995	10	225	160	4	.711	2,270	30	196.3
Jim Ballard, Mount Union	1993	10	314	229	11	*.729	3,304	37	193.2
Jason Baer, Wash. & Jeff.	1995	8	146	95	3	.650	1,536	19	192.3
Greg Lister, Rowan	1997	9	162	111	4	.685	1,688	20	191.9
Kurt Ramler, St. John's (Minn.)	1994	9	154	93	4	.603	1,560	22	187.4
Mike Bajakian, Williams	1994	8	141	92	1	.652	1,382	17	186.0
Kevin Ricca, Catholic	1997	10	306	208	6	.679	2,990	35	183.9
Mitch Sanders, Bridgeport	1973	10	151	84	7	.556	1,551	23	182.9
Pat Mayew, St. John's (Minn.)	†1991	9	247	154	4	.623	2,408	30	181.0
Guy Simons, Coe	1993	10	185	110	9	.594	1,979	21	177.1
Kyle Adamson, Allegheny	1996	10	182	119	3	.653	1,761	18	176.0
Jimbo Fisher, Samford	†1987	10	252	139	5	.551	2,394	34	175.4
Gary Collier, Emory & Henry	1987	11	249	152	10	.610	2,317	33	174.8
Paul Bell, Allegheny	1994	10	215	142	2	.660	2,137	17	173.8
Greg Lister, Rowan	1996	8	167	94	2	.562	1,711	17	173.6
James Grant, Ramapo	1989	9	147	91	7	.619	1,441	17	172.7
Chris Adams, Gettysburg	1994	10	211	139	2	.658	1,977	19	172.4
Mike Donnelly, Wittenberg	1995	10	153	92	2	.601	1,480	15	171.1
Kyle Klein, Albion	1996	9	225	151	8	.671	2,226	19	170.9
Gary Urwiler, Eureka	1991	10	171	103	5	.602	1,656	18	170.3
Kyle Adamson, Allegheny	1995	10	209	142	8	.679	2,039	17	169.1

**Record. †National champion. ‡Record for minimum 25 attempts per game.*

CAREER YARDS

Player, Team	Years	Att.	Cmp.	Int.	Pct.	Yards	TD
Kirk Baumgartner, Wis.-Stevens Point	1986-89	*1,696	*883	57	.521	*13,028	110
Mark Novara, Lakeland	1994-97	1,586	882	63	.556	11,101	100
Jim Ballard, Wilmington (Ohio)/Mount Union	1990, 91-93	1,199	743	41	.620	10,379	*115
Bill Borchert, Mount Union	1994-97	1,009	671	17	.665	10,201	141
Bryan Snyder, Albright	1994-97	1,294	763	49	.590	9,865	92
Keith Bishop, Ill. Wesleyan/Wheaton (Ill.)	1981, 83-85	1,311	772	65	.589	9,579	71
Dennis Bogacz, Wis.-Oshkosh/Wis.-Whitewater	1988-89, 90-91	1,275	654	59	.513	9,536	66
Dave Geissler, Wis.-Stevens Point	1982-85	1,346	789	57	.586	9,518	65
Kevin Ricca, Catholic	1994-97	1,190	713	56	.643	9,469	89
Eric Noble, Wilmington (Ohio)	1992-95	1,264	682	62	.540	9,260	62
John Clark, Wis.-Eau Claire	1987-90	1,119	645	42	.576	9,196	63
Tim Peterson, Wis.-Stout	1986-89	1,185	653	62	.551	8,881	59
Jordan Poznick, Principia	1990-93	1,480	765	68	.517	8,485	55
Brad Hensley, Kenyon	1991-94	1,439	718	61	.499	8,154	65
John Koz, Baldwin-Wallace	1990-93	981	609	28	.621	7,724	71
Luke Hanks, Otterbein	1990-93	1,267	715	62	.564	7,718	47
Chris Esterley, St. Thomas (Minn.)	1993-96	1,012	615	30	.608	7,709	71
Matt Jozokos, Plymouth St.	1987-90	1,003	527	39	.525	7,658	95
Chris Ings, Wabash	1992-95	1,087	569	43	.523	7,637	55

Player, Team	Years	Att.	Cmp.	Int.	Pct.	Yards	TD
Jack Ramirez, Pomona-Pitzer	1994-97	959	558	39	.582	7,523	71
Eric Rich, Ripon	1994-97	1,092	603	49	.552	7,450	67
Bill Hyland, Iona	1989-92	1,017	511	55	.502	7,382	57
Shane Fulton, Heidelberg	1983-86	1,024	587	55	.573	7,372	50
Gregg McDonald, Kalamazoo	1994-96	1,019	593	41	.582	7,339	50
Paul Brandenburg, Ripon	1984-87	1,181	607	66	.514	7,320	39

**Record.*

CAREER YARDS PER GAME

(Minimum 4,500 yards)

Player, Team	Years	G	Att.	Cmp.	Int.	Pct.	Yards	TD	Avg.
Kirk Baumgartner, Wis.-Stevens Point	1986-89	41	*1,696	*883	57	.521	*13,028	110	*317.8
Keith Bishop, Ill. Wesleyan/ Wheaton (Ill.)	1981, 83-85	31	1,311	772	65	.589	9,579	71	309.0
Mark Novara, Lakeland	1994-97	38	1,586	882	63	.556	11,101	100	292.1
Bryan Snyder, Albright	1994-97	35	1,294	763	49	.590	9,865	92	281.9
Willie Reyna, La Verne	1991-92	17	542	346	19	.638	4,712	37	277.2
Robert Farra, Claremont-M-S	1978-79	16	579	313	24	.541	4,360	31	272.5
Gregg McDonald, Kalamazoo	1994-96	27	1,019	593	41	.582	7,339	50	271.8
Jordan Poznick, Principia	1990-93	32	1,480	765	68	.517	8,485	55	265.2
Jim Ballard, Wilmington (Ohio)/ Mount Union	1990, 91-93	40	1,199	743	41	.620	10,379	115	259.5
Bill Borchert, Mount Union	1994-97	40	1,009	671	17	.665	10,201	*141	255.0
Dennis Bogacz, Wis.-Oshkosh/ Wis.-Whitewater	1988-89, 90-91	38	1,275	654	59	.513	9,536	66	250.9
Kevin Ricca, Catholic	1994-97	34	959	558	39	.582	7,523	71	221.3
Tim Peterson, Wis.-Stout	1986-89	36	1,185	653	62	.551	8,881	59	246.7
Rob Bristow, Pomona-Pitzer	1983-86	29	1,155	628	60	.544	7,120	27	245.5
Eric Noble, Wilmington (Ohio)	1992-95	38	1,264	682	62	.540	9,260	62	243.7
John Rooney, Ill. Wesleyan	1982-84	27	986	489	47	.496	6,576	55	243.6
John Clark, Wis.-Eau Claire	1987-90	38	1,119	645	42	.576	9,196	63	242.0
Brian Van Deusen, Western Md.	1992-95	30	1,129	621	40	.550	7,239	51	241.3
Tom Stallings, St. Thomas (Minn.)	1990-93	24	726	387	40	.533	5,608	44	233.7
Ed Smith, Benedictine (Ill.)	1991-93	29	862	456	41	.529	6,734	47	232.2
Kurt Ramler, St. John's (Minn.)	1994-96	28	722	420	16	.582	6,475	75	231.2
Dave Geissler, Wis.-Stevens Point	1982-85	42	1,346	789	57	.586	9,518	65	226.6
Jack Ramirez, Pomona-Pitzer	1994-97	34	959	558	39	.582	7,523	71	221.3
Chris Esterley, St. Thomas (Minn.)	1993-96	35	1,012	615	30	.608	7,709	71	220.3
Scott Scesney, St. John's (N.Y.)	1986-89	32	945	463	44	.490	6,914	72	216.1

**Record.*

SEASON YARDS

Player, Team	Year	G	Att.	Cmp.	Int.	Pct.	Yards	TD
Kirk Baumgartner, Wis.-Stevens Point	1988	11	*527	276	16	.524	*3,828	25
Kirk Baumgartner, Wis.-Stevens Point	1987	11	466	243	22	.521	3,755	31
Kirk Baumgartner, Wis.-Stevens Point	1989	10	455	247	9	.542	3,692	39
Terry Peebles, Hanover	1995	10	488	*283	10	.579	3,521	39
Mark Novara, Lakeland	1996	10	410	258	12	.629	3,405	40
John Furmaniak, Eureka	1995	10	361	210	11	.581	3,372	34
Jim Ballard, Mount Union	1993	10	314	229	11	*.729	3,304	37
Keith Bishop, Wheaton (Ill.)	1983	9	375	236	19	.629	3,274	24
Matt Bunyon, Wis.-Stout	1997	10	399	223	12	.558	3,221	33
Tom Stallings, St. Thomas (Minn.)	1993	10	395	219	20	.554	3,210	22
Bill Nietzke, Alma	1996	9	440	248	21	.563	3,197	28
Terry Peebles, Hanover	1994	10	445	252	17	.566	3,197	37
Keith Bishop, Wheaton (Ill.)	1985	9	457	262	22	.573	3,171	25
Mark Novara, Lakeland	1997	10	427	252	6	.590	3,098	23
Scott Isphording, Hanover	1992	10	359	207	19	.576	3,098	24
Gregg McDonald, Kalamazoo	1996	9	367	237	10	.645	3,089	23
Eric Noble, Wilmington (Ohio)	1994	9	398	221	17	.555	3,058	22
Dennis Bogacz, Wis.-Oshkosh	1989	10	378	219	18	.579	3,051	18
Steve Austin, Mass.-Boston	1992	9	396	181	25	.457	2,991	29
Kevin Ricca, Catholic	1997	10	306	208	6	.679	2,990	35
Bryan Snyder, Albright	1996	10	358	223	9	.622	2,983	38
Keith Bishop, Wheaton (Ill.)	1984	9	440	259	21	.589	2,968	21
Tim Peterson, Wis.-Stout	1989	10	445	256	15	.575	2,956	20
Derrin Lamker, Augsburg	1997	10	413	246	14	.595	2,946	24
Bill Borchert, Mount Union	1997	10	272	190	1	.698	2,933	*47

**Record. †National champion.*

SEASON YARDS PER GAME

Player, Team	Years	G	Att.	Cmp.	Int.	Pct.	Yards	TD	Avg.
Kirk Baumgartner, Wis.-Stevens Point	1989	10	455	247	9	.543	3,692	39	*369.2
Keith Bishop, Wheaton (Ill.)	1983	9	375	236	19	.629	3,274	24	363.8
Bill Nietzke, Alma	1996	9	440	248	21	.563	3,197	28	355.2
Keith Bishop, Wheaton (Ill.)	1985	9	457	262	22	.573	3,171	25	352.3
Terry Peebles, Hanover	1995	10	488	*283	10	.579	3,521	39	352.1
Kirk Baumgartner, Wis.-Stevens Point	1988	11	*527	276	16	.524	*3,828	25	348.0
Gregg McDonald, Kalamazoo	1996	9	367	237	10	.645	3,089	23	343.2
Kirk Baumgartner, Wis.-Stevens Point	1987	11	466	243	22	.521	3,755	31	341.4
Mark Novara, Lakeland	1996	10	410	258	12	.629	3,405	40	340.5
Eric Noble, Wilmington (Ohio)	1994	9	398	221	17	.555	3,058	22	339.8
John Furmaniak, Eureka	1995	10	361	210	11	.581	3,372	34	337.2
Steve Austin, Mass.-Boston	1992	9	396	181	25	.457	2,991	29	332.3

Player, Team	Years	G	Att.	Cmp.	Int.	Pct.	Yards	TD	Avg.
Chris Stormer, Hanover	1997	8	352	235	14	.667	2,654	20	331.8
Jim Ballard, Mount Union	1993	10	314	229	11	*.729	3,304	37	330.4
Keith Bishop, Wheaton (Ill.)	1984	9	440	259	21	.589	2,968	21	329.8
Jordan Poznick, Principia	1992	8	451	241	13	.534	2,618	21	327.3
Matt Bunyan, Wis.-Stout	1997	10	399	223	12	.558	3,221	33	322.1
Tom Stallings, St. Thomas (Minn.)	1993	10	395	219	20	.554	3,210	22	321.0
Terry Peebles, Hanover	1994	10	445	252	17	.566	3,197	37	319.7
Willie Reyna, La Verne	1991	8	267	170	6	.636	2,543	16	317.9
Bryan Snyder, Albright	1997	9	315	207	6	.657	2,808	26	312.0
Mark Novara, Lakeland	1997	10	427	252	6	.590	3,098	23	309.8
Scott Isphording, Hanover	1992	10	359	207	19	.576	3,098	24	309.8
Robert Farra, Claremont-M-S	†1978	9	359	196	15	.546	2,770	20	307.8
Dennis Bogacz, Wis.-Oshkosh	1989	10	378	219	18	.580	3,051	18	305.1

*Record. †National champion.

SINGLE-GAME YARDS

Yds.	Player, Team (Opponent)	Date
602	Tom Stallings, St. Thomas (Minn.) (Bethel [Minn.])	Nov. 13, 1993
585	Tim Lynch, Hofstra (Fordham)	Oct. 19, 1991
575	Eric Noble, Wilmington (Ohio) (Urbana)	Nov. 5, 1994
546	Bill Nietzke, Alma (Hope)	Oct. 26, 1996
533	John Love, North Park (Elmhurst)	Oct. 13, 1990
532	Bob Monroe, Knox (Cornell College)	Oct. 11, 1986
526	Jon DeVille, Menlo (Claremont-M-S)	Nov. 1, 1997
525	Chris Stormer, Hanover (Manchester)	Oct. 4, 1997
523	Kirk Baumgartner, Wis.-Stevens Point (Wis.-Stout)	Oct. 24, 1987
519	Justin Peery, Westminster (Mo.) (Bethel [Tenn.])	Nov. 8, 1997
517	Jon Nielsen, Claremont-M-S (Occidental)	Oct. 21, 1995
513	Craig Solomon, Rhodes (Rose-Hulman)	Nov. 11, 1978
510	Troy Dougherty, Grinnell (Lawrence)	Oct. 1, 1994
509	Bob Krepfle, Wis.-La Crosse (Wis.-River Falls)	Nov. 12, 1983
507	Mark Novara, Lakeland (Franklin)	Sept. 28, 1996
507	Eric Noble, Wilmington (Ohio) (Geneva)	Oct. 22, 1994
507	George Beisel, Hofstra (LIU-C. W. Post)	Sept. 28, 1991
506	Keith Bishop, Wheaton (Ill.) (Ill. Wesleyan)	Oct. 29, 1983
505	Kirk Baumgartner, Wis.-Stevens Point (Wis.-Superior)	Nov. 4, 1989
504	Jordan Poznick, Principia (Blackburn)	Oct. 10, 1992
504	Rob Shippy, Concordia (Ill.) (Concordia [Wis.])	Oct. 5, 1985

SINGLE-GAME COMPLETIONS

Cmp.	Player, Team (Opponent)	Date
50	Tim Lynch, Hofstra (Fordham)	Oct. 19, 1991
48	Jordan Poznick, Principia (Blackburn)	Oct. 10, 1992
47	Mike Wallace, Ohio Wesleyan (Denison)	Oct. 3, 1981
43	Bill Nietzke, Alma (Hope)	Oct. 26, 1996
43	Bill Nietzke, Alma (Olivet Nazarene)	Sept. 21, 1996
43	Terry Peebles, Hanover (Franklin)	Nov. 12, 1994
42	Mark Novara, Lakeland (Concordia [Wis.])	Oct. 15, 1994
42	Tim Lynch, Hofstra (Towson)	Nov. 2, 1991
42	Keith Bishop, Wheaton (Ill.) (Millikin)	Sept. 14, 1985
41	Troy Dougherty, Grinnell (Lawrence)	Oct. 1, 1994
41	Michael Doto, Hofstra (Central Conn. St.)	Sept. 14, 1991
41	Todd Monken, Knox (Cornell College)	Oct. 8, 1988
40	James Parker, Oberlin (Kenyon)	Sept. 20, 1997
40	Chris Stormer, Hanover (Otterbein)	Sept. 6, 1997
40	Dave Geissler, Wis.-Stevens Point (Wis.-Eau Claire)	Nov. 12, 1983
39	Chris Stormer, Hanover (DePauw)	Oct. 18, 1997
39	Chris Stormer, Hanover (Manchester)	Oct. 4, 1997
39	Rob Bristow, Pomona-Pitzer (La Verne)	Oct. 12, 1985
39	Steve Hendry, Wis.-Superior (Wis.-Stevens Point)	Oct. 17, 1981
38	Bill Nietzke, Alma (Kalamazoo)	Oct. 22, 1994
38	George Beisel, Hofstra (Southern Conn. St.)	Oct. 9, 1992
38	Jeff Voris, DePauw (Findlay)	Oct. 31, 1987
38	Todde Greenough, Willamette (Southern Ore. St.)	Sept. 26, 1987
38	Pat Moyer, Maryville (Tenn.) (Cumberland)	Oct. 5, 1985

ANNUAL CHAMPIONS

Year	Player, Team	Class	G	Att.	Cmp.	Avg.	Int.	Pct.	Yds.	TD
1973	Pat Clements, Kenyon	Jr.	9	239	133	14.8	17	.556	1,738	12
1974	Larry Cenotto, Pomona-Pitzer	Sr.	9	294	147	16.3	23	.500	2,024	15
1975	Ron Miller, Elmhurst	Sr.	8	205	118	14.8	15	.576	1,398	7
1976	Tom Hamilton, Occidental	Jr.	8	235	131	16.4	10	.557	1,988	10
1977	Tom Hamilton, Occidental	Sr.	9	323	171	19.0	17	.529	2,132	13
1978	Robert Farra, Claremont-M-S	Jr.	9	359	196	21.8	15	.546	2,770	20

Beginning in 1979, ranked on passing efficiency rating points, minimum 15 attempts per game (instead of per-game completions)

Year	Player, Team	Class	G	Att.	Cmp.	Int.	Pct.	Yds.	TD	Pts.
1979	David Broecker, Wabash	Fr.	9	145	81	9	.559	1,311	13	149.0
1980	George Muller, Hofstra	Sr.	10	189	115	14	.608	1,983	15	160.4
1981	Larry Atwater, Coe	Sr.	9	172	92	10	.535	1,615	15	147.2
1982	Mike Bennett, Cornell College	Sr.	9	154	83	8	.539	1,436	17	158.3
1983	Joe Shield, Trinity (Conn.)	Jr.	8	238	135	13	.567	2,185	19	149.1
1984	Cody Dearing, Randolph-Macon	Sr.	10	226	125	12	.553	2,139	27	163.4

Photo from Hofstra sports information

Hofstra quarterback Tim Lynch enjoyed a memorable afternoon October 19, 1991, when he set a Division III record with 50 completions (69 attempts). Lynch also threw for the second highest total ever—585 yards—in the Flying Dutchmen's 50-30 victory at Fordham.

Year	Player, Team	Class	G	Att.	Cmp.	Int.	Pct.	Yds.	TD	Pts.
1985	Robb Disbennett, Salisbury St.	Sr.	10	153	94	6	.614	1,462	16	168.4
1986	Gary Collier, Emory & Henry	Jr.	11	171	88	6	.514	1,509	21	158.9
1987	Jimbo Fisher, Samford	Sr.	10	252	139	5	.551	2,394	34	175.4
1988	Steve Flynn, Central (Iowa)	Jr.	8	133	82	6	.616	1,190	10	152.5
1989	Joe Blake, Simpson	††Jr.	10	144	93	3	.645	1,705	19	203.3
1990	Dan Sharley, Dayton	†††Sr.	10	149	95	2	.637	1,377	12	165.1
1991	Pat Mayew, St. John's (Minn.)	Sr.	9	247	154	4	.623	2,408	30	181.0
1992	Steve Keller, Dayton	Sr.	10	153	99	5	.647	1,350	17	168.9
1993	Willie Seiler, St. John's (Minn.)	Sr.	10	205	141	6	.687	2,648	33	224.6
1994	Mike Simpson, Eureka	So.	10	158	116	5	.734	1,988	25	*225.0
1995	Bill Borchert, Mount Union	So.	10	225	160	4	.711	2,270	30	196.3
1996	Bill Borchert, Mount Union	Jr.	10	240	165	6	.687	2,655	38	208.9
1997	Bill Borchert, Mount Union	Sr.	10	272	190	1	.698	2,933	*47	216.7

**Record. ††Declared champion; with six more pass attempts (making 15 per game), all interceptions, still would have highest efficiency (187.3). †††Declared champion; with one more attempt (making 15 per game), an interception, still would have highest efficiency (162.8).*

ANNUAL PASSING EFFICIENCY LEADERS BEFORE 1979

(Minimum 15 Attempts Per Game)

Year	Player, Team	G	Att.	Cmp.	Int.	Pct.	Yds.	TD	Pts.
1973	Mitch Sanders, Bridgeport	10	151	84	7	.556	1,551	23	182.9
1974	Tom McGuire, Benedictine (Ill.)	10	221	142	16	.643	2,206	16	157.5
1975	Jim Morrow, Wash. & Jeff.	9	137	82	7	.599	1,283	11	154.8
1976	Aaron Van Dyke, Cornell College	9	154	91	12	.591	1,611	14	161.4
1977	Matt Winslow, Middlebury	8	130	79	5	.608	919	17	155.6
1978	Matt Dillon, Cornell College	9	166	98	7	.590	1,567	16	161.7

Receiving

CAREER RECEPTIONS PER GAME

(Minimum 120 Receptions)

Player, Team	Years	G	Rec.	Yards	TD	Rec.PG
Matt Newton, Principia	1990-93	33	*287	3,646	32	*8.7
Todd Bloom, Hardin-Simmons	1995-97	28	233	2,621	14	8.3
Jeff Clay, Catholic	1994-97	36	269	4,101	44	7.5
Bill Stromberg, Johns Hopkins	1978-81	36	258	3,776	39	7.2
Tim McNamara, Trinity (Conn.)	1981-84	21	146	2,313	19	7.0
Ron Severance, Otterbein	1989-91	30	207	2,378	17	6.9
Chuck Braun, Wis.-Stevens Point	1980-81	18	124	1,914	19	6.9
Jim Jorden, Wheaton (Ill.)	1982-85	33	225	3,022	22	6.8
Ryan Ditze, Albright	1993-96	33	224	3,169	29	6.8
Mike Whitehouse, St. Norbert	1986-89	35	230	3,480	37	6.6
Kurt Barth, Eureka	1994-97	39	256	*4,311	51	6.6
Dan Daley, Pomona-Pitzer	1985-88	35	227	2,598	10	6.5
Rich Johnson, Pace	1985-87	29	188	2,614	8	6.5
Steve Wilkerson, Catholic	1993-94	19	120	1,966	17	6.3
Chris Bisaillon, Ill. Wesleyan	1989-92	36	223	3,670	*55	6.2
Rick Fry, Occidental	1974-77	33	200	3,073	18	6.1
Mike Funk, Wabash	1985, 87-89	38	228	2,858	33	6.0
Scott Faessler, Framingham St.	1989-92	34	201	2,121	8	5.9
Ted Taggart, Kenyon	1988-90	28	165	2,034	20	5.9
Pat McNamara, Trinity (Conn.)	1977-79	24	141	2,280	20	5.9
Theo Blanco, Wis.-Stevens Point	1985-88	38	223	3,139	18	5.9
Dale Amos, Frank. & Marsh.	1986-89	40	233	3,846	35	5.8
Scott Fredrickson, Wis.-Stout	1986-89	40	233	3,390	23	5.8

**Record.*

SEASON RECEPTIONS PER GAME

Player, Team	Year	G	Rec.	Yards	TD	Rec.PG
Matt Newton, Principia	†1992	8	98	1,487	14	*12.3
Matt Newton, Principia	†1993	8	96	1,080	11	12.0
Jeff Clay, Catholic	†1997	10	*112	1,625	*20	11.2
Ben Fox, Hanover	†1995	9	95	1,087	15	10.6
Sean Munroe, Mass.-Boston	1992	9	95	*1,693	17	10.6
Scott Faessler, Framingham St.	†1990	9	92	916	5	10.2
Scott Pingel, Westminster (Mo.)	1997	10	98	1,420	17	9.8
Mike Funk, Wabash	†1989	9	87	1,169	12	9.7
Jim Jorden, Wheaton (Ill.)	†1985	9	87	1,011	8	9.7
Theo Blanco, Wis.-Stevens Point	1987	11	106	1,616	8	9.6
Todd Bloom, Hardin-Simmons	†1996	10	96	1,019	6	9.6
Eric Nemec, Albright	1997	9	86	1,147	15	9.6
Jason Tincher, Wilmington (Ohio)	†1994	9	85	1,298	9	9.4
Rick Fry, Occidental	†1976	8	74	1,214	8	9.3
Mike Cook, Claremont-M-S	1995	9	83	993	7	9.2
Ron Severance, Otterbein	1990	10	92	1,049	8	9.2
Rick Fry, Occidental	†1977	9	82	1,222	5	9.1
Jim Myers, Kenyon	†1974	9	82	1,483	12	9.1
Jeff Clay, Catholic	1996	9	81	1,460	16	9.0
Steve Wilkerson, Catholic	1994	10	90	1,457	13	9.0
Bob Glanville, Lewis & Clark	1985	9	80	1,054	9	8.9
Ed Brady, Ill. Wesleyan	†1983	9	80	873	7	8.9
John Tucci, Amherst	†1986	8	70	1,025	8	8.8
Greg Lehrer, Heidelberg	1993	10	87	1,202	8	8.7
Ted Taggart, Kenyon	1989	10	87	1,004	7	8.7

**Record. †National champion.*

CAREER RECEPTIONS

Player, Team	Years	Rec.	Yards	TD
Matt Newton, Principia	1990-93	*287	3,646	32
Jeff Clay, Catholic	1994-97	269	4101	44
Bill Stromberg, Johns Hopkins	1978-81	258	3,776	39
Kurt Barth, Eureka	1994-97	256	*4311	51
Todd Bloom, Hardin-Simmons	1995-97	233	2621	14
Dale Amos, Frank. & Marsh.	1986-89	233	3,846	35
Scott Fredrickson, Wis.-Stout	1986-89	233	3,390	23
Mike Whitehouse, St. Norbert	1986-89	230	3,480	37
Mike Funk, Wabash	1985, 87-89	228	2,858	33
Dan Daley, Pomona-Pitzer	1985-88	227	2,598	10
Jim Jorden, Wheaton (Ill.)	1982-85	225	3,022	22
Ryan Ditze, Albright	1993-96	224	3,169	29
Chris Bisaillon, Ill. Wesleyan	1989-92	223	3,670	*55
Theo Blanco, Wis.-Stevens Point	1985-88	223	3,139	18
Ed Brady, Ill. Wesleyan	1981-84	220	2,907	22
Walter Kalinowski, Catholic	1983-86	219	2,430	16
Jim Bradford, Carleton	1988-91	212	3,719	32
Mike Cottle, Juniata	1985-88	212	2,607	36
John Ward, Cornell College	1979-82	211	3,085	30
Kendall Griffin, Loras	1990-93	208	3,036	26
Ron Severance, Otterbein	1989-91	207	2,378	17
Vince Dortch, Jersey City St.	1983-86	206	3,037	28
Mark Loeffler, Wheaton (Ill.)	1993-96	205	3,163	43
Manny Pina, St. John Fisher	1993-96	205	2,222	24
Mike Gundersdorf, Wilkes	1993-96	205	3,603	34
Chris Murphy, Georgetown	1989-92	205	2,817	26

**Record.*

SEASON RECEPTIONS

Player, Team	Year	G	Rec.	Yards	TD
Jeff Clay, Catholic	†1997	10	*112	1,625	*20
Theo Blanco, Wis.-Stevens Point	1987	11	106	1,616	8
Scott Pingel, Westminster (Mo.)	1997	10	98	1,420	17
Matt Newton, Principia	†1992	8	98	1,487	14
Todd Bloom, Hardin-Simmons	†1996	10	96	1,019	6
Matt Newton, Principia	†1993	8	96	1,080	11
Ben Fox, Hanover	†1995	9	95	1,087	15
Sean Munroe, Mass.-Boston	1992	9	95	*1,693	17
Ron Severance, Otterbein	1990	10	92	1,049	8
Scott Faessler, Framingham St.	†1990	9	92	916	5
Steve Wilkerson, Catholic	1994	10	90	1,457	13
Greg Lehrer, Heidelberg	1993	10	87	1,202	8
Mike Funk, Wabash	†1989	9	87	1,169	12
Ted Taggart, Kenyon	1989	10	87	1,004	7
Jim Jorden, Wheaton (Ill.)	†1985	9	87	1,011	8

Player, Team	Year	G	Rec.	Yards	TD
Eric Nemec, Albright	1997	9	86	1,147	15
Matt Plummer, Dubuque	1996	10	86	1,237	12
Jason Tincher, Wilmington (Ohio)	†1994	9	85	1,298	9
Ron Severance, Otterbein	†1991	10	85	929	4
Scott Hvistendahl, Ausburg	1997	9	84	1,329	15
Sam Williams, Defiance	1993	10	84	1,209	14
Mike Cook, Claremont-M-S	1995	9	83	993	7
Scott Fredrickson, Wis.-Stout	1989	10	83	1,102	7
Ryan Ditze, Albright	1994	10	82	1,023	5
Rick Fry, Occidental	†1977	9	82	1,222	5
Jim Myers, Kenyon	†1974	9	82	1,483	12

**Record. †National champion.*

SINGLE-GAME RECEPTIONS

No.	Player, Team (Opponent)	Date
23	Sean Munroe, Mass.-Boston (Mass. Maritime)	Oct. 10, 1992
20	Todd Bloom, Hardin-Simmons (Mississippi Col.)	Oct. 12, 1996
20	Kurt Barth, Eureka (Concordia [Wis.])	Sept. 28, 1996
20	Rich Johnson, Pace (Fordham)	Nov. 7, 1987
20	Pete Thompson, Carroll (Wis.) (Augustana [Ill.])	Nov. 4, 1978
18	Richard Wemer, Grinnell (Beloit)	Nov. 20, 1997
18	Adam Herbst, St. John's (Minn.) (St. Thomas [Minn.])	Nov. 7, 1997
18	Jeff Clay, Catholic (Albright)	Nov. 16, 1996
18	Matt Plummer, Dubuque (Buena Vista)	Oct. 12, 1996
18	Craig Antonio, Waynesburg (Bethany [W.Va.])	Oct. 16, 1993
18	Ed Sullivan, Catholic (Carnegie Mellon)	Nov. 7, 1992
17	Felix Brooks-Church, Oberlin (Allegheny)	Nov. 16, 1996
17	tied	

CAREER YARDS

Player, Team	Years	Rec.	Yards	Avg.	TD
Kurt Barth, Eureka	1994-97	256	*4,311	16.8	51
Jeff Clay, Catholic	1994-97	269	4,101	15.2	44
Dale Amos, Frank. & Marsh	1986-89	233	3,846	16.5	35
Bill Stromberg, Johns Hopkins	1978-81	258	3,776	14.6	39
Jim Bradford, Carleton	1988-91	212	3,719	17.5	32
Chris Bisaillon, Ill. Wesleyan	1989-92	223	3,670	16.5	*55
Matt Newton, Principia	1990-93	*287	3,646	12.7	32
Mike Gundersdorf, Wilkes	1993-96	205	3,603	17.6	34
Mike Whitehouse, St. Norbert	1986-89	230	3,480	15.1	37
Scott Fredrickson, Wis.-Stout	1986-89	233	3,390	14.5	23
R. J. Hoppe, Carroll (Wis.)	1993-96	152	3,295	*21.7	49
John Aromando, Col. of New Jersey	1981-84	165	3,197	19.4	39
Todd Stoner, Kenyon	1981-84	197	3,191	16.2	31
Rodd Patten, Framingham St.	1990-93	154	3,170	20.6	38
Ryan Ditze, Albright	1993-96	224	3,169	14.1	29
Mark Loeffler, Wheaton (Ill.)	1993-96	205	3,163	15.4	43
Theo Blanco, Wis.-Stevens Point	1985-88	223	3,139	14.1	18
Junior Lord, Guilford	1994-97	201	3,089	15.4	33
John Ward, Cornell College	1979-82	211	3,085	14.6	30
Rick Fry, Occidental	1974-77	200	3,073	15.4	18

**Record.*

SEASON YARDS

Player, Team	Years	Rec.	Yards	Avg.	TD
Sean Munroe, Mass.-Boston	†1992	95	*1,693	17.8	17
Jeff Clay, Catholic	†1997	*112	1,625	14.5	*20
Theo Blanco, Wis.-Stevens Point	1987	106	1,616	15.2	8
Matt Newton, Principia	1992	98	1,487	15.2	14
Jim Myers, Kenyon	1974	82	1,483	18.1	12
Jeff Clay, Catholic	†1996	81	1,460	18.0	16
Steve Wilkerson, Catholic	†1994	90	1,457	16.2	13
Scott Pingel, Westminster (Mo.)	1997	98	1,420	14.5	17
Beau Almodobar, Norwich	1984	71	1,375	19.4	10
Kurt Barth, Eureka	†1995	68	1,337	19.7	18
Scott Hvistendahl, Ausburg	1997	84	1,329	15.8	15
Chris Vogel, Knox	1987	78	1,326	17.0	15
Dale Amos, Frank. & Marsh.	1989	72	1,302	18.1	15
Jason Tincher, Wilmington (Ohio)	1994	85	1,298	15.3	9
Don Moehling, Wis.-Stevens Point	1988	72	1,290	17.9	7
Matt Surette, Worcester Tech	1997	75	1,287	17.2	16
Ed Bubonics, Mount Union	1993	74	1,286	17.4	10
Tom Buslee, St. Olaf	1993	75	1,281	17.1	10
Rob Lokerson, Muhlenberg	†1993	76	1,275	16.8	6
Mike Gundersdorf, Wilkes	1995	79	1,269	16.1	8
Jim Bradford, Carleton	1989	69	1,238	17.9	6
Jeremy Snyder, Whittier	1997	71	1,237	17.4	15
Matt Plummer, Dubuque	1996	86	1,237	14.4	12
Rick Fry, Occidental	1977	82	1,222	14.9	5
Evan Elkington, Worcester Tech	1989	52	1,220	+23.5	16

**Record. †National champion. +Record for minimum 50 receptions.*

SINGLE-GAME YARDS

Yds.	Player, Team (Opponent)	Date
364	Jeff Clay, Catholic (Albright)	Nov. 16, 1996
362	Matt Surette, Worcester Tech (Springfield)	Oct. 25, 1997
332	Ryan Pifer, Heidelberg (Marietta)	Nov. 8, 1997
332	Sean Munroe, Mass.-Boston (Mass. Maritime)	Oct. 10, 1992
310	Jeff Clay, Catholic (LaSalle)	Oct. 11, 1997
309	Dale Amos, Frank. & Marsh. (Western Md.)	Oct. 24, 1987
303	Chuck Braun, Wis.-Stevens Point (Wis.-Superior)	Oct. 17, 1981
303	Rick Fry, Occidental (Claremont-M-S)	Oct. 30, 1976
301	Jeremy Snyder, Whittier (Occidental)	Nov. 15, 1997
301	Greg Holmes, Carroll (Wis.) (North Central)	Nov. 7, 1981
296	Joe Richards, Johns Hopkins (Georgetown)	Oct. 26, 1991
296	Vince Hull, Minn.-Morris (Bemidji St.)	Oct. 10, 1981
295	Aatron Kenney, Wis.-Stevens Point (Wis.-Stout)	Oct. 24, 1987
293	Mike Stotz, Catholic (Bridgewater [Va.])	Nov. 15, 1980
292	Andy Steckel, Western Md. (Gettysburg)	Sept. 15, 1990
291	R. J. Letendre, Plymouth St. (Worcester Tech)	Nov. 12, 1994
289	Kurt Barth, Eureka (Lakeland)	Nov. 5, 1994
287	Matt Newton, Principia (Concordia [Wis.])	Nov. 7, 1992
287	Chris Bisaillon, Ill. Wesleyan (Carroll [Wis.])	Sept. 15, 1990
285	Jim Bradford, Carleton (Gust. Adolphus)	Oct. 20, 1990

ANNUAL CHAMPIONS

RECEPTIONS PER GAME

Year	Player, Team	Class	G	Rec.	Avg.	Yards	TD
1973	Ron Duckett, Trinity (Conn.)	Sr.	8	57	7.1	834	7
1974	Jim Myers, Kenyon	Sr.	9	82	9.1	1,483	12
1975	C. J. DeWitt, Bridgewater (Va.)	Sr.	9	64	7.1	836	2
1976	Rick Fry, Occidental	Jr.	8	74	9.3	1,214	8
1977	Rick Fry, Occidental	Sr.	9	82	9.1	1,222	5
1978	Pat McNamara, Trinity (Conn.)	Jr.	8	67	8.4	1,024	11
1979	Theodore Anderson, Fisk	Jr.	7	49	7.0	699	2
1980	Bill Stromberg, Johns Hopkins	Jr.	9	66	7.3	907	11
1981	Bill Stromberg, Johns Hopkins	Sr.	9	78	8.7	924	10
1982	Jim Gustafson, St. Thomas (Minn.)	Jr.	10	72	7.2	990	5
1983	Ed Brady, Ill. Wesleyan	Jr.	9	80	8.9	873	7
1984	Tim McNamara, Trinity (Conn.)	Sr.	8	67	8.4	1,004	10
1985	Jim Jorden, Wheaton (Ill.)	Sr.	9	87	9.7	1,011	8
1986	John Tucci, Amherst	Sr.	8	70	8.8	1,025	8
1987	Chris Vogel, Knox	So.	9	78	8.7	1,326	15
1988	Theo Blanco, Wis.-Stevens Point	Sr.	10	80	8.0	1,009	7
1989	Mike Funk, Wabash	Sr.	9	87	9.7	1,169	12
1990	Scott Faessler, Framingham St.	So.	9	92	10.2	916	5
1991	Ron Severance, Otterbein	Sr.	10	85	8.5	929	4
1992	Matt Newton, Principia	Jr.	8	98	*12.3	1,487	14
1993	Matt Newton, Principia	Sr.	8	96	12.0	1,080	11
1994	Jason Tincher, Wilmington (Ohio)	Sr.	9	85	9.4	1,298	9
1995	Ben Fox, Hanover	Sr.	9	95	10.6	1,087	15
1996	Todd Bloom, Hardin-Simmons	Jr.	10	96	9.6	1,019	6
1997	Jeff Clay, Catholic	Sr.	10	*112	11.2	1,625	*20

YARDS PER GAME

Year	Player, Team	Class	G	Rec.	Yards	TD	Avg.
1990	Ray Shelley, Juniata	Sr.	10	54	1,147	12	114.7
1991	Rodd Patten, Framingham St.	So.	8	49	956	13	119.5
1992	Sean Munroe, Mass.-Boston	Sr.	9	95	*1,693	17	*188.1
1993	Rob Lokerson, Muhlenberg	Jr.	9	76	1,275	6	141.7
1994	Steve Wilkerson, Catholic	Sr.	10	90	1,457	13	145.7
1995	Kurt Barth, Eureka	So.	10	68	1,337	18	133.7
1996	Jeff Clay, Catholic	Jr.	9	81	1,460	16	162.2
1997	Jeff Clay, Catholic	Sr.	10	*112	1,625	*20	162.5

**Record.*

Scoring

CAREER POINTS PER GAME

(Minimum 225 Points)

Player, Team	Years	G	TD	XPt.	FG	Pts.	Pt. PG
Ricky Gales, Simpson	1988-89	19	44	10	0	274	*14.4
Cory Christensen, Simpson	1996-97	19	44	0	0	264	13.9
Rob Marchitello, Maine Maritime	1993-95	26	59	4	0	358	13.8
Carey Bender, Coe	1991-94	39	*86	12	0	*528	13.5
Chad Hoiska, Wis.-Eau Claire	1995-97	30	58	2	0	350	11.7
Joe Dudek, Plymouth St.	1982-85	41	79	0	0	474	11.6
Chris Babirad, Wash. & Jeff.	1989-92	35	62	2	0	374	10.7
Terry Underwood, Wagner	1985-88	33	58	0	0	348	10.5
Chris Bisaillon, Ill. Wesleyan	1989-92	36	61	12	0	378	10.5
Stanley Drayton, Allegheny	1989-92	32	56	0	0	336	10.5
Greg Novarro, Bentley	1990-92	24	42	0	0	252	10.5
Mark Kacmarynski, Central (Iowa)	$1992-96	41	70	2	0	422	10.3
Ryan Kolpin, Coe	1987-90	28	48	0	0	288	10.3

Player, Team	Years	G	TD	XPt.	FG	Pts.	Pt. PG
Anthony Rice, La Verne	1994-96	27	46	0	0	276	10.2
Trent Nauholz, Simpson	1990-93	31	49	4	0	298	9.6
Dan McGovern, Rensselaer	1994-97	28	44	4	0	268	9.4
Jason Wooley, Worcester Tech	1990-93	37	55	8	0	338	9.1
R. J. Hoppe, Carroll (Wis.)	1993-96	37	54	12	0	336	9.1
A. J. Pagano, Wash. & Jeff.	1984-87	36	53	5	0	323	9.0
Heath Butler, Martin Luther	1990-93	31	44	14	0	278	9.0
Scott Tumilty, Augustana (Ill.)	1992-95	37	55	0	0	330	8.9
Matt Malmberg, St. John's (Minn.)	1991-94	31	44	12	0	276	8.9
Gary Trettel, St. Thomas (Minn.)	1988-90	29	43	0	0	258	8.9
Steve Harris, Carroll (Wis.)	1991-94	35	49	12	0	306	8.7
Vance Mueller, Occidental	1982-85	36	51	8	0	314	8.7
Brandon Steinheim, Wesley	1993-96	30	43	2	0	260	8.7

*Record. $See page 6 for explanation.

SEASON POINTS PER GAME

Player, Team	Years	G	TD	XPt.	FG	Pts.	Pt. PG
James Regan, Pomona-Pitzer	†1997	8	21	34	2	166	*20.8
Carey Bender, Coe	†1994	10	*32	2	0	*194	19.4
Chad Hoiska, Wis.-Eau Claire	1997	10	29	2	0	176	17.6
Jim Mormino, Allegheny	1997	10	29	0	0	174	17.4
Doug Steiner, Grove City	1997	10	29	0	0	174	17.4
Rob Marchitello, Maine Maritime	1994	9	25	4	0	154	17.1
Stanley Drayton, Allegheny	†1991	10	28	0	0	168	16.8
Dante Brown, Marietta	†1996	10	27	4	0	166	16.6
Ricky Gales, Simpson	†1989	10	26	10	0	166	16.6
Matt Malmberg, St. John's (Minn.)	†1993	10	27	2	0	164	16.4
Chris Babirad, Wash. & Jeff.	†1992	9	24	0	0	144	16.0
Trent Nauholz, Simpson	†1992	8	21	2	0	128	16.0
Billy Johnson, Widener	†1973	9	23	0	0	138	15.3
Cory Christensen, Simpson	1997	10	25	0	0	150	15.0
Greg Novarro, Bentley	1992	10	25	0	0	150	15.0
Bruce Naszimento, Jersey City St.	1973	10	25	0	0	150	15.0
Chris Babirad, Wash. & Jeff.	1991	9	22	2	0	134	14.9
Anthony Jones, La Verne	†1995	8	19	4	0	118	14.8
Chris Hipsley, Cornell College	†1976	9	14	42	2	132	14.7
Carey Bender, Coe	1992	9	21	4	0	130	14.4
Rob Marchitello, Maine Maritime	1995	8	19	0	0	114	14.3
Michael Waithe, Curry	†1987	8	19	0	0	114	14.3
Kelvin Gladney, Millsaps	1993	9	21	2	0	128	14.2
Rick Bell, St. John's (Minn.)	†1982	9	21	2	0	128	14.2
Trevor Shannon, Wartburg	1996	10	23	4	0	142	14.2

*Record. †National champion.

CAREER POINTS

Player, Team	Years	TD	XPt.	FG	Pts.
Carey Bender, Coe	1991-94	*86	12	0	*528
Joe Dudek, Plymouth St.	1982-85	79	0	0	474
Mark Kacmarynski, Central (Iowa)	$1992-96	70	2	0	422
Chris Bisaillon, Ill. Wesleyan	1989-92	61	12	0	378
Chris Babirad, Wash. & Jeff.	1989-92	62	2	0	374
Rob Marchitello, Maine Maritime	1993-95	59	4	0	358
Chad Hoiska, Wis.-Eau Claire	1995-97	58	2	0	350
Terry Underwood, Wagner	1985-88	58	0	0	348
Jim Romagna, Loras	1989-92	57	2	0	344
Jason Wooley, Worcester Tech	1990-93	55	8	0	338
R. J. Hoppe, Carroll (Wis.)	1993-96	54	12	0	336
Stanley Drayton, Allegheny	1989-92	56	0	0	336
Scott Tumilty, Augustana (Ill.)	1992-95	55	0	0	330
Cary Osborn, Wis.-Eau Claire	1987-90	55	0	0	330
Dante Brown, Marietta	1994-97	54	0	0	328
Matt Taylor, Catholic	1993-96	54	4	0	328
Kurt Barth, Eureka	1994-97	51	21	0	327
Tim McDaniel, Centre	1988-91	54	0	0	324
A. J. Pagano, Wash. & Jeff.	1984-87	53	5	0	323
Trevor Shannon, Wartburg#	1995-97	53	4	0	322
Greg Corning, Wis.-River Falls	1984-87	52	2	0	314
Vance Mueller, Occidental	1982-85	51	8	0	314
Scott Barnyak, Carnegie Mellon	1987-90	49	14	0	308
Shane Davis, Loras	1994-97	50	6	0	306
Steve Harris, Carroll (Wis.)	1991-94	49	12	0	306

*Record. $See page 6 for explanation.

SEASON POINTS

Player, Team	Year	TD	XPt.	FG	Pts.
Carey Bender, Coe	†1994	*32	2	0	*194
Chad Hoiska, Wis.-Eau Claire	1997	29	2	0	176
Jim Mormino, Allegheny	1997	29	0	0	174
Doug Steiner, Grove City	1997	29	0	0	174
Stanley Drayton, Allegheny	†1991	28	0	0	168
James Regan, Pomona-Pitzer	†1997	21	34	2	166
Dante Brown, Marietta	†1996	27	4	0	166
Ricky Gales, Simpson	†1989	26	10	0	166
Matt Malmberg, St. John's (Minn.)	†1993	27	2	0	164
Rob Marchitello, Maine Maritime	1994	25	4	0	154
Cory Christensen, Simpson	1997	25	0	0	150
Greg Novarro, Bentley	1992	25	0	0	150
Joe Dudek, Plymouth St.	1985	25	0	0	150
Bruce Naszimento, Jersey City St.	1973	25	0	0	150
Chris Babirad, Wash. & Jeff.	†1992	24	0	0	144
Trevor Shannon, Wartburg	1996	23	4	0	142
Scott Barnyak, Carnegie Mellon	†1990	22	6	0	138
Ryan Kolpin, Coe	†1990	23	0	0	138
Ron Corbett, Cornell College	1982	23	0	0	138
Billy Johnson, Widener	†1973	23	0	0	138
Matt Taylor, Catholic	1994	22	2	0	134
Chris Babirad, Wash. & Jeff.	1991	22	2	0	134
James Jones, Coast Guard	1996	22	0	0	132
Thomas Lee, Anderson (Ind.)	1992	22	0	0	132
Tim McDaniel, Centre	1990	22	0	0	132
Chris Hipsley, Cornell College	†1976	14	42	2	132

* Record. †National champion.

ANNUAL CHAMPIONS

Year	Player, Team	Class	G	TD	XPt.	FG	Pts.	Avg.
1973	Billy Johnson, Widener	Sr.	9	23	0	0	138	15.3
1974	Joe Thompson, Augustana (Ill.)	So.	9	17	0	0	102	11.3
1975	Ron Baker, Monmouth (Ill.)	Sr.	8	15	2	0	92	11.5
1976	Chris Hipsley, Cornell College	So.	9	14	42	2	132	14.7
1977	Chip Zawoiski, Widener	Sr.	9	18	0	0	108	12.0
1978	Roger Andrachik, Baldwin-Wallace	Sr.	8	16	0	0	96	12.0
1979	Jay Wessler, Illinois Col.	Jr.	8	16	4	0	100	12.5
1980	Daryl Johnson, Wabash	Jr.	9	20	0	0	120	13.3
1981	Scott Reppert, Lawrence	Jr.	9	15	0	0	90	10.0
	Daryl Johnson, Wabash	Sr.	9	15	0	0	90	10.0
1982	Rick Bell, St. John's (Minn.)	Sr.	9	21	2	0	128	14.2
1983	John Aromando, Col. of New Jersey	Jr.	10	20	0	0	120	12.0
1984	Joe Dudek, Plymouth St.	Jr.	10	21	0	0	126	12.6
1985	Kevin Weaver, Wash. & Lee	Jr.	8	17	8	0	110	13.8
1986	Jim Korfonta, Hamilton	Sr.	8	16	0	0	96	12.0
	Russ Kring, Mount Union	Jr.	10	20	0	0	120	12.0
1987	Michael Waithe, Curry	Sr.	8	19	0	0	114	14.3
1988	Terry Underwood, Wagner	Sr.	9	21	0	0	126	14.0
1989	Ricky Gales, Simpson	Sr.	10	26	10	0	166	16.6
1990	Scott Barnyak, Carnegie Mellon	Sr.	10	22	6	0	138	13.8
	Ryan Kolpin, Coe	Sr.	10	23	0	0	138	13.8
1991	Stanley Drayton, Allegheny	Jr.	10	28	0	0	168	16.8
1992	Chris Babirad, Wash. & Jeff.	Sr.	9	24	0	0	144	16.0
	Trent Nauholz, Simpson	Jr.	8	21	2	0	128	16.0
1993	Matt Malmberg, St. John's (Minn.)	Jr.	10	27	2	0	164	16.4
1994	Carey Bender, Coe	Sr.	10	*32	2	0	*194	19.4
1995	Anthony Jones, La Verne	Sr.	8	19	4	0	118	14.8
1996	Dante Brown, Marietta	Jr.	10	27	4	0	166	16.6
1997	James Regan, Pomona-Pitzer	Jr.	8	21	34	2	166	20.8

*Record.

Interceptions

CAREER INTERCEPTIONS

Player, Team	Years	No.	Yards	Avg.
Ralph Gebhardt, Rochester	1973-75	*29	384	13.2
Brian Fetterolf, Aurora	1986-89	28	390	13.9
Rick Bealer, Lycoming	1987-90	28	279	10.0
Andrew Ostrand, Carroll (Wis.)	1990-93	27	258	9.6
Tim Lennon, Curry	1986-89	27	190	7.0
Mike Hintz, Wis.-Platteville	1983-86	27	183	6.8
Scott Stanitous, Moravian	1985-88	27	178	6.6
Mark Dorner, Juniata	1984-87	26	*443	17.0
Cory Mabry, Susquehanna	1988-91	26	400	15.4
Jeff Hughes, Ripon	1975-78	26	333	12.8
Neal Guggemos, St. Thomas (Minn.)	1982-85	25	377	15.1
Dave Adams, Carleton	1984-87	25	327	13.1
Will Hill, Bishop	1983-86	25	261	10.4
Tom Devine, Juniata	1979-82	25	248	9.9
Gary Ellis, Rose-Hulman	1974-77	25	226	9.1

*Record.

SEASON INTERCEPTIONS

Player, Team	Year	No.	Yards
Mark Dorner, Juniata	†1987	*15	202
Steve Nappo, Buffalo	†1986	13	155
Antonio Moore, Widener	†1994	13	116
Chris McMahon, Catholic	†1984	13	105
Ralph Gebhardt, Rochester	†1973	13	105

Player, Team	Year	No.	Yards
Brian Barr, Gettysburg	†1985	12	144
John Bernard, Buffalo	†1983	12	143
Mick McConkey, Neb. Wesleyan	†1982	12	111
Chris Butts, Worcester St.	†1992	12	109
Tom Devine, Juniata	†1981	12	91

**Record. †National champion.*

ANNUAL CHAMPIONS

(Ranked on Average Per Game)

Year	Player, Team	Class	G	No.	Avg.	Yards
1973	Ralph Gebhardt, Rochester	So.	9	13	1.44	105
1974	Kevin Birkholz, Carleton	Jr.	9	11	1.22	137
1975	Mark Persichetti, Wash. & Jeff.	So.	9	10	1.11	97
1976	Gary Jantzer, Southern Ore. St.	Sr.	9	10	1.11	63
1977	Greg Jones, FDU-Madison	So.	9	10	1.11	106
	Mike Jones, Norwich	So.	9	10	1.11	98
1978	Don Sutton, San Fran. St.	Fr.	8	10	1.25	43
1979	Greg Holland, Simpson	Fr.	9	11	1.22	150
1980	Tim White, Lawrence	Sr.	8	10	1.25	131
1981	Tom Devine, Juniata	Sr.	9	12	1.33	91
1982	Mick McConkey, Neb. Wesleyan	Sr.	9	12	1.33	111
1983	John Bernard, Buffalo	Sr.	10	12	1.20	143
1984	Chris McMahon, Catholic	Sr.	9	13	1.44	140
1985	Kim McManis, Lane	Sr.	9	11	1.22	165
1986	Steve Nappo, Buffalo	Sr.	11	13	1.18	155
1987	Mark Dorner, Juniata	Sr.	10	*15	*1.50	202
1988	Tim Lennon, Curry	Jr.	9	11	1.22	86
1989	Ron Davies, Coast Guard	So.	9	11	1.22	90
1990	Craig Garritano, FDU-Madison	Jr.	9	10	1.11	158
	Brad Bohn, Neb. Wesleyan	So.	9	10	1.11	90
	Frank Greer, Sewanee	So.	9	10	1.11	67
	Harold Krebs, Merchant Marine	Sr.	9	10	1.11	19
1991	Murray Meadows, Millsaps	Sr.	9	11	1.22	46
1992	Chris Butts, Worcester St.	Jr.	9	12	1.33	109
1993	Ricky Webb, Emory & Henry	Sr.	8	8	1.00	56
1994	Antonio Moore, Widener	So.	10	13	1.30	116
1995	Mike Susi, Lebanon Valley	Sr.	8	8	1.00	153
	LeMonde Zachary, St. Lawrence	Fr.	7	7	1.00	109
1996	Peter Hinkle, Ursinus	So.	10	11	1.10	247
1997	Joel Feuerstahler, Martin Luther	Sr.	9	10	1.10	222

**Record.*

Punting

CAREER AVERAGE

(Minimum 100 Punts)

Player, Team	Years	No.	Yards	Avg.
Jeff Shea, Cal Lutheran	1994-97	183	7,939	*43.4
Mike Manson, Benedictine (Ill.)	1975-78	120	5,056	42.1
Dan Osborn, Occidental	1981-83	157	6,528	41.6
Jim Allshouse, Adrian	1973-75	163	6,718	41.2
Thomas Murray, Catholic	1983-84	122	5,028	41.2
Ryan Haley, John Carroll	1991-94	151	6,208	41.1
Scott Lanz, Bethany (W.Va.)	1975-78	235	9,592	40.8
Mitch Holloway, Millsaps	1992-93	105	4,283	40.8

**Record.*

SEASON AVERAGE

(Qualifiers for Championship)

Player, Team	Year	No.	Yards	Avg.
Justin Shively, Anderson (Ind.)	†1997	55	2,502	*45.5
Jeff Shea, Cal Lutheran	†1996	53	2,402	45.3
Jeff Shea, Cal Lutheran	†1995	43	1,933	45.0
Mario Acosta, Chapman	1996	34	1,528	44.9
Bob Burwell, Rose-Hulman	†1978	61	2,740	44.9
Charles McPherson, Clark Atlanta	1978	50	2,237	44.7
Dan Osborn, Occidental	†1982	55	2,454	44.6
Jeff Shea, Cal Lutheran	1997	43	1,910	44.4
Mike Manson, Benedictine (Ill.)	†1976	36	1,587	44.1
Linc Welles, Bloomsburg	†1973	39	1,708	43.8
Matt George, Chapman	1997	38	1,663	43.8
Kirk Seufert, Rhodes	†1983	44	1,921	43.7
Kelvin Albert, Knoxville	†1987	30	1,308	43.6

**Record. †National champion.*

ANNUAL CHAMPIONS

Year	Player, Team	Class	No.	Yards	Avg.
1973	Linc Welles, Bloomsburg	Sr.	39	1,708	43.8
1974	Sylvester Cunningham, Fort Valley St.	So.	40	1,703	42.6
1975	Larry Hersh, Shepherd	Jr.	58	2,519	43.4
1976	Mike Manson, Benedictine (Ill.)	So.	36	1,587	44.1
1977	Scott Lanz, Bethany (W.Va.)	Jr.	78	3,349	42.9
1978	Bob Burwell, Rose-Hulman	Sr.	61	2,740	44.9
1979	Jay Lenstrom, Neb. Wesleyan	Sr.	64	2,641	41.3
1980	Duane Harrison, Bridgewater (Va.)	Sr.	43	1,792	41.7
1981	Dan Paro, Denison	Jr.	54	2,223	41.2
1982	Dan Osborn, Occidental	Jr.	55	2,454	44.6
1983	Kirk Seufert, Rhodes	Jr.	44	1,921	43.7
1984	Thomas Murray, Catholic	Sr.	59	2,550	43.2
1985	Dave Lewis, Muhlenberg	So.	55	2,290	41.6
	Mike Matzen, Coe	Sr.	55	2,290	41.6
1986	Darren Estes, Millsaps	Jr.	45	1,940	43.1
1987	Kelvin Albert, Knoxville	So.	30	1,308	43.6
1988	Bobby Graves, Sewanee	So.	57	2,445	42.9
1989	Paul Becker, Kenyon	Sr.	57	2,307	40.5
1990	Bill Nolan, Carroll (Wis.)	Sr.	33	1,322	40.1
1991	Jeff Stolte, Chicago	So.	54	2,295	42.5
1992	Robert Ray, San Diego	So.	44	1,860	42.3
1993	Mitch Holloway, Millsaps	Sr.	45	1,910	42.4
1994	Ryan Haley, John Carroll	Sr.	54	2,311	42.8
1995	Jeff Shea, Cal Lutheran	So.	43	1,933	45.0
1996	Jeff Shea, Cal Lutheran	Jr.	53	2,402	45.3
1997	Justin Shively, Anderson (Ind.)	Sr.	55	2,502	*45.5

**Record.*

Punt Returns

CAREER AVERAGE

(Minimum 1.2 Returns Per Game)

Player, Team	Years	No.	Yards	Avg.
Keith Winston, Knoxville	1986-87	30	686	*22.9
Robert Middlebrook, Knoxville	1984-85	21	473	22.5
Kevin Doherty, Mass. Maritime	1976-78, 80	45	939	20.9
Chuck Downey, Stony Brook	1984-87	59	*1,198	+20.3
Mike Askew, Kean	1980-81	28	555	19.8
Willie Canady, Fort Valley St.	1979-82	41	772	18.8

**Record. +Record for minimum 50 returns.*

SEASON AVERAGE

(Minimum 1.2 Returns Per Game)

Player, Team	Year	No.	Yards	Avg.
Chuck Downey, Stony Brook	†1986	17	530	*31.2
Kevin Doherty, Mass. Maritime	†1976	11	332	30.2
Robert Middlebrook, Knoxville	†1984	9	260	28.9
Joe Troise, Kean	†1974	12	342	28.5
Melvin Dillard, Ferrum	†1990	25	*688	27.5
Eric Green, Benedictine (Ill.)	†1993	13	346	26.6
Chris Warren, Ferrum	†1989	18	421	23.4
Kevin Doherty, Mass. Maritime	1978	11	246	22.4

**Record. †National champion.*

ANNUAL CHAMPIONS

Year	Player, Team	Class	No.	Yards	‡Avg.
1973	Al Shepherd, Monmouth (Ill.)	Sr.	18	347	19.3
1974	Joe Troise, Kean	Fr.	12	342	28.5
1975	Mitch Brown, St. Lawrence	So.	25	430	17.2
1976	Kevin Doherty, Mass. Maritime	Fr.	11	332	30.2
1977	Charles Watkins, Knoxville	Sr.	15	278	18.5
1978	Dennis Robinson, Wesleyan (Conn.)	Sr.	††9	263	29.2
1979	Steve Moffett, Maryville (Tenn.)	Jr.	19	357	18.8
1980	Mike Askew, Kean	Jr.	16	304	19.0
1981	Mike Askew, Kean	Sr.	12	251	20.9
1982	Tom Southall, Colorado Col.	So.	13	281	21.6
1983	Edmond Donald, Millsaps	Jr.	15	320	21.3
1984	Robert Middlebrook, Knoxville	So.	9	260	28.9
1985	Dan Schone, Illinois Col.	Fr.	11	231	21.0
1986	Chuck Downey, Stony Brook	Jr.	17	530	*31.2
1987	Keith Winston, Knoxville	Sr.	16	343	21.4
1988	Dennis Tarr, Framingham St.	Jr.	9	178	19.8
1989	Chris Warren, Ferrum	Sr.	18	421	23.4
1990	Melvin Dillard, Ferrum	Sr.	25	*688	27.5
1991	Jordan Nixon, Augustana (Ill.)	Sr.	27	473	17.5
1992	Vic Moncato, FDU-Madison	So.	†††10	243	24.3
1993	Eric Green, Benedictine (Ill.)	Sr.	13	346	26.6
1994	Ariel Bell, Frostburg St.	Sr.	19	329	17.3
1995	Jim Wallace, Ripon	Jr.	17	305	17.9
1996	Tyrone Brown, Howard Payne	Sr.	21	415	19.8
1997	Seth Wallace, Coe	Fr.	††††10	301	30.1

**Record. ‡Ranked on minimum of 1.5 returns per game in 1973; 1.2 from 1974. ††Declared champion; with one more return (making 1.25 per game) for zero yards, still would have highest average (26.3). †††Declared champion; with one more return (making 1.22 per game) for zero yards, still would have highest average (22.1). ††††Declared champion; with one more return (making 1.22 per game) for zero yards, still would have highest average (27.4).*

Photo from Wesley sports information

Wesley running back Brandon Steinheim became the first freshman to lead Division III in kickoff returns when he averaged 42.2 yards per return in 1994.

Kickoff Returns

CAREER AVERAGE

(Minimum 1.2 Returns Per Game)

Player, Team	Years	No.	Yards	Avg.
Daryl Brown, Tufts	1974-76	38	1,111	*29.2
Darnell Rubin, Chapman	1994, 96	17	485	28.5
Mike Askew, Kean	1980-81	33	938	28.4
Chuck Downey, Stony Brook	1984-87	46	1,281	27.8
R. J. Hoppe, Carroll (Wis.)	1993-96	59	1,632	27.7
Ryan Reynolds, Thomas More	1991-94	49	1,311	26.8
LaVant King, Ohio Northern	1991, 93-95	50	1,298	26.0
Scott Reppert, Lawrence	1979-82	44	1,134	25.8
Lamont Rhim, Buffalo St.	1994-96	47	1,210	25.7
Rick Rosenfeld, Western Md.	1973-76	69	1,732	25.1

**Record.*

SEASON AVERAGE

(Minimum 1.2 Returns Per Game)

Player, Team	Year	No.	Yards	Avg.
Brandon Steinheim, Wesley	†1994	10	422	*42.2
Jason Martin, Coe	†1992	11	438	39.8
Nate Kirtman, Pomona-Pitzer	†1990	14	515	36.8
Tom Myers, Coe	†1983	11	401	36.5
Ron Scott, Occidental	1983	10	363	36.3
Alan Hill, DePauw	1980	12	434	36.2
Trevor Shannon, Wartburg	1996	14	501	35.8
Al White, Wm. Paterson	1990	12	427	35.6
Byron Womack, Iona	†1989	15	531	35.4
Derrick Brooms, Chicago	†1995	12	422	35.2
Darnell Marshall, Carroll (Wis.)	1989	17	586	34.5
Daryl Brown, Tufts	†1976	11	377	34.3
Rich Jinnette, Methodist	1992	15	514	34.3
Jeff Higgins, Ithaca	1995	12	407	33.9
Oscar Ford, Chapman	1995	11	373	33.9
Sean Healy, Coe	1989	11	372	33.8
Anthony Drakeford, Ferrum	†1987	15	507	33.8
Ryan Reynolds, Thomas More	1992	14	473	33.8
Glenn Koch, Tufts	†1986	14	472	33.7

**Record. †National champion.*

ANNUAL CHAMPIONS

Year	Player, Team	Class	No.	Yards	‡Avg.
1973	Greg Montgomery, Wis.-Whitewater	So.	17	518	30.5
1974	Tom Oleksa, Muhlenberg	Sr.	15	467	31.1
1975	Jeff Levant, Beloit	Jr.	15	434	28.9
1976	Daryl Brown, Tufts	Sr.	11	377	34.3
1977	Charlie Black, Marietta	Jr.	14	465	33.2
1978	Russ Atchison, Centre	So.	11	284	25.8
1979	Jim Iannone, Rochester	Jr.	13	411	31.6
1980	Mike Askew, Kean	So.	††10	415	41.5
1981	Gene Cote, Wesleyan (Conn.)	Sr.	16	521	32.6
1982	Jim Hachey, Bri'water (Mass.)	Jr.	16	477	29.8
1983	Tom Myers, Coe	So.	11	401	36.5
1984	Mike Doetsch, Trinity (Conn.)	Jr.	13	434	33.4
1985	Gary Newsom, Lane	So.	10	319	31.9
1986	Glenn Koch, Tufts	Sr.	14	472	33.7
1987	Anthony Drakeford, Ferrum	Sr.	15	507	33.8
1988	Harold Owens, Wis.-La Crosse	Jr.	10	508	29.9
1989	Byron Womack, Iona	Sr.	15	531	35.4
1990	Nate Kirtman, Pomona-Pitzer	Jr.	14	515	36.8
1991	Tom Reason, Albion	So.	13	423	32.5
1992	Jason Martin, Coe	So.	11	438	39.8
1993	Eric Green, Benedictine (Ill.)	Sr.	19	628	33.1
1994	Brandon Steinheim, Wesley	Fr.	10	422	*42.2
1995	Derrick Brooms, Chicago	Sr.	12	422	35.2
1996	Trevor Shannon, Wartburg	So.	14	501	35.8
1997	Qasim Ward, Mass.-Boston	Fr.	10	314	31.4

**Record. ‡Ranked on minimum of 1.5 returns per game in 1973; 1.2 from 1974. ††Declared champion; with one more return (making 1.2 per game) for zero yards, still would have highest average (37.7).*

All-Purpose Yards

CAREER YARDS PER GAME

(Minimum 3,500 Yards)

Player, Team	Years	G	Rush	Rcv.	Int.	PR	KOR	Yds.	Yd. PG
Kirk Matthieu, Maine Maritime	$1989-93	33	5,107	315	0	254	1,279	6,955	*210.8
Carey Bender, Coe	1991-94	39	*6,125	1,751	0	7	87	*7,970	204.4
Gary Trettel, St. Thomas (Minn.)	1988-90	29	3,483	834	0	0	1,407	5,724	197.4

**Record. $See page 6 for explanation.*

SEASON YARDS PER GAME

Player, Team	Year	G	Rush	Rcv.	Int.	PR	KOR	Yds.	Yd. PG
Dante Brown, Marietta	†1996	10	*2,385	174	0	46	368	*2,973	*297.3
Carey Bender, Coe	†1994	10	2,243	319	0	7	87	2,656	265.6
Kirk Matthieu, Maine Maritime	†1992	9	1,733	91	0	56	308	2,188	243.1
Ray Neosh, Coe	1996	9	1,472	273	0	0	403	2,148	238.7
Ricky Gales, Simpson	1989	10	2,035	102	0	0	248	2,385	238.5
Paul Smith, Gettsburgh	†1997	10	1.256	102	0	199	805	2,362	236.2
Gary Trettel, St. Thomas (Minn.)	1989	10	1,502	337	0	0	496	2,335	233.5
Kirk Matthieu, Maine Maritime	1990	9	1,428	77	0	99	495	2,099	233.2
Gary Trettel, St. Thomas (Minn.)	1990	10	1,620	388	0	0	319	2,327	232.7
Carey Bender, Coe	†1993	10	1,718	601	0	0	0	2,319	231.9

*Record. †National champion.

CAREER YARDS

Player, Team	Years	Rush	Rcv.	Int.	PR	KOR	Yds.
Carey Bender, Coe	1991-94	*6,125	1,751	0	7	87	*7,970
Kirk Matthieu, Maine Maritime	$1989-93	5,107	315	0	254	1,279	6,955
Eric Frees, Western Md.	1988-91	5,281	392	0	47	1,158	6,878
Joe Dudek, Plymouth St.	1982-85	5,570	348	0	0	243	6,509
Dante Brown, Marietta	1994-97	4,512	425	0	202	1,040	6,179
Adam Henry, Carleton	1990-93	3,482	601	0	186	1,839	6,108
Brad Olson, Lawrence	1994-97	5,325	590	0	14	145	6,074
Mark Kacmarnyski, Central (Iowa)	$1992-96	5,434	211	0	45	364	6,054
Gary Trettel, St. Thomas (Minn.)	1988-90	3,724	853	0	0	1,467	6,044

*Record. $See page 6 for explanation.

SEASON YARDS

Player, Team	Year	Rush	Rcv.	Int.	PR	KOR	Yds.
Dante Brown, Marietta	†1996	*2,385	174	0	46	368	*2,973
Carey Bender, Coe	†1994	2,243	319	0	7	87	2,656
Theo Blanco, Wis.-Stevens Point	1987	454	1,616	0	245	103	2,418
Ricky Gales, Simpson	1989	2,035	102	0	0	248	2,385
Paul Smith, Gettsburg	†1997	1,256	102	0	199	805	2,362
Gary Trettel, St. Thomas (Minn.)	1989	1,502	337	0	0	496	2,335
Gary Trettel, St. Thomas (Minn.)	1990	1,620	388	0	0	319	2,327
Carey Bender, Coe	†1993	1,718	601	0	0	0	2,319

*Record. †National champion.

ANNUAL CHAMPIONS

Year	Player, Team	Cl.	Rush	Rcv.	Int.	PR	KOR	Yds.	Yd. PG
1992	Kirk Matthieu, Maine Matime	Jr.	1,733	91	0	56	308	2,188	243.1
1993	Carey Bender, Coe	Jr.	1,718	601	0	0	0	2,319	231.9
1994	Carey Bender, Coe	Sr.	2,243	319	0	7	87	2,656	265.6
1995	Brad Olson, Lawrence	So.	1,760	279	0	0	0	2,039	226.6
1996	Dante Brown, Marietta	Jr.	*2,385	174	0	46	368	*2,973	*297.3
1997	Paul Smith, Gettysburg	So.	1,256	102	0	199	805	2,362	236.2

*Record.

Field Goals

CAREER FIELD GOALS

Player, Team	Years	Made	Atts.	Pct.
Ken Edelman, Mount Union (S)	1987-90	*52	*71	.732
Ted Swan, Colorado Col. (S)	1973-76	43	57	.754
Jim Hever, Rhodes (S)	1982-85	42	66	.636
Manny Matsakis, Capital (C)	1980-83	40	66	.606
Doug Hart, Grove City (S)	1985-88	40	*71	.563
Mike Duvic, Dayton (S)	1986-89	38	49	$.776
Jeff Reitz, Lawrence (C)	1974-77	37	60	.617
Dan Deneher, Montclair St. (S)	1978-79, 81-82	37	65	.569
Jim Flynn, Gettysburg (S)	1982-85	37	68	.544

*Record. $Declared record; with one more attempt (making 50), failed, still would have highest percentage (.760). (C) Conventional kicker. (S) Soccer-style kicker.

SEASON FIELD GOALS

Player, Team	Year	Made	Atts.	Pct.
Ken Edelman, Mount Union (S)	†1990	*20	27	.741
Scott Ryerson, Central Fla. (S)	†1981	18	*29	.621
Dennis Unger, Albright (S)	†1995	16	20	.800
Steve Graeca, John Carroll (S)	†1988	15	16	*.938
Ken Edelman, Mount Union (S)	1988	15	17	.882
Gary Potter, Hamline (C)	†1984	15	21	.714
Jeff Reitz, Lawrence (C)	†1975	15	26	.577

*Record. (C) Conventional kicker. (S) Soccer-style kicker. †National champion.

ANNUAL CHAMPIONS

Year	Player, Team	Class	Made	Atts.	Pct.	PG
1973	Chuck Smeltz, Susquehanna (C)	Jr.	10	14	.714	1.11
1974	Ted Swan, Colorado Col. (S)	So.	13	15	.867	1.44
1975	Jeff Reitz, Lawrence (C)	So.	15	26	.577	1.67
1976	Mark Sniegocki, Bethany (W.Va.) (C)	So.	11	14	.786	1.22
1977	Bob Unruh, Wheaton (Ill.) (S)	Jr.	11	14	.786	1.22
1978	Craig Walker, Western Md. (C)	So.	13	24	.542	1.44
1979	Jeff Holter, Concordia-M'head (S)	Jr.	12	15	.800	1.33
1980	Jeff Holter, Concordia-M'head (S)	Sr.	13	19	.684	1.30
1981	Scott Ryerson, Central Fla. (S)	So.	18	*29	.621	1.80
1982	Manny Matsakis, Capital (C)	Jr.	13	20	.650	1.44
1983	Mike Farrell, Adrian (S)	So.	12	21	.571	1.33
1984	Gary Potter, Hamline (C)	Jr.	15	21	.714	1.50
1985	Joe Bevelhimer, Wabash (C)	Sr.	14	22	.636	1.40
	Jim Hever, Rhodes (S)	Sr.	14	23	.609	1.40
1986	Tim Dewberry, Occidental (C)	Sr.	13	21	.619	1.44
1987	Doug Dickason, John Carroll (S)	Sr.	13	21	.619	1.44
1988	Steve Graeca, John Carroll (S)	Fr.	15	16	*.938	1.67
1989	Dave Bergmann, San Diego (S)	So.	14	18	.778	1.56
	Rich Egal, Merchant Marine (S)	Fr.	14	22	.636	1.56
1990	Ken Edelman, Mount Union (S)	Sr.	*20	27	.741	*2.00
1991	Greg Harrison, Union (N.Y.) (S)	So.	12	16	.750	1.33
1992	Todd Holthaus, Rose-Hulman (S)	Jr.	13	19	.684	1.30
1993	Steve Milne, Brockport St. (S)	Sr.	13	16	.813	1.30
1994	Chris Kondik, Baldwin-Wallace (S)	Fr.	13	17	.765	1.30
1995	Dennis Unger, Albright (S)	So.	16	20	.800	1.60
1996	Roger Egbert, Union (N.Y.)	Sr.	11	15	.733	1.22
1997	Ryan Boutwell, Gust. Adolphus (S)	Jr.	13	18	.722	1.30

*Record. (C) Conventional kicker. (S) Soccer-style kicker.

All-Time Longest Plays

Since 1941, official maximum length of all plays fixed at 100 yards.

RUSHING

Yds.	Player, Team (Opponent)	Year
99	Bill Casey, Mass.-Dartmouth (Norwich)	1995

Yds.	Player, Team (Opponent)	Year
99	Kelly Wilkinson, Principia (Trinity Bible)	1995
99	Arnie Boigner, Ohio Northern (Muskingum)	1992
99	Reese Wilson, MacMurray (Eureka)	1986
99	Don Patria, Rensselaer (Mass.-Lowell)	1981
99	Kevin Doherty, Mass. Maritime (New Haven)	1980
99	Sam Halliston, Albany (N.Y.) (Norwich)	1977
98	Rich Vargas, Wis.-Stout (Wis.-Oshkosh)	1992
98	Ted Pretasky, Wis.-La Crosse (Wis.-River Falls)	1987
98	Jon Hinds, Principia (Illinois Col.)	1986
98	Alex Schmidt, Muhlenberg (Lebanon Valley)	1984
98	Eric Batt, Ohio Northern (Ohio Wesleyan)	1982
98	Mike Shannon, Centre (Sewanee)	1978

PASSING

Yds.	Passer-Receiver, Team (Opponent)	Year
99	Eric Block-R. J. Hoppe, Carroll (Wis.) (Lake Forest	1996
99	Mike Schultz-R. J. Hoppe, Carroll (Wis.) (Ripon)	1995
99	Mike Magistrelli-Jason Martin, Coe (Quincy)	1994
99	Jim Connolley-Duane Martin, Wesley (FDU-Madison)	1993
99	Marc Klausner-Eric Frink, Pace (Hobart)	1992
99	Carlos Nazario-Ray Marshall, St. Peter's (Georgetown)	1991
99	Mike Jones-Warren Tweedy, Frostburg St. (Waynesburg)	1990
99	Chris Etzler-Andy Nowlin, Bluffton (Urbana)	1990
99	John Clark-Pete Balistrieri, Wis.-Eau Claire (Minn.-Duluth)	1989
99	Kelly Sandidge-Mark Green, Centre (Sewanee)	1988
99	Mike Francis-John Winter, Carleton (Trinity [Tex.])	1983
99	Rich Boling-Lewis Borsellino, DePauw (Valparaiso)	1976
99	John Wicinski-Donnell Lipford, John Carroll (Allegheny)	1975
99	Jack Berry-Mercer West, Wash. & Lee (Hampden-Sydney)	1974
99	Gary Shope-Rick Rudolph, Juniata (Moravian)	1973

INTERCEPTION RETURNS

Twenty-seven players have returned interceptions 100 yards. The most recent:

Yds.	Player, Team (Opponent)	Year
100	Terrance Oliver, Delaware Valley (Lebanon Valley)	1997
100	Randy Ames, Hope (Adrian)	1996
100	Dan Gilson, Curry (Stonehill)	1995
100	Tony Hinkle, Rose-Hulman (Millsaps)	1995
100	Mike Gerhart, Susquehanna (Moravian)	1994
100	Bruce Pritchett, Kean (Widener)	1994
100	Adam Smith, Heidelberg (Capital)	1994
100	Jason Pass, Hamline (St. John's [Minn.])	1994
100	Guy Nardulli, Elmhurst (North Central)	1994

PUNT RETURNS

Yds.	Player, Team (Opponent)	Year
99	Robert Middlebrook, Knoxville (Miles)	1985
98	Mark Griggs, Wooster (Oberlin)	1980
98	Ron Mabry, Emory & Henry (Maryville [Tenn.])	1973
97	Rob Allard, Nichols (Curry)	1991
96	Marvin Robbins, Salisbury St. (Wesley)	1987
96	Gary Martin, Muskingum (Wooster)	1976
95	Tyrone Croom, Susquehanna (Delaware Valley)	1993
95	Brian Sarver, William Penn (Dubuque)	1992
95	Stan Thompson, Knoxville (Livingstone)	1982

KICKOFF RETURNS

Forty players have returned kickoffs 100 yards. The most recent:

Yds.	Player, Team (Opponent)	Year
100	Eric Green, Benedictine (Ill.) (Carthage)	1992
100	Nate Kirtman, Pomona-Pitzer (Redlands)	1990
100	Phil Bryant, Wilmington (Ohio) (Tiffin)	1990
100	Steve Burns, Mass.-Boston (Curry)	1989
100	Wayne Morris, Hofstra (Pace)	1989

PUNTS

Yds.	Player, Team (Opponent)	Year
90	Dan Heeren, Coe (Lawrence)	1974
86	David Anastasi, Buffalo (John Carroll)	1989
86	Dana Loucks, Buffalo (Frostburg St.)	1987
86	John Pavlik, Wabash (Centre)	1978
85	Jeff Shea, Cal Lutheran (Azusa Pacific)	1996
84	Todd Whitehurst, Menlo (Cal Lutheran)	1997
84	Rob Sarvis, Norwich (Western Conn. St.)	1995
83	Jeff Shooks, Albion (Alma)	1994
83	Geoff Hansen, Gust. Adolphus (Augustana [S.D.])	1992
82	John Massab, Albion (Adrian)	1982
82	Mike Manson, Benedictine (Ill.) (Monmouth [Ill.])	1976

FIELD GOALS

Yds.	Player, Team (Opponent)	Year
62	Dom Antonini, Rowan (Salisbury St.)	1976
59	Chris Gustafson, Carroll (Wis.) (North Park)	1985
59	Hartmut Strecker, Dayton (Iowa St.)	1977
57	Scott Fritz, Wartburg (Simpson)	1982
57	Kevin Shea, St. Mary's (Cal.) (Oregon Tech)	1976

Team Champions

Annual Offense Champions

TOTAL OFFENSE

Year	Team	Avg.
1973	San Diego	441.0
1974	Ithaca	487.9
1975	Frank. & Marsh.	439.4
1976	St. John's (Minn.)	451.8
1977	St. John's (Minn.)	437.5
1978	Lawrence	432.6
1979	Norwich	465.2
1980	Widener	459.0
1981	Middlebury	446.5
1982	West Ga.	470.6
1983	Elmhurst	483.3
1984	Alma	465.1
1985	St. Thomas (Minn.)	446.9
1986	Mount Union	452.8
1987	Samford	523.1
1988	Wagner	465.9
1989	Simpson	514.0
1990	Hofstra	505.7
1991	St. John's (Minn.)	503.8
1992	Mount Union	463.7
1993	St. John's (Minn.)	549.7
1994	Allegheny	543.8
1995	Mount Union	495.8
1996	Albion	538.0
1997	Simpson	*565.3

*Record.

RUSHING OFFENSE

Year	Team	Avg.
1973	Widener	361.7
1974	Albany (N.Y.)	361.6
1975	Widener	345.8
1976	St. John's (Minn.)	348.9
1977	St. John's (Minn.)	315.3
1978	Ithaca	320.1
1979	Norwich	383.1
1980	Widener	317.5
1981	Augustana (Ill.)	313.6
1982	West Ga.	319.6
1983	Augustana (Ill.)	345.7
1984	Augustana (Ill.)	338.4
1985	Denison	351.0
1986	Wis.-River Falls	361.4
1987	Augustana (Ill.)	369.1
1988	Tufts	369.0
1989	Wis.-River Falls	388.5
1990	Ferrum	*434.7
1991	Ferrum	361.4
1992	Wis.-River Falls	315.6
1993	Chicago	324.8
1994	Wis.-River Falls	336.7
1995	Lawrence	344.0
1996	Springfield	351.2
1997	Wis.-River Falls	365.6

*Record.

PASSING OFFENSE

Year	Team	Avg.
1973	San Diego	231.7
1974	Benedictine (Ill.)	255.4
1975	St. Norbert	227.7
1976	Occidental	255.4
1977	Southwestern	257.8
1978	Claremont-M-S	331.7
1979	Claremont-M-S	250.1
1980	Occidental	255.9
1981	Wis.-Stevens Point	288.9
1982	Wheaton (Ill.)	308.7
1983	Wheaton (Ill.)	380.4
1984	Wheaton (Ill.)	351.6
1985	Wheaton (Ill.)	371.6
1986	Pace	286.9
1987	Wis.-Stout	314.6
1988	Wis.-Stevens Point	356.7
1989	Wis.-Stevens Point	380.4
1990	Hofstra	342.2
1991	St. John's (Minn.)	302.8
1992	Mass.-Boston	337.0
1993	Mount Union	352.8
1994	Hanover	351.3
1995	Hanover	362.8
1996	Alma	368.3
1997	Lakeland	357.3

SCORING OFFENSE

Year	Team	Avg.
1973	San Diego	40.1
1974	Frank. & Marsh.	45.1
1975	Frank. & Marsh.	38.2
1976	St. John's (Minn.)	42.5
1977	Lawrence	38.2
1978	Georgetown	36.5
1979	Wittenberg	39.7

Year	Team	Avg.
1980	Widener	43.3
1981	Lawrence	35.3
1982	West Ga.	42.1
1983	Elmhurst	38.1
1984	Hope	40.3
1985	Salisbury St.	39.5
1986	Dayton	40.8
1987	Samford	51.7
1988	Central (Iowa)	37.6
1989	Ferrum	46.7
1990	Ferrum	47.3
1991	Union (N.Y.)	46.1
1992	Coe	46.4
1993	St. John's (Minn.)	*61.5
1994	St. John's (Minn.)	47.1
1995	Chapman	47.2
1996	Albion	50.8
1997	Mount Union	54.5

**Record.*

Annual Defense Champions

TOTAL DEFENSE

Year	Team	Avg.
1973	Doane	144.3
1974	Alfred	153.6
1975	Lycoming	133.1
1976	Albion	129.9
1977	Knoxville	*94.0
1978	Bowie St.	112.3
1979	Catholic	116.9
1980	Maine Maritime	127.2
1981	Millsaps	147.6
1982	Plymouth St.	122.2
1983	Lycoming	154.5
1984	Swarthmore	159.2
1985	Augustana (Ill.)	149.1
1986	Augustana (Ill.)	136.2
1987	Plymouth St.	135.3
1988	Plymouth St.	143.6
1989	Frostburg St.	119.7
1990	Bentley	139.8
1991	Wash. & Jeff.	143.0
1992	Bentley	184.5
1993	Wash. & Jeff.	142.4
1994	Wash. & Jeff.	165.3
1995	Mass. Maritime	161.2
1996	Worcester St.	125.8
1997	Salve Regina	146.0

**Record.*

RUSHING DEFENSE

Year	Team	Avg.
1973	Oregon Col.	61.2
1974	Millersville	57.2
1975	Cal Lutheran	62.4
1976	Lycoming	44.3
1977	Knoxville	*-2.3
1978	Western Md.	43.4
1979	Catholic	46.4
1980	Maine Maritime	3.2
1981	Augustana (Ill.)	30.7
1982	Lycoming	34.2
1983	DePauw	41.6
1984	Swarthmore	40.0
1985	Augustana (Ill.)	35.1
1986	Dayton	13.5
1987	Lycoming	35.4
1988	Worcester St.	43.9
1989	Frostburg St.	49.7
1990	Ohio Wesleyan	18.9
1991	Wash. & Jeff.	64.6
1992	Bri'water (Mass.)	43.2
1993	Wash. & Jeff.	19.1
1994	Wash. & Jeff.	23.7
1995	Marietta	46.2
1996	Worcester St.	20.3
1997	Mount Union	48.6

**Record.*

PASSING DEFENSE

Year	Team	$Avg.
1973	Nichols	53.0
1974	Findlay	49.2
1975	Wash. & Jeff.	56.0
1976	Mass. Maritime	*48.5
1977	Hofstra	49.4
1978	Bowie St.	64.7
1979	Wagner	59.5
1980	Williams	63.8
1981	Plymouth St.	66.9
1982	Plymouth St.	48.8
1983	Muhlenberg	76.4
1984	Bri'water (Mass.)	68.7
1985	Bri'water (Mass.)	77.3
1986	Knoxville	83.2
1987	Jersey City St.	67.0
1988	Colorado Col.	78.9
1989	Frostburg St.	70.0
1990	Bentley	47.4
1991	Wash. & Jeff.	50.3
1992	St. Peter's	51.7
1993	Worcester St.	50.0
1994	Worcester St.	69.2
1995	Union (N.Y.)	54.6
1996	Worcester St.	50.6
1997	Salve Regina	57.3

**Record. $Beginning in 1990, ranked on passing efficiency defense rating points instead of per-game yardage allowed.*

SCORING DEFENSE

Year	Team	Avg.
1973	Fisk	6.4
	Slippery Rock	6.4
1974	Central (Iowa)	6.9
	Rhodes	6.9
1975	Millsaps	5.0
1976	Albion	5.4
1977	Central (Iowa)	5.0
1978	Minn.-Morris	5.9
1979	Carnegie Mellon	4.9
1980	Millsaps	*3.4
1981	Baldwin-Wallace	3.9
1982	West Ga.	4.6
1983	Carnegie Mellon	5.3
1984	Union (N.Y.)	4.6
1985	Augustana (Ill.)	4.7
1986	Augustana (Ill.)	5.1
1987	Plymouth St.	6.2
1988	Plymouth St.	6.5
1989	Millikin	4.8
1990	Bentley	4.5
1991	Mass.-Lowell	5.4
1992	Dayton	6.7
1993	Wash. & Jeff.	6.1
1994	Trinity (Tex.)	6.2
1995	Wash. & Jeff.	5.6
	Williams	5.6
1996	Amherst	8.4
1997	Mount Union	5.6

**Record.*

Other Annual Team Champions

NET PUNTING

Year	Team	Avg.
1992	San Diego	39.2
1993	Benedictine (Ill.)	38.9
1994	Redlands	37.9
1995	Hardin-Simmons	37.9
1996	Cal Lutheran	39.0
1997	John Carroll	40.7

PUNT RETURNS

Year	Team	Avg.
1992	Occidental	18.7
1993	Curry	17.9
	Wheaton (Ill.)	17.9
1994	Frostburg St.	15.2
1995	Ohio Northern	16.5
1996	Howard Payne	17.4
1997	Juniata	18.4

KICKOFF RETURNS

Year	Team	Avg.
1992	Thomas More	27.7
1993	St. John's (Minn.)	28.9
1994	Buffalo St.	26.8
1995	Howard Payne	29.5
1996	Trinity (Conn.)	30.1
1997	Western Md.	29.2

TURNOVER MARGIN

Year	Team	Avg.
1992	Illinois Col.	2.44
1993	Trinity (Conn.)	2.87
1994	Dickinson	2.70
1995	Thomas More	2.80
1996	DePauw	2.50
1997	Rensselaer	2.22

MOST IMPROVED

Year	Team	Imp.
1996	DePauw	6
1997	Grove City	6.5

1997 Most-Improved Teams

School (Coach)	1997	1996	$Games Improved
Grove City (Chris Smith)	9-2	2-8	6
Augsburg (Jack Osberg)	10-2	3-7	6
Western Md. (Tim Keating)	10-1	4-6	5
Adrian (Jim Lyall)	8-1	3-6	5
Guilford (Mike Ketchum)	8-2	3-6	4
Delaware Valley (Glen Leonard)	5-5	1-9	4
Gust. Adolphus (Jay Schoenebeck)	6-4	2-8	4
Mississippi Col. (Terry McMillan) #	8-2	4-6	4
Upper Iowa (Paul Rudolph)	7-3	3-7	4
Wesleyan (Conn.) (Frank Hauser)	7-1	3-5	4
Whittier (Bob Owens)	5-4	1-8	4
Hanover (Wayne Perry)	10-1	6-4	3
Beloit (Ed DeGeorge)	3-6	0-9	3
Methodist (Jim Sypult)	9-1	6-4	3
Neb. Wesleyan (Brian Keller)	5-5	2-8	3
Waynesburg (Dan Baranik)	5-4	2-7	3
Western New Eng. (Gerry Martin)	4-3	2-7	3
Benedictine (Ill.) (John Welty)	3-7	0-9	2
Ferrum (Dave Davis)	4-6	1-8	2
Fitchburg St. (Chris Nugai)	3-7	0-0	2

#Division II member in 1996.

$To determine games improved, add the difference in victories between the two seasons to the difference in losses, then divide by two; ties not counted. Includes postseason.

All-Time Team Won-Lost Records

Won-lost-tied record includes post-season games

BY PERCENTAGE (TOP 25)

(Minimum of 20 seasons of competition)

Team	Yrs.	Won	Lost	Tied	Pct.
Plymouth St.	28	186	76	7	.704
Wis.-La Crosse	73	452	183	40	.699
St. John's (Minn.)	87	438	203	24	.677
Ithaca	65	343	184	11	.648
Linfield	83	419	224	31	.645
Wittenberg	104	581	317	32	.642
Wis.-Whitewater	73	383	211	21	.640
Pacific Lutheran	63	357	199	29	.635
Augustana (Ill.)	85	432	245	28	.633
Concordia-M'head	78	399	227	38	.630
Baldwin-Wallace	93	462	272	30	.624
Cal Lutheran	36	216	129	7	.624
Central (Iowa)	89	451	275	26	.617
Montclair St.	67	333	203	20	.617
Williams	112	536	328	47	.614
Wash. & Jeff.	106	553	346	40	.610
Widener	117	550	351	38	.606
Millikin	92	449	289	28	.604
St. Thomas (Minn.)	92	443	285	32	.604
Gust. Adolphus	82	394	257	21	.602
Wis.-River Falls	72	352	228	32	.601
Albion	111	497	323	43	.601
Lycoming	48	248	171	11	.590
Coe	105	471	324	38	.588
Wabash	111	503	345	59	.587

ALPHABETICAL

(No minimum seasons of competition)

Team	Yrs.	Won	Lost	Tied	Pct.
Adrian	95	307	386	17	.444
Albion	111	497	323	43	.601
Albright	85	352	389	22	.476
Alfred	99	385	307	45	.553
Allegheny	103	413	340	44	.546
Alma	101	406	343	27	.541
Amherst	118	517	376	54	.574
Anderson (Ind.)	51	228	221	12	.508
Augsburg	66	161	365	18	.313
Augustana (Ill.)	85	432	245	28	.633
Aurora	12	57	45	1	.558
Austin	101	386	387	40	.499
Baldwin-Wallace	93	462	272	30	.624
Bates	102	279	433	46	.398
Beloit	107	362	433	47	.458
Benedictine (Ill.)	76	244	301	24	.450
Bethany (W.Va.)	97	299	456	34	.401
Bethel (Minn.)	45	146	249	8	.372
Blackburn	9	20	57	0	.260
Bluffton	75	240	339	23	.418
Bowdoin	104	352	406	44	.466
Bri'water (Mass.)	38	163	161	6	.503
Bridgewater (Va.)	53	126	299	11	.302
Brockport St.	51	143	263	4	.354
Buena Vista	93	356	341	28	.510
Buffalo St.	17	84	76	0	.525
Cal Lutheran	36	216	129	7	.624
Capital	74	283	299	27	.487
Carleton	103	426	326	25	.564
Carnegie Mellon	88	414	308	29	.571
Carroll (Wis.)	94	375	282	38	.567
Carthage	101	362	357	42	.503
Case Reserve	28	100	155	4	.394
Catholic	52	215	209	13	.507
Central (Iowa)	89	451	275	26	.617
Centre	105	473	350	38	.571
Chapman	4	25	10	1	.708
Chicago	78	339	319	33	.514
Claremont-M-S	40	127	221	5	.367
Coast Guard	74	262	328	49	.448
Coe	105	471	324	38	.588
Colby	104	302	415	33	.425
Colorado Col.	112	435	396	35	.523
Concordia (Ill.)	59	171	278	19	.386
Concordia-M'head	78	399	227	38	.630
Concordia (Wis.)	18	102	61	2	.624
Cornell College	107	451	354	33	.558
Cortland St.	71	298	249	28	.543
Curry	33	101	176	6	.367
Defiance	75	295	317	20	.483
Delaware Valley	50	184	236	10	.440
Denison	108	471	383	57	.548
DePauw	110	452	420	41	.518
Dickinson	109	403	468	55	.465
Dubuque	75	267	334	25	.446
Earlham	107	318	470	23	.406
Elmhurst	78	238	381	24	.389
Emory & Henry	82	433	329	19	.567
Eureka	64	155	329	26	.329
FDU-Madison	24	64	147	1	.304
Ferrum	13	78	54	1	.590
Fitchburg St.	14	14	110	1	.116
Framingham St.	24	81	131	2	.383
Franklin	97	349	417	31	.457
Frank. & Marsh.	110	528	382	47	.576
Frostburg St.	37	174	168	8	.509
Gettysburg	105	483	409	42	.540
Grinnell	107	345	473	33	.425
Grove City	103	403	403	60	.500
Guilford	92	249	480	25	.347
Gust. Adolphus	82	394	257	21	.602
Hamilton	104	336	397	47	.461
Hamline	106	375	359	30	.510
Hampden-Sydney	103	423	385	28	.523
Hanover	105	373	354	29	.513
Hardin-Simmons	61	299	214	35	.578
Hartwick	26	69	122	11	.369
Heidelberg	102	407	405	41	.501
Hiram	99	244	488	32	.340
Hobart	104	368	425	40	.466
Hope	88	341	275	38	.550
Howard Payne	92	403	374	41	.518
Illinois Col.	101	348	400	36	.467
Ill. Wesleyan	106	451	335	41	.570
Ithaca	65	343	184	11	.648
Jersey City St.	30	98	180	3	.354
John Carroll	75	354	261	37	.571
Johns Hopkins	113	373	428	57	.468
Juniata	75	313	289	22	.519
Kalamazoo	103	343	402	41	.462
Kean	26	102	140	9	.424
Kenyon	108	311	495	47	.392
King's (Pa.)	5	9	39	1	.194
Knox	104	361	445	43	.451
La Verne	72	282	302	18	.483
Lake Forest	105	345	398	55	.467
Lakeland	63	250	246	13	.504
Lawrence	104	455	317	29	.586
Lebanon Valley	97	343	445	36	.438
Lewis & Clark	51	213	195	12	.521
Linfield	83	419	224	31	.645
Loras	69	301	237	31	.556
Luther	84	362	301	21	.545
Lycoming	48	248	171	11	.590
Macalester	95	229	446	29	.346
MacMurray	13	58	66	1	.468
Maine Maritime	52	221	187	9	.541
Manchester	72	224	350	20	.394
Marietta	103	358	450	36	.446
Martin Luther	99	310	316	31	.495
Maryville (Tenn.)	100	383	410	35	.484
Mass.-Boston	10	26	63	1	.294
Mass.-Dartmouth	10	52	42	0	.553
MIT	10	32	47	1	.406
Mass. Maritime	25	125	100	1	.555
McMurry	72	289	362	36	.447
Menlo	12	43	64	2	.404
Merchant Marine	53	236	238	13	.498
Methodist	9	31	59	0	.344
Middlebury	101	341	354	42	.491
Millikin	92	449	289	28	.604
Millsaps	75	316	294	36	.517
Mississippi Col.	85	405	313	37	.561
Monmouth (Ill.)	105	422	407	39	.509
Montclair St.	67	333	203	20	.617
Moravian	64	279	252	21	.524
Mount Union	101	501	381	34	.566
Muhlenberg	98	388	440	42	.470
Muskingum	103	454	349	39	.562

Team	Yrs.	Won	Lost	Tied	Pct.
Neb. Wesleyan	89	388	350	42	.524
Col. of New Jersey	73	272	270	32	.502
Nichols	39	151	160	6	.486
North Central	93	324	369	36	.469
North Park	39	80	265	7	.237
Norwich	99	289	428	31	.407
Oberlin	107	352	479	39	.427
Occidental	96	393	341	26	.534
Ohio Northern	99	377	402	35	.485
Ohio Wesleyan	107	486	412	44	.539
Olivet	97	269	444	33	.383
Otterbein	108	341	507	43	.407
Pacific Lutheran	63	357	199	29	.635
Plymouth St.	28	186	76	7	.704
Pomona-Pitzer	100	342	374	31	.479
Principia	64	178	307	16	.371
Randolph-Macon	110	411	390	57	.512
Redlands	88	389	354	28	.523
Rensselaer	108	306	482	46	.394
Rhodes	86	305	331	38	.481
Ripon	104	426	302	46	.580
Rochester	109	437	401	38	.521
Rose-Hulman	102	345	435	29	.444
Rowan	38	199	153	8	.564
St. John Fisher	10	31	62	0	.333
St. John's (Minn.)	87	438	203	24	.677
St. Lawrence	103	344	372	29	.481
St. Norbert	64	284	243	20	.537
St. Olaf	80	355	283	20	.555
St. Thomas (Minn.)	92	443	285	32	.604
Salisbury St.	26	135	111	4	.548
Salve Regina	5	34	9	0	.791
Sewanee	103	426	385	39	.524
Simpson	92	382	418	37	.478
Springfield	104	432	386	55	.526
Susquehanna	99	356	399	38	.473
Swarthmore	117	437	440	36	.498
Thiel	93	295	387	36	.436
Thomas More	8	58	22	0	.725
Trinity (Conn.)	113	455	319	42	.583
Trinity (Tex.)	93	345	408	49	.461
Tufts	116	440	446	46	.497
Union (N.Y.)	110	417	389	62	.516
Upper Iowa	95	296	376	25	.443
Ursinus	105	317	497	54	.396
Wabash	111	503	345	59	.587
Wartburg	62	261	263	12	.498
Washington (Mo.)	100	402	403	28	.499
Wash. & Jeff.	106	553	346	40	.610
Wash. & Lee	104	401	441	39	.477
Waynesburg	94	353	333	37	.514
Wesley	12	61	52	1	.539
Wesleyan (Conn.)	116	446	431	42	.508
Western Conn. St.	26	86	158	3	.354
Western Md.	103	433	392	49	.523
Western New Eng.	17	54	94	1	.366
Westfield St.	16	68	83	1	.451
Westminster (Mo.)	35	115	105	17	.521
Wheaton (Ill.)	85	358	304	29	.539
Whittier	88	413	317	36	.563
Widener	117	550	351	38	.606
Wilkes	52	207	234	8	.470
Willamette	97	411	324	40	.556
Wm. Paterson	26	101	152	4	.401
William Penn	97	260	474	35	.361
Williams	112	536	328	47	.614
Wilmington (Ohio)	65	253	283	14	.473
Wis.-Eau Claire	79	295	313	34	.486
Wis.-La Crosse	73	452	183	40	.699
Wis.-Oshkosh	71	227	322	30	.418
Wis.-Platteville	89	300	310	31	.492
Wis.-River Falls	72	352	228	32	.601
Wis.-Stevens Point	98	384	316	43	.546
Wis.-Stout	78	215	396	33	.359
Wis.-Whitewater	73	383	211	21	.640
Wittenberg	104	581	317	32	.642
Wooster	99	417	372	41	.527
Worcester St.	13	72	48	0	.600
Worcester Tech	108	260	417	30	.389

BY VICTORIES

(Minimum of 20 seasons of competition)

Team	Wins	Team	Wins
Wittenberg	581	Denison	471
Wash. & Jeff.	553	Baldwin-Wallace	462
Widener	550	Lawrence	455
Williams	536	Trinity (Conn.)	455
Frank. & Marsh.	528	Muskingum	454
Amherst	517	DePauw	452
Wabash	503	Wis.-La Crosse	452
Mount Union	501	Central (Iowa)	451
Albion	497	Cornell College	451
Ohio Wesleyan	486	Ill. Wesleyan	451
Gettysburg	483	Millikin	449
Centre	473	Wesleyan (Conn.)	446
Coe	471		

Winningest Football Teams of 1990s

BY PERCENTAGE

School	Yrs.	Won	Lost	Tied	Pct.
1. Mount Union	8	94	6	1	.936
2. Allegheny	8	79	10	1	.883
3. Wis.-La Crosse	8	82	11	1	.878
4. Albion	8	69	9	2	.875
4. Williams	8	55	7	2	.875
6. Central (Iowa)	8	71	12	0	.855
7. Wash. & Jeff.	8	75	14	0	.843
8. St. John's (Minn.)	8	75	14	1	.839
9. Union (N.Y.)	8	66	13	0	.835
10. Coe	8	64	14	0	.821
11. Wittenberg	8	64	15	1	.806
12. Lycoming	8	72	17	1	.806
13. Rowan	8	76	18	1	.805
14. Trinity (Conn.)	8	50	13	1	.789
15. Carnegie Mellon	8	63	17	0	.788
16. Emory & Henry	8	65	18	0	.783
17. Ill. Wesleyan	8	59	16	1	.783
18. Cornell College	8	58	17	0	.773
19. Baldwin-Wallace	8	62	18	1	.772
20. John Carroll	8	61	17	4	.768
21. Dickinson	8	61	18	2	.765
21. Wis.-Whitewater	8	62	19	0	.765
23. Buffalo St.	8	62	20	0	.756
24. Simpson	8	63	20	1	.756
25. Wartburg	8	62	21	0	.747

BY VICTORIES

School	Yrs.	Won	Lost	Tied	Pct.
1. Mount Union	8	94	6	1	.936
2. Wis.-La Crosse	8	82	11	1	.878
3. Allegheny	8	79	10	1	.883
4. Rowan	8	76	18	1	.805
5. Wash. & Jeff.	8	75	14	0	.843
5. St. John's (Minn.)	8	75	14	1	.839
7. Lycoming	8	72	17	1	.806
8. Central (Iowa)	8	71	12	0	.855
9. Albion	8	69	9	2	.874
10. Union (N.Y.)	8	66	13	0	.835
11. Emory & Henry	8	65	18	0	.783
12. Coe	8	64	14	0	.821
12. Wittenberg	8	64	15	1	.806
14. Carnegie Mellon	8	63	17	0	.788
14. Simpson	8	63	20	1	.756
14. Ithaca	8	63	22	0	.741
16. Baldwin-Wallace	8	62	18	1	.772
16. Wis.-Whitewater	8	62	19	0	.765
16. Buffalo St.	8	62	20	0	.756
16. Wartburg	8	62	21	0	.747
21. John Carroll	8	61	17	4	.768
21. Dickinson	8	61	18	2	.765
21. Frostburg St.	8	61	21	2	.738
24. Ill. Wesleyan	8	59	16	1	.783
25. Cornell College	8	58	17	0	.773

National Poll Rankings

Final Poll Leaders

(Released Before Division Championship Playoffs)

Year	Team (Record*)	Coach	Record in Championship†
1975	Ithaca (8-0-0)	Jim Butterfield	2-1 Runner-up
1976	St. John's (Minn.) (7-0-1)	John Gagliardi	3-0 Champion
1977	Wittenberg (8-0-0)	Dave Maurer	Did not compete
1978	Minn.-Morris (9-0-0)	Al Molde	1-1 Lost in semifinals
1979	Wittenberg (8-0-0)	Dave Maurer	2-1 Runner-up
1980	Ithaca (10-0-0)	Jim Butterfield	2-1 Runner-up
1981	Widener (9-0-0)	Bill Manlove	3-0 Champion
1982	Baldwin-Wallace (10-0-0)	Bob Packard	0-1 Lost in first round
1983	Augustana (Ill.) (9-0-0)	Bob Reade	3-0 Champion
1984	Augustana (Ill.) (9-0-0)	Bob Reade	3-0 Champion
1985	Augustana (Ill.) (9-0-0)	Bob Reade	4-0 Champion
1986	Dayton (10-0-0)	Mike Kelly	0-1 Lost in first round
1987	Augustana (Ill.) (9-0-0)	Bob Reade	1-1 Lost in quarterfinals
1988	**East Region**		
	Cortland St. (9-0-0)	Dennis Kayser	1-1 Lost in quarterfinals
	North Region		
	Dayton (9-1-0)	Mike Kelly	0-1 Lost in first round
	South Region		
	Ferrum (9-0-0)	Hank Norton	2-1 Lost in semifinals
	West Region		
	Central (Iowa) (8-0-0)	Ron Schipper	3-1 Runner-up
1989	**East Region**		
	Union (N.Y.) (9-0-0)	Al Bagnoli	3-1 Runner-up
	North Region		
	Dayton (8-0-1)	Mike Kelly	4-0 Champion
	South Region		
	Rhodes (7-0-0)	Mike Clary	Did not compete
	West Region		
	Central (Iowa) (8-0-0)	Ron Schipper	1-1 Lost in quarterfinals
1990	**East Region**		
	Hofstra (9-0-0)	Joe Gardi	2-1 Lost in semifinals
	North Region		
	Dayton (9-0-0)	Mike Kelly	1-1 Lost in quarterfinals
	South Region		
	Ferrum (8-0-0)	Hank Norton	0-1 Lost in first round
	West Region		
	Wis.-Whitewater (9-0-0)	Bob Berezowitz	0-1 Lost in first round
1991	**East Region**		
	Ithaca (7-1-0)	Jim Butterfield	4-0 Champion
	North Region		
	Allegheny (10-0-0)	Ken O'Keefe	1-1 Lost in quarterfinals
	South Region		
	Lycoming (8-0-0)	Frank Girardi	1-1 Lost in quarterfinals
	West Region		
	St. John's (Minn.) (9-0-0)	John Gagliardi	2-1 Lost in semifinals
1992	**East Region**		
	Rowan (9-0-0)	John Bunting	2-1 Lost in semifinals
	North Region		
	Dayton (9-0-0)	Mike Kelly	0-1 Lost in first round
	South Region		
	Wash. & Jeff. (8-0-0)	John Luckhardt	3-1 Runner-up
	West Region		
	Central (Iowa) (9-0-0)	Ron Schipper	1-1 Lost in quarterfinals
1993	**East Region**		
	Rowan (7-1-0)	K. C. Keeler	3-1 Runner-up
	North Region		
	Mount Union (9-0-0)	Larry Kehres	4-0 Champion
	South Region		
	Wash. & Jeff. (8-0-0)	John Luckhardt	2-1 Lost in semifinals
	West Region		
	Wis.-La Crosse (9-0-0)	Roger Harring	1-1 Lost in quarterfinals
1994	**East Region**		
	Plymouth St. (8-0-0)	Don Brown	1-1 Lost in quarterfinals
	North Region		
	Allegheny (9-0-0)	Ken O'Keefe	0-1 Lost in first round
	South Region		
	Dickinson (9-0-0)	Darwin Breaux	0-1 Lost in first round
	West Region		
	Central (Iowa) (9-0-0)	Ron Schipper	0-1 Lost in first round
1995	**East Region**		
	Buffalo St. (8-1-0)	Jerry Boyes	0-1 Lost in first round
	North Region		
	Mount Union (9-0-0)	Larry Kehres	2-1 Lost in semifinals
	South Region		
	Wash. & Jeff. (7-0-0)	John Luckhardt	2-1 Lost in semifinals
	West Region		
	Wis.-La Crosse (9-0-0)	Roger Harring	4-0 Champion
1996	**East Region**		
	Buffalo St. (7-1)	Jerry Boyes	0-1 Lost in first round
	North Region		
	Mount Union (9-0)	Larry Kehres	4-0 Champion
	South Region		
	Lycoming (8-0)	Frank Girardi	2-1 Lost in semifinals
	West Region		
	Wis.-La Crosse (9-0)	Roger Harring	2-1 Lost in semifinals
1997	**East Region**		
	Rowan (8-0)	K.C. Keeler	2-1 Lost in semifinals
	North Region		
	Mount Union (9-0)	Larry Kehres	4-0 Champion
	South Region		
	Lycoming (8-0)	Frank Girardi	3-1 Runner-up
	West Region		
	Wis.-Whitewater (9-0)	Bob Berezowitz	0-1 Lost in first round

**Final poll record. †Number of teams in the championship: 8 (1975-84); 16 (1985-present).*

Undefeated, Untied Teams

(Regular-Season Games Only)

Following is a list of undefeated and untied teams since 1973, when College Division teams were divided into Division II and Division III under a three-division reorganization plan adopted by the special NCAA Convention in August 1973. Since 1981, conference playoff games have been included in a team's won-lost record (previously, such games were considered postseason contests). Figures indicate the regular-season wins (minimum seven games against four-year varsity opponents). A subsequent postseason win(s) in the Division III championship or a conference playoff game (before 1981) is indicated by (*), a loss by (†) and a tie by (‡).

Year	College	Wins
1973	Fisk	9
	Wittenberg	***9
1974	Albany (N.Y.)	9
	Central (Iowa)	**9
	Frank. & Marsh.	9
	Ithaca	*†9
	Towson St.	10
1975	Cal Lutheran	*†9
	Ithaca	**†8
	Widener	*†9
	Wittenberg	†***9
1976	Albion	9
1977	Central (Iowa)	†9
	Cornell College	†8
	Wittenberg	†9
1978	Baldwin-Wallace	‡***8
	Illinois Col.	9
	Minn.-Morris	*†10
	Wittenberg	‡**†8
1979	Carnegie Mellon	*†9
	Dubuque	†9
	Jamestown	7
	Tufts	8
	Widener	*†9
	Wittenberg	***†8
1980	Adrian	9
	Baldwin-Wallace	†9
	Bethany (W.Va.)	†9
	Dayton	***11
	Ithaca	**†10
	Millsaps	9
	Widener	*†10
1981	Alfred	†10
	Augustana (Ill.)	†9
	Lawrence	*†9
	West Ga.	†9
	Widener	***10
1982	Augustana (Ill.)	**†9
	Baldwin-Wallace	†10
	Plymouth St.	10
	St. John's (Minn.)	9
	St. Lawrence	*†9
	Wabash	10
	West Ga.	***9
1983	Augustana (Ill.)	***9
	Carnegie Mellon	†9
	Hofstra	†10
	Worcester Tech	8
1984	Amherst	8
	Augustana (Ill.)	***9
	Case Reserve	9
	Central (Iowa)	**†9
	Dayton	†10
	Hope	9
	Occidental	†10
	Plymouth St.	†10
1985	Augustana (Ill.)	****9
	Carnegie Mellon	†8
	Central (Iowa)	**†9
	Denison	†10
	Lycoming	†10
	Mount Union	*†10
	Union (N.Y.)	†9
1986	Central (Iowa)	*†10
	Dayton	†10
	Ithaca	**†9
	Mount Union	*†10
	Salisbury St.	***†10
	Susquehanna	*†10
	Union (N.Y.)	†9
1987	Augustana (Ill.)	*†9
	Gust. Adolphus	†10
	Wash. & Jeff.	*†9
1988	Cortland St.	*†10
	Ferrum	**†9
1989	Central (Iowa)	*†9
	Millikin	*†9
	Union (N.Y.)	***†10
	Williams	8
1990	Carnegie Mellon	†10
	Dayton	*†10
	Hofstra	**†10
	Lycoming	***†9
	Mount Union	†10
	Wash. & Jeff.	*†9
	Williams	8
	Wis.-Whitewater	†10
1991	Allegheny	*†10
	Baldwin-Wallace	†10
	Dayton	***†10
	Dickinson	†10
	Eureka	10
	Lycoming	*†9
	Mass.-Lowell	†10
	St. John's (Minn.)	**†9
	Simpson	†10
	Thomas More	10
	Union (N.Y.)	*†9
1992	Aurora	†9
	Central (Iowa)	*†9
	Cornell College	10
	Dayton	†10
	Emory & Henry	*†10
	Ill. Wesleyan	*†9
	Mount Union	**†10
	Rowan	**†10
1993	Albion	*†9
	Anderson (Ind.)	†10
	Coe	†10
	Mount Union	****10
	St. John's (Minn.)	**†10
	Trinity (Conn.)	8
	Union (N.Y.)	†9
	Wash. & Jeff.	**†9
	Wilkes	†10
	Wis.-La Crosse	*†10
1994	Albion	****9
	Allegheny	†10
	Central (Iowa)	†10
	Dickinson	†10
	La Verne	†9
	Plymouth St.	*†9
	Trinity (Tex.)	†10
	Williams	8
1995	Central (Iowa)	†10
	Hanover	†10
	La Verne	9
	Mount Union	**†10
	Plymouth St.	†9
	Thomas More	10
	Wash. & Jeff.	**†8
	Wheaton (Ill.)	*†9
	Wis.-La Crosse	****10
	Wittenberg	†10
1996	Albion	†9
	Allegheny	†10
	Ill. Wesleyan	*†9
	Lycoming	**†9
	Mount Union	****10
	St. John's (Minn.)	*†10
	Salve Regina	9
	Simpson	†10
	Worcester St.	†10
1997	Catholic	†10
	Hanover	†10
	Lakeland	10
	Lycoming	***†9
	Mount Union	****10
	Rowan	**†9
	Simpson	**†10
	Trinity (Tex.)	*†9
	Western Md.	†10
	Wis.-Whitewater	†9

The Spoilers

(Since 1973, when the three-division reorganization plan was adopted by the special NCAA Convention, creating Divisions II and III.)

Following is a list of the spoilers of Division III teams that lost their perfect (undefeated, untied) record in their **season-ending** game, including the Division III championship playoffs. An asterisk (*) indicates a Division III championship playoff game and a dagger (†) indicates the home team in a regular-season game or a conference playoff. A game involving two undefeated, untied teams is in bold face.

Date	Spoiler	Victim	Score
11-17-73	† Williams	Amherst	30-14
12-7-74	* Central (Iowa)	Ithaca	10-8
11-8-75	Cornell College	† Lawrence	17-16
11-22-75	* **Ithaca**	**Widener**	23-14
12-6-75	* Wittenberg	Ithaca	28-0
11-12-77	Norwich	† Middlebury	34-20
11-12-77	Ripon	† Cornell College	10-7
11-19-77	† Baldwin-Wallace	Wittenberg	14-7
11-19-77	* Widener	Central (Iowa)	19-0
11-25-78	* Wittenberg	Minn.-Morris	35-14
11-17-79	* Ithaca	Dubuque	27-7
11-17-79	‡ Findlay	Jamestown	41-15
11-24-79	* **Wittenberg**	**Widener**	17-14
11-24-79	* Ithaca	Carnegie Mellon	15-6
12-1-79	* Ithaca	Wittenberg	14-10
11-8-80	DePauw	† Wabash	tie 22-22
11-22-80	* **Widener**	**Bethany (W.Va.)**	43-12
11-22-80	* Dayton	Baldwin-Wallace	34-0
11-29-80	* Dayton	Widener	28-24
12-6-80	#* Dayton	Ithaca	63-0
11-14-81	† DePauw	Wabash	21-14
11-14-81	† St. Mary's (Cal.)	San Diego	31-14
11-21-81	* Widener	West Ga.	10-3
11-21-81	* Dayton	Augustana (Ill.)	19-7
11-21-81	* Montclair St.	Alfred	13-12
11-28-81	* Dayton	Lawrence	38-0
11-13-82	† Widener	Swarthmore	24-7
11-20-82	‡ Northwestern (Iowa)	St. John's (Minn.)	33-28
11-20-82	* **Augustana (Ill.)**	**Baldwin-Wallace**	28-22
11-27-82	* **Augustana (Ill.)**	**St. Lawrence**	14-0
12-4-82	* **West Ga.**	**Augustana (Ill.)**	14-0
11-19-83	* Salisbury St.	Carnegie Mellon	16-14
11-19-83	* Union (N.Y.)	Hofstra	51-19
11-10-84	St. John's (N.Y.)	† Hofstra	19-16
11-10-84	† St. Olaf	Hamline	tie 7-7
11-17-84	* Union (N.Y.)	Plymouth St.	26-14
11-17-84	* Central (Iowa)	Occidental	23-22
11-17-84	* Augustana (Ill.)	Dayton	14-13
12-8-84	* **Augustana (Ill.)**	**Central (Iowa)**	21-12
11-23-85	* Gettysburg	Lycoming	14-10

DIVISION III

Date	Spoiler	Victim	Score
11-23-85	* **Mount Union**	**Denison**	35-3
11-23-85	* Salisbury St.	Carnegie Mellon	35-22
11-23-85	* Ithaca	Union (N.Y.)	13-12
11-30-85	* **Augustana (Ill.)**	**Mount Union**	21-14
12-7-85	* **Augustana (Ill.)**	**Central (Iowa)**	14-7
11-15-86	† Lawrence	Coe	14-10
11-22-86	* **Mount Union**	**Dayton**	42-36
11-22-86	* **Ithaca**	**Union (N.Y.)**	OT 24-17
11-29-86	* Concordia-M'head	Central (Iowa)	17-14
11-29-86	* **Salisbury St.**	**Susquehanna**	31-17
11-29-86	* **Augustana (Ill.)**	**Mount Union**	16-7
12-6-86	* **Salisbury St.**	**Ithaca**	44-40
12-13-86	* **Augustana (Ill.)**	**Salisbury St.**	31-3
11-11-87	St. Norbert	† Monmouth (Ill.)	20-15
11-21-87	* St. John's (Minn.)	Gust. Adolphus	7-3
11-28-87	* Emory & Henry	Wash. & Jeff.	23-16
11-28-87	$* Dayton	Augustana (Ill.)	38-36
11-12-88	† St. Norbert	Monmouth (Ill.)	12-0
11-19-88	Coast Guard	† Plymouth St.	28-19
11-26-88	* Ithaca	Cortland St.	24-17
12-3-88	* Ithaca	Ferrum	62-28
11-11-89	† Baldwin-Wallace	John Carroll	25-19
11-11-89	† **Bri'water (Mass.)**	**Mass.-Lowell**	14-10
11-11-89	† Centre	Rhodes	13-10
11-18-89	† Alfred	Bri'water (Mass.)	30-27
11-25-89	* St. John's (Minn.)	Central (Iowa)	27-24
11-25-89	* Dayton	Millikin	28-16
12-9-89	* Dayton	Union (N.Y.)	17-7
11-10-90	Col. of New Jersey	† Ramapo	9-0
11-10-90	† Waynesburg	Frostburg St.	28-18
11-17-90	* Allegheny	Mount Union	26-15
11-17-90	* **Lycoming**	**Carnegie Mellon**	17-7
11-17-90	* St. Thomas (Minn.)	Wis.-Whitewater	24-23
11-24-90	* Allegheny	Dayton	31-23
11-24-90	* **Lycoming**	**Wash. & Jeff.**	24-0
12-1-90	* **Lycoming**	**Hofstra**	20-10
12-8-90	* Allegheny	Lycoming	OT 21-14
11-9-91	† Coe	Beloit	26-10
11-23-91	* **Union (N.Y.)**	**Mass.-Lowell**	55-16
11-23-91	* **Dayton**	**Baldwin-Wallace**	27-10
11-30-91	* **Dayton**	**Allegheny**	OT 28-25
11-30-91	* Ithaca	Union (N.Y.)	35-23
11-30-91	* Susquehanna	Lycoming	31-24
12-7-91	* **Dayton**	**St. John's (Minn.)**	19-7
12-14-91	* Ithaca	Dayton	34-20
11-7-92	Cornell College	† Coe	37-20
11-7-92	Union (N.Y.)	† Rochester	14-10
11-21-92	* **Ill. Wesleyan**	**Aurora**	21-12
11-21-92	* **Mount Union**	**Dayton**	27-10
11-28-92	* **Mount Union**	**Ill. Wesleyan**	49-27
11-28-92	* Wash. & Jeff.	Emory & Henry	51-15
11-28-92	* Wis.-La Crosse	Central (Iowa)	34-9
12-5-92	* Wash. & Jeff.	Rowan	18-13
12-5-92	* Wis.-La Crosse	Mount Union	29-24
10-30-93	Mount Senario	† Martin Luther	21-20
11-13-93	Hastings	† Colorado Col.	22-21
11-20-93	* **Albion**	**Anderson (Ind.)**	41-21
11-20-93	* **St. John's (Minn.)**	**Coe**	32-14
11-20-93	* Frostburg St.	Wilkes	26-25
11-20-93	* Wm. Paterson	Union (N.Y.)	17-7
11-27-93	* **Mount Union**	**Albion**	30-16
11-27-93	* **St. John's (Minn.)**	**Wis.-La Crosse**	47-25
12-5-93	* **Mount Union**	**St. John's (Minn.)**	56-8
12-5-93	* Rowan	Wash. & Jeff.	23-16
11-12-94	John Carroll	† Baldwin-Wallace	9-0
11-19-94	* Mount Union	Allegheny	28-19
11-19-94	* Wartburg	Central (Iowa)	22-21
11-19-94	* St. John's (Minn.)	La Verne	51-12
11-19-94	* Widener	Dickinson	14-0
11-19-94	* Wash. & Jeff.	Trinity (Tex.)	28-0
11-26-94	* Ithaca	Plymouth St.	22-7
11-11-95	Amherst	† Williams	0-0
11-18-95	* **Mount Union**	**Hanover**	52-18
Date	**Spoiler**	**Victim**	**Score**
11-18-95	* **Wheaton (Ill.)**	**Wittenberg**	63-41
11-18-95	* Wis.-River Falls	Central (Iowa)	10-7
11-18-95	* Union (N.Y.)	Plymouth St.	24-7
11-25-95	* **Mount Union**	**Wheaton (Ill.)**	40-14
12-2-95	* **Wis.-La Crosse**	**Mount Union**	20-17
12-2-95	* Rowan	Wash. & Jeff.	28-15
11-9-96	Williams	† Amherst	19-13
11-23-96	Ithaca	Worcester St.	27-21
11-23-96	* **Mount Union**	**Allegheny**	31-26
11-23-96	* **Ill. Wesleyan**	**Albion**	23-20
11-23-96	* **St. John's (Minn.)**	**Simpson**	21-18
11-30-96	* **Mount Union**	**Ill. Wesleyan**	49-14
11-30-96	* Wis.-La Crosse	St. John's (Minn.)	37-30
12-7-96	* Rowan	Lycoming	33-14
11-1-97	† Cornell College	Coe	28-21
11-8-97	† Williams	Amherst	48-46
11-15-97	† **Catholic**	**Albright**	44-22
11-22-97	* John Carroll	Hanover	30-20
11-22-97	* **Simpson**	**Wis.-Whitewater**	34-31
11-22-97	* **Lycoming**	**Western Md.**	27-13
11-22-97	* **Trinity (Tex.)**	**Catholic**	44-33
11-29-97	* **Lycoming**	**Trinity (Tex.)**	46-26
12-6-97	* **Mount Union**	**Simpson**	54-7
12-6-97	* **Lycoming**	**Rowan**	28-20
12-13-97	* **Mount Union**	**Lycoming**	61-12

‡NAIA championship playoff game. #Defeated three consecutive perfect-record teams in the Division III championship playoffs. $Ended Augustana's (Illinois) 60-game undefeated streak.

Streaks and Rivalries

Longest Winning Streaks

(Minimum Two Seasons in Division III; Includes Postseason Games)

Wins	Team	Years
37	Augustana (Ill.)	1983-85
28	Mount Union	1996-97
24	Allegheny	1990-91
23	Wis.-La Crosse	1995-96
23	Williams	1988-91
22	Dayton	1989-90
22	Augustana (Ill.)	1986-87
21	Dayton	1979-81
20	Plymouth St.	1987-88
19	Mount Union	1993-94
19	Wis.-La Crosse	1992-93
19	Plymouth St.	1981-82
18	Lawrence	1980-81
18	Ithaca	1979-80

Longest Unbeaten Streaks

(Minimum Two Seasons in Division III; Includes Postseason Games)

No.	Wins	Ties	Team	Years
60	59	1	Augustana (Ill.)	1983-87
28	28	0	Mount Union	1996-97
25	24	1	Dayton	1989-90
24	24	0	Allegheny	1990-91
24	23	1	Wis.-La Crosse	1992-93
24	23	1	Wabash	1979-81
23	23	0	Wis.-La Crosse	1995-96
23	23	0	Williams	1988-91
22	21	1	Dayton	1979-81
21	20	1	Baldwin-Wallace	1977-79
20	20	0	Plymouth St.	1987-88
20	18	2	St. John's (Minn.)	1975-76

Longest Division III Series

Games	Opponents (Series leader listed first)	Series Record	First Game
112	Williams-Amherst	62-45-5	1884
111	Albion-Kalamazoo	73-34-4	1896
109	Bowdoin-Colby	61-39-9	1892
108	Monmouth (Ill.)-Knox	49-49-10	1891
107	Coe-Cornell College	56-47-4	1891
104	Wabash-DePauw	48-47-9	1890
103	Amherst-Wesleyan (Conn.)	54-40-9	1882
103	Williams-Wesleyan (Conn.)	62-36-5	1881
103	Hampden-Sydney—Randolph-Macon	51-41-11	1893
100	Bowdoin-Bates	59-34-7	1889
100	Colby-Bates	54-38-8	1893
99	Occidental—Pomona-Pitzer	52-44-3	1895
97	Wesleyan (Conn.)-Trinity (Conn.)	50-46-1	1885
96 *	Union (N.Y.)-Hamilton	46-38-12	1890

**Did not play in 1994-97.*

Trophy Games

Following is a list of the current Division III football trophy games. The games are listed alphabetically by the trophy-object name. The date refers to the season the trophy was first exchanged and is not necessarily the start of the competition between the participants.

Trophy	Date	Colleges
Academic Bowl	1986	Carnegie Mellon-Case Reserve
Admiral's Cup	1980	Maine Maritime-Mass. Maritime
Baird Bros. Golden Stringer	1984	Case Reserve-Wooster
Bell	†1931	Franklin-Hanover
Bill Edwards Trophy	1989	Case Reserve-Wittenberg
Bridge Bowl	1990	Mt. St. Joseph-Thomas More
Bronze Turkey	1929	Knox-Monmouth (Ill.)
CBB	1966	Bates, Bowdoin, Colby
Conestoga Wagon	1963	Dickinson-Frank. & Marsh.
Cortaca Jug	1959	Cortland St.-Ithaca
Cranberry Bowl	1979	Bri'water (Mass.)-Mass. Maritime
Doehling-Heselton Helmet	1988	Lawrence-Ripon
Drum	1940	Occidental—Pomona-Pitzer
Dutchman's Shoes	1950	Rensselaer-Union (N.Y.)
Edumund Orgill	1954	Rhodes-Sewanee
Founder's	1987	Chicago-Washington (Mo.)
Goat	1931	Carleton-St. Olaf
John Wesley	1984	Ky. Wesleyan-Union (Ky.)
Keystone Cup	1981	Delaware Valley-Widener
Little Brass Bell	1947	North Central-Wheaton (Ill.)
Little Brown Bucket	1938	Dickinson-Gettysburg
Little Three	1971	Amherst, Wesleyan (Conn.), Williams
Mercer County Cup	1984	Grove City-Thiel
Monon Bell	1932	DePauw-Wabash
Mug	1931	Coast Guard-Norwich
Old Goal Post	1953	Juniata-Susquehana
Old Musket	1964	Carroll (Wis.)-Carthage
Old Rocking Chair	1980	Hamilton-Middlebury
Old Tin Cup	1954	Gettysburg-Muhlenberg
Old Water Bucket	1989	Maranatha Baptist-Martin Luther
Paint Bucket	1965	Hamline-Macalester
Pella Corporation Classic	1988	Central (Iowa)-William Penn
President's Cup	1971	Case Reserve-John Carroll
Secretary's Cup	1981	Coast Guard-Merchant Marine
Shoes	1946	Occidental-Whittier
Shot Glass	1938	Coast Guard-Rensselaer
Soup Bowl	1997	Guilford-Greensboro
Steve Dean Memorial	1976	Catholic-Georgetown
Transit	1980	Rensselaer-Worcester Tech
Victory Bell	1946	Loras-St. Thomas (Minn.)
Victory Bell	1949	Upper Iowa-Wartburg
Wadsworth	1977	Middlebury-Norwich
Wilson Brothers Cup	1986	Hamline-St. Thomas (Minn.)
Wooden Shoes	1946	Hope-Kalamazoo

Cliffhangers

Regular-season games won by Division III teams on the final play of the game in regulation time (from 1973). The extra point is listed when it provided the margin of victory after the winning touchdown.

Date	Opponents, Score	Game-Winning Play
9-22-73	Hofstra 21, Seton Hall 20	Tom Calder 15 pass from Steve Zimmer (Jim Hogan kick)
9-18-76	Ohio Wesleyan 23, DePauw 20	Tom Scurfield 48 pass from Bob Mauck
10-27-77	Albany (N.Y.) 42, Maine 39	Larry Leibowitz 19 FG
9-22-79	Augustana (Ill.) 19, Carthage 18	John Stockton 14 pass from Mark Schick
10-6-79	Carleton 17, Lake Forest 14	Tim Schoonmaker 46 FG
11-10-79	Dayton 24, St. Norbert 22	Jim Fullenkamp 21 FG
9-13-80	Cornell College 14, Lawrence 13	John Bryant 8 pass from Matt Dillon (Keith Koehler kick)
9-27-80	Muhlenberg 41, Johns Hopkins 38	Mickey Mottola 1 run
10-25-80	Mass.-Lowell 15, Marist 13	Ed Kulis 3 run
10-17-81	Carleton 22, Ripon 21	John Winter 23 pass from Billy Ford (Dave Grein kick)
10-2-82	Frostburg St. 10, Mercyhurst 7	Mike Lippold 34 FG
11-6-82	Williams 27, Wesleyan (Conn.) 24	Marc Hummon 33 pass from Robert Connolly
10-7-83	Johns Hopkins 19, Ursinus 17	John Tucker 10 pass from Mark Campbell
10-8-83	Susquehanna 17, Widener 14	Todd McCarthy 20 FG
10-29-83	Frank. & Marsh. 16, Swarthmore 15	Billy McLean 51 pass from Niall Rosenzweig
9-24-84	Muhlenberg 3, Frank. & Marsh. 0	Tom Mulroy 26 FG
9-14-85	Principia 26, Illinois Col. 22	Dan Sellers 48 pass from Jon Hinds
10-26-85	Buffalo 13, Brockport St. 11	Dan Friedman 37 FG
11-9-85	Frank. & Marsh. 29, Johns Hopkins 28	Brad Ramsey 1 run (Ken Scalet pass from John Travagline)
9-18-86	Beloit 16, Lakeland 13	Sean Saturnio 38 pass from Ed Limon
9-20-86	Susquehanna 43, Lycoming 42	Rob Sochovka 40 pass from Todd Coolidge (Randy Pozsar kick)
10-18-86	Ill. Wesleyan 25, Elmhurst 23	Dave Anderson 11 pass from Doug Moews
9-5-87	Wash. & Jeff. 17, Ohio Wesleyan 16	John Ivory 28 FG
9-26-87	Gust. Adolphus 19, Macalester 17	Dave Fuecker 8 pass from Dean Kraus
10-3-87	Wis.-Whitewater 10, Wis.-Platteville 7	Dave Emond 25 FG
10-24-87	Geneva 9, St. Francis (Pa.) 7	John Moores 19 FG
10-1-88	Canisius 17, Rochester 14	Jim Ehrig 34 FG
10-1-88	Cortland St. 24, Western Conn. St. 21	Ted Nagengast 35 FG
10-8-88	UC Santa Barb. 20, Sonoma St. 18	Harry Konstantinopoulos 52 FG
10-8-88	Hamilton 13, Bowdoin 10	Nate O'Steen 19 FG
11-5-88	Colby 20, Middlebury 18	Eric Aulenback 1 run
11-12-88	Wis.-River Falls 24, Wis.-Stout 23	Andy Feil 45 FG
10-7-89	Moravian 13, Juniata 10	Mike Howey 75 pass from Rob Light
10-21-89	Western New Eng. 17, Bentley 14	Leo Coughlin 17 FG
10-21-89	Thiel 19, Carnegie Mellon 14	Bill Barber 4 pass from Jeff Sorenson
9-8-90	Emory & Henry 22, Wash. & Lee 21	Todd Woodall 26 pass from Pat Walker
9-15-90	Otterbein 20, Capital 17	Korey Brown 39 FG
10-27-90	Hamline 26, Gust. Adolphus 24	Mike Sunnarborg 2 pass from Bob Hackney
11-10-90	Colby 23, Bowdoin 20	Paul Baisley 10 pass from Bob Ward
9-7-91	Central (Iowa) 26, Gust. Adolphus 25	Brian Krob 1 pass from Shad Flynn
9-13-91	St. John's (N.Y.) 30, Iona 27	John Ledwith 42 FG
10-5-91	Trinity (Conn.) 30, Williams 27	John Mullaney 5 pass from James Lane
10-26-91	DePauw 12, Anderson (Ind.) 7	Steve Broderick 65 pass from Brian Goodman
9-19-92	Lake Forest 9, North Park 7	Dave Mills 2 pass from Jim DeLisa
10-17-92	Elmhurst 30, North Central 28	Eric Ekstrom 2 pass from Jack Lamb
10-16-93	Union (N.Y.) 16, Rensselaer 13	Greg Harrison 38 FG
10-16-93	North Central 24, Elmhurst 22	Bryce Cann 35 FG
10-23-93	Stony Brook 21, Merchant Marine 20	Brian Hughes 44 FG
10-30-93	Thomas More 24, Defiance 18	Greg Stofko 6 blocked field goal return
9-10-94	Colorado Col. 16, Buena Vista 14	Josh Vitt 4 run
9-8-95	FDU-Madison 20, Johns Hopkins 17	Jason Herrick 37 FG
10-12-96	Difance 20, Mt. St. Joseph 19	Randy Weldman 40 pass from Jeff Edred
9-13-97	Adrian 10, Heidelberg 7	Mike Hirvela 24 FG
10-25-97	Carthage 22, Millikin 17	Kris Norton 45 pass from Eric Corbett
11-15-97	Worcester Tech 9, Plymouth St. 7	Matt Surette 2 pass from John Riccio

Regular-Season Overtime Games

In 1981, the NCAA Football Rules Committee approved an overtime tiebreaker system to decide a tie game for the purpose of determining a conference champion. The following conferences used the tiebreaker system to decide conference-only tie games. (In 1996, the tiebreaker will be mandatory in all games tied after four periods.) The number of overtimes is indicated in parentheses.

EASTERN COLLEGIATE FOOTBALL CONFERENCE

Date	Opponents, Score
10-28-95	Western New Eng. 6, Nichols 0 (4 OT)

IOWA INTERCOLLEGIATE ATHLETIC CONFERENCE

Date	Opponents, Score
9-26-81	William Penn 24, Wartburg 21 (1 OT)
9-25-82	Dubuque 16, Buena Vista 13 (1 OT)
10-2-82	Luther 25, Dubuque 22 (1 OT)
10-30-82	Wartburg 27, Dubuque 24 (3 OT)
10-4-86	Luther 28, Wartburg 21 (1 OT)
9-26-87	William Penn 19, Upper Iowa 13 (2 OT)
11-7-87	William Penn 17, Loras 10 (1 OT)
10-10-92	Simpson 20, Loras 14 (1 OT)
11-14-92	Luther 17, Buena Vista 10 (1 OT)

MIDWEST CONFERENCE

Date	Opponents, Score
10-25-86	Lake Forest 30, Chicago 23 (1 OT)
10-26-86	Lawrence 7, Beloit 0 (1 OT)
9-30-89	Illinois Col. 26, Ripon 20 (3 OT)
10-27-90	Beloit 16, St. Norbert 10 (1 OT)
11-2-91	Monmouth (Ill.) 13, Knox 7 (1 OT)
10-14-95	Beloit 20, Carroll (Wis.) 14 (1 OT)

NEW ENGLAND FOOTBALL CONFERENCE

(From 1987)

Date	Opponents, Score
10-31-87	Nichols 21, Mass.-Lowell 20 (1 OT)
9-17-88	Mass.-Lowell 22, Worcester St. 19 (2 OT)
9-30-89	Worcester St. 23, Mass.-Dartmouth 20 (1 OT)
10-27-89	Westfield St. 3, Mass.-Dartmouth 0 (3 OT)
10-28-89	Worcester St. 27, Nichols 20 (1 OT)
11-7-92	Mass.-Dartmouth 21, Westfield St. 14 (3 OT)
9-25-93	Mass. Maritime 28, Mass.-Dartmouth 21 (1 OT)
11-5-94	Mass.-Dartmouth 21, Westfield St. 14 (1 OT)

SOUTHERN CALIFORNIA INTERCOLLEGIATE ATHLETIC CONFERENCE

Date	Opponents, Score
10-18-86	La Verne 53, Occidental 52 (1 OT)
9-26-87	Claremont-M-S 33, Occidental 30 (1 OT)
10-27-90	Occidental 47, Claremont-M-S 41 (1 OT)
10-17-92	Cal Lutheran 17, Occidental 14 (1 OT)
10-30-93	Redlands 23, Cal Lutheran 17 (2 OT)

Stadiums

STADIUMS LISTED ALPHABETICALLY

School	Stadium	Year Built	Capacity	Surface
Adrian	Maple	1960	5,000	Grass
Albion	Sprankle-Sprandel	1976	5,010	Grass
Albright	Eugene L. Shirk	1925	7,000	Grass
Alfred	Merrill Field	1926	5,000	OmniTurf
Allegheny	Robertson Field	1948	5,000	Grass
Alma	Bahlke Field	1986	4,000	Turf
Amherst	Pratt Field	1891	8,000	Grass
Anderson (Ind.)	Macholtz	NA	4,200	Grass
Augsburg	Anderson-Nelson Field	1984	2,000	AstroTurf
Augustana (Ill.)	Ericson Field	1938	3,200	Grass
Aurora	Aurora Field	NA	1,500	Grass
Baldwin-Wallace	George Finnie	1971	8,100	StadiaTurf
Bates	Garcelon Field	1900	3,000	Grass
Beloit	Strong	1934	3,500	Grass
Benedictine (Ill.)	Alumni	1951	3,000	Grass
Bethany (W.Va.)	Bethany Field	1938	1,000	Grass
Bethel (Minn.)	Bremer Field	1972	3,000	Grass
Blackburn	Blackburn College	NA	1,500	Grass
Bluffton	Salzman	1993	3,000	Grass
Bowdoin	Whittier Field	NA	9,000	Grass
Bri'water (Mass.)	College	1974	3,000	Grass
Bridgewater (Va.)	Jopson Field	1971	3,000	Grass
Brockport St.	Special Olympics	1979	10,000	Grass
Buena Vista	J. Leslie Rollins	1980	3,500	Grass
Buffalo St.	Coyer Field	NA	3,000	Grass
Cal Lutheran	Mt. Clef	1962	2,000	Grass
Capital	Bernlohr	1928	2,000	Grass
Carleton	Laird	1926	7,500	Grass
Carnegie Mellon	Gesling	1990	3,500	Omni-Turf
Carroll (Wis.)	Van Male Field	1976	4,200	Grass
Carthage	Art Keller Field	1965	3,100	Grass
Case Reserve	E. L. Finningan Field	1968	3,000	Grass
Catholic	Cardinal Field	1985	3,500	Grass
Central (Iowa)	A. N. Kuyper	1977	5,000	Grass
Centre	Farris	1925	2,500	Grass
Chapman	Chapman	NA	3,000	Grass
Chicago	Stagg Field	1969	1,500	Grass
Claremont-M-S	Zinda Field	1955	3,000	Grass
Coast Guard	Cadet Memorial Field	1932	4,500	Grass
Coe	Clark Field	1989	1,100	Grass
Colby	Seaverns	1948	5,000	Grass
Colorado Col.	Washburn Field	1898	2,000	Grass
Concordia (Ill.)	Concordia	NA	1,500	Grass
Concordia-M'head	Jake Christiansen	NA	7,500	Grass
Cornell College	Ash Park Field	1922	2,500	Grass
Cortland St.	Davis Field	1959	5,000	Grass
Curry	D. Forbes Will Field	NA	1,500	Grass
Defiance	Justin F. Coressel	1994	4,000	Grass
Delaware Valley	James Work Memorial	1978	4,500	Grass
Denison	Deeds Field	1922	5,000	Grass
DePauw	Blackstock	1941	4,000	Grass
Dickinson	Biddle Field	1909	2,577	Grass
Dubuque	Chalmers Field	1942	2,800	PAT
Earlham	M. O. Ross Field	1975	1,500	Grass
Elmhurst	Langhorst Field	1920	2,500	Grass
Emory & Henry	Fullerton Field	NA	5,500	Grass
Eureka	McKinzie	1913	3,000	Grass
FDU-Madison	Jersey Devils	1973	4,000	Grass
Ferrum	W. B. Adams	1970	5,500	Grass
Fitchburg St.	Robert Elliot	1984	1,200	Grass
Framingham St.	Maple Street Field	NA	1,500	Grass
Franklin	Goodell Field	1889	2,000	Grass
Frank. & Marsh.	Sponaugle-Williamson Field	1920	4,000	Grass
Frostburg St.	Bobcat	1974	4,000	Grass
Gettysburg	Musselman	1965	6,176	Grass
Grinnell	Rosenbloom Field	1911	1,750	Grass
Grove City	Thorn Field	1981	3,500	Grass
Guilford	Armfield Athletic Center	1960	3,500	Grass
Gust. Adolphus	Hollingsworth Field	1929	5,500	Grass
Hamilton	Steuben Field	NA	2,500	Grass
Hamline	Norton	1921	2,000	Grass
Hampden-Sydney	Hundley	1964	2,400	Grass
Hanover	L. S. Ayers Field	1973	4,000	Grass
Hardin-Simmons	Shelton	1993	4,000	Grass
Hartwick	AstroTurf Field	1985	1,200	AstroTurf
Heidelberg	Columbian	1941	7,500	Grass
Hiram	Charles Henry Field	1958	3,000	Grass

School	Stadium	Year Built	Capacity	Surface
Hobart	Boswell Field	1975	4,500	Grass
Hope	Holland Municipal	1979	5,322	Grass
Howard Payne	Gordon Wood	NA	7,600	Grass
Illinois Col.	England Field	1960	2,500	Grass
Ill. Wesleyan	Ill. Wesleyan	1893	3,500	Grass
Ithaca	Jim Butterfield	1958	5,000	Grass
Jersey City St.	Tidelands Ath. Complex	1986	2,500	Grass
John Carroll	Wasmer Field	1968	3,500	Turf
Johns Hopkins	Homewood Field	1906	4,000	Turf
Juniata	Chuck Knox	1988	3,000	Grass
Kalamazoo	Angell Field	1946	3,000	Grass
Kean	Zweidinger Field	NA	2,200	Grass
Kenyon	McBride Field	1962	2,500	Grass
King's (Pa.)	Monarch Field	NA	3,000	Grass
Knox	Knox Bowl	1968	6,000	Grass
La Verne	Ortmayer	1991	1,500	Grass
Lake Forest	Farwell Field	NA	2,000	Grass
Lakeland	John Taylor Field	1958	1,500	Grass
Lawrence	Banta Bowl	1965	5,255	Grass
Lebanon Valley	Arnold Field	1969	2,500	Grass
Loras	Rock Bowl	1945	3,000	Grass
Luther	Carlson	1966	5,000	Grass
Lycoming	Person Field	1962	2,500	Grass
Macalester	Macalester	1965	4,000	Grass
MacMurray	MacMurray Field	1984	5,000	Grass
Maine Maritime	Ritchie	1965	3,500	Turf
Manchester	Burt Memorial	NA	4,500	Grass
Marietta	Don Drumm Field	1935	7,000	Grass
Martin Luther	Northwestern	1953	2,000	Grass
Maryville (Tenn.)	Thornton-Honaker Field	1951	2,500	Grass
Mass.-Boston	Clark Ath. Center	1981	750	Grass
Mass.-Dartmouth	University	NA	1,850	Grass
MIT	Henry G. Steinbrenner	1980	1,600	Grass
Mass. Maritime	Edward Ellis Field	1972	3,000	Grass
Menlo	Conner Field	1972	1,000	Grass
Merchant Marine	Captain Tomb Field	1945	5,840	Grass
Methodist	Monarch Field	1989	1,500	Grass
Middlebury	Alumni	1991	3,500	Grass
Millikin	Frank M. Lindsay Field	1987	4,000	Grass
Millsaps	Alumni Field	NA	4,000	Grass
Monmouth (Ill.)	Bobby Woll Field	1981	3,000	Grass
Montclair St.	Sprague Field	1934	6,000	AstroTurf
Moravian	Steel Field	1932	2,200	Grass
Mount Union	Mount Union	1915	5,800	Grass
Muhlenberg	Muhlenberg Field	1928	4,000	Grass
Muskingum	McConagha	1925	5,000	Grass
Neb. Wesleyan	Abel	1986	2,000	Grass
College of New Jersey	Lions	1984	5,000	AstroTurf
Nichols	Bison Bowl	1961	3,000	Grass
North Central	Kroehler Field	NA	3,000	Grass
North Park	Hedstrand Field	1955	2,500	Grass
Norwich	Sabine Field	1921	5,000	Grass
Oberlin	Dill Field	1925	3,500	Grass
Occidental	Patterson Field	1900	4,000	Grass
Ohio Northern	Ada Memorial	1948	4,000	Grass
Ohio Wesleyan	Selby	1929	9,600	Grass
Olivet	Griswold Field	1972	3,500	Grass
Otterbein	Memorial	1946	4,000	Grass
Plymouth St.	Currier Memorial Field	1970	1,000	Grass
Pomona-Pitzer	Merritt Field	1991	2,000	Grass
Principia	Clark Field	1937	1,000	Grass
Randolph-Macon	Day Field	1953	5,000	Grass
Redlands	Ted Runner	1968	7,000	Grass
Rensselaer	86 Field	1912	3,000	Grass
Rhodes	Fargason Field	NA	5,000	Grass
Ripon	Ingalls Field	1888	2,500	Grass
Rochester	Edwin Fauver	1930	5,000	All-Pro Turf
Rose-Hulman	Phil Brown Field	NA	2,500	Grass
Rowan	John Page	1969	5,000	Grass
St. John Fisher	Cardinal Field	NA	1,000	Grass
St. John's (Minn.)	St. John's	1908	5,000	Grass
St. Lawrence	Weeks Field	1906	3,000	Grass
St. Norbert	Minahan	1937	3,100	Grass
St. Olaf	Manitou Field	1930	5,000	Grass
St. Thomas (Minn.)	O'Shaughnessy	1948	5,025	Grass
Salisbury St.	Sea Gull	1980	2,500	Grass
Salve Regina	Toppa	NA	2,500	Grass
Sewanee	McGee Field	1935	1,500	Grass
Simpson	Simpson/Indianola Field	1990	5,000	Grass
Springfield	Benedum Field	1971	2,500	All-Pro Plus
Susquehanna	Amos Alonzo Stagg Field	1892	4,600	Grass
Swarthmore	Clothier	1950	2,000	Grass
Thiel	Stewart Field	1954	5,000	Grass
Thomas More	Lockland	1945	6,500	Grass
Trinity (Conn.)	Dan Jessee Field	1900	6,500	Grass
Trinity (Tex.)	E. M. Stevens	1972	3,500	Grass
Tufts	Ellis Oval	1923	6,000	Grass
Union (N.Y.)	Frank Bailey Field	1981	2,000	AstroTurf
Upper Iowa	Eischeid	1993	3,500	Grass
Ursinus	Patterson Field	1923	2,500	Grass
Wabash	Little Giant	1967	4,200	Grass
Wartburg	Schield	1956	2,500	Grass
Washington (Mo.)	Francis Field	1904	4,000	Grass
Wash. & Jeff.	College Field	1958	5,000	Grass
Wash. & Lee	Wilson Field	1930	7,000	Grass
Waynesburg	College Field	1904	1,300	Grass
Wesley	Wolverine	1989	2,000	Grass
Wesleyan (Conn.)	Andrus Field	1881	8,000	Grass
Western Conn. St.	Midtown Campus Field	NA	2,500	Turf
Western Md.	Scott S. Bair	1981	4,000	Grass
Western New Eng.	WNEC	NA	1,500	Grass
Westfield St.	Alumni Field	1982	4,800	AstroTurf
Westminster (Mo.)	Priest Field	1906	1,500	Grass
Wheaton (Ill.)	McCully Field	1956	7,000	Grass
Whittier	Memorial	NA	7,000	Grass
Widener	Leslie C. Quick Jr.	1994	4,000	Grass
Wilkes	Ralston Field	1965	4,000	Grass
Wm. Paterson	Wrightman	NA	2,000	Grass
William Penn	Community	NA	5,000	Grass
Williams	Weston Field	1875	7,500	Grass
Wilmington (Ohio)	Williams	1983	3,250	Grass
Wis.-Eau Claire	Carson Park	NA	6,500	Grass
Wis.-La Crosse	Veterans Memorial	1924	4,349	Grass
Wis.-Oshkosh	Titan	1970	9,680	Grass
Wis.-Platteville	Ralph E. Davis Pioneer	1972	10,000	Grass
Wis.-River Falls	Ramer Field	1966	4,800	Grass
Wis.-Stevens Point	Goerke Field	1932	4,000	Grass
Wis.-Stout	Nelson Field	1936	5,000	Grass
Wis.-Whitewater	Forrest Perkins	1970	11,000	Grass
Wittenberg	Edwards-Maurer	1995	2,400	StadiaTurf
Wooster	John P. Papp	1991	4,500	Grass
Worcester St.	John Coughlin Memorial	1976	2,500	Grass
Worcester Tech	Alumni Field	1916	2,800	Omni-Turf

STADIUMS LISTED BY CAPACITY (Top 35)

School	Stadium	Surface	Capacity
Wis.-Whitewater	Forrest Perkins	Grass	11,000
Brockport St.	Special Olympics	Grass	10,000
Wis.-Platteville	Ralph E. Davis Pioneer	Grass	10,000
Wis.-Oshkosh	Titan	Grass	9,680
Ohio Wesleyan	Selby	Grass	9,600
Bowdoin	Whittier Field	Grass	9,000
Baldwin-Wallace	George Finnie	StadiaTurf	8,100
Amherst	Pratt Field	Grass	8,000
Wesleyan (Conn.)	Andrus Field	Grass	8,000
Howard Payne	Gordon Wood	Grass	7,600
Carleton	Laird	Grass	7,500
Concordia-M'head	Jake Christiansen	Grass	7,500
Heidelberg	Columbian	Grass	7,500
Williams	Weston Field	Grass	7,500
Albright	Eugene L. Shirk	Grass	7,000
Marietta	Don Drumm Field	Grass	7,000
Redlands	Ted Runner	Grass	7,000
Wash. & Lee	Wilson Field	Grass	7,000
Wheaton (Ill.)	McCully Field	Grass	7,000
Whittier	Memorial	Grass	7,000
Thomas More	Lockland	Grass	6,500
Trinity (Conn.)	Dan Jessee Field	Grass	6,500
Wis.-Eau Claire	Carson Park	Grass	6,500
Gettysburg	Musselman	Grass	6,176
Knox	Knox Bowl	Grass	6,000
Montclair St.	Sprague Field	AstroTurf	6,000
Tufts	Ellis Oval	Grass	6,000
Merchant Marine	Captain Tomb Field	Grass	5,840
Mount Union	Mount Union	Grass	5,800
Ferrum	W. B. Adams	Grass	5,500
Gust. Adolphus	Hollingsworth Field	Grass	5,500
Emory & Henry	Fullerton Field	Grass	5,500
Hope	Holland Municipal	Grass	5,322
Lawrence	Banta Bowl	Grass	5,255
St. Thomas (Minn.)	O'Shaughnessy Field	Grass	5,025

PAT=Prescription Athletic Turf.

Statistics Trends

	Rushing			Passing					Total Offense			Scoring		
Year	**Plays**	**Yds.**	**Avg.**	**Att.**	**Cmp.**	**Pct.**	**Yds.**	**Av. Att.**	**Plays**	**Yds.**	**Avg.**	**TD**	**FG**	**Pts.**
1995	85.6	319.8	3.74	51.0	25.0	49.1	318.5	6.24	136.6	638.3	4.67	6.01	0.82	43.6
1996	85.6	333.8	3.90	51.7	25.6	49.4	335.5	6.48	137.3	669.3	4.87	6.41	0.85	46.6

Additional Statistics Trends

(Average Per Game, Both Teams)

			Punting		PAT Kick Attempts		Two-Point Attempts		Field Goals
Year	**Teams†**	**Games**	**No.**	**Avg.**	**Pct. Made**	**Pct. of Total Tries**	**Pct. Made**	**Pct. of Total Tries**	**Pct. Made**
1995	187	1,773	11.2	33.3	.818	.854	.456	.146	.533
1996	197	1,875	10.8	34.3	.850	.862	.483	.138	.528

†Teams reporting statistics, not the total number of teams in the division.

Classification History

The following lists show years of active membership for current and former Division III football-playing institutions. Provisional members also are shown along with the year in which they will become active memvbers.

ACTIVE MEMBERS (208)

Adrian....1973-97
Albion....1973-97
Albright....1973-97
Alfred....1973-97
Allegheny....1973-97

Alma....1973-97
Amherst....1973-97
Anderson (Ind.)....1992-97
Augsburg....1982-97
Augustana (Ill.)....1973-97

Aurora....1988-97
Austin....1973-77, 97
Baldwin-Wallace....1973-97
Bates....1973-97
Beloit....1973-97

Benedictine (Ill.)....1973-97
Bethany (W.Va.)....1973-97
Bethel (Minn.)....1983-97
Blackburn....1990-97
Bluffton....1990, 92-97

Bowdoin....1973-97
Bri'water (Mass.)....1973-97
Bridgewater (Va.)....1973-97
Brockport St. 1973-97
Buena Vista....1976-97

Buffalo St. 1981-97
Cal Lutheran....1975-77, 91-97
Capital....1973-97
Carleton....1973-97
Carnegie Mellon....1973-97

Carroll (Wis.)....1976-97
Carthage....1976-97
Case Reserve....1973-97
Catholic....1978-97
Central (Iowa)....1973-97

Centre....1973-97
Chapman....1994-97
Chicago....1973-97
Chowan....1997
Claremont-M-S....1973-97
Coast Guard....1973-97

Coe....1973-97
Colby....1973-97
Colorado Col.....1973-97
Concordia (Ill.)....1973-75, 81-97
Concordia-M'head....1977-97

Concordia (Wis.)....1997
Cornell College....1973-97
Cortland St. 1973-97
Curry....1973-97
Defiance....1973-75, 91-97

Delaware Valley....1973-97
Denison....1973-97
DePauw....1973-97
Dickinson....1973-97
Dubuque....1976-97

Earlham....1982-97

Elmhurst....1973-97
Emory & Henry....1973-97
Eureka....1978-97
FDU-Madison....1973-97

Ferrum....1985-97
Fitchburg St. 1984-97
Framingham St. 1973-97
Franklin....1992-97
Frank. & Marsh. 1973-97

Frostburg St. 1977-97
Gettysburg....1973-97
Greenville....1997
Grinnell....1973-97
Grove City....1973-97

Guilford....1990-97
Gust. Adolphus....1973-97
Hamilton....1973-97
Hamline....1973-97
Hampden-Sydney....1973-97

Hanover....1992-97
Hardin-Simmons....1990-92, 94-97
Hartwick....1992-97
Heidelberg....1973-97
Hiram....1973-97

Hobart....1973-97
Hope....1973-97
Howard Payne....1994-97
Illinois Col. 1978-97
Ill. Wesleyan....1978-97

Ithaca....1973-97
Jersey City St. 1973-97
John Carroll....1973-97
Johns Hopkins....1973-97
Juniata....1973-97

Kalamazoo....1973-97
Kean....1973-97
Kenyon....1973-97
King's (Pa.)....1994-97
Knox....1973-97

La Verne....1982-97
Lake Forest....1973-97
Lakeland....1994-97
Lawrence....1973-97
Lebanon Valley....1973-97

Loras....1986-97
Luther....1973-97
Lycoming....1973-97
Macalester....1973-97
MacMurray....1984-97

Maine Maritime....1973-97
Manchester....1992-97
Maranatha Baptist....1997
Marietta....1973-97
Martin Luther....1991-97

Maryville (Tenn.)....1973-97
Mass.-Boston....1988-97
Mass.-Dartmouth....1988-97

MIT....1988-97
Mass. Maritime....1973-97

McMurry....1997
Menlo....1986-97
Merchant Marine....1973-77, 82-97
Methodist....1989-97
Middlebury....1973-97

Millikin....1976-97
Millsaps....1973-97
Monmouth (Ill.)....1973-97
Montclair St. 1973-97
Moravian....1973-97

Mount Union....1973-97
Muhlenberg....1973-97
Muskingum....1973-97
Neb. Wesleyan....1973-97
Col. of New Jersey....1973-97

Nichols....1973-97
North Central....1973-97
North Park....1973-97
Norwich....1973-97
Oberlin....1973-97

Occidental....1973-97
Ohio Northern....1973-97
Ohio Wesleyan....1973-97
Olivet....1973-97
Otterbein....1973-97

Plymouth St. 1973-97
Pomona-Pitzer....1973-97
Principia....1973-97
Randolph-Macon....1973-97
Redlands....1973-78, 82-97

Rensselaer....1973-97
Rhodes....1984-97
Ripon....1973-97
Rochester....1973-97
Rose-Hulman....1973-97

Rowan....1973-97
St. John Fisher....1988-97
St. John's (Minn.)....1973-97
St. Lawrence....1973-97
St. Norbert....1973-97

St. Olaf....1973-97
St. Thomas (Minn.)....1973-97
Salisbury St. 1973-97
Salve Regina....1993-97
Sewanee....1973-97

Simpson....1973-97
Springfield....1995-97
Sul Ross St. 1997
Susquehanna....1973-97
Swarthmore....1973-97

Thiel....1973-97
Thomas More....1990-97
Trinity (Conn.)....1973-97
Trinity (Tex.)....1973-97
Tufts....1973-97

Union (N.Y.)....1973-97
Upper Iowa....1976-97
Upsala....1973-97
Ursinus....1973-97
Wabash....1973-97

Wartburg....1973-97
Washington (Mo.)....1973-97
Wash. & Jeff. 1973-97

Wash. & Lee....1973-97
Waynesburg....1990-97

Wesley....1986-97
Wesleyan (Conn.)....1973-97
Western Conn. St. 1977-97
Western Md. 1973-97
Western New Eng. 1981-97

Westfield St. 1982-97
Westminster (Mo.)....1997
Wheaton (Ill.)....1973-97
Whittier....1973-97
Widener....1973-97

Wilkes....1973-97
Wm. Paterson....1973-97
William Penn....1976-97
Williams....1973-97
Wilmington (Ohio)....1977-80, 90-97

Wis.-Eau Claire....1986-97
Wis.-La Crosse....1983-97
Wis.-Oshkosh....1975-97
Wis.-Platteville....1980-97
Wis.-River Falls....1977, 82-97

Wis.-Stevens Point....1980-97
Wis.-Stout....1980-97
Wis.-Whitewater....1973-77, 80-97
Wittenberg....1973-97
Wooster....1973-97

Worcester St. 1985-97
Worcester Tech....1973-97

PROVISIONAL MEMBERS (9)*

Eastern Ore. St. 1998
Lewis & Clark....1998
Linfield....1998
Mt. St. Joseph....1998
Pacific Lutheran....1998

Puget Sound....1998
Western Ore. St. 1998
Whitworth....1998
Willamette....1998

FORMER MEMBERS

UAB....1991-92
Albany (N.Y.)....1973-94
Albany St. (Ga.)....1973-75
American Int'l....1973
Ashland....1973-79

Assumption....1988-92
Bentley....1988-92
Bloomsburg....1973-79
Bowie St. 1973-79
Bridgeport....1973

Brooklyn....1978-91
Buffalo....1978-92
UC Santa Barb. 1986-90
Cal St. Chico....1973-77
Cal Tech....1973-77

Cameron....1973
Canisius....1975-92
Central Fla. 1980-81
Charleston So. 1991-92
Cheyney....1973-79

Clark Atlanta....1973-79
Colorado Mines....1973

Davidson 1990-92
Dayton 1976-92
Delaware St. 1973-77

Dist. Columbia 1978
Drake 1987-92
Duquesne 1979-92
Evansville......................1973-77, 89-92
Ferris St. 1975-76

Fisk 1973-83
Fordham...................................1973-88
Fort Valley St. 1973-80
Gallaudet 1973-79, 86-94
Gannon....................................1989-92

Georgetown 1973-92
Hillsdale 1975
Hofstra 1973-92
Humboldt St. 1975-79
Ill.-Chicago 1973

Iona 1978-92
James Madison 1977-79

Ky. Wesleyan 1983-92
Knoxville..................................1973-88
Kutztown 1973-79

Lane 1973-87
Livingston.....................................1973
Lock Haven 1973-79
LIU-C. W. Post 1975-77, 84, 89-92
Mankato St. 1977

Mansfield 1973-79
Marist......................................1978-92
Maritime (N.Y.).......................1985, 88
Mass.-Lowell............................1981-92
Mercyhurst...............................1982-92

Merrimack 1989
Miles 1973-87
Millersville................................1973-79
Minn.-Morris 1978-84
Morehouse...............................1973-80

New Haven.......................1973, 77-80
New York Tech 1973

Oswego St. 1976
Pace..1978-92
Plattsburgh St. 1973-78

Quincy 1987-92
Ramapo 1981-92
Rochester Inst. 1973-77
Sacred Heart 1991-92
St. Francis (Pa.) 1978-92

St. John's (N.Y.) 1978-92
St. Joseph's (Ind.)......................1973-78
St. Mary's (Cal.).......................1973-80
St. Peter's................................1973-92
Samford 1985-88

San Diego 1973-92
San Fran. St. 1973-78
Savannah St. 1973-80
Seton Hall.....................1973-76, 78-80
Shepherd................................1973-75

Shippensburg...........................1973-75
Siena 1988-92

Slippery Rock...........................1973-78
Sonoma St. 1980-83
Stonehill...................................1989-92

Stony Brook 1983-94
Tarleton St. 1977
Towson St. 1973-79
Valparaiso...............................1973-78
Villanova 1985-86

Wagner 1973-92
West Ga. 1981-82
Winona St. 1975
Wis.-Superior 1973-92

**Provisional members are not active members of the Association and, thus are not eligible for NCAA statistics, records and championship play. The end of the three-year provisional status and first season of active membership in Division III football is listed to the right of the school name.*

Individual Collegiate Records

Individual Collegiate Records

Individual collegiate records are determined by comparing the best records in all four divisions (I-A, I-AA, II and III) in comparable categories. Included are career records of players who played in two divisions (e.g., Dennis Shaw of San Diego St., Howard Stevens of Randolph-Macon and Louisville, and Tom Ehrhardt of LIU-C. W. Post and Rhode Island). Players who played seasons other than in the NCAA will have statistics only including NCAA seasons.

Total Offense

CAREER YARDS PER GAME

(Minimum 5,500 Yards)

Player, Team (Division[s])	Years	G	Plays	Yards	TDR‡	Yd. PG
Steve McNair, Alcorn St. (I-AA)	1991-94	42	*2,055	*16,823	152	*400.5
Aaron Flowers, Cal St. Northridge (I-AA)	1996-97	20	944	6,754	60	337.7
Terry Peebles, Hanover (III)	1992-95	23	1,140	7,672	89	333.6
Dave Dickenson, Montana (I-AA)	1992-95	35	1,539	11,523	116	329.2
Willie Totten, Mississippi Val. (I-AA)	1982-85	40	1,812	13,007	*157	325.2
Grady Benton, West Tex. A&M (II)	1994-95	18	844	5,831	55	323.9
Ty Detmer, Brigham Young (I-A)	1988-91	46	1,795	14,665	135	318.8
Neil Lomax, Portland St. (II; I-AA)	1977; 78-80	42	1,901	13,345	120	317.7
Kirk Baumgartner, Wis.-Stevens Point (III)	1986-89	41	2,007	12,767	110	311.4
Mike Perez, San Jose St. (I-A)	1986-87	20	875	6,182	37	309.1
Doug Nussmeier, Idaho (I-AA)	1990-93	39	1,556	12,054	109	309.1
Josh Wallwork, Wyoming (I-A)	1995-96	22	845	6,753	60	307.0
Oteman Sampson, Florida A&M (I-AA)	1996-97	22	906	6,751	57	306.9
Doug Gaynor, Long Beach St. (I-A)	1984-85	22	1,067	6,710	45	305.0
Tod Mayfield, West Tex. A&M (I-AA; II)	1984-85; 86	24	1,165	7,316	58	304.8
Jamie Martin, Weber St. (I-AA)	1989-92	41	1,838	12,287	93	299.7
Tony Eason, Illinois (I-A)	1981-82	22	1,016	6,589	43	299.5
Scott Otis, Glenville St. (II)	1994-95	20	755	5,911	66	295.6
Tom Proudian, Iona (I-AA)	1993-95	27	1,337	7,939	61	294.0
Robert Dougherty, Boston U. (I-AA)	1993-94	21	918	6,135	56	292.1
Keith Bishop, Ill. Wesleyan/Wheaton (Ill.) (III)	1981, 83-85	31	1,467	9,052	77	292.0
David Klingler, Houston (I-A)	1988-91	32	1,431	9,327	93	291.5
Stan Greene, Boston U. (I-AA)	1989-90	22	1,167	6,408	49	291.3
John Friesz, Idaho (I-AA)	1986-89	35	1,459	10,187	79	291.1
Steve Sarkisian, Brigham Young (I-A)	1995-96	25	953	7,253	56	290.1
Steve Young, Brigham Young (I-A)	1981-83	31	1,177	8,817	74	284.4
Mark Novara, Lakeland (III)	1994-97	38	1,653	10,801	112	284.2
Jayson Merrill, Western St. (II)	1990-91	20	641	5,619	57	281.0
Jordan Poznick, Principia (III)	1990-93	32	1,757	8,983	71	280.7
Jermaine Whitaker, N.M. Highlands (II)	1992-94	31	1,374	8,650	76	279.0
Andre Ware, Houston (I-A)	1987-89	29	1,194	8,058	81	277.9
Chris Petersen, UC Davis (II)	1985-86	20	735	5,532	52	276.6
Tim Von Dulm, Portland St. (II)	1969-70	20	989	5,501	51	275.1
Vernon Buck, Wingate (II)	1991-94	41	1,761	11,227	81	273.8
John Rooney, Ill. Wesleyan (III)	1982-84	27	1,260	7,393	71	273.8
Chris Hatcher, Valdosta St. (II)	1991-94	39	1,557	10,588	120	271.5
Pat Graham, Augustana (S.D.) (II)	1995-96	21	948	5,672	43	270.1
Tim Peterson, Wis.-Stout (III)	1986-89	36	1,558	9,701	59	269.5
Doug Flutie, Boston College (I-A)	1981-84	42	1,558	11,317	74	269.5

**Record. ‡Touchdowns-responsible-for are player's TDs scored and passed for.*

SEASON YARDS PER GAME

Player, Team (Division)	Year	G	Plays	Yards	TDR‡	Yd. PG
Steve McNair, Alcorn St. (I-AA)	†1994	11	649	*5,799	53	*527.2
David Klingler, Houston (I-A)	†1990	11	*704	5,221	55	474.6
Willie Totten, Mississippi Val. (I-AA)	†1984	10	564	4,572	*61	457.2
Andre Ware, Houston (I-A)	†1989	11	628	4,661	49	423.7
Ty Detmer, Brigham Young (I-A)	1990	12	635	5,022	45	418.5
Grady Benton, West Tex. A&M (II)	†1994	9	505	3,699	35	411.0
Steve McNair, Alcorn St. (I-AA)	†1992	10	519	4,057	39	405.7
Perry Klein, LIU-C. W. Post (II)	†1993	10	499	4,052	41	405.2
Mike Maxwell, Nevada (I-A)	†1995	9	443	3,623	34	402.6
Terry Peebles, Hanover (III)	†1995	10	572	3,981	43	398.1
Steve Young, Brigham Young (I-A)	†1983	11	531	4,346	41	395.1
Jamie Martin, Weber St. (I-AA)	†1991	11	591	4,337	37	394.3
Chris Vargas, Nevada (I-A)	†1993	11	535	4,332	35	393.8
Marty Washington, West Ala. (II)	1993	8	453	3,146	29	393.8
Wilkie Perez, Glenville St. (II)	†1997	11	509	4,301	45	391.0
Scott Mitchell, Utah (I-A)	†1988	11	589	4,299	29	390.8
Damian Poalucci, East Stroudsburg (II)	†1996	10	505	3,883	41	388.3
Jim McMahon, Brigham Young (I-A)	†1980	12	540	4,627	53	385.6
Dave Dickenson, Montana (I-AA)	†1995	11	544	4,209	41	382.6
Neil Lomax, Portland St. (I-AA)	†1980	11	550	4,157	42	377.9
Brett Salisbury, Wayne St. (Neb.) (II)	1993	10	424	3,732	32	373.2
Ty Detmer, Brigham Young (I-A)	1989	12	497	4,433	38	369.4
Troy Kopp, Pacific (Cal.) (I-A)	1990	9	485	3,276	32	364.0
Dave Dickenson, Montana (I-AA)	†1993	11	530	3,978	46	361.6
Tim Rattay, Louisiana Tech (I-A)	†1997	11	541	3,968	35	360.7

Player, Team (Division)	Year	G	Plays	Yards	TDR‡	Yd. PG
Neil Lomax, Portland St. (I-AA)	†1979	11	611	3,966	31	360.5
Jed Drenning, Glenville St. (II)	1993	10	473	3,593	32	359.3
Alfred Montez, Western N.M. (II)	1994	6	244	2,130	18	355.0
Keith Bishop, Wheaton (Ill.) (III)	†1983	9	421	3,193	24	354.8
Kirk Baumgartner, Wis.-Stevens Point (III)	†1989	10	530	3,540	39	354.0
Bill Nietzke, Alma (III)	†1996	9	468	3,185	29	353.9
Rob Tomlinson, Cal St. Chico (II)	†1989	10	534	3,525	26	352.5
Josh Wallwork, Wyoming (I-A)	†1996	12	525	4,209	35	350.8
John Furmaniak, Eureka (III)	1995	10	414	3,503	35	350.3
John Friesz, Idaho (I-AA)	†1989	11	464	3,853	31	350.3
Steve McNair, Alcorn St. (I-AA)	1993	11	493	3,830	30	348.2
Aaron Flowers, Cal St. Northridge (I-AA)	†1997	9	456	3,132	26	348.0
Todd Hammel, Stephen F. Austin (I-AA)	1989	11	487	3,822	38	347.5

**Record. †National total-offense champion. ‡Touchdowns-responsible-for are player's TDs scored and passed for.*

CAREER YARDS

Player, Team (Division[s])	Years	Plays	Yards	Avg.
Steve McNair, Alcorn St. (I-AA)	1991-94	*2,055	*16,823	8.19
Ty Detmer, Brigham Young (I-A)	1988-91	1,795	14,665	8.17
Neil Lomax, Portland St. (II; I-AA)	1977; 78-80	1,901	13,345	7.02
Willie Totten, Mississippi Val. (I-AA)	1982-85	1,812	13,007	7.18
Kirk Baumgartner, Wis.-Stevens Point (III)	1986-89	2,007	12,767	6.36
Jamie Martin, Weber St. (I-AA)	1989-92	1,838	12,287	6.68
Doug Nussmeier, Idaho (I-AA)	1990-93	1,556	12,054	7.75
Dave Dickenson, Montana (I-AA)	1992-95	1,539	11,523	7.49
Doug Flutie, Boston College (I-A)	1981-84	1,558	11,317	7.26
Vernon Buck, Wingate (II)	1991-94	1,761	11,227	6.38
Ken Hobart, Idaho (I-AA)	1980-83	1,847	11,127	6.02
Bob McLaughlin, Lock Haven (II)	1992-95	2,007	11,041	5.50
Peyton Manning, Tennessee (I-A)	1994-97	1,534	11,020	7.18
Eric Zeier, Georgia (I-A)	1991-94	1,560	10,841	6.95
Alex Van Pelt, Pittsburgh (I-A)	1989-92	1,570	10,814	6.89
Mark Novara, Lakeland (III)	1994-97	1,653	10,801	6.53
Earl Harvey, N.C. Central (II)	1985-88	2,045	10,667	5.22
Stoney Case, New Mexico (I-A)	1991-94	1,673	10,651	6.37
Chris Hatcher, Valdosta St. (II)	1991-94	1,557	10,588	6.80
Bill Borchert, Mount Union (III)	1994-97	1,274	10,639	*8.35
Jim Ballard, Wilmington (Ohio)/ Mount Union (III)	1990, 91-93	1,328	10,545	7.94
Todd Santos, San Diego St. (I-A)	1984-87	1,722	10,513	6.11
Danny Wuerffel, Florida (I-A)	1993-96	1,355	10,500	7.75
Sean Payton, Eastern Ill. (I-AA)	1983-86	1,690	10,298	6.09
Greg Wyatt, Northern Ariz. (I-AA)	1986-89	1,753	10,277	5.86
Kevin Sweeney, Fresno St. (I-A)	$1982-86	1,700	10,252	6.03
Thad Trujillo, Fort Lewis (II)	1991-94	1,787	10,209	5.71
John Friesz, Idaho (I-AA)	1986-89	1,459	10,187	6.98
Troy Kopp, Pacific (Cal.) (I-A)	1989-92	1,595	10,037	6.29
Kevin Ricca, Catholic (III)	1994-97	1,533	9,982	6.51
Rob Tomlinson, Cal St. Chico (II)	1988-91	1,656	9,921	5.99
Michael Proctor, Murray St. (I-AA)	1986-89	1,577	9,886	6.27
Jeff Wiley, Holy Cross (I-AA)	1985-88	1,428	9,877	6.92
Tom Ehrhardt, LIU-C. W. Post (II); Rhode Island (I-AA)	1981-82; 84-85	1,674	9,793	5.85
Brian McClure, Bowling Green (I-A)	1982-85	1,630	9,774	6.00
John Hebgen, Mankato St. (II)	1993-96	1,545	9,772	6.32
Jeff Lewis, Northern Ariz. (I-AA)	1992-95	1,654	9,769	5.91
Eric Noble, Wilmington (Ohio) (III)	1992-95	1,513	9,731	6.43
Jim McMahon, Brigham Young (I-A)	1977-78, 80-81	1,325	9,723	7.34
Glenn Foley, Boston College (I-A)	1990-93	1,440	9,702	6.74
Tim Peterson, Wis.-Stout (III)	1986-89	1,558	9,701	6.23
Jarrod Furgason, Fairmont St. (II)	$1993-97	1,583	9,638	6.09
John Craven, Gardner-Webb (II)	1991-94	1,666	9,630	5.78
Chris Ings, Wabash (III)	1992-95	1,532	9,608	6.27
Terrence Jones, Tulane (I-A)	1985-88	1,620	9,445	5.83
David Klingler, Houston (I-A)	1988-91	1,431	9,327	6.52
Shawn Jones, Georgia Tech (I-A)	1989-92	1,609	9,296	5.78
Matt DeGennaro, Connecticut (I-AA)	1987-90	1,619	9,269	5.73
Shane Matthews, Florida (I-A)	1989-92	1,397	9,241	6.61
Sam Mannery, Calif. (Pa.) (II)	1987-90	1,669	9,125	5.47
Spence Fischer, Duke (I-A)	1992-95	1,612	9,110	5.65
T. J. Rubley, Tulsa (I-A)	1987-89, 91	1,541	9,080	5.89
Brad Tayles, Western Mich. (I-A)	1989-92	1,675	9,071	5.42
John Elway, Stanford (I-A)	1979-82	1,505	9,070	6.03
Tom Ciaccio, Holy Cross (I-AA)	1988-91	1,283	9,066	7.07
Erik Wilhelm, Oregon St. (I-A)	1985-88	1,689	9,062	5.37

**Record. $See page 6 for explanation.*

SEASON YARDS

Player, Team (Division)	Year	G	Plays	Yards	Avg.
Steve McNair, Alcorn St. (I-AA)	†1994	11	649	*5,799	@8.94
David Klingler, Houston (I-A)	†1990	11	*704	5,221	7.42
Ty Detmer, Brigham Young (I-A)	1990	12	635	5,022	7.91
Andre Ware, Houston (I-A)	†1989	11	628	4,661	7.42
Jim McMahon, Brigham Young (I-A)	†1980	12	540	4,627	8.57
Willie Totten, Mississippi Val. (I-AA)	†1984	10	564	4,572	8.11
Ty Detmer, Brigham Young (I-A)	1989	12	497	4,433	8.92
Steve Young, Brigham Young (I-A)	†1983	11	531	4,346	8.18
Jamie Martin, Weber St. (I-AA)	†1991	11	591	4,337	7.34
Chris Vargas, Nevada (I-A)	†1993	11	535	4,332	8.10
Wilkie Perez, Glenville St. (II)	†1997	11	509	4,301	8.45
Scott Mitchell, Utah (I-A)	†1988	11	589	4,299	7.30
Josh Wallwork, Wyoming (I-A)	†1996	12	525	4,209	8.02
Dave Dickenson, Montana (I-AA)	†1995	11	544	4,209	7.74
Neil Lomax, Portland St. (I-AA)	†1980	11	550	4,157	7.56
Robbie Bosco, Brigham Young (I-A)	1985	13	578	4,141	7.16
Steve McNair, Alcorn St. (I-AA)	†1992	10	519	4,057	7.82
Perry Klein, LIU-C. W. Post (II)	†1993	10	499	4,052	8.12
Ty Detmer, Brigham Young (I-A)	†1991	12	478	4,001	8.37
Steve Sarkisian, Brigham Young (I-A)	1996	14	486	3,983	8.20
Terry Peebles, Hanover (III)	†1995	10	572	3,981	6.96
Dave Dickenson, Montana (I-AA)	†1993	11	530	3,978	7.51
Tim Rattay, Louisiana Tech (I-A)	†1997	11	541	3,968	7.33
Neil Lomax, Portland St. (I-AA)	†1979	11	611	3,966	6.49
Robbie Bosco, Brigham Young (I-A)	†1984	12	543	3,932	7.24
Damian Poalucci, East Stroudsburg (II)	†1996	10	505	3,883	7.69
Mike McCoy, Utah (I-A)	1993	12	529	3,860	7.50
John Friesz, Idaho (I-AA)	†1989	11	464	3,853	8.30
Steve McNair, Alcorn St. (I-AA)	1993	11	493	3,830	7.77
Todd Hammel, Stephen F. Austin (I-AA)	1989	11	487	3,822	7.85
Ken Hobart, Idaho (I-AA)	1983	11	578	3,800	6.57
Kirk Baumgartner, Wis.-Stevens Point (III)	†1988	11	604	3,790	6.27
Peyton Manning, Tennessee (I-A)	1997	12	526	3,789	7.20
Chris Hegg, Truman St. (II)	†1985	11	594	3,782	6.37
Jimmy Klingler, Houston (I-A)	†1992	11	544	3,768	6.93
Tim Couch, Kentucky (I-A)	1997	11	613	3,759	6.13
Dave Stireman, Weber St. (I-AA)	1985	11	502	3,759	7.49
Brian Ah Yat, Montana (I-AA)	1996	11	501	3,744	7.47
Willie Totten, Mississippi Val. (I-AA)	1985	11	561	3,742	6.67
Brett Salisbury, Wayne St. (Neb.) (II)	1993	10	424	3,732	8.80
Jeff Wiley, Holy Cross (I-AA)	†1987	11	445	3,722	8.36
Jamie Martin, Weber St. (I-AA)	1990	11	508	3,713	7.31
Anthony Dilweg, Duke (I-A)	1988	11	539	3,713	6.89
Kirk Baumgartner, Wis.-Stevens Point (III)	1987	11	561	3,712	6.62

**Record. †National total-offense champion. @ Record for minimum 3,000 yards.*

SINGLE-GAME YARDS

Yds.	Div.	Player, Team (Opponent)	Date
732	I-A	David Klingler, Houston (Arizona St.)	Dec. 2, 1990
696	I-A	Matt Vogler, Texas Christian (Houston)	Nov. 3, 1990
651	II	Wilkie Perez, Glenville St. (Concord)	Oct. 25, 1997
649	I-AA	Steve McNair, Alcorn St. (Southern U.)	Oct. 22, 1994
647	I-AA	Steve McNair, Alcorn St. (Chattanooga)	Sept. 10, 1994
643	I-AA	Jamie Martin, Weber St. (Idaho St.)	Nov. 23, 1991
633	I-AA	Steve McNair, Alcorn St. (Grambling)	Sept. 3, 1994
625	I-A	David Klingler, Houston (Texas Christian)	Nov. 3, 1990
625	I-A	Scott Mitchell, Utah (Air Force)	Oct. 15, 1988
624	I-AA	Steve McNair, Alcorn St. (Samford)	Oct. 29, 1994
623	II	Perry Klein, LIU-C. W. Post (Salisbury St.)	Nov. 6, 1993
621	I-AA	Willie Totten, Mississippi Val. (Prairie View)	Oct. 27, 1984
614	I-AA	Bryan Martin, Weber St. (Cal Poly SLO)	Sept. 23, 1995

Yds.	Div.	Player, Team (Opponent)	Date
614	II	Alfred Montez, Western N.M. (West Tex. A&M)	Oct. 8, 1994
612	I-A	Jimmy Klingler, Houston (Rice)	Nov. 28, 1992
604	I-AA	Steve McNair, Alcorn St. (Jackson St.)	Nov. 21, 1992
603	I-A	Ty Detmer, Brigham Young (San Diego St.)	Nov. 16, 1991
601	I-A	Troy Kopp, Pacific (Cal.) (New Mexico St.)	Oct. 20, 1990
599	I-A	Virgil Carter, Brigham Young (UTEP)	Nov. 5, 1966
597	II	Damian Poalucci, East Stroudsburg (Mansfield)	Nov. 2, 1996
597	I-A	John Walsh, Brigham Young (Utah St.)	Oct. 30, 1993
596	III	John Love, North Park (Elmhurst)	Oct. 13, 1990
595	I-AA	Doug Pederson, Northeast La. (Stephen F. Austin)	Nov. 11, 1989
594	II	Jarrod DeGeorgia, Wayne St., Neb. (Drake)	Nov. 9, 1996
594	I-A	Jeremy Leach, New Mexico (Utah)	Nov. 11, 1989
591	II	Marty Washington, West Ala. (Nicholls St.)	Sept. 11, 1993
590	III	Tom Stallings, St. Thomas, (Minn.) (Bethel [Minn.])	Nov. 13, 1993
587	I-AA	Vern Harris, Idaho St. (Montana)	Oct. 12, 1985
586	I-AA	Steve McNair, Alcorn St. (Troy St.)	Nov. 12, 1994
585	I-A	Dave Wilson, Illinois (Ohio St.)	Nov. 8, 1980
584	II	Tracy Kendall, Alabama A&M (Clark Atlanta)	Nov. 4, 1989
582	I-A	Marc Wilson, Brigham Young (Utah)	Nov. 5, 1977
580	II	Grady Benton, West Tex. A&M (Howard Payne)	Sept. 17, 1994
578	I-A	David Klingler, Houston (Eastern Wash.)	Nov. 17, 1990
577	III	Eric Noble, Wilmington (Ohio) (Urbana)	Nov. 5, 1994

Rushing

CAREER YARDS PER GAME

(Minimum 2,500 Yards)

Player, Team (Division[s])	Years	G	Plays	Yards	TD	Yd. PG
Arnold Mickens, Butler (I-AA)	1994-95	20	763	3,813	29	*190.7
Ed Marinaro, Cornell (I-A)	1969-71	27	918	4,715	50	174.6
Rob Marchitello, Maine Maritime (III)	1993-95	26	879	4,300	59	165.4
O. J. Simpson, Southern Cal (I-A)	1967-68	19	621	3,214	33	164.4
Kelvin Gladney, Millsaps (III)	1993-94	19	510	3,085	36	162.4
Johnny Bailey, Tex. A&M-Kingsville (II)	1986-89	39	885	*6,320	66	162.1
Herschel Walker, Georgia (I-A)	1980-82	33	994	5,259	49	159.4
Carey Bender, Coe (III)	1991-94	39	926	6,125	71	157.1
Brad Olson, Lawrence (III)	1994-97	34	792	5,325	44	156.6
Kirk Matthieu, Maine Maritime (III)	$1989-93	33	964	5,107	41	154.8
Tim Hall, Robert Morris (I-AA)	1994-95	19	393	2,908	27	153.1
Fred Lane, Lane (II)	1994-96	29	700	4,433	41	152.9
Terry Underwood, Wagner (III)	1985-88	33	742	5,010	52	151.8
LeShon Johnson, Northern Ill. (I-A)	1992-93	22	592	3,314	18	150.6
Reggie Greene, Siena (I-AA)	1994-97	36	890	5,415	45	150.4
Ole Gunderson, St. Olaf (II)	1969-71	27	639	4,060	56	150.4
Richard Huntley, Winston-Salem (II)	1992-95	42	932	6,286	57	149.7
Roger Graham, New Haven (II)	1991-94	40	821	5,953	66	148.8
Marshall Faulk, San Diego St. (I-A)	1991-93	31	766	4,589	57	148.0
George Jones, San Diego St. (I-A)	1995-96	19	486	2,810	34	147.9
Brad Hustad, Luther (II)	1957-59	27	655	3,943	25	146.0
Archie Amerson, Northern Ariz. (I-AA)	1995-96	22	526	3,196	37	145.3
Jarrett Anderson, Truman St. (II)	1993-96	43	979	6,166	69	143.4
Quincy Tillmon, Emporia St. (II)	1990-92, 94	29	790	4,141	37	142.8
Anthony Russo, St. John's (N.Y.) (III)	1990-93	41	1,152	5,834	57	142.3
Tony Dorsett, Pittsburgh (I-A)	1973-76	43	1,074	6,082	55	141.4
Troy Davis, Iowa St. (I-A)	1994-96	31	782	4,382	36	141.4
Keith Elias, Princeton (I-AA)	1991-93	30	736	4,208	49	140.3
Joe Iacone, West Chester (II)	1960-62	27	565	3,767	40	139.5

*Record. $See page 6 for explanation.

SEASON YARDS PER GAME

Player, Team (Division)	Year	G	Plays	Yards	TD	Yd. PG
Barry Sanders, Oklahoma St. (I-A)	†1988	11	344	*2,628	*37	*238.9
Dante Brown, Marietta (III)	†1996	10	314	2,385	25	238.5
Arnold Mickens, Butler (I-AA)	†1994	10	*409	2,255	18	225.5
Carey Bender, Coe (III)	†1994	10	295	2,243	29	224.3
Anthony Gray, Western N.M. (II)	†1997	10	277	2,220	12	222.0
Marcus Allen, Southern Cal (I-A)	†1981	11	403	2,342	22	212.9
Ed Marinaro, Cornell (I-A)	†1971	9	356	1,881	24	209.0
Irv Sigler, Bloomsburg (II)	1997	10	299	2,038	20	203.8
Ricky Gales, Simpson (III)	†1989	10	297	2,035	26	203.5
Tony Vinson, Towson (I-AA)	†1993	10	293	2,016	23	201.6
Terry Underwood, Wagner (III)	†1988	9	245	1,809	21	201.0
Troy Davis, Iowa St. (I-A)	†1996	11	402	2,185	21	198.6
Reggie Greene, Siena (I-AA)	†1997	9	256	1,778	18	197.6
Brad Olson, Lawrence (III)	†1995	9	242	1,760	16	195.6
Jarrett Anderson, Truman St. (II)	†1996	11	321	2,140	27	194.5
Kirk Matthieu, Maine Maritime (III)	†1992	9	327	1,733	16	192.6
Brian Shay, Emporia St. (II)	1996	11	342	2,103	18	191.2
Reggie Greene, Siena (I-AA)	†1996	9	280	1,719	12	191.0
Byron Hanspard, Texas Tech (I-A)	1996	11	339	2,084	13	189.5
Archie Amerson, Northern Ariz. (I-AA)	1996	11	333	2,079	25	189.0
Richard Huntley, Winston-Salem (II)	†1995	10	273	1,889	16	188.9
Kelvin Gladney, Millsaps (III)	1994	10	307	1,882	19	188.2
Brandon Steinheim, Wesley (III)	1996	9	319	1,684	20	187.1
Rashaan Salaam, Colorado (I-A)	†1994	11	298	2,055	24	186.8
Jon Warga, Wittenberg (III)	†1990	10	254	1,836	15	183.6
Fred Lane, Lane (II)	1995	10	273	1,833	19	183.3
Johnny Bailey, Tex. A&M-Kingsville (II)	†1986	11	271	2,011	18	182.8
Troy Davis, Iowa St. (I-A)	†1995	11	345	2,010	15	182.7
Bob White, Western N.M. (II)	†1951	9	202	1,643	20	182.6
Kevin Mitchell, Saginaw Valley (II)	1989	8	236	1,460	6	182.5
Rashaan Dumas, Southern Conn. St. (II)	1996	9	291	1,639	18	182.1
Anthony Jones, La Verne (III)	1995	8	200	1,453	19	181.6
Hank Wineman, Albion (III)	†1991	9	307	1,629	14	181.0
Charles White, Southern Cal (I-A)	†1979	10	293	1,803	18	180.3
Eric Grey, Hamilton (III)	1991	8	217	1,439	13	179.9
Mike Birosak, Dickinson (III)	1989	10	380	1,798	18	179.8
LeShon Johnson, Northern Ill. (I-A)	†1993	11	327	1,976	12	179.6
Don Aleksiewicz, Hobart (II)	†1971	9	276	1,616	19	179.6
Mike Rozier, Nebraska (I-A)	†1983	12	275	2,148	29	179.0
Aaron Stecker, Western Ill. (I-AA)	1997	11	298	1,957	24	177.9
Jim Holder, Okla. Panhandle (II)	†1963	10	275	1,775	9	177.5
Phillip Moore, North Dak. (II)	1997	10	293	1,771	14	177.1
Tony Dorsett, Pittsburgh (I-A)	†1976	11	338	1,948	21	177.1
Wilmont Perry, Livingstone (II)	1997	10	195	1,770	20	177.0
Rob Marchitello, Maine Maritime (III)	1995	8	292	1,413	19	176.6
Chris Babirad, Wash. & Jeff. (III)	1992	9	243	1,589	22	176.6
Jim Baier, Wis.-River Falls (II)	†1966	9	240	1,587	17	176.3
James Suber, Indiana (Pa.) (II)	1996	10	300	1,744	17	174.4

*Record. †National champion.

CAREER YARDS

Player, Team (Division[s])	Years	Plays	Yards	Avg.
Johnny Bailey, Tex. A&M-Kingsville (II)	1986-89	885	*6,320	7.14
Richard Huntley, Winston-Salem (II)	1992-95	932	6,286	6.74
Jarrett Anderson, Truman St. (II)	1993-96	979	6,166	6.30
Carey Bender, Coe (III)	1991-94	926	6,125	6.61
Tony Dorsett, Pittsburgh (I-A)	1973-76	1,074	6,082	5.66
Roger Graham, New Haven (II)	1991-94	821	5,953	7.25
Anthony Russo, St. John's (N.Y.) (III)	1990-93	1,152	5,834	5.06
Charles White, Southern Cal (I-A)	1976-79	1,023	5,598	5.47
Joe Dudek, Plymouth St. (III)	1982-85	785	5,570	7.10
Mark Kacmarynski, Central (Iowa) (III)	$1992-96	854	5,434	6.36
Reggie Greene, Siena (I-AA)	1994-97	890	5,415	6.08
Thomas Haskins, VMI (I-AA)	1993-96	899	5,355	5.96
Frank Hawkins, Nevada (I-AA)	1977-80	945	5,333	5.64
Howard Stevens, Randolph-Macon (II); Louisville (I-A)	1968-69; 71-72	891	5,297	5.95
Eric Frees, Western Md. (III)	1988-91	1,059	5,281	4.99
Herschel Walker, Georgia (I-A)	1980-82	994	5,259	5.29
Kenny Gamble, Colgate (I-AA)	1984-87	963	5,220	5.42
Archie Griffin, Ohio St. (I-A)	1972-75	845	5,177	6.13
Antonio Leroy, Albany St. (Ga.) (II)	1993-96	973	5,152	5.29
Markus Thomas, Eastern Ky. (I-AA)	1989-92	784	5,149	6.57
Shawn Graves, Wofford (QB) (II)	1989-92	730	5,128	7.02
Kirk Matthieu, Maine Maritime (III)	$1989-93	964	5,107	5.30
Chris Cobb, Eastern Ill. (II)	1976-79	930	5,042	5.42
Irv Sigler, Bloomsburg (II)	1994-97	820	5,034	6.14
Darren Lewis, Texas A&M (I-A)	1987-90	909	5,012	5.51
Terry Underwood, Wagner (III)	1985-88	742	5,010	6.75
Anthony Thompson, Indiana (I-A)	1986-89	1,089	4,965	4.56
George Rogers, South Caro. (I-A)	1977-80	902	4,958	5.50
Trevor Cobb, Rice (I-A)	1989-92	1,091	4,948	4.54
Paul Palmer, Temple (I-A)	1983-86	948	4,895	5.16
Harry Jackson, St. Cloud St. (II)	1986-89	915	4,890	5.34
Leonard Davis, Lenoir-Rhyne (II)	$1990-94	839	4,853	5.78
Jerry Linton, Okla. Panhandle (II)	1959-62	648	4,839	‡7.47
Erik Marsh, Lafayette (I-AA)	1991-94	1,027	4,834	4.71

*Record. ‡Record for minimum 600 carries. $See page 6 for explanation.

SEASON YARDS

Player, Team (Division)	Year	G	Plays	Yards	Avg.
Barry Sanders, Oklahoma St. (I-A)	†1988	11	344	*2,628	7.64
Dante Brown, Marietta (III)	†1996	10	314	2,385	7.60
Marcus Allen, Southern Cal (I-A)	†1981	11	403	2,342	5.81
Arnold Mickens, Butler (I-AA)	†1994	10	*409	2,255	5.51
Carey Bender, Coe (III)	†1994	10	295	2,243	7.60
Anthony Gray, Western N.M. (II)	†1997	10	277	2,220	††8.01
Troy Davis, Iowa St. (I-A)	†1996	11	402	2,185	5.44
Mike Rozier, Nebraska (I-A)	†1983	12	275	2,148	7.81
Jarrett Anderson, Truman St. (II)	†1996	11	321	2,140	6.67
Byron Hanspard, Texas Tech (I-A)	1996	11	339	2,084	6.15
Archie Amerson, Northern Ariz. (I-AA)	1996	11	333	2,079	6.24
Brian Shay, Emporia St. (II)	1996	11	342	2,103	6.15

Player, Team (Division)	Year	G	Plays	Yards	Avg.
Rashaan Salaam, Colorado (I-A)	†1994	11	298	2,055	6.90
Irv Sigler, Bloomsburg (II)	1997	10	299	2,038	6.82
Ricky Gales, Simpson (III)	†1989	10	297	2,035	6.85
Tony Vinson, Towson (I-AA)	†1993	10	293	2,016	6.89
Johnny Bailey, Tex. A&M-Kingsville (II)	†1986	11	271	2,011	7.42
Troy Davis, Iowa St. (I-A)	†1995	11	345	2,010	5.83
LeShon Johnson, Northern Ill. (I-A)	†1993	11	327	1,976	6.04
Aaron Stecker, Western Ill. (I-AA)	1997	11	298	1,957	6.57
Tony Dorsett, Pittsburgh (I-A)	†1976	11	338	1,948	5.76
Brian Shay, Emporia St. (II)	1997	11	269	1,912	7.11
Lorenzo White, Michigan St. (I-A)	†1985	11	386	1,908	4.94
Wasean Tait, Toledo (I-A)	1995	11	357	1,905	5.34
Ricky Williams, Texas (I-A)	†1997	11	279	1,893	6.78
Herschel Walker, Georgia (I-A)	†1981	11	385	1,891	4.91
Brian Pruitt, Central Mich. (I-A)	1994	11	292	1,890	6.47
Richard Huntley, Winston-Salem (II)	†1995	10	273	1,889	6.92
Rich Erenberg, Colgate (I-AA)	†1983	11	302	1,883	6.24
Kelvin Gladney, Millsaps (III)	1994	10	307	1,882	6.13
Ed Marinaro, Cornell (I-A)	†1971	9	356	1,881	5.28
Ahman Green, Nebraska (I-A)	1997	12	278	1,877	6.75
Ernest Anderson, Oklahoma St. (I-A)	†1982	11	353	1,877	5.32
Ricky Bell, Southern Cal (I-A)	†1975	11	357	1,875	5.25
Paul Palmer, Temple (I-A)	†1986	11	346	1,866	5.39
Ronald Moore, Pittsburg St. (II)	1992	11	239	1,864	7.80
Ron Dayne, Wisconsin (I-A)	1996	12	295	1,863	6.32
George Jones, San Diego St. (I-A)	1995	12	305	1,842	6.04
Jon Warga, Wittenberg (III)	†1990	10	254	1,836	7.23
Fred Lane, Lane (II)	1995	10	273	1,833	6.71
Zed Robinson, Southern Utah (II)	1991	11	254	1,828	7.20
Eddie George, Ohio St. (I-A)	1995	12	303	1,826	6.03
Kenny Gamble, Colgate (I-AA)	†1986	11	307	1,816	5.92
Richard Huntley, Winston-Salem (II)	1994	11	251	1,815	7.23
Terry Underwood, Wagner (III)	†1988	9	245	1,809	6.75
Charles White, Southern Cal (I-A)	†1979	10	293	1,803	6.15

**Record. †National champion. ††Record for minimum 214 carries.*

SINGLE-GAME YARDS

Yds.	Div.	Player, Team (Opponent)	Date
441	III	Dante Brown, Marietta (Baldwin-Wallace)	Oct. 5, 1996
436	III	A.J. Pittorino, Hartwick (Waynesboro)	Nov. 2, 1996
417	III	Carey Bender, Coe (Grinnell)	Oct. 9, 1993
413	III	Dante Brown, Marietta (Heidelberg)	Nov. 9, 1996
396	I-A	Tony Sands, Kansas (Missouri)	Nov. 23, 1991
386	I-A	Marshall Faulk, San Diego St. (Pacific [Cal.])	Sept. 14, 1991
382	III	Shane Davis, Loras (Dubuque)	Nov. 8, 1997
382	III	Pete Baranek, Carthage (North Central)	Oct. 5, 1985
382	II	Kelly Ellis, Northern Iowa (Western Ill.)	Oct. 13, 1979
379	I-AA	Reggie Greene, Siena (St. John's, N.Y.)	Nov. 2, 1996
378	I-A	Troy Davis, Iowa St. (Missouri)	Sept. 28, 1996
377	I-A	Anthony Thompson, Indiana (Wisconsin)	Nov. 11, 1989
373	I-A	Astron Whatley, Kent (Eastern Mich.)	Sept. 20, 1997
373	II	Dallas Garber, Marietta (Wash. & Jeff.)	Nov. 7, 1959
370	II	Jim Baier, Wis.-River Falls (Wis.-Stevens Point)	Nov. 5, 1966
370	II	Jim Hissam, Marietta (Bethany, [W.Va.])	Nov. 15, 1958
367	II	Don Polkinghorne, Washington (Mo.) (Wash. & Lee)	Nov. 23, 1957
364	I-AA	Tony Vinson, Towson (Bucknell)	Nov. 13, 1993
363	III	Terry Underwood, Wagner (Hofstra)	Oct. 15, 1988
363	II	Richie Weaver, Widener (Moravian)	Oct. 17, 1970
361	II	Brian Shay, Emporia St. (Washburn)	Oct. 5, 1996
361	II	Richard Huntley, Winston-Salem (Virginia Union)	Nov. 5, 1994
359	II	Anthony Gray, Western N.M. (Hardin-Simmons)	Oct. 4, 1997
357	I-A	Mike Pringle, Cal St. Fullerton (New Mexico St.)	Nov. 4, 1989
357	I-A	Rueben Mayes, Washington St. (Oregon)	Oct. 27, 1984
356	I-A	Brian Pruitt, Central Mich. (Toledo)	Nov. 5, 1994
356	I-A	Eddie Lee Ivery, Georgia Tech (Air Force)	Nov. 11, 1978
356	II	Ole Gunderson, St. Olaf (Monmouth [Ill.])	Oct. 11, 1969
354	III	Terry Underwood, Wagner (Western Conn. St.)	Oct. 3, 1986
352	III	Steve Tardif, Maine Maritime (Westfield St.)	Nov. 16, 1996
351	I-A	Scott Harley, East Caro. (North Caro. St.)	Nov. 30, 1996
350	II	Ricke Stonewall, Millersville (New Haven)	Nov. 13, 1982
350	I-A	Eric Allen, Michigan St. (Purdue)	Oct. 30, 1971

Passing

CAREER PASSING EFFICIENCY

(Minimum 475 Completions)

Player, Team (Division[s])	Years	Att.	Cmp.	Int.	Pct.	Yds.	TD	Pts.
Bill Borchert, Mount Union (III)	1994-97	1,009	671	17	.665	10,201	*141	*194.2
Dave Dickenson, Montana (I-AA)	1992-95	1,208	813	26	.673	11,080	96	166.3
Danny Wuerffel, Florida (I-A)	1993-96	1,170	708	42	.605	10,875	114	163.6
Ty Detmer, Brigham Young (I-A)	1988-91	1,530	958	65	.626	*15,031	121	162.7
Steve Sarkisian, Brigham Young (I-A)	1995-96	789	528	26	.669	7,464	53	162.0
Mike Simpson, Eureka (III)/ Eastern Ill. (I-AA)	1993-94, 96-97	724	481	25	.664	6,402	58	160.3
Jim Ballard, Wilmington (Ohio)/ Mount Union (III)	1990, 91-93	1,199	743	41	.620	10,379	115	159.5
Billy Blanton, San Diego St. (I-A)	1993-96	920	588	25	.639	8,165	67	157.1
Jim McMahon, Brigham Young (I-A)	1977-78, 80-81	1,060	653	34	.616	9,536	84	156.9
Doug Nussmeier, Idaho (I-AA)	1990-93	1,225	746	32	.609	10,824	91	154.4
Chris Hatcher, Valdosta St. (II)	1991-94	1,451	*1,001	38	.690	10,878	116	153.1
Steve Young, Brigham Young (I-A)	1981-83	908	592	33	.652	7,733	56	149.8
Jack Hull, Grand Valley St. (II)	1988-91	835	485	22	.581	7,120	64	149.7
Robbie Bosco, Brigham Young (I-A)	1983-85	997	638	36	.640	8,400	66	149.4
Elvis Grbac, Michigan (I-A)	1989-92	754	477	29	.633	5,859	64	148.9
Mike Maxwell, Nevada (I-A)	1993-95	881	560	33	.636	7,256	62	148.5
Michael Payton, Marshall (I-AA)	1989-92	876	542	32	.619	7,530	57	148.2
Chuck Long, Iowa (I-A)	$1981-85	1,072	692	46	.646	9,210	64	147.8
John Walsh, Brigham Young (I-A)	1991-94	973	587	35	.603	8,375	66	147.8
Aaron Flowers, Cal St. Northridge (I-AA)	1996-97	819	502	21	.613	6,766	54	147.3
Peyton Manning, Tennessee (I-A)	1994-97	1,381	863	33	.625	11,201	89	147.1
Willie Totten, Mississippi Val. (I-AA)	1982-85	1,555	907	75	.583	12,711	139	146.8
John Koz, Baldwin-Wallace (III)	1990-93	981	609	28	.621	7,724	71	146.4
Rob Johnson, Southern Cal (I-A)	1991-94	963	623	24	.647	7,743	52	145.1
Steve McNair, Alcorn St. (I-AA)	1991-94	1,680	929	58	.553	14,496	119	144.3
Mike Smith, Northern Iowa (I-AA)	1984-87	943	557	43	.591	8,219	58	143.5
Steve Stenstrom, Stanford (I-A)	1991-94	1,320	833	36	.631	10,531	72	142.7
Neil Lomax, Portland St. (II; I-AA)	1977; 78-80	1,606	938	55	.584	13,220	106	142.5
Lance Funderburk, Valdosta St. (II)	1993-96	1,054	689	23	.654	7,698	64	142.4
Marvin Graves, Syracuse (I-A)	1990-93	943	563	45	.597	8,466	48	142.4
Tom Ciaccio, Holy Cross (I-AA)	1988-91	1,073	658	46	.613	8,603	72	142.2
Kevin Ricca, Catholic (III)	1994-97	1,109	713	56	.643	9,469	89	142.0
Chris Esterley, St. Thomas (Minn.) (III)	1993-96	1,012	615	30	.608	7,709	71	142.0
George Bork, Northern Ill. (II)	1960-63	902	577	33	.640	6,782	60	141.8
Eric Beavers, Nevada (I-AA)	1983-86	1,094	646	37	.591	8,626	77	141.8
Doug Gaynor, Long Beach St. (I-A)	1984-85	837	569	35	.680	6,793	35	141.6
Scott Semptimphelter, Lehigh (I-AA)	1990-93	823	493	27	.599	6,668	50	141.5
Ed Hesson, Rowan (III)	1990-93	895	504	26	.563	7,053	67	141.2

Michigan sports information photo by Bob Kalmbach

Michigan quarterback Elvis Grbac ranks 15th in career passing efficiency among all passers with 475 or more completions (148.9).

Player, Team (Division[s])	Years	Att.	Cmp.	Int.	Pct.	Yds.	TD	Pts.
Danny Kanell, Florida St. (I-A)	1992-95	851	529	26	.622	6,372	57	141.1
Jack Ramirez, Pomona-Pitzer (III)	1994-97	959	558	39	.582	7,523	71	140.3
Matt Jozokos, Plymouth St. (III)	1987-90	1,003	527	39	.525	7,658	95	140.2
Dan McGwire, Iowa/San Diego St. (I-A)	1986-87, 89-90	973	575	30	.591	8,164	49	140.0
Chris Vargas, Nevada (I-AA; I-A)	1990-91; 92-93	1,017	625	42	.615	8,130	60	139.8
John Elway, Stanford (I-A)	1979-82	1,246	774	39	.621	9,349	77	139.3
Bryan Snyder, Albright (III)	1994-97	1,294	763	49	.590	9,865	92	138.9
Mike McCoy, Long Beach St./Utah (I-A)	1991, 92-94	1,069	650	26	.608	8,342	56	138.8
Jamie Martin, Weber St. (I-AA)	1989-92	1,544	934	56	.605	12,207	87	138.2
David Klingler, Houston (I-A)	1988-91	1,261	726	38	.576	9,430	91	138.2

**Record.* *$See page 6 for explanation.*

CAREER PASSING EFFICIENCY

(Minimum 325-474 Completions)

Player, Team (Division[s])	Years	Att.	Cmp.	Int.	Pct.	Yds.	TD	Pts.
John Charles, Portland St. (II)	1991-92	510	326	14	.639	5,389	56	*183.4
Shawn Knight, William & Mary (I-AA)	1991-94	558	367	15	.658	5,527	46	170.8
Tony Aliucci, Indiana (Pa.) (II)	1988-91	579	350	24	.604	5,655	53	164.4
Jayson Merrill, Western St. (II)	1990-91	580	328	25	.566	5,830	56	164.2
Chris Petersen, UC Davis (II)	1985-86	553	385	13	*.696	4,988	39	164.0
Kurt Ramler, St. John's (Minn.) (III)	1994-96	722	420	16	.582	6,475	75	163.4
Kyle Adamson, Allegheny (III)	1995-97	608	388	18	.638	5,506	48	160.0
Craig Kusick, Wis.-La Crosse (III)	1993-95	537	327	14	.609	4,767	48	159.8
Jason Baer, Wash. & Jeff. (III)	1993-96	671	406	24	.605	5,632	66	156.3
Dennis Shaw, San Diego St. (II; I-A)	1968; 69	575	333	41	.579	5,324	58	154.7
Joe Blake, Simpson (III)	1987-90	672	399	15	.594	6,183	43	153.3
Vinny Testaverde, Miami (Fla.) (I-A)	1982, 84-86	674	413	25	.613	6,058	48	152.9
Jim McMillan, Boise St. (II)	1971-74	640	382	29	.597	5,508	58	152.8
Josh Wallwork, Wyoming (I-A)	1995-96	729	449	28	.616	6,453	54	152.7
Willie Reyna, La Verne (III)	1991-92	542	346	19	.638	4,712	37	152.4
Trent Dilfer, Fresno St. (I-A)	1991-93	774	461	21	.596	6,944	51	151.2
Greg Lister, Rowan (III)	1994-97	773	454	29	.587	6,553	66	150.6
Troy Aikman, Oklahoma/UCLA (I-A)	1984-85, 87-88	637	401	18	.630	5,436	40	149.7
Jim Harbaugh, Michigan (I-A)	1983-86	582	368	19	.632	5,215	31	149.6
Koy Detmer, Colorado (I-A)	1992, 94-96	594	350	25	.589	5,390	40	148.9
Chuck Hartlieb, Iowa (I-A)	1985-88	716	461	17	.643	6,269	34	148.9
Jay Johnson, Northern Iowa (I-AA)	1989-92	744	397	25	.534	7,049	51	148.9
Danny White, Arizona St. (I-A)	1971-73	649	345	36	.532	5,932	59	148.9
Scott Otis, Glenville St. (II)	1994-95	693	421	21	.608	5,563	56	148.8
Gary Collier, Emory & Henry (III)	1984-87	738	386	33	.523	6,103	80	148.6
Bryan Martin, Weber St. (I-AA)	1992-95	606	365	14	.602	5,211	37	148.0
Jesse Showerda, New Haven (II)	1993-96	675	402	15	.596	5,175	57	147.4
Grady Benton, West Tex. A&M (II)	1994-95	686	421	22	.614	5,618	49	147.3
Kenneth Biggles, Tennessee St. (I-AA)	1981-84	701	397	28	.566	5,933	57	146.6
Bobby Hoying, Ohio St. (I-A)	1992-95	782	463	33	.592	6,751	54	146.1
Oteman Sampson, Florida A&M (I-AA)	1996-97	686	387	26	.564	6,104	46	145.7
Gifford Nielsen, Brigham Young (I-A)	1975-77	708	415	29	.586	5,833	55	145.3
Greg Heeres, Hope (III)	1981-84	630	347	21	.537	5,120	53	144.4
Tim Gutierrez, San Diego St. (I-A)	1992-94	580	357	19	.616	4,740	36	144.1
Bruce Upstill, Col. of Emporia (II)	1960-63	769	438	36	.570	6,935	48	144.0
Tom Ramsey, UCLA (I-A)	1979-82	691	411	33	.595	5,844	48	143.9
Jarrod DeGeorgia, Wayne St. (Neb.) (II)	1995-96	645	428	18	.664	5,161	31	143.9
Shawn Moore, Virginia (I-A)	1987-90	762	421	32	.552	6,629	55	143.8
Jeff Brown, Wheaton (Ill.) (III)	1992-95	767	441	30	.575	6,219	60	143.6
Moses Moreno, Colorado St. (I-A)	1994-97	787	457	28	.581	6,689	49	142.9
Jerry Rhome, Southern Methodist/Tulsa (I-A)	1961, 63-64	713	448	23	.628	5,472	47	142.6
Braniff Bonaventure, Furman (I-AA)	1993-96	672	413	17	.615	5,361	39	142.6
Lon Erickson, Ill. Wesleyan (III)	1993-96	786	461	24	.587	6,108	58	142.2
Todd Donnan, Marshall (I-AA)	1991-94	712	425	25	.597	5,566	51	142.0
Jim Zaccheo, Nevada (I-AA)	1987-88	554	326	27	.588	4,750	35	142.0
Thad Busby, Florida St. (I-A)	1994-97	715	420	27	.587	5,916	46	141.9
Ryan Leaf, Washington St. (I-A)	1995-97	845	456	23	.540	7,102	58	141.8
Charlie Ward, Florida St. (I-A)	1989, 91-93	759	474	21	.625	5,747	49	141.8
Bruce Crosthwaite, Adrian (III)	1984-87	618	368	31	.596	4,959	45	141.0

**Record.*

SEASON PASSING EFFICIENCY

(Minimum 30 Attempts Per Game)

Player, Team (Division)	Year	G	Att.	Cmp.	Int.	Pct.	Yds.	TD	Pts.
Jim Ballard, Mount Union (III)	1993	10	314	229	11	.729	3,304	37	*193.2
Jayson Merrill, Western St. (II)	†1991	10	309	195	11	.631	3,484	35	188.1
Kevin Ricca, Catholic (III)	1997	10	306	208	6	.679	2,990	35	183.9
John Charles, Portland St. (II)	1992	8	263	179	7	.681	2,770	24	181.3
Chris Hatcher, Valdosta St. (II)	†1994	11	430	321	9	*.747	3,591	50	179.0
Wilkie Perez, Glenville St. (II)	†1997	11	425	280	12	.658	4,189	45	178.0
Jim McMahon, Brigham Young (I-A)	†1980	12	445	284	18	.638	4,571	47	176.9
Ty Detmer, Brigham Young (I-A)	†1989	12	412	265	15	.643	4,560	32	175.6
Chris Boden, Villanova (I-AA)	1997	11	345	231	4	.670	3,079	36	174.0
Trent Dilfer, Fresno St. (I-A)	†1993	11	333	217	4	.652	3,276	28	173.1
Jerry Rhome, Tulsa (I-A)	†1964	10	326	224	4	.687	2,870	32	172.6
Danny Wuerffel, Florida (I-A)	1996	12	360	207	13	.575	3,625	39	170.6
Billy Blanton, San Diego St. (I-A)	1996	11	344	227	5	.660	3,221	29	169.6
Dave Dickenson, Montana (I-AA)	1995	11	455	309	9	.679	4,176	38	168.6

Player, Team (Division)	Year	G	Att.	Cmp.	Int.	Pct.	Yds.	TD	Pts.
Ty Detmer, Brigham Young (I-A)	1991	12	403	249	12	.618	4,031	35	168.5
Steve Young, Brigham Young (I-A)	†1983	11	429	306	10	.713	3,902	33	168.5
Willie Totten, Mississippi Val. (I-AA)	†1983	9	279	174	9	.624	2,566	29	167.5
Dave Dickenson, Montana (I-AA)	†1994	9	336	229	6	.682	3,053	24	164.5
Jim McMillan, Boise St. (II)	†1974	10	313	192	15	.613	2,900	33	164.4
Willie Totten, Mississippi Val. (I-AA)	†1984	10	518	324	22	.626	4,557	*56	163.6
Jeff Wiley, Holy Cross (I-AA)	†1987	11	400	265	17	.663	3,677	34	163.0
Todd Hammel, Stephen F. Austin (I-AA)	†1989	11	401	238	13	.594	3,914	34	162.8
Dennis Shaw, San Diego St. (I-A)	†1969	10	335	199	26	.594	3,185	39	162.2
Giovanni Carmazzi, Hofstra (I-AA)	1997	11	408	288	8	.706	3,554	27	161.7
John Friesz, Idaho (I-AA)	1989	11	425	260	8	.612	4,041	31	161.4
Willie Reyna, La Verne (III)	1991	8	267	170	6	.636	2,543	16	158.8
Charlie Ward, Florida St. (I-A)	1993	11	380	264	4	.695	3,032	27	157.8
Glenn Foley, Boston College (I-A)	1993	11	363	222	10	.612	3,395	25	157.0
Chris Vargas, Nevada (I-A)	1993	11	490	331	18	.676	4,265	34	156.2
George Bork, Northern Ill. (II)	1963	9	374	244	12	.652	3,077	32	156.2
John Walsh, Brigham Young (I-A)	1993	11	397	244	15	.615	3,727	28	156.0
Neil Lomax, Portland St. (I-AA)	1980	11	473	296	12	.626	4,094	37	156.0
Ty Detmer, Brigham Young (I-A)	1990	12	562	361	28	.642	*5,188	41	155.9
Rob Johnson, Southern Cal (I-A)	1993	12	405	278	5	.686	3,285	26	155.5
Doug Williams, Grambling (I-A)	1977	11	352	181	18	.514	3,286	38	155.2
Jim McMahon, Brigham Young (I-A)	†1981	10	423	272	7	.643	3,555	30	155.0
Josh Wallwork, Wyoming (I-A)	1996	12	458	286	15	.625	4,090	33	154.7
John Dutton, Nevada (I-A)	1996	11	334	222	6	.665	2,750	22	153.8
Andy Breault, Kutztown (II)	1991	10	360	225	20	.625	2,927	37	153.4
Chuck Long, Iowa (I-A)	1985	11	351	231	15	.658	2,978	26	153.0
Doug Flutie, Boston College (I-A)	1984	11	386	233	11	.604	3,454	27	152.9

**Record. †National pass-efficiency champion.*

SEASON PASSING EFFICIENCY

(Minimum 15 Attempts Per Game)

Player, Team (Division)	Year	G	Att.	Cmp.	Int.	Pct.	Yds.	TD	Pts.
Mike Simpson, Eureka (III)	†1994	10	158	116	5	.734	1,988	25	*225.0
Willie Seiler, St. John's (Minn.) (III)	†1993	10	205	141	6	.687	2,648	33	224.6
Bill Borchert, Mount Union (III)	†1997	10	272	190	1	.698	2,933	47	216.7
Boyd Crawford, Col. of Idaho (II)	†1953	8	120	72	6	.600	1,462	21	210.1
Bill Borchert, Mount Union (III)	†1996	10	240	165	6	.687	2,655	38	208.9
Shawn Knight, William & Mary (I-AA)	†1993	10	177	125	4	.706	2,055	22	204.6
Bill Borchert, Mount Union (III)	†1995	10	225	160	4	.711	2,270	30	196.3
Jason Baer, Wash. & Jeff. (III)	1995	8	146	95	3	.650	1,536	19	192.3
Greg Lister, Rowan (III)	1997	9	162	111	4	.685	1,688	20	191.9
Chuck Green, Wittenberg (II)	†1963	9	182	114	8	.626	2,181	19	189.0
Kurt Ramler, St. John's (Minn.) (III)	1994	9	154	93	4	.603	1,560	22	187.4
Jim Feeley, Johns Hopkins (II)	†1967	7	110	69	5	.627	1,264	12	186.2
Mike Bajakian, Williams (III)	1994	8	141	92	1	.652	1,382	17	186.0
John Charles, Portland St. (II)	1991	11	247	147	7	.595	2,619	32	185.7
Steve Smith, Western St. (II)	†1992	10	271	180	5	.664	2,719	30	183.5
Mitch Sanders, Bridgeport (III)	†1973	10	151	84	7	.556	1,551	23	182.9
Jim Peterson, Hanover (II)	†1948	8	125	81	12	.648	1,571	12	182.9
John Wristen, Southern Colo. (II)	†1982	8	121	68	2	.562	1,358	13	182.6
Michael Payton, Marshall (I-AA)	†1991	9	216	143	5	.622	2,333	19	181.3
Richard Basil, Savannah St. (II)	†1989	9	211	120	7	.568	2,148	29	181.1
Pat Mayew, St. John's (Minn.) (III)	†1991	9	247	154	4	.623	2,408	30	181.0
Alli Abrew, Cal Poly SLO (I-AA)	†1997	11	191	130	4	.681	1,961	17	179.5
Danny Wuerffel, Florida (I-A)	†1995	11	325	210	10	.646	3,266	35	178.4
Doug Turner, Morehead St. (I-AA)	1997	10	290	190	6	.655	2,869	29	177.5
Guy Simons, Coe (III)	1993	10	185	110	9	.594	1,979	21	177.1
Jim Cahoon, Ripon (II)	†1964	8	127	74	7	.583	1,206	19	176.4
Ted White, Howard (I-AA)	†1996	11	289	174	10	.602	2,814	36	176.2
Kyle Adamson, Allegheny (III)	1996	10	182	119	3	.653	1,761	18	176.0
Ken Suhl, New Haven (II)	1992	10	239	148	5	.619	2,336	26	175.7
Jimbo Fisher, Samford (III)	†1987	10	252	139	5	.551	2,394	34	175.4
Doug Nussmeier, Idaho (I-AA)	1993	11	304	185	5	.609	2,960	33	175.2
Brian Kadel, Dayton (I-AA)	†1995	11	183	115	6	.628	1,880	18	175.0
Gary Collier, Emory & Henry (III)	1987	11	249	152	10	.610	2,317	33	174.8
Paul Bell, Allegheny (III)	1994	10	215	142	2	.660	2,137	17	173.8
Steve Sarkisian, Brigham Young (I-A)	†1996	14	404	278	12	.688	4,027	33	173.6
Greg Lister, Rowan (III)	1996	8	167	94	2	.562	1,711	17	173.6
Kerry Collins, Penn St. (I-A)	†1994	11	264	176	7	.667	2,679	21	172.9
Kelvin Simmons, Troy St. (I-AA)	1993	11	224	143	6	.638	2,144	23	172.8
James Grant, Ramapo (III)	1989	9	147	91	7	.619	1,441	17	172.7
Tony Aliucci, Indiana (Pa.) (II)	†1990	10	181	111	10	.613	1,801	21	172.7
Chris Adams, Gettysburg (III)	1994	10	211	139	2	.658	1,977	19	172.4
James Weir, New Haven (II)	†1993	10	266	161	1	.605	2,336	31	172.0
Shawn Behr, Fort Hays St. (II)	†1995	11	318	191	6	.600	3,158	31	171.9
Frank Baur, Lafayette (I-AA)	†1988	10	256	164	11	.641	2,621	23	171.1
Mike Donnelly, Wittenberg (III)	1995	10	153	92	2	.601	1,480	15	171.1
Kyle Klein, Albion (III)	1996	9	225	151	8	.671	2,226	19	170.9
Bobby Lamb, Furman (I-AA)	†1985	11	181	106	6	.586	1,856	18	170.9
Bobby Hoying, Ohio St. (I-A)	1995	12	303	192	11	.634	3,023	28	170.4
Gary Urwiler, Eureka (III)	1991	10	171	103	5	.602	1,656	18	170.3

**Record. †National pass-efficiency champion.*

Mississippi Valley sports information photo by Mark Gall

Mississippi Valley quarterback Willie Totten threw 56 touchdown passes to set the all-time single-season mark in 1984. Totten threw 27 of his touchdown passes to a soon-to-be-famous wide receiver named Jerry Rice.

CAREER YARDS

Player, Team (Division[s])	Years	Att.	Cmp.	Int.	Pct.	Yds.	TD
Ty Detmer, Brigham Young (I-A)	1988-91	1,530	958	65	.626	*15,031	121
Steve McNair, Alcorn St. (I-AA)	1991-94	1,680	929	58	.553	14,496	119
Neil Lomax, Portland St. (II; I-AA)	1977; 78-80	1,606	938	55	.584	13,220	106
Kirk Baumgartner, Wis.-Stevens Point (III)	1986-89	1,696	883	57	.521	13,028	110
Willie Totten, Mississippi Val. (I-AA)	1982-85	1,555	907	75	.583	12,711	*139
Jamie Martin, Weber St. (I-AA)	1989-92	1,544	934	56	.605	12,207	87
Todd Santos, San Diego St. (I-A)	1984-87	1,484	910	57	.613	11,425	70
Peyton Manning, Tennessee (I-A)	1994-97	1,381	863	33	.625	11,201	89
Eric Zeier, Georgia (I-A)	1991-94	1,402	838	37	.598	11,153	67
Mark Novara, Lakeland (III)	1994-97	1,586	882	63	.556	11,101	100
Dave Dickenson, Montana (I-AA)	1992-95	1,208	813	26	.673	11,080	96
Alex Van Pelt, Pittsburgh (I-A)	1989-92	1,463	845	59	.578	10,913	64
Chris Hatcher, Valdosta St. (II)	1991-94	1,451	*1,001	38	.690	10,878	116
Danny Wuerffel, Florida (I-A)	1993-96	1,170	708	42	.605	10,875	114
Doug Nussmeier, Idaho (I-AA)	1990-93	1,225	746	32	.609	10,824	91
John Friesz, Idaho (I-AA)	1986-89	1,350	801	40	.593	10,697	77
Greg Wyatt, Northern Ariz. (I-AA)	1986-89	1,510	926	49	.613	10,697	70
Sean Payton, Eastern Ill. (I-AA)	1983-86	1,408	756	55	.537	10,655	75
Bob McLaughlin, Lock Haven (II)	1992-95	*1,719	910	*88	.529	10,640	60
Kevin Sweeney, Fresno St. (I-A)	$1982-86	1,336	731	48	.547	10,623	66
Earl Harvey, N.C. Central (II)	1985-88	1,442	690	81	.479	10,621	86
Doug Flutie, Boston College (I-A)	1981-84	1,270	677	54	.533	10,579	67
Jim Ballard, Wilmington (Ohio)/Mount Union (III)	1990, 91-93	1,199	743	41	.620	10,379	115
Tom Ehrhardt, LIU-C. W. Post (II); Rhode Island (I-AA)	1981-82; 84-85	1,489	833	63	.559	10,325	92
Brian McClure, Bowling Green (I-A)	1982-85	1,427	900	58	.631	10,280	63
Troy Kopp, Pacific (Cal.) (I-A)	1989-92	1,374	798	47	.581	10,258	87
Bill Borchert, Mount Union (III)	1994-97	1,009	671	17	.665	10,201	141
Glenn Foley, Boston College (I-A)	1990-93	1,275	703	60	.551	10,042	72
John Craven, Gardner-Webb (II)	1991-94	1,535	828	82	.539	9,934	80
Vernon Buck, Wingate (II)	1991-94	1,393	728	61	.523	9,884	72
Thad Trujillo, Fort Lewis (II)	1991-94	1,455	760	57	.522	9,873	78
Bryan Snyder, Albright (III)	1994-97	1,294	763	49	.590	9,865	92
Jarrod Furgason, Fairmont St. (II)	$1993-97	1,392	798	44	.573	9,856	101
Jeff Wiley, Holy Cross (I-AA)	1985-88	1,208	723	63	.599	9,698	71
Jeff Lewis, Northern Ariz. (I-AA)	1992-95	1,316	785	24	.597	9,655	67
Ben Bennett, Duke (I-A)	1980-83	1,375	820	57	.596	9,614	53
Keith Bishop, Ill. Wesleyan/Wheaton (Ill.) (III)	1981, 83-85	1,311	772	65	.589	9,579	71
Robbie Justino, Liberty (I-AA)	1989-92	1,267	769	51	.607	9,548	64
Dennis Bogacz, Wis.-Oshkosh/Wis.-Whitewater (III)	1988-89, 90-91	1,275	654	59	.513	9,536	66
Jim McMahon, Brigham Young (I-A)	1977-78, 80-81	1,060	653	34	.616	9,536	84
Todd Ellis, South Caro. (I-A)	1986-89	1,266	704	66	.556	9,519	97
Dave Geissler, Wis.-Stevens Point (III)	1982-85	1,346	789	57	.586	9,518	65
Kevin Ricca, Catholic (III)	1994-97	1,190	713	56	.643	9,469	89
Stoney Case, New Mexico (I-A)	1991-94	1,237	677	39	.547	9,460	67
Rob Tomlinson, Cal St. Chico (II)	1988-91	1,328	748	43	.563	9,434	52
David Klingler, Houston (I-A)	1988-91	1,261	726	38	.576	9,430	91
John Hebgen, Mankato St. (II)	1993-96	1,268	727	38	.573	9,410	71
Erik Wilhelm, Oregon St. (I-A)	1985-88	1,480	870	61	.588	9,393	52
Jeremy Leach, New Mexico (I-A)	1988-91	1,432	735	62	.513	9,382	50
John Elway, Stanford (I-A)	1979-82	1,246	774	39	.621	9,349	77

**Record. $See page 6 for explanation.*

CAREER YARDS PER GAME

(Minimum 5,000 Yards)

Player, Team (Division[s])	Years	G	Att.	Cmp.	Int.	Pct.	Yds.	TD	Yd. PG
Steve McNair, Alcorn St. (I-AA)	1991-94	42	1,680	929	58	.553	14,496	119	*345.1
Aaron Flowers, Cal St. Northridge (I-AA)	1996-97	20	819	502	21	.613	6,766	54	338.3
Ty Detmer, Brigham Young (I-A)	1988-91	46	1,530	958	65	.626	*15,031	121	326.8
Willie Totten, Mississippi Val. (I-AA)	1982-85	40	1,555	907	75	.583	12,711	*139	317.8
Kirk Baumgartner, Wis.-Stevens Point (III)	1986-89	41	1,696	883	57	.521	13,028	110	317.8
Dave Dickenson, Montana (I-AA)	1992-95	35	1,208	813	26	.673	11,080	96	316.6
Neil Lomax, Portland St. (II; I-AA)	1977; 78-80	42	1,606	938	55	.584	13,220	106	314.8
Grady Benton, West Tex. A&M (II)	1994-95	18	686	421	22	.614	5,618	49	312.1
Mike Perez, San Jose St. (I-A)	1986-87	20	792	471	30	.595	6,194	36	309.7
Keith Bishop, Ill. Wes./Wheaton (Ill.) (III)	1981, 83-85	31	1,311	772	65	.589	9,579	71	309.0
Doug Gaynor, Long Beach St. (I-A)	1984-85	22	837	569	35	.680	6,793	35	308.8
John Friesz, Idaho (I-AA)	1986-89	35	1,350	801	40	.593	10,697	77	305.6
Tony Eason, Illinois (I-A)	1981-82	22	856	526	29	.615	6,608	37	300.4

**Record.*

CAREER TOUCHDOWN PASSES

Player, Team (Division[s])	Years	Att.	Cmp.	Int.	Pct.	Yds.	TD
Bill Borchert, Mount Union (III)	1994-97	1,009	671	17	.665	10,201	*141
Willie Totten, Mississippi Val. (I-AA)	1982-85	1,555	907	75	.583	12,711	139
Ty Detmer, Brigham Young (I-A)	1988-91	1,530	958	65	.626	*15,031	121
Steve McNair, Alcorn St. (I-AA)	1991-94	1,680	929	58	.553	14,496	119
Chris Hatcher, Valdosta St. (II)	1991-94	1,451	*1,001	38	.690	10,878	116
Jim Ballard, Wilmington (Ohio)/Mount Union (III)	1990, 91-93	1,199	743	41	.620	10,379	115
Danny Wuerffel, Florida (I-A)	1993-96	1,170	708	42	.605	10,875	114
Kirk Baumgartner, Wis.-Stevens Point (III)	1986-89	1,696	883	57	.521	13,028	110
Neil Lomax, Portland St. (II; I-AA)	1977; 78-80	1,606	938	55	.584	13,220	106

Player, Team (Division[s])	Years	Att.	Cmp.	Int.	Pct.	Yds.	TD
Jarrod Furgason, Fairmont St. (II)	$1993-97	1,392	798	44	.573	9,856	101
Mark Novara, Lakeland (III)	1994-97	1,586	882	63	.556	11,101	100
Dave Dickenson, Montana (I-AA)	1992-95	1,208	813	26	.673	11,080	96
Matt Jozokos, Plymouth St. (III)	1987-90	1,003	527	39	.525	7,658	95
Doug Williams, Grambling (II; I-A)	1974-76; 77	1,009	484	52	.480	8,411	93
Bryan Snyder, Albright (III)	1994-97	1,294	763	49	.590	9,865	92
Tom Ehrhardt, LIU-C. W. Post (II); Rhode Island (I-AA)	1981-82; 84-85	1,489	833	63	.559	10,325	92
Doug Nussmeier, Idaho (I-AA)	1990-93	1,225	746	32	.609	10,824	91
David Klingler, Houston (I-A)	1988-91	1,261	726	38	.576	9,430	91
Peyton Manning, Tennessee (I-A)	1994-97	1,381	863	33	.625	11,201	89
Kevin Ricca, Catholic (III)	1994-97	1,190	713	56	.643	9,469	89
Troy Kopp, Pacific (Cal.) (I-A)	1989-92	1,374	798	47	.581	10,258	87
Jamie Martin, Weber St. (I-AA)	1989-92	1,544	934	56	.605	12,207	87
Andy Breault, Kutztown (II)	1989-92	1,259	733	63	.582	9,086	86
Earl Harvey, N.C. Central (II)	1985-88	1,442	690	81	.479	10,621	86
Rex Lamberti, Abilene Christian (II)	1984-86, 93	1,133	595	44	.525	7,934	84
Jim McMahon, Brigham Young (I-A)	1977-78, 80-81	1,060	653	34	.616	9,536	84
Darin Hinshaw, Central Fla. (I-AA)	1991-94	1,113	614	52	.552	9,000	82
Dave MacDonald, West Chester (II)	1991-94	1,123	604	46	.538	8,449	82
Dan Crowley, Towson (I-AA)	1991-94	1,170	617	54	.527	8,900	81
Joe Adams, Tennessee St. (I-A)	1977-80	1,100	604	60	.549	8,649	81
John Craven, Gardner-Webb (II)	1991-94	1,535	828	82	.539	9,934	80
Gary Collier, Emory & Henry (III)	1984-87	738	386	33	.523	6,103	80
Terry Peebles, Hanover (III)	1992-95	969	550	29	.568	6,928	79
Aaron Sparrow, Norfolk St. (II)	1992-95	1,117	615	38	.551	8,758	79
Ken Hobart, Idaho (I-AA)	1980-83	1,219	629	42	.516	9,300	79

**Record.*

SEASON YARDS

Player, Team (Division)	Year	G	Att.	Cmp.	Int.	Pct.	Yds.	TD
Ty Detmer, Brigham Young (I-A)	†1990	12	562	361	28	.642	*5,188	41
David Klingler, Houston (I-A)	1990	11	*643	*374	20	.582	5,140	54
Steve McNair, Alcorn St. (I-AA)	1994	11	530	304	17	.574	4,863	44
Andre Ware, Houston (I-A)	†1989	11	578	365	15	.631	4,699	46
Jim McMahon, Brigham Young (I-A)	†1980	12	445	284	18	.638	4,571	47
Ty Detmer, Brigham Young (I-A)	1989	12	412	265	15	.643	4,560	32
Willie Totten, Mississippi Val. (I-AA)	†1984	10	518	324	22	.626	4,557	*56
Scott Mitchell, Utah (I-A)	1988	11	533	323	15	.606	4,322	29
Chris Vargas, Nevada (I-A)	1993	11	490	331	18	.676	4,265	34
Robbie Bosco, Brigham Young (I-A)	1985	13	511	338	24	.661	4,257	30
Wilkie Perez, Glenville St. (II)	†1997	11	425	280	12	.658	4,189	45
Dave Dickenson, Montana (I-AA)	1995	11	455	309	9	.679	4,176	38
Jamie Martin, Weber St. (I-AA)	1991	11	500	310	17	.620	4,125	35
Neil Lomax, Portland St. (I-AA)	1980	11	473	296	12	.626	4,094	37
Josh Wallwork, Wyoming (I-A)	1996	12	458	286	15	.625	4,090	33
John Friesz, Idaho (I-AA)	†1989	11	425	260	8	.612	4,041	31
Ty Detmer, Brigham Young (I-A)	1991	12	403	249	12	.618	4,031	35
Steve Sarkisian, Brigham Young (I-A)	†1996	14	404	278	12	.688	4,027	33
Neil Lomax, Portland St. (I-AA)	1979	11	516	299	16	.579	3,950	26
Todd Santos, San Diego St. (I-A)	1987	12	492	306	15	.622	3,932	26
Todd Hammel, Stephen F. Austin (I-AA)	1989	11	401	238	13	.594	3,914	34
Steve Young, Brigham Young (I-A)	†1983	11	429	306	10	.713	3,902	33
Tim Couch, Kentucky (I-A)	1997	11	547	363	19	.664	3,884	37
Tim Rattay, Louisiana Tech (I-A)	1997	11	477	293	10	.614	3,881	34
Robbie Bosco, Brigham Young (I-A)	1984	12	458	283	11	.618	3,875	33
Mike McCoy, Utah (I-A)	1993	12	430	276	10	.642	3,860	21
Sean Payton, Eastern Ill. (I-AA)	1984	11	473	270	15	.571	3,843	28
Dan McGwire, San Diego St. (I-A)	1990	11	449	270	7	.601	3,833	27
Damian Poalucci, East Stroudsburg (II)	1996	10	393	214	13	.545	3,831	40
Kirk Baumgartner, Wis.-Stevens Point (III)	1988	11	527	276	16	.524	3,828	25
Anthony Dilweg, Duke (I-A)	1988	11	484	287	18	.593	3,824	24
Peyton Manning, Tennessee (I-A)	1997	12	477	287	11	.602	3,819	36
Jimmy Klingler, Houston (I-A)	1992	11	504	303	18	.601	3,818	32
Sam King, UNLV (I-A)	1981	12	433	255	19	.589	3,778	18
Troy Kopp, Pacific (Cal.) (I-A)	1991	12	449	275	16	.612	3,767	37
Perry Klein, LIU-C. W. Post (II)	1993	10	407	248	18	.609	3,757	38
Kirk Baumgartner, Wis.-Stevens Point (III)	1987	11	466	243	22	.521	3,755	31
Chris Hegg, Truman St. (II)	1985	11	503	284	20	.565	3,741	32
Lance Funderburk, Valdosta St. (II)	1996	11	459	300	10	.654	3,732	35
Brett Salisbury, Wayne St. (Neb.) (II)	1993	10	395	276	14	.699	3,729	29
John Walsh, Brigham Young (I-A)	1993	11	397	244	15	.615	3,727	28
Marc Wilson, Brigham Young (I-A)	1979	12	427	250	15	.585	3,720	29

**Record. †National pass-efficiency champion.*

SEASON YARDS PER GAME

Player, Team (Division)	Year	G	Att.	Cmp.	Int.	Pct.	Yds.	TD	Yd. PG
David Klingler, Houston (I-A)	1990	11	*643	*374	20	.582	5,140	54	*467.3
Willie Totten, Mississippi Val. (I-AA)	1984	10	518	324	22	.626	4,557	*56	455.7
Steve McNair, Alcorn St. (I-AA)	1994	11	530	304	17	.574	4,863	44	442.1
Ty Detmer, Brigham Young (I-A)	1990	12	562	361	28	.642	*5,188	41	432.3
Andre Ware, Houston (I-A)	1989	11	578	365	15	.631	4,699	46	427.2
Mike Maxwell, Nevada (I-A)	1995	9	409	277	17	.677	3,611	33	401.2
Grady Benton, West Tex. A&M (II)	1994	9	409	258	13	.631	3,541	30	393.4

Player, Team (Division)	Year	G	Att.	Cmp.	Int.	Pct.	Yds.	TD	Yd. PG
Scott Mitchell, Utah (I-A)	1988	11	533	323	15	.606	4,322	29	392.9
Chris Vargas, Nevada (I-A)	1993	11	490	331	18	.676	4,265	34	387.7
Damian Poalucci, East Stroudsburg (II)	1996	10	393	214	13	.545	3,831	40	383.1
Marty Washington, West Ala. (II)	1993	8	404	221	13	.547	3,062	26	382.8
Jim McMahon, Brigham Young (I-A)	1980	12	445	284	18	.638	4,571	47	380.9
Wilkie Perez, Glenville St. (II)	1997	11	425	280	12	.658	4,189	45	380.8
Ty Detmer, Brigham Young (I-A)	1989	12	412	265	15	.643	4,560	32	380.0

**Record.*

SEASON TOUCHDOWN PASSES

Player, Team (Division)	Year	Att.	Cmp.	Int.	Pct.	Yds.	TD
Willie Totten, Mississippi Val. (I-AA)	1984	518	324	22	.626	4,557	*56
David Klingler, Houston (I-A)	1990	*643	*374	20	.582	5,140	54
Chris Hatcher, Valdosta St. (II)	†1994	430	321	9	*.747	3,591	50
Bill Borchert, Mount Union (III)	†1997	272	190	1	.698	2,933	47
Jim McMahon, Brigham Young (I-A)	1980	445	284	18	.638	4,571	47
Andre Ware, Houston (I-A)	1989	578	365	15	.631	4,699	46
Wilkie Perez, Glenville St. (II)	†1997	425	280	12	.658	4,189	45
Bob Toledo, San Fran. St. (II)	1967	396	211	24	.533	3,513	45
Steve McNair, Alcorn St. (I-AA)	1994	530	304	17	.574	4,863	44
Brian Ah Yat, Montana (I-AA)	1996	432	265	16	.613	3,615	42
Ty Detmer, Brigham Young (I-A)	1990	562	361	28	.642	*5,188	41
Damian Poalucci, East Stroudsburg (II)	1996	393	214	13	.545	3,831	40
Mark Novara, Lakeland (III)	1996	410	258	12	.629	3,405	40
Chad Pennington, Marshall (I-AA)	1997	428	253	12	.591	3,480	39
Danny Wuerffel, Florida (I-A)	1996	360	207	13	.575	3,625	39
Terry Peebles, Hanover (III)	1995	488	283	10	.579	3,521	39
Kirk Baumgartner, Wis.-Stevens Point (III)	1989	455	247	9	.542	3,692	39
Willie Totten, Mississippi Val. (I-AA)	1985	492	295	29	.600	3,698	39
Dennis Shaw, San Diego St. (I-A)	1969	335	199	26	.594	3,185	39
Bryan Snyder, Albright (III)	1996	358	223	9	.622	2,983	38
Bill Borchert, Mount Union (III)	†1996	240	165	6	.687	2,655	38
Dave Dickenson, Montana (I-AA)	1995	455	309	9	.679	4,176	38
Perry Klein, LIU-C. W. Post (II)	1993	407	248	18	.609	3,757	38
Doug Williams, Grambling (I-A)	1977	352	181	18	.514	3,286	38
Tim Couch, Kentucky (I-A)	1997	547	363	19	.664	3,884	37
Terry Peebles, Hanover (III)	1994	445	252	17	.566	3,197	37
Jim Ballard, Mount Union (III)	1993	314	229	11	.729	3,304	37
Chris Hatcher, Valdosta St. (II)	1993	471	335	11	.711	3,651	37
Andy Breault, Kutztown (II)	1991	360	225	20	.625	2,927	37
Troy Kopp, Pacific (Cal.) (I-A)	1991	449	275	16	.613	3,767	37
Neil Lomax, Portland St. (I-AA)	1980	473	296	12	.626	4,094	37
Peyton Manning, Tennessee (I-A)	1997	477	287	11	.602	3,819	36
Chris Boden, Villanova (I-AA)	1997	345	231	4	.670	3,079	36
Ted White, Howard (I-AA)	1996	289	174	10	.602	2,814	36
Kevin Ricca, Catholic (III)	1997	306	208	6	.679	2,990	35
Lance Funderburk, Valdosta St. (II)	1996	459	300	10	.654	3,732	35
Danny Wuerffel, Florida (I-A)	1995	325	210	10	.646	3,266	35
Jarrod Furgason, Fairmont St. (II)	1995	349	222	8	.636	2,696	35
Dave MacDonald, West Chester (II)	1994	458	251	18	.548	3,308	35
Jayson Merrill, Western St. (II)	1991	309	195	11	.631	3,484	35
Ty Detmer, Brigham Young (I-A)	1991	403	249	12	.618	4,031	35
Jamie Martin, Weber St. (I-AA)	1991	500	310	17	.620	4,125	35
Tom Ehrhardt, Rhode Island (I-AA)	1985	497	283	19	.569	3,542	35

**Record. †National pass-efficiency champion.*

SINGLE-GAME YARDS

Yds.	Div.	Player, Team (Opponent)	Date
716	I-A	David Klingler, Houston (Arizona St.)	Dec. 2, 1990
690	I-A	Matt Vogler, Texas Christian (Houston)	Nov. 3, 1990
642	II	Wilkie Perez, Glenville St. (Concord)	Oct. 25, 1997
631	I-A	Scott Mitchell, Utah (Air Force)	Oct. 15, 1988
624	I-AA	Jamie Martin, Weber St. (Idaho St.)	Nov. 23, 1991
622	I-A	Jeremy Leach, New Mexico (Utah)	Nov. 11, 1989
621	I-A	Dave Wilson, Illinois (Ohio St.)	Nov. 8, 1980
619	I-A	John Walsh, Brigham Young (Utah St.)	Oct. 30, 1993
619	I-AA	Doug Pederson, Northeast La. (Stephen F. Austin)	Nov. 11, 1989
616	II	Damian Poalucci, East Stroudsburg (Mansfield)	Nov. 2, 1996
614	II	Alfred Montez, Western N.M. (West Tex. A&M)	Oct. 8, 1994
614	II	Perry Klein, LIU-C. W. Post (Salisbury St.)	Nov. 6, 1993
613	I-A	Jimmy Klingler, Houston (Rice)	Nov. 28, 1992
602	III	Tom Stallings, St. Thomas (Minn.) (Bethel [Minn.])	Nov. 13, 1993
599	II	Jarrod DeGeorgia, Wayne St. (Neb.) (Drake)	Nov. 9, 1996
599	I-A	Ty Detmer, Brigham Young (San Diego St.)	Nov. 16, 1991
599	I-AA	Willie Totten, Mississippi Val. (Prairie View)	Oct. 27, 1984
592	II	John Charles, Portland St. (Cal Poly SLO)	Nov. 16, 1991
589	I-AA	Vern Harris, Idaho St. (Montana)	Oct. 12, 1985
587	I-AA	Steve McNair, Alcorn St. (Southern U.)	Oct. 22, 1994
585	III	Tim Lynch, Hofstra (Fordham)	Oct. 19, 1991
585	I-A	Robbie Bosco, Brigham Young (New Mexico)	Oct. 19, 1985
575	III	Eric Noble, Wilmington (Ohio) (Urbana)	Nov. 5, 1994
572	I-A	David Klingler, Houston (Eastern Wash.)	Nov. 17, 1990
571	I-AA	Todd Hammel, Stephen F. Austin (Northeast La.)	Nov. 11, 1989
571	I-A	Marc Wilson, Brigham Young (Utah)	Nov. 5, 1977
568	II	Scott Otis, Glenville St. (West Va. Wesleyan)	Oct. 15, 1994
568	I-A	David Lowery, San Diego St. (Brigham Young)	Nov. 16, 1991
568	II	Bob Toledo, San Fran. St. (Cal St. Hayward)	Oct. 21, 1967
566	I-AA	Tom Ehrhardt, Rhode Island (Connecticut)	Nov. 16, 1985
565	I-A	Jim McMahon, Brigham Young (Utah)	Nov. 21, 1981
564	II	Pat Graham, Augustana (S.D.) (Mankato St.)	Oct. 28, 1995
564	I-A	Troy Kopp, Pacific (Cal.) (New Mexico St.)	Oct. 20, 1990
563	I-AA	Steve McNair, Alcorn St. (Samford)	Oct. 29, 1994
563	I-A	David Klingler, Houston (Texas Christian)	Nov. 3, 1990
561	I-A	Tony Adams, Utah St. (Utah)	Nov. 11, 1972

SINGLE-GAME ATTEMPTS

Atts.	Div.	Player, Team (Opponent)	Date
81	III	Jordan Poznick, Principia (Blackburn)	Oct. 10, 1992
79	I-A	Matt Vogler, Texas Christian (Houston)	Nov. 3, 1990
79	III	Mike Wallace, Ohio Wesleyan (Denison)	Oct. 3, 1981
78	I-A	Rusty LaRue, Wake Forest (Duke)	Oct. 28, 1995
77	I-AA	Neil Lomax, Portland St. (Northern Colo.)	Oct. 20, 1979
76	II	Jarrod DeGeorgia, Wayne St. (Neb.) (Drake)	Nov. 9, 1996
76	I-A	David Klingler, Houston (Southern Methodist)	Oct. 20, 1990
75	I-A	Chris Vargas, Nevada (McNeese St.)	Sept. 19, 1992
74	II	Jamie Sander, N.M. Highlands (Neb.-Kearney)	Nov. 9, 1996
74	II	Jermaine Whitaker, N.M. Highlands (Western St.)	Nov. 5, 1994
74	I-AA	Paul Peterson, Idaho St. (Nevada)	Oct. 1, 1983
73	I-A	Jeff Handy, Missouri (Oklahoma St.)	Oct. 17, 1992
73	I-A	Troy Kopp, Pacific (Cal.) (Hawaii)	Oct. 27, 1990
73	I-A	Shane Montgomery, North Caro. St. (Duke)	Nov. 11, 1989
72	I-AA	Dave Dickenson, Montana (Idaho)	Oct. 21, 1995
72	I-A	Matt Vogler, Texas Christian (Texas Tech)	Nov. 10, 1990
72	II	Kurt Otto, North Dak. (Tex. A&M-Kingsville)	Sept. 13, 1986
72	III	Bob Lockhart, Millikin (Franklin)	Nov. 12, 1977
72	II	Kaipo Spencer, Santa Clara (Portland St.)	Oct. 11, 1975
72	II	Joe Stetser, Cal St. Chico (Oregon Tech)	Sept. 23, 1967

SINGLE-GAME COMPLETIONS

Cmp.	Div.	Player, Team (Opponent)	Date
56	II	Jarrod DeGeorgia, Wayne St. (Neb.) (Drake)	Nov. 9, 1996
55	I-A	Rusty LaRue, Wake Forest (Duke)	Oct. 28, 1995
50	I-A	Rusty LaRue, Wake Forest (North Caro. St.)	Nov. 18, 1995
50	III	Tim Lynch, Hofstra (Fordham)	Oct. 19, 1991
48	I-AA	Clayton Millis, Cal St. Northridge (St. Mary's [Cal.])	Nov. 11, 1995
48	III	Jordan Poznick, Principia (Blackburn)	Oct. 10, 1992
48	I-A	David Klingler, Houston (Southern Methodist)	Oct. 20, 1990
47	I-AA	Jamie Martin, Weber St. (Idaho St.)	Nov. 23, 1991
47	III	Mike Wallace, Ohio Wesleyan (Denison)	Oct. 3, 1981
46	I-A	Scott Milanovich, Maryland (Florida St.)	Nov. 18, 1995
46	I-A	Jimmy Klingler, Houston (Rice)	Nov. 28, 1992
46	I-AA	Doug Pederson, Northeast La. (Stephen F. Austin)	Nov. 11, 1989
46	I-AA	Willie Totten, Mississippi Val. (Southern U.)	Sept. 29, 1984
45	II	Chris Hatcher, Valdosta St. (Mississippi Col.)	Oct. 23, 1993
45	II	Chris Hatcher, Valdosta St. (West Ga.)	Oct. 16, 1993
45	I-AA	Willie Totten, Mississippi Val. (Prairie View)	Oct. 27, 1984
45	I-A	Sandy Schwab, Northwestern (Michigan)	Oct. 23, 1982
44	II	Wilkie Perez, Glenville St. (Concord)	Oct. 25, 1997
44	I-A	Matt Vogler, Texas Christian (Houston)	Nov. 3, 1990
44	I-A	Chuck Hartlieb, Iowa (Indiana)	Oct. 29, 1988
44	II	Tom Bonds, Cal Lutheran (St. Mary's [Cal.])	Nov. 22, 1986
44	I-A	Jim McMahon, Brigham Young (Colorado St.)	Nov. 7, 1981
44	I-AA	Neil Lomax, Portland St. (Northern Colo.)	Oct. 20, 1979
43	I-AA	Aaron Flowers, Cal St. Northridge (Cal St. Sacramento)	Oct. 25, 1997
43	III	Bill Nietzke, Alma (Hope)	Oct. 26, 1996
43	III	Bill Nietzke, Alma (Olivet Nazarene)	Sept. 21, 1996
43	I-AA	Dave Dickenson, Montana (Idaho)	Oct. 21, 1995
43	III	Terry Peebles, Hanover (Franklin)	Nov. 12, 1994
43	I-A	Jeff Handy, Missouri (Oklahoma St.)	Oct. 17, 1992
43	I-A	Chris Vargas, Nevada (McNeese St.)	Sept. 19, 1992
43	I-A	Gary Schofield, Wake Forest (Maryland)	Oct. 17, 1981
43	I-A	Dave Wilson, Illinois (Ohio St.)	Nov. 8, 1980
43	I-A	Rich Campbell, California (Florida)	Sept. 13, 1980
43	II	George Bork, Northern Ill. (Central Mich.)	Nov. 9, 1963

Receiving

CAREER RECEPTIONS

Player, Team (Division[s])	Years	Rec.	Yards	Avg.	TD
Jerry Rice, Mississippi Val. (I-AA)	1981-84	*301	*4,693	15.6	50
Matt Newton, Principia (III)	1990-93	287	3,646	12.7	32
Carlos Ferralls, Glenville St. (II)	1994-97	282	4,091	14.5	53
Jeff Clay, Catholic (III)	1994-97	269	4,101	15.2	44
Kasey Dunn, Idaho (I-AA)	1988-91	268	3,847	14.4	25
Aaron Turner, Pacific (Cal.) (I-A)	1989-92	266	4,345	16.3	43
Chad Mackey, Louisiana Tech (I-A)	1993-96	264	3,789	14.4	22
Terance Mathis, New Mexico (I-A)	1985-87, 89	263	4,254	16.2	36
Mark Templeton, Long Beach St. (I-A) (RB)	1983-86	¢262	1,969	7.5	11
Jon Spinosa, Lock Haven (II)	1992-95	261	2,710	10.4	12
Howard Twilley, Tulsa (I-A)	1963-65	261	3,343	12.8	32
Marcus Harris, Wyoming (I-A)	1993-96	259	4,518	17.4	38
Bill Stromberg, Johns Hopkins (III)	1978-81	258	3,776	14.6	39
Kurt Barth, Eureka (III)	1994-97	256	4,311	16.8	51
Chris Myers, Kenyon (II)	1967-70	253	3,897	15.4	33
Brian Forster, Rhode Island (I-AA) (TE)	1983-85, 87	#245	#3,410	13.9	31
David Williams, Illinois (I-A)	1983-85	245	3,195	13.0	22
Bruce Cerone, Yankton/Emporia St. (II)	1965-66, 68-69	241	4,354	18.1	49
James Roe, Norfolk St. (II)	1992-95	239	4,468	18.7	46
Mark Didio, Connecticut (I-AA)	1988-91	239	3,535	14.8	21
Bryan McGinty, Lock Haven (II)	1993-96	238	3,100	13.0	18
Rennie Benn, Lehigh (I-AA)	1982-85	237	3,662	15.5	44
Marc Zeno, Tulane (I-A)	1984-87	236	3,725	15.8	25
Jason Wolf, Southern Methodist (I-A)	1989-92	235	2,232	9.5	17
Bryan Reeves, Nevada (I-AA; I-A)	1991; 92-93	234	3,407	14.6	32
Todd Bloom, Hardin-Simmons (III)	1995-97	233	2,621	11.2	14
Dale Amos, Frank. & Marsh. (III)	1986-89	233	3,846	16.5	35
Scott Fredrickson, Wis.-Stout (III)	1986-89	233	3,390	14.5	23
"Red" Roberts, Austin Peay (II)	1967-70	232	3,005	13.0	31
Chris George, Glenville St. (II)	1993-94	230	3,215	14.0	30
Mike Whitehouse, St. Norbert (III)	1986-89	230	3,480	15.1	37
Jerry Hendren, Idaho (II; I-A)	1967-68; 69	230	3,435	14.9	27

*Record. ¢Record for a running back. #Record for a tight end.

CAREER RECEPTIONS PER GAME

(Minimum 125 Receptions)

Player, Team (Division[s])	Years	G	Rec.	Yards	TD	Rec. PG
Chris George, Glenville St. (II)	1993-94	20	230	3,215	30	*11.5
Manny Hazard, Houston (I-A)	1989-90	21	220	2,635	31	10.5
Alex Van Dyke, Nevada (I-A)	1994-95	22	227	3,100	26	10.3
Howard Twilley, Tulsa (I-A)	1963-65	26	261	3,343	32	10.0
Jason Phillips, Houston (I-A)	1987-88	22	207	2,319	18	9.4
Matt Newton, Principia (III)	1990-93	33	287	3,646	32	8.7
Ed Bell, Idaho St. (II)	1968-69	19	163	2,608	30	8.6
Byron Chamberlain, Wayne St. (Neb.) (II)	1993-94	19	161	1,941	14	8.5
Todd Bloom, Hardin-Simmons (III)	1995-97	28	233	2,621	14	8.3
Carlos Ferralls, Glenville St. (II)	1994-97	35	282	4,091	53	8.1
Jerry Hendren, Idaho (II)	1967-69	30	230	3,435	27	7.7
Bryan Reeves, Nevada (I-AA; I-A)	1991; 92-93	31	234	3,407	32	7.6
Jeff Clay, Catholic (III)	1994-97	36	269	4,101	44	7.5
David Williams, Illinois (I-A)	1983-85	33	245	3,195	22	7.4
Gary Garrison, San Diego St. (II)	1964-65	20	148	2,188	26	7.4
Brad Bailey, West Tex. A&M (II)	1992-94	30	221	2,677	22	7.4
Jerry Rice, Mississippi Val. (I-AA)	1981-84	41	*301	*4,693	50	7.3
James Dixon, Houston (I-A)	1987-88	22	161	1,762	14	7.3

*Record.

CAREER TOUCHDOWN RECEPTIONS

Player, Team (Division[s])	Years	G	TD
Chris Bisaillon, Ill. Wesleyan (III)	1989-92	36	*55
Carlos Ferralls, Glenville St. (II)	1994-97	35	53
Kurt Barth, Eureka (III)	1994-97	39	51
Jerry Rice, Mississippi Val. (I-AA)	1981-84	41	50
Bruce Cerone, Yankton/Emporia St. (II)	1965-66, 68-69	36	49
James Roe, Norfolk St. (II)	1992-95	41	46
Randy Moss, Marshall (I-AA; I-A)	1996-97	23	44
Rennie Benn, Lehigh (I-AA)	1982-85	41	44
Aaron Turner, Pacific (Cal.) (I-A)	1989-92	44	43
R.J. Hoppe, Carroll (Wis.) (III)	1993-96	37	49
Jeff Clay, Catholic (III)	1994-97	36	44
Mark Loeffler, Wheaton (Ill.) (III)	1993-96	38	43
Sedrick Robinson, Ky. Wesleyan (II)	1993-96	38	42
Ryan Yarborough, Wyoming (I-A)	1990-93	46	42
Shannon Sharpe, Savannah St. (II)	1986-89	42	40
Dedric Ward, Northern Iowa (I-AA)	1993-96	43	41
John Aromando, Col. of New Jersey (III)	1981-84	40	39
Bill Stromberg, Johns Hopkins (III)	1978-81	40	39
Marcus Harris, Wyoming (I-A)	1993-96	46	38
Kurt Barth, Eureka (III)¢	1994-96	29	38
Rodd Patten, Framingham St. (III)	1990-93	35	38
Tony Willis, New Haven (II)	1990-93	40	38
Clarkston Hines, Duke (I-A)	1986-89	44	38
Roy Banks, Eastern Ill. (I-AA)	1983-86	38	38
Robert Clark, N.C. Central (II)	1983-86	40	38
Mike Jones, Tennessee St. (I-AA)	1979-82	42	38
Chris Holder, Tuskegee (II)	1988-91	40	37
Mike Whitehouse, St. Norbert (III)	1986-89	38	37
Terance Mathis, New Mexico (I-A)	1985-87, 89	44	36
Mike Cottle, Juniata (III)	1985-88	37	36
Joe Thomas, Mississippi Val. (I-AA)	1982-85	41	36
Willie Richardson, Jackson St. (II)	1959-62	38	36

*Record. ¢Active Player.

SEASON RECEPTIONS

Player, Team (Division)	Year	G	Rec.	Yards	TD
Manny Hazard, Houston (I-A)	†1989	11	*142	1,689	22
Howard Twilley, Tulsa (I-A)	†1965	10	134	1,779	16
Alex Van Dyke, Nevada (I-A)	†1995	11	129	1,854	16
Brad Bailey, West Tex. A&M (II)	1994	11	119	1,552	16
Chris George, Glenville St. (II)	†1993	10	117	*1,876	15
Brian Forster, Rhode Island (I-AA) (TE)	†1985	10	115	1,617	12
Damond Wilkins, Nevada (I-A)	†1996	11	114	1,121	4
Chris George, Glenville St. (II)	†1994	10	113	1,339	15
Jeff Clay, Catholic (III)	†1997	10	112	1,625	20
Sean Pender, Valdosta St. (II)	†1995	11	111	983	2
Marcus Harris, Wyoming (I-A)	1996	12	109	1,650	13
Fred Gilbert, Houston (I-A)	†1991	11	106	957	7
Barry Wagner, Alabama A&M (II)	†1989	11	106	1,812	17
Theo Blanco, Wis.-Stevens Point (III) (RB)	1987	11	#106	#1,616	8
Chris Penn, Tulsa (I-A)	†1993	11	105	1,578	12
Eugene Baker, Kent (I-A)	†1997	11	103	1,549	18
Sherman Smith, Houston (I-A)	†1992	11	103	923	6
Jerry Rice, Mississippi Val. (I-AA)	†1984	10	103	1,682	*27
Troy Edwards, Louisiana Tech (I-A)	1997	11	102	1,707	13
James Dixon, Houston (I-A)	1988	11	102	1,103	11
Jerry Rice, Mississippi Val. (I-AA)	†1983	10	102	1,450	14
Mike Healey, Valparaiso (II)	†1985	10	101	1,279	11
David Williams, Illinois (I-A)	†1984	11	101	1,278	8
Jay Miller, Brigham Young (I-A)	†1973	11	100	1,181	8
Jason Phillips, Houston (I-A)	†1987	11	99	875	3
Mark Templeton, Long Beach St. (I-A) (RB)	†1986	11	99	688	2
Scott Pingel, Westminster (Mo.) (III)	1997	10	98	1,420	17
Geoffery Noisy, Nevada (I-A)	1996	11	98	1,435	9
Alex Van Dyke, Nevada (I-A)	†1994	11	98	1,246	10
Matt Newton, Principia (III)	†1992	8	98	1,487	14
Rodney Carter, Purdue (I-A)	†1985	11	98	1,099	4
Keith Edwards, Vanderbilt (I-A)	†1983	11	97	909	0

*Record. †National champion. #Record for a running back.

SEASON RECEPTIONS PER GAME

Player, Team (Division)	Year	G	Rec.	Yards	TD	Rec. PG
Howard Twilley, Tulsa (I-A)	†1965	10	134	1,779	16	*13.4
Manny Hazard, Houston (I-A)	†1989	11	*142	1,689	22	12.9
Matt Newton, Principia (III)	†1992	8	98	1,487	14	12.3
Matt Newton, Principia (III)	†1993	8	96	1,080	11	12.0
Alex Van Dyke, Nevada (I-A)	†1995	11	129	1,854	16	11.7
Chris George, Glenville St. (II)	†1993	10	117	*1,876	15	11.7
Brian Forster, Rhode Island (I-AA) (TE)	†1985	10	115	1,617	12	11.5
Chris George, Glenville St. (II)	†1994	10	113	1,339	15	11.3
Jeff Clay, Catholic (III)	†1997	10	112	1,625	20	11.2
Brad Bailey, West Tex. A&M (II)	1994	11	119	1,552	16	10.8
Ben Fox, Hanover (III)	†1995	9	95	1,087	15	10.6
Sean Munroe, Mass.-Boston (III)	1992	9	95	1,693	17	10.6
Damond Wilkins, Nevada (I-A)	†1996	11	114	1,121	4	10.4
Jerry Rice, Mississippi Val. (I-AA)	†1984	10	103	1,682	*27	10.3
Scott Faessler, Framingham St. (III)	†1990	9	92	916	5	10.2
Jerry Rice, Mississippi Val. (I-AA)	†1983	10	102	1,450	14	10.2
Carlos Ferralls, Glenville St. (II)	†1996	8	81	965	6	10.1
Bruce Cerone, Emporia St. (II)	†1968	9	91	1,479	15	10.1
Mike Healy, Valparaiso (II)	†1985	10	101	1,279	11	10.1
Sean Pender, Valdosta St. (II)	†1995	11	111	983	2	10.1
Stuart Gaussoin, Portland St. (I-AA)	†1979	9	90	1,132	8	10.0

*Record. †National champion.

SINGLE-GAME RECEPTIONS

No.	Div.	Player, Team (Opponent)	Date
24	I-AA	Jerry Rice, Mississippi Val. (Southern U.)	Oct. 1, 1983
23	II	Chris George, Glenville St. (West Va. Wesleyan)	Oct. 15, 1994
23	I-A	Randy Gatewood, UNLV (Idaho)	Sept. 17, 1994

No.	Div.	Player, Team (Opponent)	Date
23	III	Sean Munroe, Mass.-Boston (Mass. Maritime)	Oct. 10, 1992
23	II	Barry Wagner, Alabama A&M (Clark Atlanta)	Nov. 4, 1989
22	I-AA	Marvin Walker, North Texas (Tulsa)	Nov. 20, 1982
22	I-A	Jay Miller, Brigham Young (New Mexico)	Nov. 3, 1973
21	II	Kevin Swayne, Wayne St. (Neb.) (Drake)	Nov. 9, 1996
21	II	Jarett Vito, Emporia St. (Truman St.)	Nov. 4, 1995
21#	I-AA	David Pandt, Montana St. (Eastern Wash.)	Sept. 21, 1985
20	III	Todd Bloom, Hardin-Simmons (Mississippi Col.)	Oct. 12, 1996
20	III	Kurt Barth, Eureka (Concordia, Wis.)	Sept. 28, 1996
20	I-AA	Tim Hilton, Cal St. Northridge (St. Mary's [Cal.])	Nov. 11, 1995
20	II	Sean Pender, Valdosta St. (Mississippi Col.)	Nov. 4, 1995
20	II	Keylie Martin, N.M. Highlands (Western St.)	Nov. 5, 1994
20	III	Rich Johnson, Pace (Fordham)	Nov. 7, 1987
20	III	Pete Thompson, Carroll (Wis.) (Augustana [Ill.])	Nov. 4, 1978
20	II	Harold "Red" Roberts, Austin Peay (Murray St.)	Nov. 8, 1969
20	I-A	Rick Eber, Tulsa (Idaho St.)	Oct. 7, 1967

#Record for a running back.

CAREER YARDS

Player, Team (Division[s])	Years	Rec.	Yards	Avg.	TD
Jerry Rice, Mississippi Val. (I-AA)	1981-84	*301	*4,693	15.6	50
Marcus Harris, Wyoming (I-A)	1993-96	259	4,518	17.4	38
James Roe, Norfolk St. (II)	1992-95	239	4,468	18.7	46
Ryan Yarborough, Wyoming (I-A)	1990-93	229	4,357	19.0	42
Bruce Cerone, Yankton/Emporia St. (II)	1965-66, 68-69	241	4,354	18.1	49
Aaron Turner, Pacific (Cal.) (I-A)	1989-92	266	4,345	16.3	43
Kurt Barth, Eureka (III)	1994-97	256	4,311	16.8	51
Terance Mathis, New Mexico (I-A)	1985-87, 89	263	4,254	16.2	36
Robert Clark, N.C. Central (II)	1983-86	210	4,231	‡20.1	38
Jeff Clay, Catholic (III)	1994-97	269	4,101	15.2	44
Carlos Ferralls, Glenville St. (II)	1994-97	282	4,091	14.5	53
Chris Myers, Kenyon (II)	1967-70	253	3,897	15.4	33
Dedric Ward, Northern Iowa (I-AA)	1993-96	176	3,876	22.0	41
Kasey Dunn, Idaho (I-AA)	1988-91	268	3,847	14.4	25
Dale Amos, Frank. & Marsh. (III)	1986-89	233	3,846	16.5	35
Chad Mackey, Louisiana Tech (I-A)	1993-96	264	3,789	14.4	22
Bill Stromberg, Johns Hopkins (III)	1978-81	258	3,776	14.6	39
Shannon Sharpe, Savannah St. (II)	1986-89	192	3,744	19.5	40
Marc Zeno, Tulane (I-A)	1984-87	236	3,725	15.8	25
Jim Bradford, Carleton (III)	1988-91	212	3,719	17.5	32
Tyrone Johnson, Western St. (II)	1990-93	163	3,717	22.8	35
Chris Bisaillon, Ill. Wesleyan (III)	1989-92	223	3,670	16.5	*55
Rennie Benn, Lehigh (I-AA)	1982-85	237	3,662	15.5	44
Matt Newton, Principia (III)	1990-93	287	3,646	12.7	32
Jeff Tiefenthaler, South Dak. St. (II)	1983-86	173	3,621	20.9	31
David Rhodes, Central Fla. (I-AA)	1991-94	213	3,618	17.0	29
Willie Richardson, Jackson St. (II)	1959-62	166	3,616	21.8	36
Johnny Cox, Fort Lewis (II)	1990-93	220	3,611	16.4	33
Mike Gundersdorf, Wilkes (III)	1993-96	205	3,603	17.6	34
Ron Sellers, Florida St. (I-A)	1966-68	212	3,598	17.0	23

**Record. ‡Record for minimum 180 catches.*

CAREER YARDS PER GAME

(Minimum 2,200 Yards)

Player, Team (Division[s])	Years	G	Yards	Yd. PG
Chris George, Glenville St. (II)	1993-94	20	3,215	*160.8
Alex Van Dyke, Nevada (I-A)	1994-95	22	3,100	140.9
Ed Bell, Idaho St. (II)	1968-69	19	2,608	137.3
Manny Hazard, Houston (I-A)	1989-90	21	2,635	125.5
Bruce Cerone, Yankton/Emporia St. (II)	1965-66, 68-69	36	4,354	120.9
Ron Sellers, Florida St. (I-A)	1966-68	30	3,598	119.9
Randy Moss, Marshall (I-AA; I-A)	1996-97	23	2,720	118.3
Derrick Ingram, UAB (I-AA)	1993-94	22	2,572	116.9
Carlos Ferralls, Glenville St. (II)	1994-97	35	4,091	116.9
Jerry Rice, Mississippi Val. (I-AA)	1981-84	41	*4,693	114.5
Jerry Hendren, Idaho (II)	1967-69	30	3,435	114.5
Nakia Jenkins, Utah St. (I-A)	1996-97	22	2,483	112.9
Jeff Clay, Catholic (III)	1994-97	36	4,101	113.9
Elmo Wright, Houston (I-A)	1968-70	30	3,347	111.6
Howard Twilley, Tulsa (I-A)	1963-65	30	3,343	111.4
Chris Myers, Kenyon (II)	1967-70	35	3,897	111.3
Kurt Barth, Eureka (III)	1994-97	39	4,311	110.5
Matt Newton, Principia (III)	1990-93	33	3,646	110.5
Tim McNamara, Trinity (Conn.) (III)	1981-84	21	2,313	110.1
Bryan Reeves, Nevada (I-AA; I-A)	1991; 92-93	31	3,407	109.9
James Roe, Norfolk St. (II)	1992-95	41	4,468	109.0
Chris Penn, Tulsa (I-A)	1991, 93	22	2,370	107.7
Jason Phillips, Houston (I-A)	1987-88	22	2,319	105.4
Bill Stromberg, Johns Hopkins (III)	1978-81	36	3,776	104.9
Joe Douglass, Montana (I-AA)	1995-96	22	2,301	104.6
Chris Bisaillon, Ill. Wesleyan (III)	1989-92	36	3,670	101.9

**Record.*

SEASON YARDS

Player, Team (Division)	Year	Rec.	Yards	Avg.	TD
Chris George, Glenville St. (II)	†1993	117	*1,876	16.0	15
Alex Van Dyke, Nevada (I-A)	†1995	129	1,854	14.4	16
Barry Wagner, Alabama A&M (II)	†1989	106	1,812	17.1	17
Howard Twilley, Tulsa (I-A)	†1965	134	1,779	13.3	16
Chris Perry, Adams St. (II)	†1995	88	1,719	19.5	21
Troy Edwards, Louisiana Tech (I-A)	†1997	102	1,707	16.7	13
Sean Munroe, Mass.-Boston (III)	†1992	95	1,693	17.8	17
Manny Hazard, Houston (I-A)	†1989	*142	1,689	11.9	22
Jerry Rice, Mississippi Val. (I-AA)	†1984	103	1,682	16.3	*27
Marcus Harris, Wyoming (I-A)	†1996	109	1,650	15.1	13
Randy Moss, Marshall (I-A)	1997	90	1,647	18.3	20
Jeff Clay, Catholic (III)	†1997	112	1,625	14.5	25
Brian Forster, Rhode Island (I-AA) (TE)	†1985	115	1,617	14.1	12
Theo Blanco, Wis.-Stevens Point (III) (RB)	1987	#106	#1,616	15.2	8
Aaron Turner, Pacific (Cal.) (I-A)	†1991	92	1,604	17.4	18
Dan Fulton, Neb.-Omaha (II)	1976	67	1,581	23.6	16
Chris Penn, Tulsa (I-A)	†1993	105	1,578	15.0	12
Carlos Ferralls, Glenville St. (II)	†1997	94	1,566	16.6	19
Brad Bailey, West Tex. A&M (II)	1994	119	1,552	13.0	16
Eugene Baker, Kent (I-A)	†1997	103	1,547	15.0	18
Jeff Tiefenthaler, South Dak. St. (II)	1986	73	1,534	21.0	11
Ed Bell, Idaho St. (II)	†1969	96	1,522	15.9	20
Chuck Hughes, UTEP (I-A)	1965	80	1,519	19.0	12
Ryan Yarborough, Wyoming (I-A)	1993	67	1,512	22.6	16
Henry Ellard, Fresno St. (I-A)	1982	62	1,510	††24.4	15
Rodney Robinson, Gardner-Webb (II)	†1992	89	1,496	16.8	16
Ron Sellers, Florida St. (I-A)	†1968	86	1,496	17.4	12

**Record. †National champion. ††Record for minimum 55 catches. #Record for a running back.*

SEASON YARDS PER GAME

Player, Team (Division)	Year	G	Rec.	Yards	Yd. PG
Sean Munroe, Mass.-Boston (III)	†1992	9	95	1,693	*188.1
Chris George, Glenville St. (II)	†1993	10	117	*1,876	187.6
Matt Newton, Principia (III)	†1992	8	98	1,487	185.9
Howard Twilley, Tulsa (I-A)	†1965	10	134	1,779	177.9
Chris Perry, Adams St. (II)	†1995	10	88	1,719	171.9
Alex Van Dyke, Nevada (I-A)	†1995	11	129	1,854	168.5
Jerry Rice, Mississippi Val. (I-AA)	†1984	10	103	1,682	168.2
Barry Wagner, Alabama A&M (II)	†1989	11	106	1,812	164.7
Bruce Cerone, Emporia St. (II)	†1968	9	91	1,479	164.3
Jeff Clay, Catholic (III)	†1997	10	112	1,625	162.5
Jeff Clay, Catholic (III)	†1996	9	81	1,460	162.2
Brian Forster, Rhode Island (I-AA)	†1985	10	115	1,617	161.7

**Record. †National champion.*

SEASON TOUCHDOWN RECEPTIONS

Player, Team (Division)	Year	G	TD
Jerry Rice, Mississippi Val. (I-AA)	1984	10	*27
Randy Moss, Marshall (I-A)	1997	12	25
Manny Hazard, Houston (I-A)	1989	11	22
Chris Perry, Adams St. (II)	1995	10	21
Jeff Clay, Catholic (III)	1997	10	20
John Aromando, Col. of New Jersey (III)	1983	10	20
Ed Bell, Idaho St. (II)	1969	10	20
Carlos Ferralls, Glenville St. (II)	1997	10	19
Randy Moss, Marshall (I-AA)	1996	11	19
Stanley Flanders, Valdosta St. (II)	1994	11	19
Desmond Howard, Michigan (I-A)	1991	11	19
Eugene Baker, Kent (I-A)	1997	11	18
Ryan Hinske, Wis.-Oshkosh (III)	1997	10	18
Joe Douglass, Montana (I-AA)	1996	11	18
Jamar Nailor, N.M. Highlands (II)	1996	10	18
Wayne Thomas, Miles (II)	1996	10	18
Kurt Barth, Eureka (III)	1995	10	18
Brian Penecale, West Chester (II)	1994	11	18
Aaron Turner, Pacific (Cal.) (I-A)	1991	11	18
Dennis Smith, Utah (I-A)	1989	12	18
Tom Reynolds, San Diego St. (I-A)	1971	10	18
Brian Finneran, Villanova (I-AA)	1997	11	17
Scott Pingel, Westminster (Mo.) (III)	1997	10	17
Junior Lord, Guilford (III)	1997	9	17
Terry Glenn, Ohio St. (I-A)	1995	11	17
Chris Doering, Florida (I-A)	1995	12	17
Jeremy Loretz, St. John's (Minn.) (III)	1994	10	17
James Roe, Norfolk St. (II)	1994	10	17
Robert Williams, Valdosta St. (II)	1994	11	17
Bryan Reeves, Nevada (I-A)	1993	10	17
J. J. Stokes, UCLA (I-A)	1993	11	17
Sean Munroe, Mass.-Boston (III)	1992	9	17
Chris Bisaillon, Ill. Wesleyan (III)	1991	9	17
Mario Bailey, Washington (I-A)	1991	11	17

Player, Team (Division)	Year	G	TD
Clarkston Hines, Duke (I-A)	1989	11	17
Barry Wagner, Alabama A&M (II)	1989	11	17
Mark Carrier, Nicholls St. (I-AA)	1986	11	17
Dameon Reilly, Rhode Island (I-AA)	1985	11	17
Joe Thomas, Mississippi Val. (I-AA)	1985	11	17
Roy Banks, Eastern Ill. (I-AA)	1984	11	17
Torry Holt, North Caro. St. (I-A)	1997	11	16
Ryan Bartemeyer, West Va. Wesleyan (II)	1997	9	16
Greg Dailer, West Liberty St. (II)	1997	10	16
Matt Surette, Worcester Tech (III)	1997	10	16
Wesely Bell, Upper Iowa (III)	1997	10	16
Tyrone Seabrooks, New Haven (II)	1996	10	16
Mike Mancuso, East Stroudsburg (II)	1996	10	16
Jeff Clay, Catholic (III)	1996	9	16
Ryan Ditze, Albright (III)	1996	10	16
Alex Van Dyke, Nevada (I-A)	1995	11	16
Wayne Chrebet, Hofstra (I-AA)	1994	10	16
Brad Bailey, West Tex. A&M (II)	1994	11	16
Dave Cecchini, Lehigh (I-AA)	1993	11	16
Ryan Yarborough, Wyoming (I-A)	1993	11	16
Rodney Robinson, Gardner-Webb (II)	1992	11	16
Evan Elkington, Worcester Tech (III)	1989	10	16
Dan Bitson, Tulsa (I-A)	1989	11	16
Dan Fulton, Neb.-Omaha (II)	1976	10	16
Howard Twilley, Tulsa (I-A)	1965	10	16

*Record.

SINGLE-GAME YARDS

Yds.	Div.	Player, Team (Opponent)	Date
370	I-AA	Michael Lerch, Princeton (Brown)	Oct. 12, 1991
370	II	Barry Wagner, Alabama A&M (Clark Atlanta)	Nov. 4, 1989
364	III	Jeff Clay, Catholic (Albright)	Nov. 16, 1996
363	I-A	Randy Gatewood, UNLV (Idaho)	Sept. 17, 1994
363	II	Tom Nettles, San Diego St. (Southern Miss.)	Nov. 9, 1968
362	III	Matt Surette, Worcester Tech (Springfield)	Oct. 25, 1997
354	II	Robert Clark, N.C. Central (Jackson St.)	Aug. 30, 1986
349	I-A	Chuck Hughes, UTEP (North Texas)	Sept. 18, 1965
332	III	Ryan Pifer, Heidelberg (Marietta)	Nov. 8, 1997
332	III	Sean Munroe, Mass.-Boston (Mass. Maritime)	Oct. 10, 1992
330	I-AA	Nate Singleton, Grambling (Virginia Union)	Sept. 14, 1991
327@	I-AA	Brian Forster, Rhode Island (Brown)	Sept. 28, 1985
325	II	Paul Zaeske, North Park (North Central)	Oct. 12, 1968
322	I-A	Rick Eber, Tulsa (Idaho St.)	Oct. 7, 1967
319	I-AA	Jason Cristino, Lehigh (Lafayette)	Nov. 21, 1992
318	I-A	Harry Wood, Tulsa (Idaho St.)	Oct. 7, 1967
317	II	Dan Fulton, Neb.-Omaha (South Dak.)	Sept. 4, 1976
316	I-AA	Marcus Hinton, Alcorn St. (Chattanooga)	Sept. 10, 1994
316	I-A	Jeff Evans, New Mexico St. (Southern Ill.)	Sept. 30, 1978
314	I-A	Alex Van Dyke, Nevada (San Jose St.)	Nov. 18, 1995
310	III	Jeff Clay, Catholic (La Salle)	Oct. 11, 1997
310	I-A	Chad Mackey, Louisiana Tech (Toledo)	Oct. 19, 1996
310	II	Mike Collodi, Colorado Mines (Westminster [Utah])	Oct. 3, 1970
309	III	Dale Amos, Frank. & Marsh. (Western Md.)	Oct. 24, 1987

@Record for a tight end.

Interceptions

CAREER INTERCEPTIONS

Player, Team (Division[s])	Years	No.	Yards	Avg.
Tom Collins, Indianapolis (II)	1982-85	*37	390	10.5
Ralph Gebhardt, Rochester (II; III)	1972; 73-75	34	406	11.9
Dean Diaz, Humboldt St. (II)	1980-83	31	328	10.6
Bill Grantham, Mo.-Rolla (II)	1977-80	29	263	9.1
Eugene Hunter, Fort Valley St. (II; III)	1972; 73-74	29	479	16.5
Al Brosky, Illinois (I-A)	1950-52	29	356	12.3
Jason Johnson, Shepherd (II)	1991-94	28	321	11.5
Rick Bealer, Lycoming (III)	1987-90	28	279	10.0
Brian Fetterolf, Aurora (III)	1986-89	28	390	13.9
Dave Murphy, Holy Cross (I-AA)	1986-89	28	309	11.0
Tim Lennon, Curry (III)	1986-89	27	190	7.0
Scott Stanitous, Moravian (III)	1985-88	27	178	6.6
Mike Hintz, Wis.-Platteville (III)	1983-86	27	183	6.8
Martin Bayless, Bowling Green (I-A)	1980-83	27	266	9.9
John Provost, Holy Cross (I-A)	1972-74	27	470	17.4
Cory Mabry, Susquehanna (III)	1988-91	26	400	15.4
Tony Woods, Bloomsburg (II)	1982-85	26	105	4.0
Jeff Hughes, Ripon (III)	1975-78	26	333	12.8
Buster West, Gust. Adolphus (II)	1967-70	26	192	7.4

*Record.

SEASON INTERCEPTIONS

Player, Team (Division)	Year	No.	Yards
Mark Dorner, Juniata (III)	†1987	*15	202
Eugene Hunter, Fort Valley St. (II)	†1972	14	211
Luther Howard, Delaware St. (II)	†1972	14	99
Tom Rezzuti, Northeastern (II)	†1971	14	153
Jim Blackwell, Southern U. (II)	†1970	14	196
Carl Ray Harris, Fresno St. (II)	†1970	14	98
Al Worley, Washington (I-A)	†1968	14	130

*Record. †National champion.

Punt Returns

CAREER AVERAGE

(Minimum 1.2 Returns Per Game; Minimum 30 Returns)

Player, Team (Division[s])	Years	No.	Yards	Avg.
Billy Johnson, Widener (II; III)	1971-72; 73	40	989	*24.7
Jack Mitchell, Oklahoma (I-A)	1946-48	39	922	23.6
Keith Winston, Knoxville (III)	1986-87	30	686	22.9
Kevin Doherty, Mass. Maritime (III)	1976-78, 80	45	939	20.9
Chuck Downey, Stony Brook (III)	1984-87	59	1,198	**20.3
Chuck Goehl, Monmouth (Ill.) (II)	1970-72	48	911	19.0
Eddie Macon, Pacific (Cal.) (I-A)	1949-51	48	907	18.9
Willie Canady, Fort Valley St. (III)	1979-82	41	772	18.8
Jackie Robinson, UCLA (I-A)	1939-40	37	694	18.8

*Record. **Record for minimum 50 returns.

SEASON AVERAGE

(Minimum 1.2 Returns Per Game and Qualifiers for Championship)

Player, Team (Division)	Year	No.	Yards	Avg.
Billy Johnson, Widener (II)	†1972	15	511	*34.1
Chuck Downey, Stony Brook (III)	†1986	17	530	31.2
Kevin Doherty, Mass. Maritime (III)	†1976	11	332	30.2
Dennis Robinson, Wesleyan (Conn.) (III)	†1978	9	263	29.2
Robert Middlebrook, Knoxville (III)	†1984	9	260	28.9
Joe Troise, Kean (III)	†1974	12	342	28.5
William Williams, Livingstone (II)	†1976	16	453	28.3
Terry Egerdahl, Minn.-Duluth (II)	†1975	13	360	27.7
Melvin Dillard, Ferrum (III)	†1990	25	688	27.5
Eric Green, Benedictine (Ill.) (III)	†1993	13	346	26.6
Bill Blackstock, Tennessee (I-A)	1951	12	311	25.9
Ennis Thomas, Bishop (II)	†1971	18	450	25.0
George Sims, Baylor (I-A)	1948	15	375	25.0

*Record. †National champion.

Kickoff Returns

CAREER AVERAGE

(Minimum 1.2 Returns Per Game; Minimum 30 Returns)

Player, Team (Division[s])	Years	No.	Yards	Avg.
Anthony Davis, Southern Cal (I-A)	1972-74	37	1,299	*35.1
Eric Booth, Southern Miss. (I-A)	1994	35	1,135	32.4
Overton Curtis, Utah St. (I-A)	1957-58	32	991	31.0
Fred Montgomery, New Mexico St. (I-A)	1991-92	39	1,191	30.5
Karl Evans, Mo. Southern St. (II)	1991-92	32	959	30.0
Kevin Cannon, Millersville (II)	1992-95	67	1,999	29.8
Troy Brown, Marshall (I-AA)	1991-92	32	950	29.7
Dave Ludy, Winona St. (II)	1991-94	89	2,630	29.6
Charles Swann, Indiana St. (I-AA)	1989-91	45	1,319	29.3
Altie Taylor, Utah St. (I-A)	1966-68	40	1,170	29.3
Daryl Brown, Tufts (III)	1974-76	38	1,111	29.2
Stan Brown, Purdue (I-A)	1968-70	49	1,412	28.8
Henry White, Colgate (I-A)	1974-77	41	1,180	28.8
Doug Parrish, San Fran. St. (II)	1990	35	1,002	28.6
Craig Richardson, Eastern Wash. (I-AA)	1983-86	71	2,021	28.5

*Record.

SEASON AVERAGE

(Minimum 1.2 Returns Per Game and Qualifiers for Championship)

Player, Team (Division[s])	Year	No.	Yards	Avg.
Brandon Steinheim, Wesley (III)	†1994	10	422	*42.2
Paul Allen, Brigham Young (I-A)	1961	12	481	40.1
Jason Martin, Coe (III)	†1992	11	438	39.8
Tremain Mack, Miami (Fla.)	†1996	13	514	39.5
LaVon Reis, Western St. (II)	†1993	14	552	39.4
Danny Lee, Jacksonville St. (II)	†1992	12	473	39.4
Leeland McElroy, Texas A&M (I-A)	†1993	15	590	39.3
Fran DeFalco, Assumption (II)	1993	12	461	38.4
Forrest Hall, San Francisco (I-A)	1946	15	573	@38.2

Player, Team (Division[s])	Year	No.	Yards	Avg.
David Fraterrigo, Canisius (I-AA)	†1993	13	485	37.3
Nate Kirtman, Pomona-Pitzer (III)	†1990	14	515	36.8
Kendall James, Carson-Newman (II)	1993	15	549	36.6
Kerry Hayes, Western Caro. (I-AA)	1993	16	584	36.5
Tom Myers, Coe (III)	†1983	11	401	36.5
Tony Ball, Chattanooga (I-A)	†1977	13	473	36.4
Ron Scott, Occidental (III)	1983	10	363	36.3
Alan Hill, DePauw (III)	1980	12	434	36.2
Roscoe Word, Jackson St. (II)	†1973	18	650	36.1
Steve Levenseller, Puget Sound (II)	†1978	17	610	35.9
Trevor Shannon, Wartburg (III)	†1996	14	501	35.8
George Marinkov, North Caro. St. (I-A)	1954	13	465	35.8

**Record. †National champion. @ Record for minimum 1.5 returns per game.*

Field Goals

(One-inch tees were permitted in 1949, two-inch tees were permitted in 1965, and use of tees was eliminated before the 1989 season. The goal posts were widened from 18 feet, 6 inches to 23 feet, 4 inches in 1959 and were narrowed back to 18 feet, 6 inches before the 1991 season. The hash marks were moved six feet, eight inches closer to the center of the field to 60 feet from each sideline in 1993.)

CAREER FIELD GOALS

Player, Team (Division[s])	Years	FGM	FGA	Pct.
Jeff Jaeger, Washington (S) (I-A)	1983-86	*80	99	.808
John Lee, UCLA (S) (I-A)	1982-85	79	92	*.859
Philip Doyle, Alabama (S) (I-A)	1987-90	78	*105	.743
Luis Zendejas, Arizona St. (S) (I-A)	1981-84	78	*105	.743
Max Zendejas, Arizona (S) (I-A)	1982-85	77	104	.740
Kevin Butler, Georgia (S) (I-A)	1981-84	77	98	.786
Carlos Huerta, Miami (Fla.) (S) (I-A)	1988-91	73	91	.802
Derek Schmidt, Florida St. (S) (I-A)	1984-87	73	104	.702
Marty Zendejas, Nevada (S) (I-AA)	1984-87	72	90	.800
Kirk Roach, Western Caro. (S) (I-AA)	1984-87	71	102	.696
Fuad Reveiz, Tennessee (S) (I-A)	1981-84	71	95	.747
Roman Anderson, Houston (S) (I-A)	1988-91	70	101	.693
Barry Belli, Fresno St. (S) (I-A)	1984-87	70	99	.707
Tony Zendejas, Nevada (S) (I-AA)	1981-83	70	86	.814
Collin Mackie, South Caro. (S) (I-A)	1987-90	69	95	.726
Gary Gussman, Miami (Ohio) (S) (I-A)	1984-87	68	94	.723
Larry Roach, Oklahoma St. (S) (I-A)	1981-84	68	101	.673
Michael Proctor, Alabama (S) (I-A)	1992-95	65	91	.714
Paul Woodside, West Va. (S) (I-A)	1981-84	65	81	.802

**Record. (S) Soccer-style kicker.*

SEASON FIELD GOALS

Player, Team (Division)	Year	FGM	FGA	Pct.
John Lee, UCLA (S) (I-A)	1984	*29	33	.879
Luis Zendejas, Arizona St. (S) (I-A)	1983	28	37	.757
Paul Woodside, West Va. (S) (I-A)	1982	28	31	.903
Fuad Reveiz, Tennessee (S) (I-A)	1982	27	31	.871
Brian Mitchell, Northern Iowa (S) (I-AA)	1990	26	27	*.963
Tony Zendejas, Nevada (S) (I-AA)	1982	26	33	.788
Wayne Boyer, Southwest Mo. St. (S) (I-AA)	1996	25	30	.833
Chris Jacke, UTEP (S) (I-A)	1988	25	27	.926
John Diettrich, Ball St. (S) (I-A)	1985	25	29	.862
Chuck Nelson, Washington (S) (I-A)	1982	25	26	.962
Remy Hamilton, Michigan (S) (I-A)	1994	24	29	.828
Philip Doyle, Alabama (S) (I-A)	1990	24	29	.828
Kendall Trainor, Arkansas (S) (I-A)	1988	24	27	.889
Kirk Roach, Western Caro. (S) (I-AA)	1986	24	28	.857
Carlos Reveiz, Tennessee (S) (I-A)	1985	24	28	.857
George Benyola, Louisiana Tech (S) (I-AA)	1985	24	31	.774
Chris White, Illinois (S) (I-A)	1984	24	28	.857
Mike Prindle, Western Mich. (S) (I-A)	1984	24	30	.800
Bruce Kallmeyer, Kansas (S) (I-A)	1983	24	29	.828

**Record. (S) Soccer-style kicker. (Record for attempts is 38)*

LONGEST FIELD GOALS

Yds.	Div.	Player, Team (Opponent)	Year
67	II	Tom Odle, Fort Hays St. (Washburn)	1988
67	I-A	Joe Williams, Wichita St. (Southern Ill.)	1978
67	I-A	Russell Erxleben, Texas (Rice)	1977
67	I-A	Steve Little, Arkansas (Texas)	1977
65	I-A	Tony Franklin, Texas A&M (Baylor)	1976
64	I-A	Russell Erxleben, Texas (Oklahoma)	1977
64	I-A	Tony Franklin, Texas A&M (Baylor)	1976
63	I-AA	Tim Foley, Ga. Southern (James Madison)	1987
63	I-AA	Scott Roper, Arkansas St. (North Texas)	1987
63	I-A	Morten Andersen, Michigan St. (Ohio St.)	1981
63	I-A	Clark Kemble, Colorado St. (Arizona)	1975
63	II	Joe Duren, Arkansas St. (McNeese St.)	1974
62*	I-A	Jason Hanson, Washington St. (UNLV)	1991
62	I-A	John Diettrich, Ball St. (Ohio)	1986
62	I-AA	Paul Hickert, Murray St. (Eastern Ky.)	1986
62#	I-A	Chip Lohmiller, Minnesota (Iowa)	1986
62	I-A	Tom Whelihan, Missouri (Colorado)	1986
62	I-A	Dan Christopulos, Wyoming (Colorado St.)	1977
62	I-A	Iseed Khoury, North Texas (Richmond)	1977
62	III	Dom Antonini, Rowan (Salisbury St.)	1976
62	I-A	Dave Lawson, Air Force (Iowa St.)	1975
62	II	Mike Flater, Colorado Mines (Western St.)	1973

**Longest collegiate field goal without use of a tee and also longest collegiate field goal with narrower goal posts (18 feet, 6 inches). #Longest field goal made indoors.*

Special Reference: Ove Johannson, Abilene Christian (not an NCAA-member college at the time), kicked a 69-yard field goal against East Texas State, Oct. 16, 1976, the longest collegiate field goal.

Punting

CAREER PUNTING AVERAGE

(Minimum 150 Punts)

Player, Team (Division[s])	Years	No.	Yards	Avg.
Todd Sauerbrun, West Va. (I-A)	1991-94	167	7,733	*46.3
Reggie Roby, Iowa (I-A)	1979-82	172	7,849	45.6
Greg Montgomery, Michigan St. (I-A)	1985-87	170	7,721	45.4
Tom Tupa, Ohio St. (I-A)	1984-87	196	8,854	45.2
Barry Helton, Colorado (I-A)	1984-87	153	6,873	44.9
Ray Guy, Southern Miss. (I-A)	1970-72	200	8,934	44.7
Bucky Scribner, Kansas (I-A)	1980-82	217	9,670	44.6
Terry Daniel, Auburn (I-A)	1992-94	169	7,522	44.5
Greg Horne, Arkansas (I-A)	1983-86	180	8,002	44.5
Ray Criswell, Florida (I-A)	1982-85	161	7,153	44.4
Pumpy Tudors, Chattanooga (I-AA)	1988-91	181	8,041	44.4
Mark Simon, Air Force (I-A)	1984-86	164	7,283	44.4
Bill Smith, Mississippi (I-A)	1983-86	254	11,260	44.3
Tim Baer, Colorado Mines (II)	1986-89	235	10,406	44.3
Russell Erxleben, Texas (I-A)	1975-78	214	9,467	44.2
Brad Maynard, Ball St. (I-A)	1993-96	242	10,702	44.2
Mark Simon, Air Force (I-A)	1984-86	156	6,898	44.2
Johnny Evans, North Caro. St. (I-A)	1974-77	185	8,143	44.0
Chuck Ramsey, Wake Forest (I-A)	1971-73	205	9,010	44.0

**Record.*

SEASON PUNTING AVERAGE

(Qualifiers for Championship)

Player, Team (Division)	Year	No.	Yards	Avg.
Chad Kessler, LSU (I-A)	†1997	39	1,961	*50.3
Reggie Roby, Iowa (I-A)	†1981	44	2,193	49.8
Kirk Wilson, UCLA (I-A)	†1956	30	1,479	49.3
Steve Ecker, Shippensburg (II)	†1965	32	1,570	49.1
Todd Sauerbrun, West Va. (I-A)	†1994	72	3,486	48.4
Zack Jordan, Colorado (I-A)	†1950	38	1,830	48.2
Ricky Anderson, Vanderbilt (I-A)	†1984	58	2,793	48.2
Reggie Roby, Iowa (I-A)	†1982	52	2,501	48.1
Marv Bateman, Utah (I-A)	†1971	68	3,269	48.1
Don Cockroft, Adams St. (II)	†1966	36	1,728	48.0
Owen Price, UTEP (I-A)	†1940	30	1,440	48.0
Jack Jacobs, Oklahoma (I-A)	1940	31	1,483	47.8
Bill Smith, Mississippi (I-A)	1984	44	2,099	47.7

**Record. †National champion.*

LONGEST PUNTS

Yds.	Div.	Player, Team (Opponent)	Year
99	I-A	Pat Brady, Nevada (Loyola Marymount)	1950
97	II	Earl Hurst, Emporia St. (Central Mo. St.)	1964
96	II	Alex Campbell, Morris Brown (Clark Atlanta)	1994
96	II	Gary Frens, Hope (Olivet)	1966
96	II	Jim Jarrett, North Dak. (South Dak.)	1957
96	I-A	George O'Brien, Wisconsin (Iowa)	1952
96	I-A	George O'Brien, Wisconsin (Iowa)	1952
94	I-A	John Hadl, Kansas (Oklahoma)	1959
94	I-A	Carl Knox, Texas Christian (Oklahoma St.)	1947
94	I-A	Preston Johnson, Southern Methodist (Pittsburgh)	1940
93	II	Elliot Mills, Carleton (Monmouth [Ill.])	1970
93	II	Kasper Fitins, Taylor (Georgetown [Ky.])	1966
93	II	Leeroy Sweeney, Pomona-Pitzer (UC Riverside)	1960
93	I-A	Bob Handke, Drake (Wichita St.)	1949

All-Purpose Yards

__All-purpose yardage__ is the combined net yards gained by rushing, receiving, interception (and fumble) returns, punt returns, kickoff returns and runbacks of field goal attempts. All-purpose yardage does not include forward passing yardage.

__Total offense__ is the total of net gain rushing and net gain forward passing. Receiving and runback yards are not included in total offense.

CAREER YARDS

Player, Team (Division[s])	Years	Rush	Rcv.	Int.	PR	KO	Yds.
Carey Bender, Coe (III)	1991-94	6,125	1,751	0	7	87	*7,970
Johnny Bailey, Tex. A&M-Kingsville (II)	1986-89	*6,320	452	0	20	1,011	7,803
Kenny Gamble, Colgate (I-AA)	1984-87	5,220	536	0	104	1,763	7,623
Howard Stevens, Randolph-Macon (II); Louisville (I-A)	1968-69; 71-72	5,297	738	0	781	748	7,564
Claude Mathis, Southwest Tex. St. (I-AA)	1994-97	4,691	744	0	635	1,353	7,423
Thomas Haskins, VMI (I-AA)	1993-96	5,355	179	0	216	1,661	7,411
Roger Graham, New Haven (II)	1991-94	5,953	393	0	0	870	7,216
Napoleon McCallum, Navy (I-A)	$1981-85	4,179	796	0	858	1,339	7,172
Dave Ludy, Winona St. (II)	1991-94	3,501	906	0	34	2,630	7,071
Albert Fann, Cal St. Northridge (II)	1987-90	4,090	803	0	0	2,141	7,032
Reggie Greene, Siena (I-AA)	1994-97	5,415	274	0	53	1,217	6,959
Kirk Matthieu, Maine Maritime (III)	$1989-93	5,107	315	0	254	1,279	6,955
Curtis Delgardo, Portland St. (II)	$1986-90	4,178	1,258	0	318	1,188	6,942
Jarrett Anderson, Truman St. (II)	1993-96	6,166	633	0	0	127	6,926
Darrin Nelson, Stanford (I-A)	1977-78, 80-81	4,033	2,368	0	471	13	6,885
Eric Frees, Western Md. (III)	1988-91	5,281	392	0	47	1,158	6,878
Johnny Cox, Fort Lewis (II)	1990-93	112	3,611	0	495	2,476	6,694
Steve Roberts, Butler (II)	1986-89	4,623	1,201	0	272	578	6,674
Anthony Russo, St. John's (N.Y.) (III; I-AA)	1990-92; 93	5,834	405	0	25	379	6,643
Richard Huntley, Winston-Salem (II)	1992-95	6,286	333	0	0	0	6,619
Tony Dorsett, Pittsburgh (I-A)	1973-76	6,082	406	0	0	127	6,615
Paul Palmer, Temple (I-A)	1983-86	4,895	705	0	0	997	6,609
Charles White, Southern Cal (I-A)	1976-79	5,598	507	0	0	440	6,545
Trevor Cobb, Rice (I-A)	1989-92	4,948	892	0	21	651	6,512
Mike Smith, Neb.-Kearney (II)	1994-97	348	2,975	0	932	2,255	6,510
Joe Dudek, Plymouth St. (III)	1982-85	5,570	348	0	0	243	6,509
¢Brian Shay, Emporia St. (II)	1995-97	4,693	867	0	104	818	6,482
Glyn Milburn, Oklahoma/Stanford (I-A)	1988, 90-92	2,302	1,495	0	1,145	1,246	6,188
Dante Brown, Marietta (III)	1994-97	4,512	425	0	202	1,040	6,179
Adam Henry, Carleton (III)	1990-93	3,482	601	0	186	1,839	6,108
Chris Cobb, Eastern Ill. (II)	1976-79	5,042	520	0	37	478	6,077
Brad Olson, Lawrence (III)	1994-97	5,325	590	0	14	145	6,074
Don Aleksiewicz, Hobart (II)	1969-72	4,525	470	0	320	748	6,063
Mark Kacmarynski, Central (Iowa) (III)	$1992-96	5,434	211	0	45	364	6,054
Gary Trettel, St. Thomas (Minn.) (III)	1988-90	3,724	853	0	0	1,467	6,044
Archie Griffin, Ohio St. (I-A)	1972-75	5,177	286	0	0	540	6,003
Ron "Po" James, New Mexico St. (I-A)	1968-71	3,884	217	0	8	1,870	5,979
Eric Wilkerson, Kent (I-A)	1985-88	3,830	506	0	0	1,638	5,974

**Record.* *$See page 6 for explanation.* *¢Active Player.*

CAREER YARDS PER GAME

(Minimum 3,500 Yards)

Player, Team (Division[s])	Years	G	Rush	Rcv.	Int.	PR	KO	Yds.	Yd. PG
Ryan Benjamin, Pacific (Cal.) (I-A)	1990-92	24	3,119	1,063	0	100	1,424	5,706	*237.8
Chris George, Glenville St. (II)	1993-94	20	23	3,215	0	391	1,050	4,679	234.0
Kirk Matthieu, Maine Maritime (III)	$1989-93	33	5,107	315	0	254	1,279	6,955	210.8
Sheldon Canley, San Jose St. (I-A)	1988-90	25	2,513	828	0	5	1,800	5,146	205.8
Carey Bender, Coe (III)	1991-94	39	6,125	1,751	0	7	87	*7,970	204.4
Johnny Bailey, Tex. A&M-Kingsville (II)	1986-89	39	*6,320	452	0	20	1,011	7,803	200.1
Howard Stevens, Randolph-Macon (II); Louisville (I-A)	1968-69; 71-72	38	5,297	738	0	781	748	7,564	199.1
Gary Trettel, St. Thomas (Minn.) (III)	1988-90	29	3,483	834	0	0	1,407	5,724	197.4
Arnold Mickens, Butler (I-AA)	1994-95	22	3,813	47	0	0	87	3,947	197.4
Tim Hall, Robert Morris (I-AA)	1994-95	19	2,908	793	0	0	0	3,701	194.8
Reggie Greene, Siena (I-AA)	1994-97	36	5,415	274	0	53	1,217	6,959	193.3
Billy Johnson, Widener (II; III)	1971-72; 73	28	3,737	27	0	43	989	5,404	193.0
O. J. Simpson, Southern Cal (I-A)	1967-68	19	3,124	235	0	0	307	3,666	192.9
Steve Roberts, Butler (II)	1986-89	35	4,623	1,201	0	272	578	6,674	190.7

**Record.* *$See page 6 for explanation.*

SEASON YARDS

Player, Team (Division)	Year	Rush	Rcv.	Int.	PR	KO	Yds.
Barry Sanders, Oklahoma St. (I-A)	†1988	*2,628	106	0	95	421	*3,250
Ryan Benjamin, Pacific (Cal.) (I-A)	†1991	1,581	612	0	4	798	2,995
Dante Brown, Marietta (III)	†1996	2,385	174	0	46	368	2,973
Brian Shay, Emporia St. (II)	†1996	2,103	247	0	48	340	2,738
Brian Shay, Emporia St. (II)	†1997	1,912	277	0	56	478	2,723
Mike Pringle, Cal St. Fullerton (I-A)	†1989	1,727	249	0	0	714	2,690
Steve Roberts, Butler (II)	†1989	1,450	532	0	272	415	2,669
Carey Bender, Coe (III)	†1994	2,243	319	0	7	87	2,656
Paul Palmer, Temple (I-A)	†1986	1,866	110	0	0	657	2,633
Chris George, Glenville St. (II)	†1993	23	*1,876	0	157	562	2,618
Ryan Benjamin, Pacific (Cal.) (I-A)	†1992	1,441	434	0	96	626	2,597
Marcus Allen, Southern Cal (I-A)	†1981	2,342	217	0	0	0	2,559
Sheldon Canley, San Jose St. (I-A)	1989	1,201	353	0	0	959	2,513
Mike Rozier, Nebraska (I-A)	1983	2,148	106	0	0	232	2,486
Troy Davis, Iowa St. (I-A)	†1995	2,010	159	0	0	297	2,466

Player, Team (Division)	Year	Rush	Rcv.	Int.	PR	KO	Yds.
Alex Van Dyke, Nevada (I-A)	1995	6	1,854	0	0	583	2,443
Archie Amerson, Northern Ariz. (I-AA)	1996	2,079	262	0	0	88	2,429
Johnny Bailey, Tex. A&M-Kingsville (II)	†1986	2,011	54	0	20	340	2,425
Kenny Gamble, Colgate (I-AA)	†1986	1,816	198	0	40	391	2,425
Theo Blanco, Wis.-Stevens Point (III)	1987	454	1,616	0	245	103	2,418
Rick Wegher, South Dak. St. (II)	1984	1,317	264	0	0	824	2,405
Steve Papin, Portland St. (II)	†1995	1,619	525	0	1	252	2,397
Ronald Moore, Pittsburg St. (II)	1992	1,864	141	0	0	388	2,393
Chuck Weatherspoon, Houston (I-A)	1989	1,146	735	0	415	95	2,391
Anthony Thompson, Indiana (I-A)	1989	1,793	201	0	0	394	2,388
Ricky Gales, Simpson (III)	†1989	2,035	102	0	0	248	2,385
Napoleon McCallum, Navy (I-A)	†1983	1,587	166	0	272	360	2,385
Troy Davis, Iowa St. (I-A)	†1996	2,185	61	0	0	118	2,364
Paul Smith, Gettysburg (III)	†1997	1,256	102	0	199	805	2,362
Rashaan Salaam, Colorado (I-A)	†1994	2,055	294	0	0	0	2,349
Gary Trettel, St. Thomas (Minn.) (III)	1989	1,502	337	0	0	496	2,335
Michael Clemons, William & Mary (I-AA)	1986	1,065	516	0	330	423	2,334
Napoleon McCallum, Navy (I-A)	†1985	1,327	358	0	157	488	2,330
Gary Trettel, St. Thomas (Minn.) (III)	1990	1,620	388	0	0	319	2,327
Carey Bender, Coe (III)	1993	1,718	601	0	0	0	2,319
Roger Graham, New Haven (II)	1993	1,687	116	0	0	516	2,319
Jarrett Anderson, Truman St. (II)	1996	2,140	167	0	0	0	2,307
Anthony Gray, Western N.M. (II)	1997	2,220	78	0	0	0	2,298
Brian Pruitt, Central Mich. (I-A)	1994	1,890	69	0	0	330	2,289

**Record. †National champion.*

SEASON YARDS PER GAME

Player, Team (Division)	Year	G	Rush	Rcv.	Int.	PR	KO	Yds.	Yd.PG
Dante Brown, Marietta (III)	†1996	10	2,385	174	0	46	368	2,973	*297.3
Barry Sanders, Oklahoma St. (I-A)	†1988	11	*2,628	106	0	0	95	*3,250	295.5
Steve Roberts, Butler (II)	†1989	10	1,450	532	0	272	415	2,669	266.9
Carey Bender, Coe (III)	†1994	10	2,243	319	0	7	87	2,656	265.6
Bobby Felix, Western N.M. (II)	†1994	8	439	853	0	150	667	2,109	263.6
Chris George, Glenville St. (II)	†1993	10	23	*1,876	0	157	562	2,618	261.8
Billy Johnson, Widener (II)	1972	9	1,556	40	43	511	115	2,265	251.7
Ryan Benjamin, Pacific (Cal.) (I-A)	†1991	12	1,581	612	0	4	798	2,995	249.6
Brian Shay, Emporia St. (II)	†1996	11	2,103	247	0	48	340	2,738	248.9
Brian Shay, Emporia St. (II)	†1997	11	1,912	277	0	56	478	2,723	247.5
Byron "Whizzer" White, Colorado (I-A)	†1937	8	1,121	0	103	587	159	1,970	246.3
Mike Pringle, Cal St. Fullerton (I-A)	†1989	11	1,727	249	0	0	714	2,690	244.6
Kirk Matthieu, Maine Maritime (III)	†1992	9	1,733	91	0	56	308	2,188	243.1
Paul Palmer, Temple (I-A)	†1986	11	1,866	110	0	0	657	2,633	239.4
Ray Neosh, Coe (III)	1996	9	1,472	273	0	0	403	2,148	238.7
Ricky Gales, Simpson (III)	†1989	10	2,035	102	0	0	248	2,385	238.5
Paul Smith, Gettysburg (III)	†1997	10	1,256	102	0	199	805	2,362	236.2
Ryan Benjamin, Pacific (Cal.) (I-A)	†1992	11	1,441	434	0	96	626	2,597	236.1
Reggie Greene, Siena (I-AA)	†1996	9	1,719	50	0	0	337	2,106	234.0
Gary Trettel, St. Thomas (Minn.) (III)	1989	10	1,502	337	0	0	496	2,335	233.5
Kirk Matthieu, Maine Maritime (III)	1990	9	1,428	77	0	99	495	2,099	233.2
Gary Trettel, St. Thomas (Minn.) (III)	1990	10	1,620	388	0	0	319	2,327	232.7

**Record. †National champion.*

Scoring

CAREER POINTS

Player, Team (Division[s])	Years	TD	XPt.	FG	Pts.
Carey Bender, Coe (III)	1991-94	*86	12	0	*528
Joe Dudek, Plymouth St. (III)	1982-85	79	0	0	474
Walter Payton, Jackson St. (II)	1971-74	66	53	5	464
Jarrett Anderson, Truman St. (II)	1993-96	73	2	0	440
Shawn Graves, Wofford (QB) (II)	1989-92	72	3	0	438
Johnny Bailey, Tex. A&M-Kingsville (II)	1986-89	70	3	0	426
Roger Graham, New Haven (II)	1991-94	70	2	0	424
Roman Anderson, Houston (I-A)	1988-91	0	213	70	423
Mark Kacmarynski, Central (Iowa) (III)	$1992-96	70	2	0	422
Howard Stevens, Randolph-Macon (II); Louisville (I-A)	1968-69; 71-72	69	4	0	418
Dale Mills, Truman St. (II)	1957-60	64	23	0	407
Jeremy Monroe, Michigan Tech (II)	1990-93	67	0	0	402
Carlos Huerta, Miami (Fla.) (I-A)	1988-91	0	178	73	397
Jason Elam, Hawaii (I-A)	$1988-92	0	158	79	395
Anthony Thompson, Indiana (I-A)	1986-89	65	4	0	394
Garney Henley, Huron (II)	1956-59	63	16	0	394
Derek Schmidt, Florida St. (I-A)	1984-87	0	174	73	393
Steve Roberts, Butler (II)	1986-89	63	4	0	386
Jeff Bentrim, North Dak. St. (QB) (II)	1983-86	64	2	0	386
Marty Zendejas, Nevada (I-AA)	1984-87	0	169	72	385
Leo Lewis, Lincoln (Mo.) (II)	1951-54	64	0	0	384
Chris Bisaillon, Ill. Wesleyan (III)	1989-92	61	12	0	378
Heath Sherman, Tex. A&M-Kingsville (II)	1985-88	63	0	0	378
Marshall Faulk, San Diego St. (I-A)	1991-93	62	4	0	376
Chris Babirad, Wash. & Jeff. (III)	1989-92	62	2	0	374
Billy Johnson, Widener (II; III)	1971-72; 73	62	0	0	372
Tank Younger, Grambling (II)	1945-48	60	9	0	369
¢Brian Shay, Emporia St. (II)	1995-97	59	7	0	368
Richard Huntley, Winston-Salem (II)	1992-95	60	8	0	368
Luis Zendejas, Arizona St. (I-A)	1981-84	0	134	78	368
Sherriden May, Idaho (I-AA)	1991-94	61	0	0	366
Bill Cooper, Muskingum (II)	1957-60	54	37	1	364
Charvez Foger, Nevada (I-AA)	1985-88	60	2	0	362
Ole Gunderson, St. Olaf (II)	1969-71	60	2	0	362
Rob Marchitello, Maine Maritime (III)	1993-95	59	4	0	358
Jeff Jaeger, Washington (I-A)	1983-86	0	118	*80	358
Tony Dorsett, Pittsburgh (I-A)	1973-76	59	2	0	356
Glenn Davis, Army (I-A)	1943-46	59	0	0	354

**Record. $See page 6 for explanation. ¢Active player.*

CAREER POINTS PER GAME

(Minimum 225 Points)

Player, Team (Division[s])	Years	G	TD	XPt.	FG	Pts.	Pt.PG
Cory Christensen, Simpson (III)	1996-97	19	44	0	0	264	*13.9
Rob Marchitello, Maine Maritime (III)	1993-95	26	59	4	0	358	13.8
Carey Bender, Coe (III)	1991-94	39	*86	12	0	*528	13.5
Ole Gunderson, St. Olaf (II)	1969-71	27	60	2	0	362	13.4
Billy Johnson, Widener (II; III)	1971-72; 73	28	62	0	0	372	13.3
Leon Burns, Long Beach St. (II)	1969-70	22	47	2	0	284	12.9
Marshall Faulk, San Diego St. (I-A)	1991-93	31	62	4	0	376	12.1
Ed Marinaro, Cornell (I-A)	1969-71	27	52	6	0	318	11.8

Player, Team (Division[s])	Years	G	TD	XPt.	FG	Pts.	Pt.PG
Chad Hoiska, Wis.-Eau Claire (III)	1995-97	30	58	2	0	350	11.7
Joe Dudek, Plymouth St. (III)	1982-85	41	79	0	0	474	11.6
Bill Burnett, Arkansas (I-A)	1968-70	26	49	0	0	294	11.3
Dale Mills, Truman St. (II)	1957-60	36	64	23	0	407	11.3
Steve Owens, Oklahoma (I-A)	1967-69	30	56	0	0	336	11.2
Walter Payton, Jackson St. (II)	1971-74	42	66	53	5	464	11.0
Steve Roberts, Butler (II)	1986-89	35	63	4	0	386	11.0
Jeff Bentrim, North Dak. St. (II)	1983-86	35	64	2	0	386	11.0
Shawn Graves, Wofford (II)	1989-92	40	72	3	0	438	11.0
Johnny Bailey, Tex. A&M-Kingsville (II)	1986-89	39	70	3	0	426	10.9
Eddie Talboom, Wyoming (I-A)	1948-50	28	34	99	0	303	10.8
Chris Babirad, Wash. & Jeff. (III)	1989-92	35	62	2	0	374	10.7
Keith Elias, Princeton (I-AA)	1991-93	30	52	8	0	320	10.7

**Record.*

SEASON POINTS

Player, Team (Division)	Year	TD	XPt.	FG	Pts.
Barry Sanders, Oklahoma St. (I-A)	†1988	*39	0	0	*234
¢Brian Shay, Emporia St. (II)	†1997	32	6	0	198
Carey Bender, Coe (III)	†1994	32	2	0	194
Travis Walch, Winona St. (II)	1997	30	2	0	182
Terry Metcalf, Long Beach St. (II)	1971	29	4	0	178
Chad Hoiska, Wis.-Eau Claire (III)	1997	29	2	0	176
Jim Mormino, Allegheny (III)	1997	29	0	0	174
Doug Steiner, Grove City (III)	1997	29	0	0	174
Mike Rozier, Nebraska (I-A)	†1983	29	0	0	174
Lydell Mitchell, Penn St. (I-A)	1971	29	0	0	174
Geoff Mitchell, Weber St. (I-AA)	†1991	28	2	0	170
Jarrett Anderson, Truman St. (II)	†1996	28	0	0	168
Stanley Drayton, Allegheny (III)	†1991	28	0	0	168
Jim Switzer, Col. of Emporia (II)	†1963	28	0	0	168
Carl Herakovich, Rose-Hulman (II)	†1958	25	18	0	168
Ted Scown, Sul Ross St. (II)	†1948	28	0	0	168
James Regan, Pomona-Pitzer (III)	†1997	21	34	2	166
Dante Brown, Marietta (III)	†1996	27	4	0	166
Ronald Moore, Pittsburg St. (II)	1992	27	4	0	166
Ricky Gales, Simpson (III)	†1989	26	10	0	166
Art Luppino, Arizona (I-A)	†1954	24	22	0	166
Matt Malmberg, St. John's (Minn.) (III)	†1993	27	2	0	164
Leon Burns, Long Beach St. (II)	†1969	27	2	0	164
Jerry Rice, Mississippi Val. (I-AA)	†1984	27	0	0	162
Mike Deutsch, North Dak. (II)	1972	27	0	0	162
Billy Johnson, Widener (II)	†1972	27	0	0	162
Bobby Reynolds, Nebraska (I-A)	†1950	22	25	0	157

**Record. †National champion.*

SEASON POINTS PER GAME

Player, Team (Division)	Year	G	TD	XPt.	FG	Pts.	Pt.PG
Barry Sanders, Oklahoma St. (I-A)	†1988	11	*39	0	0	*234	*21.3
Carl Herakovich, Rose-Hulman (II)	†1958	8	25	18	0	168	21.0
James Regan, Pomona-Pitzer (III)	†1997	8	21	34	2	166	20.8
Carey Bender, Coe (III)	†1994	10	32	2	0	194	19.4
Jim Switzer, Col. of Emporia (II)	†1963	9	28	0	0	168	18.7
Brian Shay, Emporia St. (II)	†1997	11	32	6	0	198	18.0
Billy Johnson, Widener (II)	†1972	9	27	0	0	162	18.0
Chad Hoiska, Wis.-Eau Claire (III)	1997	10	29	2	0	176	17.6
Carl Garrett, N.M. Highlands (II)	†1966	9	26	2	0	158	17.6
Jim Mormino, Allegheny (III)	1997	10	29	0	0	174	17.4
Doug Steiner, Grove City (III)	1997	10	29	0	0	174	17.4
Bobby Reynolds, Nebraska (I-A)	†1950	9	22	25	0	157	17.4
Rob Marchitello, Maine Maritime (III)	1994	9	25	4	0	154	17.1
Stanley Drayton, Allegheny (III)	†1991	10	28	0	0	168	16.8
Ted Scown, Sul Ross St. (II)	†1948	10	28	0	0	168	16.8
Dante Brown, Marietta (III)	†1996	10	27	4	0	166	16.6
Ricky Gales, Simpson (III)	†1989	10	26	10	0	166	16.6
Art Luppino, Arizona (I-A)	†1954	10	24	22	0	166	16.6
Ed Marinaro, Cornell (I-A)	†1971	9	24	4	0	148	16.4
Matt Malmberg, St. John's (Minn.) (III)	†1993	10	27	2	0	164	16.4
Jerry Rice, Mississippi Val. (I-AA)	†1984	10	27	0	0	162	16.2
Chris Babirad, Wash. & Jeff. (III)	†1992	9	24	0	0	144	16.0
Larry Ras, Michigan Tech (II)	†1971	9	24	0	0	144	16.0
Trent Nauholz, Simpson (III)	†1992	8	21	2	0	128	16.0
Lydell Mitchell, Penn St. (I-A)	1971	11	29	0	0	174	15.8
Marshall Faulk, San Diego St. (I-A)	†1991	9	23	2	0	140	15.6

**Record. †National champion.*

SINGLE-GAME POINTS

Pts.	Div.	Player, Team (Opponent)	Date
48	III	Carey Bender, Coe (Beloit)	Nov. 12, 1994
48	I-A	Howard Griffith, Illinois (Southern Ill.)	Sept. 22, 1990
48	II	Paul Zaeske, North Park (North Central)	Oct. 12, 1968
48	II	Junior Wolf, Okla. Panhandle (St. Mary [Kan.])	Nov. 8, 1958
44	I-A	Marshall Faulk, San Diego St. (Pacific [Cal.])	Sept. 14, 1991
43	I-A	Jim Brown, Syracuse (Colgate)	Nov. 17, 1956
42	I-A	Arnold "Showboat" Boykin, Mississippi (Mississippi St.)	Dec. 1, 1951
42	I-A	Fred Wendt, UTEP (New Mexico St.)	Nov. 25, 1948

Award Winners

Consensus All-America Selections, 1889-1997

In 1950, the National Collegiate Athletic Bureau (the NCAA's service bureau) compiled the first official comprehensive roster of all-time all-Americans. The compilation of the all-American roster was supervised by a panel of analysts working in large part with the historical records contained in the files of the Dr. Baker Football Information Service.

The roster consists of only those players who were first-team selections on one or more of the all-America teams that were selected for the national audience and received nationwide circulation. Not included are the thousands of players who received mention on all-America second or third teams, nor the numerous others who were selected by newspapers or agencies with circulations that were not primarily national and with viewpoints, therefore, that were not normally nationwide in scope.

The following chart indicates, by year (in left column), which national media and organizations selected all-America teams. The headings at the top of each column refer to the selector (see legend after chart)

All-America Selectors

	AA	AP	C	COL	CP	FBW	FC	FN	FW	INS	L	LIB	M	N	NA	NEA	SN	UP	UPI	W	WCF
1889	-	-	-	-	-	-	-	-	-	-	-	-	-	-	-	-	-	-	-	√	-
1890	-	-	-	-	-	-	-	-	-	-	-	-	-	-	-	-	-	-	-	√	-
1891	-	-	-	-	-	-	-	-	-	-	-	-	-	-	-	-	-	-	-	√	-
1892	-	-	-	-	-	-	-	-	-	-	-	-	-	-	-	-	-	-	-	√	-
1893	-	-	-	-	-	-	-	-	-	-	-	-	-	-	-	-	-	-	-	√	-
1894	-	-	-	-	-	-	-	-	-	-	-	-	-	-	-	-	-	-	-	√	-
1895	-	-	-	-	-	-	-	-	-	-	-	-	-	-	-	-	-	-	-	√	-
1896	-	-	-	-	-	-	-	-	-	-	-	-	-	-	-	-	-	-	-	√	-
1897	-	-	-	-	-	-	-	-	-	-	-	-	-	-	-	-	-	-	-	√	-
1898	-	-	√	-	-	-	-	-	-	-	-	-	-	-	-	-	-	-	-	√	-
1899	-	-	√	-	-	-	-	-	-	-	-	-	-	-	-	-	-	-	-	√	-
1900	-	-	√	-	-	-	-	-	-	-	-	-	-	-	-	-	-	-	-	√	-
1901	-	-	√	-	-	-	-	-	-	-	-	-	-	-	-	-	-	-	-	√	-
1902	-	-	√	-	-	-	-	-	-	-	-	-	-	-	-	-	-	-	-	√	-
1903	-	-	√	-	-	-	-	-	-	-	-	-	-	-	-	-	-	-	-	√	-
1904	-	-	√	-	-	-	-	-	-	-	-	-	-	-	-	-	-	-	-	√	-
1905	-	-	√	-	-	-	-	-	-	-	-	-	-	-	-	-	-	-	-	√	-
1906	-	-	√	-	-	-	-	-	-	-	-	-	-	-	-	-	-	-	-	√	-
1907	-	-	√	-	-	-	-	-	-	-	-	-	-	-	-	-	-	-	-	√	-
1908	-	-	√	-	-	-	-	-	-	-	-	-	-	-	-	-	-	-	-	√	-
1909	-	-	√	-	-	-	-	-	-	-	-	-	-	-	-	-	-	-	-	-	-
1910	-	-	√	-	-	-	-	-	-	-	-	-	-	-	-	-	-	-	-	-	-
1911	-	-	√	-	-	-	-	-	-	-	-	-	-	-	-	-	-	-	-	-	-
1912	-	-	√	-	-	-	-	-	-	-	-	-	-	-	-	-	-	-	-	-	-
1913	-	-	√	-	-	-	-	-	-	√	-	-	-	-	-	-	-	-	-	-	-
1914	-	-	√	-	-	-	-	-	-	√	-	-	-	-	-	-	-	-	-	-	-
1915	-	-	√	-	-	-	-	-	-	√	-	-	-	-	-	-	-	-	-	-	-
1916	-	-	√	-	-	-	-	-	-	√	-	-	√	-	-	-	-	-	-	-	-
1917	-	-	(*)	-	-	-	-	-	-	√	-	-	√	-	-	√	-	-	-	-	-
1918	-	-	√	-	-	-	-	-	-	-	-	-	√	-	-	-	-	-	-	-	-
1919	-	-	√	-	-	-	-	-	-	-	-	-	√	-	-	-	-	-	-	-	-
1920	-	-	√	-	-	√	-	-	-	√	-	-	√	-	-	-	-	-	-	-	-
1921	-	-	√	-	-	-	-	-	-	-	-	-	-	-	-	-	-	-	-	-	-
1922	-	-	√	-	-	-	-	-	-	-	-	-	-	-	-	-	-	-	-	-	-
1923	-	-	√	-	-	√	-	-	-	-	-	-	-	-	-	-	-	-	-	-	-
1924	√	-	√	-	-	√	-	-	-	√	-	√	-	-	-	√	-	-	-	-	-
1925	√	√	-	√	-	√	-	-	-	√	-	√	-	-	-	√	-	√	-	-	-
1926	√	√	-	√	-	-	-	-	-	√	-	-	-	-	-	√	-	√	-	-	-
1927	√	√	-	√	-	-	-	-	-	√	-	-	-	-	√	√	-	√	-	-	-
1928	√	√	-	√	-	-	-	-	-	√	-	-	-	-	√	√	-	√	-	-	-
1929	√	√	-	√	-	-	-	-	-	√	-	-	-	-	√	√	-	√	-	-	-
1930	√	√	-	√	-	-	-	-	-	√	-	-	-	-	√	√	-	√	-	-	-
1931	√	√	-	√	-	-	-	-	-	√	-	√	-	-	-	√	-	√	-	-	-
1932	√	√	-	√	-	-	-	-	-	√	-	√	-	-	√	√	-	√	-	-	-
1933	√	√	-	√	-	-	-	-	-	√	-	√	-	-	√	√	-	√	-	-	-
1934	√	√	-	√	-	-	-	-	-	√	-	√	-	-	√	√	√	√	-	-	-
1935	√	√	-	√	-	-	-	-	-	√	-	√	-	-	√	√	√	√	-	-	-
1936	√	√	-	√	-	-	-	-	-	√	-	√	-	-	√	√	√	√	-	-	-
1937	√	√	-	√	-	-	-	-	-	√	-	√	-	√	√	√	√	√	-	-	-
1938	√	√	-	√	-	-	-	-	-	√	-	√	-	√	-	√	√	√	-	-	-
1939	√	√	-	√	-	-	-	-	-	√	-	√	-	√	-	√	√	√	-	-	-
1940	√	√	-	√	-	-	-	-	-	√	-	√	-	√	-	√	√	√	-	-	-
1941	√	√	-	√	-	-	-	-	-	√	-	√	-	√	-	√	√	√	-	-	-
1942	√	√	-	√	-	-	-	-	-	√	√	-	-	√	-	√	√	√	-	-	-
1943	√	√	-	√	-	-	-	√	-	√	√	-	-	-	-	-	√	√	-	-	-
1944	√	√	-	√	-	-	-	√	√	√	√	-	-	-	-	√	√	√	-	-	-
1945	√	√	-	√	-	-	√	-	√	√	√	-	-	-	-	√	√	√	-	-	-
1946	√	√	-	√	-	-	√	-	√	√	(†)	-	-	-	-	√	√	√	-	-	-
1947	-	√	-	√	-	-	√	-	√	√	-	-	-	-	-	√	√	√	-	-	-
1948	-	√	-	(§)	-	-	√	-	√	(#)√	-	-	-	-	-	√	√	√	-	-	-
1949	√	√	-	-	-	-	√	-	√	√	-	-	-	-	-	√	√	√	-	-	-
1950	√	√	-	-	-	-	√	-	√	√	-	-	-	-	-	√	√	√	-	-	-
1951	√	√	-	-	-	-	√	-	√	√	-	-	-	-	-	√	√	√	-	-	-
1952	√	√	-	-	-	-	√	-	√	√	-	-	-	-	-	√	√	√	-	-	-
1953	√	√	-	-	-	-	√	-	√	√	-	-	-	-	-	√	√	√	-	-	-

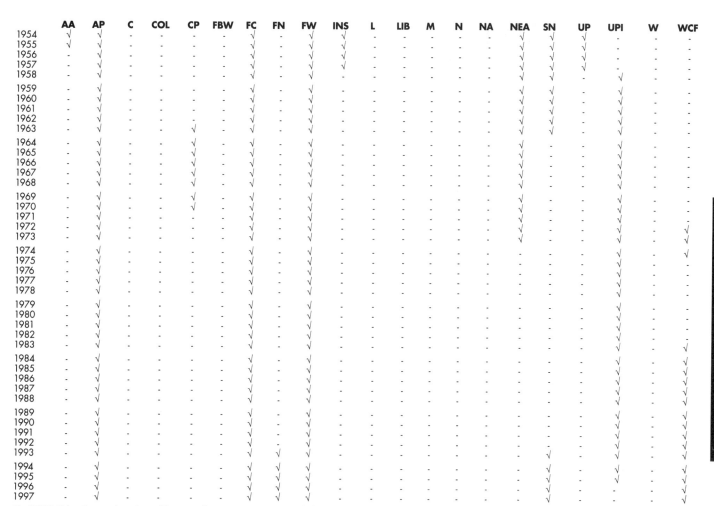

	AA	AP	C	COL	CP	FBW	FC	FN	FW	INS	L	LIB	M	N	NA	NEA	SN	UP	UPI	W	WCF
1954	√	√	-	-	-	-	√	-	√	√	-	-	-	-	-	√	√	√	-	-	-
1955	√	√	-	-	-	-	√	-	√	√	-	-	-	-	-	√	√	√	-	-	-
1956	-	√	-	-	-	-	√	-	√	√	-	-	-	-	-	√	√	√	-	-	-
1957	-	√	-	-	-	-	√	-	√	√	-	-	-	-	-	√	√	√	-	-	-
1958	-	√	-	-	-	-	√	-	√	-	-	-	-	-	-	√	√	-	√	-	-
1959	-	√	-	-	-	-	√	-	√	-	-	-	-	-	-	√	√	-	√	-	-
1960	-	√	-	-	-	-	√	-	√	-	-	-	-	-	-	√	√	-	√	-	-
1961	-	√	-	-	-	-	√	-	√	-	-	-	-	-	-	√	√	-	√	-	-
1962	-	√	-	-	-	-	√	-	√	-	-	-	-	-	-	√	√	-	√	-	-
1963	-	√	-	-	√	-	√	-	√	-	-	-	-	-	-	√	√	-	√	-	-
1964	-	√	-	-	√	-	√	-	√	-	-	-	-	-	-	√	-	-	√	-	-
1965	-	√	-	-	√	-	√	-	√	-	-	-	-	-	-	√	-	-	√	-	-
1966	-	√	-	-	√	-	√	-	√	-	-	-	-	-	-	√	-	-	√	-	-
1967	-	√	-	-	√	-	√	-	√	-	-	-	-	-	-	√	-	-	√	-	-
1968	-	√	-	-	√	-	√	-	√	-	-	-	-	-	-	√	-	-	√	-	-
1969	-	√	-	-	√	-	√	-	√	-	-	-	-	-	-	√	-	-	√	-	-
1970	-	√	-	-	√	-	√	-	√	-	-	-	-	-	-	√	-	-	√	-	-
1971	-	√	-	-	-	-	√	-	√	-	-	-	-	-	-	√	-	-	√	-	-
1972	-	√	-	-	-	-	√	-	√	-	-	-	-	-	-	√	-	-	√	-	√
1973	-	√	-	-	-	-	√	-	√	-	-	-	-	-	-	√	-	-	√	-	√
1974	-	√	-	-	-	-	√	-	√	-	-	-	-	-	-	-	-	-	√	-	√
1975	-	√	-	-	-	-	√	-	√	-	-	-	-	-	-	-	-	-	√	-	-
1976	-	√	-	-	-	-	√	-	√	-	-	-	-	-	-	-	-	-	√	-	-
1977	-	√	-	-	-	-	√	-	√	-	-	-	-	-	-	-	-	-	√	-	-
1978	-	√	-	-	-	-	√	-	√	-	-	-	-	-	-	-	-	-	√	-	-
1979	-	√	-	-	-	-	√	-	√	-	-	-	-	-	-	-	-	-	√	-	-
1980	-	√	-	-	-	-	√	-	√	-	-	-	-	-	-	-	-	-	√	-	-
1981	-	√	-	-	-	-	√	-	√	-	-	-	-	-	-	-	-	-	√	-	-
1982	-	√	-	-	-	-	√	-	√	-	-	-	-	-	-	-	-	-	√	-	-
1983	-	√	-	-	-	-	√	-	√	-	-	-	-	-	-	-	-	-	√	-	√
1984	-	√	-	-	-	-	√	-	√	-	-	-	-	-	-	-	-	-	√	-	√
1985	-	√	-	-	-	-	√	-	√	-	-	-	-	-	-	-	-	-	√	-	√
1986	-	√	-	-	-	-	√	-	√	-	-	-	-	-	-	-	-	-	√	-	√
1987	-	√	-	-	-	-	√	-	√	-	-	-	-	-	-	-	-	-	√	-	√
1988	-	√	-	-	-	-	√	-	√	-	-	-	-	-	-	-	-	-	√	-	√
1989	-	√	-	-	-	-	√	-	√	-	-	-	-	-	-	-	-	-	√	-	√
1990	-	√	-	-	-	-	√	-	√	-	-	-	-	-	-	-	-	-	√	-	√
1991	-	√	-	-	-	-	√	-	√	-	-	-	-	-	-	-	-	-	√	-	√
1992	-	√	-	-	-	-	√	-	√	-	-	-	-	-	-	-	-	-	√	-	√
1993	-	√	-	-	-	-	√	√	√	-	-	-	-	-	-	-	√	-	√	-	√
1994	-	√	-	-	-	-	√	√	√	-	-	-	-	-	-	-	√	-	√	-	√
1995	-	√	-	-	-	-	√	√	√	-	-	-	-	-	-	-	√	-	√	-	√
1996	-	√	-	-	-	-	√	√	√	-	-	-	-	-	-	-	√	-	-	-	√
1997	-	√	-	-	-	-	√	√	√	-	-	-	-	-	-	-	√	-	-	-	√

**In 1917, Walter Camp selected an all-Service, all-America team composed of military personnel. †During 1946-70, Look Magazine published the Football Writers Association of America's selections, listed under FW. §During 1948-56, Collier's Magazine published the American Football Coaches Association's selections, listed under FC. #International News Service was the first to select offensive and defensive teams.*

LEGEND FOR SELECTORS

AA—All-America Board
AP—Associated Press
C—Walter Camp (published in Harper's Weekly, 1897; in Collier's Magazine, 1898-1924)
COL—Collier's Magazine (selections by Grantland Rice, 1925-47; published American Football Coaches Association teams, 1948-56, listed under FC)
CP—Central Press
FBW—Football World Magazine
FC—American Football Coaches Association (published in Saturday Evening Post Magazine, 1945-47; in Collier's Magazine, 1948-56; sponsored by General Mills in 1957-59 and by Eastman Kodak from 1960-93)
FN—Football News
FW—Football Writers Association of America (published in Look Magazine, 1946-70)
INS—International News Service (merged with United Press in 1958 to form UPI)
L—Look Magazine (published Football Writers Association of America teams, 1946-70, listed under FW)
LIB—Liberty Magazine
M—Frank Menke Syndicate
N—Newsweek
NA—North American Newspaper Alliance
NEA—Newspaper Enterprise Association
SN—Sporting News
UP—United Press (merged with International News Service in 1958 to form UPI)
UPI—United Press International
W—Caspar Whitney (published in The Week's Sport in association with Walter Camp, 1889-90; published in Harper's Weekly, 1891-96, and in Outing Magazine, which he owned, 1898-1908; Walter Camp substituted for Whitney, who was on a world sports tour, and selected Harper's Weekly's team for 1897)
WCF—Walter Camp Foundation

All-America Selections

Listed on the following pages are the consensus all-Americans (i.e., the players who were accorded a majority of votes at their positions by the selectors). Included are the selections of 1889-97, 1909-12 and 1921-22 when there was only one selector.

1889
E—Amos Alonzo Stagg, Yale; Arthur Cumnock, Harvard; T—Hector Cowan, Princeton; Charles Gill, Yale; G—Pudge Heffelfinger, Yale; John Cranston, Harvard; C—William George, Princeton; B—Edgar Allan Poe, Princeton; Roscoe Channing, Princeton; Knowlton Ames, Princeton; James Lee, Harvard.

1890
E—Frank Hallowell, Harvard; Ralph Warren, Princeton; T—Marshall Newell, Harvard; William Rhodes, Yale; G—Pudge Heffelfinger, Yale; Jesse Riggs, Princeton; C—John Cranston, Harvard; B—Thomas McClung, Yale; Sheppard Homans, Princeton; Dudley Dean, Harvard; John Corbett, Harvard.

1891
E—Frank Hinkey, Yale; John Hartwell, Yale; T—Wallace Winter, Yale; Marshall Newell, Harvard; G—Pudge Heffelfinger, Yale; Jesse Riggs, Princeton; C—John Adams, Pennsylvania; B—Philip King, Princeton; Everett Lake, Harvard; Thomas McClung, Yale; Sheppard Homans, Princeton.

1892
E—Frank Hinkey, Yale; Frank Hallowell, Harvard; T—Marshall Newell, Harvard; A. Hamilton Wallis, Yale; G—Arthur Wheeler, Princeton; Bertram Waters, Harvard; C—William Lewis, Harvard; B—Charles Brewer, Harvard; Vance McCormick, Yale; Philip King, Princeton; Harry Thayer, Pennsylvania.

1893
E—Frank Hinkey, Yale; Thomas Trenchard, Princeton; T—Langdon Lea, Princeton; Marshall Newell, Harvard; G—Arthur Wheeler, Princeton; William Hickok, Yale; C—William Lewis, Harvard; B—Philip King, Princeton; Charles Brewer, Harvard; Franklin Morse, Princeton; Frank Butterworth, Yale.

1894
E—Frank Hinkey, Yale; Charles Gelbert, Pennsylvania; T—Bertram Waters, Harvard; Langdon Lea, Princeton; G—Arthur Wheeler, Princeton; William Hickok, Yale; C—Philip Stillman, Yale; B—George Adee, Yale; Arthur Knipe, Pennsylvania; George Brooke, Pennsylvania; Frank Butterworth, Yale.

1895
E—Norman Cabot, Harvard; Charles Gelbert, Pennsylvania; T—Langdon Lea, Princeton; Fred Murphy, Yale; G—Charles Wharton, Pennsylvania; Dudley Riggs, Princeton; C—Alfred Bull, Pennsylvania; B—Clinton Wyckoff, Cornell; Samuel Thorne, Yale; Charles Brewer, Harvard; George Brooke, Pennsylvania.

1896
E—Norman Cabot, Harvard; Charles Gelbert, Pennsylvania; T—William Church, Princeton; Fred Murphy, Yale; G—Charles Wharton, Pennsylvania; Wylie Woodruff, Pennsylvania; C—Robert Gailey, Princeton; B—Clarence Fincke, Yale; Edgar Wrightington, Harvard; Addison Kelly, Princeton; John Baird, Princeton.

1897
E—Garrett Cochran, Princeton; John Hall, Yale; T—Burr Chamberlain, Yale; John Outland, Pennsylvania; G—T. Truxton Hare, Pennsylvania; Gordon Brown, Yale; C—Alan Doucette, Harvard; B—Charles DeSaulles, Yale; Benjamin Dibblee, Harvard; Addison Kelly, Princeton; John Minds, Pennsylvania.

1898
E—Lew Palmer, Princeton; John Hallowell, Harvard; T—Arthur Hillebrand, Princeton; Burr Chamberlain, Yale; G—T. Truxton Hare, Pennsylvania; Gordon Brown, Yale; Walter Boal, Harvard; C—Pete Overfield, Pennsylvania; William Cunningham, Michigan; B—Charles Daly, Harvard; Benjamin Dibblee, Harvard; John Outland, Pennsylvania; Clarence Herschberger, Chicago; Malcolm McBride, Yale; Charles Romeyn, Army.

1899
E—David Campbell, Harvard; Arthur Poe, Princeton; T—Arthur Hillebrand, Princeton; George Stillman, Yale; G—T. Truxton Hare, Pennsylvania; Gordon Brown, Yale; C—Pete Overfield, Pennsylvania; B—Charles Daly, Harvard; Josiah McCracken, Pennsylvania; Malcolm McBride, Yale; Isaac Seneca, Carlisle; Albert Sharpe, Yale; Howard Reiter, Princeton.

1900
E—John Hallowell, Harvard; David Campbell, Harvard; William Smith, Army; T—George Stillman, Yale; James Bloomer, Yale; G—Gordon Brown, Yale; T. Truxton Hare, Pennsylvania; C—Herman Olcott, Yale; Walter Bachman, Lafayette; B—Bill Morley, Columbia; George Chadwick, Yale; Perry Hale, Yale; William Fincke, Yale; Charles Daly, Harvard; Raymond Starbuck, Cornell.

1901
E—David Campbell, Harvard; Ralph Davis, Princeton; Edward Bowditch, Harvard; Neil Snow, Michigan; T—Oliver Cutts, Harvard; Paul Bunker, Army; Crawford Blagden, Harvard; G—William Warner, Cornell; William Lee, Harvard; Charles Barnard, Harvard; Sanford Hunt, Cornell; C—Henry Holt, Yale; Walter Bachman, Lafayette; B—Robert Kernan, Harvard; Charles Daly, Army; Thomas Graydon, Harvard; Harold Weekes, Columbia; Bill Morley, Columbia.

1902
E—Thomas Shevlin, Yale; Edward Bowditch, Harvard; T—Ralph Kinney, Yale; James Hogan, Yale; Paul Bunker, Army; G—Edgar Glass, Yale; John DeWitt, Princeton; William Warner, Cornell; C—Henry Holt, Yale; Robert Boyers, Army; B—Foster Rockwell, Yale; George Chadwick, Yale; Thomas Graydon, Harvard; Thomas Barry, Brown.

1903
E—Howard Henry, Princeton; Charles Rafferty, Yale; T—Daniel Knowlton, Harvard; James Hogan, Yale; Fred Schacht, Minnesota; G—John DeWitt, Princeton; Andrew Marshall, Harvard; James Bloomer, Yale; C—Henry Hooper, Dartmouth; B—Willie Heston, Michigan; J. Dana Kafer, Princeton; James Johnson, Carlisle; Richard Smith, Columbia; Myron Witham, Dartmouth; W. Ledyard Mitchell, Yale.

1904
E—Thomas Shevlin, Yale; Fred Speik, Chicago; T—James Hogan, Yale; James Cooney, Princeton; G—Frank Piekarski, Pennsylvania; Joseph Gilman, Dartmouth; Ralph Kinney, Yale; C—Arthur Tipton, Army; B—Daniel Hurley, Harvard; Walter Eckersall, Chicago; Vincent Stevenson, Pennsylvania; Willie Heston, Michigan; Andrew Smith, Pennsylvania; Foster Rockwell, Yale; Henry Torney, Army.

1905
E—Thomas Shevlin, Yale; Ralph Glaze, Dartmouth; Mark Catlin, Chicago; T—Otis Lamson, Pennsylvania; Beaton Squires, Harvard; Karl Brill, Harvard; G—Roswell Tripp, Yale; Francis Burr, Harvard; C—Robert Torrey, Pennsylvania; B—Walter Eckersall, Chicago; Howard Roome, Yale; John Hubbard, Amherst; James McCormick, Princeton; Guy Hutchinson, Yale; Daniel Hurley, Harvard; Henry Torney, Army.

1906
E—Robert Forbes, Yale; L. Casper Wister, Princeton; T—L. Horatio Biglow, Yale; James Cooney, Princeton; Charles Osborne, Harvard; G—Francis Burr, Harvard; Elmer Thompson, Cornell; August Ziegler, Pennsylvania; C—William Dunn, Penn St.; William Newman, Cornell; B—Walter Eckersall, Chicago; Hugh Knox, Yale; Edward Dillon, Princeton; John Mayhew, Brown; William Hollenback, Pennsylvania; Paul Veeder, Yale.

1907
E—Bill Dague, Navy; Clarence Alcott, Yale; Albert Exendine, Carlisle; L. Casper Wister, Princeton; T—Dexter Draper, Pennsylvania; L. Horatio Biglow, Yale; G—August Ziegler, Pennsylvania; William Erwin, Army; C—Adolph Schulz, Michigan; Patrick Grant, Harvard; B—John Wendell, Harvard; Thomas A. D. Jones, Yale; Edwin Harlan, Princeton; James McCormick, Princeton; Edward Coy, Yale; Peter Hauser, Carlisle.

1908
E—Hunter Scarlett, Pennsylvania; George Schildmiller, Dartmouth; T—Hamilton Fish, Harvard; Frank Horr, Syracuse; Percy Northcroft, Navy; G—Clark Tobin, Dartmouth; William Goebel, Yale; Hamlin Andrus, Yale; Bernard O'Rourke, Cornell; C—Charles Nourse, Harvard; B—Edward Coy, Yale; Frederick Tibbott, Princeton; William Hollenback, Pennsylvania; Walter Steffen, Chicago; Ed Lange, Navy; Hamilton Corbett, Harvard.

1909
E—Adrian Regnier, Brown; John Kilpatrick, Yale; T—Hamilton Fish, Harvard; Henry Hobbs, Yale; G—Albert Benbrook, Michigan; Hamlin Andrus, Yale; C—Carroll Cooney, Yale; B—Edward Coy, Yale; John McGovern, Minnesota; Stephen Philbin, Yale; Wayland Minot, Harvard.

1910
E—John Kilpatrick, Yale; Stanfield Wells, Michigan; T—Robert McKay, Harvard; James Walker, Minnesota; G—Robert Fisher, Harvard; Albert Benbrook, Michigan; C—Ernest Cozens, Pennsylvania; B—E. LeRoy Mercer, Pennsylvania; Percy Wendell, Harvard; Earl Sprackling, Brown; Talbot Pendleton, Princeton.

1911
E—Douglass Bomeisler, Yale; Sanford White, Princeton; T—Edward Hart, Princeton; Leland Devore, Army; G—Robert Fisher, Harvard; Joseph Duff, Princeton; C—Henry Ketcham, Yale; B—Jim Thorpe, Carlisle; Percy Wendell, Harvard; Arthur Howe, Yale; Jack Dalton, Navy.

1912
E—Samuel Felton, Harvard; Douglass Bomeisler, Yale; T—Wesley Englehorn, Dartmouth; Robert Butler, Wisconsin; G—Stanley Pennock, Harvard; John Logan, Princeton; C—Henry Ketcham, Yale; B—Charles Brickley, Harvard; Jim Thorpe, Carlisle; George Crowther, Brown; E. LeRoy Mercer, Pennsylvania.

1913
E—Robert Hogsett, Dartmouth; Louis Merrillat, Army; T—Harold Ballin, Princeton; Nelson Talbott, Yale; Miller Pontius, Michigan; Harvey Hitchcock, Harvard; G—John Brown, Navy; Stanley Pennock, Harvard; Ray Keeler, Wisconsin; C—Paul Des Jardien, Chicago; B—Charles Brickley, Harvard; Edward Mahan, Harvard; Jim Craig, Michigan; Ellery Huntington, Colgate; Gus Dorais, Notre Dame.

1914
E—Huntington Hardwick, Harvard; John O'Hearn, Cornell; Perry Graves, Illinois; T—Harold Ballin, Princeton; Walter Trumbull, Harvard; G—Stanley Pennock, Harvard; Ralph Chapman, Illinois; Clarence Spears, Dartmouth; C—John McEwan, Army; B—John Maulbetsch, Michigan; Edward Mahan, Harvard; Charles Barrett, Cornell; John Spiegel, Wash. & Jeff.; Harry LeGore, Yale.

1915
E—Murray Shelton, Cornell; Guy Chamberlin, Nebraska; T—Joseph Gilman, Harvard; Howard Buck, Wisconsin; G—Clarence Spears, Dartmouth; Harold White, Syracuse; C—Robert Peck, Pittsburgh; B—Charles Barrett, Cornell; Edward Mahan, Harvard; Richard King, Harvard; Bart Macomber, Illinois; Eugene Mayer, Virginia; Neno Jerry DaPrato, Michigan St.

1916
E—Bert Baston, Minnesota; James Herron, Pittsburgh; T—Clarence Horning, Colgate; D. Belford West, Colgate; G—Clinton Black, Yale; Harrie Dadmun, Harvard; Frank Hogg, Princeton; C—Robert Peck, Pittsburgh; B—Elmer Oliphant, Army; Oscar Anderson, Colgate; Fritz Pollard, Brown; Charles Harley, Ohio St.

1917
E—Charles Bolen, Ohio St.; Paul Robeson, Rutgers; Henry Miller, Pennsylvania; T—Alfred Cobb, Syracuse; George Hauser, Minnesota; G—Dale Seis, Pittsburgh; John Sutherland, Pittsburgh; Eugene Neely, Dartmouth; C—Frank Rydzewski, Notre Dame; B—Elmer Oliphant, Army; Ben Boynton, Williams; Everett Strupper, Georgia Tech; Charles Harley, Ohio St.

1918
E—Paul Robeson, Rutgers; Bill Fincher, Georgia Tech; T—Wilbur Henry, Wash. & Jeff.; Leonard Hilty, Pittsburgh; Lou Usher, Syracuse; Joe Guyon, Georgia Tech; G—Joe Alexander, Syracuse; Lyman Perry, Navy; C—Ashel Day, Georgia Tech; John Depler, Illinois; B—Frank Murrey, Princeton; Tom Davies, Pittsburgh; Wolcott Roberts, Navy; George McLaren, Pittsburgh.

1919
E—Bob Higgins, Penn St.; Henry Miller, Pennsylvania; Lester Belding, Iowa; T—Wilbur Henry, Wash. & Jeff.; D. Belford West, Colgate; G—Joe Alexander, Syracuse; Adolph Youngstrom, Dartmouth; C—James Weaver, Centre; Charles Carpenter, Wisconsin; B—Charles Harley, Ohio St.; Ira Rodgers, West Va.; Edward Casey, Harvard; Bo McMillin, Centre; Ben Boynton, Williams.

1920
E—Luke Urban, Boston College; Charles Carney, Illinois; Bill Fincher, Georgia Tech; T—Stan Keck, Princeton; Ralph Scott, Wisconsin; G—Tim Callahan, Yale; Tom Woods, Harvard; Iolas Huffman, Ohio St.; C—Herb Stein, Pittsburgh; B—George Gipp, Notre Dame; Donold Lourie, Princeton; Gaylord Stinchcomb, Ohio St.; Charles Way, Penn St.

1921
E—Brick Muller, California; Eddie Anderson, Notre Dame; T—Dan McMillan, California; Iolas Huffman, Ohio St.; G—Frank Schwab, Lafayette; John Brown, Harvard; Stan Keck, Princeton; C—Herb Stein, Pittsburgh; B—Aubrey Devine, Iowa; Glenn Killinger, Penn St.; Bo McMillin, Centre; Malcolm Aldrich, Yale; Edgar Kaw, Cornell.

1922
E—Brick Muller, California; Wendell Taylor, Navy; T—C. Herbert Treat, Princeton; John Thurman, Pennsylvania; G—Frank Schwab, Lafayette; Charles Hubbard, Harvard; C—Ed Garbisch, Army; B—Harry Kipke, Michigan; Gordon Locke, Iowa; John Thomas, Chicago; Edgar Kaw, Cornell.

1923
E—Pete McRae, Syracuse; Ray Ecklund, Minnesota; Lynn Bomar, Vanderbilt; T—Century Milstead, Yale; Marty Below, Wisconsin; G—Charles Hubbard, Harvard; James McMillen, Illinois; C—Jack Blott, Michigan; B—George Pfann, Cornell; Red Grange, Illinois; William Mallory, Yale; Harry Wilson, Penn St.

Beginning in 1924, unanimous selections are indicated by (*).

1924
E—Jim Lawson, Stanford, 5-11, 190, Long Beach, Calif.; (tie) E—Dick Luman, Yale, 6-1, 176, Pinedale, Wyo.; E—Henry Wakefield, Vanderbilt, 5-10, 160, Petersburg, Tenn.; T—Ed McGinley, Pennsylvania, 5-11, 185, Swarthmore, Pa.; T—Ed Weir, Nebraska, 6-1, 194, Superior, Neb.; G—Joe Pondelik, Chicago, 5-11, 215, Cicero, Ill.; G—Carl Diehl, Dartmouth, 6-1, 205, Chicago, Ill.; C—Edwin Horrell, California, 5-11, 185, Pasadena, Calif.; B—*Red Grange, Illinois, 5-10, 170, Wheaton, Ill.; B—Harry Stuhldreher, Notre Dame, 5-7, 151, Massillon, Ohio; B—Jimmy Crowley, Notre Dame, 5-11, 162, Green Bay, Wis.; B—Elmer Layden, Notre Dame, 6-0, 162, Davenport, Iowa.

1925
E—Bennie Oosterbaan, Michigan, 6-0, 180, Muskegon, Mich.; E—George Tully, Dartmouth, 5-10, 175, Orange, N.J.; T—*Ed Weir, Nebraska, 6-1, 194, Superior, Neb.; T—Ralph Chase, Pittsburgh, 6-3, 202, Easton, Pa.; G—Carl Diehl, Dartmouth, 6-1, 205, Chicago, Ill.; G—Ed Hess, Ohio St., 6-1, 190, Cincinnati, Ohio; C—Ed McMillan, Princeton, 6-0, 208, Pittsburgh, Pa.; B—*Andy Oberlander, Dartmouth, 6-0, 197, Everett, Mass.; B—Red Grange, Illinois, 5-10, 170, Wheaton, Ill.; B—Ernie Nevers, Stanford, 6-0, 200, Superior, Wis.; (tie) B—Benny Friedman, Michigan, 5-8, 170, Cleveland, Ohio; B—George Wilson, Washington, 5-11, 190, Everett, Wash.

1926
E—Bennie Oosterbaan, Michigan, 6-0, 186, Muskegon, Mich.; E—Vic Hanson, Syracuse, 5-10, 174, Syracuse, N.Y.; T—*Frank Wickhorst, Navy, 6-0, 218, Oak Park, Ill.; T—Bud Sprague, Army, 6-2, 210, Dallas, Texas; G—Harry Connaughton, Georgetown, 6-2, 275, Philadelphia, Pa.; G—Bernie Shively, Illinois, 6-4, 208, Oliver, Ill.; C—Bud Boeringer, Notre Dame, 6-1, 186, St. Paul, Minn.; B—Benny Friedman, Michigan, 5-8, 172, Cleveland, Ohio; B—Mort Kaer, Southern Cal, 5-11, 167, Red Bluff, Calif.; B—Ralph Baker, Northwestern, 5-10, 172, Rockford, Ill.; B—Herb Joesting, Minnesota, 6-1, 192, Owatonna, Minn.

1927
E—*Bennie Oosterbaan, Michigan, 6-0, 186, Muskegon, Mich.; E—Tom Nash, Georgia, 6-3, 200, Washington, Ga.; T—Jesse Hibbs, Southern Cal, 5-11, 185, Glendale, Calif.; T—Ed Hake, Pennsylvania, 6-0, 190, Philadelphia, Pa.; G—Bill Webster, Yale, 6-0, 200, Shelton, Conn.; G—John Smith, Notre Dame, 5-9, 164, Hartford, Conn.; (tie) C—Larry Bettencourt, St. Mary's (Cal.), 5-10, 187, Centerville, Calif.; C—John Charlesworth, Yale, 5-11, 198, North Adams, Mass.; B—*Gibby Welch, Pittsburgh, 5-11, 170, Parkersburg, W. Va.; B—Morley Drury, Southern Cal, 6-0, 185, Long Beach, Calif.; B—Red Cagle, Army, 5-9, 167, Merryville, La.; B—Herb Joesting, Minnesota, 6-1, 192, Owatonna, Minn.

1928
E—Irv Phillips, California, 6-1, 188, Salinas, Calif.; E—Wes Fesler, Ohio St., 6-0, 173, Youngstown, Ohio; T—Otto Pommerening, Michigan, 6-0, 178, Ann Arbor, Mich.; T—Mike Getto, Pittsburgh, 6-2, 198, Jeannette, Pa.; G—Seraphim Post, Stanford, 6-0, 190, Berkeley, Calif.; (tie) G—Don Robesky, Stanford, 5-11, 198, Bakersfield, Calif.; G—Edward Burke, Navy, 6-0, 180, Larksville, Pa.; C—Pete Pund, Georgia Tech, 6-0, 195, Augusta, Ga.; B—*Red Cagle, Army, 5-9, 167, Merryville, La.; B—Paul Scull, Pennsylvania, 5-8, 187, Bala, Pa.; B—(tie) Ken Strong, New York U., 6-0, 201, West Haven, Conn.; Howard Harpster, Carnegie Mellon, 6-1, 160, Akron, Ohio; B—Charles Carroll, Washington, 6-0, 190, Seattle, Wash.

1929
E—*Joe Donchess, Pittsburgh, 6-0, 175, Youngstown, Ohio; E—Wes Fesler, Ohio St., 6-0, 183, Youngstown, Ohio; T—Bronko Nagurski, Minnesota, 6-2, 217, International Falls, Minn.; T—Elmer Sleight, Purdue, 6-2, 193, Morris, Ill.; G—Jack Cannon, Notre Dame, 5-11, 193, Columbus, Ohio; G—Ray Montgomery, Pittsburgh, 6-1, 188, Wheeling, W.Va.; C—Ben Ticknor, Harvard, 6-2, 193, New York, N.Y.; B—*Frank Carideo, Notre Dame, 5-7, 175, Mount Vernon, N.Y.; B—Ralph Welch, Purdue, 6-1, 189, Whitesboro, Texas; B—Red Cagle, Army, 5-9, 167, Merryville, La.; B—Gene McEver, Tennessee, 5-10, 185, Bristol, Va.

1930
E—*Wes Fesler, Ohio St., 6-0, 185, Youngstown, Ohio; E—Frank Baker, Northwestern, 6-2, 175, Cedar Rapids, Iowa; T—*Fred Sington, Alabama, 6-2, 215, Birmingham, Ala.; T—Milo Lubratovich, Wisconsin, 6-2, 216, Duluth, Minn.; G—Ted Beckett, California, 6-1, 190, Oroville, Calif.; G—Barton Koch, Baylor, 5-10, 195, Temple, Texas; C—*Ben Ticknor, Harvard, 6-2, 193, New York, N.Y.; B—*Frank Carideo, Notre Dame, 5-7, 175, Mount Vernon, N.Y.; B—Marchy Schwartz, Notre Dame, 5-11, 172, Bay St. Louis, Miss.; B—Erny Pinckert, Southern Cal, 6-0, 189, San Bernardino, Calif.; B—Leonard Macaluso, Colgate, 6-2, 210, East Aurora, N.Y.

1931
E—*Jerry Dalrymple, Tulane, 5-10, 175, Arkadelphia, Ark.; E—Vernon Smith, Georgia, 6-2, 190, Macon, Ga.; T—Jesse Quatse, Pittsburgh, 5-8, 198, Greensburg, Pa.; (tie) T—Jack Riley, Northwestern, 6-2, 218, Wilmette, Ill.; T—Dallas Marvil, Northwestern, 6-3, 227, Laurel, Del.; G—Biggie Munn, Minnesota, 5-10, 217, Minneapolis, Minn.; G—John Baker, Southern Cal, 5-10, 185, Kingsburg, Calif.; C—Tommy Yarr, Notre Dame, 5-11, 197, Chimacum, Wash.; B—Gus Shaver, Southern Cal, 5-11, 185, Covina, Calif.; B—Marchy Schwartz, Notre Dame, 5-11, 178, Bay St. Louis, Miss.; B—Pug Rentner, Northwestern, 6-1, 185, Joliet, Ill.; B—Barry Wood, Harvard, 6-1, 173, Milton, Mass.

1932
E—*Paul Moss, Purdue, 6-2, 185, Terre Haute, Ind.; E—Joe Skladany, Pittsburgh, 5-10, 185, Larksville, Pa.; T—*Joe Kurth, Notre Dame, 6-2, 204, Madison, Wis.; T—*Ernie Smith, Southern Cal, 6-2, 215, Los Angeles, Calif.; G—Milt Summerfelt, Army, 6-0, 181, Benton Harbor, Mich.; G—Bill Corbus, Stanford, 5-11, 188, Vallejo, Calif.; C—Pete Gracey, Vanderbilt, 6-0, 188, Franklin, Tenn.; B—*Harry Newman, Michigan, 5-7, 175, Detroit, Mich.; B—*Warren Heller, Pittsburgh, 6-0, 170, Steelton, Pa.; B—Don Zimmerman, Tulane, 5-10, 190, Lake Charles, La.; B—Jimmy Hitchcock, Auburn, 5-11, 172, Union Springs, Ala.

1933
E—Joe Skladany, Pittsburgh, 5-10, 190, Larksville, Pa.; E—Paul Geisler, Centenary (La.), 6-2, 189, Berwick, La.; T—Fred Crawford, Duke, 6-2, 195, Waynesville, N.C.; T—Francis Wistert, Michigan, 6-3, 212, Chicago, Ill.; G—Bill Corbus, Stanford, 5-11, 195, Vallejo, Calif.; G—Aaron Rosenberg, Southern Cal, 6-0, 210, Los Angeles, Calif.; C—*Chuck Bernard, Michigan, 6-2, 215, Benton Harbor, Mich.; B—*Cotton Warburton, Southern Cal, 5-7, 147, San Diego, Calif.; B—George Sauer, Nebraska, 6-2, 195, Lincoln, Neb.; B—Beattie Feathers, Tennessee, 5-10, 180, Bristol, Va.; B—Duane Purvis, Purdue, 6-1, 190, Mattoon, Ill.

1934
E—Don Hutson, Alabama, 6-1, 185, Pine Bluff, Ark.; E—Frank Larson, Minnesota, 6-3, 190, Duluth, Minn.; T—Bill Lee, Alabama, 6-2, 225, Eutaw, Ala.; T—Bob Reynolds, Stanford, 6-4, 220, Okmulgee, Okla.; G—Chuck Hartwig, Pittsburgh, 6-0, 190, Benwood, W.Va.; G—Bill Bevan, Minnesota, 5-11, 194, St. Paul, Minn.; C—Jack Robinson, Notre Dame, 6-3, 195, Huntington, N.Y.; B—Bobby Grayson, Stanford, 5-11, 186, Portland, Ore.; B—Pug Lund, Minnesota, 5-11, 185, Rice Lake, Wis.; B—Dixie Howell, Alabama, 5-10, 164, Hartford, Ala.; B—Fred Borries, Navy, 6-0, 175, Louisville, Ky.

1935
E—Wayne Millner, Notre Dame, 6-0, 184, Salem, Mass.; (tie) E—James Moscrip, Stanford, 6-0, 186, Adena, Ohio; E—Gaynell Tinsley, LSU, 6-0, 188, Homer, La.; T—Ed Widseth, Minnesota, 6-2, 220, McIntosh, Minn.; T—Larry Lutz, California, 6-0, 201, Santa Ana, Calif.; G—John Weller, Princeton, 6-0, 195, Wynnewood, Pa.; (tie) G—Sidney Wagner, Michigan St., 5-11, 186, Lansing, Mich.; G—J. C. Wetsel, Southern Methodist, 5-10, 185, Dallas, Texas; (tie) C—Gomer Jones, Ohio St., 5-8, 210, Cleveland, Ohio; C—Darrell Lester, Texas Christian, 6-4, 218, Jacksboro, Texas; B—*Jay Berwanger, Chicago, 6-0, 195, Dubuque, Iowa; B—*Bobby Grayson, Stanford, 5-11, 190, Portland, Ore.; B—Bobby Wilson, Southern Methodist, 5-10, 147, Corsicana, Texas; B—Riley Smith, Alabama, 6-1, 195, Columbus, Miss.

1936
E—*Larry Kelley, Yale, 6-1, 190, Williamsport, Pa.; E—*Gaynell Tinsley, LSU, 6-0, 196, Homer, La.; T—*Ed Widseth, Minnesota, 6-2, 220, McIntosh, Minn.; T—Averell Daniell, Pittsburgh, 6-3, 200, Mt. Lebanon, Pa.; G—Steve Reid, Northwestern, 5-9, 192, Chicago, Ill.; G—Max Starcevich, Washington, 5-10, 198, Duluth, Minn.; (tie) C—Alex Wojciechowicz, Fordham, 6-0, 192, South River, N.J.; C—Mike Basrak, Duquesne, 6-1, 210, Bellaire, Ohio; B—Sammy Baugh, Texas Christian, 6-2, 180, Sweetwater, Texas; B—Ace Parker, Duke, 5-11, 175, Portsmouth, Va.; B—Ray Buivid, Marquette, 6-1, 193, Port Washington, Wis.; B—Sam Francis, Nebraska, 6-1, 207, Oberlin, Kan.

1937
E—Chuck Sweeney, Notre Dame, 6-0, 190, Bloomington, Ill.; E—Andy Bershak, North Caro., 6-0, 190, Clairton, Pa.; T—Ed Franco, Fordham, 5-8, 196, Jersey City, N.J.; T—Tony Matisi, Pittsburgh, 6-0, 224, Endicott, N.Y.; G—Joe Routt, Texas A&M, 6-0, 193, Chappel Hill, Texas; G—Leroy Monsky, Alabama, 6-0, 198, Montgomery, Ala.; C—Alex Wojciechowicz, Fordham, 6-0, 196, South River, N.J.; B—*Clint Frank, Yale, 5-10, 190, Evanston, Ill.; B—Marshall Goldberg, Pittsburgh, 5-11, 185, Elkins, W.Va.; B—Byron "Whizzer" White, Colorado, 6-1, 185, Wellington, Colo.; B—Sam Chapman, California, 6-0, 190, Tiburon, Calif.

1938
E—Waddy Young, Oklahoma, 6-2, 203, Ponca City, Okla.; (tie) E—Brud Holland, Cornell, 6-1, 205, Auburn, N.Y.; E—Bowden Wyatt, Tennessee, 6-1, 190, Kingston, Tenn.; T—*Ed Beinor, Notre Dame, 6-2, 207, Harvey, Ill.; T—Alvord Wolff, Santa Clara, 6-2, 220, San Francisco, Calif.; G—*Ralph Heikkinen, Michigan, 5-10, 185, Ramsey, Mich.; G—Ed Bock, Iowa St., 6-0, 202, Fort Dodge, Iowa; C—Ki Aldrich, Texas Christian, 5-11, 195, Temple, Texas; B—*Davey O'Brien, Texas Christian, 5-7, 150, Dallas, Texas; B—*Marshall Goldberg, Pittsburgh, 6-0, 190, Elkins, W.Va.; B—Bob MacLeod, Dartmouth, 6-0, 190, Glen Ellyn, Ill.; B—Vic Bottari, California, 5-9, 182, Vallejo, Calif.

1939
E—Esco Sarkkinen, Ohio St., 6-0, 192, Fairport Harbor, Ohio; E—Ken Kavanaugh, LSU, 6-3, 203, Little Rock, Ark.; T—Nick Drahos, Cornell, 6-3, 200, Cedarhurst, N.Y.; T—Harley McCollum, Tulane, 6-4, 235, Wagoner, Okla.; G—*Harry Smith, Southern Cal, 5-11, 218, Ontario, Calif.; G—Ed Molinski, Tennessee, 5-10, 190, Massillon, Ohio; C—John Schiechl, Santa Clara, 6-2, 220, San Francisco, Calif.; B—Nile Kinnick, Iowa, 5-8,

167, Omaha, Neb.; B—Tom Harmon, Michigan, 6-0, 195, Gary, Ind.; B—John Kimbrough, Texas A&M, 6-2, 210, Haskell, Texas; B—George Cafego, Tennessee, 6-0, 174, Scarbro, W.Va.

1940

E—Gene Goodreault, Boston College, 5-10, 184, Haverhill, Mass.; E—Dave Rankin, Purdue, 6-1, 190, Warsaw, Ind.; T—Nick Drahos, Cornell, 6-3, 212, Cedarhurst, N.Y.; (tie) T—Alf Bauman, Northwestern, 6-1, 210, Chicago, Ill.; T—Urban Odson, Minnesota, 6-3, 247, Clark, S.D.; G—*Bob Suffridge, Tennessee, 6-0, 190, Knoxville, Tenn.; G—Marshall Robnett, Texas A&M, 6-1, 205, Klondike, Texas; C—Rudy Mucha, Washington, 6-2, 210, Chicago, Ill.; B—*Tom Harmon, Michigan, 6-0, 195, Gary, Ind.; B—*John Kimbrough, Texas A&M, 6-2, 221, Haskell, Texas; B—Frank Albert, Stanford, 5-9, 170, Glendale, Calif.; B—George Franck, Minnesota, 6-0, 175, Davenport, Iowa.

1941

E—Holt Rast, Alabama, 6-1, 185, Birmingham, Ala.; E—Bob Dove, Notre Dame, 6-2, 195, Youngstown, Ohio; T—Dick Wildung, Minnesota, 6-0, 210, Luverne, Minn.; T—Ernie Blandin, Tulane, 6-3, 245, Keighley, Kan.; G—*Endicott Peabody, Harvard, 6-0, 181, Syracuse, N.Y.; G—Ray Frankowski, Washington, 5-10, 210, Hammond, Ind.; C—Darold Jenkins, Missouri, 6-0, 195, Higginsville, Mo.; B—Bob Westfall, Michigan, 5-8, 190, Ann Arbor, Mich.; B—Bruce Smith, Minnesota, 6-0, 193, Faribault, Minn.; B—Frank Albert, Stanford, 5-9, 173, Glendale, Calif.; (tie) B—Bill Dudley, Virginia, 5-10, 175, Bluefield, Va.; B—Frank Sinkwich, Georgia, 5-8, 180, Youngstown, Ohio.

1942

E—*Dave Schreiner, Wisconsin, 6-2, 198, Lancaster, Wis.; E—Bob Dove, Notre Dame, 6-2, 195, Youngstown, Ohio; T—Dick Wildung, Minnesota, 6-0, 215, Luverne, Minn.; T—Albert Wistert, Michigan, 6-2, 205, Chicago, Ill.; G—Chuck Taylor, Stanford, 5-11, 200, San Jose, Calif.; (tie) G—Harvey Hardy, Georgia Tech, 5-10, 185, Thomaston, Ga.; G—Julie Franks, Michigan, 6-0, 187, Hamtramck, Mich.; C—Joe Domnanovich, Alabama, 6-1, 200, South Bend, Ind.; B—*Frank Sinkwich, Georgia, 5-8, 185, Youngstown, Ohio; B—Paul Governali, Columbia, 5-11, 186, New York, N.Y.; B—Mike Holovak, Boston College, 6-2, 214, Lansford, Pa.; B—Billy Hillenbrand, Indiana, 6-0, 195, Evansville, Ind.

1943

E—Ralph Heywood, Southern Cal, 6-2, 195, Huntington Park, Calif.; E—John Yonakor, Notre Dame, 6-4, 220, Dorchester, Mass.; T—Jim White, Notre Dame, 6-2, 210, Edgewater, N.J.; T—Don Whitmire, Navy, 5-11, 215, Decatur, Ala.; G—Alex Agase, Purdue, 5-10, 190, Evanston, Ill.; G—Pat Filley, Notre Dame, 5-8, 175, South Bend, Ind.; C—*Casimir Myslinski, Army, 5-11, 186, Steubenville, Ohio; B—*Bill Daley, Michigan, 6-2, 206, St. Cloud, Minn.; B—Angelo Bertelli, Notre Dame, 6-1, 173, West Springfield, Mass.; B—Creighton Miller, Notre Dame, 6-0, 185, Wilmington, Del.; B—Bob Odell, Pennsylvania, 5-11, 182, Sioux City, Iowa.

1944

E—Phil Tinsley, Georgia Tech, 6-1, 188, Bessemer, Ala.; (tie) E—Paul Walker, Yale, 6-3, 203, Oak Park, Ill.; E—Jack Dugger, Ohio St., 6-3, 210, Canton, Ohio; T—*Don Whitmire, Navy, 5-11, 215, Decatur, Ala.; T—John Ferraro, Southern Cal, 6-3, 235, Maywood, Calif.; G—Bill Hackett, Ohio St., 5-9, 191, London, Ohio; G—Ben Chase, Navy, 6-1, 195, San Diego, Calif.; C—John Tavener, Indiana, 6-0, 220, Granville, Ohio; B—*Les Horvath, Ohio St., 5-10, 167, Parma, Ohio; B—Glenn Davis, Army, 5-9, 170, Claremont, Calif.; B—Doc Blanchard, Army, 6-0, 205, Bishopville, S.C.; B—Bob Jenkins, Navy, 6-1, 195, Talladega, Ala.

1945

E—Dick Duden, Navy, 6-2, 203, New York, N.Y.; (tie) E—Hubert Bechtol, Texas, 6-2, 190, Lubbock, Texas; E—Bob Ravensberg, Indiana, 6-1, 180, Bellevue, Ky.; E—Max Morris, Northwestern, 6-2, 195, West Frankfort, Ill.; T—Tex Coulter, Army, 6-3, 220, Fort Worth, Texas; T—George Savitsky, Pennsylvania, 6-3, 250, Camden, N.J.; G—*Warren Amling, Ohio St., 6-0, 197, Pana, Ill.; G—John Green, Army, 5-11, 190, Shelbyville, Ky.; C—Vaughn Mancha, Alabama, 6-0, 235, Birmingham, Ala.; B—*Glenn Davis, Army, 5-9, 170, Claremont, Calif.; B—*Doc Blanchard, Army, 6-0, 205, Bishopville, S.C.; B—*Herman Wedemeyer, St. Mary's (Cal.), 5-10, 173, Honolulu, Hawaii; B—Bob Fenimore, Oklahoma St., 6-2, 188, Woodward, Okla.

1946

E—*Burr Baldwin, UCLA, 6-1, 196, Bakersfield, Calif.; E—(tie) Hubert Bechtol, Texas, 6-2, 201, Lubbock, Texas; Hank Foldberg, Army, 6-1, 200, Dallas, Texas; T—George Connor, Notre Dame, 6-3, 225, Chicago, Ill.; (tie) T—Warren Amling, Ohio St., 6-0, 197, Pana, Ill.; T—Dick Huffman, Tennessee, 6-2, 230, Charleston, W.Va.; G—Alex Agase, Illinois, 5-10, 191, Evanston, Ill.; G—Weldon Humble, Rice, 6-1, 214, San Antonio, Texas; C—Paul Duke, Georgia Tech, 6-1, 210, Atlanta, Ga.; B—*John Lujack, Notre Dame, 6-0, 180, Connellsville, Pa.; B—*Charley Trippi, Georgia, 5-11, 185, Pittston, Pa.; B—*Glenn Davis, Army, 5-9, 170, Claremont, Calif.; B—*Doc Blanchard, Army, 6-0, 205, Bishopville, S.C.

1947

E—Paul Cleary, Southern Cal, 6-1, 195, Santa Ana, Calif.; E—Bill Swiacki, Columbia, 6-2, 198, Southbridge, Mass.; T—Bob Davis, Georgia Tech, 6-4, 220, Columbus, Ga.; T—George Connor, Notre Dame, 6-3, 225, Chicago, Ill.; G—Joe Steffy, Army, 5-11, 190, Chattanooga, Tenn.; G—Bill Fischer, Notre Dame, 6-2, 230, Chicago, Ill.; C—Chuck Bednarik, Pennsylvania, 6-3, 220, Bethlehem, Pa.; B—*John Lujack, Notre Dame, 6-0, 180, Connellsville, Pa.; B—*Bob Chappuis, Michigan, 6-0, 180, Toledo, Ohio; B—Doak Walker, Southern Methodist, 5-11, 170, Dallas, Texas; (tie) B—Charley Conerly, Mississippi, 6-0, 184, Clarksdale, Miss.; B—Bobby Layne, Texas, 6-0, 191, Dallas, Texas.

1948

E—Dick Rifenburg, Michigan, 6-3, 197, Saginaw, Mich.; E—Leon Hart, Notre Dame, 6-4, 225, Turtle Creek, Pa.; T—Leo Nomellini, Minnesota, 6-2, 248, Chicago, Ill.; T—Alvin Wistert, Michigan, 6-3, 218, Chicago, Ill.; G—Buddy Burris, Oklahoma, 5-11, 214, Muskogee, Okla.; G—Bill Fischer, Notre Dame, 6-2, 233, Chicago, Ill.; C—Chuck Bednarik, Pennsylvania, 6-3, 220, Bethlehem, Pa.; B—*Doak Walker, Southern Methodist, 5-11, 168, Dallas, Texas; B—Charlie Justice, North Caro., 5-10, 165, Asheville, N.C.; B—Jackie Jensen, California, 5-11, 195, Oakland, Calif.; (tie) B—Emil Sitko, Notre Dame, 5-8, 180, Fort Wayne, Ind.; B—Clyde Scott, Arkansas, 6-0, 175, Smackover, Ark.

1949

E—*Leon Hart, Notre Dame, 6-5, 260, Turtle Creek, Pa.; E—James Williams, Rice, 6-0, 197, Waco, Texas; T—Leo Nomellini, Minnesota, 6-2, 255, Chicago, Ill.; T—Alvin Wistert, Michigan, 6-3, 223, Chicago, Ill.; G—*Rod Franz, California, 6-1, 198, San Francisco, Calif.; G—Ed Bagdon, Michigan St., 5-10, 200, Dearborn, Mich.; C—*Clayton Tonnemaker, Minnesota, 6-3, 240, Minneapolis, Minn.; B—*Emil Sitko, Notre Dame, 5-8, 180, Fort Wayne, Ind.; B—Doak Walker, Southern Methodist, 5-11, 170, Dallas, Texas; B—Arnold Galiffa, Army, 6-2, 190, Donora, Pa.; B—Bob Williams, Notre Dame, 6-1, 180, Baltimore, Md.

1950

E—*Dan Foldberg, Army, 6-1, 185, Dallas, Texas; E—Bill McColl, Stanford, 6-4, 225, San Diego, Calif.; T—Bob Gain, Kentucky, 6-3, 230, Weirton, W.Va.; T—Jim Weatherall, Oklahoma, 6-4, 220, White Deer, Texas; G—Bud McFadin, Texas, 6-3, 225, Iraan, Texas; G—Les Richter, California, 6-2, 220, Fresno, Calif.; C—Jerry Groom, Notre Dame, 6-3, 215, Des Moines, Iowa; B—*Vic Janowicz, Ohio St., 5-9, 189, Elyria, Ohio; B—Kyle Rote, Southern Methodist, 6-0, 190, San Antonio, Texas; B—Babe Parilli, Kentucky, 6-1, 183, Rochester, Pa.; B—Leon Heath, Oklahoma, 6-1, 195, Hollis, Okla.

1951

E—*Bill McColl, Stanford, 6-4, 225, San Diego, Calif.; E—Bob Carey, Michigan St., 6-5, 215, Charlevoix, Mich.; T—*Don Coleman, Michigan St., 5-10, 185, Flint, Mich.; T—*Jim Weatherall, Oklahoma, 6-4, 230, White Deer, Texas; G—*Bob Ward, Maryland, 5-10, 185, Elizabeth, N.J.; G—Les Richter, California, 6-2, 230, Fresno, Calif.; C—Dick Hightower, Southern Methodist, 6-1, 215, Tyler, Texas; B—*Dick Kazmaier, Princeton, 5-11, 171, Maumee, Ohio; B—*Hank Lauricella, Tennessee, 5-10, 169, New Orleans, La.; B—Babe Parilli, Kentucky, 6-1, 188, Rochester, Pa.; B—Johnny Karras, Illinois, 5-11, 171, Argo, Ill.

1952

E—Frank McPhee, Princeton, 6-3, 203, Youngstown, Ohio; E—Bernie Flowers, Purdue, 6-1, 189, Erie, Pa.; T—Dick Modzelewski, Maryland, 6-0, 235, West Natrona, Pa.; T—Hal Miller, Georgia Tech, 6-4, 235, Kingsport, Tenn.; G—John Michels, Tennessee, 5-10, 195, Philadelphia, Pa.; G—Elmer Wilhoite, Southern Cal, 6-2, 216, Winton, Calif.; C—Donn Moomaw, UCLA, 6-4, 220, Santa Ana, Calif.; B—*Jack Scarbath, Maryland, 6-1, 190, Baltimore, Md.; B—*Johnny Lattner, Notre Dame, 6-1, 190, Chicago, Ill.; B—Billy Vessels, Oklahoma, 6-0, 185, Cleveland, Okla.; B—Jim Sears, Southern Cal, 5-9, 167, Inglewood, Calif.

1953

E—Don Dohoney, Michigan St., 6-1, 193, Ann Arbor, Mich.; E—Carlton Massey, Texas, 6-4, 210, Rockwall, Texas; T—*Stan Jones, Maryland, 6-0, 235, Lemoyne, Pa.; T—Art Hunter, Notre Dame, 6-2, 226, Akron, Ohio; G—J. D. Roberts, Oklahoma, 5-10, 210, Dallas, Texas; G—Crawford Mims, Mississippi, 5-10, 200, Greenwood, Miss.; C—Larry Morris, Georgia Tech, 6-0, 205, Decatur, Ga.; B—*Johnny Lattner, Notre Dame, 6-1, 190, Chicago, Ill.; B—*Paul Giel, Minnesota, 5-11, 185, Winona, Minn.; B—Paul Cameron, UCLA, 6-0, 185, Burbank, Calif.; B—J. C. Caroline, Illinois, 6-0, 184, Columbia, S.C.

1954

E—Max Boydston, Oklahoma, 6-2, 207, Muskogee, Okla.; E—Ron Beagle, Navy, 6-0, 185, Covington, Ky.; T—Jack Ellena, UCLA, 6-3, 214, Susanville, Calif.; T—Sid Fournet, LSU, 5-11, 225, Baton Rouge, La.; G—*Bud Brooks, Arkansas, 5-11, 200, Wynne, Ark.; G—Calvin Jones, Iowa, 6-0, 200, Steubenville, Ohio; C—Kurt Burris, Oklahoma, 6-1, 209, Muskogee, Okla.; B—*Ralph Guglielmi, Notre Dame, 6-0, 185, Columbus, Ohio; B—*Howard Cassady, Ohio St., 5-10, 177, Columbus, Ohio; B—*Alan Ameche, Wisconsin, 6-0, 215, Kenosha, Wis.; B—Dicky Maegle, Rice, 6-0, 175, Taylor, Texas.

1955

E—*Ron Beagle, Navy, 6-0, 186, Covington, Ky.; E—Ron Kramer, Michigan, 6-3, 218, East Detroit, Mich.; T—Norman Masters, Michigan St., 6-2, 225, Detroit, Mich.; T—Bruce Bosley, West Va., 6-2, 225, Green Bank, W.Va.; G—Bo Bolinger, Oklahoma, 5-10, 206, Muskogee, Okla.; (tie) G—Calvin Jones, Iowa, 6-0, 220, Steubenville, Ohio; G—Hardiman Cureton, UCLA, 6-0, 213, Duarte, Calif.; C—*Bob Pellegrini, Maryland, 6-2, 225, Yatesboro, Pa.; B—*Howard Cassady, Ohio St., 5-10, 172, Columbus, Ohio; B—*Jim Swink, Texas Christian, 6-1, 180, Rusk, Texas; B—Earl Morrall, Michigan St., 6-1, 180, Muskegon, Mich.; B—Paul Hornung, Notre Dame, 6-2, 205, Louisville, Ky.

1956

E—*Joe Walton, Pittsburgh, 5-11, 205, Beaver Falls, Pa.; E—*Ron Kramer, Michigan, 6-3, 220, East Detroit, Mich.; T—John Witte, Oregon St., 6-2, 232, Klamath Falls, Ore.; T—Lou Michaels, Kentucky, 6-2, 229, Swoyersville, Pa.; G—*Jim Parker, Ohio St., 6-2, 251, Toledo, Ohio; G—*Bill Glass, Baylor, 6-4, 220, Corpus Christi, Texas; C—*Jerry Tubbs, Oklahoma, 6-2, 205, Breckenridge, Texas; B—*Jim Brown, Syracuse, 6-2, 212, Manhasset, N.Y.; B—*John Majors, Tennessee, 5-10, 162, Huntland, Tenn.; B—Tommy McDonald, Oklahoma, 5-9, 169, Albuquerque, N.M.; B—John Brodie, Stanford, 6-1, 190, Oakland, Calif.

1957

E—*Jimmy Phillips, Auburn, 6-2, 205, Alexander City, Ala.; E—Dick Wallen, UCLA, 6-0, 185, Alhambra, Calif.; T—Lou Michaels, Kentucky, 6-2, 235, Swoyersville, Pa.; T—Alex Karras, Iowa, 6-2, 233, Gary, Ind.; G—Bill Krisher, Oklahoma, 6-1, 213, Midwest City, Okla.; G—Al Ecuyer, Notre Dame, 5-10, 190, New Orleans, La.; C—Dan Currie, Michigan St., 6-3, 225, Detroit, Mich.; B—*John David Crow, Texas A&M, 6-2, 214, Springhill, La.; B—Walt Kowalczyk, Michigan St., 6-0, 205, Westfield, Mass.; B—Bob Anderson, Army, 6-2, 200, Cocoa, Fla.; B—Clendon Thomas, Oklahoma, 6-2, 188, Oklahoma City, Okla.

1958

E—Buddy Dial, Rice, 6-1, 185, Magnolia, Texas; E—Sam Williams, Michigan St., 6-5, 225, Dansville, Mich.; T—Ted Bates, Oregon St., 6-2, 215, Los Angeles, Calif.; T—Brock Strom, Air Force, 6-0, 217, Ironwood, Mich.; G—John Guzik, Pittsburgh, 6-3, 223, Lawrence, Pa.; (tie) G—Zeke Smith, Auburn, 6-2, 210, Uniontown, Ala.; G—George Deiderich, Vanderbilt, 6-1, 198, Toronto, Ohio; C—Bob Harrison, Oklahoma, 6-2, 206, Stamford, Texas; B—*Randy Duncan, Iowa, 6-0, 180, Des Moines, Iowa;

B—*Pete Dawkins, Army, 6-1, 197, Royal Oak, Mich.; B—*Billy Cannon, LSU, 6-1, 200, Baton Rouge, La.; B—Bob White, Ohio St., 6-2, 212, Covington, Ky.

1959

E—Bill Carpenter, Army, 6-2, 210, Springfield, Pa.; E—Monty Stickles, Notre Dame, 6-4, 225, Poughkeepsie, N.Y.; T—*Dan Lanphear, Wisconsin, 6-2, 214, Madison, Wis.; T—Don Floyd, Texas Christian, 6-3, 215, Midlothian, Texas; G—*Roger Davis, Syracuse, 6-2, 228, Solon, Ohio; G—Bill Burrell, Illinois, 6-0, 210, Chebanse, Ill.; C—Maxie Baughan, Georgia Tech, 6-1, 212, Bessemer, Ala.; B—Richie Lucas, Penn St., 6-1, 185, Glassport, Pa.; B—Billy Cannon, LSU, 6-1, 208, Baton Rouge, La.; B—Charlie Flowers, Mississippi, 6-0, 198, Marianna, Ark.; B—Ron Burton, Northwestern, 5-9, 185, Springfield, Ohio.

1960

E—*Mike Ditka, Pittsburgh, 6-3, 215, Aliquippa, Pa.; E—*Danny LaRose, Missouri, 6-4, 220, Crystal City, Mo.; T—*Bob Lilly, Texas Christian, 6-5, 250, Throckmorton, Texas; T—Ken Rice, Auburn, 6-3, 250, Bainbridge, Ga.; G—*Tom Brown, Minnesota, 6-0, 225, Minneapolis, Minn.; G—Joe Romig, Colorado, 5-10, 197, Lakewood, Colo.; C—E. J. Holub, Texas Tech, 6-4, 215, Lubbock, Texas; B—*Jake Gibbs, Mississippi, 6-0, 185, Grenada, Miss.; B—*Joe Bellino, Navy, 5-9, 181, Winchester, Mass.; B—*Bob Ferguson, Ohio St., 6-0, 217, Troy, Ohio; B—Ernie Davis, Syracuse, 6-2, 205, Elmira, N.Y.

1961

E—Gary Collins, Maryland, 6-3, 205, Williamstown, Pa.; E—Bill Miller, Miami (Fla.), 6-0, 188, McKeesport, Pa.; T—*Billy Neighbors, Alabama, 5-11, 229, Tuscaloosa, Ala.; T—Merlin Olsen, Utah St., 6-5, 265, Logan, Utah; G—*Roy Winston, LSU, 6-1, 225, Baton Rouge, La.; G—Joe Romig, Colorado, 5-10, 199, Lakewood, Colo.; C—Alex Kroll, Rutgers, 6-2, 228, Leechburg, Pa.; B—*Ernie Davis, Syracuse, 6-2, 210, Elmira, N.Y.; B—*Bob Ferguson, Ohio St., 6-0, 217, Troy, Ohio; B—*Jimmy Saxton, Texas, 5-11, 160, Palestine, Texas; B—Sandy Stephens, Minnesota, 6-0, 215, Uniontown, Pa.

1962

E—Hal Bedsole, Southern Cal, 6-5, 225, Northridge, Calif.; E—Pat Richter, Wisconsin, 6-5, 229, Madison, Wis.; T—*Bobby Bell, Minnesota, 6-4, 214, Shelby, N.C.; T—Jim Dunaway, Mississippi, 6-4, 260, Columbia, Miss.; G—*Johnny Treadwell, Texas, 6-1, 194, Austin, Texas; G—Jack Cvercko, Northwestern, 6-0, 230, Campbell, Ohio; C—*Lee Roy Jordan, Alabama, 6-2, 207, Monroeville, Ala.; B—*Terry Baker, Oregon St., 6-3, 191, Portland, Ore.; B—*Jerry Stovall, LSU, 6-2, 195, West Monroe, La.; B—Mel Renfro, Oregon, 5-11, 190, Portland, Ore.; B—George Saimes, Michigan St., 5-10, 186, Canton, Ohio.

1963

E—Vern Burke, Oregon St., 6-4, 195, Bakersfield, Calif.; E—Lawrence Elkins, Baylor, 6-1, 187, Brownwood, Texas; T—*Scott Appleton, Texas, 6-3, 235, Brady, Texas; T—Carl Eller, Minnesota, 6-6, 241, Winston-Salem, N.C.; G—*Bob Brown, Nebraska, 6-5, 259, Cleveland, Ohio; G—Rick Redman, Washington, 5-11, 210, Seattle, Wash.; C—*Dick Butkus, Illinois, 6-3, 234, Chicago, Ill.; B—*Roger Staubach, Navy, 6-2, 190, Cincinnati, Ohio; B—Sherman Lewis, Michigan St., 5-8, 154, Louisville, Ky.; B—Jim Grisham, Oklahoma, 6-2, 205, Olney, Texas; (tie) B—Gale Sayers, Kansas, 6-0, 196, Omaha, Neb.; B—Paul Martha, Pittsburgh, 6-1, 180, Wilkinsburg, Pa.

1964

E—Jack Snow, Notre Dame, 6-2, 210, Long Beach, Calif.; E—Fred Biletnikoff, Florida St., 6-1, 186, Erie, Pa.; T—*Larry Kramer, Nebraska, 6-2, 240, Austin, Minn.; T—Ralph Neely, Oklahoma, 6-5, 243, Farmington, N.M.; G—Rick Redman, Washington, 5-11, 215, Seattle, Wash.; G—Glenn Ressler, Penn St., 6-2, 230, Dornsife, Pa.; C—Dick Butkus, Illinois, 6-3, 237, Chicago, Ill.; B—John Huarte, Notre Dame, 6-0, 180, Anaheim, Calif.; B—Gale Sayers, Kansas, 6-0, 194, Omaha, Neb.; B—Lawrence Elkins, Baylor, 6-1, 187, Brownwood, Texas; B—Tucker Frederickson, Auburn, 6-2, 210, Hollywood, Fla.

Beginning in 1965, offense and defense selected.

1965

Offense E—*Howard Twilley, Tulsa, 5-10, 180, Galena Park, Texas; E—Freeman White, Nebraska, 6-5, 220, Detroit, Mich.; T—Sam Ball, Kentucky, 6-4, 241, Henderson, Ky.; T—Glen Ray Hines, Arkansas, 6-5, 235, El Dorado, Ark.; G—*Dick Arrington, Notre Dame, 5-11, 232, Erie, Pa.; G—Stas Maliszewski, Princeton, 6-1, 215, Davenport, Iowa; C—Paul Crane, Alabama, 6-2, 188, Prichard, Ala.; B—*Mike Garrett, Southern Cal, 5-9, 185, Los Angeles, Calif.; B—*Jim Grabowski, Illinois, 6-2, 211, Chicago, Ill.; B—Bob Griese, Purdue, 6-1, 185, Evansville, Ind.; B—Donny Anderson, Texas Tech, 6-3, 210, Stinnett, Texas.

Defense E—Aaron Brown, Minnesota, 6-4, 230, Port Arthur, Texas; E—Bubba Smith, Michigan St., 6-7, 268, Beaumont, Texas; T—Walt Barnes, Nebraska, 6-3, 235, Chicago, Ill.; T—Loyd Phillips, Arkansas, 6-3, 221, Longview, Texas; T—Bill Yearby, Michigan, 6-3, 222, Detroit, Mich.; LB—Carl McAdams, Oklahoma, 6-3, 215, White Deer, Texas; LB—Tommy Nobis, Texas, 6-2, 230, San Antonio, Texas; LB—Frank Emanuel, Tennessee, 6-3, 228, Newport News, Va.; B—George Webster, Michigan St., 6-4, 204, Anderson, S.C.; B—Johnny Roland, Missouri, 6-2, 198, Corpus Christi, Texas; B—Nick Rassas, Notre Dame, 6-0, 185, Winnetka, Ill.

1966

Offense E—*Jack Clancy, Michigan, 6-1, 192, Detroit, Mich.; E—Ray Perkins, Alabama, 6-0, 184, Petal, Miss.; T—*Cecil Dowdy, Alabama, 6-0, 206, Cherokee, Ala.; T—Ron Yary, Southern Cal, 6-6, 265, Bellflower, Calif.; G—Tom Regner, Notre Dame, 6-1, 245, Kenosha, Wis.; G—LaVerne Allers, Nebraska, 6-0, 209, Davenport, Iowa; C—Jim Breland, Georgia Tech, 6-2, 223, Blacksburg, Va.; B—*Steve Spurrier, Florida, 6-2, 203, Johnson City, Tenn.; B—*Nick Eddy, Notre Dame, 6-0, 195, Lafayette, Calif.; B—Mel Farr, UCLA, 6-2, 208, Beaumont, Texas; B—Clint Jones, Michigan St., 6-0, 206, Cleveland, Ohio.

Defense E—*Bubba Smith, Michigan St., 6-7, 283, Beaumont, Texas; E—Alan Page, Notre Dame, 6-5, 238, Canton, Ohio; T—*Loyd Phillips, Arkansas, 6-3, 230, Longview, Texas; T—Tom Greenlee, Washington, 6-0, 195, Seattle, Wash.; MG—Wayne Meylan, Nebraska, 6-0, 239, Bay City, Mich.; MG—John LaGrone, Southern Methodist, 5-10, 232, Borger, Texas; LB—*Jim Lynch, Notre Dame, 6-1, 225, Lima, Ohio; LB—Paul Naumoff, Tennessee, 6-1, 209, Columbus, Ohio; B—*George Webster, Michigan St., 6-4, 218, Anderson, S.C.; B—Tom Beier, Miami (Fla.), 5-11, 197, Fremont, Ohio; B—Nate Shaw, Southern Cal, 6-2, 205, San Diego, Calif.

1967

Offense E—Dennis Homan, Alabama, 6-0, 182, Muscle Shoals, Ala.; E—Ron Sellers, Florida St., 6-4, 187, Jacksonville, Fla.; T—*Ron Yary, Southern Cal, 6-6, 245, Bellflower, Calif.; T—Ed Chandler, Georgia, 6-2, 222, Cedartown, Ga.; G—Harry Olszewski, Clemson, 5-11, 237, Baltimore, Md.; G—Rich Stotter, Houston, 5-11, 225, Shaker Heights, Ohio; C—*Bob Johnson, Tennessee, 6-4, 232, Cleveland, Tenn.; B—Gary Beban, UCLA, 6-0, 191, Redwood City, Calif.; B—*Leroy Keyes, Purdue, 6-3, 199, Newport News, Va.; B—*O. J. Simpson, Southern Cal, 6-2, 205, San Francisco, Calif.; B—*Larry Csonka, Syracuse, 6-3, 230, Stow, Ohio.

Defense E—*Ted Hendricks, Miami (Fla.), 6-8, 222, Miami Springs, Fla.; E—Tim Rossovich, Southern Cal, 6-5, 235, Mountain View, Calif.; T—Dennis Byrd, North Caro. St., 6-4, 250, Lincolnton, N.C.; MG—*Granville Liggins, Oklahoma, 5-11, 216, Tulsa, Okla.; MG—Wayne Meylan, Nebraska, 6-0, 231, Bay City, Mich.; LB—Adrian Young, Southern Cal, 6-1, 210, La Puente, Calif.; LB—Don Manning, UCLA, 6-2, 204, Culver City, Calif.; B—Tom Schoen, Notre Dame, 5-11, 178, Euclid, Ohio; B—Frank Loria, Virginia Tech, 5-9, 174, Clarksburg, W.Va.; B—Bobby Johns, Alabama, 6-1, 180, Birmingham, Ala.; B—Dick Anderson, Colorado, 6-2, 204, Boulder, Colo.

1968

Offense E—*Ted Kwalick, Penn St., 6-4, 230, McKees Rocks, Pa.; E—Jerry LeVias, Southern Methodist, 5-10, 170, Beaumont, Texas; T—*Dave Foley, Ohio St., 6-5, 246, Cincinnati, Ohio; T—George Kunz, Notre Dame, 6-5, 240, Arcadia, Calif.; G—*Charles Rosenfelder, Tennessee, 6-1, 220, Humboldt, Tenn.; (tie) G—Jim Barnes, Arkansas, 6-4, 227, Pine Bluff, Ark.; G—Mike Montler, Colorado, 6-4, 235, Columbus, Ohio; C—*John Didion, Oregon St., 6-4, 242, Woodland, Calif.; B—*O. J. Simpson, Southern Cal, 6-2, 205, San Francisco, Calif.; B—*Leroy Keyes, Purdue, 6-3, 205, Newport News, Va.; B—Terry Hanratty, Notre Dame, 6-1, 200, Butler, Pa.; B—Chris Gilbert, Texas, 5-11, 176, Spring, Texas.

Defense E—*Ted Hendricks, Miami (Fla.), 6-8, 222, Miami Springs, Fla.; E—John Zook, Kansas, 6-4, 230, Larned, Kan.; T—Bill Stanfill, Georgia, 6-5, 245, Cairo, Ga.; T—Joe Greene, North Texas, 6-4, 274, Temple, Texas; MG—Ed White, California, 6-3, 245, Palm Desert, Calif.; MG—Chuck Kyle, Purdue, 6-1, 225, Fort Thomas, Ky.; LB—Steve Kiner, Tennessee, 6-1, 205, Tampa, Fla.; LB—Dennis Onkotz, Penn St., 6-2, 205, Northampton, Pa.; B—Jake Scott, Georgia, 6-1, 188, Arlington, Va.; B—Roger Wehrli, Missouri, 6-0, 184, King City, Mo.; B—Al Worley, Washington, 6-0, 175, Wenatchee, Wash.

1969

Offense E—Jim Mandich, Michigan, 6-3, 222, Solon, Ohio; (tie) E—Walker Gillette, Richmond, 6-5, 200, Capron, Va.; E—Carlos Alvarez, Florida, 5-11, 180, Miami, Fla.; T—Bob McKay, Texas, 6-6, 245, Crane, Texas; T—John Ward, Oklahoma St., 6-5, 248, Tulsa, Okla.; G—Chip Kell, Tennessee, 6-0, 255, Decatur, Ga.; G—Bill Bridges, Houston, 6-2, 230, Carrollton, Texas; C—Rodney Brand, Arkansas, 6-2, 218, Newport, Ark.; B—*Mike Phipps, Purdue, 6-3, 206, Columbus, Ind.; B—*Steve Owens, Oklahoma, 6-2, 215, Miami, Okla.; B—Jim Otis, Ohio St., 6-0, 214, Celina, Ohio; B—Bob Anderson, Colorado, 6-0, 208, Boulder, Colo.

Defense E—Jim Gunn, Southern Cal, 6-1, 210, San Diego, Calif.; E—Phil Olsen, Utah St., 6-5, 255, Logan, Utah; T—*Mike Reid, Penn St., 6-3, 240, Altoona, Pa.; T—*Mike McCoy, Notre Dame, 6-5, 274, Erie, Pa.; MG—Jim Stillwagon, Ohio St., 6-0, 216, Mount Vernon, Ohio; LB—*Steve Kiner, Tennessee, 6-1, 215, Tampa, Fla.; LB—Dennis Onkotz, Penn St., 6-2, 212, Northampton, Pa.; LB—Mike Ballou, UCLA, 6-3, 230, Los Angeles, Calif.; B—Jack Tatum, Ohio St., 6-0, 204, Passaic, N.J.; B—Buddy McClinton, Auburn, 5-11, 190, Montgomery, Ala.; B—Tom Curtis, Michigan, 6-1, 190, Aurora, Ohio.

1970

Offense E—Tom Gatewood, Notre Dame, 6-2, 208, Baltimore, Md.; E—Ernie Jennings, Air Force, 6-0, 172, Kansas City, Mo.; E—Elmo Wright, Houston, 6-0, 195, Brazoria, Texas; T—Dan Dierdorf, Michigan, 6-4, 250, Canton, Ohio; (tie) T—Bobby Wuensch, Texas, 6-3, 230, Houston, Texas; T—Bob Newton, Nebraska, 6-4, 248, LaMirada, Calif.; G—*Chip Kell, Tennessee, 6-0, 240, Decatur, Ga.; G—Larry DiNardo, Notre Dame, 6-1, 235, New York, N.Y.; C—Don Popplewell, Colorado, 6-2, 240, Raytown, Mo.; QB—Jim Plunkett, Stanford, 6-3, 204, San Jose, Calif.; RB—Steve Worster, Texas, 6-0, 210, Bridge City, Texas; RB—Don McCauley, North Caro., 6-0, 211, Garden City, N.Y.

Defense E—Bill Atessis, Texas, 6-3, 255, Houston, Texas; E—Charlie Weaver, Southern Cal, 6-2, 214, Richmond, Calif.; T—Rock Perdoni, Georgia Tech, 5-11, 236, Wellesley, Mass.; T—Dick Bumpas, Arkansas, 6-1, 225, Fort Smith, Ark.; MG—*Jim Stillwagon, Ohio St., 6-0, 220, Mount Vernon, Ohio; LB—Jack Ham, Penn St., 6-3, 212, Johnstown, Pa.; LB—Mike Anderson, LSU, 6-3, 225, Baton Rouge, La.; B—*Jack Tatum, Ohio St., 6-0, 208, Passaic, N.J.; B—Larry Willingham, Auburn, 6-1, 185, Birmingham, Ala.; B—Dave Elmendorf, Texas A&M, 6-1, 190, Houston, Texas; B—Tommy Casanova, LSU, 6-1, 191, Crowley, La.

1971

Offense E—*Terry Beasley, Auburn, 5-11, 184, Montgomery, Ala.; E—Johnny Rodgers, Nebraska, 5-10, 171, Omaha, Neb.; T—*Jerry Sisemore, Texas, 6-4, 255, Plainview, Texas; T—Dave Joyner, Penn St., 6-0, 235, State College, Pa.; G—*Royce Smith, Georgia, 6-3, 240, Savannah, Ga.; G—Reggie McKenzie, Michigan, 6-4, 232, Highland Park, Mich.; C—Tom Brahaney, Oklahoma, 6-2, 231, Midland, Texas; QB—*Pat Sullivan, Auburn, 6-0, 191, Birmingham, Ala.; RB—*Ed Marinaro, Cornell, 6-3, 210, New Milford, N.J.; RB—*Greg Pruitt, Oklahoma, 5-9, 176, Houston, Texas; RB—Johnny Musso, Alabama, 5-11, 194, Birmingham, Ala.

Defense E—*Walt Patulski, Notre Dame, 6-5, 235, Liverpool, N.Y.; E—Willie Harper, Nebraska, 6-3, 207, Toledo, Ohio; T—Larry Jacobson, Nebraska, 6-6, 250, Sioux Falls, S.D.; T—Mel Long, Toledo, 6-1, 230, Toledo, Ohio; T—Sherman White, California, 6-5, 250, Portsmouth, N.H.; LB—*Mike Taylor, Michigan, 6-2, 224, Detroit, Mich.; LB—Jeff Siemon, Stanford, 6-2, 225, Bakersfield, Calif.; B—*Bobby Majors, Tennessee, 6-1, 197, Sewanee, Tenn.; B—Clarence Ellis, Notre Dame, 6-0, 178, Grand Rapids, Mich.; B—Ernie Jackson, Duke, 5-10, 170, Hopkins, S.C.; B—Tommy Casanova, LSU, 6-2, 195, Crowley, La.

1972

Offense WR—*Johnny Rodgers, Nebraska, 5-9, 173, Omaha, Neb.; TE—*Charles Young, Southern Cal, 6-4, 228, Fresno, Calif.; T—*Jerry Sisemore, Texas, 6-4, 260, Plainview, Texas; T—Paul Seymour, Michigan, 6-5, 250, Berkley, Mich.; G—*John Hannah, Alabama, 6-3, 282, Albertville, Ala.; G—Ron Rusnak, North Caro., 6-1, 223, Prince George, Va.; C—Tom Brahaney, Oklahoma, 6-2, 227, Midland, Texas; QB—Bert Jones, LSU, 6-3, 205, Ruston, La.; RB—*Greg Pruitt, Oklahoma, 5-9, 177, Houston, Texas; RB—Otis Armstrong, Purdue, 5-11, 197, Chicago, Ill.; RB—Woody Green, Arizona St., 6-1, 190, Portland, Ore.

Defense E—Willie Harper, Nebraska, 6-2, 207, Toledo, Ohio; E—Bruce Bannon, Penn St., 6-3, 224, Rockaway, N.J.; T—*Greg Marx, Notre Dame, 6-5, 265, Redford, Mich.; T—Dave Butz, Purdue, 6-7, 279, Park Ridge, Ill.; MG—*Rich Glover, Nebraska, 6-1, 234, Jersey City, N.J.; LB—Randy Gradishar, Ohio St., 6-3, 232, Champion, Ohio; LB—John Skorupan, Penn St., 6-2, 208, Beaver, Pa.; B—*Brad VanPelt, Michigan St., 6-5, 221, Owosso, Mich.; B—Cullen Bryant, Colorado, 6-2, 215, Colorado Springs, Colo.; B—Robert Popelka, Southern Methodist, 6-1, 190, Temple, Texas; B—Randy Logan, Michigan, 6-2, 192, Detroit, Mich.

1973

Offense WR—Lynn Swann, Southern Cal, 6-0, 180, Foster City, Calif.; TE—Dave Casper, Notre Dame, 6-3, 252, Chilton, Wis.; T—*John Hicks, Ohio St., 6-3, 258, Cleveland, Ohio; T—Booker Brown, Southern Cal, 6-3, 270, Santa Barbara, Calif.; G—Buddy Brown, Alabama, 6-2, 242, Tallahassee, Fla.; G—Bill Yoest, North Caro. St., 6-0, 235, Pittsburgh, Pa.; C—Bill Wyman, Texas, 6-2, 235, Spring, Texas; QB—Dave Jaynes, Kansas, 6-2, 212, Bonner Springs, Kan.; RB—*John Cappelletti, Penn St., 6-1, 206, Upper Darby, Pa.; RB—Roosevelt Leaks, Texas, 5-11, 209, Brenham, Texas; RB—Woody Green, Arizona St., 6-1, 202, Portland, Ore.; RB—Kermit Johnson, UCLA, 6-0, 185, Los Angeles, Calif.

Defense L—*John Dutton, Nebraska, 6-7, 248, Rapid City, S.D.; L—Dave Gallagher, Michigan, 6-4, 245, Piqua, Ohio; L—*Lucious Selmon, Oklahoma, 5-11, 236, Eufaula, Okla.; L—Tony Cristiani, Miami (Fla.), 5-10, 215, Brandon, Fla.; LB—*Randy Gradishar, Ohio St., 6-3, 236, Champion, Ohio; LB—Rod Shoate, Oklahoma, 6-1, 214, Spiro, Okla.; LB—Richard Wood, Southern Cal, 6-2, 217, Elizabeth, N.J.; B—Mike Townsend, Notre Dame, 6-3, 183, Hamilton, Ohio; B—Artimus Parker, Southern Cal, 6-3, 215, Sacramento, Calif.; B—Dave Brown, Michigan, 6-1, 188, Akron, Ohio; B—Randy Rhino, Georgia Tech, 5-10, 179, Charlotte, N.C.

1974

Offense WR—Pete Demmerle, Notre Dame, 6-1, 190, New Canaan, Conn.; TE—Bennie Cunningham, Clemson, 6-5, 252, Seneca, S.C.; T—Kurt Schumacher, Ohio St., 6-4, 250, Lorain, Ohio; T—Marvin Crenshaw, Nebraska, 6-6, 240, Toledo, Ohio; G—Ken Huff, North Caro., 6-4, 261, Coronado, Calif.; G—John Roush, Oklahoma, 6-0, 252, Arvada, Colo.; G—Gerry DiNardo, Notre Dame, 6-1, 237, New York, N.Y.; C—Steve Myers, Ohio St., 6-2, 244, Kent, Ohio; QB—Steve Bartkowski, California, 6-4, 215, Santa Clara, Calif.; RB—*Archie Griffin, Ohio St., 5-9, 184, Columbus, Ohio; RB—*Joe Washington, Oklahoma, 5-10, 178, Port Arthur, Texas; RB—*Anthony Davis, Southern Cal, 5-9, 183, San Fernando, Calif.

Defense L—*Randy White, Maryland, 6-4, 238, Wilmington, Del.; L—Mike Hartenstine, Penn St., 6-4, 233, Bethlehem, Pa.; L—Pat Donovan, Stanford, 6-5, 240, Helena, Mont.; L—Jimmy Webb, Mississippi St., 6-5, 245, Florence, Miss.; L—Leroy Cook, Alabama, 6-4, 205, Abbeville, Ala.; MG—Louie Kelcher, Southern Methodist, 6-5, 275, Beaumont, Texas; MG—Rubin Carter, Miami (Fla.), 6-3, 260, Ft. Lauderdale, Fla.; LB—*Rod Shoate, Oklahoma, 6-1, 213, Spiro, Okla.; LB—Richard Wood, Southern Cal, 6-2, 213, Elizabeth, N.J.; LB—Ken Bernich, Auburn, 6-2, 240, Gretna, La.; LB—Woodrow Lowe, Alabama, 6-0, 211, Phenix City, Ala.; B—*Dave Brown, Michigan, 6-1, 188, Akron, Ohio; B—Pat Thomas, Texas A&M, 5-9, 180, Plano, Texas; B—John Provost, Holy Cross, 5-10, 180, Quincy, Mass.

1975

Offense E—Steve Rivera, California, 6-0, 185, Wilmington, Calif.; E—Larry Seivers, Tennessee, 6-4, 198, Clinton, Tenn.; T—Bob Simmons, Texas, 6-5, 245, Temple, Texas; T—Dennis Lick, Wisconsin, 6-3, 262, Chicago, Ill.; G—Randy Johnson, Georgia, 6-2, 250, Rome, Ga.; G—Ted Smith, Ohio St., 6-1, 242, Gibsonburg, Ohio; C—*Rik Bonness, Nebraska, 6-4, 223, Bellevue, Neb.; QB—John Sciarra, UCLA, 5-10, 178, Alhambra, Calif.; RB—*Archie Griffin, Ohio St., 5-9, 182, Columbus, Ohio; RB—*Ricky Bell, Southern Cal, 6-2, 215, Los Angeles, Calif.; RB—Chuck Muncie, California, 6-3, 220, Uniontown, Pa.

Defense E—*Leroy Cook, Alabama, 6-4, 205, Abbeville, Ala.; E—Jimbo Elrod, Oklahoma, 6-0, 210, Tulsa, Okla.; T—*Lee Roy Selmon, Oklahoma, 6-2, 256, Eufaula, Okla.; T—*Steve Niehaus, Notre Dame, 6-5, 260, Cincinnati, Ohio; MG—Dewey Selmon, Oklahoma, 6-1, 257, Eufaula, Okla.; LB—*Ed Simonini, Texas A&M, 6-0, 215, Las Vegas, Nev.; LB—Greg Buttle, Penn St., 6-3, 220, Linwood, N.J.; LB—Sammy Green, Florida, 6-2, 228, Ft. Meade, Fla.; B—*Chet Moeller, Navy, 6-0, 189, Kettering, Ohio; B—Tim Fox, Ohio St., 6-0, 186, Canton, Ohio; B—Pat Thomas, Texas A&M, 5-10, 180, Plano, Texas.

1976

Offense SE—Larry Seivers, Tennessee, 6-4, 200, Clinton, Tenn.; TE—Ken MacAfee, Notre Dame, 6-4, 251, Brockton, Mass.; T—Mike Vaughan, Oklahoma, 6-5, 275, Ada, Okla.; T—Chris Ward, Ohio St., 6-4, 274, Dayton, Ohio; G—Joel Parrish, Georgia, 6-3, 232, Douglas, Ga.; G—Mark Donahue, Michigan, 6-3, 245, Oak Lawn, Ill.; C—Derrel Gofourth, Oklahoma St., 6-2, 250, Parsons, Kan.; QB—Tommy Kramer, Rice, 6-2, 190, San Antonio, Texas; RB—*Tony Dorsett, Pittsburgh, 5-11, 192, Aliquippa, Pa.; RB—*Ricky Bell, Southern Cal, 6-2, 218, Los Angeles, Calif.; RB—Rob Lytle, Michigan, 6-1, 195, Fremont, Ohio; PK—Tony Franklin, Texas A&M, 5-10, 170, Fort Worth, Texas.

Defense E—*Ross Browner, Notre Dame, 6-3, 248, Warren, Ohio; E—Bob Brudzinski, Ohio St., 6-4, 228, Fremont, Ohio; T—Wilson Whitley, Houston, 6-3, 268, Brenham, Texas; T—Gary Jeter, Southern Cal, 6-5, 255, Cleveland, Ohio; T—Joe Campbell, Maryland, 6-6, 255, Wilmington, Del.; MG—Al Romano, Pittsburgh, 6-3, 230, Solvay, N.Y.; LB—*Robert Jackson, Texas A&M, 6-2, 228, Houston, Texas; LB—Jerry Robinson, UCLA, 6-3, 208, Santa Rosa, Calif.; B—*Bill Armstrong, Wake Forest, 6-4, 205, Randolph, N.J.; B—Gary Green, Baylor, 5-11, 182, San Antonio, Texas; B—Dennis Thurman, Southern Cal, 5-11, 170, Santa Monica, Calif.; B—Dave Butterfield, Nebraska, 5-10, 182, Kersey, Colo.

1977

Offense WR—John Jefferson, Arizona St., 6-1, 184, Dallas, Texas; WR—Ozzie Newsome, Alabama, 6-4, 210, Leighton, Ala.; TE—*Ken MacAfee, Notre Dame, 6-4, 250, Brockton, Mass.; T—*Chris Ward, Ohio St., 6-4, 272, Dayton, Ohio; T—Dan Irons, Texas Tech, 6-7, 260, Lubbock, Texas; G—*Mark Donahue, Michigan, 6-3, 245, Oak Lawn, Ill.; G—Leotis Harris, Arkansas, 6-1, 254, Little Rock, Ark.; C—Tom Brzoza, Pittsburgh, 6-3, 240, New Castle, Pa.; QB—Guy Benjamin, Stanford, 6-4, 202, Sepulveda, Calif.; RB—*Earl Campbell, Texas, 6-1, 220, Tyler, Texas; RB—*Terry Miller, Oklahoma St., 6-0, 196, Colorado Springs, Colo.; RB—Charles Alexander, LSU, 6-1, 215, Galveston, Texas; K—Steve Little, Arkansas, 6-0, 179, Overland Park, Kan.

Defense L—*Ross Browner, Notre Dame, 6-3, 247, Warren, Ohio; L—*Art Still, Kentucky, 6-8, 247, Camden, N.J.; L—*Brad Shearer, Texas, 6-4, 255, Austin, Texas; L—Randy Holloway, Pittsburgh, 6-6, 228, Sharon, Pa.; L—Dee Hardison, North Caro., 6-4, 252, Newton Grove, N.C.; LB—*Jerry Robinson, UCLA, 6-3, 208, Santa Rosa, Calif.; LB—Tom Cousineau, Ohio St., 6-3, 228, Fairview Park, Ohio; LB—Gary Spani, Kansas St., 6-2, 222, Manhattan, Kan.; B—*Dennis Thurman, Southern Cal, 5-11, 173, Santa Monica, Calif.; B—*Zac Henderson, Oklahoma, 6-1, 184, Burkburnett, Texas; B—Luther Bradley, Notre Dame, 6-2, 204, Muncie, Ind.; B—Bob Jury, Pittsburgh, 6-0, 190, Library, Pa.

1978

Offense WR—Emanuel Tolbert, Southern Methodist, 5-10, 180, Little Rock, Ark.; TE—Kellen Winslow, Missouri, 6-6, 235, East St. Louis, Ill.; T—*Keith Dorney, Penn St., 6-5, 257, Allentown, Pa.; T—Kelvin Clark, Nebraska, 6-4, 275, Odessa, Texas; G—*Pat Howell, Southern Cal, 6-6, 255, Fresno, Calif.; G—*Greg Roberts, Oklahoma, 6-3, 238, Nacogdoches, Texas; C—Dave Huffman, Notre Dame, 6-5, 245, Dallas, Texas; C—Jim Ritcher, North Caro. St., 6-3, 242, Hinckley, Ohio; QB—*Chuck Fusina, Penn St., 6-1, 195, McKees Rocks, Pa.; RB—*Billy Sims, Oklahoma, 6-0, 205, Hooks, Texas; RB—*Charles White, Southern Cal, 5-11, 183, San Fernando, Calif.; RB—Ted Brown, North Caro. St., 5-10, 195, High Point, N.C.; RB—Charles Alexander, LSU, 6-1, 214, Galveston, Texas.

Defense L—*Al Harris, Arizona St., 6-5, 240, Wheeler AFB, Hawaii; L—*Bruce Clark, Penn St., 6-3, 246, New Castle, Pa.; L—Hugh Green, Pittsburgh, 6-2, 215, Natchez, Miss.; L—Mike Bell, Colorado St., 6-5, 265, Wichita, Kan.; L—Marty Lyons, Alabama, 6-6, 250, St. Petersburg, Fla.; LB—*Bob Golic, Notre Dame, 6-3, 244, Willowick, Ohio; LB—*Jerry Robinson, UCLA, 6-3, 209, Santa Rosa, Calif.; LB—Tom Cousineau, Ohio St., 6-3, 227, Fairview Park, Ohio; B—*Johnnie Johnson, Texas, 6-2, 183, LaGrange, Texas; B—Kenny Easley, UCLA, 6-2, 202, Chesapeake, Va.; B—Jeff Nixon, Richmond, 6-4, 195, Glendale, Ariz.

1979

Offense WR—Ken Margerum, Stanford, 6-1, 175, Fountain Valley, Calif.; TE—*Junior Miller, Nebraska, 6-4, 222, Midland, Texas; T—*Greg Kolenda, Arkansas, 6-1, 258, Kansas City, Kan.; T—Jim Bunch, Alabama, 6-2, 240, Mechanicsville, Va.; G—*Brad Budde, Southern Cal, 6-5, 253, Kansas City, Mo.; G—Ken Fritz, Ohio St., 6-3, 238, Ironton, Ohio; C—*Jim Ritcher, North Caro. St., 6-3, 245, Hinckley, Ohio; QB—*Marc Wilson, Brigham Young, 6-5, 204, Seattle, Wash.; RB—*Charles White, Southern Cal, 6-0, 185, San Fernando, Calif.; RB—*Billy Sims, Oklahoma, 6-0, 205, Hooks, Texas; RB—Vagas Ferguson, Notre Dame, 6-1, 194, Richmond, Ind.; PK—Dale Castro, Maryland, 6-1, 170, Shady Side, Md.

Defense L—*Hugh Green, Pittsburgh, 6-2, 220, Natchez, Miss.; L—*Steve McMichael, Texas, 6-2, 250, Freer, Texas; L—Bruce Clark, Penn St., 6-3, 255, New Castle, Pa.; L—Jim Stuckey, Clemson, 6-5, 241, Cayce, S.C.; MG—Ron Simmons, Florida St., 6-1, 235, Warner Robins, Ga.; LB—*George Cumby, Oklahoma, 6-0, 205, Tyler, Texas; LB—Ron Simpkins, Michigan, 6-2, 220, Detroit, Mich.; LB—Mike Singletary, Baylor, 6-1, 224, Houston, Texas; B—*Kenny Easley, UCLA, 6-3, 204, Chesapeake, Va.; B—*Johnnie Johnson, Texas, 6-2, 190, LaGrange, Texas; B—Roland James, Tennessee, 6-2, 182, Jamestown, Ohio; P—Jim Miller, Mississippi, 5-11, 183, Ripley, Miss.

1980

Offense WR—*Ken Margerum, Stanford, 6-1, 175, Fountain Valley, Calif.; TE—*Dave Young, Purdue, 6-6, 242, Akron, Ohio; L—*Mark May, Pittsburgh, 6-6, 282, Oneonta, N.Y.; L—Keith Van Horne, Southern Cal, 6-7, 265, Fullerton, Calif.; L—Nick Eyre, Brigham Young, 6-5, 276, Las Vegas, Nev.; L—Louis Oubre, Oklahoma, 6-4, 262, New Orleans, La.; L—Randy Schleusener, Nebraska, 6-7, 242, Rapid City, S.D.; C—*John Scully, Notre Dame, 6-5, 255, Huntington, N.Y.; QB—*Mark Herrmann, Purdue, 6-4, 187, Carmel, Ind.; RB—*George Rogers, South Caro., 6-2, 220, Duluth, Ga.; RB—*Herschel Walker, Georgia, 6-2, 220, Wrightsville, Ga.; RB—Jarvis Redwine, Nebraska, 5-11, 204, Inglewood, Calif.

Defense L—*Hugh Green, Pittsburgh, 6-2, 222, Natchez, Miss.; L—*E. J. Junior, Alabama, 6-3, 227, Nashville, Tenn.; L—Kenneth Sims, Texas, 6-6, 265, Groesbeck, Texas; L—Leonard Mitchell, Houston, 6-7, 270, Houston, Texas; MG—Ron Simmons, Florida St., 6-1, 230, Warner Robins, Ga.; LB—*Mike Singletary, Baylor, 6-1, 232, Houston, Texas; LB—*Lawrence Taylor, North Caro., 6-3, 237, Williamsburg, Va.; LB—David Little, Florida, 6-1, 228, Miami, Fla.; LB—Bob Crable, Notre Dame, 6-3, 222, Cincinnati, Ohio; B—*Kenny Easley, UCLA, 6-3, 206, Chesapeake, Va.; B—*Ronnie Lott, Southern Cal, 6-2, 200, Rialto, Calif.; B—John Simmons, Southern Methodist, 5-11, 188, Little Rock, Ark.

1981

Offense WR—*Anthony Carter, Michigan, 5-11, 161, Riviera Beach, Fla.; TE—*Tim Wrightman, UCLA, 6-3, 237, San Pedro, Calif.; L—*Sean Farrell, Penn St., 6-3, 266, Westhampton Beach, N.Y.; L—Roy Foster, Southern Cal, 6-4, 265, Overland Park, Kan.; L—Terry Crouch, Oklahoma, 6-1, 275, Dallas, Texas; L—Ed Muransky, Michigan, 6-7, 275, Youngstown, Ohio; L—Terry Tausch, Texas, 6-4, 265, New Braunfels, Texas; L—Kurt Becker, Michigan, 6-6, 260, Aurora, Ill.; C—*Dave Rimington, Nebraska, 6-3, 275, Omaha, Neb.; QB—*Jim McMahon, Brigham Young, 6-0, 185, Roy, Utah; RB—*Marcus Allen, Southern Cal, 6-2, 202, San Diego, Calif.; RB—*Herschel Walker, Georgia, 6-2, 222, Wrightsville, Ga.

Defense L—*Billy Ray Smith, Arkansas, 6-4, 228, Plano, Texas; L—*Kenneth Sims, Texas, 6-6, 265, Groesbeck, Texas; L—Andre Tippett, Iowa, 6-4, 235, Newark, N.J.;

L—Tim Krumrie, Wisconsin, 6-3, 237, Mondovi, Wis.; LB—Bob Crable, Notre Dame, 6-3, 225, Cincinnati, Ohio; LB—Jeff Davis, Clemson, 6-0, 223, Greensboro, N.C.; LB—Sal Sunseri, Pittsburgh, 6-0, 220, Pittsburgh, Pa.; DB—Tommy Wilcox, Alabama, 5-11, 187, Harahan, La.; DB—Mike Richardson, Arizona St., 6-1, 192, Compton, Calif.; DB—Terry Kinard, Clemson, 6-1, 183, Sumter, S.C.; DB—Fred Marion, Miami (Fla.), 6-3, 194, Gainesville, Fla.; P—Reggie Roby, Iowa, 6-3, 215, Waterloo, Iowa.

1982

Offense WR—*Anthony Carter, Michigan, 5-11, 161, Riviera Beach, Fla.; TE—*Gordon Hudson, Brigham Young, 6-4, 224, Salt Lake City, Utah; L—*Don Mosebar, Southern Cal, 6-7, 270, Visalia, Calif.; L—*Steve Korte, Arkansas, 6-2, 270, Littleton, Colo.; L—Jimbo Covert, Pittsburgh, 6-5, 279, Conway, Pa.; L—Bruce Matthews, Southern Cal, 6-5, 265, Arcadia, Calif.; C—*Dave Rimington, Nebraska, 6-3, 290, Omaha, Neb.; QB—*John Elway, Stanford, 6-4, 202, Northridge, Calif.; RB—*Herschel Walker, Georgia, 6-2, 222, Wrightsville, Ga.; RB—*Eric Dickerson, Southern Methodist, 6-2, 215, Sealy, Texas; RB—Mike Rozier, Nebraska, 5-11, 210, Camden, N.J.; PK—*Chuck Nelson, Washington, 5-11, 178, Everett, Wash.

Defense L—*Billy Ray Smith, Arkansas, 6-3, 228, Plano, Texas; L—Vernon Maxwell, Arizona St., 6-2, 225, Carson, Calif.; L—Mike Pitts, Alabama, 6-5, 255, Baltimore, Md.; L—Wilber Marshall, Florida, 6-1, 230, Titusville, Fla.; L—Gabriel Rivera, Texas Tech, 6-3, 270, San Antonio, Texas; L—Rick Bryan, Oklahoma, 6-4, 260, Coweta, Okla.; MG—George Achica, Southern Cal, 6-5, 260, San Jose, Calif.; LB—*Darryl Talley, West Va., 6-4, 210, East Cleveland, Ohio; LB—Ricky Hunley, Arizona, 6-1, 230, Petersburg, Va.; LB—Marcus Marek, Ohio St., 6-2, 224, Masury, Ohio; DB—*Terry Kinard, Clemson, 6-1, 189, Sumter, S.C.; DB—Mike Richardson, Arizona St., 6-0, 190, Compton, Calif.; DB—Terry Hoage, Georgia, 6-3, 196, Huntsville, Texas; P—*Jim Arnold, Vanderbilt, 6-3, 205, Dalton, Ga.

1983

Offense WR—*Irving Fryar, Nebraska, 6-0, 200, Mount Holly, N.J.; TE—*Gordon Hudson, Brigham Young, 6-4, 231, Salt Lake City, Utah; L—*Bill Fralic, Pittsburgh, 6-5, 270, Penn Hills, Pa.; L—Terry Long, East Caro., 6-0, 280, Columbia, S.C.; L—Dean Steinkuhler, Nebraska, 6-3, 270, Burr, Neb.; L—Doug Dawson, Texas, 6-3, 263, Houston, Texas; C—Tony Slaton, Southern Cal, 6-4, 260, Merced, Calif.; QB—*Steve Young, Brigham Young, 6-1, 198, Greenwich, Conn.; RB—*Mike Rozier, Nebraska, 5-11, 210, Camden, N.J.; RB—Bo Jackson, Auburn, 6-1, 222, Bessemer, Ala.; RB—Greg Allen, Florida St., 6-0, 200, Milton, Fla.; RB—Napoleon McCallum, Navy, 6-2, 208, Milford, Ohio; PK—Luis Zendejas, Arizona St., 5-9, 186, Chino, Calif.

Defense L—*Rick Bryan, Oklahoma, 6-4, 260, Coweta, Okla.; L—*Reggie White, Tennessee, 6-5, 264, Chattanooga, Tenn.; L—William Perry, Clemson, 6-3, 320, Aiken, S.C.; L—William Fuller, North Caro., 6-4, 250, Chesapeake, Va.; LB—*Ricky Hunley, Arizona, 6-2, 230, Petersburg, Va.; LB—Wilber Marshall, Florida, 6-1, 230, Titusville, Fla.; LB—Ron Rivera, California, 6-3, 225, Monterey, Calif.; LB—Jeff Leiding, Texas, 6-4, 240, Tulsa, Okla.; DB—*Russell Carter, Southern Methodist, 6-3, 193, Ardmore, Pa.; DB—Jerry Gray, Texas, 6-1, 183, Lubbock, Texas; DB—Terry Hoage, Georgia, 6-3, 196, Huntsville, Texas; DB—Don Rogers, UCLA, 6-2, 208, Sacramento, Calif.; P—Jack Weil, Wyoming, 5-11, 171, Northglenn, Colo.

1984

Offense WR—*David Williams, Illinois, 6-3, 195, Los Angeles, Calif.; WR—Eddie Brown, Miami (Fla.), 6-0, 185, Miami, Fla.; TE—Jay Novacek, Wyoming, 6-4, 211, Gothenburg, Neb.; T—*Bill Fralic, Pittsburgh, 6-5, 285, Penn Hills, Pa.; T—Lomas Brown, Florida, 6-5, 277, Miami, Fla.; G—Del Wilkes, South Caro., 6-3, 255, Columbia, S.C.; G—Jim Lachey, Ohio St., 6-6, 274, St. Henry, Ohio; G—Bill Mayo, Tennessee, 6-3, 280, Dalton, Ga.; C—*Mark Traynowicz, Nebraska, 6-6, 265, Bellevue, Neb.; QB—*Doug Flutie, Boston College, 5-9, 177, Natick, Mass.; RB—*Keith Byars, Ohio St., 6-2, 233, Dayton, Ohio; RB—*Kenneth Davis, Texas Christian, 5-11, 205, Temple, Texas; RB—Rueben Mayes, Washington St., 6-0, 200, North Battleford, Saskatchewan, Canada; PK—Kevin Butler, Georgia, 6-1, 190, Stone Mountain, Ga.

Defense DL—Bruce Smith, Virginia Tech, 6-4, 275, Norfolk, Va.; DL—Tony Degrate, Texas, 6-4, 280, Snyder, Texas; DL—Ron Holmes, Washington, 6-4, 255, Lacey, Wash.; DL—Tony Casillas, Oklahoma, 6-3, 272, Tulsa, Okla.; LB—Gregg Carr, Auburn, 6-2, 215, Birmingham, Ala.; LB—Jack Del Rio, Southern Cal, 6-4, 235, Hayward, Calif.; LB—Larry Station, Iowa, 5-11, 233, Omaha, Neb.; DB—*Jerry Gray, Texas, 6-1, 183, Lubbock, Texas; DB—Tony Thurman, Boston College, 6-0, 179, Lynn, Mass.; DB—Jeff Sanchez, Georgia, 6-0, 183, Yorba Linda, Calif.; DB—David Fulcher, Arizona St., 6-3, 220, Los Angeles, Calif.; DB—Rod Brown, Oklahoma St., 6-3, 188, Gainesville, Texas; P—*Ricky Anderson, Vanderbilt, 6-2, 190, St. Petersburg, Fla.

1985

Offense WR—*David Williams, Illinois, 6-3, 195, Los Angeles, Calif.; WR—Tim McGee, Tennessee, 5-10, 181, Cleveland, Ohio; TE—Willie Smith, Miami (Fla.), 6-2, 230, Jacksonville, Fla.; L—*Jim Dombrowski, Virginia, 6-5, 290, Williamsville, N.Y.; L—Jeff Bregel, Southern Cal, 6-4, 280, Granada Hills, Calif.; L—Brian Jozwiak, West Va., 6-6, 290, Catonsville, Md.; L—John Rienstra, Temple, 6-4, 280, Colorado Springs, Colo.; L—J. D. Maarleveld, Maryland, 6-5, 300, Rutherford, N.J.; L—Jamie Dukes, Florida St., 6-0, 272, Orlando, Fla.; C—Pete Anderson, Georgia, 6-3, 264, Glen Ridge, N.J.; QB—*Chuck Long, Iowa, 6-4, 213, Wheaton, Ill.; RB—*Bo Jackson, Auburn, 6-1, 222, Bessemer, Ala.; RB—*Lorenzo White, Michigan St., 5-11, 205, Fort Lauderdale, Fla.; RB—Thurman Thomas, Oklahoma St., 5-11, 186, Missouri City, Texas; RB—Reggie Dupard, Southern Methodist, 6-0, 201, New Orleans, La.; RB—Napoleon McCallum, Navy, 6-2, 214, Milford, Ohio; PK—*John Lee, UCLA, 5-11, 187, Downey, Calif.

Defense L—*Tim Green, Syracuse, 6-2, 246, Liverpool, N.Y.; L—*Leslie O'Neal, Oklahoma St., 6-3, 245, Little Rock, Ark.; L—Tony Casillas, Oklahoma, 6-3, 280, Tulsa, Okla.; L—Mike Ruth, Boston College, 6-2, 250, Norristown, Pa.; L—Mike Hammerstein, Michigan, 6-4, 240, Wapakoneta, Ohio; LB—*Brian Bosworth, Oklahoma, 6-2, 234, Irving, Texas; LB—*Larry Station, Iowa, 5-11, 227, Omaha, Neb.; LB—Johnny Holland, Texas A&M, 6-2, 219, Hempstead, Texas; DB—David Fulcher, Arizona St., 6-3, 228, Los Angeles, Calif.; DB—Brad Cochran, Michigan, 6-3, 219, Royal Oak, Mich.; DB—Scott Thomas, Air Force, 6-0, 185, San Antonio, Texas; P—Barry Helton, Colorado, 6-3, 195, Simla, Colo.

1986

Offense WR—Cris Carter, Ohio St., 6-3, 194, Middletown, Ohio; TE—*Keith Jackson, Oklahoma, 6-3, 241, Little Rock, Ark.; L—Jeff Bregel, Southern Cal, 6-4, 280, Granada Hills, Calif.; L—Randy Dixon, Pittsburgh, 6-4, 286, Clewiston, Fla.; L—Danny Villa, Arizona St., 6-5, 284, Nogales, Ariz.; L—John Clay, Missouri, 6-5, 285, St. Louis, Mo.; C—*Ben Tamburello, Auburn, 6-3, 268, Birmingham, Ala.; QB—*Vinny Testaverde, Miami (Fla.), 6-5, 218, Elmont, N.Y.; RB—*Brent Fullwood, Auburn, 5-11, 209, St. Cloud, Fla.; RB—*Paul Palmer, Temple, 5-10, 180, Potomac, Md.; RB—Terrence Flagler, Clemson, 6-1, 200, Fernandina Beach, Fla.; RB—Brad Muster, Stanford, 6-3, 226, Novato, Calif.; RB—D. J. Dozier, Penn St., 6-1, 204, Virginia Beach, Va.; PK—Jeff Jaeger, Washington, 5-11, 191, Kent, Wash.

Defense L—*Jerome Brown, Miami (Fla.), 6-2, 285, Brooksville, Fla.; L—*Danny Noonan, Nebraska, 6-4, 280, Lincoln, Neb.; L—Tony Woods, Pittsburgh, 6-4, 240, Newark, N.J.; L—Jason Buck, Brigham Young, 6-6, 270, St. Anthony, Idaho; L—Reggie Rogers, Washington, 6-6, 260, Sacramento, Calif.; LB—*Cornelius Bennett, Alabama, 6-4, 235, Birmingham, Ala.; LB—Shane Conlan, Penn St., 6-3, 225, Frewsburg, N.Y.; LB—Brian Bosworth, Oklahoma, 6-2, 240, Irving, Texas; LB—Chris Spielman, Ohio St., 6-2, 227, Massillon, Ohio; DB—*Thomas Everett, Baylor, 5-9, 180, Daingerfield, Texas; DB—Tim McDonald, Southern Cal, 6-3, 205, Fresno, Calif.; DB—Bennie Blades, Miami (Fla.), 6-0, 207, Ft. Lauderdale, Fla.; DB—Rod Woodson, Purdue, 6-0, 195, Fort Wayne, Ind.; DB—Garland Rivers, Michigan, 6-1, 187, Canton, Ohio; P—Barry Helton, Colorado, 6-4, 200, Simla, Colo.

1987

Offense WR—*Tim Brown, Notre Dame, 6-0, 195, Dallas, Texas; WR—Wendell Davis, LSU, 6-0, 186, Shreveport, La.; TE—*Keith Jackson, Oklahoma, 6-3, 248, Little Rock, Ark.; L—*Mark Hutson, Oklahoma, 6-4, 282, Fort Smith, Ark.; L—Dave Cadigan, Southern Cal, 6-5, 280, Newport Beach, Calif.; L—John Elliott, Michigan, 6-7, 306, Lake Ronkonkoma, N.Y.; L—Randall McDaniel, Arizona St., 6-5, 261, Avondale, Ariz.; C—*Nacho Albergamo, LSU, 6-2, 257, Marrera, La.; QB—*Don McPherson, Syracuse, 6-0, 182, West Hempstead, N.Y.; RB—Lorenzo White, Michigan St., 5-11, 211, Fort Lauderdale, Fla.; RB—Craig Heyward, Pittsburgh, 6-0, 260, Passaic, N.J.; PK—David Treadwell, Clemson, 6-1, 165, Jacksonville, Fla.

Defense L—*Daniel Stubbs, Miami (Fla.), 6-4, 250, Red Bank, N.J.; L—*Chad Hennings, Air Force, 6-5, 260, Elboron, Iowa; L—Tracy Rocker, Auburn, 6-3, 258, Atlanta, Ga.; L—Ted Gregory, Syracuse, 6-1, 260, East Islip, N.Y.; L—John Roper, Texas A&M, 6-2, 215, Houston, Texas; LB—*Chris Spielman, Ohio St., 6-2, 236, Massillon, Ohio; LB—Aundray Bruce, Auburn, 6-6, 236, Montgomery, Ala.; LB—Dante Jones, Oklahoma, 6-2, 235, Dallas, Texas; DB—*Bennie Blades, Miami (Fla.), 6-0, 215, Fort Lauderdale, Fla.; DB—*Deion Sanders, Florida St., 6-0, 192, Fort Myers, Fla.; DB—Rickey Dixon, Oklahoma, 5-10, 184, Dallas, Texas; DB—Chuck Cecil, Arizona, 6-0, 185, Red Bluff, Calif.; P—*Tom Tupa, Ohio St., 6-5, 215, Brecksville, Ohio.

1988

Offense WR—Jason Phillips, Houston, 5-9, 175, Houston, Texas; WR—Hart Lee Dykes, Oklahoma St., 6-4, 220, Bay City, Texas; TE—Marv Cook, Iowa, 6-4, 243, West Branch, Iowa; L—*Tony Mandarich, Michigan St., 6-6, 315, Oakville, Ontario, Canada; L—*Anthony Phillips, Oklahoma, 6-3, 286, Tulsa, Okla.; L—Mike Utley, Washington St., 6-6, 302, Seattle, Wash.; L—Mark Stepnoski, Pittsburgh, 6-3, 265, Erie, Pa.; C—Jake Young, Nebraska, 6-5, 260, Midland, Texas; C—John Vitale, Michigan, 6-1, 273, Detroit, Mich.; QB—Steve Walsh, Miami (Fla.), 6-3, 195, St. Paul, Minn.; QB—Troy Aikman, UCLA, 6-4, 217, Henryetta, Okla.; RB—*Barry Sanders, Oklahoma St., 5-8, 197, Wichita, Kan.; RB—Anthony Thompson, Indiana, 6-0, 205, Terre Haute, Ind.; RB—Tim Worley, Georgia, 6-2, 216, Lumberton, N.C.; PK—Kendall Trainor, Arkansas, 6-2, 205, Fredonia, Kan.

Defense L—*Mark Messner, Michigan, 6-3, 244, Hartland, Mich.; L—*Tracy Rocker, Auburn, 6-3, 278, Atlanta, Ga.; L—Wayne Martin, Arkansas, 6-5, 263, Cherry Valley, Ark.; L—Frank Stams, Notre Dame, 6-4, 237, Akron, Ohio; L—Bill Hawkins, Miami (Fla.), 6-6, 260, Hollywood, Fla.; LB—*Derrick Thomas, Alabama, 6-4, 230, Miami, Fla.; LB—*Broderick Thomas, Nebraska, 6-3, 235, Houston, Texas; LB—Michael Stonebreaker, Notre Dame, 6-1, 228, River Ridge, La.; DB—*Deion Sanders, Florida St., 6-0, 195, Fort Myers, Fla.; DB—Donnell Woolford, Clemson, 5-10, 195, Fayetteville, N.C.; DB—Louis Oliver, Florida, 6-2, 222, Bell Glade, Fla.; DB—Darryl Henley, UCLA, 5-10, 165, Ontario, Calif.; P—Keith English, Colorado, 6-3, 215, Greeley, Colo.

1989

Offense WR—*Clarkston Hines, Duke, 6-1, 170, Chapel Hill, N.C.; WR—Terance Mathis, New Mexico, 5-9, 167, Stone Mountain, Ga.; TE—Mike Busch, Iowa St., 6-5, 252, Donahue, Iowa; L—Jim Mabry, Arkansas, 6-4, 262, Memphis, Tenn.; L—Bob Kula, Michigan St., 6-4, 282, West Bloomfield, Mich.; L—Mohammed Elewonibi, Brigham Young, 6-5, 290, Kamloops, British Columbia, Canada; L—Joe Garten, Colorado, 6-3, 280, Placentia, Calif.; L—*Eric Still, Tennessee, 6-3, 283, Germantown, Tenn.; C—Jake Young, Nebraska, 6-4, 270, Midland, Texas; QB—Andre Ware, Houston, 6-2, 205, Dickinson, Texas; RB—*Anthony Thompson, Indiana, 6-0, 209, Terre Haute, Ind.; RB—*Emmitt Smith, Florida, 5-10, 201, Pensacola, Fla.; PK—*Jason Hanson, Washington St., 6-0, 164, Spokane, Wash.

Defense L—Chris Zorich, Notre Dame, 6-1, 268, Chicago, Ill.; L—Greg Mark, Miami (Fla.), 6-4, 255, Pennsauken, N.J.; L—Tim Ryan, Southern Cal, 6-5, 260, San Jose, Calif.; L—*Moe Gardner, Illinois, 6-2, 250, Indianapolis, Ind.; LB—*Percy Snow, Michigan St., 6-3, 240, Canton, Ohio; LB—*Keith McCants, Alabama, 6-5, 256, Mobile, Ala.; LB—Alfred Williams, Colorado, 6-6, 230, Houston, Texas; DB—*Todd Lyght, Notre Dame, 6-1, 181, Flint, Mich.; DB—*Mark Carrier, Southern Cal, 6-1, 185, Long Beach, Calif.; DB—*Tripp Welborne, Michigan, 6-1, 193, Greensboro, N.C.; DB—LeRoy Butler, Florida St., 6-0, 194, Jacksonville, Fla.; P—Tom Rouen, Colorado, 6-3, 220, Littleton, Colo.

1990

Offense WR—*Raghib Ismail, Notre Dame, 5-10, 175, Wilkes-Barre, Pa.; WR—Herman Moore, Virginia, 6-5, 197, Danville, Va.; TE—*Chris Smith, Brigham Young, 6-4, 230, La Canada, Calif.; OL—*Antone Davis, Tennessee, 6-4, 310, Fort Valley, Ga.; OL—*Joe Garten,

Colorado, 6-3, 280, Placentia, Calif.; OL—*Ed King, Auburn, 6-4, 284, Phenix City, Ala.; OL—Stacy Long, Clemson, 6-2, 275, Griffin, Ga.; C—John Flannery, Syracuse, 6-4, 301, Pottsville, Pa.; QB—Ty Detmer, Brigham Young, 6-0, 175, San Antonio, Texas; RB—*Eric Bieniemy, Colorado, 5-7, 195, West Covina, Calif.; RB—Darren Lewis, Texas A&M, 6-0, 220, Dallas, Texas; PK—*Philip Doyle, Alabama, 6-1, 190, Birmingham, Ala.

Defense DL—*Russell Maryland, Miami (Fla.), 6-2, 273, Chicago, Ill.; DL—*Chris Zorich, Notre Dame, 6-1, 266, Chicago, Ill.; DL—Moe Gardner, Illinois, 6-2, 258, Indianapolis, Ind.; DL—David Rocker, Auburn, 6-4, 264, Atlanta, Ga.; LB—*Alfred Williams, Colorado, 6-6, 236, Houston, Texas; LB—*Michael Stonebreaker, Notre Dame, 6-1, 228, River Ridge, La.; LB—Maurice Crum, Miami (Fla.), 6-0, 222, Tampa, Fla.; DB—*Tripp Welborne, Michigan, 6-1, 201, Greensboro, N.C.; DB—*Darryll Lewis, Arizona, 5-9, 186, West Covina, Calif.; DB—*Ken Swilling, Georgia Tech, 6-3, 230, Toccoa, Ga.; DB—Todd Lyght, Notre Dame, 6-1, 184, Flint, Mich.; P—Brian Greenfield, Pittsburgh, 6-1, 210, Sherman Oaks, Calif.

1991

Offense WR—*Desmond Howard, Michigan, 5-9, 176, Cleveland, Ohio; WR—Mario Bailey, Washington, 5-9, 167, Seattle, Wash.; TE—Kelly Blackwell, Texas Christian, 6-2, 242, Fort Worth, Texas; OL—*Greg Skrepenak, Michigan, 6-8, 322, Wilkes-Barre, Pa.; OL—Bob Whitfield, Stanford, 6-7, 300, Carson, Calif.; OL—Jeb Flesch, Clemson, 6-3, 266, Morrow, Ga.; OL—(tie) Jerry Ostroski, Tulsa, 6-4, 305, Collegeville, Pa.; Mirko Jurkovic, Notre Dame, 6-4, 289, Calumet City, Ill.; C—*Jay Leeuwenburg, Colorado, 6-3, 265, Kirkwood, Mo.; QB—Ty Detmer, Brigham Young, 6-0, 175, San Antonio, Texas; RB—*Vaughn Dunbar, Indiana, 6-0, 207, Fort Wayne, Ind.; RB—(tie) Trevor Cobb, Rice, 5-9, 180, Houston, Texas; Russell White, California, 6-0, 210, Van Nuys, Calif.; PK—Carlos Huerta, Miami (Fla.), 5-9, 186, Miami, Fla.

Defense DL—*Steve Emtman, Washington, 6-4, 280, Cheney, Wash.; DL—*Santana Dotson, Baylor, 6-5, 264, Houston, Texas; DL—Brad Culpepper, Florida, 6-2, 263, Tallahassee, Fla.; DL—Leroy Smith, Iowa, 6-2, 214, Sicklerville, N. J.; LB—*Robert Jones, East Caro., 6-3, 234, Blackstone, Va.; LB—Marvin Jones, Florida St., 6-2, 220, Miami, Fla.; LB—Levon Kirkland, Clemson, 6-2, 245, Lamar, S.C.; DB—*Terrell Buckley, Florida St., 5-10, 175, Pascagoula, Miss.; DB—Dale Carter, Tennessee, 6-2, 182, Oxford, Ga.; DB—Kevin Smith, Texas A&M, 6-0, 180, Orange, Texas; DB—Darryl Williams, Miami (Fla.), 6-2, 190, Miami, Fla.; P—*Mark Bounds, Texas Tech, 5-11, 185, Stamford, Texas.

1992

Offense WR—O. J. McDuffie, Penn St., 5-11, 185, Warrensville Heights, Ohio; WR—Sean Dawkins, California, 6-4, 205, Sunnyvale, Calif.; TE—*Chris Gedney, Syracuse, 6-5, 256, Liverpool, N.Y.; OL—*Lincoln Kennedy, Washington, 6-7, 325, San Diego, Calif.; OL—*Will Shields, Nebraska, 6-1, 305, Lawton, Okla.; OL—Aaron Taylor, Notre Dame, 6-4, 294, Concord, Calif.; OL—(tie) Willie Roaf, Louisiana Tech, 6-5, 300, Pine Bluff, Ark.; Everett Lindsay, Mississippi, 6-5, 290, Raleigh, N.C.; C—Mike Compton, West Va., 6-7, 289, Richlands, Va.; QB—*Gino Torretta, Miami (Fla.), 6-3, 205, Pinole, Calif.; RB—*Marshall Faulk, San Diego St., 5-10, 200, New Orleans, La.; RB—*Garrison Hearst, Georgia, 5-11, 202, Lincolnton, Ga.; PK—Joe Allison, Memphis, 6-0, 184, Atlanta, Ga.

Defense DL—Eric Curry, Alabama, 6-6, 265, Thomasville, Ga.; DL—John Copeland, Alabama, 6-3, 261, Lanett, Ala.; DL—Chris Slade, Virginia, 6-5, 235, Tabb, Va.; DL—Rob Waldrop, Arizona, 6-2, 265, Phoenix, Ariz.; LB—*Marcus Buckley, Texas A&M, 6-4, 230, Fort Worth, Texas; LB—*Marvin Jones, Florida St., 6-2, 235, Miami, Fla.; LB—Micheal Barrow, Miami (Fla.), 6-2, 230, Homestead, Fla.; DB—*Carlton McDonald, Air Force, 6-0, 185, Jacksonville, Fla.; DB—Carlton Gray, UCLA, 6-0, 194, Cincinnati, Ohio; DB—Deon Figures, Colorado, 6-1, 195, Compton, Calif.; DB—Ryan McNeil, Miami (Fla.), 6-2, 185, Fort Pierce, Fla.; P—Sean Snyder, Kansas St., 6-1, 190, Greenville, Texas.

1993

Offense WR—*J. J. Stokes, UCLA, 6-5, 214, San Diego, Calif.; WR—Johnnie Morton, Southern Cal, 6-0, 190, Torrance, Calif.; OL—Mark Dixon, Virginia, 6-4, 283, Jamestown, N.C.; OL—Stacy Seegars, Clemson, 6-4, 320, Kershaw, S.C.; OL—*Aaron Taylor, Notre Dame, 6-4, 299, Concord, Calif.; OL—Wayne Gandy, Auburn, 6-5, 275, Haines City, Fla.; C—*Jim Pyne, Virginia Tech, 6-2, 280, Milford, Mass.; QB—*Charlie Ward, Florida St., 6-2, 190, Thomasville, Ga.; RB—*Marshall Faulk, San Diego St., 5-10, 200, New Orleans, La.; RB—*LeShon Johnson, Northern Ill., 6-0, 201, Haskell, Okla.; PK—Bjorn Merten, UCLA, 6-0, 203, Centreville, Va.; KR—David Palmer, Alabama, 5-9, 170, Birmingham, Ala.

Defense DL—*Rob Waldrop, Arizona, 6-2, 275, Phoenix, Ariz.; DL—Dan Wilkinson, Ohio St., 6-5, 300, Dayton, Ohio; DL—Sam Adams, Texas A&M, 6-4, 269, Cypress, Texas; LB—*Trev Alberts, Nebraska, 6-4, 240, Cedar Falls, Iowa; LB—*Derrick Brooks, Florida St., 6-1, 225, Pensacola, Fla.; LB—Jamir Miller, UCLA, 6-4, 233, El Cerrito, Calif.; DB—*Antonio Langham, Alabama, 6-1, 170, Town Creek, Ala.; DB—Aaron Glenn, Texas A&M, 5-10, 182, Aldine, Texas; DB—Jeff Burris, Notre Dame, 6-0, 204, Rock Hill, S.C.; DB—Corey Sawyer, Florida St., 5-11, 171, Key West, Fla.; P—Terry Daniel, Auburn, 6-1, 226, Valley, Ala.

1994

Offense WR—Jack Jackson, Florida, 5-9, 171, Moss Point, Miss.; WR—Michael Westbrook, Colorado, 6-4, 210, Detroit, Mich.; TE—Pete Mitchell, Boston College, 6-2, 238, Bloomfield Hills, Mich.; OL—*Zach Wiegert, Nebraska, 6-5, 300, Fremont, Neb.; OL—Tony Boselli, Southern Cal, 6-8, 305, Boulder, Colo.; OL—Korey Stringer, Ohio St., 6-5, 315, Warren, Ohio; OL—Brenden Stai, Nebraska, 6-4, 300, Yorba Linda, Calif.; C—Cory Raymer, Wisconsin, 6-4, 290, Fond du Lac, Wis.; QB—Kerry Collins, Penn St., 6-5, 235, West Lawn, Pa.; RB—*Rashaan Salaam, Colorado, 6-1, 210, San Diego, Calif.; RB—*Ki-Jana Carter, Penn St., 5-10, 212, Westerville, Ohio; PK—Steve McLaughlin, Arizona, 6-1, 175, Tucson, Ariz.; KR—Leeland McElroy, Texas A&M, 5-11, 200, Beaumont, Texas.

Defense DL—*Warren Sapp, Miami (Fla.), 6-3, 284, Plymouth, Fla.; DL—Tedy Bruschi, Arizona, 6-1, 255, Roseville, Calif.; DL—Luther Elliss, Utah, 6-6, 288, Mancos, Colo.; DL—Kevin Carter, Florida, 6-6, 265, Tallahassee, Fla.; LB—*Dana Howard, Illinois, 6-0, 235, East St. Louis, Ill.; LB—Ed Stewart, Nebraska, 6-1, 215, Chicago, Ill.; LB—Derrick Brooks, Florida St., 6-1, 226, Pensacola, Fla.; DB—Clifton Abraham, Florida St., 5-9, 185, Dallas, Texas; DB—Bobby Taylor, Notre Dame, 6-3, 201, Longview, Texas; DB—Chris Hudson, Colorado, 5-11, 195, Houston, Texas; DB—Brian Robinson, Auburn, 6-3, 194, Fort Lauderdale, Fla.; DB—Tony Bouie, Arizona, 5-10, 183, New Orleans, La.; P—*Todd Sauerbrun, West Va., 6-0, 205, Setauket, N.Y.

1995

Offense WR—Terry Glenn, Ohio St., 5-11, 185, Columbus, Ohio; WR—*Keyshawn Johnson, Southern Cal, 6-4, 210, Los Angeles, Calif.; TE—*Marco Battaglia, Rutgers, 6-3, 240, Queens, N.Y.; OL—*Jonathan Ogden, UCLA, 6-8, 310, Washington, D.C.; OL—*Jason Odom, Florida, 6-5, 291, Bartow, Fla.; OL—*Orlando Pace, Ohio St., 6-6, 320, Sandusky, Ohio; OL—Jeff Hartings, Penn St., 6-3, 278, St. Henry, Ohio; C—(tie) Clay Shiver, Florida St., 6-2, 285, Tifton, Ga.; Bryan Stoltenberg, Colorado, 6-2, 280, Sugarland, Texas; QB—Tommie Frazier, Nebraska, 6-2, 205, Bradenton, Fla.; RB—*Eddie George, Ohio St., 6-3, 230, Philadelphia, Pa.; RB—Troy Davis, Iowa St., 5-8, 182, Miami, Fla.; PK—Michael Reeder, Texas Christian, 6-0, 160, Sulphur, La.

Defense DL—*Tedy Bruschi, Arizona, 6-1, 253, Roseville, Calif.; DL—Cornell Brown, Virginia Tech, 6-2, 240, Lynchburg, Va.; DL—Marcus Jones, North Caro., 6-6, 270, Jacksonville, N.C.; DL—Tony Brackens, Texas, 6-4, 250, Fairfield, Texas; LB—*Zach Thomas, Texas Tech, 6-0, 232, Pampa, Texas; LB—Kevin Hardy, Illinois, 6-4, 243, Evansville, Ind.; LB—Pat Fitzgerald, Northwestern, 6-4, 228, Orland Park, Ill.; DB—Chris Canty, Kansas St., 5-10, 190, Voorhees, N.J.; DB—*Lawyer Milloy, Washington, 6-2, 200, Tacoma, Wash.; DB—Aaron Beasley, West Va., 6-0, 190, Pottstown, Pa.; DB—Greg Myers, Colorado St., 6-2, 191, Windsor, Colo.; P—Brad Maynard, Ball St., 6-1, 175, Atlanta, Ind.

1996

Offense WR—Marcus Harris, Wyoming, 6-2, 216, Senior, Minneapolis, Minn.; WR—(tie) Ike Hilliard, Florida, 5-11, 182, Junior, Patterson, La.; Reidel Anthony, Florida, 6-0, 181, Junior, South Bay, Fla.; TE—Tony Gonzalez, California, 6-6, 235, Junior, Huntington Beach, Cal.; OL—*Orlando Pace, Ohio St., 6-6, 330, Junior, Sandusky, Ohio; OL—Juan Roque, Arizona St., 6-8, 319, Senior, Ontario, Cal.; OL—Chris Naeole, Colorado, 6-4, 310, Senior, Kaaava, Hawaii; OL—Dan Neil, Texas, 6-2, 283, Senior, Cypress Creek, Tex.; OL—Benji Olson, Washington, 6-4, 310, Sophomore, Port Orchard, Wash.; C—Aaron Taylor, Nebraska, 6-1, 305, Junior, Wichita Falls, Tex.; QB—Danny Wuerffel, Florida, 6-2, 209, Senior, Fort Walton Beach, Fla.; RB—*Byron Hanspard, Texas Tech, 6-0, 193, Junior, DeSoto, Tex.; RB—Troy Davis, Iowa St., 5-8, 185, Junior, Miami, Fla.; PK—Marc Primanti, North Caro. St., 5-7, 171, Senior, Thorndale, Pa.

Defense DL—Grant Wistrom, Nebraska, 6-5, 250, Junior, Webb City, Mo.; DL—Peter Boulware, Florida St., 6-5, 255, Junior, Columbia, S. C.; DL—Reinard Wilson, Florida St., 6-2, 255, Senior, Lake City, Fla.; DL—(tie) Derrick Rodgers, Arizona St., 6-2, 220, Junior, Cordova, Tenn.; Mike Vrabel, Ohio St., 6-4, 260, Senior, Akron, Ohio; LB—#Canute Curtis, West Va., 6-2, 250, Senior, Amityville, N. Y.; LB—Pat Fitzgerald, Northwestern, 6-2, 243, Senior, Orland Park, Ill.; LB—Matt Russell, Colorado, 6-2, 245, Senior, Fairview Heights, Ill.; LB—Jarrett Irons, Michigan, 6-2, 234, Senior, The Woodlands, Tex.; DB—*Chris Canty, Kansas St., 5-10, 190, Junior, Voorhees, N. J.; DB—*Kevin Jackson, Alabama, 6-2, 206, Senior, Dothan, Ala.; DB—Dre' Bly, North Caro., 5-10, 180, Freshman, Chesapeake, Va.; DB—Shawn Springs, Ohio St., 6-0, 188, Junior, Silver Spring, Md.; P—Brad Maynard, Ball St., 6-1, 176, Senior, Atlanta, Ind.

1997

The 26-man NCAA Consensus All-America Football Team in 1997 features 13 players on both offense and defense. The players listed had the majority of votes competing against players at that position only. Three first-team votes were considered the minimum number required of the six teams available. One position had a tie and both players are listed. Four players were unanimous choices by all six teams used in the consensus chart—Associated Press, Football Writers Association of America, American Football Coaches Association, Walter Camp Foundation, The Football News and The Sporting News.

Offense WR—*Randy Moss, Marshall, 6-5, 210, Sophomore, Rand, West Va.; WR—Jacquez Green, Florida, 5-9, 168, Junior, Ft. Valley, Ga.; TE—Alonzo Mayes, Oklahoma St., 6-6, 265, Senior, Oklahoma City, Okla.; OL—***Aaron Taylor, Nebraska, 6-1, 305, Senior, Wichita Falls, Tex.;** OL—Alan Faneca, LSU, 6-5, 310, Junior, Rosenberg, Tex.; OL—Kyle Turley, San Diego St., 6-6, 305, Senior, Moreno Valley, Cal.; OL—Chad Overhauser, UCLA, 6-6, 304, Senior, Sacramento, Cal.; C—Olin Kreutz, Washington, 6-4, 290, Junior, Honolulu, Hawaii; QB—Peyton Manning, Tennessee, 6-5, 222, Senior, New Orleans, La.; RB—*Ricky Williams, Texas, 6-0, 220, Junior, San Diego, Cal.; RB—Curtis Enis, Penn St., 6-1, 233, Junior, Union City, Ohio; PK—Martin Gramatica, Kansas St., 5-9, 170, Junior, Buenos Aires, Argentina; KR—Tim Dwight, Iowa, 5-9, 185, Senior, Iowa City, Iowa.

Defense DL—Grant Wistrom, Nebraska, 6-5, 255, Senior, Webb City, Mo.; DL—Andre Wadsworth, Florida St., 6-4, 282, Senior, Miami, Fla.; DL—Greg Ellis, North Caro., 6-6, 265, Senior, Wendell, N.C.; DL—Jason Peter, Nebraska, 6-5, 285, Senior, Locust, N.J.; LB—Andy Katzenmoyer, Ohio St., 6-4, 260, Sophomore, Westerville, Ohio; LB—Sam Cowart, Florida St., 6-3, 239, Senior, Jacksonville, Fla.; LB—Anthony Simmons, Clemson, 6-1, 225, Junior, Spartanburg, S.C.; LB—Brian Simmons, North Caro., 6-4, 230, Senior, New Bern, N.C.; DB—*Charles Woodson, Michigan, 6-1, 198, Junior, Fremont, Ohio; DB—**Dre' Bly, North Caro., 5-10, 185, Sophomore, Chesapeake, Va.;** DB—Fred Weary, Florida, 5-10, 180, Senior, Jacksonville, Fla.; DB—Brian Lee, Wyoming, 6-2, 200, Senior, Arvada, Colo.; P—Chad Kessler, LSU, 6-1, 197, Senior, Longwood, Fla.

**Indicates unanimous selection. Boldface indicates consensus repeater from 1996.*

Other First-Team Selections: Offense QB—Ryan Leaf, Washington St.; RB—Skip Hicks, UCLA; Ron Dayne, Wisconsin; WR—Jerome Pathon, Washington; Bobby Shaw, California; Brian Alford, Purdue; TE—Jerame Tuman, Michigan; C—Kevin Long, Florida St.; Ben Fricke, Houston; OL—Benji Olson, Washington; Flozell Adams, Michigan St.; Matt Stinchcomb, Georgia; Victor Riley, Auburn; Rob Murphy, Ohio St.; PK—Chris Sailer, UCLA. **Defense:** DL—Lemanzer Williams, Minnesota; Jeremy Staat, Arizona St.; Glen Steele, Michigan; Kailee Wong,

Stanford; LB—Jamie Duncan, Vanderbilt; Leonard Little, Tennessee; Takeo Spikes, Auburn; Pat Tillman, Arizona St.; Ron Warner, Kansas; DB—Antoine Winfield, Ohio St.; Donovin Darius, Syracuse; Anthony Poindexter, Virginia; P—Chris Sailer, UCLA.

Other Notes: *Seven players missed being picked to all six teams by one vote (Peyton Manning, Alonzo Mayes, Alan Faneca, Grant Wistrom, Andre Wadsworth, Andy Katzenmoyer and Chad Kessler). Twenty-seven non-consensus players received at least one first-team vote on one of the six all-America teams used by the NCAA resulting in a 53-man All-American roster (UCLA's Chris Sailer had votes at both punter and placekicker). Nebraska's Grant Wistrom and Aaron Taylor as well as North Carolina's Dre' Bly are repeaters from the 1996 Consensus all-America squad.*

Consensus All-Americans by College

Beginning in 1924, unanimous selections are indicated by (*).

AIR FORCE
58— Brock Strom, T
70— Ernie Jennings, E
85— Scott Thomas, DB
87— *Chad Hennings, DL
92— *Carlton McDonald, DB

ALABAMA
30— *Fred Sington, T
34— Don Hutson, E
Bill Lee, T
Dixie Howell, B
35— Riley Smith, B
37— Leroy Monsky, G
41— Holt Rast, E
42— Joe Domnanovich, C
45— Vaughn Mancha, C
61— *Billy Neighbors, T
62— *Lee Roy Jordan, C
65— Paul Crane, C
66— Ray Perkins, E
*Cecil Dowdy, T
67— Dennis Homan, E
Bobby Johns, DB
71— Johnny Musso, B
72— *John Hannah, G
73— Buddy Brown, G
74— Leroy Cook, DL
Woodrow Lowe, LB
75— *Leroy Cook, DE
77— Ozzie Newsome, WR
78— Marty Lyons, DL
79— Jim Bunch, T
80— *E. J. Junior, DL
81— Tommy Wilcox, DB
82— Mike Pitts, DL
86— *Cornelius Bennett, LB
88— *Derrick Thomas, LB
89— *Keith McCants, LB
90— *Philip Doyle, PK
92— John Copeland, DL
Eric Curry, DL
93— David Palmer, KR
*Antonio Langham, DB
96— *Kevin Jackson, DB

AMHERST
05— John Hubbard, B

ARIZONA
82— Ricky Hunley, LB
83— *Ricky Hunley, LB
87— Chuck Cecil, DB
90— *Darryll Lewis, DB
92— Rob Waldrop, DL
93— *Rob Waldrop, DL
94— Steve McLaughlin, PK
Tedy Bruschi, DL
Tony Bouie, DB
95— *Tedy Bruschi, DL

ARIZONA ST.
72— Woody Green, B
73— Woody Green, B
77— John Jefferson, WR
78— *Al Harris, DL
81— Mike Richardson, DB
82— Mike Richardson, DB
Vernon Maxwell, DL
83— Luis Zendejas, PK
84— David Fulcher, DB
85— David Fulcher, DB
86— Danny Villa, OL
87— Randall McDaniel, OL
96— Juan Rogue, OL
Derrick Rodgers, DL

ARKANSAS
48— Clyde Scott, B
54— *Bud Brooks, G
65— Glen Ray Hines, T
Loyd Phillips, DT
66— *Loyd Phillips, DT
68— Jim Barnes, G
69— Rodney Brand, C
70— Dick Bumpas, DT
77— Leotis Harris, G
Steve Little, K
79— *Greg Kolenda, T
81— *Billy Ray Smith, DL
82— *Billy Ray Smith, DL
*Steve Korte, OL
88— Kendall Trainor, PK
Wayne Martin, DL
89— Jim Mabry, OL

ARMY
1898— Charles Romeyn, B
1900— William Smith, E
01— Paul Bunker, T
Charles Daly, B
02— Paul Bunker, T-B
Robert Boyers, C
04— Arthur Tipton, C
Henry Torney, B
05— Henry Torney, B
07— William Erwin, G
11— Leland Devore, T
13— Louis Merillat, E
14— John McEwan, C
16— Elmer Oliphant, B
17— Elmer Oliphant, B
22— Ed Garbisch, C
26— Bud Sprague, T
27— Red Cagle, B
28— *Red Cagle, B
29— Red Cagle, B
32— Milt Summerfelt, G
43— *Casimir Myslinski, C
44— Glenn Davis, B
Doc Blanchard, B
45— Tex Coulter, T
John Green, G
*Glenn Davis, B
*Doc Blanchard, B
46— Hank Foldberg, E
*Glenn Davis, B
*Doc Blanchard, B
47— Joe Steffy, G
49— Arnold Galiffa, B
50— *Dan Foldberg, E
57— Bob Anderson, B
58— *Pete Dawkins, B
59— Bill Carpenter, E

AUBURN
32— Jimmy Hitchcock, B
57— *Jimmy Phillips, E
58— Zeke Smith, G
60— Ken Rice, T
64— Tucker Frederickson, B
69— Buddy McClinton, DB
70— Larry Willingham, DB
71— *Pat Sullivan, QB
*Terry Beasley, E
74— Ken Bernich, LB
83— Bo Jackson, RB
84— Gregg Carr, LB
85— *Bo Jackson, RB
86— *Ben Tamburello, C
*Brent Fullwood, RB
87— Tracy Rocker, DL
Aundray Bruce, LB
88— *Tracy Rocker, DL

90— *Ed King, OL
David Rocker, DL
93— Wayne Gandy, OL
Terry Daniel, P
94— Brian Robinson, DB

BALL ST.
95— Brad Maynard, P
96— Brad Maynard, P

BAYLOR
30— Barton Koch, G
56— *Bill Glass, G
63— Lawrence Elkins, E
64— Lawrence Elkins, B
76— Gary Green, DB
79— Mike Singletary, LB
80— *Mike Singletary, LB
86— *Thomas Everett, DB
91— *Santana Dotson, DL

BOSTON COLLEGE
20— Luke Urban, E
40— Gene Goodreault, E
42— Mike Holovak, B
84— *Doug Flutie, QB
Tony Thurman, DB
85— Mike Ruth, DL
94— Pete Mitchell, TE

BRIGHAM YOUNG
79— *Marc Wilson, QB
80— Nick Eyre, OL
81— *Jim McMahon, QB
82— *Gordon Hudson, TE
83— *Gordon Hudson, TE
*Steve Young, QB
86— Jason Buck, DL
89— Mohammed Elewonibi, OL
90— Ty Detmer, QB
*Chris Smith, TE
91— Ty Detmer, QB

BROWN
02— Thomas Barry, B
06— John Mayhew, B
09— Adrian Regnier, E
10— Earl Sprackling, B
12— George Crowther, B
16— Fritz Pollard, B

CALIFORNIA
21— Brick Muller, E
Dan McMillan, T
22— Brick Muller, E
24— Edwin Horrell, C
28— Irv Phillips, E
30— Ted Beckett, G
35— Larry Lutz, T
37— Sam Chapman, B
38— Vic Bottari, B
48— Jackie Jensen, B
49— *Rod Franz, G
50— Les Richter, G
51— Les Richter, G
68— Ed White, MG
71— Sherman White, DT
74— Steve Bartkowski, QB
75— Chuck Muncie, RB
Steve Rivera, E
83— Ron Rivera, LB
91— Russell White, RB
92— Sean Dawkins, WR
96— Tony Gonzalez, TE

CARLISLE
1899— Isaac Seneca, B
03— James Johnson, B
07— Albert Exendine, E
Peter Hauser, B
11— Jim Thorpe, B
12— Jim Thorpe, B

CARNEGIE MELLON
28— Howard Harpster, B

CENTENARY (LA.)
33— Paul Geisler, E

CENTRE
19— James Weaver, C
Bo McMillin, B
21— Bo McMillin, B

CHICAGO
1898— Clarence Herschberger, B
04— Fred Speik, E
Walter Eckersall, B
05— Mark Catlin, E
Walter Eckersall, B
06— Walter Eckersall, B
08— Walter Steffen, B
13— Paul Des Jardien, C
22— John Thomas, B
24— Joe Pondelik, G
35— *Jay Berwanger, B

CLEMSON
67— Harry Olszewski, G
74— Bennie Cunningham, TE
79— Jim Stuckey, DL
81— Jeff Davis, LB
Terry Kinard, DB
82— *Terry Kinard, DB
83— William Perry, DL
86— Terrence Flagler, RB
87— David Treadwell, PK
88— Donnell Woolford, DB
90— Stacy Long, OL
91— Jeb Flesch, OL
Levon Kirkland, LB
93— Stacy Seegars, OL
97— Anthony Simmons, LB

COLGATE
13— Ellery Huntington, B
16— Clarence Horning, T
D. Belford West, T
Oscar Anderson, B
19— D. Belford West, T
30— Leonard Macaluso, B

COLORADO
37— Byron White, B
60— Joe Romig, G
61— Joe Romig, G
67— Dick Anderson, DB
68— Mike Montler, G
69— Bob Anderson, B
70— Don Popplewell, C
72— Cullen Bryant, DB
85— Barry Helton, P
86— Barry Helton, P
88— Keith English, P
89— Joe Garten, OL
Alfred Williams, LB
Tom Rouen, P
90— *Eric Bieniemy, RB
*Joe Garten, OL
*Alfred Williams, LB
91— *Jay Leeuwenburg, OL
92— Deon Figures, DB
94— Michael Westbrook, WR
*Rashaan Salaam, RB
Chris Hudson, DB
95— Bryan Stoltenberg, C
96— Matt Russell, LB
Chris Naeole, OL

COLORADO ST.
78— Mike Bell, DL
95— Greg Myers, DB

COLUMBIA
1900— Bill Morley, B
01— Harold Weekes, B
Bill Morley, B
03— Richard Smith, B
42— Paul Governali, B
47— Bill Swiacki, E

CORNELL
1895— Clinton Wyckoff, B
1900— Raymond Starbuck, B
01— William Warner, G
Sanford Hunt, G
02— William Warner, G
06— Elmer Thompson, G
William Newman, C
08— Bernard O'Rourke, G
14— John O'Hearn, E
Charles Barrett, B
15— Murray Shelton, E
Charles Barrett, B
21— Edgar Kaw, B
22— Edgar Kaw, B
23— George Pfann, B
38— Brud Holland, E
39— Nick Drahos, T
40— Nick Drahos, T
71— *Ed Marinaro, B

DARTMOUTH
03— Henry Hooper, C
Myron Witham, B
04— Joseph Gilman, G
05— Ralph Glaze, E
08— George Schildmiller, E
Clark Tobin, G
12— Wesley Englehorn, T
13— Robert Hogsett, E
14— Clarence Spears, G
15— Clarence Spears, G
17— Eugene Neely, G
19— Adolph Youngstrom, G
24— Carl Diehl, G
25— Carl Diehl, G
George Tully, E
*Andy Oberlander, B
38— Bob MacLeod, B

DUKE
33— Fred Crawford, T
36— Ace Parker, B
71— Ernie Jackson, DB
89—*Clarkston Hines, WR

DUQUESNE
36— Mike Basrak, C

EAST CARO.
83— Terry Long, OL
91—*Robert Jones, LB

FLORIDA
66—*Steve Spurrier, B
69— Carlos Alvarez, E
75— Sammy Green, LB
80— David Little, LB
82— Wilber Marshall, DL
83— Wilber Marshall, LB
84— Lomas Brown, OT
88— Louis Oliver, DB
89—*Emmitt Smith, RB
91— Brad Culpepper, DL
94— Jack Jackson, WR
Kevin Carter, DL
95—*Jason Odom, OL
96— Danny Wuerffel, QB
Ike Hilliard, WR
Reidel Anthony, WR
97— Jacquez Green, WR
Fred Weary, DB

FLORIDA ST.
64— Fred Biletnikoff, E
67— Ron Sellers, E
79— Ron Simmons, MG
80— Ron Simmons, MG
83— Greg Allen, RB
85— Jamie Dukes, OL
87—*Deion Sanders, DB
88—*Deion Sanders, DB
89— LeRoy Butler, DB
91—*Terrell Buckley, DB
Marvin Jones, LB
92—*Marvin Jones, LB
93—*Charlie Ward, QB
*Derrick Brooks, LB
Corey Sawyer, DB
94— Derrick Brooks, LB
Clifton Abraham, DB
95— Clay Shiver, C
96— Peter Boulware, DL
Reinard Wilson, DL
97— Andre Wadsworth, DL
Sam Cowart, LB

FORDHAM
36— Alex Wojciechowicz, C
37— Ed Franco, T
Alex Wojciechowicz, C

GEORGETOWN
26— Harry Connaughton, G

GEORGIA
27— Tom Nash, E
31— Vernon Smith, E
41— Frank Sinkwich, B
42—*Frank Sinkwich, B
46—*Charley Trippi, B
67— Ed Chandler, T
68— Bill Stanfill, DT
Jake Scott, DB
71—*Royce Smith, G
75— Randy Johnson, G
76— Joel Parrish, G
80—*Herschel Walker, RB
81—*Herschel Walker, RB
82—*Herschel Walker, RB
Terry Hoage, DB
83— Terry Hoage, DB
84— Kevin Butler, PK
Jeff Sanchez, DB
85— Pete Anderson, C
88— Tim Worley, RB
92—*Garrison Hearst, RB

GEORGIA TECH
17— Everett Strupper, B
18— Bill Fincher, E
Joe Guyon, T
Ashel Day, C
20— Bill Fincher, E
28— Pete Pund, C
42— Harvey Hardy, G
44— Phil Tinsley, E
46— Paul Duke, C
47— Bob Davis, T
52— Hal Miller, T
53— Larry Morris, C
59— Maxie Baughan, C
66— Jim Breland, C
70— Rock Perdoni, DT
73— Randy Rhino, DB
90—*Ken Swilling, DB

HARVARD
1889— Arthur Cumnock, E
John Cranston, G
James Lee, B
1890— Frank Hallowell, E
Marshall Newell, T
John Cranston, C
Dudley Dean, B
John Corbett, B
1891— Marshall Newell, T
Everett Lake, B
1892— Frank Hallowell, E
Marshall Newell, T
Bertram Waters, G
William Lewis, C
Charles Brewer, B
1893— Marshall Newell, T
William Lewis, C
Charles Brewer, B
1894— Bertram Waters, T
1895— Norman Cabot, E
Charles Brewer, B
1896— Norman Cabot, E
Edgar Wrightington, B
1897— Alan Doucette, C
Benjamin Dibblee, B
1898— John Hallowell, E
Walter Boal, G
Charles Daly, B
Benjamin Dibblee, B
1899— David Campbell, E
Charles Daly, B
1900— John Hallowell, E
David Campbell, E
Charles Daly, B
01— David Campbell, E
Edward Bowditch, E
Oliver Cutts, T
Crawford Blagden, T
William Lee, G
Charles Barnard, G
Robert Kernan, B
Thomas Graydon, B
02— Edward Bowditch, E
Thomas Graydon, B
03— Daniel Knowlton, T
Andrew Marshall, G
04— Daniel Hurley, B
05— Beaton Squires, T
Karl Brill, T
Francis Burr, G
Daniel Hurley, B
06— Charles Osborne, T
Francis Burr, G
07— Patrick Grant, C
John Wendell, B
08— Hamilton Fish, T
Charles Nourse, C
Hamilton Corbett, B
09— Hamilton Fish, T
Wayland Minot, B
10— Robert McKay, T
Robert Fisher, G
Percy Wendell, B
11— Robert Fisher, G
Percy Wendell, B
12— Samuel Felton, E
Stanley Pennock, G
Charles Brickley, B
13— Harvey Hitchcock, T
Stanley Pennock, G
Charles Brickley, B
Edward Mahan, B
14— Huntington Hardwick, E
Walter Trumbull, T
Stanley Pennock, G
Edward Mahan, B
15— Joseph Gilman, T
Edward Mahan, B
Richard King, B
16— Harrie Dadmun, G
19— Edward Casey, B
20— Tom Woods, G
21— John Brown, G
22— Charles Hubbard, G
23— Charles Hubbard, G
29— Ben Ticknor, C
30—*Ben Ticknor, C
31— Barry Wood, B
41—*Endicott Peabody, G

HOLY CROSS
74— John Provost, DB

HOUSTON
67— Rich Stotter, G
69— Bill Bridges, G
70— Elmo Wright, E
76— Wilson Whitley, DT
80— Leonard Mitchell, DL
88— Jason Phillips, WR
89— Andre Ware, QB

ILLINOIS
14— Perry Graves, E
Ralph Chapman, G
15— Bart Macomber, B
18— John Depler, C
20— Charles Carney, E
23— James McMillen, G
Red Grange, B
24—*Red Grange, B
25— Red Grange, B
26— Bernie Shively, G
46— Alex Agase, G
51— Johnny Karras, B
53— J. C. Caroline, B
59— Bill Burrell, G
63—*Dick Butkus, C
64— Dick Butkus, C
65—*Jim Grabowski, B
84—*David Williams, WR
85—*David Williams, WR
89—*Moe Gardner, DL
90— Moe Gardner, DL
94—*Dana Howard, LB
95— Kevin Hardy, LB

INDIANA
42— Billy Hillenbrand, B
44— John Tavener, C
45— Bob Ravensberg, E
88— Anthony Thompson, RB
89—*Anthony Thompson, RB
91—*Vaughn Dunbar, RB

IOWA
19— Lester Belding, E
21— Aubrey Devine, B
22— Gordon Locke, B
39— Nile Kinnick, B
54— Calvin Jones, G
55— Calvin Jones, G
57— Alex Karras, T
58—*Randy Duncan, B
81— Andre Tippett, DL
Reggie Roby, P
84— Larry Station, LB
85—*Chuck Long, QB
*Larry Station, LB
88— Marv Cook, TE
91— Leroy Smith, DL
97— Tim Dwight, KR

IOWA ST.
38— Ed Bock, G
89— Mike Busch, TE
95— Troy Davis, RB
96— Troy Davis, RB

KANSAS
63— Gale Sayers, B
64— Gale Sayers, B
68— John Zook, DE
73— David Jaynes, QB

KANSAS ST.
77— Gary Spani, LB
92— Sean Snyder, P
95— Chris Canty, DB
96—*Chris Canty, DB
97— Martin Gramatica, PK

KENTUCKY
50— Bob Gain, T
Babe Parilli, B
51— Babe Parilli, B
56— Lou Michaels, T
57— Lou Michaels, T
65— Sam Ball, T
77—*Art Still, DL

LAFAYETTE
1900— Walter Bachman, C
01— Walter Bachman, C
21— Frank Schwab, G
22— Frank Schwab, G

LSU
35— Gaynell Tinsley, E
36—*Gaynell Tinsley, E
39— Ken Kavanaugh, E
54— Sid Fournet, T
58—*Billy Cannon, B
59— Billy Cannon, B
61—*Roy Winston, G
62—*Jerry Stovall, B
70— Mike Anderson, LB
Tommy Casanova, DB
71— Tommy Casanova, DB
72— Bert Jones, QB
77— Charles Alexander, RB
78— Charles Alexander, RB
87— Wendell Davis, WR
*Nacho Albergamo, C
97— Alan Faneca, OL
Chad Kessler, P

LOUISIANA TECH
92— Willie Roaf, OL

MARQUETTE
36— Ray Buivid, B

MARSHALL
97—*Randy Moss, WR

MARYLAND
51—*Bob Ward, G
52— Dick Modzelewski, T
*Jack Scarbath, B
53—*Stan Jones, T
55—*Bob Pellegrini, C
61— Gary Collins, E
74—*Randy White, DL
76— Joe Campbell, DT
79— Dale Castro, PK
85— J. D. Maarleveld, OL

MEMPHIS
92— Joe Allison, PK

MIAMI (FLA.)
61— Bill Miller, E
66— Tom Beier, DB
67—*Ted Hendricks, DE
68—*Ted Hendricks, DE
73— Tony Cristiani, DL
74— Rubin Carter, MG
81— Fred Marion, DB
84— Eddie Brown, WR
85— Willie Smith, TE
86—*Vinny Testaverde, QB
*Jerome Brown, DL
Bennie Blades, DB
87—*Daniel Stubbs, DL
*Bennie Blades, DB
88— Steve Walsh, QB
Bill Hawkins, DL
89— Greg Mark, DL
90— Maurice Crum, LB
*Russell Maryland, DL
91— Carlos Huerta, PK
Darryl Williams, DB

92— *Gino Torretta, QB
Micheal Barrow, LB
Ryan McNeil, DB
94— *Warren Sapp, DL

MICHIGAN
1898— William Cunningham, C
1901— Neil Snow, E
03— Willie Heston, B
04— Willie Heston, B
07— Adolph Schulz, C
09— Albert Benbrook, G
10— Stanfield Wells, E
Albert Benbrook, G
13— Miller Pontius, T
Jim Craig, B
14— John Maulbetsch, B
22— Harry Kipke, B
23— Jack Blott, C
25— Bennie Oosterbaan, E
Benny Friedman, B
26— Bennie Oosterbaan, E
Benny Friedman, B
27— *Bennie Oosterbaan, E
28— Otto Pommerening, T
32— *Harry Newman, B
33— Francis Wistert, T
*Chuck Bernard, C
38— *Ralph Heikkinen, G
39— Tom Harmon, B
40— *Tom Harmon, B
41— Bob Westfall, B
42— Albert Wistert, T
Julie Franks, G
43— *Bill Daley, B
47— *Bob Chappuis, B
48— Dick Rifenburg, E
Alvin Wistert, T
49— Alvin Wistert, T
55— Ron Kramer, E
56— *Ron Kramer, E
65— Bill Yearby, DT
66— *Jack Clancy, E
69— *Jim Mandich, E
Tom Curtis, DB
70— Dan Dierdorf, T
71— Reggie McKenzie, G
*Mike Taylor, LB
72— Paul Seymour, T
Randy Logan, DB
73— Dave Gallagher, DL
Dave Brown, DB
74— *Dave Brown, DB
76— Rob Lytle, RB
Mark Donahue, G
77— *Mark Donahue, G
79— Ron Simpkins, LB
81— *Anthony Carter, WR
Ed Muransky, OL
Kurt Becker, OL
82— *Anthony Carter, WR
85— Mike Hammerstein, DL
Brad Cochran, DB
86— Garland Rivers, DB
87— John Elliott, OL
88— John Vitale, C
*Mark Messner, DL
89— *Tripp Welborne, DB
90— *Tripp Welborne, DB
91— *Desmond Howard, WR
*Greg Skrepenak, OL
96— Jarrett Irons, LB
97— *Charles Woodson, DB

MICHIGAN ST.
15— Neno Jerry DaPrato, B
35— Sidney Wagner, G
49— Ed Bagdon, G
51— Bob Carey, E
*Don Coleman, T
53— Don Dohoney, E
55— Norman Masters, T
Earl Morrall, B
57— Dan Currie, C
Walt Kowalczyk, B
58— Sam Williams, E
62— George Saimes, B
63— Sherman Lewis, B
65— Bubba Smith, DE
*George Webster, DB
66— Clint Jones, B
*Bubba Smith, DE
*George Webster, DB
72— *Brad VanPelt, DB
85— *Lorenzo White, RB
87— Lorenzo White, RB
88— Tony Mandarich, OL
89— *Percy Snow, LB
Bob Kula, OL

MINNESOTA
03— Fred Schacht, T
09— John McGovern, B
10— James Walker, T
16— Bert Baston, E
17— George Hauser, T
23— Ray Ecklund, E
26— Herb Joesting, B
27— Herb Joesting, B
29— Bronko Nagurski, T
31— Biggie Munn, G
34— Frank Larson, E
Bill Bevan, G
Pug Lund, B
35— Ed Widseth, T
36— *Ed Widseth, T
40— Urban Odson, T
George Franck, B
41— Dick Wildung, T
Bruce Smith, B
42— Dick Wildung, T
48— Leo Nomellini, T
49— Leo Nomellini, T
*Clayton Tonnemaker, C
53— *Paul Giel, B
60— *Tom Brown, G
61— Sandy Stephens, B
62— *Bobby Bell, T
63— Carl Eller, T
65— Aaron Brown, DE

MISSISSIPPI
47— Charley Conerly, B
53— Crawford Mims, G
59— Charlie Flowers, B
60— *Jake Gibbs, B
62— Jim Dunaway, T
79— Jim Miller, P
92— Everett Lindsay, OL

MISSISSIPPI ST.
74— Jimmy Webb, DL

MISSOURI
41— Darold Jenkins, C
60— *Danny LaRose, E
65— Johnny Roland, DB
68— Roger Wehrli, DB
78— Kellen Winslow, TE
86— John Clay, OL

NAVY
07— Bill Dague, E
08— Percy Northcroft, T
Ed Lange, B
11— Jack Dalton, B
13— John Brown, G
18— Lyman Perry, G
Wolcott Roberts, B
22— Wendell Taylor, T
26— *Frank Wickhorst, T
28— Edward Burke, G
34— Fred Borries, B
43— Don Whitmire, T
44— *Don Whitmire, T
Ben Chase, G
Bob Jenkins, B
45— Dick Duden, E
54— Ron Beagle, E
55— *Ron Beagle, E
60— *Joe Bellino, B
63— *Roger Staubach, B
75— *Chet Moeller, DB
83— Napoleon McCallum, RB
85— Napoleon McCallum, RB

NEBRASKA
15— Guy Chamberlin, E
24— Ed Weir, T
25— *Ed Weir, T
33— George Sauer, B
36— Sam Francis, B
63— *Bob Brown, G
64— *Larry Kramer, T
65— Freeman White, E
Walt Barnes, DT
66— LaVerne Allers, G
Wayne Meylan, MG
67— Wayne Meylan, MG
70— Bob Newton, T
71— Johnny Rodgers, FL
Willie Harper, DE
Larry Jacobson, DT
72— *Johnny Rodgers, FL
Willie Harper, DE
*Rich Glover, MG
73— *John Dutton, DL
74— Marvin Crenshaw, OT
75— *Rik Bonness, C
76— Dave Butterfield, DB
78— Kelvin Clark, OT
79— *Junior Miller, TE
80— Randy Schleusener, OL
Jarvis Redwine, RB
81— *Dave Rimington, C
82— *Dave Rimington, C
Mike Rozier, RB
83— *Irving Fryar, WR
Dean Steinkuhler, OL
*Mike Rozier, RB
84— *Mark Traynowicz, C
86— *Danny Noonan, DL
88— Jake Young, C
*Broderick Thomas, LB
89— Jake Young, C
92— *Will Shields, OL
93— *Trev Alberts, LB
94— *Zach Wiegert, OL
Brenden Stai, OL
Ed Stewart, LB
95— Tommie Frazier, QB
96— Aaron Taylor, C
Grant Wistrom, DL
97— *Aaron Taylor, OL
Grant Wistrom, DL
Jason Peter, DL

NEW MEXICO
89— Terance Mathis, WR

NEW YORK U.
28— Ken Strong, B

NORTH CARO.
37— Andy Bershak, E
48— Charlie Justice, B
70— Don McCauley, B
72— Ron Rusnak, G
74— Ken Huff, G
77— Dee Hardison, DL
80— *Lawrence Taylor, LB
83— William Fuller, DL
95— Marcus Jones, DL
96— Dre' Bly, DB
97— Greg Ellis, DL
Brian Simmons, LB
Dre' Bly, DB

NORTH CARO. ST.
67— Dennis Byrd, DT
73— Bill Yoest, G
78— Jim Ritcher, C
Ted Brown, RB
79— *Jim Ritcher, C
96— Marc Primanti, PK

NORTH TEXAS
68— Joe Greene, DT

NORTHERN ILL.
93— *LeShon Johnson, RB

NORTHWESTERN
26— Ralph Baker, B
30— Frank Baker, E
31— Jack Riley, T
Dallas Marvil, T
Pug Rentner, B
36— Steve Reid, G
40— Alf Bauman, T
45— Max Morris, E
59— Ron Burton, B
62— Jack Cvercko, G
95— Pat Fitzgerald, LB
96— Pat Fitzgerald, LB

NOTRE DAME
13— Gus Dorais, B
17— Frank Rydzewski, C
20— George Gipp, B
21— Eddie Anderson, E
24— Harry Stuhldreher, B
Jimmy Crowley, B
Elmer Layden, B
26— Bud Boeringer, C
27— John Smith, G
29— Jack Cannon, G
*Frank Carideo, B
30— *Frank Carideo, B
Marchy Schwartz, B
31— Tommy Yarr, C
Marchy Schwartz, B
32— *Joe Kurth, T
34— Jack Robinson, C
35— Wayne Millner, E
37— Chuck Sweeney, E
38— *Ed Beinor, T
41— Bob Dove, E
42— Bob Dove, E
43— John Yonakor, E
Jim White, T
Pat Filley, G
Angelo Bertelli, B
Creighton Miller, B
46— George Connor, T
*John Lujack, B
47— George Connor, T
Bill Fischer, G
*John Lujack, B
48— Leon Hart, E
Bill Fischer, G
Emil Sitko, B
49— *Leon Hart, E
*Emil Sitko, B
Bob Williams, B
50— Jerry Groom, C
52— *Johnny Lattner, B
53— Art Hunter, T
*Johnny Lattner, B
54— *Ralph Guglielmi, B
55— Paul Hornung, B
57— Al Ecuyer, G
59— Monty Stickles, E
64— Jack Snow, E
John Huarte, B
65— *Dick Arrington, G
Nick Rassas, B
66— Tom Regner, G
*Nick Eddy, B
Alan Page, DE
*Jim Lynch, LB
67— Tom Schoen, DB
68— George Kunz, T
Terry Hanratty, QB
69— *Mike McCoy, DT
70— Tom Gatewood, E
Larry DiNardo, G
71— *Walt Patulski, DE
Clarence Ellis, DB
72— *Greg Marx, DT
73— Dave Casper, TE
Mike Townsend, DB
74— Pete Demmerle, WR
Gerry DiNardo, G
75— *Steve Niehaus, DT
76— Ken MacAfee, TE
*Ross Browner, DE
77— *Ken MacAfee, TE
*Ross Browner, DL
Luther Bradley, DB
78— Dave Huffman, C
*Bob Golic, LB
79— Vagas Ferguson, RB
80— *John Scully, C
Bob Crable, LB
81— Bob Crable, LB
87— *Tim Brown, WR
88— Frank Stams, DL
Michael Stonebreaker, LB
89— *Todd Lyght, DB
Chris Zorich, DL
90— *Raghib Ismail, WR
Todd Lyght, DB
*Michael Stonebreaker, LB
*Chris Zorich, DL
91— Mirko Jurkovic, OL
92— Aaron Taylor, OL
93— *Aaron Taylor, OL
Jeff Burris, DB
94— Bobby Taylor, DB

OHIO ST.
16— Charles Harley, B

AWARD WINNERS

17— Charles Bolen, E
Charles Harley, B
19— Charles Harley, B
20— Iolas Huffman, G
Gaylord Stinchcomb, B
21— Iolas Huffman, T
25— Ed Hess, G
28— Wes Fesler, E
29— Wes Fesler, E
30—*Wes Fesler, E
35— Gomer Jones, C
39— Esco Sarkkinen, E
44— Jack Dugger, E
Bill Hackett, G
*Les Horvath, B
45—*Warren Amling, G
46— Warren Amling, T
50—*Vic Janowicz, B
54—*Howard Cassady, B
55—*Howard Cassady, B
56—*Jim Parker, G
58— Bob White, B
60—*Bob Ferguson, B
61—*Bob Ferguson, B
68—*Dave Foley, T
69— Jim Otis, B
Jim Stillwagon, MG
Jack Tatum, DB
70—*Jim Stillwagon, MG
*Jack Tatum, DB
72— Randy Gradishar, LB
73—*John Hicks, OT
*Randy Gradishar, LB
74— Kurt Schumacher, OT
Steve Myers, C
*Archie Griffin, RB
75—*Archie Griffin, RB
Ted Smith, G
Tim Fox, DB
76— Chris Ward, T
Bob Brudzinski, DE
77—*Chris Ward, T
Tom Cousineau, LB
78— Tom Cousineau, LB
79— Ken Fritz, G
82— Marcus Marek, LB
84— Jim Lachey, OG
*Keith Byars, RB
86— Cris Carter, WR
Chris Spielman, LB
87—*Chris Spielman, LB
*Tom Tupa, P
93— Dan Wilkinson, DL
94— Korey Stringer, OL
95— Terry Glenn, WR
*Orlando Pace, OL
*Eddie George, RB
96—*Orlando Pace, OL
Mike Vrabel, DL
Shawn Springs, DB
97— Andy Katzenmoyer, LB

OKLAHOMA
38— Waddy Young, E
48— Buddy Burris, G
50— Jim Weatherall, T
Leon Heath, B
51—*Jim Weatherall, T
52— Billy Vessels, B
53— J. D. Roberts, G
54— Max Boydston, E
Kurt Burris, C
55— Bo Bolinger, G
56—*Jerry Tubbs, C
Tommy McDonald, B
57— Bill Krisher, G
Clendon Thomas, B
58— Bob Harrison, C
63— Jim Grisham, B
64— Ralph Neely, T
65— Carl McAdams, LB
67—*Granville Liggins, MG
69—*Steve Owens, B
71—*Greg Pruitt, B
Tom Brahaney, C
72—*Greg Pruitt, B
Tom Brahaney, C
73—*Lucious Selmon, DL
Rod Shoate, LB
74— John Roush, G
*Joe Washington, RB
*Rod Shoate, LB
75—*Lee Roy Selmon, DT
Dewey Selmon, MG
Jimbo Elrod, DE
76—*Mike Vaughan, OT
77—*Zac Henderson, DB
78—*Greg Roberts, G
*Billy Sims, RB
79—*Billy Sims, RB
*George Cumby, LB
80— Louis Oubre, OL
81— Terry Crouch, OL
82— Rick Bryan, DL
83—*Rick Bryan, DL
84— Tony Casillas, DL
85— Tony Casillas, DL
*Brian Bosworth, LB
86—*Keith Jackson, TE
*Brian Bosworth, LB
87—*Keith Jackson, TE
*Mark Hutson, OL
Dante Jones, LB
Rickey Dixon, DB
88—*Anthony Phillips, OL

OKLAHOMA ST.
45— Bob Fenimore, B
69— John Ward, T
76— Derrel Gofourth, C
77—*Terry Miller, RB
84— Rod Brown, DB
85— Thurman Thomas, RB
*Leslie O'Neal, DL
88— Hart Lee Dykes, WR
*Barry Sanders, RB
97— Alonzo Mayes, TE

OREGON
62— Mel Renfro, B

OREGON ST.
56— John Witte, T
58— Ted Bates, T
62—*Terry Baker, B
63— Vern Burke, E
68—*John Didion, C

PENNSYLVANIA
1891— John Adams, C
1892— Harry Thayer, B
1894— Charles Gelbert, E
Arthur Knipe, B
George Brooke, B
1895— Charles Gelbert, E
Charles Wharton, G
Alfred Bull, C
George Brooke, B
1896— Charles Gelbert, E
Charles Wharton, G
Wylie Woodruff, G
1897— John Outland, T
T. Truxton Hare, G
John Minds, B
1898— T. Truxton Hare, G
Pete Overfield, C
John Outland, B
1899— T. Truxton Hare, G
Pete Overfield, C
Josiah McCracken, B
1900— T. Truxton Hare, G
04— Frank Piekarski, G
Vincent Stevenson, B
Andrew Smith, B
05— Otis Lamson, T
Robert Torrey, C
06— August Ziegler, G
William Hollenback, B
07— Dexter Draper, T
August Ziegler, G
08— Hunter Scarlett, E
William Hollenback, B
10— Ernest Cozens, C
E. LeRoy Mercer, B
12— E. LeRoy Mercer, B
17— Henry Miller, E
19— Henry Miller, E
22— John Thurman, T
24— Ed McGinley, T
27— Ed Hake, T
28— Paul Scull, B
43— Bob Odell, B
45— George Savitsky, T
47— Chuck Bednarik, C
48— Chuck Bednarik, C

PENN ST.
06— William Dunn, C
19— Bob Higgins, E
20— Charles Way, B
21— Glenn Killinger, B
23— Harry Wilson, B
59— Richie Lucas, B
64— Glenn Ressler, G
68—*Ted Kwalick, E
Dennis Onkotz, LB
69—*Mike Reid, DT
Dennis Onkotz, LB
70— Jack Ham, LB
71— Dave Joyner, T
72— Bruce Bannon, DE
John Skorupan, LB
73—*John Cappelletti, B
74— Mike Hartenstine, DL
75— Greg Buttle, LB
78—*Keith Dorney, OT
*Chuck Fusina, QB
*Bruce Clark, DL
79— Bruce Clark, DL
81—*Sean Farrell, OL
86— D. J. Dozier, RB
Shane Conlan, LB
92— O. J. McDuffie, WR
94— Kerry Collins, QB
*Ki-Jana Carter, RB
95— Jeff Hartings, OL
97— Curtis Enis, RB

PITTSBURGH
15— Robert Peck, C
16— James Herron, E
Robert Peck, C
17— Dale Seis, G
John Sutherland, G
18— Leonard Hilty, T
Tom Davies, B
George McLaren, B
20— Herb Stein, C
21— Herb Stein, C
25— Ralph Chase, T
27—*Gibby Welch, B
28— Mike Getto, T
29—*Joe Donchess, E
Ray Montgomery, G
31— Jesse Quatse, T
32— Joe Skladany, E
*Warren Heller, B
33— Joe Skladany, E
34— Chuck Hartwig, G
36— Averell Daniell, T
37— Tony Matisi, T
Marshall Goldberg, B
38—*Marshall Goldberg, B
56—*Joe Walton, E
58— John Guzik, G
60—*Mike Ditka, E
63— Paul Martha, B
76—*Tony Dorsett, RB
Al Romano, MG
77— Tom Brzoza, C
Randy Holloway, DL
Bob Jury, DB
78— Hugh Green, DL
79—*Hugh Green, DL
80—*Hugh Green, DL
*Mark May, OL
81— Sal Sunseri, LB
82— Jimbo Covert, OL
83—*Bill Fralic, OL
84—*Bill Fralic, OT
86— Randy Dixon, OL
Tony Woods, DL
87— Craig Heyward, RB
88— Mark Stepnoski, OL
90— Brian Greenfield, P

PRINCETON
1889— Hector Cowan, T
William George, C
Edgar Allan Poe, B
Roscoe Channing, B
Knowlton Ames, B
1890— Ralph Warren, E
Jesse Riggs, G
Sheppard Homans, B
1891— Jesse Riggs, G
Philip King, B
Sheppard Homans, B
1892— Arthur Wheeler, G
Philip King, B
1893— Thomas Trenchard, E
Langdon Lea, T
Arthur Wheeler, G
Philip King, B
Franklin Morse, B
1894— Langdon Lea, T
Arthur Wheeler, G
1895— Langdon Lea, T
Dudley Riggs, G
1896— William Church, T
Robert Gailey, C
Addison Kelly, B
John Baird, B
1897— Garrett Cochran, E
Addison Kelly, B
1898— Lew Palmer, E
Arthur Hillebrand, T
1899— Arthur Hillebrand, T
Arthur Poe, E
Howard Reiter, B
1901— Ralph Davis, E
02— John DeWitt, G
03— Howard Henry, E
John DeWitt, G
J. Dana Kafer, B
04— James Cooney, T
05— James McCormick, B
06— L. Casper Wister, E
James Cooney, T
Edward Dillon, B
07— L. Casper Wister, E
Edwin Harlan, B
James McCormick, B
08— Frederick Tibbott, B
10— Talbot Pendleton, B
11— Sanford White, E
Edward Hart, T
Joseph Duff, G
12— John Logan, G
13— Harold Ballin, T
14— Harold Ballin, T
16— Frank Hogg, G
18— Frank Murrey, B
20— Stan Keck, T
Donold Lourie, B
21— Stan Keck, G
22— C. Herbert Treat, T
25— Ed McMillan, C
35— John Weller, G
51—*Dick Kazmaier, B
52— Frank McPhee, E
65— Stas Maliszewski, G

PURDUE
29— Elmer Sleight, T
Ralph Welch, B
32—*Paul Moss, E
33— Duane Purvis, B
40— Dave Rankin, E
43— Alex Agase, G
52— Bernie Flowers, E
65— Bob Griese, QB
67—*Leroy Keyes, B
68—*Leroy Keyes, B
Chuck Kyle, MG
69—*Mike Phipps, QB
72— Otis Armstrong, B
Dave Butz, DT
80—*Dave Young, TE
*Mark Herrmann, QB
86— Rod Woodson, DB

RICE
46— Weldon Humble, G
49— James Williams, E
54— Dicky Maegle, B
58— Buddy Dial, E
76— Tommy Kramer, QB
91— Trevor Cobb, RB

RICHMOND
69— Walker Gillette, E
78— Jeff Nixon, DB

RUTGERS
17— Paul Robeson, E
18— Paul Robeson, E
61— Alex Kroll, C
95—*Marco Battaglia, TE

ST. MARY'S (CAL.)
27— Larry Bettencourt, C

45— *Herman Wedemeyer, B

SAN DIEGO ST.
92— *Marshall Faulk, RB
93— *Marshall Faulk, RB
97— Kyle Turley, OL

SANTA CLARA
38— Alvord Wolff, T
39— John Schiechl, C

SOUTH CARO.
80— *George Rogers, RB
84— Del Wilkes, OG

SOUTHERN CAL
26— Mort Kaer, B
27— Jesse Hibbs, T
Morley Drury, B
30— Erny Pinckert, B
31— John Baker, G
Gus Shaver, B
32— *Ernie Smith, T
33— Aaron Rosenberg, G
*Cotton Warburton, B
39— *Harry Smith, G
43— Ralph Heywood, E
44— John Ferraro, T
47— Paul Cleary, E
52— Elmer Willhoite, G
Jim Sears, B
62— Hal Bedsole, E
65— *Mike Garrett, B
66— Ron Yary, T
Nate Shaw, DB
67— *Ron Yary, T
*O. J. Simpson, B
Tim Rossovich, DE
Adrian Young, LB
68— *O. J. Simpson, B
69— Jim Gunn, DE
70— Charlie Weaver, DE
72— *Charles Young, TE
73— Lynn Swann, WR
Booker Brown, OT
Richard Wood, LB
Artimus Parker, DB
74— *Anthony Davis, RB
Richard Wood, LB
75— *Ricky Bell, RB
76— *Ricky Bell, RB
Gary Jeter, DT
Dennis Thurman, DB
77— *Dennis Thurman, DB
78— *Pat Howell, G
*Charles White, RB
79— *Brad Budde, G
*Charles White, RB
80— Keith Van Horne, OL
*Ronnie Lott, DB
81— Roy Foster, OL
*Marcus Allen, RB
82— *Don Mosebar, OL
Bruce Matthews, OL
George Achica, MG
83— Tony Slaton, C
84— Jack Del Rio, LB
85— Jeff Bregel, OL
86— Jeff Bregel, OL
Tim McDonald, DB
87— Dave Cadigan, OL
89— *Mark Carrier, DB
Tim Ryan, DL
93— Johnnie Morton, WR
94— Tony Boselli, OL
95— *Keyshawn Johnson, WR

SOUTHERN METHODIST
35— J. C. Wetsel, G
Bobby Wilson, B
47— Doak Walker, B
48— *Doak Walker, B
49— Doak Walker, B
50— Kyle Rote, B
51— Dick Hightower, C
66— John LaGrone, MG
68— Jerry LeVias, E
72— Robert Popelka, DB
74— Louie Kelcher, G
78— Emanuel Tolbert, WR
80— John Simmons, DB
82— *Eric Dickerson, RB
83— *Russell Carter, DB
85— Reggie Dupard, RB

STANFORD
24— Jim Lawson, E
25— Ernie Nevers, B
28— Seraphim Post, G
Don Robesky, G
32— Bill Corbus, G
33— Bill Corbus, G
34— Bob Reynolds, T
Bobby Grayson, B
35— James Moscrip, E
*Bobby Grayson, B
40— Frank Albert, B
41— Frank Albert, B
42— Chuck Taylor, G
50— Bill McColl, E
51— *Bill McColl, E
56— John Brodie, QB
70— Jim Plunkett, QB
71— Jeff Siemon, LB
74— Pat Donovan, DL
77— Guy Benjamin, QB
79— Ken Margerum, WR
80— *Ken Margerum, WR
82— *John Elway, QB
86— Brad Muster, RB
91— Bob Whitfield, OL

SYRACUSE
08— Frank Horr, T
15— Harold White, G
17— Alfred Cobb, T
18— Lou Usher, T
Joe Alexander, G
19— Joe Alexander, G
23— Pete McRae, E
26— Vic Hanson, E
56— *Jim Brown, B
59— *Roger Davis, G
60— Ernie Davis, B
61— *Ernie Davis, B
67— *Larry Csonka, B
85— *Tim Green, DL
87— *Don McPherson, QB
Ted Gregory, DL
90— John Flannery, C
92— *Chris Gedney, TE

TEMPLE
85— John Rienstra, OL
86— *Paul Palmer, RB

TENNESSEE
29— Gene McEver, B
33— Beattie Feathers, B
38— Bowden Wyatt, E
39— Ed Molinski, G
George Cafego, B
40— *Bob Suffridge, G
46— Dick Huffman, T
51— *Hank Lauricella, B
52— John Michels, G
56— *John Majors, B
65— Frank Emanuel, LB
66— Paul Naumoff, LB
67— *Bob Johnson, C
68— *Charles Rosenfelder, G
Steve Kiner, LB
69— Chip Kell, G
*Steve Kiner, LB
70— *Chip Kell, G
71— *Bobby Majors, DB
75— Larry Seivers, E
76— Larry Seivers, SE
79— Roland James, DB
83— *Reggie White, DL
84— Bill Mayo, OG
85— Tim McGee, WR
89— *Eric Still, OL
90— *Antone Davis, OL
91— Dale Carter, DB
97— Peyton Manning, QB

TEXAS
45— Hubert Bechtol, E
46— Hubert Bechtol, E
47— Bobby Layne, B
50— *Bud McFadin, G
53— Carlton Massey, E
61— *Jimmy Saxton, B
62— *Johnny Treadwell, G
63— *Scott Appleton, T
65— Tommy Nobis, LB
68— Chris Gilbert, B
69— Bob McKay, T
70— Bobby Wuensch, T
Steve Worster, B
Bill Atessis, DE
71— *Jerry Sisemore, T
72— *Jerry Sisemore, T
73— *Bill Wyman, C
Roosevelt Leaks, B
75— Bob Simmons, T
77— *Earl Campbell, RB
*Brad Shearer, DL
78— *Johnnie Johnson, DB
79— *Steve McMichael, DL
*Johnnie Johnson, DB
80— Kenneth Sims, DL
81— Terry Tausch, OL
*Kenneth Sims, DL
83— Doug Dawson, OL
Jeff Leiding, LB
Jerry Gray, DB
84— Tony Degrate, DL
*Jerry Gray, DB
95— Tony Brackens, DL
96— Dan Neil, OL
97— *Ricky Williams, RB

TEXAS A&M
37— Joe Routt, G
39— John Kimbrough, B
40— Marshall Robnett, G
*John Kimbrough, B
57— *John David Crow, B
70— Dave Elmendorf, DB
74— Pat Thomas, DB
75— *Ed Simonini, LB
Pat Thomas, DB
76— Tony Franklin, PK
*Robert Jackson, LB
85— Johnny Holland, LB
87— John Roper, DL
90— Darren Lewis, RB
91— Kevin Smith, DB
92— *Marcus Buckley, LB
93— Aaron Glenn, DB
Sam Adams, DL
94— Leeland McElroy, KR

TEXAS CHRISTIAN
35— Darrell Lester, C
36— Sammy Baugh, B
38— Ki Aldrich, C
*Davey O'Brien, B
55— *Jim Swink, B
59— Don Floyd, T
60— *Bob Lilly, T
84— *Kenneth Davis, RB
91— Kelly Blackwell, TE
95— Michael Reeder, PK

TEXAS TECH
60— E. J. Holub, C
65— Donny Anderson, B
77— Dan Irons, T
82— Gabriel Rivera, DL
91— *Mark Bounds, P
95— *Zach Thomas, LB
96— *Byron Hanspard, RB

TOLEDO
71— Mel Long, DT

TULANE
31— *Jerry Dalrymple, E
32— Don Zimmerman, B
39— Harley McCollum, T
41— Ernie Blandin, T

TULSA
65— *Howard Twilley, E
91— Jerry Ostroski, OL

UCLA
46— *Burr Baldwin, E
52— Donn Moomaw, C
53— Paul Cameron, B
54— Jack Ellena, T
55— Hardiman Cureton, G
57— Dick Wallen, E
66— Mel Farr, B
67— *Gary Beban, B
Don Manning, LB
69— Mike Ballou, LB
73— Kermit Johnson, B
75— John Sciarra, QB
76— Jerry Robinson, LB
77— *Jerry Robinson, LB
78— *Jerry Robinson, LB
Kenny Easley, DB
79— *Kenny Easley, DB
80— *Kenny Easley, DB
81— *Tim Wrightman, TE
83— Don Rogers, DB
85— *John Lee, PK
88— Troy Aikman, QB
Darryl Henley, DB
92— Carlton Gray, DB
93— *J. J. Stokes, WR
Bjorn Merten, PK
Jamir Miller, LB
95— *Jonathan Ogden, OL
97— Chad Overhauser, OL

UTAH
94— Luther Elliss, DL

UTAH ST.
61— Merlin Olsen, T
69— Phil Olsen, DE

VANDERBILT
23— Lynn Bomar, E
24— Henry Wakefield, E
32— Pete Gracey, C
58— George Deiderich, G
82— *Jim Arnold, P
84— *Ricky Anderson, P

VIRGINIA
15— Eugene Mayer, B
41— Bill Dudley, B
85— *Jim Dombrowski, OL
90— Herman Moore, WR
92— Chris Slade, DL
93— Mark Dixon, OL

VIRGINIA TECH
67— Frank Loria, DB
84— Bruce Smith, DL
93— *Jim Pyne, C
95— Cornell Brown, DL

WAKE FOREST
76— *Bill Armstrong, DB

WASH. & JEFF.
14— John Spiegel, B
18— Wilbur Henry, T
19— Wilbur Henry, T

WASHINGTON
25— George Wilson, B
28— Charles Carroll, B
36— Max Starcevich, G
40— Rudy Mucha, C
41— Ray Frankowski, G
63— Rick Redman, G
64— Rick Redman, G
66— Tom Greenlee, DT
68— Al Worley, DB
82— *Chuck Nelson, PK
84— Ron Holmes, DL
86— Jeff Jaeger, PK
Reggie Rogers, DL
91— *Steve Emtman, DL
Mario Bailey, WR
92— *Lincoln Kennedy, OL
95— *Lawyer Milloy, DB
96— Benji Olson, OL
97— Olin Kreutz, C

WASHINGTON ST.
84— Rueben Mayes, RB
88— Mike Utley, OL
89— *Jason Hanson, PK

WEST VA.
19— Ira Rodgers, B
55— Bruce Bosley, T
82— *Darryl Talley, LB
85— Brian Jozwiak, OL
92— Mike Compton, C
94— *Todd Sauerbrun, P
95— Aaron Beasley, DB
96— Canute Curtis, LB

WILLIAMS
17— Ben Boynton, B
19— Ben Boynton, B

WISCONSIN
12— Robert Butler, T
13— Ray Keeler, G
15— Howard Buck, T

19— Charles Carpenter, C
20— Ralph Scott, T
23— Marty Below, T
30— Milo Lubratovich, T
42— *Dave Schreiner, E
54— *Alan Ameche, B
59— *Dan Lanphear, T
62— Pat Richter, E
75— Dennis Lick, T
81— Tim Krumrie, DL
94— Cory Raymer, C

WYOMING
83— Jack Weil, P
84— Jay Novacek, TE
96— Marcus Harris, WR
97— Brian Lee, DB

YALE
1889— Amos Alonzo Stagg, E
Charles Gill, T
Pudge Heffelfinger, G
1890— William Rhodes, T
Pudge Heffelfinger, G
Thomas McClung, B
1891— Frank Hinkey, E
John Hartwell, E
Wallace Winter, T
Pudge Heffelfinger, G
Thomas McClung, B
1892— Frank Hinkey, E
A. Hamilton Wallis, T
Vance McCormick, B
1893— Frank Hinkey, E
William Hickok, G
Frank Butterworth, B
1894— Frank Hinkey, E
William Hickok, G
Philip Stillman, C
George Adee, B
Frank Butterworth, B
1895— Fred Murphy, T
Samuel Thorne, B
1896— Fred Murphy, T
Clarence Fincke, B
1897— John Hall, E
Burr Chamberlin, T
Gordon Brown, G
Charles DeSaulles, B
1898— Burr Chamberlin, T
Gordon Brown, G
Malcolm McBride, B
1899— George Stillman, T
Gordon Brown, G
Malcolm McBride, B
Albert Sharpe, B
1900— George Stillman, T
James Bloomer, T
Gordon Brown, G
Herman Olcott, C
George Chadwick, B
Perry Hale, B
William Fincke, B
01— Henry Holt, C
02— Thomas Shevlin, E
Ralph Kinney, T
James Hogan, T
Edgar Glass, G
Henry Holt, C
Foster Rockwell, B
George Chadwick, B
03— Charles Rafferty, E
James Hogan, T
James Bloomer, G
W. Ledyard Mitchell, B
04— Thomas Shevlin, E
James Hogan, T
Ralph Kinney, G
Foster Rockwell, B
05— Thomas Shevlin, E
Roswell Tripp, G
Howard Roome, B
Guy Hutchinson, B
06— Robert Forbes, E
L. Horatio Biglow, T
Hugh Knox, B
Paul Veeder, B
07— Clarence Alcott, E
L. Horatio Biglow, T
Thomas A. D. Jones, B
Edward Coy, B
08— William Goebel, G
Hamlin Andrus, G
Edward Coy, B
09— John Kilpatrick, E
Henry Hobbs, T
Hamlin Andrus, G
Carroll Cooney, C
Edward Coy, B
Stephen Philbin, B
10— John Kilpatrick, E
11— Douglass Bomeisler, E
Henry Ketcham, C
Arthur Howe, B
12— Douglass Bomeisler, E
Henry Ketcham, C
13— Nelson Talbott, T
14— Harry LeGore, B
16— Clinton Black, G
20— Tim Callahan, G
21— Malcolm Aldrich, B
23— Century Milstead, T
William Mallory, B
24— Dick Luman, E
27— Bill Webster, G
John Charlesworth, C
36— Larry Kelley, E
37— *Clint Frank, B
44— Paul Walker, E

Team Leaders in Consensus All-Americans

(Ranked on Total Number of Selections)

Team	No.	Players
Yale	100	69
Notre Dame	93	77
Harvard	89	59
Michigan	67	55
Princeton	65	49
Ohio St.	62	47
Southern Cal	60	53
Oklahoma	52	43
Nebraska	49	40
Pittsburgh	46	39
Pennsylvania	46	32
Alabama	37	36
Army	37	28
Texas	35	31
Penn St.	30	28
Minnesota	29	25
Tennessee	29	21
UCLA	28	24
Colorado	25	21
Miami (Fla.)	25	23
Stanford	25	20
Michigan St.	24	21
Auburn	23	21
Navy	23	20
Illinois	23	18
California	22	20
Florida St.	22	18
Georgia	21	17
Texas A&M	19	17
Cornell	19	15
Washington	19	18
Syracuse	18	16
Florida	18	17
LSU	18	14
Georgia Tech	17	16
Purdue	17	16
Arkansas	17	15
Dartmouth	17	15
Southern Methodist	16	14
Iowa	16	14
Clemson	15	14
Wisconsin	14	14
Arizona St.	14	11
North Caro.	13	12
Northwestern	12	12
Brigham Young	11	9
Chicago	11	9
Maryland	10	10
Texas Christian	10	10
Arizona	10	7
Oklahoma St.	10	10
Baylor	9	7
West Va.	8	8
Boston College	7	7
Houston	7	7
Mississippi	7	7
Texas Tech	7	7
Kentucky	7	5
Brown	6	6
Missouri	6	6
Rice	6	6
Vanderbilt	6	6
Virginia	6	6
Carlisle	6	5
Colgate	6	5
Col umbia	6	5
Indiana	6	5
North Caro. St.	6	5
Air Force	5	5
Oregon St.	5	5
Kansas St.	5	4

1997 First-Team All-America Teams

AMERICAN FOOTBALL COACHES ASSOCIATION

Offense QB—Peyton Manning, Tennessee; RB—Ricky Williams, Texas; RB—Skip Hicks, UCLA; WR—Randy Moss, Marshall; WR—Jerome Pathon, Washington; TE—Alonzo Mayes, Oklahoma St.; OL—Kyle Turley, San Diego St.; OL—Aaron Taylor, Nebraska; C—Kevin Long, Florida St.; OL—Victor Riley, Auburn; OL—Matt Stinchcomb, Georgia; RS—Tim Dwight, Iowa; PK—Chris Sailer, UCLA.

Defense DL—Grant Wistrom, Nebraska; DL—Andre Wadsworth, Florida St.; DL—Greg Ellis, North Caro.; DL—Glen Steele, Michigan; LB—Andy Katzenmoyer, Ohio St.; LB—Anthony Simmons, Clemson; LB—Jamie Duncan, Vanderbilt; DB—Charles Woodson, Michigan; DB—Donovin Darius, Syracuse; DB—Fred Weary, Florida; DB—Antoine Winfield, Ohio St.; P—Chad Kessler, LSU.

ASSOCIATED PRESS

Offense QB—Peyton Manning, Tennessee; RB—Curtis Enis, Penn St.; RB—Ricky Williams, Texas; WR—Jacquez Green, Florida; WR—Randy Moss, Marshall; TE—Alonzo Mayes, Oklahoma St.; G/T—Alan Faneca, LSU; G/T—Benji Olson, Washington; C—Olin Kreutz, Washington; G/T—Chad Overhauser, UCLA; G/T—Aaron Taylor, Nebraska; A/P—Tim Dwight, Iowa; PK—Martin Gramatica, Kansas St.

Defense DL—Greg Ellis, North Caro.; DL—Jason Peter, Nebraska; DL—Andre Wadsworth, Florida St.; DL—Grant Wistrom, Nebraska; LB—Sam Cowart, Florida St.; LB—Andy Katzenmoyer, Ohio St.; LB—Anthony Simmons, Clemson; LB—Brian Simmons, North Caro.; DB—Dre' Bly, North Caro.; DB—Donovin Darius, Syracuse; DB—Brian Lee, Wyoming; DB—Charles Woodson, Michigan; P—Chad Kessler, LSU.

FOOTBALL NEWS

Offense QB—Peyton Manning, Tennessee; RB—Ricky Williams, Texas; RB—Ron Dayne, Wisconsin; WR—Randy Moss, Marshall; WR—Brian Alford, Purdue; TE—Jerame Tuman, Michigan; OL—Aaron Taylor, Nebraska; OL—Alan Faneca, LSU; OL—Rob Murphy, Ohio St.; OL—Kyle Turley, San Diego St.; OL—Olin Kreutz, Washington; PK—Martin Gramatica, Kansas St.

Defense DL—Andre Wadsworth, Florida St.; DL—Greg Ellis, North Caro.; DL—Kailee Wong, Stanford; LB—Sam Cowart, Florida St.; LB—Brian Simmons, North Caro.; LB—Andy Katzenmoyer, Ohio St.; LB—Ron Warner, Kansas; DB—Charles Woodson, Michigan; DB—Fred Weary, Florida; DB—Brian Lee, Wyoming; DB—Dre' Bly, North Caro.; P—Chad Kessler, LSU.

FOOTBALL WRITERS ASSOCIATION OF AMERICA

Offense QB—Peyton Manning, Tennessee; RB—Ricky Williams, Texas; RB—Curtis Enis, Penn St.; WR—Randy Moss, Marshall; WR—Jacquez Green, Florida; TE—Alonzo Mayes, Oklahoma St.; C—Ben Fricke, Houston; OL—Aaron Taylor, Nebraska; OL—Kyle Turley, San Diego St.; OL—Chad Overhauser, UCLA; OL—Alan Faneca, LSU; KR—Tim Dwight, Iowa; PK—Martin Gramatica, Kansas St.

Defense DE—Grant Wistrom, Nebraska; DE—Lamanzer Williams, Minnesota; DT—Jason Peter, Nebraska; DT—Jeremy Staat, Arizona St.; LB—Andy Katzenmoyer, Ohio St.; LB—Sam Cowart, Florida St.; LB—Jamie Duncan, Vanderbilt; DB—Charles Woodson, Michigan; DB—Dre' Bly, North Caro.; DB—Antoine Winfield, Ohio St.; DB—Brian Lee, Wyoming; P—Chris Sailer, UCLA.

SPORTING NEWS

Offense QB—Ryan Leaf, Washington St.; RB—Skip Hicks, UCLA; RB—Ricky Williams, Texas; WR—Randy Moss, Marshall; WR—Bobby Shaw, California; TE—Alonzo Mayes, Oklahoma St.; OT—Chad Overhauser, UCLA; OT—Kyle Turley, San Diego St.; OG—Alan Faneca, LSU; OG—Aaron Taylor, Nebraska; C—Olin Kreutz, Washington; KR—Tim Dwight, Iowa; PK—Martin Gramatica, Kansas St.

Defense DE—Andre Wadsworth, Florida St.; DE—Grant Wistrom, Nebraska; DT—Jason Peter, Nebraska; OLB—Sam Cowart, Florida St.; OLB—Pat Tillman, Arizona St.; ILB—Anthony Simmons, Clemson; ILB—Takeo Spikes, Auburn; CB—Fred Weary, Florida; CB—Charles Woodson, Michigan; FS—Donovin Darius, Syracuse; SS—Anthony Poindexter, Virginia; P—Chad Kessler, LSU.

WALTER CAMP FOOTBALL FOUNDATION

Offense QB—Peyton Manning, Tennessee; RB—Ricky Williams, Texas; RB—Curtis Enis, Penn St.; WR—Randy Moss, Marshall; WR—Jacquez Green, Florida; TE—Alonzo Mayes, Oklahoma St.; OL—Flozell Adams, Michigan St.; OL—Aaron Taylor, Nebraska; OL—Alan Faneca, LSU; OL—Benji Olson, Washington; C—Olin Kreutz, Washington; PK—Chris Sailer, UCLA.

Defense DL—Jason Peter, Nebraska; DL—Grant Wistrom, Nebraska; DL—Greg Ellis, North Caro.; DL—Andre Wadsworth, Florida St.; LB—Andy Katzenmoyer, Ohio St.; LB—Leonard Little, Tennessee; LB—Brian Simmons, North Caro.; DB—Charles Woodson, Michigan; DB—Dre' Bly, North Caro.; DB—Fred Weary, Florida; DB—Brian Lee, Wyoming; P—Chad Kessler, LSU.

Special Awards

HEISMAN MEMORIAL TROPHY

Originally presented in 1935 as the DAC Trophy by the Downtown Athletic Club of New York City to the best college player east of the Mississippi River. In 1936, players across the country were eligible and the award was renamed the Heisman Memorial Trophy to honor former college coach and DAC athletics director John W. Heisman. The award now goes to the outstanding college football player in the United States. The bronze trophy was sculpted by Frank Eliscu, with the aid of Jim Crowley, one of Notre Dame's famed Four Horsemen. Crowley was then coach at Fordham, and some of his players posed as models for the trophy.

Year	Player (Winner Bold), School, Position	Points
1935	**Jay Berwanger,** Chicago, HB	84
	2nd—Monk Meyer, Army	29
	3rd—Bill Shakespeare, Notre Dame, HB	23
	4th—Pepper Constable, Princeton, FB	20
1936	**Larry Kelley,** Yale, E	219
	2nd—Sam Francis, Nebraska, FB	47
	3rd—Ray Buivid, Marquette, HB	43
	4th—Sammy Baugh, Texas Christian, HB	39
1937	**Clint Frank,** Yale, HB	524
	2nd—Byron White, Colorado, HB	264
	3rd—Marshall Goldberg, Pittsburgh, HB	211
	4th—Alex Wojciechowicz, Fordham, C	85
1938	**Davey O'Brien,** Texas Christian, QB	519
	2nd—Marshall Goldberg, Pittsburgh, HB	294
	3rd—Sid Luckman, Columbia, QB	154
	4th—Bob MacLeod, Dartmouth, HB	78
1939	**Nile Kinnick,** Iowa, HB	651
	2nd—Tom Harmon, Michigan, HB	405
	3rd—Paul Christman, Missouri, QB	391
	4th—George Cafego, Tennessee, QB	296
1940	**Tom Harmon,** Michigan, HB	1,303
	2nd—John Kimbrough, Texas A&M, FB	841
	3rd—George Franck, Minnesota, HB	102
	4th—Frankie Albert, Stanford, QB	90
1941	**Bruce Smith,** Minnesota, HB	554
	2nd—Angelo Bertelli, Notre Dame, QB	345
	3rd—Frankie Albert, Stanford, QB	336
	4th—Frank Sinkwich, Georgia, HB	249
1942	**Frank Sinkwich,** Georgia, HB	1,059
	2nd—Paul Governali, Columbia, QB	218
	3rd—Clint Castleberry, Georgia Tech, HB	99
	4th—Mike Holovak, Boston College, FB	95
1943	**Angelo Bertelli,** Notre Dame, QB	648
	2nd—Bob Odell, Pennsylvania, HB	177
	3rd—Otto Graham, Northwestern, QB	140
	4th—Creighton Miller, Notre Dame, HB	134
1944	**Les Horvath,** Ohio St., QB/HB	412
	2nd—Glenn Davis, Army, HB	287
	3rd—Doc Blanchard, Army, FB	237
	4th—Don Whitmire, Navy, T	115
1945	***Doc Blanchard,** Army, FB	860
	2nd—Glenn Davis, Army, HB	638
	3rd—Bob Fenimore, Oklahoma St., HB	187
	4th—Herman Wedemeyer, St. Mary's (Cal.), HB	152
1946	**Glenn Davis,** Army, HB	792
	2nd—Charlie Trippi, Georgia, HB	435
	3rd—Johnny Lujack, Notre Dame, QB	379
	4th—Doc Blanchard, Army, FB	267
1947	**Johnny Lujack,** Notre Dame, QB	742
	2nd—Bob Chappius, Michigan, HB	555
	3rd—Doak Walker, Southern Methodist, HB	196
	4th—Charlie Conerly, Mississippi, QB	186
1948	***Doak Walker,** Southern Methodist, HB	778
	2nd—Charlie Justice, North Caro., HB	443
	3rd—Chuck Bednarik, Pennsylvania, C	336
	4th—Jackie Jensen, California, HB	143
1949	**Leon Hart,** Notre Dame, E	995
	2nd—Charlie Justice, North Caro., HB	272
	3rd—Doak Walker, Southern Methodist, HB	229
	4th—Arnold Galiffa, Army, QB	196
1950	***Vic Janowicz,** Ohio St., HB	633
	2nd—Kyle Rote, Southern Methodist, HB	280
	3rd—Reds Bagnell, Pennsylvania, HB	231
	4th—Babe Parilli, Kentucky, QB	214
1951	**Dick Kazmaier,** Princeton, HB	1,777
	2nd—Hank Lauricella, Tennessee, HB	424
	3rd—Babe Pirilli, Kentucky, QB	344
	4th—Bill McColl, Stanford, E	313
1952	**Billy Vessels,** Oklahoma, HB	525
	2nd—Jack Scarbath, Maryland, QB	367
	3rd—Paul Giel, Minnesota, HB	329
	4th—Donn Moomaw, UCLA, C	257
1953	**Johnny Lattner,** Notre Dame, HB	1,850
	2nd—Paul Giel, Minnesota, HB	1,794
	3rd—Paul Cameron, UCLA, HB	444
	4th—Bernie Faloney, Maryland, QB	258
1954	**Alan Ameche,** Wisconsin, FB	1,068
	2nd—Kurt Burris, Oklahoma, C	838
	3rd—Howard Cassady, Ohio St., HB	810
	4th—Ralph Guglielmi, Notre Dame, QB	691
1955	**Howard Cassady,** Ohio St., HB	2,219
	2nd—Jim Swink, Texas Christian, HB	742
	3rd—George Welsh, Navy, QB	383
	4th—Earl Morrall, Michigan St., QB	323
1956	**Paul Hornung,** Notre Dame, QB	1,066
	2nd—Johnny Majors, Tennessee, HB	994
	3rd—Tommy McDonald, Oklahoma, HB	973
	4th—Jerry Tubbs, Oklahoma, C	724
1957	**John David Crow,** Texas A&M, HB	1,183
	2nd—Alex Karras, Iowa, T	693
	3rd—Walt Kowalczyk, Michigan St., HB	630
	4th—Lou Michaels, Kentucky, T	330
1958	**Pete Dawkins,** Army, HB	1,394
	2nd—Randy Duncan, Iowa, QB	1,021
	3rd—Billy Cannon, LSU, HB	975
	4th—Bob White, Ohio St., HB	365
1959	**Billy Cannon,** LSU, HB	1,929
	2nd—Richie Lucas, Penn St., QB	613
	3rd—Don Meredith, Southern Meth., QB	286
	4th—Bill Burrell, Illinois, G	196
1960	**Joe Bellino,** Navy, HB	1,793
	2nd—Tom Brown, Minnesota, G	731
	3rd—Jake Gibbs, Mississippi, QB	453
	4th—Ed Dyas, Auburn, HB	319
1961	**Ernie Davis,** Syracuse, HB	824
	2nd—Bob Ferguson, Ohio St., HB	771
	3rd—Jimmy Saxton, Texas, HB	551
	4th—Sandy Stephens, Minnesota, QB	543
1962	**Terry Baker,** Oregon St., QB	707
	2nd—Jerry Stovall, LSU, HB	618
	3rd—Bobby Bell, Minnesota, T	429
	4th—Lee Roy Jordan, Alabama, C	321
1963	***Roger Staubach,** Navy, QB	1,860
	2nd—Billy Lothridge, Georgia Tech, QB	504
	3rd—Sherman Lewis, Michigan St., HB	369
	4th—Don Trull, Baylor, QB	253
1964	**John Huarte,** Notre Dame, QB	1,026
	2nd—Jerry Rhome, Tulsa, QB	952
	3rd—Dick Butkus, Illinois, C	505
	4th—Bob Timberlake, Michigan, QB	361
1965	**Mike Garrett,** Southern Cal, HB	926
	2nd—Howard Twilley, Tulsa, E	528
	3rd—Jim Grabowski, Illinois, FB	481
	4th—Donny Anderson, Texas Tech, HB	408
1966	**Steve Spurrier,** Florida, QB	1,679
	2nd—Bob Griese, Purdue, QB	816
	3rd—Nick Eddy, Notre Dame, HB	456
	4th—Gary Beban, UCLA, QB	318
1967	**Gary Beban,** UCLA, QB	1,968
	2nd—O. J. Simpson, Southern Cal, HB	1,722
	3rd—Leroy Keyes, Purdue, HB	1,366
	4th—Larry Csonka, Syracuse, FB	136
1968	**O. J. Simpson,** Southern Cal, HB	2,853
	2nd—Leroy Keyes, Purdue, HB	1,103
	3rd—Terry Hanratty, Notre Dame, QB	387
	4th—Ted Kwalik, Penn St., TE	254
1969	**Steve Owens,** Oklahoma, HB	1,488
	2nd—Mike Phipps, Purdue, QB	1,344
	3rd—Rex Kern, Ohio St., QB	856
	4th—Archie Manning, Mississippi, QB	582
1970	**Jim Plunkett,** Stanford, QB	2,229
	2nd—Joe Theismann, Notre Dame, QB	1,410
	3rd—Archie Manning, Mississippi, QB	849
	4th—Steve Worster, Texas, RB	398

Year	Player (Winner Bold), School, Position	Points
1971	**Pat Sullivan,** Auburn, QB	1,597
	2nd—Ed Marinaro, Cornell, RB	1,445
	3rd—Greg Pruitt, Oklahoma, RB	586
	4th—Johnny Musso, Alabama, RB	365
1972	**Johnny Rodgers,** Nebraska, WR	1,310
	2nd—Greg Pruitt, Oklahoma, RB	966
	3rd—Rich Glover, Nebraska, MG	652
	4th—Bert Jones, LSU, QB	351
1973	**John Cappelletti,** Penn St., RB	1,057
	2nd—John Hicks, Ohio St., OT	524
	3rd—Roosevelt Leaks, Texas, RB	482
	4th—David Jaynes, Kansas, QB	394
1974	***Archie Griffin,** Ohio St., RB	1,920
	2nd—Anthony Davis, Southern Cal, RB	819
	3rd—Joe Washington, Oklahoma, RB	661
	4th—Tom Clements, Notre Dame, QB	244
1975	**Archie Griffin,** Ohio St., RB	1,800
	2nd—Chuck Muncie, California, RB	730
	3rd—Ricky Bell, Southern Cal, RB	708
	4th—Tony Dorsett, Pittsburgh, RB	616
1976	**Tony Dorsett,** Pittsburgh, RB	2,357
	2nd—Ricky Bell, Southern Cal, RB	1,346
	3rd—Rob Lytle, Michigan, RB	413
	4th—Terry Miller, Oklahoma St., RB	197
1977	**Earl Campbell,** Texas, RB	1,547
	2nd—Terry Miller, Oklahoma St., RB	812
	3rd—Ken MacAfee, Notre Dame, TE	343
	4th—Doug Williams, Grambling, QB	266
1978	***Billy Sims,** Oklahoma, RB	827
	2nd—Chuck Fusina, Penn St., QB	750
	3rd—Rick Leach, Michigan, QB	435
	4th—Charles White, Southern Cal, RB	354
1979	**Charles White,** Southern Cal, RB	1,695
	2nd—Billy Sims, Oklahoma, RB	773
	3rd—Marc Wilson, Brigham Young, QB	589
	4th—Art Schlichter, Ohio St., QB	251
1980	**George Rogers,** South Caro., RB	1,128
	2nd—Hugh Green, Pittsburgh, DE	861
	3rd—Herschel Walker, Georgia, RB	683
	4th—Mark Hermann, Purdue, QB	405
1981	**Marcus Allen,** Southern Cal, RB	1,797
	2nd—Herschel Walker, Georgia, RB	1,199
	3rd—Jim McMahon, Brigham Young, QB	706
	4th—Dan Marino, Pittsburgh, QB	256
1982	***Herschel Walker,** Georgia, RB	1,926
	2nd—John Elway, Stanford, QB	1,231
	3rd—Eric Dickerson, Southern Meth., RB	465
	4th—Anthony Carter, Michigan, WR	142
1983	**Mike Rozier,** Nebraska, RB	1,801
	2nd—Steve Young, Brigham Young, QB	1,172
	3rd—Doug Flutie, Boston College, QB	253
	4th—Turner Gill, Nebraska, QB	190
1984	**Doug Flutie,** Boston College, QB	2,240
	2nd—Keith Byars, Ohio St., RB	1,251
	3rd—Robbie Bosco, Brigham Young, QB	443
	4th—Bernie Kosar, Miami (Fla.), QB	320
1985	**Bo Jackson,** Auburn, RB	1,509
	2nd—Chuck Long, Iowa, QB	1,464
	3rd—Robbie Bosco, Brigham Young, QB	459
	4th—Lorenzo White, Michigan St., RB	391
1986	**Vinny Testaverde,** Miami (Fla.), QB	2,213
	2nd—Paul Palmer, Temple, RB	672
	3rd—Jim Harbaugh, Michigan, QB	458
	4th—Brian Bosworth, Oklahoma, LB	395
1987	**Tim Brown,** Notre Dame, WR	1,442
	2nd—Don McPherson, Syracuse, QB	831
	3rd—Gordie Lockbaum, Holy Cross, WR/DB	657
	4th—Lorenzo White, Michigan St., RB	632
1988	***Barry Sanders,** Oklahoma St., RB	1,878
	2nd—Rodney Peete, Southern Cal, QB	912
	3rd—Troy Aikman, UCLA, QB	582
	4th—Steve Walsh, Miami (Fla.), QB	341
1989	***Andre Ware,** Houston, QB	1,073
	2nd—Anthony Thompson, Indiana, RB	1,003
	3rd—Major Harris, West Va., QB	709
	4th—Tony Rice, Notre Dame, QB	523
1990	***Ty Detmer,** Brigham Young, QB	1,482
	2nd—Raghib Ismail, Notre Dame, WR	1,177
	3rd—Eric Bieniemy, Colorado, RB	798
	4th—Shawn Moore, Virginia, QB	465
1991	**#Desmond Howard,** Michigan, WR	2,077
	2nd—Casey Weldon, Florida St., QB	503
	3rd—Ty Detmer, Brigham Young, QB	445
	4th—Steve Emtman, Washington, DT	357
1992	**Gino Torretta,** Miami (Fla.), QB	1,400
	2nd—Marshall Faulk, San Diego St., RB	1,080
	3rd—Garrison Hearst, Georgia, RB	982
	4th—Marvin Jones, Florida St., LB	392
1993	**Charlie Ward,** Florida St., QB	2,310
	2nd—Heath Shuler, Tennessee, QB	688
	3rd—David Palmer, Alabama, RB	292
	4th—Marshall Faulk, San Diego St., RB	250
1994	***Rashaan Salaam,** Colorado, RB	1,743
	2nd—Ki-Jana Carter, Penn St., RB	901
	3rd—Steve McNair, Alcorn St., QB	655
	4th—Kerry Collins, Penn St., QB	639
1995	**Eddie George,** Ohio St., RB	1,460
	2nd—Tommie Frazier, Nebraska, QB	1,196
	3rd—Danny Wuerffel, Florida, QB	987
	4th—Darnell Autry, Northwestern, RB	535
1996	**Danny Wuerffel,** Florida, QB	1,363
	2nd—Troy Davis, Iowa St., RB	1,174
	3rd—Jake Plummer, Arizona St., QB	685
	4th—Orlando Pace, Ohio St., OL	599

**Winner as junior (all others seniors). #Had one year of eligibility remaining.*

1997 Heisman Voting

(Voting on a 3-2-1 basis)	1st	2nd	3rd	Total
1. *Charles Woodson, DB, Michigan	433	209	98	1,815
2. Peyton Manning, QB, Tennessee	281	263	174	1,543
3. *Ryan Leaf, QB, Washington St.	70	205	241	861
4. #Randy Moss, WR, Marshall	17	56	90	253
5. *Ricky Williams, RB, Texas	4	31	61	135
6. *Curtis Enis, RB, Penn St.	3	18	20	65
7. Tim Dwight, WR, Iowa	5	3	11	32
8. *Cade McNown, QB, UCLA	0	7	12	26
9. #Tim Couch, QB, Kentucky	0	5	12	22
10. Amos Zereoue, RB, West Va.	3	1	10	21

**Junior. #Sophomore. All others seniors.*

OUTLAND TROPHY

Honoring the outstanding interior lineman in the nation, first presented in 1946 by the Football Writers Association of America. The award is named for its benefactor, Dr. John H. Outland.

Year	Player, College, Position
1946	George Connor, Notre Dame, T
1947	Joe Steffy, Army, G
1948	Bill Fischer, Notre Dame, G
1949	Ed Bagdon, Michigan St., G
1950	Bob Gain, Kentucky, T
1951	Jim Weatherall, Oklahoma, T
1952	Dick Modzelewski, Maryland, T
1953	J. D. Roberts, Oklahoma, G
1954	Bill Brooks, Arkansas, G
1955	Calvin Jones, Iowa, G
1956	Jim Parker, Ohio St., G
1957	Alex Karras, Iowa, T
1958	Zeke Smith, Auburn, G
1959	Mike McGee, Duke, T
1960	Tom Brown, Minnesota, G
1961	Merlin Olsen, Utah St., T
1962	Bobby Bell, Minnesota, T
1963	Scott Appleton, Texas, T
1964	Steve DeLong, Tennessee, T
1965	Tommy Nobis, Texas, G
1966	Loyd Phillips, Arkansas, T
1967	Ron Yary, Southern Cal, T
1968	Bill Stanfill, Georgia, T
1969	Mike Reid, Penn St., DT
1970	Jim Stillwagon, Ohio St., MG
1971	Larry Jacobson, Nebraska, DT
1972	Rich Glover, Nebraska, MG
1973	John Hicks, Ohio St., OT
1974	Randy White, Maryland, DE
1975	Lee Roy Selmon, Oklahoma, DT
1976	*Ross Browner, Notre Dame, DE
1977	Brad Shearer, Texas, DT
1978	Greg Roberts, Oklahoma, G
1979	Jim Ritcher, North Caro. St., C
1980	Mark May, Pittsburgh, OT
1981	*Dave Rimington, Nebraska, C
1982	Dave Rimington, Nebraska, C
1983	Dean Steinkuhler, Nebraska, G
1984	Bruce Smith, Virginia Tech, DT
1985	Mike Ruth, Boston College, NG
1986	Jason Buck, Brigham Young, DT
1987	Chad Hennings, Air Force, DT
1988	Tracy Rocker, Auburn, DT
1989	Mohammed Elewonibi, Brigham Young, G
1990	Russell Maryland, Miami (Fla.), DT
1991	*Steve Emtman, Washington, DT
1992	Will Shields, Nebraska, G
1993	Rob Waldrop, Arizona, NG
1994	Zach Wiegert, Nebraska, OT
1995	Jonathan Ogden, UCLA, OT
1996	*Orlando Pace, Ohio St., OT
1997	Aaron Taylor, Nebraska, OG

**Junior (all others seniors).*

VINCE LOMBARDI/ROTARY AWARD

Honoring the outstanding college lineman of the year, first presented in 1970 by the Rotary Club of Houston, Texas. The award is named after professional football coach Vince Lombardi, a member of the legendary "Seven Blocks of Granite" at Fordham in the 1930s.

Year	Player, College, Position
1970	Jim Stillwagon, Ohio St., MG
1971	Walt Patulski, Notre Dame, DE
1972	Rich Glover, Nebraska, MG
1973	John Hicks, Ohio St., OT
1974	Randy White, Maryland, DT
1975	Lee Roy Selmon, Oklahoma, DT
1976	Wilson Whitley, Houston, DT
1977	Ross Browner, Notre Dame, DE
1978	Bruce Clark, Penn St., DT
1979	Brad Budde, Southern Cal, G
1980	Hugh Green, Pittsburgh, DE
1981	Kenneth Sims, Texas, DT
1982	Dave Rimington, Nebraska, C
1983	Dean Steinkuhler, Nebraska, G
1984	Tony Degrate, Texas, DT
1985	Tony Casillas, Oklahoma, NG
1986	Cornelius Bennett, Alabama, LB
1987	Chris Spielman, Ohio St., LB
1988	Tracy Rocker, Auburn, DT
1989	Percy Snow, Michigan St., LB
1990	Chris Zorich, Notre Dame, NT
1991	Steve Emtman, Washington, DT
1992	Marvin Jones, Florida St., LB
1993	Aaron Taylor, Notre Dame, OT
1994	Warren Sapp, Miami (Fla.), DT
1995	Orlando Pace, Ohio St., OT
1996	Orlando Pace, Ohio St., OT
1997	Grant Wistrom, Nebraska, DE

WALTER CAMP AWARD

Honoring the nation's outstanding college football player, first presented in 1967 by the Walter Camp Foundation in balloting by Division I-A coaches and sports information directors. The award is named after Walter Camp, one of the founders of modern American football.

Year	Player, College, Position
1967	O.J. Simpson, Southern Cal, RB
1968	O.J. Simpson, Southern Cal, RB
1969	Steve Owens, Oklahoma, RB
1970	Jim Plunkett, Stanford, QB
1971	Pat Sullivan, Auburn, QB
1972	Johnny Rodgers, Nebraska, WR
1973	John Cappelletti, Penn St., RB
1974	Archie Griffin, Ohio St., RB
1975	Archie Griffin, Ohio St., RB
1976	Tony Dorsett, Pittsburgh, RB
1977	Ken MacAfee, Notre Dame, TE
1978	Billy Sims, Oklahoma, RB
1979	Charles White, Southern Cal, RB
1980	Hugh Green, Pittsburgh, DE
1981	Marcus Allen, Southern Cal, RB

Year	Player, College, Position
1982	Herschel Walker, Georgia, RB
1983	Mike Rozier, Nebraska, RB
1984	Doug Flutie, Boston College, QB
1985	Bo Jackson, Auburn, RB
1986	Vinny Testaverde, Miami (Fla.), QB
1987	Tim Brown, Notre Dame, WR
1988	Barry Sanders, Oklahoma St., RB
1989	Andre Ware, Houston, QB
1990	Raghib Ismail, Notre Dame, RB/WR
1991	Desmond Howard, Michigan, WR
1992	Gino Torretta, Miami (Fla.), QB
1993	Charlie Ward, Florida St., QB
1994	Rashaan Salaam, Colorado, RB
1995	Eddie George, Ohio St., RB
1996	Danny Wuerffel, Florida, QB
1997	Charles Woodson, Michigan, DB

MAXWELL AWARD

Honoring the nation's outstanding college football player, first presented in 1937 by the Maxwell Memorial Football Club of Philadelphia. The award is named after Robert "Tiny" Maxwell, a Philadelphia native who played at the University of Chicago as a lineman near the turn of the century.

Year	Player, College, Position
1937	Clint Frank, Yale, HB
1938	Davey O'Brien, Texas Christian, QB
1939	Nile Kinnick, Iowa, HB
1940	Tom Harmon, Michigan, HB
1941	Bill Dudley, Virginia, HB
1942	Paul Governali, Columbia, QB
1943	Bob Odell, Pennsylvania, HB
1944	Glenn Davis, Army, HB
1945	Doc Blanchard, Army, FB
1946	Charley Trippi, Georgia, HB
1947	Doak Walker, Southern Methodist, HB
1948	Chuck Bednarik, Pennsylvania, C
1949	Leon Hart, Notre Dame, E
1950	Reds Bagnell, Pennsylvania, HB
1951	Dick Kazmaier, Princeton, HB
1952	Johnny Lattner, Notre Dame, HB
1953	Johnny Lattner, Notre Dame, HB
1954	Ron Beagle, Navy, E
1955	Howard Cassady, Ohio St., HB
1956	Tommy McDonald, Oklahoma, HB
1957	Bob Reifsnyder, Navy, T
1958	Pete Dawkins, Army, HB
1959	Rich Lucas, Penn St., QB
1960	Joe Bellino, Navy, HB
1961	Bob Ferguson, Ohio St., FB
1962	Terry Baker, Oregon St., QB
1963	Roger Staubach, Navy, QB
1964	Glenn Ressler, Penn St., C
1965	Tommy Nobis, Texas, LB
1966	Jim Lynch, Notre Dame, LB
1967	Gary Beban, UCLA, QB
1968	O. J. Simpson, Southern Cal, RB
1969	Mike Reid, Penn St., DT
1970	Jim Plunkett, Stanford, QB
1971	Ed Marinaro, Cornell, RB
1972	Brad VanPelt, Michigan St., DB
1973	John Cappelletti, Penn St., RB
1974	Steve Joachim, Temple, QB
1975	Archie Griffin, Ohio St., RB
1976	Tony Dorsett, Pittsburgh, RB
1977	Ross Browner, Notre Dame, DE
1978	Chuck Fusina, Penn St., QB
1979	Charles White, Southern Cal, RB
1980	Hugh Green, Pittsburgh, DE
1981	Marcus Allen, Southern Cal, RB
1982	Herschel Walker, Georgia, RB
1983	Mike Rozier, Nebraska, RB
1984	Doug Flutie, Boston College, QB
1985	Chuck Long, Iowa, QB
1986	Vinny Testaverde, Miami (Fla.), QB
1987	Don McPherson, Syracuse, QB
1988	Barry Sanders, Oklahoma St., RB
1989	Anthony Thompson, Indiana, RB
1990	Ty Detmer, Brigham Young, QB
1991	Desmond Howard, Michigan, WR
1992	Gino Torretta, Miami (Fla.), QB
1993	Charlie Ward, Florida St., QB
1994	Kerry Collins, Penn St., QB

Year	Player, College, Position
1995	Eddie George, Ohio St., RB
1996	Danny Wuerffel, Florida, QB
1997	Peyton Manning, Tennessee, QB

JOHNNY UNITAS GOLDEN ARM AWARD

Presented for the first time in 1987 to honor the nation's top senior quarterback. Sponsored by the Kentucky Chapter of the National Football Foundation and College Football Hall of Fame, Inc. Each year, a committee composed of NFL executives, coaches, scouts and media members selects the winner based on citizenship, scholarship, leadership and athletic accomplishments. The award is named after NFL Hall of Fame quarterback Johnny Unitas.

Year	Player, College
1987	Don McPherson, Syracuse
1988	Rodney Peete, Southern Cal
1989	Tony Rice, Notre Dame
1990	Craig Erickson, Miami (Fla.)
1991	Casey Weldon, Florida St.
1992	Gino Torretta, Miami (Fla.)
1993	Charlie Ward, Florida St.
1994	Jay Barker, Alabama
1995	Tommy Frazier, Nebraska
1996	Danny Wuerffel, Florida
1997	Peyton Manning, Tennessee

BUTKUS AWARD

First presented in 1985 to honor the nation's best collegiate linebacker by the Downtown Athletic Club of Orlando, Fla. The award is named after Dick Butkus, two-time consensus all-American at Illinois and six-time all-pro linebacker with the Chicago Bears.

Year	Player, College
1985	Brian Bosworth, Oklahoma
1986	Brian Bosworth, Oklahoma
1987	Paul McGowan, Florida St.
1988	Derrick Thomas, Alabama
1989	Percy Snow, Michigan St.
1990	Alfred Williams, Colorado
1991	Erick Anderson, Michigan
1992	Marvin Jones, Florida St.
1993	Trev Alberts, Nebraska
1994	Dana Howard, Illinois
1995	Kevin Hardy, Illinois
1996	Matt Russell, Colorado
1997	Andy Katzenmoyer, Ohio St.

JIM THORPE AWARD

First presented in 1986 to honor the nation's best defensive back by the Jim Thorpe Athletic Club of Oklahoma City. The award is named after Jim Thorpe, Olympic champion, two-time consensus all-American halfback at Carlisle and professional football player.

Year	Player, College
1986	Thomas Everett, Baylor
1987	Bennie Blades, Miami (Fla.)
	Rickey Dixon, Oklahoma
1988	Deion Sanders, Florida St.
1989	Mark Carrier, Southern Cal
1990	Darryll Lewis, Arizona
1991	Terrell Buckley, Florida St.
1992	Deon Figures, Colorado
1993	Antonio Langham, Alabama
1994	Chris Hudson, Colorado
1995	Greg Myers, Colorado St.
1996	Lawrence Wright, Florida
1997	Charles Woodson, Michigan

DAVEY O'BRIEN NATIONAL QUARTERBACK AWARD

First presented in 1977 as the O'Brien Memorial Trophy to the outstanding player in the Southwest. In 1981, the Davey O'Brien Educational and Charitable Trust of Fort Worth, Texas, renamed the award the Davey O'Brien National Quarterback Award, and it now honors the nation's best quarterback.

MEMORIAL TROPHY

Year	Player, College, Position
1977	Earl Campbell, Texas, RB

Photo from Nebraska sports information

Nebraska defensive end Grant Wistrom, winner of the Vince Lombardi/Rotary Award, which honors the nation's outstanding college lineman of the year, also earned all-America honors in 1997.

Year	Player, College, Position
1978	Billy Sims, Oklahoma, RB
1979	Mike Singletary, Baylor, LB
1980	Mike Singletary, Baylor, LB

NATIONAL QB AWARD

Year	Player, College
1981	Jim McMahon, Brigham Young
1982	Todd Blackledge, Penn St.
1983	Steve Young, Brigham Young
1984	Doug Flutie, Boston College
1985	Chuck Long, Iowa
1986	Vinny Testaverde, Miami (Fla.)
1987	Don McPherson, Syracuse
1988	Troy Aikman, UCLA
1989	Andre Ware, Houston
1990	Ty Detmer, Brigham Young
1991	Ty Detmer, Brigham Young
1992	Gino Torretta, Miami (Fla.)
1993	Charlie Ward, Florida St.
1994	Kerry Collins, Penn St.
1995	Danny Wuerffel, Florida
1996	Danny Wuerffel, Florida
1997	Peyton Manning, Tennessee

DOAK WALKER NATIONAL RUNNING BACK AWARD

Presented for the first time in 1990 to honor the nation's best running back among Division I-A juniors or seniors who combine outstanding achievements on the field, in the classroom and in the community. Sponsored by the GTE/Southern Methodist Athletic Forum in Dallas, Texas, a $10,000 scholarship is donated to the recipient's university in his name. It is voted on by a 16-member panel of media and former college football standouts. The award is named after Doak Walker, Southern Methodist's three-time consensus all-American halfback and 1948 Heisman Trophy winner.

Year	Player, College
1990	Greg Lewis, Washington
1991	Trevor Cobb, Rice
1992	Garrison Hearst, Georgia
1993	Byron Morris, Texas Tech

Year	Player, College
1994	Rashaan Salaam, Colorado
1995	Eddie George, Ohio St.
1996	Byron Hanspard, Texas Tech
1997	Ricky Williams, Texas

LOU GROZA COLLEGIATE PLACE-KICKER AWARD

Presented for the first time in 1992 to honor the nation's top collegiate place-kicker. Sponsored by the Palm Beach County Sports Authority in conjunction with the Orange Bowl Committee. The award is named after NFL Hall of Fame kicker Lou Groza.

Year	Player, College
1992	Joe Allison, Memphis
1993	Judd Davis, Florida
1994	Steve McLaughlin, Arizona
1995	Michael Reeder, Texas Christian
1996	Marc Primanti, North Caro. St.
1997	Martin Gramatica, Kansas St.

FRED BILETNIKOFF RECEIVER AWARD

First presented in 1994 to honor the nation's top collegiate pass receiver. Sponsored by the Tallahassee Quarterback Club of Tallahassee, Fla. The award is named after Fred Biletnikoff, former Florida State all-American and NFL Oakland Raider receiver, a member of both the College Football Hall of Fame and Pro Football Hall of Fame.

Year	Player, College
1994	Bobby Engram, Penn St.
1995	Terry Glenn, Ohio St.
1996	Marcus Harris, Wyoming
1997	Randy Moss, Marshall

WALTER PAYTON PLAYER OF THE YEAR AWARD

First presented in 1987 to honor the top Division I-AA football player by the Sports Network and voted on by Division I-AA sports information directors. The award is named after Walter Payton, former Jackson State player and the National Football League's all-time leading rusher.

Year	Player, College, Position
1987	Kenny Gamble, Colgate, RB
1988	Dave Meggett, Towson, RB
1989	John Friesz, Idaho, QB
1990	Walter Dean, Grambling, RB
1991	Jamie Martin, Weber St., QB
1992	Michael Payton, Marshall, QB
1993	Doug Nussmeier, Idaho, QB
1994	Steve McNair, Alcorn St., QB
1995	Dave Dickenson, Montana, QB
1996	Archie Amerson, Northern Ariz., RB
1997	Brian Finneran, Villanova, WR

ERNIE DAVIS AWARD

First presented in 1992 to honor a Division I-AA college football player who has overcome personal, athletic or academic adversity and performs in an exemplary manner. The annual award is presented by the American Sports Wire of Saugus, Calif., and is named after the late Ernie Davis, Syracuse halfback who won the Heisman Trophy in 1961.

Year	Player, College, Position
1992	Gilad Landau, Grambling, PK
1993	Jay Walker, Howard, QB
1994	Steve McNair, Alcorn St., QB
1995	Earl Holmes, Florida A&M, LB
1996	Jason DeCuir, Howard, PK
1997	DeMingo Graham, Hofstra, OL

HARLON HILL TROPHY

First presented in 1986 to honor the best Division II player by Division II sports information directors. The award is named after Harlon Hill, former receiver at North Alabama and the National Football League's most valuable player for the Chicago Bears in 1955.

Year	Player, College, Position
1986	Jeff Bentrim, North Dak. St., QB
1987	Johnny Bailey, Tex. A&M-Kingsville, RB
1988	Johnny Bailey, Tex. A&M-Kingsville, RB
1989	Johnny Bailey, Tex. A&M-Kingsville, RB
1990	Chris Simdorn, North Dak. St., QB
1991	Ronnie West, Pittsburg St., WR
1992	Ronald Moore, Pittsburg St., RB
1993	Roger Graham, New Haven, RB
1994	Chris Hatcher, Valdosta St., QB
1995	Ronald McKinnon, North Ala., LB
1996	Jarrett Anderson, Truman St., RB
1997	Irv Sigler, Bloomsburg, RB

BRONKO NAGURSKI AWARD

First presented in 1993 to honor the nation's top collegiate defensive player. Presented by the Football Writers Association of America.

Year	Player, College, Position
1993	Rob Waldrop, Arizona, DL
1994	Warren Sapp, Miami (Fla.), DT
1995	Pat Fitzgerald, Northwestern, LB
1996	Pat Fitzgerald, Northwestern, LB
1997	Charles Woodson, Michigan, CB

GAGLIARDI TROPHY

First presented in 1993 to the nation's outstanding Division III player. Presented by the St. John's (Minn.) J-Club. The award is named after John Gagliardi, St. John's head coach for 43 seasons and one of only five coaches in college football history to win 300 games.

Year	Player, College, Position
1993	Jim Ballard, Mount Union, QB
1994	Carey Bender, Coe, RB
1995	Chris Palmer, St. John's (Minn.), WR
1996	Lon Erickson, Ill. Wesleyan, QB
1997	Bill Borchert, Mount Union, QB

MELBERGER AWARD

First presented in 1995 to the nation's outstanding Division III player by the Downtown Wilkes-Barre (Pa.) Touchdown Club.

Year	Player, College, Position
1993	Jim Ballard, Mount Union, QB
1994	Carey Bender, Coe, RB
1995	Craig Kusick, Wis.-La Crosse, QB
1996	Bill Borchert, Mount Union, QB
1997	Bill Borchert, Mount Union, QB

1997 COACHING AWARDS

Eddie Robinson Coach of the Year (FWAA)—Mike Price, Washington St. (Presented by Home Depot and the Football Writers Association of America)

Bear Bryant Coach of the Year—Lloyd Carr, Michigan (Presented by the American Heart Association)

Walter Camp Coach of the Year—Lloyd Carr, Michigan (Presented by the Walter Camp Foundation)

Grant Teaff Coach of the Year Award (FCA)—Tom Osborne, Nebraska (Presented by the Fellowship of Christian Athletes, first year)

AFCA Coach of the Year (I-A)—Lloyd Carr, Michigan (Presented by the American Football Coaches Association)

AFCA Coach of the Year (I-AA)—Andy Talley, Villanova (Presented by the American Football Coaches Association)

AFCA Coach of the Year (NCAA II & NAIA I)—Joe Glenn, Northern Colo. (Presented by the American Football Coaches Association)

AFCA Coach of the Year (NCAA III & NAIA II) Larry Kehres, Mount Union (Presented by the American Football Coaches Association)

AFCA Assistant Coach of the Year (I-A)—Alan Gooch, Central Fla. (RB) (Presented by the American Football Coaches Association)

AFCA Assistant Coach of the Year (I-AA)—Alonzo Lee, Hampton (Def. Coord.) (Presented by the American Football Coaches Association)

AFCA Assistant Coach of the Year (NCAA II & NAIA I)—Richard Cundiff, Texas A&M-Kingsville (Def. Coord.) (Presented by the American Football Coaches Association)

AFCA Assistant Coach of the Year (NCAA III & NAIA II)—Roland Christensen, Wis.-La Crosse (Def. Coord.) (Presented by the American Football Coaches Association)

Eddie Robinson I-AA Coach of the Year—Andy Talley, Villanova (Presented by The Sports Network)

AFQ/Schutt I-A Coach of the Year—Lloyd Carr, Michigan (Presented by American Football Quarterly magazine)

AFQ/Schutt I-AA Coach of the Year—Paul Johnson, Ga. Southern (Presented by American Football Quarterly magazine)

AFQ/Schutt II Coach of the Year—Joe Glenn, Northern Colo. (Presented by American Football Quarterly magazine)

AFQ/Schutt III Coach of the Year—Tim Keating, Western Md. (Presented by American Football Quarterly magazine)

Grant Teaff Lifetime Achievment Award—Eddie Robinson, Grambling (Presented by the Fellowship of Christian Athletes, first year)

COLLEGE FOOTBALL HALL OF FAME

Established: In 1947, by the National Football Foundation and College Hall of Fame, Inc. The first class of enshrinement of Division I or major-college players began in 1951. In 1996, the yearly classes elected were expanded to include other than Division I players. **Eligibility:** A nominated player must be out of college at least 10 years and a first-team all-America selection by a major selector during his career. For divisional (college-division) players, the player must have been a first-team selection on a recognized all-America team in Division I-AA, II and III and the NAIA. Coaches must be retired three years. The voting is done by a 12-member panel made up of athletics directors, conference and bowl officials, and media representatives.

Member players are listed with the final year they played in college, and member coaches are listed with the schools where they coached and the inclusive years of their career. ($) Indicates college-division member. (+) Indicates deceased members. (#) Indicates dual member of the Pro Football Hall of Fame.

Hall of Fame: Only two individuals are enshrined in the College Football Hall of Fame as both a player and a coach. Amos Alonzo Stagg was an all-American at Yale (1889) and was inducted as a coach in 1951. The other two-way inductee is Bobby Dodd, who played at Tennessee (1930) and was inducted as a coach in 1993.

Class of 1997: A total of 34 former players and seven coaches were inducted by the National Football Foundation and Hall of Fame in both divisions during the past year. In Division I, 23 former players and four former coaches joined the legendary group while 11 former players and three former coaches from the divisional (college-division) group were inducted. Grambling's Eddie Robinson became the first coach to join the Hall without the usual three-year waiting period.

Division I Players (Inducted December, 1997): Ray Beck, Georgia Tech, Guard; Randy Duncan, Iowa, Quarterback; Dave Elmendorf, Texas A&M, Defensive Back; Charlie Flowers, Mississippi, Fullback; Ricky Hunley, Arizona, Linebacker; Alex Kroll, Rutgers, Center/Linebacker; Ken MacAfee, Notre Dame, Tight End; Bob Reifsnyder, Navy, Tackle; Dave Rimington, Nebraska, Center; Dave Robinson, Penn St., End; George Rogers, South Caro., Running Back; and Danny White, Arizona St., Quarterback. **Division I Coaches:** Wally Butts, Georgia; Don James, Kent and Washington; and Bowden Wyatt, Wyoming, Arkansas and Tennessee. **Divisional (College-Division) Coach:** Eddie Robinson, Grambling.

Division I Players (Inducted August, 1997): Bob Ferguson, Ohio St., Fullback; Hugh Green, Pittsburgh, Defensive End; Frank Merritt, Army, Offensive Tackle; John Michels, Tennessee, Offensive Guard; Bob Pellagrini, Maryland, Center/Linebacker; Pat Richter, Wisconsin, Wide Receiver; Jerry Robinson, UCLA, Linebacker; James Saxton, Texas, Running Back; Jerry Tubbs, Oklahoma, Center/Linebacker; Charles White, Southern Cal, Running Back; Marc Wilson, Brigham Young, Quarterback. **Division I Coach:** Henry "Red" Sanders, Vanderbilt and UCLA.

Divisional (College-Division) Players (Inducted August, 1997): Joe Cichy, North Dakota St., Defensive Back; Joe Delaney, Northwestern St., Running Back; Fred Dryer, San Diego St., Defensive End; Joe Dudek, Plymouth St., Running Back; William "John" Grinnell, Tufts, End; Frank Hawkins, Nevada, Running Back; Pierce Holt, Angelo St., Defensive Tackle; Gary Johnson, Grambling, Defensive Tackle; Ken O'Brien, UC Davis, Quarterback; Bruce Taylor, Boston U., Defensive Back; Lynn Thomsen, Augustana (Ill.), Defensive Tackle. **Divisional (College-Division) Coaches:** Jim Butterfield, Ithaca and Paul Hoernemann, Heidelberg.

Class of 1998: The National Football Foundation and Hall of Fame (NFFHF) has inducted DB Al Brosky, Illinois; OG Brad Budde, Southern Cal; OT Bill Fralic, Pittsburgh; LB Randy Gradishar, Ohio St.; RB Bo Jackson, Auburn; DT Mel Long, Toledo; QB Jim McMahon, Brigham Young; QB Jerry Rhome, Southern Methodist/Tulsa; C Jim Ritcher, North Caro. St.; RB-DB Johnny Roland, Missouri; C-LB Alex Sarkisian, Northwestern; and DT Bill Stanfill, Georgia. Also, retired Nebraska coach Tom Osborne was added to the induction list.

PLAYERS

Player, College	Year
†Earl Abell, Colgate	1915
Alex Agase, Purdue/Illinois	1946
†Harry Agganis, Boston U.	1952
Frank Albert, Stanford	1941
†Ki Aldrich, Texas Christian	1938
†Malcolm Aldrich, Yale	1921
†Joe Alexander, Syracuse	1920
Lance Alworth, Arkansas#	1961
†Alan Ameche, Wisconsin	1954
†Knowlton Ames, Princeton	1889
Warren Amling, Ohio St.	1946
Dick Anderson, Colorado	1967
Donny Anderson, Texas Tech	1965
†Hunk Anderson, Notre Dame	1921
Doug Atkins, Tennessee#	1952
Bob Babich, Miami (Ohio)	1968
†Everett Bacon, Wesleyan	1912
†Reds Bagnell, Pennsylvania	1950
†Hobey Baker, Princeton	1913
†John Baker, Southern Cal	1931
†Moon Baker, Northwestern	1926
Terry Baker, Oregon St.	1962
†Harold Ballin, Princeton	1914
†Bill Banker, Tulane	1929
Vince Banonis, Detroit	1941
†Stan Barnes, California	1921
†Charles Barrett, Cornell	1915
†Bert Baston, Minnesota	1916
†Cliff Battles, West Va. Wesleyan#	1931
Sammy Baugh, Texas Christian#	1936
Maxie Baughan, Georgia Tech	1959
†James Bausch, Wichita St./Kansas	1930
Ron Beagle, Navy	1955
Gary Beban, UCLA	1967
Hub Bechtol, Texas Tech/Texas	1946
Ray Beck, Georgia Tech	1951
†John Beckett, Oregon	1916
Chuck Bednarik, Pennsylvania#	1948
Forrest Behm, Nebraska	1940
Bobby Bell, Minnesota#	1962
Joe Bellino, Navy	1960
†Marty Below, Wisconsin	1923
†Al Benbrook, Michigan	1910
†Charlie Berry, Lafayette	1924
Angelo Bertelli, Notre Dame	1943
Jay Berwanger, Chicago	1935
†Lawrence Bettencourt, St. Mary's (Cal.)	1927
Fred Biletnikoff, Florida St.#	1964
Doc Blanchard, Army	1946
†Al Blozis, Georgetown	1941
Ed Bock, Iowa St.	1938
†Lynn Bomar, Vanderbilt	1924
†Douglas Bomeisler, Yale	1912
†Albie Booth, Yale	1931
†Fred Borries, Navy	1934
Bruce Bosley, West Va.	1955
Don Bosseler, Miami (Fla.)	1956
Vic Bottari, California	1938
†Ben Boynton, Williams	1920
Terry Bradshaw, Louisiana Tech ($)	1969
†Charles Brewer, Harvard	1895
†Johnny Bright, Drake	1951
John Brodie, Stanford	1956
†George Brooke, Swarthmore/Pennsylvania	1895
Bob Brown, Nebraska	1963
George Brown, Navy/San Diego St.	1947
†Gordon Brown, Yale	1900
Jim Brown, Syracuse#	1956
†John Brown Jr., Navy	1913
†Johnny Mack Brown, Alabama	1925
†Tay Brown, Southern Cal	1932
†Buck Buchanan, Grambling ($)	1962

Player, College	Year
†Paul Bunker, Army	1902
Chris Burford, Stanford	1959
Ron Burton, Northwestern	1959
Dick Butkus, Illinois#	1964
†Robert Butler, Wisconsin	1913
†George Cafego, Tennessee	1939
†Red Cagle, Southwestern La./Army	1929
†John Cain, Alabama	1932
Ed Cameron, Wash. & Lee	1924
†David Campbell, Harvard	1901
Earl Campbell, Texas#	1977
†Jack Cannon, Notre Dame	1929
John Cappelletti, Penn St.	1973
†Frank Carideo, Notre Dame	1930
†Charles Carney, Illinois	1921
J. C. Caroline, Illinois	1954
Bill Carpenter, Army	1959
†Hunter Carpenter, Virginia Tech/North Caro.	1905
Charles Carroll, Washington	1928
Tommy Casanova, LSU	1971
†Edward Casey, Harvard	1919
Howard Cassady, Ohio St.	1955
†Guy Chamberlin, Neb. Wesleyan/Nebraska#	1915
Sam Chapman, California	1937
Bob Chappuis, Michigan	1947
†Paul Christman, Missouri	1940
Joe Cichy, North Dakota St. ($)	1970
†Dutch Clark, Colorado Col.#	1929
Paul Cleary, Southern Cal	1947
†Zora Clevenger, Indiana	1903
Jack Cloud, William & Mary	1949
†Gary Cochran, Princeton	1897
†Josh Cody, Vanderbilt	1919
Don Coleman, Michigan St.	1951
†Charlie Conerly, Mississippi	1947
George Connor, Holy Cross/Notre Dame#	1947
†William Corbin, Yale	1888
William Corbus, Stanford	1933
†Hector Cowan, Princeton	1889
†Edward Coy, Yale	1909
†Fred Crawford, Duke	1933
John David Crow, Texas A&M	1957
†Jim Crowley, Notre Dame	1924
Larry Csonka, Syracuse#	1967
Slade Cutter, Navy	1934
†Ziggie Czarobski, Notre Dame	1947
Carroll Dale, Virginia Tech	1959
†Gerald Dalrymple, Tulane	1931
†John Dalton, Navy	1911
†Charles Daly, Harvard/Army	1902
Averell Daniell, Pittsburgh	1936
†James Daniell, Ohio St.	1941
†Tom Davies, Pittsburgh	1921
†Ernie Davis, Syracuse	1961
Glenn Davis, Army	1946
Robert Davis, Georgia Tech	1947
Pete Dawkins, Army	1958
†Joe Delaney, Northwestern St. ($)	1980
Steve DeLong, Tennessee	1964
Vern Den Herder, Central (Iowa) ($)	1970
Al DeRogatis, Duke	1948
†Paul DesJardien, Chicago	1914
†Aubrey Devine, Iowa	1921
†John DeWitt, Princeton	1903
Buddy Dial, Rice	1958
Mike Ditka, Pittsburgh#	1960
Glenn Dobbs, Tulsa	1942
†Bobby Dodd, Tennessee	1930
Holland Donan, Princeton	1950
†Joseph Donchess, Pittsburgh	1929
Tony Dorsett, Pittsburgh#	1976
†Nathan Dougherty, Tennessee	1909
Nick Drahos, Cornell	1940
†Paddy Driscoll, Northwestern#	1916
†Morley Drury, Southern Cal	1927
Fred Dryer, San Diego St. ($)	1968
Joe Dudek, Plymouth St. ($)	1985
Bill Dudley, Virginia#	1941
Randy Duncan, Iowa	1958
Kenny Easley, UCLA	1980
†Walter Eckersall, Chicago	1906
†Turk Edwards, Washington St.#	1931
†William Edwards, Princeton	1899
†Ray Eichenlaub, Notre Dame	1914

Player, College	Year
Steve Eisenhauer, Navy	1953
Lawrence Elkins, Baylor	1964
Bump Elliott, Michigan/Purdue	1947
Pete Elliott, Michigan	1948
Dave Elmendorf, Texas A&M	1970
Ray Evans, Kansas	1947
†Albert Exendine, Carlisle	1907
†Nello Falaschi, Santa Clara	1936
Tom Fears, Santa Clara/UCLA#	1947
†Beattie Feathers, Tennessee	1933
Bob Fenimore, Oklahoma St.	1946
†Doc Fenton, LSU	1909
Bob Ferguson, Ohio St.	1961
John Ferraro, Southern Cal	1947
†Wes Fesler, Ohio St.	1930
†Bill Fincher, Davidson/Georgia Tech	1920
Bill Fischer, Notre Dame	1948
†Hamilton Fish, Harvard	1909
†Robert Fisher, Harvard	1911
†Allen Flowers, Davidson/Georgia Tech	1920
Charlie Flowers, Mississippi	1959
†Danny Fortmann, Colgate#	1935
Sam Francis, Nebraska	1936
†Ed Franco, Fordham	1937
†Clint Frank, Yale	1937
Rodney Franz, California	1949
Tucker Frederickson, Auburn	1964
†Benny Friedman, Michigan	1926
Bob Ferguson, Ohio St.	1961
Roman Gabriel, North Caro. St.	1961
Bob Gain, Kentucky	1950
†Arnold Galiffa, Army	1949
Hugh Gallarneau, Stanford	1940
†Edgar Garbisch, Wash. & Jeff./Army	1924
Mike Garrett, Southern Cal	1965
†Charles Gelbert, Pennsylvania	1896
†Forest Geyer, Oklahoma	1915
Jake Gibbs, Mississippi	1960
Paul Giel, Minnesota	1953
Frank Gifford, Southern Cal#	1951
†Walter Gilbert, Auburn	1936
Harry Gilmer, Alabama	1947
†George Gipp, Notre Dame	1920
†Chet Gladchuk, Boston College	1940
Bill Glass, Baylor	1956
Rich Glover, Nebraska	1972
Marshall Goldberg, Pittsburgh	1938
Gene Goodreault, Boston College	1940
†Walter Gordon, California	1918
†Paul Governali, Columbia	1942
Jim Grabowski, Illinois	1965
Otto Graham, Northwestern#	1943
†Red Grange, Illinois#	1925
†Bobby Grayson, Stanford	1935
Hugh Green, Pittsburgh	1980
†Jack Green, Tulane/Army	1945
Joe Greene, North Texas#	1968
Bob Griese, Purdue#	1966
Archie Griffin, Ohio St.	1975
William Grinnell, Tufts ($)	1934
Jerry Groom, Notre Dame	1950
†Merle Gulick, Toledo/Hobart	1929
†Joe Guyon, Carlisle/Georgia Tech#	1918
John Hadl, Kansas	1961
†Edwin Hale, Mississippi Col.	1921
L. Parker Hall, Mississippi	1938
Jack Ham, Penn St.#	1970
Bob Hamilton, Stanford	1935
†Tom Hamilton, Navy	1926
†Vic Hanson, Syracuse	1926
†Pat Harder, Wisconsin	1942
†Tack Hardwick, Harvard	1914
†T. Truxton Hare, Pennsylvania	1900
†Chick Harley, Ohio St.	1919
†Tom Harmon, Michigan	1940
†Howard Harpster, Carnegie Mellon	1928
†Edward Hart, Princeton	1911
Leon Hart, Notre Dame	1949
Bill Hartman, Georgia	1937
Frank Hawkins, Nevada ($)	1980
†Homer Hazel, Rutgers	1924
†Matt Hazeltine, California	1954
†Ed Healey, Holy Cross/Dartmouth#	1919
†Pudge Heffelfinger, Yale	1891

Player, College	Year
†Mel Hein, Washington St.#	1930
†Don Heinrich, Washington	1952
Ted Hendricks, Miami (Fla.)#	1968
†Wilbur Henry, Wash. & Jeff.#	1919
†Clarence Herschberger, Chicago	1898
†Robert Herwig, California	1937
†Willie Heston, San Jose St./Michigan	1904
†Herman Hickman, Tennessee	1931
†William Hickok, Yale	1894
†Dan Hill, Duke	1938
†Art Hillebrand, Princeton	1899
†Frank Hinkey, Yale	1894
†Carl Hinkle, Vanderbilt	1937
†Clarke Hinkle, Bucknell#	1931
Elroy Hirsch, Wisconsin/Michigan#	1943
†James Hitchcock, Auburn	1932
†Frank Hoffmann, Notre Dame	1931
†James J. Hogan, Yale	1904
†Brud Holland, Cornell	1938
†Don Holleder, Army	1955
†Bill Hollenback, Pennsylvania	1908
Mike Holovak, Boston College	1942
Pierce Holt, Angelo St. ($)	1987
E. J. Holub, Texas Tech	1960
Paul Hornung, Notre Dame#	1956
†Edwin Horrell, California	1924
†Les Horvath, Ohio St.	1944
†Arthur Howe, Yale	1911
†Dixie Howell, Alabama	1934
†Cal Hubbard, Geneva/Centenary (La.)#	1926
†John Hubbard, Amherst	1906
†Pooley Hubert, Alabama	1925
Sam Huff, West Va.#	1955
Weldon Humble, Southwestern La./Rice	1946
Ricky Hunley, Arizona	1983
†Joel Hunt, Texas A&M	1927
†Ellery Huntington, Colgate	1913
†Don Hutson, Alabama#	1934
†Jonas Ingram, Navy	1906
†Cecil Isbell, Purdue	1937
†Harvey Jablonsky, Army/Washington (Mo.)	1933
†Vic Janowicz, Ohio St.	1951
†Darold Jenkins, Missouri	1941
†Jackie Jensen, California	1948
†Herbert Joesting, Minnesota	1927
Billy Johnson, Widener ($)	1972
Bob Johnson, Tennessee	1967
Gary Johnson, Grambling ($)	1974
†Jimmie Johnson, Carlisle/Northwestern	1905
Ron Johnson, Michigan	1968
†Calvin Jones, Iowa	1955
†Gomer Jones, Ohio St.	1935
Lee Roy Jordan, Alabama	1962
†Frank Juhan, Sewanee	1910
Charlie Justice, North Caro.	1949
†Mort Kaer, Southern Cal	1926
Alex Karras, Iowa	1957
Ken Kavanaugh, LSU	1939
†Edgar Kaw, Cornell	1922
Dick Kazmaier, Princeton	1951
†Stan Keck, Princeton	1921
Larry Kelley, Yale	1936
†Wild Bill Kelly, Montana	1926
Doug Kenna, Army	1944
†George Kerr, Boston College	1940
†Henry Ketcham, Yale	1913
Leroy Keyes, Purdue	1968
†Glenn Killinger, Penn St.	1921
†John Kilpatrick, Yale	1910
John Kimbrough, Texas A&M	1940
†Frank Kinard, Mississippi#	1937
†Phillip King, Princeton	1893
†Nile Kinnick, Iowa	1939
†Harry Kipke, Michigan	1923
†John Kitzmiller, Oregon	1930
†Barton Koch, Baylor	1930
†Walt Koppisch, Columbia	1924
Ron Kramer, Michigan	1956
Alex Kroll, Rutgers	1961
Charlie Krueger, Texas A&M	1957
Malcolm Kutner, Texas	1941
Ted Kwalick, Penn St.	1968
†Steve Lach, Duke	1941
†Myles Lane, Dartmouth	1927
Johnny Lattner, Notre Dame	1953
Hank Lauricella, Tennessee	1951
†Lester Lautenschlaeger, Tulane	1925
†Elmer Layden, Notre Dame	1924
†Bobby Layne, Texas#	1947
†Langdon Lea, Princeton	1895
Eddie LeBaron, Pacific (Cal.)	1949
†James Leech, VMI	1920
†Darrell Lester, Texas Christian	1935
Bob Lilly, Texas Christian#	1960
†Augie Lio, Georgetown	1940
Floyd Little, Syracuse	1966
†Gordon Locke, Iowa	1922
†Don Lourie, Princeton	1921
Neil Lomax, Portland St. ($)	1980
Richie Lucas, Penn St.	1959
Sid Luckman, Columbia#	1938
Johnny Lujack, Notre Dame	1947
†Pug Lund, Minnesota	1934
Jim Lynch, Notre Dame	1966
Ken MacAfee, Notre Dame	1977
Robert MacLeod, Dartmouth	1938
†Bart Macomber, Illinois	1916
Dicky Maegle, Rice	1954
†Ned Mahon, Harvard	1915
Johnny Majors, Tennessee	1956
†William Mallory, Yale	1923
Vaughn Mancha, Alabama	1947
†Gerald Mann, Southern Methodist	1927
Archie Manning, Mississippi	1970
Edgar Manske, Northwestern	1933
Ed Marinaro, Cornell	1971
Vic Markov, Washington	1937
†Bobby Marshall, Minnesota	1906
Jim Martin, Notre Dame	1949
Ollie Matson, San Francisco#	1951
Ray Matthews, Texas Christian	1927
†John Maulbetsch, Adrian/Michigan	1916
†Pete Mauthe, Penn St.	1912
†Robert Maxwell, Chicago/Swarthmore	1905
George McAfee, Duke#	1939
†Thomas McClung, Yale	1891
Bill McColl, Stanford	1951
†Jim McCormick, Princeton	1907
Tommy McDonald, Oklahoma	1956
†Jack McDowall, North Caro. St.	1927
Hugh McElhenny, Washington#	1951
†Gene McEver, Tennessee	1931
†John McEwan, Army	1916
Banks McFadden, Clemson	1939
Bud McFadin, Texas	1950
Mike McGee, Duke	1959
†Edward McGinley, Pennsylvania	1924
†John McGovern, Minnesota	1910
Thurman McGraw, Colorado St.	1949
Tyrone McGriff, Florida A&M ($)	1979
†Mike McKeever, Southern Cal	1960
†George McLaren, Pittsburgh	1918
†Dan McMillan, Southern Cal/California	1921
†Bo McMillin, Centre	1921
†Bob McWhorter, Georgia	1913
†Roy Mercer, Pennsylvania	1912
Don Meredith, Southern Methodist	1959
Frank Merritt, Army	1943
†Bert Metzger, Notre Dame	1930
†Wayne Meylan, Nebraska	1967
Lou Michaels, Kentucky	1957
John Michels, Tennessee	1952
Abe Mickal, LSU	1935
Creighton Miller, Notre Dame	1943
†Don Miller, Notre Dame	1924
†Eugene Miller, Penn St.	1913
†Fred Miller, Notre Dame	1928
†Rip Miller, Notre Dame	1924
†Wayne Millner, Notre Dame#	1935
†Century Milstead, Wabash/Yale	1923
†John Minds, Pennsylvania	1897
Skip Minisi, Pennsylvania/Navy	1947
Dick Modzelewski, Maryland	1952
†Alex Moffat, Princeton	1883
†Ed Molinski, Tennessee	1940
Cliff Montgomery, Columbia	1933
Wilbert Montgomery, Abilene Christian ($)	1976
Donn Moomaw, UCLA	1952
†William Morley, Columbia	1901
George Morris, Georgia Tech	1952
Larry Morris, Georgia Tech	1954
†Bill Morton, Dartmouth	1931
Craig Morton, California	1964
†Monk Moscrip, Stanford	1935
†Brick Muller, California	1922
†Bronko Nagurski, Minnesota#	1929
†Ernie Nevers, Stanford#	1925
†Marshall Newell, Harvard	1893
Harry Newman, Michigan	1932
Ozzie Newsome, Alabama	1977
Gifford Nielsen, Brigham Young	1977
Tommy Nobis, Texas	1965
Leo Nomellini, Minnesota#	1949
†Andrew Oberlander, Dartmouth	1925
†Davey O'Brien, Texas Christian	1938
Ken O'Brien, UC Davis ($)	1982
†Pat O'Dea, Wisconsin	1899
Bob Odell, Pennsylvania	1943
†Jack O'Hearn, Cornell	1914
Robin Olds, Army	1942
†Elmer Oliphant, Army/Purdue	1917
Merlin Olsen, Utah St.#	1961
Dennis Onkotz, Penn St.	1969
†Bennie Oosterbaan, Michigan	1927
Charles O'Rourke, Boston College	1940
†John Orsi, Colgate	1931
†Win Osgood, Cornell/Pennsylvania	1894
Bill Osmanski, Holy Cross	1938
†George Owen, Harvard	1922
Jim Owens, Oklahoma	1949
Steve Owens, Oklahoma	1969
Alan Page, Notre Dame#	1966
Jack Pardee, Texas A&M	1956
Babe Parilli, Kentucky	1951
Ace Parker, Duke#	1936
Jackie Parker, Mississippi St.	1953
Jim Parker, Ohio St.#	1956
Walter Payton, Jackson St. ($)	1974
†Vince Pazzetti, Wesleyan/Lehigh	1912
Chub Peabody, Harvard	1941
†Robert Peck, Pittsburgh	1916
Bob Pellegrini, Maryland	1955
†Stan Pennock, Harvard	1914
George Pfann, Cornell	1923
†H. D. Phillips, Sewanee	1905
Loyd Phillips, Arkansas	1966
Pete Pihos, Indiana#	1946
†Erny Pinckert, Southern Cal	1931
John Pingel, Michigan St.	1938
Jim Plunkett, Stanford	1970
†Arthur Poe, Princeton	1899
†Fritz Pollard, Brown	1916
George Poole, Mississippi/North Caro./Army	1948
Marvin Powell, Southern Cal	1976
Merv Pregulman, Michigan	1943
†Eddie Price, Tulane	1949
†Peter Pund, Georgia Tech	1928
Garrard Ramsey, William & Mary	1942
Gary Reasons, Northwestern St. ($)	1983
Rick Redman, Washington	1964
†Claude Reeds, Oklahoma	1913
Mike Reid, Penn St.	1969
Steve Reid, Northwestern	1936
†William Reid, Harvard	1899
Bob Reifsnyder, Navy	1958
Mel Renfro, Oregon#	1963
†Pug Rentner, Northwestern	1932
†Bob Reynolds, Stanford	1935
†Bobby Reynolds, Nebraska	1952
Les Richter, California	1951
Pat Richter, Wisconsin	1962
†Jack Riley, Northwestern	1931
Dave Rimington, Nebraska	1982
†Charles Rinehart, Lafayette	1897
J. D. Roberts, Oklahoma	1953
†Paul Robeson, Rutgers	1918
Dave Robinson, Penn St.	1962
Jerry Robinson, UCLA	1978
George Rogers, South Caro.	1980
†Ira Rodgers, West Va.	1919

Player, College	Year
†Edward Rogers, Carlisle/Minnesota	1903
Joe Romig, Colorado	1961
†Aaron Rosenberg, Southern Cal	1933
Kyle Rote, Southern Methodist	1950
†Joe Routt, Texas A&M	1937
†Red Salmon, Notre Dame	1903
†George Sauer, Nebraska	1933
George Savitsky, Pennsylvania	1947
James Saxton, Texas	1961
Gale Sayers, Kansas#	1964
Jack Scarbath, Maryland	1952
†Hunter Scarlett, Pennsylvania	1908
Bob Schloredt, Washington	1960
†Wear Schoonover, Arkansas	1929
†Dave Schreiner, Wisconsin	1942
†Germany Schultz, Michigan	1908
†Dutch Schwab, Lafayette	1922
†Marchy Schwartz, Notre Dame	1931
†Paul Schwegler, Washington	1931
Clyde Scott, Navy/Arkansas	1948
Richard Scott, Navy	1947
Tom Scott, Virginia	1952
†Henry Seibels, Sewanee	1900
Ron Sellers, Florida St.	1968
Lee Roy Selmon, Oklahoma#	1975
†Bill Shakespeare, Notre Dame	1935
†Murray Shelton, Cornell	1915
†Tom Shevlin, Yale	1905
†Bernie Shively, Illinois	1926
†Monk Simons, Tulane	1934
O. J. Simpson, Southern Cal#	1968
Billy Sims, Oklahoma	1979
Mike Singletary, Baylor	1980
Fred Sington, Alabama	1930
†Frank Sinkwich, Georgia	1942
†Emil Sitko, Notre Dame	1949
†Joe Skladany, Pittsburgh	1933
†Duke Slater, Iowa	1921
†Bruce Smith, Minnesota	1941
Bubba Smith, Michigan St.	1966
†Clipper Smith, Notre Dame	1927
†Ernie Smith, Southern Cal	1932
Harry Smith, Southern Cal	1939
Jim Ray Smith, Baylor	1954
Riley Smith, Alabama	1935
†Vernon Smith, Georgia	1931
†Neil Snow, Michigan	1901
Al Sparlis, UCLA	1945
†Clarence Spears, Knox/Dartmouth	1915
†W. D. Spears, Vanderbilt	1927
†William Sprackling, Brown	1911
†Bud Sprague, Army/Texas	1928
Steve Spurrier, Florida	1966
Harrison Stafford, Texas	1932
†Amos Alonzo Stagg, Yale	1889
†Max Starcevich, Washington	1936
Roger Staubach, Navy#	1964
†Walter Steffen, Chicago	1908
Joe Steffy, Tennessee/Army	1947
†Herbert Stein, Pittsburgh	1921
Bob Steuber, DePauw/Missouri	1943
†Mal Stevens, Washburn/Yale	1923
†Vincent Stevenson, Pennsylvania	1905
Jim Stillwagon, Ohio St.	1970
†Pete Stinchcomb, Ohio St.	1920
Brock Strom, Air Force	1958
†Ken Strong, New York U.#	1928
†George Strupper, Georgia Tech	1917
†Harry Stuhldreher, Notre Dame	1924
†Herb Sturhahn, Yale	1926
†Joe Stydahar, West Va.#	1935
†Bob Suffridge, Tennessee	1940
†Steve Suhey, Penn St.	1947
Pat Sullivan, Auburn	1971
†Frank Sundstrom, Cornell	1923
Lynn Swann, Southern Cal	1973
†Clarence Swanson, Nebraska	1921
†Bill Swiacki, Holy Cross/Columbia	1947
Jim Swink, Texas Christian	1956
George Taliaferro, Indiana	1948
Fran Tarkenton, Georgia#	1960
John Tavener, Indiana	1944
Bruce Taylor, Boston U. ($)	1969
†Chuck Taylor, Stanford	1942
Aurelius Thomas, Ohio St.	1957
†Joe Thompson, Geneva/Pittsburgh	1906
Lynn Thomsen, Augustana (Ill.)$	1986

Player, College	Year
†Samuel Thorne, Yale	1895
†Jim Thorpe, Carlisle#	1912
†Ben Ticknor, Harvard	1930
†John Tigert, Vanderbilt	1903
Gaynell Tinsley, LSU	1936
Eric Tipton, Duke	1938
†Clayton Tonnemaker, Minnesota	1949
†Bob Torrey, Pennsylvania	1905
†Brick Travis, Tarkio/Missouri	1920
Charley Trippi, Georgia#	1946
†Edward Tryon, Colgate	1925
Jerry Tubbs, Oklahoma	1956
Bulldog Turner, Hardin-Simmons#	1939
Howard Twilley, Tulsa	1965
†Joe Utay, Texas A&M	1907
†Norm Van Brocklin, Oregon#	1948
†Dale Van Sickel, Florida	1929
†H. Van Surdam, Wesleyan	1905
†Dexter Very, Penn St.	1912
Billy Vessels, Oklahoma	1952
†Ernie Vick, Michigan	1921
†Hube Wagner, Pittsburgh	1913
Doak Walker, Southern Methodist#	1949
†Bill Wallace, Rice	1935
†Adam Walsh, Notre Dame	1924
†Cotton Warburton, Southern Cal	1934
Bob Ward, Maryland	1951
†William Warner, Cornell	1902
†Kenny Washington, UCLA	1939
†Jim Weatherall, Oklahoma	1951
George Webster, Michigan St.	1966
Herman Wedemeyer, St. Mary's (Cal.)	1947
†Harold Weekes, Columbia	1902
Art Weiner, North Caro.	1949
†Ed Weir, Nebraska	1925
†Gus Welch, Carlisle	1914
†John Weller, Princeton	1935
†Percy Wendell, Harvard	1912
†Belford West, Colgate	1919
†Bob Westfall, Michigan	1941
†Babe Weyand, Army	1915
†Buck Wharton, Pennsylvania	1896
†Arthur Wheeler, Princeton	1894
Byron White, Colorado	1937
Charles White, Southern Cal	1979
Danny White, Arizona St.	1973
Randy White, Maryland#	1974
†Don Whitmire, Navy/Alabama	1944
†Frank Wickhorst, Navy	1926
Ed Widseth, Minnesota	1936
†Dick Wildung, Minnesota	1942
Bob Williams, Notre Dame	1950
Froggie Williams, Rice	1949
Bill Willis, Ohio St.#	1944
Bobby Wilson, Southern Methodist	1935
†George Wilson, Washington	1925
†Harry Wilson, Army/Penn St.	1927
Marc Wilson, Brigham Young	1979
Mike Wilson, Lafayette	1928
Albert Wistert, Michigan	1942
Alvin Wistert, Boston U./Michigan	1949
†Whitey Wistert, Michigan	1933
†Alex Wojciechowicz, Fordham#	1937
†Barry Wood, Harvard	1931
†Andy Wyant, Bucknell/Chicago	1894
†Bowden Wyatt, Tennessee	1938
†Clint Wyckoff, Cornell	1895
†Tommy Yarr, Notre Dame	1931
Ron Yary, Southern Cal	1967
†Lloyd Yoder, Carnegie Mellon	1926
†Buddy Young, Illinois	1946
†Harry Young, Wash. & Lee	1916
†Waddy Young, Oklahoma	1938
Jack Youngblood, Florida	1970
Jim Youngblood, Tennessee Tech ($)	1972
Gust Zarnas, Ohio St.	1937

COACHES

Coach	Year
†Joe Aillet	1989
†Bill Alexander	1951
†Ed Anderson	1971
†Ike Armstrong	1957
†Charlie Bachman	1978
Earl Banks	1992
†Harry Baujan	1990
†Matty Bell	1955

Coach	Year
†Hugo Bezdek	1954
†Dana X. Bible	1951
†Bernie Bierman	1955
Bob Blackman	1987
†Earl "Red" Blaik	1964
Frank Broyles	1983
†Paul "Bear" Bryant	1986
Harold Burry ($)	1996
Jim Butterfield ($)	1997
†Wally Butts	1997
†Charlie Caldwell	1961
†Walter Camp	1951
Len Casanova	1977
†Frank Cavanaugh	1954
†Dick Colman	1990
†Fritz Crisler	1954
†Duffy Daugherty	1984
†Bob Devaney	1981
Dan Devine	1985
†Gil Dobie	1951
†Bobby Dodd	1993
†Michael Donahue	1951
Vince Dooley	1994
†Gus Dorais	1954
†Bill Edwards	1986
†Rip Engle	1973
†Don Faurot	1961
†Jake Gaither	1975
Sid Gillman#	1989
†Ernest Godfrey	1972
Ray Graves	1990
†Andy Gustafson	1985
†Edward Hall	1951
†Jack Hardin	1980
†Richard Harlow	1954
†Harvey Harman	1981
†Jesse Harper	1971
†Percy Haughton	1951
†Woody Hayes	1983
†John W. Heisman	1954
†Robert Higgins	1954
†Paul Hoernemann ($)	1997
†Babe Hollingberry	1979
†Frank Howard	1989
†Bill Ingram	1973
Don James	1997
†Morley Jennings	1973
†Biff Jones	1954
†Howard Jones	1951
†Tad Jones	1958
†Lloyd Jordan	1978
†Ralph "Shug" Jordan	1982
†Andy Kerr	1951
Frank Kush	1995
†Frank Leahy	1970
†George Little	1955
†Lou Little	1960
†Slip Madigan	1974
Dave Maurer	1991
Charlie McClendon	1986
Herb McCracken	1973
†Dan McGugin	1951
John McKay	1988
Allyn McKeen	1991
†Tuss McLaughry	1962
†John Merritt	1994
†Dutch Meyer	1956
†Jack Mollenkopf	1988
†Bernie Moore	1954
†Scrappy Moore	1980
†Ray Morrison	1954
†George Munger	1976
†Clarence "Biggie" Munn	1959
†Bill Murray	1974
†Frank Murray	1974
†Ed "Hook" Mylin	1974
†Earle "Greasy" Neale #	1967
†Jess Neely	1971
†David Nelson	1987
†Robert Neyland	1956
†Homer Norton	1971
†Frank "Buck" O'Neill	1951
†Bennie Owen	1951
Ara Parseghian	1980
†Doyt Perry	1988
†Jimmy Phelan	1973
†Tommy Prothro	1991

Coach	Year
John Ralston	1992
†E. N. Robinson	1955
Eddie Robinson ($)	1997
†Knute Rockne	1951
†Dick Romney	1954
†Bill Roper	1951
Darrell Royal	1983
†Henry "Red" Sanders	1996
†George Sanford	1971
Glenn "Bo" Schembechler	1993
†Francis Schmidt	1971
†Ben Schwartzwalder	1982
†Clark Shaughnessy	1968
†Buck Shaw	1972
Edgar Sherman ($)	1996
†Andy Smith	1951
†Carl Snavely	1965
†Amos Alonzo Stagg	1951
†Gil Steinke ($)	1996
†Jock Sutherland	1951
†Jim Tatum	1984
†Frank Thomas	1951
†Lee Tressel ($)	1996
†Thad "Pie" Vann	1987
Johnny Vaught	1979
†Wallace Wade	1955
†Lynn "Pappy" Waldorf	1966
†Glenn "Pop" Warner	1951
†E. E. "Tad" Wieman	1956
†John Wilce	1954
†Bud Wilkinson	1969
†Henry Williams	1951
†George Woodruff	1963
†Warren Woodson	1989
†Bowden Wyatt	1997
†Fielding "Hurry Up" Yost	1951
†Bob Zuppke	1951

†Deceased

First-Team All-Americans Below Division I-A

1997 Selectors (and division[s]): American Football Coaches Association (I-AA, II, III); Associated Press (I-AA, II, III); College Sports Information Directors of America (II); Football Gazette (I-AA, II, III); Sports Network (I-AA).

Selection of Associated Press Little All-America Teams began in 1934. Early AP selectors were not bound by NCAA membership classifications; therefore, several current Division I-A teams are included in this list.

The American Football Coaches Association began selecting all-America teams below Division I-A in 1967 for two College-Division classifications. Its College-Division I team includes NCAA Division II and National Association of Intercollegiate Athletics (NAIA) Division I players. The AFCA College-Division II team includes NCAA Division III and NAIA Division II players. The AFCA added a Division I-AA team in 1979; AP began selecting a Division I-AA team in 1982; the Sports Network added a Division I-AA team in 1994; and these players are included. In 1993, the College Sports Information Directors of America Division II team was added, selected by sports information directors from every NCAA Division II institution. In 1990, the Champion USA Division III team was added, selected by a panel of 25 sports information directors and replaced by the Hewlett-Packard Division III team in 1995. In 1993, Football Gazette's team was added for Divisions I-AA, II and III.

Nonmembers of the NCAA are included in this list, as are colleges that no longer play varsity football.

Players selected to a Division I-AA all-America team are indicated by (†). Current members of Division I-A are indicated by (*).

All-Americans are listed by college, year selected and position.

ABILENE CHRISTIAN (18)
48— V. T. Smith, B
51— Lester Wheeler, OT
52— Wallace Bullington, DB
65— Larry Cox, OT
69— Chip Bennett, LB
70— Jim Lindsey, QB
73— Wilbert Montgomery, RB
74— Chip Martin, DL
77— Chuck Sitton, DB
82— Grant Feasel, C
83— Mark Wilson, DB
84— Dan Remsberg, OT
87— Richard Van Druten, OT
89— John Layfield, OG
90— Dennis Brown, PK
91— Jay Jones, LB
97— Junior Filikitonga, DL
Victor Burke, DB

ADAMS ST. (5)
79— Ronald Johnson, DB
84— Bill Stone, RB
87— Dave Humann, DB
95— Chris Perry, WR
97— Jason Van Dyke, P

AKRON* (9)
69— John Travis, OG
71— Michael Hatch, DB
76— Mark Van Horn, OG
Steve Cockerham, LB
77— Steve Cockerham, LB
80—†Brad Reece, LB
81—†Brad Reece, LB
85—†Wayne Grant, DL
86—†Mike Clark, RB

UAB* (1)
94—†Derrick Ingram, WR

ALABAMA A&M (3)
87— Howard Ballard, OL
88— Fred Garner, DB
89— Barry Wagner, WR

ALABAMA ST. (3)
90—†Eddie Robinson, LB
91—†Patrick Johnson, OL
†Eddie Robinson, LB

ALBANY (N.Y.) (2)
92— Scott Turrin, OL
94— Scott Turrin, OL

ALBANY ST. (GA.) (1)
72— Harold Little, DE

ALBION (13)
40— Walter Ptak, G
58— Tom Taylor, E
76— Steve Spencer, DL
86— Joe Felton, OG
Mike Grant, DB
91— Hank Wineman, RB
93— Ron Dawson, OL
Jeff Brooks, OL
94— Jeff Robinson, RB
Martin Heyboer, C
David Lefere, DB
95— David Lefere, DB
96— Jason Carriveau, OG

ALBRIGHT (6)
36— Richard Riffle, B
37— Richard Riffle, B
75— Chris Simcic, OL
95— Dennis Unger, PK
96— Ryan Ditze, WR
Bob Maro, DB

ALCORN ST. (13)
69— David Hadley, DB
70— Fred Carter, DT
71— Harry Gooden, LB
72— Alex Price, DT
73— Leonard Fairley, DB
74— Jerry Dismuke, OG
75— Lawrence Pillers, DE
76— Augusta Lee, RB
Larry Warren, DT
79—†Leslie Frazier, DB
84—†Issiac Holt, DB
93—†Goree White, KR
94—†Steve McNair, QB

ALFRED (7)
51— Ralph DiMicco, B
52— Ralph DiMicco, B
55— Charles Schultz, E
56— Charles Schultz, E
75— Joseph Van Cura, DE
82— Brian O'Neil, DB
92— Mark Obuszewski, DB

ALLEGHENY (21)
75— Charles Slater, OL
87— Mike Mates, OL
88— Mike Parker, DL
90— Jeff Filkovski, QB
David LaCarte, DB
John Marzca, C
91— Ron Bendekovic, OT
Stanley Drayton, RB
Tony Bifulco, DB
92— Ron Bendekovic, OT
Stanley Drayton, RB
94— Matt Allison, OL
Paul Bell, QB
Marvin Farr, DB
95— Brian Adams, C
Nick Reiser, DE
Anson Park, OL
96— Chris Conrad, KR
Nick Reiser, DL
Bob Tatsch, DL
97— Jim Mormino, RB

AMERICAN INT'L (10)
71— Bruce Laird, RB
80— Ed Cebula, C
82— Paul Thompson, DT
85— Keith Barry, OL
86— Jon Provost, OL
87— Jon Provost, OL
88— Greg Doherty, OL
89— Lamont Cato, DB
90— George Patterson, DL
91— Gabe Mokwuah, DL

AMHERST (5)
42— Adrian Hasse, E
72— Richard Murphy, QB
73— Fred Scott, FL
96— Alex Bernstein, DL
97— Devin Moriarty, DL

ANDERSON (1)
97— Justin Shively, P

ANGELO ST. (13)
75— James Cross, DB
78— Jerry Aldridge, RB
Kelvin Smith, LB
81— Clay Weishuhn, LB
82— Mike Elarms, WR
83— Mike Thomas, K
85— Henry Jackson, LB
86— Pierce Holt, DL
87— Pierce Holt, DL
88— Henry Alsbrooks, LB
92— Jimmy Morris, P
93— Anthony Hooper, DB
95— Greg Stokes, LB

APPALACHIAN ST. (22)
48— John Caskey, E
63— Greg Van Orden, G
85—†Dino Hackett, LB
87—†Anthony Downs, DE
88—†Bjorn Nittmo, PK
89—†Derrick Graham, OL
†Keith Collins, DB
91—†Harold Alexander, P
92—†Avery Hall, DL
†Harold Alexander, P
94—†Chip Miller, DL
†William Peebles, DL
†Brad Ohrt, OL
†Dexter Coakley, LB
†Matt Stevens, DB
95—†Dexter Coakley, LB
†Matt Stevens, DB
†Chip Miller, DL
†Scott Kadlub, C
96—†Scott Kadlub, C
†Dexter Coakley, LB
97—†Jackie Avery, DL

ARIZONA* (1)
41— Henry Stanton, E

ARKANSAS ST.* (17)
53— Richard Woit, B
64— Dan Summers, OG
65— Dan Summers, OG
68— Bill Bergey, LB
69— Dan Buckley, C
Clovis Swinney, DT
70— Bill Phillips, OG
Calvin Harrell, HB
71— Calvin Harrell, RB
Dennis Meyer, DB
Wayne Dorton, OG
73— Doug Lowrey, OG
84—†Carter Crawford, DL
85—†Carter Crawford, DL
86—†Randy Barnhill, OG
87—†Jim Wiseman, C
†Charlie Fredrick, DT

ARKANSAS TECH (3)
58— Edward Meador, B
61— Powell McClellan, E
95— Piotr Styczen, PK

ASHLAND (9)
70— Len Pettigrew, LB
78— Keith Dare, DL
85— Jeff Penko, OL
86— Vince Mazza, PK
89— Douglas Powell, DB
90— Morris Furman, LB

91— Ron Greer, LB
93— Bill Royce, DL
94— Sam Hohler, DE

AUGUSTANA (ILL.) (11)
72— Willie Van, DT
73— Robert Martin, OT
83— Kurt Kapischke, OL
84— Greg King, C
86— Lynn Thomsen, DL
87— Carlton Beasley, DL
88— John Bothe, OL
90— Barry Reade, PK
91— Mike Hesler, DB
92— George Annang, DL
95— Rusty Van Wetzinga, LB

AUGUSTANA (S.D.) (4)
60— John Simko, E
87— Tony Adkins, DL
88— Pete Jaros, DB
94— Bryan Schwartz, LB

AUGSBURG (1)
97— Scott Hvistendahl, WR

AUSTIN (10)
37— Wallace Johnson, C
79— Price Clifford, LB
80— Chris Luper, DB
81— Larry Shillings, QB
83— Ed Holt, DL
84— Jeff Timmons, PK
87— Otis Amy, WR
88— Otis Amy, WR
90— Jeff Cordell, DB
94— Brent Badger, P

AUSTIN PEAY (8)
65— Tim Chilcutt, DB
66— John Ogles, FB
70— Harold Roberts, OE
77— Bob Bible, LB
78— Mike Betts, DB
80— Brett Williams, DE
82— Charlie Tucker, OL
92—†Richard Darden, DL

AZUSA PACIFIC (2)
86— Christian Okoye, RB
95— Jake Wiersma, OL

BAKER (3)
83— Chris Brown, LB
85— Kevin Alewine, RB
90— John Campbell, OL

BALDWIN-WALLACE (12)
50— Norbert Hecker, E
68— Bob Quackenbush, DT
78— Jeff Jenkins, OL
80— Dan Delfino, DE
82— Pete Primeau, DL
83— Steve Varga, K
89— Doug Halbert, DL
91— John Koz, QB
Jim Clardy, LB
94— Chris Kondik, PK
Phil Sahley, DL
97— Fred Saylor, DL

BALL ST.* (4)
67— Oscar Lubke, OT
68— Amos Van Pelt, HB
72— Douglas Bell, C
73— Terry Schmidt, DB

BATES (1)
81— Larry DiGammarino, WR

BELOIT (1)
95— Maurice Redd, DB

BEMIDJI ST. (1)
83— Bruce Ecklund, TE

BENEDICTINE (ILL.) (3)
72— Mike Rogowski, LB
92— Bob McMillen, TE
93— Eric Green, KR

BENEDICTINE (KAN.) (1)
36— Leo Deutsch, E

BETHANY (W.VA.) (2)
77— Scott Lanz, P
93— Brian Darden, PK

BETHEL (KAN.) (1)
80— David Morford, C

BETHUNE-COOKMAN (2)
75— Willie Lee, DE
81— Booker Reese, DE

BIRMINGHAM-SOUTHERN (1)
37— Walter Riddle, T

BISHOP (1)
81— Carlton Nelson, DL

BLOOMSBURG (11)
79— Mike Morucci, RB
82— Mike Blake, TE
83— Frank Sheptock, LB
84— Frank Sheptock, LB
85— Frank Sheptock, LB
Tony Woods, DB
91— Eric Jonassen, OL
96— Ron Lelko, WR
Sean Smith, KR
97— Irvin Sigler, RB
Tim Baer, OL

BOISE ST. *(23)
72— Al Marshall, OE
73— Don Hutt, WR
74— Jim McMillan, QB
75— John Smith, FL
77— Chris Malmgren, DT
Terry Hutt, WR
Harold Cotton, OT
79—†Joe Aliotti, QB
†Doug Scott, DT
80—†Randy Trautman, DT
81—†Randy Trautman, DT
†Rick Woods, DB
82—†John Rade, DL
†Carl Keever, LB
84—†Carl Keever, LB
85—†Marcus Koch, DL
87—†Tom DeWitz, OG
†Pete Kwiatkowski, DT
90—†Erik Helgeson, DL
91—†Frank Robinson, DB
92—†Michael Dodd, PK
94—†Joe O'Brien, DL
†Rashid Gayle, DB

BOSTON U. (19)
67— Dick Farley, DB
68— Bruce Taylor, DB
69— Bruce Taylor, DB
79—†Mal Najarian, RB
†Tom Pierzga, DL
81—†Bob Speight, OT
†Gregg Drew, RB
82—†Mike Mastrogiacomo, OG
83—†Paul Lewis, RB
84—†Paul Lewis, RB
86—†Kevin Murphy, DT
87—†Mark Seals, DB
88—†Mark Seals, DB
89—†Daren Altieri, WR
93—†Chris Helon, DB
†Andre Maksimov, C
94—†Andre Maksimov, C
96—†Brad Costello, P
97—†Brad Costello, P

BOWDOIN (1)
77— Steve McCabe, OL

BOWIE ST. (2)
80— Victor Jackson, CB
81— Marco Tongue, DB

BOWLING GREEN* (2)
59— Bob Zimpfer, T
82—†Andre Young, DL

BRADLEY (1)
38— Ted Panish, B

BRANDEIS (2)
54— William McKenna, E
56— James Stehlin, B

BRIDGEPORT (1)
72— Dennis Paldin, DB

BRI'WATER (MASS.) (1)
92— Erik Arthur, DL

BRIDGEWATER (VA.) (1)
75— C. J. DeWitt, SE

BROCKPORT ST. (3)
90— Ed Smart, TE
93— Steve Milne, PK
97— Tom Massey, DB

BROWN (3)
96—†Paul Choquette, TE
97—†Sean Morey, WR
†Roderic Parson, DB

BUCKNELL (10)
51— George Young, DT
60— Paul Terhes, B
64— Tom Mitchell, OE
65— Tom Mitchell, OE
74— Larry Schoenberger, LB
80— Mike McDonald, OT
90—†Mike Augsberger, DB
95—†Ed Burman, DL
96—†Brandon Little, LB
97—†Willie Hill, LB

BUENA VISTA (4)
72— Joe Kotval, OG
73— Joe Kotval, OG
76— Keith Kerkhoff, DL
87— Jim Higley, LB

BUFFALO (4)
84— Gerry Quinlivan, LB
87— Steve Wojciechowski, LB
95—†Pete Conley, LB
96—†Michael Chichester, DB

BUFFALO ST. (1)
93— John Mattey, OL

BUTLER (2)
88— Steve Roberts, RB
94—†Arnold Mickens, RB

UC DAVIS (14)
72— Bob Biggs, QB
David Roberts, OT
76— Andrew Gagnon, OL
77— Chuck Fomasi, DT
78— Casey Merrill, DL
79— Jeffrey Allen, DB
82— Ken O'Brien, QB
83— Bo Eason, DB
84— Scott Barry, QB
85— Mike Wise, DL
94— Aaron Bennetts, TE
96— Josh Antstey, DE
97— Wes Terrell, TE
Kevin Daft, QB

UC RIVERSIDE (1)
75— Michael Johnson, SE

UC SANTA BARB. (3)
36— Douglas Oldershaw, G
37— Douglas Oldershaw, G
67— Paul Vallerga, DB

CALIF. (PA.) (1)
83— Perry Kemp, WR

CAL LUTHERAN (5)
72— Brian Kelley, LB
79— Mike Hagen, SE
95— Jeff Shea, P
96— Jeff Shea, P
97— Jeff Shea, P

CAL POLY (13)
53— Stan Sheriff, C
58— Charles Gonzales, G
66— David Edmondson, C
72— Mike Amos, DB
73— Fred Stewart, OG
78— Louis Jackson, RB
80— Louis Jackson, RB
Robbie Martin, FL
81— Charles Daum, OL
84— Nick Frost, DB
89— Robert Morris, DL
90— Pat Moore, DL
91— Doug O'Neill, P

CAL ST. CHICO (1)
87— Chris Verhulst, TE

CAL ST. HAYWARD (4)
75— Greg Blankenship, LB
84— Ed Lively, DT
86— Fred Williams, OL
93— Jeff Williamson, TE

CAL ST. NORTHRIDGE (6)
75— Mel Wilson, DB
82— Pat Hauser, OT
83— Pat Hauser, OT
87— Kip Dukes, DB
91— Don Goodman, OL
94—†Joe Vaughn, DB

CAL ST. SACRAMENTO (4)
64— William Fuller, OT
91— Troy Mills, RB
Jim Crouch, PK
92— Jon Kirksey, DL

CANISIUS (3)
87— Tom Doctor, LB
88— Marty Hurley, DB
94—†Aaron Fix, PR

CAPITAL (3)
74— Greg Arnold, OG
80— John Phillips, DL
Steve Wigton, C

CARLETON (1)
90— Jim Bradford, WR

CARNEGIE MELLON (4)
81— Ken Murawski, LB
85— Robert Butts, OL
91— Chuck Jackson, OT
93— Chad Wilson, LB

CARROLL (MONT.) (5)
76— Richard Dale, DB
79— Don Diggins, DL
87— Jeff Beaudry, DB
88— Paul Petrino, QB
89— Suitoa Keleti, OL

CARROLL (WIS.) (3)
74— Robert Helf, TE
90— Bill Nolan, P
93— Andy Ostrand, DB

CARSON-NEWMAN (12)
78— Tank Black, FL
80— Brad Payne, S
83— Dwight Wilson, OL
90— Robert Hardy, RB
92— Darryl Gooden, LB
93— Kendall James, KR
95— Steve Mellon, DL
Anthony Davis, LB
96— Mike Clowney, LB
97— Cedric Killings, DL
Jacques Rumph, RS
Jon Jon Simmons, DB

CASE RESERVE (4)
41— Mike Yurcheshen, E
52— Al Feeny, DE
84— Fred Manley, DE
85— Mark Raiff, OL

CATAWBA (7)
34— Charles Garland, T
35— Charles Garland, T
45— Carroll Bowen, B
72— David Taylor, OT
74— Mike McDonald, LB
96— Greg Payne, PK
97— Maurice Miller, DL

CATHOLIC (6)
84— Chris McMahon, DB
94— Steve Wilkerson, WR
96— Matt Taylor, FB
Jeff Clay, WR
97— Jeff Clay, WR
Tony Faison, OL

CENTRAL (IOWA) (15)
70— Vernon Den Herder, DT
74— Al Dorenkamp, LB
77— Donald Taylor, RB
84— Scott Froehle, DB
85— Rich Thomas, DL
88— Mike Stumberg, DL
89— Mike Estes, DL
Kris Reis, LB
92— Bill Maulder, LB
93— Jeff Helle, OL
94— Jeff Helle, OL
Mark Kacmarynski, RB
Rick Sanger, LB
95— Rick Sanger, LB
96— Mark Kacmarynski, RB

CENTRAL ARK. (5)
80— Otis Chandler, MG

84— David Burnette, DT
91— David Henson, DL
95— Bart Reynolds, DL
96— Don Struebing, C

CENTRAL CONN. ST. (4)
74— Mike Walton, C
84— Sal Cintorino, LB
88— Doug Magazu, DL
89— Doug Magazu, DL

CENTRAL FLA.* (4)
87— Bernard Ford, WR
Ed O'Brien, PK
93— †David Rhodes, WR
94— †Charlie Pierce, PK

CENTRAL MICH.* (4)
42— Warren Schmakel, G
59— Walter Beach, B
62— Ralph Soffredine, G
74— Rick Newsome, DL

CENTRAL MO. ST. (6)
68— Jim Urczyk, OT
85— Steve Huff, PK
88— Jeff Wright, DL
92— Bart Woods, DL
93— Bart Woods, DL
97— Shane Meyer, PK

CENTRAL OKLA. (6)
65— Jerome Bell, OE
78— Gary Smith, TE
94— Elton Rhoades, DB
Joe Aska, RB
96— Johnny Luter, LB
97— Dustin McNeal, OL

CENTRAL ST. (Ohio) (9)
83— Mark Corbin, RB
84— Dave Dunham, OT
85— Mark Corbin, RB
86— Terry Morrow, RB
89— Kenneth Vines, OG
90— Eric Williams, OL
92— Marvin Coleman, DB
93— Marvin Coleman, DB
94— Hugh Douglas, DL

CENTRAL WASH. (4)
48— Robert Osgood, G
50— Jack Hawkins, G
88— Mike Estes, DL
91— Eric Lamphere, OL

CENTRE (7)
55— Gene Scott, B
84— Teel Bruner, DB
85— Teel Bruner, DB
86— Jeff Leonard, OL
88— John Gohmann, DL
89— Jeff Bezold, LB
97— Montas Allen, RS

CHADRON ST. (4)
74— Dennis Fitzgerald, DB
78— Rick Mastey, OL
90— David Jones, RB
94— Scott Doyle, PK

CHATTANOOGA (22)
35— Robert Klein, E
38— Robert Sutton, G
39— Jack Gregory, T
45— Thomas Stewart, T
46— Gene Roberts, B
48— Ralph Hutchinson, T
49— Vincent Sarratore, G
51— Chester LaGod, DT
52— Chester LaGod, DT
54— Richard Young, B
57— Howard Clark, E
58— John Green, B
60— Charles Long, T
64— Jerry Harris, S
66— Harry Sorrell, OG
76— Tim Collins, LB
86— †Mike Makins, DL
89— †Pumpy Tudors, P
†Junior Jackson, LB
90— †Troy Boeck, DL
†Tony Hill, DL
†Pumpy Tudors, P

CHICAGO (4)
91— Neal Cawi, DE
Jeff Stolte, P
93— Frank Baker, FB
95— Derrick Brooms, KR

CITADEL (11)
82— Jim Ettari, DL
84— Jim Gabrish, OL
85— Jim Gabrish, OL
86— Scott Thompson, DT
88— †Carlos Avalos, OL
90— †DeRhon Robinson, OL
92— †Corey Cash, OL
†Lester Smith, DB
94— †Levi Davis, OL
95— †Brad Keeney, DL
97— †Carlos Frank, KR

CLARION (11)
78— Jeff Langhans, OL
80— Steve Scillitani, MG
Gary McCauley, TE
81— Gary McCauley, TE
83— Elton Brown, RB
85— Chuck Duffy, OL
87— Lou Weiers, DL
93— Tim Brown, TE
95— Kim Niedbala, DB
96— Chris Martin, OL
Kim Niedbala, DB

CLARK ATLANTA (1)
79— Curtis Smith, OL

CLINCH VALLEY (1)
95— Shonn Bell, TE

COAST GUARD (3)
90— Ron Davies, DB
91— Ron Davies, DB
97— Ed Hernaez, LB

COE (7)
74— Dan Schmidt, OG
76— Paul Wagner, OT
85— Mike Matzen, P
90— Richard Matthews, DB
93— Carey Bender, RB
Craig Chmelicek, OL
94— Carey Bender, RB

COLGATE (9)
82— †Dave Wolf, LB
83— †Rich Erenberg, RB
84— †Tom Stenglein, WR
85— †Tom Stenglein, WR
86— †Kenny Gamble, RB
87— †Kenny Gamble, RB
†Greg Manusky, LB
96— †Adam Sofran, LB
97— †Tim Girard, OL

COL. OF EMPORIA (1)
51— William Chai, OG

COL. OF IDAHO (2)
53— Norman Hayes, T
54— R. C. Owens, E

COLLEGE OF NEW JERSEY (5)
74— Eric Hamilton, C
83— John Aromando, WR
91— Chris Shaw, C
97— Jim Haines, OL
Tom Ruggia, DL

COLORADO COL. (4)
72— Ed Smith, DE
73— Darryl Crawford, DB
82— Ray Bridges, DL
93— Todd Mays, DL

COLORADO MINES (6)
39— Lloyd Madden, B
41— Dick Moe, T
59— Vince Tesone, B
72— Roger Cirimotich, DB
86— Tim Baer, P
94— Pat Hogelin, P

CONCORD (2)
86— Kevin Johnson, LB
92— Chris Hairston, RB

CONCORDIA-M'HEAD (4)
77— Barry Bennett, DT
90— Mike Gindorff, DT
Shayne Lindsay, NG
95— Tim Lowry, OL

CONNECTICUT (8)
45— Walter Trojanowski, B
73— Richard Foye, C
80— †Reggie Eccleston, WR
83— †John Dorsey, LB
88— †Glenn Antrum, WR
89— †Troy Ashley, LB
91— †Mark Didio, WR
97— †TaVarr Closs, OL

CORNELL (4)
82— †Dan Suren, TE
86— †Tom McHale, DE
93— †Chris Zingo, LB
96— †Chad Levitt, RB

CORNELL COLLEGE (2)
82— John Ward, WR
92— Brent Sands, DB

CORTLAND ST. (7)
67— Rodney Verkey, DE
89— Jim Cook, OL
90— Chris Lafferty, OG
Vinny Swanda, LB
91— Vinny Swanda, LB
96— Pat Lalley, OL
97— Brian McAvan, OL

CUMBERLAND (KY.) (4)
87— David Carmichael, DB
89— Ralph McWilliams, OL
93— Doug Binkley, DB
94— Doug Binkley, LB

DAKOTA WESLEYAN (1)
45— Robert Kirkman, T

DARTMOUTH (4)
91— †Al Rosier, RB
92— †Dennis Durkin, PK
96— †Brian Larsen, OL
97— †Zach Walz, LB

DAVIDSON (1)
34— John Mackorell, B

DAYTON (10)
36— Ralph Niehaus, T
78— Rick Chamberlin, LB
81— Chris Chaney, DB
84— David Kemp, LB
86— Gerry Meyer, OL
89— Mike Duvic, PK
90— Steve Harder, OL
91— Brian Olson, OG
92— Andy Pellegrino, OL
94— †Tim Duvic, PK

DEFIANCE (1)
93— Sammy Williams, WR

DELAWARE (33)
42— Hugh Bogovich, G
46— Tony Stalloni, T
54— Don Miller, B
63— Mike Brown, B
66— Herb Slattery, OT
69— John Favero, LB
70— Conway Hayman, OG
71— Gardy Kahoe, RB
72— Joe Carbone, DE
Dennis Johnson, DT
73— Jeff Cannon, DT
74— Ed Clark, LB
Ray Sweeney, OG
75— Sam Miller, DE
76— Robert Pietuszka, DB
78— Jeff Komlo, QB
79— †Herb Beck, OG
†Scott Brunner, QB
80— †Gary Kuhlman, OT
81— †Gary Kuhlman, OL
82— †George Schmitt, DB
85— †Jeff Rosen, OL
86— †Darrell Booker, LB
87— †James Anderson, WR
88— †Mike Renna, DL
89— †Mike Renna, DL
91— †Warren McIntire, DB
92— †Matt Morrill, DL
93— †Matt Morrill, DL
94— †Daryl Brown, RB
95— †Kenny Bailey, DB
96— †Kenny Bailey, DB
97— †Brian Smith, LB

DELAWARE ST. (4)
84— Gene Lake, RB
86— Joe Burton, DB
91— †Rod Milstead, OL
92— †LeRoy Thompson, DL

DELTA ST. (2)
67— Leland Hughes, OG
95— Jerome Williams, DB

DENISON (5)
47— William Hart, E
48— William Wehr, C
75— Dennis Thome, DL
79— Clay Sampson, RB
86— Dan Holland, DL

DePAUW (3)
63— Richard Dean, C
96— Scott Farnham, DB
Jay Pettigrew, TE

DETROIT TECH (1)
39— Mike Kostiuk, T

DICKINSON (3)
91— Shaughn White, DB
92— Brian Ridgway, DL
94— Jason Fox, LB

DICKINSON ST. (2)
81— Tony Moore, DL
92— Rory Farstveet, OL

DOANE (1)
66— Fred Davis, OT

DRAKE (4)
72— Mike Samples, DT
82— Pat Dunsmore, TE
Craig Wederquist, OT
95— †Matt Garvis, LB

DREXEL (2)
55— Vincent Vidas, T
56— Vincent Vidas, T

DUBUQUE (1)
96— Matt Plummer, WR

EAST CARO.* (1)
64— Bill Cline, HB

EAST CENTRAL (1)
84— Don Wilson, C

EAST STROUDSBURG (7)
65— Barry Roach, DB
75— William Stem, DB
79— Ronald Yakavonis, DL
83— Mike Reichenbach, LB
84— Andy Baranek, QB
91— Curtis Bunch, DB
94— Steve Hynes, OL

EAST TENN. ST. (9)
53— Hal Morrison, E
68— Ron Overbay, DB
70— William Casey, DB
85— George Cimadevilla, P
86— George Cimadevilla, P
94— †Jeff Johnson, WR
96— †James Russell, DL
97— †B. J. Adigun, WR
†Mario Hankerson, LB

EASTERN ILL. (18)
72— Nate Anderson, RB
76— Ted Petersen, C
78— James Warring, WR
79— Chris Cobb, RB
Pete Catan, DE
80— Pete Catan, DE
81— †Kevin Grey, DB
82— †Robert Williams, DB
†Bob Norris, OG
83— †Robert Williams, DB
†Chris Nicholson, DT
84— †Jerry Wright, WR
86— †Roy Banks, WR
88— †John Jurkovic, DL
89— †John Jurkovic, DL
90— †Tim Lance, DB
95— †Willie High, RB
†Tim Carver, LB

EASTERN KY. (27)
69— Teddy Taylor, MG
74— Everett Talbert, RB
75— Junior Hardin, MG

76— Roosevelt Kelly, OL
79— †Bob McIntyre, LB
80— †George Floyd, DB
81— †George Floyd, DB
†Kevin Greve, OG
82— †Steve Bird, WR
83— †Chris Sullivan, OL
84— †Chris Sullivan, C
85— †Joe Spadafino, OL
86— †Fred Harvey, LB
87— †Aaron Jones, DL
88— †Elroy Harris, RB
†Jessie Small, DL
89— †Al Jacevicius, OL
90— †Kelly Blount, LB
†Al Jacevicius, OL
91— †Carl Satterly, OL
†Ernest Thompson, DL
92— †Markus Thomas, RB
93— †Chad Bratzke, DL
94— †James Hand, OL
95— †James Hand, OL
†Marc Collins, P
96— †Tony McCombs, LB

EASTERN MICH.* (5)
68— John Schmidt, C
69— Robert Lints, MG
70— Dave Pureifory, DT
71— Dave Pureifory, DT
73— Jim Pietrzak, OT

EASTERN N.M. (7)
81— Brad Beck, RB
83— Kevin Kott, QB
87— Earl Jones, OL
89— Murray Garrett, DL
90— Anthony Pertile, DB
94— Conrad Hamilton, DB
95— Conrad Hamilton, DB

EASTERN ORE. (1)
96— Shea Little, OL

EASTERN WASH. (10)
57— Richard Huston, C
65— Mel Stanton, HB
73— Scott Garske, TE
81— John Tighe, OL
86— Ed Simmons, OT
87— †Eric Stein, P
91— †Kevin Sargent, OL
97— †Harry Leons, QB
†Chris Scott, DL
†Jim Buzzard, OL

EDINBORO (5)
82— Rick Ruszkiewicz, K
89— Elbert Cole, RB
90— Ernest Priester, WR
93— Mike Kegarise, OL
95— Pat Schuster, DL

ELMHURST (1)
82— Lindsay Barich, OL

ELON (9)
50— Sal Gero, T
68— Richard McGeorge, OE
69— Richard McGeorge, OE
73— Glenn Ellis, DT
76— Ricky Locklear, DT
Dan Bass, OL
77— Dan Bass, OL
80— Bobby Hedrick, RB
86— Ricky Sigmon, OL

EMORY & HENRY (15)
50— Robert Miller, B
51— Robert Miller, B
56— William Earp, C
68— Sonny Wade, B
85— Keith Furr, DB
Rob McMillen, DL
86— Sandy Rogers, RB
87— Gary Collier, QB
88— Steve Bowman, DL
89— Doug Reavis, DB
90— Billy Salyers, OL
91— Jason Grooms, DL
92— Pat Buchanan, OL
Scott Pruner, DL
97— Jamie Harless, DL

EMPORIA ST. (7)
35— James Fraley, B
37— Harry Klein, E
68— Bruce Cerone, OE
69— Bruce Cerone, OE
91— Quincy Tillmon, RB
96— Brian Shay, RB
97— Brian Shay, RB

EUREKA (1)
95— Kurt Barth, WR

EVANSVILLE (3)
46— Robert Hawkins, T
93— †Hanz Hoag, TE
94— †Hanz Hoag, TE

FDU-MADISON (4)
84— Ira Epstein, DL
86— Eric Brey, DB
87— Frank Illidge, DL
93— Vic Moncato, P

FAIRMONT ST. (3)
67— Dave Williams, DT
84— Ed Coleman, WR
88— Lou Mabin, DB

FAYETTEVILLE ST. (1)
90— Terrence Smith, LB

FERRIS ST. (6)
76— Charles Evans, RB
92— Monty Brown, LB
93— Ed Phillion, DL
94— Tyree Dye, RB
95— Bill Love, QB
96— Kelly Chisholm, DL

FERRUM (5)
87— Dave Harper, LB
88— Dave Harper, LB
89— Chris Warren, RB
90— Melvin Dillard, DB/KR
91— John Sheets, OG

FINDLAY (4)
65— Allen Smith, HB
80— Nelson Bolden, FB
85— Dana Wright, RB
90— Tim Russ, OL

FLORIDA A&M (16)
61— Curtis Miranda, C
62— Robert Paremore, B
67— Major Hazelton, DB
John Eason, OE
73— Henry Lawrence, OT
75— Frank Poole, LB
77— Tyrone McGriff, OG
78— Tyrone McGriff, OG
79— †Tyrone McGriff, OG
†Kiser Lewis, C
80— †Gifford Ramsey, DB
83— †Ray Alexander, WR
95— †Earl Holmes, LB
96— †Jamie Nails, OL
97— †Oteman Sampson, QB
†Juan Toro, PK

FLORIDA ST.* (1)
51— William Dawkins, OG

FORDHAM (1)
97— †Barry Cantrell, P

FORT HAYS ST. (2)
95— Lance Schwindt, TE
Shawn Behr, QB

FORT LEWIS (3)
89— Eric Fadness, P
92— Johnny Cox, WR
93— Johnny Cox, AP

FORT VALLEY ST. (7)
74— Fred Harris, OT
80— Willie Canady, DB
81— Willie Canady, DB
83— Tugwan Taylor, DB
92— Joseph Best, DB
93— Joseph Best, DB
94— Tyrone Poole, DB

FRANKLIN (2)
82— Joe Chester, WR
95— Michael Brouwer, DB

FRANK. & MARSH. (9)
35— Woodrow Sponaugle, C
38— Sam Roeder, B
40— Alex Schibanoff, T
47— William Iannicelli, E
50— Charles Cope, C
81— Vin Carioscia, OL
82— Vin Carioscia, OL
89— Dale Amos, WR
95— Steve DeLuca, LB

FRESNO ST.* (5)
39— Jack Mulkey, E
40— Jack Mulkey, E
60— Douglas Brown, G
68— Tom McCall, LB
Erv Hunt, DB

FROSTBURG ST. (11)
80— Terry Beamer, LB
82— Steve Forsythe, WR
83— Kevin Walsh, DL
85— Bill Bagley, WR
86— Marcus Wooley, LB
88— Ken Boyd, DB
89— Ken Boyd, DB
93— Russell Williams, DB
94— Joe Holland, DL
Ariel Bell, KR
96— Ron Wallace, DB

FURMAN (12)
82— †Ernest Gibson, DB
83— †Ernest Gibson, DB
84— †Rock Hurst, LB
85— †Gene Reeder, C
88— †Jeff Blankenship, LB
89— †Kelly Fletcher, DL
90— †Steve Duggan, C
†Kevin Kendrick, LB
91— †Eric Walter, OL
92— †Kota Suttle, LB
94— †Jim Richter, PK
97— †Bryan Dailer, DL

GALLAUDET (1)
87— Shannon Simon, OL

GARDNER-WEBB (4)
73— Richard Grissom, LB
87— Jeff Parker, PK
92— Rodney Robinson, WR
93— Gabe Wilkins, DL

GEORGETOWN (3)
73— Robert Morris, DE
74— Robert Morris, DE
91— Chris Murphy, DE

GEORGETOWN (KY.) (8)
74— Charles Pierson, DL
78— John Martinelli, OL
85— Rob McCrary, RB
87— Chris Reed, C
88— Chris Reed, OL
89— Steve Blankenbaker, DL
91— Chris Hogan, DL
92— Chris Hogan, DL

GA. SOUTHERN (19)
85— †Vance Pike, OL
†Tim Foley, PK
86— †Fred Stokes, OT
†Tracy Ham, QB
87— †Flint Matthews, LB
†Dennis Franklin, C
†Tim Foley, PK
88— †Dennis Franklin, C
†Darren Alford, DL
89— †Joe Ross, RB
†Giff Smith, DL
90— †Giff Smith, DL
91— †Rodney Oglesby, DB
92— †Alex Mash, DL
93— †Alex Mash, DL
†Franklin Stephens, OL
94— †Franklin Stephens, OL
96— †Edward Thomas, DL
97— †Roderick Russell, FB

GA. SOUTHWESTERN (2)
85— Roger Glover, LB
86— Roger Glover, LB

GETTYSBURG (5)
66— Joseph Egresitz, DE
83— Ray Condren, RB
84— Ray Condren, RB
85— Brian Barr, DB
94— Dwayne Marcus, FB

GLENVILLE ST. (7)
73— Scotty Hamilton, DB
83— Byron Brooks, RB
84— Mike Payne, DB
93— Chris George, WR
94— Chris George, WR
96— Carlos Ferralls, WR
97— Carlos Ferralls, WR

GONZAGA (2)
34— Ike Peterson, B
39— Tony Canadeo, B

GRAMBLING (28)
62— Junious Buchanan, T
64— Alphonse Dotson, OT
65— Willie Young, OG
Frank Cornish, DT
69— Billy Manning, C
70— Richard Harris, DE
Charles Roundtree, DT
71— Solomon Freelon, OG
John Mendenhall, DE
72— Steve Dennis, DB
Gary Johnson, DT
73— Gary Johnson, DT
Willie Bryant, DB
74— Gary Johnson, DT
75— Sammie White, WR
James Hunter, DB
79— †Joe Gordon, DT
†Aldrich Allen, LB
†Robert Salters, DB
80— †Trumaine Johnson, WR
†Mike Barker, DT
81— †Andre Robinson, LB
82— †Trumaine Johnson, WR
83— †Robert Smith, DL
85— †James Harris, LB
90— †Walter Dean, RB
†Jake Reed, WR
94— †Curtis Ceaser, WR

GRAND VALLEY ST. (6)
79— Ronald Essink, OL
89— Todd Tracey, DL
91— Chris Tiede, C
94— Mike Sheldon, OL
95— Diriki Mose, WR
96— Matt Potter, DE

GROVE CITY (2)
87— Doug Hart, PK
97— Doug Steiner, FB

GUILFORD (3)
75— Steve Musulin, OT
91— Rodney Alexander, DE
94— Bryan Garland, OL

GUST. ADOLPHUS (8)
37— Wendell Butcher, B
50— Calvin Roberts, T
51— Haldo Norman, OE
52— Calvin Roberts, DT
54— Gene Nei, G
67— Richard Jaeger, LB
84— Kurt Ploeger, DL
97— Ryan Boutwell, PK

HAMILTON (2)
86— Joe Gilbert, OL
91— Eric Grey, RB

HAMLINE (4)
55— Dick Donlin, E
84— Kevin Graslewicz, WR
85— Ed Hitchcock, OL
89— Jon Voss, TE

HAMPDEN-SYDNEY (8)
48— Lynn Chewning, B
54— Stokeley Fulton, C
72— Michael Leidy, LB
74— Ed Kelley, DE
75— Ed Kelley, DE
77— Robert Wilson, OL
78— Tim Smith, DL
86— Jimmy Hondroulis, PK

HAMPTON (8)
84— Ike Readon, MG
85— Ike Readon, DL
93— Emerson Martin, OL
Christopher Williams, DL
94— John Meredith, LB

95—†Hugh Hunter, DL
96—†Darrell Flythe, LB
97—†Cordell Taylor, DB

HANOVER (5)
86— Jon Pinnick, QB
88— Mike Luker, WR
95— Ben Fox, WR
Terry Peebles, QB
97— Kevin O'Donohue, LB

HARDIN-SIMMONS (6)
37— Burns McKinney, B
39— Clyde Turner, C
40— Owen Goodnight, B
42— Rudy Mobley, B
46— Rudy Mobley, B
94— Colin McCormick, WR

HARDING (3)
74— Barney Crawford, DL
91— Pat Gill, LB
94— Paul Simmons, LB

HARVARD (2)
82—†Mike Corbat, OL
84—†Roger Caron, OL

HASTINGS (2)
84— Dennis Sullivan, OL
94— Jeff Drake, DL

HAWAII* (2)
41— Nolle Smith, B
68— Tim Buchanan, LB

HENDERSON ST. (3)
90— Todd Jones, OL
93— Chris Carter, P
96— Robert Thomas, LB

HILLSDALE (9)
49— William Young, B
55— Nate Clark, B
56— Nate Clark, B
75— Mark Law, OG
81— Mike Broome, OG
82— Ron Gladnick, DE
86— Al Huge, DL
87— Al Huge, DL
88— Rodney Patterson, LB

HOBART (6)
72— Don Aleksiewicz, RB
75— Rich Kowalski, RB
86— Brian Verdon, DB
93— Bill Palmer, DB
96— Nico Karagosian, TE
97— David Russell, DL

HOFSTRA (11)
83— Chuck Choinski, DL
86— Tom Salamone, P
88— Tom Salamone, DB
90— George Tischler, LB
94—†Brian Clark, DB
95—†Dave Fiore, OL
†Dave Ettinger, PK
†Buck Buchanan, LB
96—†Eugene McAleer, LB
97—†Dave Ettinger, PK
†Lance Schulters, DB

HOLY CROSS (14)
83—†Bruce Kozerski, OT
†Steve Raquet, DL
84—†Bill McGovern, DB
†Kevin Garvey, OG
85—†Gill Fenerty, RB
86—†Gordie Lockbaum, RB-DB
87—†Jeff Wiley, QB
†Gordie Lockbaum, WR-SP
88—†Dennis Golden, OL
89—†Dave Murphy, DB
90—†Craig Callahan, LB
91—†Jerome Fuller, RB
93—†Rob Milanette, LB
95—†Tom Claro, OL

HOPE (2)
79— Craig Groendyk, OL
82— Kurt Brinks, C

HOWARD (2)
75— Ben Harris, DL
87—†Harvey Reed, RB

HOWARD PAYNE (7)
61— Ray Jacobs, T
72— Robert Woods, LB
73— Robert Woods, LB
92— Scott Lichner, QB
94— Steven Seale, OL
95— Sean Witherwax, DL
97— Sedrick Medlock, DB

HUMBOLDT ST. (6)
61— Drew Roberts, E
62— Drew Roberts, E
76— Michael Gooing, OL
82— David Rush, MG
83— Dean Diaz, DB
95— Randy Matyshock, TE

HURON (1)
76— John Aldridge, OL

IDAHO *(14)
83—†Ken Hobart, QB
85—†Eric Yarber, WR
88—†John Friesz, QB
89—†John Friesz, QB
†Lee Allen, WR
90—†Kasey Dunn, WR
91—†Kasey Dunn, WR
92—†Yo Murphy, WR
†Jeff Robinson, DL
93—†Doug Nussmeier, QB
†Mat Groshong, C
94—†Sherriden May, RB
†Jim Mills, OL
95—†Ryan Phillips, DL

IDAHO ST. (7)
69— Ed Bell, OE
77— Ray Allred, MG
81—†Case de Bruijn, P
†Mike Machurek, QB
83—†Jeff Kaiser, P
84—†Steve Anderson, DL
97—†Trevor Bell, DB

ILLINOIS COLL. (1)
81— Joe Aiello, DL

ILLINOIS ST. (5)
68— Denny Nelson, OT
85—†Jim Meyer, OL
86—†Brian Gant, LB
88—†Mike McCabe, P
93—†Todd Kurz, PK

ILL. WESLEYAN (7)
34— Tony Blazine, T
74— Caesar Douglas, OT
91— Chris Bisaillon, WR
92— Chris Bisaillon, WR
96— Adam Slotkus, C
John Munch, LB
97— John Munch, LB

INDIANA (PA.) (19)
75— Lynn Hieber, QB
76— Jim Haslett, DE
77— Jim Haslett, DE
78— Jim Haslett, DE
79— Terrence Skelley, OE
80— Joe Cuigari, DT
84— Gregg Brenner, WR
86— Jim Angelo, OL
87— Troy Jackson, LB
88— Dean Cottrill, LB
90— Andrew Hill, WR
91— Tony Aliucci, QB
93— Matt Dalverny, OL
Mike Geary, PK
Michael Mann, RB
94— Jeff Turnage, DL
95— Jon Ruff, PK
Jeff Turnage, DL
97— Barry Threats, DB

INDIANA ST. (11)
69— Jeff Keller, DE
75— Chris Hicks, OL
Vince Allen, RB
83—†Ed Martin, DE
84—†Wayne Davis, DB
85—†Vencie Glenn, DB
86—†Mike Simmonds, OL
93—†Shawn Moore, OL
94—†Dan Brandenburg, DL
95—†Dan Bradenburg, DL
†Tom Allison, PK

INDIANAPOLIS (6)
83— Mark Bless, DL
84— Paul Loggan, DB
85— Tom Collins, DB
86— Dan Jester, TE
87— Thurman Montgomery, DL
91— Greg Matheis, DL

IOWA WESLEYAN (1)
87— Mike Wiggins, P

ITHACA (12)
72— Robert Wojnar, OT
74— David Remick, RB
75— Larry Czarnecki, DT
79— John Laper, LB
80— Bob Ferrigno, HB
84— Bill Sheerin, DL
85— Tim Torrey, LB
90— Jeff Wittman, FB
91— Jeff Wittman, FB
92— Jeff Wittman, FB
Dave Brumfield, OL
95— Scott Connolly, DL

JACKSON ST. (22)
62— Willie Richardson, E
69— Joe Stephens, OG
71— Jerome Barkum, OE
74— Walter Payton, RB
Robert Brazile, LB
78— Robert Hardy, DT
80—†Larry Werts, LB
81—†Mike Fields, OT
85—†Jackie Walker, LB
86—†Kevin Dent, DB
87—†Kevin Dent, DB
88—†Lewis Tillman, RB
†Kevin Dent, DB
89—†Darion Conner, LB
90—†Robert Turner, DB
91—†Deltrich Lockridge, OL
92—†Lester Holmes, OL
95—†Picasso Nelson, DB
96—†Sean Woodson, DB
†Grailyn Pratt, QB
†Otha Evans, LB
97—†Toby Myles, OL

JACKSONVILLE ST. (9)
52— Jodie Connell, OG
66— Ray Vinson, DB
70— Jimmy Champion, C
77— Jesse Baker, DT
78— Jesse Baker, DT
82— Ed Lett, QB
86— Joe Billingsley, OT
88— Joe Billingsley, OT
95—†Darron Edwards, DB

JAMES MADISON (13)
77— Woody Bergeria, DT
78— Rick Booth, OL
85—†Charles Haley, LB
86—†Carlo Bianchini, OG
89—†Steve Bates, DL
90—†Eupton Jackson, DB
93—†David McLeod, WR
94—†Dwight Robinson, DB
95—†John Coursey, PK
†David Bailey, C
†Ed Perry, TE
96—†Ed Perry, TE
97—†Tony Booth, DB

JAMESTOWN (2)
76— Brent Tischer, OL
81— Ron Hausauer, OL

JOHN CARROLL (10)
50— Carl Taseff, B
74— Tim Barrett, RB
94— Jason Goldberg, PK
Ryan Haley, P
95— Chris Anderson, LB
96— London Fletcher, LB
Scott O'Donnell, DL
Chris Anderson, LB
97— London Fletcher, LB
David Ziegler, R

JOHNS HOPKINS (3)
80— Bill Stromberg, WR
81— Bill Stromberg, WR
96— Jim Wilson, DL

JOHNSON SMITH (2)
82— Dan Beauford, DE
88— Ronald Capers, LB

JUNIATA (3)
54— Joe Veto, T
86— Steve Yerger, OL
87— Mark Dorner, DB

KANSAS WESLEYAN (2)
35— Virgil Baker, G
56— Larry Houdek, B

KEAN (1)
87— Kevin McGuirl, TE

KENTUCKY ST. (1)
72— Wiley Epps, LB

KENYON (1)
74— Jim Myers, WR

KNOX (3)
86— Rich Schiele, TE
87— Chris Vogel, WR
96— Chris Warwick, PK

KNOXVILLE (1)
77— Dwight Treadwell, OL

KUTZTOWN (3)
77— Steve Head, OG
95— John Mobley, LB
97— Denauld Brown, DL

LA SALLE (2)
38— George Somers, T
39— Frank Loughney, G

LA VERNE (3)
72— Dana Coleman, DT
91— Willie Reyna, QB
95— Anthony Jones, RB

LAFAYETTE (7)
79—†Rich Smith, TE
81—†Joe Skladany, LB
82—†Tony Green, DL
88—†Frank Baur, QB
92—†Edward Hudak, OL
96—†B. J. Galles, DB
97—†Dan Bengele, LB

LAKELAND (1)
89— Jeff Ogiego, P

LAMAR (5)
57— Dudley Meredith, T
61— Bobby Jancik, B
67— Spergon Wynn, OG
83—†Eugene Seale, LB
85—†Burton Murchison, RB

LAMBUTH (2)
93— Jo Jo Jones, RB
94— Jo Jo Jones, RB

LANE (1)
73— Edward Taylor, DT

LANGSTON (2)
73— Thomas Henderson, DE
94— Paul Reed, DB

LAWRENCE (10)
49— Claude Radtke, E
67— Charles McKee, QB
77— Frank Bouressa, C
78— Frank Bouressa, C
80— Scott Reppert, HB
81— Scott Reppert, HB
82— Scott Reppert, RB
83— Murray McDonough, DB
86— Dan Galante, DL
95— Brad Olson, RB

LEHIGH (20)
49— Robert Numbers, C
50— Dick Doyne, B
57— Dan Nolan, B
59— Walter Meincke, T
69— Thad Jamula, OT
71— John Hill, C
73— Kim McQuilken, QB
75— Joe Sterrett, QB
77— Steve Kreider, WR
Mike Reiker, QB
79—†Dave Melone, OT
†Jim McCormick, DL
80—†Bruce Rarig, LB
83—†John Shigo, LB
85—†Rennie Benn, WR

90—†Keith Petzold, OL
93—†Dave Cecchini, WR
95—†Brian Klingerman, WR
†Rabih Abdullah, RB
96—†Ben Talbott, P

LENOIR-RHYNE (5)
52— Steve Trudnak, B
62— Richard Kemp, B
67— Eddie Joyner, OT
92— Jason Monday, PK
94— Leonard Davis, RB

LEWIS & CLARK (2)
68— Bill Bailey, DT
91— Dan Ruhl, RB

LIBERTY (4)
82— John Sanders, LB
86— Mark Mathis, DB
95—†Andrew McFadden, KR
†Tony Dews, TE

LINCOLN (MO.) (2)
53— Leo Lewis, B
54— Leo Lewis, B

LINFIELD (9)
57— Howard Morris, G
64— Norman Musser, C
72— Bernard Peterson, OE
75— Ken Cutcher, OL
78— Paul Dombroski, DB
80— Alan Schmidlin, QB
83— Steve Lopes, OL
84— Steve Boyea, OL
94— Darrin Causey, LB

LIVINGSTONE (1)
84— Jo Jo White, RB

LOCK HAVEN (1)
45— Robert Eyer, E

LONG BEACH ST. (4)
68— Bill Parks, OE
69— Leon Burns, FB
70— Leon Burns, RB
71— Terry Metcalf, RB

LIU-C. W. POST (5)
71— Gary Wichard, QB
77— John Mohring, DE
78— John Mohring, DE
81— Tom DeBona, WR
89— John Levelis, DL

LORAS (3)
47— Robert Hanlon, B
84— James Drew, P
97— Shane Davis, RB

LOS ANGELES ST. (1)
64— Walter Johnson, OG

LOUISIANA COLLEGE (1)
50— Bernard Calendar, E

LOUISIANA TECH* (15)
41— Garland Gregory, G
46— Mike Reed, G
68— Terry Bradshaw, QB
69— Terry Bradshaw, QB
72— Roger Carr, WR
73— Roger Carr, FL
74— Mike Barber, TE
Fred Dean, DT
82—†Matt Dunigan, QB
84—†Doug Landry, LB
†Walter Johnson, DE
85—†Doug Landry, LB
86—†Walter Johnson, LB-DE
87—†Glenell Sanders, LB
88—†Glenell Sanders, LB

LOUISVILLE* (1)
57— Leonard Lyles, B

LOYOLA (ILL.) (2)
35— Billy Roy, B
37— Clay Calhoun, B

LOYOLA MARYMOUNT (1)
42— Vince Pacewic, B

LUTHER (1)
57— Bruce Hartman, T

LYCOMING (8)
83— John Whalen, OL
85— Walt Zataveski, OL
89— Rick Bealer, DB
90— Rick Bealer, DB
91— Darrin Kenney, OT
Don Kinney, DL
Bill Small, LB
96— Michael Downey, OL

MacMURRAY (1)
97— Jamie Lee, RB

MAINE (6)
65— John Huard, LB
66— John Huard, LB
80—†Lorenzo Bouier, RB
89—†Carl Smith, RB
†Scott Hough, OL
90—†Claude Pettaway, DB

MAINE MARITIME (2)
92— Kirk Matthieu, RB
95— Rob Marchitello, RB

MANKATO ST. (9)
73— Marty Kranz, DB
87— Duane Goldammer, OG
91— John Kelling, DB
93— Jamie Pass, QB
94— Josh Nelsen, WR
95— Mark Erickson, AP
96— Tywan Mitchell, WR
Greg Janacek, PK
97— Tywan Mitchell, WR

MARIETTA (1)
96— Dante Brown, RB

MARS HILL (3)
78— Alan Rice, OL
79— Steven Campbell, DB
87— Lee Marchman, LB

MARSHALL *(29)
37— William Smith, E
40— Jackie Hunt, B
41— Jackie Hunt, B
87—†Mike Barber, WR
†Sean Doctor, TE
88—†Mike Barber, WR
†Sean Doctor, TE
90—†Eric Ihnat, TE
91—†Phil Ratliff, OL
92—†Michael Payton, QB
†Troy Brown, WR
†Phil Ratliff, OL
93—†Chris Deaton, OL
†William King, LB
†Roger Johnson, DB
94—†Roger Johnson, DB
†William Pannell, OL
†Travis Colquitt, P
95—†Chris Parker, RB
†William Pannell, OL
†Billy Lyon, DL
†Melvin Cunningham, DB
96—†Randy Moss, WR
†Billy Lyon, DL
†Aaron Ferguson, OL
†B. J. Cohen, DL
†Jermaine Swafford, LB
†Eugene McAleer, LB
†Melvin Cunningham, DB

MARTIN LUTHER (1)
97— John Feuersthaler, DB

MD.-EAST. SHORE (2)
64— John Smith, DT
68— Bill Thompson, DB

MARYVILLE (TENN.) (5)
67— Steve Dockery, DB
73— Earl McMahon, OG
77— Wayne Dunn, LB
92— Tom Smith, OL
93— Tom Smith, OL

MASSACHUSETTS (22)
52— Tony Chambers, OE
63— Paul Graham, T
64— Milt Morin, DE
67— Greg Landry, QB
71— William DeFlavio, MG
72— Steve Schubert, OE
73— Tim Berra, OE
75— Ned Deane, OL
76— Ron Harris, DB
77— Kevin Cummings, TE
Bruce Kimball, OL
78— Bruce Kimball, OG
80—†Bob Manning, DB
81—†Garry Pearson, RB
82—†Garry Pearson, RB
85—†Mike Dwyer, DL
88—†John McKeown, LB
90—†Paul Mayberry, OL
92—†Don Caparotti, DB
93—†Bill Durkin, OL
94—†Breon Parker, DB
95—†Rene Ingoglia, RB

MASS.-BOSTON (1)
92— Sean Munroe, WR

MASS. MARITIME (1)
95— Paul Diamantopoulos, DE

McMURRY (6)
49— Brad Rowland, B
50— Brad Rowland, B
58— Charles Davis, G
68— Telly Windham, DE
74— Randy Roemisch, OT
80— Rick Nolly, OL

McNEESE ST. (17)
52— Charles Kuehn, DE
69— Glenn Kidder, OG
72— James Moore, TE
74— James Files, OT
82—†Leonard Smith, DB
92—†Terry Irving, LB
93—†Jose Larios, PK
†Terry Irving, LB
94—†Ronald Cherry, OL
95—†Kavika Pittman, DL
†Marsh Buice, DL
†Zack Bronson, DB
†Vincent Landrum, LB
96—†Zack Bronson, DB
97—†Reggie Nelson, OL
†Chris Fontenot, TE
†Donnie Ashley, PR

MEMPHIS* (1)
54— Robert Patterson, G

MERCHANT MARINE (4)
52— Robert Wiechard, LB
69— Harvey Adams, DE
90— Harold Krebs, DB
97— Anthony Jacobs, OL

MESA ST. (8)
82— Dean Haugum, DT
83— Dean Haugum, DL
84— Don Holmes, DB
85— Mike Berk, OL
86— Mike Berk, OL
88— Tracy Bennett, PK
89— Jeff Russell, OT
90— Brian Johnson, LB

METHODIST (1)
97— Trayfer Monroe, DB

MIAMI (FLA.)* (2)
45— Ed Cameron, G
William Levitt, C

MIAMI (OHIO)* (1)
82—†Brian Pillman, MG

MICHIGAN TECH (1)
76— Jim VanWagner, RB

MIDDLE TENN. ST. (12)
64— Jimbo Pearson, S
65— Keith Atchley, LB
83—†Robert Carroll, OL
84—†Kelly Potter, PK
85—†Don Griffin, DB
88—†Don Thomas, LB
90—†Joe Campbell, RB
91—†Steve McAdoo, OL
†Joe Campbell, RB
92—†Steve McAdoo, OL
93—†Pat Hicks, OL
95—†Nathaniel Claybrooks, DL

MIDDLEBURY (2)
36— George Anderson, G
83— Jonathan Good, DL

MIDLAND LUTHERAN (2)
76— Dave Marreel, DE
79— Scott Englehardt, OL

MILLERSVILLE (7)
76— Robert Parr, DB
80— Rob Riddick, RB
81— Mark Udovich, C
86— Jeff Hannis, DL
93— Scott Martin, DL
Greg Faulkner, OL
95— Kevin Cannon, AP

MILLIKIN (2)
42— Virgil Wagner, B
92— Mike Hall, KR

MILLSAPS (12)
72— Rowan Torrey, DB
73— Michael Reams, LB
76— Rickie Haygood, QB
78— David Culpepper, LB
79— David Culpepper, LB
83— Edmond Donald, RB
85— Tommy Powell, LB
90— Sean Brewer, DL
91— Sean Brewer, DL
92— Sean Brewer, DL
93— Mitch Holloway, P
94— Kelvin Gladney, RB

MINN.-DULUTH (4)
74— Mark Johnson, DB
75— Terry Egerdahl, RB
76— Ted McKnight, RB
82— Gary Birkholz, OG

MISSISSIPPI COL. (11)
72— Ricky Herzog, FL
79— Calvin Howard, RB
80— Bert Lyles, DE
82— Major Everett, RB
83— Wayne Frazier, OL
85— Earl Conway, DL
88— Terry Fleming, DL
89— Terry Fleming, DL
90— Fred McAfee, RB
92— Johnny Poole, OL
93— Kelly Ray, C

MISSISSIPPI VAL. (7)
79—†Carl White, OG
83—†Jerry Rice, WR
84—†Jerry Rice, WR
†Willie Totten, QB
87—†Vincent Brown, LB
91—†Ashley Ambrose, DB
97—†Terry Houzah, LB

MIT (1)
97— Duane Stevens, DB

MO.-ROLLA (5)
41— Ed Kromka, T
69— Frank Winfield, OG
74— Merle Dillow, TE
80— Bill Grantham, S
93— Elvind Listerud, PK

MO. SOUTHERN ST. (3)
93— Rod Smith, WR
Ron Burton, LB
95— Yancy McKnight, OL

MISSOURI VALLEY (3)
47— James Nelson, G
48— James Nelson, G
49— Herbert McKinney, T

MONMOUTH (ILL.) (1)
75— Ron Baker, RB

MONTANA (23)
67— Bob Beers, LB
70— Ron Stein, DB
76— Greg Anderson, DB
79—†Jim Hard, FL
83—†Brian Salonen, TE
85—†Mike Rice, P
87—†Larry Clarkson, OL
88—†Tim Hauck, DB
89—†Kirk Scafford, OL
†Tim Hauck, DB
93—†Dave Dickenson, QB
†Todd Ericson, DB
94—†Scott Gragg, OL
95—†Dave Dickenson, QB
†Matt Wells, WR
†Mike Agee, OL
†Eric Simonson, OL
96—†Joe Douglass, WR

†Mike Agee, OL
†Brian Ah Yat, QB
†Jason Crebo, LB
†David Kempfert, OL
97—†Jason Crebo, LB

MONTANA ST. (12)
66— Don Hass, HB
67— Don Hass, HB
70— Gary Gustafson, LB
73— Bill Kollar, DT
75— Steve Kracher, RB
76— Lester Leininger, DL
78— Jon Borchardt, OT
81—†Larry Rubens, OL
84—†Mark Fellows, LB
†Dirk Nelson, P
93—†Sean Hill, DB
97—†Neal Smith, DL

MONTANA TECH (3)
73— James Persons, OT
80— Steve Hossler, HB
81— Craig Opatz, OL

MONTCLAIR ST. (14)
75— Barry Giblin, DB
77— Mario Benimeo, DT
79— Tom Morton, OL
80— Sam Mills, LB
81— Terrance Porter, WR
82— Mark Casale, QB
84— Jim Rennae, OL
85— Dan Zakashefski, DL
86— Dan Zakashefski, DL
89— Paul Cioffi, LB
90— Paul Cioffi, LB
93— Jeff Bargiel, DL
95— Jeff Bargiel, DL
96— Jeff Bargiel, DL

MOORHEAD ST. (2)
76— Rocky Gullickson, OG
84— Randy Sullivan, DB

MOREHEAD ST. (5)
38— John Horton, C
42— Vincent Zachem, C
69— Dave Haverdick, DT
82—†John Christopher, P
86—†Randy Poe, OG

MORGAN ST. (8)
65— Willie Lanier, LB
67— Jeff Queen, DE
70— Willie Germany, DB
72— Stan Cherry, LB
73— Eugene Simms, LB
78— Joe Fowlkes, DB
80— Mike Holston, WR
93—†Matthew Steeple, DL

MORNINGSIDE (2)
49— Connie Callahan, B
91— Jorge Diaz, PK

MOUNT UNION (20)
84— Troy Starr, LB
87— Russ Kring, RB
90— Ken Edelman, PK
Dave Lasecki, LB
92— Mike Elder, OL
Jim Ballard, QB
Chris Dattilio, LB
93— Rob Atwood, TE
Jim Ballard, QB
Ed Bubonics, WR
Mike Hallet, DL
94— Rob Rodgers, LB
95— Mike Wonderfer, OG
Matt Liggett, DL
96— Bill Borchert, QB
Joe Weimer, OL
Josh Weber, OT
Brian Wervey, LB
97— Bill Borchert, QB
Joe Weimer, OL

MUHLENBERG (3)
46— George Bibighaus, E
47— Harold Bell, B
93— Rob Lokerson, WR

MURRAY ST. (7)
37— Elmer Cochran, G
73— Don Clayton, RB
79—†Terry Love, DB
86—†Charley Wiles, OL
95—†Derrick Cullors, RB
†William Hampton, DB
96—†William Hampton, DB

MUSKINGUM (5)
40— Dave Evans, T
60— Bill Cooper, B
66— Mark DeVilling, DT
75— Jeff Heacock, DB
95— Connon Thompson, DB

NEB.-KEARNEY (4)
76— Dale Mitchell Johnson, DB
78— Doug Peterson, DL
95— Matt Bruggeman, DL
97— Mike Smith, RT

NEB.-OMAHA (9)
64— Gerald Allen, HB
68— Dan Klepper, OG
76— Dan Fulton, WR
77— Dan Fulton, OE
80— Tom Sutko, LB
82— John Walker, DT
83— Tim Carlson, LB
84— Ron Petersen, OT
86— Keith Coleman, LB

NEB. WESLEYAN (3)
90— Brad Bohn, DB
91— Darren Stohlmann, TE
92— Darren Stohlmann, TE

NEVADA* (23)
52— Neil Garrett, DB
74— Greg Grouwinkel, DB
78— James Curry, MG
Frank Hawkins, RB
79—†Frank Hawkins, RB
†Lee Fobbs, DB
80—†Frank Hawkins, RB
†Bubba Puha, DL
81—†John Ramatici, LB
†Tony Zendejas, K
82—†Tony Zendejas, K
†Charles Mann, DT
83—†Tony Zendejas, K
†Jim Werbeckes, OG
†Tony Shaw, DB
85—†Greg Rea, OL
†Marty Zendejas, PK
†Pat Hunter, DB
86—†Henry Rolling, DE-LB
88—†Bernard Ellison, DB
90—†Bernard Ellison, DB
†Treamelle Taylor, KR
91—†Matt Clafton, LB

UNLV* (3)
73— Mike Thomas, RB
74— Mike Thomas, RB
75— Joseph Ingersoll, DL

NEW HAMPSHIRE (12)
50— Ed Douglas, G
68— Al Whittman, DT
75— Kevin Martell, C
76— Bill Burnham, RB
77— Bill Burnham, RB
Grady Vigneau, OT
85—†Paul Dufault, OL
87—†John Driscoll, OL
91—†Barry Bourassa, RB
†Dwayne Sabb, LB
94—†Mike Foley, DL
97—†Jerry Azumah, RS/RB

NEW HAVEN (14)
85— David Haubner, OL
87— Erik Lesinski, LB
88— Rob Thompson, OL
90— Jay McLucas, QB
92— Scott Emmert, OL
Roger Graham, RB
93— Roger Graham, RB
George Byrd, DB
Tony Willis, WR
94— Roger Graham, RB
95— Scott Riggs, LB
96— Jesse Showerda, QB
97— Mario DiDino, OL
Cazzie Kosciolek, QB

N.M. HIGHLANDS (8)
66— Carl Garrett, HB
67— Carl Garrett, HB
68— Carl Garrett, HB
81— Jay Lewis, DL
85— Neil Windham, LB
86— Tim Salz, PK
93— Rus Bailey, WR
96— Jamar Nailor, WR

NEWBERRY (3)
40— Dominic Collangelo, B
81— Stan Stanton, DL
97— Anthony Heatley, OL

NICHOLLS ST. (7)
76— Gerald Butler, OE
77— Rusty Rebowe, LB
81—†Dwight Walker, WR
82—†Clint Conque, LB
84—†Dewayne Harrison, TE
86—†Mark Carrier, WR
94—†Darryl Pounds, DB

NICHOLS (1)
81— Ed Zywien, LB

NORFOLK ST. (5)
79— Mike Ellis, DB
89— Arthur Jimmerson, LB
94— James Roe, WR
95— James Roe, WR
Aaron Sparrow, QB

NORTH ALA. (20)
82— Don Smith, C
84— Daryl Smith, DB
85— Bruce Jones, DB
90— James Davis, LB
Mike Nord, OL
92— Harvey Summerhill, DB
93— Jeff Redcross, DL
Tyrone Rush, RB
Jeff Surbaugh, OL
Ronald McKinnon, LB
94— Jon Thompson, OL
Ronald McKinnon, LB
Marcus Keyes, DL
95— Jon Thompson, OL
Israel Raybon, DE
Ronald McKinnon, LB
Marcus Keyes, DL
96— Gerald Smith, DB
97— Reginald Ruffin, LB
Marcus Hill, DB

NORTH CARO. A&T (8)
69— Merl Code, DB
70— Melvin Holmes, OT
81—†Mike West, OL
86—†Ernest Riddick, NG
88—†Demetrius Harrison, LB
93—†Ronald Edwards, OL
95—†Jamain Stephens, OL
97—†Chris McNeil, DL

N.C. CENTRAL (5)
68— Doug Wilkerson, MG
69— Doug Wilkerson, OT
74— Charles Smith, DE
88— Earl Harvey, QB
96— Tommy Dorsey, LB

NORTH CENTRAL (1)
97— Jim Witte, OL

NORTH DAK. (23)
55— Steve Myhra, G
56— Steve Myhra, G
63— Neil Reuter, T
65— Dave Lince, DE
66— Roger Bonk, LB
71— Jim LeClair, LB
Dan Martinsen, DB
72— Mike Deutsch, RB
75— Bill Deutsch, RB
79— Paul Muckenhirn, TE
80— Todd Thomas, OT
81— Milson Jones, RB
89— Cory Solberg, PK
91— Shannon Burnell, RB
93— Shannon Burnell, RB
Kevin Robson, OL
94— Mike Mooney, LB
95— Dave Hillesheim, DE
96— Juan Gomez-Tagle, PK

Photo from St. Cloud State sports information

St. Cloud State running back Randy Martin was selected as a Division II all-American in 1995 and 1996.

Mark Callahan, DL
Tim Tibesar, LB
97— Phillip Moore, RB
Jim Kleinsasser, TE

NORTH DAK. ST. (29)
34— Melvin Hanson, B
46— Cliff Rothrock, C
66— Walt Odegaard, MG
67— Jim Ferge, LB
68— Jim Ferge, DT
Paul Hatchett, B
69— Paul Hatchett, HB
Joe Cichy, DB
70— Joe Cichy, DB
74— Jerry Dahl, DE
76— Rick Budde, LB
77— Lew Curry, OL
81— Wayne Schluchter, DB
82— Cliff Carmody, OG
Steve Garske, LB
83— Mike Whetstone, OG
84— Greg Hagfors, C
86— Jeff Bentrim, QB
Jim Dick, LB
87— Mike Favor, C
88— Matt Tracy, OL
Mike Favor, C
Yorrick Byers, LB
90— Phil Hansen, DL
Chris Simdorn, QB
93— Scott Fuchs, OL
T. R. McDonald, WR
95— Brad Servais, OL
97— Sean Fredricks, LB

NORTH PARK (2)
72— Greg Nugent, OE
90— John Love, QB

NORTH TEXAS* (6)
47— Frank Whitlow, T
51— Ray Renfro, DB
83—†Ronnie Hickman, DE
†Rayford Cooks, DL
88—†Rex Johnson, DL
90—†Mike Davis, DL

NORTHEAST LA.* (19)
67— Vic Bender, C
70— Joe Profit, RB
72— Jimmy Edwards, RB
73— Glenn Fleming, MG
74— Glenn Fleming, MG
82—†Arthur Christophe, C
†Bruce Daigle, DB
83—†Mike Grantham, OG
84—†Mike Grantham, OG
85—†Mike Turner, DB
87—†John Clement, OT
†Claude Brumfield, DT
88—†Cyril Crutchfield, DB
89—†Jackie Harris, E
92—†Jeff Blackshear, OL
†Vic Zordan, OL
†Roosevelt Potts, RB
93—†Raymond Batiste, OL
†James Folston, DL

NORTHEASTERN (3)
72— Tom Rezzuti, DB
78— Dan Ross, TE
96—†Jerome Daniels, OL

NORTHEASTERN ST. (5)
69— Manuel Britto, HB
71— Roosevelt Manning, DT
74— Kevin Goodlet, DB
82— Cedric Mack, WR
94— Ricky Ceasar, DL

NORTHERN ARIZ. (19)
66— Rick Ries, LB
67— Bill Hanna, DE
68— Larry Small, OG
77— Larry Friedrichs, OL
Tom Jurich, K
78— Jerry Lumpkin, LB
79—†Ed Judie, LB
82—†Pete Mandley, WR
83—†Pete Mandley, WR
†James Gee, DT
86—†Goran Lingmerth, PK
89—†Darrell Jordan, LB
93—†Terry Belden, P
95—†Rayna Stewart, DB
†Kevin O'Leary, P
†Ben Petrucci, DL
96—†Archie Amerson, RB
†Ricky Pearsall, PR
97—†Dan Finn, OL

NORTHERN COLO. (16)
68— Jack O'Brien, DB
80— Todd Volkart, DT
81— Brad Wimmer, OL
82— Mark Mostek, OG
Kevin Jelden, PK
89— Vance Lechman, DB
90— Frank Wainwright, TE
92— David Oliver, OL
93— Jeff Pease, LB
94— Jeff Pease, LB
95— Tony Ramirez, OL
Tim Bowie, DB
96— Tony Ramirez, OL
Delano Washington, DB
97— Aaron Smith, DL
Dirk Johnson, DB

NORTHERN ILL.* (2)
62— George Bork, B
63— George Bork, B

NORTHERN IOWA (16)
52— Lou Bohnsack, C
60— George Asleson, G
61— Wendell Williams, G
64— Randy Schultz, FB
65— Randy Schultz, FB
67— Ray Pedersen, MG
75— Mike Timmermans, OT
85— Joe Fuller, DB
87—†Carl Boyd, RB
90—†Brian Mitchell, PK
91—†Brian Mitchell, PK
92—†Kenny Shedd, WR
†William Freeney, LB
94—†Andre Allen, LB
95—†Dedric Ward, WR
96—†Dedric Ward, WR

NORTHERN MICH. (6)
75— Daniel Stencil, OL
76— Maurice Mitchell, FL
77— Joseph Stemo, DB
82— George Works, RB
87— Jerry Woods, DB
88— Jerry Woods, DB

NORTHERN ST. (1)
76— Larry Kolbo, DL

NORTHWEST MO. ST. (5)
39— Marion Rogers, G
84— Steve Hansley, WR
89— Jason Agee, DB
96— Matt Uhde, DL
97— Chris Greisen, QB

N'WESTERN (IOWA) (1)
71— Kevin Korvor, DE

NORTHWESTERN ST. (13)
66— Al Dodd, DB
80—†Warren Griffith, C
†Joe Delaney, RB
81—†Gary Reasons, LB
82—†Gary Reasons, LB
83—†Gary Reasons, LB
84—†Arthur Berry, DT
87—†John Kulakowski, DE
91—†Andre Carron, LB
92—†Adrian Hardy, DB
†Marcus Spears, OL
93—†Marcus Spears, OL
97—†Tony Maranto, DB

NORTHWOOD (2)
73— Bill Chandler, DT
74— Bill Chandler, DT

NORWICH (3)
79— Milt Williams, RB
84— Beau Almodobar, WR
85— Mike Norman, OL

OBERLIN (1)
45— James Boswell, B

OCCIDENTAL (6)
76— Rick Fry, FL
77— Rick Fry, SE
82— Dan Osborn, P
83— Ron Scott, DB
89— David Hodges, LB
90— Peter Tucker, OL

OHIO* (2)
35— Art Lewis, T
60— Dick Grecni, C

OHIO NORTHERN (2)
95— LaVant King, WR
96— Jerry Adams, DB

OHIO WESLEYAN (8)
34— John Turley, B
51— Dale Bruce, OE
71— Steve Dutton, DE
83— Eric DiMartino, LB
90— Jeff Court, OG
Neil Ringers, DL
91— Kevin Rucker, DL
96— Craig Anderson, LB

OKLA. PANHANDLE (2)
82— Tom Rollison, DB
83— Tom Rollison, DB

OTTERBEIN (3)
82— Jim Hoyle, K
90— Ron Severance, WR
91— Ron Severance, WR

OUACHITA BAPTIST (1)
79— Ezekiel Vaughn, LB

PACIFIC (CAL.) (4)
34— Cris Kjeldsen, G
47— Eddie LeBaron, B
48— Eddie LeBaron, B
49— Eddie LeBaron, B

PACIFIC LUTHERAN (9)
40— Marv Tommervik, B
41— Marv Tommervik, B
47— Dan D'Andrea, C
52— Ron Billings, DB
65— Marvin Peterson, C
78— John Zamberlin, LB
85— Mark Foege, PK
Tim Shannon, DL
88— Jon Kral, DL

PENNSYLVANIA (8)
86—†Marty Peterson, OL
88—†John Zinser, OL
90—†Joe Valerio, OL
93—†Miles Macik, WR
94—†Pat Goodwillie, LB
95—†Miles Macik, WR
†Tom McGarrity, DL
96—†Mitch Marrow, DL

PEPPERDINE (2)
47— Darwin Horn, B
55— Wixie Robinson, G

PERU ST. (4)
52— Robert Lade, OT
53— Robert Lade, T
81— Alvin Holder, RB
91— Tim Herman, DL

PILLSBURY (1)
85— Calvin Addison, RB

PITTSBURG ST. (17)
61— Gary Snadon, B
70— Mike Potchard, OT
78— Brian Byers, OL
88— Jesse Wall, OL
89— John Roderique, LB
90— Ron West, WR
91— Ron West, WR
92— Ronald Moore, RB
93— Doug Bullard, OL
94— Andy Sweet, LB
Chris Brown, DB
95— Phil Schepens, OT
B. J. McGivern, LB
Chris Brown, DB
96— Bob Goltra, OL
97— Sean McNamara, OL
Brian Moorman, P

PLYMOUTH ST. (8)
74— Robert Gibson, DB
82— Mark Barrows, LB
83— Joe Dudek, RB
84— Joe Dudek, RB
85— Joe Dudek, RB
91— Scott Allen, LB
94— Colby Compton, LB
95— Colby Compton, LB

POMONA-PITZER (1)
74— Larry Cenotto, QB

PORTLAND ST. (15)
76— June Jones, QB
77— Dave Stief, OE
79—†Stuart Gaussoin, SE
†Kurt Ijanoff, OT
80—†Neil Lomax, QB
84— Doug Mikolas, DL
88— Bary Naone, TE
Chris Crawford, QB
89— Darren Del'Andrae, QB
91— James Fuller, DB
92— John Charles, QB
93— Rick Cruz, LB
94— Sam Peoples, DB
Jesus Moreno, OT
95— Steve Papin, RB

PRAIRIE VIEW (2)
64— Otis Taylor, OE
70— Bivian Lee, DB

PRESBYTERIAN (8)
45— Andy Kavounis, G
46— Hank Caver, B
52— Joe Kirven, OE
68— Dan Eckstein, DB
71— Robert Norris, LB
78— Roy Walker, OL
79— Roy Walker, OL
83— Jimmie Turner, LB

PRINCETON (4)
87—†Dean Cain, DB
89—†Judd Garrett, RB
92—†Keith Elias, RB
93—†Keith Elias, RB

PRINCIPIA (1)
93— Matt Newton, WR

PUGET SOUND (9)
56— Robert Mitchell, G
63— Ralph Bauman, G
66— Joseph Peyton, OE
75— Bill Linnenkohl, LB
76— Dan Kuehl, DL
81— Bob Jackson, MG
82— Mike Bos, WR
83— Larry Smith, DB
87— Mike Oliphant, RB

RANDOLPH-MACON (7)
47— Albert Oley, G
57— Dave Young, G
79— Rick Eades, DL
80— Rick Eades, DL
84— Cody Dearing, QB
88— Aaron Boston, OL
96— Tim Armoska, LB

REDLANDS (2)
77— Randy Van Horn, OL
92— James Shields, DL

RENSSELAER
96— Scott Cafarelli, OL

RHODE ISLAND (9)
55— Charles Gibbons, T
82—†Richard Pelzer, OL
83—†Tony DeLuca, DL
84—†Brian Forster, TE
85—†Brian Forster, TE
†Tom Ehrhardt, QB
90—†Kevin Smith, DB
92—†Darren Rizzi, TE
96—†Frank Ferrara, DL

RHODES (5)
36— Henry Hammond, E
38— Gaylon Smith, B
76— Conrad Bradburn, DB
85— Jim Hever, PK
88— Larry Hayes, OL

RICHMOND (3)
84—†Eddie Martin, OL
97—†Shawn Barber, LB
†Marc Megna, DL

AWARD WINNERS

RIPON (6)
57— Peter Kasson, E
75— Dick Rehbein, C
76— Dick Rehbein, OL
79— Art Peters, TE
82— Bob Wallner, OL
95— Jim Wallace, DB

ROANOKE (1)
38— Kenneth Moore, E

ROCHESTER (7)
51— Jack Wilson, DE
52— Donald Bardell, DG
67— Dave Ragusa, LB
75— Ralph Gebhardt, DB
90— Craig Chodak, P
92— Brian Laudadio, DL
93— Geoff Long, DL

ROCKHURST (1)
41— Joe Kiernan, T

ROLLINS (1)
40— Charles Lingerfelt, E

ROSE-HULMAN (2)
77— Gary Ellis, DB
92— Todd Holthaus, PK

ROWAN (4)
78— Dino Hall, RB
93— Bill Fisher, DL
95— LeRoi Jones, LB
97— Terrick Grace, DB

SAGINAW VALLEY (6)
81— Eugene Marve, LB
84— Joe Rice, DL
90— David Cook, DB
92— Bill Schafer, TE
97— Paul Spicer, DL
Kent Kraatz, OT

ST. AMBROSE (5)
40— Nick Kerasiotis, G
51— Robert Flanagan, B
58— Robert Webb, B
87— Jerry Klosterman, DL
97— Craig Shepherd, OL

ST. BONAVENTURE (2)
46— Phil Colella, B
48— Frank LoVuola, E

ST. CLOUD ST. (4)
85— Mike Lambrecht, DL
95— Randy Martin, RB
96— Randy Martin, RB
97— Mike McKinney, WR

ST. JOHN'S (MINN.) (10)
65— Pat Whalin, DB
79— Ernie England, MG
82— Rick Bell, RB
83— Chris Biggins, TE
91— Pat Mayew, QB
93— Burt Chamberlin, OL
Jim Wagner, DL
94— Jim Wagner, DL
95— Chris Palmer, WR
96— Jesse Redepenning, OL

ST. JOHN'S (N.Y.) (1)
83— Todd Jamison, QB

ST. LAWRENCE (2)
51— Ken Spencer, LB
77— Mitch Brown, DB

ST. MARY (KAN.) (1)
86— Joe Brinson, RB

ST. MARY'S (CAL.) (4)
79— Fran McDermott, DB
80— Fran McDermott, DB
88— Jon Braff, TE
92— Mike Estrella, PK

ST. MARY'S (TEX.) (1)
36— Douglas Locke, B

ST. NORBERT (2)
57— Norm Jarock, B
64— Dave Jauquet, DE

ST. OLAF (3)
53— John Gustafson, E
78— John Nahorniak, LB
80— Jon Anderson, DL

ST. THOMAS (MINN.) (10)
45— Theodore Molitor, E
48— Jack Salscheider, B
84— Neal Guggemos, DB
85— Neal Guggemos, DB
90— Gary Trettel, RB
91— Kevin DeVore, OL
94— Ryan Davis, TE
95— Ryan Davis, TE
96— Ryan Collins, TE
97— Ryan Collins, TE

SALISBURY ST. (5)
82— Mark Lagowski, LB
84— Joe Mammano, OL
85— Robb Disbennett, QB
86— Tom Kress, DL
95— Mark Hannah, LB

SAM HOUSTON ST. (3)
49— Charles Williams, E
52— Don Gottlob, B
91—†Michael Bankston, DL

SAMFORD (2)
36— Norman Cooper, C
94—†Anthony Jordan, AP

SAN DIEGO (3)
73— Bob Dulich, QB
81— Dan Herbert, DB
92— Robert Ray, P

SAN DIEGO ST.* (6)
35— John Butler, G
66— Don Horn, QB
67— Steve Duich, OT
Haven Moses, OE
68— Fred Dryer, DE
Lloyd Edwards, B

SAN FRANCISCO (1)
42— John Sanchez, T

SAN FRAN. ST. (7)
51— Robert Williamson, OT
60— Charles Fuller, B
67— Joe Koontz, OE
76— Forest Hancock, LB
78— Frank Duncan, DB
82— Poncho James, RB
84— Jim Jones, TE

SAN JOSE ST.* (2)
38— Lloyd Thomas, E
39— LeRoy Zimmerman, B

SANTA CLARA (8)
64— Lou Pastorini, LB
71— Ronald Sani, C
79— Jim Leonard, C
80— Brian Sullivan, K
82— Gary Hoffman, OT
83— Alex Vlahos, C
Mike Rosselli, LB
85— Brent Jones, TE

SAVANNAH ST. (3)
79— Timothy Walker, DL
89— Shannon Sharpe, TE
96— Britt Henderson, DB

SEWANEE (8)
63— Martin Agnew, B
73— Mike Lumpkin, DE
77— Nino Austin, DB
79— John Hill, DB
80— Mallory Nimocs, TE
81— Greg Worsowicz, DB
86— Mark Kent, WR
90— Ray McGowan, DL

SHIPPENSBURG (3)
53— Robert Adams, G
91— Jeff Fickes, DB
94— Doug Seidenstricker, DB

SIENA (2)
95—†Reggie Greene, AP
97—†Reggie Greene, RB

SIMON FRASER (1)
90— Nick Mazzoli, WR

SIMPSON (4)
89— Ricky Gales, RB
96— Brent Parrott, DB
Chris Whiney, OT
97— Jeremy Whalen, DL

SLIPPERY ROCK (7)
74— Ed O'Reilly, RB
75— Jerry Skocik, TE
76— Chris Thull, LB
77— Bob Schrantz, TE
78— Bob Schrantz, TE
85— Jeff Williams, P
97— Dave Sabolcik, OL

SONOMA ST. (3)
86— Mike Henry, LB
92— Larry Allen, OL
93— Larry Allen, OL

SOUTH CARO. ST. (22)
67— Tyrone Caldwell, DE
71— James Evans, LB
72— Barney Chavous, DE
73— Donnie Shell, DB
75— Harry Carson, DE
76— Robert Sims, DL
77— Ricky Anderson, RB
79—†Phillip Murphy, DL
80—†Edwin Bailey, OG
81—†Anthony Reed, FB
†Dwayne Jackson, DL
82—†Dwayne Jackson, DE
†Anthony Reed, RB
†Ralph Green, OT
†John Courtney, DT
83—†Ralph Green, OT
89—†Eric Douglas, OL
91—†Robert Porcher, DL
93—†Anthony Cook, DE
94—†Anthony Cook, DL
96—†Raleigh Roundtree, OL
97—†Chartric Darby, DL

SOUTH DAK. (11)
68— John Kohler, OT
69— John Kohler, OT
71— Gene Macken, OG
72— Gary Kipling, OG
78— Bill Moats, DB
79— Benjamin Long, LB
83— Kurt Seibel, K
86— Jerry Glinsky, C
Todd Salat, DB
88— Doug VanderEsch, LB
97— Brent Petersen, DL

SOUTH DAK. ST. (15)
67— Darwin Gonnerman, HB
68— Darwin Gonnerman, FB
74— Lynn Boden, OT
77— Bill Matthews, DE
79— Charles Loewen, OL
84— Rick Wegher, RB
85— Jeff Tiefenthaler, WR
86— Jeff Tiefenthaler, WR
91— Kevin Tetzlaff, OL
92— Doug Miller, LB
93— Adam Timmerman, DL
94— Jake Hines, TE
Adam Vinatieri, P
Adam Timmerman, OL
96— Tom O'Brien, P

SOUTH DAK. TECH (1)
73— Charles Waite, DB

SOUTHEAST MO. ST. (4)
37— Wayne Goddard, T
94—†Doug Berg, DL
95—†Frank Russell, DB
97—†Angel Rubio, DL

SOUTHEASTERN LA. (3)
70— Ronnie Hornsby, LB
83—†Bret Wright, P
85—†Willie Shepherd, DL

SOUTHERN U. (7)
70— Isiah Robertson, LB
72— James Wright, OG
73— Godwin Turk, LB
79—†Ken Times, DL
87—†Gerald Perry, OT
93—†Sean Wallace, DB
95—†Kendell Shello, DL

SOUTHERN ARK. (3)
84— Greg Stuman, LB
85— Greg Stuman, LB
97— Fred Perry, LB

SOUTHERN CONN. ST. (9)
82— Mike Marshall, DB
83— Kevin Gray, OL
84— William Sixsmith, LB
86— Rick Atkinson, DB
91— Ron Lecointe, OL
92— Steve Lawrence, LB
94— Anthony Idone, DL
95—†Joe Andruzzi, OL
96— Joe Andruzzi, OL

SOUTHERN ILL. (5)
70— Lionel Antoine, OE
71— Lionel Antoine, OE
83—†Donnell Daniel, DB
†Terry Taylor, DB
96—†Mark Gagliano, P

SOUTHERN MISS.* (4)
53— Hugh Pepper, B
56— Don Owens, T
58— Robert Yencho, E
59— Hugh McInnis, E

SOUTHERN ORE. ST. (1)
75— Dennis Webber, LB

SOUTHERN UTAH (6)
79— Lane Martino, DL
87— Jeff McComb, P
89— Randy Bostic, C
90— Randy Bostic, C
95—†Micah Deckert, TE
97—†Jimmy Brimmer, LB

SOUTHWEST MO. ST. (11)
66— William Stringer, OG
87—†Matt Soraghan, LB
89—†Mark Christenson, OL
90—†DeAndre Smith, QB
91—†Bill Walter, DL
93—†Adrion Smith, DB
95—†DeLaun Fowler, LB
96—†Michael Cosey, RB
†Wayne Boyer, PK
†Mike Miano, DL
97—†Travis Brawner, PK

SOUTHWEST ST. (2)
87— James Ashley, WR
91— Wayne Hawkins, DE

SOUTHWEST TEX. ST. (12)
53— Pence Dacus, B
63— Jerry Cole, E
64— Jerry Cole, DB
72— Bob Daigle, C
75— Bobby Kotzur, DT
82— Tim Staskus, LB
83— Tim Staskus, LB
84—†Scott Forester, C
90—†Reggie Rivers, RB
91—†Ervin Thomas, C
94—†Don Wilkerson, RB
97—†Claude Mathis, RB

SOUTHWESTERN (KAN.) (2)
82— Tom Audley, DL
84— Jackie Jenson, RB

SOUTHWESTERN LA.* (1)
69— Glenn LaFleur, LB

SOUTHWESTERN OKLA. (2)
77— Louis Blanton, DB
82— Richard Lockman, LB

SPRINGFIELD (13)
68— Dick Dobbert, C
70— John Curtis, OE
76— Roy Samuelsen, MG
78— Jack Quinn, DB
79— Jack Quinn, DB
80— Steve Foster, OT
81— Jon Richardson, LB
83— Wally Case, DT
Ed Meachum, TE
85— Jim Anderson, LB
91— Fran Papasedero, DL
94— Matt Way, OL
96— Jamie McGourty, DL

STEPHEN F. AUSTIN (13)
51— James Terry, DE
79— Ronald Haynes, DL
85— James Noble, WR
86—†Darrell Harkless, DB
88—†Eric Lokey, LB

89—†David Whitmore, DB
93—†Cedric Walker, DB
95—†Joey Wylie, OL
†Lee Kirk, OL
†Damiyon Bell, DB
96—†Jeremiah Trotter, LB
97—†Mikhael Ricks, WR
†Jeremiah Trotter, LB

STONY BROOK (2)
87— Chuck Downey, DB
88— David Lewis, P

SUL ROSS ST. (2)
65— Tom Nelson, DE
88— Francis Jones, DB

SUSQUEHANNA (4)
51— James Hazlett, C
90— Keith Henry, DL
92— Andy Watkins, LB
96— Jeremy Ziesloft, DB

SWARTHMORE (1)
89— Marshall Happer, OL

TAMPA (5)
65— John Perry, DB
68— Ron Brown, MG
70— Leon McQuay, RB
71— Ron Mikolajczyk, OT
Sammy Gellerstedt, MG

TENN.-MARTIN (3)
68— Julian Nunnamaker, OG
88— Emanuel McNeil, DL
91— Oscar Bunch, TE

TENNESSEE ST. (17)
67— Claude Humphrey, DT
68— Jim Marsalis, DB
69— Joe Jones, DE
70— Vernon Holland, OT
71— Cliff Brooks, DB
Joe Gilliam, QB
72— Robert Woods, OT
Waymond Bryant, LB
73— Waymond Bryant, LB
Ed Jones, DE
74— Cleveland Elam, DE
81—†Mike Jones, WR
†Malcolm Taylor, DT
82—†Walter Tate, OL
86—†Onzy Elam, LB
90—†Colin Godfrey, P
93—†Brent Alexander, DB

TENNESSEE TECH (11)
52— Tom Fann, OT
59— Tom Hackler, E
60— Tom Hackler, E
61— David Baxter, T
69— Larry Schreiber, HB
71— Jim Youngblood, LB
72— Jim Youngblood, LB
74— Elois Grooms, DE
76— Ed Burns, OT
89—†Ryan Weeks, PK
96—†Robert Taylor, DB

TENN. WESLEYAN (1)
92— Derrick Scott, PK

TEXAS-ARLINGTON (5)
66— Ken Ozee, DT
67— Robert Diem, OG
Robert Willbanks, S
83—†Mark Cannon, C
84—†Bruce Collie, OL

TEX. A&M-COMMERCE (19)
38— Darrell Tully, B
53— Bruno Ashley, G
58— Sam McCord, B
59— Sam McCord, B
68— Chad Brown, OT
70— William Lewis, C
72— Curtis Wester, OG
73— Autry Beamon, DB
84— Alan Veingrad, OG
88— Kim Morton, DL
90— Terry Bagsby, DL
91— Eric Turner, DB
Dwayne Phorne, OL
92— Eric Turner, DB
Pat Williams, DB
93— Fred Woods, LB
Billy Watkins, PK
95— Kevin Mathis, DB
96— Kevin Mathis, DB

TEX. A&M-KINGSVILLE (50)
40— Stuart Clarkson, C
41— Stuart Clarkson, C
59— Gerald Lambert, G
60— William Crafts, T
62— Douglas Harvey, C
63— Sid Blanks, B
65— Randy Johnson, QB
66— Dwayne Nix, OE
67— Dwayne Nix, OE
68— Dwayne Nix, OE
Ray Hickl, OG
70— Dwight Harrison, DB
Margarito Guerrero, MG
71— Eldridge Small, OE
Levi Johnson, DB
72— Ernest Price, DE
74— Don Hardeman, RB
75— David Hill, TE
76— Richard Ritchie, QB
Larry Grunewald, LB
77— Larry Collins, RB
John Barefield, DE
78— Billy John, OT
79— Andy Hawkins, LB
80— Don Washington, CB
81— Durwood Roquemore, DB
82— Darrell Green, DB
83— Loyd Lewis, OG
84— Neal Lattue, PK
85— Charles Smith, C
86— Johnny Bailey, RB
Moses Horn, OG
87— Johnny Bailey, RB
Moses Horn, OG
88— Rod Mounts, OL
Johnny Bailey, RB
John Randle, DL
89— Johnny Bailey, RB
90— Keithen DeGrate, OL
91— Brian Nielsen, OL
92— Earl Dotson, OL
93— Anthony Phillips, DB
Moke Simon, DL
94— Jeff Rodgers, DL
Kevin Dogins, C
95— Jermane Mayberry, OT
Jaime Martinez, OG
Kevin Dogins, C
96— Todd Perkins, OT
97— Chris Hensley, LB

TEXAS LUTHERAN (3)
73— David Wehmeyer, RB
74— D. W. Rutledge, LB
75— Jerry Ellis, OL

TEXAS SOUTHERN (3)
70— Nathaniel Allen, DB
76— Freddie Dean, OL
92—†Michael Strahan, DL

TEXAS TECH* (2)
35— Herschel Ramsey, E
45— Walter Schlinkman, B

THOMAS MORE (3)
93— Mike Flesch, OL
96— Brent Moses, OL
97— Chris Wells, LB

TIFFIN (1)
93— Brian Diliberto, RB

TOLEDO* (1)
38— Dan Buckwick, G

TOWSON (11)
75— Dan Dullea, QB
76— Skip Chase, OE
77— Randy Bielski, DB
78— Ken Snoots, SE
82— Sean Landeta, P
83— Gary Rubeling, DB
84— Terry Brooks, OG
85— Stan Eisentooth, OL
86— David Haden, LB
93—†Tony Vinson, RB
94—†Mark Orlando, WR

TRINITY (CONN.) (8)
35— Mickey Kobrosky, B
36— Mickey Kobrosky, B
55— Charles Sticka, B
59— Roger LeClerc, C
70— David Kiarsis, HB
78— Pat McNamara, FL
93— Eric Mudry, DB
94— Greg Schramm, DB

TRINITY (TEX.) (7)
54— Alvin Beal, B
55— Hubert Cook, C
56— Milton Robichaux, E
67— Marvin Upshaw, DT
94— James Vallerie, LB
96— John Beckwith, LB
97— Paul Morris, PK

TROY ST. (16)
39— Sherrill Busby, E
73— Mark King, C
74— Mark King, C
76— Perry Griggs, OE
78— Tim Tucker, LB
80— Willie Tullis, QB
84— Mitch Geier, OG
86— Freddie Thomas, DB
87— Mike Turk, QB
Freddie Thomas, DB
94—†Bob Hall, OL
95—†Bob Hall, OL
96—†Pratt Lyons, DL
†Kerry Jenkins, OL
97—†Clifford Ivory, DB
†Andy Swafford, KR

TRUMAN ST. (5)
60— Dale Mills, B
65— Richard Rhodes, OT
85— Chris Hegg, QB
93— Mike Roos, DL
96— Jarrett Anderson, RB

TUFTS (6)
34— William Grinnell, E
76— Tim Whelan, RB
78— Mark Buben, DL
79— Chris Connors, QB
80— Mike Brown, OL
86— Bob Patz, DL

TULSA* (1)
34— Rudy Prochaska, C

TUSCULUM (2)
94— Matt Schults, OL
95— Eric Claridy, RB

UNION (N.Y.) (10)
39— Sam Hammerstrom, B
82— Steve Bodmer, DL
83— Tim Howell, LB
84— Brian Cox, DE
85— Anthony Valente, DL
86— Rich Romer, DL
87— Rich Romer, DL
91— Greg Harrison, PK
93— Marco Lainez, LB
96— Roger Egbert, PK

UNION (TENN.) (2)
41— James Jones, B
42— James Jones, B

U.S. INT'L (2)
72— Jerry Robinson, DB
75— Steve Matson, FL

UPSALA (1)
64— Dick Giessuebel, LB

URSINUS (1)
96— Peter Hinckle, DB

VALDOSTA ST. (8)
82— Mark Catano, OL
86— Jessie Tuggle, LB
89— Randy Fisher, WR
90— Deon Searcy, DB
93— Chris Hatcher, QB
94— Chris Hatcher, QB
96— Lance Funderburk, QB
97— Richard Freeman, DL/DE

VALPARAISO (5)
51— Joe Pahr, B
71— Gary Puetz, OT
72— Gary Puetz, OT
76— John Belskis, DB
85— Mike Healey, WR

VILLANOVA (8)
88—†Paul Berardelli, OL
89—†Bryan Russo, OL
91—†Curtis Eller, LB
92—†Curtis Eller, LB
94—†Tyrone Frazier, LB
96—†Brian Finneran, WR
97—†Brian Finneran, WR
†Chris Boden, QB

VMI (3)
88—†Mark Stock, WR
95—†Thomas Haskins, RB
96—†Thomas Haskins, RB

VIRGINIA ST. (3)
71— Larry Brooks, DT
84— John Greene, LB
85— James Ward, DL

VIRGINIA UNION (12)
73— Herb Scott, OG
74— Herb Scott, OG
75— Anthony Leonard, DB
77— Frank Dark, DB
79— Plummer Bullock, DE
80— William Dillon, DB
81— William Dillon, DB
82— William Dillon, DB
83— Larry Curtis, DT
88— Leroy Gause, LB
91— Paul DeBerry, DB
Kevin Williams, LB

WABASH (5)
76— Jimmy Parker, DB
77— David Harvey, QB
81— Pete Metzelaars, TE
88— Tim Pliske, PK
89— Mike Funk, WR

WAGNER (9)
67— John Gloistein, OT
80— Phil Theis, OL
81— Alonzo Patterson, RB
82— Alonzo Patterson, RB
83— Selwyn Davis, OT
86— Charles Stinson, DL
87— Rich Negrin, OT
88— Terry Underwood, RB
91— Walter Lopez, PK

WARTBURG (3)
94— Jamey Parker, OL
Vince Penningroth, DL
95— Vince Penningroth, DL

WASHBURN (2)
64— Robert Hardy, DB
88— Troy Slusser, WR

WASHINGTON (MO.) (7)
72— Shelby Jordan, LB
73— Stu Watkins, OE
74— Marion Stallings, DB
88— Paul Matthews, TE
94— Matt Gomric, LB
95— Chris Nalley, DB
96— Chris Nalley, DB

WASH. & JEFF. (14)
84— Ed Kusko, OL
87— A. J. Pagano, RB
91— Chris Babirad, RB
Gilbert Floyd, DB
92— Chris Babirad, RB
Todd Pivnick, OL
Kevin Pintar, OL
93— Jason Moore, OL
Shawn Prendergast, LB
94— Matt Szczypinski, DL
Mike Jones, OL
Mike Brooder, DL
95— Mike Jones, OL
96— Dan Primrose, DL

WASH. & LEE (5)
76— Tony Perry, OE
81— Mike Pressler, DL
83— Glenn Kirschner, OL
86— John Packett, OL
95— Robert Hall, DL

WAYNE ST. (NEB.) (3)
84— Herve Roussel, PK
85— Ruben Mendoza, OL

95— Brad Ottis, DL

WAYNESBURG (1)
41— Nick George, G

WEBER ST. (18)
66— Ronald McCall, DE
67— Lee White, FB
Jim Schmedding, OG
69— Carter Campbell, DE
70— Henry Reed, DE
71— David Taylor, OT
77— Dennis Duncanson, DB
78— Dennis Duncanson, DB
Randy Jordan, WR
80—†Mike Humiston, LB
89—†Peter Macon, WR
91—†Jamie Martin, QB
†Alfred Pupunu, WR
93—†Pat McNarney, TE
95—†Pokey Eckford, WR
96—†Scott Shields, DB
97—†Cameron Quayle, TE
†Scott Shields, DB/AP

WESLEY (5)
91— Fran Naselli, KR
95— Brandon Steinheim, RB
96— Brandon Steinheim, RB
Demetrius Stevenson, DL
97— Nate Casella, LB

WESLEYAN (CONN.) (6)
46— Bert VanderClute, G
48— Jack Geary, T
72— Robert Heller, C
73— Robert Heller, C
76— John McVicar, DL
77— John McVicar, DL

WEST ALA. (5)
82— Charles Martin, DT
84— Andrew Fields, WR
87— Ronnie Glanton, DL
93— Matt Carman, WR
97— John Sedely, PK

WEST CHESTER (9)
52— Charles Weber, DG
58— Richard Emerich, T
61— Joe Iacone, B
62— Joe Iacone, B
72— Tim Pierantozzi, QB
76— William Blystone, RB
87— Ralph Tamm, OL
88— Bill Hess, WR
92— Lee Woodall, DL

WEST GA. (3)
96— Byron Slack, TE
97— Corey Jarrells, DB
Chris Williams, OT

WEST LIBERTY ST. (1)
97— Greg Dailer, WR

WEST TEX. A&M (5)
86— Stan Carraway, WR
90— Mark Bounds, P
94— Brad Bailey, WR
Brian Hurley, OL
95— Jon Mason, P

WEST VA.* (1)
34— Tod Goodwin, E

WEST VA. TECH (3)
82— Elliott Washington, DB
86— Calvin Wallace, DL
89— Phil Hudson, WR

WEST VA. WESLEYAN (2)
36— George Mike, T
82— Jerry Free, T

WESTERN CARO. (13)
49— Arthur Byrd, G
71— Steve Williams, DT
73— Mark Ferguson, OT
74— Jerry Gaines, SE
Steve Yates, LB
84—†Louis Cooper, DL
†Kirk Roach, PK
†Steve Kornegay, P
85—†Clyde Simmons, DL
86—†Alonzo Carmichael, TE
†Kirk Roach, PK
87—†Kirk Roach, PK
93—†Kerry Hayes, KR/WR

WESTERN ILL. (18)
59— Bill Larson, B
61— Leroy Jackson, B
74— John Passananti, OT
76— Scott Levenhagen, TE
Greg Lee, DB
77— Craig Phalen, DT
78— Bill Huskisson, DL
80— Mike Maher, TE
Don Greco, OG
83—†Chris Gunderson, MG
84—†Chris Gunderson, T
86—†Frank Winters, C
†Todd Auer, DL
88—†Marlin Williams, DL
93—†Rodney Harrison, DB
94—†Ross Schulte, P
97—†Aaron Stecker, RB
†Jason Grott, OL

WESTERN KY. (17)
64— Dale Lindsey, LB
70— Lawrence Brame, DE
73— Mike McKoy, DB
74— John Bushong, DL
Virgil Livers, DB
75— Rick Green, LB
77— Chip Carpenter, OL
80—†Pete Walters, OG
†Tim Ford, DL
81—†Donnie Evans, DE
82—†Paul Gray, LB
83—†Paul Gray, LB
87—†James Edwards, DB
88—†Dean Tiebout, OL
†Joe Arnold, RB
95—†Brian Bixler, C
97—†Patrick Goodman, OL

WESTERN MD. (3)
51— Victor Makovitch, DG
78— Ricci Bonaccorsy, DL
79— Ricci Bonaccorsy, DL

WESTERN MICH.* (1)
82—†Matt Meares, OL

WESTERN N.M. (3)
83— Jay Ogle, WR
88— Pat Maxwell, P
97— Anthony Gray, RB

WESTERN ST. (9)
56— Bill Rhodes, B
78— Bill Campbell, DB
80— Justin Cross, OT
84— Jeff Guy, P
92— Reggie Alexander, WR
94— Derren Bryan, OL
96— Ben Kern, TE
Kurt Clay, DB
97— Shane Carwin, LB

WESTERN WASH. (3)
51— Norman Hash, DB
79— Patrick Locker, RB
95— Orlondo Steinauer, DB

WESTMINSTER (PA.) (10)
73— Robert Pontius, DB
77— Rex Macey, FL
82— Gary DeGruttola, LB
83— Scott Higgins, DB
86— Joe Keaney, LB
88— Kevin Myers, LB
89— Joe Micchia, QB
90— Brad Tokar, RB
91— Brian DeLorenzo, DL
92— Matt Raich, LB

WHEATON (ILL.) (10)
55— Dave Burnham, B
58— Robert Bakke, T
77— Larry Wagner, LB
78— Scott Hall, QB
83— Keith Bishop, QB
95— Doug Johnston, OL
Chip Parrish, LB
96— Chip Parrish, LB
Mark Loeffler, WR
97— Chris Brown, OL

WHITTIER (3)
38— Myron Claxton, T
62— Richard Peter, T
77— Michael Ciacci, DB

WHITWORTH (4)
52— Pete Swanson, OG
54— Larry Paradis, T
85— Wayne Ralph, WR
86— Wayne Ralph, WR

WIDENER (13)
72— Billy Johnson, RB
73— Billy Johnson, RB
75— John Warrington, DB
76— Al Senni, OL
77— Chip Zawoiski, RB
79— Tom Deery, DB
80— Tom Deery, DB
81— Tom Deery, DB
82— Tony Stefanoni, DL
88— Dave Duffy, DL
94— O. J. McElroy, DL
Antoine Moore, DB
95— Blaise Coleman, LB

WILKES (3)
73— Jeff Grandinetti, DT
93— Jason Feese, DL
97— J. J. Fadden, DL

WILLAMETTE (12)
34— Loren Grannis, G
35— John Oravec, B
36— Richard Weisgerber, B
46— Marvin Goodman, E
58— William Long, C
59— Marvin Cisneros, G
64— Robert Burles, DT
65— Robert Burles, DT
69— Calvin Lee, LB
75— Gary Johnson, DL
82— Richard Milroy, DB
97— Kamell Eckroth-Bernard, DB

WILLIAM & MARY (9)
83—†Mario Shaffer, OL
86—†Michael Clemons, RB
89—†Steve Christie, P
90—†Pat Crowley, DL
93—†Craig Staub, DL
95—†Darren Sharper, DB
96—†Josh Beyer, OL
†Darren Sharper, DB
97—†Ron Harrison, DB

WILLIAM JEWELL (4)
52— Al Conway, B
73— John Strada, OE
81— Guy Weber, DL
83— Mark Mundel, OL

WM. PATERSON (2)
92— Craig Paskas, DB
93— Craig Paskas, DB

WILLIAM PENN (1)
72— Bruce Polen, DB

WILLIAMS (7)
51— Charles Salmon, DG
69— Jack Maitland, HB
74— John Chandler, LB
78— Greg McAleenan, DB
90— George Rogers, DL
94— Bobby Walker, LB
95— Ethan Brooks, DL

WILMINGTON (OHIO) (2)
72— William Roll, OG
94— Jason Tincher, WR

WINGATE (1)
89— Jimmy Sutton, OT

WINONA ST. (3)
92— Dave Ludy, AP
94— Dave Ludy, AP
97— Jamey Hutchinson, DB

WINSTON-SALEM (6)
77— Cornelius Washington, DB
78— Tim Newsome, RB
84— Danny Moore, OG
87— Barry Turner, G
95— Richard Huntley, RB
96— LaTori Workman, DL

WIS.-EAU CLAIRE (1)
81— Roger Vann, RB

WIS.-LA CROSSE (16)
52— Ted Levanhagen, LB
72— Bryon Buelow, DB
78— Joel Williams, LB
83— Jim Byrne, DL
85— Tom Newberry, OL
88— Ted Pretasky, RB
89— Terry Strouf, OL
91— Jon Lauscher, LB
92— Norris Thomas, DB
Mike Breit, LB
93— Rick Schaaf, DL
95— Craig Kusick, QB
Erik Halverson, OL
96— Erik Halverson, OL
Mike Maslowski, LB
97— Ric Mathias, DB

WIS.-MILWAUKEE (1)
70— Pete Papara, LB

WIS.-PLATTEVILLE (2)
73— William Vander Velden, DE
86— Mike Hintz, DB

WIS.-RIVER FALLS (4)
80— Gerald Sonsalla, OG
82— Roland Hall, LB
87— Greg Corning, RB
95— Brian Izdepski, OT

WIS.-STEVENS POINT (6)
77— Reed Giordana, QB
81— Chuck Braun, WR
92— Randy Simpson, DB
93— Jimmy Henderson, RB
94— Randy Simpson, LB
97— Klint Kriewalt, LB

WIS.-STOUT (1)
79— Joseph Bullis, DL

WIS.-SUPERIOR (3)
66— Mel Thake, DB
83— Larry Banks, MG
85— Phil Eiting, LB

WIS.-WHITEWATER (6)
75— William Barwick, OL
79— Jerry Young, WR
82— Daryl Schleim, DE
90— Reggie White, OL
96— Derrick LeVake, OL
97— Derrick LeVake, OL

WITTENBERG (23)
62— Donald Hunt, G
63— Bob Cherry, E
64— Chuck Green, QB
68— Jim Felts, DE
73— Steve Drongowski, OT
74— Arthur Thomas, LB
75— Robert Foster, LB
76— Dean Caven, DL
78— Dave Merritt, RB
79— Joe Govern, DL
80— Mike Dowds, DE
81— Bill Beach, DB
83— Bryant Lemon, DL
87— Eric Horstman, OL
88— Ken Bonner, OT
Eric Horstman, OL
90— Jon Warga, RB
92— Taver Johnson, LB
93— Taver Johnson, LB
Greg Brame, PK
95— Ron Cunningham, OT
Jimmy Watts, PK
96— Xan Smith, OL

WOFFORD (12)
42— Aubrey Faust, E
47— Ken Dubard, T
49— Elbert Hammett, T
51— Jack Beeler, DB
57— Charles Bradshaw, B
61— Dan Lewis, G
70— Sterling Allen, OG
79— Keith Kinard, OL
90— David Wiley, OL
91— Tom Colter, OL
94— Brian Porzio, PK
97—†Dan Williams, OL/C

WOOSTER (1)
79— Blake Moore, C

WORCESTER ST. (3)
92— Chris Butts, DB
93— Chris Butts, DB
94— Brian Fitzpatrick, DB

WORCESTER TECH (1)
97— Matt Surette, TE

XAVIER (OHIO) (1)
51— Tito Carinci, LB

YALE (1)
84—†John Zanieski, DL

YOUNGSTOWN ST. (24)
74— Don Calloway, DB
75— Don Calloway, DB
78— Ed McGlasson, OL
79— James Ferranti, OE
Jeff Lear, OT
80— Jeff Gergel, LB
81—†Paris Wicks, RB
82—†Paris Wicks, RB
88—†Jim Zdelar, OL
89—†Paul Soltis, LB
90—†Tony Bowens, DL
91—†Pat Danko, DL
92—†Dave Roberts, DB
93—†Drew Garber, OL
†Tamron Smith, RB
†Jeff Wilkins, PK
94—†Randy Smith, KR
†Leon Jones, LB
†Lester Weaver, DB
†Chris Sammarone, OL
95—†Leon Jones, LB
†Jermaine Hopkins, DL
97—†Matt Hogg, OL
†Harry Deligianis, DL

NCAA Postgraduate Scholarship Winners

Following are football players who are NCAA postgraduate scholarship winners, whether or not they were able to accept the grant, plus all alternates (indicated by *) who accepted grants. The program began with the 1964 season. (Those who played in 1964 are listed as 1965 winners, those who played in 1965 as 1966 winners, etc.) To qualify, student-athletes must maintain a 3.000 grade-point average (on a 4.000 scale) during their collegiate careers and perform with distinction in varsity football.

ABILENE CHRISTIAN
71— James Lindsey
83—*Grant Feasel
85— Daniel Remsberg
86—*James Embry
Craig Huff
90— William Clayton

ADRIAN
94— Jeffrey Toner

AIR FORCE
65— Edward Fausti
67— James Hogarty
68— Kenneth Zagzebski
69—*Richard Rivers Jr.
70— Charles Longnecker
*Alfred Wurglitz
71— Ernest Jennings
Robert Parker Jr.
72— Darryl Haas
73— Mark Prill
75—*Joseph Debes
84— Jeffrey Kubiak
86— Derek Brown
88— Chad Hennings
89— David Hlatky
90— Steven Wilson
91— Christopher Howard
92— Ronald James
93— Scott Hufford
95— Preston McConnell
96— Bret Cillessen
97— Carlton Hendrix

UAB
97— John Rea

ALABAMA
69— Donald Sutton
72— John Musso Jr.
75— Randy Hall
80— Steadman Shealy

ALABAMA ST.
92— Edward Robinson Jr.

ALBANY (N.Y.)
88—*Thomas Higgins

ALBION
81— Joel Manby
94— Michael Montico
95— Jeffrey Shooks
96— Timothy Schafer
97— Kyle Klein
98— Neil Johnson

ALBRIGHT
67—*Paul Chaiet

ALLEGHENY
65— David Wion
92— Darren Hadlock
97— Nicholas Reiser

ALMA
67— Keith Bird Jr.
79— Todd Friesner

AMHERST
66— David Greenblatt
76— Geoffrey Miller
85— Raymond Nurme
96— Gregory Schneider

APPALACHIAN ST.
78— Gill Beck
93— D. J. Campbell

ARIZONA
69— William Michael Moody
78— Jon Abbott
80— Jeffrey Whitton
88— Charles Cecil
97— Wayne Wyatt

ARIZONA ST.
78— John Harris
90— Mark Tingstad
97— Devin Kendall
98— Patrick Tillman

ARKANSAS
70— Terry Stewart
71— William Burnett
79— William Bradford Shoup
85—*Mark Lee

ARKANSAS ST.
72— John Meyer
77— Thomas Humphreys

ARMY
66— Samuel Champi Jr.
68— Bohdan Neswiacheny
69— James McCall Jr.
Thomas Wheelock
70— Theodore Shadid Jr.
78— Curtis Downs
81—*Stanley March
86— Donald Smith
Douglas Black
88— William Conner
90— Michael Thorson
93— Michael McElrath
95— Eric Oliver

ASHLAND
78— Daniel Bogden
88— David Biondo
90— Douglas Powell

AUBURN
66— John Cochran
69—*Roger Giffin
85— Gregg Carr
90— James Lyle IV

AUGSBURG
90— Terry Mackenthun
98— Ted Schultz

AUGUSTANA (ILL.)
69—*Jeffrey Maurus
71— Kenneth Anderson
77— Joe Thompson
86— Steven Sanders
96— Thomas King
97— Ryan Carpenter

AUGUSTANA (S.D.)
72— Michael Olson
75— David Zelinsky
77— James Clemens
78— Dee Donlin
Roger Goebel
90—*David Gubbrud
91— Scott Boyens
97— Mitchell Pruett

BALL ST.
67—*John Hostrawser
73— Gregory Mack
77— Arthur Yaroch
84— Richard Chitwood
88— Ronald Duncan
90— Theodore Ashburn
93— Troy Hoffer

BATES
79— Christopher Howard

BAYLOR
65— Michael Kennedy
66— Edward Whiddon
94— John Eric Joe

BENEDICTINE (ILL.)
70— David Cyr
71— Thomas Danaher

BOISE ST.
72— Brent McIver
76—*Glenn Sparks
79— Samuel Miller
82— Kip Bedard
92— Larry Stayner
93— David Tingstad

BOSTON COLLEGE
66—*Lawrence Marzetti
67— Michael O'Neill
69— Gary Andrachik
70— Robert Bouley
78— Richard Scudellari
87— Michael Degnan

BOSTON U.
69— Suren Donabedian Jr.
81— David Bengtson

BOWDOIN
65— Steven Ingram
67— Thomas Allen

BOWIE ST.
92— Mark Fitzgerald

BOWLING GREEN
77— Richard Preston
78— Mark Miller
91— Patrick Jackson

BRIDGEPORT
70— Terry Sparker

BRIGHAM YOUNG
67— Virgil Carter
76— Orrin Olsen
77—*Stephen Miller
78— Gifford Nielsen
80— Marc Wilson
82— Daniel Plater
83— Bart Oates
84— Steve Young
85— Marvin Allen
89— Charles Cutler
94— Eric Drage
97— Chad Lewis

BROWN
65— John Kelly Jr.
70— James Lukens
74— Douglas Jost
75— William Taylor
77— Scott Nelson
78— Louis Cole
79— Robert Forster
82— Travis Holcombe
95— Rene Abdalah

BUCKNELL
71—*Kenneth Donahue
74— John Dailey
75— Steve Leskinen
77— Lawrence Brunt
85— David Kucera
93— David Berardinelli

BUENA VISTA
77— Steven Trost
87— Michael Habben
94— Cary Murphy

BUFFALO ST.
87— James Dunbar

BUTLER
72— George Yearsich
78— William Ginn
85— Stephen Kollias

CALIFORNIA
66— William Krum
67— John Schmidt
68— Robert Crittenden
70— James Calkins
71— Robert Richards
83— Harvey Salem
94— Douglas Brien

UC DAVIS
76— Daniel Carmazzi
David Gellerman
77— Rolf Benirschke
79— Mark Markel
86— Robert Hagenau
90—*James Tomasin
92— Robert Kincade
Michael Shepard
93— Brian Andersen
97— Mark Grieb

UC RIVERSIDE
72— Tyrone Hooks
74— Gary Van Jandegian

CAL LUTHERAN
90—*Gregory Maw

CAL POLY
69— William Creighton

CAL TECH
67— William Mitchell
68— John Frazzini
74— Frank Hobbs Jr.

CANISIUS
84— Thomas Schott

CAPITAL
84—*Michael Linton

CARLETON
67— Robert Paarlberg
73— Mark Williams
83— Paul Vaaler
93— Arthur Gilliland

CARNEGIE MELLON
80— Gusty Sunseri
91— Robert O'Toole

CARROLL (WIS.)
77— Stephen Thompson
95— Christopher Klippel

CARTHAGE
70— William Radakovitz

CASE RESERVE
89— Christopher Nutter
91— James Meek

CENTRAL (IOWA)
71— Vernon Den Herder
87— Scott Lindell

AWARD WINNERS

89— Eric Perry
92— Richard Kacmarynski
96— Rick Sanger

CENTRAL ARK.
96— Brian Barnett

CENTRAL MICH.
77— John Wunderlich
80— *Michael Ball
85— Kevin Egnatuk
88— Robert Stebbins
92— Jeffrey Bender

CENTRAL WASH.
70— Danny Collins

CENTRE
69— Glenn Shearer
86— Casteel "Teel" Bruner II
88— *Robert Clark
90— James Ellington

CHADRON ST.
96— Corey Campbell

CHATTANOOGA
67— Harvey Ouzts
72— *Frank Webb
74— John McBrayer
76— Russell Gardner

CHEYNEY
76— Steven Anderson

CHICAGO
86— *Bruce Montella
89— Paul Haar
94— Frank Baker

CINCINNATI
71— *Earl Willson

CITADEL
74— Thomas Leitner
79— Kenneth Caldwell
84— *William West IV
97— Derek Beres

CLAREMONT-M-S
68— Craig Dodel
70— *Gregory Long
71— Stephen Endemano
73— Christopher Stecher
74— Samuel Reece

CLEMSON
65— James Bell Jr.
68— James Addison
73— Benjamin Anderson
79— Stephen Fuller

COAST GUARD
73— Rodney Leis
74— Leonard Kelly
81— Bruce Hensel
89— *Ty Rinoski
*Jeffery Peters
90— Richard Schachner
91— John Freda

COE
67— Lynn Harris

COLBY
71— Ronald Lupton
Frank Apantaku

COLGATE
73— Kenneth Nelson
80— Angelo Colosimo
89— Donald Charney

COLORADO
93— James Hansen

COLORADO COL.
69— Steven Ehrhart
72— Randy Bobier
75— Bruce Kolbezen
84— Herman Motz III
97— Ryan Egeland
98— Christopher Smith

COLORADO MINES
66— Stuart Bennett
67— Michael Greensburg
Charles Kirby
75— David Chambers

COLORADO ST.
65— Russel Mowrer
76— Mark Driscoll
87— Stephan Bartalo
88— Joseph Brookhart
93— Gregory Primus
96— Gregory Myers

COLUMBIA
72— John Sefcik
80— Mario Biaggi Jr.

CONNECTICUT
77— *Bernard Palmer

CORNELL
68— Ronald Kipicki
72— Thomas Albright
84— Derrick Harmon

CORNELL COLLEGE
65— Steven Miller
72— David Hilmers
73— Robert Ash
79— Brian Farrell
Thomas Zinkula
81— *Timothy Garry
83— John Ward
93— Brent Sands
94— Matthew Miller
95— Mark McDermott

DARTMOUTH
66— Anthony Yezer
68— Henry Paulson Jr.
69— Randolph Wallick
71— Willie Bogan
73— Frederick Radke
74— Thomas Csatari
*Robert Funk
77— Patrick Sullivan
89— Paul Sorensen
95— O. Josh Bloom
98— Dominic Lanza

DAVIDSON
66— Stephen Smith
71— Rick Lyon
72— Robert Norris
86— *Louis Krempel
97— John Cowan Jr.

DAYTON
73— Timothy Quinn
76— Roy Gordon III
83— *Michael Pignatiello
91— Daniel Sharley

DELAWARE
86— Brian Farrell

DELAWARE VALLEY
85— Daniel Glowatski

DELTA ST.
76— William Hood

DENISON
70— Richard Trumball
73— Steven Smiljanich
76— *Dennis Thome
78— David Holcombe
86— Brian Gearinger
88— Grant Jones
92— Jonathan Fortkamp

DePAUW
68— Bruce Montgomerie
78— Mark Frazer
81— Jay True
85— Richard Bonaccorsi
86— Anthony deNicola
92— Thomas Beaulieu

DICKINSON
66— Robert Averback
71— *John West
75— *Gerald Urich

DOANE
68— John Lothrop
70— Richard Held

DRAKE
73— Joseph Worobec

DREXEL
72— Blake Lynn Ferguson

DUBUQUE
82— Timothy Finn

DUKE
68— Robert Lasky
71— *Curt Rawley

EAST CARO.
92— Keith Arnold

EAST TENN. ST.
82— Jay Patterson

EASTERN KY.
78— Steven Frommeyer

EASTERN N.M.
66— Richard James

EASTERN WASH.
98— Steven Mattson

ELIZABETH CITY ST.
73— Darnell Johnson
80— David Nickelson

ELMHURST
80— Richard Green

EMORY & HENRY
82— Thomas Browder Jr.

EVANSVILLE
75— David Mattingly
76— Charles Uhde Jr.
79— *Neil Saunders

FERRIS ST.
79— Robert Williams
93— Monty Brown

FLORIDA
72— Carlos Alvarez
77— Darrell Carpenter
85— Garrison Rolle
87— Bret Wiechmann
90— *Cedric Smith
91— Huey Richardson
95— Michael Gilmore
97— Danny Wuerffel

FLORIDA ST.
88— David Palmer
91— David Roberts
94— Kenneth Alexander
95— Derrick Brooks
98— Daryl Bush

FORDHAM
91— Eric Schweiker

FORT HAYS ST.
94— David Foster

FRANK. & MARSH.
69— Frank deGenova
83— *Robert Shepardson

FRESNO ST.
70— *Henry Corda
74— Dwayne Westphal
83— William Griever Jr.

FURMAN
77— Thomas Holcomb III
82— Charles Anderson
84— Ernest Gibson
86— *David Jager
87— Stephen Squire
90— Christopher Roper
92— Paul Siffri
Eric Von Walter
96— William Phillip Jones

GANNON
97— Patrick Rodkey

GEORGETOWN
75— James Chesley Jr.
98— Stephen Iorio

GEORGIA
68— Thomas Lawhorne Jr.
69— William Payne
71— Thomas Lyons
72— Thomas Nash Jr.
Raleigh Mixon Robinson
78— Jeffrey Lewis
80— Jeffrey Pyburn
81— Christopher Welton
84— Terrell Hoage
88— Kim Stephens
89— Richard Tardits

GEORGIA TECH
68— William Eastman
75— James Robinson
81— Sheldon Fox
83— Ellis Gardner
86— John Ivemeyer

GETTYSBURG
70— *Herbert Ruby III
80— Richard Swartz

GRAMBLING
73— Stephen Dennis

GRINNELL
72— Edward Hirsch
80— *Derek Muehrcke

GROVE CITY
95— Stephen Sems

GUST. ADOLPHUS
74— James Goodwin
81— *David Najarian

HAMLINE
85— Kyle Aug
91— Robert Hackney

HAMPDEN-SYDNEY
78— *Wilson Newell
80— Timothy Maxa

HARVARD
68— Alan Bersin
71— *Richard Frisbie
75— Patrick McInally
76— William Emper
81— Charles Durst
85— Brian Bergstrom
87— Scott Collins

HAWAII
68— James Roberts
73— *Don Satterlee

HIRAM
68— Sherman Riemenschneider
74— Donald Brunetti

HOLY CROSS
84— *Bruce Kozerski
89— Jeffrey Wiley
91— John Lavalette

HOPE
74— Ronald Posthuma
80— Craig Groendyk
83— Kurt Brinks
85— *Scott Jecmen
98— Brandon Graham

HOUSTON
86— Gary Schoppe
87— Robert Brezina

IDAHO
67— Michael Lavens
Joseph McCollum Jr.
84— Boyce Bailey

IDAHO ST.
76— Richard Rodgers
92— Steven Boyenger

ILLINOIS
72— Robert Bucklin
73— Laurence McCarren Jr.
91— Curtis Lovelace
92— Michael Hopkins
93— John Wright

ILL. WESLEYAN
93— Christopher Bisaillon
97— Lon Erickson

INDIANA
73— Glenn Scolnik
79— David Abrams
81— Kevin Speer

INDIANA (PA.)
78— *John Mihota
84— Kenneth Moore

INDIANA ST.
86— Jeffrey Miller

INDIANAPOLIS
76— Rodney Pawlik

IONA
81— Neal Kurtti
82— *Paul Rupp

IOWA
69— Michael Miller
76— Robert Elliott
78— Rodney Sears
86— Larry Station Jr.
88— Michael Flagg
89— Charles Hartlieb

IOWA ST.
70— William Bliss

JACKSON ST.
80— *Lester Walls

JACKSONVILLE ST.
79— Dewey Barker

JAMES MADISON
79— Warren Coleman
90— Mark Kiefer

JOHNS HOPKINS
73— Joseph Ouslander
74— Gunter Glocker
94— Steuart Markley
95— Michael House

JUNIATA
72— Maurice Taylor
87— Robert Crossey

KANSAS
65— Ronald Oelschlager
69— David Morgan
72— Michael McCoy
73— John Schroll
78— Tom Fitch
87— Mark Henderson

KANSAS ST.
66— *Larry Anderson
83— James Gale
88— Matthew Garver

KENTUCKY
76— Thomas Ranieri
79— James Kovach
84— *Keith Martin
97— Michael Schellenberger

KENTUCKY ST.
68— James Jackson

KENYON
75— Patrick Clements

KNOX
88— Robert Monroe

LAFAYETTE
71— William Sprecher
76— Michael Kline
78— Victor Angeline III

LAMAR
73— *Richard Kubiak

LAWRENCE
68— Charles McKee
83— Christopher Matheus

LEBANON VALLEY
74— *Alan Shortell

LEHIGH
66— Robert Adelaar
68— Richard Miller
73— *Thomas Benfield
75— James Addonizio
76— *Robert Liptak
77— *Michael Yaszemski
80— David Melone

LONG BEACH ST.
84— Joseph Donohue

LIU-C. W. POST
79— John Luchsinger

LSU
79— Robert Dugas
83— James Britt
88— Ignazio Albergamo
91— Solomon Graves
94— Chad Loup
95— Michael Blanchard
98— Chad Kessler

LUTHER
67— Thomas Altemeier
78— *Mark Larson
85— Larry Bonney

MANKATO ST.
70— Bernard Maczuga

MARIETTA
98— Thomas Couhig

MARYLAND
78— Jonathan Claiborne

MARYVILLE (TENN.)
67— Frank Eggers II

MIT
91— Darcy Prather
92— Rodrigo Rubiano
93— Roderick Tranum
95— Corey Foster

McNEESE ST.
81— Daryl Burckel
86— Ross Leger

MEMPHIS
77— *James Mincey Jr.

MERCHANT MARINE
70— Robert Lavinia
76— *John Castagna

MIAMI (FLA.)
90— Robert Chudzinski
91— Michael Sullivan

MICHIGAN
67— David Fisher
74— David Gallagher
81— *John Wangler
82— Norm Betts
84— Stefan Humphries
Thomas Dixon
86— Clayton Miller
87— Kenneth Higgins
93— Christopher Hutchinson
94— Marc Milia
98— Brian Griese

MICHIGAN ST.
69— Allen Brenner
70— Donald Baird
94— Steven Wasylk

MICHIGAN TECH
72— Larry Ras
74— Bruce Trusock
75— Daniel Rhude

MIDDLE TENN. ST.
73— *Edwin Zaunbrecher

MIDDLEBURY
79— Franklin Kettle

MIDLAND LUTHERAN
76— Thomas Hale

MILLERSVILLE
92— Thomas Burns III

MILLIKIN
90— *Charles Martin

MILLSAPS
67— Edward Weller
73— *Russell Gill
92— David Harrison Jr.

MINNESOTA
69— Robert Stein
71— Barry Mayer
73— Douglas Kingsriter
78— Robert Weber

MISSISSIPPI
66— Stanley Hindman
69— Steve Hindman
81— Kenneth Toler Jr.
86— Richard Austin
87— Jeffrey Noblin
88— Daniel Hoskins
89— Charles Walls
91— Todd Sandroni

MISSISSIPPI COL.
80— Stephen Johnson
98— Joseph Fulcher

MISSISSIPPI ST.
69— William Nelson
73— Frank Dowsing Jr.
75— James Webb
77— William Coltharp
93— Daniel Boyd

MISSOURI
66— Thomas Lynn
67— James Whitaker
69— *Charles Weber
71— John Weisenfels
79— Christopher Garlich
82— Van Darkow

MO.-ROLLA
69— Robert Nicodemus
73— Kim Colter
81— Paul Janke

MONMOUTH (ILL.)
72— Dale Brooks
90— Brent Thurness

MONTANA
75— Rock Svennungsen
79— Steven Fisher
84— Brian Salonen
91— Michael McGowan
96— David Dickenson
97— Michael Bouchee
Blaine McElmurry
98— Josh Branen

MONTANA ST.
65— Gene Carlson
68— Russell Dodge
71— Jay Groepper
77— Bert Markovich
79— Jon Borchardt
James Mickelson
90— Derrick Isackson
92— Travis Annette

MORAVIAN
73— Daniel Joseph
94— Judson Frank

MOREHEAD ST.
92— James Appel

MORNINGSIDE
65— Larry White

MORRIS BROWN
83— Arthur Knight Jr.

MOUNT UNION
89— Paul Hrics

MUHLENBERG
73— Edward Salo
76— Eric Butler
78— Mark Stull
81— Arthur Scavone
91— Michael Hoffman

MURRAY ST.
71— Matthew Haug
78— Edward McFarland
81— *Kris Robbins
90— Eric Crigler

NAVY
65— William Donnelly
69— William Newton
70— Daniel Pike
75— *Timothy Harden
76— Chester Moeller II
81— Theodore Dumbauld

NEBRASKA
70— Randall Reeves
71— *John Decker
72— Larry Jacobson
73— David Mason
74— Daniel Anderson
76— Thomas Heiser
77— Vince Ferragamo
78— Ted Harvey
79— James Pillen
80— Timothy Smith
81— Randy Schleusener
Jeffrey Finn
82— Eric Lindquist
85— Scott Strasburger
88— Jeffrey Jamrog
89— Mark Blazek
90— Gerald Gdowski
Jacob Young III
91— David Edeal
Patrick Tyrance Jr.
92— Patrick Engelbert
93— Michael Stigge
94— Trev Alberts
95— Robert Zatechka
96— Aaron Graham
97— Jonathan Hesse
98— Grant Wistrom

NEB.-OMAHA
84— Kirk Hutton
Clark Toner

NEB. WESLEYAN
97— Justin Rice
Bren Chambers
98— Dusten Olds
Chad Wemhoff

UNLV
95— Howard McGowan

NEW HAMPSHIRE
85— Richard Leclerc

NEW MEXICO
72— Roderick Long
76— Robert Berg
79— Robert Rumbaugh
83— George Parks

NEW MEXICO ST.
76— Ralph Jackson
77— *Joseph Fox

NORTH ALA.
82— *Warren Moore

NORTH CARO.
75— Christopher Kupec
81— William Donnalley
83— David Drechsler
91— Kevin Donnalley

N.C. CENTRAL
91— Anthony Cooley

NORTH CARO. ST.
75— Justus Everett
82— *Calvin Warren Jr.

NORTH DAK.
79— Dale Lian
81— Douglas Moen
82— Paul Franzmeier
85— Glen Kucera
88— Kurt Otto
89— Matthew Gulseth
93— Timothy Gelinske
97— Thomas Langer
Timothy Tibesar

NORTH DAK. ST.
66— James Schindler
69— *Stephen Stephens
71— Joseph Cichy
75— Paul Cichy
84— Doug Hushka
89— Charles Stock
94— Arden Beachy
98— Sean Fredricks

NORTH TEXAS
68— Ruben Draper
77— Peter Morris

NORTHEAST LA.
93— Darren Rimmer
94— Robert Cobb
Michael Young

NORTHERN ARIZ.
78— Larry Friedrichs

NORTHERN COLO.
76— Robert Bliss
91— Thomas Langer

NORTHERN IOWA
81— Owen Dockter

NORTHERN MICH.
73— Guy Falkenhagen
81— Phil Kessel
86— Keith Nelsen

NORTHWEST MO. ST.
82— Robert Gregory
97— Greg Teale

NORTHWESTERN
70— *Bruce Hubbard

74— Steven Craig
77— Randolph Dean
81— Charles Kern
96— Salvatore Valenzisi
Ryan Padgett

NORTHWESTERN ST.
95— John Dippel

NORWICH
68— Richard Starbuck
74— Matthew Hincks

NOTRE DAME
67— Frederick Schnurr
68— James Smithberger
69— George Kunz
70— Michael Oriard
71— Lawrence DiNardo
72— Thomas Gatewood
73— Gregory Marx
74— David Casper
75— Peter Demmerle
Reggie Barnett
79— Joseph Restic
81— Thomas Gibbons
82— John Krimm Jr.
86— Gregory Dingens
89— Reginald Ho
94— Timothy Ruddy

OCCIDENTAL
66— James Wanless
67— Richard Verry
69— John St. John
78— Richard Fry
80—*Timothy Bond
89—*Curtis Page
95— Davin Lundquist

OHIO
78—*Robert Weidaw
80— Mark Geisler

OHIO NORTHERN
79— Mark Palmer
82— Larry Egbert

OHIO ST.
65— Arnold Chonko
66— Donald Unverferth
67— Ray Pryor
69— David Foley
71— Rex Kern
74— Randolph Gradishar
76— Brian Baschnagel
77— William Lukens
80— James Laughlin
84— John Frank
85— David Crecelius
86— Michael Lanese
97— Greg Bellisari

OKLAHOMA
72— Larry Jack Mildren Jr.
73— Joe Wylie
81— Jay Jimerson
89— Anthony Phillips
91— Michael Sawatzky

OKLAHOMA ST.
83—*Doug Freeman

OLIVET
75— William Ziem

OREGON
79—*Willie Blasher Jr.
91— William Musgrave

OREGON ST.
69— William Enyart
69—*Jerry Belcher

PACIFIC (CAL.)
72—*Byron Cosgrove
78— Brian Peets
80— Bruce Filarsky

PENNSYLVANIA
68— Ben Mortensen
95— Michael Turner
98— John Bishop

PENN ST.
66— Joseph Bellas
67— John Runnells III
71— Robert Holuba
72— David Joyner
73— Bruce Bannon
74— Mark Markovich
75— John Baiorunos
79—*Charles Correal
80—*Michael Guman
81— John Walsh
84— Harry Hamilton
85— Douglas Strange
87— Brian Silverling
90— Roger Thomas Duffy
94— Craig Fayak
95— Charles Pittman

PITTSBURGH
79— Jeff Delaney
86— Robert Schilken
89— Mark Stepnoski

POMONA-PITZER
69—*Lee Piatek
77— Scott Borg
83—*Calvin Oishi
85—*Derek Watanabe
88— Edward Irick
93— Torin Cunningham

PORTLAND ST.
79— John Urness

PRINCETON
67— Charles Peters
69— Richard Sandler
70— Keith Mauney
76— Ronald Beible
81— Mark Bailey
83— Brent Woods
86— James Petrucci
87— John Hammond
97— Marc Washington Jr.

PUGET SOUND
68— Stephen Doolittle
79—*Patrick O'Loughlin
83—*Anthony Threlkeld

PURDUE
70— Michael Phipps
74— Robert Hoftiezer
75— Lawrence Burton

RANDOLPH-MACON
98— Joseph Seetoo

REDLANDS
65— Robert Jones
97— Morgan Bannister

RENSSELAER
67— Robert Darnall
69— John Contento

RHODES
71— John Churchill
79—*Philip Mischke
81— Jeffrey Lane
83—*Russell Ashford
85—*John Foropoulos
89— James Augustine

RICE
81—*Lamont Jefferson
91— Donald Hollas
96— James Lamy

RICHMOND
86— Leland Melvin

RIPON
65— Phillip Steans
69— Steven Thompson
80— Thomas Klofta

RUTGERS
90— Steven Tardy

ST. CLOUD ST.
90— Richard Rodgers

ST. FRANCIS (PA.)
87— Christopher Tantlinger

ST. JOHN'S (MINN.)
92— Denis McDonough
96— Christopher Palmer

ST. JOSEPH'S (IND.)
80— Michael Bettinger

ST. NORBERT
66— Michael Ryan
88— Matthew Lang

ST. PAUL'S
80— Gerald Hicks

ST. THOMAS (MINN.)
75— Mark Dienhart
97— Christopher Esterley

SAN DIEGO
96— Douglas Popovich

SANTA CLARA
72— Ronald Sani
77— Mark Tiernan
81—*David Alfaro
85— Alexis Vlahos
87— Patrick Sende

SEWANEE
65— Frank Stubblefield
66— Douglas Paschall
69— James Beene
71— John Popham IV
77— Dudley West
82— Gregory Worsowicz
Domenick Reina
83— Michael York
84— Michael Jordan
93— Jason Forrester
94— Frederick Cravens
96— Stephen Tudor

SHIPPENSBURG
77— Anthony Winter

SIMPSON
71— Richard Clogg
74— Hugh Lickiss
90— Roger Grover
94— Chad Earwood

SLIPPERY ROCK
98— David Sabolcik Jr.

SOUTH CARO.
67— Steven Stanley Juk Jr.

SOUTH DAK.
79— Michael Schurrer
87— Todd Salat
93— Jason Seurer

SOUTH DAK. ST.
80— Charles Loewen
81— Paul Kippley
88— Daniel Sonnek
95— Jacob Hines

SOUTHEASTERN LA.
74— William Percy Jr.

SOUTHERN U.
70— Alden Roche

SOUTHERN CAL
66— Charles Arrobio
69— Steven Sogge
70— Harry Khasigian
Steve Lehmer
74— Monte Doris
75— Patrick Haden
76— Kevin Bruce
78— Gary Bethel
80— Brad Budde
Paul McDonald
81— Gordon Adams
*Jeffrey Fisher
85— Duane Bickett
86— Anthony Colorito
*Matthew Koart
87— Jeffrey Bregel
90— John Jackson
96— Jeremy Hogue
97— Matthew Keneley

SOUTHERN COLO.
70— Gregory Smith
73— Collon Kennedy III

SOUTHERN METHODIST
83—*Brian O'Meara
85—*Monte Goen
87— David Adamson
93— Cary Brabham

SOUTHERN MISS.
83— Richard Thompson
84— Stephen Carmody

SOUTHERN UTAH
92— Stephen McDowell

SOUTHWEST MO. ST.
80— Richard Suchenski
Mitchel Ware
85— Michael Armentrout

SOUTHWEST TEX. ST.
82— Michael Miller

SOUTHWESTERN LA.
71—*George Coussa

STANFORD
65—*Joe Neal
66—*Terry DeSylvia
68— John Root
71— John Sande III
72— Jackie Brown
74— Randall Poltl
75—*Keith Rowen
76— Gerald Wilson
77— Duncan McColl
81— Milton McColl
84— John Bergren
85— Scott Carpenter
86— Matthew Soderlund
87— Brian Morris
88— Douglas Robison
95— Stephen Stenstrom
96— Eric Abrams
David Walker
97— Marlon Evans

STONEHILL
93— Kevin Broderick

SUSQUEHANNA
77— Gerald Huesken
82— Daniel Distasio

SWARTHMORE
72— Christopher Leinberger
83—*John Walsh

SYRACUSE
78—*Robert Avery
86— Timothy Green
94— Patrick O'Neill
95— Eric Chenoweth

TEMPLE
74— Dwight Fulton

TENNESSEE
71— Donald Denbo
Timothy Priest
77— Michael Mauck
81— Timothy Irwin
98— Peyton Manning

TEXAS
69— Corbin Robertson Jr.
71— Willie Zapalac Jr.
73—*Michael Bayer
74— Patrick Kelly
75— Wade Johnston
76— Robert Simmons
77— William Hamilton
97— Patrick Fitzgerald

TEXAS-ARLINGTON
69— Michael Baylor

UTEP
80— Eddie Forkerway
89— Patrick Hegarty
92— Robert Sesich

TEXAS A&M
69— Edward Hargett
71— David Elmendorf
72— Stephen Luebbehusen
88— Kip Corrington

TEXAS CHRISTIAN
67— John Richards
68— Eldon Gresham Jr.
73— Scott Walker
75— Terry Drennan
88— J. Clinton Hailey

TEXAS SOUTHERN
65— Leon Hardy

TEXAS TECH
65— James Ellis Jr.
68— John Scovell
75— Jeffrey Jobe
78—*Richard Arledge
85—*Bradford White
90— Thomas Mathiasmeier

THOMAS MORE
98— Michael Bramlage Jr.

TOLEDO
82— Tad Wampfler
89— Kenneth Moyer
95— Chadd Dehn
97— Craig Dues

TRINITY (CONN.)
67— *Howard Wrzosek
68— Keith Miles

TRINITY (TEX.)
84— *Peter Broderick
95— Martin Thompson
98— Mark Byarlay
Jack Doran

TROY ST.
75— Mark King

TRUMAN ST.
83— Roy Pettibone

TUFTS
65— Peter Smith
70— Robert Bass
79— *Don Leach
80— *James Ford
82— *Brian Gallagher
87— Robert Patz
92— Paulo Oliveira

TULSA
67— *Larry Williams
75— James Mack Lancaster II
98— Levi Gillen

TUSKEGEE
68— James Greene

UCLA
67— *Raymond Armstrong
Dallas Grider
70— Gregory Jones
74— Steven Klosterman
76— John Sciarra
77— Jeffrey Dankworth
78— John Fowler Jr.
83— Cormac Carney
84— Richard Neuheisel
86— Michael Hartmeier
90— Richard Meyer
93— Carlton Gray
96— George Kase

UNION (N.Y.)
88— Richard Romer

UTAH
81— James Baldwin
93— Steven Young
95— Jason Jones

UTAH ST.
67— Ronnie Edwards
68— Garth Hall
70— Gary Anderson
76— Randall Stockham

VALDOSTA ST.
95— Christopher Hatcher

VALPARAISO
75— *Richard Seall

VANDERBILT
73— Barrett Sutton Jr.
75— Douglas Martin

VILLANOVA
77— David Graziano
89— Richard Spugnardi

VIRGINIA
67— Frederick Jones
83— Patrick Chester
94— Thomas Burns Jr.
96— Patrick Jeffers
98— Stephen Phelan Jr.

VMI
79— Robert Bookmiller
80— Richard Craig Jones

VIRGINIA TECH
73— Thomas Carpenito
97— Brandon Semones

WABASH
74— *Mark Nicolini
81— *Melvin Gore
83— David Broecker
87— James Herrmann
92— William Padgett

WAKE FOREST
70— Joseph Dobner
74— *Daniel Stroup
76— Thomas Fehring
78— *Michael McGlamry
83— Philip Denfeld
87— Toby Cole Jr.

WARTBURG
75— Conrad Mandsager
76— James Charles Peterson
82— *Rod Feddersen
94— Koby Kreinbring
96— Vincent Penningroth

WASHINGTON
65— William Douglas
67— Michael Ryan
72— *James Krieg
73— John Brady
77— Scott Phillips
78— Blair Bush
80— Bruce Harrell
82— Mark Jerue
83— Charles Nelson
Mark Stewart
88— David Rill
92— Edward Cunningham
97— David Janoski

WASHINGTON (MO.)
94— Aaron Keen
98— Bradley Klein

WASH. & JEFF.
70— Edward Guna
82— Max Regula
91— David Conn
93— Raymond Cross Jr.

95— Michael Jones

WASH. & LEE
70— Michael Thornton
74— William Wallace Jr.
78— Jeffrey Slatcoff
79— Richard Wiles
80— *Scott Smith
81— Lonnie Nunley III
89— Michael Magoline

WASHINGTON ST.
67— Richard Sheron
68— A. Douglas Flansburg
83— Gregory Porter
84— Patrick Lynch Jr.
85— Daniel Lynch

WAYNE ST. (MICH.)
76— Edward Skowneski Jr.
81— Phillip Emery

WEBER ST.
68— Phillip Tuckett
74— *Douglas Smith
92— David Hall
94— Deric Gurley
98— Cameron Quayle

WESLEYAN (CONN.)
67— John Dwyer
69— Stuart Blackburn
71— James Lynch
78— John McVicar

WEST TEX. A&M
75— *Ben Bentley
82— Kevin Dennis

WEST VA.
74— Ade Dillion
*Daniel Larcamp
82— Oliver Luck

WESTERN CARO.
94— Thomas Jackson III

WESTERN ILL.
89— Paul Singer

WESTERN KY.
72— Jimmy Barber
80— Charles DeLacey

WESTERN MICH.
68— Martin Barski
71— Jonathan Bull

WESTERN N.M.
68— Richard Mahoney

WESTERN ST.
98— Jason Eves

WHEATON (ILL.)
89— David Lauber
93— Bart Moseman
96— Pedro Arruza

WHITTIER
76— John Getz
79— Mark Deven
87— *Timothy Younger

WILLAMETTE
87— *Gerry Preston

WILLIAM & MARY
78— G. Kenneth Smith
80— Clarence Gaines
85— Mark Kelso

WILLIAM JEWELL
66— Charles Scrogin
70— Thomas Dunn
John Johnston

WILLIAMS
65— Jerry Jones
72— John Murray
95— Nathan Sleeper
96— Medley Gatewood

WINONA ST.
95— Nathan Gruber

WINSTON-SALEM
84— Eddie Sauls

WISCONSIN
66— David Fronek
80— Thomas Stauss
82— *David Mohapp
83— Mathew Vanden Boom

WIS.-LA CROSSE
97— Troy Harcey

WIS.-PLATTEVILLE
87— Michael Hintz

WIS.-STEVENS POINT
98— Joel Hornby

WIS.-WHITEWATER
96— Scott Hawig

WITTENBERG
82— William Beach
98— Kent Rafey

WOOSTER
80— Edward Blake Moore

WYOMING
74— Steven Cockreham
85— Bob Gustafson
89— Randall Welniak
96— Joseph Cummings
98— Jay Korth
Cory Wedel

XAVIER (OHIO)
65— William Eastlake

YALE
66— *James Groninger
67— Howard Hilgendorf Jr.
69— Frederick Morris
71— Thomas Neville
72— David Bliss
75— John Burkus
77— *Stone Phillips
79— William Crowley
82— Richard Diana
91— Vincent Mooney
96— Matthew Siskosky

YOUNGSTOWN ST.
96— Mark Brungard

Academic All-America Hall of Fame

Since its inception in 1988, 31 former NCAA football players have been inducted into the GTE Academic All-America Hall of Fame. They were selected from among nominees by the College Sports Information Directors of America from past academic all-Americans of the 1950s, '60s and '70s. Following are the football selections by the year selected and each player's team, position and last year played:

1988
Pete Dawkins, Army, HB, 1958
Pat Haden, Southern Cal, QB, 1974
Rev. Donn Moomaw, UCLA, LB, 1953
Merlin Olsen, Utah St., T, 1961

1989
Carlos Alvarez, Florida, WR, 1971
Willie Bogan, Dartmouth, DB, 1970
Steve Bramwell, Washington, DB, 1965
Joe Romig, Colorado, G, 1961
Jim Swink, Texas Christian, B, 1956
John Wilson, Michigan St., DB, 1952

1990
Joe Theismann, Notre Dame, QB, 1970
Howard Twilley, Tulsa, TE, 1965

1991
Terry Baker, Oregon St., QB, 1962
Joe Holland, Cornell, RB, 1978
David Joyner, Penn St., OT, 1971
Brock Strom, Air Force, T, 1958

1992
Alan Ameche, Wisconsin, RB, 1954
Stephen Eisenhauer, Navy, G, 1953
Randy Gradishar, Ohio St., LB, 1973

1993
Raymond Berry, Southern Methodist, E, 1954
Dave Casper, Notre Dame, E, 1973
Jim Grabowski, Illinois, FB, 1965

1994
Richard Mayo, Air Force, QB, 1961
Lee Roy Selmon, Oklahoma, DT, 1975

1995
Pat Richter, Wisconsin, E, 1962

1996
Wade Mitchell, Georgia Tech, QB, 1956
Bob Thomas, Notre Dame, K, 1973
Byron "Whizzer" White, Colorado, HB, 1937 (honorary selection)

1997
Wade Mitchell, Georgia Tech, QB, 1956
Bob Thomas, Notre Dame, K, 1973
Byron "Whizzer" White, Colorado, HB, 1937 (honorary selection)

1998
Bernie Kosar, Miami (Fla.), QB, 1984
Jack Mildren, Oklahoma, QB, 1971
Marv Levy, Coe, RB 1949

Academic All-Americans by School

Since 1952, academic all-America teams have been selected by the College Sports Information Directors of America. To be eligible, student-athletes must be regular performers and have at least a 3.200 grade-point average (on a 4.000 scale) during their college careers. University division teams (I-A and I-AA) are complete in this list, but college division teams (II, III, NAIA) before 1970 are missing from CoSIDA archives, with few exceptions. Following are all known first-team selections:

ABILENE CHRISTIAN
63—Jack Griggs, LB
70—Jim Lindsey, QB
74—Greg Stirman, E
76—Bill Curbo, T
77—Bill Curbo, T
87—Bill Clayton, DL
88—Bill Clayton, DL
89—Bill Clayton, DL
90—Sean Grady, WR

ADRIAN
84—Steve Dembowski, QB
94—Jay Overmyer, DB

AIR FORCE
58—Brock Strom, T
59—Rich Mayo, B
60—Rich Mayo, B
70—Ernie Jennings, E
71—Darryl Haas, LB/K
72—Bob Homburg, DE
Mark Prill, LB
73—Joe Debes, OT
74—Joe Debes, OT
78—Steve Hoog, WR
81—Mike France, LB
83—Jeff Kubiak, P
86—Chad Hennings, DL
87—Chad Hennings, DL
88—David Hlatky, OL
90—Chris Howard, RB
92—Grant Johnson, LB

AKRON
80—Andy Graham, PK

UAB
97—Johnny Rea, OL

ALABAMA
61—Tommy Brooker, E
Pat Trammell, B
64—Gaylon McCollough, C
65—Steve Sloan, QB
Dennis Homan, HB
67—Steve Davis, K
Bob Childs, LB
70—Johnny Musso, HB
71—Johnny Musso, HB
73—Randy Hall, DT
74—Randy Hall, DT
75—Danny Ridgeway, KS
79—Major Ogilvie, RB

ALABAMA A&M
89—Tracy Kendall, QB
90—Tracy Kendall, QB

ALBANY (N.Y.)
86—Thomas Higgins, OT
87—Thomas Higgins, OT
94—Andy Shein, WR
95—Rich Tallarico, OL

ALBION
82—Bruce Drogosch, LB
86—Michael Grant, DB
90—Scott Bissell, DB
93—Eric Baxmann, LB
Jeffrey Shooks, P
94—Jeffrey Shooks, P
95—David Lefere, DB
96—David Lefere, DB

ALFRED
89—Mark Szynkowski, OL

ALLEGHENY
81—Kevin Baird, P
91—Adam Lechman, OL
Darren Hadlock, LB

ALMA
86—Greg Luczak, TE

AMERICAN INT'L
81—Todd Scyocurka, LB

APPALACHIAN ST.
77—Gill Beck, C
92—D. J. Campbell, QB

ARIZONA
68—Mike Moody, OG
75—Jon Abbott, LB
76—Jon Abbott, T/LB
77—Jon Abbott, T/LB
79—Jeffrey Whitton, DL
87—Charles Cecil, DB
96—Wayne Wyatt, OL

ARIZONA ST.
66—Ken Dyer, OE
88—Mark Tingstad, LB
97—Patrick Tillman, LB

ARKANSAS
57—Gerald Nesbitt, FB
61—Lance Alworth, B
64—Ken Hatfield, B
65—Randy Stewart, C
Jim Lindsey, HB
Jack Brasuell, DB
68—Bob White, K
69—Bill Burnett, HB
Terry Stewart, DB
78—Brad Shoup, DB

ARK.-MONTICELLO
85—Ray Howard, OG
88—Sean Rochelle, QB

ARKANSAS ST.
59—Larry Zabrowski, OT
61—Jim McMurray, QB

ARKANSAS TECH
90—Karl Kuhn, TE
91—Karl Kuhn, TE

ARMY
55—Ralph Chesnauskas, E
57—James Kernan, C
Pete Dawkins, HB
58—Pete Dawkins, HB
59—Don Usry, E
65—Sam Champi, DE
67—Bud Neswiacheny, DE
69—Theodore Shadid, C
89—Michael Thorson, DB
92—Mike McElrath, DB
94—Eric Oliver, LB

ASHLAND
73—Mark Gulling, DB
74—Ron Brown, LB
76—Dan Bogden, E
77—Bruce Niehm, LB
81—Mark Braun, C
91—Thomas Shiban, RB
93—Jerry Spatny, DL
96—Chad DiFranco, DB

AUBURN
57—Jimmy Phillips, E
59—Jackie Burkett, C
60—Ed Dyas, B
65—Bill Cody, LB
69—Buddy McClinton, DB
74—Bobby Davis, LB
75—Chuck Fletcher, DT
76—Chris Vacarella, RB
84—Gregg Carr, LB
94—Matt Hawkins, PK

AUGSBURG
81—Paul Elliott, DL
97—Ted Schultz, TE

AUGUSTANA (ILL.)
75—George Wesbey, T
80—Bill Dannehl, WR
84—Steve Sanders, OT
85—Steve Sanders, OT
95—Ryan Carpenter, OL
96—Ryan Carpenter, OL
97—Chris Meskan, OL

AUGUSTANA (S.D.)
72—Pat McNerney, T
73—Pat McNerney, T
74—Jim Clemens, G
75—Jim Clemens, C
77—Stan Biondi, K
86—David Gubbrud, DL
87—David Gubbrud, DL
88—David Gubbrud, LB
89—David Gubbrud, LB
96—Mitchell Pruett, TE
97—Thayne Munce, OL

AUSTIN
81—Gene Branum, PK

AUSTIN PEAY
74—Gregory Johnson, G

BAKER
61—John Jacobs, B

BALDWIN-WALLACE
70—Earl Stolberg, DB
72—John Yezerski, G
78—Roger Andrachik, RB
Greg Monda, LB
81—Chuck Krajacic, OG
88—Shawn Gorman, P
91—Tom Serdinak, P
93—Adrian Allison, DL
David Coverdale, DL
94—David Coverdale, DL

BALL ST.
83—Rich Chitwood, C
85—Ron Duncan, TE
86—Ron Duncan, TE
87—Ron Duncan, TE
88—Ted Ashburn, OL
Greg Shackelford, DL
89—Ted Ashburn, OL
David Haugh, DB
91—Troy Hoffer, DB
92—Troy Hoffer, DB

BATES
82—Neal Davidson, DB

BAYLOR
61—Ronnie Bull, RB
62—Don Trull, QB
63—Don Trull, QB
76—Cris Quinn, DE
89—Mike Welch, DB
90—Mike Welch, DB
96—Ty Atteberry, P

BELOIT
90—Shane Stadler, RB

BETHANY (KAN.)
86—Wade Gaeddert, DB

BLOOMSBURG
83—Dave Pepper, DL

BOISE ST.
71—Brent McIver, IL
73—Glenn Sparks, G
78—Sam Miller, DB

BOSTON COLLEGE
77—Richard Scudellari, LB
86—Michael Degnan, DL

BOSTON U.
83—Steve Shapiro, K
85—Brad Hokin, DB
93—Andre Maksimov, OL
94—Andre Maksimov, OL

BOWDOIN
84—Mike Siegel, P
93—Michael Turmelle, DB

BOWLING GREEN
75—John Boles, DE
89—Pat Jackson, LB
90—Pat Jackson, TE

BRIGHAM YOUNG
73—Steve Stratton, RB
80—Scott Phillips, RB
81—Dan Plater, WR
87—Chuck Cutler, WR
88—Chuck Cutler, WR
Tim Clark, DL
89—Fred Whittingham, RB
90—Andy Boyce, WR
93—Eric Drage, WR

BROCKPORT ST.
97—Tom Massey, DB

BROWN
81—Travis Holcombe, OG
82—Dave Folsom, DB
86—Marty Edwards, C
87—John Cuozzo, C

BUCKNELL
72—Douglas Nauman, T
John Ondrasik, DB
73—John Dailey, LB
74—Steve Leskinen, T
75—Larry Brunt, E
76—Larry Brunt, E
84—Rob Masonis, RB
Jim Reilly, TE
86—Mike Morrow, WR
91—David Berardinelli, WR
92—David Berardinelli, WR

BUFFALO
63—Gerry Philbin, T
84—Gerry Quinlivan, LB
85—James Dunbar, C
86—James Dunbar, C

BUFFALO ST.
87—Clint Morano, OT

BUTLER
84—Steve Kollias, L

CALIFORNIA
67—Bob Crittenden, DG
70—Robert Richards, OT
82—Harvey Salem, OT

UC DAVIS
72—Steve Algeo, LB
75—Dave Gellerman, LB
90—Mike Shepard, DL

UC RIVERSIDE
71—Tyrone Hooks, HB

CAL LUTHERAN
81—John Walsh, OT

CANISIUS
82—Tom Schott, WR
83—Tom Schott, TE
86—Mike Panepinto, RB

CAPITAL
70—Ed Coy, E
83—Mike Linton, G
85—Kevin Sheets, WR

CARLETON
92—Scott Hanks, TE

CARNEGIE MELLON
76—Rick Lackner, LB
Dave Nackoul, E
84—Roger Roble, WR
87—Bryan Roessler, DL
Chris Haupt, LB
89—Robert O'Toole, LB
90—Frank Bellante, RB
Robert O'Toole, LB
94—Aaron Neal, TE
Merle Atkinson, DL

CARROLL (WIS.)
76—Stephen Thompson, QB

CARSON-NEWMAN
61—David Dale, E
93—Chris Horton, OL
94—Chris Horton, OL

CARTHAGE
61—Bob Halsey, B
77—Mark Phelps, QB

CASE RESERVE
75—John Kosko, T
82—Jim Donnelly, RB
83—Jim Donnelly, RB
84—Jim Donnelly, RB
88—Chris Hutter, TE
90—Michael Bissler, DB
95—Doug Finefrock, LB
96—Tom Mager, LB
Kenyon Meadows, DL

CENTRAL (IOWA)
79—Chris Adkins, LB
85—Scott Lindrell, LB
86—Scott Lindrell, LB
91—Rich Kacmarynski, RB

CENTRAL MICH.
70—Ralph Burde, DL
74—Mike Franckowiak, QB
John Wunderlich, T
79—Mike Ball, WR
84—John DeBoer, WR
91—Jeff Bender, QB

CENTRAL MO. ST.
97—Shane Meyer, PK

CENTRE
84—Teel Bruner, DB
85—Teel Bruner, DB
89—Bryan Ellington, DB
91—Eric Horstmeyer, WR

CHADRON ST.
73—Jerry Sutton, LB
75—Bob Lacey, KS
79—Jerry Carder, TE
95—Corey Campbell, RB

CHAPMAN
96—Matt Hertzler, OL
97—Matt Hertzler, OL

CHEYNEY
75—Steve Anderson, G

CHICAGO
87—Paul Haar, OG
88—Paul Haar, OL
93—Frank Baker, RB

CINCINNATI
81—Kari Yli-Renko, OT
90—Kyle Stroh, DL
91—Kris Bjorson, TE
97—John Kobalka, DL

CITADEL
63—Vince Petno, E
76—Kenny Caldwell, LB
77—Kenny Caldwell, LB
78—Kenny Caldwell, LB
87—Thomas Frooman, RB
89—Thomas Frooman, RB

CLARION
96—Steve Witte, RB

CLEMSON
59—Lou Cordileone, T
78—Steve Fuller, QB

COAST GUARD
70—Charles Pike, LB
71—Bruce Melnick, DB
81—Mark Butt, DB

COE
93—Marcus Adkins, DL

COLGATE
78—Angelo Colosimo, RB
79—Angelo Colosimo, RB
85—Tom Stenglein, WR
89—Jeremy Garvey, TE

COLORADO
60—Joe Romig, G
61—Joe Romig, G
67—Kirk Tracy, OG
70—Jim Cooch, DB
73—Rick Stearns, LB
74—Rick Stearns, LB
75—Steve Young, DT
87—Eric McCarty, LB
90—Jim Hansen, OL
91—Jim Hansen, OL
92—Jim Hansen, OL
96—Ryan Olson, DL
97—Ryan Olson, DL

COLORADO COL.
96—Ryan Egeland, OL
Ryan Haygood, DL

COLORADO MINES
72—Dave Chambers, RB
83—Charles Lane, T

COLORADO ST.
55—Gary Glick, B
69—Tom French, OT
86—Steve Bartalo, RB
95—Greg Myers, DB

COLUMBIA
52—Mitch Price, B
53—John Gasella, T
56—Claude Benham, B
71—John Sefcik, HB

CORNELL
77—Joseph Holland, RB
78—Joseph Holland, RB
82—Derrick Harmon, RB
83—Derrick Harmon, RB
85—Dave Van Metre, DL

CORNELL COLLEGE
72—Rob Ash, QB
Dewey Birkhofer, S
76—Joe Lauterbach, G
Tom Zinkula, DT
77—Tom Zinkula, DT
78—Tom Zinkula, DL
82—John Ward, WR
91—Bruce Feldmann, QB
92—Brent Sands, DB
93—Mark McDermott, DB
94—Mark McDermott, DB
95—Mike Tressel, DB
97—Matt Weiss, DL

CULVER-STOCKTON
95—Mason Kaiser, DB

DARTMOUTH
70—Willie Bogan, DB
83—Michael Patsis, DB
87—Paul Sorensen, LB
88—Paul Sorensen, LB
90—Brad Preble, DB
91—Mike Bobo, WR
Tom Morrow, LB
92—Russ Torres, RB
94—David Shearer, WR
Zach Lehman, DL
97—Dominic Lanza, OL

DAYTON
71—Tim Quinn, LB
72—Tim Quinn, DT
79—Scott Terry, QB
84—Greg French, K
David Kemp, LB
Jeff Slayback, L
85—Greg French, K
86—Gerry Meyer, OT
91—Brett Cuthbert, DB
Dan Rosenbaum, DB
92—Steve Lochow, DL
Dan Rosenbaum, DB
93—Steve Lochow, DL
Brad Mager, DB
94—David Overhoiser, RB
96—Josh Lemmon, OL

DEFIANCE
80—Jill Bailey, OT
Mark Bockelman, TE

DELAWARE
70—Yancey Phillips, T
71—Robert Depew, DE
72—Robert Depew, DE

DELAWARE VALLEY
84—Dan Glowatski, WR

DELTA ST.
70—Hal Posey, RB
74—Billy Hood, E
Ricky Lewis, LB
Larry Miller, RB
75—Billy Hood, E
78—Terry Moody, DB
79—Charles Stavley, G

DENISON
75—Dennis Thome, LB
87—Grant Jones, DB

DePAUW
70—Jim Ceaser, LB
71—Jim Ceaser, LB
73—Neil Oslos, RB
80—Jay True, WR
85—Tony deNicola, QB
87—Michael Sherman, DB
90—Tom Beaulieu, DL
91—Tom Beaulieu, DL
Matt Nelson, LB
94—Mike Callahan, LB

DICKINSON
74—Gerald Urich, RB
79—Scott Mumma, RB

DRAKE
74—Todd Gaffney, KS
83—Tom Holt, RB

DREXEL
70—Lynn Ferguson, S

DUBUQUE
80—Tim Finn, RB

DUKE
66—Roger Hayes, DE
67—Bob Lasky, DT
70—Curt Rawley, DT
86—Mike Diminick, DB
87—Mike Diminick, DB
88—Mike Diminick, DB
89—Doug Key, DL
93—Travis Pearson, DL

EAST STROUDSBURG
84—Ernie Siegrist, TE

EAST TENN. ST.
71—Ken Oster, DB

EASTERN ILL.
95—Tim Carver, LB

EASTERN KY.
77—Steve Frommeyer, S

EASTERN N.M.
80—Tom Sager, DL
81—Tom Sager, DL

EASTERN WASH.
97—Jeff Ogden, WR
Steve Mattson, DL

ELON
73—John Rascoe, E
79—Bryan Burney, DB

EMORY & HENRY
71—Tom Wilson, LB

EMPORIA ST.
79—Tom Lingg, DL

EVANSVILLE
74—David Mattingly, S
76—Michael Pociask, C
87—Jeffery Willman, TE

97—Sean Bennett, RB

FERRIS ST.
81—Vic Trecha, OT
92—Monty Brown, LB

FINDLAY
97—Bo Hurley, QB

FLORIDA
65—Charles Casey, E
69—Carlos Alvarez, WR
71—Carlos Alvarez, WR
76—David Posey, KS
77—Wes Chandler, RB
80—Cris Collinsworth, WR
91—Brad Culpepper, DL
93—Michael Gilmore, DB
94—Terry Dean, QB
Michael Gilmore, DB
95—Danny Wuerffel, QB
96—Danny Wuerffel, QB

FLORIDA A&M
90—Irvin Clark, DL

FLORIDA ST.
72—Gary Huff, QB
79—William Jones, DB
Phil Williams, WR
80—William Jones, DB
81—Rohn Stark, P
94—Derrick Brooks, LB
96—Daryl Bush, LB
97—Daryl Bush, LB

FORDHAM
90—Eric Schweiker, OL

FORT HAYS ST.
75—Greg Custer, RB
82—Ron Johnson, P
85—Paul Nelson, DL
86—Paul Nelson, DL
89—Dean Gengler, OL

FORT LEWIS
72—Dee Tennison, E

FRANK. & MARSH.
77—Joe Fry, DB
78—Joe Fry, DB

FURMAN
76—Jeff Holcomb, T
85—Brian Jager, RB
88—Kelly Fletcher, DL
89—Kelly Fletcher, DL
Chris Roper, LB
91—Eric Walter, OL

GEORGETOWN
71—Gerry O'Dowd, HB
86—Andrew Phelan, OG

GEORGETOWN (KY.)
89—Eric Chumbley, OL
92—Bobby Wasson, PK

GEORGIA
60—Francis Tarkenton, QB
65—Bob Etter, K
66—Bob Etter, K
Lynn Hughes, DB
68—Bill Stanfill, DT
71—Tom Nash, OT
Mixon Robinson, DE
77—Jeff Lewis, LB
82—Terry Hoage, DB
83—Terry Hoage, DB
92—Todd Peterson, PK
97—Matt Stinchcomb, OL

GA. SOUTHERN
95—Rob Stockton, DB

GA. SOUTHWESTERN
87—Gregory Slappery, RB

GEORGIA TECH
52—Ed Gossage, T
Cecil Trainer, DE
Larry Morris, LB
55—Wade Mitchell, B
56—Allen Ecker, G
66—Jim Breland, C
W. J. Blaine, LB
Bill Eastman, DB
67—Bill Eastman, DB
80—Sheldon Fox, LB
90—Stefen Scotton, RB

GETTYSBURG
79—Richard Swartz, LB

GRAMBLING
72—Floyd Harvey, RB
93—Gilad Landau, PK

GRAND VALLEY ST.
91—Mark Smith, OL
Todd Wood, DB

GRINNELL
71—Edward Hirsch, E
81—David Smiley, TE

GROVE CITY
74—Pat McCoy, LB
89—Travis Croll, P

GUST. ADOLPHUS
80—Dave Najarian, DL
81—Dave Najarian, LB

HAMLINE
73—Thomas Dufresne, E
89—Jon Voss, TE

HAMPDEN-SYDNEY
82—John Dickinson, OG
90—W. R. Jones, OL
91—David Brickhill, PK

HAMPTON
93—Tim Benson, WR

HARVARD
97—Chris Shinnick, DB

HAWAII
97—Chris Shinnick, DB

HEIDELBERG
82—Jeff Kurtzman, DL

HILLSDALE
61—James Richendollar, T
72—John Cervini, G
81—Mark Kellogg, LB
93—Jason Ahee, DB
96—Kyle Wojciechowski, OL

HOLY CROSS
83—Bruce Kozerski, T
85—Kevin Reilly, OT
87—Jeff Wiley, QB
91—Pete Dankert, DL

HOPE
73—Ronald Posthuma, T
79—Craig Groendyk, T
80—Greg Bekius, PK
82—Kurt Brinks, C
84—Scott Jecmen, DB
86—Timothy Chase, OG

HOUSTON
64—Horst Paul, E
76—Mark Mohr, DB
Kevin Rollwage, OT
77—Kevin Rollwage, OT

IDAHO
70—Bruce Langmeade, T

IDAHO ST.
84—Brent Koetter, DB
91—Steve Boyenger, DB
96—Trevor Bell, DB

ILLINOIS
52—Bob Lenzini, DT
64—Jim Grabowski, FB
65—Jim Grabowski, FB
66—John Wright, E
70—Jim Rucks, DE
71—Bob Bucklin, DE
80—Dan Gregus, DL
81—Dan Gregus, DL
82—Dan Gregus, DL
91—Mike Hopkins, DB
92—John Wright Jr., WR
94—Brett Larsen, P

ILLINOIS COL.
80—Jay Wessler, RB
94—Warren Dodson, OL

ILLINOIS ST.
76—Tony Barnes, C
80—Jeff Hembrough, DL
89—Dan Hackman, OL
95—Keith Goodnight, RB

ILL. WESLEYAN
71—Keith Ihlanfeldt, DE
80—Jim Eaton, DL
Rick Hanna, DL
Mike Watson, DB
81—Mike Watson, DB
91—Chris Bisaillon, WR
92—Chris Udovich, DL
95—Jason Richards, TE
96—Lon Erickson, QB

INDIANA
67—Harry Gonso, HB
72—Glenn Scolnik, RB
80—Kevin Speer, C
94—John Hammerstein, DL

INDIANA (PA.)
82—Kenny Moore, DB
83—Kenny Moore, DB

INDIANA ST.
71—Gary Brown, E
72—Michael Eads, E

INDIANAPOLIS
76—William Willan, E
95—Ted Munson, DL

IONA
80—Neal Kurtti, DL

IOWA
52—Bill Fenton, DE
53—Bill Fenton, DE
75—Bob Elliott, DB
85—Larry Station, LB

IOWA ST.
52—Max Burkett, DB
82—Mark Carlson, LB

ITHACA
72—Dana Hallenbeck, LB
85—Brian Dougherty, DB
89—Peter Burns, OL

JACKSONVILLE ST.
77—Dewey Barker, E
78—Dewey Barker, TE

JAMES MADISON
78—Warren Coleman, OT

JOHN CARROLL
83—Nick D'Angelo, LB
Jim Sferra, DL
85—Joe Burrello, LB
86—Joe Burrello, LB

JOHNS HOPKINS
77—Charles Hauck, DT
93—Michael House, DL
94—Michael House, DL

JUNIATA
70—Ray Grabiak, DL
71—Ray Grabiak, DE
Maurice Taylor, IL

KALAMAZOO
92—Sean Mullendore, LB

KANSAS
64—Fred Elder, T
67—Mike Sweatman, LB
68—Dave Morgan, LB
71—Mike McCoy, C
76—Tom Fitch, S
95—Darrin Simmons, P

KANSAS ST.
74—Don Lareau, LB
77—Floyd Dorsey, OG
81—Darren Gale, DB
82—Darren Gale, DB
Mark Hundley, RB
85—Troy Faunce, P
95—Kevin Lockett, WR
96—Kevin Lockett, WR
Jason Johnson, OL

KENT
72—Mark Reiheld, DB
91—Brad Smith, RB

KENTUCKY
74—Tom Ranieri, LB
78—Mark Keene, C
Jim Kovach, LB
85—Ken Pietrowiak, C

KENYON
77—Robert Jennings, RB
85—Dan Waldeck, TE

LA VERNE
82—Scott Shier, OT

LAFAYETTE
70—William Sprecher, T
74—Mike Kline, DB
79—Ed Rogusky, RB
80—Ed Rogusky, RB

LAWRENCE
81—Chris Matheus, DL
Scott Reppert, RB
82—Chris Matheus, DL

LEHIGH
90—Shon Harker, DB

LEWIS & CLARK
61—Pat Clock, G
81—Dan Jones, WR

LONG BEACH ST.
83—Joe Donohue, LB

LIU-C. W. POST
70—Art Canario, T
75—Frank Prochilo, RB
84—Bob Jahelka, DB
93—Jim Byrne, WR

LORAS
84—John Coyle, DL
Pete Kovatisis, DB
85—John Coyle, DL
91—Mark Goedken, DL
93—Travis Michaels, LB

LSU
59—Mickey Mangham, E
60—Charles Strange, C
61—Billy Booth, T
71—Jay Michaelson, KS
73—Tyler Lafauci, OG
Joe Winkler, DB
74—Brad Davis, RB
77—Robert Dugas, OT
84—Juan Carlos Betanzos, PK
94—Michael Blanchard, OL
97—Chad Kessler, P

LUTHER
83—Larry Bonney, DL
84—Larry Bonney, DL
89—Larry Anderson, RB
90—Joel Nerem, DL
91—Joel Nerem, DL
95—Karl Borge, DL

LYCOMING
74—Thomas Vanaskie, DB
85—Mike Kern, DL

MACALESTER
82—Lee Schaefer, OG

MANKATO ST.
74—Dan Miller, C

MANSFIELD
83—John Delate, DB

MARIETTA
83—Matt Wurtzbacher, DL

MARS HILL
92—Brent Taylor, DL

MARYLAND
53—Bernie Faloney, B
75—Kim Hoover, DE
78—Joe Muffler, DL

MASS.-LOWELL
85—Don Williams, RB

MIT
89—Anthony Lapes, WR
90—Darcy Prather, LB
91—Rodrigo Rubiano, DL
92—Roderick Tranum, WR
93—Corey Foster, OL
94—Corey Foster, OL
95—Scott Vollrath, P
96—Duane Stevens, DB
Brad Gray, DL
97—Duane Stevens, DB
Mike Butville, LB
Brad Gray, DL

McGILL
87—Bruno Pietrobon, WR

McNEESE ST.
78—Jim Downing, OT
79—Jim Downing, OT
90—David Easterling, DB

MEMPHIS
92—Pat Jansen, DL

MIAMI (FLA.)
59—Fran Curci, B
84—Bernie Kosar, QB

MIAMI (OHIO)
73—Andy Pederzolli, DB

MICHIGAN
52—Dick Balzhiser, B
55—Jim Orwig, T
57—Jim Orwig, T
64—Bob Timberlake, QB
66—Dave Fisher, FB
Dick Vidmer, FB
69—Jim Mandich, OE
70—Phil Seymour, DE
71—Bruce Elliott, DB
72—Bill Hart, OG
74—Kirk Lewis, OG
75—Dan Jilek, DE
81—Norm Betts, TE
82—Stefan Humphries, OG
Robert Thompson, LB
83—Stefan Humphries, OG
85—Clay Miller, OT
86—Kenneth Higgins, WR

MICHIGAN ST.
52—John Wilson, DB
53—Don Dohoney, E
55—Buck Nystrom, G
57—Blanche Martin, HB
65—Don Bierowicz, DT
Don Japinga, DB
66—Pat Gallinagh, DT
68—Al Brenner, E/DB
69—Ron Saul, OG
Rich Saul, DE
73—John Shinsky, DT
79—Alan Davis, DB
85—Dean Altobelli, DB
86—Dean Altobelli, DB
86—Shane Bullough, LB
92—Steve Wasylk, DB
93—Steve Wasylk, DB

MICHIGAN TECH
71—Larry Ras, HB
73—Bruce Trusock, C
76—Jim Van Wagner, RB
92—Kurt Coduti, QB

MIDWESTERN ST.
95—Corby Walker, LB

MILLERSVILLE
91—Tom Burns, OL

MILLIKIN
61—Gerald Domesick, B
75—Frank Stone, G
78—Charlie Sammis, K
79—Eric Stevens, WR
83—Marc Knowles, WR
84—Tom Kreller, RB
85—Cary Bottorff, LB
Tom Kreller, RB
90—Tim Eimermann, PK

MINNESOTA
56—Bob Hobert, T
60—Frank Brixius, T
68—Bob Stein, DE
70—Barry Mayer, RB
89—Brent Herbel, P
94—Justin Conzemius, DB

MISSISSIPPI
54—Harold Easterwood, C
59—Robert Khayat, T
Charlie Flowers, B
61—Doug Elmore, B
65—Stan Hindman, G
68—Steve Hindman, HB
69—Julius Fagan, K
74—Greg Markow, DE
77—Robert Fabris, OE
George Plasketes, DE
80—Ken Toler, WR
86—Danny Hoskins, OG
87—Danny Hoskins, OG
88—Wesley Walls, TE
89—Todd Sandroni, DB

MISSISSIPPI COL.
75—Anthony Saway, S
78—Steve Johnson, OT
79—Steve Johnson, OT
83—Wayne Frazier, C
97—Kyle Fulcher, LB

MISSISSIPPI ST.
53—Jackie Parker, B
56—Ron Bennett, E
72—Frank Dowsing, DB
73—Jimmy Webb, DE
76—Will Coltharp, DE
89—Stacy Russell, DB

MISSOURI
62—Tom Hertz, G
66—Dan Schuppan, DE
Bill Powell, DT
68—Carl Garber, MG
70—John Weisenfels, LB
72—Greg Hill, KS
81—Van Darkow, LB
93—Matt Burgess, OL

MO.-ROLLA
72—Kim Colter, DB
80—Paul Janke, OG
86—Tom Reed, RB
87—Jim Pfeiffer, OT
88—Jim Pfeiffer, OL
91—Don Huff, DB
92—Don Huff, DB
94—Brian Gilmore, LB
95—Brian Gilmore, LB
96—Brian Gilmore, LB

MO. SOUTHERN ST.
85—Mike Testman, DB
93—Chris Tedford, OL
94—Chris Tedford, OL

MONMOUTH (ILL.)
83—Robb Long, QB

MONTANA
77—Steve Fisher, DE
79—Ed Cerkovnik, DB
88—Michael McGowan, LB
89—Michael McGowan, LB
90—Michael McGowan, LB
93—Dave Dickenson, QB
95—Matt Wells, WR
96—Josh Branen, RB
Blaine McElmurry, DB

MONTANA ST.
84—Dirk Nelson, P
88—Anders Larsson, PK
96—Devlan Geddes, DL

MONTCLAIR ST.
70—Bill Trimmer, DL
82—Daniel Deneher, KS

MOORHEAD ST.
88—Brad Shamla, DL

MORAVIAN
87—Jeff Pollock, WR
96—Mike Paciulli, DB

MOREHEAD ST.
74—Don Russell, KS
90—James Appel, OL
91—James Appel, OL
96—Mike Appel, OL

MORGAN ST.
96—Willie Thompson, DL

MOUNT UNION
71—Dennis Montgomery, QB
84—Rick Marabito, L
86—Scott Gindlesberger, QB
87—Paul Hrics, C

MUHLENBERG
70—Edward Salo, G
71—Edward Salo, IL
72—Edward Salo, C
75—Keith Ordemann, LB
80—Arthur Scavone, OT
89—Joe Zeszotarski, DL
90—Mike Hoffman, DB

MURRAY ST.
76—Eddie McFarland, DB

MUSKINGUM
78—Dan Radalia, DL
79—Dan Radalia, DL

NAVY
53—Steve Eisenhauer, G
57—Tom Forrestal, QB
58—Joe Tranchini, B
69—Dan Pike, RB
80—Ted Dumbauld, LB

NEBRASKA
62—James Huge, E
63—Dennis Calridge, B
66—Marv Mueller, DB
69—Randy Reeves, DB
71—Larry Jacobson, DT
Jeff Kinney, HB
73—Frosty Anderson, E
75—Rik Bonness, C
Tom Heiser, RB
76—Vince Ferragamo, QB
Ted Harvey, DB
77—Ted Harvey, DB
78—George Andrews, DL
James Pillen, DB
79—Rod Horn, DL
Kelly Saalfeld, C
Randy Schleusener, OG
80—Jeff Finn, TE
Randy Schleusener, OG
81—Eric Lindquist, DB
David Rimington, C
Randy Theiss, OT
82—David Rimington, C
83—Scott Strasburger, DL
Rob Stuckey, DL
84—Scott Strasburger, DL
Rob Stuckey, DL
Mark Traynowicz, C
86—Dale Klein, K
Thomas Welter, OT
87—Jeffrey Jamrog, DL
Mark Blazek, DB
88—Mark Blazek, DB
John Kroeker, P
89—Gerry Gdowski, QB
Jake Young, OL
90—David Edeal, OL
Pat Tyrance, LB
Jim Wanek, OL
91—Pat Engelbert, DL
Mike Stigge, P
92—Mike Stigge, P
93—Rob Zatechka, OL
Terry Connealy, DL
Trev Alberts, LB
94—Matt Shaw, TE
Rob Zatechka, OL
Terry Connealy, DL
95—Aaron Graham, OL
96—Grant Wistrom, LB
97—Joel Mackovicka, RB
Grant Wistrom, DL

NEB.-KEARNEY
70—John Makovicka, RB
75—Tim Brodahl, E

NEB.-OMAHA
82—Kirk Hutton, DB
Clark Toner, LB
83—Kirk Hutton, DB
84—Jerry Kripal, QB

NEB. WESLEYAN
87—Pat Sweeney, DB
88—Pat Sweeney, DB
Mike Surls, LB
89—Scott Shaffer, RB
Scott Shipman, DB
95—Justin Rice, DL
96—Justin Rice, DL
97—Chad Wemhoff, WR

NEVADA
82—David Heppe, P

NEW HAMPSHIRE
52—John Driscoll, T
84—Dave Morton, OL

NEW MEXICO
75—Bob Johnson, S
77—Robert Rumbaugh, DT
78—Robert Rumbaugh, DL
93—Justin Hall, OL

NEW MEXICO ST.
66—Jim Bohl, B
74—Ralph Jackson, OG
75—Ralph Jackson, OG
85—Andy Weiler, KS
92—Todd Cutler, TE
Shane Hackney, OL
Tim Mauck, LB
93—Tim Mauck, LB
96—David Patterson, WR
97—David Patterson, WR

NICHOLS
89—David Kane, DB

NORTH CARO.
64—Ken Willard, QB
85—Kevin Anthony, QB

NORTH CARO. ST.
60—Roman Gabriel, QB
63—Joe Scarpati, B
67—Steve Warren, OT
71—Craig John, OG
73—Justus Everett, C
Stan Fritts, RB
74—Justus Everett, C
80—Calvin Warren, P

NORTH DAK.
87—Kurt Otto, QB
88—Chuck Clairmont, OL
Matt Gulseth, DB
92—Tim Gelinske, WR
Mark Ewen, LB
96—Tim Tibesar, LB

NORTH DAK. ST.
71—Tomm Smail, DT
93—T. R. McDonald, WR

NORTH PARK
83—Mike Lilgegren, DB
85—Scott Love, WR
86—Todd Love, WR
87—Todd Love, WR

NORTH TEXAS
75—Pete Morris, LB
76—Pete Morris, LB

NORTHEAST LA.
70—Tom Miller, KS
74—Mike Bialas, T

NORTHEASTERN
85—Shawn O'Malley, LB

NORTHERN ARIZ.
89—Chris Baniszewski, WR

NORTHERN COLO.
71—Charles Putnik, OG
81—Duane Hirsch, DL
Ray Sperger, DB
82—Jim Bright, RB
89—Mike Yonkovich, DL
Tom Langer, LB
90—Tom Langer, LB

NORTHERN MICH.
83—Bob Stefanski, WR

NORTHWEST MO. ST.
81—Robert "Chip" Gregory, LB

NORTHWESTERN
56—Al Viola, G
58—Andy Cvercko, T
61—Larry Onesti, C
62—Paul Flatley, B
63—George Burman, E
70—Joe Zigulich, OG
76—Randolph Dean, E
80—Jim Ford, OT
86—Michael Baum, OT
Bob Dirkes, DL
Todd Krehbiel, DB
87—Mike Baum, OL
88—Mike Baum, OL

90—Ira Adler, PK
95—Sam Valenzisi, PK

N'WESTERN (IOWA)
83—Mark Muilenberg, RB
92—Joel Bundt, OL

N'WESTERN (OKLA.)
61—Stewart Arthurs, B

NORTHWESTERN ST.
92—Guy Hedrick, RB
94—John Dippel, OL

NORWICH
70—Gary Fry, RB

NOTRE DAME
52—Joe Heap, B
53—Joe Heap, B
54—Joe Heap, B
55—Don Schaefer, B
58—Bob Wetoska, E
63—Bob Lehmann, G
66—Tom Regner, OG
Jim Lynch, LB
67—Jim Smithberger, DB
68—George Kunz, OT
69—Jim Reilly, OT
70—Tom Gatewood, E
Larry DiNardo, OG
Joe Theismann, QB
71—Greg Marx, DT
Tom Gatewood, E
72—Michael Creaney, E
Greg Marx, DT
73—David Casper, E
Gary Potempa, LB
Bob Thomas, K
74—Reggie Barnett, DB
Pete Demmerle, E
77—Ken MacAfee, E
Joe Restic, S
Dave Vinson, OG
78—Joe Restic, DB
80—Bob Burger, OG
Tom Gibbons, DB
81—John Krimm, DB
85—Greg Dingens, DL
87—Ted Gradel, PK
Vince Phelan, P
92—Tim Ruddy, OL
93—Tim Ruddy, OL

OCCIDENTAL
88—Curtis Page, DL

OHIO
71—John Rousch, HB

OHIO NORTHERN
76—Jeff McFarlin, S
79—Robert Coll, WR
86—David Myers, DL
90—Chad Hummell, OL
97—Andy Roecker, OL

OHIO ST.
52—John Borton, B
54—Dick Hilinski, T
58—Bob White, B
61—Tom Perdue, E
65—Bill Ridder, MG
66—Dave Foley, OT
68—Dave Foley, OT
Mark Stier, LB
69—Bill Urbanik, DT
71—Rick Simon, OG
73—Randy Gradishar, LB
74—Brian Baschnagel, RB
75—Brian Baschnagel, RB
76—Pete Johnson, RB
Bill Lukens, OG
77—Jeff Logan, RB
80—Marcus Marek, LB
82—John Frank, TE
Joseph Smith, OT
83—John Frank, TE
84—David Crecelius, DL
Michael Lanese, WR
85—Michael Lanese, WR
89—Joseph Staysniak, OL
92—Leonard Hartman, OL
Gregory Smith, DL
95—Greg Bellisari, LB
96—Greg Bellisari, LB

OHIO WESLEYAN
70—Tony Heald, LB
Tom Liller, E
81—Ric Kinnan, WR
85—Kevin Connell, OG
94—Craig Anderson, LB
95—Craig Anderson, LB
96—Craig Anderson, LB

OKLAHOMA
52—Tom Catlin, C
54—Carl Allison, E
56—Jerry Tubbs, C
57—Doyle Jenning, T
58—Ross Coyle, E
62—Wayne Lee, C
63—Newt Burton, G
64—Newt Burton, G
66—Ron Shotts, HB
67—Ron Shotts, HB
68—Eddie Hinton, DB
70—Joe Wylie, RB
71—Jack Mildren, QB
72—Joe Wylie, RB
74—Randy Hughes, S
75—Dewey Selmon, LB
Lee Roy Selmon, DT
80—Jay Jimerson, DB
86—Brian Bosworth, LB

OKLA. PANHANDLE
76—Larry Johnson, G

OKLAHOMA ST.
54—Dale Meinert, G
72—Tom Wolf, OT
73—Doug Tarrant, LB
74—Tom Wolf, OT
77—Joe Avanzini, DE

OREGON
62—Steve Barnett, T
65—Tim Casey, LB
86—Mike Preacher, P
90—Bill Musgrave, QB

OREGON ST.
62—Terry Baker, B
67—Bill Enyart, FB
68—Bill Enyart, FB
93—Chad Paulson, RB

OUACHITA BAPTIST
78—David Cowling, OG

PACIFIC (CAL.)
78—Bruce Filarsky, OG
79—Bruce Filarsky, DL

PACIFIC LUTHERAN
82—Curt Rodin, TE

PENNSYLVANIA
86—Rich Comizio, RB

PENN ST.
65—Joe Bellas, T
John Runnells, LB
66—John Runnells, LB
67—Rich Buzin, OT
69—Charlie Pittman, HB
Dennis Onkotz, LB
71—Dave Joyner, OT
72—Bruce Bannon, DE
73—Mark Markovich, OG
76—Chuck Benjamin, OT
78—Keith Dorney, OT
82—Todd Blackledge, QB
Harry Hamilton, DB
Scott Radicec, LB
83—Harry Hamilton, LB
84—Lance Hamilton, DB
Carmen Masciantonio, LB
85—Lance Hamilton, DB
86—John Shaffer, QB
94—Jeff Hartings, OL
Tony Pittman, DB
95—Jeff Hartings, OL

PITTSBURG ST.
72—Jay Sperry, RB
89—Brett Potts, DL
91—Mike Brockel, OL
92—Mike Brockel, OL
96—Brian Moorman, P
97—Brian Moorman, P

PITTSBURGH
52—Dick Deitrick, DT
54—Lou Palatella, T
56—Joe Walton, E
58—John Guzik, G
76—Jeff Delaney, LB
80—Greg Meisner, DL
81—Rob Fada, OG
82—Rob Fada, OG
J. C. Pelusi, DL
88—Mark Stepnoski, OL

PORTLAND ST.
72—Bill Dials, T
77—John Urness, WR
78—John Urness, WR

PRINCETON
68—Dick Sandler, DT
76—Kevin Fox, OG
82—Kevin Guthrie, WR
83—Kevin Guthrie, WR

PUGET SOUND
82—Buster Crook, DB

PURDUE
56—Len Dawson, QB
60—Jerry Beabout, T
65—Sal Ciampi, G
67—Jim Beirne, E
Lance Olssen, DT
68—Tim Foley, DB
69—Tim Foley, DB
Mike Phipps, QB
Bill Yanchar, DT
73—Bob Hoftiezer, DE
79—Ken Loushin, DL
80—Tim Seneff, DB
81—Tim Seneff, DB
89—Bruce Brineman, OL

RENSSELAER
95—Alic Scott, OL
96—Dan McGovern, RB
97—Chris Cochran, DL

RHODE ISLAND
76—Richard Moser, RB
77—Richard Moser, RB

RHODES
90—Robert Heck, DL

RICE
52—Richard Chapman, DG
53—Richard Chapman, DG
54—Dicky Maegle, B
69—Steve Bradshaw, DG
79—LaMont Jefferson, LB
83—Brian Patterson, DB
95—Jay Lamy, DB

ROCHESTER
82—Bob Cordaro, LB
92—Jeremy Hurd, RB
93—Jeremy Hurd, RB

ROSE-HULMAN
78—Rick Matovich, DL
79—Scott Lindner, DL
80—Scott Lindner, DL
Jim Novacek, P
83—Jack Grote, LB
84—Jack Grote, LB
88—Greg Kremer, LB
Shawn Ferron, PK
89—Shawn Ferron, PK
90—Ed Huonden, WR
92—Greg Hubbard, OL
93—Greg Hubbard, OL

SAGINAW VALLEY
93—Troy Hendrickson, PK

ST. CLOUD ST.
88—Rick Rodgers, DB
89—Rick Rodgers, DB

ST. FRANCIS (PA.)
93—Todd Eckenroad, WR

ST. JOHN'S (MINN.)
72—Jim Kruzich, E
79—Terry Geraghty, DB
94—Chris Palmer, WR
Matthew Malmberg, RB
95—Chris Palmer, WR
97—Matt Emmerich, DB

ST. JOHN'S (N.Y.)
93—Anthony Russo, RB

ST. JOSEPH'S (IND.)
77—Mike Bettinger, DB
78—Mike Bettinger, DB
79—Mike Bettinger, DB
85—Ralph Laura, OT
88—Keith Woodason, OL
89—Jeff Fairchild, P

ST. NORBERT
86—Matthew Lang, LB
Karl Zacharias, P
87—Karl Zacharias, PK
Matthew Lang, LB
88—Mike Whitehouse, WR
89—Mike Whitehouse, WR

ST. OLAF
61—Dave Hindermann, T

ST. THOMAS (MINN.)
73—Mark Dienhart, T
74—Mark Dienhart, T
77—Tom Kelly, OG
80—Doug Groebner, C
94—Curt Behrns, DB

SAM HOUSTON ST.
72—Walter Anderson, KS
73—Walter Anderson, KS
93—Kevin Riley, DB

SAN DIEGO
87—Bryan Day, DB
88—Bryan Day, DB
94—Doug Popovich, DB
95—Doug Popovich, DB
96—Jeb Dougherty, DB

SAN JOSE ST.
75—Tim Toews, OG

SANTA CLARA
71—Ron Sani, IL
73—Alex Damascus, RB
74—Steve Lagorio, LB
75—Mark Tiernan, LB
76—Lou Marengo, KS
Mark Tiernan, LB
80—Dave Alfaro, QB

SHIPPENSBURG
76—Tony Winter, LB
82—Dave Butler, DL
94—Joel Yohn, PK
95—Joel Yohn, PK

SOUTH CARO.
87—Mark Fryer, OL
88—Mark Fryer, OL
91—Joe Reeves, LB

SOUTH DAK.
78—Scott Pollock, QB
82—Jerus Campbell, DL
83—Jeff Sime, T
87—Dan Sonnek, RB

SOUTH DAK. ST.
74—Bob Gissler, E
75—Bill Matthews, T
77—Bill Matthews, DE
79—Tony Harris, PK
Paul Kippley, DB

SOUTHERN CAL
52—Dick Nunis, DB
59—Mike McKeever, G
60—Mike McKeever, G
Marlin McKeever, E
65—Charles Arrobio, T
67—Steve Sogge, QB
68—Steve Sogge, QB
69—Harry Khasigian, OG
73—Pat Haden, QB
74—Pat Haden, QB
78—Rich Dimler, DL
79—Brad Budde, OG
Paul McDonald, QB
Keith Van Horne, T
84—Duane Bickett, LB
85—Matt Koart, DL
86—Jeffrey Bregel, OG
88—John Jackson, WR
89—John Jackson, WR
95—Jeremy Hogue, OL

Matt Keneley, DL
96—Matt Keneley, DL

SOUTHERN COLO.
83—Dan DeRose, LB

SOUTHERN CONN. ST.
84—Gerald Carbonaro, OL

SOUTHERN ILL.
70—Sam Finocchio, G
88—Charles Harmke, RB
91—Dwayne Summers, DL
Jon Manley, LB

SOUTHERN METHODIST
52—Dave Powell, E
53—Darrell Lafitte, G
54—Raymond Berry, E
55—David Hawk, G
57—Tom Koenig, G
58—Tom Koenig, G
62—Raymond Schoenke, T
66—John LaGrone, MG
Lynn Thornhill, OG
68—Jerry LeVias, OE
72—Cleve Whitener, LB
83—Brian O'Meara, T

SOUTHERN MISS.
92—James Singleton, DL
97—Jeremy Lindley, OL

SOUTHERN ORE.
97—Ian Reid, OL

SOUTHERN UTAH
88—Jim Andrus, RB
90—Steve McDowell, P

SOUTHWEST MO. ST.
73—Kent Stringer, QB
75—Kent Stringer, QB
78—Steve Newbold, WR

SOUTHWEST ST.
88—Bruce Saugstad, DB

SOUTHWEST TEX. ST.
72—Jimmy Jowers, LB
73—Jimmy Jowers, LB
78—Mike Ferris, OG
79—Mike Ferris, G
Allen Kiesling, DL
81—Mike Miller, QB

SPRINGFIELD
71—Bruce Rupert, LB
84—Sean Flanders, DL
85—Sean Flanders, DL

STANFORD
70—John Sande, C
Terry Ewing, DB
75—Don Stevenson, RB
76—Don Stevenson, RB
77—Guy Benjamin, QB
78—Vince Mulroy, WR
Jim Stephens, OG
79—Pat Bowe, TE
Milt McColl, LB
Joe St. Geme, DB
81—John Bergren, DL
Darrin Nelson, RB
82—John Bergren, DL
83—John Bergren, DL
85—Matt Soderlund, LB
87—Brad Muster, RB
90—Ed McCaffrey, WR
91—Tommy Vardell, RB
94—Justin Armour, WR

SUL ROSS ST.
73—Archie Nexon, RB

SUSQUEHANNA
75—Gerry Huesken, T
76—Gerry Huesken, T
80—Dan Distasio, LB

SYRACUSE
60—Fred Mautino, E
71—Howard Goodman, LB
83—Tony Romano, LB
84—Tim Green, DL
85—Tim Green, DL

TARLETON ST.
81—Ricky Bush, RB
90—Mike Loveless, OL

TENNESSEE
56—Charles Rader, T
57—Bill Johnson, G
65—Mack Gentry, DT
67—Bob Johnson, C
70—Tim Priest, DB
80—Timothy Irwin, OT
82—Mike Terry, DL
97—Peyton Manning, QB

TENN.-MARTIN
74—Randy West, E

TENNESSEE TECH
87—Andy Rittenhouse, DL

TEXAS
59—Maurice Doke, G
61—Johnny Treadwell, G
62—Johnny Treadwell, G
Pat Culpepper, B
63—Duke Carlisle, B
66—Gene Bledsoe, OT
67—Mike Perrin, DE
Corby Robertson, LB
68—Corby Robertson, LB
Scott Henderson, LB
69—Scott Henderson, LB
Bill Zapalac, DE
70—Scott Henderson, LB
Bill Zapalac, LB
72—Mike Bayer, DB
Tommy Keel, S
Steve Oxley, T
73—Tommy Keel, S
83—Doug Dawson, G
88—Lee Brockman, DL
95—Pat Fitzgerald, TE
96—Pat Fitzgerald, TE
97—Dusty Renfro, LB

UTEP
88—Pat Hegarty, QB

TEXAS A&M
56—Jack Pardee, B
71—Steve Luebbehusen, LB
76—Kevin Monk, LB
77—Kevin Monk, LB
85—Kip Corrington, DB
86—Kip Corrington, DB
87—Kip Corrington, DB

TEX. A&M-COMMERCE
77—Mike Hall, OT

TEX. A&M-KINGSVILLE
72—Floyd Goodwin, T
73—Johnny Jackson, E
76—Wade Whitmer, DL
77—Joe Henke, LB
Wade Whitmer, DL
78—Wade Whitmer, DL

TEXAS CHRISTIAN
52—Marshall Harris, T
55—Hugh Pitts, C
Jim Swink, B
56—Jim Swink, B
57—John Nikkel, E
68—Jim Ray, G
72—Scott Walker, C
74—Terry Drennan, DB
80—John McClean, DL

TEXAS TECH
72—Jeff Jobe, E
79—Maury Buford, P
83—Chuck Alexander, DB
93—Robert King, P

THOMAS MORE
97—Mike Bramlage Jr., DB

TOLEDO
83—Michael Matz, DL
95—Craig Dues, LB

TRINITY (CONN.)
96—Joseph DeAngelis, OL

TRINITY (TEX.)
92—Jeff Bryan, OL
97—Mark Byarlay, RB

TRUMAN ST.
73—Tom Roberts, T
78—Keith Driscoll, LB
79—Keith Driscoll, LB

92—K. C. Conaway, P

TUFTS
70—Bruce Zinsmeister, DL
81—Brian Gallagher, OG
83—Richard Guiunta, G

TULANE
71—David Hebert, DB

TULSA
64—Howard Twilley, E
65—Howard Twilley, E
74—Mack Lancaster, T
95—David Millwee, OL
96—Levi Gillen, DB
97—Levi Gillen, DB

UCLA
52—Ed Flynn, G
Donn Moomaw, LB
53—Ira Pauly, C
54—Sam Boghosian, G
66—Ray Armstrong, E
75—John Sciarra, QB
77—John Fowler, LB
81—Cormac Carney, WR
Tim Wrightman, TE
82—Cormac Carney, WR
85—Mike Hartmeier, OG
92—Carlton Gray, DB
95—George Kase, DL

UNION (N.Y.)
71—Tom Anacher, LB
73—Dave Ricks, DB
87—Richard Romer, DL
93—Greg Oswitt, OL
96—Roger Egbert, PK

URSINUS
86—Chuck Odgers, DB
87—Chuck Odgers, LB

UTAH
64—Mel Carpenter, T
71—Scott Robbins, DB
73—Steve Odom, RB
76—Dick Graham, E

UTAH ST.
61—Merlin Olsen, T
69—Gary Anderson, LB
74—Randy Stockham, DE
75—Randy Stockham, DE

VALDOSTA ST.
93—Chris Hatcher, QB
94—Chris Hatcher, QB

VANDERBILT
58—Don Donnell, C
68—Jim Burns, DB
74—Doug Martin, E
75—Damon Regen, LB
77—Greg Martin, K
83—Phil Roach, WR

VILLANOVA
86—Ron Sency, RB
88—Peter Lombardi, RB
92—Tim Matas, DL

VIRGINIA
72—Tom Kennedy, OG
75—Bob Meade, DT
92—Tom Burns, LB
93—Tom Burns, LB
95—Tiki Barber, RB
96—Tiki Barber, RB
97—Stephen Phelan, DB

VMI
78—Craig Jones, PK
79—Craig Jones, PK
84—David Twillie, OL
86—Dan Young, DL
88—Anthony McIntosh, DB

VIRGINIA TECH
67—Frank Loria, DB
72—Tommy Carpenito, LB

WABASH
70—Roscoe Fouts, DB
71—Kendrick Shelburne, DT
82—Dave Broecker, QB

WARTBURG
75—James Charles Peterson, DB

76—Randy Groth, DB
77—Neil Mandsager, LB
90—Jerrod Staack, OL
93—Koby Kreinbring, LB
94—Vince Penningroth, DL
95—Vince Penningroth, DL

WASHINGTON
55—Jim Houston, E
63—Mike Briggs, T
64—Rick Redman, G
65—Steve Bramwell, DB
79—Bruce Harrell, LB
81—Mark Jerue, LB
Chuck Nelson, PK
82—Chuck Nelson, PK
86—David Rill, LB
87—David Rill, LB
91—Ed Cunningham, OL

WASHINGTON (MO.)
97—Brad Klein, LB

WASH. & JEFF.
92—Raymond Cross, DL
93—Michael Jones, OL
94—Michael Jones, OL

WASH. & LEE
75—John Cocklereece, DB
78—George Ballantyne, LB
92—Evans Edwards, OL

WASHINGTON ST.
89—Jason Hanson, PK
90—Lee Tilleman, DL
Jason Hanson, PK
91—Jason Hanson, PK

WAYNE ST. (MICH.)
71—Gary Schultz, DB
72—Walt Stasinski, DB

WAYNESBURG
77—John Culp, RB
78—John Culp, RB
89—Andrew Barrish, OL
90—Andrew Barrish, OL
91—Karl Petrof, OL

WEBER ST.
97—Cameron Quayle, TE

WEST CHESTER
83—Eric Wentling, K
86—Gerald Desmond, K

WEST VA.
52—Paul Bischoff, E
54—Fred Wyant, B
55—Sam Huff, T
70—Kim West, K
80—Oliver Luck, QB
81—Oliver Luck, QB
83—Jeff Hostetler, QB
92—Mike Compton, OL
94—Matt Taffoni, LB

WESTERN CARO.
75—Mike Wade, E
76—Mike Wade, LB
84—Eddie Maddox, RB

WESTERN ILL.
61—Jerry Blew, G
85—Jeff McKinney, RB
91—David Fierke, OL

WESTERN KY.
71—James Barber, LB
81—Tim Ford, DL
84—Mark Fatkin, OL
85—Mark Fatkin, OG
95—Brian Bixler, OL

WESTERN MD.
73—Chip Chaney, S

WESTERN MICH.
70—Jon Bull, OT
94—Rich Kaiser, DL
95—Rich Kaiser, DL

WESTERN OREGON
61—Francis Tresler, C

WESTERN ST.
78—Bill Campbell, DB
88—Damon Lockhart, RB

WESTMINSTER (PA.)
73—Bob Clark, G
77—Scott McLuckey, LB
93—Brian Wilson, OL

WHEATON (ILL.)
73—Bill Hyer, E
75—Eugene Campbell, RB
76—Eugene Campbell, RB
88—Paul Sternenberg, DL
92—Bart Moseman, DB
94—Pedro Arruza, RB
95—Jeff Brown, QB
Pedro Arruzo, RB

WHITTIER
86—Brent Kane, DL

WILKES
70—Al Kenney, C

WILLAMETTE
61—Stuart Hall

WILLIAM & MARY
74—John Gerdelman, RB
75—Ken Smith, DB
77—Ken Smith, DB
78—Robert Muscalus, TE
84—Mark Kelso, DB
88—Chris Gessner, DB
90—Jeff Nielsen, LB
93—Craig Staub, DL

WM. PATERSON
92—John Trust, RB

WINONA ST.
93—Nathan Gruber, DB
94—Nathan Gruber, DB
97—Travis Walch, RB

WISCONSIN
52—Bob Kennedy, DG
53—Alan Ameche, B
54—Alan Ameche, B
58—Jon Hobbs, B
59—Dale Hackbart, B
62—Pat Richter, E
63—Ken Bowman, C
72—Rufus Ferguson, RB
82—Kyle Borland, LB
87—Don Davey, DL
88—Don Davey, DL
89—Don Davey, DL
90—Don Davey, DL

WIS.-EAU CLAIRE
74—Mark Anderson, RB
80—Mike Zeihen, DB

WIS.-LA CROSSE
95—Troy Harcey, WR
96—Troy Harcey, WR

WIS.-OSHKOSH
96—Rob Stoltz, WR
97—Ryan Hinske, WR

WIS.-PLATTEVILLE
85—Mark Hintz, DB
Mark Rae, P
86—Mike Hintz, QB
87—Mark Rae, P

WIS.-RIVER FALLS
91—Mike Olson, LB
95—Brian Izdepski, OT

WIS.-STEVENS POINT
97—Joel Hornby, DL

WIS.-WHITEWATER
95—Scott Hawig, OL

WITTENBERG
80—Bill Beach, DB
81—Bill Beach, DB
82—Tom Jones, OT
88—Paul Kungl, WR
90—Victor Terebuh, DB

WOOSTER
73—Dave Foy, LB
77—Blake Moore, C
78—Blake Moore, C
79—Blake Moore, C
80—Dale Fortner, DB
John Weisensell, OG

WYOMING
65—Bob Dinges, DE
67—George Mills, OG
73—Mike Lopiccolo, OT
84—Bob Gustafson, OT
87—Patrick Arndt, OG
94—Ryan Christopherson, RB
95—Joe Cummings, DL
96—Jay Korth, OL
Cory Wedel, PK
97—Jay Korth, OL
Cory Wedel, PK
Brian Lee, DB

YALE
68—Fred Morris, C
70—Tom Neville, DT
78—William Crowley, LB
81—Rich Diana, RB
Frederick Leone, DL
89—Glover Lawrence, DL
91—Scott Wagner, DB

YOUNGSTOWN ST.
93—John Quintana, TE

Bowl/All-Star Game Records

1998-99 Bowl Schedule

(All Starting Times Eastern; Conference Affiliations as of June 15, 1997)

AMERICAN GENERAL MUSIC CITY BOWL
Nashville, Tennessee
December 29, 1998, at 5 p.m.
Scott Ramsey, executive director
Nashville Area Chamber of Commerce
401 Church Street, Suite 2700
Nashville, TN 37219
(615) 880-1900 Fax: (615) 244-3540
Televising Network: ESPN
Facility: Vanderbilt Stadium
Capacity: 65,000
Sponsor: American General Music City Bowl
Teams: SEC #6 vs. At-Large

AXA/EQUITABLE LIBERTY BOWL
Memphis, Tennessee
December 31, 1998, at 1:30 p.m.
Steve Ehrhart, managing partner
AXA/Equitable
3767 New Getwell Road
Memphis, TN 38118
(901) 795-7700 Fax: (901) 795-7826
Televising Network: ESPN
Facility: Liberty Bowl Memorial Stadium
Capacity: 62,921
Title Sponsor: AXA Equitable
Teams: CUSA Champion vs. SEC #7

BUILDERS SQUARE ALAMO BOWL
San Antonio, Texas
December 29, 1998, at 8 p.m.
Derrick S. Fox, executive director
San Antonio Bowl Association, Inc.
100 Montana Street, Suite 3D01
San Antonio, TX 78203-1031
(210) 226-2695 Fax: (210) 704-6399
Televising Network: ESPN Radio or Host Communications
Facility: Alamodome
Capacity: 65,000
Title Sponsor: Builders Square
Teams: Big Ten #4 vs. Big 12 #4

CHICK-FIL-A PEACH BOWL
Atlanta, Georgia
December 31, 1998, at 5 p.m.
Peach Bowl, Inc.
235 International Boulevard
Atlanta, GA 30303
(404) 586-8500 Fax: (404) 586-8508
Televising Network: ESPN
Facility: Georgia Dome
Capacity: 71,228
Sponsor: Chick-Fil-A
Teams: ACC #3 vs. SEC #4

COMPUSA FLORIDA CITRUS BOWL
Orlando, Florida
January 1, 1999, at 1 p.m.
Charles H. Rohe, executive director
Florida Citrus Sports Association, Inc.
One Citrus Bowl Place
Orlando, FL 32805-2451
(407) 423-2476 Fax: (407) 425-8451
Televising Network: ABC
Facility: Florida Citrus Bowl
Capacity: 70,000
Title Sponsor: CompUSA & Florida Department of Citrus
Teams: SEC #2 vs. Big Ten #2

CULLIGAN HOLIDAY BOWL
San Diego, California
December 30, 1998, at 8 p.m.
John K. Reid, executive director
San Diego Bowl Game Association
P.O. Box 601400
San Diego, CA 92160
(619) 283-5808 Fax: (619) 281-7947
Televising Network: ESPN
Facility: Qualcomm Stadium
Capacity: 70,000
Title Sponsor: Culligan
Teams: WAC Champion/Pac-10 #2 vs. Big 12 #3

FEDEX ORANGE BOWL
Miami, Florida
January 2, 1999, at 8 p.m.
Keith R. Tribble, executive director
Orange Bowl Committee
601 Brickell Key Drive, Suite 206
Miami, FL 33131
(305) 371-4600 Fax: (305) 371-4318
Televising Network: ABC
Facility: Pro Player Stadium
Capacity: 75,014
Title Sponsor: Federal Express
Teams: ACC Champion/Big East Champion vs. At-Large

HUMANITARIAN BOWL
Boise, Idaho
December 30, 1998, at 4 p.m.
Steven Wood Schmader, president
Sports Humanitarian Bowl Association
7032 S. Eisenman Road
Boise, Idaho 83716
(208) 338-8887 Fax: (208) 338-3833
Televising Network: ESPN2
Facility: Bronco Stadium
Capacity: 30,000
Title Sponsor: TBD
Teams: Big West Champion vs. At-Large

INSIGHT.COM BOWL
Tucson, Arizona
December 26, 1998, at 7 p.m.
John Junker, executive director
Tucson Bowl Foundation
120 South Ash Avenue
Tempe, AZ 85281
(602) 350-0900 Fax: (602) 350-0915
Televising Network: ESPN
Facility: Arizona Stadium
Capacity: 55,883
Title Sponsor: Insight
Teams: Big East #2/Notre Dame vs. Big 12 #5

JEEP ALOHA CHRISTMAS FOOTBALL CLASSICS
Honolulu, Hawaii
December 25, 1998, at 3:30 and 8:30 p.m.
Marcia J. Klompus, executive director
Aloha Sports, Inc.
1110 University Avenue, Suite 403
Honolulu, HI 96826
(808) 947-4141 Fax: (808) 941-9911
Televising Network: ABC
Facility: Aloha Stadium
Capacity: 50,000
Title Sponsor: Jeep Division of Chrysler Corporation
Teams: Game No. 1 (3:30 p.m.) Pac-10 #4 vs. At-Large
Game No. 2 (8:30 p.m.) Pac-10 #5 vs. WAC #3

LAS VEGAS BOWL
Las Vegas, Nevada
December 19, 1998, at 6 p.m.
Manuel Cortez, president
Las Vegas Convention & Visitors Authority
3150 Paradise Road
Las Vegas, NV 89109-9096
(702) 892-0711 Fax: (702) 892-7515
Televising Network: ESPN
Facility: Sam Boyd Stadium
Capacity: 40,000
Sponsor: Las Vegas Convention & Visitor's Authority
Teams: WAC #2 vs. At-Large

MOTOR CITY BOWL
Pontiac, Michigan
December 23, 1998, at 8 p.m.
George Perles, executive director
Ford Division (Ford Motor Company)
1200 Featherstone Drive
Pontiac, MI 48342
(248) 456-1694 or 858-7358 Fax: (248) 456-1691
Televising Network: ESPN (ESPN2)
Facility: Pontiac Silverdome
Capacity: 79,083
Sponsor: Ford Division (Ford Motor Company)
Teams: MAC Champion vs. At-Large

NOKIA SUGAR BOWL
New Orleans, Louisiana
January 1, 1999, at 8:30 p.m.
Paul J. Hoolahan, executive director
The Sugar Bowl Committee
1500 Sugar Bowl Drive
New Orleans, LA 70112
(504) 525-8573 Fax: (504) 525-4867
Televising Network: ABC
Facility: Louisiana Superdome
Capacity: 71,023
Title Sponsor: Nokia Mobile Telephones
Teams: SEC Champion vs. At-Large

NORWEST SUN BOWL
El Paso, Texas
December 31, 1998, at 2 p.m.
Joyce E. Feinberg, executive director
Sun Bowl Association
4100 Rio Bravo, Suite 303
El Paso, TX 79902-1049
(915) 533-4416 Fax: (915) 533-0661
Televising Network: CBS
Facility: Sun Bowl Stadium
Capacity: 51,270
Sponsor: Norwest Corporation
Teams: PAC-10 #3 vs. Big Ten #5

OUTBACK BOWL
Tampa, Florida
January 1, 1999, at 11 a.m.
James P. McVay, executive director
Tampa Bay Bowl Association, Inc.
4511 North Himes Avenue, Suite 260
Tampa, Florida 33614
(813) 874-2695 Fax: (813) 873-1959
Televising Network: ESPN
Facility: Tampa Community
Capacity: 65,000
Title Sponsor: Outback Steakhouse, Inc.
Teams: SEC #3 vs. Big Ten #3

ROSE BOWL
Pasadena, California
January 1, 1999, at 5 p.m.
John H.B. "Jack" French, executive director
Pasadena Tournament of Roses Association
391 South Orange Grove Boulevard
Pasadena, CA 91184
(818) 449-4100 Fax: (818) 449-9066
Televising Network: ABC
Facility: Rose Bowl
Capacity: 96,576
Sponsor: TBD
Teams: Pac-10 Champion vs. Big Ten Champion

SANFORD INDEPENDENCE BOWL
Shreveport, Louisiana
December 31, 1998, at 8:30 p.m.
Glen Krupica, executive director
Independence Bowl Foundation
P.O. Box 1723
Shreveport, LA 71166
(318) 221-0712 Fax: (318) 221-7366
Televising Network: ESPN
Facility: Independence Stadium
Capacity: 50,459
Title Sponsor: TBD
Teams: SEC #5 vs. At-Large

SOUTHWESTERN BELL COTTON BOWL
Dallas, Texas
January 1, 1999, at 1:30 p.m.
Rick Baker, executive director
Cotton Bowl Athletic Association
P.O. Box 569420
Dallas, TX 75356
(214) 634-7525 Fax: (214) 634-7764
Televising Network: Fox Sports Net/Fox Network
Facility: Cotton Bowl
Capacity: 68,252
Sponsor: Southwestern Bell
Teams: Pac-10 #2/WAC Champion vs. Big 12 #2

SUNSHINE FOOTBALL CLASSIC BOWL
Miami, Florida
December 26 or 29, 1998, at 7:30 p.m.
Mitch Morrall, executive director

Sunshine Football Classic
915 Middle River Drive, Suite 120
Fort Lauderdale, FL 33304
(954) 564-5000 Fax: (954) 564-8902
Televising Network: Raycom/Turner Sports
Facility: Pro Player Stadium
Capacity: 75,014
Title Sponsor: TBD
Teams: ACC #4 vs. Big Ten #6

TOSTITOS FIESTA BOWL

Tempe, Arizona
January 4, 1999, at 7:30 p.m.
John Junker, executive director
Arizona Sports Foundation
120 South Ash Avenue
Tempe, AZ 85281
(602) 350-0900 Fax: (602) 350-0915
Televising Network: ABC
Facility: Sun Devil Stadium
Capacity: 73,259
Title Sponsor: Tostitos
Teams: No. 1 vs. No. 2 (National Championship)

TOYOTA GATOR BOWL

Jacksonville, Florida
January 1, 1999, at 12:30 p.m.
Richard M. Catlett, executive director
Toyota Motor Sales/Southeast Toyota
One Gator Bowl Boulevard
Jacksonville, FL 32202
(904) 798-1700 Fax: (904) 632-2080
Televising Network: NBC
Facility: Gator Bowl/Alltel Stadium
Capacity: 76,976
Sponsor: Toyota Motor Sales, USA, Inc.
Teams: Notre Dame/Big East #2 vs. ACC #2

POSTSEASON BOWL GAME INVOLVING DIV. I-AA TEAMS

McDONALD'S HERITAGE BOWL

Atlanta, Georgia
December 26, 1998, Time—TBD
Mr. Kyle Shields, Historically Black College Coalition (HBCC)
Game Coordinator
1401 Peachtree Street, Suite M102
Atlanta, Georgia 30309
(404) 870-8414
Televising Network: ESPN
Facility: Georgia Dome
Capacity: 71,228
Title Sponsor: McDonald's Corporation
Teams: SWAC Champion vs. MEAC Champion

1997-98 Bowl Results

Game-by-Game Summaries

LAS VEGAS BOWL

December 20, 1997
Sam Boyd Stadium
Las Vegas, Nevada

Oregon	13	13	8	7	41
Air Force	0	0	13	0	13

OR—Johnson 69 pass from Akili Smith (Frankel kick)
OR—McCullough 76 rush (kick failed)
OR—Parker blocked punt return (Frankel kick)
OR—Hartley 7 pass from Maas (Joshua Smith kick)
AF—Morgan 1 rush (Wright kick)
OR—Hartley 21 pass from Maas (Spence pass from Maas)
AF—Fisher 45 fumble return (pass failed)
OR—Johnson 78 pass from Maas (Joshua Smith kick)

Game Statistics	OR	AF
First Downs	22	11
Rushes-Yards	43-266	41-152
Passing Yards	317	59
Comp.-Att.-Int.	16-30-1	6-21-1
Punts-Avg.	6-38.7	10-36.6
Fumbles-Lost	3-2	1-1
Penalties-Yards	19-166	7-57
Time of Possession	30:22	29:38

Weather: Partly cloudy, 58 degrees
Attendance: 21,514

EAGLE ALOHA BOWL

December 25, 1997
Aloha Stadium
Honolulu, Hawaii

Washington	14	17	13	7	51
Michigan St.	7	3	7	6	23

WAS—Shehee 33 rush (Lentz kick)
WAS—Coleman 15 pass from Huard (Lentz kick)
MSU—Scott 12 pass from Schultz (Edinger kick)
WAS—Coleman 22 pass from Huard (Lentz kick)
WAS—Lentz 41 field goal
MSU—Edinger 43 field goal
WAS—Parrish 56 interception return (Lentz kick)
WAS—Shehee 10 rush (Lentz kick)
MSU—Scott 28 pass from Schultz (Edinger kick)
WAS—Reed 64 rush (kick failed)
WAS—Towns 66 interception return (Lentz kick)
MSU—Richardson 21 pass from Burke (kick failed)

Game Statistics	WAS	MSU
First Downs	25	24
First Downs	23	15
Rushes-Yards	43-298	29-47
Passing Yards	179	296
Comp.-Att.-Int.	18-30-0	20-35-3
Punts-Avg.	6-39.8	3-40.0
Fumbles-Lost	2-1	6-2
Penalties-Yards	13-126	4-28
Time of Possession	36:14	23:46

Weather: Partly cloudy, 76 degrees
Attendance: 44,598

FORD MOTOR CITY BOWL

December 26, 1997
Pontiac Silverdome
Pontiac, Michigan

Mississippi	7	0	14	13	34
Marshall	10	7	0	14	31

MIS—Avery 1 rush (Lindsey kick)
MAR—Moss 80 pass from Pennington (Malashevich kick)
MAR—Malashevich 36 field goal
MAR—Colclough 19 pass from Pennington (Malashevich kick)
MIS—Rone 13 pass from Patridge (Lindsey kick)
MIS—McAllister 20 pass from Patridge (Lindsey kick)
MAR—Chapman 6 pass from Pennington (Malashevich kick)
MIS—Heard 19 pass from Patridge (kick failed)
MAR—Chapman 9 rush (Malashevich kick)
MIS—McAllister 1 rush (Lindsey kick)

Game Statistics	MIS	MAR
First Downs	29	23
Rushes-Yards	39-179	23-170
Passing Yards	332	337
Comp.-Att.-Int.	29-48-1	23-45-0
Punts-Avg.	4-41.8	7-39.7
Fumbles-Lost	0-0	3-2
Penalties-Yards	7-71	10-93
Time of Possession	34:21	25:39

Weather: Indoors, perfect
Attendance: 43,340

INSIGHT.COM BOWL

December 27, 1997
Arizona Stadium
Tucson, Arizona

New Mexico	0	7	7	0	14
Arizona	7	6	7	0	20

AR—Eafon 15 rush (McDonald kick)
NM—Thomas 15 pass from Leigh (Cason kick)
AR—Canidate 3 rush (kick failed)
AR—Eafon 1 rush (McDonald kick)
NM—Leigh 4 rush (Cason kick)

Game Statistics	NM	AR
First Downs	16	19
Rushes-Yards	35-140	59-209
Passing Yards	150	89
Comp.-Att.-Int.	12-32-4	7-22-2
Punts-Avg.	7-40.7	9-38.7
Fumbles-Lost	0-0	0-0
Penalties-Yards	9-60	5-39
Time of Possession	24:15	35:45

Weather: Clear, 58 degrees
Attendance: 49,385

POULAN/WEED EATER INDEPENDENCE BOWL

December 28, 1997
Independence Stadium
Shreveport, Louisiana

Notre Dame	3	3	0	3	9
LSU	0	3	10	14	27

ND—Cengia 33 field goal
LSU—Richey 37 field goal
ND—Cengia 21 field goal
LSU—Richey 42 field goal
LSU—Booty 12 pass from Tyler (Richey kick)
ND—Cengia 33 field goal
LSU—Mealey 2 rush (Richey kick)
LSU—Mealey 1 rush (Richey kick)

Game Statistics	ND	LSU
First Downs	19	19
Rushes-Yards	41-128	52-265
Passing Yards	115	61
Comp.-Att.-Int.	13-25-0	5-12-0
Punts-Avg.	5-45.0	4-35.8
Fumbles-Lost	1-1	0-0
Penalties-Yards	5-30	5-55
Time of Possession	29:56	30:04

Weather: Cloudy, showers, 40 degrees
Attendance: 50,459

PLYMOUTH HOLIDAY BOWL

December 29, 1997
Qualcomm Stadium
San Diego, California

Colorado St.	7	7	14	7	35
Missouri	3	14	7	0	24

CSU—Hall 14 rush (Franz kick)
MIS—Knickman 32 field goal
MIS—Jones 4 rush (Knickman kick)
CSU—McCoy 22 pass from Moreno (Franz kick)
MIS—Blackwell 7 rush (Knickman kick)
CSU—Hall 85 punt return (Franz kick)
CSU—Davis 47 pass from Moreno (Franz kick)
MIS—Olivo 3 rush (Knickman kick)
CSU—Eslinger 23 rush (Franz kick)

Game Statistics	MIS	CSU
First Downs	17	22
Rushes-Yards	46-314	43-214
Passing Yards	68	206
Comp.-Att.-Int.	7-17-1	18-24-0
Punts-Avg.	4-44.3	5-30.6
Fumbles-Lost	3-2	1-1
Penalties-Yards	5-39	5-59
Time of Possession	27:18	32:42

Weather: Overcast, 61 degrees
Attendance: 50,761

CARQUEST BOWL

December 29, 1997
Pro Player Stadium
Miami, Florida

Georgia Tech	14	14	0	7	35
West Va.	7	7	10	6	30

GT—Wilder 1 rush (Chambers kick)
WV—Zereoue 14 rush (Taylor kick)
GT—Hamilton 30 rush (Chambers kick)
GT—Lillis 3 pass from Hamilton (Chambers kick)
WV—Porter 21 pass from Bulger (Taylor kick)
GT—Hamilton 9 rush (Chambers kick)
WV—Zereoue 19 rush (Taylor kick)
WV—Taylor 21 field goal
GT—Wiley 5 rush (Chambers kick)

WV—Porter 74 pass from Bulger (pass failed)

Game Statistics	GT	WV
First Downs	28	24
Rushes-Yards	53-210	22-56
Passing Yards	274	353
Comp.-Att.-Int.	19-36-0	25-40-1
Punts-Avg.	4-42.0	3-43.3
Fumbles-Lost	1-1	1-1
Penalties-Yards	10-86	9-75
Time of Possession	35:02	24:58

Weather: Partly cloudy, 64 degrees
Attendance: 28,262

SPORTS HUMANITARIAN BOWL

December 29, 1997
Bronco Stadium
Boise, Idaho

Cincinnati	7	14	14	0	— 35
Utah St.	0	0	13	6	— 19

CIN—Bonner 14 pass from Plummer (Judge kick)
CIN—Bonner 14 pass from Kenner (Judge kick)
CIN—Smith 1 rush (Judge kick)
CIN—Plummer 15 rush (Judge kick)
USU—Smith 75 pass from Sauk (Bohn Kick)
CIN—O. Smith 7 rush (Judge kick)
USU—Blue 3 rush (kick failed)
USU—Passey 10 fumble return (pass failed)

Game Statistics	CIN	USU
First Downs	23	15
Rushes-Yards	65-225	20-76
Passing Yards	186	253
Comp.-Att.-Int.	15-25-0	12-30-3
Punts-Avg.	5-36.8	6-32.3
Fumbles-Lost	2-1	1-1
Penalties-Yards	7-84	3-13
Time of Possession	42:17	17:43

Weather: Partly cloudy, 43 degrees
Attendance: 16,131

BUILDERS SQUARE ALAMO BOWL

December 30, 1997
The Alamodome
San Antonio, Texas

Purdue	7	3	20	3	— 33
Oklahoma St.	3	3	7	7	— 20

OSU—Sydnes 34 field goal
PUR—Alford 18 pass from Dicken (Ryan kick)
OSU—Sydnes 22 field goal
PUR—Ryan 42 field goal
PUR—Dicken 1 rush (Ryan kick)
OSU—Fobbs 21 rush (Sydnes kick)
PUR—Sutherland 16 rush (Ryan kick)
PUR—Daniels 69 pass from Dicken (Ryan kick)
PUR—Ryan 37 field goal
OSU—McQuarters 17 pass from Lindsey (Sydnes kick)

Game Statistics	PUR	OSU
First Downs	20	24
Rushes-Yards	28-129	37-162
Passing Yards	325	206
Comp.-Att.-Int.	18-36-3	17-35-3
Punts-Avg.	2-45.5	4-44.8
Fumbles-Lost	1-0	2-1
Penalties-Yards	9-81	8-70
Time of Possession	25:35	34:25

Weather: Indoor, perfect
Attendance: 55,552

NORWEST SUN BOWL

December 31, 1997
Sun Bowl
El Paso, Texas

Arizona St.	0	10	7	0	— 17
Iowa	0	0	0	7	— 7

ASU—Jackson 35 pass from Campbell (Nycz kick)
ASU—Nycz 20 field goal
ASU—Martin 1 rush (Nycz kick)
IA—Carter 26 pass from Reiners (Bromert kick)

Game Statistics	ASU	IA
First Downs	18	10
Rushes-Yards	61-268	30-19
Passing Yards	109	190
Comp.-Att.-Int.	5-11-0	12-27-0
Punts-Avg.	9-36.0	8-49.0
Fumbles-Lost	2-0	2-1
Penalties-Yards	11-90	7-44
Time of Possession	35:29	24:31

Weather: Sunny, 59 degrees
Attendance: 49,104

AXA EQUITABLE LIBERTY BOWL

December 31, 1997
Liberty Bowl
Memphis, Tennessee

Pittsburgh	0	7	0	0	— 7
Southern Miss.	7	7	14	13	— 41

USM—Gideon 31 pass from Roberts (Hardaway kick)
USM—Gideon 8 pass from Roberts (Hardaway kick)
PITT—Hoffart 89 pass from Gonzalez (Ferencik kick)
USM—Phenix 16 fumble return (Hardaway kick)
USM—Gideon 5 pass from Roberts (Hardaway kick)
USM—Thomas 26 interception return (Hardaway kick)
USM—Parrish 63 interception return (kick failed)

Game Statistics	PITT	USM
First Downs	16	15
Rushes-Yards	38-150	31-125
Passing Yards	190	227
Comp.-Att.-Int.	16-41-2	18-27-1
Punts-Avg.	7-40.3	7-36.3
Fumbles-Lost	1-1	0-0
Penalties-Yards	8-72	6-40
Time of Possession	32:55	27:05

Weather: Sunny, 43 degrees
Attendance: 50,209

OUTBACK BOWL

January 1, 1998
Houlihan's Stadium
Tampa, Florida

Wisconsin	0	0	0	6	— 6
Georgia	12	7	7	7	— 33

GA—Edwards 2 rush (kick failed)
GA—Edwards 40 rush (pass failed)
GA—Gary 3 rush (Hines kick)
GA—Edwards 13 rush (Hines kick)
GA—Allen 7 pass from Bobo (Hines kick)
WIS—Retzlaff 12 pass from Kavanaugh (kick failed)

Game Statistics	WIS	GA
First Downs	18	25
Rushes-Yards	29-74	41-207
Passing Yards	160	267
Comp.-Att.-Int.	14-36-2	26-29-0
Punts-Avg.	5-43.6	3-35.7
Fumbles-Lost	0-0	2-1
Penalties-Yards	7-71	5-59
Time of Possession	25:55	34:05

Weather: Partly cloudy, 75 degrees
Attendance: 56,186

TOYOTA GATOR BOWL

January 1, 1998
Gator Bowl
Jacksonville, Florida

Virginia Tech	0	0	3	0	— 3
North Caro.	16	6	6	14	— 42

NC—McGee 29 field goal
NC—Barnes 62 pass from Keldorf (McGee kick)
NC—Bly 6 blocked punt return (kick failed)
NC—Ellie fumble recovery in end zone (pass failed)
NC—Linton 1 rush (kick failed)
VT—Graham 40 field goal
NC—Barnes 14 pass from Keldorf (McGee kick)
NC—Carrick 4 pass from Keldorf (McGee kick)

Game Statistics	NC	VT
First Downs	18	14
Rushes-Yards	37-109	40-95
Passing Yards	318	90
Comp.-Att.-Int.	18-29-0	13-25-0
Punts-Avg.	3-40.3	6-30.8
Fumbles-Lost	0-0	6-3
Penalties-Yards	6-61	4-36
Time of Possession	29:31	30:29

Weather: Sunny, 50 degrees
Attendance: 54,116

COMPUSA FLORIDA CITRUS BOWL

January 1, 1998
Florida Citrus Bowl
Orlando, Florida

Penn St.	0	3	3	0	— 6
Florida	14	0	0	7	— 21

FLA—Brindise 1 rush (Cooper kick)
FLA—Green 35 pass from Johnson (Cooper kick)
PSU—Forney 42 field goal
PSU—Forney 30 field goal
FLA—Green 37 pass from Palmer (Cooper kick)

Game Statistics	PSU	FLA
First Downs	9	23
Rushes-Yards	29-47	59-254
Passing Yards	92	143
Comp.-Att.-Int.	10-32-3	9-19-2
Punts-Avg.	7-42.1	5-36.4
Fumbles-Lost	0-0	2-1
Penalties-Yards	1-5	5-46
Time of Possession	24:53	35:07

Weather: Partly sunny, 57 degrees
Attendance: 72,940

SOUTHWESTERN BELL COTTON BOWL

January 1, 1998
The Cotton Bowl
Dallas, Texas

UCLA	0	7	14	8	— 29
Texas A&M	7	9	7	0	— 23

A&M—Jennings 64 interception return (Bryant kick)
A&M—Team Safety
A&M—Hall 74 rush (Bryant kick)
UCLA—McElroy 22 pass from McNown (Sailer kick)
UCLA—Hicks 41 pass from McNown (Sailer kick)
A&M—Cole 43 rush (Bryant kick)
UCLA—McNown 20 rush (Sailer kick)
UCLA—Neufeld 5 rush (McNown run)

Game Statistics	UCLA	A&M
First Downs	23	10
Rushes-Yards	48-154	40-192
Passing Yards	239	55
Comp.-Att.-Int.	16-30-1	7-14-1
Punts-Avg.	8-43.6	9-45.3
Fumbles-Lost	3-0	1-0
Penalties-Yards	7-73	4-38
Time of Possession	33:04	26:56

Weather: Partly cloudy, 53 degrees
Attendance: 59,215

ROSE BOWL

January 1, 1998
The Rose Bowl
Pasadena, California

Washington St.	7	0	6	3	— 16
Michigan	0	7	7	7	— 21

WSU—McKenzie 15 pass from Leaf (Lindell kick)
MICH—Streets 53 pass from Griese (Baker kick)
WSU—Tims 14 rush (kick blocked)
MICH—Streets 58 pass from Griese (Baker kick)
MICH—Tuman 23 pass from Griese (Baker kick)
WSU—Lindell 48 field goal

Game Statistics	WSU	MICH
First Downs	18	22
Rushes-Yards	28-67	41-128
Passing Yards	331	251
Comp.-Att.-Int.	17-35-1	18-30-1
Punts-Avg.	6-40.3	6-30.5
Fumbles-Lost	2-0	0-0
Penalties-Yards	4-43	4-40
Time of Possession	27:46	32;14

Weather: Hazy, 75 degrees
Attendance: 101,219

CHICK-FIL-A PEACH BOWL

January 2, 1998
Georgia Dome
Atlanta, Georgia

Clemson	0	7	10	0	— 17
Auburn	3	3	0	15	— 21

AUB—Holmes 52 field goal
CLEM—Speck 18 blocked punt return (Richardson kick)
AUB—Holmes 24 field goal
CLEM—Witherspoon 2 rush (Richardson kick)
CLEM—Richardson 48 field goal
AUB—Craig 22 rush (pass failed)
AUB—Williams 7 rush (pass failed)
AUB—Holmes 22 field goal

Game Statistics	CLEM	AUB
First Downs	4	18
Rushes-Yards	27-60	36-108
Passing Yards	86	258
Comp.-Att.-Int.	11-25-1	15-45-0
Punts-Avg.	9-43.7	6-25.8

Fumbles-Lost	1-0	1-1
Penalties-Yards	5-59	7-63
Time of Possession	27:59	32:01

Weather: Indoors, perfect
Attendance: 71,212

ALLIANCE BOWLS 1997-98:

TOSTITOS FIESTA BOWL

December 31, 1997
Sun Devil Stadium
Tempe, Arizona

Kansas St.	0	21	9	14	— 35
Syracuse	3	12	0	3	— 18

SYR—Trout 27 field goal
KSU—McDonald 19 pass from Bishop (Gramatica kick)
KSU—Bishop 12 rush (Gramatica kick)
KSU—Swift 28 pass from Bishop (Gramatica kick)
SYR—Brown 24 rush (Trout kick)
SYR—Team safety
SYR—Trout 33 field goal
KSU—McDonald 77 pass from Bishop (Gramatica kick)
SYR—Trout 40 field goal
KSU—McDonald 41 pass from Bishop (Gramatica kick)

Game Statistics	KSU	SYR
First Downs	21	24
Rushes-Yards	40-140	38-176
Passing Yards	317	271
Comp.-Att.-Int.	14-23-1	16-39-1
Punts-Avg.	3-44.0	5-43.0
Fumbles-Lost	0-0	1-1
Penalties-Yards	7-58	8-68
Time of Possession	29:30	30:30

Weather: Partly cloudy, 72 degrees
Attendance: 69,367

NOKIA SUGAR BOWL

January 1, 1998
Louisiana Superdome
New Orleans, Louisiana

Ohio St.	3	0	5	6	— 14
Florida St.	7	14	0	10	— 31

OSU—Stultz 40 field goal
FSU—E. G. Green 27 pass from Busby (Janikowski kick)
FSU—Busby 9 rush (Janikowski kick)
FSU—McCray 1 rush (Janikowski kick)
OSU—Stultz 34 field goal
OSU—Team safety
FSU—Janikowski 35 field goal
OSU—Lumpkin 50 pass from Germaine (pass failed)
FSU—McCray 1 rush (Janikowski kick)

Game Statistics	OSU	FSU
First Downs	21	18
Rushes-Yards	44-118	27-60
Passing Yards	207	334
Comp.-Att.-Int.	16-36-3	22-33-2
Punts-Avg.	7-45.4	6-42.7
Fumbles-Lost	1-0	0-0
Penalties-Yards	10-70	9-74
Time of Possession	35:04	24:56

Weather: Indoors, perfect
Attendance: 67,289

FEDEX ORANGE BOWL

January 2, 1998
Pro Player Stadium
Miami, Florida

Tennessee	0	3	6	8	— 17
Nebraska	7	7	21	7	— 42

NEB—Green 1 rush (Brown kick)
NEB—Wiggins 10 rush (Brown kick)
TENN—Hall 44 field goal
NEB—Frost 1 rush (Brown kick)
NEB—Frost 11 rush (Brown kick)
TENN—Price 5 pass from Manning (pass failed)
NEB—Green 22 rush (Brown kick)
NEB—Frost 9 rush (Brown kick)
TENN—McCullough 3 pass from Martin (Stephens pass from Martin)

Game Statistics	TENN	NEB
First Downs	16	30
Rushes-Yards	21-128	68-409
Passing Yards	187	125
Comp.-Att.-Int.	25-35-1	9-12-0
Punts-Avg.	6-52.3	4-39.0
Fumbles-Lost	2-2	3-2
Penalties-Yards	5-37	8-63
Time of Possession	23:57	36:03

Weather: Cool, cloudy, 57 degrees
Attendance: 72,385

All-Time Bowl-Game Results

Major Bowl Games

ROSE BOWL

Present Site: Pasadena, Calif.
Stadium (Capacity): Rose Bowl (96,576)
Playing Surface: Grass
Playing Sites: Tournament Park, Pasadena (1902, 1916-22); Rose Bowl, Pasadena (1923-41); Duke Stadium, Durham, N.C. (1942); Rose Bowl (since 1943)

1-1-02—Michigan 49, Stanford 0
1-1-16—Washington St. 14, Brown 0
1-1-17—Oregon 14, Pennsylvania 0
1-1-18—Mare Island 19, Camp Lewis 7
1-1-19—Great Lakes 17, Mare Island 0

1-1-20—Harvard 7, Oregon 6
1-1-21—California 28, Ohio St. 0
1-2-22—California 0, Wash. & Jeff. 0
1-1-23—Southern Cal 14, Penn St. 3
1-1-24—Navy 14, Washington 14

1-1-25—Notre Dame 27, Stanford 10
1-1-26—Alabama 20, Washington 19
1-1-27—Alabama 7, Stanford 7
1-2-28—Stanford 7, Pittsburgh 6
1-1-29—Georgia Tech 8, California 7

1-1-30—Southern Cal 47, Pittsburgh 14
1-1-31—Alabama 24, Washington St. 0
1-1-32—Southern Cal 21, Tulane 12
1-2-33—Southern Cal 35, Pittsburgh 0
1-1-34—Columbia 7, Stanford 0

1-1-35—Alabama 29, Stanford 13
1-1-36—Stanford 7, Southern Methodist 0
1-1-37—Pittsburgh 21, Washington 0
1-1-38—California 13, Alabama 0
1-2-39—Southern Cal 7, Duke 3

1-1-40—Southern Cal 14, Tennessee 0
1-1-41—Stanford 21, Nebraska 13
1-1-42—Oregon St. 20, Duke 16 (at Durham)
1-1-43—Georgia 9, UCLA 0
1-1-44—Southern Cal 29, Washington 0

1-1-45—Southern Cal 25, Tennessee 0
1-1-46—Alabama 34, Southern Cal 14
1-1-47—Illinois 45, UCLA 14
1-1-48—Michigan 49, Southern Cal 0
1-1-49—Northwestern 20, California 14

1-2-50—Ohio St. 17, California 14
1-1-51—Michigan 14, California 6
1-1-52—Illinois 40, Stanford 7
1-1-53—Southern Cal 7, Wisconsin 0
1-1-54—Michigan St. 28, UCLA 20

1-1-55—Ohio St. 20, Southern Cal 7
1-2-56—Michigan St. 17, UCLA 14
1-1-57—Iowa 35, Oregon St. 19
1-1-58—Ohio St. 10, Oregon 7
1-1-59—Iowa 38, California 12

1-1-60—Washington 44, Wisconsin 8
1-2-61—Washington 17, Minnesota 7
1-1-62—Minnesota 21, UCLA 3
1-1-63—Southern Cal 42, Wisconsin 37
1-1-64—Illinois 17, Washington 7

1-1-65—Michigan 34, Oregon St. 7
1-1-66—UCLA 14, Michigan St. 12
1-2-67—Purdue 14, Southern Cal 13
1-1-68—Southern Cal 14, Indiana 3
1-1-69—Ohio St. 27, Southern Cal 16

1-1-70—Southern Cal 10, Michigan 3
1-1-71—Stanford 27, Ohio St. 17
1-1-72—Stanford 13, Michigan 12
1-1-73—Southern Cal 42, Ohio St. 17
1-1-74—Ohio St. 42, Southern Cal 21

1-1-75—Southern Cal 18, Ohio St. 17
1-1-76—UCLA 23, Ohio St. 10
1-1-77—Southern Cal 14, Michigan 6
1-2-78—Washington 27, Michigan 20
1-1-79—Southern Cal 17, Michigan 10

1-1-80—Southern Cal 17, Ohio St. 16
1-1-81—Michigan 23, Washington 6
1-1-82—Washington 28, Iowa 0
1-1-83—UCLA 24, Michigan 14
1-2-84—UCLA 45, Illinois 9

1-1-85—Southern Cal 20, Ohio St. 17
1-1-86—UCLA 45, Iowa 28
1-1-87—Arizona St. 22, Michigan 15
1-1-88—Michigan St. 20, Southern Cal 17
1-2-89—Michigan 22, Southern Cal 14

1-1-90—Southern Cal 17, Michigan 10
1-1-91—Washington 46, Iowa 34
1-1-92—Washington 34, Michigan 14
1-1-93—Michigan 38, Washington 31
1-1-94—Wisconsin 21, UCLA 16

1-2-95—Penn St. 38, Oregon 20
1-1-96—Southern Cal 41, Northwestern 32
1-1-97—Ohio St. 20, Arizona St. 17
1-1-98—Michigan 21, Washington St. 16

ORANGE BOWL

Present Site: Miami, Fla.
Stadium (Capacity): Pro Player Stadium (75,014)
Playing Surface: Prescription Athletic Turf
Name Changes: Orange Bowl (1935-88); Federal Express Orange Bowl (since 1989)
Playing Sites: Miami Field Stadium (1935-37); Orange Bowl (1938-96); renamed Pro Player Stadium (since 1997)

1-1-35—Bucknell 26, Miami (Fla.) 0
1-1-36—Catholic 20, Mississippi 19
1-1-37—Duquesne 13, Mississippi St. 12
1-1-38—Auburn 6, Michigan St. 0
1-2-39—Tennessee 17, Oklahoma 0

1-1-40—Georgia Tech 21, Missouri 7
1-1-41—Mississippi St. 14, Georgetown 7
1-1-42—Georgia 40, Texas Christian 26
1-1-43—Alabama 37, Boston College 21
1-1-44—LSU 19, Texas A&M 14

1-1-45—Tulsa 26, Georgia Tech 12
1-1-46—Miami (Fla.) 13, Holy Cross 6
1-1-47—Rice 8, Tennessee 0
1-1-48—Georgia Tech 20, Kansas 14
1-1-49—Texas 41, Georgia 28

1-2-50—Santa Clara 21, Kentucky 13
1-1-51—Clemson 15, Miami (Fla.) 14
1-1-52—Georgia Tech 17, Baylor 14
1-1-53—Alabama 61, Syracuse 6
1-1-54—Oklahoma 7, Maryland 0

1-1-55—Duke 34, Nebraska 7
1-2-56—Oklahoma 20, Maryland 6
1-1-57—Colorado 27, Clemson 21
1-1-58—Oklahoma 48, Duke 21
1-1-59—Oklahoma 21, Syracuse 6

1-1-60—Georgia 14, Missouri 0
1-2-61—Missouri 21, Navy 14
1-1-62—LSU 25, Colorado 7
1-1-63—Alabama 17, Oklahoma 0
1-1-64—Nebraska 13, Auburn 7

1-1-65—Texas 21, Alabama 17
1-1-66—Alabama 39, Nebraska 28
1-2-67—Florida 27, Georgia Tech 12
1-1-68—Oklahoma 26, Tennessee 24
1-1-69—Penn St. 15, Kansas 14

1-1-70—Penn St. 10, Missouri 3
1-1-71—Nebraska 17, LSU 12
1-1-72—Nebraska 38, Alabama 6
1-1-73—Nebraska 40, Notre Dame 6
1-1-74—Penn St. 16, LSU 9

1-1-75—Notre Dame 13, Alabama 11
1-1-76—Oklahoma 14, Michigan 6
1-1-77—Ohio St. 27, Colorado 10
1-2-78—Arkansas 31, Oklahoma 6
1-1-79—Oklahoma 31, Nebraska 24

1-1-80—Oklahoma 24, Florida St. 7
1-1-81—Oklahoma 18, Florida St. 17
1-1-82—Clemson 22, Nebraska 15
1-1-83—Nebraska 21, LSU 20

1-2-84—Miami (Fla.) 31, Nebraska 30

1-1-85—Washington 28, Oklahoma 17
1-1-86—Oklahoma 25, Penn St. 10
1-1-87—Oklahoma 42, Arkansas 8
1-1-88—Miami (Fla.) 20, Oklahoma 14
1-2-89—Miami (Fla.) 23, Nebraska 3

1-1-90—Notre Dame 21, Colorado 6
1-1-91—Colorado 10, Notre Dame 9
1-1-92—Miami (Fla.) 22, Nebraska 0
1-1-93—Florida St. 27, Nebraska 14
1-1-94—Florida St. 18, Nebraska 16

1-1-95—Nebraska 24, Miami (Fla.) 17
1-1-96—Florida St. 31, Notre Dame 26
12-31-96—Nebraska 41, Virginia Tech 21
1-2-98—Nebraska 42, Tennessee 17

SUGAR BOWL

Present Site: New Orleans, La.
Stadium (Capacity): Louisiana Superdome (71,023)
Playing Surface: AstroTurf
Name Changes: Sugar Bowl (1935-87); USF&G Sugar Bowl (1988-95); Nokia Sugar Bowl (since 1996)
Playing Sites: Tulane Stadium, New Orleans (1935-74); Louisiana Superdome (since 1975)

1-1-35—Tulane 20, Temple 14
1-1-36—Texas Christian 3, LSU 2
1-1-37—Santa Clara 21, LSU 14
1-1-38—Santa Clara 6, LSU 0
1-2-39—Texas Christian 15, Carnegie Mellon 7

1-1-40—Texas A&M 14, Tulane 13
1-1-41—Boston College 19, Tennessee 13
1-1-42—Fordham 2, Missouri 0
1-1-43—Tennessee 14, Tulsa 7
1-1-44—Georgia Tech 20, Tulsa 18

1-1-45—Duke 29, Alabama 26
1-1-46—Oklahoma St. 33, St. Mary's (Cal.) 13
1-1-47—Georgia 20, North Caro. 10
1-1-48—Texas 27, Alabama 7
1-1-49—Oklahoma 14, North Caro. 6

1-2-50—Oklahoma 35, LSU 0
1-1-51—Kentucky 13, Oklahoma 7
1-1-52—Maryland 28, Tennessee 13
1-1-53—Georgia Tech 24, Mississippi 7
1-1-54—Georgia Tech 42, West Va. 19

1-1-55—Navy 21, Mississippi 0
1-2-56—Georgia Tech 7, Pittsburgh 0
1-1-57—Baylor 13, Tennessee 7
1-1-58—Mississippi 39, Texas 7
1-1-59—LSU 7, Clemson 0

1-1-60—Mississippi 21, LSU 0
1-2-61—Mississippi 14, Rice 6
1-1-62—Alabama 10, Arkansas 3
1-1-63—Mississippi 17, Arkansas 13
1-1-64—Alabama 12, Mississippi 7

1-1-65—LSU 13, Syracuse 10
1-1-66—Missouri 20, Florida 18
1-2-67—Alabama 34, Nebraska 7
1-1-68—LSU 20, Wyoming 13
1-1-69—Arkansas 16, Georgia 2

1-1-70—Mississippi 27, Arkansas 22
1-1-71—Tennessee 34, Air Force 13
1-1-72—Oklahoma 40, Auburn 22
12-31-72—Oklahoma 14, Penn St. 0
12-31-73—Notre Dame 24, Alabama 23

12-31-74—Nebraska 13, Florida 10
12-31-75—Alabama 13, Penn St. 6
1-1-77—Pittsburgh 27, Georgia 3
1-2-78—Alabama 35, Ohio St. 6
1-1-79—Alabama 14, Penn St. 7

1-1-80—Alabama 24, Arkansas 9
1-1-81—Georgia 17, Notre Dame 10
1-1-82—Pittsburgh 24, Georgia 20
1-1-83—Penn St. 27, Georgia 23
1-2-84—Auburn 9, Michigan 7

1-1-85—Nebraska 28, LSU 10
1-1-86—Tennessee 35, Miami (Fla.) 7
1-1-87—Nebraska 30, LSU 15
1-1-88—Auburn 16, Syracuse 16
1-2-89—Florida St. 13, Auburn 7

1-1-90—Miami (Fla.) 33, Alabama 25
1-1-91—Tennessee 23, Virginia 22
1-1-92—Notre Dame 39, Florida 28
1-1-93—Alabama 34, Miami (Fla.) 13
1-1-94—Florida 41, West Va. 7

1-2-95—Florida St. 23, Florida 17
12-31-95—Virginia Tech 28, Texas 10
1-2-97—Florida 52, Florida St. 20
1-1-98—Florida St. 31, Ohio St. 14

COTTON BOWL

Present Site: Dallas, Tex.
Stadium (Capacity): Cotton Bowl (68,252)
Playing Surface: Grass
Name Changes: Cotton Bowl (1937-88, 1996); Mobil Cotton Bowl (1989-95); Southwestern Bell Cotton Bowl (since 1997)
Playing Sites: Fair Park Stadium, Dallas (1937); Cotton Bowl (since 1938)

1-1-37—Texas Christian 16, Marquette 6
1-1-38—Rice 28, Colorado 14
1-2-39—St. Mary's (Cal.) 20, Texas Tech 13
1-1-40—Clemson 6, Boston College 3
1-1-41—Texas A&M 13, Fordham 12

1-1-42—Alabama 29, Texas A&M 21
1-1-43—Texas 14, Georgia Tech 7
1-1-44—Randolph Field 7, Texas 7
1-1-45—Oklahoma St. 34, Texas Christian 0
1-1-46—Texas 40, Missouri 27

1-1-47—Arkansas 0, LSU 0
1-1-48—Penn St. 13, Southern Methodist 13
1-1-49—Southern Methodist 21, Oregon 13
1-2-50—Rice 27, North Caro. 13
1-1-51—Tennessee 20, Texas 14

1-1-52—Kentucky 20, Texas Christian 7
1-1-53—Texas 16, Tennessee 0
1-1-54—Rice 28, Alabama 6
1-1-55—Georgia Tech 14, Arkansas 6
1-2-56—Mississippi 14, Texas Christian 13

1-1-57—Texas Christian 28, Syracuse 27
1-1-58—Navy 20, Rice 7
1-1-59—Air Force 0, Texas Christian 0
1-1-60—Syracuse 23, Texas 14
1-2-61—Duke 7, Arkansas 6

1-1-62—Texas 12, Mississippi 7
1-1-63—LSU 13, Texas 0
1-1-64—Texas 28, Navy 6
1-1-65—Arkansas 10, Nebraska 7
1-1-66—LSU 14, Arkansas 7

12-31-66—Georgia 24, Southern Methodist 9
1-1-68—Texas A&M 20, Alabama 16
1-1-69—Texas 36, Tennessee 13
1-1-70—Texas 21, Notre Dame 17
1-1-71—Notre Dame 24, Texas 11

1-1-72—Penn St. 30, Texas 6
1-1-73—Texas 17, Alabama 13
1-1-74—Nebraska 19, Texas 3
1-1-75—Penn St. 41, Baylor 20
1-1-76—Arkansas 31, Georgia 10

1-1-77—Houston 30, Maryland 21
1-2-78—Notre Dame 38, Texas 10
1-1-79—Notre Dame 35, Houston 34
1-1-80—Houston 17, Nebraska 14
1-1-81—Alabama 30, Baylor 2

1-1-82—Texas 14, Alabama 12
1-1-83—Southern Methodist 7, Pittsburgh 3
1-2-84—Georgia 10, Texas 9
1-1-85—Boston College 45, Houston 28
1-1-86—Texas A&M 36, Auburn 16

1-1-87—Ohio St. 28, Texas A&M 12
1-1-88—Texas A&M 35, Notre Dame 10
1-2-89—UCLA 17, Arkansas 3
1-1-90—Tennessee 31, Arkansas 27
1-1-91—Miami (Fla.) 46, Texas 3

1-1-92—Florida St. 10, Texas A&M 2
1-1-93—Notre Dame 28, Texas A&M 3
1-1-94—Notre Dame 24, Texas A&M 21
1-2-95—Southern Cal 55, Texas Tech 14
1-1-96—Colorado 38, Oregon 6
1-1-97—Brigham Young 19, Kansas St. 15
1-1-98—UCLA 29, Texas A&M 23

NORWEST SUN BOWL

Present Site: El Paso, Tex.
Stadium (Capacity): Sun Bowl (51,270)
Playing Surface: AstroTurf
Name Changes: Sun Bowl (1936-86, 1994-95); John Hancock Sun Bowl (1987-88); John Hancock Bowl (1989-93); Norwest Bank Sun Bowl (1996); Norwest Sun Bowl (since 1997)
Playing Sites: Kidd Field, UTEP, El Paso (1936-62); Sun Bowl (since 1963)

1-1-36—Hardin-Simmons 14, New Mexico St. 14
1-1-37—Hardin-Simmons 34, UTEP 6
1-1-38—West Va. 7, Texas Tech 6
1-2-39—Utah 26, New Mexico 0
1-1-40—Arizona St. 0, Catholic 0

1-1-41—Case Reserve 26, Arizona St. 13
1-1-42—Tulsa 6, Texas Tech 0
1-1-43—Second Air Force 13, Hardin-Simmons 7
1-1-44—Southwestern (Tex.) 7, New Mexico 0
1-1-45—Southwestern (Tex.) 35, U. of Mexico 0

1-1-46—New Mexico 34, Denver 24
1-1-47—Cincinnati 18, Virginia Tech 6
1-1-48—Miami (Ohio) 13, Texas Tech 12
1-1-49—West Va. 21, UTEP 12
1-2-50—UTEP 33, Georgetown 20

1-1-51—West Tex. A&M 14, Cincinnati 13
1-1-52—Texas Tech 25, Pacific (Cal.) 14
1-1-53—Pacific (Cal.) 26, Southern Miss. 7
1-1-54—UTEP 37, Southern Miss. 14
1-1-55—UTEP 47, Florida St. 20

1-2-56—Wyoming 21, Texas Tech 14
1-1-57—Geo. Washington 13, UTEP 0
1-1-58—Louisville 34, Drake 20
12-31-58—Wyoming 14, Hardin-Simmons 6
12-31-59—New Mexico St. 28, North Texas 8

12-31-60—New Mexico St. 20, Utah St. 13
12-30-61—Villanova 17, Wichita St. 9
12-31-62—West Tex. A&M 15, Ohio 14
12-31-63—Oregon 21, Southern Methodist 14
12-26-64—Georgia 7, Texas Tech 0

12-31-65—UTEP 13, Texas Christian 12
12-24-66—Wyoming 28, Florida St. 20
12-30-67—UTEP 14, Mississippi 7
12-28-68—Auburn 34, Arizona 10
12-20-69—Nebraska 45, Georgia 6

12-19-70—Georgia Tech 17, Texas Tech 9
12-18-71—LSU 33, Iowa St. 15
12-30-72—North Caro. 32, Texas Tech 28
12-29-73—Missouri 34, Auburn 17
12-28-74—Mississippi St. 26, North Caro. 24

12-26-75—Pittsburgh 33, Kansas 19
1-2-77—Texas A&M 37, Florida 14
12-31-77—Stanford 24, LSU 14
12-23-78—Texas 42, Maryland 0
12-22-79—Washington 14, Texas 7

12-27-80—Nebraska 31, Mississippi St. 17
12-26-81—Oklahoma 40, Houston 14
12-25-82—North Caro. 26, Texas 10
12-24-83—Alabama 28, Southern Methodist 7
12-22-84—Maryland 28, Tennessee 27

12-28-85—Arizona 13, Georgia 13
12-25-86—Alabama 28, Washington 6
12-25-87—Oklahoma St. 35, West Va. 33
12-24-88—Alabama 29, Army 28
12-30-89—Pittsburgh 31, Texas A&M 28

12-31-90—Michigan St. 17, Southern Cal 16
12-31-91—UCLA 6, Illinois 3
12-31-92—Baylor 20, Arizona 15
12-24-93—Oklahoma 41, Texas Tech 10
12-30-94—Texas 35, North Caro. 31

12-29-95—Iowa 38, Washington 18
12-31-96—Stanford 38, Michigan St. 0
12-31-97—Arizona St. 17, Iowa 7

GATOR BOWL

Present Site: Jacksonville, Fla.
Stadium (Capacity): Alltel Stadium (76,976)
Playing Surface: Grass
Name Changes: Gator Bowl (1946-85, 1991); Mazda Gator Bowl (1986-90); Outback Steakhouse Gator Bowl (1992-94); Toyota Gator Bowl (since 1995)
Playing Sites: Gator Bowl name changed to Alltel Stadium 1998; Gator Bowl (1946-93, 1996, since 1997); Ben Hill Griffin Stadium, Gainesville, Fla. (1994); Jacksonville Municipal Stadium (1997)

1-1-46—Wake Forest 26, South Caro. 14
1-1-47—Oklahoma 34, North Caro. St. 13
1-1-48—Georgia 20, Maryland 20
1-1-49—Clemson 24, Missouri 23
1-2-50—Maryland 20, Missouri 7

1-1-51—Wyoming 20, Wash. & Lee 7
1-1-52—Miami (Fla.) 14, Clemson 0
1-1-53—Florida 14, Tulsa 13
1-1-54—Texas Tech 35, Auburn 13
12-31-54—Auburn 33, Baylor 13

12-31-55—Vanderbilt 25, Auburn 13
12-29-56—Georgia Tech 21, Pittsburgh 14
12-28-57—Tennessee 3, Texas A&M 0
12-27-58—Mississippi 7, Florida 3
1-2-60—Arkansas 14, Georgia Tech 7

12-31-60—Florida 13, Baylor 12
12-30-61—Penn St. 30, Georgia Tech 15
12-29-62—Florida 17, Penn St. 7
12-28-63—North Caro. 35, Air Force 0
1-2-65—Florida St. 36, Oklahoma 19

12-31-65—Georgia Tech 31, Texas Tech 21
12-31-66—Tennessee 18, Syracuse 12
12-30-67—Florida St. 17, Penn St. 17
12-28-68—Missouri 35, Alabama 10
12-27-69—Florida 14, Tennessee 13

1-2-71—Auburn 35, Mississippi 28
12-31-71—Georgia 7, North Caro. 3
12-30-72—Auburn 24, Colorado 3
12-29-73—Texas Tech 28, Tennessee 19
12-30-74—Auburn 27, Texas 3

12-29-75—Maryland 13, Florida 0
12-27-76—Notre Dame 20, Penn St. 9
12-30-77—Pittsburgh 34, Clemson 3
12-29-78—Clemson 17, Ohio St. 15
12-28-79—North Caro. 17, Michigan 15

12-29-80—Pittsburgh 37, South Caro. 9
12-28-81—North Caro. 31, Arkansas 27
12-30-82—Florida St. 31, West Va. 12
12-30-83—Florida 14, Iowa 6
12-28-84—Oklahoma St. 21, South Caro. 14

12-30-85—Florida St. 34, Oklahoma St. 23
12-27-86—Clemson 27, Stanford 21
12-31-87—LSU 30, South Caro. 13
1-1-89—Georgia 34, Michigan St. 27
12-30-89—Clemson 27, West Va. 7

1-1-91—Michigan 35, Mississippi 3
12-29-91—Oklahoma 48, Virginia 14
12-31-92—Florida 27, North Caro. St. 10
12-31-93—Alabama 24, North Caro. 10
12-30-94—Tennessee 45, Virginia Tech 23 (at Gainesville)

1-1-96—Syracuse 41, Clemson 0
1-1-97—North Caro. 20, West Va. 13
1-1-98—North Caro. 42, Virginia Tech 3

FLORIDA CITRUS BOWL

Present Site: Orlando, Fla.
Stadium (Capacity): Florida Citrus Bowl (70,000)
Playing Surface: Grass
Name Changes: Tangerine Bowl (1947-82); Florida Citrus Bowl (1983-93); CompUSA Florida Citrus Bowl (since 1994)
Playing Sites: Tangerine Bowl, Orlando (1947-72); Florida Field, Gainesville (1973); Tangerine Bowl (now Florida Citrus Bowl) (1974-82); Orlando Stadium (now Florida Citrus Bowl) (1983-85); Florida Citrus Bowl (since 1986)

1-1-47—Catawba 31, Maryville (Tenn.) 6
1-1-48—Catawba 7, Marshall 0
1-1-49—Murray St. 21, Sul Ross St. 21
1-2-50—St. Vincent 7, Emory & Henry 6
1-1-51—Morris Harvey 35, Emory & Henry 14

1-1-52—Stetson 35, Arkansas St. 20
1-1-53—East Tex. St. 33, Tennessee Tech 0
1-1-54—Arkansas St. 7, East Tex. St. 7
1-1-55—Neb.-Omaha 7, Eastern Ky. 6
1-2-56—Juniata 6, Missouri Valley 6

1-1-57—West Tex. A&M 20, Southern Miss. 13
1-1-58—East Tex. St. 10, Southern Miss. 9
12-27-58—East Tex. St. 26, Missouri Valley 7
1-1-60—Middle Tenn. St. 21, Presbyterian 12
12-30-60—Citadel 27, Tennessee Tech 0

12-29-61—Lamar 21, Middle Tenn. St. 14
12-22-62—Houston 49, Miami (Ohio) 21
12-28-63—Western Ky. 27, Coast Guard 0
12-12-64—East Caro. 14, Massachusetts 13
12-11-65—East Caro. 31, Maine 0

12-10-66—Morgan St. 14, West Chester 6
12-16-67—Tenn.-Martin 25, West Chester 8
12-27-68—Richmond 49, Ohio 42
12-26-69—Toledo 56, Davidson 33
12-28-70—Toledo 40, William & Mary 12

12-28-71—Toledo 28, Richmond 3
12-29-72—Tampa 21, Kent 18
12-22-73—Miami (Ohio) 16, Florida 7
12-21-74—Miami (Ohio) 21, Georgia 10
12-20-75—Miami (Ohio) 20, South Caro. 7

12-18-76—Oklahoma St. 49, Brigham Young 21
12-23-77—Florida St. 40, Texas Tech 17
12-23-78—North Caro. St. 30, Pittsburgh 17
12-22-79—LSU 34, Wake Forest 10
12-20-80—Florida 35, Maryland 20

12-19-81—Missouri 19, Southern Miss. 17
12-18-82—Auburn 33, Boston College 26
12-17-83—Tennessee 30, Maryland 23
12-22-84—Florida St. 17, Georgia 17
12-28-85—Ohio St. 10, Brigham Young 7

1-1-87—Auburn 16, Southern Cal 7
1-1-88—Clemson 35, Penn St. 10
1-2-89—Clemson 13, Oklahoma 6
1-1-90—Illinois 31, Virginia 21
1-1-91—Georgia Tech 45, Nebraska 21

1-1-92—California 37, Clemson 13
1-1-93—Georgia 21, Ohio St. 14
1-1-94—Penn St. 31, Tennessee 13
1-2-95—Alabama 24, Ohio St. 17
1-1-96—Tennessee 20, Ohio St. 14

1-1-97—Tennessee 48, Northwestern 28
1-1-98—Florida 21, Penn St. 6

Note: No classified major teams participated in games from January 1, 1947, through January 1, 1960, or in 1961 and 1963 through 1967.

LIBERTY BOWL

Present Site: Memphis, Tenn.
Stadium (Capacity): Liberty Bowl Memorial Stadium (62,921)
Playing Surface: Prescription Athletic Turf
Name Changes: Liberty Bowl (1959-92); St. Jude Liberty Bowl (1993-96); AXA Equitable Liberty Bowl (since 1997)
Playing Sites: Municipal Stadium, Philadelphia (1959-63); Convention Hall, Atlantic City, N.J. (1964); Liberty Bowl Memorial Stadium (since 1965)

12-19-59—Penn St. 7, Alabama 0
12-17-60—Penn St. 41, Oregon 12
12-16-61—Syracuse 15, Miami (Fla.) 14
12-15-62—Oregon St. 6, Villanova 0
12-21-63—Mississippi St. 16, North Caro. St. 12

12-19-64—Utah 32, West Va. 6
12-18-65—Mississippi 13, Auburn 7
12-10-66—Miami (Fla.) 14, Virginia Tech 7
12-16-67—North Caro. St. 14, Georgia 7
12-14-68—Mississippi 34, Virginia Tech 17

12-13-69—Colorado 47, Alabama 33
12-12-70—Tulane 17, Colorado 3
12-20-71—Tennessee 14, Arkansas 13
12-18-72—Georgia Tech 31, Iowa St. 30
12-17-73—North Caro. St. 31, Kansas 18

12-16-74—Tennessee 7, Maryland 3
12-22-75—Southern Cal 20, Texas A&M 0
12-20-76—Alabama 36, UCLA 6
12-19-77—Nebraska 21, North Caro. 17
12-23-78—Missouri 20, LSU 15

12-22-79—Penn St. 9, Tulane 6
12-27-80—Purdue 28, Missouri 25
12-30-81—Ohio St. 31, Navy 28
12-29-82—Alabama 21, Illinois 15
12-29-83—Notre Dame 19, Boston College 18

12-27-84—Auburn 21, Arkansas 15
12-27-85—Baylor 21, LSU 7
12-29-86—Tennessee 21, Minnesota 14
12-29-87—Georgia 20, Arkansas 17
12-28-88—Indiana 34, South Caro. 10

12-28-89—Mississippi 42, Air Force 29
12-27-90—Air Force 23, Ohio St. 11
12-29-91—Air Force 38, Mississippi St. 15
12-31-92—Mississippi 13, Air Force 0
12-28-93—Louisville 18, Michigan St. 7

12-31-94—Illinois 30, East Caro. 0
12-30-95—East Caro. 19, Stanford 13
12-27-96—Syracuse 30, Houston 17
12-31-97—Southern Miss. 41, Pittsburgh 7

PEACH BOWL

Present Site: Atlanta, Ga.
Stadium (Capacity): Georgia Dome (71,228)
Name Changes: Peach Bowl (1968-96); Chick-Fil-A Peach Bowl (since 1997)
Playing Surface: AstroTurf
Playing Sites: Grant Field, Atlanta (1968-70); Atlanta/Fulton County (1971-92); Georgia Dome (since 1993)

12-30-68—LSU 31, Florida St. 27
12-30-69—West Va. 14, South Caro. 3
12-30-70—Arizona St. 48, North Caro. 26
12-30-71—Mississippi 41, Georgia Tech 18
12-29-72—North Caro. St. 49, West Va. 13

12-28-73—Georgia 17, Maryland 16
12-28-74—Texas Tech 6, Vanderbilt 6
12-31-75—West Va. 13, North Caro. St. 10
12-31-76—Kentucky 21, North Caro. 0
12-31-77—North Caro. St. 24, Iowa St. 14

12-25-78—Purdue 41, Georgia Tech 21
12-31-79—Baylor 24, Clemson 18
1-2-81—Miami (Fla.) 20, Virginia Tech 10
12-31-81—West Va. 26, Florida 6
12-31-82—Iowa 28, Tennessee 22

12-30-83—Florida St. 28, North Caro. 3
12-31-84—Virginia 27, Purdue 24
12-31-85—Army 31, Illinois 29
12-31-86—Virginia Tech 25, North Caro. St. 24
1-2-88—Tennessee 27, Indiana 22

12-31-88—North Caro. St. 28, Iowa 23
12-30-89—Syracuse 19, Georgia 18
12-29-90—Auburn 27, Indiana 23
1-1-92—East Caro. 37, North Caro. St. 34
1-2-93—North Caro. 21, Mississippi St. 17

12-31-93—Clemson 14, Kentucky 13
1-1-95—North Caro. St. 28, Mississippi St. 24
12-30-95—Virginia 34, Georgia 27
12-28-96—LSU 10, Clemson 7
1-2-98—Auburn 21, Clemson 17

FIESTA BOWL

Present Site: Tempe, Ariz.
Stadium (Capacity): Sun Devil Stadium (73,259)
Playing Surface: Grass
Name Changes: Fiesta Bowl (1971-85, 1991-92); Sunkist Fiesta Bowl (1986-90); IBM OS/2 Fiesta Bowl (1993-95); Tostitos Fiesta Bowl (since 1996)
Playing Sites: Sun Devil Stadium (since 1971)

12-27-71—Arizona St. 45, Florida St. 38
12-23-72—Arizona St. 49, Missouri 35
12-21-73—Arizona St. 28, Pittsburgh 7
12-28-74—Oklahoma St. 16, Brigham Young 6
12-26-75—Arizona St. 17, Nebraska 14

12-25-76—Oklahoma 41, Wyoming 7
12-25-77—Penn St. 42, Arizona St. 30
12-25-78—Arkansas 10, UCLA 10
12-25-79—Pittsburgh 16, Arizona 10
12-26-80—Penn St. 31, Ohio St. 19

1-1-82—Penn St. 26, Southern Cal 10
1-1-83—Arizona St. 32, Oklahoma 21
1-2-84—Ohio St. 28, Pittsburgh 23
1-1-85—UCLA 39, Miami (Fla.) 37
1-1-86—Michigan 27, Nebraska 23

1-2-87—Penn St. 14, Miami (Fla.) 10
1-1-88—Florida St. 31, Nebraska 28
1-2-89—Notre Dame 34, West Va. 21
1-1-90—Florida St. 41, Nebraska 17
1-1-91—Louisville 34, Alabama 7

1-1-92—Penn St. 42, Tennessee 17
1-1-93—Syracuse 26, Colorado 22
1-1-94—Arizona 29, Miami (Fla.) 0
1-2-95—Colorado 41, Notre Dame 24
1-2-96—Nebraska 62, Florida 24

1-1-97—Penn St. 38, Texas 15
12-31-97—Kansas St. 35, Syracuse 18

INDEPENDENCE BOWL

Present Site: Shreveport, La.
Stadium (Capacity): Independence Stadium (50,459)
Playing Surface: Grass
Name Changes: Independence Bowl (1976-89); Poulan Independence Bowl (1990); Poulan/Weed Eater Independence Bowl (since 1991)
Playing Sites: Independence Stadium (since 1976)

12-13-76—McNeese St. 20, Tulsa 16
12-17-77—Louisiana Tech 24, Louisville 14
12-16-78—East Caro. 35, Louisiana Tech 13
12-15-79—Syracuse 31, McNeese St. 7
12-13-80—Southern Miss. 16, McNeese St. 14

12-12-81—Texas A&M 33, Oklahoma St. 16
12-11-82—Wisconsin 14, Kansas St. 3
12-10-83—Air Force 9, Mississippi 3
12-15-84—Air Force 23, Virginia Tech 7
12-21-85—Minnesota 20, Clemson 13

12-20-86—Mississippi 20, Texas Tech 17
12-19-87—Washington 24, Tulane 12

12-23-88—Southern Miss. 38, UTEP 18
12-16-89—Oregon 27, Tulsa 24
12-15-90—Louisiana Tech 34, Maryland 34

12-29-91—Georgia 24, Arkansas 15
12-31-92—Wake Forest 39, Oregon 35
12-31-93—Virginia Tech 45, Indiana 20
12-28-94—Virginia 20, Texas Christian 10
12-29-95—LSU 45, Michigan St. 26

12-31-96—Auburn 32, Army 29
12-28-97—LSU 27, Notre Dame 9

HOLIDAY BOWL

Present Site: San Diego, Calif.
Stadium (Capacity): Qualcomm Stadium (70,000))
Playing Surface: Grass
Name Changes: Holiday Bowl (1978-85); Sea World Holiday Bowl (1986-90); Thrifty Car Rental Holiday Bowl (1991-94); Plymouth Holiday Bowl (1995-97); Culligan Holiday Bowl (since 1998)
Playing Sites: San Diego Jack Murphy Stadium; renamed Qualcomm Stadium in 1997 (since 1978)

12-22-78—Navy 23, Brigham Young 16
12-21-79—Indiana 38, Brigham Young 37
12-19-80—Brigham Young 46, Southern Methodist 45
12-18-81—Brigham Young 38, Washington St. 36
12-17-82—Ohio St. 47, Brigham Young 17

12-23-83—Brigham Young 21, Missouri 17
12-21-84—Brigham Young 24, Michigan 17
12-22-85—Arkansas 18, Arizona St. 17
12-30-86—Iowa 39, San Diego St. 38
12-30-87—Iowa 20, Wyoming 19

12-30-88—Oklahoma St. 62, Wyoming 14
12-29-89—Penn St. 50, Brigham Young 39
12-29-90—Texas A&M 65, Brigham Young 14
12-30-91—Brigham Young 13, Iowa 13
12-30-92—Hawaii 27, Illinois 17

12-30-93—Ohio St. 28, Brigham Young 21
12-30-94—Michigan 24, Colorado St. 14
12-29-95—Kansas St. 54, Colorado St. 21
12-30-96—Colorado 33, Washington 21
12-29-97—Colorado St. 35, Missouri 24

ALOHA BOWL

Present Site: Honolulu, Hawaii
Stadium (Capacity): Aloha Stadium (50,000)
Playing Surface: AstroTurf
Name Changes: Aloha Bowl (1982-84); Eagle Aloha Bowl (1985-88); Jeep Eagle Aloha Bowl (1989-96); Eagle Aloha Bowl Football Classic (since 1997)
Playing Sites: Aloha Stadium (since 1982)

12-25-82—Washington 21, Maryland 20
12-26-83—Penn St. 13, Washington 10
12-29-84—Southern Methodist 27, Notre Dame 20
12-28-85—Alabama 24, Southern Cal 3
12-27-86—Arizona 30, North Caro. 21

12-25-87—UCLA 20, Florida 16
12-25-88—Washington St. 24, Houston 22
12-25-89—Michigan St. 33, Hawaii 13
12-25-90—Syracuse 28, Arizona 0
12-25-91—Georgia Tech 18, Stanford 17

12-25-92—Kansas 23, Brigham Young 20
12-25-93—Colorado 41, Fresno St. 30
12-25-94—Boston College 12, Kansas St. 7
12-25-95—Kansas 51, UCLA 30
12-25-96—Navy 42, California 38

12-25-97—Washington 51, Michigan St. 23

OUTBACK BOWL (Formerly Hall of Fame)

Present Site: Tampa, Fla.
Stadium (Capacity): Tampa Community (55,883)
Playing Surface: Grass
Name Changes: Hall of Fame Bowl (1986-95); Outback Bowl (since 1996)
Playing Sites: Tampa Stadium, renamed Houlihan's Stadium in 1997 (1986-97); Tampa Community Stadium (since 1998)

12-23-86—Boston College 27, Georgia 24
1-2-88—Michigan 28, Alabama 24
1-2-89—Syracuse 23, LSU 10
1-1-90—Auburn 31, Ohio St. 14
1-1-91—Clemson 30, Illinois 0

1-1-92—Syracuse 24, Ohio St. 17
1-1-93—Tennessee 38, Boston College 23
1-1-94—Michigan 42, North Caro. St. 7
1-2-95—Wisconsin 34, Duke 20
1-1-96—Penn St. 43, Auburn 14

1-1-97—Alabama 17, Michigan 14
1-1-98—Georgia 33, Wisconsin 6

INSIGHT.com BOWL

Present Site: Tucson, Ariz.
Stadium (Capacity): Arizona Stadium (57,000)
Playing Surface: Grass
Name Changes: Copper Bowl (1989, 1996); Domino's Pizza Copper Bowl (1990-91); Weiser Lock Copper Bowl (1992-95); Insight.com Bowl (since 1997)
Playing Sites: Arizona Stadium (since 1989)

12-31-89—Arizona 17, North Caro. St. 10
12-31-90—California 17, Wyoming 15
12-31-91—Indiana 24, Baylor 0
12-29-92—Washington St. 31, Utah 28
12-29-93—Kansas St. 52, Wyoming 17

12-29-94—Brigham Young 31, Oklahoma 6
12-27-95—Texas Tech 55, Air Force 41
12-27-96—Wisconsin 38, Utah 10
12-27-97—Arizona 20, New Mexico 14

SUNSHINE FOOTBALL CLASSIC BOWL (Formerly Carquest)

Present Site: Miami, Fla.
Stadium (Capacity): Pro Player Stadium (75,014)
Playing Surface: Prescription Athletic Turf
Name Changes: Blockbuster Bowl (1990-93); Carquest Bowl (1994-97); Sunshine Football Classic (since 1998)
Playing Sites: Joe Robbie Stadium (1990-95); renamed Pro Player Stadium (since 1996)

12-28-90—Florida St. 24, Penn St. 17
12-28-91—Alabama 30, Colorado 25
1-1-93—Stanford 24, Penn St. 3
1-1-94—Boston College 31, Virginia 13
1-2-95—South Caro. 24, West Va. 21

12-30-95—North Caro. 20, Arkansas 10
12-27-96—Miami (Fla.) 31, Virginia 21
12-29-97—Georgia Tech 35, West Va. 30

LAS VEGAS BOWL

Present Site: Las Vegas, Nev.
Stadium (Capacity): Sam Boyd Stadium (40,000)
Playing Surface: Monsanto Turf (retractable)
Playing Sites: Sam Boyd Stadium (since 1992)

12-18-92—Bowling Green 35, Nevada 34
12-17-93—Utah St. 42, Ball St. 33
12-15-94—UNLV 52, Central Mich. 24
12-14-95—Toledo 40, Nevada 37 (OT)
12-19-96—Nevada 18, Ball St. 15
12-20-97—Oregon 41, Air Force 13

ALAMO BOWL

Present Site: San Antonio, Tex.
Stadium (Capacity): Alamodome (65,000)
Playing Surface: AstroTurf
Playing Sites: Alamodome (since 1993)

12-31-93—California 37, Iowa 3
12-31-94—Washington St. 10, Baylor 3
12-28-95—Texas A&M 22, Michigan 20
12-29-96—Iowa 27, Texas Tech 0
12-30-97—Purdue 33, Oklahoma St. 20

HUMANITARIAN BOWL

Present Site: Boise, Idaho
Stadium (Capacity): Bronco Stadium (30,000)
Playing Surface: Blue AstroTurf
Playing Sites: Bronco Stadium (since 1997)

12-29-97—Cincinnati 35, Utah St. 19

MOTOR CITY BOWL

Present Site: Pontiac, Mich.
Stadium (Capacity): Pontiac Silverdome (79,083)
Playing Surface: AstroTurf
Playing Sites: Pontiac Silverdome (since 1997)

12-26-97—Mississippi 34, Marshall 31

Bowl-Game Title Sponsors

Bowl	Title Sponsor (Year Began)	Bowl Name (Years)
Alamo	Builders Square (since 1993)	Builders Square Alamo (since 1993)
Aloha	Jeep Division of Chrysler (since 1985)	Aloha (1982-84) Eagle Aloha (1985-88) Jeep Eagle Aloha (1989-96) Eagle Aloha Bowl Football Classic (1997) Jeep Aloha Christmas Football Classics (since 1998)
Insight.com	Domino's Pizza (1990-91) Weiser Lock (1992-95) Insight.com (since 1997)	Copper (1989, since 1996) Domino's Pizza Copper (1990-91) Weiser Lock Copper (1992-95) Insight.com (since 1997)
Cotton	Mobil (1989-95) Southwestern Bell (since 1997)	Cotton (1937-88, 1996) Mobil Cotton (1989-95) Southwestern Bell (since 1997)
Fiesta	Sunkist (1986-90) IBM (1993-95) Tostitos (since 1996)	Fiesta (1971-85; 1991-92) Sunkist Fiesta (1986-90) IBM OS/2 Fiesta (1993-95) Tostitos Fiesta (since 1996)
Florida Citrus	CompUSA (since 1994)	Tangerine (1947-82) Florida Citrus (1983-93) CompUSA Florida Citrus (since 1994)
Gator	Mazda (1986-91) Outback Steakhouse (1992-95) Toyota (since 1995)	Gator (1946-85) Mazda Gator (1986-91) Outback Steakhouse Gator (1992-94) Toyota Gator (since 1995)
Holiday	Sea World (1986-90) Thrifty Car Rental (1991-95) Plymouth (1995-97) Culligan (since 1998)	Holiday (1978-85) Sea World Holiday (1986-90) Thrifty Car Rental Holiday (1991-94) Plymouth Holiday (1995-97) Culligan Holiday (since 1998)
Humanitarian	Humanitarian Bowl Association (since 1997)	Sports Humanitarian (1997) Humanitarian (since 1998)
Independence	Poulan (1990-97) Sanford (since 1998)	Independence (1976-89) Poulan Independence (1990) Poulan/Weed Eater Independence (since 1991) Sanford Independence (since 1998)
Las Vegas	None (1992-97) Las Vegas Convention & Visitor's Authority (since 1998)	Las Vegas (since 1992) Las Vegas Convention & Visitor's Authority (since 1998)
Liberty	St. Jude (1993-96) AXA/Equitable (since 1997)	Liberty (1959-92) St. Jude Liberty (1993-96) AXA/Equitable Liberty (since 1997)
Motor City	Motor City Bowl, Inc. (1997) Ford Division (Ford Motor Company) (since 1998)	Ford Motor City (1997) Motor City (since 1998)

Bowl	Title Sponsor (Year Began)	Bowl Name (Years)
Orange	Federal Express (since 1989)	Orange (1935-88) Federal Express Orange (since 1989)
Outback	None (1986-95) Outback Steakhouse (since 1996)	Hall of Fame (1986-95) Outback (since 1996)
Peach	None (1968-96) Chick-Fil-A (since 1997)	Peach (1968-96) Chick-Fil-A Peach (since 1997)
Rose	Pasadena Tournament of Roses Association (1902, since 1916)	Rose (since 1902)
Sugar	USF&G Sugar (1988-95) Nokia Mobile Telephones (since 1996)	Sugar (1935-87) USF&G Sugar (1988-95) Nokia Sugar (since 1996)
Sun	John Hancock (1987-93) Norwest Corporation (since 1996)	John Hancock Sun (1987-88) John Hancock (1989-93) Sun (1936-86, 1994-95) Norwest Bank Sun (1996) Norwest Sun (since 1997)
Sunshine Football Classic	Blockbuster (1990-93) Carquest Auto Parts (since 1994) None (since 19980	Blockbuster (1990-93) Carquest (since 1994) Sunshine Football Classic (since 1998)

Bowl Financial Analysis, 1976-98

Year	No. Bowls	No. Teams	Total Payout	Per-Game Payout	Per-Team Payout
1976-77	11	22	$11,345,851	$515,714	$257,857
1977-78	12	24	13,323,638	1,110,303	555,152
1978-79	13	26	15,506,516	1,192,809	596,405
1979-80	13	26	17,219,624	1,324,586	662,293
1980-81	13	26	19,517,938	1,501,380	750,690
1981-82	14	28	21,791,222	1,556,516	778,258
1982-83	15	30	26,682,486	1,778,832	889,416
1983-84	15	30	32,535,788	2,169,052	1,084,526
1984-85	16	32	36,666,738	2,291,671	1,145,836
1985-86	16	32	36,995,864	2,312,242	1,156,121
1986-87	17	34	45,830,906	2,695,936	1,347,968
1987-88	17	34	48,251,516	2,838,324	1,419,162
1988-89	17	34	52,905,426	3,112,084	1,556,042
1989-90	18	36	58,208,058	3,233,781	1,616,891
1990-91	19	38	60,378,362	3,177,809	1,588,904
1991-92	18	36	63,494,554	3,527,475	1,763,738
1992-93	18	36	67,950,000	3,775,000	1,887,500
1993-94	19	38	71,006,000	3,737,158	1,868,579
1994-95	19	38	72,416,000	3,811,368	1,905,684
1995-96	18	36	101,390,000	5,632,778	2,816,389
1996-97	18	36	101,316,000	5,628,667	2,814,333
1997-98	20	40	108,750,000	5,437,500	2,718,750

27 Former Major Bowl Games

(Games in which at least one team was classified major that season)

ALAMO
(San Antonio, Texas)

1-4-47—Hardin-Simmons 20, Denver 0

ALL-AMERICAN
(Called Hall of Fame Classic, 1977-85)
(Birmingham, Ala.)

12-22-77—Maryland 17, Minnesota 7
12-20-78—Texas A&M 28, Iowa St. 12
12-29-79—Missouri 24, South Caro. 14
12-27-80—Arkansas 34, Tulane 15
12-31-81—Mississippi St. 10, Kansas 0

12-31-82—Air Force 36, Vanderbilt 28
12-22-83—West Va. 20, Kentucky 16
12-29-84—Kentucky 20, Wisconsin 19
12-31-85—Georgia Tech 17, Michigan St. 14
12-31-86—Florida St. 27, Indiana 13

12-22-87—Virginia 22, Brigham Young 16
12-29-88—Florida 14, Illinois 10
12-28-89—Texas Tech 49, Duke 21
12-28-90—North Caro. St. 31, Southern Miss. 27

AVIATION
(Dayton, Ohio)

12-9-61—New Mexico 28, Western Mich. 12

BACARDI
(Cuban National Sports Festival at Havana)

1-1-37—Auburn 7, Villanova 7

BLUEBONNET
(Houston, Texas)

12-19-59—Clemson 23, Texas Christian 7
12-17-60—Alabama 3, Texas 3
12-16-61—Kansas 33, Rice 7
12-22-62—Missouri 14, Georgia Tech 10
12-21-63—Baylor 14, LSU 7

12-19-64—Tulsa 14, Mississippi 7
12-18-65—Tennessee 27, Tulsa 6
12-17-66—Texas 19, Mississippi 0
12-23-67—Colorado 31, Miami (Fla.) 21
12-31-68—Southern Methodist 28, Oklahoma 27

12-31-69—Houston 36, Auburn 7
12-31-70—Alabama 24, Oklahoma 24
12-31-71—Colorado 29, Houston 17
12-30-72—Tennessee 24, LSU 17

12-29-73—Houston 47, Tulane 7

12-23-74—Houston 31, North Caro. St. 31
12-27-75—Texas 38, Colorado 21
12-31-76—Nebraska 27, Texas Tech 24
12-31-77—Southern Cal 47, Texas A&M 28
12-31-78—Stanford 25, Georgia 22

12-31-79—Purdue 27, Tennessee 22
12-31-80—North Caro. 16, Texas 7
12-31-81—Michigan 33, UCLA 14
12-31-82—Arkansas 28, Florida 24
12-31-83—Oklahoma St. 24, Baylor 14

12-31-84—West Va. 31, Texas Christian 14
12-31-85—Air Force 24, Texas 16
12-31-86—Baylor 21, Colorado 9
12-31-87—Texas 32, Pittsburgh 27

BLUEGRASS
(Louisville, Ky.)

12-13-58—Oklahoma St. 15, Florida St. 6

CALIFORNIA
(Fresno, Calif.)

12-19-81—Toledo 27, San Jose St. 25
12-18-82—Fresno St. 29, Bowling Green 28
12-17-83—Northern Ill. 20, Cal St. Fullerton 13
12-15-84—UNLV 30, *Toledo 13
12-14-85—Fresno St. 51, Bowling Green 7

12-13-86—San Jose St. 37, Miami (Ohio) 7
12-12-87—Eastern Mich. 30, San Jose St. 27
12-10-88—Fresno St. 35, Western Mich. 30
12-9-89—Fresno St. 27, Ball St. 6
12-8-90—San Jose St. 48, Central Mich. 24

12-14-91—Bowling Green 28, Fresno St. 21

Won by forfeit.

CAMELLIA
(Lafayette, La.)

12-30-48—Hardin-Simmons 49, Wichita St. 12

CHERRY
(Pontiac, Mich.)

12-22-84—Army 10, Michigan St. 6
12-21-85—Maryland 35, Syracuse 18

DELTA
(Memphis, Tenn.)

1-1-48—Mississippi 13, Texas Christian 9
1-1-49—William & Mary 20, Oklahoma St. 0

DIXIE BOWL
(Birmingham, Ala.)

1-1-48—Arkansas 21, William & Mary 19
1-1-49—Baylor 20, Wake Forest 7

DIXIE CLASSIC
(Dallas, Texas)

1-2-22—Texas A&M 22, Centre 14
1-1-25—West Va. Wesleyan 9, Southern Methodist 7
1-1-34—Arkansas 7, Centenary (La.) 7

FORT WORTH CLASSIC
(Fort Worth, Texas)

1-1-21—Centre 63, Texas Christian 7

FREEDOM BOWL
(Anaheim, Calif.)

12-26-84—Iowa 55, Texas 17
12-30-85—Washington 20, Colorado 17
12-30-86—UCLA 31, Brigham Young 10
12-30-87—Arizona St. 33, Air Force 28
12-29-88—Brigham Young 20, Colorado 17

12-30-89—Washington 34, Florida 7
12-29-90—Colorado St. 32, Oregon 31
12-30-91—Tulsa 28, San Diego St. 17
12-29-92—Fresno St. 24, Southern Cal 7
12-30-93—Southern Cal 28, Utah 21

12-27-94—Utah 16, Arizona 13

GARDEN STATE
(East Rutherford, N.J.)

12-16-78—Arizona St. 34, Rutgers 18
12-15-79—Temple 28, California 17
12-14-80—Houston 35, Navy 0
12-13-81—Tennessee 28, Wisconsin 21

GOTHAM
(New York, N.Y.)

12-9-61—Baylor 24, Utah St. 9
12-15-62—Nebraska 36, Miami (Fla.) 34

GREAT LAKES
(Cleveland, Ohio)

12-6-47—Kentucky 24, Villanova 14

HARBOR
(San Diego, Calif.)

1-1-47—Montana St. 13, New Mexico 13
1-1-48—Hardin-Simmons 53, San Diego St. 0
1-1-49—Villanova 27, Nevada 7

LOS ANGELES CHRISTMAS FESTIVAL
(Los Angeles, Calif.)

12-25-24—Southern Cal 20, Missouri 7

MERCY
(Los Angeles, Calif.)

11-23-61—Fresno St. 36, Bowling Green 6

OIL
(Houston, Texas)

1-1-46—Georgia 20, Tulsa 6
1-1-47—Georgia Tech 41, St. Mary's (Cal.) 19

PASADENA
(Called Junior Rose in 1967)
(Pasadena, Calif.)

12-2-67—West Tex. A&M 35, Cal St. Northridge 13
12-6-69—San Diego St. 28, Boston U. 7
12-19-70—Long Beach St. 24, Louisville 24
12-18-71—Memphis 28, San Jose St. 9

PRESIDENTIAL CUP
(College Park, Md.)

12-9-50—Texas A&M 40, Georgia 20

RAISIN
(Fresno, Calif.)

1-1-46—Drake 13, Fresno St. 12
1-1-47—San Jose St. 20, Utah St. 0
1-1-48—Pacific (Cal.) 26, Wichita St. 14
1-1-49—Occidental 21, Colorado St. 20
12-31-49—San Jose St. 20, Texas Tech 13

SALAD
(Phoenix, Ariz.)

1-1-48—Nevada 13, North Texas 6
1-1-49—Drake 14, Arizona 13
1-1-50—Xavier (Ohio) 33, Arizona St. 21
1-1-51—Miami (Ohio) 34, Arizona St. 21
1-1-52—Houston 26, Dayton 21

SAN DIEGO EAST-WEST CHRISTMAS CLASSIC
(San Diego, Calif.)

12-26-21—Centre 38, Arizona 0
12-25-22—West Va. 21, Gonzaga 13

SHRINE
(Little Rock, Ark.)

12-18-48—Hardin-Simmons 40, Ouachita Baptist 12

Other Major Postseason Games

There was a proliferation of postseason benefit games specially scheduled at the conclusion of the regular season during the Great Depression (principally in 1931) to raise money for relief of the unemployed in response to the President's Committee on Mobilization of Relief Resources and for other charitable causes.

The exact number of these games is unknown, but it is estimated that more than 100 college games were played nationwide during this period, often irrespective of the competing teams' records.

Most notable among these postseason games were the Tennessee-New York University game of 1931 and the Army-Navy contests of 1930 and 1931 (the two academies had severed athletics relations during 1928-31 and did not meet in regular-season play). All three games were played before huge crowds in New York City's Yankee Stadium.

Following is a list of the principal postseason benefit and charity games involving at least one major college. Not included (nor included in all-time team won-lost records) are several special feature, same-day double-header tournaments in 1931 in which four participating teams were paired to play halves or modified quarters.

Date	Site	Opposing Teams
12-6-30	New York	Colgate 7, New York U. 0
12-13-30	New York	Army 6, Navy 0
11-28-31	Kansas City	Temple 38, Missouri 6
11-28-31	Chicago	Purdue 7, Northwestern 0
11-28-31	Minneapolis	Minnesota 19, Ohio St. 7
11-28-31	Ann Arbor	Michigan 16, Wisconsin 0
11-28-31	Philadelphia	Penn St. 31, Lehigh 0
12-2-31	Chattanooga	Alabama 49, Tenn.-Chatt. 0
12-3-31	Brooklyn	Manhattan 7, Rutgers 6
12-5-31	Denver	Nebraska 20, Colorado St. 7
12-5-31	Pittsburgh	Carnegie Mellon 0, Duquesne 0
12-5-31	New York	Tennessee 13, New York U. 0
12-5-31	St. Louis	St. Louis 31, Missouri 6
12-5-31	Topeka	Kansas 6, Washburn 0
12-5-31	Wichita	Kansas St. 20, Wichita St. 6
12-5-31	Columbia	Centre 9, South Caro. 7
12-5-31	Norman	Oklahoma City 6, Oklahoma 0
12-12-31	New York	Army 17, Navy 7
12-12-31	Tulsa	Oklahoma 20, Tulsa 7
1-2-33	El Paso	Southern Methodist 26, UTEP 0
12-8-34	St. Louis	Southern Methodist 7, Washington (Mo.) 0

Team-by-Team Bowl Results

All-Time Bowl-Game Records

This list includes all bowls played by a current major team, providing its opponent was classified as a major that season or it was a major team then. The list excludes games in which a home team served as a predetermined, preseason host regardless of its record and/or games scheduled before the season, thus eliminating the old Pineapple, Glass and Palm Festival. Following is the alphabetical list showing the record of each current major team in all major bowls.

Team	W	L	T
Air Force	6	7	1
Alabama	28	17	3
Arizona	4	7	1
Arizona St.	10	6	1
Arkansas	9	16	3
Army	2	2	0
Auburn	14	10	2
Ball St.	0	3	0
Baylor	8	8	0
Boston College	5	5	0
Bowling Green	2	3	0
Brigham Young	7	12	1
California	5	7	1
Central Mich.	0	2	0
Cincinnati	2	1	0
Clemson	12	10	0
Colorado	9	12	0
Colorado St.	2	3	0
Duke	3	5	0
East Caro.	3	1	0
Eastern Mich.	1	0	0
Florida	12	13	0
Florida St.	16	8	2
Fresno St.	6	3	0
Georgia	16	14	3
Georgia Tech	18	8	0
Hawaii	1	1	0
Houston	7	6	1
Illinois	5	7	0
Indiana	3	5	0
Iowa	8	7	1
Iowa St.	0	4	0
Kansas	3	5	0
Kansas St.	3	3	0
Kent	0	1	0
Kentucky	5	3	0
LSU	14	16	1
Louisiana Tech	1	1	1
Louisville	3	1	1
Marshall	0	1	0
Maryland	6	9	2
Memphis	1	0	0
Miami (Fla.)	11	11	0
Miami (Ohio)	5	2	0
Michigan	14	15	0
Michigan St.	5	9	0
Minnesota	2	3	0
Mississippi	15	11	0
Mississippi St.	4	5	0
Missouri	8	12	0
Navy	4	4	1
Nebraska	18	18	0
Nevada	2	3	0
UNLV	#2	0	0
New Mexico	2	3	1
New Mexico St.	2	0	1
North Caro.	10	12	0
North Caro. St.	8	8	1
North Texas	0	2	0
Northern Ill.	1	0	0
Northwestern	1	2	0
Notre Dame	13	9	0
Ohio	0	2	0
Ohio St.	13	17	0
Oklahoma	20	11	1
Oklahoma St.	9	4	0
Oregon	4	8	0
Oregon St.	2	2	0
Penn St.	21	11	2
Pittsburgh	8	11	0
Purdue	5	1	0
Rice	4	3	0
Rutgers	0	1	0
San Diego St.	1	3	0
San Jose St.	4	3	0
South Caro.	1	8	0
Southern Cal	25	13	0
Southern Methodist	4	6	1
Southern Miss.	3	4	0
Stanford	9	8	1
Syracuse	10	7	1
Temple	1	1	0
Tennessee	21	17	0
Texas	17	18	2
UTEP	5	4	0
Texas A&M	12	11	0
Texas Christian	4	10	1
Texas Tech	5	16	1
Toledo	5	1	0
Tulane	2	6	0
Tulsa	4	7	0
UCLA	11	9	1
Utah	3	3	0
Utah St.	2	3	0
Vanderbilt	1	1	1
Virginia	4	5	0
Virginia Tech	3	8	0
Wake Forest	2	2	0
Washington	13	10	1
Washington St.	4	3	0
West Va.	8	11	0
Western Mich.	0	2	0
Wisconsin	4	6	0
Wyoming	4	6	0
TOTALS	**665**	**665**	**42**

#Later lost game by forfeit.

The following current Division I-A teams have not played in a major bowl game: Akron, UAB, Arkansas St., Central Fla., Idaho, Northeast La. and Southwestern La.

Major Bowl Records of Non-Division I-A Teams

Boston U. 0-1-0; Brown 0-1-0; Bucknell 1-0-0; Cal St. Fullerton 0-1-0; Cal St. Northridge 0-1-0; Carnegie Mellon 0-1-0; Case Reserve 1-0-0; Catholic 1-0-1; Centenary (La.) 0-0-1; Centre 2-1-0; Citadel 1-0-0; Columbia 1-0-0; Davidson 0-1-0; Dayton 0-1-0; Denver 0-2-0; Drake 2-1-0; Duquesne 1-0-0; Fordham 1-1-0; Geo. Washington 1-0-0; Georgetown 0-2-0; Gonzaga 0-1-0; Hardin-Simmons 5-2-1; Harvard 1-0-0; Holy Cross 0-1-0; Long Beach St. 0-0-1; Marquette 0-1-0; McNeese St. 1-2-0; Montana St. 0-0-1; Occidental 1-0-0; Ouachita Baptist 0-1-0; Pacific (Cal.) 2-1-0; Pennsylvania 0-1-0; Randolph Field 0-0-1; Richmond 1-1-0; St. Mary's (Cal.) 1-2-0; Santa Clara 3-0-0; Second Air Force 1-0-0; Southwestern (Tex.) 2-0-0; Tampa 1-0-0; Tennessee Tech 0-1-0; U. of Mexico 0-1-0; Villanova 2-2-1; Wash. & Jeff. 0-0-1; Wash. & Lee 0-1-0; West Tex. A&M 3-0-0; West Va. Wesleyan 1-0-0; Wichita St. 0-3-0; William & Mary 1-2-0; Xavier (Ohio) 1-0-0. TOTALS: 39-37-8

All-Time Bowl Appearances

(Must be classified as a major bowl game where one team was considered a major college at the time.)

Team	Appearances	Team	Appearances
Alabama	48	Clemson	22
Southern Cal	38	Miami (Fla.)	22
Tennessee	38	North Caro.	22
Texas	37	Notre Dame	22
Nebraska	36	Texas Tech	22
Penn St.	34	Colorado	21
Georgia	33	UCLA	21
Oklahoma	32	Brigham Young	20
LSU	31	Missouri	20
Ohio St.	30	Pittsburgh	19
Michigan	29	West Va.	19
Arkansas	28	Stanford	18
Auburn	26	Syracuse	18
Florida St.	26	Arizona St.	17
Georgia Tech	26	Maryland	17
Mississippi	26	North Caro. St.	17
Florida	25	Baylor	16
Washington	24	Iowa	16
Texas A&M	23		

All-Time Bowl Victories

(Includes bowls where at least one team was classified a major college at the time.)

Team	Victories	Team	Victories
Alabama	28	Notre Dame	13
Southern Cal	25	Ohio St.	13
Penn St.	21	Washington	13
Tennessee	21	Clemson	12
Oklahoma	20	Florida St.	12
Oklahoma St.	20	Texas A&M	12
Georgia Tech	18	Miami (Fla.)	11
Nebraska	18	UCLA	11
Texas	17	Arizona St.	10
Florida St.	16	North Caro.	10
Georgia	16	Syracuse	10
Mississippi	15	Arkansas	9
Auburn	14	Colorado	9
LSU	14	Oklahoma St.	9
Michigan	14	Stanford	9

Team-by-Team Major Bowl Scores With Coach of Each Bowl Team

Listed below are the 104 I-A teams that have participated in history's 728 major bowl games (the term "major bowl" is defined above the alphabetical list of team bowl records). The teams are listed alphabetically, with each coach listed along with the bowl participated in, date played, opponent, score and team's all-time bowl-game record. Following the I-A list is a group of 49 teams that played in a major bowl game or games but are no longer classified as I-A.

School/Coach	Bowl/Date	Opponent/Score
AIR FORCE		
Ben Martin	Cotton 1-1-59	Texas Christian 0-0
Ben Martin	Gator 12-28-63	North Caro. 0-35
Ben Martin	Sugar 1-1-71	Tennessee 13-34
Ken Hatfield	Hall of Fame 12-31-82	Vanderbilt 36-28
Ken Hatfield	Independence 12-10-83	Mississippi 9-3
Fisher DeBerry	Independence 12-15-84	Virginia Tech 23-7
Fisher DeBerry	Bluebonnet 12-31-85	Texas 24-16
Fisher DeBerry	Freedom 12-30-87	Arizona St. 28-33
Fisher DeBerry	Liberty 12-28-89	Mississippi 29-42
Fisher DeBerry	Liberty 12-27-90	Ohio St. 23-11
Fisher DeBerry	Liberty 12-29-91	Mississippi St. 38-15
Fisher DeBerry	Liberty 12-31-92	Mississippi 0-13
Fisher DeBerry	Copper 12-27-95	Texas Tech 41-55
Fisher DeBerry	Las Vegas 12-20-97	Oregon 13-41
All bowls 6-7-1		
ALABAMA		
Wallace Wade	Rose 1-1-26	Washington 20-19
Wallace Wade	Rose 1-1-27	Stanford 7-7
Wallace Wade	Rose 1-1-31	Washington St. 24-0
Frank Thomas	Rose 1-1-35	Stanford 29-13
Frank Thomas	Rose 1-1-38	California 0-13
Frank Thomas	Cotton 1-1-42	Texas A&M 29-21
Frank Thomas	Orange 1-1-43	Boston College 37-21
Frank Thomas	Sugar 1-1-45	Duke 26-29
Frank Thomas	Rose 1-1-46	Southern Cal 34-14
Harold "Red" Drew	Sugar 1-1-48	Texas 7-27
Harold "Red" Drew	Orange 1-1-53	Syracuse 61-6
Harold "Red" Drew	Cotton 1-1-54	Rice 6-28
Paul "Bear" Bryant	Liberty 12-19-59	Penn St. 0-7
Paul "Bear" Bryant	Bluebonnet 12-17-60	Texas 3-3
Paul "Bear" Bryant	Sugar 1-1-62	Arkansas 10-3
Paul "Bear" Bryant	Orange 1-1-63	Oklahoma 17-0
Paul "Bear" Bryant	Sugar 1-1-64	Mississippi 12-7
Paul "Bear" Bryant	Orange 1-1-65	Texas 17-21
Paul "Bear" Bryant	Orange 1-1-66	Nebraska 39-28
Paul "Bear" Bryant	Sugar 1-2-67	Nebraska 34-7
Paul "Bear" Bryant	Cotton 1-1-68	Texas A&M 16-20
Paul "Bear" Bryant	Gator 12-28-68	Missouri 10-35
Paul "Bear" Bryant	Liberty 12-13-69	Colorado 33-47
Paul "Bear" Bryant	Bluebonnet 12-31-70	Oklahoma 24-24
Paul "Bear" Bryant	Orange 1-1-72	Nebraska 6-38
Paul "Bear" Bryant	Cotton 1-1-73	Texas 13-17
Paul "Bear" Bryant	Sugar 12-31-73	Notre Dame 23-24
Paul "Bear" Bryant	Orange 1-1-75	Notre Dame 11-13
Paul "Bear" Bryant	Sugar 12-31-75	Penn St. 13-6
Paul "Bear" Bryant	Liberty 12-20-76	UCLA 36-6
Paul "Bear" Bryant	Sugar 1-2-78	Ohio St. 35-6
Paul "Bear" Bryant	Sugar 1-1-79	Penn St. 14-7
Paul "Bear" Bryant	Sugar 1-1-80	Arkansas 24-9
Paul "Bear" Bryant	Cotton 1-1-81	Baylor 30-2
Paul "Bear" Bryant	Cotton 1-1-82	Texas 12-14
Paul "Bear" Bryant	Liberty 12-29-82	Illinois 21-15
Ray Perkins	Sun 12-24-83	Southern Methodist 28-7
Ray Perkins	Aloha 12-28-85	Southern Cal 24-3
Ray Perkins	Sun 12-25-86	Washington 28-6
Bill Curry	Hall of Fame 1-2-88	Michigan 24-28
Bill Curry	Sun 12-24-88	Army 29-28
Bill Curry	Sugar 1-1-90	Miami (Fla.) 25-33
Gene Stallings	Fiesta 1-1-91	Louisville 7-34
Gene Stallings	Blockbuster 12-28-91	Colorado 30-25
Gene Stallings	Sugar 1-1-93	Miami (Fla.) 34-13
Gene Stallings	Gator 12-31-93	North Caro. 24-10
Gene Stallings	Florida Citrus 1-2-95	Ohio St. 24-17
Gene Stallings	Outback 1-1-97	Michigan 17-14
All bowls 28-17-3		
ARIZONA		
J. F. "Pop" McKale	San Diego East-West Christmas Classic 12-26-21	Centre 0-38
Miles Casteel	Salad 1-1-49	Drake 13-14
Darrell Mudra	Sun 12-28-68	Auburn 10-34
Tony Mason	Fiesta 12-25-79	Pittsburgh 10-16
Larry Smith	Sun 12-28-85	Georgia 13-13
Larry Smith	Aloha 12-27-86	North Caro. 30-21
Dick Tomey	Copper 12-31-89	North Caro. St. 17-10
Dick Tomey	Aloha 12-25-90	Syracuse 0-28
Dick Tomey	John Hancock 12-31-92	Baylor 15-20
Dick Tomey	Fiesta 1-1-94	Miami (Fla.) 29-0
Dick Tomey	Freedom 12-27-94	Utah 13-16
Dick Tomey	Insight.com 12-27-97	New Mexico 20-14
All bowls 4-7-1		
ARIZONA ST.		
Millard "Dixie" Howell	Sun 1-1-40	Catholic 0-0
Millard "Dixie" Howell	Sun 1-1-41	Case Reserve 13-26
Ed Doherty	Salad 1-1-50	Xavier (Ohio) 21-33
Ed Doherty	Salad 1-1-51	Miami (Ohio) 21-34
Frank Kush	Peach 12-30-70	North Caro. 48-26
Frank Kush	Fiesta 12-27-71	Florida St. 45-38
Frank Kush	Fiesta 12-23-72	Missouri 49-35
Frank Kush	Fiesta 12-21-73	Pittsburgh 28-7
Frank Kush	Fiesta 12-26-75	Nebraska 17-14
Frank Kush	Fiesta 12-25-77	Penn St. 30-42
Frank Kush	Garden State 12-16-78	Rutgers 34-18
Darryl Rogers	Fiesta 1-1-83	Oklahoma 32-21
John Cooper	Holiday 12-22-85	Arkansas 17-18
John Cooper	Rose 1-1-87	Michigan 22-15
John Cooper	Freedom 12-30-87	Air Force 33-28
Bruce Snyder	Rose 1-1-97	Ohio St. 17-20
Bruce Snyder	Sun 12-31-97	Iowa 17-7
All bowls 10-6-1		
ARKANSAS		
Fred Thomsen	Dixie Classic 1-1-34	Centenary (La.) 7-7
John Barnhill	Cotton 1-1-47	LSU 0-0
John Barnhill	Dixie 1-1-48	William & Mary 21-19
Bowden Wyatt	Cotton 1-1-55	Georgia Tech 6-14
Frank Broyles	Gator 1-2-60	Georgia Tech 14-7
Frank Broyles	Cotton 1-2-61	Duke 6-7

School/Coach	Bowl/Date	Opponent/Score
Frank Broyles	Sugar 1-1-62	Alabama 3-10
Frank Broyles	Sugar 1-1-63	Mississippi 13-17
Frank Broyles	Cotton 1-1-65	Nebraska 10-7
Frank Broyles	Cotton 1-1-66	LSU 7-14
Frank Broyles	Sugar 1-1-69	Georgia 16-2
Frank Broyles	Sugar 1-1-70	Mississippi 22-27
Frank Broyles	Liberty 12-20-71	Tennessee 13-14
Frank Broyles	Cotton 1-1-76	Georgia 31-10
Lou Holtz	Orange 1-2-78	Oklahoma 31-6
Lou Holtz	Fiesta 12-25-78	UCLA 10-10
Lou Holtz	Sugar 1-1-80	Alabama 9-24
Lou Holtz	Hall of Fame 12-27-80	Tulane 34-15
Lou Holtz	Gator 12-28-81	North Caro. 27-31
Lou Holtz	Bluebonnet 12-31-82	Florida 28-24
Ken Hatfield	Liberty 12-27-84	Auburn 15-21
Ken Hatfield	Holiday 12-22-85	Arizona St. 18-17
Ken Hatfield	Orange 1-1-87	Oklahoma 8-42
Ken Hatfield	Liberty 12-29-87	Georgia 17-20
Ken Hatfield	Cotton 1-2-89	UCLA 3-17
Ken Hatfield	Cotton 1-1-90	Tennessee 27-31
Jack Crowe	Independence 12-29-91	Georgia 15-24
Danny Ford	Carquest 12-30-95	North Caro. 10-20
All bowls 9-16-3		
ARMY		
Jim Young	Cherry 12-22-84	Michigan St. 10-6
Jim Young	Peach 12-31-85	Illinois 31-29
Jim Young	Sun 12-24-88	Alabama 28-29
Bob Sutton	Independence 12-31-96	Auburn 29-32
All bowls 2-2-0		
AUBURN		
Jack Meagher	Bacardi, Cuba 1-1-37	Villanova 7-7
Jack Meagher	Orange 1-1-38	Michigan St. 6-0
Ralph "Shug" Jordan	Gator 1-1-54	Texas Tech 13-35
Ralph "Shug" Jordan	Gator 12-31-54	Baylor 33-13
Ralph "Shug" Jordan	Gator 12-31-55	Vanderbilt 13-25
Ralph "Shug" Jordan	Orange 1-1-64	Nebraska 7-13
Ralph "Shug" Jordan	Liberty 12-18-65	Mississippi 7-13
Ralph "Shug" Jordan	Sun 12-28-68	Arizona 34-10
Ralph "Shug" Jordan	Bluebonnet 12-31-69	Houston 7-36
Ralph "Shug" Jordan	Gator 1-2-71	Mississippi 35-28
Ralph "Shug" Jordan	Sugar 1-1-72	Oklahoma 22-40
Ralph "Shug" Jordan	Gator 12-30-72	Colorado 24-3
Ralph "Shug" Jordan	Sun 12-29-73	Missouri 17-34
Ralph "Shug" Jordan	Gator 12-30-74	Texas 27-3
Pat Dye	Tangerine 12-18-82	Boston College 33-26
Pat Dye	Sugar 1-2-84	Michigan 9-7
Pat Dye	Liberty 12-27-84	Arkansas 21-15
Pat Dye	Cotton 1-1-86	Texas A&M 16-36
Pat Dye	Florida Citrus 1-1-87	Southern Cal 16-7
Pat Dye	Sugar 1-1-88	Syracuse 16-16
Pat Dye	Sugar 1-2-89	Florida St. 7-13
Pat Dye	Hall of Fame 1-1-90	Ohio St. 31-24
Pat Dye	Peach 12-29-90	Indiana 27-23
Terry Bowden	Outback 1-1-96	Penn St. 14-43
Terry Bowden	Independence 12-31-96	Army 33-29
Terry Bowden	Peach 1-2-98	Clemson 21-17
All bowls 14-10-2		
BALL ST.		
Paul Schudel	California 12-9-89	Fresno St. 6-27
Paul Schudel	Las Vegas 12-17-93	Utah St. 33-42
Bill Lynch	Las Vegas 12-19-96	Nevada 15-18
All bowls 0-3-0		
BAYLOR		
Bob Woodruff	Dixie 1-1-49	Wake Forest 20-7
George Sauer	Orange 1-1-52	Georgia Tech 14-17
George Sauer	Gator 12-31-54	Auburn 13-33
Sam Boyd	Sugar 1-1-57	Tennessee 13-7
John Bridgers	Gator 12-31-60	Florida 12-13
John Bridgers	Gotham 12-9-61	Utah St. 24-9
John Bridgers	Bluebonnet 12-21-63	LSU 14-7
Grant Teaff	Cotton 1-1-75	Penn St. 20-41
Grant Teaff	Peach 12-31-79	Clemson 24-18
Grant Teaff	Cotton 1-1-81	Alabama 2-30
Grant Teaff	Bluebonnet 12-31-83	Oklahoma St. 14-24
Grant Teaff	Liberty 12-27-85	LSU 21-7
Grant Teaff	Bluebonnet 12-31-86	Colorado 21-9
Grant Teaff	Copper 12-31-91	Indiana 0-24
Grant Teaff	John Hancock 12-31-92	Arizona 20-15
Chuck Reedy	Alamo 12-31-94	Washington St. 3-10
All bowls 8-8-0		

School/Coach	Bowl/Date	Opponent/Score
BOSTON COLLEGE		
Frank Leahy	Cotton 1-1-40	Clemson 3-6
Frank Leahy	Sugar 1-1-41	Tennessee 19-13
Denny Myers	Orange 1-1-43	Alabama 21-37
Jack Bicknell	Tangerine 12-18-82	Auburn 26-33
Jack Bicknell	Liberty 12-29-83	Notre Dame 18-19
Jack Bicknell	Cotton 1-1-85	Houston 45-28
Jack Bicknell	Hall of Fame 12-23-86	Georgia 27-24
Tom Coughlin	Hall of Fame 1-1-93	Tennessee 23-38
Tom Coughlin	Carquest 1-1-94	Virginia 31-13
Dan Henning	Aloha 12-25-94	Kansas St. 12-7
All bowls 5-5-0		
BOWLING GREEN		
Doyt Perry	Mercy 11-23-61	Fresno St. 6-36
Denny Stolz	California 12-18-82	Fresno St. 28-29
Denny Stolz	California 12-14-85	Fresno St. 7-51
Gary Blackney	California 12-14-91	Fresno St. 28-21
Gary Blackney	Las Vegas 12-18-92	Nevada 35-34
All bowls 2-3-0		
BRIGHAM YOUNG		
LaVell Edwards	Fiesta 12-28-74	Oklahoma St. 6-16
LaVell Edwards	Tangerine 12-18-76	Oklahoma St. 21-49
LaVell Edwards	Holiday 12-22-78	Navy 16-23
LaVell Edwards	Holiday 12-21-79	Indiana 37-38
LaVell Edwards	Holiday 12-19-80	Southern Methodist 46-45
LaVell Edwards	Holiday 12-18-81	Washington St. 38-36
LaVell Edwards	Holiday 12-17-82	Ohio St. 17-47
LaVell Edwards	Holiday 12-23-83	Missouri 21-17
LaVell Edwards	Holiday 12-21-84	Michigan 24-17
LaVell Edwards	Florida Citrus 12-28-85	Ohio St. 7-10
LaVell Edwards	Freedom 12-30-86	UCLA 10-31
LaVell Edwards	All-American 12-22-87	Virginia 16-22
LaVell Edwards	Freedom 12-29-88	Colorado 20-17
LaVell Edwards	Holiday 12-29-89	Penn St. 39-50
LaVell Edwards	Holiday 12-29-90	Texas A&M 14-65
LaVell Edwards	Holiday 12-30-91	Iowa 13-13
LaVell Edwards	Aloha 12-25-92	Kansas 20-23
LaVell Edwards	Holiday 12-30-93	Ohio St. 21-28
LaVell Edwards	Copper 12-29-94	Oklahoma 31-6
LaVell Edwards	Cotton 1-1-97	Kansas St. 19-15
All bowls 7-12-1		
CALIFORNIA		
Andy Smith	Rose 1-1-21	Ohio St. 28-0
Andy Smith	Rose 1-2-22	Wash. & Jeff. 0-0
Clarence "Nibs" Price	Rose 1-1-29	Georgia Tech 7-8
Leonard "Stub" Allison	Rose 1-1-38	Alabama 13-0
Lynn "Pappy" Waldorf	Rose 1-1-49	Northwestern 14-20
Lynn "Pappy" Waldorf	Rose 1-2-50	Ohio St. 14-17
Lynn "Pappy" Waldorf	Rose 1-1-51	Michigan 6-14
Pete Elliott	Rose 1-1-59	Iowa 12-38
Roger Theder	Garden State 12-15-79	Temple 17-28
Bruce Snyder	Copper 12-31-90	Wyoming 17-15
Bruce Snyder	Florida Citrus 1-1-92	Clemson 37-13
Keith Gilbertson	Alamo 12-31-93	Iowa 37-3
Steve Mariucci	Aloha 12-25-96	Navy 38-42
All bowls 5-7-1		
CENTRAL MICH.		
Herb Deromedi	California 12-8-90	San Jose St. 24-48
Dick Flynn	Las Vegas 12-15-94	UNLV 24-52
All bowls 0-2-0		
CINCINNATI		
Ray Nolting	Sun 1-1-47	Virginia Tech 18-6
Sid Gillman	Sun 1-1-51	West Tex. A&M 13-14
Rick Minter	Humanitarian 12-29-97	Utah St. 35-19
All bowls 2-1-0		
CLEMSON		
Jess Neely	Cotton 1-1-40	Boston College 6-3
Frank Howard	Gator 1-1-49	Missouri 24-23
Frank Howard	Orange 1-1-51	Miami (Fla.) 15-14
Frank Howard	Gator 1-1-52	Miami (Fla.) 0-14
Frank Howard	Orange 1-1-57	Colorado 21-27
Frank Howard	Sugar 1-1-59	LSU 0-7
Frank Howard	Bluebonnet 12-19-59	Texas Christian 23-7
Charley Pell	Gator 12-30-77	Pittsburgh 3-34
Danny Ford	Gator 12-29-78	Ohio St. 17-15
Danny Ford	Peach 12-31-79	Baylor 18-24
Danny Ford	Orange 1-1-82	Nebraska 22-15
Danny Ford	Independence 12-21-85	Minnesota 13-20
Danny Ford	Gator 12-27-86	Stanford 27-21
Danny Ford	Florida Citrus 1-1-88	Penn St. 35-10
Danny Ford	Florida Citrus 1-2-89	Oklahoma 23-6

School/Coach	Bowl/Date	Opponent/Score
Danny Ford	Gator 12-30-89	West Va. 27-7
Ken Hatfield	Hall of Fame 1-1-91	Illinois 30-0
Ken Hatfield	Florida Citrus 1-1-92	California 13-37
Tommy West	Peach 12-31-93	Kentucky 14-13
Tommy West	Gator 1-1-96	Syracuse 0-41
Tommy West	Peach 12-28-96	LSU 7-10
Tommy West	Peach 1-2-98	Auburn 17-21
All bowls 12-10-0		

COLORADO

School/Coach	Bowl/Date	Opponent/Score
Bernard "Bunnie" Oaks	Cotton 1-1-38	Rice 14-28
Dallas Ward	Orange 1-1-57	Clemson 27-21
Sonny Grandelius	Orange 1-1-62	LSU 7-25
Eddie Crowder	Bluebonnet 12-23-67	Miami (Fla.) 31-21
Eddie Crowder	Liberty 12-13-69	Alabama 47-33
Eddie Crowder	Liberty 12-12-70	Tulane 3-17
Eddie Crowder	Bluebonnet 12-31-71	Houston 29-17
Eddie Crowder	Gator 12-30-72	Auburn 3-24
Bill Mallory	Bluebonnet 12-27-75	Texas 21-38
Bill Mallory	Orange 1-1-77	Ohio St. 10-27
Bill McCartney	Freedom 12-30-85	Washington 17-20
Bill McCartney	Bluebonnet 12-31-86	Baylor 9-21
Bill McCartney	Freedom 12-29-88	Brigham Young 17-20
Bill McCartney	Orange 1-1-90	Notre Dame 6-21
Bill McCartney	Orange 1-1-91	Notre Dame 10-9
Bill McCartney	Blockbuster 12-28-91	Alabama 25-30
Bill McCartney	Fiesta 1-1-93	Syracuse 22-26
Bill McCartney	Aloha 12-25-93	Fresno St. 41-30
Bill McCartney	Fiesta 1-2-95	Notre Dame 41-24
Rick Neuheisel	Cotton 1-1-96	Oregon 38-6
Rick Neuheisel	Holiday 12-30-96	Washington 33-21
All bowls 9-12-0		

COLORADO ST.

School/Coach	Bowl/Date	Opponent/Score
Bob Davis	Raisin 1-1-49	Occidental 20-21
Earle Bruce	Freedom 12-24-90	Oregon 32-31
Sonny Lubick	Holiday 12-30-94	Michigan 14-24
Sonny Lubick	Holiday 12-29-95	Kansas St. 21-54
Sonny Lubick	Holiday 12-29-97	Missouri 35-24
All bowls 2-3-0		

DUKE

School/Coach	Bowl/Date	Opponent/Score
Wallace Wade	Rose 1-2-39	Southern Cal 3-7
Wallace Wade	Rose 1-1-42	Oregon St. 16-20
Eddie Cameron	Sugar 1-1-45	Alabama 29-26
Bill Murray	Orange 1-1-55	Nebraska 34-7
Bill Murray	Orange 1-1-58	Oklahoma 21-48
Bill Murray	Cotton 1-2-61	Arkansas 7-6
Steve Spurrier	All-American 12-28-89	Texas Tech 21-49
Fred Goldsmith	Hall of Fame 1-2-95	Wisconsin 20-34
All bowls 3-5-0		

EAST CARO.

School/Coach	Bowl/Date	Opponent/Score
Pat Dye	Independence 12-16-78	Louisiana Tech 35-13
Bill Lewis	Peach 1-1-92	North Caro. St. 37-34
Steve Logan	Liberty 12-31-94	Illinois 0-30
Steve Logan	Liberty 12-30-95	Stanford 19-13
All bowls 3-1-0		

EASTERN MICH.

School/Coach	Bowl/Date	Opponent/Score
Jim Harkema	California 12-12-87	San Jose St. 30-27
All bowls 1-0-0		

FLORIDA

School/Coach	Bowl/Date	Opponent/Score
Bob Woodruff	Gator 1-1-53	Tulsa 14-13
Bob Woodruff	Gator 12-27-58	Mississippi 3-7
Ray Graves	Gator 12-31-60	Baylor 13-12
Ray Graves	Gator 12-29-62	Penn St. 17-7
Ray Graves	Sugar 1-1-66	Missouri 18-20
Ray Graves	Orange 1-2-67	Georgia Tech 27-12
Ray Graves	Gator 12-27-69	Tennessee 14-13
Doug Dickey	Tangerine 12-22-73	Miami (Ohio) 7-16
Doug Dickey	Sugar 12-31-74	Nebraska 10-13
Doug Dickey	Gator 12-29-75	Maryland 0-13
Doug Dickey	Sun 1-2-77	Texas A&M 14-37
Charley Pell	Tangerine 12-20-80	Maryland 35-20
Charley Pell	Peach 12-31-81	West Va. 6-26
Charley Pell	Bluebonnet 12-31-82	Arkansas 24-28
Charley Pell	Gator 12-30-83	Iowa 14-6
Galen Hall	Aloha 12-25-87	UCLA 16-20
Galen Hall	All-American 12-29-88	Illinois 14-10
Gary Darnell	Freedom 12-30-89	Washington 7-34
Steve Spurrier	Sugar 1-1-92	Notre Dame 28-39
Steve Spurrier	Gator 12-31-92	North Caro. St. 27-10
Steve Spurrier	Sugar 1-1-94	West Va. 41-7
Steve Spurrier	Sugar 1-2-95	Florida St. 17-23
Steve Spurrier	Fiesta 1-2-96	Nebraska 24-62
Steve Spurrier	Sugar 1-2-97	Florida St. 52-20
Steve Spurrier	Florida Citrus 1-1-98	Penn St. 21-6
All bowls 12-13-0		

FLORIDA ST.

School/Coach	Bowl/Date	Opponent/Score
Tom Nugent	Sun 1-1-55	UTEP 20-47
Tom Nugent	Bluegrass 12-13-58	Oklahoma St. 6-15
Bill Peterson	Gator 1-2-65	Oklahoma 36-19
Bill Peterson	Sun 12-24-66	Wyoming 20-28
Bill Peterson	Gator 12-30-67	Penn St. 17-17
Bill Peterson	Peach 12-30-68	LSU 27-31
Larry Jones	Fiesta 12-27-71	Arizona St. 38-45
Bobby Bowden	Tangerine 12-23-77	Texas Tech 40-17
Bobby Bowden	Orange 1-1-80	Oklahoma 7-24
Bobby Bowden	Orange 1-1-81	Oklahoma 17-18
Bobby Bowden	Gator 12-30-82	West Va. 31-12
Bobby Bowden	Peach 12-30-83	North Caro. 28-3
Bobby Bowden	Florida Citrus 12-22-84	Georgia 17-17
Bobby Bowden	Gator 12-30-85	Oklahoma St. 34-23
Bobby Bowden	All-American 12-31-86	Indiana 27-13
Bobby Bowden	Fiesta 1-1-88	Nebraska 31-28
Bobby Bowden	Sugar 1-2-89	Auburn 13-7
Bobby Bowden	Fiesta 1-1-90	Nebraska 41-17
Bobby Bowden	Blockbuster 12-28-90	Penn St. 24-17
Bobby Bowden	Cotton 1-1-92	Texas A&M 10-2
Bobby Bowden	Orange 1-1-93	Nebraska 27-14
Bobby Bowden	Orange 1-1-94	Nebraska 18-16
Bobby Bowden	Sugar 1-2-95	Florida 23-17
Bobby Bowden	Orange 1-1-96	Notre Dame 31-26
Bobby Bowden	Sugar 1-2-97	Florida 20-52
Bobby Bowden	Sugar 1-1-98	Ohio St. 31-14
All bowls 16-8-2		

FRESNO ST.

School/Coach	Bowl/Date	Opponent/Score
Alvin "Pix" Pierson	Raisin 1-1-46	Drake 12-13
Cecil Coleman	Mercy 11-23-61	Bowling Green 36-6
Jim Sweeney	California 12-18-82	Bowling Green 29-28
Jim Sweeney	California 12-14-85	Bowling Green 51-7
Jim Sweeney	California 12-10-88	Western Mich. 35-30
Jim Sweeney	California 12-9-89	Ball St. 27-6
Jim Sweeney	California 12-14-91	Bowling Green 21-28
Jim Sweeney	Freedom 12-29-92	Southern Cal 24-7
Jim Sweeney	Aloha 12-25-93	Colorado 30-41
All bowls 6-3-0		

GEORGIA

School/Coach	Bowl/Date	Opponent/Score
Wally Butts	Orange 1-1-42	Texas Christian 40-26
Wally Butts	Rose 1-1-43	UCLA 9-0
Wally Butts	Oil 1-1-46	Tulsa 20-6
Wally Butts	Sugar 1-1-47	North Caro. 20-10
Wally Butts	Gator 1-1-48	Maryland 20-20
Wally Butts	Orange 1-1-49	Texas 28-41
Wally Butts	Presidential 12-9-50	Texas A&M 20-40
Wally Butts	Orange 1-1-60	Missouri 14-0
Vince Dooley	Sun 12-26-64	Texas Tech 7-0
Vince Dooley	Cotton 12-31-66	Southern Methodist 24-9
Vince Dooley	Liberty 12-16-67	North Caro. St. 7-14
Vince Dooley	Sugar 1-1-69	Arkansas 2-16
Vince Dooley	Sun 12-20-69	Nebraska 6-45
Vince Dooley	Gator 12-31-71	North Caro. 7-3
Vince Dooley	Peach 12-28-73	Maryland 17-16
Vince Dooley	Tangerine 12-21-74	Miami (Ohio) 10-21
Vince Dooley	Cotton 1-1-76	Arkansas 10-31
Vince Dooley	Sugar 1-1-77	Pittsburgh 3-27
Vince Dooley	Bluebonnet 12-31-78	Stanford 22-25
Vince Dooley	Sugar 1-1-81	Notre Dame 17-10
Vince Dooley	Sugar 1-1-82	Pittsburgh 20-24
Vince Dooley	Sugar 1-1-83	Penn St. 23-27
Vince Dooley	Cotton 1-2-84	Texas 10-9
Vince Dooley	Florida Citrus 12-22-84	Florida St. 17-17
Vince Dooley	Sun 12-28-85	Arizona 13-13
Vince Dooley	Hall of Fame 12-23-86	Boston College 24-27
Vince Dooley	Liberty 12-29-87	Arkansas 20-17
Vince Dooley	Gator 1-1-89	Michigan St. 34-27
Ray Goff	Peach 12-30-89	Syracuse 18-19
Ray Goff	Independence 12-29-91	Arkansas 24-15
Ray Goff	Florida Citrus 1-1-93	Ohio St. 21-14
Ray Goff	Peach 12-30-95	Virginia 27-34
Jim Donnan	Outback 1-1-98	Wisconsin 33-6
All bowls 16-14-3		

GEORGIA TECH

School/Coach	Bowl/Date	Opponent/Score
Bill Alexander	Rose 1-1-29	California 8-7
Bill Alexander	Orange 1-1-40	Missouri 21-7
Bill Alexander	Cotton 1-1-43	Texas 7-14
Bill Alexander	Sugar 1-1-44	Tulsa 20-18

School/Coach	Bowl/Date	Opponent/Score
Bill Alexander	Orange 1-1-45	Tulsa 12-26
Bobby Dodd	Oil 1-1-47	St. Mary's (Cal.) 41-19
Bobby Dodd	Orange 1-1-48	Kansas 20-14
Bobby Dodd	Orange 1-1-52	Baylor 17-14
Bobby Dodd	Sugar 1-1-53	Mississippi 24-7
Bobby Dodd	Sugar 1-1-54	West Va. 42-19
Bobby Dodd	Cotton 1-1-55	Arkansas 14-6
Bobby Dodd	Sugar 1-2-56	Pittsburgh 7-0
Bobby Dodd	Gator 12-29-56	Pittsburgh 21-14
Bobby Dodd	Gator 1-2-60	Arkansas 7-14
Bobby Dodd	Gator 12-30-61	Penn St. 15-30
Bobby Dodd	Bluebonnet 12-22-62	Missouri 10-14
Bobby Dodd	Gator 12-31-65	Texas Tech 31-21
Bobby Dodd	Orange 1-2-67	Florida 12-27
Bud Carson	Sun 12-19-70	Texas Tech 17-9
Bud Carson	Peach 12-30-71	Mississippi 18-41
Bill Fulcher	Liberty 12-18-72	Iowa St. 31-30
Pepper Rodgers	Peach 12-25-78	Purdue 21-41
Bill Curry	Hall of Fame 12-31-85	Michigan St. 17-14
Bobby Ross	Florida Citrus 1-1-91	Nebraska 45-21
Bobby Ross	Aloha 12-25-91	Stanford 18-17
George O'Leary	Carquest 12-29-97	West Va. 35-30
All bowls 18-8-0		
HAWAII		
Bob Wagner	Aloha 12-25-89	Michigan St. 13-33
Bob Wagner	Holiday 12-30-92	Illinois 27-17
All bowls 1-1-0		
HOUSTON		
Clyde Lee	Salad 1-1-52	Dayton 26-21
Bill Yeoman	Tangerine 12-22-62	Miami (Ohio) 49-21
Bill Yeoman	Bluebonnet 12-31-69	Auburn 36-7
Bill Yeoman	Bluebonnet 12-31-71	Colorado 17-29
Bill Yeoman	Bluebonnet 12-29-73	Tulane 47-7
Bill Yeoman	Bluebonnet 12-23-74	North Caro. St. 31-31
Bill Yeoman	Cotton 1-1-77	Maryland 30-21
Bill Yeoman	Cotton 1-1-79	Notre Dame 34-35
Bill Yeoman	Cotton 1-1-80	Nebraska 17-14
Bill Yeoman	Garden State 12-14-80	Navy 35-0
Bill Yeoman	Sun 12-26-81	Oklahoma 14-40
Bill Yeoman	Cotton 1-1-85	Boston College 28-45
Jack Pardee	Aloha 12-25-88	Washington St. 22-24
Kim Helton	Liberty 12-27-96	Syracuse 17-30
All bowls 7-6-1		
ILLINOIS		
Ray Eliot	Rose 1-1-47	UCLA 45-14
Ray Eliot	Rose 1-1-52	Stanford 40-7
Pete Elliott	Rose 1-1-64	Washington 17-7
Mike White	Liberty 12-29-82	Alabama 15-21
Mike White	Rose 1-2-84	UCLA 9-45
Mike White	Peach 12-31-85	Army 29-31
John Mackovic	All-American 12-29-88	Florida 10-14
John Mackovic	Florida Citrus 1-1-90	Virginia 31-21
John Mackovic	Hall of Fame 1-1-91	Clemson 0-30
Lou Tepper	John Hancock 12-31-91	UCLA 3-6
Lou Tepper	Holiday 12-30-92	Hawaii 17-27
Lou Tepper	Liberty 12-31-94	East Caro. 30-0
All bowls 5-7-0		
INDIANA		
John Pont	Rose 1-1-68	Southern Cal 3-14
Lee Corso	Holiday 12-21-79	Brigham Young 38-37
Bill Mallory	All-American 12-31-86	Florida St. 13-27
Bill Mallory	Peach 1-2-88	Tennessee 22-27
Bill Mallory	Liberty 12-28-88	South Caro. 34-10
Bill Mallory	Peach 12-29-90	Auburn 23-27
Bill Mallory	Copper 12-31-91	Baylor 24-0
Bill Mallory	Independence 12-31-93	Virginia Tech 20-45
All bowls 3-5-0		
IOWA		
Forest Evashevski	Rose 1-1-57	Oregon St. 35-19
Forest Evashevski	Rose 1-1-59	California 38-12
Hayden Fry	Rose 1-1-82	Washington 0-28
Hayden Fry	Peach 12-31-82	Tennessee 28-22
Hayden Fry	Gator 12-30-83	Florida 6-14
Hayden Fry	Freedom 12-26-84	Texas 55-17
Hayden Fry	Rose 1-1-86	UCLA 28-45
Hayden Fry	Holiday 12-30-86	San Diego St. 39-38
Hayden Fry	Holiday 12-30-87	Wyoming 20-19
Hayden Fry	Peach 12-31-88	North Caro. St. 23-28
Hayden Fry	Rose 1-1-91	Washington 34-46
Hayden Fry	Holiday 12-30-91	Brigham Young 13-13
Hayden Fry	Alamo 12-31-93	California 3-37

School/Coach	Bowl/Date	Opponent/Score
Hayden Fry	Sun 12-29-95	Washington 38-18
Hayden Fry	Alamo 12-29-96	Texas Tech 27-0
Hayden Fry	Sun 12-31-97	Arizona St. 7-17
All bowls 8-7-1		
IOWA ST.		
Johnny Majors	Sun 12-18-71	LSU 15-33
Johnny Majors	Liberty 12-18-72	Georgia Tech 30-31
Earle Bruce	Peach 12-31-77	North Caro. St. 14-24
Earle Bruce	Hall of Fame 12-20-78	Texas A&M 12-28
All bowls 0-4-0		
KANSAS		
George Sauer	Orange 1-1-48	Georgia Tech 14-20
Jack Mitchell	Bluebonnet 12-16-61	Rice 33-7
Pepper Rodgers	Orange 1-1-69	Penn St. 14-15
Don Fambrough	Liberty 12-17-73	North Caro. St. 18-31
Bud Moore	Sun 12-26-75	Pittsburgh 19-33
Don Fambrough	Hall of Fame 12-31-81	Mississippi St. 0-10
Glen Mason	Aloha 12-25-92	Brigham Young 23-20
Glen Mason	Aloha 12-25-95	UCLA 51-30
All bowls 3-5-0		
KANSAS ST.		
Jim Dickey	Independence 12-11-82	Wisconsin 3-14
Bill Snyder	Copper 12-29-93	Wyoming 52-17
Bill Snyder	Aloha 12-25-94	Boston College 7-12
Bill Snyder	Holiday 12-29-95	Colorado St. 54-21
Bill Snyder	Cotton 1-1-97	Brigham Young 15-19
Bill Snyder	Fiesta 12-31-97	Syracuse 35-18
All bowls 3-3-0		
KENT		
Don James	Tangerine 12-29-72	Tampa 18-21
All bowls 0-1-0		
KENTUCKY		
Paul "Bear" Bryant	Great Lakes 12-6-47	Villanova 24-14
Paul "Bear" Bryant	Orange 1-2-50	Santa Clara 13-21
Paul "Bear" Bryant	Sugar 1-1-51	Oklahoma 13-7
Paul "Bear" Bryant	Cotton 1-1-52	Texas Christian 20-7
Fran Curci	Peach 12-31-76	North Caro. 21-0
Jerry Claiborne	Hall of Fame 12-22-83	West Va. 16-20
Jerry Claiborne	Hall of Fame 12-29-84	Wisconsin 20-19
Bill Curry	Peach 12-31-93	Clemson 13-14
All bowls 5-3-0		
LSU		
Bernie Moore	Sugar 1-1-36	Texas Christian 2-3
Bernie Moore	Sugar 1-1-37	Santa Clara 14-21
Bernie Moore	Sugar 1-1-38	Santa Clara 0-6
Bernie Moore	Orange 1-1-44	Texas A&M 19-14
Bernie Moore	Cotton 1-1-47	Arkansas 0-0
Gaynell Tinsley	Sugar 1-2-50	Oklahoma 0-35
Paul Dietzel	Sugar 1-1-59	Clemson 7-0
Paul Dietzel	Sugar 1-1-60	Mississippi 0-21
Paul Dietzel	Orange 1-1-62	Colorado 25-7
Charlie McClendon	Cotton 1-1-63	Texas 13-0
Charlie McClendon	Bluebonnet 12-21-63	Baylor 7-14
Charlie McClendon	Sugar 1-1-65	Syracuse 13-10
Charlie McClendon	Cotton 1-1-66	Arkansas 14-7
Charlie McClendon	Sugar 1-1-68	Wyoming 20-13
Charlie McClendon	Peach 12-30-68	Florida St. 31-27
Charlie McClendon	Orange 1-1-71	Nebraska 12-17
Charlie McClendon	Sun 12-18-71	Iowa St. 33-15
Charlie McClendon	Bluebonnet 12-30-72	Tennessee 17-24
Charlie McClendon	Orange 1-1-74	Penn St. 9-16
Charlie McClendon	Sun 12-31-77	Stanford 14-24
Charlie McClendon	Liberty 12-23-78	Missouri 15-20
Charlie McClendon	Tangerine 12-22-79	Wake Forest 34-10
Jerry Stovall	Orange 1-1-83	Nebraska 20-21
Bill Arnsparger	Sugar 1-1-85	Nebraska 10-28
Bill Arnsparger	Liberty 12-27-85	Baylor 7-21
Bill Arnsparger	Sugar 1-1-87	Nebraska 15-30
Mike Archer	Gator 12-31-87	South Caro. 30-13
Mike Archer	Hall of Fame 1-2-89	Syracuse 10-23
Gerry DiNardo	Independence 12-29-95	Michigan St. 45-26
Gerry DiNardo	Peach 12-28-96	Clemson 10-7
Gerry DiNardo	Independence 12-28-97	Notre Dame 27-9
All bowls 14-16-1		
LOUISIANA TECH		
Maxie Lambright	Independence 12-17-77	Louisville 24-14
Maxie Lambright	Independence 12-16-78	East Caro. 13-35
Joe Raymond Peace	Independence 12-15-90	Maryland 34-34
All bowls 1-1-1		

School/Coach	Bowl/Date	Opponent/Score
LOUISVILLE		
Frank Camp	Sun 1-1-58	Drake 34-20
Lee Corso	Pasadena 12-19-70	Long Beach St. 24-24
Vince Gibson	Independence 12-17-77	Louisiana Tech 14-24
Howard Schnellenberger	Fiesta 1-1-91	Alabama 34-7
Howard Schnellenberger	Liberty 12-28-93	Michigan St. 18-7
All bowls 3-1-1		
MARSHALL		
Bob Pruett	Motor City 12-26-97	Mississippi 31-34
MARYLAND		
Jim Tatum	Gator 1-1-48	Georgia 20-20
Jim Tatum	Gator 1-2-50	Missouri 20-7
Jim Tatum	Sugar 1-1-52	Tennessee 28-13
Jim Tatum	Orange 1-1-54	Oklahoma 0-7
Jim Tatum	Orange 1-2-56	Oklahoma 6-20
Jerry Claiborne	Peach 12-28-73	Georgia 16-17
Jerry Claiborne	Liberty 12-16-74	Tennessee 3-7
Jerry Claiborne	Gator 12-29-75	Florida 13-0
Jerry Claiborne	Cotton 1-1-77	Houston 21-30
Jerry Claiborne	Hall of Fame 12-22-77	Minnesota 17-7
Jerry Claiborne	Sun 12-23-78	Texas 0-42
Jerry Claiborne	Tangerine 12-20-80	Florida 20-35
Bobby Ross	Aloha 12-25-82	Washington 20-21
Bobby Ross	Florida Citrus 12-17-83	Tennessee 23-30
Bobby Ross	Sun 12-22-84	Tennessee 27-26
Bobby Ross	Cherry 12-21-85	Syracuse 35-18
Joe Krivak	Independence 12-15-90	Louisiana Tech 34-34
All bowls 6-9-2		
MEMPHIS		
Billy Murphy	Pasadena 12-18-71	San Jose St. 28-9
All bowls 1-0-0		
MIAMI (FLA.)		
Tom McCann	Orange 1-1-35	Bucknell 0-26
Jack Harding	Orange 1-1-46	Holy Cross 13-6
Andy Gustafson	Orange 1-1-51	Clemson 14-15
Andy Gustafson	Gator 1-1-52	Clemson 14-0
Andy Gustafson	Liberty 12-16-61	Syracuse 14-15
Andy Gustafson	Gotham 12-15-62	Nebraska 34-36
Charlie Tate	Liberty 12-10-66	Virginia Tech 14-7
Charlie Tate	Bluebonnet 12-31-67	Colorado 21-31
Howard Schnellenberger	Peach 1-2-81	Virginia Tech 20-10
Howard Schnellenberger	Orange 1-2-84	Nebraska 31-30
Jimmy Johnson	Fiesta 1-1-85	UCLA 37-39
Jimmy Johnson	Sugar 1-1-86	Tennessee 7-35
Jimmy Johnson	Fiesta 1-2-87	Penn St. 10-14
Jimmy Johnson	Orange 1-1-88	Oklahoma 20-14
Jimmy Johnson	Orange 1-2-89	Nebraska 23-3
Dennis Erickson	Sugar 1-1-90	Alabama 33-25
Dennis Erickson	Cotton 1-1-91	Texas 46-3
Dennis Erickson	Orange 1-1-92	Nebraska 22-0
Dennis Erickson	Sugar 1-1-93	Alabama 13-34
Dennis Erickson	Fiesta 1-1-94	Arizona 0-29
Dennis Erickson	Orange 1-1-95	Nebraska 17-24
Butch Davis	Carquest 12-27-96	Virginia 31-21
All bowls 11-11-0		
MIAMI (OHIO)		
Sid Gillman	Sun 1-1-48	Texas Tech 13-12
Woody Hayes	Salad 1-1-51	Arizona St. 34-21
John Pont	Tangerine 12-22-62	Houston 21-49
Bill Mallory	Tangerine 12-22-73	Florida 16-7
Dick Crum	Tangerine 12-21-74	Georgia 21-10
Dick Crum	Tangerine 12-20-75	South Caro. 20-7
Tim Rose	California 12-13-86	San Jose St. 7-37
All bowls 5-2-0		
MICHIGAN		
Fielding "Hurry Up" Yost	Rose 1-1-02	Stanford 49-0
H. O. "Fritz" Crisler	Rose 1-1-48	Southern Cal 49-0
Bennie Oosterbaan	Rose 1-1-51	California 14-6
Chalmers "Bump" Elliott	Rose 1-1-65	Oregon St. 34-7
Glenn "Bo" Schembechler	Rose 1-1-70	Southern Cal 3-10
Glenn "Bo" Schembechler	Rose 1-1-72	Stanford 12-13
Glenn "Bo" Schembechler	Orange 1-1-76	Oklahoma 6-14
Glenn "Bo" Schembechler	Rose 1-1-77	Southern Cal 6-14
Glenn "Bo" Schembechler	Rose 1-2-78	Washington 20-27
Glenn "Bo" Schembechler	Rose 1-1-79	Southern Cal 10-17
Glenn "Bo" Schembechler	Gator 12-28-79	North Caro. 15-17
Glenn "Bo" Schembechler	Rose 1-1-81	Washington 23-6
Glenn "Bo" Schembechler	Bluebonnet 12-31-81	UCLA 33-14
Glenn "Bo" Schembechler	Rose 1-1-83	UCLA 14-24
Glenn "Bo" Schembechler	Sugar 1-2-84	Auburn 7-9
Glenn "Bo" Schembechler	Holiday 12-21-84	Brigham Young 17-24
Glenn "Bo" Schembechler	Fiesta 1-1-86	Nebraska 27-23
Glenn "Bo" Schembechler	Rose 1-1-87	Arizona St. 15-22
Glenn "Bo" Schembechler	Hall of Fame 1-2-88	Alabama 28-24
Glenn "Bo" Schembechler	Rose 1-2-89	Southern Cal 22-14
Glenn "Bo" Schembechler	Rose 1-1-90	Southern Cal 10-17
Gary Moeller	Gator 1-1-91	Mississippi 35-3
Gary Moeller	Rose 1-1-92	Washington 14-34
Gary Moeller	Rose 1-1-93	Washington 38-31
Gary Moeller	Hall of Fame 1-1-94	North Caro. St. 42-7
Gary Moeller	Holiday 12-30-94	Colorado St. 24-14
Lloyd Carr	Alamo 12-28-95	Texas A&M 20-22
Lloyd Carr	Outback 1-1-97	Alabama 14-17
Lloyd Carr	Rose 1-1-98	Washington St. 21-16
All bowls 14-15-0		
MICHIGAN ST.		
Charlie Bachman	Orange 1-1-38	Auburn 0-6
Clarence "Biggie" Munn	Rose 1-1-54	UCLA 28-20
Duffy Daugherty	Rose 1-2-56	UCLA 17-14
Duffy Daugherty	Rose 1-1-66	UCLA 12-14
George Perles	Cherry 12-22-84	Army 6-10
George Perles	Hall of Fame 12-31-85	Georgia Tech 14-17
George Perles	Rose 1-1-88	Southern Cal 20-17
George Perles	Gator 1-1-89	Georgia 27-34
George Perles	Aloha 12-25-89	Hawaii 33-13
George Perles	John Hancock 12-31-90	Southern Cal 17-6
George Perles	Liberty 12-28-93	Louisville 7-18
Nick Saban	Independence 12-29-95	LSU 26-45
Nick Saban	Sun 12-31-96	Stanford 0-38
Nick Saban	Aloha 12-25-97	Washington 23-51
All bowls 5-9-0		
MINNESOTA		
Murray Warmath	Rose 1-2-61	Washington 7-17
Murray Warmath	Rose 1-1-62	UCLA 21-3
Cal Stoll	Hall of Fame 12-22-77	Maryland 7-17
John Gutekunst	Independence 12-21-85	Clemson 20-13
John Gutekunst	Liberty 12-29-86	Tennessee 14-21
All bowls 2-3-0		
MISSISSIPPI		
Ed Walker	Orange 1-1-36	Catholic 19-20
John Vaught	Delta 1-1-48	Texas Christian 13-9
John Vaught	Sugar 1-1-53	Georgia Tech 7-24
John Vaught	Sugar 1-1-55	Navy 0-21
John Vaught	Cotton 1-2-56	Texas Christian 14-13
John Vaught	Sugar 1-1-58	Texas 39-7
John Vaught	Gator 12-27-58	Florida 7-3
John Vaught	Sugar 1-1-60	LSU 21-0
John Vaught	Sugar 1-2-61	Rice 14-6
John Vaught	Cotton 1-1-62	Texas 7-12
John Vaught	Sugar 1-1-63	Arkansas 17-13
John Vaught	Sugar 1-1-64	Alabama 7-12
John Vaught	Bluebonnet 12-19-64	Tulsa 7-14
John Vaught	Liberty 12-18-65	Auburn 13-7
John Vaught	Bluebonnet 12-17-66	Texas 0-19
John Vaught	Sun 12-30-67	UTEP 7-14
John Vaught	Liberty 12-14-68	Virginia Tech 34-17
John Vaught	Sugar 1-1-70	Arkansas 27-22
John Vaught	Gator 1-2-71	Auburn 28-35
Billy Kinard	Peach 12-30-71	Georgia Tech 41-18
Billy Brewer	Independence 12-10-83	Air Force 3-9
Billy Brewer	Independence 12-20-86	Texas Tech 20-17
Billy Brewer	Liberty 12-28-89	Air Force 42-29
Billy Brewer	Gator 1-1-91	Michigan 3-35
Billy Brewer	Liberty 12-31-92	Air Force 13-0
Tommy Turberville	Motor City 12-26-97	Marshall 34-31
All bowls 15-11-0		
MISSISSIPPI ST.		
Ralph Sasse	Orange 1-1-37	Duquesne 12-13
Allyn McKeen	Orange 1-1-41	Georgetown 14-7
Paul Davis	Liberty 12-21-63	North Caro. St. 16-12
Bob Tyler	Sun 12-28-74	North Caro. 26-24
Emory Bellard	Sun 12-27-80	Nebraska 17-31
Emory Bellard	Hall of Fame 12-31-81	Kansas 10-0
Jackie Sherrill	Liberty 12-29-91	Air Force 15-38
Jackie Sherrill	Peach 1-2-93	North Caro. 17-21
Jackie Sherrill	Peach 1-1-95	North Caro. St. 24-28
All bowls 4-5-0		
MISSOURI		
Gwinn Henry	Los Angeles Christmas Festival 12-25-24	Southern Cal 7-20
Don Faurot	Orange 1-1-40	Georgia Tech 7-21
Don Faurot	Sugar 1-1-42	Fordham 0-2
Chauncey Simpson	Cotton 1-1-46	Texas 27-40

BOWL/ALL-STAR RECORDS

School/Coach	Bowl/Date	Opponent/Score
Don Faurot	Gator 1-1-49	Clemson 23-24
Don Faurot	Gator 1-2-50	Maryland 7-20
Dan Devine	Orange 1-1-60	Georgia 0-40
Dan Devine	Orange 1-2-61	Navy 21-14
Dan Devine	Bluebonnet 12-22-62	Georgia Tech 14-10
Dan Devine	Sugar 1-1-66	Florida 20-18
Dan Devine	Gator 12-28-68	Alabama 35-10
Dan Devine	Orange 1-1-70	Penn St. 3-10
Al Onofrio	Fiesta 12-23-72	Arizona St. 35-49
Al Onofrio	Sun 12-29-73	Auburn 34-17
Warren Powers	Liberty 12-23-78	LSU 20-15
Warren Powers	Hall of Fame 12-29-79	South Caro. 24-14
Warren Powers	Liberty 12-27-80	Purdue 25-28
Warren Powers	Tangerine 12-19-81	Southern Miss. 19-17
Warren Powers	Holiday 12-23-83	Brigham Young 17-21
Larry Smith	Holiday 12-29-97	Colorado St. 24-35

All bowls 8-12-0

NAVY

School/Coach	Bowl/Date	Opponent/Score
Bob Folwell	Rose 1-1-24	Washington 14-14
Eddie Erdelatz	Sugar 1-1-55	Mississippi 21-0
Eddie Erdelatz	Cotton 1-1-58	Rice 20-7
Wayne Hardin	Orange 1-1-61	Missouri 14-21
Wayne Hardin	Cotton 1-1-64	Texas 6-28
George Welsh	Holiday 12-22-78	Brigham Young 23-16
George Welsh	Garden State 12-14-80	Houston 0-35
George Welsh	Liberty 12-30-81	Ohio St. 28-31
Charlie Weatherbie	Aloha 12-25-96	California 42-38

All bowls 4-4-1

NEBRASKA

School/Coach	Bowl/Date	Opponent/Score
Lawrence McC. "Biff" Jones	Rose 1-1-41	Stanford 13-21
Bill Glassford	Orange 1-1-55	Duke 7-34
Bob Devaney	Gotham 12-15-62	Miami (Fla.) 36-34
Bob Devaney	Orange 1-1-64	Auburn 13-7
Bob Devaney	Cotton 1-1-65	Arkansas 7-10
Bob Devaney	Orange 1-1-66	Alabama 28-39
Bob Devaney	Sugar 1-2-67	Alabama 7-34
Bob Devaney	Sun 12-20-69	Georgia 45-6
Bob Devaney	Orange 1-1-71	LSU 17-12
Bob Devaney	Orange 1-1-72	Alabama 38-6
Bob Devaney	Orange 1-1-73	Notre Dame 40-6
Tom Osborne	Cotton 1-1-74	Texas 19-3
Tom Osborne	Sugar 12-31-74	Florida 13-10
Tom Osborne	Fiesta 12-26-75	Arizona St. 14-17
Tom Osborne	Bluebonnet 12-31-76	Texas Tech 27-24
Tom Osborne	Liberty 12-19-77	North Caro. 21-17
Tom Osborne	Orange 1-1-79	Oklahoma 24-31
Tom Osborne	Cotton 1-1-80	Houston 14-17
Tom Osborne	Sun 12-27-80	Mississippi St. 31-17
Tom Osborne	Orange 1-1-82	Clemson 15-22
Tom Osborne	Orange 1-1-83	LSU 21-20
Tom Osborne	Orange 1-2-84	Miami (Fla.) 30-31
Tom Osborne	Sugar 1-1-85	LSU 28-10
Tom Osborne	Fiesta 1-1-86	Michigan 23-27
Tom Osborne	Sugar 1-1-87	LSU 30-15
Tom Osborne	Fiesta 1-1-88	Florida St. 28-31
Tom Osborne	Orange 1-2-89	Miami (Fla.) 3-23
Tom Osborne	Fiesta 1-1-90	Florida St. 17-41
Tom Osborne	Florida Citrus 1-1-91	Georgia Tech 21-45
Tom Osborne	Orange 1-1-92	Miami (Fla.) 0-22
Tom Osborne	Orange 1-1-93	Florida St. 14-27
Tom Osborne	Orange 1-1-94	Florida St. 16-18
Tom Osborne	Orange 1-1-95	Miami (Fla.) 24-17
Tom Osborne	Fiesta 1-2-96	Florida 62-24
Tom Osborne	Orange 12-31-96	Virginia Tech 41-21
Tom Osborne	Orange 1-2-98	Tennessee 42-17

All bowls 18-18-0

NEVADA

School/Coach	Bowl/Date	Opponent/Score
Joe Sheeketski	Salad 1-1-48	North Texas 13-6
Joe Sheeketski	Harbor 1-1-49	Villanova 7-27
Chris Ault	Las Vegas 12-18-92	Bowling Green 34-35
Chris Ault	Las Vegas 12-14-95	Toledo 37-40 (OT)
Jeff Tisdel	Las Vegas 12-29-96	Ball St. 18-15

All bowls 2-3-0

UNLV

School/Coach	Bowl/Date	Opponent/Score
Harvey Hyde	California 12-15-84	Toledo 30-13
Jeff Horton	Las Vegas 12-15-94	Central Mich. 52-24

All bowls 2-0-0

NEW MEXICO

School/Coach	Bowl/Date	Opponent/Score
Ted Shipkey	Sun 1-2-39	Utah 0-26
Willis Barnes	Sun 1-1-44	Southwestern (Tex.) 0-7
Willis Barnes	Sun 1-1-46	Denver 34-24
Willis Barnes	Harbor 1-1-47	Montana St. 13-13
Bill Weeks	Aviation 12-9-61	Western Mich. 28-12
Dennis Franchione	Insight.com 12-27-97	Arizona 14-20

All bowls 2-3-1

NEW MEXICO ST.

School/Coach	Bowl/Date	Opponent/Score
Jerry Hines	Sun 1-1-36	Hardin-Simmons 14-14
Warren Woodson	Sun 12-31-59	North Texas 28-8
Warren Woodson	Sun 12-31-60	Utah St. 20-13

All bowls 2-0-1

NORTH CARO.

School/Coach	Bowl/Date	Opponent/Score
Carl Snavely	Sugar 1-1-47	Georgia 10-20
Carl Snavely	Sugar 1-1-49	Oklahoma 6-14
Carl Snavely	Cotton 1-2-50	Rice 13-27
Jim Hickey	Gator 12-28-63	Air Force 35-0
Bill Dooley	Peach 12-30-70	Arizona St. 26-48
Bill Dooley	Gator 12-31-71	Georgia 3-7
Bill Dooley	Sun 12-30-72	Texas Tech 32-28
Bill Dooley	Sun 12-28-74	Mississippi St. 24-26
Bill Dooley	Peach 12-31-76	Kentucky 0-21
Bill Dooley	Liberty 12-19-77	Nebraska 17-21
Dick Crum	Gator 12-28-79	Michigan 17-15
Dick Crum	Bluebonnet 12-31-80	Texas 16-7
Dick Crum	Gator 12-28-81	Arkansas 31-27
Dick Crum	Sun 12-25-82	Texas 26-10
Dick Crum	Peach 12-30-83	Florida St. 3-28
Dick Crum	Aloha 12-27-86	Arizona 21-30
Mack Brown	Peach 1-2-93	Mississippi St. 21-17
Mack Brown	Gator 12-31-93	Alabama 10-24
Mack Brown	Sun 12-30-94	Texas 31-35
Mack Brown	Carquest 12-30-95	Arkansas 20-10
Mack Brown	Gator 1-1-97	West Va. 20-13
Carl Torbush	Gator 1-1-98	Virginia Tech 42-3

All bowls 10-12-0

NORTH CARO. ST.

School/Coach	Bowl/Date	Opponent/Score
Beattie Feathers	Gator 1-1-47	Oklahoma 13-34
Earle Edwards	Liberty 12-21-63	Mississippi St. 12-16
Earle Edwards	Liberty 12-16-67	Georgia 14-7
Lou Holtz	Peach 12-29-72	West Va. 49-13
Lou Holtz	Liberty 12-17-73	Kansas 31-18
Lou Holtz	Bluebonnet 12-23-74	Houston 31-31
Lou Holtz	Peach 12-31-75	West Va. 10-13
Bo Rein	Peach 12-31-77	Iowa St. 24-14
Bo Rein	Tangerine 12-23-78	Pittsburgh 30-17
Dick Sheridan	Peach 12-31-86	Virginia Tech 24-25
Dick Sheridan	Peach 12-31-88	Iowa 28-23
Dick Sheridan	Copper 12-31-89	Arizona 10-17
Dick Sheridan	All-American 12-28-90	Southern Miss. 31-27
Dick Sheridan	Peach 1-1-92	East Caro. 34-37
Dick Sheridan	Gator 12-31-92	Florida 10-27
Mike O'Cain	Hall of Fame 1-1-94	Michigan 7-42
Mike O'Cain	Peach 1-1-95	Mississippi St. 28-24

All bowls 8-8-1

NORTH TEXAS

School/Coach	Bowl/Date	Opponent/Score
Odus Mitchell	Salad 1-1-48	Nevada 6-13
Odus Mitchell	Sun 12-31-59	New Mexico St. 8-28

All bowls 0-2-0

NORTHERN ILL.

School/Coach	Bowl/Date	Opponent/Score
Bill Mallory	California 12-17-83	Cal St. Fullerton 20-13

All bowls 1-0-0

NORTHWESTERN

School/Coach	Bowl/Date	Opponent/Score
Bob Voigts	Rose 1-1-49	California 20-14
Gary Barnett	Rose 1-1-96	Southern Cal 32-41
Gary Barnett	Florida Citrus 1-1-97	Tennessee 28-48

All bowls 1-2-0

NOTRE DAME

School/Coach	Bowl/Date	Opponent/Score
Knute Rockne	Rose 1-1-25	Stanford 27-10
Ara Parseghian	Cotton 1-1-70	Texas 17-21
Ara Parseghian	Cotton 1-1-71	Texas 24-11
Ara Parseghian	Orange 1-1-73	Nebraska 6-40
Ara Parseghian	Sugar 12-31-73	Alabama 24-23
Ara Parseghian	Orange 1-1-75	Alabama 13-11
Dan Devine	Gator 12-27-76	Penn St. 20-9
Dan Devine	Cotton 1-2-78	Texas 38-10
Dan Devine	Cotton 1-1-79	Houston 35-34
Dan Devine	Sugar 1-1-81	Georgia 10-17
Gerry Faust	Liberty 12-29-83	Boston College 19-18
Gerry Faust	Aloha 12-29-84	Southern Methodist 20-27
Lou Holtz	Cotton 1-1-88	Texas A&M 10-35
Lou Holtz	Fiesta 1-2-89	West Va. 34-21
Lou Holtz	Orange 1-1-90	Colorado 21-6

School/Coach	Bowl/Date	Opponent/Score
Lou Holtz	Orange 1-1-91	Colorado 9-10
Lou Holtz	Sugar 1-1-92	Florida 39-28
Lou Holtz	Cotton 1-1-93	Texas A&M 28-3
Lou Holtz	Cotton 1-1-94	Texas A&M 24-21
Lou Holtz	Fiesta 1-2-95	Colorado 24-41
Lou Holtz	Orange 1-1-96	Florida St. 26-31
Bob Davie	Independence 12-28-97	LSU 9-27
All bowls 13-9-0		
OHIO		
Bill Hess	Sun 12-31-62	West Tex. A&M 14-15
Bill Hess	Tangerine 12-27-68	Richmond 42-49
All bowls 0-2-0		
OHIO ST.		
John Wilce	Rose 1-1-21	California 0-28
Wes Fesler	Rose 1-2-50	California 17-14
Woody Hayes	Rose 1-1-55	Southern Cal 20-7
Woody Hayes	Rose 1-1-58	Oregon 10-7
Woody Hayes	Rose 1-1-69	Southern Cal 27-16
Woody Hayes	Rose 1-1-71	Stanford 17-27
Woody Hayes	Rose 1-1-73	Southern Cal 17-42
Woody Hayes	Rose 1-1-74	Southern Cal 42-21
Woody Hayes	Rose 1-1-75	Southern Cal 17-18
Woody Hayes	Rose 1-1-76	UCLA 10-23
Woody Hayes	Orange 1-1-77	Colorado 27-10
Woody Hayes	Sugar 1-2-78	Alabama 6-35
Woody Hayes	Gator 12-29-78	Clemson 15-17
Earle Bruce	Rose 1-1-80	Southern Cal 16-17
Earle Bruce	Fiesta 12-26-80	Penn St. 19-31
Earle Bruce	Liberty 12-30-81	Navy 31-28
Earle Bruce	Holiday 12-17-82	Brigham Young 47-17
Earle Bruce	Fiesta 1-2-84	Pittsburgh 28-23
Earle Bruce	Rose 1-1-85	Southern Cal 17-20
Earle Bruce	Florida Citrus 12-28-85	Brigham Young 10-7
Earle Bruce	Cotton 1-1-87	Texas A&M 28-12
John Cooper	Hall of Fame 1-1-90	Auburn 14-31
John Cooper	Liberty 12-27-90	Air Force 11-23
John Cooper	Hall of Fame 1-1-92	Syracuse 17-24
John Cooper	Florida Citrus 1-1-93	Georgia 14-21
John Cooper	Holiday 12-30-93	Brigham Young 28-21
John Cooper	Florida Citrus 1-2-95	Alabama 17-24
John Cooper	Florida Citrus 1-1-96	Tennessee 14-20
John Cooper	Rose 1-1-97	Arizona St. 20-17
John Cooper	Sugar 1-1-98	Florida St. 14-31
All bowls 13-17-0		
OKLAHOMA		
Tom Stidham	Orange 1-2-39	Tennessee 0-17
Jim Tatum	Gator 1-1-47	North Caro. St. 34-13
Bud Wilkinson	Sugar 1-1-49	North Caro. 14-6
Bud Wilkinson	Sugar 1-2-50	LSU 35-0
Bud Wilkinson	Sugar 1-1-51	Kentucky 7-13
Bud Wilkinson	Orange 1-1-54	Maryland 7-0
Bud Wilkinson	Orange 1-2-56	Maryland 20-6
Bud Wilkinson	Orange 1-1-58	Duke 48-21
Bud Wilkinson	Orange 1-1-59	Syracuse 21-6
Bud Wilkinson	Orange 1-1-63	Alabama 0-17
Gomer Jones	Gator 1-2-65	Florida St. 19-36
Chuck Fairbanks	Orange 1-1-68	Tennessee 26-24
Chuck Fairbanks	Bluebonnet 12-31-68	Southern Methodist 27-28
Chuck Fairbanks	Bluebonnet 12-31-70	Alabama 24-24
Chuck Fairbanks	Sugar 1-1-72	Auburn 40-22
Chuck Fairbanks	Sugar 12-31-72	Penn St. 14-0
Barry Switzer	Orange 1-1-76	Michigan 14-6
Barry Switzer	Fiesta 12-25-76	Wyoming 41-7
Barry Switzer	Orange 1-2-78	Arkansas 6-31
Barry Switzer	Orange 1-1-79	Nebraska 31-24
Barry Switzer	Orange 1-1-80	Florida St. 24-7
Barry Switzer	Orange 1-1-81	Florida St. 18-17
Barry Switzer	Sun 12-26-81	Houston 40-14
Barry Switzer	Fiesta 1-1-83	Arizona St. 21-32
Barry Switzer	Orange 1-1-85	Washington 17-28
Barry Switzer	Orange 1-1-86	Penn St. 25-10
Barry Switzer	Orange 1-1-87	Arkansas 42-8
Barry Switzer	Orange 1-1-88	Miami (Fla.) 14-20
Barry Switzer	Florida Citrus 1-2-89	Clemson 6-13
Gary Gibbs	Gator 12-29-91	Virginia 48-14
Gary Gibbs	John Hancock 12-24-93	Texas Tech 41-10
Gary Gibbs	Copper 12-29-94	Brigham Young 6-31
All bowls 20-11-1		
OKLAHOMA ST.		
Jim Lookabaugh	Cotton 1-1-45	Texas Christian 34-0
Jim Lookabaugh	Sugar 1-1-46	St. Mary's (Cal.) 33-13
Jim Lookabaugh	Delta 1-1-49	William & Mary 0-20

School/Coach	Bowl/Date	Opponent/Score
Cliff Speegle	Bluegrass 12-13-58	Florida St. 15-6
Jim Stanley	Fiesta 12-28-74	Brigham Young 16-6
Jim Stanley	Tangerine 12-18-76	Brigham Young 49-12
Jimmy Johnson	Independence 12-12-81	Texas A&M 16-33
Jimmy Johnson	Bluebonnet 12-31-83	Baylor 24-14
Pat Jones	Gator 12-28-84	South Caro. 21-14
Pat Jones	Gator 12-30-85	Florida St. 23-34
Pat Jones	Sun 12-25-87	West Va. 35-33
Pat Jones	Holiday 12-30-88	Wyoming 62-14
Bob Simmons	Alamo 12-30-97	Purdue 20-33
All bowls 9-4-0		
OREGON		
Hugo Bezdek	Rose 1-1-17	Pennsylvania 14-0
Charles "Shy" Huntington	Rose 1-1-20	Harvard 6-7
Jim Aiken	Cotton 1-1-49	Southern Methodist 13-21
Len Casanova	Rose 1-1-58	Ohio St. 7-10
Len Casanova	Liberty 12-17-60	Penn St. 12-41
Len Casanova	Sun 12-31-63	Southern Methodist 21-14
Rich Brooks	Independence 12-16-89	Tulsa 27-24
Rich Brooks	Freedom 12-29-90	Colorado St. 31-32
Rich Brooks	Independence 12-31-92	Wake Forest 35-39
Rich Brooks	Rose 1-2-95	Penn St. 20-38
Mike Bellotti	Cotton 1-1-96	Colorado 6-38
Mike Bellotti	Las Vegas 12-20-97	Air Force 41-13
All bowls 4-8-0		
OREGON ST.		
Lon Stiner	Rose 1-1-42	Duke 20-16
Tommy Prothro	Rose 1-1-57	Iowa 19-35
Tommy Prothro	Liberty 12-15-62	Villanova 6-0
Tommy Prothro	Rose 1-1-65	Michigan 7-34
All bowls 2-2-0		
PENN ST.		
Hugo Bezdek	Rose 1-1-23	Southern Cal 3-14
Bob Higgins	Cotton 1-1-48	Southern Methodist 13-13
Charles "Rip" Engle	Liberty 12-19-59	Alabama 7-0
Charles "Rip" Engle	Liberty 12-17-60	Oregon 41-12
Charles "Rip" Engle	Gator 12-30-61	Georgia Tech 30-15
Charles "Rip" Engle	Gator 12-29-62	Florida 7-17
Joe Paterno	Gator 12-30-67	Florida St. 17-17
Joe Paterno	Orange 1-1-69	Kansas 15-14
Joe Paterno	Orange 1-1-70	Missouri 10-3
Joe Paterno	Cotton 1-1-72	Texas 30-6
Joe Paterno	Sugar 12-31-72	Oklahoma 0-14
Joe Paterno	Orange 1-1-74	LSU 16-9
Joe Paterno	Cotton 1-1-75	Baylor 41-20
Joe Paterno	Sugar 12-31-75	Alabama 6-13
Joe Paterno	Gator 12-27-76	Notre Dame 9-20
Joe Paterno	Fiesta 12-25-77	Arizona St. 42-30
Joe Paterno	Sugar 1-1-79	Alabama 7-14
Joe Paterno	Liberty 12-22-79	Tulane 9-6
Joe Paterno	Fiesta 12-26-80	Ohio St. 31-19
Joe Paterno	Fiesta 1-1-82	Southern Cal 26-10
Joe Paterno	Sugar 1-1-83	Georgia 27-23
Joe Paterno	Aloha 12-26-83	Washington 13-10
Joe Paterno	Orange 1-1-86	Oklahoma 10-25
Joe Paterno	Fiesta 1-2-87	Miami (Fla.) 14-10
Joe Paterno	Florida Citrus 1-1-88	Clemson 10-35
Joe Paterno	Holiday 12-29-89	Brigham Young 50-39
Joe Paterno	Blockbuster 12-28-90	Florida St. 17-24
Joe Paterno	Fiesta 1-1-92	Tennessee 42-17
Joe Paterno	Blockbuster 1-1-93	Stanford 3-24
Joe Paterno	Florida Citrus 1-1-94	Tennessee 31-13
Joe Paterno	Rose 1-2-95	Oregon 38-20
Joe Paterno	Outback 1-1-96	Auburn 43-14
Joe Paterno	Fiesta 1-1-97	Texas 38-15
Joe Paterno	Flordia Citrus 1-1-98	Florida 6-21
All bowls 21-11-2		
PITTSBURGH		
Jock Sutherland	Rose 1-2-28	Stanford 6-7
Jock Sutherland	Rose 1-1-30	Southern Cal 14-47
Jock Sutherland	Rose 1-2-33	Southern Cal 0-35
Jock Sutherland	Rose 1-1-37	Washington 21-0
John Michelosen	Sugar 1-2-56	Georgia Tech 0-7
John Michelosen	Gator 12-29-56	Georgia Tech 14-21
Johnny Majors	Fiesta 12-21-73	Arizona St. 7-28
Johnny Majors	Sun 12-26-75	Kansas 33-19
Johnny Majors	Sugar 1-1-77	Georgia 27-3
Jackie Sherrill	Gator 12-30-77	Clemson 34-3
Jackie Sherrill	Tangerine 12-23-78	North Caro. St. 17-30
Jackie Sherrill	Fiesta 12-25-79	Arizona 16-10
Jackie Sherrill	Gator 12-29-80	South Caro. 37-9
Jackie Sherrill	Sugar 1-1-82	Georgia 24-20

BOWL/ALL-STAR RECORDS

School/Coach	Bowl/Date	Opponent/Score
Foge Fazio	Cotton 1-1-83	Southern Methodist 3-7
Foge Fazio	Fiesta 1-2-84	Ohio St. 23-28
Mike Gottfried	Bluebonnet 12-31-87	Texas 27-32
Paul Hackett	John Hancock 12-30-89	Texas A&M 31-28
Walt Harris	Liberty 12-31-97	Southern Miss. 7-41
All bowls 8-11-0		

PURDUE

School/Coach	Bowl/Date	Opponent/Score
Jack Mollenkopf	Rose 1-2-67	Southern Cal 14-13
Jim Young	Peach 12-25-78	Georgia Tech 41-21
Jim Young	Bluebonnet 12-31-79	Tennessee 27-22
Jim Young	Liberty 12-27-80	Missouri 28-25
Leon Burtnett	Peach 12-31-84	Virginia 24-27
Joe Tiller	Alamo 12-30-97	Oklahoma St. 33-20
All bowls 5-1-0		

RICE

School/Coach	Bowl/Date	Opponent/Score
Jimmy Kitts	Cotton 1-1-38	Colorado 28-14
Jess Neely	Orange 1-1-47	Tennessee 8-0
Jess Neely	Cotton 1-2-50	North Caro. 27-13
Jess Neely	Cotton 1-1-54	Alabama 28-6
Jess Neely	Cotton 1-1-58	Navy 7-20
Jess Neely	Sugar 1-2-61	Mississippi 6-14
Jess Neely	Bluebonnet 12-16-61	Kansas 7-33
All bowls 4-3-0		

RUTGERS

School/Coach	Bowl/Date	Opponent/Score
Frank Burns	Garden State 12-16-78	Arizona St. 18-34
All bowls 0-1-0		

SAN DIEGO ST.

School/Coach	Bowl/Date	Opponent/Score
Bill Schutte	Harbor 1-1-48	Hardin-Simmons 0-53
Don Coryell	Pasadena 12-6-69	Boston U. 28-7
Denny Stolz	Holiday 12-30-86	Iowa 38-39
Al Luginbill	Freedom 12-30-91	Tulsa 17-28
All bowls 1-3-0		

SAN JOSE ST.

School/Coach	Bowl/Date	Opponent/Score
Bill Hubbard	Raisin 1-1-47	Utah St. 20-0
Bill Hubbard	Raisin 12-31-49	Texas Tech 20-13
Dewey King	Pasadena 12-18-71	Memphis 9-28
Jack Elway	California 12-19-81	Toledo 25-27
Claude Gilbert	California 12-31-86	Miami (Ohio) 37-7
Claude Gilbert	California 12-12-87	Eastern Mich. 27-30
Terry Shea	California 12-8-90	Central Mich. 48-24
All bowls 4-3-0		

SOUTH CARO.

School/Coach	Bowl/Date	Opponent/Score
Johnny McMillan	Gator 1-1-46	Wake Forest 14-26
Paul Dietzel	Peach 12-30-69	West Va. 3-14
Jim Carlen	Tangerine 12-20-75	Miami (Ohio) 7-20
Jim Carlen	Hall of Fame 12-29-79	Missouri 14-24
Jim Carlen	Gator 12-29-80	Pittsburgh 9-37
Joe Morrison	Gator 12-28-84	Oklahoma St. 14-21
Joe Morrison	Gator 12-31-87	LSU 13-30
Joe Morrison	Liberty 12-28-88	Indiana 10-34
Brad Scott	Carquest 1-2-95	West Va. 24-21
All bowls 1-8-0		

SOUTHERN CAL

School/Coach	Bowl/Date	Opponent/Score
Elmer "Gus" Henderson	Rose 1-1-23	Penn St. 14-3
Elmer "Gus" Henderson	Los Angeles Christmas Festival 12-25-24	Missouri 20-7
Howard Jones	Rose 1-1-30	Pittsburgh 47-14
Howard Jones	Rose 1-1-32	Tulane 21-12
Howard Jones	Rose 1-2-33	Pittsburgh 35-0
Howard Jones	Rose 1-2-39	Duke 7-3
Howard Jones	Rose 1-1-40	Tennessee 14-0
Jeff Cravath	Rose 1-1-44	Washington 29-0
Jeff Cravath	Rose 1-1-45	Tennessee 25-0
Jeff Cravath	Rose 1-1-46	Alabama 14-34
Jeff Cravath	Rose 1-1-48	Michigan 0-49
Jess Hill	Rose 1-1-53	Wisconsin 7-0
Jess Hill	Rose 1-1-55	Ohio St. 7-20
John McKay	Rose 1-1-63	Wisconsin 42-37
John McKay	Rose 1-2-67	Purdue 13-14
John McKay	Rose 1-1-68	Indiana 14-3
John McKay	Rose 1-1-69	Ohio St. 16-27
John McKay	Rose 1-1-70	Michigan 10-3
John McKay	Rose 1-1-73	Ohio St. 42-17
John McKay	Rose 1-1-74	Ohio St. 21-42
John McKay	Rose 1-1-75	Ohio St. 18-17
John McKay	Liberty 12-22-75	Texas A&M 20-0
John Robinson	Rose 1-1-77	Michigan 14-6
John Robinson	Bluebonnet 12-31-77	Texas A&M 47-28
John Robinson	Rose 1-1-79	Michigan 17-10
John Robinson	Rose 1-1-80	Ohio St. 17-16
John Robinson	Fiesta 1-1-82	Penn St. 10-26
Ted Tollner	Rose 1-1-85	Ohio St. 20-17
Ted Tollner	Aloha 12-28-85	Alabama 3-24
Ted Tollner	Florida Citrus 1-1-87	Auburn 7-16
Larry Smith	Rose 1-1-88	Michigan St. 17-20
Larry Smith	Rose 1-2-89	Michigan 14-22
Larry Smith	Rose 1-1-90	Michigan 17-10
Larry Smith	John Hancock 12-31-90	Michigan St. 16-17
Larry Smith	Freedom 12-29-92	Fresno St. 7-24
John Robinson	Freedom 12-30-93	Utah 28-21
John Robinson	Cotton 1-2-95	Texas Tech 55-14
John Robinson	Rose 1-1-96	Northwestern 41-32
All bowls 25-13-0		

SOUTHERN METHODIST

School/Coach	Bowl/Date	Opponent/Score
Ray Morrison	Dixie Classic 1-1-25	West Va. Wesleyan 7-9
Matty Bell	Rose 1-1-36	Stanford 0-7
Matty Bell	Cotton 1-1-48	Penn St. 13-13
Matty Bell	Cotton 1-1-49	Oregon 21-13
Hayden Fry	Sun 12-31-63	Oregon 14-21
Hayden Fry	Cotton 12-31-66	Georgia 9-24
Hayden Fry	Bluebonnet 12-31-68	Oklahoma 28-27
Ron Meyer	Holiday 12-19-80	Brigham Young 45-46
Bobby Collins	Cotton 1-1-83	Pittsburgh 7-3
Bobby Collins	Sun 12-24-83	Alabama 7-28
Bobby Collins	Aloha 12-29-84	Notre Dame 27-20
All bowls 4-6-1		

SOUTHERN MISS.

School/Coach	Bowl/Date	Opponent/Score
Thad "Pie" Vann	Sun 1-1-53	Pacific (Cal.) 7-26
Thad "Pie" Vann	Sun 1-1-54	UTEP 14-37
Bobby Collins	Independence 12-13-80	McNeese St. 16-14
Bobby Collins	Tangerine 12-19-81	Missouri 17-19
Curley Hallman	Independence 12-23-88	UTEP 38-18
Jeff Bower	All-American 12-28-90	North Caro. St. 27-31
Jeff Bower	Liberty 12-31-97	Pittsburgh 41-7
All bowls 3-4-0		

STANFORD

School/Coach	Bowl/Date	Opponent/Score
Charlie Fickert	Rose 1-1-02	Michigan 0-49
Glenn "Pop" Warner	Rose 1-1-25	Notre Dame 10-27
Glenn "Pop" Warner	Rose 1-1-27	Alabama 7-7
Glenn "Pop" Warner	Rose 1-2-28	Pittsburgh 7-6
Claude "Tiny" Thornhill	Rose 1-1-34	Columbia 0-7
Claude "Tiny" Thornhill	Rose 1-1-35	Alabama 13-29
Claude "Tiny" Thornhill	Rose 1-1-36	Southern Methodist 7-0
Clark Shaughnessy	Rose 1-1-41	Nebraska 21-13
Chuck Taylor	Rose 1-1-52	Illinois 7-40
John Ralston	Rose 1-1-71	Ohio St. 27-17
John Ralston	Rose 1-1-72	Michigan 13-12
Bill Walsh	Sun 12-31-77	LSU 24-14
Bill Walsh	Bluebonnet 12-31-78	Georgia 25-22
Jack Elway	Gator 12-27-86	Clemson 21-27
Dennis Green	Aloha 12-25-91	Georgia Tech 17-18
Bill Walsh	Blockbuster 1-1-93	Penn St. 24-3
Tyrone Willingham	Liberty 12-30-95	East Caro. 13-19
Tyrone Willingham	Sun 12-31-96	Michigan St. 38-0
All bowls 9-8-1		

SYRACUSE

School/Coach	Bowl/Date	Opponent/Score
Ben Schwartzwalder	Orange 1-1-53	Alabama 6-61
Ben Schwartzwalder	Cotton 1-1-57	Texas Christian 27-28
Ben Schwartzwalder	Orange 1-1-59	Oklahoma 6-21
Ben Schwartzwalder	Cotton 1-1-60	Texas 23-14
Ben Schwartzwalder	Liberty 12-16-61	Miami (Fla.) 15-14
Ben Schwartzwalder	Sugar 1-1-65	LSU 10-13
Ben Schwartzwalder	Gator 12-31-66	Tennessee 12-18
Frank Maloney	Independence 12-15-79	McNeese St. 31-7
Dick MacPherson	Cherry 12-21-85	Maryland 18-35
Dick MacPherson	Sugar 1-1-88	Auburn 16-16
Dick MacPherson	Hall of Fame 1-2-89	LSU 23-10
Dick MacPherson	Peach 12-30-89	Georgia 19-18
Dick MacPherson	Aloha 12-25-90	Arizona 28-0
Paul Pasqualoni	Hall of Fame 1-1-92	Ohio St. 24-17
Paul Pasqualoni	Fiesta 1-1-93	Colorado 26-22
Paul Pasqualoni	Gator 1-1-96	Clemson 41-0
Paul Pasqualoni	Liberty 12-27-96	Houston 30-17
Paul Pasqualoni	Fiesta 12-31-97	Kansas St. 18-35
All bowls 10-7-1		

TEMPLE

School/Coach	Bowl/Date	Opponent/Score
Glenn "Pop" Warner	Sugar 1-1-35	Tulane 14-20
Wayne Hardin	Garden State 12-15-79	California 28-17
All bowls 1-1-0		

TENNESSEE

School/Coach	Bowl/Date	Opponent/Score
Bob Neyland	Orange 1-2-39	Oklahoma 17-0
Bob Neyland	Rose 1-1-40	Southern Cal 0-14
Bob Neyland	Sugar 1-1-41	Boston College 13-19
John Barnhill	Sugar 1-1-43	Tulsa 14-7
John Barnhill	Rose 1-1-45	Southern Cal 0-25
Bob Neyland	Orange 1-1-47	Rice 0-8
Bob Neyland	Cotton 1-1-51	Texas 20-14
Bob Neyland	Sugar 1-1-52	Maryland 13-28
Bob Neyland	Cotton 1-1-53	Texas 0-16
Bowden Wyatt	Sugar 1-1-57	Baylor 7-13
Bowden Wyatt	Gator 12-28-57	Texas A&M 3-0
Doug Dickey	Bluebonnet 12-18-65	Tulsa 27-6
Doug Dickey	Gator 12-31-66	Syracuse 18-12
Doug Dickey	Orange 1-1-68	Oklahoma 24-26
Doug Dickey	Cotton 1-1-69	Texas 13-36
Doug Dickey	Gator 12-27-69	Florida 13-14
Bill Battle	Sugar 1-1-71	Air Force 34-13
Bill Battle	Liberty 12-20-71	Arkansas 14-13
Bill Battle	Bluebonnet 12-30-72	LSU 24-17
Bill Battle	Gator 12-29-73	Texas Tech 19-28
Bill Battle	Liberty 12-16-74	Maryland 7-3
Johnny Majors	Bluebonnet 12-31-79	Purdue 22-27
Johnny Majors	Garden State 12-13-81	Wisconsin 28-21
Johnny Majors	Peach 12-31-82	Iowa 22-28
Johnny Majors	Florida Citrus 12-17-83	Maryland 30-23
Johnny Majors	Sun 12-24-84	Maryland 26-27
Johnny Majors	Sugar 1-1-86	Miami (Fla.) 35-7
Johnny Majors	Liberty 12-29-86	Minnesota 21-14
Johnny Majors	Peach 1-2-88	Indiana 27-22
Johnny Majors	Cotton 1-1-90	Arkansas 31-27
Johnny Majors	Sugar 1-1-91	Virginia 23-22
Johnny Majors	Fiesta 1-1-92	Penn St. 17-42
Phillip Fulmer	Hall of Fame 1-1-93	Boston College 38-23
Phillip Fulmer	Florida Citrus 1-1-94	Penn St. 13-31
Phillip Fulmer	Gator 12-30-94	Virginia Tech 45-23
Phillip Fulmer	Florida Citrus 1-1-96	Ohio St. 20-14
Phillip Fulmer	Florida Citrus 1-1-97	Northwestern 48-28
Phillip Fulmer	Orange 1-2-98	Nebraska 17-42
All bowls 21-17-0		

TEXAS

School/Coach	Bowl/Date	Opponent/Score
Dana Bible	Cotton 1-1-43	Georgia Tech 14-7
Dana Bible	Cotton 1-1-44	Randolph Field 7-7
Dana Bible	Cotton 1-1-46	Missouri 40-27
Blair Cherry	Sugar 1-1-48	Alabama 27-7
Blair Cherry	Orange 1-1-49	Georgia 41-28
Blair Cherry	Cotton 1-1-51	Tennessee 14-20
Ed Price	Cotton 1-1-53	Tennessee 16-0
Darrell Royal	Sugar 1-1-58	Mississippi 7-39
Darrell Royal	Cotton 1-1-60	Syracuse 14-23
Darrell Royal	Bluebonnet 12-17-60	Alabama 3-3
Darrell Royal	Cotton 1-1-62	Mississippi 12-7
Darrell Royal	Cotton 1-1-63	LSU 0-13
Darrell Royal	Cotton 1-1-64	Navy 28-6
Darrell Royal	Orange 1-1-65	Alabama 21-17
Darrell Royal	Bluebonnet 12-17-66	Mississippi 19-0
Darrell Royal	Cotton 1-1-69	Tennessee 36-13
Darrell Royal	Cotton 1-1-70	Notre Dame 21-17
Darrell Royal	Cotton 1-1-71	Notre Dame 11-24
Darrell Royal	Cotton 1-1-72	Penn St. 6-30
Darrell Royal	Cotton 1-1-73	Alabama 17-13
Darrell Royal	Cotton 1-1-74	Nebraska 3-19
Darrell Royal	Gator 12-30-74	Auburn 3-27
Darrell Royal	Bluebonnet 12-27-75	Colorado 38-21
Fred Akers	Cotton 1-2-78	Notre Dame 10-38
Fred Akers	Sun 12-23-78	Maryland 42-0
Fred Akers	Sun 12-22-79	Washington 7-14
Fred Akers	Bluebonnet 12-31-80	North Caro. 7-16
Fred Akers	Cotton 1-1-82	Alabama 14-12
Fred Akers	Sun 12-25-82	North Caro. 10-26
Fred Akers	Cotton 1-2-84	Georgia 9-10
Fred Akers	Freedom 12-26-84	Iowa 17-55
Fred Akers	Bluebonnet 12-31-85	Air Force 16-24
David McWilliams	Bluebonnet 12-31-87	Pittsburgh 32-27
David McWilliams	Cotton 1-1-91	Miami (Fla.) 3-46
John Mackovic	Sun 12-30-94	North Caro. 35-31
John Mackovic	Sugar 12-31-95	Virginia Tech 10-28
John Mackovic	Fiesta 1-1-97	Penn St. 15-38
All bowls 17-18-2		

UTEP

School/Coach	Bowl/Date	Opponent/Score
Mack Saxon	Sun 1-1-37	Hardin-Simmons 6-34
Jack "Cactus Jack" Curtice	Sun 1-1-49	West Va. 12-21
Jack "Cactus Jack" Curtice	Sun 1-2-50	Georgetown 33-20
Mike Brumbelow	Sun 1-1-54	Southern Miss. 37-14
Mike Brumbelow	Sun 1-1-55	Florida St. 47-20
Mike Brumbelow	Sun 1-1-57	Geo. Washington 0-13
Bobby Dobbs	Sun 12-31-65	Texas Christian 13-12
Bobby Dobbs	Sun 12-30-67	Mississippi 14-7
Bob Stull	Independence 12-23-88	Southern Miss. 18-38
All bowls 5-4-0		

TEXAS A&M

School/Coach	Bowl/Date	Opponent/Score
Dana Bible	Dixie Classic 1-2-22	Centre 22-14
Homer Norton	Sugar 1-1-40	Tulane 14-13
Homer Norton	Cotton 1-1-41	Fordham 13-12
Homer Norton	Cotton 1-1-42	Alabama 21-29
Homer Norton	Orange 1-1-44	LSU 14-19
Harry Stiteler	Presidential 12-9-50	Georgia 40-20
Paul "Bear" Bryant	Gator 12-28-57	Tennessee 0-3
Gene Stallings	Cotton 1-1-68	Alabama 20-16
Emory Bellard	Liberty 12-22-75	Southern Cal 0-20
Emory Bellard	Sun 1-2-77	Florida 37-14
Emory Bellard	Bluebonnet 12-31-77	Southern Cal 28-47
Tom Wilson	Hall of Fame 12-20-78	Iowa St. 28-12
Tom Wilson	Independence 12-12-81	Oklahoma St. 33-16
Jackie Sherrill	Cotton 1-1-86	Auburn 36-16
Jackie Sherrill	Cotton 1-1-87	Ohio St. 12-28
Jackie Sherrill	Cotton 1-1-88	Notre Dame 35-10
R. C. Slocum	John Hancock 12-30-89	Pittsburgh 28-31
R. C. Slocum	Holiday 12-29-90	Brigham Young 65-14
R. C. Slocum	Cotton 1-1-92	Florida St. 2-10
R. C. Slocum	Cotton 1-1-93	Notre Dame 3-28
R. C. Slocum	Cotton 1-1-94	Notre Dame 21-24
R. C. Slocum	Alamo 12-28-95	Michigan 22-20
R. C. Slocum	Cotton 1-1-98	UCLA 23-29
All bowls 12-11-0		

TEXAS CHRISTIAN

School/Coach	Bowl/Date	Opponent/Score
Bill Driver	Fort Worth Classic 1-1-21	Centre 7-63
Leo "Dutch" Meyer	Sugar 1-1-36	LSU 3-2
Leo "Dutch" Meyer	Cotton 1-1-37	Marquette 16-6
Leo "Dutch" Meyer	Sugar 1-2-39	Carnegie Mellon 15-7
Leo "Dutch" Meyer	Orange 1-1-42	Georgia 26-40
Leo "Dutch" Meyer	Cotton 1-1-45	Oklahoma St. 0-34
Leo "Dutch" Meyer	Delta 1-1-48	Mississippi 9-13
Leo "Dutch" Meyer	Cotton 1-1-52	Kentucky 7-20
Abe Martin	Cotton 1-2-56	Mississippi 13-14
Abe Martin	Cotton 1-1-57	Syracuse 28-27
Abe Martin	Cotton 1-1-59	Air Force 0-0
Abe Martin	Bluebonnet 12-19-59	Clemson 7-23
Abe Martin	Sun 12-31-65	UTEP 12-13
Jim Wacker	Bluebonnet 12-31-84	West Va. 14-31
Pat Sullivan	Independence 12-28-94	Virginia 10-20
All bowls 4-10-1		

TEXAS TECH

School/Coach	Bowl/Date	Opponent/Score
Pete Cawthon	Sun 1-1-38	West Va. 6-7
Pete Cawthon	Cotton 1-2-39	St. Mary's (Cal.) 13-20
Dell Morgan	Sun 1-1-42	Tulsa 0-6
Dell Morgan	Sun 1-1-48	Miami (Ohio) 12-13
Dell Morgan	Raisin 12-31-49	San Jose St. 13-20
DeWitt Weaver	Sun 1-1-52	Pacific (Cal.) 25-14
DeWitt Weaver	Gator 1-1-54	Auburn 35-13
DeWitt Weaver	Sun 1-2-56	Wyoming 14-21
J. T. King	Sun 12-26-64	Georgia 0-7
J. T. King	Gator 12-31-65	Georgia Tech 21-31
Jim Carlen	Sun 12-19-70	Georgia Tech 9-17
Jim Carlen	Sun 12-30-72	North Caro. 28-32
Jim Carlen	Gator 12-29-73	Tennessee 28-19
Jim Carlen	Peach 12-28-74	Vanderbilt 6-6
Steve Sloan	Bluebonnet 12-31-76	Nebraska 24-27
Steve Sloan	Tangerine 12-23-77	Florida St. 17-40
Spike Dykes	Independence 12-20-86	Mississippi 17-20
Spike Dykes	All-American 12-28-89	Duke 49-21
Spike Dykes	John Hancock 12-24-93	Oklahoma 10-41
Spike Dykes	Cotton 1-2-95	Southern Cal 14-55
Spike Dykes	Copper 12-27-95	Air Force 55-41
Spike Dykes	Alamo 12-29-96	Iowa 0-27
All bowls 5-16-1		

TOLEDO

School/Coach	Bowl/Date	Opponent/Score
Frank Lauterbur	Tangerine 12-26-69	Davidson 56-33
Frank Lauterbur	Tangerine 12-28-70	William & Mary 40-12
Jack Murphy	Tangerine 12-28-71	Richmond 28-3
Chuck Stobart	California 12-19-81	San Jose St. 27-25
Dan Simrell	California 12-15-84	UNLV 13-30
Gary Pinkel	Las Vegas 12-14-95	Nevada 40-37 (OT)
All bowls 5-1-0		

School/Coach	Bowl/Date	Opponent/Score
TULANE		
Bernie Bierman	Rose 1-1-32	Southern Cal 12-21
Ted Cox	Sugar 1-1-35	Temple 20-14
Lowell "Red" Dawson	Sugar 1-1-40	Texas A&M 13-14
Jim Pittman	Liberty 12-12-70	Colorado 17-3
Bennie Ellender	Bluebonnet 12-29-73	Houston 7-47
Larry Smith	Liberty 12-22-79	Penn St. 6-9
Vince Gibson	Hall of Fame 12-27-80	Arkansas 15-34
Mack Brown	Independence 12-19-87	Washington 12-24
All bowls 2-6-0		
TULSA		
Henry Frnka	Sun 1-1-42	Texas Tech 6-0
Henry Frnka	Sugar 1-1-43	Tennessee 7-14
Henry Frnka	Sugar 1-1-44	Georgia Tech 18-20
Henry Frnka	Orange 1-1-45	Georgia Tech 26-12
Henry Frnka	Oil 1-1-46	Georgia 6-20
J. O. "Buddy" Brothers	Gator 1-1-53	Florida 13-14
Glenn Dobbs	Bluebonnet 12-19-64	Mississippi 14-7
Glenn Dobbs	Bluebonnet 12-18-65	Tennessee 6-27
F. A. Dry	Independence 12-13-76	McNeese St. 16-20
Dave Rader	Independence 12-16-89	Oregon 24-27
Dave Rader	Freedom 12-30-91	San Diego St. 28-17
All bowls 4-7-0		
UCLA		
Edwin "Babe" Horrell	Rose 1-1-43	Georgia 0-9
Bert LaBrucherie	Rose 1-1-47	Illinois 14-45
Henry "Red" Sanders	Rose 1-1-54	Michigan St. 20-28
Henry "Red" Sanders	Rose 1-2-56	Michigan St. 14-17
Bill Barnes	Rose 1-1-62	Minnesota 3-21
Tommy Prothro	Rose 1-1-66	Michigan St. 14-12
Dick Vermeil	Rose 1-1-76	Ohio St. 23-10
Terry Donahue	Liberty 12-20-76	Alabama 6-36
Terry Donahue	Fiesta 12-25-78	Arkansas 10-10
Terry Donahue	Bluebonnet 12-31-81	Michigan 14-33
Terry Donahue	Rose 1-1-83	Michigan 24-14
Terry Donahue	Rose 1-2-84	Illinois 45-9
Terry Donahue	Fiesta 1-1-85	Miami (Fla.) 39-37
Terry Donahue	Rose 1-1-86	Iowa 45-28
Terry Donahue	Freedom 12-30-86	Brigham Young 31-10
Terry Donahue	Aloha 12-25-87	Florida 20-16
Terry Donahue	Cotton 1-1-89	Arkansas 17-3
Terry Donahue	John Hancock 12-31-91	Illinois 6-3
Terry Donahue	Rose 1-1-94	Wisconsin 16-21
Terry Donahue	Aloha 12-25-95	Kansas 30-51
Bob Toledo	Cotton 1-1-98	Texas A&M 29-23
All bowls 11-9-1		
UTAH		
Ike Armstrong	Sun 1-2-39	New Mexico 26-0
Ray Nagel	Liberty 12-19-64	West Va. 32-6
Ron McBride	Copper 12-29-92	Washington St. 28-31
Ron McBride	Freedom 12-30-93	Southern Cal 21-28
Ron McBride	Freedom 12-27-94	Arizona 16-13
Ron McBride	Copper 12-27-96	Wisconsin 10-38
All bowls 3-3-0		
UTAH ST.		
E. L. "Dick" Romney	Raisin 1-1-47	San Jose St. 0-20
John Ralston	Sun 12-31-60	New Mexico St. 13-20
John Ralston	Gotham 12-9-61	Baylor 9-24
Charlie Weatherbie	Las Vegas 12-17-93	Ball St. 42-33
John L. Smith	Humanitarian 12-29-97	Cincinnati 19-35
All bowls 1-4-0		
VANDERBILT		
Art Guepe	Gator 12-31-55	Auburn 25-13
Steve Sloan	Peach 12-28-74	Texas Tech 6-6
George MacIntyre	Hall of Fame 12-31-82	Air Force 28-36
All bowls 1-1-1		
VIRGINIA		
George Welsh	Peach 12-31-84	Purdue 27-24
George Welsh	All-American 12-22-87	Brigham Young 22-16
George Welsh	Florida Citrus 1-1-90	Illinois 21-31
George Welsh	Sugar 1-1-91	Tennessee 22-23
George Welsh	Gator 12-29-91	Oklahoma 14-48
George Welsh	Carquest 1-1-94	Boston College 13-31
George Welsh	Independence 12-28-94	Texas Christian 20-10
George Welsh	Peach 12-30-95	Georgia 34-27
George Welsh	Carquest 12-27-96	Miami (Fla.) 21-31
All bowls 4-5-0		
VIRGINIA TECH		
Jimmy Kitts	Sun 1-1-47	Cincinnati 6-18
Jerry Claiborne	Liberty 12-10-66	Miami (Fla.) 7-14

School/Coach	Bowl/Date	Opponent/Score
Jerry Claiborne	Liberty 12-14-68	Mississippi 17-34
Bill Dooley	Peach 1-2-81	Miami (Fla.) 10-20
Bill Dooley	Independence 12-15-84	Air Force 7-23
Bill Dooley	Peach 12-31-86	North Caro. St. 25-24
Frank Beamer	Independence 12-31-93	Indiana 45-20
Frank Beamer	Gator 12-30-94	Tennessee 23-45
Frank Beamer	Sugar 12-31-95	Texas 28-10
Frank Beamer	Orange 12-31-96	Nebraska 21-41
Frank Beamer	Gator 1-1-98	North Caro. 3-42
All bowls 3-8-0		
WAKE FOREST		
D. C. "Peahead" Walker	Gator 1-1-46	South Caro. 26-14
D. C. "Peahead" Walker	Dixie 1-1-49	Baylor 7-20
John Mackovic	Tangerine 12-22-79	LSU 10-34
Bill Dooley	Independence 12-31-92	Oregon 39-35
All bowls 2-2-0		
WASHINGTON		
Enoch Bagshaw	Rose 1-1-24	Navy 14-14
Enoch Bagshaw	Rose 1-1-26	Alabama 19-20
Jimmy Phelan	Rose 1-1-37	Pittsburgh 0-21
Ralph "Pest" Welch	Rose 1-1-44	Southern Cal 0-29
Jim Owens	Rose 1-1-60	Wisconsin 44-8
Jim Owens	Rose 1-2-61	Minnesota 17-7
Jim Owens	Rose 1-1-64	Illinois 7-17
Don James	Rose 1-2-78	Michigan 27-20
Don James	Sun 12-22-79	Texas 14-7
Don James	Rose 1-1-81	Michigan 6-23
Don James	Rose 1-1-82	Iowa 28-0
Don James	Aloha 12-25-82	Maryland 21-20
Don James	Aloha 12-26-83	Penn St. 10-13
Don James	Orange 1-1-85	Oklahoma 28-17
Don James	Freedom 12-30-85	Colorado 20-17
Don James	Sun 12-25-86	Alabama 6-28
Don James	Independence 12-19-87	Tulane 24-12
Don James	Freedom 12-30-89	Florida 34-7
Don James	Rose 1-1-91	Iowa 46-34
Don James	Rose 1-1-92	Michigan 34-14
Don James	Rose 1-1-93	Michigan 31-38
Jim Lambright	Sun 12-29-95	Iowa 18-38
Jim Lambright	Holiday 12-30-96	Colorado 21-33
Jim Lambright	Aloha 12-25-97	Michigan St. 51-23
All bowls 13-10-1		
WASHINGTON ST.		
Bill "Lone Star" Dietz	Rose 1-1-16	Brown 14-0
Orin "Babe" Hollingbery	Rose 1-1-31	Alabama 0-24
Jim Walden	Holiday 12-18-81	Brigham Young 36-38
Dennis Erickson	Aloha 12-25-88	Houston 24-22
Mike Price	Copper 12-29-92	Utah 31-28
Mike Price	Alamo 12-31-94	Baylor 10-3
Mike Price	Rose 1-1-98	Michigan 16-21
All bowls 4-3-0		
WEST VA.		
Clarence "Doc" Spears	San Diego East-West Christmas Classic 12-25-22	Gonzaga 21-13
Marshall "Little Sleepy" Glenn	Sun 1-1-38	Texas Tech 7-6
Dud DeGroot	Sun 1-1-49	UTEP 21-12
Art Lewis	Sugar 1-1-54	Georgia Tech 19-42
Gene Corum	Liberty 12-19-64	Utah 6-32
Jim Carlen	Peach 12-30-69	South Caro. 14-3
Bobby Bowden	Peach 12-29-72	North Caro. St. 13-49
Bobby Bowden	Peach 12-31-75	North Caro. St. 13-10
Don Nehlen	Peach 12-31-81	Florida 26-6
Don Nehlen	Gator 12-30-82	Florida St. 12-31
Don Nehlen	Hall of Fame 12-22-83	Kentucky 20-16
Don Nehlen	Bluebonnet 12-31-84	Texas Christian 31-14
Don Nehlen	Sun 12-25-87	Oklahoma St. 33-35
Don Nehlen	Fiesta 1-2-89	Notre Dame 21-34
Don Nehlen	Gator 12-30-89	Clemson 7-27
Don Nehlen	Sugar 1-1-94	Florida 7-41
Don Nehlen	Carquest 1-2-95	South Caro. 21-24
Don Nehlen	Gator 1-1-97	North Caro. 13-20
Don Nehlen	Carquest 12-29-97	Georgia Tech 30-35
All bowls 8-11-0		
WESTERN MICH.		
Merle Schlosser	Aviation 12-9-61	New Mexico 12-28
Al Molde	California 12-10-88	Fresno St. 30-35
All bowls 0-2-0		
WISCONSIN		
Ivy Williamson	Rose 1-1-53	Southern Cal 0-7
Milt Bruhn	Rose 1-1-60	Washington 8-44

School/Coach	Bowl/Date	Opponent/Score
Milt Bruhn	Rose 1-2-63	Southern Cal 37-42
Dave McClain	Garden State 12-13-81	Tennessee 21-28
Dave McClain	Independence 12-11-82	Kansas St. 14-3
Dave McClain	Hall of Fame 12-29-84	Kentucky 19-20
Barry Alvarez	Rose 1-1-94	UCLA 21-16
Barry Alvarez	Hall of Fame 1-2-95	Duke 34-20
Barry Alvarez	Copper 12-27-96	Utah 38-10
Barry Alvarez	Outback 1-1-98	Georgia 6-33
All bowls 4-6-0		
WYOMING		
Bowden Wyatt	Gator 1-1-51	Wash. & Lee 20-7
Phil Dickens	Sun 1-2-56	Texas Tech 21-14
Bob Devaney	Sun 12-31-58	Hardin-Simmons 14-6
Lloyd Eaton	Sun 12-24-66	Florida St. 28-20
Lloyd Eaton	Sugar 1-1-68	LSU 13-20
Fred Akers	Fiesta 12-25-76	Oklahoma 7-41
Paul Roach	Holiday 12-30-87	Iowa 19-20
Paul Roach	Holiday 12-30-88	Oklahoma St. 14-62
Paul Roach	Copper 12-31-90	California 15-17
Joe Tiller	Copper 12-29-93	Kansas St. 17-52
All bowls 4-6-0		

Played in Major Bowl—No Longer I-A

School/Coach	Bowl/Date	Opponent/Score
BOSTON U.		
Larry Naviaux	Pasadena 12-6-69	San Diego St. 7-28
All bowls 0-1-0		
BROWN		
Ed Robinson	Rose 1-1-16	Washington St. 0-14
All bowls 0-1-0		
BUCKNELL		
Edward "Hook" Mylin	Orange 1-1-35	Miami (Fla.) 26-0
All bowls 1-0-0		
CAL ST. FULLERTON		
Gene Murphy	California 12-17-83	Northern Ill. 13-20
All bowls 0-1-0		

School/Coach	Bowl/Date	Opponent/Score
CAL ST. NORTHRIDGE		
Sam Winningham	Pasadena 12-2-67	West Tex. A&M 13-35
All bowls 0-1-0		
CARNEGIE MELLON		
Bill Kern	Sugar 1-2-39	Texas Christian 7-15
All bowls 0-1-0		
CASE RESERVE		
Bill Edwards	Sun 1-1-41	Arizona St. 26-13
All bowls 1-0-0		
CATHOLIC		
Arthur "Dutch" Bergman	Orange 1-1-36	Mississippi 20-19
Arthur "Dutch" Bergman	Sun 1-1-40	Arizona St. 0-0
All bowls 1-0-1		
CENTENARY (LA.)		
Homer Norton	Dixie Classic 1-1-34	Arkansas 7-7
All bowls 0-0-1		
CENTRE		
Charley Moran	Fort Worth Classic 1-1-21	Texas Christian 63-7
Charley Moran	San Diego East-West Christmas Classic 12-26-21	Arizona 38-0
Charley Moran	Dixie Classic 1-2-22	Texas A&M 14-22
All bowls 2-1-0		
CITADEL		
Eddie Teague	Tangerine 12-30-60	Tennessee Tech 27-0
All bowls 1-0-0		
COLUMBIA		
Lou Little	Rose 1-1-34	Stanford 7-0
All bowls 1-0-0		
DAVIDSON		
Homer Smith	Tangerine 12-26-69	Toledo 33-56
All bowls 0-1-0		
DAYTON		
Joe Gavin	Salad 1-1-52	Houston 21-26
All bowls 0-1-0		

School/Coach	Bowl/Date	Opponent/Score
DENVER		
Clyde "Cac" Hubbard	Sun 1-1-46	New Mexico 24-34
Clyde "Cac" Hubbard	Alamo 1-4-47	Hardin-Simmons 0-20
All bowls 0-2-0		
DRAKE		
Vee Green	Raisin 1-1-46	Fresno St. 13-12
Al Kawal	Salad 1-1-49	Arizona 14-13
Warren Gaer	Sun 1-1-58	Louisville 20-34
All bowls 2-1-0		
DUQUESNE		
John "Little Clipper" Smith	Orange 1-1-37	Mississippi St. 13-12
All bowls 1-0-0		
FORDHAM		
Jim Crowley	Cotton 1-1-41	Texas A&M 12-13
Jim Crowley	Sugar 1-1-42	Missouri 2-0
All bowls 1-1-0		
GEO. WASHINGTON		
Eugene "Bo" Sherman	Sun 1-1-57	UTEP 13-0
All bowls 1-0-0		
GEORGETOWN		
Jack Hagerty	Orange 1-1-41	Mississippi St. 7-14
Bob Margarita	Sun 1-2-50	UTEP 20-33
All bowls 0-2-0		
GONZAGA		
Charles "Gus" Dorais	San Diego East-West Christmas Classic 12-15-22	West Va. 13-21
All bowls 0-1-0		
HARDIN-SIMMONS		
Frank Kimbrough	Sun 1-1-36	New Mexico St. 14-14
Frank Kimbrough	Sun 1-1-37	UTEP 34-6
Warren Woodson	Sun 1-1-43	Second Air Force 7-13
Warren Woodson	Alamo 1-4-47	Denver 20-6
Warren Woodson	Harbor 1-1-48	San Diego St. 53-0
Warren Woodson	Shrine 12-18-48	Ouachita Baptist 40-12
Warren Woodson	Camellia 12-30-48	Wichita St. 29-12
Sammy Baugh	Sun 12-31-58	Wyoming 6-14
All bowls 5-2-1		
HARVARD		
Robert Fisher	Rose 1-1-20	Oregon 7-6
All bowls 1-0-0		
HOLY CROSS		
John "Ox" Da Grosa	Orange 1-1-46	Miami (Fla.) 6-13
All bowls 0-1-0		
LONG BEACH ST.		
Jim Stangeland	Pasadena 12-19-70	Louisville 24-24
All bowls 0-0-1		
MARQUETTE		
Frank Murray	Cotton 1-1-37	Texas Christian 6-16
All bowls 0-1-0		
McNEESE ST.		
Jack Doland	Independence 12-13-76	Tulsa 20-16
Ernie Duplechin	Independence 12-15-79	Syracuse 7-31
Ernie Duplechin	Independence 12-13-80	Southern Miss. 14-16
All bowls 1-2-0		
MONTANA ST.		
Clyde Carpenter	Harbor 1-1-47	New Mexico 13-13
All bowls 0-0-1		
OCCIDENTAL		
Roy Dennis	Raisin 1-1-49	Colorado St. 21-20
All bowls 1-0-0		
OUACHITA BAPTIST		
Wesley Bradshaw	Shrine 12-18-48	Hardin-Simmons 12-40
All bowls 0-1-0		
PACIFIC (CAL.)		
Larry Siemering	Raisin 1-1-48	Wichita St. 26-14
Ernie Jorge	Sun 1-1-52	Texas Tech 14-25
Ernie Jorge	Sun 1-1-53	Southern Miss. 26-7
All bowls 2-1-0		
PENNSYLVANIA		
Bob Folwell	Rose 1-1-17	Oregon 0-14
All bowls 0-1-0		

School/Coach	Bowl/Date	Opponent/Score
RANDOLPH FIELD		
Frank Tritico	Cotton 1-1-44	Texas 7-7
All bowls 0-0-1		
RICHMOND		
Frank Jones	Tangerine 12-27-68	Ohio 49-42
Frank Jones	Tangerine 12-28-71	Toledo 3-28
All bowls 1-1-0		
ST. MARY'S (CAL.)		
Edward "Slip" Madigan	Cotton 1-2-39	Texas Tech 20-13
Jimmy Phelan	Sugar 1-1-46	Oklahoma St. 13-33
Jimmy Phelan	Oil 1-1-47	Georgia Tech 19-41
All bowls 1-2-0		
SANTA CLARA		
Lawrence "Buck" Shaw	Sugar 1-1-37	LSU 21-14
Lawrence "Buck" Shaw	Sugar 1-1-38	LSU 6-0
Len Casanova	Orange 1-2-50	Kentucky 21-13
All bowls 3-0-0		
SECOND AIR FORCE		
Red Reese	Sun 1-1-43	Hardin-Simmons 13-7
All bowls 1-0-0		
SOUTHWESTERN (TEX.)		
Randolph R. M. Medley	Sun 1-1-44	New Mexico 7-0
Randolph R. M. Medley	Sun 1-1-45	U. of Mexico 35-0
All bowls 2-0-0		
TAMPA		
Earle Bruce	Tangerine 12-29-72	Kent 21-18
All bowls 1-0-0		
TENNESSEE TECH		
Wilburn Tucker	Tangerine 12-30-60	Citadel 0-27
All bowls 0-1-0		
U. OF MEXICO		
Bernard A. Hoban	Sun 1-1-45	Southwestern (Tex.) 0-35
All bowls 0-1-0		

School/Coach	Bowl/Date	Opponent/Score
VILLANOVA		
Maurice "Clipper" Smith	Bacardi, Cuba 1-1-37	Auburn 7-7
Jordan Olivar	Great Lakes 12-6-47	Kentucky 14-24
Jordan Olivar	Harbor 1-1-49	Nevada 27-7
Alex Bell	Sun 12-30-61	Wichita St. 17-9
Alex Bell	Liberty 12-15-62	Oregon St. 0-6
All bowls 2-2-1		
WASH. & JEFF.		
Earle "Greasy" Neale	Rose 1-2-22	California 0-0
All bowls 0-0-1		
WASH. & LEE		
George Barclay	Gator 1-1-51	Wyoming 7-20
All bowls 0-1-0		
WEST TEX. A&M		
Frank Kimbrough	Sun 1-1-51	Cincinnati 14-13
Joe Kerbel	Sun 12-31-62	Ohio 15-14
Joe Kerbel	Pasadena 12-2-67	Cal St. Northridge 35-13
All bowls 3-0-0		
WEST VA. WESLEYAN		
Bob Higgins	Dixie Classic 1-1-25	Southern Methodist 9-7
All bowls 1-0-0		
WICHITA ST.		
Ralph Graham	Raisin 1-1-48	Pacific (Cal.) 14-26
Jim Trimble	Camellia 12-30-48	Hardin-Simmons 12-49
Hank Foldberg	Sun 12-30-61	Villanova 9-17
All bowls 0-3-0		
WILLIAM & MARY		
Rube McCray	Dixie 1-1-48	Arkansas 19-21
Rube McCray	Delta 1-1-49	Oklahoma St. 20-0
Lou Holtz	Tangerine 12-28-70	Toledo 12-40
All bowls 1-2-0		
XAVIER (OHIO)		
Ed Kluska	Salad 1-1-50	Arizona St. 33-21
All bowls 1-0-0		

Average Bowl-Game Attendance, By Decade

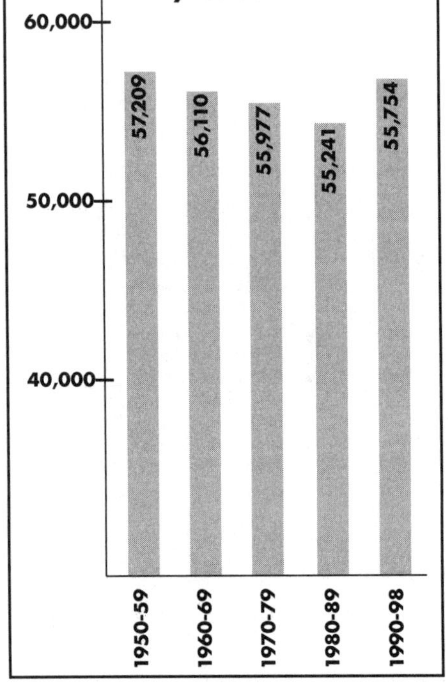

Major Bowl-Game Attendance

Total Yearly Attendance

Year	No. Bowls	Total Attendance	Per/Game Average
1902	1	8,000	8,000
1916	1	7,000	7,000
1917	1	26,000	26,000
1920	1	30,000	30,000
1921	2	51,000	25,500
1922	3	57,000	19,000
1923	2	48,000	24,000
1924	1	40,000	40,000
1925	3	107,000	35,667
1926	1	50,000	50,000
1927	1	57,417	57,417
1928	1	65,000	65,000
1929	1	66,604	66,604
1930	1	72,000	72,000
1931	1	60,000	60,000
1932	1	75,562	75,562
1933	1	78,874	78,874
1934	2	47,000	23,500
1935	3	111,634	37,211
1936	4	137,042	34,261
1937	6	176,396	29,399
1938	5	202,972	40,594
1939	5	224,643	44,929
1940	5	226,478	45,296
1941	5	253,735	50,747
1942	5	215,786	43,157
1943	5	240,166	48,033
1944	5	195,203	39,041
1945	5	236,279	47,256
1946	8	308,071	38,509
1947	10	304,316	30,432
1948	12	404,772	33,731
1949	13	442,531	34,041

Year	No. Bowls	Total Attendance	Per/Game Average
1950	8	384,505	48,063
1951	8	392,548	49,069
1952	7	388,588	55,513
1953	6	366,299	61,050
1954	6	359,285	59,881
1955	6	357,871	59,645
1956	6	379,723	63,287
1957	6	369,162	61,527
1958	6	385,427	64,238
1959	7	392,394	56,056
1960	8	481,814	60,227
1961	9	490,113	54,457
1962	11	509,654	46,332
1963	10	481,722	48,172
1964	8	460,720	57,590
1965	8	448,541	56,068
1966	8	482,106	60,263
1967	8	521,427	65,178
1968	9	532,113	59,124
1969	10	585,621	58,562
1970	11	649,915	59,083
1971	11	623,072	56,643
1972	12	668,031	55,669
1973	11	668,461	60,769
1974	11	631,229	57,384
1975	11	597,079	54,280
1976	11	650,881	59,171
1977	12	660,429	55,036
1978	13	730,078	56,160
1979	15	726,064	48,404
1980	15	865,236	57,682
1981	15	856,730	57,115
1982	16	871,594	54,475
1983	16	919,193	57,450
1984	16	867,319	54,207
1985	18	977,374	54,299
1986	18	975,756	54,209
1987	18	958,933	53,274
1988	18	995,830	55,324
1989	17	937,323	55,137
1990	18	1,047,772	58,210
1991	19	1,048,306	55,174
1992	18	1,049,694	58,316
1993	18	973,570	54,087
1994	19	1,036,950	54,576
1995	19	1,064,640	56,034
1996	18	1,021,466	56,748
1997	18	985,292	54,738
1998	20	1,083,244	54,162

Bowl-by-Bowl Attendance

(Current site and stadium capacity in parentheses. For participating teams, refer to pages 250-255.)

ROSE BOWL

(Rose Bowl, Pasadena, Calif.; Capacity: 96,576)

Date	Attendance
1-1-02	8,000
1-1-16	7,000
1-1-17	26,000
1-1-20	30,000
1-1-21	42,000
1-2-22	40,000
1-1-23	43,000
1-1-24	40,000
1-1-25	53,000
1-1-26	50,000
1-1-27	57,417
1-2-28	65,000
1-1-29	66,604
1-1-30	72,000
1-1-31	60,000
1-1-32	75,562
1-2-33	78,874
1-1-34	35,000
1-1-35	84,474
1-1-36	84,474
1-1-37	87,196
1-1-38	90,000
1-2-39	89,452
1-1-40	92,200
1-1-41	91,500
1-1-42#	56,000
1-1-43	93,000
1-1-44	68,000
1-1-45	91,000
1-1-46	93,000
1-1-47	90,000
1-1-48	93,000
1-1-49	93,000
1-2-50	100,963
1-1-51	98,939
1-1-52	96,825
1-1-53	101,500
1-1-54	101,000
1-1-55	89,191
1-2-56	100,809
1-1-57	97,126
1-1-58	98,202
1-1-59	98,297
1-1-60	100,809
1-2-61	97,314
1-1-62	98,214
1-1-63	98,698
1-1-64	96,957
1-1-65	100,423
1-1-66	100,087
1-2-67	100,807
1-1-68	102,946
1-1-69	102,063
1-1-70	103,878
1-1-71	103,839
1-1-72	103,154
1-1-73	*106,869
1-1-74	105,267
1-1-75	106,721
1-1-76	105,464
1-1-77	106,182
1-2-78	105,312
1-1-79	105,629
1-1-80	105,526
1-1-81	104,863
1-1-82	105,611
1-1-83	104,991
1-2-84	103,217
1-1-85	102,594
1-1-86	103,292
1-1-87	103,168
1-1-88	103,847
1-2-89	101,688
1-1-90	103,450
1-1-91	101,273
1-1-92	103,566
1-1-93	94,236
1-1-94	101,237
1-2-95	102,247
1-1-96	100,102
1-1-97	100,635
1-1-98	101,219

**Record attendance. #Game held at Duke, Durham, N.C., due to war-time West Coast restrictions.*

ORANGE BOWL

(Pro Player Stadium, Miami, Fla.; Capacity: 75,014)

Date	Attendance
1-1-35	5,134
1-1-36	6,568
1-1-37	9,210
1-1-38	18,972
1-2-39	32,191
1-1-40	29,278
1-1-41	29,554
1-1-42	35,786
1-1-43	25,166
1-1-44	25,203
1-1-45	23,279
1-1-46	35,709
1-1-47	36,152
1-1-48	59,578
1-1-49	60,523
1-2-50	64,816
1-1-51	65,181
1-1-52	65,839
1-1-53	66,280
1-1-54	68,640
1-1-55	68,750
1-2-56	76,561
1-1-57	73,280
1-1-58	76,561
1-1-59	75,281
1-1-60	72,186
1-2-61	72,212
1-1-62	68,150
1-1-63	72,880
1-1-64	72,647
1-1-65	72,647
1-1-66	72,214
1-2-67	72,426
1-1-68	77,993
1-1-69	77,719
1-1-70	77,282
1-1-71	80,699
1-1-72	78,151
1-1-73	80,010
1-1-74	60,477
1-1-75	71,801
1-1-76	76,799
1-1-77	65,537
1-2-78	60,987
1-1-79	66,365
1-1-80	66,714
1-1-81	71,043
1-1-82	72,748
1-1-83	68,713
1-2-84	72,549
1-1-85	56,294
1-1-86	74,178
1-1-87	52,717
1-1-88	74,760
1-2-89	79,480
1-1-90	81,190
1-1-91	77,062
1-1-92	77,747
1-1-93	57,324
1-1-94	81,536
1-1-95	*81,753
1-1-96	72,198
12-31-96	51,212
1-2-98	72,385

**Record attendance.*

SUGAR BOWL

(Louisiana Superdome, New Orleans, La.; Capacity: 71,023)

Date	Attendance
1-1-35	22,026
1-1-36	35,000
1-1-37	41,000
1-1-38	45,000
1-2-39	50,000
1-1-40	73,000
1-1-41	73,181
1-1-42	72,000
1-1-43	70,000
1-1-44	69,000
1-1-45	72,000
1-1-46	75,000
1-1-47	73,300
1-1-48	72,000
1-1-49	82,000
1-2-50	82,470
1-1-51	82,000
1-1-52	82,000
1-1-53	82,000
1-1-54	76,000
1-1-55	82,000
1-2-56	80,175
1-1-57	81,000
1-1-58	82,000
1-1-59	82,000
1-1-60	83,000
1-2-61	82,851
1-1-62	82,910
1-1-63	82,900
1-1-64	80,785
1-1-65	65,000

Date	Attendance
1-1-66	67,421
1-2-67	82,000
1-1-68	78,963
1-1-69	82,113
1-1-70	82,500
1-1-71	78,655
1-1-72	84,031
12-31-72	80,123
12-31-73	*85,161
12-31-74	67,890
12-31-75	75,212
1-1-77	76,117
1-2-78	76,811
1-1-79	76,824
1-1-80	77,486
1-1-81	77,895
1-1-82	77,224
1-1-83	78,124
1-2-84	77,893
1-1-85	75,608
1-1-86	77,432
1-1-87	76,234
1-1-88	75,495
1-2-89	61,934
1-1-90	77,452
1-1-91	75,132
1-1-92	76,447
1-1-93	76,789
1-1-94	75,437
1-2-95	76,224
12-31-95	70,283
1-2-97	78,344
1-1-98	67,289

**Record attendance.*

COTTON BOWL

(Cotton Bowl, Dallas, Texas; Capacity: 68,252)

Date	Attendance
1-1-37	17,000
1-1-38	37,000
1-2-39	40,000
1-1-40	20,000
1-1-41	45,500
1-1-42	38,000
1-1-43	36,000
1-1-44	15,000
1-1-45	37,000
1-1-46	45,000
1-1-47	38,000
1-1-48	43,000
1-1-49	69,000
1-2-50	75,347
1-1-51	75,349
1-1-52	75,347
1-1-53	75,504
1-1-54	75,504
1-1-55	75,504
1-2-56	75,504
1-1-57	68,000
1-1-58	75,504
1-1-59	75,504
1-1-60	75,504
1-2-61	74,000
1-1-62	75,504
1-1-63	75,504
1-1-64	75,504
1-1-65	75,504
1-1-66	76,200
12-31-66	75,400
1-1-68	75,504
1-1-69	72,000
1-1-70	73,000
1-1-71	72,000
1-1-72	72,000
1-1-73	72,000
1-1-74	67,500
1-1-75	67,500
1-1-76	74,500
1-1-77	54,500
1-2-78	*76,601
1-1-79	32,500
1-1-80	72,032
1-1-81	74,281
1-1-82	73,243
1-1-83	60,359
1-2-84	67,891
1-1-85	56,522
1-1-86	73,137
1-1-87	74,188
1-1-88	73,006
1-2-89	74,304
1-1-90	74,358
1-1-91	73,521
1-1-92	73,728
1-1-93	71,615
1-1-94	69,855
1-2-95	70,218
1-1-96	58,214
1-1-97	71,928
1-1-98	59,215

**Record attendance.*

SUN BOWL#

(Sun Bowl, El Paso, Texas; Capacity: 51,270)

Date	Attendance
1-1-36	11,000
1-1-37	10,000
1-1-38	12,000
1-2-39	13,000
1-1-40	12,000
1-1-41	14,000
1-1-42	14,000
1-1-43	16,000
1-1-44	18,000
1-1-45	13,000
1-1-46	15,000
1-1-47	10,000
1-1-48	18,000
1-1-49	13,000
1-2-50	15,000
1-1-51	16,000
1-1-52	17,000
1-1-53	11,000
1-1-54	9,500
1-1-55	14,000
1-2-56	14,500
1-1-57	13,500
1-1-58	12,000
12-31-58	13,000
12-31-59	14,000
12-31-60	16,000
12-30-61	15,000
12-31-62	16,000
12-31-63	26,500
12-26-64	28,500
12-31-65	27,450
12-24-66	24,381
12-30-67	34,685
12-28-68	32,307
12-20-69	29,723
12-19-70	30,512
12-18-71	33,503
12-30-72	31,312
12-29-73	30,127
12-28-74	30,131
12-26-75	33,240
1-2-77	33,252
12-31-77	31,318
12-23-78	33,122
12-22-79	33,412
12-27-80	34,723
12-26-81	33,816
12-25-82	31,359
12-24-83	41,412
12-22-84	50,126
12-28-85	*52,203
12-25-86	48,722
12-25-87	43,240
12-24-88	48,719
12-30-89	44,887
12-31-90	50,562
12-31-91	42,821
12-31-92	41,622
12-24-93	43,848
12-30-94	50,612
12-29-95	49,116
12-31-96	42,721
12-31-97	49,104

**Record attendance. #Named John Hancock, 1989-93.*

GATOR BOWL

(AllTel Stadium, Jacksonville, Fla.; Capacity: 76,976)

Date	Attendance
1-2-46	7,362
1-1-47	10,134
1-1-48	16,666
1-1-49	32,939
1-2-50	18,409
1-1-51	19,834
1-1-52	34,577
1-1-53	30,015
1-1-54	28,641
12-31-54	28,426
12-31-55	32,174
12-29-56	36,256
12-28-57	41,160
12-27-58	41,312
1-2-60	45,104
12-31-60	50,112
12-30-61	50,202
12-29-62	50,026
12-28-63	50,018
1-2-65	50,408
12-31-65	60,127
12-31-66	60,312
12-30-67	68,019
12-28-68	68,011
12-27-69	72,248
1-2-71	71,136
12-31-71	71,208
12-30-72	71,114
12-29-73	62,109
12-30-74	63,811
12-29-75	64,012
12-27-76	67,827
12-30-77	72,289
12-29-78	72,011
12-28-79	70,407
12-29-80	72,297
12-28-81	71,009
12-30-82	80,913
12-30-83	81,293
12-28-84	82,138
12-30-85	79,417
12-27-86	80,104
12-31-87	82,119
1-1-89	76,236
12-30-89	*82,911
1-1-91	68,927
12-29-91	62,003
12-31-92	71,233
12-31-93	67,205
12-30-94†	62,200
1-1-96	45,202
1-1-97	52,103
1-1-98	54,116

**Record attendance. †Played at Gainesville, Fla.*

LIBERTY BOWL†

(Liberty Bowl Memorial Stadium, Memphis, Tenn.; Capacity: 62,921)

Date	Attendance
12-19-59	36,211
12-17-60	16,624
12-16-61	15,712
12-15-62	17,048
12-31-63	8,309
12-19-64	6,059
12-18-65	38,607
12-10-66	39,101
12-16-67	35,045
12-14-68	46,206
12-13-69	50,042
12-12-70	44,640
12-20-71	51,410
12-18-72	50,021
12-17-73	50,011
12-16-74	51,284

Date	Attendance
12-22-75	52,129
12-20-76	52,736
12-19-77	49,456
12-23-78	53,064
12-22-79	50,021
12-27-80	53,667
12-30-81	43,216
12-29-82	54,123
12-29-83	38,229
12-27-84	50,108
12-27-85	40,186
12-29-86	51,327
12-29-87	53,249
12-28-88	39,210
12-28-89	60,128
12-27-90	13,144
12-29-91	*61,497
12-31-92	32,107
12-28-93	21,097
12-31-94	33,280
12-30-95	47,398
12-27-96	49,163
12-31-97	50,209

**Record attendance. †Played at Philadelphia, 1959-63; Atlantic City, 1964; Memphis, from 1965.*

FLORIDA CITRUS BOWL#

(Florida Citrus Bowl, Orlando, Fla.; Capacity: 70,000)

Date	Attendance
12-30-60	13,000
12-22-62	7,500
12-27-68	16,114
12-26-69	16,311
12-28-70	15,164
12-28-71	16,750
12-29-72	20,062
12-22-73@	37,234
12-21-74	20,246
12-20-75	20,247
12-18-76	37,812
12-23-77	44,502
12-23-78	31,356
12-22-79	38,666
12-20-80	52,541
12-19-81	50,045
12-18-82	51,296
12-17-83	50,183
12-22-84	51,821
12-28-85	50,920
1-1-87	51,113
1-1-88	53,152
1-2-89	53,571
1-1-90	60,016
1-1-91	72,328
1-1-92	64,192
1-1-93	65,861
1-1-94	72,456
1-2-95	71,195
1-1-96	70,797
1-1-97	63,467
1-1-98	*72,940

**Record attendance. #Named Tangerine Bowl before 1982. The first 14 games in the Tangerine Bowl, through 1-1-60, are not listed because no major teams were involved. The same is true for those games played in December 1961, 1963, 1964, 1965, 1966 and 1967. @ Played at Gainesville, Fla.*

PEACH BOWL

(Georgia Dome, Atlanta, Ga.; Capacity: 71,228)

Date	Attendance
12-30-68	35,545
12-30-69	48,452
12-30-70	52,126
12-30-71	36,771
12-29-72	52,671
12-28-73	38,107
12-28-74	31,695
12-31-75	45,134
12-31-76	54,132
12-31-77	36,733
12-25-78	20,277
12-31-79	57,371
1-2-81	45,384
12-31-81	37,582
12-31-82	50,134
12-30-83	25,648
12-31-84	41,107
12-31-85	29,857
12-31-86	53,668
1-2-88	58,737
12-31-88	44,635
12-30-89	44,991
12-29-90	38,912
1-1-92	59,322
1-2-93	69,125
12-31-93	63,416
1-1-95	64,902
12-30-95	70,825
12-28-96	63,622
1-2-98	*71,212

**Record attendance.*

FIESTA BOWL

(Sun Devil Stadium, Tempe, Ariz.; Capacity: 73,259)

Date	Attendance
12-27-71	51,089
12-23-72	51,318
12-21-73	50,878
12-28-74	50,878
12-26-75	51,396
12-25-76	48,174
12-25-77	57,727
12-25-78	55,227
12-25-79	55,347
12-26-80	66,738
1-1-82	71,053
1-1-83	70,533
1-2-84	66,484
1-1-85	60,310
1-1-86	72,454
1-2-87	73,098
1-1-88	72,112
1-2-89	74,911
1-1-90	73,953
1-1-91	69,098
1-1-92	71,133
1-1-93	70,224
1-1-94	72,260
1-2-95	73,968
1-2-96	*79,864
1-1-97	65,106
12-31-97	69,367

**Record attendance.*

INDEPENDENCE BOWL

(Independence Stadium, Shreveport, La.; Capacity: 50,459)

Date	Attendance
12-13-76	15,542
12-17-77	18,500
12-16-78	18,200
12-15-79	27,234
12-13-80	45,000
12-12-81	47,300
12-11-82	49,503
12-10-83	41,274
12-15-84	41,000
12-21-85	42,800
12-20-86	46,369
12-19-87	41,683
12-23-88	20,242
12-16-89	30,333
12-15-90	48,325
12-29-91	46,932
12-31-92	31,337
12-31-93	33,819
12-28-94	27,242
12-29-95	48,835
12-31-96	41,366
12-28-97	*50,459

**Record attendance.*

HOLIDAY BOWL

(Qualcomm Stadium, San Diego, Calif.; Capacity: 70,000)

Date	Attendance
12-28-78	52,500
12-21-79	52,200
12-19-80	50,214
12-18-81	52,419
12-17-82	52,533
12-23-83	51,480
12-21-84	61,243
12-22-85	42,324
12-30-86	59,473
12-30-87	*61,892
12-30-88	60,718
12-29-89	61,113
12-29-90	61,441
12-30-91	60,646
12-30-92	44,457
12-30-93	52,108
12-30-94	59,453
12-29-95	51,051
12-30-96	54,749
12-29-97	50,761

**Record attendance.*

ALOHA BOWL

(Aloha Stadium, Honolulu, Hawaii; Capacity: 50,000)

Date	Attendance
12-25-82	30,055
12-26-83	37,212
12-29-84	41,777
12-28-85	35,183
12-27-86	26,743
12-25-87	24,839
12-25-88	35,132
12-25-89	*50,000
12-25-90	14,185
12-25-91	34,433
12-25-92	42,933
12-25-93	44,009
12-25-94	44,862
12-25-95	41,112
12-25-96	43,380
12-25-97	44,598

**Record attendance.*

OUTBACK BOWL (Formerly Hall of Fame)

(Tampa Community Stadium, Tampa, Fla.; Capacity: 65,000)

Date	Attendance
12-23-86	25,368
1-2-88	60,156
1-2-89	51,112
1-1-90	52,535
1-1-91	63,154
1-1-92	57,789
1-1-93	52,056
1-1-94	52,649
1-2-95	61,384
1-1-96	*65,313
1-1-97	53,161
1-1-98	56,186

**Record attendance.*

INSIGHT.com BOWL

(Arizona Stadium, Tucson, Ariz.; Capacity: 55,883)

Date	Attendance
12-31-89	37,237
12-31-90	36,340
12-31-91	35,752
12-29-92	40,876
12-29-93	49,075
12-29-94	45,122
12-27-95	41,004
12-27-96	42,122
12-27-97	*49,385

**Record attendance.*

SUNSHINE BOWL#

(Pro Player Stadium, Miami, Fla.; Capacity: 75,014)

Date	Attendance
12-28-90	*74,021
12-28-91	52,644
1-1-93	45,554
1-1-94	38,516

Date	Attendance
1-2-95	50,833
12-30-95	34,428
12-27-96	46,418
12-29-97	28,262

**Record attendance. #Named Blockbuster Bowl before 1993 and named Carquest Bowl 1994-97.*

LAS VEGAS BOWL
(Sam Boyd Stadium, Las Vegas, Nev.; Capacity: 40,000)

Date	Attendance
12-18-92	15,476
12-17-93	15,508
12-15-94	17,562
12-14-95	11,127
12-19-96	10,118
12-20-97	*21,514

**Record attendance.*

ALAMO BOWL
(Alamodome, San Antonio, Texas; Capacity: 65,000)

Date	Attendance
12-31-93	45,716
12-31-94	44,106
12-28-95	*64,597
12-29-96	55,677
12-30-97	55,552

MOTOR CITY BOWL
(Pontiac Silverdome, Pontiac, Mich.; Capacity: 79,083)

Date	Attendance
12-26-97	43,340

HUMANITARIAN BOWL
(Bronco Stadium, Boise, Idaho; Capacity: 30,000)

Date	Attendance
12-29-97	16,131

Former Major Bowl Games

ALAMO
(San Antonio, Texas)

Date	Attendance
1-4-47	3,730

ALL-AMERICAN
(Birmingham, Ala.)

Date	Attendance
12-22-77	47,000
12-20-78	41,500
12-29-79	62,785
12-27-80	30,000
12-31-81	41,672
12-31-82	75,000
12-22-83	42,000
12-29-84	47,300
12-31-85	45,000
12-31-86	30,000
12-22-87	37,000
12-29-88	48,218
12-28-89	47,750
12-28-90	44,000

(Named Hall of Fame Classic until 1986 and then discontinued after 1990 game; played at Legion Field, capacity 75,952)

AVIATION
(Dayton, Ohio)

Date	Attendance
12-9-61	3,694

BACARDI
(Havana, Cuba)

Date	Attendance
1-1-37	12,000

BLUEBONNET
(Houston, Texas)

Date	Attendance
12-19-59	55,000
12-17-60	68,000
12-16-61	52,000
12-22-62	55,000
12-21-63	50,000
12-19-64	50,000
12-18-65	40,000
12-17-66	67,000
12-23-67	30,156
12-31-68	53,543
12-31-69	55,203
12-31-70	53,829
12-31-71	54,720
12-30-72	52,961
12-29-73	44,358
12-23-74	35,122
12-27-75	52,748
12-31-76	48,618
12-31-77	52,842
12-31-78	34,084
12-31-79	40,542
12-31-80	36,667
12-31-81	40,309
12-31-82	31,557
12-31-83	50,090
12-31-84	43,260
12-31-85	42,000
12-31-86	40,476
12-31-87	23,282

(Played at Rice Stadium 1959-67 and 1985, Astrodome 1968-84 and from 1986; Astrodome capacity 60,000)

BLUEGRASS
(Louisville, Ky.)

Date	Attendance
12-13-58	7,000

CALIFORNIA
(Fresno, Calif.)

Date	Attendance
12-19-81	15,565

Date	Attendance
12-18-82	30,000
12-17-83	20,464
12-15-84	21,741
12-14-85	32,554
12-13-86	10,743
12-12-87	24,000
12-10-88	31,272
12-9-89	31,610
12-8-90	25,431
12-14-91	34,825

CAMELLIA
(Lafayette, La.)

Date	Attendance
12-30-48	4,500

CHERRY
(Pontiac, Mich.)

Date	Attendance
12-22-84	70,332
12-21-85	51,858

DELTA
(Memphis, Tenn.)

Date	Attendance
1-1-48	28,120
1-1-49	15,069

DIXIE BOWL
(Birmingham, Ala.)

Date	Attendance
1-1-48	22,000
1-1-49	20,000

DIXIE CLASSIC
(Dallas, Texas)

Date	Attendance
1-2-22	12,000
1-1-25	7,000
1-1-34	12,000

FORT WORTH CLASSIC
(Fort Worth, Texas)

Date	Attendance
1-1-21	9,000

FREEDOM BOWL
(Anaheim, Calif.)

Date	Attendance
12-26-84	24,093
12-30-85	30,961
12-30-86	55,422
12-30-87	33,261
12-29-88	35,941
12-30-89	33,858
12-29-90	41,450
12-30-91	34,217
12-29-92	50,745
12-30-93	37,203
12-27-94	27,477

GARDEN STATE
(East Rutherford, N.J.)

Date	Attendance
12-16-78	33,402
12-15-79	55,493
12-14-80	41,417
12-13-81	38,782

GOTHAM
(New York, N.Y.)

Date	Attendance
12-9-61	15,123
12-15-62	6,166

GREAT LAKES
(Cleveland, Ohio)

Date	Attendance
12-6-47	14,908

HARBOR
(San Diego, Calif.)

Date	Attendance
1-1-47	7,000
1-1-48	12,000
1-1-49	20,000

LOS ANGELES CHRISTMAS FESTIVAL
(Los Angeles, Calif.)

Date	Attendance
12-25-24	47,000

MERCY
(Los Angeles, Calif.)

Date	Attendance
11-23-61	33,145

OIL
(Houston, Texas)

Date	Attendance
1-1-46	27,000
1-1-47	23,000

PASADENA
(Pasadena, Calif.)

Date	Attendance
12-2-67	28,802
12-6-69	41,276
12-19-70	20,472
12-18-71	15,244

PRESIDENTIAL CUP
(College Park, Md.)

Date	Attendance
12-9-50	12,245

RAISIN
(Fresno, Calif.)

Date	Attendance
1-1-46	10,000
1-1-47	13,000
1-1-48	13,000
1-1-49	10,000
12-31-49	9,000

SALAD
(Phoenix, Ariz.)

Date	Attendance
1-1-48	12,500
1-1-49	17,500
1-1-50	18,500
1-1-51	23,000
1-1-52	17,000

SAN DIEGO EAST-WEST CHRISTMAS CLASSIC
(San Diego, Calif.)

Date	Attendance
12-26-21	5,000
12-25-22	5,000

SHRINE
(Little Rock, Ark.)

Date	Attendance
12-18-48	5,000

Individual Records

Only official records after 1937 are included. Prior records are included if able to be substantiated. Each team's score is in parentheses after the team name. The year listed is the actual (calendar) year the game was played; the date is included if the bowl was played twice (i.e., January and December) during one calendar year. The list also includes discontinued bowls, marked with (D). Bowls are listed by the name of the bowl at the time it was played: The Florida Citrus Bowl was the Tangerine Bowl in 1947-82; the first Hall of Fame Bowl (1977-85) was called the All-American Bowl in 1986-90; the second Hall of Fame Bowl (1986-95) is now called the Outback Bowl and is played in Tampa, Fla.; the Sun Bowl was called the John Hancock Bowl in 1989-93, the John Hancock Sun Bowl in 1987-88, and reverted to Sun Bowl in 1994; the Blockbuster Bowl changed its name to Carquest Bowl in 1993 and then to Sunshine Bowl in 1998 and the Copper Bowl changed its name to Insight.com Bowl in 1997. The NCAA Statistics Service thanks former staff member Steve Boda for his valuable assistance in compiling these records.

Total Offense

MOST TOTAL PLAYS
74—(D) Tony Kimbrough, Western Mich. (30) vs. Fresno St. (35) (California, 1988) (431 yards)

MOST TOTAL YARDS
594—Ty Detmer, Brigham Young (39) vs. Penn St. (50) (Holiday, 1989) (576 passing yards, 67 plays)

HIGHEST AVERAGE PER PLAY (Min. 10 Plays)
24.1—Dicky Maegle, Rice (28) vs. Alabama (6) (Cotton, 1954) (11 for 265)

MOST TOUCHDOWNS RESPONSIBLE FOR (TDs Scored & Passed For)
6—(D) Chuck Long, Iowa (55) vs. Texas (17) (Freedom, 1984) (6 pass); Bobby Layne, Texas (40) vs. Missouri (27) (Cotton, 1946) (3 rush, 2 pass, 1 catch)

Rushing

MOST RUSHING ATTEMPTS
46—(D) Ron Jackson, Tulsa (28) vs. San Diego St. (17) (Freedom, 1991) (211 yards)

MOST NET RUSHING YARDS
280—(D) James Gray, Texas Tech (49) vs. Duke (21) (All-American, 1989) (33 carries)

MOST NET RUSHING YARDS BY A QUARTERBACK
199—Tommie Frazier, Nebraska (62) vs. Florida (24) (Fiesta, 1996) (16 carries)

HIGHEST AVERAGE PER RUSH (Min. 9 Carries)
24.1—Dicky Maegle, Rice (28) vs. Alabama (6) (Cotton, 1954) (11 for 265)

MOST NET RUSHING YARDS BY TWO RUSHERS, SAME TEAM, OVER 100 YARDS RUSHING EACH
373—Woody Green (202) & Brent McClanahan (171), Arizona St. (49) vs. Missouri (35) (Fiesta, 1972)

MOST RUSHING TOUCHDOWNS
5—Barry Sanders, Oklahoma St. (62) vs. Wyoming (14) (Holiday, 1988) (runs of 33, 2, 67, 1, 10 yards); Neil Snow, Michigan (49) vs. Stanford (0) (Rose, 1902) (touchdowns counted as five-point scores)

Passing

MOST PASS ATTEMPTS
63—Trent Dilfer, Fresno St. (30) vs. Colorado (41) (Aloha, 1993) (completed 37)

MOST PASS COMPLETIONS
43—(D) Steve Clarkson, San Jose St. (25) vs. Toledo (27) (California, 1981) (attempted 62)

MOST CONSECUTIVE PASS COMPLETIONS
10—Danny Wuerffel, Florida (17) vs. Florida St. (23) (Sugar, Jan. 2, 1995); Rick Neuheisel, UCLA (45) vs. Illinois (9) (Rose, 1984)

MOST NET PASSING YARDS
576—Ty Detmer, Brigham Young (39) vs. Penn St. (50) (Holiday, 1989) (42 of 59 with 2 interceptions)

MOST NET PASSING YARDS, ONE QUARTER
223—Browning Nagle, Louisville (34) vs. Alabama (7) (Fiesta, 1991) (1st quarter, 9 of 16)

MOST TOUCHDOWN PASSES THROWN
6—(D) Chuck Long, Iowa (55) vs. Texas (17) (Freedom, 1984) (29 of 39 with no interceptions) (touchdown passes of 6, 11, 33, 49, 4, 15 yards)

MOST PASSES HAD INTERCEPTED
6—Bruce Lee, Arizona (10) vs. Auburn (34) (Sun, 1968) (6 of 24)

HIGHEST COMPLETION PERCENTAGE (Min. 10 Attempts)
.929—Mike Bobo, Georgia (33) vs. Wisconsin (6) (Outback, 1998) (26 of 28 with no interceptions)

MOST YARDS PER PASS ATTEMPT (Min. 10 Attempts)
21.3—Chris McCoy, Navy (42) vs. California (38) (Aloha, 1996) (13 for 277 yards)

MOST YARDS PER PASS COMPLETION (Min. 7 Completions)
30.8—Chris McCoy, Navy (42) vs. California (38) (Aloha, 1996) (9 for 277 yards)

Receiving

MOST PASS RECEPTIONS
20—(D) Norman Jordan, Vanderbilt (28) vs. Air Force (36) (Hall of Fame, 1982) (173 yards); Walker Gillette, Richmond (49) vs. Ohio (42) (Tangerine, 1968) (242 yards)

MOST PASS RECEIVING YARDS
252—Andre Rison, Michigan St. (27) vs. Georgia (34) (Gator, Jan. 1, 1989) (9 catches)

HIGHEST AVERAGE PER CATCH (Min. 3 Receptions)
52.3—Phil Harris, Texas (28) vs. Navy (6) (Cotton, 1964) (3 for 157 yards)

MOST TOUCHDOWNS RECEIVING
4—Fred Biletnikoff, Florida St. (36) vs. Oklahoma (19) (Gator, Jan. 2, 1965) (13 catches); (D) Bob McChesney, Hardin-Simmons (49) vs. Wichita St. (12) (Camellia, 1948) (8 catches)

Scoring

MOST POINTS SCORED
30—(D) Sheldon Canley, San Jose St. (48) vs. Central Mich. (24) (California, 1990) (5 touchdowns); Barry Sanders, Oklahoma St. (62) vs. Wyoming (14) (Holiday, 1988) (5 touchdowns)

MOST POINTS RESPONSIBLE FOR (TDs SCORED & PASSED FOR, EXTRA POINTS, AND FGs)
40—Bobby Layne, Texas (40) vs. Missouri (27) (Cotton, 1946) (18 rushing, 12 passing, 6 receiving and 4 PATs)

MOST TOUCHDOWNS SCORED
5—(D) Sheldon Canley, San Jose St. (48) vs. Central Mich. (24) (California, 1990) (4 rushing, 1 receiving); Barry Sanders, Oklahoma St. (62) vs. Wyoming (14) (Holiday, 1988) (5 rushing); Neil Snow, Michigan (49) vs. Stanford (0) (Rose, 1902) (5 rushing five-point TDs)

MOST TWO-POINT CONVERSIONS
2—Ernie Davis, Syracuse (23) vs. Texas (14) (Cotton, 1960) (2 receptions)

Kicking

MOST FIELD GOALS ATTEMPTED
6—Kyle Bryant, Texas A&M (22) vs. Michigan (20) (Alamo, 1995) (Made 5)

MOST FIELD GOALS MADE
5—Kyle Bryant, Texas A&M (22) vs. Michigan (20) (Alamo, 1995) (27, 49, 47, 31, 37 yards); Tim Rogers, Mississippi St. (24) vs. North Caro. St. (28) (Peach, Jan. 1, 1995) (37, 21, 29, 36, 30 yards); Arden Czyzewski, Florida (28) vs. Notre Dame (39) (Sugar, 1992) (26, 24, 36, 37, 24 yards); Jess Atkinson, Maryland (23) vs. Tennessee (30) (Florida Citrus, 1983) (18, 48, 31, 22, 26 yards)

MOST EXTRA-POINT KICK ATTEMPTS
9—Layne Talbot, Texas A&M (65) vs. Brigham Young (14) (Holiday, 1990) (9 made); Bobby Luna, Alabama (61) vs. Syracuse (6) (Orange, 1953) (7 made); (D) James Weaver, Centre (63) vs. Texas Christian (7) (Fort Worth Classic, 1921) (9 made)

MOST EXTRA-POINT KICKS MADE
9—Layne Talbot, Texas A&M (65) vs. Brigham Young (14) (Holiday, 1990) (9 attempts); (D) James Weaver, Centre (63) vs. Texas Christian (7) (Fort Worth Classic, 1921) (9 attempts)

MOST POINTS BY A KICKER
16—Kyle Bryant, Texas A&M (22) vs. Michigan (20)

(Alamo, 1995) (5 FGs, 1 PAT); Tim Rogers, Mississippi St. (24) vs. North Caro. St. (28) (Peach, Jan. 1, 1995) (5 FGs, 1 PAT); Arden Czyzewski, Florida (28) vs. Notre Dame (39) (Sugar, 1992) (5 FGs, 1 PAT)

Punting

MOST PUNTS
21—Everett Sweeney, Michigan (49) vs. Stanford (0) (Rose, 1902)

HIGHEST AVERAGE PER PUNT (Min. 5 Punts)
52.7—Des Koch, Southern Cal (7) vs. Wisconsin (0) (Rose, 1953) (7 for 369 yards)

Punt Returns

MOST PUNT RETURNS
9—Buzy Rosenberg, Georgia (7) vs. North Caro. (3) (Gator, Dec. 31, 1971) (54 yards); Paddy Driscoll, Great Lakes (17) vs. Mare Island (0) (Rose, 1919) (115 yards)

MOST PUNT RETURN YARDS
136—Johnny Rodgers, Nebraska (38) vs. Alabama (6) (Orange, 1972) (6 returns)

HIGHEST PUNT RETURN AVERAGE (Min. 3 Returns)
40.7—George Fleming, Washington (44) vs. Wisconsin (8) (Rose, 1960) (3 for 122 yards)

MOST TOUCHDOWNS ON PUNT RETURNS
2—James Henry, Southern Miss. (38) vs. UTEP (18) (Independence, 1988) (65 and 45 yards)

Kickoff Returns

MOST KICKOFF RETURNS
7—Dale Carter, Tennessee (17) vs. Penn St. (42) (Fiesta, 1992) (132 yards); Jeff Sydner, Hawaii (13) vs. Michigan St. (33) (Aloha, 1989) (174 yards); Homer Jones, Brigham Young (37) vs. Indiana (38) (Holiday, 1979) (126 yards)

MOST KICKOFF RETURN YARDS
203—Mike Fink, Missouri (35) vs. Arizona St. (49) (Fiesta, 1972) (6 returns)

HIGHEST KICKOFF RETURN AVERAGE (Min. 2 Returns)
60.5—(D) Bob Smith, Texas A&M (40) vs. Georgia (20) (Presidential Cup, 1950) (2 for 121 yards)

MOST TOUCHDOWNS ON KICKOFF RETURNS
1—Many players tied

Interceptions

MOST INTERCEPTIONS MADE
4—Jim Dooley, Miami (Fla.) (14) vs. Clemson (0) (Gator, 1952); (D) Manuel Aja, Arizona St. (21) vs. Xavier (Ohio) (33) (Salad, 1950)

MOST INTERCEPTION RETURN YARDAGE
148—Elmer Layden, Notre Dame (27) vs. Stanford (10) (Rose, 1925) (2 interceptions)

All-Purpose Yards

(Includes All Runs From Scrimmage, Pass Receptions and All Returns)

MOST ALL-PURPOSE PLAYS (Must Have at Least One Reception or Return)
47—(D) Ron Jackson, Tulsa (28) vs. San Diego St. (17) (Freedom, 1991) (46 rushes, 1 reception)

MOST ALL-PURPOSE YARDS GAINED (Must Have at Least One Reception or Return)
359—Sherman Williams, Alabama (24) vs. Ohio St. (17) (Florida Citrus, 1995) (166 rushing, 155 receiving, 38 kickoff returns)

Defensive Statistics

MOST TOTAL TACKLES MADE (Includes Assists)
31—Lee Roy Jordan, Alabama (17) vs. Oklahoma (0) (Orange, 1963)

MOST UNASSISTED TACKLES
18—Rod Smith, Notre Dame (39) vs. Florida (28) (Sugar, 1992)

MOST TACKLES MADE FOR LOSSES
5—(D) Michael Jones, Colorado (17) vs. Brigham Young (20) (Freedom, 1988) (20 yards in losses); Jimmy Walker, Arkansas (10) vs. UCLA (10) (Fiesta, 1978)

MOST QUARTERBACK SACKS
4—Rusty Medearis, Miami (Fla.) (22) vs. Nebraska (0) (Orange, 1992); Bobby Bell, Missouri (17) vs. Brigham Young (21) (Holiday, 1983)

MOST FUMBLE RECOVERIES
2—Randall Brown, Ohio St. (17) vs. Alabama (24) (Florida Citrus, 1995); (D) Michael Stewart, Fresno St. (51) vs. Bowling Green (7) (California, 1985); Rod Kirby, Pittsburgh (7) vs. Arizona St. (28) (Fiesta, 1973)

MOST BLOCKED KICKS
2—Carlton Williams, Pittsburgh (7) vs. Arizona St. (28) (Fiesta, 1973) (2 PATKs)

MOST BLOCKED PUNTS
2—Bracey Walker, North Caro (21) vs. Mississippi St. (17) (Peach, 1992)

MOST PASSES BROKEN UP
4—Chris Cummings, LSU (27) vs. Notre Dame (9) (Independence, 1997)

Team Records

Totals for each team in both-team records are in brackets after the team's score.

Total Offense

MOST TOTAL PLAYS
96—North Caro. St. (10) vs. Arizona (17) (Copper, 1989) (310 yards)

MOST TOTAL PLAYS, BOTH TEAMS
175—Toledo (40) [95] & Nevada (37) [80] (OT) (Las Vegas, 1995) (974 yards)

MOST YARDS GAINED
718—Arizona St. (49) vs. Missouri (35) (Fiesta, 1972) (452 rush, 266 pass)

MOST YARDS GAINED, BOTH TEAMS
1,143—(D) Southern Cal (47) [624] & Texas A&M (28) [519] (Bluebonnet, 1977) (148 plays)

HIGHEST AVERAGE GAINED PER PLAY
9.5—Louisville (34) vs. Alabama (7) (Fiesta, 1991) (60 plays for 571 yards)

FEWEST PLAYS
35—Tennessee (0) vs. Texas (16) (Cotton, 1953) (29 rush, 6 pass)

FEWEST PLAYS, BOTH TEAMS
107—Texas Christian (16) [54] & Marquette (6) [53] (Cotton, 1937)

FEWEST YARDS
Minus 21—U. of Mexico (0) vs. Southwestern (Tex.) (35) (Sun, 1945) (29 rush, -50 pass)

FEWEST YARDS, BOTH TEAMS
260—Randolph Field (7) [150] & Texas (7) [110] (Cotton, 1944)

LOWEST AVERAGE GAINED PER PLAY
0.9—Tennessee (0) vs. Texas (16) (Cotton, 1953) (35 plays for 32 yards)

Rushing

MOST RUSHING ATTEMPTS
87—Oklahoma (40) vs. Auburn (22) (Sugar, Jan. 1, 1972) (439 yards)

MOST RUSHING ATTEMPTS, BOTH TEAMS
122—(D) Southern Cal (47) [50] & Texas A&M (28) [72] (Bluebonnet, 1977) (864 yards); Mississippi St. (26) [68] & North Caro. (24) [54] (Sun, 1974) (732 yards)

MOST NET RUSHING YARDS
524—Nebraska (62) vs. Florida (24) (Fiesta, 1996) (68 attempts)

MOST NET RUSHING YARDS, BOTH TEAMS
864—(D) Southern Cal (47) [378] & Texas A&M (28) [486] (Bluebonnet, 1977) (122 attempts)

HIGHEST RUSHING AVERAGE (Min. 30 Attempts)
9.3—Texas Tech (55) vs. Air Force (41) (Copper, 1995) (39 for 361 yards)

FEWEST RUSHING ATTEMPTS
12—(D) Vanderbilt (28) vs. Air Force (36) (Hall of Fame, 1982) (35 yards)

FEWEST RUSHING ATTEMPTS, BOTH TEAMS
57—Iowa (20) [36] & Wyoming (19) [21] (Holiday, 1987)

FEWEST RUSHING YARDS
Minus 61—Kansas St. (7) vs. Boston College (12) (Aloha, 1994) (23 attempts)

FEWEST RUSHING YARDS, BOTH TEAMS
51—(D) Utah (16) [6] & Arizona (13) [45] (Freedom, 1994)

LOWEST RUSHING AVERAGE (Min. 20 Attempts)
Minus 2.7—Kansas St. (7) vs. Boston College (12) (Aloha, 1994) (23 for -61 yards)

RUSHING DEFENSE, FEWEST YARDS ALLOWED
Minus 61—Boston College (12) vs. Kansas St. (7) (Aloha, 1994) (23 attempts)

Passing

MOST PASS ATTEMPTS
63—(D) San Jose St. (25) vs. Toledo (27) (California, 1981) (43 completions, 5 interceptions, 467 yards)

MOST PASS ATTEMPTS, BOTH TEAMS
93—Mississippi (34) [48] & Marshall (31) [45] (Motor City, 1997) (52 completions)

MOST PASS COMPLETIONS
43—(D) San Jose St. (25) vs. Toledo (27) (California, 1981) (63 attempts, 5 interceptions, 467 yards)

MOST PASS COMPLETIONS, BOTH TEAMS
61—Penn St. (38) [20] & Oregon (20) [41] (Rose, 1995) (92 attempts)

MOST PASSING YARDS
576—Brigham Young (39) vs. Penn St. (50) (Holiday, 1989) (42 completions, 59 attempts, 2 interceptions)

MOST PASSING YARDS, BOTH TEAMS
808—Washington St. (31) [492] & Utah (28) [316] (Copper, 1992) (88 attempts)

MOST PASSES HAD INTERCEPTED
8—Arizona (10) vs. Auburn (34) (Sun, 1968)

MOST PASSES HAD INTERCEPTED, BOTH TEAMS
12—Auburn (34) [4] & Arizona (10) [8] (Sun, 1968)

MOST PASSES ATTEMPTED WITHOUT AN INTERCEPTION
57—(D) Western Mich. (30) vs. Fresno St. (35) (California, 1988) (24 completions)

MOST PASSES ATTEMPTED BY BOTH TEAMS WITHOUT AN INTERCEPTION
90—Bowling Green (35) [49] & Nevada (34) [41] (Las Vegas, 1992) (54 completions)

HIGHEST COMPLETION PERCENTAGE (Min. 10 Attempts)
.929—Texas (40) vs. Missouri (27) (Cotton, 1946) (13 of 14, no interceptions, 234 yards)

MOST YARDS PER ATTEMPT (Min. 10 Attempts)
21.7—Southern Cal (47) vs. Pittsburgh (14) (Rose, 1930) (13 for 282 yards)

MOST YARDS PER COMPLETION (Min. 8 Completions)
35.2—Southern Cal (47) vs. Pittsburgh (14) (Rose, 1930) (8 for 282 yards)

FEWEST PASS ATTEMPTS
2—Air Force (38) vs. Mississippi St. (15) (Liberty, 1991) (1 completion); (D) Army (10) vs. Michigan St. (6) (Cherry, 1984) (1 completion); West Va. (14) vs. South Caro. (3) (Peach, 1969) (1 completion)

FEWEST PASS ATTEMPTS, BOTH TEAMS
9—Fordham (2) [4] & Missouri (0) [5] (Sugar, 1942)

FEWEST PASS COMPLETIONS
0—13 teams tied (see Team Record Lists)

FEWEST PASS COMPLETIONS, BOTH TEAMS
3—Arizona St. (0) [0] & Catholic (0) [3] (Sun, 1940)

FEWEST PASSING YARDS
Minus 50—U. of Mexico (0) vs. Southwestern (Tex.) (35) (Sun, 1945) (2 completions, 9 attempts, 3 interceptions)

FEWEST PASSING YARDS, BOTH TEAMS
15—Rice (8) [-17] & Tennessee (0) [32] (Orange, 1947)

LOWEST COMPLETION PERCENTAGE
.000—13 teams tied (see Team Record Lists)

FEWEST YARDS PER PASS ATTEMPT
Minus 5.6—U. of Mexico (0) vs. Southwestern (Tex.) (35) (Sun, 1945) (9 for -50 yards)

FEWEST YARDS PER PASS COMPLETION (Min. 1 Completion)
Minus 25.0—U. of Mexico (0) vs. Southwestern (Tex.) (35) (Sun, 1945) (2 for -50 yards)

Scoring

MOST TOUCHDOWNS
9—Texas A&M (65) vs. Brigham Young (14) (Holiday, 1990) (5 rush, 4 pass); Alabama (61) vs. Syracuse (6) (Orange, 1953) (4 rush, 3 pass, 1 punt return, 1 interception return); (D) Centre (63) vs. Texas Christian (7) (Fort Worth Classic, 1921) (8 rush, 1 blocked punt recovery in end zone)

MOST TOUCHDOWNS, BOTH TEAMS
13—Texas Tech (55) [7] & Air Force (41) [6] (Copper, 1995); Richmond (49) [7] & Ohio (42) [6] (Tangerine, 1968)

MOST TOUCHDOWNS RUSHING
8—(D) Centre (63) vs. Texas Christian (7) (Fort Worth Classic, 1921)

MOST TOUCHDOWNS RUSHING, BOTH TEAMS
12—Texas Tech (55) [6] & Air Force (41) [6] (Copper, 1995)

MOST TOUCHDOWNS PASSING
6—(D) Iowa (55) vs. Texas (17) (Freedom, 1984)

MOST TOUCHDOWNS PASSING, BOTH TEAMS
8—(D) Iowa (55) [6] & Texas (17) [2] (Freedom, 1984); Richmond (49) [4] & Ohio (42) [4] (Tangerine, 1968)

MOST FIELD GOALS MADE
5—Texas A&M (22) vs. Michigan (20) (Alamo, 1995) (27, 49, 47, 31, 37 yards); Mississippi St. (24) vs. North Caro. St. (28) (Peach, Jan. 1, 1995) (37, 21, 29, 36, 30 yards); Florida (28) vs. Notre Dame (39) (Sugar, 1992) (26, 24, 36, 37, 24 yards); Maryland (23) vs. Tennessee (30) (Florida Citrus, 1983) (18, 48, 31, 22, 26 yards)

MOST FIELD GOALS MADE, BOTH TEAMS
7—Texas A&M (22) [5] & Michigan (20) [2] (Alamo, 1995); North Caro. St. (28) [2] & Mississippi St. (24) [5] (Peach, Jan. 1, 1995)

MOST POINTS, WINNING TEAM
65—Texas A&M vs. Brigham Young (14) (Holiday, 1990)

MOST POINTS, LOSING TEAM
45—Southern Methodist vs. Brigham Young (46) (Holiday, 1980)

MOST POINTS, BOTH TEAMS
96—Texas Tech (55) & Air Force (41) (Copper, 1995)

LARGEST MARGIN OF VICTORY
55—Alabama (61) vs. Syracuse (6) (Orange, 1953)

FEWEST POINTS, WINNING TEAM
2—Fordham vs. Missouri (0) (Sugar, 1942)

FEWEST POINTS, LOSING TEAM
0—By many teams

FEWEST POINTS, BOTH TEAMS
0—Air Force (0) & Texas Christian (0) (Cotton, 1959); Arkansas (0) & LSU (0) (Cotton, 1947); Arizona St. (0) & Catholic (0) (Sun, 1940); California (0) & Wash. & Jeff. (0) (Rose, 1922)

MOST POINTS SCORED IN FIRST HALF
42—Toledo (56) vs. Davidson (33) (Tangerine, 1969)

MOST POINTS SCORED IN SECOND HALF
45—Oklahoma St. (62) vs. Wyoming (14) (Holiday, 1988)

MOST POINTS SCORED IN FIRST HALF, BOTH TEAMS
63—Navy (42) [28] vs. California (38) [35] (Aloha, 1996)

MOST POINTS SCORED IN SECOND HALF, BOTH TEAMS
64—Kansas (51) [34] & UCLA (30) [30] (Aloha, 1995); Penn St. (50) [38] & Brigham Young (39) [26] (Holiday, 1989)

MOST POINTS SCORED EACH QUARTER
1st: 28—Southern Cal (55) vs. Texas Tech (14) (Cotton, 1995)
2nd: 29—Nebraska (62) vs. Florida (24) (Fiesta, 1996)
3rd: 31—(D) Iowa (55) vs. Texas (17) (Freedom, 1984)
4th: 30—Oklahoma (40) vs. Houston (14) (Sun, 1981)

MOST POINTS SCORED EACH QUARTER, BOTH TEAMS
1st: 28—Texas Tech (55) [21] & Air Force (41) [7] (Copper, 1995); Southern Cal (55) [28] & Texas Tech (14) [0] (Cotton, 1995); Indiana (38) [14] & Brigham Young (37) [14] (Holiday, 1979); Louisiana Tech (24) [21] & Louisville (14) [7] (Independence, 1977)
2nd: 43—Navy (42) [21] vs. California (38) [22] (Aloha, 1996)
3rd: 35—Kansas St. (54) [21] & Colorado St. (21) [14] (Holiday, 1995); Oklahoma St. (62) [28] & Wyoming (14) [7] (Holiday, 1988)
4th: 37—Kansas (51) [14] & UCLA (30) [23] (Aloha, 1995); Oklahoma (40) [30] & Houston (14) [7] (Sun, 1981)

First Downs

MOST FIRST DOWNS
36—Oklahoma (48) vs. Virginia (14) (Gator, Dec. 29, 1991) (16 rush, 18 pass, 2 penalty)

MOST FIRST DOWNS, BOTH TEAMS
61—Penn St. (50) [26] & Brigham Young (39) [35] (Holiday, 1989)

MOST FIRST DOWNS RUSHING
26—Oklahoma (40) vs. Auburn (22) (Sugar, Jan. 1, 1972)

MOST FIRST DOWNS RUSHING, BOTH TEAMS
36—Miami (Fla.) (46) [16] & Texas (3) [20] (Cotton, 1991); Colorado (47) [24] & Alabama (33) [12] (Liberty, 1969)

MOST FIRST DOWNS PASSING
27—Brigham Young (39) vs. Penn St. (50) (Holiday, 1989)

MOST FIRST DOWNS PASSING, BOTH TEAMS
36—Tennessee (48) [23] vs. Northwestern (28) [13] (Florda Citrus, 1997)

MOST FIRST DOWNS BY PENALTY
6—Florida (52) vs. Florida St. (20) (Sugar, 1997); Texas (3) vs. Miami (Fla.) (46) (Cotton, 1991)

MOST FIRST DOWNS BY PENALTY, BOTH TEAMS
8—Florida (52) [6] vs. Florida St. (20) [2] (Sugar, 1997); Texas A&M (22) [4] & Michigan (20) [4] (Alamo, 1995); Miami (Fla.) (46) [2] & Texas (3) [6] (Cotton, 1991)

FEWEST FIRST DOWNS
1—Arkansas (0) vs. LSU (0) (Cotton, 1947) (1 rush); Alabama (29) vs. Texas A&M (21) (Cotton, 1942) (1 pass)

FEWEST FIRST DOWNS, BOTH TEAMS
10—Randolph Field (7) [7] & Texas (7) [3] (Cotton, 1944)

FEWEST FIRST DOWNS RUSHING
0—Florida (18) vs. Missouri (20) (Sugar, 1966); Navy (6) vs. Texas (28) (Cotton, 1964); Alabama (29) vs. Texas A&M (21) (Cotton, 1942)

FEWEST FIRST DOWNS RUSHING, BOTH TEAMS
3—Alabama (29) [0] & Texas A&M (21) [3] (Cotton, 1942)

FEWEST FIRST DOWNS PASSING
0—By 13 teams (see Team Record Lists)

FEWEST FIRST DOWNS PASSING, BOTH TEAMS
1—Alabama (10) [0] & Arkansas (3) [1] (Sugar, 1962)

Punting

MOST PUNTS
17—Duke (3) vs. Southern Cal (7) (Rose, 1939)

MOST PUNTS, BOTH TEAMS
28—Rice (8) [13] & Tennessee (0) [15] (Orange, 1947); Santa Clara (6) [14] & LSU (0) [14] (Sugar, 1938)

HIGHEST PUNTING AVERAGE (Min. 5 Punts)
53.9—Southern Cal (7) vs. Wisconsin (0) (Rose, 1953) (8 for 431)

FEWEST PUNTS
0—Oklahoma St. (62) vs. Wyoming (14) (Holiday, 1988); Oklahoma (41) vs. Wyoming (7) (Fiesta, 1976)

LOWEST PUNTING AVERAGE (Min. 3 Punts)
17.0—Nevada (34) vs. Bowling Green (35) (Las Vegas, 1992) (4 for 68 yards)

MOST PUNTS BLOCKED BY ONE TEAM
2—North Caro. (21) vs. Mississippi St. (17) (Peach, 1992); North Caro. St. (14) vs. Georgia (7) (Liberty, 1967)

Punt Returns

MOST PUNT RETURNS
9—Georgia (7) vs. North Caro. (3) (Gator, Dec. 31, 1971) (6.8 average)

MOST PUNT RETURN YARDS
136—Nebraska (38) vs. Alabama (6) (Orange, 1972) (6 returns)

HIGHEST PUNT RETURN AVERAGE (Min. 3 Returns)
33.0—Kent (18) vs. Tampa (21) (Tangerine, 1972) (3 for 99 yards)

Kickoff Returns

MOST KICKOFF RETURNS
10—Florida (24) vs. Nebraska (62) (Fiesta, 1996) (26.8 average); Wyoming (14) vs. Oklahoma St. (62) (Holiday, 1988) (20.5 average)

MOST KICKOFF RETURN YARDS
268—Florida (24) vs. Nebraska (62) (Fiesta, 1996) (10 returns)

HIGHEST KICKOFF RETURN AVERAGE (Min. 3 Returns)
42.5—Tennessee (27) vs. Maryland (28) (Sun, 1984) (4 for 170 yards)

Fumbles

MOST FUMBLES
11—Mississippi (7) vs. Alabama (12) (Sugar, 1964) (lost 6)

MOST FUMBLES, BOTH TEAMS
17—Alabama (12) [6] & Mississippi (7) [11] (Sugar, 1964) (lost 9)

MOST FUMBLES LOST
6—By five teams (see Team Record Lists)

MOST FUMBLES LOST, BOTH TEAMS
9—Alabama (12) [3] & Mississippi (7) [6] (Sugar, 1964) (17 fumbles)

Penalties

MOST PENALTIES
20—(D) Fresno St. (35) vs. Western Mich. (30) (California, 1988) (166 yards)

MOST PENALTIES, BOTH TEAMS
29—Florida (52) [15] vs. Florida St. (20) [14] (Sugar, 1997) (217 yards); McNeese St. (20) [13] & Tulsa (16) [16] (Independence, 1976) (205 yards)

MOST YARDS PENALIZED
202—Miami (Fla.) (46) vs. Texas (3) (Cotton, 1991) (16 penalties)

MOST YARDS PENALIZED, BOTH TEAMS
270—Miami (Fla.) (46) [202] & Texas (3) [68] (Cotton, 1991)

FEWEST PENALTIES
0—By eight teams (see Team Record Lists)

FEWEST PENALTIES, BOTH TEAMS
3—In five games (see Team Record Lists)

FEWEST YARDS PENALIZED
0—By eight teams (see Team Record Lists)

FEWEST YARDS PENALIZED, BOTH TEAMS
10—Duquesne (13) [5] & Mississippi St. (12) [5] (Orange, 1937)

Individual Record Lists

Only official records after 1937 are included. Prior records are included if able to be substantiated. Each team's score is in parentheses after the team name. The year listed is the actual (calendar) year the game was played; the date is included if the bowl was played twice (i.e., January and December) during one calendar year. The list also includes discontinued bowls, marked with (D). Bowls are listed by the name of the bowl at the time it was played: The Florida Citrus Bowl was the Tangerine Bowl in 1947-82; the first Hall of Fame Bowl (1977-85) was called the All-American Bowl in 1986-90; the second Hall of Fame Bowl (1986-95) is now called the Outback Bowl and is played in Tampa, Fla.; the Sun Bowl was called the John Hancock Bowl in 1989-93, the John Hancock Sun Bowl in 1987-88, and reverted to the Sun Bowl in 1994; the Blockbuster Bowl changed its name to Carquest Bowl in 1993 and then to Sunshine Bowl in 1998; and the Copper Bowl changed its name to Insight.com Bowl in 1997.

Photo from Fresno St. sports information

Trent Dilfer compiled 474 total yards against Colorado in the 1993 Aloha Bowl to rank fourth in Division I bowl history.

Total Offense

MOST PLAYS
74—(D) Tony Kimbrough, Western Mich. (30) vs. Fresno St. (35) (California, 1988)
68—Hines Ward, Georgia (27) vs. Virginia (34) (Peach, Dec. 30, 1995)
67—Ty Detmer, Brigham Young (39) vs. Penn St. (50) (Holiday, 1989)
65—Shane Matthews, Florida (28) vs. Notre Dame (39) (Sugar, 1992)
65—Tony Eason, Illinois (15) vs. Alabama (21) (Liberty, 1982)
65—Buster O'Brien, Richmond (49) vs. Ohio (42) (Tangerine, 1968)
63—(D) Steve Clarkson, San Jose St. (25) vs. Toledo (27) (California, 1981)
62—Mark Young, Mississippi (20) vs. Texas Tech (17) (Independence, 1986)
62—Jack Trudeau, Illinois (29) vs. Army (31) (Peach, 1985)
62—Dennis Sproul, Arizona St. (30) vs. Penn St. (42) (Fiesta, 1977)
61—Jeff Blake, East Caro. (37) vs. North Caro. St. (34) (Peach, 1992)
61—Shawn Halloran, Boston College (27) vs. Georgia (24) (Hall of Fame, 1986)
61—Kim Hammond, Florida St. (17) vs. Penn St. (17) (Gator, 1967)
59—Vinny Testaverde, Miami (Fla.) (10) vs. Penn St. (14) (Fiesta, 1987)
59—Jim McMahon, Brigham Young (46) vs. Southern Methodist (45) (Holiday, 1980)
58—Terrence Jones, Tulane (12) vs. Washington (24) (Independence, 1987)
58—(D) Jerry Rhome, Tulsa (14) vs. Mississippi (7) (Bluebonnet, 1964)

MOST TOTAL YARDS
594—Ty Detmer, Brigham Young (39) vs. Penn St. (50) (Holiday, 1989) (576 pass)
486—Buster O'Brien, Richmond (49) vs. Ohio (42) (Tangerine, 1968) (447 pass)
481—(D) Chuck Long, Iowa (55) vs. Texas (17) (Freedom, 1984) (461 pass)
474—Trent Dilfer, Fresno St. (30) vs. Colorado (41) (Aloha, 1993) (523 pass)
469—Hines Ward, Georgia (27) vs. Virginia (34) (Peach, Dec. 30, 1995) (413 pass)
464—(D) Steve Clarkson, San Jose St. (25) vs. Toledo (27) (California, 1981) (467 pass)
454—John Walsh, Brigham Young (31) vs. Oklahoma (6) (Copper, 1994) (454 pass)
446—(D) Whit Taylor, Vanderbilt (28) vs. Air Force (36) (Hall of Fame, 1982) (452 pass)
446—Jim McMahon, Brigham Young (46) vs. Southern Methodist (45) (Holiday, 1980) (446 pass)
431—Browning Nagle, Louisville (34) vs. Alabama (7) (Fiesta, 1991) (451 pass)
431—(D) Tony Kimbrough, Western Mich. (30) vs. Fresno St. (35) (California, 1988) (366 pass)
420—(D) Ralph Martini, San Jose St. (48) vs. Central Mich. (24) (California, 1990) (404 pass)
414—Peter Tom Willis, Florida St. (41) vs. Nebraska (17) (Fiesta, 1990) (422 pass)
413—Tony Eason, Illinois (15) vs. Alabama (21) (Liberty, 1982) (423 pass)
412—David Smith, Alabama (29) vs. Army (28) (John Hancock Sun, 1988) (412 pass)
410—Chuck Hartlieb, Iowa (23) vs. North Caro. St. (28) (Peach, Dec. 31, 1988) (428 pass)
408—Marc Wilson, Brigham Young (37) vs. Indiana (38) (Holiday, 1979) (380 pass)
407—Jack Trudeau, Illinois (29) vs. Army (31) (Peach, 1985) (401 pass)

HIGHEST AVERAGE PER PLAY (Minimum 10 Plays)
24.1—Dicky Maegle, Rice (28) vs. Alabama (6) (Cotton, 1954) (11 for 265 yards)
14.1—Marcus Dupree, Oklahoma (21) vs. Arizona St. (32) (Fiesta, 1983) (17 for 239 yards)
14.0—Bucky Richardson, Texas A&M (65) vs. Brigham Young (14) (Holiday, 1990) (23 for 322 yards)
13.2—Kordell Stewart, Colorado (41) vs. Notre Dame (24) (Fiesta, 1995) (28 for 369)
12.2—Ger Schwedes, Syracuse (23) vs. Texas (14) (Cotton, 1960) (10 for 122 yards)
12.0—Tony Rice, Notre Dame (34) vs. West Va. (21) (Fiesta, 1989) (24 for 288 yards)
11.3—Rob Johnson, Southern Cal (55) vs. Texas Tech (14) (Cotton, 1995) (24 for 271 yards)
11.2—(D) Dwight Ford, Southern Cal (47) vs. Texas A&M (28) (Bluebonnet, 1977) (14 for 157 yards)
11.1—Browning Nagle, Louisville (34) vs. Alabama (7) (Fiesta, 1991) (39 for 431 yards)
10.8—Byron Hanspard, Texas Tech (55) vs. Air Force (41) (Copper, 1995) (24 for 260 yards)
10.8—Danny White, Arizona St. (49) vs. Missouri (35) (Fiesta, 1972) (27 for 291 yards)
10.8—(D) Ralph Martini, San Jose St. (48) vs. Central Mich. (24) (California, 1990) (39 for 420 yards)
10.5—(D) Chuck Long, Iowa (55) vs. Texas (17) (Freedom, 1984) (46 for 481 yards)
10.4—Frank Sinkwich, Georgia (40) vs. Texas Christian (26) (Orange, 1942) (35 for 365 yards)

10.3—Chuck Curtis, Texas Christian (28) vs. Syracuse (27) (Cotton, 1957) (18 for 185 yards)

MOST TOUCHDOWNS RESPONSIBLE FOR (TDS SCORED & PASSED FOR)
6—(D) Chuck Long, Iowa (55) vs. Texas (17) (Freedom, 1984) (6 pass)
6—Bobby Layne, Texas (40) vs. Missouri (27) (Cotton, 1946) (3 rush, 2 pass, 1 catch)
5—Michael Bishop, Kansas St. (35) vs. Syracuse (18) (Fiesta, 1997) (4 pass, 1 rush)
5—Jeff Blake, East Caro. (37) vs. North Caro. St. (34) (Peach, 1992) (4 pass, 1 rush)
5—Peter Tom Willis, Florida St. (41) vs. Nebraska (17) (Fiesta, 1990) (5 pass)
5—(D) Sheldon Canley, San Jose St. (48) vs. Central Mich. (24) (California, 1990) (4 rush, 1 pass)
5—Buster O'Brien, Richmond (49) vs. Ohio (42) (Tangerine, 1968) (4 pass, 1 rush)
5—Steve Tensi, Florida St. (36) vs. Oklahoma (19) (Gator, Jan. 2, 1965) (5 pass)
5—Neil Snow, Michigan (49) vs. Stanford (0) (Rose, 1902) (5 rush)

Rushing

MOST RUSHING ATTEMPTS
46—(D) Ron Jackson, Tulsa (28) vs. San Diego St. (17) (Freedom, 1991) (211 yards)
43—Fred Taylor, Florida (21) vs. Penn St. (6) (Florida Citrus, 1998) (234 yards)
41—Blake Ezor, Michigan St. (33) vs. Hawaii (13) (Aloha, 1989) (179 yards)
39—Terrell Fletcher, Wisconsin (34) vs. Duke (20) (Hall of Fame, 1995) (241 yards)
39—Raymont Harris, Ohio St. (28) vs. Brigham Young (21) (Holiday, 1993) (235 yards)
39—Errict Rhett, Florida (27) vs. North Caro. St. (10) (Gator, 1992) (182 yards)
39—Charlie Wysocki, Maryland (20) vs. Florida (35) (Tangerine, 1980) (159 yards)
39—Charles White, Southern Cal (17) vs. Ohio St. (16) (Rose, 1980) (247 yards)
37—(D) Charles Davis, Colorado (29) vs. Houston (17) (Bluebonnet, 1971) (202 yards)
36—Brent Moss, Wisconsin (21) vs. UCLA (16) (Rose, 1994) (158 yards)
36—Herschel Walker, Georgia (17) vs. Notre Dame (10) (Sugar, 1981) (150 yards)
36—Don McCauley, North Caro. (26) vs. Arizona St. (48) (Peach, 1970) (143 yards)
35—Blair Thomas, Penn St. (50) vs. Brigham Young (39) (Holiday, 1989) (186 yards)
35—Lorenzo White, Michigan St. (20) vs. Southern Cal (17) (Rose, 1988) (113 yards)
35—(D) Robert Newhouse, Houston (17) vs. Colorado (29) (Bluebonnet, 1971) (168 yards)
35—Ed Williams, West Va. (14) vs. South Caro. (3) (Peach, 1969) (208 yards)
35—Bob Anderson, Colorado (47) vs. Alabama (33) (Liberty, 1969) (254 yards)
34—Rondell Mealey, LSU (27) vs. Notre Dame (9) (Independence, 1997) (222 yards)
34—(D) Curtis Dickey, Texas A&M (28) vs. Iowa St. (12) (Hall of Fame, 1978) (276 yards)
34—Vic Bottari, California (13) vs. Alabama (0) (Rose, 1938) (137 yards)
34—Ernie Nevers, Stanford (10) vs. Notre Dame (27) (Rose, 1925) (114 yards)

MOST NET RUSHING YARDS
280—(D) James Gray, Texas Tech (49) vs. Duke (21) (All-American, 1989) (33 carries)
276—(D) Curtis Dickey, Texas A&M (28) vs. Iowa St. (12) (Hall of Fame, 1978) (34 carries)
266—(D) Gaston Green, UCLA (31) vs. Brigham Young (10) (Freedom, 1986) (33 carries)
265—Dicky Maegle, Rice (28) vs. Alabama (6) (Cotton, 1954) (11 carries)
260—Byron Hanspard, Texas Tech (55) vs. Air Force (41) (Copper, 1995) (24 carries)
254—Bob Anderson, Colorado (47) vs. Alabama (33) (Liberty, 1969) (35 carries)
250—Chuck Webb, Tennessee (31) vs. Arkansas (27) (Cotton, 1990) (26 carries)
247—Charles White, Southern Cal (17) vs. Ohio St. (16) (Rose, 1980) (39 carries)
246—Ron Dayne, Wisconsin (38) vs. Utah (10) (Copper, 1996) (30 carries)
241—Terrell Fletcher, Wisconsin (34) vs. Duke (20) (Hall of Fame, 1995) (39 carries)
239—Marcus Dupree, Oklahoma (21) vs. Arizona St. (32) (Fiesta, 1983) (17 carries)
235—Tyrone Wheatley, Michigan (38) vs. Washington (31) (Rose, 1993) (15 carries)
235—Raymont Harris, Ohio St. (28) vs. Brigham Young (21) (Holiday, 1993) (39 carries)
234—Fred Taylor, Florida (21) vs. Penn St. (6) (Florida Citrus, 1998) (43 carries)
234—Kevin Faulk, LSU (45) vs. Michigan St. (26) (Independence, 1995) (25 carries)
234—Jamie Morris, Michigan (28) vs. Alabama (24) (Hall of Fame, 1988) (23 carries)
227—Eric Ball, UCLA (45) vs. Iowa (28) (Rose, 1986) (22 carries)
225—Craig James, Southern Methodist (45) vs. Brigham Young (46) (Holiday, 1980) (23 carries)
222—Rondell Mealey, LSU (27) vs. Notre Dame (9) (Independence, 1997) (34 carries)
222—Barry Sanders, Oklahoma St. (62) vs. Wyoming (14) (Holiday, 1988) (29 carries)
216—Floyd Little, Syracuse (12) vs. Tennessee (18) (Gator, 1966) (29 carries)
211—(D) Ron Jackson, Tulsa (28) vs. San Diego St. (17) (Freedom, 1991) (46 carries)
208—Ed Williams, West Va. (14) vs. South Caro. (3) (Peach, 1969) (35 carries)
206—Ahman Green, Nebraska (42) vs. Tennessee (17) (Orange, 1998) (29 carries)
205—(D) Sammie Smith, Florida St. (27) vs. Indiana (13) (All-American, 1986) (25 carries)
205—Roland Sales, Arkansas (31) vs. Oklahoma (6) (Orange, 1978) (22 carries)
202—Tony Dorsett, Pittsburgh (27) vs. Georgia (3) (Sugar, 1977) (32 carries)
202—Woody Green, Arizona St. (49) vs. Missouri (35) (Fiesta, 1972) (25 carries)
202—(D) Charles Davis, Colorado (29) vs. Houston (17) (Bluebonnet, 1971) (37 carries)
201—Malcolm Thomas, Syracuse (30) vs. Houston (17) (Liberty, 1996) (24 carries)

MOST NET RUSHING YARDS BY A QUARTERBACK
199—Tommie Frazier, Nebraska (62) vs. Florida (24) (Fiesta, 1996) (16 carries)
180—(D) Mike Mosley, Texas A&M (28) vs. Southern Cal (47) (Bluebonnet, 1977) (20 carries)
164—Eddie Phillips, Texas (11) vs. Notre Dame (24) (Cotton, 1971) (23 carries)
149—Jack Mildren, Oklahoma (40) vs. Auburn (22) (Sugar, 1972) (30 carries)
143—Kordell Stewart, Colorado (41) vs. Notre Dame (24) (Fiesta, 1995) (7 carries)
136—(D) Nate Sassaman, Army (10) vs. Michigan St. (6) (Cherry, 1984) (28 carries)
133—(D) Eddie Wolgast, Arizona (13) vs. Drake (14) (Salad, 1949) (22 carries) (listed in newspaper accounts as halfback but also attempted 15 passes in game)
132—Corby Jones, Missouri (24) vs. Colorado St. (35) (Holiday, 1997) (20 carries)
129—Beau Morgan, Air Force (41) vs. Texas Tech (55) (Copper, 1995) (22 carries)
129—Rex Kern, Ohio St. (17) vs. Stanford (27) (Rose, 1971) (20 carries)
127—J. C. Watts, Oklahoma (24) vs. Florida St. (7) (Orange, 1980) (12 carries)
119—Bucky Richardson, Texas A&M (65) vs. Brigham Young (14) (Holiday, 1990) (12 carries)
113—Harry Gilmer, Alabama (34) vs. Southern Cal (14) (Rose, 1946)
107—Darrell Shepard, Oklahoma (40) vs. Houston (14) (Sun, 1981) (12 carries)
103—Major Harris, West Va. (33) vs. Oklahoma St. (35) (John Hancock Sun, 1987)

HIGHEST AVERAGE PER RUSH
(Minimum 9 Carries)
24.1—Dicky Maegle, Rice (28) vs. Alabama (6) (Cotton, 1954) (11 for 265 yards)
21.6—Bob Jeter, Iowa (38) vs. California (12) (Rose, 1959) (9 for 194 yards)
15.7—Tyrone Wheatley, Michigan (38) vs. Washington (31) (Rose, 1993) (15 for 235 yards)
14.2—(D) Gary Anderson, Arkansas (34) vs. Tulane (15) (Hall of Fame, 1980) (11 for 156 yards)
14.1—Mike Holovak, Boston College (21) vs. Alabama (37) (Orange, 1943) (10 for 141 yards)
14.1—Marcus Dupree, Oklahoma (21) vs. Arizona St. (32) (Fiesta, 1983) (17 for 239 yards)
12.6—Randy Baldwin, Mississippi (42) vs. Air Force (29) (Liberty, 1989) (14 for 177 yards)
12.6—Ben Barnett, Army (28) vs. Alabama (29) (John Hancock Sun, 1988) (14 for 177 yards)
12.4—Tommie Frazier, Nebraska (62) vs. Florida (24) (Fiesta, 1996) (16 for 199 yards)
12.3—George Smith, Texas Tech (28) vs. North Caro. (32) (Sun, 1972) (14 for 172 yards)
11.2—(D) Dwight Ford, Southern Cal (47) vs. Texas A&M (28) (Bluebonnet, 1977) (14 for 157 yards)
11.2—Elliott Walker, Pittsburgh (33) vs. Kansas (19) (Sun, 1975) (11 for 123 yards)
10.9—Rodney Hampton, Georgia (34) vs. Michigan St. (27) (Gator, Jan. 1, 1989) (10 for 109 yards)
10.8—Bobby Cavazos, Texas Tech (35) vs. Auburn (13) (Gator, Jan. 1, 1954) (13 for 141 yards)
10.8—Byron Hanspard, Texas Tech (55) vs. Air Force (41) (Copper, 1995) (24 for 260 yards)
10.6—J. C. Watts, Oklahoma (24) vs. Florida St. (7) (Orange, 1980) (12 for 127 yards)
10.5—Ray Brown, Mississippi (39) vs. Texas (7) (Sugar, 1958) (15 for 157 yards)
10.3—Eric Ball, UCLA (45) vs. Iowa (28) (Rose, 1986) (22 for 227 yards)
10.2—(D) Bill Tobin, Missouri (14) vs. Georgia Tech (10) (Bluebonnet, 1962) (11 for 112 yards)
10.2—Jamie Morris, Michigan (28) vs. Alabama (24) (Hall of Fame, 1988) (23 for 234 yards)

THREE RUSHERS, SAME TEAM, GAINING MORE THAN 100 YARDS
366—Tony Dorsett (142), Elliott Walker (123) & Robert Haygood (QB) (101), Pittsburgh (33) vs. Kansas (19) (Sun, 1975)

TWO RUSHERS, SAME TEAM, GAINING MORE THAN 100 YARDS
373—Woody Green (202) & Brent McClanahan (171), Arizona St. (49) vs. Missouri (35) (Fiesta, 1972)
365—(D) George Woodard (185) & Mike Mosley (QB) (180), Texas A&M (28) vs. Southern Cal (47) (Bluebonnet, 1977)
365—Bob Anderson (254) & Jim Bratten (111), Colorado (47) vs. Alabama (33) (Liberty, 1969)
364—Tommie Frazier (QB) (199) & Lawrence Phillips (165), Nebraska (62) vs. Florida (24) (Fiesta, 1996)
347—Walter Packer (183) & Terry Vitrano (164), Mississippi St. (26) vs. North Caro. (24) (Sun, 1974)
343—(D) Charles White (186) & Dwight Ford (157), Southern Cal (47) vs. Texas A&M (28) (Bluebonnet, 1977)
330—Floyd Little (216) & Larry Csonka (114), Syracuse (12) vs. Tennessee (18) (Gator, 1966)
297—Monroe Eley (173) & Bob Thomas (124), Arizona St. (48) vs. North Caro. (26) (Peach, 1970)
292—Kelvin Bryant (148) & Ethan Horton (144), North Caro. (31) vs. Arkansas (27) (Gator, 1981)
291—Billy Sims (164) & J. C. Watts (QB) (127), Oklahoma (24) vs. Florida St. (7) (Orange, 1980)
288—Billy Sims (181) & Darrell Shepard (QB) (107), Oklahoma (40) vs. Houston (14) (Sun, 1981)
277—Danta Johnson (148) & Beau Morgan (QB) (129), Air Force (41) vs. Texas Tech (55) (Copper, 1995)
277—Willie Heston (170) & Neil Snow (107), Michigan (49) vs. Stanford (0) (Rose, 1902)
270—Anthony Brown (167) & Major Harris (QB) (103), West Va. (33) vs. Oklahoma St. (35) (John Hancock Sun, 1987)
257—Sedrick Shaw (135) & Tavian Banks (122), Iowa (38) vs. Washington (18) (Sun, 1995)
253—Alois Blackwell (149) & Dyral Thomas (104), Houston (30) vs. Maryland (21) (Cotton, 1977)
246—T. Robert Hopkins (125) & Leonard Brown (121), Missouri (27) vs. Texas (40) (Cotton, 1946)

240—Jon Vaughn (128) & Ricky Powers (112), Michigan (35) vs. Mississippi (3) (Gator, Jan. 1, 1991)
237—James Rouse (134) & Barry Foster (103), Arkansas (27) vs. Tennessee (31) (Cotton, 1990)
237—Raymond Bybee (127) & Thomas Reamon (110), Missouri (34) vs. Auburn (17) (Sun, 1973)
236—Corby Jones (132) & Devin West (104), Missouri (24) vs. Colorado St. (35) (Holiday, 1997)
230—Rex Kern (QB) (129) & John Brockington (101), Ohio St. (17) vs. Stanford (27) (Rose, 1971)
223—Bucky Richardson (QB) (119) & Darren Lewis (104), Texas A&M (65) vs. Brigham Young (14) (Holiday, 1990)
222—(D) Marshall Johnson (114) & Donnie McGraw (108), Houston (47) vs. Tulane (7) (Bluebonnet, 1973)
218—Travis Sims (113) & Michael Carter (105), Hawaii (27) vs. Illinois (17) (Holiday, 1992)
218—Steve Giese (111) & Bob Torrey (107), Penn St. (42) vs. Arizona St. (30) (Fiesta, 1977)
215—Jeff Atkins (112) & Reggie Dupard (103), Southern Methodist (27) vs. Notre Dame (20) (Aloha, 1984)
215—Allen Pinkett (111) & Chris Smith (104), Notre Dame (19) vs. Boston College (18) (Liberty, 1983)
204—Johnny "Ham" Jones (104) & Johnny "Jam" Jones (100), Texas (42) vs. Maryland (0) (Sun, 1978)
201—Jerome Heavens (101) & Vagas Ferguson (100), Notre Dame (38) vs. Texas (10) (Cotton, 1978)

MOST RUSHING TOUCHDOWNS
5—Barry Sanders, Oklahoma St. (62) vs. Wyoming (14) (Holiday, 1988) (runs of 33, 2, 67, 1, 10)
5—Neil Snow, Michigan (49) vs. Stanford (0) (Rose, 1902) (five-point scores)
4—Byron Hanspard, Texas Tech (55) vs. Air Force (41) (Copper, 1995) (runs of 2, 11, 2, 29)
4—Wasean Tait, Toledo (40) vs. Nevada (37) (OT) (Las Vegas, 1995) (runs of 18, 31, 26, 3)
4—(D) Ron Jackson, Tulsa (28) vs. San Diego St. (17) (Freedom, 1991) (runs of 10, 6, 3, 4)
4—(D) Sheldon Canley, San Jose St. (48) vs. Central Mich. (24) (California, 1990) (runs of 5, 22, 59, 5)
4—(D) James Gray, Texas Tech (49) vs. Duke (21) (All-American, 1989) (runs of 2, 54, 18, 32)
4—Thurman Thomas, Oklahoma St. (35) vs. West Va. (33) (John Hancock Sun, 1987) (runs of 5, 9, 4, 4)
4—Eric Ball, UCLA (45) vs. Iowa (28) (Rose, 1986) (runs of 30, 40, 6, 32)
4—Terry Miller, Oklahoma St. (49) vs. Brigham Young (21) (Tangerine, 1976) (runs of 3, 78, 6, 1)
4—Sam Cunningham, Southern Cal (42) vs. Ohio St. (17) (Rose, 1973) (runs of 2, 1, 1, 1)
4—Woody Green, Arizona St. (49) vs. Missouri (35) (Fiesta, 1972) (runs of 2, 12, 17, 21)
4—Charles Cole, Toledo (56) vs. Davidson (33) (Tangerine, 1969) (runs of 1, 11, 16, 1)
4—(D) Gene Shannon, Houston (26) vs. Dayton (21) (Salad, 1952) (runs of 15, 19, 1, 10)

Passing

MOST PASS ATTEMPTS
63—Trent Dilfer, Fresno St. (30) vs. Colorado (41) (Aloha, 1993)
62—(D) Steve Clarkson, San Jose St. (25) vs. Toledo (27) (California, 1981)
61—Danny O'Neil, Oregon (20) vs. Penn St. (38) (Rose, 1995)
61—(D) Sean Covey, Brigham Young (16) vs. Virginia (22) (All-American, 1987)
59—Hines Ward, Georgia (27) vs. Virginia (34) (Peach, Dec. 30, 1995)
59—Ty Detmer, Brigham Young (39) vs. Penn St. (50) (Holiday, 1989)
58—Shane Matthews, Florida (28) vs. Notre Dame (39) (Sugar, 1992)
58—Buster O'Brien, Richmond (49) vs. Ohio (42) (Tangerine, 1968)
57—(D) Tony Kimbrough, Western Mich. (30) vs. Fresno St. (35) (California, 1988)
56—Gino Torretta, Miami (Fla.) (13) vs. Alabama (34) (Sugar, 1993)
55—Jack Trudeau, Illinois (29) vs. Army (31) (Peach, 1985)
55—Tony Eason, Illinois (15) vs. Alabama (21) (Liberty, 1982)
53—Tim Cowan, Washington (21) vs. Maryland (20) (Aloha, 1982)
53—Kim Hammond, Florida St. (17) vs. Penn St. (17) (Gator, 1967)
52—David Smith, Alabama (29) vs. Army (28) (John Hancock Sun, 1988)
52—Shawn Halloran, Boston College (27) vs. Georgia (24) (Hall of Fame, 1986)
51—Jeff Blake, East Caro. (37) vs. North Caro. St. (34) (Peach, 1992)
51—Danny McManus, Florida St. (31) vs. Nebraska (28) (Fiesta, 1988)
51—Chuck Hartlieb, Iowa (23) vs. North Caro. St. (28) (Peach, Dec. 31, 1988)
51—Craig Burnett, Wyoming (19) vs. Iowa (20) (Holiday, 1987)
51—(D) Whit Taylor, Vanderbilt (28) vs. Air Force (36) (Hall of Fame, 1982)

MOST PASS COMPLETIONS
43—(D) Steve Clarkson, San Jose St. (25) vs. Toledo (27) (California, 1981)
42—Ty Detmer, Brigham Young (39) vs. Penn St. (50) (Holiday, 1989)
41—Danny O'Neil, Oregon (20) vs. Penn St. (38) (Rose, 1995)
39—Buster O'Brien, Richmond (49) vs. Ohio (42) (Tangerine, 1968)
38—Jack Trudeau, Illinois (29) vs. Army (31) (Peach, 1985)
38—(D) Whit Taylor, Vanderbilt (28) vs. Air Force (36) (Hall of Fame, 1982)
37—Trent Dilfer, Fresno St. (30) vs. Colorado (41) (Aloha, 1993)
37—(D) Sean Covey, Brigham Young (16) vs. Virginia (22) (All-American, 1987)
37—Kim Hammond, Florida St. (17) vs. Penn St. (17) (Gator, 1967)
35—Tony Eason, Illinois (15) vs. Alabama (21) (Liberty, 1982)
33—David Smith, Alabama (29) vs. Army (28) (John Hancock Sun, 1988)
33—Tim Cowan, Washington (21) vs. Maryland (20) (Aloha, 1982)
33—Ron VanderKelen, Wisconsin (37) vs. Southern Cal (42) (Rose, 1963)
32—Jim McMahon, Brigham Young (46) vs. Southern Methodist (45) (Holiday, 1980)
31—Hines Ward, Georgia (27) vs. Virginia (34) (Peach, Dec. 30, 1995)
31—John Walsh, Brigham Young (31) vs. Oklahoma (6) (Copper, 1994)
31—Jeff Blake, East Caro. (37) vs. North Caro. St. (34) (Peach, 1992)
31—Stan White, Auburn (27) vs. Indiana (23) (Peach, 1990)
31—Shawn Halloran, Boston College (27) vs. Georgia (24) (Hall of Fame, 1986)
31—Mark Young, Mississippi (20) vs. Texas Tech (17) (Independence, 1986)
31—Bernie Kosar, Miami (Fla.) (37) vs. UCLA (39) (Fiesta, 1985)
31—John Congemi, Pittsburgh (23) vs. Ohio St. (28) (Fiesta, 1984)
31—(D) Jeff Tedford, Fresno St. (29) vs. Bowling Green (28) (California, 1982)

MOST CONSECUTIVE PASS COMPLETIONS
19—Mike Bobo, Georgia (33) vs. Wisconsin (6) (Outback, 1998)
10—Danny Wuerffel, Florida (17) vs. Florida St. (23) (Sugar, Jan. 2, 1995)
10—Rick Neuheisel, UCLA (45) vs. Illinois (9) (Rose, 1984)
9—(D) Rob Johnson, Southern Cal (28) vs. Utah (21) (Freedom, 1993)
9—Bill Montgomery, Arkansas (16) vs. Georgia (2) (Sugar, 1969)
9—Glenn Dobbs, Tulsa (7) vs. Tennessee (14) (Sugar, 1943)
8—Billy Roland, Houston (49) vs. Miami (Ohio) (21) (Tangerine, 1962)
8—Bobby Layne, Texas (40) vs. Missouri (27) (Cotton, 1946)
8—Harry Gilmer, Alabama (26) vs. Duke (29) (Sugar, 1945)
7—(D) Daniel Ford, Arizona St. (33) vs. Air Force (28) (Freedom, 1987)

MOST NET PASSING YARDS
(Followed by Comp.-Att.-Int.)
576—Ty Detmer, Brigham Young (39) vs. Penn St. (50) (Holiday, 1989) (42-59-2)
523—Trent Dilfer, Fresno St. (30) vs. Colorado (41) (Aloha, 1993) (37-63-1)
476—Drew Bledsoe, Washington St. (31) vs. Utah (28) (Copper, 1992) (30-46-1)
467—(D) Steve Clarkson, San Jose St. (25) vs. Toledo (27) (California, 1981) (43-62-5)
461—(D) Chuck Long, Iowa (55) vs. Texas (17) (Freedom, 1984) (29-39-0)
456—Danny O'Neil, Oregon (20) vs. Penn St. (38) (Rose, 1995) (41-61-2)
454—John Walsh, Brigham Young (31) vs. Oklahoma (6) (Copper, 1994) (31-45-0)
452—(D) Whit Taylor, Vanderbilt (28) vs. Air Force (36) (Hall of Fame, 1982) (38-51-3)
451—Browning Nagle, Louisville (34) vs. Alabama (7) (Fiesta, 1991) (20-33-1)
447—Buster O'Brien, Richmond (49) vs. Ohio (42) (Tangerine, 1968) (39-58-2)
446—Jim McMahon, Brigham Young (46) vs. Southern Methodist (45) (Holiday, 1980) (32-49-1)
428—Chuck Hartlieb, Iowa (23) vs. North Caro. St. (28) (Peach, Dec. 31, 1988) (30-51-4)
423—Tony Eason, Illinois (15) vs. Alabama (21) (Liberty, 1982) (35-55-4)
422—Peter Tom Willis, Florida St. (41) vs. Nebraska (17) (Fiesta, 1990) (25-40-0)
413—Hines Ward, Georgia (27) vs. Virginia (34) (Peach, Dec. 30, 1995) (31-59-2)
412—David Smith, Alabama (29) vs. Army (28) (John Hancock Sun, 1988) (33-52-1)
408—Peyton Manning, Tennessee (48) vs. Northwestern (28) (Florida Citrus, 1997) (27-39-0)
404—(D) Ralph Martini, San Jose St. (48) vs. Central Mich. (24) (California, 1990) (27-36-1)
401—Jack Trudeau, Illinois (29) vs. Army (31) (Peach, 1985) (38-55-2)
401—Ron VanderKelen, Wisconsin (37) vs. Southern Cal (42) (Rose, 1963) (33-48-3)

MOST NET PASSING YARDS, ONE QUARTER
223—Browning Nagle, Louisville (34) vs. Alabama (7) (Fiesta, 1991) (1st, 9 of 16)
202—(D) Bret Stafford, Texas (32) vs. Pittsburgh (27) (Bluebonnet, 1987) (1st)

MOST TOUCHDOWN PASSES THROWN
6—(D) Chuck Long, Iowa (55) vs. Texas (17) (Freedom, 1984) (29-39-0) (6, 11, 33, 49, 4, 15 yards)
5—Peter Tom Willis, Florida St. (41) vs. Nebraska (17) (Fiesta, 1990)
5—Steve Tensi, Florida St. (36) vs. Oklahoma (19) (Gator, Jan. 2, 1965)
4—Michael Bishop, Kansas St. (35) vs. Syracuse (18) (Fiesta, 1997)
4—Peyton Manning, Tennessee (48) vs. Northwestern (28) (Florida Citrus, 1997)
4—Danny Kanell, Florida St. (31) vs. Notre Dame (26) (Orange, 1996)
4—Wally Richardson, Penn St. (43) vs. Auburn (14) (Outback, 1996)
4—Brian Kavanagh, Kansas St. (54) vs. Colorado St. (21) (Holiday, 1995)
4—Johnny Johnson, Illinois (30) vs. East Caro. (0) (Liberty, 1994)
4—John Walsh, Brigham Young (31) vs. Oklahoma (6) (Copper, 1994)
4—Tony Sacca, Penn St. (42) vs. Tennessee (17) (Fiesta, 1992)
4—Jeff Blake, East Caro. (37) vs. North Caro. St. (34) (Peach, 1992)
4—Elvis Grbac, Michigan (35) vs. Mississippi (3) (Gator, Jan. 1, 1991)
4—Rick Neuheisel, UCLA (45) vs. Illinois (9) (Rose, 1984)
4—Jim McMahon, Brigham Young (46) vs. Southern Methodist (45) (Holiday, 1980)
4—Mark Herrmann, Purdue (28) vs. Missouri (25) (Liberty, 1980)
4—(D) Rob Hertel, Southern Cal (47) vs. Texas A&M (28) (Bluebonnet, 1977)
4—Matt Cavanaugh, Pittsburgh (34) vs. Clemson (3) (Gator, 1977)
4—Gordon Slade, Davidson (33) vs. Toledo (55) (Tangerine, 1969)
4—Buster O'Brien, Richmond (49) vs. Ohio (42) (Tangerine, 1968)
4—Cleve Bryant, Ohio (42) vs. Richmond (49) (Tangerine, 1968)
4—Pete Beathard, Southern Cal (42) vs. Wisconsin (37) (Rose, 1963)

MOST PASSES HAD INTERCEPTED
(Followed by Comp.-Att.-Int.)

6—Bruce Lee, Arizona (10) vs. Auburn (34) (Sun, 1968) (6-24-6)
5—Wade Hill, Arkansas (15) vs. Georgia (24) (Independence, 1991) (12-31-5)
5—Kevin Murray, Texas A&M (12) vs. Ohio St. (28) (Cotton, 1987) (12-31-5)
5—Vinny Testaverde, Miami (Fla.) (10) vs. Penn St. (14) (Fiesta, 1987) (26-50-5)
5—Jeff Wickersham, LSU (10) vs. Nebraska (28) (Sugar, 1985) (20-38-5)
5—(D) Steve Clarkson, San Jose St. (25) vs. Toledo (27) (California, 1981) (43-62-5)
5—Terry McMillan, Missouri (3) vs. Penn St. (10) (Orange, 1970) (6-28-5)
5—Paul Gilbert, Georgia (6) vs. Nebraska (45) (Sun, 1969) (10-30-5)

HIGHEST COMPLETION PERCENTAGE
(Minimum 10 Attempts) (Followed by Comp.-Att.-Int.)

.929—Mike Bobo, Georgia (33) vs. Wisconsin (6) (Outback, 1998) (26-28-0)
.917—Bobby Layne, Texas (40) vs. Missouri (27) (Cotton, 1946) (11-12-0)
.900—Ken Ploen, Iowa (35) vs. Oregon St. (19) (Rose, 1957) (9-10-0)
.846—Tom Sorley, Nebraska (21) vs. North Caro. (17) (Liberty, 1977) (11-13-0)
.833—Mike Gundy, Oklahoma St. (62) vs. Wyoming (14) (Holiday, 1988) (20-24-0)
.833—Richard Todd, Alabama (13) vs. Penn St. (6) (Sugar, 1975) (10-12-0)
.818—Bucky Richardson, Texas A&M (65) vs. Brigham Young (14) (Holiday, 1990) (9-11-0)
.806—Cale Gundy, Oklahoma (48) vs. Virginia (14) (Gator, Dec. 29, 1991) (25-31-0)
.800—Art Schlichter, Ohio St. (15) vs. Clemson (17) (Gator, 1978) (16-20-1)
.800—Jim Stevens, Georgia Tech (31) vs. Iowa St. (30) (Liberty, 1972) (12-15-0)
.800—Don Altman, Duke (7) vs. Arkansas (6) (Cotton, 1961) (12-15-0)
.800—Chuck Curtis, Texas Christian (28) vs. Syracuse (27) (Cotton, 1957) (12-15-0)
.789—Charles Ortmann, Michigan (14) vs. California (6) (Rose, 1951) (15-19-0)
.786—Chad Hutchinson, Stanford (38) vs. Michigan St. (0) (Sun, 1996) (22-28-1)
.786—Mark Herrmann, Purdue (28) vs. Missouri (25) (Liberty, 1980) (22-28-0)

MOST YARDS PER PASS ATTEMPT
(Minimum 10 Attempts)

21.3—Chris McCoy, Navy (42) vs. California (38) (Aloha, 1996) (13 for 277)
19.4—Tony Rice, Notre Dame (34) vs. West Va. (21) (Fiesta, 1989) (11 for 213)
18.7—Frank Sinkwich, Georgia (40) vs. Texas Christian (26) (Orange, 1942) (13 for 243)
18.5—Bucky Richardson, Texas A&M (65) vs. Brigham Young (14) (Holiday, 1990) (11 for 203)
17.3—Don Rumley, New Mexico (34) vs. Denver (24) (Sun, 1946) (12 for 207)
16.4—(D) Rob Hertel, Southern Cal (47) vs. Texas A&M (28) (Bluebonnet, 1977) (15 for 246)
15.4—James Street, Texas (36) vs. Tennessee (13) (Cotton, 1969) (13 for 200)
14.2—Danny White, Arizona St. (28) vs. Pittsburgh (7) (Fiesta, 1973) (19 for 269)
13.8—Michael Bishop, Kansas St. (35) vs. Syracuse (18) (Fiesta, 1997) (23 for 317)
13.8—Rob Johnson, Southern Cal (55) vs. Texas Tech (14) (Cotton, 1995) (21 for 289)
13.7—Browning Nagle, Louisville (34) vs. Alabama (7) (Fiesta, 1991) (33 for 451)
13.6—Bob Churchich, Nebraska (28) vs. Alabama (39) (Orange, 1966) (17 for 232)
13.4—Donovan McNabb, Syracuse (41) vs. Clemson (0) (Gator, 1996) (23 for 309)
13.2—Bobby Layne, Texas (40) vs. Missouri (27) (Cotton, 1946) (12 for 158)

MOST YARDS PER PASS COMPLETION
(Minimum 7 Completions)

30.8—Chris McCoy, Navy (42) vs. California (38) (Aloha, 1996) (9 for 277)
30.4—Tony Rice, Notre Dame (34) vs. West Va. (21) (Fiesta, 1989) (7 for 213)
30.4—Duke Carlisle, Texas (28) vs. Navy (6) (Cotton, 1964) (7 for 213)
28.6—James Street, Texas (36) vs. Tennessee (13) (Cotton, 1969) (7 for 200)
27.0—Frank Sinkwich, Georgia (40) vs. Texas Christian (26) (Orange, 1942) (9 for 243)

Receiving

MOST PASS RECEPTIONS

20—(D) Norman Jordan, Vanderbilt (28) vs. Air Force (36) (Hall of Fame, 1982) (173 yards)
20—Walker Gillette, Richmond (49) vs. Ohio (42) (Tangerine, 1968) (242 yards)
18—(D) Gerald Willhite, San Jose St. (25) vs. Toledo (27) (California, 1981) (124 yards)
15—(D) Stephone Paige, Fresno St. (29) vs. Bowling Green (28) (California, 1982) (246 yards)
14—Alex Van Dyke, Nevada (37) vs. Toledo (40) (OT) (Las Vegas, 1995) (176 yards)
14—J. J. Stokes, UCLA (16) vs. Wisconsin (21) (Rose, 1994) (176 yards)
14—Ron Sellers, Florida St. (17) vs. Penn St. (17) (Gator, 1967) (145 yards)
13—Fred Biletnikoff, Florida St. (36) vs. Oklahoma (19) (Gator, Jan. 2, 1965) (192 yards)
12—Hines Ward, Georgia (33) vs. Wisconsin (6) (Outback, 1998) (122 yards)
12—Keyshawn Johnson, Southern Cal (41) vs. Northwestern (32) (Rose, 1996) (216 yards)
12—Luke Fisher, East Caro. (37) vs. North Caro. St. (34) (Peach, 1992) (144 yards)
12—Chuck Dicus, Arkansas (16) vs. Georgia (2) (Sugar, 1969) (169 yards)
12—Bill Moremen, Florida St. (17) vs. Penn St. (17) (Gator, 1967) (106 yards)
11—Josh Wilcox, Oregon (20) vs. Penn St. (38) (Rose, 1995) (135 yards)
11—Bill Khayat, Duke (20) vs. Wisconsin (34) (Hall of Fame, 1995) (109 yards)
11—(D) Mark Szlachcic, Bowling Green (28) vs. Fresno St. (21) (California, 1991) (189 yards)
11—Ronnie Harmon, Iowa (28) vs. UCLA (45) (Rose, 1986) (102 yards)
11—David Mills, Brigham Young (24) vs. Michigan (17) (Holiday, 1984) (103 yards)
11—(D) Chip Otten, Bowling Green (28) vs. Fresno St. (29) (California, 1982) (76 yards)
11—(D) Anthony Hancock, Tennessee (28) vs. Wisconsin (21) (Garden State, 1981) (196 yards)
11—Pat Richter, Wisconsin (37) vs. Southern Cal (42) (Rose, 1963) (163 yards)
11—(D) James Ingram, Baylor (14) vs. LSU (7) (Bluebonnet, 1963) (163 yards)
10—Willie Gosha, Auburn (32) vs. Army (29) (Independence, 1996) (132 yards)
10—Damon Wilkins, Nevada (18) vs. Ball St. (15) (Las Vegas, 1996) (106 yards)
10—Larry Bowie, Georgia (27) vs. Virginia (34) (Peach, Dec. 30, 1995) (156 yards)
10—Johnnie Morton, Southern Cal (28) vs. Utah (21) (Freedom, 1993) (147 yards)
10—Mike Blair, Ball St. (33) vs. Utah St. (42) (Las Vegas, 1993) (66 yards)
10—Matt Bellini, Brigham Young (39) vs. Penn St. (50) (Holiday, 1989) (124 yards)
10—Hart Lee Dykes, Oklahoma St. (62) vs. Wyoming (14) (Holiday, 1988) (163 yards)
10—(D) David Miles, Brigham Young (16) vs. Virginia (22) (All-American, 1987) (188 yards)
10—Lakei Heimuli, Brigham Young (7) vs. Ohio St. (10) (Florida Citrus, 1985)
10—Bobby Joe Edmonds, Arkansas (15) vs. Auburn (21) (Liberty, 1984)
10—David Williams, Illinois (9) vs. UCLA (45) (Rose, 1984)
10—Kelly Smith, Brigham Young (24) vs. Michigan (17) (Holiday, 1984) (88 yards)
10—Paul Skansi, Washington (21) vs. Maryland (20) (Aloha, 1982) (87 yards)
10—(D) Tim Kearse, San Jose St. (25) vs. Toledo (27) (California, 1981) (104 yards)
10—Scott Phillips, Brigham Young (46) vs. Southern Methodist (45) (Holiday, 1980) (81 yards)
10—Gordon Jones, Pittsburgh (34) vs. Clemson (3) (Gator, 1977) (163 yards)
10—Bobby Crockett, Arkansas (7) vs. LSU (14) (Cotton, Jan. 1, 1966)
10—Ron Stover, Oregon (7) vs. Ohio St. (10) (Rose, 1958) (144 yards)

MOST PASS RECEIVING YARDS

252—Andre Rison, Michigan St. (27) vs. Georgia (34) (Gator, Jan. 1, 1989) (9 catches)
246—(D) Stephone Paige, Fresno St. (29) vs. Bowling Green (28) (California, 1982) (15 catches)
242—(D) Tony Jones, Texas (32) vs. Pittsburgh (27) (Bluebonnet, 1987) (8 catches)
242—Walker Gillette, Richmond (49) vs. Ohio (42) (Tangerine, 1968) (20 catches)
222—Keyshawn Johnson, Southern Cal (55) vs. Texas Tech (14) (Cotton, 1995) (8 catches)
216—Keyshawn Johnson, Southern Cal (41) vs. Northwestern (32) (Rose, 1996) (12 catches)
212—Phillip Bobo, Washington St. (31) vs. Utah (28) (Copper, 1992) (7 catches)
206—Darnell McDonald, Kansas St. (35) vs. Syracuse (18) (Fiesta, 1997) (7 catches)
201—(D) Bob McChesney, Hardin-Simmons (49) vs. Wichita St. (12) (Camellia, 1948) (8 catches)
196—(D) Anthony Hancock, Tennessee (28) vs. Wisconsin (21) (Garden State, 1981) (11 catches)
194—Cory Schemm, Navy (42) vs. California (38) (Aloha, 1996) (5 catches)
192—Fred Biletnikoff, Florida St. (36) vs. Oklahoma (19) (Gator, Jan. 2, 1965) (13 catches)
189—(D) Mark Szlachcic, Bowling Green (28) vs. Fresno St. (21) (California, 1991) (11 catches)
188—(D) David Miles, Brigham Young (16) vs. Virginia (22) (All-American, 1987) (10 catches)
186—Greg Hudson, Arizona St. (28) vs. Pittsburgh (7) (Fiesta, 1973) (8 catches)
182—Rob Turner, Indiana (34) vs. South Caro. (10) (Liberty, 1988) (5 catches)
178—Ray Perkins, Alabama (34) vs. Nebraska (7) (Sugar, 1967) (7 catches)
177—Thomas Lewis, Indiana (20) vs. Virginia Tech (45) (Independence, 1993) (6 catches)
176—E. G. Green, Florida St. (31) vs. Ohio St. (14) (Sugar, 1998) (7 catches)
176—Alex Van Dyke, Nevada (37) vs. Toledo (40) (OT) (Las Vegas, 1995) (14 catches)
176—J. J. Stokes, UCLA (16) vs. Wisconsin (21) (Rose, 1994) (14 catches)
173—Marvin Harrison, Syracuse (41) vs. Clemson (0) (Gator, 1996) (7 catches)
173—(D) Norman Jordan, Vanderbilt (28) vs. Air Force (36) (Hall of Fame, 1982) (20 catches)
172—Cris Carter, Ohio St. (17) vs. Southern Cal (20) (Rose, 1985) (9 catches)

HIGHEST AVERAGE PER RECEPTION
(Minimum 3 Receptions)

52.3—Phil Harris, Texas (28) vs. Navy (6) (Cotton, 1964) (3 for 157 yards)
39.7—Ike Hilliard, Florida (17) vs. Florida St. (23) (Sugar, Jan. 2, 1995) (3 for 119 yards)
38.8—Cory Schemm, Navy (42) vs. California (38) (Aloha, 1996) (5 for 194 yards)
36.4—Rob Turner, Indiana (34) vs. South Caro. (10) (Liberty, 1988) (5 for 182 yards)
36.3—Clarence Cannon, Boston College (31) vs. Virginia (13) (Carquest, 1994) (3 for 109 yards)
35.5—Rodney Harris, Kansas (23) vs. Brigham Young (20) (Aloha, 1992) (4 for 142 yards)
35.3—Anthony Carter, Michigan (15) vs. North Caro. (17) (Gator, 1979) (4 for 141 yards)
34.3—(D) Andre Alexander, Fresno St. (35) vs. Western Mich. (30) (California, 1988) (3 for 103 yards)
34.3—Ron Beverly, Arizona St. (49) vs. Missouri (35) (Fiesta, 1972) (3 for 103 yards)
34.0—Jimmy Cefalo, Penn St. (41) vs. Baylor (20) (Cotton, 1975) (3 for 102 yards)
33.7—Justin Shull, Colorado St. (14) vs. Michigan (24) (Holiday, 1994) (3 for 101 yards)
33.7—J. D. Hill, Arizona St. (48) vs. North Caro. (26) (Peach, 1970) (3 for 101 yards)
33.3—Tony Buford, Indiana (34) vs. South Caro. (10) (Liberty, 1988) (3 for 100 yards)
33.2—Melvin Bonner, Baylor (20) vs. Arizona (15) (John Hancock, 1992) (5 for 166 yards)
33.2—Todd Dixon, Wake Forest (39) vs. Oregon (35) (Independence, 1992) (5 for 166 yards)
33.0—Ed Hervey, Southern Cal (55) vs. Texas Tech (14) (Cotton, 1995) (3 for 99 yards)
32.2—Cotton Speyrer, Texas (36) vs. Tennessee (13) (Cotton, 1969) (5 for 161 yards)
31.0—Olanda Truitt, Pittsburgh (31) vs. Texas A&M (28) (John Hancock, 1989) (4 for 124 yards)
31.0—Clay Brown, Brigham Young (46) vs. Southern Methodist (45) (Holiday, 1980) (5 for 155 yards)

MOST TOUCHDOWNS RECEIVING

4—Fred Biletnikoff, Florida St. (36) vs. Oklahoma (19) (Gator, Jan. 2, 1965) (13 catches)
4—(D) Bob McChesney, Hardin-Simmons (49) vs. Wichita St. (12) (Camellia, 1948) (8 catches)
3—Darnell McDonald, Kansas St. (35) vs. Syracuse (18) (Fiesta, 1997) (7 catches)
3—Ike Hilliard, Florida (52) vs. Florida St. (20) (Sugar, 1997) (7 catches)
3—Keyshawn Johnson, Southern Cal (55) vs. Texas Tech (14) (Cotton, 1995) (8 catches)
3—(D) Ken Ealy, Central Mich. (24) vs. San Jose St. (48) (California, 1990) (7 catches)
3—Wendell Davis, LSU (30) vs. South Caro. (13) (Gator, 1987) (9 catches)
3—Anthony Allen, Washington (21) vs. Maryland (20) (Aloha, 1982) (8 catches)
3—(D) Norman Jordan, Vanderbilt (28) vs. Air Force (36) (Hall of Fame, 1982) (20 catches)
3—(D) Dwayne Dixon, Florida (24) vs. Arkansas (28) (Bluebonnet, 1982) (8 catches)
3—(D) Mervyn Fernandez, San Jose St. (25) vs. Toledo (27) (California, 1981) (9 catches)
3—Clay Brown, Brigham Young (46) vs. Southern Methodist (45) (Holiday, 1980) (5 catches)
3—Elliott Walker, Pittsburgh (34) vs. Clemson (3) (Gator, 1977) (6 catches)
3—Rhett Dawson, Florida St. (38) vs. Arizona St. (45) (Fiesta, 1971) (8 catches)
3—George Hannen, Davidson (33) vs. Toledo (56) (Tangerine, 1969)
3—Todd Snyder, Richmond (49) vs. Ohio (42) (Tangerine, 1968)

Scoring

MOST POINTS SCORED

30—(D) Sheldon Canley, San Jose St. (48) vs. Central Mich. (24) (California, 1990) (5 TDs)
30—Barry Sanders, Oklahoma St. (62) vs. Wyoming (14) (Holiday, 1988) (5 TDs)
28—Bobby Layne, Texas (40) vs. Missouri (27) (Cotton, 1946) (4 TDs, 4 PATs)
25—Neil Snow, Michigan (49) vs. Stanford (0) (Rose, 1902) (5 five-point TDs)
24—Byron Hanspard, Texas Tech (55) vs. Air Force (41) (Copper, 1995) (4 TDs)
24—Wasean Tait, Toledo (40) vs. Nevada (37) (OT) (Las Vegas, 1995) (4 TDs)
24—(D) Ron Jackson, Tulsa (28) vs. San Diego St. (17) (Freedom, 1991) (4 TDs)
24—(D) James Gray, Texas Tech (49) vs. Duke (21) (All-American, 1989) (4 TDs)
24—Thurman Thomas, Oklahoma St. (35) vs. West Va. (33) (John Hancock Sun, 1987) (4 TDs)
24—Eric Ball, UCLA (45) vs. Iowa (28) (Rose, 1986) (4 TDs)
24—Terry Miller, Oklahoma St. (49) vs. Brigham Young (21) (Tangerine, 1976) (4 TDs)
24—Sam Cunningham, Southern Cal (42) vs. Ohio St. (17) (Rose, 1973) (4 TDs)
24—Johnny Rodgers, Nebraska (40) vs. Notre Dame (6) (Orange, 1973) (4 TDs)
24—Woody Green, Arizona St. (49) vs. Missouri (35) (Fiesta, 1972) (4 TDs)
24—Charles Cole, Toledo (56) vs. Davidson (33) (Tangerine, 1969) (4 TDs)
24—Fred Biletnikoff, Florida St. (36) vs. Oklahoma (19) (Gator, Jan. 2, 1965) (4 TDs)
24—Joe Lopasky, Houston (49) vs. Miami (Ohio) (21) (Tangerine, 1962) (4 TDs)
24—(D) Gene Shannon, Houston (26) vs. Dayton (21) (Salad, 1952) (4 TDs)
24—(D) Bob McChesney, Hardin-Simmons (49) vs. Wichita St. (12) (Camellia, 1948) (4 TDs)

MOST POINTS RESPONSIBLE FOR (TDs Scored & Passed For, Extra Points, and FGs)

40—Bobby Layne, Texas (40) vs. Missouri (27) (Cotton, 1946) (18 rush, 12 pass, 6 receiving and 4 PATs)
36—(D) Chuck Long, Iowa (55) vs. Texas (17) (Freedom, 1984) (36 pass)
30—Michael Bishop, Kansas St., (35) vs. Syracuse (18) (Fiesta, 1997) (24 pass, 6 rush)
30—Jeff Blake, East Caro. (37) vs. North Caro. St. (34) (Peach, 1992) (24 pass, 6 rush)
30—(D) Sheldon Canley, San Jose St. (48) vs. Central Mich. (24) (California, 1990) (24 rush, 6 receiving)
30—Peter Tom Willis, Florida St. (41) vs. Nebraska (17) (Fiesta, 1990) (30 pass)
30—Barry Sanders, Oklahoma St. (62) vs. Wyoming (14) (Holiday, 1988) (30 rush)
30—Johnny Rodgers, Nebraska (40) vs. Notre Dame (6) (Orange, 1973) (18 rush, 6 pass, 6 receiving)
30—Steve Tensi, Florida St. (36) vs. Oklahoma (19) (Gator, Jan. 2, 1965) (30 pass)

MOST TOUCHDOWNS

5—(D) Sheldon Canley, San Jose St. (48) vs. Central Mich. (24) (California, 1990) (4 rush, 1 catch)
5—Barry Sanders, Oklahoma St. (62) vs. Wyoming (14) (Holiday, 1988) (5 rush)
5—Neil Snow, Michigan (49) vs. Stanford (0) (Rose, 1902) (5 rush five-point TDs)
4—Byron Hanspard, Texas Tech (55) vs. Air Force (41) (Copper, 1995) (4 rush)
4—Wasean Tait, Toledo (40) vs. Nevada (37) (OT) (Las Vegas, 1995) (4 rush)
4—(D) Ron Jackson, Tulsa (28) vs. San Diego St. (17) (Freedom, 1991) (4 rush)
4—(D) James Gray, Texas Tech (49) vs. Duke (21) (All-American, 1989) (4 rush)
4—Thurman Thomas, Oklahoma St. (35) vs. West Va. (33) (John Hancock Sun, 1987) (4 rush)
4—Eric Ball, UCLA (45) vs. Iowa (28) (Rose, 1986) (4 rush)
4—Terry Miller, Oklahoma St. (49) vs. Brigham Young (21) (Tangerine, 1976) (4 rush)
4—Sam Cunningham, Southern Cal (42) vs. Ohio St. (17) (Rose, 1973) (4 rush)
4—Johnny Rodgers, Nebraska (40) vs. Notre Dame (6) (Orange, 1973) (3 rush, 1 catch)
4—Woody Green, Arizona St. (49) vs. Missouri (35) (Fiesta, 1972) (4 rush)
4—Charles Cole, Toledo (56) vs. Davidson (33) (Tangerine, 1969) (4 rush)
4—Fred Biletnikoff, Florida St. (36) vs. Oklahoma (19) (Gator, Jan. 2, 1965) (4 catch)
4—Joe Lopasky, Houston (49) vs. Miami (Ohio) (21) (Tangerine, 1962) (2 rush, 1 catch, 1 punt return)
4—(D) Gene Shannon, Houston (26) vs. Dayton (21) (Salad, 1952) (4 rush)
4—(D) Bob McChesney, Hardin-Simmons (49) vs. Wichita St. (12) (Camellia, 1948) (4 catch)
4—Bobby Layne, Texas (40) vs. Missouri (27) (Cotton, 1946) (3 rush, 1 catch)
4—(D) Alvin McMillin, Centre (63) vs. Texas Christian (7) (Fort Worth Classic, 1921) (4 rush)

MOST TWO-POINT CONVERSIONS

2—Ernie Davis, Syracuse (23) vs. Texas (14) (Cotton, 1960) (2 pass receptions)

Kicking

MOST FIELD GOALS ATTEMPTED

6—Kyle Bryant, Texas A&M (22) vs. Michigan (20) (Alamo, 1995) (5 made)
5—Chad Holcomb, East Caro. (19) vs. Stanford (13) (Liberty, 1995) (4 made)
5—Dan Mowrey, Florida St. (23) vs. Florida (17) (Sugar, Jan. 2, 1995) (3 made)
5—Tim Rogers, Mississippi St. (24) vs. North Caro. St. (28) (Peach, Jan. 1, 1995) (5 made)
5—Scott Bentley, Florida St. (18) vs. Nebraska (16) (Orange, 1994) (4 made)
5—Arden Czyzewski, Florida (28) vs. Notre Dame (39) (Sugar, 1992) (5 made)
5—Jess Atkinson, Maryland (23) vs. Tennessee (30) (Florida Citrus, 1983) (5 made)
5—Bob White, Arkansas (16) vs. Georgia (2) (Sugar, 1969) (3 made)
5—Tim Davis, Alabama (12) vs. Mississippi (7) (Sugar, 1964) (4 made)
4—Brett Conway, Penn St. (43) vs. Auburn (14) (Outback, 1996) (3 made)
4—Kanon Parkman, Georgia (27) vs. Virginia (34) (Peach, Dec. 30, 1995) (4 made)
4—Carlos Huerta, Miami (Fla.) (22) vs. Nebraska (0) (Orange, 1992) (3 made)
4—Greg Worker, Wyoming (19) vs. Iowa (20) (Holiday, 1987) (2 made)
4—Tim Lashar, Oklahoma (25) vs. Penn St. (10) (Orange, 1986) (4 made)
4—Kent Bostrom, Arizona St. (17) vs. Arkansas (18) (Holiday, 1985) (3 made)
4—(D) Todd Gregoire, Wisconsin (19) vs. Kentucky (20) (Hall of Fame, 1984) (4 made)
4—Bill Capece, Florida St. (17) vs. Oklahoma (18) (Orange, 1981) (1 made)
4—David Hardy, Texas A&M (33) vs. Oklahoma St. (16) (Independence, 1981) (4 made)
4—Bob Lucchesi, Missouri (19) vs. Southern Miss. (17) (Tangerine, 1981) (4 made)
4—Paul Woodside, West Va. (26) vs. Florida (6) (Peach, Dec. 31, 1981) (4 made)
4—(D) Fuad Reveiz, Tennessee (28) vs. Wisconsin (21) (Garden State, 1981) (2 made)
4—Dale Castro, Maryland (20) vs. Florida (35) (Tangerine, 1980) (4 made)
4—Brent Johnson, Brigham Young (37) vs. Indiana (38) (Holiday, 1979) (3 made)
4—Ricky Townsend, Tennessee (19) vs. Texas Tech (28) (Gator, 1973) (2 made)
4—Paul Rogers, Nebraska (45) vs. Georgia (6) (Sun, 1969) (4 made)

MOST FIELD GOALS MADE

5—Kyle Bryant, Texas A&M (22) vs. Michigan (20) (Alamo, 1995) (27, 49, 47, 31, 37 yards)
5—Tim Rogers, Mississippi St. (24) vs. North Caro. St. (28) (Peach, Jan. 1, 1995) (37, 21, 29, 36, 30 yards)
5—Arden Czyzewski, Florida (28) vs. Notre Dame (39) (Sugar, 1992) (26, 24, 36, 37, 24 yards)
5—Jess Atkinson, Maryland (23) vs. Tennessee (30) (Florida Citrus, 1983) (18, 48, 31, 22, 26 yards)
4—Chad Holcomb, East Caro. (19) vs. Stanford (13) (Liberty, 1995) (46, 26, 41, 34 yards)
4—Kanon Parkman, Georgia (27) vs. Virginia (34) (Peach, Dec. 30, 1995) (36, 37, 20, 42 yards)
4—Scott Bentley, Florida St. (18) vs. Nebraska (16) (Orange, 1994) (34, 25, 39, 22 yards)
4—Tim Lashar, Oklahoma (25) vs. Penn St. (10) (Orange, 1986) (26, 31, 21, 22 yards)
4—(D) Todd Gregoire, Wisconsin (19) vs. Kentucky (20) (Hall of Fame, 1984) (40, 27, 20, 40 yards)
4—David Hardy, Texas A&M (33) vs. Oklahoma St. (16) (Independence, 1981) (33, 32, 50, 18 yards)
4—Paul Woodside, West Va. (26) vs. Florida (6) (Peach, Dec. 31, 1981) (35, 42, 49, 24 yards)
4—Bob Lucchesi, Missouri (19) vs. Southern Miss. (17) (Tangerine, 1981) (45, 41, 30, 28 yards)
4—Dale Castro, Maryland (20) vs. Florida (35) (Tangerine, 1980) (35, 27, 27, 43 yards)
4—Paul Rogers, Nebraska (45) vs. Georgia (6) (Sun, 1969) (50, 32, 42, 37 yards, all in 1st quarter)
4—Tim Davis, Alabama (12) vs. Mississippi (7) (Sugar, 1964) (31, 46, 22, 48 yards)

MOST EXTRA-POINT KICK ATTEMPTS

9—Layne Talbot, Texas A&M (65) vs. Brigham Young (14) (Holiday, 1990) (9 made)
9—Bobby Luna, Alabama (61) vs. Syracuse (6) (Orange, 1953) (7 made)
9—(D) James Weaver, Centre (63) vs. Texas Christian (7) (Fort Worth Classic, 1921) (9 made)
8—Cary Blanchard, Oklahoma St. (62) vs. Wyoming (14) (Holiday, 1988) (8 made)
8—Ken Crots, Toledo (56) vs. Davidson (33) (Tangerine, 1969) (8 made)
7—Martin Gramatica, Kansas St. (54) vs. Colorado St. (21) (Holiday, 1995) (6 made)
7—Tony Rogers, Texas Tech (55) vs. Air Force (41) (Copper, 1995) (7 made)
7—Cole Ford, Southern Cal (55) vs. Texas Tech (14) (Cotton, 1995) (7 made)
7—Scott Blanton, Oklahoma (48) vs. Virginia (14) (Gator, Dec. 29, 1991) (6 made)
7—(D) Barry Belli, Fresno St. (51) vs. Bowling Green (7) (California, 1985) (7 made)
7—(D) Tom Nichol, Iowa (55) vs. Texas (17) (Freedom, 1984) (7 made)
7—Juan Cruz, Arizona St. (49) vs. Missouri (35) (Fiesta, 1972) (7 made)
7—Ron Sewell, North Caro. St. (49) vs. West Va. (13) (Peach, 1972) (7 made)
7—Don Ekstrand, Arizona St. (48) vs. North Caro. (26) (Peach, 1970) (6 made)
7—Bill McMillan, Houston (49) vs. Miami (Ohio) (21) (Tangerine, 1962) (7 made)
7—Jesse Whittenton, UTEP (47) vs. Florida St. (20) (Sun, 1955) (5 made)

7—Jim Brieske, Michigan (49) vs. UCLA (0) (Rose, 1948) (7 made)
7—(D) Pat Bailey, Hardin-Simmons (49) vs. Wichita St. (12) (Camellia, 1948) (7 made)

MOST EXTRA-POINT KICKS MADE

9—Layne Talbot, Texas A&M (65) vs. Brigham Young (14) (Holiday, 1990) (9 attempts)
9—(D) James Weaver, Centre (63) vs. Texas Christian (7) (Fort Worth Classic, 1921) (9 attempts)
8—Cary Blanchard, Oklahoma St. (62) vs. Wyoming (14) (Holiday, 1988) (8 attempts)
8—Ken Crots, Toledo (56) vs. Davidson (33) (Tangerine, 1969) (8 attempts)
7—Tony Rogers, Texas Tech (55) vs. Air Force (41) (Copper, 1995) (7 attempts)
7—Cole Ford, Southern Cal (55) vs. Texas Tech (14) (Cotton, 1995) (7 attempts)
7—(D) Barry Belli, Fresno St. (51) vs. Bowling Green (7) (California, 1985) (7 attempts)
7—(D) Tom Nichol, Iowa (55) vs. Texas (17) (Freedom, 1984) (7 attempts)
7—Juan Cruz, Arizona St. (49) vs. Missouri (35) (Fiesta, 1972) (7 attempts)
7—Ron Sewell, North Caro. St. (49) vs. West Va. (13) (Peach, 1972) (7 attempts)
7—Bill McMillan, Houston (49) vs. Miami (Ohio) (21) (Tangerine, 1962) (7 attempts)
7—Bobby Luna, Alabama (61) vs. Syracuse (6) (Orange, 1953) (9 attempts)
7—Jim Brieske, Michigan (49) vs. UCLA (0) (Rose, 1948) (7 attempts)
7—(D) Pat Bailey, Hardin-Simmons (49) vs. Wichita St. (12) (Camellia, 1948) (7 attempts)

MOST POINTS BY A KICKER

16—Kyle Bryant, Texas A&M (22) vs. Michigan (20) (Alamo, 1995) (5 FGs, 1 PAT)
16—Tim Rogers, Mississippi St. (24) vs. North Caro. St. (28) (Peach, Jan. 1, 1995) (5 FGs, 1 PAT)
16—Arden Czyzewski, Florida (28) vs. Notre Dame (39) (Sugar, 1992) (5 FGs, 1 PAT)
15—Jess Atkinson, Maryland (23) vs. Tennessee (30) (Florida Citrus, 1983) (5 FGs)
15—David Hardy, Texas A&M (33) vs. Oklahoma St. (16) (Independence, 1981) (4 FGs, 3 PATs)
15—Paul Rogers, Nebraska (45) vs. Georgia (6) (John Hancock, 1969) (4 FGs, 3 PATs)
14—Cary Blanchard, Oklahoma St. (62) vs. Wyoming (14) (Holiday, 1988) (2 FGs, 8 PATs)
14—Paul Woodside, West Va. (26) vs. Florida (6) (Peach, Dec. 31, 1981) (4 FGs, 2 PATs)
13—Chad Holcomb, East Caro. (19) vs. Stanford (13) (Liberty, 1995) (4 FGs, 1 PAT)
13—Kanon Parkman, Georgia (27) vs. Virginia (34) (Peach, Dec. 30, 1995) (4 FGs, 1 PAT)
13—Tony Rogers, Texas Tech (55) vs. Air Force (41) (Copper, 1995) (2 FGs, 7 PATs)
13—Damon Shea, Nevada (37) vs. Toledo (40) (OT) (Las Vegas, 1995) (3 FGs, 4 PATs)
13—Cole Ford, Southern Cal (55) vs. Texas Tech (14) (Cotton, 1995) (2 FGs, 7 PATs)
13—Tim Lashar, Oklahoma (25) vs. Penn. St. (10) (Orange, 1986) (4 FGs, 1 PAT)
13—John Lee, UCLA (39) vs. Miami (Fla.) (37) (Fiesta, 1985) (3 FGs, 4 PATs)
13—(D) Tom Nichol, Iowa (55) vs. Texas (17) (Freedom, 1984) (2 FGs, 7 PATs)
13—(D) Todd Gregoire, Wisconsin (19) vs. Kentucky (20) (Hall of Fame, 1984) (4 FGs, 1 PAT)
13—Bob Lucchesi, Missouri (19) vs. Southern Miss. (17) (Tangerine, 1981) (4 FGs, 1 PAT)
13—Dave Johnson, Brigham Young (37) vs. Indiana (38) (Holiday, 1979) (3 FGs, 4 PATs)
12—Scott Bentley, Florida St. (18) vs. Nebraska (16) (Orange, 1994) (4 FGs)
12—Chris Gardocki, Clemson (30) vs. Illinois (0) (Hall of Fame, 1991) (3 FGs, 3 PATs)
12—Ray Tarasi, Penn St. (50) vs. Brigham Young (39) (Holiday, 1989) (3 FGs, 3 PATs)
12—Luis Zendejas, Arizona St. (32) vs. Oklahoma (21) (Fiesta, 1983) (3 FGs, 3 PATs)
12—Dale Castro, Maryland (20) vs. Florida (35) (Tangerine, 1980) (4 FGs)
12—Nathan Ritter, North Caro. St. (30) vs. Pittsburgh (17) (Tangerine, 1978) (3 FGs, 3 PATs)
12—Buckey Berrey, Alabama (36) vs. UCLA (6) (Liberty, 1976) (3 FGs, 3 PATs)
12—Al Vitiello, Penn St. (30) vs. Texas (6) (Cotton, 1972) (3 FGs, 3 PATs)
12—Frank Fontes, Florida St. (38) vs. Arizona St. (45) (Fiesta, 1971) (3 FGs, 3 PATs)

Punting

MOST PUNTS

21—Everett Sweeney, Michigan (49) vs. Stanford (0) (Rose, 1902)
16—Lem Pratt, New Mexico St. (14) vs. Hardin-Simmons (14) (Sun, 1936) (38.4 average)
14—Sammy Baugh, Texas Christian (3) vs. LSU (2) (Sugar, 1936)
13—Hugh Keeney, Rice (8) vs. Tennessee (0) (Orange, 1947)
13—N. A. Keithley, Tulsa (6) vs. Texas Tech (0) (Sun, 1942) (37.0 average)
13—Hugh McCullough, Oklahoma (0) vs. Tennessee (17) (Orange, 1939) (40.6 average)
13—Tyler, Hardin-Simmons (14) vs. New Mexico St. (14) (Sun, 1936) (45.2 average)
13—(D) Tom Murphy, Arkansas (7) vs. Centenary (La.) (7) (Dixie Classic, 1934) (44.0 average)
12—Mitch Berger, Colorado (25) vs. Alabama (30) (Blockbuster, 1991) (41.0 average)
12—Bob Parsons, Penn St. (10) vs. Missouri (3) (Orange, 1970) (42.6 average)
12—Jim Callahan, Texas Tech (0) vs. Tulsa (6) (Sun, 1942) (43.0 average)
12—Mike Palm, Penn St. (3) vs. Southern Cal (14) (Rose, 1923)

HIGHEST AVERAGE PER PUNT
(Minimum 5 Punts)

52.7—Des Koch, Southern Cal (7) vs. Wisconsin (0) (Rose, 1953) (7 for 369 yards) (adjusted to current statistical rules)
52.4—Mike Sochko, Maryland (21) vs. Houston (30) (Cotton, 1977) (5 for 262 yards)
52.0—Nick Gallery, Iowa (27) vs. Texas Tech (0) (Alamo, 1996) (5 for 260 yards)
51.0—Chris Clauss, Penn St. (10) vs. Clemson (35) (Florida Citrus, 1988) (5 for 255 yards)
50.0—Dana Moore, Mississippi St. (17) vs. Nebraska (31) (Sun, 1980) (5 for 250 yards)
49.3—Chris McInally, Clemson (0) vs. Syracuse (41) (Gator, 1996) (6 for 296)
49.2—(D) Mark Simon, Air Force (24) vs. Texas (16) (Bluebonnet, 1985) (11 for 541 yards)
49.2—Allen Meacham, Arkansas (3) vs. UCLA (17) (Cotton, 1989) (6 for 295 yards)
49.0—Jim DiGuilio, Indiana (24) vs. Baylor (0) (Copper, 1991) (6 for 294 yards)
49.0—(D) Dana Moore, Mississippi St. (10) vs. Kansas (0) (Hall of Fame, 1981) (9 for 441 yards)
48.1—Robby Stevenson, Florida (52) vs. Florida St. (20) (Sugar, 1997) (7 for 337 yards)
48.1—Brent Bartholomew, Ohio St. (14) vs. Tennessee (20) (Florida Citrus, 1996) (7 for 337)
48.0—Dan Eichloff, Kansas (23) vs. Brigham Young (20) (Aloha, 1992) (8 for 384 yards)
47.9—Doug Helkowski, Penn St. (42) vs. Tennessee (17) (Fiesta, 1992) (9 for 431 yards)
47.8—(D) Kevin Buenafe, UCLA (14) vs. Michigan (33) (Bluebonnet, 1981) (8 for 382 yards)
47.6—Todd Thomsen, Oklahoma (42) vs. Arkansas (8) (Orange, 1987) (5 for 238 yards)
47.5—Jerry Dowd, St. Mary's (Cal.) (20) vs. Texas Tech (13) (Cotton, 1939) (11 for 523 yards)
47.4—Jason Bender, Georgia Tech (18) vs. Stanford (17) (Aloha, 1991) (7 for 332 yards)
47.4—(D) Mike Mancini, Fresno St. (51) vs. Bowling Green (7) (California, 1985) (7 for 332 yards)
47.4—(D) Jimmy Colquitt, Tennessee (28) vs. Wisconsin (21) (Garden State, 1981) (5 for 237 yards)

Punt Returns

MOST PUNT RETURNS

9—Buzy Rosenberg, Georgia (7) vs. North Caro. (3) (Gator, Dec. 31, 1971) (54 yards)
9—Paddy Driscoll, Great Lakes (17) vs. Mare Island (0) (Rose, 1919) (115 yards)
8—Thomas Lewis, Indiana (20) vs. Virginia Tech (45) (Independence, 1993) (58 yards)
6—Dale Carter, Tennessee (17) vs. Penn St. (42) (Fiesta, 1992)
6—Joey Smith, Louisville (34) vs. Alabama (7) (Fiesta, 1991) (35 yards)
6—David Palmer, Alabama (30) vs. Colorado (25) (Blockbuster, 1991) (74 yards)
6—(D) Hesh Colar, San Jose St. (48) vs. Central Mich. (24) (California, 1990)
6—David Kintigh, Miami (Fla.) (10) vs. Penn St. (14) (Fiesta, 1987) (32 yards)
6—(D) Eric Metcalf, Texas (16) vs. Air Force (24) (Bluebonnet, 1985) (49 yards)
6—Vai Sikahema, Brigham Young (7) vs. Ohio St. (10) (Florida Citrus, 1985)
6—Ray Horton, Washington (21) vs. Maryland (20) (Aloha, 1982) (28 yards)
6—Bill Gribble, Washington St. (36) vs. Brigham Young (38) (Holiday, 1981) (39 yards)
6—Johnny Rodgers, Nebraska (38) vs. Alabama (6) (Orange, 1972) (136 yards)
6—Rick Sygar, Michigan (34) vs. Oregon St. (7) (Rose, 1965) (50 yards)
6—Billy Hair, Clemson (0) vs. Miami (Fla.) (14) (Gator, 1952) (73 yards)
6—Don Zimmerman, Tulane (12) vs. Southern Cal (21) (Rose, 1932)

MOST PUNT RETURN YARDS

136—Johnny Rodgers, Nebraska (38) vs. Alabama (6) (Orange, 1972) (6 returns)
122—George Fleming, Washington (44) vs. Wisconsin (8) (Rose, 1960) (3 returns)
122—Bobby Kellogg, Tulane (13) vs. Texas A&M (14) (Sugar, 1940) (5 returns)
115—Paddy Driscoll, Great Lakes (17) vs. Mare Island (0) (Rose, 1919) (9 returns)
110—James Henry, Southern Miss. (38) vs. UTEP (18) (Independence, 1988) (2 returns, touchdowns of 65 and 45 yards)
106—Kevin Baugh, Penn St. (27) vs. Georgia (23) (Sugar, 1983) (5 returns)
106—Steve Holden, Arizona St. (45) vs. Florida St. (38) (Fiesta, 1971) (3 returns)
104—Leo Daniels, Texas A&M (21) vs. Alabama (29) (Cotton, 1942) (5 returns)
103—Jon Staggers, Missouri (3) vs. Penn St. (10) (Orange, 1970)
89—Lawrence Williams, Texas Tech (28) vs. North Caro. (32) (Sun, 1972) (5 returns)
87—Vai Sikahema, Brigham Young (46) vs. Southern Methodist (45) (Holiday, 1980) (2 returns)
86—Bobby Majors, Tennessee (34) vs. Air Force (13) (Sugar, 1971) (4 returns)
86—Aramis Dandoy, Southern Cal (7) vs. Ohio St. (20) (Rose, 1955) (1 return)
82—Marcus Wall, North Caro. (31) vs. Texas (35) (Sun, 1994) (1 return)
82—Willie Drewrey, West Va. (12) vs. Florida St. (31) (Gator, 1982) (1 return)
80—(D) Gary Anderson, Arkansas (34) vs. Tulane (15) (Hall of Fame, 1980) (2 returns)
80—Cecil Ingram, Alabama (61) vs. Syracuse (6) (Orange, 1953) (1 return)

HIGHEST PUNT RETURN AVERAGE
(Minimum 3 Returns)

40.7—George Fleming, Washington (44) vs. Wisconsin (8) (Rose, 1960) (3 for 122 yards)
35.3—Steve Holden, Arizona St. (45) vs. Florida St. (38) (Fiesta, 1971) (3 for 106 yards)
24.4—Bobby Kellogg, Tulane (13) vs. Texas A&M (14) (Sugar, 1940) (5 for 122 yards)
24.0—Shayne Wasden, Auburn (31) vs. Ohio St. (14) (Hall of Fame, 1990) (3 for 72 yards)
22.7—Johnny Rodgers, Nebraska (38) vs. Alabama (6) (Orange, 1972) (6 for 136 yards)
21.5—Bobby Majors, Tennessee (34) vs. Air Force (13) (Sugar, 1971) (4 for 86 yards)
21.0—Tiki Barber, Virginia (34) vs. Georgia (27) (Peach, Dec. 30, 1995) (3 for 63 yards)
21.0—(D) Brian Williams, Kentucky (16) vs. West Va. (20) (Hall of Fame, 1983) (3 for 63 yards)
20.8—Leo Daniels, Texas A&M (21) vs. Alabama (29) (Cotton, 1942) (5 for 104 yards)
19.5—(D) Zippy Morocco, Georgia (20) vs. Texas A&M (40) (Presidential Cup, 1950) (4 for 78 yards)
19.3—Dave Liegi, Nebraska (14) vs. Houston (17) (Cotton, 1980) (3 for 58 yards)
19.0—Gary Moss, Georgia (10) vs. Texas (9) (Cotton, 1984) (3 for 57 yards)

Kickoff Returns

MOST KICKOFF RETURNS

7—Dale Carter, Tennessee (17) vs. Penn St. (42) (Fiesta, 1992) (132 yards)
7—Jeff Sydner, Hawaii (13) vs. Michigan St. (33) (Aloha, 1989) (174 yards)
7—Homer Jones, Brigham Young (37) vs. Indiana (38) (Holiday, 1979) (126 yards)
6—Deltha O'Neal, California (38) vs. Navy (42) (Aloha, 1996) (186 yards)
6—Dave Beazley, Northwestern (28) vs. Tennessee (48) (Florida Citrus, 1997) (137 yards)
6—Eugene Napoleon, West Va. (21) vs. Notre Dame (34) (Fiesta, 1989) (107 yards)
6—Tim Brown, Notre Dame (10) vs. Texas A&M (35) (Cotton, 1988) (129 yards)
6—Leroy Thompson, Penn St. (10) vs. Clemson (35) (Florida Citrus, 1988)
6—(D) Anthony Roberson, Air Force (28) vs. Arizona St. (33) (Freedom, 1987) (109 yards)
6—Casey Tiumalu, Brigham Young (17) vs. Ohio St. (47) (Holiday, 1982) (116 yards)
6—Brian Nelson, Texas Tech (17) vs. Florida St. (40) (Tangerine, 1977) (143 yards)
6—Wally Henry, UCLA (6) vs. Alabama (36) (Liberty, 1976)
6—Steve Williams, Alabama (6) vs. Nebraska (38) (Orange, 1972)
6—Mike Fink, Missouri (35) vs. Arizona St. (49) (Fiesta, 1972) (203 yards)

MOST KICKOFF RETURN YARDS

203—Mike Fink, Missouri (35) vs. Arizona St. (49) (Fiesta, 1972) (6 returns)
186—Deltha O'Neal, California (38) vs. Navy (42) (Aloha, 1996) (6 returns)
178—Al Hoisch, UCLA (14) vs. Illinois (45) (Rose, 1947) (4 returns)
174—Jeff Sydner, Hawaii (13) vs. Michigan St. (33) (Aloha, 1989) (7 returns)
166—Willie Jones, Iowa St. (30) vs. Georgia Tech (31) (Liberty, 1972) (4 returns)
154—Dave Lowery, Brigham Young (21) vs. Oklahoma St. (49) (Tangerine, 1976) (4 returns)
154—(D) Martin Mitchell, Tulane (7) vs. Houston (47) (Bluebonnet, 1973) (5 returns)
148—Earl Allen, Houston (28) vs. Boston College (45) (Cotton, 1985) (4 returns)
147—Carlos Snow, Ohio St. (17) vs. Syracuse (24) (Hall of Fame, 1992) (4 returns)
144—Clint Johnson, Notre Dame (39) vs. Florida (28) (Sugar, 1992) (5 returns)
143—Brian Nelson, Texas Tech (17) vs. Florida St. (40) (Tangerine, 1977) (6 returns)
143—Barry Smith, Florida St. (38) vs. Arizona St. (45) (Fiesta, 1971) (5 returns)

HIGHEST KICKOFF RETURN AVERAGE
(Minimum 2 Returns)

60.5—(D) Bob Smith, Texas A&M (40) vs. Georgia (20) (Presidential Cup, 1950) (2 for 121 yards)
60.0—Jerome Pathon, Washington (21) vs. Colorado (33) (Holiday, 1996) (2 for 120 yards)
58.0—Eddie Kennison, LSU (45) vs. Michigan St. (26) (Independence, 1995) (2 for 116 yards)
57.5—Pete Panuska, Tennessee (27) vs. Maryland (28) (Sun, 1984) (2 for 115 yards)
55.5—Todd Snyder, Ohio (42) vs. Richmond (49) (Tangerine, 1968) (2 for 111 yards)
46.7—(D) Cal Beck, Utah (16) vs. Arizona (13) (Freedom, 1994) (3 for 140 yards)
44.5—Al Hoisch, UCLA (14) vs. Illinois (45) (Rose, 1947) (4 for 178 yards)
43.7—Larry Key, Florida St. (40) vs. Texas Tech (17) (Tangerine, 1977) (3 for 131 yards)
41.5—Willie Jones, Iowa St. (30) vs. Georgia Tech (31) (Liberty, 1972) (4 for 166 yards)
41.0—Kevin Williams, Miami (Fla.) (46) vs. Texas (3) (Cotton, 1991) (2 for 82 yards)
40.3—(D) Willie Gault, Tennessee (28) vs. Wisconsin (21) (Garden State, 1981) (3 for 121 yards)
39.0—Damon Dunn, Stanford (13) vs. East Caro. (19) (Liberty, 1995) (3 for 117 yards)
37.0—Earl Allen, Houston (28) vs. Boston College (45) (Cotton, 1985) (4 for 148 yards)
36.8—Carlos Snow, Ohio St. (17) vs. Syracuse (24) (Hall of Fame, 1992) (4 for 147 yards)
33.8—Mike Fink, Missouri (35) vs. Arizona St. (49) (Fiesta, 1972) (6 for 203 yards)
33.8—Demetrius Allen, Virginia (34) vs. Georgia (27) (Peach, Dec. 30, 1995) (4 for 135)
33.2—Hudhaifa Ismaeli, Northwestern (32) vs. Southern Cal (41) (Rose, 1996) (5 for 166)
33.0—Derrick Mason, Michigan St. (26) vs. LSU (45) (Independence, 1995) (4 for 132)
32.6—Jim McElroy, UCLA (30) vs. Kansas (51) (Aloha, 1995) (5 for 163)
32.5—Reidel Anthony, Florida (24) vs. Nebraska (62) (Fiesta, 1996) (6 for 195)
32.0—(D) Eric Alozie, Washington (34) vs. Florida (7) (Freedom, 1989) (2 for 64 yards)
32.0—Jim Brown, Syracuse (27) vs. Texas Christian (28) (Cotton, 1957) (3 for 96 yards)
32.0—Harry Jones, Kentucky (20) vs. Texas Christian (7) (Cotton, 1952) (2 for 64 yards)

Interceptions

MOST INTERCEPTIONS MADE

4—Jim Dooley, Miami (Fla.) (14) vs. Clemson (0) (Gator, 1952)
4—(D) Manuel Aja, Arizona St. (21) vs. Xavier (Ohio) (33) (Salad, 1950)
3—Michael Brooks, North Caro. St. (28) vs. Iowa (23) (Peach, Dec. 31, 1988)
3—Bud Hebert, Oklahoma (24) vs. Florida St. (7) (Orange, 1980)
3—Louis Campbell, Arkansas (13) vs. Tennessee (14) (Liberty, 1971)
3—Bud McClinton, Auburn (34) vs. Arizona (10) (Sun, 1968)
3—(D) Les Derrick, Texas (19) vs. Mississippi (0) (Bluebonnet, 1966)
3—(D) Tommy Luke, Mississippi (0) vs. Texas (19) (Bluebonnet, 1966)
3—Jerry Cook, Texas (12) vs. Mississippi (7) (Cotton, 1962)
3—Ray Brown, Mississippi (39) vs. Texas (7) (Sugar, 1958)
3—Bill Paulman, Stanford (7) vs. Southern Methodist (0) (Rose, 1936)
3—Shy Huntington, Oregon (14) vs. Pennsylvania (0) (Rose, 1917)

MOST INTERCEPTION RETURN YARDAGE

148—Elmer Layden, Notre Dame (27) vs. Stanford (10) (Rose, 1925) (2 interceptions)
94—David Baker, Oklahoma (48) vs. Duke (21) (Orange, 1958) (1 interception)
90—Norm Beal, Missouri (21) vs. Navy (14) (Orange, 1961) (1 interception)
90—Charlie Brembs, South Caro. (14) vs. Wake Forest (26) (Gator, 1946) (1 interception)
89—Al Hudson, Miami (Fla.) (13) vs. Holy Cross (6) (Orange, 1946) (1 interception)
88—Dwayne Rudd, Alabama (17) vs. Michigan (14) (Outback, 1997) (1 interception)
81—Gary Moss, Georgia (24) vs. Boston College (27) (Hall of Fame, 1986) (1 interception)
80—(D) Russ Meredith, West Va. (21) vs. Gonzaga (13) (San Diego East-West Christmas Classic, 1922) (1 interception)
77—George Halas, Great Lakes (17) vs. Mare Island (0) (Rose, 1919) (1 interception)
75—Hugh Morrow, Alabama (26) vs. Duke (29) (Sugar, 1945) (1 interception)
72—Alton Montgomery, Houston (22) vs. Washington St. (24) (Aloha, 1988) (1 interception)
70—Robert Bailey, Mississippi (34) vs. Virginia Tech (17) (Liberty, 1968) (1 interception)
70—(D) Mel McGaha, Arkansas (21) vs. William & Mary (19) (Dixie, 1948) (1 interception)
69—Chris Carter, Texas (35) vs. North Caro. (31) (Sun, 1994) (1 interception)
69—Howard Ehler, Florida St. (36) vs. Oklahoma (19) (Gator, Jan. 2, 1965) (1 interception)
67—John Matsock, Michigan St. (28) vs. UCLA (20) (Rose, 1954) (2 interceptions)

All-Purpose Yards

(Includes All Runs From Scrimmage, Pass Receptions and All Returns)

MOST ALL-PURPOSE PLAYS
(Must Have at Least One Reception or Return)

47—(D) Ron Jackson, Tulsa (28) vs. San Diego St. (17) (Freedom, 1991) (46 rush, 1 reception)
46—Errict Rhett, Florida (27) vs. North Caro. St. (10) (Gator, 1992) (39 rush, 7 receptions)
42—Blake Ezor, Michigan St. (33) vs. Hawaii (13) (Aloha, 1989) (41 rush, 1 reception)
41—Terrell Fletcher, Wisconsin (34) vs. Duke (20) (Hall of Fame, 1995) (39 rush, 1 reception, 1 kickoff return)
39—(D) Marshall Faulk, San Diego St. (17) vs. Tulsa (28) (Freedom, 1991) (30 rush, 9 receptions)
37—Wasean Tait, Toledo (40) vs. Nevada (37) (OT) (Las Vegas, 1995) (31 rush, 6 receptions)
37—Sherman Williams, Alabama (24) vs. Ohio St. (17) (Florida Citrus, 1995) (27 rush, 8 receptions, 2 kickoff returns)
37—O. J. Simpson, Southern Cal (16) vs. Ohio St. (27) (Rose, 1969) (28 rush, 8 receptions, 1 kickoff return)
36—Rondell Mealey, LSU (27) vs. Notre Dame (9) (Independence, 1997) (34 rush, 2 kickoff returns)
36—Thurman Thomas, Oklahoma St. (35) vs. West Va. (33) (John Hancock Sun, 1987) (33 rush, 6 receptions)
36—Bob Anderson, Colorado (47) vs. Alabama (33) (Liberty, 1969) (35 rush, 1 kickoff return)
35—Ricky Ervins, Southern Cal (17) vs. Michigan (10) (Rose, 1990) (30 rush, 5 receptions)
35—(D) Eric Bieniemy, Colorado (17) vs. Brigham Young (20) (Freedom, 1988) (33 rush, 2 receptions)
33—Leon Johnson, North Caro. (20) vs. West Va. (13) (Gator, 1996) (25 rush, 3 receptions, 1 punt return, 4 kickoff returns)
33—Shaumbe Wright-Fair, Washington St. (31) vs. Utah (28) (Copper, 1992) (27 rush, 6 receptions)
33—(D) Greg Lewis, Washington (34) vs. Florida (7) (Freedom, 1989) (27 rush, 6 receptions)
33—Bo Jackson, Auburn (16) vs. Texas A&M (36) (Cotton, 1986) (31 rush, 2 receptions)

MOST ALL-PURPOSE YARDS GAINED
(Must Have at Least One Reception or Return)

359—Sherman Williams, Alabama (24) vs. Ohio St. (17) (Florida Citrus, 1995) (166 rush, 155 receptions, 38 kickoff returns)
303—(D) Bob Smith, Texas A&M (40) vs. Georgia (20) (Presidential Cup, 1950) (160 rush, 22 receptions, 121 kickoff returns)
283—Andre Coleman, Kansas St. (52) vs. Wyoming (17) (Copper, 1993) (7 rush, 144 receptions, 73 punt returns, 54 kickoff returns)
278—Byron Hanspard, Texas Tech (55) vs. Air Force (41) (Copper, 1995) (260 rush, 18 receptions)
277—Bob Anderson, Colorado (47) vs. Alabama (33) (Liberty, 1969) (254 rush, 23 kickoff returns)
276—O. J. Simpson, Southern Cal (16) vs. Ohio St. (27) (Rose, 1969) (171 rush, 85 receptions, 20 kickoff returns)
272—Pat Johnson, Oregon (41) vs. Air Force (13) (Las Vegas, 1997) (169 receptions, 49 punt returns, 54 kickoff returns)
256—Rondell Mealey, LSU (27) vs. Notre Dame (9) (Independence, 1997) (222 rush, 34 kickoff returns)
256—Terrell Fletcher, Wisconsin (34) vs. Duke (20) (Hall of Fame, 1995) (241 rush, 8 receptions, 7 kickoff returns)
247—(D) Wilford White, Arizona St. (21) vs. Miami (Ohio) (34) (Salad, 1951) (106 rush, 87 receptions, 54 kickoff returns)
246—Demetrius Allen, Virginia (34) vs. Georgia (27) (Peach, Dec. 30, 1995) (111 receiving, 135 kickoff returns)
246—Ernie Jones, Indiana (22) vs. Tennessee (27) (Peach, 1987) (15 rush, 150 receptions, 81 kickoff returns)

242—Errict Rhett, Florida (27) vs. North Caro. St. (10) (Gator, 1992) (182 rush, 60 receptions)
239—Tyrone Wheatley, Michigan (38) vs. Washington (31) (Rose, 1993) (235 rush, 4 receptions)
238—Wasean Tait, Toledo (40) vs. Nevada (37) (OT) (Las Vegas, 1995) (185 rush, 53 receptions)
237—Ahman Green, Nebraska (42) vs. Tennessee (17) (Orange, 1998) (206 rush, 31 receptions)
236—(D) Gary Anderson, Arkansas (34) vs. Tulane (15) (Hall of Fame, 1980) (156 rush, 80 punt returns)
230—Jamie Morris, Michigan (28) vs. Alabama (24) (Hall of Fame, 1987) (234 rush, -4 receptions)
228—Phillip Bobo, Washington St. (31) vs. Utah (28) (Copper, 1992) (16 rush, 212 receptions)
227—Marcus Wall, North Caro. (31) vs. Texas (35) (Sun, 1994) (30 rush, 82 receptions, 82 punt returns, 33 kickoff returns)
225—(D) Ron Jackson, Tulsa (28) vs. San Diego St. (17) (Freedom, 1991) (211 rush, 14 receptions)
223—Donny Anderson, Texas Tech (21) vs. Georgia Tech (31) (Gator, 1966) (85 rush, 138 receptions)
212—Troy Stradford, Boston College (45) vs. Houston (28) (Cotton, 1985) (196 rush, 16 receptions)
211—(D) Charles White, Southern Cal (47) vs. Texas A&M (28) (Bluebonnet, 1977) (186 rush, 25 receptions)
208—(D) Sheldon Canley, San Jose St. (48) vs. Central Mich. (24) (California, 1990) (164 rush, 44 receptions)

Defensive Statistics

MOST TOTAL TACKLES MADE (Includes Assists)

31—Lee Roy Jordan, Alabama (17) vs. Oklahoma (0) (Orange, 1963)
22—Bubba Brown, Clemson (17) vs. Ohio St. (15) (Gator, 1978)
22—Gordy Ceresino, Stanford (24) vs. LSU (14) (Sun, Dec. 31, 1977)
20—Vada Murray, Michigan (10) vs. Southern Cal (17) (Rose, 1990)
20—(D) Gordy Ceresino, Stanford (25) vs. Georgia (22) (Bluebonnet, 1978)
18—Allen Stansberry, LSU (45) vs. Michigan St. (26) (Independence, 1995)
18—Ted Johnson, Colorado (41) vs. Notre Dame (24) (Fiesta, 1995)
18—Rod Smith, Notre Dame (39) vs. Florida (28) (Sugar, 1992)
18—Erick Anderson, Michigan (10) vs. Southern Cal (17) (Rose, 1990)
18—(D) Yepi Pauu, San Jose St. (27) vs. Eastern Mich. (30) (California, 1987)
18—Garland Rivers, Michigan (17) vs. Brigham Young (24) (Holiday, 1984)
18—(D) Terry Hubbard, Cal St. Fullerton (13) vs. Northern Ill. (20) (California, 1983)
18—(D) Don Turner, Fresno St. (29) vs. Bowling Green (28) (California, 1982)
18—Matt Millen, Penn St. (42) vs. Arizona St. (30) (Fiesta, 1977)

MOST UNASSISTED TACKLES

18—Rod Smith, Notre Dame (39) vs. Florida (28) (Sugar, 1992)
17—Garland Rivers, Michigan (17) vs. Brigham Young (24) (Holiday, 1984)
15—Randy Neal, Virginia (13) vs. Boston College (31) (Carquest, 1994)
15—(D) Ken Norton Jr., UCLA (31) vs. Brigham Young (10) (Freedom, 1986)
15—Lynn Evans, Missouri (35) vs. Arizona St. (49) (Fiesta, 1972)

MOST TACKLES MADE FOR LOSSES

5—(D) Michael Jones, Colorado (17) vs. Brigham Young (20) (Freedom, 1988) (20 yards)
5—Jimmy Walker, Arkansas (10) vs. UCLA (10) (Fiesta, 1978)
4—Clint Bruce, Navy (42) vs. California (38) (Aloha, 1996)
4—Montae Reagor, Texas Tech (0) vs. Iowa (27) (Alamo, 1996)
4—Reggie Garnett, Michigan St. (0) vs. Stanford (38) (Sun, 1996)
4—Corey Terry, Tennessee (48) vs. Northwestern (28) (Florida Citrus, 1997)
4—Matt Finkes, Ohio St. (14) vs. Tennessee (20) (Florida Citrus, 1996)
4—(D) Ken Norton Jr., UCLA (31) vs. Brigham Young (10) (Freedom, 1986)
3—James Hamilton, North Caro. (20) vs. West Va. (13) (Gator, 1996)
3—Mike Vrabel, Ohio St. (14) vs. Tennessee (20) (Florida Citrus, 1996)
3—Nate Hemsley, Syracuse (41) vs. Clemson (0) (Gator, 1996)
3—Marcus Jones, North Caro. (20) vs. Arkansas (10) (Carquest, Dec. 30, 1995)
3—(D) Guy Boliaux, Wisconsin (21) vs. Tennessee (28) (Garden State, 1981)

MOST QUARTERBACK SACKS

6—Shay Muirbrook, Brigham Young (19) vs. Kansas St. (15) (Cotton, 1997)
4—Rusty Medearis, Miami (Fla.) (22) vs. Nebraska (0) (Orange, 1992)
4—Bobby Bell, Missouri (17) vs. Brigham Young (21) (Holiday, 1983)
3—Andy Katzenmoyer, Ohio St. (20) vs. Arizona St. (17) (Rose, 1997)
3—Travis Ochs, Kansas St. (15) vs. Brigham Young (19) (Cotton, 1997)
3—Trevor Pryce, Clemson (7) vs. LSU (10) (Peach 1996)
3—Jamie Sharper, Virginia (21) vs. Miami (Fla.) (31) (Carquest, 1996)
3—Mike Crawford, Nevada (18) vs. Ball St. (15) (Las Vegas, 1996)
3—Gabe Northern, LSU (45) vs. Michigan St. (26) (Independence, 1995)
3—James Gillyard, LSU (45) vs. Michigan St. (26) (Independence, 1995)
3—Dewayne Harris, Nebraska (24) vs. Miami (Fla.) (17) (Orange, 1995)
3—Trev Alberts, Nebraska (16) vs. Florida St. (18) (Orange, 1994)
3—(D) Alfred Williams, Colorado (17) vs. Brigham Young (20) (Freedom, 1988)
3—(D) Jim Wahler, UCLA (31) vs. Brigham Young (10) (Freedom, 1986)
3—James Mosley, Texas Tech (17) vs. Mississippi (20) (Independence, 1986)
3—(D) Ernie Barnes, Mississippi St. (10) vs. Kansas (0) (Hall of Fame, 1981)

FUMBLE RECOVERIES

2—Randall Brown, Ohio St. (17) vs. Alabama (24) (Florida Citrus, 1995)
2—(D) Michael Stewart, Fresno St. (51) vs. Bowling Green (7) (California, 1985)
2—Rod Kirby, Pittsburgh (7) vs. Arizona St. (28) (Fiesta, 1973)

BLOCKED KICKS

2—Bracey Walker, North Caro. (21) vs. Mississippi St. (17) (Peach, Jan. 2, 1993)
2—Carlton Williams, Pittsburgh (7) vs. Arizona St. (28) (Fiesta, 1973)

PASSES BROKEN UP

4—Chris Cummings, LSU (27) vs. Notre Dame (9) (Independence, 1997)
3—Robert Williams, North Caro. (20) vs. West Va. (13) (Gator, 1996)
3—Mark Tate, Penn St. (43) vs. Auburn (14) (Outback, 1996)
3—Kwame Ellis, Stanford (13) vs. East Caro. (19) (Liberty, 1995)
3—Mickey Dalton, Air Force (41) vs. Texas Tech (55) (Copper, 1995)
3—Barron Miles, Nebraska (24) vs. Miami (Fla.) (17) (Orange, 1995)
3—Sam McKiver, Virginia (20) vs. Texas Christian (10) (Independence, 1994)
3—Percy Ellsworth, Virginia (20) vs. Texas Christian (10) (Independence, 1994)
3—Tyrone Williams, Nebraska (16) vs. Florida St. (18) (Orange, 1994)
3—(D) John Herpin, Southern Cal (28) vs. Utah (21) (Freedom, 1993)
3—Demouy Williams, Washington (24) vs. Tulane (12) (Independence, 1987)

Team Record Lists

Only official records after 1937 are included. Prior records are included if able to be substantiated. Each team's score is in parentheses after the team name. Totals for each team in both-team records are in brackets after the team's score. The year listed is the actual (calendar) year the game was played; the date is included if the bowl was played twice (i.e., January and December) during one calendar year. The list also includes discontinued bowls, marked with (D). Bowls are listed by the name of the bowl at the time it was played: The Florida Citrus Bowl was the Tangerine Bowl in 1947-82; the first Hall of Fame Bowl (1977-85) was called the All-American Bowl in 1986-90; the second Hall of Fame Bowl (1986-95) is now called the Outback Bowl and is played in Tampa, Fla.; the Sun Bowl was called the John Hancock Bowl in 1989-93, the John Hancock Sun Bowl in 1987-88, and reverted to the Sun Bowl in 1994; the Blockbuster Bowl changed its name to Carquest Bowl in 1993 and then to Sunshine Bowl in 1998; and the Copper Bowl changed its name to Insight.com Bowl in 1997.

Total Offense

MOST TOTAL PLAYS

96—North Caro. St. (10) vs. Arizona (17) (Copper, 1989) (310 yards)
95—Georgia (27) vs. Virginia (34) (Peach, Dec. 30, 1995) (525 yards)
95—Toledo (40) vs. Nevada (37) (OT) (Las Vegas, 1995) (561 yards)
95—North Caro. St. (28) vs. Iowa (23) (Peach, Dec. 31, 1988) (431 yards)
94—Arkansas (27) vs. Tennessee (31) (Cotton, 1990) (568 yards)
93—Miami (Fla.) (10) vs. Penn St. (14) (Fiesta, 1987) (445 yards)
92—Oregon (20) vs. Penn St. (38) (Rose, 1995) (501 yards)
92—Washington St. (24) vs. Houston (22) (Aloha, 1988) (460 yards)
92—(D) Western Mich. (30) vs. Fresno St. (35) (California, 1988) (503 yards)
92—(D) Purdue (27) vs. Tennessee (22) (Bluebonnet, 1979) (483 yards)
92—Arizona St. (30) vs. Penn St. (42) (Fiesta, 1977) (426 yards)
91—Florida (28) vs. Notre Dame (39) (Sugar, 1992) (511 yards)
91—Baylor (21) vs. LSU (7) (Liberty, 1985) (489 yards)
90—Virginia Tech (25) vs. North Caro. St. (24) (Peach, 1986) (487 yards)
90—Maryland (0) vs. Texas (42) (Sun, 1978) (248 yards)
90—Nebraska (40) vs. Notre Dame (6) (Orange, 1973) (560 yards)
90—(D) Oklahoma (27) vs. Southern Methodist (28) (Bluebonnet, 1968)
90—Richmond (49) vs. Ohio (42) (Tangerine, 1968) (556 yards)

MOST TOTAL PLAYS, BOTH TEAMS

175—Toledo (40) [95] & Nevada (37) [80] (OT) (Las Vegas, 1995) (974 yards)
171—Auburn (34) [82] & Arizona (10) [89] (Sun, 1968) (537 yards)
167—(D) Fresno St. (35) [75] & Western Mich. (30) [92] (California, 1988) (943 yards)
167—Arizona St. (45) [86] & Florida St. (38) [81] (Fiesta, 1971) (863 yards)
166—Colorado (47) [86] & Alabama (33) [80] (Liberty, 1969) (930 yards)
165—North Caro. St. (28) [95] & Iowa (23) [70] (Peach, Dec. 31, 1988)
165—East Caro. (35) [80] & Louisiana Tech (13) [85] (Independence, 1978) (607 yards)
165—Penn St. (42) [73] & Arizona St. (30) [92] (Fiesta, 1977) (777 yards)
163—Nebraska (45) [88] & Georgia (6) [75] (Sun, 1969) (540 yards)
162—Penn St. (38) [70] & Oregon (20) [92] (Rose, 1995) (931 yards)
161—Ohio St. (28) [78] & Pittsburgh (23) [83] (Fiesta, 1984) (897 yards)
161—Auburn (35) [84] & Mississippi (28) [77] (Gator, Jan. 2, 1971) (1,024 yards)
160—Texas (35) [76] vs. North Caro. (31) [84] (Sun, 1994) (903 yards)
160—Texas Tech (55) [80] & Air Force (41) [80] (Copper, 1995) (1,120 yards)
160—Mississippi (42) [78] & Air Force (29) [82] (Liberty, 1989) (1,047 yards)
159—Notre Dame (39) [68] & Florida (28) [91] (Sugar, 1992) (944 yards)
159—Notre Dame (38) [85] & Texas (10) [74] (Cotton, 1978) (690 yards)
159—Texas (42) [69] & Maryland (0) [90] (Sun, 1978) (517 yards)

MOST YARDS GAINED
718—Arizona St. (49) vs. Missouri (35) (Fiesta, 1972) (452 rush, 266 pass)
715—Michigan (35) vs. Mississippi (3) (Gator, Jan. 1, 1991) (324 rush, 391 pass)
698—Oklahoma St. (62) vs. Wyoming (14) (Holiday, 1988) (320 rush, 378 pass)
680—Texas A&M (65) vs. Brigham Young (14) (Holiday, 1989) (356 rush, 324 pass)
655—(D) Houston (47) vs. Tulane (7) (Bluebonnet, 1973) (402 rush, 253 pass)
651—Brigham Young (39) vs. Penn St. (50) (Holiday, 1989) (75 rush, 576 pass)
646—Navy (42) vs. California (38) (Aloha, 1996) (251 rush, 395 pass)
642—(D) San Jose St. (48) vs. Central Mich. (24) (California, 1990) (200 rush, 442 pass)
629—Nebraska (62) vs. Florida (24) (Fiesta, 1996) (524 rush, 105 pass)
624—(D) Southern Cal (47) vs. Texas A&M (28) (Bluebonnet, 1977) (378 rush, 246 pass)
618—Oklahoma (48) vs. Virginia (14) (Gator, Dec. 29, 1991) (261 rush, 357 pass)
606—Texas Tech (55) vs. Air Force (41) (Copper, 1995) (361 rush, 245 pass)
596—Alabama (61) vs. Syracuse (6) (Orange, 1953) (296 rush, 300 pass)
589—UNLV (52) vs. Central Mich. (24) (Las Vegas, 1994) (301 rush, 288 pass)
583—Oregon (41) vs. Air Force (13) (Las Vegas, 1997) (266 rush, 317 pass)
578—Southern Cal (55) vs. Texas Tech (14) (Cotton, 1995) (143 rush, 435 pass)
575—Indiana (34) vs. South Caro. (10) (Liberty, 1988) (185 rush, 390 pass)
571—Louisville (34) vs. Alabama (7) (Fiesta, 1991) (113 rush, 458 pass)
569—Florida St. (34) vs. Oklahoma St. (23) (Gator, 1985) (231 rush, 338 pass)
568—Arkansas (27) vs. Tennessee (31) (Cotton, 1990) (361 rush, 207 pass)
566—Pittsburgh (34) vs. Clemson (3) (Gator, 1977) (179 rush, 387 pass)

MOST YARDS GAINED, BOTH TEAMS
1,143—(D) Southern Cal (47) [624] & Texas A&M (28) [519] (Bluebonnet, 1977) (148 plays)
1,129—Arizona St. (49) [718] & Missouri (35) [411] (Fiesta, 1972) (134 plays)
1,120—Texas Tech (55) [606] & Air Force (41) [514] (Copper, 1995) (160 plays)
1,115—Penn St. (50) [464] & Brigham Young (39) [651] (Holiday, 1989) (157 plays)
1,080—Navy (42) [646] & California (38) [434] (Aloha, 1996) (147 plays)
1,048—Michigan (35) [715] & Mississippi (3) [333] (Gator, Jan. 1, 1991) (153 plays)
1,047—Mississippi (42) [533] & Air Force (29) [514] (Liberty, 1989) (160 plays)
1,038—Tennessee (31) [470] & Arkansas (27) [568] (Cotton, 1990) (155 plays)
1,024—Auburn (35) [559] & Mississippi (28) [465] (Gator, Jan. 2, 1971) (161 plays)
1,018—Mississippi (34) [511] & Marshall (31) [507] (Motor City, 1997) (155 plays)
1,007—(D) Toledo (27) [486] & San Jose St. (25) [521] (California, 1981) (158 plays)
978—Pittsburgh (31) [530] & Texas A&M (28) [448] (John Hancock, 1989) (158 plays)
974—Toledo (40) [561] & Nevada (37) [413] (OT) (Las Vegas, 1995) (175 plays)
965—UNLV (52) [589] & Central Mich. (24) [376] (Las Vegas, 1994) (145 plays)
954—Mississippi (27) [427] & Arkansas (22) [527] (Sugar, 1970)
950—Texas (40) [436] & Missouri (27) [514] (Cotton, 1946)
944—Notre Dame (39) [433] & Florida (28) [511] (Sugar, 1992) (159 plays)

HIGHEST AVERAGE GAINED PER PLAY
9.5—Louisville (34) vs. Alabama (7) (Fiesta, 1991) (60 for 571 yards)
9.1—Navy (42) vs. California (38) (Aloha, 1996) (71 for 646 yards)
8.7—Oklahoma St. (62) vs. Wyoming (14) (Holiday, 1988) (80 for 698 yards)
8.4—Michigan (35) vs. Mississippi (3) (Gator, Jan. 1, 1991) (85 for 715 yards)
8.3—Texas A&M (65) vs. Brigham Young (14) (Holiday, 1990) (82 for 680 yards)
8.1—Arizona St. (49) vs. Missouri (35) (Fiesta, 1972) (89 for 718 yards)
8.0—Oregon (41) vs. Air Force (13) (Las Vegas, 1997) (73 for 583 yards)
7.9—Brigham Young (39) vs. Penn St. (50) (Holiday, 1989) (82 for 651 yards)
7.7—Alabama (61) vs. Syracuse (6) (Orange, 1953) (77 for 596 yards)
7.7—(D) Vanderbilt (28) vs. Air Force (36) (Hall of Fame, 1982) (63 for 487 yards)
7.7—Kansas (51) vs. UCLA (30) (Aloha, 1995) (71 for 548 yards)
7.7—Tennessee (31) vs. Arkansas (27) (Cotton, 1990) (61 for 470 yards)
7.6—Florida St. (41) vs. Nebraska (17) (Fiesta, 1990) (65 for 494 yards)
7.6—Nebraska (62) vs. Florida (24) (Fiesta, 1996) (83 for 629 yards)
7.6—Texas Tech (55) vs. Air Force (41) (Copper, 1995) (80 for 606 yards)
7.5—Kansas St. (52) vs. Wyoming (17) (Copper, 1993) (71 for 536 yards)
7.5—(D) Houston (47) vs. Tulane (7) (Bluebonnet, 1973) (87 for 655 yards)
7.5—Iowa (38) vs. California (12) (Rose, 1959) (69 for 516 yards)
7.5—Marshall (31) vs. Mississippi (34) (68 for 507 yards)
7.4—(D) UCLA (31) vs. Brigham Young (10) (Freedom, 1986) (70 for 518 yards)
7.3—(D) UNLV (30) vs. Toledo (13) (California, 1984) (56 for 409 yards)
7.3—(D) San Jose St. (48) vs. Central Mich. (24) (California, 1990) (88 for 642 yards)

FEWEST PLAYS
35—Tennessee (0) vs. Texas (16) (Cotton, 1953) (29 rush, 6 pass)
36—Arkansas (3) vs. UCLA (17) (Cotton, 1989) (22 rush, 14 pass)
37—Texas Christian (0) vs. Oklahoma St. (34) (Cotton, 1945) (27 rush, 10 pass)
38—Iowa (3) vs. California (37) (Alamo, 1993) (21 rush, 17 pass)

FEWEST PLAYS, BOTH TEAMS
107—Texas Christian (16) [54] & Marquette (6) [53] (Cotton, 1937)

FEWEST YARDS
-21—U. of Mexico (0) vs. Southwestern (Tex.) (35) (Sun, 1945) (29 rush, -50 pass)
23—Alabama (10) vs. Missouri (35) (Gator, 1968) (-45 rush, 68 pass)
32—Tennessee (0) vs. Texas (16) (Cotton, 1953) (-14 rush, 46 pass)
38—Miami (Fla.) (0) vs. Bucknell (26) (Orange, 1935) (20 rush, 18 pass)
41—Southern Cal (14) vs. Alabama (34) (Rose, 1946) (6 rush, 35 pass)
42—Arkansas (3) vs. UCLA (17) (Cotton, 1989) (21 rush, 21 pass)
48—New Mexico (0) vs. Southwestern (Tex.) (7) (Sun, 1944) (38 rush, 10 pass)
54—Arkansas (0) vs. LSU (0) (Cotton, 1947) (54 rush, 0 pass)
57—Michigan St. (0) vs. Auburn (6) (Orange, 1938) (32 rush, 25 pass)

FEWEST YARDS, BOTH TEAMS
260—Randolph Field (7) [150] & Texas (7) [110] (Cotton, 1944)
263—LSU (19) [92] & Texas A&M (14) [171] (Orange, 1944)

Rushing

MOST RUSHING ATTEMPTS
87—Oklahoma (40) vs. Auburn (22) (Sugar, Jan. 1, 1972) (439 yards)
82—Missouri (35) vs. Alabama (10) (Gator, 1968) (402 yards)
79—West Va. (14) vs. South Caro. (3) (Peach, 1969) (356 yards)
79—Georgia Tech (31) vs. Texas Tech (21) (Gator, Dec. 31, 1965) (364 yards)
78—(D) Houston (35) vs. Navy (0) (Garden State, 1980) (405 yards)
78—Texas (16) vs. Tennessee (0) (Cotton, 1953) (296 yards)
76—Oklahoma (14) vs. Penn St. (0) (Sugar, Dec. 31, 1972) (278 yards)
74—Oklahoma (41) vs. Wyoming (7) (Fiesta, 1976) (415 yards)
74—Michigan (12) vs. Stanford (13) (Rose, 1972) (264 yards)
74—Ohio St. (20) vs. Southern Cal (7) (Rose, 1955) (305 yards)
73—Syracuse (31) vs. McNeese St. (7) (Independence, 1979) (276 yards)
73—Penn St. (41) vs. Oregon (12) (Liberty, 1960) (301 yards)
72—Arkansas (27) vs. Tennessee (31) (Cotton, 1990) (361 yards)
72—North Caro. St. (28) vs. Iowa (23) (Peach, Dec. 31, 1988) (236 yards)
72—(D) Texas A&M (28) vs. Southern Cal (47) (Bluebonnet, 1977) (486 yards)

MOST RUSHING ATTEMPTS, BOTH TEAMS
122—(D) Southern Cal (47) [50] & Texas A&M (28) [72] (Bluebonnet, 1977) (864 yards)
122—Mississippi St. (26) [68] & North Caro. (24) [54] (Sun, 1974) (732 yards)
120—Pittsburgh (33) [53] & Kansas (19) [67] (Sun, 1975) (714 yards)
117—Oklahoma (14) [65] & Michigan (6) [52] (Orange, 1976) (451 yards)
117—West Va. (14) [79] & South Caro. (3) [38] (Peach, 1969) (420 yards)
116—Oklahoma (41) [74] & Wyoming (7) [42] (Fiesta, 1976) (568 yards)
116—Colorado (47) [70] & Alabama (33) [46] (Liberty, 1969) (628 yards)
115—Southern Cal (7) [47] & Wisconsin (0) [68] (Rose, 1953) (259 yards)
113—Oklahoma (40) [54] & Houston (14) [59] (Sun, 1981) (566 yards)
113—(D) Houston (35) [78] & Navy (0) [35] (Garden State, 1980) (540 yards)
113—Missouri (34) [71] & Auburn (17) [42] (Sun, 1973) (408 yards)
112—Arkansas (31) [65] & Georgia (10) [47] (Cotton, 1976) (426 yards)
112—(D) Colorado (29) [62] & Houston (17) [50] (Bluebonnet, 1971) (552 yards)

MOST NET RUSHING YARDS
524—Nebraska (62) vs. Florida (24) (Fiesta, 1996) (68 attempts)
486—(D) Texas A&M (28) vs. Southern Cal (47) (Bluebonnet, 1977) (72 attempts)
473—Colorado (47) vs. Alabama (33) (Liberty, 1969) (70 attempts)
455—Mississippi St. (26) vs. North Caro. (24) (Sun, 1974) (68 attempts)
452—Arizona St. (49) vs. Missouri (35) (Fiesta, 1972) (65 attempts)
439—Oklahoma (40) vs. Auburn (22) (Sugar, Jan. 1, 1972) (87 attempts)
434—Oklahoma (41) vs. Wyoming (7) (Fiesta, 1976) (74 attempts)
431—Air Force (41) vs. Texas Tech (55) (Copper, 1995) (67 attempts)
429—Iowa (38) vs. California (12) (Rose, 1959) (55 attempts)
423—(D) UCLA (31) vs. Brigham Young (10) (Freedom, 1986) (49 attempts)
423—Auburn (33) vs. Baylor (13) (Gator, Dec. 31, 1954) (48 attempts)
417—Oklahoma (21) vs. Arizona St. (32) (Fiesta, 1983) (63 attempts)
411—Oklahoma (24) vs. Florida St. (7) (Orange, 1980) (62 attempts)
409—Nebraska (42) vs. Tennessee (17) (Orange, 1998) (68 attempts)
409—Oklahoma (40) vs. Houston (14) (Sun, 1981) (54 attempts)
408—Missouri (27) vs. Texas (40) (Cotton, 1946)
405—(D) Houston (35) vs. Navy (0) (Garden State, 1980) (78 attempts)
402—(D) Houston (47) vs. Tulane (7) (Bluebonnet, 1973) (58 attempts)

MOST NET RUSHING YARDS, BOTH TEAMS
864—(D) Southern Cal (47) [378] & Texas A&M (28) [486] (Bluebonnet, 1977) (122 attempts)
792—Texas Tech (55) [361] & Air Force (41) [431] (Copper, 1995) (107 attempts)
732—Mississippi St. (26) [455] & North Caro. (24) [277] (Sun, 1974) (122 attempts)
714—Pittsburgh (33) [372] & Kansas (19) [342] (Sun, 1975) (120 attempts)
701—Arizona St. (49) [453] & Missouri (35) [248] (Fiesta, 1972) (109 attempts)
681—Tennessee (31) [320] & Arkansas (27) [361] (Cotton, 1990) (110 attempts)
643—Iowa (38) [429] & California (12) [214] (Rose, 1959) (108 attempts)
628—Colorado (47) [473] & Alabama (33) [155] (Liberty, 1969) (116 attempts)
616—Oklahoma (41) [434] & Wyoming (7) [182] (Fiesta, 1976) (116 attempts)
610—Texas (40) [202] & Missouri (27) [408] (Cotton, 1946)

HIGHEST RUSHING AVERAGE
(Minimum 30 Attempts)
9.3—Texas Tech (55) vs. Air Force (41) (Copper, 1995) (39 for 361 yards)
8.6—(D) UCLA (31) vs. Brigham Young (10) (Freedom, 1986) (49 for 423 yards)
8.6—Michigan (38) vs. Washington (31) (Rose, 1993) (36 for 308 yards)
8.4—Tennessee (31) vs. Arkansas (27) (Cotton, 1990) (38 for 320 yards)
8.0—Toledo (56) vs. Davidson (33) (Tangerine, 1969) (42 for 334 yards)
7.8—Iowa (38) vs. California (12) (Rose, 1959) (55 for 429 yards)
7.7—Texas Tech (28) vs. North Caro. (32) (Sun, 1972) (38 for 293 yards)
7.7—Nebraska (62) vs. Florida (24) (Fiesta, 1996) (68 for 524 yards)
7.6—Oklahoma (42) vs. Arkansas (8) (Orange, 1987) (48 for 366 yards)
7.6—Oklahoma (40) vs. Houston (14) (Sun, 1981) (54 for 409 yards)
7.6—(D) Southern Cal (47) vs. Texas A&M (28) (Bluebonnet, 1977) (50 for 378 yards)
7.4—Michigan (35) vs. Mississippi (3) (Gator, Jan. 1, 1991) (53 for 391 yards)
7.1—Boston College (45) vs. Houston (28) (Cotton, 1985) (50 for 353 yards)

7.0—Pittsburgh (33) vs. Kansas (19) (Sun, 1975) (53 for 372 yards)
7.0—Arizona St. (49) vs. Missouri (35) (Fiesta, 1972) (65 for 453 yards)

FEWEST RUSHING ATTEMPTS
12—(D) Vanderbilt (28) vs. Air Force (36) (Hall of Fame, 1982) (35 yards)
16—Florida (18) vs. Missouri (20) (Sugar, 1966) (-2 yards)
16—Colorado (7) vs. LSU (25) (Orange, 1962) (24 yards)
17—(D) Duke (21) vs. Texas Tech (49) (All-American, 1989) (67 yards)
17—Illinois (9) vs. UCLA (45) (Rose, 1984) (0 yards)
18—Brigham Young (46) vs. Southern Methodist (45) (Holiday, 1980) (-2 yards)
19—Iowa (23) vs. North Caro. St. (28) (Peach, Dec. 31, 1988) (46 yards)
19—Baylor (13) vs. Auburn (33) (Gator, Dec. 31, 1954) (108 yards)
20—Utah St. (19) vs. Cincinnati (35) (Humanitarian, 1997) (76 yards)
20—(D) San Jose St. (27) vs. Eastern Mich. (30) (California, 1987) (81 yards)
20—Tulane (6) vs. Penn St. (9) (Liberty, 1979) (-8 yards)
21—Tennessee (17) vs. Nebraska (42) (Orange, 1998) (128 yards)
21—Florida (24) vs. Nebraska (62) (Fiesta, 1996) (-28 yards)
21—Iowa (3) vs. California (37) (Alamo, 1993) (20 yards)
21—Brigham Young (14) vs. Texas A&M (65) (Holiday, 1990) (-12 yards)
21—Houston (22) vs. Washington St. (24) (Aloha, 1988) (68 yards)
21—Wyoming (19) vs. Iowa (20) (Holiday, 1987) (43 yards)
21—(D) San Jose St. (25) vs. Toledo (27) (California, 1981) (54 yards)

FEWEST RUSHING ATTEMPTS, BOTH TEAMS
57—Iowa (20) [36] & Wyoming (19) [21] (Holiday, 1987)
62—Mississippi (34) [39] vs. Marshall (31) [23] (Motor City, 1997)
63—Auburn (21) [36] & Clemson (17) [27] (Peach, 1998)
63—(D) Southern Cal (28) [38] & Utah (21) [25] (Freedom, 1993)
65—Purdue (33) [28] & Oklahoma St. (20) [37] (Alamo, 1997)
66—Southern Cal (41) [27] & Northwestern (32) [39] (Rose, 1996)
66—Brigham Young (13) [33] & Iowa (13) [33] (Holiday, 1991)
66—Miami (Fla.) (23) [28] & Nebraska (3) [38] (Orange, 1989)
66—Texas Christian (16) [34] & Marquette (6) [32] (Cotton, 1937)
67—UCLA (6) [41] & Illinois (3) [26] (John Hancock, 1991)
67—Southern Cal (7) [39] & Duke (3) [28] (Rose, 1939)
68—Tennessee (20) [32] & Ohio St. (14) [36] (Florida Citrus, 1996)
68—(D) Fresno St. (29) [24] & Bowling Green (28) [44] (California, 1982)
69—Michigan (21) [41] & Washington St. (16) [28] (Rose, 1998)
69—(D) Utah (16) [32] & Arizona (13) [37] (Freedom, 1994)
70—Georgia (33) [41] vs. Wisconsin (6) [29] (Outback, 1998)
70—Colorado (38) [41] & Oregon (6) [29] (Cotton, 1996)
70—Arizona (29) [50] & Miami (Fla.) (0) [20] (Fiesta, 1994)
70—Florida St. (41) [24] & Nebraska (17) [46] (Fiesta, 1990)
70—Florida St. (24) [39] & Penn St. (17) [31] (Blockbuster, 1990)

FEWEST RUSHING YARDS
-61—Kansas St. (7) vs. Boston College (12) (Aloha, 1994) (23 attempts)
-45—Alabama (10) vs. Missouri (35) (Gator, 1968) (29 attempts)
-30—Florida (6) vs. West Va. (26) (Peach, Dec. 31, 1981) (34 attempts)
-28—Florida (24) vs. Nebraska (62) (Fiesta, 1996) (21 attempts)
-21—Florida St. (20) vs. Wyoming (28) (Sun, 1966) (31 attempts)
-15—LSU (0) vs. Mississippi (20) (Sugar, 1960)
-14—Navy (6) vs. Texas (28) (Cotton, 1964) (29 attempts)
-14—Tennessee (0) vs. Texas (16) (Cotton, 1953) (29 attempts)
-12—Brigham Young (14) vs. Texas A&M (65) (Holiday, 1990) (21 attempts)
-12—Air Force (13) vs. Tennessee (34) (Sugar, 1971)
-11—Colorado (25) vs. Alabama (30) (Blockbuster, 1991) (30 attempts)
-8—Tulane (6) vs. Penn St. (9) (Liberty, 1979) (20 attempts)
-8—Navy (14) vs. Missouri (21) (Orange, 1961) (24 attempts)
-2—Brigham Young (46) vs. Southern Methodist (45) (Holiday, 1980) (24 attempts)
-2—Florida (18) vs. Missouri (20) (Sugar, 1966) (16 attempts)

FEWEST RUSHING YARDS, BOTH TEAMS
51—(D) Utah (16) [6] & Arizona (13) [45] (Freedom, 1994)
74—Tennessee (34) [86] & Air Force (13) [-12] (Sugar, 1971)
81—Florida St. (23) [76] & Florida (17) [5] (Sugar, Jan. 2, 1995)
81—Washington St. (10) [7] & Baylor (3) [74] (Alamo, 1994)
88—Boston College (12) [149] & Kansas St. (7) [-61] (Aloha, 1994)
137—Iowa (20) [94] & Wyoming (19) [43] (Holiday, 1987)
143—Brigham Young (31) [71] & Oklahoma (6) [72] (Copper, 1994)
145—Arkansas (10) [45] & Nebraska (7) [100] (Cotton, 1965)
147—(D) San Jose St. (37) [123] & Miami (Ohio) (7) [24] (California, 1986)

LOWEST RUSHING AVERAGE
(Minimum 20 Attempts)
-2.7—Kansas St. (7) vs. Boston College (12) (Aloha, 1994) (23 for -61 yards)
-1.6—Alabama (10) vs. Missouri (35) (Gator, 1968) (29 for -45 yards)
-1.3—Florida (24) vs. Nebraska (62) (Fiesta, 1996) (21 for -28 yards)
-0.9—Florida (6) vs. West Va. (26) (Peach, Dec. 31, 1981) (32 for -30 yards)
-0.7—Florida St. (20) vs. Wyoming (28) (Sun, 1966) (31 for -21 yards)
-0.6—Brigham Young (14) vs. Texas A&M (65) (Holiday, 1990) (21 for -12 yards)
-0.5—Navy (6) vs. Texas (28) (Cotton, 1964) (29 for -14 yards)
-0.5—Tennessee (0) vs. Texas (16) (Cotton, 1953) (29 for -14 yards)
-0.4—Colorado (25) vs. Alabama (30) (Blockbuster, 1991) (30 for -11 yards)
-0.3—Navy (14) vs. Missouri (21) (Orange, 1961) (24 for -8 yards)

RUSHING DEFENSE, FEWEST YARDS ALLOWED
-61—Boston College (12) vs. Kansas St. (7) (Aloha, 1994) (23 attempts)
-45—Missouri (35) vs. Alabama (10) (Gator, 1968) (29 attempts)
-30—West Va. (26) vs. Florida (6) (Peach, Dec. 31, 1981) (32 attempts)
-28—Nebraska (62) vs. Florida (24) (Fiesta, 1996) (21 attempts)
-21—Wyoming (28) vs. Florida St. (20) (Sun, 1966) (31 attempts)
-15—Mississippi (20) vs. LSU (0) (Sugar, 1960)
-14—Texas (28) vs. Navy (6) (Cotton, 1964) (29 attempts)
-14—Texas (16) vs. Tennessee (0) (Cotton, 1953) (29 attempts)
-12—Texas A&M (65) vs. Brigham Young (14) (Holiday, 1990) (21 attempts)
-12—Tennessee (34) vs. Air Force (13) (Sugar, 1971)
-11—Alabama (30) vs. Colorado (25) (Blockbuster, 1991) (30 attempts)
-8—Penn St. (9) vs. Tulane (6) (Liberty, 1979) (20 attempts)
-8—Missouri (21) vs. Navy (14) (Orange, 1961) (24 attempts)
-2—Southern Methodist (45) vs. Brigham Young (46) (Holiday, 1980) (24 attempts)
-2—Missouri (20) vs. Florida (18) (Sugar, 1966) (16 attempts)

Passing

MOST PASS ATTEMPTS
(Followed by Comp.-Att.-Int. and Yardage)
63—Fresno St. (30) vs. Colorado (41) (Aloha, 1993) (37-63-1, 523 yards)
63—(D) San Jose St. (25) vs. Toledo (27) (California, 1981) (43-63-5, 467 yards)
61—Oregon (20) vs. Penn St. (38) (Rose, 1995) (41-61-2, 456 yards)
61—(D) Brigham Young (16) vs. Virginia (22) (All-American, 1987) (37-61-1, 394 yards)
59—Georgia (27) vs. Virginia (34) (Peach, Dec. 30, 1995) (31-59-2, 413 yards)
59—Brigham Young (39) vs. Penn St. (50) (Holiday, 1989) (42-59-2, 576 yards)
58—Florida (28) vs. Notre Dame (39) (Sugar, 1992) (28-58-2, 370 yards)
58—Illinois (15) vs. Alabama (21) (Liberty, 1982) (35-58-7, 423 yards)
58—Richmond (49) vs. Ohio (42) (Tangerine, 1968) (39-58-2, 447 yards)
57—(D) Western Mich. (30) vs. Fresno St. (35) (California, 1988) (24-57-0, 366 yards)
56—Miami (Fla.) (13) vs. Alabama (34) (Sugar, 1993) (24-56-3, 278 yards)
56—Washington (21) vs. Maryland (20) (Aloha, 1982) (35-56-0, 369 yards)
55—Illinois (29) vs. Army (31) (Peach, 1985) (38-55-2, 401 yards)
55—Florida St. (17) vs. Penn St. (17) (Gator, 1967) (38-55-4, 363 yards)
52—Alabama (29) vs. Army (28) (John Hancock Sun, 1988) (33-52-1, 412 yards)
52—Louisiana Tech (13) vs. East Caro. (35) (Independence, 1978) (18-52-3, 263 yards)

MOST PASS ATTEMPTS, BOTH TEAMS
93—Mississippi (34) [48] & Marshall (31) [45] (Motor City, 1997) (52 completed)
92—Toledo (40) [41] & Nevada (37) [51] (OT) (Las Vegas, 1995) (50 completed)
92—Penn St. (38) [31] & Oregon (20) [61] (Rose, 1995) (61 completed)
92—Tennessee (34) [46] & Air Force (13) [46] (Sugar, 1971) (47 completed)
91—Richmond (49) [58] & Ohio (42) [33] (Tangerine, 1968) (56 completed)
90—Bowling Green (35) [41] & Nevada (34) [49] (Las Vegas, 1992) (54 completed)
90—Mississippi (20) [50] & Texas Tech (17) [40] (Independence, 1986) (48 completed)
88—Washington St. (31) [48] & Utah (28) [40] (Copper, 1992) (53 completed)
88—Washington (21) [56] & Maryland (20) [32] (Aloha, 1982) (54 completed)
86—(D) Fresno St. (35) [29] & Western Mich. (30) [57] (California, 1988) (39 completed)
86—Iowa (20) [35] & Wyoming (19) [51] (Holiday, 1987) (49 completed)
85—Ohio St. (10) [35] & Brigham Young (7) [50] (Florida Citrus, 1985) (45 completed)
85—(D) Toledo (27) [22] & San Jose St. (25) [63] (California, 1981) (54 completed)
84—Florida St. (23) [41] & Florida (17) [43] (Sugar, Jan. 2, 1995) (54 completed)
84—(D) Southern Cal (28) [44] & Utah (21) [40] (Freedom, 1993) (53 completed)
83—Southern Cal (41) [44] & Northwestern (32) [39] (Rose, 1996) (52 completed)
83—Auburn (35) [44] & Mississippi (28) [39] (Gator, Jan. 2, 1971) (50 completed)
82—(D) Fresno St. (29) [50] & Bowling Green (28) [32] (California, 1982) (53 completed)
80—Penn St. (50) [21] & Brigham Young (39) [59] (Holiday, 1989) (53 completed)
80—(D) Virginia (22) [19] & Brigham Young (16) [61] (All-American, 1987) (47 completed)
80—(D) San Jose St. (37) [39] & Miami (Ohio) (7) [41] (California, 1986) (40 completed)

MOST PASS COMPLETIONS
(Followed by Comp.-Att.-Int. and Yardage)
43—(D) San Jose St. (25) vs. Toledo (27) (California, 1981) (43-63-5, 467 yards)
42—Brigham Young (39) vs. Penn St. (50) (Holiday, 1989) (42-59-2, 576 yards)
41—Oregon (20) vs. Penn St. (38) (Rose, 1995) (41-61-2, 456 yards)
39—Richmond (49) vs. Ohio (42) (Tangerine, 1968) (39-58-2, 447 yards)
38—Illinois (29) vs. Army (31) (Peach, 1985) (38-55-2, 401 yards)
38—(D) Vanderbilt (28) vs. Air Force (36) (Hall of Fame, 1982) (38-51-3, 452 yards)
38—Florida St. (17) vs. Penn St. (17) (Gator, 1967) (38-55-4, 363 yards)
37—Fresno St. (30) vs. Colorado (41) (Aloha, 1993) (37-63-1, 523 yards)
37—(D) Brigham Young (16) vs. Virginia (22) (All-American, 1987) (37-61-1, 394 yards)
35—Brigham Young (24) vs. Michigan (17) (Holiday, 1984) (35-49-3, 371 yards)
35—Illinois (15) vs. Alabama (21) (Liberty, 1982) (35-58-7, 423 yards)
35—Washington (21) vs. Maryland (20) (Aloha, 1982) (35-56-0, 369 yards)
34—Wisconsin (37) vs. Southern Cal (42) (Rose, 1963) (34-49-3, 419 yards)
33—Alabama (29) vs. Army (28) (John Hancock Sun, 1988) (33-52-1, 412 yards)

MOST PASS COMPLETIONS, BOTH TEAMS
61—Penn St. (38) [20] & Oregon (20) [41] (Rose, 1995) (92 attempted)
56—Richmond (49) [39] & Ohio (42) [17] (Tangerine, 1968) (91 attempted)
54—Florida St. (23) [24] & Florida (17) [30] (Sugar, Jan. 2, 1995) (84 attempted)

54—Bowling Green (35) [25] & Nevada (34) [29] (Las Vegas, 1992) (90 attempted)
54—Washington (21) [35] & Maryland (20) [19] (Aloha, 1982) (88 attempted)
54—(D) Toledo (27) [11] & San Jose St. (25) [43] (California, 1981) (85 attempted)
53—(D) Southern Cal (28) [30] & Utah (21) [23] (Freedom, 1993) (84 attempted)
53—Washington St. (31) [32] & Utah (28) [21] (Copper, 1992) (88 attempted)
53—Penn St. (50) [11] & Brigham Young (39) [42] (Holiday, 1989) (80 attempted)
53—(D) Fresno St. (29) [31] & Bowling Green (28) [22] (California, 1982) (82 attempted)
52—Mississippi (34) [29] & Marshall (31) [23] (Motor City, 1997) (93 attempted)
52—Southern Cal (41) [29] & Northwestern (32) [23] (Rose, 1996) (83 attempted)
50—Kansas St. (52) [19] vs. Wyoming (17) [31] (Copper, 1993) (79 attempted)
50—Toledo (40) [23] & Nevada (37) [27] (OT) (Las Vegas, 1995) (92 attempted)
50—Auburn (35) [27] & Mississippi (28) [23] (Gator, Jan. 2, 1971) (83 attempted)
49—Iowa (20) [21] & Wyoming (19) [28] (Holiday, 1987) (86 attempted)
49—UCLA (39) [18] & Miami (Fla.) (37) [31] (Fiesta, 1985) (71 attempted)
49—(D) Air Force (36) [11] & Vanderbilt (28) [38] (Hall of Fame, 1982) (68 attempted)
48—Brigham Young (13) [29] & Iowa (13) [19] (Holiday, 1991) (72 attempted)
48—LSU (30) [20] & South Caro. (13) [28] (Gator, 1987) (79 attempted)
48—Mississippi (20) [31] & Texas Tech (17) [17] (Independence, 1986) (90 attempted)

MOST PASSING YARDS
(Followed by Comp.-Att.-Int.)

576—Brigham Young (39) vs. Penn St. (50) (Holiday, 1989) (42-59-2)
523—Fresno St. (30) vs. Colorado (41) (Aloha, 1993) (37-63-1)
492—Washington St. (31) vs. Utah (28) (Copper, 1992) (32-48-1)
485—Brigham Young (31) vs. Oklahoma (6) (Copper, 1994) (23-46-0)
469—(D) Iowa (55) vs. Texas (17) (Freedom, 1984) (30-40-0)
467—(D) San Jose St. (25) vs. Toledo (27) (California, 1981) (43-63-5)
458—Louisville (34) vs. Alabama (7) (Fiesta, 1991) (21-39-3)
456—Oregon (20) vs. Penn St. (38) (Rose, 1995) (41-61-2)
455—Florida St. (40) vs. Texas Tech (17) (Tangerine, 1977) (25-35-0)
452—(D) Vanderbilt (28) vs. Air Force (36) (Hall of Fame, 1982) (38-51-3)
449—Florida (17) vs. Florida St. (23) (Sugar, Jan. 2, 1995) (30-43-1)
447—Richmond (49) vs. Ohio (42) (Tangerine, 1968) (39-58-2)
446—Brigham Young (46) vs. Southern Methodist (45) (Holiday, 1980) (32-49-1)
442—(D) San Jose St. (48) vs. Central Mich. (24) (California, 1990) (32-43-1)
435—Southern Cal (55) vs. Texas Tech (14) (Cotton, 1995) (24-35-0)
428—Iowa (23) vs. North Caro. St. (28) (Peach, Dec. 31, 1988) (30-51-4)
423—Illinois (15) vs. Alabama (21) (Liberty, 1982) (35-58-7)
422—Florida St. (41) vs. Nebraska (17) (Fiesta, 1990) (25-41-0)
419—Wisconsin (37) vs. Southern Cal (42) (Rose, 1963) (34-49-3)
413—Georgia (27) vs. Virginia (34) (Peach, Dec. 30, 1995) (31-59-2)
412—Alabama (29) vs. Army (28) (John Hancock Sun, 1988) (33-52-1)

MOST PASSING YARDS, BOTH TEAMS

808—Washington St. (31) [492] & Utah (28) [316] (Copper, 1992) (88 attempted)
791—Penn St. (50) [215] & Brigham Young (39) [576] (Holiday, 1989) (80 attempted)
774—Florida St. (23) [325] & Florida (17) [449] (Sugar, Jan. 2, 1995) (84 attempted)
734—Florida St. (40) [455] & Texas Tech (17) [279] (Tangerine, 1977) (63 attempted)
732—(D) Toledo (27) [265] & San Jose St. (25) [467] (California, 1981) (85 attempted)
727—Southern Cal (41) [391] & Northwestern (32) [336] (Rose, 1996) (83 attempted)
708—Navy (42) [395] & California (38) [313] (Aloha, 1996) (59 attempted)
672—Southern Cal (42) [253] & Wisconsin (37) [419] (Rose, 1963) (69 attempted)
669—Mississippi (34) [332] & Marshall (31) [337] (Motor City, 1997) (93 attempted)
662—(D) San Jose St. (48) [442] & Central Mich. (24) [220] (California, 1990) (68 attempted)
658—Penn St. (38) [202] & Oregon (20) [456] (Rose, 1995) (92 attempted)
654—(D) Iowa (55) [469] & Texas (17) [185] (Freedom, 1984) (74 attempted)
648—Brigham Young (31) [485] & Oklahoma (6) [163] (Copper, 1994) (76 attempted)
647—Colorado (41) [124] & Fresno St. (30) [523] (Aloha, 1993) (78 attempted)
640—Southern Cal (55) [435] & Texas Tech (14) [205] (Cotton, 1995) (72 attempted)
631—(D) Southern Cal (28) [345] & Utah (21) [286] (Freedom, 1993) (84 attempted)
629—Florida St. (41) [422] & Nebraska (17) [207] (Fiesta, 1990) (67 attempted)
627—Georgia Tech (35) [274] & West Va. (30) [353] (Carquest, 1997) (76 attempted)
623—North Caro. St. (28) [195] & Iowa (23) [428] (Peach, Dec. 31, 1988) (74 attempted)
620—Washington (21) [369] & Maryland (20) [251] (Aloha, 1982) (88 attempted)
619—(D) Fresno St. (29) [373] & Bowling Green (28) [246] (California, 1982) (82 attempted)
611—Arizona St. (45) [250] & Florida St. (38) [361] (Fiesta, 1971) (77 attempted)
611—Mississippi (27) [273] & Arkansas (22) [338] (Sugar, 1970) (70 attempted)
607—Auburn (35) [351] & Mississippi (28) [256] (Gator, Jan. 2, 1971) (83 attempted)
606—(D) Fresno St. (35) [240] & Western Mich. (30) [366] (California, 1988) (86 attempted)

MOST PASSES HAD INTERCEPTED

8—Arizona (10) vs. Auburn (34) (Sun, 1968)
7—Illinois (15) vs. Alabama (21) (Liberty, 1982)
7—Missouri (3) vs. Penn St. (10) (Orange, 1970)
7—Texas A&M (21) vs. Alabama (29) (Cotton, 1942)
6—Georgia (6) vs. Nebraska (45) (Sun, 1969)
6—Texas Christian (26) vs. Georgia (40) (Orange, 1942)
6—Southern Methodist (0) vs. Stanford (7) (Rose, 1936)

MOST PASSES HAD INTERCEPTED, BOTH TEAMS

12—Auburn (34) [4] & Arizona (10) [8] (Sun, 1968)
10—Georgia (40) [6] & Texas Christian (26) [4] (Orange, 1942)
9—Alabama (21) [2] & Illinois (15) [7] (Liberty, 1982)
8—Ohio St. (28) [3] & Texas A&M (12) [5] (Cotton, 1987)
8—Nebraska (28) [3] & LSU (10) [5] (Sugar, 1985)
8—Penn St. (10) [1] & Missouri (3) [7] (Orange, 1970)
8—Nebraska (45) [2] & Georgia (6) [6] (Sun, 1969)
8—Texas (12) [3] & Mississippi (7) [5] (Cotton, 1962)

MOST PASSES ATTEMPTED WITHOUT AN INTERCEPTION
(Followed by Comp.-Att.-Int. and Yardage)

57—(D) Western Mich. (30) vs. Fresno St. (35) (California, 1988) (24-57-0, 366 yards)
51—Nevada (37) vs. Toledo (40) (OT) (Las Vegas, 1995) (27-51-0, 330 yards)

MOST PASSES ATTEMPTED BY BOTH TEAMS WITHOUT AN INTERCEPTION
(Followed by Comp.-Att.-Int. and Yardage)

90—Bowling Green (35) [49] & Nevada (34) [41] (Las Vegas, 1992) (54-90-0, 597 yards)

HIGHEST COMPLETION PERCENTAGE
(Minimum 10 Attempts) (Followed by Comp.-Att.-Int. and Yardage)

.929—Texas (40) vs. Missouri (27) (Cotton, 1946) (13-14-0, 234 yards)
.900—Mississippi (13) vs. Air Force (0) (Liberty, 1992) (9-10-0, 163 yards)
.897—Georgia (33) vs. Wisconsin (6) (Outback, 1998) (26-29-0, 267 yards)
.889—Texas A&M (65) vs. Brigham Young (14) (Holiday, 1990) (16-18-0, 324 yards)
.833—Alabama (13) vs. Penn St. (6) (Sugar, 1975) (10-12-0, 210 yards)
.828—Oklahoma St. (62) vs. Wyoming (14) (Holiday, 1988) (24-29-0, 378 yards)
.824—Nebraska (21) vs. North Caro. (17) (Liberty, 1977) (14-17-2, 161 yards)
.813—Texas Christian (28) vs. Syracuse (27) (Cotton, 1957) (13-16-0, 202 yards)
.800—Ohio St. (15) vs. Clemson (17) (Gator, 1978) (16-20-1, 205 yards)
.800—Georgia Tech (31) vs. Iowa St. (30) (Liberty, 1972) (12-15-1, 157 yards)
.778—Tennessee (27) vs. Indiana (22) (Peach, 1987) (21-27-0, 230 yards)
.771—Washington St. (10) vs. Baylor (3) (Alamo, 1994) (27-35-0, 286 yards)
.765—Illinois (17) vs. Hawaii (27) (Holiday, 1992) (26-34-1, 248 yards)
.765—Duke (7) vs. Arkansas (6) (Cotton, 1961) (13-17-1, 93 yards)
.763—Iowa (28) vs. UCLA (45) (Rose, 1986) (29-38-1, 319 yards)
.750—Colorado St. (35) vs. Missouri (24) (Holiday, 1997) (18-24-0, 206 yards)
.750—Kansas St. (54) vs. Colorado St. (21) (Holiday, 1995) (24-32-1, 324 yards)
.750—Oklahoma (48) vs. Virginia (14) (Gator, Dec. 29, 1991) (27-36-0, 357 yards)
.750—(D) Iowa (55) vs. Texas (17) (Freedom, 1984) (30-40-0, 469 yards)

MOST YARDS PER ATTEMPT
(Minimum 10 Attempts)

21.7—Southern Cal (47) vs. Pittsburgh (14) (Rose, 1930) (13 for 282 yards)
18.8—Navy (42) vs. California (38) (Aloha, 1996) (21 for 295 yards)
18.0—Texas A&M (65) vs. Brigham Young (14) (Holiday, 1990) (18 for 324 yards)
17.5—Alabama (13) vs. Penn St. (6) (Sugar, 1975) (12 for 210 yards)
16.7—Texas (36) vs. Tennessee (13) (Cotton, 1969) (14 for 234 yards)
16.7—Texas (40) vs. Missouri (27) (Cotton, 1946) (14 for 234 yards)
13.8—Kansas St. (35) vs. Syracuse (18) (Fiesta, 1997) (23 for 317 yards)

MOST YARDS PER COMPLETION
(Minimum 8 Completions)

35.2—Southern Cal (47) vs. Pittsburgh (14) (Rose, 1930) (8 for 282 yards)
29.3—Texas (36) vs. Tennessee (13) (Cotton, 1969) (8 for 234 yards)
29.3—Texas (28) vs. Navy (6) (Cotton, 1964) (8 for 234 yards)

FEWEST PASS ATTEMPTS

2—Air Force (38) vs. Mississippi St. (15) (Liberty, 1991) (completed 1)
2—(D) Army (10) vs. Michigan St. (6) (Cherry, 1984) (completed 1)
2—West Va. (14) vs. South Caro. (3) (Peach, 1969) (completed 1)
3—Air Force (23) vs. Ohio St. (11) (Liberty, 1990) (completed 1)
3—Oklahoma (31) vs. Nebraska (24) (Orange, 1979) (completed 2)
3—Georgia Tech (21) vs. Pittsburgh (14) (Gator, 1956) (completed 3)
3—Georgia Tech (7) vs. Pittsburgh (0) (Sugar, 1956) (completed 0)
3—Miami (Fla.) (14) vs. Clemson (0) (Gator, 1952) (completed 2)
3—Hardin-Simmons (7) vs. Second Air Force (13) (Sun, 1943) (completed 1)
3—Catholic (20) vs. Mississippi (19) (Orange, 1936) (completed 1)

FEWEST PASS ATTEMPTS, BOTH TEAMS

9—Fordham (2) [4] & Missouri (0) [5] (Sugar, 1942)
13—Colorado (27) [9] & Clemson (21) [4] (Orange, 1957)
14—Texas (16) [8] & Tennessee (0) [6] (Cotton, 1953)
15—LSU (7) [11] & Clemson (0) [4] (Sugar, 1959)
15—Utah (26) [4] & New Mexico (0) [11] (Sun, 1939)

FEWEST PASS COMPLETIONS
(Followed by Comp.-Att.-Int.)

0—Army (28) vs. Alabama (29) (John Hancock Sun, 1988) (0-6-1)
0—Missouri (35) vs. Alabama (10) (Gator, 1968) (0-6-2)
0—(D) Missouri (14) vs. Georgia Tech (10) (Bluebonnet, 1962) (0-7-2)
0—(D) New Mexico (28) vs. Western Mich. (12) (Aviation, 1961) (0-4-0)
0—Utah St. (13) vs. New Mexico St. (20) (Sun, 1960) (0-4-0)
0—Georgia Tech (7) vs. Pittsburgh (0) (Sugar, 1956) (0-3-1)
0—Arkansas (0) vs. LSU (0) (Cotton, 1947) (0-4-1)
0—Rice (8) vs. Tennessee (0) (Orange, 1947) (0-6-2)
0—Miami (Fla.) (13) vs. Holy Cross (6) (Orange, 1946) (0-10-3)
0—Fordham (2) vs. Missouri (0) (Sugar, 1942) (0-4-0)
0—Arizona St. (0) vs. Catholic (0) (Sun, 1940) (0-7-2)
0—Tulane (13) vs. Texas A&M (14) (Sugar, 1940) (0-4-0)
0—West Va. (7) vs. Texas Tech (6) (Sun, 1938) (0-7-0)

FEWEST PASS COMPLETIONS, BOTH TEAMS

3—Arizona St. (0) [0] & Catholic (0) [3] (Sun, 1940)
4—Penn St. (7) [2] & Alabama (0) [2] (Liberty, 1959)
5—Oklahoma (14) [3] & Michigan (6) [2] (Orange, 1976)
5—Kentucky (21) [2] & North Caro. (0) [3] (Peach, 1976)
5—Texas (16) [2] & Tennessee (0) [3] (Cotton, 1953)
5—Arkansas (0) [0] & LSU (0) [5] (Cotton, 1947)
5—Wake Forest (26) [1] & South Caro. (14) [4] (Gator, 1946)
5—Utah (26) [1] & New Mexico (0) [4] (Sun, 1939)

FEWEST PASSING YARDS
(Followed by Comp.-Att.-Int.)

-50—U. of Mexico (0) vs. Southwestern (Tex.) (35) (Sun, 1945) (2-9-3)
-17—Rice (8) vs. Tennessee (0) (Orange, 1947) (0-6-2)
-2—Oklahoma (40) vs. Houston (14) (Sun, 1981) (1-5-1)
0—Army (28) vs. Alabama (29) (John Hancock Sun, 1988) (0-6-1)
0—Missouri (35) vs. Alabama (10) (Gator, 1968) (0-6-2)
0—(D) Missouri (14) vs. Georgia Tech (10) (Bluebonnet, 1962) (0-7-2)
0—(D) New Mexico (28) vs. Western Mich. (12) (Aviation, 1961) (0-4-0)
0—Utah St. (13) vs. New Mexico St. (20) (Sun, 1960)
0—Georgia Tech (7) vs. Pittsburgh (0) (Sugar, 1956) (0-3-1)
0—Arkansas (0) vs. LSU (0) (Cotton, 1947) (0-4-1)
0—Miami (Fla.) (13) vs. Holy Cross (6) (Orange, 1946) (0-10-3)
0—Fordham (2) vs. Missouri (0) (Sugar, 1942) (0-4-0)
0—Tulane (13) vs. Texas A&M (14) (Sugar, 1940)
0—Arizona St. (0) vs. Catholic (0) (Sun, 1940) (0-7-2)
0—West Va. (7) vs. Texas Tech (6) (Sun, 1938) (0-7-0)
0—California (0) vs. Wash. & Jeff. (0) (Rose, 1922)
0—Oregon (6) vs. Harvard (7) (Rose, 1920)

FEWEST PASSING YARDS, BOTH TEAMS

15—Rice (8) [-17] & Tennessee (0) [32] (Orange, 1947)
16—Arkansas (0) [0] & LSU (0) [16] (Cotton, 1947)
16—Arizona St. (0) [0] & Catholic (0) [16] (Sun, 1940)
21—Fordham (2) [0] & Missouri (0) [21] (Sugar, 1942)
40—Kentucky (21) [16] vs. North Caro. (0) [24] (Peach, 1976)
52—Colorado (27) [25] & Clemson (21) [27] (Orange, 1957)
59—Miami (Fla.) (13) [0] & Holy Cross (6) [59] (Orange, 1946)
60—North Caro. (26) [10] vs. Texas (10) [50] (Sun, 1982)
68—Missouri (35) [0] & Alabama (10) [68] (Gator, 1968)
68—Penn St. (7) [41] & Alabama (0) [27] (Liberty, 1959)
74—Oklahoma (41) [23] & Wyoming (7) [51] (Fiesta, 1976)
75—Southwestern (Tex.) (7) [65] & New Mexico (0) [10] (Sun, 1944)
77—Utah (26) [18] & New Mexico (0) [59] (Sun, 1939)
78—Texas (16) [32] & Tennessee (0) [46] (Cotton, 1953)

LOWEST COMPLETION PERCENTAGE
(Followed by Comp.-Att.-Int.)

.000—Army (28) vs. Alabama (29) (John Hancock Sun, 1988) (0-6-1)
.000—Missouri (35) vs. Alabama (10) (Gator, 1968) (0-6-2)
.000—(D) Missouri (14) vs. Georgia Tech (10) (Bluebonnet, 1962) (0-7-2)
.000—(D) New Mexico (28) vs. Western Mich. (12) (Aviation, 1961) (0-4-0)
.000—Utah St. (13) vs. New Mexico St. (20) (Sun, 1960) (0-4-0)
.000—Georgia Tech (7) vs. Pittsburgh (0) (Sugar, 1956) (0-3-1)
.000—Arkansas (0) vs. LSU (0) (Cotton, 1947) (0-4-1)
.000—Rice (8) vs. Tennessee (0) (Orange, 1947) (0-6-2)
.000—Miami (Fla.) (13) vs. Holy Cross (6) (Orange, 1946) (0-10-3)
.000—Fordham (2) vs. Missouri (0) (Sugar, 1942) (0-4-0)
.000—Arizona St. (0) vs. Catholic (0) (Sun, 1940) (0-7-2)
.000—Tulane (13) vs. Texas A&M (14) (Sugar, 1940) (0-4-0)
.000—West Va. (7) vs. Texas Tech (6) (Sun, 1938) (0-7-0)

FEWEST YARDS PER PASS ATTEMPT

-5.6—U. of Mexico (0) vs. Southwestern (Tex.) (35) (Sun, 1945) (9 for -50 yards)
-2.8—Rice (8) vs. Tennessee (0) (Orange, 1947) (6 for -17 yards)
-0.4—Oklahoma (40) vs. Houston (14) (Sun, 1981) (5 for -2 yards)
0.0—Army (28) vs. Alabama (29) (John Hancock Sun, 1988) (6 for 0 yards)
0.0—Missouri (35) vs. Alabama (10) (Gator, 1968) (6 for 0 yards)
0.0—(D) Missouri (14) vs. Georgia Tech (10) (Bluebonnet, 1962) (7 for 0 yards)
0.0—(D) New Mexico (28) vs. Western Mich. (12) (Aviation, 1961) (4 for 0 yards)
0.0—Utah St. (13) vs. New Mexico St. (20) (Sun, 1960) (4 for 0 yards)
0.0—Georgia Tech (7) vs. Pittsburgh (0) (Sugar, 1956) (3 for 0 yards)
0.0—Arkansas (0) vs. LSU (0) (Cotton, 1947) (4 for 0 yards)
0.0—Miami (Fla.) (13) vs. Holy Cross (6) (Orange, 1946) (10 for 0 yards)
0.0—Fordham (2) vs. Missouri (0) (Sugar, 1942) (4 for 0 yards)
0.0—Arizona St. (0) vs. Catholic (0) (Sun, 1940) (7 for 0 yards)
0.0—Tulane (13) vs. Texas A&M (14) (Sugar, 1940) (4 for 0 yards)
0.0—West Va. (7) vs. Texas Tech (6) (Sun, 1938) (7 for 0 yards)

FEWEST YARDS PER PASS COMPLETION
(Minimum 1 completion)

-25.0—U. of Mexico (0) vs. Southwestern (Tex.) (35) (Sun, 1945) (2 for -50 yards)
-2.0—Oklahoma (40) vs. Houston (14) (Sun, 1981) (1 for -2 yards)
3.0—West Va. (14) vs. South Caro. (3) (Peach, 1969) (1 for 3 yards)
3.2—LSU (0) vs. Arkansas (0) (Cotton, 1947) (5 for 16 yards)
3.3—North Caro. (26) vs. Texas (10) (Sun, 1982) (3 for 10 yards)
3.3—New Mexico (0) vs. Southwestern (Tex.) (7) (Sun, 1944) (3 for 10 yards)
4.5—Alabama (34) vs. Miami (Fla.) (13) (Sugar, 1993) (4 for 18 yards)
4.6—Texas (14) vs. Georgia Tech (7) (Cotton, 1943) (5 for 23 yards)
4.8—UTEP (33) vs. Georgetown (20) (Sun, 1950) (5 for 24 yards)
5.3—Case Reserve (26) vs. Arizona St. (13) (Sun, 1941) (3 for 16 yards)
5.3—Arkansas (3) vs. UCLA (17) (Cotton, 1989) (4 for 21 yards)

Scoring

MOST TOUCHDOWNS

9—Texas A&M (65) vs. Brigham Young (14) (Holiday, 1990) (5 rush, 4 pass)
9—Alabama (61) vs. Syracuse (6) (Orange, 1953) (4 rush, 3 pass, 1 punt return, 1 interception return)
9—(D) Centre (63) vs. Texas Christian (7) (Fort Worth Classic, 1921) (8 rush, 1 blocked punt recovery in end zone)
8—Nebraska (62) vs. Florida (24) (Fiesta, 1996) (6 rush, 1 pass, 1 interception return)
8—Kansas St. (54) vs. Colorado St. (21) (Holiday, 1995) (4 rush, 4 pass)
8—Oklahoma St. (62) vs. Wyoming (14) (Holiday, 1988) (6 rush, 2 pass)
8—Toledo (56) vs. Davidson (33) (Tangerine, 1969) (4 rush, 3 pass, 1 fumble return)
7—Washington (51) vs. Michigan St. (23) (Aloha, 1997) (3 rush, 2 pass, 2 interception returns)
7—Texas Tech (55) vs. Air Force (41) (Copper, 1995) (6 rush, 1 pass)
7—Southern Cal (55) vs. Texas Tech (14) (Cotton, 1995) (1 rush, 5 pass, 1 interception retrun)
7—UNLV (52) vs. Central Mich. (24) (Las Vegas, 1994) (3 rush, 3 pass, 1 fumble return)
7—Kansas St. (52) vs. Wyoming (17) (Copper, 1993) (3 rush, 2 pass, 1 punt return, 1 interception return)
7—Oklahoma (48) vs. Virginia (14) (Gator, Dec. 29, 1991) (4 rush, 2 pass, 1 blocked punt return)
7—(D) Texas Tech (49) vs. Duke (21) (All-American, 1989) (6 rush, 1 pass)
7—(D) Fresno St. (51) vs. Bowling Green (7) (California, 1985) (4 rush, 3 pass)
7—(D) Iowa (55) vs. Texas (17) (Freedom, 1984) (1 rush, 6 pass)
7—(D) Houston (47) vs. Tulane (7) (Bluebonnet, 1973) (7 rush)
7—Arizona St. (49) vs. Missouri (35) (Fiesta, 1972) (5 rush, 2 pass)
7—North Caro. St. (49) vs. West Va. (13) (Peach, 1972) (4 rush, 3 pass)
7—Arizona St. (48) vs. North Caro. (26) (Peach, 1970) (6 rush, 1 pass)
7—Houston (49) vs. Miami (Ohio) (21) (Tangerine, 1962) (4 rush, 2 pass, 1 punt return)
7—Oklahoma (48) vs. Duke (21) (Orange, 1958) (3 rush, 2 pass, 1 pass interception return, 1 intercepted lateral return)
7—UTEP (47) vs. Florida St. (20) (Sun, 1955) (4 rush, 3 pass)
7—Michigan (49) vs. Southern Cal (0) (Rose, 1948) (3 rush, 4 pass)
7—Illinois (45) vs. UCLA (14) (Rose, 1947) (5 rush, 2 pass interception returns)

MOST TOUCHDOWNS, BOTH TEAMS

13—Texas Tech (55) [7] & Air Force (41) [6] (Copper, 1995)
13—Richmond (49) [7] & Ohio (42) [6] (Tangerine, 1968)
11—Navy (42) [6] & California (38) [5] (Aloha, 1996)
11—Nebraska (62) [8] & Florida (24) [3] (Fiesta, 1996)
11—Kansas St. (54) [8] & Colorado St. (21) [3] (Holiday, 1995)
11—Washington (46) [6] & Iowa (34) [5] (Rose, 1991)
11—Texas A&M (65) [9] & Brigham Young (14) [2] (Holiday, 1990)
11—Penn St. (50) [6] & Brigham Young (39) [5] (Holiday, 1989)
11—Arizona St. (49) [7] & Missouri (35) [4] (Fiesta, 1971)
11—Arizona St. (48) [7] & North Caro. (26) [4] (Peach, 1970)
11—Southern Cal (42) [6] & Wisconsin (37) [5] (Rose, 1963)
10—Washington (51) [7] & Michigan St. (23) [3] (Aloha, 1997)
10—UNLV (52) [7] & Central Mich. (24) [3] (Las Vegas, 1994)
10—Utah St. (42) [6] & Ball St. (33) [4] (Las Vegas, 1993)
10—East Caro. (37) [5] & North Caro. St. (34) [5] (Peach, 1992)
10—(D) Texas Tech (49) [7] & Duke (21) [3] (All-American, 1989)
10—Mississippi (42) [6] & Air Force (29) [4] (Liberty, 1989)
10—Oklahoma St. (62) [8] & Wyoming (14) [2] (Holiday, 1988)
10—Boston College (45) [6] & Houston (28) [4] (Cotton, 1985)
10—Colorado (47) [6] & Alabama (33) [4] (Liberty, 1969)
10—(D) Nebraska (36) [5] & Miami (Fla.) (34) [5] (Gotham, 1962)
10—UTEP (47) [7] & Florida St. (20) [3] (Sun, 1955)
10—Alabama (61) [9] & Syracuse (6) [1] (Orange, 1953)

MOST TOUCHDOWNS RUSHING

8—(D) Centre (63) vs. Texas Christian (7) (Fort Worth Classic, 1921)
7—(D) Houston (47) vs. Tulane (7) (Bluebonnet, 1973)
6—Nebraska (42) vs. Tennessee (17) (Orange, 1998)
6—Navy (42) vs. California (38) (Aloha, 1996)
6—Nebraska (62) vs. Florida (24) (Fiesta, 1996)
6—Texas Tech (55) vs. Air Force (41) (Copper, 1995)
6—Air Force (41) vs. Texas Tech (55) (Copper, 1995)
6—(D) Texas Tech (49) vs. Duke (21) (All-American, 1989)
6—Oklahoma St. (62) vs. Wyoming (14) (Holiday, 1988)
6—Oklahoma (42) vs. Arkansas (8) (Orange, 1987)
6—Ohio St. (47) vs. Brigham Young (17) (Holiday, 1982)
6—Oklahoma St. (49) vs. Brigham Young (21) (Tangerine, 1976)
6—Arizona St. (48) vs. North Caro. (26) (Peach, 1970)
6—Michigan (49) vs. Stanford (0) (Rose, 1902)

MOST TOUCHDOWNS RUSHING, BOTH TEAMS

12—Texas Tech (55) [6] & Air Force (41) [6] (Copper, 1995)

9—Arizona St. (48) [6] & North Caro. (26) [3] (Peach, 1970)
8—Oklahoma St. (62) [6] & Wyoming (14) [2] (Holiday, 1988)
8—Colorado (47) [5] & Alabama (33) [3] (Liberty, 1969)
7—Navy (42) [6] & California (38) [1] (Aloha, 1996)
7—Nebraska (62) [6] & Florida (24) [1] (Fiesta, 1996)
7—Kansas St. (54) [4] & Colorado St. (21) [3] (Holiday, 1995)
7—Oklahoma (42) [6] & Arkansas (8) [1] (Orange, 1987)
7—Oklahoma St. (35) [4] & West Va. (33) [3] (John Hancock Sun, 1987)
7—UCLA (45) [5] & Iowa (28) [2] (Rose, 1986)
7—Oklahoma St. (49) [6] & Brigham Young (21) [1] (Tangerine, 1976)
7—Arizona St. (49) [5] & Missouri (35) [2] (Fiesta, 1972)
7—Penn St. (41) [5] & Oregon (12) [2] (Liberty, 1960)

MOST TOUCHDOWNS PASSING
6—(D) Iowa (55) vs. Texas (17) (Freedom, 1984)
5—Southern Cal (55) vs. Texas Tech (14) (Cotton, 1995)
5—Florida St. (41) vs. Nebraska (17) (Fiesta, 1990)
5—Florida St. (36) vs. Oklahoma (19) (Gator, Jan. 2, 1965)
4—Kansas St. (35) vs. Syracuse (18) (Fiesta, 1997)
4—Florida St. (31) vs. Notre Dame (26) (Orange, 1996)
4—Penn St. (43) vs. Auburn (14) (Outback, 1996)
4—Kansas St. (54) vs. Colorado St. (21) (Holiday, 1995)
4—East Caro. (37) vs. North Caro. St. (34) (Peach, 1992)
4—Miami (Fla.) (46) vs. Texas (3) (Cotton, 1991)
4—Michigan (35) vs. Mississippi (3) (Gator, Jan. 1, 1991)
4—Texas A&M (65) vs. Brigham Young (14) (Holiday, 1990)
4—UCLA (45) vs. Illinois (9) (Rose, 1984)
4—Purdue (28) vs. Missouri (25) (Liberty, 1980)
4—Pittsburgh (34) vs. Clemson (3) (Gator, 1977)
4—Florida St. (40) vs. Texas Tech (17) (Tangerine, 1977)
4—Davidson (33) vs. Toledo (56) (Tangerine, 1969)
4—Richmond (49) vs. Ohio (42) (Tangerine, 1968)
4—Ohio (42) vs. Richmond (49) (Tangerine, 1968)
4—Southern Cal (42) vs. Wisconsin (37) (Rose, 1963)
4—Michigan (49) vs. Southern Cal (0) (Rose, 1948)
4—Georgia (40) vs. Texas Christian (26) (Orange, 1942)
4—Southern Cal (47) vs. Pittsburgh (14) (Rose, 1930)

MOST TOUCHDOWNS PASSING, BOTH TEAMS
8—(D) Iowa (55) [6] & Texas (17) [2] (Freedom, 1984)
8—Richmond (49) [4] & Ohio (42) [4] (Tangerine, 1968)
7—Florida St. (31) [4] & Notre Dame (26) [3] (Orange, 1996)
7—East Caro. (37) [4] & North Caro. St. (34) [3] (Peach, 1992)
7—Toledo (56) [3] & Davidson (33) [4] (Tangerine, 1969)
7—Georgia (40) [4] & Texas Christian (26) [3] (Orange, 1942)
6—Mississippi (34) [3] & Marshall (31) [3] (Motor City, 1997)
6—Southern Cal (55) [5] & Texas Tech (14) [1] (Cotton, 1995)
6—Kansas (51) [3] & UCLA (30) [3] (Aloha, 1995)
6—Utah St. (42) [3] & Ball St. (33) [3] (Las Vegas, 1993)
6—Miami (Fla.) (33) [3] & Alabama (25) [3] (Sugar, 1990)
6—Florida St. (41) [5] & Nebraska (17) [1] (Fiesta, 1990)
6—Texas A&M (65) [4] & Brigham Young (14) [2] (Holiday, 1990)
6—Florida St. (36) [5] & Oklahoma (19) [1] (Gator, Jan. 2, 1965)
6—Southern Cal (42) [4] & Wisconsin (37) [2] (Rose, 1963)

MOST FIELD GOALS MADE
5—Texas A&M (22) vs. Michigan (20) (Alamo, 1995) (27, 49, 47, 31, 37 yards)
5—Mississippi St. (24) vs. North Caro. St. (28) (Peach, Jan. 1, 1995) (37, 21, 29, 36, 30 yards)
5—Florida (28) vs. Notre Dame (39) (Sugar, 1992) (26, 24, 36, 37, 24 yards)
5—Maryland (23) vs. Tennessee (30) (Florida Citrus, 1983) (18, 48, 31, 22, 26 yards)
4—East Caro. (19) vs. Stanford (13) (Liberty, 1995) (46, 26, 41, 34 yards)
4—Oklahoma (25) vs. Penn St. (10) (Orange, 1986) (26, 31, 21, 22 yards)
4—North Caro. (26) vs. Texas (10) (Sun, 1982) (53, 47, 24, 42 yards)
4—Texas A&M (33) vs. Oklahoma St. (16) (Independence, 1981) (33, 32, 50, 18 yards)
4—West Va. (26) vs. Florida (6) (Peach, Dec. 31, 1981) (35, 42, 49, 24 yards)
4—Missouri (19) vs. Southern Miss. (17) (Tangerine, 1981) (45, 41, 30, 28 yards)
4—Nebraska (45) vs. Georgia (6) (Sun, 1969) (50, 32, 42, 37 yards)
4—Alabama (12) vs. Mississippi (7) (Sugar, 1964) (46, 31, 34, 48 yards)

MOST FIELD GOALS MADE, BOTH TEAMS
7—Texas A&M (22) [5] & Michigan (20) [2] (Alamo, 1995)
7—North Caro. St. (28) [2] & Mississippi St. (24) [5] (Peach, Jan. 1, 1995)
6—Notre Dame (39) [1] & Florida (28) [5] (Sugar, 1992)
6—Syracuse (16) [3] & Auburn (16) [3] (Sugar, 1988)
6—Tennessee (30) [1] & Maryland (23) [5] (Florida Citrus, 1983)
5—LSU (27) [2] & Notre Dame (9) [3] (Independence, 1997)
5—Penn St. (50) [3] & Brigham Young (39) [2] (Holiday, 1989)
5—Oklahoma (25) [4] & Penn St. (10) [1] (Orange, 1986)
5—North Caro. (26) [4] & Texas (10) [1] (Sun, 1982)
5—Texas A&M (33) [4] & Oklahoma St. (16) [1] (Independence, 1981)
5—Missouri (19) [4] & Southern Miss. (17) [1] (Tangerine, 1981)
5—Penn St. (9) [3] & Tulane (6) [2] (Liberty, 1979)
5—Penn St. (30) [3] & Texas (6) [2] (Cotton, 1972)

MOST POINTS, WINNING TEAM
65—Texas A&M vs. Brigham Young (14) (Holiday, 1990)
62—Nebraska vs. Florida (24) (Fiesta, 1996)
62—Oklahoma St. vs. Wyoming (14) (Holiday, 1988)
61—Alabama vs. Syracuse (6) (Orange, 1953)
56—Toledo vs. Davidson (33) (Tangerine, 1969)
55—Texas Tech vs. Air Force (41) (Copper, 1995)
55—Southern Cal vs. Texas Tech (14) (Cotton, 1995)
55—(D) Iowa vs. Texas (17) (Freedom, 1984)
54—Kansas St. vs. Colorado St. (21) (Holiday, 1995)
52—Florida vs. Florida St. (20) (Sugar, 1997)
52—UNLV vs. Central Mich. (24) (Las Vegas, 1994)
52—Kansas St. vs. Wyoming (17) (Copper, 1993)
51—Washington vs. Michigan St. (23) (Aloha, 1997)
51—Kansas vs. UCLA (30) (Aloha, 1995)
51—(D) Fresno St. vs. Bowling Green (7) (California, 1985)
50—Penn St. vs. Brigham Young (39) (Holiday, 1989)
49—(D) Texas Tech vs. Duke (21) (All-American, 1989)
49—Oklahoma St. vs. Brigham Young (21) (Tangerine, 1976)
49—North Caro. St. vs. West Va. (13) (Peach, 1972)
49—Arizona St. vs. Missouri (35) (Fiesta, 1972)
49—Richmond vs. Ohio (42) (Tangerine, 1968)
49—Michigan vs. Southern Cal (0) (Rose, 1948)

MOST POINTS, LOSING TEAM
45—Southern Methodist vs. Brigham Young (46) (Holiday, 1980)
42—Ohio vs. Richmond (49) (Tangerine, 1968)
41—Air Force vs. Texas Tech (55) (Copper, 1995)
39—Brigham Young vs. Penn St. (50) (Holiday, 1989)
38—California vs. Navy (42) (Aloha, 1996)
38—San Diego St. vs. Iowa (39) (Holiday, 1986)
38—Florida St. vs. Arizona St. (45) (Fiesta, 1971)
37—Nevada vs. Toledo (40) (OT) (Las Vegas, 1995)
37—Miami (Fla.) vs. UCLA (39) (Fiesta, 1985)
37—Brigham Young vs. Indiana (38) (Holiday, 1979)
37—Wisconsin vs. Southern Cal (42) (Rose, 1963)
36—Washington St. vs. Brigham Young (38) (Holiday, 1981)
35—Oregon vs. Wake Forest (39) (Independence, 1992)
35—Missouri vs. Arizona St. (49) (Fiesta, 1972)
34—Nevada vs. Bowling Green (35) (Las Vegas, 1992)
34—North Caro. St. vs. East Caro. (37) (Peach, 1992)
34—Iowa vs. Washington (46) (Rose, 1991)
34—Houston vs. Notre Dame (35) (Cotton, 1979)
34—(D) Miami (Fla.) vs. Nebraska (36) (Gotham, 1962)

MOST POINTS, BOTH TEAMS
96—Texas Tech (55) & Air Force (41) (Copper, 1995)
91—Brigham Young (46) & Southern Methodist (45) (Holiday, 1980)
91—Richmond (49) & Ohio (42) (Tangerine, 1968)
89—Penn St. (50) & Brigham Young (39) (Holiday, 1989)
89—Toledo (56) & Davidson (33) (Tangerine, 1969)
86—Nebraska (62) & Florida (24) (Fiesta, 1996)
84—Arizona St. (49) & Missouri (35) (Fiesta, 1972)
83—Arizona St. (45) & Florida St. (38) (Fiesta, 1971)
81—Kansas (51) & UCLA (30) (Aloha, 1995)
80—Navy (42) vs. California (38) (Aloha, 1996)
80—Washington (46) & Iowa (34) (Rose, 1991)
80—Colorado (47) & Alabama (33) (Liberty, 1969)
79—Texas A&M (65) & Brigham Young (14) (Holiday, 1990)
79—Southern Cal (42) & Wisconsin (37) (Rose, 1963)
77—Toledo (40) & Nevada (37) (OT) (Las Vegas, 1995)
77—Iowa (39) & San Diego St. (38) (Holiday, 1986)
76—Tennessee (48) vs. Northwestern (28) (Florida Citrus, 1997)
76—UNLV (52) & Central Mich. (24) (Las Vegas, 1994)
76—Oklahoma St. (62) & Wyoming (14) (Holiday, 1988)
76—UCLA (39) & Miami (Fla.) (37) (Fiesta, 1985)
75—Kansas St. (54) & Colorado St. (21) (Holiday, 1995)
75—Utah St. (42) & Ball St. (33) (Las Vegas, 1993)
75—Indiana (38) & Brigham Young (37) (Holiday, 1979)
75—Houston (47) & Miami (Ohio) (28) (Tangerine, 1962)

LARGEST MARGIN OF VICTORY
55—Alabama (61) vs. Syracuse (6) (Orange, 1953)
51—Texas A&M (65) vs. Brigham Young (14) (Holiday, 1990)
48—Oklahoma St. (62) vs. Wyoming (14) (Holiday, 1988)
44—(D) Fresno St. (51) vs. Bowling Green (7) (California, 1985)
43—Miami (Fla.) (46) vs. Texas (3) (Cotton, 1991)
42—Texas (42) vs. Maryland (0) (Sun, 1978)
41—Syracuse (41) vs. Clemson (0) (Gator, 1996)
41—Southern Cal (55) vs. Texas Tech (14) (Cotton, 1995)
40—(D) Houston (47) vs. Tulane (7) (Bluebonnet, 1973)
39—North Caro. (42) vs. Virginia Tech (3) (Gator, 1998)
39—Nebraska (45) vs. Georgia (6) (Sun, 1969)
38—Stanford (38) vs. Michigan St. (0) (Sun, 1996)
38—Nebraska (62) vs. Florida (24) (Fiesta, 1996)
38—(D) Iowa (55) vs. Texas (17) (Freedom, 1984)
36—North Caro. St. (49) vs. West Va. (13) (Peach, 1972)
35—Michigan (42) vs. North Caro. St. (7) (Hall of Fame, 1994)
35—Kansas St. (52) vs. Wyoming (17) (Copper, 1993)

35—(D) Houston (35) vs. Navy (0) (Garden State, 1980)
35—North Caro. (35) vs. Air Force (0) (Gator, 1963)
35—Oklahoma (35) vs. LSU (0) (Sugar, 1950)
35—Southwestern (Tex.) (35) vs. U. of Mexico (0) (Sun, 1945)

FEWEST POINTS, WINNING TEAM
2—Fordham vs. Missouri (0) (Sugar, 1942)
3—Tennessee vs. Texas A&M (0) (Gator, 1957)
3—Texas Christian vs. LSU (2) (Sugar, 1936)
6—UCLA vs. Illinois (3) (John Hancock, 1991)
6—Oregon St. vs. Villanova (0) (Liberty, 1962)
6—Tulsa vs. Texas Tech (0) (Sun, 1942)
6—Clemson vs. Boston College (3) (Cotton, 1940)
6—Auburn vs. Michigan St. (0) (Orange, 1938)
6—Santa Clara vs. LSU (0) (Sugar, 1938)

FEWEST POINTS, LOSING TEAM
0—By many teams

FEWEST POINTS, BOTH TEAMS
0—Air Force (0) & Texas Christian (0) (Cotton, 1959)
0—Arkansas (0) & LSU (0) (Cotton, 1947)
0—Arizona St. (0) & Catholic (0) (Sun, 1940)
0—California (0) & Wash. & Jeff. (0) (Rose, 1922)

MOST POINTS SCORED IN ONE HALF
45—Oklahoma St. (62) vs. Wyoming (14) (Holiday, 1988) (2nd half)
42—Toledo (56) vs. Davidson (33) (Tangerine, 1969) (1st half)
40—Alabama (61) vs. Syracuse (6) (Orange, 1953) (2nd half)
38—Penn St. (50) vs. Brigham Young (39) (Holiday, 1989) (2nd half)
38—Penn St. (41) vs. Baylor (20) (Cotton, 1975) (2nd half)
38—Mississippi (41) vs. Georgia Tech (18) (Peach, 1971) (1st half)
37—Texas A&M (65) vs. Brigham Young (14) (Holiday, 1990) (1st half)
35—California (38) vs. Navy (42) (Aloha, 1996) (1st half)
35—Nebraska (62) vs. Florida (24) (Fiesta, 1996) (1st half)
35—Tennessee (45) vs. Virginia Tech (23) (Gator, 1994) (1st half)
35—Penn St. (42) vs. Tennessee (17) (Fiesta, 1992) (2nd half)
35—Southern Cal (42) vs. Ohio St. (17) (Rose, 1973) (2nd half)
35—North Caro. St. (49) vs. West Va. (13) (Peach, 1972) (2nd half)
35—Houston (49) vs. Miami (Ohio) (21) (Tangerine, 1962) (1st half)
34—Kansas (51) vs. UCLA (30) (Aloha, 1995) (2nd half)
34—Southern Cal (55) vs. Texas Tech (14) (Cotton, 1995) (1st half)
34—Oklahoma (48) vs. Virginia (14) (Gator, Dec. 29, 1991) (1st half)
34—Purdue (41) vs. Georgia Tech (21) (Peach, 1978) (1st half)
34—Oklahoma (48) vs. Duke (21) (Orange, 1958) (2nd half)
34—UTEP (47) vs. Florida St. (20) (Sun, 1955) (1st half)

MOST POINTS SCORED IN ONE HALF, BOTH TEAMS
64—Kansas (51) [34] & UCLA (30) [30] (Aloha, 1995) (2nd half)
64—Penn St. (50) [38] & Brigham Young (39) [26] (Holiday, 1989) (2nd half)
63—Navy (42) [28] vs. California (38) [35] (Aloha, 1996) (1st half)
54—Utah St. (42) [21] & Ball St. (33) [33] (Las Vegas, 1993) (2nd half)
52—Tennessee (48) [31] vs. Northwestern (28) [21] (Florida Citrus, 1997) (1st half)
52—Texas Tech (55) [24] & Air Force (41) [28] (Copper, 1995) (2nd half)
52—Oklahoma St. (62) [45] & Wyoming (14) [7] (Holiday, 1988) (2nd half)
51—Penn St. (41) [38] & Baylor (20) [13] (Cotton, 1975) (2nd half)
49—Brigham Young (46) [33] & Southern Methodist (45) [16] (Holiday, 1980) (2nd half)
49—(D) Houston (31) [28] & North Caro. St. (31) [21] (Bluebonnet, 1974) (2nd half)
49—Arizona St. (49) [21] & Missouri (35) [28] (Fiesta, 1972) (2nd half)
49—Arizona St. (45) [21] & Florida St. (38) [28] (Fiesta, 1971) (1st half)
49—Toledo (56) [42] & Davidson (33) [7] (Tangerine, 1969) (1st half)
49—Richmond (49) [28] & Ohio (42) [21] (Tangerine, 1968) (1st half)
48—Oklahoma (48) [34] & Duke (21) [14] (Orange, 1958) (2nd half)
47—Arizona St. (48) [21] & North Caro. (26) [26] (Peach, 1970) (1st half)
45—Colorado (33) [24] vs. Washington (21) [21] (Holiday, 1996) (1st half)
45—LSU (45) [21] & Michigan St. (26) [24] (Independence, 1995) (1st half)
45—Tennessee (45) [35] & Virginia Tech (23) [10] (Gator, 1994) (1st half)
45—Boston College (45) [31] & Houston (28) [14] (Cotton, 1985) (1st half)
45—Southern Cal (42) [35] & Ohio St. (17) [10] (Rose, 1973) (2nd half)

MOST POINTS SCORED IN ONE QUARTER
31—(D) Iowa (55) vs. Texas (17) (Freedom, 1984) (3rd quarter)
30—Oklahoma (40) vs. Houston (14) (Sun, 1981) (4th quarter)
29—Nebraska (62) vs. Florida (24) (Fiesta, 1996) (2nd quarter)
28—Southern Cal (55) vs. Texas Tech (14) (Cotton, 1995) (1st quarter)
28—Oklahoma St. (62) vs. Wyoming (14) (Holiday, 1988) (3rd quarter)
28—Missouri (34) vs. Auburn (17) (Sun, 1973) (2nd quarter)
28—Mississippi (41) vs. Georgia Tech (18) (Peach, 1971) (2nd quarter)
28—Toledo (56) vs. Davidson (33) (Tangerine, 1969) (2nd quarter)
28—Houston (49) vs. Miami (Ohio) (21) (Tangerine, 1962) (2nd quarter)
27—Penn St. (43) vs. Auburn (14) (Outback, 1996) (3rd quarter)
27—Oklahoma (48) vs. Virginia (14) (Gator, Dec. 29, 1991) (2nd quarter)
27—Brigham Young (46) vs. Southern Methodist (45) (Holiday, 1980) (4th quarter)
27—Oklahoma (48) vs. Duke (21) (Orange, 1958) (4th quarter)
27—UTEP (47) vs. Florida St. (20) (Sun, 1955) (2nd quarter)
27—Illinois (40) vs. Stanford (7) (Rose, 1952) (4th quarter)
26—North Caro. (26) vs. Arizona St. (48) (Peach, 1970) (2nd quarter)
25—Louisville (34) vs. Alabama (7) (Fiesta, 1991) (1st quarter)

MOST POINTS SCORED IN ONE QUARTER, BOTH TEAMS
43—Navy (42) [21] vs. California (38) [22] (Aloha, 1996) (2nd quarter)
40—Arizona St. (48) [14] & North Caro. (26) [26] (Peach, 1970) (2nd quarter)
38—Missouri (34) [28] & Auburn (17) [10] (Sun, 1973) (2nd quarter)
37—Kansas (51) [14] & UCLA (30) [23] (Aloha, 1995) (4th quarter)
37—Oklahoma (40) [30] & Houston (14) [7] (Sun, 1981) (4th quarter)
35—Kansas St. (54) [21] & Colorado St. (21) [14] (Holiday, 1995) (3rd quarter)
35—Oklahoma St. (62) [28] & Wyoming (14) [7] (Holiday, 1988) (3rd quarter)
35—Oklahoma St. (49) [21] & Brigham Young (21) [14] (Tangerine, 1976) (2nd quarter)
35—(D) Houston (31) [21] & North Caro. St. (31) [14] (Bluebonnet, 1974) (4th quarter)
35—Arizona St. (49) [21] & Missouri (35) [14] (Fiesta, 1972) (4th quarter)
35—Richmond (49) [21] & Ohio (42) [14] (Tangerine, 1968) (2nd quarter)
34—Oklahoma (48) [27] & Virginia (14) [7] (Gator, Dec. 29, 1991) (2nd quarter)
34—Penn St. (50) [21] & Brigham Young (39) [13] (Holiday, 1989) (4th quarter)
34—Brigham Young (46) [27] & Southern Methodist (45) [7] (Holiday, 1980) (4th quarter)
34—Penn St. (42) [18] & Arizona St. (30) [16] (Fiesta, 1977) (4th quarter)
34—Mississippi (41) [28] & Georgia Tech (18) [6] (Peach, 1971) (2nd quarter)
34—Oklahoma (48) [27] & Duke (21) [7] (Orange, 1958) (4th quarter)

First Downs

MOST FIRST DOWNS
36—Oklahoma (48) vs. Virginia (14) (Gator, Dec. 29, 1991) (16 rush, 18 pass, 2 penalty)
35—Michigan (35) vs. Mississippi (3) (Gator, Jan. 1, 1991) (20 rush, 14 pass, 1 penalty)
35—Brigham Young (39) vs. Penn St. (50) (Holiday, 1989) (8 rush, 27 pass, 0 penalty)
34—Fresno St. (30) vs. Colorado (41) (Aloha, 1993) (4 rush, 25 pass, 5 penalty)
34—Oklahoma St. (62) vs. Wyoming (14) (Holiday, 1988) (15 rush, 17 pass, 2 penalty)
34—(D) Miami (Fla.) (34) vs. Nebraska (36) (Gotham, 1962)
33—Toledo (40) vs. Nevada (37) (OT) (Las Vegas, 1995) (19 rush, 12 pass, 2 penalty)
33—Arizona St. (49) vs. Missouri (35) (Fiesta, 1972) (22 rush, 11 pass, 0 penalty)
32—Brigham Young (24) vs. Michigan (17) (Holiday, 1984)
32—Richmond (49) vs. Ohio (42) (Tangerine, 1968) (8 rush, 24 pass, 0 penalty)
32—Wisconsin (37) vs. Southern Cal (42) (Rose, 1963) (7 rush, 23 pass, 2 penalty)
31—UCLA (16) vs. Wisconsin (21) (Rose, 1994)
31—Arkansas (27) vs. Tennessee (31) (Cotton, 1990) (21 rush, 10 pass, 0 penalty)
31—Florida St. (34) vs. Oklahoma St. (23) (Gator, 1985) (10 rush, 21 pass, 0 penalty)
31—Brigham Young (37) vs. Indiana (38) (Holiday, 1979) (9 rush, 21 pass, 1 penalty)
31—(D) Purdue (27) vs. Tennessee (22) (Bluebonnet, 1979)
31—(D) Houston (26) vs. Dayton (21) (Salad, 1952) (25 rush, 6 pass, 0 penalty)

MOST FIRST DOWNS, BOTH TEAMS
61—Penn St. (50) [26] & Brigham Young (39) [35] (Holiday, 1989)
56—Toledo (40) [33] & Nevada (37) [23] (OT) (Las Vegas, 1995)
56—Mississippi (42) [30] & Air Force (29) [26] (Liberty, 1989)
55—Michigan (35) [35] & Mississippi (3) [20] (Gator, Jan. 1, 1991)
54—UCLA (45) [29] & Iowa (28) [25] (Rose, 1986)
54—Florida St. (34) [31] & Oklahoma St. (23) [23] (Gator, 1985)
53—Texas Tech (55) [28] & Air Force (41) [25] (Copper, 1995)
53—Colorado (41) [19] & Fresno St. (30) [34] (Aloha, 1993)
53—Tennessee (23) [28] & Virginia (22) [25] (Sugar, 1991)
53—Colorado (47) [29] & Alabama (33) [24] (Liberty, 1969)
52—Mississippi (34) [29] & Marshall (31) [23] (Motor City, 1997)
52—Georgia Tech (35) [28] & West Va. (30) [24] (Carquest, 1997)
52—Wisconsin (21) [21] & UCLA (16) [31] (Rose, 1994)
52—Notre Dame (39) [23] & Florida (28) [29] (Sugar, 1992)
52—Indiana (38) [21] & Brigham Young (37) [31] (Holiday, 1979)
51—Tennessee (48) [29] vs. Northwestern (28) [22] (Florida Citrus, 1997)
51—Texas (35) & North Caro. (31) (Sun, 1994)
51—(D) Arkansas (28) [28] & Florida (24) [23] (Bluebonnet, 1982)
50—(D) Toledo (27) [21] & San Jose St. (25) [29] (California, 1981)
50—Texas (21) [25] & Notre Dame (17) [25] (Cotton, 1970)

MOST FIRST DOWNS RUSHING
26—Oklahoma (40) vs. Auburn (22) (Sugar, Jan. 1, 1972)
25—(D) Houston (26) vs. Dayton (21) (Salad, 1952)
24—Colorado (47) vs. Alabama (33) (Liberty, 1969)
23—Georgia Tech (31) vs. Texas Tech (21) (Gator, Dec. 31, 1965)
22—Syracuse (30) vs. Houston (17) (Liberty, 1996)
22—(D) Arkansas (28) vs. Florida (24) (Bluebonnet, 1982)
22—Oklahoma (41) vs. Wyoming (7) (Fiesta, 1976)
22—Arizona St. (49) vs. Missouri (35) (Fiesta, 1972)
21—Nebraska (62) vs. Florida (24) (Fiesta, 1996)
21—Arkansas (27) vs. Tennessee (31) (Cotton, 1990)
21—Florida St. (7) vs. Oklahoma (24) (Orange, 1980)
21—(D) Houston (35) vs. Navy (0) (Garden State, 1980)
21—Mississippi St. (26) vs. North Caro. (24) (Sun, 1974)
21—Missouri (35) vs. Alabama (10) (Gator, 1968)

MOST FIRST DOWNS RUSHING, BOTH TEAMS
36—Miami (Fla.) (46) [16] & Texas (3) [20] (Cotton, 1991)
36—Colorado (47) [24] & Alabama (33) [12] (Liberty, 1969)
32—Texas Tech (55) [15] & Air Force (41) [17] (Copper, 1995)
32—Tennessee (31) [11] & Arkansas (27) [21] (Cotton, 1990)
32—Oklahoma (41) [22] & Wyoming (7) [10] (Fiesta, 1976)
32—Arizona St. (49) [22] & Missouri (35) [10] (Fiesta, 1972)

32—Texas (21) [19] & Notre Dame (17) [13] (Cotton, 1970)
31—Air Force (38) [18] & Mississippi St. (15) [13] (Liberty, 1991)

MOST FIRST DOWNS PASSING

27—Brigham Young (39) vs. Penn St. (50) (Holiday, 1989)
25—Fresno St. (30) vs. Colorado (41) (Aloha, 1993)
24—Richmond (49) vs. Ohio (42) (Tangerine, 1968)
23—Tennessee (48) vs. Northwestern (28) (Florida Citrus, 1997)
23—(D) San Jose St. (25) vs. Toledo (27) (California, 1981)
23—Wisconsin (37) vs. Southern Cal (42) (Rose, 1963)
21—Southern Cal (41) vs. Northwestern (32) (Rose, 1996)
21—(D) Fresno St. (29) vs. Bowling Green (28) (California, 1982)
21—Brigham Young (46) vs. Southern Methodist (45) (Holiday, 1980)
21—Brigham Young (37) vs. Indiana (38) (Holiday, 1979)
20—Nevada (18) vs. Ball St. (15) (Las Vegas, 1996)
20—Mississippi (20) vs. Texas Tech (17) (Independence, 1986)
20—Brigham Young (24) vs. Michigan (17) (Holiday, 1984)
20—(D) Vanderbilt (28) vs. Air Force (36) (Hall of Fame, 1982)
19—Brigham Young (21) vs. Ohio St. (28) (Holiday, 1993)
19—(D) Oregon (31) vs. Colorado St. (32) (Freedom, 1990)
19—Florida St. (31) vs. Nebraska (28) (Fiesta, 1988)
19—Florida St. (34) vs. Oklahoma (23) (Gator, 1985)
19—Illinois (29) vs. Army (31) (Peach, 1985)

MOST FIRST DOWNS PASSING, BOTH TEAMS

36—Tennessee (48) [23] vs. Northwestern (28) [13] (Florida Citrus, 1997)
32—Southern Cal (41) [21] & Northwestern (32) [11] (Rose, 1996)
30—Georgia Tech (35) [15] & West Va. (30) [15] (Carquest, 1997)
30—Colorado (41) [5] & Fresno St. (30) [25] (Aloha, 1993)
30—(D) Fresno St. (29) [21] & Bowling Green (28) [9] (California, 1982)
30—Richmond (49) [24] & Ohio (42) [6] (Tangerine, 1968)
29—Navy (42) [12] vs. California (38) [17] (Aloha, 1996)
29—Mississippi (42) [17] & Air Force (29) [12] (Liberty, 1989)
29—Indiana (38) [8] & Brigham Young (37) [21] (Holiday, 1979)
28—Ohio St. (28) [12] & Pittsburgh (23) [16] (Fiesta, 1984)
27—Florida St. (23) [12] & Florida (17) [15] (Sugar, Jan. 2, 1995)
27—Brigham Young (31) [18] & Oklahoma (6) [9] (Copper, 1994)
27—Arizona St. (45) [13] & Florida St. (38) [14] (Fiesta, 1971)
26—Boston College (31) [16] & Virginia (13) [10] (Carquest, 1994)
26—(D) Southern Cal (28) [15] & Utah (21) [11] (Freedom, 1993)
26—Brigham Young (24) [20] & Michigan (17) [6] (Holiday, 1984)
26—Washington (21) [15] & Maryland (20) [11] (Aloha, 1982)
26—(D) Air Force (36) [6] & Vanderbilt (28) [20] (Hall of Fame, 1982)
25—Nevada (18) [20] vs. Ball St. (15) [5] (Las Vegas, 1996)
25—Wisconsin (34) [8] & Duke (20) [17] (Hall of Fame, 1995)
25—Texas (35) [9] & North Caro. (31) [16] (Sun, 1994)
25—Oklahoma St. (62) [17] & Wyoming (14) [8] (Holiday, 1988)
25—Florida St. (31) [19] & Nebraska (28) [6] (Fiesta, 1988)
25—Miami (Fla.) (31) [15] & Nebraska (30) [10] (Orange, 1984)
25—Brigham Young (46) [21] & Southern Methodist (45) [4] (Holiday, 1980)

MOST FIRST DOWNS BY PENALTY

6—Florida (52) vs. Florida St. (20) (Sugar, 1997)
6—Texas (3) vs. Miami (Fla.) (46) (Cotton, 1991)
5—Iowa (27) vs. Texas Tech (0) (Alamo, 1996)
5—(D) Arizona (13) vs. Utah (16) (Freedom, 1994)
5—Fresno St. (30) vs. Colorado (41) (Aloha, 1993)
5—West Va. (21) vs. Notre Dame (34) (Fiesta, 1989)
5—(D) Washington (34) vs. Florida (7) (Freedom, 1989)
5—(D) Western Mich. (30) vs. Fresno St. (35) (California, 1988)
5—Miami (Fla.) (7) vs. Tennessee (35) (Sugar, 1986)
5—(D) Miami (Ohio) (7) vs. San Jose St. (37) (California, 1986)
4—Syracuse (18) vs. Kansas St. (35) (Fiesta, 1997)
4—Northwestern (28) vs. Tennessee (48) (Florida Citrus, 1997)
4—Texas A&M (22) vs. Michigan (20) (Alamo, 1995)
4—Michigan (20) vs. Texas A&M (22) (Alamo, 1995)
4—Texas (35) vs. North Caro. (31) (Sun, 1994)
4—Alabama (25) vs. Miami (Fla.) (33) (Sugar, 1990)
4—Brigham Young (14) vs. Texas A&M (65) (Holiday, 1990)
4—Georgia (10) vs. Texas (9) (Cotton, 1984)
4—(D) Iowa (55) vs. Texas (17) (Freedom, 1984)
4—(D) Vanderbilt (28) vs. Air Force (36) (Hall of Fame, 1982)
4—Maryland (20) vs. Florida (35) (Tangerine, 1980)
4—Baylor (20) vs. Penn St. (41) (Cotton, 1975)
4—Arkansas (13) vs. Tennessee (14) (Liberty, 1971)
4—Arizona St. (45) vs. Florida St. (38) (Fiesta, 1971)
4—Alabama (33) vs. Colorado (47) (Liberty, 1969)
4—Texas A&M (21) vs. Alabama (29) (Cotton, 1942)

MOST FIRST DOWNS BY PENALTY, BOTH TEAMS

8—Florida (52) [6] vs. Florida St. (20) [2] (Sugar, 1997)
8—Texas A&M (22) [4] & Michigan (20) [4] (Alamo, 1995)
8—Miami (Fla.) (46) [2] & Texas (3) [6] (Cotton, 1991)
7—Iowa (27) [5] vs. Texas Tech (0) [2] (Alamo, 1996)
7—(D) Washington (34) [5] & Florida (7) [2] (Freedom, 1989)
7—Tennessee (35) [2] & Miami (Fla.) (7) [5] (Sugar, 1986)
6—Tennessee (48) [2] vs. Northwestern (28) [4] (Florida Citrus, 1997)
6—Colorado (41) [1] & Fresno St. (30) [5] (Aloha, 1993)
6—Miami (Fla.) (33) [2] & Alabama (25) [4] (Sugar, 1990)
5—North Caro. (20) [3] vs. West Va. (13) [2] (Gator, 1996)
5—Texas (35) [4] & North Caro. (31) [1] (Sun, 1994)
5—(D) Utah (16) [0] & Arizona (13) [5] (Freedom, 1994)
5—Florida (41) [3] & West Va. (7) [2] (Sugar, 1994)
5—Texas A&M (65) [1] & Brigham Young (14) [4] (Holiday, 1990)
5—Notre Dame (34) [0] & West Va. (21) [5] (Fiesta, 1989)
5—Georgia (10) [4] & Texas (9) [1] (Cotton, 1984)
5—Southern Methodist (7) [3] & Pittsburgh (3) [2] (Cotton, 1983)
5—Pittsburgh (16) [3] & Arizona (10) [2] (Fiesta, 1979)
5—Penn St. (41) [1] & Baylor (20) [4] (Cotton, 1975)

FEWEST FIRST DOWNS

1—Arkansas (0) vs. LSU (0) (Cotton, 1947) (rushing)
1—Alabama (29) vs. Texas A&M (21) (Cotton, 1942) (passing)
2—Michigan St. (0) vs. Auburn (6) (Orange, 1938) (1 rushing, 1 passing)

FEWEST FIRST DOWNS, BOTH TEAMS

10—Texas (7) [3] & Randolph Field (7) [7] (Cotton, 1944)
12—LSU (19) [4] & Texas A&M (14) [8] (Orange, 1944)

FEWEST FIRST DOWNS RUSHING

0—Florida (18) vs. Missouri (20) (Sugar, 1966)
0—Navy (6) vs. Texas (28) (Cotton, 1964)
0—Alabama (29) vs. Texas A&M (21) (Cotton, 1942)

FEWEST FIRST DOWNS RUSHING, BOTH TEAMS

3—Alabama (29) [0] & Texas A&M (21) [3] (Cotton, 1942)
8—(D) Southern Cal (28) [4] & Utah (21) [4] (Freedom, 1993)
9—Florida St. (41) [2] & Nebraska (17) [7] (Fiesta, 1990)
9—Texas (28) [9] & Navy (6) [0] (Cotton, 1964)

FEWEST FIRST DOWNS PASSING

0—Army (28) vs. Alabama (29) (John Hancock Sun, 1988)
0—Oklahoma (40) vs. Houston (10) (Sun, 1981)
0—West Va. (14) vs. South Caro. (3) (Peach, 1969)
0—Missouri (35) vs. Alabama (10) (Gator, 1968)
0—Virginia Tech (7) vs. Miami (Fla.) (14) (Liberty, 1966)
0—Auburn (7) vs. Mississippi (13) (Liberty, 1965)
0—Alabama (10) vs. Arkansas (3) (Sugar, 1962)
0—(D) Missouri (14) vs. Georgia Tech (10) (Bluebonnet, 1962)
0—Utah St. (13) vs. New Mexico St. (20) (Sun, 1960)
0—Arkansas (0) vs. LSU (0) (Cotton, 1947)
0—Fordham (2) vs. Missouri (0) (Sugar, 1942)
0—Arizona St. (0) vs. Catholic (0) (Sun, 1940)
0—West Va. (7) vs. Texas Tech (6) (Sun, 1938)

FEWEST FIRST DOWNS PASSING, BOTH TEAMS

1—Alabama (10) [0] & Arkansas (3) [1] (Sugar, 1962)
4—Oklahoma (41) [1] & Wyoming (7) [3] (Fiesta, 1976)
4—Texas (16) [2] & Tennessee (0) [2] (Cotton, 1953)
4—Rice (28) [3] & Colorado (14) [1] (Cotton, 1938)

Punting

MOST PUNTS

17—Duke (3) vs. Southern Cal (7) (Rose, 1939)
16—Alabama (29) vs. Texas A&M (21) (Cotton, 1942)
16—New Mexico St. (14) vs. Hardin-Simmons (14) (Sun, 1936)
15—Tennessee (0) vs. Rice (8) (Orange, 1947)
14—Tulsa (7) vs. Tennessee (14) (Sugar, 1943)
14—Santa Clara (6) vs. LSU (0) (Sugar, 1938)
14—LSU (0) vs. Santa Clara (6) (Sugar, 1938)
14—Texas Christian (3) vs. LSU (2) (Sugar, 1936)
13—Rice (8) vs. Tennessee (0) (Orange, 1947)
13—Tennessee (0) vs. Southern Cal (25) (Rose, 1945)
13—Oklahoma (0) vs. Tennessee (17) (Orange, 1939)
13—Catholic (20) vs. Mississippi (19) (Orange, 1936)
13—LSU (2) vs. Texas Christian (3) (Sugar, 1936)
13—Miami (Fla.) (0) vs. Bucknell (26) (Orange, 1935)

MOST PUNTS, BOTH TEAMS

28—Rice (8) [13] & Tennessee (0) [15] (Orange, 1947)
28—Santa Clara (6) [14] & LSU (0) [14] (Sugar, 1938)
27—Texas Christian (3) [14] & LSU (2) [13] (Sugar, 1936)
25—Tennessee (17) [12] & Oklahoma (0) [13] (Orange, 1939)
24—Catholic (20) [13] & Mississippi (19) [11] (Orange, 1936)
23—UTEP (14) [12] & Mississippi (7) [11] (Sun, 1967)
22—Auburn (6) [10] & Michigan St. (0) [12] (Orange, 1938)

HIGHEST PUNTING AVERAGE
(Minimum 5 Punts)

53.9—Southern Cal (7) vs. Wisconsin (0) (Rose, 1953) (8 for 431 yards)
52.3—Tennessee (17) vs. Nebraska (42) (Orange, 1998) (6 for 314 yards)
52.0—Iowa (27) vs. Texas Tech (0) (Alamo, 1996) (5 for 260 yards)
51.0—Penn St. (10) vs. Clemson (35) (Florida Citrus, 1988) (5 for 255 yards)
50.0—Nevada (37) vs. Toledo (40) (OT) (Las Vegas, 1995) (5 for 250 yards)
50.0—Mississippi St. (17) vs. Nebraska (31) (Sun, 1980) (5 for 250 yards)
49.3—Clemson (0) vs. Syracuse (41) (Gator, 1996) (6 for 296 yards)

49.2—(D) Air Force (24) vs. Texas (16) (Bluebonnet, 1985) (11 for 541 yards)
49.2—Arkansas (3) vs. UCLA (17) (Cotton, 1989) (6 for 295 yards)
49.0—Iowa (7) vs. Arizona St. (17) (Sun, 1997) (8 for 392 yards)
49.0—Indiana (24) vs. Baylor (0) (Copper, 1991) (6 for 294 yards)
49.0—(D) Mississippi St. (10) vs. Kansas (0) (Hall of Fame, 1981) (9 for 441 yards)
48.1—Florida (52) vs. Florida St. (20) (Sugar, 1997) (7 for 337 yards)
48.1—Ohio St. (14) vs. Tennessee (20) (Florida Citrus, 1996) (7 for 337 yards)
48.0—Oklahoma (41) vs. Texas Tech (10) (John Hancock, 1993) (7 for 336 yards)
48.0—Kansas (23) vs. Brigham Young (20) (Aloha, 1992) (8 for 384 yards)
47.9—Penn St. (42) vs. Tennessee (17) (Fiesta, 1992) (9 for 431 yards)
47.9—Oregon St. (20) vs. Duke (16) (Rose, 1942) (7 for 335 yards)
47.6—Oklahoma (42) vs. Arkansas (8) (Orange, 1987) (5 for 238 yards)
47.5—St. Mary's (Cal.) (20) vs. Texas Tech (13) (Cotton, 1939) (11 for 523 yards)
47.4—Georgia Tech (18) vs. Stanford (17) (Aloha, 1991) (7 for 332 yards)
47.4—(D) Fresno St. (51) vs. Bowling Green (7) (California, 1985) (7 for 332 yards)
47.4—(D) Tennessee (28) vs. Wisconsin (21) (Garden State, 1981) (5 for 237 yards)

FEWEST PUNTS
0—Oklahoma St. (62) vs. Wyoming (14) (Holiday, 1988)
0—Oklahoma (41) vs. Wyoming (7) (Fiesta, 1976)
1—Nebraska (62) vs. Florida (24) (Fiesta, 1996)
1—Brigham Young (39) vs. Penn St. (50) (Holiday, 1989)
1—Nebraska (21) vs. LSU (20) (Orange, 1983)
1—North Caro. St. (31) vs. Kansas (18) (Liberty, 1973)
1—Utah (32) vs. West Va. (6) (Liberty, 1964)
1—(D) Miami (Fla.) (34) vs. Nebraska (36) (Gotham, 1962)
1—Georgia Tech (42) vs. West Va. (19) (Sugar, 1954)
1—West Va. (19) vs. Georgia Tech (42) (Sugar, 1954)
1—Missouri (23) vs. Clemson (24) (Gator, 1949)

LOWEST PUNTING AVERAGE
(Minimum 3 Punts)
17.0—Nevada (34) vs. Bowling Green (35) (Las Vegas, 1992) (4 for 68 yards)
19.0—Cincinnati (18) vs. Virginia Tech (6) (Sun, 1947) (6 for 114 yards)
22.0—Mississippi St. (16) vs. North Caro. St. (12) (Liberty, 1963) (3 for 66 yards)
23.0—Bowling Green (35) vs. Nevada (34) (Las Vegas, 1992) (5 for 115 yards)
25.5—Houston (34) vs. Notre Dame (35) (Cotton, 1979) (10 for 255 yards)
26.1—Michigan (14) vs. Alabama (17) (Outback, 1997) (7 for 183 yards)
26.3—Oklahoma St. (34) vs. Texas Christian (0) (Cotton, 1945) (6 for 158 yards)
26.3—Notre Dame (35) vs. Houston (34) (Cotton, 1979) (7 for 184 yards)
26.3—Rice (28) vs. Alabama (6) (Cotton, 1954) (8 for 210 yards)

MOST PUNTS BLOCKED BY ONE TEAM
2—North Caro. (21) vs. Mississippi St. (17) (Peach, Jan. 2, 1993)
2—North Caro. St. (14) vs. Georgia (7) (Liberty, 1967)
2—LSU (25) vs. Colorado (7) (Orange, 1962)

Punt Returns

MOST PUNT RETURNS
9—Georgia (7) vs. North Caro. (3) (Gator, Dec. 31, 1971) (6.8 average)
8—Indiana (20) vs. Virginia Tech (45) (Independence, 1993) (7.3 average)
8—Tennessee (34) vs. Air Force (13) (Sugar, 1971) (10.8 average)
8—Mississippi (7) vs. UTEP (14) (Sun, 1967) (9.4 average)
8—Michigan (34) vs. Oregon St. (7) (Rose, 1965) (10.6 average)
7—Stanford (38) vs. Michigan St. (0) (Sun, 1996) (13.4 average)
7—Louisville (34) vs. Alabama (7) (Fiesta, 1991) (7.3 average)
6—UCLA (29) vs. Texas A&M (23) (Cotton, 1998) (11.0 average)
6—Florida (52) vs. Florida St. (20) (Sugar, 1997) (11.5 average)
6—Ohio St. (14) vs. Tennessee (20) (Florida Citrus, 1996) (5.0 average)
6—Tennessee (17) vs. Penn St. (42) (Fiesta, 1992) (8.2 average)
6—Clemson (30) vs. Illinois (0) (Hall of Fame, 1991)
6—(D) San Jose St. (48) vs. Central Mich. (24) (California, 1990)
6—Brigham Young (7) vs. Ohio St. (10) (Florida Citrus, 1985)
6—Texas (9) vs. Georgia (10) (Cotton, 1984) (2.5 average)
6—Washington (21) vs. Maryland (20) (Aloha, 1982) (4.7 average)
6—(D) Vanderbilt (28) vs. Air Force (36) (Hall of Fame, 1982)
6—Washington St. (36) vs. Brigham Young (38) (Holiday, 1981)
6—Nebraska (38) vs. Alabama (6) (Orange, 1972) (22.7 average)
6—Miami (Fla.) (14) vs. Syracuse (15) (Liberty, 1961) (13.0 average)
6—Air Force (0) vs. Texas Christian (0) (Cotton, 1959) (5.8 average)
6—Tulane (13) vs. Texas A&M (14) (Sugar, 1940) (21.0 average)
6—Tulane (20) vs. Temple (14) (Sugar, 1935)
6—Tulane (12) vs. Southern Cal (21) (Rose, 1932)

MOST PUNT RETURN YARDS
136—Nebraska (38) vs. Alabama (6) (Orange, 1972) (6 returns)
128—Oklahoma (48) vs. Duke (21) (Orange, 1958)
126—Tulane (13) vs. Texas A&M (14) (Sugar, 1940) (6 returns)
124—California (37) vs. Clemson (13) (Florida Citrus, 1992) (5 returns)
124—Washington (44) vs. Wisconsin (8) (Rose, 1960) (4 returns)
108—Southern Miss. (38) vs. UTEP (18) (Independence, 1988) (2 returns)
107—Arizona St. (45) vs. Florida St. (38) (Fiesta, 1971) (5 returns)
104—Texas A&M (21) vs. Alabama (29) (Cotton, 1942) (5 returns)
100—Virginia (34) vs. Georgia (27) (Peach, Dec. 30, 1995) (4 returns)
99—Kent (18) vs. Tampa (21) (Tangerine, 1972) (3 returns)
98—Brigham Young (46) vs. Southern Methodist (45) (Holiday, 1980) (3 returns)
94—Stanford (38) vs. Michigan St. (0) (Sun, 1996) (7 returns)
94—Denver (24) vs. New Mexico (34) (Sun, 1946)
93—Auburn (35) vs. Mississippi (28) (Gator, Jan. 2, 1971) (4 returns)
92—Southern Cal (7) vs. Ohio St. (20) (Rose, 1955) (2 returns)
89—Nebraska (28) vs. Florida St. (31) (Fiesta, 1988) (3 returns)
88—Penn St. (42) vs. Arizona St. (30) (Fiesta, 1977) (2 returns)

HIGHEST PUNT RETURN AVERAGE
(Minimum 3 Returns)
33.0—Kent (18) vs. Tampa (21) (Tangerine, 1972) (3 for 99 yards)
32.7—Brigham Young (46) vs. Southern Methodist (45) (Holiday, 1980) (3 for 98 yards)
31.0—Washington (44) vs. Wisconsin (8) (Rose, 1960) (4 for 124 yards)
30.7—Michigan (42) vs. North Caro. St. (7) (Hall of Fame, 1994) (3 for 92 yards)
29.7—Nebraska (28) vs. Florida St. (31) (Fiesta, 1988) (3 for 89 yards)
27.6—Kansas St. (52) vs. Wyoming (17) (Copper, 1993) (3 for 83 yards)
25.0—Virginia (34) vs. Georgia (27) (Peach, Dec. 30, 1995) (4 for 100 yards)
24.8—California (37) vs. Clemson (13) (Florida Citrus, 1992) (5 for 124 yards)
24.0—Auburn (31) vs. Ohio St. (14) (Hall of Fame, 1990) (3 for 72 yards)
23.3—Auburn (35) vs. Mississippi (28) (Gator, Jan. 2, 1971) (4 for 93 yards)
22.7—Nebraska (38) vs. Alabama (6) (Orange, 1972) (6 for 136 yards)
21.4—Arizona St. (45) vs. Florida St. (38) (Fiesta, 1971) (5 for 107 yards)
21.0—Arkansas (6) vs. Duke (7) (Cotton, 1961) (3 for 63 yards)
21.0—Tulane (13) vs. Texas A&M (14) (Sugar, 1940) (6 for 126 yards)
20.8—Texas A&M (21) vs. Alabama (29) (Cotton, 1942) (5 for 104 yards)
19.5—(D) Georgia (20) vs. Texas A&M (40) (Presidential Cup, 1950) (4 for 78 yards)
19.3—Nebraska (14) vs. Houston (17) (Cotton, 1980) (3 for 58 yards)

Kickoff Returns

MOST KICKOFF RETURNS
10—Florida (24) vs. Nebraska (62) (Fiesta, 1996) (26.8 average)
10—Wyoming (14) vs. Oklahoma St. (62) (Holiday, 1988) (20.5 average)
9—Brigham Young (14) vs. Texas A&M (65) (Holiday, 1990) (18.2 average)
8—Virginia Tech (3) vs. North Caro. (42) (Gator, 1998) (19.4 average)
8—Florida St. (20) vs. Florida (52) (Sugar, 1997) (19.0 average)
8—Northwestern (32) vs. Southern Cal (41) (Rose, 1996) (28.1 average)
8—Nebraska (21) vs. Georgia Tech (45) (Florida Citrus, 1991) (23.6 average)
8—Notre Dame (10) vs. Texas A&M (35) (Cotton, 1988) (18.9 average)
8—Texas Tech (17) vs. Florida St. (40) (Tangerine, 1977)
8—UCLA (6) vs. Alabama (36) (Liberty, 1976) (17.6 average)
8—Brigham Young (21) vs. Oklahoma St. (49) (Tangerine, 1976)
8—(D) Tulane (7) vs. Houston (47) (Bluebonnet, 1973) (28.1 average)
8—Missouri (35) vs. Arizona St. (49) (Fiesta, 1972) (32.3 average)
8—Arizona St. (45) vs. Florida St. (38) (Fiesta, 1971) (16.4 average)
8—Florida St. (38) vs. Arizona St. (45) (Fiesta, 1971) (23.0 average)
8—Colorado (47) vs. Alabama (33) (Liberty, 1969) (27.8 average)
8—Ohio (42) vs. Richmond (49) (Tangerine, 1968)
8—Florida St. (20) vs. UTEP (47) (Sun, 1955)
8—UCLA (14) vs. Illinois (45) (Rose, 1947) (32.4 average)

MOST KICKOFF RETURN YARDS
268—Florida (24) vs. Nebraska (62) (Fiesta, 1996) (10 returns)
259—UCLA (14) vs. Illinois (45) (Rose, 1947) (8 returns)
258—Missouri (35) vs. Arizona St. (49) (Fiesta, 1972) (8 returns)
225—Northwestern (32) vs. Southern Cal (41) (Rose, 1996) (8 returns)
225—(D) Tulane (7) vs. Houston (47) (Bluebonnet, 1973) (8 returns)
222—Colorado (47) vs. Alabama (33) (Liberty, 1969) (8 returns)
207—California (38) vs. Navy (42) (Aloha, 1996) (7 returns)
205—Wyoming (14) vs. Oklahoma (62) (Holiday, 1988) (10 returns)
204—Brigham Young (21) vs. Oklahoma St. (49) (Tangerine, 1976) (8 returns)
191—Houston (22) vs. Washington St. (24) (Aloha, 1988) (5 returns)
189—Nebraska (21) vs. Georgia Tech (45) (Florida Citrus, 1991) (8 returns)
188—Stanford (13) vs. East Caro. (19) (Liberty, 1995) (6 returns)
187—Houston (28) vs. Boston College (45) (Cotton, 1985) (7 returns)
184—Florida St. (38) vs. Arizona St. (45) (Fiesta, 1971) (8 returns)
179—Washington (21) vs. Colorado (33) (Holiday, 1996) (5 returns)
174—Hawaii (13) vs. Michigan St. (33) (Aloha, 1989) (7 returns)
170—Tennessee (27) vs. Maryland (28) (John Hancock, 1984) (4 returns)
169—Oregon St. (19) vs. Iowa (35) (Rose, 1957) (5 returns)
164—Brigham Young (14) vs. Texas A&M (65) (Holiday, 1990) (9 returns)

HIGHEST KICKOFF RETURN AVERAGE
(Minimum 3 Returns)
42.5—Tennessee (27) vs. Maryland (28) (John Hancock, 1984) (4 for 170 yards)
38.3—Fresno St. (30) vs. Colorado (41) (Aloha, 1993) (3 for 115 yards)
38.3—Ohio St. (28) vs. Pittsburgh (23) (Fiesta, 1984) (4 for 153 yards)
38.2—Houston (22) vs. Washington St. (24) (Aloha, 1988) (5 for 191 yards)
37.5—LSU (45) vs. Michigan St. (26) (Independence, 1995) (4 for 150 yards)
37.5—Notre Dame (24) vs. Alabama (23) (Sugar, 1973) (4 for 150 yards)
36.8—Ohio St. (17) vs. Syracuse (24) (Hall of Fame, 1992) (4 for 147 yards)
36.7—Indiana (20) vs. Virginia Tech (45) (Independence, 1993) (3 for 110 yards)
35.8—Washington (21) vs. Colorado (33) (Holiday, 1996) (5 for 179 yards)
33.8—Oregon St. (19) vs. Iowa (35) (Rose, 1957) (5 for 169 yards)
32.8—Florida St. (40) vs. Texas Tech (17) (Tangerine, 1977) (4 for 131 yards)
32.6—UCLA (30) vs. Kansas (51) (Aloha, 1995) (5 for 163 yards)
32.4—UCLA (14) vs. Illinois (45) (Rose, 1947) (8 for 259 yards)

32.3—Missouri (35) vs. Arizona St. (49) (Fiesta, 1972) (8 for 258 yards)
31.7—Penn St. (41) vs. Baylor (20) (Cotton, 1975) (3 for 95 yards)
31.6—Virginia Tech (21) vs. Nebraska (41) (Orange, 1996) (3 for 95 yards)
31.3—Penn St. (38) vs. Texas (15) (Fiesta, 1997) (4 for 125 yards)
31.3—Stanford (13) vs. East Caro. (19) (Liberty, 1995) (6 for 188 yards)
29.5—California (38) vs. Navy (42) (Aloha, 1996) (7 for 207 yards)
29.4—Virginia (34) vs. Georgia (27) (Peach, Dec. 30, 1995) (5 for 147 yards)
29.0—Mississippi St. (17) vs. Nebraska (31) (Sun, 1980) (4 for 116 yards)
28.1—Northwestern (32) vs. Southern Cal (41) (Rose, 1996) (8 for 225 yards)
27.8—Brigham Young (21) vs. Ohio St. (28) (Holiday, 1993) (5 for 139 yards)
27.6—Houston (17) vs. Syracuse (30) (Liberty, 1996) (5 for 138 yards)
27.2—West Va. (30) vs. Georgia Tech (35) (Carquest, 1997) (6 for 163 yards)
27.0—Arizona St. (17) vs. Arkansas (18) (Holiday, 1985) (3 for 81 yards)
26.8—Florida (24) vs. Nebraska (62) (Fiesta, 1996) (10 for 268 yards)
26.7—Houston (28) vs. Boston College (45) (Cotton, 1985) (7 for 187 yards)

Fumbles

MOST FUMBLES
11—Mississippi (7) vs. Alabama (12) (Sugar, 1964) (lost 6)
9—Texas (11) vs. Notre Dame (24) (Cotton, 1971) (lost 5)
8—North Caro. St. (28) vs. Iowa (23) (Peach, Dec. 31, 1988) (lost 5)
8—(D) Houston (35) vs. Navy (0) (Garden State, 1980) (lost 3)
8—Louisville (14) vs. Louisiana Tech (24) (Independence, 1977) (lost 3)
8—North Texas (8) vs. New Mexico St. (28) (Sun, 1959) (lost 6)
8—Texas Christian (0) vs. Air Force (0) (Cotton, 1959) (lost 3)
8—Colorado (27) vs. Clemson (21) (Orange, 1957) (lost 3)
7—(D) Florida (7) vs. Washington (34) (Freedom, 1989) (lost 3)
7—Hawaii (13) vs. Michigan St. (33) (Aloha, 1989) (lost 4)
7—(D) Toledo (27) vs. San Jose St. (25) (California, 1981) (lost 2)
7—(D) Texas A&M (28) vs. Southern Cal (47) (Bluebonnet, 1977) (lost 5)
7—Auburn (27) vs. Texas (3) (Gator, 1974) (lost 5)
7—Tennessee (34) vs. Air Force (13) (Sugar, 1971) (lost 4)
7—Air Force (13) vs. Tennessee (34) (Sugar, 1971) (lost 3)
7—Georgia (2) vs. Arkansas (16) (Sugar, 1969) (lost 5)
7—Alabama (0) vs. Penn St. (7) (Liberty, 1959) (lost 4)
7—Southern Cal (7) vs. Ohio St. (20) (Rose, 1955) (lost 3)
7—Wash. & Lee (7) vs. Wyoming (20) (Gator, 1951) (lost 2)
7—Missouri (7) vs. Maryland (20) (Gator, 1950) (lost 5)
7—(D) Georgia (20) vs. Texas A&M (40) (Presidential Cup, 1950)
7—(D) Arizona St. (21) vs. Xavier (Ohio) (33) (Salad, 1950) (lost 6)

MOST FUMBLES, BOTH TEAMS
17—Alabama (12) [6] & Mississippi (7) [11] (Sugar, 1964) (lost 9)
14—Louisiana Tech (24) [6] & Louisville (14) [8] (Independence, 1977) (lost 6)
14—Tennessee (34) [7] & Air Force (13) [7] (Sugar, 1971) (lost 7)
13—Texas Christian (0) [8] & Air Force (0) [5] (Cotton, 1959) (lost 6)
12—North Caro. St. (28) [8] & Iowa (23) [4] (Peach, Dec. 31, 1988) (lost 8)
12—(D) Houston (35) [8] & Navy (0) [4] (Garden State, 1980) (lost 6)
12—New Mexico St. (28) [4] & North Texas (8) [8] (Sun, 1959) (lost 8)
11—(D) Toledo (27) [7] & San Jose St. (25) [4] (California, 1981) (lost 3)
11—Oklahoma (41) [6] & Wyoming (7) [5] (Fiesta, 1976)
10—Alabama (30) [5] & Baylor (2) [5] (Cotton, 1981) (lost 5)
10—(D) Houston (31) [5] & North Caro. St. (31) [5] (Bluebonnet, 1974) (lost 4)
10—Notre Dame (24) [1] & Texas (11) [9] (Cotton, 1971) (lost 6)
10—Illinois (17) [5] & Washington (7) [5] (Rose, 1964) (lost 6)
10—Navy (20) [5] & Rice (7) [5] (Cotton, 1958) (lost 8)
10—Mississippi (7) [5] & Florida (3) [5] (Gator, 1958) (lost 5)
10—Texas (16) [5] & Tennessee (0) [5] (Cotton, 1953) (lost 6)

MOST FUMBLES LOST
6—Texas A&M (2) vs. Florida St. (10) (Cotton, 1992) (6 fumbles)
6—East Caro. (31) vs. Maine (0) (Tangerine, 1965) (6 fumbles)
6—Mississippi (7) vs. Alabama (12) (Sugar, 1964) (11 fumbles)
6—North Texas (8) vs. New Mexico St. (28) (Sun, 1959) (8 fumbles)
6—(D) Arizona St. (21) vs. Xavier (Ohio) (33) (Salad, 1950) (7 fumbles)
5—UCLA (16) vs. Wisconsin (21) (Rose, 1994) (5 fumbles)
5—North Caro. St. (28) vs. Iowa (23) (Peach, Dec. 31, 1988) (8 fumbles)
5—North Caro. (21) vs. Arizona (30) (Aloha, 1986) (5 fumbles)
5—(D) Bowling Green (7) vs. Fresno St. (51) (California, 1985) (6 fumbles)
5—(D) Georgia (22) vs. Stanford (25) (Bluebonnet, 1978) (6 fumbles)
5—(D) Texas A&M (28) vs. Southern Cal (47) (Bluebonnet, 1977) (7 fumbles)
5—Auburn (27) vs. Texas (3) (Gator, 1974) (7 fumbles)
5—Texas (11) vs. Notre Dame (24) (Cotton, 1971) (9 fumbles)
5—Georgia (2) vs. Arkansas (16) (Sugar, 1969) (7 fumbles)
5—(D) Utah St. (9) vs. Baylor (24) (Gotham, 1961) (5 fumbles)
5—Rice (7) vs. Navy (20) (Cotton, 1958) (5 fumbles)
5—Auburn (13) vs. Vanderbilt (25) (Gator, 1955) (5 fumbles)
5—Oklahoma (7) vs. Kentucky (13) (Sugar, 1951)
5—Missouri (7) vs. Maryland (20) (Gator, 1950) (7 fumbles)
5—Texas A&M (21) vs. Alabama (29) (Cotton, 1942) (6 fumbles)

MOST FUMBLES LOST, BOTH TEAMS
9—Alabama (12) [3] & Mississippi (7) [6] (Sugar, 1964) (17 fumbles)
8—North Caro. St. (28) [5] & Iowa (23) [3] (Peach, Dec. 31, 1988) (12 fumbles)
8—New Mexico St. (28) [2] & North Texas (8) [6] (Sun, 1959) (12 fumbles)
8—Navy (20) [3] & Rice (7) [5] (Cotton, 1958) (10 fumbles)
7—Florida St. (10) [1] & Texas A&M (2) [6] (Cotton, 1992) (7 fumbles)
7—Texas A&M (37) [3] & Florida (14) [4] (Sun, Jan. 2, 1977) (8 fumbles)
7—Arizona St. (28) [3] & Pittsburgh (7) [4] (Fiesta, 1973) (9 fumbles)
7—Tennessee (34) [4] & Air Force (13) [3] (Sugar, 1971) (14 fumbles)
7—Michigan St. (28) [4] & UCLA (20) [3] (Rose, 1954) (8 fumbles)

Penalties

MOST PENALTIES
20—(D) Fresno St. (35) vs. Western Mich. (30) (California, 1988) (166 yards)
19—Oregon (41) vs. Air Force (13) (Las Vegas, 1997) (166 yards)
18—Washington St. (31) vs. Utah (28) (Copper, 1992) (136 yards)
17—Tennessee (17) vs. Oklahoma (0) (Orange, 1939) (157 yards)
16—Miami (Fla.) (46) vs. Texas (3) (Cotton, 1991) (202 yards)
16—Tulsa (16) vs. McNeese St. (20) (Independence, 1976) (100 yards)
15—Florida (52) vs. Florida St. (20) (Sugar, 1997) (102 yards)
15—Washington St. (10) vs. Baylor (3) (Alamo, 1994) (110 yards)
15—Illinois (30) vs. East Caro. (0) (Liberty, 1994) (164 yards)
15—Utah St. (42) vs. Ball St. (33) (Las Vegas, 1993) (150 yards)
15—Miami (Fla.) (7) vs. Tennessee (35) (Sugar, 1986) (120 yards)
15—(D) Michigan (33) vs. UCLA (14) (Bluebonnet, 1981) (148 yards)
14—Florida St. (20) vs. Florida (52) (Sugar, 1997) (115 yards)
14—(D) San Jose St. (37) vs. Miami (Ohio) (7) (California, 1986) (163 yards)
13—Washington (51) vs. Michigan St. (23) (Aloha, 1997) (126 yards)
13—Tennessee (48) vs. Northwestern (28) (Florida Citrus, 1997) (112 yards)
13—Florida St. (41) vs. Nebraska (17) (Fiesta, 1990) (135 yards)
13—(D) San Jose St. (27) vs. Eastern Mich. (30) (California, 1987) (103 yards)
13—(D) Washington (20) vs. Colorado (17) (Freedom, 1985) (88 yards)
13—Miami (Fla.) (31) vs. Nebraska (30) (Orange, 1984) (101 yards)
13—McNeese St. (20) vs. Tulsa (16) (Independence, 1976) (105 yards)
13—Lamar (21) vs. Middle Tenn. St. (14) (Tangerine, 1961) (140 yards)

MOST PENALTIES, BOTH TEAMS
29—Florida (52) [15] & Florida St. (20) [14] (Sugar, 1997) (217 yards)
29—McNeese St. (20) [13] & Tulsa (16) [16] (Independence, 1976) (205 yards)
28—(D) Fresno St. (35) [20] & Western Mich. (30) [8] (California, 1988) (231 yards)
26—Oregon (41) [19] & Air Force (13) [7] (Las Vegas, 1997) (223 yards)
26—Tennessee (35) [11] & Miami (Fla.) (7) [15] (Sugar, 1986) (245 yards)
26—Tennessee (17) [17] & Oklahoma (0) [9] (Orange, 1939) (221 yards)
25—Washington St. (31) [18] & Utah (28) [7] (Copper, 1992) (191 yards)
24—Miami (Fla.) (46) [16] & Texas (3) [8] (Cotton, 1991) (270 yards)
24—(D) San Jose St. (37) [14] & Miami (Ohio) (7) [10] (California, 1986) (264 yards)
24—(D) Michigan (33) [15] & UCLA (14) [9] (Bluebonnet, 1981) (242 yards)
23—Kansas St. (54) [12] & Colorado St. (21) [11] (Holiday, 1995) (219 yards)
23—(D) Fresno St. (51) [12] & Bowling Green (7) [11] (California, 1985) (183 yards)
22—(D) Eastern Mich. (30) [9] & San Jose St. (27) [13] (California, 1987) (162 yards)
21—Illinois (30) [15] & East Caro. (0) [6] (Liberty, 1994) (204 yards)
21—Florida St. (18) [10] & Nebraska (16) [11] (Orange, 1994) (184 yards)
21—Ohio St. (47) [12] & Brigham Young (17) [9] (Holiday, 1982) (184 yards)
21—Oklahoma St. (16) [12] & Brigham Young (6) [9] (Fiesta, 1974) (150 yards)
20—Virginia Tech (28) [11] & Texas (10) [9] (Sugar, Dec. 31, 1995) (190 yards)
20—Iowa (38) [12] & Washington (18) [8] (Sun, 1995) (164 yards)
20—Utah St. (42) [15] & Ball St. (33) [5] (Las Vegas, 1993) (180 yards)
20—Penn St. (50) [10] & Brigham Young (39) [10] (Holiday, 1989) (181 yards)
20—Washington St. (24) [11] & Houston (22) [9] (Aloha, 1988) (153 yards)
20—Brigham Young (24) [9] & Michigan (17) [11] (Holiday, 1984) (194 yards)

MOST YARDS PENALIZED
202—Miami (Fla.) (46) vs. Texas (3) (Cotton, 1991) (16 penalties)
166—Oregon (41) vs. Air Force (13) (Las Vegas, 1997) (19 penalties)
166—(D) Fresno St. (35) vs. Western Mich. (30) (California, 1988) (20 penalties)
164—Illinois (30) vs. East Caro. (0) (Liberty, 1994) (15 penalties)
163—(D) San Jose St. (37) vs. Miami (Ohio) (7) (California, 1986) (14 penalties)
150—Utah St. (42) vs. Ball St. (33) (Las Vegas, 1993) (15 penalties)
150—Oklahoma (48) vs. Duke (21) (Orange, 1958) (12 penalties)
148—(D) Michigan (33) vs. UCLA (14) (Bluebonnet, 1981) (15 penalties)
143—Miami (Fla.) (22) vs. Nebraska (0) (Orange, 1992) (12 penalties)
140—Lamar (21) vs. Middle Tenn. St. (14) (Tangerine, 1961) (13 penalties)
136—Washington St. (31) vs. Utah (28) (Copper, 1992) (18 penalties)
135—Florida St. (41) vs. Nebraska (17) (Fiesta, 1990) (13 penalties)
130—LSU (15) vs. Nebraska (30) (Sugar, 1987) (12 penalties)
130—Tennessee (17) vs. Oklahoma (0) (Orange, 1939)
128—Oklahoma (48) vs. Virginia (14) (Gator, Dec. 29, 1991) (12 penalties)
126—Washington (51) vs. Michigan St. (23) (Aloha, 1997) (13 penalties)
126—Penn St. (42) vs. Arizona St. (30) (Fiesta, 1977) (12 penalties)
125—Tennessee (35) vs. Miami (Fla.) (7) (Sugar, 1986) (11 penalties)
124—Kansas St. (54) vs. Colorado St. (21) (Holiday, 1995) (12 penalties)
122—Mississippi St. (16) vs. North Caro. St. (12) (Liberty, 1963) (11 penalties)

MOST YARDS PENALIZED, BOTH TEAMS
270—Miami (Fla.) (46) [202] & Texas (3) [68] (Cotton, 1991)
264—(D) San Jose St. (37) [163] & Miami (Ohio) (7) [101] (California, 1986)
245—Tennessee (35) [125] & Miami (Fla.) (7) [120] (Sugar, 1986)
242—(D) Michigan (33) [148] & UCLA (14) [94] (Bluebonnet, 1981)
231—(D) Fresno St. (35) [166] & Western Mich. (30) [65] (California, 1988)

223—Oregon (41) [166] & Air Force (13) [57] (Las Vegas, 1997)
221—Tennessee (17) [130] & Oklahoma (0) [91] (Orange, 1939)
219—Kansas St. (54) [124] & Colorado St. (21) [95] (Holiday, 1995)
217—Florida (52) [102] vs. Florida St. (20) [115] (Sugar, 1997)
205—McNeese St. (20) [105] & Tulsa (16) [100] (Independence, 1976)
204—Illinois (30) [164] & East Caro. (0) [40] (Liberty, 1994)
194—Brigham Young (24) [82] & Michigan (17) [112] (Holiday, 1984)
191—Washington St. (31) [136] & Utah (28) [55] (Copper, 1992)
190—Virginia Tech (28) [99] & Texas (10) [91] (Sugar, Dec. 31, 1995)
184—Florida St. (18) [69] & Nebraska (16) [115] (Orange, 1994)
183—Florida St. (41) [135] & Nebraska (17) [48] (Fiesta, 1990)
183—(D) Fresno St. (51) [112] & Bowling Green (7) [71] (California, 1985)
181—Penn St. (50) [93] & Brigham Young (39) [88] (Holiday, 1989)
180—Utah St. (42) [150] & Ball St. (33) [30] (Las Vegas, 1993)
179—Miami (Fla.) (22) [143] & Nebraska (0) [36] (Orange, 1992)
176—Oklahoma (48) [128] & Virginia (14) [48] (Gator, Dec. 29, 1991)
175—Oklahoma (48) [150] & Duke (21) [25] (Orange, 1958)

FEWEST PENALTIES
0—Southern Methodist (7) vs. Alabama (28) (Sun, 1983)
0—Louisiana Tech (13) vs. East Caro. (35) (Independence, 1978)
0—Texas (17) vs. Alabama (13) (Cotton, 1973)
0—(D) Rice (7) vs. Kansas (33) (Bluebonnet, 1961)
0—Pittsburgh (14) vs. Georgia Tech (21) (Gator, 1956)
0—Clemson (0) vs. Miami (Fla.) (14) (Gator, 1952)
0—Texas (7) vs. Randolph Field (7) (Cotton, 1944)
0—Alabama (20) vs. Washington (19) (Rose, 1926)

FEWEST PENALTIES, BOTH TEAMS
3—Alabama (28) [3] & Southern Methodist (7) [0] (Sun, 1983)
3—Penn St. (30) [2] & Texas (6) [1] (Cotton, 1972)
3—Texas (21) [1] & Notre Dame (17) [2] (Cotton, 1970)
3—Penn St. (15) [1] & Kansas (14) [2] (Orange, 1969)
3—(D) Kansas (33) [3] & Rice (7) [0] (Bluebonnet, 1961)

FEWEST YARDS PENALIZED
0—Southern Methodist (7) vs. Alabama (28) (Sun, 1983)
0—Louisiana Tech (13) vs. East Caro. (35) (Independence, 1978)
0—Texas (17) vs. Alabama (13) (Cotton, 1973)
0—(D) Rice (7) vs. Kansas (33) (Bluebonnet, 1961)
0—Pittsburgh (14) vs. Georgia Tech (21) (Gator, 1956)
0—Clemson (0) vs. Miami (Fla.) (14) (Gator, 1952)
0—Texas (7) vs. Randolph Field (7) (Cotton, 1944)
0—Alabama (20) vs. Washington (19) (Rose, 1926)

FEWEST YARDS PENALIZED, BOTH TEAMS
10—Duquesne (13) [5] & Mississippi St. (12) [5] (Orange, 1937)
15—Texas (21) [5] & Notre Dame (17) [10] (Cotton, 1970)
15—(D) Kansas (33) [15] vs. Rice (7) [0] (Bluebonnet, 1961)

Miscellaneous Records

SCORELESS TIES#
1959—Air Force 0, Texas Christian 0 (Cotton)
1947—Arkansas 0, LSU 0 (Cotton)
1940—Arizona St. 0, Catholic 0 (Sun)
1922—California 0, Wash. & Jeff. 0 (Rose)

TIE GAMES#
(Not Scoreless)
1991—Brigham Young 13, Iowa 13 (Holiday)
1990—Louisiana Tech 34, Maryland 34 (Independence)
1988—Auburn 16, Syracuse 16 (Sugar)
1985—Arizona 13, Georgia 13 (Sun)
1984—Florida St. 17, Georgia 17 (Florida Citrus)
1978—Arkansas 10, UCLA 10 (Fiesta)
1977—(D) Maryland 17, Minnesota 17 (Hall of Fame)
1974—Texas Tech 6, Vanderbilt 6 (Peach)
1974—(D) Houston 31, North Caro. St. 31 (Bluebonnet)
1970—(D) Alabama 24, Oklahoma 24 (Bluebonnet)
1970—(D) Long Beach St. 24, Louisville 24 (Pasadena)
1967—Florida St. 17, Penn St. 17 (Gator)
1960—(D) Alabama 3, Texas 3 (Bluebonnet)
1948—Georgia 20, Maryland 20 (Gator)
1948—Penn St. 13, Southern Methodist 13 (Cotton)
1947—(D) Montana St. 13, New Mexico 13 (Harbor)
1944—Randolph Field 7, Texas 7 (Cotton)
1937—(D) Auburn 7, Villanova 7 (Bacardi)
1936—Hardin-Simmons 14, New Mexico St. 14 (Sun)
1934—(D) Arkansas 7, Centenary (La.) 7 (Dixie Classic)
1927—Alabama 7, Stanford 7 (Rose)
1924—Navy 14, Washington 14 (Rose)

LARGEST DEFICIT OVERCOME TO WIN
22—Brigham Young (46) vs. Southern Methodist (45) (Holiday, 1980) (trailed 35-13 in 3rd quarter and then trailed 45-25 with four minutes remaining in the game)
22—Notre Dame (35) vs. Houston (34) (Cotton, 1979) (trailed 34-12 in 4th quarter)
21—(D) Fresno St. (29) vs. Bowling Green (28) (California, 1982) (trailed 21-0 in 2nd quarter)
19—Wake Forest (39) vs. Oregon (35) (Independence, 1992) (trailed 29-10 in 3rd quarter)
14—Colorado (33) vs. Washington (21) (Holiday, 1996) (trailed 14-0 with 3:10 remaining in first quarter)
14—Rice (28) vs. Colorado (14) (Cotton, 1938) (trailed 14-0 in 2nd quarter)
13—Mississippi (14) vs. Texas Christian (13) (Cotton, 1956) (trailed 13-0 in 2nd quarter)
11—Michigan (27) vs. Nebraska (23) (Fiesta, 1986) (trailed 14-3 in 3rd quarter)

OVERTIME GAMES#
1995—Toledo (40) vs. Nevada (37) (Las Vegas) (1 OT)

#Beginning in 1995-96, tied bowl games were allowed to use a tiebreaker system.

Longest Plays

(D) Denotes discontinued bowl. Year listed is actual year bowl was played.

LONGEST RUNS FROM SCRIMMAGE

Yds.	Player, Team (Score) vs. Opponent (Score)	Bowl, Year
99*	Terry Baker (QB), Oregon St. (6) vs. Villanova (0)	Liberty, 1962
95*#	Dicky Maegle, Rice (28) vs. Alabama (6)	Cotton, 1954
94*(D)	Dwight Ford, Southern Cal (47) vs. Texas A&M (28)	Bluebonnet, 1977
94*	Larry Smith, Florida (27) vs. Georgia Tech (12)	Orange, 1967
94*	Hascall Henshaw, Arizona St. (13) vs. Case Reserve (26)	Sun, 1941

*#Famous bench-tackle play; Maegle tackled on Alabama 40-yard line by Tommy Lewis, awarded touchdown. *Scored touchdown on play.*

LONGEST PASS PLAYS

Yds.	Player, Team (Score) vs. Opponent (Score)	Bowl, Year
95*	Ronnie Fletcher to Ben Hart, Oklahoma (19) vs. Florida St. (36)	Gator, Jan. 2, 1965
93*(D)	Stan Heath to Tommy Kalminir, Nevada (13) vs. North Texas (6)	Salad, 1948
91*(D)	Mark Barsotti to Stephen Shelley, Fresno St. (27) vs. Ball St. (6)	California, 1989
89*	Pete Gonzalez to Jake Hoffart, Pittsburgh (7) vs. Southern Miss. (41)	Liberty, 1997
88*	Dave Schnell to Rob Turner, Indiana (34) vs. South Caro. (10)	Liberty, 1988
87*	Mike Thomas to L. C. Stevens, North Caro. (20) vs. Arkansas (10)	Carquest, Dec. 30, 1995
87*	Drew Bledsoe to Phillip Bobo, Washington St. (31) vs. Utah (28)	Copper, 1992

Photo from Brigham Young sports information

Jim Machon's "Hail Mary" pass to Clay Brown rallied Brigham Young from a 22-point deficit to a last-second, 46-45 victory over Southern Methodist in the 1980 Holiday Bowl.

Yds.	Player, Team (Score) vs. Opponent (Score)	Bowl, Year
87*	Randy Wright to Tim Stracka, Wisconsin (14) vs. Kansas St. (3)	Independence, 1982
87*	Ger Schwedes to Ernie Davis, Syracuse (23) vs. Texas (14)	Cotton, 1960
86*	Brad Otton to Keyshawn Johnson, Southern Cal (55) vs. Texas Tech (14)	Cotton, 1995

Scored touchdown on play.

LONGEST FIELD GOALS

Yds.	Player, Team (Score) vs. Opponent (Score)	Bowl, Year
62	Tony Franklin, Texas A&M (37) vs. Florida (14)	Sun, Jan. 2, 1977
56	Greg Cox, Miami (Fla.) (20) vs. Oklahoma (14)	Orange, 1988
55(D)	Russell Erxleben, Texas (38) vs. Colorado (21)	Bluebonnet, 1975
54	Carlos Huerta, Miami (Fla.) (22) vs. Nebraska (0)	Orange, 1992
54	Quin Rodriguez, Southern Cal (16) vs. Michigan St. (17)	John Hancock, 1990
54	Luis Zendejas, Arizona St. (32) vs. Oklahoma (21)	Fiesta, 1983

LONGEST PUNTS

Yds.	Player, Team (Score) vs. Opponent (Score)	Bowl, Year
84$	Kyle Rote, Southern Methodist (21) vs. Oregon (13)	Cotton, 1949
82	Ike Pickle, Mississippi St. (12) vs. Duquesne (13)	Orange, 1937
80	Elmer Layden, Notre Dame (27) vs. Stanford (10)	Rose, 1925
79$	Doak Walker, Southern Methodist (21) vs. Oregon (13)	Cotton, 1949
77	Mike Sochko, Maryland (21) vs. Houston (30)	Cotton, 1977
73	Sean Reali, Syracuse (41) vs. Clemson (0)	Gator, 1996

$Quick kick.

LONGEST PUNT RETURNS

Yds.	Player, Team (Score) vs. Opponent (Score)	Bowl, Year
86*	Aramis Dandoy, Southern Cal (7) vs. Ohio St. (20)	Rose, 1955
85*	Darran Hall, Colorado St. (35) vs. Missouri (24)	Holiday, 1997
83*	Vai Sikahema, Brigham Young (46) vs. Southern Methodist (45)	Holiday, 1980
82*	Marcus Wall, North Caro. (31) vs. Texas (35)	Sun, 1994
82	Willie Drewrey, West Va. (12) vs. Florida St. (31)	Gator, 1982
80*(D)	Gary Anderson, Arkansas (34) vs. Tulane (15)	Hall of Fame, 1980
80*	Cecil Ingram, Alabama (61) vs. Syracuse (6)	Orange, 1953

Scored touchdown on play.

LONGEST KICKOFF RETURNS

Yds.	Player, Team (Score) vs. Opponent (Score)	Bowl, Year
100*	Deltha O'Neal, California (38) vs. Navy (42)	Aloha, 1996
100*	Derrick Mason, Michigan St. (26) vs. LSU (45)	Independence, 1995
100*	Kirby Dar Dar, Syracuse (26) vs. Colorado (22)	Fiesta, 1993
100*	Pete Panuska, Tennessee (27) vs. Maryland (28)	Sun, 1984
100*	Dave Lowery, Brigham Young (21) vs. Oklahoma St. (49)	Tangerine, 1976
100*	Mike Fink, Missouri (35) vs. Arizona St. (49)	Fiesta, 1972
100*(D)	Bob Smith, Texas A&M (40) vs. Georgia (20)	Presidential Cup, 1950
100*!	Al Hoisch, UCLA (14) vs. Illinois (45)	Rose, 1947

Scored touchdown on play. !Rose Bowl records carry as 103-yard return.

LONGEST INTERCEPTION RETURNS

Yds.	Player, Team (Score) vs. Opponent (Score)	Bowl, Year
95*	Marcus Washington, Colorado (38) vs. Oregon (6)	Cotton, 1996
94*	David Baker, Oklahoma (48) vs. Duke (21)	Orange, 1958
91*	Don Hoover, Ohio (14) vs. West Tex. A&M (15)	Sun, 1962
90*	Norm Beal, Missouri (21) vs. Navy (14)	Orange, 1961
90*	Charlie Brembs, South Caro. (14) vs. Wake Forest (26)	Gator, 1946
90*(D)	G. P. Jackson, Texas Christian (7) vs. Centre (63)	Fort Worth Classic, 1921

Scored touchdown on play.

LONGEST MISCELLANEOUS RETURNS

Yds.	Player, Team (Score) vs. Opponent (Score)	Bowl, Year
98	Greg Mather, Navy (14) vs. Missouri (21) (Int. Lat.)	Orange, 1961
80	Antonio Banks, Virginia Tech (45) vs. Indiana (20) (Blocked field goal return)	Independence, 1993
79	Tremain Mack, Miami (Fla.) (31) vs. Virginia (21) (Live Fum.)	Carquest, 1996
73	Dick Carpenter, Oklahoma (48) vs. Duke (21) (Int. Lat.)	Orange, 1958
65	Steve Manstedt, Nebraska (19) vs. Texas (3) (Live Fum.)	Cotton, 1974

Bowl Coaching Records

All-Time Bowl Appearances

(Ranked by Most Bowl Games Coached)

Coach (Teams Taken to Bowl)	G	W-L-T	Pct.
Bear Bryant, Alabama, Texas A&M, Kentucky	29	15-12-2	.552
*Joe Paterno, Penn St.	28	18-9-1	.661
Tom Osborne, Nebraska	25	12-13-0	.480
*Bobby Bowden, West Va., Florida St.	21	16-4-1	.786
Lou Holtz, William & Mary, North Caro. St., Arkansas, Notre Dame	20	10-8-2	.550
Vince Dooley, Georgia	20	8-10-2	.450
*LaVell Edwards, Brigham Young	20	7-12-1	.375
John Vaught, Mississippi	18	10-8-0	.556
Bo Schembechler, Michigan	17	5-12-0	.294
*Hayden Fry, Southern Methodist, Iowa	17	7-9-1	.441
Johnny Majors, Iowa St., Pittsburgh, Tennessee	16	9-7-0	.563
Darrell Royal, Texas	16	8-7-1	.531
Don James, Kent, Washington	15	10-5-0	.667
Bobby Dodd, Georgia Tech	13	9-4-0	.692
Terry Donahue, UCLA	13	8-4-1	.654
Barry Switzer, Oklahoma	13	8-5-0	.615
Charlie McClendon, LSU	13	7-6-0	.538
Earle Bruce, Ohio St., Colorado St.	12	7-5-0	.583
Woody Hayes, Miami (Ohio), Ohio St.	12	6-6-0	.500
Shug Jordan, Auburn	12	5-7-0	.417
*George Welsh, Navy, Virginia	12	5-7-0	.417
Jerry Claiborne, Virginia Tech, Maryland, Kentucky	11	3-8-0	.273
Bill Yeoman, Houston	11	6-4-1	.591

Active coach.

All-Time Bowl Victories

Coach	Wins	Record	Coach	Wins	Record
*Joe Paterno	18	18-9-1	Darrell Royal	8	8-7-1
*Bobby Bowden	16	16-4-1	Vince Dooley	8	8-10-2
Bear Bryant	15	15-12-2	John Robinson	7	7-1-0
Tom Osborne	12	12-13-0	Bob Devaney	7	7-3-0
Don James	10	10-5-0	Dan Devine	7	7-3-0
John Vaught	10	10-8-0	Earle Bruce	7	7-5-0
Lou Holtz	10	10-8-2	Charlie McClendon	7	7-6-0
Bobby Dodd	9	9-4-0	*LaVell Edwards	7	7-9-1
Johnny Majors	9	9-7-0	*Hayden Fry	7	7-9-1
Terry Donahue	8	8-4-1	Pat Dye	7	7-2-1
Barry Switzer	8	8-5-0			

Active coach.

All-Time Bowl Winning Percentage

(Minimum 11 Games)

Coach, Last Team Coached	G	W-L-T	Pct.
*Bobby Bowden, Florida St.	21	16-4-1	.786
Bobby Dodd, Georgia Tech	13	9-4-0	.692
Don James, Washington	15	10-5-0	.667
*Joe Paterno, Penn St.	28	18-9-1	.661
Terry Donahue, UCLA	13	8-4-1	.654
Barry Switzer, Oklahoma	13	8-5-0	.615
Bill Yeoman, Houston	11	6-4-1	.591
Earle Bruce, Colorado St.	12	7-5-0	.583
Johnny Majors, Pittsburgh	16	9-7-0	.563
John Vaught, Mississippi	18	10-8-0	.556
Bear Bryant, Alabama	29	15-12-2	.552
Lou Holtz, Notre Dame	20	10-8-2	.550
Charlie McClendon, LSU	13	7-6-0	.538
Darrell Royal, Texas	16	8-7-1	.531
Woody Hayes, Ohio St.	12	6-6-0	.500
Tom Osborne, Nebraska	25	12-13-0	.480
Vince Dooley, Georgia	20	8-10-2	.450
*Hayden Fry, Iowa	17	7-9-1	.441
*George Welsh, Virginia	12	5-7-0	.417
Shug Jordan, Auburn	12	5-7-0	.417
*LaVell Edwards, Brigham Young	20	7-12-1	.375
Bo Schembechler, Michigan	17	5-12-0	.294
Jerry Claiborne, Kentucky	11	3-8-0	.273

Active coach.

All-Time Bowl Coaching History

A total of 441 coaches have head-coached in history's 728 major bowl games (the term "major bowl" is defined above the alphabetical list of team bowl records). Below is an alphabetical list of all 441 bowl coaches, with their alma mater and year, their birth date, and their game-by-game bowl records, with name and date of each bowl, opponent, final score (own score first) and opposing coach (in parentheses). A handful coached service teams or colleges never in the major category but are included because they coached against a major team in a major bowl.

Coach/School	Bowl/Date	Opponent/Score (Coach)
JIM AIKEN, 0-1-0 (Wash. & Jeff. '22) Born 5-26-1899		
Oregon	Cotton 1-1-49	Southern Methodist 12-21 (Matty Bell)
FRED AKERS, 2-8-0 (Arkansas '60) Born 3-17-38		
Wyoming	Fiesta 12-19-76	Oklahoma 7-41 (Barry Switzer)
Texas	Cotton 1-2-78	Notre Dame 10-38 (Dan Devine)
Texas	Sun 12-23-78	Maryland 42-0 (Jerry Claiborne)
Texas	Sun 12-22-79	Washington 7-14 (Don James)
Texas	Bluebonnet 12-31-80	North Caro. 7-16 (Dick Crum)
Texas	Cotton 1-1-82	Alabama 14-12 (Paul "Bear" Bryant)
Texas	Sun 12-25-82	North Caro. 10-26 (Dick Crum)
Texas	Cotton 1-2-84	Georgia 9-10 (Vince Dooley)
Texas	Freedom 12-26-84	Iowa 17-55 (Hayden Fry)
Texas	Bluebonnet 12-31-85	Air Force 16-24 (Fisher DeBerry)
BILL ALEXANDER, 3-2-0 (Georgia Tech '12) Born 6-6-1889		
Georgia Tech	Rose 1-1-29	California 8-7 (Clarence "Nibs" Price)
Georgia Tech	Orange 1-1-40	Missouri 21-7 (Don Faurot)
Georgia Tech	Cotton 1-1-43	Texas 7-14 (Dana Bible)
Georgia Tech	Sugar 1-1-44	Tulsa 20-18 (Henry Frnka)
Georgia Tech	Orange 1-1-45	Tulsa 12-26 (Henry Frnka)
LEONARD "STUB" ALLISON, 1-0-0 (Carleton '17) Born 1892		
California	Rose 1-1-38	Alabama 13-0 (Frank Thomas)
BARRY ALVAREZ, 3-1-0 (Nebraska '69) Born 12-30-46		
Wisconsin	Rose 1-1-94	UCLA 21-16 (Terry Donahue)
Wisconsin	Hall of Fame 1-2-95	Duke 34-20 (Fred Goldsmith)
Wisconsin	Copper 12-27-96	Utah 38-10 (Ron McBride)
Wisconsin	Outback 1-1-98	Georgia 6-33 (Jim Donnan)
MIKE ARCHER, 1-1-0 (Miami, Fla. '75) Born 7-26-53		
LSU	Gator 12-31-87	South Caro. 30-13 (Joe Morrison)
LSU	Hall of Fame 1-2-89	Syracuse 10-23 (Dick MacPherson)
IKE ARMSTRONG, 1-0-0 (Drake '23) Born 6-8-1895		
Utah	Sun 1-2-39	New Mexico 16-0 (Ted Shipkey)
BILL ARNSPARGER, 0-3-0 (Miami, Ohio '50) Born 12-16-26		
LSU	Sugar 1-1-85	Nebraska 10-28 (Tom Osborne)
LSU	Liberty 12-27-85	Baylor 7-21 (Grant Teaff)
LSU	Sugar 1-1-87	Nebraska 15-30 (Tom Osborne)
CHRIS AULT, 0-2-0 (Nevada '68) Born 11-8-47		
Nevada	Las Vegas 12-18-92	Bowling Green 34-35 (Gary Blackney)
Nevada	Las Vegas 12-14-95	Toledo 37-40 OT (Gary Pinkel)
CHARLEY BACHMAN, 0-1-0 (Notre Dame '17) Born 12-1-92		
Michigan St.	Orange 1-1-38	Auburn 0-6 (Jack Meagher)
ENOCH BAGSHAW, 0-1-1 (Washington '08) Born 1884		
Washington	Rose 1-1-24	Navy 14-14 (Bob Folwell)
Washington	Rose 1-1-26	Alabama 19-20 (Wallace Wade)
GEORGE BARCLAY, 0-1-0 (North Caro. '35) Born 5-14-11		
Wash. & Lee	Gator 1-1-51	Wyoming 7-20 (Bowden Wyatt)
BILL BARNES, 0-1-0 (Tennessee '41) Born 10-20-17		
UCLA	Rose 1-1-62	Minnesota 3-21 (Murray Warmath)
WILLIS BARNES, 1-1-1 (Nebraska) Born 10-22-1900		
New Mexico	Sun 1-1-44	Southwestern (Tex.) 0-7 (R. M. Medley)
New Mexico	Sun 1-1-46	Denver 34-24 (Clyde "Cac" Hubbard)
New Mexico	Harbor 1-1-47	Montana St. 13-13 (Clyde Carpenter)
GARY BARNETT, 0-2-0 (Missouri '69) Born 5-23-46		
Northwestern	Rose 1-1-96	Southern Cal 32-41 (John Robinson)
Northwestern	Fla. Citrus 1-1-97	Tennessee 28-48 (Phillip Fulmer)
JOHN BARNHILL, 2-1-1 (Tennessee '28) Born 2-21-03		
Tennessee	Sugar 1-1-43	Tulsa 14-7 (Henry Frnka)
Tennessee	Rose 1-1-45	Southern Cal 0-25 (Jeff Cravath)
Arkansas	Cotton 1-1-47	LSU 0-0 (Bernie Moore)
Arkansas	Dixie 1-1-48	William & Mary 21-19 (Rube McCray)
BILL BATTLE, 4-1-0 (Alabama '63) Born 12-8-41		
Tennessee	Sugar 1-1-71	Air Force 34-13 (Ben Martin)
Tennessee	Liberty 12-20-71	Arkansas 14-13 (Frank Broyles)
Tennessee	Bluebonnet 12-30-72	LSU 24-17 (Charlie McClendon)
Tennessee	Gator 12-29-73	Texas Tech 19-28 (Jim Carlen)
Tennessee	Liberty 12-16-74	Maryland 7-3 (Jerry Claiborne)
SAMMY BAUGH, 0-1-0 (Texas Christian '37) Born 3-17-14		
Hardin-Simmons	Sun 12-31-58	Wyoming 6-14 (Bob Devaney)
FRANK BEAMER, 2-3-0 (Virginia Tech '69) Born 10-18-46		
Virginia Tech	Independence 12-31-93	Indiana 45-20 (Bill Mallory)
Virginia Tech	Gator 12-30-94	Tennessee 23-45 (Phillip Fulmer)
Virginia Tech	Sugar 12-31-95	Texas 28-10 (John Mackovic)
Virginia Tech	Orange 12-31-96	Nebraska 21-41 (Tom Osborne)
Virginia Tech	Gator 1-1-98	North Caro. 3-42 (Carl Torbush)
ALEX BELL, 1-1-0 (Villanova '38) Born 8-12-15		
Villanova	Sun 12-20-61	Wichita St. 17-9 (Hank Foldberg)
Villanova	Liberty 12-15-62	Oregon St. 0-6 (Tommy Prothro)
MATTY BELL, 1-1-1 (Centre '20) Born 2-22-1899		
Southern Methodist	Rose 1-1-36	Stanford 0-7 (Claude "Tiny" Thornhill)
Southern Methodist	Cotton 1-1-48	Penn St. 13-13 (Bob Higgins)
Southern Methodist	Cotton 1-1-49	Oregon 21-13 (Jim Aiken)
EMORY BELLARD, 2-3-0 (Southwest Tex. St. '49) Born 12-17-27		
Texas A&M	Liberty 12-22-75	Southern Cal 0-20 (John McKay)
Texas A&M	Sun 1-2-77	Florida 37-14 (Doug Dickey)
Texas A&M	Bluebonnet 12-31-77	Southern Cal 28-47 (John Robinson)
Mississippi St.	Sun 12-27-80	Nebraska 17-31 (Tom Osborne)
Mississippi St.	Hall of Fame 12-31-81	Kansas 10-0 (Don Fambrough)
MIKE BELLOTTI, 1-1-0 (UC Davis '73) Born 12-21-50		
Oregon	Cotton 1-1-96	Colorado 6-38 (Rick Neuheisel)
Oregon	Las Vegas 12-20-97	Air Force 41-13 (Fisher DeBerry)
ARTHUR "DUTCH" BERGMAN, 1-0-1 (Notre Dame '20) Born 2-23-1895		
Catholic	Orange 1-1-36	Mississippi 20-19 (Ed Walker)
Catholic	Sun 1-1-40	Arizona St. 0-0 (Millard "Dixie" Howell)
HUGO BEZDEK, 1-1-0 (Chicago '06) Born 4-1-1884		
Oregon	Rose 1-1-17	Pennsylvania 14-0 (Bob Folwell)
Penn St.	Rose 1-1-23	Southern Cal 3-14 (Elmer "Gus" Henderson)
DANA BIBLE, 3-0-1 (Carson-Newman '12) Born 10-8-1891		
Texas A&M	Dixie Classic 1-2-22	Centre 22-14 (Charley Moran)
Texas	Cotton 1-1-43	Georgia Tech 14-7 (Bill Alexander)
Texas	Cotton 1-1-44	Randolph Field 7-7 (Frank Tritico)
Texas	Cotton 1-1-46	Missouri 40-27 (Chauncey Simpson)
JACK BICKNELL, 2-2-0 (Montclair St. '60) Born 2-20-38		
Boston College	Tangerine 12-18-82	Auburn 26-33 (Pat Dye)
Boston College	Liberty 12-29-83	Notre Dame 18-19 (Gerry Faust)
Boston College	Cotton 1-1-85	Houston 45-28 (Bill Yeoman)
Boston College	Hall of Fame 12-23-86	Georgia 27-24 (Vince Dooley)
BERNIE BIERMAN, 0-1-0 (Minnesota '16) Born 3-11-1894		
Tulane	Rose 1-1-32	Southern Cal 12-21 (Howard Jones)
GARY BLACKNEY, 2-0-0 (Connecticut '67) Born 12-10-55		
Bowling Green	California 12-14-91	Fresno St. 28-21 (Jim Sweeney)
Bowling Green	Las Vegas 12-18-92	Nevada 35-34 (Chris Ault)
BOBBY BOWDEN, 16-4-1 (Samford '53) Born 11-8-29		
West Va.	Peach 12-29-72	North Caro. St. 13-49 (Lou Holtz)
West Va.	Peach 12-31-75	North Caro. St. 13-10 (Lou Holtz)
Florida St.	Tangerine 12-23-77	Texas Tech 40-17 (Steve Sloan)
Florida St.	Orange 1-1-80	Oklahoma 7-24 (Barry Switzer)
Florida St.	Orange 1-1-81	Oklahoma 17-18 (Barry Switzer)
Florida St.	Gator 12-30-82	West Va. 31-12 (Don Nehlen)
Florida St.	Peach 12-30-83	North Caro. 28-3 (Dick Crum)
Florida St.	Fla. Citrus 12-22-84	Georgia 17-17 (Vince Dooley)
Florida St.	Gator 12-30-85	Oklahoma St. 34-23 (Pat Jones)
Florida St.	All-American 12-31-86	Indiana 27-13 (Bill Mallory)
Florida St.	Fiesta 1-1-88	Nebraska 31-28 (Tom Osborne)
Florida St.	Sugar 1-2-89	Auburn 13-7 (Pat Dye)
Florida St.	Fiesta 1-1-90	Nebraska 41-17 (Tom Osborne)
Florida St.	Blockbuster 12-28-90	Penn St. 24-17 (Joe Paterno)
Florida St.	Cotton 1-1-92	Texas A&M 10-2 (R. C. Slocum)
Florida St.	Orange 1-1-93	Nebraska 27-14 (Tom Osborne)
Florida St.	Orange 1-1-94	Nebraska 18-16 (Tom Osborne)
Florida St.	Sugar 1-2-95	Florida 23-17 (Steve Spurrier)
Florida St.	Orange 1-1-96	Notre Dame 31-26 (Lou Holtz)
Florida St.	Sugar 1-2-97	Florida 20-52 (Steve Spurrier)
Florida St.	Sugar 1-1-98	Ohio St. 31-14 (John Cooper)
TERRY BOWDEN, 2-1-0 (West Va. '78) Born 2-24-56		
Auburn	Outback 1-1-96	Penn St. 14-43 (Joe Paterno)
Auburn	Independence 12-31-96	Army 32-29 (Bob Sutton)
Auburn	Peach 1-2-98	Clemson 21-17 (Tommy West)
JEFF BOWER, 1-1-0 (Southern Miss. '76) Born 5-28-53		
Southern Miss.	All-American 12-28-90	North Caro. St. 27-31 (Dick Sheridan)
Southern Miss	Liberty 12-31-97	Pittsburgh 41-7 (Walt Harris)
SAM BOYD, 1-0-0 (Baylor '38) Born 8-12-15		
Baylor	Sugar 1-1-57	Tennessee 13-7 (Bowden Wyatt)
WESLEY BRADSHAW, 0-1-0 (Baylor '23) Born 11-26-1898		
Ouachita Baptist	Shrine 12-18-48	Hardin-Simmons 12-40 (Warren Woodson)
BILLY BREWER, 3-2-0 (Mississippi '61) Born 10-8-35		
Mississippi	Independence 12-10-83	Air Force 3-9 (Ken Hatfield)
Mississippi	Independence 12-20-86	Texas Tech 20-17 (Spike Dykes)
Mississippi	All-American 12-29-89	Air Force 42-29 (Fisher DeBerry)
Mississippi	Gator 1-1-91	Michigan 3-35 (Gary Moeller)
Mississippi	Liberty 12-31-92	Air Force 13-0 (Fisher DeBerry)

Coach/School	Bowl/Date	Opponent/Score (Coach)
JOHN BRIDGERS, 2-1-0 (Auburn '47) Born 1-13-22		
Baylor	Gator 12-31-60	Florida 12-13 (Ray Graves)
Baylor	Gotham 12-9-61	Utah St. 24-9 (John Ralston)
Baylor	Bluebonnet 12-21-63	LSU 14-7 (Charlie McClendon)
RICH BROOKS, 1-3-0 (Oregon St. '63) Born 8-20-41		
Oregon	Independence 12-16-89	Tulsa 27-24 (Dave Rader)
Oregon	Freedom 12-29-90	Colorado St. 31-32 (Earle Bruce)
Oregon	Independence 12-31-92	Wake Forest 35-39 (Bill Dooley)
Oregon	Rose 1-2-95	Penn St. 20-38 (Joe Paterno)
J. O. "BUDDY" BROTHERS, 0-1-0 (Texas Tech '31) Born 5-29-09		
Tulsa	Gator 1-1-53	Florida 13-14 (Bob Woodruff)
MACK BROWN, 3-3-0 (Florida St. '74) Born 8-27-51		
Tulane	Independence 12-19-87	Washington 12-24 (Don James)
North Caro.	Peach 1-2-93	Mississippi St. 21-17 (Jackie Sherrill)
North Caro.	Gator 12-31-93	Alabama 10-24 (Gene Stallings)
North Caro.	Sun 12-30-94	Texas 31-35 (John Mackovic)
North Caro.	Carquest 12-30-95	Arkansas 20-10 (Danny Ford)
North Caro.	Gator 1-1-97	West Va. 20-13 (Don Nehlen)
FRANK BROYLES, 4-6-0 (Georgia Tech '47) Born 12-26-24		
Arkansas	Gator 1-2-60	Georgia Tech 14-7 (Bobby Dodd)
Arkansas	Cotton 1-2-61	Duke 6-7 (Bill Murray)
Arkansas	Sugar 1-1-62	Alabama 3-10 (Paul "Bear" Bryant)
Arkansas	Sugar 1-1-63	Mississippi 13-17 (John Vaught)
Arkansas	Cotton 1-1-65	Nebraska 10-7 (Bob Devaney)
Arkansas	Cotton 1-1-66	LSU 7-14 (Charlie McClendon)
Arkansas	Sugar 1-1-69	Georgia 16-2 (Vince Dooley)
Arkansas	Sugar 1-1-70	Mississippi 22-27 (John Vaught)
Arkansas	Liberty 12-20-71	Tennessee 13-14 (Bill Battle)
Arkansas	Cotton 1-1-76	Georgia 31-10 (Vince Dooley)
EARLE BRUCE, 7-5-0 (Ohio St. '53) Born 3-8-31		
Tampa	Tangerine 12-29-72	Kent 21-18 (Don James)
Iowa St.	Peach 12-31-77	North Caro. St. 14-24 (Bo Rein)
Iowa St.	Hall of Fame 12-20-78	Texas A&M 12-28 (Tom Wilson)
Ohio St.	Rose 1-1-80	Southern Cal 16-17 (John Robinson)
Ohio St.	Fiesta 12-26-80	Penn St. 19-31 (Joe Paterno)
Ohio St.	Liberty 12-30-81	Navy 31-28 (George Welsh)
Ohio St.	Holiday 12-17-82	Brigham Young 47-17 (LaVell Edwards)
Ohio St.	Fiesta 1-2-84	Pittsburgh 28-23 (Foge Fazio)
Ohio St.	Rose 1-1-85	Southern Cal 17-20 (Ted Tollner)
Ohio St.	Fla. Citrus 12-28-85	Brigham Young 10-7 (LaVell Edwards)
Ohio St.	Cotton 1-1-87	Texas A&M 28-12 (Jackie Sherrill)
Colorado St.	Freedom 12-29-90	Oregon 32-31 (Rich Brooks)
MILT BRUHN, 0-2-0 (Minnesota '35) Born 7-28-12		
Wisconsin	Rose 1-1-60	Washington 8-44 (Jim Owens)
Wisconsin	Rose 1-2-63	Southern Cal 37-42 (John McKay)
MIKE BRUMBELOW, 2-1-0 (Texas Christian '30) Born 7-13-06		
UTEP	Sun 1-1-54	Southern Miss. 37-14 (Thad "Pie" Vann)
UTEP	Sun 1-1-55	Florida St. 47-20 (Tom Nugent)
UTEP	Sun 1-1-57	Geo. Washington 0-13 (Eugene "Bo" Sherman)
PAUL "BEAR" BRYANT, 15-12-2 (Alabama '36) Born 9-11-13		
Kentucky	Great Lakes 12-6-47	Villanova 24-14 (Jordan Oliver)
Kentucky	Orange 1-2-50	Santa Clara 13-21 (Len Casanova)
Kentucky	Sugar 1-1-51	Oklahoma 13-7 (Bud Wilkinson)
Kentucky	Cotton 1-1-52	Texas Christian 20-7 (Leo "Dutch" Meyer)
Texas A&M	Gator 12-28-57	Tennessee 0-3 (Bowden Wyatt)
Alabama	Liberty 12-19-59	Penn St. 0-7 (Charles "Rip" Engle)
Alabama	Bluebonnet 12-17-60	Texas 3-3 (Darrell Royal)
Alabama	Sugar 1-1-62	Arkansas 10-3 (Frank Broyles)
Alabama	Orange 1-1-63	Oklahoma 17-0 (Bud Wilkinson)
Alabama	Sugar 1-1-64	Mississippi 12-7 (John Vaught)
Alabama	Orange 1-1-65	Texas 17-21 (Darrell Royal)
Alabama	Orange 1-1-66	Nebraska 39-28 (Bob Devaney)
Alabama	Sugar 1-2-67	Nebraska 34-7 (Bob Devaney)
Alabama	Cotton 1-1-68	Texas A&M 16-20 (Gene Stallings)
Alabama	Gator 12-28-68	Missouri 10-35 (Dan Devine)
Alabama	Liberty 12-13-69	Colorado 33-47 (Eddie Crowder)
Alabama	Bluebonnet 12-31-70	Oklahoma 24-24 (Chuck Fairbanks)
Alabama	Orange 1-1-72	Nebraska 6-38 (Bob Devaney)
Alabama	Cotton 1-1-73	Texas 13-17 (Darrell Royal)
Alabama	Sugar 12-31-73	Notre Dame 23-24 (Ara Parseghian)
Alabama	Orange 1-1-75	Notre Dame 11-13 (Ara Parseghian)
Alabama	Sugar 12-31-75	Penn St. 13-6 (Joe Paterno)
Alabama	Liberty 12-20-76	UCLA 36-6 (Terry Donahue)
Alabama	Sugar 1-2-78	Ohio St. 35-6 (Woody Hayes)
Alabama	Sugar 1-1-79	Penn St. 14-7 (Joe Paterno)
Alabama	Sugar 1-1-80	Arkansas 24-9 (Lou Holtz)
Alabama	Cotton 1-1-81	Baylor 30-2 (Grant Teaff)
Alabama	Cotton 1-1-82	Texas 12-14 (Fred Akers)
Alabama	Liberty 12-29-82	Illinois 21-15 (Mike White)
FRANK BURNS, 0-1-0 (Rutgers '49) Born 3-16-28		
Rutgers	Garden State 12-16-78	Arizona St. 18-34 (Frank Kush)
LEON BURTNETT, 0-1-0 (Southwestern, Kan. '65) Born 5-30-43		
Purdue	Peach 12-31-84	Virginia 24-27 (George Welsh)
WALLY BUTTS, 5-2-1 (Mercer '28) Born 2-7-05		
Georgia	Orange 1-1-42	Texas Christian 40-26 (Leo "Dutch" Meyer)
Georgia	Rose 1-1-43	UCLA 9-0 (Edwin "Babe" Horrell)
Georgia	Oil 1-1-46	Tulsa 20-6 (Henry Frnka)
Georgia	Sugar 1-1-47	North Caro. 20-10 (Carl Snavely)
Georgia	Gator 1-1-48	Maryland 20-20 (Jim Tatum)
Georgia	Orange 1-1-49	Texas 28-41 (Blair Cherry)
Georgia	Presidential Cup 12-9-50	Texas A&M 20-40 (Harry Stiteler)
Georgia	Orange 1-1-60	Missouri 14-0 (Dan Devine)
EDDIE CAMERON, 1-0-0 (Wash. & Lee '24) Born 4-22-02		
Duke	Sugar 1-1-45	Alabama 29-26 (Frank Thomas)
FRANK CAMP, 1-0-0 (Transylvania '30) Born 12-23-05		
Louisville	Sun 1-1-58	Drake 34-20 (Warren Gaer)
JIM CARLEN, 2-5-1 (Georgia Tech '55) Born 7-11-33		
West Va.	Peach 12-30-69	South Caro. 14-3 (Paul Dietzel)
Texas Tech	Sun 12-19-70	Georgia Tech 9-17 (Bud Carson)
Texas Tech	Sun 12-30-72	North Caro. 28-32 (Bill Dooley)
Texas Tech	Gator 12-29-73	Tennessee 28-19 (Bill Battle)
Texas Tech	Peach 12-28-74	Vanderbilt 6-6 (Steve Sloan)
South Caro.	Tangerine 12-20-75	Miami (Ohio) 7-20 (Dick Crum)
South Caro.	Hall of Fame 12-29-79	Missouri 14-24 (Warren Powers)
South Caro.	Gator 12-29-80	Pittsburgh 8-37 (Jackie Sherrill)
CLYDE CARPENTER, 0-0-1 (Montana '32) Born 4-17-08		
Montana St.	Harbor 1-1-47	New Mexico 13-13 (Willis Barnes)
LLOYD CARR, 1-2-0 (Northern Mich. '68) Born 7-30-45		
Michigan	Alamo 12-28-95	Texas A&M 20-22 (R. C. Slocum)
Michigan	Outback 1-1-97	Alabama 14-17 (Gene Stallings)
Michigan	Rose 1-1-98	Washington St. 21-16 (Mike Price)
BUD CARSON, 1-1-0 (North Caro. '52) Born 4-28-30		
Georgia Tech	Sun 12-19-70	Texas Tech 17-9 (Jim Carlen)
Georgia Tech	Peach 12-30-71	Mississippi 18-41 (Billy Kinard)
LEN CASANOVA, 2-2-0 (Santa Clara '27) Born 6-12-05		
Santa Clara	Orange 1-2-50	Kentucky 21-13 (Paul "Bear" Bryant)
Oregon	Rose 1-1-58	Ohio St. 7-10 (Woody Hayes)
Oregon	Liberty 12-17-60	Penn St. 12-41 (Charles "Rip" Engle)
Oregon	Sun 12-31-63	Southern Methodist 21-14 (Hayden Fry)
MILES CASTEEL, 0-1-0 (Kalamazoo '25) Born 12-30-1896		
Arizona	Salad 1-1-49	Drake 13-14 (Al Kawal)
PETE CAWTHON, 0-2-0 (Southwestern, Tex. '20) Born 8-24-1898		
Texas Tech	Sun 1-1-38	West Va. 6-7 (Marshall "Little Sleepy" Glenn)
Texas Tech	Cotton 1-2-39	St. Mary's (Cal.) 13-20 (Edward "Slip" Madigan)
BLAIR CHERRY, 2-1-0 (Texas Christian '24) Born 9-7-01		
Texas	Sugar 1-1-48	Alabama 27-7 (Harold "Red" Drew)
Texas	Orange 1-1-49	Georgia 41-28 (Wally Butts)
Texas	Cotton 1-1-51	Tennessee 14-20 (Bob Neyland)
JERRY CLAIBORNE, 3-8-0 (Kentucky '50) Born 8-26-28		
Virginia Tech	Liberty 12-10-66	Miami (Fla.) 7-14 (Charlie Tate)
Virginia Tech	Liberty 12-14-68	Mississippi 17-34 (John Vaught)
Maryland	Peach 12-28-73	Georgia 16-17 (Vince Dooley)
Maryland	Liberty 12-16-74	Tennessee 3-7 (Bill Battle)
Maryland	Gator 12-29-75	Florida 13-0 (Doug Dickey)
Maryland	Cotton 1-1-77	Houston 21-30 (Bill Yeoman)
Maryland	Hall of Fame 12-22-77	Minnesota 17-7 (Cal Stoll)
Maryland	Sun 12-23-78	Texas 0-42 (Fred Akers)
Maryland	Tangerine 12-20-80	Florida 20-35 (Charley Pell)
Kentucky	Hall of Fame 12-22-83	West Va. 16-20 (Don Nehlen)
Kentucky	Hall of Fame 12-29-84	Wisconsin 20-19 (Dave McClain)
CECIL COLEMAN, 1-0-0 (Arizona St. '50) Born 4-12-26		
Fresno St.	Mercy 11-23-61	Bowling Green 36-6 (Doyt Perry)
BOBBY COLLINS, 3-2-0 (Mississippi St. '55) Born 10-25-33		
Southern Miss.	Independence 12-13-70	McNeese St. 16-14 (Ernie Duplechin)
Southern Miss.	Tangerine 12-19-81	Missouri 17-19 (Warren Powers)
Southern Methodist	Cotton 1-1-83	Pittsburgh 7-3 (Foge Fazio)
Southern Methodist	Sun 12-24-83	Alabama 7-28 (Ray Perkins)
Southern Methodist	Aloha 12-29-84	Notre Dame 27-20 (Gerry Faust)
JOHN COOPER, 4-8-0 (Iowa St. '62) Born 7-2-37		
Arizona St.	Holiday 12-22-85	Arkansas 17-18 (Ken Hatfield)
Arizona St.	Rose 1-1-87	Michigan 22-15 (Glenn "Bo" Schembechler)
Arizona St.	Freedom 12-30-87	Air Force 33-28 (Fisher DeBerry)
Ohio St.	Hall of Fame 1-1-90	Auburn 14-31 (Pat Dye)
Ohio St.	Liberty 12-27-90	Air Force 11-23 (Fisher DeBerry)
Ohio St.	Hall of Fame 1-1-92	Syracuse 17-24 (Paul Pasqualoni)
Ohio St.	Fla. Citrus 1-1-93	Georgia 14-21 (Ray Goff)
Ohio St.	Holiday 12-30-93	Brigham Young 28-21 (LaVell Edwards)
Ohio St.	Fla. Citrus 1-2-95	Alabama 17-24 (Gene Stallings)
Ohio St.	Fla. Citrus 1-1-96	Tennessee 14-20 (Phillip Fulmer)
Ohio St.	Rose 1-1-97	Arizona St. 20-17 (Bruce Snyder)
Ohio St.	Sugar 1-1-98	Florida St. 14-31 (Bobby Bowden)

Coach/School	Bowl/Date	Opponent/Score (Coach)
LEE CORSO, 1-0-1 (Florida St. '57) Born 8-7-35		
Louisville	Pasadena 12-19-70	Long Beach St. 24-24 (Jim Stangeland)
Indiana	Holiday 12-21-79	Brigham Young 38-37 (LaVell Edwards)
GENE CORUM, 0-1-0 (West Va. '48) Born 5-29-21		
West Va.	Liberty 12-19-64	Utah 6-32 (Ray Nagel)
DON CORYELL, 1-0-0 (Washington '50) Born 10-17-24		
San Diego St.	Pasadena 12-6-69	Boston U. 28-7 (Larry Naviaux)
TOM COUGHLIN, 1-1-0 (Syracuse '68) Born 8-31-46		
Boston College	Hall of Fame 1-1-93	Tennessee 23-38 (Phillip Fulmer)
Boston College	Carquest 1-1-94	Virginia 31-13 (George Welsh)
TED COX, 1-0-0 (Minnesota '26) Born 6-30-03		
Tulane	Sugar 1-1-35	Temple 20-14 (Glenn "Pop" Warner)
JEFF CRAVATH, 2-2-0 (Southern Cal '27) Born 2-5-05		
Southern Cal	Rose 1-1-44	Washington 29-0 (Ralph "Pest" Welch)
Southern Cal	Rose 1-1-45	Tennessee 25-0 (John Barnhill)
Southern Cal	Rose 1-1-46	Alabama 14-34 (Frank Thomas)
Southern Cal	Rose 1-1-48	Michigan 0-49 (H. O. "Fritz" Crisler)
H. O. "FRITZ" CRISLER, 1-0-0 (Chicago '22) Born 1-2-1899		
Michigan	Rose 1-1-48	Southern Cal 49-0 (Jeff Cravath)
EDDIE CROWDER, 3-2-0 (Oklahoma '55) Born 8-26-31		
Colorado	Bluebonnet 12-23-67	Miami (Fla.) 31-21 (Charlie Tate)
Colorado	Liberty 12-13-69	Alabama 47-33 (Paul "Bear" Bryant)
Colorado	Liberty 12-12-70	Tulane 3-17 (Jim Pittman)
Colorado	Bluebonnet 12-31-71	Houston 29-17 (Bill Yeoman)
Colorado	Gator 12-20-72	Auburn 3-24 (Ralph "Shug" Jordan)
JACK CROWE, 0-1-0 (Ala.-Birmingham '70) Born 4-6-48		
Arkansas	Independence 12-29-91	Georgia 15-24 (Ray Goff)
JIM CROWLEY, 1-1-0 (Notre Dame '25) Born 9-10-02		
Fordham	Cotton 1-1-41	Texas A&M 12-13 (Homer Norton)
Fordham	Sugar 1-1-42	Missouri 2-0 (Don Faurot)
DICK CRUM, 6-2-0 (Mount Union '57) Born 4-29-34		
Miami (Ohio)	Tangerine 12-21-74	Georgia 21-10 (Vince Dooley)
Miami (Ohio)	Tangerine 12-20-75	South Caro. 20-7 (Jim Carlen)
North Caro.	Gator 12-28-79	Michigan 17-15 (Glenn "Bo" Schembechler)
North Caro.	Bluebonnet 12-31-80	Texas 16-7 (Fred Akers)
North Caro.	Gator 12-28-81	Arkansas 31-27 (Lou Holtz)
North Caro.	Sun 12-25-82	Texas 26-10 (Fred Akers)
North Caro.	Peach 12-30-83	Florida St. 3-28 (Bobby Bowden)
North Caro.	Aloha 12-27-86	Arizona 21-30 (Larry Smith)
FRAN CURCI, 1-0-0 (Miami, Fla. '60) Born 6-11-38		
Kentucky	Peach 12-31-76	North Caro. 21-0 (Bill Dooley)
BILL CURRY, 2-3-0 (Georgia Tech '65) Born 10-21-42		
Georgia Tech	Hall of Fame 12-31-85	Michigan St. 17-14 (George Perles)
Alabama	Hall of Fame 1-2-88	Michigan 24-28 (Glenn "Bo" Schembechler)
Alabama	Sun 12-24-88	Army 29-28 (Jim Young)
Alabama	Sugar 1-1-90	Miami (Fla.) 25-33 (Dennis Erickson)
Kentucky	Peach 12-31-93	Clemson 13-14 (Tommy West)
JACK "CACTUS JACK" CURTICE, 1-1-0 (Transylvania '30) Born 5-24-07		
UTEP	Sun 1-1-49	West Va. 12-21 (Dud DeGroot)
UTEP	Sun 1-2-50	Georgetown 33-20 (Bob Margarita)
JOHN "OX" Da GROSA, 0-1-0 (Colgate '26) Born 2-17-02		
Holy Cross	Orange 1-1-46	Miami (Fla.) 6-13 (Jack Harding)
GARY DARNELL, 0-1-0 (Oklahoma St. '71) Born 10-15-48		
Florida	Freedom 12-29-89	Washington 7-34 (Don James)
DUFFY DAUGHERTY, 1-1-0 (Syracuse '40) Born 9-8-15		
Michigan St.	Rose 1-2-56	UCLA 17-14 (Henry "Red" Sanders)
Michigan St.	Rose 1-1-66	UCLA 12-14 (Tommy Prothro)
BOB DAVIE, 0-1-0 (Youngstown St. '76) Born 9-30-54		
Notre Dame	Independence 12-28-97	LSU 9-27 (Gerry DiNardo)
BOB DAVIS, 0-1-0 (Utah '30) Born 2-13-08		
Colorado St.	Raisin 1-1-49	Occidental 20-21 (Roy Dennis)
BUTCH DAVIS, 1-0-0 (Arkansas '74) Born 11-17-51		
Miami (Fla.)	Carquest 12-27-96	Virginia 31-21 (Geroge Welsh)
PAUL DAVIS, 1-0-0 (Mississippi '47) Born 2-3-22		
Mississippi St.	Liberty 12-21-63	North Caro. St. 16-12 (Earle Edwards)
LOWELL "RED" DAWSON, 0-1-0 (Tulane '30) Born 12-26-06		
Tulane	Sugar 1-1-40	Texas A&M 13-14 (Homer Norton)
FISHER DeBERRY, 4-5-0 (Wofford '60) Born 9-9-38		
Air Force	Independence 12-15-84	Virginia Tech 23-7 (Bill Dooley)
Air Force	Bluebonnet 12-31-85	Texas 24-16 (Fred Akers)
Air Force	Freedom 12-30-87	Arizona St. 28-33 (John Cooper)
Air Force	Liberty 12-29-89	Mississippi 29-42 (Billy Brewer)
Air Force	Liberty 12-27-90	Ohio St. 23-11 (John Cooper)
Air Force	Liberty 12-29-91	Mississippi St. 38-15 (Jackie Sherrill)
Air Force	Liberty 12-31-92	Mississippi 0-13 (Billy Brewer)
Air Force	Copper 12-27-95	Texas Tech 41-55 (Spike Dykes)

Coach/School	Bowl/Date	Opponent/Score (Coach)
Air Force	Las Vegas 12-20-97	Oregon 13-41 (Mike Bellotti)
DUD DeGROOT, 1-0-0 (Stanford '24) Born 11-20-1895		
West Va.	Sun 1-1-49	UTEP 21-12 (Jack "Cactus Jack" Curtice)
ROY DENNIS, 1-0-0 (Occidental '33) Born 5-13-05		
Occidental	Raisin 1-1-49	Colorado St. 21-20 (Bob Davis)
HERB DEROMEDI, 0-1-0 (Michigan '60) Born 5-26-39		
Central Mich.	California 12-8-90	San Jose St. 24-48 (Terry Shea)
BOB DEVANEY, 7-3-0 (Alma '39) Born 4-2-15		
Wyoming	Sun 12-31-58	Hardin-Simmons 14-6 (Sammy Baugh)
Nebraska	Gotham 12-15-62	Miami (Fla.) 36-34 (Andy Gustafson)
Nebraska	Orange 1-1-64	Auburn 13-7 (Ralph "Shug" Jordan)
Nebraska	Cotton 1-1-65	Arkansas 7-10 (Frank Broyles)
Nebraska	Orange 1-1-66	Alabama 28-39 (Paul "Bear" Bryant)
Nebraska	Sugar 1-2-67	Alabama 7-34 (Paul "Bear" Bryant)
Nebraska	Sun 12-20-69	Georgia 45-6 (Vince Dooley)
Nebraska	Orange 1-1-71	LSU 17-12 (Charlie McClendon)
Nebraska	Orange 1-1-72	Alabama 38-6 (Paul "Bear" Bryant)
Nebraska	Orange 1-1-73	Notre Dame 40-6 (Ara Parseghian)
DAN DEVINE, 7-3-0 (Minn.-Duluth '48) Born 12-23-24		
Missouri	Orange 1-1-60	Georgia 0-14 (Wally Butts)
Missouri	Orange 1-2-61	Navy 21-14 (Wayne Hardin)
Missouri	Bluebonnet 12-22-62	Georgia Tech 14-10 (Bobby Dodd)
Missouri	Sugar 1-1-66	Florida 20-18 (Ray Graves)
Missouri	Gator 12-28-68	Alabama 35-10 (Paul "Bear" Bryant)
Missouri	Orange 1-1-70	Penn St. 3-10 (Joe Paterno)
Notre Dame	Gator 12-27-76	Penn St. 20-9 (Joe Paterno)
Notre Dame	Cotton 1-2-78	Texas 38-10 (Fred Akers)
Notre Dame	Cotton 1-1-79	Houston 35-34 (Bill Yeoman)
Notre Dame	Sugar 1-1-81	Georgia 10-17 (Vince Dooley)
PHIL DICKENS, 1-0-0 (Tennessee '37) Born 6-29-14		
Wyoming	Sun 1-2-56	Texas Tech 21-14 (DeWitt Weaver)
DOUG DICKEY, 2-7-0 (Florida '54) Born 6-24-32		
Tennessee	Bluebonnet 12-18-65	Tulsa 27-6 (Glenn Dobbs)
Tennessee	Gator 12-31-66	Syracuse 18-12 (Ben Schwartzwalder)
Tennessee	Orange 1-1-68	Oklahoma 24-26 (Chuck Fairbanks)
Tennessee	Cotton 1-1-69	Texas 13-35 (Darrell Royal)
Tennessee	Gator 12-27-69	Florida 13-14 (Ray Graves)
Florida	Tangerine 12-22-73	Miami (Ohio) 7-16 (Bill Mallory)
Florida	Sugar 12-31-74	Nebraska 10-13 (Tom Osborne)
Florida	Gator 12-29-75	Maryland 0-13 (Jerry Claiborne)
Florida	Sun 1-2-77	Texas A&M 14-37 (Emory Bellard)
JIM DICKEY, 0-1-0 (Houston '56) Born 3-22-34		
Kansas St.	Independence 12-11-82	Wisconsin 3-14 (Dave McClain)
BILL "LONE STAR" DIETZ, 1-0-0 (Carlisle '12) Born 8-15-1885		
Washington St.	Rose 1-1-16	Brown 14-0 (Ed Robinson)
PAUL DIETZEL, 2-2-0 (Miami, Ohio '48) Born 9-5-24		
LSU	Sugar 1-1-59	Clemson 7-0 (Frank Howard)
LSU	Sugar 1-1-60	Mississippi 0-21 (John Vaught)
LSU	Orange 1-1-62	Colorado 25-7 (Sonny Grandelius)
South Caro.	Peach 12-20-69	West Va. 3-14 (Jim Carlen)
GERRY DiNARDO, 3-0-0 (Notre Dame '75) Born 11-10-52		
LSU	Independence 12-29-95	Michigan St. 45-26 (Nick Saban)
LSU	Peach 12-28-96	Clemson 10-7 (Tommy West)
LSU	Independence 12-28-97	Notre Dame 27-9 (Bob Davie)
BOBBY DOBBS, 2-0-0 (Army '46) Born 10-13-22		
UTEP	Sun 12-31-65	Texas Christian 13-12 (Abe Martin)
UTEP	Sun 12-30-67	Mississippi 14-7 (John Vaught)
GLENN DOBBS, 1-1-0 (Tulsa '43) Born 7-12-20		
Tulsa	Bluebonnet 12-19-64	Mississippi 14-7 (John Vaught)
Tulsa	Bluebonnet 12-18-65	Tennessee 6-27 (Doug Dickey)
BOBBY DODD, 9-4-0 (Tennessee '31) Born 11-11-08		
Georgia Tech	Oil 1-1-47	St. Mary's (Cal.) 41-19 (Jimmy Phelan)
Georgia Tech	Orange 1-1-48	Kansas 20-14 (George Sauer)
Georgia Tech	Orange 1-1-52	Baylor 17-14 (George Sauer)
Georgia Tech	Sugar 1-1-53	Mississippi 24-7 (John Vaught)
Georgia Tech	Sugar 1-1-54	West Va. 42-19 (Art Lewis)
Georgia Tech	Cotton 1-1-55	Arkansas 14-6 (Bowden Wyatt)
Georgia Tech	Sugar 1-2-56	Pittsburgh 7-0 (John Michelosen)
Georgia Tech	Gator 12-29-56	Pittsburgh 21-14 (John Michelosen)
Georgia Tech	Gator 1-2-60	Arkansas 7-14 (Frank Broyles)
Georgia Tech	Gator 12-30-61	Penn St. 15-30 (Charles "Rip" Engle)
Georgia Tech	Bluebonnet 12-22-62	Missouri 10-14 (Dan Devine)
Georgia Tech	Gator 12-31-65	Texas Tech 31-21 (J. T. King)
Georgia Tech	Orange 1-2-67	Florida 12-27 (Ray Graves)
ED DOHERTY, 0-2-0 (Boston College '44) Born 7-25-18		
Arizona St.	Salad 1-1-50	Xavier (Ohio) 21-33 (Ed Kluska)
Arizona St.	Salad 1-1-51	Miami (Ohio) 21-34 (Woody Hayes)
JACK DOLAND, 1-0-0 (Tulane '50) Born 3-3-28		
McNeese St.	Independence 12-13-76	Tulsa 20-16 (F. A. Dry)
TERRY DONAHUE, 8-4-1 (UCLA '67) Born 6-24-44		
UCLA	Liberty 12-30-76	Alabama 6-36 (Paul "Bear" Bryant)

Coach/School	Bowl/Date	Opponent/Score (Coach)
UCLA	Fiesta 12-25-78	Arkansas 10-10 (Lou Holtz)
UCLA	Bluebonnet 12-31-81	Michigan 14-33 (Glenn "Bo" Schembechler)
UCLA	Rose 1-1-83	Michigan 24-14 (Glenn "Bo" Schembechler)
UCLA	Rose 1-2-84	Illinois 45-9 (Mike White)
UCLA	Fiesta 1-1-85	Miami (Fla.) 39-37 (Jimmy Johnson)
UCLA	Rose 1-1-86	Iowa 45-28 (Hayden Fry)
UCLA	Freedom 12-30-86	Brigham Young 31-10 (LaVell Edwards)
UCLA	Aloha 12-25-87	Florida 20-16 (Galen Hall)
UCLA	Cotton 1-2-89	Arkansas 17-3 (Ken Hatfield)
UCLA	John Hancock 12-31-91	Illinois 6-3 (Lou Tepper)
UCLA	Rose 1-1-94	Wisconsin 16-21 (Barry Alvarez)
UCLA	Aloha 12-25-95	Kansas 30-51 (Glen Mason)
JIM DONNAN, 1-0-0 (North Caro. St. '68) Born 1-29-45		
Georgia	Outback 1-1-98	Wisconsin 33-6 (Barry Alvarez)
BILL DOOLEY, 3-7-0 (Mississippi St. '56) Born 5-19-34		
North Caro.	Peach 12-30-70	Arizona St. 26-48 (Frank Kush)
North Caro.	Gator 12-31-71	Georgia 3-7 (Vince Dooley)
North Caro.	Sun 12-30-72	Texas Tech 32-28 (Jim Carlen)
North Caro.	Sun 12-28-74	Mississippi St. 24-26 (Bob Tyler)
North Caro.	Peach 12-31-76	Kentucky 0-21 (Fran Curci)
North Caro.	Liberty 12-19-77	Nebraska 17-21 (Tom Osborne)
Virginia Tech	Peach 1-2-81	Miami (Fla.) 10-20 (Howard Schnellenberger)
Virginia Tech	Independence 12-15-84	Air Force 7-23 (Fisher DeBerry)
Virginia Tech	Peach 12-31-86	North Caro. St. 25-24 (Dick Sheridan)
Wake Forest	Independence 12-31-92	Oregon 39-35 (Rich Brooks)
VINCE DOOLEY, 8-10-2 (Auburn '54) Born 9-4-32		
Georgia	Sun 12-26-64	Texas Tech 7-0 (J. T. King)
Georgia	Cotton 12-31-66	Southern Methodist 24-9 (Hayden Fry)
Georgia	Liberty 12-16-67	North Caro. St. 7-14 (Earle Edwards)
Georgia	Sugar 1-1-69	Arkansas 2-16 (Frank Broyles)
Georgia	Sun 12-20-69	Nebraska 6-45 (Bob Devaney)
Georgia	Gator 12-31-71	North Caro. 7-3 (Bill Dooley)
Georgia	Peach 12-28-73	Maryland 17-16 (Jerry Claiborne)
Georgia	Tangerine 12-21-74	Miami (Ohio) 10-21 (Dick Crum)
Georgia	Cotton 1-1-76	Arkansas 10-31 (Frank Broyles)
Georgia	Sugar 1-1-77	Pittsburgh 3-27 (Johnny Majors)
Georgia	Bluebonnet 12-31-78	Stanford 22-25 (Bill Walsh)
Georgia	Sugar 1-1-81	Notre Dame 17-10 (Dan Devine)
Georgia	Sugar 1-1-82	Pittsburgh 20-24 (Jackie Sherrill)
Georgia	Sugar 1-1-83	Penn St. 23-27 (Joe Paterno)
Georgia	Cotton 1-2-84	Texas 10-9 (Fred Akers)
Georgia	Fla. Citrus 12-22-84	Florida St. 17-17 (Bobby Bowden)
Georgia	Sun 12-28-85	Arizona 13-13 (Larry Smith)
Georgia	Hall of Fame 12-23-86	Boston College 24-27 (Jack Bicknell)
Georgia	Liberty 12-29-87	Arkansas 20-17 (Ken Hatfield)
Georgia	Gator 1-1-89	Michigan St. 34-27 (George Perles)
CHARLES "GUS" DORAIS, 0-1-0 (Notre Dame '14) Born 7-21-1891		
Gonzaga	San Diego East-West Christmas Classic 12-25-22	West Va. 13-21 (Clarence "Doc" Spears)
HAROLD "RED" DREW, 1-2-0 (Bates '16) Born 11-9-1894		
Alabama	Sugar 1-1-48	Texas 7-27 (Blair Cherry)
Alabama	Orange 1-1-53	Syracuse 61-6 (Ben Schwartzwalder)
Alabama	Cotton 1-1-54	Rice 6-28 (Jess Neely)
BILL DRIVER, 0-1-0 (Missouri '09) Born 11-7-1883		
Texas Christian	Fort Worth Classic 1-1-21	Centre 7-63 (Charley Moran)
F. A. DRY, 0-1-0 (Oklahoma St. '53) Born 9-2-31		
Tulsa	Independence 12-13-76	McNeese St. 16-20 (Jack Doland)
ERNIE DUPLECHIN, 0-2-0 (Louisiana Col. '55) Born 7-19-32		
McNeese St.	Independence 12-15-79	Syracuse 7-31 (Frank Maloney)
McNeese St.	Independence 12-13-80	Southern Miss. 14-16 (Bobby Collins)
PAT DYE, 7-2-1 (Georgia '62) Born 11-6-39		
East Caro.	Independence 12-16-78	Louisiana Tech 35-13 (Maxie Lambright)
Auburn	Tangerine 12-18-82	Boston College 33-26 (Jack Bicknell)
Auburn	Sugar 1-2-84	Michigan 9-7 (Glenn "Bo" Schembechler)
Auburn	Liberty 12-27-84	Arkansas 21-15 (Ken Hatfield)
Auburn	Cotton 1-1-86	Texas A&M 16-36 (Jackie Sherrill)
Auburn	Fla. Citrus 1-1-87	Southern Cal 16-7 (Ted Tollner)
Auburn	Sugar 1-1-88	Syracuse 16-16 (Dick MacPherson)
Auburn	Sugar 1-2-89	Florida St. 7-13 (Bobby Bowden)
Auburn	Hall of Fame 1-1-90	Ohio St. 31-14 (John Cooper)
Auburn	Peach 12-29-90	Indiana 27-23 (Bill Mallory)
SPIKE DYKES, 2-4-0 (Stephen F. Austin '59) Born 4-15-38		
Texas Tech	Independence 12-20-86	Mississippi 17-20 (Billy Brewer)
Texas Tech	All-American 12-28-89	Duke 49-21 (Steve Spurrier)
Texas Tech	John Hancock 12-24-93	Oklahoma 10-41 (Gary Gibbs)
Texas Tech	Cotton 1-2-95	Southern Cal 14-55 (John Robinson)
Texas Tech	Copper 12-27-95	Air Force 55-41 (Fisher DeBerry)
Texas Tech	Alamo 12-29-96	Iowa 0-27 (Hayden Fry)

Coach/School	Bowl/Date	Opponent/Score (Coach)
LLOYD EATON, 1-1-0 (Black Hills St. '40) Born 3-23-18		
Wyoming	Sun 12-24-66	Florida St. 28-20 (Bill Peterson)
Wyoming	Sugar 1-1-68	LSU 13-20 (Charlie McClendon)
BILL EDWARDS, 1-0-0 (Wittenberg '31) Born 6-21-05		
Case Reserve	Sun 1-1-41	Arizona St. 26-13 (Millard "Dixie" Howell)
EARLE EDWARDS, 1-1-0 (Penn St. '31) Born 11-10-08		
North Caro. St.	Liberty 12-21-63	Mississippi St. 12-16 (Paul Davis)
North Caro. St.	Liberty 12-16-67	Georgia 14-7 (Vince Dooley)
LaVELL EDWARDS, 7-12-1 (Utah St. '52) Born 10-11-30		
Brigham Young	Fiesta 12-28-74	Oklahoma St. 6-16 (Jim Stanley)
Brigham Young	Tangerine 12-18-76	Oklahoma St. 21-49 (Jim Stanley)
Brigham Young	Holiday 12-22-78	Navy 16-23 (George Welsh)
Brigham Young	Holiday 12-21-79	Indiana 37-38 (Lee Corso)
Brigham Young	Holiday 12-19-80	Southern Methodist 46-45 (Ron Meyer)
Brigham Young	Holiday 12-18-81	Washington St. 38-36 (Jim Walden)
Brigham Young	Holiday 12-17-82	Ohio St. 17-47 (Earle Bruce)
Brigham Young	Holiday 12-23-83	Missouri 21-17 (Warren Powers)
Brigham Young	Holiday 12-21-84	Michigan 24-17 (Glenn "Bo" Schembechler)
Brigham Young	Fla. Citrus 12-28-85	Ohio St. 7-10 (Earle Bruce)
Brigham Young	Freedom 12-30-86	UCLA 10-31 (Terry Donahue)
Brigham Young	All-American 12-22-87	Virginia 16-22 (George Welsh)
Brigham Young	Freedom 12-29-88	Colorado 20-17 (Bill McCartney)
Brigham Young	Holiday 12-29-89	Penn St. 39-50 (Joe Paterno)
Brigham Young	Holiday 12-29-90	Texas A&M 14-65 (R. C. Slocum)
Brigham Young	Holiday 12-30-91	Iowa 13-13 (Hayden Fry)
Brigham Young	Aloha 12-25-92	Kansas 20-23 (Glen Mason)
Brigham Young	Holiday 12-30-93	Ohio St. 21-28 (John Cooper)
Brigham Young	Copper 12-29-94	Oklahoma 31-6 (Gary Gibbs)
Brigham Young	Cotton 1-1-97	Kansas St. 19-15 (Bill Snyder)
RAY ELIOT, 2-0-0 (Illinois '32) Born 6-13-05		
Illinois	Rose 1-1-47	UCLA 45-14 (Bert LaBrucherie)
Illinois	Rose 1-1-52	Stanford 40-7 (Chuck Taylor)
BENNIE ELLENDER, 0-1-0 (Tulane '48) Born 3-2-25		
Tulane	Bluebonnet 12-29-73	Houston 7-47 (Bill Yeoman)
CHALMERS "BUMP" ELLIOTT, 1-0-0 (Michigan '48) Born 1-30-25		
Michigan	Rose 1-1-65	Oregon St. 34-7 (Tommy Prothro)
PETE ELLIOTT, 1-1-0 (Michigan '49) Born 9-29-26		
California	Rose 1-1-59	Iowa 12-38 (Forest Evashevski)
Illinois	Rose 1-1-64	Washington 17-7 (Jim Owens)
JACK ELWAY, 0-2-0 (Washington St. '53) Born 5-30-31		
San Jose St.	California 12-19-81	Toledo 25-27 (Chuck Stobart)
Stanford	Gator 12-27-86	Clemson 21-27 (Danny Ford)
CHARLES "RIP" ENGLE, 3-1-0 (Western Md. '30) Born 3-26-06		
Penn St.	Liberty 12-19-53	Alabama 7-0 (Paul "Bear" Bryant)
Penn St.	Liberty 12-17-60	Oregon 41-12 (Len Casanova)
Penn St.	Gator 12-30-61	Georgia Tech 30-15 (Bobby Dodd)
Penn St.	Gator 12-29-62	Florida 7-17 (Ray Graves)
EDDIE ERDELATZ, 2-0-0 (St. Mary's, Cal. '36) Born 4-21-13		
Navy	Sugar 1-1-55	Mississippi 21-0 (John Vaught)
Navy	Cotton 1-1-58	Rice 20-7 (Jess Neely)
DENNIS ERICKSON, 4-3-0 (Montana St. '70) Born 3-24-47		
Washington St.	Aloha 12-25-88	Houston 24-22 (Jack Pardee)
Miami (Fla.)	Sugar 1-1-90	Alabama 33-25 (Bill Curry)
Miami (Fla.)	Cotton 1-1-91	Texas 46-3 (David McWilliams)
Miami (Fla.)	Orange 1-1-92	Nebraska 22-0 (Tom Osborne)
Miami (Fla.)	Sugar 1-1-93	Alabama 13-34 (Gene Stallings)
Miami (Fla.)	Fiesta 1-1-94	Arizona 0-24 (Dick Tomey)
Miami (Fla.)	Orange 1-1-95	Nebraska 17-24 (Tom Osborne)
FOREST EVASHEVSKI, 2-0-0 (Michigan '41) Born 2-19-18		
Iowa	Rose 1-1-57	Oregon St. 35-19 (Tommy Prothro)
Iowa	Rose 1-1-59	California 38-12 (Pete Elliott)
CHUCK FAIRBANKS, 3-1-1 (Michigan St. '55) Born 6-10-33		
Oklahoma	Orange 1-1-68	Tennessee 26-24 (Doug Dickey)
Oklahoma	Bluebonnet 12-31-68	Southern Methodist 27-28 (Hayden Fry)
Oklahoma	Bluebonnet 12-31-70	Alabama 24-24 (Paul "Bear" Bryant)
Oklahoma	Sugar 1-1-72	Auburn 40-22 (Ralph "Shug" Jordan)
Oklahoma	Sugar 12-31-72	Penn St. 14-0 (Joe Paterno)
DON FAMBROUGH, 0-2-0 (Kansas '48) Born 10-19-22		
Kansas	Liberty 12-17-73	North Caro. St. 18-31 (Lou Holtz)
Kansas	Hall of Fame 12-31-81	Mississippi St. 0-10 (Emory Bellard)
DON FAUROT, 0-4-0 (Missouri '25) Born 6-23-02		
Missouri	Orange 1-1-40	Georgia Tech 7-21 (Bill Alexander)
Missouri	Sugar 1-1-42	Fordham 0-2 (Jim Crowley)
Missouri	Gator 1-1-49	Clemson 23-24 (Frank Howard)
Missouri	Gator 1-2-50	Maryland 7-21 (Jim Tatum)
GERRY FAUST, 1-1-0 (Dayton '58) Born 5-21-35		
Notre Dame	Liberty 12-29-83	Boston College 19-18 (Jack Bicknell)
Notre Dame	Aloha 12-29-84	Southern Methodist 20-27 (Bobby Collins)

Coach/School	Bowl/Date	Opponent/Score (Coach)
FOGE FAZIO, 0-2-0 (Pittsburgh '60) Born 2-28-39		
Pittsburgh	Cotton 1-1-83	Southern Methodist 3-7 (Bobby Collins)
Pittsburgh	Fiesta 1-2-84	Ohio St. 23-28 (Earle Bruce)
BEATTIE FEATHERS, 0-1-0 (Tennessee '34) Born 6-1-12		
North Caro. St.	Gator 1-1-47	Oklahoma 13-34 (Jim Tatum)
WES FESLER, 1-0-0 (Ohio St. '32) Born 6-29-08		
Ohio St.	Rose 1-2-50	California 17-14 (Lynn "Pappy" Waldorf)
CHARLIE FICKERT, 0-1-0 (Stanford '98) Born 2-23-1873		
Stanford	Rose 1-1-02	Michigan 0-49 (Fielding "Hurry Up" Yost)
ROBERT FISHER, 1-0-0 (Harvard '12) Born 12-3-1888		
Harvard	Rose 1-1-20	Oregon 7-6 (Charles "Shy" Huntington)
DICK FLYNN, 0-1-0 (Michigan St. '65) Born 7-17-43		
Central Mich.	Las Vegas 12-15-94	UNLV 24-52 (Jeff Horton)
HANK FOLDBERG, 0-1-0 (Army '48) Born 3-12-23		
Wichita St.	Sun 12-30-61	Villanova 9-17 (Alex Bell)
BOB FOLWELL, 0-1-1 (Pennsylvania '08) Born 1885		
Pennsylvania	Rose 1-1-17	Oregon 0-14 (Hugo Bezdek)
Navy	Rose 1-1-24	Washington 14-14 (Enoch Bagshaw)
DANNY FORD, 6-3-0 (Alabama '70) Born 4-2-48		
Clemson	Gator 12-29-78	Ohio St. 17-15 (Woody Hayes)
Clemson	Peach 12-31-79	Baylor 18-24 (Grant Teaff)
Clemson	Orange 1-1-82	Nebraska 22-15 (Tom Osborne)
Clemson	Independence 12-21-85	Minnesota 13-20 (John Gutekunst)
Clemson	Gator 12-27-86	Stanford 27-21 (Jack Elway)
Clemson	Fla. Citrus 1-1-88	Penn St. 35-10 (Joe Paterno)
Clemson	Fla. Citrus 1-2-89	Oklahoma 23-6 (Barry Switzer)
Clemson	Gator 12-30-89	West Va. 27-7 (Don Nehlen)
Arkansas	Carquest 12-30-95	North Caro. 10-20 (Mack Brown)
DENNIS FRANCHIONE, 0-1-0 (Pittsburgh St. '73) Born 3-28-51		
New Mexico	Insight.com 12-27-97	Arizona 14-20 (Dick Tomey)
HENRY FRNKA, 2-3-0 (Austin '26) Born 3-16-03		
Tulsa	Sun 1-1-42	Texas Tech 6-0 (Dell Morgan)
Tulsa	Sugar 1-1-43	Tennessee 7-14 (John Barnhill)
Tulsa	Sugar 1-1-44	Georgia Tech 18-20 (Bill Alexander)
Tulsa	Orange 1-1-45	Georgia Tech 26-12 (Bill Alexander)
Tulsa	Oil 1-1-46	Georgia 6-20 (Wally Butts)
HAYDEN FRY, 7-9-1 (Baylor '51) Born 2-28-29		
Southern Methodist	Sun 12-31-63	Oregon 13-21 (Len Casanova)
Southern Methodist	Cotton 12-31-66	Georgia 9-24 (Vince Dooley)
Southern Methodist	Bluebonnet 12-31-68	Oklahoma 28-27 (Chuck Fairbanks)
Iowa	Rose 1-1-82	Washington 0-28 (Don James)
Iowa	Peach 12-31-82	Tennessee 28-22 (Johnny Majors)
Iowa	Gator 12-30-83	Florida 6-14 (Charley Pell)
Iowa	Freedom 12-26-84	Texas 55-17 (Fred Akers)
Iowa	Rose 1-1-86	UCLA 28-45 (Terry Donahue)
Iowa	Holiday 12-30-86	San Diego St. 39-38 (Denny Stolz)
Iowa	Holiday 12-30-87	Wyoming 20-19 (Paul Roach)
Iowa	Peach 12-31-88	North Caro. St. 23-29 (Dick Sheridan)
Iowa	Rose 1-1-91	Washington 34-46 (Don James)
Iowa	Holiday 12-30-91	Brigham Young 13-13 (LaVell Edwards)
Iowa	Alamo 12-31-93	California 3-37 (Keith Gilbertson)
Iowa	Sun 12-29-95	Washington 38-18 (Jim Lambright)
Iowa	Alamo 12-29-96	Texas Tech 27-0 (Spike Dykes)
Iowa	Sun 12-31-97	Arizona St. 7-17 (Bruce Snyder)
BILL FULCHER, 1-0-0 (Georgia Tech '57) Born 2-9-34		
Georgia Tech	Liberty 12-18-72	Iowa St. 31-30 (Johnny Majors)
PHILLIP FULMER, 4-2-0 (Tennessee '72) Born 9-1-50		
Tennessee	Hall of Fame 1-1-93	Boston College 38-23 (Tom Coughlin)
Tennessee	Fla. Citrus 1-1-94	Penn St. 13-31 (Joe Paterno)
Tennessee	Gator 12-30-94	Virginia Tech 45-23 (Frank Beamer)
Tennessee	Fla. Citrus 1-1-96	Ohio St. 20-14 (John Cooper)
Tennessee	Fla. Citrus 1-1-97	Northwestern 48-28 (Gary Barnett)
Tennessee	Orange 1-2-98	Nebraska 17-42 (Tom Osborne)
WARREN GAER, 0-1-0 (Drake '35) Born 2-7-12		
Drake	Sun 1-1-58	Louisville 20-34 (Frank Camp)
JOE GAVIN, 0-1-0 (Notre Dame '31) Born 3-20-08		
Dayton	Salad 1-1-52	Houston 21-26 (Clyde Lee)
GARY GIBBS, 2-1-0 (Oklahoma '75) Born 8-13-52		
Oklahoma	Gator 12-29-91	Virginia 48-14 (George Welsh)
Oklahoma	John Hancock 12-24-93	Texas Tech 41-10 (Spike Dykes)
Oklahoma	Copper 12-29-94	Brigham Young 6-31 (LaVell Edwards)
VINCE GIBSON, 0-2-0 (Florida St. '55) Born 3-27-33		
Louisville	Independence 12-17-77	Louisiana Tech 14-24 (Maxie Lambright)
Tulane	Hall of Fame 12-27-80	Arkansas 15-34 (Lou Holtz)
CLAUDE GILBERT, 1-1-0 (San Jose St. '59) Born 7-10-32		
San Jose St.	California 12-13-86	Miami (Ohio) 37-7 (Tim Rose)
San Jose St.	California 12-12-87	Eastern Mich. 27-30 (Jim Harkema)
KEITH GILBERTSON, 1-0-0 (Central Wash. '71) Born 5-15-48		
California	Alamo 12-31-93	Iowa 37-3 (Hayden Fry)

Coach/School	Bowl/Date	Opponent/Score (Coach)
SID GILLMAN, 1-1-0 (Ohio St. '34) Born 10-26-11		
Miami (Ohio)	Sun 1-1-48	Texas Tech 13-12 (Dell Morgan)
Cincinnati	Sun 1-1-51	West Tex. A&M 13-14 (Frank Kimbrough)
BILL GLASSFORD, 0-1-0 (Pittsburgh '37) Born 3-8-14		
Nebraska	Orange 1-1-55	Duke 7-34 (Bill Murray)
MARSHALL "LITTLE SLEEPY" GLENN, 1-0-0 (West Va. '31) Born 4-22-08		
West Va.	Sun 1-1-38	Texas Tech 7-6 (Pete Cawthon)
RAY GOFF, 2-2-0 (Georgia '78) Born 7-10-55		
Georgia	Peach 12-30-89	Syracuse 18-19 (Dick MacPherson)
Georgia	Independence 12-29-91	Arkansas 24-15 (Jack Crowe)
Georgia	Fla. Citrus 1-1-93	Ohio St. 21-14 (John Cooper)
Georgia	Peach 12-30-95	Virginia 27-34 (George Welsh)
FRED GOLDSMITH, 0-1-0 (Florida '67) Born 3-3-44		
Duke	Hall of Fame 1-2-95	Wisconsin 20-34 (Barry Alvarez)
MIKE GOTTFRIED, 0-1-0 (Morehead St. '66) Born 12-17-44		
Pittsburgh	Bluebonnet 12-31-87	Texas 27-32 (David McWilliams)
RALPH GRAHAM, 0-1-0 (Kansas St. '34) Born 8-16-10		
Wichita St.	Raisin 1-1-48	Pacific (Cal.) 14-26 (Larry Siemering)
SONNY GRANDELIUS, 0-1-0 (Michigan St. '51) Born 4-16-29		
Colorado	Orange 1-1-62	LSU 7-25 (Paul Dietzel)
RAY GRAVES, 4-1-0 (Tennessee '43) Born 12-31-18		
Florida	Gator 12-31-60	Baylor 13-12 (John Bridgers)
Florida	Gator 12-29-62	Penn St. 17-7 (Charles "Rip" Engle)
Florida	Sugar 1-1-66	Missouri 18-20 (Dan Devine)
Florida	Orange 1-2-67	Georgia Tech 27-12 (Bobby Dodd)
Florida	Gator 12-27-69	Tennessee 14-13 (Doug Dickey)
DENNIS GREEN, 0-1-0 (Iowa '71) Born 2-17-49		
Stanford	Aloha 12-25-91	Georgia Tech 17-18 (Bobby Ross)
VEE GREEN, 1-0-0 (Illinois '24) Born 10-9-1900		
Drake	Raisin 1-1-46	Fresno St. 13-12 (Alvin "Pix" Pierson)
ART GUEPE, 1-0-0 (Marquette '37) Born 1-28-15		
Vanderbilt	Gator 12-31-55	Auburn 25-13 (Ralph "Shug" Jordan)
ANDY GUSTAFSON, 1-3-0 (Pittsburgh '26) Born 4-3-03		
Miami (Fla.)	Orange 1-1-51	Clemson 14-15 (Frank Howard)
Miami (Fla.)	Gator 1-1-52	Clemson 14-0 (Frank Howard)
Miami (Fla.)	Liberty 12-16-61	Syracuse 14-15 (Ben Schwartzwalder)
Miami (Fla.)	Gotham 12-15-62	Nebraska 34-36 (Bob Devaney)
JOHN GUTEKUNST, 1-1-0 (Duke '66) Born 4-13-44		
Minnesota	Independence 12-21-85	Clemson 20-13 (Danny Ford)
Minnesota	Liberty 12-29-86	Tennessee 14-21 (Johnny Majors)
PAUL HACKETT, 1-0-0 (UC Davis '69) Born 6-5-47		
Pittsburgh	John Hancock 12-30-89	Texas A&M 31-28 (R. C. Slocum)
JACK HAGERTY, 0-1-0 (Georgetown '26) Born 7-3-03		
Georgetown	Orange 1-1-41	Mississippi St. 7-14 (Alvin McKeen)
GALEN HALL, 1-1-0 (Penn St. '62) Born 8-14-40		
Florida	Aloha 12-25-87	UCLA 16-20 (Terry Donahue)
Florida	All-American 12-29-88	Illinois 14-10 (John Mackovic)
CURLEY HALLMAN, 1-0-0 (Texas A&M '70) Born 9-3-47		
Southern Miss.	Independence 12-23-88	UTEP 38-18 (Bob Stull)
WAYNE HARDIN, 1-2-0 (Pacific, Cal. '50) Born 3-23-27		
Navy	Orange 1-2-61	Missouri 14-21 (Dan Devine)
Navy	Cotton 1-1-64	Texas 6-28 (Darrell Royal)
Temple	Garden State 12-15-79	California 28-17 (Roger Theder)
JACK HARDING, 1-0-0 (Pittsburgh '26) Born 1-5-1898		
Miami (Fla.)	Orange 1-1-48	Holy Cross 13-6 (John "Ox" Da Grosa)
JIM HARKEMA, 1-0-0 (Kalamazoo '64) Born 6-25-42		
Eastern Mich.	California 12-12-87	San Jose St. 30-27 (Claude Gilbert)
WALT HARRIS, 0-1-0 (Pacific, Cal. '68) Born 11-9-46		
Pittsburgh	Liberty 12-31-97	Southern Miss. 7-41 (Jeff Bower)
KEN HATFIELD, 4-6-0 (Arkansas '65) Born 6-8-43		
Air Force	Hall of Fame 12-31-82	Vanderbilt 36-28 (George MacIntyre)
Air Force	Independence 12-10-83	Mississippi 9-3 (Billy Brewer)
Arkansas	Liberty 12-27-84	Auburn 15-21 (Pat Dye)
Arkansas	Holiday 12-22-85	Arizona St. 18-17 (John Cooper)
Arkansas	Orange 1-1-87	Oklahoma 8-42 (Barry Switzer)
Arkansas	Liberty 12-29-87	Georgia 17-20 (Vince Dooley)
Arkansas	Cotton 1-2-89	UCLA 3-17 (Terry Donahue)
Arkansas	Cotton 1-1-90	Tennessee 27-31 (Johnny Majors)
Clemson	Hall of Fame 1-1-91	Illinois 30-0 (John Mackovic)
Clemson	Fla. Citrus 1-1-92	California 13-37 (Bruce Snyder)
WOODY HAYES, 6-6-0 (Denison '35) Born 2-14-13		
Miami (Ohio)	Salad 1-1-51	Arizona St. 34-21 (Ed Doherty)
Ohio St.	Rose 1-1-55	Southern Cal 20-7 (Jess Hill)
Ohio St.	Rose 1-1-58	Oregon 10-7 (Len Casanova)
Ohio St.	Rose 1-1-69	Southern Cal 27-16 (John McKay)
Ohio St.	Rose 1-1-71	Stanford 17-27 (John Ralston)

BOWL/ALL-STAR RECORDS

Coach/School	Bowl/Date	Opponent/Score (Coach)
Ohio St.	Rose 1-1-73	Southern Cal 17-42 (John McKay)
Ohio St.	Rose 1-1-74	Southern Cal 42-21 (John McKay)
Ohio St.	Rose 1-1-75	Southern Cal 17-18 (John McKay)
Ohio St.	Rose 1-1-76	UCLA 10-23 (Dick Vermeil)
Ohio St.	Orange 1-1-77	Colorado 27-10 (Bill Mallory)
Ohio St.	Sugar 1-2-78	Alabama 6-35 (Paul "Bear" Bryant)
Ohio St.	Gator 12-29-78	Clemson 15-17 (Danny Ford)
KIM HELTON, 0-1-0 (Florida '70) Born 7-28-48		
Houston	Liberty 12-27-96	Syracuse 17-30 (Paul Pasqualoni)
ELMER "GUS" HENDERSON, 2-0-0 (Oberlin '12) Born 3-10-1889		
Southern Cal	Rose 1-1-23	Penn St. 14-3 (Hugo Bezdek)
Southern Cal	L.A. Christmas Festival 12-25-24	Missouri 20-7 (Gwinn Henry)
DAN HENNING, 1-0-0 (William & Mary '64) Born 7-21-42		
Boston College	Aloha 12-25-94	Kansas St. 12-7 (Bill Snyder)
GWINN HENRY, 0-1-0 (Howard Payne '17) Born 8-5-1887		
Missouri	L.A. Christmas Festival 12-25-24	Southern Cal 7-20 (Elmer "Gus" Henderson)
BILL HESS, 0-2-0 (Ohio '47) Born 2-5-23		
Ohio	Sun 12-31-62	West Tex. A&M 14-15 (Joe Kerbel)
Ohio	Tangerine 12-27-68	Richmond 42-49 (Frank Jones)
JIM HICKEY, 1-0-0 (William & Mary '42) Born 1-22-20		
North Caro.	Gator 12-28-63	Air Force 35-0 (Ben Martin)
BOB HIGGINS, 1-0-1 (Penn St. '20) Born 12-24-1893		
West Va. Wesleyan	Dixie Classic 1-1-25	Southern Methodist 9-7 (Ray Morrison)
Penn St.	Cotton 1-1-48	Southern Methodist 13-13 (Matty Bell)
JESS HILL, 1-1-0 (Southern Cal '30) Born 1-20-07		
Southern Cal	Rose 1-1-53	Wisconsin 7-0 (Ivy Williamson)
Southern Cal	Rose 1-1-55	Ohio St. 7-20 (Woody Hayes)
JERRY HINES, 0-0-1 (New Mexico St. '26) Born 10-11-03		
New Mexico St.	Sun 1-1-36	Hardin-Simmons 14-14 (Frank Kimbrough)
BERNARD A. HOBAN, 0-1-0 (Dartmouth '12) Born 4-21-1890		
U. of Mexico	Sun 1-1-45	Southwestern (Tex.) 0-35 (Randolph R. M. Medley)
ORIN "BABE" HOLLINGBERY, 0-1-0 (No college) Born 7-15-1893		
Washington St.	Rose 1-1-31	Alabama 0-24 (Wallace Wade)
LOU HOLTZ, 10-8-2 (Kent '59) Born 1-6-37		
William & Mary	Tangerine 12-28-70	Toledo 12-40 (Frank Lauterbur)
North Caro. St.	Peach 12-29-72	West Va. 49-13 (Bobby Bowden)
North Caro. St.	Liberty 12-17-73	Kansas 31-18 (Don Fambrough)
North Caro. St.	Bluebonnet 12-23-74	Houston 31-31 (Bill Yeoman)
North Caro. St.	Peach 12-31-75	West Va. 10-13 (Bobby Bowden)
Arkansas	Orange 1-2-78	Oklahoma 31-6 (Barry Switzer)
Arkansas	Fiesta 12-25-78	UCLA 10-10 (Terry Donahue)
Arkansas	Sugar 1-1-80	Alabama 9-24 (Paul "Bear" Bryant)
Arkansas	Hall of Fame 12-27-80	Tulane 34-15 (Vince Gibson)
Arkansas	Gator 12-28-81	North Caro. 27-31 (Dick Crum)
Arkansas	Bluebonnet 12-31-82	Florida 28-24 (Charley Pell)
Notre Dame	Cotton 1-1-88	Texas A&M 10-35 (Jackie Sherrill)
Notre Dame	Fiesta 1-2-89	West Va. 34-21 (Don Nehlen)
Notre Dame	Orange 1-1-90	Colorado 21-6 (Bill McCartney)
Notre Dame	Orange 1-1-91	Colorado 9-10 (Bill McCartney)
Notre Dame	Sugar 1-1-92	Florida 39-28 (Steve Spurrier)
Notre Dame	Cotton 1-1-93	Texas A&M 28-3 (R. C. Slocum)
Notre Dame	Cotton 1-1-94	Texas A&M 24-21 (R. C. Slocum)
Notre Dame	Fiesta 1-2-95	Colorado 24-41 (Bill McCartney)
Notre Dame	Orange 1-1-96	Florida St. 26-31 (Bobby Bowden)
EDWIN "BABE" HORRELL, 0-1-0 (California '26) Born 9-29-02		
UCLA	Rose 1-1-43	Georgia 0-9 (Wally Butts)
JEFF HORTON, 1-0-0 (Nevada '81) Born 7-13-57		
UNLV	Las Vegas 12-15-94	Central Mich. 52-24 (Dick Flynn)
FRANK HOWARD, 3-3-0 (Alabama '31) Born 3-25-09		
Clemson	Gator 1-1-49	Missouri 24-23 (Don Faurot)
Clemson	Orange 1-1-51	Miami (Fla.) 15-14 (Andy Gustafson)
Clemson	Gator 1-1-52	Miami (Fla.) 0-14 (Andy Gustafson)
Clemson	Orange 1-1-57	Colorado 21-27 (Dallas Ward)
Clemson	Sugar 1-1-59	LSU 0-7 (Paul Dietzel)
Clemson	Bluebonnet 12-19-59	Texas Christian 23-7 (Abe Martin)
MILLARD "DIXIE" HOWELL, 0-1-1 (Alabama '35) Born 11-24-12		
Arizona St.	Sun 1-1-40	Catholic 0-0 (Arthur "Dutch" Bergman)
Arizona St.	Sun 1-1-41	Case Reserve 13-26 (Bill Edwards)
BILL HUBBARD, 2-0-0 (Stanford '30) Born 2-5-07		
San Jose St.	Raisin 1-1-47	Utah St. 20-0 (E. L. "Dick" Romney)
San Jose St.	Raisin 12-31-49	Texas Tech 20-13 (Dell Morgan)
CLYDE "CAC" HUBBARD, 0-2-0 (Oregon St. '21) Born 9-13-1897		
Denver	Sun 1-1-46	New Mexico 24-34 (Willis Barnes)
Denver	Alamo 1-4-47	Hardin-Simmons 0-20 (Warren Woodson)
CHARLES "SHY" HUNTINGTON, 0-1-0 (Oregon) Born 7-7-1891		
Oregon	Rose 1-1-20	Harvard 6-7 (Robert Fisher)
HARVEY HYDE, 1-0-0 (Redlands '62) Born 7-13-39		
UNLV	California 12-15-84	Toledo 30-13 (Dan Simrell)
DON JAMES, 10-5-0 (Miami, Fla. '54) Born 12-31-32		
Kent	Tangerine 12-29-72	Tampa 18-21 (Earle Bruce)
Washington	Rose 1-2-78	Michigan 27-20 (Glenn "Bo" Schembechler)
Washington	Sun 12-22-79	Texas 14-7 (Fred Akers)
Washington	Rose 1-1-81	Michigan 6-23 (Glenn "Bo" Schembechler)
Washington	Rose 1-1-82	Iowa 28-0 (Hayden Fry)
Washington	Aloha 12-25-82	Maryland 21-20 (Bobby Ross)
Washington	Aloha 12-26-83	Penn St. 10-13 (Joe Paterno)
Washington	Orange 1-1-85	Oklahoma 28-17 (Barry Switzer)
Washington	Freedom 12-30-85	Colorado 20-17 (Bill McCartney)
Washington	Sun 12-25-86	Alabama 6-28 (Ray Perkins)
Washington	Independence 12-18-87	Tulane 24-12 (Mack Brown)
Washington	Freedom 12-29-89	Florida 34-7 (Gary Darnell)
Washington	Rose 1-1-91	Iowa 46-34 (Hayden Fry)
Washington	Rose 1-1-92	Michigan 34-14 (Gary Moeller)
Washington	Rose 1-1-93	Michigan 31-38 (Gary Moeller)
JIMMY JOHNSON, 3-4-0 (Arkansas '65) Born 7-16-43		
Oklahoma St.	Independence 12-12-81	Texas A&M 16-33 (Tom Wilson)
Oklahoma St.	Bluebonnet 12-31-83	Baylor 24-14 (Grant Teaff)
Miami (Fla.)	Fiesta 1-1-85	UCLA 37-39 (Terry Donahue)
Miami (Fla.)	Sugar 1-1-86	Tennessee 7-35 (Johnny Majors)
Miami (Fla.)	Fiesta 1-2-87	Penn St. 10-14 (Joe Paterno)
Miami (Fla.)	Orange 1-1-88	Oklahoma 20-14 (Barry Switzer)
Miami (Fla.)	Orange 1-2-89	Nebraska 23-3 (Tom Osborne)
FRANK JONES, 1-1-0 (North Caro. '48) Born 8-30-21		
Richmond	Tangerine 12-27-68	Ohio 49-42 (Bill Hess)
Richmond	Tangerine 12-28-71	Toledo 3-28 (John Murphy)
GOMER JONES, 0-1-0 (Ohio St. '36) Born 2-26-14		
Oklahoma	Gator 1-2-65	Florida St. 19-36 (Bill Peterson)
HOWARD JONES, 5-0-0 (Yale '08) Born 8-23-1885		
Southern Cal	Rose 1-1-30	Pittsburgh 47-14 (Jock Sutherland)
Southern Cal	Rose 1-1-32	Tulane 21-12 (Bernie Bierman)
Southern Cal	Rose 1-2-33	Pittsburgh 35-0 (Jock Sutherland)
Southern Cal	Rose 1-2-39	Duke 7-3 (Wallace Wade)
Southern Cal	Rose 1-1-40	Tennessee 14-0 (Bob Neyland)
LARRY JONES, 0-1-0 (LSU '54) Born 12-18-33		
Florida St.	Fiesta 12-27-71	Arizona St. 38-45 (Frank Kush)
LAWRENCE McC. "BIFF" JONES, 0-1-0 (Army '17) Born 10-8-95		
Nebraska	Rose 1-1-41	Stanford 13-21 (Clark Shaughnessy)
PAT JONES, 3-1-0 (Arkansas '69) Born 11-4-47		
Oklahoma St.	Gator 12-28-84	South Caro. 21-14 (Joe Morrison)
Oklahoma St.	Gator 12-30-85	Florida St. 23-34 (Bobby Bowden)
Oklahoma St.	Sun 12-25-87	West Va. 35-33 (Don Nehlen)
Oklahoma St.	Holiday 12-30-88	Wyoming 62-14 (Paul Roach)
RALPH "SHUG" JORDAN, 5-7-0 (Auburn '32) Born 9-25-10		
Auburn	Gator 1-1-54	Texas Tech 13-35 (DeWitt Weaver)
Auburn	Gator 12-31-54	Baylor 33-13 (George Sauer)
Auburn	Gator 12-31-55	Vanderbilt 13-25 (Art Guepe)
Auburn	Orange 1-1-64	Nebraska 7-13 (Bob Devaney)
Auburn	Liberty 12-18-65	Mississippi 7-13 (John Vaught)
Auburn	Sun 12-28-68	Arizona 34-10 (Darrell Mudra)
Auburn	Bluebonnet 12-31-69	Houston 7-36 (Bill Yeoman)
Auburn	Gator 1-2-71	Mississippi 35-28 (John Vaught)
Auburn	Sugar 1-1-72	Oklahoma 22-40 (Chuck Fairbanks)
Auburn	Gator 12-30-72	Colorado 24-3 (Eddie Crowder)
Auburn	Sun 12-29-73	Missouri 17-34 (Al Onofrio)
Auburn	Gator 12-30-74	Texas 27-3 (Darrell Royal)
ERNIE JORGE, 1-1-0 (St. Mary's, Cal. '36) Born 10-7-14		
Pacific (Cal.)	Sun 1-1-52	Texas Tech 14-25 (DeWitt Weaver)
Pacific (Cal.)	Sun 1-1-53	Southern Miss. 26-7 (Thad "Pie" Vann)
AL KAWAL, 1-0-0 (Northwestern '35) Born 7-4-12		
Drake	Salad 1-1-49	Arizona 14-13 (Miles Casteel)
JOE KERBEL, 2-0-0 (Oklahoma '47) Born 5-3-21		
West Tex. A&M	Sun 12-21-62	Ohio 15-14 (Bill Hess)
West Tex. A&M	Pasadena 12-2-67	Cal St. Northridge 35-13 (Sam Winningham)
BILL KERN, 0-1-0 (Pittsburgh '28) Born 9-2-06		
Carnegie Mellon	Sugar 1-2-39	Texas Christian 7-15 (Leo "Dutch" Meyer)
FRANK KIMBROUGH, 2-0-1 (Hardin-Simmons '26) Born 6-24-04		
Hardin-Simmons	Sun 1-1-36	New Mexico St. 14-14 (Jerry Hines)
Hardin-Simmons	Sun 1-1-37	UTEP 34-6 (Max Saxon)
West Tex. A&M	Sun 1-1-51	Cincinnati 14-13 (Sid Gillman)
BILLY KINARD, 1-0-0 (Mississippi '56) Born 12-16-33		
Mississippi	Peach 12-30-71	Georgia Tech 41-18 (Bud Carson)
DEWEY KING, 0-1-0 (North Dak. '50) Born 10-1-25		
San Jose St.	Pasadena 12-18-71	Memphis 9-28 (Billy Murphy)

Coach/School	Bowl/Date	Opponent/Score (Coach)
J. T. KING, 0-2-0 (Texas '38) Born 10-22-12		
Texas Tech	Sun 12-26-64	Georgia 0-7 (Vince Dooley)
Texas Tech	Gator 12-31-65	Georgia Tech 21-31 (Bobby Dodd)
JIMMY KITTS, 1-1-0 (Southern Methodist) Born 6-14-1900		
Rice	Cotton 1-1-38	Colorado 28-14 (Bernard "Bunnie" Oakes)
Virginia Tech	Sun 1-1-47	Cincinnati 6-18 (Ray Nolting)
ED KLUSKA, 1-0-0 (Xavier, Ohio '40) Born 5-21-18		
Xavier (Ohio)	Salad 1-1-50	Arizona St. 33-21 (Ed Doherty)
JOE KRIVAK, 0-0-1 (Syracuse '57) Born 3-20-35		
Maryland	Independence 12-15-90	Louisiana Tech 34-34 (Joe Raymond Peace)
FRANK KUSH, 6-1-0 (Michigan St. '53) Born 1-20-29		
Arizona St.	Peach 12-30-70	North Caro. 48-26 (Bill Dooley)
Arizona St.	Fiesta 12-27-71	Florida St. 45-38 (Larry Jones)
Arizona St.	Fiesta 12-23-72	Missouri 49-35 (Al Onofrio)
Arizona St.	Fiesta 12-21-73	Pittsburgh 28-7 (Johnny Majors)
Arizona St.	Fiesta 12-26-75	Nebraska 17-14 (Tom Osborne)
Arizona St.	Fiesta 12-25-77	Penn St. 30-42 (Joe Paterno)
Arizona St.	Garden State 12-16-78	Rutgers 34-18 (Frank Burns)
BERT LaBRUCHERIE, 0-1-0 (UCLA '29) Born 1-19-05		
UCLA	Rose 1-1-47	Illinois 14-45 (Ray Eliot)
JIM LAMBRIGHT, 1-2-0 (Washington '65) Born 4-26-42		
Washington	Sun 12-29-95	Iowa 18-38 (Hayden Fry)
Washington	Holiday 12-30-96	Colorado 21-33 (Rick Neuheisel)
Washington	Aloha 12-25-97	Michigan St. 51-23 (Nick Saban)
MAXIE LAMBRIGHT, 1-1-0 (Southern Miss. '49) Born 6-3-24		
Louisiana Tech	Independence 12-17-77	Louisville 24-14 (Vince Gibson)
Louisiana Tech	Independence 12-16-78	East Caro. 13-35 (Pat Dye)
FRANK LAUTERBUR, 2-0-0 (Mount Union '49) Born 8-8-25		
Toledo	Tangerine 12-26-69	Davidson 56-33 (Homer Smith)
Toledo	Tangerine 12-28-70	William & Mary 40-12 (Lou Holtz)
FRANK LEAHY, 1-1-0 (Notre Dame '31) Born 8-27-08		
Boston College	Cotton 1-1-40	Clemson 3-6 (Jess Neely)
Boston College	Sugar 1-1-41	Tennessee 19-13 (Bob Neyland)
CLYDE LEE, 1-0-0 (Centenary, La. '32) Born 2-11-08		
Houston	Salad 1-1-52	Dayton 26-21 (Joe Gavin)
ART LEWIS, 0-1-0 (Ohio '36) Born 2-18-11		
West Va.	Sugar 1-1-54	Georgia Tech 19-42 (Bobby Dodd)
BILL LEWIS, 1-0-0 (East Stroudsburg '63) Born 8-5-41		
East Caro.	Peach 1-1-92	North Caro. St. 37-34 (Dick Sheridan)
LOU LITTLE, 1-0-0 (Pennsylvania '20) Born 12-6-1893		
Columbia	Rose 1-1-34	Stanford 7-0 (Claude "Tiny" Thornhill)
STEVE LOGAN, 1-1-0 (Tulsa '75) Born 2-3-53		
East Caro.	Liberty 12-31-94	Illinois 0-30 (Lou Tepper)
East Caro.	Liberty 12-30-95	Stanford 19-13 (Tyrone Willingham)
JIM LOOKABAUGH, 2-1-0 (Oklahoma St. '25) Born 6-15-02		
Oklahoma St.	Cotton 1-1-45	Texas Christian 34-0 (Leo "Dutch" Meyer)
Oklahoma St.	Sugar 1-1-46	St. Mary's (Cal.) 33-13 (Jimmy Phelan)
Oklahoma St.	Delta 1-1-49	William & Mary 0-20 (Rube McCray)
SONNY LUBICK, 1-2-0 (Western Mont. '60) Born 3-12-37		
Colorado St.	Holiday 12-30-94	Michigan 14-24 (Gary Moeller)
Colorado St.	Holiday 12-29-95	Kansas St. 21-54 (Bill Snyder)
Colorado St.	Holiday 12-29-97	Missouri 35-24 (Larry Smith)
AL LUGINBILL, 0-1-0 (Cal Poly Pomona '67) Born 11-3-46		
San Diego St.	Freedom 12-30-91	Tulsa 17-28 (Dave Rader)
BILL LYNCH, 0-1-0 (Butler '77) Born 6-12-54		
Ball St.	Las Vegas 12-19-96	Nevada 15-18 (Jeff Tisdel)
GEORGE MacINTYRE, 0-1-0 (Miami, Fla. '61) Born 4-30-39		
Vanderbilt	Hall of Fame 12-31-82	Air Force 28-36 (Ken Hatfield)
JOHN MACKOVIC, 2-5-0 (Wake Forest '65) Born 10-1-43		
Wake Forest	Tangerine 12-22-79	LSU 10-34 (Charlie McClendon)
Illinois	All-American 12-29-88	Florida 10-14 (Galen Hall)
Illinois	Fla. Citrus 1-1-90	Virginia 31-21 (George Welsh)
Illinois	Hall of Fame 1-1-91	Clemson 0-30 (Ken Hatfield)
Texas	Sun 12-30-94	North Caro. 35-31 (Mack Brown)
Texas	Sugar 12-31-95	Virginia Tech 10-28 (Frank Beamer)
Texas	Fiesta 1-1-97	Penn St. 15-38 (Joe Paterno)
DICK MacPHERSON, 3-1-1 (Springfield '58) Born 11-4-30		
Syracuse	Cherry 12-21-85	Maryland 18-35 (Bobby Ross)
Syracuse	Sugar 1-1-88	Auburn 16-16 (Pat Dye)
Syracuse	Hall of Fame 1-2-89	LSU 23-10 (Mike Archer)
Syracuse	Peach 12-30-89	Georgia 19-18 (Ray Goff)
Syracuse	Aloha 12-25-90	Arizona 28-0 (Dick Tomey)
EDWARD "SLIP" MADIGAN, 1-0-0 (Notre Dame '20) Born 11-18-1895		
St. Mary's (Cal.)	Cotton 1-2-39	Texas Tech 20-13 (Pete Cawthon)

Coach/School	Bowl/Date	Opponent/Score (Coach)
JOHNNY MAJORS, 9-7-0 (Tennessee '57) Born 5-21-35		
Iowa St.	Sun 12-18-71	LSU 15-33 (Charlie McClendon)
Iowa St.	Liberty 12-18-72	Georgia Tech 30-31 (Bill Fulcher)
Pittsburgh	Fiesta 12-21-73	Arizona St. 7-28 (Frank Kush)
Pittsburgh	Sun 12-26-75	Kansas 33-19 (Bud Moore)
Pittsburgh	Sugar 1-1-77	Georgia 27-3 (Vince Dooley)
Tennessee	Bluebonnet 12-31-79	Purdue 22-27 (Jim Young)
Tennessee	Garden State 12-13-81	Wisconsin 28-21 (Dave McClain)
Tennessee	Peach 12-31-82	Iowa 22-28 (Hayden Fry)
Tennessee	Fla. Citrus 12-17-83	Maryland 30-23 (Bobby Ross)
Tennessee	Sun 12-24-84	Maryland 26-27 (Bobby Ross)
Tennessee	Sugar 1-1-86	Miami (Fla.) 35-7 (Jimmy Johnson)
Tennessee	Liberty 12-29-86	Minnesota 21-14 (John Gutekunst)
Tennessee	Peach 1-2-88	Indiana 27-22 (Bill Mallory)
Tennessee	Cotton 1-1-90	Arkansas 31-27 (Ken Hatfield)
Tennessee	Sugar 1-1-91	Virginia 23-22 (George Welsh)
Tennessee	Fiesta 1-1-92	Penn St. 17-42 (Joe Paterno)
BILL MALLORY, 4-6-0 (Miami, Ohio '57) Born 5-30-35		
Miami (Ohio)	Tangerine 12-22-73	Florida 16-7 (Doug Dickey)
Colorado	Bluebonnet 12-27-75	Texas 21-38 (Darrell Royal)
Colorado	Orange 1-1-77	Ohio St. 10-27 (Woody Hayes)
Northern Ill.	California 12-17-83	Cal St. Fullerton 20-13 (Gene Murphy)
Indiana	All-American 12-31-86	Florida St. 13-27 (Bobby Bowden)
Indiana	Peach 1-2-88	Tennessee 22-27 (Johnny Majors)
Indiana	Liberty 12-28-88	South Caro. 34-10 (Joe Morrison)
Indiana	Peach 12-29-90	Auburn 23-27 (Pat Dye)
Indiana	Copper 12-31-91	Baylor 24-0 (Grant Teaff)
Indiana	Independence 12-31-93	Virginia Tech 20-45 (Frank Beamer)
FRANK MALONEY, 1-0-0 (Michigan '62) Born 9-26-40		
Syracuse	Independence 12-15-79	McNeese St. 31-7 (Ernie Duplechin)
BOB MARGARITA, 0-1-0 (Brown '44) Born 11-3-20		
Georgetown	Sun 1-2-50	UTEP 20-33 (Jack "Cactus Jack" Curtice)
STEVE MARIUCCI, 0-1-0 (Northern Mich. '77) Born 11-4-55		
California	Aloha 12-25-96	Navy 38-42 (Charlie Weatherbie)
ABE MARTIN, 1-3-1 (Texas Christian '32) Born 10-8-08		
Texas Christian	Cotton 1-2-56	Mississippi 13-14 (John Vaught)
Texas Christian	Cotton 1-1-57	Syracuse 28-27 (Ben Schwartzwalder)
Texas Christian	Cotton 1-1-59	Air Force 0-0 (Ben Martin)
Texas Christian	Bluebonnet 12-19-59	Clemson 7-23 (Frank Howard)
Texas Christian	Sun 12-31-65	UTEP 12-13 (Bobby Dobbs)
BEN MARTIN, 0-2-1 (Navy '46) Born 6-28-21		
Air Force	Cotton 1-1-59	Texas Christian 0-0 (Abe Martin)
Air Force	Gator 12-28-63	North Caro. 0-35 (Jim Hickey)
Air Force	Sugar 1-1-71	Tennessee 13-34 (Bill Battle)
GLEN MASON, 2-0-0 (Ohio St. '72) Born 4-9-50		
Kansas	Aloha 12-25-92	Brigham Young 23-20 (LaVell Edwards)
Kansas	Aloha 12-25-95	UCLA 51-30 (Terry Donahue)
TONY MASON, 0-1-0 (Clarion '50) Born 3-2-30		
Arizona	Fiesta 12-25-79	Pittsburgh 10-16 (Jackie Sherrill)
RON McBRIDE, 1-3-0 (San Jose St. '63) Born 10-14-39		
Utah	Copper 12-29-92	Washington St. 28-31 (Mike Price)
Utah	Freedom 12-30-93	Southern Cal 21-28 (John Robinson)
Utah	Freedom 12-27-94	Arizona 16-13 (Dick Tomey)
Utah	Copper 12-27-96	Wisconsin 10-38 (Barry Alvarez)
TOM McCANN, 0-1-0 (Illinois '24) Born 11-7-1898		
Miami (Fla.)	Orange 1-1-35	Bucknell 0-26 (Edward "Hook" Mylin)
BILL McCARTNEY, 3-6-0 (Missouri '62) Born 8-22-40		
Colorado	Freedom 12-30-85	Washington 17-20 (Don James)
Colorado	Bluebonnet 12-31-86	Baylor 9-21 (Grant Teaff)
Colorado	Freedom 12-29-88	Brigham Young 17-20 (LaVell Edwards)
Colorado	Orange 1-1-90	Notre Dame 6-21 (Lou Holtz)
Colorado	Orange 1-1-91	Notre Dame 10-9 (Lou Holtz)
Colorado	Blockbuster 12-28-91	Alabama 25-30 (Gene Stallings)
Colorado	Fiesta 1-1-93	Syracuse 22-26 (Paul Pasqualoni)
Colorado	Aloha 12-25-93	Fresno St. 41-30 (Jim Sweeney)
Colorado	Fiesta 1-2-95	Notre Dame 41-24 (Lou Holtz)
DAVE McCLAIN, 1-2-0 (Bowling Green '60) Born 1-28-38		
Wisconsin	Garden State 12-13-81	Tennessee 21-28 (Johnny Majors)
Wisconsin	Independence 12-11-82	Kansas St. 14-3 (Jim Dickey)
Wisconsin	Hall of Fame 12-29-84	Kentucky 19-20 (Jerry Claiborne)
CHARLIE McCLENDON, 7-6-0 (Kentucky '50) Born 10-17-22		
LSU	Cotton 1-1-63	Texas 13-0 (Darrell Royal)
LSU	Bluebonnet 12-21-63	Baylor 7-14 (John Bridgers)
LSU	Sugar 1-1-65	Syracuse 13-10 (Ben Schwartzwalder)
LSU	Cotton 1-1-66	Arkansas 14-7 (Frank Broyles)
LSU	Sugar 1-1-68	Wyoming 20-13 (Lloyd Eaton)
LSU	Peach 12-30-68	Florida St. 31-27 (Bill Peterson)
LSU	Orange 1-1-71	Nebraska 12-17 (Bob Devaney)
LSU	Sun 12-18-71	Iowa St. 33-15 (Johnny Majors)
LSU	Bluebonnet 12-30-72	Tennessee 17-24 (Bill Battle)
LSU	Orange 1-1-74	Penn St. 9-16 (Joe Paterno)
LSU	Sun 12-31-77	Stanford 14-24 (Bill Walsh)
LSU	Liberty 12-23-78	Missouri 15-20 (Warren Powers)

Coach/School	Bowl/Date	Opponent/Score (Coach)
LSU	Tangerine 12-22-79	Wake Forest 34-10 (John Mackovic)
RUBE McCRAY, 1-1-0 (Ky. Wesleyan '30)		Born 6-13-05
William & Mary	Dixie 1-1-48	Arkansas 19-21 (John Barnhill)
William & Mary	Delta 1-1-49	Oklahoma St. 20-0 (Jim Lookabaugh)
J. F. "POP" McKALE, 0-1-0 (Albion '10)		Born 6-12-1887
Arizona	San Diego East-West Christmas Classic 12-26-21	Centre 0-38 (Charley Moran)
JOHN McKAY, 6-3-0 (Oregon St. '50)		Born 7-5-23
Southern Cal	Rose 1-2-63	Wisconsin 42-37 (Milt Bruhn)
Southern Cal	Rose 1-2-67	Purdue 13-14 (Jack Mollenkopf)
Southern Cal	Rose 1-1-68	Indiana 14-3 (John Pont)
Southern Cal	Rose 1-1-69	Ohio St. 16-27 (Woody Hayes)
Southern Cal	Rose 1-1-70	Michigan 10-3 (Glenn "Bo" Schembechler)
Southern Cal	Rose 1-1-73	Ohio St. 42-17 (Woody Hayes)
Southern Cal	Rose 1-1-74	Ohio St. 21-42 (Woody Hayes)
Southern Cal	Rose 1-1-75	Ohio St. 18-17 (Woody Hayes)
Southern Cal	Liberty 12-22-75	Texas A&M 20-0 (Emory Bellard)
ALLYN McKEEN, 1-0-0 (Tennessee '29)		Born 1-26-05
Mississippi St.	Orange 1-1-41	Georgetown 14-7 (Jack Hagerty)
JOHNNIE McMILLAN, 0-1-0 (South Caro. '41)		Born 1-27-19
South Caro.	Gator 1-1-46	Wake Forest 14-26 (D. C. "Peahead" Walker)
DAVID McWILLIAMS, 1-1-0 (Texas '64)		Born 4-18-42
Texas	Bluebonnet 12-31-87	Pittsburgh 32-27 (Mike Gottfried)
Texas	Cotton 1-1-91	Miami (Fla.) 3-46 (Dennis Erickson)
JACK MEAGHER, 1-0-1 (Notre Dame '17)		Born 7-4-1894
Auburn	Bacardi, Cuba 1-1-37	Villanova 7-7 (Maurice "Clipper" Smith)
Auburn	Orange 1-1-38	Michigan St. 6-0 (Charlie Bachman)
RANDOLPH R. M. MEDLEY, 2-0-0 (Mo. Wesleyan '21)		Born 9-22-1898
Southwestern (Tex.)	Sun 1-1-44	New Mexico 7-0 (Willis Barnes)
Southwestern (Tex.)	Sun 1-1-45	U. of Mexico 35-0 (Bernard A. Hoban)
LEO "DUTCH" MEYER, 3-4-0 (Texas Christian '22)		Born 1-15-1898
Texas Christian	Sugar 1-1-36	LSU 3-2 (Bernie Moore)
Texas Christian	Cotton 1-1-37	Marquette 16-6 (Frank Murray)
Texas Christian	Sugar 1-2-39	Carnegie Mellon 15-7 (Bill Kern)
Texas Christian	Orange 1-1-42	Georgia 26-40 (Wally Butts)
Texas Christian	Cotton 1-1-45	Oklahoma St. 0-34 (Jim Lookabaugh)
Texas Christian	Delta 1-1-48	Mississippi 9-13 (John Vaught)
Texas Christian	Cotton 1-1-52	Kentucky 7-20 (Paul "Bear" Bryant)
RON MEYER, 0-1-0 (Purdue '63)		Born 2-17-41
Southern Methodist	Holiday 12-19-80	Brigham Young 45-46 (LaVell Edwards)
RICK MINTER, 1-0-0 (Henderson St. '77)		Born 10-4-54
Cincinnati	Humanitarian 12-29-97	Utah St. 35-19 (John L. Smith)
JOHN MICHELOSEN, 0-2-0 (Pittsburgh '38)		Born 2-13-16
Pittsburgh	Sugar 1-2-56	Georgia Tech 0-7 (Bobby Dodd)
Pittsburgh	Gator 12-29-56	Georgia Tech 14-21 (Bobby Dodd)
JACK MITCHELL, 1-0-0 (Oklahoma '49)		Born 12-3-24
Kansas	Bluebonnet 12-16-61	Rice 33-7 (Jess Neely)
ODUS MITCHELL, 0-2-0 (West Tex. A&M '25)		Born 6-29-1899
North Texas	Salad 1-1-48	Nevada 6-13 (Joe Sheeketski)
North Texas	Sun 12-31-59	New Mexico St. 8-28 (Warren Woodson)
GARY MOELLER, 4-1-0 (Ohio St. '63)		Born 1-26-41
Michigan	Gator 1-1-91	Mississippi 35-3 (Billy Brewer)
Michigan	Rose 1-1-92	Washington 14-34 (Don James)
Michigan	Rose 1-1-93	Washington 38-31 (Don James)
Michigan	Hall of Fame 1-1-94	North Caro. St. 42-7 (Mike O'Cain)
Michigan	Holiday 12-30-94	Colorado St. 24-14 (Sonny Lubick)
AL MOLDE, 0-1-0 (Gust. Adolphus '66)		Born 11-15-43
Western Mich.	California 12-10-88	Fresno St. 30-35 (Jim Sweeney)
JACK MOLLENKOPF, 1-0-0 (Bowling Green '31)		Born 11-24-05
Purdue	Rose 1-2-67	Southern Cal 14-13 (John McKay)
BERNIE MOORE, 1-3-1 (Carson-Newman '17)		Born 4-30-1895
LSU	Sugar 1-1-36	Texas Christian 2-3 (Leo "Dutch" Meyer)
LSU	Sugar 1-1-37	Santa Clara 14-21 (Lawrence "Buck" Shaw)
LSU	Sugar 1-1-38	Santa Clara 0-6 (Lawrence "Buck" Shaw)
LSU	Orange 1-1-44	Texas A&M 19-14 (Homer Norton)
LSU	Cotton 1-1-47	Arkansas 0-0 (John Barnhill)
BUD MOORE, 0-1-0 (Alabama '61)		Born 10-16-39
Kansas	Sun 12-26-75	Pittsburgh 19-33 (Johnny Majors)
CHARLEY MORAN, 2-1-0 (Tennessee '98)		Born 2-22-1878
Centre	Fort Worth Classic 1-1-21	Texas Christian 63-7 (Bill Driver)
Centre	San Diego East-West Christmas Classic 12-26-21	Arizona 38-0 (J. F. "Pop" McKale)
Centre	Dixie Classic 1-2-22	Texas A&M 14-22 (Dana Bible)

Coach/School	Bowl/Date	Opponent/Score (Coach)
DELL MORGAN, 0-3-0 (Austin '25)		Born 2-14-02
Texas Tech	Sun 1-1-42	Tulsa 0-6 (Henry Frnka)
Texas Tech	Sun 1-1-48	Miami (Ohio) 12-13 (Sid Gillman)
Texas Tech	Raisin 12-31-49	San Jose St. 13-20 (Bill Hubbard)
JOE MORRISON, 0-3-0 (Cincinnati '59)		Born 8-21-37
South Caro.	Gator 12-28-84	Oklahoma St. 14-21 (Pat Jones)
South Caro.	Gator 12-31-87	LSU 13-30 (Mike Archer)
South Caro.	Liberty 12-28-88	Indiana 10-34 (Bill Mallory)
RAY MORRISON, 0-1-0 (Vanderbilt '12)		Born 2-28-1885
Southern Methodist	Dixie Classic 1-1-25	West Va. Wesleyan 7-9 (Bob Higgins)
DARRELL MUDRA, 0-1-0 (Peru St. '51)		Born 1-4-29
Arizona	Sun 12-28-68	Auburn 10-34 (Ralph "Shug" Jordan)
CLARENCE "BIGGIE" MUNN, 1-0-0 (Minnesota '32)		Born 9-11-08
Michigan St.	Rose 1-1-54	UCLA 28-20 (Henry "Red" Sanders)
BILLY MURPHY, 1-0-0 (Mississippi St. '47)		Born 1-13-21
Memphis	Pasadena 12-18-71	San Jose St. 28-9 (Dewey King)
GENE MURPHY, 0-1-0 (North Dak. '62)		Born 8-6-39
Cal St. Fullerton	California 12-17-83	Northern Ill. 13-20 (Bill Mallory)
JACK MURPHY, 1-0-0 (Heidelberg '54)		Born 8-6-32
Toledo	Tangerine 12-28-71	Richmond 28-3 (Frank Jones)
BILL MURRAY, 2-1-0 (Duke '31)		Born 9-9-08
Duke	Orange 1-1-55	Nebraska 34-7 (Bill Glassford)
Duke	Orange 1-1-58	Oklahoma 21-48 (Bud Wilkinson)
Duke	Cotton 1-2-61	Arkansas 7-6 (Frank Broyles)
FRANK MURRAY, 0-1-0 (Tufts '08)		Born 2-12-85
Marquette	Cotton 1-1-37	Texas Christian 6-16 (Leo "Dutch" Meyer)
DENNY MYERS, 0-1-0 (Iowa '30)		Born 11-10-05
Boston College	Orange 1-1-43	Alabama 21-37 (Frank Thomas)
EDWARD "HOOK" MYLIN, 1-0-0 (Frank. & Marsh.)		Born 10-23-1897
Bucknell	Orange 1-1-35	Miami (Fla.) 26-0 (Tom McCann)
RAY NAGEL, 1-0-0 (UCLA '50)		Born 5-18-27
Utah	Liberty 12-19-64	West Va. 32-6 (Gene Corum)
LARRY NAVIAUX, 0-1-0 (Nebraska '59)		Born 12-17-36
Boston U.	Pasadena 12-6-69	San Diego St. 7-28 (Don Coryell)
EARLE "GREASY" NEALE, 0-0-1 (West Va. Wesleyan '14)		Born 11-5-1891
Wash. & Jeff.	Rose 1-2-22	California 0-0 (Andy Smith)
JESS NEELY, 4-3-0 (Vanderbilt '23)		Born 1-4-1898
Clemson	Cotton 1-1-40	Boston College 6-3 (Frank Leahy)
Rice	Orange 1-1-47	Tennessee 8-0 (Bob Neyland)
Rice	Cotton 1-2-50	North Caro. 27-13 (Carl Snavely)
Rice	Cotton 1-1-54	Alabama 28-6 (Harold "Red" Drew)
Rice	Cotton 1-1-58	Navy 7-20 (Eddie Erdelatz)
Rice	Sugar 1-2-61	Mississippi 6-14 (John Vaught)
Rice	Bluebonnet 12-16-61	Kansas 7-33 (Jack Mitchell)
DON NEHLEN, 3-8-0 (Bowling Green '58)		Born 1-1-36
West Va.	Peach 12-31-81	Florida 26-6 (Charley Pell)
West Va.	Gator 12-30-82	Florida St. 12-31 (Bobby Bowden)
West Va.	Hall of Fame 12-22-83	Kentucky 20-16 (Jerry Claiborne)
West Va.	Bluebonnet 12-31-84	Texas Christian 31-14 (Jim Wacker)
West Va.	Sun 12-25-87	Oklahoma St. 33-35 (Pat Jones)
West Va.	Fiesta 1-2-89	Notre Dame 21-34 (Lou Holtz)
West Va.	Gator 12-30-89	Clemson 7-27 (Danny Ford)
West Va.	Sugar 1-1-94	Florida 7-41 (Steve Spurrier)
West Va.	Carquest 1-2-95	South Caro. 21-24 (Brad Scott)
West Va.	Gator 1-1-97	North Caro. 13-20 (Mack Brown)
West Va.	Carquest 12-29-97	Georgia Tech 30-35 (George O'Leary)
RICK NEUHEISEL, 2-0-0 (UCLA '84)		Born 2-7-61
Colorado	Cotton 1-1-96	Oregon 38-6 (Mike Bellotti)
Colorado	Holiday 12-30-96	Washington 33-21 (Jim Lambright)
BOB NEYLAND, 2-5-0 (Army '16)		Born 2-17-1892
Tennessee	Orange 1-2-39	Oklahoma 17-0 (Tom Stidham)
Tennessee	Rose 1-1-40	Southern Cal 0-14 (Howard Jones)
Tennessee	Sugar 1-1-41	Boston College 13-19 (Frank Leahy)
Tennessee	Orange 1-1-47	Rice 0-8 (Jess Neely)
Tennessee	Cotton 1-1-51	Texas 20-14 (Blair Cherry)
Tennessee	Sugar 1-1-52	Maryland 13-28 (Jim Tatum)
Tennessee	Cotton 1-1-53	Texas 0-16 (Ed Price)
RAY NOLTING, 1-0-0 (Cincinnati '36)		Born 11-8-13
Cincinnati	Sun 1-1-47	Virginia Tech 18-6 (Jimmy Kitts)
HOMER NORTON, 2-2-1 (Birmingham Southern '16)		Born 12-30-1896
Centenary (La.)	Dixie Classic 1-1-34	Arkansas 7-7 (Fred Thomsen)
Texas A&M	Sugar 1-1-40	Tulane 14-13 (Lowell "Red" Dawson)
Texas A&M	Cotton 1-1-41	Fordham 13-12 (Jim Crowley)
Texas A&M	Cotton 1-1-42	Alabama 21-29 (Frank Thomas)
Texas A&M	Orange 1-1-44	LSU 14-19 (Bernie Moore)
TOM NUGENT, 0-2-0 (Ithaca '36)		Born 2-24-16
Florida St.	Sun 1-1-55	UTEP 20-47 (Mike Brumbelow)
Florida St.	Bluegrass 12-13-58	Oklahoma St. 6-15 (Cliff Speegle)

Coach/School	Bowl/Date	Opponent/Score (Coach)
MIKE O'CAIN, 1-1-0 (Clemson '77) Born 7-20-54		
North Caro. St.	Hall of Fame 1-1-94	Michigan 7-42 (Gary Moeller)
North Caro. St.	Peach 1-1-95	Mississippi St. 28-24 (Jackie Sherrill)
GEORGE O'LEARY, 1-0-0 (New Hampshire '68) Born 8-17-46		
Georgia Tech	Carquest 12-29-97	West Va. 35-30 (Don Nehlen)
BERNARD "BUNNIE" OAKES, 0-1-0 (Illinois '24) Born 9-15-1898		
Colorado	Cotton 1-1-38	Rice 14-28 (Jimmy Kitts)
JORDAN OLIVAR, 1-1-0 (Villanova '38) Born 1-30-15		
Villanova	Great Lakes 12-6-47	Kentucky 14-24 (Paul "Bear" Bryant)
Villanova	Harbor 1-1-49	Nevada 27-7 (Joe Sheeketski)
AL ONOFRIO, 1-1-0 (Arizona St. '43) Born 3-15-21		
Missouri	Fiesta 12-23-72	Arizona St. 35-49 (Frank Kush)
Missouri	Sun 12-29-73	Auburn 34-17 (Ralph "Shug" Jordan)
BENNIE OOSTERBAAN, 1-0-0 (Michigan '28) Born 2-24-06		
Michigan	Rose 1-1-51	California 14-6 (Lynn "Pappy" Waldorf)
TOM OSBORNE, 12-13-0 (Hastings '59) Born 2-23-37		
Nebraska	Cotton 1-1-74	Texas 19-3 (Darrell Royal)
Nebraska	Sugar 12-31-74	Florida 13-10 (Doug Dickey)
Nebraska	Fiesta 12-26-75	Arizona St. 14-17 (Frank Kush)
Nebraska	Bluebonnet 12-31-76	Texas Tech 27-24 (Steve Sloan)
Nebraska	Liberty 12-19-77	North Caro. 21-17 (Bill Dooley)
Nebraska	Orange 1-1-79	Oklahoma 24-31 (Barry Switzer)
Nebraska	Cotton 1-1-80	Houston 14-17 (Bill Yeoman)
Nebraska	Sun 12-27-80	Mississippi St. 31-17 (Emory Bellard)
Nebraska	Orange 1-1-82	Clemson 15-22 (Danny Ford)
Nebraska	Orange 1-1-83	LSU 21-20 (Jerry Stovall)
Nebraska	Orange 1-2-84	Miami (Fla.) 30-31 (Howard Schnellenberger)
Nebraska	Sugar 1-1-85	LSU 28-10 (Bill Arnsparger)
Nebraska	Fiesta 1-1-86	Michigan 23-27 (Glenn "Bo" Schembechler)
Nebraska	Sugar 1-1-87	LSU 30-15 (Bill Arnsparger)
Nebraska	Fiesta 1-1-88	Florida St. 28-31 (Bobby Bowden)
Nebraska	Orange 1-2-89	Miami (Fla.) 3-23 (Jimmy Johnson)
Nebraska	Fiesta 1-1-90	Florida St. 17-41 (Bobby Bowden)
Nebraska	Fla. Citrus 1-1-91	Georgia Tech 21-45 (Bobby Ross)
Nebraska	Orange 1-1-92	Miami (Fla.) 0-22 (Dennis Erickson)
Nebraska	Orange 1-1-93	Florida St. 14-27 (Bobby Bowden)
Nebraska	Orange 1-1-94	Florida St. 16-18 (Bobby Bowden)
Nebraska	Orange 1-1-95	Miami (Fla.) 24-17 (Dennis Erickson)
Nebraska	Fiesta 1-2-96	Florida 62-24 (Steve Spurrier)
Nebraska	Orange 12-31-96	Virginia Tech 41-21 (Frank Beamer)
Nebraska	Orange 1-2-98	Tennessee 42-17 (Phillip Fulmer)
JIM OWENS, 2-1-0 (Oklahoma '50) Born 3-6-27		
Washington	Rose 1-1-60	Wisconsin 44-8 (Milt Bruhn)
Washington	Rose 1-2-61	Minnesota 17-7 (Murray Warmath)
Washington	Rose 1-1-64	Illinois 7-17 (Pete Elliott)
JACK PARDEE, 0-1-0 (Texas A&M '57) Born 4-9-36		
Houston	Aloha 12-25-88	Washington St. 22-24 (Dennis Erickson)
ARA PARSEGHIAN, 3-2-0 (Miami, Ohio '49) Born 5-21-23		
Notre Dame	Cotton 1-1-70	Texas 17-21 (Darrell Royal)
Notre Dame	Cotton 1-1-71	Texas 24-11 (Darrell Royal)
Notre Dame	Orange 1-1-73	Nebraska 6-40 (Bob Devaney)
Notre Dame	Sugar 12-31-73	Alabama 24-23 (Paul "Bear" Bryant)
Notre Dame	Orange 1-1-75	Alabama 13-11 (Paul "Bear" Bryant)
PAUL PASQUALONI, 4-1-0 (Penn St. '72) Born 8-16-49		
Syracuse	Hall of Fame 1-1-92	Ohio St. 24-17 (John Cooper)
Syracuse	Fiesta 1-1-93	Colorado 26-22 (Bill McCartney)
Syracuse	Gator 1-1-96	Clemson 41-0 (Tommy West)
Syracuse	Liberty 12-27-96	Houston 30-17 (Kim Helton)
Syracuse	Fiesta 12-31-97	Kansas St. 18-35 (Bill Snyder)
JOE PATERNO, 18-9-1 (Brown '50) Born 12-21-26		
Penn St.	Gator 12-30-67	Florida St. 17-17 (Bill Peterson)
Penn St.	Orange 1-1-69	Kansas 15-14 (Pepper Rodgers)
Penn St.	Orange 1-1-70	Missouri 10-3 (Dan Devine)
Penn St.	Cotton 1-1-72	Texas 30-6 (Darrell Royal)
Penn St.	Sugar 12-31-72	Oklahoma 0-14 (Chuck Fairbanks)
Penn St.	Orange 1-1-74	LSU 16-9 (Charlie McClendon)
Penn St.	Cotton 1-1-75	Baylor 41-20 (Grant Teaff)
Penn St.	Sugar 12-31-75	Alabama 6-13 (Paul "Bear" Bryant)
Penn St.	Gator 12-27-76	Notre Dame 9-20 (Dan Devine)
Penn St.	Fiesta 12-25-77	Arizona St. 42-30 (Frank Kush)
Penn St.	Sugar 1-1-79	Alabama 7-14 (Paul "Bear" Bryant)
Penn St.	Liberty 12-22-79	Tulane 9-6 (Larry Smith)
Penn St.	Fiesta 12-26-80	Ohio St. 31-19 (Earle Bruce)
Penn St.	Fiesta 1-1-82	Southern Cal 26-10 (John Robinson)
Penn St.	Sugar 1-1-83	Georgia 27-23 (Vince Dooley)
Penn St.	Aloha 12-26-83	Washington 13-10 (Don James)
Penn St.	Orange 1-1-86	Oklahoma 10-25 (Barry Switzer)
Penn St.	Fiesta 1-1-87	Miami (Fla.) 14-10 (Jimmy Johnson)
Penn St.	Fla. Citrus 1-1-88	Clemson 10-35 (Danny Ford)
Penn St.	Holiday 12-29-89	Brigham Young 50-39 (LaVell Edwards)
Penn St.	Blockbuster 12-28-90	Florida St. 17-24 (Bobby Bowden)
Penn St.	Fiesta 1-1-92	Tennessee 42-17 (Johnny Majors)
Penn St.	Blockbuster 1-1-93	Stanford 3-24 (Bill Walsh)
Penn St.	Fla. Citrus 1-1-94	Tennessee 31-13 (Phillip Fulmer)
Penn St.	Rose 1-2-95	Oregon 38-20 (Rich Brooks)
Penn St.	Outback 1-1-96	Auburn 43-14 (Terry Bowden)
Penn St.	Fiesta 1-1-97	Texas 38-15 (John Mackovic)
Penn St.	Fla. Citrus 1-1-98	Florida 6-21 (Steve Spurrier)
JOE RAYMOND PEACE, 0-0-1 (Louisiana Tech '68) Born 6-5-45		
Louisiana Tech	Independence 12-15-90	Maryland 34-34 (Joe Krivak)
CHARLEY PELL, 2-3-0 (Alabama '64) Born 2-27-41		
Clemson	Gator 12-30-77	Pittsburgh 3-34 (Jackie Sherrill)
Florida	Tangerine 12-20-80	Maryland 35-20 (Jerry Claiborne)
Florida	Peach 12-31-81	West Va. 6-26 (Don Nehlen)
Florida	Bluebonnet 12-31-82	Arkansas 24-28 (Lou Holtz)
Florida	Gator 12-30-83	Iowa 14-6 (Hayden Fry)
RAY PERKINS, 3-0-0 (Alabama '67) Born 11-6-41		
Alabama	Sun 12-24-83	Southern Methodist 28-7 (Bobby Collins)
Alabama	Aloha 12-28-85	Southern Cal 24-3 (Ted Tollner)
Alabama	Sun 12-26-86	Washington 28-6 (Don James)
GEORGE PERLES, 3-4-0 (Michigan St. '60) Born 7-16-34		
Michigan St.	Cherry 12-22-84	Army 6-10 (Jim Young)
Michigan St.	Hall of Fame 12-31-85	Georgia Tech 14-17 (Bill Curry)
Michigan St.	Rose 1-1-88	Southern Cal 20-17 (Larry Smith)
Michigan St.	Gator 1-1-89	Georgia 27-34 (Vince Dooley)
Michigan St.	Aloha 12-25-89	Hawaii 33-13 (Bob Wagner)
Michigan St.	John Hancock 12-31-90	Southern Cal 17-16 (Larry Smith)
Michigan St.	Liberty 12-28-93	Louisville 7-18 (Howard Schnellenberger)
DOYT PERRY, 0-1-0 (Bowling Green '32) Born 1-6-10		
Bowling Green	Mercy 11-23-61	Fresno St. 6-36 (Cecil Coleman)
BILL PETERSON, 1-2-1 (Ohio Northern '46) Born 5-14-20		
Florida St.	Gator 1-2-65	Oklahoma 36-19 (Gomer Jones)
Florida St.	Sun 12-24-66	Wyoming 20-28 (Lloyd Eaton)
Florida St.	Gator 12-30-67	Penn St. 17-17 (Joe Paterno)
Florida St.	Peach 12-30-68	LSU 27-31 (Charlie McClendon)
JIMMY PHELAN, 0-3-0 (Notre Dame '19) Born 12-5-1892		
Washington	Rose 1-1-37	Pittsburgh 0-21 (Jock Sutherland)
St. Mary's (Cal.)	Sugar 1-1-46	Oklahoma St. 12-33 (Jim Lookabaugh)
St. Mary's (Cal.)	Oil 1-1-47	Georgia Tech 19-41 (Bobby Dodd)
ALVIN "PIX" PIERSON, 0-1-0 (Nevada '22) Born 7-25-1898		
Fresno St.	Raisin 1-1-46	Drake 12-13 (Vee Green)
GARY PINKEL, 1-0-0 (Kent '75) Born 4-27-52		
Toledo	Las Vegas 12-14-95	Nevada 40-37 OT (Chris Ault)
JIM PITTMAN, 1-0-0 (Mississippi St. '50) Born 8-28-25		
Tulane	Liberty 12-12-70	Colorado 17-3 (Eddie Crowder)
JOHN PONT, 0-2-0 (Miami, Ohio '52) Born 11-13-27		
Miami (Ohio)	Tangerine 12-22-52	Houston 21-49 (Bill Yeoman)
Indiana	Rose 1-1-68	Southern Cal 3-14 (John McKay)
WARREN POWERS, 3-2-0 (Nebraska '63) Born 2-19-41		
Missouri	Liberty 12-23-78	LSU 20-15 (Charlie McClendon)
Missouri	Hall of Fame 12-29-79	South Caro. 24-14 (Jim Carlen)
Missouri	Liberty 12-27-80	Purdue 25-28 (Jim Young)
Missouri	Tangerine 12-19-81	Southern Miss. 19-17 (Bobby Collins)
Missouri	Holiday 12-23-83	Brigham Young 17-21 (LaVell Edwards)
CLARENCE "NIBS" PRICE, 0-1-0 (California '14) Born 1889		
California	Rose 1-1-29	Georgia Tech 7-8 (Bill Alexander)
ED PRICE, 1-0-0 (Texas '33) Born 1-12-09		
Texas	Cotton 1-1-53	Tennessee 16-0 (Bob Neyland)
MIKE PRICE, 2-1-0 (Puget Sound '69) Born 4-6-46		
Washington St.	Copper 12-29-92	Utah 31-28 (Ron McBride)
Washington St.	Alamo 12-31-94	Baylor 10-3 (Chuck Reedy)
Washington St.	Rose 1-1-98	Michigan 16-21 (Lloyd Carr)
TOMMY PROTHRO, 2-2-0 (Duke '42) Born 7-20-20		
Oregon St.	Rose 1-1-57	Iowa 19-35 (Forest Evashevski)
Oregon St.	Liberty 12-15-62	Villanova 6-0 (Alex Bell)
Oregon St.	Rose 1-1-65	Michigan 7-34 (Chalmers "Bump" Elliott)
UCLA	Rose 1-1-66	Michigan St. 14-12 (Duffy Daugherty)
BOB PRUETT, 0-1-0 (Marshall '65) Born 6-30-43		
Marshall	Motor City 12-26-97	Mississippi 31-34 (Tommy Tuberville)
DAVE RADER, 1-1-0 (Tulsa '80) Born 3-9-57		
Tulsa	Independence 12-16-89	Oregon 24-27 (Rich Brooks)
Tulsa	Freedom 12-30-91	San Diego St. 28-17 (Al Luginbill)
JOHN RALSTON, 2-2-0 (California '54) Born 4-25-27		
Utah St.	Sun 12-31-60	New Mexico St. 13-20 (Warren Woodson)
Utah St.	Gotham 12-9-61	Baylor 9-24 (John Bridgers)
Stanford	Rose 1-1-71	Ohio St. 27-17 (Woody Hayes)
Stanford	Rose 1-1-72	Michigan 13-12 (Glenn "Bo" Schembechler)
CHUCK REEDY, 0-1-0 (Appalachian St. '71) Born 5-31-49		
Baylor	Alamo 12-31-94	Washington St. 3-10 (Mike Price)

Coach/School	Bowl/Date	Opponent/Score (Coach)
RED REESE, 1-0-0 (Washington St. '25) Born 3-2-1899		
Second Air Force	Sun 1-1-43	Hardin-Simmons 13-7 (Warren Woodson)
BO REIN, 2-0-0 (Ohio St. '68) Born 7-20-45		
North Caro. St.	Peach 12-31-77	Iowa St. 24-14 (Earle Bruce)
North Caro. St.	Tangerine 12-23-78	Pittsburgh 30-17 (Jackie Sherrill)
PAUL ROACH, 0-3-0 (Black Hills St. '52) Born 10-24-27		
Wyoming	Holiday 12-30-87	Iowa 19-20 (Hayden Fry)
Wyoming	Holiday 12-30-88	Oklahoma St. 14-62 (Pat Jones)
Wyoming	Copper 12-31-90	California 15-17 (Bruce Snyder)
ED ROBINSON, 0-1-0 (Brown '96) Born 10-15-73		
Brown	Rose 1-1-16	Washington St. 0-14 (Bill "Lone Star" Dietz)
JOHN ROBINSON, 7-1-0 (Oregon '58) Born 7-25-35		
Southern Cal	Rose 1-1-77	Michigan 14-6 (Glenn "Bo" Schembechler)
Southern Cal	Bluebonnet 12-31-77	Texas A&M 47-28 (Emory Bellard)
Southern Cal	Rose 1-1-79	Michigan 17-10 (Glenn "Bo" Schembechler)
Southern Cal	Rose 1-1-80	Ohio St. 17-16 (Earle Bruce)
Southern Cal	Fiesta 1-1-82	Penn St. 10-26 (Joe Paterno)
Southern Cal	Freedom 12-30-93	Utah 28-21 (Ron McBride)
Southern Cal	Cotton 1-2-95	Texas Tech 55-14 (Spike Dykes)
Southern Cal	Rose 1-1-96	Northwestern 41-32 (Gary Barnett)
KNUTE ROCKNE, 1-0-0 (Notre Dame '14) Born 3-4-1888		
Notre Dame	Rose 1-1-25	Stanford 27-10 (Glenn "Pop" Warner)
PEPPER RODGERS, 0-2-0 (Georgia Tech '55) Born 10-8-31		
Kansas	Orange 1-1-69	Penn St. 14-15 (Joe Paterno)
Georgia Tech	Peach 12-25-78	Purdue 21-41 (Jim Young)
DARRYL ROGERS, 1-0-0 (Fresno St. '57) Born 5-28-34		
Arizona St.	Fiesta 1-1-83	Oklahoma 32-21 (Barry Switzer)
E. L. "DICK" ROMNEY, 0-1-0 (Utah '17) Born 2-12-1895		
Utah St.	Raisin 1-1-47	San Jose St. 0-20 (Bill Hubbard)
TIM ROSE, 0-1-0 (Xavier, Ohio '62) Born 10-14-41		
Miami (Ohio)	California 12-13-86	San Jose St. 7-37 (Claude Gilbert)
BOBBY ROSS, 4-2-0 (VMI '59) Born 12-23-36		
Maryland	Aloha 12-25-82	Washington 20-21 (Don James)
Maryland	Fla. Citrus 12-17-83	Tennessee 23-30 (Johnny Majors)
Maryland	Sun 12-22-84	Tennessee 27-26 (Johnny Majors)
Maryland	Cherry 12-21-85	Syracuse 35-18 (Dick MacPherson)
Georgia Tech	Fla. Citrus 1-1-91	Nebraska 45-21 (Tom Osborne)
Georgia Tech	Aloha 12-25-91	Stanford 18-17 (Dennis Green)
DARRELL ROYAL, 8-7-1 (Oklahoma '50) Born 7-6-24		
Texas	Sugar 1-1-58	Mississippi 7-39 (John Vaught)
Texas	Cotton 1-1-60	Syracuse 14-23 (Ben Schwartzwalder)
Texas	Bluebonnet 12-17-60	Alabama 3-3 (Paul "Bear" Bryant)
Texas	Cotton 1-1-62	Mississippi 12-7 (John Vaught)
Texas	Cotton 1-1-63	LSU 0-13 (Charlie McClendon)
Texas	Cotton 1-1-64	Navy 28-6 (Wayne Hardin)
Texas	Orange 1-1-65	Alabama 21-17 (Paul "Bear" Bryant)
Texas	Bluebonnet 12-17-66	Mississippi 19-0 (John Vaught)
Texas	Cotton 1-1-69	Tennessee 36-13 (Doug Dickey)
Texas	Cotton 1-1-70	Notre Dame 21-17 (Ara Parseghian)
Texas	Cotton 1-1-71	Notre Dame 11-24 (Ara Parseghian)
Texas	Cotton 1-1-72	Penn St. 6-30 (Joe Paterno)
Texas	Cotton 1-1-73	Alabama 17-13 (Paul "Bear" Bryant)
Texas	Cotton 1-1-74	Nebraska 3-19 (Tom Osborne)
Texas	Gator 12-30-74	Auburn 3-27 (Ralph "Shug" Jordan)
Texas	Bluebonnet 12-27-75	Colorado 38-21 (Bill Mallory)
NICK SABAN, 0-3-0 (Kent '73) Born 10-31-51		
Michigan St.	Independence 12-29-95	LSU 26-45 (Gerry DiNardo)
Michigan St.	Sun 12-31-96	Stanford 0-38 (Tyrone Willingham)
Michigan St.	Aloha 12-25-97	Washington 23-51 (Jim Lambright)
HENRY "RED" SANDERS, 0-2-0 (Vanderbilt '27) Born 3-7-05		
UCLA	Rose 1-1-54	Michigan St. 20-28 (Clarence "Biggie" Munn)
UCLA	Rose 1-2-56	Michigan St. 14-17 (Duffy Daugherty)
RALPH SASSE, 0-1-0 (Army '10) Born 7-19-89		
Mississippi St.	Orange 1-1-37	Duquesne 12-13 (John Smith)
GEORGE SAUER, 0-3-0 (Nebraska '34) Born 12-11-10		
Kansas	Orange 1-1-48	Georgia Tech 14-20 (Bobby Dodd)
Baylor	Orange 1-1-52	Georgia Tech 14-17 (Bobby Dodd)
Baylor	Gator 12-31-54	Auburn 13-33 (Ralph "Shug" Jordan)
MACK SAXON, 0-1-0 (Texas) Born 1901		
UTEP	Sun 1-1-37	Hardin-Simmons 6-34 (Frank Kimbrough)
GLENN "BO" SCHEMBECHLER, 5-12-0 (Miami, Ohio '51) Born 4-1-29		
Michigan	Rose 1-1-70	Southern Cal 3-10 (John McKay)
Michigan	Rose 1-1-72	Stanford 12-13 (John Ralston)
Michigan	Orange 1-1-76	Oklahoma 6-14 (Barry Switzer)
Michigan	Rose 1-1-77	Southern Cal 6-14 (John Robinson)
Michigan	Rose 1-2-78	Washington 20-27 (Don James)
Michigan	Rose 1-1-79	Southern Cal 10-17 (John Robinson)
Michigan	Gator 12-28-79	North Caro. 15-17 (Dick Crum)
Michigan	Rose 1-1-81	Washington 23-6 (Don James)
Michigan	Bluebonnet 12-31-81	UCLA 33-14 (Terry Donahue)
Michigan	Rose 1-1-83	UCLA 14-24 (Terry Donahue)
Michigan	Sugar 1-2-84	Auburn 7-9 (Pat Dye)
Michigan	Holiday 12-21-84	Brigham Young 17-24 (LaVell Edwards)
Michigan	Fiesta 1-1-86	Nebraska 27-23 (Tom Osborne)
Michigan	Rose 1-1-87	Arizona St. 15-22 (John Cooper)
Michigan	Hall of Fame 1-2-88	Alabama 28-24 (Bill Curry)
Michigan	Rose 1-2-89	Southern Cal 22-14 (Larry Smith)
Michigan	Rose 1-1-90	Southern Cal 10-17 (Larry Smith)
MERLE SCHLOSSER, 0-1-0 (Illinois '50) Born 10-14-27		
Western Mich.	Aviation 12-9-61	New Mexico 12-28 (Bill Weeks)
HOWARD SCHNELLENBERGER, 4-0-0 (Kentucky '56) Born 3-16-34		
Miami (Fla.)	Peach 1-2-81	Virginia Tech 20-10 (Bill Dooley)
Miami (Fla.)	Orange 1-2-84	Nebraska 31-30 (Tom Osborne)
Louisville	Fiesta 1-1-91	Alabama 34-7 (Gene Stallings)
Louisville	Liberty 12-28-93	Michigan St. 18-7 (George Perles)
PAUL SCHUDEL, 0-2-0 (Miami, Ohio '66) Born 7-2-44		
Ball St.	California 12-9-89	Fresno St. 6-27 (Jim Sweeney)
Ball St.	Las Vegas 12-17-93	Utah St. 33-42 (Charlie Weatherbie)
BILL SCHUTTE, 0-1-0 (Idaho '33) Born 5-7-10		
San Diego St.	Harbor 1-1-48	Hardin-Simmons 0-53 (Warren Woodson)
BEN SCHWARTZWALDER, 2-5-0 (West Va. '35) Born 6-2-09		
Syracuse	Orange 1-1-53	Alabama 6-61 (Harold "Red" Drew)
Syracuse	Cotton 1-1-57	Texas Christian 27-28 (Abe Martin)
Syracuse	Orange 1-1-59	Oklahoma 6-21 (Bud Wilkinson)
Syracuse	Cotton 1-1-60	Texas 23-14 (Darrell Royal)
Syracuse	Liberty 12-16-61	Miami (Fla.) 15-14 (Andy Gustafson)
Syracuse	Sugar 1-1-65	LSU 10-13 (Charlie McClendon)
Syracuse	Gator 12-31-66	Tennessee 12-18 (Doug Dickey)
BRAD SCOTT, 1-0-0 (Mo.-Rolla '76) Born 9-30-54		
South Caro.	Carquest 1-2-95	West Va. 24-21 (Don Nehlen)
CLARK SHAUGHNESSY, 1-0-0 (Minnesota '14) Born 3-6-1892		
Stanford	Rose 1-1-41	Nebraska 21-13 (Lawrence McC. "Biff" Jones)
LAWRENCE "BUCK" SHAW, 2-0-0 (Notre Dame '22) Born 3-28-99		
Santa Clara	Sugar 1-1-37	LSU 21-14 (Bernie Moore)
Santa Clara	Sugar 1-1-38	LSU 6-0 (Bernie Moore)
TERRY SHEA, 1-0-0 (Oregon '68) Born 6-12-46		
San Jose St.	California 12-8-90	Central Mich. 48-24 (Herb Deromedi)
JOE SHEEKETSKI, 1-1-0 (Notre Dame '33) Born 4-15-09		
Nevada	Salad 1-1-48	North Texas 13-6 (Odus Mitchell)
Nevada	Harbor 1-1-49	Villanova 7-27 (Jordan Olivar)
DICK SHERIDAN, 2-4-0 (South Caro. '64) Born 8-9-41		
North Caro. St.	Peach 12-31-86	Virginia Tech 24-25 (Bill Dooley)
North Caro. St.	Peach 12-31-88	Iowa 28-23 (Hayden Fry)
North Caro. St.	Copper 12-31-89	Arizona 10-17 (Dick Tomey)
North Caro. St.	All-American 12-28-90	Southern Miss. 31-27 (Jeff Bower)
North Caro. St.	Peach 1-1-92	East Caro. 34-37 (Bill Lewis)
North Caro. St.	Gator 12-31-92	Florida 10-27 (Steve Spurrier)
EUGENE "BO" SHERMAN, 1-0-0 (Henderson St. '30) Born 7-5-08		
Geo. Washington	Sun 1-1-57	UTEP 13-0 (Mike Brumbelow)
JACKIE SHERRILL, 6-5-0 (Alabama '66) Born 11-28-43		
Pittsburgh	Gator 12-30-77	Clemson 34-3 (Charley Pell)
Pittsburgh	Tangerine 12-23-78	North Caro. St. 17-30 (Bo Rein)
Pittsburgh	Fiesta 12-25-79	Arizona 16-10 (Tony Mason)
Pittsburgh	Gator 12-29-80	South Caro. 37-9 (Jim Carlen)
Pittsburgh	Sugar 1-1-82	Georgia 24-20 (Vince Dooley)
Texas A&M	Cotton 1-1-86	Auburn 36-16 (Pat Dye)
Texas A&M	Cotton 1-1-87	Ohio St. 12-28 (Earle Bruce)
Texas A&M	Cotton 1-1-88	Notre Dame 35-10 (Lou Holtz)
Mississippi St.	Liberty 12-29-91	Air Force 15-38 (Fisher DeBerry)
Mississippi St.	Peach 1-2-93	North Caro. 17-21 (Mack Brown)
Mississippi St.	Peach 1-1-95	North Caro. St. 24-28 (Mike O'Cain)
TED SHIPKEY, 0-1-0 (Stanford '27) Born 9-28-04		
New Mexico	Sun 1-2-39	Utah 0-28 (Ike Armstrong)
LARRY SIEMERING, 1-0-0 (San Francisco '35) Born 11-24-10		
Pacific (Cal.)	Raisin 1-1-48	Wichita St. 26-14 (Ralph Graham)
BOB SIMMONS, 0-1-0 (Bowling Green '71) Born 6-13-48		
Oklahoma St.	Alamo 12-30-97	Purdue 20-33 (Joe Tiller)
CHAUNCEY SIMPSON, 0-1-0 (Missouri '25) Born 12-21-02		
Missouri	Cotton 1-1-46	Texas 27-40 (Dana Bible)
DAN SIMRELL, 0-1-0 (Toledo '65) Born 4-9-43		
Toledo	California 12-15-84	UNLV 13-30 (Harvey Hyde)
STEVE SLOAN, 0-2-1 (Alabama '66) Born 8-19-44		
Vanderbilt	Peach 12-28-74	Texas Tech 6-6 (Jim Carlen)
Texas Tech	Bluebonnet 12-31-76	Nebraska 24-27 (Tom Osborne)

Coach/School	Bowl/Date	Opponent/Score (Coach)
Texas Tech	Tangerine 12-23-77	Florida St. 17-40 (Bobby Bowden)
R. C. SLOCUM, 2-5-0 (McNeese St. '67) Born 11-7-44		
Texas A&M	John Hancock 12-30-89	Pittsburgh 28-31 (Paul Hackett)
Texas A&M	Holiday 12-29-90	Brigham Young 65-14 (LaVell Edwards)
Texas A&M	Cotton 1-1-92	Florida St. 2-10 (Bobby Bowden)
Texas A&M	Cotton 1-1-93	Notre Dame 3-28 (Lou Holtz)
Texas A&M	Cotton 1-1-94	Notre Dame 21-24 (Lou Holtz)
Texas A&M	Alamo 12-28-95	Michigan 22-20 (Lloyd Carr)
Texas A&M	Cotton 1-1-98	UCLA 23-29 (Bob Toledo)
ANDY SMITH, 1-0-1 (Pennsylvania '06) Born 9-10-1883		
California	Rose 1-1-21	Ohio St. 28-0 (John Wilce)
California	Rose 1-2-22	Wash. & Jeff. 0-0 (Earle "Greasy" Neale)
HOMER SMITH, 0-1-0 (Princeton '54) Born 10-9-31		
Davidson	Tangerine 12-26-69	Toledo 33-56 (Frank Lauterbur)
JOHN L. SMITH, 0-1-0 (Weber St. '71) Born 11-5-48		
Utah St.	Humanitarian 12-29-97	Cincinnati 19-35 (Rick Minter)
JOHN "LITTLE CLIPPER" SMITH, 1-0-0 (Notre Dame '29) Born 12-12-04		
Duquesne	Orange 1-1-37	Mississippi St. 13-12 (Ralph Sasse)
LARRY SMITH, 2-6-1 (Bowling Green '62) Born 9-12-39		
Tulane	Liberty 12-22-79	Penn St. 6-9 (Joe Paterno)
Arizona	Sun 12-28-85	Georgia 13-13 (Vince Dooley)
Arizona	Aloha 12-27-86	North Caro. 30-21 (Dick Crum)
Southern Cal	Rose 1-1-88	Michigan St. 17-20 (George Perles)
Southern Cal	Rose 1-2-89	Michigan 14-22 (Glenn "Bo" Schembechler)
Southern Cal	Rose 1-1-90	Michigan 17-10 (Glenn "Bo" Schembechler)
Southern Cal	John Hancock 12-31-90	Michigan St. 16-17 (George Perles)
Southern Cal	Freedom 12-29-92	Fresno St. 7-24 (Jim Sweeney)
Missouri	Holiday 12-29-97	Colorado St. 24-35 (Sonny Lubick)
MAURICE "CLIPPER" SMITH, 0-0-1 (Notre Dame '21) Born 10-15-1898		
Villanova	Bacardi, Cuba 1-1-37	Auburn 7-7 (Jack Meagher)
CARL SNAVELY, 0-3-0 (Lebanon Valley '15) Born 7-30-1894		
North Caro.	Sugar 1-1-47	Georgia 10-20 (Wally Butts)
North Caro.	Sugar 1-1-49	Oklahoma 6-14 (Bud Wilkinson)
North Caro.	Cotton 1-2-50	Rice 13-27 (Jess Neely)
BILL SNYDER, 3-2-0 (William Jewell '63) Born 10-7-41		
Kansas St.	Copper 12-29-93	Wyoming 52-17 (Joe Tiller)
Kansas St.	Aloha 12-25-94	Boston College 7-12 (Dan Henning)
Kansas St.	Holiday 12-29-95	Colorado St. 54-21 (Sonny Lubick)
Kansas St.	Cotton 1-1-97	Brigham Young 15-19 (LaVell Edwards)
Kansas St.	Fiesta 12-31-97	Syracuse 35-18 (Paul Pasqualoni)
BRUCE SNYDER, 3-1-0 (Oregon '62) Born 3-14-40		
California	Copper 12-31-90	Wyoming 17-15 (Paul Roach)
California	Fla. Citrus 1-1-92	Clemson 37-13 (Ken Hatfield)
Arizona St.	Rose 1-1-97	Ohio St. 17-20 (John Cooper)
Arizona St.	Sun 12-31-97	Iowa 17-7 (Hayden Fry)
CLARENCE "DOC" SPEARS, 1-0-0 (Dartmouth '16) Born 7-24-1894		
West Va.	San Diego East-West Christmas Classic 12-25-22	Gonzaga 21-13 (Charles "Gus" Dorais)
CLIFF SPEEGLE, 1-0-0 (Oklahoma '41) Born 11-4-17		
Oklahoma St.	Bluegrass 12-13-58	Florida St. 15-6 (Tom Nugent)
STEVE SPURRIER, 4-4-0 (Florida '67) Born 4-20-45		
Duke	All-American 12-28-89	Texas Tech 21-49 (Spike Dykes)
Florida	Sugar 1-1-92	Notre Dame 28-39 (Lou Holtz)
Florida	Gator 12-31-92	North Caro. St. 27-10 (Dick Sheridan)
Florida	Sugar 1-1-94	West Va. 41-7 (Don Nehlen)
Florida	Sugar 1-2-95	Florida St. 17-23 (Bobby Bowden)
Florida	Fiesta 1-2-96	Nebraska 24-62 (Tom Osborne)
Florida	Sugar 1-2-97	Florida St. 52-20 (Bobby Bowden)
Florida	Fla. Citrus 1-1-98	Penn St. 21-6 (Joe Paterno)
GENE STALLINGS, 6-1-0 (Texas A&M '57) Born 3-2-35		
Texas A&M	Cotton 1-1-68	Alabama 20-16 (Paul "Bear" Bryant)
Alabama	Fiesta 1-1-91	Louisville 7-34 (Howard Schnellenberger)
Alabama	Blockbuster 12-28-91	Colorado 30-25 (Bill McCartney)
Alabama	Sugar 1-1-93	Miami (Fla.) 34-13 (Dennis Erickson)
Alabama	Gator 12-31-93	North Caro. 24-10 (Mack Brown)
Alabama	Fla. Citrus 1-2-95	Ohio St. 24-17 (John Cooper)
Alabama	Outback 1-1-97	Michigan 17-14 (Lloyd Carr)
JIM STANGELAND, 0-0-1 (Arizona St. '48) Born 12-21-21		
Long Beach St.	Pasadena 12-19-70	Louisville 24-24 (Lee Corso)
JIM STANLEY, 2-0-0 (Texas A&M '59) Born 5-22-35		
Oklahoma St.	Fiesta 12-28-74	Brigham Young 16-6 (LaVell Edwards)
Oklahoma St.	Tangerine 12-18-76	Brigham Young 49-12 (LaVell Edwards)
TOM STIDHAM, 0-1-0 (Haskell '27) Born 3-27-04		
Oklahoma	Orange 1-2-39	Tennessee 0-17 (Bob Neyland)
LON STINER, 1-0-0 (Nebraska '27) Born 6-20-03		
Oregon St.	Rose 1-1-42	Duke 20-16 (Wallace Wade)

Coach/School	Bowl/Date	Opponent/Score (Coach)
HARRY STITELER, 1-0-0 (Texas A&M '31) Born 9-17-09		
Texas A&M	Presidential Cup 12-9-50	Georgia 40-20 (Wally Butts)
CHUCK STOBART, 1-0-0 (Ohio '59) Born 10-27-34		
Toledo	California 12-19-81	San Jose St. 27-25 (Jack Elway)
CAL STOLL, 0-1-0 (Minnesota '50) Born 12-12-23		
Minnesota	Hall of Fame 12-22-77	Maryland 7-17 (Jerry Claiborne)
DENNY STOLZ, 0-3-0 (Alma '55) Born 9-12-34		
Bowling Green	California 12-18-82	Fresno St. 28-29 (Jim Sweeney)
Bowling Green	California 12-14-85	Fresno St. 7-51 (Jim Sweeney)
San Diego St.	Holiday 12-30-86	Iowa 38-39 (Hayden Fry)
JERRY STOVALL, 0-1-0 (LSU '63) Born 4-30-41		
LSU	Orange 1-1-83	Nebraska 20-21 (Tom Osborne)
BOB STULL, 0-1-0 (Kansas St. '68) Born 11-21-45		
UTEP	Independence 12-23-88	Southern Miss. 18-38 (Curley Hallman)
PAT SULLIVAN, 0-1-0 (Auburn '72) Born 1-18-50		
Texas Christian	Independence 12-28-94	Virginia 10-20 (George Welsh)
JOCK SUTHERLAND, 1-3-0 (Pittsburgh '18) Born 3-21-1889		
Pittsburgh	Rose 1-1-28	Stanford 6-7 (Glenn "Pop" Warner)
Pittsburgh	Rose 1-1-30	Southern Cal 14-47 (Howard Jones)
Pittsburgh	Rose 1-2-33	Southern Cal 0-35 (Howard Jones)
Pittsburgh	Rose 1-1-37	Washington 21-0 (Jimmy Phelan)
BOB SUTTON, 0-1-0 (Eastern Mich. '74) Born 1-28-51		
Army	Independence 12-31-96	Auburn 29-32 (Terry Bowden)
JIM SWEENEY, 5-2-0 (Portland '51) Born 9-1-29		
Fresno St.	California 12-18-82	Bowling Green 29-28 (Denny Stolz)
Fresno St.	California 12-14-85	Bowling Green 51-7 (Denny Stolz)
Fresno St.	California 12-10-88	Western Mich. 35-30 (Al Molde)
Fresno St.	California 12-9-89	Ball St. 27-8 (Paul Schudel)
Fresno St.	California 12-13-91	Bowling Green 21-28 (Gary Blackney)
Fresno St.	Freedom 12-29-92	Southern Cal 24-7 (Larry Smith)
Fresno St.	Aloha 12-25-93	Colorado 30-41 (Bill McCartney)
BARRY SWITZER, 8-5-0 (Arkansas '60) Born 10-5-37		
Oklahoma	Orange 1-1-76	Michigan 14-6 (Glenn "Bo" Schembechler)
Oklahoma	Fiesta 12-25-76	Wyoming 41-7 (Fred Akers)
Oklahoma	Orange 1-2-78	Arkansas 6-31 (Lou Holtz)
Oklahoma	Orange 1-1-79	Nebraska 31-24 (Tom Osborne)
Oklahoma	Orange 1-1-80	Florida St. 24-7 (Bobby Bowden)
Oklahoma	Orange 1-1-81	Florida St. 18-17 (Bobby Bowden)
Oklahoma	Sun 12-26-81	Houston 40-14 (Bill Yeoman)
Oklahoma	Fiesta 1-1-83	Arizona St. 21-32 (Darryl Rogers)
Oklahoma	Orange 1-1-85	Washington 17-28 (Don James)
Oklahoma	Orange 1-1-86	Penn St. 25-10 (Joe Paterno)
Oklahoma	Orange 1-1-87	Arkansas 42-8 (Ken Hatfield)
Oklahoma	Orange 1-1-88	Miami (Fla.) 14-20 (Jimmy Johnson)
Oklahoma	Fla. Citrus 1-2-89	Clemson 6-13 (Danny Ford)
CHARLIE TATE, 1-1-0 (Florida '42) Born 2-20-21		
Miami (Fla.)	Liberty 12-10-66	Virginia Tech 14-7 (Jerry Claiborne)
Miami (Fla.)	Bluebonnet 12-23-67	Colorado 21-31 (Eddie Crowder)
JIM TATUM, 3-2-1 (North Caro. '35) Born 7-22-13		
Oklahoma	Gator 1-1-47	North Caro. St. 34-13 (Beattie Feathers)
Maryland	Gator 1-1-48	Georgia 20-20 (Wally Butts)
Maryland	Gator 1-2-50	Missouri 20-7 (Don Faurot)
Maryland	Sugar 1-1-52	Tennessee 28-13 (Bob Neyland)
Maryland	Orange 1-1-54	Oklahoma 0-7 (Bud Wilkinson)
Maryland	Orange 1-2-56	Oklahoma 6-20 (Bud Wilkinson)
CHUCK TAYLOR, 0-1-0 (Stanford '43) Born 1-24-20		
Stanford	Rose 1-1-52	Illinois 7-40 (Ray Eliot)
GRANT TEAFF, 4-4-0 (McMurry '56) Born 11-12-33		
Baylor	Cotton 1-1-75	Penn St. 20-41 (Joe Paterno)
Baylor	Peach 12-31-79	Clemson 24-18 (Danny Ford)
Baylor	Cotton 1-1-81	Alabama 2-30 (Paul "Bear" Bryant)
Baylor	Bluebonnet 12-31-83	Oklahoma St. 14-24 (Jimmy Johnson)
Baylor	Liberty 12-27-85	LSU 21-7 (Bill Arnsparger)
Baylor	Bluebonnet 12-31-86	Colorado 21-9 (Bill McCartney)
Baylor	Copper 12-31-91	Indiana 0-24 (Bill Mallory)
Baylor	John Hancock 12-31-92	Arizona 20-15 (Dick Tomey)
EDDIE TEAGUE, 1-0-0 (North Caro. '44) Born 12-14-21		
Citadel	Tangerine 12-30-60	Tennessee Tech 27-0 (Wilburn Tucker)
LOU TEPPER, 1-2-0 (Rutgers '67) Born 7-21-45		
Illinois	John Hancock 12-31-91	UCLA 3-6 (Terry Donahue)
Illinois	Holiday 12-30-92	Hawaii 17-27 (Bob Wagner)
Illinois	Liberty 12-31-94	East Caro. 30-0 (Steve Logan)
ROBERT THEDER, 0-1-0 (Western Mich. '63) Born 9-22-39		
California	Garden State 12-15-79	Temple 17-28 (Wayne Hardin)
FRANK THOMAS, 4-2-0 (Notre Dame '23) Born 11-14-1898		
Alabama	Rose 1-1-35	Stanford 29-13 (Claude "Tiny" Thornhill)
Alabama	Rose 1-1-38	California 0-13 (Leonard "Stub" Allison)
Alabama	Cotton 1-1-42	Texas A&M 29-21 (Homer Norton)

Coach/School	Bowl/Date	Opponent/Score (Coach)
Alabama	Orange 1-1-43	Boston College 37-21 (Denny Myers)
Alabama	Sugar 1-1-45	Duke 26-29 (Eddie Cameron)
Alabama	Rose 1-1-46	Southern Cal 34-14 (Jeff Cravath)
FRED THOMSEN, 0-0-1 (Nebraska '25) Born 4-25-1897		
Arkansas	Dixie Classic 1-1-34	Centenary (La.) 7-7 (Homer Norton)
CLAUDE "TINY" THORNHILL, 1-2-0 (Pittsburgh '17) Born 4-14-1893		
Stanford	Rose 1-1-34	Columbia 0-7 (Lou Little)
Stanford	Rose 1-1-35	Alabama 13-29 (Frank Thomas)
Stanford	Rose 1-1-36	Southern Methodist 7-0 (Matty Bell)
JOE TILLER, 1-1-0 (Montana St. '64) Born 12-7-42		
Wyoming	Copper 12-29-93	Kansas St. 17-52 (Bill Snyder)
Purdue	Alamo 12-30-97	Oklahoma St. 33-20 (Bob Simmons)
GAYNELL TINSLEY, 0-1-0 (LSU '37) Born 2-1-15		
LSU	Sugar 1-2-50	Oklahoma 0-35 (Bud Wilkinson)
JEFF TISDEL, 1-0-0 (Nevada '77) Born 1-10-56		
Nevada	Las Vegas 12-19-96	Ball St. 18-15 (Bill Lynch)
BOB TOLEDO, 1-0-0 (San Francisco St. '68) Born 3-4-46		
UCLA	Cotton 1-1-98	Texas A&M 29-23 (R. C. Slocum)
TED TOLLNER, 1-2-0 (Cal Poly SLO '62) Born 5-29-40		
Southern Cal	Rose 1-1-85	Ohio St. 20-17 (Earle Bruce)
Southern Cal	Aloha 12-28-85	Alabama 3-24 (Ray Perkins)
Southern Cal	Fla. Citrus 1-1-87	Auburn 7-16 (Pat Dye)
DICK TOMEY, 3-3-0 (DePauw '61) Born 6-20-38		
Arizona	Copper 12-30-89	North Caro. St. 17-10 (Dick Sheridan)
Arizona	Aloha 12-28-90	Syracuse 0-28 (Dick MacPherson)
Arizona	John Hancock 12-31-92	Baylor 15-20 (Grant Teaff)
Arizona	Fiesta 1-1-94	Miami (Fla.) 29-0 (Dennis Erickson)
Arizona	Freedom 12-27-94	Utah 13-16 (Ron McBride)
Arizona	Insight.com 12-27-97	New Mexico 20-14 (Dennis Franchione)
CARL TORBUSH, 1-0-0 (Carson-Newman '74) Born 10-11-51		
North Caro.	Gator 1-1-98	Virginia Tech 42-3 (Frank Beamer)
JIM TRIMBLE, 0-1-0 (Indiana '42) Born 5-29-18		
Wichita St.	Camellia 12-30-48	Hardin-Simmons 12-49 (Warren Woodson)
FRANK TRITICO, 0-0-1 (Southwestern La. '34) Born 3-25-09		
Randolph Field	Cotton 1-1-44	Texas 7-7 (Dana Bible)
TOMMY TUBERVILLE, 1-0-0 (Southern Ark. '76) Born 9-18-54		
Mississippi	Motor City 12-26-97	Marshall 34-31 (Bob Pruett)
WILBURN TUCKER, 0-1-0 (Tennessee Tech '43) Born 8-11-20		
Tennessee Tech	Tangerine 12-30-60	Citadel 0-27 (Eddie Teague)
BOB TYLER, 1-0-0 (Mississippi '58) Born 7-4-32		
Mississippi St.	Sun 12-28-74	North Caro. 26-24 (Bill Dooley)
THAD "PIE" VANN, 0-2-0 (Mississippi '28) Born 9-22-07		
Southern Miss.	Sun 1-1-53	Pacific (Cal.) 7-26 (Ernie Jorge)
Southern Miss.	Sun 1-1-54	UTEP 14-37 (Mike Brumbelow)
JOHN VAUGHT, 10-8-0 (Texas Christian '33) Born 5-6-08		
Mississippi	Delta 1-1-48	Texas Christian 13-9 (Leo "Dutch" Meyer)
Mississippi	Sugar 1-1-53	Georgia Tech 7-24 (Bobby Dodd)
Mississippi	Sugar 1-1-55	Navy 0-21 (Eddie Erdelatz)
Mississippi	Cotton 1-2-56	Texas Christian 14-13 (Abe Martin)
Mississippi	Sugar 1-1-58	Texas 39-7 (Darrell Royal)
Mississippi	Gator 12-27-58	Florida 7-3 (Bob Woodruff)
Mississippi	Sugar 1-1-60	LSU 21-0 (Paul Dietzel)
Mississippi	Sugar 1-2-61	Rice 14-6 (Jess Neely)
Mississippi	Cotton 1-1-62	Texas 7-12 (Darrell Royal)
Mississippi	Sugar 1-1-63	Arkansas 17-13 (Frank Broyles)
Mississippi	Sugar 1-1-64	Alabama 7-12 (Paul "Bear" Bryant)
Mississippi	Bluebonnet 12-19-64	Tulsa 7-14 (Glenn Dobbs)
Mississippi	Liberty 12-18-65	Auburn 13-7 (Ralph "Shug" Jordan)
Mississippi	Bluebonnet 12-17-66	Texas 0-19 (Darrell Royal)
Mississippi	Sun 12-30-67	UTEP 7-14 (Bobby Dobbs)
Mississippi	Liberty 12-14-68	Virginia Tech 34-17 (Jerry Claiborne)
Mississippi	Sugar 1-1-70	Arkansas 27-22 (Frank Broyles)
Mississippi	Gator 1-2-71	Auburn 28-35 (Ralph "Shug" Jordan)
DICK VERMEIL, 1-0-0 (San Jose St. '58) Born 10-30-36		
UCLA	Rose 1-1-76	Ohio St. 23-10 (Woody Hayes)
BOB VOIGTS, 1-0-0 (Northwestern '39) Born 3-29-16		
Northwestern	Rose 1-1-49	California 20-14 (Lynn "Pappy" Waldorf)
JIM WACKER, 0-1-0 (Valparaiso '60) Born 4-28-37		
Texas Christian	Bluebonnet 12-31-84	West Va. 14-31 (Don Nehlen)
WALLACE WADE, 2-2-1 (Brown '17) Born 6-15-1892		
Alabama	Rose 1-1-26	Washington 20-19 (Enoch Bagshaw)
Alabama	Rose 1-1-27	Stanford 7-7 (Glenn "Pop" Warner)
Alabama	Rose 1-1-31	Washington St. 24-0 (Orin "Babe" Hollingbery)
Duke	Rose 1-2-39	Southern Cal 3-7 (Howard Jones)
Duke	Rose 1-1-42	Oregon St. 16-20 (Lon Stiner)
BOB WAGNER, 1-1-0 (Wittenberg '69) Born 5-16-47		
Hawaii	Aloha 12-25-89	Michigan St. 13-33 (George Perles)
Hawaii	Holiday 12-30-92	Illinois 27-17 (Lou Tepper)
JIM WALDEN, 0-1-0 (Wyoming '60) Born 4-10-38		
Washington St.	Holiday 12-18-81	Brigham Young 36-38 (LaVell Edwards)
LYNN "PAPPY" WALDORF, 0-3-0 (Syracuse '25) Born 10-3-02		
California	Rose 1-1-49	Northwestern 14-20 (Bob Voigts)
California	Rose 1-2-50	Ohio St. 14-17 (Wes Fesler)
California	Rose 1-1-51	Michigan 6-14 (Bennie Oosterbaan)
D. C. "PEAHEAD" WALKER, 1-1-0 (Samford '22) Born 2-17-1900		
Wake Forest	Gator 1-1-46	South Caro. 26-14 (Johnnie McMillan)
Wake Forest	Dixie 1-1-49	Baylor 7-20 (Bob Woodruff)
ED WALKER, 0-1-0 (Stanford '27) Born 3-25-01		
Mississippi	Orange 1-1-36	Catholic 19-20 (Arthur "Dutch" Bergman)
BILL WALSH, 3-0-0 (San Jose St. '54) Born 11-30-31		
Stanford	Sun 12-31-77	LSU 24-14 (Charlie McClendon)
Stanford	Bluebonnet 12-31-78	Georgia 25-22 (Vince Dooley)
Stanford	Blockbuster 1-1-93	Penn St. 24-3 (Joe Paterno)
DALLAS WARD, 1-0-0 (Oregon St. '27) Born 8-11-06		
Colorado	Orange 1-1-57	Clemson 27-21 (Frank Howard)
MURRAY WARMATH, 1-1-0 (Tennessee '35) Born 12-26-13		
Minnesota	Rose 1-2-61	Washington 7-17 (Jim Owens)
Minnesota	Rose 1-1-62	UCLA 21-3 (Bill Barnes)
GLENN "POP" WARNER, 1-2-1 (Cornell '95) Born 4-5-1871		
Stanford	Rose 1-1-25	Notre Dame 10-27 (Knute Rockne)
Stanford	Rose 1-1-27	Alabama 7-7 (Wallace Wade)
Stanford	Rose 1-2-28	Pittsburgh 7-6 (Jock Sutherland)
Temple	Sugar 1-1-35	Tulane 14-20 (Ted Cox)
CHARLIE WEATHERBIE, 2-0-0 (Oklahoma St. '77) Born 1-17-55		
Utah St.	Las Vegas 12-17-93	Ball St. 42-33 (Paul Schudel)
Navy	Aloha 12-25-96	California 42-38 (Steve Mariucci)
DeWITT WEAVER, 2-1-0 (Tennessee '37) Born 5-11-12		
Texas Tech	Sun 1-1-52	Pacific (Cal.) 25-14 (Ernie Jorge)
Texas Tech	Gator 1-1-54	Auburn 35-13 (Ralph "Shug" Jordan)
Texas Tech	Sun 1-2-56	Wyoming 14-21 (Phil Dickens)
BILL WEEKS, 1-0-0 (Iowa St. '51) Born 10-20-29		
New Mexico	Aviation 12-9-61	Western Mich. 28-12 (Merle Schlosser)
RALPH "PEST" WELCH, 0-1-0 (Purdue '30) Born 8-11-07		
Washington	Rose 1-1-44	Southern Cal 0-29 (Jeff Cravath)
GEORGE WELSH, 5-7-0 (Navy '56) Born 8-26-33		
Navy	Holiday 12-22-78	Brigham Young 23-16 (LaVell Edwards)
Navy	Garden State 12-14-80	Houston 0-35 (Bill Yeoman)
Navy	Liberty 12-30-81	Ohio St. 28-31 (Earle Bruce)
Virginia	Peach 12-31-84	Purdue 27-24 (Leon Burtnett)
Virginia	All-American 12-22-87	Brigham Young 22-16 (LaVell Edwards)
Virginia	Fla. Citrus 1-1-90	Illinois 21-31 (John Mackovic)
Virginia	Sugar 1-1-91	Tennessee 22-23 (Johnny Majors)
Virginia	Gator 12-29-91	Oklahoma 14-48 (Gary Gibbs)
Virginia	Carquest 1-1-94	Boston College 13-31 (Tom Coughlin)
Virginia	Independence 12-28-94	Texas Christian 20-10 (Pat Sullivan)
Virginia	Peach 12-30-95	Georgia 34-27 (Ray Goff)
Virginia	Carquest 12-27-96	Miami (Fla.) 21-31 (Butch Davis)
TOMMY WEST, 1-3-0 (Tennessee '75) Born 7-31-54		
Clemson	Peach 12-31-93	Kentucky 14-13 (Bill Curry)
Clemson	Gator 1-1-96	Syracuse 0-41 (Paul Pasqualoni)
Clemson	Peach 12-28-96	LSU 7-10 (Gerry DiNardo)
Clemson	Peach 1-2-98	Auburn 17-21 (Terry Bowden)
MIKE WHITE, 0-3-0 (California '58) Born 1-3-36		
Illinois	Liberty 12-29-82	Alabama 15-21 (Paul "Bear" Bryant)
Illinois	Rose 1-2-84	UCLA 9-45 (Terry Donahue)
Illinois	Peach 12-31-85	Army 29-31 (Jim Young)
JOHN WILCE, 0-1-0 (Wisconsin '10) Born 5-12-88		
Ohio St.	Rose 1-1-21	California 0-28 (Andy Smith)
BUD WILKINSON, 6-2-0 (Minnesota '37) Born 4-12-16		
Oklahoma	Sugar 1-1-49	North Caro. 14-6 (Carl Snavely)
Oklahoma	Sugar 1-2-50	LSU 35-0 (Gaynell Tinsley)
Oklahoma	Sugar 1-1-51	Kentucky 7-13 (Paul "Bear" Bryant)
Oklahoma	Orange 1-1-54	Maryland 7-0 (Jim Tatum)
Oklahoma	Orange 1-2-56	Maryland 20-6 (Jim Tatum)
Oklahoma	Orange 1-1-58	Duke 48-21 (Bill Murray)
Oklahoma	Orange 1-1-59	Syracuse 21-6 (Ben Schwartzwalder)
Oklahoma	Orange 1-1-63	Alabama 0-17 (Paul "Bear" Bryant)
IVY WILLIAMSON, 0-1-0 (Michigan '33) Born 2-4-11		
Wisconsin	Rose 1-1-53	Southern Cal 0-7 (Jess Hill)
TYRONE WILLINGHAM, 1-1-0 (Michigan St. '77) Born 12-30-53		
Stanford	Liberty 12-30-95	East Caro. 13-19 (Steve Logan)
Stanford	Sun 12-31-96	Michigan St. 38-0 (Nick Saban)
TOM WILSON, 2-0-0 (Texas Tech '66) Born 2-24-44		

Coach/School	Bowl/Date	Opponent/Score (Coach)
Texas A&M	Hall of Fame 12-20-78	Iowa St. 28-12 (Earle Bruce)
Texas A&M	Independence 12-12-81	Oklahoma St. 33-16 (Jimmy Johnson)
SAM WINNINGHAM, 0-1-0 (Colorado '50) Born 10-11-26		
Cal St. Northridge	Pasadena 12-2-67	West Tex. A&M 13-35 (Joe Kerbel)
BOB WOODRUFF, 2-1-0 (Tennessee '39) Born 3-14-16		
Baylor	Dixie 1-1-49	Wake Forest 20-7 (D. C. "Peahead" Walker)
Florida	Gator 1-1-53	Tulsa 14-13 (J. O. "Buddy" Brothers)
Florida	Gator 12-27-58	Mississippi 3-7 (John Vaught)
WARREN WOODSON, 6-1-0 (Baylor '24) Born 2-24-03		
Hardin-Simmons	Sun 1-1-43	Second Air Force 7-13 (Red Reese)
Hardin-Simmons	Alamo 1-4-47	Denver 20-6 (Clyde "Cac" Hubbard)
Hardin-Simmons	Harbor 1-1-48	San Diego St. 53-0 (Bill Schutte)
Hardin-Simmons	Shrine 12-18-48	Ouachita Baptist 40-12 (Wesley Bradshaw)
Hardin-Simmons	Camellia 12-30-48	Wichita St. 49-12 (Jim Trimble)
New Mexico St.	Sun 12-31-59	North Texas 28-8 (Odus Mitchell)
New Mexico St.	Sun 12-31-60	Utah St. 20-13 (John Ralston)
BOWDEN WYATT, 2-2-0 (Tennessee '39) Born 11-3-17		
Wyoming	Gator 1-1-51	Wash. & Lee 20-7 (George Barclay)
Arkansas	Cotton 1-1-55	Georgia Tech 6-14 (Bobby Dodd)
Tennessee	Sugar 1-1-57	Baylor 7-13 (Sam Boyd)
Tennessee	Gator 12-26-57	Texas A&M 3-0 (Paul "Bear" Bryant)
BILL YEOMAN, 6-4-1 (Army '50) Born 12-26-27		
Houston	Tangerine 12-22-62	Miami (Ohio) 49-21 (John Pont)
Houston	Bluebonnet 12-31-69	Auburn 36-7 (Ralph "Shug" Jordan)
Houston	Bluebonnet 12-31-71	Colorado 17-29 (Eddie Crowder)
Houston	Bluebonnet 12-29-73	Tulane 47-7 (Bennie Ellender)
Houston	Bluebonnet 12-23-74	North Caro. St. 31-31 (Lou Holtz)
Houston	Cotton 1-1-77	Maryland 30-21 (Jerry Claiborne)
Houston	Cotton 1-1-79	Notre Dame 34-35 (Dan Devine)
Houston	Cotton 1-1-80	Nebraska 17-14 (Tom Osborne)
Houston	Garden State 12-14-80	Navy 35-0 (George Welsh)
Houston	Sun 12-26-81	Oklahoma 14-40 (Barry Switzer)
Houston	Cotton 1-1-85	Boston College 28-45 (Jack Bicknell)
FIELDING "HURRY UP" YOST, 1-0-0 (Lafayette '97) Born 4-30-1871		
Michigan	Rose 1-1-02	Stanford 49-0 (Charlie Fickert)
JIM YOUNG, 5-1-0 (Bowling Green '57) Born 4-21-35		
Purdue	Peach 12-25-78	Georgia Tech 41-21 (Pepper Rodgers)
Purdue	Bluebonnet 12-31-79	Tennessee 27-22 (Johnny Majors)
Purdue	Liberty 12-27-80	Missouri 28-25 (Warren Powers)
Army	Cherry 12-22-84	Michigan St. 10-6 (George Perles)
Army	Peach 12-31-85	Illinois 31-29 (Mike White)
Army	Sun 12-24-88	Alabama 28-29 (Bill Curry)

Coaches Who Have Taken More Than One Team to a Bowl Game

FOUR TEAMS (4)

Earle Bruce: Tampa, Iowa St., Ohio St. & Colorado St.
Lou Holtz: William & Mary, North Caro. St., Arkansas & Notre Dame
Bill Mallory: Miami (Ohio), Colorado, Northern Ill. & Indiana
*Larry Smith: Tulane, Arizona, Southern Cal & Missouri

THREE TEAMS (10)

Bear Bryant: Kentucky, Texas A&M & Alabama
Jim Carlen: West Va., Texas Tech & South Caro.
Jerry Claiborne: Virginia Tech, Maryland & Kentucky
Bill Curry: Georgia Tech, Alabama & Kentucky
Bill Dooley: North Caro., Virginia Tech & Wake Forest

*Ken Hatfield: Air Force, Arkansas & Clemson
John Mackovic: Wake Forest, Illinois & Texas
Johnny Majors: Iowa St., Pittsburgh & Tennessee
*Jackie Sherrill: Pittsburgh, Texas A&M & Mississippi St.

Bowden Wyatt: Wyoming, Arkansas & Tennessee

TWO TEAMS (56)

Fred Akers: Wyoming & Texas
John Barnhill: Tennessee & Arkansas
Emory Bellard: Texas A&M & Mississippi St.
Hugo Bezdek: Oregon & Penn St.
Dana X. Bible: Texas A&M & Texas

*Bobby Bowden: West Va. & Florida St.
*Mack Brown: Tulane & North Caro.
Len Casanova: Santa Clara & Oregon
Bobby Collins: Southern Miss. & Southern Methodist
*John Cooper: Arizona St. & Ohio St.

Lee Corso: Louisville & Indiana
Dick Crum: Miami (Ohio) & North Caro.
Bob Devaney: Wyoming & Nebraska
Dan Devine: Missouri & Notre Dame
Doug Dickey: Tennessee & Florida

Paul Dietzel: LSU & South Caro.
Pat Dye: East Caro. & Auburn
Pete Elliott: California & Illinois
Jack Elway: San Jose St. & Stanford
Dennis Erickson: Washington St. & Miami (Fla.)

Bob Folwell: Pennsylvania & Navy
Danny Ford: Clemson & Arkansas
*Hayden Fry: Southern Methodist & Iowa
Vince Gibson: Louisville & Tulane
Sid Gillman: Miami (Ohio) & Cincinnati

Wayne Hardin: Navy & Temple
Woody Hayes: Miami (Ohio) & Ohio St.
Bob Higgins: West Va. Wesleyan & Penn St.
Don James: Kent & Washington
Jimmy Johnson: Oklahoma St. & Miami (Fla.)

Frank Kimbrough: Hardin-Simmons & West Tex. A&M
Jimmy Kitts: Rice & Virginia Tech
Jess Neely: Clemson & Rice
Homer Norton: Centenary (La.) & Texas A&M
Charley Pell: Clemson & Florida

Jimmy Phelan: Washington & St. Mary's (Cal.)
John Pont: Miami (Ohio) & Indiana
Tommy Prothro: Oregon St. & UCLA
John Ralston: Utah St. & Stanford
Pepper Rodgers: Kansas & Georgia Tech

Bobby Ross: Maryland & Georgia Tech
George Sauer: Kansas & Baylor
Howard Schnellenberger: Miami (Fla.) & Louisville
Steve Sloan: Vanderbilt & Texas Tech
*Bruce Snyder: California & Arizona St.

*Steve Spurrier: Duke & Florida
Gene Stallings: Texas A&M & Alabama
Denny Stolz: Bowling Green & San Diego St.
Jim Tatum: Oklahoma & Maryland
Wallace Wade: Alabama & Duke

Pop Warner: Stanford & Temple
*Charlie Weatherbie: Utah St. & Navy
*George Welsh: Navy & Virginia
Bob Woodruff: Baylor & Florida
Warren Woodson: Hardin-Simmons & New Mexico St.

Jim Young: Purdue & Army

*Active coach.

Coaches With the Most Years Taking One College to a Bowl Game

Coach, Team Taken	Bowls	Consecutive Years
*Joe Paterno, Penn St.	28	13 (1971-83)
Tom Osborne, Nebraska	25	25 (1973-97)
Bear Bryant, Alabama	24	24 (1959-82)
Vince Dooley, Georgia	20	9 (1980-88)
*LaVell Edwards, Brigham Young	20	17 (1978-94)
John Vaught, Mississippi	18	14 (1957-70)
*Bobby Bowden, Florida St.	18	16 (1982-97)
Bo Schembechler, Michigan	17	15 (1975-89)
Darrell Royal, Texas	16	8 (1968-75)
Don James, Washington	14	9 (1979-87)
Bobby Dodd, Georgia Tech	13	6 (1951-56)
Terry Donahue, UCLA	13	8 (1981-88)
*Hayden Fry, Iowa	14	8 (1981-88)
Charlie McClendon, LSU	13	4 (1970-73)
Barry Switzer, Oklahoma	13	8 (1975-82)
Ralph Jordan, Auburn	12	7 (1968-74)
Woody Hayes, Ohio St.	11	7 (1972-78)
Johnny Majors, Tennessee	11	7 (1981-87)
Bill Yeoman, Houston	11	4 (1978-81)
Frank Broyles, Arkansas	10	4 (1959-62)
*Don Nehlen, West Va.	10	4 (1981-84)
Fred Akers, Texas	9	9 (1977-85)
Bob Devaney, Nebraska	9	5 (1962-66)
Pat Dye, Auburn	9	9 (1982-90)
Lou Holtz, Notre Dame	9	9 (1987-95)
Bill McCartney, Colorado	9	7 (1988-94)
John McKay, Southern Cal	9	4 (1966-69; 1972-75)
*George Welsh, Virginia	9	4 (1993-96)
*Fisher DeBerry, Air Force	9	4 (1989-92)
Earle Bruce, Ohio St.	8	8 (1979-86)
Wally Butts, Georgia	8	4 (1945-48)
Danny Ford, Clemson	8	5 (1985-89)
John Robinson, Southern Cal	8	4 (1976-79)
Grant Teaff, Baylor	8	2 (1979-80; 1985-86; 1991-92)
Bud Wilkinson, Oklahoma	8	3 (1948-50)

*Active coach.

Coaches Who Have Coached in a Bowl Game and Also Coached a Team in the NCAA Basketball Tournament

Coach, School	Bowl	NCAA Tournament
Clarence "Nibs" Price, California	Rose 1-1-29	NCAA 1946
E. L. "Dick" Romney, Utah St.	Raisin 1-1-47	NCAA 1939

Conference Bowl Records

1997-98 Bowl Records by Conference

Conference (Teams in Bowls)	W-L-T	Pct.
Conference USA (2)	2-0-0	1.000
Pacific-10 (6)	5-1-0	.833
Southeastern (6)	5-1-0	.833
Atlantic Coast (4)	3-1-0	.750
Big 12 (5)	2-3-0	.400
Western Atletic (3)	1-2-0	.333
Big Ten (7)	2-5-0	.286
Big East (4)	0-4-0	.000
Big West (1)	0-1-0	.000
Mid-American (1)	0-1-0	.000
I-A Independents (1)	0-1-0	.000

All-Time Conference Bowl Records

(Through 1997-98 Bowls, Using Present Conference Alignments)

ATLANTIC COAST CONFERENCE

School	Bowls	W-L-T	Pct.	Last Appearance
Clemson	22	12-10-0	.545	1998 Peach
Duke	8	3-5-0	.375	1995 Hall of Fame
Florida St.	26	16-8-2	.654	1998 Sugar
Georgia Tech	26	18-8-0	.692	1997 Carquest
Maryland	17	6-9-2	.412	1990 Independence
North Caro.	22	10-12-0	.455	1998 Gator
North Caro. St.	17	8-8-1	.500	1995 Peach (Jan. 1)
Virginia	9	4-5-0	.444	1996 Carquest
Wake Forest	4	2-2-0	.500	1992 Independence
Current Members	**151**	**79-67-5**	**.540**	

BIG EAST CONFERENCE

School	Bowls	W-L-T	Pct.	Last Appearance
Boston College	10	5-5-0	.500	1994 Aloha
Miami (Fla.)	22	11-11-0	.500	1996 Carquest
Pittsburgh	19	8-11-0	.421	1989 John Hancock
Rutgers	1	0-1-0	.000	1978 Garden State
Syracuse	18	10-7-1	.583	1997 Fiesta (Dec. 31)
Temple	2	1-1-0	.500	1979 Garden State
Virginia Tech	11	3-8-0	.273	1998 Gator
West Va.	19	8-11-0	.421	1997 Carquest
Current Members	**102**	**46-55-1**	**.456**	

BIG 12 CONFERENCE

School	Bowls	W-L-T	Pct.	Last Appearance
North				
Colorado	21	9-12-0	.429	1996 Holiday
Iowa St.	4	0-4-0	.000	1978 Hall of Fame
Kansas	8	3-5-0	.375	1995 Aloha
Kansas St.	6	3-3-0	.500	1997 Fiesta (Dec. 31)
Missouri	19	8-11-0	.421	1997 Holiday
Nebraska	36	18-18-0	.500	1998 Orange
South				
Baylor	16	8-8-0	.500	1994 Alamo
Oklahoma	32	20-11-1	.641	1994 Copper
Oklahoma St.	13	9-4-0	.692	1997 Alamo
Texas	37	17-18-2	.486	1997 Fiesta
Texas A&M	23	12-11-0	.522	1998 Cotton
Texas Tech	22	5-16-1	.250	1996 Alamo
Current Members	**237**	**112-121-4**	**.481**	

BIG TEN CONFERENCE

School	Bowls	W-L-T	Pct.	Last Appearance
Illinois	12	5-7-0	.417	1994 Liberty
Indiana	8	3-5-0	.375	1993 Independence
Iowa	16	8-7-1	.531	1997 Sun
Michigan	29	14-15-0	.483	1998 Rose
Michigan St.	14	5-9-0	.357	1997 Aloha
Minnesota	5	2-3-0	.400	1986 Liberty
Northwestern	3	1-2-0	.333	1997 Florida Citrus
Ohio St.	30	13-17-0	.433	1998 Sugar
Penn St.	34	21-11-2	.647	1998 Florida Citrus
Purdue	6	5-1-0	.833	1997 Alamo
Wisconsin	10	4-6-0	.400	1997 Outback
Current Members	**167**	**81-83-3**	**.494**	

BIG WEST CONFERENCE

School	Bowls	W-L-T	Pct.	Last Appearance
Arkansas St.	0	0-0-0	.000	Has never appeared
Boise St.	0	0-0-0	.000	Has never appeared
Idaho	0	0-0-0	.000	Has never appeared
Nevada	5	2-3-0	.400	1996 Las Vegas
New Mexico St.	3	2-0-1	.833	1960 Sun
North Texas	2	0-2-0	.000	1959 Sun
Utah St.	5	1-4-0	.200	1997 Humanitarian
Current Members	**15**	**5-9-1**	**.357**	

CONFERENCE USA

School	Bowls	W-L-T	Pct.	Last Appearance
Army	4	2-2-0	.500	1996 Independence
Cincinnati	3	2-1-0	.667	1997 Humanitarian
East Caro.	4	3-1-0	.750	1995 Liberty
Houston	14	7-6-1	.536	1996 Liberty
Louisville	5	3-1-1	.700	1993 Liberty
Memphis	1	1-0-0	1.000	1971 Pasadena
Southern Miss.	7	3-4-0	.429	1997 Liberty
Tulane	8	2-6-0	.250	1987 Independence
Current Members	**46**	**23-21-2**	**.522**	

MID-AMERICAN CONFERENCE

School	Bowls	W-L-T	Pct.	Last Appearance
East				
Akron	0	0-0-0	.000	Has never appeared
Bowling Green	5	2-3-0	.400	1992 Las Vegas
Kent	1	0-1-0	.000	1972 Tangerine
Marshall	1	0-1-0	.000	1997 Motor City
Miami (Ohio)	7	5-2-0	.714	1986 California
Ohio	2	0-2-0	.000	1968 Tangerine
West				
Ball St.	3	0-3-0	.000	1996 Las Vegas
Central Mich.	2	0-2-0	.000	1994 Las Vegas
Eastern Mich.	1	1-0-0	1.000	1987 California
Northern Ill.	1	1-0-0	1.000	1983 California
Toledo	6	5-1-0	.833	1995 Las Vegas
Western Mich.	2	0-2-0	.000	1988 California
Current Members	**31**	**14-17-0**	**.452**	

PACIFIC-10 CONFERENCE

School	Bowls	W-L-T	Pct.	Last Appearance
Arizona	12	4-7-1	.375	1997 Insight.com
Arizona St.	17	10-6-1	.618	1997 Sun
California	13	5-7-1	.423	1996 Aloha
Oregon	12	4-8-0	.333	1997 Las Vegas
Oregon St.	4	2-2-0	.500	1965 Rose
Southern Cal	38	25-13-0	.658	1996 Rose
Stanford	18	9-8-1	.528	1996 Sun
UCLA	21	11-9-1	.548	1998 Cotton
Washington	24	13-10-1	.563	1997 Aloha
Washington St.	7	4-3-0	.571	1998 Rose
Current Members	**166**	**87-73-6**	**.542**	

SOUTHEASTERN CONFERENCE

School	Bowls	W-L-T	Pct.	Last Appearance
Eastern				
Florida	25	12-13-0	.480	1998 Florida Citrus
Georgia	33	16-14-3	.530	1998 Outback
Kentucky	8	5-3-0	.625	1993 Peach (Dec. 31)
South Caro.	9	1-8-0	.111	1995 Carquest
Tennessee	38	21-17-0	.553	1998 Orange
Vanderbilt	3	1-1-1	.500	1982 Hall of Fame
Western				
Alabama	48	28-17-3	.615	1997 Outback
Arkansas	28	9-16-3	.375	1995 Carquest (Dec. 30)
Auburn	26	14-10-2	.577	1998 Peach
LSU	31	14-16-1	.468	1997 Independence
Mississippi	26	15-11-0	.577	1997 Motor City
Mississippi St.	9	4-5-0	.444	1995 Peach (Jan. 1)
Current Members	**284**	**140-131-13**	**.516**	

WESTERN ATHLETIC CONFERENCE

School	Bowls	W-L-T	Pct.	Last Appearance
Mountain				
Brigham Young	20	7-12-1	.375	1997 Cotton
New Mexico	6	2-3-1	.417	1997 Insight.com
Rice	7	4-3-0	.571	1961 Bluebonnet

School	Bowls	W-L-T	Pct.	Last Appearance
Southern Methodist	11	4-6-1	.409	1984 Aloha
Texas Christian	15	4-10-1	.300	1994 Independence
Tulsa	11	4-7-0	.364	1991 Freedom
UTEP	9	5-4-0	.556	1988 Independence
Utah	6	3-3-0	.500	1996 Copper
Pacific				
Air Force	14	6-7-1	.464	1997 Las Vegas
Colorado St.	5	2-3-0	.400	1997 Holiday
Fresno St.	9	6-3-0	.667	1993 Aloha
Hawaii	2	1-1-0	.500	1992 Holiday
UNLV	2	2-0-0	1.000	1994 Las Vegas
San Diego St.	4	1-3-0	.250	1991 Freedom
San Jose St.	7	4-3-0	.571	1990 California
Wyoming	10	4-6-0	.400	1993 Copper
Current Members	**138**	**59-74-5**	**.446**	

INDEPENDENTS

School	Bowls	W-L-T	Pct.	Last Appearance
UAB	0	0-0-0	.000	Has never appeared
Central Fla.	0	0-0-0	.000	Has never appeared
Louisiana Tech	3	1-1-1	.500	1990 Independence
Navy	9	4-4-1	.500	1996 Aloha
Northeast La.	0	0-0-0	.000	Has never appeared
Notre Dame	22	13-9-0	.591	1997 Independence
Southwestern La.	0	0-0-0	.000	Has never appeared
Current Members	**34**	**18-14-2**	**.559**	

Award Winners in Bowl Games

Most Valuable Players in Major Bowls

Bowls that are played twice in the same calendar year (i.e., January and December) are listed in chronological order.

ALAMO BOWL

Year Player, Team, Position
1993 Dave Barr, California, quarterback (offense)
Jerrott Willard, California, linebacker (defense)
Larry Blue, Iowa, defensive tackle (sportsmanship award)
1994 Chad Davis, Washington St., quarterback (offense)
Ron Childs, Washington St., linebacker (defense)
Adrian Robinson, Baylor, defensive back (sportsmanship award)
1995 Kyle Bryant, Texas A&M, kicker (offense)
Keith Mitchell, Texas A&M, linebacker (defense)
Jarrett Irons, Michigan, linebacker (sportsmanship award)
1996 Sedrick Shaw, Iowa, running back (offense)
James DeVries, Iowa, defensive lineman (defense)
Shane Dunn, Texas Tech (sportsmanship award)
1997 Billy Dicken, Purdue, quarterback (offense)
Adrian Beasley, Purdue, safety (defense)
Kevin Williams, Oklahoma St., cornerback (sportsmanship award)

ALOHA BOWL

Year Player, Team, Position
1982 Offense—Tim Cowan, Washington, quarterback
Defense—Tony Caldwell, Washington, linebacker
1983 Offense—Danny Greene, Washington, wide receiver
Defense—George Reynolds, Penn St., punter
1984 Offense—Jeff Atkins, Southern Methodist, running back
Defense—Jerry Ball, Southern Methodist, nose guard
1985 Offense—Gene Jelks, Alabama, running back
Defense—Cornelius Bennett, Alabama, linebacker
1986 Offense—Alfred Jenkins, Arizona, quarterback
Defense—Chuck Cecil, Arizona, safety
1987* Troy Aikman, UCLA, quarterback
Emmitt Smith, Florida, running back
1988 David Dacus, Houston, quarterback
Victor Wood, Washington St., wide receiver
1989 Blake Ezor, Michigan St., tailback
Chris Roscoe, Hawaii, wide receiver
1990 Todd Burden, Arizona, cornerback
Marvin Graves, Syracuse, quarterback
1991 Tommy Vardell, Stanford, running back
Shawn Jones, Georgia Tech, quarterback
1992 Tom Young, Brigham Young, quarterback
Dana Stubblefield, Kansas, defensive tackle
1993 Rashaan Salaam, Colorado, tailback
Trent Dilfer, Fresno St., quarterback
1994 David Green, Boston College, running back (offense)
Mike Mamula, Boston College, defensive end (defense)
Joe Gordon, Kansas St., cornerback
1995 Mark Williams, Kansas, quarterback
Karim Abdul-Jabbar, UCLA, running back
1996 Chris McCoy, Navy, quarterback
Pat Barnes, California, quarterback
1997 Rashaan Shehee, Washington, running back

**Began selecting one MVP for each team.*

INSIGHT.com BOWL
(Named Copper Bowl, 1989-96)

Year Player, Team, Position
1989 Shane Montgomery, North Caro. St., quarterback
Scott Geyer, Arizona, defensive back
1990 Mike Pawlawski, California, quarterback
Robert Midgett, Wyoming, linebacker
1991 Vaughn Dunbar, Indiana, tailback
Mark Hagen, Indiana, linebacker
1992 Drew Bledsoe, Washington St., quarterback (overall)
Phillip Bobo, Washington St., wide receiver (offense)
Kareem Leary, Utah, defensive back (defense)
1993 Andre Coleman, Kansas St., wide receiver (offense)
Kenny McEntyre, Kansas St., cornerback (defense)
1994 John Walsh, Brigham Young, quarterback (overall)
Jamal Willis, Brigham Young, running back (offense)
Broderick Simpson, Oklahoma, linebacker (defense)
1995 Byron Hanspard, Texas Tech, running back (overall)
Zebbie Lethridge, Texas Tech, quarterback (offense)
Mickey Dalton, Air Force, cornerback (defense)
1996 Ron Dayne, Wisconsin, running back

COTTON BOWL

Year Player, Team, Position
1937 Ki Aldrich, Texas Christian, center
Sammy Baugh, Texas Christian, quarterback
L. D. Meyer, Texas Christian, end
1938 Ernie Lain, Rice, back
Byron "Whizzer" White, Colorado, quarterback
1939 Jerry Dowd, St. Mary's (Tex.), center
Elmer Tarbox, Texas Tech, back
1940 Banks McFadden, Clemson, back
1941 Charles Henke, Texas A&M, guard
John Kimbrough, Texas A&M, fullback
Chip Routt, Texas A&M, tackle
Lou De Filippo, Fordham, center
Joe Ungerer, Fordham, tackle
1942 Martin Ruby, Texas A&M, tackle
Jimmy Nelson, Alabama, halfback
Holt Rast, Alabama, end
Don Whitmire, Alabama, tackle
1943 Jack Freeman, Texas, guard
Roy McKay, Texas, fullback
Stanley Mauldin, Texas, tackle
Harvey Hardy, Georgia Tech, guard
Jack Marshall, Georgia Tech, end
1944 Joe Parker, Texas, end
Martin Ruby, Randolph Field, tackle
Glenn Dobbs, Randolph Field, quarterback
1945 Neil Armstrong, Oklahoma St., end
Bob Fenimore, Oklahoma St., back
Ralph Foster, Oklahoma St., tackle
1946 Hub Bechtol, Texas, end
Bobby Layne, Texas, back
Jim Kekeris, Missouri, tackle
1947 Alton Baldwin, Arkansas, end
Y. A. Tittle, LSU, quarterback
1948 Doak Walker, Southern Methodist, back
Steve Suhey, Penn St., guard
1949 Kyle Rote, Southern Methodist, back
Doak Walker, Southern Methodist, back
Brad Ecklund, Oregon, center
Norm Van Brocklin, Oregon, quarterback
1950 Billy Burkhalter, Rice, halfback
Joe Watson, Rice, center
James "Froggie" Williams, Rice, end
1951 Bud McFadin, Texas, guard
Andy Kozar, Tennessee, fullback
Hank Lauricella, Tennessee, halfback
Horace "Bud" Sherrod, Tennessee, defensive end
1952 Keith Flowers, Texas Christian, fullback
Emery Clark, Kentucky, halfback
Ray Correll, Kentucky, guard
Vito "Babe" Parilli, Kentucky, quarterback
1953 Richard Ochoa, Texas, fullback
Harley Sewell, Texas, guard
Bob Griesbach, Tennessee, linebacker
1954 Richard Chapman, Rice, tackle
Dan Hart, Rice, end
Dicky Maegle, Rice, halfback
1955 Bud Brooks, Arkansas, guard
George Humphreys, Georgia Tech, fullback
1956 Buddy Alliston, Mississippi, guard
Eagle Day, Mississippi, quarterback
1957 Norman Hamilton, Texas Christian, tackle
Jim Brown, Syracuse, halfback
1958 Tom Forrestal, Navy, quarterback
Tony Stremic, Navy, guard
1959 Jack Spikes, Texas Christian, fullback
Dave Phillips, Air Force, tackle
1960 Maurice Doke, Texas, guard
Ernie Davis, Syracuse, halfback

Year Player, Team, Position
1961 Lance Alworth, Arkansas, halfback
Dwight Bumgarner, Duke, tackle
1962 Mike Cotten, Texas, quarterback
Bob Moser, Texas, end
1963 Johnny Treadwell, Texas, guard
Lynn Amedee, LSU, quarterback
1964 Scott Appleton, Texas, tackle
Duke Carlisle, Texas, quarterback
1965 Ronnie Caveness, Arkansas, linebacker
Fred Marshall, Arkansas, quarterback
1966 Joe Labruzzo, LSU, tailback
David McCormick, LSU, tackle
1966 Kent Lawrence, Georgia, tailback
George Patton, Georgia, tackle
1968 Grady Allen, Texas A&M, defensive end
Edd Hargett, Texas A&M, quarterback
Bill Hobbs, Texas A&M, linebacker
1969 Tom Campbell, Texas, linebacker
Charles "Cotton" Speyrer, Texas, wide receiver
James Street, Texas, quarterback
1970 Steve Worster, Texas, fullback
Bob Olson, Notre Dame, linebacker
1971 Eddie Phillips, Texas, quarterback
Clarence Ellis, Notre Dame, cornerback
1972 Bruce Bannon, Penn St., defensive end
Lydell Mitchell, Penn St., running back
1973 Randy Braband, Texas, linebacker
Alan Lowry, Texas, quarterback
1974 Wade Johnston, Texas, linebacker
Tony Davis, Nebraska, tailback
1975 Ken Quesenberry, Baylor, safety
Tom Shuman, Penn St., quarterback
1976 Ike Forte, Arkansas, running back
Hal McAfee, Arkansas, linebacker
1977 Alois Blackwell, Houston, running back
Mark Mohr, Houston, cornerback
1978 Vagas Ferguson, Notre Dame, running back
Bob Golic, Notre Dame, linebacker
1979 David Hodge, Houston, linebacker
Joe Montana, Notre Dame, quarterback
1980 Terry Elston, Houston, quarterback
David Hodge, Houston, linebacker
1981 Warren Lyles, Alabama, nose guard
Major Ogilvie, Alabama, running back
1982 Robert Brewer, Texas, quarterback
Robbie Jones, Alabama, linebacker
1983 Wes Hopkins, Southern Methodist, strong safety
Lance McIlhenny, Southern Methodist, quarterback
1984 Jeff Leiding, Texas, linebacker
John Lastinger, Georgia, quarterback
1985 Bill Romanowski, Boston College, linebacker
Steve Strachan, Boston College, fullback
1986 Domingo Bryant, Texas A&M, strong safety
Bo Jackson, Auburn, tailback
1987 Chris Spielman, Ohio St., linebacker
Roger Vick, Texas A&M, fullback
1988 Adam Bob, Texas A&M, linebacker
Bucky Richardson, Texas A&M, quarterback
1989 LaSalle Harper, Arkansas, linebacker
Troy Aikman, UCLA, quarterback
1990 Carl Pickens, Tennessee, free safety
Chuck Webb, Tennessee, tailback
1991 Craig Erickson, Miami (Fla.), quarterback
Russell Maryland, Miami (Fla.), defensive lineman
1992 Sean Jackson, Florida St., running back
Chris Crooms, Texas A&M, safety
1993 Rick Mirer, Notre Dame, quarterback
Devon McDonald, Notre Dame, defensive end
1994 Lee Becton, Notre Dame, running back
Antonio Shorter, Texas A&M, linebacker
1995 Keyshawn Johnson, Southern Cal, wide receiver
John Herpin, Southern Cal, cornerback
1996 Herchell Troutman, Colorado, running back
Marcus Washington, Colorado, defensive back
1997 Steve Sarkisian, Brigham Young, quarterback
Kevin Lockett, Kansas St., wide receiver
Shay Muirbrook, Brigham Young, linebacker
1998 Cade McNown, UCLA, quarterback
Dat Nguyen, Texas A&M, linebacker

FIESTA BOWL

Year Player, Team, Position
1971 Gary Huff, Florida St., quarterback
Junior Ah You, Arizona St., defensive end
1972 Woody Green, Arizona St., halfback
Mike Fink, Missouri, defensive back
1973 Greg Hudson, Arizona St., split end
Mike Haynes, Arizona St., cornerback
1974 Kenny Walker, Oklahoma St., running back
Phillip Dokes, Oklahoma St., defensive tackle

Year Player, Team, Position
1975 John Jefferson, Arizona St., split end
Larry Gordon, Arizona St., linebacker
1976 Thomas Lott, Oklahoma, quarterback
Terry Peters, Oklahoma, cornerback
1977 Matt Millen, Penn St., linebacker
Dennis Sproul, Arizona St., quarterback (sportsmanship award)
1978 James Owens, UCLA, running back
Jimmy Walker, Arkansas, defensive tackle
Kenny Easley, UCLA, safety (sportsmanship award)
1979 Mark Schubert, Pittsburgh, kicker
Dave Liggins, Arizona, safety
Dan Fidler, Pittsburgh, offensive guard (sportsmanship award)
1980 Curt Warner, Penn St., running back
Frank Case, Penn St., defensive end (sportsmanship award)
1982 Curt Warner, Penn St., running back
Leo Wisniewski, Penn St., nose tackle
George Achica, Southern Cal, nose guard (sportsmanship award)
1983 Marcus Dupree, Oklahoma, running back
Jim Jeffcoat, Arizona St., defensive lineman
Paul Ferrer, Oklahoma, center (sportsmanship award)
1984 John Congemi, Pittsburgh, quarterback
Rowland Tatum, Ohio St., linebacker (sportsmanship award)
1985 Gaston Green, UCLA, tailback
James Washington, UCLA, defensive back
Bruce Fleming, Miami (Fla.), linebacker (sportsmanship award)
1986 Jamie Morris, Michigan, running back
Mark Messner, Michigan, defensive tackle
Mike Mallory, Michigan, linebacker (sportsmanship award)
1987 D. J. Dozier, Penn St., running back
Shane Conlan, Penn St., linebacker
Paul O'Connor, Miami (Fla.), offensive guard (sportsmanship award)
1988 Danny McManus, Florida St., quarterback
Neil Smith, Nebraska, defensive lineman
Steve Forch, Nebraska, linebacker (sportsmanship award)
1989 Tony Rice, Notre Dame, quarterback
Frank Stams, Notre Dame, defensive end
Chris Parker, West Va., defensive lineman (sportsmanship award)
1990 Peter Tom Willis, Florida St., quarterback
Odell Haggins, Florida St., nose guard
Jake Young, Nebraska, center (sportsmanship award)
1991 Browning Nagle, Louisville, quarterback
Ray Buchanan, Louisville, free safety
1992 O. J. McDuffie, Penn St., wide receiver
Reggie Givens, Penn St., outside linebacker
1993 Marvin Graves, Syracuse, quarterback
Kevin Mitchell, Syracuse, nose guard
1994 Chuck Levy, Arizona, running back
Tedy Bruschi, Arizona, defensive end
Paul White, Miami (Fla.), cornerback (sportsmanship award)
1995 Kordell Stewart, Colorado, quarterback
Shannon Clavelle, Colorado, defensive tackle
Oliver Gibson, Notre Dame, nose guard (sportsmanship award)
1996 Tommie Frazier, Nebraska, quarterback
Michael Booker, Nebraska, cornerback
Danny Wuerffel, Florida, quarterback (sportsmanship award)
1997 Curtis Enis, Penn St., tailback
Brandon Noble, Penn St., defensive tackle
Ryan Fiebiger, Texas, center (sportsmanship award)
1998 Michael Bishop, Kansas St., quarterback
Travis Ochs, Kansas St., linebacker
Jason Walters, Syracuse, end (sportsmanship)

FLORIDA CITRUS BOWL
(Named Tangerine Bowl, 1947-82)

Players of the Game (Pre-1977)
Year Player, Team, Position
1949 Dale McDaniels, Murray St.
Ted Scown, Sul Ross St.
1950 Don Henigan, St. Vincent
Chick Davis, Emory & Henry
1951 Pete Anania, Morris Harvey
Charles Hubbard, Morris Harvey
1952 Bill Johnson, Stetson
Dave Laude, Stetson

Year Player, Team, Position
1953 Marvin Brown, East Tex. St.
1954 Billy Ray Norris, East Tex. St.
Bobby Spann, Arkansas St.
1955 Bill Englehardt, Nebraska-Omaha
1956 Pat Tarquinio, Juniata
1957 Ron Mills, West Tex. A&M
1958 Garry Berry, East Tex. St.
Neal Hinson, East Tex. St.
1958 Sam McCord, East Tex. St.
1960 Bucky Pitts, Middle Tenn. St.
Bob Waters, Presbyterian
1960 Jerry Nettles, Citadel
1961 Win Herbert, Lamar
1962 Joe Lopasky, Houston
Billy Roland, Houston
1963 Sharon Miller, Western Ky.
1964 Bill Cline, East Caro.
Jerry Whelchel, Massachusetts
1965 Dave Alexander, East Caro.
1966 Willie Lanier, Morgan St.
1967 Errol Hook, Tenn.-Martin
Gordon Lambert, Tenn.-Martin
1968 Buster O'Brien, Richmond, back
Walker Gillette, Richmond, lineman
1969 Chuck Ealy, Toledo, back
Dan Crockett, Toledo, lineman
1970 Chuck Ealy, Toledo, back
Vince Hubler, William & Mary, lineman
1971 Chuck Ealy, Toledo, back
Mel Long, Toledo, lineman
1972 Freddie Solomon, Tampa, back
Jack Lambert, Kent, lineman
1973 Chuck Varner, Miami (Ohio), back
Brad Cousino, Miami (Ohio), lineman
1974 Sherman Smith, Miami (Ohio), back
Brad Cousino, Miami (Ohio), lineman (tie)

Players of the Game (Pre-1977)
John Roudebush, Miami (Ohio), lineman (tie)
1975 Rob Carpenter, Miami (Ohio), back
Jeff Kelly, Miami (Ohio), lineman
1976 Terry Miller, Oklahoma St., back
Phillip Dokes, Oklahoma St., lineman

Most Valuable Player (1977-Present)
Year Player, Team, Position
1977 Jimmy Jordan, Florida St., quarterback
1978 Ted Brown, North Caro. St., running back
1979 David Woodley, LSU, quarterback
1980 Cris Collinsworth, Florida, wide receiver
1981 Jeff Gaylord, Missouri, linebacker
1982 Randy Campbell, Auburn, quarterback
1983 Johnnie Jones, Tennessee, running back
1984 James Jackson, Georgia, quarterback
1985 Larry Kolic, Ohio St., middle guard
1987 Aundray Bruce, Auburn, linebacker
1988 Rodney Williams, Clemson, quarterback
1989 Terry Allen, Clemson, tailback
1990 Jeff George, Illinois, quarterback
1991 Shawn Jones, Georgia Tech, quarterback
1992 Mike Pawlawski, California, quarterback
1993 Garrison Hearst, Georgia, running back
1994 Bobby Engram, Penn St., wide receiver (overall)
Charlie Garner, Tennessee, tailback (offense)
Lee Rubin, Penn St., free safety (defense)
Raymond Austin, Tennessee, strong safety (defense)
1995 Sherman Williams, Alabama, running back (overall)
Joey Galloway, Ohio St., wide receiver (offense)
Dameian Jeffries, Alabama, defensive end (defense)
Matt Finkes, Ohio St., defensive end (defense)
1996 Jay Graham, Tennessee, running back (overall)
Rickey Dudley, Ohio St., tight end (offense)
Leonard Little, Tennessee, defensive end (defense)
Matt Finkes, Ohio St., defensive end (defense)
1997 Peyton Manning, Tennessee, quarterback (overall)
Brian Musso, Northwestern, wide receiver (offense)
Tyrone Hines, Tennessee, linebacker (defense)
Mike Nelson, Northwestern, linebacker (defense)
1998 Fred Taylor, Florida, tailback (overall)
Fred Weary, Florida, cornerback (defense)
Chris Eberly, Penn St., tailback (offense)
Brandon Short, Penn St., linebacker (defense)

GATOR BOWL

Year Player, Team
1946 Nick Sacrinty, Wake Forest
1947 Joe Golding, Oklahoma
1948 Lu Gambino, Maryland
1949 Bobby Gage, Clemson

Year	Player, Team
1950	Bob Ward, Maryland
1951	Eddie Talboom, Wyoming
1952	Jim Dooley, Miami (Fla.)
1953	Marv Matuszak, Tulsa
	John Hall, Florida
1954	Vince Dooley, Auburn
	Bobby Cavazos, Texas Tech
1954	Billy Hooper, Baylor
	Joe Childress, Auburn
1955	Joe Childress, Auburn
	Don Orr, Vanderbilt
1956	Corny Salvaterra, Pittsburgh
	Wade Mitchell, Georgia Tech
1957	John David Crow, Texas A&M
	Bobby Gordon, Tennessee
1958	Dave Hudson, Florida
	Bobby Franklin, Mississippi
1960	Maxie Baughan, Georgia Tech
	Jim Mooty, Arkansas
1960	Bobby Ply, Baylor
	Larry Libertore, Florida
1961	Joe Auer, Georgia Tech
	Galen Hall, Penn St.
1962	Dave Robinson, Penn St.
	Tom Shannon, Florida
1963	David Sicks, Air Force
	Ken Willard, North Caro.
1965	Carl McAdams, Oklahoma
	Fred Biletnikoff, Florida St.
	Steve Tensi, Florida
1965	Donny Anderson, Texas Tech
	Lenny Snow, Georgia Tech
1966	Floyd Little, Syracuse
	Dewey Warren, Tennessee
1967	Tom Sherman, Penn St.
	Kim Hammond, Florida St.
1968	Mike Hall, Alabama
	Terry McMillan, Missouri
1969	Curt Watson, Tennessee
	Mike Kelley, Florida
1971	Archie Manning, Mississippi
	Pat Sullivan, Auburn
1971	James Webster, North Caro.
	Jimmy Poulos, Georgia
1972	Mark Cooney, Colorado
	Wade Whatley, Auburn
1973	Haskell Stanback, Tennessee
	Joe Barnes, Texas Tech
1974	Earl Campbell, Texas
	Phil Gargis, Auburn
1975	Sammy Green, Florida
	Steve Atkins, Maryland
1976	Jim Cefalo, Penn St.
	Al Hunter, Notre Dame
1977	Jerry Butler, Clemson
	Matt Cavanaugh, Pittsburgh
1978	Art Schlichter, Ohio St.
	Steve Fuller, Clemson
1979	John Wangler, Michigan
	Anthony Carter, Michigan
	Matt Kupec, North Caro.
	Amos Lawrence, North Caro.
1980	George Rogers, South Caro.
	Rick Trocano, Pittsburgh
1981	Gary Anderson, Arkansas
	Kelvin Bryant, North Caro.
	Ethan Horton, North Caro.
1982	Paul Woodside, West Va.
	Greg Allen, Florida St.
1983	Owen Gill, Iowa
	Tony Lilly, Florida
1984	Mike Hold, South Caro.
	Thurman Thomas, Oklahoma St.
1985	Thurman Thomas, Oklahoma St.
	Chip Ferguson, Florida St.
1986	Brad Muster, Stanford
	Rodney Williams, Clemson
1987	Harold Green, South Caro.
	Wendell Davis, LSU
1989	Andre Rison, Michigan St.
	Wayne Johnson, Georgia
1989	Mike Fox, West Va.
	Levon Kirkland, Clemson
1991	Tyrone Ashley, Mississippi
	Michigan offensive line: Tom Dohring, Matt Elliott, Steve Everitt, Dean Dingman, Greg Skrepenak
1991	Cale Gundy, Oklahoma
	Tyrone Lewis, Virginia
1992	Errict Rhett, Florida
	Reggie Lawrence, North Caro. St.
1993	Brian Burgdorf, Alabama
	Corey Holliday, North Caro.
1994	James Stewart, Tennessee
	Dwayne Thomas, Virginia Tech
1996	Donovan McNabb, Syracuse, quarterback
	Peter Ford, Clemson, cornerback
1997	Oscar Davenport, North Caro., quarterback
	David Saunders, West Va., wide receiver
1998	Chris Keldorf, North Caro., quarterback
	Al Clark, Virginia Tech, quarterback

HOLIDAY BOWL

Year	Player, Team, Position
1978	Phil McConkey, Navy, wide receiver
1979	Marc Wilson, Brigham Young, quarterback
	Tim Wilbur, Indiana, cornerback
1980	Jim McMahon, Brigham Young, quarterback
	Craig James, Southern Methodist, running back
1981	Jim McMahon, Brigham Young, quarterback
	Kyle Whittingham, Brigham Young, linebacker
1982	Tim Spencer, Ohio St., running back
	Garcia Lane, Ohio St., cornerback
1983	Steve Young, Brigham Young, quarterback
	Bobby Bell, Missouri, defensive end
1984	Robbie Bosco, Brigham Young, quarterback
	Leon White, Brigham Young, linebacker
1985	Bobby Joe Edmonds, Arkansas, running back
	Greg Battle, Arizona St., linebacker
1986	Todd Santos, San Diego St., quarterback (co-offensive)
	Mark Vlasic, Iowa, quarterback (co-offensive)
	Richard Brown, San Diego St., linebacker
1987	Craig Burnett, Wyoming, quarterback
	Anthony Wright, Iowa, cornerback
1988	Barry Sanders, Oklahoma St., running back
	Sim Drain, Oklahoma St., linebacker
1989	Blair Thomas, Penn St., running back
	Ty Detmer, Brigham Young, quarterback
1990	Bucky Richardson, Texas A&M, quarterback
	William Thomas, Texas A&M, linebacker
1991	Ty Detmer, Brigham Young, quarterback
	Josh Arnold, Brigham Young, defensive back (co-defensive)
	Carlos James, Iowa, defensive back (co-defensive)
1992	Michael Carter, Hawaii, quarterback
	Junior Tagoai, Hawaii, defensive tackle
1993	John Walsh, Brigham Young, quarterback (co-offensive)
	Raymont Harris, Ohio St., running back (co-offensive)
	Lorenzo Styles, Ohio St., linebacker
1994	Todd Collins, Michigan, quarterback (co-offensive)
	Anthoney Hill, Colorado St., quarterback (co-offensive)
	Matt Dyson, Michigan, linebacker
1995	Brian Kavanagh, Kansas St., quarterback (offense)
	Mario Smith, Kansas St., defensive back (defense)
1996	Koy Detmer, Colorado, quarterback (offense)
	Nick Ziegler, Colorado, defensive end (defense)
1997	Moses Moreno, Colorado St., quarterback
	Darran Hall, Colorado St., wide receiver

HUMANITARIAN BOWL

Year	Player, Team, Position
1997	Steve Smith, Utah St., wide receiver
	Chad Plummer, Cincinnati, quarterback

INDEPENDENCE BOWL

Year	Player, Team, Position
1976	Terry McFarland, McNeese St., quarterback
	Terry Clark, Tulsa, cornerback
1977	Keith Thibodeaux, Louisiana Tech, quarterback
	Otis Wilson, Louisville, linebacker
1978	Theodore Sutton, East Caro., fullback
	Zack Valentine, East Caro., defensive end
1979	Joe Morris, Syracuse, running back
	Clay Carroll, McNeese St., defensive tackle
1980	Stephan Starring, McNeese St., quarterback
	Jerald Baylis, Southern Miss., nose guard
1981	Gary Kubiak, Texas A&M, quarterback
	Mike Green, Oklahoma St., linebacker
1982	Randy Wright, Wisconsin, quarterback
	Tim Krumrie, Wisconsin, nose guard
1983	Marty Louthan, Air Force, quarterback
	Andre Townsend, Mississippi, defensive tackle
1984	Bart Weiss, Air Force, quarterback
	Scott Thomas, Air Force, safety
1985	Rickey Foggie, Minnesota, quarterback
	Bruce Holmes, Minnesota, linebacker
1986	Mark Young, Mississippi, quarterback
	James Mosley, Texas Tech, defensive end
1987	Chris Chandler, Washington, quarterback
	David Rill, Washington, linebacker
1988	James Henry, Southern Miss., punt returner/cornerback
1989	Bill Musgrave, Oregon, quarterback
	Chris Oldham, Oregon, defensive back
1990	Mike Richardson, Louisiana Tech, running back
	Lorenzo Baker, Louisiana Tech, linebacker
1991	Andre Hastings, Georgia, flanker
	Torrey Evans, Georgia, linebacker
1992	Todd Dixon, Wake Forest, split end
1993	Maurice DeShazo, Virginia Tech, quarterback
	Antonio Banks, Virginia Tech, safety
1994	Mike Groh, Virginia, quarterback
	Mike Frederick, Virginia, defensive end
1995	Kevin Faulk, LSU, running back
	Gabe Northern, LSU, defensive end
1996	Dameyune Craig, Auburn, quarterback
	Takeo Spikes, Auburn, linebacker
	Ben Kotwica, Army, linebacker
1997	Rondell Mealey, LSU, running back
	Arnold Miller, LSU, defensive end

LAS VEGAS BOWL

Year	Player, Team, Position
1992	Chris Vargas, Nevada, quarterback
1993	Anthony Calvillo, Utah St., quarterback
	Mike Neu, Ball St., quarterback
1994	Henry Bailey, UNLV, running back
1995	Wasean Tait, Toledo, running back
	Alex Van Dyke, Nevada, wide receiver
1996	Brad Maynard, Ball St., punter
	Mike Crawford, Nevada, linebacker
1997	Pat Johnson, Oregon, wide receiver
	Bryce Fisher, Air Force, defensive tackle

LIBERTY BOWL

Year	Player, Team
1959	Jay Huffman, Penn St.
1960	Dick Hoak, Penn St.
1961	Ernie Davis, Syracuse
1962	Terry Baker, Oregon St.
1963	Ode Burrell, Mississippi St.
1964	Ernest Adler, Utah
1965	Tom Bryan, Auburn
1966	Jimmy Cox, Miami (Fla.)
1967	Jim Donnan, North Caro. St.
1968	Steve Hindman, Mississippi
1969	Bob Anderson, Colorado
1970	Dave Abercrombie, Tulane
1971	Joe Ferguson, Arkansas
1972	Jim Stevens, Georgia Tech
1973	Stan Fritts, North Caro. St.
1974	Randy White, Maryland
1975	Ricky Bell, Southern Cal
1976	Barry Krauss, Alabama
1977	Matt Kupec, North Caro.
1978	James Wilder, Missouri
1979	Roch Hontas, Tulane
1980	Mark Herrmann, Purdue
1981	Eddie Meyers, Navy
1982	Jeremiah Castille, Alabama
1983	Doug Flutie, Boston College
1984	Bo Jackson, Auburn
1985	Cody Carlson, Baylor
1986	Jeff Francis, Tennessee
1987	Greg Thomas, Arkansas
1988	Dave Schnell, Indiana
1989	Randy Baldwin, Mississippi
1990	Rob Perez, Air Force
1991	Rob Perez, Air Force
1992	Cassius Ware, Mississippi
1993	Jeff Brohm, Louisville
1994	Johnny Johnson, Illinois
1995	Kwame Ellis, Stanford, cornerback
1996	Malcolm Thomas, Syracuse, running back
1997	Sherrod Gideon, Southern Miss., wide receiver

MOTOR CITY BOWL

Year	Player, Team, Position
1997	Deuce McCallister, Mississippi, running back
	B. J. Cohen, Marshall, defensive end

ORANGE BOWL

Year	Player, Team, Position
1965	Joe Namath, Alabama, quarterback
1966	Steve Sloan, Alabama, quarterback
1967	Larry Smith, Florida, tailback
1968	Bob Warmack, Oklahoma, quarterback
1969	Donnie Shanklin, Kansas, halfback
1970	Chuck Burkhart, Penn St., quarterback
	Mike Reid, Penn St., defensive tackle
1971	Jerry Tagge, Nebraska, quarterback
	Willie Harper, Nebraska, defensive end
1972	Jerry Tagge, Nebraska, quarterback
	Rich Glover, Nebraska, defensive guard
1973	Johnny Rodgers, Nebraska, wingback
	Rich Glover, Nebraska, defensive guard
1974	Tom Shuman, Penn St., quarterback
	Randy Crowder, Penn St., defensive tackle
1975	Wayne Bullock, Notre Dame, fullback
	Leroy Cook, Alabama, defensive end
1976	Steve Davis, Oklahoma, quarterback
	Lee Roy Selmon, Oklahoma, defensive tackle
1977	Rod Gerald, Ohio St., quarterback
	Tom Cousineau, Ohio St., linebacker
1978	Roland Sales, Arkansas, running back
	Reggie Freeman, Arkansas, nose guard
1979	Billy Sims, Oklahoma, running back
	Reggie Kinlaw, Oklahoma, nose guard
1980	J. C. Watts, Oklahoma, quarterback
	Bud Hebert, Oklahoma, free safety
1981	J. C. Watts, Oklahoma, quarterback
	Jarvis Coursey, Florida St., defensive end
1982	Homer Jordan, Clemson, quarterback
	Jeff Davis, Clemson, linebacker
1983	Turner Gill, Nebraska, quarterback
	Dave Rimington, Nebraska, center
1984	Bernie Kosar, Miami (Fla.), quarterback
	Jack Fernandez, Miami (Fla.), linebacker
1985	Jacque Robinson, Washington, tailback
	Ron Holmes, Washington, defensive tackle
1986	Sonny Brown, Oklahoma, defensive back
	Tim Lashar, Oklahoma, kicker
1987	Dante Jones, Oklahoma, linebacker
	Spencer Tillman, Oklahoma, halfback
1988	Bernard Clark, Miami (Fla.), linebacker
	Darrell Reed, Oklahoma, defensive end
1989	Steve Walsh, Miami (Fla.), quarterback
	Charles Fryar, Nebraska, cornerback
1990	Raghib Ismail, Notre Dame, tailback/wide receiver
	Darian Hagan, Colorado, quarterback
1991	Charles Johnson, Colorado, quarterback
	Chris Zorich, Notre Dame, nose guard
1992	Larry Jones, Miami (Fla.), running back
	Tyrone Leggett, Nebraska, cornerback
1993	Charlie Ward, Florida St., quarterback
	Corey Dixon, Nebraska, split end
1994	Tommie Frazier, Nebraska, quarterback
	Charlie Ward, Florida St., quarterback
1995	Tommie Frazier, Nebraska, quarterback
	Chris T. Jones, Miami (Fla.), cornerback
1996	Andre Cooper, Florida St., wide receiver
	Derrick Mayes, Notre Dame, wide receiver
1997	Damon Benning, Nebraska, running back
	Ken Oxendine, Virginia Tech, running back
1998	Ahman Green, Nebraska, running back

OUTBACK BOWL (Formerly Hall of Fame, 1986-95)

Year	Player, Team, Position
1986	Shawn Halloran, Boston College, quarterback
	James Jackson, Georgia, quarterback
1988	Jamie Morris, Michigan, tailback
	Bobby Humphrey, Alabama, tailback
1989	Robert Drummond, Syracuse, running back
1990	Reggie Slack, Alabama, quarterback
	Derek Isaman, Ohio St., linebacker
1991	DeChane Cameron, Clemson, quarterback
1992	Marvin Graves, Syracuse, quarterback
1993	Heath Shuler, Tennessee, quarterback
1994	Tyrone Wheatley, Michigan, running back
1995	Terrell Fletcher, Wisconsin, running back
1996	Bobby Engram, Penn St., wide receiver
1997	Dwayne Rudd, Alabama, linebacker
1998	Mike Bobo, Georgia, quarterback

PEACH BOWL

Year	Player, Team, Position
1968	Mike Hillman, LSU (offense)
	Buddy Millican, Florida St. (defense)
1969	Ed Williams, West Va. (offense)
	Carl Crennel, West Va. (defense)
1970	Monroe Eley, Arizona St. (offense)
	Junior Ah You, Arizona St. (defense)
1971	Norris Weese, Mississippi (offense)
	Crowell Armstrong, Mississippi (defense)
1972	Dave Buckey, North Caro. St. (offense)
	George Bell, North Caro. St. (defense)
1973	Louis Carter, Maryland (offense)
	Sylvester Boler, Georgia (defense)
1974	Larry Isaac, Texas Tech (offense)
	Dennis Harrison, Vanderbilt (defense)
1975	Dan Kendra, West Va. (offense)
	Ray Marshall, West Va. (defense)
1976	Rod Stewart, Kentucky (offense)
	Mike Martin, Kentucky (defense)
1977	Johnny Evans, North Caro. St. (offense)
	Richard Carter, North Caro. St. (defense)
1978	Mark Herrmann, Purdue (offense)
	Calvin Clark, Purdue (defense)
1979	Mike Brannan, Baylor (offense)
	Andrew Melontree, Baylor (defense)
1980	Jim Kelly, Miami (Fla.) (offense)
	Jim Burt, Miami (Fla.) (defense)
1981	Mickey Walczak, West Va. (offense)
	Don Stemple, West Va. (defense)
1982	Chuck Long, Iowa (offense)
	Clay Uhlenhake, Iowa (defense)
1983	Eric Thomas, Florida St. (offense)
	Alphonso Carreker, Florida St. (defense)
1984	Howard Petty, Virginia (offense)
	Ray Daly, Virginia (defense)
1985	Rob Healy, Army (offense)
	Peel Chronister, Army (defense)
1986	Erik Kramer, North Caro. St. (offense)
	Derrick Taylor, North Caro. St. (defense)
1987	Reggie Cobb, Tennessee (offense)
	Van Waiters, Indiana (defense)
1988	Shane Montgomery, North Caro. St. (offense)
	Michael Brooks, North Caro. St. (defense)
1989	Michael Owens, Syracuse (offense)
	Rodney Hampton, Georgia (offense)
	Terry Wooden, Syracuse (defense)
	Morris Lewis, Georgia (defense)
1990	Stan White, Auburn (offense)
	Vaughn Dunbar, Indiana (offense)
	Darrel Crawford, Auburn (defense)
	Mike Dumas, Indiana (defense)
1991	Jeff Blake, East Caro. (offense)
	Terry Jordan, North Caro. St. (offense)
	Robert Jones, East Caro. (defense)
	Billy Ray Haynes, North Caro. St. (defense)
1993	Natrone Means, North Caro., running back (offense)
	Greg Plump, Mississippi St., quarterback (offense)
	Bracey Walker, North Caro., strong safety (defense)
	Marc Woodard, Mississippi St., linebacker (defense)
1993	Emory Smith, Clemson, fullback (offense)
	Pookie Jones, Kentucky, quarterback (offense)
	Brentson Buckner, Clemson, tackle (defense)
	Zane Beehn, Kentucky, end (defense)
1995	Treymayne Stephens, North Caro. St., running back
1995	Tiki Barber, Virginia, running back (offense)
	Hines Ward, Georgia, quarterback (offense)
	Skeet Jones, Virginia, linebacker (defense)
	Whit Marshall, Georgia, linebacker (defense)
1996	Herb Tyler, LSU, quarterback (offense)
	Raymond Priester, Clemson, running back (offense)
	Anthony McFarland, LSU, defensive lineman (defense)
	Trevor Pryce, Clemson, defensive lineman (defense)
1998	Dameyune Craig, Auburn, quarterback
	Takeo Spikes, Auburn, linebacker
	Raymond Priester, Clemson, running back
	Rahim Abdullah, Clemson, linebacker

ROSE BOWL

Year	Player, Team, Position
1902	Neil Snow, Michigan, fullback
1916	Carl Dietz, Washington St., fullback
1917	John Beckett, Oregon, tackle
1918	Hollis Huntington, Mare Island, fullback
1919	George Halas, Great Lakes, end
1920	Edward Casey, Harvard, halfback
1921	Harold "Brick" Muller, California, end
1922	Russell Stein, Wash. & Jeff., tackle
1923	Leo Calland, Southern Cal, guard
1924	Ira McKee, Navy, quarterback
1925	Elmer Layden, Notre Dame, fullback
	Ernie Nevers, Stanford, fullback
1926	Johnny Mack Brown, Alabama, halfback
	George Wilson, Washington, halfback
1927	Fred Pickhard, Alabama, tackle
1928	Clifford Hoffman, Stanford, fullback
1929	Benjamin Lom, California, halfback
1930	Russell Saunders, Southern Cal, quarterback
1931	John "Monk" Campbell, Alabama, quarterback
1932	Ernie Pinckert, Southern Cal, halfback
1933	Homer Griffith, Southern Cal, quarterback
1934	Cliff Montgomery, Columbia, quarterback
1935	Millard "Dixie" Howell, Alabama, halfback
1936	James "Monk" Moscrip, Stanford, end
	Keith Topping, Stanford, end
1937	William Daddio, Pittsburgh, end
1938	Victor Bottari, California, halfback
1939	Doyle Nave, Southern Cal, quarterback
	Alvin Krueger, Southern Cal, end
1940	Ambrose Schindler, Southern Cal, quarterback
1941	Peter Kmetovic, Stanford, halfback
1942	Donald Durdan, Oregon St., halfback
1943	Charles Trippi, Georgia, halfback
1944	Norman Verry, Southern Cal, guard
1945	James Hardy, Southern Cal, quarterback
1946	Harry Gilmer, Alabama, halfback
1947	Claude "Buddy" Young, Illinois, halfback
	Julius Rykovich, Illinois, halfback
1948	Robert Chappius, Michigan, halfback
1949	Frank Aschenbrenner, Northwestern, halfback
1950	Fred Morrison, Ohio St., fullback
1951	Donald Dufek, Michigan, fullback
1952	William Tate, Illinois, halfback
1953	Rudy Bukich, Southern Cal, quarterback
1954	Billy Wells, Michigan St., halfback
1955	Dave Leggett, Ohio St., quarterback
1956	Walter Kowalczyk, Michigan St., halfback
1957	Kenneth Ploen, Iowa, quarterback
1958	Jack Crabtree, Oregon, quarterback
1959	Bob Jeter, Iowa, halfback
1960	Bob Schloredt, Washington, quarterback
	George Fleming, Washington, halfback
1961	Bob Schloredt, Washington, quarterback
1962	Sandy Stephens, Minnesota, quarterback
1963	Pete Beathard, Southern Cal, quarterback
	Ron VanderKelen, Wisconsin, quarterback
1964	Jim Grabowski, Illinois, fullback
1965	Mel Anthony, Michigan, fullback
1966	Bob Stiles, UCLA, defensive back
1967	John Charles, Purdue, halfback
1968	O. J. Simpson, Southern Cal, tailback
1969	Rex Kern, Ohio St., quarterback
1970	Bob Chandler, Southern Cal, flanker
1971	Jim Plunkett, Stanford, quarterback
1972	Don Bunce, Stanford, quarterback
1973	Sam Cunningham, Southern Cal, fullback
1974	Cornelius Greene, Ohio St., quarterback
1975	Pat Haden, Southern Cal, quarterback
	John McKay Jr., Southern Cal, split end
1976	John Sciarra, UCLA, quarterback
1977	Vince Evans, Southern Cal, quarterback
1978	Warren Moon, Washington, quarterback
1979	Charles White, Southern Cal, tailback
	Rick Leach, Michigan, quarterback
1980	Charles White, Southern Cal, tailback
1981	Butch Woolfolk, Michigan, running back
1982	Jacque Robinson, Washington, running back
1983	Don Rogers, UCLA, free safety
	Tom Ramsey, UCLA, quarterback
1984	Rick Neuheisel, UCLA, quarterback
1985	Tim Green, Southern Cal, quarterback
	Jack Del Rio, Southern Cal, linebacker
1986	Eric Ball, UCLA, tailback
1987	Jeff Van Raaphorst, Arizona St., quarterback
1988	Percy Snow, Michigan St., linebacker
1989	Leroy Hoard, Michigan, fullback
1990	Ricky Ervins, Southern Cal, tailback
1991	Mark Brunell, Washington, quarterback
1992	Steve Emtman, Washington, defensive tackle
	Billy Joe Hobert, Washington, quarterback
1993	Tyrone Wheatley, Michigan, running back
1994	Brent Moss, Wisconsin, tailback
1995	Danny O'Neil, Oregon, quarterback
	Ki-Jana Carter, Penn St., running back
1996	Keyshawn Johnson, Southern Cal, wide receiver
1997	Joe Germaine, Ohio St., quarterback
1998	Brian Griese, Michigan, quarterback

SUGAR BOWL

Miller-Digby Memorial Trophy

Year	Player, Team, Position
1948	Bobby Layne, Texas, quarterback
1949	Jack Mitchell, Oklahoma, quarterback
1950	Leon Heath, Oklahoma, fullback
1951	Walt Yowarsky, Kentucky, tackle
1952	Ed Modzelewski, Maryland, fullback
1953	Leon Hardemann, Georgia Tech, halfback
1954	"Pepper" Rodgers, Georgia Tech, quarterback
1955	Joe Gattuso, Navy, fullback
1956	Franklin Brooks, Georgia Tech, guard
1957	Del Shofner, Baylor, halfback
1958	Raymond Brown, Mississippi, quarterback
1959	Billy Cannon, LSU, halfback
1960	Bobby Franklin, Mississippi, quarterback
1961	Jake Gibbs, Mississippi, quarterback
1962	Mike Fracchia, Alabama, fullback
1963	Glynn Griffing, Mississippi, quarterback
1964	Tim Davis, Alabama, kicker
1965	Doug Moreau, LSU, flanker
1966	Steve Spurrier, Florida, quarterback
1967	Kenny Stabler, Alabama, quarterback
1968	Glenn Smith, LSU, halfback
1969	Chuck Dicus, Arkansas, flanker
1970	Archie Manning, Mississippi, quarterback
1971	Bobby Scott, Tennessee, quarterback
1972	Jack Mildren, Oklahoma, quarterback
1972	Tinker Owens, Oklahoma, flanker
1973	Tom Clements, Notre Dame, quarterback
1974	Tony Davis, Nebraska, fullback
1975	Richard Todd, Alabama, quarterback
1977	Matt Cavanaugh, Pittsburgh, quarterback
1978	Jeff Rutledge, Alabama, quarterback
1979	Barry Krauss, Alabama, linebacker
1980	Major Ogilvie, Alabama, running back
1981	Herschel Walker, Georgia, running back
1982	Dan Marino, Pittsburgh, quarterback
1983	Todd Blackledge, Penn St., quarterback
1984	Bo Jackson, Auburn, running back
1985	Craig Sundberg, Nebraska, quarterback
1986	Daryl Dickey, Tennessee, quarterback
1987	Steve Taylor, Nebraska, quarterback
1988	Don McPherson, Syracuse, quarterback
1989	Sammie Smith, Florida St., running back
1990	Craig Erickson, Miami (Fla.), quarterback
1991	Andy Kelly, Tennessee, quarterback
1992	Jerome Bettis, Notre Dame, fullback
1993	Derrick Lassic, Alabama, running back
1994	Errict Rhett, Florida, running back
1995	Warrick Dunn, Florida St., running back
1995	Bryan Still, Virginia Tech, wide receiver
1997	Danny Wuerffel, Florida, quarterback
1998	E. G. Green, Florida St., wide receiver

SUN BOWL

(Named Sun Bowl, 1936-86, 1994-95; John Hancock Sun Bowl, 1987-88; John Hancock Bowl, 1989-93); Norwest Bank Sun Bowl (since 1996)

C. M. Hendricks Most Valuable Player Trophy (1954-Present)
Jimmy Rogers Jr. Most Valuable Lineman Trophy (1961-Present)
John Folmer Most Valuable Special Teams Trophy (1994)

Year	Player, Team, Position
1950	Harvey Gabriel, UTEP, halfback
1951	Bill Cross, West Tex. A&M, end
1952	Junior Arteburn, Texas Tech, quarterback
1953	Tom McCormick, Pacific (Cal.), halfback
1954	Dick Shinaut, UTEP, quarterback
1955	Jesse Whittenton, UTEP, quarterback
1956	Jim Crawford, Wyoming, halfback
1957	Claude Austin, Geo. Washington
1958	Leonard Kucewski, Wyoming, guard
1959	Charley Johnson, New Mexico St., quarterback
1960	Charley Johnson, New Mexico St., quarterback
1961	Billy Joe, Villanova, fullback
	Richie Ross, Villanova, guard
1962	Jerry Logan, West Tex. A&M, halfback
	Don Hoovler, Ohio, guard
1963	Bob Berry, Oregon, quarterback
	John Hughes, Southern Methodist, guard
1964	Preston Ridlehuber, Georgia, quarterback
	Jim Wilson, Georgia, tackle
1965	Billy Stevens, UTEP, quarterback
	Ronny Nixon, Texas Christian, tackle
1966	Jim Kiick, Wyoming, tailback
	Jerry Durling, Wyoming, middle guard
1967	Billy Stevens, UTEP, quarterback
	Fred Carr, UTEP, linebacker
1968	Buddy McClintock, Auburn, defensive back
	David Campbell, Auburn, tackle
1969	Paul Rogers, Nebraska, halfback
	Jerry Murtaugh, Nebraska, linebacker
1970	Rock Perdoni, Georgia Tech, defensive tackle
	Bill Flowers, Georgia Tech, linebacker
1971	Bert Jones, LSU, quarterback
	Matt Blair, Iowa St., linebacker
1972	George Smith, Texas Tech, halfback
	Ecomet Burley, Texas Tech, defensive tackle
1973	Ray Bybee, Missouri, fullback
	John Kelsey, Missouri, tight end
1974	Terry Vitrano, Mississippi St., fullback
	Jimmy Webb, Mississippi St., defensive tackle
1975	Robert Haygood, Pittsburgh, quarterback
	Al Romano, Pittsburgh, middle guard
1977	Tony Franklin, Texas A&M, kicker
	Edgar Fields, Texas A&M, defensive tackle
1977	Charles Alexander, LSU, tailback
	Gordy Ceresino, Stanford, linebacker
1978	Johnny "Ham" Jones, Texas, running back
	Dwight Jefferson, Texas, defensive end
1979	Paul Skansi, Washington, flanker
	Doug Martin, Washington, defensive tackle
1980	Jeff Quinn, Nebraska, quarterback
	Jimmy Williams, Nebraska, defensive end
1981	Darrell Shepard, Oklahoma, quarterback
	Rick Bryan, Oklahoma, defensive tackle
1982	Ethan Horton, North Caro., tailback
	Ronnie Mullins, Texas, defensive end
1983	Walter Lewis, Alabama, quarterback
	Wes Neighbors, Alabama, center
1984	Rick Badanjek, Maryland, fullback
	Carl Zander, Tennessee, linebacker
1985	Max Zendejas, Arizona, kicker
	Peter Anderson, Georgia, center
1986	Cornelius Bennett, Alabama, defensive end
	Steve Alvord, Washington, middle guard
1987	Thurman Thomas, Oklahoma St., running back
	Darnell Warren, West Va., linebacker
1988	David Smith, Alabama, quarterback
	Derrick Thomas, Alabama, linebacker
1989	Alex Van Pelt, Pittsburgh, quarterback
	Anthony Williams, Texas A&M, linebacker
1990	Courtney Hawkins, Michigan St., wide receiver
	Craig Hartsuyker, Southern Cal, linebacker
1991	Arnold Ale, UCLA, inside linebacker
	Jimmy Rogers Jr., Illinois, lineman
1992	Melvin Bonner, Baylor, flanker
1993	Jerald Moore, Oklahoma, running back
1994	Priest Holmes, Texas, running back
	Blake Brockermeyer, Texas, offensive lineman
	Marcus Wall, North Caro., wide receiver
1995	Sedrick Shaw, Iowa, running back
	Jared DeVries, Iowa, defensive tackle
	Brion Hurley, Iowa, kicker
1996	Troy Walters, Stanford, flanker
	Kailee Wong, Stanford, defensive end
	Chad Hutchinson, Stanford, quarterback
1997	Mike Martin, Arizona St., running back

SUNSHINE BOWL

(Named Blockbuster Bowl, 1990-92; Carquest Bowl, 1993-97))

Brian Piccolo Most Valuable Player Award

Year	Player, Team, Position
1990	Amp Lee, Florida St., running back
1991	David Palmer, Alabama, wide receiver
1992	Darrien Gordon, Stanford, cornerback
1993	Glenn Foley, Boston College, quarterback
1995	Steve Taneyhill, South Caro., quarterback
1995	Leon Johnson, North Caro., running back
1996	Tremain Mack, Miami (Fla.), strong safety
1997	Joe Hamilton, Georgia Tech, quarterback

Most Valuable Players in Former Major Bowls

ALL-AMERICAN BOWL

(Birmingham, Ala.; Known as Hall of Fame Classic, 1977-85)

Year	Player, Team, Position
1977	Chuck White, Maryland, split end
	Charles Johnson, Maryland, defensive tackle
1978	Curtis Dickey, Texas A&M, running back
1979	Phil Bradley, Missouri, quarterback
1980	Gary Anderson, Arkansas, running back
	Billy Ray Smith, Arkansas, linebacker
1981	John Bond, Mississippi St., quarterback
	Johnie Cooks, Mississippi St., linebacker
1982	Whit Taylor, Vanderbilt, quarterback
	Carl Dieudonne, Air Force, defensive end
1983	Jeff Hostetler, West Va., quarterback
1984	Mark Logan, Kentucky, running back
	Todd Gregoire, Wisconsin, placekicker
1985	Mark Ingram, Michigan St., wide receiver
1986	Sammie Smith, Florida St., running back
1987	Scott Secules, Virginia, quarterback
1988	Emmitt Smith, Florida, running back
1989	Jerry Gray, Texas Tech, running back
1990	Brett Favre, Southern Miss., quarterback

AVIATION BOWL

(Dayton, Ohio)

Year	Player, Team, Position
1961	Bobby Santiago, New Mexico, running back
	Chuck Cummings, New Mexico, guard

BLUEBONNET BOWL

(Houston, Texas)

Year	Player, Team
1959	Lowndes Shingles, Clemson
	Bob Lilly, Texas Christian
1960	James Saxton, Texas
	Lee Roy Jordan, Alabama
1961	Ken Coleman, Kansas
	Elvin Basham, Kansas
1962	Bill Tobin, Missouri
	Conrad Hitchler, Missouri
1963	Don Trull, Baylor
	James Ingram, Baylor
1964	Jerry Rhome, Tulsa
	Willy Townes, Tulsa
1965	Dewey Warren, Tennessee
	Frank Emanuel, Tennessee
1966	Chris Gilbert, Texas
	Fred Edwards, Texas
1967	Bob Anderson, Colorado
	Ted Hendricks, Miami (Fla.)
1968	Joe Pearce, Oklahoma
	Rufus Cormier, Southern Methodist
1969	Jim Strong, Houston
	Jerry Drones, Houston
1970	Greg Pruitt, Oklahoma
	Jeff Rouzie, Alabama
1971	Charlie Davis, Colorado
	Butch Brezina, Houston
1972	Condredge Holloway, Tennessee
	Carl Johnson, Tennessee
1973	D. C. Nobles, Houston
	Deryl McGallion, Houston
1974	John Housmann, Houston
	Mack Mitchell, Houston
1975	Earl Campbell, Texas
	Tim Campbell, Texas
1976	Chuck Malito, Nebraska
	Rodney Allison, Texas Tech
1977	Rob Hertel, Southern Cal
	Walt Underwood, Southern Cal
1978	Steve Dils, Stanford
	Gordy Ceresino, Stanford
1979	Mark Herrmann, Purdue
	Roland James, Tennessee
1980	Amos Lawrence, North Caro.
	Steve Streater, North Caro.
1981	Butch Woolfolk, Michigan
	Ben Needham, Michigan
1982	Gary Anderson, Arkansas
	Dwayne Dixon, Florida
1983	Rusty Hilger, Oklahoma St.
	Alfred Anderson, Baylor
1984	Willie Drewrey, West Va.
1985	Pat Evans, Air Force
	James McKinney, Texas
1986	Ray Berry, Baylor
	Mark Hatcher, Colorado
1987	Tony Jones, Texas
	Zeke Gadson, Pittsburgh

BLUEGRASS BOWL
(Louisville, Ky.)

Year	Player, Team
1958	Forrest Campbell, Oklahoma St.

CALIFORNIA RAISIN BOWL
(Beginning in 1992, Mid-American Conference and Big West Conference winners met in Las Vegas Bowl)

Year	Player, Team, Position
1981	Arnold Smiley, Toledo, running back
	Marlin Russell, Toledo, linebacker
1982	Chip Otten, Bowling Green, tailback
	Jac Tomasello, Bowling Green, defensive back
1983	Lou Wicks, Northern Ill., fullback
	James Pruitt, Cal St. Fullerton, wide receiver
1984	Randall Cunningham, UNLV, quarterback
	Steve Morgan, Toledo, tailback
1985	Mike Mancini, Fresno St., punter
	Greg Meehan, Bowling Green, flanker
1986	Mike Perez, San Jose St., quarterback
	Andrew Marlatt, Miami (Ohio), defensive tackle
1987	Gary Patton, Eastern Mich., tailback
	Mike Perez, San Jose St., quarterback
1988	Darrell Rosette, Fresno St., running back
	Tony Kimbrough, Western Mich., quarterback
1989	Ron Cox, Fresno St., linebacker
	Sean Jones, Ball St., wide receiver
1990	Sheldon Canley, San Jose St., tailback
	Ken Ealy, Central Mich., wide receiver
1991	Mark Szlachcic, Bowling Green, wide receiver
	Mark Barsotti, Fresno St., quarterback

CHERRY BOWL
(Pontiac, Mich.)

Year	Player, Team
1984	Nate Sassaman, Army
1985	Stan Gelbaugh, Maryland
	Scott Shankweiler, Maryland

DELTA BOWL
(Memphis, Tenn.)

Year	Player, Team
1948	Charlie Conerly, Mississippi

FREEDOM BOWL
(Anaheim, Calif.)

Year	Player, Team, Position
1984	Chuck Long, Iowa, quarterback
	William Harris, Texas, tight end
1985	Chris Chandler, Washington, quarterback
	Barry Helton, Colorado, punter
1986	Gaston Green, UCLA, tailback
	Shane Shumway, Brigham Young, defensive back
1987	Daniel Ford, Arizona St., quarterback
	Chad Hennings, Air Force, defensive tackle
1988	Ty Detmer, Brigham Young, quarterback
	Eric Bieniemy, Colorado, halfback
1989	Cary Conklin, Washington, quarterback
	Huey Richardson, Florida, linebacker
1990	Todd Yert, Colorado St., running back
	Bill Musgrave, Oregon, quarterback
1991	Marshall Faulk, San Diego St., running back
	Ron Jackson, Tulsa, running back
1992	Lorenzo Neal, Fresno St., fullback
	Estrus Crayton, Southern Cal, tailback
1993	Johnnie Morton, Southern Cal, wide receiver
	Henry Lusk, Utah, wide receiver
1994	Tedy Bruschi, Arizona, defensive end
	Cal Beck, Utah, kick returner

GARDEN STATE BOWL
(East Rutherford, N.J.)

Year	Player, Team
1978	John Mistler, Arizona St.
1979	Mark Bright, Temple
1980	Terald Clark, Houston
1981	Steve Alatorre, Tennessee
	Anthony Hancock, Tennessee
	Randy Wright, Wisconsin

GOTHAM BOWL
(New York, N.Y.)

Year	Player, Team
1961	Don Trull, Baylor
1962	Willie Ross, Nebraska
	George Mira, Miami (Fla.)

HARBOR BOWL
(San Diego, Calif.)

Year	Player, Team
1947	Bryan Brock, New Mexico
	Bill Nelson, Montana St.

MERCY BOWL
(Los Angeles, Calif.)

Year	Player, Team
1961	Beau Carter, Fresno St.

PASADENA BOWL
(Pasadena, Calif.; called Junior Rose Bowl in 1967)

Year	Player, Team
1967	Eugene "Mercury" Morris, West Tex. A&M
	Albie Owens, West Tex. A&M
1969	John Featherstone, San Diego St.
1970	Leon Burns, Long Beach St.
	Paul Mattingly, Louisville
1971	Tom Carlsen, Memphis
	Dornell Harris, Memphis

PRESIDENTIAL CUP
(College Park, Md.)

Year	Player, Team
1950	Bob Smith, Texas A&M
	Zippy Morocco, Georgia

SALAD BOWL
(Phoenix, Ariz.)

Year	Player, Team
1950	Bob McQuade, Xavier (Ohio)
	Wilford White, Arizona St.
1951	Jim Bailey, Miami (Ohio)
1952	Gene Shannon, Houston

Heisman Trophy Winners in Bowl Games

YEAR-BY-YEAR BOWL RESULTS FOR HEISMAN WINNERS

(Includes bowl games immediately after award of Heisman Trophy)

Of the 62 winners of the 63 Heisman Trophies (Archie Griffin won twice), 38 played in bowl games after they received their prize. Of those 38 players, only 18 were on the winning team in the bowl.

Houston's Andre Ware is the only Heisman recipient to miss a bowl date since 1969. The Cougars were on probation during the 1989 season and were ineligible for selection to a bowl. Before that lapse, Oklahoma's Steve Owens in 1969 was the last Heisman awardee not to participate in a bowl game.

Only three of the first 22 Heisman Trophy winners played in bowl games after receiving the award—Texas Christian's Davey O'Brien in 1938, Georgia's Frank Sinkwich in 1942 and Southern Methodist's Doak Walker in 1948.

Year	Heisman Winner, Team, Position	Bowl (Opponent, Result)
1935	Jay Berwanger, Chicago, HB	Did not play in bowl
1936	Larry Kelley, Yale, E	Did not play in bowl
1937	Clint Frank, Yale, HB	Did not play in bowl
1938	Davey O'Brien, Texas Christian, QB	Sugar (Carnegie Mellon, W 15-7)
1939	Nile Kinnick, Iowa, HB	Did not play in bowl
1940	Tom Harmon, Michigan, HB	Did not play in bowl
1941	Bruce Smith, Minnesota, HB	Did not play in bowl
1942	Frank Sinkwich, Georgia, HB	Rose (UCLA, W 9-0)
1943	Angelo Bertelli, Notre Dame, QB	Did not play in bowl
1944	Les Horvath, Ohio St., QB	Did not play in bowl
1945	Doc Blanchard, Army, FB	Did not play in bowl
1946	Glenn Davis, Army, HB	Did not play in bowl
1947	Johnny Lujack, Notre Dame, QB	Did not play in bowl
1948	Doak Walker, Southern Methodist, HB	Cotton (Oregon, W 21-13)
1949	Leon Hart, Notre Dame, E	Did not play in bowl
1950	Vic Janowicz, Ohio St., HB	Did not play in bowl
1951	Dick Kazmeier, Princeton, HB	Did not play in bowl
1952	Billy Vessels, Oklahoma, HB	Did not play in bowl
1953	John Lattner, Notre Dame, HB	Did not play in bowl
1954	Alan Ameche, Wisconsin, FB	Did not play in bowl
1955	Howard Cassady, Ohio St., HB	Did not play in bowl
1956	Paul Hornung, Notre Dame, QB	Did not play in bowl
1957	John David Crow, Texas A&M, HB	Gator (Tennessee, L 3-0)
1958	Pete Dawkins, Army, HB	Did not play in bowl
1959	Billy Cannon, LSU, HB	Sugar (Mississippi, L 21-0)
1960	Joe Bellino, Navy, HB	Orange (Missouri, L 21-14)
1961	Ernie Davis, Syracuse, HB	Liberty (Miami, Fla., W 15-14)
1962	Terry Baker, Oregon St., QB	Liberty (Villanova, W 6-0)
1963	Roger Staubach, Navy, QB	Cotton (Texas, L 28-6)
1964	John Huarte, Notre Dame, QB	Did not play in bowl
1965	Mike Garrett, Southern Cal, HB	Did not play in bowl
1966	Steve Spurrier, Florida, QB	Orange (Georgia Tech, W 27-12)
1967	Gary Beban, UCLA, QB	Did not play in bowl
1968	O. J. Simpson, Southern Cal, HB	Rose (Ohio St., L 27-16)
1969	Steve Owens, Oklahoma, HB	Did not play in bowl
1970	Jim Plunkett, Stanford, QB	Rose (Ohio St., W 27-17)
1971	Pat Sullivan, Auburn, QB	Sugar (Oklahoma, L 40-22)
1972	Johnny Rodgers, Nebraska, FL	Orange (Notre Dame, W 40-6)
1973	John Cappelletti, Penn St., HB	Orange (LSU, W 16-9)
1974	Archie Griffin, Ohio St., HB	Rose (Southern Cal, L 18-17)
1975	Archie Griffin, Ohio St., HB	Rose (UCLA, L 23-10)
1976	Tony Dorsett, Pittsburgh, HB	Sugar (Georgia, W 27-3)
1977	Earl Campbell, Texas, HB	Cotton (Notre Dame, L 38-10)
1978	Billy Sims, Oklahoma, HB	Orange (Nebraska, W 31-24)
1979	Charles White, Southern Cal, HB	Rose (Ohio St., W 17-16)
1980	George Rogers, South Caro., HB	Gator (Pittsburgh, L 37-9)
1981	Marcus Allen, Southern Cal, HB	Fiesta (Penn St., L 26-10)
1982	Herschel Walker, Georgia, HB	Sugar (Penn St., L 27-23)
1983	Mike Rozier, Nebraska, HB	Orange (Miami, Fla., L 31-30)
1984	Doug Flutie, Boston College, QB	Cotton (Houston, W 45-28)
1985	Bo Jackson, Auburn, HB	Cotton (Texas A&M, L 36-16)
1986	Vinny Testaverde, Miami (Fla.), QB	Fiesta (Penn St., L 14-10)
1987	Tim Brown, Notre Dame, WR	Cotton (Texas A&M, L 35-10)
1988	Barry Sanders, Oklahoma St., RB	Holiday (Wyoming, W 62-14)
1989	Andre Ware, Houston, QB	Did not play in bowl
1990	Ty Detmer, Brigham Young, QB	Holiday (Texas A&M, L 65-14)
1991	Desmond Howard, Michigan, WR	Rose (Washington, L 34-14)
1992	Gino Torretta, Miami (Fla.), QB	Sugar (Alabama, L 34-13)

Year	Heisman Winner, Team, Position	Bowl (Opponent, Result)
1993	Charlie Ward, Florida St., QB	Orange (Nebraska, W 18-16)
1994	Rashaan Salaam, Colorado, RB	Fiesta (Notre Dame, W 41-24)
1995	Eddie George, Ohio St., RB	Fla. Citrus (Tennessee, L 20-14)
1996	Danny Wuerffel, Florida, QB	Sugar (Florida St., W 52-20)
1997	Charles Woodson, Michigan, CB	Rose (Washington St., 21-16)

TOP BOWLS FOR HEISMAN WINNERS

Bowl	Heisman Winner Year	Heisman Winners
Rose	1942, 1968, 1970, 1974, 1975, 1979, 1991, 1998	8
Orange	1960, 1966, 1972, 1973, 1978, 1983, 1993	7
Sugar	1938, 1959, 1971, 1976, 1982, 1992, 1997	7
Cotton	1948, 1963, 1977, 1984, 1985, 1987	6
Fiesta	1981, 1986, 1995	3
Gator	1957, 1980	2
Holiday	1988, 1990	2
Liberty	1961, 1962	2

HEISMAN TROPHY WINNERS WHO WERE BOWL-GAME MVPs

Heisman Winner, Team (Year Won)	Bowl, Year Played
Doak Walker, Southern Methodist (1948)	Cotton, 1948
Doak Walker, Southern Methodist (1948)	Cotton, 1949
John David Crow, Texas A&M (1957)	Gator, 1957
Billy Cannon, LSU (1959)	Sugar, 1959
Ernie Davis, Syracuse (1961)	Cotton, 1960
Ernie Davis, Syracuse (1961)	Liberty, 1961
Terry Baker, Oregon St. (1962)	Liberty, 1962
Steve Spurrier, Florida (1966)	Sugar, 1966
O. J. Simpson, Southern Cal (1968)	Rose, 1968
Jim Plunkett, Stanford (1970)	Rose, 1971
Pat Sullivan, Auburn (1971)	Gator, 1971
Johnny Rodgers, Nebraska (1972)	Orange, 1973
Earl Campbell, Texas (1977)	Gator, 1974
Earl Campbell, Texas (1977)	Bluebonnet, 1975*
Billy Sims, Oklahoma (1978)	Orange, 1979
Charles White, Southern Cal (1979)	Rose, 1979
Charles White, Southern Cal (1979)	Rose, 1980
George Rogers, South Caro. (1980)	Gator, 1980
Herschel Walker, Georgia (1982)	Sugar, 1981
Doug Flutie, Boston College (1984)	Liberty, 1983
Bo Jackson, Auburn (1985)	Sugar, 1984
Bo Jackson, Auburn (1985)	Liberty, 1984
Bo Jackson, Auburn (1985)	Cotton, 1986
Barry Sanders, Oklahoma St. (1988)	Holiday, 1988
Ty Detmer, Brigham Young (1990)	Freedom, 1988*
Ty Detmer, Brigham Young (1990)	Holiday, 1989
Ty Detmer, Brigham Young (1990)	Holiday, 1991
Charlie Ward, Florida St. (1993)	Orange, 1994
Danny Wuerffel, Florida (1996)	Sugar, 1997

**Discontinued bowl.*

Bowls and Polls

Associated Press No. 1 Teams Defeated in Bowl Games

Date	Bowl	Teams Involved	Score	New No. 1
1-1-51	Sugar	No. 7 Kentucky beat No. 1 Oklahoma	13-7	Same
1-1-52	Sugar	No. 3 Maryland beat No. 1 Tennessee	28-13	Same
1-1-54	Orange	No. 4 Oklahoma beat No. 1 Maryland	7-0	Same
1-1-61	Rose	No. 6 Washington beat No. 1 Minnesota	17-7	Same
1-1-65	Orange	No. 5 Texas beat No. 1 Alabama	21-17	Same
1-1-71	Cotton	No. 6 Notre Dame beat No. 1 Texas	24-11	Nebraska
12-31-73	Sugar	No. 3 Notre Dame beat No. 1 Alabama	24-23	Notre Dame
1-1-76	Rose	No. 11 UCLA beat No. 1 Ohio St.	23-10	Oklahoma
1-2-78	Cotton	No. 5 Notre Dame beat No. 1 Texas	38-10	Notre Dame
1-1-79	Sugar	No. 2 Alabama beat No. 1 Penn St.	14-7	Alabama
1-1-83	Sugar	No. 2 Penn St. beat No. 1 Georgia	27-23	Penn St.
1-2-84	Orange	No. 5 Miami (Fla.) beat No. 1 Nebraska	31-30	Miami (Fla.)
1-1-86	Orange	No. 3 Oklahoma beat No. 1 Penn St.	25-10	Oklahoma
1-2-87	Fiesta	No. 2 Penn St. beat No. 1 Miami (Fla.)	14-10	Penn St.
1-1-88	Orange	No. 2 Miami (Fla.) beat No. 1 Oklahoma	20-14	Miami (Fla.)
1-1-90	Orange	No. 4 Notre Dame beat No. 1 Colorado	21-6	Miami (Fla.)
1-1-93	Sugar	No. 2 Alabama beat No. 1 Miami (Fla.)	34-13	Alabama
1-2-97	Sugar	No. 3 Florida beat No. 1 Florida St.	52-20	Florida

Associated Press No. 1 Vs. No. 2 in Bowl Games

Date	Bowl	Teams, Score
1-1-63	Rose	No. 1 Southern Cal 42, No. 2 Wisconsin 37
1-1-64	Cotton	No. 1 Texas 28, No. 2 Navy 6
1-1-69	Rose	No. 1 Ohio St. 27, No. 2 Southern Cal 16
1-1-72	Orange	No. 1 Nebraska 38, No. 2 Alabama 6
1-1-79	Sugar	No. 2 Alabama 14, No. 1 Penn St. 7
1-1-83	Sugar	No. 2 Penn St. 27, No. 1 Georgia 23
1-2-87	Fiesta	No. 2 Penn St. 14, No. 1 Miami (Fla.) 10
1-1-88	Orange	No. 2 Miami (Fla.) 20, No. 1 Oklahoma 14
1-1-93	Sugar*	No. 2 Alabama 34, No. 1 Miami (Fla.) 13
1-1-94	Orange*	No. 1 Florida St. 18, No. 2 Nebraska 16
1-2-96	Fiesta*	No. 1 Nebraska 62, No. 2 Florida 24

**Bowl alliance matched the No. 1 and No. 2 teams.*

Bowl Games and the National Championship

(How the bowl games determined the national champion from 1965 to present. Year listed is the football season before the bowl games.)

Note: The national champion was selected before the bowl games as follows: Associated Press (1936-64 and 1966-67); United Press International (1950-73); Football Writers Association of America (1954), and National Football Foundation and Hall of Fame (1959-70).

1965 The Associated Press (AP) selected Alabama as national champion after it defeated Nebraska, 39-28, in the Orange Bowl on January 1, 1966.

1968 AP selected Ohio State as national champion after it defeated Southern California, 27-16, in the Rose Bowl on January 1, 1969.

1969 AP selected Texas as national champion after it defeated Notre Dame, 21-17, in the Cotton Bowl on January 1, 1970.

1970 AP selected Nebraska as national champion after it defeated LSU, 17-12, in the Orange Bowl on January 1, 1971.

1971 AP selected Nebraska as national champion after it defeated Alabama, 38-6, in the Orange Bowl on January 1, 1972.

1972 AP selected Southern California as national champion after it defeated Ohio State, 42-17, in the Rose Bowl on January 1, 1973.

1973 AP selected Notre Dame as national champion after it defeated Alabama, 24-23, in the Sugar Bowl on December 31, 1973.

Beginning in 1974, all four of the national polls waited until after the bowl-game results before selecting a national champion. The following list shows how the bowl games figured in the final national championship polls for AP and UPI:

1974 First year of the agreement between the American Football Coaches Association (AFCA) and the UPI Board of Coaches to declare any teams on NCAA probation ineligible for the poll. AP—Oklahoma (11-0-0) did not participate in a bowl game because of NCAA probation. UPI—Southern California (10-1-1) defeated Ohio State, 18-17, in the Rose Bowl on January 1, 1975.

1975 AP and UPI both selected Oklahoma (11-1-0). Coach Barry Switzer's Sooners defeated Michigan, 14-6, in the Orange Bowl on January 1, 1976. Ohio State had led the AP poll for nine consecutive weeks until a 23-10 loss to UCLA in the Rose Bowl on January 1, 1976. Oklahoma had led the AP poll for the first four weeks of the year.

1976 AP and UPI both selected Tony Dorsett-led Pittsburgh (12-0-0). Pittsburgh whipped Georgia, 27-3, in the Sugar Bowl on January 1, 1977. Pittsburgh took over the No. 1 position from Michigan in the ninth week of the season en route to an undefeated year.

1977 AP and UPI were in agreement again, picking Notre Dame as national titlist. The Irish crushed previously undefeated and top-ranked Texas, 38-10, in the Cotton Bowl on January 2, 1978. Notre Dame was the sixth team to be ranked No. 1 during the 1977 season in the AP poll.

1978 This was the last time until the 1991 season that the two polls split on a national champion, with AP selecting Alabama (11-1-0) and UPI going for Southern California (12-1-0). Alabama, ranked No. 2 in the AP poll, upset No. 1 Penn State, 14-7, in the Sugar Bowl on January 1, 1979. Alabama had been ranked No. 1 in the first two weeks of the season until a 24-14 loss to Southern California.

1979 Unbeaten Alabama (12-0-0) was the unanimous choice of both polls. Bear Bryant's Tide whipped Arkansas easily, 24-9, in the Sugar Bowl on January 1, 1980, to claim the title.

1980 Georgia made it three No. 1's in a row for the Southeastern Conference with an undefeated season (12-0-0) to take the top spot in both polls. Vince Dooley's Bulldogs downed Notre Dame, 17-10, behind freshman phenom Herschel Walker in the Sugar Bowl on January 1, 1981.

1981 Both polls selected unbeaten Clemson (12-0-0). The Tigers gave coach Danny Ford the first Clemson national football championship with a 22-15 victory over Nebraska in the Orange Bowl on January 1, 1982. Clemson did not take over the AP No. 1 slot until the next-to-last poll of the year.

1982 AP and UPI both selected Penn State (11-1-0). The Nittany Lions were No. 2 in the AP poll but knocked off No. 1 Georgia, 27-23, in the Sugar Bowl on January 1, 1983. Georgia had led the AP poll for the final five weeks of the season.

1983 AP and UPI had no choice but to select Miami (Florida) as the unanimous champion after the No. 2 Hurricanes downed No. 1 Nebraska, 31-30, in the Orange Bowl on January 2, 1984. Many observers felt this may have been the most exciting Orange Bowl ever played as the Cornhuskers failed on a two-point conversion attempt with 48 seconds remaining. Nebraska had led the AP poll since the first week of the season.

1984 Unknown and a victim of the Mountain time zone, Brigham Young (13-0-0) overcame many obstacles to ascend to No. 1 in both polls. Coach LaVell Edwards' Cougars downed Michigan, 24-17, in the Holiday Bowl on December 21, 1984. BYU took over the top spot in the AP poll with three weeks left in the season after four other teams came and went as the top-rated team.

1985 Oklahoma (11-1-0) returned as the unanimous choice of both polls. Barry Switzer's Sooners knocked off top-rated Penn State, 25-10, in the Orange Bowl on January 1, 1986, to claim the national title.

1986 Penn State (12-0-0) had to battle top-rated Miami (Florida) in the Fiesta Bowl to take the top slot in both polls. Joe Paterno's No. 2 Nittany Lions upset the Hurricanes, 14-10, on January 2, 1987, to claim the championship. Miami (Florida) had been ranked No. 1 for the final 10 weeks of the season.

1987 Miami (Florida) (12-0-0) bounced back to a similar scenario as Jimmy Johnson's Hurricanes played underdog and finished ranked first in both polls. The No. 2 Hurricanes beat No. 1-ranked Oklahoma, 20-14, in the Orange Bowl on January 1, 1988. The Sooners had been the top-rated AP team for 13 of the season's 15 polls.

1988 Notre Dame (12-0-0) finished as the top team in both polls and gave the Fiesta Bowl its second national title game in three seasons. Lou Holtz's Irish whipped West Virginia, 34-21, on January 2, 1989, to claim their eighth AP title. Notre Dame took over the top spot in the poll from UCLA in the ninth week of the season.

1989 Miami (Florida) (11-1-0) claimed its second national title in three years in both polls. The Hurricanes downed Alabama, 33-25, in the Sugar Bowl on January 1, 1990, while No. 1-ranked Colorado lost to Notre Dame, 21-6, in the Orange Bowl to clear the way. Notre Dame led the AP poll for 12 of the 15 weeks.

1990 Colorado (11-1-0) and Georgia Tech (11-0-1) split the polls for the first time since 1978 with the Buffs taking the AP vote and the Jackets the UPI. Colorado bounced back from a disappointing 1989 title march to edge Notre Dame, 10-9, in the Orange Bowl on January 1, 1991. Georgia Tech had little trouble with Nebraska, 45-21, in the Florida Citrus Bowl on January 1, 1991, to finish as Division I-A's only undefeated team.

1991 Miami (Florida) (12-0-0) and Washington (12-0-0) kept Division I-A playoff talk alive with a split in the national polls for the second consecutive year. The Hurricanes took the AP vote, while the Huskies took both the USA Today/CNN and UPI polls. If either had stumbled in a bowl, then the other would have been a unanimous selection. However, Washington drubbed Michigan, 34-14, in the Rose Bowl, and Miami (Florida) had little trouble shutting out Nebraska, 22-0, in the Orange Bowl later that evening.

1992 No. 2 Alabama (13-0-0) turned in a magnificent performance in the Sugar Bowl by upsetting No. 1 Miami (Florida), 34-13, in a game dominated by the Crimson Tide. It marked the first year of the bowl coalition, and the bowlmeisters managed to match the top two teams for the national championship. It also marked the 17th time that a No. 1 team in the AP poll was knocked off in a bowl game since 1951. Alabama was named No. 1 in all polls after the January 1, 1993, matchup.

1993 No. 1 Florida State downed No. 2 Nebraska, 18-16, in the Orange Bowl to become a unanimous national champion. Notre Dame, winner over Texas A&M (24-21) in the Cotton Bowl, wanted to claim the title after beating the Seminoles in the regular season. But a late-season loss to Boston College cost the Irish in the polls. Florida State was No. 1 in all polls after the bowls.

1994 No. 1 Nebraska halted a seven-game bowl losing streak by posting a come-from-behind victory, 24-17, over Miami (Florida) in the Orange Bowl to cap a perfect 13-0 season with the national title. No. 2 Penn State, also undefeated at 12-0, downed Oregon, 38-20, in the Rose Bowl but had to settle for second place in the polls. Nebraska was No. 1 in all polls after the bowls.

1995 Another unanimous year for undefeated and No. 1 Nebraska. The Cornhuskers posted back-to-back national titles with a convincing 62-24 victory over No. 2 Florida in the bowl alliance's Fiesta Bowl matchup.

1996 No. 3 Florida took the national crown in all polls after meeting and beating No. 1 Florida State, 52-20, in the bowl alliance matchup in the Sugar Bowl. Just a month earlier, the Seminoles had knocked off No. 1 Florida and the Gators returned the favor. No. 2 Arizona State was defeated, 20-17, by Ohio State in the non-alliance Rose Bowl and dropped out of national championship consideration.

1997 In the last year before the bowl alliance would include the Rose Bowl, the two top-ranked teams—Michigan and Nebraska—never met for the title. Michigan, the final No. 1 in the Associated Press media poll defeated Washington State, 21-16, in the Rose Bowl while Nebraska, No. 1 in the final USA Today/ESPN coaches' poll, rolled over Tennessee, 42-17, in the Orange Bowl. Both teams were rewarded with a piece of the national title. It was the fourth time in the 1990s that the national champion was either shared or unclear.

Bowl Results of Teams Ranked in The Associated Press Poll

The bowls and national polls have been perpetually linked since 1936, when The Associated Press introduced its weekly college football poll. The final AP poll was released at the end of the regular season until 1965, when bowl results were included for one year, dropped for two more and then added again in 1968 until the present. This is a list of the key bowl games as they related to the AP poll since 1936 (with pertinent references made to other polls where applicable).

(Key to polls: AP, Associated Press; UPI, United Press International; FW, Football Writers; NFF, National Football Foundation and Hall of Fame; USA/CNN, USA Today/Cable News Network; USA/NFF, USA Today/National Football Foundation and Hall of Fame; UPI/NFF, United Press International/National Football Foundation and Hall of Fame.)

1936 SUGAR—No. 6 Santa Clara beat No. 2 LSU, 21-14; ROSE—No. 3 Pittsburgh beat No. 5 Washington, 21-0; ORANGE—No. 14 Duquesne beat unranked Mississippi St., 13-12; COTTON—No. 16 Texas Christian beat No. 20 Marquette, 16-6. (Minnesota selected No. 1 but did not play in a bowl)

1937 ROSE—No. 2 California beat No. 4 Alabama, 13-0; SUGAR—No. 9 Santa Clara beat No. 8 LSU, 6-0; COTTON—No. 18 Rice beat No. 17 Colorado, 28-14. (Pittsburgh selected No. 1 but did not play in a bowl)

1938 SUGAR—No. 1 Texas Christian beat No. 6 Carnegie Mellon, 15-7; ORANGE—No. 2 Tennessee beat No. 4 Oklahoma, 17-0; ROSE—No. 7 Southern Cal beat No. 3 Duke, 7-3; COTTON—Unranked St. Mary's (Cal.) beat No. 11 Texas Tech, 20-13. (Texas Christian selected No. 1)

1939 SUGAR—No. 1 Texas A&M beat No. 5 Tulane, 14-13; ROSE—No. 3 Southern Cal beat No. 2 Tennessee, 14-0; ORANGE—No. 16 Georgia Tech beat No. 6 Missouri, 21-7; COTTON—No. 12 Clemson beat No. 11 Boston College, 6-3. (Texas A&M selected No. 1)

1940 ROSE—No. 2 Stanford beat No. 7 Nebraska, 21-13; SUGAR—No. 5 Boston College beat No. 4 Tennessee, 19-13; COTTON—No. 6 Texas A&M beat No. 12 Fordham, 13-12; ORANGE—No. 9 Mississippi St. beat No. 13 Georgetown, 14-7. (Minnesota selected No. 1 but did not play in a bowl)

1941 ROSE—No. 12 Oregon St. beat No. 2 Duke, 20-16 (played at Durham, N.C., because of World War II); SUGAR—No. 6 Fordham beat No. 7 Missouri, 2-0; COTTON—No. 20 Alabama beat No. 9 Texas A&M, 29-21; ORANGE—No. 14 Georgia beat unranked Texas Christian, 40-26. (Minnesota selected No. 1 but did not play in a bowl)

1942 ROSE—No. 2 Georgia beat No. 13 UCLA, 9-0; SUGAR—No. 7 Tennessee beat No. 4 Tulsa, 14-7; COTTON—No. 11 Texas beat No. 5 Georgia Tech, 14-7; ORANGE—No. 10 Alabama beat No. 8 Boston College, 37-21. (Ohio St. selected No. 1 but did not play in a bowl)

1943 ROSE—Unranked Southern Cal beat No. 12 Washington, 29-0; COTTON—No. 14 Texas tied unranked Randolph Field, 7-7; SUGAR—No. 13 Georgia Tech beat No. 15 Tulsa, 20-18. (Notre Dame selected No. 1 but did not play in a bowl)

1944 ROSE—No. 7 Southern Cal beat No. 12 Tennessee, 25-0; ORANGE—Unranked Tulsa beat No. 13 Georgia Tech, 26-12; No. 3 Randolph Field beat No. 20 Second Air Force, 13-6, in a battle of military powers. (Army selected No. 1 but did not play in a bowl)

1945 ROSE—No. 2 Alabama beat No. 11 Southern Cal, 34-14; COTTON—No. 10 Texas beat unranked Missouri, 40-27; ORANGE—Unranked Miami (Fla.) beat No. 16 Holy Cross, 13-6; SUGAR—No. 5 Oklahoma St. beat No. 7 St. Mary's (Cal.), 33-13. (Army selected No. 1 but did not play in a bowl)

1946 COTTON—No. 8 LSU tied No. 16 Arkansas, 0-0; ROSE—No. 5 Illinois beat No. 4 UCLA, 45-14; SUGAR—No. 3 Georgia beat No. 9 North Caro., 20-10; ORANGE—No. 10 Rice beat No. 7 Tennessee, 8-0. (Notre Dame selected No. 1 but did not play in a bowl)

1947 ORANGE—No. 10 Georgia Tech beat No. 12 Kansas, 20-14; ROSE—No. 2 Michigan beat No. 8 Southern Cal, 49-0; SUGAR—No. 5 Texas beat No. 6 Alabama, 27-7; COTTON—No. 3 Southern Methodist tied No. 4 Penn St., 13-13. (Notre Dame selected No. 1 but did not play in a bowl; Michigan also declared champion in vote after Rose Bowl victory but AP kept Notre Dame as vote of record)

1948 ROSE—No. 7 Northwestern beat No. 4 California, 20-14; COTTON—No. 10 Southern Methodist beat No. 9 Oregon, 21-13; SUGAR—No. 5 Oklahoma beat No. 3 North Caro., 14-6; ORANGE—Unranked Texas beat No. 8 Georgia, 41-28. (Michigan selected No. 1 but did not play in a bowl)

1949 ORANGE—No. 15 Santa Clara beat No. 11 Kentucky, 21-13; COTTON—No. 5 Rice beat No. 16 North Caro., 27-13; ROSE—No. 6 Ohio St. beat No. 3 California, 17-14; SUGAR—No. 2 Oklahoma beat No. 9 LSU, 35-0. (Notre Dame selected No. 1 but did not play in a bowl)

1950 ROSE—No. 9 Michigan beat No. 5 California, 14-6; SUGAR—No. 7 Kentucky beat No. 1 Oklahoma, 13-7; ORANGE—No. 10 Clemson beat No. 15 Miami (Fla.), 15-14; COTTON—No. 4 Tennessee beat No. 3 Texas, 20-14. (Oklahoma selected No. 1 in vote before losing in Sugar Bowl)

1951 COTTON—No. 15 Kentucky beat No. 11 Texas Christian, 20-7; ORANGE—No. 5 Georgia Tech beat No. 9 Baylor, 17-14; ROSE—No. 4 Illinois beat No. 7 Stanford, 40-7; SUGAR—No. 3 Maryland beat No. 1 Tennessee, 28-13. (Tennessee selected No. 1 in vote before losing in Sugar Bowl)

1952 ROSE—No. 5 Southern Cal beat No. 11 Wisconsin, 7-0; SUGAR—No. 2 Georgia Tech beat No. 7 Mississippi, 24-7; ORANGE—No. 9 Alabama beat No. 14 Syracuse, 61-6; COTTON—No. 10 Texas beat No. 8 Tennessee, 16-0. (Michigan St. selected No. 1 but did not play in a bowl)

1953 SUGAR—No. 8 Georgia Tech beat No. 10 West Va., 42-19; ORANGE—No. 4 Oklahoma beat No. 1 Maryland, 7-0; COTTON—No. 5 Rice beat No. 13 Alabama, 28-6; ROSE—No. 3 Michigan St. beat No. 5 UCLA, 28-20. (Maryland selected No. 1 before losing in Orange Bowl)

1954 ROSE—No. 1 Ohio St. beat No. 17 Southern Cal, 20-7; ORANGE—No. 14 Duke beat unranked Nebraska, 34-7; SUGAR—No. 5 Navy beat No. 6 Mississippi, 21-0; COTTON—Unranked Georgia Tech beat No. 10 Arkansas, 14-6. (Ohio St. remained No. 1 but UCLA named in UPI and FW polls)

1955 GATOR—Unranked Vanderbilt beat No. 8 Auburn, 25-13; ROSE—No. 2 Michigan St. beat No. 4 UCLA, 17-14; ORANGE—No. 1 Oklahoma beat No. 3 Maryland, 20-6; COTTON—No. 10 Mississippi beat No. 6 Texas Christian, 14-13; SUGAR—No. 7 Georgia Tech beat No. 11 Pittsburgh, 7-0. (Oklahoma remained No. 1)

1956 SUGAR—No. 11 Baylor beat No. 2 Tennessee, 13-7; ORANGE—No. 20 Colorado beat No. 19 Clemson, 27-21; GATOR—No. 4 Georgia Tech beat No. 13 Pittsburgh, 21-14; ROSE—No. 3 Iowa beat No. 10 Oregon St., 35-19; COTTON—No. 14 Texas Christian beat No. 8 Syracuse, 28-27. (Oklahoma selected No. 1 but did not play in a bowl)

1957 GATOR—No. 13 Tennessee beat No. 9 Texas A&M, 3-0; ROSE—No. 2 Ohio St. beat unranked Oregon, 10-7; COTTON—No. 5 Navy beat No. 8 Rice, 20-7; ORANGE—No. 4 Oklahoma beat No. 16 Duke, 48-21; SUGAR—No. 7 Mississippi beat No. 11 Texas, 39-7. (Auburn selected No. 1 but did not play in a bowl; Ohio St. selected No. 1 in both UPI and FW polls)

1958 SUGAR—No. 1 LSU beat No. 12 Clemson, 7-0; COTTON—No. 6 Air Force tied No. 10 Texas Christian, 0-0; ROSE—No. 2 Iowa beat No. 16 California, 38-12; ORANGE—No. 5 Oklahoma beat No. 9 Syracuse, 21-6. (LSU remained No. 1 in AP and UPI but Iowa selected in FW poll)

1959 COTTON—No. 1 Syracuse beat No. 4 Texas, 23-14; ROSE—No. 8 Washington beat No. 6 Wisconsin, 44-8; ORANGE—No. 5 Georgia beat No. 18 Missouri, 14-0; SUGAR—No. 2 Mississippi beat No. 3 LSU, 21-0; BLUEBONNET—No. 11 Clemson beat No. 7 Texas Christian, 23-7; LIBERTY—No. 12 Penn St. beat No. 10 Alabama, 7-0; GATOR—No. 9 Arkansas beat unranked Georgia Tech, 14-7. (Syracuse selected No. 1 by all four polls)

1960 ROSE—No. 6 Washington beat No. 1 Minnesota, 17-7; COTTON—No. 10 Duke beat No. 7 Arkansas, 7-6; SUGAR—No. 2 Mississippi beat unranked Rice, 14-6; ORANGE—No. 5 Missouri beat No. 4 Navy, 21-14; BLUEBONNET—No. 9 Alabama tied unranked Texas, 3-3. (Minnesota selected No. 1 by AP, UPI and NFF before losing in Rose Bowl; Mississippi named No. 1 in FW poll)

1961 COTTON—No. 3 Texas beat No. 5 Mississippi, 12-7; SUGAR—No. 1 Alabama beat No. 9 Arkansas, 10-3; ORANGE—No. 4 LSU beat No. 7 Colorado, 25-7; GOTHAM—Unranked Baylor beat No. 10 Utah St., 24-9; ROSE—No. 6 Minnesota beat No. 16 UCLA, 21-3. (Alabama selected No. 1 in AP, UPI and NFF, but Ohio St. picked by FW poll)

1962 ROSE—No. 1 Southern Cal beat No. 2 Wisconsin, 42-37; SUGAR—No. 3 Mississippi beat No. 6 Arkansas, 17-13; COTTON—No. 7 LSU beat No. 4 Texas, 13-0; GATOR—Unranked Florida beat No. 9 Penn St., 17-7; ORANGE—No. 5 Alabama beat No. 8 Oklahoma, 17-0. (Southern Cal selected No. 1 by all four polls)

1963 COTTON—No. 1 Texas beat No. 2 Navy, 28-6; ORANGE—No. 6 Nebraska beat No. 5 Auburn, 13-7; ROSE—No. 3 Illinois beat unranked Washington, 17-7; SUGAR—No. 8 Alabama beat No. 7 Mississippi, 12-7. (Texas selected No. 1 by all four polls)

1964 ORANGE—No. 5 Texas beat No. 1 Alabama, 21-17; ROSE—No. 4 Michigan beat No. 8 Oregon St., 34-7; COTTON—No. 2 Arkansas beat No. 6 Nebraska, 10-7; SUGAR—No. 7 LSU beat unranked Syracuse, 13-10. (Alabama selected No. 1 by AP and UPI before losing in the Orange Bowl, while Arkansas No. 1 in FW poll and Notre Dame No. 1 in NFF poll)

1965 ***(First year final poll taken after bowl games)*** ROSE—No. 5 UCLA beat No. 1 Michigan St., 14-12; COTTON—Unranked LSU beat No. 2 Arkansas, 14-7; SUGAR—No. 6 Missouri beat unranked Florida, 20-18; ORANGE—No. 4 Alabama beat No. 3 Nebraska, 39-28; BLUEBONNET—No. 7 Tennessee beat unranked Tulsa, 27-6; GATOR—Unranked Georgia Tech beat No. 10 Texas Tech, 31-21. (Alabama selected No. 1 in final poll but Michigan St. named by UPI and NFF polls and they tied in FW poll)

1966 ***(Returned to final poll taken before bowls)*** SUGAR—No. 3 Alabama beat No. 6 Nebraska, 34-7; ROSE—No. 7 Purdue beat unranked Southern Cal, 14-13; COTTON—No. 4 Georgia beat No. 10 Southern Methodist, 24-9; ORANGE—Unranked Florida beat No. 8 Georgia Tech, 27-12; LIBERTY—No. 9 Miami (Fla.) beat unranked Virginia Tech, 14-7. (Notre Dame selected No. 1 by AP, UPI and FW polls and tied with Michigan St. in NFF poll; neither team played in a bowl game and they tied in a regular-season game)

1967 ROSE—No. 1 Southern Cal beat No. 4 Indiana, 14-3; SUGAR—Unranked LSU beat No. 6 Wyoming, 20-13; ORANGE—No. 3 Oklahoma beat No. 2 Tennessee, 26-24; COTTON—Unranked Texas A&M beat No. 8 Alabama, 20-16; GATOR—No. 10 Penn St. tied unranked Florida St., 17-17. (Southern Cal selected No. 1 in all four polls)

1968 ***(Returned to final poll taken after bowl games)*** ROSE—No. 1 Ohio St. beat No. 2 Southern Cal, 27-16; SUGAR—No. 9 Arkansas beat No. 4 Georgia, 16-2; ORANGE—No. 3 Penn St. beat No. 6 Kansas, 15-14; COTTON—No. 5 Texas beat No. 8 Tennessee, 36-13; BLUEBONNET—No. 20 Southern Methodist beat No. 10 Oklahoma, 28-27; GATOR—No. 16 Missouri beat No. 12 Alabama, 35-10. (Ohio St. remained No. 1)

1969 COTTON—No. 1 Texas beat No. 9 Notre Dame, 21-17; SUGAR—No. 13 Mississippi beat No. 3 Arkansas, 27-22; ORANGE—No. 2 Penn St. beat No. 6 Missouri, 10-3; ROSE—No. 5 Southern Cal beat No. 7 Michigan, 10-3. (Texas remained No. 1)

1970 ROSE—No. 12 Stanford beat No. 2 Ohio St., 27-17; COTTON—No. 6 Notre Dame beat No. 1 Texas, 24-11; ROSE—No. 12 Stanford beat No. 2 Ohio St., 27-17; SUGAR—No. 5 Tennessee beat No. 11 Air Force, 34-13; ORANGE—No. 3 Nebraska beat No. 8 LSU, 17-12; PEACH—No. 9 Arizona St. beat unranked North Caro., 48-26. (Nebraska selected No. 1 in AP and FW polls while Texas was No. 1 in UPI and tied with Ohio St. in NFF poll)

1971 ORANGE—No. 1 Nebraska beat No. 2 Alabama, 38-6; SUGAR—No. 3 Oklahoma beat No. 5 Auburn, 40-22; ROSE—No. 16 Stanford beat No. 4 Michigan, 13-12; GATOR—No. 6 Georgia beat unranked North Caro., 7-3; COTTON—No. 10 Penn St. beat No. 12 Texas, 30-6; FIESTA—No. 8 Arizona St. beat unranked Florida St., 45-38; BLUEBONNET—No. 7 Colorado beat No. 15 Houston, 29-17. (Nebraska remained No. 1 in all four polls)

1972 ROSE—No. 1 Southern Cal beat No. 3 Ohio St., 42-17; COTTON—No. 7 Texas beat No. 4 Alabama, 17-13; SUGAR—No. 2 Oklahoma beat No. 5 Penn St., 14-0; ORANGE—No. 9 Nebraska beat No. 12 Notre Dame, 40-6; GATOR—No. 6 Auburn beat No. 13 Colorado, 24-3; BLUEBONNET—No. 11 Tennessee beat No. 10 LSU, 24-17. (Southern Cal remained No. 1 in all four polls)

1973 SUGAR—No. 3 Notre Dame beat No. 1 Alabama, 24-23; ROSE—No. 4 Ohio St. beat No. 7 Southern Cal, 42-21; ORANGE—No. 6 Penn St. beat No. 13 LSU, 16-9; COTTON—No. 12 Nebraska beat No. 8 Texas, 19-3; FIESTA—No. 10 Arizona St. beat unranked Pittsburgh, 28-7; BLUEBONNET—No. 14 Houston beat No. 17 Tulane, 47-7. (Notre Dame selected No. 1 in AP, FW and NFF polls, Alabama named No. 1 by UPI but No. 2 Oklahoma was on probation and could not go to a bowl game)

1974 ROSE—No. 5 Southern Cal beat No. 3 Ohio St., 18-17; ORANGE—No. 9 Notre Dame beat No. 2 Alabama, 13-11; GATOR—No. 6 Auburn beat No. 11 Texas, 27-3; COTTON—No. 7 Penn St. beat No. 12 Baylor, 41-20; SUGAR—No. 8 Nebraska beat No. 18 Florida, 13-10; LIBERTY—Unranked Tennessee beat No. 10 Maryland, 7-3. (Oklahoma selected No. 1 in AP poll despite being on probation and not able to participate in bowl game; Southern Cal named No. 1 by UPI, FW and NFF polls)

1975 ROSE—No. 11 UCLA beat No. 1 Ohio St., 23-10; ORANGE—No. 3 Oklahoma beat No. 5 Michigan, 14-6; LIBERTY—No. 17 Southern Cal beat No. 2 Texas A&M, 20-0; SUGAR—No. 4 Alabama beat No. 8 Penn St., 13-6; FIESTA—No. 7 Arizona St. beat No. 6 Nebraska, 17-14; COTTON—No. 18 Arkansas beat No. 12 Georgia, 31-10; BLUEBONNET—No. 9 Texas beat No. 10 Colorado, 38-21. (Oklahoma selected No. 1 in all four polls)

1976 SUGAR—No. 1 Pittsburgh beat No. 5 Georgia, 27-3; ROSE—No. 3 Southern Cal beat No. 2 Michigan, 14-6; COTTON—No. 6 Houston beat No. 4 Maryland, 30-21; LIBERTY—No. 16 Alabama beat No. 7 UCLA, 36-6; ORANGE—No. 11 Ohio St. beat No. 12 Colorado, 27-10; FIESTA—No. 8 Oklahoma beat unranked Wyoming, 41-7; SUN—No. 10 Texas A&M beat unranked Florida, 37-14; BLUEBONNET—No. 13 Nebraska beat No. 9 Texas Tech, 27-24. (Pittsburgh remained No. 1 in all four polls)

1977 COTTON—No. 5 Notre Dame beat No. 1 Texas, 38-10; ORANGE—No. 6 Arkansas beat No. 2 Oklahoma, 31-6; SUGAR—No. 3 Alabama beat No. 9 Ohio St., 35-6; ROSE—No. 13 Washington beat No. 4 Michigan, 27-20; FIESTA—No. 8 Penn St. beat No. 15 Arizona St., 42-30; GATOR—No. 10 Pittsburgh beat No. 11 Clemson, 34-3. (Notre Dame selected No. 1 in all four polls)

1978 SUGAR—No. 2 Alabama beat No. 1 Penn St., 14-7; ROSE—No. 3 Southern Cal beat No. 5 Michigan, 17-10; ORANGE—No. 4 Oklahoma beat No. 6 Nebraska, 31-24; COTTON—No. 10 Notre Dame beat No. 9 Houston, 35-34; GATOR—No. 7 Clemson beat No. 20 Ohio St., 17-15; FIESTA—No. 8 Arkansas tied No. 15 UCLA, 10-10. (Alabama selected No. 1 in AP, FW and NFF polls, while Southern Cal named in UPI)

1979 ROSE—No. 3 Southern Cal beat No. 1 Ohio St., 17-16; SUGAR—No. 2 Alabama beat No. 6 Arkansas, 24-9; ORANGE—No. 5 Oklahoma beat No. 4 Florida St., 24-7; COTTON—No. 8 Houston beat No. 7 Nebraska, 17-14; SUN—No. 13 Washington beat No. 11 Texas, 14-7; FIESTA—No. 10 Pittsburgh beat unranked Arizona, 16-10. (Alabama selected No. 1 in all four polls)

1980 SUGAR—No. 1 Georgia beat No. 7 Notre Dame, 17-10; ORANGE—No. 4 Oklahoma beat No. 2 Florida St., 18-17; ROSE—No. 5 Michigan beat No. 16 Washington, 23-6; COTTON—No. 9 Alabama beat No. 6 Baylor, 30-2; GATOR—No. 3 Pittsburgh beat No. 18 South Caro., 37-9; SUN—No. 8 Nebraska beat No. 17 Mississippi St., 31-17; FIESTA—No. 10 Penn St. beat No. 11 Ohio St., 31-19; BLUEBONNET—No. 13 North Caro. beat unranked Texas, 16-7. (Georgia remained No. 1 in all four polls)

1981 ORANGE—No. 1 Clemson beat No. 4 Nebraska, 22-15; SUGAR—No. 10 Pittsburgh beat No. 2 Georgia, 24-20; COTTON—No. 6 Texas beat No. 3 Alabama, 14-12; GATOR—No. 11 North Caro. beat unranked Arkansas, 31-27; ROSE—No. 12 Washington beat No. 13 Iowa, 28-0; FIESTA—No. 7 Penn St. beat No. 8 Southern Cal, 26-10. (Clemson remained No. 1 in all four polls)

1982 SUGAR—No. 2 Penn St. beat No. 1 Georgia, 27-23; ORANGE—No. 3 Nebraska beat No. 13 LSU, 21-20; COTTON—No. 4 Southern Methodist beat No. 6 Pittsburgh, 7-3; ROSE—No. 5 UCLA beat No. 19 Michigan, 24-14; ALOHA—No. 9 Washington beat No. 16 Maryland, 21-20; FIESTA—No. 11 Arizona St. beat No. 12 Oklahoma, 32-21; BLUEBONNET—No. 14 Arkansas beat unranked Florida, 28-24. (Penn St. selected No. 1 in all four polls)

1983 ORANGE—No. 5 Miami (Fla.) beat No. 1 Nebraska, 31-30; COTTON—No. 7 Georgia beat No. 2 Texas, 10-9; SUGAR—No. 3 Auburn beat No. 8 Michigan, 9-7; ROSE—Unranked UCLA beat No. 4 Illinois, 45-9; HOLIDAY—No. 9 Brigham Young beat unranked Missouri, 21-17; GATOR—No. 11 Florida beat No. 10 Iowa, 14-6; FIESTA—No. 14 Ohio St. beat No. 15 Pittsburgh, 28-23. (Miami, Fla., selected No. 1 in all four polls)

1984 HOLIDAY—No. 1 Brigham Young beat unranked Michigan, 24-17; ORANGE—No. 4 Washington beat No. 2 Oklahoma, 28-17; SUGAR—No. 5 Nebraska beat No. 11 LSU, 28-10; ROSE—No. 18 Southern Cal beat No. 6 Ohio St., 20-17; COTTON—No. 8 Boston College beat unranked Houston, 45-28; GATOR—No. 9 Oklahoma St. beat No. 7 South Caro., 21-14; ALOHA—No. 10 Southern Methodist beat No. 17 Notre Dame, 27-20. (Brigham Young remained No. 1 in all four polls)

1985 ORANGE—No. 3 Oklahoma beat No. 1 Penn St., 25-10; SUGAR—No. 8 Tennessee beat No. 2 Miami (Fla.), 35-7; ROSE—No. 13 UCLA beat No. 4 Iowa, 45-28; COTTON—No. 11 Texas A&M beat No. 16 Auburn, 36-16; FIESTA—No. 5 Michigan beat No. 7 Nebraska, 27-23; BLUEBONNET—No. 10 Air Force beat unranked Texas, 24-16. (Oklahoma selected No. 1 in all four polls)

1986 FIESTA—No. 2 Penn St. beat No. 1 Miami (Fla.), 14-10; ORANGE—No. 3 Oklahoma beat No. 9 Arkansas, 42-8; ROSE—No. 7 Arizona St. beat No. 4 Michigan, 22-15; SUGAR—No. 6 Nebraska beat No. 5 LSU, 30-15; COTTON—No. 11 Ohio St. beat No. 8 Texas A&M, 28-12; CITRUS—No. 10 Auburn beat unranked Southern Cal, 16-7; SUN—No. 13 Alabama beat No. 12 Washington, 28-6. (Penn St. selected No. 1 in all four polls)

1987 ORANGE—No. 2 Miami (Fla.) beat No. 1 Oklahoma, 20-14; FIESTA—No. 3 Florida St. beat No. 5 Nebraska, 31-28; SUGAR—No. 4 Syracuse tied No. 6 Auburn, 16-16; ROSE—No. 8 Michigan St. beat No. 16 Southern Cal, 20-17; COTTON—No. 13 Texas A&M beat No. 12 Notre Dame, 35-10; GATOR—No. 7 LSU beat No. 9 South Caro., 30-13; ALOHA—No. 10 UCLA beat unranked Florida, 20-16. (Miami, Fla., selected No. 1 in all four polls)

1988 FIESTA—No. 1 Notre Dame beat No. 3 West Va., 34-21; ORANGE—No. 2 Miami (Fla.) beat No. 6 Nebraska, 23-3; SUGAR—No. 4 Florida St. beat No. 7 Auburn,

unranked Michigan St., 18-7; ALOHA—No. 17 Colorado beat No. 25 Fresno St., 41-30; JOHN HANCOCK—No. 19 Oklahoma beat unranked Texas Tech, 41-10. (Florida St. selected in all four major polls—AP, FW, USA/CNN and USA/NFF)

1994 ORANGE—No. 1 Nebraska beat No. 3 Miami (Fla.), 24-17; ROSE—No. 2 Penn St. beat No. 12 Oregon, 38-20; FIESTA—No. 4 Colorado beat unranked Notre Dame, 41-24; SUGAR—No. 7 Florida St. beat No. 5 Florida, 23-17; FLORIDA CITRUS—No. 6 Alabama beat No. 13 Ohio St., 24-17; FREEDOM—No. 14 Utah beat No. 15 Arizona, 16-13; ALOHA—Unranked Boston College beat No. 11 Kansas St., 12-7; HOLIDAY—No. 20 Michigan beat No. 10 Colorado St., 24-14; PEACH—No. 23 North Caro. St. beat No. 16 Mississippi St., 28-24; INDEPENDENCE—No. 18 Virginia beat unranked Texas Christian, 20-10; SUN—Unranked Texas beat No. 19 North Caro., 35-31; GATOR—Unranked Tennessee beat No. 17 Virginia Tech, 45-23. (Nebraska selected in all four major polls—AP, UPI, USA/CNN and FW)

1995 FIESTA—No. 1 Nebraska beat No. 2 Florida, 62-24; ROSE—No. 17 Southern Cal beat No. 3 Northwestern, 41-32; FLORIDA CITRUS—No. 4 Tennessee beat No. 4 Ohio St., 20-14; ORANGE—No. 8 Florida St. beat No. 6 Notre Dame, 31-26; COTTON—No. 7 Colorado beat No. 12 Oregon, 38-6; SUGAR—No. 13 Virginia Tech beat No. 9 Texas, 28-10; HOLIDAY—No. 10 Kansas St. beat unranked Colorado St., 54-21; ALOHA—No. 11 Kansas beat unranked UCLA, 51-30; ALAMO—No. 19 Texas A&M beat No. 14 Michigan, 22-20; OUTBACK—No. 15 Penn St. beat No. 16 Auburn, 43-14; PEACH—No. 18 Virginia beat unranked Georgia, 34-27. (Nebraska selected in all four major polls—AP, UPI, USA/CNN and FW)

1996 SUGAR—No. 3 Florida beat No. 1 Florida St., 52-20; FIESTA—No. 7 Penn St. beat No. 20 Texas, 38-15; ROSE—No. 4 Ohio St. beat No. 2 Arizona St., 20-17; COTTON—No. 5 Brigham Young beat No. 14 Kansas St., 19-15; FLORIDA CITRUS—No. 9 Tennessee beat No. 11 Northwestern, 48-28; GATOR—No. 12 North Caro. beat No. 25 West Va., 20-13; OUTBACK—No. 16 Alabama beat No. 15 Michigan, 17-14; ORANGE—No. 6 Nebraska beat No. 10 Virginia Tech, 41-21; INDEPENDENCE—Unranked Auburn beat No. 24 Army, 32-29; SUN—Unranked Stanford beat unranked Michigan St., 38-0; HOLIDAY—No. 8 Colorado beat No. 13 Washington, 33-21; ALAMO—No. 21 Iowa beat unranked Texas Tech, 27-0; PEACH—No. 17 LSU beat unranked Clemson, 10-7; COPPER—Unranked Wisconsin beat unranked Utah, 38-10; CARQUEST—No. 19 Miami (Fla.) beat unranked Virginia, 31-21; LIBERTY—No. 23 Syracuse beat unranked Houston, 30-17; ALOHA—Unranked Navy beat unranked California, 42-38; LAS VEGAS—Unranked Nevada beat unranked Ball St., 18-15. (Florida selected in all four major polls—AP, USA/CNN, FW and NFF/HOF)

1997 ROSE—No. 1 Michigan beat No. 9 Washington St., 21-16; ORANGE—No. 2 Nebraska beat No. 7 Tennessee, 42-17; SUGAR—No. 3 Florida St. beat No. 12 Ohio St., 31-14; FIESTA—No. 8 Kansas St. beat No. 21 Syracuse, 35-18; COTTON—No. 5 UCLA beat No. 20 Texas A&M, 29-23; FLORIDA CITRUS—No. 4 Florida beat No. 16 Penn St., 21-6; ALAMO—No. 15 Purdue beat No. 24 Oklahoma St., 33-20; GATOR—No. 6 North Caro. beat unranked Virginia Tech, 42-3; HOLIDAY—No. 17 Colorado St. beat No. 23 Missouri, 35-24; PEACH—No. 11 Auburn beat unranked Clemson, 21-17; LAS VEGAS—Unranked Oregon beat unranked Air Force, 41-13; ALOHA—No. 18 Washington beat unranked Michigan St., 51-23; MOTOR CITY—No. 22 Mississippi beat unranked Marshall, 34-31; INSIGHT.COM—Unranked Arizona beat unranked New Mexico, 20-14; INDEPENDENCE—No. 13 LSU beat unranked Notre Dame, 27-9; CARQUEST—No. 25 Georgia Tech beat unranked West Va., 35-30; HUMANITARIAN—Unranked Cincinnati beat unranked Utah St., 35-19; SUN—No. 14 Arizona St. beat unranked Iowa, 17-7; LIBERTY—No. 19 Southern Miss. beat unranked Pittsburgh, 41-7; OUTBACK—No. 10 Georgia beat unranked Wisconsin, 33-6. (Michigan selected by AP (media), FW and NFF/HOF while Nebraska was picked by the USA/ESPN (coaches)

Most Consecutive Bowl-Game Victories

(Bowls do not have to be in consecutive years; year listed is calendar year in which bowl was played)

College	Victories (Years)
Florida St.	11 (1985-86-88-89-90-90-92-93-94-95-96)
Southern Cal	9 (1923-24-30-32-33-39-40-44-45)
UCLA	8 (1983-84-85-86-86-87-89-91)
Georgia Tech	8 (1947-48-52-53-54-55-56-56)
Syracuse	7 (1989-89-90-92-93-96-97)
Alabama	6 (1975-76-78-79-80-81)
Nebraska	6 (1969-71-72-73-74-74)
Arizona St.	5 (1970-71-72-73-75)
Alabama	5 (1991-93-93-95-97)
Notre Dame	5 (1973-75-76-78-79)
Air Force	4 (1982-83-84-85)
Alabama	4 (1982-83-85-86)
Colorado	4 (1993-95-96-97)
North Caro.	4 (1979-80-81-82)
Team	**No. Faced**
Michigan	4 (1902-48-51-65)
Penn St.	4 (1994-95-96-97)
Southern Cal	3 (1993-95-96)
California	3 (1990-92-93)
Notre Dame	3 (1992-93-94)

Most Consecutive Seasons With Bowl-Game Victories

11 Florida St.—85 Gator, Oklahoma St. 34-23; 86 All-American, Indiana 27-13; 87 Fiesta, Nebraska 31-28; 88 Sugar, Auburn 13-7; 89 Fiesta, Nebraska 41-17; 90 Blockbuster, Penn St. 24-17; 92 Cotton, Texas A&M 10-2; 93 Orange, Nebraska 27-14; 94 Orange, Nebraska 18-16; 95 Sugar, Florida 23-17; 96 Orange, Notre Dame 31-26. Coach: Bobby Bowden.

7 UCLA—83 Rose, Michigan 24-14; 84 Rose, Illinois 45-9; 85 Fiesta, Miami (Fla.) 39-37; 86 Rose, Iowa 45-28; 86 Freedom, Brigham Young 31-10; 87 Aloha, Florida 20-16; 89 Cotton, Arkansas, 17-3. Coach: Terry Donahue.

6 Alabama—75 Sugar, Penn St. 13-6; 76 Liberty, UCLA 36-6; 78 Sugar, Ohio St. 35-6; 79 Sugar, Penn St. 14-7; 80 Sugar, Arkansas 24-9; 81 Cotton, Baylor 30-2. Coach: Paul "Bear" Bryant.

6 Nebraska—69 Sun, Georgia 45-6; 71 Orange, LSU 17-12; 72 Orange, Alabama 38-6; 73 Orange, Notre Dame 40-6; 74 Cotton, Texas 19-3; 74 Sugar, Florida 13-10. Coaches: Bob Devaney first 4 games, Tom Osborne last 2.

6 Georgia Tech—52 Orange, Baylor 17-14; 53 Sugar, Mississippi 24-7; 54 Sugar, West Va. 42-19; 55 Cotton, Arkansas 14-6; 56 Sugar, Pittsburgh 7-0; 56 Gator, Pittsburgh 21-14. Coach: Bobby Dodd.

Active Consecutive Appearances in Bowl Games

(Must have appeared in 1997-98 bowls)

Team	Appearances	Team	Appearances
Nebraska	29	Penn St.	9
Michigan	23	Tennessee	9
Florida St.	16	Ohio St.	9

Most Bowl Teams Faced in 1997

(Teams that faced the most 1997-98 bowl teams during their 1996 regular-season schedule)

Team	No. Faced	Team	No. Faced
Illinois	8	Arkansas	5
Colorado	7	Auburn	5
Indiana	7	Baylor	5
Minnesota	7	California	5
Northwestern	7	Georgia	5
Southern Cal	7	Kentucky	5
Stanford	7	LSU	5
Arizona	6	Michigan St.	5
Boston College	6	Oklahoma	5
Florida	6	Oregon	5
Iowa St.	6	Pittsburgh	5
Miami (Fla.)	6	Purdue	5
Michigan	6	Temple	5
Ohio St.	6	Texas Tech	5
Oregon St.	6	UCLA	5
Penn St.	6	Vanderbilt	5
San Diego St.	6	Washington St.	5
Tennessee	6	West Va.	5
Washington	6	Wisconsin	5
Alabama	5		

Undefeated, Untied Team Matchups in Bowl Games

Bowl	Date	Winner (Record Going In, Coach)	Loser (Record Going In, Coach)
Rose	1-1-21	California 28 (8-0, Andy Smith)	Ohio St. 0 (7-0, John Wilce)
Rose	1-2-22	0-0 tie: California (9-0, Andy Smith); Wash. & Jeff. (10-0, Earle "Greasy" Neale)	
Rose	1-1-27	7-7 tie: Alabama (9-0, Wallace Wade); Stanford (10-0, Glenn "Pop" Warner)	
Rose	1-1-31	Alabama 24 (9-0, Wallace Wade)	Washington St. 0 (9-0, Orin "Babe" Hollingbery)
Orange	1-2-39	Tennessee 17 (10-0, Bob Neyland)	Oklahoma 0 (10-0, Tom Stidham)
Sugar	1-1-41	Boston College 19 (10-0, Frank Leahy)	Tennessee 13 (10-0, Bob Neyland)
Sugar	1-1-52	Maryland 28 (9-0, Jim Tatum)	Tennessee 13 (10-0, Bob Neyland)
Orange	1-2-56	Oklahoma 20 (10-0, Bud Wilkinson)	Maryland 6 (10-0, Jim Tatum)
Orange	1-1-72	Nebraska 38 (12-0, Bob Devaney)	Alabama 6 (11-0, Paul "Bear" Bryant)
Sugar	12-31-73	Notre Dame 24 (10-0, Ara Parseghian)	Alabama 23 (11-0, Paul "Bear" Bryant)
Fiesta	1-2-87	Penn St. 14 (11-0, Joe Paterno)	Miami (Fla.) 10 (11-0, Jimmy Johnson)
Orange	1-1-88	Miami (Fla.) 20 (11-0, Jimmy Johnson)	Oklahoma 14 (11-0, Barry Switzer)
Fiesta	1-2-89	Notre Dame 34 (11-0, Lou Holtz)	West Va. 21 (11-0, Don Nehlen)
Sugar	1-1-93	Alabama 34 (12-0, Gene Stallings)	Miami (Fla.) 13 (11-0, Dennis Erickson)
Fiesta	1-2-96	Nebraska 62 (11-0, Tom Osborne)	Florida 24 (12-0, Steve Spurrier)

Undefeated Team Matchups in Bowl Games

(Both teams were undefeated but one or both was tied one or more times)

Bowl	Date	Winner (Record Going In, Coach)	Loser (Record Going In, Coach)
Rose	1-1-25	Notre Dame 27 (9-0, Knute Rockne)	Stanford 10 (7-0-1, Glenn "Pop" Warner)
Rose	1-1-26	Alabama 20 (9-0, Wallace Wade)	Washington 19 (10-0-1, Enoch Bagshaw)
Rose	1-2-33	Southern Cal 35 (9-0, Howard Jones)	Pittsburgh 0 (8-0-2, Jock Sutherland)
Rose	1-1-35	Alabama 29 (9-0, Frank Thomas)	Stanford 13 (9-0-1, Claude "Tiny" Thornhill)
Rose	1-1-38	California 13 (9-0-1, Leonard "Stub" Allison)	Alabama 0 (9-0, Frank Thomas)
Rose	1-1-40	Southern Cal 14 (7-0-2, Howard Jones)	Tennessee 0 (10-0, Bob Neyland)
Sugar	1-1-40	Texas A&M 14 (10-0, Homer Norton)	Tulane 13 (8-0-1, Lowell "Red" Dawson)
Rose	1-1-45	Southern Cal 25 (7-0-2, Jeff Cravath)	Tennessee 0 (7-0-1, John Barnhill)
Cotton	1-1-48	13-13 tie: Penn St. (9-0, Bob Higgins); Southern Methodist (9-0-1, Matty Bell)	
Orange	1-1-51	Clemson 15 (8-0-1, Frank Howard)	Miami (Fla.) 14 (9-0-1, Andy Gustafson)
Sugar	1-1-53	Georgia Tech 24 (11-0, Bobby Dodd)	Mississippi 7 (8-0-2, John Vaught)
Rose	1-1-69	Ohio St. 27 (9-0, Woody Hayes)	Southern Cal 16 (9-0-1, John McKay)
Rose	1-1-80	Southern Cal 17 (10-0-1, John Robinson)	Ohio St. 16 (11-0, Earle Bruce)
California	12-14-85	Fresno St. 51 (10-0-1, Jim Sweeney)	Bowling Green 7 (11-0, Denny Stolz)

Bowl Rematches of Regular-Season Opponents

Date	Regular Season	Date	Bowl-Game Rematch
10-9-43	Texas A&M 28, LSU 13	1-1-44	(Orange) LSU 19, Texas A&M 14
11-22-45	South Caro. 13, Wake Forest 13	1-1-46	(Gator) Wake Forest 26, South Caro. 14
10-6-56	Iowa 14, Oregon St. 13	1-1-57	(Rose) Iowa 35, Oregon St. 19
10-31-59	LSU 7, Mississippi 3	1-1-60	(Sugar) Mississippi 21, LSU 0
9-18-65	Michigan St. 13, UCLA 3	1-1-66	(Rose) UCLA 14, Michigan St. 12
10-4-75	Ohio St. 41, UCLA 20	1-1-76	(Rose) UCLA 23, Ohio St. 10
11-11-78	Nebraska 17, Oklahoma 14	1-1-79	(Orange) Oklahoma 31, Nebraska 24
9-25-82	UCLA 31, Michigan 27	1-1-83	(Rose) UCLA 24, Michigan 14
9-7-87	Michigan St. 27, Southern Cal 13	1-1-88	(Rose) Michigan St. 20, Southern Cal 17
11-26-94	Florida 31, Florida St. 31	1-2-95	(Sugar) Florida St. 23, Florida 17
9-23-95	Toledo 49, Nevada 35	12-14-95	(Las Vegas) Toledo 40, Nevada 37 (OT)
11-30-96	Florida St. 24, Florida 21	1-2-97	(Sugar) Florida 52, Florida St. 20
11-15-97	Notre Dame 24, LSU 6	12-28-97	(Independence) LSU 27, Notre Dame 9

Bowl-Game Facts

The Bowl/Basketball Connection

Nine times in history, a football bowl winner also won the NCAA men's basketball championship during the same academic year. They are as follows:

Year	School	Bowl	Date of Bowl
1992-93	North Caro.	Peach	1-2-93
1988-89	Michigan	Rose	1-2-89
1981-82	North Caro.	Gator	12-28-81
1973-74	North Caro. St.	Liberty	12-17-73
1965-66	UTEP	Sun	12-31-65
1950-51	Kentucky	Sugar	1-1-51
1947-48	Kentucky	Great Lakes	12-6-47
1945-46	Oklahoma St.	Sugar	1-1-46
1944-45	Oklahoma St.	Cotton	1-1-45

One-Time Wonders

Seven major-college teams have played in only one bowl game in their football history, and three of those have posted victories. The winners were Eastern Michigan, Memphis and Northern Illinois. The one-time bowlers are as follows:

School	Date	Bowl	Opponent (Score)
Eastern Mich.	12-12-87	California	San Jose St. (30-27)
Kent	12-29-72	Tangerine	Tampa (18-21)
Long Beach St.	12-19-70	Pasadena	Louisville (24-24)
Marshall	12-26-97	Motor City	Mississippi (31-34)
Memphis	12-18-71	Pasadena	San Jose St. (28-9)
Northern Ill.	12-17-83	California	Cal St. Fullerton (20-13)
Rutgers	12-16-78	Garden State	Arizona St. (18-34)

Year-by-Year Bowl Facts

(A note about bowl-game dates: Traditionally, bowl games have been played on January 1, but as more bowl games joined the holiday lineup, schedule adjustments were made whereby some bowl games are now played as early as mid-December. In the interest of avoiding confusion, all years referred to in bowl records are the actual calendar year in which the bowl game was played.)

1917 Coach Hugo Bezdek led the first of three teams to the Rose Bowl from 1917 to 1923. His Oregon team beat Pennsylvania, 14-0, in 1917; his Mare Island squad defeated Camp Lewis, 19-7, in 1918; and his Penn State team lost to Southern California, 14-3, in 1923. In his 1923 trip with the Nittany Lions, Bezdek almost came to blows with Southern California coach Elmer "Gloomy Gus" Henderson because Penn State did not arrive for the game until an hour after the scheduled kickoff time. Henderson accused

Bezdek of not taking the field until the hot California sun had gone down to give his winterized Easterners an advantage.

1919 George Halas (yes, "Papa Bear") was the player of the game for Great Lakes Naval Training Station in Chicago as the Sailors shut out Mare Island, 17-0, in another of the wartime Rose Bowls.

1923 The first Rose Bowl game actually played in the stadium in Pasadena saw Southern California defeat Penn State, 14-3.

1926 Johnny Mack Brown, one of Hollywood's most famous movie cowboys, also was one of college football's most exciting players at Alabama. He was selected player of the game for the Rose Bowl in the Crimson Tide's 20-19 victory over Washington.

1927 The Rose Bowl becomes the first coast-to-coast radio broadcast of a sporting event.

1929 The Rose Bowl game became one of the most famous in bowl history because of California player Roy Riegels' now-legendary wrong-way run. Early in the second quarter, with each team just changing possessions, Georgia Tech was on its own 20. Tech halfback Stumpy Thompson broke for a seven-yard run, fumbled, and Riegels picked up the ball, momentarily headed for the Tech goal, then reversed his field and started running the wrong way. Teammate Benny Lom tried to stop him and finally did on the California one-yard line, where the dazed Riegels was pounced on by a group of Tech tacklers. Lom went back to punt on the next play and the kick was blocked out of the end zone for a safety, which decided the contest, eventually won by Tech, 8-7.

1938 The first Orange Bowl played in Miami's new stadium, which seated 22,000 at the time, saw Auburn edge Michigan State, 6-0. Also, in the second annual Cotton Bowl, Colorado's do-it-all standout Byron "Whizzer" White, the Rhodes Scholar and future U.S. Supreme Court justice, passed for one score and returned a pass interception for another, but the Buffs lost to Rice, 28-14.

1941 On December 6, 1941, Hawaii defeated Willamette, 20-6, but a second postseason game, scheduled with San Jose State for the next week, was cancelled after the attack on Pearl Harbor.

1942 You would think a team making only one first down and gaining only 75 yards to its opponent's 309 yards could not come out of a game a 29-21 victor, but it happened in the Cotton Bowl as Alabama downed Texas A&M. The Tide intercepted seven of A&M's 42 passes and recovered five Aggie fumbles. Also, the Rose Bowl was moved for one year to Durham, N.C., because of wartime considerations that precluded large gatherings on the West Coast, and Oregon State downed Duke, 20-16.

1946 The first and only bowl game decided after time expired was the Orange Bowl when Miami (Florida) downed Holy Cross, 13-6. Time expired as Miami halfback Al Hudson returned an 89-yard intercepted pass for the deciding score.

1949 A Pacific Coast team had never been allowed to play in a major bowl other than the Rose Bowl, but the conference leadership let Oregon play in the Cotton Bowl against Southern Methodist. Doak Walker and Kyle Rote led Southern Methodist to a 20-13 victory over the Ducks and quarterback Norm Van Brocklin. John McKay, later the head coach at Southern California, also was on the Oregon roster.

1953 The Rose, Cotton, Sugar and Orange Bowls were televised nationally for the first time.

1954 Dicky Maegle of Rice may be the best-remembered bowl player, not because of his 265 yards rushing and three touchdowns vs. Alabama in 1954, but because of what happened on a 95-yard scoring run. Alabama's Tommy Lewis became infamous by coming off the bench to tackle Maegle in the Cotton Bowl, won by Rice, 28-6.

1960 In one of those pupil-vs.-teacher battles, former Georgia Tech player and assistant coach Frank Broyles led his Arkansas Razorbacks to a 14-7 Gator Bowl victory over his former coach, Bobby Dodd, and the Yellow Jackets.

1962 Oregon State quarterback Terry Baker turned in the longest run in bowl history with a 99-yard scamper to down Villanova, 6-0, in the Liberty Bowl. Baker, an outstanding athlete, became the only Heisman Trophy winner to play in an NCAA Final Four basketball game later that academic year (1963).

1964 Utah and West Virginia became the first teams to play a major bowl game indoors when they met in the Atlantic City Convention Hall. Utah won, 32-6, beneath the bright indoor lights.

1965 The first Orange Bowl played under the lights in Miami saw Texas stun national champion Alabama and quarterback Joe Namath, 21-17.

1968 It was the student beating the teacher in the Cotton Bowl as Texas A&M head coach Gene Stallings saw his Aggies hold on for a 20-16 victory over Alabama and legendary head coach Paul "Bear" Bryant. Stallings had played (at Texas A&M) and coached (at Alabama) under Bryant. The "Bear" met Stallings at midfield after the contest and lifted the 6-foot-3 Aggie coach up in admiration. Also, the Astro-Bluebonnet Bowl (also known as the Bluebonnet Bowl) became the first bowl game to be played in a domed stadium as the Astrodome served as the site of the December 31, 1968, game between Southern Methodist (28) and Oklahoma (27).

1970 Three of the four legendary Four Horsemen of Notre Dame came to Dallas to watch the Fighting Irish drop a 21-17 Cotton Bowl game to Texas. The only other time Notre Dame had played in a bowl game was the 1925 Rose Bowl, when the Four Horsemen led the Irish to a 27-10 victory over Stanford.

1971 Notre Dame snapped the second-longest winning streak going into a bowl game by halting Texas' 30-game string, 24-11, in the Cotton Bowl. In 1951, Kentucky had stopped Oklahoma's 31-game streak in the Sugar Bowl, 13-7.

1976 Archie Griffin started his fourth straight Rose Bowl for Ohio State (1973-76), totaling 412 yards on 79 carries in the four games. The Buckeyes, under legendary head coach Woody Hayes, won only the 1974 contest, but Griffin is the only player to win two Heisman Trophies (1974-75).

1989 Texas Tech's James Gray set a college bowl record with 280 yards rushing in the All-American Bowl against Duke. Brigham Young's Ty Detmer set the bowl passing mark with 576 yards versus Penn State in the Holiday Bowl.

Special Regular- and Postseason Games

Postseason Games

UNSANCTIONED OR OTHER BOWLS

The following bowl and/or postseason games were unsanctioned by the NCAA or otherwise had no team classified as major college at the time of the bowl. Most are postseason games; in many cases, complete dates and/or statistics are not available and the scores are listed only to provide a historical reference. Attendance of the game, if known, is listed in parentheses after the score.

ALL-SPORTS BOWL
(Oklahoma City, Okla.)
12-9-61—Okla. Panhandle 28, Langston 14 (8,000)
12-8-62—Neb.-Omaha 34, East Central 21 (2,500)
12-7-63—Northeastern St. 59, Slippery Rock 12
12-5-64—Sul Ross St. 21, East Central 13

ALUMINUM BOWL (NAIA Title Game)
(Little Rock, Ark.)
12-22-56—Montana St. 0, St. Joseph's (Ind.) 0

ANGEL BOWL
(Los Angeles, Calif.)
12-28-46—Florida A&M 6, Wiley 6 (12,000)

AZALEA BOWL
(Orlando, Fla.)
1-1-46—Knoxville 18, Florida Normal 0 (4,000)

AZALEA CLASSIC
(Mobile, Ala.)
12-4-71—Jackson St. 40, Alabama A&M 21
12-7-74—Bethune-Cookman 19, Langston 3 (1,000)

AZTEC BOWL
(Mexico City, Mexico)
12-50—Whittier 27, Mexico All-Stars 14
12-53—Mexico City 45, Eastern N.M. 26

BEAN BOWL
(Scottsbluff, Neb.)
11-24-49—Idaho St. 20, Chadron St. 2
11-23-50—Doane 14, Northern Colo. 6

BEAVER BOWL
(Corry, Pa.)
11-15-58—Slippery Rock 6, Edinboro 0 (3,000)

BICENTENNIAL BOWL
(Little Rock, Ark.)
11-29-75—Henderson St. 27, East Central 14 (2,000)

BICENTENNIAL BOWL
(Richmond, Va.)
12-11-76—South Caro. St. 26, Norfolk St. 10 (7,500)

BOOT HILL BOWL
(Dodge City, Kan.)
12-70—Cameron 13, N.M. Highlands 12
12-4-71—Dakota St. 23, Northwestern Okla. 20 (2,000)
12-2-72—William Penn 17, Emporia St. 14 (2,000)
12-1-73—Millikin 51, Bethany (Kan.) 7 (1,600)
11-30-74—Washburn 21, Millikin 7 (2,500)
11-22-75—Buena Vista 24, St. Mary's (Kan.) 21 (2,700)
11-20-76—Benedictine 29, Washburn 14 (3,000)
11-19-77—Mo. Western St. 35, Benedictine 30 (1,000)
11-18-78—Chadron St. 30, Baker (Kan.) 19 (3,000)
11-17-79—Pittsburg St. 43, Peru St. 14 (2,800)
11-21-80—Cameron 34, Adams St. 16

BOTANY BOWL
11-24-55—Neb.-Kearney 34, Northern St. 13

BOY'S RANCH BOWL
(Abilene, Texas)
12-13-47—Missouri Valley 20, McMurry (Tex.) 13 (2,500)

BURLEY BOWL
(Johnson City, Tenn.)
1-1-46—High Point 7, Milligan 7 (3,500)
11-28-46—Southeastern La. 21, Milligan 13 (7,500)
11-27-47—West Chester 20, Carson-Newman 6 (10,000)
11-25-48—West Chester 7, Appalachian St. 2 (12,000)
11-24-49—Emory & Henry 32, Hanover 0 (12,000)
11-23-50—Emory & Henry 26, Appalachian St. 6 (12,000)
11-22-51—Morris Harvey (now Charleston) 27, Lebanon Valley 20 (9,000)
11-27-52—East Tenn. St. 34, Emory & Henry 16
11-26-53—East Tenn. St. 48, Emory & Henry 12
11-25-54—Appalachian St. 28, East Tenn. St. 13
11-24-55—East Tenn. St. 7, Appalachian St. 0
11-22-56—Memphis 32, East Tenn. St. 12

CAJUN BOWL
12-47—McNeese St. 0, Southern Ark. 0

CATTLE BOWL
(Fort Worth, Texas)
1-1-47—Ark.-Pine Bluff 7, Lane 0 (1,000)
1-1-48—Samuel Huston 7, Philander Smith 0 (800)

CEMENT BOWL
(Allentown, Pa.)
12-8-62—West Chester 46, Hofstra 12

CHARITY BOWL
(Los Angeles, Calif.)
12-25-37—Fresno St. 27, Central Ark. 26 (5,000)

CHRISTMAS BOWL
(Natchitoches, La.)
12-6-58—Northwestern St. 18, Sam Houston St. 11
12-5-59—Delta St. 19, East Central 0

CIGAR BOWL
(Tampa, Fla.)
1-1-47—Delaware 21, Rollins 7 (9,500)
1-1-48—Missouri Valley 26, West Chester 7 (10,000)
1-1-49—Missouri Valley 13, St. Thomas (Minn.) 13 (11,000)
1-2-50—Florida St. 19, Wofford 6 (14,000)
1-1-51—Wis.-La Crosse 47, Valparaiso 14 (12,000)
12-29-51—Brooke Army Medical 20, Camp LeJeune Marines 0 (7,500) (see Cigar Bowl in Service Games)
12-13-52—Tampa 21, Lenoir-Rhyne 12 (7,500)

1-1-54—Missouri Valley 12, Wis.-La Crosse 12 (5,000)
12-17-54—Tampa 21, Morris Harvey (now Charleston) 0

CITRACADO BOWL
(see Citracado Bowl in Service Games)

COCONUT BOWL
(Miami, Fla.)
1-1-42—Florida Normal 0, Miami All-Stars 0 (9,000)
1-1-46—Bethune-Cookman 32, Albany St. (Ga.) 0 (5,000)
1-1-47—Bethune-Cookman 13, Columbia (S.C.) Sporting Club 0 (5,000)

CORN BOWL
(Bloomington, Ill.)
11-27-47—Southern Ill. 21, North Central 0 (5,500)
11-25-48—Ill. Wesleyan 6, Eastern Ill. 0 (8,500)
11-24-49—Western Ill. 13, Wheaton (Ill.) 0 (4,567)
11-23-50—Mo.-Rolla 7, Illinois St. 6 (2,500)
11-22-51—Lewis 21, William Jewell 12 (2,000)
11-26-53—Western Ill. 32, Iowa Wesleyan 0
11-24-55—Luther 24, Western Ill. 20 (3,100)

COSMOPOLITAN BOWL
(Alexandria, La.)
12-51—McNeese St. 13, Louisiana Col. 6

COTTON-TOBACCO BOWL
(Greensboro, N.C.)
1-1-46—Johnson Smith 18, Allen 6
1-1-47—Norfolk St. 0, Richmond 0 (10,000)

COWBOY BOWL
(Lawton, Okla.)
12-11-71—Howard Payne 16, Cameron 13
12-9-72—Harding 30, Langston 27

DIXIE CLASSIC
(Dallas, Texas)
1-1-34—Arkansas 7, Centenary 7 (12,000)

DOLL AND TOY CHARITY GAME
(Gulfport, Miss.)
12-3-37—Southern Miss. 7, Appalachian St. 0 (2,000)

EASTERN BOWL
(Allentown, Pa.)
12-14-63—East Caro. 27, Northeastern 6 (2,700)

ELKS BOWL
1-2-54—Morris Harvey (now Charleston) 12, East Caro. 0 (4,500) (at Greenville, N.C.)
12-11-54—Newberry 20, Appalachian St. 13 (at Raleigh, N.C.)

FISH BOWL
(Corpus Christi, Texas)
11-48—Southwestern (Tex.) 7, Corpus Christi 0

FISH BOWL
(Norfolk, Va.)
12-4-48—Hampton 20, Central St. 19

FLOWER BOWL
(Jacksonville, Fla.)
1-1-42—Johnson Smith 13, Lane 0 (4,500)
1-1-43—North Caro. A&T 14, Southern U. 6 (2,000)
1-1-44—Allen 33, Winston-Salem 0 (2,000)
1-1-45—Texas College 18, North Caro. A&T 0 (5,000)
1-1-46—Grambling 19, Lane 6 (6,000)
1-1-47—Delaware St. 7, Florida Normal 6 (3,000)
1-1-48—Bethune-Cookman 6, Lane 0 (3,000)

FRUIT BOWL
(San Francisco, Calif.)
12-14-47—Central St. 26, Prairie View 0 (9,000)
12-5-48—Southern U. 30, San Fran. St. 0 (5,000)

GATE CITY BOWL
(Atlanta, Ga.)
12-21-74—Tuskegee 15, Norfolk St. 14 (6,252)

GLASS BOWL
(Toledo, Ohio)
12-7-46—Toledo 21, Bates 12 (12,000)
12-6-47—Toledo 20, New Hampshire 14 (13,500)
12-4-48—Toledo 27, Oklahoma City 14 (8,500)
12-3-49—Cincinnati 33, Toledo 13

GOLD BOWL
(Richmond, Va.)
12-3-77—South Caro. St. 10, Winston-Salem 7 (14,000)
12-2-78—Virginia Union 21, North Caro. A&T 6 (7,500)
12-1-79—South Caro. St. 39, Norfolk St. 7 (8,000)
12-6-80—North Caro. A&T 37, N.C. Central 0 (3,374)

GOLDEN ISLES BOWL
(Brunswick, Ga.)
12-1-62—McNeese St. 21, Samford 14

GRAPE BOWL
(Lodi, Calif.)
12-13-47—Pacific (Cal.) 35, Utah St. 21 (12,000)
12-11-48—Hardin-Simmons 35, Pacific (Cal.) 35 (10,000)

GREAT LAKES BOWL
(Cleveland, Ohio)
12-5-48—John Carroll 14, Canisius 13 (18,000)

GREAT SOUTHWEST BOWL
(Grand Prairie, Texas)
12-31-60—Tex. A&M-Kingsville 45, Arkansas Tech 14 (3,900)

HOLIDAY BOWL
(St. Petersburg, Fla.)
12-21-57—Pittsburg St. 27, Hillsdale 26
12-20-58—Northeastern St. 19, Northern Ariz. 13
12-19-59—Tex. A&M-Kingsville 20, Lenoir-Rhyne 7 (9,500)
12-10-60—Lenoir-Rhyne 15, Humboldt St. 14 (also served as NAIA national title game)

HOOSIER BOWL
(See Turkey Bowl)

INTERNATIONAL BOWL
12-52—Tex. A&M-Kingsville 49, Hereico Colegio Military 0

IODINE BOWL
(Charleston, S.C.)
12-3-49—Johnson Smith 20, Allen 12
12-9-50—Allen 20, Bethune-Cookman 0 (1,000)
12-1-51—Allen 33, Morris College 14 (3,000)
12-5-53—Allen 33, Paul Quinn 6

KICKAPOO BOWL
(Wichita Falls, Texas)
12-5-47—Midwestern St. 39, Central Ark. 20 (5,000)

LIONS BOWL
(Ruston, La.)
12-46—Grambling 69, Miss. Industrial 12
12-5-47—Grambling 47, Bethune-Cookman 6
12-49—Grambling 21, Texas College 18
12-2-50—Bishop 35, Grambling 0
12-1-51—Grambling 52, Bishop 0 (at Shreveport, La.)
12-6-52—Grambling 27, Alcorn St. 13 (at Monroe, La.)

LIONS BOWL
(Salisbury, N.C.)
12-13-52—Clarion 13, East Caro. 6 (3,000)

MERCY BOWL II
(Anaheim, Calif.)
12-11-71—Cal St. Fullerton 17, Fresno St. 14 (16,854)

MINERAL WATER BOWL
(Excelsior Springs, Mo.)
11-25-54—Hastings 20, Col. of Emporia 14 (4,000)
11-24-55—Missouri Valley 31, Hastings 7
11-22-56—St. Benedict's 14, Northeastern St. 13 (2,000)
11-30-57—William Jewell 33, Hastings 14 (2,000)
11-22-58—Lincoln (Mo.) 21, Emporia St. 0 (2,500)
11-28-59—Col. of Emporia 21, Austin (Tex.) 20 (3,000)
11-26-60—Hillsdale 17, Northern Iowa 6 (6,000)
11-25-61—Truman St. 22, Parsons 8 (8,000)
11-24-62—Adams St. 23, Northern Ill. 20
11-30-63—Northern Ill. 21, Southwest Mo. St. 14
11-28-64—North Dak. St. 14, Western St. 13 (4,500)
11-27-65—North Dak. 37, Northern Ill. 20
11-26-66—Adams St. 14, Southwest Mo. St. 8 (5,500)
11-25-67—Doane 14, William Jewell 14 (6,500)
11-30-68—Doane 10, Central Mo. St. 0 (6,000)
11-29-69—St. John's (Minn.) 21, Simpson 0 (5,000)
11-28-70—Franklin 40, Wayne St. (Neb.) 12 (2,500)
12-4-71—Bethany (Kan.) 17, Missouri Valley 14 (2,500)
11-18-72—Ottawa 27, Friends 20 (4,500)
11-73—William Jewell 20, St. Mary's (Kan.) 9
11-23-74—Midland 32, Friends 6 (1,500)
11-22-75—Mo. Western St. 44, Graceland (Ia.) 0 (3,300)

MIRZA SHRINE BOWL
(Pittsburg, Kan.)
12-1-50—Central Mo. St. 32, Pittsburg St. 21

MISSOURI-KANSAS BOWL
(Kansas City, Mo.)
12-4-48—Emporia St. 34, Southwest Mo. St. 20

MOILA SHRINE CLASSIC
(St. Joseph, Mo.)
11-24-79—Mo. Western St. 72, William Jewell 44 (1,600)
11-22-80—Truman St. 17, Pittsburg St. 14 (500)

NATIONAL CLASSIC
(Greensboro, N.C.)
12-4-54—N.C. Central 19, Tennessee St. 6

NEW YEAR'S CLASSIC
(Honolulu, Hawaii)
1-1-34—Santa Clara 26, Hawaii 7
1-1-35—Hawaii 14, California 0 (later called Poi Bowl)

OIL BOWL
(Houston, Texas)
1-1-44—Southwestern La. 24, Ark.-Monticello 7 (12,000)

OLEANDER BOWL
(Galveston, Texas)
1-2-50—McMurry 19, Missouri Valley 13 (7,500)

OLYMPIAN BOWL
(see Pythian Bowl)

OPTIMIST BOWL
(Houston, Texas)
12-21-46—North Texas 14, Pacific (Cal.) 13 (5,000)

ORANGE BLOSSOM CLASSIC
(Miami, Fla.)
12-2-33—Florida A&M 9, Howard 6
12-13-34—Florida A&M 13, Virginia St. 12
12-12-35—Kentucky St. 19, Florida A&M 10
12-5-36—Prairie View 25, Florida A&M 0
12-9-37—Florida A&M 25, Hampton 20
12-8-38—Florida A&M 9, Kentucky St. 7
12-9-39—Florida A&M 42, Wiley 0
12-7-40—Central St. 0, Florida A&M 0
12-6-41—Florida A&M 15, Tuskegee 7
12-12-42—Florida A&M 12, Texas College 6
12-4-43—Hampton 39, Florida A&M 0
12-9-44—Virginia St. 19, Florida A&M 6
12-8-45—Wiley 32, Florida A&M 6
12-7-46—Lincoln (Pa.) 20, Florida A&M 0 (at Tampa)
12-6-47—Florida A&M 7, Hampton 0
12-4-48—Virginia Union 10, Florida A&M 6 (16,000)
12-10-49—North Caro. A&T 20, Florida A&M 14
12-2-50—Central St. 13, Florida A&M 6
12-1-51—Florida A&M 67, N.C. Central 6
12-6-52—Florida A&M 29, Virginia St. 7
12-5-53—Prairie View 33, Florida A&M 27
12-4-54—Florida A&M 67, Md.-East. Shore 19
12-3-55—Grambling 28, Florida A&M 21
12-1-56—Tennessee St. 41, Florida A&M 39
12-14-57—Florida A&M 27, Md.-East. Shore 21
12-13-58—Prairie View 26, Florida A&M 8
12-5-59—Florida A&M 28, Prairie View 7
12-10-60—Florida A&M 40, Langston 26
12-9-61—Florida A&M 14, Jackson St. 8 (47,791)
12-8-62—Jackson St. 22, Florida A&M 6
12-14-63—Morgan St. 30, Florida A&M 7
12-5-64—Florida A&M 42, Grambling 15
12-4-65—Morgan St. 36, Florida A&M 7
12-3-66—Florida A&M 43, Alabama A&M 26
12-2-67—Grambling 28, Florida A&M 25
12-7-68—Alcorn St. 36, Florida A&M 9 (37,398)
12-6-69—Florida A&M 23, Grambling 19 (36,784) (at Tallahassee, Fla.)
12-12-70—Jacksonville St. 21, Florida A&M 7 (31,184)
12-11-71—Florida A&M 27, Kentucky St. 9 (26,161)
12-2-72—Florida A&M 41, Md.-East. Shore 21 (21,606)
12-8-73—Florida A&M 23, South Caro. St. 12 (18,996)
12-7-74—Florida A&M 17, Howard 13 (20,166)
12-6-75—Florida A&M 40, Kentucky St. 13 (27,875)
12-4-76—Florida A&M 26, Central St. 21 (18,000)
12-3-77—Florida A&M 37, Delaware St. 15 (29,493)
12-2-78—Florida A&M 31, Grambling 7

ORCHID BOWL
(Mexico City, Mexico)
1-1-42—Louisiana Col. 10, U. of Mexico 0 (8,000)
12-28-46—Mississippi Col. 43, U. of Mexico 7 (7,500)

PALM FESTIVAL
(Miami, Fla.)
1-2-33—Miami (Fla.) 7, Manhattan 0 (6,000)
1-1-34—Duquesne 33, Miami (Fla.) 7 (3,500) (forerunner to Orange Bowl)

PALMETTO SHRINE
(Columbia, S.C.)
12-10-55—Lenoir-Rhyne 14, Newberry 13 (6,000)

PAPER BOWL
(Pensacola, Fla.)
12-18-48—Jacksonville St. 19, Troy St. 0
12-16-49—Jacksonville St. 12, West Ala. 7 (3,000)
12-2-50—Pensacola Alumni Cardinals 7, Jacksonville St. 6 (3,600)

PEACH BLOSSOM CLASSIC
(Atlanta, Ga.)
12-9-39—Morris Brown 13, Virginia St. 7
12-6-40—Morris Brown 28, Kentucky St. 6 (1,500)
12-6-41—Morris Brown 7, N.C. Central 6 (6,000) (at

Columbus, Ga.)
12-4-42—Morris Brown 20, Lane 0 (3,000) (at Columbus, Ga.)

PEACH BOWL
(Macon, Ga.)
12-13-46—Tenn. Wesleyan 14, Ga. Military 13 (5,000)
12-6-47—Virginia St. 48, Morris Brown 0
12-3-49—Morris Brown 33, Texas College 28 (at Atlanta, Ga.)

PEANUT BOWL
(Dothan, Ala.)
12-21-68—Ouachita Baptist 39, West Ala. 6

PEAR BOWL
(Medford, Ore.)
11-28-46—Southern Ore. St. 13, Central Wash. 8 (3,000) (at Ashland, Ore.)
11-27-47—Pacific Lutheran 27, Southern Ore. St. 21
11-25-48—Col. of Idaho 27, Southern Ore. St. 20 (2,500)
11-24-49—Pacific (Ore.) 33, UC Davis 15 (4,000)
11-23-50—Lewis & Clark 61, San Fran. St. 7 (4,000)
11-24-51—Pacific (Ore.) 25, UC Davis 7 (4,000)

PECAN BOWL
(Orangeburg, S.C.)
12-7-46—South Caro. St. 13, Johnson Smith 6
12-13-47—South Caro. St. 7, Allen 0 (3,000)

PELICAN BOWL
(New Orleans, La.)
12-2-72—Grambling 56, N.C. Central 6 (22,500) (at Durham, N.C.)
12-7-74—Grambling 28, South Caro. St. 7 (30,120)
12-27-75—Southern U. 15, South Caro. St. 12 (6,748)

PENINSULA BOWL
(Charleston, S.C.)
12-2-50—Allen 47, South Caro. St. 13 (7,500)

PHILLIPS FIELD BOWL
(Tampa, Fla.)
12-8-51—Tampa 7, Brandeis 0

PIEDMONT TOBACCO BOWL
(Fayetteville, N.C.)
12-7-46—Allen 40, Fayetteville St. 6 (900)

PINEAPPLE BOWL
(Honolulu, Hawaii)
1-1-40—Oregon St. 39, Hawaii 6 (formerly called Poi Bowl)
1-1-41—Fresno St. 3, Hawaii 0
1-1-47—Hawaii 19, Utah 16 (25,000)
1-1-48—Hawaii 33, Redlands 32 (12,000)
1-1-49—Oregon St. 47, Hawaii 27 (15,000)
1-2-50—Stanford 74, Hawaii 20
1-1-51—Hawaii 28, Denver 27
1-1-52—San Diego St. 34, Hawaii 13

PITTSBURGH CHARITY GAME
(Pittsburgh, Pa.)
12-5-31—Carnegie Mellon 0, Duquesne 0 (42,539) (see Other Postseason Games)

POI BOWL
(Honolulu, Hawaii)
1-1-36—Southern Cal 38, Hawaii 6
1-2-37—Hawaii 18, Honolulu All-Stars 12
1-1-38—Washington 53, Hawaii 13 (13,500)
1-2-39—UCLA 32, Hawaii 7 (later called Pineapple Bowl)

POULTRY BOWL
(Gainesville, Ga.)
12-8-73—Stephen F. Austin 31, Gardner-Webb 10 (2,500)
12-7-74—Guilford 7, William Penn 7 (1,000) (at Greensboro, N.C.) (Guilford awarded win on 10-8 edge in first downs)

PRAIRIE VIEW BOWL
(Also called Bayou City Bowl)
(Houston, Texas)
1-1-29—Atlanta 7, Prairie View 0
1-1-30—Fisk 20, Prairie View 0
1-1-31—Tuskegee 19, Prairie View 7
1-1-32—Prairie View 27, Alabama St. 2
1-1-33—Prairie View 14, Tuskegee 0
1-1-34—Prairie View 20, Langston 7
1-1-35—Tuskegee 15, Prairie View 6
1-1-36—Wiley 7, Prairie View 6
1-1-37—Tuskegee 6, Prairie View 0 (3,000)
1-1-38—Prairie View 27, Florida A&M 14
1-2-39—Prairie View 34, Tuskegee 0
1-1-40—Prairie View 7, Xavier (La.) 6
1-1-41—Prairie View 7, Alabama St. 6
1-1-42—Kentucky St. 19, Prairie View 13
1-1-43—Langston 18, Prairie View 13
1-1-44—Prairie View 6, Wiley 0 (5,000)
1-1-45—Wiley 26, Prairie View 0 (4,000)
1-1-46—Prairie View 12, Tuskegee 0 (10,000)
1-1-47—Prairie View 14, Lincoln (Mo.) 0 (1,500) (called Houston Bowl)
1-1-48—Texas Southern 13, Prairie View 0
1-1-49—Central St. 6, Prairie View 0 (9,000)
1-2-50—Prairie View 27, Fisk 6 (4,718)
1-1-51—Prairie View 6, Bishop 0
1-1-52—Prairie View 27, Ark.-Pine Bluff 26
1-1-53—Texas Southern 13, Prairie View 12 (13,000)
1-1-54—Prairie View 33, Texas Southern 8
1-1-55—Prairie View 14, Texas Southern 12 (10,000)
1-2-56—Prairie View 59, Fisk 0 (7,500)
1-1-57—Prairie View 27, Texas Southern 6
1-1-58—Prairie View 6, Texas Southern 6 (3,500)
1-1-59—Prairie View 34, Langston 8
1-1-60—Prairie View 47, Wiley 10 (1,200)
12-31-60—Prairie View 19, Ark.-Pine Bluff 8 (1,400)
12-1-62—Prairie View 37, Central St. 16

PRETZEL BOWL
(Reading, Pa.)
11-24-51—West Chester 32, Albright 9 (7,500)

PYTHIAN BOWL
(Salisbury, N.C.)
11-26-49—Appalachian St. 21, Catawba 7
12-9-50—West Liberty St. 28, Appalachian St. 26
12-8-51—Lenoir-Rhyne 13, Calif. (Pa.) 7 (4,500)

REFRIGERATOR BOWL
(Evansville Ind.)
12-4-48—Evansville 13, Missouri Valley 7 (7,500)
12-3-49—Evansville 22, Hillsdale 7
12-2-50—Abilene Christian 13, Gust. Adolphus 7 (8,000)
12-2-51—Arkansas St. 46, Camp Breckinridge 12 (10,000)
12-7-52—Western Ky. 34, Arkansas St. 19 (9,500)
12-6-53—Sam Houston St. 14, Col. of Idaho 12 (7,500)
12-5-54—Delaware 19, Kent 7 (4,500)
12-4-55—Jacksonville St. 12, Rhode Island 10 (7,000)
12-1-56—Sam Houston St. 27, Middle Tenn. St. 13 (3,000)

RICE BOWL
(Stuggart, Ark.)
12-57—Arkansas Tech 19, Ark.-Monticello 7
12-58—Louisiana Col. 39, Arkansas Tech 12
12-2-60—East Central 25, Henderson St. 7

ROCKET BOWL
(Huntsville, Ala.)
11-19-60—Maryville (Tenn.) 19, Millsaps 0

SAN JACINTO SHRINE BOWL
(Pasadena, Texas)
12-4-76—Abilene Christian 22, Harding 12 (8,000)

SHARE BOWL
(Knoxville, Tenn.)
12-11-71—Carson-Newman 54, Fairmont St. 3 (1,200)

SHRIMP BOWL
(Galveston, Texas)
12-27-52—Sam Houston St. 41, Northeastern St. 20 (3,500)

SHRINE BOWL
(Ardmore, Okla.)
12-9-72—Southwestern Okla. 28, Angelo St. 6

SILVER BOWL
(Mexico City, Mexico)
12-20-47—Mexico All-Stars 24, Randolph Field 19
12-11-48—Pacific Fleet 33, Mexico All-Stars 26
12-17-49—Trinity (Tex.) 52, Mexico 6

SMOKY MOUNTAIN BOWL
(Bristol, Tenn.)
11-24-49—West Liberty St. 20, Western Caro. 0 (1,000)

SPACE CITY BOWL
(Huntsville, Ala.)
11-24-66—Jacksonville St. 41, Ark.-Monticello 30
12-9-67—Samford 20, Ark.-Monticello 7

STEEL BOWL
(Birmingham, Ala.)
1-1-41—Morris Brown 19, Central St. 3 (8,000)
1-1-42—Southern College All-Stars 26, Nashville Pros 13
1-1-52—Bethune-Cookman 27, Texas College 13 (1,500) (see Vulcan Bowl)

SUGAR CUP CLASSIC
(New Orleans, La.)
11-28-64—Grambling 42, Bishop 6

TANGERINE BOWL#
(Orlando, Fla.)
1-1-47—Catawba 31, Maryville (Tenn.) 6
1-1-48—Catawba 7, Marshall 0
1-1-49—Murray St. 21, Sul Ross St. 21
1-2-50—St. Vincent (Pa.) 7, Emory & Henry 6
1-1-51—Morris Harvey (now Charleston) 35, Emory & Henry 14
1-1-52—Stetson 35, Arkansas St. 20 (12,500)
1-1-53—East Tex. St. 33, Tennessee Tech 0 (12,340)
1-1-54—Arkansas St. 7, East Tex. St. 7
1-1-55—Neb.-Omaha 7, Eastern Ky. 6
1-2-56—Juniata 6, Missouri Valley 6 (10,000)
1-1-57—West Tex. A&M 20, Southern Miss. 13 (11,000)
1-1-58—East Tex. St. 10, Southern Miss. 9
12-27-58—East Tex. St. 26, Missouri Valley 7 (4,000)
1-1-60—Middle Tenn. St. 21, Presbyterian 12 (12,500)
12-29-61—Lamar 21, Middle Tenn. St. 14
12-28-63—Western Ky. 27, Coast Guard 0 (7,500)
12-12-64—East Caro. 14, Massachusetts 13
12-11-65—East Caro. 31, Maine 0 (8,350)
12-10-66—Morgan St. 14, West Chester 6
12-16-67—Tenn.-Martin 25, West Chester 8

TEXHOMA BOWL
(Denison, Texas)
12-10-48—Ouachita Baptist 7, Southeastern Okla. 0
11-25-49—Austin (Tex.) 27, East Central 6

TEXTILE BOWL
(Spartanburg, S.C.)
11-30-74—Wofford 20, South Caro. St. 0 (3,000)

TOBACCO BOWL
(Lexington, Ky.)
12-14-46—Muhlenberg 26, St. Bonaventure 25 (3,000)

TROPICAL BOWL
12-18-51—Morris Brown 21, Alcorn St. 0
12-13-52—Bethune-Cookman 54, Albany St. (Ga.) 0
12-12-53—Virginia Union 13, Bethune-Cookman 0

TURKEY BOWL
11-28-46—Evansville 19, Northern Ill. 7 (12,000) (also called Hoosier Bowl)

VULCAN BOWL
(Birmingham, Ala.)
1-1-42—Langston 13, Morris Brown 0 (7,000)
1-1-43—Texas College 13, Tuskegee 10 (6,000)
1-1-44—Tuskegee 12, Clark (Ga.) 7 (6,000)
1-1-45—Tennessee St. 13, Tuskegee 0 (5,000)
1-1-46—Tennessee St. 33, Texas College 6 (9,000)
1-1-47—Tennessee St. 32, Louisville Municipal 0 (4,000)
1-2-48—Central St. 27, Grambling 21 (8,000)
1-1-49—Kentucky St. 23, North Caro. A&T 13 (5,000)
1-1-52—Bethune-Cookman 27, Texas College 13 (1,500) (see Steel Bowl)

WILL ROGERS BOWL
(Oklahoma City, Okla.)
1-1-47—Pepperdine 38, Neb. Wesleyan 13 (800)

YAM BOWL
(Dallas, Texas)
12-25-46—Texas Southern 64, Tuskegee 7 (5,000)
12-25-47—Southern U. 46, Fort Valley St. 0 (1,200)

#Became Florida Citrus Bowl (no classified major teams participated in games from January 1, 1947, through January 1, 1960, or in 1961 and 1963 through 1967.

SERVICE GAMES

AIRBORNE BOWL
12-15-57—101st Airborne 20, 82nd Airborne 14
12-5-59—Fort Campbell 26, Fort Bragg 7

ARAB BOWL
(Oran, Africa)
1-1-44—Army 10, Navy 7 (15,000)

ARMY ALL-STAR GAMES
8-30-42—Washington Redskins 26, Western Army All-Stars 7 (at Los Angeles, Calif.)
9-6-42—Western Army All-Stars 16, Chicago Cardinals 10 (at Denver, Colo.)
9-9-42—Western Army All-Stars 12, Detroit Lions 0 (at Detroit, Mich.)
9-12-42—Eastern Army All-Stars 16, New York Giants 0 (at New York, N.Y.)
9-13-42—Green Bay Packers 36, Western Army All-Stars 21 (at Milwaukee, Wis.)
9-16-42—Eastern Army All-Stars 13, Brooklyn Dodgers 7 (at Baltimore, Md.)
9-19-42—New York Giants 10, Western Army All-Stars 7 (at New York, N.Y.)
9-20-42—Chicago Bears 14, Eastern Army All-Stars 7 (at Boston, Mass.)

ARMY PACIFIC OLYMPICS
(Osaka, Japan)
1-13-46—11th Airborne Angels 27, Clark Field 6
1-27-46—11th Airborne Angels 18, Honolulu All-Stars 0

ARMY-NAVY BENEFIT BOWL
(Tallahassee, Fla.)
12-20-52—Parris Island 49, Fort Benning 0

ATOM BOWL
(Nagasaki, Japan)
12-45—Nishahaya Tigers 14, Bertelli's Bears 13 (2,000)

BAMBINO BOWL
(Bari, Italy)
11-23-44—Technical School 13, Playboys 0 (5,000)

BAMBOO BOWL
(Manila, Philippines)
1-1-46—Clark Field Acpacs 14, Leyte Base 12 (40,000)
1-1-47—Manila Raiders 13, Scofield Barracks 6 (12,000)
12-47—Ryukgus Command Sea Horses 21, Hawaiian Mid-Pacific Commandos 0
1-1-50—All-Navy Guam 19, Clark Air Force Base 7

BLUEBONNET BOWL
(Houston, Texas)
12-25-46—Texas Southern 49, Camp Hood 0

CHERRY BOWL
(Yokohama, Japan)
1-1-52—Camp Drake 26, Yoksuka Naval Base 12

CHIGGER BOWL
(Dutch Guiana)
1-1-45—Army Air Base Bonecrushers 6, Army Airway Rams 0 (1,200)

CHINA BOWL
(Shanghai)
1-27-46—Navy All-Stars 12, Army All-Stars 0
1-1-47—11th Airborne 12, Army-Navy All-Stars 6
1-1-48—Marines (Guam) 45, China All-Stars 0

CIGAR BOWL
12-29-51—Brooke Army Medical 20, Camp LeJeune 0 (7,500)

CITRICADO BOWL
12-56—San Diego Marines 25, UC Santa Barb. 14

COCONUT BOWL
(New Guinea)
1-6-45—Bulldogs 18, Crimson Tide 7 (3,000)

COFFEE BOWL
(London, England)
3-19-44—United States 18, Canada 0

CONCH BOWL
(Key West, Fla.)
11-24-57—Keesler Air Force Base 27, Maxwell Air Force Base 7
11-28-58—Keesler Air Force Base 14, Maxwell Air Force Base 8

COSMOPOLITAN BOWL
(Alexandria, La.)
12-50—Camp Polk 26, Louisiana Col. 7
12-52—Louisiana Col. 14, Alexander Air Base 0

ELECTRONICS BOWL
(Biloxi, Miss.)
12-9-51—Keesler Air Force Base 13, Camp LeJeune 0
12-53—Eglin Air Force Base 19, Keesler Air Force Base 8
12-54—Shaw Air Force Base 20, Keesler Air Force Base 19

EUROPEAN "ORANGE BOWL"
(Heidelberg, Germany)
12-7-46—1st Division Artillery 27, 60th Infantry 13

EUROPEAN "ROSE BOWL"
(Augsburg, Germany)
12-7-46—9th Division 20, 16th Infantry 7 (3,000)

EUROPEAN "SUGAR BOWL"
(Nuremberg, Germany)
12-7-46—Grafenwohr Military 0, 39th Infantry 0

G. I. BOWL
(London, England)
11-12-44—Army G.I.'s 20, Navy Bluejackets 0 (60,000)

ICE BOWL
(Fairbanks, Alaska)
1-1-49—Ladd Air Force Base 0, University of Alaska 0 (500)
1-2-50—University of Alaska 3, Ladd Air Force Base 0
1-1-51—University of Alaska 0, Ladd Air Force Base 0
12-30-52—Ladd Air Force Base 47, University of Alaska 0

IRANIAN BOWL
(Teheran, Iran)
12-12-44—Camp Amirabad 20, Camp Khorramsahr 0 (9,000)

JUNGLE BOWL
(Southwest Pacific)
1-1-45—American All-Stars 49, Marines 0 (6,400)

LILY BOWL
(Hamilton, Bermuda)
1-3-43—Army 19, Navy 18
1-1-44—Navy 19, Army 0
1-7-45—Navy 39, Army 6 (11,000)
1-5-47—Army 7, Navy 7 (9,000)
1-1-48—Air Force 12, Navy 12
1-1-49—Navy All-Stars 25, Kindley Fliers 6

MARINE BOWL
(Pritchard Field, Southwest Pacific)
12-24-44—4th Marines 0, 29th Marines 0 (7,000)

MISSILE BOWL
(Orlando, Fla.)
12-3-60—Quantico Marines 36, Pensacola Air Force Base 6
12-9-61—Fort Eustis 25, Quantico Marines 24
12-15-62—Fort Campbell 14, Lackland Air Force Base 10
12-14-63—Quantico Marines 13, San Diego Marines 10
12-5-64—Fort Benning 9, Fort Eustis 3

PALMETTO SHRINE
(Charleston, S.C.)
1-1-55—Fort Jackson 26, Shaw Air Force Base 21

PARC DES PRINCES BOWL
(Paris, France)
12-19-44—9th Air Force 6, 1st General Hospital 0 (20,000)

POI BOWL
(Honolulu, Hawaii)
(Pacific Ocean Areas Service Championship)
1-8-45—Navy 14, Army Air Force 0 (29,000)

POINSETTIA BOWL
(San Diego, Calif.)
12-20-52—Bolling Air Force Base 35, San Diego NTC 14
12-19-53—Fort Ord 55, Quantico Marines 19
12-19-54—Fort Sill 27, Bolling Air Force Base 6
12-17-55—Fort Ord 35, Pensacola NAS 13

POTATO BOWL
(Belfast, Ireland)
1-1-44—Galloping Gaels 0, Wolverines 0

RICE BOWL
(Tokyo, Japan)
1-1-46—11th Airborne Angels 25, 41st Division 12 (15,000)
12-46—Yokota Air Base 13, 1st AD 8 (7,000)
1-1-48—Korea All-Stars 19, Japan All-Stars 13
1-1-49—Army Ground Forces 13, Air Force 7 (20,000)
1-1-50—Air Force All-Stars 18, Army All-Stars 14
1-1-53—Camp Drake 25, Yokosuka Naval Base 6
1-1-54—Camp Fisher 19, Nagoya Air Base 13
1-1-55—Air Force 21, Marines 14
12-31-55—Air Force 33, Army 14 (40,000)
12-30-56—Army 21, Air Force 6
12-7-57—Johnson Air Base Vanguards 6, Marine Corps Sukiran Streaks 0
12-20-58—Air Force 20, Army 0

RIVIERA BOWL
(Marseille, France)
1-1-45—Railway Shop Battalion Unit 37, Army All-Stars 0 (18,000)

SALAD BOWL
(Phoenix, Ariz.)
1-1-53—San Diego Navy 81, 101st Airborne 20
1-1-54—Fort Ord 67, Great Lakes 12

SATELLITE BOWL
(Cocoa, Fla.)
12-29-57—Fort Carson 12, Fort Dix 6

SHRIMP BOWL
(Galveston, Texas)
1-1-55—Fort Ord 36, Fort Hood 0
12-18-55—Fort Hood 33, Little Creek 13
12-8-56—Bolling Air Force Base 29, Fort Hood 14
12-15-57—Bolling Air Force Base 28, San Diego Marines 7
12-14-58—Eglin Air Force Base 15, Brooke Medics 7
12-13-59—Quantico Marines 90, McClellan Air Force Base 0

SHURI BOWL
12-58—Air Force 60, Marine Corps 0

SPAGHETTI BOWL
(Florence, Italy)
1-1-45—5th Army 20, 12th Air Force 0 (20,000)
1-1-53—Salzburg Army 12, Wiesbaden AFC 7 (at Leghorn, Italy)

SUKIYAKI BOWL
12-56—Air Force 29, Marines 7

TEA BOWL
(London, England)
2-13-44—Canada 16, United States 6 (30,000)
12-31-44—Air Service Command Warriors 13, 8th Air Force Shuttle Raiders 0 (12,000)

TREASURY BOWL
(New York, N.Y.)
12-16-44—Randolph Field 13, 2nd Air Force 6 (8,356)

TYPHOON BOWL
12-56—Army 13, Marines 0

VALOR BOWL
(Chattanooga, Tenn.)
12-7-57—Hamilton Air Force Base 12, Quantico Marines 6

POSTSEASON BOWL INVOLVING NON-I-A TEAMS

HERITAGE BOWL
Site: Atlanta, Ga.
Stadium (Capacity): Georgia Dome (71,228)
Name Changes: Alamo Heritage Bowl (1991); Heritage Bowl (1993-94; 96); Jim Walters Heritage Bowl (1995); McDonald's Heritage Bowl (since 1997)
Playing Surface: AstroTurf
Playing Sites: Joe Robbie Stadium, Miami (1991); Bragg Memorial Stadium, Tallahassee (1993); Georgia Dome, Atlanta (since 1994)

Date	Score (Attendance)
12-21-91	Alabama St. 36, North Caro. A&T 13 (7,724)
1-2-93	Grambling 45, Florida A&M 15 (11,273)
1-1-94	Southern U. 11, South Caro. St. 0 (36,128)
12-30-94	South Caro. St. 31, Grambling 27 (22,179)
12-29-95	Southern U. 30, Florida A&M 25 (25,164)
12-31-96	Howard 27, Southern U. 24 (18,126)
12-27-97	Southern U. 34, South Caro. St. 28 (32,629)

NCAA-CERTIFIED ALL-STAR GAMES

EAST-WEST SHRINÉ CLASSIC
Present Site: Palo Alto, Calif.
Stadium (Capacity): Stanford (85,500)
Playing Surface: Grass
Playing Sites: Ewing Field, San Francisco (1925); Kezar Stadium, San Francisco (1927-41); Sugar Bowl, New Orleans (1942); Kezar Stadium, San Francisco (1943-66); Candlestick Park, San Francisco (1967-68); Stanford Stadium, Palo Alto (1969); Oakland Coliseum (1971); Candlestick Park, San Francisco (1971-73); Stanford Stadium, Palo Alto (since 1974)

Date	Score (Attendance)
12-26-25	West 7-0 (20,000)
1-1-27	West 7-3 (15,000)
12-26-27	West 16-6 (27,500)
12-29-28	East 20-0 (55,000)
1-1-30	East 19-7 (58,000)
12-27-30	West 3-0 (40,000)
1-1-32	East 6-0 (45,000)
1-2-33	West 21-13 (45,000)
1-1-34	West 12-0 (35,000)
1-1-35	West 19-13 (52,000)
1-1-36	East 19-3 (55,000)
1-1-37	East 3-0 (38,000)
1-1-38	Tie 0-0 (55,000)
1-2-39	West 14-0 (60,000)
1-1-40	West 28-11 (50,000)
1-1-41	West 20-14 (60,000)
1-3-42	Tie 6-6 (35,000)
1-1-43	East 13-12 (57,000)
1-1-44	Tie 13-13 (55,000)
1-1-45	West 13-7 (60,000)
1-1-46	Tie 7-7 (60,000)
1-1-47	West 13-9 (60,000)
1-1-48	East 40-9 (60,000)
1-1-49	East 14-12 (59,000)
12-31-49	East 28-6 (60,000)

Date	Score (Attendance)
12-30-50	West 16-7 (60,000)
12-29-51	East 15-14 (60,000)
12-27-52	East 21-20 (60,000)
1-2-54	West 31-7 (60,000)
1-1-55	East 13-12 (60,000)
12-31-55	East 29-6 (60,000)
12-29-56	West 7-6 (60,000)
12-28-57	West 27-13 (60,000)
12-27-58	East 26-14 (60,000)
1-2-60	West 21-14 (60,000)
12-31-60	East 7-0 (60,000)
12-30-61	West 21-8 (60,000)
12-29-62	East 25-19 (60,000)
12-28-63	Tie 6-6 (60,000)
1-2-65	West 11-7 (60,000)
12-31-65	West 22-7 (47,000)
12-31-66	East 45-22 (46,000)
12-30-67	East 16-14 (29,000)
12-28-68	West 18-7 (29,000)
12-27-69	West 15-0 (70,000)
1-2-71	West 17-13 (50,000)
12-31-71	West 17-13 (35,000)
12-30-72	East 9-3 (37,000)
12-29-73	East 35-7 (30,000)
12-28-74	East 16-14 (35,000)
1-3-76	West 21-14 (75,000)
1-2-77	West 30-14 (45,000)
12-31-77	West 23-3 (65,000)
1-6-79	East 56-17 (72,000)
1-5-80	West 20-10 (75,000)
1-10-81	East 21-3 (76,000)
1-9-82	West 20-13 (75,000)
1-15-83	East 26-25 (72,999)
1-7-84	East 27-19 (77,000)
1-5-85	West 21-10 (72,000)
1-11-86	East 18-7 (77,000)
1-10-87	West 24-21 (74,000)
1-16-88	West 16-13 (62,000)
1-15-89	East 24-6 (76,000)
1-21-90	West 22-21 (78,000)
1-26-91	West 24-21 (70,000)
1-19-92	West 14-6 (83,000)
1-24-93	East 31-17 (84,000)
1-15-94	West 29-28 (60,000)
1-14-95	West 30-28 (35,079)
1-13-96	West 34-18 (68,500)
1-11-97	East 17, West 13 (62,500)
1-10-98	West 24, East 7 (68,329)

Series record: West won 39, East 29, 5 ties.

BLUE-GRAY ALL-STAR CLASSIC
Present Site: Montgomery, Ala.
Stadium (Capacity): Cramton Bowl (24,600)
Playing Surface: Grass
Playing Sites: Cramton Bowl, Montgomery (since 1939)

Date	Score (Attendance)
1-2-39	Blue 7-0 (8,000)
12-30-39	Gray 33-20 (10,000)
12-28-40	Blue 14-12 (14,000)
12-27-41	Gray 16-0 (15,571)
12-26-42	Gray 24-0 (16,000)
1943	No Game
12-30-44	Gray 24-7 (16,000)
12-29-45	Blue 26-0 (20,000)
12-28-46	Gray 20-13 (22,500)
12-27-47	Gray 33-6 (22,500)
12-25-48	Blue 19-13 (15,000)
12-31-49	Gray 27-13 (21,500)
12-30-50	Gray 31-6 (21,000)
12-29-51	Gray 20-14 (22,000)
12-27-52	Gray 28-7 (22,000)
12-26-53	Gray 40-20 (18,500)
12-25-54	Blue 14-7 (18,000)
12-31-55	Gray 20-19 (19,000)
12-29-56	Blue 14-0 (21,000)
12-28-57	Gray 21-20 (16,000)
12-27-58	Blue 16-0 (16,000)
12-26-59	Blue 20-8 (20,000)
12-31-60	Blue 35-7 (18,000)
12-30-61	Gray 9-7 (18,000)
12-29-62	Blue 10-6 (20,000)
12-28-63	Gray 21-14 (20,000)
12-26-64	Blue 10-6 (16,000)
12-25-65	Gray 23-19 (18,000)
12-24-66	Blue 14-9 (18,000)
12-30-67	Blue 22-16 (23,350)
12-28-68	Gray 28-7 (18,000)
12-27-69	Tie 6-6 (21,500)
12-28-70	Gray 38-7 (23,000)
12-28-71	Gray 9-0 (24,000)
12-27-72	Gray 27-15 (20,000)
12-18-73	Blue 20-14 (21,000)
12-17-74	Blue 29-24 (12,000)
12-19-75	Blue 14-13 (10,000)
12-24-76	Gray 31-10 (16,000)
12-30-77	Blue 20-16 (5,000)
12-29-78	Gray 28-24 (18,380)
12-25-79	Blue 22-13 (18,312)
12-25-80	Blue 24-23 (25,000)
12-25-81	Blue 21-9 (19,000)
12-25-82	Gray 20-10 (21,000)
12-25-83	Gray 17-13 (2,000)
12-25-84	Gray 33-6 (24,080)
12-25-85	Blue 27-20 (18,500)
12-25-86	Blue 31-7 (18,500)
12-25-87	Gray 12-10 (20,300)
12-25-88	Blue 22-21 (20,000)
12-25-89	Gray 28-10 (16,000)
12-25-90	Blue 17-14 (17,500)
12-25-91	Gray 20-12 (21,000)
12-25-92	Gray 27-17 (20,500)
12-25-93	Gray 17-10 (18,500)
12-25-94	Blue 38-27 (23,500)
12-25-95	Blue 26, Gray 7 (18,500)
12-25-96	Blue 44, Gray 34 (17,000)
12-25-97	Gray 31, Blue 24 (25,214)

Series record: Gray won 31, Blue 27, 1 tie.

HULA BOWL
Present Site: Honolulu, Hawaii
Stadium (Capacity): Aloha (50,000)
Playing Surface: AstroTurf
Format: From 1947 through 1950, the College All-Stars played the Hawaii All-Stars. Beginning in 1951, the Hawaiian team was augmented by players from the National Football League. This format, however, was changed to an all-collegiate contest—first between the East and West, then between North and South (in 1963), and then back to East and West in 1974 and 1995-96. In 1994, the format went to a collection of collegiate all-stars versus a collection of Hawaiian former collegiate players. In 1997, it reverted back to North-South.
Playing Sites: Honolulu Stadium (1960-74); Aloha Stadium (since 1975)

Date	Score (Attendance)
1-10-60	East 34-8 (23,000)
1-8-61	East 14-7 (17,017)
1-7-62	Tie 7-7 (20,598)
1-6-63	North 20-13 (20,000)
1-4-64	North 20-13 (18,177)
1-9-65	South 16-14 (22,100)
1-8-66	North 27-26 (25,000)
1-7-67	North 28-27 (23,500)
1-6-68	North 50-6 (21,000)
1-4-69	North 13-7 (23,000)
1-10-70	South 35-13 (25,000)
1-9-71	North 42-32 (23,500)
1-8-72	North 24-7 (23,000)
1-6-73	South 17-3 (23,000)
1-5-74	East 24-14 (23,000)
1-4-75	East 34-25 (22,000)
1-10-76	East 16-0 (45,458)
1-8-77	West 20-17 (45,579)
1-7-78	West 42-22 (48,197)
1-6-79	East 29-24 (49,132)
1-5-80	East 17-10 (47,096)
1-10-81	West 24-17 (39,010)
1-9-82	West 26-23 (43,002)
1-15-83	East 30-14 (39,456)
1-7-84	West 21-16 (34,216)
1-5-85	East 34-14 (30,767)
1-11-86	West 23-10 (29,564)
1-10-87	West 16-14 (17,775)
1-16-88	West 20-18 (26,737)
1-7-89	East 21-10 (25,000)
1-13-90	West 21-13 (28,742)
1-19-91	East 23-10 (21,926)
1-11-92	West 27-20 (23,112)
1-16-93	West 13-10 (25,479)
1-22-94	College All-Stars 28-15 (33,947)
1-22-95	East 20-9 (19,074)
1-21-96	East 17-10 (25,112)
1-19-97	South 26, North 13 (24,725)
1-18-98	South 20, North 19 (20,079)

Series records: North-South (1963-73, 97-98)—North won 8, South 5; East-West (1960-62, 1974-93 and 1995-96)—East won 13, West 11, 1 tie; College All-Stars vs. Hawaiian All-Stars (1994)—College All-Stars won 1, Hawaiian All-Stars 0.

SENIOR BOWL
Played at Ladd Memorial Stadium in Mobile, Ala., since 1951 under the auspices of the National Football League. North and South teams are composed of senior players who have used all of their collegiate eligibility. In 1991, the teams switched from North and South to AFC and NFC; in 1994, the teams switched back to North and South.

Date	Score (Attendance)
1-7-50	South 22, North 13 (at Jacksonville, Fla.)
1-6-51	South 19, North 18
1-5-52	North 20, South 6
1-3-53	North 28, South 13
1-9-54	North 20, South 14
1-8-55	South 12, North 6
1-7-56	South 12, North 2
1-5-57	South 21, North 7
1-11-58	North 15, South 13
1-3-59	South 21, North 12
1-9-60	North 26, South 7 (40,119)
1-7-61	South 33, North 26
1-6-62	South 42, North 7
1-5-63	South 33, North 27
1-4-64	South 28, North 21 (37,094)
1-9-65	Tie 7-7 (40,605)
1-8-66	South 27, North 18
1-7-67	North 35, South 13
1-6-68	South 34, North 21
1-11-69	North 27, South 16
1-10-70	Tie 37-37
1-9-71	North 31, South 13 (40,646)
1-8-72	North 26, South 21 (40,646)
1-6-73	South 33, North 30 (40,646)
1-12-74	North 16, South 13 (40,646)
1-11-75	Tie 17-17 (40,646)
1-10-76	North 42, South 35 (40,646)
1-9-77	North 27, South 24 (40,646)
1-7-78	Tie 17-17 (40,646)
1-13-79	South 41, North 21 (40,100)
1-12-80	North 57, South 3 (40,646)
1-17-81	North 23, South 10 (40,102)
1-16-82	South 27, North 10 (39,410)
1-22-83	North 14, South 6 (37,511)
1-14-84	South 21, North 20 (38,254)
1-12-85	South 23, North 7 (33,500)
1-18-86	North 31, South 17 (40,646)
1-17-87	South 42, North 38
1-23-88	North 21, South 7
1-21-89	South 13, North 12 (39,742)
1-20-90	North 41, South 0 (42,400)
1-19-91	AFC 38, NFC 28 (37,500)
1-18-92	AFC 13, NFC 10 (37,100)
1-16-93	NFC 21, AFC 6 (37,124)
1-22-94	South 35, North 32 (39,200)
1-21-95	South 14, North 7 (40,007)
1-20-96	North 25, South 10 (40,700)
1-18-97	North 35, South 14 (40,646)
1-17-98	South 31, North 8 (40,820)

Series records: North-South (1950-90 and 1994 to present)—South won 22, North 20, 4 ties; AFC-NFC (1991-93)—AFC won 2, NFC 1.

DISCONTINUED ALL-STAR FOOTBALL GAMES

Many of these games were identified without complete information such as scores, teams, sites or dates. Please send any updates or additional information to: NCAA Statistics Service, 6201 College Boulevard, Overland Park, Kansas 66211-2422.

ALL-AMERICAN BOWL (1969-77) (Tampa, Fla.)

Date	Score (Attendance)
1-4-69	North 21, South 15 (16,380)

Date	Score (Attendance)
1-3-70	South 24, North 23 (17,642)
1-10-71	North 39, South 2 (12,000)
1-9-72	North 27, South 8 (20,137)
1-7-73	North 10, South 6 (23,416)
1-6-74	North 28, South 7 (24,536)
1-5-75	South 28, North 22 (19,246)
1-10-76	North 21, South 14 (15,321)
1-2-77	North 21, South 20 (14,207)

AMERICAN COLLEGE ALL-STAR GAME (1948)
(Los Angeles, Calif.)

Date	Score
12-18-48	American All-Stars 43, Canadian All-Stars 0
12-26-48	American All-Stars 14, Hawaiian All-Stars 0

BLACK COLLEGE ALL-STAR BOWL (1979-82)

Date	Score (Location, Attendance)
1-7-79	East 25, West 20 (at New Orleans, La.)
1-5-80	West 27, East 21 (OT) (at New Orleans, La.)
1-17-81	West 19, East 10 (at Jackson, Miss., 7,500)
1-16-82	West 7, East 0 (at Jackson, Miss.)

CAMP FOOTBALL FOUNDATION BOWL (1974)

CANADIAN-AMERICAN BOWL (1978-79)
(Tampa, Fla.)

Date	Score (Attendance)
1-8-78	U.S. All-Stars 22, Canadian All-Stars 7 (11,328)
1-6-79	U.S. All-Stars 34, Canadian All-Stars 14 (11,033)

CHALLENGE BOWL (1978-79)
(Seattle, Wash.)

Date	Score (Attendance)
1-14-78	Pacific-8 27, Big Ten 20 (20,578)
1-13-79	Pacific-10 36, Big Eight 23 (23,961)

CHICAGO COLLEGE ALL-STAR FOOTBALL GAME (1934-76)

An all-star team composed of the top senior collegiate players met the National Football League champions (1933-66) or the Super Bowl champions (1967-75) from the previous season, beginning in 1934. The only time the all-stars did not play the league champions was in 1935. All games except 1943 and 1944 were played at Soldier Field, Chicago, Ill. The 1943 and 1944 games were played at Dyche Stadium, Evanston, Ill.

Date	Score (Attendance)
8-31-34	(Tie) Chicago Bears 0-0 (79,432)
8-29-35	Chicago Bears 5, All-Stars 0 (77,450)
9-2-36	(Tie) Detroit 7-7 (76,000)
9-1-37	All-Stars 6, Green Bay 0 (84,560)
8-31-38	All-Stars 28, Washington 16 (74,250)
8-30-39	New York Giants 9, All-Stars 0 (81,456)
8-29-40	Green Bay 45, All-Stars 28 (84,567)
8-28-41	Chicago Bears 37, All-Stars 13 (98,203)
8-28-42	Chicago Bears 21, All-Stars 0 (101,100)
8-25-43	All-Stars 27, Washington 7 (48,471)
8-30-44	Chicago Bears 24, All-Stars 21 (48,769)
8-30-45	Green Bay 19, All-Stars 7 (92,753)
8-23-46	All-Stars 16, Los Angeles 0 (97,380)
8-22-47	All-Stars 16, Chicago Bears 0 (105,840)
8-20-48	Chicago Cardinals 28, All-Stars 0 (101,220)
8-12-49	Philadelphia 38, All-Stars 0 (93,780)
8-11-50	All-Stars 17, Philadelphia 7 (88,885)
8-17-51	Cleveland 33, All-Stars 0 (92,180)
8-15-52	Los Angeles 10, All-Stars 7 (88,316)
8-14-53	Detroit 24, All-Stars 10 (93,818)
8-13-54	Detroit 31, All-Stars 6 (93,470)
8-12-55	All-Stars 30, Cleveland 27 (75,000)
8-10-56	Cleveland 26, All-Stars 0 (75,000)
8-9-57	New York Giants 22, All-Stars 12 (75,000)
8-15-58	All-Stars 35, Detroit 19 (70,000)
8-14-59	Baltimore 29, All-Stars 0 (70,000)
8-12-60	Baltimore 32, All-Stars 7 (70,000)
8-4-61	Philadelphia 28, All-Stars 14 (66,000)
8-3-62	Green Bay 42, All-Stars 20 (65,000)
8-2-63	All-Stars 20, Green Bay 17 (65,000)
8-7-64	Chicago Bears 28, All-Stars 17 (65,000)
8-6-65	Cleveland 24, All-Stars 16 (68,000)
8-5-66	Green Bay 38, All-Stars 0 (72,000)
8-4-67	Green Bay 27, All-Stars 0 (70,934)
8-2-68	Green Bay 34, All-Stars 17 (69,917)
8-1-69	New York Jets 26, All-Stars 24 (74,208)
7-31-70	Kansas City 24, All-Stars 3 (69,940)
7-30-71	Baltimore 24, All-Stars 17 (52,289)
7-28-72	Dallas 20, All-Stars 7 (54,162)
7-27-73	Miami 14, All-Stars 3 (54,103)
1974	No game played
8-1-75	Pittsburgh 21, All-Stars 14 (54,103)
7-23-76	*Pittsburgh 24, All-Stars 0 (52,895)

**Game was not completed due to thunderstorms.*

CHRISTIAN BOWL (1955)
(Murfreesboro, Tenn.)

Date	Score (Attendance)
12-26-55	East 21, West 10 (4,000)

COACHES ALL-AMERICAN GAME (1961-76)

Date	Score (Attendance)
at Buffalo, N.Y.	
6-23-61	West 30, East 20 (12,913)
6-29-62	East 13, West 8 (22,759)
6-29-63	West 22, East 21 (20,840)
6-27-64	East 18, West 15 (21,112)
6-26-65	East 34, West 14 (25,501)
at Atlanta, Ga.	
7-9-66	West 24, East 7 (38,236)
7-9-67	East 12, West 9 (29,145)
6-28-68	West 34, East 20 (21,120)
6-28-69	West 14, East 10 (17,008)
at Lubbock, Texas	
6-28-70	East 34, West 27 (42,150)
6-26-71	West 33, East 28 (43,320)
6-24-72	East 42, West 20 (42,314)
6-23-73	West 20, East 6 (43,272)
6-22-74	West 36, East 6 (42,368)
6-21-75	East 23, West 21 (36,108)
6-19-76	West 35, East 17 (36,504)

COPPER BOWL (1958-60)
(Tempe, Ariz.)

Date	Score (Attendance)
12-20-58	Southwest All-Stars 22, National All-Stars 13 (12,000)
12-26-59	National All-Stars 21, Southwest All-Stars 6 (16,000)
12-31-60	National All-Stars 27, Southwest All-Stars 8 (8,000)

CRUSADE BOWL (1963)
(Baltimore, Md.)

Date	Score (Attendance)
1-6-63	East 38, West 10 (2,400)

DALLAS ALL-STAR GAME (1936-39)
(Dallas, Texas)

Date	Score
9-7-36	Southwest All-Stars 7, Chicago Bears 6
9-6-37	Southwest All-Stars 6, Chicago Bears 0
9-5-38	Southwest All-Stars 13, Washington Redskins 7
9-4-39	Green Bay Packers 31, Southwest All-Stars 20

DIXIE CLASSIC (1928-31)
(Dallas, Texas)

Date	Score (Attendance)
12-29-28	Southwest Conference 14, Small Texas Schools 6
1-1-29	Big Six Conference 14, Southwest Conference 6 (10,000)
1-1-30	Midwest 25, Southwest Conference 12 (15,000)
1-1-31	Southwest Conference 18, Midwest 0 (14,000)

EAST-WEST BLACK ALL-STAR GAME (1971)
(Houston, Texas)

Date	Score (Attendance)
12-11-71	East 19, West 10 (5,156)

EAST-WEST COLLEGE ALL-STAR GAME (1932)

(Demonstrated at Tenth Olympiad, Los Angeles, Calif.; East team composed of players from Harvard, Princeton and Yale, West team composed of players from California, Southern Cal and Stanford)

Date	Score (Attendance)
8-8-32	West 7, East 6 (50,000)

FREEDOM BOWL ALL-STAR CLASSIC (1984-86)
(Atlanta, Ga.)

Southwestern Athletic Conference vs. Mid-Eastern Athletic Conference.

Date	Score (Attendance)
1-14-84	SWAC 36, MEAC 22 (16,097)
1-12-85	SWAC 14, MEAC 0 (18,352)
1-11-86	SWAC 16, MEAC 14 (10,200)

FREEDOM BOWL ALL-STAR CLASSIC (1990)
(Houston, Texas)

Date	Score
1-13-90	North 14, South 13

FREEDOM CLASSIC (1976)

Year	Score (Attendance)
1976	West 12, East 9 (6,654)

JAPAN BOWL
(Yokohama, Japan)

Date	Score (Attendance)
1-18-76	West 27-18 (68,000)
1-16-77	West 21-10 (58,000)
1-15-78	East 26-10 (32,500)
1-14-79	East 33-14 (55,000)
1-13-80	West 28-17 (27,000)
1-17-81	West 25-13 (30,000)
1-16-82	West 28-17 (28,000)
1-23-83	West 30-21 (30,000)
1-15-84	West 26-21 (26,000)
1-13-85	West 28-14 (30,000)
1-11-86	East 31-14 (30,000)
1-11-87	West 24-17 (30,000)
1-10-88	West 17-3 (30,000)
1-15-89	East 30-7 (29,000)
1-13-90	East 24-10 (27,000)
1-12-91	West 20-14 (30,000)
1-11-92	East 14-13 (50,000)
1-9-93	East 27-13 (46,000)

LOS ANGELES ALL-STAR GAME (1948)
(Los Angeles, Calif.)

Date	Score
1-18-48	West 34, East 20

MARTIN LUTHER KING ALL-AMERICA CLASSIC (1990-91)
(Division I-A vs. all other divisions)

Date	Score (Attendance)
1-15-90	All Div. All-Stars 35, I-A All-Stars 24 (350) (at San Jose, Calif.)
1-14-91	I-A All-Stars 21, All Div. All-Stars 14 (6,272) (at St. Petersburg, Fla.)

NORTH-SOUTH ALL-STAR SHRINE GAME (1930-34, 1948-73, 1976)

Date	Score (Attendance)
1-1-30	North 21, South 12 (20,000) (at Atlanta, Ga.) (Southern Conference All-Star Game)
12-28-30	South 7, North 0 (2,000) (at New York, N.Y.)
12-10-32	South 7, North 6 (500) (at Baltimore, Md.)
12-24-33	North 3, South 0 (5,000) (at New York, N.Y.)
1-1-34	North 7, South 0 (12,000) (at Knoxville, Tenn.) (Southeastern Conference All-Star Game)
at Miami, Fla.	
12-25-48	South 24, North 14 (33,056)
12-25-49	North 20, South 14 (37,378)
12-25-50	South 14, North 9 (39,132)
12-25-51	South 35, North 7 (39,995)
12-25-52	North 21, South 21 (42,866)
12-25-53	South 20, North 0 (44,715)
12-25-54	South 20, North 17 (37,847)
12-26-55	South 20, North 7 (42,179)
12-26-56	North 17, South 7 (39,181)
12-25-57	North 23, South 20 (28,303)
12-27-58	South 49, North 20 (35,519)
12-26-59	North 27, South 17 (35,185)
12-26-60	North 41, South 14 (26,146)
12-25-61	South 35, North 16 (18,892)
12-22-62	South 15, North 14 (16,952)
12-21-63	South 23, North 14 (19,120)
12-25-64	North 37, South 30 (29,124)
12-25-65	South 21, North 14 (25,640)
12-26-66	North 27, South 14 (28,569)
12-25-67	North 24, South 0 (17,400)
12-25-68	North 3, South 0 (18,063)
12-25-69	North 31, South 10 (23,527)
12-25-70	North 28, South 7 (15,402)
12-27-71	South 7, North 6 (18,640)
12-25-72	North 17, South 10 (18,013)
12-25-73	South 27, North 6 (10,672)

at Pontiac, Mich.

Date	Score
12-17-76	South 24, North 0 (41,627)

OHIO SHRINE BOWL (1972-76)
(Columbus, Ohio)

Date	Score
12-9-72	East 20, West 7
12-1-73	East 8, West 6
12-7-74	East 27, West 6
1975	West 17, East 7
12-4-76	East 24, West 8 (played elsewhere)

OLYMPIA GOLD BOWL (1982)
(San Diego, Calif.)

Date	Score (Attendance)
1-16-82	National All-Stars 30, American All-Stars 21 (22,316)

OLYMPIC GAME (1933)
(Chicago, Ill.)

Date	Score (Attendance)
8-24-33	East 13, West 7 (50,000)

OPTIMIST ALL-AMERICA BOWL (1958-62)
(Tucson, Ariz.)

Date	Score (Attendance)
1-4-58	College All-Stars 56, Tucson Cowboys 28
1-3-59	Major-College 14, Small-College 12 (10,000)
1-2-60	Major College 53, Small-College 0 (14,500)
12-26-60	Major-College 25, Small-College 12
12-30-61	Major-College 31, Small-College 0 (14,000)
12-29-62	Small-College 14, Major-College 13

POTATO BOWL (1967)
(Bakersfield, Calif.)

Date	Score (Attendance)
12-23-67	North 23, South 7 (5,600)

ROCKY MOUNTAIN CONFERENCE-NORTH CENTRAL CONFERENCE GAME (1930)
(Elks Charity Bowl)
(Denver, Colo.)

Date	Score
1-1-30	North Central 13, Rocky Mountain 6

SALAD BOWL ALL-STAR GAME (1955)
(Phoenix, Ariz.)

Date	Score (Attendance)
1-1-55	Skyline Conference 20, Border Conference 13 (8,000)
12-31-55	Border Conference 13, Skyline Conference 10

SHERIDAN BLACK ALL-STAR GAME (1979-82)
(See Black College All-Star Bowl)

SMOKE BOWL (1941)
(Richmond, Va.)

Date	Score (Attendance)
1-1-41	Norfolk All-Stars 16, Richmond All-Stars 2 (5,000)

SOUTHWEST CHALLENGE BOWL (1963-64)
(Corpus Christi, Texas)

Date	Score (Attendance)
1-5-63	National 33, Southwest 13
1-4-64	National 66, Southwest 14 (10,200)

U.S. BOWL (1962)
(Washington, D. C.)
(Teams were composed of players selected in the recent NFL draft)

Date	Score
1-7-62	West 33, East 19

Special Regular-Season Games

REGULAR-SEASON GAMES PLAYED IN USA

EDDIE ROBINSON CLASSIC
Present Site: Lincoln, Neb.
Stadium (Capacity): Memorial (72,700)
Playing Surface: AstroTurf-8
Playing Sites: Memorial Stadium (1998)

Date	Teams
8-29-98	Louisiana Tech vs. Nebraska

BCA CLASSIC
Present Site: East Lansing, Mich.
Stadium (Capacity): Spartan (72,027)
Playing Surface: Artificial Turf
Sponsor: Black Coaches' Association
Playing Site: Spartan Stadium (1998)

Date	Teams
8-29-98	Colorado St. vs. Michigan St.

KICKOFF CLASSIC
Present Site: East Rutherford, N.J.
Stadium (Capacity): Giants Stadium (76,000)
Playing Surface: AstroTurf
Sponsor: National Association of Collegiate Directors of Athletics (NACDA). It is a permitted 12th regular-season game.
Playing Sites: Giants Stadium (since 1983)

Date	Teams, Score (Attendance)
8-29-83	Nebraska 44, Penn St. 6 (71,123)
8-27-84	Miami (Fla.) 20, Auburn 18 (51,131)
8-29-85	Brigham Young 28, Boston College 14 (51,227)
8-27-86	Alabama 16, Ohio St. 10 (68,296)
8-30-87	Tennessee 23, Iowa 22 (54,681)
8-27-88	Nebraska 23, Texas A&M 14 (58,172)
8-31-89	Notre Dame 36, Virginia 13 (77,323)
8-31-90	Southern Cal 34, Syracuse 16 (57,293)
8-28-91	Penn St. 34, Georgia Tech 22 (77,409)
8-29-92	North Caro. St. 24, Iowa 14 (46,251)
8-28-93	Florida St. 42, Kansas 0 (51,734)
8-28-94	Nebraska 31, West Va. 0 (58,233)
8-27-95	Ohio St. 38, Boston College 6 (62,711)
8-25-96	Penn St. 24, Southern Cal 7 (77,716)
8-24-97	Syracuse 34, Wisconsin) (51,185)
8-31-98	Florida St. vs. Texas A&M

PIGSKIN CLASSIC
Present Site: Los Angeles, Cal.
Stadium (Capacity): L. A. Memorial Coliseum (92,000)
Playing Surface: Grass
Sponsor: None. It is a permitted 12th regular-season game.
Playing Sites: Anaheim Stadium (1990-94); Michigan Stadium (1995); Cougar Stadium (1996); Soldier Field (1997); L. A. Memorial Coliseum (1998)

Date	Teams, Score (Attendance)
8-26-90	Colorado 31, Tennessee 31 (33,458)
8-29-91	Florida St. 44, Brigham Young 28 (38,363)
8-26-92	Texas A&M 10, Stanford 7 (35,240)
8-29-93	North Caro. 31, Southern Cal 9 (49,309)
8-29-94	Ohio St. 34, Fresno St. 10 (28,513)
8-26-95	Michigan 18, Virginia 17 (101,444)
8-24-96	Brigham Young 41, Texas A&M 37 (55,229)
8-23-97	Northwestern 24, Oklahoma 0 (36,804)
8-30-98	Purdue vs. Southern Cal

BIG 12 CONFERENCE CHAMPIONSHIP
Present Site: San Antonio, Tex.
Stadium (Capacity): Alamodome (65,000)
Playing Surface: AstroTurf
Playing Sites: Trans World Dome, St. Louis, Mo. (1996); Alamodome, San Antonio, Tex. (since 1997)

Date	Teams, Score (Attendance)
12-7-96	Texas (South Div.) 37, Nebraska (North Div.) 27 (63,109)
12-6-97	Nebraska (North Div.) 54, Texas A&M (South Div.) 15 (64,824)

MID-AMERICAN CONFERENCE CHAMPIONSHIP
Present Site: Huntington, W. Va.
Stadium (Capacity): Marshall University (30,000)
Playing Surface: Poly Turf
Playing Sites: Marshall University Stadium (1997)

Date	Teams Score (Attendance)
12-5-97	Marshall (East Div.) 34, Toledo (West Div.) 14 (28,021)
	Nebraska (North Div.) 54, Texas A&M (South Div.) 15, (64,824)

SOUTHEASTERN CONFERENCE CHAMPIONSHIP
Present Site: Atlanta, Ga.
Stadium (Capacity): Georgia Dome (71,228)
Playing Surface: AstroTurf
Playing Sites: Legion Field (1992-93); Georgia Dome (since 1994)

Date	Teams, Score (Attendance)
12-5-92	Alabama (Western Div.) 28, Florida (Eastern Div.) 21 (83,091) (at Birmingham, Ala.)
12-4-93	Florida (Eastern Div.) 28, Alabama (Western Div.) 13 (76,345) (at Birmingham, Ala.)
12-3-94	Florida (Eastern Div.) 24, Alabama (Western Div.) 23 (74,751)
12-2-95	Florida (Eastern Div.) 34, Arkansas (Western Div.) 3 (71,325)
12-7-96	Florida (Eastern Div.) 45, Alabama (Western Div.) 30 (74,132)
12-6-97	Tennessee (Eastern Div.) 30, Auburn (Western Div.) 29 (74,896)

WESTERN ATHLETIC CONFERENCE CHAMPIONSHIP
Present Site: Las Vegas, Nev.
Stadium (Capacity): Sam Boyd (32,000)
Playing Surface: Monsanto Turf
Playing Sites: Sam Boyd Stadium, Las Vegas, Nev. (since 1996)

Date	Teams, Score (Attendance)
12-7-96	Brigham Young (Mountain Div.) 28, Wyoming (Pacific Div.) 25 (41,238)
12-6-97	Colorado St. (Pacific Div.) 41, New Mexico (Mountain Div.) 13 (12,706)

REGULAR-SEASON GAMES PLAYED IN FOREIGN COUNTRIES

TOKYO, JAPAN
(Called Mirage Bowl 1976-85, Coca-Cola Classic from 1986. Played at Tokyo Olympic Memorial Stadium 1976-87, Tokyo Dome from 1988-93.)

Date	Teams, Score (Attendance)
9-4-76	Grambling 42, Morgan St. 16 (50,000)
12-11-77	Grambling 35, Temple 32 (50,000)
12-10-78	Temple 28, Boston College 24 (55,000)
11-24-79	Notre Dame 40, Miami (Fla.) 15 (62,574)
11-30-80	UCLA 34, Oregon St. 3 (86,000)
11-28-81	Air Force 21, San Diego St. 16 (80,000)
11-27-82	Clemson 21, Wake Forest 17 (64,700)
11-26-83	Southern Methodist 34, Houston 12 (70,000)
11-17-84	Army 45, Montana 31 (60,000)
11-30-85	Southern Cal 20, Oregon 6 (65,000)
11-30-86	Stanford 29, Arizona 24 (55,000)
11-28-87	California 17, Washington St. 17 (45,000)
12-3-88	Oklahoma St. 45, Texas Tech 42 (56,000)
12-4-89	Syracuse 24, Louisville 13 (50,000)
12-2-90	Houston 62, Arizona St. 45 (50,000)
11-30-91	Clemson 33, Duke 21 (50,000)
12-6-92	Nebraska 38, Kansas St. 24 (50,000)
12-5-93	Wisconsin 41, Michigan St. 20 (51,500)

MELBOURNE, AUSTRALIA

Date	Teams, Score (Attendance)
12-6-85*	Wyoming 24, UTEP 21 (22,000)
12-4-87†	Brigham Young 30, Colorado St. 26 (76,652)

**Played at V.F.L. Park. †Played at Princes Park.*

YOKOHAMA, JAPAN

Date	Teams, Score (Attendance)
12-2-78	Brigham Young 28, UNLV 24 (27,500)

OSAKA, JAPAN

Date	Teams, Score (Attendance)
9-3-78	Utah St. 10, Idaho St. 0 (15,000)

DUBLIN, IRELAND
#(Called Emerald Isle Classic. Played at Lansdowne Road Stadium.) ¢Played at Croke Park.

Date	Teams, Score (Attendance)
11-19-88	Boston College 38, Army 24 (45,525)#
12-2-89	Pittsburgh 46, Rutgers 29 (19,800)#
11-2-96	Notre Dame 54, Navy 27 (38,651)¢

LONDON, ENGLAND

Date	Teams, Score (Attendance)
10-16-88	Richmond 20, Boston U. 17 (6,000)

MILAN, ITALY
(Played at The Arena.)

Date	Teams, Score (Attendance)
10-28-89	Villanova 28, Rhode Island 25 (5,000)

LIMERICK, IRELAND
(Wild Geese Classic. Played at Limerick Gaelic Grounds.)

Date	Teams, Score (Attendance)
11-16-91	Holy Cross 24, Fordham 19 (17,411)

FRANKFURT, GERMANY
(Played at Wald Stadium.)

Date	Teams, Score (Attendance)
9-19-92	Heidelberg 7, Otterbein 7 (4,351)

GALWAY, IRELAND
(Called Christopher Columbus Classic.)

Date	Teams, Score (Attendance)
11-29-92	Bowdoin 7, Tufts 6 (2,500)

HAMILTON, BERMUDA
(Played at Bermuda National Soccer Stadium.)

Date	Teams, Score (Attendance)
11-20-93	Georgetown 17, Wash. & Lee 14 (3,218)
11-19-94	Davidson 28, Sewanee 14 (2,000)
10-28-95	Fordham 17, Holy Cross 10 (2,436)

EXHIBITION GAMES PLAYED IN FOREIGN COUNTRIES

(Games involving an active NCAA member versus a team from another country. Not counted as a regular-season game.)

KYOTO, JAPAN
(Played at Nishi Kyogoku Stadium)

Date	Teams, Score (Attendance)
3-29-97	Harvard 42, Kyoto 35 (16,000)

COLLEGE FOOTBALL TROPHY GAMES

Following is a list of the current college football trophy games. The games are listed alphabetically by the trophy-object name. The date refers to the season the trophy was first exchanged and is not necessarily the start of competition between the participants. A game involving interdivision teams is listed in the higher-division classification.

DIVISION I-A

Trophy	Date	Colleges
Anniversary Award	1985	Bowling Green-Kent
Apple Cup	1962	Washington-Washington St.
Axe	1933	California-Stanford
Bayou Bucket	1974	Houston-Rice
Beehive Boot	1971	Brigham Young, Utah, Weber St.
Beer Barrel	1925	Kentucky-Tennessee
Bell	1927	Missouri-Nebraska
Bell Clapper	1931	Oklahoma-Oklahoma St.
Big Game	1979	Arizona-Arizona St.
Blue Key Victory Bell	1940	Ball St.-Indiana St.
Bourbon Barrel	1967	Indiana-Kentucky
Brass Spittoon	1950	Indiana-Michigan St.
Brass Spittoon	1981	New Mexico St.-UTEP
Bronze Boot	1968	Colorado St.-Wyoming
Cannon	1943	Illinois-Purdue
Commander in Chief's	1972	Air Force, Army, Navy
Cy-Hawk	1977	Iowa-Iowa St.
Floyd of Rosedale	1935	Iowa-Minnesota
Foy-O.D.K.	1948	Alabama-Auburn
Fremont Cannon	1970	Nevada-UNLV
Golden Egg	1927	Mississippi-Mississippi St.
Golden Hat	1941	Oklahoma-Texas
Governor's	1969	Kansas-Kansas St.
Governor's Cup	1958	Florida-Florida St.
Governor's Cup	1983	Colorado-Colorado St.
Governor's Flag*	1953	Arizona-Arizona St.
Governor's Victory Bell	1993	Minnesota-Penn St.
Illibuck	1925	Illinois-Ohio St.
Indian War Drum	1935	Kansas-Missouri
Iron Bowl	1983	Alabama-Auburn
Keg of Nails	1950	Cincinnati-Louisville
Kit Carson Rifle	1938	Arizona-New Mexico
Land Grant Trophy	1993	Michigan St.-Penn St.
Little Brown Jug	1909	Michigan-Minnesota
Mayor's Cup	1981	Bethune-Cookman—Central Fla.
Megaphone	1949	Michigan St.-Notre Dame
Old Oaken Bucket	1925	Indiana-Purdue
Old Wagon Wheel	1948	Brigham Young-Utah St.
Paniolo Trophy	1979	Hawaii-Wyoming
Paul Bunyan Axe	1948	Minnesota-Wisconsin
Paul Bunyan-Governor of Michigan	1953	Michigan-Michigan St.
Peace Pipe	1929	Missouri-Oklahoma
Peace Pipe	1955	Miami (Ohio)-Western Mich.
Peace Pipe	1980	Bowling Green-Toledo
Ram-Falcon	1980	Air Force-Colorado St.
Sabine Shoe	1937	Lamar-Southwestern La.
Shillelagh	1952	Notre Dame-Southern Cal
Shillelagh	1958	Notre Dame-Purdue
Silver Spade	1955	New Mexico St.-UTEP
Steel Tire	1976	Akron-Youngstown St.
Telephone	1960	Iowa St.-Missouri
Textile Bowl	1981	Clemson-North Caro. St.
Tomahawk	1945	Illinois-Northwestern
Victory Bell	1942	Southern Cal-UCLA
Victory Bell	1948	Cincinnati-Miami (Ohio)
Victory Bell	1948	Duke-North Caro.
Wagon Wheel	1946	Akron-Kent

DIVISION I-AA

Trophy	Date	Colleges
Bill Knight	1986	Massachusetts-New Hampshire
Brice-Colwell Musket	1946	Maine-New Hampshire
Chief Caddo	1962	Northwestern St.-Stephen F. Austin
Field Cup	1983	Evansville-Ky. Wesleyan
Gem State	1978	Boise St., Idaho, Idaho St.
Governor's	1979	Central Conn. St.-Southern Conn. St.
Governor's Cup	1972	Brown-Rhode Island
Governor's Cup	1975	Dartmouth-Princeton
Governor's Cup	1984	Eastern Wash.-Idaho
Grizzly-Bobcat Painting	1984	Montana-Montana St.
Harvey—Shin-A-Ninny Totem Pole	1961	Middle Tenn. St.-Tennessee Tech
Little Brown Stein	1938	Idaho-Montana
Mare's	1987	Murray St.—Tenn.-Martin
Ol' Mountain Jug	1937	Appalachian St.-Western Caro.
Ol' School Bell	1988	Jacksonville St.-Troy St.
Red Belt	1978	Murray St.-Western Ky.
Ron Rogerson Memorial	1988	Maine-Rhode Island
Silver Shako	1976	Citadel-VMI
Team of Game's MVP	1960	Lafayette-Lehigh
Top Dog	1971	Butler-Indianapolis
Victory Carriage	1960	UC Davis-Cal St. Sacramento

DIVISION II

Trophy	Date	Colleges
Axe	1946	Cal St. Chico-Humboldt St.
Axe Bowl	1975	Northwood-Saginaw Valley
Backyard Bowl	1987	Cheyney-West Chester
Battle Axe	1948	Bemidji St.-Moorhead St.
Battle of the Ravine	1976	Henderson St.-Ouachita Baptist
Bishop's	1970	Lenoir-Rhyne—Newberry
Bronze Derby	1946	Newberry-Presbyterian
Eagle-Rock	1980	Black Hills St.-Chadron St.
East Meets West	1987	Chadron St.-Peru St.
Elm City	1983	New Haven-Southern Conn. St.
Field Cup	1983	Ky. Wesleyan-Evansville
Governor's	1979	Southern Conn. St.-Central Conn. St.
Heritage Bell	1979	Delta St.-Mississippi Col.
John Wesley	1984	Ky. Wesleyan-Union (Ky.)
KTEN Savage-Tiger	1979	East Central-Southeastern Okla.
Miner's Bowl	1986	Mo. Southern St.-Pittsburg St.
Nickel	1938	North Dak.-North Dak. St.
Old Hickory Stick	1931	Northwest Mo. St.-Truman St.
Old Settler's Musket	1975	Adams St.-Fort Lewis
Sitting Bull	1953	North Dak.-South Dak.
Springfield Mayor's	1941	American Int'l-Springfield
Textile	1960	Clark Atlanta-Fort Valley St.
Top Dog	1971	Indianapolis-Butler
Traveling	1976	Ashland-Hillsdale
Traveling Training Kit	1978	Mankato St.-St. Cloud St.
Victory Carriage	1960	UC Davis-Cal St. Sacramento
Wagon Wheel	1986	Eastern N.M.-West Tex. A&M
Wooden Shoes	1977	Grand Valley St.-Wayne St. (Mich.)

DIVISION III

Trophy	Date	Colleges
Academic Bowl	1986	Carnegie Mellon-Case Reserve
Admiral's Cup	1980	Maine Maritime-Mass. Maritime
Baird Bros. Golden Stringer	1984	Case Reserve-Wooster
Baptist Bible Bowl	1982	Maranatha Baptist-Pillsbury
Bell	†1931	Franklin-Hanover
Bill Edwards Trophy	1989	Case Reserve-Wittenberg
Bridge Bowl	1990	Mt. St. Joseph-Thomas More
Bronze Turkey	1929	Knox-Monmouth (Ill.)
CBB	1966	Bates, Bowdoin, Colby
Conestoga Wagon	1963	Dickinson-Frank. & Marsh.
Cortaca Jug	1959	Cortland St.-Ithaca
Cranberry Bowl	1979	Bri'water (Mass.)-Mass. Maritime
Doehling-Heselton Helmet	1988	Lawrence-Ripon
Drum	1940	Occidental—Pomona-Pitzer
Dutchman's Shoes	1950	Rensselaer-Union (N.Y.)
Edmund Orgill	1954	Rhodes-Sewanee
Founder's	1987	Chicago-Washington (Mo.)
Goal Post	1953	Juniata-Susquehanna
Goat	1931	Carleton-St. Olaf
Keystone Cup	1981	Delaware Valley-Widener
Little Brass Bell	1947	North Central-Wheaton (Ill.)
Little Brown Bucket	1938	Dickinson-Gettysburg
Little Three	1971	Amherst, Wesleyan (Conn.), Williams
Mercer County Cup	1984	Grove City-Thiel
Monon Bell	1932	DePauw-Wabash
Mug	1931	Coast Guard-Norwich
Old Goal Post	1953	Juniata-Susquehanna
Old Musket	1964	Carroll (Wis.)-Carthage

Trophy	Date	Colleges
Old Rocking Chair	1980	Hamilton-Middlebury
Old Tin Cup	1954	Gettysburg-Muhlenberg
Old Water Bucket	1989	Maranatha Baptist-Martin Luther
Paint Bucket	1965	Hamline-Macalester
Pella Corporation Classic	1988	Central (Iowa)-William Penn
President's Cup	1971	Case Reserve-John Carroll
Secretary's Cup	1981	Coast Guard-Merchant Marine
Shoes	1946	Occidental-Whittier
Shot Glass	1938	Coast Guard-Rensselaer
Stagg Hat Trophy	1993	Susquehanna-Lycoming
Steve Dean Memorial	1976	Catholic-Georgetown
Transit	1980	Rensselaer-Worcester Tech
Victory Bell	1946	Loras-St. Thomas (Minn.)
Victory Bell	1949	Upper Iowa-Wartburg
Wadsworth	1977	Middlebury-Norwich
Wilson Brothers Cup	1986	Hamline-St. Thomas (Minn.)
Wooden Shoes	1946	Hope-Kalamazoo

NON-NCAA MEMBERS

Trophy	Date	Colleges
Home Stake-Gold Mine	1950	Black Hills St.-South Dak. Tech
Paint Bucket	1961	Jamestown-Valley City St.
Wagon Wheel	1957	Lewis & Clark-Willamette

**Changed to Big Game Trophy. †Was reinstated in 1988 after a 17-year lapse.*

Coaching Records

All-Division Coaching Records

Coaches With Career Winning Percentage of .800 or Better

This list includes all coaches in history with a winning percentage of at least .800 over a career of at least 10 seasons at four-year colleges (regardless of division or association). Bowl and playoff games included.

Coach (Alma Mater) (Colleges Coached, Tenure)	Years	Won	Lost	Tied	Pct.
Knute Rockne (Notre Dame '14) (Notre Dame 1918-30)	13	105	12	5	.881
#Larry Kehres (Mount Union '71) (Mount Union 1986—)	†12	124	16	3	.878
Frank Leahy (Notre Dame '31) (Boston College 1939-40; Notre Dame 1941-43, 1946-53)	13	107	13	9	.864
Bob Reade (Cornell College '54) (Augustana [Ill.] 1979-94)	†16	146	23	1	.862
Doyt Perry (Bowling Green '32) (Bowling Green 1955-64)	†10	77	11	5	.855
#Mike Kelly (Manchester '70) (Dayton 1981—)	†17	165	28	1	.853
#Dick Farley (Boston U. '68) (Williams 1987—)	†11	73	12	3	.847
George Woodruff (Yale '89) (Pennsylvania 1892-1901; Illinois 1903; Carlisle 1905)	12	142	25	2	.846
Jake Gaither (Knoxville '27) (Florida A&M 1945-69)	†25	203	36	4	.844
Dave Maurer (Denison '54) (Wittenberg 1969-83)	†15	129	23	3	.842
Paul Hoereman (Heidelberg '38) (Heidelberg 1946-59)	†14	102	18	4	.839
Barry Switzer (Arkansas '60) (Oklahoma 1973-88)	16	157	29	4	.837
Tom Osborne (Hastings '59) (Nebraska 1973-97)	25	255	49	3	.836
Don Coryell (Washington '50) (Whittier 1957-59; San Diego St. 1961-72)	†15	127	24	3	.834
Percy Haughton (Harvard '99) (Cornell 1899-1900; Harvard 1908-16; Columbia 1923-24)	13	96	17	6	.832
Bob Neyland (Army '16) (Tennessee 1926-34, 1936-40, 1946-52)	21	173	31	12	.829
Fielding Yost (Lafayette '97) (Ohio Wesleyan 1897; Nebraska 1898; Kansas 1899; Stanford 1900; Michigan 1901-23, 1925-26)	29	196	36	12	.828
Bud Wilkinson (Minnesota '37) (Oklahoma 1947-63)	17	145	29	4	.826
Chuck Klausing (Slippery Rock '48) (Indiana [Pa.] 1964-69; Carnegie Mellon 1976-85)	†16	123	26	2	.821
Vernon McCain (Langston '31) (Md.-East. Shore 1948-63)	†16	102	21	5	.816
Jock Sutherland (Pittsburgh '18) (Lafayette 1919-23; Pittsburgh 1924-38)	20	144	28	14	.812
Ron Schipper (Hope '52) (Central [Iowa] 1961-96)	†36	287	67	3	.808
Bob Devaney (Alma '39) (Wyoming 1957-61; Nebraska 1962-72)	16	136	30	7	.806
Biggie Munn (Minnesota '32) (Albright 1935-36; Syracuse 1946; Michigan St. 1947-53)	10	71	16	3	.805
Sid Gillman (Ohio St. '34) (Miami [Ohio] 1944-47; Cincinnati 1949-54)	†10	81	19	2	.804

†Zero to nine years in Division I-A. #Active coach.

Coaches With 200 or More Career Victories

This list includes all coaches who have won at least 200 games at four-year colleges (regardless of classification or association). Bowl and playoff games included.

Coach (Alma Mater) (Colleges Coached, Tenure)	Years	Won	Lost	Tied	Pct.
Eddie Robinson (Leland '41) (Grambling 1941-42, 1945-97)	†55	408	165	15	.707
#John Gagliardi (Colorado Col. '49) (Carroll, Mont. 1949-52; St. John's [Minn.] 1953—)	†49	342	104	11	.760
Bear Bryant (Alabama '36) (Maryland 1945; Kentucky 1946-53; Texas A&M 1954-57; Alabama 1958-82)	38	323	85	17	.780
Pop Warner (Cornell '95) (Georgia 1895-96; Cornell 1897-98; Carlisle 1899-1903; Cornell 1904-06; Carlisle 1907-14; Pittsburgh 1915-23; Stanford 1924-32; Temple 1933-38)	44	319	106	32	.733
Amos Alonzo Stagg (Yale '88) (Springfield 1890-91; Chicago 1892-1932; Pacific [Cal.] 1933-46)	57	314	199	35	.605
#Joe Paterno (Brown '50) (Penn St. 1966—)	32	298	77	3	.792
Ron Schipper (Hope '52) (Central [Iowa] 1961-96)	†36	287	67	3	.808
#Bobby Bowden (Samford '53) (Samford 1959-62; West Va. 1970-75; Florida St. 1976—)	32	281	83	4	.769
#Roy Kidd (Eastern Ky. '54) (Eastern Ky. 1964—)	†34	280	103	8	.726
#Tubby Raymond (Michigan '50) (Delaware 1966—)	†32	270	103	3	.722
Tom Osborne (Hastings '59) (Nebraska 1973-97)	25	255	49	3	.836
#Jim Malosky (Minnesota '51) (Minn.-Duluth 1958—)	†40	255	125	13	.665
#Roger Harring (Wis.-La Crosse '58) (Wis.-La Crosse 1969—)	†29	250	66	7	.785
Woody Hayes (Denison '35) (Denison 1946-48; Miami [Ohio] 1949-50; Ohio St. 1951-78)	33	238	72	10	.759
Bo Schembechler (Miami [Ohio] '51) (Miami, Ohio 1963-68; Michigan 1969-89)	27	234	65	8	.775
Arnett Mumford (Wilberforce '24) (Jarvis 1924-26; Bishop 1927-29; Texas College 1931-35; Southern U. 1936-42, 1944-61)	†36	233	85	23	.717
††John Merritt (Kentucky St. '50) (Jackson St. 1953-62; Tennessee St. 1963-83)	†31	232	65	11	.771
#LaVell Edwards (Utah St. '52) (Brigham Young 1972—)	26	234	86	3	.729
Fred Long (Millikin '18) (Paul Quinn 1921-22; Wiley 1923-47; Prairie View 1948; Texas College 1949-55; Wiley 1956-65)	†45	227	151	31	.593
#Hayden Fry (Baylor '51) (Southern Methodist 1962-72; North Texas 1973-78; Iowa 1979—)	36	229	170	10	.572
Fred Martinelli (Otterbein '51) (Ashland 1959-93)	†35	217	119	12	.641
Lou Holtz (Kent '59) (William & Mary 1969-71; North Caro. St. 1972-75; Arkansas 1977-83; Minnesota 1984-85; Notre Dame 1986-96)	27	216	95	7	.690
Jess Neely (Vanderbilt '24) (Southwestern [Tenn.] 1924-27; Clemson 1931-39; Rice 1940-66)	40	207	176	19	.539
Jim Butterfield (Maine '53) (Ithaca 1967-93)	†27	206	71	1	.743
Jake Gaither (Knoxville '27) (Florida A&M 1945-69)	†25	203	36	4	.844
Warren Woodson (Baylor '24) (Conway St. 1935-40; Hardin-Simmons 1941-42, 1946-51; Arizona 1952-56; New Mexico St. 1958-67; Trinity [Tex.] 1972-73)	31	203	95	14	.673
#Jim Christopherson (Concordia-M'head '60) (Concordia-M'head 1969—)	29	203	86	7	.698
#Ron Harms (Valparaiso '59) (Concordia, Neb. 1964-69; Adams St. 1970-73; Texas A&M-Kingsville 1979—)	29	203	103	4	.661
Vince Dooley (Auburn '54) (Georgia 1964-88)	25	201	77	10	.715
Eddie Anderson (Notre Dame '22) (Loras 1922-24; DePaul 1925-31; Holy Cross 1933-38; Iowa 1939-42, 1946-49; Holy Cross 1950-64)	39	201	128	15	.606
Darrell Mudra (Peru St. '51) (Adams St. 1959-62; North Dak. St. 1963-65; Arizona 1967-68; Western Ill. 1969-73; Florida St. 1974-75; Eastern Ill. 1978-82; Northern Iowa 1983-87)	†26	200	81	4	.709
Jim Sweeney (Portland '51) (Montana St. 1963-67; Washington St. 1968-75; Fresno St. 1976-96)	32	200	154	4	.564

†Zero to nine years in Division I-A. ††Tennessee State's participation in 1981 and 1982 Division I-AA championships (1-2 record) vacated by action of the NCAA Committee on Infractions. #Active coach.

Matchups of Coaches Each With 200 Victories

Date	Coaches, Teams (Victories Going In)	Winner (Score)
11-11-61	Arnett Mumford, Southern U. (232)	
	Fred Long, Wiley (215)	Wiley (21-19)
1-1-78	Bear Bryant, Alabama (272)	Alabama (35-6)
Sugar Bowl	Woody Hayes, Ohio St. (231)	
10-11-80	Eddie Robinson, Grambling (284)	Grambling (52-27)
	John Merritt, Tennessee St. (200)	
10-10-81	Eddie Robinson, Grambling (294)	
	John Merritt, Tennessee St. (209)	Tennessee St. (14-10)
10-9-82	Eddie Robinson, Grambling (301)	
	John Merritt, Tennessee St. (218)	Tennessee St. (22-8)
10-8-83	Eddie Robinson, Grambling (308)	Tie (7-7)
	John Merritt, Tennessee St. (228)	
11-28-87	John Gagliardi, St. John's (Minn.) (251)	
	Ron Schipper, Central (Iowa) (202)	Central (Iowa) (13-3)
11-25-89	John Gagliardi, St. John's (Minn.) (268)	St. John's (Minn.) (27-24)
	Ron Schipper, Central (Iowa) (224)	
12-28-90	Joe Paterno, Penn St. (229)	
Blockbuster Bowl	Bobby Bowden, Florida St. (204)	Florida St. (24-17)
11-27-93	John Gagliardi, St. John's (Minn.) (305)	St. John's (Minn.) (47-25)
	Roger Harring, Wis.-La Crosse (210)	
1-1-94	Bobby Bowden, Florida St. (238)	Florida St. (18-16)
Orange Bowl	Tom Osborne, Nebraska (206)	
9-17-94	Joe Paterno, Penn St. (258)	Penn St. (61-21)
	Hayden Fry, Iowa (202)	
10-21-95	Joe Paterno, Penn St. (273)	Penn St. (41-27)
	Hayden Fry, Iowa (210)	
1-1-96	Bobby Bowden, Florida St. (258)	Florida St. (31-26)
Orange Bowl	Lou Holtz, Notre Dame (208)	
10-19-96	Joe Paterno, Penn St. (284)	
	Hayden Fry, Iowa (217)	Iowa (21-20)
11-17-96	Jim Malosky, Minn.-Duluth (250)	Minn.-Duluth (17-3)
	Roger Harring, Wis.-La Crosse (241)	
11-30-96	John Gagliardi, St. John 's (Minn.) (336)	
	Roger Harring, Wis.-La Crosse (242)	Wis.-La Crosse (37-30)

Coaches With 200 or More Victories at One College

(Bowl and Playoff Games Included)

Coach (College, Tenure)	Years	Won	Lost	Tied	Pct.
Eddie Robinson, Grambling (1941-42, 45-97)	†55	408	165	15	.707
#John Gagliardi, St. John's (Minn.) (1953–)	†45	317	98	10	.758
#Joe Paterno, Penn St. (1966–)	32	298	77	3	.792
Ron Schipper, Central (Iowa) (1961-96)	†36	287	67	3	.808
#Roy Kidd, Eastern Ky. (1964–)	†34	280	103	8	.726
#Tubby Raymond, Delaware (1966–)	†32	270	103	3	.722
Tom Osborne, Nebraska (1973-97)	25	255	49	3	.836
#Jim Malosky, Minn.-Duluth (1958–)	†40	255	125	13	.665
#Roger Harring, Wis.-La Crosse (1969–)	†29	250	66	7	.785
Amos Alonzo Stagg, Chicago (1892-1932)	41	244	111	27	.674
#LaVell Edwards, Brigham Young (1972–)	26	234	86	3	.729
Bear Bryant, Alabama (1958-82)	25	232	46	9	.824
Fred Martinelli, Ashland (1959-93)	†35	217	119	12	.641
#Bobby Bowden, Florida St. (1976–)	22	208	51	4	.798
Jim Butterfield, Ithaca (1967-93)	†27	206	71	1	.743
Woody Hayes, Ohio St. (1951-78)	28	205	61	10	.761
Jake Gaither, Florida A&M (1945-69)	†25	203	36	4	.844
Vince Dooley, Georgia (1964-88)	25	201	77	10	.715

†Zero to nine years in Division I-A. #Active coach.

Division I-A Coaching Records

Winningest Active Division I-A Coaches

(Minimum five years as Division I-A head coach; record at four-year colleges only.)

BY PERCENTAGE

Coach, College	Years	Won	Lost	Tied	†Pct.	Bowls W-L-T
Phillip Fulmer, Tennessee$	6	54	11	0	.83077	4-2-0
Joe Paterno, Penn St.	32	298	77	3	.79233	18-9-1
Steve Spurrier, Florida	11	103	29	2	.77612	4-4-0
Bobby Bowden, Florida St.!	32	281	83	4	.76902	16-4-1
R. C. Slocum, Texas A&M	9	83	25	2	.76364	2-5-0
LaVell Edwards, Brigham Young	26	234	86	3	.72910	7-12-1
Paul Pasqualoni, Syracuse	12	94	39	1	.70522	*4-2-0
Terry Bowden, Auburn	14	110	48	2	.69375	*4-5-0
John Cooper, Ohio St.	21	167	73	6	.69106	4-8-0
Dennis Franchione, Texas Christian	15	113	55	2	.67059	*6-6-0
Jim Lambright, Washington	5	38	19	1	.66379	1-2-0
Gary Pinkel, Toledo	7	50	26	3	.65190	1-0-0
Bill Snyder, Kansas St.	9	66	37	1	.63942	3-2-0
Jackie Sherrill, Mississippi St.$	20	146	82	4	.63793	6-5-0
Fisher DeBerry, Air Force	14	108	63	1	.63081	4-5-0
Gary Blackney, Bowling Green	7	48	29	2	.62025	2-0-0
Sonny Lubick, Colorado St.	9	62	38	0	.62000	1-2-0
Don Nehlen, West Va.	27	183	112	8	.61716	3-8-0
Ken Hatfield, Rice	19	134	84	4	.61261	4-6-0
Joe Tiller, Purdue	7	48	33	1	.59146	1-1-0
Randy Walker, Miami (Ohio)	8	49	34	5	.58523	0-0-0
Ron McBride, Utah	8	55	39	0	.58511	1-3-0
George Welsh, Virginia	25	167	118	4	.58478	5-7-0
Frank Beamer, Virginia Tech	17	110	79	4	.58031	2-4-0
Dick Tomey, Arizona	21	135	97	7	.57950	3-3-0
Hayden Fry, Iowa	36	229	170	10	.57213	7-9-1
Gerry DiNardo, LSU	7	45	34	1	.56875	3-0-0
Ted Tollner, San Diego St.	8	51	41	1	.55376	1-2-0
Jeff Bower, Southern Miss.	8	43	35	1	.55063	1-1-0
Spike Dykes, Texas Tech#	12	69	57	1	.54724	2-4-0
Bruce Snyder, Arizona St.	18	107	89	6	.54455	3-1-0
Larry Smith, Missouri	21	128	107	7	.54339	2-6-1
Barry Alvarez, Wisconsin	8	49	41	4	.54255	3-1-0
Tommy West, Clemson	6	32	27	0	.54237	1-3-0
Mack Brown, North Caro.	14	86	74	1	.53727	3-3-0
Steve Logan, East Caro.	6	36	32	0	.52941	1-1-0
Charlie Weatherbie, Navy	6	36	32	0	.52941	2-0-0
Mike Price, Washington St.	17	99	93	0	.51563	*3-2-0
Bob Toledo, UCLA	8	44	44	0	.50000	1-0-0
Bob Sutton, Army	7	38	39	1	.49359	0-1-0
Mike O'Cain, North Caro. St.	5	28	29	0	.49123	1-1-0
Gary Barnett, Northwestern^	8	41	46	2	.47191	1-1-0
Glen Mason, Minnesota	12	62	73	1	.45956	2-0-0
Nelson Stokley, Southwestern La.	12	60	71	1	.45833	0-0-0
Dave Rader, Tulsa	10	44	67	1	.39732	1-1-0
Fred Goldsmith, Duke	10	38	70	1	.35321	0-1-0
Jeff Horton, UNLV	5	20	37	0	.35088	1-0-0
Watson Brown, UAB	13	47	95	1	.33217	0-0-0
Charlie Bailey, UTEP	8	23	58	2	.28916	0-0-0
Woody Widenhofer, Vanderbilt	5	15	39	1	.28182	0-0-0
Kim Helton, Houston	5	14	41	1	.25893	0-1-0
Jim Caldwell, Wake Forest	5	14	41	0	.25455	0-0-0

Less than five years in Division I-A (school followed by years in I-A, includes record at all four-year colleges):

Coach, College	Years	Won	Lost	Tied	†Pct.	Bowls W-L-T
Jim Donnan, Georgia (2)	8	79	29	0	.73148	*16-4-0
Terry Allen, Kansas (1)	9	80	32	0	.71429	*6-7-0
Bobby Wallace, Temple (0)	10	82	36	1	.69328	*13-3-0
Hal Mumme, Kentucky (1)	9	70	33	1	.67788	*2-2-0
Bill Lynch, Ball St. (3)	8	56	26	3	.67647	*0-2-0
John L. Smith, Louisville (3)	9	69	39	0	.63889	*3-6-0
Houston Nutt, Arkansas (1)	5	35	23	0	.60345	*1-2-0
Mike Cavan, Southern Methodist (0)	12	73	54	2	.57480	*1-1-0
Mike Bellotti, Oregon (3)	8	43	38	2	.53012	1-1-0
Dave Arslanian, Utah St. (0)	9	53	47	0	.53000	*0-1-0
Dave Roberts, Baylor (1)	11	65	59	3	.52362	*2-5-0
Rip Scherer, Memphis (3)	7	40	41	0	.49383	*2-2-0
Gary Darnell, Western Mich. (1)	5	14	36	0	.28000	0-1-0

*†Ties computed as half won and half lost. Overall record includes bowl and playoff games. *Includes record in NCAA and/or NAIA championships. @Win in Gator Bowl in first game. #Loss in Independence Bowl in first game. ! Includes games forfeited by action of NCAA Committee on Infractions. $Includes forfeit victory over Alabama in 1993 by action of NCAA Committee on Infractions. ^Includes forfeit victory over Michigan State by action of NCAA Committee on Infractions.*

BY VICTORIES

(Minimum 100 Victories)

Coach, College, Win Pct.	Won
Joe Paterno, Penn St. (.792)	298
Bobby Bowden, Florida St. (.769)	281
LaVell Edwards, Brigham Young (.729)	234
Hayden Fry, Iowa (.572)	229
Don Nehlen, West Va. (.617)	183
John Cooper, Ohio St. (.691)	167
George Welsh, Virginia (.585)	167
Jackie Sherrill, Miss. St. (638)	146
Dick Tomey, Arizona (.580)	135
Ken Hatfield, Rice (.613)	134
Larry Smith, Missouri (.543)	128
Dennis Franchione, Texas Christian (.671)	113
Terry Bowden, Auburn (.694)	110
Frank Beamer, Virginia Tech (.580)	110
Fisher DeBerry, Air Force (.631)	108
Bruce Snyder, Arizona St. (.545)	107
Steve Spurrier, Florida (.776)	103

Winningest All-Time Division I-A Coaches

Minimum 10 years as head coach at Division I institutions; record at four-year colleges only; bowl games included; ties computed as half won, half lost. Active coaches indicated by (*). College Football Hall of Fame members indicated by (†).

BY PERCENTAGE

Coach (Alma Mater) (Colleges Coached, Tenure)	Years	Won	Lost	Tied	Pct.
Knute Rockne (Notre Dame '14)† (Notre Dame 1918-30)	13	105	12	5	.881
Frank Leahy (Notre Dame '31)† (Boston College 1939-40; Notre Dame 1941-43, 1946-53)	13	107	13	9	.864
George Woodruff (Yale 1889)† (Pennsylvania 1892-01; Illinois 1903; Carlisle 1905)	12	142	25	2	.846
Barry Switzer (Arkansas '60) (Oklahoma 1973-88)	16	157	29	4	.837
Tom Osborne (Hastings '59)† (Nebraska 1973-97)	25	255	49	3	.836
Percy Haughton (Harvard 1899)† (Cornell 1899-00; Harvard 1908-16; Columbia 1923-24)	13	96	17	6	.832
Bob Neyland (Army '16)† (Tennessee 1926-34, 1936-40, 1946-52)	21	173	31	12	.829
Fielding Yost (West Va. 1895)† (Ohio Wesleyan 1897; Nebraska 1898; Kansas 1899; Stanford 1900; Michigan 1901-23, 1925-26)	29	196	36	12	.828
Bud Wilkinson (Minnesota '37)† (Oklahoma 1947-63)	17	145	29	4	.826
Jock Sutherland (Pittsburgh '18)† (Lafayette 1919-23; Pittsburgh 1924-38)	20	144	28	14	.812
Bob Devaney (Alma '39)† (Wyoming 1957-61; Nebraska 1962-72)	16	136	30	7	.806
Frank Thomas (Notre Dame '23)† (Chattanooga 1925-28; Alabama 1931-42, 1944-46)	19	141	33	9	.795
*Joe Paterno (Brown '50) (Penn St. 1966—)	32	298	77	3	.792
Henry Williams (Yale 1891)† (Army 1891; Minnesota 1900-21)	23	141	34	12	.786
Gil Dobie (Minnesota '02)† (North Dak. St. 1906-07; Washington 1908-16; Navy 1917-19; Cornell 1920-35; Boston College 1936-38)	33	180	45	15	.781
Bear Bryant (Alabama '36)† (Maryland 1945; Kentucky 1946-53; Texas A&M 1954-57; Alabama 1958-82)	38	323	85	17	.780
Fred Folsom (Dartmouth 1895) (Colorado 1895-99, 1901-02; Dartmouth 1903-06; Colorado 1908-15)	19	106	28	6	.779
*Steve Spurrier (Florida '67) (Duke 1987-89; Florida 1990—)	11	103	29	2	.776
Bo Schembechler (Miami, Ohio '51)† (Miami, Ohio 1963-68; Michigan 1969-89)	27	234	65	8	.775
*Bobby Bowden (Samford '53)√ (Samford 1959-62; West Va. 1970-75; Florida St. 1976—)	32	281	83	4	.769
Fritz Crisler (Chicago '22)† (Minnesota 1930-31; Princeton 1932-37; Michigan 1938-47)	18	116	32	9	.768
Charley Moran (Tennessee 1898) (Texas A&M 1909-14; Centre 1919-23; Bucknell 1924-26; Catawba 1930-33)	18	122	33	12	.766
Wallace Wade (Brown '17)† (Alabama 1923-30; Duke 1931-41, 1946-50)	24	171	49	10	.765
Frank Kush (Michigan St. '53)† (Arizona St. 1958-79)	22	176	54	1	.764
Dan McGugin (Michigan '04)† (Vanderbilt 1904-17, 1919-34)	30	197	55	19	.762
Jimmy Crowley (Notre Dame '25)# (Michigan St. 1929-32; Fordham 1933-41)	13	78	21	10	.761
Andy Smith (Penn St., Pennsylvania '05)† (Pennsylvania 1909-12; Purdue 1913-15; California 1916-25)	17	116	32	13	.761
Woody Hayes (Denison '35)† (Denison 1946-48; Miami, Ohio 1949-50; Ohio St. 1951-78)	33	238	72	10	.759
Red Blaik (Miami, Ohio '18; Army '20)† (Dartmouth 1934-40; Army 1941-58)	25	166	48	14	.759
Darrell Royal (Oklahoma '50)† (Mississippi St. 1954-55; Washington 1956; Texas 1957-76)	23	184	60	5	.749
John McKay (Oregon '50)† (Southern Cal 1960-75)	16	127	40	8	.749
John Vaught (Texas Christian '33)† (Mississippi 1947-70, 1973)	25	190	61	12	.745
Dan Devine (Minn.-Duluth '48)† (Arizona St. 1955-57; Missouri 1958-70; Notre Dame 1975-80)	22	172	57	9	.742
John Robinson (Oregon '58) (Southern Cal 1976-82, 1993-97)	12	104	35	4	.741
Gus Henderson (Oberlin '12) (Southern Cal 1919-24; Tulsa 1925-35; Occidental 1940-42)	20	126	42	7	.740
Ara Parseghian (Miami, Ohio '49)† (Miami, Ohio 1951-55; Northwestern 1956-63; Notre Dame 1964-74)	24	170	58	6	.739
Elmer Layden (Notre Dame '25)# (Loras 1925-26; Duquesne 1927-33; Notre Dame 1934-40)	16	103	34	11	.733
Pop Warner (Cornell 1895)† (Georgia 1895-96; Cornell 1897-98; Carlisle 1899-1903; Cornell 1904-06; Carlisle 1907-14; Pittsburgh 1915-23; Stanford 1924-32; Temple 1933-38)	44	319	106	32	.733
Howard Jones (Yale '08)† (Syracuse 1908; Yale 1909; Ohio St. 1910; Yale 1913; Iowa 1916-23; Duke 1924; Southern Cal 1925-40)	29	194	64	21	.733
Frank Cavanaugh (Dartmouth 1897)† (Cincinnati 1898; Holy Cross 1903-05; Dartmouth 1911-16; Boston College 1919-26; Fordham 1927-32)	24	145	48	17	.731
*LaVell Edwards (Utah St. '52) (Brigham Young 1972—)	26	234	86	3	.729
Jim Tatum (North Caro. '35)† (North Caro. 1942; Oklahoma 1946; Maryland 1947-55; North Caro. 1956-58)	14	100	35	7	.729
Francis Schmidt (Nebraska '14)† (Tulsa 1919-21; Arkansas 1922-28; Texas Christian 1929-33; Ohio St. 1934-40; Idaho 1941-42)	24	158	57	11	.723
Bill Roper (Princeton '03)† (Va. Military 1903-04; Princeton 1906-08; Missouri 1909; Princeton 1910-11; Swarthmore 1915-16; Princeton 1919-30)	22	112	37	19	.723
Doc Kennedy (Kansas & Pennsylvania '03) (Kansas 1904-10; Haskell 1911-16)	13	85	31	7	.720
Tad Jones (Yale '08)† (Syracuse 1909-10; Yale 1916, 1920-27)	11	66	24	6	.719
Vince Dooley (Auburn '54)† (Georgia 1964-88)	25	201	77	10	.715
Dana Bible (Carson-Newman '12)† (Mississippi Col. 1913-15; LSU 1916; Texas A&M 1917, 1919-28; Nebraska 1929-36; Texas 1937-46)	33	198	72	23	.715
Bobby Dodd (Tennessee '31)†# (Georgia Tech 1945-66)	22	165	64	8	.713
John Heisman (Brown 1890, Pennsylvania 1892)† (Oberlin 1892; Akron 1893; Oberlin 1894; Auburn 1895-99; Clemson 1900-03; Georgia Tech 1904-19; Pennsylvania 1920-22; Wash. & Jeff. 1923; Rice 1924-27)	36	185	70	17	.711
Jumbo Stiehm (Wisconsin '09) (Ripon 1910; Nebraska 1911-15; Indiana 1916-21)	12	59	23	4	.709
Red Sanders (Vanderbilt '27)† (Vanderbilt 1940-42, 1946-48; UCLA 1949-57)	15	102	41	3	.709
Pat Dye (Georgia '62) (East Caro. 1974-79; Wyoming 1980; Auburn 1981-92)	19	153	62	5	.707
Chick Meehan (Syracuse '18) (Syracuse 1920-24; New York U. 1925-31; Manhattan 1932-37)	18	115	44	14	.705
John McEwan (Army '17) (Army 1923-25; Oregon 1926-29; Holy Cross 1930-32)	10	59	23	6	.705
Bennie Owen (Kansas '00)† (Washburn 1900; Bethany, Kan. 1901-04; Oklahoma 1905-26)	27	155	60	19	.703
Ike Armstrong (Drake '23)† (Utah 1925-49)	25	140	55	15	.702
Frank Broyles (Georgia Tech '47)† (Missouri 1957; Arkansas 1958-76)	20	149	62	6	.700
Biff Jones (Army '17)† (Army 1926-29; LSU 1932-34; Oklahoma 1935-36; Nebraska 1937-41)	14	87	33	15	.700

#Member of College Football Hall of Fame as a player. ‡Last game of 1978 season counted as full season. √Includes games forfeited, team and/or individual statistics abrogated, and coaching records changed by action of the NCAA Committee on Infractions.

All-Time Division I-A Coaching Victories

Minimum 10 years as head coach at Division I institutions; record at four-year colleges only; bowl games included. After each coach's name is his alma mater, year graduated, total years coached, won-lost record and percentage, tenure at each college coached, and won-lost record there. Active coaches are denoted by an asterisk (*).

(Minimum 150 Victories)

323 Bear Bryant (Born 9-11-13 Moro Bottoms, Ark.; Died 1-26-83)
Alabama 1936 (38: 323-85-17 .780)
Maryland 1945 (6-2-1); Kentucky 1946-53 (60-23-5); Texas A&M 1954-57 (25-14-2); Alabama 1958-82 (232-46-9)

319 Pop Warner (Born 4-5-1871 Springville, N.Y.; Died 9-7-54)
Cornell 1895 (44: 319-106-32 .733)
Georgia 1895-96 (7-4-0); Cornell 1897-98, 1904-06 (36-13-3); Carlisle 1899-1903, 1907-14 (114-42-8); Pittsburgh 1915-23 (60-12-4); Stanford 1924-32 (71-17-8); Temple 1933-38 (31-18-9)

314 Amos Alonzo Stagg (Born 8-16-1862 West Orange, N.J.; Died 3-17-65)
Yale 1888 (57: 314-199-35 .605)
Springfield 1890-91 (10-11-1); Chicago 1892-1932 (244-111-27); Pacific (Cal.) 1933-46 (60-77-7)

298 *Joe Paterno (Born 12-21-26 Brooklyn, N.Y.)
Brown 1951 (32: 298-77-3 .792)
Penn St. 1966-97 (298-77-3)

281 *Bobby Bowden (Born 11-8-29 Birmingham, Ala.)
Samford 1953 (√32: 281-83-4 .769)
Samford 1959-62 (31-6-0); West Va. 1970-75 (√42-26-0); Florida St. 1976-97 (208-51-4)

255 Tom Osborne (Born 2-23-37 Hastings, Neb.)
Hastings 1959 (25: 255-49-3 .836)
Nebraska 1973-97 (255-49-3)

238 Woody Hayes (Born 2-13-14 Clifton, Ohio; Died 3-12-87)
Denison 1935 (33: 238-72-10 .759)
Denison 1946-48 (19-6-0); Miami (Ohio) 1949-50 (14-5-0); Ohio St. 1951-78 (205-61-10)

234 Bo Schembechler (Born 9-1-29 Barberton, Ohio)
Miami (Ohio) 1951 (27: 234-65-8 .775)
Miami (Ohio) 1963-68 (40-17-3); Michigan 1969-89 (194-48-5)

234 *LaVell Edwards (Born 10-11-30 Provo, Utah)
Utah St. 1952 (26: 234-86-3 .729)
Brigham Young 1972-97 (234-86-3)

229 *Hayden Fry (Born 2-28-29 Odessa, Texas)
Baylor 1951 (√36: 229-120-10 .572)
Southern Methodist 1962-72 (49-66-1); North Texas 1973-78 (√40-23-3); Iowa 1979-97 (139-81-6)

216 Lou Holtz (Born 1-6-37 Follansbee, W.Va.)
Kent 1959 (27: 216-95-7 .690)
William & Mary 1969-71 (13-20-0); North Caro. St. 1972-75 (33-12-3); Arkansas 1977-83 (60-21-2); Minnesota 1984-85 (10-12-0); Notre Dame 1986-96 (100-30-2)

207 Jess Neely (Born 1-4-1898 Smyrna, Tenn.; Died 4-9-83)
Vanderbilt 1924 (40: 207-176-19 .539)
Rhodes 1924-27 (20-17-2); Clemson 1931-39 (43-35-7); Rice 1940-66 (144-124-10)

203 Warren Woodson (Born 2-24-03 Fort Worth, Texas; Died 2-22-98)
Baylor 1924 (31: 203-95-14 .673)
Central Ark. 1935-39 (40-8-3); Hardin-Simmons 1941-42, 1946-51 (58-24-6); Arizona 1952-56 (26-22-2); New Mexico St. 1958-67 (63-36-3); Trinity (Tex.) 1972-73 (16-5-0)

201 Vince Dooley (Born 9-4-32 Mobile, Ala.)
Auburn 1954 (25: 201-77-10 .715)
Georgia 1964-88 (201-77-10)

201 Eddie Anderson (Born 11-13-1900 Mason City, Iowa; Died 4-26-74)
Notre Dame 1922 (39: 201-128-15 .606)
Loras 1922-24 (16-6-2); DePaul 1925-31 (21-22-3); Holy Cross 1933-38, 1950-64 (129-67-8); Iowa 1939-42, 1946-49 (35-33-2)

200 Jim Sweeney (Born 9-1-29 Butte, Mont.)
Portland 1951 (32: 200-154-4 .564)
Montana St. 1963-67 (31-20-0); Washington St. 1968-75 (26-59-1); Fresno St. 1976-77, 1980-96 (143-75-3)

198 Dana X. Bible (Born 10-8-1891 Jefferson City, Tenn.; Died 1-19-80)
Carson-Newman 1912 (33: 198-72-23 .715)
Mississippi Col. 1913-15 (12-7-2); LSU 1916 (1-0-2); Texas A&M 1917, 1919-28 (72-19-9); Nebraska 1929-36 (50-15-7); Texas 1937-46 (63-31-3)

197 Dan McGugin (Born 7-29-1879 Tingley, Iowa; Died 1-19-36)
Michigan 1904 (30: 197-55-19 .762)
Vanderbilt 1904-17, 1919-34 (197-55-19)

196 Fielding Yost (Born 4-30-1871 Fairview, W.Va.; Died 8-20-46)
West Va. '95 (29: 196-36-12 .828)
Ohio Wesleyan 1897 (7-1-1); Nebraska 1898 (7-4-0); Kansas 1899 (10-0-0); Stanford 1900 (7-2-1); Michigan 1901-23, 1925-26 (165-29-10)

194 Howard Jones (Born 8-23-1885 Excello, Ohio; Died 7-27-41)
Yale 1908 (29: 194-64-21 .733)
Syracuse 1908 (6-3-1); Yale 1909, 1913 (15-2-3); Ohio St. 1910 (6-1-3); Iowa 1916-23 (42-17-1); Duke 1924 (4-5-0); Southern Cal 1925-40 (121-36-13)

190 John Vaught (Born 5-6-08 Olney, Texas)
Texas Christian 1933 (25: 190-61-12 .745)
Mississippi 1947-70, 1973 (190-61-12)

185 John Heisman (Born 10-23-1869 Cleveland, Ohio; Died 10-3-36)
Brown 1890 (36: 185-70-17 .711)
Oberlin 1892, 1894 (11-3-1); Akron 1893 (5-2-0); Auburn 1895-99 (12-4-2); Clemson 1900-03 (19-3-2); Georgia Tech 1904-19 (102-29-6); Pennsylvania 1920-22 (16-10-2); Wash. & Jeff. 1923 (6-1-1); Rice 1924-27 (14-18-3)

185 Johnny Majors (Born 5-21-35 Lynchburg, Tenn.)
Tennessee 1957 (29: 185-137-10 .572)
Iowa St. 1968-72 (24-30-1); Pittsburgh 1973-76, 1993-96 (45-45-1); Tennessee 1977-92 (116-62-8)

184 Darrell Royal (Born 7-6-24 Hollis, Okla.)
Oklahoma 1950 (23: 184-60-5 .749)
Mississippi St. 1954-55 (12-8-0); Washington 1956 (5-5-0); Texas 1957-76 (167-47-5)

183 *Don Nehlen (Born 1-1-36 Canton, Ohio)
Bowling Green 1958 (27: 183-112-8 .617)
Bowling Green 1968-76 (53-35-4); West Va. 1980-97 (130-77-4)

180 Gil Dobie (Born 1-31-1879 Hastings, Minn.; Died 12-24-48)
Minnesota 1902 (33: 180-45-15 .781)
North Dak. St. 1906-07 (7-0-0); Washington 1908-16 (58-0-3); Navy 1917-19 (17-3-0); Cornell 1920-35 (82-36-7); Boston College 1936-38 (16-6-5)

180 Carl Snavely (Born 7-30-1894 Omaha, Neb.; Died 7-12-75)
Lebanon Valley 1915 (32: 180-96-16 .644)
Bucknell 1927-33 (42-16-8); North Caro. 1934-35, 1945-52 (59-35-5); Cornell 1936-44 (46-26-3); Washington (Mo.) 1953-58 (33-19-0)

179 Jerry Claiborne (Born 8-26-28 Hopkinsville, Ky.)
Kentucky 1950 (28: 179-122-8 .592)
Virginia Tech 1961-70 (61-39-2); Maryland 1972-81 (77-37-3); Kentucky 1982-89 (41-46-3)

178 Ben Schwartzwalder (Born 6-2-09 Point Pleasant, W.Va.; Died 4-28-93)
West Va. 1933 (28: 178-96-3 .648)
Muhlenberg 1946-48 (25-5-0); Syracuse 1949-73 (153-91-3)

176 Frank Kush (Born 1-20-29 Windber, Pa.)
Michigan St. 1953 (22: 176-54-1 .764)
Arizona St. 1958-79 (176-54-1)

176 Don James (Born 12-31-32 Massillon, Ohio)
Miami (Fla.) 1954 (22: 176-78-3 .691)
Kent 1971-74 (25-19-1); Washington 1975-92 (151-59-2)

176 Ralph Jordan (Born 9-25-10 Selma, Ala.; Died 7-17-80)
Auburn 1932 (√25: 176-83-6 .675)
Auburn 1951-75 (√176-83-6)

174 Pappy Waldorf (Born 10-3-02 Clifton Springs, N.Y.; Died 8-15-81)
Syracuse 1925 (31: 174-100-22 .625)
Oklahoma City 1925-27 (17-11-3); Oklahoma St. 1929-33 (34-10-7); Kansas St. 1934 (7-2-1); Northwestern 1935-46 (49-45-7); California 1947-56 (67-32-4)

173 Bob Neyland (Born 2-17-92 Greenville, Texas; Died 3-28-62)
Army 1916 (21: 173-31-12 .829)
Tennessee 1926-34, 1936-40, 1946-52 (173-31-12)

172 Dan Devine (Born 12-23-24 Augusta, Wis.)
Minn.-Duluth 1948 (22: 172-57-9 .742)
Arizona St. 1955-57 (27-3-1); Missouri 1958-70 (92-38-7); Notre Dame 1975-80 (53-16-1)

171 Wallace Wade (Born 6-15-1892 Trenton, Tenn.; Died 10-7-86)
Brown 1917 (24: 171-49-10 .765)
Alabama 1923-30 (61-13-3); Duke 1931-41, 1946-50 (110-36-7)

170 Ara Parseghian (Born 5-21-23 Akron, Ohio)
Miami (Ohio) 1949 (24: 170-58-6 .739)
Miami (Ohio) 1951-55 (39-6-1); Northwestern 1956-63 (36-35-1); Notre Dame 1964-74 (95-17-4)

170 Grant Teaff (Born 11-12-33 Hermleigh, Texas)
McMurry 1956 (30: 170-151-8 .529)
McMurry 1960-65 (23-35-2); Angelo St. 1969-71 (19-11-0); Baylor 1972-92 (128-105-6)

168 Al Molde (Born 11-15-43 Montevideo, Minn.)
Gust. Adolphus 1966 (26: 168-104-8 .614)
Sioux Falls 1971-72 (5-12-1); Minn.-Morris 1973-79 (52-21-1); Central Mo. St. 1980-82 (17-9-4); Eastern Ill. 1983-86 (32-15-0); Western Mich. 1987-96 (62-47-2)

168 Bob Blackman (Born 7-7-18 De Soto, Iowa)
Southern Cal 1941 (30: 168-112-7 .598)
Denver 1953-54 (12-6-2); Dartmouth 1955-70 (104-37-3); Illinois 1971-76 (29-36-1); Cornell 1977-82 (23-33-1)

167 *George Welsh (Born 8-26-33 Coaldale, Pa.)
Navy 1960 (25: 167-118-4 .585)
Navy 1973-81 (55-46-1); Virginia 1982-97 (112-72-3)

167 *John Cooper (Born 7-2-37 Powell, Tenn.)
Iowa St. 1962 (21: 167-73-6 .691)
Tulsa 1977-84 (56-32-0); Arizona St. 1985-87 (25-9-2); Ohio St. 1988-97 (86-32-4)

167 Bill Mallory (Born 5-30-35 Sandusky, Ohio)
Miami (Ohio) 1957 (27:167-130-4 .561)
Miami (Ohio) 1969-73 (39-12-0); Colorado 1974-78 (35-21-1); Northern Ill. 1980-83 (25-19-0); Indiana 1984-96 (68-78-3)

166 Red Blaik (Born 2-17-1897 Detroit, Mich.; Died 5-6-89)
Miami (Ohio) 1918; Army 1920 (25: 166-48-14 .759)
Dartmouth 1934-40 (45-15-4); Army 1941-58 (121-33-10)

165 Bobby Dodd (Born 11-11-08 Galax, Va.; Died 6-21-88)
Tennessee 1931 (22: 165-64-8 .713)
Georgia Tech 1945-66 (165-64-8)

165 Frank Howard (Born 3-25-09 Barlow Bend, Ala.; Died 1-25-96)
Alabama 1931 (30: 165-118-12 .580)
Clemson 1940-69 (165-118-12)

163 Don Faurot (Born 6-23-02 Mountain Grove, Mo.; Died 10-18-95)
Missouri 1925 (28: 163-93-13 .630)
Truman St. 1926-34 (63-13-3); Missouri 1935-42, 1946-56 (100-80-10)

162 Ossie Solem (Born 12-13-1891 Minneapolis, Minn.; Died 10-26-70)
Minnesota 1915 (37: 162-117-20 .575)
Luther 1920 (5-1-1); Drake 1921-31 (54-35-2); Iowa 1932-36 (15-21-4); Syracuse 1937-45 (30-27-6); Springfield 1946-57 (58-33-7)

161 Bill Dooley (Born 5-19-34 Mobile, Ala.)
Mississippi St. 1956 (26: 161-127-5 .558)
North Caro. 1967-77 (69-53-2); Virginia Tech 1978-86 (64-37-1); Wake Forest 1987-92 (29-36-2)

160 Bill Yeoman (Born 12-26-27 Elnora, Ind.)
Army 1949 (25: 160-108-8 .595)
Houston 1962-86 (160-108-8)

160 Jim Wacker (Born 4-28-37 Detroit, Mich.)
Valparaiso 1960 (26: 160-130-3 .551)
Texas Lutheran 1971-75 (38-16-0); North Dak. St. 1976-78 (24-9-1); Southwest Tex. St. 1979-82 (42-8-0); Texas Christian 1983-91 (40-58-2); Minnesota 1992-96 (16-39-0)

158 Francis Schmidt (Born 12-3-1885 Downs, Kan.; Died 9-19-44)
Nebraska 1914 (24: 158-57-11 .723)
Tulsa 1919-21 (24-3-2); Arkansas 1922-28 (42-20-3); Texas Christian 1929-33 (46-6-5); Ohio St. 1934-40 (39-16-1); Idaho 1941-42 (7-12-0)

157 Barry Switzer (Born 10-5-37 Crossett, Ark.)
Arkansas 1960 (16: 157-29-4 .837)
Oklahoma 1973-88 (157-29-4)

157 Edward Robinson (Born 10-15-1873 Lynn, Miss.; Died 3-10-45)
Brown 1896 (27: 157-88-13 .632)
Nebraska 1896-97 (11-4-1); Brown 1898-1901, 1904-07, 1910-1925 (140-82-12); Maine 1902 (6-2-0)

155 Bennie Owen (Born 7-24-1875 Chicago, Ill.; Died 2-9-70)
Kansas 1900 (27: 155-60-19 .703)
Washburn 1900 (6-2-0); Bethany (Kan.) 1901-04 (27-4-3); Oklahoma 1905-26 (122-54-16)

155 Ray Morrison (Born 2-28-1885 Switzerland Co., Ind.; Died 11-19-82)
Vanderbilt 1912 (34: 155-130-33 .539)
Southern Methodist 1915-16, 1922-34 (84-44-22); Vanderbilt 1918, 1935-39 (29-22-2); Temple 1940-48 (31-38-9); Austin 1949-52 (11-26-0)

154 Earle Bruce (Born 3-8-31 Massillon, Ohio)
Ohio St. 1953 (21: 154-90-2 .630)
Tampa 1972 (10-2-0); Iowa St. 1973-78 (36-32-0); Ohio St. 1979-87 (81-26-1); Northern Iowa 1988 (5-6-0); Colorado St. 1989-92 (22-24-1)

153 Pat Dye (Born 11-6-39 Augusta, Ga.)
Georgia 1962 (19: 153-62-5 .707)
East Caro. 1974-79 (48-18-1); Wyoming 1980 (6-5-0); Auburn 1981-92 (99-39-4)

153 Morley Jennings (Born 1-23-1885 Holland, Mich.; Died 5-13-85)
Mississippi St. 1912 (29: 153-75-18 .658)
Ouachita Baptist 1912-25 (70-15-12); Baylor 1926-40 (83-60-6)

153 Matty Bell (Born 2-22-1899 Baylor Co., Texas; Died 6-30-83)
Centre 1920 (26: 153-87-16 .630)
Haskell 1920-21 (13-6-0); Carroll (Wis.) 1922 (4-3-0); Texas Christian 1923-28 (33-17-5); Texas A&M 1929-33 (24-21-3); Southern Methodist 1935-41, 1945-49 (79-40-8)

151 Lou Little (Born 12-6-1893 Leominster, Mass.; Died 5-28-79)
Pennsylvania 1920 (33: 151-128-13 .539)
Georgetown 1924-29 (41-12-3); Columbia 1930-56 (110-116-10)

√*Includes games forfeited, team and/or individual statistics abrogated, and coaching records changed by action of the NCAA Committee on Infractions.*

Division I-A Best Career Starts by Wins

(Head coaches with at least half their seasons at major college at the time and minimum five years coached)

1 SEASON

Coach, Team	Season	W	L	T	Pct.
George Woodruff, Pennsylvania	1892	15	1	0	.938
Walter Camp, Yale	1888	13	0	0	1.000
Bill Battle, Tennessee	1970	11	1	0	.917
*Gary Blackney, Bowling Green	1991	11	1	0	.917
John Robinson, Southern Cal	1976	11	1	0	.917
Dick Crum, Miami (Ohio)	1974	10	0	1	.955
Barry Switzer, Oklahoma	1973	10	0	1	.955
Chuck Fairbanks, Oklahoma	1967	10	1	0	.909
Larry Siemering, Pacific (Cal.)	1947	10	1	0	.909
Dwight Wallace, Ball St.	1978	10	1	0	.909
Mike Archer, LSU	1987	10	1	1	.875

2 SEASONS

Coach, Team	Seasons	W	L	T	Pct.
Walter Camp, Yale	1888-89	28	1	0	.966
George Woodruff, Pennsylvania	1892-93	27	4	0	.871
Barry Switzer, Oklahoma	1973-74	21	0	1	.977
Dick Crum, Miami (Ohio)	1974-75	21	1	1	.935
Bill Battle, Tennessee	1970-71	21	3	0	.875
*Gary Blackney, Bowling Green	1991-92	21	3	0	.875
Frank Leahy, Boston College	1939-40	20	2	0	.909
Ron Meyer, UNLV	1973-74	20	4	0	.833
*Fisher DeBerry, Air Force	1984-85	20	5	0	.800
Dutch Meyer, Texas Christian	1934-35	20	5	0	.800
Herb Deromedi, Central Mich.	1978-79	19	2	1	.886
John Robinson, Southern Cal	1976-77	19	5	0	.792

3 SEASONS

Coach, Team(s)	Seasons	W	L	T	Pct.
Walter Camp, Yale	1888-90	41	2	0	.953
George Woodruff, Pennsylvania	1892-94	39	4	0	.907
Barry Switzer, Oklahoma	1973-75	32	1	1	.956
Bill Battle, Tennessee	1970-72	31	5	0	.861
John Robinson, Southern Cal	1976-78	31	6	0	.838
Dutch Meyer, Texas Christian	1934-36	29	7	2	.789
Frank Leahy, Boston College, Notre Dame	1939-41	28	2	1	.919
Larry Siemering, Pacific (Cal.)	1947-49	28	2	2	.906
Bud Wilkinson, Oklahoma	1947-49	28	3	1	.891
Herb Deromedi, Central Mich.	1978-80	28	4	1	.864
Tom Osborne, Nebraska	1973-75	28	7	1	.792

4 SEASONS

Coach, Team(s)	Seasons	W	L	T	Pct.
Walter Camp, Yale	1888-91	54	2	0	.964
George Woodruff, Pennsylvania	1892-95	53	4	0	.930
John Robinson, Southern Cal	1976-79	42	6	1	.867
Barry Switzer, Oklahoma	1973-76	41	3	2	.935
Bill Battle, Tennessee	1970-73	39	9	0	.813
*R. C. Slocum, Texas A&M	1989-92	39	10	1	.790
Bud Wilkinson, Oklahoma	1947-50	38	4	1	.895
Tom Osborne, Nebraska	1973-76	37	10	2	.776
*Gary Blackney, Bowling Green	1991-94	36	8	2	.804
Frank Leahy, Boston College, Notre Dame	1939-42	35	4	3	.869
Larry Siemering, Pacific (Cal.)	1947-50	35	5	3	.849
*Joe Paterno, Penn St.	1966-69	35	7	1	.826
Claude Gilbert, San Diego St.	1973-76	35	7	2	.818
Herb Deromedi, Central Mich.	1978-81	35	8	1	.807
*Fisher DeBerry, Air Force	1984-87	35	14	0	.714

5 SEASONS

Coach, Team(s)	Seasons	W	L	T	Pct.
Walter Camp, Yale, Stanford	1888-92	69	2	2	.959
George Woodruff, Pennsylvania	1892-96	67	5	0	.931
Barry Switzer, Oklahoma	1973-77	51	5	2	.896
John Robinson, Southern Cal	1976-80	50	8	2	.850
*R. C. Slocum, Texas A&M	1989-93	49	12	1	.798
Henry Williams, Army, Minnesota	1891, 1900-03	47	4	6	.877
Bud Wilkinson, Oklahoma	1947-51	46	6	1	.877
Bill Battle, Tennessee	1970-74	46	12	2	.783
Tom Osborne, Nebraska	1973-77	46	13	2	.770
Claude Gilbert, San Diego St.	1973-77	45	8	2	.836

6 SEASONS

Coach, Team(s)	Seasons	W	L	T	Pct.
George Woodruff, Pennsylvania	1892-97	82	5	0	.943
Walter Camp, Yale, Stanford	1888-92, 94	75	5	2	.927
Barry Switzer, Oklahoma	1973-78	62	6	2	.900
Henry Williams, Army, Minnesota	1891, 1900-04	60	4	6	.900
John Robinson, Southern Cal	1976-81	59	11	2	.833
*R. C. Slocum, Texas A&M	1989-94	59	12	2	.822
Tom Osborne, Nebraska	1973-78	55	16	2	.767
*Phillip Fulmer, Tennessee	1992-97	54	11	0	.841
Bud Wilkinson, Oklahoma	1947-52	54	7	2	.873
Fielding Yost, Ohio Wesleyan, Nebraska, Kansas, Stanford, Michigan	1897-1902	53	7	2	.871
*Joe Paterno, Penn St.	1966-71	53	11	1	.823
*Jackie Sherrill, Washington St., Pittsburgh	1976-81	53	17	1	.754
Bill Battle, Tennessee	1970-75	53	17	2	.750

7 SEASONS

Coach, Team(s)	Seasons	W	L	T	Pct.
George Woodruff, Pennsylvania	1892-98	94	6	0	.940
Walter Camp, Yale, Stanford	1888-92, 94-95	79	5	3	.925
Barry Switzer, Oklahoma	1973-79	73	7	2	.902
Henry Williams, Army, Minnesota	1891, 1900-05	70	5	6	.901
*R. C. Slocum, Texas A&M	1989-95	68	15	2	.812
John Robinson, Southern Cal	1976-82	67	14	2	.819
Tom Osborne, Nebraska	1973-79	65	18	2	.776
Fielding Yost, Ohio Wesleyan, Nebraska, Kansas, Stanford, Michigan	1897-1903	64	7	3	.897
Bud Wilkinson, Oklahoma	1947-53	63	8	3	.872
*Joe Paterno, Penn St.	1966-72	63	13	1	.825
Amos Alonzo Stagg, Springfield, Chicago	1890-96	63	31	7	.658

8 SEASONS

Coach, Team(s)	Seasons	W	L	T	Pct.
George Woodruff, Pennsylvania	1892-99	102	9	2	.912
Barry Switzer, Oklahoma	1973-80	83	9	2	.894
*Joe Paterno, Penn St.	1966-73	75	13	1	.848
John Robinson, Southern Cal	1976-82, 93	75	19	2	.792
Tom Osborne, Nebraska	1973-80	75	20	2	.784
Fielding Yost, Ohio Wesleyan, Nebraska, Kansas, Stanford, Michigan	1897-1904	74	7	3	.898
Henry Williams, Army, Minnesota	1891, 1900-06	74	6	6	.895
*R. C. Slocum, Texas A&M	1989-96	74	21	2	.773
Amos Alonzo Stagg, Springfield, Chicago	1890-97	74	32	7	.686
Bud Wilkinson, Oklahoma	1947-54	73	8	3	.887
Frank Leahy, Boston College, Notre Dame	1939-43, 46-48	70	5	5	.882

9 SEASONS

Coach, Team(s)	Seasons	W	L	T	Pct.
George Woodruff, Pennsylvania	1892-1900	114	10	2	.913
Barry Switzer, Oklahoma	1973-81	90	13	3	.863
Fielding Yost, Ohio Wesleyan, Nebraska, Kansas, Stanford, Michigan	1897-1905	86	8	3	.902
*Joe Paterno, Penn St.	1966-74	85	15	1	.847
Bud Wilkinson, Oklahoma	1947-55	84	8	3	.900
Tom Osborne, Nebraska	1973-81	84	23	2	.780
*R. C. Slocum, Texas A&M	1989-97	83	25	2	.764
John Robinson, Southern Cal	1976-82, 93-94	83	22	3	.782
Amos Alonzo Stagg, Springfield, Chicago	1890-98	83	34	7	.698
*Steve Spurrier, Duke, Florida	1987-95	81	26	2	.752
Frank Leahy, Boston College, Notre Dame	1939-43, 46-49	80	5	5	.917
Bob Neyland, Tennessee	1926-34	76	7	5	.892
Henry Williams, Army, Minnesota	1891, 1900-07	76	8	7	.874
Dick Crum, Miami (Ohio), North Caro.	1974-82	76	26	2	.740
Fred Akers, Wyoming, Texas	1975-83	76	30	1	.715

10 SEASONS

Coach, Team(s)	Seasons	W	L	T	Pct.
George Woodruff, Pennsylvania	1892-1901	124	15	2	.887
Barry Switzer, Oklahoma	1973-82	98	17	3	.843
Tom Osborne, Nebraska	1973-82	96	24	2	.795
Amos Alonzo Stagg, Springfield, Chicago	1890-99	95	34	9	.721
Bud Wilkinson, Oklahoma	1947-56	94	8	3	.910
*Joe Paterno, Penn St.	1966-75	94	18	1	.836
*Steve Spurrier, Duke, Florida	1987-96	93	27	2	.770
John Robinson, Southern Cal	1976-82, 93-95	92	24	4	.783
Fielding Yost, Ohio Wesleyan, Nebraska, Kansas, Stanford, Michigan	1897-1906	90	9	3	.897
Frank Leahy, Boston College, Notre Dame	1939-43, 46-50	84	9	6	.879
Dick Crum, Miami (Ohio), North Caro.	1974-83	84	30	2	.733
Dennis Erickson, Idaho, Wyoming, Washington St., Miami (Fla.)	1982-91	83	34	1	.708
Fred Akers, Wyoming, Texas	1975-84	83	34	2	.706

11 SEASONS

Coach, Team(s)	Seasons	W	L	T	Pct.
George Woodruff, Pennsylvania, Illinois	1892-1901, 03	132	21	2	.858
Tom Osborne, Nebraska	1973-83	108	25	2	.807
Barry Switzer, Oklahoma	1973-83	106	21	3	.827
Bud Wilkinson, Oklahoma	1947-57	104	9	3	.909
*Steve Spurrier, Duke, Florida	1987-97	103	29	2	.776
Amos Alonzo Stagg, Springfield, Chicago	1890-1900	102	39	10	.709
*Joe Paterno, Penn St.	1966-76	101	23	1	.812
John Robinson, Southern Cal	1976-82, 93-96	98	30	4	.758
Fielding Yost, Ohio Wesleyan, Nebraska, Kansas, Stanford, Michigan	1897-1907	95	10	3	.894
Dennis Erickson, Idaho, Wyoming, Washington St., Miami (Fla.)	1982-92	94	35	1	.727
Frank Leahy, Boston College, Notre Dame	1939-43, 46-51	91	11	7	.867
Bobby Dodd, Georgia Tech	1945-55	91	27	3	.764
Fred Akers, Wyoming, Texas	1975-85	91	38	2	.702

12 SEASONS

Coach, Team(s)	Seasons	W	L	T	Pct.
George Woodruff, Pennsylvania, Illinois, Carlisle	1892-1901, 03, 05	142	25	2	.846
Tom Osborne, Nebraska	1973-84	118	27	2	.810
Barry Switzer, Oklahoma	1973-84	115	23	4	.824
Bud Wilkinson, Oklahoma	1947-58	114	10	3	.909
*Joe Paterno, Penn St.	1966-77	112	24	1	.821
Amos Alonzo Stagg, Springfield, Chicago	1890-1901	107	44	12	.693
John Robinson, Southern Cal	1976-82, 93-97	104	35	4	.741
Dennis Erickson, Idaho, Wyoming, Washington St., Miami (Fla.)	1982-93	103	38	1	.729
Bobby Dodd, Georgia Tech	1945-56	101	28	3	.777
Fielding Yost, Ohio Wesleyan, Nebraska, Kansas, Stanford, Michigan	1897-1908	100	12	4	.879
Bob Neyland, Tennessee	1926-34, 36-38	99	12	8	.866

13 SEASONS

Coach, Team(s)	Seasons	W	L	T	Pct.
Tom Osborne, Nebraska	1973-85	127	30	2	.805
Barry Switzer, Oklahoma	1973-85	126	24	4	.831
*Joe Paterno, Penn St.	1966-78	123	25	1	.829
Bud Wilkinson, Oklahoma	1947-59	121	13	3	.894
*LaVell Edwards, Brigham Young	1972-84	118	37	1	.760
Amos Alonzo Stagg, Springfield, Chicago	1890-1902	118	45	12	.709
Dennis Erickson, Idaho, Wyoming, Washington St., Miami (Fla.)	1982-94	113	40	1	.737
Bob Neyland, Tennessee	1926-34, 36-39	109	13	8	.869
Terry Donahue, UCLA	1976-88	108	38	7	.729
Frank Leahy, Boston College, Notre Dame	1939-43, 46-53	107	13	9	.864

14 SEASONS

Coach, Team(s)	Seasons	W	L	T	Pct.
Barry Switzer, Oklahoma	1973-86	137	25	4	.837
Tom Osborne, Nebraska	1973-86	137	32	2	.807
*Joe Paterno, Penn St.	1966-79	131	29	1	.817
*LaVell Edwards, Brigham Young	1972-85	129	40	1	.762
Amos Alonzo Stagg, Springfield, Chicago.	1890-1903	128	47	13	.715
Bud Wilkinson, Oklahoma	1947-60	124	19	4	.857
Bob Neyland, Tennessee	1926-34, 36-40	119	14	8	.872
Bo Schembechler, Miami (Ohio), Michigan	1963-76	116	28	6	.793
Pat Dye, East Caro., Wyoming, Auburn	1974-87	115	44	3	.719
Bob Devaney, Wyoming, Nebraska	1957-70	114	28	6	.791

15 SEASONS

Coach, Team(s)	Seasons	W	L	T	Pct.
Barry Switzer, Oklahoma	1973-87	148	26	4	.843
Tom Osborne, Nebraska	1973-87	147	34	2	.809
*Joe Paterno, Penn St.	1966-80	141	31	1	.818
*LaVell Edwards, Brigham Young	1972-86	137	45	1	.751
Amos Alonzo Stagg, Springfield, Chicago	1890-1904	136	48	14	.722
Bud Wilkinson, Oklahoma	1947-61	129	24	4	.834
Bob Neyland, Tennessee	1926-34, 36-40, 46	128	16	8	.868
Bob Devaney, Wyoming, Nebraska	1957-71	127	28	6	.807
Bo Schembechler, Miami (Ohio), Michigan	1963-77	126	30	6	.796
Pat Dye, East Caro., Wyoming, Auburn	1974-88	125	46	3	.727

16 SEASONS

Coach, Team(s)	Seasons	W	L	T	Pct.
Tom Osborne, Nebraska	1973-88	158	36	2	.811
Barry Switzer, Oklahoma	1973-88	157	29	4	.837
*Joe Paterno, Penn St.	1966-81	151	33	1	.819
*LaVell Edwards, Brigham Young	1972-87	146	49	1	.747
Amos Alonzo Stagg, Springfield, Chicago	1890-1905	146	48	14	.736
Bud Wilkinson, Oklahoma	1947-62	137	27	4	.827
Bob Devaney, Wyoming, Nebraska	1957-72	136	30	7	.806
Bo Schembechler, Miami (Ohio), Michigan	1963-78	136	32	6	.799
Pat Dye, East Caro., Wyoming, Auburn	1974-89	135	48	3	.734
Bob Neyland, Tennessee	1926-34, 36-40, 46-47	133	21	8	.846

17 SEASONS

Coach, Team(s)	Seasons	W	L	T	Pct.
Tom Osborne, Nebraska	1973-89	168	38	2	.813
*Joe Paterno, Penn St.	1966-82	162	34	1	.825
*LaVell Edwards, Brigham Young	1972-88	155	53	1	.744
Amos Alonzo Stagg, Springfield, Chicago	1890-1906	150	49	15	.736
Bud Wilkinson, Oklahoma	1947-63	145	29	4	.826
Bo Schembechler, Miami (Ohio), Michigan	1963-79	144	36	6	.790
Pat Dye, East Caro., Wyoming, Auburn	1974-90	143	51	4	.732
Frank Kush, Arizona St.	1958-74	139	39	1	.779
Bob Neyland, Tennessee	1926-34, 36-40, 46-48	137	25	10	.826
Johnny Vaught, Mississippi	1947-63	137	32	9	.795
Tony Knap, Utah St., Boise St., UNLV	1963-66, 68-80	137	47	4	.739

18 SEASONS

Coach, Team(s)	Seasons	W	L	T	Pct.
Tom Osborne, Nebraska	1973-90	177	41	2	.809
*Joe Paterno, Penn St.	1966-83	170	38	2	.814
*LaVell Edwards, Brigham Young	1972-89	165	56	1	.745
Bo Schembechler, Miami (Ohio), Michigan	1963-80	154	38	6	.793
Amos Alonzo Stagg, Springfield, Chicago	1890-1907	154	50	15	.737
Frank Kush, Arizona St.	1958-75	151	39	1	.793
Pat Dye, East Caro., Wyoming, Auburn	1974-91	148	57	4	.718
Bob Neyland, Tennessee	1926-34, 36-40, 46-49	144	27	11	.821
Darrell Royal, Mississippi St., Washington, Texas	1954-71	143	45	4	.755
Tony Knap, Utah St., Boise St., UNLV	1963-66, 68-81	143	53	4	.725

19 SEASONS

Coach, Team(s)	Seasons	W	L	T	Pct.
Tom Osborne, Nebraska	1973-91	186	43	3	.808
*Joe Paterno, Penn St.	1966-84	176	43	2	.801
*LaVell Edwards, Brigham Young	1972-90	175	59	1	.747
Bo Schembechler, Miami (Ohio), Michigan	1963-81	163	41	6	.790
Amos Alonzo Stagg, Springfield, Chicago	1890-1908	159	50	16	.742
Bob Neyland, Tennessee	1926-34, 36-40, 46-50	155	28	11	.827
Frank Kush, Arizona St.	1958-76	155	46	1	.770
Darrell Royal, Mississippi St., Washington, Texas	1954-72	153	46	4	.764
Pat Dye, East Caro., Wyoming, Auburn	1974-92	153	62	5	.707
Pop Warner, Georgia, Cornell, Carlisle	1895-1913	152	50	10	.741

20 SEASONS

Coach, Team(s)	Seasons	W	L	T	Pct.
Tom Osborne, Nebraska	1973-92	195	46	3	.805
*Joe Paterno, Penn St.	1966-85	187	44	2	.807
*LaVell Edwards, Brigham Young	1972-91	183	62	3	.744
Bo Schembechler, Miami (Ohio), Michigan	1963-82	171	45	6	.784
Bob Neyland, Tennessee	1926-34, 36-40, 46-51	165	29	11	.832
Frank Kush, Arizona St.	1958-77	164	49	1	.769
Amos Alonzo Stagg, Springfield, Chicago	1890-1909	163	51	18	.741
Darrell Royal, Mississippi St., Washington, Texas	1954-73	161	49	4	.762
Vince Dooley, Georgia	1964-83	161	60	7	.721
Johnny Vaught, Mississippi	1947-66	157	44	10	.768
Pop Warner, Georgia, Cornell, Carlisle	1895-1914	157	59	11	.716
*John Cooper, Tulsa, Arizona, Ohio St.	1977-96	157	70	6	.687

21 SEASONS

Coach, Team(s)	Seasons	W	L	T	Pct.
Tom Osborne, Nebraska	1973-93	206	47	3	.811
*Joe Paterno, Penn St.	1966-86	199	44	2	.816
*LaVell Edwards, Brigham Young	1972-92	191	67	3	.738
Bo Schembechler, Miami (Ohio), Michigan	1963-83	180	48	6	.782
Bob Neyland, Tennessee	1926-34, 36-40, 46-52	173	31	12	.829
Frank Kush, Arizona St.	1958-78	173	52	1	.768
Darrell Royal, Mississippi St., Washington, Texas	1954-74	169	53	4	.757
Vince Dooley, Georgia	1964-84	168	64	8	.717
*John Cooper, Tulsa, Arizona, Ohio St.	1977-97	167	73	6	.691
Don James, Kent, Washington	1971-91	167	75	3	.688
Amos Alonzo Stagg, Springfield, Chicago	1890-1910	165	56	18	.728
Pop Warner, Georgia, Cornell, Carlisle, Pittsburgh	1895-1915	165	59	11	.726

22 SEASONS

Coach, Team(s)	Seasons	W	L	T	Pct.
Tom Osborne, Nebraska	1973-94	219	47	3	.820
*Joe Paterno, Penn St.	1966-87	207	48	2	.809
*LaVell Edwards, Brigham Young	1972-93	197	73	3	.727
Bo Schembechler, Miami (Ohio), Michigan	1963-84	186	54	6	.768
Darrell Royal, Mississippi St., Washington, Texas	1954-75	179	55	4	.761
Frank Kush, Arizona St.	1958-79	176	54	1	.764
Don James, Kent, Washington	1971-92	176	78	3	.691
Vince Dooley, Georgia	1964-85	175	67	10	.714
*Bobby Bowden, Samford, West Va., Florida St.	1959-62, 70-87	174	69	3	.713
Pop Warner, Georgia, Cornell, Carlisle, Pittsburgh	1895-1916	173	59	11	.735

23 SEASONS

Coach, Team(s)	Seasons	W	L	T	Pct.
Tom Osborne, Nebraska	1973-95	231	47	3	.827
*Joe Paterno, Penn St.	1966-88	212	54	2	.795
*LaVell Edwards, Brigham Young	1972-94	207	76	3	.729
Bo Schembechler, Miami (Ohio), Michigan	1963-85	196	55	7	.773
*Bobby Bowden, Samford, West Va., Florida St.	1959-62, 70-88	185	70	3	.723
Darrell Royal, Mississippi St., Washington, Texas	1954-76	184	60	5	.749
Pop Warner, Georgia, Cornell, Carlisle, Pittsburgh	1895-1917	183	59	11	.745
Vince Dooley, Georgia	1964-86	183	71	10	.712
Lou Holtz, William & Mary, North Caro. St., Arkansas, Minnesota, Notre Dame	1969-92	182	83	6	.683
Bear Bryant, Maryland, Kentucky, Texas A&M, Alabama	1945-67	179	53	15	.755
Johnny Vaught, Mississippi	1947-69	178	54	12	.754

24 SEASONS

Coach, Team(s)	Seasons	W	L	T	Pct.
Tom Osborne, Nebraska	1973-96	242	49	3	.828
*Joe Paterno, Penn St.	1966-89	220	57	3	.791
*LaVell Edwards, Brigham Young	1972-95	214	80	3	.726
Bo Schembechler, Miami (Ohio), Michigan	1963-86	207	57	7	.777
*Bobby Bowden, Samford, West Va., Florida St.	1959-62, 70-89	195	72	3	.728
Lou Holtz, William & Mary, North Caro. St., Arkansas, Minnesota, Notre Dame	1969-93	193	84	6	.693
Vince Dooley, Georgia	1964-87	192	74	10	.714
Bear Bryant, Maryland, Kentucky, Texas A&M, Alabama	1945-68	187	56	15	.754
Pop Warner, Georgia, Cornell, Carlisle, Pittsburgh	1895-1918	187	60	11	.746
Johnny Vaught, Mississippi	1947-70	185	58	12	.749
Amos Alonzo Stagg, Springfield, Chicago	1890-1913	184	58	18	.742

25 SEASONS

Coach, Team(s)	Seasons	W	L	T	Pct.
Tom Osborne, Nebraska	1973-97	255	49	3	.836
*Joe Paterno, Penn St.	1966-90	229	60	3	.789
*LaVell Edwards, Brigham Young	1972-96	228	81	3	.736
Bo Schembechler, Miami (Ohio), Michigan	1963-87	215	61	7	.772
*Bobby Bowden, Samford, West Va., Florida St.	1959-62, 70-90	205	74	3	.732
Vince Dooley, Georgia	1964-88	201	77	10	.715
Lou Holtz, William & Mary, North Caro. St., Arkansas, Minnesota, Notre Dame	1969-94	199	89	7	.686
Bear Bryant, Maryland, Kentucky, Texas A&M, Alabama	1945-69	193	61	15	.745
Pop Warner, Georgia, Cornell, Carlisle, Pittsburgh	1895-1919	193	62	12	.745
Johnny Vaught, Mississippi	1947-70, 73	190	61	12	.745
Amos Alonzo Stagg, Springfield, Chicago	1890-1914	188	60	19	.740

26 SEASONS

Coach, Team(s)	Seasons	W	L	T	Pct.
*Joe Paterno, Penn St.	1966-91	240	62	3	.792
*LaVell Edwards, Brigham Young	1972-97	234	86	3	.729
Bo Schembechler, Miami (Ohio), Michigan	1963-88	224	63	8	.773
*Bobby Bowden, Samford, West Va., Florida St.	1959-62, 70-91	216	76	3	.737
Lou Holtz, William & Mary, North Caro. St., Arkansas, Minnesota, Notre Dame	1969-95	208	92	7	.689
Pop Warner, Georgia, Cornell, Carlisle, Pittsburgh	1895-1920	199	62	14	.749
Bear Bryant, Maryland, Kentucky, Texas A&M, Alabama	1945-70	199	66	16	.737
Amos Alonzo Stagg, Springfield, Chicago	1890-1915	193	62	19	.739

27 SEASONS

Coach, Team(s)	Seasons	W	L	T	Pct.
*Joe Paterno, Penn St.	1966-92	247	67	3	.784
Bo Schembechler, Miami (Ohio), Michigan	1963-89	234	65	8	.775
*Bobby Bowden, Samford, West Va., Florida St.	1959-62, 70-92	227	77	3	.744
Bear Bryant, Maryland, Kentucky, Texas A&M, Alabama	1945-71	210	67	16	.744
Pop Warner, Georgia, Cornell, Carlisle, Pittsburgh	1895-1921	204	65	15	.745
Amos Alonzo Stagg, Springfield, Chicago	1890-1916	196	66	19	.731

28 SEASONS

Coach, Team(s)	Seasons	W	L	T	Pct.
*Joe Paterno, Penn St.	1966-93	257	69	3	.786
*Bobby Bowden, Samford, West Va., Florida St.	1959-62, 70-93	239	78	3	.752
Bear Bryant, Maryland, Kentucky, Texas A&M, Alabama	1945-72	220	69	16	.748
Pop Warner, Georgia, Cornell, Carlisle, Pittsburgh	1895-1922	212	67	15	.747
Amos Alonzo Stagg, Springfield, Chicago	1890-1917	199	68	20	.728
Woody Hayes, Denison, Miami (Ohio), Ohio St.	1946-73	192	60	8	.754
Howard Jones, Syracuse, Yale, Ohio St., Iowa, Duke, Southern Cal	1908-10, 13, 16-39	191	60	19	.743

29 SEASONS

Coach, Team(s)	Seasons	W	L	T	Pct.
*Joe Paterno, Penn St.	1966-94	269	69	3	.793
*Bobby Bowden, Samford, West Va., Florida St.	1959-62, 70-94	249	79	4	.756
Bear Bryant, Maryland, Kentucky, Texas A&M, Alabama	1945-73	231	70	16	.754

Coach, Team(s)	Seasons	W	L	T	Pct.
Pop Warner, Georgia, Cornell, Carlisle, Pittsburgh	1895-1923	217	71	15	
.741Woody Hayes, Denison, Miami (Ohio), Ohio St.	1946-74	202	62	8	.757
Amos Alonzo Stagg, Springfield, Chicago	1890-1918	199	74	20	.713
Fielding Yost, Ohio Wesleyan, Nebraska, Kansas, Stanford, Michigan	1897-1923, 25-26	196	36	12	.828
Howard Jones, Syracuse, Yale, Ohio St., Iowa, Duke, Southern Cal	1908-10, 13, 16-40	194	64	21	.733
Dan McGugin, Vanderbilt	1904-17, 19-33	191	52	19	.765

30 SEASONS

Coach, Team(s)	Seasons	W	L	T	Pct.
*Joe Paterno, Penn St.	1966-95	278	72	3	.792
*Bobby Bowden, Samford, West Va., Florida St.	1959-62, 70-95	259	81	4	.759
Bear Bryant, Maryland, Kentucky, Texas A&M, Alabama	1945-74	242	71	16	.760
Pop Warner, Georgia, Cornell, Carlisle, Pittsburgh, Stanford	1895-1924	224	72	16	.744
Woody Hayes, Denison, Miami (Ohio), Ohio St.	1946-75	213	63	8	.764
Amos Alonzo Stagg, Springfield, Chicago	1890-1919	204	76	20	.713

31 SEASONS

Coach, Team(s)	Seasons	W	L	T	Pct.
*Joe Paterno, Penn St.	1966-96	289	74	3	.794
*Bobby Bowden, Samford, West Va., Florida St.	1959-62, 70-96	270	82	4	.764
Bear Bryant, Maryland, Kentucky, Texas A&M, Alabama	1945-75	253	72	16	.765
Pop Warner, Georgia, Cornell, Carlisle, Pittsburgh, Stanford	1895-1925	231	74	16	.745
Woody Hayes, Denison, Miami (Ohio), Ohio St.	1946-76	222	65	9	.765
Amos Alonzo Stagg, Springfield, Chicago	1890-1920	207	80	20	.707
Warren Woodson, Central Ark., Hardin-Simmons, Arizona, New Mexico St., Trinity (Tex.)	1935-42, 46-56, 58-67, 72-73	203	95	14	.673
Dana X. Bible, Mississippi Col., LSU, Texas A&M, Nebraska, Texas	1913-17, 19-44	180	69	23	.704

32 SEASONS

Coach, Team(s)	Seasons	W	L	T	Pct.
*Joe Paterno, Penn St.	1966-97	298	77	3	.792
*Bobby Bowden, Stamford, West Va. Florida St.	1959-62, 70-97	281	83	4	.769
Bear Bryant, Maryland, Kentucky, Texas A&M, Alabama	1945-76	262	75	16	.765
Pop Warner, Georgia, Cornell, Carlisle, Pittsburgh, Stanford	1895-1926	241	74	17	.752
Woody Hayes, Denison, Miami (Ohio), Ohio St.	1946-77	231	68	9	.765
Amos Alonzo Stagg, Springfield, Chicago	1890-1921	213	81	20	.710
*Hayden Fry, Southern Methodist, North Texas, Iowa	1962-93	200	153	9	.565
Dana X. Bible, Mississippi Col., LSU, Texas A&M, Nebraska, Texas	1913-17, 19-45	190	70	23	.712

33 SEASONS

Coach, Team(s)	Seasons	W	L	T	Pct.
Bear Bryant, Maryland, Kentucky, Texas A&M, Alabama	1945-77	273	76	16	.770
Pop Warner, Georgia, Cornell, Carlisle, Pittsburgh, Stanford	1895-1927	249	76	18	.752
Woody Hayes, Denison, Miami (Ohio), Ohio St.	1946-78	238	72	10	.759
Amos Alonzo Stagg, Springfield, Chicago	1890-1922	219	82	20	.713
*Hayden Fry, Southern Methodist, North Texas, Iowa	1962-94	205	158	10	.563
Dana X. Bible, Mississippi Col., LSU, Texas A&M, Nebraska, Texas	1913-17, 19-46	198	72	23	.715

34 SEASONS

Coach, Team(s)	Seasons	W	L	T	Pct.
Bear Bryant, Maryland, Kentucky, Texas A&M, Alabama	1945-78	284	77	16	.775
Pop Warner, Georgia, Cornell, Carlisle, Pittsburgh, Stanford	1895-1928	257	79	19	.751
Amos Alonzo Stagg, Springfield, Chicago	1890-1923	226	83	20	.717
*Hayden Fry, Southern Methodist, North Texas, Iowa	1962-95	213	162	10	.566

35 SEASONS

Coach, Team(s)	Seasons	W	L	T	Pct.
Bear Bryant, Maryland, Kentucky, Texas A&M, Alabama	1945-79	296	77	16	.781
Pop Warner, Georgia, Cornell, Carlisle, Pittsburgh, Stanford	1895-1929	266	81	19	.753
Amos Alonzo Stagg, Springfield, Chicago	1890-1924	230	84	23	.717
*Hayden Fry, Southern Methodist, North Texas, Iowa	1962-96	222	165	10	.572

36 SEASONS

Coach, Team(s)	Seasons	W	L	T	Pct.
Bear Bryant, Maryland, Kentucky, Texas A&M, Alabama	1945-80	306	79	16	.783
Pop Warner, Georgia, Cornell, Carlisle, Pittsburgh, Stanford	1895-1930	275	82	20	.756
Amos Alonzo Stagg, Springfield, Chicago	1890-1925	233	88	24	.710
*Hayden Fry, Southern Methodist, North Texas, Iowa	1962-97	229	170	10	.572

37 SEASONS

Coach, Team(s)	Seasons	W	L	T	Pct.
Bear Bryant, Maryland, Kentucky, Texas A&M, Alabama	1945-81	315	81	17	.783
Pop Warner, Georgia, Cornell, Carlisle, Pittsburgh, Stanford	1895-1931	282	84	22	.755
Amos Alonzo Stagg, Springfield, Chicago	1890-1926	235	94	24	.700

38 SEASONS

Coach, Team(s)	Seasons	W	L	T	Pct.
Bear Bryant, Maryland, Kentucky, Texas A&M, Alabama	1945-82	323	85	17	.780
Pop Warner, Georgia, Cornell, Carlisle, Pittsburgh, Stanford	1895-1932	288	88	23	.751
Amos Alonzo Stagg, Springfield, Chicago	1890-1927	239	98	24	.695
Jess Neely, Rhodes, Clemson, Rice	1924-27, 31-64	203	160	19	.556

39 SEASONS

Coach, Team(s)	Seasons	W	L	T	Pct.
Pop Warner, Georgia, Cornell, Carlisle, Pittsburgh, Stanford, Temple	1895-1933	293	91	23	.748
Amos Alonzo Stagg, Springfield, Chicago	1890-1928	241	105	24	.684
Jess Neely, Rhodes, Clemson, Rice	1924-27, 31-65	205	168	19	.539
Eddie Anderson, Loras, DePaul, Holy Cross, Iowa	1922-42, 46-64	201	128	15	.606

40 SEASONS

Coach, Team(s)	Seasons	W	L	T	Pct.
Pop Warner, Georgia, Cornell, Carlisle, Pittsburgh, Stanford, Temple	1895-1934	300	92	25	.749
Amos Alonzo Stagg, Springfield, Chicago	1890-1929	248	108	24	.684
Jess Neely, Rhodes, Clemson, Rice	1924-27, 31-66	207	176	19	.539

41 SEASONS

Coach, Team(s)	Seasons	W	L	T	Pct.
Pop Warner, Georgia, Cornell, Carlisle, Pittsburgh, Stanford, Temple	1895-1935	307	95	25	.748
Amos Alonzo Stagg, Springfield, Chicago	1890-1930	249	113	26	.675

42 SEASONS

Coach, Team(s)	Seasons	W	L	T	Pct.
Pop Warner, Georgia, Cornell, Carlisle, Pittsburgh, Stanford, Temple	1895-1936	313	98	27	.745
Amos Alonzo Stagg, Springfield, Chicago	1890-1931	251	118	27	.668

43 SEASONS

Coach, Team(s)	Seasons	W	L	T	Pct.
Pop Warner, Georgia, Cornell, Carlisle, Pittsburgh, Stanford, Temple	1895-1937	316	100	31	.742
Amos Alonzo Stagg, Springfield, Chicago	1890-1932	254	122	28	.663

44 SEASONS

Coach, Team(s)	Seasons	W	L	T	Pct.
Pop Warner, Georgia, Cornell, Carlisle, Pittsburgh, Stanford, Temple	1895-1938	319	106	32	.733
Amos Alonzo Stagg, Springfield, Chicago, Pacific (Cal.)	1890-1933	259	127	28	.659

*Active coach.

Division I-A Best Career Starts by Percentage

(Head coaches with at least half their seasons at major college at the time and minimum five years coached)

1 SEASON

Coach, Team	Season	W	L	T	Pct.
Walter Camp, Yale	1888	13	0	0	1.000
Dan McGugin, Vanderbilt	1904	9	0	0	1.000
Bennie Oosterbaan, Michigan	1948	9	0	0	1.000
Carroll Widdoes, Ohio St.	1944	9	0	0	1.000
Galen Hall, Florida	1984	8	0	0	1.000
William Dietz, Washington St.	1915	7	0	0	1.000
John Heisman, Oberlin	1892	7	0	0	1.000
Dick Crum, Miami (Ohio)	1974	10	0	1	.955
Barry Switzer, Oklahoma	1973	10	0	1	.955
Aldo Donelli, Duquesne	1939	8	0	1	.944
Francis Schmidt, Tulsa	1919	8	0	1	.944

2 SEASONS

Coach, Team	Seasons	W	L	T	Pct.
Barry Switzer, Oklahoma	1973-74	21	0	1	.977
Walter Camp, Yale	1888-89	28	1	0	.966
Francis Schmidt, Tulsa	1919-20	18	0	2	.950
John Bateman, Rutgers	1960-61	17	1	0	.944
Dan McGugin, Vanderbilt	1904-05	16	1	0	.941
Dick Crum, Miami (Ohio)	1974-75	21	1	1	.935
Galen Hall, Florida	1984-85	17	1	1	.921
Bob Neyland, Tennessee	1926-27	16	1	1	.917
Aldo Donelli, Duquesne	1939-40	15	1	1	.912
Charley Moran, Texas A&M	1909-10	15	1	1	.912

3 SEASONS

Coach, Team(s)	Seasons	W	L	T	Pct.
Barry Switzer, Oklahoma	1973-75	32	1	1	.956
Walter Camp, Yale	1888-90	41	2	0	.953
Aldo Donelli, Duquesne	1939-41	23	1	1	.940
Bob Neyland, Tennessee	1926-28	25	1	2	.929
Dan McGugin, Vanderbilt	1904-06	24	2	0	.923
Frank Leahy, Boston College, Notre Dame	1939-41	28	2	1	.919
Knute Rockne, Notre Dame	1918-20	21	1	2	.917
Elmer Henderson, Southern Cal	1919-21	20	2	0	.909
George Woodruff, Pennsylvania	1892-94	39	4	0	.907
Larry Siemering, Pacific (Cal.)	1947-49	28	2	2	.906

4 SEASONS

Coach, Team(s)	Seasons	W	L	T	Pct.
Gil Dobie, North Dak. St., Washington	1906-09	20	0	1	.976
Walter Camp, Yale	1888-91	54	2	0	.964
Barry Switzer, Oklahoma	1973-76	41	3	2	.935
Bob Neyland, Tennessee	1926-29	34	1	3	.934
George Woodruff, Pennsylvania	1892-95	53	4	0	.930
Knute Rockne, Notre Dame	1918-21	31	2	2	.914
Elmer Henderson, Southern Cal	1919-22	30	3	0	.909
Wallace Wade, Alabama	1923-26	34	3	2	.897
William Murray, Delaware	1940-42, 46	30	3	1	.897
Bud Wilkinson, Oklahoma	1947-50	38	4	1	.895

5 SEASONS

Coach, Team(s)	Seasons	W	L	T	Pct.
Gil Dobie, North Dak. St., Washington	1906-10	26	0	1	.981
Walter Camp, Yale, Stanford	1888-92	69	2	2	.959
George Woodruff, Pennsylvania	1892-96	67	5	0	.931
Bob Neyland, Tennessee	1926-30	43	2	3	.927
Knute Rockne, Notre Dame	1918-22	39	3	3	.900
Barry Switzer, Oklahoma	1973-77	51	5	2	.896
Elmer Henderson, Southern Cal	1919-23	36	5	0	.878
Bud Wilkinson, Oklahoma	1947-51	46	6	1	.877
Henry Williams, Army, Minnesota	1891, 1900-03	47	4	6	.877
Frank Leahy, Boston College, Notre Dame	1939-43	44	5	3	.875

6 SEASONS

Coach, Team(s)	Seasons	W	L	T	Pct.
Gil Dobie, North Dak. St., Washington	1906-11	33	0	1	.985
George Woodruff, Pennsylvania	1892-97	82	5	0	.943
Bob Neyland, Tennessee	1926-31	52	2	4	.931
Walter Camp, Yale, Stanford	1888-92, 94	75	5	2	.927
Knute Rockne, Notre Dame	1918-23	48	4	3	.900
Barry Switzer, Oklahoma	1973-78	62	6	2	.900
Henry Williams, Army, Minnesota	1891, 1900-04	60	4	6	.900
Frank Leahy, Boston College, Notre Dame	1939-43, 46	52	5	4	.885
Bud Wilkinson, Oklahoma	1947-52	54	7	2	.873
Fielding Yost, Ohio Wesleyan, Nebraska, Kansas, Stanford, Michigan	1897-1902	53	7	2	.871

7 SEASONS

Coach, Team(s)	Seasons	W	L	T	Pct.
Gil Dobie, North Dak. St., Washington	1906-12	39	0	1	.988
George Woodruff, Pennsylvania	1892-98	94	6	0	.940
Bob Neyland, Tennessee	1926-32	61	2	5	.934
Walter Camp, Yale, Stanford	1888-92, 94-95	79	5	3	.925
Knute Rockne, Notre Dame	1918-24	58	4	3	.915
Barry Switzer, Oklahoma	1973-79	73	7	2	.902
Henry Williams, Army, Minnesota	1891, 1900-05	70	5	6	.901
Frank Leahy, Boston College, Notre Dame	1939-43, 46-47	61	5	4	.900
Fielding Yost, Ohio Wesleyan, Nebraska, Kansas, Stanford, Michigan	1897-1903	64	7	3	.897
Bud Wilkinson, Oklahoma	1947-53	63	8	3	.872

8 SEASONS

Coach, Team(s)	Seasons	W	L	T	Pct.
Gil Dobie, North Dak. St., Washington	1906-13	46	0	1	.989
George Woodruff, Pennsylvania	1892-99	102	9	2	.912
Bob Neyland, Tennessee	1926-33	68	5	5	.904
Fielding Yost, Ohio Wesleyan, Nebraska, Kansas, Stanford, Michigan	1897-1904	74	7	3	.898
Henry Williams, Army, Minnesota	1891, 1900-06	74	6	6	.895
Barry Switzer, Oklahoma	1973-80	83	9	2	.894
Knute Rockne, Notre Dame	1918-25	65	6	4	.893
Bud Wilkinson, Oklahoma	1947-54	73	8	3	.887
Frank Leahy, Boston College, Notre Dame	1939-43, 46-48	70	5	5	.882
Percy Haughton, Cornell, Harvard	1899-1900, 08-13	66	8	3	.877

9 SEASONS

Coach, Team(s)	Seasons	W	L	T	Pct.
Gil Dobie, North Dak. St., Washington	1906-14	52	0	2	.981
Frank Leahy, Boston College, Notre Dame	1939-43, 46-49	80	5	5	.917
George Woodruff, Pennsylvania	1892-1900	114	10	2	.913
Fielding Yost, Ohio Wesleyan, Nebraska, Kansas, Stanford, Michigan	1897-1905	86	8	3	.902
Bud Wilkinson, Oklahoma	1947-55	84	8	3	.900
Knute Rockne, Notre Dame	1918-26	74	7	4	.894
Bob Neyland, Tennessee	1926-34	76	7	5	.892
Percy Haughton, Cornell, Harvard	1899-1900, 08-14	73	8	5	.878
Henry Williams, Army, Minnesota	1891, 1900-07	76	8	7	.874
Barry Switzer, Oklahoma	1973-81	90	13	3	.863

10 SEASONS

Coach, Team(s)	Seasons	W	L	T	Pct.
Gil Dobie, North Dak. St., Washington	1906-15	59	0	2	.984
Bud Wilkinson, Oklahoma	1947-56	94	8	3	.910
Fielding Yost, Ohio Wesleyan, Nebraska, Kansas, Stanford, Michigan	1897-1906	90	9	3	.897
Knute Rockne, Notre Dame	1918-27	81	8	5	.888
George Woodruff, Pennsylvania	1892-1901	124	15	2	.887
Percy Haughton, Cornell, Harvard	1899-1900, 08-15	81	9	5	.879
Frank Leahy, Boston College, Notre Dame	1939-43, 46-50	84	9	6	.879
Bob Neyland, Tennessee	1926-34, 36	82	9	7	.872
Henry Williams, Army, Minnesota	1891, 1900-08	79	10	8	.856
Barry Switzer, Oklahoma	1973-82	98	17	3	.843

11 SEASONS

Coach, Team(s)	Seasons	W	L	T	Pct.
Gil Dobie, North Dak. St., Washington	1906-16	65	0	3	.978
Bud Wilkinson, Oklahoma	1947-57	104	9	3	.909
Fielding Yost, Ohio Wesleyan, Nebraska, Kansas, Stanford, Michigan	1897-1907	95	10	3	.894
Frank Leahy, Boston College, Notre Dame	1939-43, 46-51	91	11	7	.867
Percy Haughton, Cornell, Harvard	1899-1900, 08-16	88	12	5	.862
Knute Rockne, Notre Dame	1918-28	86	12	5	.859
George Woodruff, Pennsylvania, Illinois	1892-1901, 03	132	21	2	.858
Henry Williams, Army, Minnesota	1891, 1900-09	85	11	8	.856
Bob Neyland, Tennessee	1926-34, 36-37	88	12	8	.852
Charley Moran, Texas A&M, Centre	1909-14, 19-23	80	14	5	.833

12 SEASONS

Coach, Team(s)	Seasons	W	L	T	Pct.
Gil Dobie, North Dak. St., Washington, Navy	1906-17	72	1	3	.967
Bud Wilkinson, Oklahoma	1947-58	114	10	3	.909
Fielding Yost, Ohio Wesleyan, Nebraska, Kansas, Stanford, Michigan	1897-1908	100	12	4	.879

Coach, Team(s)	Seasons	W	L	T	Pct.
Knute Rockne, Notre Dame	1918-29	95	12	5	.871
Bob Neyland, Tennessee	1926-34, 36-38	99	12	8	.866
Frank Leahy, Boston College, Notre Dame	1939-43, 46-52	98	13	8	.857
Henry Williams, Army, Minnesota	1891, 1900-10	91	12	8	.856
George Woodruff, Pennsylvania, Illinois, Carlisle	1892-1901, 03, 05	142	25	2	.846
Percy Haughton, Cornell, Harvard, Columbia	1899-1900, 08-16, 23	92	16	6	.833
Charley Moran, Texas A&M, Centre, Bucknell	1909-14, 19-24	88	16	5	.830

13 SEASONS

Coach, Team(s)	Seasons	W	L	T	Pct.
Gil Dobie, North Dak. St., Washington, Navy	1906-18	76	2	3	.957
Bud Wilkinson, Oklahoma	1947-59	121	13	3	.894
Knute Rockne, Notre Dame	1918-30	105	12	5	.881
Fielding Yost, Ohio Wesleyan, Nebraska, Kansas, Stanford, Michigan	1897-1909	106	13	4	.878
Bob Neyland, Tennessee	1926-34, 36-39	109	13	8	.869
Frank Leahy, Boston College, Notre Dame	1939-43, 46-53	107	13	9	.864
Henry Williams, Army, Minnesota	1891, 1900-11	97	12	9	.860
Percy Haughton, Cornell, Harvard, Columbia	1899-1900, 08-16, 23-24	96	17	6	.832
Barry Switzer, Oklahoma	1973-85	126	24	4	.831
*Joe Paterno, Penn St.	1966-78	123	25	1	.829

14 SEASONS

Coach, Team(s)	Seasons	W	L	T	Pct.
Gil Dobie, North Dak. St., Washington, Navy	1906-19	82	3	3	.949
Bob Neyland, Tennessee	1926-34, 36-40	119	14	8	.872
Fielding Yost, Ohio Wesleyan, Nebraska, Kansas, Stanford, Michigan	1897-1910	109	13	7	.872
Bud Wilkinson, Oklahoma	1947-60	124	19	4	.857
Henry Williams, Army, Minnesota	1891, 1900-12	101	15	9	.844
Barry Switzer, Oklahoma	1973-86	137	25	4	.837
*Joe Paterno, Penn St.	1966-79	131	29	1	.817
Fred Folsom, Colorado, Dartmouth	1895-99, 1901-06, 08-10	83	17	5	.814
Elmer Henderson, Southern Cal, Tulsa	1919-32	101	23	3	.807
Tom Osborne, Nebraska	1973-86	137	32	2	.807

15 SEASONS

Coach, Team(s)	Seasons	W	L	T	Pct.
Gil Dobie, North Dak. St., Washington, Navy, Cornell	1906-20	88	5	3	.932
Bob Neyland, Tennessee	1926-34, 36-40, 46	128	16	8	.868
Fielding Yost, Ohio Wesleyan, Nebraska, Kansas, Stanford, Michigan	1897-1911	114	14	9	.858
Barry Switzer, Oklahoma	1973-87	148	26	4	.843
Henry Williams, Army, Minnesota	1891, 1900-13	106	17	9	.837
Bud Wilkinson, Oklahoma	1947-61	129	24	4	.834
Fred Folsom, Colorado, Dartmouth	1895-99, 1901-06, 08-11	89	17	5	.824
*Joe Paterno, Penn St.	1966-80	141	31	1	.818
Elmer Henderson, Southern Cal, Tulsa	1919-33	107	24	3	.810
Tom Osborne, Nebraska	1973-87	147	34	2	.809

16 SEASONS

Coach, Team(s)	Seasons	W	L	T	Pct.
Gil Dobie, North Dak. St., Washington, Navy, Cornell	1906-21	96	5	3	.938
Fielding Yost, Ohio Wesleyan, Nebraska, Kansas, Stanford, Michigan	1897-1912	119	16	9	.858
Bob Neyland, Tennessee	1926-34, 36-40, 46-47	133	21	8	.846
Henry Williams, Army, Minnesota	1891, 1900-14	112	18	9	.838
Barry Switzer, Oklahoma	1973-88	157	29	4	.837
Bud Wilkinson, Oklahoma	1947-62	137	27	4	.827
*Joe Paterno, Penn St.	1966-81	151	33	1	.819
Fred Folsom, Colorado, Dartmouth	1895-99, 1901-06, 08-12	95	20	5	.813
Tom Osborne, Nebraska	1973-88	158	36	2	.811
Bob Devaney, Wyoming, Nebraska	1957-72	136	30	7	.806

17 SEASONS

Coach, Team(s)	Seasons	W	L	T	Pct.
Gil Dobie, North Dak. St., Washington, Navy, Cornell	1906-22	104	5	3	.942
Fielding Yost, Ohio Wesleyan, Nebraska, Kansas, Stanford, Michigan	1897-1913	125	17	9	.858
Henry Williams, Army, Minnesota	1891, 1900-15	118	18	10	.842
Bud Wilkinson, Oklahoma	1947-63	145	29	4	.826

Photo from Oklahoma sports information

Bud Wilkinson's 17-year coaching career at Oklahoma resulted in an .826 winning percentage (145-29-4)—the fourth best mark in Division I-A history during that time span.

Coach, Team(s)	Seasons	W	L	T	Pct.
Bob Neyland, Tennessee	1926-34, 36-40, 46-48	137	25	10	.826
*Joe Paterno, Penn St.	1966-82	162	34	1	.825
Tom Osborne, Nebraska	1973-89	168	38	2	.813
Fred Folsom, Colorado, Dartmouth	1895-99, 1901-06, 08-13	100	21	6	.811
Wallace Wade, Alabama, Duke	1923-39	130	29	6	.806
Red Blaik, Dartmouth, Army	1934-50	120	26	10	.801
Jock Sutherland, Lafayette, Pittsburgh	1919-35	119	25	12	.801

18 SEASONS

Coach, Team(s)	Seasons	W	L	T	Pct.
Gil Dobie, North Dak. St., Washington, Navy, Cornell	1906-23	112	5	3	.946
Fielding Yost, Ohio Wesleyan, Nebraska Kansas, Stanford, Michigan	1897-1914	131	20	9	.847
Henry Williams, Army, Minnesota	1891, 1900-16	124	19	10	.843
Bob Neyland, Tennessee	1926-34, 36-40, 46-49	144	27	11	.821
*Joe Paterno, Penn St.	1966-83	170	38	2	.814
Fred Folsom, Colorado, Dartmouth	1895-99, 1901-06, 08-14	105	22	6	.812
Tom Osborne, Nebraska	1973-90	177	41	2	.809
Frank Thomas, Chattanooga, Alabama	1925-28, 31-42, 44-45	134	29	9	.805
Wallace Wade, Alabama, Duke	1923-40	137	31	6	.805
Jock Sutherland, Lafayette, Pittsburgh	1919-36	127	26	13	.804

19 SEASONS

Coach, Team(s)	Seasons	W	L	T	Pct.
Gil Dobie, North Dak. St., Washington, Navy, Cornell	1906-24	116	9	3	.918
Henry Williams, Army, Minnesota	1891, 1900-17	128	20	10	.842
Fielding Yost, Ohio Wesleyan, Nebraska, Kansas, Stanford, Michigan	1897-1915	135	23	10	.833
Bob Neyland, Tennessee	1926-34, 36-40, 46-50	155	28	11	.827
Jock Sutherland, Lafayette, Pittsburgh	1919-37	136	26	14	.813
Wallace Wade, Alabama, Duke	1923-41	146	32	6	.810
Tom Osborne, Nebraska	1973-91	186	43	3	.808
*Joe Paterno, Penn St.	1966-84	176	43	2	.801
Frank Thomas, Chattanooga, Alabama	1925-28, 31-42, 44-46	141	33	9	.795
Bo Schembechler, Miami (Ohio), Michigan	1963-81	163	41	6	.790

20 SEASONS

Coach, Team(s)	Seasons	W	L	T	Pct.
Gil Dobie, North Dak. St., Washington, Navy, Cornell	1906-25	122	11	3	.908
Henry Williams, Army, Minnesota	1891, 1900-18	133	22	11	.834
Bob Neyland, Tennessee	1926-34, 36-40, 46-51	165	29	11	.832
Fielding Yost, Ohio Wesleyan, Nebraska, Kansas, Stanford, Michigan	1897-1916	142	25	10	.831
Jock Sutherland, Lafayette, Pittsburgh	1919-38	144	28	14	.812
*Joe Paterno, Penn St.	1966-85	187	44	2	.807
Tom Osborne, Nebraska	1973-92	195	46	3	.805
Wallace Wade, Alabama, Duke	1923-41, 46	150	37	6	.793
Bo Schembechler, Miami (Ohio), Michigan	1963-82	171	45	6	.784
Dan McGugin, Vanderbilt	1904-17, 19-24	131	33	12	.778

21 SEASONS

Coach, Team(s)	Seasons	W	L	T	Pct.
Gil Dobie, North Dak. St., Washington, Navy, Cornell	1906-26	128	12	4	.903
Fielding Yost, Ohio Wesleyan, Nebraska, Kansas, Stanford, Michigan	1897-1917	150	27	10	.829
Bob Neyland, Tennessee	1926-34, 36-40, 46-52	173	31	12	.829
Henry Williams, Army, Minnesota	1891, 1900-19	137	24	12	.827
*Joe Paterno, Penn St.	1966-86	199	44	2	.816
Tom Osborne, Nebraska	1973-93	206	47	3	.811
Wallace Wade, Alabama, Duke	1923-41, 46-47	154	40	8	.782
Bo Schembechler, Miami (Ohio), Michigan	1963-83	180	48	6	.782
Howard Jones, Syracuse, Yale, Ohio St., Iowa, Duke, Southern Cal	1908-10, 13, 16-32	147	38	10	.779
Dan McGugin, Vanderbilt	1904-17, 19-25	137	36	12	.773

22 SEASONS

Coach, Team(s)	Seasons	W	L	T	Pct.
Gil Dobie, North Dak. St., Washington, Navy, Cornell	1906-27	131	15	6	.882
Fielding Yost, Ohio Wesleyan, Nebraska, Kansas, Stanford, Michigan	1897-1918	155	27	10	.833
Tom Osborne, Nebraska	1973-94	219	47	3	.820
*Joe Paterno, Penn St.	1966-87	207	48	2	.809
Henry Williams, Army, Minnesota	1891, 1900-20	138	30	12	.800
Howard Jones, Syracuse, Yale, Ohio St., Iowa, Duke, Southern Cal	1908-10, 13, 16-33	157	39	11	.785
Dan McGugin, Vanderbilt	1904-17, 19-26	145	37	12	.778
Wallace Wade, Alabama, Duke	1923-41, 46-48	158	43	10	.773
Bo Schembechler, Miami (Ohio), Michigan	1963-84	186	54	6	.768
Bear Bryant, Maryland, Kentucky, Texas A&M, Alabama	1945-66	171	51	14	.767

23 SEASONS

Coach, Team(s)	Seasons	W	L	T	Pct.
Gil Dobie, North Dak. St., Washington, Navy, Cornell	1906-28	134	18	8	.863
Tom Osborne, Nebraska	1973-95	231	47	3	.827
Fielding Yost, Ohio Wesleyan, Nebraska, Kansas, Stanford, Michigan	1897-1919	158	31	10	.819
*Joe Paterno, Penn St.	1966-88	212	54	2	.795
Henry Williams, Army, Minnesota	1891, 1900-21	141	34	12	.786
Dan McGugin, Vanderbilt	1904-17, 19-27	153	38	14	.780
Bo Schembechler, Miami (Ohio), Michigan	1963-85	196	55	7	.773
Wallace Wade, Alabama, Duke	1923-41, 46-49	164	46	10	.768
Howard Jones, Syracuse, Yale, Ohio St., Iowa, Duke, Southern Cal	1908-10, 13, 16-34	161	45	12	.766
Bear Bryant, Maryland, Kentucky, Texas A&M, Alabama	1945-67	179	53	15	.755
Johnny Vaught, Mississippi	1947-69	178	54	12	.754

24 SEASONS

Coach, Team(s)	Seasons	W	L	T	Pct.
Gil Dobie, North Dak. St., Washington, Navy, Cornell	1906-29	140	20	8	.857
Tom Osborne, Nebraska	1973-96	242	49	3	.828
Fielding Yost, Ohio Wesleyan, Nebraska, Kansas, Stanford, Michigan	1897-1920	163	33	10	.816
*Joe Paterno, Penn St.	1966-89	220	57	3	.791
Dan McGugin, Vanderbilt	1904-17, 19-28	161	40	14	.781
Bo Schembechler, Miami (Ohio), Michigan	1963-86	207	57	7	.777
Wallace Wade, Alabama, Duke	1923-41, 46-50	171	49	10	.765
Bear Bryant, Maryland, Kentucky, Texas A&M, Alabama	1945-68	187	56	15	.754
Red Blaik, Dartmouth, Army	1934-57	158	48	13	.751
Johnny Vaught, Mississippi	1947-70	185	58	12	.749
Howard Jones, Syracuse, Yale, Ohio St., Iowa, Duke, Southern Cal	1908-10, 13, 16-35	166	52	12	.748

25 SEASONS

Coach, Team(s)	Seasons	W	L	T	Pct.
Gil Dobie, North Dak. St., Washington, Navy, Cornell	1906-30	146	22	8	.852
Tom Osborne, Nebraska	1973-97	255	49	3	.836
Fielding Yost, Ohio Wesleyan, Nebraska, Kansas, Stanford, Michigan	1897-1921	168	34	11	.815
*Joe Paterno, Penn St.	1966-90	229	60	3	.789
Dan McGugin, Vanderbilt	1904-17, 19-29	168	42	14	.781
Bo Schembechler, Miami (Ohio), Michigan	1963-87	215	61	7	.772
Red Blaik, Dartmouth, Army	1934-58	166	48	14	.759
John Heisman, Oberlin, Akron, Auburn, Clemson, Georgia Tech	1892-1916	127	37	11	.757
Howard Jones, Syracuse, Yale, Ohio St., Iowa, Duke, Southern Cal	1908-10, 13, 16-36	170	54	15	.755
Woody Hayes, Denison, Miami (Ohio), Ohio St.	1946-70	167	54	7	.748
Bear Bryant, Maryland, Kentucky, Texas A&M, Alabama	1945-69	193	61	15	.745

26 SEASONS

Coach, Team(s)	Seasons	W	L	T	Pct.
Gil Dobie, North Dak. St., Washington, Navy, Cornell	1906-31	153	23	8	.853
Fielding Yost, Ohio Wesleyan, Nebraska, Kansas, Stanford, Michigan	1897-1922	174	34	12	.818
*Joe Paterno, Penn St.	1966-91	240	62	3	.792
Dan McGugin, Vanderbilt	1904-17, 19-30	176	44	14	.782
Bo Schembechler, Miami (Ohio), Michigan	1963-88	224	63	8	.773
John Heisman, Oberlin, Akron, Auburn, Clemson, Georgia Tech	1892-1917	136	37	11	.769
Pop Warner, Georgia, Cornell, Carlisle, Pittsburgh	1895-1920	199	62	14	.749
Woody Hayes, Denison, Miami (Ohio), Ohio St.	1946-71	173	58	7	.742
Amos Alonzo Stagg, Springfield, Chicago	1890-1915	193	62	19	.739
*Bobby Bowden, Samford, West Va., Florida St.	1959-62, 70-91	216	76	3	.737

27 SEASONS

Coach, Team(s)	Seasons	W	L	T	Pct.
Gil Dobie, North Dak. St., Washington, Navy, Cornell	1906-32	158	25	9	.846
Fielding Yost, Ohio Wesleyan, Nebraska, Kansas, Stanford, Michigan	1897-1923	182	34	12	.825
*Joe Paterno, Penn St.	1966-92	247	67	3	.784
Bo Schembechler, Miami (Ohio), Michigan	1963-89	234	65	8	.775
Dan McGugin, Vanderbilt	1904-17, 19-31	181	48	14	.774
John Heisman, Oberlin, Akron, Auburn, Clemson, Georgia Tech	1892-1918	142	38	11	.772
Woody Hayes, Denison, Miami (Ohio), Ohio St.	1946-72	182	60	7	.745
Pop Warner, Georgia, Cornell, Carlisle, Pittsburgh	1895-1921	204	65	15	.745
*Bobby Bowden, Samford, West Va., Florida St.	1959-62, 70-92	227	77	3	.744
Bear Bryant, Maryland, Kentucky, Texas A&M, Alabama	1945-71	210	67	16	.744

28 SEASONS

Coach, Team(s)	Seasons	W	L	T	Pct.
Gil Dobie, North Dak. St., Washington, Navy, Cornell	1906-33	162	28	9	.837
Fielding Yost, Ohio Wesleyan, Nebraska, Kansas, Stanford, Michigan	1897-1923, 25	189	35	12	.826
*Joe Paterno, Penn St.	1966-93	257	69	3	.786
Dan McGugin, Vanderbilt	1904-17, 19-32	187	49	16	.774
John Heisman, Oberlin, Akron, Auburn, Clemson, Georgia Tech	1892-1919	149	41	11	.769
Woody Hayes, Denison, Miami (Ohio), Ohio St.	1946-73	192	60	8	.754
*Bobby Bowden, Samford, West Va., Florida St.	1959-62, 70-93	239	78	3	.752
Bear Bryant, Maryland, Kentucky, Texas A&M, Alabama	1945-72	220	69	16	.748
Pop Warner, Georgia, Cornell, Carlisle, Pittsburgh	1895-1922	212	67	15	.747
Howard Jones, Syracuse, Yale, Ohio St., Iowa, Duke, Southern Cal	1908-10, 13, 16-39	191	60	19	.743

29 SEASONS

Coach, Team(s)	Seasons	W	L	T	Pct.
Fielding Yost, Ohio Wesleyan, Nebraska, Kansas, Stanford, Michigan	1897-1923, 25-26	196	36	12	.828
Gil Dobie, North Dak. St., Washington, Navy, Cornell	1906-34	164	33	9	.818

Coach, Team(s)	Seasons	W	L	T	Pct.
*Joe Paterno, Penn St.	1966-94	269	69	3	.793
Dan McGugin, Vanderbilt	1904-17, 19-33	191	52	19	.765
John Heisman, Oberlin, Akron, Auburn, Clemson, Georgia Tech, Pennsylvania	1892-1920	155	45	11	.761
Woody Hayes, Denison, Miami (Ohio), Ohio St.	1946-74	202	62	8	.757
*Bobby Bowden, Samford, West Va., Florida St.	1959-62, 70-94	249	79	4	.756
Bear Bryant, Maryland, Kentucky, Texas A&M, Alabama	1945-73	231	70	16	.754
Pop Warner, Georgia, Cornell, Carlisle, Pittsburgh	1895-1923	217	71	15	.741
Howard Jones, Syracuse, Yale, Ohio St., Iowa, Duke, Southern Cal	1908-10, 13, 16-40	194	64	21	.733

30 SEASONS

Coach, Team(s)	Seasons	W	L	T	Pct.
Gil Dobie, North Dak. St., Washington, Navy, Cornell	1906-35	164	39	10	.793
*Joe Paterno, Penn St.	1966-95	278	72	3	.792
Woody Hayes, Denison, Miami (Ohio), Ohio St.	1946-75	213	63	8	.764
Dan McGugin, Vanderbilt	1904-17, 19-34	197	55	19	.762
Bear Bryant, Maryland, Kentucky, Texas A&M, Alabama	1945-74	242	71	16	.760
*Bobby Bowden, Samford, West Va., Florida St.	1959-62, 70-95	259	81	4	.759
John Heisman, Oberlin, Akron, Auburn, Clemson, Georgia Tech, Pennsylvania	1892-1921	159	48	13	.752
Pop Warner, Georgia, Cornell, Carlisle, Pittsburgh, Stanford	1895-1924	224	72	16	.744
Amos Alonzo Stagg, Springfield, Chicago	1890-1919	204	76	20	.713
Dana X. Bible, Mississippi Col., LSU, Texas A&M, Nebraska, Texas	1913-17, 19-43	175	67	23	.704

31 SEASONS

Coach, Team(s)	Seasons	W	L	T	Pct.
*Joe Paterno, Penn St.	1966-96	289	74	3	.794
Gil Dobie, North Dak. St., Washington, Navy, Cornell, Boston College	1906-36	170	40	12	.793
Bear Bryant, Maryland, Kentucky, Texas A&M, Alabama	1945-75	253	72	16	.765
Woody Hayes, Denison, Miami (Ohio), Ohio St.	1946-76	222	65	9	.765
*Bobby Bowden, Samford, West Va., Florida St.	1959-62, 70-96	270	82	4	.764
John Heisman, Oberlin, Akron, Auburn, Clemson, Georgia Tech, Pennsylvania	1892-1922	165	51	13	.749
Pop Warner, Georgia, Cornell, Carlisle, Pittsburgh, Stanford	1895-1925	231	74	16	.745
Amos Alonzo Stagg, Springfield, Chicago	1890-1920	207	80	20	.707
Dana X. Bible, Mississippi Col., LSU, Texas A&M, Nebraska, Texas	1913-17, 19-44	180	69	23	.704

32 SEASONS

Coach, Team(s)	Seasons	W	L	T	Pct.
*Joe Paterno, Penn St.	1966-97	298	77	3	.792
Gil Dobie, North Dak. St., Washington, Navy, Cornell, Boston College	1906-37	174	44	13	.781
*Bobby Bowden, Stamford, West Va., Florida St.	1959-62, 70-97	281	83	4	.769
Bear Bryant, Maryland, Kentucky, Texas A&M, Alabama	1945-76	262	75	16	.765
Woody Hayes, Denison, Miami (Ohio), Ohio St.	1946-77	231	68	9	.765
Pop Warner, Georgia, Cornell, Carlisle, Pittsburgh, Stanford	1895-1926	241	74	17	.752
John Heisman, Oberlin, Akron, Auburn, Clemson, Georgia Tech, Pennsylvania, Wash. & Jeff.	1892-1923	171	52	14	.751
Dana X. Bible, Mississippi Col., LSU, Texas A&M, Nebraska, Texas	1913-17, 19-45	190	70	23	.712
Amos Alonzo Stagg, Springfield, Chicago	1890-1921	213	81	20	.710

33 SEASONS

Coach, Team(s)	Seasons	W	L	T	Pct.
Gil Dobie, North Dak. St., Washington, Navy, Cornell, Boston College	1906-38	180	45	15	.781
Bear Bryant, Maryland, Kentucky, Texas A&M, Alabama	1945-77	273	76	16	.770
Woody Hayes, Denison, Miami (Ohio), Ohio St.	1946-78	238	72	10	.759
Pop Warner, Georgia, Cornell, Carlisle, Pittsburgh, Stanford	1895-1927	249	76	18	.752
John Heisman, Oberlin, Akron, Auburn, Clemson, Georgia Tech, Pennsylvania, Wash. & Jeff., Rice	1892-1924	175	56	14	.743
Dana X. Bible, Mississippi Col., LSU, Texas A&M, Nebraska, Texas	1913-17, 19-46	198	72	23	.715
Amos Alonzo Stagg, Springfield, Chicago	1890-1922	219	82	20	.713

34 SEASONS

Coach, Team(s)	Seasons	W	L	T	Pct.
Bear Bryant, Maryland, Kentucky, Texas A&M, Alabama	1945-78	284	77	16	.775
Pop Warner, Georgia, Cornell, Carlisle, Pittsburgh, Stanford	1895-1928	257	79	19	.751
John Heisman, Oberlin, Akron, Auburn, Clemson, Georgia Tech, Pennsylvania, Wash. & Jeff., Rice	1892-1925	179	60	15	.734
Amos Alonzo Stagg, Springfield, Chicago.	1890-1923	226	83	20	.717

35 SEASONS

Coach, Team(s)	Seasons	W	L	T	Pct.
Bear Bryant, Maryland, Kentucky, Texas A&M, Alabama	1945-79	296	77	16	.781
Pop Warner, Georgia, Cornell, Carlisle, Pittsburgh, Stanford	1895-1929	266	81	19	.753
John Heisman, Oberlin, Akron, Auburn, Clemson, Georgia Tech, Pennsylvania, Wash. & Jeff., Rice	1892-1926	183	64	16	.726
Amos Alonzo Stagg, Springfield, Chicago.	1890-1924	230	84	23	.717

36 SEASONS

Coach, Team(s)	Seasons	W	L	T	Pct.
Bear Bryant, Maryland, Kentucky, Texas A&M, Alabama	1945-80	306	79	16	.783
Pop Warner, Georgia, Cornell, Carlisle, Pittsburgh, Stanford	1895-1930	275	82	20	.756
John Heisman, Oberlin, Akron, Auburn, Clemson, Georgia Tech, Pennsylvania, Wash. & Jeff., Rice	1892-1927	185	70	17	.711
Amos Alonzo Stagg, Springfield, Chicago.	1890-1925	233	88	24	.710

37 SEASONS

Coach, Team(s)	Seasons	W	L	T	Pct.
Bear Bryant, Maryland, Kentucky, Texas A&M, Alabama	1945-81	315	81	17	.783
Pop Warner, Georgia, Cornell, Carlisle, Pittsburgh, Stanford	1895-1931	282	84	22	.755
Amos Alonzo Stagg, Springfield, Chicago.	1890-1926	235	94	24	.700
Eddie Anderson, Loras, DePaul, Holy Cross, Iowa	1922-31, 33-42, 46-62	194	117	14	.618

38 SEASONS

Coach, Team(s)	Seasons	W	L	T	Pct.
Bear Bryant, Maryland, Kentucky, Texas A&M, Alabama	1945-82	323	85	17	.780
Pop Warner, Georgia, Cornell, Carlisle, Pittsburgh, Stanford	1895-1932	288	88	23	.751
Amos Alonzo Stagg, Springfield, Chicago	1890-1927	239	98	24	.695
Eddie Anderson, Loras, DePaul, Holy Cross, Iowa	1922-31, 33-42, 46-63	196	123	15	.609

39 SEASONS

Coach, Team(s)	Seasons	W	L	T	Pct.
Pop Warner, Georgia, Cornell, Carlisle, Pittsburgh, Stanford, Temple	1895-1933	293	91	23	.748
Amos Alonzo Stagg, Springfield, Chicago	1890-1928	241	105	24	.684
Eddie Anderson, Loras, DePaul, Holy Cross, Iowa	1922-31, 33-42, 46-64	201	128	15	.606

40 SEASONS

Coach, Team(s)	Seasons	W	L	T	Pct.
Pop Warner, Georgia, Cornell, Carlisle, Pittsburgh, Stanford, Temple	1895-1934	300	92	25	.749
Amos Alonzo Stagg, Springfield, Chicago	1890-1929	248	108	24	.684

41 SEASONS

Coach, Team(s)	Seasons	W	L	T	Pct.
Pop Warner, Georgia, Cornell, Carlisle, Pittsburgh, Stanford, Temple	1895-1935	307	95	25	.748
Amos Alonzo Stagg, Springfield, Chicago	1890-1930	249	113	26	.675

42 SEASONS

Coach, Team(s)	Seasons	W	L	T	Pct.
Pop Warner, Georgia, Cornell, Carlisle, Pittsburgh, Stanford, Temple	1895-1936	313	98	27	.745
Amos Alonzo Stagg, Springfield, Chicago	1890-1931	251	118	27	.668

43 SEASONS

Coach, Team(s)	Seasons	W	L	T	Pct.
Pop Warner, Georgia, Cornell, Carlisle, Pittsburgh, Stanford, Temple	1895-1937	316	100	31	.742
Amos Alonzo Stagg, Springfield, Chicago	1890-1932	254	122	28	.663

44 SEASONS

Coach, Team(s)	Seasons	W	L	T	Pct.
Pop Warner, Georgia, Cornell, Carlisle, Pittsburgh, Stanford, Temple	1895-1938	319	106	32	.733
Amos Alonzo Stagg, Springfield, Chicago, Pacific (Cal.)	1890-1933	259	127	28	.659

**Active coach.*

Coaches to Reach 100, 200 and 300 Victories

(Must have five years or 50 victories at a school that was classified as a major college at the time)

100 VICTORIES

Coach (Date Reached Milestone) (Schools Coached and Years)	WHEN MILESTONE REACHED Age in Yrs.-Days	Career Game (Record)	Career Yr.-Game
FRED AKERS (9-17-88) (Wyoming 1975-76, Texas 1977-86, Purdue 1987-90)	50-184	155th (100-52-3)	14-2
WILLIAM ALEXANDER (11-18-39) (Georgia Tech 1920-44)	49-233	189th (100-74-15)	20-7
EDDIE ANDERSON (10-12-46) (Loras 1922-24, DePaul 1925-31, Holy Cross 1933-38, Iowa 1939-42, 1946-49, Holy Cross 1950-64)	45-333	160th (100-50-10)	21-4
IKE ARMSTRONG (10-17-42) (Utah 1925-49)	47-131	141st (100-30-11)	18-4
#FRANK BEAMER (11-9-96) (Murray St. 1981-86, Virginia Tech 1987-97)	50-22	177th (100-73-4)	16-8
MATTY BELL (11-5-38) (Haskell 1920-21, Carroll [Wis.] 1922, Texas Christian 1923-28, Texas A&M 1929-33, Southern Methodist 1935-41, 1945-49)	39-256	169th (100-60-9)	18-6
HUGO BEZDEK (11-22-24) (Oregon 1906, Arkansas 1908-12, Oregon 1913-17, Penn St. 1918-29, Delaware Valley 1949)	40-120	147th (100-34-13)	18-9
DANA X. BIBLE (11-21-31) (Mississippi Col. 1913-15, LSU 1916, Texas A&M 1917, 1919-28, Nebraska 1929-36, Texas 1937-46)	40-44	149th (100-31-18)	18-8
BERNIE BIERMAN (11-11-39) (Montana St. 1919-21, Mississippi St. 1925-26, Tulane 1927-31, Minnesota 1932-41, 1945-50)	45-245	149th (100-38-11)	18-6
BOB BLACKMAN (9-27-69) (Denver 1953-54, Dartmouth 1955-70, Illinois 1971-76, Cornell 1977-82)	51-82	147th (100-42-5)	17-1
RED BLAIK (10-23-48) (Dartmouth 1934-40, Army 1941-58)	51-249	134th (100-25-9)	15-5
#BOBBY BOWDEN (10-7-78) (Samford 1959-62, West Va. 1970-75, Florida St. 1976-97)	48-333	144th (100-44-0)	14-5
#TERRY BOWDEN (12-31-96) (Teikyo Salem 1983-85, Samford 1987-92, Auburn 1993-97)	40-280	147th (100-45-2)	13-12
BILLY BREWER (10-6-90) (Southeast La. 1974-79, Louisiana Tech 1980-82, Mississippi 1983-93)	54-363	184th (100-78-6)	17-5
FRANK BROYLES (11-27-69) (Missouri 1957, Arkansas 1958-76)	44-336	138th (100-36-2)	13-9
EARLE BRUCE (11-3-84) (Tampa 1972, Iowa St. 1973-78, Ohio St. 1979-87, Northern Iowa 1988, Colorado St. 1989-92)	53-240	149th (100-49-0)	13-9
BEAR BRYANT (11-7-59) (Maryland 1945, Kentucky 1946-53, Texas A&M 1954-57, Alabama 1958-82)	46-57	154th (100-44-10)	15-7
WALLY BUTTS (11-15-52) (Georgia 1939-60)	47-281	151st (100-44-7)	14-9
CHARLIE CALDWELL (10-21-50) (Williams 1928-42, Princeton 1945-56)	48-80	163rd (100-55-8)	21-4
FRANK CAMP (10-23-65) (Louisville 1946-68)	60-39	182nd (100-80-2)	20-6
JIM CARLEN (11-8-80) (West Va. 1966-69, Texas Tech 1970-74, South Caro. 1975-81)	47-120	167th (100-61-6)	15-9
LEN CASANOVA (10-2-65) (Santa Clara 1946-49, Pittsburgh 1950, Oregon 1951-66)	59-263	192nd (100-82-10)	20-3
FRANK CAVANAUGH (10-3-25) (Cincinnati 1898, Holy Cross 1903-05, Dartmouth 1911-16, Boston College 1919-26, Fordham 1927-32)	49-158	143rd (100-32-11)	17-1
JERRY CLAIBORNE (11-6-76) (Virginia Tech 1961-70, Maryland 1972-81, Kentucky 1982-89)	48-72	158th (100-54-4)	15-9
#JOHN COOPER (11-17-90) (Tulsa 1977-84, Arizona St. 1985-87, Ohio St. 1988-97)	53-137	162nd (100-57-5)	14-10
FRITZ CRISLER (11-24-45) (Minnesota 1930-31, Princeton 1932-37, Michigan 1938-47)	46-316	138th (100-30-8)	16-10
DICK CRUM (11-15-86) (Miami [Ohio] 1974-77, North Caro. 1978-87, Kent 1988-90)	52-200	148th (100-44-4)	13-10

Coach (Date Reached Milestone) (Schools Coached and Years)	WHEN MILESTONE REACHED Age in Yrs.-Days	Career Game (Record)	Career Yr.-Game
JACK CURTICE (10-3-64) (West Tex. A&M 1940-41, UTEP 1946-49, Utah 1950-57, Stanford 1958-61, UC Santa Barb. 1962-69)	56-118	202nd (100-95-7)	21-1
DUFFY DAUGHERTY (9-25-71) (Michigan St. 1954-72)	56-17	164th (100-60-4)	18-3
#FISHER DeBERRY (9-6-97) (Air Force 1984-97)	59-89	161st (100-60-1)	14-2
DUDLEY DeGROOT (9-17-49) (UC Santa Barb. 1926-28, San Jose St. 1932-39, Rochester 1940-43, West Va. 1948-49, New Mexico 1950-52)	49-302	152nd (100-44-8)	17-1
HERB DEROMEDI (11-16-91) (Central Mich. 1978-93)	52-171	153rd (100-43-10)	14-11
BOB DEVANEY (11-8-69) (Wyoming 1957-61, Nebraska 1962-72)	54-209	133rd (100-28-5)	13-8
DAN DEVINE (10-12-68) (Arizona St. 1955-57, Missouri 1958-70, Notre Dame 1975-80)	43-293	139th (100-31-8)	14-4
DOUG DICKEY (11-27-77) (Tennessee 1964-69, Florida 1970-78)	45-202	156th (100-50-6)	14-10
PAUL DIETZEL (10-6-73) (LSU 1955-61, Army 1962-65, South Caro. 1966-74)	47-188	191st (100-86-5)	19-4
GIL DOBIE (10-20-22) (North Dak. St. 1906-07, Washington 1908-16, Navy 1917-19, Cornell 1920-35, Boston College 1936-38)	43-262	108th (100-5-3)	17-4
BOBBY DODD (12-1-56) (Georgia Tech 1945-66)	48-20	131st (100-28-3)	12-10
MIKE DONAHUE (9-29-23) (Auburn 1904-06, 1908-22, LSU 1923-27)	42-111	140th (100-35-5)	19-1
TERRY DONAHUE (9-10-88) (UCLA 1976-95)	44-78	143rd (100-36-7)	13-2
ALDO DONELLI (10-16-65) (Duquesne 1939-42, Boston U. 1947-56, Columbia 1957-67)	58-86	197th (100-89-8)	23-4
BILL DOOLEY (11-27-82) (North Caro. 1967-77, Virginia Tech 1978-86, Wake Forest 1987-92)	48-192	180th (100-78-2)	16-11
VINCE DOOLEY (9-24-77) (Georgia 1964-88)	45-20	149th (100-44-5)	14-3
FRED DUNLAP (10-29-83) (Lehigh 1965-75, Colgate 1976-87)	55-194	195th (100-91-4)	19-8
PAT DYE (10-4-86) (East Caro. 1974-79, Wyoming 1980, Auburn 1981-92)	46-332	142nd (100-41-1)	13-4
LLOYD EATON (10-4-69) (Alma 1949-55, Northern Mich. 1956, Wyoming 1962-70)	51-101	145th (100-40-5)	16-3
#LaVELL EDWARDS (10-22-83) (Brigham Young 1972-97)	53-11	138th (100-37-1)	12-7
RAY ELIOT (10-10-59) (Illinois Col. 1933-36, Illinois 1942-59)	54-119	191st (100-79-12)	22-3
RIP ENGLE (10-21-61) (Brown 1944-49, Penn St. 1950-65)	55-209	161st (100-53-8)	18-5
DENNIS ERICKSON (10-30-93) (Idaho 1982-85, Wyoming 1986, Washington St. 1987-88, Miami [Fla.] 1989-94)	46-334	137th (100-36-1)	12-7
DON FAUROT (11-1-41) (Northeast Mo. St. 1926-34, Missouri 1935-42, 1946-56)	39-131	171st (100-63-8)	16-6
FRED FOLSOM (11-1-13) (Colorado 1895-1902, Dartmouth 1903-06, Colorado 1908-15)	41-357	126th (100-20-6)	17-6
DANNY FORD (11-13-93) (Clemson 1978-89, Arkansas 1993-97)	45-225	139th (100-34-5)	13-9
#DENNIS FRANCHIONE (9-7-96) (Southwestern Ks. 1981-82, Pittsburg St. 1985-89; Southwest Tex. St. 1990-91, New Mexico 1992-97)	45-163	148th (100-46-2)	14-2
#HAYDEN FRY (9-26-81) (Southern Methodist 1962-72, North Texas 1973-78, Iowa 1979-97)	52-185	207th (100-103-4)	20-3
ANDY GUSTAFSON (9-29-61) (Virginia Tech 1926-29, Miami [Fla.] 1948-63)	58-179	168th (100-64-4)	18-3
WAYNE HARDIN (10-13-79) (Navy 1959-64, Temple 1970-82)	52-204	159th (100-54-5)	16-6
JIM HARKEMA (9-16-89) (Grand Valley St. 1973-82, Eastern Mich. 1983-92)	47-83	167th (100-63-4)	17-3
DICK HARLOW (11-3-34) (Penn St. 1915-17, Colgate 1922-25, Western Md. 1926-34, Harvard 1935-42, 1945-47)	44-67	142nd (100-31-11)	16-5
HARVEY HARMAN (10-4-47) (Haverford 1922-29, Sewanee 1930, Pennsylvania 1931-37, Rutgers 1938-55)	46-334	177th (100-70-7)	22-2
#KEN HATFIELD (11-20-91) (Air Force 1979-83, Arkansas 1984-89, Clemson 1990-93, Rice 1994-97)	48-174	155th (100-52-3)	13-11
WOODY HAYES (10-21-61) (Denison 1946-48, Miami, Ohio 1949-50, Ohio St. 1951-78)	48-249	140th (100-34-6)	16-4
JOHN HEISMAN (9-27-13) (Oberlin 1892, Akron 1893, Oberlin 1894, Auburn 1895-99, Clemson 1900-03, Georgia Tech 1904-19, Pennsylvania 1920-22, Wash. & Jeff. 1923, Rice 1924-27)	43-339	142nd (100-33-9)	22-1
GUS HENDERSON (11-24-32) (Southern Cal 1919-24, Tulsa 1925-35, Occidental 1940-42)	43-259	126th (100-23-3)	14-8
BILL HESS (9-4-76) (Ohio 1958-77)	51-106	182nd (100-78-4)	19-1

Coach (Date Reached Milestone) (Schools Coached and Years)	WHEN MILESTONE REACHED Age in Yrs.-Days	Career Game (Record)	Career Yr.-Game
JIM HESS (9-5-87) (Angelo St. 1974-81, Stephen F. Austin 1982-88, New Mexico St. 1990-96)	50-278	147th (100-43-4)	14-1
LOU HOLTZ (12-31-82) (William & Mary 1969-71, North Caro. St. 1972-75, Arkansas 1977-83, Minnesota 1984-85, Notre Dame 1986-96)	45-359	153rd (100-48-5)	13-12
FRANK HOWARD (9-27-58) (Clemson 1940-69)	49-186	175th (100-65-10)	19-2
DON JAMES (9-15-84) (Kent 1971-74, Washington 1975-92)	51-258	153rd (100-52-1)	14-2
MORLEY JENNINGS (10-3-31) (Ouachita Baptist 1912-25, Baylor 1926-40)	46-253	136th (100-33-3)	20-1
HOWARD JONES (12-3-27) (Syracuse 1908, Yale 1909, Ohio St. 1910, Yale 1913, Iowa 1916-23, Duke 1924, Southern Cal 1925-40)	42-102	142nd (100-33-9)	16-10
LLOYD JORDAN (10-27-56) (Amherst 1932-49, Harvard 1950-56)	55-317	172nd (100-65-7)	22-4
SHUG JORDAN (10-9-65) (Auburn 1951-75)	55-14	148th (100-43-5)	15-4
FRANK KIMBROUGH (9-29-56) (Hardin-Simmons 1935-40, Baylor 1941-42, 1945-46, West Tex. A&M 1947-57)	52-97	181st (100-73-8)	20-3
TONY KNAP (10-2-76) (Utah St. 1963-66, Boise St. 1968-75, UNLV 1976-81)	61-298	135th (100-33-2)	13-4
FRANK KUSH (12-30-70) (Arizona St. 1958-79)	41-344	131st (100-30-1)	13-11
ELMER LAYDEN (10-26-40) (Loras 1925-26, Duquesne 1927-33, Notre Dame 1934-40)	37-175	143rd (100-32-11)	16-4
FRANK LEAHY (10-3-53) (Boston College 1939-40, Notre Dame 1941-53)	45-37	121st (100-13-8)	13-2
LOU LITTLE (9-26-42) (Georgetown 1924-29, Columbia 1930-56)	48-294	161st (100-49-12)	19-1
DICK MacPHERSON (10-28-89) (Massachusetts 1971-77, Syracuse 1981-90)	58-358	171st (100-68-3)	16-7
JOHNNY MAJORS (11-19-83) (Iowa St. 1968-72, Pittsburgh 1973-76, Tennessee 1977-92, Pittsburgh 1993-96)	48-181	185th (100-81-4)	16-10
BILL MALLORY (9-14-85) (Miami, Ohio 1969-73, Colorado 1974-78, Northern Ill. 1980-83, Indiana 1984-96)	50-107	164th (100-63-1)	16-1
BEN MARTIN (11-20-76) (Virginia 1956-57, Air Force 1958-77)	55-145	217th (100-108-9)	21-11
CHARLIE McCLENDON (11-2-74) (LSU 1962-79)	46-222	141st (100-35-6)	13-7
DAN McGUGIN (11-15-19) (Vanderbilt 1904-34)	40-78	132nd (100-25-7)	15-7
JOHN McKAY (1-1-73) (Southern Cal 1960-75)	49-209	139th (100-33-6)	13-12
TUSS McLAUGHRY (10-25-41) (Westminster 1916-18, 1921, Amherst 1922-25, Brown 1926-40, Dartmouth 1941-42, 1945-54)	48-109	196th (100-86-10)	23-5
CHICK MEEHAN (9-28-35) (Syracuse 1920-24, New York U. 1925-31, Manhattan 1932-37)	42-23	146th (100-34-12)	16-2
DUTCH MEYER (9-29-51) (Texas Christian 1934-52)	53-204	182nd (100-71-11)	18-2
CHUCK MILLS (9-15-84) (Pomona-Pitzer 1959-61, Indiana [Pa.] 1962-63, Merchant Marine 1964, Utah St. 1967-72, Wake Forest 1973-77, Southern Ore. St. 1980-88, Coast Guard 1997)	55-287	213th (100-109-4)	22-2
ODUS MITCHELL (11-25-61) (North Texas 1946-66)	59-116	167th (100-59-8)	16-10
AL MOLDE (10-11-86) (Sioux Falls 1971-72, Minn.-Morris 1973-79, Central Mo. St. 1980-82, Eastern Ill. 1983-86, Western Mich. 1987-96)	42-330	162nd (100-56-6)	16-6
CHARLEY MORAN (9-27-30) (Texas A&M 1909-14, Centre 1919-23, Bucknell 1924-26, Catawba 1930-33)	52-217	131st (100-24-7)	15-1
JOE MORRISON (10-29-88) (Chattanooga 1973-79, New Mexico 1980-82, South Caro. 1983-88)	51-69	176th (100-69-7)	16-8
RAY MORRISON (10-2-37) (Southern Methodist 1915-16, Vanderbilt 1918, Southern Methodist 1922-34, Vanderbilt 1935-39, Temple 1940-48, Austin College 1949-52)	52-216	177th (100-54-23)	19-2
BILL MURRAY (11-22-58) (Delaware 1940-42, 1946-50, Duke 1951-65)	50-74	149th (100-40-9)	16-10
JESS NEELY (10-19-46) (Rhodes 1924-27, Clemson 1931-39, Rice 1940-66)	48-288	190th (100-79-11)	20-4
#DON NEHLEN (11-16-85) (Bowling Green 1968-76, West Va. 1980-97)	48-319	162nd (100-57-5)	15-10
BOB NEYLAND (9-29-39) (Tennessee 1926-34, 1936-40, 1946-52)	47-224	120th (100-12-8)	13-1
BOB ODELL (9-24-77) (Bucknell 1958-64, Pennsylvania 1965-70, Williams 1971-86)	55-203	166th (100-64-2)	20-1
JORDAN OLIVAR (10-15-60) (Villanova 1943-48, Loyola Marymount 1949-51, Yale 1952-60)	45-258	159th (100-53-6)	18-4
TOM OSBORNE (9-24-83) (Nebraska 1973-97)	46-211	126th (100-24-2)	11-4

Coach (Date Reached Milestone) (Schools Coached and Years)	WHEN MILESTONE REACHED Age in Yrs.-Days	Career Game (Record)	Career Yr.-Game
BENNIE OWEN (10-4-15) (Washburn 1900, Bethany [Kan.] 1901-04, Oklahoma 1905-26)	40-72	136th (100-28-8)	16-5
ARA PARSEGHIAN (11-26-66) (Miami [Ohio] 1951-55, Northwestern 1956-63, Notre Dame 1964-74)	43-189	147th (100-43-4)	16-10
#JOE PATERNO (11-6-76) (Penn St. 1966-97)	49-320	122nd (100-21-1)	11-9
TOMMY PROTHRO (9-19-70) (Oregon St. 1955-64, UCLA 1965-70)	50-38	155th (100-50-5)	16-2
EDWARD ROBINSON (11-6-15) (Nebraska 1896-97, Brown 1898-1901, Maine 1902, Brown 1904-07, 1910-25)	41-344	165th (100-56-9)	17-7
KNUTE ROCKNE (11-1-30) (Notre Dame 1918-30)	42-242	117th (100-12-5)	13-5
DARRYL ROGERS (9-12-81) (Cal St. Hayward 1965, Fresno St. 1966-72, San Jose St. 1973-75, Michigan St. 1976-79, Arizona St. 1980-84)	47-106	176th (100-70-6)	17-1
BILL ROPER (10-8-27) (VMI 1903-04, Princeton 1906-08, Missouri 1909, Princeton 1910-11, Swarthmore 1915-16, Princeton 1919-30)	47-47	141st (100-26-15)	19-2
DARRELL ROYAL (10-7-67) (Mississippi St. 1954-55, Washington 1956, Texas 1957-76)	43-93	141st (100-38-3)	14-3
RED SANDERS (11-9-57) (Vanderbilt 1940-48, UCLA 1949-57)	52-216	144th (100-41-3)	15-8
PHILIP SARBOE (12-1-60) (Central Wash. 1941-42, Washington St. 1945-49, Humboldt St. 1951-65, Hawaii 1966)	48-233	160th (100-53-7)	17-11
BO SCHEMBECHLER (10-4-75) (Miami [Ohio] 1963-68, Michigan 1969-89)	46-33	130th (100-24-6)	13-4
FRANCIS SCHMIDT (11-5-32) (Tulsa 1919-21, Arkansas 1922-28, Texas Christian 1929-33, Ohio St. 1934-40, Idaho 1941-42)	46-336	136th (100-27-9)	14-8
HOWARD SCHNELLENBERGER (10-28-95) (Miami [Fla.] 1979-83, Louisville 1985-94, Oklahoma 1995)	61-226	177th (100-74-3)	16-8
BEN SCHWARTZWALDER (9-30-65) (Muhlenberg 1946-48, Syracuse 1949-73)	52-120	143rd (100-41-2)	16-2
CLARK SHAUGHNESSY (10-20-34) (Tulane 1915-20, 1922-26, Loyola, Ill. 1927-32, Chicago 1933-39, Stanford 1940-41, Maryland 1942, Pittsburgh 1943-45, Maryland 1946, Hawaii 1965)	42-228	164th (100-50-14)	19-3
DICK SHERIDAN (10-6-90) (Furman 1978-85, North Caro. St. 1986-92)	49-58	147th (100-43-4)	13-6
#JACKIE SHERRILL (10-8-88) (Washington St. 1976, Pittsburgh 1977-81, Texas A&M 1982-88, Mississippi St. 1991-97)	44-314	145th (100-43-2)	13-5
ANDY SMITH (11-10-23) (Pennsylvania 1909-12, Purdue 1913-15, California 1916-25)	40-71	140th (100-29-11)	15-8
CLIPPER SMITH (11-6-42) (Gonzaga 1925-28, Santa Clara 1929-35, Villanova 1936-42, San Francisco 1946, Lafayette 1949-51)	44-81	159th (100-47-12)	18-5
#LARRY SMITH (11-10-90) (Tulane 1976-79, Arizona 1980-86, Southern Cal 1987-92, Missouri 1994-97)	51-59	170th (100-65-5)	15-10
CARL SNAVELY (9-30-44) (Bucknell 1927-33, North Caro. 1934-35, Cornell 1936-44, North Caro. 1945-52, Washington [Mo.] 1953-58)	50-60	152nd (100-40-12)	18-2
#BRUCE SNYDER (9-13-97) (Utah St. 1976-82, California 1987-91, Arizona St. 1992-97)	57-183	192nd (100-86-6)	18-2
OSSIE SOLEM (10-24-42) (Luther 1920, Drake 1921-31, Iowa 1932-36, Syracuse 1937-45, Springfield 1946-57)	50-315	183rd (100-71-12)	23-5
#STEVE SPURRIER (11-8-97) (Duke 1987-89, Florida 1990-97)	52-202	131st (100-29-2)	11-9
AMOS ALONZO STAGG (10-6-1900) (Springfield 1890-91, Chicago 1892-1932, Pacific [Cal.] 1933-46)	38-51	143rd (100-34-9)	11-6
DENNY STOLZ (9-14-85) (Alma 1965-70, Michigan St. 1973-75, Bowling Green 1977-85, San Diego St. 1986-88)	51-2	175th (100-73-2)	18-2
ABE STUBER (10-16-48) (Westminster [Mo.] 1929-31, Southeast Mo. St. 1932-44, 1946, Iowa St. 1947-52)	43-338	162nd (100-54-8)	19-5
JOCK SUTHERLAND (10-14-33) (Lafayette 1919-23, Pittsburgh 1924-38)	44-207	132nd (100-22-10)	15-4
JIM SWEENEY (9-8-84) (Montana St. 1963-67, Washington St. 1968-75, Fresno St. 1976-77, 1980-96)	55-7	206th (100-105-1)	20-2
BARRY SWITZER (9-24-83) (Oklahoma 1973-88)	45-353	122nd (100-18-4)	11-3
JIM TATUM (11-8-58) (North Caro. 1942, Oklahoma 1946, Maryland 1947-55, North Caro. 1956-58)	45-78	140th (100-33-7)	14-8
GRANT TEAFF (9-25-82) (McMurry 1960-65, Angelo St. 1969-71, Baylor 1972-92)	48-317	206th (100-101-5)	20-3
FRANK THOMAS (11-9-40) (Chattanooga 1925-28, Alabama 1931-42, 1944-46)	41-359	128th (100-21-7)	14-6
#DICK TOMEY (9-4-93) (Hawaii 1977-86, Arizona 1987-97)	55-76	182nd (100-75-7)	17-1

Coach (Date Reached Milestone) (Schools Coached and Years)	WHEN MILESTONE REACHED Age in Yrs.-Days	Career Game (Record)	Career Yr.-Game
PIE VANN (10-6-62) (Southern Miss. 1949-68)	55-14	137th (100-36-1)	14-4
JOHNNY VAUGHT (11-28-59) (Mississippi 1947-73)	51-206	135th (100-29-6)	13-10
JIM WACKER (11-14-81) (Texas Lutheran 1971-75, North Dak. St. 1976-78, Southwest Tex. St. 1979-82, Texas Christian 1983-91, Minnesota 1992-96)	44-200	134th (100-33-1)	12-10
WALLACE WADE (10-3-36) (Alabama 1923-30, Duke 1931-41, 1946-50)	44-110	129th (100-24-5)	14-3
PAPPY WALDORF (10-27-45) (Oklahoma City 1925-27, Oklahoma St. 1929-33, Kansas St. 1934, Northwestern 1935-46, California 1947-56)	43-24	173rd (100-56-17)	20-5
POP WARNER (11-26-08) (Georgia 1895-96, Cornell 1897-98, Carlisle 1899-1903, Cornell 1904-06, Carlisle 1907-14, Pittsburgh 1915-23, Stanford 1924-32, Temple 1933-38)	37-235	145th (100-38-7)	14-11
#GEORGE WELSH (10-14-89) (Navy 1973-81, Virginia 1982-97)	56-49	188th (100-85-3)	17-7
BUD WILKINSON (11-2-57) (Oklahoma 1947-63)	41-193	111th (100-8-3)	11-6
HENRY WILLIAMS (10-2-12) (Army 1891, Minnesota 1900-21)	43-98	122nd (100-13-9)	14-4
GEORGE WOODRUFF (11-11-1898) (Pennsylvania 1892-1901, Illinois 1903, Carlisle 1905)	35-261	109th (100-9-0)	8-11
WARREN WOODSON (9-27-52) (Conway 1935-40, Hardin-Simmons 1941-51, Arizona St. 1952-56, New Mexico St. 1958-67, Trinity, Tex. 1972-73)	49-215	141st (100-32-9)	15-2
BILL YEOMAN (9-12-77) (Houston 1962-86)	49-260	161st (100-56-5)	16-1
FIELDING YOST (11-7-08) (Ohio Wesleyan 1897, Nebraska 1898, Kansas 1899, Stanford 1900, Michigan 1901-23, 1925-26)	37-191	114th (100-10-4)	12-6
JIM YOUNG (9-10-88) (Arizona 1973-76, Purdue 1977-81, Army 1983-90)	53-142	160th (100-58-2)	15-1
JOHN YOVICSIN (11-16-68) (Gettysburg 1952-56, Harvard 1957-70)	50-131	150th (100-45-5)	17-8
JOSEPH YUKICA (11-20-82) (New Hampshire 1966-67, Boston College 1968-77, Dartmouth 1978-86)	51-177	169th (100-68-1)	17-10
ROBERT ZUPPKE (11-12-32) (Illinois 1913-41)	53-102	152nd (100-44-8)	20-9

#Active coach.

200 VICTORIES

Coach (Date Reached Milestone)	WHEN MILESTONE REACHED Age in Yrs.-Days	Career Game (Record)	Career Yr.-Game
Eddie Anderson (11-14-64)	64-1	342nd (200-127-15)	39-8
#Bobby Bowden (10-27-90)	60-353	279th (200-76-3)	25-7
Bear Bryant (9-10-71)	57-364	282nd (200-66-16)	27-1
Vince Dooley (11-26-88)	56-84	286th (200-76-10)	25-11
#LaVell Edwards (9-24-94)	64-348	277th (200-74-3)	23-4
#Hayden Fry (11-20-93)	64-265	361st (200-152-9)	32-11
Woody Hayes (11-2-74)	61-261	268th (200-60-8)	29-8

EDDIE ROBINSON
A Coach For The Ages

Because Grambling is not a Division I-A member, most football historians agree that Grambling's Eddie Robinson not be listed in the major college coaches' section. But there is no denying that the Tigers' former head coach belongs in any mention of great collegiate coaches.

Robinson, who retired following the 1997 season, compiled one of the most impressive coaching legacies in collegiate history. He is the only college football coach with more than 400 victories (408) and he has coached in more games (588) than any other coach in the 129 years of college football.

Only the legendary Amos Alonzo Stagg had more years as a college head coach (57) than Robinson's 55 seasons at Grambling (he coached two war years at Grambling High School). Robinson began his career in 1941, at the start of World War II and continued through more than half a century of change.

Here is a breakdown of the milestone victories in his career:

Victory No.	(Date Reached Milestone)	Age in Yrs.-Days	Career Game (Record)	Career Yr.-Game
100th	(11-9-57)	38-270	146th (100-39-7)	15-6
200th	(10-16-71)	52-246	285th (200-74-11)	29-6
300th	(9-25-82)	63-225	411th (300-98-13)	40-3
400th	(10-7-95)	76-237	560th (400-145-15)	53-5

	WHEN MILESTONE REACHED		
Coach (Date Reached Milestone)	**Age in Yrs.-Days**	**Career Game (Record)**	**Career Yr.-Game**
Lou Holtz (9-9-95)	58-243	297th (200-90-7)	26-2
Jess Neely (9-26-64)	66-265	373rd (200-155-18)	38-1
Tom Osborne (10-7-93)	56-224	249th (200-46-3)	21-5
#Joe Paterno (9-5-87)	60-258	246th (200-44-2)	22-1
Bo Schembechler (10-4-86)	57-33	262nd (200-55-7)	24-4
Jim Sweeney (11-2-96)	67-62	326th (200-158-4)	32-8
Amos Alonzo Stagg (10-11-19)	57-56	294th (200-74-20)	30-1
Pop Warner (9-24-21)	50-172	276th (200-62-14)	28-1
Warren Woodson (10-13-73)	70-231	307th (200-93-14)	31-6

#Active coach.

300 VICTORIES

	WHEN MILESTONE REACHED		
Coach (Date Reached Milestone)	**Age in Yrs.-Days**	**Career Game (Record)**	**Career Yr.-Game**
Bear Bryant (10-3-80)	67-22	393rd (300-77-16)	36-4
Amos Alonzo Stagg (11-6-43)	81-82	507th (300-173-34)	54-7
Pop Warner (11-24-34)	63-233	415th (300-91-24)	41-8

Other Coaching Milestones

(Must have five years or 50 victories at a school that was classified as a major college at the time)

YOUNGEST COACHES TO REACH 100 VICTORIES

Coach	Age in Yrs.-Days
George Woodruff	35-261
Elmer Layden	37-175
Fielding Yost	37-191
Pop Warner	37-235
Amos Alonzo Stagg	38-51
Don Faurot	39-131
Matty Bell	39-256
Dana Bible	40-44
Andy Smith	40-71
Bennie Owen	40-72
Dan McGugin	40-78
Hugo Bezdek	40-120
*Terry Bowden	40-280

**Active coach.*

YOUNGEST COACHES TO REACH 200 VICTORIES

Coach	Age in Yrs.-Days
Pop Warner	50-172
Vince Dooley	56-84
Tom Osborne	56-224
Bo Schembechler	57-33
Amos Alonzo Stagg	57-56
Bear Bryant	57-364
Lou Holtz	58-243

YOUNGEST COACHES TO REACH 300 VICTORIES

Coach	Age in Yrs.-Days
Pop Warner	63-233
Bear Bryant	67-22
Amos Alonzo Stagg	81-82

FEWEST GAMES TO REACH 100 VICTORIES

Coach	Career Game (Record at Time)
Gil Dobie	108 (100-5-3)
George Woodruff	109 (100-9-0)
Bud Wilkinson	111 (100-8-3)
Fielding Yost	114 (100-10-4)
Knute Rockne	117 (100-12-5)
Bob Neyland	120 (100-12-8)
Frank Leahy	121 (100-13-8)
*Joe Paterno	122 (100-21-1)
Barry Switzer	122 (100-18-4)
Henry Williams	122 (100-13-9)
Fred Folsom	126 (100-20-6)
Gus Henderson	126 (100-23-3)
Tom Osborne	126 (100-24-2)
Frank Thomas	128 (100-21-7)
Wallace Wade	129 (100-24-5)
Bo Schembechler	130 (100-24-6)
Bobby Dodd	131 (100-28-3)
*Steve Spurrier	131 (100-29-2)
Frank Kush	131 (100-30-1)
Charley Moran	131 (100-24-7)
Dan McGugin	132 (100-25-7)
Jock Sutherland	132 (100-22-10)
Bob Devaney	133 (100-28-5)
Red Blaik	134 (100-25-9)
Jim Wacker	134 (100-33-1)
Tony Knap	135 (100-33-2)
Johnny Vaught	135 (100-29-6)
Morley Jennings	136 (100-33-3)
Bennie Owen	136 (100-28-8)
Francis Schmidt	136 (100-27-9)
Dennis Erickson	137 (100-36-1)
Pie Vann	137 (100-36-1)
Frank Broyles	138 (100-36-2)
Fritz Crisler	138 (100-30-8)
*LaVell Edwards	138 (100-37-1)
Dan Devine	139 (100-31-8)
Danny Ford	139 (100-34-5)
John McKay	139 (100-33-6)

**Active coach.*

FEWEST GAMES TO REACH 200 VICTORIES

Coach	Career Game (Record at Time)
*Joe Paterno	246 (200-44-2)
Tom Osborne	249 (200-46-3)
Bo Schembechler	262 (200-55-7)
Woody Hayes	268 (200-60-8)
Pop Warner	276 (200-62-14)
*LaVell Edwards	277 (200-74-3)
*Bobby Bowden	279 (200-76-3)
Bear Bryant	282 (200-66-16)
Vince Dooley	286 (200-76-10)
Amos Alonzo Stagg	294 (200-74-20)

**Active coach.*

FEWEST GAMES TO REACH 300 VICTORIES

Coach	Career Game (Record at Time)
Bear Bryant	393 (300-77-16)
Pop Warner	415 (300-91-24)
Amos Alonzo Stagg	507 (300-173-34).

All-Time Division I Coaching Longevity Records

(Minimum 10 Head-Coaching Seasons in Division I; Bowl Games Included)

MOST GAMES

Games	Coach, School(s) and Years
548	Amos Alonzo Stagg, Springfield 1890-91, Chicago 1892-1932, Pacific (Cal.) 1933-46
457	Pop Warner, Georgia 1895-96, Cornell 1897-98 and 1904-06, Carlisle 1899-1903 and 1907-14, Pittsburgh 1915-23, Stanford 1924-32, Temple 1933-38
425	Bear Bryant, Maryland 1945, Kentucky 1946-53, Texas A&M 1954-57, Alabama 1958-82

Games	Coach, School(s) and Years
409	*Hayden Fry, Southern Methodist 1962-72, North Texas 1973-78, Iowa 1979-97
402	Jess Neely, Rhodes 1924-27, Clemson 1931-39, Rice 1940-66
378	*Joe Paterno, Penn St. 1966-97
368	*Bobby Bowden, Samford 1959-62, West Va. 1970-75, Florida St. 1976-97
368	Jim Sweeney, Montana St. 1963-67, Washington St. 1968-75, Fresno St. 1976-77 and 1980-96
344	Eddie Anderson, Loras 1922-24, DePaul 1925-31, Holy Cross 1933-38 and 1950-64, Iowa 1939-42 and 1946-49
332	Johnny Majors, Iowa St. 1968-72, Pittsburgh 1973-76 and 1993-96, Tennessee 1977-92
329	Grant Teaff, McMurry 1960-65, Angelo St. 1969-71, Baylor 1972-92
323	*LaVell Edwards, Brigham Young 1972-97
320	Woody Hayes, Denison 1946-48, Miami (Ohio) 1949-50, Ohio St. 1951-78
318	Ray Morrison, Southern Methodist 1915-16 and 1922-34, Vanderbilt 1918 and 1935-39, Temple 1940-48, Austin 1949-52
318	Lou Holtz, William & Mary 1969-71, North Caro. St. 1972-75, Arkansas 1977-83, Minnesota 1984-85, Notre Dame 1986-96
312	Warren Woodson, Central Ark. 1935-39, Hardin-Simmons 1941-42 and 1946-51, Arizona 1952-56, New Mexico St. 1958-67, Trinity (Tex.) 1972-73
309	Jerry Claiborne, Virginia Tech 1961-70, Maryland 1972-81, Kentucky 1982-89
307	Bo Schembechler, Miami (Ohio) 1963-68, Michigan 1969-89
307	Tom Osborne, Nebraska 1973-97
303	Don Nehlen, Bowling Green 1968-76, West Va. 1980-97
301	Bill Mallory, Miami (Ohio) 1969-73, Colorado 1974-78, Northern Ill. 1980-83, Indiana 1984-96
299	Ossie Solem, Luther 1920, Drake 1921-31, Iowa 1932-36, Syracuse 1937-42 and 1944-45, Springfield 1946-57
296	Tuss McLaughry, Westminster 1916, 1918 and 1921, Amherst 1922-25, Brown 1926-40, Dartmouth 1941-54
296	Pappy Waldorf, Oklahoma City 1925-27, Oklahoma St. 1929-33, Kansas St. 1934, Northwestern 1935-46, California 1947-56
295	Frank Howard, Clemson 1940-69
293	Dana X. Bible, Mississippi Col. 1913-15, LSU 1916, Texas A&M 1917 and 1919-28, Nebraska 1929-36, Texas 1937-46
293	Bill Dooley, North Caro. 1967-77, Virginia Tech 1978-86, Wake Forest 1987-92
293	Jim Wacker, Texas Lutheran 1971-75, North Dak. St. 1976-78, Southwest Tex. St. 1979-82, Texas Christian 1983-91, Minnesota 1992-95
292	Lou Little, Georgetown 1924-29, Columbia 1930-56
292	Carl Snavely, Bucknell 1927-33, North Caro. 1934-35 and 1945-52, Cornell 1936-44, Washington (Mo.) 1953-58
289	*George Welsh, Navy 1973-81, Virginia 1982-97
288	Vince Dooley, Georgia 1964-88
287	Bob Blackman, Denver 1953-54, Dartmouth 1955-70, Illinois 1971-76, Cornell 1977-82
282	Clark Shaughnessy, Tulane 1915-20 and 1922-26, Loyola (Ill.) 1927-32, Chicago 1933-39, Stanford 1940-41, Maryland 1942 and 1946, Pittsburgh 1943-45, Hawaii 1965
279	Howard Jones, Syracuse 1908, Yale 1909 and 1913, Ohio St. 1910, Iowa 1916-23, Duke 1924, Southern Cal 1925-40
277	Ben Schwartzwalder, Muhlenberg 1946-48, Syracuse 1949-73
276	Bill Yeoman, Houston 1962-86
272	John Heisman, Oberlin 1892 and 1894, Akron 1893, Auburn 1895-99, Clemson 1900-03, Georgia Tech 1904-19, Pennsylvania 1920-22, Wash. & Jeff. 1923, Rice 1924-27
271	Dan McGugin, Vanderbilt 1904-17 and 1919-34
271	Chuck Mills, Pomona-Pitzer 1959-61, Indiana (Pa.) 1962-63, Merchant Marine 1964, Utah St. 1967-72, Wake Forest 1973-77, Southern Ore. St. 1980-88, Coast Guard 1997
269	Don Faurot, Truman St. 1926-34, Missouri 1935-42 and 1946-56
265	Shug Jordan, Auburn 1951-75
263	John Vaught, Mississippi 1947-70 and 1973
260	Jack Curtice, West Tex. A&M 1940-41, UTEP 1946-49, Utah 1950-57, Stanford 1958-61, UC Santa Barb. 1962-69
260	Frank Dobson, Georgia 1909, Clemson 1910-12, Richmond 1913-17 and 1919-33, South Caro. 1918, Maryland 1935-39
258	Edward Robinson, Nebraska 1896-97, Brown 1898-1901, 1904-07 and 1910-25
257	Don James, Kent 1971-74, Washington 1975-92
256	Matty Bell, Haskell 1920-21, Carroll (Wis.) 1922, Texas Christian 1923-28, Texas A&M 1929-33, Southern Methodist 1935-41 and 1945-49
252	Harvey Harman, Haverford 1922-29, Sewanee 1930, Pennsylvania 1931-37, Rutgers 1938-55

*Active.

MOST YEARS

Years	Coach, School(s) and Years
57	Amos Alonzo Stagg, Springfield 1890-91, Chicago 1892-1932, Pacific (Cal.) 1933-46
44	Pop Warner, Georgia 1895-96, Cornell 1897-98 and 1904-06, Carlisle 1899-1903 and 1907-14, Pittsburgh 1915-23, Stanford 1924-32, Temple 1933-38
40	Jess Neely, Rhodes 1924-27, Clemson 1931-39, Rice 1940-66
39	Eddie Anderson, Loras 1922-24, DePaul 1925-31, Holy Cross 1933-38 and 1950-54, Iowa 1939-42 and 1946-49
38	Bear Bryant, Maryland 1945, Kentucky 1946-53, Texas A&M 1954-57, Alabama 1958-82
37	Ossie Solem, Luther 1920, Drake 1921-31, Iowa 1932-36, Syracuse 1937-45, Springfield 1946-57
36	John Heisman, Oberlin 1892 and 1894, Akron 1893, Auburn 1895-99, Clemson 1900-03, Georgia Tech 1904-19, Pennsylvania 1920-22, Wash. & Jeff. 1923, Rice 1924-27
36	*Hayden Fry, Southern Methodist 1962-72, North Texas 1973-78, Iowa 1979-97
34	Tuss McLaughry, Westminster 1916, 1918 and 1921, Amherst 1922-25, Brown 1926-40, Dartmouth 1941-54
34	Ray Morrison, Southern Methodist 1915-16 and 1922-34, Vanderbilt 1918 and 1935-39, Temple 1940-48, Austin 1949-52
33	Dana X. Bible, Mississippi Col. 1913-15, LSU 1916, Texas A&M 1917 and 1919-28, Nebraska 1929-36, Texas 1937-46
33	Gil Dobie, North Dak. St. 1906-07, Washington 1908-16, Navy 1917-19, Cornell 1920-35, Boston College 1936-38
33	Woody Hayes, Denison 1946-48, Miami (Ohio) 1949-50, Ohio St. 1951-78
33	Lou Little, Georgetown 1924-29, Columbia 1930-56
32	Clark Shaughnessy, Tulane 1915-20 and 1922-26, Loyola (Ill.) 1927-32, Chicago 1933-39, Stanford 1940-41, Maryland 1942 and 1946, Pittsburgh 1943-45, Hawaii 1965
32	Carl Snavely, Bucknell 1927-33, North Caro. 1934-35 and 1945-52, Cornell 1936-44, Washington (Mo.) 1953-58
32	William Spaulding, Western Mich. 1907-21, Minnesota 1922-24, UCLA 1925-38
32	Jim Sweeney, Montana St. 1963-67, Washington St. 1968-75, Fresno St. 1976-77 and 1980-96
32	*Bobby Bowden, Samford 1959-62, West Va. 1970-75, Florida St. 1976-97
32	*Joe Paterno, Penn St. 1966-97
31	Pappy Waldorf, Oklahoma City 1925-27, Oklahoma St. 1929-33, Kansas St. 1934, Northwestern 1935-46, California 1947-56
31	Warren Woodson, Central Ark. 1935-39, Hardin-Simmons 1941-42 and 1946-51, Arizona 1952-56, New Mexico St. 1958-67, Trinity (Tex.) 1972-73
30	Bob Blackman, Denver 1953-54, Dartmouth 1955-70, Illinois 1971-76, Cornell 1977-82
30	Frank Dobson, Georgia 1909, Clemson 1910-12, Richmond 1913-17 and 1919-33, South Caro. 1918, Maryland 1935-39
30	Harvey Harman, Haverford 1922-29, Sewanee 1930, Pennsylvania 1931-37, Rutgers 1938-55
30	Frank Howard, Clemson 1940-69
30	Dan McGugin, Vanderbilt 1904-17 and 1919-34
30	Grant Teaff, McMurry 1960-65, Angelo St. 1969-71, Baylor 1972-92

*Active.

MOST SCHOOLS

(Must Have Coached at Least One Division I or Major-College Team)

Schools	Coach, Schools and Years
8	John Heisman, Oberlin 1892 and 1894, Akron 1893, Auburn 1895-99, Clemson 1900-03, Georgia Tech 1904-19, Pennsylvania 1920-22, Wash. & Jeff. 1923, Rice 1924-27
7	Darrell Mudra, Adams St. 1959-62, North Dak. St. 1963-65, Arizona 1967-68, Western Ill. 1969-73, Florida St. 1974-75, Eastern Ill. 1978-82, Northern Iowa 1983-87
7	Lou Saban, Case Reserve 1950-52, Northwestern 1955, Western Ill. 1957-59, Maryland 1966, Miami (Fla.) 1977-78, Army 1979, Central Fla. 1983-84
7	Clark Shaughnessy, Tulane 1915-20 and 1922-26, Loyola (Ill.) 1927-32, Chicago 1933-39, Stanford 1940-41, Maryland 1942 and 1946, Pittsburgh 1943-45, Hawaii 1965
7	Clarence Spears, Dartmouth 1917-20, West Va. 1921-24, Minnesota 1925-29, Oregon 1930-31, Wisconsin 1932-35, Toledo 1936-42, Maryland 1943-44
7	Chuck Mills, Pomona-Pitzer 1959-61, Indiana (Pa.) 1962-63, Merchant Marine 1964, Utah St. 1967-72, Wake Forest 1973-77, Southern Ore. St. 1980-88, Coast Guard 1997
6	Howard Jones, Syracuse 1908, Yale 1909 and 1913, Ohio St. 1910, Iowa 1916-23, Duke 1924, Southern Cal 1925-40
6	Pop Warner, Georgia 1895-96, Cornell 1897-98 and 1904-06, Carlisle 1899-1903 and 1907-14, Pittsburgh 1915-23, Stanford 1924-32, Temple 1933-38
5	Matty Bell, Haskell 1920-21, Carroll (Wis.) 1922, Texas Christian 1923-28, Texas A&M 1929-33, Southern Methodist 1935-41 and 1945-49
5	Dana X. Bible, Mississippi Col. 1913-15, LSU 1916, Texas A&M 1917 and 1919-28, Nebraska 1929-36, Texas 1937-46
5	*Watson Brown, Austin Peay 1979-80, Cincinnati 1983, Rice 1984-85, Vanderbilt 1986-90, UAB 1995-97
5	Earle Bruce, Tampa 1972, Iowa St. 1973-78, Ohio St. 1979-87, Northern Iowa 1988, Colorado St. 1989-92
5	Frank Cavanaugh, Cincinnati 1898, Holy Cross 1903-05, Dartmouth 1911-16, Boston College 1919-26, Fordham 1927-32
5	Jack Curtice, West Tex. A&M 1940-41, UTEP 1946-49, Utah 1950-57, Stanford 1958-61, UC Santa Barb. 1962-69
5	Dudley DeGroot, UC Santa Barb. 1926-28, San Jose St. 1932-39, Rochester 1940-43, West Va. 1948-49, New Mexico 1950-52
5	Gil Dobie, North Dak. St. 1906-07, Washington 1908-16, Navy 1917-19, Cornell 1920-35, Boston College 1936-38
5	Frank Dobson, Georgia 1909, Clemson 1910-12, Richmond 1913-17 and 1919-33, South Caro. 1918, Maryland 1935-39

Schools	Coach, Schools and Years
5	Ed Doherty, Arizona St. 1947-50, Rhode Island 1951, Arizona 1957-58, Xavier (Ohio) 1959-61, Holy Cross 1971-75
5	Red Drew, Trinity (Conn.) 1921-23, Birmingham So. 1924-27, Chattanooga 1929-30, Mississippi 1946, Alabama 1947-54
5	*Dennis Franchione, S'western (Kan.) 1981-82, Pittsburg St. 1985-89, Southwest Tex. St. 1990-91, New Mexico 1992-97, Texas Christian 1998
5	Stuart Holcomb, Findlay 1932-35, Muskingum 1936-40, Wash. & Jeff. 1941, Miami (Ohio) 1942-43, Purdue 1947-55
5	Lou Holtz, William & Mary 1969-71, North Caro. St. 1972-75, Arkansas 1977-83, Minnesota 1984-85, Notre Dame 1986-96
5	Al Molde, Sioux Falls 1971-72, Minn.-Morris 1973-79, Central Mo. St. 1980-82, Eastern Ill. 1983-86, Western Mich. 1987-96
5	Darryl Rogers, Cal St. Hayward 1965, Fresno St. 1966-72, San Jose St. 1973-75, Michigan St. 1976-79, Arizona St. 1980-84
5	John Rowland, Henderson St. 1925-30, Ouachita Baptist 1931, Citadel 1940-42, Oklahoma City 1946-47, Geo. Washington 1948-51
5	Francis Schmidt, Tulsa 1919-21, Arkansas 1922-28, Texas Christian 1929-33, Ohio St. 1934-40, Idaho 1941-42
5	Clipper Smith, Gonzaga 1925-28, Santa Clara 1929-35, Villanova 1936-42, San Francisco 1946, Lafayette 1949-51
5	Ossie Solem, Luther 1920, Drake 1921-31, Iowa 1932-36, Syracuse 1937-45, Springfield 1946-57
5	Skip Stahley, Delaware 1934, Brown 1941-43, Geo. Washington 1946-47, Toledo 1948-49, Idaho 1954-60
5	Jim Wacker, Texas Lutheran 1971-75, North Dak. St. 1976-78, Southwest Tex. St. 1979-82, Texas Christian 1983-91, Minnesota 1992-96
5	Pappy Waldorf, Oklahoma City 1925-27, Oklahoma St. 1929-33, Kansas St. 1934, Northwestern 1935-46, California 1947-56
5	Warren Woodson, Central Ark. 1935-39, Hardin-Simmons 1941-42, Arizona 1952-56, New Mexico St. 1958-67, Trinity (Tex.) 1972-73
5	Fielding Yost, Ohio Wesleyan 1897, Nebraska 1898, Kansas 1899, Stanford 1900, Michigan 1901-23 and 1925-26
4	Eddie Anderson, Loras 1922-24, DePaul 1925-31, Holy Cross 1933-38 and 1950-64, Iowa 1939-42 and 1946-49
4	Charles Bachman, Northwestern 1919, Kansas St. 1920-27, Florida 1928-32, Michigan St. 1933-42 and 1944-46
4	Jerry Berndt, DePauw 1979-80, Pennsylvania 1981-85, Rice 1986-88, Temple 1989-92
4	Bob Blackman, Denver 1953-54, Dartmouth 1955-70, Illinois 1971-76, Cornell 1977-82
4	Bear Bryant, Maryland 1945, Kentucky 1946-53, Texas A&M 1954-57, Alabama 1958-82
4	Pete Elliott, Nebraska 1956, California 1957-59, Illinois 1960-66, Miami (Fla.) 1973-74
4	Dennis Erickson, Idaho 1982-85, Wyoming 1986, Washington St. 1987-88, Miami (Fla.) 1989-94
4	Wesley Fesler, Wesleyan (Conn.) 1941-42, Pittsburgh 1946, Ohio St. 1947-50, Minnesota 1951-53
4	Mike Gottfried, Murray St. 1978-80, Cincinnati 1981-82, Kansas 1983-85, Pittsburgh 1986-89
4	Harvey Harman, Haverford 1922-29, Sewanee 1930, Pennsylvania 1931-37, Rutgers 1938-55
4	*Ken Hatfield, Air Force 1979-83, Arkansas 1984-89, Clemson 1990-93, Rice 1994-97
4	Bill Mallory, Miami (Ohio) 1969-73, Colorado 1974-78, Northern Ill. 1980-83, Indiana 1984-96
4	Tuss McLaughry, Westminster 1916, 1918 and 1921, Amherst 1922-25, Brown 1926-40, Dartmouth 1941-54
4	Joe McMullen, Stetson 1950-51, Wash. & Jeff. 1952-53, Akron 1954-60, San Jose St. 1969-70
4	Bill Meek, Kansas St. 1951-54, Houston 1955-56, Southern Methodist 1957-61, Utah 1968-73
4	Charley Moran, Texas A&M 1909-14, Centre 1919-23, Bucknell 1924-26, Catawba 1930-31
4	Ray Morrison, Southern Methodist 1915-16 and 1922-34, Vanderbilt 1918 and 1935-39, Temple 1940-48, Austin 1949-52
4	Frank Navarro, Williams 1963-67, Columbia 1968-73, Wabash 1974-77, Princeton 1978-84
4	John Pont, Miami (Ohio) 1956-62, Yale 1963-64, Indiana 1965-72, Northwestern 1973-77
4	Bill Roper, Va. Military 1903-04, Princeton 1906-08, 1910-11 and 1919-30, Missouri 1909, Swarthmore 1915-16
4	Philip Sarboe, Central Wash. 1941-42, Washington St. 1945-49, Humboldt St. 1951-65, Hawaii 1966
4	George Sauer, New Hampshire 1937-41, Kansas 1946-47, Navy 1948-49, Baylor 1950-55
4	*Jackie Sherrill, Washington St. 1976, Pittsburgh 1977-81, Texas A&M 1982-88, Mississippi St. 1991-97
4	Steve Sloan, Vanderbilt 1973-74, Texas Tech 1975-77, Mississippi 1978-82, Duke 1983-86
4	*Larry Smith, Tulane 1976-79, Arizona 1980-86, Southern Cal 1987-92, Missouri 1994-97
4	Carl Snavely, Bucknell 1927-33, North Caro. 1934-35 and 1945-52, Cornell 1936-44, Washington (Mo.) 1953-58
4	Denny Stolz, Alma 1965-70, Michigan St. 1973-75, Bowling Green 1977-85, San Diego St. 1986-88

**Active.*

MOST YEARS COACHED AT ONE COLLEGE

(Minimum 15 Years)

Coach, College (Years)	Years	School W-L-T	Overall W-L-T
Amos Alonzo Stagg, Chicago (1892-1932)	41	244-111-27	314-199-35
*Joe Paterno, Penn St. (1966-97)	32 #	298-77-3	298-77-3
Frank Howard, Clemson (1940-69)	30 #	165-118-12	165-118-12
Dan McGugin, Vanderbilt (1904-17, 1919-34)	30 #	197-55-19	197-55-19
Robert Zuppke, Illinois (1913-41)	29 #	131-81-13	131-81-13
Woody Hayes, Ohio St. (1951-78)	28	205-61-10	238-72-10
Lou Little, Columbia (1930-56)	27	110-116-10	151-128-13
Jess Neely, Rice (1940-66)	27	144-124-10	207-176-19
*LaVell Edwards, Brigham Young (1972-97)	26 #	234-86-3	234-86-3
William Alexander, Georgia Tech (1920-44)	25 #	134-95-15	134-95-15
Ike Armstrong, Utah (1925-49)	25 #	140-55-15	140-55-15
Bear Bryant, Alabama (1958-82)	25	232-46-9	323-85-17
Vince Dooley, Georgia (1964-88)	25 #	201-77-10	201-77-10
Ralph Jordan, Auburn (1951-75)	25 #	176-83-6	176-83-6
Ben Schwartzwalder, Syracuse (1949-73)	25	153-91-3	178-96-3
John Vaught, Mississippi (1947-70, 1973)	25 #	190-61-12	190-61-12
Bill Yeoman, Houston (1962-86)	25 #	160-108-8	160-108-8
Fielding Yost, Michigan (1901-23, 1925-26)	25	165-29-10	196-36-12
Tom Osborne, Nebraska (1973-97)	25 #	255-49-3	255-49-3
Edward Robinson, Brown (1898-1901, 1904-07, 1910-25)	24	140-82-12	157-88-13
Frank Camp, Louisville (1946-68)	23 #	118-96-2	118-96-2
*Bobby Bowden, Florida St. (1976-97)	22	208-51-4	281-83-4
Wally Butts, Georgia (1939-60)	22 #	140-86-9	140-86-9
Bobby Dodd, Georgia Tech (1945-66)	22 #	165-64-8	165-64-8
Frank Kush, Arizona St. (1958-79)	22 #	176-54-1	176-54-1
Bennie Owen, Oklahoma (1905-26)	22	122-54-16	155-60-19
Henry Williams, Minnesota (1900-21)	22	140-33-11	141-34-12
Eddie Anderson, Holy Cross (1933-38, 1950-64)	21	129-67-8	201-128-15
Bob Neyland, Tennessee (1926-34, 1936-40, 1946-52)	21 #	173-31-12	173-31-12
Bo Schembechler, Michigan (1969-89)	21	194-48-5	234-65-8

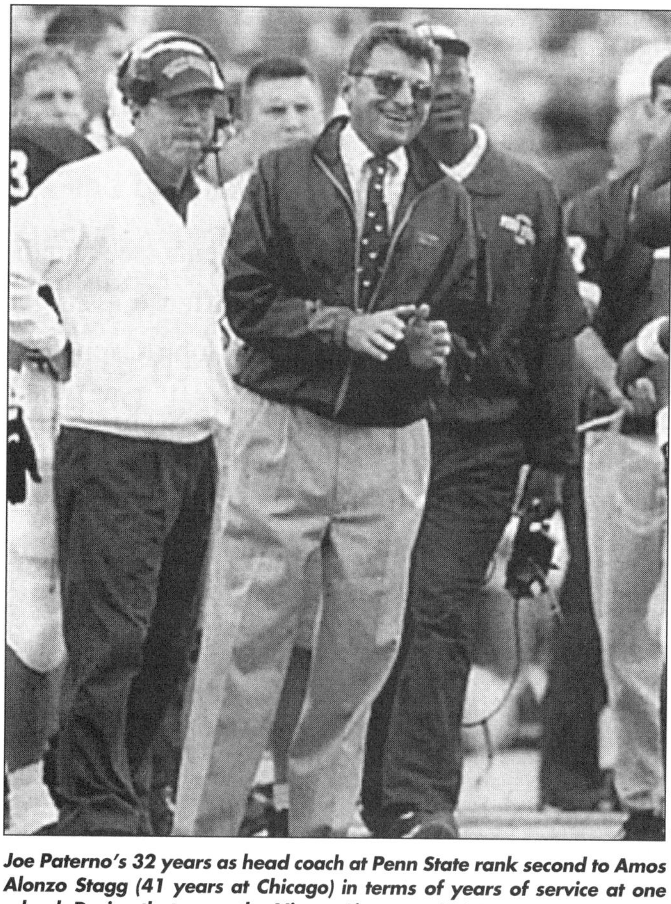

Photo from Penn State sports information

Joe Paterno's 32 years as head coach at Penn State rank second to Amos Alonzo Stagg (41 years at Chicago) in terms of years of service at one school. During that span, the Nittany Lions are 298-77-3.

Coach, College (Years)	Years	School W-L-T	Overall W-L-T
Grant Teaff, Baylor (1972-92)	21	128-105-6	170-151-8
Terry Donahue, UCLA (1976-95)	20 #	151-74-8	151-74-8
Bill Hess, Ohio (1958-77)	20 #	107-92-4	107-92-4
Ben Martin, Air Force (1958-77)	20	96-103-9	102-116-10
Darrell Royal, Texas (1957-76)	20	167-47-5	184-60-5
Pie Vann, Southern Miss. (1949-68)	20 #	139-59-2	139-59-2
Chris Ault, Nevada (1976-92, 1994-95)	19 #	163-63-1	163-63-1
Frank Broyles, Arkansas (1958-76)	19	144-58-5	149-62-6
Robert Higgins, Penn St. (1930-48)	19	91-57-10	123-79-18
*Hayden Fry, Iowa (1979-97)	19	140-81-6	229-170-10
Jim Sweeney, Fresno St. (1976-77, 1980-96)	19	143-75-3	200-154-4
*Don Nehlen, West Va. (1980-97)	18	130-77-4	183-112-8
Red Blaik, Army (1941-58)	18	121-33-10	166-48-14
Rich Brooks, Oregon (1977-94)	18 #	91-109-4	91-109-4
Ray Eliot, Illinois (1942-59)	18	83-73-11	102-82-13
Don James, Washington (1975-92)	18	151-59-2	176-78-3
Charlie McClendon, LSU (1962-79)	18 #	137-59-7	137-59-7
Jim Owens, Washington (1957-74)	18 #	99-82-6	99-82-6
Murray Warmath, Minnesota (1954-71)	18	87-78-7	97-84-10
Johnny Majors, Tennessee (1977-92)	17	120-69-8	185-137-10
Earle Edwards, North Caro. St. (1954-70)	17 #	77-88-8	77-88-8
Bud Wilkinson, Oklahoma (1947-63)	17 #	145-29-4	145-29-4
Bob Blackman, Dartmouth (1955-70)	16	104-37-3	168-112-7
Len Casanova, Oregon (1951-66)	16	82-73-8	104-94-11
Herb Deromedi, Central Mich. (1978-93)	16 #	110-55-10	110-55-10
Gil Dobie, Cornell (1920-35)	16	82-36-7	180-45-15
Rip Engle, Penn St. (1950-65)	16	104-48-4	132-68-8
Andy Gustafson, Miami (Fla.) (1948-63)	16	93-65-3	115-78-4
John Heisman, Georgia Tech (1904-19)	16	102-29-6	185-70-17
Howard Jones, Southern Cal (1925-40)	16	121-36-13	194-64-21
John McKay, Southern Cal (1960-75)	16 #	127-40-8	127-40-8
Barry Switzer, Oklahoma (1973-88)	16 #	157-29-4	157-29-4
Wallace Wade, Duke (1931-41, 1946-50)	16	110-36-7	171-49-10
*George Welsh, Virginia (1982-97)	16	112-72-3	167-118-4
Rex Enright, South Caro. (1938-42, 1946-55)	15 #	64-69-7	64-69-7
Morley Jennings, Baylor (1926-40)	15	83-60-6	153-75-18
Ray Morrison, Southern Methodist (1915-16, 1922-34)	15	84-44-22	155-130-33
Bill Murray, Duke (1951-65)	15	83-51-9	142-67-11
Jock Sutherland, Pittsburgh (1924-38)	15	111-20-12	144-28-14
Frank Thomas, Alabama (1931-42, 1944-46)	15	115-24-7	141-33-9

**Active coach. #Never coached at any other college.*

Active Coaching Longevity Records

(Minimum Five Years as a Division I-A Head Coach; Includes Bowl Games)

MOST GAMES

Games	Coach, School(s) and Years
409	Hayden Fry, Southern Methodist 1962-72, North Texas 1973-78, Iowa 1979-97
378	Joe Paterno, Penn St., 1966-97
368	Bobby Bowden, Samford 1959-62, West Va. 1970-75, Florida St. 1976-97
323	LaVell Edwards, Brigham Young 1972-97
303	Don Nehlen, Bowling Green 1968-76, West Va. 1980-97
289	George Welsh, Navy 1973-81, Virginia 1982-97
246	John Cooper, Tulsa 1977-84, Arizona St. 1985-87, Ohio St. 1988-97
242	Larry Smith, Tulane 1976-79, Arizona 1980-86, Southern Cal 1987-92, Missouri 94-97
239	Dick Tomey, Hawaii 1977-86, Arizona 1987-97
232	Jackie Sherrill, Washington St. 1976, Pittsburgh 1977-81, Texas A&M 1982-88, Mississippi St. 1991-97
222	Ken Hatfield, Air Force 1979-83, Arkansas 1984-89, Clemson 1990-93, Rice 1994-97
202	Bruce Snyder, Utah St. 1976-82, California 1987-91, Arizona St. 1992-97
193	Frank Beamer, Murray St. 1981-86, Virginia Tech 1987-97
192	Mike Price, Weber St. 1981-88, Washington St. 1989-97

MOST YEARS

Years	Coach, School(s) and Years
36	Hayden Fry, Southern Methodist 1962-72, North Texas 1973-78, Iowa 1979-97
32	Bobby Bowden, Samford 1959-62, West Va. 1970-75, Florida St. 1976-97
32	Joe Paterno, Penn St. 1966-97
27	Don Nehlen, Bowling Green 1968-76, West Va. 1980-97
26	LaVell Edwards, Brigham Young 1972-97
25	George Welsh, Navy 1973-81, Virginia 1982-97
21	John Cooper, Tulsa 1977-84, Arizona 1985-87, Ohio St. 1988-97
21	Larry Smith, Tulane 1976-79, Arizona 1980-86, Southern Cal 1987-92, Missouri 1994-97
21	Dick Tomey, Hawaii 1977-86, Arizona 1987-97
20	Jackie Sherrill, Washington St. 1976, Pittsburgh 1977-81, Texas A&M 1982-88, Mississippi St. 1991-97
19	Ken Hatfield, Air Force 1979-83, Arkansas 1984-89, Clemson 1990-93, Rice 1994-97
18	Bruce Snyder, Utah St. 1976-82, California 1987-91, Arizona St. 1992-97
17	Frank Beamer, Murray St. 1981-86, Virginia Tech 1987-97
17	Mike Price, Weber St. 1981-88, Washington St. 1989-97

MOST YEARS AT CURRENT SCHOOL

Years	Coach, School and Years
32	Joe Paterno, Penn St. 1966-97
26	LaVell Edwards, Brigham Young 1972-97
22	Bobby Bowden, Florida St. 1976-97
19	Hayden Fry, Iowa 1979-97
18	Don Nehlen, West Va. 1980-97
16	George Welsh, Virginia 1982-97
14	Fisher DeBerry, Air Force 1984-97
12	Spike Dykes, Texas Tech 1986-97
12	Nelson Stokley, Southwestern La. 1986-97

MOST SCHOOLS

Schools	Coach, Schools and Years
5	Watson Brown, Austin Peay 1979-80, Cincinnati 1983, Rice 1984-85, Vanderbilt 1986-90, UAB 1995-97
5	Dennis Franchione, S'western (Kan.) 1981-82, Pittsburg St. 1985-89, Southwest Tex. St. 1990-91, New Mexico 1992-97, Texas Christian 1998
4	Ken Hatfield, Air Force 1979-83, Arkansas 1984-89, Clemson 1990-93, Rice 1994-97
4	Jackie Sherrill, Washington St. 1976, Pittsburgh 1977-81, Texas A&M 1982-88, Mississippi St. 1991-97
4	Larry Smith, Tulane 1976-79, Arizona 1980-86, Southern Cal 1987-92, Missouri 1994-97
4	Mack Brown, Appalachian St. 1983, Tulane 1985-87, North Caro. 1988-97, Texas 1998
3	Bobby Bowden, Samford 1959-62, West Va. 1970-75, Florida St. 1976-97
3	Terry Bowden, Salem Teikyo 1984-86, Samford 1987-92, Auburn 1993-97
3	John Cooper, Tulsa 1977-84, Arizona St. 1985-87, Ohio St. 1988-97
3	Hayden Fry, Southern Methodist 1962-72, North Texas 1973-78, Iowa 1979-97
3	Fred Goldsmith, Slippery Rock 1981, Rice 1989-93, Duke 1994-97
3	Bruce Snyder, Utah St. 1976-82, California 1987-91, Arizona St. 1992-97
3	Glen Mason, Kent 1986-87, Kansas 1988-96, Minnesota 1997

Major-College Brother vs. Brother Coaching Matchups

(Thanks to Tex Noel of Bedford, Indiana)
(Each brother's victories in parentheses)

Mack Brown, Tulane (2), vs. Watson, Vanderbilt (0), 1986-87

Vince Dooley, Georgia (1), vs. Bill, North Caro. (0), 1971 Gator Bowl

Bump Elliott, Michigan (6), vs. Pete, Illinois (1), 1960-66

Howard Jones, Yale 1909 and Iowa 1922 (2), vs. Tad, Syracuse 1909 and Yale 1922 (0)

Pop Warner, Cornell (0) vs. Bill, Colgate (0) (tie), 1906

Annual Division I-A Head-Coaching Changes

Year	Changes	Teams	Pct.
1947	27	125	.216
1948	24	121	.198
1949	22	114	.193
1950	23	119	.193
1951	23	115	.200
1952	15	113	.133
1953	18	111	.162
1954	14	103	.136
1955	23	103	.223
1956	19	105	.181
1957	22	108	.204
1958	18	109	.165
1959	18	110	.164
1960	18	114	.158
1961	11	112	.098
1962	20	119	.168
1963	12	118	.102
1964	14	116	.121
1965	16	114	.140
1966	16	116	.138
1967	21	114	.184
1968	14	114	.123
1969	22	118	.186
1970	13	118	.110
1971	27	119	.227
1972	17	121	.140
1973	36	126	†.286
1974	28	128	.219
1975	18	134	.134
1976	23	137	.168
1977	27	144	.188
1978	27	139	.194
1979	26	139	.187
1980	27	139	.194

Year	Changes	Teams	Pct.
1981	17	137	.123
1982	17	97	.175
1983	22	105	.210
1984	16	105	.152
1985	15	105	.143
1986	22	105	.210
1987	24	104	.231
1988	9	104	.087
1989	19	106	.179
1990	20	106	.189
1991	16	106	.151
1992	16	107	.150
1993	15	106	.142
1994	15	107	.140
1995	21	108	.194
1996	9	111	*.081
1997	24	112	.214
1998	14	112	.125

*Record low. †Record high.

Records of Division I-A First-Year Head Coaches

(Coaches with no previous head-coaching experience at a four-year college.)

							Team's Previous Season Record				
Year	No.	Won	Lost	Tied	Pct.	Bowl Record	Won	Lost	Tied	Pct.	Bowl Record
1948	14	56	68	7	.454	0-1	76	52	8	.588	2-1
1949	8	26	49	3	.353	0-1	35	41	4	.463	0-0
1950	10	37	56	4	.402	0-0	49	42	6	.536	2-0
1951	13	60	67	4	.473	1-2	39	88	7	.317	1-1
1952	8	31	42	3	.428	0-0	38	40	0	.487	0-0
1953	8	29	45	5	.399	0-0	48	28	7	.620	1-2
1954	8	31	43	4	.423	0-0	40	33	7	.543	1-0
1955	9	36	50	4	.422	0-1	36	52	1	.410	0-0
1956	14	47	80	11	.380	1-0	61	68	6	.474	0-1
1957	9	32	50	6	.398	0-0	44	42	2	.511	0-0
1958	7	26	44	0	.371	0-0	37	31	2	.543	0-0
1959	8	34	43	2	.443	0-0	41	35	2	.538	0-1
1960	14	54	80	5	.406	1-0	57	78	2	.423	0-0
1961	8	26	50	0	.342	0-0	38	38	2	.500	0-0
1962	12	40	74	4	.356	2-0	52	66	2	.442	1-1
1963	8	23	49	6	.333	0-0	32	46	1	.411	0-1
1964	12	45	67	7	.408	1-1	42	71	4	.376	0-0
1965	8	28	47	2	.377	0-0	36	42	1	.462	0-0
1966	10	46	50	3	.480	0-0	38	56	5	.409	0-0
1967	18	58	114	5	.342	1-0	60	116	4	.344	0-1
1968	6	19	40	1	.325	0-0	20	38	2	.350	0-0
1969	15	49	90	1	.353	0-0	62	85	3	.423	0-1
1970	10	45	61	1	.425	1-0	46	54	0	.460	0-2
1971	12	57	72	0	.442	1-1	64	61	0	.512	0-1
1972	11	57	64	1	.471	1-0	53	64	2	.454	1-0
1973	14	84	63	8	.568	1-0	83	71	2	.538	3-0
1974	17	63	116	5	.356	1-0	78	105	1	.427	1-0
1975	10	38	72	0	.345	0-1	43	67	0	.391	0-0
1976	15	57	109	2	.345	3-1	72	91	5	.443	3-1
1977	14	55	94	5	.373	1-0	66	88	3	.430	0-2
1978	16	68	104	3	.397	0-0	77	96	3	.446	0-1
1979	11	53	66	3	.447	0-0	66	57	1	.536	2-2
1980	12	54	75	2	.420	0-0	60	68	3	.469	1-0
1981	6	25	40	0	.385	0-0	31	35	1	.470	0-1
1982	10	51	59	1	.464	0-1	58	57	2	.504	2-2
1983	12	51	82	2	.385	1-0	60	73	1	.451	1-1
1984	7	47	28	1	*.625	2-1	45	35	1	.562	3-0
1985	5	19	37	0	.339	0-0	20	32	4	.393	0-0
1986	12	53	81	0	.396	0-1	56	76	3	.426	1-1
1987	9	51	49	3	.510	1-1	52	50	1	.510	0-2
1988	4	25	20	0	.556	1-0	22	23	1	.489	1-1
1989	7	32	49	1	.396	0-2	39	43	0	.476	1-2
1990	9	46	42	2	.522	1-1	41	48	1	.461	0-1
1991	10	38	72	1	.347	1-0	46	64	2	.420	0-2
1992	4	15	20	1	.431	0-0	32	14	0	.696	1-1
1993	8	29	58	2	.337	0-1	41	51	1	.446	2-2
1994	7	30	40	2	.431	2-1	40	39	0	.506	1-0
1995	10	57	56	2	.504	1-2	45	65	3	.412	2-1
1996	6	27	42	0	.391	1-1	29	38	1	.434	0-1
1997	11	47	79	0	.373	0-1	56	70	0	.444	1-1

*Record percentage for first-year coaches. 1984 coaches and their records, with bowl game indicated by an asterisk (*): Pat Jones, Oklahoma St. (*10-2-0); Galen Hall, Florida (8-0-0, took over from Charley Pell after three games); Bill Arnsparger, LSU (8-*3-1); Fisher DeBerry, Air Force (*8-4-0); Dick Anderson, Rutgers (7-3-0); Mike Sheppard, Long Beach St. (4-7-0); Ron Chismar, Wichita St. (2-9-0).

Most Victories by First-Year Head Coaches

Coach, College, Year	W	L	T
Gary Blackney, Bowling Green, 1991	*11	1	0
John Robinson, Southern Cal, 1976	*11	1	0
Bill Battle, Tennessee, 1970	*11	1	0
Dick Crum, Miami (Ohio), 1974	*10	0	1
Barry Switzer, Oklahoma, 1973	10	0	1
John Jenkins, Houston, 1990	10	1	0
Dwight Wallace, Ball St., 1978	10	1	0
Chuck Fairbanks, Oklahoma, 1967	*10	1	0
Mike Archer, LSU, 1987	*10	1	1
Rick Neuheisel, Colorado, 1995	*10	2	0
Curley Hallman, Southern Miss., 1988	*10	2	0
Pat Jones, Oklahoma St., 1984	*10	2	0
Earle Bruce, Tampa, 1972	*10	2	0
Billy Kinard, Mississippi, 1971	*10	2	0

*Bowl game victory included.
Only first-year coach to win a national championship: Bennie Oosterbaan, Michigan, 1948 (9-0-0).

Division I-AA Coaching Records

Winningest Active Division I-AA Coaches

(Minimum five years as Division I-A and/or Division I-AA head coach; record at four-year colleges only.)

BY PERCENTAGE

Coach, College	Years	Won	Lost	Tied	†Pct.	Playoffs# W-L-T
Mike Kelly, Dayton	17	165	28	1	.85309	13-8-0
Al Bagnoli, Pennsylvania$	16	125	39	0	.76220	7-6-0
Pete Richardson, Southern U.	10	87	27	1	.76087	2-4-0
Larry Blakeney, Troy St.	7	63	21	1	.74706	4-4-0
John Lyons, Dartmouth	6	44	15	1	.74167	0-0-0
Roy Kidd, Eastern Ky.	34	280	103	8	.72634	17-16-0
Walt Hamelin, Wagner	17	129	48	2	.72626	6-2-0
Tubby Raymond, Delaware	32	270	103	3	.72207	20-14-0
Joe Gardi, Hofstra	8	62	24	2	.71591	2-3-0
Greg Gattuso, Duquesne	5	37	15	0	.71154	1-1-0
Jim Tressel, Youngstown St.	12	108	46	2	.69872	20-4-0
James Carson, Jackson St.	6	47	21	1	.68891	0-3-0
Bobby Keasler, McNeese St.	8	69	31	2	.68627	8-6-0
Bill Hayes, North Caro. A&T	22	156	85	2	.64609	1-5-0
Steve Tosches, Princeton$	11	70	38	2	.64545	0-0-0
Rob Ash, Drake	18	114	63	5	.64011	0-0-0
John Pearce, Stephen F. Austin	6	43	24	2	.63768	2-2-0
Mike Rasmussen, St. Mary's (Cal.)	8	50	29	1	.63125	0-0-0
Bill Bowes, New Hampshire	26	171	99	5	.63091	1-4-0
Boots Donnelly, Middle Tenn. St.	21	149	89	1	.62552	6-7-0
Bob Benson, Georgetown	5	30	18	0	.62500	0-1-0
Bob Ricca, St. John's (N.Y.)	20	127	76	1	.62500	1-0-0
Andy Talley, Villanova	18	115	69	2	.62366	2-6-0
Steve Wilson, Howard	9	61	40	0	.60396	1-1-0
Gordy Combs, Towson	6	36	24	0	.60000	0-0-0
Jimmye Laycock, William & Mary	18	122	81	2	.60000	2-5-0
Willie Jeffries, South Caro. St.	25	161	107	6	.59854	3-4-0
Sam Rutigliano, Liberty	9	58	40	0	.59184	0-0-0
Jim Parady, Marist	6	35	24	1	.59167	0-0-0
Randy Ball, Western Ill.	8	53	38	1	.58152	1-3-0
Ron Randleman, Sam Houston St.	29	175	128	6	.57605	3-5-1
Bob Spoo, Eastern Ill.	11	68	56	1	.54800	1-3-0
Bill Thomas, Texas Southern	9	52	45	3	.53500	1-1-0
Bill Russo, Lafayette	20	111	98	4	.53052	0-1-0
Jerry Moore, Appalachian St.	16	96	85	2	.53005	2-5-0
Jim Reid, Richmond	9	51	46	3	.52500	0-2-0
Sam Goodwin, Northwestern St.	17	96	89	4	.51852	1-2-0
Ken LaRose, Butler	6	30	30	0	.50000	0-0-0
Jack Harbaugh, Western Ky.	14	72	77	3	.48355	1-1-0
Cliff Hysell, Montana St.	6	31	35	0	.46970	0-0-0
Larry Dorsey, Mississippi Val.	8	36	44	3	.45181	0-0-0
Dan Allen, Holy Cross	8	41	50	0	.45055	1-2-0
Floyd Keith, Rhode Island	9	41	53	2	.43750	0-0-0
Tim Murphy, Harvard	11	51	66	1	.43644	0-1-0
Barry Gallup, Northeastern	7	31	45	1	.40909	0-0-0
John Mumford, Southeast Mo. St.	8	34	54	0	.38636	0-0-0

Coach, College	Years	Won	Lost	Tied	†Pct.	Playoffs# W-L-T
Tom Horne, Valparaiso	12	46	74	2	.38525	0-0-0
Tim Landis, Davidson	5	19	31	1	.38235	0-0-0
Jack Cosgrove, Maine	5	21	34	0	.38182	0-0-0
Ray Tellier, Columbia$	14	45	80	3	.36328	0-1-0
Sal Cintorino, Central Conn. St.	6	20	39	0	.33898	0-0-0
Jim Marshall, Tenn.-Martin	7	20	57	0	.25974	0-0-0
David Dowd, Charleston So.	7	12	59	0	.16901	0-0-0
Ron Dickerson, Alabama St.	5	8	47	0	.14545	0-0-0

Less than five years as Division I-A and/or Division I-AA head coach (school followed by years in I-A or I-AA, includes record at all four-year colleges):

Coach, College	Years	Won	Lost	Tied	†Pct.	Playoffs# W-L-T
Ken O'Keefe, Fordham (0)	8	79	10	1	.88333	5-5-0
Mike Dunbar, Northern Iowa (0)	7	61	13	1	.82000	3-3-0
Joe Taylor, Hampton (3)	15	115	44	4	.71779	1-6-0
Billy Joe, Florida A&M (4)	24	184	76	4	.70455	12-8-0
Mark Whipple, Massachusetts (4)$	10	72	33	0	.68571	3-2-0
Bill Manlove, La Salle (1)	28	193	90	1	.68134	9-5-0
Jack Siedlecki, Yale (1)$	10	58	29	2	.66292	0-1-0
Mick Dennehy, Montana (2)	5	32	18	0	.64000	4-4-0
Lee Hardman, Ark.-Pine Bluff (0)	5	33	22	0	.60000	0-0-0
Tim Walsh, Portland St. (0)	9	59	40	0	.59596	2-3-0
Mike Ayers, Wofford (3)	13	71	70	2	.50350	0-2-0
Matt Ballard, Morehead St.. (4)	10	50	51	1	.49510	0-0-0
Kevin Kiesel, Fairfield (2)	5	23	25	1	.47959	1-0-0
Greg Johnson, Prairie View (1)	7	35	39	0	.47297	1-2-0
Steve Gilbert, Jacksonville (0)	9	41	48	0	.46067	0-1-0
Bill Schmitz, Austin Peay (1)	5	20	29	0	.40816	0-1-0

+Ties computed as half won and half lost. Overall records includes bowl and playoff games. #Playoffs include all divisional championships as well as bowl games, conference playoff games and NAIA playoffs. $Includes a forfeit from Pennsylvania by order of NCAA Committee on Infractions.

BY VICTORIES

(Minimum 100 Victories)

Coach, College, Win Pct.	Won
Roy Kidd, Eastern Ky. (.726)	280
Tubby Raymond, Delaware (.722)	270
Ron Randleman, Sam Houston St. (.576)	175
Bill Bowes, New Hampshire (.631)	171
Mike Kelly, Dayton (.853)	165
Willie Jeffries, South Caro. St. (.599)	161
Bill Hayes, North Caro. A&T (.646)	156
Boots Donnelly, Middle Tenn. St. (.626)	149
Walt Hamelin, Wagner (.726)	129
Bob Ricca, St. John's (N.Y.) (.625)	127
Al Bagnoli, Pennsylvania (.762)	125
Jimmye Laycock, William & Mary (.600)	122
Andy Talley, Villanova (.624)	115
Rob Ash, Drake (.640)	114
Bill Russo, Lafayette (.531)	111
Jim Tressel, Youngstown St. (.699)	108
Less than five years in Division I-A and/or I-AA:	
Bill Manlove, La Salle (.681)	193
Bill Joe, Florida A&M (.705)	184
Joe Taylor, Hampton (.718)	115

Annual Division I-AA Head-Coaching Changes

(From the 1982 reorganization of the division for parallel comparisons)

Year	Changes	Teams	Pct.
1982	7	92	.076
1983	17	84	.202
1984	14	87	.161
1985	11	87	.126
1986	18	86	.209
1987	13	87	.149
1988	12	88	.136
1989	21	89	†.236
1990	16	89	.180
1991	6	87	*.069
1992	14	89	.157
1993	13	#115	.113
1994	17	116	.147
1995	11	119	.092
1996	11	116	.095
1997	20	118	.169
1998	14	119	.118

**Record low. †Record high. #Twenty-seven teams switched from Divisions II & III to I-AA.*

Division I-AA Championship Coaches

All coaches who have coached teams in the Division I-AA championship playoffs since 1978 are listed here with their playoff record, alma mater and year graduated, team, year coached, opponent, and score.

Dan Allen (1-2) (Hanover '78)
Boston U. 93 Northern Iowa 27-21 (2 OT)
Boston U. 93 Idaho 14-21
Boston U. 94 Eastern Ky. 23-30

Pokey Allen (3-1) (Utah '65)
Boise St. 94 North Texas 42-20
Boise St. 94 Appalachian St. 17-14
Boise St. 94 Marshall 28-24
Boise St. 94 Youngstown St. 14-28

Terry Allen (6-7) (Northern Iowa '79)
Northern Iowa 90 Boise St. 3-20
Northern Iowa 91 Weber St. 38-21
Northern Iowa 91 Marshall 13-41
Northern Iowa 92 Eastern Wash. 17-14
Northern Iowa 92 McNeese St. 29-7
Northern Iowa 92 Youngstown St. 7-19
Northern Iowa 93 Boston U. 21-27 (2 OT)
Northern Iowa 94 Montana 20-23
Northern Iowa 95 Murray St. 35-34
Northern Iowa 95 Marshall 24-41
Northern Iowa 96 Eastern Ill. 21-14
Northern Iowa 96 William & Mary 38-35
Northern Iowa 96 Marshall 14-31

Dave Arnold (3-0) (Drake '67)
Montana St. 84 Arkansas St. 31-24
Montana St. 84 Rhode Island 32-20
Montana St. 84* Louisiana Tech 19-6

Dave Arslanian (0-1) (Weber St. '72)
Weber St. 91 Northern Iowa 21-38

Chris Ault (9-7) (Nevada '68)
Nevada 78 Massachusetts 21-44
Nevada 79 Eastern Ky. 30-33
Nevada 83 Idaho St. 27-20
Nevada 83 North Texas 20-17 (OT)
Nevada 83 Southern Ill. 7-23
Nevada 85 Arkansas St. 24-23
Nevada 85 Furman 12-35
Nevada 86 Idaho 27-7
Nevada 86 Tennessee St. 33-6
Nevada 86 Ga. Southern 38-48
Nevada 90 Northeast La. 27-14
Nevada 90 Furman 42-35 (3 OT)
Nevada 90 Boise St. 59-52 (3 OT)
Nevada 90 Ga. Southern 13-36
Nevada 91 McNeese St. 22-16
Nevada 91 Youngstown St. 28-30

Stephen Axman (0-1) (LIU-C. W. Post '69)
Northern Ariz. 96 Furman 31-42

Randy Ball (1-3) (Truman St. '73)
Western Ill. 91 Marshall 17-20 (OT)
Western Ill. 96 Murray St. 6-34
Western Ill. 97 Jackson St. 31-24
Western Ill. 97 McNeese St. 12-14

Darren Barbier (0-1) (Nicholls St. '82)
Nicholls St. 96 Montana 3-48

Frank Beamer (0-1) (Virginia Tech '69)
Murray St. 86 Eastern Ill. 21-28

Dick Biddle (0-1) (Duke '71)
Colgate 97 Villanova 28-49

Larry Blakeney (4-4) (Auburn '70)
Troy St. 93 Stephen F. Austin 42-20
Troy St. 93 McNeese St. 35-28
Troy St. 93 Marshall 21-24
Troy St. 94 James Madison 26-45
Troy St. 95 Ga. Southern 21-24
Troy St. 96 Florida A&M 29-25
Troy St. 96 Murray St. 31-3
Troy St. 96 Montana 7-70

Terry Bowden (2-2) (West Va. '78)
Samford 91 New Hampshire 29-13
Samford 91 James Madison 24-21

Terry Bowden (2-2) (West Va. '78)
Samford 91 Youngstown St. 0-10
Samford 92 Delaware 21-56

Bill Bowes (0-2) (Penn St. '65)
New Hampshire 91 Samford 13-29
New Hampshire 94 Appalachian St. 10-17 (OT)

Jesse Branch (1-2) (Arkansas '64)
Southwest Mo. St. 89 Maine 38-35
Southwest Mo. St. 89 Stephen F. Austin 25-55
Southwest Mo. St. 90 Idaho 35-41

Billy Brewer (1-1) (Mississippi '61)
Louisiana Tech 82 South Caro. St. 38-3
Louisiana Tech 82 Delaware 0-17

James Carson (0-3) (Jackson St. '63)
Jackson St. 95 Marshall 8-38
Jackson St. 96 William & Mary 6-45
Jackson St. 97 Western Ill. 24-31

Rick Carter (0-1) (Earlham '65)
Holy Cross 83 Western Caro. 21-28

Marino Casem (0-1) (Xavier [La.] '56)
Alcorn St. 84 Louisiana Tech 21-44

Mike Cavan (1-1) (Georgia '72)
East Tenn. St. 96 Villanova 35-29
East Tenn. St. 96 Montana 14-44

George Chaump (4-2) (Bloomsburg '58)
Marshall 87 James Madison 41-12
Marshall 87 Weber St. 51-23
Marshall 87 Appalachian St. 24-10
Marshall 87 Northeast La. 42-43
Marshall 88 North Texas 7-0
Marshall 88 Furman 9-13

Pat Collins (4-0) (Louisiana Tech '63)
Northeast La. 87 North Texas 30-9
Northeast La. 87 Eastern Ky. 33-32
Northeast La. 87 Northern Iowa 44-41 (OT)
Northeast La. 87* Marshall 43-42

Archie Cooley Jr. (0-1) (Jackson St. '62)
Mississippi Val. 84 Louisiana Tech 19-66

Bruce Craddock (0-1) (Truman St. '66)
Western Ill. 88 Western Ky. 32-35

Jim Criner (3-1) (Cal Poly Pomona '61)
Boise St. 80 Grambling 14-9
Boise St. 80* Eastern Ky. 31-29
Boise St. 81 Jackson St. 19-7
Boise St. 81 Eastern Ky. 17-23

Bill Davis (2-2) (Johnson Smith '65)
South Caro. St. 81 Tennessee St. 26-25
South Caro. St. 81 Idaho St. 12-41
South Caro. St. 82 Furman 17-0
South Caro. St. 82 Louisiana Tech 3-38

Rey Dempsey (3-0) (Geneva '58)
Southern Ill. 83 Indiana St. 23-7
Southern Ill. 83 Nevada 23-7
Southern Ill. 83* Western Caro. 43-7

Mick Dennehy (3-2) (Montana '73)
Montana 96 Nicholls St. 48-3
Montana 96 East Tenn. St. 44-14
Montana 96 Troy St. 70-7
Montana 96 Marshall 29-49
Montana 97 McNeese St. 14-19

Jim Dennison (0-1) (Wooster '60)

Akron	85	Rhode Island 27-35

Jim Donnan (15-4) (North Caro. St. '67)

Marshall	91	Western Ill. 20-17 (OT)
Marshall	91	Northern Iowa 41-13
Marshall	91	Eastern Ky. 14-7
Marshall	91	Youngstown St. 17-25
Marshall	92	Eastern Ky. 44-0
Marshall	92	Middle Tenn. St. 35-21
Marshall	92	Delaware 28-7
Marshall	92*	Youngstown St. 31-28
Marshall	93	Howard 28-14
Marshall	93	Delaware 34-31
Marshall	93	Troy St. 24-21
Marshall	93	Youngstown St. 5-17
Marshall	94	Middle Tenn. St. 49-14
Marshall	94	James Madison 28-21 (OT)
Marshall	94	Boise St. 24-28
Marshall	95	Jackson St. 38-8
Marshall	95	Northern Iowa 41-24
Marshall	95	McNeese St. 25-13
Marshall	95	Montana 20-22

Boots Donnelly (6-7) (Middle Tenn. St. '65)

Middle Tenn. St.	84	Eastern Ky. 27-10
Middle Tenn. St.	84	Indiana St. 42-41 (3 OT)
Middle Tenn. St.	84	Louisiana Tech 13-21
Middle Tenn. St.	85	Ga. Southern 21-28
Middle Tenn. St.	89	Appalachian St. 24-21
Middle Tenn. St.	89	Ga. Southern 3-45
Middle Tenn. St.	90	Jackson St. 28-7
Middle Tenn. St.	90	Boise St. 13-20
Middle Tenn. St.	91	Sam Houston St. 20-19 (OT)
Middle Tenn. St.	91	Eastern Ky. 13-23
Middle Tenn. St.	92	Appalachian St. 35-10
Middle Tenn. St.	92	Marshall 21-35
Middle Tenn. St.	94	Marshall 14-49

Larry Donovan (0-1) (Nebraska '64)

Montana	82	Idaho 7-21

Fred Dunlap (1-2) (Colgate '50)

Colgate	82	Boston U. 21-7
Colgate	82	Delaware 13-20
Colgate	83	Western Caro. 23-24

Dennis Erickson (1-2) (Montana St. '70)

Idaho	82	Montana 21-7
Idaho	82	Eastern Ky. 30-38
Idaho	85	Eastern Wash. 38-42

Mo Forte (0-1) (Minnesota '71)

North Caro. A&T	86	Ga. Southern 21-52

Joe Gardi (0-2) (Maryland '60)

Hofstra	95	Delaware 17-38
Hofstra	97	Delaware 14-24

Keith Gilbertson (2-3) (Central Wash. '71)

Idaho	86	Nevada 7-27
Idaho	87	Weber St. 30-59
Idaho	88	Montana 38-19
Idaho	88	Northwestern St. 38-30
Idaho	88	Furman 7-38

Sam Goodwin (1-2) (Henderson St. '66)

Northwestern St.	88	Boise St. 22-13
Northwestern St.	88	Idaho 30-38
Northwestern St.	97	Eastern Wash. 10-40

W. C. Gorden (0-9) (Tennessee St. '52)

Jackson St.	78	Florida A&M 10-15
Jackson St.	81	Boise St. 7-19
Jackson St.	82	Eastern Ill. 13-16 (OT)
Jackson St.	85	Ga. Southern 0-27
Jackson St.	86	Tennessee St. 23-32
Jackson St.	87	Arkansas St. 32-35
Jackson St.	88	Stephen F. Austin 0-24
Jackson St.	89	Montana 7-48
Jackson St.	90	Middle Tenn. St. 7-28

Mike Gottfried (0-1) (Morehead St. '66)

Murray St.	79	Lehigh 9-28

Lynn Graves (%3-1) (Stephen F. Austin '65)

Stephen F. Austin	89%	Grambling 59-56
Stephen F. Austin	89%	Southwest Mo. St. 55-25
Stephen F. Austin	89%	Furman 21-19
Stephen F. Austin	89%	Ga. Southern 34-37

Bob Griffin (2-3) (Southern Conn. St. '63)

Rhode Island	81	Idaho St. 0-51
Rhode Island	84	Richmond 23-17
Rhode Island	84	Montana St. 20-32
Rhode Island	85	Akron 35-27
Rhode Island	85	Furman 15-59

Skip Hall (2-2) (Concordia-M'head '66)

Boise St.	88	Northwestern St. 13-22
Boise St.	90	Northern Iowa 20-3
Boise St.	90	Middle Tenn. St. 20-13
Boise St.	90	Nevada 52-59 (3 OT)

Jack Harbaugh (1-1) (Bowling Green '61)

Western Ky.	97	Eastern Ky. 42-14
Western Ky.	97	Eastern Wash. 21-38

Bill Hayes (0-1) (N.C. Central '64)

North Caro. A&T	92	Citadel 0-44

Jim Hess (1-1) (Southeastern Okla. '59)

Stephen F. Austin	88	Jackson St. 24-0
Stephen F. Austin	88	Ga. Southern 6-27

Rudy Hubbard (2-0) (Ohio St. '68)

Florida A&M	78	Jackson St. 15-10
Florida A&M	78*	Massachusetts 35-28

Sonny Jackson (1-1) (Nicholls St. '63)

Nicholls St.	86	Appalachian St. 28-26
Nicholls St.	86	Ga. Southern 31-55

Billy Joe (0-2) (Villanova '63)

Florida A&M	96	Troy St. 25-29
Florida A&M	97	Ga. Southern 37-52

Bobby Johnson (1-1) (Clemson '73)

Furman	96	Northern Ariz. 42-31
Furman	96	Marshall 0-54

Paul Johnson (1-1) (Western Caro. '79)

Ga. Southern	97	Florida A&M 52-37
Ga. Southern	97	Delaware 7-16

Cardell Jones (0-2) (Alcorn St. '65)

Alcorn St.	92	Northeast La. 27-78
Alcorn St.	94	Youngstown St. 20-63

Bobby Keasler (8-6) (Northeast La. '70)

McNeese St.	91	Nevada 16-22
McNeese St.	92	Idaho 23-20
McNeese St.	92	Northern Iowa 7-29
McNeese St.	93	William & Mary 34-28
McNeese St.	93	Troy St. 28-35
McNeese St.	94	Idaho 38-21
McNeese St.	94	Montana 28-30
McNeese St.	95	Idaho 33-3
McNeese St.	95	Delaware 52-18
McNeese St.	95	Marshall 13-25
McNeese St.	97	Montana 19-14
McNeese St.	97	Western Ill. 14-12
McNeese St.	97	Delaware 23-21
McNeese St.	97	Youngstown St. 9-10

Roy Kidd (16-15) (Eastern Ky. '54)

Eastern Ky.	79	Nevada 33-30
Eastern Ky.	79*	Lehigh 30-7
Eastern Ky.	80	Lehigh 23-20
Eastern Ky.	80	Boise St. 29-31
Eastern Ky.	81	Delaware 35-28
Eastern Ky.	81	Boise St. 23-17
Eastern Ky.	81	Idaho St. 23-34
Eastern Ky.	82	Idaho St. 38-30
Eastern Ky.	82	Tennessee St. 13-7
Eastern Ky.	82*	Delaware 17-14
Eastern Ky.	83	Boston U. 20-24
Eastern Ky.	84	Middle Tenn. St. 10-27
Eastern Ky.	86	Furman 23-10
Eastern Ky.	86	Eastern Ill. 24-22
Eastern Ky.	86	Arkansas St. 10-24
Eastern Ky.	87	Western Ky. 40-17
Eastern Ky.	87	Northeast La. 32-33
Eastern Ky.	88	Massachusetts 28-17
Eastern Ky.	88	Western Ky. 41-24
Eastern Ky.	88	Ga. Southern 17-21
Eastern Ky.	89	Youngstown St. 24-28
Eastern Ky.	90	Furman 17-45
Eastern Ky.	91	Appalachian St. 14-3
Eastern Ky.	91	Middle Tenn. St. 23-13
Eastern Ky.	91	Marshall 7-14
Eastern Ky.	92	Marshall 0-44
Eastern Ky.	93	Ga. Southern 12-14
Eastern Ky.	94	Boston U. 30-23
Eastern Ky.	94	Youngstown St. 15-18
Eastern Ky.	95	Montana 0-48
Eastern Ky.	97	Western Ky. 14-42

Jim Koetter (0-1) (Idaho St. '61)

Idaho St.	83	Nevada 20-27

Dave Kragthorpe (3-0) (Utah St. '55)

Idaho St.	81	Rhode Island 51-0
Idaho St.	81	South Caro. St. 41-12
Idaho St.	81*	Eastern Ky. 34-23

Mike Kramer (2-1) (Idaho '77)

Eastern Wash.	97	Northwestern St. 40-10
Eastern Wash.	97	Western Ky. 38-21
Eastern Wash.	97	Youngstown St. 14-25

Larry Lacewell (6-4) (Ark.-Monticello '59)

Arkansas St.	84	Chattanooga 37-10
Arkansas St.	84	Montana St. 14-31
Arkansas St.	85	Grambling 10-7
Arkansas St.	85	Nevada 23-24
Arkansas St.	86	Sam Houston St. 48-7
Arkansas St.	86	Delaware 55-14
Arkansas St.	86	Eastern Ky. 24-10
Arkansas St.	86	Ga. Southern 21-48
Arkansas St.	87	Jackson St. 35-32
Arkansas St.	87	Northern Iowa 28-49

Jimmye Laycock (2-5) (William & Mary '70)

William & Mary	86	Delaware 17-51
William & Mary	89	Furman 10-24
William & Mary	90	Massachusetts 38-0
William & Mary	90	Central Fla. 38-52
William & Mary	93	McNeese St. 28-34
William & Mary	96	Jackson St. 45-6
William & Mary	96	Northern Iowa 35-38

Tom Lichtenberg (0-1) (Louisville '62)

Maine	89	Southwest Mo. St. 35-38

Gene McDowell (2-2) (Florida St. '63)

Central Fla.	90	Youngstown St. 20-17
Central Fla.	90	William & Mary 52-38
Central Fla.	90	Ga. Southern 7-44
Central Fla.	93	Youngstown St. 30-56

John Merritt (†1-2) (Kentucky St. '50)

Tennessee St.	81†	South Caro. St. 25-26 (OT)
Tennessee St.	82†	Eastern Ill. 20-19
Tennessee St.	82†	Eastern Ky. 7-13

Al Molde (1-2) (Gust. Adolphus '66)

Eastern Ill.	83	Indiana St. 13-16 (2 OT)
Eastern Ill.	86	Murray St. 28-21
Eastern Ill.	86	Eastern Ky. 22-24

Jerry Moore (2-5) (Baylor '61)

Appalachian St.	89	Middle Tenn. St. 21-24
Appalachian St.	91	Eastern Ky. 3-14
Appalachian St.	92	Middle Tenn. St. 10-35
Appalachian St.	94	New Hampshire 17-10 (OT)
Appalachian St.	94	Boise St. 14-17
Appalachian St.	95	James Madison 31-24
Appalachian St.	95	Stephen F. Austin 17-27

Darrell Mudra (4-3) (Peru St. '51)

Eastern Ill.	82	Jackson St. 16-13 (OT)
Eastern Ill.	82	Tennessee St. 19-20
Northern Iowa	85	Eastern Wash. 17-14
Northern Iowa	85	Ga. Southern 33-40
Northern Iowa	87	Youngstown St. 31-28
Northern Iowa	87	Arkansas St. 49-28
Northern Iowa	87	Northeast La. 41-44 (OT)

Tim Murphy (0-1) (Springfield '78)

Maine	87	Ga. Southern 28-31 (OT)

Corky Nelson (0-3) (Southwest Tex. St. '64)

North Texas	83	Nevada 17-20 (OT)
North Texas	87	Northeast La. 9-30
North Texas	88	Marshall 0-7

Buddy Nix (0-1) (West Ala. '61)

Chattanooga	84	Arkansas St. 10-37

Houston Nutt (1-2) (Oklahoma St. '81)

Murray St.	95	Northern Iowa 34-35
Murray St.	96	Western Ill. 34-6
Murray St.	96	Troy St. 3-31

John Pearce (2-2) (Tex. A&M-Commerce '70)

Stephen F. Austin	93	Troy St. 20-42
Stephen F. Austin	95	Eastern Ill. 34-29
Stephen F. Austin	95	Appalachian St. 27-17
Stephen F. Austin	95	Montana 14-70

Bob Pickett (1-1) (Maine '59)

Massachusetts	78	Nevada 44-21
Massachusetts	78	Florida A&M 28-35

Mike Price (1-1) (Puget Sound '69)

Weber St.	87	Idaho 59-30
Weber St.	87	Marshall 23-51

Bob Pruett (4-0) (Marshall '65)

Marshall	96	Delaware 59-14
Marshall	96	Furman 54-0
Marshall	96	Northern Iowa 31-14
Marshall	96*	Montana 49-29

Joe Purzycki (0-1) (Delaware '71)
James Madison....... 87 Marshall 12-41

Dennis Raetz (1-2) (Nebraska '68)
Indiana St. .... 83 Eastern Ill. 16-13 (2 OT)
Indiana St. .... 83 Southern Ill. 7-23
Indiana St. .... 84 Middle Tenn. St. 41-42 (3 OT)

Ron Randleman (0-2) (William Penn '64)
Sam Houston St. .... 86 Arkansas St. 7-48
Sam Houston St. .... 91 Middle Tenn. St. 19-20 (OT)

Tubby Raymond (9-10) (Michigan '50)
Delaware.............. 81 Eastern Ky. 28-35
Delaware.............. 82 Colgate 20-13
Delaware.............. 82 Louisiana Tech 17-0
Delaware.............. 82 Eastern Ky. 14-17
Delaware.............. 86 William & Mary 51-17
Delaware.............. 86 Arkansas St. 14-55
Delaware.............. 88 Furman 7-21
Delaware.............. 91 James Madison 35-42 (2 OT)
Delaware.............. 92 Samford 56-21
Delaware.............. 92 Northeast La. 41-18
Delaware.............. 92 Marshall 7-28
Delaware.............. 93 Montana 49-48
Delaware.............. 93 Marshall 31-34
Delaware.............. 95 Hofstra 38-17
Delaware.............. 95 McNeese St. 18-52
Delaware.............. 96 Marshall 14-59
Delaware.............. 97 Hofstra 24-14
Delaware.............. 97 Ga. Southern 16-7
Delaware.............. 97 McNeese St. 21-23

Don Read (8-4) (Cal St. Sacramento '59)
Montana................ 88 Idaho 19-38
Montana................ 89 Jackson St. 48-7
Montana................ 89 Eastern Ill. 25-19
Montana................ 89 Ga. Southern 15-45
Montana................ 93 Delaware 48-49
Montana................ 94 Northern Iowa 23-20
Montana................ 94 McNeese St. 30-28
Montana................ 94 Youngstown St. 9-28
Montana................ 95 Eastern Ky. 48-0
Montana................ 95 Ga. Southern 45-0
Montana................ 95 Stephen F. Austin 70-14
Montana................ 95* Marshall 22-20

Jim Reid (0-2) (Maine '73)
Massachusetts......... 88 Eastern Ky. 17-28
Massachusetts......... 90 William & Mary 0-38

Dave Roberts (2-5) (Western Caro. '68)
Western Ky. .... 87 Eastern Ky. 17-40
Western Ky. .... 88 Western Ill. 35-32
Western Ky. .... 88 Eastern Ky. 24-41
Northeast La. .... 90 Nevada 14-27
Northeast La. .... 92 Alcorn St. 78-27
Northeast La. .... 92 Delaware 18-41
Northeast La. .... 93 Idaho 31-34

Eddie Robinson (0-3) (Leland '41)
Grambling.............. 80 Boise St. 9-14
Grambling.............. 85 Arkansas St. 7-10
Grambling.............. 89 Stephen F. Austin 56-59

Erk Russell (16-2) (Auburn '49)
Ga. Southern.......... 85 Jackson St. 27-0
Ga. Southern.......... 85 Middle Tenn. St. 28-21
Ga. Southern.......... 85 Northern Iowa 40-33
Ga. Southern.......... 85* Furman 44-42
Ga. Southern.......... 86 North Caro. A&T 52-21
Ga. Southern.......... 86 Nicholls St. 55-31

Erk Russell (16-2) (Auburn '49)
Ga. Southern.......... 86 Nevada 48-38
Ga. Southern.......... 86* Arkansas St. 48-21
Ga. Southern.......... 87 Maine 31-28 (OT)
Ga. Southern.......... 87 Appalachian St. 0-19
Ga. Southern.......... 88 Citadel 38-20
Ga. Southern.......... 88 Stephen F. Austin 27-6
Ga. Southern.......... 88 Eastern Ky. 21-17
Ga. Southern.......... 88 Furman 12-17
Ga. Southern.......... 89 Villanova 52-36
Ga. Southern.......... 89 Middle Tenn. St. 45-3
Ga. Southern.......... 89 Montana 45-15
Ga. Southern.......... 89* Stephen F. Austin 37-34

Jimmy Satterfield (7-3) (South Caro. '62)
Furman .... 86 Eastern Ky. 10-23
Furman .... 88 Delaware 21-7
Furman .... 88 Marshall 13-9
Furman .... 88 Idaho 38-7
Furman .... 88* Ga. Southern 17-12
Furman .... 89 William & Mary 24-10
Furman .... 89 Youngstown St. 42-23
Furman .... 89 Stephen F. Austin 19-21
Furman .... 90 Eastern Ky. 45-17
Furman .... 90 Nevada 35-42 (3 OT)

Rip Scherer (2-2) (William & Mary '74)
James Madison....... 91 Delaware 42-35 (2 OT)
James Madison....... 91 Samford 21-24
James Madison....... 94 Troy St. 45-26
James Madison....... 94 Marshall 21-28 (OT)

Dal Shealy (1-2) (Carson-Newman '60)
Richmond.............. 84 Boston U. 35-33
Richmond.............. 84 Rhode Island 17-23
Richmond.............. 87 Appalachian St. 3-20

Dick Sheridan (3-3) (South Caro. '64)
Furman .... 82 South Caro. St. 0-17
Furman .... 83 Boston U. 35-16
Furman .... 83 Western Caro. 7-14
Furman .... 85 Rhode Island 59-15
Furman .... 85 Nevada 35-12
Furman .... 85 Ga. Southern 42-44

Matt Simon (0-1) (Eastern N.M. '76)
North Texas........... 94 Boise St. 20-24

John L. Smith (3-5) (Weber St. '71)
Idaho.................... 89 Eastern Ill. 21-38
Idaho.................... 90 Southwest Mo. St. 41-35
Idaho.................... 90 Ga. Southern 27-28
Idaho.................... 92 McNeese St. 20-23
Idaho.................... 93 Northeast La. 34-31
Idaho.................... 93 Boston U. 21-14
Idaho.................... 93 Youngstown St. 16-35
Idaho.................... 94 McNeese St. 21-38

Bob Spoo (1-3) (Purdue '60)
Eastern Ill. .... 89 Idaho 38-21
Eastern Ill. .... 89 Montana 19-25
Eastern Ill. .... 95 Stephen F. Austin 29-34
Eastern Ill. .... 96 Northern Iowa 14-21

Tim Stowers (6-2) (Auburn '79)
Ga. Southern.......... 90 Citadel 31-0
Ga. Southern.......... 90 Idaho 28-27
Ga. Southern.......... 90 Central Fla. 44-7
Ga. Southern.......... 90* Nevada 36-13
Ga. Southern.......... 93 Eastern Ky. 14-12
Ga. Southern.......... 93 Youngstown St. 14-34
Ga. Southern.......... 95 Troy St. 24-21
Ga. Southern.......... 95 Montana 0-45

Charlie Taaffe (1-3) (Siena '73)
Citadel.................. 88 Ga. Southern 20-38
Citadel.................. 90 Ga. Southern 0-31
Citadel.................. 92 North Caro. A&T 44-0
Citadel.................. 92 Youngstown St. 17-42

Andy Talley (1-5) (Southern Conn. St. '67)
Villanova............... 89 Ga. Southern 36-52
Villanova............... 91 Youngstown St. 16-17
Villanova............... 92 Youngstown St. 20-23
Villanova............... 96 East Tenn. St. 29-35
Villanova............... 97 Colgate 49-28
Villanova............... 97 Youngstown St. 34-37

Joe Taylor (0-1) (Western Ill. '72)
Hampton............... 97 Youngstown St. 13-28

Rick Taylor (1-3) (Gettysburg '64)
Boston U. .... 82 Colgate 7-21
Boston U. .... 83 Eastern Ky. 24-20
Boston U. .... 83 Furman 16-35
Boston U. .... 84 Richmond 33-35

Bill Thomas (1-1) (Tennessee St. '71)
Tennessee St. .... 86 Jackson St. 32-23
Tennessee St. .... 86 Nevada 6-33

Chris Tormey (0-1) (Idaho '78)
Idaho..................... 95 McNeese St. 3-33

Jim Tressel (20-4) (Baldwin-Wallace '75)
Youngstown St. ...... 87 Northern Iowa 28-31
Youngstown St. ...... 89 Eastern Ky. 28-24
Youngstown St. ...... 89 Furman 23-42
Youngstown St. ...... 90 Central Fla. 17-20
Youngstown St. ...... 91 Villanova 17-16
Youngstown St. ...... 91 Nevada 30-28
Youngstown St. ...... 91 Samford 10-0
Youngstown St. ...... 91* Marshall 25-17
Youngstown St. ...... 92 Villanova 23-20
Youngstown St. ...... 92 Citadel 42-17
Youngstown St. ...... 92 Northern Iowa 19-7
Youngstown St. ...... 92 Marshall 28-31
Youngstown St. ...... 93 Central Fla. 56-30
Youngstown St. ...... 93 Ga. Southern 34-14
Youngstown St. ...... 93 Idaho 35-16
Youngstown St. ...... 93* Marshall 17-5
Youngstown St. ...... 94 Alcorn St. 63-20
Youngstown St. ...... 94 Eastern Ky. 18-15
Youngstown St. ...... 94 Montana 28-9
Youngstown St. ...... 94* Boise St. 28-14
Youngstown St........ 97 Hampton 28-13
Youngstown St........ 97 Villanova 37-34
Youngstown St........ 97 Eastern Wash. 25-14
Youngstown St........ 97* McNeese St. 10-9

Bob Waters (3-1) (Presbyterian '60)
Western Caro......... 83 Colgate 24-23
Western Caro......... 83 Holy Cross 28-21
Western Caro......... 83 Furman 14-7
Western Caro......... 83 Southern Ill. 7-43

John Whitehead (1-2) (East Stroudsburg '50)
Lehigh.................... 79 Murray St. 28-9
Lehigh.................... 79 Eastern Ky. 7-30
Lehigh.................... 80 Eastern Ky. 20-23

A. L. Williams (3-1) (Louisiana Tech '57)
Louisiana Tech........ 84 Mississippi Val. 66-19
Louisiana Tech........ 84 Alcorn St. 44-21
Louisiana Tech........ 84 Middle Tenn. St. 21-13
Louisiana Tech........ 84 Montana St. 6-19

Steve Wilson (0-1) (Howard '79)
Howard .... 93 Marshall 14-28

Alex Wood (0-1) (Iowa '79)
James Madison....... 95 Appalachian St. 24-31

Sparky Woods (2-2) (Carson-Newman '76)
Appalachian St....... 86 Nicholls St. 26-28
Appalachian St....... 87 Richmond 20-3
Appalachian St....... 87 Ga. Southern 19-0
Appalachian St....... 87 Marshall 10-24

Dick Zornes (1-2) (Eastern Wash. '68)
Eastern Wash......... 85 Idaho 42-38
Eastern Wash......... 85 Northern Iowa 14-17
Eastern Wash......... 92 Northern Iowa 14-17

**National championship. †Tennessee State's participation vacated by action of the NCAA Committee on Infractions. %Stephen F. Austin's participation vacated by action of the NCAA Committee on Infractions.*

Division II Coaching Records

Winningest Active Division II Coaches

(Minimum five years as college head coach; record at four-year colleges only.)

BY PERCENTAGE

Coach, College	Years	Won	Lost	Tied	†Pct.	Playoffs# W-L-T
Chuck Broyles, Pittsburg St.	8	86	13	2	.86139	12-7-0
Ken Sparks, Carson-Newman	18	172	43	2	.79724	6-5-0
Gene Nicholson, Westminster (Pa.)	7	61	17	2	.77500	0-0-0
Peter Yetten, Bentley	10	72	21	1	.77128	0-0-0
Danny Hale, Bloomsburg	10	80	27	1	.74537	0-2-0
Brian Kelly, Grand Valley St.	7	56	21	2	.72152	0-2-0
Gene Carpenter, Millersville	29	197	81	6	.70423	1-2-0
Connie Driscoll, Stonehill	5	35	15	0	.70000	0-0-0
Frank Cignetti, Indiana (Pa.)	16	130	56	1	.69786	12-8-0
Rob Smith, Western Wash.	9	61	28	1	.68333	0-0-0
Mike Isom, Central Ark.	8	59	27	4	.67778	0-0-0
Tom Hollman, Edinboro	14	95	45	3	.67483	1-5-0
Carl Iverson, Western St.	14	94	45	3	.67254	0-3-0
Bob Biggs, UC Davis	5	39	19	1	.66949	5-3-0
Eric Holm, Northern Mich.	8	58	29	0	.66667	0-3-0
Jim Malosky, Minn.-Duluth	40	255	125	13	.66539	0-0-0
Ron Harms, Tex. A&M-Kingsville	29	203	103	4	.66129	10-8-0
Joe Glenn, Northern Colo.	13	96	50	1	.65646	8-3-0
Jerry Vandergriff, Angelo St.	16	112	59	2	.65318	3-4-0
Lou Anderson, Virginia St.	7	47	25	0	.65278	0-0-0
Brad Smith, Chadron St.	11	75	40	1	.65086	0-1-0
Willard Bailey, Virginia Union	25	167	92	7	.64098	0-6-0
Stan McGarvey, West Tex. A&M	13	86	51	4	.62411	0-0-0
Hampton Smith, Albany St. (Ga.)	22	141	85	4	.62174	1-5-0
George Mihalik, Slippery Rock	10	64	39	4	.61682	1-1-0
Claire Boroff, Neb.-Kearney	26	157	98	5	.61346	0-0-0
Rick Daniels, West Chester	9	59	38	1	.60714	0-2-0
Mel Tjeerdsma, Northwest Mo. St.	14	88	58	4	.60000	2-2-0
Gary Howard, Central Okla.	21	127	84	6	.59908	1-1-0
Malen Luke, Clarion	10	61	41	0	.59804	2-1-0
Dennis Douds, East Stroudsburg	24	143	97	3	.59465	0-1-0
Morris Sloan, Southeastern Okla.	9	52	35	4	.59341	0-0-0
Steve Patton, Gardner-Webb	6	38	26	1	.59231	0-0-0
Bill Davis, Johnson Smith	18	113	80	1	.58505	0-1-0
Monte Cater, Shepherd	17	96	70	2	.57738	0-0-0
Jimmy Parker, Ouachita Baptist	25	153	112	2	.57678	0-0-0
Tom Eckert, Northwestern Okla.	11	67	49	3	.57563	0-0-0
Roger Thomas, North Dak.	14	82	63	2	.56463	4-4-0
Robert Ford, Albany (N.Y.)	29	157	121	1	.56452	0-0-0
Tony DeMeo, Washburn	15	76	59	4	.56115	0-0-0
Ricky Rees, Shippensburg	13	77	62	2	.55319	1-1-0
Noel Martin, St. Cloud St.	15	88	73	0	.54658	1-1-0
Pat Behrns, Neb.-Omaha	10	58	49	0	.54206	0-1-0
Paul Sharp, Southwestern Okla.	12	65	55	1	.54132	0-0-0
Tim Clifton, Mars Hill	5	27	24	0	.52941	0-0-0
Fred Whitmire, Humboldt St.	7	37	33	2	.52778	0-0-0
Eddie Vowell, Tex. A&M-Commerce	12	70	64	1	.52222	2-3-0
Kermit Blount, Winston-Salem	5	26	24	3	.51887	0-0-0
Joe Kimball, Mercyhurst	13	62	59	2	.51220	0-0-0
Bud Elliott, Eastern N. M.	30	157	152	9	.50786	0-1-0
Sam Kornhauser, Stony Brook	14	67	66	2	.50370	0-0-0
Bob Mullett, Concord	9	45	45	2	.50000	0-0-0
Dennis Rolando, Southwest Baptist	5	25	26	0	.49020	0-0-0
Dan Runkle, Mankato St.	17	92	96	2	.48947	2-3-0
Larry Little, N. C. Central	14	71	76	1	.48311	0-0-0
Tom Herman, Gannon	9	40	44	2	.47674	0-0-0
Bill Struble, West Va. Wesleyan	15	71	78	0	.47651	0-0-0
Richard Cavanaugh, Southern Conn.	13	62	69	1	.47348	0-0-0
Rick Comegy, Tuskegee	6	30	35	0	.46154	0-0-0
Bob Eaton, West Liberty St.	8	36	43	1	.45625	0-0-0
Doug Sams, Fairmont St.	7	32	39	0	.45070	0-0-0
Bernie Anderson, Michigan Tech	11	48	60	0	.44444	0-0-0
Ralph Micheli, Moorhead St.	15	60	81	2	.42657	0-0-0
Jim Heinitz, Augustana (S.D.)	10	45	63	1	.41743	0-2-0
Mike Taylor, Newberry	6	27	38	0	.41538	0-0-0
Todd Knight, Delta St.	5	20	29	2	.41176	0-0-0
Ron Cooper, Alabama A&M	5	22	33	0	.40000	0-0-0
Hank Walbrick, East Central	8	32	50	1	.39157	0-0-0
Maurice Hunt, Lane	19	71	120	4	.37436	0-0-0
Pat Riepma, Northwood	5	16	34	2	.32692	0-0-0
Sherman Wood, Bowie St.	5	16	34	1	.32353	0-0-0
Jim Anderson, Mo.-Rolla	6	17	46	1	.27344	0-0-0

#Record in Division II championship. †Ties computed as half won and half lost.

BY VICTORIES

(Minimum 100 Victories)

Coach, College, Win Pct.	Won
Jim Malosky, Minn.-Duluth .665	255
Ron Harms, Tex. A&M-Kingsville .661	203
Gene Carpenter, Millersville .704	197
Ken Sparks, Carson-Newman .797	172
Willard Bailey, Virginia Union .641	167
Claire Boroff, Neb.-Kearney .613	157
Robert Ford, Albany (N.Y.) .565	157
Bud Elliott, Eastern N. M. .508	157
Jimmy Parker, Ouachita Baptist .577	153
Dennis Douds, East Stroudsburg .595	143
Hampton Smith, Albany St. (Ga.) .622	141
Frank Cignetti, Indiana (Pa.) .698	130
Gary Howard, Central Okla. .599	127
Bill Davis, Johnson Smith .585	113
Jerry Vandergriff, Angelo St. .653	112

Division II Championship Coaches

All coaches who have coached teams in the Division II championship playoffs since 1973 are listed here with their playoff record, alma mater and year graduated, team, year coached, opponent, and score.

Phil Albert (1-3) (Arizona '66)
Towson St. .... 83 North Dak. St. 17-24
Towson St. .... 84 Norfolk St. 31-21
Towson St. .... 84 Troy St. 3-45
Towson St. .... 86 Central St. 0-31

Pokey Allen (10-5) (Utah '65)
Portland St. .... 87 Mankato St. 27-21
Portland St. .... 87 Northern Mich. 13-7
Portland St. .... 87 Troy St. 17-31
Portland St. .... 88 Bowie St. 34-17
Portland St. .... 88 Jacksonville St. 20-13
Portland St. .... 88 Tex. A&M-Kingsville 35-27
Portland St. .... 88 North Dak. St. 21-35
Portland St. .... 89 West Chester 56-50 (3 OT)
Portland St. .... 89 Indiana (Pa.) 0-17
Portland St. .... 91 Northern Colo. 28-24
Portland St. .... 91 Mankato St. 37-27
Portland St. .... 91 Pittsburg St. 21-53
Portland St. .... 92 UC Davis 42-28
Portland St. .... 92 Tex. A&M-Kingsville 35-30
Portland St. .... 92 Pittsburg St. 38-41

Mike Ayers (0-2) (Georgetown [Ky.] '74)
Wofford .... 90 Mississippi Col. 19-70
Wofford .... 91 Mississippi Col. 15-28

Bob Babich (0-1) (Tulsa '84)
North Dak. St. .... 97 Northwest Mo. St. 28-39

Willard Bailey (0-6) (Norfolk St. '62)
Virginia Union .... 79 Delaware 28-58
Virginia Union .... 80 North Ala. 8-17
Virginia Union .... 81 Shippensburg 27-40
Virginia Union .... 82 North Dak. St. 20-21
Virginia Union .... 83 North Ala. 14-16
Norfolk St. .... 84 Towson St. 21-31

Bob Bartolomeo (0-1) (Butler '77)
Butler .... 91 Pittsburg St. 16-26

Tom Beck (0-2) (Northern Ill. '61)
Grand Valley St. .... 89 Indiana (Pa.) 24-34
Grand Valley St. ..... 90 Texas A&M-Commerce 14-20

Pat Behrns (0-1) (Dakota St. '72)
Neb.-Omaha .... 96 Northwest Mo. St. 21-22

Bob Biggs (5-3) (UC Davis '73)
UC Davis .... 93 Fort Hays St. 37-34
UC Davis .... 93 Tex. A&M-Kingsville 28-51
UC Davis .... 96 Tex. A&M-Kingsville 17-14
UC Davis .... 96 Central Okla. 26-6
UC Davis .... 96 Carson-Newman 26-29
UC Davis .... 97 Tex. A&M-Kingsville 37-34
UC Davis .... 97 Angelo St. 50-33
UC Davis .... 97 New Haven 25-27

Bob Blasi (0-1) (Colorado St. '53)
Northern Colo. .... 80 Eastern Ill. 14-21

Bill Bowes (1-2) (Penn St. '65)
New Hampshire ..... 75 Lehigh 35-21
New Hampshire ..... 75 Western Ky. 3-14
New Hampshire ..... 76 Montana St. 16-17

Chuck Broyles (12-7) (Pittsburg St. '70)
Pittsburg St. .... 90 Truman St. 59-3
Pittsburg St. .... 90 Tex. A&M-Commerce 60-28
Pittsburg St. .... 90 North Dak. St. 29-39
Pittsburg St. .... 91 Butler 26-16
Pittsburg St. .... 91 Tex. A&M-Commerce 38-28
Pittsburg St. .... 91 Portland St. 53-21
Pittsburg St. .... 91* Jacksonville St. 23-6
Pittsburg St. .... 92 North Dak. 26-21
Pittsburg St. .... 92 North Dak. St. 38-37 (OT)
Pittsburg St. .... 92 Portland St. 41-38
Pittsburg St. .... 92 Jacksonville St. 13-17
Pittsburg St. .... 93 North Dak. 14-17
Pittsburg St. .... 94 North Dak. St. 12-18 (3 OT)
Pittsburg St. .... 95 Northern Colo. 36-17
Pittsburg St. .... 95 North Dak. St. 9-7
Pittsburg St. .... 95 Tex. A&M-Kingsville 28-25 (OT)
Pittsburg St. .... 95 North Ala. 7-27
Pittsburg St. .... 96 Northern Colo. 21-24
Pittsburg St. .... 97 Northern Colo. 16-24

Sandy Buda (1-2) (Kansas '67)
Neb.-Omaha .... 78 Youngstown St. 14-21
Neb.-Omaha .... 84 Northwest Mo. St. 28-15
Neb.-Omaha .... 84 North Dak. St. 14-25

Bill Burgess (12-4) (Auburn '63)
Jacksonville St. .... 88 West Chester 63-24
Jacksonville St. .... 88 Portland St. 13-20

Jacksonville St. 89 Alabama A&M 33-9

Jacksonville St. 89 North Dak. St. 21-17

Jacksonville St. 89 Angelo St. 34-16

Jacksonville St. 89 Mississippi Col. 0-3

Jacksonville St. 90 North Ala. 38-14

Jacksonville St. 90 Mississippi Col. 7-14

Jacksonville St. 91 Winston-Salem 49-24

Jacksonville St. 91 Mississippi Col. 35-7

Jacksonville St. 91 Indiana (Pa.) 27-20

Jacksonville St. 91 Pittsburg St. 6-23

Jacksonville St. 92 Savannah St. 41-16

Jacksonville St. 92 North Ala. 14-12

Jacksonville St. 92 New Haven 46-35

Jacksonville St. 92* Pittsburg St. 17-13

Bob Burt (0-1) (Cal St. Los Angeles '62)

Cal St. Northridge 90 Cal Poly SLO 7-14

Gene Carpenter (1-2) (Huron '63)

Millersville 88 Indiana (Pa.) 27-24

Millersville 88 North Dak. St. 26-36

Millersville 95 Ferris St. 26-36

Marino Casem (0-1) (Xavier [La.] '56)

Alcorn St. 74 UNLV 22-35

Frank Cignetti (12-8) (Indiana [Pa.] '60)

Indiana (Pa.) 87 Central Fla. 10-12

Indiana (Pa.) 88 Millersville 24-27

Indiana (Pa.) 89 Grand Valley St. 34-24

Indiana (Pa.) 89 Portland St. 17-0

Indiana (Pa.) 89 Mississippi Col. 14-26

Indiana (Pa.) 90 Winston-Salem 48-0

Indiana (Pa.) 90 Edinboro 14-7

Indiana (Pa.) 90 Mississippi Col. 27-8

Indiana (Pa.) 90 North Dak. St. 11-51

Indiana (Pa.) 91 Virginia Union 56-7

Indiana (Pa.) 91 Shippensburg 52-7

Indiana (Pa.) 91 Jacksonville St. 20-27

Indiana (Pa.) 93 Ferris St. 28-21

Indiana (Pa.) 93 New Haven 38-35

Indiana (Pa.) 93 North Dak. 21-6

Indiana (Pa.) 93 North Ala. 34-41

Indiana (Pa.) 94 Grand Valley St. 35-27

Indiana (Pa.) 94 Ferris St. 21-17

Indiana (Pa.) 94 Tex. A&M-Kingsville 20-46

Indiana (Pa.) 96 Ferris St. 23-24

Bob Cortese (0-2) (Colorado '67)

Fort Hays St. 93 UC Davis 34-37

Fort Hays St. 95 Tex. A&M-Kingsville 28-59

Bruce Craddock (0-1) (Truman St. '66)

Truman St. 82 Jacksonville St. 21-34

Rick Daniels (0-3) (West Chester '75)

West Chester 89 Portland St. 50-56 (3 OT)

West Chester 92 New Haven 26-38

West Chester 94 Ferris St. 40-43

Bill Davis (0-1) (Johnson Smith '65)

Savannah St. 92 Jacksonville St. 16-41

Rey Dempsey (0-1) (Geneva '58)

Youngstown St. 74 Delaware 14-35

Jim Dennison (2-1) (Wooster '60)

Akron 76 UNLV 26-6

Akron 76 Northern Mich. 29-26

Akron 76 Montana St. 13-24

Dennis Douds (0-1) (Slippery Rock '63)

East Stroudsburg 91 Shippensburg 33-34

Fred Dunlap (0-2) (Colgate '50)

Lehigh 73 Western Ky. 16-25

Lehigh 75 New Hampshire 21-35

Bud Elliott (0-1) (Baker '53)

Northwest Mo. St. 89 Pittsburg St. 7-28

Jimmy Feix (4-2) (Western Ky. '53)

Western Ky. 73 Lehigh 25-16

Western Ky. 73 Grambling 28-20

Western Ky. 73 Louisiana Tech 0-34

Western Ky. 75 Northern Iowa 14-12

Western Ky. 75 New Hampshire 14-3

Western Ky. 75 Northern Mich. 14-16

Charlie Fisher (0-2) (Springfield '81)

West Ga. 95 Carson-Newman 26-37

West Ga. 96 Carson-Newman 7-41

Bob Foster (0-2) (UC Davis '62)

UC Davis 89 Angelo St. 23-28

UC Davis 92 Portland St. 28-42

Dennis Franchione (1-1) (Pittsburg St. '73)

Pittsburg St. 89 Northwest Mo. St. 28-7

Pittsburg St. 89 Angelo St. 21-24

Fred Freeman (0-1) (Mississippi Val. '66)

Hampton 85 Bloomsburg 28-38

Jim Fuller (3-5) (Alabama '67)

Jacksonville St. 77 Northern Ariz. 35-0

Jacksonville St. 77 North Dak. St. 31-7

Jacksonville St. 77 Lehigh 0-33

Jacksonville St. 78 Delaware 27-42

Jacksonville St. 80 Cal Poly SLO 0-15

Jacksonville St. 81 Southwest Tex. St. 22-38

Jacksonville St. 82 Truman St. 34-21

Jacksonville St. 82 Southwest Tex. St. 14-19

Chan Gailey (3-0) (Florida '74)

Troy St. 84 Central St. 31-21

Troy St. 84 Towson St. 45-3

Troy St. 84* North Dak. St. 18-17

Joe Glenn (8-3) (South Dak. '71)

Northern Colo. 90 North Dak. St. 7-17

Northern Colo. 91 Portland St. 24-28

Northern Colo. 95 Pittsburg St. 17-36

Northern Colo. 96 Pittsburg St. 24-21

Northern Colo. 96 Northwest Mo. St. 27-26

Northern Colo. 96 Clarion 19-18

Northern Colo. 96* Carson-Newman 23-14

Northern Colo. 97 Pittsburg St. 24-16

Northern Colo. 97 Northwest Mo. St. 35-19

Northern Colo. 97 Carson-Newman 30-29

Northern Colo. 97* New Haven 51-0

Ray Greene (1-1) (Akron '63)

Alabama A&M 79 Morgan St. 27-7

Alabama A&M 79 Youngstown St. 0-52

John Gregory (0-1) (Northern Iowa '61)

South Dak. St. 79 Youngstown St. 7-50

Herb Grenke (1-1) (Wis.-Milwaukee '63)

Northern Mich. 87 Angelo St. 23-20 (OT)

Northern Mich. 87 Portland St. 7-13

Wayne Grubb (4-3) (Tennessee '61)

North Ala. 80 Virginia Union 17-8

North Ala. 80 Eastern Ill. 31-56

North Ala. 83 Virginia Union 16-14

North Ala. 83 Central St. 24-27

North Ala. 85 Fort Valley St. 14-7

North Ala. 85 Bloomsburg 34-0

North Ala. 85 North Dak. St. 7-35

Rocky Hager (12-5) (Minot St. '74)

North Dak. St. 88 Augustana (S.D.) 49-7

North Dak. St. 88 Millersville 36-26

North Dak. St. 88 Cal St. Sacramento 42-20

North Dak. St. 88* Portland St. 35-21

North Dak. St. 89 Edinboro 45-32

North Dak. St. 89 Jacksonville St. 17-21

North Dak. St. 90 Northern Colo. 17-7

North Dak. St. 90 Cal Poly SLO 47-0

North Dak. St. 90 Pittsburg St. 39-29

North Dak. St. 90* Indiana (Pa.) 51-11

North Dak. St. 91 Mankato St. 7-27

North Dak. St. 92 Truman St. 42-7

North Dak. St. 92 Pittsburg St. 37-38 (OT)

North Dak. St. 94 Pittsburg St. 18-12 (3 OT)

North Dak. St. 94 North Dak. 7-14

North Dak. St. 95 North Dak. 41-10

North Dak. St. 95 Pittsburg St. 7-9

Danny Hale (0-2) (West Chester '68)

West Chester 88 Jacksonville St. 24-63

Bloomsburg 96 Clarion 29-42

Ron Harms (10-8) (Valparaiso '59)

Tex. A&M-Kingsville 88 Mississippi Col. 39-15

Tex. A&M-Kingsville 88 Tenn.-Martin 34-0

Tex. A&M-Kingsville 88 Portland St. 27-35

Tex. A&M-Kingsville 89 Mississippi Col. 19-34

Tex. A&M-Kingsville 92 Western St. 22-13

Tex. A&M-Kingsville 92 Portland St. 30-35

Tex. A&M-Kingsville 93 Portland St. 50-15

Tex. A&M-Kingsville 93 UC Davis 51-28

Tex. A&M-Kingsville 93 North Ala. 25-27

Tex. A&M-Kingsville 94 Western St. 43-7

Tex. A&M-Kingsville 94 Portland St. 21-16

Tex. A&M-Kingsville 94 Indiana (Pa.) 46-20

Tex. A&M-Kingsville 94 North Ala. 10-16

Tex. A&M-Kingsville 95 Fort Hays St. 59-28

Tex. A&M-Kingsville 95 Portland St. 30-3

Tex. A&M-Kingsville 95 Pittsburg St. 25-28 (OT)

Tex. A&M-Kingsville 96 UC Davis 14-17

Tex. A&M-Kingsville 97 UC Davis 34-37

Joe Harper (3-1) (UCLA '59)

Cal Poly SLO 78 Winston-Salem 0-17

Cal Poly SLO 80 Jacksonville St. 15-0

Cal Poly SLO 80 Santa Clara 38-14

Cal Poly SLO 80* Eastern Ill. 21-13

Bill Hayes (1-2) (N.C. Central '64)

Winston-Salem 78 Cal Poly SLO 17-0

Winston-Salem 78 Delaware 0-41

Winston-Salem 87 Troy St. 14-45

Jim Heinitz (0-2) (South Dak. St. '72)

Augustana (S.D.) 88 North Dak. St. 7-49

Augustana (S.D.) 89 St. Cloud St. 20-27

Andy Hinson (0-1) (Bethune-Cookman '53)

Bethune-Cookman 77 UC Davis 16-34

Sonny Holland (3-0) (Montana St. '60)

Montana St. 76 New Hampshire 17-16

Montana St. 76 North Dak. St. 10-3

Montana St. 76* Akron 24-13

Tom Hollman (1-5) (Ohio Northern '68)

Edinboro 89 North Dak. St. 32-45

Edinboro 90 Virginia Union 38-14

Edinboro 90 Indiana (Pa.) 7-14

Edinboro 92 Ferris St. 15-19

Edinboro 93 New Haven 28-48

Edinboro 95 New Haven 12-27

Eric Holm (0-3) (Truman St. '81)

Truman St. 90 Pittsburg St. 3-59

Truman St. 92 North Dak. St. 7-42

Truman St. 94 North Dak. 6-18

Gary Howard (1-1) (Arkansas '64)

Central Okla. 96 Chadron St. 23-21

Central Okla. 96 UC Davis 6-26

Carl Iverson (0-3) (Whitman '62)

Western St. 92 Tex. A&M-Kingsville 13-22

Western St. 94 Tex. A&M-Kingsville 7-43

Western St. 97 Angelo St. 12-46

Billy Joe (3-4) (Villanova '63)

Central St. 83 Southwest Tex. St. 24-16

Central St. 83 North Ala. 27-24

Central St. 83 North Dak. St. 21-41

Central St. 84 Troy St. 21-31

Central St. 85 South Dak. 10-13 (2 OT)

Central St. 86 Towson St. 31-0

Central St. 86 North Dak. St. 12-35

Gary Keller (0-1) (Bluffton '73)

Ashland 97 Slippery Rock 20-30

Brian Kelly (0-2) (Assumption '83)

Grand Valley St. 91 Tex. A&M-Commerce 15-36

Grand Valley St. 94 Indiana (Pa.) 27-35

Roy Kidd (0-1) (Eastern Ky. '54)

Eastern Ky. 76 North Dak. St. 7-10

Jim King (1-1)

West Ala. 75 North Dak. 34-14

West Ala. 75 Northern Mich. 26-28

Tony Knap (1-4) (Idaho '39)

Boise St. 73 South Dak. 53-10

Boise St. 73 Louisiana Tech 34-38

Boise St. 74 Central Mich. 6-20

Boise St. 75 Northern Mich. 21-24

UNLV 76 Akron 6-26

Roy Kramer (3-0) (Maryville [Tenn.] '53)

Central Mich. 74 Boise St. 20-6

Central Mich. 74 Louisiana Tech 35-14

Central Mich. 74* Delaware 54-14

Gil Krueger (4-2) (Marquette '52)

Northern Mich. 75 Boise St. 24-21

Northern Mich. 75 West Ala. 28-26

Northern Mich. 75* Western Ky. 16-14

Northern Mich. 76 Delaware 28-17

Northern Mich. 76 Akron 26-29

Northern Mich. 77 North Dak. St. 6-20

Maxie Lambright (4-1) (Southern Miss. '49)

Louisiana Tech 73 Western Ill. 18-13

Louisiana Tech 73 Boise St. 38-34

Louisiana Tech 73* Western Ky. 34-0

Louisiana Tech 74 Western Caro. 10-7

Louisiana Tech 74 Central Mich. 14-35

George Landis (1-1) (Penn St. '71)

Bloomsburg 85 Hampton 38-28

Bloomsburg 85 North Ala. 0-34

Jon Lantz (0-1) (Okla. Panhandle '74)
Mo. Southern St. .... 93 Mankato St. 13-34

Henry Lattimore (1-1) (Jackson St. '57)
N.C. Central .... 88 Winston-Salem 31-16
N.C. Central .... 88 Cal St. Sacramento 7-56

Malen Luke (2-1) (Westminster [Pa.] '76)
Clarion .... 96 Bloomsburg 42-29
Clarion .... 96 Ferris St. 23-21
Clarion .... 96 Northern Colo. 18-19

Bill Lynch (0-1) (Butler '77)
Butler .... 88 Tenn.-Martin 6-23

Dick MacPherson (0-1) (Springfield '58)
Massachusetts......... 77 Lehigh 23-30

George Mahalik (1-1) (Slippery Rock '74)
Slippery Rock .... 97 Ashland 30-20
Slippery Rock .... 97 New Haven 21-49

Pat Malley (1-1) (Santa Clara '53)
Santa Clara............ 80 Northern Mich. 27-26
Santa Clara............ 80 Cal Poly SLO 14-38

Noel Martin (1-1) (Nebraska '63)
St. Cloud St. .... 89 Augustana (S.D.) 27-20
St. Cloud St. .... 89 Mississippi Col. 24-55

Fred Martinelli (0-1) (Otterbein '51)
Ashland .... 86 North Dak. St. 0-50

Bob Mattos (2-1) (Cal St. Sacramento '64)
Cal St. Sacramento.. 88 UC Davis 35-14
Cal St. Sacramento.. 88 N.C. Central 56-7
Cal St. Sacramento.. 88 North Dak. St. 20-42

Gene McDowell (1-1) (Florida St. '65)
Central Fla. .... 87 Indiana (Pa.) 12-10
Central Fla. .... 87 Troy St. 10-31

Don McLeary (1-1) (Tennessee '70)
Tenn.-Martin .... 88 Butler 23-6
Tenn.-Martin .... 88 Tex. A&M-Kingsville 0-34

Terry McMillan (1-1) (Southern Miss. '69)
Mississippi Col. ..... 91 Wofford 28-15
Mississippi Col. ..... 91 Jacksonville St. 7-35

Ron Meyer (1-1) (Purdue '63)
UNLV...................... 74 Alcorn St. 35-22
UNLV...................... 74 Delaware 11-49

Don Morton (8-3) (Augustana [Ill.] '69)
North Dak. St. .... 81 Puget Sound 24-10
North Dak. St. .... 81 Shippensburg 18-6
North Dak. St. .... 81 Southwest Tex. St. 13-42
North Dak. St. .... 82 Virginia Union 21-20
North Dak. St. .... 82 UC Davis 14-19
North Dak. St. .... 83 Towson St. 24-17
North Dak. St. .... 83 UC Davis 26-17
North Dak. St. .... 83* Central St. 41-21
North Dak. St. .... 84 UC Davis 31-23
North Dak. St. .... 84 Neb.-Omaha 25-14
North Dak. St. .... 84 Troy St. 17-18

Darrell Mudra (5-2) (Peru St. '51)
Western Ill. .... 73 Louisiana Tech 13-18
Eastern Ill. .... 78 UC Davis 35-31
Eastern Ill. .... 78 Youngstown St. 26-22
Eastern Ill. .... 78* Delaware 10-9
Eastern Ill. .... 80 Northern Colo. 21-14
Eastern Ill. .... 80 North Ala. 56-31
Eastern Ill. .... 80 Cal Poly SLO 13-21

Hal Mumme (2-2) (Tarleton St. '75)
Valdosta St. .... 94 Albany St. (Ga.) 14-7
Valdosta St. .... 94 North Ala. 24-27 (2 OT)
Valdosta St. .... 96 Albany St. (Ga.) 38-28
Valdosta St. .... 96 Carson-Newman 19-24

Gene Murphy (0-1) (North Dak. '62)
North Dak. .... 79 Mississippi Col. 15-35

Bill Narduzzi (3-2) (Miami [Ohio] '59)
Youngstown St. ...... 78 Neb.-Omaha 21-14
Youngstown St. ...... 78 Eastern Ill. 22-26
Youngstown St. ...... 79 South Dak. St. 50-7
Youngstown St. ...... 79 Alabama A&M 52-0
Youngstown St. ...... 79 Delaware 21-38

John O'Hara (0-1) (Okla. Panhandle '67)
Southwest Tex. St. .. 83 Central St. 16-24

Jerry Olson (0-1) (Valley City St. '55)
North Dak. .... 75 West Ala. 14-34

Keith Otterbein (3-2) (Ferris St. '79)
Ferris St. .... 92 Edinboro 19-15
Ferris St. .... 92 New Haven 13-35
Ferris St. .... 93 Indiana (Pa.) 21-28
Ferris St. .... 94 West Chester 43-40
Ferris St. .... 94 Indiana (Pa.) 17-21

Jeff Pierce (3-2) (Ferris St. '79)
Ferris St. .... 95 Millersville 36-26
Ferris St. .... 95 New Haven 17-9
Ferris St. .... 95 North Ala. 7-45
Ferris St. .... 96 Indiana (Pa.) 24-23
Ferris St. .... 96 Clarion 21-23

Doug Porter (0-1) (Xavier [La.] '52)
Fort Valley St. .... 82 Southwest Tex. St. 6-27

George Pugh (0-1) (Alabama '76)
Alabama A&M....... 89 Jacksonville St. 9-33

Bill Rademacher (1-3) (Northern Mich. '63)
Northern Mich. ...... 80 Santa Clara 6-27
Northern Mich. ...... 81 Elizabeth City St. 55-6
Northern Mich. ...... 81 Southwest Tex. St. 0-62
Northern Mich. ...... 82 UC Davis 21-42

Vito Ragazzo (1-1) (William & Mary '51)
Shippensburg .... 81 Virginia Union 40-27
Shippensburg .... 81 North Dak. St. 6-18

Tubby Raymond (7-4) (Michigan '50)
Delaware .... 73 Grambling 8-17
Delaware .... 74 Youngstown St. 35-14
Delaware .... 74 UNLV 49-11
Delaware .... 74 Central Mich. 14-54
Delaware .... 76 Northern Mich. 17-28
Delaware .... 78 Jacksonville St. 42-27
Delaware .... 78 Winston-Salem 41-0
Delaware .... 78 Eastern Ill. 9-10
Delaware .... 79 Virginia Union 58-28
Delaware .... 79 Mississippi Col. 60-10
Delaware .... 79* Youngstown St. 38-21

Rocky Rees (1-1) (West Chester '71)
Shippensburg .... 91 East Stroudsburg 34-33
Shippensburg .... 91 Indiana (Pa.) 7-52

Rick Rhodes (4-1)
Troy St. .... 86 Virginia Union 31-7
Troy St. .... 86 South Dak. 28-42
Troy St. .... 87 Winston-Salem 45-14
Troy St. .... 87 Central Fla. 31-10
Troy St. .... 87* Portland St. 31-17

Pete Richardson (0-3) (Dayton '68)
Winston-Salem........ 88 N.C. Central 16-31
Winston-Salem........ 90 Indiana (Pa.) 0-48
Winston-Salem........ 91 Jacksonville St. 24-49

Steve Roberts (0-1) (Ouachita Bapt. '87)
Southern Ark. .... 97 Albany St. (Ga.) 6-10

Eddie Robinson (1-1) (Leland '41)
Grambling.............. 73 Delaware 17-8
Grambling.............. 73 Western Ky. 20-28

Warren Ruggerio (0-1) (Delaware '88)
Glenville St. .... 97 New Haven 7-47

Dan Runkle (2-3) (Illinois Col. '68)
Mankato St. .... 87 Portland St. 21-27
Mankato St. .... 91 North Dak. St. 27-7
Mankato St. .... 91 Portland St. 27-37
Mankato St. .... 93 Mo. Southern St. 34-13
Mankato St. .... 93 North Dak. 21-54

Joe Salem (0-2) (Minnesota '61)
South Dak. .... 73 Boise St. 10-53
Northern Ariz. .... 77 Jacksonville St. 0-35

Lyle Setencich (1-1) (Fresno St. '68)
Cal Poly SLO.......... 90 Cal St. Northridge 14-7
Cal Poly SLO.......... 90 North Dak. St. 0-47

Stan Sheriff (0-1) (Cal Poly SLO '54)
Northern Iowa .... 75 Western Ky. 12-14

Sanders Shiver (0-1) (Carson-Newman '76)
Bowie St. .... 88 Portland St. 17-34

Ron Simonson (0-1) (Portland St. '65)
Puget Sound .... 81 North Dak. St. 10-24

Brad Smith (0-1) (Western Ill. '72)
Chadron St. .... 96 Central Okla. 21-23

Hampton Smith (1-5) (Mississippi Val. '57)
Albany St. (Ga.) ..... 93 Hampton 7-33
Albany St. (Ga.) ..... 94 Valdosta St. 7-14
Albany St. (Ga.) ..... 95 North Ala. 28-38
Albany St. (Ga.) ..... 96 Valdosta St. 28-38
Albany St. (Ga.) ..... 97 Southern Ark. 10-6
Albany St. (Ga.) ..... 97 Carson-Newman 22-23

Jim Sochor (4-8) (San Fran. St. '60)
UC Davis .... 77 Bethune-Cookman 34-16
UC Davis .... 77 Lehigh 30-39
UC Davis .... 78 Eastern Ill. 31-35
UC Davis .... 82 Northern Mich. 42-21
UC Davis .... 82 North Dak. St. 19-14
UC Davis .... 82 Southwest Tex. St. 9-34
UC Davis .... 83 Butler 25-6
UC Davis .... 83 North Dak. St. 17-26
UC Davis .... 84 North Dak. St. 23-31
UC Davis .... 85 North Dak. St. 12-31
UC Davis .... 86 South Dak. 23-26
UC Davis .... 88 Cal St. Sacramento 14-35

Earle Solomonson (6-0) (Augsburg '69)
North Dak. St. .... 85 UC Davis 31-12
North Dak. St. .... 85 South Dak. 16-7
North Dak. St. .... 85* North Ala. 35-7
North Dak. St. .... 86 Ashland 50-0
North Dak. St. .... 86 Central St. 35-12
North Dak. St. .... 86* South Dak. 27-7

Tony Sparano (4-2) (New Haven '82)
New Haven............ 95 Edinboro 27-12
New Haven............ 95 Ferris St. 9-17
New Haven .... 97 Glenville St. 47-7
New Haven............ 97 Slippery Rock 49-21
New Haven............ 97 UC Davis 27-25
New Haven............ 97 Northern Colo. 0-51

Ken Sparks (6-5) (Carson-Newman '68)
Carson-Newman..... 93 North Ala. 28-38
Carson-Newman..... 94 North Ala. 13-17
Carson-Newman..... 95 West Ga. 37-26
Carson-Newman..... 95 North Ala. 7-28
Carson-Newman..... 96 West Ga. 41-7
Carson-Newman..... 96 Valdosta St. 24-19
Carson-Newman..... 96 UC Davis 29-26
Carson-Newman..... 96 Northern Colo. 14-23
Carson-Newman..... 97 North Ala. 21-7
Carson-Newman..... 97 Albany St. (Ga.) 23-22
Carson-Newman..... 97 Northern Colo. 29-30

Bill Sylvester (0-1) (Butler '50)
Butler .... 83 UC Davis 6-25

Joe Taylor (1-5) (Western Ill. '72)
Virginia Union .... 86 Troy St. 7-31
Virginia Union .... 90 Edinboro 14-38
Virginia Union .... 91 Indiana (Pa.) 7-56
Hampton .... 92 North Ala. 21-33
Hampton .... 93 Albany St. (Ga.) 33-7
Hampton .... 93 North Ala. 20-45

Clarence Thomas (0-1)
Morgan St. .... 79 Alabama A&M 7-27

Roger Thomas (4-4) (Augustana [Ill.] '69)
North Dak. .... 92 Pittsburg St. 21-26
North Dak. .... 93 Pittsburg St. 17-14
North Dak. .... 93 Mankato St. 54-21
North Dak. .... 93 Indiana (Pa.) 6-21
North Dak. .... 94 Truman St. 18-6
North Dak. .... 94 North Dak. St. 14-7
North Dak. .... 94 North Ala. 7-35
North Dak. .... 95 North Dak. St. 10-41

Vern Thomsen (0-1) (Peru St. '61)
Northwest Mo. St. .. 84 Neb.-Omaha 15-28

Mel Tjeerdsma (2-2) (Southern St. '67)
Northwest Mo. St. .. 96 Neb.-Omaha 22-21
Northwest Mo. St. .. 96 Northern Colo. 26-27
Northwest Mo. St.... 97 North Dakota St. 39-28
Northwest Mo. St.... 97 Northern Colo. 19-35

Dave Triplett (3-2) (Iowa '72)
South Dak. .... 85 Central St. 13-10 (2 OT)
South Dak. .... 85 North Dak. St. 7-16
South Dak. .... 86 UC Davis 26-23
South Dak. .... 86 Troy St. 42-28
South Dak. .... 86 North Dak. St. 7-27

Jerry Vandergriff (3-4) (Corpus Christi '65)
Angelo St. .... 87 Northern Mich. 20-23 (OT)
Angelo St. .... 89 UC Davis 28-23
Angelo St. .... 89 Pittsburg St. 24-21
Angelo St. .... 89 Jacksonville St. 16-34
Angelo St. .... 94 Portland St. 0-29
Angelo St. .... 97 Western St. 46-12
Angelo St. .... 97 UC Davis 33-50

Eddie Vowell (2-3) (Southwestern Okla. '69)
Tex. A&M-Commerce 90 Grand Valley St. 20-14
Tex. A&M-Commerce 90 Pittsburg St. 28-60
Tex. A&M-Commerce 91 Grand Valley St. 36-15
Tex. A&M-Commerce 91 Pittsburg St. 28-38
Tex. A&M-Commerce 95 Portland St. 35-56

Jim Wacker (8-2) (Valparaiso '60)
North Dak. St. .... 76 Eastern Ky. 10-7
North Dak. St. .... 76 Montana St. 3-10
North Dak. St. .... 77 Northern Mich. 20-6
North Dak. St. .... 77 Jacksonville St. 7-31
Southwest Tex. St. .. 81 Jacksonville St. 38-22
Southwest Tex. St. .. 81 Northern Mich. 62-0
Southwest Tex. St. .. 81* North Dak. St. 42-13
Southwest Tex. St. .. 82 Fort Valley St. 27-6
Southwest Tex. St. .. 82 Jacksonville St. 19-14
Southwest Tex. St. .. 82* UC Davis 34-9

Gerald Walker (0-1) (Lincoln [Mo.] '62)
Fort Valley St. .... 85 North Ala. 7-14

Bobby Wallace (13-3) (Mississippi St. '76)
North Ala. .... 90 Jacksonville St. 14-38
North Ala. .... 92 Hampton 33-21
North Ala. .... 92 Jacksonville St. 12-14
North Ala. .... 93 Carson-Newman 38-28
North Ala. .... 93 Hampton 45-20
North Ala. .... 93 Tex. A&M-Kingsville 27-25
North Ala. .... 93* Indiana (Pa.) 41-34
North Ala. .... 94 Carson-Newman 17-13
North Ala. .... 94 Valdosta St. 27-24 (2 OT)
North Ala. .... 94 North Dak. 35-7
North Ala. .... 94* Tex. A&M-Kingsville 16-10
North Ala. .... 95 Albany St. (Ga.) 38-28
North Ala. .... 95 Carson-Newman 28-7
North Ala. .... 95 Ferris St. 45-7
North Ala. .... 95* Pittsburg St. 27-7
North Ala. .... 97 Carson-Newman 7-21

Tim Walsh (2-3) (UC Riverside '77)
Portland St. .... 93 Tex. A&M-Kingsville 15-50
Portland St. .... 94 Angelo St. 29-0
Portland St. .... 94 Tex. A&M-Kingsville 16-21
Portland St. .... 95 Tex. A&M-Commerce 56-35
Portland St. .... 95 Tex. A&M-Kingsville 3-30

Johnnie Walton (0-1) (Elizabeth City St. '69)
Elizabeth City St. ... 81 Northern Mich. 6-55

Bob Waters (0-1) (Presbyterian '60)
Western Caro. ...... 74 Louisiana Tech 7-10

Mark Whipple (3-2) (Brown '79)
New Haven........... 92 West Chester 38-26
New Haven........... 92 Ferris St. 35-13
New Haven........... 92 Jacksonville St. 35-46
New Haven........... 93 Edinboro 48-28
New Haven........... 93 Indiana (Pa.) 35-38

John Whitehead (3-0) (East Stroudsburg '50)
Lehigh.................... 77 Massachusetts 30-23
Lehigh.................... 77 UC Davis 39-30
Lehigh.................... 77* Jacksonville St. 33-0

John Williams (†7-3) (Mississippi Col. '57)
Mississippi Col. ..... 79 North Dak. 35-15
Mississippi Col. ..... 79 Delaware 10-60
Mississippi Col. ..... 88 Tex. A&M-Kingsville 15-39
Mississippi Col. ..... 89† Tex. A&M-Kingsville 34-19
Mississippi Col. ..... 89† St. Cloud St. 55-24
Mississippi Col. ..... 89† Indiana (Pa.) 26-14
Mississippi Col. ..... 89†* Jacksonville St. 3-0
Mississippi Col. ..... 90† Wofford 70-19
Mississippi Col. ..... 90† Jacksonville St. 14-7
Mississippi Col. ..... 90† Indiana (Pa.) 8-27

**National championship. †Mississippi College's participation vacated by action of the NCAA Committee on Infractions.*

Division III Coaching Records

Winningest Active Division III Coaches

(Minimum five years as college head coach; record at four-year colleges only.)

BY PERCENTAGE

Coach, College	Years	Won	Lost	Tied	+Pct.	Playoffs# W-L-T
Larry Kehres, Mount Union	12	124	16	3	.87762	18-5-0
Dick Farley, Williams	11	73	12	3	.84659	0-0-0
Tim Coen, Salve Regina	5	36	9	0	.80000	0-0-0
John Luckhardt, Wash. & Jeff.	16	132	33	2	.79641	13-11-0
K. C. Keeler, Rowan	5	48	12	7	.79508	11-4-0
Roger Harring, Wis.-La Crosse	29	250	66	7	.78483	13-4-0
Bob Packard, Baldwin-Wallace	17	130	40	2	.76163	0-2-0
John Gagliardi, St. John's (Minn.)	49	342	104	11	.76039	13-8-0
Tony DeCarlo, John Carroll	11	82	25	4	.75676	1-2-0
Rich Lackner, Carnegie Mellon	12	88	29	2	.74790	0-1-0
Frank Girardi, Lycoming	26	192	64	5	.74521	11-8-0
Mike Drass, Wesley	5	37	13	1	.73529	0-0-0
Jim Williams, Simpson	11	83	31	1	.72609	2-5-0
Vic Clark, Thomas More	8	58	22	0	.72500	0-1-0
D. J. LeRoy, Coe	15	112	42	2	.72436	0-3-0
Lou Wacker, Emory & Henry	16	122	47	0	.72189	3-4-0
John Audino, Union (N.Y.)	8	57	24	0	.70370	1-2-0
Don Miller, Trinity (Conn.)	31	172	71	5	.70363	0-0-0
Darwin Breaux, Dickinson	5	36	15	1	.70192	0-1-0
Jim Christopherson, Concordia-M'head	29	203	86	7	.69764	2-4-0
Joe King, Rensselaer	9	58	25	2	.69412	0-0-0
Jimmie Keeling, Hardin-Simmons	8	60	27	0	.68966	0-0-0
Scot Dapp, Moravian	11	77	35	1	.68584	1-2-0
Norm Eash, Ill. Wesleyan	11	70	32	1	.68447	2-2-0
Bob Berezowitz, Wis.-Whitewater	13	91	41	4	.68382	1-3-0
C. Wayne Perry, Hanover	16	108	50	2	.68125	0-2-0
John Miech, Wis.-Stevens Point	10	67	31	2	.68000	0-0-0
Tom Gilburg, Frank. & Marsh.	23	149	73	2	.66964	0-0-0
Mike Maynard, Redlands	10	61	30	1	.66848	0-2-0
Bob Nielson, Wis.-Eau Claire	9	60	30	1	.66484	1-2-0
Steve Briggs, Susquehanna	8	55	28	0	.66265	2-1-0
Rick Giancola, Montclair St.	15	101	51	2	.66234	3-3-0
Vance Gibson, Howard Payne	6	39	20	0	.66102	0-0-0
Doug Neibhur, Millikin	9	57	29	1	.66092	0-1-0
Greg Carlson, Wabash	15	92	47	2	.65957	0-0-0
John O'Grady, Wis.-River Falls	9	58	31	3	.64674	1-2-0
Ron Earnst, Ripon	7	42	23	0	.64615	0-0-0
Charlie Pravata, Merchant Marine	7	42	23	2	.64179	0-1-0
Jeffrey Gabrielson, Concordia (Wis.)	8	46	27	0	.63014	0-0-0
Eric Hamilton, Col. of New Jersey	21	131	76	6	.62911	3-3-0
Nick Mourouzis, DePauw	17	103	62	4	.62130	0-0-0
Brien Cullen, Worcester St.	13	76	47	0	.61789	0-0-0
Bob Bierie, Loras	18	111	69	5	.61351	0-0-0
Dale Widolff, Occidental	16	90	57	2	.61074	1-3-0
Steve Miller, Cornell College	19	104	69	3	.59943	0-1-0
Dick Tressel, Hamline	20	117	78	2	.59898	0-0-0
Ed Sweeney, Frostburg St.	13	77	54	4	.58519	0-2-0
Bill Kavanaugh, Mass.-Dartmouth	8	45	32	0	.58442	0-0-0
Steve Johnson, Bethel (Minn.)	9	51	37	1	.57865	0-0-0
Larry Kindbom, Washington (Mo.)	15	84	63	1	.57095	0-0-0
Jim Margraff, Johns Hopkins	8	44	33	3	.56875	0-0-0
Barry Streeter, Gettysburg	20	112	86	5	.56404	2-1-0
Ken Visser, Chapman	7	35	27	1	.56349	0-0-0
Craig Rundle, Albion	12	63	49	1	.56195	0-0-0
Jerry Boyes, Buffalo St.	12	66	52	0	.55932	1-5-0
Jim Scott, Aurora	12	57	45	3	.55714	0-1-0
Mike Hollway, Ohio Wesleyan	15	82	65	2	.55705	0-0-0
Tim Keating, Western Md.	10	53	42	3	.55612	0-1-0
Steven Mohr, Trinity (Tex.)	8	45	36	0	.55556	1-2-0
Don Ruggeri, Mass. Maritime	25	125	100	1	.55531	0-0-0
Mickey Heinecken, Middlebury	25	110	88	2	.55500	0-0-0
Scott Duncan, Rose-Hulman	12	66	53	1	.55417	0-0-0
Jim Moretti, Alfred	13	70	57	3	.55000	0-0-0
Peter Mazzaferro, Bri'water St. (Mass.)	34	163	135	11	.54531	0-0-0
Steve Frank, Hamilton	13	55	48	1	.53365	0-0-0
Dave Murray, Lebanon Valley	8	44	40	1	.53012	0-1-0
Jim Cole, Alma	7	33	30	0	.52381	0-0-0
Terry McMillan, Mississippi Col.	7	35	32	5	.52083	0-0-0
Frank Hauser, Wesleyan (Conn.)	6	25	23	0	.52083	0-0-0
Kelly Kane, Monmouth (Ill.)	14	67	62	0	.51938	0-0-0
Bob Sullivan, Carleton	19	96	89	0	.51892	0-1-0
Merle Masonholder, Carroll (Wis.)	16	74	70	0	.51389	0-0-0
Mike DeLong, Springfield	16	78	74	2	.51299	0-0-0
Ed DeGeorge, Beloit	21	97	94	1	.50781	0-0-0
Terry Price, Maranatha Bapt.	21	100	97	1	.50758	0-0-0
Mike Ketchum, Guilford	7	34	34	0	.50000	0-0-0
A. Wallace Hood, Otterbein	21	97	97	8	.50000	0-0-0
Jeff Heacock, Muskingum	17	81	82	4	.49701	0-0-0
Rich Johanningmeier, Illinois Col.	13	64	65	5	.49627	0-0-0
Randy Awrey, Lakeland	8	38	40	1	.48734	0-0-0
Jim Sypult, Methodist	6	29	31	0	.48333	0-0-0
Bill Samko, Tufts	11	45	49	1	.47895	0-0-0
Jack Osberg, Augsburg	7	34	37	0	.47887	1-1-0
Phil Wilks, Maryville (Tenn.)	10	46	52	0	.46939	0-0-0
Steve Marino, Westfield St.	8	36	41	1	.46795	0-0-0
Dave Warmack, Kalamazoo	8	33	38	1	.46528	0-0-0
Dick West, Heidelberg	14	64	74	2	.46429	0-0-0
Steve Campos, Bethany (W. Va.)	5	21	25	1	.45745	0-0-0
Paul Rudolph, Upper Iowa	7	32	38	0	.45714	0-0-0
Brian Carlson, Kean	6	24	29	4	.45614	0-0-0
Tom Kaczkowski, Ohio Northern	12	53	64	2	.45378	0-0-0
Jim Lyall, Adrian	8	32	39	1	.45139	0-0-0
Tom Austin, Colby	12	42	53	1	.44271	0-0-0
Mike Manley, Anderson (Ind.)	16	68	86	3	.44268	0-1-0
Howard Vandersea, Bowdoin	22	82	104	3	.44180	0-0-0
Gene Epley, Marietta	11	47	61	3	.43694	0-0-0
Rick Candaele, Claremont-M-S	6	24	31	0	.43636	0-0-0
Steve Stetson, Hartwick	12	47	61	2	.43636	0-0-0
Ron Jurney, Millsaps	5	23	30	0	.43396	0-0-0
Kevin Morris, Worcester Tech	5	20	27	0	.42553	0-0-0
Roy Miller, Jersey City St.	13	53	73	0	.42063	0-0-0
Carlin Carpenter, Bluffton	19	73	103	1	.41525	0-0-0
John Cervino, Western Conn. St.	6	24	35	1	.40833	0-0-0
Chris Smith, Grove City	14	52	76	2	.40769	0-0-0
Dwight Smith, MIT	10	32	47	1	.40625	0-0-0

Coach, College	Years	Won	Lost	Tied	+Pct.	Playoffs# W-L-T
Dennis Riccio, St. Lawrence	11	42	62	0	.40385	0-0-0
Dennis Gorsline, Martin Luther	27	93	147	1	.38797	0-0-0
Ed Meierkort, Wis.-Stout	5	19	31	0	.38000	0-0-0
Ron Cardo, Wis.-Oshkosh	14	51	85	4	.37857	0-0-0
Dale Sprague, Blackburn	12	39	66	2	.37383	0-0-0
Mike Wallace, Wilmington (Ohio)	7	23	44	1	.34559	0-0-0
Ralph Young, Westminster (Mo.)	10	33	66	0	.33333	0-0-0
Bill Unsworth, Franklin	8	25	51	1	.33117	0-0-0
Bill Wentworth, Denison	5	16	33	1	.33000	0-0-0
Greg Quick, St. Norbert	9	27	58	0	.31765	0-0-0
Rick Coles, Lawrence	5	14	31	0	.31111	0-0-0
Tim Rucks, Carthage	8	20	48	4	.30556	0-0-0

Coach, College	Years	Won	Lost	Tied	+Pct.	Playoffs# W-L-T
Jim Kinder, Wis.-Platteville	5	15	35	0	.30000	0-0-0
Joe Rotellini, Salisbury St.	8	22	52	0	.29730	0-0-0
Gerry Martin, Western N. Eng.	7	17	42	1	.29167	0-0-0
Paul Vosburgh, St. John Fisher	10	29	65	1	.27692	0-0-0
Greg Polnasek, Colorado Col.	5	13	34	0	.27660	0-0-0
Greg Wallace, Grinnell	10	24	65	1	.27222	0-0-0
Frank Carr, Earlham	13	33	92	0	.26400	0-0-0
Robert Thomas, Hiram	6	14	46	0	.23333	0-0-0
Steve Keenum, McMurry	5	11	37	0	.22917	0-0-0
Dallas Hilliar, Olivet	5	10	35	0	.22222	0-0-0
Paul Krohn, Elmhurst	5	9	35	1	.21111	0-0-0
Rich Mannello, King's (Pa.)	5	9	39	1	.19388	0-0-0

#Record in Division III Championship. +Ties computed as half won and half lost.

BY VICTORIES

(Minimum 100 Victories)

Coach, College, Win Pct.	Won
John Gagliardi, St. John's (Minn.) .760	342
Roger Harring, Wis.-La Crosse .785	250
Jim Christopherson, Concordia-M'head .698	203
Frank Girardi, Lycoming .745	192
Don Miller, Trinity (Conn.) .704	172
Peter Mazzaferro, Bri'water (Mass.) .545	163
Tom Gilburg, Frank. & Marsh. .670	149
John Luckhardt, Wash. & Jeff. .796	132
Eric Hamilton, Col. of New Jersey .629	131
Bob Packard, Baldwin-Wallace .762	130
Don Ruggeri, Mass. Maritime .555	125
Larry Kehres, Mount Union .878	124
Lou Wacker, Emory & Henry .722	122
Dick Tressel, Hamline .599	117
D. J. LeRoy, Coe .724	112
Barry Streeter, Gettysburg .564	112
Bob Bierie, Loras .614	111
Mickey Heinecken, Middlebury .555	110
C. Wayne Perry, Hanover .681	108
Steve Miller, Cornell College .599	104
Nick Mourouzis, DePauw .621	103
Rick Giancola, Montclair St. .662	101
Terry Price, Maranatha Bapt. .508	100

Division III Championship Coaches

All coaches who have coached teams in the Division III championship playoffs since 1973 are listed here with their playoff record, alma mater and year graduated, team, year coached, opponent, and score.

Phil Albert (2-1) (Arizona '66)
Towson St. ... 76 LIU-C. W. Post 14-10
Towson St. ... 76 St. Lawrence 38-36
Towson St. ... 76 St. John's (Minn.) 28-31

Dom Anile (0-1) (LIU-C. W. Post '59)
LIU-C. W. Post ... 76 Towson St. 10-14

John Audino (1-2) (Notre Dame '75)
Union (N.Y.) ... 93 Wm. Paterson 7-17
Union (N.Y.) ... 95 Plymouth St. 24-7
Union (N.Y.) ... 95 Rowan 7-38

Don Ault (0-1) (West Liberty St. '52)
Bethany (W.Va.) ... 80 Widener 12-43

Al Bagnoli (7-6) (Central Conn. St. '74)
Union (N.Y.) ... 83 Hofstra 51-19
Union (N.Y.) ... 83 Salisbury St. 23-21
Union (N.Y.) ... 83 Augustana (Ill.) 17-21
Union (N.Y.) ... 84 Plymouth St. 26-14
Union (N.Y.) ... 84 Augustana (Ill.) 6-23
Union (N.Y.) ... 85 Ithaca 12-13
Union (N.Y.) ... 86 Ithaca 17-24 (OT)
Union (N.Y.) ... 89 Cortland St. 42-14
Union (N.Y.) ... 89 Montclair St. 45-6
Union (N.Y.) ... 89 Ferrum 37-21
Union (N.Y.) ... 89 Dayton 7-17
Union (N.Y.) ... 91 Mass.-Lowell 55-16
Union (N.Y.) ... 91 Ithaca 23-35

Bob Berezowitz (1-3) (Wis.-Whitewater '67)
Wis.-Whitewater ... 88 Simpson 29-27
Wis.-Whitewater ... 88 Central (Iowa) 13-16
Wis.-Whitewater ... 90 St. Thomas (Minn.) 23-24
Wis.-Whitewater ... 97 Simpson 31-34

Don Birmingham (0-2) (Westmar '62)
Dubuque ... 79 Ithaca 7-27
Dubuque ... 80 Minn.-Morris 35-41

J. R. Bishop (1-1) (Franklin '61)
Wheaton (Ill.) ... 95 Wittenberg 63-41
Wheaton (Ill.) ... 95 Mount Union 14-40

Jim Blackburn (0-1) (Virginia '71)
Randolph-Macon ... 84 Wash. & Jeff. 21-22

Bill Bless (0-1) (Indianapolis '63)
Indianapolis ... 75 Wittenberg 13-17

Jerry Boyes (1-5) (Ithaca '76)
Buffalo St. ... 92 Ithaca 28-26
Buffalo St. ... 92 Rowan 19-28
Buffalo St. ... 93 Rowan 6-29
Buffalo St. ... 94 Ithaca 7-10 (2 OT)
Buffalo St. ... 95 Rowan 7-46
Buffalo St. ... 96 Rowan 20-21

Darwin Breaux (0-1) (West Chester '77)
Dickinson ... 94 Widener 0-14

Steve Briggs (2-1) (Springfield '84)
Susquehanna ... 91 Dickinson 21-20
Susquehanna ... 91 Lycoming 31-24
Susquehanna ... 91 Ithaca 13-49

Don Brown (1-2) (Norwich '77)
Plymouth St. ... 94 Merchant Marine 19-18
Plymouth St. ... 94 Ithaca 7-22
Plymouth St. ... 95 Union (N.Y.) 7-24

John Bunting (2-2) (North Caro. '72)
Rowan ... 91 Ithaca 10-31
Rowan ... 92 Worcester Tech 41-14
Rowan ... 92 Buffalo St. 28-19
Rowan ... 92 Wash. & Jeff. 13-18

Jim Butterfield (21-8) (Maine '53)
Ithaca ... 74 Slippery Rock 27-14
Ithaca ... 74 Central (Iowa) 8-10
Ithaca ... 75 Fort Valley St. 41-12
Ithaca ... 75 Widener 23-14
Ithaca ... 75 Wittenberg 0-28
Ithaca ... 78 Wittenberg 3-6
Ithaca ... 79 Dubuque 27-7
Ithaca ... 79 Carnegie Mellon 15-6
Ithaca ... 79* Wittenberg 14-10
Ithaca ... 80 Wagner 41-13
Ithaca ... 80 Minn.-Morris 36-0
Ithaca ... 80 Dayton 0-63
Ithaca ... 85 Union (N.Y.) 13-12
Ithaca ... 85 Montclair St. 50-28
Ithaca ... 85 Gettysburg 34-0
Ithaca ... 85 Augustana (Ill.) 7-20
Ithaca ... 86 Union (N.Y.) 24-17 (OT)
Ithaca ... 86 Montclair St. 29-15
Ithaca ... 86 Salisbury St. 40-44
Ithaca ... 88 Wagner 34-31 (OT)
Ithaca ... 88 Cortland St. 24-17
Ithaca ... 88 Ferrum 62-28
Ithaca ... 88* Central (Iowa) 39-24
Ithaca ... 90 Col. of New Jersey 14-24
Ithaca ... 91 Rowan 31-10
Ithaca ... 91 Union (N.Y.) 35-23
Ithaca ... 91 Susquehanna 49-13
Ithaca ... 91* Dayton 34-20
Ithaca ... 92 Buffalo St. 26-28

Jim Byers (0-1) (Michigan '59)
Evansville ... 74 Central (Iowa) 16-17

Don Canfield (0-1)
Wartburg ... 82 Bishop 7-32

Jerry Carle (0-1) (Northwestern '48)
Colorado Col. ... 75 Millsaps 21-28

Gene Carpenter (0-1) (Huron '63)
Millersville ... 79 Wittenberg 14-21

Rick Carter (3-1) (Earlham '65)
Dayton ... 78 Carnegie Mellon 21-24
Dayton ... 80 Baldwin-Wallace 34-0
Dayton ... 80 Widener 28-24
Dayton ... 80* Ithaca 63-0

Don Charlton (0-1) (Lock Haven '65)
Hiram ... 87 Augustana (Ill.) 0-53

Jim Christopherson (2-4) (Concordia-M'head '60)
Concordia-M'head ... 86 Wis.-Stevens Point 24-15
Concordia-M'head ... 86 Central (Iowa) 17-14
Concordia-M'head ... 86 Augustana (Ill.) 7-41
Concordia-M'head ... 88 Central (Iowa) 0-7
Concordia-M'head ... 95 Wis.-La Crosse 7-45
Concordia-M'head ... 97 Augsburg 22-34

Tom Clark (0-1) (Maryland '86)
Catholic ... 97 Trinity (Tex.) 33-44

Vic Clark (0-1) (Indiana St. '71)
Thomas More ... 92 Emory & Henry 0-17

Mike Clary (0-1) (Rhodes '77)
Rhodes ... 88 Ferrum 10-35

Jay Cottone (0-1) (Norwich '71)
Plymouth St. ... 84 Union (N.Y.) 14-26

Bill Cubit (1-2) (Delaware '75)
Widener ... 94 Dickinson 14-0
Widener ... 94 Wash. & Jeff. 21-37
Widener ... 95 Lycoming 27-31

Scot Dapp (1-2) (West Chester '73)
Moravian ... 88 Widener 17-7
Moravian ... 88 Ferrum 28-49
Moravian ... 93 Wash. & Jeff. 7-27

Harper Davis (1-1) (Mississippi St. '49)
Millsaps ... 75 Colorado Col. 28-21
Millsaps ... 75 Wittenberg 22-55

Tony DeCarlo (1-2) (Kent '62)
John Carroll ... 89 Dayton 10-35
John Carroll ... 97 Hanover 30-20
John Carroll ... 97 Mount Union 7-59

Joe DeMelfi (0-1) (Delta St. '66)
Wilkes ... 93 Frostburg St. 25-26

Bob Di Spirito (0-1) (Rhode Island '53)
Slippery Rock ... 74 Ithaca 14-27

Norm Eash (2-2) (Ill. Wesleyan '75)
Ill. Wesleyan ... 92 Aurora 21-12
Ill. Wesleyan ... 92 Mount Union 27-49
Ill. Wesleyan ... 96 Albion 23-20
Ill. Wesleyan ... 96 Mount Union 14-49

Ed Farrell (0-1) (Rutgers '56)
Bridgeport ... 73 Juniata 14-35

Bob Ford (1-1) (Springfield '59)
Albany (N.Y.) ... 77 Hampden-Sydney 51-45
Albany (N.Y.) ... 77 Widener 15-33

Stokeley Fulton (0-1) (Hampden-Sydney '55)
Hampden-Sydney ... 77 Albany (N.Y.) 45-51

John Gagliardi (13-8) (Colorado Col. '49)
St. John's (Minn.) ... 76 Augustana (Ill.) 46-7
St. John's (Minn.) ... 76 Buena Vista 61-0
St. John's (Minn.) ... 76* Towson St. 31-28
St. John's (Minn.) ... 77 Wabash 9-20
St. John's (Minn.) ... 85 Occidental 10-28
St. John's (Minn.) ... 87 Gust. Adolphus 7-3
St. John's (Minn.) ... 87 Central (Iowa) 3-13
St. John's (Minn.) ... 89 Simpson 42-35
St. John's (Minn.) ... 89 Central (Iowa) 27-24

St. John's (Minn.) .... 89 Dayton 0-28
St. John's (Minn.) .... 91 Coe 75-2
St. John's (Minn.) .... 91 Wis.-La Crosse 29-10
St. John's (Minn.) .... 91 Dayton 7-19
St. John's (Minn.) .... 93 Coe 32-14
St. John's (Minn.) .... 93 Wis.-La Crosse 47-25
St. John's (Minn.) .... 93 Mount Union 8-56
St. John's (Minn.) .... 94 La Verne 51-12
St. John's (Minn.) .... 94 Wartburg 42-14
St. John's (Minn.) .... 94 Albion 16-19
St. John's (Minn.) .... 96 Simpson 21-18
St. John's (Minn.) .... 96 Wis.-La Crosse 30-37

Gerry Gallagher (1-1) (Wm. Paterson '74)
Wm. Paterson......... 93 Union (N.Y.) 17-7
Wm. Paterson......... 93 Rowan 0-37

Joe Gardi (2-1) (Maryland '60)
Hofstra.................. 90 Cortland St. 35-9
Hofstra.................. 90 Col. of New Jersey 38-3
Hofstra.................. 90 Lycoming 10-20

Rick Giancola (3-3) (Rowan '68)
Montclair St. .... 85 Western Conn. St. 28-0
Montclair St. .... 85 Ithaca 28-50
Montclair St. .... 86 Hofstra 24-21
Montclair St. .... 86 Ithaca 15-29
Montclair St. .... 89 Hofstra 23-6
Montclair St. .... 89 Union (N.Y.) 6-45

Steve Gilbert (0-1) (West Chester '79)
Ursinus.................. 96 Lycoming 24-31

Frank Girardi (11-8) (West Chester '61)
Lycoming............... 85 Gettysburg 10-14
Lycoming............... 89 Dickinson 21-0
Lycoming............... 89 Ferrum 24-49
Lycoming............... 90 Carnegie Mellon 17-7
Lycoming............... 90 Wash. & Jeff. 24-0
Lycoming............... 90 Hofstra 20-10
Lycoming............... 90 Allegheny 14-21 (OT)
Lycoming............... 91 Wash. & Jeff. 18-16
Lycoming............... 91 Susquehanna 24-31
Lycoming............... 92 Wash. & Jeff. 0-33
Lycoming............... 95 Widener 31-27
Lycoming............... 95 Wash. & Jeff. 0-48
Lycoming............... 96 Ursinus 31-24
Lycoming............... 96 Albright 31-13
Lycoming............... 96 Rowan 14-33
Lycoming............... 97 Western Md. 27-13
Lycoming............... 97 Trinity (Tex.) 46-26
Lycoming............... 97 Rowan 28-20
Lycoming............... 97 Mount Union 12-61

Larry Glueck (1-1) (Villanova '63)
Fordham .... 87 Hofstra 41-6
Fordham .... 87 Wagner 0-21

Walt Hameline (4-2) (Brockport St. '75)
Wagner................. 82 St. Lawrence 34-43
Wagner................. 87 Rochester 38-14
Wagner................. 87 Fordham 21-0
Wagner................. 87 Emory & Henry 20-15
Wagner................. 87* Dayton 19-3
Wagner................. 88 Ithaca 31-34 (OT)

Eric Hamilton (3-3) (Col. of New Jersey '75)
Col. of New Jersey.. 90 Ithaca 24-14
Col. of New Jersey.. 90 Hofstra 3-38
Col. of New Jersey.. 96 Coast Guard 17-16
Col. of New Jersey.. 96 Rowan 3-7
Col. of New Jersey.. 97 Cortland St. 34-30
Col. of New Jersey.. 97 Rowan 7-13

Roger Harring (13-4) (Wis.-La Crosse '58)
Wis.-La Crosse........ 83 Occidental 43-42
Wis.-La Crosse........ 83 Augustana (Ill.) 15-21
Wis.-La Crosse........ 91 Simpson 28-13
Wis.-La Crosse........ 91 St. John's (Minn.) 10-29
Wis.-La Crosse........ 92 Redlands 47-26
Wis.-La Crosse........ 92 Central (Iowa) 34-9
Wis.-La Crosse........ 92 Mount Union 29-24
Wis.-La Crosse........ 92* Wash. & Jeff. 16-12
Wis.-La Crosse........ 93 Wartburg 55-26
Wis.-La Crosse........ 93 St. John's (Minn.) 25-47
Wis.-La Crosse........ 95 Concordia-M'head 45-7
Wis.-La Crosse........ 95 Wis.-River Falls 28-14
Wis.-La Crosse........ 95 Mount Union 20-17
Wis.-La Crosse........ 95* Rowan 36-7
Wis.-La Crosse........ 96 Wis.-River Falls 44-0
Wis.-La Crosse........ 96 St. John's (Minn.) 37-30
Wis.-La Crosse........ 96 Mount Union 21-39

Jim Hershberger (1-2) (Northern Iowa '57)
Buena Vista........... 76 Carroll (Wis.) 20-14 (OT)
Buena Vista........... 76 St. John's (Minn.) 0-61
Buena Vista........... 86 Central (Iowa) 0-37

Fred Hill (1-1) (Upsala '57)
Montclair St. .... 81 Alfred 13-12
Montclair St. .... 81 Widener 12-23

Rex Huigens (0-1) (La Verne '70)
La Verne .... 94 St. John's (Minn.) 12-51

James Jones (1-1) (Bishop '49)
Bishop .... 82 Wartburg 32-7
Bishop .... 82 West Ga. 6-27

Frank Joranko (0-1) (Albion '52)
Albion................... 77 Minn.-Morris 10-13

Dennis Kayser (1-2) (Ithaca '74)
Cortland St. .... 88 Hofstra 32-27
Cortland St. .... 88 Ithaca 17-24
Cortland St. .... 89 Union (N.Y.) 14-42

Tim Keating (0-1) (Bethany [W.Va.] '75)
Western Md. .... 97 Lycoming 13-27

K. C. Keeler (11-4) (Delaware '81)
Rowan .... 93 Buffalo St. 29-6
Rowan .... 93 Wm. Paterson 37-0
Rowan .... 93 Wash. & Jeff. 23-16
Rowan .... 93 Mount Union 24-34
Rowan .... 95 Buffalo St. 46-7
Rowan .... 95 Union (N.Y.) 38-7
Rowan .... 95 Wash. & Jeff. 28-15
Rowan .... 95 Wis.-La Crosse 7-36
Rowan .... 96 Buffalo St. 21-20
Rowan .... 96 Col. of New Jersey 7-3
Rowan .... 96 Lycoming 33-14
Rowan .... 96 Mount Union 24-56
Rowan .... 97 Coast Guard 43-0
Rowan .... 97 Col. of New Jersey 13-7
Rowan .... 97 Lycoming 20-28

Larry Kehres (18-5) (Mount Union '71)
Mount Union .... 86 Dayton 42-36
Mount Union .... 86 Augustana (Ill.) 7-16
Mount Union .... 90 Allegheny 15-26
Mount Union .... 92 Dayton 27-10
Mount Union .... 92 Ill. Wesleyan 49-27
Mount Union .... 92 Wis.-La Crosse 24-29
Mount Union .... 93 Allegheny 40-7
Mount Union .... 93 Albion 30-16
Mount Union .... 93 St. John's (Minn.) 56-8
Mount Union .... 93* Rowan 34-24
Mount Union .... 94 Allegheny 28-19
Mount Union .... 94 Albion 33-34
Mount Union .... 95 Hanover 52-18
Mount Union .... 95 Wheaton (Ill.) 40-14
Mount Union .... 95 Wis.-La Crosse 17-20
Mount Union .... 96 Allegheny 31-26
Mount Union .... 96 Ill. Wesleyan 49-14
Mount Union .... 96 Wis.-La Crosse 39-21
Mount Union .... 96* Rowan 56-24
Mount Union .... 97 Allegheny 34-30
Mount Union .... 97 John Carroll 59-7
Mount Union .... 97 Simpson 54-7
Mount Union .... 97* Lycoming 61-12

Mike Kelly (13-8) (Manchester '70)
Dayton.................. 81 Augustana (Ill.) 19-7
Dayton.................. 81 Lawrence 38-0
Dayton.................. 81 Widener 10-17
Dayton.................. 84 Augustana (Ill.) 13-14
Dayton.................. 86 Mount Union 36-42
Dayton.................. 87 Capital 52-28
Dayton.................. 87 Augustana (Ill.) 38-36
Dayton.................. 87 Central (Iowa) 34-0
Dayton.................. 87 Wagner 3-19
Dayton.................. 88 Wittenberg 28-35 (2 OT)
Dayton.................. 89 John Carroll 35-10
Dayton.................. 89 Millikin 28-16
Dayton.................. 89 St. John's (Minn.) 28-0
Dayton.................. 89* Union (N.Y.) 17-7
Dayton.................. 90 Augustana (Ill.) 24-14
Dayton.................. 90 Allegheny 23-31
Dayton.................. 91 Baldwin-Wallace 27-10
Dayton.................. 91 Allegheny 28-25 (OT)
Dayton.................. 91 St. John's (Minn.) 19-7
Dayton.................. 91 Ithaca 20-34
Dayton.................. 92 Mount Union 10-27

Chuck Klausing (2-4) (Slippery Rock '48)
Carnegie Mellon..... 78 Dayton 24-21
Carnegie Mellon..... 78 Baldwin-Wallace 6-31
Carnegie Mellon..... 79 Minn.-Morris 31-25
Carnegie Mellon..... 79 Ithaca 6-15
Carnegie Mellon..... 83 Salisbury St. 14-16
Carnegie Mellon..... 85 Salisbury St. 22-35

Mickey Kwiatkowski (0-5) (Delaware '70)
Hofstra.................. 83 Union (N.Y.) 19-51
Hofstra.................. 86 Montclair St. 21-24
Hofstra.................. 87 Fordham 6-41
Hofstra.................. 88 Cortland St. 27-32
Hofstra.................. 89 Montclair St. 6-23

Ron Labadie (0-2) (Adrian '71)
Adrian .... 83 Augustana (Ill.) 21-22
Adrian .... 88 Augustana (Ill.) 7-25

Rich Lackner (0-1) (Carnegie Mellon '79)
Carnegie Mellon..... 90 Lycoming 7-17

Don LaViolette (0-1) (St. Norbert '54)
St. Norbert............ 89 Central (Iowa) 7-55

D. J. LeRoy (0-3) (Wis.-Eau Claire '79)
Wis.-Stevens Point... 86 Concordia-M'head 15-24
Coe....................... 91 St. John's (Minn.) 2-75
Coe....................... 93 St. John's (Minn.) 14-32

Leon Lomax (0-1) (Fort Valley St. '43)
Fort Valley St. .... 75 Ithaca 12-41

John Luckhardt (13-11) (Purdue '67)
Wash. & Jeff. .... 84 Randolph-Macon 22-21
Wash. & Jeff. .... 84 Central (Iowa) 0-20
Wash. & Jeff. .... 86 Susquehanna 20-28
Wash. & Jeff. .... 87 Allegheny 23-17 (OT)
Wash. & Jeff. .... 87 Emory & Henry 16-23
Wash. & Jeff. .... 89 Ferrum 7-41
Wash. & Jeff. .... 90 Ferrum 10-7
Wash. & Jeff. .... 90 Lycoming 0-24
Wash. & Jeff. .... 91 Lycoming 16-18
Wash. & Jeff. .... 92 Lycoming 33-0
Wash. & Jeff. .... 92 Emory & Henry 51-15
Wash. & Jeff. .... 92 Rowan 18-13
Wash. & Jeff. .... 92 Wis.-La Crosse 12-16
Wash. & Jeff. .... 93 Moravian 27-7
Wash. & Jeff. .... 93 Frostburg St. 28-7
Wash. & Jeff. .... 93 Rowan 16-23
Wash. & Jeff. .... 94 Trinity (Tex.) 28-0
Wash. & Jeff. .... 94 Widener 37-21
Wash. & Jeff. .... 94 Ithaca 23-19
Wash. & Jeff. .... 94 Albion 15-38
Wash. & Jeff. .... 95 Emory & Henry 35-16
Wash. & Jeff. .... 95 Lycoming 48-0
Wash. & Jeff. .... 95 Rowan 15-28
Wash. & Jeff. .... 96 Albright 17-31

Dan MacNeil (0-1) (Cortland St. '79)
Cortland St. .... 97 Col. of New Jersey 30-34

Ron Maier (1-1) (Bentley '86)
Albright................. 96 Wash. & Jeff. 31-17
Albright................. 96 Lycoming 13-31

Mike Manley (0-1) (Anderson [Ind.] '73)
Anderson (Ind.)....... 93 Albion 21-41

Bill Manlove (9-5) (Temple '58)
Widener .... 75 Albright 14-6
Widener .... 75 Ithaca 14-23
Widener .... 77 Central (Iowa) 19-0
Widener .... 77 Albany (N.Y.) 33-15
Widener .... 77* Wabash 39-36
Widener .... 79 Baldwin-Wallace 29-8
Widener .... 79 Wittenberg 14-17
Widener .... 80 Bethany (W.Va.) 43-12
Widener .... 80 Dayton 24-28
Widener .... 81 West Ga. 10-3
Widener .... 81 Montclair St. 23-12
Widener .... 81* Dayton 17-10
Widener .... 82 West Ga. 24-31 (3 OT)
Widener .... 88 Moravian 7-17

Dave Maurer (9-2) (Denison '54)
Wittenberg............ 73 San Diego 21-14
Wittenberg............ 73* Juniata 41-0
Wittenberg............ 75 Indianapolis 17-13
Wittenberg............ 75 Millsaps 55-22
Wittenberg............ 75* Ithaca 28-0
Wittenberg............ 78 Ithaca 6-3
Wittenberg............ 78 Minn.-Morris 35-14
Wittenberg............ 78 Baldwin-Wallace 10-24
Wittenberg............ 79 Millersville 21-14
Wittenberg............ 79 Widener 17-14
Wittenberg............ 79 Ithaca 10-14

Mike Maynard (0-2) (Ill. Wesleyan '80)
Redlands .... 90 Central (Iowa) 14-24
Redlands .... 92 Wis.-La Crosse 26-47

Mike McGlinchey (6-4) (Delaware '67)
Salisbury St. .... 83 Carnegie Mellon 16-14
Salisbury St. .... 83 Union (N.Y.) 21-23
Salisbury St. .... 85 Carnegie Mellon 35-22
Salisbury St. .... 85 Gettysburg 6-22
Salisbury St. .... 86 Emory & Henry 34-20
Salisbury St. .... 86 Susquehanna 31-17
Salisbury St. .... 86 Ithaca 44-40
Salisbury St. .... 86 Augustana (Ill.) 3-31
Frostburg St. .... 93 Wilkes 26-25
Frostburg St. .... 93 Wash. & Jeff. 7-28

Steve Miller (0-1) (Cornell College '65)
Carroll (Wis.) .... 76 Buena Vista 14-20 (OT)

Chuck Mills (0-1) (Illinois St. '50)
Coast Guard .... 97 Rowan 0-43

Steve Mohr (1-2) (Denison '76)
Trinity (Tex.) .... 94 Wash. & Jeff. 0-28
Trinity (Tex.) .... 97 Catholic 44-33
Trinity (Tex.) .... 97 Lycoming 26-46

Al Molde (2-3) (Gust. Adolphus '66)
Minn.-Morris .... 77 Albion 13-10
Minn.-Morris .... 77 Wabash 21-37
Minn.-Morris .... 78 St. Olaf 23-10
Minn.-Morris .... 78 Wittenberg 14-35
Minn.-Morris .... 79 Carnegie Mellon 25-31

Ron Murphy (1-1) (Wittenberg '60)
Wittenberg .... 88 Dayton 35-28 (2 OT)
Wittenberg .... 88 Augustana (Ill.) 14-28

Dave Murray (0-1) (Springfield '81)
Cortland St. .... 90 Hofstra 9-35

Walt Nadzak (1-1) (Denison '57)
Juniata .... 73 Bridgeport 35-14
Juniata .... 73 Wittenberg 0-41

Frank Navarro (2-1) (Maryland '53)
Wabash .... 77 St. John's (Minn.) 20-9
Wabash .... 77 Minn.-Morris 37-21
Wabash .... 77 Widener 36-39

Doug Neibuhr (0-1) (Millikin '75)
Wittenberg .... 95 Wheaton (Ill.) 41-63

Ben Newcomb (0-1) (Augustana [S.D.] '57)
Augustana (Ill.) .... 76 St. John's (Minn.) 7-46

Bob Nielson (1-2) (Wartburg '81)
Wartburg .... 93 Wis.-La Crosse 26-55
Wartburg .... 94 Central (Iowa) 22-21
Wartburg .... 94 St. John's (Minn.) 14-42

Hank Norton (4-4) (Lynchburg '51)
Ferrum .... 87 Emory & Henry 7-49
Ferrum .... 88 Rhodes 35-10
Ferrum .... 88 Moravian 49-28
Ferrum .... 88 Ithaca 28-62
Ferrum .... 89 Wash. & Jeff. 41-7
Ferrum .... 89 Lycoming 49-24
Ferrum .... 89 Union (N.Y.) 21-37
Ferrum .... 90 Wash. & Jeff. 7-10

John O'Grady (1-2) (Wis.-River Falls '79)
Wis.-River Falls .... 95 Central (Iowa) 10-7
Wis.-River Falls .... 95 Wis.-La Crosse 14-28
Wis.-River Falls .... 96 Wis.-La Crosse 0-44

Ken O'Keefe (5-5) (John Carroll '75)
Allegheny .... 90 Mount Union 26-15
Allegheny .... 90 Dayton 31-23
Allegheny .... 90 Central (Iowa) 24-7
Allegheny .... 90* Lycoming 21-14 (OT)
Allegheny .... 91 Albion 24-21 (OT)
Allegheny .... 91 Dayton 25-28 (OT)
Allegheny .... 93 Mount Union 7-40
Allegheny .... 94 Mount Union 19-28
Allegheny .... 96 Mount Union 26-31
Allegheny .... 97 Mount Union 30-34

Jack Osberg (1-1) (Ausburg '62)
Augsburg .... 97 Concordia-M'head 34-22
Augsburg .... 97 Simpson 21-61

Bob Packard (0-2) (Baldwin-Wallace '65)
Baldwin-Wallace .... 82 Augustana (Ill.) 22-28
Baldwin-Wallace .... 91 Dayton 10-27

Paul Pasqualoni (0-1) (Penn St. '72)
Western Conn. St. .... 85 Montclair St. 0-28

Bobby Pate (3-1) (Georgia '63)
West Ga. .... 81 Widener 3-10
West Ga. .... 82 Widener 31-24 (3 OT)
West Ga. .... 82 Bishop 27-6
West Ga. .... 82* Augustana (Ill.) 14-0

C. Wayne Perry (0-2) (DePauw '72)
Hanover .... 95 Mount Union 18-52
Hanover .... 97 John Carroll 20-30

Keith Piper (0-1) (Baldwin-Wallace '48)
Denison .... 85 Mount Union 3-35

Carl Poelker (1-1) (Millikin '68)
Millikin .... 89 Augustana (Ill.) 21-12
Millikin .... 89 Dayton 16-28

Tom Porter (0-1) (St. Olaf '51)
St. Olaf .... 78 Minn.-Morris 10-23

John Potsklan (0-2) (Penn St. '49)
Albright .... 75 Widener 6-14
Albright .... 76 St. Lawrence 7-26

Charlie Pravata (0-1) (Adelphi '72)
Merchant Marine .... 94 Plymouth St. 18-19

Steve Raarup (0-1) (Gust. Adolphus '53)
Gust. Adolphus .... 87 St. John's (Minn.) 3-7

Bob Reade (19-7) (Cornell College '54)
Augustana (Ill.) .... 81 Dayton 7-19
Augustana (Ill.) .... 82 Baldwin-Wallace 28-22
Augustana (Ill.) .... 82 St. Lawrence 14-0
Augustana (Ill.) .... 82 West Ga. 0-14
Augustana (Ill.) .... 83 Adrian 22-21
Augustana (Ill.) .... 83 Wis.-La Crosse 21-15
Augustana (Ill.) .... 83* Union (N.Y.) 21-17
Augustana (Ill.) .... 84 Dayton 14-13
Augustana (Ill.) .... 84 Union (N.Y.) 23-6
Augustana (Ill.) .... 84* Central (Iowa) 21-12
Augustana (Ill.) .... 85 Albion 26-10
Augustana (Ill.) .... 85 Mount Union 21-14
Augustana (Ill.) .... 85 Central (Iowa) 14-7
Augustana (Ill.) .... 85* Ithaca 20-7
Augustana (Ill.) .... 86 Hope 34-10
Augustana (Ill.) .... 86 Mount Union 16-7
Augustana (Ill.) .... 86 Concordia-M'head 41-7
Augustana (Ill.) .... 86* Salisbury St. 31-3
Augustana (Ill.) .... 87 Hiram 53-0
Augustana (Ill.) .... 87 Dayton 36-38
Augustana (Ill.) .... 88 Adrian 25-7
Augustana (Ill.) .... 88 Wittenberg 28-14
Augustana (Ill.) .... 88 Central (Iowa) 17-23 (2 OT)
Augustana (Ill.) .... 89 Millikin 12-21
Augustana (Ill.) .... 90 Dayton 14-24
Augustana (Ill.) .... 94 Albion 21-28

Rocky Rees (1-1) (West Chester '71)
Susquehanna .... 86 Wash. & Jeff. 28-20
Susquehanna .... 86 Salisbury St. 17-31

Ron Roberts (1-1) (Wisconsin '54)
Lawrence .... 81 Minn.-Morris 21-14 (OT)
Lawrence .... 81 Dayton 0-38

Bill Russo (0-1)
Wagner .... 80 Ithaca 13-41

Sam Sanders (0-1) (Buffalo '60)
Alfred .... 81 Montclair St. 12-13

Dennis Scannell (0-1) (Villanova '74)
Mass.-Lowell .... 91 Union (N.Y.) 16-55

Ron Schipper (16-11) (Hope '52)
Central (Iowa) .... 74 Evansville 17-16
Central (Iowa) .... 74* Ithaca 10-8
Central (Iowa) .... 77 Widener 0-19
Central (Iowa) .... 84 Occidental 23-22
Central (Iowa) .... 84 Wash. & Jeff. 20-0
Central (Iowa) .... 84 Augustana (Ill.) 12-21
Central (Iowa) .... 85 Coe 27-7
Central (Iowa) .... 85 Occidental 71-0
Central (Iowa) .... 85 Augustana (Ill.) 7-14
Central (Iowa) .... 86 Buena Vista 37-0
Central (Iowa) .... 86 Concordia-M'head 14-17
Central (Iowa) .... 87 Menlo 17-0
Central (Iowa) .... 87 St. John's (Minn.) 13-3
Central (Iowa) .... 87 Dayton 0-34
Central (Iowa) .... 88 Concordia-M'head 7-0
Central (Iowa) .... 88 Wis.-Whitewater 16-13
Central (Iowa) .... 88 Augustana (Ill.) 23-17 (2 OT)
Central (Iowa) .... 88 Ithaca 24-39
Central (Iowa) .... 89 St. Norbert 55-7
Central (Iowa) .... 89 St. John's (Minn.) 24-27
Central (Iowa) .... 90 Redlands 24-14
Central (Iowa) .... 90 St. Thomas (Minn.) 33-32
Central (Iowa) .... 90 Allegheny 7-24
Central (Iowa) .... 92 Carleton 20-8
Central (Iowa) .... 92 Wis.-La Crosse 9-34
Central (Iowa) .... 94 Wartburg 21-22
Central (Iowa) .... 95 Wis.-River Falls 7-10

Pete Schmidt (5-4) (Alma '70)
Albion .... 85 Augustana (Ill.) 10-26
Albion .... 91 Allegheny 21-24 (OT)
Albion .... 93 Anderson (Ind.) 41-21
Albion .... 93 Mount Union 16-30
Albion .... 94 Augustana (Ill.) 28-21
Albion .... 94 Mount Union 34-33
Albion .... 94 St. John's (Minn.) 19-16
Albion .... 94* Wash. & Jeff. 38-15
Albion .... 96 Ill. Wesleyan 20-23

Bill Schmitz (0-1) (Coast Guard '76)
Coast Guard .... 96 Col. of New Jersey 16-17

Jim Scott (0-1) (Luther '61)
Aurora .... 92 Ill. Wesleyan 12-21

Jack Siedlecki (0-1) (Union [N.Y.] '73)
Worcester Tech .... 92 Rowan 14-41

Dick Smith (1-2) (Coe '68)
Minn.-Morris .... 80 Dubuque 41-35
Minn.-Morris .... 80 Ithaca 0-36
Minn.-Morris .... 81 Lawrence 14-21 (OT)

Ray Smith (0-1) (UCLA '61)
Hope .... 86 Augustana (Ill.) 10-34

Ray Solari (0-1) (California '51)
Menlo .... 87 Central (Iowa) 0-17

Ted Stratford (1-2) (St. Lawrence '57)
St. Lawrence .... 76 Albright 26-7
St. Lawrence .... 76 Towson St. 36-38
St. Lawrence .... 78 Baldwin-Wallace 7-71

Barry Streeter (2-1) (Lebanon Valley '71)
Gettysburg .... 85 Lycoming 14-10
Gettysburg .... 85 Salisbury St. 22-6
Gettysburg .... 85 Ithaca 0-34

Bob Sullivan (0-1) (St. John's [Minn.] '59)
Carleton .... 92 Central (Iowa) 8-20

Ed Sweeney (0-2) (LIU-C. W. Post '71)
Dickinson .... 89 Lycoming 0-21
Dickinson .... 91 Susquehanna 20-21

Andy Talley (1-1) (Southern Conn. St. '67)
St. Lawrence .... 82 Wagner 43-34
St. Lawrence .... 82 Augustana (Ill.) 0-14

Ray Tellier (0-1) (Connecticut '73)
Rochester .... 87 Wagner 14-38

Bob Thurness (0-1) (Coe '62)
Coe .... 85 Central (Iowa) 7-27

Lee Tressel (3-2) (Baldwin-Wallace '48)
Baldwin-Wallace .... 78 St. Lawrence 71-7
Baldwin-Wallace .... 78 Carnegie Mellon 31-6
Baldwin-Wallace .... 78* Wittenberg 24-10
Baldwin-Wallace .... 79 Widener 8-29
Baldwin-Wallace .... 80 Dayton 0-34

Peter Vaas (0-1) (Holy Cross '74)
Allegheny .... 87 Wash. & Jeff. 17-23 (OT)

Andy Vinci (0-1) (Cal St. Los Angeles '63)
San Diego .... 73 Wittenberg 14-21

Ken Wable (1-1) (Muskingum '52)
Mount Union .... 85 Denison 35-3
Mount Union .... 85 Augustana (Ill.) 14-21

Lou Wacker (3-4) (Richmond '56)
Emory & Henry .... 86 Salisbury St. 20-34
Emory & Henry .... 87 Ferrum 49-7
Emory & Henry .... 87 Wash. & Jeff. 23-16
Emory & Henry .... 87 Wagner 15-20
Emory & Henry .... 92 Thomas More 17-0
Emory & Henry .... 92 Wash. & Jeff. 15-51
Emory & Henry .... 95 Wash. & Jeff. 16-35

Vic Wallace (1-1) (Cornell College '65)
St. Thomas (Minn.) .... 90 Wis.-Whitewater 24-23
St. Thomas (Minn.) .... 90 Central (Iowa) 32-33

Michael Welch (2-1) (Ithaca '73)
Ithaca .... 94 Buffalo St. 10-7 (2 OT)
Ithaca .... 94 Plymouth St. 22-7
Ithaca .... 94 Wash. & Jeff. 19-23

Roger Welsh (0-1) (Muskingum '64)
Capital .... 87 Dayton 28-52

Dale Widolff (1-3) (Indiana Central '75)
Occidental .... 83 Wis.-La Crosse 42-43

Occidental	84	Central (Iowa) 22-23
Occidental	85	St. John's (Minn.) 28-10
Occidental	85	Central (Iowa) 0-71

Jim Williams (2-5) (Northern Iowa '60)

Simpson	88	Wis.-Whitewater 27-29
Simpson	89	St. John's (Minn.) 35-42
Simpson	91	Wis.-La Crosse 13-28
Simpson	96	St. John's (Minn.) 18-21
Simpson	97	Wis.-Whitewater 34-31
Simpson	97	Augsburg 61-21
Simpson	97	Mount Union 7-54

*National championship.

Coaching Honors

Division I-A Coach-of-the-Year Award

(Selected by the American Football Coaches Association and the Football Writers Association of America)

AFCA

1935 Lynn Waldorf, Northwestern
1936 Dick Harlow, Harvard
1937 Edward Mylin, Lafayette
1938 Bill Kern, Carnegie Mellon
1939 Eddie Anderson, Iowa
1940 Clark Shaughnessy, Stanford
1941 Frank Leahy, Notre Dame
1942 Bill Alexander, Georgia Tech
1943 Amos Alonzo Stagg, Pacific (Cal.)
1944 Carroll Widdoes, Ohio St.
1945 Bo McMillin, Indiana
1946 Red Blaik, Army
1947 Fritz Crisler, Michigan
1948 Bennie Oosterbaan, Michigan
1949 Bud Wilkinson, Oklahoma
1950 Charlie Caldwell, Princeton
1951 Chuck Taylor, Stanford
1952 Biggie Munn, Michigan St.
1953 Jim Tatum, Maryland
1954 Red Sanders, UCLA
1955 Duffy Daugherty, Michigan St.
1956 Bowden Wyatt, Tennessee
1957 Woody Hayes, Ohio St.
1958 Paul Dietzel, LSU
1959 Ben Schwartzwalder, Syracuse
1960 Murray Warmath, Minnesota
1961 Bear Bryant, Alabama
1962 John McKay, Southern Cal
1963 Darrell Royal, Texas
1964 Frank Broyles, Arkansas, and Ara Parseghian, Notre Dame
1965 Tommy Prothro, UCLA
1966 Tom Cahill, Army
1967 John Pont, Indiana
1968 Joe Paterno, Penn St.
1969 Bo Schembechler, Michigan
1970 Charlie McClendon, LSU, and Darrell Royal, Texas
1971 Bear Bryant, Alabama
1972 John McKay, Southern Cal
1973 Bear Bryant, Alabama
1974 Grant Teaff, Baylor
1975 Frank Kush, Arizona St.
1976 Johnny Majors, Pittsburgh
1977 Don James, Washington
1978 Joe Paterno, Penn St.
1979 Earle Bruce, Ohio St.
1980 Vince Dooley, Georgia
1981 Danny Ford, Clemson
1982 Joe Paterno, Penn St.
1983 Ken Hatfield, Air Force
1984 LaVell Edwards, Brigham Young
1985 Fisher DeBerry, Air Force
1986 Joe Paterno, Penn St.
1987 Dick MacPherson, Syracuse
1988 Don Nehlen, West Va.
1989 Bill McCartney, Colorado
1990 Bobby Ross, Georgia Tech
1991 Bill Lewis, East Caro.
1992 Gene Stallings, Alabama
1993 Barry Alvarez, Wisconsin
1994 Tom Osborne, Nebraska
1995 Gary Barnett, Northwestern
1996 Bruce Snyder, Arizona St.
1997 Lloyd Carr, Michigan

FWAA

1957 Woody Hayes, Ohio St.
1958 Paul Dietzel, LSU
1959 Ben Schwartzwalder, Syracuse
1960 Murray Warmath, Minnesota
1961 Darrell Royal, Texas
1962 John McKay, Southern Cal
1963 Darrell Royal, Texas
1964 Ara Parseghian, Notre Dame
1965 Duffy Daugherty, Michigan St.
1966 Tom Cahill, Army
1967 John Pont, Indiana
1968 Woody Hayes, Ohio St.
1969 Bo Schembechler, Michigan
1970 Alex Agase, Northwestern
1971 Bob Devaney, Nebraska
1972 John McKay, Southern Cal
1973 Johnny Majors, Pittsburgh
1974 Grant Teaff, Baylor
1975 Woody Hayes, Ohio St.
1976 Johnny Majors, Pittsburgh
1977 Lou Holtz, Arkansas
1978 Joe Paterno, Penn St.
1979 Earle Bruce, Ohio St.
1980 Vince Dooley, Georgia
1981 Danny Ford, Clemson
1982 Joe Paterno, Penn St.
1983 Howard Schnellenberger, Miami (Fla.)
1984 LaVell Edwards, Brigham Young
1985 Fisher DeBerry, Air Force
1986 Joe Paterno, Penn St.
1987 Dick MacPherson, Syracuse
1988 Lou Holtz, Notre Dame
1989 Bill McCartney, Colorado
1990 Bobby Ross, Georgia Tech
1991 Don James, Washington
1992 Gene Stallings, Alabama
1993 Terry Bowden, Auburn
1994 Rich Brooks, Oregon
1995 Gary Barnett, Northwestern
1996 Bruce Snyder, Arizona St.
1997 Mike Price, Washington St.

Division I-AA Coach-of-the-Year Award

(Selected by the American Football Coaches Association)

1983 Rey Dempsey, Southern Ill.
1984 Dave Arnold, Montana St.
1985 Dick Sheridan, Furman
1986 Erk Russell, Ga. Southern
1987 Mark Duffner, Holy Cross
1988 Jimmy Satterfield, Furman
1989 Erk Russell, Ga. Southern
1990 Tim Stowers, Ga. Southern
1991 Mark Duffner, Holy Cross
1992 Charlie Taafe, Citadel
1993 Dan Allen, Boston U.
1994 Jim Tressel, Youngstown St.
1995 Don Read, Montana
1996 Ray Tellier, Columbia
1997 Andy Talley, Villanova

Small College Coach-of-the-Year Awards

(Selected by the American Football Coaches Association)

COLLEGE DIVISION

1960 Warren Woodson, New Mexico St.
1961 Jake Gaither, Florida A&M
1962 Bill Edwards, Wittenberg
1963 Bill Edwards, Wittenberg
1964 Clarence Stasavich, East Caro.
1965 Jack Curtice, UC Santa Barb.
1966 Dan Jessee, Trinity (Conn.)
1967 Scrappy Moore, Chattanooga
1968 Jim Root, New Hampshire
1969 Larry Naviaux, Boston U.
1970 Bennie Ellender, Arkansas St.
1971 Tubby Raymond, Delaware
1972 Tubby Raymond, Delaware
1973 Dave Maurer, Wittenberg
1974 Roy Kramer, Central Mich.
1975 Dave Maurer, Wittenberg
1976 Jim Dennison, Akron
1977 Bill Manlove, Widener
1978 Lee Tressel, Baldwin-Wallace
1979 Bill Narduzzi, Youngstown St.
1980 Rick Carter, Dayton
1981 Vito Ragazzo, Shippensburg
1982 Jim Wacker, Southwest Tex. St.

COLLEGE DIVISION I

(NCAA Division II and NAIA Division I)

1983 Don Morton, North Dak. St.
1984 Chan Gailey, Troy St.
1985 George Landis, Bloomsburg
1986 Earle Solomonson, North Dak. St.
1987 Rick Rhoades, Troy St.
1988 Rocky Hager, North Dak. St.
1989 John Williams, Mississippi Col.
1990 Rocky Hager, North Dak. St.
1991 Frank Cignetti, Indiana (Pa.)
1992 Bill Burgess, Jacksonville St.
1993 Bobby Wallace, North Ala.
1994 Bobby Wallace, North Ala.
1995 Bobby Wallace, North Ala.
1996 Joe Glenn, Northern Colo.
1997 Joe Glenn, Northern Colo.

COLLEGE DIVISION II

(NCAA Division III and NAIA Division II)

1983 Bob Reade, Augustana (Ill.)
1984 Bob Reade, Augustana (Ill.)
1985 Bob Reade, Augustana (Ill.)
1986 Bob Reade, Augustana (Ill.)
1987 Walt Hameline, Wagner
1988 Jim Butterfield, Ithaca
1989 Mike Kelly, Dayton
1990 Ken O'Keefe, Allegheny
1991 Mike Kelly, Dayton
1992 John Luckhardt, Wash. & Jeff.
1993 Larry Kehres, Mount Union
1994 Pete Schmidt, Albion
1995 Roger Harring, Wis.-La Crosse
1996 Larry Kehres, Mount Union
1997 Larry Kehres, Mount Union

Added and Discontinued Programs

Nationally Prominent Teams That Permanently Dropped Football

Listed alphabetically at right are the all-time records of teams formerly classified as major college that permanently discontinued football. Also included are those teams that, retroactively, are considered to have been major college (before the advent of official classification in 1937) by virtue of their schedules (i.e., at least half of their games versus other major-college opponents). All schools listed were considered to have been major college or classified in either Division I-A or I-AA for a minimum of 10 consecutive seasons.

Team	Inclusive Seasons	Years	Won	Lost	Tied	Pct.†
Cal St. Fullerton	1970-1992	23	107	150	3	.417
Carlisle Indian School	1893-1917	25	167	88	13	.647
Centenary (La.)	1894-1947	36	148	100	21	.589
Creighton	1900-1942	43	183	139	27	.563
Denver	1885-1960	73	273	262	40	.510
Detroit	1896-1964	64	305	200	25	.599
Geo. Washington	1890-1966	58	209	240	34	.468
Gonzaga	1892-1941	39	130	99	20	.562
Haskell Institute	1896-1938	43	199	166	18	.543
Lamar	1951-1989	39	171	225	9	.433
Long Beach St.	1955-1991	37	199	183	4	.521
Manhattan	1923-1942	20	77	75	11	.506
Marquette	1892-1960	68	273	220	38	.550
New York U.	1873-1952	66	201	231	32	.468
Pacific (Cal.)	1919-1995	77	346	397	23	.467
Saint Louis	1899-1949	49	235	179	33	.563
San Francisco	*1924-1951; 1959-1971	38	133	169	20	.444
Texas-Arlington	1959-1985	27	129	150	2	.463
Wichita St.	1897-1986	89	375	402	47	.484
Xavier (Ohio)	1900-1973	61	302	223	21	.572

*†Ties computed as half won and half lost. *Discontinued football during 1952 after having been classified major college. Resumed at the Division II level during 1959-71, when it was discontinued again.*

Added or Resumed Programs Since 1968

NCAA Member Colleges

1968 (4)
Boise St.; *Chicago; Jersey City St.; UNLV.

1969 (2)
*Adelphi (dropped 1972); Towson

1970 (6)
Cal St. Fullerton (dropped 1993); *Fordham; *Georgetown; Plattsburgh St. (dropped 1979); Plymouth St.; *St. Mary's (Cal.).

1971 (6)
Boston St. (dropped 1982); D.C. Teachers (dropped 1974); Federal City (dropped 1975); *New England Col. (dropped 1973); Rochester Tech (dropped 1978); St. Peter's (suspended after one game 1984, resumed 1985, dropped 1988, resumed 1989).

1972 (6)
Kean; *Lake Forest; Nicholls St.; Salisbury St.; *San Diego; Wm. Paterson.

1973 (7)
Albany St. (N.Y.); *Benedictine; Bowie St.; James Madison; New Haven; New York Tech (dropped 1984); Seton Hall (dropped 1982).

1974 (2)
FDU-Madison; Framingham St.

1975 (2)
*Brooklyn (dropped 1991); *Canisius.

1976 (1)
Oswego St. (dropped 1977).

1977 (2)
*Catholic; *Mankato St.

1978 (7)
*Buffalo; Dist. Columbia; Iona; Marist; Pace; *St. Francis (Pa.); *St. John's (N.Y.).

1979 (2)
Central Fla.; *Duquesne.

1980 (5)
*Loras; Mass.-Lowell; *Miles (dropped 1989, resumed 1990); Ramapo (dropped 1993); *Sonoma St. (dropped 1997)

1981 (4)
Buffalo St.; Mercyhurst; *West Ga.; Western New Eng.

1982 (2)
Valdosta St.; Westfield St.

1983 (2)
*Ky. Wesleyan; Stony Brook.

1984 (3)
Fitchburg St.; *Ga. Southern; *Samford.

1985 (6)
Ferrum; MacMurray; N.Y. Maritime (dropped 1986, resumed 1987, dropped 1989); *St. Peter's (dropped 1988, resumed 1989); *Villanova; Worcester St.

1986 (4)
*UC Santa Barb.; Menlo; *Quincy; Wesley.

1987 (5)
*Aurora; *Drake; Gallaudet; *N.Y. Maritime (dropped 1989); St. John Fisher.

1988 (7)
Assumption; Bentley; Mass.-Boston; Mass.-Dartmouth; *MIT (last team was in 1901); Siena; Stonehill.

1989 (4)
*Gannon; Methodist; *St. Peter's; *Southern Methodist.

1990 (3)
*Hardin-Simmons; *Miles; Thomas More.

1991 (3)
UAB; Charleston So.; Sacred Heart.

1992 (1)
*West Tex. A&M.

1993 (3)
*King's (Pa.); Monmouth; Salve Regina.

1994 (2)
Chapman; Robert Morris.

1996 (3)
Fairfield; Merrimack.; Westminster (Mo.)

1997 (2)
*La Salle; South Fla.

1998 (1)
Jacksonville (Fla.)

**Previously dropped football.*

Non-NCAA Senior Colleges

1968 (2)
#Mo. Southern St.; #Southwest St.

1970 (1)
#Mo. Western St.

1971 (3)
Concordia (St. Paul); #Gardner-Webb; #Grand Valley St.

1972 (5)
Dr. Martin Luther; #Mars Hill; N'western (Minn.); Pillsbury; #Western Conn. St.

1973 (2)
#Liberty; #Mass. Maritime.

1974 (3)
#*N.M. Highlands; #Northeastern Ill. (dropped 1988); #Saginaw Valley.

1976 (2)
#Maranatha Baptist; #Mesa St.

1977 (2)
Evangel; Olivet Nazarene.

1978 (3)
*Baptist Christian (dropped 1983); *St. Ambrose; *Yankton (dropped 1984).

1979 (2)
Fort Lauderdale (dropped 1982); Lubbock Christian (dropped 1983).

1980 (1)
Mid-America Nazarene.

1983 (2)
Ga. Southwestern (dropped 1989); #Loras.

1984 (3)
St. Paul Bible; #Southwest Baptist; *Union (Ky.).

1985 (4)
*Cumberland (Ky.); *Lambuth; *Tenn. Wesleyan; Tiffin.

1986 (4)
*#St. Francis (Ill.); Trinity Bible (N.D.); Urbana; #Wingate.

1987 (1)
#Greenville.

1988 (5)
Campbellsville; Mary; #Midwestern St.; Trinity (Ill.); *Western Mont.

1990 (3)
*Cumberland; Lindenwood; Mt. St. Joseph (Ohio).

1991 (3)
Clinch Valley; #Lees-McRae (dropped 1994); #*Tusculum.

1993 (6)
#Ark.-Pine Bluff; *Bethel (Tenn.); #Chowan; Malone; St. Xavier (Ill.); Sue Bennett.

1996 (1)
*McKendree

1998 (1)
#Texas Lutheran (dropped 1988)

**Previously dropped football. #Now NCAA member.*

Discontinued Programs Since 1950

(Includes NCAA member colleges and non-member colleges; also colleges that closed or merged with other institutions.)

1950 (9)
Alliance; Canisius (resumed 1975); Huntington; Oklahoma City; *Portland; Rio Grande; Rollins; *Saint Louis; Steubenville.

1951 (38)
Arkansas Col.; Atlantic Christian; Canterbury; Catholic (resumed 1977); CCNY; Corpus Christi (resumed 1954, dropped 1967); Daniel Baker; Detroit Tech; *Duquesne (resumed 1979); East Tex. Baptist; Gannon (resumed 1989); *Georgetown (resumed 1970); Glassboro St. (resumed 1964—name changed to Rowan in 1992); Hartwick; High Point; LeMoyne-Owen; Lowell Textile; Lycoming (resumed 1954); McKendree (resumed 1996); Milligan; Mt. St. Mary's (Md.); Nevada (resumed 1952); New Bedford Textile; New England Col. (resumed 1971, dropped 1973); Niagara; Northern Idaho; Panzer; St. Mary's (Cal.) (resumed 1970); St. Michael's (N.M.); Shurtleff (resumed 1953, dropped 1954); Southern Idaho; Southwestern (Tenn.) (resumed 1952—name changed to Rhodes in 1986); Southwestern (Tex.); Tillotson; Tusculum (resumed 1991); Washington (Md.); West Va. Wesleyan (resumed 1953); William Penn (resumed 1953).

1952 (13)
Aquinas; Clarkson; Erskine; Louisville Municipal; *Loyola Marymount; Nebraska Central; Rider; Samuel Huston; *San Francisco (resumed 1959, dropped 1972); Shaw (resumed 1953, dropped 1979); St. Bonaventure; St. Martin's; Teikyo Westmar (resumed 1953).

1953 (10)
Arnold; Aurora; Bethel (Tenn.) (resumed 1993); Cedarville; Champlain; Davis & Elkins (resumed 1955, dropped 1962); Georgetown (Ky.) (resumed 1955); *New York U.; *Santa Clara (resumed 1959, dropped 1993); Union (Tenn.).

1954 (8)
Adelphi (resumed 1969, dropped 1972); Case Tech (resumed 1955); Quincy (resumed 1986); St. Francis (Pa.) (resumed 1978); St. Michael's (Vt.); Shurtleff; *Wash. & Lee (resumed 1955); York (Neb.).

1955 (2)
*Fordham (resumed 1970); St. Mary's (Minn.).

1956 (4)
Brooklyn (resumed 1975, dropped 1991); Hendrix (resumed 1957, dropped 1961); William Carey; Wisconsin Extension.

1957 (4)
Lewis; Midwestern (Iowa) (resumed 1966); Morris Harvey; Stetson.

1959 (2)
Florida N&I; West Ga. (resumed 1981).

1960 (5)
Brandeis; Leland; Loras (resumed 1980); St. Ambrose (resumed 1978); Xavier (La.).

1961 (9)
*Denver; Hawaii (resumed 1962); Hendrix; Lincoln (Pa.); *Marquette; Paul Quinn; Scranton; Texas College; Tougaloo.

1962 (5)
Azusa Pacific (resumed 1965); Davis & Elkins; San Diego (resumed 1972); Southern Cal Col.; Westminster (Utah) (resumed 1965, dropped 1979).

1963 (3)
Benedictine (resumed 1973); *Hardin-Simmons (resumed 1990); St. Vincent (Pa.).

1964 (2)
King's (Pa.) (resumed 1993); Paine.

1965 (7)
Claflin; *Detroit; Dillard; Miss. Industrial; Morris; Philander Smith; Rust.

1966 (1)
St. Augustine's.

1967 (6)
Benedict; Corpus Christi; *Geo. Washington; Jarvis Christian; Ozarks; South Caro. Trade.

1968 (2)
Edward Waters; Frederick.

1969 (6)
Allen; Case Tech and Western Reserve merged to form Case Western Reserve; George Fox; Louisiana Col.; UC San Diego; Wiley.

1971 (5)
Bradley; *Buffalo (resumed 1978); Hiram Scott; Lake Forest (resumed 1972); Parsons.

1972 (8)
Adelphi; UC Santa Barb. (resumed 1986); Haverford; North Dak.-Ellendale; Northern Mont.; Northwood (Tex.); San Francisco; Sonoma St. (resumed 1980).

1973 (2)
New England Col.; N.M. Highlands (resumed 1974).

1974 (6)
Col. of Emporia; D.C. Teachers; Drexel; Ill.-Chicago; Samford (resumed 1984); *Xavier (Ohio).

1975 (6)
Baptist Christian (resumed 1978, dropped 1983); Bridgeport; Federal City; *Tampa; Vermont; Wis.-Milwaukee.

1976 (3)
UC Riverside; Mankato St. (resumed 1977); Northland.

1977 (4)
Cal Tech; Oswego St.; Whitman; Yankton (resumed 1978, dropped 1984).

1978 (3)
Cal St. Los Angeles; Col. of Idaho; Rochester Tech.

1979 (5)
Miles (resumed 1980, dropped 1989, resumed 1990); Mont. St.-Billings; Plattsburgh St.; Shaw; Westminster (Utah).

1980 (3)
†Gallaudet; Md.-East. Shore; U.S. Int'l.

1981 (2)
Bluefield St.; *Villanova (resumed 1985).

1982 (4)
Boston St.; Fort Lauderdale; Milton; Seton Hall.

1983 (3)
Baptist Christian; Cal Poly Pomona; Lubbock Christian.

1984 (5)
Fisk; New York Tech; St. Peter's (suspended after one game, resumed 1985, dropped 1988, resumed 1989); So. Dak.-Springfield; Yankton.

1985 (1)
Southern Colo.

1986 (4)
Drake (resumed 1987); N.Y. Maritime (resumed 1987, dropped 1989); Southeastern La.; *Texas-Arlington.

1987 (4)
Bishop; *Southern Methodist (resumed 1989); Western Mont. (resumed 1988); *Wichita St.

1988 (4)
Northeastern Ill.; St. Paul's; St. Peter's (resumed 1989); Texas Lutheran (resumed 1998).

1989 (3)
Ga. Southwestern; Miles (resumed 1990); N.Y. Maritime.

1990 (2)
*Lamar; Lincoln (Mo.).

1991 (3)
Brooklyn; Tarkio; West Tex. A&M (resumed 1992).

1992 (3)
*Long Beach St.; Pacific (Ore.); St. Mary of the Plains.

1993 (5)
*Cal St. Fullerton; Cameron; Ramapo; Santa Clara; Wis.-Superior.

1994 (4)
Cal St. Hayward; Lees-McRae; Oregon Tech; Upsala.

1995 (1)
San Fran St.

1996 (1)
*Pacific (Cal.).

1997 (2)
Cal St. Chico; Sonoma St.

1998 (2)
Boston U.; Evansville

**Classified major college previous year. †Did not play a 7-game varsity schedule, 1980-86, and returned to club status in 1995.*

Championship Results

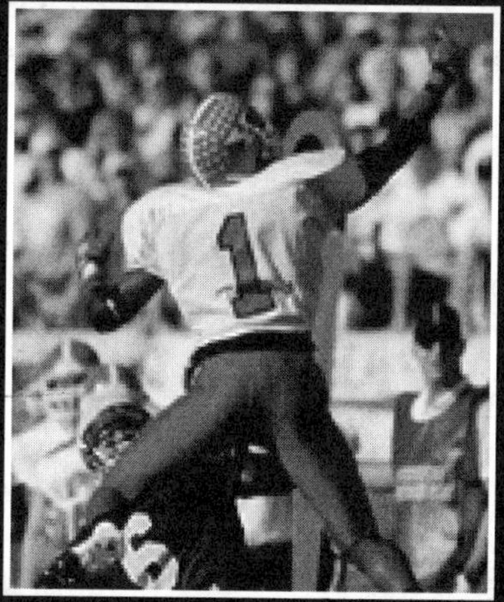

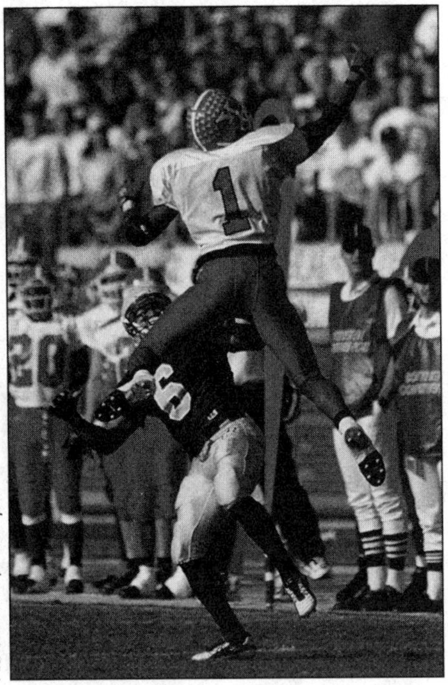

Alex McMahan/NCAA photos

Youngstown State defensive back Dwyte Smiley leaped to deflect a pass from McNeese State wide receiver Damien Morris in the 1997 NCAA Division I-AA Championship game. Youngstown State defeated McNeese State, 10-9, to win its fourth national title.

Division I-AA Championship

1997 Title Game Summary

FINLEY STADIUM/DAVENPORT FIELD, CHATTANOOGA, TENNESSEE; DECEMBER 20

		Youngstown St.		McNeese St.
First Downs		12		11
Rushing Yardage		73		58
Passing Yardage		127		143
Return Yardage		5		28
Passes (Comp.-Att.-Int.)		12-21-0		14-28-1
Punts (Number-Average)		9-33.1		5-36.6
Fumbles (Number-Lost)		0-0		0-0
Penalties (Number-Yards)		3-20		3-35
Youngstown St.	0	3	0	7—10
McNeese St.	3	0	6	0— 9

FIRST QUARTER

McNeese St.—Shonz LaFrenz 22 field goal (54 yards in 10 plays, 5:30 left)

SECOND QUARTER

Youngstown St.—Mark Griffith 21 field goal (52 yards in 14 plays, 2:19 left)

THIRD QUARTER

McNeese St.—LaFrenz 37 field goal (28 yards in 5 plays, 8:08 left)
McNeese St.—LaFrenz 46 field goal (38 yards in 9 plays, :51 left)

FOURTH QUARTER

Youngstown St.—Renauld Ray 9 pass from Demond Tidwell (Griffith kick) (66 yards in 9 plays, 8:08 left)

INDIVIDUAL LEADERS

Rushing—Youngstown St.: Jake Andreadis, 35 yards on 16 carries; McNeese St.: William Davis, 54 yards on 19 carries.

Passing—Youngstown St.: Tidwell, 11 of 20 for 110 yards; McNeese St.: Blake Prejean, 14 of 28 for 143 yards.

Receiving—Youngstown St.: Tim Tyrell, 4 catches for 54 yards, and Ray, 3 catches for 38 yards; McNeese St.: Donnie Ashley, 4 catches for 45 yards, and Andre Perkins, 4 catches for 44 yards.

NCAA I-AA Football Championship History

1978 At the 72nd NCAA Convention (January 1978) in Atlanta, Ga., the membership voted to establish the Division I-AA Football Championship and a statistics program for the division. The format for the first I-AA championship, held in Wichita Falls, Texas, was a single-elimination, four-team tournament. Florida A&M defeated Massachusetts, 35-28, in the title game. The game was televised by ABC.

1981 The championship expanded to include eight teams in a single-elimination tournament.

1982 The championship expanded to include 12 teams. Eight teams played first-round games at campus sites, and the top four teams, seeded by the Division I-AA Football Committee, received byes.

1986 The championship field expanded to its current format of 16 teams with each team playing a first-round game.

1987 Northeast Louisiana defeated Marshall, 43-42, in the closest game in championship history.

1989 A then-record 25,725 fans watched Georgia Southern down Stephen F. Austin, 37-34, in the championship game at Allen E. Paulson Stadium in Statesboro, Ga.

1990 Georgia Southern won its fourth I-AA championship, adding to its titles in 1985, 1986 and 1989.

1991 Youngstown State won its first national championship with a 25-17 victory over Marshall. Penguin head coach Jim Tressel joined his father, Lee, as the only father-son combination to win NCAA football titles. Lee Tressel won the 1978 Division III championship at Baldwin-Wallace.

1992 A then-record crowd of 31,304 in Huntington, W.Va., saw Marshall return the favor with a 31-28 win over Youngstown State for its first I-AA title.

1993 The I-AA championship provided for a maximum field of 16 teams. Six member conferences (Big Sky, Gateway, Ohio Valley, Southern, Southland and Yankee) were granted automatic qualification for their respective winners. Youngstown State won its second I-AA title with a 17-5 victory over Marshall before a crowd of 29,218 in Huntington, W. Va.

1994 Youngstown State won its third national title in four years with a 28-14 victory over Boise State.

1995 Montana won its first Division I-AA title before a championship record crowd of 32,106 in Huntington, W.Va.

1996 Marshall, making its fifth visit to the championship game since 1991, won its second Division I-AA title with a 49-29 victory over defending champion Montana before 30,052 in Huntington, W. Va.

1997 Youngstown State won its fourth national title in the 1990s with a 10-9 victory over McNeese State in Chattanooga, Tennessee.

Division I-AA All-Time Championship Results

Year	Champion	Coach	Score	Runner-Up	Site	Attendance
1978	Florida A&M	Rudy Hubbard	35-28	Massachusetts	Wichita Falls, Texas	13,604
1979	Eastern Ky.	Roy Kidd	30-7	Lehigh	Orlando, Fla.	5,500
1980	Boise St.	Jim Criner	31-29	Eastern Ky.	Sacramento, Calif.	8,157
1981	Idaho St.	Dave Kragthorpe	34-23	Eastern Ky.	Wichita Falls, Texas	11,003
1982	Eastern Ky.	Roy Kidd	17-14	Delaware	Wichita Falls, Texas	11,257
1983	Southern Ill.	Rey Dempsey	43-7	Western Caro.	Charleston, S.C.	15,950
1984	Montana St.	Dave Arnold	19-6	Louisiana Tech	Charleston, S.C.	9,125
1985	Ga. Southern	Erk Russell	44-42	Furman	Tacoma, Wash.	5,306
1986	Ga. Southern	Erk Russell	48-21	Arkansas St.	Tacoma, Wash.	4,419
1987	Northeast La.	Pat Collins	43-42	Marshall	Pocatello, Idaho	11,513
1988	Furman	Jimmy Satterfield	17-12	Ga. Southern	Pocatello, Idaho	11,500
1989	Ga. Southern	Erk Russell	37-34	*Stephen F. Austin	Statesboro, Ga.	25,725
1990	Ga. Southern	Tim Stowers	36-13	Nevada	Statesboro, Ga.	23,204
1991	Youngstown St.	Jim Tressel	25-17	Marshall	Statesboro, Ga.	12,667
1992	Marshall	Jim Donnan	31-28	Youngstown St.	Huntington, W.Va.	31,304
1993	Youngstown St.	Jim Tressel	17-5	Marshall	Huntington, W.Va.	29,218
1994	Youngstown St.	Jim Tressel	28-14	Boise St.	Huntington, W.Va.	27,674
1995	Montana	Don Read	22-20	Marshall	Huntington, W.Va.	32,106
1996	Marshall	Bob Pruett	49-29	Montana	Huntington, W.Va.	30,052
1997	Youngstown St.	Jim Tressel	10-9	McNeese St.	Chattanooga, Tenn.	14,771

**Stephen F. Austin's participation in 1989 Division I-AA championship vacated.*

1997 Division I-AA Championship Results

(Attendance in parentheses)

FIRST ROUND

Villanova 49, Colgate 28 (8,875)
Youngstown St. 28, Hampton 13 (12,431)
Western Ky. 42, Eastern Ky. 14 (9,000)
Eastern Wash. 40, Northwestern St. 10 (6,384)
Delaware 24, Hofstra 14 (14,075)
Ga. Southern 52, Florida A&M 37 (10,409)
McNeese St. 19, Montana 14 (13,681)
Western Ill. 31, Jackson St. 24 (8,980)

QUARTERFINALS

Youngstown St. 37, Villanova 34 (7,591)
Eastern Wash. 38, Western Ky. 21 (6,829)
Delaware 16, Ga. Southern 7 (11,203)
McNeese St. 14, Western Ill. 12 (5,000)

SEMIFINALS

Youngstown St. 25, Eastern Wash. 14 (8,529)
McNeese St. 23, Delaware 21 (14,461

CHAMPIONSHIP

Youngstown St. 10, McNeese St. 9 (14,771)

Championship Records

INDIVIDUAL: SINGLE GAME

NET YARDS RUSHING
250—Greg Robinson, Northeast La. (78) vs. Alcorn St. (27), 11-28-92.

RUSHES ATTEMPTED
46—Tamron Smith, Youngstown St. (10) vs. Samford (0), 12-14-91.

TOUCHDOWNS BY RUSHING
6—Sean Sanders, Weber St. (59) vs. Idaho (30), 11-28-87.

NET YARDS PASSING
517—Todd Hammel, Stephen F. Austin (59) vs. Grambling (56), 11-25-89.

PASSES ATTEMPTED
82—Steve McNair, Alcorn St. (20) vs. Youngstown St. (63), 11-25-94.

PASSES COMPLETED
52—Steve McNair, Alcorn St. (20) vs. Youngstown St. (63), 11-25-94.

PASSES HAD INTERCEPTED
7—Jeff Gilbert, Western Caro. (7) vs. Southern Ill. (43), 12-17-83.

TOUCHDOWN PASSES COMPLETED
6—Mike Smith, Northern Iowa (41) vs. Northeast La. (44), 12-12-87; Clemente Gordon, Grambling (56) vs. Stephen F. Austin (59), 11-25-89.

COMPLETION PERCENTAGE (Min. 15 Attempts)
.841—Dave Dickenson, Montana (48) vs. Delaware (49), 11-27-93 (37 of 44).

NET YARDS RUSHING AND PASSING
539—Todd Hammel, Stephen F. Austin (59) vs. Grambling (56), 11-25-89 (517 passing, 22 rushing).

NUMBER OF RUSHING AND PASSING PLAYS
91—Steve McNair, Alcorn St. (20) vs. Youngstown St. (63), 11-25-94.

PUNTING AVERAGE (Min. 3 Punts)
50.3—Steve Rowe, Eastern Ky. (38) vs. Idaho (30), 12-4-82 (3 for 151).

NUMBER OF PUNTS
14—Fred McRae, Jackson St. (0) vs. Stephen F. Austin (24), 11-26-88.

PASSES CAUGHT
18—Brian Forster, Rhode Island (23) vs. Richmond (17), 12-1-84.

NET YARDS RECEIVING
288—Randy Moss, Marshall (49) vs. Montana (29), 12-21-96 (8 catches).

TOUCHDOWN PASSES CAUGHT
4—Randy Moss, Marshall (49) vs. Montana (29), 12-21-96; Tony DiMaggio, Rhode Island (35) vs. Akron (27), 11-30-85.

PASSES INTERCEPTED
4—Greg Shipp, Southern Ill. (43) vs. Western Caro. (7), 12-17-83.

YARDS GAINED ON INTERCEPTION RETURNS
117—Kevin Sullivan, Massachusetts (44) vs. Nevada (21), 12-9-78.

YARDS GAINED ON PUNT RETURNS
121—Darren Sharper, William & Mary (45) vs. Jackson St. (6), 11-30-96.

YARDS GAINED ON KICKOFF RETURNS
232—Mike Cadore, Eastern Ky. (32) vs. Northeast La. (33), 12-5-87, 6 returns, 1 for 99-yard TD.

YARDS GAINED ON FUMBLE RETURNS
95—Randy Smith, Youngstown St. (63) vs. Alcorn St. (20), 11-25-94.

POINTS
36—Sean Sanders, Weber St. (59) vs. Idaho (30), 11-28-87.

TOUCHDOWNS
6—Sean Sanders, Weber St. (59) vs. Idaho (30), 11-28-87.

EXTRA POINTS
10—Andy Larson, Montana (70) vs. Stephen F. Austin (14), 12-9-95.

FIELD GOALS
4—Jeff Wilkins, Youngstown St. (19) vs. Northern Iowa (7), 12-12-92; Jose Larios, McNeese St. (33) vs. Idaho (3), 11-25-95.

INDIVIDUAL: TOURNAMENT

NET YARDS RUSHING
661—Tracy Ham, Ga. Southern, 1986 (128 vs. North Caro. A&T, 191 vs. Nicholls St., 162 vs. Nevada, 180 vs. Arkansas St.).

RUSHES ATTEMPTED
123—Ray Whalen, Nevada, 1990 (21 vs. Northeast La., 34 vs. Furman, 44 vs. Boise St., 24 vs. Ga. Southern).

NET YARDS PASSING
1,500—Dave Dickenson, Montana, 1995 (441 vs. Eastern Ky., 408 vs. Ga. Southern, 370 vs. Stephen F. Austin, 281 vs. Marshall).

PASSES ATTEMPTED
177—Brian Ah Yat, Montana, 1996 (48 vs. Nicholls St., 34 vs. East Tenn. St., 40 vs. Troy St., 55 vs. Marshall); Jeff Gilbert, Western Caro., 1983 (47 vs. Colgate, 52 vs. Holy Cross, 45 vs. Furman, 33 vs. Southern Ill.).

PASSES COMPLETED
122—Dave Dickenson, Montana, 1995 (31 vs. Eastern Ky., 37 vs. Ga. Southern, 25 vs. Stephen F. Austin, 29 vs. Marshall).

TOUCHDOWN PASSES COMPLETED
14—Todd Hammel, Stephen F. Austin, 1989 (5 vs. Grambling, 4 vs. Southwest Mo. St., 2 vs. Furman, 3 vs. Ga. Southern).

COMPLETION PERCENTAGE (Min. 50 Completions)
.722—Dave Dickenson, Montana, 1995, 122 of 169 (31-39 vs. Eastern Ky., 37-46 vs. Ga. Southern, 25-36 vs. Stephen F. Austin, 29-48 vs. Marshall).

PASSES HAD INTERCEPTED
11—Todd Hammel, Stephen F. Austin, 1989 (0 vs. Grambling, 4 vs. Southwest Mo. St., 2 vs. Furman, 5 vs. Ga. Southern).

PASSES CAUGHT
41—Joe Douglass, Montana, 1996 (10 vs. Nicholls St., 10 vs. East Tenn. St., 8 vs. Troy St., 13 vs. Marshall).

NET YARDS RECEIVING
636—Randy Moss, Marshall, 1996 (288 vs. Delaware, 82 vs. Furman, 46 vs. Northern Iowa, 220 vs. Montana).

TOUCHDOWN PASSES CAUGHT
10—Randy Moss, Marshall, 1996 (3 vs. Delaware, 2 vs. Furman, 1 vs. Northern Iowa, 4 vs. Montana).

POINTS
66—Gerald Harris, Ga. Southern, 1986 (30 vs. North Caro. A&T, 18 vs. Nicholls St., 12 vs. Nevada, 6 vs. Arkansas St.).

TOUCHDOWNS
11—Gerald Harris, Ga. Southern, 1986 (5 vs. North Caro. A&T 18 vs. Nicholls St., 12 vs. Nevada, 6 vs. Arkansas St.).

INDIVIDUAL: LONGEST PLAYS

LONGEST RUSH
90—Henry Fields, McNeese St. (38) vs. Idaho (21), 11-26-94.

LONGEST PASS (INCLUDING RUN)
90—Paul Singer 22 pass to Derek Swanson and 68 fumble recovery advancement by Steve Williams, Western Ill. (32) vs. Western Ky. (35), 11-26-88.

LONGEST FIELD GOAL
56—Tony Zendejas, Nevada (27) vs. Idaho St. (20), 11-26-83.

LONGEST PUNT
88—Mike Cassidy, Rhode Island (20) vs. Montana St. (32), 12-8-84.

LONGEST PUNT RETURN
84—Rob Friese, Eastern Wash. (14) vs. Northern Iowa (17), 12-7-85, TD.

LONGEST KICKOFF RETURN
100—Chris Fontenette, McNeese St. (7) vs. Northern Iowa (29), 12-5-92, TD.

LONGEST FUMBLE RETURN
95—Randy Smith, Youngstown St. (63) vs. Alcorn St. (20), 11-25-94.

LONGEST INTERCEPTION RETURN
100—Melvin Cunningham, Marshall (28) vs. James Madison (21), OT, 12-3-94, TD; Paul Williams, Delaware (38) vs. Hofstra (17), 11-25-95, TD.

TEAM: SINGLE GAME

FIRST DOWNS
41—Montana (45) vs. Ga. Southern (0), 12-2-95.

FIRST DOWNS BY RUSHING
29—Alcorn St. (20) vs. Youngstown St. (63), 11-25-94.

FIRST DOWNS BY PASSING
29—Alcorn St. (20) vs. Youngstown St. (63), 11-25-94.

RUSHES ATTEMPTED
81—Youngstown St. (10) vs. Samford (0), 12-14-91.

NET YARDS RUSHING
518—Arkansas St. (55) vs. Delaware (14), 12-6-86.

NET YARDS PASSING
537—Montana (30) vs. McNeese St. (28), 12-3-94.

PASSES ATTEMPTED
90—Rhode Island (15) vs. Furman (59), 12-7-85.

PASSES COMPLETED
52—Alcorn St. (20) vs. Youngstown St. (63), 11-25-94.

COMPLETION PERCENTAGE
(Min. 10 Attempts)
.841—Montana (48) vs. Delaware (49), 11-27-93 (37 of 44).

PASSES HAD INTERCEPTED
7—Western Caro. (7) vs. Southern Ill. (43), 12-17-83; Rhode Island (15) vs. Furman (59), 12-7-85; Weber St. (23) vs. Marshall (51), 12-5-87.

NET YARDS RUSHING AND PASSING
742—Northeast La. (78) vs. Alcorn St. (27), 11-28-92.

RUSHING AND PASSING PLAYS
114—Nevada (42) vs. Furman (35), 3 OT, 12-1-90 (47 rushing, 67 passing).

PUNTING AVERAGE
(Min. 4 Punts)
50.2—Montana St. (32) vs. Rhode Island (20), 12-8-84.

NUMBER OF PUNTS
14—Jackson St. (0) vs. Stephen F. Austin (24), 11-26-88.

PUNTS HAD BLOCKED
2—Florida A&M (35) vs. Massachusetts (28), 12-16-78; Boise St. (14) vs. Grambling (9), 12-13-80.

YARDS GAINED ON PUNT RETURNS
128—William & Mary (45) vs. Jackson St. (6), 11-30-96.

YARDS GAINED ON KICKOFF RETURNS
232—Eastern Ky. (32) vs. Northeast La. (33), 12-5-87.

YARDS GAINED ON INTERCEPTION RETURNS
164—Marshall (51) vs. Weber St. (23), 12-5-87.

YARDS PENALIZED
172—Tennessee St. (32) vs. Jackson St. (23), 11-29-86.

FUMBLES LOST
7—Jackson St. (8) vs. Marshall (38), 11-25-95.

POINTS
78—Northeast La. vs. Alcorn St. (27), 11-28-92.

TEAM: TOURNAMENT

FIRST DOWNS
125—Montana, 1995 (25 vs. Eastern Ky., 41 vs. Ga. Southern, 38 vs. Stephen F. Austin, 21 vs. Marshall).

NET YARDS RUSHING
1,522—Ga. Southern, 1986 (442 vs. North Caro. A&T, 317 vs. Nicholls St., 466 vs. Nevada, 297 vs. Arkansas St.).

NET YARDS PASSING
1,703—Montana, 1996 (447 vs. Nicholls St., 467 vs. East Tenn. St., 454 vs. Troy St., 335 vs. Marshall).

NET YARDS RUSHING AND PASSING
2,241—Ga. Southern, 1986 (541 vs. North Caro. A&T, 484 vs. Nicholls St., 613 vs. Nevada, 603 vs. Arkansas St.).

PASSES ATTEMPTED
197—Montana, 1996 (53 vs. Nicholls St., 44 vs. East Tenn. St., 45 vs. Troy St., 55 vs. Marshall).

PASSES COMPLETED
137—Montana, 1995 (35 vs. Eastern Ky., 42 vs. Ga. Southern, 31 vs. Stephen F. Austin, 29 vs. Marshall).

PASSES HAD INTERCEPTED
11—Stephen F. Austin, 1989 (0 vs. Grambling, 4 vs. Southwest Mo. St., 2 vs. Furman, 5 vs. Ga. Southern).

NUMBER OF PUNTS
29—Northern Iowa, 1992 (11 vs. Eastern Wash., 10 vs. McNeese St., 8 vs. Youngstown St.).

YARDS PENALIZED
350—Ga. Southern, 1986 (106 vs. North Caro. A&T, 104 vs. Nicholls St., 75 vs. Nevada, 65 vs. Arkansas St.).

FUMBLES LOST
9—Nevada, 1983 (3 vs. Idaho St., 4 vs. North Texas, 2 vs. Southern Ill.); Youngstown St., 1991 (3 vs. Villanova, 1 vs. Nevada, 4 vs. Samford, 1 vs. Marshall).

POINTS
203—Ga. Southern, 1986 (52 vs. North Caro. A&T, 55 vs. Nicholls St., 48 vs. Nevada, 48 vs. Arkansas St.).

INDIVIDUAL: CHAMPIONSHIP GAME

NET YARDS RUSHING
207—Mike Solomon, Florida A&M (35) vs. Massachusetts (28), 1978 (27 carries).

RUSHES ATTEMPTED
31—Joe Ross, Ga. Southern (37) vs. Stephen F. Austin (34), 1989 (152 yards); Raymond Gross, Ga. Southern (36) vs. Nevada (13), 1990 (145 yards).

TOUCHDOWNS BY RUSHING
4—John Bagwell, Furman (42) vs. Ga. Southern (44), 1985.

NET YARDS PASSING
474—Tony Peterson, Marshall (42) vs. Northeast La. (43), 1987 (28 of 54).

PASSES ATTEMPTED
57—Kelly Bradley, Montana St. (19) vs. Louisiana Tech (6), 1984 (32 completions).

PASSES COMPLETED
56—Brian Ah Yat, Montana (29) vs. Marshall (49), 1996 (55 attempts).

PASSES HAD INTERCEPTED
7—Jeff Gilbert, Western Caro. (7) vs. Southern Ill. (43), 1983.

TOUCHDOWN PASSES COMPLETED
4—Eric Kresser, Marshall (49) vs. Montana (29), 1996; Tracy Ham, Ga. Southern (44) vs. Furman (42), 1985; Tony Peterson, Marshall (42) vs. Northeast La. (43), 1987.

COMPLETION PERCENTAGE
(Min. 8 Attempts)
.875—Mark Brungard, Youngstown St. (17) vs. Marshall (5), 1993 (7 of 8).

NET YARDS RUSHING AND PASSING
509—Tracy Ham, Ga. Southern (44) vs. Furman (42), 1985 (56 plays).

NUMBER OF RUSHING AND PASSING PLAYS
67—Brian Ah Yat, Montana (29) vs. Marshall (49), 1996 (12 rush, 55 pass, 301 yards).

PUNTING AVERAGE
(Min. 3 Punts)
48.3—Todd Fugate, Marshall (42) vs. Northeast La. (43), 1987 (3 punts).

NUMBER OF PUNTS
10—Rick Titus, Delaware (14) vs. Eastern Ky. (17), 1982 (41.6 average).

PASSES CAUGHT
13—Joe Douglass, Montana (29) vs. Marshall (49), 1996 (117 yards).

NET YARDS RECEIVING
220—Randy Moss, Marshall (49) vs. Montana (29), 1996 (9 catches).

TOUCHDOWN PASSES CAUGHT
4—Randy Moss, Marshall (49) vs. Montana (29), 1996 (9 catches for 220 yards).

PASSES INTERCEPTED
4—Greg Shipp, Southern Ill. (43) vs. Western Caro. (7), 1983.

YARDS GAINED ON INTERCEPTION RETURNS
58—Chris Cook, Boise St. (14) vs. Youngstown St. (28), 1994 (1 interception).

YARDS GAINED ON PUNT RETURNS
67—Rodney Oglesby, Ga. Southern (36) vs. Nevada (13), 1990 (6 returns).

YARDS GAINED ON KICKOFF RETURNS
207—Eric Rasheed, Western Caro. (7) vs. Southern Ill. (43), 1983 (6 returns).

POINTS
24—Randy Moss, Marshall (49) vs. Montana (29), 1996; John Bagwell, Furman (42) vs. Ga. Southern (44), 1985.

TOUCHDOWNS
4—Randy Moss, Marshall (49) vs. Montana (29), 1996; John Bagwell, Furman (42) vs. Ga. Southern (44), 1985.

EXTRA POINTS
6—Keven Esval, Furman (42) vs. Ga. Southern (44), 1985.

FIELD GOALS
4—Tim Foley, Ga. Southern (48) vs. Arkansas St. (21), 1986.

LONGEST RUSH
61—Doug Chapman, Marshall (49) vs. Montana (29), 1996.

LONGEST PASS COMPLETION
79—Tracy Ham to Ricky Harris, Ga. Southern (48) vs. Arkansas St. (21), 1986.

LONGEST FIELD GOAL
55—David Cool, Ga. Southern (12) vs. Furman (17), 1988.

LONGEST PUNT
72—Rick Titus, Delaware (14) vs. Eastern Ky. (17), 1982.

TEAM: CHAMPIONSHIP GAME

FIRST DOWNS
31—Montana (29) vs. Marshall (49), 1996 (11 rush, 17 pass, 3 penalty).

FIRST DOWNS BY RUSHING
19—Florida A&M (35) vs. Massachusetts (28), 1978.

FIRST DOWNS BY PASSING
19—Marshall (42) vs. Northeast La. (43), 1987.

FIRST DOWNS BY PENALTY
3—Montana (29) vs. Marshall (49), 1996; Eastern Ky. (23) vs. Idaho St. (34), 1981; Furman (42) vs. Ga. Southern (44), 1985; Northeast La. (43) vs. Marshall (42), 1987.

NET YARDS RUSHING
470—Florida A&M (35) vs. Massachusetts (28), 1978 (76 attempts).

RUSHES ATTEMPTED
76—Florida A&M (35) vs. Massachusetts (28), 1978 (470 yards).

NET YARDS PASSING
474—Marshall (42) vs. Northeast La. (43), 1987 (28 of 54).

PASSES ATTEMPTED
57—Montana St. (19) vs. Louisiana Tech (6), 1984 (32 completions).

PASSES COMPLETED
36—Montana (29) vs. Marshall (49), 1996 (55 attempts).

COMPLETION PERCENTAGE (Min. 10 Attempts)
.760—Southern Ill. (43) vs. Western Caro. (7), 1983 (19 of 25).

PASSES HAD INTERCEPTED
7—Western Caro. (7) vs. Southern Ill. (43), 1983.

NET YARDS RUSHING AND PASSING
640—Ga. Southern (44) vs. Furman (42), 1985 (77 plays).

RUSHING AND PASSING PLAYS
90—Montana (29) vs. Marshall (49), 1996 (430 yards).

PUNTING AVERAGE (Min. 3 Punts)
48.3—Marshall (42) vs. Northeast La. (43), 1987 (3 punts).

NUMBER OF PUNTS
10—Delaware (14) vs. Eastern Ky. (17), 1982 (41.6 average).

YARDS GAINED ON PUNT RETURNS
67—Ga. Southern (36) vs. Nevada (13), 1990 (6 returns).

YARDS GAINED ON KICKOFF RETURNS
229—Western Caro. (7) vs. Southern Ill. (43), 1983 (8 returns).

YARDS GAINED ON INTERCEPTION RETURNS
70—Marshall (31) vs. Youngstown St. (28), 1992 (2 interceptions).

YARDS PENALIZED
162—Idaho St. (34) vs. Eastern Ky. (23), 1981 (12 penalties).

FUMBLES
5—Eastern Ky. (17) vs. Delaware (14), 1982; Western Caro. (7) vs. Southern Ill. (43), 1983; Louisiana Tech (6) vs. Montana St. (19), 1984; Northeast La. (43) vs. Marshall (42), 1987; Ga. Southern (12) vs. Furman (17), 1988; Ga. Southern (36) vs. Nevada (13), 1990.

FUMBLES LOST
4—Northeast La. (43) vs. Marshall (42), 1987; Ga. Southern (36) vs. Nevada (13), 1990.

POINTS
49—Marshall vs. Montana (29), 1996.

ATTENDANCE
32,106—Marshall University Stadium, Huntington, W.Va., 1995.

CHAMPIONSHIP RESULTS

Year-by-Year Division I-AA Championship Results

Year (Number of Teams)	Coach	Record	Result
1978 (4)			
Florida A&M	Rudy Hubbard	2-0	Champion
Massachusetts	Bob Pickett	1-1	Second
Jackson St.	W. C. Gorden	0-1	Lost 1st Round
Nevada	Chris Ault	0-1	Lost 1st Round
1979 (4)			
Eastern Ky.	Roy Kidd	2-0	Champion
Lehigh	John Whitehead	1-1	Second
Murray St.	Mike Gottfried	0-1	Lost 1st Round
Nevada	Chris Ault	0-1	Lost 1st Round
1980 (4)			
Boise St.	Jim Criner	2-0	Champion
Eastern Ky.	Roy Kidd	1-1	Second
Grambling	Eddie Robinson	0-1	Lost 1st Round
Lehigh	John Whitehead	0-1	Lost 1st Round
1981 (8)			
Idaho St.	Dave Kragthorpe	3-0	Champion
Eastern Ky.	Roy Kidd	2-1	Second
Boise St.	Jim Criner	1-1	Semifinalist
South Caro. St.	Bill Davis	1-1	Semifinalist
Delaware	Tubby Raymond	0-1	Lost 1st Round
Jackson St.	W. C. Gorden	0-1	Lost 1st Round
Rhode Island	Bob Griffin	0-1	Lost 1st Round
*Tennessee St.	John Merritt	0-1	Vacated
1982 (12)			
Eastern Ky.	Roy Kidd	3-0	Champion
Delaware	Tubby Raymond	2-1	Second
Louisiana Tech	Billy Brewer	1-1	Semifinalist
*Tennessee St.	John Merritt	1-1	Vacated
Colgate	Fred Dunlap	1-1	Quarterfinalist
Eastern Ill.	Darrell Mudra	1-1	Quarterfinalist
Idaho	Dennis Erickson	1-1	Quarterfinalist
South Caro. St.	Bill Davis	1-1	Quarterfinalist
Boston U.	Rick Taylor	0-1	Lost 1st Round
Furman	Dick Sheridan	0-1	Lost 1st Round
Jackson St.	W. C. Gorden	0-1	Lost 1st Round
Montana	Larry Donovan	0-1	Lost 1st Round
1983 (12)			
Southern Ill.	Rey Dempsey	3-0	Champion
Western Caro.	Bob Waters	3-1	Second
Furman	Dick Sheridan	1-1	Semifinalist
Nevada	Chris Ault	2-1	Semifinalist
Boston U.	Rick Taylor	1-1	Quarterfinalist
Holy Cross	Rick Carter	0-1	Quarterfinalist
Indiana St.	Dennis Raetz	1-1	Quarterfinalist
North Texas	Corky Nelson	0-1	Quarterfinalist
Colgate	Fred Dunlap	0-1	Lost 1st Round
Eastern Ill.	Al Molde	0-1	Lost 1st Round
Eastern Ky.	Roy Kidd	0-1	Lost 1st Round
Idaho St.	Jim Koetter	0-1	Lost 1st Round
1984 (12)			
Montana St.	Dave Arnold	3-0	Champion
Louisiana Tech	A. L. Williams	3-1	Second
Middle Tenn. St.	James Donnelly	2-1	Semifinalist
Rhode Island	Bob Griffin	1-1	Semifinalist
Alcorn St.	Marino Casem	0-1	Quarterfinalist
Arkansas St.	Larry Lacewell	1-1	Quarterfinalist
Indiana St.	Dennis Raetz	0-1	Quarterfinalist
Richmond	Dal Shealy	1-1	Quarterfinalist
Boston U.	Rick Taylor	0-1	Lost 1st Round
Eastern Ky.	Roy Kidd	0-1	Lost 1st Round
Mississippi Val.	Archie Cooley Jr.	0-1	Lost 1st Round
Chattanooga	Buddy Nix	0-1	Lost 1st Round
1985 (12)			
Ga. Southern	Erk Russell	4-0	Champion
Furman	Dick Sheridan	2-1	Second
Nevada	Chris Ault	1-1	Semifinalist
Northern Iowa	Darrell Mudra	1-1	Semifinalist
Arkansas St.	Larry Lacewell	1-1	Quarterfinalist
Eastern Wash.	Dick Zornes	1-1	Quarterfinalist
Middle Tenn. St.	James Donnelly	0-1	Quarterfinalist
Rhode Island	Bob Griffin	1-1	Quarterfinalist
Akron	Jim Dennison	0-1	Lost 1st Round
Grambling	Eddie Robinson	0-1	Lost 1st Round
Idaho	Dennis Erickson	0-1	Lost 1st Round
Jackson St.	W. C. Gorden	0-1	Lost 1st Round
1986 (16)			
Ga. Southern	Erk Russell	4-0	Champion
Arkansas St.	Larry Lacewell	3-1	Second
Eastern Ky.	Roy Kidd	2-1	Semifinalist
Nevada	Chris Ault	2-1	Semifinalist
Delaware	Tubby Raymond	1-1	Quarterfinalist
Eastern Ill.	Al Molde	1-1	Quarterfinalist
Nicholls St.	Sonny Jackson	1-1	Quarterfinalist
Tennessee St.	William Thomas	1-1	Quarterfinalist
Appalachian St.	Sparky Woods	0-1	Lost 1st Round
Furman	Jimmy Satterfield	0-1	Lost 1st Round
Idaho	Keith Gilbertson	0-1	Lost 1st Round
Jackson St.	W. C. Gorden	0-1	Lost 1st Round
Murray St.	Frank Beamer	0-1	Lost 1st Round
North Caro. A&T	Maurice Forte	0-1	Lost 1st Round
Sam Houston St.	Ron Randleman	0-1	Lost 1st Round
William & Mary	Jimmye Laycock	0-1	Lost 1st Round
1987 (16)			
Northeast La.	Pat Collins	4-0	Champion
Marshall	George Chaump	3-1	Second
Appalachian St.	Sparky Woods	2-1	Semifinalist
Northern Iowa	Darrell Mudra	2-1	Semifinalist
Arkansas St.	Larry Lacewell	1-1	Quarterfinalist

Year (Number of Teams)	Coach	Record	Result
Eastern Ky.	Roy Kidd	1-1	Quarterfinalist
Ga. Southern	Erk Russell	1-1	Quarterfinalist
Weber St.	Mike Price	1-1	Quarterfinalist
Idaho	Keith Gilbertson	0-1	Lost 1st Round
Jackson St.	W. C. Gorden	0-1	Lost 1st Round
James Madison	Joe Purzycki	0-1	Lost 1st Round
Maine	Tim Murphy	0-1	Lost 1st Round
North Texas	Corky Nelson	0-1	Lost 1st Round
Richmond	Dal Shealy	0-1	Lost 1st Round
Western Ky.	Dave Roberts	0-1	Lost 1st Round
Youngstown St.	Jim Tressel	0-1	Lost 1st Round

1988 (16)

Furman	Jimmy Satterfield	4-0	Champion
Ga. Southern	Erk Russell	3-1	Second
Eastern Ky.	Roy Kidd	2-1	Semifinalist
Idaho	Keith Gilbertson	2-1	Semifinalist
Marshall	George Chaump	1-1	Quarterfinalist
Northwestern St.	Sam Goodwin	1-1	Quarterfinalist
Stephen F. Austin	Jim Hess	1-1	Quarterfinalist
Western Ky.	Dave Roberts	1-1	Quarterfinalist
Boise St.	Skip Hall	0-1	Lost 1st Round
Citadel	Charlie Taaffe	0-1	Lost 1st Round
Delaware	Tubby Raymond	0-1	Lost 1st Round
Jackson St.	W. C. Gorden	0-1	Lost 1st Round
Massachusetts	Jim Reid	0-1	Lost 1st Round
Montana	Don Read	0-1	Lost 1st Round
North Texas	Corky Nelson	0-1	Lost 1st Round
Western Ill.	Bruce Craddock	0-1	Lost 1st Round

1989 (16)

Ga. Southern	Erk Russell	4-0	Champion
*Stephen F. Austin	Lynn Graves	3-1	Vacated
Furman	Jimmy Satterfield	2-1	Semifinalist
Montana	Don Read	2-1	Semifinalist
Eastern Ill.	Bob Spoo	1-1	Quarterfinalist
Middle Tenn. St.	James Donnelly	1-1	Quarterfinalist
Southwest Mo. St.	Jesse Branch	1-1	Quarterfinalist
Youngstown St.	Jim Tressel	1-1	Quarterfinalist
Appalachian St.	Jerry Moore	0-1	Lost 1st Round
Eastern Ky.	Roy Kidd	0-1	Lost 1st Round
Grambling	Eddie Robinson	0-1	Lost 1st Round
Idaho	John L. Smith	0-1	Lost 1st Round
Jackson St.	W. C. Gorden	0-1	Lost 1st Round
Maine	Tom Lichtenberg	0-1	Lost 1st Round
Villanova	Andy Talley	0-1	Lost 1st Round
William & Mary	Jimmye Laycock	0-1	Lost 1st Round

1990 (16)

Ga. Southern	Tim Stowers	4-0	Champion
Nevada	Chris Ault	3-1	Second
Boise St.	Skip Hall	2-1	Semifinalist
Central Fla.	Gene McDowell	2-1	Semifinalist
Furman	Jimmy Satterfield	1-1	Quarterfinalist
Idaho	John L. Smith	1-1	Quarterfinalist
Middle Tenn. St.	James Donnelly	1-1	Quarterfinalist
William & Mary	Jimmye Laycock	1-1	Quarterfinalist
Citadel	Charlie Taaffe	0-1	Lost 1st Round
Eastern Ky.	Roy Kidd	0-1	Lost 1st Round
Jackson St.	W. C. Gorden	0-1	Lost 1st Round
Massachusetts	Jim Reid	0-1	Lost 1st Round
Northeast La.	Dave Roberts	0-1	Lost 1st Round
Northern Iowa	Terry Allen	0-1	Lost 1st Round
Southwest Mo. St.	Jesse Branch	0-1	Lost 1st Round
Youngstown St.	Jim Tressel	0-1	Lost 1st Round

1991 (16)

Youngstown St.	Jim Tressel	4-0	Champion
Marshall	Jim Donnan	3-1	Second
Eastern Ky.	Roy Kidd	2-1	Semifinalist
Samford	Terry Bowden	2-1	Semifinalist
James Madison	Rip Scherer	1-1	Quarterfinalist
Middle Tenn. St.	James Donnelly	1-1	Quarterfinalist
Nevada	Chris Ault	1-1	Quarterfinalist
Northern Iowa	Terry Allen	1-1	Quarterfinalist
Appalachian St.	Jerry Moore	0-1	Lost 1st Round
Delaware	Tubby Raymond	0-1	Lost 1st Round
McNeese St.	Bobby Keasler	0-1	Lost 1st Round
New Hampshire	Bill Bowes	0-1	Lost 1st Round
Sam Houston St.	Ron Randleman	0-1	Lost 1st Round
Villanova	Andy Talley	0-1	Lost 1st Round
Weber St.	Dave Arslanian	0-1	Lost 1st Round
Western Ill.	Randy Ball	0-1	Lost 1st Round

1992 (16)

Marshall	Jim Donnan	4-0	Champion
Youngstown St.	Jim Tressel	3-1	Second
Delaware	Tubby Raymond	2-1	Semifinalist

Year (Number of Teams)	Coach	Record	Result
Northern Iowa	Terry Allen	2-1	Semifinalist
Citadel	Charlie Taaffe	1-1	Quarterfinalist
McNeese St.	Bobby Keasler	1-1	Quarterfinalist
Middle Tenn. St.	James Donnelly	1-1	Quarterfinalist
Northeast La.	Dave Roberts	1-1	Quarterfinalist
Alcorn St.	Cardell Jones	0-1	Lost 1st Round
Appalachian St.	Jerry Moore	0-1	Lost 1st Round
Eastern Ky.	Roy Kidd	0-1	Lost 1st Round
Eastern Wash.	Dick Zornes	0-1	Lost 1st Round
Idaho	John L. Smith	0-1	Lost 1st Round
North Caro. A&T	Bill Hayes	0-1	Lost 1st Round
Samford	Terry Bowden	0-1	Lost 1st Round
Villanova	Andy Talley	0-1	Lost 1st Round

1993 (16)

Youngstown St.	Jim Tressel	4-0	Champion
Marshall	Jim Donnan	3-1	Second
Idaho	John L. Smith	2-1	Semifinalist
Troy St.	Larry Blakeney	2-1	Semifinalist
Boston U.	Dan Allen	1-1	Quarterfinalist
Delaware	Tubby Raymond	1-1	Quarterfinalist
Ga. Southern	Tim Stowers	1-1	Quarterfinalist
McNeese St.	Bobby Keasler	1-1	Quarterfinalist
Central Fla.	Gene McDowell	0-1	Lost 1st Round
Eastern Ky.	Roy Kidd	0-1	Lost 1st Round
Howard	Steve Wilson	0-1	Lost 1st Round
Montana	Don Read	0-1	Lost 1st Round
Northeast La.	Dave Roberts	0-1	Lost 1st Round
Northern Iowa	Terry Allen	0-1	Lost 1st Round
Stephen F. Austin	John Pearce	0-1	Lost 1st Round
William & Mary	Jimmye Laycock	0-1	Lost 1st Round

1994 (16)

Youngstown St.	Jim Tressel	4-0	Champion
Boise St.	Pokey Allen	3-1	Second
Marshall	Jim Donnan	2-1	Semifinalist
Montana	Don Read	2-1	Semifinalist
Appalachian St.	Jerry Moore	1-1	Quarterfinalist
Eastern Ky.	Roy Kidd	1-1	Quarterfinalist
James Madison	Rip Scherer	1-1	Quarterfinalist
McNeese St.	Bobby Keasler	1-1	Quarterfinalist
Alcorn St.	Cardell Jones	0-1	Lost 1st Round
Boston U.	Dan Allen	0-1	Lost 1st Round
Idaho	John L. Smith	0-1	Lost 1st Round
Middle Tenn. St.	James Donnelly	0-1	Lost 1st Round
New Hampshire	Bill Bowes	0-1	Lost 1st Round
North Texas	Matt Simon	0-1	Lost 1st Round
Northern Iowa	Terry Allen	0-1	Lost 1st Round
Troy St.	Larry Blakeney	0-1	Lost 1st Round

1995 (16)

Montana	Don Read	4-0	Champion
Marshall	Jim Donnan	3-1	Second
McNeese St.	Bobby Keasler	2-1	Semifinalist
Stephen F. Austin	John Pearce	2-1	Semifinalist
Appalachian St.	Jerry Moore	1-1	Quarterfinalist
Delaware	Tubby Raymond	1-1	Quarterfinalist
Ga. Southern	Tim Stowers	1-1	Quarterfinalist
Northern Iowa	Terry Allen	1-1	Quarterfinalist
Eastern Ill.	Bob Spoo	0-1	Lost 1st Round
Eastern Ky.	Roy Kidd	0-1	Lost 1st Round
Hofstra	Joe Gardi	0-1	Lost 1st Round
Idaho	Chris Tormey	0-1	Lost 1st Round
Jackson St.	James Carson	0-1	Lost 1st Round
James Madison	Alex Wood	0-1	Lost 1st Round
Murray St.	Houston Nutt	0-1	Lost 1st Round
Troy St.	Larry Blakeney	0-1	Lost 1st Round

1996 (16)

Marshall	Bob Pruett	4-0	Champion
Montana	Mick Dennehy	3-1	Second
Troy St.	Larry Blakeney	2-1	Semifinalist
Northern Iowa	Terry Allen	2-1	Semifinalist
East Tenn. St.	Mike Cavan	1-1	Quarterfinalist
Murray St.	Houston Nutt	1-1	Quarterfinalist
Furman	Bobby Johnson	1-1	Quarterfinalist
William & Mary	Jimmye Laycock	1-1	Quarterfinalist
Nicholls St.	Darren Barbier	0-1	Lost 1st Round
Villanova	Andy Talley	0-1	Lost 1st Round
Florida A&M	Billy Joe	0-1	Lost 1st Round
Western Ill.	Randy Ball	0-1	Lost 1st Round
Delaware	Tubby Raymond	0-1	Lost 1st Round
Northern Ariz.	Stephen Axman	0-1	Lost 1st Round
Eastern Ill.	Bob Spoo	0-1	Lost 1st Round
Jackson St.	James Carson	0-1	Lost 1st Round

1997 (16)

Year (Number of Teams)	Coach	Record	Result
Youngstown St.	Jim Tressel	4-0	Champion
McNeese St.	Bobby Keasler	3-1	Second
Delaware	Tubby Raymond	2-1	Semifinalist
Eastern Wash.	Mike Kramer	2-1	Semifinalist
Ga. Southern	Paul Johnson	1-1	Quarterfinalist
Villanova	Andy Talley	1-1	Quarterfinalist
Western Ill.	Randy Ball	1-1	Quarterfinalist
Western Ky.	Jack Harbaugh	1-1	Quarterfinalist
Colgate	Dick Biddle	0-1	Lost 1st Round
Eastern Ky.	Roy Kidd	0-1	Lost 1st Round
Florida A&M	Billy Joe	0-1	Lost 1st Round
Hampton	Joe Taylor	0-1	Lost 1st Round
Hofstra	Joe Gardi	0-1	Lost 1st Round
Jackson St.	James Carson	0-1	Lost 1st Round
Montana	Mick Dennehy	0-1	Lost 1st Round
Northwestern St.	Sam Goodwin	0-1	Lost 1st Round

**Competition in championship vacated by action of the NCAA Committee on Infractions.*

Division I-AA Championship Record of Each College by Coach

(65 Colleges; 1978-97)

	Yrs	Won	Lost	CH	2D
AKRON					
Jim Dennison (Wooster '60) 85	1	0	1	0	0
ALCORN ST.					
Marino Casem (Xavier, La. '56) 84	1	0	1	0	0
Cardell Jones (Alcorn St. '65) 92, 94	2	0	2	0	0
TOTAL	3	0	3	0	0
APPALACHIAN ST.					
Sparky Woods (Carson-Newman '76) 86, 87	2	2	2	0	0
Jerry Moore (Baylor '61) 89, 91, 92, 94, 95	5	2	5	0	0
TOTAL	7	4	7	0	0
ARKANSAS ST.					
Larry Lacewell (Ark.-Monticello '59) 84, 85, 86-2D, 87	4	6	4	0	1
BOISE ST.					
Jim Criner (Cal Poly Pomona '61) 80-CH, 81	2	3	1	1	0
Skip Hall (Concordia-M'head '66) 88, 90	2	2	2	0	0
Pokey Allen (Utah '65) 94-2D	1	3	1	0	1
TOTAL	5	8	4	1	1
BOSTON U.					
Rick Taylor (Gettysburg '64) 82, 83, 84	3	1	3	0	0
Dan Allen (Hanover '78) 93, 94	2	1	2	0	0
TOTAL	5	2	5	0	0
CENTRAL FLA.					
Gene McDowell (Florida St. '63) 90, 93	2	2	2	0	0
CHATTANOOGA					
Buddy Nix (West Ala. '61) 84	1	0	1	0	0
CITADEL					
Charlie Taaffe (Siena '73) 88, 90, 92	3	1	3	0	0
COLGATE					
Fred Dunlap (Colgate '50) 82, 83	2	1	2	0	0
Dick Biddle (Duke '71)	1	0	1	0	0
TOTAL	3	1	3	0	0
DELAWARE					
Harold "Tubby" Raymond (Michigan '50) 81, 82-2D, 86, 88, 91, 92, 93, 95, 96, 97	10	9	10	0	1
EAST TENN. ST.					
Mike Cavan (Georgia '72) 96	1	1	1	0	0
EASTERN ILL.					
Darrell Mudra (Peru St. '51) 82	1	1	1	0	0
Al Molde (Gust. Adolphus '66) 83, 86	2	1	2	0	0
Bob Spoo (Purdue '60) 89, 95, 96	3	1	3	0	0
TOTAL	6	3	6	0	0
EASTERN KY.					
Roy Kidd (Eastern Ky. '54) 79-CH, 80-2D, 81-2D, 82-CH, 83, 84, 86, 87, 88, 89, 90, 91, 92, 93, 94, 95, 97	17	16	15	2	2
EASTERN WASH.					
Dick Zornes (Eastern Wash. '68) 85, 92	2	1	2	0	0
Mike Kramer (Idaho '77) 97	1	2	1	0	0
TOTAL	3	3	3	0	0
FLORIDA A&M					
Rudy Hubbard (Ohio St. '68) 78-CH	1	2	0	1	0
Billy Joe (Villanova '63) 96, 97	2	0	2	0	0
TOTAL	3	2	2	1	0
FURMAN					
Dick Sheridan (South Caro. '64) 82, 83, 85-2D	3	3	3	0	1
Jimmy Satterfield (South Caro. '62) 86, 88-CH, 89, 90	4	7	3	1	0
Bobby Johnson (Clemson '73) 96	1	1	1	0	0
TOTAL	8	11	7	1	1
GA. SOUTHERN					
Erk Russell (Auburn '49) 85-CH, 86-CH, 87, 88-2D, 89-CH	5	16	2	3	1
Tim Stowers (Auburn '79) 90-CH, 93, 95	3	6	2	1	0
Paul Johnson (Western Caro. '74)	1	1	1	0	0
TOTAL	9	23	5	4	1
GRAMBLING					
Eddie Robinson (Leland '41) 80, 85, 89	3	0	3	0	0
HOFSTRA					
Joe Gardi (Maryland '60) 95, 97	2	0	2	0	0
HOLY CROSS					
Rick Carter (Earlham '65) 83	1	0	1	0	0
HOWARD					
Steve Wilson (Howard '79) 93	1	0	1	0	0
IDAHO					
Dennis Erickson (Montana St. '70) 82, 85	2	1	2	0	0
Keith Gilbertson (Central Wash. '71) 86, 87, 88	3	2	3	0	0
John L. Smith (Weber St. '71) 89, 90, 92, 93, 94	5	3	5	0	0
Chris Tormey (Idaho '78) 95	1	0	1	0	0
TOTAL	11	6	11	0	0
IDAHO ST.					
Dave Kragthorpe (Utah St. '55) 81-CH	1	3	0	1	0
Jim Koetter (Idaho St. '61) 83	1	0	1	0	0
TOTAL	2	3	1	1	0
INDIANA ST.					
Dennis Raetz (Nebraska '68) 83, 84	2	1	2	0	0
JACKSON ST.					
W. C. Gorden (Tennessee St. '52) 78, 81, 82, 85, 86, 87, 88, 89, 90	9	0	9	0	0
James Carson (Jackson St. '63) 95, 96, 97	3	0	3	0	0
TOTAL	12	0	12	0	0
JAMES MADISON					
Joe Purzycki (Delaware '71) 87	1	0	1	0	0
Rip Scherer (William & Mary '74) 91, 94	2	2	2	0	0
Alex Wood (Iowa '79) 95	1	0	1	0	0
TOTAL	4	2	4	0	0
LEHIGH					
John Whitehead (East Stroudsburg '50) 79-2D, 80	2	1	2	0	1
LOUISIANA TECH					
Billy Brewer (Mississippi '61) 82	1	1	1	0	0
A. L. Williams (Louisiana Tech '57) 84-2D	1	3	1	0	1
TOTAL	2	4	2	0	1
MAINE					
Tim Murphy (Springfield '78) 87	1	0	1	0	0
Tom Lichtenberg (Louisville '62) 89	1	0	1	0	0
TOTAL	2	0	2	0	0
MARSHALL					
George Chaump (Bloomsburg '58) 87-2D, 88	2	4	2	0	1
Jim Donnan (North Caro. St. '67) 91-2D, 92-CH, 93-2D, 94, 95-2D	5	15	4	1	3
Bob Pruett (Marshall '65) 96-CH	1	4	0	1	0
TOTAL	8	23	6	2	4
MASSACHUSETTS					
Bob Pickett (Maine '59) 78-2D	1	1	1	0	1
Jim Reid (Maine '73) 88, 90	2	0	2	0	0
TOTAL	3	1	3	0	1
McNEESE ST.					
Bobby Keasler (Northeast La. '70) 91, 92, 93, 94, 95, 97-2D	6	8	6	0	1
MIDDLE TENN. ST.					
James "Boots" Donnelly (Middle Tenn. St. '65) 84, 85, 89, 90, 91, 92, 94	7	6	7	0	0
MISSISSIPPI VAL.					
Archie Cooley Jr. (Jackson St. '62) 84	1	0	1	0	0
MONTANA					
Larry Donovan (Nebraska '64) 82	1	0	1	0	0
Don Read (Cal St. Sacramento '59) 88, 89, 93, 94, 95-CH	5	8	4	1	0
Mick Dennehy (Montana '73) 96-2D, 97	2	3	2	0	1
TOTAL	8	11	7	1	1

	Yrs	Won	Lost	CH	2D
MONTANA ST.					
Dave Arnold (Drake '67) 84-CH	1	3	0	1	0
MURRAY ST.					
Mike Gottfried (Morehead St. '66) 79	1	0	1	0	0
Frank Beamer (Virginia Tech '69) 86	1	0	1	0	0
Houston Nutt (Oklahoma St. '81) 95, 96	2	1	2	0	0
TOTAL	4	1	4	0	0
NEVADA					
Chris Ault (Nevada '68) 78, 79, 83, 85, 86, 90-2D, 91	7	9	7	0	1
NEW HAMPSHIRE					
Bill Bowes (Penn St. '65) 91, 94	2	0	2	0	0
NICHOLLS ST.					
Sonny Jackson (Nicholls St. '63) 86	1	1	1	0	0
Darren Barbier (Nicholls St. '82) 96	1	0	1	0	0
TOTAL	2	1	2	0	0
NORTH CARO. A&T					
Maurice "Mo" Forte (Minnesota '71) 86	1	0	1	0	0
Bill Hayes (N.C. Central '64) 92	1	0	1	0	0
TOTAL	2	0	2	0	0
NORTH TEXAS					
Corky Nelson (Southwest Tex. St. '64) 83, 87, 88	3	0	3	0	0
Matt Simon (Eastern N.M. '76) 94	1	0	1	0	0
TOTAL	4	0	4	0	0
NORTHEAST LA.					
Pat Collins (Louisiana Tech '63) 87-CH	1	4	0	1	0
Dave Roberts (Western Caro. '68) 90, 92, 93	3	1	3	0	0
TOTAL	4	5	3	1	0
NORTHERN IOWA					
Darrell Mudra (Peru St. '51) 85, 87	2	3	2	0	0
Terry Allen (Northern Iowa '79) 90, 91, 92, 93, 94, 95, 96	7	6	7	0	0
TOTAL	9	9	9	0	0
NORTHERN ARIZ.					
Stephen Axman (LIU-C. W. Post '69) 96	1	0	1	0	0
NORTHWESTERN ST.					
Sam Goodwin (Henderson St. '66) 88, 97	2	1	2	0	0
RHODE ISLAND					
Bob Griffin (Southern Conn. St. '63) 81, 84, 85	3	2	3	0	0
RICHMOND					
Dal Shealy (Carson-Newman '60) 84, 87	2	1	2	0	0
SAM HOUSTON ST.					
Ron Randleman (William Penn '64) 86, 91	2	0	2	0	0
SAMFORD					
Terry Bowden (West Va. '78) 91, 92	2	2	2	0	0
SOUTH CARO. ST.					
Bill Davis (Johnson Smith '65) 81, 82	2	2	2	0	0
SOUTHERN ILL.					
Rey Dempsey (Geneva '58) 83-CH	1	3	0	1	0
SOUTHWEST MO. ST.					
Jesse Branch (Arkansas '64) 89, 90	2	1	2	0	0
STEPHEN F. AUSTIN¢					
Jim Hess (Southeastern Okla. '59) 88	1	1	1	0	0
Lynn Graves (Stephen F. Austin '65) 89-2D	1	3	1	0	1
John Pearce (East Tex. St. '70) 93, 95	2	2	2	0	0
TOTAL	4	6	4	0	1
TENNESSEE ST.*					
John Merritt (Kentucky St. '50) 81, 82	2	1	2	0	0
Bill Thomas (Tennessee St. '71) 86	1	1	1	0	0
TOTAL	3	2	3	0	0
TROY ST.					
Larry Blakeney (Auburn '70) 93, 94, 95, 96	4	4	4	0	0
VILLANOVA					
Andy Talley (Southern Conn. St. '67) 89, 91, 92, 96, 97	5	1	5	0	0
WEBER ST.					
Mike Price (Puget Sound '69) 87	1	1	1	0	0
Dave Arslanian (Weber St. '72) 91	1	0	1	0	0
TOTAL	2	1	2	0	0
WESTERN CARO.					
Bob Waters (Presbyterian '60) 83-2D	1	3	1	0	1
WESTERN ILL.					
Bruce Craddock (Truman St. '66) 88	1	0	1	0	0
Randy Ball (Truman St. '73) 91, 96, 97	3	1	3	0	0
TOTAL	4	1	4	0	0
WESTERN KY.					
Dave Roberts (Western Caro. '68) 87, 88	2	1	2	0	0
Jack Harbaugh (Bowling Green '61) 97	1	1	1	0	0
TOTAL	3	2	3	0	0
WILLIAM & MARY					
Jimmye Laycock (William & Mary '70) 86, 89, 90, 93, 96	5	2	5	0	0
YOUNGSTOWN ST.					
Jim Tressel (Baldwin-Wallace '75) 87, 89, 90, 91-CH, 92-2D, 93-CH, 94-CH, 97-CH	8	20	4	4	1

Tennessee State's competition in the 1981 and 1982 Division I-AA championships was vacated by action of the NCAA Committee on Infractions (official record is 1-1). ¢Stephen F. Austin's competition in the 1989 Division I-AA championship was vacated by action of the NCAA Committee on Infractions (official record is 1-2).

Division I-AA Championship Attendance History

Year	Teams	G	Total Attend.	Avg. PG
1978	4	3	34,630	11,543
1979	4	3	20,300	6,767
1980	4	3	36,957	12,319
1981	8	7	81,455	11,636
1982	12	11	106,801	9,709
1983	12	11	103,631	9,421
1984	12	11	122,142	11,104
1985	12	11	86,996	7,909
1986	16	15	153,832	10,255
1987	16	15	133,956	8,930
1988	16	15	146,782	9,785
1989	16	15	145,198	9,680
1990	16	15	180,027	12,002
1991	16	15	169,605	11,307
1992	16	15	199,450	13,297
1993	16	15	178,884	11,926
1994	16	15	209,761	13,984
1995	16	15	209,367	13,958
1996	16	15	178,768	11,918
1997	16	15	152,219	10,418

1978		
First Round (12/9):		
Florida A&M 15, Jackson St. 10	Jackson, Miss.	7,000
Massachusetts 44, Nevada 21	Reno, Nev.	14,026
Championship (12/16):		
Florida A&M 35, Massachusetts 28	Wichita Falls, Tex.	13,604
1979		
First Round (12/8):		
Lehigh 28, Murray St. 9	Murray, Ky.	10,000
Eastern Ky. 33, Nevada 30 (2 OT)	Richmond, Ky.	5,100
Championship (12/15):		
Eastern Ky. 30, Lehigh 7	Orlando, Fla.	5,200
1980		
First Round (12/13):		
Eastern Ky. 23, Lehigh 20	Bethlehem, Pa.	11,500
Boise St. 14, Grambling 9	Boise, Id.	17,300
Championship (12/20):		
Boise St. 31, Eastern Ky. 29	Sacramento, Cal.	8,157
1981		
First Round (12/5):		
Eastern Ky. 35, Delaware 28	Richmond, Ky.	8,100
Boise St. 19, Jackson St. 7	Jackson, Miss.	11,500
Idaho St. 51, Rhode Island 0	Pocatello, Id.	12,153
South Caro. St. 26, Tennessee St. 25 (OT)	Orangeburg, S. C.	6,224
Semifinals (12/12):		
Eastern Ky. 23, Boise St. 17	Boise, Id.	20,176
Idaho St. 41, South Caro. St. 12	Pocatello, Id.	12,300
Championship (12/19):		
Idaho St. 34, Eastern Ky. 23	Wichita Falls, Tex.	11,002
1982		
First Round (11/27):		
Idaho 21, Montana 7	Moscow, Id.	8,000
Eastern Ill. 16, Jackson St. 13 (OT)	Charleston, Ill.	5,000
South Caro. St. 17, Furman 0	Greenville, S. C.	13,865
Colgate 21, Boston U. 7	Hamilton, N. Y.	5,000
Quarterfinals (12/4):		
Eastern Ky. 38, Idaho 30	Richmond, Ky.	10,893
Tennessee St. 20, Eastern Ill. 19	Nashville, Tenn.	8,000
Louisiana Tech 38, South Caro. St. 3	Ruston, La.	13,000
Delaware 20, Colgate 13	Newark, Del.	11,448
Semifinals (12/11):		
Eastern Ky. 13, Tennessee St. 7	Richmond, Ky.	7,338
Delaware 17, Louisiana Tech 0	Ruston, La.	13,000
Championship (12/18):		
Eastern Ky. 17, Delaware 14	Wichita Falls, Tex.	11,257

1983

First Round (11/27):		
Indiana St. 16, Eastern Ill. 13 (2 OT)	Terre Haute, Ind.	6,222
Nevada 27, Idaho St. 20	Pocatello, Id.	10,333
Western Caro. 24, Colgate 23	Cullowhee, N. C.	6,500
Boston U. 24, Eastern Ky. 20	Richmond, Ky.	4,800
Quarterfinals (12/3):		
Southern Ill. 23, Indiana St. 7	Carbondale, Ill.	8,000
Nevada 20, North Texas 17 (OT)	Reno, Nev.	7,878
Western Caro. 28, Holy Cross 21	Worcester, Mass.	10,814
Furman 35, Boston U. 16	Greenville, S. C.	7,600
Semifinals (12/10):		
Southern Ill. 23, Nevada 7	Carbondale, Ill.	12,500
Western Caro. 14, Furman 7	Greenville, S. C.	13,034
Championship (12/17):		
Southern Ill. 43, Western Caro. 7	Charleston, S. C.	15,950

1984

First Round (11/24):		
Louisiana Tech 66, Mississippi Val. 19	Ruston, La.	17,500
Middle Tenn. St. 27, Eastern Ky. 10	Richmond, Ky.	4,800
Richmond 35, Boston U. 33	Richmond, Va.	11,236
Arkansas St. 37, Chattanooga 10	Jonesboro, Ark.	10,872
Quarterfinals (12/1):		
Louisiana Tech 44, Alcorn St. 21	Jackson, Miss.	16,204
Middle Tenn. St. 42, Indiana St. 41 (3OT)	Terre Haute, Ind.	6,225
Rhode Island 23, Richmond 17	Kingston, R. I.	10,446
Montana St. 31, Arkansas St. 14	Bozeman, Mont.	12,037
Semifinals (12/8):		
Louisiana Tech 21, Middle Tenn. St. 13	Murfreesboro, Tenn.	11,000
Montana St. 32, Rhode Island 20	Bozeman, Mont.	12,697
Championship (12/15):		
Montana St. 19, Louisiana Tech 6	Charleston, S. C.	9,125

1985

First Round (11/30):		
Ga. Southern 27, Jackson St. 0	Statesboro, Ga.	4,128
Eastern Wash. 42, Idaho 38	Moscow, Id.	6,500
Rhode Island 35, Akron 27	Kingston, R. I.	7,317
Arkansas St. 10, Grambling 7	Jonesboro, Ark.	5,730
Quarterfinals (12/7):		
Ga. Southern 28, Middle Tenn. St. 21	Murfreesboro, Tenn.	9,500
Northern Iowa 17, Eastern Wash. 14	Cedar Falls, Ia.	6,220
Furman 59, Rhode Island 15	Greenville, S. C.	9,454
Nevada 24, Arkansas St. 23	Reno, Nev.	10,241
Semifinals (12/14):		
Ga. Southern 40, Northern Iowa 33	Cedar Falls, Ia.	12,300
Furman 35, Nevada 12	Greenville, S. C.	10,300
Championship (12/21):		
Ga. Southern 44, Furman 42	Tacoma, Wash.	5,306

1986

First Round (11/29):		
Nevada 27, Idaho 7	Reno, Nev.	13,715
Tennessee St. 32, Jackson St. 23	Jackson, Miss.	24,000
Ga. Southern 52, North Caro. A&T 21	Statesboro, Ga.	7,767
Nicholls St. 28, Appalachian St. 26	Boone, N. C.	6,250
Arkansas St. 48, Sam Houston St. 7	Jonesboro, Ark.	4,500
Delaware 51, William & Mary 17	Williamsburg, Va.	6,340
Eastern Ill. 28, Murray St. 21	Charleston, Ill.	9,500
Eastern Ky. 23, Furman 10	Greenville, S. C.	8,000
Quarterfinals (12/6):		
Nevada 33, Tennessee St. 6	Reno, Nev.	13,102
Ga. Southern 55, Nicholls St. 31	Statesboro, Ga.	9,121
Arkansas St. 55, Delaware 14	Newark, Del.	12,018
Eastern Ky. 24, Eastern Ill. 22	Charleston, Ill.	9,500
Semifinals (12/13):		
Ga. Southern 48, Nevada 38	Reno. Nev.	15,100
Arkansas St. 24, Eastern Ky. 10	Jonesboro, Ark.	10,500
Championship (12/20):		
Ga. Southern 48, Arkansas St. 21	Tacoma, Wash.	4,419

1987

First Round (11/28):		
Appalachian St. 20, Richmond 3	Boone, N. C.	4,138
Ga. Southern 31, Maine 28 (OT)	Statesboro, Ga.	9,440
Weber St. 59, Idaho 30	Moscow, Id.	4,900
Marshall 41, James Madison 12	Huntington, W. Va.	15,584
Northeast La. 30, North Texas 9	Monroe, La.	9,500
Eastern Ky. 40, Western Ky. 17	Richmond, Ky.	4,050
Northern Iowa 31, Youngstown St. 28	Cedar Falls, Ia.	3,887
Arkansas St. 35, Jackson St. 32	Jackson, Miss.	7,500
Quarterfinals (12/5):		
Appalachian St. 19, Ga. Southern 0	Boone, N. C.	9,229
Marshall 51, Weber St. 23	Huntington, W. Va.	13,197
Nortrheast La. 33, Eastern Ky. 32	Monroe, La.	10,475
Northern Iowa 49, Arkansas St. 28	Cedar Falls, Ia.	6,100
Semifinals (12/12):		
Marshall 24, Appalachian St. 10	Boone, N. C.	10,000
Northeast La. 44, Northern Iowa 41 (2OT)	Monroe, La.	14,443
Championship (12/19):		
Northeast La. 43, Marshall 42	Pocatello, Id.	11,513

1988

First Round (11/26):		
Idaho 38, Montana 19	Moscow, Id.	5,500
Northwestern St. 22, Boise St. 13	Boise, Id.	10,537
Furman 21, Delaware 7	Greenville, S. C.	7,487
Marshall 7, North Texas 0	Huntington, W. Va.	15,086
Ga. Southern 38, Citadel 20	Statesboro, Ga.	11,011
Stephen F. Austin 24, Jackson St. 0	Nacogdoches, Tex.	5,384
Western Ky. 35, Western Ill. 32	Macomb, Ill.	6,000
Eastern Ky. 28, Massachusetts 17	Richmond, Ky.	4,600
Quarterfinals (12/3):		
Idaho 38, Northwestern St. 30	Moscow, Id.	6,800
Furman 13, Marshall 9	Huntington, W. Va.	16,820
Ga. Southern 27, Stephen F. Austin 6	Statesboro, Ga.	12,289
Eastern Ky. 41, Western Ky. 24	Richmnond, Ky.	8,100
Semifinals (12/10):		
Furman 38, Idaho 7	Greenville, S. C.	11,645
Ga. Southern 21, Eastern Ky. 17	Statesboro, Ga.	14,023
Championship (12/17):		
Furman 17, Ga. Southern 12	Pocatello, Id.	11,500

1989

First Round (11/25):		
Ga. Southern 52, Villanova 36	Statesboro, Ga.	10,161
Middle Tenn. St. 24, Appalachian St. 21	Murfreesboro, Tenn.	5,000
Eastern Ill. 38, Idaho 21	Moscow, Id.	6,025
Montana 48, Jackson St. 7	Missoula, Mont.	11,854
Furman 24, William & Mary 10	Greenville, S. C.	8,642
Youngstown St. 28, Eastern Ky. 24	Richmond, Ky.	3,898
Stephen F. Austin 59, Grambling 56	Nacogdoches, Tex.	7,106
Southwest Mo. St. 38, Maine 35	Springfield, Mo.	7,270
Quarterfinals (12/2):		
Ga. Southern 45, Middle Tenn. St. 3	Statesboro, Ga.	11,272
Montana 25, Eastern Ill. 19	Missoula, Mont.	12,285
Furman 42, Youngstown St. 23	Greenville, S. C.	8,033
Stephen F. Austin 55, Southwest Mo. St. 25	Nacogdoches, Tex.	10,491
Semifinals (12/9):		
Ga. Southern 45, Montana 15	Statesboro, Ga.	10,421
Stephen F. Austin 21, Furman 19	Greenville, S. C.	7,015
Championship (12/16):		
Ga. Southern 37, Stephen F. Austin 34	Statesboro, Ga.	25,725

1990

First Round (11/24):		
Middle Tenn. St. 28, Jackson St. 7	Murfreesboro, Tenn.	7,000
Boise St. 20, Northern Iowa 3	Boise, Id.	11,691
Nevada 27, Northeast La. 14	Reno, Nev.	11,008
Furman 45, Eastern Ky. 17	Richmond, Ky.	4,528
Central Fla. 20, Youngstown St. 17	Youngstown, Ohio	5,000
William & Mary 38, Massachusetts 0	Williamsburg, Va.	5,000
Ga. Southern 31, Citadel 0	Statesboro, Ga.	11,881
Idaho 41, Southwest Mo. St. 35	Springfield, Mo.	8,750
Quarterfinals (12/1):		
Boise St. 20, Middle Tenn. St. 13	Boise, Id.	15,849
Nevada 42, Furman 35 (3OT)	Reno, Nev.	11,519
Central Fla. 52, William & Mary 38	Orlando, Fla.	20,067
Ga. Southern 28, Idaho 27	Statesboro, Ga.	11,571
Semifinals (12/8):		
Nevada 59, Boise St. 52 (3OT)	Reno, Nev.	19,776
Ga. Southern 44, Central Fla. 7	Statesboro, Ga.	13,183
Championship (12/15):		
Ga. Southern 36, Nevada 13	Statesboro, Ga.	23,204

1991

First Round (11/30):		
Nevada 22, McNeese St. 16	Reno, Nev.	15,000
Youngstown St. 17, Villanova 16	Youngstown, Ohio	9,556
James Madison 42, Delaware 35 (2OT)	Newark, Del.	14,905
Samford 29, New Hampshire 13	Durham, N. H.	6,034
Eastern Ky. 14, Appalachian St. 3	Richmond, Ky.	2,750
Middle Tenn. St. 20, Sam Houston St. 19 (OT)	Murfreesboro, Tenn.	2,000
Northern Iowa 38, Weber St. 21	Cedar Falls, Ia.	8,723
Marshall 20, Western Ill. 17 (OT)	Huntington, W. Va.	16,840
Quarterfinals (12/7):		
Youngstown St. 30, Nevada 28	Reno, Nev.	13,476
Samford 24, James Madison 21	Harrisonburg, Va.	9,028
Eastern Ky. 23, Middle Tenn. St. 13	Richmond, Ky.	3,650
Marshall 41, Northern Iowa 13	Huntington, W. Va.	16,889
Semifinals (12/14):		
Youngstown St. 10, Samford 0	Youngstown, Ohio	17,003
Marshall 14, Eastern Ky. 7	Huntington, W. Va.	21,084
Championship (12/21):		
Youngstown St. 25, Marshall 17	Statesboro, Ga.	12,667

1992

First Round (11/28):		
Northeast La. 78, Alcorn St. 27	Monroe, La.	14,416
Delaware 56, Samford 21	Newark, Del.	11,364
Middle Tenn. St. 35, Appalachian St. 10	Murfreesboro, Tenn.	4,000
Marshall 44, Eastern Ky. 0	Huntington, W. Va.	16,598
Citadel 44, North Caro. A&T 0	Charleston, S. C.	12,300
Youngstown St. 23, Villanova 20	Youngstown, Ohio	9,465

Northern Iowa 17, Eastern Wash. 14	Cedar Falls, Ia.	13,149
McNeese St. 23, Idaho 20	Moscow, Id.	6,000
Quarterfinals (12/5):		
Delaware 41, Northeast La. 18	Monroe, La.	10,172
Marshall 35, Middle Tenn. St. 21	Huntington, W. Va.	14,011
Youngstown St. 42, Citadel 17	Charleston, S. C.	12,300
Northern Iowa 29, McNeese St. 7	Cedar Falls, Ia.	13,375
Semifinals (12/12):		
Marshall 28, Delaware 7	Huntington, W. Va.	16,323
Youngstown St. 19, Northern Iowa 7	Cedar Falls, Ia.	14,682
Championship (12/19):		
Marshall 31, Youngstown St. 28	Huntington, W. Va.	31,304
1993		
First Round (11/27):		
Ga. Southern 14, Eastern Ky. 12	Statesboro, Ga.	7,278
Youngstown St. 56, Central Fla. 30	Youngstown, Ohio	7,408
Boston U. 27, Northern Iowa 21 (2OT)	Boston, Mass.	6,882
Idaho 34, Northeast La. 31	Monroe, La.	5,500
Delaware 49, Montana 48	Missoula, Mont.	11,271
Marshall 28, Howard 14	Huntington, W. Va.	13,554
McNeese St. 34, William & Mary 28	Lake Charles, La.	17,167
Troy St. 42, Stephen F. Austin 20	Troy, Ala.	4,500
Quarterfinals (12/4):		
Youngstown St. 34, Ga. Southern 14	Youngstown, Ohio	9,503
Idaho 21, Boston U. 14	Moscow, Id.	8,800
Marshall 34, Delaware 31	Huntington, W. Va.	13,687
Troy St. 35, McNeese St. 28	Lake Charles, La.	20,000
Semifinals (12/11):		
Youngstown St. 35, Idaho 16	Youngstown, Ohio	9,644
Marshall 24, Troy St. 21	Huntington, W. Va.	14,472
Championship (12/18):		
Youngstown St. 17, Marshall 5	Huntington, W. Va.	29,218
1994		
First Round (11/26):		
Youngstown St. 63, Alcorn St. 20	Youngstown, Ohio	17,795
Eastern Ky. 30, Boston U. 23	Richmond, Ky.	4,111
McNeese St. 38, Idaho 21	Lake Charles, La.	16,000
Montana 23, Northern Iowa 20	Missoula, Mont.	7,958
Marshall 49, Middle Tenn. St. 14	Huntington, W. Va.	17,349
James Madison 45, Troy St. 26	Harrisonburg, Va.	5,200
Boise St. 24, North Texas 20	Boise, Id.	14,706
Appalachian St. 17, New Hampshire 10 (OT)	Durham, N. H.	7,329
Quarterfinals (12/3):		
Youngstown St. 18, Eastern Ky. 15	Youngstown, Ohio	16,023
Montana 30, McNeese St. 28	Missoula, Mont.	8,419
Marshall 28, James Madison 21 (OT)	Huntington, W. Va.	16,494
Boise St. 17, Appalachian St. 14	Boise, Id.	15,302
Semifinals (12/10):		
Youngstown St. 28, Montana 9	Youngstown, Ohio	15,333
Boise St. 28, Marshall 24	Boise, Id.	20,068
Championship (12/17):		
Youngstown St. 28, Boise St. 14	Huntington, W. Va.	27,674
1995		
First Round (11/25):		
McNeese St. 33, Idaho 3	Lake Charles, La.	15,736
Delaware 38, Hofstra 17	Newark, Del.	13,295
Northern Iowa 35, Murray St. 34	Murray, Ky.	7,635
Marshall 38, Jackson St. 8	Huntington, W. Va.	13,035
Appalachian St. 31, James Madison 24	Boone, N. C.	9,467
Stephen F. Austin 34, Eastern Ill. 29	Nacogdoches, Tex.	3,552
Ga. Southern 24, Troy St. 21	Troy, Ala.	6,000
Montana 48, Eastern Ky. 0	Missoula, Mont.	13,830
Quarterfinals (12/2):		
McNeese St. 52, Delaware 18	Lake Charles, La.	17,239
Marshall 41, Northern Iowa 24	Huntington, W. Va.	14,472
Stephen F. Austin 27, Appalachian St. 17	Boone, N. C.	8,941
Montana 45, Ga. Southern 0	Missoula, Mont.	18,518
Semifinals (12/9):		
Marshall 25, McNeese St. 13	Lake Charles, La.	18,018
Montana 70, Stephen F. Austin 14	Missoula, Mont.	18,523
Championship (12/16):		
Montana 22, Marshall 20	Huntington, W. Va.	32,106
1996		
First Round (11/30):		
Montana 48, Nicholls St. 3	Missoula, Mont.	13,438
East Tenn. St. 35, Villanova 29	Johnson City, Tenn.	4,939
Troy St. 29, Florida A&M 25	Troy, Ala.	10,200
Murray St. 34, Western Ill. 6	Murray, Ky.	2,753
Marshall 59, Delaware 14	Huntington, W. Va.	15,429
Furman 42, Northern Ariz. 31	Flagstaff, Ariz.	8,700
Northern Iowa 21, Eastern Ill. 14	Cedar Falls, Ia.	10,402
William & Mary 45, Jackson St. 6	Williamsburg, Va.	4,057
Quarterfinals (12/7):		
Montana 44, East Tenn. St. 14	Missoula, Mont.	15,025
Troy St. 31, Murray St. 3	Troy, Ala.	6,100
Marshall 54, Furman 0	Huntington, W. Va.	14,096
Northern Iowa 38, William & Mary 35	Cedar Falls, Ia.	10,796
Semifinals (12/14):		
Montana 70, Troy St. 7	Missoula, Mont.	18,367
Marshall 31, Northern Iowa 14	Huntington, W. Va.	14,414
Championship (12/21):		
Marshall 49, Montana 29	Huntington, W. Va.	30,052
1997	**Site**	**Attend.**
First Round (11/29):		
Villanova 49, Colgate 28	Villanova, Pa.	8,875
Youngstown St. 28, Hampton 13	Youngstown, Ohio	12,431
Western Ky. 42, Eastern Ky. 14	Bowling Green, Ky.	9,000
Eastern Wash. 40, Northwestern St. 10	Cheney, Wash.	6,384
Delaware 24, Hofstra 14	Newark, Del.	14,075
Ga. Southern 52, Florida A&M 37	Statesboro, Ga.	10,409
McNeese St. 19, Montana 14	Lake Charles, La.	13,681
Western Ill. 31, Jackson St. 24	Macomb, Ill.	8,980
Quarterfinals (12/6):		
Youngstown St. 37, Villanova 34	Villanova, Pa.	7,591
Eastern Wash. 38, Western Ky. 21	Cheney, Wash.	6,829
Delaware 16, Ga. Southern 7	Newark, Del.	11,203
McNeese St. 14, Western Ill. 12	Macomb, Ill.	5,000
Semifinals(12/13):		
Youngstown St. 25, Eastern Wash. 14	Cheney, Wash.	8,529
McNeese St. 23, Delaware 21	Newark, Del.	14,461
Championship (12/20):		
Youngstown St. 10, McNeese St. 9	Chattanooga, Tenn.	14,771

All-Time Results

1978 First Round: Florida A&M 15, Jackson St. 10; Massachusetts 44, Nevada 21. **Championship:** Florida A&M 35, Massachusetts 28.

1979 First Round: Lehigh 28, Murray St. 9; Eastern Ky. 33, Nevada 30 (2 OT). **Championship:** Eastern Ky. 30, Lehigh 7.

1980 First Round: Eastern Ky. 23, Lehigh 20; Boise St. 14, Grambling 9. **Championship:** Boise St. 31, Eastern Ky. 29.

1981 First Round: Eastern Ky. 35, Delaware 28; Boise St. 19, Jackson St. 7; Idaho St. 51, Rhode Island 0; South Caro. St. 26, *Tennessee St. 25 (OT). **Semifinals:** Eastern Ky. 23, Boise St. 17; Idaho St. 41, South Caro. St. 12. **Championship:** Idaho St. 34, Eastern Ky. 23.

**Tennessee State's participation in 1981 playoff vacated.*

1982 First Round: Idaho 21, Montana 7; Eastern Ill. 16, Jackson St. 13 (OT); South Caro. St. 17, Furman 0; Colgate 21, Boston U. 7. **Quarterfinals:** Eastern Ky. 38, Idaho 30; *Tennessee St. 20, Eastern Ill. 19; Louisiana Tech 38, South Caro. St. 3; Delaware 20, Colgate 13. **Semifinals:** Eastern Ky. 13, *Tennessee St. 7; Delaware 17, Louisiana Tech 0. **Championship:** Eastern Ky. 17, Delaware 14.

**Tennessee State's participation in 1982 playoff vacated.*

1983 First Round: Indiana St. 16, Eastern Ill. 13 (2 OT); Nevada 27, Idaho St. 20; Western Caro. 24, Colgate 23; Boston U. 24, Eastern Ky. 20. **Quarterfinals:** Southern Ill. 23, Indiana St. 7; Nevada 20, North Texas 17 (OT); Western Caro. 28, Holy Cross 21; Furman 35, Boston U. 16. **Semifinals:** Southern Ill. 23, Nevada 7; Western Caro. 14, Furman 7. **Championship:** Southern Ill. 43, Western Caro. 7.

1984 First Round: Louisiana Tech 66, Mississippi Val. 19; Middle Tenn. St. 27, Eastern Ky. 10; Richmond 35, Boston U. 33; Arkansas St. 37, Chattanooga 10. **Quarterfinals:** Louisiana Tech 44, Alcorn St. 21; Middle Tenn. St. 42, Indiana St. 41 (3 OT); Rhode Island 23, Richmond 17; Montana St. 31, Arkansas St. 14. **Semifinals:** Louisiana Tech 21, Middle Tenn. St. 13; Montana St. 32, Rhode Island 20. **Championship:** Montana St. 19, Louisiana Tech 6.

1985 First Round: Ga. Southern 27, Jackson St. 0; Eastern Wash. 42, Idaho 38; Rhode Island 35, Akron 27; Arkansas St. 10, Grambling 7. **Quarterfinals:** Ga. Southern 28, Middle Tenn. St. 21; Northern Iowa 17, Eastern Wash. 14; Furman 59, Rhode Island 15; Nevada 24, Arkansas St. 23. **Semifinals:** Ga. Southern 40, Northern Iowa 33; Furman 35, Nevada 12. **Championship:** Ga. Southern 44, Furman 42.

1986 First Round: Nevada 27, Idaho 7; Tennessee St. 32, Jackson St. 23; Ga. Southern 52, North Caro. A&T 21; Nicholls St. 28, Appalachian St. 26; Arkansas St. 48, Sam Houston St. 7; Delaware 51, William & Mary 17; Eastern Ill. 28, Murray St. 21; Eastern Ky. 23, Furman 10. **Quarterfinals:** Nevada 33, Tennessee St. 6; Ga. Southern 55, Nicholls St. 31; Arkansas St. 55, Delaware 14; Eastern Ky. 24, Eastern Ill. 22. **Semifinals:** Ga. Southern 48, Nevada 38; Arkansas St. 24, Eastern Ky. 10. **Championship:** Ga. Southern 48, Arkansas St. 21.

1987 First Round: Appalachian St. 20, Richmond 3; Ga. Southern 31, Maine 28 (OT); Weber St. 59, Idaho 30; Marshall 41, James Madison 12; Northeast La. 30, North Texas 9; Eastern Ky. 40, Western Ky. 17; Northern Iowa 31, Youngstown St. 28; Arkansas St. 35, Jackson St. 32. **Quarterfinals:** Appalachian St. 19, Ga. Southern 0; Marshall 51, Weber St. 23; Northeast La. 33, Eastern Ky. 32; Northern Iowa 49, Arkansas St. 28. **Semifinals:** Marshall 24, Appalachian St. 10; Northeast La. 44, Northern Iowa 41 (2 OT). **Championship:** Northeast La. 43, Marshall 42.

1988 First Round: Idaho 38, Montana 19; Northwestern St. 22, Boise St. 13; Furman 21, Delaware 7; Marshall 7, North Texas 0; Ga. Southern 38, Citadel 20; Stephen F. Austin 24, Jackson St. 0; Western Ky. 35, Western Ill. 32; Eastern Ky. 28, Massachusetts 17. **Quarterfinals:** Idaho 38, Northwestern St. 30; Furman 13, Marshall 9; Ga. Southern 27, Stephen F. Austin 6; Eastern Ky. 41, Western Ky. 24. **Semifinals:** Furman 38, Idaho 7; Ga. Southern 21, Eastern Ky. 17. **Championship:** Furman 17, Ga. Southern 12.

1989 First Round: Ga. Southern 52, Villanova 36; Middle Tenn. St. 24, Appalachian St. 21; Eastern Ill. 38,

Idaho 21; Montana 48, Jackson St. 7; Furman 24, William & Mary 10; Youngstown St. 28, Eastern Ky. 24; ¢Stephen F. Austin 59, Grambling 56; Southwest Mo. St. 38, Maine 35. **Quarterfinals:** Ga. Southern 45, Middle Tenn. St. 3; Montana 25, Eastern Ill. 19; Furman 42, Youngstown St. 23; ¢Stephen F. Austin 55, Southwest Mo. St. 25. **Semifinals:** Ga. Southern 45, Montana 15; ¢Stephen F. Austin 21, Furman 19. **Championship:** Ga. Southern 37, ¢Stephen F. Austin 34.

¢Stephen F. Austin's participation in 1989 playoff vacated.

1990 First Round: Middle Tenn. St. 28, Jackson St. 7; Boise St. 20, Northern Iowa 3; Nevada 27, Northeast La. 14; Furman 45, Eastern Ky. 17; Central Fla. 20, Youngstown St. 17; William & Mary 38, Massachusetts 0; Ga. Southern 31, Citadel 0; Idaho 41, Southwest Mo. St. 35. **Quarterfinals:** Boise St. 20, Middle Tenn. St. 13; Nevada 42, Furman 35 (3 OT); Central Fla. 52, William & Mary 38; Ga. Southern 28, Idaho 27. **Semifinals:** Nevada 59, Boise St. 52 (3 OT); Ga. Southern 44, Central Fla. 7. **Championship:** Ga. Southern 36, Nevada 13.

1991 First Round: Nevada 22, McNeese St. 16; Youngstown St. 17, Villanova 16; James Madison 42, Delaware 35 (2 OT); Samford 29, New Hampshire 13; Eastern Ky. 14, Appalachian St. 3; Middle Tenn. St. 20, Sam Houston St. 19 (OT); Northern Iowa 38, Weber St. 21; Marshall 20, Western Ill. 17 (OT). **Quarterfinals:** Youngstown St. 30, Nevada 28; Samford 24, James Madison 21; Eastern Ky. 23, Middle Tenn. St. 13; Marshall 41, Northern Iowa 13. **Semifinals:** Youngstown St. 10, Samford 0; Marshall 14, Eastern Ky. 7. **Championship:** Youngstown St. 25, Marshall 17.

1992 First Round: Northeast La. 78, Alcorn St. 27; Delaware 56, Samford 21; Middle Tenn. St. 35, Appalachian St. 10; Marshall 44, Eastern Ky. 0; Citadel 44, North Caro. A&T 0; Youngstown St. 23, Villanova 20; Northern Iowa 17, Eastern Wash. 14; McNeese St. 23, Idaho 20. **Quarterfinals:** Delaware 41, Northeast La. 18; Marshall 35, Middle Tenn. St. 21; Youngstown St. 42, Citadel 17; Northern Iowa 29, McNeese St. 7. **Semifinals:** Marshall 28, Delaware 7; Youngstown St. 19, Northern Iowa 7. **Championship:** Marshall 31, Youngstown St. 28.

1993 First Round: Ga. Southern 14, Eastern Ky. 12; Youngstown St. 56, Central Fla. 30; Boston U. 27, Northern Iowa 21 (2 OT); Idaho 34, Northeast La. 31; Delaware 49, Montana 48; Marshall 28, Howard 14; McNeese St. 34, William & Mary 28; Troy St. 42, Stephen F. Austin 20. **Quarterfinals:** Youngstown St. 34, Ga. Southern 14; Idaho 21, Boston U. 14; Marshall 34, Delaware 31; Troy St. 35, McNeese St. 28. **Semifinals:** Youngstown St. 35, Idaho 16; Marshall 24, Troy St. 21. **Championship:** Youngstown St. 17, Marshall 5.

1994 First Round: Youngstown St. 63, Alcorn St. 20; Eastern Ky. 30, Boston U. 23; McNeese St. 38, Idaho 21; Montana 23, Northern Iowa 20; Marshall 49, Middle Tenn. St. 14; James Madison 45, Troy St. 26; Boise St. 24, North Texas 20; Appalachian St. 17, New Hampshire 10 (OT). **Quarterfinals:** Youngstown St. 18, Eastern Ky. 15; Montana 30, McNeese St. 28; Marshall 28, James Madison 21 (OT); Boise St. 17, Appalachian St. 14. **Semifinals:** Youngstown St. 28, Montana 9; Boise St. 28, Marshall 24. **Championship:** Youngstown St. 28, Boise St. 14.

1995 First Round: McNeese St. 33, Idaho 3; Delaware 38, Hofstra 17; Northern Iowa 35, Murray St. 34; Marshall 38, Jackson St. 8; Appalachian St. 31, James Madison 24; Stephen F. Austin 34, Eastern Ill. 29; Ga. Southern 24, Troy St. 21; Montana 48, Eastern Ky. 0. **Quarterfinals:** McNeese St. 52, Delaware 18; Marshall 41, Northern Iowa 24; Stephen F. Austin 27, Appalachian St. 17; Montana 45, Ga. Southern 0. **Semifinals:** Marshall 25, McNeese St. 13; Montana 70, Stephen F. Austin 14. **Championship:** Montana 22, Marshall 20.

1996 First Round: Montana 48, Nicholls St. 3;East Tenn. St. 35, Villanova 29; Troy St. 29, Florida A&M 25 Murray St. 34, Western Ill. 6; Marshall 59, Delaware 14; Furman 42, Northern Ariz. 31; Northern Iowa 21, Eastern Ill. 14; William & Mary 45, Jackson St. 6. **Quarterfinals:** Montana 44, East Tenn. St. 14; Troy St. 31, Murray St. 3; Marshall 54, Furman 0; Northern Iowa 28, William & Mary 35. **Semifinals:** Montana 70, Troy St. 7; Marshall 31, Northern Iowa 14. **Championship:** Marshall 49, Montana 29.

1997 First Round: Villanova 49, Colgate 28; Youngstown St. 28, Hampton 13; Western Ky. 42, Eastern Ky. 14; Eastern Wash. 40, Northwestern St. 10; Delaware 24, Hofstra 14; Ga. Southern 52, Florida A&M 37; McNeese St. 19, Montana 14; Western Ill. 31, Jackson St. 24. **Quarterfinals:** Youngstown St. 37, Villanova 34; Eastern Wash. 38, Western Ky. 21; Delaware 16, Ga. Southern 7; McNeese St. 14, Western Ill. 12. **Semifinals:** Youngstown St. 25, Eastern Wash. 14; McNeese St. 23, Delaware 21. **Championship:** Youngstown St. 10, McNeese St. 9.

Division II Championship

1997 Title Game Summary

BRALY MUNICIPAL STADIUM, FLORENCE, ALABAMA; DECEMBER 13

	New Haven	Northern Colo.
First Downs	14	19
Rushing Yardage	22	266
Passing Yardage	182	187
Return Yardage	-2	36
Passes (Comp.-Att.-Int.)	20-39-3	11-17-0
Punts (Number-Average)	5-35.6	7-37.0
Fumbles (Number-Lost)	2-2	3-0
Penalties (Number-Yards)	4-27	11-90

New Haven	0	0	0	0— 0
Northern Colo.	14	21	2	14—51

FIRST QUARTER
Northern Colo.—Dillon Micus 20 pass from Corte McGuffey (Mike Schauer kick) (72 yards in 6 plays, 12:36 left)
Northern Colo.—Billy Holmes 3 run (Schauer kick) (50 yards in 6 plays, 8:37 left)

SECOND QUARTER
Northern Colo.—Andy Haase 40 pass from McGuffey (Schauer kick) (71 yards in 6 plays, 13:42 left)
Northern Colo.—Holmes 7 run (kick failed) (57 yards in 6 plays, 1:52 left)
Northern Colo.—Brian Lusk 7 pass from Dean Grable (Keith Grable pass from McGuffey) (60 yards in 5 plays, :01 left)

THIRD QUARTER
Northern Colo.—Cazzie Kosciolek tackled in end zone (2:43 left)

FOURTH QUARTER
Northern Colo.—Holmes 11 run (Schauer kick) (53 yards in 7 plays, 14:15 left)
Northern Colo.—Grable 8 run (Schauer kick) (28 yards in 5 plays, 1:22 left)

INDIVIDUAL LEADERS
Rushing—New Haven: Donald Highsmith, 52 yards on 13 carries; Northern Colo.: Holmes, 195 yards on 30 carries.
Passing—New Haven: Kosciolek, 20 of 39 for 182 yards; Northern Colo.: McGuffey, 8 of 11 for 165 yards.
Receiving—New Haven: Diallo Freeman, 5 catches for 41 yards, and Elvert Eden, 5 catches for 37 yards; Northern Colo.: Micus, 2 catches for 56 yards, and Haase, 2 catches for 44 yards.

Josh Gibson/NCAA photos

Northern Colorado quarterback Corte McGuffey hit on 8 of 11 passes for 165 yards to lead the Bears to a 51-0 victory over New Haven in the 1997 NCAA Division II Championship title game. The victory marked Northern Colorado's second straight championship title.

Division II All-Time Championship Results

Year	Champion	Coach	Score	Runner-Up	Site
1973	Louisiana Tech	Maxie Lambright	34-0	Western Ky.	Sacramento, Calif.
1974	Central Mich.	Roy Kramer	54-14	Delaware	Sacramento, Calif.
1975	Northern Mich.	Gil Krueger	16-14	Western Ky.	Sacramento, Calif.

Year	Champion	Coach	Score	Runner-Up	Site
1976	Montana St.	Sonny Holland	24-13	Akron	Wichita Falls, Texas
1977	Lehigh	John Whitehead	33-0	Jacksonville St.	Wichita Falls, Texas
1978	Eastern Ill.	Darrell Mudra	10-9	Delaware	Longview, Texas
1979	Delaware	Tubby Raymond	38-21	Youngstown St.	Albuquerque, N.M.
1980	Cal Poly	Joe Harper	21-13	Eastern Ill.	Albuquerque, N.M.
1981	Southwest Tex. St.	Jim Wacker	42-13	North Dak. St.	McAllen, Texas
1982	Southwest Tex. St.	Jim Wacker	34-9	UC Davis	McAllen, Texas
1983	North Dak. St.	Don Morton	41-21	Central St.	McAllen, Texas
1984	Troy St.	Chan Gailey	18-17	North Dak. St.	McAllen, Texas
1985	North Dak. St.	Earle Solomonson	35-7	North Ala.	McAllen, Texas
1986	North Dak. St.	Earle Solomonson	27-7	South Dak.	Florence, Ala.
1987	Troy St.	Rick Rhoades	31-17	Portland St.	Florence, Ala.
1988	North Dak. St.	Rocky Hager	35-21	Portland St.	Florence, Ala.
1989	*Mississippi Col.	John Williams	3-0	Jacksonville St.	Florence, Ala.
1990	North Dak. St.	Rocky Hager	51-11	Indiana (Pa.)	Florence, Ala.
1991	Pittsburg St.	Chuck Broyles	23-6	Jacksonville St.	Florence, Ala.
1992	Jacksonville St.	Bill Burgess	17-13	Pittsburg St.	Florence, Ala.
1993	North Ala.	Bobby Wallace	41-34	Indiana (Pa.)	Florence, Ala.
1994	North Ala.	Bobby Wallace	16-10	Tex. A&M-Kingsville	Florence, Ala.
1995	North Ala.	Bobby Wallace	27-7	Pittsburg St.	Florence, Ala.
1996	Northern Colo.	Joe Glenn	23-14	Carson-Newman	Florence, Ala.
1997	Northern Colo.	Joe Glenn	51-0	New Haven	Florence, Ala.

**Mississippi College's participation in the 1989 Division II championship vacated by the NCAA Committee on Infractions.*

Regional Championship Results

Before 1973, there was no Division II Football Championship. Instead, four regional bowl games were played in order to provide postseason action for what then were called NCAA College Division member institutions. Following are the results of those bowl games:

Year	Champion	Coach	Score	Runner-Up	Site
EAST (TANGERINE BOWL)					
1964	East Caro.	Clarence Stasavich	14-13	Massachusetts	Orlando, Fla.
1965	East Caro.	Clarence Stasavich	31-0	Maine	Orlando, Fla.
1966	Morgan St.	Earl Banks	14-6	West Chester	Orlando, Fla.
1967	Tenn.-Martin	Robert Carroll	25-8	West Chester	Orlando, Fla.
EAST (BOARDWALK BOWL)					
1968	Delaware	Tubby Raymond	31-24	Indiana (Pa.)	Atlantic City, N.J.
1969	Delaware	Tubby Raymond	31-13	N.C. Central	Atlantic City, N.J.
1970	Delaware	Tubby Raymond	38-23	Morgan St.	Atlantic City, N.J.
1971	Delaware	Tubby Raymond	72-22	LIU-C. W. Post	Atlantic City, N.J.
1972	Massachusetts	Dick MacPherson	35-14	UC Davis	Atlantic City, N.J.
MIDEAST (GRANTLAND RICE BOWL)					
1964	Middle Tenn. St.	Charles Murphy	20-0	Muskingum	Murfreesboro, Tenn.
1965	Ball St.	Ray Louthen	14-14	—	Murfreesboro, Tenn.
	Tennessee St.	John Merritt			
1966	Tennessee St.	John Merritt	34-7	Muskingum	Murfreesboro, Tenn.
1967	Eastern Ky.	Roy Kidd	27-13	Ball St.	Murfreesboro, Tenn.
1968	Louisiana Tech	Maxie Lambright	33-13	Akron	Murfreesboro, Tenn.
1969	East Tenn. St.	John Bell	34-14	Louisiana Tech	Baton Rouge, La.
1970	Tennessee St.	John Merritt	26-25	Southwestern La.	Baton Rouge, La.
1971	Tennessee St.	John Merritt	26-23	McNeese St.	Baton Rouge, La.
1972	Louisiana Tech	Maxie Lambright	35-0	Tennessee Tech	Baton Rouge, La.
MIDWEST (PECAN BOWL)					
1964	Northern Iowa	Stan Sheriff	19-17	Lamar	Abilene, Texas
1965	North Dak. St.	Darrell Mudra	20-7	Grambling	Abilene, Texas
1966	North Dak.	Marv Helling	42-24	Parsons	Abilene, Texas
1967	Texas-Arlington	Burley Bearden	13-0	North Dak. St.	Abilene, Texas
1968	North Dak. St.	Ron Erhardt	23-14	Arkansas St.	Arlington, Texas
1969	Arkansas St.	Bennie Ellender	29-21	Drake	Arlington, Texas
1970	Arkansas St.	Bennie Ellender	38-21	Central Mo. St.	Arlington, Texas
MIDWEST (PIONEER BOWL)					
1971	Louisiana Tech	Maxie Lambright	14-3	Eastern Mich.	Wichita Falls, Texas
1972	Tennessee St.	John Merritt	29-7	Drake	Wichita Falls, Texas
WEST (CAMELLIA BOWL)					
1964	Montana St.	Jim Sweeney	28-7	Cal St. Sacramento	Sacramento, Calif.
1965	Cal St. Los Angeles	Homer Beatty	18-10	UC Santa Barb.	Sacramento, Calif.
1966	San Diego St.	Don Coryell	28-7	Montana St.	Sacramento, Calif.
1967	San Diego St.	Don Coryell	27-6	San Fran. St.	Sacramento, Calif.
1968	Humboldt St.	Frank VanDeren	29-14	Fresno St.	Sacramento, Calif.
1969	North Dak. St.	Ron Erhardt	30-3	Montana	Sacramento, Calif.
1970	North Dak. St.	Ron Erhardt	31-16	Montana	Sacramento, Calif.
1971	Boise St.	Tony Knap	32-28	Cal St. Chico	Sacramento, Calif.
1972	North Dak.	Jerry Olson	38-21	Cal Poly	Sacramento, Calif.

1997 Division II Championship Results

FIRST ROUND
UC Davis 37, Tex. A&M-Kingsville 34
Angelo St. 46, Western St. 12
New Haven 47, Glenville St. 7
Slippery Rock 30, Ashland 20
Northwest Mo. St. 39, North Dak. St. 28
Northern Colo. 24, Pittsburg St. 16
Carson-Newman 21, North Ala. 7
Albany St. (Ga.) 10, Southern Ark. 6

QUARTERFINALS
UC Davis 50, Angelo St. 33
New Haven 49, Slippery Rock 21
Northern Colo. 35, Northwest Mo. St. 28
Carson-Newman 23, Albany St. (Ga.) 22

SEMIFINALS
New Haven 27, UC Davis 25
Northern Colo. 30, Carson-Newman 29

CHAMPIONSHIP
Northern Colo. 51, New Haven 0

Championship Records

INDIVIDUAL: SINGLE GAME

NET YARDS RUSHING
379—Ronald Moore, Pittsburg St. (41) vs. Portland St. (38), 12-5-92.

RUSHES ATTEMPTED
51—Terry Morrow, Central St. (31) vs. Towson (0), 11-28-86.

TOUCHDOWNS BY RUSHING
5—Ronald Moore, Pittsburg St. (38) vs. North Dak. St. (37), OT, 11-28-92; Ronald Moore, Pittsburg St. (41) vs. Portland St. (38), 12-5-92.

NET YARDS PASSING
482—Kevin Daft, UC Davis (25) vs. New Haven (27), 12-6-97.

PASSES ATTEMPTED
64—Kevin Daft, UC Davis (25) vs. New Haven (27), 12-6-97.

PASSES COMPLETED
43—Kevin Daft, UC Davis (25) vs. New Haven (27), 12-6-97.

PASSES HAD INTERCEPTED
7—George Coussan, Southwestern La. (25) vs. Tennessee St. (26), 12-12-70.

TOUCHDOWN PASSES COMPLETED
6—Darren Del'Andrae, Portland St. (56) vs. West Chester (50), 3 OT, 11-18-89.

COMPLETION PERCENTAGE (Min. 8 Attempts)
.909—Kevin Feeney, North Dak. St. (41) vs. North Dak. (10), 10-11, 11-18-95.

NET YARDS RUSHING AND PASSING
505—Kevin Daft, UC Davis (25) vs. New Haven (27), 12-6-97.

NUMBER OF RUSHING AND PASSING PLAYS
69—Kevin Daft, UC Davis (25) vs. New Haven (27), 12-6-97.

PUNTING AVERAGE (Min. 3 Punts)
53.7—Chris Humes, UC Davis (23) vs. Angelo St. (28), 11-18-89.

NUMBER OF PUNTS
12—Dan Gentry, Tennessee Tech (0) vs. Louisiana Tech (35), 12-9-72.

PASSES CAUGHT
14—Don Hutt, Boise St. (34) vs. Louisiana Tech (38), 12-8-73.

NET YARDS RECEIVING
220—Steve Hansley, Northwest Mo. St. (15) vs. Neb.-Omaha (28), 11-24-84.

TOUCHDOWN PASSES CAUGHT
4—Steve Kreider, Lehigh (30) vs. Massachusetts (23), 11-26-77; Scott Asman, West Chester (50) vs. Portland St. (56), 3 OT, 11-18-89; Brian Penecale, West Chester (40) vs. Ferris St. (43), 11-19-94.

PASSES INTERCEPTED
5—Don Pinson, Tennessee St. (26) vs. Southwestern La. (25), 12-12-70.

YARDS GAINED ON INTERCEPTION RETURNS
113—Darren Ryals, Millersville (27) vs. Indiana (Pa.) (24), 2 returns for 53- and 60-yard TDs, 11-19-88.

YARDS GAINED ON PUNT RETURNS
138—Rick Caswell, Western Ky. (14) vs. New Hampshire (3), 12-6-75.

YARDS GAINED ON KICKOFF RETURNS
215—Sean Smith, Bloomsburg (29) vs. Clarion (42), 11-23-96.

POINTS
32—Ronald Moore, Pittsburg St. (38) vs. North Dak. St. (37), OT, 11-28-92; Ronald Moore, Pittsburg St. (41) vs. Portland St. (38), 12-5-92.

TOUCHDOWNS
5—Ronald Moore, Pittsburg St. (38) vs. North Dak. St. (37), OT, 11-28-92; Ronald Moore, Pittsburg St. (41) vs. Portland St. (38), 12-5-92; Dexter Deese, Tex. A&M-Kingsville (43) vs. Western St. (7), 11-19-94.

EXTRA POINTS
10—Larry Washington, Delaware (72) vs. LIU-C. W. Post (22), 12-11-71.

FIELD GOALS
4—Mario Ferretti, Northern Mich. (55) vs. Elizabeth City St. (6), 11-28-81; Ken Kubisz, North Dak. St. (26) vs. UC Davis (17), 12-3-83.

INDIVIDUAL: TOURNAMENT

NET YARDS RUSHING
721—Ronald Moore, Pittsburg St., 1992 (108 vs. North Dak., 151 vs. North Dak. St., 379 vs. Portland St., 83 vs. Jacksonville St.).

RUSHES ATTEMPTED
117—Ronald Moore, Pittsburg St., 1992 (29 vs. North Dak., 31 vs. North Dak. St., 37 vs. Portland St., 20 vs. Jacksonville St.).

NET YARDS PASSING
1,226—Chris Crawford, Portland St., 1988 (248 vs. Bowie St., 375 vs. Jacksonville St., 270 vs. Tex. A&M-Kingsville, 333 vs. North Dak. St.).

PASSES ATTEMPTED
140—Kevin Daft, UC Davis, 1997 (44 vs. Tex. A&M-Kingsville, 32 vs. Angelo St., 64 vs. New Haven).

PASSES COMPLETED
94—Chris Crawford, Portland St., 1988 (20 vs. Bowie St., 27 vs. Jacksonville St., 25 vs. Tex. A&M-Kingsville, 22 vs. North Dak. St.).

TOUCHDOWN PASSES COMPLETED
12—Kevin Daft, UC Davis, 1997 (5 vs. Tex. A&M-Kingsville, 4 vs. Angelo St., 3 vs. New Haven).

COMPLETION PERCENTAGE (Min. 2 Games)
.824—Mike Turk, Troy St., 1984, 14 of 17 (4-5 vs. Central St., 5-5 vs. Towson, 5-7 vs. North Dak. St.).

PASSES HAD INTERCEPTED
9—Dennis Tomek, Western Ky., 1973 (0 vs. Lehigh, 6 vs. Grambling, 3 vs. Louisiana Tech).

PASSES CAUGHT
27—Don Hutt, Boise St., 1973 (13 vs. South Dak., 14 vs. Louisiana Tech).

NET YARDS RECEIVING
452—Henry Newson, Portland St., 1991 (94 vs. Northern Colo., 209 vs. Mankato St., 149 vs. Pittsburg St.).

TOUCHDOWN PASSES CAUGHT
7—Steve Kreider, Lehigh, 1977 (4 vs. Massachusetts, 1 vs. UC Davis, 2 vs. Jacksonville St.).

POINTS
88—Ronald Moore, Pittsburg St., 1992 (18 vs. North Dak., 32 vs. North Dak. St., 32 vs. Portland St., 6 vs. Jacksonville St.).

TOUCHDOWNS
14—Ronald Moore, Pittsburg St., 1992 (3 vs. North Dak., 5 vs. North Dak. St., 5 vs. Portland St., 1 vs. Jacksonville St.).

INDIVIDUAL: LONGEST PLAYS

LONGEST RUSH
98—Wesley Whiten, Tex. A&M-Kingsville (59) vs. Fort Hays St. (28), 11-18-95.

LONGEST PASS COMPLETION
99—Ken Suhl to Tony Willis, New Haven (35) vs. Ferris St. (13), 11-28-92, TD.

LONGEST FIELD GOAL
50—Ted Clem, Troy St. (18) vs. North Dak. St. (17), 12-8-84.

LONGEST PUNT
76—Chris Humes, UC Davis (23) vs. Angelo St. (28), 11-18-89.

LONGEST PUNT RETURN
91—Winford Wilborn, Louisiana Tech (14) vs. Eastern Mich. (3), 12-11-71, TD.

LONGEST KICKOFF RETURN
100—Ken Bowles, UNLV (6) vs. Akron (26), 11-26-76, TD.

LONGEST INTERCEPTION RETURN
100—Charles Harris, Jacksonville St. (34) vs. Truman St. (21), 11-27-82, TD.

LONGEST FUMBLE RETURN
93—Ray Neal, Middle Tenn. St. (20) vs. Muskingum (0), 12-12-64, TD.

TEAM: SINGLE GAME

FIRST DOWNS
34—Delaware (60) vs. Mississippi Col. (10), 12-1-79; Cal St. Sacramento (56) vs. N.C. Central (7), 11-26-88.

FIRST DOWNS BY RUSHING
27—Delaware (72) vs. LIU-C. W. Post (22), 12-11-71.

FIRST DOWNS BY PASSING
25—UC Davis (25) vs. New Haven (27), 12-6-97.

NET YARDS RUSHING
566—Jacksonville St. (63) vs. West Chester (24), 11-19-88.

RUSHES ATTEMPTED
84—Southwest Tex. St. (34) vs. UC Davis (9), 12-11-82.

NET YARDS PASSING
482—UC Davis (25) vs. New Haven (27), 12-6-97.

PASSES ATTEMPTED
64—UC Davis (25) vs. New Haven (27), 12-6-97.

PASSES COMPLETED
43—UC Davis (25) vs. New Haven (27), 12-6-97.

COMPLETION PERCENTAGE (Min. 10 Attempts)
.909—North Dak. St. (41) vs. North Dak. (10), 10-11, 11-18-95.

PASSES HAD INTERCEPTED
8—Southwestern La. (25) vs. Tennessee St. (26), 12-12-70.

NET YARDS RUSHING AND PASSING
695—Northern Mich. (55) vs. Elizabeth City St. (6), 11-28-81.

RUSHING AND PASSING PLAYS
98—Northern Mich. (55) vs. Elizabeth City St. (6), 11-28-81.

PUNTING AVERAGE
53.7—UC Davis (23) vs. Angelo St. (28), 11-18-89.

NUMBER OF PUNTS
12—Delaware (8) vs. Grambling (17), 12-1-73; Western Ky. (0) vs. Louisiana Tech (34), 12-15-73.

PUNTS HAD BLOCKED
2—Truman St. (21) vs. Jacksonville St. (34), 11-27-82.

YARDS GAINED ON PUNT RETURNS
140—Southwest Tex. St. (62) vs. Northern Mich. (0), 12-5-81.

YARDS GAINED ON KICKOFF RETURNS
251—LIU-C. W. Post (22) vs. Delaware (72), 12-11-71.

YARDS GAINED ON INTERCEPTION RETURNS
131—Millersville (27) vs. Indiana (Pa.) (24), 11-19-88.

YARDS PENALIZED
185—Tex. A&M-Kingsville (30) vs. Portland St. (3), 11-25-95.

NUMBER OF PENALTIES
21—San Diego St. (27) vs. San Fran. St. (6), 12-9-67.

FUMBLES
10—Winston-Salem (0) vs. Delaware (41), 12-2-78.

FUMBLES LOST
7—Louisiana Tech (10) vs. Western Caro. (7), 11-30-74.

POINTS
*63—Jacksonville St. vs. West Chester (24), 11-19-88.
**Mississippi Col. defeated Wofford, 70-19, on 11-17-90, but its participation was vacated.*

TEAM: TOURNAMENT

FIRST DOWNS
99—North Ala., 1993 (25 vs. Carson-Newman, 30 vs. Hampton, 23 vs. Tex. A&M-Kingsville, 21 vs. Indiana, Pa.).

NET YARDS RUSHING
1,660—North Dak. St., 1988 (474 vs. Augustana [S.D.], 434 vs. Millersville, 413 vs. Cal St. Sacramento, 339 vs. Portland St.).

NET YARDS PASSING
1,226—Portland St., 1988 (248 vs. Bowie St., 375 vs. Jacksonville St., 270 vs. Tex. A&M-Kingsville, 333 vs. North Dak. St.).

NET YARDS RUSHING AND PASSING
2,032—North Ala., 1993 (455 vs. Carson-Newman, 570 vs. Hampton, 470 vs. Tex. A&M-Kingsville, 537 vs. Indiana, Pa.).

PASSES ATTEMPTED
143—UC Davis, 1997 (44 vs. Tex. A&M-Kingsville, 35 vs. Angelo St., 64 vs. New Haven).

PASSES COMPLETED
94—Portland St., 1988 (20 vs. Bowie St., 27 vs. Jacksonville St., 25 vs. Tex. A&M-Kingsville, 22 vs. North Dak. St.).

PASSES HAD INTERCEPTED
10—Western Ky., 1973 (0 vs. Lehigh, 6 vs. Grambling, 4 vs. Louisiana Tech).

NUMBER OF PUNTS
29—Western Ky., 1973 (6 vs. Lehigh, 11 vs. Grambling, 12 vs. Louisiana Tech).

YARDS PENALIZED
355—New Haven, 1992 (114 vs. West Chester, 146 vs. Ferris St., 95 vs. Jacksonville St.).

FUMBLES
16—Delaware, 1978 (8 vs. Jacksonville St., 2 vs. Winston-Salem, 6 vs. Eastern Ill.).

FUMBLES LOST
12—Delaware, 1978 (6 vs. Jacksonville St., 2 vs. Winston-Salem, 4 vs. Eastern Ill.).

POINTS
162—North Dak. St., 1988 (49 vs. Augustana [S.D.], 36 vs. Millersville, 42 vs. Cal St. Sacramento, 35 vs. Portland St.).

Year-by-Year Division II Championship Results

Year (Number of Teams)	Coach	Record	Result
1973 (8)			
Louisiana Tech	Maxie Lambright	3-0	Champion
Western Ky.	Jimmy Feix	2-1	Second
Boise St.	Tony Knap	1-1	Semifinalist
Grambling	Eddie Robinson	1-1	Semifinalist
Delaware	Tubby Raymond	0-1	Lost 1st Round
Lehigh	Fred Dunlap	0-1	Lost 1st Round
South Dak.	Joe Salem	0-1	Lost 1st Round
Western Ill.	Darrell Mudra	0-1	Lost 1st Round
1974 (8)			
Central Mich.	Roy Kramer	3-0	Champion
Delaware	Tubby Raymond	2-1	Second
Louisiana Tech	Maxie Lambright	1-1	Semifinalist
UNLV	Ron Meyer	1-1	Semifinalist
Alcorn St.	Marino Casem	0-1	Lost 1st Round
Boise St.	Tony Knap	0-1	Lost 1st Round
Western Caro.	Bob Waters	0-1	Lost 1st Round
Youngstown St.	Rey Dempsey	0-1	Lost 1st Round
1975 (8)			
Northern Mich.	Gil Krueger	3-0	Champion
Western Ky.	Jimmy Feix	2-1	Second
New Hampshire	Bill Bowes	1-1	Semifinalist
West Ala.	Jim King	1-1	Semifinalist
Boise St.	Tony Knap	0-1	Lost 1st Round
Lehigh	Fred Dunlap	0-1	Lost 1st Round
North Dak.	Jerry Olson	0-1	Lost 1st Round
Northern Iowa	Stan Sheriff	0-1	Lost 1st Round
1976 (8)			
Montana St.	Sonny Holland	3-0	Champion
Akron	Jim Dennison	2-1	Second
North Dak. St.	Jim Wacker	1-1	Semifinalist
Northern Mich.	Gil Krueger	1-1	Semifinalist
Delaware	Tubby Raymond	0-1	Lost 1st Round
Eastern Ky.	Roy Kidd	0-1	Lost 1st Round
UNLV	Tony Knap	0-1	Lost 1st Round
New Hampshire	Bill Bowes	0-1	Lost 1st Round
1977 (8)			
Lehigh	John Whitehead	3-0	Champion
Jacksonville St.	Jim Fuller	2-1	Second
UC Davis	Jim Sochor	1-1	Semifinalist
North Dak. St.	Jim Wacker	1-1	Semifinalist
Bethune-Cookman	Andy Hinson	0-1	Lost 1st Round
Massachusetts	Dick MacPherson	0-1	Lost 1st Round
Northern Ariz.	Joe Salem	0-1	Lost 1st Round
Northern Mich.	Gil Krueger	0-1	Lost 1st Round
1978 (8)			
Eastern Ill.	Darrell Mudra	3-0	Champion
Delaware	Tubby Raymond	2-1	Second
Winston-Salem	Bill Hayes	1-1	Semifinalist
Youngstown St.	Bill Narduzzi	1-1	Semifinalist
UC Davis	Jim Sochor	0-1	Lost 1st Round
Cal Poly	Joe Harper	0-1	Lost 1st Round
Jacksonville St.	Jim Fuller	0-1	Lost 1st Round
Neb.-Omaha	Sandy Buda	0-1	Lost 1st Round
1979 (8)			
Delaware	Tubby Raymond	3-0	Champion
Youngstown St.	Bill Narduzzi	2-1	Second
Alabama A&M	Ray Greene	1-1	Semifinalist
Mississippi Col.	John Williams	1-1	Semifinalist
Morgan St.	Clarence Thomas	0-1	Lost 1st Round
North Dak.	Gene Murphy	0-1	Lost 1st Round
South Dak. St.	John Gregory	0-1	Lost 1st Round
Virginia Union	Willard Bailey	0-1	Lost 1st Round
1980 (8)			
Cal Poly	Joe Harper	3-0	Champion
Eastern Ill.	Darrell Mudra	2-1	Second
North Ala.	Wayne Grubb	1-1	Semifinalist
Santa Clara	Pat Malley	1-1	Semifinalist
Jacksonville St.	Jim Fuller	0-1	Lost 1st Round
Northern Colo.	Bob Blasi	0-1	Lost 1st Round
Northern Mich.	Bill Rademacher	0-1	Lost 1st Round
Virginia Union	Willard Bailey	0-1	Lost 1st Round
1981 (8)			
Southwest Tex. St.	Jim Wacker	3-0	Champion
North Dak. St.	Don Morton	2-1	Second
Northern Mich.	Bill Rademacher	1-1	Semifinalist
Shippensburg	Vito Ragazzo	1-1	Semifinalist
Elizabeth City St.	Johnnie Walton	0-1	Lost 1st Round
Jacksonville St.	Jim Fuller	0-1	Lost 1st Round
Puget Sound	Ron Simonson	0-1	Lost 1st Round
Virginia Union	Willard Bailey	0-1	Lost 1st Round
1982 (8)			
Southwest Tex. St.	Jim Wacker	3-0	Champion
UC Davis	Jim Sochor	2-1	Second
Jacksonville St.	Jim Fuller	1-1	Semifinalist
North Dak. St.	Don Morton	1-1	Semifinalist
Fort Valley St.	Doug Porter	0-1	Lost 1st Round
Northern Mich.	Bill Rademacher	0-1	Lost 1st Round
Truman St.	Bruce Craddock	0-1	Lost 1st Round
Virginia Union	Willard Bailey	0-1	Lost 1st Round
1983 (8)			
North Dak. St.	Don Morton	3-0	Champion
Central St.	Billy Joe	2-1	Second
UC Davis	Jim Sochor	1-1	Semifinalist
North Ala.	Wayne Grubb	1-1	Semifinalist
Butler	Bill Sylvester	0-1	Lost 1st Round
Southwest Tex. St.	John O'Hara	0-1	Lost 1st Round
Towson	Phil Albert	0-1	Lost 1st Round
Virginia Union	Willard Bailey	0-1	Lost 1st Round
1984 (8)			
Troy St.	Chan Gailey	3-0	Champion
North Dak. St.	Don Morton	2-1	Second
Neb.-Omaha	Sandy Buda	1-1	Semifinalist
Towson	Phil Albert	1-1	Semifinalist

Year (Number of Teams)	Coach	Record	Result
UC Davis	Jim Sochor	0-1	Lost 1st Round
Central St.	Billy Joe	0-1	Lost 1st Round
Norfolk St.	Willard Bailey	0-1	Lost 1st Round
Northwest Mo. St.	Vern Thomsen	0-1	Lost 1st Round

1985 (8)

Year (Number of Teams)	Coach	Record	Result
North Dak. St.	Earle Solomonson	3-0	Champion
North Ala.	Wayne Grubb	2-1	Second
Bloomsburg	George Landis	1-1	Semifinalist
South Dak.	Dave Triplett	1-1	Semifinalist
UC Davis	Jim Sochor	0-1	Lost 1st Round
Central St.	Billy Joe	0-1	Lost 1st Round
Fort Valley St.	Gerald Walker	0-1	Lost 1st Round
Hampton	Fred Freeman	0-1	Lost 1st Round

1986 (8)

Year (Number of Teams)	Coach	Record	Result
North Dak. St.	Earle Solomonson	3-0	Champion
South Dak.	Dave Triplett	2-1	Second
Central St.	Billy Joe	1-1	Semifinalist
Troy St.	Rick Rhodes	1-1	Semifinalist
Ashland	Fred Martinelli	0-1	Lost 1st Round
UC Davis	Jim Sochor	0-1	Lost 1st Round
Towson	Phil Albert	0-1	Lost 1st Round
Virginia Union	Joe Taylor	0-1	Lost 1st Round

1987 (8)

Year (Number of Teams)	Coach	Record	Result
Troy St.	Rick Rhodes	3-0	Champion
Portland St.	Pokey Allen	2-1	Second
Central Fla.	Gene McDowell	1-1	Semifinalist
Northern Mich.	Herb Grenke	1-1	Semifinalist
Angelo St.	Jerry Vandergriff	0-1	Lost 1st Round
Indiana (Pa.)	Frank Cignetti	0-1	Lost 1st Round
Mankato St.	Dan Runkle	0-1	Lost 1st Round
Winston-Salem	Bill Hayes	0-1	Lost 1st Round

1988 (16)

Year (Number of Teams)	Coach	Record	Result
North Dak. St.	Rocky Hager	4-0	Champion
Portland St.	Pokey Allen	3-1	Second
Cal St. Sacramento	Bob Mattos	2-1	Semifinalist
Tex. A&M-Kingsville	Ron Harms	2-1	Semifinalist
Jacksonville St.	Bill Burgess	1-1	Quarterfinalist
Millersville	Gene Carpenter	1-1	Quarterfinalist
N.C. Central	Henry Lattimore	1-1	Quarterfinalist
Tenn.-Martin	Don McLeary	1-1	Quarterfinalist
Augustana (S.D.)	Jim Heinitz	0-1	Lost 1st Round
Bowie St.	Sanders Shiver	0-1	Lost 1st Round
Butler	Bill Lynch	0-1	Lost 1st Round
UC Davis	Jim Sochor	0-1	Lost 1st Round
Indiana (Pa.)	Frank Cignetti	0-1	Lost 1st Round
Mississippi Col.	John Williams	0-1	Lost 1st Round
West Chester	Danny Hale	0-1	Lost 1st Round
Winston-Salem	Pete Richardson	0-1	Lost 1st Round

1989 (16)

Year (Number of Teams)	Coach	Record	Result
*Mississippi Col.	John Williams	4-0	Champion
Jacksonville St.	Bill Burgess	3-1	Second
Angelo St.	Jerry Vandergriff	2-1	Semifinalist
Indiana (Pa.)	Frank Cignetti	2-1	Semifinalist
North Dak. St.	Rocky Hager	1-1	Quarterfinalist
Pittsburg St.	Dennis Franchione	1-1	Quarterfinalist
Portland St.	Pokey Allen	1-1	Quarterfinalist
St. Cloud St.	Noel Martin	1-1	Quarterfinalist
Alabama A&M	George Pugh	0-1	Lost 1st Round
Augustana (S.D.)	Jim Heinitz	0-1	Lost 1st Round
UC Davis	Bob Foster	0-1	Lost 1st Round
Edinboro	Tom Hollman	0-1	Lost 1st Round
Grand Valley St.	Tom Beck	0-1	Lost 1st Round
Northwest Mo. St.	Bud Elliott	0-1	Lost 1st Round
Tex. A&M-Kingsville	Ron Harms	0-1	Lost 1st Round
West Chester	Rick Daniels	0-1	Lost 1st Round

1990 (16)

Year (Number of Teams)	Coach	Record	Result
North Dak. St.	Rocky Hager	4-0	Champion
Indiana (Pa.)	Frank Cignetti	3-1	Second
*Mississippi Col.	John Williams	2-1	Semifinalist
Pittsburg St.	Chuck Broyles	2-1	Semifinalist
Cal Poly	Lyle Setencich	1-1	Quarterfinalist
East Tex. St.	Eddie Vowell	1-1	Quarterfinalist
Edinboro	Tom Hollman	1-1	Quarterfinalist
Jacksonville St.	Bill Burgess	1-1	Quarterfinalist
Cal St. Northridge	Bob Burt	0-1	Lost 1st Round
Grand Valley St.	Tom Beck	0-1	Lost 1st Round
North Ala.	Bobby Wallace	0-1	Lost 1st Round
Northern Colo.	Joe Glenn	0-1	Lost 1st Round
Truman St.	Eric Holm	0-1	Lost 1st Round
Virginia Union	Joe Taylor	0-1	Lost 1st Round
Winston-Salem	Pete Richardson	0-1	Lost 1st Round
Wofford	Mike Ayers	0-1	Lost 1st Round

1991 (16)

Year (Number of Teams)	Coach	Record	Result
Pittsburg St.	Chuck Broyles	4-0	Champion
Jacksonville St.	Bill Burgess	3-1	Second
Indiana (Pa.)	Frank Cignetti	2-1	Semifinalist
Portland St.	Pokey Allen	2-1	Semifinalist
East Tex. St.	Eddie Vowell	1-1	Quarterfinalist
Mankato St.	Dan Runkle	1-1	Quarterfinalist
Mississippi Col.	Terry McMillan	1-1	Quarterfinalist
Shippensburg	Rocky Rees	1-1	Quarterfinalist
Butler	Bob Bartolomeo	0-1	Lost 1st Round
East Stroudsburg	Dennis Douds	0-1	Lost 1st Round
Grand Valley St.	Brian Kelly	0-1	Lost 1st Round
North Dak. St.	Rocky Hager	0-1	Lost 1st Round
Northern Colo.	Joe Glenn	0-1	Lost 1st Round
Virginia Union	Joe Taylor	0-1	Lost 1st Round
Winston-Salem	Pete Richardson	0-1	Lost 1st Round
Wofford	Mike Ayers	0-1	Lost 1st Round

1992 (16)

Year (Number of Teams)	Coach	Record	Result
Jacksonville St.	Bill Burgess	4-0	Champion
Pittsburg St.	Chuck Broyles	3-1	Second
New Haven	Mark Whipple	2-1	Semifinalist
Portland St.	Pokey Allen	2-1	Semifinalist
Ferris St.	Keith Otterbein	1-1	Quarterfinalist
North Ala.	Bobby Wallace	1-1	Quarterfinalist
North Dak. St.	Rocky Hager	1-1	Quarterfinalist
Tex. A&M-Kingsville	Ron Harms	1-1	Quarterfinalist
UC Davis	Bob Foster	0-1	Lost 1st Round
Edinboro	Tom Hollman	0-1	Lost 1st Round
Hampton	Joe Taylor	0-1	Lost 1st Round
North Dak.	Roger Thomas	0-1	Lost 1st Round
Savannah St.	Bill Davis	0-1	Lost 1st Round
Truman St.	Eric Holm	0-1	Lost 1st Round
West Chester	Rick Daniels	0-1	Lost 1st Round
Western St.	Carl Iverson	0-1	Lost 1st Round

1993 (16)

Year (Number of Teams)	Coach	Record	Result
North Ala.	Bobby Wallace	4-0	Champion
Indiana (Pa.)	Frank Cignetti	3-1	Second
North Dak.	Roger Thomas	2-1	Semifinalist
Tex. A&M-Kingsville	Ron Harms	2-1	Semifinalist
UC Davis	Bob Biggs	1-1	Quarterfinalist
Hampton	Joe Taylor	1-1	Quarterfinalist
Mankato St.	Dan Runkle	1-1	Quarterfinalist
New Haven	Mark Whipple	1-1	Quarterfinalist
Albany St. (Ga.)	Hampton Smith	0-1	Lost 1st Round
Carson-Newman	Ken Sparks	0-1	Lost 1st Round
Edinboro	Tom Hollman	0-1	Lost 1st Round
Ferris St.	Keith Otterbein	0-1	Lost 1st Round
Fort Hays St.	Bob Cortese	0-1	Lost 1st Round
Mo. Southern St.	Jon Lantz	0-1	Lost 1st Round
Pittsburg St.	Chuck Broyles	0-1	Lost 1st Round
Portland St.	Tim Walsh	0-1	Lost 1st Round

1994 (16)

Year (Number of Teams)	Coach	Record	Result
North Ala.	Bobby Wallace	4-0	Champion
Tex. A&M-Kingsville	Ron Harms	3-1	Second
Indiana (Pa.)	Frank Cignetti	2-1	Semifinalist
North Dak.	Roger Thomas	2-1	Semifinalist
Ferris St.	Keith Otterbein	1-1	Quarterfinalist
North Dak. St.	Rocky Hager	1-1	Quarterfinalist
Portland St.	Tim Walsh	1-1	Quarterfinalist
Valdosta St.	Hal Mumme	1-1	Quarterfinalist
Albany St. (Ga.)	Hampton Smith	0-1	Lost 1st Round
Angelo St.	Jerry Vandergriff	0-1	Lost 1st Round
Carson-Newman	Ken Sparks	0-1	Lost 1st Round
Grand Valley St.	Brian Kelly	0-1	Lost 1st Round
Pittsburg St.	Chuck Broyles	0-1	Lost 1st Round
Truman St.	Eric Holm	0-1	Lost 1st Round
West Chester	Rick Daniels	0-1	Lost 1st Round
Western St.	Carl Iverson	0-1	Lost 1st Round

1995 (16)

Year (Number of Teams)	Coach	Record	Result
North Ala.	Bobby Wallace	4-0	Champion
Pittsburg St.	Chuck Broyles	3-1	Second
Ferris St.	Jeff Pierce	2-1	Semifinalist
Tex. A&M-Kingsville	Ron Harms	2-1	Semifinalist
Carson-Newman	Ken Sparks	1-1	Quarterfinalist
New Haven	Tony Sparano	1-1	Quarterfinalist
North Dak. St.	Rocky Hager	1-1	Quarterfinalist
Portland St.	Tim Walsh	1-1	Quarterfinalist
Albany St. (Ga.)	Hampton Smith	0-1	Lost 1st Round
East Tex. St.	Eddie Vowell	0-1	Lost 1st Round
Edinboro	Tom Hollman	0-1	Lost 1st Round
Fort Hays St.	Bob Cortese	0-1	Lost 1st Round
Millersville	Gene Carpenter	0-1	Lost 1st Round

Year (Number of Teams)	Coach	Record	Result
North Dak.	Roger Thomas	0-1	Lost 1st Round
Northern Colo.	Joe Glenn	0-1	Lost 1st Round
West Ga.	Charlie Fisher	0-1	Lost 1st Round
1996 (16)			
Northern Colo.	Joe Glenn	4-0	Champion
Carson-Newman	Ken Sparks	3-1	Second
Clarion	Malen Luke	2-1	Semifinalist
UC Davis	Bob Biggs	2-1	Semifinalist
Ferris St.	Jeff Pierce	1-1	Quarterfinalist
Northwest Mo. St.	Mel Tjeerdsma	1-1	Quarterfinalist
Valdosta St.	Hal Mumme	1-1	Quarterfinalist
Central Okla.	Gary Howard	1-1	Quarterfinalist
Bloomsburg	Danny Hale	0-1	Lost 1st Round
Indiana (Pa.)	Frank Cignetti	0-1	Lost 1st Round
Pittsburg St.	Chuck Broyles	0-1	Lost 1st Round
Neb.-Omaha	Pat Behrns	0-1	Lost 1st Round
Albany St. (Ga.)	Hampton Smith	0-1	Lost 1st Round
West Ga.	Charlie Fisher	0-1	Lost 1st Round
Chadron St.	Brad Smith	0-1	Lost 1st Round
Tex. A&M-Kingsville	Ron Harms	0-1	Lost 1st Round
1997 (16)			
Northern Colo.	Joe Glenn	4-0	Champion
New Haven	Tony Sparano	3-1	Second
UC Davis	Bob Biggs	2-1	Semifinalist
Carson-Newman	Ken Sparks	2-1	Semifinalist
Angelo St.	Jerry Vandergriff	1-1	Quarterfinalist
Slippery Rock	George Mahalik	1-1	Quarterfinalist
Northwest Mo. St.	Mel Tjeerdsma	1-1	Quarterfinalist
Albany St. (Ga.)	Hampton Smith	1-1	Quarterfinalist
Tex. A&M-Kingsville	Ron Harms	0-1	Lost 1st Round
Western St.	Carl Iverson	0-1	Lost 1st Round
Glenville St.	Warren Ruggerio	0-1	Lost 1st Round
Ashland	Gary Keller	0-1	Lost 1st Round
North Dak. St.	Bob Babich	0-1	Lost 1st Round
Pittsburg St.	Chuck Broyles	0-1	Lost 1st Round
North Ala.	Bobby Wallace	0-1	Lost 1st Round
Southern Ark.	Steve Roberts	0-1	Lost 1st Round

**Competition in championship vacated by action of the NCAA Committee on Infractions.*

Division II Championship Record of Each College by Coach

(91 Colleges; 1973-97)

	Yrs	Won	Lost	CH	2D
AKRON					
Jim Dennison (Wooster '60) 76-2D	1	2	1	0	1
ALABAMA A&M					
Ray Green (Akron '63) 79	1	1	1	0	0
George Pugh (Alabama '76) 89	1	0	1	0	0
TOTAL	2	1	2	0	0
ALBANY ST. (GA.)					
Hampton Smith (Mississippi Val. '57) 93, 94, 95, 96, 97	5	1	5	0	0
ALCORN ST.					
Marino Casem (Xavier [La.] '56) 74	1	0	1	0	0
ANGELO ST.					
Jerry Vandergriff (Corpus Christi '65) 87, 89, 94, 97	4	3	4	0	0
ASHLAND					
Fred Martinelli (Otterbein '51) 86	1	0	1	0	0
Gary Keller (Bluffton '73) 97	1	0	1	0	0
TOTAL	2	0	2	0	0
AUGUSTANA (S.D.)					
Jim Heinitz (South Dak. St. '72) 88, 89	2	0	2	0	0
BETHUNE-COOKMAN					
Andy Hinson (Bethune-Cookman '53) 77	1	0	1	0	0
BLOOMSBURG					
George Landis (Penn St. '71) 85	1	1	1	0	0
Danny Hale (West Chester '68) 96	1	0	1	0	0
TOTAL	2	1	2	0	0
BOISE ST.					
Tony Knap (Idaho '39) 73, 74, 75	3	1	3	0	0
BOWIE ST.					
Sanders Shiver (Carson-Newman '76) 88	1	0	1	0	0
BUTLER					
Bill Sylvester (Butler '50) 83	1	0	1	0	0
Bill Lynch (Butler '77) 88	1	0	1	0	0
Bob Bartolomeo (Butler '77) 91	1	0	1	0	0
TOTAL	3	0	3	0	0
UC DAVIS					
Jim Sochor (San Fran. St. '60) 77, 78, 82-2D, 83, 84, 85, 86, 88	8	4	8	0	1
Bob Foster (UC Davis '62) 89, 92	2	0	2	0	0
Bob Biggs (UC Davis '73) 93, 96, 97	3	5	3	0	0
TOTAL	13	9	13	0	1
CAL POLY					
Joe Harper (UCLA '59) 78, 80-CH	2	3	1	1	0
Lyle Setencich (Fresno St. '68) 90	1	1	1	0	0
TOTAL	3	4	2	1	0
CAL ST. NORTHRIDGE					
Bob Burt (Cal St. Los Angeles '62) 90	1	0	1	0	0
CAL ST. SACRAMENTO					
Bob Mattos (Cal St. Sacramento '64) 88	1	2	1	0	0
CARSON-NEWMAN					
Ken Sparks (Carson-Newman '68) 93, 94, 95, 96-2D, 97	5	6	5	0	1
CENTRAL FLA.					
Gene McDowell (Florida St. '65) 87	1	1	1	0	0
CENTRAL MICH.					
Roy Kramer (Maryville [Tenn.] '53) 74-CH	1	3	0	1	0
CENTRAL OKLA.					
Gary Howard (Arkansas '64) 96	1	1	1	0	0
CENTRAL ST.					
Billy Joe (Villanova '63) 83-2D, 84, 85, 86	4	3	4	0	1
CHADRON ST.					
Brad Smith (Western Ill. '72) 96	1	0	1	0	0
CLARION					
Malen Luke (Westminster [Pa.] '76)	1	2	1	0	0
DELAWARE					
Harold "Tubby" Raymond (Michigan '50) 73, 74-2D, 76, 78-2D, 79-CH	5	7	4	1	2
EAST STROUDSBURG					
Dennis Douds (Slippery Rock '63) 91	1	0	1	0	0
EASTERN ILL.					
Darrell Mudra (Peru St. '51) 78-CH, 80-2D	2	5	1	1	1
EASTERN KY.					
Roy Kidd (Eastern Ky. '54) 76	1	0	1	0	0
EDINBORO					
Tom Hollman (Ohio Northern '68) 89, 90, 92, 93, 95	5	1	5	0	0
ELIZABETH CITY ST.					
Johnnie Walton (Elizabeth City St. '69) 81	1	0	1	0	0
FERRIS ST.					
Keith Otterbein (Ferris St. '79) 92, 93, 94	3	2	3	0	0
Jeff Pierce (Ferris St. '79) 95, 96	2	3	2	0	0
TOTAL	5	5	5	0	0
FORT HAYS ST.					
Bob Cortese (Colorado '67) 93, 95	2	0	2	0	0
FORT VALLEY ST.					
Doug Porter (Xavier [La.] '52) 82	1	0	1	0	0
Gerald Walker (Lincoln [Mo.] '62) 85	1	0	1	0	0
TOTAL	2	0	2	0	0
GLENVILLE ST.					
Warren Ruggerio (Delaware '88) 97	1	0	1	0	0
GRAMBLING					
Eddie Robinson (Leland '41) 73	1	1	1	0	0
GRAND VALLEY ST.					
Tom Beck (Northern Ill. '61) 89, 90	2	0	2	0	0
Brian Kelly (Assumption '83) 91, 94	2	0	2	0	0
TOTAL	4	0	4	0	0
HAMPTON					
Fred Freeman (Mississippi Val. '66) 85	1	0	1	0	0
Joe Taylor (Western Ill. '72) 92, 93	2	1	2	0	0
TOTAL	3	1	3	0	0
INDIANA (PA.)					
Frank Cignetti (Indiana [Pa.] '60) 87, 88, 89, 90-2D, 91, 93-2D, 94, 96	8	12	8	0	2
JACKSONVILLE ST.					
Jim Fuller (Alabama '67) 77-2D, 78, 80, 81, 82	5	3	5	0	1
Bill Burgess (Auburn '63) 88, 89-2D, 90, 91-2D, 92-CH	5	12	4	1	2
TOTAL	10	15	9	1	3
LEHIGH					
Fred Dunlap (Colgate '50) 73, 75	2	0	2	0	0
John Whitehead (East Stroudsburg '50) 77-CH	1	3	0	1	0
TOTAL	3	3	2	1	0

	Yrs	Won	Lost	CH	2D
LOUISIANA TECH					
Maxie Lambright (Southern Miss. '49) 73-CH, 74	2	4	1	1	0
MANKATO ST.					
Dan Runkle (Illinois Col. '68) 87, 91, 93	3	2	3	0	0
MASSACHUSETTS					
Dick MacPherson (Springfield '58) 77	1	0	1	0	0
MILLERSVILLE					
Gene Carpenter (Huron '63) 88, 95	2	1	2	0	0
MISSISSIPPI COL.*					
John Williams (Mississippi Col. '57) 79, 88, 89-CH, 90	4	7	3	1	0
Terry McMillan (Southern Miss. '69) 91	1	1	1	0	0
TOTAL	5	8	4	1	0
MO. SOUTHERN ST.					
Jon Lantz (Okla. Panhandle '74) 93	1	0	1	0	0
MONTANA ST.					
Sonny Holland (Montana St. '60) 76-CH	1	3	0	1	0
MORGAN ST.					
Clarence Thomas 79	1	0	1	0	0
NEB.-OMAHA					
Sandy Buda (Kansas '67) 78, 84	2	1	2	0	0
Pat Behrns (Dakota St. '72) 96	1	0	1	0	0
TOTAL	3	1	3	0	0
UNLV					
Ron Meyer (Purdue '63) 74	1	1	1	0	0
Tony Knap (Idaho '39) 76	1	0	1	0	0
TOTAL	2	1	2	0	0
NEW HAMPSHIRE					
Bill Bowes (Penn St. '65) 75, 76	2	1	2	0	0
NEW HAVEN					
Mark Whipple (Brown '79) 92, 93	2	3	2	0	0
Tony Sparano (New Haven '82) 95, 97-2D	2	4	2	0	1
TOTAL	4	7	4	0	1
NORFOLK ST.					
Willard Bailey (Norfolk St. '62) 84	1	0	1	0	0
NORTH ALA.					
Wayne Grubb (Tennessee '61) 80, 83, 85-2D	3	4	3	0	1
Bobby Wallace (Mississippi St. '76) 90, 92, 93-CH, 94-CH, 95-CH, 97	6	13	3	3	0
TOTAL	9	17	6	3	1
N.C. CENTRAL					
Henry Lattimore (Jackson St. '57) 88	1	1	1	0	0
NORTH DAK.					
Jerry Olson (Valley City St. '55) 75	1	0	1	0	0
Gene Murphy (North Dak. '62) 79	1	0	1	0	0
Roger Thomas (Augustana [Ill.] '69) 92, 93, 94, 95	4	4	4	0	0
TOTAL	6	4	6	0	0
NORTH DAK. ST.					
Jim Wacker (Valparaiso '60) 76, 77	2	2	2	0	0
Don Morton (Augustana [Ill.] '69) 81-2D, 82, 83-CH, 84-2D	4	8	3	1	2
Earle Solomonson (Augsburg '69) 85-CH, 86-CH	2	6	0	2	0
Rocky Hager (Minot St. '74) 88-CH, 89, 90-CH, 91, 92, 94, 95	7	12	5	2	0
Bob Babich (Tulsa '84) 97	1	0	1	0	0
TOTAL	16	28	11	5	2
NORTHERN ARIZ.					
Joe Salem (Minnesota '61) 77	1	0	1	0	0
NORTHERN COLO.					
Bob Blasi (Colorado St. '53) 80	1	0	1	0	0
Joe Glenn (South Dak. '71) 90, 91, 95, 96-CH, 97-CH	5	8	3	2	0
TOTAL	6	8	4	2	0
NORTHERN IOWA					
Stan Sheriff (Cal Poly '54) 75	1	0	1	0	0
NORTHERN MICH.					
Gil Krueger (Marquette '52) 75-CH, 76, 77	3	4	2	1	0
Bill Rademacher (Northern Mich. '63) 80, 81, 82	3	1	3	0	0
Herb Grenke (Wis.-Milwaukee '63) 87	1	1	1	0	0
TOTAL	7	6	6	1	0
NORTHWEST MO. ST.					
Vern Thomsen (Peru St. '61) 84	1	0	1	0	0
Bud Elliott (Baker '53) 89	1	0	1	0	0
Mel Tjeerdsma (Southern St. [S.D.] '67) 96, 97	2	2	2	0	0
TOTAL	4	2	4	0	0

	Yrs	Won	Lost	CH	2D
PITTSBURG ST.					
Dennis Franchione (Pittsburg St. '73) 89	1	1	1	0	0
Chuck Broyles (Pittsburg St. '70) 90, 91-CH, 92-2D, 93, 94, 95-2D, 96, 97	8	12	7	1	2
TOTAL	9	13	8	1	2
PORTLAND ST.					
Pokey Allen (Utah '65) 87-2D, 88-2D, 89, 91, 92	5	10	5	0	2
Tim Walsh (UC Riverside '77) 93, 94, 95	3	2	3	0	0
TOTAL	8	12	8	0	2
PUGET SOUND					
Ron Simonson (Portland St. '65) 81	1	0	1	0	0
ST. CLOUD ST.					
Noel Martin (Nebraska '63) 89	1	1	1	0	0
SANTA CLARA					
Pat Malley (Santa Clara '53) 80	1	1	1	0	0
SAVANNAH ST.					
Bill Davis (Johnson Smith '65) 92	1	0	1	0	0
SHIPPENSBURG					
Vito Ragazzo (William & Mary '51) 81	1	1	1	0	0
Rocky Rees (West Chester '71) 91	1	1	1	0	0
TOTAL	2	2	2	0	0
SLIPPERY ROCK					
George Mahalik (Slippery Rock '74) 97	1	1	1	0	0
SOUTH DAK.					
Joe Salem (Minnesota '61) 73	1	0	1	0	0
Dave Triplett (Iowa '72) 85, 86-2D	2	3	2	0	1
TOTAL	3	3	3	0	1
SOUTH DAK. ST.					
John Gregory (Northern Iowa '61) 79	1	0	1	0	0
SOUTHERN ARK.					
Steve Roberts (Ouachita Baptist '87) 97	1	0	1	0	0
SOUTHWEST TEX. ST.					
Jim Wacker (Valparaiso '60) 81-CH, 82-CH	2	6	0	2	0
John O'Hara (Okla. Panhandle '67) 83	1	0	1	0	0
TOTAL	3	6	1	2	0
TENN.-MARTIN					
Don McLeary (Tennessee '70) 88	1	1	1	0	0
TEX. A&M-COMMERCE					
Eddie Vowell (Southwestern Okla. '69) 90, 91, 95	3	2	3	0	0
TEX. A&M-KINGSVILLE					
Ron Harms (Valparaiso '59) 88, 89, 92, 93, 94-2D, 95, 96, 97	8	10	8	0	1
TOWSON					
Phil Albert (Arizona '66) 83, 84, 86	3	1	3	0	0
TROY ST.					
Chan Gailey (Florida '74) 84-CH	1	3	0	1	0
Rick Rhodes 86, 87-CH	2	4	1	1	0
TOTAL	3	7	1	2	0
TRUMAN ST.					
Bruce Craddock (Truman St. '66) 82	1	0	1	0	0
Eric Holm (Truman St. '81) 90, 92, 94	3	0	3	0	0
TOTAL	4	0	4	0	0
VALDOSTA ST.					
Hal Mumme (Tarleton St. '75) 94, 96	2	2	2	0	0
VIRGINIA UNION					
Willard Bailey (Norfolk St. '62) 79, 80, 81, 82, 83	5	0	5	0	0
Joe Taylor (Western Ill. '72) 86, 90, 91	3	0	3	0	0
TOTAL	8	0	8	0	0
WEST ALA.					
Jim King 75	1	1	1	0	0
WEST CHESTER					
Danny Hale (West Chester '68) 88	1	0	1	0	0
Rick Daniels (West Chester '75) 89, 92, 94	3	0	3	0	0
TOTAL	4	0	4	0	0
WEST GA.					
Charlie Fisher (Springfield '81) 95, 96	2	0	2	0	0
WESTERN CARO.					
Bob Waters (Presbyterian '60) 74	1	0	1	0	0
WESTERN ILL.					
Darrell Mudra (Peru St. '51) 73	1	0	1	0	0
WESTERN KY.					
Jimmy Feix (Western Ky. '53) 73-2D, 75-2D	2	4	2	0	2
WESTERN ST.					
Carl Iverson (Whitman '62) 92, 94, 97	3	0	3	0	0

	Yrs	Won	Lost	CH	2D
WINSTON-SALEM					
Bill Hayes (N.C. Central '64) 78, 87	2	1	2	0	0
Pete Richardson (Dayton '68) 88, 90, 91	3	0	3	0	0
TOTAL	5	1	5	0	0
WOFFORD					
Mike Ayers (Georgetown [Ky.] '74) 90, 91	2	0	2	0	0

	Yrs	Won	Lost	CH	2D
YOUNGSTOWN ST.					
Rey Dempsey (Geneva '58) 74	1	0	1	0	0
Bill Narduzzi (Miami [Ohio] '59) 78, 79-2D	2	3	2	0	1
TOTAL	3	3	3	0	1

Mississippi College's competition in the 1989 and 1990 Division II championships was vacated by action of the NCAA Committee on Infractions (official record is 2-3).

All-Time Results

1973 First Round: Grambling 17, Delaware 8; Western Ky. 25, Lehigh 16; Louisiana Tech 18, Western Ill. 13; Boise St. 53, South Dak. 10. **Semifinals:** Western Ky. 28, Grambling 20; Louisiana Tech 38, Boise St. 34. **Championship:** Louisiana Tech 34, Western Ky. 0.

1974 First Round: Central Mich. 20, Boise St. 6; Louisiana Tech 10, Western Caro. 7; UNLV 35, Alcorn St. 22; Delaware 35, Youngstown St. 14. **Semifinals:** Central Mich. 35, Louisiana Tech 14; Delaware 49, UNLV 11. **Championship:** Central Mich. 54, Delaware 14.

1975 First Round: Northern Mich. 24, Boise St. 21; West Ala. 34, North Dak. 14; Western Ky. 14, Northern Iowa 12; New Hampshire 35, Lehigh 21. **Semifinals:** Northern Mich. 28, West Ala. 26; Western Ky. 14, New Hampshire 3. **Championship:** Northern Mich. 16, Western Ky. 14.

1976 First Round: Akron 26, UNLV 6; Northern Mich. 28, Delaware 17; North Dak. St. 10, Eastern Ky. 7; Montana St. 17, New Hampshire 16. **Semifinals:** Akron 29, Northern Mich. 26; Montana St. 10, North Dak. St. 3. **Championship:** Montana St. 24, Akron 13.

1977 First Round: UC Davis 34, Bethune-Cookman 16; Lehigh 30, Massachusetts 23; North Dak. St. 20, Northern Mich. 6; Jacksonville St. 35, Northern Ariz. 0. **Semifinals:** Lehigh 39, UC Davis 30; Jacksonville St. 31, North Dak. St. 7. **Championship:** Lehigh 33, Jacksonville St. 0.

1978 First Round: Winston-Salem 17, Cal Poly 0; Delaware 42, Jacksonville St. 27; Youngstown St. 21, Neb.-Omaha 14; Eastern Ill. 35, UC Davis 31. **Semifinals:** Delaware 41, Winston-Salem 0; Eastern Ill. 26, Youngstown St. 22. **Championship:** Eastern Ill. 10, Delaware 9.

1979 First Round: Delaware 58, Virginia Union 28; Mississippi Col. 35, North Dak. 15; Youngstown St. 50, South Dak. St. 7; Alabama A&M 27, Morgan St. 7. **Semifinals:** Delaware 60, Mississippi Col. 10; Youngstown St. 52, Alabama A&M 0. **Championship:** Delaware 38, Youngstown St. 21.

1980 First Round: Eastern Ill. 21, Northern Colo. 14; North Ala. 17, Virginia Union 8; Santa Clara 27, Northern Mich. 26; Cal Poly 15, Jacksonville St. 0. **Semifinals:** Eastern Ill. 56, North Ala. 31; Cal Poly 38, Santa Clara 14. **Championship:** Cal Poly 21, Eastern Ill. 13.

1981 First Round: Northern Mich. 55, Elizabeth City St. 6; Southwest Tex. St. 38, Jacksonville St. 22; North Dak. St. 24, Puget Sound 10; Shippensburg 40, Virginia Union 27. **Semifinals:** Southwest Tex. St. 62, Northern Mich. 0; North Dak. St. 18, Shippensburg 6. **Championship:** Southwest Tex. St. 42, North Dak. St. 13.

1982 First Round: Southwest Tex. St. 27, Fort Valley St. 6; Jacksonville St. 34, Truman St. 21; North Dak. St. 21, Virginia Union 20; UC Davis 42, Northern Mich. 21. **Semifinals:** Southwest Tex. St. 19, Jacksonville St. 14; UC Davis 19, North Dak. St. 14. **Championship:** Southwest Tex. St. 34, UC Davis 9.

1983 First Round: UC Davis 25, Butler 6; North Dak. St. 24, Towson 17; North Ala. 16, Virginia Union 14; Central St. 24, Southwest Tex. St. 16. **Semifinals:** North Dak. St. 26, UC Davis 17; Central St. 27, North Ala. 24. **Championship:** North Dak. St. 41, Central St. 21.

1984 First Round: North Dak. St. 31, UC Davis 23; Neb.-Omaha 28, Northwest Mo. St. 15; Troy St. 31, Central St. 21; Towson 31, Norfolk St. 21. **Semifinals:** North Dak. St. 25, Neb.-Omaha 14; Troy St. 45, Towson 3. **Championship:** Troy St. 18, North Dak. St. 17.

1985 First Round: North Dak. St. 31, UC Davis 12; South Dak. 13, Central St. 10 (2 OT); Bloomsburg 38, Hampton 28; North Ala. 14, Fort Valley St. 7. **Semifinals:** North Dak. St. 16, South Dak. 7; North Ala. 34, Bloomsburg 0. **Championship:** North Dak. St. 35, North Ala. 7.

1986 First Round: North Dak. St. 50, Ashland 0; Central St. 31, Towson 0; Troy St. 31, Virginia Union 7; South Dak. 26, UC Davis 23. **Semifinals:** North Dak. St. 35, Central St. 12; South Dak. 42, Troy St. 28. **Championship:** North Dak. St. 27, South Dak. 7.

1987 First Round: Portland St. 27, Mankato St. 21; Northern Mich. 23, Angelo St. 20 (OT); Central Fla. 12, Indiana (Pa.) 10; Troy St. 45, Winston-Salem 14. **Semifinals:** Portland St. 13, Northern Mich. 7; Troy St. 31, Central Fla. 10. **Championship:** Troy St. 31, Portland St. 17.

1988 First Round: North Dak. St. 49, Augustana (S.D.) 7; Millersville 27, Indiana (Pa.) 24; Cal St. Sacramento 35, UC Davis 14; N.C. Central 31, Winston-Salem 16; Tex. A&M-Kingsville 39, Mississippi Col. 15; Tenn.-Martin 23, Butler 6; Portland St. 34, Bowie St. 17; Jacksonville St. 63, West Chester 24. **Quarterfinals:** North Dak. St. 36, Millersville 26; Cal St. Sacramento 56, N.C. Central 7; Tex. A&M-Kingsville 34, Tenn.-Martin 0; Portland St. 20, Jacksonville St. 13. **Semifinals:** North Dak. St. 42, Cal St. Sacramento 20; Portland St. 35, Tex. A&M-Kingsville 27. **Championship:** North Dak. St. 35, Portland St. 21.

1989 First Round: *Mississippi Col. 34, Tex. A&M-Kingsville 19; St. Cloud St. 27, Augustana (S.D.) 20; Portland St. 56, West Chester 50 (3 OT); Indiana (Pa.) 34, Grand Valley St. 24; Pittsburg St. 28, Northwest Mo. St. 7; Angelo St. 28, UC Davis 23; North Dak. St. 45, Edinboro 32; Jacksonville St. 33, Alabama A&M 9. **Quarterfinals:** *Mississippi Col. 55, St. Cloud St. 24; Indiana (Pa.) 17, Portland St. 0; Angelo St. 24, Pittsburg St. 21; Jacksonville St. 21, North Dak. St. 17. **Semifinals:** *Mississippi Col. 26, Indiana (Pa.) 14; Jacksonville St. 34, Angelo St. 16. **Championship:** *Mississippi Col. 3, Jacksonville St. 0.

Mississippi College's participation in 1989 playoff vacated.

1990 First Round: *Mississippi Col. 70, Wofford 19; Jacksonville St. 38, North Ala. 14; Indiana (Pa.) 48, Winston-Salem 0; Edinboro 38, Virginia Union 14; North Dak. St. 17, Northern Colo. 7; Cal Poly 14, Cal St. Northridge 7; Pittsburg St. 59, Truman St. 3; East Tex. St. 20, Grand Valley St. 14. **Quarterfinals:** *Mississippi Col. 14, Jacksonville St. 7; Indiana (Pa.) 14, Edinboro 7; North Dak. St. 47, Cal Poly 0; Pittsburg St. 60, East Tex. St. 28. **Semifinals:** Indiana (Pa.) 27, *Mississippi Col. 8; North Dak. St. 39, Pittsburg St. 29. **Championship:** North Dak. St. 51, Indiana (Pa.) 11.

Mississippi College's participation in 1990 playoff vacated.

1991 First Round: Pittsburg St. 26, Butler 16; East Tex. St. 36, Grand Valley St. 15; Portland St. 28, Northern Colo. 24; Mankato St. 27, North Dak. St. 7; Jacksonville St. 49, Winston-Salem 24; Mississippi Col. 28, Wofford 15; Indiana (Pa.) 56, Virginia Union 7; Shippensburg 34, East Stroudsburg 33 (OT). **Quarterfinals:** Pittsburg St. 38, East Tex. St. 28; Portland St. 37, Mankato St. 27; Jacksonville St. 35, Mississippi Col. 7; Indiana (Pa.) 52, Shippensburg 7. **Semifinals:** Pittsburg St. 53, Portland St. 21; Jacksonville St. 27, Indiana (Pa.) 20. **Championship:** Pittsburg St. 23, Jacksonville St. 6.

1992 First Round: Ferris St. 19, Edinboro 15; New Haven 38, West Chester 26; Jacksonville St. 41, Savannah St. 16; North Ala. 33, Hampton 21; Tex. A&M-Kingsville 22, Western St. 13; Portland St. 42, UC Davis 28; Pittsburg St. 26, North Dak. 21; North Dak. St. 42, Truman St. 7. **Quarterfinals:** New Haven 35, Ferris St. 13; Jacksonville St. 14, North Ala. 12; Portland St. 35, Tex. A&M-Kingsville 30; Pittsburg St. 38, North Dak. St. 37 (OT). **Semifinals:** Jacksonville St. 46, New Haven 35; Pittsburg St. 41, Portland St. 38. **Championship:** Jacksonville St. 17, Pittsburg St. 13.

1993 First Round: North Ala. 38, Carson-Newman 28; Hampton 33, Albany St. (Ga.) 7; Tex. A&M-Kingsville 50, Portland St. 15; UC Davis 37, Fort Hays St. 34; Mankato St. 34, Mo. Southern St. 13; North Dak. 17, Pittsburg St. 14; New Haven 48, Edinboro 28; Indiana (Pa.) 28, Ferris St. 21. **Quarterfinals:** North Ala. 45, Hampton 20; Tex. A&M-Kingsville 51, UC Davis 28; North Dak. 54, Mankato St. 21; Indiana (Pa.) 38, New Haven 35. **Semifinals:** North Ala. 27, Tex. A&M-Kingsville 25; Indiana (Pa.) 21, North Dak. 6. **Championship:** North Ala. 41, Indiana (Pa.) 34.

1994 First Round: Ferris St. 43, West Chester 40; Indiana (Pa.) 35, Grand Valley St. 27; Tex. A&M-Kingsville 43, Western St. 7; Portland St. 29, Angelo St. 0; North Dak. St. 18, Pittsburg St. 12 (3 OT); North Dak. 18, Truman St. 6; North Ala. 17, Carson-Newman 13; Valdosta St. 14, Albany St. (Ga.) 7. **Quarterfinals:** Indiana (Pa.) 21, Ferris St. 17; Tex. A&M-Kingsville 21, Portland St. 16; North Dak. 14, North Dak. St. 7; North Ala. 27, Valdosta St. 24 (2 OT). **Semifinals:** Tex. A&M-Kingsville 46, Indiana (Pa.) 20; North Ala. 35, North Dak. 7. **Championship:** North Ala. 16, Tex. A&M-Kingsville 10.

1995 First Round: Ferris St. 36, Millersville 26; New Haven 27, Edinboro 12; North Ala. 38, Albany St. (Ga.) 28; Carson-Newman 37, West Ga. 26; Pittsburg St. 36, Northern Colo. 17; North Dak. St. 41, North Dak. 10; Tex. A&M-Kingsville 59, Fort Hays St. 28; Portland St. 56, East Tex. St. 35. **Quarterfinals:** Ferris St. 17, New Haven 9; North Ala. 28, Carson-Newman 7; Pittsburg St. 9, North Dak. St. 7; Tex. A&M-Kingsville 30, Portland St. 3. **Semifinals:** North Ala. 45, Ferris St. 7; Pittsburg St. 28, Tex. A&M-Kingsville 25 (OT). **Championship:** North Ala. 27, Pittsburg St. 7.

1996 First Round: Clarion 42, Bloomsburg 29; Ferris St. 24, Indiana (Pa.) 23; Northern Colo. 24, Pittsburg St. 21; Northwest Mo. St. 22, Neb.-Omaha 21; Valdosta St. 38, Albany St. (Ga.) 28; Carson-Newman 41, West Ga. 7; Central Okla. 23, Chadron St. 21; UC Davis 17, Tex. A&M-Kingsville 14. **Quarterfinals:** Clarion 23, Ferris St. 21; Northern Colo. 27, Northwest Mo. St. 26; Carson-Newman 24, Valdosta St. 19; UC Davis 26, Central Okla. 7. **Semifinals:** Northern Colo. 19, Clarion 18; Carson-Newman 29, UC Davis 26. **Championship:** Northern Colo. 23, Carson-Newman 14.

1997 First Round: UC Davis 37, Tex. A&M-Kingsville 34; Angelo St. 46, Western St. 12; New Haven 47, Glenville St. 7; Slippery Rock 30, Ashland 20; Northwest Mo. St. 39, North Dak. St. 28; Northern Colo. 24, Pittsburg St. 16; Carson-Newman 21, North Ala. 7; Albany St. (Ga.) 10, Southern Ark. 6. **Quarterfinals:** UC Davis 50, Angelo St. 33; New Haven 49, Slippery Rock 21; Northern Colo. 35, Northwest Mo. St. 19; Carson-Newman 23, Albany St. (Ga.) 22. **Semifinals:** New Haven 27, UC Davis 25; Northern Colo. 30, Carson-Newman 29. **Championship:** Northern Colo. 51, New Haven 0.

Division III Championship

1997 Title Game Summary

AMOS ALONZO STAGG BOWL, SALEM STADIUM, SALEM, VA.; DECEMBER 13, 1997

	Lycoming	Mount Union
First Downs	11	33
Rushing Yardage	67	258

	Lycoming	Mount Union
Passing Yardage	116	439
Return Yardage	16	56
Passes (Comp.-Att.-Int.)	7-16-1	25-41-0
Punts (Number-Average)	10-31.3	1-43.0
Fumbles (Number-Lost)	1-0	2-2
Penalties (Number-Yards)	2-20	9-102
Lycoming	0 6	0 6—12
Mount Union	14 14	21 12—61

FIRST QUARTER
Mount Union—Ryan Gorius 20 run (Bill Andrea kick) (78 yards in 6 plays, 13:11 left)
Mount Union—Marc Lantos 23 pass from Bill Borchert (Andrea kick) (67 yards in 11 plays, 3:47 left)

SECOND QUARTER
Lycoming—Joe Spang 5 pass from Jason Marraccini (kick failed) (65 yards in 11 plays, 10:30 left)
Mount Union—Reiko Gollate 36 pass from Borchert (Andrea kick) (81 yards in 5 plays, 8:00 left)
Mount Union—Brian Tyla 3 pass from Borchert (Andrea kick) (75 yards in 7 plays, 4:48 left)

THIRD QUARTER
Mount Union—Borchert 10 run (Andrea kick) (10 yards in 1 play, 12:50 left)
Mount Union—Tyla 18 pass from Borchert (Andrea kick) (45 yards in 4 plays, 8:05 left)
Mount Union—Gorius 14 pass from Borchert (Andrea kick) (58 yards in 4 plays, 4:33 left)

FOURTH QUARTER
Mount Union—Gollate 11 pass from Borchert (kick failed) (68 yards in 9 plays, 12:06 left)
Mount Union—Steve Evans 2 run (kick failed) (81 yards in 10 plays, 5:30 left)
Lycoming—Tim Dumas 34 pass from Andy Showalter (pass failed) (34 yards in 1 play, 2:07 left)

INDIVIDUAL LEADERS
Rushing—Lycoming: Brian Thompson, 80 yards on 19 carries; Mount Union: Gorius, 86 yards on 7 carries.
Passing—Lycoming: Marraccini, 6 of 14 for 82 yards; Mount Union: Borchert, 24 of 40 for 411 yards.
Receiving—Lycoming: Dumas, 4 catches for 69 yards, and Jake Maskerines, 1 catch for 28 yards; Mount Union: Tyla, 7 catches for 102 yards, and Kevin Knestrick, 6 catches for 163 yards.

David Gonzales/NCAA photos

Mount Union quarterback Bill Borchert capped his outstanding career with 411 passing yards en route to the Raiders' second consecutive NCAA Division III Football Championship title. Mount Union's 61-12 victory over Lycoming was the third title in five years for the Raiders.

Division III All-Time Championship Results

Year	Champion	Coach	Score	Runner-Up	Site
1973	Wittenberg	Dave Maurer	41-0	Juniata	Phenix City, Ala.
1974	Central (Iowa)	Ron Schipper	10-8	Ithaca	Phenix City, Ala.
1975	Wittenberg	Dave Maurer	28-0	Ithaca	Phenix City, Ala.
1976	St. John's (Minn.)	John Gagliardi	31-28	Towson	Phenix City, Ala.
1977	Widener	Bill Manlove	39-36	Wabash	Phenix City, Ala.
1978	Baldwin-Wallace	Lee Tressel	24-10	Wittenberg	Phenix City, Ala.
1979	Ithaca	Jim Butterfield	14-10	Wittenberg	Phenix City, Ala.
1980	Dayton	Rick Carter	63-0	Ithaca	Phenix City, Ala.
1981	Widener	Bill Manlove	17-10	Dayton	Phenix City, Ala.
1982	West Ga.	Bobby Pate	14-0	Augustana (Ill.)	Phenix City, Ala.
1983	Augustana (Ill.)	Bob Reade	21-17	Union (N.Y.)	Kings Island, Ohio
1984	Augustana (Ill.)	Bob Reade	21-12	Central (Iowa)	Kings Island, Ohio
1985	Augustana (Ill.)	Bob Reade	20-7	Ithaca	Phenix City, Ala.
1986	Augustana (Ill.)	Bob Reade	31-3	Salisbury St.	Phenix City, Ala.
1987	Wagner	Walt Hameline	19-3	Dayton	Phenix City, Ala.
1988	Ithaca	Jim Butterfield	39-24	Central (Iowa)	Phenix City, Ala.
1989	Dayton	Mike Kelly	17-7	Union (N.Y.)	Phenix City, Ala.
1990	Allegheny	Ken O'Keefe	21-14 (OT)	Lycoming	Bradenton, Fla.
1991	Ithaca	Jim Butterfield	34-20	Dayton	Bradenton, Fla.
1992	Wis.-La Crosse	Roger Harring	16-12	Wash. & Jeff.	Bradenton, Fla.
1993	Mount Union	Larry Kehres	34-24	Rowan	Salem, Va.
1994	Albion	Pete Schmidt	38-15	Wash. & Jeff.	Salem, Va.
1995	Wis.-La Crosse	Roger Harring	36-7	Rowan	Salem, Va.
1996	Mount Union	Larry Kehres	56-24	Rowan	Salem, Va.
1997	Mount Union	Larry Kehres	61-12	Lycoming	Salem, Va.

Regional Championship Results

(Before Division III Championship)

Year	Champion	Coach	Score	Runner-Up	Site
EAST (KNUTE ROCKNE BOWL)					
1969	Randolph-Macon	Ted Keller	47-28	Bridgeport	Bridgeport, Conn.
1970	Montclair St.	Clary Anderson	7-6	Hampden-Sydney	Atlantic City, N.J.
1971	Bridgeport	Ed Farrell	17-12	Hampden-Sydney	Atlantic City, N.J.
1972	Bridgeport	Ed Farrell	27-22	Slippery Rock	Atlantic City, N.J.
WEST (AMOS ALONZO STAGG BOWL)					
1969	Wittenberg	Dave Maurer	27-21	William Jewell	Springfield, Ohio
1970	Capital	Gene Slaughter	34-21	Luther	Columbus, Ohio
1971	Samford*		20-10	Ohio Wesleyan	Phenix City, Ala.
1972	Heidelberg	Pete Riesen	28-16	Fort Valley St.	Phenix City, Ala.

**Samford's participation in the Amos Alonzo Stagg Bowl vacated by the NCAA Committee in Infractions.*

1997 Division III Championship Results

FIRST ROUND
Mount Union 34, Allegheny 30
John Carroll 30, Hanover 20
Simpson 34, Wis.-Whitewater 31
Augsburg 34, Concordia-M'head 22
Lycoming 27, Western Md. 13
Trinity (Tex.) 44, Catholic 33
Rowan 43, Coast Guard 0
Col. of New Jersey 34, Cortland St. 30

QUARTERFINALS
Mount Union 59, John Carroll 7
Simpson 61, Augsburg 21
Lycoming 46, Trinity (Tex.) 26
Rowan 13, Col. of New Jersey 7

SEMIFINALS
Mount Union 54, Simpson 7
Lycoming 28, Rowan 20

CHAMPIONSHIP
Mount Union 61, Lycoming 12

Championship Records

INDIVIDUAL: SINGLE GAME

NET YARDS RUSHING
389—Ricky Gales, Simpson (35) vs. St. John's (Minn.) (42), 11-18-89.

RUSHES ATTEMPTED
51—Ricky Gales, Simpson (35) vs. St. John's (Minn.) (42), 11-18-89.

TOUCHDOWNS BY RUSHING
5—Jeff Norman, St. John's (Minn.) (46) vs. Augustana (Ill.) (7), 11-20-76; Mike Coppa, Salisbury St. (44) vs. Ithaca (40), 12-6-86; Paul Parker, Ithaca (62) vs. Ferrum (28), 12-3-88; Kevin Hofacre, Dayton (35) vs. John Carroll (10), 11-18-89.

NET YARDS PASSING
584—Bill Borchert, Mount Union (52) vs. Hanover (18), 11-18-95.

PASSES ATTEMPTED
67—Terry Peebles, Hanover (18) vs. Mount Union (52), 11-18-95; Vic Ameye, Widener (27) vs. Lycoming (31), 11-18-95.

PASSES COMPLETED
37—Bill Borchert, Mount Union (52) vs. Hanover (18), 11-18-95.

PASSES HAD INTERCEPTED
7—Rick Steil, Dubuque (7) vs. Ithaca (27), 11-17-79.

TOUCHDOWN PASSES COMPLETED
8—Jim Ballard, Mount Union (56) vs. St. John's (Minn.) (8), 12-4-93.

COMPLETION PERCENTAGE
(Min. 8 Attempts)
.900—Robb Disbennett, Salisbury St. (16) vs. Carnegie Mellon (14), 11-19-83 (18 of 20).

NET YARDS RUSHING AND PASSING
595—Bill Borchert, Mount Union (52) vs. Hanover (18) 11-18-95.

NUMBER OF RUSHING AND PASSING PLAYS
77—Terry Peebles, Hanover (18) vs. Mount Union (52), 11-18-95.

PUNTING AVERAGE
(Min. 3 Punts)
48.5—Phil Macken, Minn.-Morris (25) vs. Carnegie Mellon (31), 11-17-79.

NUMBER OF PUNTS
14—Tim Flynn, Gettysburg (14) vs. Lycoming (10), 11-23-85.

PASSES CAUGHT
17—Jeff Clay, Catholic (33) vs. Trinity (Tex.) (44), 11-22-97

NET YARDS RECEIVING
265—Todd Zufra, Mount Union (52) vs. Hanover (18), 11-18-95.

TOUCHDOWN PASSES CAUGHT
4—Kirk Liesimer, Ill. Wesleyan (27) vs. Mount Union (49), 11-28-92; Rob Atwood, Mount Union (56) vs. St. John's (Minn.) (8), 12-4-93.

PASSES INTERCEPTED
3—By nine players. Most recent: Arnell Palmer, Rowan (28) vs. Wash. & Jeff. (15), 12-2-95.

YARDS GAINED ON INTERCEPTION RETURNS
100—Jay Zunic, Ithaca (31) vs. Rowan (10), 11-23-91 (2 interceptions, 1 for 100-yard TD).

YARDS GAINED ON PUNT RETURNS
140—David Ziegler, John Carroll (30) vs. Hanover (20), 11-22-97.

YARDS GAINED ON KICKOFF RETURNS
190—George Day, Susquehanna (31) vs. Lycoming (24), 11-30-91.

POINTS
36—Mike Coppa, Salisbury St. (44) vs. Ithaca (40), 12-6-86.

TOUCHDOWNS
6—Mike Coppa, Salisbury St. (44) vs. Ithaca (40), 12-6-86.

EXTRA POINTS
9—Tim Robinson, Baldwin-Wallace (71) vs. St. Lawrence (7), 11-18-78.

INDIVIDUAL: TOURNAMENT

NET YARDS RUSHING
882—Chris Babirad, Wash. & Jeff., 1992 (285 vs. Lycoming, 286 vs. Emory & Henry, 207 vs. Rowan, 104 vs. Wis.-La Crosse).

RUSHES ATTEMPTED
129—Chris Babirad, Wash. & Jeff., 1992 (37 vs. Lycoming, 31 vs. Emory & Henry, 36 vs. Rowan, 25 vs. Wis.-La Crosse).

NET YARDS PASSING
1,402—Bill Borchert, Mount Union, 1997 (317 vs. Allegheny, 278 vs. John Carroll, 396 vs. Simpson, 411 vs. Lycoming).

PASSES ATTEMPTED
141—Brett Russ, Union (N.Y.), 1989 (23 vs. Cortland St., 37 vs. Montclair St., 38 vs. Ferrum, 43 vs. Dayton); Jim Ballard, Mount Union, 1993 (40 vs. Allegheny, 28 vs. Albion, 28 vs. St. John's [Minn.], 45 vs. Rowan).

PASSES COMPLETED
90—Jim Ballard, Mount Union, 1993 (26 vs. Allegheny, 16 vs. Albion, 20 vs. St. John's [Minn.], 28 vs. Rowan).

TOUCHDOWN PASSES COMPLETED
17—Bill Borchert, Mount Union, 1996 (4 vs. Allegheny, 3 vs. Ill. Wesleyan, 3 vs. Wis.-LaCrosse, 7 vs. Rowan); Jim Ballard, Mount Union, 1993 (5 vs. Allegheny, 1 vs. Albion, 8 vs. St. John's [Minn.], 3 vs. Rowan).

COMPLETION PERCENTAGE
(Min. 2 Games)
.676—Bill Borchert, Mount Union, 1994, 46 of 68 (23-34 vs. Allegheny, 23-34 vs. Albion).

PASSES HAD INTERCEPTED
9—Rollie Wiebers, Buena Vista, 1976 (4 vs. Carroll [Wis.], 5 vs. St. John's [Minn.]).

PASSES CAUGHT
39—Nick Ismailoff, Ithaca, 1991 (12 vs. Rowan, 6 vs. Union [N.Y.], 11 vs. Susquehanna, 10 vs. Dayton).

NET YARDS RECEIVING
599—Nick Ismailoff, Ithaca, 1991 (179 vs. Rowan, 122 vs. Union [N.Y.], 105 vs. Susquehanna, 193 vs. Dayton).

TOUCHDOWN PASSES CAUGHT
6—Chris Begley, Wash & Jeff., 1995 (3 vs. Emory & Henry, 2 vs. Lycoming, 1 vs. Rowan); Rob Atwood, Mount Union, 1993 (0 vs. Allegheny, 0 vs. Albion, 4 vs. St. John's [Minn.], 2 vs. Rowan).

POINTS
60—By four players. Most recent: Chris Babirad, Wash. & Jeff., 1992 (18 vs. Lycoming, 24 vs. Emory & Henry, 12 vs. Rowan, 6 vs. Wis.-La Crosse).

TOUCHDOWNS
10—Brad Price, Augustana (Ill.), 1986 (4 vs. Hope, 1 vs. Mount Union, 2 vs. Concordia-M'head, 3 vs. Salisbury St.); Mike Coppa, Salisbury St., 1986 (1 vs. Emory & Henry, 3 vs. Susquehanna, 6 vs. Ithaca, 0 vs. Augustana [Ill.]); Chris Babirad, Wash. & Jeff., 1992 (3 vs. Lycoming, 4 vs. Emory & Henry, 2 vs. Rowan, 1 vs. Wis.-La Crosse).

INDIVIDUAL: LONGEST PLAYS

LONGEST RUSH
93—Rick Papke, Augustana (Ill.) (17) vs. Central (Iowa) (23), 12-3-88, TD.

LONGEST PASS COMPLETION
96—Mark Blom to Tom McDonald, Central (Iowa) (37) vs. Buena Vista (0), 11-22-86, TD.

LONGEST FIELD GOAL
52—Rod Vesling, St. Lawrence (43) vs. Wagner (34), 11-20-82.

LONGEST PUNT
79—Tom Hansen, Ithaca (3) vs. Wittenberg (6), 11-18-78.

LONGEST PUNT RETURN
84—David Ziegler, John Carroll (30) vs. Hanover (20), 11-22-97, TD.

LONGEST KICKOFF RETURN
100—Tom Deery, Widener (23) vs. Montclair St. (12), 11-30-81, TD.

LONGEST INTERCEPTION RETURN
100—Jay Zunic, Ithaca (31) vs. Rowan (10), 11-23-91, TD.

TEAM: SINGLE GAME

FIRST DOWNS
40—Mount Union (52) vs. Hanover (18), 11-18-95.

FIRST DOWNS BY RUSHING
30—Central (Iowa) (71) vs. Occidental (0), 12-7-85.

FIRST DOWNS BY PASSING
34—Mount Union (52) vs. Hanover (18), 11-18-95.

NET YARDS RUSHING
530—St. John's (Minn.) (46) vs. Augustana (Ill.) (7), 11-20-76.

RUSHES ATTEMPTED
83—Capital (34) vs. Luther (21), 11-28-70; Baldwin-Wallace (31) vs. Carnegie Mellon (6), 11-25-78.

NET YARDS PASSING
697—Mount Union (61) vs. Lycoming (12), 12-13-97.

PASSES ATTEMPTED
67—Hanover (18) vs. Mount Union (52), 11-18-95; Widener (27) vs. Lycoming (31), 11-18-95.

PASSES COMPLETED
39—Mount Union (52) vs. Hanover (18), 11-18-95.

COMPLETION PERCENTAGE
(Min. 10 Attempts)
.857—Salisbury St. (16) vs. Carnegie Mellon (14), 11-19-83 (18 of 21).

PASSES HAD INTERCEPTED
9—Dubuque (7) vs. Ithaca (27), 11-17-79.

NET YARDS RUSHING AND PASSING
773—Mount Union (52) vs. Hanover (18), 11-18-95.

RUSHING AND PASSING PLAYS
101—Union (N.Y.) (45) vs. Montclair St. (6), 11-25-89.

PUNTING AVERAGE
48.5—Minn.-Morris (25) vs. Carnegie Mellon (31), 11-17-79.

NUMBER OF PUNTS
14—Gettysburg (14) vs. Lycoming (10), 11-23-85.

YARDS GAINED ON PUNT RETURNS
140—John Carroll (30) vs. Hanover, 11-22-97.

YARDS GAINED ON KICKOFF RETURNS
234—Ithaca (40) vs. Salisbury St. (44), 12-6-86.

YARDS GAINED ON INTERCEPTION RETURNS
176—Augustana (Ill.) (14) vs. St. Lawrence (0), 11-27-82.

YARDS PENALIZED
166—Ferrum (49) vs. Moravian (28), 11-26-88.

FUMBLES LOST
6—Albright (7) vs. St. Lawrence (26), 11-20-76; St. John's (Minn.) (7) vs. Dayton (19), 12-7-91.

POINTS
75—St. John's (Minn.) vs. Coe (2), 11-23-91.

TEAM: TOURNAMENT

FIRST DOWNS
112—Mount Union, 1997 (24 vs. Allegheny, 32 vs. John Carroll, 23 vs. Simpson, 33 vs. Lycoming).

NET YARDS RUSHING
1,377—Ithaca, 1988 (251 vs. Wagner, 293 vs. Cortland St., 425 vs. Ferrum, 408 vs. Central [Iowa]).

NET YARDS PASSING
1,441—Mount Union, 1997 (317 vs. Allegheny, 289 vs. John Carroll, 396 vs. Simpson, 439 vs. Lycoming.)

NET YARDS RUSHING AND PASSING
2,470—Mount Union, 1997 (528 vs. Allegheny, 601 vs. John Carroll, 644 vs. Simpson, 697 vs. Lycoming.)

PASSES ATTEMPTED
150—Hofstra, 1990 (51 vs. Cortland St., 50 vs. Col. of New Jersey, 49 vs. Lycoming).

PASSES COMPLETED
92—Mount Union, 1993 (26 vs. Allegheny, 16 vs. Albion, 22 vs. St. John's [Minn.], 28 vs. Rowan).

PASSES HAD INTERCEPTED
11—Hofstra, 1990 (5 vs. Cortland St., 3 vs. Col. of New Jersey, 3 vs. Lycoming).

NUMBER OF PUNTS
30—Central (Iowa), 1988 (12 vs. Concordia-M'head, 8 vs. Wis.-Whitewater, 5 vs. Augustana [Ill.], 5 vs. Ithaca).

YARDS PENALIZED
331—Wagner, 1987 (61 vs. Rochester, 80 vs. Fordham, 87 vs. Emory & Henry, 103 vs. Dayton).

FUMBLES LOST
10—Wittenberg, 1978 (4 vs. Ithaca, 2 vs. Minn.-Morris, 4 vs. Baldwin-Wallace).

POINTS
208—Mount Union, 1997 (34 vs. Allegheny, 59 vs. John Carroll, 54 vs. Simpson, 61 vs. Lycoming).

Year-by-Year Division III Championship Results

Year (Number of Teams)	Coach	Record	Result
1973 (4)			
Wittenberg	Dave Maurer	2-0	Champion
Juniata	Walt Nadzak	1-1	Second
Bridgeport	Ed Farrell	0-1	Semifinalist
San Diego	Andy Vinci	0-1	Semifinalist
1974 (4)			
Central (Iowa)	Ron Schipper	2-0	Champion
Ithaca	Jim Butterfield	1-1	Second
Evansville	Jim Byers	0-1	Semifinalist
Slippery Rock	Bob Di Spirito	0-1	Semifinalist
1975 (8)			
Wittenberg	Dave Maurer	3-0	Champion
Ithaca	Jim Butterfield	2-1	Second
Millsaps	Harper Davis	1-1	Semifinalist
Widener	Bill Manlove	1-1	Semifinalist
Albright	John Potsklan	0-1	Lost 1st Round
Colorado Col.	Jerry Carle	0-1	Lost 1st Round
Fort Valley St.	Leon Lomax	0-1	Lost 1st Round
Indianapolis	Bill Bless	0-1	Lost 1st Round
1976 (8)			
St. John's (Minn.)	John Gagliardi	3-0	Champion
Towson	Phil Albert	2-1	Second
Buena Vista	Jim Hershberger	1-1	Semifinalist
St. Lawrence	Ted Stratford	1-1	Semifinalist
Albright	John Potsklan	0-1	Lost 1st Round
Augustana (Ill.)	Ben Newcomb	0-1	Lost 1st Round
Carroll (Wis.)	Steve Miller	0-1	Lost 1st Round
LIU-C. W. Post	Dom Anile	0-1	Lost 1st Round
1977 (8)			
Widener	Bill Manlove	3-0	Champion
Wabash	Frank Navarro	2-1	Second
Albany (N.Y.)	Bob Ford	1-1	Semifinalist
Minn.-Morris	Al Molde	1-1	Semifinalist
Albion	Frank Joranko	0-1	Lost 1st Round
Central (Iowa)	Ron Schipper	0-1	Lost 1st Round
Hampden-Sydney	Stokeley Fulton	0-1	Lost 1st Round
St. John's (Minn.)	John Gagliardi	0-1	Lost 1st Round
1978 (8)			
Baldwin-Wallace	Lee Tressel	3-0	Champion
Wittenberg	Dave Maurer	2-1	Second
Carnegie Mellon	Chuck Klausing	1-1	Semifinalist
Minn.-Morris	Al Molde	1-1	Semifinalist
Dayton	Rick Carter	0-1	Lost 1st Round
Ithaca	Jim Butterfield	0-1	Lost 1st Round
St. Lawrence	Ted Stratford	0-1	Lost 1st Round
St. Olaf	Tom Porter	0-1	Lost 1st Round
1979 (8)			
Ithaca	Jim Butterfield	3-0	Champion
Wittenberg	Dave Maurer	2-1	Second
Carnegie Mellon	Chuck Klausing	1-1	Semifinalist
Widener	Bill Manlove	1-1	Semifinalist
Baldwin-Wallace	Lee Tressel	0-1	Lost 1st Round
Dubuque	Don Birmingham	0-1	Lost 1st Round
Millersville	Gene Carpenter	0-1	Lost 1st Round
Minn.-Morris	Al Molde	0-1	Lost 1st Round
1980 (8)			
Dayton	Rick Carter	3-0	Champion
Ithaca	Jim Butterfield	2-1	Second
Minn.-Morris	Dick Smith	1-1	Semifinalist
Widener	Bill Manlove	1-1	Semifinalist
Baldwin-Wallace	Lee Tressel	0-1	Lost 1st Round
Bethany (W.Va.)	Don Ault	0-1	Lost 1st Round
Dubuque	Don Birmingham	0-1	Lost 1st Round
Wagner	Bill Russo	0-1	Lost 1st Round
1981 (8)			
Widener	Bill Manlove	3-0	Champion
Dayton	Mike Kelly	2-1	Second
Lawrence	Ron Roberts	1-1	Semifinalist
Montclair St.	Fred Hill	1-1	Semifinalist
Alfred	Sam Sanders	0-1	Lost 1st Round
Augustana (Ill.)	Bob Reade	0-1	Lost 1st Round
Minn.-Morris	Dick Smith	0-1	Lost 1st Round
West Ga.	Bobby Pate	0-1	Lost 1st Round
1982 (8)			
West Ga.	Bobby Pate	3-0	Champion
Augustana (Ill.)	Bob Reade	2-1	Second
Bishop	James Jones	1-1	Semifinalist
St. Lawrence	Andy Talley	1-1	Semifinalist
Baldwin-Wallace	Bob Packard	0-1	Lost 1st Round
Wagner	Walt Hameline	0-1	Lost 1st Round
Wartburg	Don Canfield	0-1	Lost 1st Round
Widener	Bill Manlove	0-1	Lost 1st Round
1983 (8)			
Augustana (Ill.)	Bob Reade	3-0	Champion
Union (N.Y.)	Al Bagnoli	2-1	Second
Salisbury St.	Mike McGlinchey	1-1	Semifinalist
Wis.-La Crosse	Roger Harring	1-1	Semifinalist
Adrian	Ron Labadie	0-1	Lost 1st Round
Carnegie Mellon	Chuck Klausing	0-1	Lost 1st Round
Hofstra	Mickey Kwiatkowski	0-1	Lost 1st Round
Occidental	Dale Widolff	0-1	Lost 1st Round
1984 (8)			
Augustana (Ill.)	Bob Reade	3-0	Champion
Central (Iowa)	Ron Schipper	2-1	Second
Union (N.Y.)	Al Bagnoli	1-1	Semifinalist
Wash. & Jeff.	John Luckhardt	1-1	Semifinalist
Dayton	Mike Kelly	0-1	Lost 1st Round
Occidental	Dale Widolff	0-1	Lost 1st Round
Plymouth St.	Jay Cottone	0-1	Lost 1st Round
Randolph-Macon	Jim Blackburn	0-1	Lost 1st Round
1985 (16)			
Augustana (Ill.)	Bob Reade	4-0	Champion
Ithaca	Jim Butterfield	3-1	Second
Central (Iowa)	Ron Schipper	2-1	Semifinalist
Gettysburg	Barry Streeter	2-1	Semifinalist
Montclair St.	Rick Giancola	1-1	Quarterfinalist
Mount Union	Ken Wable	1-1	Quarterfinalist
Occidental	Dale Widolff	1-1	Quarterfinalist
Salisbury St.	Mike McGlinchey	1-1	Quarterfinalist
Albion	Pete Schmidt	0-1	Lost 1st Round
Carnegie Mellon	Chuck Klausing	0-1	Lost 1st Round
Coe	Bob Thurness	0-1	Lost 1st Round
Denison	Keith Piper	0-1	Lost 1st Round
Lycoming	Frank Girardi	0-1	Lost 1st Round
St. John's (Minn.)	John Gagliardi	0-1	Lost 1st Round
Union (N.Y.)	Al Bagnoli	0-1	Lost 1st Round
Western Conn. St.	Paul Pasqualoni	0-1	Lost 1st Round

1986 (16)

Augustana (Ill.)	Bob Reade	4-0	Champion
Salisbury St.	Mike McGlinchey	3-1	Second
Concordia-M'head	Jim Christopherson	2-1	Semifinalist
Ithaca	Jim Butterfield	2-1	Semifinalist
Central (Iowa)	Ron Schipper	1-1	Quarterfinalist
Montclair St.	Rick Giancola	1-1	Quarterfinalist
Mount Union	Larry Kehres	1-1	Quarterfinalist
Susquehanna	Rocky Rees	1-1	Quarterfinalist
Buena Vista	Jim Hershberger	0-1	Lost 1st Round
Dayton	Mike Kelly	0-1	Lost 1st Round
Emory & Henry	Lou Wacker	0-1	Lost 1st Round
Hofstra	Mickey Kwiatkowski	0-1	Lost 1st Round
Hope	Ray Smith	0-1	Lost 1st Round
Union (N.Y.)	Al Bagnoli	0-1	Lost 1st Round
Wash. & Jeff.	John Luckhardt	0-1	Lost 1st Round
Wis.-Stevens Point	D. J. LeRoy	0-1	Lost 1st Round

1987 (16)

Wagner	Walt Hameline	4-0	Champion
Dayton	Mike Kelly	3-1	Second
Central (Iowa)	Ron Schipper	2-1	Semifinalist
Emory & Henry	Lou Wacker	2-1	Semifinalist
Augustana (Ill.)	Bob Reade	1-1	Quarterfinalist
Fordham	Larry Glueck	1-1	Quarterfinalist
St. John's (Minn.)	John Gagliardi	1-1	Quarterfinalist
Wash. & Jeff.	John Luckhardt	1-1	Quarterfinalist
Allegheny	Peter Vaas	0-1	Lost 1st Round
Capital	Roger Welsh	0-1	Lost 1st Round
Ferrum	Hank Norton	0-1	Lost 1st Round
Gust. Adolphus	Steve Raarup	0-1	Lost 1st Round
Hiram	Don Charlton	0-1	Lost 1st Round
Hofstra	Mickey Kwiatkowski	0-1	Lost 1st Round
Menlo	Ray Solari	0-1	Lost 1st Round
Rochester	Ray Tellier	0-1	Lost 1st Round

1988 (16)

Ithaca	Jim Butterfield	4-0	Champion
Central (Iowa)	Ron Schipper	3-1	Second
Augustana (Ill.)	Bob Reade	2-1	Semifinalist
Ferrum	Hank Norton	2-1	Semifinalist
Cortland St.	Dennis Kayser	1-1	Quarterfinalist
Moravian	Scot Dapp	1-1	Quarterfinalist
Wis.-Whitewater	Bob Berezowitz	1-1	Quarterfinalist
Wittenberg	Ron Murphy	1-1	Quarterfinalist
Adrian	Ron Labadie	0-1	Lost Regionals
Concordia-M'head	Jim Christopherson	0-1	Lost Regionals
Dayton	Mike Kelly	0-1	Lost Regionals
Hofstra	Mickey Kwiatkowski	0-1	Lost Regionals
Rhodes	Mike Clary	0-1	Lost Regionals
Simpson	Jim Williams	0-1	Lost Regionals
Wagner	Walt Hameline	0-1	Lost Regionals
Widener	Bill Manlove	0-1	Lost Regionals

1989 (16)

Dayton	Mike Kelly	4-0	Champion
Union (N.Y.)	Al Bagnoli	3-1	Second
Ferrum	Hank Norton	2-1	Semifinalist
St. John's (Minn.)	John Gagliardi	2-1	Semifinalist
Central (Iowa)	Ron Schipper	1-1	Quarterfinalist
Lycoming	Frank Girardi	1-1	Quarterfinalist
Millikin	Carl Poelker	1-1	Quarterfinalist
Montclair St.	Rick Giancola	1-1	Quarterfinalist
Augustana (Ill.)	Bob Reade	0-1	Lost Regionals
Cortland St.	Dennis Kayser	0-1	Lost Regionals
Dickinson	Ed Sweeney	0-1	Lost Regionals
Hofstra	Mickey Kwiatkowski	0-1	Lost Regionals
John Carroll	Tony DeCarlo	0-1	Lost Regionals
St. Norbert	Don LaViolette	0-1	Lost Regionals
Simpson	Jim Williams	0-1	Lost Regionals
Wash. & Jeff.	John Luckhardt	0-1	Lost Regionals

1990 (16)

Year (Number of Teams)	Coach	Record	Result
Allegheny	Ken O'Keefe	4-0	Champion
Lycoming	Frank Girardi	3-1	Second
Central (Iowa)	Ron Schipper	2-1	Semifinalist
Hofstra	Joe Gardi	2-1	Semifinalist
Dayton	Mike Kelly	1-1	Quarterfinalist
St. Thomas (Minn.)	Vic Wallace	1-1	Quarterfinalist
Col. of New Jersey	Eric Hamilton	1-1	Quarterfinalist
Wash. & Jeff.	John Luckhardt	1-1	Quarterfinalist
Augustana (Ill.)	Bob Reade	0-1	Lost Regionals
Carnegie Mellon	Rich Lackner	0-1	Lost Regionals
Cortland St.	Dave Murray	0-1	Lost Regionals
Ferrum	Hank Norton	0-1	Lost Regionals
Ithaca	Jim Butterfield	0-1	Lost Regionals
Mount Union	Larry Kehres	0-1	Lost Regionals
Redlands	Mike Maynard	0-1	Lost Regionals
Wis.-Whitewater	Bob Berezowitz	0-1	Lost Regionals

1991 (16)

Ithaca	Jim Butterfield	4-0	Champion
Dayton	Mike Kelly	3-1	Second
St. John's (Minn.)	John Gagliardi	2-1	Semifinalist
Susquehanna	Steve Briggs	2-1	Semifinalist
Allegheny	Ken O'Keefe	1-1	Quarterfinalist
Lycoming	Frank Girardi	1-1	Quarterfinalist
Union (N.Y.)	Al Bagnoli	1-1	Quarterfinalist
Wis.-La Crosse	Roger Harring	1-1	Quarterfinalist
Albion	Pete Schmidt	0-1	Lost Regionals
Baldwin-Wallace	Bob Packard	0-1	Lost Regionals
Coe	D. J. LeRoy	0-1	Lost Regionals
Dickinson	Ed Sweeney	0-1	Lost Regionals
Mass.-Lowell	Dennis Scannell	0-1	Lost Regionals
Rowan	John Bunting	0-1	Lost Regionals
Simpson	Jim Williams	0-1	Lost Regionals
Wash. & Jeff.	John Luckhardt	0-1	Lost Regionals

1992 (16)

Wis.-La Crosse	Roger Harring	4-0	Champion
Wash. & Jeff.	John Luckhardt	3-1	Second
Mount Union	Larry Kehres	2-1	Semifinalist
Rowan	John Bunting	2-1	Semifinalist
Buffalo St.	Jerry Boyes	1-1	Quarterfinalist
Central (Iowa)	Ron Schipper	1-1	Quarterfinalist
Emory & Henry	Lou Wacker	1-1	Quarterfinalist
Ill. Wesleyan	Norm Eash	1-1	Quarterfinalist
Aurora	Jim Scott	0-1	Lost Regionals
Carleton	Bob Sullivan	0-1	Lost Regionals
Dayton	Mike Kelly	0-1	Lost Regionals
Ithaca	Jim Butterfield	0-1	Lost Regionals
Lycoming	Frank Girardi	0-1	Lost Regionals
Redlands	Mike Maynard	0-1	Lost Regionals
Thomas More	Vic Clark	0-1	Lost Regionals
Worcester Tech	Jack Siedlecki	0-1	Lost Regionals

1993 (16)

Mount Union	Larry Kehres	4-0	Champion
Rowan	K. C. Keeler	3-1	Second
St. John's (Minn.)	John Gagliardi	2-1	Semifinalist
Wash. & Jeff.	John Luckhardt	2-1	Semifinalist
Albion	Pete Schmidt	1-1	Quarterfinalist
Frostburg St.	Mike McGlinchey	1-1	Quarterfinalist
Wm. Paterson	Gerry Gallagher	1-1	Quarterfinalist
Wis.-La Crosse	Roger Harring	1-1	Quarterfinalist
Allegheny	Ken O'Keefe	0-1	Lost Regionals
Anderson (Ind.)	Mike Manley	0-1	Lost Regionals
Buffalo St.	Jerry Boyes	0-1	Lost Regionals
Coe	D. J. LeRoy	0-1	Lost Regionals
Moravian	Scot Dapp	0-1	Lost Regionals
Union (N.Y.)	John Audino	0-1	Lost Regionals
Wartburg	Bob Nielson	0-1	Lost Regionals
Wilkes	Joe DeMelfi	0-1	Lost Regionals

1994 (16)

Albion	Pete Schmidt	4-0	Champion
Wash. & Jeff.	John Luckhardt	3-1	Second
Ithaca	Michael Welch	2-1	Semifinalist
St. John's (Minn.)	John Gagliardi	2-1	Semifinalist
Mount Union	Larry Kehres	1-1	Quarterfinalist
Plymouth St.	Don Brown	1-1	Quarterfinalist
Wartburg	Bob Nielson	1-1	Quarterfinalist
Widener	Bill Cubit	1-1	Quarterfinalist
Allegheny	Ken O'Keefe	0-1	Lost Regionals
Augustana (Ill.)	Bob Reade	0-1	Lost Regionals
Buffalo St.	Jerry Boyes	0-1	Lost Regionals
Central (Iowa)	Ron Schipper	0-1	Lost Regionals
Dickinson	Darwin Breaux	0-1	Lost Regionals
La Verne	Rex Huigens	0-1	Lost Regionals
Merchant Marine	Charlie Pravata	0-1	Lost Regionals
Trinity (Tex.)	Steven Mohr	0-1	Lost Regionals

1995 (16)

Wis.-La Crosse	Roger Harring	4-0	Champion
Rowan	K. C. Keeler	3-1	Second
Mount Union	Larry Kehres	2-1	Semifinalist
Wash. & Jeff.	John Luckhardt	2-1	Semifinalist
Lycoming	Frank Girardi	1-1	Quarterfinalist
Union (N.Y.)	John Audino	1-1	Quarterfinalist
Wheaton (Ill.)	J. R. Bishop	1-1	Quarterfinalist
Wis.-River Falls	John O'Grady	1-1	Quarterfinalist
Buffalo St.	Jerry Boyes	0-1	Lost Regionals
Central (Iowa)	Ron Schipper	0-1	Lost Regionals

Year (Number of Teams)	Coach	Record	Result
Concordia-M'head	Jim Christopherson	0-1	Lost Regionals
Emory & Henry	Lou Wacker	0-1	Lost Regionals
Hanover	C. Wayne Perry	0-1	Lost Regionals
Plymouth St.	Don Brown	0-1	Lost Regionals
Widener	Bill Cubit	0-1	Lost Regionals
Wittenberg	Doug Neibuhr	0-1	Lost Regionals
1996 (16)			
Mount Union	Larry Kehres	4-0	Champion
Rowan	K. C. Keeler	3-1	Second
Wis.-La Crosse	Roger Harring	2-1	Semifinalist
Lycoming	Frank Girardi	2-1	Semifinalist
Ill. Wesleyan	Norm Eash	1-1	Quarterfinalist
St. John's (Minn.)	John Gagliardi	1-1	Quarterfinalist
Albright	Ron Maier	1-1	Quarterfinalist
Col. of New Jersey	Eric Hamilton	1-1	Quarterfinalist
Allegheny	Ken O'Keefe	0-1	Lost 1st Round
Albion	Pete Schmidt	0-1	Lost 1st Round
Wis.-River Falls	John O'Grady	0-1	Lost 1st Round
Simpson	Jim Williams	0-1	Lost 1st Round
Ursinus	Steve Gilbert	0-1	Lost 1st Round
Wash. & Jeff.	John Luckhardt	0-1	Lost 1st Round
Buffalo St.	Jerry Boyes	0-1	Lost 1st Round
Coast Guard	Bill Schmitz	0-1	Lost 1st Round
1997 (16)			
Mount Union	Larry Kehres	4-0	Champion
Lycoming	Frank Girardi	3-1	Second
Simpson	Jim Williams	2-1	Semifinalist
Rowan	K. C. Keeler	2-1	Semifinalist
John Carroll	Tony DeCarlo	1-1	Quarterfinalist
Augsburg	Jack Osberg	1-1	Quarterfinalist
Trinity (Tex.)	Steven Mohr	1-1	Quarterfinalist
Col. of New Jersey	Eric Hamilton	1-1	Quarterfinalist
Allegheny	Ken O'Keefe	0-1	Lost 1st Round
Hanover	C. Wayne Perry	0-1	Lost 1st Round
Wis.-Whitewater	Bob Berezowitz	0-1	Lost 1st Round
Concordia-M'head	Jim Christopherson	0-1	Lost 1st Round
Westrn Md.	Tim Keating	0-1	Lost 1st Round
Catholic	Tom Clark	0-1	Lost 1st Round
Coast Guard	Chuck Mills	0-1	Lost 1st Round
Cortland St.	Dan MacNeil	0-1	Lost 1st Round

Division III Championship Record of Each College by Coach

(103 Colleges; 1973-97)

	Yrs	Won	Lost	CH	2D
ADRIAN					
Ron Labadie (Adrian '71) 83, 88	2	0	2	0	0
ALBANY (N.Y.)					
Bob Ford (Springfield '59) 77	1	1	1	0	0
ALBION					
Frank Joranko (Albion '52) 77	1	0	1	0	0
Pete Schmidt (Alma '70) 85, 91, 93, 94-CH, 96	5	5	4	1	0
TOTAL	6	5	5	1	0
ALBRIGHT					
John Potsklan (Penn St. '49) 75, 76	2	0	2	0	0
Ron Maier (Bentley '86) 96	1	1	1	0	0
TOTAL	3	1	3	0	0
ALFRED					
Sam Sanders (Buffalo '60) 81	1	0	1	0	0
ALLEGHENY					
Peter Vaas (Holy Cross '74) 87	1	0	1	0	0
Ken O'Keefe (John Carroll '75) 90-CH, 91, 93, 94, 96, 97	6	5	5	1	0
TOTAL	7	5	6	1	0
ANDERSON (IND.)					
Mike Manley (Anderson [Ind.] '73) 93	1	0	1	0	0
AUGSBURG					
Jack Osberg (Augsburg '62) 97	1	1	1	0	0
AUGUSTANA (ILL.)					
Ben Newcomb 76	1	0	1	0	0
Bob Reade (Cornell College '54) 81, 82-2D, 83-CH, 84-CH, 85-CH, 86-CH, 87, 88, 89, 90, 94	11	19	7	4	1
TOTAL	12	19	8	4	1
AURORA					
Jim Scott (Luther '61) 92	1	0	1	0	0
BALDWIN-WALLACE					
Lee Tressel (Baldwin-Wallace '48) 78-CH, 79, 80	3	3	2	1	0
Bob Packard (Baldwin-Wallace '65) 82, 91	2	0	2	0	0
TOTAL	5	3	4	1	0
BETHANY (W.VA.)					
Don Ault (West Liberty St. '52) 80	1	0	1	0	0
BISHOP					
James Jones (Bishop '49) 82	1	1	1	0	0
BRIDGEPORT					
Ed Farrell (Rutgers '56) 73	1	0	1	0	0
BUENA VISTA					
Jim Hershberger (Northern Iowa '57) 76, 86	2	1	2	0	0
BUFFALO ST.					
Jerry Boyes (Ithaca '76) 92, 93, 94, 95, 96	5	1	5	0	0
CAPITAL					
Roger Welsh (Muskingum '64) 87	1	0	1	0	0
CARLETON					
Bob Sullivan (St. John's [Minn.] '59) 92	1	0	1	0	0
CARNEGIE MELLON					
Chuck Klausing (Slippery Rock '48) 78, 79, 83, 85	4	2	4	0	0
Rich Lackner (Carnegie Mellon '79) 90	1	0	1	0	0
TOTAL	5	2	5	0	0
CARROLL (WIS.)					
Steve Miller (Cornell College '65) 76	1	0	1	0	0
CATHOLIC					
Tom Clark (Maryland '86) 97	1	0	1	0	0
CENTRAL (IOWA)					
Ron Schipper (Hope '52) 74-CH, 77, 84-2D, 85, 86, 87, 88-2D, 89, 90, 92, 94, 95	12	16	11	1	2
COAST GUARD					
Bill Schmitz (Coast Guard '76) 96	1	0	1	0	0
Chuck Mills 97	1	0	1	0	0
TOTAL	2	0	2	0	0
COE					
Bob Thurness (Coe '62) 85	1	0	1	0	0
D. J. LeRoy (Wis.-Eau Claire '79) 91, 93	2	0	2	0	0
TOTAL	3	0	3	0	0
COLORADO COL.					
Jerry Carle (Northwestern '48) 75	1	0	1	0	0
CONCORDIA-M'HEAD					
Jim Christopherson (Concordia-M'head '60) 86, 88, 95, 97	4	2	4	0	0
CORTLAND ST.					
Dennis Kayser (Ithaca '74) 88, 89	2	1	2	0	0
Dave Murray (Springfield '81) 90	1	0	1	0	0
Dan MacNeil (Cortland St. '79) 97	1	0	1	0	0
TOTAL	4	1	4	0	0
DAYTON					
Rick Carter (Earlham '65) 78, 80-CH	2	3	1	1	0
Mike Kelly (Manchester '70) 81-2D, 84, 86, 87-2D, 88, 89-CH, 90, 91-2D, 92	9	13	8	1	3
TOTAL	11	16	9	2	3
DENISON					
Keith Piper (Baldwin-Wallace '48) 85	1	0	1	0	0
DICKINSON					
Ed Sweeney (LIU-C. W. Post '71) 89, 91	2	0	2	0	0
Darwin Breaux (West Chester '77) 94	1	0	1	0	0
TOTAL	3	0	3	0	0
DUBUQUE					
Don Birmingham (Westmar '62) 79, 80	2	0	2	0	0
EMORY & HENRY					
Lou Wacker (Richmond '56) 86, 87, 92, 95	4	3	4	0	0
EVANSVILLE					
Jim Byers (Michigan '59) 74	1	0	1	0	0
FERRUM					
Hank Norton (Lynchburg '51) 87, 88, 89, 90	4	4	4	0	0
FORDHAM					
Larry Glueck (Villanova '63) 87	1	1	1	0	0
FORT VALLEY ST.					
Leon Lomax (Fort Valley St. '43) 75	1	0	1	0	0
FROSTBURG ST.					
Mike McGlinchey (Delaware '67) 93	1	1	1	0	0
GETTYSBURG					
Barry Streeter (Lebanon Valley '71) 85	1	2	1	0	0

	Yrs	Won	Lost	CH	2D
GUST. ADOLPHUS					
Steve Raarup (Gust. Adolphus '53) 87	1	0	1	0	0
HAMPDEN-SYDNEY					
Stokeley Fulton (Hampden-Sydney '55) 77	1	0	1	0	0
HANOVER					
C. Wayne Perry (DePauw '72) 95, 97	2	0	2	0	0
HIRAM					
Don Charlton (Lock Haven '65) 87	1	0	1	0	0
HOFSTRA					
Mickey Kwiatkowski (Delaware '70) 83, 86, 87, 88, 89	5	0	5	0	0
Joe Gardi (Maryland '60) 90	1	2	1	0	0
TOTAL	6	2	6	0	0
HOPE					
Ray Smith (UCLA '61) 86	1	0	1	0	0
ILL. WESLEYAN					
Norm Eash (Ill. Wesleyan '75) 92, 96	2	2	2	0	0
INDIANAPOLIS					
Bill Bless (Indianapolis '63) 75	1	0	1	0	0
ITHACA					
Jim Butterfield (Maine '53) 74-2D, 75-2D, 78, 79-CH, 80-2D, 85-2D, 86, 88-CH, 90, 91-CH, 92	11	21	8	3	4
Michael Welch (Ithaca '73) 94	1	2	1	0	0
TOTAL	12	23	9	3	4
JOHN CARROLL					
Tony DeCarlo (Kent '62) 89, 97	2	1	2	0	0
JUNIATA					
Walt Nadzak (Denison '57) 73-2D	1	1	1	0	1
LA VERNE					
Rex Huigens (La Verne '70) 94	1	0	1	0	0
LAWRENCE					
Ron Roberts (Wisconsin '54) 81	1	1	1	0	0
LIU-C. W. POST					
Dom Anile (LIU-C. W. Post '59) 76	1	0	1	0	0
LYCOMING					
Frank Girardi (West Chester '61) 85, 89, 90-2D, 91, 92, 95, 96, 97-2D	8	11	8	0	1
MASS.-LOWELL					
Dennis Scannell (Villanova '74) 91	1	0	1	0	0
MENLO					
Ray Solari (California '51) 87	1	0	1	0	0
MERCHANT MARINE					
Charlie Pravata (Adelphi '72) 94	1	0	1	0	0
MILLERSVILLE					
Gene Carpenter (Huron '63) 79	1	0	1	0	0
MILLIKIN					
Carl Poelker (Millikin '68) 89	1	1	1	0	0
MILLSAPS					
Harper Davis (Mississippi St. '49) 75	1	1	1	0	0
MINN.-MORRIS					
Al Molde (Gust. Adolphus '66) 77, 78, 79	3	2	3	0	0
Dick Smith (Coe '68) 80, 81	2	1	2	0	0
TOTAL	5	3	5	0	0
MONTCLAIR ST.					
Fred Hill (Upsala '57) 81	1	1	1	0	0
Rick Giancola (Rowan '68) 85, 86, 89	3	3	3	0	0
TOTAL	4	4	4	0	0
MORAVIAN					
Scot Dapp (West Chester '73) 88, 93	2	1	2	0	0
MOUNT UNION					
Ken Wable (Muskingum '52) 85	1	1	1	0	0
Larry Kehres (Mount Union '71) 86, 90, 92, 93-CH, 94, 95, 96-CH, 97-CH	8	18	5	2	0
TOTAL	9	19	6	2	0
COL. OF NEW JERSEY					
Eric Hamilton (Col. of New Jersey '75) 90, 96, 97	3	3	3	0	0
OCCIDENTAL					
Dale Widolff (Indiana Central '75) 83, 84, 85	3	1	3	0	0
PLYMOUTH ST.					
Jay Cottone (Norwich '71) 84	1	0	1	0	0
Don Brown (Norwich '77) 94, 95	2	1	2	0	0
TOTAL	3	1	3	0	0
RANDOLPH-MACON					
Jim Blackburn (Virginia '71) 84	1	0	1	0	0
REDLANDS					
Mike Maynard (Ill. Wesleyan '80) 90, 92	2	0	2	0	0
RHODES					
Mike Clary (Rhodes '77) 88	1	0	1	0	0
ROCHESTER					
Ray Tellier (Connecticut '73) 87	1	0	1	0	0
ROWAN					
John Bunting (North Caro. '72) 91, 92	2	2	2	0	0
K. C. Keeler (Delaware '81) 93-2D, 95-2D, 96-2D, 97	4	11	4	0	3
TOTAL	6	13	6	0	3
ST. JOHN'S (MINN.)					
John Gagliardi (Colorado Col. '49) 76-CH, 77, 85, 87, 89, 91, 93, 94, 96	9	13	8	1	0
ST. LAWRENCE					
Ted Stratford (St. Lawrence '57) 76, 78	2	1	2	0	0
Andy Talley (Southern Conn. St. '67) 82	1	1	1	0	0
TOTAL	3	2	3	0	0
ST. NORBERT					
Don LaViolette (St. Norbert '54) 89	1	0	1	0	0
ST. OLAF					
Tom Porter (St. Olaf '51) 78	1	0	1	0	0
ST. THOMAS (MINN.)					
Vic Wallace (Cornell College '65) 90	1	1	1	0	0
SALISBURY ST.					
Mike McGlinchey (Delaware '67) 83, 85, 86-2D	3	5	3	0	1
SAN DIEGO					
Andy Vinci (Cal St. Los Angeles '63) 73	1	0	1	0	0
SIMPSON					
Jim Williams (Northern Iowa '60) 88, 89, 91, 96, 97	5	2	5	0	0
SLIPPERY ROCK					
Bob Di Spirito (Rhode Island '53) 74	1	0	1	0	0
SUSQUEHANNA					
Rocky Rees (West Chester '71) 86	1	1	1	0	0
Steve Briggs (Springfield '84) 91	1	2	1	0	0
TOTAL	2	3	2	0	0
THOMAS MORE					
Vic Clark (Indiana St. '71) 92	1	0	1	0	0
TOWSON					
Phil Albert (Arizona '66) 76-2D	1	2	1	0	1
TRINITY (TEX.)					
Steven Mohr (Denison '76) 94, 97	2	1	2	0	0
UNION (N.Y.)					
Al Bagnoli (Central Conn. St. '74) 83-2D, 84, 85, 86, 89-2D, 91	6	7	6	0	2
John Audino (Notre Dame '75) 93, 95	2	1	2	0	0
TOTAL	8	8	8	0	2
URSINUS					
Steve Gilbert (West Chester '79) 96	1	0	1	0	0
WABASH					
Frank Navarro (Maryland '53) 77-2D	1	2	1	0	1
WAGNER					
Bill Russo 80	1	0	1	0	0
Walt Hameline (Brockport St. '75) 82, 87-CH, 88	3	4	2	1	0
TOTAL	4	4	3	1	0
WARTBURG					
Don Canfield 82	1	0	1	0	0
Bob Nielson (Wartburg '81) 93, 94	2	1	2	0	0
TOTAL	3	1	3	0	0
WASH. & JEFF.					
John Luckhardt (Purdue '67) 84, 86, 87, 89, 90, 91 92-2D, 93, 94-2D, 95, 96	11	13	11	0	2
WEST GA.					
Bobby Pate (Georgia '63) 81, 82-CH	2	3	1	1	0
WESTERN CONN. ST.					
Paul Pasqualoni (Penn St. '72) 85	1	0	1	0	0
WESTERN MD.					
Tim Keating (Bethany, W. Va. '75) 97	1	0	1	0	0
WHEATON (ILL.)					
J. R. Bishop (Franklin '61) 95	1	1	1	0	0
WIDENER					
Bill Manlove (Temple '58) 75, 77-CH, 79, 80, 81-CH, 82, 88	7	9	5	2	0
Bill Cubit (Delaware '75) 94, 95	2	1	2	0	0
TOTAL	9	10	7	2	0

	Yrs	Won	Lost	CH	2D
WILKES					
Joe DeMelfi (Delta St. '66) 93	1	0	1	0	0
WM. PATERSON					
Gerry Gallagher (Wm. Paterson '74) 93	1	1	1	0	0
WIS.-LA CROSSE					
Roger Harring (Wis.-La Crosse '58) 83, 91, 92-CH, 93, 95-CH, 96	6	13	4	2	0
WIS.-RIVER FALLS					
John O'Grady (Wis.-River Falls '79) 95, 96	2	1	2	0	0
WIS.-STEVENS POINT					
D. J. LeRoy (Wis.-Eau Claire '79) 86	1	0	1	0	0
WIS.-WHITEWATER					
Bob Berezowitz (Wis.-Whitewater '67) 88, 90, 97	3	1	3	0	0
WITTENBERG					
Dave Maurer (Denison '54) 73-CH, 75-CH, 78-2D, 79-2D	4	9	2	2	2
Ron Murphy 88	1	1	1	0	0
Doug Neibuhr (Millikin '75) 95	1	0	1	0	0
TOTAL	6	10	4	2	2
WORCESTER TECH					
Jack Siedlecki (Union [N.Y.] '73) 92	1	0	1	0	0

All-Time Results

1973 Semifinals: Juniata 35, Bridgeport 14; Wittenberg 21, San Diego 14. **Championship:** Wittenberg 41, Juniata 0.

1974 Semifinals: Central (Iowa) 17, Evansville 16; Ithaca 27, Slippery Rock 14. **Championship:** Central (Iowa) 10, Ithaca 8.

1975 First Round: Widener 14, Albright 6; Ithaca 41, Fort Valley St. 12; Wittenberg 17, Indianapolis 13; Millsaps 28, Colorado Col. 21. **Semifinals:** Ithaca 23, Widener 14; Wittenberg 55, Millsaps 22. **Championship:** Wittenberg 28, Ithaca 0.

1976 First Round: St. John's (Minn.) 46, Augustana (Ill.) 7; Buena Vista 20, Carroll (Wis.) 14 (OT); St. Lawrence 26, Albright 7; Towson 14, LIU-C. W. Post 10. **Semifinals:** St. John's (Minn.) 61, Buena Vista 0; Towson 38, St. Lawrence 36. **Championship:** St. John's (Minn.) 31, Towson 28.

1977 First Round: Minn.-Morris 13, Albion 10; Wabash 20, St. John's (Minn.) 9; Widener 19, Central (Iowa) 0; Albany (N.Y.) 51, Hampden-Sydney 45. **Semifinals:** Wabash 37, Minn.-Morris 21; Widener 33, Albany (N.Y.) 15. **Championship:** Widener 39, Wabash 36.

1978 First Round: Minn.-Morris 23, St. Olaf 10; Wittenberg 6, Ithaca 3; Carnegie Mellon 24, Dayton 21, Baldwin-Wallace 71, St. Lawrence 7. **Semifinals:** Wittenberg 35, Minn.-Morris 14; Baldwin-Wallace 31, Carnegie Mellon 6. **Championship:** Baldwin-Wallace 24, Wittenberg 10.

1979 First Round: Wittenberg 21, Millersville 14; Widener 29, Baldwin-Wallace 8; Carnegie Mellon 31, Minn.-Morris 25; Ithaca 27, Dubuque 7. **Semifinals:** Wittenberg 17, Widener 14; Ithaca 15, Carnegie Mellon 6. **Championship:** Ithaca 14, Wittenberg 10.

1980 First Round: Ithaca 41, Wagner 13; Minn.-Morris 41, Dubuque 35; Dayton 34, Baldwin-Wallace 0; Widener 43, Bethany (W.Va.) 12. **Semifinals:** Ithaca 36, Minn.-Morris 0; Dayton 28, Widener 24. **Championship:** Dayton 63, Ithaca 0.

1981 First Round: Dayton 19, Augustana (Ill.) 7; Lawrence 21, Minn.-Morris 14 (OT); Montclair St. 13, Alfred 12; Widener 10, West Ga. 3. **Semifinals:** Dayton 38, Lawrence 0; Widener 23, Montclair St. 12. **Championship:** Widener 17, Dayton 10.

1982 First Round: Augustana (Ill.) 28, Baldwin-Wallace 22; St. Lawrence 43, Wagner 34; Bishop 32, Wartburg 7; West Ga. 31, Widener 24 (3 OT). **Semifinals:** Augustana (Ill.) 14, St. Lawrence 0; West Ga. 27, Bishop 6. **Championship:** West Ga. 14, Augustana (Ill.) 0.

1983 First Round: Union (N.Y.) 51, Hofstra 19; Salisbury St. 16, Carnegie Mellon 14; Augustana (Ill.) 22, Adrian 21; Wis.-La Crosse 43, Occidental 42. **Semifinals:** Union (N.Y.) 23, Salisbury St. 21; Augustana (Ill.) 21, Wis.-La Crosse 15. **Championship:** Augustana (Ill.) 21, Union (N.Y.) 17.

1984 First Round: Union (N.Y.) 26, Plymouth St. 14; Augustana (Ill.) 14, Dayton 13; Wash. & Jeff. 22, Randolph-Macon 21; Central (Iowa) 23, Occidental 22. **Semifinals:** Augustana (Ill.) 23, Union (N.Y.) 6; Central (Iowa) 20, Wash. & Jeff. 0. **Championship:** Augustana (Ill.) 21, Central (Iowa) 12.

1985 First Round: Ithaca 13, Union (N.Y.) 12; Montclair St. 28, Western Conn. St. 0; Salisbury St. 35, Carnegie Mellon 22; Gettysburg 14, Lycoming 10; Augustana (Ill.) 26, Albion 10; Mount Union 35, Denison 3; Central (Iowa) 27, Coe 7; Occidental 28, St. John's (Minn.) 10. **Quarterfinals:** Ithaca 50, Montclair St. 28; Gettysburg 22, Salisbury St. 6; Augustana (Ill.) 21, Mount Union 14; Central (Iowa) 71, Occidental 0. **Semifinals:** Ithaca 34, Gettysburg 0; Augustana (Ill.) 14, Central (Iowa) 7. **Championship:** Augustana (Ill.) 20, Ithaca 7.

1986 First Round: Ithaca 24, Union (N.Y.) 17 (OT); Montclair St. 24, Hofstra 21; Susquehanna 28, Wash. & Jeff. 20; Salisbury St. 34, Emory & Henry 20; Mount Union 42, Dayton 36; Augustana (Ill.) 34, Hope 10; Central (Iowa) 37, Buena Vista 0; Concordia-M'head 24, Wis.-Stevens Point 15. **Quarterfinals:** Ithaca 29, Montclair St. 15; Salisbury St. 31, Susquehanna 17; Augustana (Ill.) 16, Mount Union 7; Concordia-M'head 17, Central (Iowa) 14. **Semifinals:** Salisbury St. 44, Ithaca 40; Augustana (Ill.) 41, Concordia-M'head 7. **Championship:** Augustana (Ill.) 31, Salisbury St. 3.

1987 First Round: Wagner 38, Rochester 14; Fordham 41, Hofstra 6; Wash. & Jeff. 23, Allegheny 17 (OT); Emory & Henry 49, Ferrum 7; Dayton 52, Capital 28; Augustana (Ill.) 53, Hiram 0; St. John's (Minn.) 7, Gust. Adolphus 3; Central (Iowa) 17, Menlo 0. **Quarterfinals:** Wagner 21, Fordham 0; Emory & Henry 23, Wash. & Jeff. 16; Dayton 38, Augustana (Ill.) 36; Central (Iowa) 13, St. John's (Minn.) 3. **Semifinals:** Wagner 20, Emory & Henry 15; Dayton 34, Central (Iowa) 0. **Championship:** Wagner 19, Dayton 3.

1988 Regionals: Cortland St. 32, Hofstra 27; Ithaca 34, Wagner 31 (OT); Ferrum 35, Rhodes 10; Moravian 17, Widener 7; Wittenberg 35, Dayton 28 (OT); Augustana (Ill.) 25, Adrian 7; Central (Iowa) 7, Concordia-M'head 0; Wis.-Whitewater 29, Simpson 27. **Quarterfinals:** Ithaca 24, Cortland St. 17; Ferrum 49, Moravian 28; Augustana (Ill.) 28, Wittenberg 14; Central (Iowa) 16, Wis.-Whitewater 13. **Semifinals:** Ithaca 62, Ferrum 28; Central (Iowa) 23, Augustana (Ill.) 17 (2 OT). **Championship:** Ithaca 39, Central (Iowa) 24.

1989 Regionals: Union (N.Y.) 42, Cortland St. 14; Montclair St. 23, Hofstra 6; Lycoming 21, Dickinson 0; Ferrum 41, Wash. & Jeff. 7; Dayton 35, John Carroll 10; Millikin 21, Augustana (Ill.) 12; Central (Iowa) 55, St. Norbert 7; St. John's (Minn.) 42, Simpson 35. **Quarterfinals:** Union (N.Y.) 45, Montclair St. 6; Ferrum 49, Lycoming 24; Dayton 28, Millikin 16; St. John's (Minn.) 27, Central (Iowa) 24. **Semifinals:** Union (N.Y.) 37, Ferrum 21; Dayton 28, St. John's (Minn.) 0. **Championship:** Dayton 17, Union (N.Y.) 7.

1990 Regionals: Hofstra 35, Cortland St. 9; Col. of New Jersey 24, Ithaca 14; Wash. & Jeff. 10, Ferrum 7; Lycoming 17, Carnegie Mellon 7; Dayton 24, Augustana (Ill.) 14; Allegheny 26, Mount Union 15; St. Thomas (Minn.) 24, Wis.-Whitewater 23; Central (Iowa) 24, Redlands 14. **Quarterfinals:** Hofstra 38, Col. of New Jersey 3; Lycoming 24, Wash. & Jeff. 0; Allegheny 31, Dayton 23; Central (Iowa) 33, St. Thomas (Minn.) 32. **Semifinals:** Lycoming 20, Hofstra 10; Allegheny 24, Central (Iowa) 7. **Championship:** Allegheny 21, Lycoming 14 (OT).

1991 Regionals: St. John's (Minn.) 75, Coe 2; Wis.-La Crosse 28, Simpson 13; Allegheny 24, Albion 21 (OT); Dayton 27, Baldwin-Wallace 10; Ithaca 31, Rowan 10; Union (N.Y.) 55, Mass.-Lowell 16; Lycoming 18, Wash. & Jeff. 16; Susquehanna 21, Dickinson 20. **Quarterfinals:** St. John's (Minn.) 29, Wis.-La Crosse 10; Dayton 28, Allegheny 25 (OT); Ithaca 35, Union (N.Y.) 23; Susquehanna 31, Lycoming 24. **Semifinals:** Dayton 19, St. John's (Minn.) 7; Ithaca 49, Susquehanna 13. **Championship:** Ithaca 34, Dayton 20.

1992 Regionals: Mount Union 27, Dayton 10; Ill. Wesleyan 21, Aurora 12; Central (Iowa) 20, Carleton 8; Wis.-La Crosse 47, Redlands 26; Emory & Henry 17, Thomas More 0; Wash. & Jeff. 33, Lycoming 0; Rowan 41, Worcester Tech 14; Buffalo St. 28, Ithaca 26. **Quarterfinals:** Mount Union 49, Ill. Wesleyan 27; Wis.-La Crosse 34, Central (Iowa) 9; Wash. & Jeff. 51, Emory & Henry 15; Rowan 28, Buffalo St. 19. **Semifinals:** Wis.-La Crosse 29, Mount Union 24; Wash. & Jeff. 18, Rowan 13. **Championship:** Wis.-La Crosse 16, Wash. & Jeff. 12.

1993 Regionals: Mount Union 40, Allegheny 7; Albion 41, Anderson (Ind.) 21; Wis.-La Crosse 55, Wartburg 26; St. John's (Minn.) 32, Coe 14; Wash. & Jeff. 27, Moravian 7; Frostburg St. 26, Wilkes 25; Rowan 29, Buffalo St. 6; Wm. Paterson 17, Union (N.Y.) 7. **Quarterfinals:** Mount Union 30, Albion 16; St. John's (Minn.) 47, Wis.-La Crosse 25; Wash. & Jeff. 28, Frostburg St. 7; Rowan 37, Wm. Paterson 0. **Semifinals:** Mount Union 56, St. John's (Minn.) 8; Rowan 23, Wash. & Jeff. 16. **Championship:** Mount Union 34, Rowan 24.

1994 Regionals: Mount Union 28, Allegheny 19; Albion 28, Augustana (Ill.) 21; Wartburg 22, Central (Iowa) 21; St. John's (Minn.) 51, La Verne 12; Widener 14, Dickinson 0; Wash. & Jeff. 28, Trinity (Tex.) 0; Plymouth St. 19, Merchant Marine 18; Ithaca 10, Buffalo St. 7 (2 OT). **Quarterfinals:** Albion 34, Mount Union 33; St. John's (Minn.) 42, Wartburg 14; Wash. & Jeff. 37, Widener 21; Ithaca 22, Plymouth St. 7. **Semifinals:** Albion 19, St. John's (Minn.) 16; Wash. & Jeff. 23, Ithaca 19. **Championship:** Albion 38, Wash. & Jeff. 15.

1995 Regionals: Mount Union 52, Hanover 18; Wheaton (Ill.) 63, Wittenberg 41; Wis.-La Crosse 45, Concordia-M'head 7; Wis.-River Falls 10, Central (Iowa) 7; Wash. & Jeff. 35, Emory & Henry 16; Lycoming 31, Widener 27; Rowan 46, Buffalo St. 7; Union (N.Y.) 24, Plymouth St. 7. **Quarterfinals:** Mount Union 40, Wheaton (Ill.) 14; Wis.-La Crosse 28, Wis.-River Falls 14; Wash. & Jeff. 48, Lycoming 0; Rowan 38, Union (N.Y.) 7. **Semifinals:** Wis.-La Crosse 20, Mount Union 17; Rowan 28, Wash. & Jeff. 15. **Championship:** Wis.-La Crosse 36, Rowan 7.

1996 Regionals: Mount Union 31, Allegheny 26; Ill. Wesleyan 23, Albion 20; Wis.-La Crosse 44, Wis.-River Falls 0; St John's (Minn.) 21, Simpson 18; Lycoming 31, Ursinus 24; Albright 31, Wash. & Jeff. 17; Rowan 21, Buffalo St. 20; Col. of New Jersey 17, Coast Guard 16. **Quarterfinals:** Mount Union 49, Ill. Wesleyan 14; Wis.-La Crosse 37, St. John's (Minn.) 30; Lycoming 31, Albright 13; Rowan 7, Col. of New Jersey 3. **Semifinals:** Mount Union 39, Wis.-La Crosse 21; Rowan 33, Lycoming 14. **Championship:** Mount Union 56, Rowan 24.

1997 First Round: Mount Union 34, Allegheny 30; John Carroll 30, Hanover 20; Simpson 34, Wis.-Whitewater 31; Augsburg 34, Concordia-M'head 22; Lycoming 27, Western Md. 13; Trinity (Tex.) 44, Catholic 33; Rowan 43, Coast Guard 0; Col. of New Jersey 34, Cortland St. 30. **Quarterfinals:** Mount Union 59, John Carroll 7; Simpson 61, Augsburg 21; Lycoming 46, Trinity (Tex.) 26; Rowan 13, Col. of New Jersey 7. **Semifinals:** Mount Union 54, Simpson 7; Lycoming 28, Rowan 20. **Championship:** Mount Union 61, Lycoming 12.

Attendance Records

All-Time College Football Attendance

(Includes all divisions and non-NCAA teams)

Year	No. Teams	G	Total Attendance	P/G Avg.	Yearly Change Total	Yearly Change Percent
1948	685	—	19,134,159	—	—	—
1949	682	—	19,651,995	—	Up 517,836	+2.71
1950	674	—	18,961,688	—	Dn 690,307	-3.51
1951	635	—	17,480,533	—	Dn 1,481,155	-7.81
1952	625	—	17,288,062	—	Dn 192,471	-1.10
1953	618	—	16,681,731	—	Dn 606,331	-3.51
1954	614	—	17,048,603	—	Up 366,872	+2.20
1955	621	—	17,266,556	—	Up 217,953	+1.28
1956	618	—	18,031,805	—	Up 765,249	+4.43
1957	618	2,586	18,290,724	7,073	Up 258,919	+1.44
1958	618	2,673	19,280,709	7,213	Up 989,985	+5.41
1959	623	2,695	19,615,344	7,278	Up 334,635	+1.74
1960	620	2,711	20,403,409	7,526	Up 788,065	+4.02
1961	616	2,697	20,677,604	7,667	Up 274,195	+1.34
1962	610	2,679	21,227,162	7,924	Up 549,558	+2.66
1963	616	2,686	22,237,094	8,279	Up 1,009,932	+4.76
1964	622	2,745	23,354,477	8,508	Up 1,117,383	+5.02
1965	616	2,749	24,682,572	8,979	Up 1,328,095	+5.69
1966	616	2,768	25,275,899	9,131	Up 593,327	+2.40
1967	610	2,764	26,430,639	9,562	Up 1,154,740	+4.57
1968	612	2,786	27,025,846	9,701	Up 595,207	+2.25
1969	615	2,820	27,626,160	9,797	Up 600,314	+2.22
1970	617	2,895	29,465,604	10,178	Up 1,839,444	+6.66
1971	618	2,955	30,455,442	10,306	Up 989,838	+3.36
1972	620	2,997	30,828,802	10,287	Up 373,360	+1.23
1973	630	3,062	31,282,540	10,216	Up 453,738	+1.47
1974	634	3,101	31,234,855	10,073	Dn 47,685	-0.15
1975	634	3,089	31,687,847	10,258	Up 452,992	+1.45
1976	637	3,108	32,012,008	10,299	Up 324,161	+1.02
1977	638	3,145	32,905,178	10,463	Up 893,170	+2.79

Beginning in 1978, attendance includes NCAA teams only.

All-Time NCAA Attendance

Annual Total NCAA Attendance

(Includes Only NCAA Teams, All Divisions)

Year	No. Teams	G	Total Attendance	P/G Avg.	Yearly Change Total	Yearly Change Percent
1978	484	2,422	32,369,730	13,365	—	—
1979	478	2,381	32,874,755	13,807	Up 505,025	+1.56
1980	485	2,451	33,707,772	13,753	Up 833,017	+2.53
1981	497	2,505	34,230,471	13,665	Up 522,699	+1.55
1982	510	2,569	35,176,195	13,693	Up 945,724	+2.76
1983	505	2,557	34,817,264	13,616	Dn 358,931	-1.02
1984	501	2,542	35,211,076	*13,852	Up 393,812	+1.13
1985	509	2,599	34,951,548	13,448	Dn 259,528	-0.74
1986	510	2,605	35,030,902	13,448	Up 79,354	+2.27
1987	507	2,589	35,007,541	13,522	Dn 23,361	-0.07
1988	524	2,644	34,323,842	12,982	Dn 683,699	-1.95
1989	524	2,630	35,116,188	13,352	Up 792,346	-2.31
1990	533	2,704	35,329,946	13,066	Up 213,758	+0.61
1991	548	2,776	35,528,220	12,798	Up 198,274	+0.56
1992	552	2,824	35,225,431	12,474	Dn 302,789	-0.65
1993	560	2,888	34,870,634	12,074	Dn 354,797	-1.01
1994	568	2,907	36,459,896	12,542	*Up 1,591,352	*+4.56
1995	565	2,923	35,637,784	12,192	Dn 822,112	-2.25
1996	566	2,925	36,083,053	12,336	Up 445,269	+1.25
1997	*581	*2,998	*36,857,849	12,294	Up 774,796	+2.15

**Record.*

Annual Division I-A Attendance

Year	Teams	G	Attendance	Avg.
1976	137	796	23,917,522	30,047
1977	144	799	24,613,285	30,805
1978	139	772	25,017,915	32,407
1979	139	774	25,862,801	33,414
1980	139	776	26,499,022	34,148
1981	137	768	26,588,688	34,621
1982	97	567	24,771,855	*43,689
1983	105	602	25,381,761	42,162
1984	105	606	25,783,807	42,548
1985	105	605	25,434,412	42,040
1986	105	611	25,692,095	42,049
1987	104	607	25,471,744	41,963
1988	104	605	25,079,490	41,454
1989	106	603	25,307,915	41,970
1990	106	615	25,513,098	41,485
1991	106	610	25,646,067	42,043
1992	107	617	25,402,046	41,170
1993	106	613	25,305,438	41,281
1994	107	614	25,590,190	41,678
1995	108	623	25,836,469	41,471
1996	111	644	26,620,942	41,337
1997	112	655	*27,565,959	42,085

**Record.*

Annual Division I-AA Attendance

Year	Teams	G	Attendance	Avg.
1978	38	201	2,032,766	10,113
1979	39	211	2,073,890	9,829
1980	46	251	2,617,932	10,430
1981	50	270	2,950,156	10,927
1982	92	483	5,655,519	*11,709
1983	84	450	4,879,709	10,844
1984	87	465	5,061,480	10,885
1985	87	471	5,143,077	10,919
1986	86	456	5,044,992	11,064
1987	87	460	5,129,250	11,151
1988	88	465	4,801,637	10,326
1989	89	471	5,278,520	11,020
1990	87	473	5,328,477	11,265
1991	89	490	5,386,425	10,993
1992	88	485	5,057,955	10,429
1993	115	623	5,356,873	8,599
1994	117	643	*6,193,989	9,633
1995	119	647	5,660,329	8,749
1996	116	629	5,255,033	8,355
1997	118	642	5,212,048	8,118

**Record.*

Annual Division II Attendance

Year	Teams	G	Attendance	Avg.
1978	103	518	*2,871,683	*5,544
1979	105	526	2,775,569	5,277
1980	111	546	2,584,765	4,734
1981	121	589	2,726,537	4,629
1982	126	618	2,745,964	4,443
1983	122	611	2,705,892	4,429
1984	114	568	2,413,947	4,250
1985	114	569	2,475,325	4,350
1986	111	551	2,404,852	4,365
1987	107	541	2,424,041	4,481
1988	117	580	2,570,964	4,493
1989	116	579	2,572,496	4,428
1990	120	580	2,472,811	4,263
1991	128	622	2,490,929	4,005
1992	129	643	2,733,094	4,251
1993	142	718	2,572,053	3,582
1994	142	704	2,791,074	3,965
1995	138	705	2,459,792	3,489
1996	139	701	2,514,241	3,587
1997	142	710	2,349,442	3,309

**Record.*

Annual Division III Attendance

Year	Teams	G	Attendance	Avg.
1978	204	931	*2,447,366	*2,629
1979	195	870	2,162,495	2,486
1980	189	878	2,006,053	2,285
1981	189	878	1,965,090	2,238
1982	195	901	2,002,857	2,223
1983	194	894	1,849,902	2,069
1984	195	903	1,951,842	2,162
1985	203	954	1,898,734	1,990
1986	208	987	1,888,963	1,914
1987	209	981	1,982,506	2,021
1988	215	994	1,871,751	1,883

Year	Teams	G	Attendance	Avg.
1989	213	977	1,957,257	1,948
1990	220	1,036	2,015,560	1,946
1991	225	1,054	2,004,799	1,902
1992	228	1,079	2,032,336	1,884
1993	197	934	1,636,270	1,752
1994	202	946	1,884,643	1,992
1995	200	948	1,681,194	1,773
1996	200	951	1,692,837	1,780
1997	209	991	1,730,400	1,746

**Record.*

Annual Conference Attendance Leaders

(Based on per-game average; minimum 20 games)

Division I-A

Year	Conference	Teams	Attendance	P/G Avg.
1978	Big Ten	10	3,668,926	61,149
1979	Big Ten	10	3,865,170	63,363
1980	Big Ten	10	3,781,232	64,089
1981	Big Ten	10	3,818,728	63,645
1982	Big Ten	10	3,935,722	66,707
1983	Big Ten	10	3,710,931	67,471
1984	Big Ten	10	3,943,802	*67,997
1985	Big Ten	10	4,015,693	66,928
1986	Big Ten	10	4,006,845	65,686
1987	Big Ten	10	3,990,524	65,418
1988	Southeastern	10	3,912,241	63,101
1989	Southeastern	10	4,123,005	65,445
1990	Southeastern	10	4,215,400	63,870
1991	Southeastern	10	4,063,190	66,610
1992	Southeastern	12	4,844,014	63,737
1993	Big Ten	11	4,320,397	63,535
1994	Big Ten	11	4,452,839	66,460
1995	Big Ten	11	4,592,499	67,537
1996	Big Ten	11	4,321,276	67,520
1997	Big Ten	11	4,744,211	67,774

**Record. Note: The total attendance record is 5,005,126 by the Southeastern Conference in 1997.*

Division I-AA

Year	Conference	Teams	Attendance	P/G Avg.
1978	Southwestern Athletic	5	483,159	17,895
1979	Southwestern Athletic	6	513,768	16,055
1980	Southwestern Athletic	7	611,234	16,085
1981	Southwestern Athletic	7	662,221	18,921
1982	Southwestern Athletic	7	634,505	18,129
1983	Southwestern Athletic	8	709,160	16,117
1984	Southwestern Athletic	8	702,186	17,555
1985	Southwestern Athletic	8	790,296	17,961
1986	Southwestern Athletic	8	621,584	16,357
1987	Southwestern Athletic	8	697,534	16,608
1988	Southwestern Athletic	8	541,127	14,240
1989	Southwestern Athletic	8	796,844	18,110
1990	Southwestern Athletic	7	828,169	20,704
1991	Southwestern Athletic	8	856,491	18,223
1992	Southwestern Athletic	8	873,772	20,804
1993	Southwestern Athletic	8	772,714	18,398
1994	Southwestern Athletic	8	*958,508	*23,378
1995	Southwestern Athletic	8	628,702	16,545
1996	Southwestern Athletic	8	600,798	15,405
1997	Southwestern Athletic	8	567,929	15,776

**Record.*

Division II

Year	Conference	Teams	Attendance	P/G Avg.
1978	Mid-Continent	6	237,458	9,133
1979	Mid-Continent	6	313,790	9,509
1980	Southern Intercollegiate	12	356,744	7,280
1981	Lone Star	8	340,876	7,575
1982	Lone Star	8	348,780	8,507
1983	Lone Star	8	296,350	7,228
1984	Central Intercollegiate	12	418,075	6,743
1985	Central Intercollegiate	12	378,160	6,099
1986	Central Intercollegiate	12	380,172	6,670
1987	Lone Star	6	208,709	6,325
1988	Central Intercollegiate	12	343,070	6,473
1989	Lone Star	8	249,570	5,942
1990	Southern Intercollegiate	9	264,741	6,967
1991	Central Intercollegiate	11	349,962	6,603
1992	Southern Intercollegiate	9	344,504	7,489
1993	Southern Intercollegiate	9	342,446	8,352
1994	Southern Intercollegiate	9	*456,289	*10,140
1995	Southern Intercollegiate	10	321,751	6,846
1996	Southern Intercollegiate	10	310,491	6,750
1997	Southern Intercollegiate	10	314,975	6,562

**Record.*

Division III

Year	Conference	Teams	Attendance	P/G Avg.
1979	Great Lakes	6	90,531	3,482
1980	Great Lakes	7	113,307	3,333
1981	Ohio Athletic	14	*196,640	2,979
1982	New Jersey State	7	98,502	2,985
1983	Heartland	7	121,825	3,384
1984	Heartland	7	107,500	2,986
1985	Ohio Athletic	9	125,074	2,719
1986	Heartland	7	91,793	2,550
1987	Heartland	6	84,815	3,029
1988	Heartland	5	82,966	2,963
1989	Old Dominion	5	70,676	2,945
1990	Old Dominion	6	86,238	2,974
1991	Old Dominion	6	101,774	3,283
1992	Old Dominion	6	100,132	3,338
1993	Old Dominion	6	96,526	3,218
1994	Old Dominion	6	111,334	*3,976
1995	Old Dominion	6	105,819	3,527
1996	Old Dominion	6	90,277	3,113
1997	Old Dominion	6	92,810	3,094

**Record. Note: 1978 figures not available.*

All-time Division I-A Conference Attendance

(Since 1978)

ATLANTIC COAST CONFERENCE

Season	Teams	Games	Attendance	P/G	Change in Pct.	Avg.
1978	7	39	1,475,410	37,831	Up	3.88
1979	7	40	1,620,776	40,519	Up	7.11
1980	7	41	1,590,495	38,793	Dn	4.26
1981	7	40	1,589,152	39,729	Up	2.41
1982	7	41	1,706,451	41,621	Up	4.76
1983	8	49	2,087,800	42,608	Up	3.71
1984	8	46	1,998,274	43,441	Up	1.96
1985	8	48	2,029,574	42,283	Dn	2.67
1986	8	45	1,848,949	41,088	Dn	2.83
1987	8	47	1,970,198	41,919	Up	2.02
1988	8	47	1,911,949	40,680	Dn	2.96
1989	8	49	2,010,317	41,027	Up	0.85
1990	8	47	1,988,781	42,314	Up	3.14
1991	8	51	2,257,413	44,263	Up	4.61
1992	9	53	2,332,674	44,013	Dn	4.62
1993	9	54	2,379,045	44,056	Up	0.10
1994	9	51	2,248,700	44,092	Up	0.08
1995	9	51	2,329,868	45,684	Up	3.61
1996	9	50	2,203,849	44,077	Dn	3.52
1997	9	52	2,333,784	44,880	Up	1.82

BIG EAST CONFERENCE

Season	Teams	Games	Attendance	P/G	Change in Pct.	Avg.
1991	8	47	1,788,611	38,056	Dn	7.00
1992	8	48	1,847,269	38,485	Up	1.13
1993	8	47	1,787,843	38,039	Dn	1.16
1994	8	46	1,902,096	41,350	Up	8.70
1995	8	44	1,679,043	38,160	Dn	7.71
1996	8	47	1,825,870	38,848	Up	1.80
1997	8	46	1,657,056	36,023	Dn	7.27

BIG TEN CONFERENCE

Season	Teams	Games	Attendance	P/G	Change in Pct.	Avg.
1978	10	60	3,668,926	61,149	Up	2.87

Season	Teams	Games	Attendance	P/G	Change in Pct.	Avg.
1979	10	61	3,865,170	63,363	Up	3.62
1980	10	59	3,781,232	64,089	Up	1.15
1981	10	60	3,818,728	63,645	Dn	0.69
1982	10	59	3,935,722	66,707	Up	4.81
1983	10	55	3,710,931	67,471	Up	1.15
1984	10	58	3,943,802	67,997	Up	0.78
1985	10	60	4,015,693	66,928	Dn	1.57
1986	10	61	4,006,845	65,686	Dn	1.86
1987	10	61	3,990,524	65,418	Dn	0.41
1988	10	59	3,714,231	62,953	Dn	3.77
1989	10	59	3,492,647	59,197	Dn	5.97
1990	10	60	3,533,504	58,892	Dn	0.52
1991	10	61	3,674,654	60,240	Up	2.29
1992	10	60	3,600,410	60,007	Dn	0.39
1993	11	68	4,320,397	63,535	Up	0.60
1994	11	67	4,452,839	66,460	Up	4.60
1995	11	68	4,592,499	67,537	Up	1.62
1996	11	64	4,321,276	67,520	Dn	0.03
1997	11	70	4,744,211	67,774	Up	0.04

BIG 12 CONFERENCE

Season	Teams	Games	Attendance	P/G	Change in Pct.	Avg.
1996	12	69	3,549,474	51,442	Up	3.39
1997	12	71	3,640,692	51,277	Dn	0.03

BIG WEST CONFERENCE

Season	Teams	Games	Attendance	P/G	Change in Pct.	Avg.
1988	8	38	570,533	15,014	Up	2.58
1989	8	37	528,921	14,295	Dn	4.79
1990	8	41	650,800	15,873	Up	11.04
1991	8	37	570,332	15,414	Dn	2.89
1992	7	36	515,291	14,314	Up	4.44
1993	10	48	778,224	16,213	Up	6.49
1994	10	49	705,539	14,399	Dn	11.19
1995	10	51	793,452	15,558	Up	8.05
1996	6	34	554,684	16,314	Dn	14.87
1997	6	32	584,020	18,251	Up	11.87

CONFERENCE USA

Season	Teams	Games	Attendance	P/G	Change in Pct.	Avg.
1996	6	33	825,899	25,027	Up	12.87
1997	7	38	963,239	25,348	Dn	0.09

MID-AMERICAN CONFERENCE

Season	Teams	Games	Attendance	P/G	Change in Pct.	Avg.
1978	10	51	722,026	14,157	Up	14.36
1979	10	52	696,784	13,400	Dn	5.35
1980	10	51	714,415	14,008	Up	4.54
1981	10	53	804,158	15,173	Up	8.32
1982@	10	51	980,087	19,217	Up	26.65
1983	10	51	884,888	17,351	Dn	9.71
1984	10	53	918,133	17,323	Dn	0.16
1985	10	49	719,024	14,674	Dn	15.29
1986	9	47	679,866	14,465	Up	2.18
1987	9	45	652,285	14,495	Up	0.21
1988	9	46	765,563	16,643	Up	14.82
1989	9	44	689,698	15,675	Dn	5.82
1990	9	45	744,368	16,542	Up	5.53
1991	9	45	608,485	13,522	Dn	18.26
1992	10	49	704,233	14,372	Up	5.97
1993	10	51	726,847	14,252	Dn	0.83
1994	10	51	754,296	14,790	Up	3.77
1995	10	50	748,138	14,963	Up	1.17
1996	10	50	787,035	15,741	Up	5.18
1997	12	63	1,130,939	17,951	Up	13.44

PACIFIC-10 CONFERENCE

Season	Teams	Games	Attendance	P/G	Change in Pct.	Avg.
1978	10	57	2,632,755	46,189	Up	5.56
1979	10	59	2,741,656	46,469	Up	0.61
1980	10	58	2,777,146	47,882	Up	3.04
1981	10	59	2,772,237	46,987	Dn	1.87
1982	10	59	2,745,676	46,537	Dn	0.96
1983	10	58	2,740,406	47,248	Up	1.53
1984	10	63	2,976,655	47,248	No Change	
1985	10	56	2,665,356	47,596	Up	0.74
1986	10	59	2,856,910	48,422	Up	1.74
1987	10	57	2,866,723	50,293	Up	3.86
1988	10	60	3,058,637	50,977	Up	1.36
1989	10	60	3,006,176	50,103	Dn	1.71
1990	10	58	2,872,173	49,520	Dn	1.16

Season	Teams	Games	Attendance	P/G	Change in Pct.	Avg.
1991	10	59	2,851,991	48,339	Dn	2.38
1992	10	60	2,825,401	47,090	Dn	2.58
1993	10	57	2,731,361	47,919	Up	1.76
1994	10	59	2,785,373	47,210	Dn	1.48
1995	10	57	2,680,510	47,026	Dn	0.39
1996	10	58	2,761,006	47,604	Up	1.23
1997	10	60	2,891,522	48,192	Up	1.24

SOUTHEASTERN CONFERENCE

Season	Teams	Games	Attendance	P/G	Change in Pct.	Avg.
1978	10	61	3,464,112	56,789	Up	2.62
1979	10	59	3,376,833	57,234	Up	0.78
1980	10	66	3,951,104	59,865	Up	4.60
1981	10	61	3,846,492	63,057	Up	5.33
1982	10	66	4,206,507	63,735	Up	1.08
1983	10	65	4,214,702	64,842	Up	1.74
1984	10	63	4,007,351	63,609	Dn	1.90
1985	10	63	4,017,104	63,764	Up	0.24
1986	10	69	4,351,832	63,070	Dn	1.09
1987	10	64	4,117,046	64,329	Up	2.00
1988	10	62	3,912,241	63,101	Dn	1.91
1989	10	63	4,123,005	65,445	Up	3.71
1990	10	66	4,215,400	63,870	Dn	2.41
1991	10	61	4,063,190	66,610	Up	4.29
1992	12	76	4,844,014	63,737	Dn	1.26
1993	12	78	4,897,564	62,789	Dn	1.49
1994	12	77	4,891,615	63,527	Up	1.18
1995	12	76	4,827,834	63,524	Dn	0.01
1996	12	76	4,932,802	64,905	Up	2.17
1997	12	76	5,005,126	65,857	Up	1.47

WESTERN ATHLETIC CONFERENCE

Season	Teams	Games	Attendance	P/G	Change in Pct.	Avg.
1978	7	37	906,518	24,500	Dn	1.84
1979	8	47	1,349,156	28,705	Up	7.02
1980	9	51	1,354,492	26,559	Dn	5.41
1981	9	51	1,443,515	28,304	Up	6.57
1982	9	53	1,605,684	30,296	Up	7.04
1983	9	52	1,567,062	30,136	Dn	0.53
1984	9	55	1,741,793	31,669	Up	5.09
1985	9	55	1,744,123	31,711	Up	0.13
1986	9	51	1,748,857	34,291	Up	8.14
1987	9	54	1,927,572	35,696	Up	4.10
1988	9	54	1,795,735	33,254	Dn	6.84
1989	9	55	1,844,999	33,545	Up	0.88
1990	9	55	1,784,807	32,451	Dn	3.26
1991	9	55	1,883,861	34,252	Up	5.55
1992	10	60	2,111,587	35,193	Up	2.85
1993	10	61	2,109,441	34,581	Dn	1.74
1994	10	61	2,090,620	34,272	Dn	0.89
1995	10	63	1,987,860	31,553	Dn	7.93
1996	16	91	2,615,219	28,739	Up	2.38
1997	16	92	2,758,817	29,987	Up	4.34

@Mid-American and Missouri Valley divided between I-A and I-AA.

ALL-TIME ATTENDANCE OTHER CONFERENCES

(Conferences that either discontinued or changed names)

BIG EIGHT CONFERENCE

(All members went into Big 12 Conference after 1995 season)

Season	Teams	Games	Attendance	P/G	Change in Pct.	Avg.
1978	8	48	2,549,553	53,116	Dn	1.45
1979	8	46	2,457,633	53,427	Up	0.59
1980	8	49	2,629,195	53,657	Up	0.43
1981	8	50	2,559,480	51,190	Dn	4.60
1982	8	48	2,377,389	49,529	Dn	3.24
1983	8	49	2,398,184	48,943	Dn	1.18
1984	8	45	2,247,010	49,934	Up	2.02
1985	8	54	2,504,509	46,380	Dn	7.12
1986	8	49	2,242,082	45,757	Dn	1.34
1987	8	49	2,182,199	44,535	Dn	2.67
1988	8	49	2,184,333	44,578	Up	0.10
1989	8	49	2,362,465	48,214	Up	8.16
1990	8	49	2,257,825	46,078	Dn	4.43
1991	8	49	2,308,238	47,107	Up	2.23
1992	8	47	2,247,907	47,828	Up	1.53
1993	8	48	2,126,247	44,297	Dn	7.38
1994	8	46	2,194,545	47,708	Up	7.70
1995	8	50	2,414,804	48,296	Up	1.23

IVY GROUP

(Went into Division I-AA after 1981 season)

Season	Teams	Games	Attendance	P/G	Change in Pct.	Avg.
1978	8	40	547,395	13,685	Up	4.87
1979	8	40	534,597	13,365	Dn	2.34
1980	8	43	514,433	11,964	Dn	10.48
1981	8	41	564,059	13,758	Up	14.99

MISSOURI VALLEY CONFERENCE

(Conference discontinued after 1985 season)

Season	Teams	Games	Attendance	P/G	Change in Pct.	Avg.
1978	7	39	523,565	13,425	Up	5.83
1979	7	37	481,706	13,019	Dn	3.02
1980	7	35	473,462	13,527	Up	3.90
1981	8	43	575,174	13,376	Up	3.34
1982@	8	40	594,515	14,863	Up	11.12
1983@	7	37	412,412	11,146	Dn	23.63
1984@	7	37	427,112	11,544	Up	3.57
1985@	5	26	308,137	11,851	Dn	8.32

PACIFIC COAST CONFERENCE

(Became Big West Conference after 1987 season)

Season	Teams	Games	Attendance	P/G	Change in Pct.	Avg.
1978	6	29	279,772	9,647	Dn	3.81
1979	6	25	322,305	12,892	Up	33.64
1980	6	28	353,022	12,608	Dn	2.20
1981	6	27	360,005	13,334	Up	5.76
1982	7	34	487,638	14,342	Dn	6.98
1983	7	35	500,380	14,297	Dn	0.31
1984	8	39	597,420	15,318	Up	5.52
1985	8	40	654,045	16,351	Up	6.74
1986	8	42	753,466	17,940	Up	9.72
1987	8	41	600,129	14,637	Dn	18.41

SOUTHERN CONFERENCE

(Went into Division I-AA after 1981 season)

Season	Teams	Games	Attendance	P/G	Change in Pct.	Avg.
1978	7	34	372,009	10,941	Up	11.20
1979	8	47	478,107	10,172	Up	0.64
1980	8	40	484,727	12,118	Up	19.13
1981	8	42	459,576	10,942	Dn	9.70

SOUTHLAND CONFERENCE

(Went into Division I-AA after 1981 season)

Season	Teams	Games	Attendance	P/G	Change in Pct.	Avg.
1978	6	37	467,915	12,646	Dn	13.67
1979	6	31	491,917	15,868	Up	25.48
1980	6	32	452,311	14,135	Dn	10.92
1981	6	30	427,106	14,237	Up	0.72

SOUTHWEST CONFERENCE

(Discontinued after 1995 season; teams went to Big Twelve and Western Athletic Conferences)

Season	Teams	Games	Attendance	P/G	Change in Pct.	Avg.
1978	9	45	2,033,212	45,182	Up	15.46
1979	9	52	2,301,148	44,253	Dn	2.06
1980	9	54	2,263,881	41,924	Dn	5.26
1981	9	54	2,232,757	41,347	Dn	1.38
1982	9	52	2,226,009	42,808	Up	3.53
1983	9	56	2,292,540	40,938	Dn	4.37
1984	9	53	2,177,507	41,085	Up	0.36
1985	9	51	2,077,717	40,740	Dn	0.84
1986	9	53	2,006,663	37,862	Dn	7.06
1987	8	48	1,859,454	38,739	Up	2.32
1988	8	46	1,774,120	38,568	Dn	0.44
1989	9	51	1,914,608	37,541	Dn	2.66
1990	9	53	2,087,248	39,382	Up	4.90
1991	9	50	2,062,309	41,246	Up	4.73
1992	8	47	1,697,152	36,110	Dn	10.52
1993	8	45	1,587,652	35,281	Dn	2.30
1994	8	43	1,588,955	36,952	Up	4.74
1995	8	43	1,653,888	38,463	Up	4.09

All-time Division I-AA Conference Attendance

(Since 1978)

BIG SKY CONFERENCE

Season	Teams	Games	Attendance	P/G	Change in Pct.	Avg.
1978	7	36	393,274	10,924	Up	4.16
1979	8	47	463,920	9,871	Dn	7.70
1980	8	45	520,250	11,561	Up	17.12
1981	8	47	538,920	11,466	Dn	0.82
1982	8	43	463,393	10,777	Dn	6.01
1983	8	44	474,167	10,777	No change	
1984	8	47	475,645	10,120	Dn	6.10
1985	8	48	481,015	10,021	Dn	0.98
1986	8	46	469,368	10,204	Up	1.83
1987	9	52	537,300	10,333	Up	7.37
1988	9	50	513,467	10,269	Dn	0.62
1989	9	52	550,975	10,596	Up	3.18
1990	9	50	531,060	10,621	Up	0.24
1991	9	56	623,326	11,131	Up	4.80
1992	8	46	437,592	9,513	Dn	1.13
1993	8	48	460,613	9,596	Up	0.87
1994	8	47	530,089	11,278	Up	17.53
1995	8	46	530,022	11,522	Up	2.16
1996	8	44	360,082	8,184	Up	4.63
1997	8	47	385,728	8,207	Up	0.03

GATEWAY FOOTBALL CONFERENCE

Season	Teams	Games	Attendance	P/G	Change in Pct.	Avg.
1985	6	35	281,632	8,047	Up	8.01
1986	7	37	351,972	9,513	Up	16.03
1987	7	36	315,318	8,759	Dn	7.93
1988	7	36	332,800	9,244	Up	5.54
1989	7	40	315,633	7,891	Dn	14.64
1990	7	36	313,409	8,706	Up	10.33
1991	7	38	332,482	8,750	Up	0.51
1992	7	40	345,823	8,646	Dn	1.19
1993	7	36	285,921	7,942	Dn	8.14
1994	7	40	293,437	7,336	Dn	7.63
1995	7	41	317,344	7,740	Up	5.51
1996	6	33	294,724	8,931	Up	11.37
1997	7	41	399,221	9,737	Up	6.24

IVY GROUP

Season	Teams	Games	Attendance	P/G	Change in Pct.	Avg.
1982	8	44	602,857	13,701	Dn	0.41
1983	8	43	653,263	15,192	Up	10.88
1984	8	39	591,562	15,168	Dn	0.16
1985	8	41	562,184	13,712	Dn	9.60
1986	8	43	543,983	12,651	Dn	7.74
1987	8	42	602,480	14,345	Up	13.39
1988	8	42	513,674	12,230	Dn	14.74
1989	8	43	557,872	12,974	Up	6.08
1990	8	41	471,245	11,494	Dn	11.41
1991	8	39	466,928	11,973	Up	4.17
1992	8	40	401,980	10,050	Dn	16.06
1993	8	42	420,915	10,022	Dn	0.28
1994	8	42	445,900	10,617	Up	5.94
1995	8	42	396,539	9,441	Dn	11.08
1996	8	40	413,112	10,328	Up	9.40
1997	8	39	284,650	7,299	Dn	29.33

METRO ATLANTIC ATHLETIC CONFERENCE

Season	Teams	Games	Attendance	P/G	Change in Pct.	Avg.
1993	6	29	34,483	1,189	Up	13.02
1994	7	35	41,364	1,182	Dn	2.72
1995	8	37	51,549	1,393	Dn	4.74
1996	9	41	57,742	1,408	Up	1.08
1997	9	46	69,249	1,505	Up	6.89

MID-EASTERN ATHLETIC CONFERENCE

Season	Teams	Games	Attendance	P/G	Change in Pct.	Avg.
1978	4	19	141,234	7,433	Dn	2.96
1979	4	24	131,942	5,498	Dn	26.03
1980	6	29	308,530	10,639	Up	10.20
1981	6	35	357,982	10,228	Dn	3.86
1982	6	35	358,315	10,238	Up	0.10
1983	6	34	335,664	9,872	Dn	3.57
1984	5	27	209,612	7,763	Dn	8.30
1985	5	23	263,687	11,465	Up	47.69
1986	6	32	270,405	8,450	Dn	22.56
1987	6	30	354,899	11,830	Up	40.00
1988	7	39	466,030	11,948	Dn	2.34
1989	7	41	521,529	12,720	Up	6.45
1990	7	36	475,909	13,220	Up	3.93
1991	7	40	578,412	14,460	Up	9.38
1992	7	38	450,962	11,867	Dn	17.93
1993	7	40	440,012	11,000	Dn	7.31
1994	7	40	556,159	13,904	Up	26.40
1995	8	37	350,770	9,480	Dn	21.02

Season	Teams	Games	Attendance	P/G	Change in Pct.	Avg.
1996	8	41	445,672	10,870	Up	20.00
1997	9	42	427,794	10,186	Dn	10.22

NORTHEAST CONFERENCE

Season	Teams	Games	Attendance	P/G	Change in Pct.	Avg.
1996	5	27	40,800	1,511	Dn	10.70
1997	5	24	37,014	1,542	Up	2.05

OHIO VALLEY CONFERENCE

Season	Teams	Games	Attendance	P/G	Change in Pct.	Avg.
1978	7	37	355,893	9,619	Dn	8.47
1979	7	36	349,165	9,699	Up	0.83
1980	8	45	470,001	10,444	Dn	0.59
1981	9	47	428,182	9,110	Dn	7.99
1982	8	43	367,591	8,549	Dn	2.48
1983	8	44	356,124	8,094	Dn	5.32
1984	8	45	377,991	8,400	Up	3.78
1985	8	44	420,016	9,546	Up	13.64
1986	8	44	379,014	8,614	Dn	9.76
1987	7	35	277,978	7,942	Up	7.95
1988	7	38	302,609	7,963	Dn	23.00
1989	7	34	296,739	8,728	Up	9.61
1990	7	40	465,183	11,630	Up	33.25
1991	8	42	316,755	7,542	Dn	30.54
1992	9	49	395,264	8,067	Up	8.83
1993	9	49	294,714	6,015	Dn	25.44
1994	9	49	354,903	7,243	Up	20.42
1995	9	50	373,967	7,479	Up	3.26
1996	9	49	363,860	7,426	Dn	4.64
1997	8	42	265,345	6,318	Dn	23.99

PATRIOT LEAGUE

Season	Teams	Games	Attendance	P/G	Change in Pct.	Avg.
1990	6	30	223,893	7,463	Up	3.15
1991	6	32	231,155	7,224	Dn	3.20
1992	6	31	202,187	6,522	Dn	9.72
1993	6	29	165,581	5,710	Dn	12.45
1994	6	32	198,274	6,196	Up	8.51
1995	6	29	157,625	5,435	Dn	12.28
1996	6	32	185,275	5,790	Up	6.53
1997	7	38	175,992	4,631	Dn	13.94

PIONEER FOOTBALL LEAGUE

Season	Teams	Games	Attendance	P/G	Change in Pct.	Avg.
1993	6	32	94,995	2,969	Dn	16.15
1994	6	32	129,678	4,052	Up	36.48
1995	6	32	115,148	3,598	Dn	11.20
1996	6	31	117,406	3,787	Up	5.25
1997	6	30	109,234	3,641	Dn	3.86

SOUTHERN CONFERENCE

Season	Teams	Games	Attendance	P/G	Change in Pct.	Avg.
1982	8	42	451,214	10,743	Dn	1.82
1983	9	47	442,328	9,411	Dn	3.63
1984	9	49	497,040	10,144	Up	7.79
1985	9	49	501,420	10,233	Up	0.88
1986	9	47	484,589	10,310	Up	0.75
1987	8	47	516,773	10,995	Dn	1.29
1988	8	43	479,649	11,155	Up	1.46
1989	8	44	495,918	11,271	Up	1.04
1990	8	44	504,248	11,415	Up	1.28
1991	8	46	574,059	12,480	Up	9.33
1992	9	55	700,613	12,738	Dn	1.25
1993	9	51	617,620	12,110	Dn	4.93
1994	9	53	667,283	12,590	Up	3.96
1995	9	47	532,530	11,330	Dn	10.01
1996	9	51	578,350	11,340	Up	0.09
1997	9	52	491,680	9,455	Dn	1.44

SOUTHLAND FOOTBALL LEAGUE
(Formerly Southland Conference)

Season	Teams	Games	Attendance	P/G	Change in Pct.	Avg.
1982	6	31	438,147	14,134	Up	0.63
1983	7	35	469,010	13,400	Dn	1.60
1984	7	38	458,259	12,059	Dn	10.01
1985	7	35	408,960	11,685	Dn	3.10
1986	6	30	395,515	13,184	Up	3.82
1987	7	35	412,898	11,797	Up	3.67
1988	7	40	441,301	11,033	Dn	6.48
1989	7	38	423,772	11,152	Up	1.08
1990	7	38	436,110	11,477	Up	2.91

Season	Teams	Games	Attendance	P/G	Change in Pct.	Avg.
1991	8	41	392,513	9,573	Dn	9.65
1992	8	45	429,971	9,555	Dn	0.19
1993	8	43	403,508	9,384	Dn	1.79
1994	7	43	435,078	10,118	Up	19.87
1995	6	33	316,426	9,589	Up	5.53
1996	8	46	411,357	8,943	Dn	10.29
1997	8	46	388,593	8,448	Dn	5.54

SOUTHWESTERN ATHLETIC CONFERENCE

Season	Teams	Games	Attendance	P/G	Change in Pct.	Avg.
1978	5	27	483,159	17,895	Dn	5.30
1979	6	32	513,768	16,055	Dn	1.02
1980	7	38	611,234	16,085	Up	4.58
1981	7	35	662,221	18,921	Up	17.63
1982	7	35	634,505	18,129	Dn	4.19
1983	8	44	709,160	16,117	Dn	5.11
1984	8	40	702,186	17,555	Up	8.92
1985	8	44	790,296	17,961	Up	2.31
1986	8	38	621,584	16,357	Dn	8.93
1987	8	42	697,534	16,608	Up	1.53
1988	8	38	541,127	14,240	Dn	14.26
1989	8	44	796,844	18,110	Up	27.18
1990	7	40	828,169	20,704	Up	10.85
1991	8	47	856,491	18,223	Dn	11.98
1992	8	42	873,772	20,804	Up	14.16
1993	8	42	772,714	18,398	Dn	11.57
1994	8	41	958,508	23,378	Up	27.04
1995	8	38	628,702	16,545	Dn	29.23
1996	8	39	600,798	15,405	Dn	6.35
1997	8	36	567,929	15,776	Up	2.41

ATLANTIC 10 CONFERENCE

Season	Teams	Games	Attendance	P/G	Change in Pct.	Avg.
1978	6	32	207,502	6,484	Dn	9.81
1979	6	29	197,293	6,803	Up	4.92
1980	6	32	211,822	6,619	Dn	2.70
1981	6	29	233,680	8,058	Up	21.74
1982	6	32	254,789	7,962	Dn	1.19
1983	6	30	218,186	7,273	Dn	8.65
1984	6	31	284,709	9,184	Up	26.28
1985	6	36	257,170	7,144	Dn	22.21
1986	8	44	486,299	11,052	Up	13.48
1987	8	43	408,170	9,492	Dn	14.12
1988	9	47	447,641	9,524	Dn	0.27
1989	9	48	460,683	9,598	Up	0.78
1990	9	49	423,459	8,642	Dn	9.96
1991	9	48	431,522	8,990	Up	4.03
1992	9	53	461,366	8,705	Dn	3.17
1993	12	67	550,245	8,213	Dn	7.09
1994	12	67	630,847	9,416	Up	14.65
1995	12	66	578,742	8,769	Dn	6.87
1996	12	64	526,442	8,226	Dn	6.19
1997	12	65	486,798	7,489	Dn	8.96

ALL-TIME ATTENDANCE OTHER CONFERENCES
(Conferences that either discontinued or changed names)

AMERICAN WEST CONFERENCE

Season	Teams	Games	Attendance	P/G	Change in Pct.	Avg.
1994	4	20	82,986	4,149	Dn	8.77
1995	4	23	97,798	4,252	Up	2.48

COLONIAL ATHLETIC ASSOCIATION

Season	Teams	Games	Attendance	P/G	Change in Pct.	Avg.
1986	5	24	241,192	10,050	Up	23.97
1987	6	29	241,831	8,339	Dn	5.39
1988	6	31	195,686	6,312	Dn	24.31
1989	5	26	196,767	7,568	Up	3.25

GULF STAR CONFERENCE
(Teams went to Southland Conference)

Season	Teams	Games	Attendance	P/G	Change in Pct.	Avg.
1984	4	20	149,516	7,476	Dn	9.23
1985	4	22	166,046	7,548	Up	0.96
1986	5	25	211,094	8,444	Up	17.72

MID-CONTINENT CONFERENCE
(Discontinued after 1984 season; Four members went to Gateway)

Season	Teams	Games	Attendance	P/G	Change in Pct.	Avg.
1981	3	17	140,506	8,265	Up	4.74
1982	4	23	191,975	8,347	Up	7.73
1983	4	21	167,219	7,963	Dn	4.60
1984	4	24	175,181	7,299	Dn	8.34

Largest Regular-Season Crowds

Largest Regular-Season Crowds*

Crowd	Date	Home Visitor
107,608	9-21-96	Tennessee 29, Florida 35
107,073	11-8-97	Tennessee 44, Southern Miss. 20
106,986	11-22-97	Michigan 20, Ohio St. 14
106,867	11-20-93	Michigan 28, Ohio St. 0
106,851	9-11-93	Michigan 23, Notre Dame 27
106,832	10-15-94	Michigan 24, Penn St. 31
106,788	10-10-92	Michigan 35, Michigan St. 10
106,700	10-26-96	Tennessee 20, Alabama 13
106,683	11-29-97	Tennessee 17, Vanderbilt 10
106,656	10-11-97	Tennessee 38, Georgia 13
106,579	10-24-92	Michigan 63, Minnesota 13
106,577	11-1-97	Michigan 24, Minnesota 3
106,505	10-18-97	Michigan 28, Iowa 24
106,481	11-14-92	Michigan 22, Illinois 22
106,474	9-13-97	Michigan 27, Colorado 3
106,427	9-24-94	Michigan 26, Colorado 27
106,385	10-23-93	Michigan 21, Illinois 24
106,381	11-2-96	Michigan 45, Michigan St. 29
106,301	11-1-97	Tennessee 22, South Caro. 7
106,297	9-7-96	Tennessee 35, UCLA 20
106,288	11-25-95	Michigan 31, Ohio St. 23
106,285	8-30-97	Tennessee 52, Texas Tech 17
106,272	10-8-94	Michigan 40, Michigan St. 20
106,255	11-17-79	Michigan 15, Ohio St. 18
106,229	10-4-97	Tennessee 31, Mississippi 17
106,212	8-31-96	Tennessee 62, UNLV 3
106,209	10-29-94	Michigan 19, Wisconsin 31
106,208	10-8-88	Michigan 17, Michigan St. 3

**In the 50 seasons official national attendance records have been maintained.*

WEEKS WITH LARGEST TOTAL ATTENDANCE FOR THE TOP-10 ATTENDED GAMES

Total	Date
862,941	9-4-93
857,115	10-10-92
855,722	11-22-97
854,835	9-30-95
853,640	9-21-96
848,356	9-7-96
847,327	11-18-97
843,076	11-11-97
842,043	11-2-96
834,370	10-8-94
833,285	10-22-83
831,666	9-13-97
829,425	11-1-97
828,869	10-28-95
828,516	11-4-97
828,253	10-2-93
828,034	9-24-94
827,402	11-23-96
827,232	9-16-89
825,455	9-22-84
825,260	9-9-95
822,941	10-19-96
821,793	9-20-97
820,668	11-18-89
820,545	11-19-94

1997 Top Ten Regular-Season Crowds

Attend.	Home Team vs. Opponent Score	Date	Site
107,073	Tennessee 44, So. Miss. 20	11-8	Knoxville, Tenn.
106,986	Michigan 20, Ohio St. 14	11-22	Ann Arbor, Mich.
106,683	Tennessee 17, Vanderbilt 10	11-29	Knoxville, Tenn.
106,656	Tennessee 38, Georgia 13	10-11	Knoxville, Tenn.
106,577	Michigan 24, Minnesota 3	11-1	Ann Arbor, Mich.
106,508	Michigan 21, Notre Dame 14	9-27	Ann Arbor, Mich.
106,505	Michigan 28, Iowa 24	10-18	Ann Arbor, Mich.
106,474	Michigan 27, Colorado 3	9-13	Ann Arbor, Mich.
106,301	Tennessee 22, South Caro. 7	11-1	Knoxville, Tenn.
106,285	Tennessee 52, Texas Tech 17	8-30	Knoxville, Tenn.

**Largest All-Time Regular-Season Crowd.*

Pre-1948 Regular-Season Crowds in Excess of 100,000

Crowd	Date	Site	Opponents, Score
120,000*	11-26-27	Soldier Field, Chicago	Notre Dame 7, Southern Cal 6
120,000*	10-13-28	Soldier Field, Chicago	Notre Dame 7, Navy 0
112,912	11-16-29	Soldier Field, Chicago	Notre Dame 13, Southern Cal 12
110,000*	11-27-26	Soldier Field, Chicago	Army 21, Navy 21
110,000*	11-29-30	Soldier Field, Chicago	Notre Dame 7, Army 6
104,953	12-6-47	Los Angeles	Notre Dame 38, Southern Cal 7

**Estimated attendance; others are audited figures.*

Additional Records

Highest Average Attendance Per Home Game: 106,538, Tennessee, 1997 (639,227 in 6)

Highest Total Home Attendance: 745,139, Michigan, 1997 (7 games)

Highest Total Attendance, Home and Away: 1,044,370, Michigan, 1997 (11 games)

Highest Bowl Game Attendance: 106,869, 1973 Rose Bowl (Southern Cal 42, Ohio St. 17)

Most Consecutive Home Sellout Crowds: 219, Nebraska (current, from Nov. 3, 1962)

Most Consecutive 100,000-Plus Crowds: 142, Michigan (current, from Nov. 8, 1975)

1997 Attendance

Division I-A

	Games	Attendance	Average	Change in Avg.	
1. Tennessee	6	639,227	106,538	Up	1,120
2. Michigan	7	745,139	106,448	Up	516
3. Penn St.	6	582,517	97,086	Up	919
4. Ohio St.	8	731,884	91,486	Dn	2,542
5. Florida	6	512,775	85,463	Up	59
6. Auburn	6	501,267	83,545	Up	1,077
7. Georgia	6	494,375	82,396	Up	3,124
8. Notre Dame	6	481,350	80,225	Up	21,150
9. LSU	7	561,016	80,145	Up	626
10. South Caro.	6	480,041	80,007	Up	472
11. Wisconsin	6	467,281	77,880	Dn	69
12. Nebraska	6	453,610	75,602	Up	164
13. Michigan St.	6	447,903	74,651	Up	4,928
14. Florida St.	5	372,001	74,400	Dn	3,118
15. Texas	5	370,200	74,040	Dn	705
16. Washington	6	441,534	73,589	Up	2,320
17. Alabama	7	492,883	70,412	Dn	5,034
18. Oklahoma	6	417,697	69,616	Up	2,715
19. Clemson	6	409,918	68,320	Up	1,088
20. Iowa	6	405,788	67,631	Dn	1,773
21. Brigham Young	6	388,115	64,686	Up	1,933
22. Southern Cal	6	376,732	62,789	Up	2,588
23. Arizona St.	6	374,749	62,458	Dn	1,902
24. Texas A&M	6	371,512	61,919	Dn	1,353
25. Kentucky	6	354,662	59,110	Up	18,463
26. North Caro.	6	345,900	57,650	Up	10,150
27. Stanford	6	341,624	56,937	Up	21,154
28. UCLA	6	327,531	54,589	Dn	2,943
29. West Va.	6	317,126	52,854	Dn	2,842
30. Missouri	6	314,904	52,484	Up	13,314
31. Purdue	6	310,141	51,690	Up	6,334
32. Colorado	6	303,218	50,536	Dn	1,562
33. Arkansas	6	280,724	46,787	Up	2,235
34. North Caro. St.	6	275,636	45,939	Up	4,611
35. Syracuse	6	275,188	45,865	Dn	2,312
36. Minnesota	6	269,385	44,898	Up	1,379
37. Air Force	7	304,494	43,499	Dn	3,909
38. Georgia Tech	5	216,607	43,321	Dn	1,534
39. Illinois	6	259,577	43,263	Dn	7,892
40. Virginia Tech	6	259,057	43,176	Dn	2,541
41. Kansas St.	6	255,422	42,570	Dn	911
42. Texas Tech	6	251,433	41,906	Dn	3,411
43. Oregon	5	209,242	41,848	Dn	114
44. Virginia	7	290,600	41,514	Up	264
45. Northwestern	7	288,016	41,145	Dn	817
46. Oklahoma St.	6	237,100	39,517	Up	1,093
47. Indiana	6	236,580	39,430	Up	1,015

	Games	Attendance	Average	Change in Avg.	
48. Arizona	6	234,168	39,028	Dn	8,423
49. Pittsburgh	6	233,350	38,892	Up	8,096
50. Baylor	6	224,463	37,411	Up	5,517
51. California	5	185,946	37,189	Dn	3,906
52. Iowa St.	5	184,433	36,887	Dn	6,484
53. Kansas	7	256,700	36,671	Dn	5,429
54. Army	6	216,687	36,115	Dn	1,192
55. Rice	5	177,547	35,509	Up	15,339
56. Vanderbilt	6	211,792	35,299	Dn	2,971
57. Mississippi	6	208,795	34,799	Dn	1,733
58. Boston College	6	206,937	34,490	Dn	9,671
59. Fresno St.	6	205,606	34,268	Dn	3,105
60. Mississippi St.*	7	234,259	33,466	Dn	1,096
61. East Caro.	5	164,375	32,875	Up	3,610
62. Hawaii	9	295,296	32,811	Dn	187
63. Washington St.	7	225,678	32,240	Up	3,182
64. Louisville	6	190,287	31,715	Dn	2,057
65. Central Fla.	4	121,393	30,348	Up	14,686
66. New Mexico	7	209,614	29,945	Up	7,672
67. Colorado St.	6	178,645	29,774	Up	889
68. Utah	5	144,789	28,958	Dn	2,464
69. Rutgers	5	146,259	29,252	Up	2,995
70. Miami (Fla.)	6	173,495	28,916	Dn	12,696
71. Maryland	6	165,349	27,558	Dn	2,011
72. Houston	5	137,446	27,489	Up	12,107
73. Navy*	6	164,174	27,362	Dn	1,894
74. Marshall	6	158,410	26,402	Up	6,144
75. Toledo	6	153,205	25,534	Up	3,006
76. San Diego St.	5	125,109	25,022	Dn	2,213
77. Oregon St.	7	174,318	24,903	Dn	293
78. Nevada	6	147,086	24,514	Up	1,610
79. Duke	6	145,058	24,176	Up	478
80. Boise St.	6	144,537	24,090	Up	4,833
81. Southern Miss.	4	95,692	23,923	Up	1,526
82. Texas Christian	5	117,718	23,544	Dn	3,709
83. Tulane	6	139,113	23,186	Up	3,332
84. Wake Forest	5	112,715	22,543	Up	4.503
85. Ball St.	5	107,986	21,597	Up	3,487
86. Southern Methodist	5	107,419	21,484	Up	7,318
87. UTEP	5	105,545	21,109	Up	2,786
88. UNLV	5	105,219	21,044	Up	1,253
89. Louisiana Tech	6	125,435	20,906	Up	1,669
90. Ohio	6	125,400	20,900	Up	17
91. Memphis	6	119,130	19,855	Dn	15,897
92. Wyoming	6	120,752	20,125	Up	97
93. Central Mich.	5	99,195	19,839	Dn	708
94. Bowling Green	4	78,771	19,693	Up	8,869
95. Cincinnati	6	117,196	19,533	Dn	4,721
96. Tulsa	5	96,661	19,332	Dn	5,482
97. North Texas	4	77,057	19,264	Up	5,021
98. Utah St.	5	93,067	18,613	Dn	2,921
99. Western Mich.	5	85,489	17,098	Up	2,376
100. UAB	4	67,150	16,788	Up	137
101. Miami (Ohio)	6	92,992	15,499	Up	3,170
102. San Jose St.	5	76,288	15,258	Up	3,123
103. Southwestern La.	6	89,762	14,960	Dn	6,750
104. Arkansas St.	5	73,491	14,698	Up	133
105. Eastern Mich.	5	70,380	14,076	Up	2,399
106. Northeast La.	4	52,400	13,100	Dn	2,243
107. Idaho	5	62,139	12,428	Up	1,272
108. Northern Ill.	6	72,259	12,043	Up	1,440
109. Akron	4	45,682	11,421	Up	5,258
110. New Mexico St.	6	60,134	10,022	Up	3,038
111. Temple	5	45,644	9,129	Up	2,713
112. Kent	5	41,170	8,234	Dn	12,967

**Mississippi State later changed total from 8 games for 267,569.*

Division I-AA

	Games	Attendance	Average	Change in Avg.	
1. Jackson St.	5	194,366	38,873	Up	17,896
2. South Fla.	7	231,271	33,039	No Change	
3. Southern U.	5	119,637	23,927	Up	3,763
4. Montana	6	107,926	17,988	Up	171
5. North Caro. A&T	4	70,794	17,699	Dn	3,189
6. Delaware	5	86,587	17,317	Up	900
7. Florida A&M	6	101,387	16,898	Dn	3,699
8. Yale	6	90,558	15,093	Dn	5,700
9. Youngstown St.	8	119,442	14,930	Up	4,378
10. Texas Southern	6	78,900	13,150	Up	2,184
11. Southwest Mo. St.	6	77,698	12,950	Dn	231
12. Ga. Southern	6	75,397	12,566	Up	434
13. Appalachian St.	6	73,582	12,264	Dn	2,025
14. South Caro. St.	5	61,191	12,238	Up	2,180
15. Citadel	6	73,036	12,173	Dn	637
16. McNeese St.	6	69,509	11,585	Up	2,817
17. Northern Iowa	5	55,591	11,118	Dn	2,318
18. Northern Ariz.	6	66,531	11,089	Up	785
19. Howard	3	31,754	10,585	Dn	1,554
20. Western Ky.	5	52,600	10,520	Up	860
21. Norfolk St.	6	62,343	10,391	Dn	5,285
22. Pennsylvania	5	51,930	10,386	Dn	2,301
23. Eastern Ky.	5	51,800	10,360	Dn	423
24. Chattanooga	7	72,082	10,297	Up	4,615
25. Alcorn St.	5	50,535	10,107	Dn	11,429
26. James Madison	6	60,300	10,050	Dn	1,117
27. Southwest Tex. St.	6	60,246	10,041	Up	4,069
28. Tennessee St.	4	40,090	10,023	Dn	4,555
29. Alabama St.	4	38,758	9,690	Up	132
30. Lehigh	5	47,898	9,580	Up	1,676
31. Western Caro.	5	47,486	9,497	Up	645
32. Western Ill.	6	56,409	9,402	Up	1,574
33. Mississippi Val.	4	37,369	9,342	Up	2,193
34. William & Mary	5	45,863	9,173	Up	361
35. Hampton	4	36,512	9,128	Up	1,089
36. Northwestern St.	6	54,670	9,112	Dn	1,672
37. Richmond	5	45,398	9,080	Dn	2,249
38. Sam Houston St.	6	53,569	8,928	Dn	2,948
39. Troy St.	5	44,500	8,900	Dn	2,985
40. Furman	5	43,343	8,669	Dn	2,362
41. Montana St.	6	51,902	8,650	Up	1,863
42. Illinois St.	5	43,035	8,607	Up	515
43. Stephen F. Austin	8	67,876	8,485	Dn	1,268
44. Villanova	7	58,690	8,384	Dn	221
45. Weber St.	6	50,194	8,366	Dn	620
46. Connecticut	6	49,377	8,230	Dn	849
47. Liberty	5	40,307	8,061	Up	2,133
48. Massachusetts	7	55,424	7,918	Dn	2,021
49. Harvard	5	38,062	7,612	Dn	4,561
50. Buffalo	7	53,187	7,598	Up	1,757
51. Grambling	3	22,374	7,458	Dn	2,724
52. Wofford	5	36,581	7,316	Up	1,037
53. Dayton	5	35,557	7,111	Up	368
54. Bucknell	4	28,090	7,023	Up	1,651
55. Cal Poly SLO	6	39,718	6,620	Up	1,314
56. Murray St.	6	39,504	6,584	Dn	2,209
57. Prairie View	4	25,990	6,498	Dn	11,152
58. East Tenn. St.	7	42,570	6,081	Dn	1,806
59. Eastern Ill.	5	30,200	6,040	Dn	1,222
60. Dartmouth	5	29,814	5,963	Dn	1,232
61. Idaho St.	6	35,835	5,973	Dn	420
62. Middle Tenn. St.	4	23,559	5,890	Dn	3,335
63. Jacksonville St.	4	23,370	5,843	Dn	4,398
64. Cornell	6	34,079	5,680	Dn	1,688
65. Southern Ill.	5	28,200	5,640	Dn	531
66. Southern Utah	6	33,766	5,628	Up	627
67. VMI	5	27,603	5,521	Dn	990
68. Morgan St.	3	16,404	5,468	Up	2,338
69. Cal St. Sacramento	5	26,978	5,396	Up	1,145
70. Holy Cross	6	29,266	4,878	Dn	2,382
71. Tennessee Tech	4	19,444	4,861	Up	570
72. Maine	4	19,182	4,796	Up	277
73. Hofstra	5	23,602	4,720	Up	785
74. Bethune-Cookman	5	23,547	4,709	Dn	1,217
75. Southeast Mo. St.	7	30,993	4,428	Dn	61
76. Morehead St.	6	26,502	4,417	Up	2,593
77. Samford	6	26,194	4,366	Dn	117
78. Tenn.-Martin	7	29,755	4,251	Up	986
79. New Hampshire	5	20,940	4,188	Dn	680
80. Cal St. Northridge	5	20,934	4,187	Dn	74
81. La Salle	5	20,603	4,121	No Change	
82. Lafayette	6	24,341	4,057	Dn	2,372
83. Delaware St.	6	23,862	3,977	Up	311
84. Eastern Wash.	7	25,428	3,633	Dn	1,325
85. San Diego	6	21,783	3,631	Up	50
86. Drake	5	17,883	3,577	Dn	720
87. Columbia	6	21,126	3,521	Dn	2,131
88. Rhode Island	5	17,464	3,493	Dn	267
89. Northeastern	5	17,069	3,414	Dn	227
90. Brown	6	19,081	3,180	Dn	2,403
91. Indiana St.	6	18,846	3,141	Dn	1,940
92. Valparaiso	4	12,290	3,073	Up	282
93. Nicholls St.	5	14,853	2,971	Dn	688
94. St. Mary's (Cal.)	5	14,757	2,951	Up	972
95. Butler	5	14,720	2,944	Dn	718
96. Fordham	6	17,661	2,944	Dn	424
97. Duquesne	5	13,884	2,777	Dn	10

	Games	Attendance	Average	Change in Avg.	
98. Austin Peay	4	11,067	2,767	Up	1,272
99. Colgate	6	16,421	2,737	Dn	1,373
100. Monmouth (N. J.)	4	10,887	2,722	Up	222
101. Towson	5	12,315	2,463	Dn	723
102. Davidson	5	12,271	2,454	Up	436
103. Fairfield	5	12,260	2,452	Up	216
104. Charleston So.	4	9,147	2,287	Up	547
105. Boston U.	5	10,504	2,101	Dn	2,342
106. Robert Morris	5	10,116	2,023	Dn	469
107. St. Peter's	6	11,556	1,926	Up	569
108. Georgetown	4	7,646	1,912	Up	52
109. Wagner	5	8,151	1,630	Up	1,003
110. Evansville	5	7,001	1,400	Up	340
111. St. John's (N. Y.)	6	6,853	1,142	Up	92
112. Marist	5	5,467	1,093	Up	529
113. Central Conn. St.	5	5,435	1,087	Dn	307
114. Siena	4	3,362	841	Up	65
115. Iona	5	3,880	776	Dn	16
116. Canisius	6	4,341	724	Dn	29
117. St. Francis (Pa.)	5	2,425	485	Dn	54
118. Princeton	0	000	000	Dn	10,240

Division II

	Games	Attendance	Average	Change in Avg.	
1. North Dak. St.	6	75,069	12,512	Dn	2,250
2. Tuskegee	4	45,184	11,296	Dn	1,977
3. Alabama A&M	5	47,460	9,492	Up	2,935
4. Tex. A&M-Kingsville	4	36,800	9,200	Up	117
5. Angelo St.	5	44,700	8,940	Up	540
6. North Dak.	5	44,049	8,810	Up	2,726
7. Portland St.	5	42,159	8,432	Dn	864
8. North Ala.	5	41,420	8,284	Dn	847
9. Albany St. (Ga.)	4	29,708	7,427	No Change	
10. Morehouse	6	42,168	7,028	No Change	
11. Pittsburg St.	5	34,150	6,830	Dn	620
12. South Dak.	6	40,404	6,734	No Change	
13. Fort Valley St.	5	32,588	6,518	Up	1,045
14. Northwest Mo. St.	5	32,425	6,485	Up	1,002
15. Winston-Salem	6	38,033	6,339	Up	823
16. Miles	5	30,901	6,180	No Change	
17. Neb.-Omaha	5	30,800	6,160	Up	346
18. Morris Brown	5	30,116	6,023	Up	1,050
19. UC Davis	6	35,845	5,974	Dn	743
20. Elon	5	29,768	5,954	Up	1,926
21. Mo. Southern St.	5	27,939	5,588	Up	1,542
22. N. C. Central	4	21,604	5,401	Dn	979
23. Clark Atlanta	4	20,800	5,200	Dn	3.145
24. Arkansas Tech	5	25,623	5,125	No Change	
25. Harding	5	25,524	5,105	No Change	

Division III

	Games	Attendance	Average	Change in Avg.	
1. Emory & Henry	5	29,267	5,853	Up	454
2. St. John's (Minn.)	4	21,231	5,308	Dn	1,526
3. Mississippi Col.	6	29,287	4,881	Dn	31
4. Baldwin-Wallace	5	23,050	4,610	Up	1,610
5. Williams	4	17,344	4,336	No Change	
6. Trinity (Conn.)	4	17,211	4,303	Dn	281
7. Wis.-Whitewater	5	21,173	4,235	Dn	747
8. Hope	5	20,742	4,148	Up	1,104
9. Amherst	4	16,572	4,143	Dn	486
10. Wis.-La Crosse	4	15,394	3,849	Up	521
11. Ithaca	5	18,228	3,646	Up	551
12. Grove City	5	17,200	3,440	Up	1,809
13. Bethel (Minn.)	5	16,700	3,340	Up	915
14. Randolph-Macon	5	16,650	3,330	Up	1,090
15. Wartburg	5	16,300	3,260	Dn	190
16. Hampden-Sydney	5	16,171	3,234	Dn	1,571
17. Simpson	5	15,941	3,188	Up	314
18. Catholic	5	15,755	3,151	Up	582
19. Millsaps	4	12,500	3,125	Up	2,042
20. Adrian	4	12,338	3,085	Up	245
21. Wittenberg	6	18,164	3,027	Up	409
22. Gust. Adolphus	5	14,850	2,970	Dn	64
23. St. Thomas (Minn.)	5	14,200	2,840	Up	740
24. Wis.-Eau Claire	4	11,000	2,750	Up	890
25. Wooster	5	13,586	2,717	Up	420

Divisions I-A and I-AA Conferences and Independent Groups

	Total Teams	Games	1997 Attend.	Avg. PG	Change† In Avg.		Change† In Total	
1. Big Ten (I-A)	11	70	*4,744,211	67,774	Up	254	Up	422,935
2. Southeastern (I-A)	12	76	*5,005,126	*65,857	Up	952	Up	72,324
3. Big 12 (I-A)	12	71	*3,640,692	51,277	Dn	165	Up	91,218
4. Pacific-10 (I-A)	10	60	2,891,522	48,192	Up	588	Up	130,516
5. Atlantic Coast (I-A)	9	52	2,333,784	44,880	Up	803	Up	129,935
6. Big East (I-A)	8	46	1,657,056	36,023	Dn	2,825	Dn	168,814
7. Western Atl. (I-A)	16	92	*2,758,817	29,987	Up	1,248	Up	143,598
8. I-A Independents#	9	47	1,391,842	29,614	Up	3,689	Up	147,389
9. Conf. USA (I-A)#	7	38	*963,239	*25,348	Dn	237	Dn	8,984
10. Big West (I-A)	6	32	584,020	*18,251	Up	1,937	Up	29,336
11. Mid-American (I-A)#	12	63	*1,130,939	17,951	Up	2,115	Up	149,085
12. Southwestern (I-AA)	8	36	567,929	15,776	Up	371	Dn	32,869
13. Mid-Eastern (I-AA)#	9	42	427,794	10,186	Dn	1,111	Dn	80,582
14. Gateway (I-AA)#	7	41	*399,221	*9,737	Up	557	Up	41,183
15. Southern (I-AA)#	9	52	491,680	9,455	Dn	163	Up	30,020
16. Southland (I-AA)	8	46	388,593	8,448	Dn	495	Dn	22,764
17. Big Sky (I-AA)#^	8	47	385,728	8,207	Up	23	Up	25,421
18. I-AA Independents#	14	76	594,992	7,829	Up	3,693	Up	322,007
19. Atlantic 10 (I-AA)	12	65	486,798	7,489	Dn	737	Dn	39,644
20. Ivy (I-AA)	8	39	284,650	7,299	Dn	3,029	Dn	128,462
21. Ohio Valley (I-AA)#	8	42	265,345	6,318	Dn	1,782	Dn	91,040
22. Patriot (I-AA)#	7	38	175,992	4,631	Dn	807	Dn	25,211
23. Pioneer (I-AA)	6	30	109,234	3,641	Dn	146	Dn	8,172
24. Northeast (I-AA)@	5	24	37,014	*1,542	Up	31	Dn	3,786
25. Metro Atlantic (I-AA)	9	46	*69,249	*1,505	Up	97	Up	11,507
I-A Neutral Sites		8	464,711	58,089	-	-	-	-
I-AA Neutral Sites		18	527,829	29,324	-	-	-	-
DIVISION I-A#	112	655	27,565,959	42,085	Up	748	Up	945,017
DIVISION I-AA#	118	642	5,212,048	8,118	Dn	237	Dn	42,985
I-A & I-AA Combined	230	1,297	32,778,007	25,272	Up	232	Up	902,032
DIVISION II#	142	710	2,349,442	3,309	Dn	278	Dn	164,799
DIVISION III#	209	991	1,730,400	1,746	Dn	34	Up	37,563
ALL NCAA TEAMS	**581**	**2,998**	**36,857,849**	**12,294**	**Dn**	**42**	**Up**	**774,796**

By Percentage of Capacity: Div. I-A: 77.6 percent - Southeastern 91.1, Big Ten 89.8, Atlantic Coast 86.6, Big 12 85.1, Mid-American 73.1, Pacific-10 71.3, I-A Independents 63.1, Western Athletic 62.7, Big West 62.1, Big East

60.8, Conference USA 50.9. **Div. I-AA:** 47.3 percent - Metro Atlantic 60.0, Southern 60.0, Big Sky 59.1, Gateway 57.9, Southland 53.6, Atlantic 10 52.7, I-AA Independents 50.5, Ohio Valley 37.6, Mid-Eastern 36.9, Patriot 36.3, Northeast 36.1, Southwestern Athletic 32.6, Pioneer 29.8, Ivy 20.9.

*# Did not have same lineup in 1997 as in 1996. @ New conference. * Record high for this conference. + The 1997 figures used for comparison reflect changes in conference and division lineups to provide parallel, valid comparisons. ^Does not include Division II member Portland State.*

Conferences and Independent Groups Below Division I-AA

	Total Teams	Games	1996 Attend.	Avg. PG	Change† In Avg		Change In Total	
1. Southern Intercoll. (II)	10	48	314,975	6,562	Dn	188	Up	4,484
2. North Central (II)	10	53	277,861	5,243	Dn	392	Dn	20,791
3. Lone Star (II)#	11	54	243,518	4,510	Dn	35	Dn	20,064
4. Gulf South (II)#	10	47	197,334	4,199	Dn	729	Dn	44,147
5. Mid-America Intercoll. (II)	10	53	196,315	3,849	Dn	16	Dn	8,518
6. Central Intercoll. (II)#	9	44	162,792	3,700	Dn	943	Dn	22,920
7. Old Dominion (III)	6	30	92,810	3,094	Dn	19	Up	2,533
8. Pennsylvania (II)	14	69	209,399	3,035	Up	189	Up	13,010
9. Midwest Intercoll. (II)	11	58	166,609	2,873	Up	401	Up	25,703
10. Div. II Indep.#	13	59	158,110	2,680	Dn	177	Dn	7,578
11. Amer. Southwest (III)@	6	30	79,174	2,639	Up	156	Up	9,641
12. New Eng. Small Coll. (III)	10	40	103,762	2,594	Dn	265	Dn	10,605
13. South Atlantic (II)#	8	45	116,629	2,592	Dn	336	Dn	6,356
14. Wisconsin (III)	8	36	92,069	2,557	Up	259	Up	4,740
15. Minnesota Intercoll. (III)	10	47	112,261	2,389	Dn	151	Up	480
16. Michigan Intercoll. (III)	6	27	62,152	2,302	Up	235	Up	6,345
17. Ohio Athletic (III)	10	51	116,382	2,282	Up	233	Up	15,970
18. Iowa Intercoll. (III)	9	46	92,528	2,011	Up	53	Up	8,351
19. Indiana Collegiate (III)	7	35	66,616	1,903	Dn	352	Dn	12,292
20. Presidents' Athletic (III)#	6	28	52,940	1,891	Up	85	Dn	1,230
21. New Jersey (III)	6	25	46,567	1,863	Up	659	Up	14,051
22. Rocky Mountain (II)	9	50	92,139	1,843	Dn	249	Dn	1,992
23. Middle Atlantic (III)	11	55	99,123	1,802	Dn	180	Dn	11,857
24. Upstate Colleg. (III)	5	25	44,898	1,796	Dn	180	Up	1,436
25. Southern Collegiate (III)	5	22	38,017	1,728	Up	394	Up	6,003
26. Freedom FB (III)	7	34	58,371	1,717	Dn	26	Dn	2,640
27. Northern Sun (II)	7	36	59,021	1,639	Up	20	Up	5,608
28. University Ath. (III)	5	24	38,028	1,585	Dn	224	Dn	5,381
29. West Va. Intercoll. (II)#	8	37	57,889	1,565	Dn	77	Dn	6,150
30. North Coast (III)	9	47	73,280	1,559	Dn	32	Up	4,885
31. Illinois & Wisconsin (III)	8	36	55,325	1,537	Dn	65	Dn	3,935
32. Centennial FB (III)	8	39	57,290	1,469	Dn	223	Dn	10,386
33. Div. III Indep.#	34	155	220,224	1,421	Up	48	Dn	4,900
34. Eastern FB (II)#	12	59	76,851	1,303	Dn	15	Dn	4,892
35. Midwest (III)#	10	47	48,563	1,033	Dn	190	Dn	7,717
36. Southern Calif. (III)	6	30	30,303	1,010	Dn	150	Up	132
37. St. Louis (III)#	5	24	18,837	785	Dn	67	Dn	757
38. New England FB (III)#	14	67	47,538	710	Dn	100	Dn	7,529

@ New conference. # Did not have the same lineup in 1997 as in 1996. $Rochester is a member of both the University Athletic Association and the Upstate Collegiate Athletic Conference. Case Reserve is a member of both the University Athletic Association and the North Coast Athletic Conference. Their attendance figures are included in each conference figure but counted only once for division totals. † The figures used for comparison reflect changes in conference and division lineups to provide parallel, valid comparison.

Annual Team Attendance Leaders

Annual Leading Division I-A Teams in Per-Game Home Attendance

Year/Teams	G	Attendance	Avg.
1949			
Michigan	6	563,363	93,894
Ohio St.	5	382,146	76,429
Southern Methodist	8	484,000	60,500
1950			
Michigan	6	493,924	82,321
Ohio St.	5	368,021	73,604
Southern Methodist	5	309,000	61,800
1951			
Ohio St.	6	455,737	75,956
Michigan	6	445,635	74,273
Illinois	4	237,035	59,259
1952			
Ohio St.	6	453,911	75,652
Michigan	6	395,907	65,985
Texas	#5	311,160	62,232
1953			
Ohio St.	5	397,998	79,600
Southern Cal	6	413,617	68,936
Michigan	6	353,860	58,977
1954			
Ohio St.	6	479,840	79,973
Michigan	6	409,454	68,242
UCLA	5	318,371	63,674
1955			
Michigan	7	544,838	77,834
Ohio St.	7	493,178	70,454
Southern Cal	7	467,085	66,726
1956			
Ohio St.	6	494,575	82,429
Michigan	7	566,145	80,878
Minnesota	6	375,407	62,568
1957			
Michigan	6	504,954	84,159
Ohio St.	6	484,118	80,686
Minnesota	5	319,942	63,988
1958			
Ohio St.	6	499,352	82,225
Michigan	6	405,115	67,519
LSU	5	296,576	59,315
1959			
Ohio St.	6	495,536	82,589
Michigan	6	456,385	76,064
LSU	7	408,727	58,390
1960			
Ohio St.	5	413,583	82,717
Michigan St.	4	274,367	68,592
Michigan	6	374,682	62,447
1961			
Ohio St.	5	414,712	82,942
Michigan	7	514,924	73,561
LSU	6	381,409	63,651
1962			
Ohio St.	6	497,644	82,941
Michigan St.	4	272,568	68,142
LSU	6	397,701	66,284
1963			
Ohio St.	5	416,023	83,205
LSU	6	396,846	66,141
Michigan St.	5	326,597	65,319
1964			
Ohio St.	7	583,740	83,391
Michigan St.	4	284,933	71,233
Michigan	6	388,829	64,805
1965			
Ohio St.	5	416,282	83,256
Michigan	6	480,487	80,081
Michigan St.	5	346,296	69,259

Year/Teams	G	Attendance	Avg.
1966			
Ohio St.	6	488,399	81,400
Michigan St.	6	426,750	71,125
Michigan	6	413,599	68,933
1967			
Ohio St.	5	383,502	76,700
Michigan	6	447,289	74,548
Michigan St.	6	411,916	68,653
1968			
Ohio St.	6	482,564	80,427
Southern Cal	5	354,945	70,989
Michigan St.	6	414,177	69,030
1969			
Ohio St.	5	431,175	86,235
Michigan	6	428,780	71,463
Michigan St.	5	352,123	70,425
1970			
Ohio St.	5	432,451	86,490
Michigan	6	476,164	79,361
Purdue	5	340,090	68,018
1971			
Ohio St.	6	506,699	84,450
Michigan	7	564,376	80,625
Wisconsin	6	408,885	68,148
1972			
Michigan	6	513,398	85,566
Ohio St.	6	509,420	84,903
Nebraska	6	456,859	76,143
1973			
Ohio St.	6	523,369	87,228
Michigan	7	595,171	85,024
Nebraska	6	456,726	76,121
1974			
Michigan	6	562,105	93,684
Ohio St.	6	525,314	87,552
Nebraska	7	534,388	76,341
1975			
Michigan	7	689,146	98,449
Ohio St.	6	527,141	87,856
Nebraska	7	533,368	76,195
1976			
Michigan	7	722,113	103,159
Ohio St.	6	526,216	87,702
Tennessee	7	564,922	80,703
1977			
Michigan	7	729,418	104,203
Ohio St.	6	525,535	87,589
Tennessee	7	582,979	83,283
1978			
Michigan	6	629,690	104,948
Ohio St.	7	614,881	87,840
Tennessee	†8	627,381	78,422
1979			
Michigan	7	730,315	104,331
Ohio St.	7	611,794	87,399
Tennessee	6	512,139	85,357
1980			
Michigan	6	625,750	104,292
Tennessee	†8	709,193	88,649
Ohio St.	7	615,476	87,925
1981			
Michigan	6	632,990	105,498
Tennessee	6	558,996	93,166
Ohio St.	6	521,760	86,960
1982			
Michigan	6	631,743	105,291
Tennessee	6	561,102	93,517
Ohio St.	7	623,152	89,022
1983			
Michigan	6	626,916	104,486
Ohio St.	6	534,110	89,018
Tennessee	†8	679,420	84,928
1984			
Michigan	7	726,734	103,819
Tennessee	7	654,602	93,515
Ohio St.	6	536,691	89,449
1985			
Michigan	6	633,530	105,588
Tennessee	7	658,690	94,099
Ohio St.	6	535,284	89,214
1986			
Michigan	6	631,261	105,210
Tennessee	7	643,317	91,902
Ohio St.	6	536,210	89,368
1987			
Michigan	7	731,281	104,469
Tennessee	‡8	705,434	88,179
Ohio St.	6	511,772	85,295
1988			
Michigan	6	628,807	104,801
Tennessee	6	551,677	91,946
Ohio St.	6	516,972	86,162
1989			
Michigan	6	632,136	105,356
Tennessee	6	563,502	93,917
Ohio St.	6	511,812	85,302
1990			
Michigan	6	627,046	104,508
Tennessee	7	666,540	95,220
Ohio St.	6	536,297	89,383
1991			
Michigan	6	632,024	105,337
Tennessee	6	578,389	96,398
Penn St.	6	575,077	95,846
1992			
Michigan	6	635,201	105,867
Tennessee	6	575,544	95,924
Penn St.	6	569,195	94,866
1993			
Michigan	7	739,620	105,660
Tennessee	7	667,280	95,326
Penn St.	6	564,190	94,032
1994			
Michigan	6	637,300	106,217
Penn St.	6	577,731	96,289
Tennessee	6	573,821	95,637
1995			
Michigan	7	726,368	103,767
Tennessee	7	662,857	94,694
Penn St.	6	561,546	93,591
1996			
Michigan	6	635,589	105,932
Tennessee	6	632,509	105,418
Penn St.	6	577,001	96,167
1997			
Tennessee	6	639,227	*106,538
Michigan	7	*745,139	106,448
Penn St.	6	582,517	97,086

**Record. #Includes neutral-site game (Oklahoma) at Dallas counted as a home game (75,500). †Includes neutral-site game at Memphis counted as a home game. Attendance: 1978 (40,879), 1980 (50,003), 1983 (20,135). ‡Includes neutral-site game at East Rutherford (54,681).*

Annual Leading Division I-AA Teams in Per-Game Home Attendance

Year	Team	Avg.
1978	Southern U.	28,333
1979	Grambling	29,900
1980	Southern U.	29,708
1981	Grambling	30,835
1982	Southern U.	32,265
1983	Jackson St.	29,117
1984	Jackson St.	29,215
1985	Yale	29,347
1986	Jackson St.	25,177
1987	Jackson St.	32,734
1988	Jackson St.	26,500
1989	Jackson St.	32,269
1990	Grambling	30,152
1991	Grambling	27,181
1992	Southern U.	28,906
1993	Jackson St.	28,917
1994	Alcorn St.	26,203
1995	Jackson St.	34,849
1996	Alcorn St.	21,536
1997	Jackson St.	*38,873

**Record.*

Annual Leading Division II Teams in Per-Game Home Attendance

Year	Team	Avg.
1958	Southern Miss.	11,998
1959	Southern Miss.	13,964
1960	Florida A&M	12,083
1961	Akron	12,988
1962	Mississippi Col.	13,125
1963	San Diego St.	14,200
1964	Southern U.	12,633
1965	San Diego St.	15,227
1966	San Diego St.	15,972
1967	San Diego St.	*41,030
1968	San Diego St.	36,969
1969	Grambling	27,680
1970	Tampa	24,204
1971	Grambling	29,341
1972	Grambling	22,663
1973	Morgan St.	22,371
1974	Southern U.	33,563
1975	Texas Southern	22,800
1976	Southern U.	25,864
1977	Florida A&M	21,376
1978	Delaware	18,981
1979	Delaware	19,644
1980	Alabama A&M	15,820
1981	Norfolk St.	19,750
1982	Norfolk St.	16,183
1983	Norfolk St.	15,417
1984	Norfolk St.	18,500
1985	Norfolk St.	18,430
1986	Norfolk St.	13,836
1987	North Dak. St.	14,120
1988	Central Fla.	21,905
1989	North Dak. St.	16,833
1990	Norfolk St.	14,904
1991	Norfolk St.	16,779
1992	Norfolk St.	14,196
1993	Norfolk St.	15,346
1994	Clark Atlanta	20,223
1995	Norfolk St.	16,593
1996	Norfolk St.	15,676
1997	North Dak. St.	12,512

**Record.*

Annual Leading Division III Teams in Per-Game Home Attendance

Year	Team	Avg.
1974	Albany St. (Ga.)	9,380
1975	Wittenberg	7,000
1976	Morehouse	11,600
1977	Dayton	10,315
1978	Dayton	9,827
1979	Central Fla.	11,240
1980	Central Fla.	10,450
1981	Dayton	10,025
1982	Dayton	7,906
1983	Dayton	6,542
1984	Dayton	8,332
1985	Villanova	11,740
1986	Villanova	*11,883
1987	Trinity (Conn.)	6,254
1988	St. John's (Minn.)	5,788
1989	Dayton	5,962
1990	Dayton	6,185
1991	Dayton	7,657
1992	Dayton	6,098
1993	St. John's (Minn.)	6,655
1994	Hampden-Sydney	6,614
1995	St. John's (Minn.)	6,574
1996	St. John's (Minn.)	6,834
1997	Emory & Henry	5,853

**Record.*

1997 Statistical Leaders

1997 Division I-A Individual Leaders

UCLA sports information photo by Scott Quintard

UCLA quarterback Cade McNown, Division I-A's 1997 leader in passing efficiency, accounted for nearly 264 yards per game in total offense last year.

Rushing

	1997 Class	G	Car.	Yards	Avg.	TD	Yds.PG
Ricky Williams, Texas	Jr	11	279	1893	6.8	25	172.09
Ahman Green, Nebraska	Jr	12	278	1877	6.8	22	156.42
Amos Zereoue, West Va.	So	10	264	1505	5.7	16	150.50
Tavian Banks, Iowa	Sr	11	246	1639	6.7	17	149.00
Ron Dayne, Wisconsin	So	10	249	1421	5.7	15	142.10
Travis Prentice, Miami (Ohio)	So	11	296	1549	5.2	25	140.82
Dwayne Harris, Toledo	Jr	10	254	1278	5.0	10	127.80
Kevin Faulk, LSU	Jr	9	205	1144	5.6	15	127.11
Demond Parker, Oklahoma	So	9	194	1143	5.9	6	127.00
Chris McCoy, Navy	Sr	11	246	1370	5.6	20	124.55
Curtis Enis, Penn St.	Jr	11	228	1363	6.0	19	123.91
Fred Taylor, Florida	Sr	11	214	1292	6.0	13	117.45
Robert Holcombe, Illinois	Sr	11	294	1253	4.3	4	113.91
Jamal Lewis, Tennessee	Fr	12	232	1364	5.9	7	113.67
Darren Davis, Iowa St.	So	9	212	1005	4.7	5	111.67
Sedrick Irvin, Michigan St.	So	11	231	1211	5.2	9	110.09
Edgerrin James, Miami (Fla.)	So	10	184	1098	6.0	13	109.80
Saladin McCullough, Oregon	Sr	11	250	1193	4.8	8	108.45
Autry Denson, Notre Dame	Jr	12	264	1268	4.8	12	105.67
Michael Black, Washington St.	Sr	11	235	1157	4.9	11	105.18

Passing Efficiency

(Min. 15 att. per game)	1997 Class	G	Att.	Cmp.	Cmp. Pct.	Int.	Int. Pct.	Yards	Yds./ Att.	TD	TD Pct.	Rating Points
Cade McNown, UCLA	Jr	11	283	173	61.13	5	1.77	2877	10.17	22	7.77	168.6
Ryan Leaf, Washington St.	Jr	11	375	210	56.00	10	2.67	3637	9.70	33	8.80	161.2
Joe Germaine, Ohio St.	Sr	12	184	119	64.67	7	3.80	1674	9.10	15	8.15	160.4
John Dutton, Nevada	Sr	11	367	225	61.31	6	1.63	3526	9.61	20	5.45	156.7
Brock Huard, Washington	So	10	244	146	59.84	10	4.10	2140	8.77	23	9.43	156.4
Mike Bobo, Georgia	Sr	11	306	199	65.03	8	2.61	2751	8.99	19	6.21	155.8
Donovan McNabb, Syracuse	Jr	12	265	145	54.72	6	2.26	2488	9.39	20	7.55	154.0
Graham Leigh, New Mexico	Jr	12	276	166	60.14	8	2.90	2318	8.40	24	8.70	153.6
Moses Moreno, Colorado St.	Sr	12	257	157	61.09	9	3.50	2257	8.78	20	7.78	153.5
Chad Pennington, Marshall	So	12	428	253	59.11	12	2.80	3480	8.13	39	9.11	151.9
Aaron Brooks, Virginia	Jr	11	270	164	60.74	7	2.59	2282	8.45	20	7.41	151.0
Tim Rattay, Louisiana Tech	So	11	477	293	61.43	10	2.10	3881	8.14	34	7.13	149.1
Thad Busby, Florida St.	Sr	11	390	235	60.26	10	2.56	3317	8.51	25	6.41	147.7
Peyton Manning, Tennessee	Sr	12	477	287	60.17	11	2.31	3819	8.01	36	7.55	147.7
Daunte Culpepper, Central Fla	Jr	11	381	238	62.47	10	2.62	3086	8.10	25	6.56	146.9
Pete Gonzalez, Pittsburgh	Sr	11	345	198	57.39	7	2.03	2657	7.70	30	8.70	146.7
Joe Hamilton, Georgia Tech	So	11	268	173	64.55	7	2.61	2314	8.63	12	4.48	146.6
Jason Maas, Oregon	Jr	9	172	95	55.23	8	4.65	1443	8.39	15	8.72	145.2
Nealon Greene, Clemson	Sr	11	265	169	63.77	8	3.02	2126	8.02	16	6.04	145.1
Mike McQueary, Penn St.	Sr	11	255	146	57.25	9	3.53	2211	8.67	17	6.67	145.0

Total Offense

	RUSHING				PASSING		TOTAL OFFENSE				
	Car.	Gain	Loss	Net	Att.	Yards	Plays	Yards	Avg.	TDR*	Yds.PG
Tim Rattay, Louisiana Tech	64	233	146	87	477	3881	541	3968	7.33	35	360.73
Tim Couch, Kentucky	66	139	264	-125	547	3884	613	3759	6.13	40	341.73
Ryan Leaf, Washington St.	72	176	230	-54	375	3637	447	3583	8.02	39	325.73
Daunte Culpepper, Central Fla.	136	677	239	438	381	3086	517	3524	6.82	30	320.36
John Dutton, Nevada	44	134	138	-4	367	3526	411	3522	8.57	21	320.18
Peyton Manning, Tennessee	49	103	133	-30	477	3819	526	3789	7.20	39	315.75
Charlie Batch, Eastern Mich.	85	327	217	110	434	3280	519	3390	6.53	24	308.18
Thad Busby, Florida St.	57	132	148	-16	390	3317	447	3301	7.38	27	300.09
Jose Davis, Kent	50	305	129	176	365	2707	415	2883	6.95	35	288.30
Jon Denton, UNLV	64	204	199	5	374	2586	438	2591	5.92	21	287.89
Chad Pennington, Marshall	55	104	163	-59	428	3480	483	3421	7.08	40	285.08
Billy Dicken, Purdue	89	428	120	308	373	2811	462	3119	6.75	24	283.55
Shaun King, Tulane	124	601	90	511	363	2567	487	3078	6.32	29	279.82
Dameyune Craig, Auburn	96	312	312	0	403	3277	499	3277	6.57	22	273.08
Chris Redman, Louisville	47	952	16	-121	445	3079	492	2958	6.01	18	268.91
Brian Brennan, Idaho	46	122	162	-40	387	2708	433	2668	6.16	20	266.80
Chris Wallace, Toledo	98	458	226	232	433	2955	531	3187	6.00	29	265.58
Cade McNown, UCLA	65	217	192	25	283	2877	348	2902	8.34	25	263.82
Matt Sauk, Utah St.	64	180	178	2	378	2896	442	2898	6.56	22	263.45
Pete Gonzalez, Pittsburgh	91	364	195	169	345	2657	436	2826	6.48	33	256.91

Touchdowns responsible for are players' TDs scored and passed for.

Receptions Per Game

	1997 Class	G	Rec.	Yards	TD	Rec.PG
Eugene Baker, Kent	Jr.	11	103	1549	18	9.36
Troy Edwards, Louisiana Tech	Jr.	11	102	1707	13	9.27
Troy Walters, Stanford	Jr.	11	86	1206	8	7.82
Geoff Noisy, Nevada	Jr.	11	86	1184	5	7.82
Randy Moss, Marshall	So.	12	90	1647	25	7.50
Siaha Burley, Central Fla.	Jr.	11	77	1106	7	7.00
Antonio Wilson, Idaho	Sr.	11	77	9101	0	7.00
Bobby Shaw, California	Sr.	11	75	1093	10	6.82
Nakia Jenkins, Utah St.	Sr.	11	73	1086	6	6.64
Craig Yeast, Kentucky	Jr.	11	73	873	10	6.64
Desmond Clark, Wake Forest	Jr.	11	72	950	5	6.55
Marcus Nash, Tennessee	Sr.	12	76	1170	13	6.33

Receiving Yards Per Game

	1997 Class	G	Rec.	Yards	TD	Yds.PG
Troy Edwards, Louisiana Tech	Jr.	11	102	1707	13	155.18
Eugene Baker, Kent	Jr.	11	103	1549	18	140.82
Randy Moss, Marshall	So.	12	90	1647	25	137.25
Jerome Pathon, Washington	Sr.	11	69	1245	8	113.18
Troy Walters, Stanford	Jr.	11	86	1206	8	109.64
Geoff Noisy, Nevada	Jr.	11	86	1184	5	107.64
Brian Alford, Purdue	Sr.	11	59	1167	9	106.09
Trevor Insley, Nevada	So.	11	59	1151	6	104.64
Pascal Volz, New Mexico	Sr.	12	69	1229	13	102.42
Siaha Burley, Central Fla.	Jr.	11	77	1106	7	100.55
Torry Holt, North Caro. St.	Jr.	11	62	1099	16	99.91

Interceptions

	1997 Class	G	Int.	Yards	TD	Int.PG
Brian Lee, Wyoming	Sr.	11	8	103	1	.73
Cedric Donaldson, LSU	Sr.	11	7	192	2	.64
John Noel, Louisiana Tech	Sr.	11	7	93	0	.64
Omarr Smith, San Jose St.	Jr.	11	7	80	0	.64
Tevell Jones, Ohio	Sr.	11	7	36	0	.64
Samari Rolle, Florida St.	Sr.	11	7	32	0	.64
Charles Woodson, Michigan	Jr.	11	7	7	0	.64
Donovin Darius, Syracuse	Sr.	12	7	56	0	.58
Paul Jackson, Maryland	Jr.	9	5	14	0	.56

Scoring

	1997 Class	G	TD	XP	FG	Pts.	Pts.PG
Ricky Williams, Texas	Jr.	11	25	2	0	152	13.82
Skip Hicks, UCLA	Sr.	11	25	0	0	150	13.64
Travis Prentice, Miami (Ohio)	So.	11	25	0	0	150	13.64
Randy Moss, Marshall	So.	12	25	2	0	152	12.67
Curtis Enis, Penn St.	Jr.	11	20	2	0	122	11.09
Ahman Green, Nebraska	Jr.	12	22	0	0	132	11.00
Chris McCoy, Navy	Sr.	11	20	0	0	120	10.91
Tavian Banks, Iowa	Sr.	11	19	0	0	114	10.36
Chris Lemon, Nevada	So.	11	19	0	0	114	10.36
Eugene Baker, Kent	Jr.	11	18	2	0	110	10.00
Kevin Faulk, LSU	Jr.	9	15	0	0	90	10.00
Brad Palazzo, Tulane	Jr.	11	0	40	23	109	9.91
Kris Brown, Nebraska	Jr.	12	0	62	18	116	9.67
Chris Sailer, UCLA	Jr.	11	0	49	19	106	9.64
Benji Wood, Rice	Sr.	10	16	0	0	96	9.60
Amos Zereoue, West Va.	So.	10	16	0	0	96	9.60
Scott Frost, Nebraska	Sr.	12	19	0	0	114	9.50
Ron Dayne, Wisconsin	So.	10	15	0	0	90	9.00
Torry Holt, North Caro. St.	Jr.	11	16	2	0	98	8.91
Harold Shaw, Southern Miss.	Sr.	11	16	0	0	96	8.73
Troy Edwards, Louisiana Tech	Jr.	11	16	0	0	96	8.73
Edgerrin James, Miami (Fla.)	So.	10	14	2	0	86	8.60
Colby Cason, New Mexico	Sr.	12	04	0	21	103	8.58
Martin Gramatica, Kansas St.	Jr.	11	0	37	19	94	8.55
Kyle Bryant, Texas A&M	Sr.	12	0	48	18	102	8.50

All-Purpose Yards

	1997 Class	G	Rush	Rec.	PR	KOR	Total Yards	Yds.PG
Troy Edwards, Louisiana Tech	Jr.	11	190	1707	6	241	2144	194.91
Ricky Williams, Texas	Jr.	11	1893	150	0	0	2043	185.73
Kevin Faulk, LSU	Jr.	9	1144	93	192	217	1646	182.89
Randy Moss, Marshall	So.	12	2	1647	266	263	2178	181.50
Michael Perry, Rice	Jr.	10	1034	44	26	680	1784	178.40
Tutu Atwell, Minnesota	Sr.	12	77	924	296	776	2073	172.75
Jerome Pathon, Washington	Sr.	11	0	1245	209	386	1840	167.27
Tavian Banks, Iowa	Sr.	11	1639	200	0	0	1839	167.18
Ahman Green, Nebraska	Jr.	12	1877	105	0	0	1982	165.17
Sedrick Irvin, Michigan St.	So.	11	1211	339	263	0	1813	164.82
Saladin McCullough, Oregon	Sr.	11	1193	160	0	441	1794	163.09
J.R. Redmond, Arizona St.	So.	10	865	186	236	303	1590	159.00
Amos Zereoue, West Va.	So.	10	1505	76	0	0	1581	158.10
Savon Edwards, Eastern Mich.	Sr.	10	627	444	0	486	1557	155.70
Tony Horne, Clemson	Sr.	11	7	897	298	491	1693	153.91
Ron Dayne, Wisconsin	So.	10	142	1117	0	0	1538	153.80
Tyrone Watley, Iowa St.	Sr.	11	0	827	12	852	1691	153.73
Dwayne Harris, Toledo	Jr.	10	1278	229	0	28	1535	153.50
Travis Prentice, Miami (Ohio)	So.	11	1549	138	0	0	1687	153.36
Troy Walters, Stanford	Jr.	11	-7	1206	424	41	1664	151.27

Punt Returns

(Min. 1.2 per game)	1997 Class	No.	Yds.	TD	Avg.
Tim Dwight, Iowa	Sr.	19	367	3	19.32
R.W. McQuarters, Oklahoma St.	Jr.	32	521	1	16.28
Steve Smith, Utah St.	Sr.	22	344	2	15.64
Nod Washington, Miami (Ohio)	Jr.	12	185	0	15.42
Geoff Turner, Colorado St.	Sr.	20	304	1	15.20

Kickoff Returns

(Min. 1.2 per game)	1997 Class	No.	Yds.	TD	Avg.
Eric Booth, Southern Miss.	Sr.	22	766	2	34.82
Ben Kelly, Colorado	Fr.	25	777	1	31.08
Pat McGrew, Navy	Sr.	15	441	0	29.40
Boo Williams, South Caro.	So.	18	527	2	29.28
Pat Johnson, Oregon	Sr.	16	462	0	28.88

Punting

(Min. 3.6 per game)	1997 Class	No.	Avg.
Chad Kessler, LSU	Sr.	39	50.28
John Baker, North Texas	So.	62	47.18
Shane Lechler, Texas A&M	So.	56	46.98
Brad Hill, Tulane	Sr.	42	46.19
Chad Shrout, Hawaii	So.	68	46.07

Field Goals

	1997 Class	G	FGA	FG	Pct.	FGPG
Brad Palazzo, Tulane	Jr.	11	28	23	.821	2.09
Colby Cason, New Mexico	Sr.	12	30	21	.700	1.75
Martin Gramatica, Kansas St.	Jr.	11	20	19	.950	1.73
Shayne Graham, Virginia Tech	So.	11	23	19	.826	1.73
Chris Sailer, UCLA	Jr.	11	24	19	.792	1.73
Brian Gowins, Northwestern	Sr.	12	27	20	.741	1.67
Kris Brown, Nebraska	Jr.	12	21	18	.857	1.50
Kyle Bryant, Texas A&M	Sr.	12	22	18	.818	1.50

1997 Division I-A Team Leaders

Total Offense

	G	Plays	Yds.	Avg.	TD*	Yds.PG
Nebraska	12	937	6164	6.6	71	513.67
Washington St.	11	808	5524	6.8	60	502.18
Louisiana Tech	11	813	5456	6.7	48	496.00
Tennessee	12	890	5794	6.5	50	482.83
Nevada	11	796	5272	6.6	45	479.27
Kentucky	11	876	5214	6.0	45	474.00
Purdue	11	794	5056	6.4	42	459.64
Florida St.	11	784	4973	6.3	49	452.09
Utah St.	11	835	4933	5.9	45	448.45
Marshall	12	832	5339	6.4	58	444.92
Miami (Ohio)	11	827	4876	5.9	49	443.27
Kent	11	815	4866	6.0	45	442.36
UCLA	11	741	4763	6.4	53	433.00
Georgia	11	758	4759	6.3	43	432.64
Syracuse	12	829	5127	6.2	48	427.25
Eastern Mich.	11	808	4687	5.8	41	426.09

Touchdowns scored by rushing/passing only.

Total Defense

	G	Plays	Yds.	Avg.	TD*	Yds.PG
Michigan	11	660	2276	3.4	10	206.9
North Caro.	11	693	2302	3.3	12	209.3
Florida St.	11	717	2655	3.7	22	241.4
Kansas St.	11	702	2825	4.0	17	256.8
Nebraska	12	717	3088	4.3	25	257.3
Navy	11	642	2863	4.5	24	260.3
Iowa	11	733	2927	4.0	18	266.1
Ohio St.	12	820	3215	3.9	13	267.9
Vanderbilt	11	704	3026	4.3	22	275.1
Air Force	12	756	3471	4.6	16	289.3
Syracuse	12	769	3482	4.5	23	290.2
Florida	11	754	3195	4.2	23	290.5
Michigan St.	11	716	3312	4.6	17	301.1
Oklahoma St.	11	678	3330	4.9	26	302.7
Miami (Ohio)	11	745	3374	4.5	29	306.7

Touchdowns scored by rushing or passing only.

Rushing Offense

	G	Car.	Yds.	Avg.	TD	Yds.PG
Nebraska	12	755	4711	6.2	66	392.6
Rice	11	690	3660	5.3	38	332.7
Navy	11	618	3370	5.5	36	306.4
Ohio	11	649	3321	5.1	32	301.9
Army	11	670	3247	4.8	24	295.2
Missouri	11	592	2899	4.9	35	263.5
LSU	11	521	2823	5.4	34	256.6
Iowa	11	492	2585	5.3	25	235.0
Air Force	12	688	2791	4.1	22	232.6
Oklahoma St.	11	592	2486	4.2	25	226.0
Akron	11	504	2431	4.8	22	221.0
Kansas St.	11	541	2422	4.5	29	220.2
Colorado St.	12	484	2631	5.4	30	219.3
Cincinnati	11	593	2371	4.0	22	215.5
Virginia Tech	11	548	2368	4.3	22	215.3

Rushing Defense

	G	Car.	Yds.	Avg.	TD	Yds.PG
Florida St.	11	379	571	1.5	10	51.9
Florida	11	362	778	2.1	12	70.7
Nebraska	12	407	881	2.2	12	73.4
North Caro.	11	371	857	2.3	5	77.9
Cincinnati	11	338	930	2.8	10	84.5
Clemson	11	362	971	2.7	10	88.3
Michigan	11	368	1001	2.7	6	91.0
Tennessee	12	382	1119	2.9	11	93.3
Southern Cal	11	381	1032	2.7	12	93.8
Wake Forest	11	364	1057	2.9	11	96.1
Iowa	11	408	1161	2.8	6	105.5
Arizona	11	411	1164	2.8	17	105.8
Vanderbilt	11	415	1169	2.8	8	106.3
Southern Miss.	11	367	1184	3.2	8	107.6
UCLA	11	380	1191	3.1	11	108.3

Scoring Offense

	G	Pts.	Avg.
Nebraska	12	565	47.1
Washington St.	11	467	42.5
UCLA	11	448	40.7
Florida St.	11	437	39.7
Marshall	12	453	37.8
Miami (Ohio)	11	412	37.5
Florida	11	409	37.2
Colorado St.	12	442	36.8
Iowa	11	404	36.7
Navy	11	398	36.2
Syracuse	12	423	35.3
Texas A&M	12	422	35.2
Kansas St.	11	383	34.8
Tennessee	12	411	34.3
Tulane	11	375	34.1
Central Fla.	11	374	34.0
Utah St.	11	370	33.6
Washington	11	369	33.5

Scoring Defense

	G	Pts.	Avg.
Michigan	11	98	8.9
Ohio St.	12	139	11.6
Air Force	12	149	12.4
Iowa	11	142	12.9
North Caro.	11	143	13.0
Kansas St.	11	159	14.5
Colorado St.	12	179	14.9
Florida St.	11	167	15.2

	G	Pts.	Avg.
Syracuse	12	191	15.9
Ohio	11	177	16.1
LSU	11	179	16.3
Nebraska	12	197	16.4
Virginia Tech	11	185	16.8
Michigan St.	11	186	16.9
Georgia	11	189	17.2
Texas A&M	12	207	17.3
Wyoming	13	227	17.5
Clemson	11	198	18.0

Passing Offense

	G	Att.	Cmp.	Int.	Pct.	Yards	Yds./ Att.	TD	Yds.PG
Nevada	11	443	265	11	59.8	4072	9.2	21	370.2
Kentucky	11	562	374	19	66.5	4019	7.2	37	365.4
Louisiana Tech	11	495	301	11	60.8	3965	8.0	34	360.5
Washington St.	11	400	223	12	55.8	3789	9.5	34	344.5
Florida St.	11	440	262	11	59.5	3740	8.5	30	340.0
Tennessee	12	492	296	12	60.2	3981	8.1	37	331.8
Marshall	12	450	264	13	58.7	3688	8.2	41	307.3
Eastern Mich.	11	438	250	11	57.1	3314	7.6	23	301.3
Louisville	11	473	276	14	58.4	3282	6.9	19	298.4
Kent	11	451	235	16	52.1	3243	7.2	35	294.8
Central Fla.	11	394	243	10	61.7	3187	8.1	26	289.7
UNLV	11	471	249	24	52.9	3140	6.7	21	285.5
Purdue	11	421	228	14	54.2	3097	7.4	20	281.5
Utah St.	11	397	200	10	50.4	3085	7.8	17	280.5
Florida	11	394	211	18	53.6	3039	7.7	32	276.3
Auburn	12	406	217	13	53.4	3282	8.1	18	273.5
Idaho	11	457	246	6	53.8	2999	6.6	22	272.6
UCLA	11	291	176	5	60.5	2929	10.1	23	266.3
Georgia	11	324	209	8	64.5	2890	8.9	20	262.7
Oregon	11	371	206	14	55.5	2883	7.8	28	262.1

Pass Efficiency Defense

	G	Att.	Cmp.	Cmp. Pct.	Int.	Int. Pct.	Yards	Yds./ Att.	TD	TD Pct.	Rating Points
Michigan	11	292	145	49.66	22	7.53	1275	4.37	4	1.37	75.79
Ohio St.	12	360	160	44.44	19	5.28	1724	4.79	6	1.67	79.62
North Caro.	11	322	148	45.96	15	4.66	1445	4.49	7	2.17	81.52
Iowa	11	325	146	44.92	22	6.77	1766	5.43	12	3.69	89.21
Kansas St.	11	239	99	41.42	5	2.09	1396	5.84	4	1.67	91.83
Wyoming	13	374	169	45.19	24	6.42	2358	6.30	11	2.94	95.02
Marshall	12	322	146	45.34	15	4.66	1948	6.05	8	2.48	95.04
New Mexico	12	333	153	45.95	16	4.80	1989	5.97	10	3.00	96.42
UAB	11	337	159	47.18	17	5.04	1912	5.67	12	3.56	96.50
Florida St.	11	338	164	48.52	22	6.51	2084	6.17	12	3.55	99.01
Southern Miss.	11	429	225	52.45	17	3.96	2278	5.31	13	3.03	99.13
Texas A&M	12	295	155	52.54	11	3.73	1804	6.12	3	1.02	99.81
Florida	11	392	192	48.98	18	4.59	2417	6.17	11	2.81	100.85
Tulane	11	368	197	53.53	26	7.07	2288	6.22	11	2.99	101.49
UCLA	11	442	221	50.00	21	4.75	2783	6.30	14	3.17	103.84
Michigan St.	11	326	170	52.15	18	5.52	2043	6.27	10	3.07	103.87
Washington St.	11	414	200	48.31	18	4.35	2353	5.68	21	5.07	104.09
Colorado St.	12	390	201	51.54	18	4.62	2451	6.28	11	2.82	104.41
Western Mich.	11	362	178	49.17	9	2.49	2215	6.12	10	2.76	104.71
LSU	11	404	203	50.25	14	3.47	2547	6.30	11	2.72	105.26

Photo from Iowa sports information

Iowa's Tim Dwight averaged 19.3 yards per punt return and returned three for touchdowns last season to lead Division I-A in punt returns.

Net Punting

	Punts	Avg.	No. Ret.	Yds. Ret.	Net Avg.
LSU	54	46.0	17	150	43.3
Wyoming	79	45.2	28	181	42.9
Texas A&M	56	47.0	28	316	41.3
Mississippi St.	58	43.0	20	102	41.3
North Texas	63	46.4	33	327	41.2
Georgia Tech	47	45.6	19	220	41.0
Oklahoma St.	51	43.9	16	155	40.8
Arizona St.	69	43.1	32	173	40.6
Penn St.	55	42.6	23	130	40.2
Idaho	60	42.4	25	137	40.1
Tulane	42	46.2	25	256	40.1
Central Fla.	56	42.6	23	154	39.8
Utah	40	43.2	16	141	39.7
Virginia Tech	54	42.0	18	141	39.4
Utah St.	57	44.1	27	271	39.3
UCLA	54	43.3	25	221	39.2

Punt Returns

	G	No.	Yds.	TD	Avg.
Iowa	11	34	620	4	18.2
Oklahoma St.	11	32	521	1	16.3
Syracuse	12	34	531	4	15.6
Colorado St.	12	33	506	2	15.3
Utah St.	11	24	362	2	15.1
Washington St.	11	36	525	1	14.6
Cincinnati	11	40	582	4	14.6
Stanford	11	32	460	3	14.4
San Diego St.	12	22	309	2	14.0
Florida St.	11	45	632	2	14.0
Texas A&M	12	24	327	2	13.6
Tennessee	12	29	388	0	13.4
Kansas St.	11	43	560	2	13.0
Minnesota	12	23	296	0	12.9
Ohio	11	18	222	1	12.3
Florida	11	38	458	2	12.1
Memphis	11	24	288	1	12.0

Kickoff Returns

	G	No.	Yds.	TD	Avg.
Southern Miss.	11	31	873	2	28.2
Colorado	11	36	958	1	26.6
Syracuse	12	31	823	2	26.5
Kansas St.	11	18	470	1	26.1
Stanford	11	34	845	0	24.9
Minnesota	12	51	1,257	2	24.6
Nebraska	12	29	706	0	24.3
Oregon	11	47	1,144	1	24.3
Northern Ill.	11	54	1,299	1	24.1
Miami (Ohio)	11	31	745	1	24.0
Air Force	12	26	618	0	23.8
Wake Forest	11	31	732	1	23.6
Colorado St.	12	28	659	0	23.5
Clemson	11	38	887	0	23.3
Washington	11	27	626	1	23.2
Texas Tech	11	32	741	1	23.2
New Mexico	12	33	758	0	23.0

Turnover Margin

	TURNOVERS GAINED			TURNOVERS LOST			Margin/
	Fum.	Int.	Total	Fum.	Int.	Total	Game
Colorado St.	20	18	38	4	9	13	2.08
UCLA	18	21	39	14	5	19	1.82
Texas A&M	22	11	33	1	14	15	1.50
Florida St.	10	22	32	6	11	17	1.36
Tulane	8	26	34	6	14	20	1.27
Southern Methodist	12	15	27	7	7	14	1.18
Oklahoma St.	14	15	29	8	8	16	1.18
Navy	13	14	27	6	8	14	1.18

Longest Division I-A Plays of 1997

Rushing

Player, Team (Opponent)	Yards
Eric Vann, Kansas (Oklahoma)	99
John Avery, Mississippi (Arkansas)	97
Trung Canidate, Arizona (San Diego St.)	96
Astron Whatley, Kent (Eastern Mich.)	91
Travis Minor, Florida St. (Virginia)	87
Rickey Williams, Texas (Baylor)	87
LeAndre Moore, Ball St. (James Madison)	85
Ron Dayne, Wisconsin (San Jose St.)	80
Sirr Parker, Texas A&M (Iowa St.)	80
Eric Moore, Oklahoma (Baylor)	80
Robert Edwards, Georgia (Kentucky)	80
Marquis Williams, Northeast La. (Western Mich.)	80

*Did not score.

Passing

Passer-Receiver, Team (Opponent)	Yards
Jose Davis to Eugene Baker, Kent (Central Fla.)	98
Billy Dicken to Brian Alford, Purdue (Minnesota)	93
Chad Pennington to Randy Moss, Marshall (Army)	90
Billy Dicken to Brian Alford, Purdue (Minnesota)	89
Chris Redmon to Arnold Jackson, Louisville (Utah)	86
John Dutton to Trevor Insley, Nevada (Boise St.)	82
Tim Rattay to Troy Edwards, Louisiana Tech (Southwestern La.)	82
Todd Bandhauer to Ed Williams, Iowa St. (Minnesota)	81
Cleo Lemon to Lennie Johnson, Arkansas St. (Southwest Mo. St.)	81
Thad Busby to Peter Warrick, Florida St. (Clemson)	80
Ryan Leaf to Kevin McKenzie, Washington St. (Illinois)	80
John Rayborn to Jim Carpenter, UTEP (Tulsa)	80
Clint Stoerner to Anthony Lucas, Arkansas (LSU)	80
Clint Stoerner to Anthony Eubanks, Arkansas (LSU)	80

*Did not score.

Interception Returns

Player, Team (Opponent)	Yards
Dwight Henry, East Caro. (Louisville)	98
Jermaine Smith, Washington (Arizona)	91
Tony George, Florida (Tennessee)	89
Izell Reese, UAB (Arkansas St.)	85
Lorenzo Ferguson, Virginia Tech (Arkansas St.)	84
Barrett Green, West Va. (Rutgers)	*83
Ahmed Plummer, Ohio St. (Illinois)	83
Armon Hatcher, Oregon St. (Arizona St.)	76
Ross Farris, Boise St. (New Mexico St.)	73
Fernando Bryant, Alabama (Houston)	66

*Did not score.

Punt Returns

Player, Team (Opponent)	Yards
Lamar Chapman, Kansas St. (Ohio)	94
Peter Warrick, Florida St. (Clemson)	90
Jacquez Green, Florida (South Caro.)	86
Duane Starks, Miami (Fla.) (Baylor)	85
Arnold Jackson, Louisville (Illinois)	85
Craig Yeast, Kentucky (South Caro.)	85
Quinton Spotwood, Syracuse (Oklahoma)	84
Steve Neal, Western Mich. (Kent)	84
LaDouphyous McCalla, Rice (Texas Christian)	84
R. W. McQuarters, Oklahoma St. (Northeast La.)	*82

*Did not score.

Kickoff Returns

Player, Team (Opponent)	Yards
Nate Terry, West Va. (East Caro.)	100
Michael Wiley, Ohio St. (Bowling Green)	100
Eric Vann, Kansas (Oklahoma)	100
John Avery, Mississippi (Alabama)	100
Boo Williams, South Caro. (Vanderbilt)	100
Ben Kelly, Colorado (Wyoming)	99
Gerald Neasman, Kansas St. (Kansas)	99
Myles Savage, Wake Forest (Maryland)	98
Deshawn Williams, Oregon St. (Stanford)	96
Eric Booth, Southern Miss. (Tennessee)	96

Field Goals

Player, Team (Opponent)	Yards
Rian Lindell, Washington St. (Boise St.)	57
Chris Sailer, UCLA (Oregon)	56
Brian Huston, Ohio (Bowling Green)	56
Sebastian Janikowski, Florida St. (Wake Forest)	56
Martin Gramatica, Kansas St. (Ohio)	55
Dan Stultz, Ohio St. (Indiana)	55
James Anderson, Tulsa (Cinsinnati)	54
Phil Dawson, Texas (Rutgers)	54
Brian Hazelwood, Mississippi St. (Memphis)	53
Sixteen tied at	52

Punts

Player, Team (Opponent)	Yards
Dean Royal, Kansas (Missouri)	82
Chris Hunter, Utah (Tulsa)	80
James Garcia, Kansas St. (Missouri)	76
Nick Cecava, New Mexico St. (North Texas)	76
Jason Bloom, New Mexico (Northern Ariz.)	75
Chris Hunter, Utah (Southern Methodist)	75
Jason McLean, Nevada (UNLV)	74
Jason Davis, Oklahoma St. (Fresno St.)	74
Doug Johnson, Cincinnati (Memphis)	72
David Leaverton, Tennessee (UCLA)	71
Chad Shrout, Hawaii (Colorado St.)	71
Tim Hughes, Northwestern (Michigan)	71

Fumble Returns

Player, Team (Opponent)	Yards
Dennis Gibbs, Idaho (Boise St.)	99
Greg Van Leer, Wyoming (San Jose St.)	90
Nick Ward, Miami (Fla.) (Arizona St.)	85
Amar Brisco, UNLV (Wyoming)	*84
Rahim Abdullah, Clemson (North Caro. St.)	74
Jeff Popovich, Miami (Fla. (Baylor)	72
Rashad Holman, Louisville (Memphis)	70
Hamilton Mee, Arizona St. (Washington St.)	69
Clarence Lawson, Utah (Rice)	68
Heron O'Neal, Western Mich. (Kent)	67
Scott Patton, UNLV (Wyoming)	67

*Did not score.

1997 Division I-AA Individual Leaders

Rushing

	1997 Class	G	Car.	Yards	Avg.	TD	Yds.PG
Reggie Greene, Siena	Sr.	9	256	1778	6.9	18	197.56
Aaron Stecker, Western Ill.	Jr.	11	298	1957	6.6	24	177.91
Sean Bennett, Evansville	Jr.	10	235	1668	7.1	16	166.80
Rex Prescott, Eastern Wash.	Sr.	10	212	1494	7.0	12	149.40
Claude Mathis, Southwest Tex.	Sr.	11	311	1595	5.1	14	145.00
Jerry Azumah, New Hampshire	Jr.	11	269	1572	5.8	13	142.91
Stan House, Central Conn. St.	Sr.	10	294	1413	4.8	12	141.30
Rick Sarille, Wagner	Jr.	10	245	1285	5.2	13	128.50
Steve Wofford, Southern U.	Jr.	10	243	1274	5.2	12	127.40
Chris Menick, Harvard	So.	10	247	1267	5.1	13	126.70
Jason Grove, Drake	Jr.	11	283	1374	4.9	16	124.91
Rabih Abdullah, Lehigh	Sr.	10	244	1225	5.0	15	122.50
Willie Taggart, Western Ky.	Sr.	10	152	1217	8.0	15	121.70
Roger Harriott, Boston U.	So.	11	260	1333	5.1	7	121.18
Anthony Ravizee, Morehead St.	Sr.	10	210	1197	5.7	13	119.70
Alvin Porch, William & Mary	Sr.	11	261	1316	5.0	6	119.64
Naim Sanders, Butler	Jr.	10	267	1122	4.2	9	112.20
Brook Madsen, Southern Utah	Jr.	11	234	1214	5.2	10	110.36
Jason Corle, Towson	So.	10	239	1075	4.5	6	107.50
Ed Weiss, Colgate	So.	10	178	1069	6.0	7	106.90
Roderick Russell, Ga. Southern	Sr.	11	215	1171	5.4	11	106.45

Passing Efficiency

(Min. 15 att. per game)	1997 Class	G	Att.	Cmp.	Cmp. Pct.	Int.	Int. Pct.	Yards	Yds./ Att.	TD	TD Pct.	Rating Points
Alli Abrew, Cal Poly	Sr.	11	191	130	68.06	4	2.09	1961	10.27	17	8.90	179.5
Doug Turner, Morehead St.	Sr.	10	290	190	65.52	6	2.07	2869	9.89	29	10.00	177.5
Chris Boden, Villanova	So.	11	345	231	66.96	4	1.16	3079	8.92	36	10.43	174.0
Harry Leons, Eastern Wash.	Sr.	10	257	159	61.87	5	1.95	2588	10.07	21	8.17	169.5
Simon Fuentes, Eastern Ky.	Sr.	11	189	116	61.38	2	1.06	1932	10.22	13	6.88	167.8
Giovanni Carmazzi, Hofstra	Jr.	11	408	288	70.59	8	1.96	3554	8.71	27	6.62	161.7
Mike Stadler, San Diego	So.	11	262	152	58.02	10	3.82	2287	8.73	30	11.45	161.5
Todd Wells, East Tenn. St.	Fr.	11	247	144	58.30	9	3.64	2404	9.73	17	6.88	155.5
Shane Stafford, Connecticut	Sr.	11	296	164	55.41	10	3.38	2814	9.51	23	7.77	154.1
Brian Ginn, Delaware	So.	10	178	97	54.49	3	1.69	1622	9.11	14	7.87	153.6
Ben Anderson, Liberty	Sr.	11	268	152	56.72	10	3.73	2505	9.35	18	6.72	149.9
Rob Compson, Montana St.	Jr.	11	295	179	60.68	9	3.05	2388	8.09	22	7.46	147.2
Kevin Johns, Dayton	Sr.	10	175	92	52.57	7	4.00	1531	8.75	15	8.57	146.3
Blake Prejean, McNeese St.	So.	11	265	160	60.38	9	3.40	2412	9.10	13	4.91	146.2
Oteman Sampson, Florida A&M	Sr.	11	379	215	56.73	10	2.64	3290	8.68	25	6.60	146.1
Aaron Flowers, CS Northridge	Sr.	9	4042	55	63.12	10	2.48	3226	7.99	24	5.94	144.8
Mike Simpson, Eastern Ill.	Sr.	11	246	168	68.29	8	3.25	1914	7.78	13	5.28	144.6
Ryan Vena, Colgate	So.	11	222	129	58.11	12	5.41	1882	8.48	17	7.66	143.8
Demond Tidwell, Youngstown St.	Sr.	11	178	113	63.48	6	3.37	1583	8.89	6	3.37	142.6
Brian Ah Yat, Montana	Jr.	10	357	216	60.50	6	1.68	2691	7.54	21	5.88	139.9

Total Offense

	RUSHING				PASSING		TOTAL OFFENSE				
	Car.	Gain	Loss	Net	Att.	Yards	Plays	Yards	Avg.	TDR*	Yds.PG
Aaron Flowers, CS Northridge	52	761	70	-94	404	3226	456	3132	6.87	26	348.00
Giovanni Carmazzi, Hofstra	116	351	198	153	408	3554	524	3707	7.07	36	337.00
Oteman Sampson, Florida A&M	113	551	216	335	379	3290	492	3625	7.37	27	329.55
Travis Brown, Northern Ariz.	49	98	130	-32	474	3395	523	3363	6.43	23	305.73
James Perry, Brown	50	181	114	67	397	2873	447	2940	6.58	25	294.00
Mickey Fein, Maine	55	105	138	-33	414	2912	469	2879	6.14	30	287.90
Chris Boden, Villanova	55	164	163	1	345	3079	400	3080	7.70	36	280.00
Chad Salisbury, Buffalo	24	8	100	-92	384	2889	408	2797	6.86	16	279.70
Doug Turner, Morehead St.	54	94	177	-83	290	2869	344	2786	8.10	30	278.60
Montressa Kirby, Jacksnvlle St	75	247	139	108	419	2817	494	2925	5.92	19	265.91
Brian Ah Yat, Montana	55	107	217	-110	357	2691	412	2581	6.26	23	258.10
Todd Wells, East Tenn. St.	123	499	140	359	247	2404	370	2763	7.47	23	251.18
Harry Leons, Eastern Wash.	30	10	88	-78	257	2588	287	2510	8.75	21	251.00
Steve Buck, Weber St.	77	352	239	113	299	2393	376	2506	6.66	17	250.60
Shane Stafford, Connecticut	41	59	144	-85	296	2814	337	2729	8.10	23	248.09
Shane Fortney, Northern Iowa	62	219	122	97	349	2558	411	2655	6.46	16	241.36
Bake Baker, Appalachian St.	76	240	173	67	347	2550	423	2617	6.19	24	237.91
Jonathan Quinn, Middle Tenn. S	66	305	135	170	293	2209	359	2379	6.63	20	237.90
Rich Linden, Harvard	99	352	143	209	286	2099	385	2308	5.99	21	230.80
Darnell Kennedy, Alabama St.	72	261	153	108	388	2395	460	2503	5.44	172	227.55

*Touchdowns responsible for are players' TDs scored and passed for.

Receptions Per Game

	1997 Class	G	Rec.	Yards	TD	Rec.PG
Eric Krawczyk, Cornell	Sr.	10	89	1042	11	8.90
Rameek Wright, Maine	Sr.	11	88	1176	7	8.00
Mike Furrey, Northern Iowa	Jr.	11	82	1291	7	7.45
Bryan Kish, Hofstra	Sr.	11	82	1084	7	7.45
Sean Morey, Brown	Jr.	10	73	1427	15	7.30
Shane Sullivan, St Mary's (Cal)	Sr.	10	72	832	6	7.20
Jerome Henry, Cal St. Northridge	Sr.	10	71	827	8	7.10
Wayne Yearwood, Hofstra	Sr.	11	76	973	12	6.91
Brian Finneran, Villanova	Sr.	11	75	1151	17	6.82
Eric Wise, Fairfield	So.	10	67	698	4	6.70

Receiving Yards Per Game

	1997 Class	G	Rec.	Yards	TD	Yds.PG
Sean Morey, Brown	Jr.	10	73	1427	15	142.70
B.J. Adigun, East Tenn. St.	Sr.	11	68	1389	12	126.27
Mikhael Ricks, Stephen F. Austin	Sr.	11	47	1358	13	123.45
Mike Furrey, Northern Iowa	Jr.	11	82	1291	7	117.36
Carl Bond, Connecticut	Sr.	11	51	1178	6	107.09
Rameek Wright, Maine	Sr.	11	88	1176	7	106.91
Brian Finneran, Villanova	Sr.	11	75	1151	17	104.64
Jeff Ogden, Eastern Wash.	Sr.	11	57	1148	13	104.36
Eric Krawczyk, Cornell	Sr.	10	89	1042	11	104.20
Chris Berry, Morehead St.	Sr.	10	54	1016	7	101.60
Bryan Kish, Hofstra	Sr.	11	82	1084	7	98.55
Rondel Menendez, Eastern Ky.	Jr.	11	49	1073	8	97.55

Interceptions

	1997 Class	G	Int.	Yards	TD	Int.PG
Roderic Parson, Brown	Sr.	8	8	93	0	1.00
Tony Booth, James Madison	Jr.	10	8	77	1	.80
Paul Serie, Siena	Jr.	9	7	36	1	.78
Trevor Bell, Idaho St.	Sr.	11	8	148	0	.73
Derek Carter, Maine	Sr.	11	8	137	0	.73
Chris Tillotson, Columbia	Jr.	10	7	156	2	.70
Brian Dunn, Robert Morris	Sr.	10	7	92	0	.70
Reid Ruberti, Georgetown	Sr.	9	6	150	0	.67

Scoring

	1997 Class	G	TD	XP	FG	Pts.	Pts.PG
Aaron Stecker, Western Ill.	Jr.	11	25	0	0	150	13.64
Reggie Greene, Siena	Sr.	9	18	2	0	110	12.22
Sean Bennett, Evansville	Jr.	10	20	2	0	122	12.20
Stan House, Central Conn. St.	Sr.	10	18	2	0	110	11.00
Rabih Abdullah, Lehigh	Sr.	10	18	0	0	108	10.80
Brian Finneran, Villanova	Sr.	11	17	10	0	112	10.18
Adrian Brown, Youngstown St.	So.	9	15	0	0	90	10.00
Jerry Azumah, New Hampshire	Jr.	11	17	2	0	104	9.45
Rick Sarille, Wagner	Jr.	10	15	4	0	94	9.40
Anthony Ravizee, Morehead St.	Sr.	10	15	4	0	94	9.40
Willie Taggart, Western Ky.	Sr.	10	15	0	0	90	9.00
Sean Morey, Brown	Jr.	10	15	0	0	90	9.00
Jason Grove, Drake	Jr.	11	16	0	0	96	8.73
Chris Berry, Morehead St.	Sr.	10	14	2	0	86	8.60
Chris Menick, Harvard	So.	10	14	2	0	86	8.60
Dave Ettinger, Hofstra	Sr.	11	0	42	17	93	8.45
Stacy Nobles, Liberty	So.	10	14	0	0	84	8.40
Juan Toro, Florida A&M	Jr.	11	0	40	17	91	8.27
Daymon Smith, Colgate	Sr.	11	15	0	0	90	8.18
Shonz Lafrenz, McNeese St.	So.	11	0	37	17	88	8.00
Scott Shields, Weber St.	Jr.	11	22	4	17	87	7.91
Travis Brawner, Southwest Mo. St.	So.	11	0	23	21	86	7.82
Jeff Poisel, Western Ky.	So.	10	0	45	11	78	7.80
James Finn, Pennsylvania	Jr.	10	13	0	0	78	7.80

All-Purpose Yards

	1997 Class	G	Rush	Rec.	PR	KOR	Total Yards	Yds.PG
Reggie Greene, Siena	Sr.	9	1778	73	0	158	2009	223.22
Sean Bennett, Evansville	Jr.	10	1668	260	81	34	2043	204.30
Aaron Stecker, Western Ill.	Jr.	11	1957	288	0	0	2245	204.09
Jerry Azumah, New Hampshire	Jr.	11	1572	297	0	351	2220	201.82
Sean Morey, Brown	Jr.	10	15	1427	15	465	1922	192.20
Rick Sarille, Wagner	Jr.	10	1285	85	0	514	1884	188.40
Stan House, Central Conn. St.	Sr.	10	1413	357	16	23	1809	180.90
Chris Berry, Morehead St.	Sr.	10	401	1016	273	115	1805	180.50
Delvin Joyce, James Madison	Fr.	9	422	197	289	656	1564	173.78
Rex Prescott, Eastern Wash.	Sr.	10	1494	223	0	0	1717	171.70
Tom Reali, St. Peter's	Sr.	10	893	257	0	535	1685	168.50
Claude Mathis, Southwest Tex.	Sr.	11	1595	42	0	162	1799	163.55
Kino Carson, Northern Ariz.	Sr.	11	1099	169	165	362	1795	163.18
Chris Menick, Harvard	So.	10	1267	123	0	214	1604	160.40
T. Butterfield, Tennessee St.	Jr.	11	-13	1053	44	619	1703	154.82
Ed Williams, St. Mary's (Cal.)	Sr.	10	744	219	162	384	1509	150.90
Joe Rosato, Duquesne	Sr.	10	-4	698	391	418	1503	150.30
Jason Corle, Towson	So.	10	1075	390	0	0	1465	146.50
Anthony Ravizee, Morehead St.	Sr.	10	1197	220	0	0	1417	141.70
Mike Furrey, Northern Iowa	Jr.	11	7	1291	146	106	1550	140.91

Punt Returns

(Min. 1.2 per game)	1997 Class	No.	Yds.	TD	Avg.
Chris Berry, Morehead St.	Sr.	13	273	1	21.00
Delvin Joyce, James Madison	Fr.	17	289	0	17.00
Lydell Finley, Norfolk St.	Sr.	18	286	0	15.89
Chris Caldwell, North Caro A&T	Fr.	23	361	1	15.70
Byron Plummer, Alabama St.	Jr.	14	219	1	15.64

Kickoff Returns

(Min. 1.2 per game)	1997 Class	No.	Yds.	TD	Avg.
Andy Swafford, Troy St.	Sr.	14	440	1	31.43
Sylvester Miller, St. Peter's	Fr.	15	442	2	29.47
Marq Cerqua, Furman	So.	12	350	1	29.17
Rick Sarille, Wagner	Jr.	18	514	2	28.56
James Banks, Ga. Southern	So.	12	335	1	27.92

Punting

(Min. 3.6 per game)	1997 Class	No.	Avg.
Barry Cantrell, Fordham	Sr.	65	45.85
Chad Stanley, Stephen F. Austin	Jr.	62	44.69
Brad Costello, Boston U.	Sr.	73	44.37
Ken Hinsley, Western Caro.	Jr.	46	44.17
Steve Thorns, Cal St. Sacramento	Jr.	66	44.05

Field Goals

	1997 Class	G	FGA	FG	Pct.	FGPG
Travis Brawner, Southwest Mo. St.	So.	11	28	21	.750	1.91
Alex Sierk, Princeton	Jr.	10	21	18	.857	1.80
Juan Toro, Florida A&M	Jr.	11	21	17	.810	1.55
Dave Ettinger, Hofstra	Sr.	11	22	17	.773	1.55
Scott Shields, Weber St.	Jr.	11	25	17	.680	1.55
Shonz Lafrenz, McNeese St.	So.	11	26	17	.654	1.55
Brian Shallcross, Wm. & Mary	Sr.	11	18	15	.833	1.36
Steve Riggs, South Fla.	Sr.	11	22	15	.682	1.36
Ryan Smith, Stephen F. Austin	Sr.	11	18	14	.778	1.27
Mark Goldstein, Northern Ariz.	Fr.	10	21	12	.571	1.20

1997 Division I-AA Team Leaders

Total Offense

	G	Plays	Yds.	Avg.	TD*	Yds.PG
Eastern Wash.	11	775	5562	7.2	48	505.64
Morehead St.	10	743	4955	6.7	58	495.50
Brown	10	821	4753	5.8	33	475.30
Florida A&M	11	787	5213	6.6	45	473.91
Cal St. Northridge	12	920	5480	6.0	45	456.67
Western Ky.	10	724	4566	6.3	47	456.60
Cal Poly	11	734	5010	6.8	49	455.45
Hofstra	11	795	4993	6.3	46	453.91
Northern Ariz.	11	876	4927	5.6	38	447.91
Colgate	11	786	4857	6.2	51	441.55
Dayton	10	671	4394	6.5	46	439.40
Jackson St.	11	772	4809	6.2	46	437.18
East Tenn. St.	11	764	4755	6.2	42	432.27
Western Ill.	11	778	4731	6.1	45	430.09
Villanova	11	732	4693	6.4	57	426.64
Southern Utah	11	857	4689	5.5	42	426.27

*Touchdowns scored by rushing or passing only.

Total Defense

	G	Plays	Yds.	Avg.	TD*	Yds.PG
Marist	10	642	2136	3.3	16	213.6
Murray St.	11	707	2613	3.7	20	237.5
Hampton	11	675	2623	3.9	17	238.5
McNeese St.	11	715	2698	3.8	11	245.3
Troy St.	11	679	2734	4.0	17	248.5
St. John's (N.Y.)	11	742	2739	3.7	18	249.0
Drake	11	669	2775	4.1	19	252.3
Grambling	11	662	2799	4.2	30	254.5
South Fla.	11	655	2800	4.3	20	254.5
Princeton	10	673	2584	3.8	12	258.4
Northwestern St.	11	650	2865	4.4	20	260.5
Richmond	11	718	2881	4.0	19	261.9
Harvard	10	680	2648	3.9	15	264.8
Georgetown	10	646	2660	4.1	17	266.0
Youngstown St.	11	693	2947	4.3	19	267.9
Northeastern	11	699	3027	4.3	29	275.2

*Touchdowns scored by rushing or passing only.

Rushing Offense

	G	Car.	Yds.	Avg.	TD	Yds.PG
Western Ky.	10	610	3660	6.0	39	366.0
Southern Utah	11	700	3563	5.1	35	323.9
Wofford	10	640	2922	4.6	22	292.2
Ga. Southern	11	592	3087	5.2	31	280.6
Dayton	10	492	2804	5.7	31	280.4
Cal Poly	11	530	2929	5.5	31	266.3
Colgate	11	552	2879	5.2	34	261.7
Western Ill.	11	509	2686	5.3	35	244.2
Siena	9	368	2045	5.6	21	227.2
Eastern Wash.	11	458	2489	5.4	22	226.3
Youngstown St.	11	565	2488	4.4	37	226.2
Drake	11	558	2483	4.4	30	225.7
Hampton	11	533	2460	4.6	19	223.6
New Hampshire	11	525	2375	4.5	19	215.9
Harvard	10	482	2077	4.3	22	207.7

Rushing Defense

	G	Car.	Yds.	Avg.	TD	Yds.PG
Marist	10	319	404	1.3	3	40.4
Northeastern	11	355	721	2.0	14	65.5
Dartmouth	10	331	773	2.3	9	77.3
Eastern Wash.	11	342	896	2.6	10	81.5
Harvard	10	308	819	2.7	4	81.9
Murray St.	11	417	916	2.2	12	83.3
Pennsylvania	10	364	833	2.3	5	83.3
Western Ky.	10	299	848	2.8	9	84.8
Southern U.	11	370	933	2.5	7	84.8
Drake	11	351	961	2.7	4	87.4
Delaware	11	386	999	2.6	6	90.8
Richmond	11	426	1032	2.4	5	93.8

Troy St.	11	402	1058	2.6	8	96.2
Northwestern St.	11	360	1059	2.9	8	96.3
Hampton	11	385	1067	2.8	7	97.0

Scoring Offense

	G	Pts.	Avg.
Morehead St.	10	419	41.9
Villanova	11	442	40.2
Dayton	10	366	36.6
Western Ky.	10	366	36.6
Connecticut	11	398	36.2
Eastern Wash.	11	389	35.4
Florida A&M	11	388	35.3
Colgate	11	386	35.1
Hofstra	11	383	34.8
Cal Poly	11	382	34.7
Eastern Ky.	11	369	33.5
San Diego	11	369	33.5
Western Ill.	11	364	33.1
Ga. Southern	11	364	33.1
Jackson St.	11	363	33.0
Youngstown St.	11	360	32.7
Liberty	11	356	32.4
Delaware	11	355	32.3

Scoring Defense

	G	Pts.	Avg.
McNeese St.	11	116	10.5
Harvard	10	123	12.3
Hampton	11	139	12.6
St. John's (N.Y.)	11	145	13.2
Princeton	10	132	13.2
Duquesne	10	132	13.2
Eastern Ky.	11	147	13.4
Marist	10	141	14.1
Troy St.	11	157	14.3
Georgetown	10	143	14.3
Drake	11	158	14.4
Youngstown St.	11	160	14.5
Murray St.	11	172	15.6
Delaware	11	174	15.8
Tennessee Tech	11	174	15.8
Ga. Southern	11	176	16.0
South Fla.	11	181	16.5
Dartmouth	10	165	16.5

Passing Offense

	G	Att.	Cmp.	Int.	Pct.	Yards	Yds./Att.	TD	Yds.PG
Cal St. Northridge	12	551	344	16	62.4	4297	7.8	30	358.1
Hofstra	11	415	293	8	70.6	3618	8.7	28	328.9
Brown	10	438	229	20	52.3	3192	7.3	26	319.2
Montana	11	476	286	12	60.1	3488	7.3	28	317.1
Florida A&M	11	388	220	10	56.7	3466	8.9	28	315.1
Northern Ariz.	11	483	278	19	57.6	3449	7.1	21	313.5
Villanova	11	374	251	4	67.1	3331	8.9	39	302.8
Buffalo	11	453	246	19	54.3	3275	7.2	18	297.7
Maine	11	454	257	14	56.6	3209	7.1	27	291.7
Morehead St.	10	296	192	6	64.9	2914	9.8	29	291.4
Eastern Wash.	11	317	198	7	62.5	3073	9.7	26	279.4
Weber St.	11	422	203	14	48.1	3060	7.3	17	278.2
Tennessee St.	11	371	186	18	50.1	2917	7.9	21	265.2
Jacksonville St.	11	429	221	22	51.5	2897	6.8	18	263.4
Northern Iowa	11	387	203	13	52.5	2881	7.4	19	261.9
Connecticut	11	308	169	10	54.9	2871	9.3	23	261.0
Northeastern	11	386	228	11	59.1	2841	7.4	20	258.3
Jackson St.	11	341	190	17	55.7	2826	8.3	22	256.9
William & Mary	11	361	199	11	55.1	2795	7.7	21	254.1

Pass Efficiency Defense

	G	Att.	Cmp.	Cmp. Pct.	Int.	Int. Pct.	Yards	Yds./Att.	TD	TD Pct.	Rating Points
McNeese St.	11	325	157	48.31	26	8.00	1612	4.96	5	1.54	79.05
Brown	10	326	136	41.72	29	8.90	1771	5.43	11	3.37	80.69
Alcorn St.	11	224	96	42.86	11	4.91	1159	5.17	5	2.23	83.86
Princeton	10	299	131	43.81	18	6.02	1609	5.38	8	2.68	85.80
Harvard	10	372	165	44.35	17	4.57	1829	4.92	11	2.96	86.27
Eastern Ky.	11	298	131	43.96	15	5.03	1661	5.57	6	2.01	87.36
Georgetown	10	277	138	49.82	24	8.66	1544	5.57	8	2.89	88.84
Canisius	10	251	112	44.62	17	6.77	1497	5.96	6	2.39	89.06
St. John's (N.Y.)	11	265	125	47.17	11	4.15	1332	5.03	7	2.64	89.81
Hampton	11	290	132	45.52	15	5.17	1556	5.37	10	3.45	91.62
Marist	10	323	142	43.96	16	4.95	1732	5.36	13	4.02	92.38
South Fla.	11	139	63	45.32	10	7.19	826	5.94	5	3.60	92.72
William & Mary	11	284	135	47.54	14	4.93	1553	5.47	8	2.82	92.91
Fairfield	10	238	103	43.28	9	3.78	1278	5.37	10	4.20	94.69
Bethune-Cookman	11	268	113	42.16	15	5.60	1529	5.71	13	4.85	94.90
Duquesne	10	261	123	47.13	18	6.90	1584	6.07	9	3.45	95.69
Siena	9	292	138	47.26	16	5.48	1712	5.86	9	3.08	95.72
Northwestern St.	11	290	133	45.86	21	7.24	1806	6.23	12	4.14	97.35
Morgan St.	10	282	112	39.72	11	3.90	1766	6.26	11	3.90	97.39

Net Punting

	Punts	Avg.	No. Ret.	Yds. Ret.	Net Avg.
James Madison	72	42.8	38	166	40.5
Middle Tenn. St.	42	40.9	18	73	39.1
Eastern Wash.	47	41.6	16	119	39.0
Boston U.	74	43.8	31	400	38.4
Southeast Mo. St.	74	42.9	47	340	38.3
Southern Ill.	71	42.8	34	330	38.2
Weber St.	69	41.7	29	247	38.1
Cal St. Sacramento	69	42.3	31	293	38.0
Southwest Mo. St.	73	40.0	25	143	38.0
Dartmouth	72	40.6	44	209	37.7
Nicholls St.	66	40.7	28	201	37.6
Ga. Southern	48	39.9	23	122	37.4
Western Ill.	40	39.8	13	109	37.1
Fordham	70	43.1	37	425	37.0
Delaware	57	42.0	36	285	37.0

Punt Returns

	G	No.	Yds.	TD	Avg.
Morehead St.	10	15	291	1	19.4
James Madison	11	24	446	1	18.6
North Caro. A&T	11	34	504	2	14.8
Valparaiso	10	25	355	2	14.2
Norfolk St.	10	26	341	0	13.1
Western Ill.	11	24	312	2	13.0
Delaware	11	35	450	3	12.9
Idaho St.	11	19	242	1	12.7
South Caro. St.	11	32	401	2	12.5
Weber St.	11	23	288	0	12.5
Mississippi Val.	10	23	279	0	12.1
Wofford	10	16	194	2	12.1
Alcorn St.	11	30	362	1	12.1
Colgate	11	25	300	1	12.0
Furman	11	34	405	2	11.9

Kickoff Returns

	G	No.	Yds.	TD	Avg.
Furman	11	30	814	2	27.1
Robert Morris	10	31	828	1	26.7
Troy St.	11	30	784	1	26.1
Ga. Southern	11	28	715	2	25.5
Appalachian St.	11	30	706	0	23.5
Dayton	10	30	703	0	23.4
Eastern Wash.	11	27	632	2	23.4
Murray St.	11	33	762	1	23.1
South Fla.	11	37	853	1	23.1
Cal Poly	11	34	764	0	22.5
Wagner	10	33	731	2	22.2
Southern U.	11	35	770	0	22.0
Western Ky.	10	32	704	0	22.0
James Madison	11	47	1,031	1	21.9
Chattanooga	11	32	698	0	21.8
Morehead St.	10	47	1,025	0	21.8
McNeese St.	11	13	283	0	21.8

Turnover Margin

	TURNOVERS GAINED			TURNOVERS LOST			Margin/
	Fum.	Int.	Total	Fum.	Int.	Total	Game
Texas Southern	18	18	36	10	5	15	1.91
Liberty	22	18	40	10	10	20	1.82
Georgetown	12	24	36	8	11	19	1.70
Indiana St.	12	18	30	9	6	15	1.36
Idaho St.	15	17	32	8	11	19	1.18
St. John's (N.Y.)	20	11	31	11	7	18	1.18
Dayton	4	20	24	6	7	13	1.10
Central Conn. St.	14	17	31	10	10	20	1.10
Ga. Southern	21	13	34	14	8	22	1.09
Bucknell	9	17	26	4	10	14	1.09

Longest Division I-AA Plays of 1997

Rushing

Player, Team (Opponent)	Yards
Brian Edwards, East Tenn. St. (Appalachian St.)	91
Jerome Tillman, Tennessee Tech (Middle Tenn. St.)	87
Lorenzo Moll, Davidson (Sewanee)	86
Barry Chandler, Connecticut (Buffalo)	86
Lorenzo Moll, Davidson (Sewanee)	85
Rex Prescott, Eastern Wash. (Idaho St.)	85
Joey Stockton, Western Ky. (Southern Ill.)	84
Reggie Greene, Siena (Duquesne)	82
Kennedy Nkeyasen, Idaho St. (Portland St.)	82
Josh Branen, Montana (Stephen F. Austin)	79
Reggie Greene, Siena (Georgetown)	79

Passing

Passer-Receiver, Team (Opponent)	Yards
Brian Hampton to Stepfon Hawkins, Chattanooga (Ga. Southern)	94
Montressa Kirby to Joey Hamilton, Jacksonville St. (Southwest Mo. St.)	93
Brian Ah Yat to Jim Farris, Montana (Portland St.)	93
Jeremy Swords to Sam Campoli, St. Francis (Pa.) (Mercyhurst)	92
James Perry to Sean Morey, Brown (Fordham)	92
Bill Ward to Rob Rosentahl, Georgetown (Siena)	*88
Dan Sabella to William Holder, Monmouth (Wagner)	88
Todd Welk to Anthony Stringfield, East Tenn. St. (Appalachian St.)	86
Ben Anderson to Courtney Freeman, Liberty (Elon)	86
Harry Leons to Jeff Ogden, Eastern Wash. (Montana)	86

Interception Returns

Player, Team (Opponent)	Yards
John Keith, Furman (Chattanooga)	99
Josh Symonette, Tennessee Tech (Austin Peay)	98
Keian Davis, Cal St. Sacramento (Cal St. Northridge)	95
Marcus Harvey, Liberty (Appalachian St.)	95
Kujanga Jackson, San Diego (Evansville)	93
Lance Schulters, Hofstra (Liberty)	92
Sean Gorius, Dayton (San Diego)	90
Chris Guyton, Eastern Ky. (Eastern Ill.)	80
Louis Waggoner, Connecticut (Buffalo)	77
Clifford Ivory, Troy St. (Nicholls St.)	76

Punt Returns

Player, Team (Opponent)	Yards
Steve Clancy, Valparaiso (San Diego)	87
Salecia Sanford, Middle Tenn. St. (Chattanooga)	85
Earnest Payton, James Madison (Boston U.)	77
Mario Wilson, Marist (St. Peter's)	75
Ed Conti, Delware (New Hampshire)	68
Chris Tillotson, Columbia (Holy Cross)	68
Lamont Williams, Western Caro. (Citadel)	65
Terrance Smith, Tenn.-Martin (Austin Peay)	54

Kickoff Returns

Player, Team (Opponent)	Yards
Darriel Ruffin, Tenn.-Martin (Murray St.)	100
Jerry Azumah, New Hampshire (Rhode Island)	99
Roland Williams, Davidson (Emory & Henry)	98
Reginald Swinton, Murray St. (Austin Peay)	98
Steve Correa, Eastern Wash. (Portland St.)	97
James Banks, Ga. Southern (William & Mary)	94
Antonio Lee, Robert Morris (Towson)	93
Marq Cerqua, Furman (East Tenn. St.)	90
Desmond Kitchings, Furman (Chattanooga)	90
Tyrone Taylor, Cal St. Sacramento (Cal St. Northridge)	89

Field Goals

Player, Team (Opponent)	Yards
Kris Heppner, Montana (Idaho St.)	54
Ryan Smith, Stephen F. Austin (Jacksonville St.)	53
Dave Ettinger, Hofstra (Youngstown St.)	53
Ramon Rivera, Texas Southern (Ark.-Pine Bluff)	53
Scott Brown, Cal St. Sacramento (Montana)	52
Justin Skinner, Citadel (East Tenn. St.)	52
Dave Ettinger, Hofstra (Liberty)	52
Keegan Ray, Middle Tenn. St. (Tennessee St.)	52
Ramon Rivera, Texas Southern (Ark.-Pine Bluff)	52
Travis Brawner, Southwest Mo. St. (Indiana St.)	51
Ryan Smith, Stephen F. Austin (Nicholls St.)	51
Mike Harris, VMI (Richmond)	51
Scott Shields, Weber St. (Portland St.)	51

Punts

Player, Team (Opponent)	Yards
Jade Stillings, Tenn.-Martin (Tennessee Tech)	80
Charles Watson, Cornell (Princeton)	74
Justin Terrill, Southeast Mo. St. (Tennessee Tech)	74
Stephen Brown, Eastern Ky. (Appalachian St.)	73
Scott Shields, Weber St. (Southern Utah)	72
Ben Simpson, Idaho St. (Montana)	68
Brian Holmes, Samford (Austin Peay)	67
Jade Stillings, Tenn.-Martin (Southwest Mo. St.)	67
Erich Kutschke, Colgate (Princeton)	66
Scott Shields, Weber St. (Portland St.)	66

Fumble Returns

Player, Team (Opponent)	Yards
Justin Gaines, Montana (Idaho St.)	95
Matt Wilson, Rhode Island (Hofstra)	95
Max Kerry, Canisius (Fairfield)	87
Joe Huber, La Salle (Monmouth)	85
Derrick Williams, Alcorn St. (Mississippi Val.)	*81
Mike McHoney, Charleston So. (Wofford)	80
Jeff DeLucia, Connecticut (Buffalo)	74
Vinnie Sasso, Monmouth (Wagner)	*74
Freddie Taylor, Southern Ill. (Southwest Mo. St.)	71
Mike Gallagher, Drake (Aurora)	70

*Did not score.

1997 Division II Individual Leaders

Rushing

	1997 Class	G	Car.	Yards	TD	Yds.PG
Anthony Gray, Western N.M.	Jr.	10	277	2220	12	222.0
Irv Sigler, Bloomsburg	Sr.	10	299	2038	20	203.8
Phillip Moore, North Dak.	Jr.	10	293	1771	14	177.1
Wilmont Perry, Livingstone	Jr.	10	195	1770	20	177.0
Brian Shay, Emporia St.	Jr.	11	269	1912	29	173.8
Damian Beane, Shepherd	So.	10	258	1590	18	159.0
Jake Morris, North Dak. St.	Sr.	11	280	1710	15	155.5
Conan Smith, N.M. Highlands	Sr.	11	277	1599	18	145.4
Tracy Bowen, Wingate	So.	9	179	1274	13	141.6
Chris Pierson, Harding	Sr.	10	196	1306	10	130.6
Matt Rapoza, Bentley	Jr.	9	225	1154	11	128.2
Andre Braxton, Virginia Union	Fr.	11	251	1383	10	125.7
Emneko Sweeney, Kutztown	Jr.	9	193	1113	11	123.7
Grover Moore, Moorhead St.	Jr.	10	175	1235	12	123.5
Emile Fann, LIU-C.W. Post	Sr.	8	185	941	6	117.6
Tregnel Thomas, Delta St.	So.	10	215	1145	9	114.5
Justin Johnson, Pittsburg St.	Sr.	10	170	1125	14	112.5
Thomas Fulton, West Chester	Sr.	11	261	1228	6	111.6
Stewart Ford, East Stroudsburg	Fr.	10	175	1109	11	110.9
Rashaan Dumas, Southern Conn. St.	So.	9	184	987	12	109.7
Chris Meyer, Bemidji St.	So.	10	280	1091	8	109.1
Anthony Simmons, Chadron St.	So.	10	175	1060	8	106.0
Jeff Klopf, Saginaw Valley	Jr.	11	196	1161	15	105.5
Tyrone Westmoreland, Carson-Newman	Sr.	9	119	946	17	105.1
Matt Otero, Ashland	Fr.	10	155	1030	6	103.0

Passing Efficiency

(Min. 15 att. per game)	1997 Class	G	Att.	Cmp.	Pct.	Int.	Yards	TD	Rating Points
Wilkie Perez, Glenville St.	Jr.	11	425	280	65.8	12	4189	45	178.0
Jake Goettl, Winona St.	Jr.	11	259	153	59.0	13	2504	23	159.6
Joe Savino, Albany (N.Y.)	Sr.	12	256	150	58.5	11	2377	22	156.4
Justin Coleman, Neb.-Kearney	Fr.	11	309	177	57.2	13	2804	29	156.0
Chris Greisen, Northwest Mo. St.	Jr.	11	272	155	56.9	7	2456	23	155.6
Cazzie Kosciolek, New Haven	Sr.	10	271	162	59.7	6	2327	23	155.5
J.D. Meyers, Ky. Wesleyan	So.	10	247	134	54.2	8	2172	22	151.0
Corte McGuffey, Northern Colo.	So.	11	169	104	61.5	8	1518	12	150.9
Pete Jelovic, Emporia St.	Sr.	11	276	178	64.4	9	2422	15	149.6
Chad Broadwater, Shepherd	Sr.	10	200	110	55.0	12	1837	16	146.6
Kevin Klancher, North Dak.	Sr.	10	162	935	7.43	11	85	15	145.7
Jeff Fox, Grand Valley St.	Jr.	11	298	172	57.7	8	2422	18	140.6
Erik Hartman, Angelo St.	Sr.	10	255	118	46.2	12	2315	20	139.0
Toby Strange, West Ga.	Sr.	10	277	169	61.0	15	2164	18	137.2
Frank Ramirez, West Liberty St.	Sr.	10	252	131	51.9	11	2064	19	136.9
Drew Folmar, Millersville	Fr.	10	294	173	58.8	10	2152	19	134.9
Kevin Feeney, North Dak. St.	Jr.	11	186	101	54.3	7	1321	16	134.8
Antonio Hawkins, Virginia St.	Fr.	9	198	99	50.0	10	1550	17	134.0
Chad Roanhaus, N.M. Highlands	Jr.	10	282	152	53.9	15	2295	19	133.9
Ricky Hebert, American Int'l	So.	11	217	120	55.3	5	1515	16	133.7
Mike Mason, Bentley	Sr.	9	202	114	56.4	8	1566	12	133.2
Eric Miller, Bloomsburg	Fr.	10	176	94	53.4	7	1378	10	130.0
Matt Kissell, Mercyhurst	Jr.	8	125	60	48.0	2	874	10	129.9
Brian VanderLuitgaren, St. Francis	Sr.	11	277	165	59.5	9	1980	14	129.8
Kevin Daft, UC Davis	Jr.	11	347	190	54.7	12	2497	21	128.3

Total Offense

	1997 Class	G	Plays	Yards	Yds.PG
Wilkie Perez, Glenville St.	Jr.	11	509	4301	391.0
Erik Hartman, Angelo St.	Sr.	10	381	2744	274.4
Jeff Fox, Grand Valley St.	Jr.	11	440	2904	264.0
Damian Poalucci, East Stroudsburg	Sr.	10	447	2635	263.5
Mike Lazo, Concord	Jr.	10	234	2504	250.4
Jake Goettl, Winona St.	Jr.	11	321	2663	242.1
Jaime Jones, Wayne St. (Neb.)	So.	10	501	2383	238.3
Justin Coleman, Neb.-Kearney	Fr.	11	373	2601	236.5
Eric Hannah, Western St.	Jr.	11	390	2585	235.0
Trevor Moon, Chadron St.	Jr.	11	410	2583	234.8
Chad Cole, Tarleton St.	Sr.	11	402	2582	234.7
Chad Roanhaus, N.M. Highlands	Jr.	10	326	2331	233.1
Cazzie Kosciolek, New Haven	Sr.	10	324	2304	230.4
Joe Savino, Albany (N.Y.)	Sr.	12	352	2752	229.3
Chris Greisen, Northwest Mo. St.	Jr.	11	325	2505	227.7

	1997 Class	G	Plays	Yards	Yds.PG
J.D. Meyers, Ky. Wesleyan	So.	10	315	2253	225.3
Kevin Daft, UC Davis	Jr.	11	409	2473	224.8
Drew Folmar, Millersville	Fr.	10	375	2228	222.8
Anthony Gray, Western N.M.	Jr.	10	277	2220	222.0
Brad Cornelsen, Mo. Southern St.	Jr.	10	393	2194	219.4
Chris Freeman, Central Ark.	Sr.	10	349	2194	219.4
Josh Penry, Mesa St.	Jr.	11	409	2349	213.5
Toby Strange, West Ga.	Sr.	10	312	2099	209.9
Pete Jelovic, Emporia St.	Sr.	11	307	2273	206.6
Irv Sigler, Bloomsburg	Sr.	10	299	2038	203.8

Receptions Per Game

	1997 Class	G	Rec.	Yards	TD	Rec.PG
Jamar Nailor, N.M. Highlands	Sr.	10	82	1149	19	8.2
Shon King, Wayne St. (Neb.)	Sr.	9	72	1166	9	8.0
Ryan Bartemeyer, West Va. Wesleyan	Sr.	9	70	1243	16	7.8
Chad Gomarko, Augustana (S.D.)	Sr.	11	78	1037	8	7.1
Mike McFetridge, Millersville	Jr.	10	70	770	6	7.0
Mark DeBrito, Bentley	So.	9	60	1013	13	6.7
Mike McKinney, St. Cloud St.	Jr.	11	73	1145	10	6.6
Brett Witmer, East Stroudsburg	Sr.	10	63	1040	6	6.3
Lewis Hicks, Indiana (Pa.)	Sr.	10	59	819	3	5.9
Dameon Porter, Wayne St. (Neb.)	Sr.	10	59	545	3	5.9
Ron Lelko, Bloomsburg	Sr.	10	57	870	7	5.7
Tywan Mitchell, Mankato St.	So.	11	62	794	4	5.6
Jason Trice, Grand Valley St.	Jr.	11	62	853	7	5.6
Anthony Giovingo, Ark.-Monticello	Jr.	10	56	866	6	5.6
Mike Mancuso, East Stroudsburg	Sr.	10	56	981	9	5.6
Adam Roman, New Haven	Jr.	10	53	726	5	5.3
Greg Dailer, West Liberty St.	Sr.	10	53	1073	16	5.3
Wayne Thomas, Miles	Sr.	10	53	957	11	5.3
Thomas Stevens, Adams St.	Sr.	11	58	748	7	5.3
Bryan Fisher, Arkansas Tech	Jr.	11	58	721	5	5.3
Neal Mozdzierz, Ferris St.	So.	10	52	640	1	5.2
Jeremy Wilkinson, Northern Mich.	Jr.	11	57	950	9	5.2
Chad Fitzsimmons, Winona St.	Jr.	11	57	1048	10	5.2
Jovelle Tillman, Virginia St.	Sr.	10	51	880	12	5.1
Mike Joseph, Fairmont St.	Sr.	11	56	502	4	5.1

Receiving Yards Per Game

	1997 Class	G	Rec.	Yards	TD	Yds.PG
Carlos Ferralls, Glenville St.	Sr.	10	94	1566	19	156.6
Ryan Bartemeyer, West Va. Wesleyan	Sr.	9	70	1243	16	138.1
Shon King, Wayne St. (Neb.)	Sr.	9	72	1166	9	129.6
Jamar Nailor, N.M. Highlands	Sr.	10	82	1149	9	114.9
Mark DeBrito, Bentley	So.	9	60	1013	13	112.6
Chris Brazzell, Angelo St.	Sr.	10	47	1091	13	109.1
Greg Dailer, West Liberty St.	Sr.	10	53	1073	16	107.3
Mike McKinney, St. Cloud St.	Jr.	11	73	1145	10	104.1
Brett Witmer, East Stroudsburg	Sr.	10	63	1040	6	104.0
Mike Mancuso, East Stroudsburg	Sr.	10	56	981	9	98.1
Wayne Thomas, Miles	Sr.	10	53	957	11	95.7
Chad Fitzsimmons, Winona St.	Jr.	11	57	1048	10	95.3
Chad Gomarko, Augustana (S.D.)	Sr.	11	78	1037	8	94.3
Dan Gmelin, Albany (N.Y.)	Sr.	12	57	1070	10	89.2
Jovelle Tillman, Virginia St.	Sr.	10	51	880	12	88.0
Ron Lelko, Bloomsburg	Sr.	10	57	870	7	87.0
Bryan Uhl, Fort Lewis	Sr.	9	44	780	4	86.7
Anthony Giovingo, Ark.-Monticello	Jr.	10	56	866	6	86.6
Jeremy Wilkinson, Northern Mich.	Jr.	11	57	950	9	86.4
Mike Smith, Neb.-Kearney	Sr.	11	55	915	7	83.2
Marquis Churchwell, Ky. Wesleyan	Sr.	10	42	829	10	82.9
Lewis Hicks, Indiana (Pa.)	Sr.	10	59	819	3	81.9
Lee Castana, Gannon	Jr.	10	48	807	4	80.7
Chad Beam, Lenoir-Rhyne	Jr.	10	50	807	7	80.7
Enrico Grayer, Central Ark.	Sr.	9	42	715	9	79.4

All-Purpose Yards

	1997 Class	GRush	Rec.	PR	KOR	Total Int.	Yards	Yds.PG
Brian Shay, Emporia St.	Jr.	11 1912	277	56	478	0	2723	247.55
Anthony Gray, Western N.M.	Jr.	10 2220	78	0	0	0	2298	229.80
Irv Sigler, Bloomsburg	Sr.	10 2038	37	0	56	0	2131	213.10
Wilmont Perry, Livingstone	Jr.	10 1770	92	0	0	0	1862	186.20
Travis Walch, Winona St.	Sr.	11 1103	534	128	272	0	2037	185.18
Phillip Moore, North Dak.	Jr.	10 1771	7	0	0	0	1778	177.80
Mike Mancuso, East Stroudsburg	Sr.	10 14	981	161	599	0	1755	175.50
Grover Moore, Moorhead St.	Jr.	10 1235	46	34	420	0	1735	173.50
Mike Smith, Neb.-Kearney	Sr.	11 38	915	310	604	0	1867	169.73
Tracy Bowen, Wingate	So.	9 1274	152	0	85	0	1511	167.89
Carlos Ferralls, Glenville St.	Sr.	10 27	1566	85	0	0	1678	167.80
Jake Morris, North Dak. St.	Sr.	11 1710	76	0	58	0	1844	167.64
Damian Beane, Shepherd	So.	10 1590	77	0	0	0	1667	166.70
Charles Turner, Clark Atlanta	So.	10 615	202	268	559	0	1644	164.40
Conan Smith, N.M. Highlands	Sr.	11 1599	105	0	0	0	1704	154.91
Andre Braxton, Virginia Union	Fr.	11 1383	48	0	257	0	1688	153.45
Chad Gomarko, Augustana (S.D.)	Sr.	11 24	1037	1-	627	0	1687	153.36
Chris Pierson, Harding	Sr.	10 1306	212	0	0	0	1518	151.80
Emneko Sweeney, Kutztown	Jr.	9 1113	112	0	109	0	1334	148.22
Tink Stennett, Indiana (Pa.)	Fr.	8 728	264	13	166	0	1171	146.38
Thomas Fulton, West Chester	Sr.	11 1228	212	0	150	0	1590	144.55
Shon King, Wayne St. (Neb.)	Sr.	9 0	1166	67	58	0	1291	143.44
Matt Rapoza, Bentley	Jr.	9 1154	81	0	47	0	1282	142.44
Emile Fann, LIU-C.W. Post	Sr.	8 941	182	0	15	0	1138	142.25
Dan Gmelin, Albany (N.Y.)	Sr.	12 42	1070	368	225	0	1705	142.08

Includes 25 yards in interception returns.

Interceptions

	1997 Class	G	No.	Yards	Int.PG
Jamey Hutchinson, Winona St.	Jr.	11	11	125	1.0
Tim Bednarski, Mercyhurst	Jr.	9	9	59	1.0
Victor Burke, Abilene Christian	Sr.	11	10	229	.9
Jarvis Davis, Fayetteville St.	So.	10	8	84	.8
Marcus Dover, Kentucky St.	Sr.	9	7	83	.8
Roddrick Dunlap, Livingstone	Sr.	8	6	180	.8
Chris Gillam, Savannah St.	Sr.	11	8	202	.7
Nolan Peterson, Catawba	Sr.	11	8	171	.7
Danny Johnson, Central Ark.	Jr.	10	7	21	.7
Telley Priester, Virginia St.	Sr.	10	7	5	.7
Jon Jon Simmons, Carson-Newman	Sr.	9	6	112	.7
Larry Miller, St. Cloud St.	So.	11	7	100	.6
Chuck Richmond, Wingate	Sr.	11	7	10	.6
Jason Matthews, West Va. Wesleyan	Fr.	10	6	112	.6
Patrick Johnson, Mars Hill	Jr.	10	6	37	.6
Dennis Burney, New Haven	Jr.	10	6	150	.6
Ray Cannon, Bowie St.	Sr.	10	6	268	.6
Ryan Buchanan, Fort Hays St.	Sr.	10	6	55	.6
Bobby Jones, Carson-Newman	Sr.	9	5	32	.6
Jake Oates, Bentley	Sr.	9	5	32	.6

Scoring

	1997 Class	G	TD	XP	FG	Pts.	Pts.PG
Brian Shay, Emporia St.	Jr.	11	32	6	0	198	18.0
Travis Walch, Winona St.	Sr.	11	30	2	0	182	16.5
Wilmont Perry, Livingstone	Jr.	10	21	2	0	128	12.8
Irv Sigler, Bloomsburg	Sr.	10	20	0	0	120	12.0
Carlos Ferralls, Glenville St.	Jr.	10	20	0	0	120	12.0
Tyrone Westmoreland, Carson-Newman	Sr.	9	17	4	0	106	11.8
Mike Joseph, Fairmont St.	Sr.	11	20	6	0	126	11.5
Damian Beane, Shepherd	So.	10	19	0	0	114	11.4
Ryan Bartemeyer, West Va. Wesleyan	Sr.	9	16	2	0	98	10.9
Derek Lane, Northwest Mo. St.	Jr.	9	16	0	0	96	10.7
Greg Dailer, West Liberty St.	Sr.	10	16	4	0	100	10.0
Conan Smith, N.M. Highlands	Sr.	11	18	2	0	110	10.0
Tracy Bowen, Wingate	So.	9	14	2	0	86	9.6
Tim Neelands, Saginaw Valley	Jr.	11	17	0	0	102	9.3
Don Highsmith, New Haven	Sr.	10	15	0	0	90	9.0
Stan Kennedy, Slippery Rock	Fr.	11	16	0	0	96	8.7
Dave Purnell, Northwest Mo. St.	So.	11	0	54	14	96	8.7
Mark DeBrito, Bentley	So.	9	13	0	0	78	8.7
Leo Loiacano, Saginaw Valley	Sr.	11	0	53	14	95	8.6
Justin Johnson, Pittsburg St.	Sr.	10	14	2	0	86	8.6
Phillip Moore, North Dak.	Jr.	10	14	0	0	84	8.4
Greg Manson, North Ala.	Jr.	11	15	0	0	90	8.2
Jake Morris, North Dak. St.	Sr.	11	15	0	0	90	8.2
Jeff Klopf, Saginaw Valley	Jr.	11	15	0	0	90	8.2
Rashaan Dumas, Southern Conn. St.	So.	9	12	0	0	72	8.0

Punt Returns

(Min. 1.2 per game)	1997 Class	No.	Yds.	Avg.
Bootsie Washington, Shepherd	Sr.	19	461	24.3
John Humphrey, Tex. A&M-Kingsville	Jr.	15	309	20.6
Kareem Jordan, Gardner-Webb	Sr.	21	400	19.0
Brian Pinks, Northern Mich.	Sr.	28	533	19.0
Chaka Smith, Wayne St. (Neb.)	So.	12	206	17.2
Lance Voegely, Fort Lewis	So.	21	326	15.5
Dan Gmelin, Albany (N.Y.)	Sr.	24	368	15.3
Mac Whitehead, Mo. Southern St.	Sr.	13	191	14.7
Mitch Allner, Morningside	So.	16	234	14.6
Tramel Gilmore, Morris Brown	Jr.	17	243	14.3
Adrian Perez, Mesa St.	Fr.	20	283	14.2
Mike Smith, Neb.-Kearney	Sr.	22	310	14.1
Derrick Reese, Miles	Jr.	11	151	13.7
Adam Roman, New Haven	Jr.	24	322	13.4
Dedrick Weddington, Western N.M.	Jr.	13	172	13.2
Tiquon Murry, Bowie St.	So.	18	237	13.2
Adam DeSanctis, Merrimack	So.	15	195	13.0
Troy Gamble, Presbyterian	Jr.	36	463	12.9
Charles Turner, Clark Atlanta	So.	21	268	12.8
Miles Keel, Western St.	Sr.	28	355	12.7

Kickoff Returns

(Min. 1.2 per game)	1997 Class	No.	Yds.	Avg.
Boobie Thornton, Midwestern St.	Fr.	12	426	35.5
Brian Outlaw, St. Joseph's (Ind.)	Jr.	14	426	30.4
Adrian Jones, N.C. Central	Sr.	17	502	29.5
Charlie Pugh, Northwest Mo. St.	So.	14	413	29.5
Kevin Wimberly, Kutztown	Jr.	11	319	29.0
Andre Rawlings, Wingate	Jr.	16	464	29.0
Chris Schrantz, North Dak.	Sr.	15	422 2	8.1
Charlie Ragle, Eastern N.M.	Sr.	21	579	27.6
Brian Bengston, Colorado Mines	Jr.	22	596	27.1
Chris Jackson, Central Mo. St.	Sr.	24	631	26.3
Steve Eichert, Bloomsburg	Fr.	11	289	26.3
Ed Starks, Mo.-Rolla	Jr.	15	392	26.1
Bill Bussey, Concord	Jr.	22	572	26.0
Traco Rachel, Tex. A&M-Commerce	Jr.	15	388	25.9
Bret Geishauser, Slippery Rock	Sr.	13	336	25.8
Trokya Bates, Newberry	Jr.	14	361	25.8
DeWayne Thomas, Elon	So.	20	509	25.5
Jeffrey Greider, Mass.-Lowell	Fr.	16	407	25.4
Deyea Jones, Northwood	Fr.	12	303	25.3
Tony Colenburg, Mo. Southern St.	Jr.	19	479	25.2
Ed Bailey, Mercyhurst	Fr.	11	277	25.2
Travis Whelan, Northern Mich.	Sr.	17	428	25.2
Brian Shay, Emporia St.	Jr.	19	478	25.2
Patrick Johnson, Mars Hill	Jr.	15	377	25.1

Punting

(Min. 3.6 per game)	1997 Class	No.	Avg.
Brian Moorman, Pittsburg St.	Jr.	36	46.0
Tom O'Brien, South Dak. St.	Jr.	50	44.8
Jason Van Dyke, Adams St.	Jr.	71	43.6
Jeff Works, Ouachita Baptist	So.	60	43.3
Caleb Lewis, Mo. Southern St.	Jr.	37	42.4
Tony Faggioni, North Ala.	Jr.	43	42.0
Trei Oliver, N.C. Central	Sr.	67	41.7
Craig Goodson, West Ala.	So.	57	41.6
John Torrance, North Dak. St.	Sr.	42	41.5
Will Schale, Tex. A&M-Commerce	So.	78	41.2
Ryan Corn, Western St.	Fr.	64	41.2
Jonathan Thomas, Clark Atlanta	So.	79	41.1
Rob Buffington, Glenville St.	Sr.	43	41.1
Chris Heathcock, Northwood	Sr.	48	41.0
Tim Duncan, Kentucky St.	Fr.	54	41.0
Warner Jones, Virginia Union	Sr.	50	40.8
Trey Greene, Gardner-Webb	Sr.	57	40.7
Sean Hegarty, N.M. Highlands	Sr.	51	40.4
Eric Wicks, Mercyhurst	Sr.	50	40.3
Scott Juengst, Colorado Mines	So.	67	40.2

Field Goals

	1997 Class	G	FGA	FG	Pct.	FGPG
Shane Meyer, Central Mo. St.	Jr.	11	25	18	72.0	1.64
Tim Seder, Ashland	Sr.	10	19	14	73.7	1.40
John Sedely, West Ala.	Sr.	10	17	13	76.5	1.30
Dave Purnell, Northwest Mo. St.	So.	11	16	14	87.5	1.27
Leo Loiacano, Saginaw Valley	Sr.	11	18	14	77.8	1.27
Geoff Christian, Wingate	So.	11	15	13	86.7	1.18
John Duginski, Northern Mich.	Jr.	11	20	13	65.0	1.18
Neil Fish, St. Cloud St.	So.	11	19	13	68.4	1.18
Ryan Hicks, Western St.	Sr.	11	15	13	86.7	1.18
Garron Spickard, Southern Ark.	So.	10	18	11	61.1	1.10
Doug Kochanski, Grand Valley St.	Jr.	11	21	12	57.1	1.09
Matt Fishburn, Wayne St. (Mich.)	Sr.	11	18	12	66.7	1.09
Jay Glymph, Indiana (Pa.)	Jr.	10	15	10	66.7	1.00
Toby Sheers, Mesa St.	Fr.	11	13	11	84.6	1.00
Marcus Shaw, Morehouse	Jr.	9	19	9	47.4	1.00
Sammy Bridges, Angelo St.	Sr.	10	13	10	76.9	1.00
Greg Payne, Catawba	Sr.	11	15	10	66.7	.91
Brandon Risner, Mo.-Rolla	Sr.	11	22	10	45.5	.91
Abdul Rashad, Savannah St.	Fr.	11	14	10	71.4	.91
Paul Kosel, Neb.-Omaha	Jr.	11	17	10	58.8	.91
Jeremy Thompson, Harding	So.	10	13	9	69.2	.90
Peter Baldwin, Humboldt St.	Jr.	10	16	9	56.3	.90
Michael Becker, West Tex. A&M	Fr.	10	13	9	69.2	.90
Josh Barcus, Pittsburg St.	Jr.	10	12	9	75.0	.90
Tyson Cook, Edinboro	So.	10	18	9	50.0	.90

1997 Division II Team Leaders

Total Offense

	G	Plays	Yds.	Yds.PG
Emporia St.	11	857	5846	531.5
N.M. Highlands	11	830	5348	486.2
Winona St.	11	740	5122	465.6
Glenville St.	11	651	5058	459.8
Neb.-Omaha	11	844	4762	432.9
Concord	10	561	4324	432.4
Carson-Newman	9	577	3863	429.2
Saginaw Valley	11	770	4697	427.0
Livingstone	10	646	4244	424.4
Shepherd	10	662	4213	421.3
Bloomsburg	10	677	4207	420.7
Albany (N.Y.)	12	814	5035	419.6
East Stroudsburg	10	712	4167	416.7
Western N.M.	10	681	4162	416.2
West Va. Wesleyan	10	748	4161	416.1

Total Defense

	G	Plays	Yds.	Yds.PG
Livingstone	10	584	1715	171.5
Tex. A&M-Kingsville	10	576	1776	177.6
Albany St. (Ga.)	10	610	2013	201.3
Bentley	9	521	1826	202.9
Kentucky St.	11	704	2369	215.4
LIU-C.W. Post	10	685	2198	219.8
Catawba	11	701	2562	232.9
Southern Ark.	10	626	2374	237.4
Stony Brook	10	680	2383	238.3
Virginia Union	11	660	2681	243.7

Rushing Offense

	G	Car.	Yds.	Yds.PG
Saginaw Valley	11	624	3683	334.8
Livingstone	10	511	3160	316.0
Neb.-Omaha	11	662	3452	313.8
Pittsburg St.	10	591	3048	304.8
North Ala.	11	557	3278	298.0
Elon	11	586	3091	281.0
Bloomsburg	10	494	2777	277.7
Western N.M.	10	467	2766	276.6
St. Joseph's (Ind.)	11	544	2967	269.7
North Dak. St.	11	572	2963	269.4

Rushing Defense

	G	Car.	Yds.	Yds.PG
Livingstone	10	295	528	52.8
Tex. A&M-Kingsville	10	352	662	66.2
Bentley	9	334	725	80.6
Albany St. (Ga.)	10	330	824	82.4
Catawba	11	431	963	87.5
Virginia Union	11	381	1000	90.9
Slippery Rock	11	406	1002	91.1
Pittsburg St.	10	380	924	92.4
North Dak. St.	11	380	1076	97.8
Carson-Newman	9	348	895	99.4

Scoring Offense

	G	TD	XP	2XP	DXP	FG	SAF	Pts.	Avg.
New Haven	10	58	49	1	00	8	5	433	43.3
Emporia St.	11	67	25	13	00	4	0	465	42.3
Livingstone	10	61	42	4	00	0	1	418	41.8
Glenville St.	11	63	52	4	00	6	1	458	41.6
Saginaw Valley	11	60	53	1	00	14	0	457	41.5
Winona St.	11	61	50	3	00	8	0	446	40.5
Northwest Mo. St.	11	57	54	1	00	14	0	440	40.0
Albany (N.Y.)	12	67	45	3	00	5	0	468	39.0
Carson-Newman	9	48	33	3	00	4	0	339	37.7
Tex. A&M-Kingsville	10	49	39	3	00	8	0	363	36.3
N.M. Highlands	11	53	45	2	00	4	1	381	34.6
West Va. Wesleyan	10	46	27	10	00	5	2	342	34.2
Shepherd	10	50	25	3	01	1	2	340	34.0
North Dak. St.	11	48	40	3	00	9	1	363	33.0
Angelo St.	10	44	34	0	00	10	1	330	33.0
Neb.-Kearney	11	50	41	2	00	5	1	362	32.9
Northern Colo.	11	43	36	3	00	15	2	349	31.7
Western St.	11	44	35	4	00	13	1	348	31.6
St. Joseph's (Ind.)	11	46	38	2	01	9	0	347	31.5
Pittsburg St.	10	41	34	3	00	9	1	315	31.5

Scoring Defense

	G	TD	XP	2XP	DXP	FG	SAF	Pts.	Avg.
Albany St. (Ga.)	10	10	7	0	0	2	0	73	7.3
New Haven	10	12	11	0	0	5	0	98	9.8
Carson-Newman	9	12	7	1	0	4	0	93	10.3
Tex. A&M-Kingsville	10	15	11	0	0	1	0	104	10.4
Bloomsburg	10	14	9	0	0	4	1	107	10.7
Southern Ark.	10	13	13	0	1	5	0	108	10.8
LIU-C.W. Post	10	12	9	1	0	8	1	109	10.9
Ashland	10	14	10	1	0	7	0	117	11.7
Livingstone	10	16	10	2	0	3	1	121	12.1
Catawba	11	19	13	0	1	4	0	141	12.8
Western St.	11	18	10	2	0	8	0	146	13.3
Virginia St.	10	19	13	3	0	1	0	136	13.6
North Dak. St.	11	19	16	1	0	6	0	150	13.6
Northwest Mo. St.	11	18	12	2	0	9	0	151	13.7
Pittsburg St.	10	17	9	4	0	5	2	138	13.8
Bentley	9	18	5	1	0	4	0	127	14.1
Albany (N.Y.)	12	24	9	3	0	3	2	172	14.3
Stony Brook	10	19	11	1	0	5	1	144	14.4
Chadron St.	11	19	17	0	0	8	2	159	14.5
Central Okla.	11	19	12	1	0	9	2	159	14.5
West Ga.	10	20	11	1	0	4	1	147	14.7
Fort Valley St.	11	24	15	0	0	4	0	171	15.5
Slippery Rock	11	23	12	2	0	5	1	171	15.5
Presbyterian	11	24	14	2	0	5	0	177	16.1
Winston-Salem	10	24	13	1	0	2	0	165	16.5

Passing Offense

	G	Att.	Cmp.	Pct.	Int.	Yards	Yds.PG
Glenville St.	11	429	282	65.7	12	4201	381.9
Winona St.	11	335	189	56.4	17	3196	290.5
Emporia St.	11	357	223	62.5	11	3099	281.7
East Stroudsburg	10	361	195	54.0	18	2813	281.3
UC Davis	11	416	229	55.0	16	2987	271.5
N.M. Highlands	11	365	186	51.0	20	2962	269.3
Ky. Wesleyan	10	340	171	50.3	16	2632	263.2
Neb.-Kearney	11	323	181	56.0	16	2893	263.0
Tarleton St.	11	382	197	51.6	17	2802	254.7
Chadron St.	11	378	190	50.3	12	2786	253.3
New Haven	10	288	170	59.0	6	2508	250.8
Virginia St.	10	350	165	47.1	15	2482	248.2
West Va. Wesleyan	10	347	180	51.9	9	2481	248.1
Western St.	11	361	181	50.1	15	2672	242.9
Wayne St. (Neb.)	10	417	216	51.8	21	2367	236.7
Millersville	10	326	191	58.6	11	2354	235.4
Angelo St.	10	262	118	45.0	12	2330	233.0
West Liberty St.	10	293	147	50.2	14	2312	231.2
Concord	10	299	144	48.2	9	2290	229.0
Northwest Mo. St.	11	290	161	55.5	7	2515	228.6
Central Ark.	10	315	176	55.9	11	2255	225.5
West Ga.	10	293	176	60.1	16	2250	225.0
Grand Valley St.	11	302	174	57.6	8	2470	224.5
Indiana (Pa.)	10	314	182	58.0	10	2240	224.0
Albany (N.Y.)	12	282	170	60.3	12	2651	220.9

Pass Efficiency Defense

	G	Att.	Cmp.	Pct.	Int.	Yards	TD	Rating Points
Kentucky St.	11	243	90	37.0	18	946	7	64.4
Livingstone	10	289	116	40.1	20	1187	7	68.8
Albany St. (Ga.)	10	280	102	36.4	10	1189	4	69.7
Tex. A&M-Kingsville	10	224	82	36.6	15	1114	7	75.3
Stony Brook	10	236	104	44.0	13	1007	7	78.7
Western St.	11	309	124	40.1	22	1516	12	79.9
Virginia St.	10	236	96	40.6	19	1275	8	81.1
Gardner-Webb	11	266	109	40.9	18	1382	9	82.3
Abilene Christian	11	244	94	38.5	17	1324	9	82.3
Northwest Mo. St.	11	289	122	42.2	10	1418	6	83.4
Fort Valley St.	11	252	109	43.2	20	1301	10	83.8
New Haven	10	307	149	48.5	19	1546	6	84.9
Millersville	10	250	109	43.6	9	1249	5	85.0
Carson-Newman	9	286	136	47.5	16	1442	6	85.6
LIU-C.W. Post	10	261	139	53.2	14	1188	4	85.8
Bloomsburg	10	320	139	43.4	16	1644	9	85.9
Winona St.	11	302	133	44.0	26	1752	12	88.7
Bentley	9	187	76	40.6	12	1101	7	89.6
Tuskegee	11	297	127	42.7	16	1653	10	89.8
Albany (N.Y.)	12	327	140	42.8	16	1903	8	90.0
Ashland	10	276	125	45.2	9	1440	7	91.0
South Dak. St.	10	203	110	54.1	10	1029	3	91.8
Pace	10	207	92	44.4	13	1170	8	92.1
Shepherd	10	328	140	42.6	8	1732	11	93.2
Southern Ark.	10	262	132	50.3	13	1360	8	94.1

Net Punting

	Punts	Yds.	Avg.	No. Ret.	Yds. Ret.	Net Avg.
North Ala.	43	1807	42.02	15	110	39.46
Pittsburg St.	37	1657	44.78	19	222	38.78
Virginia St.	57	2286	40.10	20	165	37.21
South Dak. St.	53	2318	43.73	26	353	37.07
Mercyhurst	50	2014	40.28	24	161	37.06
N.C. Central	70	2813	40.18	28	233	36.85

	Punts	Yds.	Avg.	No. Ret.	Yds. Ret.	Net Avg.
West Ala.	59	2424	41.08	27	252	36.81
Adams St.	73	3119	42.72	38	433	36.79
Mo. Southern St.	39	1628	41.74	24	199	36.64
North Dak. St.	43	1771	41.18	26	196	36.62
Virginia Union	50	2040	40.80	23	211	36.58
UC Davis	67	2596	38.74	25	158	36.38
Northern Colo.	47	1848	39.31	18	140	36.34
Presbyterian	69	2601	37.69	25	107	36.14
Humboldt St.	71	2700	38.02	22	155	35.84
Northern Mich.	57	2253	39.52	26	213	35.78
Angelo St.	49	1852	37.79	17	100	35.75
Glenville St.	43	1767	41.09	24	234	35.65
Tex. A&M-Commerce	79	3225	40.82	34	415	35.56
Truman St.	38	1434	37.73	11	90	35.36
Albany St. (Ga.)	56	2023	36.12	16	44	35.33
LIU-C.W. Post	78	2961	37.96	38	214	35.21
Mesa St.	63	2400	38.09	26	192	35.04
Morningside	74	2816	38.05	32	226	35.00
Mankato St.	51	1988	38.98	26	207	34.92

Punt Returns

	G	No.	Yds.	TD	Avg.
Gardner-Webb	11	24	474	2	19.75
Shepherd	10	32	624	4	19.50
Northern Mich.	11	30	563	2	18.76
Tex. A&M-Kingsville	10	30	481	4	16.03
Ky. Wesleyan	10	11	172	0	15.63
Bowie St.	10	29	446	2	15.37
Cheyney	11	8	122	1	15.25
New Haven	10	36	548	1	15.22
Concord	10	14	211	1	15.07
Miles	10	19	275	1	14.47
Fort Lewis	11	24	341	2	14.20
Johnson Smith	9	16	226	1	14.12
Albany (N.Y.)	12	33	445	1	13.48
Tex. A&M-Commerce	11	21	283	0	13.47
Morningside	11	23	307	1	13.34
Angelo St.	10	19	253	1	13.31
Presbyterian	11	46	612	0	13.30
Mesa St.	11	26	344	1	13.23
Wayne St. (Neb.)	10	24	315	3	13.12
N.C. Central	11	39	504	1	12.92
Mo. Southern St.	10	16	206	1	12.87
Morris Brown	11	31	397	0	12.80
Harding	10	26	321	1	12.34
Fayetteville St.	11	27	333	0	12.33
Delta St.	10	29	355	0	12.24

Kickoff Returns

	G	No.	Yds.	TD	Avg.
Carson-Newman	9	14	425	0	30.35
Northwest Mo. St.	11	23	664	0	28.86
Elon	11	36	895	3	24.86
Fort Hays St.	11	30	727	0	24.23
Tex. A&M-Kingsville	10	22	532	0	24.18
Clarion	10	40	956	0	23.90
Wingate	11	47	1123	2	23.89
North Dak.	10	26	620	1	23.84
Alabama A&M	11	32	761	2	23.78
West Tex. A&M	11	28	664	0	23.71
Slippery Rock	11	33	777	0	23.54
Mo. Southern St.	10	40	939	1	23.47
Midwestern St.	10	45	1047	1	23.26
West Ga.	10	24	545	1	22.70
N.C. Central	11	37	839	1	22.67
Eastern N.M.	11	32	722	1	22.56
Miles	10	46	1036	2	22.52
Northern Colo.	11	27	604	0	22.37
Bentley	9	25	559	2	22.36
Colorado Mines	11	43	950	0	22.09
Valdosta St.	11	32	705	0	22.03
Chadron St.	1	34	740	0	21.76
Central Mo. St.	11	45	976	1	21.68
Southern Ark.	10	21	454	0	21.61
Presbyterian	11	22	475	0	21.59

Turnover Margin

		TURNOVERS GAINED			TURNOVERS LOST			Margin/
	G	Fum.	Int.	Total	Fum.	Int.	Total	Game
North Dak. St.	11	12	23	35	5	8	13	2.00
Central Ark.	10	17	19	36	7	11	18	1.80
Mercyhurst	9	9	20	29	7	6	13	1.77
Fort Valley St.	11	17	20	37	6	12	18	1.72
New Haven	10	15	19	34	13	6	19	1.50
American Int'l	11	18	13	31	10	5	15	1.45
Northern Colo.	11	15	18	33	6	12	18	1.36
Indianapolis	11	11	16	27	6	7	13	1.27
Johnson Smith	9	18	12	30	12	8	20	1.11
Tex. A&M-Kingsville	10	14	15	29	12	6	18	1.10
Mars Hill	10	17	18	35	11	14	25	1.00
Albany (N.Y.)	12	19	16	35	11	12	23	1.00
Grand Valley St.	11	11	14	25	6	8	14	1.00
Alabama A&M	11	15	26	41	17	13	30	1.00

Longest Division II Plays of 1997

Rushing

Player, Team (Opponent)	Yards
Mark Chicarelli, Northern Colo. (Morningside)	93
Anthony Gray, Western N.M. (N.M. Highlands)	93
Tracy Bowen, Wingate (Tusculum)	91
Jerry Reitan, St. Cloud St. (Augustana, S.D.)	91
Stewart Ford, East Stroudsburg (West Chester)	90
Amos Myles, Gardner-Webb (Tusculum)	90
Stephan Clegg, LIU-C.W. Post (Sacred Heart)	89
Derrick Moore, Elon (Lenoir-Rhyne)	89
Emile Fann, LIU-C.W. Post (Southern Conn. St.)	87
Damian Beane, Shepherd (West Liberty St.)	86
Jerit Siedor, Shepherd (West Va. St.)	86
Ward Turner, Alabama A&M (Tuskegee)	85
Stan Kennedy, Slippery Rock (Calif., Pa.)	81

Passing

Passer-Receiver, Team (Opponent)	Yards
Justin Coleman-Mike Smith, Neb.-Kearney (Wayne St., Neb.)	99
Antonio Hawkins-Jovelle Tillman, Virginia St. (Fayetteville St.)	99
Matt Morris-Casey Cowan, Tex. A&M-Commerce (Midwestern St.)	99
Scott Moore-Marty Corley, St. Joseph's, Ind. (Calif., Pa.)	96
Chad Roanhaus-Jamar Nailor, N.M. Highlands (Colorado Mines)	96
Matt Kissell-Tim Brediger, Mercyhurst (Gannon)	95
Travis Carswell-James Moore, North Ala. (Arkansas Tech)	94
Parnell Wilder-Matthew Allen, Livingstone (Fayetteville St.)	94
Corte McGuffey-Dollon Micus, Northern Colo. (South Dak.)	92
Jeff Orihel-William Jefferson, LIU-C.W. Post (Bentley)	91
Brad Beard-Michael James, West Ala. (West Ga.)	90
J.D. Meyers-Corey Jordan, Ky. Wesleyan (Maryville, Tenn.)	90
Damian Poalucci-Mike Mancuso, East Stroudsburg (Elon)	90
Zack Siegrist-Douglas Hix, Pittsburg St. (Mo.-Rolla)	90

Interception Returns

Player, Team (Opponent)	Yards
Ray Cannon, Bowie St. (N.C. Central)	100
Victor Burke, Abilene Christian (Tex. A&M-Commerce)	95
Jason Matthews, West Va. Wesleyan (Fairmont St.)	95
Donell Wade, Tuskegee (Morehouse)	95
Kelly Snell, Ferris St. (Northern Mich.)	92
Asinia Knight, Mars Hill (Wingate)	90
Jeremy Davis, Saginaw Valley (Northwood)	89
Nate Neuhaus, Neb.-Kearney (Wayne St., Neb.)	89
Marcus Wilson, Winston-Salem (Elizabeth City St.)	80
Corey Harris, North Ala. (Alabama A&M)	78
Chris Gillam, Savannah St. (Kentucky St.)	76
Shawn Harrison, Fayetteville St. (Bowie St.)	75

Punt Returns

Player, Team (Opponent)	Yards
Derek Deuvall, Southwest Baptist (Washburn)	90
Brian Pinks, Northern Mich. (Michigan Tech)	89
Joe Kostro, St. Francis, Ill. (Northwood	87
Mitch Allner, Morningside (South Dak. St.)	86
Dillon Micus, Northern Colo. (South Dak.)	86
Gabe Rodriguez, Stony Brook (Pace)	85
Bill Bussey, Concord (West Va. Wesleyan)	84
Tony Miles, Northwest Mo. St. (Southwest Baptist)	84
Dondre Gilliam, Cheyney (Virginia Union)	83
Adam DeSanctis, Merrimack (Bentley)	80
Stanley Johnson, Angelo St. (Sam Houston St.)	80
Adrian Jones, N.C. Central (Fayetteville St.)	80
Corey Jordan, Ky. Wesleyan (Mt. St. Joseph)	79
Bootsie Washington, Shepherd (Concord)	79
Bootsie Washington, Shepherd (Concord)	79

Kickoff Returns

Player, Team (Opponent)	Yards
Mike Erlandson, Shippensburg (Bloomsburg)	100
Bret Hartman, Pace (Southern Conn. St.)	99
Brian Outlaw, St. Joseph's, Ind. (Ky. Wesleyan)	99
Bill Bussey, Concord (Newport News App.)	97
Brian Shay, Emporia St. (Washburn)	97
Jason Donadi, Mansfield (Lock Haven)	96
Chris Schrantz, North Dak. (South Dak. St.)	96
Justin Taylor, Mo. Southern St. (Truman St.)	96
Demeco Archangel, Fayetteville St. (Benedict)	95
Darrell Erby, Catawba (Presbyterian)	95
Kevin Wimberly, Kutztown (East Stroudsburg)	95
Adrian Jones, N.C. Central (Gardner-Webb)	94
DeWayne Thomas, Elon (East Stroudsburg)	94
Boobie Thornton, Midwestern St. (Eastern N.M.)	94

Field Goals

Player, Team (Opponent)	Yards
Ken Johnson, North Dak. St. (South Dak. St.)	55
Lenny Laguardia, Adams St. (Western St.)	53
Tyson Cook, Edinboro (Hillsdale)	52
Doug Kochanski, Grand Valley St. (UC Davis)	52
James Lightfoot, Valdosta St. (Ark.-Monticello)	52
Leo Loiacano, Saginaw Valley (Ashland)	52
Tyson Maples, Carson-Newman (Valdosta St.)	52
Shane Meyer, Central Mo. St. (Truman St.)	52
Scott Nolan, Northwood (Indianapolis)	52
Mike Schauer, Northern Colo. (North Dak. St.)	52
Eric Wicks, Mercyhurst (St. Francis, Pa.)	52
Greg Payne, Catawba (Elon)	51
Michael Mayeux, Central Ark. (Northeastern St.)	50
Brandon Risner, Mo.-Rolla (Washburn)	50
Jeremy Thompson, Harding (East Central)	50

Punts

Player, Team (Opponent)	Yards
Cullen Garrity, Bemidji St. (Southwest St.)	85
Adam Ryan, Fort Hays St. (Chadron St.)	84
Scott Juengst, Colorado Mines (N.M. Highlands)	82
Scott Juengst, Colorado Mines (Chadron St.)	80
Jaime Jones, Wayne St., Neb. (Southwest St.)	76
Scott Stephens, Central Ark. (Arkansas St.)	76
Rob Buffington, Glenville St. (West Liberty St.)	74
Doc Proctor, Ferris St. (Northern Mich.)	74
Adam Ryan, Fort Hays St. (Adams St.)	74
Tim Duncan, Kentucky St. (Albany St., Ga.)	73
Adam Ryan, Fort Hays St. (Western St.)	73
John Cerra, New Haven (Monmouth, N.J.)	72
Tony Palazzi, Sacred Heart (LIU-C.W. Post)	72

1997 Division III Individual Leaders

Rushing

	1997 Class	G	Car.	Yards	TD	Yds.PG
Jamie Lee, MacMurray	Sr.	8	207	1639	11	204.9
Shane Davis, Loras	Sr.	10	267	1774	18	177.4
Brandon Graham, Hope	Sr.	9	275	1516	20	168.4
Ray Neosh, Coe	Jr.	9	183	1447	14	160.8
Jason Scott, Concordia (Wis.)	Sr.	10	254	1593	17	159.3
Steve Tardif, Maine Maritime	So.	10	342	1543	12	154.3
Dante Brown, Marietta	Sr.	10	280	1528	15	152.8
Brad Olson, Lawrence	Sr.	9	221	1349	16	149.9
Doug Steiner, Grove City	Sr.	10	257	1490	29	149.0
David Glisson, Mississippi Col.	Sr.	10	214	1443	10	144.3
Mark Byarlay, Trinity (Tex.)	Sr.	8	155	1145	5	143.1
Jason Brader, Muhlenberg	Jr.	10	271	1406	10	140.6
John Damato, Wis.-Whitewater	Sr.	9	168	1265	11	140.6
Jim Mormino, Allegheny	Sr.	10	233	1393	25	139.3
Mike Hankins, Wilkes	So.	10	272	1390	8	139.0
Oliver Jordan, Emory & Henry	So.	10	216	1380	13	138.0
James Regan, Pomona-Pitzer	Jr.	8	174	1102	19	137.8
Cory Christensen, Simpson	Sr.	10	208	1370	25	137.0
Matt Wichlinski, Susquehanna	Jr.	10	233	1322	18	132.2
Jeff Rohlwing, Luther	Jr.	9	222	1180	9	131.1
Andrew Notarfrancesco, Catholic	So.	10	241	1307	19	130.7
Jeff Brock, Heidelberg	So.	9	279	1166	7	129.6
Trevor Shannon, Wartburg	Jr.	9	245	1162	18	129.1
Paul Smith, Gettysburg	So.	10	163	1256	13	125.6

Passing Efficiency

(Min. 15 att. per game)	1997 Class	G	Att.	Cmp.	Pct.	Int.	Yards	TD	Rating Points
Bill Borchert, Mount Union	Sr.	10	272	190	69.8	1	2933	47	216.7
Greg Lister, Rowan	Sr.	9	162	111	68.5	4	1688	20	191.9
Kevin Ricca, Catholic	Sr.	10	306	208	67.9	6	2990	35	183.9
Jack Ramirez, Pomona-Pitzer	Sr.	8	196	109	55.6	9	2013	20	166.4
Bryan Snyder, Albright	Sr.	9	315	207	65.7	6	2808	26	164.0
Shaun Brown, Wittenberg	So.	10	205	109	53.1	8	1869	24	160.6
Sean Hoolihan, Wis.-Eau Claire	Jr.	10	262	158	60.3	7	2574	18	160.1
Jesse Willis, Upper Iowa	Jr.	8	125	69	55.2	3	1042	15	160.1

(Min. 15 att. per game)	1997 Class	G	Att.	Cmp.	Pct.	Int.	Yards	TD	Rating Points
Jeff Baker, Wis.-La Crosse	Sr.	9	243	136	55.9	9	2508	18	159.7
Rodger Guy, Mississippi Col.	Sr.	8	152	90	59.2	3	1324	14	158.8
Matt Delly, Hartwick	Sr.	9	267	137	51.3	8	2474	26	155.3
Mike Burton, Trinity (Tex.)	So.	9	215	123	57.2	5	1811	20	154.0
Joel Parrett, Bluffton	So.	10	158	90	56.9	8	1507	12	152.0
Troy Dougherty, Grinnell	So.	10	351	208	59.2	11	2790	32	149.9

Total Offense

	1997 Class	G	Plays	Yards	Yds.PG
Matt Bunyan, Wis.-Stout	Jr.	10	422	3216	321.6
Chris Stormer, Hanover	Jr.	8	403	2563	320.4
Kevin Ricca, Catholic	Sr.	10	392	3200	320.0
Sidney Chappell, Randolph-Macon	Sr.	10	463	3149	314.9
Sean Hoolihan, Wis.-Eau Claire	Jr.	10	369	3148	314.8
Mark Novara, Lakeland	Sr.	10	469	3064	306.4
Bill Borchert, Mount Union	Sr.	10	313	3049	304.9
Bryan Snyder, Albright	Sr.	9	365	2691	299.0
Derrin Lamker, Augsburg	Sr.	10	462	2976	297.6
Jack Ramirez, Pomona-Pitzer	Sr.	8	287	2373	296.6
Jason VanDerMaas, Alma	Jr.	9	426	2659	295.4
Troy Dougherty, Grinnell	So.	10	457	2950	295.0
Jeff Baker, Wis.-La Crosse	Sr.	9	305	2557	284.1
Steve Luce, Whittier	Jr.	8	335	2254	281.8
Brian Tomalak, Wis.-Oshkosh	Jr.	10	444	2816	281.6
Bob Southworth, Gust. Adolphus	Jr.	10	411	2788	278.8
Justin Peery, Westminster (Mo.)	So.	10	434	2770	277.0
Matt Lundeen, Bethel (Minn.)	Sr.	10	403	2691	269.1
Danny Strelkauskas, Guilford	Sr.	10	363	2662	266.2
Matt Delly, Hartwick	Sr.	9	318	2374	263.8
Michael O'Donovan, Ithaca	Jr.	10	383	2603	260.3
Joe Zarlinga, Ohio Northern	Jr.	10	349	2454	245.4
Greg Kaiser, St. Thomas (Minn.)	So.	10	325	2453	245.3
Eric Rich, Ripon	Sr.	9	399	2183	242.6

Receptions Per Game

	1997 Class	G	Rec.	Yards	TD	Rec.PG
Jeff Clay, Catholic	Sr.	10	112	1625	20	11.2
Scott Pingel, Westminster (Mo.)	So.	10	98	1420	17	9.8
Eric Nemec, Albright	Jr.	9	86	1147	15	9.6
Felix Brooks-Church, Oberlin	Jr.	8	68	698	8	8.5
Fred Rau, McMurry	So.	9	76	775	5	8.4
Scott Hvistendahl, Augsburg	Jr.	10	84	1329	15	8.4
Jeremy Snyder, Whittier	Jr.	9	71	1237	15	7.9
Tarrik Wilson, Hanover	So.	9	71	903	8	7.9
Anthony Johnson, Oberlin	Jr.	10	78	986	5	7.8
Richard Wemer, Grinnell	Jr.	10	76	925	13	7.6
Matt Surette, Worcester Tech	Jr.	10	75	1287	16	7.5
Craig Carreiro, Hartwick	Sr.	9	67	1166	9	7.4
Ryan Hinske, Wis.-Oshkosh	Sr.	10	74	1093	18	7.4
Shane Fouch, Capital	Sr.	10	73	777	2	7.3
Todd Bloom, Hardin-Simmons	Sr.	9	65	858	4	7.2
Junior Lord, Guilford	Sr.	9	64	1094	17	7.1
Joe Rettler, Ripon	So.	9	64	778	7	7.1
Dan Ragsdale, Redlands	Jr.	9	63	673	4	7.0
Andrew Husband, Middlebury	Jr.	8	54	659	3	6.8
Bill Wilcox, Hanover	So.	9	60	567	4	6.7
Ryan Pifer, Heidelberg	Sr.	10	66	1077	9	6.6
Brian O'Sullivan, Colorado Col.	Sr.	8	52	441	3	6.5
Kurt Barth, Eureka	Sr.	0	64	939	13	6.4

Receiving Yards Per Game

	1997 Class	G	Rec.	Yards	TD	Yds.PG
Jeff Clay, Catholic	Sr.	10	112	1625	20	162.5
Scott Pingel, Westminster (Mo.)	So.	10	98	1420	17	142.0
Jeremy Snyder, Whittier	Jr.	9	71	1237	15	137.4
Scott Hvistendahl, Augsburg	Jr.	10	84	1329	15	132.9
Craig Carreiro, Hartwick	Sr.	9	67	1166	9	129.6
Matt Surette, Worcester Tech	Jr.	10	75	1287	16	128.7

	1997 Class	G	Rec.	Yards	TD	Yds.PG
Eric Nemec, Albright	Jr.	9	86	1147	15	127.4
Junior Lord, Guilford	Sr.	9	64	1094	17	121.6
Kirk Aikens, Hartwick	Jr.	9	48	1063	11	118.1
Jeremy Earp, Wis.-La Crosse	Sr.	8	38	936	5	117.0
Eric Larsen, Ill. Wesleyan	Sr.	9	51	1019	11	113.2
Bryan Keats, Worcester St.	Sr.	10	53	1129	11	112.9
William Rochelle, Guilford	Sr.	10	59	1094	7	109.4
Ryan Hinske, Wis.-Oshkosh	Sr.	10	74	1093	18	109.3
Matt Plummer, Dubuque	So.	10	62	1090	13	109.0
Ben Fortkamp, Denison	Jr.	10	54	1086	11	108.6
Tim Kirksey, Cal Lutheran	Jr.	9	51	977	10	108.6
Ryan Pifer, Heidelberg	Sr.	10	66	1077	9	107.7
Aaron Fuller, Emory & Henry	Sr.	10	58	1010	6	101.0
Tarrik Wilson, Hanover	So.	9	71	903	8	100.3
Scott Wojcik, Wis.-Stout	Sr.	10	61	1002	9	100.2
Anthony Johnson, Oberlin	Jr.	10	78	986	5	98.6
David Hutchison, Adrian	Sr.	9	38	879	5	97.7
Mark Jacobson, Martin Luther	Jr.	9	38	871	5	96.8
Matt Perceval, Wesleyan (Conn.)	So.	8	37	772	8	96.5
Russ Fedyk, Wittenberg	Jr.	10	53	954	10	95.4
Todd Bloom, Hardin-Simmons	Sr.	9	65	858	4	95.3

Interceptions

	1997 Class	G	No.	Yards	Int.PG
Joel Feuerstahler, Martin Luther	Sr.	9	10	222	1.1
Duane Stevens, MIT	Sr.	9	9	69	1.0
Tom Massey, Brockport St.	Jr.	10	9	99	.9
Erik Schiller, Hobart	Sr.	9	8	54	.9
Anthony Sullivan, Cal Lutheran	Jr.	9	8	103	.9
Damon Sefa, Olivet	Jr.	9	8	168	.9
Keith Beaulieu, Maine Maritime	Jr.	10	8	52	.8
Ryan Burress, Franklin	Sr.	10	8	129	.8
Jon Goldie, Ill. Wesleyan	Jr.	9	7	59	.8
Mike Scheuer, Wis.-La Crosse	Jr.	9	7	34	.8
Jack Prall, Carthage	Jr.	9	7	53	.8
Jason Exley, Augsburg	Sr.	8	6	55	.8
Sedrick Madlock, Howard Payne	Jr.	10	7	202	.7

Scoring

	1997 Class	G	TD	XP	FG	Pts.	Pts.PG
James Regan, Pomona-Pitzer	Jr.	8	21	34	2	166	20.8
Chad Hoiska, Wis.-Eau Claire	Sr.	10	29	2	0	176	17.6
Jim Mormino, Allegheny	Sr.	10	29	0	0	174	17.4
Doug Steiner, Grove City	Sr.	10	29	0	0	174	17.4
Cory Christensen, Simpson	Sr.	10	25	0	0	150	15.0
Virgil Petty, Albion	Jr.	9	21	0	0	126	14.0
Brandon Graham, Hope	Sr.	9	20	0	0	120	13.3
Trevor Shannon, Wartburg	Jr.	9	20	0	0	120	13.3
Andrew Notarfrancesco, Catholic	So.	10	21	4	0	130	13.0
Junior Lord, Guilford	Sr.	9	18	2	0	110	12.2
Jeff Clay, Catholic	Sr.	10	20	0	0	120	12.0
Ray Dawood, Alma	Sr.	9	18	0	0	108	12.0
Scott Pingel, Westminster (Mo.)	So.	10	17	16	0	118	11.8
DeCarlos West, Methodist	Sr.	9	17	0	0	102	11.3
Jason Barr, Wash. & Jeff.	Jr.	7	13	0	0	78	11.1
Ryan Hinske, Wis.-Oshkosh	Sr.	10	18	2	0	110	11.0
Ray Neosh, Coe	Jr.	9	16	2	0	98	10.9
Jason Scott, Concordia (Wis.)	Sr.	10	18	0	0	108	10.8
Shane Davis, Loras	Sr.	10	18	0	0	108	10.8
Matt Wichlinski, Susquehanna	Jr.	10	18	0	0	108	10.8

All-Purpose Yards

	1997 Class	G	Rush	Rec.	PR	KOR	Total Int.	Yards	Yds.PG
Paul Smith, Gettysburg	So.	10	1256	102	199	805	0	2362	236.20
Ray Neosh, Coe	Jr.	9	1447	252	0	282	0	1981	220.11
Shane Davis, Loras	Sr.	10	1774	37	0	305	0	2116	211.60
Jamie Lee, MacMurray	Sr.	8	1639	6	0	17	0	1662	207.75
R.J. Bowers, Grove City	Fr.	10	1239	253	46	488	0	2026	202.60
Dante Brown, Marietta	Sr.	10	1528	191	78	201	0	1998	199.80
Tim Caldwell, Bethany (W.Va.)	Jr.	10	1120	178	184	480	0	1962	196.20
Cory Christensen, Simpson	Sr.	10	1370	117	331	134	0	1952	195.20
Damon Lynch, Upper Iowa	Sr.	10	1201	135	133	474	0	1943	194.30
Steve Tardif, Maine Maritime	So.	10	1543	85	0	287	0	1915	191.50
Trevor Shannon, Wartburg	Jr.	9	1162	265	0	225	0	1652	183.56
Ray Dawood, Alma	Sr.	9	718	552	8	361	7	1646	182.89
James Regan, Pomona-Pitzer	Jr.	8	1102	99	0	242	0	1443	180.38
Jim Mormino, Allegheny	Sr.	10	1393	354	0	56	0	1803	180.30
Jason Scott, Concordia (Wis.)	Sr.	10	1593	191	0	0	0	1784	178.40
Jason Brader, Muhlenberg	Jr.	10	1406	231	0	131	0	1768	176.80
William Rochelle, Guilford	Sr.	10	18	1094	276	357	0	1745	174.50
Brandon Graham, Hope	Sr.	9	1516	53	0	0	0	1569	174.33
Russ Fedyk, Wittenberg	Jr.	10	120	954	312	352	0	1738	173.80
Mark Byarlay, Trinity (Tex.)	Sr.	8	1145	244	0	0	0	1389	173.63
Oliver Jordan, Emory & Henry	So.	10	1380	82	0	270	0	1732	173.20
Matt Perceval, Wesleyan (Conn.)	So.	8	55	772	106	452	0	1385	173.13
David Glisson, Mississippi Col.	Sr.	10	1443	228	0	45	0	1716	171.60
Jeff Rohlwing, Luther	Jr.	9	1180	181	6	132	0	1499	166.56
Chad Hoiska, Wis.-Eau Claire	Sr.	10	1167	367	126	0	0	1660	166.00

Punt Returns

(Min. 1.2 per game)	1997 Class	No.	Yds.	Avg.
Seth Wallace, Coe	Fr.	10	301	30.1
David Ziegler, John Carroll	So.	32	626	19.6
Russ Fedyk, Wittenberg	Jr.	16	312	19.5
Darin Kershner, Mount Union	Jr.	18	293	16.3
Adrian Young, Dickinson	Jr.	14	226	16.1
Qasim Ward, Mass.-Boston	Fr.	12	191	15.9
Chris Moore, St. John's (Minn.)	Fr.	30	464	15.5
Ryan Rausch, Wartburg	Fr.	15	226	15.1
Cory Christensen, Simpson	Sr.	23	331	14.4
Marvin Deal, Western Md.	So.	42	591	14.1

Kickoff Returns

(Min. 1.2 per game)	1997 Class	No.	Yds.	Avg.
Qasim Ward, Mass.-Boston	Fr.	10	314	31.4
Mike Mott, Rochester	Jr.	10	304	30.4
Mario Thompson, Occidental	So.	16	476	29.8
Russ Fedyk, Wittenberg	JR.	12	352	29.3
Scott Larsen, Cornell College	Jr.	14	407	29.1
Dan Reading, Mass. Maritime	So.	18	515	28.6
Shane Thielke, Gust. Adolphus	Sr.	14	396	28.3
Matt Gudorf, Adrian	Jr.	11	310	28.2
Tyler Gerry, Westfield St.	Sr.	13	362	27.8
Dave DeHommel, Hope	Jr.	11	300	27.3
Ryan Hollom, St. Olaf	So.	15	403	26.9
Drew Sherman, Knox	So.	21	562	26.8
Andrew Woosley, La Verne	So.	11	287	26.1

Punting

(Min. 3.6 per game)	1997 Class	No.	Avg.
Justin Shively, Anderson (Ind.)	Jr.	55	45.5
Jeff Shea, Cal Lutheran	Sr.	43	44.4
Matt George, Chapman	Sr.	38	43.8
Jeff Floyd, Centre	Sr.	48	42.8
Richard Harr, Ferrum	So.	66	42.5
Josh Schneider, John Carroll	Fr.	45	42.3
Mike Zappia, Buffalo St.	Jr.	50	41.6
Brandon Pierceall, Greensboro	Jr.	54	41.5
Matt Mahaffey, Wooster	So.	44	40.5
Vince Coley, Allegheny	Sr.	40	40.3
Dan Hildebrandt, St. Olaf	Fr.	78	40.3
Mark McGonagle, Ursinus	Sr.	47	40.1
Jerry Faust, Wis.-La Crosse	Sr.	37	40.0
Erik Berendsen, Wis.-Stevens Point	Jr.	60	40.0

Field Goals

	1997 Class	G	FGA	FG	Pct.	FGPG
Ryan Boutwell, Gust. Adolphus	Jr.	10	18	13	72.2	1.30
Paul Morris, Trinity (Tex.)	So.	9	14	11	78.6	1.22
Rick Brands, Alma	Jr.	9	19	11	57.9	1.22
Paul Boehms, Wheaton (Ill.)	Sr.	9	13	10	76.9	1.11
Chase Young, Buena Vista	Fr.	9	18	10	55.6	1.11
Ben Arnold, Wooster	So.	10	13	10	76.9	1.00
Keith Scranton, Brockport St.	So.	10	19	10	52.6	1.00
A.J. Pilato, Hartwick	So.	9	13	9	69.2	1.00
Ryan Geisler, Cal Lutheran	Fr.	9	14	9	64.3	1.00
Nick DePaola, Buffalo St.	So.	9	14	9	64.3	1.00
Chris Warwick, Knox	Jr.	9	14	9	64.3	1.00
Adam Clark, Worcester Tech	Jr.	10	14	10	71.4	1.00
Joel Buseman, Central (Iowa)	Sr.	10	18	10	55.6	1.00
Matt George, Chapman	Sr.	9	15	9	60.0	1.00
Mike Stoehr, Montclair St.	So.	10	14	10	71.4	1.00
Tom Riley, Hanover	Jr.	10	14	10	71.4	1.00
Scott Hainlen, Claremont-M-S	Jr.	9	15	9	60.0	1.00

1997 Division III Team Leaders

Total Offense

	G	Plays	Yds.	Yds.PG
Simpson	10	869	5653	565.3
Wis.-Eau Claire	10	771	5418	541.8
Mount Union	10	920	5265	526.5
Pomona-Pitzer	8	578	4102	512.8
Catholic	10	717	4894	489.4
Wis.-Whitewater	9	630	4396	488.4
Lakeland	10	785	4853	485.3
Ohio Northern	10	737	4818	481.8
Wis.-La Crosse	9	649	4163	462.6

Total Defense

	G	Plays	Yds.	Yds.PG
Salve Regina	9	502	1314	146.0
Western Md.	10	631	1755	175.5
Mount Union	10	652	1812	181.2
Rowan	9	550	1643	182.6
Wesley	9	516	1790	198.9
Amherst	8	523	1727	215.9

Rushing Offense

	G	Car.	Yds.	Yds.PG
Wis.-River Falls	10	586	3656	365.6
Simpson	10	598	3387	338.7
Wis.-Whitewater	9	486	3008	334.2
Grove City	10	568	3315	331.5
Augustana (Ill.)	9	600	2970	330.0
Coe	9	487	2887	320.8
Sewanee	9	545	2793	310.3
North Central	9	524	2581	286.8
Lawrence	9	503	2529	281.0

Rushing Defense

	G	Car.	Yds.	Yds.PG
Mount Union	10	342	486	48.6
Western Md.	10	351	530	53.0
Rensselaer	9	294	531	59.0
Emory & Henry	10	317	616	61.6
Amherst	8	308	528	66.0
Rowan	9	316	618	68.7
Salve Regina	9	340	639	71.0
La Verne	9	294	677	75.2
Albright	9	330	693	77.0
Frostburg St.	9	335	700	77.8
Wesley	9	329	717	79.7
Worcester St.	10	340	798	79.8
Catholic	10	346	802	80.2
Wabash	10	322	813	81.3
Susquehanna	10	329	825	82.5

Scoring Offense

	G	TD	XP	2XP	DXP	FG	SAF	Pts.	Avg.
Mount Union	10	74	71	0	00	9	1	544	54.4
Simpson	10	70	60	1	00	3	1	493	49.3
Wittenberg	10	66	54	1	00	7	0	473	47.3
Pomona-Pitzer	8	53	37	6	00	2	0	373	46.6
Wis.-Eau Claire	10	59	43	10	00	8	0	441	44.1
Lakeland	10	58	45	3	00	9	1	428	42.8
Catholic	10	61	45	5	00	1	1	426	42.6
Wis.-Whitewater	9	51	46	2	00	7	1	379	42.1
Allegheny	10	56	44	3	00	5	3	407	40.7
Ohio Northern	10	56	43	3	00	1	0	388	38.8
Rowan	9	48	38	0	00	4	0	338	37.6
Grove City	10	54	33	1	00	5	0	374	37.4
Central (Iowa)	10	49	38	2	00	10	1	368	36.8
Trinity (Tex.)	9	42	37	1	00	11	2	328	36.4
Mass.-Dartmouth	10	52	36	1	00	2	0	356	35.6
Wis.-La Crosse	9	45	38	1	00	2	1	318	35.3
Coe	9	46	27	7	00	0	0	317	35.2

Scoring Defense

	G	TD	XP	2XP	DXP	FG	SAF	Pts.	Avg.
Mount Union	0	8	8	0	0	0	0	56	5.6
Rowan	9	7	4	0	0	4	1	60	6.7
Western Md.	10	9	6	1	0	3	1	73	7.3
Salve Regina	9	10	2	0	0	3	0	71	7.9
Concordia-M'head	10	12	8	1	0	5	0	97	9.7
Plymouth St.	10	14	6	0	0	5	0	105	10.5
Wesley	9	13	11	0	0	3	0	98	10.9
Wittenberg	10	15	13	0	0	2	0	109	10.9
Lycoming	9	14	5	1	0	4	0	103	11.4
Rensselaer	9	13	7	0	0	6	0	103	11.4
Lakeland	10	17	11	0	0	1	0	116	11.6
Amherst	8	12	10	1	0	3	0	93	11.6
Hanover	10	17	15	0	0	1	0	120	12.0
Catholic	10	17	11	3	0	1	0	122	12.2
Wabash	10	17	11	1	0	3	0	124	12.4
Coast Guard	10	16	13	1	0	5	0	126	12.6
DePauw	10	17	15	0	0	4	0	129	12.9
Jersey City St.	10	16	13	0	0	7	1	132	13.2
Trinity (Tex.)	9	16	10	2	0	4	0	122	13.6
Western New Eng.	7	13	6	0	0	3	1	95	13.6

Passing Offense

	G	Att.	Cmp.	Pct.	Int.	Yards	Yds.PG
Lakeland	10	478	280	58.6	8	3573	357.3
Hanover	10	460	293	63.7	16	3390	339.0
Hartwick	9	360	179	49.7	16	3039	337.7
Wis.-Stout	10	410	228	55.6	14	3295	329.5
Albright	9	332	214	64.5	6	2858	317.6
Mount Union	10	311	212	68.2	3	3171	317.1
Whittier	9	346	185	53.5	12	2809	312.1
Catholic	10	322	216	67.1	6	3104	310.4
Westminster (Mo.)	10	419	244	58.2	14	3077	307.7
Guilford	10	389	198	50.9	18	3067	306.7
Augsburg	10	420	250	59.5	14	2999	299.9
Wis.-Oshkosh	10	403	217	53.8	5	2945	294.5
Redlands	9	383	223	58.2	16	2627	291.9
Randolph-Macon	10	363	199	54.8	13	2914	291.4
Wis.-La Crosse	9	255	141	55.3	10	2622	291.3
Bethel (Minn.)	10	374	215	57.5	12	2855	285.5
Grinnell	10	354	211	59.6	11	2813	281.3
Wis.-Eau Claire	10	285	174	61.1	8	2798	279.8
Gust. Adolphus	10	336	204	60.7	12	2776	277.6
Menlo	10	376	202	53.7	18	2765	276.5

Pass Efficiency Defense

	G	Att.	Cmp.	Pct.	Int.	Yards	TD	Rating Points
Salve Regina	9	162	59	36.4	18	675	4	57.3
Western Md.	10	280	103	36.7	19	1225	5	65.9
Western New Eng.	7	147	54	36.7	8	602	5	71.5
Lakeland	10	319	131	41.0	22	1527	4	71.6
Mount Union	10	310	145	46.7	19	1326	4	74.7
Rowan	9	234	103	44.0	15	1025	5	75.0
Albion	9	333	143	42.9	17	1624	5	78.7
Martin Luther	9	273	116	42.4	20	1457	8	82.3

Net Punting

	Punts	Yds.	Avg.	No. Ret.	Yds. Ret.	Net Avg.
John Carroll	45	1905	42.33	21	72	40.73
Chapman	45	1949	43.31	19	161	39.73
Anderson (Ind.)	59	2655	45.00	27	345	39.15
Centre	52	2126	40.88	17	115	38.67
Cal Lutheran	45	1925	42.77	24	208	38.15
Allegheny	40	1612	40.30	20	107	37.62
La Verne	65	2574	39.60	20	145	37.36
St. John's (Minn.)	64	2428	37.93	16	55	37.07
Central (Iowa)	45	1708	37.95	15	66	36.48
Claremont M-S	65	2576	39.63	25	207	36.44
Wis-Stevens Point	60	2398	39.96	30	219	36.31
Wesleyan (Conn.)	39	1497	38.38	15	85	36.20
Wooster	47	1888	40.17	22	203	35.85
Adrian	41	1591	38.80	13	123	35.80
Albion	53	2062	38.90	26	169	35.71
Buffalo St.	50	2082	41.64	32	297	35.70
Moravian	58	2131	36.74	26	65	35.62
Menlo	51	2011	39.43	28	206	35.39
Loras	56	2219	39.62	21	239	35.35
Bridgewater (Va.)	64	2461	38.45	27	204	35.26

Punt Returns

	G	No.	Yds.	TD	Avg.
Juniata	10	19	350	2	18.42
John Carroll	10	39	710	2	18.20
Coe	9	27	445	1	16.48
Nichols	9	16	260	1	16.25
Wittenberg	10	37	597	3	16.13
Springfield	9	14	220	2	15.71
Bluffton	10	20	306	1	15.30
St. John's (Minn.)	10	36	527	1	14.63
Greenville	10	19	267	0	14.05
Western Md.	10	52	717	3	13.78
Simpson	10	27	370	0	13.70
Allegheny	10	30	411	1	13.70
Wartburg	10	19	260	0	13.68
Dubuque	10	12	164	1	13.66
Martin Luther	9	23	304	3	13.21
Wis.-Whitewater	9	27	356	0	13.18
Gust. Adolphus	10	27	354	0	13.11
Hobart	10	38	494	1	13.00
Ithaca	10	54	699	1	12.94
Mass. Maritime	10	21	268	1	12.76

Kickoff Returns

	G	No.	Yds.	TD	Avg.
Western Md.	10	18	526	1	29.22
Mount Union	10	17	487	0	28.64
Hartwick	9	24	630	3	26.25
Gust. Adolphus	10	31	794	0	25.61
John Carroll	10	23	588	0	25.56
Howard Payne	10	16	388	1	24.25
Adrian	9	22	531	2	24.13
Wittenberg	10	21	488	0	23.23
Hope	9	25	576	0	23.04
Knox	9	32	735	0	22.96
Occidental	9	44	992	0	22.54
Simpson	10	28	631	0	22.53
Mass. Maritime	10	41	921	1	22.46
Hardin-Simmons	10	18	401	0	22.27
Allegheny	10	32	712	2	22.25
Bluffton	10	51	1128	1	22.11
Greenville	10	21	464	0	22.09
Sewanee	9	32	706	1	22.06
Hanover	10	19	418	0	22.00
Rowan	9	18	394	1	21.88

Turnover Margin

		TURNOVERS GAINED			TURNOVERS LOST			Margin/
	G	Fum.	Int.	Total	Fum.	Int.	Total	Game
Rensselaer	9	10	25	35	10	5	15	2.22
Wittenberg	10	17	20	37	7	9	16	2.10
Lakeland	10	13	22	35	10	8	18	1.70
Wis-Stevens Point	10	17	16	33	5	11	16	1.70
Rowan	9	16	15	31	12	4	16	1.66
Wesley	9	14	17	31	6	10	16	1.66
Mount Union	10	10	19	29	10	3	13	1.60
Western Md.	10	11	19	30	12	3	15	1.50
Brockport St.	10	14	22	36	13	8	21	1.50
North Central	9	11	19	30	13	4	17	1.44
Coe	9	14	16	30	9	8	17	1.44
Grove City	10	13	14	27	5	8	13	1.40
Central (Iowa)	10	10	24	34	10	10	20	1.40
St. Thomas (Minn.)	10	16	13	29	7	8	15	1.40
Concordia (Wis.)	10	13	20	33	9	11	20	1.30
Wabash	10	10	21	31	9	9	18	1.30
Hamline	10	7	18	25	6	6	12	1.30
Carnegie Mellon	10	11	17	28	11	4	15	1.30
John Carroll	10	13	17	30	6	11	17	1.30
Methodist	10	19	15	34	13	8	21	1.30
Howard Payne	10	10	15	25	9	3	12	1.30
Allegheny	10	14	19	33	12	9	21	1.20
Upper Iowa	10	16	23	39	17	10	27	1.20
Guilford	10	17	27	44	14	18	32	1.20
Jersey City St.	10	15	17	32	10	10	20	1.20

Longest Division III Plays of 1997

Rushing

Player, Team (Opponent)	Yards
David Glisson, Mississippi Col. (Sul Ross St.)	98
Eugene Foster, Rowan (Jersey City St.)	98
Mike Gooden, Benedictine (Ill.) (Wabash)	97
Merrell Middleton, Greenville (Blackburn)	96
Richard Holmes, Ohio Wesleyan (Denison)	95
John Damato, Wis.-Whitewater (Carroll [Wis.])	95
Ben Snell, Ohio Northern (Hiram)	90
Krishaun Gilmore, Rensselaer (St. Lawrence)	90
William Castleberry, Thomas More (Wilmington [Ohio])	89
Joe Becker, Wabash (Wilmington [Ohio])	89

Passing

Passer-Receiver, Team (Opponent)	Yards
Matt Bunyan-Jesse Witcraft, Wis.-Stout (Moorhead St.)	98
Hayes MacArthur-Steve Lafond, Bowdoin (Tufts)	90
Shawn Tate-Matt Plummer, Dubuque (Cornell College)	90
Brian Turner-William Ray, Methodist (Apprentice)	90
Chad Beaty-Eric Larsen, Ill. Wesleyan (Thomas More)	88
Jeremy Belisle-Matt Lundeen, Bethel (Minn.) (Trinity [Ill.])	87
Dennis Flaherty-Jeff Closz, Gettysburg (Muhlenberg)	87
Chris Stormer-Tarrik Wilson, Hanover (Manchester)	87
Ethan Pole-Mike Rice, Concordia (Wis.) (Hamline)	86
Michael O'Donovan-Abe Ceesay, Ithaca (Cortland St.)	86

Interception Returns

Player, Team (Opponent)	Yards
Terrance Oliver, Delaware Valley (Lebanon Valley)	100
Sedrick Medlock, Howard Payne (Austin)	99
Frank Bennett, Wilkes (Lycoming)	99
Kyle Bennett, Hamilton (Trinity [Conn.])	98
Mark Rendell, Hobart (Hartwick)	95
Ken Pope, Wittenberg (Denison)	91

Punt Returns

Player, Team (Opponent)	Yards
Ryan Hollom, St. Olaf (Hamline)	91
Terrence King, Kean (Col. of New Jersey)	90
Adrian Young, Dickinson (Frank. & Marsh.)	89
Matt Eisenberg, Juniata (Widener)	86
Scott Schoffner, Wilkes (King's [Pa.])	86
Player, Team (Opponent)	**Yards**
Ken Pope, Wittenberg (Earlham)	86
Qasim Ward, Mass.-Boston (Worcester St.)	85
Jim Larkin, Franklin (Manchester)	82
Matt Buddenhagen, Ithaca (Springfield)	81

Kickoff Returns

Player, Team (Opponent)	Yards
Erick Bernard, Cortland St. (Kean)	99
Matt Gudorf, Adrian (Albion)	97
Clyde Morgan, Thiel (Allegheny)	97
Bert Martin, La Verne (Occidental)	96
Jay Gilmore, Adrian (Ill. Benedictine)	95
Lamarr Renshaw, Bluffton (Sue Bennett)	95
John Harris, Frostburg St. (Greensboro)	95
Terrick Grace, Rowan (Col. of New Jersey)	95
Demetrius Dunn, Springfield (Worcester Tech)	94
Montas Allen, Centre (Maryville [Tenn.])	93
Dan Reading, Mass. Maritime (Fitchburg St.)	93
Jason Hamilton, Sewanee (Trinity [Tex.])	93

Field Goals

Player, Team (Opponent)	Yards
Ryan Geisler, Cal Luthern (Pacific Lutheran)	57
Nate Solmose, Grinnell (Knox)	55
Matt George, Chapman (Howard Payne)	52
Ryan Boutwell, Gust. Adolphus (Macalester)	52
Bryan Mader, Wis.-Whitewater (South Dak. Tech)	52
Joel Buseman, Central (Iowa) (Wartburg)	51
Todd Bencivenni, Johns Hopkins (Swarthmore)	51
Mark Oberholtzer, McMurry (Hardin-Simmons)	50
Scott Hainlen, Claremont-M-S (Redlands)	49
Matt George, Chapman (La Verne)	48
Jason Gardner, DePauw (Franklin)	48
Mike Stoehr, Montclair St. (Wilkes)	48

Punts

Player, Team (Opponent)	Yards
Todd Whitehurst, Menlo (Cal Lutheran)	84
Nathan Bradley, Colby (Wesleyan [Conn.])	81
Jerry Faust, Wis.-La Crosse (Wis.-Stout)	81
Joe Warren, St. Thomas (Minn.) (Concordia-M'head)	78
Jeff Timmons, Monmouth (Ill.) (MacMurray)	77
Phil Barry, St. John's (Minn.) (Gust. Adolphus)	76
Rob Stager, Wesleyan (Conn.) (Tufts)	76
Jeff Shea, Cal Lutheran (Pacific Lutheran)	75
Bart Vanlandingham, Hardin-Simmons (Sul Ross St.)	74
John Manley, Hamilton (Colby)	73

Conference Standings and Champions

1997 Conference Standings

(Full-season records do not include postseason play; ties in standings broken by full-season records unless otherwise noted.)

Division I-A

ATLANTIC COAST CONFERENCE

	Conference			Full Season		
Team	**W**	**L**	**Pct.**	**W**	**L**	**Pct.**
Florida St.	8	0	1.000	10	1	.909
North Caro.	7	1	.875	10	1	.909
Virginia	5	3	.625	7	4	.636
Georgia Tech	5	3	.625	6	5	.545
Clemson	4	4	.500	7	4	.636
North Caro. St.	3	5	.375	6	5	.545
Wake Forest	3	5	.375	5	6	.455
Maryland	1	7	.125	2	9	.182
Duke	0	8	.000	2	9	.182

Bowl Games (3-1): Florida St. (1-0, defeated Ohio St., 31-14, in Sugar Bowl); North Caro. (1-0, defeated Virginia Tech, 42-3, in Gator Bowl); Georgia Tech (1-0, defeated West Va., 35-30, in Carquest Bowl); Clemson (0-1, lost to Auburn, 21-17, in Peach Bowl)

BIG EAST CONFERENCE

	Conference			Full Season		
Team	**W**	**L**	**Pct.**	**W**	**L**	**Pct.**
Syracuse	6	1	.857	9	3	.750
Virginia Tech	5	2	.714	7	4	.636
West Va.	4	3	.571	7	4	.636
Pittsburgh	4	3	.571	6	5	.545
Miami (Fla.)	3	4	.429	5	6	.455
Boston College	3	4	.429	4	7	.364
Temple	3	4	.429	3	8	.273
Rutgers	0	7	.000	0	11	.000

Bowl Games (0-4): Syracuse (0-1, lost to Kansas St., 35-18, in Fiesta Bowl); Virginia Tech (0-1, lost to North Caro., 42-3, in Gator Bowl); West Va. (0-1, lost to Georgia Tech, 35-30, in Carquest Bowl); Pittsburgh (0-1, lost to Southern Miss., 41-7, in Liberty Bowl)

BIG TEN CONFERENCE

	Conference			Full Season		
Team	**W**	**L**	**Pct.**	**W**	**L**	**Pct.**
Michigan	8	0	1.000	11	0	1.000
Ohio St.	6	2	.750	10	2	.833
Penn St.	6	2	.750	9	2	.818
Purdue	6	2	.750	8	3	.727
Wisconsin	5	3	.625	8	4	.667
Iowa	4	4	.500	7	4	.636
Michigan St.	4	4	.500	7	4	.636
Northwestern	3	5	.375	5	7	.417
Minnesota	1	7	.125	3	9	.250
Indiana	1	7	.125	2	9	.182
Illinois	0	8	.000	0	11	.000

Bowl Games (2-5): Michigan (1-0, defeated Washington St., 21-16, in Rose Bowl); Ohio St. (0-1, lost to Florida St., 31-14, in Sugar Bowl); Penn St. (0-1, lost to Florida, 21-6, in Florida Citrus Bowl); Purdue (1-0, defeated Oklahoma St., 33-20, in Alamo Bowl); Wisconsin (0-1, lost to Georgia, 33-6, in Outback Bowl); Iowa (0-1, lost to Arizona St., 17-7, in Sun Bowl); Michigan St. (0-1, lost to Washington, 51-23, in Aloha Bowl)

BIG 12 CONFERENCE

	Conference			Full Season		
Team	**W**	**L**	**Pct.**	**W**	**L**	**Pct.**
North Division						
Nebraska#	8	0	1.000	12	0	1.000
Kansas St.	7	1	.875	10	1	.909
Missouri	5	3	.625	7	4	.636
Colorado*	3	5	.375	5	6	.455
Kansas*	3	5	.375	5	6	.455
Iowa St.	1	7	.125	1	10	.091
South Division						
Texas A&M#	6	2	.750	9	3	.818
Oklahoma St.	5	3	.625	8	3	.727
Texas Tech	5	3	.625	6	5	.545
Texas	2	6	.250	4	7	.364
Oklahoma	2	6	.250	4	8	.333
Baylor	1	7	.125	2	9	.182

**Colorado defeated Kansas, 42-6, on October 18. #Overall record includes Big 12 championship game on December 6 in which Nebraska defeated Texas A&M, 54-15, in The Alamodome, San Antonio, Texas.*

Bowl Games (2-3): Nebraska (1-0, defeated Tennessee, 42-17, in Orange Bowl); Kansas St. (1-0, defeated Syracuse, 35-18, in Fiesta Bowl); Missouri (0-1, lost to Colorado St., 35-24, in Holiday Bowl); Texas A&M (0-1, lost to UCLA, 29-23, in Cotton Bowl); Oklahoma St. (0-1, lost to Purdue, 33-20, in Alamo Bowl)

BIG WEST CONFERENCE

	Conference			Full Season		
Team	**W**	**L**	**Pct.**	**W**	**L**	**Pct.**
Utah St.	4	1	.800	6	5	.545
Nevada	4	1	.800	5	6	.455
Boise St.	3	2	.600	4	7	.364
Idaho	2	3	.400	5	6	.455
North Texas	2	3	.400	4	7	.364
New Mexico St.	0	5	.000	2	9	.182

Bowl Games (0-1): Utah St. (0-1, lost to Cincinnati, 35-19, in Humanitarian Bowl)

CONFERENCE USA

	Conference			Full Season		
Team	**W**	**L**	**Pct.**	**W**	**L**	**Pct.**
Southern Miss.	6	0	1.000	8	3	.727
Tulane	5	1	.833	7	4	.636
East Caro.	4	2	.667	5	6	.455
Cincinnati	2	4	.333	7	4	.636
Memphis	2	4	.333	4	7	.364
Houston	2	4	.333	3	8	.273
Louisville	0	6	.000	1	10	.091

Bowl Games (2-0): Southern Miss. (1-0, defeated Pittsburgh, 41-7, in Liberty Bowl); Cincinnati (1-0, defeated Utah St., 35-19, in Humanitarian Bowl)

MID-AMERICAN ATHLETIC CONFERENCE

	Conference			Full Season		
Team	**W**	**L**	**Pct.**	**W**	**L**	**Pct.**
East Division						
Marshall#	7	1	.875	10	2	.818
Miami (Ohio)*	6	2	.750	8	3	.727
Ohio*	6	2	.750	8	3	.727
Bowling Green	3	5	.375	3	8	.273
Kent	3	5	.375	3	8	.273
Akron	2	6	.250	2	9	.182
West Division						
Toledo#	7	1	.875	9	3	.818
Western Mich.	6	2	.750	8	3	.727
Ball St.	4	4	.500	5	6	.455
Eastern Mich.	3	5	.375	4	7	.364
Central Mich.	1	7	.125	2	9	.182
Northern Ill.	0	8	.000	0	11	.000

*#Overall record includes Mid-American Conference championship game on December 5 in which Marshall defeated Toledo, 34-14, in Marshall Stadium, Huntington, West Virginia. *Miami (Ohio) defeated Ohio, 45-21, on November 8.*

Bowl Games (0-1): Marshall (0-1, lost to Mississippi, 34-31, in Motor City Bowl)

PACIFIC-10 CONFERENCE

	Conference			Full Season		
Team	**W**	**L**	**Pct.**	**W**	**L**	**Pct.**
Washington St.	7	1	.875	10	1	.909
UCLA	7	1	.875	9	2	.818
Arizona St.	6	2	.750	8	3	.727
Washington	5	3	.625	7	4	.636
Arizona	4	4	.500	6	5	.545
Southern Cal	4	4	.500	6	5	.545
Oregon	3	5	.375	6	5	.545
Stanford	3	5	.375	5	6	.455
California	1	7	.125	3	8	.273
Oregon St.	0	8	.000	3	8	.273

Bowl Games (5-1): Washington St. (0-1, lost to Michigan, 21-16, in Rose Bowl); UCLA (1-0, defeated Texas A&M, 29-23, in Cotton Bowl); Arizona St. (1-0, defeated Iowa, 17-7, in Sun Bowl); Washington (1-0, defeated Michigan St., 51-23, in Aloha Bowl); Arizona (1-0, defeated New Mexico, 20-14, in Insight.com Bowl); Oregon (1-0, defeated Air Force, 41-13, in Las Vegas Bowl)

SOUTHEASTERN CONFERENCE

	Conference			Full Season		
Team	**W**	**L**	**Pct.**	**W**	**L**	**Pct.**
East Division						
Tennessee#	7	1	.875	11	1	.909
Florida	6	2	.750	9	2	.818
Georgia	6	2	.750	9	2	.818
South Caro.	3	5	.375	5	6	.455
Kentucky	2	6	.250	5	6	.455
Vanderbilt	0	8	.000	3	8	.273
West Division						
Alabama#*	6	2	.750	9	3	.750
Auburn#	6	2	.750	9	3	.818
LSU	6	2	.750	8	3	.727
Mississippi*	4	4	.500	7	4	.636
Mississippi St.*	4	4	.500	7	4	.636
Arkansas$	2	6	.250	4	7	.364
Alabama$	2	6	.250	4	7	.364

**Mississippi defeated Mississippi St., 15-14, on November 29. $Arkansas defeated Alabama, 17-16, on September 20. #Overall record includes Southeastern Conference championship game on December 6 in which Tennessee defeated Auburn, 30-29, in the Georgia Dome, Atlanta, Georgia.*

Bowl Games (5-1): Tennessee (0-1, lost to Nebraska, 42-17, in Orange Bowl); Florida (1-0, defeated Penn St., 21-6, in Florida Citrus Bowl); Georgia (1-0, defeated Wisconsin, 33-6, in Outback Bowl); Auburn (1-0, defeated Clemson, 21-17, in Peach Bowl); LSU (1-0, defeated Notre Dame, 27-9, in Independence Bowl); Mississippi (1-0, defeated Marshall, 34-31, in Motor City Bowl)

WESTERN ATHLETIC CONFERENCE

	Conference			Full Season		
Team	**W**	**L**	**Pct.**	**W**	**L**	**Pct.**
Mountain Division						
New Mexico#	6	2	.750	9	3	.818
Rice	5	3	.625	7	4	.636
Southern Methodist*	5	3	.625	6	5	.545
Utah*	5	3	.625	6	5	.545
Brigham Young	4	4	.500	6	5	.545
UTEP	3	5	.375	4	7	.364
Tulsa	2	6	.250	2	9	.182
Texas Christian	1	7	.125	1	10	.091
Pacific Division						
Colorado St.#	7	1	.875	10	2	.818
Air Force	6	2	.750	10	2	.833
Fresno St.	5	3	.625	6	6	.500
Wyoming	4	4	.500	7	6	.538
San Diego St.	4	4	.500	5	7	.417
San Jose St.	4	4	.500	4	7	.364
UNLV	2	6	.250	3	8	.273
Hawaii	1	7	.125	3	9	.250

**Southern Methodist defeated Utah, 20-19, on October 11. #Overall record includes Western Athletic Conference championship game on December 6 in which Colorado St. defeated New Mexico, 41-13, in Sam Boyd Stadium, Las Vegas, Nevada.*

Bowl Games (1-2): New Mexico (0-1, lost to Arizona, 20-14, in Insight.com Bowl); Colorado St. (1-0, defeated Missouri, 35-24, in Holiday Bowl); Air Force (0-1, lost to Oregon, 41-13, in Las Vegas Bowl)

DIVISION I-A INDEPENDENTS

	Full Season		
Team	**W**	**L**	**Pct.**
Louisiana Tech	9	2	.818
Navy	7	4	.636
Notre Dame	7	5	.583
UAB	5	6	.455
Central Fla.	5	6	.455
Northeast La.	5	7	.417
Army	4	7	.364
Arkansas St.	2	9	.182
Southwestern La.	1	10	.091

Bowl Games (0-1): Notre Dame (0-1, lost to LSU, 27-9, in Independence Bowl)

Division I-AA

ATLANTIC 10 CONFERENCE

	Conference			Full Season		
Team	**W**	**L**	**Pct.**	**W**	**L**	**Pct.**
New England Division						
New Hampshire*	5	3	.625	5	6	.454
Connecticut	4	4	.500	7	4	.636
Maine	4	4	.500	5	6	.454
Rhode Island	2	6	.250	2	9	.182
Massachusetts	1	7	.125	2	9	.182
Boston U.	1	7	.125	1	10	.091
Mid-Atlantic Division						
Villanova*#	8	0	1.000	11	0	1.000
Delaware	7	1	.875	10	1	.909
Northeastern	5	3	.625	8	3	.727
William & Mary	4	4	.500	7	4	.636
Richmond	4	4	.500	6	5	.545
James Madison	3	5	.375	5	6	.454

*#Atlantic 10 champion. *Division champion.*

NCAA Division I-AA Playoffs (3-2): Villanova (1-1, defeated Colgate, 49-28, in first round; lost to Youngstown St., 37-34, in quarterfinals); Delaware (2-1, defeated Hofstra, 24-14, in first round; defeated Ga. Southern, 16-7, in quarterfinals; lost to McNeese St., 23-21, in semifinals)

BIG SKY CONFERENCE

	Conference			Full Season		
Team	**W**	**L**	**Pct.**	**W**	**L**	**Pct.**
Eastern Wash.	7	1	.875	10	1	.909
Montana	6	2	.750	8	3	.727
Montana St.	5	3	.625	6	5	.545
Weber St.*	4	4	.500	6	5	.545
Northern Ariz.*	4	4	.500	6	5	.545
Cal St. Northridge	4	4	.500	6	6	.500
Portland St.#	3	5	.375	4	7	.364
Idaho St.	2	6	.250	3	8	.272
Cal St. Sacramento	1	7	.125	1	10	.091

**Weber St. defeated Northern Ariz., 36-23, on October 4. #Portland St. is Division II.*

NCAA Division I-AA Playoffs (2-2): Eastern Wash. (2-1, defeated Northwestern St., 40-10, in first round; defeated Western Ky., 38-21, in quarterfinals; lost to Youngstown St., 25-14, in semifinals); Montana (0-1, lost to McNeese St., 19-14, in first round)

GATEWAY FOOTBALL CONFERENCE

	Conference			Full Season		
Team	**W**	**L**	**Pct.**	**W**	**L**	**Pct.**
Western Ill.	6	0	1.000	10	1	.909
Northern Iowa	5	1	.833	7	4	.636
Youngstown St.	4	2	.667	9	2	.818
Southwest Mo. St.	3	3	.500	5	6	.455
Indiana St.	2	4	.333	3	8	.273
Southern Ill.	1	5	.167	3	8	.273
Illinois St.	0	6	.000	2	9	.182

NCAA Division I-AA Playoffs (5-1): Western Ill. (1-1, defeated Jackson St., 31-24, in first round; lost to McNeese St., 14-12, in quarterfinals); Youngstown St. (4-0, defeated Hampton, 28-13, in first round; defeated Villanova, 37-34, in quarterfinals; defeated Eastern Wash., 25-14, in semifinals; defeated McNeese St., 10-9, in championship game)

IVY GROUP

	Conference			Full Season		
Team	**W**	**L**	**Pct.**	**W**	**L**	**Pct.**
Harvard	7	0	1.000	9	1	.900
Dartmouth	6	1	.857	8	2	.800
Pennsylvania	5	2	.714	6	4	.600
Brown	3	4	.429	6	4	.600
Cornell	3	4	.429	5	5	.500
Princeton	2	5	.286	5	5	.500
Columbia	2	5	.286	3	7	.300
Yale	0	7	.000	1	9	.100

METRO ATLANTIC ATHLETIC CONFERENCE

	Conference			Full Season		
Team	**W**	**L**	**Pct.**	**W**	**L**	**Pct.**
Georgetown*	7	0	1.000	8	2	.800
Duquesne	6	1	.857	7	3	.700
Fairfield	4	3	.571	7	3	.700
Siena	4	3	.571	6	3	.667
Marist	4	3	.571	6	4	.600
Canisius	2	5	.286	3	7	.300
St. Peter's	1	6	.143	1	9	.100
Iona	0	7	.000	0	10	.000
St. John's (N.Y.)#	–	–	–	8	3	.727

*#St. John's (N. Y.) not eligible for MAAC title this year and its games do not count in the league standings. *Does not include 35-13 loss to Robert Morris in ECAC I-AA Bowl on November 22.*

MID-EASTERN ATHLETIC CONFERENCE

	Conference			Full Season		
Team	**W**	**L**	**Pct.**	**W**	**L**	**Pct.**
Hampton	7	0	1.000	10	1	.909
Florida A&M*	5	2	.714	9	2	.818
South Caro. St.*	5	2	.714	9	2	.818
Howard	4	3	.571	7	4	.636
North Caro. A&T	3	4	.429	7	4	.636
Morgan St.	2	5	.286	3	7	.300
Bethune-Cookman	1	6	.143	4	7	.364
Delaware St.	1	6	.143	3	8	.273
Norfolk St.#	–	–	–	3	7	.300

**Florida A&M defeated South Caro. St., 22-20, on November 15. #Norfolk St. did not compete for league title.*

NCAA Division I-AA Playoffs (0-2): Hampton (0-1, lost to Youngstown St., 28-13, in first round; Florida A&M (0-1, lost to Ga. Southern, 52-37, in first round)

Heritage Bowl: South Caro. St. lost to Southern U., 34-28, on December 27

NORTHEAST CONFERENCE

	Conference			Full Season		
Team	**W**	**L**	**Pct.**	**W**	**L**	**Pct.**
Robert Morris*	4	0	1.000	7	3	.700
Monmouth (N.J.)	3	1	.750	5	4	.556
Wagner	2	2	.500	6	4	.600
Central Conn. St.	1	3	.250	5	5	.500
St. Francis (Pa.)	0	4	.000	2	9	.182

**Does not include 35-13 victory over Georgetown in ECAC I-AA Bowl on November 22.*

OHIO VALLEY CONFERENCE

	Conference			Full Season		
Team	**W**	**L**	**Pct.**	**W**	**L**	**Pct.**
Eastern Ky.	7	0	1.000	8	4	.667
Eastern Ill.#	5	2	.714	8	3	.727
Murray St.	5	2	.714	7	4	.636
Tennessee Tech	4	3	.571	6	5	.545
Tennessee St.#	4	3	.571	4	7	.364
Middle Tenn. St.	2	5	.286	4	6	.400
Southeast Mo. St.	1	6	.143	4	7	.364
Tenn.-Martin	0	7	.000	1	10	.091

#Eastern Ill. defeated Indiana St., 21-14, on November 1, and Tennessee St. lost to Chattanooga, 28-7, on October 18, in designated conference games.

NCAA Division I-AA Playoffs (0-1): Eastern Ky. (0-1, lost to Western Ky., 42-14, in first round)

PATRIOT LEAGUE

	Conference			Full Season		
Team	**W**	**L**	**Pct.**	**W**	**L**	**Pct.**
Colgate	6	0	1.000	7	4	.636
Bucknell	5	1	.833	10	1	.909
Fordham	4	2	.667	5	6	.455
Lehigh	2	4	.333	4	7	.364
Lafayette	2	4	.333	3	8	.273
Holy Cross*	2	4	.333	4	7	.273
Towson*	0	6	.000	2	8	.200

**Includes Towson forfeit of 27-7 victory over Holy Cross on September 13 for ineligible player.*

NCAA Division I-AA Playoffs (0-1): Colgate (0-1, lost to Villanova, 49-28, in first round)

PIONEER FOOTBALL LEAGUE

	Conference			Full Season		
Team	**W**	**L**	**Pct.**	**W**	**L**	**Pct.**
Dayton	5	0	1.000	9	1	.900
San Diego	4	1	.800	8	3	.727
Drake	2	3	.400	8	3	.727
Butler	2	3	.400	6	4	.600
Valparaiso	2	3	.400	3	7	.300
Evansville	0	5	.000	2	8	.200

SOUTHERN CONFERENCE

	Conference			Full Season		
Team	**W**	**L**	**Pct.**	**W**	**L**	**Pct.**
Ga. Southern	7	1	.875	9	2	.818
Appalachian St.	6	2	.750	7	4	.636
East Tenn. St.*	5	3	.625	7	4	.636
Furman*	5	3	.625	7	4	.636
Chattanooga	4	4	.500	7	4	.636
Citadel	4	4	.500	6	5	.545
Western Caro.	3	5	.375	3	8	.273
Wofford	2	6	.250	3	7	.300
VMI	0	8	.000	0	11	.000

**East Tenn. St. defeated Furman, 58-28, on October 25.*

NCAA Division I-AA Playoffs (1-1): Ga. Southern (1-1, defeated Florida A&M, 52-37, in first round; lost to Delaware, 16-7, in quarterfinals)

SOUTHLAND FOOTBALL LEAGUE

	Conference			Full Season		
Team	**W**	**L**	**Pct.**	**W**	**L**	**Pct.**
McNeese St.*	6	1	.857	10	1	.909
Northwestern St.*	6	1	.857	8	3	.727
Stephen F. Austin	5	2	.714	8	3	.727
Sam Houston St.#	3	4	.429	5	6	.455
Nicholls St.#	3	4	.429	5	6	.455
Southwest Tex. St.	2	5	.286	5	6	.455
Troy St.	2	5	.286	5	6	.455
Jacksonville St.	1	6	.143	1	10	.091

**Southland Conference cochampions. #Sam Houston St. defeated Nicholls St., 24-17, on October 18.*

NCAA Division I-AA Playoffs (3-2): McNeese St. (3-1, defeated Montana, 19-14, in first round; defeated Western Ill., 14-12, in quarterfinals; defeated Delaware, 23-21, in semifinals; lost to Youngstown St., 10-9, in championship game); Northwestern St. (0-1, lost to Eastern Wash., 40-10, in first round)

SOUTHWESTERN ATHLETIC CONFERENCE

	Conference			Full Season		
Team	**W**	**L**	**Pct.**	**W**	**L**	**Pct.**
Southern U.	8	0	1.000	10	1	.909
Jackson St.	7	1	.875	9	2	.818
Ark.-Pine Bluff*	6	2	.750	8	3	.727
Texas Southern	4	4	.500	5	6	.455
Alcorn St.	4	4	.500	4	7	.364
Mississippi Val.	3	5	.375	4	6	.400
Alabama St.#	2	6	.250	3	8	.273
Grambling #	2	6	.250	3	8	.273
Prairie View	0	8	.000	0	9	.000

**Ark-Pine Bluff's games count in the standings but not eligible for league championship. #Alabama State defeated Grambling, 20-13, on November 9.*

NCAA Division I-AA Playoffs (0-1): Jackson St. (0-1, lost to Western Ill., 31-24, in first round)

Heritage Bowl: Southern U. defeated South Caro. St., 34-28, on December 27

DIVISION I-AA INDEPENDENTS

	Full Season		
Team	**W**	**L**	**Pct.**
Cal Poly	10	1	.909
Western Ky.	9	1	.900
Liberty	9	2	.818
Hofstra	9	2	.818
Morehead St.	7	3	.700
Samford	7	4	.636
South Fla.	5	6	.455
Southern Utah	5	6	.455
St. Mary's (Cal.)	4	6	.400
Davidson	3	8	.273
Buffalo	2	9	.182
La Salle	1	8	.111
Charleston So.	1	9	.100
Austin Peay	0	10	.000

NCAA Division I-AA Playoffs (1-2): Hofstra (0-1, lost to Delaware, 24-14, in first round); Western Ky. (1-1, defeated Eastern Ky., 42-14, in first round; lost to Eastern Wash., 38-21, in quarterfinals)

Division II

CENTRAL INTERCOLLEGIATE ATHLETIC ASSOCIATION

	Conference			Full Season		
Team	W	L	Pct.	W	L	Pct.
Livingstone*#	5	2	.714	8	2	.800
Virginia St.	5	2	.714	8	2	.800
Virginia Union	5	2	.714	7	4	.636
Winston-Salem	4	3	.571	6	4	.600
N. C. Central	4	3	.571	4	7	.364
Fayetteville St.	3	4	.429	4	7	.364
Bowie St.	2	5	.286	5	5	.500
Elizabeth City St.	1	6	.143	2	8	.200
Johnson Smith	1	6	.143	2	8	.200

**Conference champion. #Livingstone forfeited conference games to Virginia Union and Bowie St. Note: The CIAA plays some designated nonconference games.*

EASTERN FOOTBALL CONFERENCE

	Conference			Full Season		
Team	W	L	Pct.	W	L	Pct.
Atlantic Division						
Albany (N.Y.)#	8	0	1.000	11	1	.917
Southern Conn. St.	6	2	.750	7	4	.636
LIU-C. W. Post	5	3	.625	6	4	.600
Pace	4	4	.500	5	5	.500
Stony Brook	4	4	.500	4	6	.400
Sacred Heart	1	7	.125	1	9	.100
Bay State Division						
American Int'l#	8	0	1.000	8	3	.727
Bentley	5	3	.625	6	3	.667
Stonehill	3	5	.375	4	6	.400
Merrimack	3	5	.375	3	6	.333
Mass.-Lowell	1	7	.125	2	8	.200
Assumption	0	8	.000	0	10	.000

#Overall record includes EFC championship game in which Albany (N. Y.) defeated American Int'l, 27-20, on November 22.

GULF SOUTH CONFERENCE

	Conference			Full Season		
Team	W	L	Pct.	W	L	Pct.
Southern Ark.*	6	1	.857	9	1	.900
West Ga.*	6	1	.857	8	2	.800
North Ala.	6	2	.750	9	2	.818
Central Ark.	5	3	.625	6	4	.600
Valdosta St.	5	3	.625	6	5	.545
Arkansas Tech	4	4	.500	4	7	.364
Henderson St.	3	5	.375	4	6	.400
Delta St.	3	6	.333	3	7	.300
West Ala.	1	6	.143	4	6	.400
Ark.-Monticello	0	8	.000	0	10	.000

**GSC Conference cochampions.*

NCAA Division II Playoffs (0-2): Southern Ark. (0-1, lost to Albany St., Ga., 10-6, in first round); North Ala. (0-1, lost to Carson-Newman, 21-7, in first round)

LONE STAR CONFERENCE*

	Conference			Full Season		
Team	W	L	Pct.	W	L	Pct.
Tex. A&M-Kingsville	9	0	1.000	9	1	.900
Angelo St.	8	1	.889	9	1	.900
Central Okla.	7	2	.778	9	2	.818
West Tex. A&M	6	3	.667	7	4	.636
Abilene Christian	5	4	.556	7	4	.636
Southwestern Okla.	5	4	.556	5	5	.500
Northeastern Okla.	4	4	.500	4	7	.364
Harding	3	5	.375	5	5	.500
Ouachita Baptist	3	5	.375	4	6	.400
Southeastern Okla.	3	5	.375	3	7	.300
Eastern N. M.	3	6	.333	5	6	.455
Tex. A&M-Commerce	3	6	.333	3	8	.273
Tarleton St.	3	6	.333	4	7	.364
Midwestern St.	3	6	.333	3	7	.300
East Central Okla.	0	8	.000	0	10	.000

**The LSC is divided into North and South Divisions but does not have a playoff for the championship. The champion is based on overall conference record.*

NCAA Division II Playoffs (1-2): Tex. A&M-Kingsville (0-1, lost to UC Davis, 37-34, in first round); Angelo St. (1-1, defeated Western St., 46-12, in first round; lost to UC Davis, 50-33, in quarterfinals)

MID-AMERICAN INTERCOLLEGIATE ATHLETICS ASSOCIATION

	Conference			Full Season		
Team	W	L	Pct.	W	L	Pct.
Northwest Mo. St.	9	0	1.000	11	0	1.000
Pittsburg St.	8	1	.889	9	1	.900
Mo. Southern St.	6	3	.667	7	3	.700
Truman St.	6	3	.667	6	4	.600
Emporia St.	5	4	.556	7	4	.636
Central Mo. St.	4	5	.444	5	6	.455
Mo. Western St.	3	6	.333	5	6	.455
Washburn*	2	7	.222	3	8	.273
Mo.-Rolla*	2	7	.222	3	8	.273
Southwest Bapt.	0	9	.000	0	10	.000

**Washburn defeated Mo.-Rolla, 27-13, on September 27.*

NCAA Division II Playoffs (1-2): Northwest Mo. St. (1-1, defeated North Dak. St., 39-28, in first round; lost to Northern Colo., 35-19, in quarterfinals); Pittsburg St. (0-1, lost to Northern Colo., 24-16, in first round)

MIDWEST INTERCOLLEGIATE FOOTBALL CONFERENCE

	Conference			Full Season		
Team	W	L	Pct.	W	L	Pct.
Grand Valley St.#	9	1	.900	9	2	.818
Ashland#	9	1	.900	9	1	.900
Saginaw Valley	8	2	.800	9	2	.818
Indianapolis	7	3	.700	8	3	.727
Northern Mich.	6	4	.600	7	4	.636
Hillsdale	4	6	.400	4	7	.364
Ferris St.*	3	7	.300	3	7	.300
Northwood*	3	7	.300	3	7	.300
Wayne St. (Mich.)	3	7	.300	3	8	.273
Michigan Tech	2	8	.200	2	8	.200
St. Francis (Ill.)	1	9	.100	2	9	.182

*#Grand Valley St. defeated Ashland, 31-20, on September 13. *Ferris St. defeated Northwood, 31-17, on October 11.*

NCAA Division II Playoffs (0-1): Ashland (0-1, lost to Slippery Rock, 30-20, in first round)

NORTH CENTRAL INTERCOLLEGIATE ATHLETIC CONFERENCE

	Conference			Full Season		
Team	W	L	Pct.	W	L	Pct.
Northern Colo.	8	1	.889	9	2	.818
North Dak. St.	7	2	.778	9	2	.818
North Dak.	7	2	.778	8	2	.800
Neb.-Omaha	6	3	.667	8	3	.727
St. Cloud St.	5	4	.556	6	5	.545
South Dak.*	3	6	.333	5	6	.454
Augustana (S. D.)*	3	6	.333	5	6	.454
South Dak. St.	3	6	.333	4	6	.400
Mankato St.	3	6	.333	4	7	.364
Morningside	0	9	.000	0	11	.000

**South Dak. defeated Augustana (S.D.), 35-23, on October 25.*

NCAA Division II Playoffs (4-1): Northern Colo. (4-0, defeated Pittsburg St., 24-16, in first round; defeated Northwest Mo. St., 35-19, in quarterfinals; defeated Carson-Newman, 30-29, in semifinals; defeated New Haven, 51-0, in championship game); North Dak. St. (0-1, lost to Northwest Mo. St., 39-28, in first round)

NORTHERN SUN INTERCOLLEGIATE ATHLETIC CONFERENCE

	Conference			Full Season		
Team	W	L	Pct.	W	L	Pct.
Winona St.	6	0	1.000	9	2	.818
Minn.-Duluth	4	2	.667	4	6	.400
Moorhead St.	3	3	.500	5	5	.500
Southwest St.	3	3	.500	5	6	.455
Northern St.	3	3	.500	4	7	.364
Minn.-Morris	1	5	.167	3	7	.300
Bemidji St.	1	5	.167	2	8	.200

PENNSYLVANIA STATE ATHLETIC CONFERENCE

	Conference			Full Season		
Team	W	L	Pct.	W	L	Pct.
Eastern Division						
Bloomsburg	6	0	1.000	8	2	.800
Millersville	4	2	.667	7	3	.700
West Chester	4	2	.667	5	6	.455
Kutztown	3	3	.500	6	4	.600
East Stroudsburg	3	3	.500	4	6	.400
Mansfield	1	5	.167	1	10	.091
Cheyney	0	6	.000	0	11	.000
Western Division						
Slippery Rock	6	0	1.000	10	1	.909
Shippensburg	4	2	.667	6	4	.600
Indiana (Pa.)	4	2	.667	5	5	.500
Edinboro	2	4	.333	4	6	.400
Clarion	2	4	.333	3	7	.300
Lock Haven	2	4	.333	3	8	.273
California (Pa.)	1	5	.167	2	8	.200

NCAA Division II Playoffs (1-1): Slippery Rock (1-1, defeated Ashland, 30-20, in first round; lost to New Haven, 49-21, in quarterfinals)

ROCKY MOUNTAIN ATHLETIC CONFERENCE

	Conference			Full Season		
Team	W	L	Pct.	W	L	Pct.
Western St.	7	1	.875	9	2	.818
N. M. Highlands*	6	2	.750	8	3	.727
Chadron St.*	6	2	.750	8	3	.727
Neb.-Kearney	6	2	.750	7	4	.636
Fort Hays St.	4	4	.500	5	6	.455
Fort Lewis	3	5	.375	4	7	.364
Mesa St.	2	6	.250	3	8	.273
Colorado Mines	1	7	.125	3	8	.273
Adams St.	1	7	.125	1	10	.090

**N. M. Highlands defeated Chadron St., 16-14, on October 11.*

NCAA Division II Playoffs (0-1): Western St. (0-1, lost to Angelo St., 46-12, in first round)

SOUTH ATLANTIC CONFERENCE

	Conference			Full Season		
Team	W	L	Pct.	W	L	Pct.
Carson-Newman	7	0	1.000	9	0	1.000
Catawba	5	2	.714	8	3	.727
Wingate*	4	3	.571	8	3	.727
Gardner-Webb*	4	3	.571	8	3	.727
Mars Hill	3	4	.429	5	5	.500
Presbyterian	3	4	.429	5	6	.455
Newberry	2	5	.286	4	7	.364
Lenoir-Rhyne	0	7	.000	0	10	.000

**Wingate defeated Gardner-Webb, 54-34, on October 4.*

NCAA Division II Playoffs (2-1): Carson-Newman (2-1, defeated North Ala., 21-7, in first round; defeated Albany St., Ga., 23-22, in quarterfinals; lost to Northern Colo., 30-29, in semifinals)

SOUTHERN INTERCOLLEGIATE ATHLETIC CONFERENCE

	Conference			Full Season		
Team	W	L	Pct.	W	L	Pct.
Albany St. (Ga.)	6	0	1.000	10	0	1.000
Alabama A&M*	4	2	.667	7	4	.636
Kentucky St.	4	2	.667	6	5	.545
Fort Valley St.	4	2	.667	5	6	.455
Tuskegee	3	3	.500	6	4	.600
Morris Brown	3	3	.500	6	5	.545
Miles	3	3	.500	4	6	.400
Clark Atlanta	2	4	.333	4	7	.364
Savannah St.	1	5	.167	3	8	.273
Morehouse	0	6	.000	3	8	.273

*Note: The SIAC plays some designated league games. *Alabama A&M not eligible for the SIAC title but games count in standings.*

NCAA Division II Playoffs (1-1): Albany St., Ga. (1-1, defeated Southern Ark., 10-6, in first round; lost to Carson-Newman, 23-22, in quarterfinals)

WEST VIRGINIA INTERCOLLEGIATE ATHLETIC CONFERENCE

	Conference			Full Season		
Team	W	L	Pct.	W	L	Pct.
Shepherd*	6	1	.857	9	1	.900
Glenville St.*	6	1	.857	9	2	.818
West Va. Wesleyan	5	2	.714	5	5	.500
Concord	3	4	.429	5	5	.500
West Va. St.	3	4	.429	5	6	.455
Fairmont St.	3	4	.429	5	6	.455
West Liberty St.	2	5	.286	4	8	.333

Team	Conference W	L	Pct.	Full Season W	L	Pct.
West Va. Tech	0	7	.000	0	11	.000

**WVIAC cochampions.*

NCAA Division II Playoffs (0-1): Glenville St. (0-1, lost to New Haven, 47-7, in first round)

DIVISION II INDEPENDENTS

Team	Full Season W	L	Pct.
New Haven	9	1	.900
Mercyhurst	6	3	.667
UC Davis	7	4	.636
Elon	7	4	.636
Ky. Wesleyan	5	4	.556
St. Joseph's (Ind.)	5	6	.455
Western N. M.	4	5	.444
Gannon	4	6	.400
Portland St.#	4	7	.364
Wayne St. (Neb.)	3	7	.300
Humboldt St.*	2	8	.200
Quincy	0	10	.000
Lane	0	10	.000

**Member of NAIA Columbia Football Association. #Member of NCAA I-AA Big Sky Conference.*

NCAA Division II Playoffs (0-1): New Haven (3-1, defeated Glenville St., 47-7, in first round; defeated Slippery Rock, 49-21, in quarterfinals; defeated UC Davis, 27-25, in semifinals; lost to Northern Colo., 51-0, in championship game); UC Davis (2-1, defeated Tex. A&M-Kingsville, 37-34, in first round; defeated Angelo St., 50-33, in quarterfinals, lost to New Haven, 27-25, in semifinals)

Division III

AMERICAN SOUTHWEST CONFERENCE

Team	Conference W	L	Pct.	Full Season W	L	Pct.
Mississippi Col.	4	1	.800	8	2	.800
Howard Payne	3	2	.600	7	3	.700
Hardin-Simmons	2	3	.400	7	3	.700
McMurry	2	3	.400	5	5	.500
Sul Ross St.	2	3	.400	4	6	.400
Austin College	2	3	.400	4	6	.400

CENTENNIAL FOOTBALL CONFERENCE

Team	Conference W	L	Pct.	Full Season W	L	Pct.
Western Md.	7	0	1.000	10	0	1.000
Dickinson	6	1	.857	7	3	.700
Johns Hopkins	5	2	.714	7	3	.700
Frank. & Marsh.	4	3	.571	4	6	.400
Ursinus	3	4	.429	4	6	.400
Gettysburg	2	5	.286	4	6	.400
Muhlenberg	1	6	.143	1	9	.100
Swarthmore	0	7	.000	0	10	.000

NCAA Division III Playoffs (0-1): Western Md. (0-1, lost to Lycoming, 27-13, in first round)

COLLEGE CONFERENCE OF ILLINOIS AND WISCONSIN

Team	Conference W	L	Pct.	Full Season W	L	Pct.
Augustana (Ill.)	6	1	.857	7	2	.778
Ill. Wesleyan	5	2	.714	7	2	.778
Carthage*	4	3	.571	5	4	.556
North Central*	4	3	.571	5	4	.556
Millikin$	4	3	.571	4	5	.444
Wheaton (Ill.)$	4	3	.571	4	5	.444
Elmhurst	1	6	.143	1	8	.111
North Park	0	7	.000	0	9	.000

**Carthage defeated North Central, 23-13, on October 4. $Millikin defeated Wheaton (Ill.), 30-26, on October 18.*

EASTERN COLLEGIATE FOOTBALL CONFERENCE

Team	Conference W	L	Pct.	Full Season W	L	Pct.
Salve Regina	4	0	1.000	7	2	.778
Western New Eng.	3	1	.750	4	3	.571
MIT	2	2	.500	5	4	.556
Nichols	1	3	.250	2	7	.222
Curry	0	4	.000	0	9	.000

FREEDOM FOOTBALL CONFERENCE

Team	Conference W	L	Pct.	Full Season W	L	Pct.
Coast Guard	6	0	1.000	9	1	.900
Merchant Marine*	4	2	.667	7	2	.778
Plymouth St.#	4	2	.667	7	3	.700
Springfield	3	3	.500	4	5	.444
Worcester Tech	2	4	.333	4	6	.400
Western Conn. St.	1	5	.167	4	6	.400
Norwich	1	5	.167	2	8	.200

**Does not include 25-12 victory over Grove City in ECAC Southwest playoff game on November 22. #Does not include 21-17 loss to Buffalo St. in ECAC Northwest playoff game on November 22.*

NCAA Division III Playoffs (0-1): Coast Guard (0-1, lost to Rowan, 43-0, in first round)

ILLINI-BADGER CONFERENCE

Team	Conference W	L	Pct.	Full Season W	L	Pct.
Lakeland (Wis.)	5	0	1.000	10	0	1.000
Concordia (Wis.)	4	1	.800	7	3	.700
MacMurray#	3	2	.600	8	2	.800
Eureka	2	3	.400	5	5	.500
Concordia (Ill.)	1	4	.200	2	7	.222
Greenville (Ill.)	0	5	.000	2	8	.200

#Also a member of St. Louis Intercollegiate Athletic Confernce.

INDIANA COLLEGIATE ATHLETIC CONFERENCE

Team	Conference W	L	Pct.	Full Season W	L	Pct.
Hanover	6	0	1.000	10	0	1.000
DePauw	5	1	.833	8	2	.800
Wabash	4	2	.667	6	4	.600
Manchester	2	4	.333	6	4	.600
Rose-Hulman	2	4	.333	3	7	.300
Franklin*	1	5	.167	2	8	.200
Anderson*	1	5	.167	2	8	.200

**Franklin defeated Anderson, 26-23 (2OT), on October 18.*

NCAA Division III Playoffs (0-1): Hanover (0-1, lost to John Carroll, 30-20, in first round)

IOWA INTERCOLLEGIATE ATHLETIC CONFERENCE

Team	Conference W	L	Pct.	Full Season W	L	Pct.
Simpson	8	0	1.000	10	0	1.000
Central (Iowa)	7	1	.875	8	2	.800
Wartburg*	5	3	.675	7	3	.700
Upper Iowa*	5	3	.625	7	3	.700
Loras	4	4	.500	6	4	.600
Luther	3	5	.375	5	6	.455
Buena Vista	3	5	.375	3	7	.300
Dubuque	1	7	.125	3	7	.300
William Penn	0	8	.000	1	9	.100

**Wartburg defeated Upper Iowa, 13-10, on September 27.*

NCAA Division III Playoffs (2-1): Simpson (2-1, defeated Wis.-Whitewater, 34-31, in first round; defeated Augsburg, 61-21, in quarterfinals; lost to Mount Union, 54-7, in semifinals)

MICHIGAN INTERCOLLEGIATE ATHLETIC CONFERENCE

Team	Conference W	L	Pct.	Full Season W	L	Pct.
Adrian*	4	1	.800	8	1	.889
Hope*	4	1	.800	6	3	.667
Albion	3	2	.600	6	3	.667
Alma	3	2	.600	6	3	.667
Kalamazoo	1	4	.200	4	5	.444
Olivet	0	5	.000	1	7	.125
Defiance#	–	–	–	1	8	.111

**Adrian defeated Hope, 26-19, on October 18. #Defiance did not compete for the league title.*

MIDDLE ATLANTIC STATES COLLEGIATE ATHLETIC CONFERENCE

Team	Conference W	L	Pct.	Full Season W	L	Pct.
Commonwealth League						
Albright	5	0	1.000	8	1	.889
Moravian	4	1	.800	7	3	.700
Widener	3	2	.600	7	3	.700
Susquehanna	2	3	.400	6	4	.600
Juniata	1	4	.200	3	7	.300
Lebanon Valley	0	5	.000	0	10	.000
Freedom League						
Lycoming	4	0	1.000	9	0	1.000
Wilkes	3	1	.750	5	5	.500
Delaware Valley	2	2	.500	5	5	.500
King's (Pa.)	1	3	.250	3	7	.300
FDU-Madison	0	4	.000	0	10	.000

NCAA Division III Playoffs (3-1): Lycoming (3-1, defeated Western Md., 27-13, in first round; defeated Trinity, Tex., 46-26, in quarterfinals; defeated Rowan, 28-20, in semifinals; lost to Mount Union, 61-12, in championship game)

MIDWEST COLLEGIATE ATHLETIC CONFERENCE

Team	Conference W	L	Pct.	Full Season W	L	Pct.
North Division						
Carroll (Wis.)*#$	4	1	.800	5	5	.500
Ripon*	4	1	.800	6	3	.667
Lawrence	2	3	.400	4	5	.444
St. Norbert	2	3	.400	4	5	.444
Beloit	2	3	.400	3	6	.333
Lake Forest	1	4	.200	2	7	.222
South Division						
Grinnell#$	3	0	1.000	5	5	.500
Knox	2	1	.667	5	4	.556
Monmouth (Ill.)	1	2	.333	2	7	.222
Illinois Col.	0	3	.000	1	8	.111

**Carroll (Wis.) defeated Ripon, 32-3, on October 25 for North Division title. #Division champion. $Carroll (Wis.) 20-15 defeated Grinnell on November 8 for MCAC championship.*

MINNESOTA INTERCOLLEGIATE ATHLETIC CONFERENCE

Team	Conference W	L	Pct.	Full Season W	L	Pct.
Augsburg	8	1	.889	9	1	.900
Concordia-M'head*	7	2	.778	8	2	.800
St. Thomas (Minn.)*	7	2	.778	8	2	.800
St. John's (Minn.)	6	3	.667	6	4	.600
Gust. Adolphus#	5	4	.556	6	4	.600
Bethel#	5	4	.556	6	4	.600
Hamline	4	5	.444	5	5	.500
St. Olaf	2	7	.222	2	8	.200
Carleton	1	8	.111	2	8	.200
Macalester	0	9	.000	1	9	.100

**Concordia-M'head defeated St. Thomas (Minn.), 28-7, on October 11. #Gust. Adolphus defeated Bethel, 31-21, on September 27.*

NCAA Division III Playoffs (1-2):): Augsburg (1-1, defeated Concordia-M'head, 34-22, in first round; lost to Simpson, 61-21, in quarterfinals); Concordia-M'head (0-1, lost to Augsburg, 34-22, in first round)

NEW ENGLAND FOOTBALL CONFERENCE

Team	Conference W	L	Pct.	Full Season W	L	Pct.
Worcester St.*	7	1	.875	8	2	.800
Bri'water (Mass.)	7	1	.875	7	3	.700
Mass.-Dartmouth	6	2	.750	8	2	.800
Westfield St.	4	4	.500	4	6	.400
Maine Maritime	4	4	.500	4	6	.400
Mass.-Boston	3	5	.375	3	6	.333
Mass. Maritime	3	5	.375	3	7	.300
Fitchburg St.	1	7	.125	3	7	.300
Framingham St.	1	7	.125	2	8	.200

**Does not include 14-13 loss to Rensselaer in ECAC Northeast playoff game on November 22.*

NEW ENGLAND SMALL COLLEGE ATHLETIC FOOTBALL CONFERENCE#

Team	Full Season W	L	Pct.
Amherst	7	1	.875
Wesleyan (Conn.)	7	1	.875
Williams	7	1	.875
Trinity (Conn.)	5	3	.625
Bowdoin	4	4	.500
Middlebury	4	4	.500
Tufts	3	5	.375
Hamilton	2	6	.250
Bates	1	7	.125
Colby	0	8	.000

#New England Small College Athletic Conference does not keep standings.

NEW JERSEY ATHLETIC CONFERENCE

Team	Conference W	L	Pct.	Full Season W	L	Pct.
Rowan	5	0	1.000	9	0	1.000
Col. of New Jersey	4	1	.800	8	2	.800
Montclair St.	3	2	.600	6	4	.600
Jersey City St.	2	3	.400	5	5	.500
Kean	1	4	.200	1	9	.100
William Paterson	0	5	.000	0	10	.000

NCAA Division III Playoffs (3-2): Rowan (2-1, defeated Coast Guard, 43-0, in first round; defeated Col. of New Jersey, 13-7, in quarterfinals; lost to Lycoming, 28-20, in semifinals); Col. of New Jersey (1-1, defeated Cortland St., 34-30, in first round; lost to Rowan, 13-7, in quarterfinals)

NORTH COAST ATHLETIC CONFERENCE*

Team	Conference W	L	Pct.	Full Season W	L	Pct.
Allegheny	7	1	.875	9	1	.900
Wittenberg	7	1	.875	9	1	.900
Wooster	7	1	.875	9	1	.900
Denison	3	4	.429	4	6	.400
Ohio Wesleyan	3	4	.429	4	6	.400
Kenyon	3	5	.375	3	7	.300
Case Reserve$	2	4	.333	3	7	.300
Earlham	2	6	.250	2	8	.200
Oberlin	0	8	.000	1	9	.100

*$Also a member of University Athletic Association. *Standings based on winning percentage since teams do not play same number of league games.*

NCAA Division III Playoffs (0-1): Allegheny (0-1, lost to Mount Union, 34-30, in first round)

OHIO ATHLETIC CONFERENCE

Team	Conference W	L	Pct.	Full Season W	L	Pct.
Mount Union	9	0	1.000	10	0	1.000
John Carroll	8	1	.889	9	1	.900
Ohio Northern	7	2	.778	8	2	.800
Baldwin-Wallace	6	3	.667	7	3	.700
Heidelberg	5	4	.556	5	5	.500
Marietta	3	6	.333	4	6	.400
Capital	2	7	.222	3	7	.300
Muskingum*	2	7	.222	2	8	.200
Otterbein*	2	7	.222	2	8	.200
Hiram	1	8	.111	2	8	.200

**Muskingum defeated Otterbein, 21-17, on November 8.*

NCAA Division III Playoffs (5-1): Mount Union (4-0, defeated Allegheny, 34-30, in first round; defeated John Carroll, 59-7, in quarterfinals; defeated Simpson, 54-7, in semifinals; defeated Lycoming, 61-12, in championship game); John Carroll (1-1, defeated Hanover, 30-20, in first round; lost to Mount Union, 59-7, in quarterfinals)

OLD DOMINION ATHLETIC CONFERENCE

Team	Conference W	L	Pct.	Full Season W	L	Pct.
Emory & Henry*	4	1	.800	8	2	.800
Guilford*	4	1	.800	8	2	.800
Randolph-Macon*	4	1	.800	8	2	.800
Wash. & Lee	2	3	.400	4	6	.400
Bridgewater (Va.)	1	4	.200	2	8	.200
Hampden-Sydney	0	5	.000	0	10	.000

**Old Dominion Athletic Conference tri-champions.*

PRESIDENTS' ATHLETIC CONFERENCE

Team	Conference W	L	Pct.	Full Season W	L	Pct.
Grove City*	5	0	1.000	9	1	.900
Wash. & Jeff.	4	1	.800	6	3	.667
Waynesburg	3	2	.600	5	4	.556
Bethany (W. Va.)	2	3	.400	4	6	.400
Alfred	1	4	.200	2	8	.200
Thiel	0	5	.000	1	9	.100

**Does not include 25-12 loss to Merchant Marine in ECAC Southwest playoff game on November 22.*

ST. LOUIS INTERCOLLEGIATE ATHLETIC CONFERENCE

Team	Conference W	L	Pct.	Full Season W	L	Pct.
MacMurray#	4	0	1.000	8	2	.800
Westminster (Mo.)	3	1	.750	6	4	.600
Greenville (Ill.)	2	2	.500	2	8	.200
Blackburn	1	3	.250	1	8	.111
Principia	0	4	.000	0	8	.000

#Also a member of Illini-Badger Conference.

SOUTHERN CALIFORNIA INTERCOLLEGIATE ATHLETIC CONFERENCE

Team	Conference W	L	Pct.	Full Season W	L	Pct.
Redlands*	4	1	.800	7	2	.778
Cal Lutheran*	4	1	.800	5	4	.556
Whittier*	4	1	.800	5	4	.556
La Verne	2	3	.400	2	7	.222
Occidental	1	4	.200	1	8	.111
Claremont-M-S	0	5	.000	0	9	.000

**SCIAC tri-champions.*

SOUTHERN COLLEGIATE ATHLETIC CONFERENCE

Team	Conference W	L	Pct.	Full Season W	L	Pct.
Trinity (Tex.)	4	0	1.000	9	0	1.000
Centre	3	1	.750	6	3	.667
Sewanee	1	3	.250	5	4	.556
Millsaps	1	3	.250	3	7	.300
Rhodes	1	3	.250	2	7	.222

NCAA Division III Playoffs (1-1): Trinity (Tex.) (1-1, defeated Catholic, 44-33, in first round; lost to Lycoming, 46-26, in quarterfinals)

UNIVERSITY ATHLETIC ASSOCIATION

Team	Conference W	L	Pct.	Full Season W	L	Pct.
Carnegie Mellon	4	0	1.000	8	2	.800
Washington (Mo.)	3	1	.750	6	4	.600
Chicago	1	3	.250	5	4	.556
Case Reserve$	1	3	.250	3	7	.300
Rochester^	1	3	.250	1	8	.111

$Also a member of the North Coast Athletic Conference. ^Also a member of the Upstate Collegiate Athletic Conference.

UPSTATE COLLEGIATE ATHLETIC CONFERENCE

Team	Conference W	L	Pct.	Full Season W	L	Pct.
Rensselaer*	4	0	1.000	8	1	.889
Union (N.Y.)	3	1	.750	7	2	.778
Hobart	2	2	.500	6	4	.600
St. Lawrence	1	3	.250	2	7	.222
Rochester^	0	4	.000	1	8	.111

**Does not include 14-13 victory over Worcester St. in ECAC Northeast playoff game on November 22. ^Also a member of the University Athletic Association.*

WISCONSIN STATE UNIVERSITY CONFERENCE

Team	Conference W	L	Pct.	Full Season W	L	Pct.
Wis.-Whitewater	7	0	1.000	9	0	1.000
Wis.-La Crosse	5	2	.714	7	2	.778
Wis.-Stout	5	2	.714	6	4	.600
Wis.-Eau Claire	4	3	.571	7	3	.700
Wis.-Stevens Point	3	4	.429	6	4	.600
Wis.-River Falls	3	4	.429	5	5	.500
Wis.-Oshkosh	1	6	.143	3	7	.300
Wis.-Platteville	0	7	.000	1	9	.100

NCAA Division III Playoffs (0-1): Wis.-Whitewater (0-1, lost to Simpson, 34-31, in first round)

DIVISION III INDEPENDENTS

Team	Full Season W	L	Pct.
Catholic	10	0	1.000
Methodist	9	1	.900
Coe	8	1	.889
Cortland St.	8	2	.800
Buffalo St.	7	2	.778
Hartwick	7	2	.778
Wesley	7	2	.778
Pomona-Pitzer	6	2	.750
Ithaca	7	3	.700
Cornell (Iowa)	6	3	.667
Martin Luther%	6	3	.667
Brockport St.	6	4	.600
Frostburg St.	5	4	.556
Mt. St. Joseph's	5	4	.556
Menlo	5	5	.500
Neb. Wesleyan#	5	5	.500
Thomas More	5	5	.500
Aurora	4	5	.444
Chapman	4	5	.444
Bluffton	4	6	.400
Ferrum	4	6	.400
Wilmington (Ohio)	4	6	.400
Salisbury St.	3	6	.333
Benedictine (Ill.)	3	7	.300
Maryville (Tenn.)	3	7	.300
Colorado College	2	6	.250
St. Lawrence	2	7	.222
Chowan	2	8	.200
Defiance*	1	8	.111
St. John Fisher	1	8	.111
SW Assembly of God	0	5	.000
Greensboro	0	9	.000

**Defiance is a member of the Michigan Intercollegiate Athletic Conference but did not compete for the league title. % Martin Luther is a member of the Upper Midwest Athletic Conference (NAIA). #Nebraska Wesleyan is a member of the Nebraska-Iowa Athletic Conference (NAIA).*

NCAA Division III Playoffs (0-2): Catholic (0-1, lost to Trinity, Tex., 44-33, in first round); Cortland St. (0-1, lost to Col. of New Jersey, 34-30, in first round)

All-Time Conference Champions

Division I-A

ATLANTIC COAST CONFERENCE

Founded: In 1953 when charter members all left the Southern Conference to form the ACC. **Charter members** (7): Clemson, Duke, Maryland, North Caro., North Caro. St., South Caro. and Wake Forest. **Admitted later** (3): Virginia (1953), Georgia Tech (1978) and Florida St. (1992). **Withdrew later** (1): South Caro. (1971). **Current members** (9): Clemson, Duke, Florida St., Georgia Tech, Maryland, North Caro., North Caro. St., Virginia and Wake Forest.

Year	Champion (Record)
1953	Duke (4-0) & Maryland (3-0)
1954	Duke (4-0)
1955	Maryland (4-0) & Duke (4-0)
1956	Clemson (4-0-1)
1957	North Caro. St. (5-0-1)
1958	Clemson (5-1)
1959	Clemson (6-1)
1960	Duke (5-1)
1961	Duke (5-1)
1962	Duke (6-0)
1963	North Caro. (6-1) & North Caro. St. (6-1)
1964	North Caro. St. (5-2)
1965	Clemson (5-2) & North Caro. St. (5-2)
1966	Clemson (6-1)
1967	Clemson (6-0)
1968	North Caro. St. (6-1)
1969	South Caro. (6-0)
1970	Wake Forest (5-1)
1971	North Caro. (6-0)
1972	North Caro. (6-0)
1973	North Caro. St. (6-0)
1974	Maryland (6-0)
1975	Maryland (5-0)
1976	Maryland (5-0)
1977	North Caro. (5-0-1)
1978	Clemson (6-0)
1979	North Caro. St. (5-1)
1980	North Caro. (6-0)
1981	Clemson (6-0)
1982	Clemson (6-0)
1983	Maryland (5-0)
1984	Maryland (5-0)
1985	Maryland (6-0)
1986	Clemson (5-1-1)
1987	Clemson (6-1)
1988	Clemson (6-1)
1989	Virginia (6-1) & Duke (6-1)
1990	Georgia Tech (6-0-1)
1991	Clemson (6-0-1)
1992	Florida St. (8-0)
1993	Florida St. (8-0)
1994	Florida St. (8-0)
1995	Virginia (7-1) & Florida St. (7-1)
1996	Florida St. (8-0)
1997	Florida St. (8-0)

BIG EAST CONFERENCE

Founded: In 1991 when eight charter members all went from independent status to form the Big East. **Charter members** (8): Boston College, Miami (Fla.), Pittsburgh, Rutgers (football only), Syracuse, Temple (football only), Virginia Tech (football only) and West Va. (football only). **Current members** (8): Boston College, Miami (Fla.), Pittsburgh, Rutgers, Syracuse, Temple, Virginia Tech and West Va. **Note:** In 1991 and 1992, the team ranked highest in the USA Today/CNN coaches poll was declared champion. Beginning in 1993, the champion was decided by a seven-game round-robin schedule.

Year	Champion (Record)
1991	Miami (Fla.) (2-0, No. 1) & Syracuse (5-0, No. 16)
1992	Miami (Fla.) (4-0, No. 1)
1993	West Va. (7-0)
1994	Miami (Fla.) (7-0)
1995	Virginia Tech (6-1) & Miami (Fla.) (6-1)
1996	Virginia Tech (6-1), Miami (Fla.) (6-1) & Syracuse (6-1)
1997	Syracuse (6-1)

BIG TEN CONFERENCE

Founded: In 1895 as the Intercollegiate Conference of Faculty Representatives, better known as the Western Conference. **Charter members** (7): Chicago, Illinois, Michigan, Minnesota, Northwestern, Purdue and Wisconsin. **Admitted later** (5): Indiana (1899), Iowa (1899), Ohio St. (1912), Michigan St. (1950) and Penn St. (1993). **Withdrew later** (2): Michigan (1907, rejoined in 1917) and Chicago (1940). **Note:** Iowa belonged to both the Missouri Valley and Western Conferences from 1907 to 1910. Unofficially called the Big Ten from 1912 until after 1939, then Big Nine from 1940 until Michigan St. began conference play in 1953. Formally renamed **Big Ten** in 1984. **Current members** (11): Illinois, Indiana, Iowa, Michigan, Michigan St., Minnesota, Northwestern, Ohio St., Penn St., Purdue and Wisconsin.

Year	Champion (Record)
1896	Wisconsin (2-0-1)
1897	Wisconsin (3-0)
1898	Michigan (3-0)
1899	Chicago (4-0)
1900	Iowa (3-0-1) & Minnesota (3-0-1)
1901	Michigan (4-0) & Wisconsin (2-0)
1902	Michigan (5-0)
1903	Michigan (3-0-1), Minnesota (3-0-1) & Northwestern (1-0-2)
1904	Minnesota (3-0) & Michigan (2-0)
1905	Chicago (7-0)
1906	Wisconsin (3-0), Minnesota (2-0) & Michigan (1-0)
1907	Chicago (4-0)
1908	Chicago (5-0)
1909	Minnesota (3-0)
1910	Illinois (4-0) & Minnesota (2-0)
1911	Minnesota (3-0-1)
1912	Wisconsin (6-0)
1913	Chicago (7-0)
1914	Illinois (6-0)
1915	Minnesota (3-0-1) & Illinois (3-0-2)
1916	Ohio St. (4-0)
1917	Ohio St. (4-0)
1918	Illinois (4-0), Michigan (2-0) & Purdue (1-0)
1919	Illinois (6-1)
1920	Ohio St. (5-0)
1921	Iowa (5-0)
1922	Iowa (5-0) & Michigan (4-0)
1923	Illinois (5-0) & Michigan (4-0)
1924	Chicago (3-0-3)
1925	Michigan (5-1)
1926	Michigan (5-0) & Northwestern (5-0)
1927	Illinois (5-0)
1928	Illinois (4-1)
1929	Purdue (5-0)
1930	Michigan (5-0) & Northwestern (5-0)
1931	Purdue (5-1), Michigan (5-1) & Northwestern (5-1)
1932	Michigan (6-0)
1933	Michigan (5-0-1)
1934	Minnesota (5-0)
1935	Minnesota (5-0) & Ohio St. (5-0)
1936	Northwestern (6-0)
1937	Minnesota (5-0)
1938	Minnesota (4-1)
1939	Ohio St. (5-1)
1940	Minnesota (6-0)
1941	Minnesota (5-0)
1942	Ohio St. (5-1)
1943	Purdue (6-0) & Michigan (6-0)
1944	Ohio St. (6-0)
1945	Indiana (5-0-1)
1946	Illinois (6-1)
1947	Michigan (6-0)
1948	Michigan (6-0)
1949	Ohio St. (4-1-1) & Michigan (4-1-1)
1950	Michigan (4-1-1)
1951	Illinois (5-0-1)
1952	Wisconsin (4-1-1) & Purdue (4-1-1)
1953	Michigan St. (5-1) & Illinois (5-1)
1954	Ohio St. (7-0)
1955	Ohio St. (6-0)
1956	Iowa (5-1)
1957	Ohio St. (7-0)
1958	Iowa (5-1)
1959	Wisconsin (5-2)
1960	Minnesota (5-1) & Iowa (5-1)
1961	Ohio St. (6-0)
1962	Wisconsin (6-1)
1963	Illinois (5-1-1)
1964	Michigan (6-1)
1965	Michigan St. (7-0)
1966	Michigan St. (7-0)
1967	Indiana (6-1), Purdue (6-1) & Minnesota (6-1)
1968	Ohio St. (7-0)
1969	Ohio St. (6-1) & Michigan (6-1)
1970	Ohio St. (7-0)
1971	Michigan (8-0)
1972	Ohio St. (8-0) & Michigan (7-1)
1973	Ohio St. (7-0-1) & Michigan (7-0-1)
1974	Ohio St. (7-1) & Michigan (7-1)
1975	Ohio St. (8-0)
1976	Michigan (7-1) & Ohio St. (7-1)
1977	Michigan (7-1) & Ohio St. (7-1)
1978	Michigan (7-1) & Michigan St. (7-1)
1979	Ohio St. (8-0)
1980	Michigan (8-0)
1981	Iowa (6-2) & Ohio St. (6-2)
1982	Michigan (8-1)
1983	Illinois (9-0)
1984	Ohio St. (7-2)
1985	Iowa (7-1)
1986	Michigan (7-1) & Ohio St. (7-1)
1987	Michigan St. (7-0-1)
1988	Michigan (7-0-1)
1989	Michigan (8-0)
1990	Iowa (6-2), Michigan (6-2), Michigan St. (6-2) & Illinois (6-2)
1991	Michigan (8-0)
1992	Michigan (6-0-2)
1993	Ohio St. (6-1-1) & Wisconsin (6-1-1)
1994	Penn St. (8-0)
1995	Northwestern (8-0)
1996	Ohio St. (7-1) & Northwestern (7-1)
1997	Michigan (8-0)

BIG 12 CONFERENCE

Founded: In 1996 when 12 charter members combined eight members of Big Eight Conference with four former Southwest Conference members. **Charter members** (12): Baylor, Colorado, Iowa St., Kansas, Kansas St., Missouri, Nebraska, Oklahoma, Oklahoma St., Texas, Texas A&M and Texas Tech. **Current members** (12): Baylor, Colorado, Iowa St., Kansas, Kansas St., Missouri, Nebraska, Oklahoma, Oklahoma St., Texas, Texas A&M and Texas Tech.

Year	Champion (Record)
1996	Texas (6-2)
1997	Nebraska (8-0)

In 1996, the Big 12 conducted a championship game to determine the league's representative in the alliance bowls. Following are the results of the North Division Champion (N) vs. the South Division Champion (S):

1996	Texas (S) 37, Nebraska (N) 27
1997	Nebraska (N) 54, Texas A&M (S) 15

BIG WEST CONFERENCE

Founded: In 1969 as the Pacific Coast Athletic Association (PCAA). **Charter members** (7): UC Santa Barb., Cal St. Los Angeles, Fresno St., Long Beach St., Pacific (Cal.), San Diego St. and San Jose St. **Admitted later** (12): Cal St. Fullerton (1974), Utah St. (1977), UNLV (1982), New Mexico St. (1983), Nevada (1992), Arkansas St. (1993), Louisiana Tech (1993), Northern Ill. (1993), Southwestern La. (1993), Boise St. (1996), Idaho (1996), North Texas (1996) and Arkansas St. (1998). **Withdrew later** (13): UC Santa Barb. (1972), Cal St. Los Angeles (1974), San Diego St. (1976), Fresno St. (1991), Long Beach St. (1991, dropped football), Cal St. Fullerton (1992, dropped football), Arkansas St. (1996), Louisiana Tech (1996), UNLV (1996), Northern Ill. (1996), Pacific (Cal.) (1996, dropped football), San Jose St. (1996) and Southwestern La. (1996). Renamed **Big West** in 1988. **Current members** (7): Arkansas St., Boise St., Idaho, Nevada, New Mexico St., North Texas and Utah St.

Year	Champion (Record)
1969	San Diego St. (6-0)
1970	Long Beach St. (5-1) & San Diego St. (5-1)
1971	Long Beach St. (5-1)

Year	Champion (Record)
1972	San Diego St. (4-0)
1973	San Diego St. (3-0-1)
1974	San Diego St. (4-0)
1975	San Jose St. (5-0)
1976	San Jose St. (4-0)
1977	Fresno St. (4-0)
1978	San Jose St. (4-1) & Utah St. (4-1)
1979	Utah St. (5-0)
1980	Long Beach St. (5-0)
1981	San Jose St. (5-0)
1982	Fresno St. (6-0)
1983	Cal St. Fullerton (5-1)
1984	Cal St. Fullerton (6-1)#
1985	Fresno St. (7-0)
1986	San Jose St. (7-0)
1987	San Jose St. (7-0)
1988	Fresno St. (7-0)
1989	Fresno St. (7-0)
1990	San Jose St. (7-0)
1991	Fresno St. (6-1) & San Jose St. (6-1)
1992	Nevada (5-1)
1993	Southwestern La. (5-1) & Utah St. (5-1)
1994	Nevada (5-1), Southwestern La. (5-1) & UNLV (5-1)
1995	Nevada (6-0)
1996	Nevada (4-1) & Utah St. (4-1)*
1997	Utah St. (4-1) & Nevada (4-1)

*#UNLV forfeited title. *Nevada defeated Utah St., 54-27, on Nov. 9.*

CONFERENCE USA

Founded: In 1996 when five charter members went from independent status and one former Southwest Conference member combined to form Conference USA. **Charter members** (6): Cincinnati, Houston, Louisville, Memphis, Southern Miss. and Tulane. **Admitted later** (2): East Caro. (1997) and Army (1998). **Current members** (8): Army, Cincinnati, East Caro., Houston, Louisville, Memphis, Southern Miss. and Tulane.

Year	Champion (Record)
1996	Houston (4-1) & Southern Miss. (4-1)*
1997	Southern Miss. (6-0)

**Houston defeated Southern Miss., 56-49, on Nov. 9.*

MID-AMERICAN ATHLETIC CONFERENCE

Founded: In 1946. **Charter members** (6): Butler, Cincinnati, Miami (Ohio), Ohio, Western Mich. and Western Reserve (now Case Reserve). **Admitted later** (11): Kent St. (now Kent) (1951), Toledo (1951), Bowling Green (1952), Marshall (1954 and 1997), Central Mich. (1972), Eastern Mich. (1972), Ball St. (1973), Northern Ill. (1973 and 1997) and Akron (1992). **Withdrew later** (5): Butler (1950), Cincinnati (1953), Case Reserve (1955), Marshall (1969) and Northern Ill. (1986). **Current members** (12): Akron, Ball St., Bowling Green, Central Mich., Eastern Mich., Kent, Marshall, Miami (Ohio), Northern Ill., Ohio, Toledo and Western Mich.

Year	Champion (Record)
1947	Cincinnati (3-1)
1948	Miami (Ohio) (4-0)
1949	Cincinnati (4-0)
1950	Miami (Ohio) (4-0)
1951	Cincinnati (3-0)
1952	Cincinnati (3-0)
1953	Ohio (5-0-1)
1954	Miami (Ohio) (4-0)
1955	Miami (Ohio) (5-0)
1956	Bowling Green (5-0-1)
1957	Miami (Ohio) (5-0)
1958	Miami (Ohio) (5-0)
1959	Bowling Green (6-0)
1960	Ohio (6-0)
1961	Bowling Green (5-1)
1962	Bowling Green (5-0-1)
1963	Ohio (5-1)
1964	Bowling Green (5-1)
1965	Bowling Green (5-1) & Miami (Ohio) (5-1)
1966	Miami (Ohio) (5-1) & Western Mich. (5-1)
1967	Toledo (5-1) & Ohio (5-1)
1968	Ohio (6-0)
1969	Toledo (5-0)
1970	Toledo (5-0)
1971	Toledo (5-0)
1972	Kent (4-1)
1973	Miami (Ohio) (5-0)
1974	Miami (Ohio) (5-0)
1975	Miami (Ohio) (6-0)
1976	Ball St. (4-1)
1977	Miami (Ohio) (5-0)
1978	Ball St. (8-0)
1979	Central Mich. (8-0-1)
1980	Central Mich. (7-2)
1981	Toledo (8-1)
1982	Bowling Green (7-2)
1983	Northern Ill. (8-1)
1984	Toledo (7-1-1)
1985	Bowling Green (9-0)
1986	Miami (Ohio) (6-2)
1987	Eastern Mich. (7-1)
1988	Western Mich. (7-1)
1989	Ball St. (6-1-1)
1990	Central Mich. (7-1)
1991	Bowling Green (8-0)
1992	Bowling Green (8-0)
1993	Ball St. (7-0-1)
1994	Central Mich. (8-1)
1995	Toledo (7-0-1)
1996	Ball St. (7-1)
1997	Marshall (7-1) & Toledo (7-1)

Since 1997, the MAC has conducted a championship game between the East and West division champion to determine a league champion. Following are the results of the East Division champion (E) vs. the West Division champion (W):

1997 Marshall (E) 34, Toledo (W) 14

PACIFIC-10 CONFERENCE

Founded: In 1915 as the **Pacific Coast Conference** by group of four charter members. **Charter members** (4): California, Oregon, Oregon St. and Washington. **Admitted later** (6): Washington St. (1917), Stanford (1918), Idaho (1922), Southern Cal (1922), Montana (1924) and UCLA (1928). **Withdrew later** (2): Montana (1950) and Idaho (1958).

The Pacific Coast Conference dissolved in 1959 and the Athletic Association of Western Universities was founded with five charter members. **Charter members** (5): California, Southern Cal, Stanford, UCLA and Washington. **Admitted later** (5): Washington St. (1962), Oregon (1964), Oregon St. (1964), Arizona (1978) and Arizona St. (1978). Conference renamed **Pacific-8** in 1968 and **Pacific-10** in 1978. **Current members** (10): Arizona, Arizona St., California, Oregon, Oregon St., Southern Cal, Stanford, UCLA, Washington and Washington St.

Year	Champion (Record)
1916	Washington (3-0-1)
1917	Washington (3-0)
1918	California (3-0)
1919	Oregon (2-1) & Washington (2-1)
1920	California (3-0)
1921	California (5-0)
1922	California (3-0)
1923	California (5-0)
1924	Stanford (3-0-1)
1925	Washington (5-0)
1926	Stanford (4-0)
1927	Southern Cal (4-0-1) & Stanford (4-0-1)
1928	Southern Cal (4-0-1)
1929	Southern Cal (6-1)
1930	Washington St. (6-0)
1931	Southern Cal (7-0)
1932	Southern Cal (6-0)
1933	Oregon (4-1) & Stanford (4-1)
1934	Stanford (5-0)
1935	California (4-1), Stanford (4-1) & UCLA (4-1)
1936	Washington (6-0-1)
1937	California (6-0-1)
1938	Southern Cal (6-1) & California (6-1)
1939	Southern Cal (5-0-2) & UCLA (5-0-3)
1940	Stanford (7-0)
1941	Oregon St. (7-2)
1942	UCLA (6-1)
1943	Southern Cal (4-0)
1944	Southern Cal (3-0-2)
1945	Southern Cal (6-0)
1946	UCLA (7-0)
1947	Southern Cal (6-0)
1948	California (6-0) & Oregon (6-0)
1949	California (7-0)
1950	California (5-0-1)
1951	Stanford (6-1)
1952	Southern Cal (6-0)
1953	UCLA (6-1)
1954	UCLA (6-0)
1955	UCLA (6-0)
1956	Oregon St. (6-1-1)
1957	Oregon (6-2) & Oregon St. (6-2)
1958	California (6-1)
1959	Washington (3-1), Southern Cal (3-1) & UCLA (3-1)
1960	Washington (4-0)
1961	UCLA (3-1)
1962	Southern Cal (4-0)
1963	Washington (4-1)
1964	Oregon St. (3-1) & Southern Cal (3-1)
1965	UCLA (4-0)
1966	Southern Cal (4-1)
1967	Southern Cal (6-1)
1968	Southern Cal (6-0)
1969	Southern Cal (6-0)
1970	Stanford (6-1)
1971	Stanford (6-1)
1972	Southern Cal (7-0)
1973	Southern Cal (7-0)
1974	Southern Cal (6-0-1)
1975	UCLA (6-1) & California (6-1)
1976	Southern Cal (7-0)
1977	Washington (6-1)
1978	Southern Cal (6-1)
1979	Southern Cal (6-0-1)
1980	Washington (6-1)
1981	Washington (6-2)
1982	UCLA (5-1-1)
1983	UCLA (6-1-1)
1984	Southern Cal (7-1)
1985	UCLA (6-2)
1986	Arizona St. (5-1-1)
1987	Southern Cal (7-1) & UCLA (7-1)
1988	Southern Cal (8-0)
1989	Southern Cal (6-0-1)
1990	Washington (7-1)
1991	Washington (8-0)
1992	Stanford (6-2) & Washington (6-2)
1993	UCLA (6-2), Arizona (6-2) & Southern Cal (6-2)
1994	Oregon (7-1)
1995	Southern Cal (6-1-1) & Washington (6-1-1)*
1996	Arizona St. (8-0)
1997	Washington St. (7-1) & UCLA (7-1)

**Southern Cal tied Washington, 21-21, on October 28.*

SOUTHEASTERN CONFERENCE

Founded: In 1933 when charter members all left the **Southern Conference** to become the SEC. **Charter members** (13): Alabama, Auburn, Florida, Georgia, Georgia Tech, Kentucky, LSU, Mississippi, Mississippi St., Sewanee, Tennessee, Tulane and Vanderbilt. **Admitted later** (2): Arkansas (1992) and South Caro. (1992). **Withdrew later** (3): Sewanee (1940), Georgia Tech (1964) and Tulane (1966). **Current members** (12): Alabama, Arkansas, Auburn, Florida, Georgia, Kentucky, LSU, Mississippi, Mississippi St., South Caro., Tennessee and Vanderbilt.

Year	Champion (Record)
1933	Alabama (5-0-1)
1934	Tulane (8-0) & Alabama (7-0)
1935	LSU (5-0)
1936	LSU (6-0)
1937	Alabama (6-0)
1938	Tennessee (7-0)
1939	Tennessee (6-0), Georgia Tech (6-0) & Tulane (5-0)
1940	Tennessee (5-0)
1941	Mississippi St. (4-0-1)
1942	Georgia (6-1)
1943	Georgia Tech (4-0)
1944	Georgia Tech (4-0)
1945	Alabama (6-0)
1946	Georgia (5-0) & Tennessee (5-0)
1947	Mississippi (6-1)
1948	Georgia (6-0)
1949	Tulane (5-1)
1950	Kentucky (5-1)
1951	Georgia Tech (7-0) & Tennessee (5-0)
1952	Georgia (6-0)
1953	Alabama (4-0-3)
1954	Mississippi (5-1)
1955	Mississippi (5-1)
1956	Tennessee (6-0)
1957	Auburn (7-0)
1958	LSU (6-0)
1959	Georgia (7-0)
1960	Mississippi (5-0-1)
1961	Alabama (7-0) & LSU (6-0)
1962	Mississippi (6-0)
1963	Mississippi (5-0-1)
1964	Alabama (8-0)

Year	Champion (Record)
1965	Alabama (6-1-1)
1966	Alabama (6-0) & Georgia (6-0)
1967	Tennessee (6-0)
1968	Georgia (5-0-1)
1969	Tennessee (5-1)
1970	LSU (5-0)
1971	Alabama (7-0)
1972	Alabama (7-1)
1973	Alabama (8-0)
1974	Alabama (6-0)
1975	Alabama (6-0)
1976	Georgia (5-1) & Kentucky (5-1)
1977	Alabama (7-0) & Kentucky (6-0)
1978	Alabama (6-0)
1979	Alabama (6-0)
1980	Georgia (6-0)
1981	Georgia (6-0) & Alabama (6-0)
1982	Georgia (6-0)
1983	Auburn (6-0)
1984	Florida (5-0-1)#
1985	Tennessee (5-1)*
1986	LSU (5-1)
1987	Auburn (5-0-1)
1988	Auburn (6-1) & LSU (6-1)
1989	Alabama (6-1), Tennessee (6-1) & Auburn (6-1)
1990	Tennessee (5-1-1)*
1991	Florida (7-0)
1992	Alabama (8-0)
1993	Florida (7-1)*
1994	Florida (7-1)
1995	Florida (8-0)
1996	Florida (8-0)
1997	Tennessee (7-1)

*#Title vacated. *Ineligible for title (probation): Florida (5-1) in 1985, Florida (6-1) in 1990 and Auburn (8-0) in 1993.*

Since 1992, the SEC has conducted a championship game to determine the league's representative in the alliance bowls. Following are the results year-by-year of the Western Division champion (W) vs. the Eastern Division champion (E):

1992	Alabama (W) 28, Florida (E) 21
1993	Florida (E) 28, Alabama (W) 13
1994	Florida (E) 24, Alabama (W) 23
1995	Florida (E) 34, Arkansas (W) 3
1996	Florida (E) 45, Alabama (W) 30
1997	Tennessee (E) 30, Auburn (W) 29

WESTERN ATHLETIC CONFERENCE

Founded: In 1962 when charter members left the Skyline and Border Conferences to form the WAC. In 1996, three former Southwest Conference members joined two former Big West members and one former independent team to form a 16-team league, the largest conference alignment ever in Division I-A. The league will be divided into Mountain and Pacific divisions. **Charter members** (6): Arizona (from Border), Arizona St. (from Border), Brigham Young (from Skyline), New Mexico (from Skyline), Utah (from Skyline) and Wyoming (from Skyline). **Admitted later** (12): Colorado St. (1968), UTEP (1968), San Diego St. (1978), Hawaii (1979), Air Force (1980), Fresno St. (1992), UNLV (1996), Rice (1996), San Jose St. (1996), Southern Methodist (1996), Texas Christian (1996) and Tulsa (1996). **Withdrew later** (2): Arizona (1978) and Arizona St. (1978). **Current members** (16): Air Force, Brigham Young, Colorado St., Fresno St., Hawaii, UNLV, New Mexico, Rice, San Diego St., San Jose St., Southern Methodist, UTEP, Texas Christian, Tulsa, Utah and Wyoming.

Year	Champion (Record)
1962	New Mexico (2-1-1)
1963	New Mexico (3-1)
1964	Arizona (3-1), Utah (3-1) & New Mexico (3-1)
1965	Brigham Young (4-1)
1966	Wyoming (5-0)
1967	Wyoming (5-0)
1968	Wyoming (6-1)
1969	Arizona St. (6-1)
1970	Arizona St. (7-0)
1971	Arizona St. (7-0)
1972	Arizona St. (5-1)
1973	Arizona (6-1) & Arizona St. (6-1)
1974	Brigham Young (6-0-1)
1975	Arizona St. (7-0)
1976	Brigham Young (6-1) & Wyoming (6-1)
1977	Arizona St. (6-1) & Brigham Young (6-1)
1978	Brigham Young (5-1)
1979	Brigham Young (7-0)
1980	Brigham Young (6-1)
1981	Brigham Young (7-1)
1982	Brigham Young (7-1)
1983	Brigham Young (7-0)
1984	Brigham Young (8-0)
1985	Air Force (7-1) & Brigham Young (7-1)
1986	San Diego St. (7-1)
1987	Wyoming (8-0)
1988	Wyoming (8-0)
1989	Brigham Young (7-1)
1990	Brigham Young (7-1)
1991	Brigham Young (7-0-1)
1992	Hawaii (6-2), Fresno St. (6-2) & Brigham Young (6-2)
1993	Wyoming (6-2), Fresno St. (6-2) & Brigham Young (6-2)
1994	Colorado St. (7-1)
1995	Colorado St. (6-2), Air Force (6-2), Utah (6-2) & Brigham Young (6-2)
1996	Brigham Young (8-0)
1997	Colorado St. (7-1)

In 1996, the WAC conducted a championship game to determine the league's representative in the alliance bowls. Following are the results of the Mountain Division Champion (M) vs. the Pacific Division Champion (P):

1996	Brigham Young (M) 28, Wyoming (P) 25
1997	Colorado St. (P) 41, New Mexico (M) 13

Division I-AA

ATLANTIC 10 FOOTBALL CONFERENCE

Founded: In 1947 as the Yankee Conference by six institutions from the old New England College Conference. **Charter members** (6): Connecticut, Maine, Massachusetts, New Hampshire, Rhode Island and Vermont. **Admitted later** (8): Boston U. (1971), Holy Cross (1971), Delaware (1983), Richmond (1984), Villanova (1985), James Madison (1993), Northeastern (1993) and William & Mary (1993). **Withdrew later** (3): Holy Cross (1972), Vermont (1974, dropped football) and Boston U. (1997, dropped football). **Current members** (11): Connecticut, Delaware, James Madison, Maine, Massachusetts, New Hampshire, Northeastern, Rhode Island, Richmond, Villanova and William & Mary. **Note:** The league officially changed its name to Atlantic 10 Football Conference in 1997 and is divided into the New England and Mid-Atlantic Divisions.

Year	Champion (Record)
1947	New Hampshire (4-0)
1948	New Hampshire (3-1)
1949	Connecticut (2-0-1) & Maine (2-0-1)
1950	New Hampshire (4-0)
1951	Maine (3-0-1)
1952	Connecticut (3-1), Maine (3-1) & Rhode Island (3-1)
1953	New Hampshire (3-1) & Rhode Island (3-1)
1954	New Hampshire (4-0)
1955	Rhode Island (4-0-1)
1956	Connecticut (3-0-1)
1957	Connecticut (3-0-1) & Rhode Island (3-0-1)
1958	Connecticut (4-0)
1959	Connecticut (4-0)
1960	Connecticut (3-1)
1961	Maine (5-0)
1962	New Hampshire (4-0-1)
1963	Massachusetts (5-0)
1964	Massachusetts (5-0)
1965	Maine (5-0)
1966	Massachusetts (5-0)
1967	Massachusetts (5-0)
1968	Connecticut (4-1) & New Hampshire (4-1)
1969	Massachusetts (5-0)
1970	Connecticut (4-0-1)
1971	Connecticut (3-1-1) & Massachusetts (3-1-1)
1972	Massachusetts (5-0)
1973	Connecticut (5-0-1)
1974	Maine (4-2) & Massachusetts (4-2)
1975	New Hampshire (5-0)
1976	New Hampshire (4-1)
1977	Massachusetts (5-0)
1978	Massachusetts (5-0)*
1979	Massachusetts (4-1)
1980	Boston U. (5-0)
1981	Rhode Island (4-1) & Massachusetts (4-1)
1982	Boston U. (3-2)*, Connecticut (3-2), Maine (3-2) and Massachusetts (3-2)
1983	Boston U. (4-1)* & Connecticut (4-1)
1984	Boston U. (4-1)* & Rhode Island (4-1)*
1985	Rhode Island (5-0)*
1986	Connecticut (5-2), Delaware (5-2)* & Massachusetts (5-2)
1987	Maine (6-1)* & Richmond (6-1)*
1988	Delaware (6-2)* & Massachusetts (6-2)*
1989	Connecticut (6-2), Maine (6-2)* & Villanova (6-2)*
1990	Massachusetts (7-1)*
1991	Delaware (7-1)* & Villanova (7-1)*
1992	Delaware (7-1)*
1993	Boston U. (9-0)*
1994	New Hampshire (8-0)*
1995	Delaware (8-0)*
1996	William & Mary (7-1)*
1997	Villanova (8-0)*

**Participated in NCAA Division I-AA Championship.*

BIG SKY CONFERENCE

Founded: In 1963 when six charter members—Gonzaga, Idaho, Idaho St., Montana, Montana St. and Weber St.—banded together to form the Big Sky. **Admitted later** (7): Boise St. (1970), Northern Ariz. (1970), Nevada (1979, replacing charter member Gonzaga), Eastern Wash. (1987), Cal St. Northridge (1996), Cal St. Sacramento (1996) and Portland St. (1996). **Withdrew later** (4): Gonzaga (1979), Nevada (1992), Boise St. (1996) and Idaho (1996). **Current members** (9): Cal St. Northridge, Cal St. Sacramento, Eastern Wash., Idaho St., Montana, Montana St., Northern Ariz., Portland St. and Weber St.

Year	Champion (Record)
1963	Idaho St. (3-1)
1964	Montana St. (3-0)
1965	Weber St. (3-1) & Idaho (3-1)
1966	Montana St. (4-0)
1967	Montana St. (4-0)
1968	Weber St. (3-1), Montana St. (3-1) & Idaho (3-1)
1969	Montana (4-0)#
1970	Montana (5-0)
1971	Idaho (4-1)
1972	Montana St. (5-1)
1973	Boise St. (6-0)#
1974	Boise St. (6-0)#
1975	Boise St. (5-0-1)#
1976	Montana St. (6-0)#
1977	Boise St. (6-0)
1978	Northern Ariz. (6-0)
1979	Montana St. (6-1)
1980	Boise St. (6-1)
1981	Idaho St. (6-1)*
1982	Montana (5-2)*
1983	Nevada (6-1)*
1984	Montana St. (6-1)*
1985	Idaho (6-1)*
1986	Nevada (7-0)*
1987	Idaho (7-1)*
1988	Idaho (7-1)*
1989	Idaho (8-0)*
1990	Nevada (7-1)*
1991	Nevada (8-0)*
1992	Idaho (6-1)* & Eastern Wash. (6-1)*
1993	Montana (7-0)*
1994	Boise St. (6-1)*
1995	Montana (6-1)*
1996	Montana (7-0)*
1997	Eastern Wash. (7-1)*

#Participated in NCAA Division II Championship.
**Participated in NCAA Division I-AA Championship.*

GATEWAY FOOTBALL CONFERENCE

Founded: In 1982 as a women's athletics organization by 10 Midwestern universities. Six members started as a football conference in 1985. **Charter members** (6): (Football) Eastern Ill., Illinois St., Northern Iowa, Southern Ill., Southwest Mo. St. and Western Ill. Four members—Eastern Ill., Northern Iowa, Southwest Mo. St. and Western Ill.—were members of the Mid-Continent Conference for football. **Admitted later** (2): Indiana St. (1986) and Youngstown St. (1997). **Withdrew later** (1): Eastern Ill. (1996). **Current members** (7): Illinois St., Indiana St., Northern Iowa, Southern Ill., Southwest Mo. St., Western Ill. and Youngstown St.

Year	Champion (Record)
1985	Northern Iowa (5-0)*
1986	Eastern Ill. (5-1)*
1987	Northern Iowa (6-0)*
1988	Western Ill. (6-0)*

Year Champion (Record)
1989 Southwest Mo. St. (5-1)*
1990 Northern Iowa (5-1)*
1991 Northern Iowa (5-1)*
1992 Northern Iowa (5-1)*
1993 Northern Iowa (5-1)*
1994 Northern Iowa (6-0)*
1995 Northern Iowa (5-1)* & Eastern Ill. (5-1)*#
1996 Northern Iowa (5-0)*
1997 Western Ill. (6-0)*

**Participated in NCAA Division I-AA Championship.*
#Northern Iowa defeated Eastern Ill., 17-7, on October 7.

IVY GROUP

Founded: In 1956 by a group of eight charter members. **Charter members** (8): Brown, Columbia, Cornell, Dartmouth, Harvard, Pennsylvania, Princeton and Yale. **Current members** (8): Brown, Columbia, Cornell, Dartmouth, Harvard, Pennsylvania, Princeton and Yale.

Year Champion (Record)
1956 Yale (7-2)
1957 Princeton (6-1)
1958 Dartmouth (6-1)
1959 Pennsylvania (6-1)
1960 Yale (7-0)
1961 Columbia (6-1) & Harvard (6-1)
1962 Dartmouth (7-0)
1963 Dartmouth (5-2) & Princeton (5-2)
1964 Princeton (7-0)
1965 Dartmouth (7-0)
1966 Dartmouth (6-1), Harvard (6-1) & Princeton (6-1)
1967 Yale (7-0)
1968 Harvard (6-0-1) & Yale (6-0-1)
1969 Dartmouth (6-1), Yale (6-1) & Princeton (6-1)
1970 Dartmouth (7-0)
1971 Cornell (6-1) & Dartmouth (6-1)
1972 Dartmouth (5-1-1)
1973 Dartmouth (6-1)
1974 Harvard (6-1) & Yale (6-1)
1975 Harvard (6-1)
1976 Brown (6-1) & Yale (6-1)
1977 Yale (6-1)
1978 Dartmouth (6-1)
1979 Yale (6-1)
1980 Yale (6-1)
1981 Yale (6-1) & Dartmouth (6-1)
1982 Harvard (5-2), Pennsylvania (5-2) & Dartmouth (5-2)
1983 Harvard (5-1-1) & Pennsylvania (5-1-1)
1984 Pennsylvania (7-0)
1985 Pennsylvania (6-1)
1986 Pennsylvania (7-0)
1987 Harvard (6-1)
1988 Pennsylvania (6-1) & Cornell (6-1)
1989 Princeton (6-1) & Yale (6-1)
1990 Cornell (6-1) & Dartmouth (6-1)
1991 Dartmouth (6-0-1)
1992 Dartmouth (6-1) & Princeton (6-1)
1993 Pennsylvania (7-0)
1994 Pennsylvania (7-0)
1995 Princeton (5-1-1)
1996 Dartmouth (7-0)
1997 Harvard (7-0)

METRO ATLANTIC ATHLETIC CONFERENCE

Founded: Began in Division I-AA in 1993 with Canisius, Georgetown, Iona, St. John's (N.Y.), St. Peter's and Siena as charter members. **Admitted later** (3): Duquesne (1994), Marist (1994) and Fairfield (1996). **Withdrew later** (0): None. **Current members** (9): Canisius, Duquesne, Fairfield, Georgetown, Iona, Marist, St. John's (N.Y.), St. Peter's and Siena.

Year Champion (Record)
1993 Iona (5-0)
1994 Marist (6-1) & St. John's (N.Y.) (6-1)
1995 Duquesne (7-0)
1996 Duquesne (8-0)
1997 Georgetown (7-0)

MID-EASTERN ATHLETIC CONFERENCE

Founded: In 1970 with first playing season in 1971 by six charter members. **Charter members** (6): Delaware St., Howard, Morgan St., North Caro. A&T, N.C. Central and South Caro. St. **Admitted later** (3): Bethune-Cookman (1979), Florida A&M (1979), Hampton (1996) and Norfolk St. (1997). **Withdrew later** (3): Morgan St. (1979), N.C. Central (1979) and Florida A&M (1984). **Readmitted** (2): Morgan St. (1984) and Florida A&M (1986). **Current members** (9): Bethune-Cookman, Delaware St., Florida A&M, Hampton, Howard, Morgan St., Norfolk St., North Caro. A&T and South Caro. St.

Year Champion (Record)
1971 Morgan St. (5-0-1)
1972 N.C. Central (5-1)
1973 N.C. Central (5-1)
1974 South Caro. St. (5-1)
1975 South Caro. St. (5-1)
1976 South Caro. St. (5-1)
1977 South Caro. St. (6-0)
1978 South Caro. St. (5-0-1)
1979 Morgan St. (5-0)#
1980 South Caro. St. (5-0)
1981 South Caro. St. (5-0)*
1982 South Caro. St. (4-1)*
1983 South Caro. St. (4-0)
1984 Bethune-Cookman (4-0)
1985 Delaware St. (4-0)
1986 North Caro. A&T (4-1)*
1987 Howard (5-0)
1988 Bethune-Cookman (4-2), Florida A&M (4-2) & Delaware St. (4-2)
1989 Delaware St. (5-1)
1990 Florida A&M (6-0)
1991 North Caro. A&T (5-1)√
1992 North Caro. A&T (5-1)*
1993 Howard (6-0)*
1994 South Caro. St. (6-0)√
1995 Florida A&M (6-0)√
1996 Florida A&M (7-0)*
1997 Hampton (7-0)*

#Participated in NCAA Division II Championship.
**Participated in NCAA Division I-AA Championship.*
√Participated in Division I-AA Heritage Bowl.

NORTHEAST CONFERENCE

Founded: In 1996 when five charter members all went from independent status to form the Northeast Conference. **Charter members** (5): Central Conn. St., Monmouth, Robert Morris, St. Francis (Pa.) and Wagner. **Current members** (5): Central Conn. St., Monmouth, Robert Morris, St. Francis (Pa.) and Wagner.

Year Champion (Record)
1996 Robert Morris (3-1) & Monmouth (3-1)
1997 Robert Morris (4-0)

OHIO VALLEY CONFERENCE

Founded: In 1948 by six charter members, five of which withdrew from the Kentucky Intercollegiate Athletic Conference (Eastern Ky., Louisville, Morehead St., Murray St. and Western Ky.), plus Evansville. **Charter members** (6): Eastern Ky., Evansville, Louisville, Morehead St., Murray St. and Western Ky. **Admitted later** (11): Marshall (1949), Tennessee Tech (1949), Middle Tenn. St. (1952), East Tenn. St. (1957), Austin Peay (1962), Akron (1979), Youngstown St. (1980), Tennessee St. (1988), Southeast Mo. St. (1991), Tenn.-Martin (1992) and Eastern Ill. (1996). **Withdrew later** (8): Louisville (1949), Evansville (1952), Marshall (1952), East Tenn. St. (1979), Western Ky. (1982), Akron (1987), Youngstown St. (1988), Morehead St. (1996) and Austin Peay (1997). **Current members** (8): Eastern Ill., Eastern Ky., Middle Tenn. St., Murray St., Southeast Mo. St., Tenn.-Martin, Tennessee St. and Tennessee Tech.

Team Champion (Record)
1948 Murray St. (3-1)
1949 Evansville (3-1)
1950 Murray St. (5-0-1)
1951 Murray St. (5-1)
1952 Tennessee St. (4-1) & Western Ky. (4-1)
1953 Tennessee Tech (5-0)
1954 Eastern Ky. (5-0)
1955 Tennessee Tech (5-0)
1956 Middle Tenn. St. (5-0)
1957 Middle Tenn. St. (5-0)
1958 Middle Tenn. St. (5-1) & Tennessee Tech (5-1)
1959 Middle Tenn. St. (5-0-1) & Tennessee Tech (5-0-1)
1960 Tennessee Tech (6-0)
1961 Tennessee Tech (6-0)
1962 East Tenn. St. (4-2)
1963 Western Ky. (7-0)
1964 Middle Tenn. St. (6-1)#
1965 Middle Tenn. St. (7-0)
1966 Morehead St. (6-1)
1967 Eastern Ky. (5-0-2)#
1968 Eastern Ky. (7-0)
1969 East Tenn. St. (6-0-1)#
1970 Western Ky. (5-1-1)
1971 Western Ky. (5-2)
1972 Tennessee Tech (7-0)#
1973 Western Ky. (7-0)#
1974 Eastern Ky. (6-1)
1975 Tennessee Tech (6-1) & Western Ky. (6-1)#
1976 Eastern Ky. (6-1)#
1977 Austin Peay (6-1)
1978 Western Ky. (6-0)
1979 Murray St. (6-0)*
1980 Western Ky. (6-1)
1981 Eastern Ky. (8-0)*
1982 Eastern Ky. (7-0)*
1983 Eastern Ky. (6-1)*
1984 Eastern Ky. (6-1)*
1985 Middle Tenn. St. (7-0)*
1986 Murray St. (5-2)
1987 Eastern Ky. (5-1)* & Youngstown St. (5-1)
1988 Eastern Ky. (6-0)*
1989 Middle Tenn. St. (6-0)*
1990 Middle Tenn. St. (5-1)* & Eastern Ky. (5-1)*
1991 Eastern Ky. (7-0)*
1992 Middle Tenn. St. (8-0)*
1993 Eastern Ky. (8-0)*
1994 Eastern Ky. (8-0)*
1995 Murray St. (8-0)*
1996 Murray St. (8-0)*
1997 Eastern Ky. (7-0)*

#Participated in NCAA Division II Championship.
**Participated in NCAA Division I-AA Championship.*

PATRIOT LEAGUE

Founded: In 1984 originally as the Colonial League with six charter members. **Charter members** (6): Bucknell, Colgate, Davidson, Holy Cross, Lafayette and Lehigh. **Admitted later** (2): Fordham (1990) and Towson (1997). **Withdrew later** (1): Davidson (1989). **Current members** (7): Bucknell, Colgate, Fordham, Holy Cross, Lafayette, Lehigh and Towson.

Year Champion (Record)
1986 Holy Cross (4-0)
1987 Holy Cross (4-0)
1988 Lafayette (5-0)
1989 Holy Cross (4-0)
1990 Holy Cross (5-0)
1991 Holy Cross (5-0)
1992 Lafayette (5-0)
1993 Lehigh (4-1)
1994 Lafayette (5-0)
1995 Lehigh (5-0)
1996 Bucknell (4-1)
1997 Colgate (6-0)*

**Participated in NCAA I-AA Championship.*

PIONEER FOOTBALL LEAGUE

Founded: Started in 1993 with Division I-AA charter members Butler, Dayton, Drake, Evansville, San Diego and Valparaiso. **Admitted later** (0): None. **Withdrew later** (0): None. **Current members** (6): Butler, Dayton, Drake, Evansville, San Diego and Valparaiso.

Year Champion (Record)
1993 Dayton (5-0)
1994 Dayton (4-1) & Butler (4-1)
1995 Drake (5-0)
1996 Dayton (5-0)
1997 Dayton (5-0)

SOUTHERN CONFERENCE

Founded: In 1921 by 14 institutions to form the Southern Intercollegiate Conference. Roots for the conference can actually be traced back to 1894 when several football-playing schools formed a confederation known as the Southeastern Intercollegiate Athletic Association. **Charter members** (14): Alabama, Auburn, Clemson, Georgia, Georgia Tech, Kentucky, Maryland, Mississippi St., North Caro., North Caro. St., Tennessee, Virginia, Virginia Tech and Wash. & Lee. **Admitted later** (17): Florida (1922), LSU (1922), Mississippi (1922), South Caro. (1922), Tulane (1922), Vanderbilt (1922), VMI (1924), Citadel (1936), Furman (1936), West Va. (1951), Appalachian St. (1971), Marshall (1976), Chattanooga (1976), Western Caro. (1976), East Tenn. St. (1978), Ga. Southern (1992) and Wofford (1997). **Withdrew**

later: Since 1922, membership has changed drastically, with a total of 39 schools having been affiliated with the league, including 11 of the 12 schools currently comprising the Southeastern Conference and eight of the nine schools currently comprising the Atlantic Coast Conference. **Current members** (9): Appalachian St., Chattanooga, Citadel, East Tenn. St., Furman, Ga. Southern, VMI, Western Caro. and Wofford.

Year	Champion (Record√)
1922	Georgia Tech
1923	Vanderbilt
1924	Alabama
1925	Alabama
1926	Alabama
1927	Georgia Tech
1928	Georgia Tech
1929	Tulane
1930	Alabama & Tulane
1931	Tulane
1932	Tennessee & Auburn
1933	Duke (4-0)
1934	Wash. & Lee (4-0)
1935	Duke (5-0)
1936	Duke (7-0)
1937	Maryland (2-0)
1938	Duke (5-0)
1939	Clemson (4-0)
1940	Clemson (4-0)
1941	Duke (5-0)
1942	William & Mary (4-0)
1943	Duke (4-0)
1944	Duke (4-0)
1945	Duke (4-0)
1946	North Caro. (4-0-1)
1947	William & Mary (7-1)
1948	Clemson (5-0)
1949	North Caro. (5-0)
1950	Wash. & Lee (6-0)
1951	Maryland (5-0) & VMI (5-0)
1952	Duke (5-0)
1953	West Va. (4-0)
1954	West Va. (3-0)
1955	West Va. (4-0)
1956	West Va. (5-0)
1957	VMI (6-0)
1958	West Va. (4-0)
1959	VMI (6-0-1)
1960	VMI (4-1)
1961	Citadel (5-1)
1962	VMI (6-0)
1963	Virginia Tech (5-0)
1964	West Va. (5-0)
1965	West Va. (4-0)
1966	East Caro. (4-1-1) & William & Mary (4-1-1)
1967	West Va. (4-0-1)
1968	Richmond (6-0)
1969	Davidson (5-1) & Richmond (5-1)
1970	William & Mary (3-1)
1971	Richmond (5-1)
1972	East Caro. (7-0)
1973	East Caro. (7-0)
1974	VMI (5-1)
1975	Richmond (5-1)
1976	East Caro. (4-1)
1977	Chattanooga (4-1) & VMI (4-1)
1978	Furman (4-1) & Chattanooga (4-1)
1979	Chattanooga (5-1)
1980	Furman (7-0)
1981	Furman (5-2)
1982	Furman (6-1)*
1983	Furman (6-0-1)*
1984	Chattanooga (5-1)*
1985	Furman (6-0)*
1986	Appalachian St. (6-0-1)*
1987	Appalachian St. (7-0)*
1988	Furman (6-1)* & Marshall (6-1)*
1989	Furman (7-0)*
1990	Furman (6-1)*
1991	Appalachian St. (6-1)*
1992	Citadel (6-1)*
1993	Ga. Southern (7-1)*
1994	Marshall (7-1)*
1995	Appalachian St. (8-0)*
1996	Marshall (8-0)*
1997	Ga. Southern (7-1)*

**Participated in NCAA Division I-AA Championship. √No records available until 1933.*

SOUTHLAND FOOTBALL LEAGUE

Founded: In 1963 by a group of five institutions. **Charter members** (5): Abilene Christian, Arkansas St., Lamar, Texas-Arlington and Trinity (Tex.). **Admitted later** (12): Louisiana Tech (1971), Southwestern La. (1971), McNeese St. (1972), North Texas (1982), Northeast La. (1982), Northwestern St. (1987), Sam Houston St. (1987), Southwest Tex. St. (1987), Stephen F. Austin (1987), Nicholls St. (1992), Jacksonville St. (1996) and Troy St. (1996). **Withdrew later** (9): Trinity (Tex.) (1972), Abilene Christian (1973), Southwestern La. (1982), Texas-Arlington (1986, dropped football), Arkansas St. (1987), Lamar (1987), Louisiana Tech (1987), North Texas (1995) and Northeast La. (1996). **Current members** (8): Jacksonville St., McNeese St., Nicholls St., Northwestern St., Sam Houston St., Southwest Tex. St., Stephen F. Austin and Troy St.

Year	Champion (Record)
1964	Lamar (3-0-1)
1965	Lamar (3-1)
1966	Texas-Arlington (3-1)
1967	Texas-Arlington (4-0)
1968	Arkansas St. (3-0-1)
1969	Arkansas St. (4-0)
1970	Arkansas St. (4-0)
1971	Louisiana Tech (4-1)
1972	Louisiana Tech (5-0)
1973	Louisiana Tech (5-0)
1974	Louisiana Tech (5-0)
1975	Arkansas St. (5-0)
1976	McNeese St. (4-1) & Southwestern La. (4-1)
1977	Louisiana Tech (4-0-1)
1978	Louisiana Tech (4-1)
1979	McNeese St. (5-0)
1980	McNeese St. (5-0)
1981	Texas-Arlington (4-1)
1982	Louisiana Tech (5-0)*
1983	North Texas (5-1)* & Northeast La. (5-1)
1984	Louisiana Tech (5-1)*
1985	Arkansas St. (5-1)*
1986	Arkansas St. (5-0)*
1987	Northeast La. (6-0)*
1988	Northwestern St. (6-0)*
1989	Stephen F. Austin (5-0-1)*
1990	Northeast La. (5-1)*
1991	McNeese St. (4-1-2)*
1992	Northeast La. (7-0)*
1993	McNeese St. (7-0)*
1994	North Texas (5-0-1)*
1995	McNeese St. (5-0)*
1996	Troy St. (5-1)*
1997	McNeese St. (6-1)* & Northwestern St. (6-1)*

**Participated in NCAA Division I-AA Championship.*

SOUTHWESTERN ATHLETIC CONFERENCE

Founded: In 1920 by a group of six institutions. **Charter members** (6): Bishop, Paul Quinn, Prairie View, Sam Houston College, Texas College and Wiley. **Admitted later** (10): Langston (1931), Southern U. (1934), Arkansas AM&N (1936), Texas Southern (1954), Grambling (1958), Jackson St. (1958), Alcorn St. (1962), Mississippi Val. (1968), Alabama St. (1982) and Ark.-Pine Bluff (1998). **Withdrew later** (8): Paul Quinn (1929), Bishop (1956), Langston (1957), Sam Houston College (1959), Texas College (1961), Wiley (1968), Arkansas AM&N (1970) and Prairie View (1990, dropped program, readmitted 1991). **Current members** (9): Alabama St., Alcorn St., Ark.-Pine Bluff, Grambling, Jackson St., Mississippi Val., Prairie View, Southern U. and Texas Southern.

Year	Champion (Record√)
1921	Wiley
1922	Paul Quinn
1923	Wiley
1924	Paul Quinn
1925	Bishop
1926	Sam Houston College
1927	Wiley
1928	Wiley
1929	Wiley
1930	Wiley
1931	Prairie View
1932	Wiley
1933	Langston & Prairie View
1934	Texas College
1935	Texas College
1936	Texas College & Langston
1937	Southern U. & Langston
1938	Southern U. & Langston
1939	Langston
1940	Southern U. & Langston
1941	No champion
1942	Texas College
1943	No champion
1944	Wiley (5-1), Texas College (5-1) & Langston (5-1)
1945	Wiley (6-0)
1946	Southern U. (5-1)
1947	Southern U. (7-0)
1948	Southern U. (7-0)
1949	Southern U. (6-0-1) & Langston (6-0-1)
1950	Southern U. (7-0)
1951	Prairie View (6-1)
1952	Prairie View (6-0)
1953	Prairie View (6-0)
1954	Prairie View (6-0)
1955	Southern U. (6-1)
1956	Texas Southern (5-1) & Langston (5-1)
1957	Wiley (6-0)
1958	Prairie View (5-0)
1959	Southern U. (7-0)
1960	Southern U. (6-1), Prairie View (6-1) & Grambling (6-1)
1961	Jackson St. (6-1)
1962	Jackson St. (6-1)
1963	Prairie View (7-0)
1964	Prairie View (7-0)
1965	Grambling (6-1)
1966	Southern U. (4-2-1), Grambling (4-2-1), Texas Southern (4-2-1) & Arkansas AM&N (4-2-1)
1967	Grambling (6-1)
1968	Alcorn St. (6-1), Grambling (6-1) & Texas Southern (6-1)
1969	Alcorn St. (6-0-1)
1970	Alcorn St. (6-0)
1971	Grambling (5-1)
1972	Grambling (5-1) & Jackson St. (5-1)
1973	Grambling (5-1) & Jackson St. (5-1)
1974	Alcorn St. (5-1) & Grambling (5-1)
1975	Grambling (4-2) & Southern U. (4-2)
1976	Alcorn St. (5-1)
1977	Grambling (6-0)
1978	Grambling (5-0-1)
1979	Grambling (5-1) & Alcorn St. (5-1)
1980	Grambling (5-1)* & Jackson St. (5-1)
1981	Jackson St. (5-1)*
1982	Jackson St. (6-0)*
1983	Grambling (6-0-1)
1984	Alcorn St. (7-0)*
1985	Jackson St. (6-1)* & Grambling (6-1)*
1986	Jackson St. (7-0)*
1987	Jackson St. (7-0)*
1988	Jackson St. (7-0)*
1989	Jackson St. (7-0)*
1990	Jackson St. (5-1)*
1991	Alabama St. (6-0-1)#
1992	Alcorn St. (7-0)*
1993	Southern U. (7-0)#
1994	Grambling (6-1)# & Alcorn St. (6-1)*
1995	Jackson St. (7-0)*
1996	Jackson St. (6-1)*
1997	Southern U. (8-0)#

*√No records available until 1944. *Participated in NCAA Division I-AA Championship. #Participated in Division I-AA Heritage Bowl.*

Discontinued Conferences

Division I-A

BIG EIGHT CONFERENCE

Founded: Originally founded in 1907 as the Missouri Valley Intercollegiate Athletic Association. Charter members were Iowa, Kansas, Missouri, Nebraska and Washington (Mo.). Six schools were admitted later: Drake (1908), Iowa St. (1908), Kansas St. (1913), Grinnell (1919), Oklahoma (1920) and Oklahoma St. (1925). Iowa withdrew in 1911. The Big Six Conference was founded in 1928 when charter members left the MVIAA. Iowa St., Kansas, Kansas St., Missouri, Nebraska and Oklahoma were joined by Colorado (1948) (known as Big Seven) and Oklahoma St. (1958) (known as Big Eight until 1996). All eight members of Big Eight joined four former Southwest Conference members (Baylor, Texas, Texas A&M and Texas Tech) to form Big 12 Conference in 1996.

Year	Champion (Record)
1907	Iowa (1-0) & Nebraska (1-0)
1908	Kansas (4-0)
1909	Missouri (4-0-1)
1910	Nebraska (2-0)
1911	Iowa St. (2-0-1) & Nebraska (2-0-1)
1912	Iowa St. (2-0) & Nebraska (2-0)
1913	Missouri (4-0) & Nebraska (3-0)
1914	Nebraska (3-0)
1915	Nebraska (4-0)
1916	Nebraska (3-1)
1917	Nebraska (2-0)
1918	No Champion—War
1919	Missouri (4-0-1)
1920	Oklahoma (4-0-1)
1921	Nebraska (3-0)
1922	Nebraska (5-0)
1923	Nebraska (3-0-2)
1924	Missouri (5-1)
1925	Missouri (5-1)
1926	Oklahoma St. (3-0-1)
1927	Missouri (5-1)
1928	Nebraska (4-0)
1929	Nebraska (3-0-2)
1930	Kansas (4-1)
1931	Nebraska (5-0)
1932	Nebraska (5-0)
1933	Nebraska (5-0)
1934	Kansas St. (5-0)
1935	Nebraska (4-0-1)
1936	Nebraska (5-0)
1937	Nebraska (3-0-2)
1938	Oklahoma (5-0)
1939	Missouri (5-0)
1940	Nebraska (5-0)
1941	Missouri (5-0)
1942	Missouri (4-0-1)
1943	Oklahoma (5-0)
1944	Oklahoma (4-0-1)
1945	Missouri (5-0)
1946	Oklahoma (4-1) & Kansas (4-1)
1947	Kansas (4-0-1) & Oklahoma (4-0-1)
1948	Oklahoma (5-0)
1949	Oklahoma (5-0)
1950	Oklahoma (6-0)
1951	Oklahoma (6-0)
1952	Oklahoma (5-0-1)
1953	Oklahoma (6-0)
1954	Oklahoma (6-0)
1955	Oklahoma (6-0)
1956	Oklahoma (6-0)
1957	Oklahoma (6-0)
1958	Oklahoma (6-0)
1959	Oklahoma (5-1)
1960	Missouri (7-0)
1961	Colorado (7-0)
1962	Oklahoma (7-0)
1963	Nebraska (7-0)
1964	Nebraska (6-1)
1965	Nebraska (7-0)
1966	Nebraska (6-1)
1967	Oklahoma (7-0)
1968	Kansas (6-1) & Oklahoma (6-1)
1969	Missouri (6-1) & Nebraska (6-1)
1970	Nebraska (7-0)
1971	Nebraska (7-0)
1972	Nebraska (5-1-1)*
1973	Oklahoma (7-0)
1974	Oklahoma (7-0)
1975	Nebraska (6-1) & Oklahoma (6-1)
1976	Colorado (5-2), Oklahoma (5-2) & Oklahoma St. (5-2)
1977	Oklahoma (7-0)
1978	Nebraska (6-1) & Oklahoma (6-1)
1979	Oklahoma (7-0)
1980	Oklahoma (7-0)
1981	Nebraska (7-0)
1982	Nebraska (7-0)
1983	Nebraska (7-0)
1984	Oklahoma (6-1) & Nebraska (6-1)
1985	Oklahoma (7-0)
1986	Oklahoma (7-0)
1987	Oklahoma (7-0)
1988	Nebraska (7-0)
1989	Colorado (7-0)
1990	Colorado (7-0)
1991	Colorado (6-0-1) & Nebraska (6-0-1)
1992	Nebraska (6-1)
1993	Nebraska (7-0)
1994	Nebraska (7-0)
1995	Nebraska (7-0)

**Oklahoma (5-1-1) forfeited title.*

BORDER INTERCOLLEGIATE ATHLETIC ASSOCIATION

Founded: In 1931 as Border Intercollegiate Athletic Association. Charters members were Arizona, Arizona St. Teachers' (Flagstaff) (now Northern Ariz.), Arizona St. Teachers' (Tempe) (now Arizona St.), New Mexico and New Mexico A&M (now New Mexico St.). Texas Tech admitted in 1932, Texas Mines (now UTEP) admitted in 1935, and Hardin-Simmons and West Texas St. Teachers' (now West Tex. A&M) in 1941.

Year	Champion (Record)
1931	Arizona St. (3-1)
1932	Texas Tech (2-0)*
1933	Texas Tech (1-0)*
1934	Texas Tech (1-0)*
1935	Arizona (4-0)
1936	Arizona (3-0-1)
1937	Texas Tech (3-0)
1938	New Mexico St. (4-1)** New Mexico (4-2)**
1939	Arizona St. (4-0)
1940	Arizona St. (3-0-1)
1941	Arizona (5-0)
1942	Hardin-Simmons (3-0-1) Texas Tech (3-0-1)
1943	No full conference program
1944	Texas Tech (2-0)
1945	Arizona (1-0)
1946	Hardin-Simmons (6-0)
1947	Texas Tech (4-0)

**Texas Tech has been listed by some as conference champion for the years 1932, 1933 and 1934, but conference rules forbade an official conference championship. This was due to the fact that the conference covered such a large area that games between all members were not practical.*

***Texas Tech won its two conference games in 1938 but did not win the official championship since it did not meet the conference three-game requirement. Its victory over New Mexico did not count toward the championship, permitting New Mexico to share championship honors with New Mexico St.*

MISSOURI VALLEY CONFERENCE

Founded: Originally founded as the Missouri Valley Intercollegiate Athletic Association. Several charter members left in 1928 to form the Big Six Conference, which became the Big Eight later. But Drake, Grinnell, Iowa St., Kansas St., Oklahoma, Oklahoma A&M (now Oklahoma St.) and Washington (Mo.) continued the MVIAA. Creighton joined in 1928, Butler in 1932, Tulsa and Washburn in 1935, St. Louis in 1937, Wichita St. in 1947, Bradley and Detroit in 1949, Houston in 1951, North Texas in 1957, Cincinnati in 1957, West Tex. A&M in 1972, Memphis in 1968, and Louisville in 1964.

Year	Champion
1928	Drake
1929	Drake
1930	Drake & Oklahoma St.
1931	Drake
1932	Oklahoma St.
1933	Drake & Oklahoma St.
1934	Washington (Mo.)
1935	Washington (Mo.) & Tulsa
1936	Tulsa & Creighton
1937	Tulsa
1938	Tulsa
1939	Washington (Mo.)
1940	Tulsa
1941	Tulsa
1942	Tulsa
1943	Tulsa
1944	Oklahoma St.
1945	Oklahoma St.
1946	Tulsa
1947	Tulsa
1948	Oklahoma St.
1949	Detroit
1950	Tulsa
1951	Tulsa
1952	Houston
1953	Oklahoma St. & Detroit
1954	Wichita St.
1955	Wichita St. & Detroit
1956	Houston
1957	Houston
1958	North Texas
1959	North Texas & Houston
1960	Wichita St.
1961	Wichita St.
1962	Tulsa
1963	Cincinnati & Wichita St.
1964	Cincinnati
1965	Tulsa
1966	North Texas & Tulsa
1967	North Texas
1968	Memphis
1969	Memphis
1970	Louisville
1971	Memphis
1972	Louisville, West Tex. A&M & Drake
1973	North Texas
1974	Tulsa
1975	Tulsa
1976	Tulsa & New Mexico St.
1977	West Tex. A&M
1978	New Mexico St.
1979	West Tex. A&M
1980	Tulsa
1981	Drake & Tulsa
1982	Tulsa
1983	Tulsa
1984	Tulsa
1985	Tulsa

OLD ROCKY MOUNTAIN CONFERENCE
(Mountain States Athletic Conference and Big Seven Conference)

Founded: This conference predates every conference except the Big Ten and consisted of Brigham Young (1922), Colorado (1900), Colorado Agricultural College (now Colorado St.) (1900), Colorado St. College (1900), Denver (1900), Utah (1902), Utah St. (1902) and Wyoming (1905). Before 1938, these schools were part of the Rocky Mountain Conference, other members of which, at that time, were Colorado College, Colorado Mines, Greeley St. Teachers' (now Northern Colo.), Montana St. (1917) and Western St. Teachers' (now Western St.) (1925). A split took place in 1938, when the Mountain States Athletic Conference or "Big Seven" was formed. The name Rocky Mountain Conference was retained by the last six schools after 1938. Some members went into the Western Athletic Conference when the RMC was dissolved in 1962.

Year	Champion
1900	Colorado College
1901	Colorado
1902	Colorado
1903	Colorado
1904	Colorado Mines
1905	Colorado Mines
1906	Colorado Mines
1907	Colorado Mines

Year	Champion
1908	Denver
1909	Denver
1910	Colorado
1911	Colorado
1912	Colorado Mines
1913	Colorado
1914	Colorado Mines
1915	Colorado Aggies
1916	Colorado Aggies
1917	Denver
1918	Colorado Mines
1919	Colorado Aggies
1920	Colorado Aggies
1921	Utah St.
1922	Utah
1923	Colorado
1924	Colorado
1925	Colorado Aggies
1926	Utah
1927	Colorado Aggies
1928	Utah
1929	Utah
1930	Utah
1931	Utah
1932	Utah
1933	Utah, Denver* & Colorado St.*
1934	Colorado, Northern Colo. & Colorado St.*
1935	Colorado & Utah St.*
1936	Utah St.
1937	Colorado
1938	Utah (4-0-2)
1939	Colorado (5-1-0)
1940	Utah (5-1-0)
1941	Utah (4-0-2)
1942	Colorado & Utah (5-1-0)
1943	Colorado (2-0-0)
1944	Colorado (2-0-0)
1945	Denver (4-1-0)
1946	Utah St. & Denver (4-1-1)
1947	Utah (6-0-0)
1948	Utah
1949	Wyoming
1950	Wyoming
1951	Utah
1952	Utah
1953	Utah
1954	Denver
1955	Colorado St.
1956	Wyoming
1957	Utah
1958	Wyoming
1959	Wyoming
1960	Wyoming & Utah St.
1961	Wyoming & Utah St.

**In final ratings, according to conference rules, tie games were not counted in awarding championships. Thus, teams marked with * shared the championship because one or more ties were not counted in their conference records.*

SOUTHLAND CONFERENCE
(I-A only 1975-79, now I-AA conference)

SOUTHWEST CONFERENCE

Founded: In 1914 as the Southwest Athletic Conference with charter members Arkansas, Baylor, Oklahoma, Oklahoma St., Rice, Southwestern (Tex.), Texas and Texas A&M. Five teams were added: Southern Methodist (1918), Phillips (1920), Texas Christian (1923), Texas Tech (1960) and Houston (1976). Five withdrew: Southwestern (Texas) (1917), Oklahoma (1920), Phillips (1921), Oklahoma St. (1925) and Arkansas (1992). Of the eight members in the final (1995) season, four (Baylor, Texas, Texas A&M and Texas Tech) joined with eight members of the Big Eight Conference to form the Big 12 Conference in 1996. The other members in 1996: Houston (to Conference USA), Rice (to Western Athletic Conference), Southern Methodist (to Western Athletic Conference) and Texas Christian (to Western Athletic Conference).

Year	Champion (Record)
1914	No champion
1915	Oklahoma (3-0)*
1916	No champion
1917	Texas A&M (2-0)
1918	No champion
1919	Texas A&M (4-0)
1920	Texas (5-0)
1921	Texas A&M (3-0-2)
1922	Baylor (5-0)
1923	Southern Methodist (5-0)
1924	Baylor (4-0-1)
1925	Texas A&M (4-1)
1926	Southern Methodist (5-0)
1927	Texas A&M (4-0-1)
1928	Texas (5-1)
1929	Texas Christian (4-0-1)
1930	Texas (4-1)
1931	Southern Methodist (5-0-1)
1932	Texas Christian (6-0)
1933	No champion*
1934	Rice (5-1)
1935	Southern Methodist (6-0)
1936	Arkansas (5-1)
1937	Rice (4-1-1)
1938	Texas Christian (6-0)
1939	Texas A&M (6-0)
1940	Texas A&M (5-1)
1941	Texas A&M (5-1)
1942	Texas (5-1)
1943	Texas (5-0)
1944	Texas Christian (3-1-1)
1945	Texas (5-1)
1946	Rice (5-1) & Arkansas (5-1)
1947	Southern Methodist (5-0-1)
1948	Southern Methodist (5-0-1)
1949	Rice (6-0)
1950	Texas (6-0)
1951	Texas Christian (5-1)
1952	Texas (6-0)
1953	Rice (5-1) & Texas (5-1)
1954	Arkansas (5-1)
1955	Texas Christian (5-1)
1956	Texas A&M (6-0)
1957	Rice (5-1)
1958	Texas Christian (5-1)
1959	Texas (5-1), Texas Christian (5-1) & Arkansas (5-1)
1960	Arkansas (6-1)
1961	Texas (6-1) & Arkansas (6-1)
1962	Texas (6-0-1)
1963	Texas (7-0)
1964	Arkansas (7-0)
1965	Arkansas (7-0)
1966	Southern Methodist (6-1)
1967	Texas A&M (6-1)
1968	Texas (6-1) & Arkansas (6-1)
1969	Texas (7-0)
1970	Texas (7-0)
1971	Texas (6-1)
1972	Texas (7-0)
1973	Texas (7-0)
1974	Baylor (6-1)
1975	Arkansas (6-1), Texas A&M (6-1) & Texas (6-1)
1976	Houston (7-1) & Texas Tech (7-1)
1977	Texas (8-0)
1978	Houston (7-1)
1979	Houston (7-1) & Arkansas (7-1)
1980	Baylor (8-0)
1981	Southern Methodist (7-1)¢
1982	Southern Methodist (7-0-1)
1983	Texas (8-0)
1984	Southern Methodist (6-2) & Houston (6-2)
1985	Texas A&M (7-1)
1986	Texas A&M (7-1)
1987	Texas A&M (6-1)
1988	Arkansas (7-0)
1989	Arkansas (7-1)
1990	Texas (8-0)
1991	Texas A&M (8-0)
1992	Texas A&M (7-0)
1993	Texas A&M (7-0)
1994	Baylor (4-3), Rice (4-3), Texas (4-3), Texas Christian (4-3) & Texas Tech (4-3)*
1995	Texas (7-0)

**Forfeited title: Baylor (3-0) in 1915, Arkansas (4-1) in 1933 and Texas A&M (6-0-1) in 1994 on probation. ¢Southern Methodist on probation; did not forfeit championship.*

Division I-AA

AMERICAN WEST CONFERENCE

Founded: Started Division I-AA play in 1993 with charter members Cal St. Northridge, Cal St. Sacramento and Southern Utah. Other members were UC Davis and Cal Poly SLO (both Division II members at the time). Cal Poly SLO became a Division I-AA member in 1994, and UC Davis withdrew in 1994. Last-year members were Cal Poly SLO (became independent), Cal St. Northridge (to Big Sky Conference), Cal St. Sacramento (to Big Sky Conference) and Southern Utah (became independent).

Year	Champion (Record)
1993	Southern Utah (3-1) & UC Davis (3-1)#
1994	Cal Poly SLO (3-0)
1995	Cal St. Sacramento (3-0)

#Participated in NCAA Division II Championship.

1998 Conference Alignment Changes

Division I-A

In Division I-A, there are no big changes for 1998. The division boasts 112 teams and 10 conferences for 1998 with only seven independent teams remaining.

Two former I-A independent teams will make a move into conferences. Army, a long-time independent, joins the Conference USA fold giving the league eight members while Arkansas State rejoins the Big West Conference, upping its membership to seven.

Division I-AA

Three new members in the division and two dropping its football program brings I-AA to 119 teams and 13 conferences for 1998.

Jacksonville (Florida) is starting a brand new football program this season while Portland State is jumping from Division II and Arkansas-Pine Bluff, a provisional member, will be upgraded to full-time status this fall. Boston University and Evansville dropped its football programs following the final game in 1997 because of financial concerns.

Portland State is already a member of the Big Sky Conference while Arkansas-Pine Bluff joins the Southwestern Athletic Conference, bringing its total to nine members. Jacksonville will play as an independent in its first football season, becoming the 15th I-AA independent team in 1998.

Division II

Nine schools joined Division II in 1998 and one departed to I-AA to bring the total to 150 teams and 13 conferences,

The new schools, all former provisional members, are Central Washington, East Central Oklahoma, Northeastern Oklahoma State, Oklahoma Panhandle, Southeastern Oklahoma State, Southwestern Oklahoma State, Tusculum, Western Washington and Westminster (Pennsylvania). Portland State moved from II to I-AA.

In conference alignments, Northeastern Oklahoma State, Southeastern Oklahoma State each joined The Lone Star Conference, bringing its membership to 13 teams. Westminster (Pennsylvania) joined The Midwest Conference, bringing its league total to 12 teams. The remainder of new teams will play as Division II independents, bringing that total to 17 teams.

Division III

Seven new teams have joined the division to bring the total to 213 for the 1998 season. The new teams, all former provisional members, are Greenville, Lewis & Clark, Linfield, Mount St. Joseph, Pacific Lutheran and Willamette.

1998 Schedules/ 1997 Results

1998 Schedules and 1997 Results for All Divisions

Listed alphabetically in this section are 1998 schedules and 1997 results for all football-playing NCAA member institutions. The division designation for each school is indicated to the right of the school location.

Coaching records (below head coaches' names) are for all seasons as the head coach at any four-year collegiate institution.

Game dates and starting times are subject to change.
■ Designates home games.
*** Designates night games. Neutral sites are listed in brackets.**

ABILENE CHRISTIAN

Abilene, TX 79699 II

Coach: Jack Kiser, Ab. Christian 1971
Record: 2 Years, 13-8-0

1998 SCHEDULE

Southwestern Okla.	*Sept. 5
Central Okla.	Sept. 19
East Central ■	*Sept. 26
Eastern N.M. ■	*Oct. 3
Midwestern St.	Oct. 10
Angelo St. ■	Oct. 17
Tarleton St.	Oct. 24
Tex. A&M-Commerce ■	Oct. 31
Texas A&M-Kingsville	*Nov. 7
West Tex. A&M ■	Nov. 14

1997 RESULTS (7-4-0)

25	Southwestern Okla.	17
26	Tex. A&M-Commerce	10
0	Central Okla.	28
20	East Central	7
40	Eastern N.M.	7
34	Midwestern St.	14
10	Angelo St.	42
23	Tarleton St.	17
19	Tex. A&M-Commerce	9
7	Texas A&M-Kingsville	54
0	West Tex. A&M	20
204		**225**

Nickname: Wildcats.
Stadium: Shotwell (1959), 15,000 capacity. Natural turf.
Colors: Purple & White.
Conference: Lone Star Conference.
SID: Garner Roberts, 915-674-2693.
AD: Stan D. Lambert.

ADAMS ST.

Alamosa, CO 81102 II

Coach: David Elsenrath, Mo.-Rolla 1985
Record: 1 Year, 1-10-0

1998 SCHEDULE

Northern Colo.	Sept. 5
Western N. Mex. ■	Sept. 12
Neb.-Kearney ■	Sept. 19
N. M. Highlands	Sept. 26
Mesa St.	*Oct. 3
Western St. (Colo.) ■	Oct. 17
Colorado Mines ■	Oct. 24
Chadron St.	Oct. 31
Fort Lewis	Nov. 7
Fort Hays St. ■	Nov. 14

1997 RESULTS (1-10-0)

0	West Tex. A&M	48
7	Western N. Mex.	26
7	N. M. Highlands	33
30	Mesa St.	46
21	Northwestern Okla.	33
15	Western St. (Colo.)	50
24	Colorado Mines	18
14	Chadron St.	36
12	Fort Lewis	14
15	Fort Hays St.	41
7	Neb.-Kearney	35
152		**380**

Nickname: Indians.
Stadium: Rex Field (1949), 2,800 capacity. Natural turf.
Colors: Green & White.
Conference: Rocky Mountain Athletic Conf.
SID: Jeff Storm, 719-589-7825.
AD: Rodger Jehlicka.

ADRIAN

Adrian, MI 49221 III

Coach: Jim Lyall, Michigan 1974
Record: 8 Years, 32-39-1

1998 SCHEDULE

Defiance ■	Sept. 5
Heidelberg	Sept. 12
Buffalo St. ■	Sept. 19
Anderson (Ind.)	Sept. 26
Alma	Oct. 10
Hope ■	Oct. 17
Olivet	Oct. 24
Albion ■	Oct. 31
Kalamazoo	Nov. 7

1997 RESULTS (8-1-0)

10	Heidelberg	7
28	Defiance	7
41	Anderson (Ind.)	14
30	Benedictine (Ill.)	6
27	Alma	24
26	Hope	19
29	Olivet	12
13	Albion	31
17	Kalamazoo	6
221		**126**

Nickname: Bulldogs.
Stadium: Maple (1960), 5,000 capacity. Natural turf.
Colors: Gold & Black.
Conference: Michigan Intercoll Athl Assn.
SID: Darcy Gifford, 517-264-3176.
AD: C. Henry Mensing.

AIR FORCE

USAF Academy, CO 80840 ..... I-A

Coach: Fisher DeBerry, Wofford 1960
Record: 14 Years, 108-63-1

1998 SCHEDULE

Wake Forest ■	Sept. 5
UNLV	*Sept. 12
Colorado St. ■	*Sept. 17
Texas Christian	*Sept. 26
New Mexico ■	Oct. 3
Navy ■	Oct. 10
Tulsa	Oct. 24
Southern Methodist ■	Oct. 31
Army	Nov. 7
Wyoming	Nov. 14
Rice ■	Nov. 21

1997 RESULTS (10-2-0)

14	Idaho	10
41	Rice	12
25	UNLV	24
24	Colorado St.	0
24	San Diego St.	18
17	Citadel	3
10	Navy	7
17	Fresno St.	20
22	San Jose St.	25
34	Hawaii	27
24	Army	0
14	Wyoming	3
266		**149**

Las Vegas Bowl

13	Oregon	41

Nickname: Falcons.
Stadium: Falcon (1962), 52,480 capacity. Natural turf.
Colors: Blue & Silver.
Conference: Western Athletic.
SID: Dave Kellogg, 719-472-2313.
AD: Randall W. Spetman.

AKRON

Akron, OH 44325 ..... I-A

Coach: Lee Owens, Bluffton 1977
Record: 3 Years, 8-25-0

1998 SCHEDULE

Marshall ■	*Sept. 5
Temple	*Sept. 12
Ball St. ■	*Sept. 26
Pittsburgh	Oct. 3
Kent	Oct. 10
Ohio	Oct. 17
Toledo ■	Oct. 24
Central Mich.	Oct. 31
Bowling Green	Nov. 7
Eastern Mich. ■	Nov. 14
Miami (Ohio) ■	Nov. 21

1997 RESULTS (2-9-0)

14	Nebraska	59
20	Miami (Ohio)	49
28	Bowling Green	31
0	LSU	56
53	Central Mich.	14
17	Marshall	52
0	Eastern Mich.	45
17	Ohio	21
14	Ball St.	31
45	Kent	35
10	Toledo	42
218		**435**

Nickname: Zips.
Stadium: Rubber Bowl (1940), 35,202 capacity. Artificial turf.
Colors: Blue & Gold.
Conference: Mid-American.
SID: Jeff Brewer, 330-972-7468.
AD: Michael A. Bobinski.

ALABAMA

Tuscaloosa, AL 35487 ..... I-A

Coach: Mike DuBose, Alabama 1975
Record: 1 Year, 4-7-0

1998 SCHEDULE

Brigham Young ■	Sept. 5
Vanderbilt [Birmingham, Ala.]	Sept. 12
Arkansas	*Sept. 26
Florida ■	Oct. 3
Mississippi ■	Oct. 10
East Caro. [Birmingham, Ala.]	Oct. 17
Tennessee	Oct. 24
Southern Miss. ■	Oct. 31
LSU	*Nov. 7
Mississippi St.	Nov. 14
Auburn ■	*Nov. 21

1997 RESULTS (4-7-0)

42	Houston	17
20	Vanderbilt	0
16	Arkansas	17
27	Southern Miss.	13
34	Kentucky	40
21	Tennessee	38
29	Mississippi	20
20	Louisiana Tech	26
0	LSU	27
20	Mississippi St.	32
17	Auburn	18
246		**248**

Nickname: Crimson Tide.

Stadium: Bryant-Denny (1929), 70,123 capacity. Natural turf.
Colors: Crimson & White.
Conference: Southeastern.
SID: Larry White, 205-348-6084.
AD: Robert L. Bockrath.

ALABAMA A&M

Normal, AL 35762 II

Coach: Ron Cooper, Jacksonville St. 1983
Record: 5 Years, 22-33-0

1998 SCHEDULE

Jacksonville St. ■ ....*Sept. 5
Grambling ■ ....*Sept. 12
Mississippi Val. ■ ....*Sept. 19
Morris Brown ....*Sept. 26
Tennessee St. ....Oct. 3
Southern U. ■ ....*Oct. 10
Tuskegee ....Oct. 17
Miles ■ ....Oct. 24
Alabama St. [Birmingham, Ala.] ....Oct. 31
Alcorn St. ■ ....Nov. 14
Ark.-Pine Bluff ....Nov. 21

1997 RESULTS (7-4-0)

20	North Ala.	49
9	Clark Atlanta	7
23	Mississippi Val.	8
10	Morris Brown	6
38	Morehouse	14
13	Albany St. (Ga.)	25
33	Fort Valley St.	26
13	Alabama St.	20
31	Miles	26
26	Tuskegee	15
20	Kentucky St.	27
236		**223**

Nickname: Bulldogs.
Stadium: Bulldog 20,000 capacity. Natural turf.
Colors: Maroon & White.
Conference: Southern Intercol. Ath. Conf.
SID: Ashley Balch, 205-851-5368.
AD: James A. Martin Sr.

ALABAMA ST.

Montgomery, AL 36101 ....I-AA

Coach: Ron Dickerson Sr., Kansas St. 1971
Record: 5 Years, 8-47-0

1998 SCHEDULE

Troy St. ....*Sept. 5
Texas Southern ■ ....*Sept. 12
Alcorn St. ....*Sept. 19
Southern U. ....*Sept. 26
Ark.-Pine Bluff ■ ....*Oct. 3
Jackson St. [Mobile, Ala.] ....*Oct. 10
Prairie View ....*Oct. 17
Alabama A&M [Birmingham, Ala.] ....Oct. 31
Grambling ....Nov. 7
Mississippi Val. ■ ....Nov. 14
Tuskegee ■ ....Nov. 26

1997 RESULTS (3-8-0)

11	Jackson St.	38
6	Texas Southern	31
13	Troy St.	20
6	Alcorn St.	20
10	Ark.-Pine Bluff	18
16	Southern U.	27
56	Prairie View	7
20	Alabama A&M	13
20	Grambling	13
10	Mississippi Val.	34
16	Tuskegee	21
184		**242**

Nickname: Hornets.
Stadium: Cramton (1922), 24,600 capacity. Natural turf.
Colors: Black & Gold.
Conference: Southwestern.
SID: Kevin J. Manns, 205-293-4511.
AD: W. Curtis Williams.

UAB

Birmingham, AL 35294 ....I-A

Coach: Watson Brown, Vanderbilt 1973
Record: 13 Years, 47-95-1

1998 SCHEDULE

Nebraska ....Sept. 5
Tennessee Tech ■ ....*Sept. 19
Kansas ■ ....*Sept. 26
Southwestern La. ■ ....*Oct. 3
East Caro. ....Oct. 10
Louisiana Tech ....*Oct. 17
Virginia Tech ■ ....*Oct. 24
Northeast La. ....*Oct. 31
Tennessee ....Nov. 7
Middle Tenn. St. ■ ....Nov. 14
Tenn.-Martin ■ ....Nov. 21

1997 RESULTS (5-6-0)

0	Kansas	24
7	Memphis	28
10	Arizona	24
34	Jacksonville St.	16
42	Southwestern La.	7
20	Western Ky.	16
29	Cincinnati	33
0	Virginia Tech	37
29	Louisiana Tech	32
38	Tennessee Tech	14
13	Arkansas St.	7
222		**238**

Nickname: Blazers.
Stadium: Legion Field (1927), 83,091 capacity. Natural turf.
Colors: Green, Gold & White.
Conference: Independent.
SID: Grant Shingleton, 205-934-0722.
AD: B. Gene Bartow.

ALBANY ST. (GA.)

Albany, GA 31705 II

Coach: Hampton Smith, Mississippi Val. 1951
Record: 22 Years, 141-85-4

1998 SCHEDULE

Valdosta St. ■ ....*Aug. 29
Miles ■ ....Sept. 5
Kentucky St. ....*Sept. 12
Morehouse ....Sept. 19
N.C. Central ■ ....*Sept. 26
Savannah St. ■ ....*Oct. 3
Mississippi Val. ....Oct. 17
Clark Atlanta ■ ....Oct. 24
Morris Brown ....Oct. 31
Livingstone ■ ....Nov. 7
Fort Valley St. [Columbus, GA.] ....Nov. 14

1997 RESULTS (10-0-0)

22	Miles	12
10	Kentucky St.	7
17	Morehouse	7
18	Tuskegee	7
41	Savannah St.	3
25	Alabama A&M	13
14	Clark Atlanta	10
20	Morris Brown	7
20	N.C. Central	0
12	Fort Valley St.	7
199		**73**

II Championship

10	Southern Ark.	0
22	Carson-Newman	23

Nickname: Golden Rams.
Stadium: Mills Memorial (1957), 11,000 capacity. Natural turf.
Colors: Blue & Gold.
Conference: Southern Intercol. Ath. Conf.
SID: Edythe Y. Bradley, 912-430-4672.
AD: Craig B. Curry.

ALBANY (N.Y.)

Albany, NY 12222 II

Coach: Robert Ford, Springfield 1959
Record: 29 Years, 157-121-1

1998 SCHEDULE

Central Conn. St. ■ ....*Sept. 4
American Int'l ....Sept. 12
Monmouth ■ ....*Sept. 19
LIU-C.W. Post ■ ....*Sept. 26
Merrimack ....Oct. 10
Stony Brook ....Oct. 17
Mass.-Lowell ■ ....Oct. 24
Stonehill ■ ....Oct. 31
Pace ■ ....Nov. 7
Southern Conn. St. ....Nov. 14

1997 RESULTS (11-1-0)

26	Central Conn. St.	33
42	Sacred Heart	0
49	St. Lawrence	0
44	LIU-C.W. Post	7
42	Merrimack	3
48	Pace	14
30	Stony Brook	23
22	Mass.-Lowell	6
42	Stonehill	26
54	Union (N.Y.)	0
42	Southern Conn. St.	40
27	American Int'l	20
468		**172**

Nickname: Great Danes.
Stadium: University Field (1967), 10,000 capacity. Natural turf.
Colors: Purple & Gold.
Conference: Eastern Football.
SID: Brian DePasquale, 518-442-3072.
AD: Milton E. Richards.

ALBION

Albion, MI 49224 III

Coach: Craig Rundle, Albion 1974
Record: 12 Years, 63-49-1

1998 SCHEDULE

Butler ....Sept. 5
Mount Union ■ ....Sept. 12
Manchester ....Sept. 26
Defiance ....Oct. 3
Olivet ....Oct. 10
Alma ■ ....Oct. 17
Kalamazoo ■ ....Oct. 24
Adrian ....Oct. 31
Hope ■ ....Nov. 7

1997 RESULTS (6-3-0)

33	Tiffin	10
14	Wabash	19
24	DePauw	10
61	Olivet	6
16	Alma	56
49	Kalamazoo	0
31	Adrian	13
25	Hope	28
31	Thomas More	13
284		**155**

Nickname: Britons.
Stadium: Sprankle-Sprandel (1976), 5,010 capacity. Natural turf.
Colors: Purple & Gold.
Conference: Michigan Intercoll Athl Assn.
SID: Robin Hartman, 517-629-0434.
AD: Jim Conway.

ALBRIGHT

Reading, PA 19612 III

Coach: E. J. Sandusky, Penn St. 1993
Record: 1 Year, 9-1-0

1998 SCHEDULE

Wm. Paterson ....Sept. 5

Delaware Valley ■	*Sept. 12
Lebanon Valley ■	*Sept. 19
Moravian	Sept. 26
King's (Pa.) ■	Oct. 10
Widener	Oct. 17
FDU-Madison ■	Oct. 24
Juniata	Oct. 31
Susquehanna	Nov. 7
Catholic ■	Nov. 14

1997 RESULTS (8-1-0)

39	Delaware Valley	17
31	Lebanon Valley	7
46	Moravian	0
38	King's (Pa.)	20
28	Widener	21
37	FDU-Madison	0
14	Juniata	6
35	Susquehanna	14
22	Catholic	44
290		**129**

ECAC III Playoff

10	Wesley	0

Nickname: Lions.
Stadium: Eugene L. Shirk (1925), 7,000 capacity. Natural turf.
Colors: Cardinal & White.
Conference: Middle Atlantic States Conf.
SID: Stan Hyman, 610-921-7833.
AD: Sally Ann Stetler.

ALCORN ST.

Lorman, MS 39096 .... I-AA

Coach: Johnny Thomas, Alcorn St. 1978
(First year as head coach)

1998 SCHEDULE

Grambling	*Sept. 5
Alabama St. ■	*Sept. 19
Ark.-Pine Bluff ■	Sept. 26
Morehouse	Oct. 3
Prairie View	Oct. 10
Texas Southern ■	Oct. 17
Southern U. ■	Oct. 24
Mississippi Val.	Nov. 7
Alabama A&M	Nov. 14
Jackson St. ■	Nov. 21

1997 RESULTS (4-7-0)

0	Troy St.	30
44	Grambling	20
17	Western Ill.	31
20	Alabama St.	6
16	Samford	21
10	Ark.-Pine Bluff	20
24	Prairie View	9
7	Texas Southern	10
16	Southern U.	25
23	Mississippi Val.	18
15	Jackson St.	54
192		**244**

Nickname: Braves.
Stadium: Jack Spinks (1992), 22,500 capacity. Natural turf.
Colors: Purple & Gold.
Conference: Southwestern.
SID: Derick Hackett, 601-877-6466.
AD: Lloyd N. Hill.

ALFRED

Alfred, NY 14802 III

Coach: David Murray, Springfield 1981
Record: 8 Years, 44-40-1

1998 SCHEDULE

Susquehanna ■	*Sept. 5
Salisbury St. ■	Sept. 12
St. Lawrence	Sept. 19
Carnegie Mellon ■	Sept. 26
Union (N.Y.) ■	Oct. 3
Hartwick	Oct. 10
Thiel	Oct. 17
Hobart	Oct. 24
Grove City	Oct. 31
Bethany (W. Va.) ■	Nov. 7

1997 RESULTS (2-8-0)

30	King's (Pa.)	0
27	Waynesburg	43
7	Ithaca	52
26	Bethany (W. Va.)	38
42	Thiel	6
20	Canisius	23
19	Hobart	58
35	Grove City	56
3	Wash. & Jeff.	27
0	Union (N.Y.)	43
209		**346**

Nickname: Saxons.
Stadium: Merrill Field (1926), 5,000 capacity. Artificial turf.
Colors: Purple & Gold.
Conference: Presidents' Athletic Conf.
SID: R. J. Hydorn, 607-871-2103.
AD: James M. Moretti.

ALLEGHENY

Meadville, PA 16335 III

Coach: Blair Hrovat
(First year as head coach)

1998 SCHEDULE

Wash. & Jeff. ■	Sept. 12
Denison	Sept. 19
Susquehanna	Sept. 26
Wittenberg	Oct. 3
Kenyon ■	Oct. 10
Earlham ■	Oct. 17
Wooster	Oct. 24
Ohio Wesleyan	Oct. 31
Gannon ■	Nov. 7
Oberlin ■	Nov. 14

1997 RESULTS (9-1-0)

45	Thiel	19
17	Wittenberg	29
37	Ohio Wesleyan	21
34	Denison	3
55	Case Reserve	20
28	Wooster	27
35	Earlham	21
43	Brockport St.	10
38	Kenyon	10
75	Oberlin	16
407		**176**

III Championship

30	Mount Union	34

Nickname: Gators.
Stadium: Robertson Field (1948), 5,000 capacity. Natural turf.
Colors: Blue & Gold.
Conference: North Coast Athletic Conf.
SID: Steven Mest, 814-332-6755.
AD: Richard A. Creehan.

ALMA

Alma, MI 48801 III

Coach: Jim Cole, Alma 1974
Record: 7 Years, 33-30-0

1998 SCHEDULE

Thomas More ■	Sept. 5
Defiance	Sept. 12
Olivet Nazarene	Sept. 19
Franklin ■	Sept. 26
Adrian ■	Oct. 10
Albion	Oct. 17
Hope ■	Oct. 24
Kalamazoo	Oct. 31
Olivet ■	Nov. 7

1997 RESULTS (6-3-0)

45	Valparaiso	28
39	Olivet Nazarene	36
48	Elmhurst	7
24	Defiance	29
24	Adrian	27
56	Albion	16
13	Hope	51
20	Kalamazoo	16
31	Olivet	0
300		**210**

Nickname: Scots.
Stadium: Bahlke Field (1986), 4,000 capacity. Artificial turf.
Colors: Maroon & Cream.
Conference: Michigan Intercoll Athl Assn.
SID: To be named, 517-463-7323.
AD: Denny Griffin.

AMERICAN INT'L

Springfield, MA 01109 II

Coach: Art Wilkins, Bucknell 1972
Record: 4 Years, 19-22-0

1998 SCHEDULE

Albany (N.Y.) ■	Sept. 12
Stonehill ■	Sept. 19
Bentley	*Sept. 25
Merrimack	Oct. 3
Assumption ■	Oct. 10
Southern Conn. St.	Oct. 17
Ithaca ■	Oct. 24
Pace	Oct. 31
Stony Brook	Nov. 7
Mass.-Lowell ■	Nov. 14

1997 RESULTS (8-3-0)

14	Springfield	31
26	Stonehill	24
33	Bentley	24
41	Assumption	9
21	Merrimack	8
26	Southern Conn. St.	23
13	Ithaca	40
20	Pace	0
30	Stony Brook	7
27	Mass.-Lowell	0
20	Albany (N.Y.)	27
271		**193**

Nickname: Yellow Jackets.
Stadium: J. H. Miller Field (1964), 5,000 capacity. Natural turf.
Colors: Gold, White & Black.
Conference: Eastern Football.
SID: Chris Herman, 413-747-6544.
AD: Robert E. Burke.

AMHERST

Amherst, MA 01002 III

Coach: E. J. Mills, Dayton 1988
Record: 1 Year, 7-1-0

1998 SCHEDULE

Bates ■	Sept. 26
Bowdoin	Oct. 3
Middlebury	Oct. 10
Colby ■	Oct. 17
Wesleyan (Conn.)	Oct. 24
Tufts ■	Oct. 31
Trinity (Conn.)	Nov. 7
Williams ■	Nov. 14

1997 RESULTS (7-1-0)

38	Hamilton	0
30	Bowdoin	0
22	Middlebury	17
35	Colby	0
36	Wesleyan (Conn.)	14
14	Tufts	6
35	Trinity (Conn.)	8
46	Williams	48
256		**93**

Nickname: Lord Jeffs.
Stadium: Pratt Field (1891), 8,000 capacity. Natural turf.
Colors: Purple & White.
Conference: NESCAC
SID: Rotating, 413-542-2390.
AD: Peter J. Gooding.

ANDERSON (IND.)

Anderson, IN 46012 ... III

Coach: Joe Williams
(First year as head coach)

1998 SCHEDULE

Taylor (Ind.) ■ ... Sept. 12
Wheaton (Ill.) ... Sept. 19
Adrian ■ ... Sept. 26
Wabash ■ ... Oct. 3
Mount Saint Joseph ... Oct. 10
Bluffton ■ ... Oct. 17
Franklin ■ ... Oct. 24
Hanover ... Oct. 31
Wilmington (Ohio) ... Nov. 7
Manchester ■ ... Nov. 14

1997 RESULTS (2-8-0)

23 Taylor (Ind.) ... 24
13 Olivet ... 30
14 Adrian ... 41
7 DePauw ... 21
24 Rose-Hulman ... 10
23 Franklin ... 26
0 Hanover ... 21
29 Benedictine (Ill.) ... 10
12 Wabash ... 37
15 Manchester ... 28
160 **248**

Nickname: Ravens.
Stadium: Macholtz 4,200 capacity. Natural turf.
Colors: Orange & Black.
Conference: Heartland College Athletic Conference.
SID: Brett Marhanka, 317-641-4479.
AD: A. Barrett Bates.

ANGELO ST.

San Angelo, TX 76909 ... II

Coach: Jerry Vandergriff, Corpus Christi 1964
Record: 16 Years, 111-60-2

1998 SCHEDULE

Sam Houston St. ■ ... *Sept. 5
Northeastern St. ■ ... *Sept. 19
Ouachita Baptist ... *Sept. 26
West Tex. A&M ... *Oct. 3
Eastern N.M. ■ ... *Oct. 10
Abilene Christian ... Oct. 17
Midwestern St. ■ ... *Oct. 24
Tarleton St. ... Oct. 31
Tex. A&M-Commerce ... Nov. 7
Texas A&M-Kingsville ■ ... Nov. 14

1997 RESULTS (9-1-0)

24 Sam Houston St. ... 17
34 Northeastern St. ... 30
41 Ouachita Baptist ... 14
31 West Tex. A&M ... 23
16 Eastern N.M. ... 7
42 Abilene Christian ... 10
30 Midwestern St. ... 9
47 Tarleton St. ... 13
40 Tex. A&M-Commerce ... 21
25 Texas A&M-Kingsville ... 35
330 **179**

II Championship

46 Western St. (Colo.) ... 12
33 UC Davis ... 50

Nickname: Rams.
Stadium: San Angelo (1962), 17,500 capacity. Natural turf.
Colors: Blue & Gold.
Conference: Lone Star Conference.
SID: M. L. Stark Hinkle, 915-942-2248.
AD: Jerry Vandergriff.

APPALACHIAN ST.

Boone, NC 28608 ... I-AA

Coach: Jerry Moore, Baylor 1961
Record: 16 Years, 96-85-2

1998 SCHEDULE

Liberty ■ ... *Sept. 5
East Tenn. St. ... *Sept. 12
Citadel ■ ... Sept. 26
Wake Forest ... *Oct. 3
Furman ■ ... Oct. 10
Ga. Southern ... Oct. 17
Wofford ■ ... Oct. 24
Chattanooga ... Oct. 31
VMI ■ ... Nov. 7
Eastern Ky. ... Nov. 14
Western Caro. ... Nov. 21

1997 RESULTS (7-4-0)

12 Clemson ... 23
27 Eastern Ky. ... 23
40 Citadel ... 15
28 East Tenn. St. ... 51
22 Furman ... 24
24 Ga. Southern ... 12
26 Wofford ... 21
41 Chattanooga ... 7
42 VMI ... 7
13 Western Caro. ... 7
19 Liberty ... 25
294 **215**

Nickname: Mountaineers.
Stadium: Kidd Brewer (1962), 16,650 capacity. Artificial turf.
Colors: Black & Gold.
Conference: Southern.
SID: Rick Covington, 704-262-3080.
AD: Roachel Laney.

ARIZONA

Tucson, AZ 85721 ... I-A

Coach: Dick Tomey, De Pauw 1961
Record: 21 Years, 135-97-7

1998 SCHEDULE

Hawaii ... Sept. 3
Stanford ... Sept. 12
Iowa ■ ... *Sept. 19
San Diego St. ... Sept. 24
Washington ... *Oct. 3
UCLA ■ ... *Oct. 10
Oregon St. ... Oct. 17
Northeast La. ■ ... Oct. 24
Oregon ■ ... *Oct. 31
Washington St. ■ ... *Nov. 7
California ... Nov. 14
Arizona St. ■ ... Nov. 27

1997 RESULTS (6-5-0)

9 Oregon ... 16
24 UAB ... 10
20 Ohio St. ... 28
27 UCLA ... 40
31 San Diego St. ... 28
28 Stanford ... 22
28 Washington ... 58
34 Washington St. ... 35
27 Oregon St. ... 7
41 California ... 38
28 Arizona St. ... 16
297 **298**

Insight.com Bowl

20 New Mexico ... 14

Nickname: Wildcats.
Stadium: Arizona (1928), 57,803 capacity. Natural turf.
Colors: Cardinal & Navy.
Conference: Pacific-10.
SID: Tom Duddleston Jr., 602-621-4163.
AD: Jim Livengood.

ARIZONA ST.

Tempe, AZ 85287 ... I-A

Coach: Bruce Snyder, Oregon 1963
Record: 18 Years, 107-89-6

1998 SCHEDULE

Washington ■ ... *Sept. 5
Brigham Young ... *Sept. 12
North Texas ■ ... *Sept. 19
Oregon St. ■ ... *Sept. 26
Southern Cal ... Oct. 3
Notre Dame ■ ... Oct. 10
Stanford ■ ... *Oct. 22
Washington St. ... Oct. 31
California ■ ... Nov. 7
Oregon ... Nov. 14
Arizona ... Nov. 27

1997 RESULTS (8-3-0)

41 New Mexico St. ... 10
23 Miami (Fla.) ... 12
10 Brigham Young ... 13
13 Oregon St. ... 10
14 Washington ... 26
35 Southern Cal ... 7
31 Stanford ... 14
44 Washington St. ... 31
28 California ... 21
52 Oregon ... 31
16 Arizona ... 28
307 **203**

Sun Bowl

17 Iowa ... 7

Nickname: Sun Devils.
Stadium: Sun Devil (1959), 73,379 capacity. Natural turf.
Colors: Maroon & Gold.
Conference: Pacific-10.
SID: Mark Brand, 602-965-6592.
AD: Kevin M. White.

ARKANSAS

Fayetteville, AR 72701 ... I-A

Coach: Houston Nutt, Oklahoma 1981
Record: 5 Years, 35-23-0

1998 SCHEDULE

Southwestern La. ■ ... *Sept. 5
Southern Methodist [Little Rock, Ark.] ... *Sept. 19
Alabama ■ ... *Sept. 26
Kentucky [Little Rock, Ark.] ... *Oct. 3
Memphis ... *Oct. 10
South Caro. ... Oct. 17
Auburn ... Oct. 31
Mississippi ■ ... Nov. 7
Tennessee ... Nov. 14
Mississippi St. ... Nov. 21
LSU [Little Rock, Ark.] ... Nov. 27

1997 RESULTS (4-7-0)

28 Northeast La. ... 16
9 Southern Methodist ... 31
17 Alabama ... 16
17 Louisiana Tech ... 13
7 Florida ... 56
13 South Caro. ... 39
21 Auburn ... 26
9 Mississippi ... 19
22 Tennessee ... 30
17 Mississippi St. ... 7
21 LSU ... 31
181 **284**

Nickname: Razorbacks.
Stadium: Razorback (1938), 51,000 capacity. Natural turf.
Colors: Cardinal & White.
Conference: Southeastern.
SID: Rick Schaeffer, 501-575-2751.
AD: J. Frank Broyles.

ARKANSAS ST.

State University, AR 72467 ... I-A

Coach: Joe Hollis, Auburn 1969
Record: 2 Years, 6-14-1

1998 SCHEDULE

Minnesota ... Sept. 5
LSU ... *Sept. 12

Southwest Mo. St. ■	Sept. 19
Hawaii	*Sept. 26
New Mexico St. ■	Oct. 3
Idaho ■	Oct. 10
Southwestern La.	Oct. 17
Mississippi	Oct. 24
Memphis	Oct. 31
Louisiana Tech ■	Nov. 7
Northeast La. ■	Nov. 14
Cincinnati ■	Nov. 21

1997 RESULTS (2-9-0)

7	Georgia	38
36	Central Ark.	35
24	Southern Utah	34
0	Virginia Tech	50
38	Southwestern La.	41
9	Memphis	38
14	Louisiana Tech	42
20	New Mexico St.	34
10	Miami (Fla.)	42
35	Southwest Mo. St.	27
7	UAB	13
200		**394**

Nickname: Indians.
Stadium: Indian (1974), 33,410 capacity. Natural turf.
Colors: Scarlet & Black.
Conference: Big West.
SID: Gina Bowman, 501-972-2541.
AD: D. Barry Dowd.

ARKANSAS TECH

Russellville, AR 72801 II

Coach: Steve Mullins, Ark.-Monticello 1980
Record: 1 Year, 4-7-0

1998 SCHEDULE

Southwest Baptist	Sept. 5
Delta St. ■	*Sept. 12
West Ala. ■	Sept. 19
Valdosta St.	Sept. 26
Henderson St. ■	Oct. 3
Central Ark.	Oct. 17
Ark.-Monticello ■	Oct. 24
North Ala.	Oct. 31
West Ga. ■	Nov. 7
Southern Ark.	Nov. 14

1997 RESULTS (4-7-0)

10	Harding	28
41	West Ala.	17
23	Delta St.	20
14	Valdosta St.	31
24	North Ala.	45
7	McNeese St.	55
7	Southern Ark.	42
50	Ark.-Monticello	47
10	Northwestern St.	49
29	Henderson St.	22
36	Central Ark.	53
251		**409**

Nickname: Wonder Boys.
Stadium: Buerkle Field, 6,000 capacity. Natural turf.
Colors: Green & Gold.
Conference: Gulf South Conference.
SID: Larry Smith, 501-968-0645.
AD: Earle Doman.

ARK.-MONTICELLO

Monticello, AR 71656.................................II

Coach: Carl Preston, Ark.-Monticello 1964
Record: 1 Year, 0-10-0

1998 SCHEDULE

Harding ■	*Sept. 5
West Ga.	*Sept. 12
Southern Ark. ■	*Sept. 19
McNeese St.	*Sept. 26
North Ala. ■	Oct. 3
Central Ark.	Oct. 10
Henderson St. ■	Oct. 17
Arkansas Tech	Oct. 24
Valdosta St. ■	Oct. 31
West Ala.	Nov. 7
Delta St. ■	Nov. 14

1997 RESULTS (0-10-0)

14	Harding	48
7	West Ga.	39
0	Sam Houston St.	55
10	West Ala.	31
14	Valdosta St.	58
47	Arkansas Tech	50
28	Central Ark.	41
17	Southern Ark.	20
21	Henderson St.	31
14	Delta St.	31
172		**404**

Nickname: Boll Weevils.
Stadium: Cotton Boll, 5,000 capacity. Natural tuf.
Colors: Kelly Green & White.
Conference: Gulf South Conference.
SID: Rob Rodgers, 501-460-1074.
AD: Alvy Early.

ARK.-PINE BLUFF

Pine Bluff, AR 71611...............................I-AA

Coach: Lee Hardman, Ark.-Pine Bluff 1971
Record: 5 Years, 33-22-0

1998 SCHEDULE

Mississippi Val.	*Sept. 5
Southern U. ■	*Sept. 12
Howard [St. Louis, Mo.]	Sept. 19
Alcorn St.	Sept. 26
Alabama St.	*Oct. 3
Texas Southern	*Oct. 10
Grambling [Shreveport, La.]	*Oct. 17
Langston	*Oct. 24
Jackson St. [Little Rock, Ark.]	*Oct. 31
Prairie View ■	Nov. 7
Alabama A&M ■	Nov. 21

1997 RESULTS (8-3-0)

55	Lane	10
15	Mississippi Val.	7
33	Southern U.	36
21	Howard	32
18	Alabama St.	10
36	Texas Southern	16
20	Alcorn St.	10
22	Grambling	16
44	Langston	0
8	Jackson St.	37
48	Prairie View	14
320		**188**

Nickname: Golden Lions.
Stadium: Pumphrey (1951), 6,000 capacity. Natural turf.
Colors: Black & Gold.
Conference: Southwestern.
SID: Carl Wimper, 501-543-8675.
AD: H. O. Clemmons.

ARMY

West Point, NY 10996..............................I-A

Coach: Bob Sutton, Eastern Mich. 1974
Record: 7 Years, 38-39-1

1998 SCHEDULE

Miami (Ohio) ■	Sept. 12
Cincinnati ■	Sept. 19
Rutgers	*Sept. 26
East Caro.	Oct. 3
Houston	Oct. 10
Southern Miss. ■	Oct. 17
Notre Dame	Oct. 24
Air Force ■	Nov. 7
Tulane ■	Nov. 14
Louisville	Nov. 21
Navy [Philadelphia, PA.]	Dec. 5

1997 RESULTS (4-7-0)

25	Marshall	35
41	Lafayette	14
17	Duke	20
14	Miami (Ohio)	38
0	Tulane	41
37	Rutgers	35
35	Colgate	27
0	Air Force	24
25	North Texas	14
20	Boston College	24
7	Navy	39
221		**311**

Nickname: Cadets/Black Knights.
Stadium: Michie (1924), 39,929 capacity. Artificial turf.
Colors: Black, Gold & Gray.
Conference: Conference USA.
SID: Bob Beretta, 914-938-3303.
AD: Albert Vanderbush.

ASHLAND

Ashland, OH 44805.................................II

Coach: Gary Keller, Bluffton 1973
Record: 4 Years, 21-21-0

1998 SCHEDULE

Grand Valley St.	*Sept. 3
Hillsdale ■	*Sept. 12
Northern Mich. ■	*Sept. 19
Wayne St. (Mich.)	Sept. 26
Westminster (Pa.) ■	Oct. 3
Michigan Tech	Oct. 10
Ferris St. ■	*Oct. 17
Mercyhurst	Oct. 24
Indianapolis ■	Nov. 7
Findlay	Nov. 14

1997 RESULTS (9-1-0)

26	Ferris St.	7
31	Michigan Tech	7
20	Grand Valley St.	31
24	Northwood	7
27	Hillsdale	3
27	Saginaw Valley	20
21	Wayne St. (Mich.)	13
27	Northern Mich.	22
28	St. Francis (Ill.)	0
15	Indianapolis	7
246		**117**

II Championship

20	Slippery Rock	30

Nickname: Eagles.
Stadium: Community (1963), 5,700 capacity. Natural turf.
Colors: Purple & Gold.
Conference: Midwest Intercollegiate.
SID: Al King, 419-289-5442.
AD: William Weidner.

ASSUMPTION

Worcester, MA 01615 II

Coach: To be named

1998 SCHEDULE

LIU-C.W. Post	Sept. 12
Merrimack ■	Sept. 19
Bryant	Sept. 26
Stony Brook ■	Oct. 3
American Int'l	Oct. 10
Stonehill	Oct. 17
Bentley ■	Oct. 31
Mass.-Lowell ■	Nov. 7
Pace	Nov. 14

1997 RESULTS (0-10-0)

7	Stonehill	27
7	Merrimack	33
0	Sacred Heart	27
9	American Int'l	41
30	MIT	34
7	LIU-C.W. Post	42
0	Salve Regina	10
0	Bentley	25
14	Mass.-Lowell	29
0	Pace	8
74		**276**

Nickname: Greyhounds.
Stadium: Rocheleau Field (1961), 1,200 capacity. Natural turf.
Colors: Royal Blue & White.

Conference: Eastern Football.
SID: Steve Morris, 508-767-7240.
AD: Rita M. Castagna.

AUBURN

Auburn Univ., AL 36849 .... I-A

Coach: Terry Bowden, West Va. 1978
Record: 14 Years, 110-48-2

1998 SCHEDULE

Virginia ■	*Sept. 3
Mississippi	*Sept. 12
LSU ■	Sept. 19
Tennessee ■	Oct. 3
Mississippi St.	*Oct. 10
Florida	Oct. 17
Louisiana Tech ■	Oct. 24
Arkansas ■	Oct. 31
Central Fla. ■	Nov. 7
Georgia ■	Nov. 14
Alabama	*Nov. 21

1997 RESULTS (9-3-0)

28	Virginia	17
19	Mississippi	9
31	LSU	28
41	Central Fla.	14
23	South Caro.	6
49	Louisiana Tech	13
10	Florida	24
26	Arkansas	21
0	Mississippi St.	20
45	Georgia	34
18	Alabama	17
29	Tennessee	30
319		**233**

Peach Bowl

21	Clemson	17

Nickname: Tigers.
Stadium: Jordan-Hare (1939), 85,214 capacity. Natural turf.
Colors: Orange & Blue.
Conference: Southeastern.
SID: Kent Partridge, 334-844-9800.
AD: David E. Housel.

AUGSBURG

Minneapolis, MN 55454 III

Coach: Jack Osberg, Augsburg 1962
Record: 7 Years, 34-37-0

1998 SCHEDULE

Mayville St. ■	*Sept. 12
Hamline ■	Sept. 19
St. Olaf	Sept. 26
St. John's (Minn.) ■	*Oct. 3
Gust. Adolphus	Oct. 10
Macalester ■	Oct. 17
St. Thomas (Minn.)	Oct. 24
Carleton	Oct. 31
Bethel (Minn.) ■	Nov. 7
Concordia-M'head [Minneapolis, MINN.]	Nov. 13

1997 RESULTS (9-1-0)

24	Valley City St.	20
12	St. Thomas (Minn.)	28
20	St. John's (Minn.)	10
42	St. Olaf	0
26	Hamline	7
35	Carleton	21
41	Gust. Adolphus	35
13	Concordia-M'head	10
24	Macalester	7
56	Bethel (Minn.)	22
293		**160**

III Championship

34	Concordia-M'head	22
21	Simpson	61

Nickname: Auggies.
Stadium: Anderson-Nelson Field (1984), 2,000 capacity. Artificial turf.
Colors: Maroon & Gray.
Conference: Minn. Intercol. Athletic Conf.
SID: Don Stoner, 612-330-1677.
AD: Paul Grauer.

AUGUSTANA (ILL.)

Rock Island, IL 61201 III

Coach: Tom Schmulbach, Western Ill. 1969
Record: 3 Years, 18-9-0

1998 SCHEDULE

Hope ■	Sept. 12
Wis.-Platteville	*Sept. 19
Millikin	Oct. 3
Ill. Wesleyan	Oct. 10
Elmhurst ■	Oct. 17
North Central	*Oct. 24
North Park ■	Oct. 31
Carthage	Nov. 7
Wheaton (Ill.) ■	Nov. 14

1997 RESULTS (7-2-0)

30	Wartburg	33
51	Benedictine (Ill.)	0
21	Wheaton (Ill.)	16
28	Carthage	21
28	North Park	3
42	North Central	14
2	Ill. Wesleyan	28
50	Elmhurst	14
18	Millikin	0
270		**129**

Nickname: Vikings.
Stadium: Ericson Field (1938), 3,200 capacity. Natural turf.
Colors: Gold & Blue.
Conference: College Conf. of Ill. & Wisc.
SID: Dave Wrath, 309-794-7265.
AD: John Farwell.

AUGUSTANA (S.D.)

Sioux Falls, SD 57197 II

Coach: Jim Heinitz, South Dak. St. 1972
Record: 10 Years, 47-61-1

1998 SCHEDULE

Northern St.	*Sept. 5
Southwest St.	*Sept. 12
Northern Colo.	Sept. 19
North Dak. St. ■	*Sept. 26
Morningside	Oct. 3
Neb.-Omaha	Oct. 10
St. Cloud St. ■	Oct. 17
South Dak. ■	Oct. 24
South Dak. St.	Oct. 31
North Dak. ■	Nov. 7
Mankato St. ■	Nov. 14

1997 RESULTS (5-6-0)

21	Washburn	17
35	Southwest St.	3
40	Northern Colo.	49
0	North Dak. St.	37
10	Morningside	6
6	Neb.-Omaha	35
28	St. Cloud St.	43
23	South Dak.	35
28	South Dak. St.	22
14	North Dak.	42
43	Mankato St.	10
248		**299**

Nickname: Vikings.
Stadium: Howard Wood (1957), 10,000 capacity. Natural turf.
Colors: Navy & Yellow.
Conference: No. Central Intercoll Ath Conf.
SID: Karen Madsen, 605-336-4335.
AD: Bill Gross.

AURORA

Aurora, IL 60506 III

Coach: Jim Scott, Luther 1961
Record: 12 Years, 57-45-3

1998 SCHEDULE

Urbana	Sept. 12
Millikin ■	Sept. 19
MacMurray ■	Sept. 26
Eureka	Oct. 3
Benedictine (Ill.) ■	Oct. 10
Concordia (Ill.)	Oct. 17
Concordia (Wis.) ■	Oct. 24
Greenville	Oct. 31
Lakeland ■	Nov. 7
Valparaiso	Nov. 14

1997 RESULTS (4-5-0)

20	Coe	21
32	Wheaton (Ill.)	25
14	Kalamazoo	15
37	Concordia (Wis.)	7
27	Benedictine (Ill.)	16
27	Upper Iowa	34
18	Simpson	37
0	Drake	45
33	Valparaiso	7
208		**207**

Nickname: Spartans.
Stadium: Aurora Field 1,500 capacity. Natural turf.
Colors: Royal Blue & White.
Conference: Independent.
SID: Dave Beyer, 708-844-5479.
AD: Rita Yerkes.

AUSTIN

Sherman, TX 75090 III

Coach: David Norman, Austin 1983
Record: 4 Years, 15-25-0

1998 SCHEDULE

Millsaps ■	Sept. 5
Neb. Wesleyan	Sept. 12
Trinity (Tex.)	*Sept. 19
Texas Lutheran ■	*Oct. 3
Howard Payne	Oct. 10
Hardin-Simmons ■	Oct. 17
Mary Hardin-Baylor	Oct. 24
McMurry ■	Oct. 31
Sul Ross St.	Nov. 7
Mississippi Col. ■	Nov. 14

1997 RESULTS (4-6-0)

15	Millsaps	44
9	Neb. Wesleyan	35
21	Rhodes	13
10	Trinity (Tex.)	37
30	Colorado Col.	7
17	Mississippi Col.	15
21	McMurry	20
13	Hardin-Simmons	35
20	Sul Ross St.	24
13	Howard Payne	27
169		**257**

Nickname: Kangaroos.
Stadium: Lewis Calder (1960), 2,800 capacity. Natural turf.
Colors: Crimson & Gold.
Conference: American Southwest.
SID: Chuck Sadowski, 214-892-9101.
AD: Timothy P. Millerick.

AUSTIN PEAY

Clarksville, TN 37044 .... I-AA

Coach: Bill Schmitz, Coast Guard 1976
Record: 5 Years, 20-29-0

1998 SCHEDULE

Campbellsville ■	*Aug. 29
Morehead St. ■	*Sept. 3
Samford	*Sept. 12
Dayton ■	*Sept. 19
Western Ky.	*Sept. 26
Jacksonville	Oct. 3
Charleston So. ■	Oct. 17
Cumberland (Tenn.)	Oct. 31
Tusculum ■	Nov. 7

Georgetown ....Nov. 14
Valparaiso ....Nov. 21

1997 RESULTS (0-10-0)

43 Morehead St. 55
13 Samford 21
7 Western Ky. 53
3 Eastern Ky. 56
3 Tennessee Tech 36
0 Murray St. 51
14 Eastern Ill. 42
0 Southeast Mo. St. 31
10 Middle Tenn. St. 59
26 Tenn.-Martin 36
119 **440**

Nickname: Governors.
Stadium: Governors (1946), 10,000 capacity. Artificial turf.
Colors: Red & White.
Conference: Independent.
SID: Brad Kirtley, 615-648-7561.
AD: Dave Loos.

BALDWIN-WALLACE

Berea, OH 44017 III

Coach: Bob Packard, Baldwin-Wallace 1965
Record: 17 Years, 130-40-2

1998 SCHEDULE

Wittenberg ■ ....*Sept. 12
Otterbein ■ ....*Sept. 19
Marietta ....*Sept. 26
Hiram ....Oct. 3
Ohio Northern ■ ....Oct. 10
John Carroll ....Oct. 17
Capital ■ ....Oct. 24
Muskingum ■ ....Oct. 31
Heidelberg ....Nov. 7
Mount Union ■ ....Nov. 14

1997 RESULTS (7-3-0)

30 Mercyhurst 13
14 Mount Union 56
20 Heidelberg 13
35 Marietta 17
63 Capital 6
31 Otterbein 17
47 Hiram 20
16 Muskingum 10
17 Ohio Northern 31
17 John Carroll 20
290 **203**

Nickname: Yellow Jackets.
Stadium: George Finnie (1971), 8,100 capacity. Artificial turf.
Colors: Brown & Gold.
Conference: Ohio Athletic Conference.
SID: Kevin Ruple, 216-826-2327.
AD: Stephen Bankson.

BALL ST.

Muncie, IN 47306 ....I-A

Coach: Bill Lynch, Butler 1977
Record: 8 Years, 56-26-3

1998 SCHEDULE

South Caro. ....*Sept. 5
Eastern Mich. ■ ....Sept. 12
Iowa St. ....Sept. 19
Akron ....*Sept. 26
Northern Ill. ■ ....Oct. 3
Toledo ....Oct. 10
Miami (Ohio) ■ ....Oct. 17
Marshall ....Oct. 24
Western Mich. ■ ....Nov. 7
Central Fla. ....Nov. 14
Central Mich. ....Nov. 21

1997 RESULTS (5-6-0)

10 Miami (Ohio) 27
24 James Madison 6
6 Indiana 33
14 Purdue 28
16 Marshall 42
13 Western Mich. 21
32 Eastern Mich. 38
37 Central Mich. 34
21 Northern Ill. 14
31 Akron 14
35 Toledo 3
239 **260**

Nickname: Cardinals.
Stadium: Ball State (1967), 21,581 capacity. Natural turf.
Colors: Cardinal & White.
Conference: Mid-American.
SID: Joe Hernandez, 317-285-8242.
AD: Andrea Seger.

BATES

Lewiston, ME 04240 III

Coach: Mark Harriman, Springfield 1980
(First year as head coach)

1998 SCHEDULE

Amherst ....Sept. 26
Tufts ....Oct. 3
Williams ■ ....Oct. 10
Wesleyan (Conn.) ■ ....Oct. 17
Middlebury ....Oct. 24
Colby ■ ....Oct. 31
Bowdoin ....Nov. 7
Hamilton ■ ....Nov. 14

1997 RESULTS (1-7-0)

6 Trinity (Conn.) 31
0 Tufts 24
16 Williams 36
14 Wesleyan (Conn.) 17
20 Middlebury 35
22 Colby 21
19 Bowdoin 28
7 Hamilton 17
104 **209**

Nickname: Bobcats.
Stadium: Garcelon Field (1900), 3,000 capacity. Natural turf.
Colors: Garnet.
Conference: NESCAC.
SID: Adam Levin, 207-786-6411.
AD: Suzanne R. Coffey.

BAYLOR

Waco, TX 76798 ....I-A

Coach: Dave Roberts, Western Caro. 1968
Record: 11 Years, 65-59-3

1998 SCHEDULE

Oregon St. ....Sept. 12
North Caro. St. ■ ....*Sept. 19
Colorado ....Sept. 26
Texas Tech ....*Oct. 3
Kansas ■ ....*Oct. 10
Texas A&M ■ ....*Oct. 17
Texas ....Oct. 24
Notre Dame ....Oct. 31
Kansas St. ■ ....Nov. 7
Oklahoma ■ ....Nov. 14
Oklahoma St. ....Nov. 21

1997 RESULTS (2-9-0)

14 Miami (Fla.) 45
37 Fresno St. 35
3 Michigan 38
14 Texas Tech 35
21 Nebraska 49
23 Oklahoma 24
17 Iowa St. 24
23 Texas 21
10 Texas A&M 38
24 Missouri 42
14 Oklahoma St. 24
200 **375**

Nickname: Bears.
Stadium: Floyd Casey (1950), 50,000 capacity. Artificial turf.
Colors: Green & Gold.
Conference: Big 12.
SID: Brian McCallum, 817-755-2743.
AD: Tom Stanton.

BELOIT

Beloit, WI 53511 III

Coach: Ed DeGeorge, Colorado Col. 1964
Record: 21 Years, 97-94-1

1998 SCHEDULE

Concordia (Wis.) ....Sept. 12
Grinnell ....Sept. 19
Monmouth (Ill.) ■ ....Sept. 26
Lake Forest ....Oct. 3
Lawrence ■ ....Oct. 10
Illinois Col. ....Oct. 17
Knox ■ ....Oct. 24
Carroll (Wis.) ■ ....Oct. 31
St. Norbert ....Nov. 7
Ripon ■ ....Nov. 14

1997 RESULTS (3-6-0)

7 Knox 35
0 Concordia (Wis.) 40
17 Grinnell 38
28 Cornell College 20
26 Ripon 32
12 Carroll (Wis.) 43
34 Lawrence 27
21 St. Norbert 20
19 Lake Forest 31
164 **286**

Nickname: Buccaneers.
Stadium: Strong (1934), 3,500 capacity. Natural turf.
Colors: Navy Blue & Gold.
Conference: Midwest Conference.
SID: Nate Llewellyn, 608-363-2229.
AD: Edward J. De George.

BEMIDJI ST.

Bemidji, MN 56601 II

Coach: Jeff Tesch, Moorhead St. 1978
Record: 2 Years, 4-16-0

1998 SCHEDULE

Crookston ....Sept. 5
St. Thomas (Minn.) ■ ....Sept. 12
Mayville St. ....*Sept. 19
Moorhead St. ■ ....Sept. 26
Winona St. ....Oct. 3
Minn.-Morris ■ ....Oct. 10
Northern St. ....Oct. 17
Minn.-Duluth ■ ....Oct. 31
Southwest St. ....Nov. 7
Wis.-River Falls [Minneapolis, Minn.] ....Nov. 14

1997 RESULTS (2-8-0)

25 St. John's (Minn.) 21
6 Wis.-Stout 43
0 Wis.-Stevens Point 47
0 Southwest St. 16
17 Moorhead St. 36
14 Winona St. 58
28 Minn.-Morris 45
25 Northern St. 22
0 Minn.-Duluth 41
34 Minn.-Morris 41
149 **370**

Nickname: Beavers.
Stadium: BSU (1937), 4,000 capacity. Natural turf.
Colors: Kelly Green & White.
Conference: Northern Sun.
SID: Ron Christian, 218-755-2763.
AD: Robert H. Peters.

BENEDICTINE (ILL.)

Lisle, IL 60532 III

Coach: Rob Boras, De Pauw 1992
(First year as head coach)

1998 SCHEDULE

Blackburn ■ ....Sept. 5

North Central ■ .... Sept. 12
Elmhurst .... Sept. 19
Eureka .... Sept. 26
Concordia (Ill.) ■ .... Oct. 3
Aurora .... Oct. 10
Concordia (Wis.) ■ .... Oct. 17
Greenville .... Oct. 24
Lakeland .... Oct. 31
MacMurray ■ .... Nov. 7

1997 RESULTS (3-7-0)

15 Loras 23
0 Hope 27
10 Elmhurst 7
0 Augustana (Ill.) 51
6 Adrian 30
16 Aurora 27
22 Wabash 18
27 Bethel (Tenn.) 21
10 Anderson (Ind.) 29
9 DePauw 24
115 **257**

Nickname: Eagles.
Stadium: Alumni Memorial (1910), 2,500 capacity. Natural turf.
Colors: Cardinal & White.
Conference: Independent.
SID: Renee Kanak, 708-960-1500.
AD: Florence Grebner.

BENTLEY

Waltham, MA 02154 II

Coach: Peter Yetten, Boston U. 1971
Record: 10 Years, 72-21-1

1998 SCHEDULE

Merrimack .... Sept. 12
Southern Conn. St. ■ .... *Sept. 18
American Int'l ■ .... *Sept. 25
Mass.-Lowell .... *Oct. 3
Stony Brook ■ .... Oct. 10
Pace ■ .... Oct. 17
Plymouth St. .... Oct. 24
Assumption .... Oct. 31
LIU-C.W. Post .... Nov. 7
Stonehill ■ .... Nov. 14

1997 RESULTS (6-3-0)

14 Merrimack 12
24 American Int'l 33
45 La Salle 0
9 Stony Brook 35
47 Mass.-Lowell 14
35 Sacred Heart 0
25 Assumption 0
7 LIU-C.W. Post 9
49 Stonehill 24
255 **127**

Nickname: Falcons.
Stadium: Bentley College (1990), 3,100 capacity. Natural turf.
Colors: Royal Blue & Gold.
Conference: Eastern Football.
SID: Dick Lipe, 617-891-2334.
AD: Robert De Felice.

BETHANY (W. VA.)

Bethany, WV 26032 III

Coach: Steve Campos, Indiana (Pa.) 1982
Record: 5 Years, 21-25-1

1998 SCHEDULE

Bluffton .... Sept. 5
Carnegie Mellon .... *Sept. 19
Grove City ■ .... Sept. 26
Waynesburg .... Oct. 3
Madison Tech ■ .... Oct. 10
Wash. & Jeff. ■ .... Oct. 17
Thiel ■ .... Oct. 24
Maryville (Tenn.) .... Oct. 31
Alfred .... Nov. 7
Greensboro .... Nov. 14

1997 RESULTS (4-6-0)

16 Capital 20
56 Swarthmore 0
45 Greensboro 13
23 Waynesburg 29
38 Alfred 26
21 Wash. & Jeff. 38
26 Thiel 7
21 Grove City 35
14 Wilmington (Ohio) 30
14 Carnegie Mellon 49
274 **247**

Nickname: Bison.
Stadium: Bethany Field (1938), 1,000 capacity. Natural turf.
Colors: Green & White.
Conference: Presidents' Athletic Conf.
SID: John Stroh, 304-829-7292.
AD: Wallace B. Neel.

BETHEL (MINN.)

St. Paul, MN 55112 III

Coach: Steve Johnson, Bethel (Minn.) 1980
Record: 9 Years, 51-37-1

1998 SCHEDULE

Trinity (Ill.) .... Sept. 12
Concordia-M'head ■ .... Sept. 19
Hamline .... Sept. 26
St. Olaf ■ .... Oct. 3
St. John's (Minn.) .... Oct. 10
Gust. Adolphus ■ .... Oct. 17
Macalester .... Oct. 24
St. Thomas (Minn.) ■ .... Oct. 31
Augsburg .... Nov. 7
Carleton [Minneapolis, Minn.] .... *Nov. 13

1997 RESULTS (6-4-0)

32 Trinity (Ill.) 30
39 Hamline 10
62 Carleton 14
21 Gust. Adolphus 31
14 Concordia-M'head 22
35 Macalester 0
52 St. Olaf 10
33 St. Thomas (Minn.) 27
14 St. John's (Minn.) 17
22 Augsburg 56
324 **217**

Nickname: Royals.
Stadium: Bremer Field (1972), 3,000 capacity. Natural turf.
Colors: Royal Blue & Gold.
Conference: Minn. Intercol. Athletic Conf.
SID: Greg Peterson, 612-638-6394.
AD: David A. Klostreich.

BETHUNE-COOKMAN

Daytona Beach, FL 32114 .... I-AA

Coach: Alvin Wyatt Sr., Bethune-Cookman 1970
Record: 1 Year, 4-7-0

1998 SCHEDULE

Savannah St. [Jacksonville, Fla.] .... Sept. 5
Morgan St. .... Sept. 12
Virginia St. ■ .... *Sept. 26
Howard [Indianapolis, Ind.] .... Oct. 3
Delaware St. ■ .... Oct. 10
South Caro. St. .... Oct. 17
North Caro. A&T .... Oct. 31
Hampton .... Nov. 7
Norfolk St. ■ .... Nov. 14
Florida A&M [Orlando, Fla.] .... *Nov. 21

1997 RESULTS (4-7-0)

35 Morris Brown 20
15 Morgan St. 18
14 Fayetteville St. 0
44 Cheyney 0
14 Delaware St. 35
7 Howard 14
10 South Caro. St. 17
26 North Caro. A&T 25
0 Hampton 27
7 Norfolk St. 21
35 Florida A&M 52
207 **229**

Nickname: Wildcats.
Stadium: Municipal, 10,000 capacity. Natural turf.
Colors: Maroon & Gold.
Conference: Mid-Eastern.
SID: Charles D. Jackson, 904-255-1401.
AD: Lynn W. Thompson.

BLACKBURN

Carlinville, IL 62626 III

Coach: Dale Sprague, American Intl 1976
Record: 12 Years, 40-66-2

1998 SCHEDULE

Benedictine (Ill.) .... Sept. 5
MacMurray ■ .... Sept. 12
Franklin ■ .... Sept. 19
Millikin ■ .... Sept. 26
Westminster (Mo.) .... Oct. 3
Greenville ■ .... Oct. 10
Principia .... Oct. 24
Maranatha Baptist ■ .... Nov. 7
Culver-Stockton .... Nov. 14

1997 RESULTS (1-8-0)

10 Greenville 17
16 Eureka 42
0 North Central 44
13 Westminster (Mo.) 33
34 Principia 14
0 McKendree 48
0 Wartburg 48
23 MacMurray 31
16 Culver-Stockton 34
112 **311**

Nickname: Battlin' Beavers.
Stadium: Blackburn College (1989), 1,500 capacity. Natural turf.
Colors: Scarlet & Black.
Conference: St. Louis Intercol. Ath. Conf.
SID: Tom Emery, 217-854-3231.
AD: Ira Zeff.

BLOOMSBURG

Bloomsburg, PA 17815 II

Coach: Danny Hale, West Chester 1968
Record: 10 Years, 80-27-1

1998 SCHEDULE

New Haven .... Sept. 5
Shippensburg .... Sept. 12
Lock Haven ■ .... Sept. 19
Indiana (Pa.) ■ .... Sept. 26
Kutztown ■ .... Oct. 3
Millersville .... *Oct. 10
West Chester .... Oct. 17
Cheyney ■ .... Oct. 24
East Stroudsburg ■ .... Oct. 31
Mansfield .... Nov. 7
Edinboro .... Nov. 14

1997 RESULTS (8-2-0)

22 Wayne St. (Mich.) 0
13 Indiana (Pa.) 18
17 Lock Haven 3
68 Cheyney 6
55 Mansfield 0
24 Millersville 8
29 Shippensburg 34
17 Kutztown 7
24 West Chester 14
42 East Stroudsburg 17
311 **107**

Nickname: Huskies.
Stadium: Redman (1974), 5,000 capacity. Natural turf.
Colors: Maroon & Gold.
Conference: Pennsylvania State Athl. Conf.
SID: Tom McGuire, 717-389-4413.
AD: Mary Gardner.

BLUFFTON

Bluffton, OH 45817 III

Coach: Carlin Carpenter, Defiance 1964
Record: 19 Years, 73-103-1

1998 SCHEDULE

Bethany (W. Va.) ■ ....Sept. 5
Hiram ■ ....Sept. 12
Grove City ....Sept. 19
Hanover ....Oct. 3
Wabash ■ ....Oct. 10
Anderson (Ind.) ....Oct. 17
Manchester ....Oct. 24
Mount Saint Joseph ■ ....Oct. 31
Franklin ....Nov. 7
Wilmington (Ohio) ■ ....Nov. 14

1997 RESULTS (4-6-0)

0	Wittenberg	52
0	Ohio Northern	55
27	Thiel	33
24	Manchester	31
14	Thomas More	38
30	Sue Bennett	0
21	Grove City	71
40	Mount Saint Joseph	35
21	Wilmington (Ohio)	17
31	Defiance	6
208		**338**

Nickname: Beavers.
Stadium: Salzman (1993), 3,000 capacity. Natural turf.
Colors: Northwestern Purple & White.
Conference: Independent.
SID: Ron Geiser, 419-358-3241.
AD: Carlin B. Carpenter.

BOISE ST.

Boise, ID 83725 ....I-A

Coach: Dirk Koetter, Idaho St. 1981
(First year as head coach)

1998 SCHEDULE

Cal St. Northridge ■ ....*Sept. 5
Washington St. ■ ....*Sept. 12
Portland St. ■ ....*Sept. 19
Utah ....*Sept. 26
Louisiana Tech ....Oct. 3
North Texas ■ ....*Oct. 10
Weber St. ■ ....*Oct. 17
Utah St. ■ ....*Oct. 24
Nevada ....Oct. 31
New Mexico St. ....*Nov. 7
Idaho ■ ....Nov. 21

1997 RESULTS (4-7-0)

23	Cal St. Northridge	63
24	Wisconsin	28
26	Central Mich.	44
24	Weber St.	7
0	Washington St.	58
52	New Mexico St.	10
17	North Texas	14
27	Louisiana Tech	31
20	Utah St.	24
42	Nevada	56
30	Idaho	23
285		**358**

Nickname: Broncos.
Stadium: Bronco (1970), 30,000 capacity. Artificial turf.
Colors: Orange & Blue.
Conference: Big West.
SID: Max Corbet, 208-385-1515.
AD: Gene Bleymaier.

BOSTON COLLEGE

Chestnut Hill, MA 02167 ....I-A

Coach: Tom O'Brien, Navy 1971
Record: 1 Year, 4-7-0

1998 SCHEDULE

Georgia Tech ....Sept. 5
Rutgers ■ ....Sept. 12
Temple ■ ....Sept. 19
Louisville ....Sept. 26
Virginia Tech ■ ....*Oct. 8
Syracuse ■ ....Oct. 17
Navy ■ ....Oct. 24
Miami (Fla.) ....Oct. 31
Notre Dame ■ ....Nov. 7
Pittsburgh ....Nov. 14
West Va. ....Nov. 21

1997 RESULTS (4-7-0)

21	Temple	28
31	West Va.	24
35	Rutgers	21
6	Cincinnati	24
14	Georgia Tech	42
7	Virginia Tech	17
44	Miami (Fla.)	45
20	Notre Dame	52
22	Pittsburgh	21
13	Syracuse	20
24	Army	20
237		**314**

Nickname: Eagles.
Stadium: Alumni (1957), 44,500 capacity. Artificial turf.
Colors: Maroon & Gold.
Conference: Big East.
SID: Chris Cameron, 617-552-3004.
AD: Gene De Filippo.

BOSTON U.

Boston, MA 02215 ....I-AA

Coach: Tom Masella, Wagner 1981

1998 SCHEDULE

Dropped program following 1997 season.

1997 RESULTS (1-10-0)

14	Hofstra	24
7	Youngstown St.	28
17	William & Mary	20
17	Delaware	49
17	Rhode Island	20
29	Maine	62
7	Northeastern	28
7	Connecticut	45
33	Massachusetts	8
0	New Hampshire	38
14	James Madison	31
162		**353**

Nickname: Terriers.
Stadium: Nickerson Field (1930), 17,369 capacity. Artificial turf.
Colors: Scarlet & White.
Conference: Atlantic 10.
SID: Ed Carpenter, 617-353-2872.
AD: Gary Strickler.

BOWDOIN

Brunswick, ME 04011 III

Coach: Howard Vandersea, Bates 1963
Record: 22 Years, 82-104-3

1998 SCHEDULE

Williams ....Sept. 26
Amherst ■ ....Oct. 3
Tufts ■ ....Oct. 10
Hamilton ....Oct. 17
Trinity (Conn.) ■ ....Oct. 24
Wesleyan (Conn.) ....Oct. 31
Bates ■ ....Nov. 7
Colby ....Nov. 14

1997 RESULTS (4-4-0)

0	Middlebury	43
0	Amherst	30
28	Tufts	20
33	Hamilton	14
7	Trinity (Conn.)	38
17	Wesleyan (Conn.)	24
28	Bates	19
27	Colby	19
140		**207**

Nickname: Polar Bears.
Stadium: Whittier Field (1896), 6,000 capacity. Natural turf.
Colors: White.
Conference: NESCAC.
SID: Jac Coyne, 207-725-3254.
AD: Jeffrey H. Ward.

BOWIE ST.

Bowie, MD 20715 II

Coach: Sherman Wood, Salisbury St. 1984
Record: 5 Years, 16-34-1

1998 SCHEDULE

Cheyney ....Sept. 5
Johnson Smith ■ ....Sept. 19
Livingstone ....Sept. 26
Virginia Union ■ ....Oct. 3
Gannon ■ ....Oct. 10
Elizabeth City St. ■ ....Oct. 17
N.C. Central ....Oct. 24
Fayetteville St. ....Oct. 31
Virginia St. ■ ....Nov. 7

1997 RESULTS (4-6-0)

9	Livingstone	40
13	Johnson Smith	19
27	Cheyney	6
14	Virginia Union	38
10	Gannon	7
32	Elizabeth City St.	26
20	N.C. Central	14
7	Fayetteville St.	14
22	Virginia St.	31
0	Winston-Salem	21
154		**216**

Nickname: Bulldogs.
Stadium: Bulldog (1992), 6,000 capacity. Natural turf.
Colors: Black & Gold.
Conference: Central Intercol. Ath. Assn.
SID: Scott Rouch, 301-464-7710.
AD: David Y. Thomas.

BOWLING GREEN

Bowling Green, OH 43403 ....I-A

Coach: Gary Blackney, Connecticut 1967
Record: 7 Years, 48-29-2

1998 SCHEDULE

Missouri ....*Sept. 5
Penn St. ....Sept. 12
Central Fla. ■ ....Sept. 26
Ohio ■ ....Oct. 3
Miami (Ohio) ....Oct. 10
Toledo ....*Oct. 17
Kent ■ ....Oct. 24
Marshall ■ ....Oct. 31
Akron ■ ....Nov. 7
Western Mich. ....Nov. 14
Northern Ill. ....Nov. 21

1997 RESULTS (3-8-0)

23	Louisiana Tech	30
28	Miami (Ohio)	21
13	Ohio St.	44
31	Akron	28
0	Kansas St.	58
35	Northern Ill.	10
21	Western Mich.	34
0	Ohio	24
20	Toledo	35
20	Kent	29
0	Marshall	28
191		**341**

Nickname: Falcons.
Stadium: Doyt Perry (1966), 30,599 capacity. Natural turf.
Colors: Orange & Brown.
Conference: Mid-American.
SID: Steve Barr, 419-372-7075.
AD: Ronald E. Zwierlein.

BRI'WATER (MASS.)

Bridgewater, MA 02325 III

Coach: Peter Mazzaferro, Centre 1954
Record: 24 Years, 163-135-11

1998 SCHEDULE

Springfield ■ .... Sept. 12
Salve Regina .... *Sept. 19
Worcester St. .... Sept. 26
Framingham St. ■ .... Oct. 3
Maine Maritime .... Oct. 10
MIT ■ .... Oct. 17
Westfield St. .... Oct. 24
Mass.-Dartmouth ■ .... Oct. 31
Fitchburg St. .... Nov. 7
Mass. Maritime ■ .... Nov. 14

1997 RESULTS (7-3-0)

7	Western Conn. St.	45
28	Maine Maritime	27
32	Mass.-Boston	14
39	Fitchburg St.	7
42	Framingham St.	0
55	Westfield St.	21
9	Plymouth St.	15
6	Worcester St.	23
33	Mass. Maritime	14
44	Mass.-Dartmouth	28
295		**194**

Nickname: Bears.
Stadium: College (1974), 3,000 capacity. Natural turf.
Colors: Crimson & White.
Conference: New England FB.
SID: Michael Storey, 617-697-1352.
AD: John C. Harper.

BRIDGEWATER (VA.)

Bridgewater, VA 22812 III

Coach: Michael Clark, Cincinnati 1979
Record: 3 Years, 7-22-1

1998 SCHEDULE

Western Md. .... Sept. 5
Catholic .... Sept. 12
Emory & Henry .... Sept. 19
Ferrum ■ .... Sept. 26
Hampden-Sydney ■ .... Oct. 3
Guilford .... Oct. 17
Johns Hopkins ■ .... Oct. 24
Wash. & Lee ■ .... Oct. 31
Randolph-Macon .... Nov. 7
Davidson ■ .... Nov. 14

1997 RESULTS (2-8-0)

17	Western Md.	21
0	Catholic	35
7	Emory & Henry	31
24	Hampden-Sydney	0
0	Methodist	18
14	Guilford	30
10	Johns Hopkins	21
10	Wash. & Lee	22
20	Randolph-Macon	37
13	Davidson	10
115		**225**

Nickname: Eagles.
Stadium: Jopson Field (1971), 3,000 capacity. Natural turf.
Colors: Crimson & Gold.
Conference: Old Dominion Athletic Conf.
SID: Douglas Barton, 703-828-5360.
AD: Thomas M. Kinder.

BRIGHAM YOUNG

Provo, UT 84602 ....I-A

Coach: LaVell Edwards, Utah St. 1952
Record: 26 Years, 234-86-3

1998 SCHEDULE

Alabama .... Sept. 5
Arizona St. ■ .... *Sept. 12
Washington .... Sept. 19
Murray St. ■ .... Sept. 26
Fresno St. .... *Oct. 3
UNLV ■ .... Oct. 10
Hawaii .... *Oct. 17
San Jose St. ■ .... Oct. 24
San Diego St. ■ .... *Oct. 29
New Mexico ■ .... Nov. 7
UTEP .... Nov. 14
Utah .... Nov. 21

1997 RESULTS (6-5-0)

20	Washington	42
13	Arizona St.	10
19	Southern Methodist	16
42	Utah St.	35
14	Rice	27
17	Hawaii	3
31	Texas Christian	10
3	UTEP	14
49	Tulsa	39
28	New Mexico	38
14	Utah	20
250		**254**

Nickname: Cougars.
Stadium: Cougar (1964), 65,000 capacity. Natural turf.
Colors: Royal Blue & White.
Conference: Western Athletic.
SID: Ralph Zobell, 801-378-4911.
AD: Rondo Fehlberg.

BROCKPORT ST.

Brockport, NY 14420 III

Coach: Rocco Salomone, Brockport St. 1988
Record: 3 Years, 16-13-1

1998 SCHEDULE

New Jersey City .... Sept. 12
Plymouth St. .... Sept. 19
Montclair St. .... Sept. 26
Buffalo St. ■ .... Oct. 3
Ithaca ■ .... Oct. 10
Frostburg St. .... Oct. 17
St. John Fisher ■ .... Oct. 24
Col. of New Jersey ■ .... Nov. 7
Cortland St. .... Nov. 14

1997 RESULTS (6-4-0)

12	New Jersey City	7
10	Plymouth St.	9
33	Montclair St.	27
10	Buffalo St.	13
14	Ithaca	21
33	Frostburg St.	22
17	St. John Fisher	0
10	Allegheny	43
7	Col. of New Jersey	42
30	Cortland St.	28
176		**212**

Nickname: Golden Eagles.
Stadium: Special Olympics (1979), 10,000 capacity. Natural turf.
Colors: Green & Gold.
Conference: Independent
SID: Mike Andriatch, 716-395-2218.
AD: Linda J. Case.

BROWN

Providence, RI 02912 ....I-AA

Coach: Phil Estes, New Hampshire 1981
(First year as head coach)

1998 SCHEDULE

Yale ■ .... Sept. 19
Lafayette .... Sept. 26
Rhode Island .... Oct. 3
Princeton .... Oct. 10
Fordham ■ .... Oct. 17
Pennsylvania ■ .... Oct. 24
Cornell .... Oct. 31
Harvard .... Nov. 7
Dartmouth ■ .... Nov. 14
Columbia .... Nov. 21

1997 RESULTS (6-4-0)

52	Yale	14
35	Lafayette	27
45	Fordham	14
13	Princeton	30
23	Rhode Island	15
10	Pennsylvania	31
37	Cornell	12
10	Harvard	27
7	Dartmouth	13
42	Columbia	11
274		**194**

Nickname: Bears.
Stadium: Brown (1925), 20,000 capacity. Natural turf.
Colors: Seal Brown, Cardinal & White.
Conference: Ivy.
SID: Christopher Humm, 401-863-2219.
AD: David T. Roach.

BUCKNELL

Lewisburg, PA 17837 ....I-AA

Coach: Tom Gadd, UC Riverside 1970
Record: 3 Years, 23-10-0

1998 SCHEDULE

Duquesne .... *Sept. 5
St. Mary's (Cal.) ■ .... Sept. 12
Fordham ■ .... Sept. 19
Columbia ■ .... Sept. 26
Pennsylvania .... Oct. 3
Cornell .... Oct. 17
Lafayette ■ .... Oct. 24
Colgate ■ .... Oct. 31
Holy Cross .... Nov. 7
Lehigh .... Nov. 14
Towson ■ .... Nov. 21

1997 RESULTS (10-1-0)

23	Duquesne	16
23	Lafayette	21
20	Pennsylvania	16
24	Harvard	20
25	Yale	24
36	Fordham	10
18	Holy Cross	6
21	Lehigh	14
45	St. Mary's (Cal.)	38
33	Towson	0
14	Colgate	48
282		**213**

Nickname: Bison.
Stadium: Christy Mathewson (1924), 13,100 capacity. Natural turf.
Colors: Orange & Blue.
Conference: Patriot.
SID: Pat Farabaugh, 717-524-1227.
AD: Rick R. Hartzell.

BUENA VISTA

Storm Lake, IA 50588 III

Coach: Joe Hadachek, Northern Iowa 1985
Record: 2 Years, 8-12-0

1998 SCHEDULE

Upper Iowa .... Sept. 5
William Penn ■ .... Sept. 12
Wartburg .... Sept. 19
Cornell College ■ .... Oct. 3
Loras ■ .... Oct. 10
Simpson .... Oct. 17
Luther ■ .... Oct. 24
Dubuque .... Oct. 31
Coe .... Nov. 7
Central (Iowa) ■ .... Nov. 14

1997 RESULTS (3-7-0)

22	Northwestern (Iowa)	27
29	William Penn	6
13	Luther	14
24	Dana	31
33	Dubuque	13
24	Wartburg	14
31	Upper Iowa	35

0	Loras	13
14	Simpson	57
0	Central (Iowa)	35
190		**245**

Nickname: Beavers.
Stadium: J. Leslie Rollins (1980), 3,500 capacity. Natural turf.
Colors: Blue & Gold.
Conference: Iowa Intercol. Athletic Conf.
SID: Paul Misner, 712-749-2633.
AD: Roger Egland.

BUFFALO

Buffalo, NY 14260 ....I-AA

Coach: Craig Cirbus, Buffalo 1980
Record: 3 Years, 13-20-0

1998 SCHEDULE

Maine [Portland, Me.]	*Sept. 3
Lock Haven ■	*Sept. 12
Lafayette	Sept. 19
Massachusetts	Sept. 26
Cornell	Oct. 3
Morgan St. ■	Oct. 10
Canisius ■	*Oct. 17
Liberty	Oct. 24
Western Ill. ■	Oct. 31
Villanova	Nov. 14
Hofstra	Nov. 21

1997 RESULTS (2-9-0)

30	Lock Haven	7
28	Illinois St.	40
40	Delaware St.	30
0	Ohio	50
27	West Chester	30
0	Connecticut	55
17	Youngstown St.	52
20	Massachusetts	26
26	Hofstra	37
13	Maine	52
28	Villanova	42
229		**421**

Nickname: Bulls.
Stadium: UB Stadium (1993), 17,200 capacity. Natural turf.
Colors: Royal Blue & White.
Conference: Independent.
SID: Paul Vecchio, 716-645-6311.
AD: Nelson E. Townsend.

BUFFALO ST.

Buffalo, NY 14222 III

Coach: Jerry Boyes, Ithaca 1976
Record: 12 Years, 66-52-0

1998 SCHEDULE

Robert Morris ■	Sept. 5
Rochester ■	Sept. 12
Adrian	Sept. 19
Cortland St. ■	Sept. 26
Brockport St.	Oct. 3
Rowan ■	Oct. 10
St. John Fisher	Oct. 17
Kean	Oct. 24
Wash. & Jeff. ■	Oct. 31
Ithaca	Nov. 14

1997 RESULTS (7-2-0)

23	Robert Morris	35
19	St. John Fisher	13
16	Wash. & Jeff.	7
9	Cortland St.	38
13	Brockport St.	10
16	Mercyhurst	14
38	Kean	0
43	Rochester	19
13	Ithaca	10
190		**146**

ECAC III Playoff

21	Plymouth St.	17

Nickname: Bengals.
Stadium: Coyer Field (1964), 3,000 capacity. Natural turf.
Colors: Orange & Black.
Conference: Independent.
SID: Chris Rollman, 716-878-6030.
AD: Alfonso Scandrett Jr.

BUTLER

Indianapolis, IN 46208 ....I-AA

Coach: Ken LaRose, Butler 1980
Record: 6 Years, 30-30-0

1998 SCHEDULE

Albion ■	Sept. 5
Morehead St.	*Sept. 12
St. Francis (Pa.) ■	Sept. 19
Wesley	Sept. 26
Dayton ■	Oct. 3
San Diego ■	Oct. 10
Valparaiso	Oct. 17
Catawba	Oct. 24
Drake	Oct. 31
Quincy	Nov. 7
Lindenwood ■	Nov. 14

1997 RESULTS (6-4-0)

10	Howard Payne	9
21	Robert Morris	26
38	St. Francis (Pa.)	12
17	Clinch Valley	3
7	Dayton	42
14	San Diego	24
17	Valparaiso	19
38	Evansville	35
14	Drake	13
20	St. Joseph's (Ind.)	13
196		**196**

Nickname: Bulldogs.
Stadium: Butler Bowl (1927), 19,000 capacity. Natural turf.
Colors: Blue & White.
Conference: Pioneer.
SID: Jim McGrath, 317-940-9671.
AD: John C. Parry.

CALIFORNIA

Berkeley, CA 94720.................................I-A

Coach: Tom Holmoe, Brigham Young 1983
Record: 1 Year, 3-8-0

1998 SCHEDULE

Houston ■	Sept. 5
Nebraska ■	Sept. 12
Oklahoma	*Sept. 19
Washington St. ■	Sept. 26
Southern Cal	Oct. 10
Washington	Oct. 17
UCLA ■	Oct. 24
Oregon St.	Oct. 31
Arizona St.	Nov. 7
Arizona ■	Nov. 14
Stanford ■	Nov. 21

1997 RESULTS (3-8-0)

35	Houston	3
40	Oklahoma	36
17	Southern Cal	27
34	Louisiana Tech	41
3	Washington	30
37	Washington St.	63
17	UCLA	35
33	Oregon St.	14
21	Arizona St.	28
38	Arizona	41
20	Stanford	21
295		**339**

Nickname: Golden Bears.
Stadium: Memorial (1923), 74,909 capacity. Natural turf.
Colors: Blue & Gold.
Conference: Pacific-10.
SID: Kevin Reneau, 510-642-5363.
AD: John V. Kasser.

UC DAVIS

Davis, CA 95616 II

Coach: Bob Biggs, UC Davis 1973
Record: 5 Years, 39-19-1

1998 SCHEDULE

Tex. A&M-Commerce	*Sept. 5
South Dak. St.	Sept. 12
Cal St. Sacramento ■	*Sept. 19
New Haven ■	*Sept. 26
Cal Poly	Oct. 3
Central Wash.	Oct. 10
Western Wash.	Oct. 17
St. Mary's (Cal.) ■	Oct. 24
Grand Valley St.	Oct. 31
Western Ore. U. ■	Nov. 7
Southern Utah ■	Nov. 14

1997 RESULTS (7-4-0)

19	Cal Poly	20
7	South Dak. St.	17
36	Cal St. Sacramento	28
35	Clarion	28
32	Central Wash.	6
14	Idaho	44
16	Western Wash.	7
19	St. Mary's (Cal.)	9
27	Southern Utah	37
21	Grand Valley St.	19
40	Western Ore. U.	16
266		**231**

II Championship

37	Texas A&M-Kingsville	33
50	Angelo St.	33
25	New Haven	27

Nickname: Aggies.
Stadium: Toomey Field (1949), 10,111 capacity. Natural turf.
Colors: Yale Blue & Gold.
Conference: Independent.
SID: Doug Dull, 916-752-3505.
AD: Greg Warzecka.

CAL LUTHERAN

Thousand Oaks, CA 91360 III

Coach: Scott Squires, Pacific Luth. 1988
Record: 2 Years, 8-10-0

1998 SCHEDULE

Menlo ■	Sept. 5
Pacific Lutheran	Sept. 12
Whittier	*Sept. 19
San Diego ■	Sept. 26
Chapman ■	Oct. 10
Claremont-M-S	*Oct. 17
Occidental ■	Oct. 31
La Verne ■	Nov. 7
Redlands	*Nov. 14

1997 RESULTS (5-4-0)

21	Menlo	32
23	Pacific Lutheran	45
39	San Diego	32
21	Redlands	28
34	La Verne	7
28	Whittier	16
59	Occidental	35
16	Chapman	23
33	Claremont-M-S	10
274		**228**

Nickname: Kingsmen.
Stadium: Mt. Clef (1962), 2,000 capacity. Natural turf.
Colors: Purple & Gold.
Conference: So Calif Intercol Ath Conf.
SID: John Czimbal, 805-493-3153.
AD: Bruce D. Bryde.

CAL POLY

San Luis Obispo, CA 93407....................I-AA

Coach: Larry Welsh, Northern Ariz. 1966
Record: 1 Year, 10-1-0

1998 SCHEDULE

Northern Ariz. ■ ....*Sept. 5
Cal St. Sacramento....*Sept. 12
Montana....Sept. 19
St. Mary's (Cal.) ■ ....*Sept. 26
UC Davis ■ ....Oct. 3
Northern Iowa....Oct. 17
Western N. Mex. ■....Oct. 24
Portland St. ....*Oct. 31
Southern Utah ....Nov. 7
Nevada....Nov. 14
Liberty ■....Nov. 21

1997 RESULTS (10-1-0)

20 UC Davis....19
45 Western Mont....3
24 Western N. Mex....14
24 St. Mary's (Cal.)....14
38 New Mexico St....35
52 Simon Fraser....12
38 Northern Iowa 24
32 Liberty....49
20 Montana St....19
44 Dayton....24
45 Cal St. Sacramento 0
382 **213**

Nickname: Mustangs.
Stadium: Mustang (1935), 8,500 capacity. Natural turf.
Colors: Green & Gold.
Conference:Independent.
SID: Jason Sullivan, 805-756-6531.
AD: John F. Mc Cutcheon.

CAL ST. NORTHRIDGE

Northridge, CA 91330 ....I-AA

Coach: Ron Ponciano, Azusa Pacific 1983
(First year as head coach)

1998 SCHEDULE

Boise St. ....*Sept. 5
Northern Ariz....*Sept. 19
Eastern Wash. ■....Sept. 26
Southern Utah ■....Oct. 3
Montana ■....Oct. 10
Cal St. Sacramento....*Oct. 17
Montana St. ■ ....Oct. 24
Weber St....Oct. 31
Portland St. ■....Nov. 7
Southwest Mo. St....Nov. 14
Idaho St....*Nov. 21

1997 RESULTS (6-6-0)

63 Boise St....23
21 Hawaii....34
18 New Mexico St....28
63 Azusa Pacific....21
13 Portland St....26
30 Weber St....20
20 Montana St....31
45 Cal St. Sacramento 38
13 Montana 21
31 Idaho St....22
32 Eastern Wash....39
21 Northern Ariz. 13
370 **316**

Nickname: Matadors.
Stadium: North Campus (1971), 6,000 capacity. Natural turf.
Colors: Red, White & Black.
Conference: Big Sky.
SID: Ryan Finney, 818-677-3243.
AD: Paul A. Bubb.

CAL ST. SACRAMENTO

Sacramento, CA 95819 ....I-AA

Coach: John Volek, UC Riverside 1968
Record: 3 Years, 6-26-1

1998 SCHEDULE

St. Mary's (Cal.)....Sept. 5
Cal Poly ■....*Sept. 12
UC Davis....*Sept. 19
Montana St. ....Sept. 26
Weber St. ■ ....*Oct. 3
Portland St. ....*Oct. 10
Cal St. Northridge ■ ....*Oct. 17
Northern Ariz....Oct. 24
Eastern Wash. ■....Oct. 31
Idaho St. ....*Nov. 7
Montana ■ ....Nov. 14

1997 RESULTS (1-10-0)

14 Southwest Tex. St. 24
28 UC Davis....36
10 Montana 52
23 Idaho St....19
17 Eastern Wash. 30
25 Northern Ariz. 48
38 Cal St. Northridge....45
13 Portland St....27
14 Weber St. 52
6 Montana St....30
0 Cal Poly 45
188 **408**

Nickname: Hornets.
Stadium: Hornet Field (1964), 21,418 capacity. Natural turf.
Colors: Green & Gold.
Conference: Big Sky.
SID: Jeff Minahan, 916-278-6896.
AD: Judith A. Davidson.

CALIF. (PA.)

California, PA 15419 II

Coach: Mike Kolakowski, Ohio Northern 1979
Record: 1 Year, 2-8-0

1998 SCHEDULE

Glenville St. ■ ....*Aug. 29
Fairmont St....Sept. 12
Geneva ....*Sept. 19
Mansfield....Sept. 26
Cheyney ■....*Oct. 3
Lock Haven ....*Oct. 10
Slippery Rock ■....*Oct. 17
Edinboro....Oct. 24
Indiana (Pa.) ■....Oct. 31
Shippensburg ■....Nov. 7
Clarion ....Nov. 14

1997 RESULTS (2-8-0)

14 Fairmont St. 16
21 West Va. Wesleyan 16
21 St. Joseph's (Ind.) 42
10 Indiana (Pa.)....20
22 Edinboro 38
30 Clarion....0
3 Lock Haven....17
26 Shippensburg....31
7 Kutztown 12
6 Slippery Rock....27
160 **219**

Nickname: Vulcans.
Stadium: Adamson (1970), 5,000 capacity. Natural turf.
Colors: Red & Black.
Conference: Pennsylvania State Athl. Conf.
SID: Bruce Wald, 412-938-4552.
AD: Thomas G. Pucci.

CANISIUS

Buffalo, NY 14208 ....I-AA

Coach: Chuck Williams, Brockport St. 1955
Record: 3 Years, 12-17-0

1998 SCHEDULE

Gannon ....Sept. 12
St. Peter's ■ ....Sept. 19
Siena ■....Sept. 26
Iona....Oct. 3
Georgetown....Oct. 10
Buffalo....*Oct. 17
Fairfield ....Oct. 24
St. John's (N.Y.) ■....Oct. 31
Marist....Nov. 7
Duquesne ■....Nov. 14

1997 RESULTS (3-7-0)

9 Gannon....27
10 St. Peter's 7
38 Siena 41
14 Iona 7
10 Georgetown 24
23 Alfred....20
14 Fairfield....21
0 St. John's (N.Y.) 6
6 Marist 20
7 Duquesne 32
131 **205**

Nickname: Golden Griffins.
Stadium: Demske Sports Complex (1989), 1,000 capacity. Artificial turf.
Colors: Blue & Gold.
Conference: Metro Atlantic.
SID: John Maddock, 716-888-2977.
AD: Daniel P. Starr.

CAPITAL

Columbus, OH 43209 III

Coach: Jim Collins, Wittenberg 1988
Record: 4 Years, 7-33-0

1998 SCHEDULE

Thiel ■....Sept. 5
John Carroll ....Sept. 19
Muskingum ■....Sept. 26
Heidelberg....Oct. 3
Otterbein ■....Oct. 10
Hiram....Oct. 17
Baldwin-Wallace ....Oct. 24
Mount Union ■ ....Oct. 31
Marietta....Nov. 7
Ohio Northern ■....Nov. 14

1997 RESULTS (3-7-0)

20 Bethany (W. Va.) 16
28 Marietta....18
27 Ohio Northern....61
10 Muskingum 6
6 Baldwin-Wallace....63
6 Heidelberg 34
0 John Carroll....55
42 Hiram....54
0 Mount Union....62
13 Otterbein....20
152 **389**

Nickname: Crusaders.
Stadium: Bernlohr (1928), 2,000 capacity. Natural turf.
Colors: Purple & White.
Conference: Ohio Athletic Conference.
SID: Barry Katz, 614-236-6174.
AD: Roger Welsh.

CARLETON

Northfield, MN 55057....III

Coach: Bob Sullivan, St. John's (Minn.) 1959
Record: 19 Years, 96-89-0

1998 SCHEDULE

Northwestern (Minn.) ....Sept. 12
Gust. Adolphus ■....Sept. 19
Concordia-M'head....Sept. 26
Macalester ■ ....Oct. 3
Hamline....Oct. 10
St. Thomas (Minn.) ■ ....Oct. 17
St. Olaf....Oct. 24
Augsburg ■....Oct. 31
St. John's (Minn.)....Nov. 7
Bethel (Minn.) [Minneapolis, Minn.]....*Nov. 13

1997 RESULTS (2-8-0)

29 Lawrence....19
21 Macalester....3
14 Bethel (Minn.) 62
8 St. Thomas (Minn.) 36
6 St. John's (Minn.)....55
21 Augsburg 35
7 Hamline 36
12 St. Olaf....14

SCHEDULES/RESULTS

6 Gust. Adolphus 44
10 Concordia-M'head 39
134 **343**

Nickname: Knights.
Stadium: Laird (1926), 7,500 capacity. Natural turf.
Colors: Maize & Blue.
Conference: Minn. Intercol. Athletic Conf.
SID: Eric Sieger, 507-663-4045.
AD: Leon Lunder.

CARNEGIE MELLON

Pittsburgh, PA 15213 III

Coach: Rich Lackner, Carnegie Mellon 1979
Record: 12 Years, 88-29-2

1998 SCHEDULE

Denison ....Sept. 5
Case Reserve ....Sept. 12
Bethany (W. Va.) ■ ....*Sept. 19
Alfred ....Sept. 26
Dickinson ....Oct. 3
Chicago ■ ....Oct. 17
Washington (Mo.) ....Oct. 24
Rochester ■ ....Oct. 31
Juniata ■ ....Nov. 7
Thomas More ■ ....Nov. 14

1997 RESULTS (8-2-0)

32 Denison 7
16 Case Reserve 7
7 Grove City 26
20 Rhodes 13
37 Dickinson 44
13 Washington (Mo.) 10
35 Chicago 34
14 Rochester 0
28 Muhlenberg 13
49 Bethany (W. Va.) 14
251 **168**

Nickname: Tartans.
Stadium: Gesling (1990), 3,500 capacity. Artificial turf.
Colors: Cardinal, White & Grey.
Conference: University Athletic Assoc.
SID: Jon Surmacz, 412-268-3087.
AD: John H. Harvey.

CARROLL (WIS.)

Waukesha, WI 53186 III

Coach: Merle Masonholder, Northern Iowa 1966
Record: 16 Years, 74-70-0

1998 SCHEDULE

North Park ....Sept. 12
St. Norbert ....Sept. 19
Ripon ■ ....Sept. 26
Grinnell ....Oct. 3
Monmouth (Ill.) ■ ....Oct. 10
Knox ....Oct. 17
Lawrence ■ ....Oct. 24
Beloit ....Oct. 31
Illinois Col. ■ ....Nov. 7
Lake Forest ■ ....Nov. 14

1997 RESULTS (5-5-0)

0 Wis.-Whitewater 53
12 Carthage 28
14 Knox 21
21 Coe 28
33 Lawrence 21
43 Beloit 12
28 Lake Forest 16
32 Ripon 3
17 St. Norbert 18
20 Grinnell 15
220 **215**

Nickname: Pioneers.
Stadium: Van Male Field (1976), 4,200 capacity. Natural turf.
Colors: Orange & White.
Conference: Midwest Conference.
SID: Shawn Ama, 414-524-7376.
AD: Merle Masonholder.

CARSON-NEWMAN

Jefferson City, TN 37760 II

Coach: Ken Sparks, Carson-Newman 1968
Record: 18 Years, 172-43-2

1998 SCHEDULE

North Ala. [Rome, GA.] ....*Sept. 5
Edinboro ....Sept. 12
Presbyterian ■ ....Sept. 19
Tusculum ■ ....Sept. 26
Catawba ....Oct. 3
Wingate ■ ....Oct. 10
Mars Hill ....Oct. 17
Gardner-Webb ■ ....Oct. 24
Lenoir-Rhyne ....*Oct. 31
Newberry ■ ....Nov. 7

1997 RESULTS (9-0-0)

28 Valdosta St. 7
33 Edinboro 10
21 Presbyterian 3
26 Catawba 7
55 Wingate 17
31 Mars Hill 20
35 Gardner-Webb 14
76 Lenoir-Rhyne 3
34 Newberry 12
339 **93**

II Championship

21 North Ala. 7
23 Albany St. (Ga.) 22
29 Northern Colo. 30

Nickname: Eagles.
Stadium: Burke-Tarr (1966), 5,000 capacity. Natural turf.
Colors: Orange & Blue.
Conference: South Atlantic Conference.
SID: Buddy Pearson, 423-471-3477.
AD: David W. Barger.

CARTHAGE

Kenosha, WI 53140 III

Coach: Tim Rucks, Carthage 1983
Record: 8 Years, 20-48-4

1998 SCHEDULE

St. Olaf ■ ....Sept. 12
Lakeland ....Sept. 19
North Park ■ ....Oct. 3
Wheaton (Ill.) ■ ....*Oct. 10
Ill. Wesleyan ....Oct. 17
Millikin ■ ....*Oct. 24
Elmhurst ....Oct. 31
Augustana (Ill.) ■ ....Nov. 7
North Central ....Nov. 14

1997 RESULTS (5-4-0)

28 Carroll (Wis.) 12
26 Lakeland 32
23 North Central 13
21 Augustana (Ill.) 28
41 Elmhurst 0
22 Millikin 17
14 Wheaton (Ill.) 25
7 Ill. Wesleyan 30
14 North Park 0
196 **157**

Nickname: Redmen.
Stadium: Art Keller Field (1965), 3,100 capacity. Natural turf.
Colors: Red, White & Black.
Conference: College Conf. of Ill. & Wisc.
SID: Steve Marovich, 414-551-5740.
AD: Robert R. Bonn.

CASE RESERVE

Cleveland, OH 44106 III

Coach: Regis Scafe, Case Reserve 1971
Record: 4 Years, 11-29-0

1998 SCHEDULE

Carnegie Mellon ■ ....Sept. 12
Rochester ....Sept. 19
Washington (Mo.) ....Sept. 26
Ohio Wesleyan ....Oct. 3
Earlham ■ ....Oct. 10
Denison ■ ....Oct. 17
Wittenberg ....Oct. 24
Oberlin ■ ....Oct. 31
Wooster ....Nov. 7
Chicago ■ ....Nov. 14

1997 RESULTS (3-7-0)

7 Carnegie Mellon 16
32 Washington (Mo.) 37
14 Wooster 21
31 Earlham 6
20 Allegheny 55
27 Kenyon 34
42 Oberlin 6
21 Wittenberg 49
9 Chicago 14
21 Rochester 6
224 **244**

Nickname: Spartans.
Stadium: E.L. Finnigan Field (1968), 3,000 capacity. Natural turf.
Colors: Blue, Gray & White.
Conference: North Coast Athletic Conf.
SID: Sue Herdle Penicka, 216-368-6517.
AD: David M. Hutter.

CATAWBA

Salisbury, NC 28144 II

Coach: David Bennett, Presbyterian 1984
Record: 3 Years, 24-8-0

1998 SCHEDULE

Winston-Salem ■ ....Sept. 5
Tusculum ■ ....Sept. 12
Mars Hill ....Sept. 19
West Va. Wesleyan ....Sept. 26
Carson-Newman ■ ....Oct. 3
Presbyterian ....Oct. 10
Gardner-Webb ....*Oct. 17
Butler ■ ....Oct. 24
Newberry ....*Oct. 31
Wingate ....Nov. 7
Lenoir-Rhyne ■ ....Nov. 14

1997 RESULTS (8-3-0)

48 Tusculum 0
56 West Va. Tech 0
37 Mars Hill 3
38 Charleston So. 13
7 Carson-Newman 26
7 Presbyterian 10
34 Gardner-Webb 6
9 Elon 23
36 Newberry 17
31 Wingate 22
24 Lenoir-Rhyne 21
327 **141**

Nickname: Indians.
Stadium: Shuford Field (1926), 4,000 capacity. Natural turf.
Colors: Blue & White.
Conference: South Atlantic Conference.
SID: Jim Lewis, 704-637-4720.
AD: Dennis Davidson.

CATHOLIC

Washington, DC 20064 III

Coach: Tom Clark, Maryland 1986
Record: 4 Years, 31-7-1

1998 SCHEDULE

Greensboro ■ ....Sept. 5
Bridgewater (Va.) ■ ....Sept. 12
Randolph-Macon ■ ....Sept. 19
Dickinson ....Sept. 26
Frank. & Marsh. ....Oct. 3
La Salle ■ ....Oct. 10
FDU-Madison ■ ....Oct. 17

Hampden-Sydney .... Oct. 24
Newport News ■ .... Oct. 31
Albright .... Nov. 14

1997 RESULTS (10-0-0)

49 Greensboro 7
35 Bridgewater (Va.) 0
34 Randolph-Macon 21
35 Dickinson 6
35 Frank. & Marsh. 21
61 La Salle 21
51 FDU-Madison 14
40 Hampden-Sydney 10
42 Thiel 0
44 Albright 22
426 **122**

III Championship

33 Trinity (Tex.) 44

Nickname: Cardinals.
Stadium: Cardinal Field (1985), 3,500 capacity. Natural turf.
Colors: Cardinal Red & Black.
Conference: Independent.
SID: Chris McManes, 202-319-5610.
AD: Robert J. Talbot.

CENTRAL (IOWA)

Pella, IA 50219 III

Coach: Rich Kacmarynski, Central (Iowa) 1992
Record: 1 Year, 8-2-0

1998 SCHEDULE

Cornell College ■ .... Sept. 5
Loras .... Sept. 12
Simpson ■ .... Sept. 19
Luther .... Sept. 26
Dubuque ■ .... Oct. 3
Coe .... Oct. 10
Upper Iowa ■ .... Oct. 24
William Penn .... Oct. 31
Wartburg ■ .... Nov. 7
Buena Vista .... Nov. 14

1997 RESULTS (8-2-0)

9 Marietta 10
35 Wartburg 6
55 Dubuque 25
55 William Penn 13
38 Loras 14
27 Simpson 31
48 Luther 8
44 Upper Iowa 22
22 Washington (Mo.) 12
35 Buena Vista 0
368 **141**

Nickname: Flying Dutchmen.
Stadium: Kuyper (1977), 5,000 capacity. Natural turf.
Colors: Red & White.
Conference: Iowa Intercol. Athletic Conf.
SID: Larry Happel, 515-628-5278.
AD: John Edwards.

CENTRAL ARK.

Conway, AR 72035 II

Coach: Mike Isom, Central Ark. 1970
Record: 8 Years, 60-27-4

1998 SCHEDULE

West Tex. A&M ■ .... *Sept. 5
West Ga. ■ .... *Sept. 19
North Ala. .... Sept. 26
Southern Ark. .... *Oct. 3
Ark.-Monticello ■ .... Oct. 10
Arkansas Tech ■ .... Oct. 17
Valdosta St. .... Oct. 24
West Ala. ■ .... Oct. 31
Delta St. .... Nov. 7
Henderson St. ■ .... Nov. 14

1997 RESULTS (6-4-0)

20 Northeastern St. 14
35 Arkansas St. 36
20 Southern Ark. 13
37 Delta St. 12
13 West Ga. 17
36 Henderson St. 21
41 Ark.-Monticello 28
6 North Ala. 35
22 Valdosta St. 31
53 Arkansas Tech 36
283 **243**

Nickname: Bears.
Stadium: Estes (1939), 7,000 capacity. Natural turf.
Colors: Purple & Gray.
Conference: Gulf South Conference.
SID: Steve East, 501-450-5743.
AD: Bill E. Stephens.

CENTRAL CONN. ST.

New Britain, CT 06050 .... I-AA

Coach: Sal Cintorio, Cent. Conn. St. 1986
Record: 6 Years, 20-39-0

1998 SCHEDULE

Albany (N.Y.) .... *Sept. 4
St. John's (N.Y.) ■ .... Sept. 12
Robert Morris .... Sept. 26
San Diego .... *Oct. 3
St. Francis (Pa.) ■ .... Oct. 10
Wagner ■ .... Oct. 17
Sacred Heart .... Oct. 24
Southern Conn. St. .... Nov. 7
Monmouth .... Nov. 14
Fairfield ■ .... Nov. 21

1997 RESULTS (5-5-0)

33 Albany (N.Y.) 26
7 St. John's (N.Y.) 13
37 Frostburg St. 17
21 Robert Morris 44
10 Fairfield 17
25 St. Francis (Pa.) 18
23 Wagner 34
55 La Salle 14
24 Southern Conn. St. 0
17 Monmouth 31
252 **214**

Nickname: Blue Devils.
Stadium: Arute Field (1969), 5,000 capacity. Natural turf.
Colors: Blue & White.
Conference: Northeast.
SID: Brent Rutkowski, 203-832-3089.
AD: Charles Jones Jr.

CENTRAL FLA.

Orlando, FL 32816 .... I-A

Coach: Mike Kruczek, Boston College 1976
(First year as head coach)

1998 SCHEDULE

Louisiana Tech .... *Sept. 5
Eastern Ill. ■ .... *Sept. 12
Purdue .... Sept. 19
Bowling Green .... Sept. 26
Toledo .... *Oct. 3
Northern Ill. ■ .... *Oct. 10
Southwestern La. .... *Oct. 24
Youngstown St. ■ .... *Oct. 31
Auburn .... Nov. 7
Ball St. ■ .... Nov. 14
New Mexico ■ .... Nov. 21

1997 RESULTS (5-6-0)

23 Mississippi 24
31 South Caro. 33
24 Nebraska 38
41 Idaho 10
14 Auburn 41
59 Kent 43
52 Samford 7
28 Mississippi St. 35
41 Northeast La. 45
27 Eastern Mich. 10
34 Toledo 17
374 **303**

Nickname: Golden Knights.
Stadium: Florida Citrus (1936), 70,188 capacity. Natural turf.
Colors: Black & Gold.
Conference: Independent.
SID: John Marini, 407-823-2729.
AD: Steve Sloan.

CENTRAL MICH.

Mount Pleasant, MI 48859 .... I-A

Coach: Dick Flynn, Michigan St. 1965
Record: 4 Years, 20-25-0

1998 SCHEDULE

Iowa .... Sept. 5
Western Ill. ■ .... Sept. 12
Kent ■ .... Sept. 26
Michigan St. .... Oct. 3
Eastern Mich. .... *Oct. 10
Northern Ill. .... Oct. 17
Western Mich. ■ .... Oct. 24
Akron ■ .... Oct. 31
Marshall .... Nov. 7
Toledo .... Nov. 14
Ball St. ■ .... Nov. 21

1997 RESULTS (2-9-0)

44 Northern Ill. 10
6 Florida 82
44 Boise St. 26
28 Louisiana Tech 56
24 Eastern Mich. 31
14 Akron 53
10 Toledo 41
34 Ball St. 37
37 Kent 60
17 Marshall 45
24 Western Mich. 38
282 **479**

Nickname: Chippewas.
Stadium: Kelly-Shorts (1972), 20,086 capacity. Artificial turf.
Colors: Maroon & Gold.
Conference: Mid-American.
SID: Fred Stabley Jr., 517-774-3277.
AD: Herb Deromedi.

CENTRAL MO. ST.

Warrensburg, MO 64093 II

Coach: Willie Fritz, Pittsburg St. 1983
Record: 1 Year, 5-6-0

1998 SCHEDULE

Neb.-Omaha ■ .... *Sept. 3
St. Cloud St. ■ .... *Sept. 12
Mo.-Rolla ■ .... Sept. 19
Truman St. .... Sept. 26
Southwest Baptist ■ .... Oct. 3
Mo. Southern St. .... *Oct. 10
Pittsburg St. .... *Oct. 15
Emporia St. ■ .... Oct. 24
Northwest Mo. St. ■ .... Oct. 31
Washburn .... Nov. 7
Mo. Western St. ■ .... *Nov. 12

1997 RESULTS (5-6-0)

12 Neb.-Omaha 41
53 Menlo 13
44 Mo.-Rolla 14
34 Truman St. 37
52 Southwest Baptist 17
31 Mo. Southern St. 10
29 Pittsburg St. 30
10 Emporia St. 50
9 Northwest Mo. St. 41
20 Washburn 14
24 Mo. Western St. 27
318 **294**

Nickname: Mules.
Stadium: Audrey J. Walton (1995), 10,000 capacity. Natural turf.
Colors: Cardinal & Black.
Conference: MIAA.

SID: Bill Turnage, 816-543-4312.
AD: Jerry M. Hughes.

CENTRAL OKLA.

Edmond, OK 73034 II

Coach: Gary Howard, Arkansas 1964
Record: 21 Years, 127-84-6

1998 SCHEDULE

Northwestern Okla.	*Sept. 5
Texas A&M-Kingsville ■	Sept. 12
Abilene Christian ■	Sept. 19
Tarleton St.	*Sept. 26
Langston ■	Oct. 3
East Central ■	Oct. 10
Harding	Oct. 17
Ouachita Baptist ■	Oct. 24
Southwestern Okla.	Oct. 31
Southeastern Okla. ■	Nov. 7
Northeastern St.	Nov. 14

1997 RESULTS (9-2-0)

23	Northwestern Okla.	0
7	Texas A&M-Kingsville	33
28	Abilene Christian	0
28	Tarleton St.	19
51	Langston	0
42	East Central	7
35	Harding	19
31	Ouachita Baptist	14
17	Southwestern Okla.	33
23	Southeastern Okla.	18
17	Northeastern St.	16
302		**159**

Nickname: Bronchos.
Stadium: Wantland (1965), 10,000 capacity. Natural turf.
Colors: Bronze & Blue.
Conference: Lone Star Conference.
SID: Mike Kirk, 405-341-2980.
AD: John E. Wagnon.

CENTRAL WASH.

Ellensburg, WA 98926 II

Coach: John Zamberlin, Pacific Luth. 1979
Record: 1 Year, 5-4-0

1998 SCHEDULE

Azusa Pacific ■	Sept. 19
Willamette	Sept. 26
Simon Fraser	Oct. 3
UC Davis ■	Oct. 10
Southern Ore.	Oct. 17
Western Ore. U. ■	Oct. 24
Eastern Ore. U. ■	Oct. 31
Western Wash.	Nov. 7
Humboldt St.	Nov. 14

1997 RESULTS (5-4-0)

50	Simon Fraser	16
32	Eastern Ore. U.	21
21	Willamette	34
6	UC Davis	32
24	Southern Ore.	21
34	Western Ore. U.	47
28	Azusa Pacific	7
36	Western Wash.	22
30	Humboldt St.	40
261		**240**

Nickname: Wildcats.
Stadium: Tomlinson Field, 4,000 capacity. Natural turf.
Colors: Crimson & Black.
Conference: Independent.
SID: Bob Guptill, 509-963-1485.
AD: Gary C. Frederick.

CENTRE

Danville, KY 40422 III

Coach: Andy Frye, Muskingum 1981
(First year as head coach)

1998 SCHEDULE

Kenyon ■	Sept. 12
Rhodes	Sept. 19
Wash. & Lee ■	Sept. 26
Sewanee ■	Oct. 3
Millsaps	Oct. 10
Maryville (Tenn.)	Oct. 17
Trinity (Tex.) ■	Oct. 24
DePauw ■	Oct. 31
Davidson	Nov. 7
Rose-Hulman	Nov. 14

1997 RESULTS (6-3-0)

10	Wooster	31
17	Hanover	22
30	Wash. & Lee	14
30	Sewanee	0
43	Millsaps	21
36	Maryville (Tenn.)	22
21	Trinity (Tex.)	42
19	Davidson	14
38	Rhodes	14
244		**180**

Nickname: Colonels.
Stadium: Farris (1925), 2,500 capacity. Natural turf.
Colors: Gold & White.
Conference: Southern Collegiate Ath. Conf.
SID: Glenn Osborne, 606-238-8746.
AD: Ray K. Hammond.

CHADRON ST.

Chadron, NE 69337 II

Coach: Brad Smith, Western Ill. 1972
Record: 11 Years, 75-40-1

1998 SCHEDULE

Western Mont.	Sept. 5
Sam Houston St.	*Sept. 12
Fort Lewis ■	Sept. 19
Mesa St.	Sept. 26
Neb.-Kearney ■	Oct. 3
Western St. (Colo.) ■	Oct. 10
N. M. Highlands	Oct. 17
Wayne St. (Neb.) ■	Oct. 24
Adams St. ■	Oct. 31
Fort Hays St.	Nov. 7
Colorado Mines	Nov. 14

1997 RESULTS (8-3-0)

34	Western Mont.	10
14	Montana St.	24
20	Mesa St.	18
40	Neb.-Kearney	34
14	Western St. (Colo.)	16
14	N. M. Highlands	16
30	Peru St.	13
36	Adams St.	14
40	Fort Hays St.	0
43	Colorado Mines	0
51	Fort Lewis	14
336		**159**

Nickname: Eagles.
Stadium: Elliott Field (1930), 2,500 capacity. Natural turf.
Colors: Cardinal & White.
Conference: Rocky Mountain Athletic Conf.
SID: Con Marshall, 308-432-6212.
AD: Bradley Roy Smith.

CHAPMAN

Orange, CA 92866 III

Coach: Ken Visser, Occidental 1968
Record: 7 Years, 35-27-1

1998 SCHEDULE

Western Wash. ■	Sept. 12
Hardin-Simmons ■	Sept. 19
Whittier	*Sept. 26
Azusa Pacific	Oct. 3
Cal Lutheran	Oct. 10
Occidental ■	*Oct. 17
Menlo	Oct. 24
La Verne ■	Oct. 31
St. Mary's (Cal.)	Nov. 14

1997 RESULTS (4-5-0)

0	Western Wash.	35
6	Willamette	40
14	Hardin-Simmons	19
20	Howard Payne	28
24	Menlo	21
20	St. Mary's (Cal.)	36
24	La Verne	20
23	Cal Lutheran	16
17	Azusa Pacific	12
148		**227**

Nickname: Panthers.
Stadium: Chapman (0000), 3,000 capacity. Natural turf.
Colors: Cardinal & Gray.
Conference: Independent.
SID: Jim Moore, 714-997-6900.
AD: David Currey.

CHARLESTON SO.

Charleston, SC 29423 ....I-AA

Coach: David Dowd, Guilford 1976
Record: 7 Years, 12-59-0

1998 SCHEDULE

South Caro. St. ■	Sept. 5
Presbyterian	Sept. 12
North Greenville ■	Sept. 19
Wofford	*Sept. 26
Liberty	*Oct. 3
Newberry ■	Oct. 10
Austin Peay	Oct. 17
South Fla. ■	Oct. 31
Morehead St. ■	Nov. 7
Bethel (Tenn.) ■	Nov. 14
East Tenn. St.	*Nov. 21

1997 RESULTS (1-9-0)

7	East Tenn. St.	30
12	South Caro. St.	13
7	Presbyterian	16
12	Tusculum	3
13	Catawba	38
14	Newberry	48
14	Liberty	48
6	South Fla.	24
27	Morehead St.	55
21	Wofford	51
133		**326**

Nickname: Buccaneers.
Stadium: CSU (1970), 3,000 capacity. Natural turf.
Colors: Blue & Gold.
Conference: Independent.
SID: Ken Gerlinger, 803-863-7688.
AD: W. Howard Bagwell.

CHATTANOOGA

Chattanooga, TN 37403 ....I-AA

Coach: Buddy Green, North Caro. St. 1976
Record: 4 Years, 17-27-0

1998 SCHEDULE

Samford ■	*Sept. 3
East Caro.	Sept. 12
Troy St. ■	*Sept. 19
Ga. Southern ■	*Sept. 26
Wofford	Oct. 3
VMI ■	*Oct. 17
Western Caro.	Oct. 24
Appalachian St. ■	Oct. 31
Citadel	Nov. 7
East Tenn. St. ■	Nov. 14
Furman	Nov. 21

1997 RESULTS (7-4-0)

13	Tennessee Tech	10
33	Middle Tenn. St.	24
10	Ga. Southern	37
20	Wofford	17
27	VMI	24
28	Tennessee St.	7

24 Western Caro. 21
7 Appalachian St. 41
3 Citadel 7
17 East Tenn. St. 13
21 Furman 43
203 **244**

Nickname: Mocs.
Stadium: Finley/Davenport Field (1997), 20,000 capacity. Natural turf.
Colors: Navy Blue & Gold.
Conference: Southern.
SID: Jeff Romero, 423-755-4618.
AD: L. Oval Jaynes.

CHEYNEY

Cheyney, PA 19319 II

Coach: John Parker
(First year as head coach)

1998 SCHEDULE

Bowie St. ■ .....Sept. 5
Virginia Union .....*Sept. 12
Elizabeth City St. ■ .....Sept. 19
Lock Haven ■ .....Sept. 26
Calif. (Pa.) .....*Oct. 3
Kutztown .....Oct. 10
East Stroudsburg ■ .....Oct. 17
Bloomsburg .....Oct. 24
Mansfield ■ .....Oct. 31
West Chester .....Nov. 7
Millersville ■ .....Nov. 14

1997 RESULTS (0-11-0)

18 Delaware St. 50
7 Virginia Union 29
6 Bowie St. 27
0 Bethune-Cookman 44
6 Bloomsburg 68
6 Kutztown 50
20 West Chester 54
16 East Stroudsburg 39
0 Edinboro 44
7 Mansfield 20
14 Millersville 39
100 **464**

Nickname: Wolves.
Stadium: O'Shield-Stevenson, 3,500 capacity. Natural turf.
Colors: Blue & White.
Conference: Pennsylvania State Athl. Conf.
SID: To be named, 610-399-2287.
AD: Andrew Hinson

CHICAGO

Chicago, IL 60637 III

Coach: Dick Maloney, Mass.-Boston 1974
Record: 4 Years, 22-16-0

1998 SCHEDULE

Lake Forest .....Sept. 12
Rose-Hulman ■ .....Sept. 19
North Central .....*Sept. 26
DePauw .....Oct. 3
Carnegie Mellon .....Oct. 17
Rochester ■ .....Oct. 24
Washington (Mo.) ■ .....Oct. 31
Madison Tech ■ .....Nov. 7
Case Reserve .....Nov. 14

1997 RESULTS (5-4-0)

0 DePauw 25
26 Concordia (Ill.) 6
16 Rose-Hulman 14
33 Kalamazoo 23
18 Rochester 28
34 Carnegie Mellon 35
26 Washington (Mo.) 55
14 Case Reserve 9
12 Kenyon 0
179 **195**

Nickname: Maroons.
Stadium: Stagg Field (1969), 1,500 capacity. Natural turf.
Colors: White & Maroon.
Conference: University Athletic Assoc.
SID: Dave Hilbert, 312-702-4638.
AD: Thomas Weingartner.

CHOWAN

Murfreesboro, NC 27855 III

Coach: Steve Lee, Lock Haven 1978
(First year as head coach)

1998 SCHEDULE

Methodist ■ .....Sept. 5
Greensboro .....Sept. 12
Jacksonville ■ .....Sept. 19
Randolph-Macon .....Sept. 26
Frostburg St. ■ .....Oct. 3
Salisbury St. .....Oct. 10
Ferrum .....Oct. 17
Wesley ■ .....Oct. 31
Newport News .....Nov. 7
Guilford ■ .....Nov. 14

1997 RESULTS (2-8-0)

20 Methodist 25
38 Greensboro 7
3 Clinch Valley 27
3 Randolph-Macon 38
0 Frostburg St. 21
17 Salisbury St. 28
0 Ferrum 19
6 Wesley 41
28 Newport News 19
0 Guilford 61
115 **286**

Nickname: Braves.
Stadium: Garrison (1964), 3,500 capacity. Natural turf.
Colors: Columbia Blue & White.
Conference: Atlantic Central FB.
SID: To be named.
AD: Diane M. Morea.

CINCINNATI

Cincinnati, OH 45221 .....I-A

Coach: Rick Minter, Henderson St. 1977
Record: 4 Years, 22-22-1

1998 SCHEDULE

Tulane ■ .....*Sept. 5
Miami (Fla.) ■ .....Sept. 12
Army .....Sept. 19
Indiana ■ .....*Sept. 26
Louisville .....Oct. 3
Syracuse .....Oct. 10
Memphis .....*Oct. 17
Miami (Ohio) ■ .....Oct. 24
East Caro. ■ .....Nov. 7
Houston ■ .....Nov. 14
Arkansas St. .....Nov. 21

1997 RESULTS (7-4-0)

34 Tulsa 24
17 Tulane 31
34 Kansas 7
24 Boston College 6
20 Memphis 17
33 UAB 29
38 Houston 41
34 Miami (Ohio) 31
17 Southern Miss. 24
28 Louisville 9
7 East Caro. 14
286 **233**

Humanitarian Bowl

35 Utah St. 19

Nickname: Bearcats.
Stadium: Nippert (1916), 35,000 capacity. Artificial turf.
Colors: Red & Black.
Conference: Conference USA.
SID: Tom Hathaway, 513-556-5191.
AD: Bob Goin.

CITADEL

Charleston, SC 29409 .....I-AA

Coach: Don Powers, Western Caro. 1966
Record: 2 Years, 10-12-0

1998 SCHEDULE

Florida .....*Sept. 5
Wofford .....*Sept. 12
Western Caro. ■ .....*Sept. 19
Appalachian St. .....Sept. 26
South Fla. .....*Oct. 3
East Tenn. St. ■ .....Oct. 10
Furman .....Oct. 17
Ga. Southern ■ .....Oct. 24
Hofstra ■ .....Oct. 31
Chattanooga ■ .....Nov. 7
VMI .....Nov. 14

1997 RESULTS (6-5-0)

33 Newberry 13
10 South Fla. 7
25 Western Caro. 45
15 Appalachian St. 40
3 Air Force 17
23 East Tenn. St. 20
7 Furman 21
7 Ga. Southern 49
7 Wofford 3
7 Chattanooga 3
28 VMI 6
165 **224**

Nickname: Bulldogs.
Stadium: Johnson Hagood (1948), 22,500 capacity. Natural turf.
Colors: Blue & White.
Conference: Southern.
SID: Art Chase, 803-953-5120.
AD: Walt Nadzak.

CLAREMONT-M-S

Claremont, CA 91711 III

Coach: Rick Candaele, Coll. of Idaho 1969
Record: 6 Years, 24-31-0

1998 SCHEDULE

Puget Sound ■ .....*Sept. 12
Colorado Col. .....Sept. 19
La Verne ■ .....*Oct. 3
Occidental .....*Oct. 10
Cal Lutheran ■ .....*Oct. 17
Whittier ■ .....*Oct. 24
Redlands .....*Oct. 31
Pomona-Pitzer .....Nov. 7
Lewis & Clark ■ .....Nov. 14

1997 RESULTS (0-9-0)

16 Merchant Marine 41
3 Puget Sound 20
2 Whittier 38
6 La Verne 17
3 Redlands 56
12 Occidental 31
22 Menlo 58
7 Pomona-Pitzer 74
10 Cal Lutheran 33
81 **368**

Nickname: Stags.
Stadium: Zinda Field (1955), 3,000 capacity. Natural turf.
Colors: Maroon, Gold & White.
Conference: So Calif Intercol Ath Conf.
SID: Kelly Beck, 909-607-3138.
AD: David Wells.

CLARION

Clarion, PA 16214 II

Coach: Malen Luke, Westminster (Pa.) 1976
Record: 10 Years, 61-41-0

1998 SCHEDULE

Youngstown St. .....*Sept. 3

Millersville ■	Sept. 12
Shepherd	Sept. 19
Kutztown	Sept. 26
Slippery Rock	Oct. 3
Edinboro ■	Oct. 10
Shippensburg ■	Oct. 17
Indiana (Pa.)	Oct. 24
West Chester ■	Oct. 31
Lock Haven	Nov. 7
Calif. (Pa.) ■	Nov. 14

1997 RESULTS (3-7-0)

25	Millersville	31
0	Glenville St.	51
28	UC Davis	35
32	Lock Haven	33
14	Shippensburg	37
0	Calif. (Pa.)	30
7	Slippery Rock	28
21	Indiana (Pa.)	6
28	Edinboro	0
17	Mansfield	0
172		**251**

Nickname: Golden Eagles.
Stadium: Memorial Field (1965), 5,000 capacity. Natural turf.
Colors: Blue & Gold.
Conference: Pennsylvania State Athl. Conf.
SID: Rich Herman, 814-226-2334.
AD: Robert Carlson.

CLARK ATLANTA

Atlanta, GA 30314 II

Coach: Elmer Mixon, Clark Atlanta 1964
Record: 1 Year, 4-7-0

1998 SCHEDULE

Morris Brown	*Sept. 6
Savannah St. ■	*Sept. 12
Kentucky St. ■	*Sept. 19
Miles ■	*Sept. 26
Lane [Memphis, Tenn.]	*Oct. 3
Benedict ■	Oct. 10
Fort Valley St. ■	*Oct. 17
Albany St. (Ga.)	Oct. 24
Tuskegee [LaGrange, Ga.]	Oct. 31
Morehouse ■	Nov. 7

1997 RESULTS (4-7-0)

14	Morris Brown	0
25	Lane	0
7	Alabama A&M	9
25	Kentucky St.	32
17	Miles	32
6	Fort Valley St.	27
31	Benedict	12
23	Savannah St.	22
10	Albany St. (Ga.)	14
7	Tuskegee	16
3	Morehouse	24
168		**188**

Nickname: Panthers.
Stadium: Georgia Dome (1992), 71,000 capacity. Artificial turf.
Colors: Red, Black & Grey.
Conference: Southern Intercol. Ath. Conf.
SID: Tammy A. Bagby, 404-880-8029.
AD: Richard Cosby.

CLEMSON

Clemson, SC 29634 .... I-A

Coach: Tommy West, Tennessee 1976
Record: 6 Years, 32-27-0

1998 SCHEDULE

Furman ■	Sept. 5
Virginia Tech ■	Sept. 12
Virginia	Sept. 19
Wake Forest ■	Sept. 26
North Caro.	Oct. 3
Maryland ■	Oct. 10
Florida St.	Oct. 17
Duke	Oct. 24
North Caro. St. ■	Oct. 31
Georgia Tech ■	*Nov. 12
South Caro. ■	Nov. 21

1997 RESULTS (7-4-0)

23	Appalachian St.	12
19	North Caro. St.	17
28	Florida St.	35
20	Georgia Tech	23
39	UTEP	7
7	Virginia	21
20	Maryland	9
33	Wake Forest	16
29	Duke	20
10	North Caro.	17
47	South Caro.	21
275		**198**

Peach Bowl

17	Auburn	21

Nickname: Tigers.
Stadium: Memorial (1942), 81,474 capacity. Natural turf.
Colors: Purple & Orange.
Conference: Atlantic Coast.
SID: Tim Bourret, 803-656-2114.
AD: Robert W. Robinson.

COAST GUARD

New London, CT 06320 III

Coach: Bob Estock, Colorado St. 1968
(First year as head coach)

1998 SCHEDULE

Mass. Maritime ■	Sept. 12
Rensselaer ■	Sept. 19
Springfield	Sept. 26
Norwich	Oct. 3
Western Conn. St. ■	Oct. 17
Union (N.Y.)	Oct. 24
Plymouth St. ■	Oct. 31
Worcester Tech	Nov. 7
Merchant Marine	Nov. 14

1997 RESULTS (9-1-0)

22	Rensselaer	16
13	Mass. Maritime	8
26	Springfield	20
27	Norwich	10
44	Westfield St.	28
21	Western Conn. St.	14
6	Union (N.Y.)	14
19	Plymouth St.	0
44	Worcester Tech	0
34	Merchant Marine	16
256		**126**

III Championship

0	Rowan	43

Nickname: Bears.
Stadium: Cadet Memorial Field (1932), 4,500 capacity. Natural turf.
Colors: Blue, White & Orange.
Conference: Freedom FB.
SID: Jason Southard, 860-437-6800.
AD: Chuck Mills.

COE

Cedar Rapids, IA 52402 III

Coach: D. J. LeRoy, Wis.-Eau Claire 1979
Record: 15 Years, 112-42-2

1998 SCHEDULE

Loras ■	Sept. 5
Simpson	Sept. 12
Luther ■	Sept. 19
Dubuque	Sept. 26
Central (Iowa) ■	Oct. 10
Upper Iowa	Oct. 17
William Penn ■	Oct. 24
Wartburg	Oct. 31
Buena Vista ■	Nov. 7
Cornell College	Nov. 14

1997 RESULTS (8-1-0)

21	Aurora	20
35	Eureka	28
70	Lawrence	7
28	Carroll (Wis.)	21
20	Grinnell	13
67	Illinois Col.	0
34	Monmouth (Ill.)	7
21	Knox	14
21	Cornell College	28
317		**138**

Nickname: Kohawks.
Stadium: Clark (1989), 1,100 capacity. Natural turf.
Colors: Crimson & Gold.
Conference: Independent.
SID: Alice Davidson, 319-399-8570.
AD: J. Barron Bremner.

COLBY

Waterville, ME 04901 III

Coach: Tom Austin, Maine 1963
Record: 12 Years, 42-53-1

1998 SCHEDULE

Trinity (Conn.)	Sept. 26
Middlebury ■	Oct. 3
Wesleyan (Conn.) ■	Oct. 10
Amherst	Oct. 17
Hamilton ■	Oct. 24
Bates	Oct. 31
Tufts	Nov. 7
Bowdoin ■	Nov. 14

1997 RESULTS (0-8-0)

6	Williams	26
15	Middlebury	27
13	Wesleyan (Conn.)	20
0	Amherst	35
0	Hamilton	28
21	Bates	22
12	Tufts	21
19	Bowdoin	27
86		**206**

Nickname: White Mules.
Stadium: Seaverns (1948), 5,000 capacity. Natural turf.
Colors: Blue & Gray.
Conference: NESCAC
SID: To be named, 207-872-3227.
AD: Richard L. Whitmore Jr.

COLGATE

Hamilton, NY 13346 .... I-AA

Coach: Dick Biddle, Duke 1971
Record: 2 Years, 13-10-0

1998 SCHEDULE

Connecticut ■	Sept. 5
Towson	Sept. 19
Harvard ■	Sept. 26
Yale	Oct. 3
Dartmouth ■	Oct. 10
Navy	Oct. 17
Fordham	Oct. 24
Bucknell	Oct. 31
Lehigh	Nov. 7
Lafayette ■	Nov. 14
Holy Cross ■	Nov. 21

1997 RESULTS (7-4-0)

7	Richmond	23
27	Fordham	14
44	Cornell	38
61	Lehigh	28
44	Lafayette	6
28	Princeton	31
27	Army	35
42	Holy Cross	7
34	Towson	3
24	Navy	52
48	Bucknell	14
386		**251**

I-AA Championship

28	Villanova	49

Nickname: Red Raiders.
Stadium: Andy Kerr (1937), 10,221 capacity. Natural turf.
Colors: Maroon, Gray & White.
Conference: Patriot.
SID: Bob Cornell, 315-824-7616.
AD: Mark H. Murphy.

COLORADO

Boulder, CO 80309 .... I-A

Coach: Rick Neuheisel, UCLA 1984
Record: 3 Years, 25-10-0

1998 SCHEDULE

Colorado St. [Denver, Colo.]	*Sept. 5
Fresno St. ■	Sept. 12
Utah St. ■	Sept. 19
Baylor ■	Sept. 26
Oklahoma	*Oct. 3
Kansas St. ■	Oct. 10
Texas Tech ■	Oct. 17
Kansas	Oct. 24
Missouri	Nov. 7
Iowa St. ■	Nov. 14
Nebraska	Nov. 27

1997 RESULTS (5-6-0)

31	Colorado St.	21
3	Michigan	27
20	Wyoming	19
10	Texas A&M	16
29	Oklahoma St.	33
42	Kansas	6
47	Texas	30
31	Missouri	41
43	Iowa St.	38
20	Kansas St.	37
24	Nebraska	27
300		**295**

kname: Golden Buffaloes.
Stadium: Folsom (1924), 51,808 capacity. Artificial turf.
Colors: Silver, Gold & Black.
Conference: Big 12.
SID: David Plati, 303-492-5626.
AD: Richard A. Tharp.

COLORADO COL.

Colorado Springs, CO 80903 III

Coach: Greg Polnasek, Wis.-Eau Claire 1979
Record: 5 Years, 13-34-0

1998 SCHEDULE

Pomona-Pitzer ■	Sept. 5
Willamette ■	Sept. 12
Claremont-M-S ■	Sept. 19
Millsaps	*Sept. 26
Crown ■	Oct. 10
Southwestern Aly God ■	Oct. 17
Rhodes	Oct. 24
McPherson ■	Oct. 31
Washington (Mo.)	Nov. 7

1997 RESULTS (2-6-0)

0	Gust. Adolphus	34
7	Pomona-Pitzer	31
31	Neb. Wesleyan	30
13	Trinity (Tex.)	24
7	Austin	30
54	Trinity Bible (N.D.)	0
3	McPherson	21
19	Black Hills St.	34
134		**204**

Nickname: Tigers.
Stadium: Washburn Field (1898), 2,000 capacity. Natural turf.
Colors: Black & Gold.
Conference: Independent.
SID: Dave Moross, 719-389-6755.
AD: V. Martin Scarano.

COLORADO MINES

Golden, CO 80401 II

Coach: Versie Wallace, NW Oklahoma St. 1981
Record: 3 Years, 7-25-0

1998 SCHEDULE

South Dak. Tech	Sept. 5
Montana Tech ■	Sept. 12
Fort Hays St. ■	Sept. 19
Neb.-Kearney	Sept. 26
Fort Lewis	Oct. 3
N. M. Highlands ■	Oct. 10
Mesa St. ■	Oct. 17
Adams St.	Oct. 24
Western St. (Colo.)	Oct. 31
Chadron St. ■	Nov. 14

1997 RESULTS (3-8-0)

38	South Dak. Tech	0
20	Hastings	17
15	Neb.-Kearney	50
16	Fort Lewis	28
0	N. M. Highlands	66
21	Mesa St.	18
18	Adams St.	24
7	Okla. Panhandle St.	10
0	Western St. (Colo.)	40
0	Chadron St.	43
14	Fort Hays St.	17
149		**313**

Nickname: Orediggers.
Stadium: Brooks Field (1922), 5,000 capacity. Natural turf.
Colors: Silver & Blue.
Conference: Rocky Mountain Athletic Conf.
SID: Jeff Duggan, 303-273-3300.
AD: Marvin L. Kay.

COLORADO ST.

Fort Collins, CO 80523 .... I-A

Coach: Sonny Lubick, Western Mont. 1960
Record: 9 Years, 62-38-0

1998 SCHEDULE

Michigan St.	Aug. 29
Colorado [Denver, Colo.]	*Sept. 5
Nevada	Sept. 12
Air Force	*Sept. 17
UNLV ■	Sept. 26
UTEP	*Oct. 3
Tulsa ■	Oct. 10
New Mexico St.	*Oct. 17
Texas Christian ■	Oct. 24
Rice	Oct. 31
Wyoming ■	Nov. 7
Southern Methodist	Nov. 14

1997 RESULTS (10-2-0)

45	Nevada	13
21	Colorado	31
35	Utah St.	24
0	Air Force	24
63	Hawaii	0
55	San Jose St.	20
14	Wyoming	7
44	Tulsa	8
45	UNLV	19
41	Fresno St.	3
38	San Diego St.	17
41	New Mexico	13
442		**179**

Holiday Bowl

35	Missouri	24

Nickname: Rams.
Stadium: Hughes (1968), 30,000 capacity. Natural turf.
Colors: Green & Gold.
Conference: Western Athletic.
SID: Gary Ozzello, 303-491-5067.
AD: Tim L. Weiser.

COLUMBIA

New York, NY 10027 .... I-AA

Coach: Ray Tellier, Connecticut 1973
Record: 14 Years, 48-87-3

1998 SCHEDULE

Harvard ■	Sept. 19
Bucknell	Sept. 26
St. Mary's (Cal.)	Oct. 3
Lehigh ■	Oct. 10
Pennsylvania	Oct. 17
Yale	Oct. 24
Princeton ■	Oct. 31
Dartmouth	Nov. 7
Cornell ■	Nov. 14
Brown ■	Nov. 21

1997 RESULTS (3-7-0)

7	Harvard	45
16	Towson	6
3	Lafayette	31
16	Holy Cross	45
7	Pennsylvania	24
21	Yale	10
17	Princeton	0
21	Dartmouth	23
22	Cornell	33
11	Brown	42
141		**259**

Nickname: Lions.
Stadium: Lawrence A. Wien (1984), 17,000 capacity. Artificial turf.
Colors: Columbia Blue & White.
Conference: Ivy.
SID: Brian Bodine, 212-854-2534.
AD: John A. Reeves.

CONCORD

Athens, WV 24712 II

Coach: Bob Mullett, Concord (W. Va.) 197
Record: 9 Years, 45-44-2

1998 SCHEDULE

Lenoir-Rhyne ■	Aug. 29
Mars Hill	Sept. 12
Newport News ■	Sept. 19
Clinch Valley	Sept. 26
West Va. Tech	Oct. 3
Shepherd	Oct. 10
West Liberty St. ■	Oct. 17
Glenville St. ■	Oct. 24
West Va. Wesleyan	Oct. 31
West Va. St.	Nov. 7
Fairmont St. ■	Nov. 14

1997 RESULTS (5-5-0)

25	Mars Hill	35
24	Newport News	20
55	Tusculum	28
25	West Va. Tech	10
20	Shepherd	64
49	West Liberty St.	21
26	Glenville St.	71
27	West Va. Wesleyan	57
20	West Va. St.	18
15	Fairmont St.	50
286		**374**

Nickname: Mountain Lions.
Stadium: Callahan, 5,000 capacity. Natural turf.
Colors: Maroon & Gray.
Conference: WV Intercollegiate Athletic.
SID: Don Christie, 304-384-5347.
AD: Donald P. Christie.

CONCORDIA (ILL.)

River Forest, IL 60305 III

Coach: Rod Olson, Peru St. 1989
Record: 1 Year, 2-7-0

1998 SCHEDULE

Principia ■	Sept. 5
Maranatha Baptist	Sept. 12
North Park ■	Sept. 19
Benedictine (Ill.)	Oct. 3
Lakeland	Oct. 10
Aurora ■	Oct. 17
MacMurray ■	Oct. 24
Concordia (Wis.)	Oct. 31

Eureka ■ ....Nov. 7
Greenville ....Nov. 14

1997 RESULTS (2-7-0)

3	Maranatha Baptist	23
39	Lawrence	41
6	Chicago	26
37	Principia	6
0	Eureka	34
26	Greenville	19
0	Lakeland	67
0	MacMurray	32
15	Concordia (Wis.)	49
126		**297**

Nickname: Cougars.
Stadium: Concordia, 1,500 capacity. Natural turf.
Colors: Maroon & Gold.
Conference: Independent.
SID: Jim Egan, 708-209-3116.
AD: Janet L. Fisher.

CONCORDIA (WIS.)

Mequon, WI 53097 III

Coach: Jeffrey Gabrielsen, Ripon 1980
Record: 8 Years, 46-27-0

1998 SCHEDULE

Mt. Senario ■ ....Sept. 5
Beloit ■ ....Sept. 12
Concordia (Neb.) ....Sept. 19
Lakeland ■ ....Sept. 26
MacMurray ....Oct. 3
Eureka ■ ....Oct. 10
Benedictine (Ill.) ....Oct. 17
Aurora ....Oct. 24
Concordia (Ill.) ■ ....Oct. 31
Greenville ■ ....Nov. 7

1997 RESULTS (7-3-0)

20	Wis.-Platteville	28
40	Beloit	0
48	Concordia (Neb.)	43
31	Eureka	0
7	Aurora	37
33	Lakeland	41
26	MacMurray	6
48	Greenville	20
49	Concordia (Ill.)	15
41	Mt. Senario	14
343		**204**

Nickname: Falcons.
Stadium: Century, 2,500 capacity. Natural turf.
Colors: Royal Blue & White.
Conference: Independent..
SID: Mike Bartholomew, 414-243-4404.
AD: Kenneth L. Witte.

CONCORDIA-M'HEAD

Moorhead, MN 56562 III

Coach: Jim Christopherson, Concordia-M'head 1960
Record: 29 Years, 203-86-7

1998 SCHEDULE

Moorhead St. ....Sept. 5
Bethel (Minn.) ....Sept. 19
Carleton ■ ....Sept. 26
Hamline ■ ....Oct. 3
St. Olaf ....Oct. 10
St. John's (Minn.) ■ ....Oct. 17
Gust. Adolphus ....Oct. 24
Macalester ■ ....Oct. 31
St. Thomas (Minn.) ....Nov. 7
Augsburg [Minneapolis, Minn.] ....Nov. 13

1997 RESULTS (8-2-0)

17	Moorhead St.	7
28	Gust. Adolphus	7
38	St. Olaf	0
28	Macalester	0
22	Bethel (Minn.)	14
28	St. Thomas (Minn.)	7
12	St. John's (Minn.)	20
10	Augsburg	13
45	Hamline	19
39	Carleton	10
267		**97**

III Championship

22	Augsburg	34

Nickname: Cobbers.
Stadium: Jake Christiansen, 7,500 capacity. Natural turf.
Colors: Maroon & Gold.
Conference: Minn. Intercol. Athletic Conf.
SID: Jerry Pyle, 218-299-3194.
AD: Armin Pipho.

CONNECTICUT

Storrs, CT 06269 ....I-AA

Coach: Skip Holtz, Notre Dame 1986
Record: 4 Years, 23-20-0

1998 SCHEDULE

Colgate ....Sept. 5
Maine ■ ....Sept. 19
Yale ....Sept. 26
New Hampshire ....Oct. 3
Hofstra ■ ....Oct. 10
Massachusetts ■ ....Oct. 17
Rhode Island ■ ....Oct. 24
Northeastern ....Oct. 31
Delaware ■ ....Nov. 7
William & Mary ....Nov. 14
Massachusetts ....Nov. 21

1997 RESULTS (7-4-0)

38	Northeastern	26
35	Hofstra	31
28	Yale	0
55	Buffalo	0
47	Maine	49
17	William & Mary	38
37	Rhode Island	21
45	Boston U.	7
29	Delaware	37
49	Massachusetts	16
18	New Hampshire	21
398		**246**

Nickname: Huskies.
Stadium: Memorial (1953), 16,200 capacity. Natural turf.
Colors: Blue & White.
Conference: Atlantic 10.
SID: Kyle Muncy, 203-486-3531.
AD: Lewis Perkins.

CORNELL

Ithaca, NY 14853 ....I-AA

Coach: Pete Mangurian, LSU 1978
(First year as head coach)

1998 SCHEDULE

Princeton ....Sept. 19
Holy Cross ....Sept. 26
Buffalo ■ ....Oct. 3
Harvard ....Oct. 10
Bucknell ■ ....Oct. 17
Dartmouth ■ ....Oct. 24
Brown ■ ....Oct. 31
Yale ....Nov. 7
Columbia ....Nov. 14
Pennsylvania ■ ....Nov. 21

1997 RESULTS (5-5-0)

14	Princeton	10
38	Colgate	44
20	Dartmouth	24
9	Harvard	34
41	Lafayette	34
45	Fordham	13
12	Brown	37
37	Yale	10
33	Columbia	22
20	Pennsylvania	33
269		**261**

Nickname: Big Red.
Stadium: Schoellkopf (1915), 27,000 capacity. Artificial turf.
Colors: Carnelian & White.
Conference: Ivy.
SID: Dave Wohlhueter, 607-255-3753.
AD: Charles H. Moore.

CORNELL COLLEGE

Mt. Vernon, IA 52314 III

Coach: Steve Miller, Cornell College 1965
Record: 19 Years, 104-69-3

1998 SCHEDULE

Central (Iowa) ....Sept. 5
Upper Iowa ■ ....Sept. 12
William Penn ....Sept. 19
Wartburg ■ ....Sept. 26
Buena Vista ....Oct. 3
Loras ....Oct. 17
Simpson ■ ....Oct. 24
Luther ....Oct. 31
Dubuque ■ ....Nov. 7
Coe ■ ....Nov. 14

1997 RESULTS (6-3-0)

20	Simpson	54
34	Dubuque	35
28	Ripon	14
20	Beloit	28
33	Knox	28
48	Monmouth (Ill.)	14
49	Grinnell	48
31	Illinois Col.	23
28	Coe	21
291		**265**

Nickname: Rams.
Stadium: Ash Park Field (1922), 2,500 capacity. Natural turf.
Colors: Purple & White.
Conference: Independent.
SID: Darren Miller, 319-895-4483.
AD: Stephen Miller.

CORTLAND ST.

Cortland, NY 13045 III

Coach: Dan MacNeill, Cortland St. 1979
Record: 1 Year, 8-3-0

1998 SCHEDULE

St. Lawrence ■ ....Sept. 5
Montclair St. ....Sept. 12
Kean ■ ....Sept. 19
Buffalo St. ....Sept. 26
Col. of New Jersey ....Oct. 10
Rowan ....Oct. 17
Wm. Paterson ■ ....Oct. 24
Springfield ....Oct. 31
Ithaca ■ ....Nov. 7
Brockport St. ■ ....Nov. 14

1997 RESULTS (8-2-0)

42	St. Lawrence	0
28	Montclair St.	14
47	Kean	21
38	Buffalo St.	9
43	Col. of New Jersey	22
6	Rowan	41
31	Wm. Paterson	0
24	Springfield	8
33	Ithaca	28
28	Brockport St.	30
320		**173**

III Championship

30	Col. of New Jersey	34

Nickname: Red Dragons.
Stadium: Davis Field (1959), 5,000 capacity. Natural turf.
Colors: Red & White.
Conference: Independent.
SID: Fran Elia, 607-753-5673.
AD: Lee Roberts.

CURRY

Milton, MA 02186 III

Coach: Steve Nelson, North Dak. St. 1974
(First year as head coach)

1998 SCHEDULE

Norwich	Sept. 5
Maine Maritime ■	Sept. 19
Framingham St.	Sept. 26
MIT ■	Oct. 3
Nichols	Oct. 10
Western New Eng.	Oct. 17
Salve Regina ■	Oct. 24
Fitchburg St.	Oct. 31
Mass.-Boston	Nov. 7
Mass.-Dartmouth ■	Nov. 14

1997 RESULTS (0-10-0)

0	Norwich	21
12	Mass.-Dartmouth	39
0	Hartwick	57
6	Framingham St.	7
6	Western New Eng.	28
6	Nichols	42
0	MIT	31
12	Salve Regina	52
0	Plymouth St.	42
6	Fitchburg St.	25
48		**344**

Nickname: Colonels.
Stadium: D. Forbes Will Field, 1,500 capacity. Natural turf.
Colors: Purple & White.
Conference: New England FB.
SID: Michael P. King, 617-333-2324.
AD: Pamela S. Samuelson.

DARTMOUTH

Hanover, NH 03755 .....I-AA

Coach: John Lyons, Pennsylvania 1974
Record: 6 Years, 44-15-1

1998 SCHEDULE

Pennsylvania ■	Sept. 19
Maine	Sept. 26
Lafayette ■	Oct. 3
Colgate	Oct. 10
Yale ■	Oct. 17
Cornell	Oct. 24
Harvard ■	Oct. 31
Columbia ■	Nov. 7
Brown	Nov. 14
Princeton	Nov. 21

1997 RESULTS (8-2-0)

23	Pennsylvania	15
35	Holy Cross	6
24	Cornell	20
31	Fordham	10
21	Yale	7
26	Lehigh	46
0	Harvard	24
23	Columbia	21
13	Brown	7
12	Princeton	9
208		**165**

Nickname: Big Green.
Stadium: Memorial Field (1923), 20,416 capacity. Natural turf.
Colors: Green & White.
Conference: Ivy.
SID: Kathy Slattery, 603-646-2468.
AD: Richard Jaeger.

DAVIDSON

Davidson, NC 28036 .....I-AA

Coach: Tim Landis, Randolph-Macon 1986
Record: 5 Years, 19-31-1

1998 SCHEDULE

Jacksonville	Sept. 12
Sewanee	Sept. 19
Emory & Henry ■	Sept. 26
Guilford ■	*Oct. 3
Wash. & Lee ■	Oct. 10
Methodist	Oct. 17
Randolph-Macon ■	Oct. 24
Hampden-Sydney	Oct. 31
Centre ■	Nov. 7
Bridgewater (Va.)	Nov. 14

1997 RESULTS (3-8-0)

41	Maryville (Tenn.)	25
42	Sewanee	14
35	Emory & Henry	49
22	Guilford	25
22	Wash. & Lee	32
16	Methodist	19
15	Randolph-Macon	22
43	Hampden-Sydney	0
14	Centre	19
10	Bridgewater (Va.)	13
3	South Fla.	48
263		**266**

Nickname: Wildcats.
Stadium: Richardson Field (1924), 5,200 capacity. Natural turf.
Colors: Red & Black.
Conference: Independent.
SID: Emil Parker, 704-892-2374.
AD: James E. Murphy III.

DAYTON

Dayton, OH 45469 .....I-AA

Coach: Mike Kelly, Manchester 1970
Record: 17 Years, 165-28-1

1998 SCHEDULE

Monmouth	Sept. 5
Robert Morris ■	Sept. 12
Austin Peay	*Sept. 19
Morehead St. ■	*Sept. 26
Butler	Oct. 3
Drake ■	Oct. 10
St. Joseph's (Ind.) ■	*Oct. 17
Valparaiso	Oct. 24
Towson ■	Nov. 7
San Diego	*Nov. 14

1997 RESULTS (9-1-0)

45	Georgetown (Ky.)	21
51	Monmouth	16
16	Robert Morris	13
42	Morehead St.	28
42	Butler	7
14	Drake	13
49	San Diego	25
34	Valparaiso	13
49	Evansville	7
24	Cal Poly	44
366		**187**

Nickname: Flyers.
Stadium: Welcome (1949), 11,000 capacity. Artificial turf.
Colors: Red & Blue.
Conference: Pioneer.
SID: Doug Hauschild, 513-229-4460.
AD: Ted Kissell.

DEPAUW

Greencastle, IN 46135 III

Coach: Nick Mourouzis, Miami (Ohio) 1959
Record: 17 Years, 103-62-4

1998 SCHEDULE

Rhodes	Sept. 5
Ill. Wesleyan	Sept. 12
Hope ■	Sept. 19
Trinity (Tex.) ■	Sept. 26
Chicago ■	Oct. 3
Sewanee ■	Oct. 10
Millsaps	*Oct. 24
Centre	Oct. 31
Rose-Hulman ■	Nov. 7
Wabash	Nov. 14

1997 RESULTS (8-2-0)

25	Chicago	0
33	Hope	20
10	Albion	24
21	Anderson (Ind.)	7
30	Franklin	7
7	Hanover	34
17	Rose-Hulman	14
21	Manchester	7
24	Benedictine (Ill.)	9
14	Wabash	7
202		**129**

Nickname: Tigers.
Stadium: Blackstock (1941), 4,000 capacity. Natural turf.
Colors: Old Gold & Black.
Conference: Heartland College. Ath. Conf.
SID: Bill Wagner, 317-658-4630.
AD: Page Cotton Jr.

DEFIANCE

Defiance, OH 43512 III

Coach: Greg Pscodna, Adrian 1986
Record: 2 Years, 4-14-0

1998 SCHEDULE

Adrian	Sept. 5
Alma ■	Sept. 12
Kalamazoo ■	Sept. 19
Olivet	Sept. 26
Albion ■	Oct. 3
Ohio Wesleyan ■	Oct. 17
Thomas More	Oct. 31
Thiel	Nov. 7
Hope	Nov. 14

1997 RESULTS (1-8-0)

0	Mount Union	58
7	Adrian	28
14	Olivet	41
29	Alma	24
0	Mount Saint Joseph	28
14	Thomas More	21
26	Manchester	51
6	Bluffton	31
0	Wash. & Jeff.	30
96		**312**

Nickname: Yellow Jackets.
Stadium: Justin F. Coressel (1994), 4,176 capacity. Natural turf.
Colors: Purple & Gold.
Conference: Independent.
SID: Holli Stone, 419-783-2346.
AD: D. Marvin Hohenberger.

DELAWARE ST.

Dover, DE 19901 .....I-AA

Coach: John McKenzie, Jackson St. 1985
Record: 1 Year, 3-8-0

1998 SCHEDULE

Hofstra	Sept. 5
Elon	*Sept. 12
Norfolk St.	*Sept. 19
Florida A&M ■	Oct. 3
Bethune-Cookman	Oct. 10
Liberty ■	Oct. 17
Morgan St.	Oct. 24
South Caro. St. ■	Oct. 31
North Caro. A&T ■	Nov. 7
Hampton ■	Nov. 14
Howard	Nov. 21

1997 RESULTS (3-8-0)

50	Cheyney	18
30	Buffalo	40
24	Norfolk St.	21
17	Liberty	33
35	Bethune-Cookman	14
0	Florida A&M	49
7	Morgan St.	14
17	South Caro. St.	37

14	North Caro. A&T	22
20	Hampton	24
21	Howard	40
235		**312**

Nickname: Hornets.
Stadium: Alumni Field (1957), 4,200 capacity. Natural turf.
Colors: Red & Columbia Blue.
Conference: Mid-Eastern.
SID: Dennis Jones, 302-739-4926.
AD: William Collick.

DELAWARE VALLEY

Doylestown, PA 18901 III

Coach: Glen Leonard, Ursinus 1981
Record: 1 Year, 5-5-0

1998 SCHEDULE

West Va. Tech	Sept. 5
Albright	*Sept. 12
La Salle ■	Sept. 26
Moravian ■	Oct. 3
FDU-Madison	Oct. 10
Lycoming ■	Oct. 17
King's (Pa.) ■	Oct. 24
Wilkes	Oct. 31
Widener ■	Nov. 7
Lebanon Valley	Nov. 14

1997 RESULTS (5-5-0)

17	Albright	39
14	Salisbury St.	12
43	La Salle	0
10	Moravian	28
47	FDU-Madison	44
3	Lycoming	49
38	King's (Pa.)	33
12	Wilkes	32
7	Widener	34
40	Lebanon Valley	27
231		**298**

Nickname: Aggies.
Stadium: James Work (1978), 4,500 capacity. Natural turf.
Colors: Green & Gold.
Conference: Middle Atlantic States Conf.
SID: Matthew Levy, 215-345-1500.
AD: Frank Wolfgang.

DELAWARE

Newark, DE 19716 ....I-AA

Coach: Harold Raymond, Michigan 1950
Record: 32 Years, 270-103-3

1998 SCHEDULE

Massachusetts ■	*Sept. 3
Villanova	Sept. 12
West Chester ■	Sept. 19
New Hampshire ■	Sept. 26
Northeastern ■	Oct. 3
William & Mary	Oct. 10
Youngstown St.	Oct. 17
Maine ■	Oct. 31
Connecticut	Nov. 7
Richmond	Nov. 14
James Madison ■	Nov. 21

1997 RESULTS (10-1-0)

27	New Hampshire	10
25	Villanova	35
28	West Chester	7
38	Northeastern	14
49	Boston U.	17
24	Richmond	7
49	James Madison	27
40	Massachusetts	9
14	William & Mary	0
37	Connecticut	29
24	Lehigh	19
355		**174**

I-AA Championship

24	Hofstra	14
16	Ga. Southern	7
21	McNeese St.	23

Nickname: Fightin' Blue Hens.
Stadium: Delaware (1952), 23,000 capacity. Natural turf.
Colors: Blue & Gold.
Conference: Atlantic 10.
SID: Scott Selheimer, 302-831-2186.
AD: Edgar N. Johnson.

DELTA ST.

Cleveland, MS 38733 II

Coach: Todd Knight, Ouachita Bapt. 1986
Record: 5 Years, 20-29-2

1998 SCHEDULE

Southwest Tex. St.	*Sept. 3
Arkansas Tech	*Sept. 12
Valdosta St. ■	*Sept. 19
West Ala. ■	Oct. 3
Henderson St.	*Oct. 10
North Ala.	Oct. 17
West Ga. ■	Oct. 24
Southern Ark.	Oct. 31
Central Ark. ■	Nov. 7
Ark.-Monticello	Nov. 14

1997 RESULTS (3-7-0)

3	Stephen F. Austin	38
20	Arkansas Tech	23
12	Central Ark.	37
6	Southern Ark.	24
20	Henderson St.	41
10	North Ala.	17
9	West Ga.	28
27	Valdosta St.	23
27	West Ala.	13
31	Ark.-Monticello	14
165		**258**

Nickname: Statesmen.
Stadium: Travis E. Parker Field (1970), 8,000 capacity. Natural turf.
Colors: Green & White.
Conference: Gulf South Conference.
SID: Bryan Roller, 601-846-4677.
AD: James H. Jordan.

DENISON

Granville, OH 43023 III

Coach: Bill Wentworth, Purdue 1980
Record: 5 Years, 16-33-1

1998 SCHEDULE

Carnegie Mellon ■	Sept. 5
Muskingum	Sept. 12
Allegheny ■	Sept. 19
Wooster ■	Sept. 26
Oberlin	Oct. 3
Case Reserve	Oct. 17
Ohio Wesleyan ■	Oct. 24
Kenyon	Oct. 31
Wittenberg ■	Nov. 7
Earlham	Nov. 14

1997 RESULTS (4-6-0)

7	Carnegie Mellon	32
24	Muskingum	16
22	Wooster	45
30	Earlham	0
3	Allegheny	34
31	Kenyon	21
54	Oberlin	18
14	Wittenberg	57
28	Ohio Wesleyan	30
29	Grove City	41
242		**294**

Nickname: Big Red.
Stadium: Deeds Field (1922), 5,000 capacity. Natural turf.
Colors: Red & White.
Conference: North Coast Athletic Conf.
SID: Jack Hire, 614-587-6546.
AD: Larry Scheiderer.

DICKINSON

Carlisle, PA 17013 III

Coach: Darwin Breaux, West Chester 1977
Record: 5 Years, 36-15-1

1998 SCHEDULE

Hobart	Sept. 12
Muhlenberg ■	Sept. 19
Catholic ■	Sept. 26
Carnegie Mellon ■	Oct. 3
Frank. & Marsh. ■	Oct. 10
Western Md.	Oct. 17
Swarthmore ■	Oct. 24
Johns Hopkins	Oct. 31
Gettysburg ■	Nov. 7
Ursinus	Nov. 14

1997 RESULTS (7-3-0)

13	Hobart	26
21	Muhlenberg	14
6	Catholic	35
44	Carnegie Mellon	37
24	Frank. & Marsh.	6
7	Western Md.	41
43	Swarthmore	0
13	Johns Hopkins	7
35	Gettysburg	14
32	Ursinus	3
238		**183**

Nickname: Red Devils.
Stadium: Biddle Field (1909), 2,577 capacity. Natural turf.
Colors: Red & White.
Conference: Centennial Conference.
SID: Matt Howell, 717-245-1652.
AD: Leslie J. Poolman.

DRAKE

Des Moines, IA 50311 ....I-AA

Coach: Rob Ash, Cornell College 1973
Record: 18 Years, 114-63-5

1998 SCHEDULE

Morningside ■	Sept. 5
St. Ambrose	*Sept. 12
Wis.-La Crosse ■	Sept. 19
Quincy	Sept. 26
Valparaiso ■	Oct. 3
Dayton	Oct. 10
San Diego ■	Oct. 24
Butler ■	Oct. 31
St. Mary's (Cal.)	Nov. 7
Towson	Nov. 14

1997 RESULTS (8-3-0)

7	Morningside	0
48	St. Norbert	7
23	South Fla.	22
27	Valparaiso	7
35	Wayne St. (Neb.)	17
13	Dayton	14
28	Evansville	18
30	San Diego	39
45	Aurora	0
13	Butler	14
27	Northwestern (Iowa)	20
296		**158**

Nickname: Bulldogs.
Stadium: Drake (1925), 18,000 capacity. Natural turf.
Colors: Blue & White.
Conference: Pioneer.
SID: Mike Mahon, 515-271-3012.
AD: Lynn H. King.

DUBUQUE

Dubuque, IA 52001 III

Coach: Mike Murray, Ill. Wesleyan 1984
Record: 1 Year, 3-7-0

1998 SCHEDULE

Simpson ■	Sept. 5
Luther	Sept. 12

Coe ■	Sept. 26
Central (Iowa)	Oct. 3
Upper Iowa ■	Oct. 10
William Penn	Oct. 17
Wartburg ■	Oct. 24
Buena Vista ■	Oct. 31
Cornell College	Nov. 7
Loras	Nov. 14

1997 RESULTS (3-7-0)

35	Cornell College	34
46	Concordia-St. Paul	21
25	Central (Iowa)	55
26	Luther	27
13	Buena Vista	33
35	William Penn	27
21	Wartburg	40
20	Simpson	62
15	Loras	52
6	Upper Iowa	46
242		**397**

Nickname: Spartans.
Stadium: Chalmers Field (1942), 2,800 capacity. Natural turf.
Colors: Blue and White.
Conference: Iowa Intercol. Athletic Conf.
SID: Greg Yoko, 319-589-3225.
AD: Connie Bandy Hodge.

DUKE

Durham, NC 27708 .... I-A

Coach: Fred Goldsmith, Florida 1967
Record: 10 Years, 38-70-1

1998 SCHEDULE

Western Caro. ■	*Sept. 5
Northwestern	Sept. 12
Florida St.	Sept. 19
Virginia ■	Sept. 26
Georgia Tech	Oct. 3
Wake Forest	*Oct. 10
North Caro. St.	Oct. 17
Clemson ■	Oct. 24
Vanderbilt	Oct. 31
Maryland ■	Nov. 14
North Caro. ■	Nov. 21

1997 RESULTS (2-9-0)

14	North Caro. St.	45
20	Northwestern	24
20	Army	17
26	Navy	17
10	Maryland	16
27	Florida St.	51
10	Virginia	13
24	Wake Forest	38
20	Clemson	29
38	Georgia Tech	41
14	North Caro.	50
223		**341**

Nickname: Blue Devils.
Stadium: Wallace Wade (1929), 33,941 capacity. Natural turf.
Colors: Royal Blue & White.
Conference: Atlantic Coast.
SID: Mike Cragg, 919-684-2633.
AD: Joe Alleva.

DUQUESNE

Pittsburgh, PA 15282 .... I-AA

Coach: Greg Gattuso, Penn St. 1983
Record: 5 Years, 37-15-0

1998 SCHEDULE

Bucknell ■	*Sept. 5
St. Francis (Pa.)	Sept. 12
Siena	Sept. 19
St. John's (N.Y.)	Sept. 26
Fairfield ■	Oct. 3
Marist ■	Oct. 10
Georgetown ■	Oct. 24
Iona ■	Oct. 31
St. Peter's	Nov. 7
Canisius	Nov. 14
Robert Morris ■	Nov. 21

1997 RESULTS (7-3-0)

16	Bucknell	23
51	St. Francis (Pa.)	3
38	Siena	14
27	Marist	24
28	Fairfield	23
11	St. John's (N.Y.)	14
0	Georgetown	24
41	Iona	0
40	St. Peter's	0
32	Canisius	7
284		**132**

Nickname: Dukes.
Stadium: Arthur J. Rooney Field (1993), 2,500 capacity. Artificial turf.
Colors: Red & Blue.
Conference: Metro Atlantic.
SID: To be named, 412-396-5861.
AD: Brian Colleary.

EARLHAM

Richmond, IN 47374 III

Coach: Frank Carr, Albion 1978
Record: 13 Years, 33-92-0

1998 SCHEDULE

Franklin	Sept. 12
Wooster ■	Sept. 19
Wittenberg	Sept. 26
Kenyon ■	Oct. 3
Case Reserve	Oct. 10
Allegheny	Oct. 17
Oberlin ■	Oct. 24
Rose-Hulman ■	Oct. 31
Ohio Wesleyan	Nov. 7
Denison ■	Nov. 14

1997 RESULTS (2-8-0)

0	Manchester	26
23	Ohio Wesleyan	21
0	Denison	30
6	Case Reserve	31
0	Wooster	38
7	Wilmington (Ohio)	43
21	Allegheny	35
3	Kenyon	20
64	Oberlin	18
14	Wittenberg	50
138		**312**

Nickname: Quakers.
Stadium: M. O. Ross Field (1975), 1,500 capacity. Natural turf.
Colors: Maroon & White.
Conference: North Coast Athletic Conf.
SID: David Knight, 317-983-1416.
AD: Porter Miller.

EAST CARO.

Greenville, NC 27858 .... I-A

Coach: Steve Logan, Tulsa 1975
Record: 6 Years, 36-32-0

1998 SCHEDULE

Virginia Tech	Sept. 5
Chattanooga ■	Sept. 12
Ohio	Sept. 19
Army ■	Oct. 3
UAB ■	Oct. 10
Alabama [Birmingham, Ala.]	Oct. 17
Southern Miss.	Oct. 24
Houston ■	Oct. 31
Cincinnati	Nov. 7
Louisville ■	Nov. 14
Memphis	Nov. 21

1997 RESULTS (5-6-0)

17	West Va.	24
25	Wake Forest	24
0	South Caro.	26
0	Syracuse	56
13	Southern Miss.	23
16	Tulane	33
32	Memphis	10
45	Louisville	31
28	Houston	27
14	Cincinnati	7
24	North Caro. St.	37
214		**298**

Nickname: Pirates.
Stadium: Dowdy-Ficklen (1963), 43,000 capacity. Natural turf.
Colors: Purple & Gold.
Conference: Conference USA.
SID: Norm Reilly, 919-328-4522.
AD: Mike Hamrick.

EAST CENTRAL

Ada, OK 74820 II

Coach: Hank Walbrick, East Central 1975
Record: 8 Years, 32-50-1

1998 SCHEDULE

Southern Ark.	*Sept. 3
Northwestern Okla. ■	*Sept. 12
West Tex. A&M ■	Sept. 19
Abilene Christian	*Sept. 26
Northeastern St. ■	*Oct. 3
Central Okla.	Oct. 10
Harding ■	Oct. 24
Ouachita Baptist	Oct. 31
Southwestern Okla. ■	Nov. 7
Southeastern Okla.	Nov. 14

1997 RESULTS (0-10-0)

9	Southern Ark.	37
0	Northwestern Okla.	27
0	West Tex. A&M	48
7	Abilene Christian	20
0	Northeastern St.	35
7	Central Okla.	42
21	Harding	41
13	Ouachita Baptist	21
14	Southwestern Okla.	20
14	Southeastern Okla.	35
85		**326**

Nickname: Tigers.
Stadium: Norris Field, 5,000 capacity. Natural turf.
Colors: Orange & Black.
Conference: Lone Star Conference.
SID: Justin Tinder, 405-436-5212.
AD: Tim Green.

EAST STROUDSBURG

East Stroudsburg, PA 18301 II

Coach: Dennis Douds, Slippery Rock 1963
Record: 24 Years, 143-97-3

1998 SCHEDULE

Shepherd ■	Sept. 12
New Hampshire	Sept. 19
Slippery Rock ■	Sept. 26
West Chester ■	Oct. 3
Shippensburg	Oct. 10
Cheyney	Oct. 17
Kutztown ■	Oct. 24
Bloomsburg	Oct. 31
Millersville	Nov. 7
Mansfield ■	Nov. 14

1997 RESULTS (4-6-0)

0	New Haven	38
34	Elon	41
25	Slippery Rock	40
45	Kutztown	20
31	West Chester	32
33	Indiana (Pa.)	31
39	Cheyney	16
23	Mansfield	21
13	Millersville	47
17	Bloomsburg	42
260		**328**

Nickname: Warriors.
Stadium: Eiler-Martin (1969), 6,000 capacity. Natural turf.

Colors: Red & Black.
Conference: Pennsylvania State Athl. Conf.
SID: Peter Nevins, 717-422-3312.
AD: Earl W. Edwards.

EAST TENN. ST.

Johnson City, TN 37614 .... I-AA

Coach: Paul Hamilton, Appalachian St. 1981
Record: 1 Year, 7-4-0

1998 SCHEDULE

Miami (Fla.) .... *Sept. 5
Appalachian St. ■ .... *Sept. 12
VMI ■ .... *Sept. 19
Western Caro. .... *Sept. 26
Citadel .... Oct. 10
Mississippi St. .... Oct. 17
Furman ■ .... Oct. 24
Ga. Southern .... Oct. 31
Wofford ■ .... *Nov. 7
Chattanooga .... Nov. 14
Charleston So. ■ .... *Nov. 21

1997 RESULTS (7-4-0)

30	Charleston So.	7
35	Elon	16
27	James Madison	32
28	Western Caro.	18
51	Appalachian St.	28
20	Citadel	23
58	Furman	28
30	Ga. Southern	38
31	Wofford	28
13	Chattanooga	17
17	VMI	7
340		**242**

Nickname: Buccaneers.
Stadium: Memorial (1977), 12,000 capacity. Artificial turf.
Colors: Blue & Gold.
Conference: Southern.
SID: Annabelle Vaughan, 615-929-4220.
AD: Frank S. Pergolizzi.

EASTERN ILL.

Charleston, IL 61920 .... I-AA

Coach: Bob Spoo, Purdue 1960
Record: 11 Years, 68-56-1

1998 SCHEDULE

St. Joseph's (Ind.) ■ .... Sept. 3
Central Fla. .... *Sept. 12
Northern Ill. .... *Sept. 19
Tennessee Tech ■ .... Sept. 26
Southeast Mo. St. ■ .... Oct. 3
Illinois St. ■ .... Oct. 17
Middle Tenn. St. .... *Oct. 24
Tennessee St. ■ .... Oct. 31
Murray St. ■ .... Nov. 7
Tenn.-Martin .... Nov. 14
Eastern Ky. .... Nov. 21

1997 RESULTS (8-3-0)

0	Western Ill.	41
42	Tenn.-Martin	6
41	St. Joseph's (Ind.)	20
25	Illinois St.	14
10	Tennessee Tech	7
32	Southeast Mo. St.	7
30	Middle Tenn. St.	17
42	Austin Peay	14
21	Indiana St.	14
17	Murray St.	24
7	Eastern Ky.	49
267		**213**

Nickname: Panthers.
Stadium: O'Brien (1970), 10,000 capacity. Natural turf.
Colors: Blue & Gray.
Conference: Ohio Valley.
SID: Dave Kidwell, 217-581-6408.
AD: Richard A. Mc Duffie.

EASTERN KY.

Richmond, KY 40475 .... I-AA

Coach: Roy Kidd, Eastern Ky. 1954
Record: 34 Years, 280-103-8

1998 SCHEDULE

Kentucky St. ■ .... Sept. 5
Kentucky .... Sept. 12
Western Ky. .... *Sept. 19
Middle Tenn. St. .... *Sept. 26
Tennessee St. ■ .... *Oct. 10
Murray St. ■ .... Oct. 17
Tennessee Tech .... Oct. 24
Tenn.-Martin .... Oct. 31
Southeast Mo. St. ■ .... Nov. 7
Appalachian St. ■ .... Nov. 14
Eastern Ill. ■ .... Nov. 21

1997 RESULTS (8-3-0)

12	Troy St.	21
21	Western Ky.	37
23	Appalachian St.	27
56	Austin Peay	3
49	Tennessee St.	7
29	Murray St.	8
26	Tennessee Tech	7
49	Tenn.-Martin	0
20	Southeast Mo. St.	10
35	Middle Tenn. St.	20
49	Eastern Ill.	7
369		**147**

I-AA Championship

14	Western Ky.	42

Nickname: Colonels.
Stadium: Roy Kidd (1969), 20,000 capacity. Natural turf.
Colors: Maroon & White.
Conference: Ohio Valley.
SID: Karl Park, 606-622-1253.
AD: Robert Baugh.

EASTERN MICH.

Ypsilanti, MI 48197 .... I-A

Coach: Rick Rasnick, San Jose St. 1982
Record: 3 Years, 13-20-0

1998 SCHEDULE

Northern Iowa ■ .... *Sept. 3
Ball St. .... Sept. 12
Michigan .... Sept. 19
Marshall ■ .... Sept. 26
Kent .... *Oct. 3
Central Mich. ■ .... *Oct. 10
Western Mich. .... Oct. 17
Northern Ill. ■ .... *Oct. 24
Ohio .... Nov. 7
Akron .... Nov. 14
Toledo ■ .... Nov. 21

1997 RESULTS (4-7-0)

24	Missouri	44
35	Toledo	38
38	Kent	41
31	Central Mich.	24
7	Ohio	47
38	Ball St.	32
45	Akron	0
25	Marshall	48
38	Western Mich.	41
38	Northern Ill.	10
10	Central Fla.	27
329		**352**

Nickname: Eagles.
Stadium: Rynearson (1969), 30,200 capacity. Artificial turf.
Colors: Green & White.
Conference: Mid-American.
SID: Jim Streeter, 313-487-0317.
AD: Carole J. Huston.

EASTERN N.M.

Portales, NM 88130 II

Coach: Bud Elliott, Baker (Kan.) 1953
Record: 30 Years, 157-152-9

1998 SCHEDULE

Western N. Mex. ■ .... *Sept. 5
N. M. Highlands .... *Sept. 12
Southwestern Okla. .... *Sept. 19
Southeastern Okla. ■ .... Sept. 26
Abilene Christian .... *Oct. 3
Angelo St. .... *Oct. 10
Tarleton St. ■ .... *Oct. 17
Tex. A&M-Commerce .... Oct. 24
Texas A&M-Kingsville ■ .... *Oct. 31
West Tex. A&M .... Nov. 7
Midwestern St. ■ .... Nov. 14

1997 RESULTS (5-6-0)

3	Western N. Mex.	0
34	N. M. Highlands	31
21	Southwestern Okla.	12
7	Southeastern Okla.	21
7	Abilene Christian	40
7	Angelo St.	16
26	Tarleton St.	20
10	Tex. A&M-Commerce	9
14	Texas A&M-Kingsville	56
34	West Tex. A&M	35
7	Midwestern St.	24
170		**264**

Nickname: Greyhounds.
Stadium: Greyhound (1969), 6,500 capacity. Natural turf.
Colors: Green & Silver.
Conference: Lone Star Conference.
SID: Judy Willson, 505-562-4309.
AD: Rosemarie Stallman.

EASTERN WASH.

Cheney, WA 99004 .... I-AA

Coach: Mike Kramer, Idaho 1977
Record: 4 Years, 25-22-0

1998 SCHEDULE

Idaho .... Sept. 5
Portland St. ■ .... *Sept. 12
Cal St. Northridge .... Sept. 26
Northern Ariz. ■ .... *Oct. 3
Western Wash. ■ .... Oct. 10
Idaho St. .... Oct. 17
Montana ■ .... Oct. 24
Cal St. Sacramento .... Oct. 31
Montana St. ■ .... Nov. 7
Weber St. .... Nov. 14
Southern Utah .... Nov. 21

1997 RESULTS (10-1-0)

63	Rocky Mountain	7
38	Eastern Ore. U.	14
31	Portland St.	14
35	Weber St.	11
7	Montana St.	17
30	Cal St. Sacramento	17
40	Montana	35
51	Idaho St.	7
24	Idaho	21
31	Northern Ariz.	14
39	Cal St. Northridge	32
389		**189**

I-AA Championship

40	Northwestern St.	10
38	Western Ky.	21
14	Youngstown St.	25

Nickname: Eagles.
Stadium: Woodward (1967), 6,000 capacity. Natural turf.
Colors: Red & White.
Conference: Big Sky.
SID: Dave Cook, 509-359-6334.
AD: Richard L. Zornes.

EDINBORO

Edinboro, PA 16444 ... II

Coach: Tom Hollman, Ohio Northern 1968
Record: 14 Years, 95-45-3

1998 SCHEDULE

Hillsdale ... *Sept. 5
Carson-Newman ■ ... Sept. 12
Glenville St. ... Sept. 19
Millersville ... *Sept. 26
Shippensburg ■ ... Oct. 3
Clarion ... Oct. 10
Lock Haven ■ ... Oct. 17
Calif. (Pa.) ■ ... Oct. 24
Slippery Rock ... Oct. 31
Indiana (Pa.) ... Nov. 7
Bloomsburg ■ ... Nov. 14

1997 RESULTS (4-6-0)

21 Hillsdale ... 17
10 Carson-Newman ... 33
27 Glenville St. ... 35
3 Shippensburg ... 17
38 Calif. (Pa.) ... 22
10 Slippery Rock ... 30
20 Indiana (Pa.) ... 25
44 Cheyney ... 0
0 Clarion ... 28
29 Lock Haven ... 23
202 **230**

Nickname: Fighting Scots.
Stadium: Sox Harrison (1965), 5,000 capacity. Natural turf.
Colors: Red & White.
Conference: Pennsylvania State Athl. Conf.
SID: Shawn Ahearn, 814-732-2811.
AD: Bruce R. Baumgartner.

ELIZABETH CITY ST.

Elizabeth City, NC 27909 ... II

Coach: Elisha Harris, Norfolk St. 1978
Record: 2 Years, 6-14-0

1998 SCHEDULE

Savannah St. ■ ... *Aug. 29
Fayetteville St. [Rocky Mount, N.C.] ... Sept. 12
Cheyney ... Sept. 19
Benedict ... Sept. 26
N.C. Central ... Oct. 3
Virginia Union ■ ... Oct. 10
Bowie St. ... Oct. 17
Livingstone ... Oct. 24
Winston-Salem ■ ... Nov. 7
Virginia St. ■ ... Nov. 14
Johnson Smith ... Nov. 21

1997 RESULTS (2-8-0)

0 Fayetteville St. ... 19
15 Benedict ... 12
12 Johnson Smith ... 10
6 N.C. Central ... 37
6 Virginia Union ... 13
26 Bowie St. ... 32
16 Livingstone ... 41
0 New Haven ... 59
0 Winston-Salem ... 48
12 Virginia St. ... 22
93 **293**

Nickname: Vikings.
Stadium: Roebuck, 6,500 capacity. Natural turf.
Colors: Royal Blue & White.
Conference: Central Intercol. Ath. Assn.
SID: Kirt Campbell, 919-335-3278.
AD: Edward Mc Lean.

ELMHURST

Elmhurst, IL 60126 ... III

Coach: Paul Krohn, Mankato St. 1976
Record: 5 Years, 9-35-1

1998 SCHEDULE

Ripon ... Sept. 12
Benedictine (Ill.) ■ ... Sept. 19
Ill. Wesleyan ■ ... Oct. 3
North Central ■ ... Oct. 10
Augustana (Ill.) ... Oct. 17
North Park ... Oct. 24
Carthage ■ ... Oct. 31
Wheaton (Ill.) ... Nov. 7
Millikin ... Nov. 14

1997 RESULTS (1-8-0)

7 Benedictine (Ill.) ... 10
7 Alma ... 48
7 Millikin ... 51
20 Wheaton (Ill.) ... 59
0 Carthage ... 41
28 North Park ... 25
7 North Central ... 48
14 Augustana (Ill.) ... 50
0 Ill. Wesleyan ... 7
90 **339**

Nickname: Bluejays.
Stadium: Langhorst (1920), 2,500 capacity. Natural turf.
Colors: Blue & White.
Conference: College Conf. of Ill. & Wisc.
SID: John Quigley, 708-617-3380.
AD: Christopher Ragsdale.

ELON

Elon College, NC 27244 ... II

Coach: Al Seagraves, Shippensburg 1975
Record: 2 Years, 11-11-0

1998 SCHEDULE

Ga. Southern ... *Sept. 5
Delaware St. ■ ... *Sept. 12
Western Ill. ■ ... Sept. 19
James Madison ... *Sept. 26
Morehead St. ... *Oct. 3
South Fla. ... *Oct. 10
Presbyterian ■ ... Oct. 17
Western Ky. ... Oct. 24
Liberty ■ ... Oct. 31
Western Caro. ... Nov. 7
Samford ■ ... Nov. 14

1997 RESULTS (7-4-0)

63 Lenoir-Rhyne ... 13
16 East Tenn. St. ... 35
52 Newberry ... 20
41 East Stroudsburg ... 34
9 Liberty ... 41
41 South Fla. ... 13
24 Presbyterian ... 3
23 Catawba ... 9
20 Furman ... 38
17 Western Caro. ... 16
32 Samford ... 46
338 **268**

Nickname: Fightin' Christians.
Stadium: Burlington Memorial (1949), 10,000 capacity. Natural turf.
Colors: Maroon & Gold.
Conference: Independent.
SID: David Hibbard, 910-584-2316.
AD: Alan J. White.

EMORY & HENRY

Emory, VA 24327 ... III

Coach: Lou Wacker, Richmond 1956
Record: 16 Years, 122-47-0

1998 SCHEDULE

Wash. & Jeff. ... Sept. 5
Bridgewater (Va.) ■ ... Sept. 19
Davidson ... Sept. 26
Greensboro ■ ... Oct. 3
Hampden-Sydney ... Oct. 10
Randolph-Macon ■ ... Oct. 17
Guilford ... Oct. 24
Ferrum ■ ... Oct. 31
Wash. & Lee ... Nov. 7
Maryville (Tenn.) ■ ... Nov. 14

1997 RESULTS (8-2-0)

38 Wash. & Jeff. ... 10
31 Bridgewater (Va.) ... 7
49 Davidson ... 35
37 Greensboro ... 3
33 Hampden-Sydney ... 10
20 Randolph-Macon ... 27
35 Guilford ... 27
13 Ferrum ... 10
27 Wash. & Lee ... 17
24 Maryville (Tenn.) ... 27
307 **173**

Nickname: Wasps.
Stadium: Fullerton Field, 5,500 capacity. Natural turf.
Colors: Blue & Gold.
Conference: Old Dominion Athletic Conf.
SID: Nathan Graybeal, 540-944-6830.
AD: Louis Wacker.

EMPORIA ST.

Emporia, KS 66801 ... II

Coach: Manny Matsakis, Capital 1984
Record: 3 Years, 17-16-0

1998 SCHEDULE

North Dak. St. ... *Aug. 27
Fort Hays St. ■ ... *Sept. 3
Pittsburg St. ■ ... *Sept. 19
Southwest Baptist ... Sept. 26
Truman St. ■ ... Oct. 3
Mo. Western St. ... *Oct. 8
Mo. Southern St. ■ ... Oct. 17
Central Mo. St. ... Oct. 24
Washburn ... *Oct. 29
Mo.-Rolla ■ ... Nov. 7
Northwest Mo. St. ... Nov. 14

1997 RESULTS (7-4-0)

23 Northwestern Okla. ... 16
51 Fort Hays St. ... 35
22 Pittsburg St. ... 32
46 Southwest Baptist ... 7
28 Truman St. ... 44
27 Mo. Western St. ... 15
39 Mo. Southern St. ... 40
50 Central Mo. St. ... 10
64 Washburn ... 35
77 Mo.-Rolla ... 20
38 Northwest Mo. St. ... 44
465 **298**

Nickname: Hornets.
Stadium: Welch (1937), 7,000 capacity. Natural turf.
Colors: Black & Gold.
Conference: MIAA.
SID: J. D. Campbell, 316-341-5454.
AD: William W. Quayle.

EUREKA

Eureka, IL 61530 ... III

Coach: Nicholas Fletcher, Johns Hopkins 1976
Record: 3 Years, 19-10-0

1998 SCHEDULE

Bethel (Tenn.) ... Sept. 5
Monmouth (Ill.) ■ ... Sept. 12
Hanover ... Sept. 19
Benedictine (Ill.) ■ ... Sept. 26
Aurora ■ ... Oct. 3
Concordia (Wis.) ... Oct. 10
Greenville ■ ... Oct. 17
Lakeland ■ ... Oct. 24
MacMurray ... Oct. 31
Concordia (Ill.) ... Nov. 7

1997 RESULTS (5-5-0)

35 Monmouth (Ill.) ... 12
28 Coe ... 35
42 Blackburn ... 16
0 Concordia (Wis.) ... 31
21 MacMurray ... 35
34 Concordia (Ill.) ... 0
17 Bethel (Tenn.) ... 14
13 McKendree ... 28
13 Lakeland ... 24

35	Greenville	29
238		**224**

Nickname: Red Devils.
Stadium: McKinzie (1913), 3,000 capacity. Natural turf.
Colors: Maroon & Gold.
Conference: Independent.
SID: Shellie Schwanke, 309-467-6370.
AD: Marty Stromberger.

EVANSVILLE

Evansville, IN 47722 ... I-AA

Coach: Robin Cooper, Ill. Wesleyan 1975

1998 SCHEDULE

Dropped program following 1997 season.

1997 RESULTS (2-8-0)

22	Cumberland (Tenn.)	31
41	Quincy	14
26	McKendree	30
20	San Diego	55
10	Valparaiso	12
18	Drake	28
35	Butler	38
7	Dayton	49
48	Ky. Wesleyan	6
27	Morehead St.	54
254		**317**

Nickname: Aces.
Stadium: Arad McCutchan (1984), 3,000 capacity. Natural turf.
Colors: Purple & White.
Conference: Pioneer.
SID: Bob Boxell, 812-479-2350.
AD: James A. Byers.

FAIRFIELD

Fairfield, CT 06430 ... I-AA

Coach: Kevin Kiesel, Gettysburg 1981
Record: 5 Years, 23-25-1

1998 SCHEDULE

Holy Cross	Sept. 5
Iona ■	Sept. 12
Marist	Sept. 19
Georgetown ■	Sept. 26
Duquesne	Oct. 3
San Diego	Oct. 17
Canisius ■	Oct. 24
Siena	Oct. 31
St. John's (N.Y.)	Nov. 6
St. Peter's ■	Nov. 14
Central Conn. St.	Nov. 21

1997 RESULTS (7-3-0)

34	La Salle	10
34	St. John's (N.Y.)	21
9	Georgetown	34
17	Central Conn. St.	10
23	Duquesne	28
34	Marist	14
21	Canisius	14
6	Siena	16
28	Iona	7
38	St. Peter's	34
244		**188**

Nickname: Stags.
Stadium: Alumni, 3,000 capacity. Natural turf.
Colors: Cardinal Red.
Conference: Metro Atlantic.
SID: Jack Jones, 203-254-4000.
AD: Eugene Doris.

FDU-MADISON

Madison, NJ 07940 ... III

Coach: Larry Arico, Lehigh 1992
Record: 1 Year, 0-10-0

1998 SCHEDULE

Col. of New Jersey ■	*Sept. 11
Widener	Sept. 19
Wilkes ■	*Sept. 25
Lycoming	Oct. 3
Delaware Valley ■	Oct. 10
Catholic	Oct. 17
Albright	Oct. 24
Moravian	Oct. 31
King's (Pa.) ■	*Nov. 7
Juniata ■	Nov. 14

1997 RESULTS (0-10-0)

0	Col. of New Jersey	24
14	Widener	27
3	Wilkes	29
19	Lycoming	35
44	Delaware Valley	47
14	Catholic	51
0	Albright	37
8	Moravian	21
31	King's (Pa.)	34
33	Juniata	34
166		**339**

Nickname: Devils.
Stadium: Devils (1973), 4,000 capacity. Natural turf.
Colors: Black, FDU Blue & White.
Conference: Middle Atlantic States Conf.
SID: Alan Wickstrom, 201-443-8965.
AD: William T. Klika.

FAIRMONT ST.

Fairmont, WV 26554 ... II

Coach: Doug Sams, Oregon St. 1978
Record: 7 Years, 32-39-0

1998 SCHEDULE

Saginaw Valley	*Sept. 5
Calif. (Pa.) ■	Sept. 12
Slippery Rock	Sept. 19
West Va. St. ■	Oct. 3
West Va. Tech ■	Oct. 10
Glenville St.	Oct. 17
Shepherd	Oct. 24
West Liberty St. ■	Oct. 31
West Va. Wesleyan ■	Nov. 7
Concord	Nov. 14

1997 RESULTS (5-6-0)

30	Indiana (Pa.)	29
16	Calif. (Pa.)	14
14	Slippery Rock	42
7	Saginaw Valley	56
28	West Va. St.	33
52	West Va. Tech	0
14	Glenville St.	23
27	Shepherd	39
48	West Liberty St.	15
0	West Va. Wesleyan	31
50	Concord	15
286		**297**

Nickname: Falcons.
Stadium: Rosier Field (1929), 6,000 capacity. Natural turf.
Colors: Maroon & White.
Conference: WV Intercollegiate Athletic.
SID: Jim Brinkman, 304-367-4264.
AD: David W. Cooper.

FAYETTEVILLE ST.

Fayetteville, NC 28301 ... II

Coach: James Toon, North Caro. A&T 1959
Record: 1 Year, 4-7-0

1998 SCHEDULE

Elizabeth City St. [Rocky Mount, N.C.]	Sept. 12
Benedict ■	*Sept. 19
North Caro. A&T	Sept. 26
Winston-Salem	Oct. 3
N.C. Central ■	*Oct. 10
Virginia St. ■	*Oct. 17
Johnson Smith	Oct. 24
Bowie St. ■	Oct. 31
Virginia Union	Nov. 7
Livingstone ■	Nov. 14

1997 RESULTS (4-7-0)

26	Benedict	32
19	Elizabeth City St.	0
12	Wingate	48
0	Bethune-Cookman	14
18	Winston-Salem	16
13	N.C. Central	38
29	Virginia St.	51
38	Johnson Smith	27
14	Bowie St.	7
0	Virginia Union	46
13	Livingstone	67
182		**346**

Nickname: Broncos.
Stadium: Jeralds Ath. Complex (1993), 6,100 capacity. Natural turf.
Colors: White & Royal Blue.
Conference: Central Intercol. Ath. Assn.
SID: Marion Crowe Jr., 910-486-1349.
AD: Horace T. Small.

FERRIS ST.

Big Rapids, MI 49307 ... II

Coach: Jeff Pierce, Ferris St. 1979
Record: 3 Years, 25-10-0

1998 SCHEDULE

Winona St.	Sept. 5
Saginaw Valley ■	Sept. 12
Findlay	Sept. 19
Northwood	Sept. 26
Northern Mich. ■	Oct. 3
Wayne St. (Mich.) ■	Oct. 10
Ashland	*Oct. 17
Michigan Tech	Oct. 24
Hillsdale ■	Oct. 31
St. Francis (Ill.)	Nov. 7
Grand Valley St. ■	Nov. 14

1997 RESULTS (3-7-0)

7	Ashland	26
21	Indianapolis	32
35	Hillsdale	21
18	Grand Valley St.	21
21	Northern Mich.	23
26	Wayne St. (Mich.)	30
31	Northwood	17
24	Michigan Tech	34
24	Saginaw Valley	23
15	St. Francis (Ill.)	16
222		**243**

Nickname: Bulldogs.
Stadium: Top Taggart Field (1957), 9,100 capacity. Natural turf.
Colors: Crimson & Gold.
Conference: Midwest Intercoll.
SID: Joe Gorby, 616-592-2336.
AD: Larry Marfise.

FERRUM

Ferrum, VA 24088 ... III

Coach: Dave Davis, Elon 1971
Record: 4 Years, 15-23-0

1998 SCHEDULE

Newport News	Sept. 5
Greensboro ■	Sept. 19
Bridgewater (Va.)	Sept. 26
Methodist	Oct. 3
Guilford	Oct. 10
Chowan ■	Oct. 17
Frostburg St. ■	Oct. 24
Emory & Henry	Oct. 31
Salisbury St. ■	Nov. 7
Wesley	Nov. 14

1997 RESULTS (4-6-0)

0	Wesley	23
0	Clinch Valley	7
6	Rowan	54
34	Greensboro	0
24	Newport News	14
22	Guilford	28
19	Chowan	0

31	Methodist	12
10	Emory & Henry	13
0	Frostburg St.	31
146		**182**

Nickname: Panthers.
Stadium: Adams (1970), 5,500 capacity. Natural turf.
Colors: Black & Gold.
Conference: Atlantic Central FB.
SID: Gary Holden, 540-365-4306.
AD: T. Michael Kinder.

FITCHBURG ST.

Fitchburg, MA 01420 III

Coach: To be named

1998 SCHEDULE

Mass.-Boston	Sept. 12
Nichols ■	Sept. 19
Westfield St.	Sept. 26
Worcester St. ■	Oct. 3
Mass. Maritime ■	Oct. 10
Framingham St.	Oct. 17
Maine Maritime	Oct. 24
Curry ■	Oct. 31
Bri'water (Mass.) ■	Nov. 7
Western New Eng.	Nov. 14

1997 RESULTS (3-7-0)

17	Western New Eng.	7
31	Framingham St.	33
35	Westfield St.	13
7	Bri'water (Mass.)	39
9	Worcester St.	47
22	Mass. Maritime	45
10	Mass.-Dartmouth	32
6	Maine Maritime	23
6	Mass.-Boston	27
25	Curry	6
168		**272**

Nickname: Falcons.
Stadium: Robert Elliot (1984), 1,200 capacity. Natural turf.
Colors: Green, Gold & White.
Conference: New England FB.
SID: David Marsh, 508-665-3343.
AD: Sue E. Lauder.

FLORIDA

Gainesville, FL 32611 ....I-A

Coach: Steve Spurrier, Florida 1967
Record: 11 Years, 103-29-2

1998 SCHEDULE

Citadel ■	*Sept. 5
Northeast La. ■	*Sept. 12
Tennessee	*Sept. 19
Kentucky ■	Sept. 26
Alabama	Oct. 3
LSU ■	Oct. 10
Auburn ■	Oct. 17
Georgia [Jacksonville, Fla.]	Oct. 31
Vanderbilt	Nov. 7
South Caro. ■	Nov. 14
Florida St.	Nov. 21

1997 RESULTS (9-2-0)

21	Southern Miss.	6
82	Central Mich.	6
33	Tennessee	20
55	Kentucky	28
56	Arkansas	7
21	LSU	28
24	Auburn	10
17	Georgia	37
20	Vanderbilt	7
48	South Caro.	21
32	Florida St.	29
409		**199**

Florida Citrus Bowl

21	Penn St.	6

Nickname: Gators.
Stadium: Florida Field (1929), 83,000 capacity. Natural turf.
Colors: Orange & Blue.
Conference: Southeastern.
SID: John Humenik, 352-375-4683.
AD: Jeremy Foley.

FLORIDA A&M

Tallahassee, FL 32307 ....I-AA

Coach: Billy Joe, Villanova 1963
Record: 24 Years, 184-76-4

1998 SCHEDULE

Hampton ■	*Sept. 5
Norfolk St.	*Sept. 12
Jackson St.	*Sept. 19
Tennessee St. [Atlanta, Ga.]	Sept. 26
Delaware St.	Oct. 3
North Caro. A&T ■	Oct. 10
Howard [Jacksonville, Fla.]	Oct. 17
Morgan St. ■	*Oct. 31
Southern U.	*Nov. 7
South Caro. St. ■	*Nov. 14
Bethune-Cookman [Orlando, Fla.]	*Nov. 21

1997 RESULTS (9-2-0)

43	Tennessee St.	28
41	Norfolk St.	26
30	Jackson St.	14
24	Howard	15
15	Hampton	18
37	North Caro. A&T	40
49	Delaware St.	0
42	Morgan St.	13
33	Southern U.	3
22	South Caro. St.	20
52	Bethune-Cookman	35
388		**212**

I-AA Championship

37	Ga. Southern	52

Nickname: Rattlers.
Stadium: Bragg Memorial (1957), 25,500 capacity. Natural turf.
Colors: Orange & Green.
Conference: Mid-Eastern.
SID: Alvin Hollins, 904-599-3200.
AD: Kenneth Riley.

FLORIDA ST.

Tallahassee, FL 32306 ....I-A

Coach: Bobby Bowden, Samford 1953
Record: 32 Years, 281-83-4

1998 SCHEDULE

Texas A&M [East Rutherford, N. J.]	Aug. 31
North Caro. St.	Sept. 12
Duke ■	Sept. 19
Southern Cal ■	Sept. 26
Maryland	Oct. 3
Miami (Fla.)	Oct. 10
Clemson ■	Oct. 17
Georgia Tech	Oct. 24
North Caro. ■	Oct. 31
Virginia ■	Nov. 7
Wake Forest	Nov. 14
Florida ■	Nov. 21

1997 RESULTS (10-1-0)

14	Southern Cal	7
50	Maryland	7
35	Clemson	28
47	Miami (Fla.)	0
51	Duke	27
38	Georgia Tech	0
47	Virginia	21
48	North Caro. St.	35
20	North Caro.	3
58	Wake Forest	7
29	Florida	32
437		**167**

Sugar Bowl

31	Ohio St.	14

Nickname: Seminoles.
Stadium: Doak S. Campbell (1950), 80,000 capacity. Natural turf.
Colors: Garnet & Gold.
Conference: Atlantic Coast.
SID: Rob Wilson, 904-644-1403.
AD: David R. Hart Jr.

FORDHAM

Bronx, NY 10458 ....I-AA

Coach: Ken O'Keefe, John Carroll 1975
Record: 8 Years, 79-10-1

1998 SCHEDULE

Lehigh	Sept. 12
Bucknell	Sept. 19
Towson	Sept. 26
Princeton ■	Oct. 3
Pennsylvania ■	Oct. 10
Brown	Oct. 17
Colgate ■	Oct. 24
Villanova ■	Oct. 31
Lafayette ■	Nov. 7
Holy Cross	Nov. 14
Georgetown ■	Nov. 21

1997 RESULTS (5-6-0)

23	Lafayette	0
42	Lehigh	35
14	Colgate	27
7	Princeton	9
14	Brown	45
10	Dartmouth	31
10	Bucknell	36
13	Cornell	45
12	Towson	7
42	Georgetown	0
28	Holy Cross	12
215		**247**

Nickname: Rams.
Stadium: Jack Coffey Field (1930), 7,000 capacity. Natural turf.
Colors: Maroon & White.
Conference: Patriot.
SID: Joe DiBari, 718-817-4240.
AD: Francis X. Mc Laughlin.

FORT HAYS ST.

Hays, KS 67601 II

Coach: Jeff Leiker, Washburn 1985
(First year as head coach)

1998 SCHEDULE

Emporia St.	*Sept. 3
Washburn ■	*Sept. 12
Colorado Mines	Sept. 19
Fort Lewis ■	Sept. 26
Wayne St. (Neb.)	Oct. 3
Mesa St. ■	*Oct. 10
Neb.-Kearney	Oct. 17
Western St. (Colo.)	Oct. 24
N. M. Highlands ■	Oct. 31
Chadron St. ■	Nov. 7
Adams St.	Nov. 14

1997 RESULTS (5-6-0)

35	Emporia St.	51
14	Washburn	31
23	Fort Lewis	30
62	Wayne St. (Neb.)	12
34	Mesa St.	19
20	Neb.-Kearney	23
28	Western St. (Colo.)	15
28	N. M. Highlands	35
0	Chadron St.	40
41	Adams St.	15
17	Colorado Mines	14
302		**285**

Nickname: Tigers.
Stadium: Lewis Field (1936), 7,000 capacity. Artificial turf.
Colors: Black & Gold.
Conference: Rocky Mountain Athletic Conf.
SID: Jack Kuestermeyer, 913-628-5903.
AD: Thomas E. Spicer.

FORT LEWIS

Durango, CO 81301 II

Coach: Todd Wash, North Dak. St. 1994
Record: 2 Years, 9-12-0

1998 SCHEDULE

Montana St.	Sept. 5
Chadron St.	Sept. 19
Fort Hays St.	Sept. 26
Colorado Mines ■	Oct. 3
Neb.-Kearney ■	Oct. 10
Southern Utah	Oct. 17
N. M. Highlands	Oct. 24
Mesa St.	Oct. 31
Adams St. ■	Nov. 7
Western St. (Colo.) ■	Nov. 14

1997 RESULTS (4-7-0)

14	Southern Utah	27
14	Montana Tech	27
30	Fort Hays St.	23
28	Colorado Mines	16
36	Neb.-Kearney	50
56	Okla. Panhandle St.	21
22	N. M. Highlands	35
16	Mesa St.	52
14	Adams St.	12
17	Western St. (Colo.)	66
14	Chadron St.	51
261		380

Nickname: Skyhawks.
Stadium: Ray Dennison Memorial (1958), 4,000 capacity. Natural turf.
Colors: Blue & Gold.
Conference: Rocky Mountain Athletic Conf.
SID: Chris Aaland, 970-247-7441.
AD: Joel R. Smith Jr.

FORT VALLEY ST.

Fort Valley, GA 31030 II

Coach: Kent Schoolfield, Florida A&M 1970
Record: 1 Year, 5-6-0

1998 SCHEDULE

Morehouse ■	*Aug. 29
Valdosta St.	*Sept. 5
Lane	Sept. 12
Morris Brown	*Sept. 19
Kentucky St. ■	*Sept. 26
Miles	Oct. 10
Clark Atlanta	*Oct. 17
Tuskegee ■	Oct. 24
Savannah St.	Oct. 31
Benedict ■	Nov. 7
Albany St. (Ga.) [Columbus, Ga.]	Nov. 14

1997 RESULTS (5-6-0)

16	Morehouse	27
0	Valdosta St.	10
15	Morris Brown	12
7	Kentucky St.	38
27	Clark Atlanta	6
9	Miles	7
26	Alabama A&M	33
0	Tuskegee	10
12	Savannah St.	3
41	Benedict	13
7	Albany St. (Ga.)	12
160		171

Nickname: Wildcats.
Stadium: Wildcat (1957), 7,500 capacity. Natural turf.
Colors: Old Gold & Blue.
Conference: Southern Intercol. Ath. Conf.
SID: Russell Boone Jr., 912-825-6437.
AD: To be named.

FRAMINGHAM ST.

Framingham, MA 01701 III

Coach: Michael Strachan, Swedish Sports 1990
Record: 4 Years, 6-30-1

1998 SCHEDULE

Nichols	Sept. 12
Mass.-Boston ■	Sept. 19
Curry ■	Sept. 26
Bri'water (Mass.)	Oct. 3
Westfield St. ■	Oct. 10
Fitchburg St. ■	Oct. 17
Worcester St.	Oct. 24
Western New Eng. ■	Oct. 31
Mass. Maritime	Nov. 7
Maine Maritime ■	Nov. 14

1997 RESULTS (2-8-0)

18	MIT	27
33	Fitchburg St.	31
7	Curry	6
22	Westfield St.	28
0	Bri'water (Mass.)	42
15	Worcester St.	44
0	Mass. Maritime	21
7	Mass.-Dartmouth	26
14	Maine Maritime	27
21	Mass.-Boston	24
137		276

Nickname: Rams.
Stadium: Maple Street Field, 1,500 capacity. Natural turf.
Colors: Black & Gold.
Conference: New England FB.
SID: Elizabeth Rieb, 508-626-4612.
AD: Thomas M. Kelley.

FRANKLIN

Franklin, IN 46131 III

Coach: Bill Unsworth, Franklin 1971
Record: 8 Years, 25-51-1

1998 SCHEDULE

Earlham ■	Sept. 12
Blackburn	Sept. 19
Alma	Sept. 26
Manchester	Oct. 3
Wilmington (Ohio) ■	Oct. 10
Mount Saint Joseph ■	Oct. 17
Anderson (Ind.)	Oct. 24
Wabash ■	Oct. 31
Bluffton ■	Nov. 7
Hanover	Nov. 14

1997 RESULTS (2-8-0)

21	Mount Saint Joseph	27
17	Kalamazoo	21
6	Lakeland	40
14	Olivet	11
7	DePauw	30
26	Anderson (Ind.)	23
3	Wabash	24
6	Rose-Hulman	22
21	Manchester	46
6	Hanover	19
127		263

Nickname: Grizzlies.
Stadium: Goodell Field (1889), 2,000 capacity. Natural turf.
Colors: Navy Blue & Old Gold.
Conference: Heartland College Ath. Conf.
SID: Kevin Elixman, 317-738-8184.
AD: Kerry N. Prather.

FRANK. & MARSH.

Lancaster, PA 17604 III

Coach: Tom Gilburg, Syracuse 1961
Record: 23 Years, 149-73-2

1998 SCHEDULE

Randolph-Macon	Sept. 12
Ursinus ■	Sept. 19
Muhlenberg	Sept. 26
Catholic ■	Oct. 3
Dickinson	Oct. 10
Hobart ■	Oct. 17
Western Md. ■	Oct. 24
Swarthmore	Oct. 31
Johns Hopkins ■	Nov. 7
Gettysburg	Nov. 14

1997 RESULTS (4-6-0)

25	Randolph-Macon	37
27	Ursinus	15
14	Muhlenberg	10
21	Catholic	35
6	Dickinson	24
7	Hobart	10
12	Western Md.	28
41	Swarthmore	0
21	Johns Hopkins	35
27	Gettysburg	18
201		212

Nickname: Diplomats.
Stadium: Sponaugle-Williamson (1920), 4,000 capacity. Natural turf.
Colors: Blue & White.
Conference: Centennial Conference.
SID: Tom Byrnes, 717-291-3838.
AD: William A. Marshall.

FRESNO ST.

Fresno, CA 93740 .... I-A

Coach: Pat Hill, UC Riverside 1973
Record: 1 Year, 6-6-0

1998 SCHEDULE

Colorado	Sept. 12
Texas Tech	*Sept. 19
Nevada ■	*Sept. 26
Brigham Young ■	*Oct. 3
Texas Christian	*Oct. 10
Utah	Oct. 17
UTEP ■	*Oct. 24
New Mexico	Oct. 31
San Diego St.	*Nov. 7
Hawaii ■	Nov. 14
San Jose St. ■	Nov. 21

1997 RESULTS (6-6-0)

35	Portland St.	7
35	Baylor	37
0	Oklahoma St.	35
40	Oregon	43
27	Utah	13
16	Hawaii	28
20	Air Force	17
46	UNLV	28
53	San Jose St.	12
3	Colorado St.	41
19	San Diego St.	20
24	Wyoming	7
318		288

Nickname: Bulldogs.
Stadium: Bulldog (1980), 41,031 capacity. Natural turf.
Colors: Cardinal & Blue.
Conference: Western Athletic.
SID: To be named, 209-278-2509.
AD: Allen R. Bohl.

FROSTBURG ST.

Frostburg, MD 21532 III

Coach: Ed Sweeney, LIU-C. W. Post 1971
Record: 13 Years, 77-54-4

1998 SCHEDULE

Salve Regina	Sept. 12
West Va. Tech ■	Sept. 19
Salisbury St. ■	Sept. 26
Chowan	Oct. 3
Greensboro	Oct. 10
Brockport St. ■	Oct. 17
Ferrum	Oct. 24
Ky. Wesleyan ■	Oct. 31
Waynesburg	Nov. 7
Methodist ■	Nov. 14

1997 RESULTS (6-3-0)

24	Salve Regina	7
17	Central Conn. St.	37
16	Salisbury St.	7
21	Chowan	0

60	Greensboro	3
22	Brockport St.	33
14	Waynesburg	7
31	Ferrum	0
12	Methodist	40
217		**134**

Nickname: Bobcats.
Stadium: Bobcat (1974), 4,000 capacity. Natural turf.
Colors: Red, White & Black.
Conference: Atlantic Central FB.
SID: Jeffrey P. Krone, 301-687-4371.
AD: Loyal K. PArk.

FURMAN

Greenville, SC 29613 .... I-AA

Coach: Bobby Johnson, Clemson 1973
Record: 4 Years, 25-21-0

1998 SCHEDULE

Clemson	Sept. 5
South Caro. St. ■	Sept. 12
Samford ■	*Sept. 19
VMI	Sept. 26
Western Caro. ■	Oct. 3
Appalachian St.	Oct. 10
Citadel ■	Oct. 17
East Tenn. St.	Oct. 24
Ga. Southern ■	Nov. 7
Wofford	Nov. 14
Chattanooga ■	Nov. 21

1997 RESULTS (7-4-0)

29	Samford	10
6	South Caro. St.	17
35	VMI	14
16	Western Caro.	17
24	Appalachian St.	22
21	Citadel	7
28	East Tenn. St.	58
38	Elon	20
13	Ga. Southern	30
28	Wofford	7
43	Chattanooga	21
281		**223**

Nickname: Paladins.
Stadium: Paladin (1981), 16,000 capacity. Natural turf.
Colors: Purple & White.
Conference: Southern.
SID: Hunter Reid, 864-294-2061.
AD: John M. Block.

GANNON

Erie, PA 16541 II

Coach: Tom Herman, Edinboro 1972
Record: 9 Years, 40-44-2

1998 SCHEDULE

Pace ■	Sept. 5
Canisius ■	Sept. 12
Waynesburg	Sept. 19
St. John Fisher	Sept. 26
Wash. & Jeff. ■	Oct. 3
Bowie St.	Oct. 10
Thomas More	Oct. 24
Thiel ■	Oct. 31
Allegheny	Nov. 7
St. Francis (Pa.) ■	Nov. 14

1997 RESULTS (4-6-0)

9	John Carroll	23
27	Canisius	9
6	Tiffin	27
7	Bowie St.	10
18	Mercyhurst	35
19	Pace	3
26	St. Francis (Pa.)	41
42	Thiel	14
35	St. John Fisher	12
13	Robert Morris	17
202		**191**

Nickname: Golden Knights.
Stadium: Erie Veterans Mem. (1958), 10,500 capacity. Artificial turf.
Colors: Maroon & Gold.
Conference: Independent.
SID: Bob Shreve, 814-871-7418.
AD: Kathleen M. Mc Nally.

GARDNER-WEBB

Boiling Springs, NC 28017 II

Coach: Steve Patton, Furman 1977
Record: 6 Years, 38-26-1

1998 SCHEDULE

Johnson Smith	Sept. 5
N.C. Central ■	*Sept. 12
West Va. St.	Sept. 19
Newberry	*Sept. 26
Wingate ■	Oct. 3
Lenoir-Rhyne	*Oct. 10
Catawba ■	*Oct. 17
Carson-Newman	Oct. 24
Tusculum	Oct. 31
Presbyterian ■	Nov. 7
Mars Hill ■	Nov. 14

1997 RESULTS (8-3-0)

38	Johnson Smith	13
20	N.C. Central	12
53	West Va. St.	28
35	Newberry	10
34	Wingate	54
32	Lenoir-Rhyne	0
6	Catawba	34
14	Carson-Newman	35
66	Tusculum	6
16	Presbyterian	13
25	Mars Hill	15
339		**220**

Nickname: Runnin' Bulldogs.
Stadium: Spangler (1969), 5,000 capacity. Natural turf.
Colors: Scarlet, White & Black.
Conference: South Atlantic Conference.
SID: Mark Wilson, 704-434-4355.
AD: Chuck Burch.

GEORGETOWN

Washington, DC 20057 .... I-AA

Coach: Bob Benson, Vermont 1986
Record: 5 Years, 30-18-0

1998 SCHEDULE

Marist ■	Sept. 12
Holy Cross ■	Sept. 19
Fairfield	Sept. 26
Siena	Oct. 3
Canisius ■	Oct. 10
St. John's (N.Y.)	Oct. 17
Duquesne	Oct. 24
St. Peter's ■	Oct. 31
Iona ■	Nov. 7
Austin Peay ■	Nov. 14
Fordham	Nov. 21

1997 RESULTS (8-2-0)

19	Marist	13
21	Holy Cross	25
34	Fairfield	9
41	Siena	10
24	Canisius	10
33	Iona	2
24	Duquesne	0
40	St. Peter's	32
27	St. John's (N.Y.)	0
0	Fordham	42
263		**143**

ECAC I-AA Playoff

13	Robert Morris	35

Nickname: Hoyas.
Stadium: Kehoe Field (1979), 2,400 capacity. Artificial turf.
Colors: Blue & Gray.
Conference: Metro Atlantic.
SID: Bill Hurd, 202-687-2492.
AD: Joseph C. Lang.

GEORGIA

Athens, GA 30602 .... I-A

Coach: Jim Donnan, North Caro. St. 1968
Record: 8 Years, 79-29-0

1998 SCHEDULE

Kent ■	Sept. 5
South Caro.	*Sept. 12
Wyoming ■	Sept. 19
LSU	*Oct. 3
Tennessee ■	Oct. 10
Vanderbilt ■	Oct. 17
Kentucky	*Oct. 24
Florida [Jacksonville, Fla.]	Oct. 31
Auburn	Nov. 14
Mississippi ■	Nov. 21
Georgia Tech ■	Nov. 28

1997 RESULTS (9-2-0)

38	Arkansas St.	7
31	South Caro.	15
42	Northeast La.	3
47	Mississippi St.	0
13	Tennessee	38
34	Vanderbilt	13
23	Kentucky	13
37	Florida	17
34	Auburn	45
21	Mississippi	14
27	Georgia Tech	24
347		**189**

Outback Bowl

33	Wisconsin	6

Nickname: Bulldogs.
Stadium: Sanford (1929), 86,117 capacity. Natural turf.
Colors: Red & Black.
Conference: Southeastern.
SID: Claude Felton, 706-542-1621.
AD: Vincent J. Dooley.

GA. SOUTHERN

Statesboro, GA 30460 .... I-AA

Coach: Paul Johnson, Western Caro. 1979
Record: 1 Year, 10-3-0

1998 SCHEDULE

Elon ■	*Sept. 5
Jacksonville St. ■	Sept. 12
Wofford ■	Sept. 19
Chattanooga	*Sept. 26
VMI ■	Oct. 3
Western Caro.	*Oct. 10
Appalachian St. ■	Oct. 17
Citadel	Oct. 24
East Tenn. St. ■	Oct. 31
Furman	Nov. 7
South Fla. ■	Nov. 14

1997 RESULTS (9-2-0)

45	Valdosta St.	26
28	William & Mary	29
22	Wofford	7
37	Chattanooga	10
49	VMI	0
30	Western Caro.	7
12	Appalachian St.	24
49	Citadel	7
38	East Tenn. St.	30
30	Furman	13
24	South Fla.	23
364		**176**

I-AA Championship

52	Florida A&M	37
7	Delaware	16

Nickname: Eagles.
Stadium: Paulson (1984), 18,000 capacity. Natural turf.
Colors: Blue & White.
Conference: Southern.
SID: Tom McClellan, 912-681-5239.
AD: Sam Baker.

GEORGIA TECH

Atlanta, GA 30332 ..... I-A

Coach: George O'Leary, New Hampshire 1968
Record: 4 Years, 18-19-0

1998 SCHEDULE

Boston College ■	Sept. 5
New Mexico St. ■	*Sept. 12
North Caro.	*Sept. 26
Duke ■	Oct. 3
North Caro. St.	Oct. 10
Virginia ■	Oct. 17
Florida St. ■	Oct. 24
Maryland [Baltimore, MD.]	Oct. 31
Clemson	*Nov. 12
Wake Forest ■	Nov. 21
Georgia	Nov. 28

1997 RESULTS (6-5-0)

13	Notre Dame	17
28	Wake Forest	26
23	Clemson	20
42	Boston College	14
27	North Caro. St.	17
0	Florida St.	38
13	North Caro.	16
31	Virginia	35
41	Duke	38
37	Maryland	18
24	Georgia	27
279		**266**

Carquest Bowl

35	West Va.	30

Nickname: Yellow Jackets.
Stadium: Bobby Dodd/Grant Field (1913), 46,000 capacity. Natural turf.
Colors: Old Gold & White.
Conference: Atlantic Coast.
SID: Mike Finn, 404-894-5445.
AD: David T. Braine.

GETTYSBURG

Gettysburg, PA 17325 III

Coach: Barry Streeter, Lebanon Valley 1971
Record: 20 Years, 112-86-5

1998 SCHEDULE

Hampden-Sydney ■	Sept. 12
Western Md.	Sept. 19
Swarthmore ■	Sept. 26
Johns Hopkins	*Oct. 2
Randolph-Macon	Oct. 10
Ursinus ■	Oct. 17
Muhlenberg	Oct. 24
Lebanon Valley ■	Oct. 31
Dickinson	Nov. 7
Frank. & Marsh. ■	Nov. 14

1997 RESULTS (4-6-0)

33	Hampden-Sydney	7
7	Western Md.	55
64	Swarthmore	15
12	Johns Hopkins	20
13	Randolph-Macon	44
2	Ursinus	13
45	Muhlenberg	33
19	Lebanon Valley	6
14	Dickinson	35
18	Frank. & Marsh.	27
227		**255**

Nickname: Bullets.
Stadium: Musselman (1965), 6,176 capacity. Natural turf.
Colors: Orange & Blue.
Conference: Centennial Conference.
SID: Robert Kenworthy, 717-337-6527.
AD: Charles W. Winters.

GLENVILLE ST.

Glenville, WV 26351 II

Coach: Warren Ruggerio, Delaware 1988
Record: 1 Year, 9-3-0

1998 SCHEDULE

Calif. (Pa.)	*Aug. 29
Indiana (Pa.)	*Sept. 12
Edinboro ■	Sept. 19
Liberty	*Sept. 26
West Liberty St.	Oct. 3
West Va. Wesleyan	Oct. 10
Fairmont St. ■	Oct. 17
Concord	Oct. 24
West Va. Tech ■	Oct. 31
Shepherd	Nov. 7
West Va. St. ■	Nov. 14

1997 RESULTS (9-2-0)

36	Geneva	35
7	Liberty	56
51	Clarion	0
35	Edinboro	27
42	West Liberty St.	18
46	West Va. Wesleyan	50
23	Fairmont St.	14
71	Concord	26
49	West Va. Tech	10
44	Shepherd	14
54	West Va. St.	14
458		**264**

II Championship

7	New Haven	47

Nickname: Pioneers.
Stadium: Pioneer (1977), 5,000 capacity. Natural turf.
Colors: Royal Blue & White.
Conference: WV Intercollegiate Athletic.
SID: Jed Drenning, 304-462-4102.
AD: Steven Harold.

GRAMBLING

Grambling, LA 71245 ..... I-AA

Coach: Doug Williams, Grambling 1978
Record: 1 Year, 3-8-0

1998 SCHEDULE

Alcorn St. ■	*Sept. 5
Alabama A&M	*Sept. 12
Hampton [East Rutherford, N. J.]	Sept. 26
Prairie View [Dallas, Tex.]	*Oct. 3
Mississippi Val.	*Oct. 10
Ark.-Pine Bluff [Shreveport, La.]	*Oct. 17
Jackson St. ■	Oct. 24
Texas Southern	*Oct. 31
Alabama St. ■	Nov. 7
Winston-Salem [San Diego, Cal.]	Nov. 14
Southern U. [New Orleans, La.]	Nov. 28

1997 RESULTS (3-8-0)

20	Alcorn St.	44
20	Langston	0
7	Hampton	42
33	Prairie View	6
20	Mississippi Val.	13
16	Ark.-Pine Bluff	22
0	Jackson St.	23
16	Texas Southern	21
13	Alabama St.	20
35	North Caro. A&T	37
7	Southern U.	30
187		**258**

Nickname: Tigers.
Stadium: Robinson (1983), 19,600 capacity. Natural turf.
Colors: Black & Gold.
Conference: Southwestern.
SID: T. Scott Boatright, 318-274-2479.
AD: Robert L. Piper.

GRAND VALLEY ST.

Allendale, MI 49401 II

Coach: Brian Kelly, Assumption 1983
Record: 7 Years, 56-21-2

1998 SCHEDULE

Ashland ■	*Sept. 3
Northwood ■	Sept. 12
Indianapolis	Sept. 19
Findlay ■	Sept. 26
St. Francis (Ill.) ■	Oct. 3
Mercyhurst	Oct. 10
Saginaw Valley	Oct. 17
Northern Mich. ■	Oct. 24
UC Davis ■	Oct. 31
Michigan Tech	Nov. 7
Ferris St.	Nov. 14

1997 RESULTS (9-2-0)

38	St. Francis (Ill.)	29
31	Ashland	20
21	Ferris St.	18
45	Wayne St. (Mich.)	30
14	Hillsdale	12
49	Michigan Tech	21
39	Northern Mich.	22
27	Saginaw Valley	30
24	Northwood	20
19	UC Davis	21
23	Indianapolis	14
330		**237**

Nickname: Lakers.
Stadium: Arend D. Lubbers (1979), 4,146 capacity. Natural turf.
Colors: Blue, Black & White.
Conference: Midwest Intercoll.
SID: Don Thomas, 616-895-3275.
AD: Tim W. Selgo.

GREENSBORO

Greensboro, NC 27401 III

Coach: Marion Kirby, Lenoir-Rhyne 1964
Record: 1 Year, 0-9-0

1998 SCHEDULE

Catholic	Sept. 5
Chowan ■	Sept. 12
Ferrum	Sept. 19
Emory & Henry	Oct. 3
Frostburg St. ■	Oct. 10
Jacksonville ■	Oct. 17
Newport News	Oct. 24
Methodist ■	Oct. 31
Guilford	Nov. 7
Bethany (W. Va.) ■	Nov. 14

1997 RESULTS (0-9-0)

7	Catholic	49
7	Chowan	38
13	Bethany (W. Va.)	45
0	Ferrum	34
3	Emory & Henry	37
3	Frostburg St.	60
27	Newport News	30
12	Methodist	41
7	Guilford	46
79		**380**

Nickname: The Pride.
Stadium: Greensboro Field, 800 capacity. Natural turf.
Colors: Green & White.
Conference: Independent.
SID: Robert McKinney, 910-272-7102.
AD: Kim A. Strable.

GREENVILLE

Greenville, IL 62246 III

Coach: Rob Harley,
(First year as head coach)

1998 SCHEDULE

MacMurray	Sept. 5
Westminster (Mo.) ■	*Sept. 19
Principia ■	Sept. 26
Lakeland	Oct. 3
Blackburn	Oct. 10
Eureka	Oct. 17
Benedictine (Ill.) ■	Oct. 24

Aurora ■ ... Oct. 31
Concordia (Wis.) ... Nov. 7
Concordia (Ill.) ■ ... Nov. 14

1997 RESULTS (2-8-0)

14	Bethel (Tenn.)	21
17	Blackburn	10
20	Westminster (Mo.)	27
12	Millsaps	56
7	Lakeland	59
14	MacMurray	42
19	Concordia (Ill.)	26
46	Principia	0
20	Concordia (Wis.)	48
29	Eureka	35
198		**324**

Nickname: Panthers.
Stadium: Francis Field, 2,000 capacity.
Colors: Orange & Black.
Conference: St. Louis Intercol. Ath. Conf.
SID: Sharon Alger, 618-664-1840.
AD: Jack D. Trager.

GRINNELL

Grinnell, IA 50112 ... III

Coach: Greg Wallace, Mo. Valley 1970
Record: 10 Years, 24-65-1

1998 SCHEDULE

Principia ■ ... Sept. 12
Beloit ■ ... Sept. 19
Lake Forest ... Sept. 26
Carroll (Wis.) ■ ... Oct. 3
Illinois Col. ... Oct. 10
Ripon ■ ... Oct. 17
St. Norbert ... Oct. 24
Knox ... Oct. 31
Monmouth (Ill.) ... Nov. 7
Lawrence ... Nov. 14

1997 RESULTS (5-5-0)

20	Pomona-Pitzer	55
48	Principia	0
38	Beloit	17
14	Ripon	17
13	Coe	20
38	Knox	24
48	Cornell College	49
38	Monmouth (Ill.)	7
64	Illinois Col.	49
15	Carroll (Wis.)	20
336		**258**

Nickname: Pioneers.
Stadium: Rosenbloom (1911), 1,750 capacity. Natural turf.
Colors: Scarlet & Black.
Conference: Midwest Conference.
SID: Andy Hamilton, 515-269-3832.
AD: Diane Fairchild.

GROVE CITY

Grove City, PA 11127 ... III

Coach: Chris Smith, Grove City 1972
Record: 14 Years, 52-76-2

1998 SCHEDULE

Wooster ... Sept. 5
Ohio Wesleyan ... Sept. 12
Bluffton ■ ... Sept. 19
Bethany (W. Va.) ... Sept. 26
Thiel ■ ... Oct. 3
Wash. & Jeff. ... Oct. 10
Waynesburg ... Oct. 17
Kenyon ■ ... Oct. 24
Alfred ■ ... Oct. 31
Muhlenberg ... Nov. 7

1997 RESULTS (9-1-0)

37	Kenyon	30
3	Wooster	10
26	Carnegie Mellon	7
32	Thiel	9
31	Wash. & Jeff.	28
42	Waynesburg	30
71	Bluffton	21
35	Bethany (W. Va.)	21
56	Alfred	35
41	Denison	29
374		**220**

ECAC III Playoff

12	Merchant Marine	25

Nickname: Wolverines.
Stadium: Thorn Field (1981), 3,500 capacity. Natural turf.
Colors: Crimson & White.
Conference: Presidents' Athletic Conf.
SID: Joe Klimchak, 412-458-3365.
AD: Christopher Smith.

GUILFORD

Greensboro, NC 27410 ... III

Coach: Mike Ketchum, Guilford 1978
Record: 7 Years, 34-34-0

1998 SCHEDULE

Methodist ... Sept. 12
Wash. & Lee ■ ... Sept. 19
Hampden-Sydney ... Sept. 26
Davidson ... *Oct. 3
Ferrum ■ ... Oct. 10
Bridgewater (Va.) ■ ... Oct. 17
Emory & Henry ■ ... Oct. 24
Randolph-Macon ... Oct. 31
Greensboro ■ ... Nov. 7
Chowan ... Nov. 14

1997 RESULTS (8-2-0)

19	Methodist	26
34	Wash. & Lee	20
34	Hampden-Sydney	7
25	Davidson	22
28	Ferrum	22
30	Bridgewater (Va.)	14
27	Emory & Henry	35
35	Randolph-Macon	21
46	Greensboro	7
61	Chowan	0
339		**174**

Nickname: Quakers.
Stadium: Armfield Athletic (1960), 3,500 capacity. Natural turf.
Colors: Crimson & Gray.
Conference: Old Dominion Athletic Conf.
SID: Dave Walters, 910-316-2107.
AD: Michael R. Ketchum.

GUST. ADOLPHUS

St. Peter, MN 56082 ... III

Coach: Jay Schoenebeck, Gust. Adolphus 1980
Record: 4 Years, 14-26-0

1998 SCHEDULE

Martin Luther ■ ... Sept. 12
Carleton ... Sept. 19
Macalester ■ ... Sept. 26
St. Thomas (Minn.) ... Oct. 3
Augsburg ■ ... Oct. 10
Bethel (Minn.) ... Oct. 17
Concordia-M'head ■ ... Oct. 24
Hamline ... Oct. 31
St. Olaf ■ ... Nov. 7
St. John's (Minn.) [Minneapolis, Minn.] ... Nov. 13

1997 RESULTS (6-4-0)

34	Colorado Col.	0
7	Concordia-M'head	28
34	Macalester	3
31	Bethel (Minn.)	21
31	St. Thomas (Minn.)	34
24	St. John's (Minn.)	16
35	Augsburg	41
28	Hamline	31
44	Carleton	6
37	St. Olaf	6
305		**186**

Nickname: Golden Gusties.
Stadium: Hollingsworth Field (1929), 5,500 capacity. Natural turf.
Colors: Black & Gold.
Conference: Minn. Intercol. Athletic Conf.
SID: Tim Kennedy, 507-933-7647.
AD: Alan Molde.

HAMILTON

Clinton, NY 13323 ... III

Coach: Steve Frank, Bridgeport 1972
Record: 13 Years, 55-48-1

1998 SCHEDULE

Tufts ... Sept. 26
Wesleyan (Conn.) ... Oct. 3
Trinity (Conn.) ■ ... Oct. 10
Bowdoin ■ ... Oct. 17
Colby ... Oct. 24
Williams ■ ... Oct. 31
Middlebury ■ ... Nov. 7
Bates ... Nov. 14

1997 RESULTS (2-6-0)

0	Amherst	38
15	Wesleyan (Conn.)	16
7	Trinity (Conn.)	28
14	Bowdoin	33
28	Colby	0
14	Williams	21
7	Middlebury	41
17	Bates	7
102		**184**

Nickname: Continentals.
Stadium: Steuben Field, 2,500 capacity. Natural turf.
Colors: Buff & Blue.
Conference: NESAC.
SID: Nico Karagosian, 315-859-4685.
AD: Thomas E. Murphy.

HAMLINE

St. Paul, MN 55104 ... III

Coach: Dick Tressel, Baldwin-Wallace 1970
Record: 20 Years, 117-78-2

1998 SCHEDULE

Jamestown ... Sept. 12
Augsburg ... Sept. 19
Bethel (Minn.) ■ ... Sept. 26
Concordia-M'head ... Oct. 3
Carleton ■ ... Oct. 10
St. Olaf ■ ... Oct. 17
St. John's (Minn.) ... Oct. 24
Gust. Adolphus ■ ... Oct. 31
Macalester ... Nov. 7
St. Thomas (Minn.) [Minneapolis, Minn.] ... *Nov. 12

1997 RESULTS (5-5-0)

35	Lake Forest	12
10	Bethel (Minn.)	39
0	St. Thomas (Minn.)	14
0	St. John's (Minn.)	21
7	Augsburg	26
27	St. Olaf	21
36	Carleton	7
31	Gust. Adolphus	28
19	Concordia-M'head	45
16	Macalester	6
181		**219**

Nickname: Pipers.
Stadium: Norton (1921), 2,000 capacity. Natural turf.
Colors: Red & Grey.
Conference: Minn. Intercol. Athletic Conf.
SID: Tom Gilles, 612-641-2242.
AD: Richard Tressel.

HAMPDEN-SYDNEY

Hampden-Sydney, VA 23943 ... III

Coach: Phil Culicerto, Virginia Tech 1984
Record: 1 Year, 0-10-0

1998 SCHEDULE

Sewanee ... Sept. 5

Gettysburg ... Sept. 12
Guilford ■ ... Sept. 26
Bridgewater (Va.) ... Oct. 3
Emory & Henry ■ ... Oct. 10
Wash. & Lee ... Oct. 17
Catholic ■ ... Oct. 24
Davidson ■ ... Oct. 31
Methodist ... Nov. 7
Randolph-Macon ■ ... Nov. 14

1997 RESULTS (0-10-0)

7	Sewanee	31
7	Gettysburg	33
7	Guilford	34
0	Bridgewater (Va.)	24
10	Emory & Henry	33
7	Wash. & Lee	29
10	Catholic	40
0	Davidson	43
0	Methodist	7
18	Randolph-Macon	49
66		**323**

Nickname: Tigers.
Stadium: Hundley (1964), 2,400 capacity. Natural turf.
Colors: Garnet & Gray.
Conference: Old Dominion Athletic Conf.
SID: Trip Tepper, 804-223-6156.
AD: Joseph E. Bush.

HAMPTON

Hampton, VA 23668 ... I-AA

Coach: Joe Taylor, Western Ill. 1972
Record: 15 Years, 115-44-4

1998 SCHEDULE

Florida A&M ... *Sept. 5
Howard ... Sept. 12
North Caro. A&T ■ ... Sept. 19
Grambling [East Rutherford, N. J.] ... Sept. 26
Liberty ■ ... Oct. 10
Norfolk St. ■ ... Oct. 17
South Caro. St. ... Oct. 24
William & Mary ■ ... Oct. 31
Bethune-Cookman ■ ... Nov. 7
Delaware St. ... Nov. 14
Morgan St. ... Nov. 21

1997 RESULTS (10-1-0)

6	William & Mary	31
49	Howard	21
7	North Caro. A&T	2
42	Grambling	7
18	Florida A&M	15
33	Liberty	27
9	Norfolk St.	2
20	South Caro. St.	14
27	Bethune-Cookman	0
24	Delaware St.	20
10	Morgan St.	0
245		**139**

I-AA Championship

13 Youngstown St. ... 28

Nickname: Pirates.
Stadium: Armstrong Field (1928), 11,000 capacity. Natural turf.
Colors: Royal Blue & White.
Conference: Mid-Eastern.
SID: LeCounte Conaway, 804-727-5757.
AD: Dennis E. Thomas.

HANOVER

Hanover, IN 47243 ... III

Coach: C. Wayne Perry, De Pauw 1972
Record: 16 Years, 108-50-2

1998 SCHEDULE

Thomas More ... Sept. 12
Eureka ■ ... Sept. 19
Wash. & Jeff. ... Sept. 26
Bluffton ■ ... Oct. 3
Manchester ■ ... Oct. 10
Wilmington (Ohio) ... Oct. 17
Mount Saint Joseph ... Oct. 24
Anderson (Ind.) ■ ... Oct. 31
Wabash ... Nov. 7
Franklin ■ ... Nov. 14

1997 RESULTS (10-0-0)

35	Otterbein	28
24	North Central	7
22	Centre	17
25	Mount Saint Joseph	21
45	Manchester	7
34	DePauw	7
21	Anderson (Ind.)	0
10	Wabash	7
47	Rose-Hulman	20
19	Franklin	6
282		**120**

III Championship

20 John Carroll ... 30

Nickname: Panthers.
Stadium: L. S. Ayers Field (1973), 4,000 capacity. Natural turf.
Colors: Red & Blue.
Conference: Heartland College Ath. Conf.
SID: Carter Cloyd, 812-866-7010.
AD: Dick Naylor.

HARDIN-SIMMONS

Abilene, TX 79698 ... III

Coach: Jimmie Keeling, Howard Payne 1958
Record: 8 Years, 60-27-0

1998 SCHEDULE

Midwestern St. ... *Sept. 12
Chapman ... Sept. 19
Azusa Pacific ■ ... Sept. 26
Sul Ross St. ... Oct. 3
Mississippi Col. ■ ... Oct. 10
Austin ... Oct. 17
Howard Payne ■ ... Oct. 24
Texas Lutheran ■ ... Oct. 31
Mary Hardin-Baylor ... Nov. 7
McMurry ■ ... Nov. 14

1997 RESULTS (7-3-0)

28	Azusa Pacific	21
35	Sul Ross St.	14
19	Chapman	14
33	Western N. Mex.	29
41	Langston	0
34	McMurry	25
12	Howard Payne	30
35	Austin	13
14	Mississippi Col.	17
21	Sul Ross St.	27
272		**190**

Nickname: Cowboys.
Stadium: Shelton (1993), 4,000 capacity. Natural turf.
Colors: Purple & Gold.
Conference: American Southwest.
SID: Kevin Carmody, 915-670-1273.
AD: John Neese.

HARDING

Searcy, AR 72149 ... II

Coach: Randy Tribble, Harding 1977
Record: 4 Years, 20-19-1

1998 SCHEDULE

Ark.-Monticello ... *Sept. 5
Southwest Mo. St. ... *Sept. 12
Tarleton St. ■ ... *Sept. 19
Texas A&M-Kingsville ... *Sept. 26
Southeastern Okla. ■ ... *Oct. 3
Northeastern St. ... *Oct. 10
Central Okla. ■ ... Oct. 17
East Central ... Oct. 24
Langston ■ ... Oct. 31
Ouachita Baptist ■ ... Nov. 7
Southwestern Okla. ... Nov. 14

1997 RESULTS (5-5-0)

28	Arkansas Tech	10
48	Ark.-Monticello	14
46	Tarleton St.	49
7	Texas A&M-Kingsville	33
17	Southeastern Okla.	14
10	Northeastern St.	35
19	Central Okla.	35
41	East Central	21
31	Ouachita Baptist	28
33	Southwestern Okla.	42
280		**281**

Nickname: Bisons.
Stadium: Alumni Field (1959), 4,500 capacity. Natural turf.
Colors: Black & Gold.
Conference: Lone Star Conference.
SID: Ted Lloyd, 501-279-4760.
AD: Greg Harnden.

HARTWICK

Oneonta, NY 13820 ... III

Coach: Steve Stetson, Dartmouth 1973
Record: 12 Years, 47-61-2

1998 SCHEDULE

Muhlenberg ... Sept. 5
Westfield St. ... Sept. 12
Kean ■ ... *Sept. 25
King's (Pa.) ... Oct. 3
Alfred ■ ... Oct. 10
Norwich ■ ... Oct. 17
Rensselaer ... Oct. 24
Union (N.Y.) ■ ... Oct. 31
Sacred Heart ■ ... Nov. 7
St. Lawrence ■ ... Nov. 14

1997 RESULTS (7-2-0)

42	Muhlenberg	17
38	Westfield St.	25
57	Curry	0
35	Nichols	28
41	Norwich	19
24	Rensselaer	25
3	Union (N.Y.)	13
31	Hobart	30
35	St. Lawrence	0
306		**157**

Nickname: Hawks.
Stadium: AstroTurf Field (1985), 1,200 capacity. Artificial turf.
Colors: Royal Blue & White.
Conference: Independent.
SID: Dave Caspole, 607-431-4703.
AD: Kenneth Kutler.

HARVARD

Cambridge, MA 02138 ... I-AA

Coach: Tim Murphy, Springfield 1978
Record: 11 Years, 51-66-1

1998 SCHEDULE

Columbia ... Sept. 19
Colgate ... Sept. 26
Lehigh ■ ... Oct. 3
Cornell ■ ... Oct. 10
Holy Cross ■ ... Oct. 17
Princeton ... Oct. 24
Dartmouth ... Oct. 31
Brown ■ ... Nov. 7
Pennsylvania ... Nov. 14
Yale ■ ... Nov. 21

1997 RESULTS (9-1-0)

45	Columbia	7
35	Lehigh	30
20	Bucknell	24
34	Cornell	9
52	Holy Cross	24
14	Princeton	12
24	Dartmouth	0
27	Brown	10
33	Pennsylvania	0
17	Yale	7
301		**123**

Nickname: Crimson.
Stadium: Harvard (1903), 37,289 capacity. Natural turf.
Colors: Crimson, Black & White.
Conference: Ivy.
SID: John Veneziano, 617-495-2206.
AD: William J. Cleary Jr.

HAWAII

Honolulu, HI 96822 ... I-A

Coach: Fred vonAppen, Linfield 1964
Record: 2 Years, 5-19-0

1998 SCHEDULE

Arizona ■	Sept. 3
Utah	*Sept. 19
Arkansas St. ■	*Sept. 26
Southern Methodist ■	*Oct. 3
San Diego St.	*Oct. 10
Brigham Young ■	*Oct. 17
New Mexico ■	*Oct. 24
UTEP	Oct. 31
San Jose St. ■	*Nov. 7
Fresno St.	Nov. 14
Northwestern ■	*Nov. 21
Michigan ■	*Nov. 28

1997 RESULTS (3-9-0)

17	Minnesota	3
34	Cal St. Northridge	21
6	Wyoming	35
15	UNLV	25
0	Colorado St.	63
28	Fresno St.	16
3	Brigham Young	17
3	San Diego St.	10
27	Air Force	34
14	San Jose St.	38
20	Northeast La.	23
22	Notre Dame	23
189		**308**

Nickname: Rainbows.
Stadium: Aloha (1975), 50,000 capacity. Artificial turf.
Colors: Green & White.
Conference: Western Athletic.
SID: Lois Manin, 808-956-7523.
AD: Hugh Yoshida.

HEIDELBERG

Tiffin, OH 44883 ... III

Coach: Larry Shank
(First year as head coach)

1998 SCHEDULE

Adrian ■	Sept. 12
Ohio Northern ■	Sept. 19
Hiram	Sept. 26
Capital ■	Oct. 3
Mount Union	Oct. 10
Marietta	Oct. 17
Otterbein ■	Oct. 24
John Carroll	Oct. 31
Baldwin-Wallace ■	Nov. 7
Muskingum	Nov. 14

1997 RESULTS (5-5-0)

7	Adrian	10
14	Muskingum	7
13	Baldwin-Wallace	20
24	Hiram	7
7	Mount Union	48
34	Capital	6
19	Otterbein	14
10	John Carroll	35
52	Marietta	37
7	Ohio Northern	49
187		**233**

Nickname: Student Princes.
Stadium: Columbian (1941), 7,500 capacity. Natural turf.
Colors: Red, Orange & Black.
Conference: Ohio Athletic Conference.
SID: Dick Edmond, 419-448-2140.
AD: John D. Hill.

HENDERSON ST.

Arkadelphia, AR 71999 ... II

Coach: Ronnie Kerr, Henderson St. 1966
Record: 4 Years, 17-25-1

1998 SCHEDULE

Ouachita Baptist ■	*Sept. 5
Valdosta St. ■	*Sept. 12
Northwestern St.	*Sept. 19
West ALa.	Sept. 26
Arkansas Tech	Oct. 3
Delta St. ■	*Oct. 10
Ark.-Monticello	Oct. 17
North ALa. ■	Oct. 24
West Ga.	Oct. 31
Southern Ark. ■	Nov. 7
Central Ark.	Nov. 14

1997 RESULTS (4-6-0)

36	Ouachita Baptist	23
7	Northwestern St.	42
18	West Ga.	36
24	West ALa.	16
41	Delta St.	20
21	Central Ark.	36
20	North ALa.	42
22	Arkansas Tech	29
31	Ark.-Monticello	21
14	Southern Ark.	19
234		**284**

Nickname: Reddies.
Stadium: Carpenter-Haygood (1968), 9,600 capacity. Natural turf.
Colors: Red & Gray.
Conference: Gulf South Conference.
SID: David Worlock, 501-230-5197.
AD: Kenneth J. Turner.

HILLSDALE

Hillsdale, MI 49242 ... II

Coach: Dave Dye, Baldwin-Wallace 1967
Record: 1 Year, 4-7-0

1998 SCHEDULE

Edinboro ■	*Sept. 5
Ashland	*Sept. 12
Michigan Tech	Sept. 19
Westminster (Pa.) ■	Sept. 26
Mercyhurst	Oct. 3
St. Francis (Ill.) ■	Oct. 10
Findlay ■	Oct. 17
Wayne St. (Mich.)	Oct. 24
Ferris St.	Oct. 31
Saginaw Valley ■	Nov. 7
Indianapolis ■	Nov. 14

1997 RESULTS (4-7-0)

27	St. Francis (Ill.)	15
17	Edinboro	21
21	Ferris St.	35
10	Indianapolis	17
3	Ashland	27
12	Grand Valley St.	14
0	Northern Mich.	10
10	Wayne St. (Mich.)	6
43	Northwood	40
35	Michigan Tech	19
13	Saginaw Valley	30
191		**234**

Nickname: Chargers.
Stadium: Frank Waters (1982), 8,500 capacity. Natural turf.
Colors: Royal Blue & White.
Conference: Midwest Intercoll.
SID: Greg Younger, 517-437-7364.
AD: Michael J. Kovalchik.

HIRAM

Hiram, OH 44234 ... III

Coach: Bobby Thomas, Hiram 1979
Record: 6 Years, 14-46-0

1998 SCHEDULE

Bluffton	Sept. 12
Mount Union	*Sept. 19
Heidelberg ■	Sept. 26
Baldwin-Wallace ■	Oct. 3
Muskingum	Oct. 10
Capital ■	Oct. 17
Ohio Northern ■	Oct. 24
Marietta	Oct. 31
Otterbein ■	Nov. 7
John Carroll	Nov. 14

1997 RESULTS (2-8-0)

48	Oberlin	12
28	Otterbein	50
27	Muskingum	35
7	Heidelberg	24
0	Ohio Northern	68
10	Marietta	55
20	Baldwin-Wallace	47
54	Capital	42
14	John Carroll	54
0	Mount Union	63
208		**450**

Nickname: Terriers.
Stadium: Charles Henry Field (1963), 3,500 capacity. Natural turf.
Colors: Red & Blue.
Conference: Ohio Athletic Conference.
SID: Tom Cammett, 216-569-5495.
AD: Bobby Thomas.

HOBART

Geneva, NY 14456 ... III

Coach: Mike Cragg, Slippery Rock 1981
Record: 3 Years, 15-15-0

1998 SCHEDULE

Dickinson ■	Sept. 12
Union (N.Y.)	Sept. 26
St. Lawrence ■	Oct. 3
Rochester	Oct. 10
Frank. & Marsh.	Oct. 17
Alfred ■	Oct. 24
Ithaca ■	Oct. 31
St. John Fisher	Nov. 7
Rensselaer ■	Nov. 14

1997 RESULTS (6-4-0)

26	Dickinson	13
38	St. John Fisher	7
17	Union (N.Y.)	28
57	St. Lawrence	0
48	Rochester	14
10	Frank. & Marsh.	7
58	Alfred	19
13	Ithaca	35
30	Hartwick	31
14	Rensselaer	16
311		**170**

Nickname: Statesmen.
Stadium: Boswell (1975), 4,500 capacity. Natural turf.
Colors: Orange & Purple.
Conference: Upstate Collegiate Athl Assn.
SID: Eric T. Reuscher, 315-781-3538.
AD: Michael J. Hanna.

HOFSTRA

Hempstead, NY 11549 ... I-AA

Coach: Joe Gardi, Maryland 1960
Record: 8 Years, 62-24-2

1998 SCHEDULE

Delaware St. ■	Sept. 5
James Madison	*Sept. 12
Southwest Tex. St.	*Sept. 19
Massachusetts ■	Oct. 3
Connecticut	Oct. 10
Rhode Island ■	Oct. 17
South FLa. ■	Oct. 24
Citadel	Oct. 31

New Hampshire ■ ....Nov. 7
Liberty ■ ....Nov. 14
Buffalo ■ ....Nov. 21

1997 RESULTS (9-2-0)

24 Boston U. 14
28 Southwest Tex. St. 24
31 Connecticut....................35
22 Youngstown St. 27
28 Rhode Island....................21
33 New Hampshire 14
45 Lehigh....................38
37 Buffalo 26
51 Massachusetts....................13
40 Liberty....................27
44 Maine....................32
383 **271**

I-AA Championship

14 Delaware 24

Nickname: Flying Dutchmen.
Stadium: Hofstra (1963), 15,000 capacity. Artificial turf.
Colors: Blue, White & Gold.
Conference: Independent.
SID: Jim Sheehan, 516-463-6764.
AD: Harry H. Royle.

HOLY CROSS

Worcester, MA 01610....................I-AA

Coach: Dan Allen, Hanover 1978
Record: 8 Years, 41-50-0

1998 SCHEDULE

Fairfield ■....................Sept. 5
Georgetown....................Sept. 19
Cornell ■....................Sept. 26
Towson ■ ....Oct. 3
Yale ....Oct. 10
Harvard....................Oct. 17
Lehigh ■....................Oct. 24
Lafayette ....Oct. 31
Bucknell ■....................Nov. 7
Fordham ■ ....Nov. 14
Colgate ....Nov. 21

1997 RESULTS (3-8-0)

7 Towson 27
25 Georgetown 21
6 Dartmouth....................35
7 Princeton 21
45 Columbia 16
24 Harvard 52
6 Bucknell....................18
7 Colgate....................42
20 Lehigh....................14
23 Lafayette....................34
12 Fordham....................28
182 **308**

Nickname: Crusaders.
Stadium: Fitton Field (1924), 23,500 capacity. Natural turf.
Colors: Royal Purple.
Conference: Patriot.
SID: Frank Mastrandrea, 203-870-4750.
AD: Richard M. Regan Jr.

HOPE

Holland, MI 49422....................III

Coach: Dean Kreps, Monmouth 1983
Record: 3 Years, 12-15-0

1998 SCHEDULE

Augustana (Ill.) ....Sept. 12
DePauw....................Sept. 19
Ill. Wesleyan ■ ....Sept. 26
Kalamazoo ■....................Oct. 10
Adrian....................Oct. 17
Alma ....Oct. 24
Olivet ■....................Oct. 31
Albion ....Nov. 7
Defiance ■ ....Nov. 14

1997 RESULTS (6-3-0)

34 Valparaiso....................35
27 Benedictine (Ill.)....................0
20 DePauw 33
14 Wabash....................13
28 Kalamazoo....................0
19 Adrian 26
51 Alma....................13
37 Olivet....................8
28 Albion....................25
258 **153**

Nickname: Flying Dutchmen.
Stadium: Holland Municipal (1979), 5,322 capacity. Natural turf.
Colors: Blue & Orange.
Conference: Michigan Intercoll Athl Assn.
SID: Tom Renner, 616-395-7860.
AD: Raymond E. Smith.

HOUSTON

Houston, TX 77204 ....I-A

Coach: Kim Helton, Florida 1970
Record: 5 Years, 14-41-1

1998 SCHEDULE

California....................Sept. 5
Minnesota ■ ....*Sept. 12
UCLA ■....................Sept. 19
Tennessee ....*Sept. 26
Memphis ■ ....Oct. 3
Army ■....................Oct. 10
North Texas ....*Oct. 24
East Caro....................Oct. 31
Southern Miss. ■ ....Nov. 7
Cincinnati ....Nov. 14
Tulane....................Nov. 21

1997 RESULTS (3-8-0)

17 Alabama 42
3 California 35
24 Pittsburgh....................35
45 Minnesota 43
10 UCLA 66
41 Cincinnati....................38
36 Louisville....................22
3 Memphis 24
27 East Caro. 28
0 Southern Miss. 33
10 Tulane....................44
216 **410**

Nickname: Cougars.
Stadium: Robertson (1942), 20,800 capacity. Natural turf.
Colors: Scarlet & White.
Conference: Conference USA.
SID: Donna Turner, 713-743-9404.
AD: Chester S. Gladchuk.

HOWARD

Washington, DC 20059....................I-AA

Coach: Steve Wilson, Howard 1979
(9 years, 61-40-0)

1998 SCHEDULE

Jackson St. [Columbus, Ohio] ....Sept. 5
Hampton ■....................Sept. 12
Ark.-Pine Bluff [St. Louis, Mo.] ....Sept. 19
Texas Southern ....*Sept. 26
Bethune-Cookman [Indianapolis, Ind.]....................Oct. 3
Florida A&M [Jacksonville, Fla.]....................Oct. 17
North Caro. A&T ■....................Oct. 24
Norfolk St. ■....................Oct. 31
South Caro. St. ....Nov. 7
Morgan St. ■....................Nov. 14
Delaware St. ■....................Nov. 21

1997 RESULTS (7-4-0)

33 Jackson St.....................35
21 Hampton 49
32 Ark.-Pine Bluff....................21
15 Florida A&M....................24
14 Bethune-Cookman 7
52 Morehouse 0
21 North Caro. A&T 13
32 Norfolk St.....................24
18 South Caro. St. 27
30 Morgan St. 27
40 Delaware St.....................21
308 **248**

Nickname: Bison.
Stadium: Greene (1986), 7,500 capacity. Artificial turf.
Colors: Blue, White & Red.
Conference: Mid-Eastern.
SID: Edward Hill, 202-806-9200.
AD: Hank Ford.

HOWARD PAYNE

Brownwood, TX 76801 III

Coach: Vance Gibson, Austin 1975
Record: 6 Years, 40-21-0

1998 SCHEDULE

Midland Lutheran....................Sept. 5
Prairie View ■....................*Sept. 12
La Verne ■....................Sept. 26
Mississippi Col. ....Oct. 3
Austin ■ ....Oct. 10
Texas Lutheran ■....................Oct. 17
Hardin-Simmons ....Oct. 24
Mary Hardin-Baylor ■....................Oct. 31
McMurry....................Nov. 7
Sul Ross St. ■....................Nov. 14

1997 RESULTS (7-3-0)

9 Butler 10
28 Sul Ross St.....................18
21 La Verne....................18
28 Chapman 20
25 Thomas More....................5
27 Sul Ross St.....................9
30 Hardin-Simmons....................12
0 Mississippi Col.....................13
23 McMurry 26
27 Austin....................13
218 **144**

Nickname: Yellow Jackets.
Stadium: Gordon Wood, 7,600 capacity. Natural turf.
Colors: Gold & Blue.
Conference: American Southwest.
SID: Scott Jeffries, 915-649-8034.
AD: Phil Fuller.

HUMBOLDT ST.

Arcata, CA 95521 II

Coach: Fred Whitmire, Humboldt St. 1964
Record: 7 years, 37-33-2

1998 SCHEDULE

Weber St. ....*Sept. 12
Willamette ■....................Sept. 19
Western Wash. ....Oct. 3
Menlo....................Oct. 31
Central Wash. ■ ....Nov. 14

1997 RESULTS (2-8-0)

17 Montana Tech....................34
14 Willamette....................42
33 Western Mont.....................20
12 Azusa Pacific....................16
6 St. Mary's (Cal.)....................44
7 Western Wash. 45
16 Simon Fraser....................21
21 Western Ore. U. 31
7 Southern Ore.....................49
40 Central Wash. 30
173 **332**

Nickname: Lumberjacks.
Stadium: Redwood Bowl (1946), 7,000 capacity. Natural turf.
Colors: Green & Gold.
Conference: Independent.
SID: Dan Pambianco, 707-826-3631.
AD: Scott Barnes.

IDAHO

Moscow, ID 83843 ..... I-A

Coach: Chris Tormey, Idaho 1978
Record: 3 Years, 17-16-0

1998 SCHEDULE

Eastern Wash. ■	Sept. 5
San Jose St.	*Sept. 12
Washington St.	Sept. 19
LSU	*Sept. 26
Idaho St. ■	Oct. 3
Arkansas St.	Oct. 10
Utah St.	Oct. 17
Nevada ■	Oct. 24
North Texas	*Oct. 31
New Mexico St. ■	Nov. 14
Boise St.	Nov. 21

1997 RESULTS (5-6-0)

10	Air Force	14
46	Portland St.	0
43	Idaho St.	0
10	Central Fla.	41
30	North Texas	17
44	UC Davis	14
23	Nevada	42
17	Utah St.	63
21	Eastern Wash.	24
35	New Mexico St.	18
23	Boise St.	30
302		**263**

Nickname: Vandals.
Stadium: Kibbie (1975), 16,000 capacity. Artificial turf.
Colors: Silver & Gold.
Conference: Big West.
SID: Becky Paull, 208-885-0211.
AD: Mike R. Bohn.

IDAHO ST.

Pocatello, ID 83209 ..... I-AA

Coach: Tom Walsh, UC Santa Barb. 1971
Record: 2 Years, 11-11-0

1998 SCHEDULE

New Mexico	*Sept. 5
Weber St. ■	*Sept. 19
Portland St.	*Sept. 26
Idaho	Oct. 3
Northern Ariz.	Oct. 10
Eastern Wash. ■	Oct. 17
Southern Utah ■	*Oct. 24
Montana	Oct. 31
Cal St. Sacramento ■	*Nov. 7
Montana St.	Nov. 14
Cal St. Northridge ■	*Nov. 21

1997 RESULTS (3-8-0)

7	Utah St.	41
0	Idaho	43
13	Montana St.	14
19	Cal St. Sacramento	23
0	Montana	48
46	Southern Utah	31
7	Eastern Wash.	51
41	Northern Ariz.	24
22	Cal St. Northridge	31
26	Portland St.	24
7	Weber St.	26
188		**356**

Nickname: Bengals.
Stadium: Holt Arena (1970), 12,000 capacity. Artificial turf.
Colors: Orange & Black.
Conference: Big Sky.
SID: To be named, 208-236-3651.
AD: Irvin A. Cross.

ILLINOIS

Champaign, IL 61820 ..... I-A

Coach: Ron Turner, Pacific (Cal.) 1977
Record: 2 Years, 7-15-0

1998 SCHEDULE

Washington St.	Sept. 5
Middle Tenn. St. ■	*Sept. 12
Louisville ■	Sept. 19
Iowa ■	Sept. 26
Northwestern	Oct. 3
Ohio St. ■	Oct. 10
Wisconsin ■	Oct. 17
Purdue	Oct. 24
Penn St.	Oct. 31
Indiana ■	Nov. 7
Michigan St.	Nov. 21

1997 RESULTS (0-11-0)

7	Southern Miss.	24
14	Louisville	26
22	Washington St.	35
10	Iowa	38
6	Penn St.	41
7	Wisconsin	31
3	Purdue	48
6	Indiana	23
21	Northwestern	34
6	Ohio St.	41
17	Michigan St.	27
119		**368**

Nickname: Fighting Illini.
Stadium: Memorial (1923), 70,904 capacity. Artificial turf.
Colors: Orange & Blue.
Conference: Big Ten.
SID: Dave Johnson, 217-333-1391.
AD: Ronald E. Guenther.

ILLINOIS COL.

Jacksonville, IL 62650 III

Coach: Rich Johanningmeier, Southwest Mo. St. 1964
Record: 13 Years, 64-65-5

1998 SCHEDULE

Westminster (Mo.)	Sept. 5
Lawrence ■	Sept. 19
Knox	Sept. 26
Monmouth (Ill.)	Oct. 3
Grinnell ■	Oct. 10
Beloit ■	Oct. 17
Lake Forest	Oct. 24
Ripon ■	Oct. 31
Carroll (Wis.)	Nov. 7
St. Norbert	Nov. 14

1997 RESULTS (1-8-0)

27	Principia	7
7	Washington (Mo.)	77
18	Lake Forest	46
13	St. Norbert	70
14	Monmouth (Ill.)	17
0	Coe	67
30	Knox	50
23	Cornell College	31
49	Grinnell	64
181		**429**

Nickname: Blueboys.
Stadium: England Field (1960), 2,500 capacity. Natural turf.
Colors: Blue & White.
Conference: Midwest Conference.
SID: James T. Murphy, 217-245-3048.
AD: Richard A. Johanningmeier.

ILLINOIS ST.

Normal, IL 61761 ..... I-AA

Coach: Todd Berry, Tulsa 1983
Record: 2 Years, 5-17-0

1998 SCHEDULE

St. Francis (Ill.) ■	*Sept. 12
Kansas	*Sept. 19
Southern Ill. ■	Sept. 26
Indiana St.	Oct. 3
Northern Iowa	*Oct. 10
Eastern Ill.	Oct. 17
Western Ill.	Oct. 24
Southern Utah ■	Oct. 31
Southwest Mo. St. ■	Nov. 7
Youngstown St. ■	Nov. 14
Kentucky St. ■	Nov. 21

1997 RESULTS (2-9-0)

13	Southern Utah	44
40	Buffalo	28
41	Southeast Mo. St.	7
14	Eastern Ill.	25
6	UNLV	41
34	Northern Iowa	50
29	Southern Ill.	31
7	Southwest Mo. St.	41
13	Indiana St.	16
0	Youngstown St.	13
23	Western Ill.	37
220		**333**

Nickname: Redbirds.
Stadium: Hancock (1967), 15,000 capacity. Artificial turf.
Colors: Red & White.
Conference: Gateway.
SID: Kenny Mossman, 309-438-3825.
AD: Richard Greenspan.

ILL. WESLEYAN

Bloomington, IL 61702 III

Coach: Norm Eash, Ill. Wesleyan 1975
Record: 11 Years, 70-32-1

1998 SCHEDULE

DePauw ■	Sept. 12
Hope	Sept. 26
Elmhurst	Oct. 3
Augustana (Ill.) ■	Oct. 10
Carthage ■	Oct. 17
Wheaton (Ill.)	Oct. 24
North Central ■	Oct. 31
Millikin ■	Nov. 7
North Park	Nov. 14

1997 RESULTS (7-2-0)

37	Thomas More	6
50	Washington (Mo.)	21
64	North Park	13
13	Millikin	17
28	North Central	20
29	Wheaton (Ill.)	39
28	Augustana (Ill.)	2
30	Carthage	7
7	Elmhurst	0
286		**125**

Nickname: Titans.
Stadium: Wesleyan (1893), 3,500 capacity. Natural turf.
Colors: Green & White.
Conference: College Conf. of Ill. & Wisc.
SID: Stew Salowitz, 309-556-3206.
AD: Dennis Bridges.

INDIANA

Bloomington, IN 47405 ..... I-A

Coach: Cam Cameron, Indiana 1983
Record: 1 Year, 2-9-0

1998 SCHEDULE

Western Mich. ■	*Sept. 12
Kentucky	Sept. 19
Cincinnati	*Sept. 26
Wisconsin ■	Oct. 3
Michigan St.	Oct. 10
Iowa ■	Oct. 17
Michigan	Oct. 24
Ohio St. ■	Oct. 31
Illinois	Nov. 7
Minnesota ■	Nov. 14
Purdue	Nov. 21

1997 RESULTS (2-9-0)

6	North Caro.	23
33	Ball St.	6

7	Kentucky	49
26	Wisconsin	27
0	Michigan	37
6	Michigan St.	38
0	Ohio St.	31
0	Iowa	62
23	Illinois	6
12	Minnesota	24
7	Purdue	56
120		**359**

Nickname: Hoosiers.
Stadium: Memorial (1960), 52,354 capacity. Artificial turf.
Colors: Cream & Crimson.
Conference: Big Ten.
SID: Kit Klingelhoffer, 812-855-9610.
AD: Clarence Doninger.

INDIANA (PA.)

Indiana, PA 15705 II

Coach: Frank Cignetti, Indiana (Pa.) 1960
Record: 16 Years, 130-56-1

1998 SCHEDULE

West Chester	Sept. 5
Glenville St. ■	*Sept. 12
West Va. Wesleyan ■	*Sept. 19
Bloomsburg	Sept. 26
Lock Haven ■	Oct. 3
Slippery Rock	Oct. 10
Millersville ■	Oct. 17
Clarion ■	Oct. 24
Calif. (Pa.)	Oct. 31
Edinboro ■	Nov. 7
Shippensburg	Nov. 14

1997 RESULTS (5-5-0)

29	Fairmont St.	30
18	Bloomsburg	13
14	New Haven	43
20	Calif. (Pa.)	10
9	Slippery Rock	16
31	East Stroudsburg	33
25	Edinboro	20
6	Clarion	21
48	Lock Haven	21
44	Shippensburg	26
244		**233**

Nickname: Indians.
Stadium: Miller (1962), 6,500 capacity. Artificial turf.
Colors: Crimson & Gray.
Conference: Pennsylvania State Athl. Conf.
SID: Mike Hoffman, 412-357-2747.
AD: Frank Cignetti.

INDIANA ST.

Terre Haute, IN 47809 .... I-AA

Coach: Tim McGuire, Nebraska 1975
Record: 2 Years, 7-15-0

1998 SCHEDULE

Kansas St.	*Sept. 5
Southeast Mo. St.	*Sept. 12
Youngstown St.	*Sept. 19
St. Joseph's (Ind.) ■	*Sept. 24
Illinois St. ■	Oct. 3
Southwest Mo. St. ■	Oct. 17
Southern Ill.	Oct. 24
Northern Iowa ■	Oct. 31
Western Ill.	Nov. 7
Western Ky.	Nov. 14
Murray St. ■	Nov. 21

1997 RESULTS (3-8-0)

0	Murray St.	13
19	Kentucky St.	6
6	North Texas	41
19	Southern Ill.	14
0	Youngstown St.	31
7	Southwest Mo. St.	22
3	Western Ill.	37
16	Illinois St.	13
14	Eastern Ill.	21
14	Western Ky.	21
21	Northern Iowa	29
119		**248**

Nickname: Sycamores.
Stadium: Memorial (1970), 12,764 capacity. Artificial turf.
Colors: Blue & White.
Conference: Gateway.
SID: Chris Burkhalter, 812-237-4160.
AD: Andrea Myers.

INDIANAPOLIS

Indianapolis, IN 46227 II

Coach: Joe Polizzi, Hillsdale 1976
Record: 4 Years, 17-25-1

1998 SCHEDULE

Westminster (Pa.)	Sept. 5
Grand Valley St. ■	Sept. 19
Mercyhurst ■	Sept. 26
Findlay ■	Oct. 3
Northwood	Oct. 10
Wayne St. (Mich.) ■	Oct. 17
St. Francis (Ill.)	*Oct. 24
Northern Mich. ■	Oct. 31
Ashland	Nov. 7
Hillsdale	Nov. 14

1997 RESULTS (8-3-0)

26	St. Joseph's (Ind.)	13
32	Ferris St.	21
28	Wayne St. (Mich.)	9
17	Hillsdale	10
35	Michigan Tech	29
12	Northern Mich.	10
17	Saginaw Valley	31
24	Northwood	19
50	St. Francis (Ill.)	24
7	Ashland	15
14	Grand Valley St.	23
262		**204**

Nickname: Greyhounds.
Stadium: Key (1971), 5,500 capacity. Natural turf.
Colors: Crimson & Grey.
Conference: Midwest Intercoll.
SID: Joe Gentry, 317-788-3494.
AD: David J. Huffman.

IONA

New Rochelle, NY 10801 .... I-AA

Coach: Fred Mariani, St. Joseph's (Ind.) 1974
(First year as head coach)

1998 SCHEDULE

Fairfield	Sept. 12
La Salle ■	Sept. 19
Sacred Heart	Sept. 26
Canisius ■	Oct. 3
Siena ■	Oct. 10
Marist	Oct. 17
St. Peter's ■	Oct. 24
Duquesne	Oct. 31
Georgetown	Nov. 7
St. John's (N.Y.) ■	Nov. 14

1997 RESULTS (0-10-0)

0	Wagner	33
12	Marist	31
0	Pace	26
7	Canisius	14
7	Siena	50
2	Georgetown	33
12	St. Peter's	14
0	Duquesne	41
7	Fairfield	28
7	St. John's (N.Y.)	37
54		**307**

Nickname: Gaels.
Stadium: Mazzella Field (1989), 1,200 capacity. Artificial turf.
Colors: Maroon & Gold.
Conference: Metro Atlantic.
SID: Dave Cagianello, 914-633-2334.
AD: Rich Petriccione.

IOWA

Iowa City, IA 52242 .... I-A

Coach: Hayden Fry, Baylor 1951
Record: 36 Years, 229-170-10

1998 SCHEDULE

Central Mich. ■	Sept. 5
Iowa St. ■	Sept. 12
Arizona	*Sept. 19
Illinois	Sept. 26
Michigan ■	Oct. 3
Northwestern ■	Oct. 10
Indiana	Oct. 17
Wisconsin ■	Oct. 24
Purdue	Oct. 31
Ohio St. ■	Nov. 14
Minnesota	Nov. 21

1997 RESULTS (7-4-0)

66	Northern Iowa	0
54	Tulsa	16
63	Iowa St.	20
38	Illinois	10
7	Ohio St.	23
24	Michigan	28
62	Indiana	0
35	Purdue	17
10	Wisconsin	13
14	Northwestern	15
31	Minnesota	0
404		**142**

Sun Bowl

7	Arizona St.	17

Nickname: Hawkeyes.
Stadium: Kinnick (1929), 70,397 capacity. Natural turf.
Colors: Old Gold & Black.
Conference: Big Ten.
SID: Phil Haddy, 319-335-9411.
AD: Robert A. Bowlsby.

IOWA ST.

Ames, IA 50011 .... I-A

Coach: Dan McCarney, Iowa 1975
Record: 3 Years, 6-27-0

1998 SCHEDULE

Texas Christian ■	*Sept. 5
Iowa	Sept. 12
Ball St. ■	Sept. 19
Texas Tech ■	Sept. 26
Texas	Oct. 3
Missouri ■	Oct. 10
Kansas St.	Oct. 24
Oklahoma	Oct. 31
Nebraska ■	Nov. 7
Colorado	Nov. 14
Kansas ■	Nov. 21

1997 RESULTS (1-10-0)

14	Oklahoma St.	21
10	Wyoming	56
29	Minnesota	53
20	Iowa	63
21	Missouri	45
17	Texas A&M	56
24	Baylor	17
24	Kansas	34
38	Colorado	43
14	Nebraska	77
3	Kansas St.	28
214		**493**

Nickname: Cyclones.
Stadium: Cyclone-Jack Trice (1975), 50,000 capacity. Natural turf.
Colors: Cardinal & Gold.
Conference: Independent.
SID: Tom Kroeschell, 515-294-3372.
AD: Eugene D. Smith.

ITHACA

Ithaca, NY 14850 ... III

Coach: Michael Welch, Ithaca 1973
Record: 4 Years, 29-13-0

1998 SCHEDULE

St. John Fisher ... Sept. 12
Mansfield ■ ... Sept. 19
Col. of New Jersey ■ ... Sept. 26
Springfield ■ ... Oct. 3
Brockport St. ... Oct. 10
St. Lawrence ■ ... Oct. 17
American Int'l ... Oct. 24
Hobart ... Oct. 31
Cortland St. ... Nov. 7
Buffalo St. ■ ... Nov. 14

1997 RESULTS (7-3-0)

5 Mercyhurst ... 10
42 Mansfield ... 17
52 Alfred ... 7
42 Springfield ... 15
21 Brockport St. ... 14
41 St. Lawrence ... 6
40 American Int'l ... 13
35 Hobart ... 13
28 Cortland St. ... 33
10 Buffalo St. ... 13
316 **141**

Nickname: Bombers.
Stadium: Butterfield (1958), 5,000 capacity. Natural turf.
Colors: Blue & Gold.
Conference: Independent.
SID: Pete Moore, 607-274-3825.
AD: Elizabeth A. Alden.

JACKSON ST.

Jackson, MS 39217 ... I-AA

Coach: James Carson, Jackson St. 1963
Record: 6 Years, 47-21-1

1998 SCHEDULE

Howard [Columbus, Ohio] ... Sept. 5
Tennessee St. [Memphis, Tenn.] ... *Sept. 12
Florida A&M ■ ... *Sept. 19
Mississippi Val. ■ ... *Sept. 26
Texas Southern ■ ... Oct. 3
Alabama St. [Mobile, Ala.] ... *Oct. 10
Southern U. ... *Oct. 17
Grambling ... Oct. 24
Ark.-Pine Bluff [Little Rock, Ark.] ... *Oct. 31
Prairie View ■ ... Nov. 14
Alcorn St. ... Nov. 21

1997 RESULTS (9-2-0)

38 Alabama St. ... 11
35 Howard ... 33
31 Tennessee St. ... 28
14 Florida A&M ... 30
48 Mississippi Val. ... 31
55 Texas Southern ... 49
8 Southern U. ... 28
23 Grambling ... 0
37 Ark.-Pine Bluff ... 8
20 Prairie View ... 7
54 Alcorn St. ... 15
363 **240**

I-AA Championship

24 Western Ill. ... 31

Nickname: Tigers.
Stadium: Mississippi Memorial (1949), 62,512 capacity. Natural turf.
Colors: Blue & White.
Conference: Southwestern.
SID: Samuel Jefferson, 601-968-2273.
AD: Paul E. Covington.

JACKSONVILLE

Jacksonville, FL 32211 ... I-AA

Coach: Steve Gilbert, West Chester 1979
Record: 9 years, 41-48-0

1998 SCHEDULE

Davidson ■ ... Sept. 12
Chowan ... Sept. 19
Mississippi Col ... Sept. 26
Austin Peay ■ ... Oct. 3
Methodist ■ ... Oct. 10
Greensboro ... Oct. 17
Clinch Valley ... Oct. 24
La Salle ■ ... Nov. 7
Wagner ■ ... Nov. 14

1997

Did not play in 1997.

Nickname: Dolphins
Stadium: Jacksonville, 4,500 capacity. Natural turf.
Colors: Green & White.
Conference: Independent.
SID: Rob Ervin, 904-745-7402.
AD: Tom Seitz.

JACKSONVILLE ST.

Jacksonville, AL 36265 ... I-AA

Coach: Mike Williams, Troy St. 1977
Record: 1 Year, 1-10-0

1998 SCHEDULE

Alabama A&M ... *Sept. 5
Ga. Southern ... Sept. 12
Middle Tenn. St. ■ ... *Sept. 19
Nicholls St. ... *Sept. 26
Stephen F. Austin ■ ... Oct. 1
McNeese St. ... *Oct. 10
Samford ■ ... Oct. 17
Sam Houston St. ■ ... Oct. 24
Northwestern St. ■ ... Nov. 7
Southwest Tex. St. ... Nov. 14
Troy St. ■ ... *Nov. 21

1997 RESULTS (1-10-0)

42 Southwest Mo. St. ... 47
28 Sam Houston St. ... 21
16 UAB ... 34
6 McNeese St. ... 27
16 Middle Tenn. St. ... 27
15 Stephen F. Austin ... 41
14 Nicholls St. ... 16
14 Samford ... 17
21 Northwestern St. ... 42
27 Southwest Tex. St. ... 35
0 Troy St. ... 49
199 **356**

Nickname: Gamecocks.
Stadium: Paul Snow (1947), 15,000 capacity. Natural turf.
Colors: Red & White.
Conference: Southland.
SID: Mike Galloway, 205-782-5377.
AD: Joe Davidson.

JAMES MADISON

Harrisonburg, VA 22807 ... I-AA

Coach: Alex Wood, Iowa 1979
Record: 3 Years, 20-14-0

1998 SCHEDULE

Maryland ... *Sept. 5
Hofstra ■ ... *Sept. 12
Villanova ■ ... Sept. 19
Elon ■ ... *Sept. 26
Richmond ... Oct. 3
Massachusetts ... Oct. 10
William & Mary ■ ... Oct. 17
Maine ■ ... Oct. 24
Rhode Island ... Oct. 31
Northeastern ■ ... Nov. 7
Delaware ... Nov. 21

1997 RESULTS (5-6-0)

6 Ball St. ... 24
32 East Tenn. St. ... 27
13 Massachusetts ... 10
24 Maine ... 22
17 Villanova ... 49
25 William & Mary ... 38
27 Delaware ... 49
21 Richmond ... 26
17 Northeastern ... 41
39 Rhode Island ... 37
31 Boston U. ... 14
252 **337**

Nickname: Dukes.
Stadium: Bridgeforth (1974), 12,500 capacity. Artificial turf.
Colors: Purple & Gold.
Conference: Atlantic 10.
SID: Gary Michael, 540-568-6154.
AD: Donald L. Lemish.

JOHN CARROLL

University Hgts., OH 44118 ... III

Coach: Tony DeCarlo, Kent 1962
Record: 11 Years, 82-25-4

1998 SCHEDULE

Stonehill ... Sept. 5
Capital ■ ... Sept. 19
Otterbein ... Sept. 26
Mount Union ... Oct. 3
Marietta ■ ... Oct. 10
Baldwin-Wallace ■ ... Oct. 17
Muskingum ... Oct. 24
Heidelberg ■ ... Oct. 31
Ohio Northern ... Nov. 7
Hiram ■ ... Nov. 14

1997 RESULTS (9-1-0)

23 Gannon ... 9
28 Ohio Northern ... 21
18 Marietta ... 12
50 Otterbein ... 8
36 Muskingum ... 7
14 Mount Union ... 42
55 Capital ... 0
35 Heidelberg ... 10
54 Hiram ... 14
20 Baldwin-Wallace ... 17
333 **140**

III Championship

30 Hanover ... 20
7 Mount Union ... 59

Nickname: Blue Streaks.
Stadium: Wasmer Field (1968), 3,500 capacity. Artificial turf.
Colors: Blue & Gold.
Conference: Ohio Athletic Conference.
SID: Chris Wenzler, 216-397-4676.
AD: Anthony J. DeCarlo.

JOHNS HOPKINS

Baltimore, MD 21218 ... III

Coach: Jim Margraff, Johns Hopkins 1982
Record: 8 Years, 44-33-3

1998 SCHEDULE

Wash. & Lee ... Sept. 12
Swarthmore ... Sept. 19
Merchant Marine ■ ... Sept. 26
Gettysburg ■ ... *Oct. 2
Ursinus ... Oct. 10
Muhlenberg ■ ... *Oct. 16
Bridgewater (Va.) ... Oct. 24
Dickinson ■ ... Oct. 31
Frank. & Marsh. ... Nov. 7
Western Md. ■ ... Nov. 14

1997 RESULTS (7-3-0)

34 Wash. & Lee ... 28
73 Swarthmore ... 0
14 Merchant Marine ... 27
20 Gettysburg ... 12
33 Ursinus ... 6

24	Muhlenberg	21
21	Bridgewater (Va.)	10
7	Dickinson	13
35	Frank. & Marsh.	21
3	Western Md.	21
264		**159**

Nickname: Blue Jays.
Stadium: Homewood Field (1906), 4,000 capacity. Artificial turf.
Colors: Blue & Black.
Conference: Centennial Conference.
SID: Ernie Larossa, 410-889-4636.
AD: Thomas P. Calder.

JOHNSON SMITH

Charlotte, NC 28216 II

Coach: William Davis, Johnson Smith 1965
Record: 18 Years, 113-80-1

1998 SCHEDULE

Gardner-Webb ■	Sept. 5
Virginia St. ■	Sept. 12
Bowie St.	Sept. 19
South Caro. St.	*Sept. 26
Benedict ■	Oct. 3
Livingstone	Oct. 17
Fayetteville St. ■	Oct. 24
Winston-Salem ■	Oct. 31
N.C. Central	Nov. 7
Virginia Union	Nov. 14
Elizabeth City St. ■	Nov. 21

1997 RESULTS (2-8-0)

13	Gardner-Webb	38
0	Virginia St.	31
19	Bowie St.	13
10	Elizabeth City St.	12
44	Benedict	15
21	Livingstone	42
27	Fayetteville St.	38
7	Winston-Salem	40
0	N.C. Central	28
11	Virginia Union	19
152		**276**

Nickname: Golden Bulls.
Stadium: Bullpit (1990), 7,500 capacity. Natural turf.
Colors: Blue & Gold.
Conference: Central Intercol. Ath. Assn.
SID: To be named, 704-378-1205.
AD: William R. Davis.

JUNIATA

Huntingdon, PA 16652 III

Coach: To be named.

1998 SCHEDULE

Western Md. ■	Sept. 12
Moravian	Sept. 19
King's (Pa.) ■	Sept. 26
Widener ■	Oct. 3
Lycoming	Oct. 10
Lebanon Valley ■	Oct. 17
Susquehanna	Oct. 24
Albright ■	Oct. 31
Carnegie Mellon	Nov. 7
FDU-Madison	Nov. 14

1997 RESULTS (3-7-0)

8	Western Md.	30
28	Moravian	29
12	King's (Pa.)	24
20	Widener	56
16	Lycoming	20
30	Lebanon Valley	15
14	Susquehanna	45
6	Albright	14
26	Waynesburg	23
34	FDU-Madison	33
194		**289**

Nickname: Eagles.
Stadium: Chuck Knox (1988), 3,000 capacity. Natural turf.
Colors: Yale Blue & Old Gold.
Conference: Middle Atlantic States Conf.
SID: Bub Parker, 814-643-4310.
AD: Lawrence R. Bock.

KALAMAZOO

Kalamazoo, MI 49006 III

Coach: Tim Rogers
(First year as head coach)

1998 SCHEDULE

Oberlin	Sept. 5
Wooster ■	Sept. 12
Defiance	Sept. 19
Rose-Hulman	Sept. 26
Hope	Oct. 10
Olivet ■	Oct. 17
Albion	Oct. 24
Alma ■	Oct. 31
Adrian ■	Nov. 7

1997 RESULTS (4-5-0)

21	Wheaton (Ill.)	20
21	Franklin	17
15	Aurora	14
23	Chicago	33
0	Hope	28
12	Olivet	7
0	Albion	49
16	Alma	20
6	Adrian	17
114		**205**

Nickname: Hornets.
Stadium: Angell Field (1946), 3,000 capacity. Natural turf.
Colors: Orange & Black.
Conference: Michigan Intercoll Athl Assn.
SID: Geoff Brown, 616-337-7287.
AD: Robert L. Kent.

KANSAS

Lawrence, KS 66045 ....I-A

Coach: Terry Allen, Northern Iowa 1979
Record: 9 Years, 80-32-0

1998 SCHEDULE

Oklahoma St. ■	Sept. 5
Missouri	*Sept. 12
Illinois St. ■	*Sept. 19
UAB	*Sept. 26
Texas A&M ■	Oct. 3
Baylor	*Oct. 10
Nebraska	Oct. 17
Colorado ■	Oct. 24
Kansas St. ■	Oct. 31
North Texas ■	Nov. 7
Iowa St.	Nov. 21

1997 RESULTS (5-6-0)

24	UAB	0
17	Texas Christian	10
15	Missouri	7
7	Cincinnati	34
20	Oklahoma	17
7	Texas Tech	17
6	Colorado	42
0	Nebraska	35
34	Iowa St.	24
16	Kansas St.	48
31	Texas	45
177		**279**

Nickname: Jayhawks.
Stadium: Memorial (1921), 50,250 capacity. Artificial turf.
Colors: Crimson & Blue.
Conference: Big 12.
SID: Doug Vance, 913-864-3417.
AD: Robert E. Frederick.

KANSAS ST.

Manhattan, KS 66506 ....I-A

Coach: Bill Snyder, William Jewell 1963
Record: 9 Years, 66-37-1

1998 SCHEDULE

Indiana St. ■	*Sept. 5
Northern Ill. ■	Sept. 12
Texas ■	Sept. 19
Northeast La. ■	Sept. 26
Colorado	Oct. 10
Oklahoma St. ■	Oct. 17
Iowa St. ■	Oct. 24
Kansas	Oct. 31
Baylor	Nov. 7
Nebraska ■	Nov. 14
Missouri	Nov. 21

1997 RESULTS (10-1-0)

47	Northern Ill.	7
23	Ohio	20
58	Bowling Green	0
26	Nebraska	56
41	Missouri	11
36	Texas A&M	17
26	Oklahoma	7
13	Texas Tech	2
48	Kansas	16
37	Colorado	20
28	Iowa St.	3
383		**159**

Fiesta Bowl

35	Syracuse	18

Nickname: Wildcats.
Stadium: K S U (1968), 42,000 capacity. Artificial turf.
Colors: Purple & White.
Conference: Big 12.
SID: Kent Brown, 913-532-6735.
AD: Max F. Urick.

KEAN

Union, NJ 07083.......................................III

Coach: Brian Carlson, Montclair St. 1982
Record: 6 Years, 24-29-4

1998 SCHEDULE

Rensselaer ■	Sept. 12
Cortland St.	Sept. 19
Hartwick	*Sept. 25
Wm. Paterson	Oct. 3
Montclair St. ■	Oct. 10
New Jersey City	Oct. 17
Buffalo St. ■	Oct. 24
Rowan ■	Oct. 31
Plymouth St.	Nov. 7
Col. of New Jersey	Nov. 14

1997 RESULTS (1-9-0)

14	Susquehanna	31
7	Wesley	34
21	Cortland St.	47
14	Rensselaer	20
21	Wm. Paterson	9
3	Montclair St.	30
0	New Jersey City	7
0	Buffalo St.	38
0	Rowan	40
18	Col. of New Jersey	33
98		**289**

Nickname: Cougars.
Stadium: Zweidinger Field, 2,200 capacity. Natural turf.
Colors: Royal Blue & Silver.
Conference: New Jersey Athletic Conference.
SID: John Stallings, 908-527-2939.
AD: Glenn Hedden.

KENT

Kent, OH 44242 ....I-A

Coach: Dean Pees, Bowling Green 1971
(First year as head coach)

1998 SCHEDULE

Georgia	Sept. 5
Youngstown St. ■	*Sept. 12
Navy	*Sept. 19

Central Mich.	Sept. 26
Eastern Mich. ■	*Oct. 3
Akron ■	Oct. 10
Marshall	*Oct. 17
Bowling Green	Oct. 24
Western Mich. ■	Oct. 31
Miami (Ohio)	Nov. 14
Ohio ■	Nov. 21

1997 RESULTS (3-8-0)

7	Ohio	31
23	Youngstown St.	44
17	Marshall	42
41	Eastern Mich.	38
43	Central FLa.	59
26	Miami (Ohio)	62
27	Western Mich.	50
60	Central Mich.	37
29	Bowling Green	20
35	Akron	45
29	Navy	62
337		**490**

Nickname: Golden Flashes.
Stadium: Dix (1969), 30,520 capacity. Artificial turf.
Colors: Navy Blue & Gold.
Conference: Mid-American.
SID: Dale Gallagher, 330-672-2110.
AD: Laing E. Kennedy.

KENTUCKY

Lexington, KY 40506 ... I-A

Coach: Hal Mumme, Tarleton St. 1975
Record: 9 Years, 70-33-1

1998 SCHEDULE

Louisville	Sept. 5
Eastern Ky. ■	Sept. 12
Indiana ■	Sept. 19
Florida	Sept. 26
Arkansas [Little Rock, Ark.]	*Oct. 3
South Caro. ■	*Oct. 10
LSU	*Oct. 17
Georgia ■	*Oct. 24
Mississippi St. ■	Nov. 7
Vanderbilt ■	Nov. 14
Tennessee	Nov. 21

1997 RESULTS (5-6-0)

38	Louisville	24
27	Mississippi St.	35
49	Indiana	7
28	Florida	55
40	Alabama	34
24	South Caro.	38
49	Northeast La.	14
13	Georgia	23
28	LSU	63
21	Vanderbilt	10
31	Tennessee	59
348		**362**

Nickname: Wildcats.
Stadium: Commonwealth (1973), 57,800 capacity. Natural turf.
Colors: Blue & White.
Conference: Southeastern.
SID: Tony Neely, 606-257-3838.
AD: C. M. Newton.

KENTUCKY ST.

Frankfort, KY 40601 ... II

Coach: George Small, North Caro. A&T 1979
Record: 3 Years, 19-15-0

1998 SCHEDULE

Miles	Aug. 29
Eastern Ky.	Sept. 5
Albany St. (Ga.) ■	*Sept. 12
Clark Atlanta	*Sept. 19
Fort Valley St.	*Sept. 26
Tuskegee	Oct. 3
Lane ■	Oct. 10
Savannah St.	Oct. 24
Morehouse ■	Oct. 31
Morris Brown ■	Nov. 7
Illinois St.	Nov. 21

1997 RESULTS (7-5-0)

15	Miles	28
6	Indiana St.	19
7	Albany St. (Ga.)	10
32	Clark Atlanta	25
38	Fort Valley St.	7
21	Tuskegee	42
45	Lane	12
28	Savannah St.	10
9	Morehouse	7
17	Morris Brown	30
27	Alabama A&M	20
30	Livingstone	26
275		**236**

Nickname: Thorobreds.
Stadium: Alumni Field (1978), 6,000 capacity. Natural turf.
Colors: Green & Gold.
Conference: Southern Intercol. Ath. Conf.
SID: Ron Braden, 502-227-6011.
AD: Donald W. Lyons.

KY. WESLEYAN

Owensboro, KY 42302 ... II

Coach: John Johnson, Northern Mich. 1984
Record: 4 Years, 19-22-0

1998 SCHEDULE

Tennessee Tech	*Sept. 3
Cumberland (Tenn.) ■	*Sept. 12
Thomas More ■	Sept. 19
Westminster (Mo.) ■	Sept. 26
Concordia-St. Paul	Oct. 3
St. Joseph's (Ind.)	Oct. 10
Quincy ■	Oct. 17
Madison Tech	Oct. 24
Frostburg St.	Oct. 31
Morehead St.	Nov. 14

1997 RESULTS (6-4-0)

3	South FLa.	80
55	Bethel (Tenn.)	17
45	Maryville (Tenn.)	24
42	Sue Bennett	14
42	Quincy	20
39	Westminster (Mo.)	34
31	St. Joseph's (Ind.)	37
6	Evansville	48
0	Lakeland	51
43	Mount Saint Joseph	14
306		**339**

Nickname: Panthers.
Stadium: Apollo (1989), 3,000 capacity. Natural turf.
Colors: Purple & White.
Conference: Independent.
SID: Roy Pickerill, 502-926-3111.
AD: William J. Meadors.

KENYON

Gambier, OH 43022 ... III

Coach: Vince Arduini, Norwich 1977
Record: 3 Years, 10-19-1

1998 SCHEDULE

Centre	Sept. 12
Thiel ■	Sept. 19
Ohio Wesleyan ■	Sept. 26
Earlham	Oct. 3
Allegheny	Oct. 10
Wooster ■	Oct. 17
Grove City	Oct. 24
Denison ■	Oct. 31
Oberlin	Nov. 7
Wittenberg ■	Nov. 14

1997 RESULTS (3-7-0)

30	Grove City	37
53	Oberlin	35
10	Wittenberg	62
12	Ohio Wesleyan	13
21	Denison	31
34	Case Reserve	27
3	Wooster	47
20	Earlham	3
10	Allegheny	38
0	Chicago	12
193		**305**

Nickname: Lords.
Stadium: McBride Field (1962), 2,500 capacity. Natural turf.
Colors: Purple & White.
Conference: North Coast Athletic Conf.
SID: Joe Wasiluk, 614-427-5471.
AD: Robert Bunnell.

KING'S (PA.)

Wilkes-Barre, PA 18711 ... III

Coach: Richard Mannello, Springfield 1983
Record: 5 Years, 9-39-1

1998 SCHEDULE

Susquehanna ■	Sept. 12
Lycoming ■	Sept. 19
Juniata	Sept. 26
Hartwick ■	Oct. 3
Albright	Oct. 10
Wilkes ■	Oct. 17
Delaware Valley	Oct. 24
Widener ■	Oct. 31
FDU-Madison	*Nov. 7
New Jersey City	Nov. 14

1997 RESULTS (3-7-0)

0	Alfred	30
14	Susquehanna	35
3	Lycoming	42
24	Juniata	12
20	Albright	38
0	Wilkes	23
33	Delaware Valley	38
20	Widener	34
34	FDU-Madison	31
7	New Jersey City	6
155		**289**

Nickname: Monarchs.
Stadium: Monarch Fields, 3,000 capacity. Natural turf.
Colors: Red & Gold.
Conference: Middle Atlantic States Conf.
SID: Bob Ziadie, 717-826-5934.
AD: John J. Dorish.

KNOX

Galesburg, IL 61401 ... III

Coach: Andy Gibbons, Culver Stockton 1990
Record: 2 years, 11-7-0

1998 SCHEDULE

Ripon	Sept. 19
Illinois Col. ■	Sept. 26
Lawrence	Oct. 3
St. Norbert ■	Oct. 10
Carroll (Wis.) ■	Oct. 17
Beloit	Oct. 24
Grinnell ■	Oct. 31
Lake Forest ■	Nov. 7
Monmouth (Ill.)	Nov. 14

1997 RESULTS (5-4-0)

35	Beloit	7
23	Lake Forest	6
21	Carroll (Wis.)	14
36	Lawrence	38
28	Cornell College	33
24	Grinnell	38
50	Illinois Col.	30
14	Coe	21
14	Monmouth (Ill.)	7
245		**194**

Nickname: Prairie Fire.
Stadium: Knox Bowl (1968), 6,000 capacity. Natural turf.
Colors: Purple & Gold.
Conference: Midwest Conference.

SID: Andy Gibbons, 309-341-7379.
AD: Harlan D. Knosher.

KUTZTOWN

Kutztown, PA 19530 ... II

Coach: David Keeny, Kutztown 1983
(First year as head coach)

1998 SCHEDULE

Lock Haven	*Sept. 3
Shippensburg ■	Sept. 19
Clarion ■	Sept. 26
Bloomsburg	Oct. 3
Cheyney ■	Oct. 10
Mansfield	Oct. 17
East Stroudsburg	Oct. 24
Millersville ■	Oct. 31
Slippery Rock	Nov. 7
West Chester ■	Nov. 14

1997 RESULTS (6-4-0)

44	West Va. Wesleyan	26
22	Lock Haven	11
14	Shippensburg	21
20	East Stroudsburg	45
50	Cheyney	6
44	Mansfield	0
24	Millersville	21
7	Bloomsburg	17
12	Calif. (Pa.)	7
12	West Chester	24
249		**178**

Nickname: Golden Bears.
Stadium: University Field (1987), 5,600 capacity. Natural turf.
Colors: Maroon & Gold.
Conference: Pennsylvania State Athl. Conf.
SID: Matt Santos, 610-683-4182.
AD: Clark Yeager.

LA SALLE

Philadelphia, PA 19141 ... I-AA

Coach: Bill Manlove, Temple 1958
Record: 28 Years, 193-90-1

1998 SCHEDULE

St. Peter's ■	Sept. 12
Iona	Sept. 19
Delaware Valley	Sept. 26
Monmouth ■	Oct. 3
Catholic	Oct. 10
Bryant ■	Oct. 17
St. Francis (Pa.)	Oct. 24
Waynesburg ■	Oct. 31
Jacksonville	Nov. 7

1997 RESULTS (1-8-0)

10	Fairfield	34
25	St. Peter's	16
20	Monmouth	42
0	Delaware Valley	43
0	Bentley	45
21	Catholic	61
14	Central Conn. St.	55
7	Waynesburg	41
7	St. Francis (Pa.)	30
104		**367**

Nickname: Explorers.
Stadium: McCarthy, 8,500 capacity. Natural turf.
Colors: Blue & Gold.
Conference: Independent.
SID: Scott Leightman, 215-951-1605.
AD: Thomas M. Brennan.

LA VERNE

La Verne, CA 91750 ... III

Coach: Don Morel, La Verne 1987
Record: 3 Years, 18-9-0

1998 SCHEDULE

Occidental ■	Sept. 19
Howard Payne	Sept. 26
Claremont-M-S	*Oct. 3
Whittier	*Oct. 10
Azusa Pacific	*Oct. 17
Redlands ■	Oct. 24
Chapman	Oct. 31
Cal Lutheran	Nov. 7
Menlo ■	Nov. 14

1997 RESULTS (2-7-0)

13	Whittier	34
41	Occidental	14
18	Howard Payne	21
17	Claremont-M-S	6
7	Cal Lutheran	34
14	Azusa Pacific	23
20	Chapman	24
13	Menlo	42
14	Redlands	42
157		**240**

Nickname: Leopards, Leos.
Stadium: Ortmayer (1991), 1,500 capacity. Natural turf.
Colors: Orange & Green.
Conference: So Calif Intercol Ath Conf.
SID: Daniel Mulville, 909-593-3511.
AD: Jimmy M. Paschal.

LAFAYETTE

Easton, PA 18042 ... I-AA

Coach: Bill Russo, Brown 1969
Record: 20 Years, 111-98-4

1998 SCHEDULE

Northeastern	Sept. 12
Buffalo ■	Sept. 19
Brown ■	Sept. 26
Dartmouth	Oct. 3
Towson	Oct. 10
Princeton ■	Oct. 17
Bucknell	Oct. 24
Holy Cross ■	Oct. 31
Fordham	Nov. 7
Colgate	Nov. 14
Lehigh ■	Nov. 21

1997 RESULTS (3-8-0)

0	Fordham	23
14	Army	41
21	Bucknell	23
27	Brown	35
31	Columbia	3
6	Colgate	44
34	Cornell	41
38	Towson	0
0	New Haven	38
34	Holy Cross	23
31	Lehigh	43
236		**314**

Nickname: Leopards.
Stadium: Fisher Field (1926), 13,750 capacity. Natural turf.
Colors: Maroon & White.
Conference: Patriot.
SID: Scott D. Morse, 610-250-5122.
AD: Eve Atkinson.

LAKE FOREST

Lake Forest, IL 60045 ... III

Coach: Randy Moore, Iowa 1984
Record: 3 Years, 4-23-0

1998 SCHEDULE

Chicago ■	Sept. 12
Monmouth (Ill.)	Sept. 19
Grinnell ■	Sept. 26
Beloit ■	Oct. 3
Ripon	Oct. 10
Lawrence	Oct. 17
Illinois Col. ■	Oct. 24
St. Norbert ■	Oct. 31
Knox	Nov. 7
Carroll (Wis.)	Nov. 14

1997 RESULTS (2-7-0)

12	Hamline	35
6	Knox	23
46	Illinois Col.	18
7	Monmouth (Ill.)	14
21	St. Norbert	28
19	Ripon	45
16	Carroll (Wis.)	28
30	Lawrence	51
31	Beloit	19
188		**261**

Nickname: Foresters.
Stadium: Farwell Field, 2,000 capacity. Natural turf.
Colors: Red & Black.
Conference: Midwest Conference.
SID: Stephanie Hojan, 708-735-6011.
AD: Jackie A. Slaats.

LAKELAND

Sheboygan, WI 53082 ... III

Coach: Randy Awrey, Northern Mich. 1978
Record: 8 Years, 38-40-1

1998 SCHEDULE

Wis.-Platteville ■	Sept. 5
Carthage ■	Sept. 19
Concordia (Wis.)	Sept. 26
Greenville ■	Oct. 3
Concordia (Ill.) ■	Oct. 10
MacMurray ■	Oct. 17
Eureka	Oct. 24
Benedictine (Ill.) ■	Oct. 31
Aurora	Nov. 7
Mt. Senario	Nov. 14

1997 RESULTS (10-0-0)

48	Ripon	0
42	Maranatha Baptist	14
32	Carthage	26
40	Franklin	6
59	Greenville	7
41	Concordia (Wis.)	33
24	MacMurray	17
67	Concordia (Ill.)	0
24	Eureka	13
51	Ky. Wesleyan	0
428		**116**

Nickname: Muskies.
Stadium: Taylor Field (1958), 1,500 capacity. Natural turf.
Colors: Navy & Gold.
Conference: Independent.
SID: Dave Moyer, 414-565-1411.
AD: Jane Bouche.

LANE

Jackson, TN 38301 ... II

Coach: Leonard Anderson
(First year as head coach)

1998 SCHEDULE

Virginia St.	Aug. 29
Morehouse	Sept. 5
Fort Valley St. ■	Sept. 12
Savannah St. ■	*Sept. 19
West Va. St. ■	Sept. 26
Clark Atlanta [Memphis, Tenn.]	*Oct. 3
Kentucky St.	Oct. 10
Miles ■	Oct. 17
Benedict	Oct. 31
Tuskegee	Nov. 7
Morris Brown ■	Nov. 14

1997 RESULTS (0-10-0)

10	Ark.-Pine Bluff	55
0	Clark Atlanta	25
14	West Ala.	37
10	Savannah St.	32
16	West Va. St.	44
12	Kentucky St.	45
14	Mississippi Val.	17
14	Benedict	19
0	Texas Southern	38

0	Virginia St.	30
90		**342**

Nickname: Dragons.
Stadium: Rothrock (1930), 3,500 capacity. Natural turf.
Colors: Blue & Red.
Conference: Southern Intercol. Ath. Conf.
SID: Darrius Brown, 901-426-7651.
AD: J. L. Perry.

LAWRENCE

Appleton, WI 54912 III

Coach: Rick Coles, Coe 1979
Record: 5 Years, 14-31-0

1998 SCHEDULE

Pomona-Pitzer	Sept. 12
Illinois Col.	Sept. 19
St. Norbert ■	Sept. 26
Knox ■	Oct. 3
Beloit	Oct. 10
Lake Forest ■	Oct. 17
Carroll (Wis.)	Oct. 24
Monmouth (Ill.) ■	Oct. 31
Ripon	Nov. 7
Grinnell ■	Nov. 14

1997 RESULTS (4-5-0)

19	Carleton	29
41	Concordia (Ill.)	39
7	Coe	70
38	Knox	36
21	Carroll (Wis.)	33
27	St. Norbert	24
27	Beloit	34
51	Lake Forest	30
24	Ripon	43
255		**338**

Nickname: Vikings.
Stadium: Banta Bowl (1965), 5,255 capacity. Natural turf.
Colors: Navy & White.
Conference: Midwest Conference.
SID: Shelly Burzinski, 414-832-7346.
AD: Amy Proctor.

LEBANON VALLEY

Annville, PA 17003 III

Coach: To be named.

1998 SCHEDULE

Ursinus	Sept. 12
Albright	*Sept. 19
Widener	Sept. 26
Wilkes ■	Oct. 3
Susquehanna ■	Oct. 10
Juniata	Oct. 17
Moravian ■	Oct. 24
Gettysburg	Oct. 31
Lycoming ■	Nov. 7
Delaware Valley ■	Nov. 14

1997 RESULTS (0-10-0)

16	Ursinus	42
7	Albright	31
6	Widener	28
0	Wilkes	32
13	Susquehanna	34
15	Juniata	30
6	Moravian	21
6	Gettysburg	19
7	Lycoming	26
27	Delaware Valley	40
103		**303**

Nickname: Flying Dutchmen.
Stadium: Arnold Field (1969), 2,500 capacity. Natural turf.
Colors: Royal Blue & White.
Conference: Middle Atlantic States Conf.
SID: Tom Hanrahan, 717-867-6033.
AD: Louis A. Sorrentino.

LEHIGH

Bethlehem, PA 18015 ....I-AA

Coach: Kevin Higgins, West Chester 1977
Record: 4 Years, 22-21-1

1998 SCHEDULE

Fordham ■	Sept. 12
St. Mary's (Cal.)	Sept. 19
Princeton ■	Sept. 26
Harvard	Oct. 3
Columbia	Oct. 10
Towson ■	Oct. 17
Holy Cross	Oct. 24
Wofford ■	Oct. 31
Colgate ■	Nov. 7
Bucknell ■	Nov. 14
Lafayette	Nov. 21

1997 RESULTS (4-7-0)

35	Fordham	42
16	Towson	14
30	Harvard	35
28	Colgate	61
24	Pennsylvania	7
38	Hofstra	45
46	Dartmouth	26
14	Bucknell	21
14	Holy Cross	20
19	Delaware	24
43	Lafayette	31
307		**326**

Nickname: Mountain Hawks.
Stadium: Goodman (1988), 16,000 capacity. Natural turf.
Colors: Brown & White.
Conference: Patriot.
SID: Glenn Hofmann, 610-758-3174.
AD: Joseph D. Sterrett.

LENOIR-RHYNE

Hickory, NC 28603 II

Coach: Bill Hart, Rowan 1973
Record: 1 Year, 0-10-0

1998 SCHEDULE

Concord	Aug. 29
VMI	Sept. 5
Livingstone	*Sept. 12
Tusculum	*Sept. 19
Presbyterian	Sept. 26
Gardner-Webb ■	*Oct. 10
Wingate	Oct. 17
Newberry ■	Oct. 24
Carson-Newman ■	*Oct. 31
Mars Hill ■	*Nov. 7
Catawba	Nov. 14

1997 RESULTS (0-10-0)

13	Elon	63
12	Livingstone	35
16	Shepherd	45
13	Presbyterian	26
0	Gardner-Webb	32
21	Wingate	22
23	Newberry	49
3	Carson-Newman	76
7	Mars Hill	27
21	Catawba	24
129		**399**

Nickname: Bears.
Stadium: Moretz (1923), 8,500 capacity. Natural turf.
Colors: Red & Black.
Conference: South Atlantic Conference.
SID: Michael MacEachern, 704-328-7174.
AD: Jane Jenkins.

LEWIS & CLARK

Portland, OR 97219 III

Coach: Chuck Solberg, Valley City St. 1959
Record: 4 Years, 13-24-0

1998 SCHEDULE

Occidental	*Sept. 26
Claremont-M-S	Nov. 14
Simon Fraser ■	Sept. 12
Pacific Lutheran ■	Oct. 3
Willamette	Oct. 10
Puget Sound	Oct. 17
Linfield ■	Oct. 24
Whitworth	Oct. 31
Eastern Ore. U. ■	Nov. 7

1997 RESULTS (3-6-0)

25	Redlands	33
9	Southern Ore.	39
28	Occidental	21
16	Pacific Lutheran	53
14	Willamette	34
34	Puget Sound	0
0	Linfield	49
20	Whitworth	7
12	Eastern Ore. U.	55
158		**291**

Nickname: Pioneers.
Stadium: Griswold, 3,700 capacity. Natural turf.
Colors: Orange & Black.
Conference: NCIC.
SID: Julie Lapomarda, 503-768-7067.
AD: Steve Wallo.

LIBERTY

Lynchburg, VA 24502 ....I-AA

Coach: Sam Rutigliano, Tulsa 1956
Record: 9 Years, 58-40-0

1998 SCHEDULE

Appalachian St.	*Sept. 5
South Fla. ■	*Sept. 19
Glenville St. ■	*Sept. 26
Charleston So. ■	*Oct. 3
Hampton	Oct. 10
Delaware St.	Oct. 17
Buffalo ■	Oct. 24
Elon	Oct. 31
Norfolk St. ■	Nov. 7
Hofstra	Nov. 14
Cal Poly	Nov. 21

1997 RESULTS (9-2-0)

56	Glenville St.	7
17	Western Caro.	10
33	Delaware St.	17
41	Elon	9
27	Hampton	33
16	Virginia Union	8
48	Charleston So.	14
49	Cal Poly	32
17	Norfolk St.	6
27	Hofstra	40
25	Appalachian St.	19
356		**195**

Nickname: Flames.
Stadium: Williams (1989), 12,000 capacity. Artificial turf.
Colors: Red, White & Blue.
Conference: Independent.
SID: Mike Montoro, 804-582-2292.
AD: Kim Graham.

LINFIELD

Mc Minnville, OR 97128 III

Coach: Jay Locey, Oregon State 1976
Record: 2 Years, 11-7-0

1998 SCHEDULE

Redlands	*Sept. 12
Western Ore. U.	Sept. 19
Southern Ore. ■	Oct. 3
Whitworth ■	Oct. 10
Willamette ■	Oct. 17
Lewis & Clark	Oct. 24
Pacific Lutheran	Oct. 31
Puget Sound ■	Nov. 7
Eastern Ore. U.	Nov. 14

1997 RESULTS (6-3-0)

15	Southern Ore.	14
10	Western Ore. U.	24
17	Western Wash.	28
28	Whitworth	3
0	Willamette	27
49	Lewis & Clark	0
28	Pacific Lutheran	12
31	Puget Sound	14
33	Eastern Ore. U.	20
211		**142**

Nickname: Wildcats.
Stadium: Memorial (Maxwell Field), 1,800 capacity. Natural turf.
Colors: Purple & Red.
Conference: NCIC.
SID: Kelly Bird, 503-434-2439.
AD: Scott Carnahan.

LIVINGSTONE

Salisbury, NC 28144 II

Coach: Rudy Abhrams, Livingstone 1964
Record: 4 Years, 28-12-1

1998 SCHEDULE

Lenoir-Rhyne ■	*Sept. 12
Virginia Union	Sept. 19
Bowie St. ■	Sept. 26
Virginia St.	Oct. 3
Winston-Salem	Oct. 10
Johnson Smith ■	Oct. 17
Elizabeth City St. ■	Oct. 24
N.C. Central ■	Oct. 31
Albany St. (Ga.)	Nov. 7
Fayetteville St.	Nov. 14

1997 RESULTS (10-1-0)

56	Virginia Union	6
40	Bowie St.	9
35	Lenoir-Rhyne	12
48	Benedict	16
28	Virginia St.	14
41	Winston-Salem	7
42	Johnson Smith	21
41	Elizabeth City St.	16
20	N.C. Central	7
67	Fayetteville St.	13
26	Kentucky St.	30
444		**151**

Nickname: Fighting Bears.
Stadium: Alumni, 4,000 capacity. Natural turf.
Colors: Columbia Blue & Black.
Conference: Central Intercol. Ath. Assn.
SID: Adrian Ferguson, 704-638-5586.
AD: Clifton Huff.

LOCK HAVEN

Lock Haven, PA 17745 II

Coach: Nick Polk, Lock Haven 1986
Record: 2 Years, 4-18-0

1998 SCHEDULE

Kutztown ■	*Sept. 3
Buffalo	*Sept. 12
Bloomsburg	Sept. 19
Cheyney	Sept. 26
Indiana (Pa.)	Oct. 3
Calif. (Pa.) ■	*Oct. 10
Edinboro	Oct. 17
Mansfield ■	Oct. 24
Shippensburg	Oct. 31
Clarion ■	Nov. 7
Slippery Rock ■	Nov. 14

1997 RESULTS (3-8-0)

7	Buffalo	30
11	Kutztown	22
3	Bloomsburg	17
34	Mansfield	19
33	Clarion	32
6	Millersville	21
0	Shippensburg	26
17	Calif. (Pa.)	3
6	Slippery Rock	38
21	Indiana (Pa.)	48
23	Edinboro	29
161		**285**

Nickname: Bald Eagles.
Stadium: Hubert Jack, 3,000 capacity. Artificial turf.
Colors: Crimson & White.
Conference: Pennsylvania State Athl. Conf.
SID: Will Adair, 717-893-2350.
AD: Sharon E. Taylor.

LIU-C.W. POST

Brookville, NY 11548 II

Coach: Bryan Collins, St. John's (N. Y.) 1987
(First year as head coach)

1998 SCHEDULE

Assumption ■	Sept. 12
Rowan	*Sept. 19
Albany (N.Y.)	*Sept. 26
Stonehill	Oct. 3
Monmouth ■	Oct. 10
Merrimack ■	Oct. 17
Pace	Oct. 24
Southern Conn. St. ■	Oct. 31
Bentley ■	Nov. 7
Stony Brook	Nov. 14

1997 RESULTS (6-4-0)

34	Wm. Paterson	3
12	Wagner	13
7	Albany (N.Y.)	44
16	Stonehill	0
62	Sacred Heart	10
42	Assumption	7
7	Pace	8
7	Southern Conn. St.	17
9	Bentley	7
7	Stony Brook	0
203		**109**

Nickname: Pioneers.
Stadium: Hickox Field (1966), 5,000 capacity. Natural turf.
Colors: Green & Gold.
Conference: Eastern Football.
SID: Jeremy Kniffin, 516-299-4156.
AD: Vincent Salamone.

LORAS

Dubuque, IA 52004 III

Coach: Bob Bierie, Loras 1965
Record: 18 Years, 111-69-5

1998 SCHEDULE

Coe	Sept. 5
Central (Iowa) ■	Sept. 12
Upper Iowa	Sept. 19
William Penn ■	Sept. 26
Wartburg	Oct. 3
Buena Vista	Oct. 10
Cornell College ■	Oct. 17
Simpson	Oct. 31
Luther ■	Nov. 7
Dubuque ■	Nov. 14

1997 RESULTS (6-4-0)

23	Benedictine (Ill.)	15
17	Wis.-Platteville	10
14	Upper Iowa	17
10	Wartburg	23
14	Central (Iowa)	38
35	Luther	28
20	William Penn	14
13	Buena Vista	0
52	Dubuque	15
28	Simpson	42
226		**202**

Nickname: Duhawks.
Stadium: Rock Bowl (1945), 3,000 capacity. Natural turf.
Colors: Purple & Gold.
Conference: Iowa Intercol. Athletic Conf.
SID: Howard Thomas, 319-588-7407.
AD: Dennis O'Connor.

LSU

Baton Rouge, LA 70803 ....I-A

Coach: Gerry DiNardo, Notre Dame 1975
Record: 7 Years, 45-34-1

1998 SCHEDULE

Arkansas St. ■	*Sept. 12
Auburn	Sept. 19
Idaho ■	*Sept. 26
Georgia ■	*Oct. 3
Florida	Oct. 10
Kentucky ■	*Oct. 17
Mississippi St. ■	*Oct. 24
Mississippi	Oct. 31
Alabama ■	*Nov. 7
Notre Dame	Nov. 21
Arkansas [Little Rock, Ark.]	Nov. 27

1997 RESULTS (8-3-0)

55	UTEP	3
24	Mississippi St.	9
28	Auburn	31
56	Akron	0
7	Vanderbilt	6
28	Florida	21
21	Mississippi	36
63	Kentucky	28
27	Alabama	0
6	Notre Dame	24
31	Arkansas	21
346		**179**

Independence Bowl

27	Notre Dame	9

Nickname: Fighting Tigers.
Stadium: Tiger (1924), 79,940 capacity. Natural turf.
Colors: Purple & Gold.
Conference: Independent.
SID: Herb Vincent, 504-388-8226.
AD: Joe Dean.

LOUISIANA TECH

Ruston, LA 71272 ....I-A

Coach: Gary Crowton, Brigham Young 1983
Record: 2 Years, 15-7-0

1998 SCHEDULE

Nebraska	Aug. 29
Central Fla. ■	*Sept. 5
Texas A&M	*Sept. 12
Southwestern La. ■	*Sept. 19
Wyoming	Sept. 26
Boise St. ■	Oct. 3
Northeast La.	*Oct. 10
UAB ■	*Oct. 17
Auburn	Oct. 24
Nicholls St. ■	Oct. 31
Arkansas St.	Nov. 7
Tulane	*Nov. 26

1997 RESULTS (9-2-0)

30	Bowling Green	23
17	Northeast La.	16
56	Central Mich.	28
13	Arkansas	17
41	California	34
13	Auburn	49
42	Arkansas St.	14
31	Boise St.	27
26	Alabama	20
32	UAB	29
63	Southwestern La.	24
364		**281**

Nickname: Bulldogs.
Stadium: Joe Aillet (1968), 30,600 capacity. Natural turf.
Colors: Red & Blue.
Conference: Independent.
SID: Byron Avery, 318-257-3144.
AD: Jim M. Oakes.

LOUISVILLE

Louisville, KY 40292 .... I-A

Coach: John L. Smith, Weber St. 1971
Record: 9 Years, 69-39-0

1998 SCHEDULE

Kentucky ■	Sept. 5
Utah	*Sept. 12
Illinois	Sept. 19
Boston College ■	Sept. 26
Cincinnati ■	Oct. 3
Southern Miss.	Oct. 10
Tulane	Oct. 17
Memphis ■	Oct. 24
Western Ky. ■	Oct. 31
East Caro.	Nov. 14
Army ■	Nov. 21

1997 RESULTS (1-10-0)

24	Kentucky	38
21	Utah	27
26	Illinois	14
21	Penn St.	57
14	Oklahoma	35
24	Southern Miss.	42
33	Tulane	64
22	Houston	36
31	East Caro.	45
9	Cincinnati	28
20	Memphis	21
245		**407**

Nickname: Cardinals.
Stadium: Papa John's Cardinal (1998), 45,000 capacity. Artificial turf.
Colors: Red, Black & White.
Conference: Conference USA.
SID: Kenny Klein, 502-852-6581.
AD: Tom Jurich.

LUTHER

Decorah, IA 52101 III

Coach: Brad Pole, Rocky Mountain 1979
Record: 2 Years, 7-13-0

1998 SCHEDULE

Dubuque ■	Sept. 12
Coe	Sept. 19
Central (Iowa) ■	Sept. 26
Upper Iowa	Oct. 3
William Penn	Oct. 10
Wartburg ■	Oct. 17
Buena Vista	Oct. 24
Cornell College ■	Oct. 31
Loras	Nov. 7
Simpson ■	Nov. 14

1997 RESULTS (4-6-0)

19	St. Olaf	12
14	Martin Luther	21
6	Simpson	61
14	Buena Vista	13
27	Dubuque	26
28	Loras	35
8	Central (Iowa)	48
24	William Penn	13
24	Upper Iowa	40
15	Wartburg	49
179		**318**

Nickname: Norse.
Stadium: Carlson (1966), 5,000 capacity. Natural turf.
Colors: Blue & White.
Conference: Iowa Intercol. Athletic Conf.
SID: Dave Blanchard, 319-387-1586.
AD: Joe Thompson.

LYCOMING

Williamsport, PA 17701 III

Coach: Frank Girardi, West Chester 1961
Record: 26 Years, 192-64-5

1998 SCHEDULE

Moravian ■	Sept. 12
King's (Pa.)	Sept. 19
FDU-Madison ■	Oct. 3
Juniata ■	Oct. 10
Delaware Valley	Oct. 17
Widener	Oct. 24
Susquehanna ■	Oct. 31
Lebanon Valley	Nov. 7
Wilkes ■	Nov. 14

1997 RESULTS (9-0-0)

17	Moravian	14
42	King's (Pa.)	3
35	FDU-Madison	19
20	Juniata	16
49	Delaware Valley	3
19	Widener	17
21	Susquehanna	12
26	Lebanon Valley	7
26	Wilkes	12
255		**103**

III Championship

27	Western Md.	13
46	Trinity (Tex.)	26
28	Rowan	20
12	Mount Union	61

Nickname: Warriors.
Stadium: Person Field (1962), 2,500 capacity. Natural turf.
Colors: Blue & Gold.
Conference: Middle Atlantic States Conf.
SID: Jeff Michaels, 717-321-4028.
AD: Frank L. Girardi.

MACMURRAY

Jacksonville, IL 62650 III

Coach: Bob Frey, Mount Union 1985
Record: 3 Years, 18-12-0

1998 SCHEDULE

Greenville ■	Sept. 5
Blackburn	Sept. 12
Aurora	Sept. 26
Concordia (Wis.) ■	Oct. 3
Principia ■	Oct. 10
Lakeland	Oct. 17
Concordia (Ill.)	Oct. 24
Eureka ■	Oct. 31
Benedictine (Ill.)	Nov. 7
Westminster (Mo.)	Nov. 14

1997 RESULTS (8-2-0)

28	William Penn	14
34	Monmouth (Ill.)	6
59	Principia	13
35	Eureka	21
42	Greenville	14
17	Lakeland	24
6	Concordia (Wis.)	26
32	Concordia (Ill.)	0
31	Blackburn	23
48	Westminster (Mo.)	16
332		**157**

Nickname: Highlanders.
Stadium: Highlander (1984), 5,000 capacity. Natural turf.
Colors: Scarlet & Navy.
Conference: St. Louis Intercol. Ath. Conf.
SID: Tom Lenz, 217-479-7143.
AD: Robert E. Gay.

MACALESTER

St. Paul, MN 55105 III

Coach: Dennis Czech, Macalester 1983
(First year as head coach)

1998 SCHEDULE

Crown	Sept. 5
St. John's (Minn.) ■	Sept. 19
Gust. Adolphus	Sept. 26
Carleton	Oct. 3
St. Thomas (Minn.) ■	Oct. 10
Augsburg	Oct. 17
Bethel (Minn.) ■	Oct. 24
Concordia-M'head	Oct. 31
Hamline ■	Nov. 7
St. Olaf [Minneapolis, Minn.]	*Nov. 12

1997 RESULTS (1-9-0)

28	Crown	20
3	Carleton	21
3	Gust. Adolphus	34
0	Concordia-M'head	28
3	St. Olaf	19
0	Bethel (Minn.)	35
3	St. Thomas (Minn.)	30
7	St. John's (Minn.)	47
7	Augsburg	24
6	Hamline	16
60		**274**

Nickname: Scots.
Stadium: Macalester (1965), 4,000 capacity. Natural turf.
Colors: Orange & Blue.
Conference: Minn. Intercol. Athletic Conf.
SID: Andy Johnson, 612-696-6533.
AD: Kenneth W. Andrews.

MAINE

Orono, ME 04469 .... I-AA

Coach: Jack Cosgrove, Maine 1978
Record: 5 Years, 21-34-0

1998 SCHEDULE

Buffalo [Portland, Me.]	*Sept. 3
New Hampshire ■	*Sept. 12
Connecticut	Sept. 19
Dartmouth ■	Sept. 26
Villanova ■	Oct. 3
Rhode Island ■	Oct. 10
Richmond ■	Oct. 17
James Madison	Oct. 24
Delaware	Oct. 31
Massachusetts	Nov. 14
Northeastern ■	Nov. 21

1997 RESULTS (5-6-0)

30	Rhode Island	14
49	Massachusetts	6
14	Villanova	34
22	James Madison	24
14	Richmond	17
49	Connecticut	47
62	Boston U.	29
7	New Hampshire	24
52	Buffalo	13
17	Northeastern	23
32	Hofstra	44
348		**275**

Nickname: Black Bears.
Stadium: Morse Field/Al Fond, 10,000 capacity. Artificial turf.
Colors: Blue & White.
Conference: Atlantic 10.
SID: Joe Roberts, 207-581-1086.
AD: Suzanne J. Tyler.

MAINE MARITIME

Castine, ME 04421 III

Coach: Mike Hodgson, Maine 1979
Record: 4 Years, 23-16-0

1998 SCHEDULE

Plymouth St. ■	Sept. 12
Curry	Sept. 19
Mass. Maritime ■	Sept. 26
Mass.-Dartmouth	Oct. 3
Bri'water (Mass.) ■	Oct. 10
Westfield St.	Oct. 17
Fitchburg St. ■	Oct. 24
Salve Regina	Oct. 31
Worcester St. ■	Nov. 7
Framingham St.	Nov. 14

1997 RESULTS (4-6-0)

6	Plymouth St.	44
27	Bri'water (Mass.)	28
6	Worcester St.	31
13	Mass. Maritime	20
7	Mass.-Dartmouth	34
0	Salve Regina	10
12	Mass.-Boston	0
23	Fitchburg St.	6
27	Framingham St.	14
54	Westfield St.	28
175		**215**

Nickname: Mariners.
Stadium: Ritchie (1965), 3,500 capacity. Artificial turf.
Colors: Royal Blue & Gold.
Conference: New England FB.
SID: To be named, 207-326-2259.
AD: William J. MottoLa.

MANCHESTER

North Manchester, IN 46962 ... III

Coach: Dave Harms, Drake 1980
Record: 3 Years, 14-16-0

1998 SCHEDULE

Walsh	Sept. 12
Olivet	Sept. 19
Albion ■	Sept. 26
Franklin ■	Oct. 3
Hanover	Oct. 10
Wabash	Oct. 17
Bluffton ■	Oct. 24
Wilmington (Ohio) ■	Oct. 31
Mount Saint Joseph	Nov. 7
Anderson (Ind.)	Nov. 14

1997 RESULTS (6-4-0)

26	Earlham	0
13	Mount Saint Joseph	10
31	Bluffton	24
7	Hanover	45
7	Wabash	24
28	Rose-Hulman	29
51	Defiance	26
7	DePauw	21
46	Franklin	21
28	Anderson (Ind.)	15
244		**215**

Nickname: Spartans.
Stadium: Burt Memorial, 4,500 capacity. Natural turf.
Colors: Black & Gold.
Conference: Heartland Colleg. Ath. Conf.
SID: Rob Nichols, 219-982-5035.
AD: Tom Jarman.

MANKATO ST.

Mankato, MN 56002 ... II

Coach: Dan Runkle, Illinois Col. 1968
Record: 17 Years, 92-96-2

1998 SCHEDULE

Minn.-Duluth ■	Sept. 5
Mo. Western St.	*Sept. 12
South Dak.	Sept. 19
South Dak. St. ■	Sept. 26
St. Cloud St. ■	Oct. 3
North Dak.	Oct. 10
Northern Colo. ■	Oct. 17
Morningside	Oct. 24
Neb.-Omaha ■	Oct. 31
North Dak. St.	*Nov. 7
Augustana (S.D.)	Nov. 14

1997 RESULTS (4-7-0)

31	Minn.-Duluth	20
15	Northern Iowa	39
24	South Dak.	20
21	South Dak. St.	7
6	St. Cloud St.	13
7	North Dak.	21
0	Northern Colo.	31
26	Morningside	14
16	Neb.-Omaha	30
20	North Dak. St.	47
10	Augustana (S.D.)	43
176		**285**

Nickname: Mavericks.
Stadium: Blakeslee Field (1962), 7,500 capacity. Natural turf.
Colors: Purple & Gold.
Conference: No. Central Intercoll Ath Conf.
SID: Paul Allan, 507-389-2625.
AD: Don Amiot.

MANSFIELD

Mansfield, PA 16933 ... II

Coach: Joe Viadella, Rhode Island 1983
Record: 3 Years, 5-27-0

1998 SCHEDULE

West Liberty St.	Sept. 5
Westminster (Pa.) ■	Sept. 12
Ithaca	Sept. 19
Calif. (Pa.) ■	Sept. 26
Millersville ■	Oct. 3
West Chester	Oct. 10
Kutztown ■	Oct. 17
Lock Haven	Oct. 24
Cheyney	Oct. 31
Bloomsburg ■	Nov. 7
East Stroudsburg	Nov. 14

1997 RESULTS (1-10-0)

7	Southern Conn. St.	20
12	Westminster (Pa.)	34
17	Ithaca	42
19	Lock Haven	34
6	Millersville	42
0	Bloomsburg	55
0	Kutztown	44
9	West Chester	38
21	East Stroudsburg	23
20	Cheyney	7
0	Clarion	17
111		**356**

Nickname: Mountaineers.
Stadium: Van Norman Field, 4,000 capacity. Natural turf.
Colors: Red & Black.
Conference: Pennsylvania State Athl. Conf.
SID: Steve McCloskey, 717-662-4845.
AD: Roger N. Maisner.

MARIETTA

Marietta, OH 45750 ... III

Coach: Gene Epley, Indiana (Pa.) 1965
Record: 11 Years, 47-61-3

1998 SCHEDULE

Waynesburg ■	*Sept. 5
Muskingum	*Sept. 19
Baldwin-Wallace ■	*Sept. 26
Ohio Northern	Oct. 3
John Carroll	Oct. 10
Heidelberg ■	Oct. 17
Mount Union	Oct. 24
Hiram ■	Oct. 31
Capital ■	Nov. 7
Otterbein	Nov. 14

1997 RESULTS (4-6-0)

10	Central (Iowa)	9
18	Capital	28
12	John Carroll	18
17	Baldwin-Wallace	35
51	Otterbein	34
55	Hiram	10
17	Ohio Northern	20
7	Mount Union	69
37	Heidelberg	52
14	Muskingum	12
238		**287**

Nickname: Pioneers.
Stadium: Don Drumm Field (1935), 7,000 capacity. Natural turf.
Colors: Navy Blue & White.
Conference: Ohio Athletic Conference.
SID: Tom Perry, 614-376-4891.
AD: Debora Lazorik.

MARIST

Poughkeepsie, NY 12601 ... I-AA

Coach: Jim Parady, Maine 1984
Record: 6 Years, 35-24-1

1998 SCHEDULE

Georgetown	Sept. 12
Fairfield ■	Sept. 19
St. Peter's	*Sept. 26
St. John's (N.Y.) ■	Oct. 3
Duquesne	Oct. 10
Iona ■	Oct. 17
Wagner	Oct. 24
St. Francis (Pa.) ■	Oct. 31
Canisius ■	Nov. 7
Siena	Nov. 14

1997 RESULTS (6-4-0)

13	Georgetown	19
31	Iona	12
42	St. Peter's	0
24	Duquesne	27
7	St. John's (N.Y.)	24
14	Fairfield	34
21	Wagner	0
26	St. Francis (Pa.)	10
20	Canisius	6
34	Siena	9
232		**141**

Nickname: Red Foxes.
Stadium: Leonidoff Field (1972), 2,500 capacity. Natural turf.
Colors: Red & White.
Conference: Metro Atlantic.
SID: Dawn DeRosa, 914-575-3000.
AD: Timothy S. Murray.

MARS HILL

Mars Hill, NC 28754 ... II

Coach: Tim Clifton, Mercer 1976
Record: 5 Years, 27-24-0

1998 SCHEDULE

West Ga. ■	Sept. 5
Concord ■	Sept. 12
Catawba ■	Sept. 19
Wingate	Sept. 26
Newberry	*Oct. 3
Tusculum	Oct. 10
Carson-Newman ■	Oct. 17
Presbyterian ■	Oct. 24
Samford	Oct. 31
Lenoir-Rhyne	*Nov. 7
Gardner-Webb	Nov. 14

1997 RESULTS (5-5-0)

12	West Ga.	37
35	Concord	25
3	Catawba	37
28	Wingate	7
21	Newberry	17
44	Tusculum	17
20	Carson-Newman	31
14	Presbyterian	24
27	Lenoir-Rhyne	7
15	Gardner-Webb	25
219		**227**

Nickname: Lions.
Stadium: Meares (1965), 5,000 capacity. Natural turf.
Colors: Blue & Gold.
Conference: South Atlantic Conference.
SID: Rick Baker, 704-689-1373.
AD: Ed Hoffmeyer.

MARSHALL

Huntington, WV 25755 ... I-A

Coach: Bob Pruett, Marshall 1965

Record: 2 Years, 25-3-0

1998 SCHEDULE

Akron	*Sept. 5
Troy St. ■	*Sept. 12
South Caro.	*Sept. 19
Eastern Mich.	Sept. 26
Miami (Ohio) ■	*Oct. 3
Ohio	Oct. 10
Kent ■	*Oct. 17
Ball St. ■	Oct. 24
Bowling Green	Oct. 31
Central Mich. ■	Nov. 7
Wofford ■	Nov. 21

1997 RESULTS (10-2-0)

31	West Va.	42
35	Army	25
42	Kent	17
48	Western Ill.	7
42	Ball St.	16
52	Akron	17
21	Miami (Ohio)	45
48	Eastern Mich.	25
45	Central Mich.	17
28	Bowling Green	0
27	Ohio	0
34	Toledo	14
453		**225**

Motor City Bowl

31	Mississippi	34

Nickname: Thundering Herd.
Stadium: Marshall University (1991), 30,000 capacity. Artificial turf.
Colors: Green & White.
Conference: Mid-American.
SID: Clark Haptonstall, 304-696-5275.
AD: Lance West.

MARTIN LUTHER

New Ulm, MN 56073 III

Coach: Dennis Gorsline, Northern Mich. 1965
Record: 27 Years, 93-147-1

1998 SCHEDULE

Trinity Bible (N.D.) ■	Sept. 5
Gust. Adolphus	Sept. 12
Dakota St. ■	Sept. 19
Concordia-St. Paul	Sept. 26
Madison Tech ■	Oct. 3
Northwestern (Minn.) ■	Oct. 10
Mt. Senario ■	Oct. 17
Maranatha Baptist	Oct. 24
Crown	Oct. 31

1997 RESULTS (6-3-0)

70	Trinity Bible (N.D.)	0
21	Luther	14
13	Minn.-Crookston	47
26	Concordia-St. Paul	28
41	Northwestern (Minn.)	12
26	Mt. Senario	29
42	Crown	6
26	Maranatha Baptist	10
41	Crown	21
306		**167**

Nickname: Knights.
Stadium: Martin Luther, 2,200 capacity. Natural turf.
Colors: Black, Red & White.
Conference: Independent.
SID: Nick Guillaume, 507-354-8221.
AD: James M. Unke.

MARYLAND

College Park, MD 20740.......................... I-A

Coach: Ron Vanderlinden, Albion 1978
Record: 1 Year, 2-9-0

1998 SCHEDULE

James Madison ■	*Sept. 5
Virginia	Sept. 12
West Va.	Sept. 19
Temple ■	*Sept. 26
Florida St. ■	Oct. 3
Clemson	Oct. 10
Wake Forest ■	Oct. 17
Georgia Tech [Baltimore, Md.]	Oct. 31
North Caro.	Nov. 7
Duke	Nov. 14
North Caro. St. ■	Nov. 21

1997 RESULTS (2-9-0)

14	Ohio	21
7	Florida St.	50
14	North Caro.	40
24	Temple	21
16	Duke	10
14	West Va.	31
17	Wake Forest	35
9	Clemson	20
0	Virginia	45
28	North Caro. St.	45
18	Georgia Tech	37
161		**355**

Nickname: Terps.
Stadium: Byrd (1950), 48,055 capacity. Natural turf.
Colors: Red, White, Black & Gold.
Conference: Atlantic Coast.
SID: Dave Haglund, 301-314-7064.
AD: Deborah A. Yow.

MARYVILLE (TENN.)

Maryville, TN 37804 III

Coach: Phil Wilks, Marshall 1970
Record: 10 years, 46-52-0

1998 SCHEDULE

Tusculum	Sept. 5
Wilmington (Ohio)	Sept. 19
Rhodes	Sept. 26
Millsaps ■	Oct. 3
Centre ■	Oct. 17
Bethany (W. Va.) ■	Oct. 31
Thomas More	Nov. 7
Emory & Henry	Nov. 14

1997 RESULTS (2-7-0)

24	Thomas More	30
25	Davidson	41
24	Ky. Wesleyan	45
0	Sewanee	31
38	Rhodes	26
22	Centre	36
19	Wilmington (Ohio)	26
27	Emory & Henry	24
14	Tusculum	28
193		**287**

Nickname: Scots.
Stadium: Lloyd Thorton (1951), 2,500 capacity. Natural turf.
Colors: Orange & Garnet.
Conference: Independent.
SID: Eric Etchison, 615-981-8283.
AD: Randy Lambert.

MASSACHUSETTS

Amherst, MA 01003 .... I-AA

Coach: Mark Whipple, Brown 1979
Record: 10 Years, 71-34-0

1998 SCHEDULE

Delaware	*Sept. 3
Richmond	Sept. 12
Buffalo ■	Sept. 26
Hofstra	Oct. 3
James Madison ■	Oct. 10
Connecticut	Oct. 17
Villanova ■	Oct. 24
New Hampshire	Oct. 31
Rhode Island	Nov. 7
Maine ■	Nov. 14
Connecticut ■	Nov. 21

1997 RESULTS (2-9-0)

6	Richmond	21
6	Maine	49
10	James Madison	13
18	Rhode Island	14
10	New Hampshire	28
27	Villanova	49
26	Buffalo	20
9	Delaware	40
13	Hofstra	51
8	Boston U.	33
16	Connecticut	49
149		**367**

Nickname: Minutemen.
Stadium: Warren McGuirk (1965), 17,000 capacity. Natural turf.
Colors: Maroon & White.
Conference: Atlantic 10.
SID: Scott McConnell, 413-545-2439.
AD: Robert K. Marcum.

MIT

Cambridge, MA 02139 III

Coach: Dwight Smith, Bates 1975
Record: 10 Years, 32-47-1

1998 SCHEDULE

Mass. Maritime	Sept. 19
Salve Regina ■	Sept. 26
Curry	Oct. 3
Mass.-Dartmouth ■	Oct. 10
Bri'water (Mass.)	Oct. 17
Nichols	Oct. 24
Worcester St. ■	Oct. 31
Western New Eng.	Nov. 7
Mass.-Boston ■	Nov. 14

1997 RESULTS (5-4-0)

27	Framingham St.	18
10	Western New Eng.	25
23	Worcester Tech	24
7	Salve Regina	28
34	Assumption	30
31	Curry	0
16	Nichols	13
20	Mass.-Boston	15
13	Siena	17
181		**170**

Nickname: Engineers.
Stadium: Steinbrenner (1980), 1,600 capacity. Natural turf.
Colors: Cardinal & Gray.
Conference: New England FB.
SID: Roger F. Crosley, 617-253-7946.
AD: Richard A. Hill.

MASS. MARITIME

Buzzards Bay, MA 02532.......................... III

Coach: Don Ruggeri, Springfield 1962
Record: 25 Years, 125-100-1

1998 SCHEDULE

Coast Guard	Sept. 12
MIT ■	Sept. 19
Maine Maritime	Sept. 26
Westfield St. ■	Oct. 3
Fitchburg St.	Oct. 10
Worcester St. ■	Oct. 17
Mass.-Boston ■	Oct. 24
Nichols	Oct. 31
Framingham St. ■	Nov. 7
Bri'water (Mass.)	Nov. 14

1997 RESULTS (3-7-0)

9	Nichols	20
8	Coast Guard	13
29	Mass.-Dartmouth	41
20	Maine Maritime	13
6	Mass.-Boston	27
45	Fitchburg St.	22
21	Framingham St.	0
26	Westfield St.	28
14	Bri'water (Mass.)	33
28	Worcester St.	49
206		**246**

Nickname: Buccaneers.
Stadium: Commander Ellis (1972), 3,000 capacity.

Natural turf.
Colors: Blue & Gold.
Conference: New England FB.
SID: Leroy Thompson, 508-830-5054.
AD: Robert Corradi.

MASS.-BOSTON

Boston, MA 02125 III

Coach: Gus Giardi, Syracuse 1964
Record: 4 Years, 7-29-0

1998 SCHEDULE

Fitchburg St. ■ ....Sept. 12
Framingham St. ....Sept. 19
Mass.-Dartmouth ■ ....Sept. 26
Nichols ....Oct. 3
Western New Eng. ■ ....Oct. 10
Salve Regina ....Oct. 17
Mass. Maritime ....Oct. 24
Westfield St. ■ ....Oct. 31
Curry ■ ....Nov. 7
MIT ....Nov. 14

1997 RESULTS (3-6-0)

18	Westfield St.	26
14	Bri'water (Mass.)	32
32	Worcester St.	34
27	Mass. Maritime	6
6	Mass.-Dartmouth	43
0	Maine Maritime	12
15	MIT	20
27	Fitchburg St.	6
24	Framingham St.	21
163		**200**

Nickname: Beacons.
Stadium: Clark Field (1981), 750 capacity. Natural turf.
Colors: Blue & White.
Conference: New England FB.
SID: Chuck Sullivan, 617-287-7815.
AD: Charlie Titus.

MASS.-DARTMOUTH

North Dartmouth, MA 02747 III

Coach: Bill Kavanaugh, Stonehill 1972
Record: 8 Years, 45-32-0

1998 SCHEDULE

Western Conn. St. ■ ....Sept. 12
Worcester St. ■ ....Sept. 19
Mass.-Boston ....Sept. 26
Maine Maritime ■ ....Oct. 3
MIT ....Oct. 10
Nichols ■ ....Oct. 17
Western New Eng. ■ ....Oct. 24
Bri'water (Mass.) ....Oct. 31
Salve Regina ■ ....Nov. 7
Curry ....Nov. 14

1997 RESULTS (8-2-0)

39	Curry	12
16	Worcester St.	25
41	Mass. Maritime	29
48	Nichols	14
34	Maine Maritime	7
43	Mass.-Boston	6
32	Fitchburg St.	10
26	Framingham St.	7
48	Westfield St.	23
28	Bri'water (Mass.)	44
355		**177**

Nickname: Corsairs.
Stadium: University, 1,850 capacity. Natural turf.
Colors: Blue, White & Gold.
Conference: New England FB.
SID: Bill Gathright, 508-999-8727.
AD: Robert A. Dowd.

MASS.-LOWELL

Lowell, MA 01854 II

Coach: Sandy Ruggles, Northeastern 1973
Record: 2 Years, 8-12-0

1998 SCHEDULE

New Jersey City ....Sept. 5
Pace ■ ....*Sept. 11
Norwich ■ ....*Sept. 18
Southern Conn. St. ....*Sept. 25
Bentley ■ ....*Oct. 3
Stonehill ■ ....*Oct. 9
Albany (N.Y.) ....Oct. 24
Merrimack ■ ....Oct. 31
Assumption ....Nov. 7
American Int'l ....Nov. 14

1997 RESULTS (2-8-0)

7	New Jersey City	10
7	Pace	29
42	Norwich	13
20	Southern Conn. St.	24
9	Stonehill	21
14	Bentley	47
6	Albany (N.Y.)	22
13	Merrimack	27
29	Assumption	14
0	American Int'l	27
147		**234**

Nickname: River Hawks.
Stadium: Cawley Memorial (1934), 7,000 capacity. Natural turf.
Colors: Red, White & Blue.
Conference: Eastern Football.
SID: Jim Seavey, 508-934-2306.
AD: Dana K. Skinner.

MCMURRY

Abilene, TX 79697 III

Coach: Steve Keenum, McMurry 1980
Record: 5 Years, 11-37-0

1998 SCHEDULE

Trinity (Tex.) ■ ....*Sept. 12
Millsaps ....*Sept. 19
Okla. Panhandle St. ■ ....Sept. 26
Mary Hardin-Baylor ■ ....Oct. 3
Texas Lutheran ....Oct. 10
Sul Ross St. ....Oct. 17
Mississippi Col. ■ ....Oct. 24
Austin ....Oct. 31
Howard Payne ■ ....Nov. 7
Hardin-Simmons ....Nov. 14

1997 RESULTS (5-5-0)

7	Trinity (Tex.)	38
35	Southwestern Aly God	7
32	Okla. Panhandle St.	27
38	Millsaps	7
14	Sul Ross St.	34
25	Hardin-Simmons	34
20	Austin	21
49	Sul Ross St.	29
26	Howard Payne	23
22	Mississippi Col.	45
268		**265**

Nickname: Indians.
Stadium: Indian (1935), 4,500 capacity. Natural turf.
Colors: Maroon & White.
Conference: American Southwest.
SID: Trenten Hilburn, 915-691-6376.
AD: Marvin Stringfellow.

MCNEESE ST.

Lake Charles, LA 70609 ....I-AA

Coach: Bobby Keasler, Northeast La. 1970
Record: 8 Years, 69-31-2

1998 SCHEDULE

Southeastern Okla. ■ ....*Sept. 5
Northern Iowa ....*Sept. 12
Southern Utah ....*Sept. 19
Ark.-Monticello ■ ....*Sept. 26
Jacksonville St. ■ ....*Oct. 10
Northwestern St. ....*Oct. 15
Stephen F. Austin ■ ....*Oct. 24
Sam Houston St. ....Oct. 31
Southwest Tex. St. ■ ....*Nov. 7
Troy St. ....Nov. 14
Nicholls St. ■ ....*Nov. 21

1997 RESULTS (10-1-0)

31	Southeastern Okla.	0
28	Southwest Mo. St.	16
22	Northern Iowa	5
27	Jacksonville St.	6
55	Arkansas Tech	7
50	Northwestern St.	7
7	Stephen F. Austin	13
38	Sam Houston St.	21
31	Southwest Tex. St.	21
10	Troy St.	7
31	Nicholls St.	13
330		**116**

I-AA Championship

19	Montana	14
14	Western Ill.	12
23	Delaware	21
9	Youngstown St.	10

Nickname: Cowboys.
Stadium: Cowboy (1965), 17,500 capacity. Natural turf.
Colors: Blue & Gold.
Conference: Southland.
SID: Louis Bonnette, 318-475-5207.
AD: Sonny Watkins.

MEMPHIS

Memphis, TN 38152 ....I-A

Coach: Rip Scherer, William & Mary 1974
Record: 7 Years, 40-41-0

1998 SCHEDULE

Mississippi ....Sept. 5
Mississippi St. ■ ....Sept. 12
Minnesota ....Sept. 19
Houston ....Oct. 3
Arkansas ■ ....*Oct. 10
Cincinnati ■ ....*Oct. 17
Louisville ....Oct. 24
Arkansas St. ■ ....Oct. 31
Tulane ■ ....Nov. 7
Southern Miss. ....*Nov. 14
East Caro. ■ ....Nov. 21

1997 RESULTS (4-7-0)

10	Mississippi St.	13
28	UAB	7
21	Michigan St.	51
17	Minnesota	20
17	Cincinnati	20
38	Arkansas St.	9
10	East Caro.	32
24	Houston	3
14	Tulane	26
21	Louisville	20
18	Southern Miss.	42
218		**243**

Nickname: Tigers.
Stadium: Liberty Bowl (1965), 62,380 capacity. Natural turf.
Colors: Blue & Gray.
Conference: Conference USA.
SID: Bob Winn, 901-678-2337.
AD: R. C. Johnson.

MENLO

Atherton, CA 94027 III

Coach: Ken Margerum, Stanford 1981
Record: 1 Year, 5-5-0

1998 SCHEDULE

Cal Lutheran ....Sept. 5
Whittier ■ ....Sept. 12
Wis.-Oshkosh ■ ....Sept. 19
Southern Ore. ....Sept. 26
Redlands ....*Oct. 10
Merchant Marine ■ ....Oct. 17
Chapman ■ ....Oct. 24
Humboldt St. ■ ....Oct. 31
Whitworth ....Nov. 7

La Verne ....Nov. 14

1997 RESULTS (5-5-0)

32	Cal Lutheran	21
13	Central Mo. St.	53
20	Whittier	26
20	Southern Ore.	44
41	Occidental	7
21	Chapman	24
20	Redlands	26
35	Pomona-Pitzer	28
58	Claremont-M-S	22
42	La Verne	13
302		**264**

Nickname: Oaks.
Stadium: Connor Field (1972), 1,000 capacity. Natural turf.
Colors: Navy Blue & White.
Conference: Independent.
SID: Matt Monroe, 415-688-3780.
AD: Craig Walsh.

MERCHANT MARINE

Kings Point, NY 11024 III

Coach: Charlie Pravata, Adelphi 1972
Record: 7 Years, 42-23-2

1998 SCHEDULE

Norwich ....Sept. 12
Springfield ■ ....Sept. 19
Johns Hopkins ....Sept. 26
Worcester Tech ....Oct. 3
Plymouth St. ■ ....Oct. 10
Menlo ....Oct. 17
Ursinus ■ ....Oct. 24
Western Conn. St. ....Nov. 7
Coast Guard ■ ....Nov. 14

1997 RESULTS (7-2-0)

41	Claremont-M-S	16
25	Norwich	0
42	Springfield	28
27	Johns Hopkins	14
20	Plymouth St.	33
22	Worcester Tech	19
61	Ursinus	18
36	Western Conn. St.	0
16	Coast Guard	34
290		**162**

ECAC III Playoff

25	Grove City	12

Nickname: Mariners.
Stadium: Capt. Tomb Field (1945), 5,840 capacity. Natural turf.
Colors: Blue & Gray.
Conference: Freedom FB.
SID: Kim Robinson, 516-773-5455.
AD: Susan Petersen-Lubow.

MERCYHURST

Erie, PA 16546 II

Coach: Joe Kimball, Syracuse 1975
Record: 13 Years, 62-59-2

1998 SCHEDULE

Wayne St. (Mich.) ....Sept. 5
Michigan Tech ■ ....Sept. 12
St. Francis (Ill.) ....*Sept. 19
Indianapolis ....Sept. 26
Hillsdale ■ ....Oct. 3
Grand Valley St. ■ ....Oct. 10
Westminster (Pa.) ....Oct. 17
Ashland ■ ....Oct. 24
Saginaw Valley ....Oct. 31
Findlay ■ ....Nov. 7

1997 RESULTS (6-3-0)

13	Baldwin-Wallace	30
10	Ithaca	5
14	Findlay	44
14	St. John Fisher	7
45	St. Francis (Pa.)	13
35	Gannon	18
14	Buffalo St.	16
17	Robert Morris	10
31	Ohio Wesleyan	7
193		**150**

Nickname: Lakers.
Stadium: Erie Veteran Memorial (1958), 10,500 capacity. Artificial turf.
Colors: Blue & Green.
Conference: Independent.
SID: John Leisering, 814-824-2525.
AD: Peter J. Russo.

MERRIMACK

North Andover, MA 01845 II

Coach: Thomas Caito, Boston U. 1960
Record: 2 Years, 8-10-0

1998 SCHEDULE

St. John Fisher ■ ....Sept. 5
Bentley ■ ....Sept. 12
Assumption ....Sept. 19
Stonehill ....Sept. 26
American Int'l ■ ....Oct. 3
Albany (N.Y.) ■ ....Oct. 10
LIU-C.W. Post ....Oct. 17
Stony Brook ■ ....Oct. 24
Mass.-Lowell ....Oct. 31

1997 RESULTS (3-6-0)

12	Bentley	14
33	Assumption	7
13	Stonehill	16
3	Albany (N.Y.)	42
8	American Int'l	21
17	Sacred Heart	7
6	Stony Brook	17
27	Mass.-Lowell	13
12	Western New Eng.	14
131		**151**

Nickname: Warriors.
Stadium: Merrimack, 2,000 capacity. Natural turf.
Colors: Navy Blue & Gold.
Conference: Eastern Football.
SID: Tom Caraccioli, 508-837-5341.
AD: Robert M. De Gregorio Jr.

MESA ST.

Grand Junction, CO 81501 II

Coach: Joe Ramunno, Wyoming 1984
(First year as head coach)

1998 SCHEDULE

OkLa. Panhandle St. ....*Sept. 5
Western Mont. ■ ....*Sept. 12
Western St. (Colo.) ....Sept. 19
Chadron St. ■ ....Sept. 26
Adams St. ■ ....*Oct. 3
Fort Hays St. ....*Oct. 10
Colorado Mines ....Oct. 17
Neb.-Kearney ■ ....Oct. 24
Fort Lewis ■ ....Oct. 31
N. M. Highlands ....Nov. 7
Western N. Mex. ....Nov. 14

1997 RESULTS (3-8-0)

7	Northern Colo.	28
47	OkLa. Panhandle St.	13
18	Chadron St.	20
46	Adams St.	30
19	Fort Hays St.	34
18	Colorado Mines	21
22	Neb.-Kearney	46
52	Fort Lewis	16
7	N. M. Highlands	34
41	Western N. Mex.	43
3	Western St. (Colo.)	27
280		**312**

Nickname: Mavericks.
Stadium: Stocker (1949), 8,000 capacity. Natural turf.
Colors: Cardinal, Gold & White.
Conference: Rocky Mountain Athletic Conf.
SID: Tish Elliott, 970-248-1143.
AD: Doug Schakel.

METHODIST

Fayetteville, NC 28311 III

Coach: Jim Sypult, West Va. 1967
Record: 6 Years, 29-31-0

1998 SCHEDULE

Chowan ....Sept. 5
Guilford ■ ....Sept. 12
Salisbury St. ■ ....Sept. 19
Newport News ....Sept. 26
Ferrum ■ ....Oct. 3
Jacksonville ....Oct. 10
Davidson ■ ....Oct. 17
Greensboro ....Oct. 31
Hampden-Sydney ■ ....Nov. 7
Frostburg St. ....Nov. 14

1997 RESULTS (9-1-0)

25	Chowan	20
26	Guilford	19
27	Newport News	13
29	Salisbury St.	22
18	Bridgewater (Va.)	0
19	Davidson	16
12	Ferrum	31
41	Greensboro	12
7	Hampden-Sydney	0
40	Frostburg St.	12
244		**145**

Nickname: Monarchs.
Stadium: Monarch Field (1989), 1,500 capacity. Natural turf.
Colors: Green & Gold.
Conference: Atlantic Central FB.
SID: Matt Eviston, 910-630-7172.
AD: Rita Wiggs.

MIAMI (FLA.)

Coral Gables, FL 33146 ....I-A

Coach: Butch Davis, Arkansas 1974
Record: 3 Years, 22-12-0

1998 SCHEDULE

East Tenn. St. ■ ....*Sept. 5
Cincinnati ....Sept. 12
Virginia Tech ■ ....*Sept. 19
UCLA ■ ....Sept. 26
Rutgers ....Oct. 3
Florida St. ■ ....Oct. 10
West Va. ....Oct. 24
Boston College ■ ....Oct. 31
Temple ....Nov. 14
Pittsburgh ■ ....*Nov. 19
Syracuse ....Nov. 28

1997 RESULTS (5-6-0)

45	Baylor	14
12	Arizona St.	23
17	Pittsburgh	21
17	West Va.	28
0	Florida St.	47
45	Boston College	44
47	Temple	15
42	Arkansas St.	10
25	Virginia Tech	27
51	Rutgers	23
13	Syracuse	33
314		**285**

Nickname: Hurricanes.
Stadium: Orange Bowl (1935), 74,476 capacity. Natural turf.
Colors: Orange, Green & White.
Conference: Big East.
SID: Bob Burda, 305-284-3244.
AD: Paul T. Dee.

MIAMI (OHIO)

Oxford, OH 45056 ....I-A

Coach: Randy Walker, Miami (Ohio) 1976
Record: 8 Years, 49-34-5

1998 SCHEDULE

North Caro.	*Sept. 5
Army	Sept. 12
Toledo ■	Sept. 26
Marshall	*Oct. 3
Bowling Green ■	Oct. 10
Ball St.	Oct. 17
Cincinnati	Oct. 24
Ohio ■	Oct. 31
Northern Ill.	Nov. 7
Kent ■	Nov. 14
Akron	Nov. 21

1997 RESULTS (8-3-0)

27	Ball St.	10
21	Bowling Green	28
49	Akron	20
38	Army	14
24	Virginia Tech	17
62	Kent	26
45	Marshall	21
31	Cincinnati	34
28	Toledo	35
45	Ohio	21
42	Northern Ill.	0
412		**226**

Nickname: RedHawks.
Stadium: Fred C. Yager (1983), 30,012 capacity. Natural turf.
Colors: Red & White.
Conference: Mid-American.
SID: Mike Wolf, 513-529-4327.
AD: Joel Maturi.

MICHIGAN

Ann Arbor, MI 48109 ....I-A

Coach: Lloyd Carr, Northern Mich. 1968
Record: 3 Years, 29-8-0

1998 SCHEDULE

Notre Dame	Sept. 5
Syracuse ■	Sept. 12
Eastern Mich. ■	Sept. 19
Michigan St. ■	Sept. 26
Iowa	Oct. 3
Northwestern	*Oct. 17
Indiana ■	Oct. 24
Minnesota	Oct. 31
Penn St. ■	Nov. 7
Wisconsin ■	Nov. 14
Ohio St.	Nov. 21
Hawaii	*Nov. 28

1997 RESULTS (11-0-0)

27	Colorado	3
38	Baylor	3
21	Notre Dame	14
37	Indiana	0
23	Northwestern	6
28	Iowa	24
23	Michigan St.	7
24	Minnesota	3
34	Penn St.	8
26	Wisconsin	16
20	Ohio St.	14
301		**98**

Rose Bowl

21	Washington St.	16

Nickname: Wolverines.
Stadium: Michigan (1927), 102,501 capacity. Natural turf.
Colors: Maize & Blue.
Conference: Big Ten.
SID: Bruce Madej, 313-763-4423.
AD: Tom A. Goss.

MICHIGAN ST.

East Lansing, MI 48824 ....I-A

Coach: Nick Saban, Kent 1973
Record: 4 Years, 28-18-1

1998 SCHEDULE

Colorado St. ■	Aug. 29
Oregon	Sept. 5
Notre Dame ■	*Sept. 12
Michigan	Sept. 26
Central Mich. ■	Oct. 3
Indiana ■	Oct. 10
Minnesota	Oct. 24
Northwestern ■	Oct. 31
Ohio St.	Nov. 7
Purdue ■	Nov. 14
Illinois ■	Nov. 21
Penn St.	Nov. 28

1997 RESULTS (7-4-0)

42	Western Mich.	10
51	Memphis	21
23	Notre Dame	7
31	Minnesota	10
38	Indiana	6
17	Northwestern	19
7	Michigan	23
13	Ohio St.	37
21	Purdue	22
27	Illinois	17
49	Penn St.	14
319		**186**

Aloha Bowl

23	Washington	51

Nickname: Spartans.
Stadium: Spartan (1957), 72,027 capacity. Artificial turf.
Colors: Green & White.
Conference: Big Ten.
SID: Ken Hoffman, 517-355-2271.
AD: Merritt J. Norvell Jr.

MICHIGAN TECH

Houghton, MI 49931 II

Coach: Bernie Anderson, Northern Mich. 1978
Record: 11 Years, 48-60-0

1998 SCHEDULE

Northwood	*Sept. 3
Mercyhurst	Sept. 12
Hillsdale ■	Sept. 19
St. Francis (Ill.)	*Sept. 26
Saginaw Valley	Oct. 3
Ashland ■	Oct. 10
Northern Mich.	Oct. 17
Ferris St. ■	Oct. 24
Wayne St. (Mich.)	Oct. 31
Grand Valley St. ■	Nov. 7

1997 RESULTS (2-8-0)

14	Northwood	52
7	Ashland	31
28	Saginaw Valley	45
29	Indianapolis	35
52	St. Francis (Ill.)	28
21	Grand Valley St.	49
34	Ferris St.	24
28	Wayne St. (Mich.)	35
19	Hillsdale	35
12	Northern Mich.	17
244		**351**

Nickname: Huskies.
Stadium: Sherman Field (1954), 3,000 capacity. Natural turf.
Colors: Silver, Gold & Black.
Conference: Midwest Intercoll.
SID: Dave Fischer, 906-487-2350.
AD: J. Richard Yeo.

MIDDLE TENN. ST.

Murfreesboro, TN 37132 ....I-AA

Coach: Boots Donnelly, Middle Tenn. 1965
Record: 21 Years, 149-89-1

1998 SCHEDULE

Tennessee St. ■	*Sept. 5
Illinois	*Sept. 12
Jacksonville St.	*Sept. 19
Eastern Ky. ■	*Sept. 26
Tennessee Tech	Oct. 3
Murray St. ■	*Oct. 10
Eastern Ill. ■	*Oct. 24
Southeast Mo. St.	Oct. 31
Tenn.-Martin	Nov. 7
UAB	Nov. 14

1997 RESULTS (4-6-0)

16	Tennessee St.	25
24	Chattanooga	33
17	Murray St.	35
27	Jacksonville St.	16
37	Tenn.-Martin	24
17	Eastern Ill.	30
55	Southeast Mo. St.	6
59	Austin Peay	10
20	Eastern Ky.	35
20	Tennessee Tech	30
292		**244**

Nickname: Blue Raiders.
Stadium: Johnny Floyd (1969), 31,000 capacity. Artificial turf.
Colors: Blue & White.
Conference: Ohio Valley.
SID: Ed Given, 615-898-2450.
AD: Lee G. Fowler.

MIDDLEBURY

Middlebury, VT 05753 III

Coach: Mickey Heinecken, Delaware 1961
Record: 25 Years, 110-88-2

1998 SCHEDULE

Wesleyan (Conn.) ■	Sept. 26
Colby	Oct. 3
Amherst ■	Oct. 10
Williams	Oct. 17
Bates ■	Oct. 24
Trinity (Conn.)	Oct. 31
Hamilton	Nov. 7
Tufts ■	Nov. 14

1997 RESULTS (4-4-0)

43	Bowdoin	0
27	Colby	15
17	Amherst	22
22	Williams	25
35	Bates	20
22	Trinity (Conn.)	27
41	Hamilton	7
15	Tufts	17
222		**133**

Nickname: Panthers.
Stadium: Alumni (1991), 3,500 capacity. Natural turf.
Colors: Blue & White.
Conference: NESCAC.
SID: Brad Nadeau, 802-443-5193.
AD: Russell Reilly.

MIDWESTERN ST.

Wichita Falls, TX 76308 II

Coach: Hank McClung, Eastern N. M. 1986
Record: 3 Years, 8-16-0

1998 SCHEDULE

Northwest Mo. St.	Sept. 5
Hardin-Simmons ■	*Sept. 12
Ouachita Baptist ■	Sept. 19
Northeastern St.	Sept. 26
Tex. A&M-Commerce ■	*Oct. 3
Abilene Christian ■	Oct. 10
Texas A&M-Kingsville	*Oct. 17
Angelo St.	*Oct. 24
West Tex. A&M ■	Oct. 31
Tarleton St. ■	Nov. 7
Eastern N.M.	Nov. 14

1997 RESULTS (3-7-0)

14	Northwest Mo. St.	52
30	Ouachita Baptist	28
13	Northeastern St.	10
7	Tex. A&M-Commerce	49
14	Abilene Christian	34

7	Texas A&M-Kingsville	30
9	Angelo St.	30
7	West Tex. A&M	51
28	Tarleton St.	29
24	Eastern N.M.	7
153		**320**

Nickname: Indians.
Stadium: Memorial, 14,500 capacity. Artificial turf.
Colors: Maroon & Gold.
Conference: Lone Star Conference.
SID: Stan Wagnon, 817-689-4769.
AD: Robert D. Mc Bee.

MILES

Birmingham, AL 35208 ... II

Coach: Cecil Leonard, Tuskegee 1969
Record: 4 Years, 16-22-1

1998 SCHEDULE

Kentucky St. ■	Aug. 29
Albany St. (Ga.)	Sept. 5
Morehouse ■	Sept. 12
Tuskegee	Sept. 19
Clark Atlanta	*Sept. 26
Morris Brown ■	Oct. 3
Fort Valley St. ■	Oct. 10
Lane	Oct. 17
Alabama A&M	Oct. 24
Savannah St. ■	Nov. 7

1997 RESULTS (4-6-0)

28	Kentucky St.	15
12	Albany St. (Ga.)	22
36	Morehouse	9
20	Tuskegee	17
32	Clark Atlanta	17
30	Morris Brown	32
7	Fort Valley St.	9
41	Morehead St.	56
26	Alabama A&M	31
28	Savannah St.	34
260		**242**

Nickname: Golden Bears.
Stadium: Alumni, 3,400 capacity. Natural turf.
Colors: Purple & Gold.
Conference: Southern Intercol. Ath. Conf.
SID: Willie K. Patterson Jr., 205-923-8323.
AD: Augustus James.

MILLERSVILLE

Millersville, PA 17551 ... II

Coach: Gene Carpenter, Huron 1963
Record: 29 Years, 197-81-6

1998 SCHEDULE

Clarion	Sept. 12
New Haven ■	Sept. 19
Edinboro ■	*Sept. 26
Mansfield	Oct. 3
Bloomsburg ■	*Oct. 10
Indiana (Pa.)	Oct. 17
West Chester ■	Oct. 24
Kutztown	Oct. 31
East Stroudsburg ■	Nov. 7
Cheyney	Nov. 14

1997 RESULTS (7-3-0)

31	Clarion	25
10	New Haven	53
37	Shippensburg	27
42	Mansfield	6
21	Lock Haven	6
8	Bloomsburg	24
21	Kutztown	24
21	West Chester	7
47	East Stroudsburg	13
39	Cheyney	14
277		**199**

Nickname: Marauders.
Stadium: Biemesderfer (1970), 6,500 capacity. Natural turf.
Colors: Black & Gold.
Conference: Pennsylvania State Athl. Conf.
SID: Greg Wright, 717-872-3100.
AD: Daniel N. Audette.

MILLIKIN

Decatur, IL 62522 ... III

Coach: Doug Neibuhr, Millikin 1975
Record: 9 Years, 57-29-1

1998 SCHEDULE

Aurora	Sept. 19
Blackburn	Sept. 26
Augustana (Ill.) ■	Oct. 3
North Park ■	Oct. 10
North Central	Oct. 17
Carthage	*Oct. 24
Wheaton (Ill.) ■	Oct. 31
Ill. Wesleyan	Nov. 7
Elmhurst ■	Nov. 14

1997 RESULTS (4-5-0)

11	Trinity (Tex.)	20
17	Iowa Wesleyan	21
51	Elmhurst	7
17	Ill. Wesleyan	13
30	Wheaton (Ill.)	26
17	Carthage	22
31	North Park	0
6	North Central	44
0	Augustana (Ill.)	18
180		**171**

Nickname: Big Blue.
Stadium: Frank M. Lindsay Field (1987), 4,000 capacity. Natural turf.
Colors: Royal & White.
Conference: College Conf. of Ill. & Wisc.
SID: David Johnson, 217-424-6350.
AD: Lori Kerans.

MILLSAPS

Jackson, MS 39210 ... III

Coach: Ron Jurney, Millsaps 1977
Record: 5 Years, 23-30-0

1998 SCHEDULE

Austin	Sept. 5
McMurry ■	*Sept. 19
Colorado Col. ■	*Sept. 26
Maryville (Tenn.)	Oct. 3
Centre ■	Oct. 10
Rose-Hulman	Oct. 17
DePauw ■	*Oct. 24
Sewanee	Oct. 31
Rhodes	Nov. 7
Trinity (Tex.) ■	Nov. 14

1997 RESULTS (3-7-0)

44	Austin	15
19	Rhodes	22
17	Rose-Hulman	37
56	Greenville	12
7	McMurry	38
21	Centre	43
34	Tusculum	51
30	Sewanee	56
36	Rhodes	26
13	Trinity (Tex.)	45
277		**345**

Nickname: Majors.
Stadium: Alumni Field (1920), 4,000 capacity. Natural turf.
Colors: Purple & White.
Conference: Southern Collegiate Ath. Conf.
SID: Richard Moser, 601-974-1195.
AD: Ron Jurney.

MINNESOTA

Minneapolis, MN 55455 ... I-A

Coach: Glen Mason, Ohio St. 1972
Record: 12 Years, 62-73-1

1998 SCHEDULE

Arkansas St. ■	Sept. 5
Houston	*Sept. 12
Memphis ■	Sept. 19
Purdue	Oct. 3
Penn St. ■	Oct. 10
Ohio St.	Oct. 17
Michigan St. ■	Oct. 24
Michigan ■	Oct. 31
Wisconsin	Nov. 7
Indiana	Nov. 14
Iowa ■	Nov. 21

1997 RESULTS (3-9-0)

3	Hawaii	17
53	Iowa St.	29
20	Memphis	17
43	Houston	45
10	Michigan St.	31
43	Purdue	59
15	Penn St.	16
21	Wisconsin	22
3	Michigan	24
3	Ohio St.	31
24	Indiana	12
0	Iowa	31
238		**334**

Nickname: Golden Gophers.
Stadium: Metrodome (1982), 63,669 capacity. Artificial turf.
Colors: Maroon & Gold.
Conference: Big Ten.
SID: Marc Ryan, 612-625-4090.
AD: Mark C. Dienhart.

MINN.-DULUTH

Duluth, MN 55812 ... II

Coach: James Malosky, Minnesota 1951
Record: 40 Years, 255-125-13

1998 SCHEDULE

Mankato St.	Sept. 5
Northern Mich.	*Sept. 12
Wis.-Eau Claire ■	*Sept. 19
Southwest St. ■	Sept. 26
Moorhead St.	Oct. 3
Winona St. ■	Oct. 10
Minn.-Morris	Oct. 17
Northern St. ■	Oct. 24
Bemidji St.	Oct. 31
Wayne St. (Neb.) ■	Nov. 7
Moorhead St. [Minneapolis, Minn.]	Nov. 14

1997 RESULTS (4-6-0)

7	Northern Mich.	24
20	Mankato St.	31
13	St. Cloud St.	25
6	Northern Ariz.	40
14	Southwest St.	20
31	Moorhead St.	14
35	Winona St.	63
48	Minn.-Morris	7
35	Northern St.	7
41	Bemidji St.	0
250		**231**

Nickname: Bulldogs.
Stadium: Griggs Field (1966), 4,000 capacity. Artificial turf.
Colors: Maroon & Gold.
Conference: Northern Sun.
SID: Bob Nygaard, 218-726-8191.
AD: Robert Corran.

MINN.-MORRIS

Morris, MN 56267 ... II

Coach: Ken Crandall, Fort Hays St. 1990
(First year as head coach)

1998 SCHEDULE

Wis.-Stout	*Sept. 12
Minn.-Crookston ■	Sept. 19
Wis.-Eau Claire	Sept. 26
Northern St. ■	Oct. 3
Bemidji St.	Oct. 10
Minn.-Duluth ■	Oct. 17
Southwest St.	Oct. 24

Moorhead St. ■ ....Oct. 31
Winona St. ....Nov. 7
Mayville St. [Minneapolis, Minn.] ....Nov. 14

1997 RESULTS (3-7-0)

34 Minn.-Crookston 54
22 Northwestern (Iowa) 19
19 Winona St. 52
10 Minot St. 35
19 Northern St. 33
45 Bemidji St. 28
7 Minn.-Duluth 48
7 Southwest St. 32
14 Moorhead St. 50
41 Bemidji St. 34
218 **385**

Nickname: Cougars.
Stadium: UMM Field, 5,000 capacity. Natural turf.
Colors: Maroon & Gold.
Conference: Northern Sun.
SID: Broderick Powell, 612-589-6423.
AD: Mark Fohl.

MISSISSIPPI

University, MS 38677 ....I-A

Coach: Tommy Tuberville, Southern Ark. 1976
Record: 3 Years, 19-15-0

1998 SCHEDULE

Memphis ■ ....Sept. 5
Auburn ■ ....*Sept. 12
Vanderbilt ....Sept. 19
Southern Methodist ....Sept. 26
South Caro. ■ ....Oct. 3
Alabama ....Oct. 10
Arkansas St. ■ ....Oct. 24
LSU ■ ....Oct. 31
Arkansas ....Nov. 7
Georgia ....Nov. 21
Mississippi St. ■ ....*Nov. 26

1997 RESULTS (7-4-0)

24 Central Fla. 23
23 Southern Methodist 15
9 Auburn 19
15 Vanderbilt 3
17 Tennessee 31
36 LSU 21
20 Alabama 29
19 Arkansas 9
41 Tulane 24
14 Georgia 21
15 Mississippi St. 14
233 **209**

Motor City Bowl

34 Marshall 31

Nickname: Rebels.
Stadium: Vaught-Hemingway (1941), 50,577 capacity. Natural turf.
Colors: Red & Blue.
Conference: Southeastern.
SID: Langston Rogers, 601-232-7522.
AD: James T. Boone.

MISSISSIPPI COL.

Clinton, MS 39058 III

Coach: Terry McMillan, Southern Miss. 1969
Record: 7 Years, 35-32-5

1998 SCHEDULE

Georgetown (Ky.) ■ ....Sept. 12
Bethel (Tenn.) ....Sept. 19
Jacksonville ■ ....Sept. 26
Howard Payne ■ ....Oct. 3
Hardin-Simmons ....Oct. 10
Mary Hardin-Baylor ■ ....Oct. 17
McMurry ....Oct. 24
Sul Ross St. ■ ....Oct. 31
Texas Lutheran ....Nov. 7
Austin ....Nov. 14

1997 RESULTS (8-2-0)

26 Tusculum 19
56 Bethel (Tenn.) 10
37 Lambuth 10
41 Georgetown (Ky.) 32
21 West Ala. 38
15 Austin 17
31 Sul Ross St. 26
13 Howard Payne 0
17 Hardin-Simmons 14
45 McMurry 22
302 **188**

Nickname: Choctaws.
Stadium: Robinson-Hale (1985), 8,500 capacity. Natural turf.
Colors: Blue & Gold.
Conference: American Southwest.
SID: Pete Smith, 601-925-3255.
AD: Terry Mc Millan.

MISSISSIPPI ST.

Miss. State, MS 39762 ....I-A

Coach: Jackie Sherrill, Alabama 1966
Record: 20 Years, 146-82-4

1998 SCHEDULE

Vanderbilt ■ ....*Sept. 5
Memphis ....Sept. 12
Oklahoma St. ....*Sept. 19
South Caro. ....*Sept. 26
Auburn ■ ....*Oct. 10
East Tenn. St. ■ ....Oct. 17
LSU ....*Oct. 24
Kentucky ....Nov. 7
Alabama ■ ....Nov. 14
Arkansas ■ ....Nov. 21
Mississippi ....*Nov. 26

1997 RESULTS (7-4-0)

13 Memphis 10
35 Kentucky 27
9 LSU 24
37 South Caro. 17
0 Georgia 47
24 Northeast La. 10
35 Central Fla. 28
20 Auburn 0
32 Alabama 20
7 Arkansas 17
14 Mississippi 15
226 **215**

Nickname: Bulldogs.
Stadium: Scott Field (1935), 40,656 capacity. Natural turf.
Colors: Maroon & White.
Conference: Southeastern.
SID: Mike Nemeth, 601-325-2703.
AD: Larry Templeton.

MISSISSIPPI VAL.

Itta Bena, MS 38941 ....I-AA

Coach: Larry Dorsey, Tennessee St. 1976
Record: 8 Years, 36-44-3

1998 SCHEDULE

Ark.-Pine Bluff ■ ....*Sept. 5
Nicholls St. ....*Sept. 12
Alabama A&M ....*Sept. 19
Jackson St. ....*Sept. 26
Southern U. ....*Oct. 3
Grambling ■ ....*Oct. 10
Albany St. (Ga.) ■ ....Oct. 17
Texas Southern ....*Oct. 24
Prairie View ■ ....Oct. 31
Alcorn St. ■ ....Nov. 7
Alabama St. ....Nov. 14

1997 RESULTS (4-6-0)

30 Southern U. 51
7 Ark.-Pine Bluff 15
8 Alabama A&M 23
31 Jackson St. 48
13 Grambling 20
17 Lane 14
13 Texas Southern 10
27 Prairie View 0
18 Alcorn St. 23
34 Alabama St. 10
198 **214**

Nickname: Delta Devils.
Stadium: Magnolia (1958), 10,500 capacity. Natural turf.
Colors: Green & White.
Conference: Southwestern.
SID: Chuck Prophet, 601-254-3551.
AD: Charles Prophet.

MISSOURI

Columbia, MO 65211 ....I-A

Coach: Larry Smith, Bowling Green 1962
Record: 21 Years, 128-107-7

1998 SCHEDULE

Bowling Green ■ ....*Sept. 5
Kansas ■ ....*Sept. 12
Ohio St. ....Sept. 19
Northwestern St. ■ ....Oct. 3
Iowa St. ....Oct. 10
Oklahoma ■ ....Oct. 17
Nebraska ....Oct. 24
Texas Tech ....Oct. 31
Colorado ■ ....Nov. 7
Texas A&M ....Nov. 14
Kansas St. ■ ....Nov. 21

1997 RESULTS (7-4-0)

44 Eastern Mich. 24
7 Kansas 15
42 Tulsa 21
10 Ohio St. 31
45 Iowa St. 21
11 Kansas St. 41
37 Texas 29
51 Oklahoma St. 50
41 Colorado 31
38 Nebraska 45
42 Baylor 24
368 **332**

Holiday Bowl

24 Colorado St. 35

Nickname: Tigers.
Stadium: Memorial/Faurot Fld (1926), 62,000 capacity. Natural turf.
Colors: Old Gold & Black.
Conference: Big 12.
SID: Bob Brendel, 573-882-0712.
AD: Michael F. Alden.

MO. SOUTHERN ST.

Joplin, MO 64801 II

Coach: Greg Gregory, Richmond 1980
(First year as head coach)

1998 SCHEDULE

Northeastern St. ....*Sept. 12
Northwest Mo. St. ■ ....*Sept. 17
Pittsburg St. ....*Sept. 26
Mo. Western St. ■ ....*Oct. 3
Central Mo. St. ■ ....*Oct. 10
Emporia St. ....Oct. 17
Washburn ■ ....Oct. 24
Mo.-Rolla ....Oct. 31
Southwest Baptist ■ ....*Nov. 5
Truman St. ....Nov. 14

1997 RESULTS (7-3-0)

24 Northeastern St. 16
26 Northwest Mo. St. 31
14 Pittsburg St. 42
35 Mo. Western St. 22
10 Central Mo. St. 31
40 Emporia St. 39
17 Washburn 14
35 Mo.-Rolla 3
35 Southwest Baptist 10
40 Truman St. 32
276 **240**

Nickname: Lions.
Stadium: Fred G. Hughes (1975), 7,000 capacity. Artificial turf.
Colors: Green & Gold.
Conference: MIAA.
SID: Joe Moore, 417-625-9359.
AD: Jim Frazier.

MO. WESTERN ST.

St. Joseph, MO 64507 II

Coach: Jerry Partridge, Mo. Western St. 1985
Record: 1 Year, 5-6-0

1998 SCHEDULE

Neb.-Kearney ....Sept. 5
Mankato St. ■ ....*Sept. 12
Truman St. ■ ....*Sept. 19
Northwest Mo. St. ....Sept. 26
Mo. Southern St. ....*Oct. 3
Emporia St. ■ ....*Oct. 8
Washburn ....Oct. 17
Mo.-Rolla ■ ....Oct. 24
Southwest Baptist ....Oct. 31
Pittsburg St. ■ ....Nov. 7
Central Mo. St. ....*Nov. 12

1997 RESULTS (5-6-0)

39 Neb.-Kearney 16
49 Quincy 7
17 Truman St. 31
13 Northwest Mo. St. 52
22 Mo. Southern St. 35
15 Emporia St. 27
13 Washburn 12
0 Mo.-Rolla 17
31 Southwest Baptist 6
14 Pittsburg St. 21
27 Central Mo. St. 24
240 **248**

Nickname: Griffons.
Stadium: Spratt (1979), 6,000 capacity. Natural turf.
Colors: Black & Gold.
Conference: MIAA.
SID: Pat Madden, 816-271-4257.
AD: Don Kaverman.

MO.-ROLLA

Rolla, MO 65401 II

Coach: Jim Anderson, Missouri 1969
Record: 6 Years, 17-46-1

1998 SCHEDULE

Quincy ■ ....Sept. 5
Missouri Valley ■ ....Sept. 12
Central Mo. St. ....Sept. 19
Washburn ■ ....Sept. 26
Pittsburg St. ■ ....Oct. 3
Northwest Mo. St. ....Oct. 10
Truman St. ■ ....Oct. 17
Mo. Western St. ....Oct. 24
Mo. Southern St. ■ ....Oct. 31
Emporia St. ....Nov. 7
Southwest Baptist ....Nov. 14

1997 RESULTS (3-8-0)

40 Quincy 0
10 Missouri Valley 14
14 Central Mo. St. 44
13 Washburn 27
7 Pittsburg St. 42
3 Northwest Mo. St. 38
7 Truman St. 56
17 Mo. Western St. 0
3 Mo. Southern St. 35
20 Emporia St. 77
19 Southwest Baptist 0
153 **333**

Nickname: Miners.
Stadium: Jackling Field (1967), 8,000 capacity. Natural turf.
Colors: Silver & Gold.
Conference: MIAA.
SID: John Kean, 314-341-4140.
AD: Mark Mullin.

MONMOUTH (ILL.)

Monmouth, IL 61462 III

Coach: Kelly Kane, Ill. Wesleyan 1970
Record: 14 Years, 67-62-0

1998 SCHEDULE

Eureka ....Sept. 12
Lake Forest ■ ....Sept. 19
Beloit ....Sept. 26
Illinois Col. ■ ....Oct. 3
Carroll (Wis.) ....Oct. 10
St. Norbert ■ ....Oct. 17
Ripon ....Oct. 24
Lawrence ....Oct. 31
Grinnell ■ ....Nov. 7
Knox ■ ....Nov. 14

1997 RESULTS (2-7-0)

12 Eureka 35
6 MacMurray 34
14 St. Norbert 41
14 Lake Forest 7
17 Illinois Col. 14
14 Cornell College 48
7 Coe 34
7 Grinnell 38
7 Knox 14
98 **265**

Nickname: Fighting Scots.
Stadium: Bobby Woll Field (1981), 3,000 capacity. Natural turf.
Colors: Crimson & White.
Conference: Midwest Conference.
SID: Chris Pio, 309-457-2173.
AD: Terry L. Glasgow.

MONMOUTH

West Long Branch, NJ 07764 ....I-AA

Coach: Kevin Callahan, Rochester 1977
Record: 4 Years, 26-12-0

1998 SCHEDULE

Dayton ■ ....Sept. 5
Towson ■ ....Sept. 12
Albany (N.Y.) ....*Sept. 19
La Salle ....Oct. 3
LIU-C.W. Post ....Oct. 10
St. Francis (Pa.) ■ ....Oct. 17
Robert Morris ....Oct. 24
Sacred Heart ■ ....Oct. 31
Wagner ....Nov. 7
Central Conn. St. ■ ....Nov. 14

1997 RESULTS (5-4-0)

21 Towson 22
16 Dayton 51
42 La Salle 20
3 New Haven 49
27 St. Francis (Pa.) 7
20 Robert Morris 41
43 Sacred Heart 0
51 Wagner 7
31 Central Conn. St. 17
254 **214**

Nickname: Hawks.
Stadium: Kessler Field (1993), 4,600 capacity. Natural turf.
Colors: Royal Blue & White.
Conference: Northeast.
SID: Brian Ierardi, 908-728-7103.
AD: Marilyn A. Mc Neil.

MONTANA

Missoula, MT 59812 ....I-AA

Coach: Mick Dennehy, Montana 1973
Record: 5 Years, 32-18-0

1998 SCHEDULE

Stephen F. Austin ....*Sept. 5
Southern Utah ■ ....Sept. 12
Cal Poly ■ ....Sept. 19
Weber St. ....*Sept. 26
Portland St. ■ ....Oct. 3
Cal St. Northridge ....Oct. 10
Northern Ariz. ■ ....Oct. 17
Eastern Wash. ....Oct. 24
Idaho St. ■ ....Oct. 31
Cal St. Sacramento ....Nov. 14
Montana St. ■ ....Nov. 21

1997 RESULTS (8-3-0)

24 Stephen F. Austin 10
35 St. Mary's (Cal.) 14
52 Cal St. Sacramento 10
13 Wyoming 28
48 Idaho St. 0
35 Eastern Wash. 40
24 Northern Ariz. 27
21 Cal St. Northridge 13
37 Portland St. 7
38 Weber St. 13
27 Montana St. 25
354 **187**

I-AA Championship

14 McNeese St. 19

Nickname: Grizzlies.
Stadium: Washington-Grizzly (1986), 18,845 capacity. Natural turf.
Colors: Copper, Silver, Gold.
Conference: Big Sky.
SID: Dave Guffey, 406-243-6899.
AD: Wayne Hogan.

MONTANA ST.

Bozeman, MT 59717 ....I-AA

Coach: Cliff Hysell, Montana St. 1966
Record: 6 Years, 31-35-0

1998 SCHEDULE

Fort Lewis ■ ....Sept. 5
Wyoming ....Sept. 12
Western Wash. ■ ....Sept. 19
Cal St. Sacramento ■ ....Sept. 26
Weber St. ....*Oct. 10
Portland St. ■ ....Oct. 17
Cal St. Northridge ....Oct. 24
Northern Ariz. ■ ....Oct. 31
Eastern Wash. ....Nov. 7
Idaho St. ■ ....Nov. 14
Montana ....Nov. 21

1997 RESULTS (6-5-0)

24 Chadron St. 14
26 Southwest Tex. St. 28
14 Idaho St. 13
17 Eastern Wash. 7
13 Northern Ariz. 14
31 Cal St. Northridge 20
0 Portland St. 44
28 Weber St. 14
19 Cal Poly 20
30 Cal St. Sacramento 6
25 Montana 27
227 **207**

Nickname: Bobcats.
Stadium: Reno H. Sales (1973), 15,197 capacity. Natural turf.
Colors: Blue & Gold.
Conference: Big Sky.
SID: Bill Lamberty, 406-994-5133.
AD: Chuck Lindemenn.

MONTCLAIR ST.

Upper Montclair, NJ 07043 III

Coach: Rick Giancola, Rowan 1968
Record: 15 Years, 101-51-2

1998 SCHEDULE

Cortland St. ■ ....Sept. 12
Wesley ....Sept. 19
Brockport St. ■ ....Sept. 26
St. John Fisher ....Oct. 3

Kean ....Oct. 10
Wm. Paterson ■ ....*Oct. 17
Western Conn. St. ....Oct. 24
Col. of New Jersey ■ ....*Oct. 31
New Jersey City ....Nov. 7
Rowan ■ ....Nov. 14

1997 RESULTS (6-4-0)

14 Cortland St. 28
14 Wesley....7
27 Brockport St. 33
21 St. John Fisher....0
30 Kean....3
28 Wm. Paterson....7
15 Wilkes 12
7 Col. of New Jersey....31
20 New Jersey City....7
7 Rowan 19
183 **147**

Nickname: Red Hawks.
Stadium: Sprague (1934), 6,000 capacity. Artificial turf.
Colors: Scarlet & White.
Conference: New Jersey Athletic Conference.
SID: Al Langer, 201-655-5249.
AD: Holly P. Gera.

MOORHEAD ST.

Moorhead, MN 56563 II

Coach: Ralph Micheli, Macalester 1970
Record: 15 Years, 60-81-2

1998 SCHEDULE

Concordia-M'head ■ ....Sept. 5
North Dak. ....Sept. 12
Bemidji St. ....Sept. 26
Minn.-Duluth ■ ....Oct. 3
Southwest St. ....Oct. 10
Wayne St. (Neb.) ....Oct. 17
Winona St. ■ ....Oct. 24
Minn.-Morris ....Oct. 31
Northern St. ■ ....Nov. 7
Minn.-Duluth [Minneapolis, Minn.] ....Nov. 14

1997 RESULTS (5-5-0)

7 Concordia-M'head 17
14 North Dak. 45
30 Wayne St. (Neb.) 21
17 Northern St. 20
36 Bemidji St. 17
14 Minn.-Duluth 31
10 Southwest St. 6
10 Winona St. 28
50 Minn.-Morris 14
30 Wis.-Stout 21
218 **220**

Nickname: Dragons.
Stadium: Alex Nemzek (1960), 5,000 capacity. Natural turf.
Colors: Scarlet & White.
Conference: Northern Sun.
SID: Larry Scott, 218-236-2113.
AD: Katy Wilson.

MORAVIAN

Bethlehem, PA 18018 III

Coach: Scot Dapp, West Chester 1973
Record: 11 Years, 77-35-1

1998 SCHEDULE

Lycoming ....Sept. 12
Juniata ■ ....Sept. 19
Albright ■ ....Sept. 26
Delaware Valley ....Oct. 3
Widener ■ ....Oct. 10
Susquehanna ....Oct. 17
Lebanon Valley ....Oct. 24
FDU-Madison ■ ....Oct. 31
Wilkes ....Nov. 7
Muhlenberg ■ ....Nov. 14

1997 RESULTS (7-3-0)

14 Lycoming 17
29 Juniata 28
0 Albright 46
28 Delaware Valley 10
27 Widener....24
31 Susquehanna 24
21 Lebanon Valley 6
21 FDU-Madison 8
21 Wilkes 27
21 Muhlenberg 16
213 **206**

Nickname: Greyhounds.
Stadium: Steel Field (1932), 2,200 capacity. Natural turf.
Colors: Blue & Grey.
Conference: Middle Atlantic States Conf.
SID: Mark Fleming, 610-861-1472.
AD: Richard M. Dull.

MOREHEAD ST.

Morehead, KY 40351 ....I-AA

Coach: Matt Ballard, Gardner-Webb 1979
Record: 10 Years, 50-51-1

1998 SCHEDULE

Austin Peay ....*Sept. 3
Butler ■ ....*Sept. 12
Valparaiso ....Sept. 19
Dayton....*Sept. 26
Elon ■ ....*Oct. 3
Thomas More ■ ....Oct. 17
VMI ....Oct. 24
Bethel (Tenn.) ■ ....Oct. 31
Charleston So. ....Nov. 7
Ky. Wesleyan ■ ....Nov. 14
South FLa. ....*Nov. 21

1997 RESULTS (7-3-0)

55 Austin Peay....43
56 Valparaiso....24
28 Dayton 42
17 South FLa....33
37 Wofford 35
56 Miles....41
37 St. Joseph's (Ind.) 7
24 Western Ky. 38
55 Charleston So. 27
54 Evansville....27
419 **317**

Nickname: Eagles.
Stadium: Jayne (1964), 10,000 capacity. Artificial turf.
Colors: Blue & Gold.
Conference: Independent.
SID: Randy Stacy, 606-783-2500.
AD: Michael Mincey.

MOREHOUSE

Atlanta, GA 30314 II

Coach: Frank Hickson, Tuskegee 1982
(First year as head coach)

1998 SCHEDULE

Fort Valley St. ....*Aug. 29
Lane ■ ....Sept. 5
Miles ....Sept. 12
Albany St. (Ga.) ■ ....Sept. 19
Savannah St. ....Sept. 26
Alcorn St. ■ ....Oct. 3
Tuskegee [Columbus, Ga.] ....*Oct. 10
Virginia Union ■ ....Oct. 17
Morris Brown [Augusta, Ga.] ....Oct. 24
Kentucky St. ....Oct. 31
Clark Atlanta ....Nov. 7

1997 RESULTS (3-8-0)

24 Morgan St. 14
27 Fort Valley St. 16
9 Miles....36
7 Albany St. (Ga.)....17
0 Savannah St. 3
14 Alabama A&M 38
26 Tuskegee 29
0 Howard....52
16 Morris Brown 17
7 Kentucky St. 9
24 Clark Atlanta 3
154 **234**

Nickname: Tigers.
Stadium: B. T. Harvey (1983), 9,850 capacity. Natural turf.
Colors: Maroon & White.
Conference: Southern Intercol. Ath. Conf.
SID: James E. Nix, 404-681-2800.
AD: Josh Culbreath.

MORGAN ST.

Baltimore, MD 21239 ....I-AA

Coach: Stump Mitchell, Citadel 1981
Record: 2 Years, 7-14-0

1998 SCHEDULE

Towson ....*Sept. 3
Bethune-Cookman ■ ....Sept. 12
Norfolk St. ■ ....Sept. 26
South Caro. St. ....*Oct. 3
Buffalo ....Oct. 10
North Caro. A&T ....Oct. 17
Delaware St. ■ ....Oct. 24
Florida A&M ....*Oct. 31
Samford ....Nov. 7
Howard ....Nov. 14
Hampton ■ ....Nov. 21

1997 RESULTS (3-7-0)

14 Morehouse 24
18 Bethune-Cookman 15
24 Texas Southern....17
6 Norfolk St. 48
27 South Caro. St. 34
6 North Caro. A&T 7
14 Delaware St. 7
13 Florida A&M....42
27 Howard....30
0 Hampton 10
149 **234**

Nickname: Bears.
Stadium: Hughes (1934), 10,000 capacity. Natural turf.
Colors: Blue & Orange.
Conference: Mid-Eastern.
SID: Joe McIver, 410-319-3831.
AD: Garnett H. Purnell.

MORNINGSIDE

Sioux City, IA 51106 II

Coach: Dave Elliott, Michigan 1975
Record: 2 Years, 1-21-0

1998 SCHEDULE

Drake ....Sept. 5
Quincy ■ ....Sept. 12
St. Cloud St. ....Sept. 19
North Dak. ....Sept. 26
Augustana (S.D.) ■ ....Oct. 3
North Dak. St. ■ ....Oct. 10
South Dak. ....Oct. 17
Mankato St. ■ ....Oct. 24
Northern Colo. ....Oct. 31
Neb.-Omaha ■ ....Nov. 7
South Dak. St. ■ ....Nov. 14

1997 RESULTS (0-11-0)

0 Drake 7
13 Wis.-Stevens Point 34
13 St. Cloud St. 16
14 North Dak. 28
6 Augustana (S.D.) 10
0 North Dak. St. 35
0 South Dak. 22
14 Mankato St. 26
7 Northern Colo. 41
14 Neb.-Omaha 31
20 South Dak. St. 35
101 **285**

Nickname: Chiefs.
Stadium: Roberts (1939), 9,000 capacity. Natural turf.
Colors: Maroon & White.
Conference: No. Central Intercoll Ath Conf.
SID: Dave Rebstock, 712-274-5127.
AD: Bill Goldring.

MORRIS BROWN

Atlanta, GA 30314 II

Coach: Joseph C. Crosby Jr., North Caro. A&T 1977
Record: 4 Years, 22-19-2

1998 SCHEDULE

Clark Atlanta ■	*Sept. 6
Tuskegee	Sept. 12
Fort Valley St. ■	*Sept. 19
Alabama A&M ■	*Sept. 26
Miles	Oct. 3
Savannah St. ■	Oct. 10
Benedict ■	Oct. 17
Morehouse [Augusta, Ga.]	Oct. 24
Albany St. (Ga.) ■	Oct. 31
Kentucky St.	Nov. 7
Lane	Nov. 14

1997 RESULTS (6-5-0)

0	Clark Atlanta	14
20	Bethune-Cookman	35
36	Tuskegee	27
12	Fort Valley St.	15
6	Alabama A&M	10
32	Miles	30
24	Savannah St.	23
7	Benedict	6
17	Morehouse	16
7	Albany St. (Ga.)	20
30	Kentucky St.	17
191		**213**

Nickname: Wolverines.
Stadium: A.F. Herndon, 20,000 capacity. Natural turf.
Colors: Purple & Black.
Conference: Southern Intercol. Ath. Conf.
SID: Charles E. Mooney, 404-220-3628.
AD: Gene Bright.

MOUNT SAINT JOSEPH

Cincinnati, OH 45233 III

Coach: Ron Corradini, Miami (Ohio) 1961
Record: 5 Years, 20-28-1

1998 SCHEDULE

Olivet	Sept. 5
Otterbein ■	Sept. 12
Urbana ■	Sept. 19
Wabash	Sept. 26
Wilmington (Ohio) ■	Oct. 3
Anderson (Ind.) ■	Oct. 10
Franklin	Oct. 17
Hanover ■	Oct. 24
Bluffton	Oct. 31
Manchester ■	Nov. 7

1997 RESULTS (3-5-2)

27	Franklin	21
0	Urbana	0
10	Manchester	13
21	Hanover	25
0	Sue Bennett	0
28	Defiance	0
35	Bluffton	40
7	Wash. & Jeff.	20
31	Wilmington (Ohio)	25
14	Ky. Wesleyan	43
173		**187**

Nickname: Lions.
Stadium: Galbreath Field, 12,000 capacity. Natural turf.
Colors: Blue & Gold.
Conference: Independent.
SID: Bridget Pilot, 513-244-4311
AD: Steven F. Radcliffe.

MOUNT UNION

Alliance, OH 44601 III

Coach: Larry Kehres, Mount Union 1971
Record: 12 Years, 124-16-3

1998 SCHEDULE

Albion	Sept. 12
Hiram ■	*Sept. 19
Ohio Northern	Sept. 26
John Carroll ■	Oct. 3
Heidelberg ■	Oct. 10
Otterbein	Oct. 17
Marietta ■	Oct. 24
Capital	Oct. 31
Muskingum ■	Nov. 7
Baldwin-Wallace	Nov. 14

1997 RESULTS (10-0-0)

58	Defiance	0
56	Baldwin-Wallace	14
49	Otterbein	0
38	Ohio Northern	14
48	Heidelberg	7
42	John Carroll	14
59	Muskingum	0
69	Marietta	7
62	Capital	0
63	Hiram	0
544		**56**

III Championship

34	Allegheny	30
59	John Carroll	7
54	Simpson	7
61	Lycoming	12

Nickname: Purple Raiders.
Stadium: Mt. Union (1915), 5,800 capacity. Natural turf.
Colors: Purple & White.
Conference: Ohio Athletic Conference.
SID: Michael De Matteis, 216-823-6093.
AD: Larry Kehres.

MUHLENBERG

Allentown, PA 18104.................................III

Coach: Mike Donnelly, Ithaca 1975
Record: 1 Year, 1-9-0

1998 SCHEDULE

Hartwick ■	Sept. 5
Dickinson	Sept. 19
Frank. & Marsh. ■	Sept. 26
Western Md.	Oct. 3
Swarthmore ■	Oct. 10
Johns Hopkins	*Oct. 16
Gettysburg ■	Oct. 24
Ursinus	Oct. 31
Grove City ■	Nov. 7
Moravian	Nov. 14

1997 RESULTS (1-9-0)

17	Hartwick	42
14	Dickinson	21
10	Frank. & Marsh.	14
9	Western Md.	44
60	Swarthmore	14
21	Johns Hopkins	24
33	Gettysburg	45
7	Ursinus	9
13	Carnegie Mellon	28
16	Moravian	21
200		**262**

Nickname: Mules.
Stadium: Muhlenberg Field (1928), 4,000 capacity. Natural turf.
Colors: Cardinal & Gray.
Conference: Centennial Conference.
SID: Mike Falk, 610-821-3232.
AD: Stephen P. Erber.

MURRAY ST.

Murray, KY 42071.................................I-AA

Coach: Denver Johnson, Tulsa 1981
Record: 1 Year, 7-4-0

1998 SCHEDULE

Southern Ill. ■	*Sept. 5
Western Ky. ■	*Sept. 12
Southeast Mo. St.	*Sept. 19
Brigham Young	Sept. 26
Tenn.-Martin ■	Oct. 3
Middle Tenn. St.	*Oct. 10
Eastern Ky.	Oct. 17
Tennessee Tech ■	Oct. 31
Eastern Ill.	Nov. 7
Tennessee St. ■	Nov. 14
Indiana St.	Nov. 21

1997 RESULTS (7-4-0)

13	Indiana St.	0
50	Western Ky.	52
20	Southern Ill.	24
17	Southeast Mo. St.	3
35	Middle Tenn. St.	17
45	Tenn.-Martin	7
51	Austin Peay	0
8	Eastern Ky.	29
13	Tennessee Tech	16
24	Eastern Ill.	17
13	Tennessee St.	7
289		**172**

Nickname: Racers.
Stadium: Stewart (1973), 16,800 capacity. Artificial turf.
Colors: Blue & Gold.
Conference: Ohio Valley.
SID: Steve Parker, 502-762-4271.
AD: E. W. Dennison.

MUSKINGUM

New Concord, OH 43762..........................III

Coach: Jeff Heacock, Muskingum 1976
Record: 17 Years, 81-82-4

1998 SCHEDULE

Denison ■	Sept. 12
Marietta ■	*Sept. 19
Capital	Sept. 26
Otterbein	Oct. 3
Hiram ■	Oct. 10
Ohio Northern	Oct. 17
John Carroll ■	Oct. 24
Baldwin-Wallace	Oct. 31
Mount Union	Nov. 7
Heidelberg ■	Nov. 14

1997 RESULTS (2-8-0)

16	Denison	24
7	Heidelberg	14
35	Hiram	27
6	Capital	10
7	John Carroll	36
7	Ohio Northern	41
0	Mount Union	59
10	Baldwin-Wallace	16
21	Otterbein	17
12	Marietta	14
121		**258**

Nickname: Fighting Muskies.
Stadium: Mc Conagha (1925), 5,000 capacity. Natural turf.
Colors: Black & Magenta.
Conference: Ohio Athletic Conference.
SID: Bobby Lee, 614-826-8022.
AD: Jeffrey W. Heacock.

NAVY

Annapolis, MD 21402...............................I-A

Coach: Charlie Weatherbie, Oklahoma St. 1977
Record: 6 Years, 36-32-0

1998 SCHEDULE

Wake Forest	*Sept. 10
Kent ■	*Sept. 19
Tulane	*Sept. 26
West Va. ■	Oct. 3
Air Force	Oct. 10
Colgate ■	Oct. 17
Boston College	Oct. 24
Rutgers ■	Nov. 7
Notre Dame [Raljon, Md.]	Nov. 14
Southern Methodist ■	Nov. 21
Army [Philadelphia, Pa.]	Dec. 5

1997 RESULTS (7-4-0)

31 San Diego St. 45
36 Rutgers 7
46 Southern Methodist....16
17 Duke 26
7 Air Force 10
42 VMI 7
17 Notre Dame 21
49 Temple 17
52 Colgate 24
62 Kent 29
39 Army 7
398 **209**

Nickname: Midshipmen.
Stadium: Navy-Marine Corps Mem. (1959), 30,000 capacity. Natural turf.
Colors: Navy Blue & Gold.
Conference: Independent.
SID: Scott Strasemeier, 410-268-6226.
AD: Jack Lengyel.

NEBRASKA

Lincoln, NE 68588 ....I-A

Coach: Frank Solich, Nebraska 1966
(First year as head coach)

1998 SCHEDULE

Louisiana Tech ■ ....Aug. 29
UAB ■ ....Sept. 5
California ....Sept. 12
Washington ■ ....Sept. 26
Oklahoma St. [Kansas City, Mo.] ....Oct. 3
Texas A&M ....Oct. 10
Kansas ■ ....Oct. 17
Missouri ■ ....Oct. 24
Texas ■ ....Oct. 31
Iowa St. ....Nov. 7
Kansas St. ....Nov. 14
Colorado ■ ....Nov. 27

1997 RESULTS (12-0-0)

59 Akron 14
38 Central FLa. 24
27 Washington 14
56 Kansas St. 26
49 Baylor 21
29 Texas Tech 0
35 Kansas 0
69 Oklahoma 7
45 Missouri 38
77 Iowa St. 14
27 Colorado 24
54 Texas A&M 15
565 **197**

Orange Bowl

42 Tennessee 17

Nickname: Cornhuskers.
Stadium: Memorial (1923), 72,700 capacity. Artificial turf.
Colors: Scarlet & Cream.
Conference: Big 12.
SID: Chris Anderson, 402-472-2263.
AD: C. William Byrne Jr.

NEB. WESLEYAN

Lincoln, NE 68504 III

Coach: Brian Keller, Neb. Wesleyan 1983
Record: 2 Years, 7-13-0

1998 SCHEDULE

Austin ■ ....Sept. 12
Iowa Wesleyan ■ ....Sept. 19
Doane ....Sept. 26
Midland Lutheran ■ ....Oct. 3
Concordia (Neb.) ■ ....Oct. 10
Northwestern (Iowa) ....Oct. 17
Hastings ■ ....Oct. 24
Dana ....Oct. 31
Sioux Falls ....Nov. 7
Peru St. ....Nov. 14

1997 RESULTS (5-5-0)

35 Austin 9
30 Colorado Col. 31
35 Midland Lutheran 28
20 Concordia (Neb.) 7
27 Northwestern (Iowa) 37
7 Hastings 42
20 Dana 7
13 Sioux Falls 35
20 Doane 44
38 Peru St. 32
245 **272**

Nickname: Plainsmen.
Stadium: Abel (1986), 2,000 capacity. Natural turf.
Colors: Yellow & Brown.
Conference: Independent.
SID: Larry Cain, 402-465-2151.
AD: Mary Beth Kennedy.

NEB.-KEARNEY

Kearney, NE 68849 II

Coach: Claire Boroff, Neb.-Kearney 1959
Record: 26 Years, 157-98-5

1998 SCHEDULE

Mo. Western St. ■ ....Sept. 5
Neb.-Omaha ....Sept. 12
Adams St. ....Sept. 19
Colorado Mines ■ ....Sept. 26
Chadron St. ....Oct. 3
Fort Lewis ....Oct. 10
Fort Hays St. ■ ....Oct. 17
Mesa St. ....Oct. 24
Western St. (Colo.) ■ ....Nov. 7
N. M. Highlands ■ ....Nov. 14

1997 RESULTS (7-4-0)

16 Mo. Western St. 39
13 Neb.-Omaha 15
50 Colorado Mines 15
34 Chadron St. 40
50 Fort Lewis 36
23 Fort Hays St. 20
46 Mesa St. 22
40 Wayne St. (Neb.) 18
6 Western St. (Colo.) 34
49 N. M. Highlands 48
35 Adams St. 7
362 **294**

Nickname: Antelopes, Lopers.
Stadium: Foster Field (1929), 6,500 capacity. Natural turf.
Colors: Royal Blue & Light Old Gold.
Conference: Rocky Mountain Athletic Conf.
SID: Aaron Babcock, 308-865-8334.
AD: Michael L. Sumpter.

NEB.-OMAHA

Omaha, NE 68182 II

Coach: Pat Behrns, Dakota St. 1972
Record: 10 Years, 58-49-0

1998 SCHEDULE

Central Mo. St. ....*Sept. 3
Neb.-Kearney ■ ....Sept. 12
North Dak. St. ■ ....Sept. 19
South Dak. ....Sept. 26
North Dak. ■ ....Oct. 3
Augustana (S.D.) ■ ....Oct. 10
South Dak. St. ....Oct. 17
Northern Colo. ■ ....Oct. 24
Mankato St. ....Oct. 31
Morningside ....Nov. 7
St. Cloud St. ■ ....Nov. 14

1997 RESULTS (8-3-0)

41 Central Mo. St. 12
15 Neb.-Kearney 13
27 North Dak. St. 21
38 South Dak. 14
24 North Dak. 35
35 Augustana (S.D.) 6
31 South Dak. St. 21
17 Northern Colo. 37
30 Mankato St. 16
31 Morningside 14
7 St. Cloud St. 46
296 **235**

Nickname: Mavericks.
Stadium: Al F. Caniglia Field (1949), 9,500 capacity. Artificial turf.
Colors: Black & Crimson.
Conference: No. Central Intercoll Ath Conf.
SID: Gary Anderson, 402-554-2305.
AD: Bob Danenhauer.

NEVADA

Reno, NV 89557 ....I-A

Coach: Jeff Tisdel, Nevada 1977
Record: 2 Years, 14-9-0

1998 SCHEDULE

Oregon St. ....Sept. 5
Colorado St. ■ ....Sept. 12
Fresno St. ....*Sept. 26
UNLV ....*Oct. 3
New Mexico St. ■ ....Oct. 10
North Texas ....*Oct. 17
Idaho ....Oct. 24
Boise St. ■ ....Oct. 31
Utah St. ....Nov. 7
Cal Poly ■ ....Nov. 14
Southern Miss. ■ ....Nov. 21

1997 RESULTS (5-6-0)

13 Colorado St. 45
31 UNLV 14
20 Oregon 24
19 Southern Miss. 35
13 Toledo 31
30 Wyoming 34
42 Idaho 23
65 North Texas 10
45 New Mexico St. 24
56 Boise St. 42
19 Utah St. 38
353 **320**

Nickname: Wolf Pack.
Stadium: Mackay (1967), 31,545 capacity. Natural turf.
Colors: Silver & Blue.
Conference: Big West.
SID: Paul Stuart, 702-784-4600.
AD: Chris Ault.

UNLV

Las Vegas, NV 89154 ....I-A

Coach: Jeff Horton, Nevada 1981
Record: 5 Years, 20-37-0

1998 SCHEDULE

Northwestern ....Sept. 5
Air Force ■ ....*Sept. 12
Wisconsin ....Sept. 19
Colorado St. ....Sept. 26
Nevada ■ ....*Oct. 3
Brigham Young ....Oct. 10
Wyoming ■ ....Oct. 17
Southern Methodist ....Oct. 24
Tulsa ■ ....Oct. 31
Rice ....Nov. 14
Texas Christian ■ ....Nov. 21

1997 RESULTS (3-8-0)

14 Nevada 31
24 Air Force 25
25 Hawaii 15
41 Illinois St. 6
21 Southern Cal 35
21 Texas Christian 19
17 San Diego St. 20
28 Fresno St. 46
19 Colorado St. 45
23 Wyoming 35
48 San Jose St. 55
281 **332**

Nickname: Rebels.
Stadium: Sam Boyd (1971), 32,000 capacity. Artificial turf.

Colors: Scarlet & Gray.
Conference: Western Athletic.
SID: Mark Wallington, 702-895-4472.
AD: Charles W. Cavagnaro.

NEW HAMPSHIRE

Durham, NH 03824 ....I-AA

Coach: Bill Bowes, Penn State 1965
Record: 26 Years, 171-99-5

1998 SCHEDULE

Northeastern ....Sept. 5
Maine....*Sept. 12
East Stroudsburg ■....Sept. 19
Delaware....Sept. 26
Connecticut ■....Oct. 3
Richmond ■....Oct. 10
Northeastern ■....Oct. 17
William & Mary....Oct. 24
Massachusetts ■....Oct. 31
Hofstra....Nov. 7
Rhode Island ■....Nov. 14

1997 RESULTS (5-6-0)

10	Delaware	27
21	Rhode Island	35
24	William & Mary	22
14	Stephen F. Austin	17
28	Massachusetts	10
14	Hofstra	33
19	Northeastern	34
24	Maine	7
20	Villanova	23
38	Boston U.	0
21	Connecticut	18
233		**226**

Nickname: Wildcats.
Stadium: Cowell (1936), 9,571 capacity. Natural turf.
Colors: Blue & White.
Conference: Atlantic 10.
SID: Scott Stapin, 603-862-2585.
AD: Judith L. Ray.

NEW HAVEN

West Haven, CT 06516..............II

Coach: Tony Sparano, New Haven 1982
Record: 4 Years, 36-9-1

1998 SCHEDULE

Bloomsburg ■....Sept. 5
West Chester ■....Sept. 12
Millersville....Sept. 19
UC Davis....*Sept. 26
Western Ky.....*Oct. 3
Southern Conn. St. ■....Oct. 10
Youngstown St.....Oct. 24
St. Joseph's (Ind.) ■....Oct. 31
Western N. Mex. ....Nov. 7
Robert Morris ....Nov. 14

1997 RESULTS (9-1-0)

32	West Chester	26
38	East Stroudsburg	0
53	Millersville	10
43	Indiana (Pa.)	14
49	Monmouth	3
44	Southern Conn. St.	7
21	Western Ky.	24
59	Elizabeth City St.	0
38	Lafayette	0
56	St. Joseph's (Ind.)	14
433		**98**

II Championship

47	Glenville St.	7
49	Slippery Rock	21
27	UC Davis	25
0	Northern Colo.	51

Nickname: Chargers.
Stadium: Robert B. Dodds, 3,500 capacity. Natural turf.
Colors: Blue & Gold.
Conference: Independent.
SID: Vinnie DiCarlo, 203-932-7025.
AD: Deborah Chin.

NEW JERSEY CITY

(Formerly Jersey City St.)

Jersey City, NJ 07305..............III

Coach: Roy Miller, New Jersey City 1969
Record: 13 Years, 53-73-0

1998 SCHEDULE

Mass.-Lowell ■....Sept. 5
Brockport St. ■....Sept. 12
Western Conn. St. ....Sept. 19
Rowan....*Sept. 25
St. John Fisher ■....Oct. 10
Kean ■....Oct. 17
Col. of New Jersey....Oct. 24
Wm. Paterson....*Oct. 30
Montclair St. ■....Nov. 7
King's (Pa.) ■....Nov. 14

1997 RESULTS (5-5-0)

10	Mass.-Lowell	7
7	Brockport St.	12
14	Western Conn. St.	13
6	Rowan	35
22	St. John Fisher	12
7	Kean	0
12	Col. of New Jersey	24
7	Wm. Paterson	2
7	Montclair St.	20
6	King's (Pa.)	7
98		**132**

Nickname: Gothic Knights.
Stadium: Thomas Gerrity Ath. Cmplx (1986), 3,000 capacity. Natural turf.
Colors: Green & Gold.
Conference: New Jersey Athletic Conference.
SID: Tracy King, 201-200-3301.
AD: Lawrence R. Schiner.

COL. OF NEW JERSEY

(formerly Trenton St.)

Ewing, NJ 08628..............III

Coach: Eric Hamilton, Col. of New Jersey 1975
Record: 21 Years, 131-76-6

1998 SCHEDULE

FDU-Madison ....*Sept. 11
Wm. Paterson ■....*Sept. 18
Ithaca....Sept. 26
Rowan ■....*Oct. 2
Cortland St. ■....Oct. 10
Salisbury St.....Oct. 17
New Jersey City ■....Oct. 24
Montclair St.....*Oct. 31
Brockport St.....Nov. 7
Kean ■....Nov. 14

1997 RESULTS (8-2-0)

24	FDU-Madison	0
42	Wm. Paterson	7
31	Wesley	14
7	Rowan	30
22	Cortland St.	43
35	Salisbury St.	7
24	New Jersey City	12
31	Montclair St.	7
42	Brockport St.	7
33	Kean	18
291		**145**

III Championship

34	Cortland St.	30
7	Rowan	13

Nickname: Lions.
Stadium: Lions (1984), 5,000 capacity. Artificial turf.
Colors: Blue & Gold.
Conference: New Jersey Athletic Conference.
SID: Ann Bready, 609-771-2517.
AD: Kevin A. Mc Hugh.

NEW MEXICO

Albuquerque, NM 87131..............I-A

Coach: Rocky Long, New Mexico 1974
(First year as head coach)

1998 SCHEDULE

Idaho St. ■....*Sept. 5
Utah St. ■....*Sept. 12
New Mexico St. ....*Sept. 19
San Jose St.....*Sept. 26
Air Force....Oct. 3
UTEP ■....*Oct. 10
San Diego St. ■....*Oct. 17
Hawaii ....*Oct. 24
Fresno St. ■....Oct. 31
Brigham Young....Nov. 7
Utah ■....Nov. 14
Central Fla.....Nov. 21

1997 RESULTS (9-3-0)

33	Northern Ariz.	10
61	New Mexico St.	24
38	UTEP	20
25	Utah St.	22
22	Southern Methodist	15
36	San Diego St.	21
23	Rice	35
10	Utah	15
40	Texas Christian	10
38	Brigham Young	28
51	Tulsa	13
13	Colorado St.	41
390		**254**

Insight.com Bowl

14	Arizona	20

Nickname: Lobos.
Stadium: University (1960), 31,218 capacity. Natural turf.
Colors: Cherry & Silver.
Conference: Western Athletic.
SID: Greg Remington, 505-277-2026.
AD: Rudy Davalos.

N. M. HIGHLANDS

Las Vegas, NM 87701 II

Coach: Carl Ferrill, N. M. Highlands 1969
Record: 2 Years, 16-6-0

1998 SCHEDULE

Tarleton St.....*Sept. 3
Eastern N.M. ■....*Sept. 12
Western N. Mex. ....*Sept. 19
Adams St. ■....Sept. 26
Western St. (Colo.) ....Oct. 3
Colorado Mines ....Oct. 10
Chadron St. ■....Oct. 17
Fort Lewis ■....Oct. 24
Fort Hays St.....Oct. 31
Mesa St. ■....Nov. 7
Neb.-Kearney....Nov. 14

1997 RESULTS (8-3-0)

34	Tarleton St.	29
31	Eastern N.M.	34
33	Adams St.	7
21	Western St. (Colo.)	27
66	Colorado Mines	0
16	Chadron St.	14
35	Fort Lewis	22
35	Fort Hays St.	28
34	Mesa St.	7
48	Neb.-Kearney	49
28	Western N. Mex.	21
381		**238**

Nickname: Cowboys.
Stadium: Perkins, 5,000 capacity. Natural turf.
Colors: Purple & White.
Conference: Rocky Mountain Athletic Conf.
SID: Jesse Gallegos, 505-454-3387.
AD: Joe L. Singleton.

NEW MEXICO ST.

Las Cruces, NM 88003 .... I-A

Coach: Tony Samuel, Nebraska 1979
Record: 1 Year, 2-9-0

1998 SCHEDULE

Texas	*Sept. 5
Georgia Tech	*Sept. 12
New Mexico ■	*Sept. 19
UTEP ■	*Sept. 26
Arkansas St.	Oct. 3
Nevada	Oct. 10
Colorado St. ■	*Oct. 17
Utah St. ■	Oct. 31
Boise St. ■	*Nov. 7
Idaho	Nov. 14
North Texas	Nov. 21

1997 RESULTS (2-9-0)

10	Arizona St.	41
24	New Mexico	61
28	Cal St. Northridge	18
16	UTEP	24
35	Cal Poly	38
10	Boise St.	52
7	Utah St.	38
34	Arkansas St.	20
24	Nevada	45
15	North Texas	26
18	Idaho	35
221		**398**

Nickname: Aggies.
Stadium: Aggie Memorial (1978), 30,343 capacity. Natural turf.
Colors: Crimson & White.
Conference: Big West.
SID: Steve Shutt, 505-646-3929.
AD: James E. Paul Jr.

NEWBERRY

Newberry, SC 29108 II

Coach: Mike Taylor, Newberry 1976
Record: 6 Years, 27-38-0

1998 SCHEDULE

North Greenville ■	*Sept. 5
Benedict	*Sept. 12
Wingate	Sept. 19
Gardner-Webb ■	*Sept. 26
Mars Hill ■	*Oct. 3
Charleston So.	Oct. 10
Tusculum ■	Oct. 17
Lenoir-Rhyne	Oct. 24
Catawba ■	*Oct. 31
Carson-Newman	Nov. 7
Presbyterian	Nov. 14

1997 RESULTS (4-7-0)

45	North Greenville	0
13	Citadel	33
20	Elon	52
38	Wingate	43
10	Gardner-Webb	35
17	Mars Hill	21
48	Charleston So.	14
49	Lenoir-Rhyne	23
17	Catawba	36
12	Carson-Newman	34
28	Presbyterian	22
297		**313**

Nickname: Indians.
Stadium: Setzler Field (1930), 4,000 capacity. Natural turf.
Colors: Scarlet & Gray.
Conference: South Atlantic Conference.
SID: Darrell Orand, 803-321-5667.
AD: Grafton Young.

NICHOLLS ST.

Thibodaux, LA 70310 .... I-AA

Coach: Darren Barbier, Nicholls St. 1982
Record: 3 Years, 13-21-0

1998 SCHEDULE

Northeast La.	*Sept. 5
Mississippi Val. ■	*Sept. 12
Jacksonville St. ■	*Sept. 26
Samford	Oct. 3
Sam Houston St. ■	*Oct. 8
Southwest Tex. St.	Oct. 17
Northwestern St. ■	*Oct. 24
Louisiana Tech	Oct. 31
Troy St.	*Nov. 7
Stephen F. Austin ■	*Nov. 14
McNeese St.	*Nov. 21

1997 RESULTS (5-6-0)

0	Northeast La.	28
33	Southern Ill.	0
22	Troy St.	20
0	Northwestern St.	19
17	Samford	14
29	Southwest Tex. St.	28
17	Sam Houston St.	24
16	Jacksonville St.	14
14	Southern U.	21
7	Stephen F. Austin	39
13	McNeese St.	31
168		**238**

Nickname: Colonels.
Stadium: John L. Guidry (1972), 12,800 capacity. Natural turf.
Colors: Red & Gray.
Conference: Southland.
SID: Ron Mears, 504-448-4282.
AD: Michael G. Knight.

NICHOLS

Dudley, MA 01571 III

Coach: Jim Foster, Oklahoma 1969
Record: 2 Years, 4-15-0

1998 SCHEDULE

Framingham St. ■	Sept. 12
Fitchburg St.	Sept. 19
Western New Eng.	Sept. 26
Mass.-Boston ■	Oct. 3
Curry ■	Oct. 10
Mass.-Dartmouth	Oct. 17
MIT ■	Oct. 24
Mass. Maritime ■	Oct. 31
Westfield St.	Nov. 7
Salve Regina	*Nov. 14

1997 RESULTS (2-7-0)

20	Mass. Maritime	9
0	Salve Regina	34
28	Hartwick	35
14	Mass.-Dartmouth	48
42	Curry	6
20	St. John Fisher	29
13	MIT	16
7	Western New Eng.	20
20	Worcester St.	33
164		**230**

Nickname: Bison.
Stadium: Bison Bowl (1961), 3,000 capacity. Natural turf.
Colors: Black & Green.
Conference: New England FB.
SID: Mike Serijan, 508-943-1560.
AD: Thomas R. Cafaro.

NORFOLK ST.

Norfolk, VA 23504 .... I-AA

Coach: Darnell Moore, Elizabeth City 1970
Record: 4 Years, 24-17-0

1998 SCHEDULE

Virginia St. ■	*Sept. 5
Florida A&M ■	*Sept. 12
Delaware St. ■	*Sept. 19
Morgan St.	Sept. 26
North Caro. A&T	Oct. 3
South Caro. St. ■	Oct. 10
Hampton	Oct. 17
Virginia Union ■	Oct. 24
Howard	Oct. 31
Liberty	Nov. 7
Bethune-Cookman	Nov. 14

1997 RESULTS (3-7-0)

7	Virginia St.	36
26	Virginia Union	0
26	Florida A&M	41
21	Delaware St.	24
48	Morgan St.	6
25	South Caro. St.	28
2	Hampton	9
24	Howard	32
6	Liberty	17
21	Bethune-Cookman	7
206		**200**

Nickname: Spartans.
Stadium: Price (1997), 30,000 capacity. Natural turf.
Colors: Green & Gold.
Conference: Mid-Eastern.
SID: Traci L. Allen, 804-683-8444.
AD: William L. Price.

NORTH ALA.

Florence, AL 35632 II

Coach: Bill Hyde, Samford 1962
(First year as head coach)

1998 SCHEDULE

Carson-Newman [Rome, Ga.]	*Sept. 5
Southern Ark.	*Sept. 12
Central Ark. ■	Sept. 26
Ark.-Monticello	Oct. 3
West Ga.	*Oct. 10
Delta St. ■	Oct. 17
Henderson St.	Oct. 24
Arkansas Tech ■	Oct. 31
Valdosta St.	Nov. 7
West ALa. ■	Nov. 14

1997 RESULTS (9-2-0)

49	Alabama A&M	20
7	Southern Ark.	16
17	Texas A&M-Kingsville	12
45	Arkansas Tech	24
0	Valdosta St.	21
48	Southwestern La.	42
17	Delta St.	10
42	Henderson St.	20
35	Central Ark.	6
21	West Ga.	18
56	West ALa.	14
337		**203**

II Championship

7	Carson-Newman	21

Nickname: Lions.
Stadium: Braly (1940), 13,000 capacity. Natural turf.
Colors: Purple & Gold.
Conference: Gulf South Conference.
SID: Jeff Hodges, 205-760-4595.
AD: K. Dan Summy.

NORTH CARO.

Chapel Hill, NC 27514 .... I-A

Coach: Carl Torbush, Carson-Newman 1974
Record: 2 Years, 4-8-0

1998 SCHEDULE

Miami (Ohio) ■	*Sept. 5
Stanford	Sept. 19
Georgia Tech ■	*Sept. 26
Clemson ■	Oct. 3
Pittsburgh ■	Oct. 10
Wake Forest	Oct. 24
Florida St.	Oct. 31
Maryland ■	Nov. 7
Virginia	Nov. 14
Duke	Nov. 21
North Caro. St. [Charlotte, N. C.]	Nov. 28

1997 RESULTS (10-1-0)

23	Indiana	6
28	Stanford	17
40	Maryland	14

48 Virginia ... 20
31 Texas Christian ... 10
30 Wake Forest ... 12
20 North Caro. St. ... 7
16 Georgia Tech ... 13
3 Florida St. ... 20
17 Clemson ... 10
50 Duke ... 14
306 **143**

Gator Bowl

42 Virginia Tech ... 3

Nickname: Tar Heels.
Stadium: Kenan (1927), 60,000 capacity. Natural turf.
Colors: Carolina Blue & White.
Conference: Atlantic Coast.
SID: Steve Kirschner, 919-962-2123.
AD: Richard A. Baddour.

NORTH CARO. A&T

Greensboro, NC 27411 ... I-AA

Coach: Bill Hayes, N. C. Central 1965
Record: 22 Years, 156-85-2

1998 SCHEDULE

N.C. Central [Raleigh, N. C.] ... Sept. 5
Winston-Salem ■ ... Sept. 12
Hampton ... Sept. 19
Fayetteville St. ■ ... Sept. 26
Norfolk St. ■ ... Oct. 3
Florida A&M ... Oct. 10
Morgan St. ■ ... Oct. 17
Howard ... Oct. 24
Bethune-Cookman ■ ... Oct. 31
Delaware St. ... Nov. 7
South Caro. St. [Charlotte, N. C.] ... Nov. 21

1997 RESULTS (7-4-0)

36 N.C. Central ... 7
27 Winston-Salem ... 7
2 Hampton ... 7
49 Tennessee St. ... 37
40 Florida A&M ... 37
7 Morgan St. ... 6
13 Howard ... 21
25 Bethune-Cookman ... 26
22 Delaware St. ... 14
37 Grambling ... 35
18 South Caro. St. ... 33
276 **230**

Nickname: Aggies.
Stadium: Aggie (1981), 21,000 capacity. Natural turf.
Colors: Blue & Gold.
Conference: Mid-Eastern.
SID: Bradford Evans Jr., 919-334-7141.
AD: Willie J. Burden.

N.C. CENTRAL

Durham, NC 27707 ... II

Coach: Larry Little, Bethune-Cookman 1967
Record: 14 Years, 71-76-1

1998 SCHEDULE

North Caro. A&T [Raleigh, N. C.] ... Sept. 5
Gardner-Webb ... *Sept. 12
Virginia St. ■ ... Sept. 19
Albany St. (Ga.) ... *Sept. 26
Elizabeth City St. ■ ... Oct. 3
Fayetteville St. ... *Oct. 10
Winston-Salem ■ ... Oct. 17
Bowie St. ■ ... Oct. 24
Livingstone ... Oct. 31
Johnson Smith ■ ... Nov. 7

1997 RESULTS (4-7-0)

7 North Caro. A&T ... 36
12 Gardner-Webb ... 20
6 Virginia St. ... 13
0 West Ga. ... 27
37 Elizabeth City St. ... 6
38 Fayetteville St. ... 13
30 Winston-Salem ... 29
14 Bowie St. ... 20
7 Livingstone ... 20
28 Johnson Smith ... 0
0 Albany St. (Ga.) ... 20
179 **204**

Nickname: Eagles.
Stadium: O'Kelly-Riddick (1975), 11,500 capacity. Natural turf.
Colors: Maroon & Gray.
Conference: Central Intercol. Ath. Assn.
SID: Kyle Serba, 919-560-5427.
AD: William E. Lide.

NORTH CARO. ST.

Raleigh, NC 27695 ... I-A

Coach: Mike O'Cain, Clemson 1977
Record: 5 Years, 28-29-0

1998 SCHEDULE

Ohio ■ ... *Sept. 3
Florida St. ■ ... Sept. 12
Baylor ... *Sept. 19
Syracuse ■ ... Oct. 1
Georgia Tech ■ ... Oct. 10
Duke ■ ... Oct. 17
Virginia ... Oct. 24
Clemson ... Oct. 31
Wake Forest ■ ... Nov. 7
Maryland ... Nov. 21
North Caro. [Charlotte, N. C.] ... Nov. 28

1997 RESULTS (6-5-0)

32 Syracuse ... 31
45 Duke ... 14
17 Clemson ... 19
41 Northern Ill. ... 14
18 Wake Forest ... 19
17 Georgia Tech ... 27
7 North Caro. ... 20
35 Florida St. ... 48
45 Maryland ... 28
31 Virginia ... 24
37 East Caro. ... 24
325 **268**

Nickname: Wolfpack.
Stadium: Carter-Finley (1966), 51,500 capacity. Natural turf.
Colors: Red & White.
Conference: Atlantic Coast.
SID: Joan von Thron, 919-515-2102.
AD: Leslie G. Robinson.

NORTH CENTRAL

Naperville, IL 60566 ... III

Coach: Joe DeGeorge, Beloit 1988
(First year as head coach)

1998 SCHEDULE

Benedictine (Ill.) ... Sept. 12
Chicago ■ ... *Sept. 26
Wheaton (Ill.) ... Oct. 3
Elmhurst ... Oct. 10
Millikin ■ ... Oct. 17
Augustana (Ill.) ■ ... *Oct. 24
Ill. Wesleyan ... Oct. 31
North Park ... Nov. 7
Carthage ■ ... Nov. 14

1997 RESULTS (5-4-0)

7 Hanover ... 24
44 Blackburn ... 0
13 Carthage ... 23
42 North Park ... 6
20 Ill. Wesleyan ... 28
14 Augustana (Ill.) ... 42
48 Elmhurst ... 7
44 Millikin ... 6
20 Wheaton (Ill.) ... 7
252 **143**

Nickname: Cardinals.
Stadium: Kroehler Field, 7,500 capacity. Natural turf.
Colors: Cardinal & White.
Conference: College Conf. of Ill. & Wisc.
SID: Mike Koon, 708-637-5302.
AD: Walter J. Johnson.

NORTH DAK.

Grand Forks, ND 58202 ... II

Coach: Roger Thomas, Augustana (Ill.) 1969
Record: 14 Years, 82-63-2

1998 SCHEDULE

Moorhead St. ■ ... Sept. 12
South Dak. St. ... Sept. 19
Morningside ■ ... Sept. 26
Neb.-Omaha ... Oct. 3
Mankato St. ■ ... Oct. 10
North Dak. St. ... *Oct. 17
St. Cloud St. ... Oct. 24
South Dak. ■ ... Oct. 31
Augustana (S.D.) ... Nov. 7
Northern Colo. ■ ... Nov. 14

1997 RESULTS (8-2-0)

45 Moorhead St. ... 14
28 South Dak. St. ... 7
28 Morningside ... 14
35 Neb.-Omaha ... 24
21 Mankato St. ... 7
10 North Dak. St. ... 31
41 St. Cloud St. ... 21
20 South Dak. ... 19
42 Augustana (S.D.) ... 14
7 Northern Colo. ... 34
277 **185**

Nickname: Fighting Sioux.
Stadium: Memorial (1927), 10,000 capacity. Artificial turf.
Colors: Green & White.
Conference: No. Central Intercoll Ath Conf.
SID: Matt Schmidt, 701-777-2985.
AD: Terry L. Wanless.

NORTH DAK. ST.

Fargo, ND 58105 ... II

Coach: Bob Babich, Tulsa 1984
Record: 1 Year, 9-3-0

1998 SCHEDULE

Emporia St. ■ ... *Aug. 27
Texas A&M-Kingsville ■ ... *Sept. 3
Neb.-Omaha ... Sept. 19
Augustana (S.D.) ... *Sept. 26
Northern Colo. ■ ... Oct. 3
Morningside ... Oct. 10
North Dak. ■ ... *Oct. 17
South Dak. St. ■ ... *Oct. 24
St. Cloud St. ... Oct. 31
Mankato St. ■ ... *Nov. 7
South Dak. ■ ... *Nov. 14

1997 RESULTS (9-2-0)

31 West Ga. ... 14
51 Tex. A&M-Commerce ... 0
21 Neb.-Omaha ... 27
37 Augustana (S.D.) ... 0
28 Northern Colo. ... 24
35 Morningside ... 0
31 North Dak. ... 10
27 South Dak. St. ... 34
31 St. Cloud St. ... 0
47 Mankato St. ... 20
24 South Dak. ... 21
363 **150**

II Championship

28 Northwest Mo. St. ... 39

Nickname: Bison.
Stadium: FargoDome (1992), 18,700 capacity. Artificial turf.
Colors: Yellow & Green.
Conference: No. Central Intercoll Ath Conf.
SID: George Ellis, 701-231-8331.
AD: Robert Entzion.

NORTH PARK

Chicago, IL 60625....................................III

Coach: Mike Liljegren, North Park 1985
Record: 3 Years, 2-25-0

1998 SCHEDULE

Carroll (Wis.) ■ ....Sept. 12
Concordia (Ill.) ....Sept. 19
Carthage ....Oct. 3
Millikin ....Oct. 10
Wheaton (Ill.) ■ ....Oct. 17
Elmhurst ■ ....Oct. 24
Augustana (Ill.) ....Oct. 31
North Central ■ ....Nov. 7
Ill. Wesleyan ■ ....Nov. 14

1997 RESULTS (0-9-0)

7 Ripon 14
15 Mt. Senario 31
13 Ill. Wesleyan 64
6 North Central 42
3 Augustana (Ill.) 28
25 Elmhurst 28
0 Millikin 31
7 Wheaton (Ill.) 33
0 Carthage 14
76 **285**

Nickname: Vikings.
Stadium: Hedstrand Field (1955), 2,500 capacity. Natural turf.
Colors: Blue & Gold.
Conference: College Conf. of Ill. & Wisc.
SID: Chris Nelson, 312-244-5675.
AD: Jack Surridge.

NORTH TEXAS

Denton, TX 76203....................................I-A

Coach: Darrell Dickey, Kansas St. 1984
(First year as head coach)

1998 SCHEDULE

Oklahoma....................*Sept. 5
Texas Tech [Irving, Tex.]....................*Sept. 12
Arizona St. ....*Sept. 19
Texas A&M....................*Sept. 26
Boise St. ....*Oct. 10
Nevada ■ ....*Oct. 17
Houston ■ ....*Oct. 24
Idaho ■....................*Oct. 31
Kansas....................Nov. 7
Utah St. ....Nov. 14
New Mexico St. ■ ....Nov. 21

1997 RESULTS (4-7-0)

12 Vanderbilt....................29
7 Oregon St. 33
41 Indiana St....................6
30 Texas Tech 27
10 Texas A&M 36
17 Idaho 30
14 Boise St. 17
10 Nevada 65
26 New Mexico St....................15
14 Army....................25
51 Utah St. 48
232 **331**

Nickname: Mean Green Eagles.
Stadium: Fouts Field (1952), 30,500 capacity. Artificial turf.
Colors: Green & White.
Conference: Big West.
SID: Sean Johnson, 817-565-2476.
AD: Craig P. Helwig.

NORTHEAST LA.

Monroe, LA 71209 ....I-A

Coach: Ed Zaunbrecher, Middle Tenn. St. 1971
Record: 4 Years, 15-30-0

1998 SCHEDULE

Nicholls St. ■....................*Sept. 5
Florida....................*Sept. 12
Stephen F. Austin ■....................*Sept. 19
Kansas St....................Sept. 26
Western Mich....................*Oct. 3
Louisiana Tech ■....................*Oct. 10
Arizona ....Oct. 24
UAB ■....................*Oct. 31
Southwestern La. ■....................*Nov. 7
Arkansas St....................Nov. 14
Portland St. ■....................*Nov. 21

1997 RESULTS (5-7-0)

28 Nicholls St. 0
16 Arkansas 28
16 Louisiana Tech 17
3 Georgia 42
7 Oklahoma St. 38
17 Northwestern St. 7
10 Mississippi St. 24
14 Kentucky....................49
28 Southwestern La. 21
45 Central FLa. 41
19 Western Mich. 32
23 Hawaii 20
226 **319**

Nickname: Indians.
Stadium: Malone (1978), 30,427 capacity. Natural turf.
Colors: Maroon & Gold.
Conference: Independent.
SID: Robby Edwards, 318-342-5460.
AD: Richard C. Giannini.

NORTHEASTERN

Boston, MA 02115 ....I-AA

Coach: Barry Gallup, Boston College 1969
Record: 7 Years, 31-45-1

1998 SCHEDULE

New Hampshire ■ ....Sept. 5
Lafayette ■....................Sept. 12
William & Mary ....Sept. 19
Rhode Island ■....................Sept. 26
Delaware....................Oct. 3
Villanova ■....................Oct. 10
New Hampshire....................Oct. 17
Richmond ■....................Oct. 24
Connecticut ■ ....Oct. 31
James Madison....................Nov. 7
Maine....................Nov. 21

1997 RESULTS (8-3-0)

24 St. Mary's (Cal.)....................16
26 Connecticut....................38
41 Rhode Island....................13
14 Delaware 38
33 William & Mary....................12
34 New Hampshire....................19
28 Boston U....................7
21 Richmond 17
41 James Madison 17
23 Maine 17
35 Villanova 49
320 **243**

Nickname: Huskies.
Stadium: E.S. Parsons (1933), 7,000 capacity. Artificial turf.
Colors: Red & Black.
Conference: Atlantic 10.
SID: Jack Grinold, 617-373-2691.
AD: Ian Mc Caw.

NORTHEASTERN ST.

Tahlequah, OK 74464....................................II

Coach: Tom Eckert, Northeastern St. 1966
Record: 11 Years, 67-49-3

1998 SCHEDULE

Ouachita Baptist....................Oct. 17
Southeastern OkLa....................Oct. 31
Southwestern OkLa. ■....................Oct. 24
Angelo St....................*Sept. 19
Mo. Southern St. ■....................*Sept. 12
OkLa. Panhandle St. ....Nov. 7
East Central....................*Oct. 3
Harding ■ ....*Oct. 10
Midwestern St. ■....................Sept. 26
Central OkLa. ■....................Nov. 14

1997 RESULTS (4-7-0)

14 Central Ark....................20
16 Mo. Southern St. 24
30 Angelo St. 34
10 Midwestern St....................13
35 East Central 0
35 Harding 10
10 Ouachita Baptist 28
7 Southwestern OkLa....................6
20 Southeastern OkLa. 0
7 Southern Ark....................10
16 Central OkLa. 17
200 **162**

Nickname: Redmen.
Stadium: Gable Field, 12,000 capacity. Natural turf.
Colors: Green & White.
Conference: Lone Star Conference.
SID: Scott Pettus, 918-458-2339.
AD: Gil Cloud.

NORTHERN ARIZ.

Flagstaff, AZ 86011 ....I-AA

Coach: Jerome Souers, Oregon 1983
(First year as head coach)

1998 SCHEDULE

Cal Poly....................*Sept. 5
Southwest Tex. St. ■....................*Sept. 12
Cal St. Northridge ■ ....*Sept. 19
Western St. (Colo.) ■....................Sept. 26
Eastern Wash....................*Oct. 3
Idaho St. ■ ....Oct. 10
Montana....................Oct. 17
Cal St. Sacramento ■....................Oct. 24
Montana St. ....Oct. 31
Weber St. ■ ....Nov. 7
Portland St. ....*Nov. 14

1997 RESULTS (6-5-0)

10 New Mexico 33
33 St. Cloud St. 10
40 Minn.-Duluth 6
56 Portland St....................21
23 Weber St. 36
14 Montana St....................13
48 Cal St. Sacramento 25
27 Montana 24
24 Idaho St. 41
14 Eastern Wash. 31
13 Cal St. Northridge....................21
302 **261**

Nickname: Lumberjacks.
Stadium: Walkup Skydome (1977), 15,300 capacity. Artificial turf.
Colors: Blue & Gold.
Conference: Big Sky.
SID: Kevin Klintworth, 520-523-6792.
AD: Steven P. Holton.

NORTHERN COLO.

Greeley, CO 80639 II

Coach: Joe Glenn, South Dak. 1971
Record: 13 Years, 96-50-1

1998 SCHEDULE

Adams St. ■ ....Sept. 5
Western St. (Colo.) ■....................Sept. 12
Augustana (S.D.) ■....................Sept. 19
St. Cloud St....................Sept. 26
North Dak. St. ....Oct. 3
South Dak. ■ ....Oct. 10
Mankato St. ....Oct. 17
Neb.-Omaha....................Oct. 24
Morningside ■....................Oct. 31
South Dak. St. ■....................Nov. 7
North Dak....................Nov. 14

1997 RESULTS (9-2-0)

28 Mesa St. 7
13 Western St. (Colo.) 14
49 Augustana (S.D.) 40
30 St. Cloud St. 27
24 North Dak. St. 28
45 South Dak. 31
31 Mankato St. 0
37 Neb.-Omaha 17
41 Morningside 7
17 South Dak. St. 7
34 North Dak. 7
349 **185**

II Championship

24 Pittsburg St. 16
35 Northwest Mo. St. 19
30 Carson-Newman 29
51 New Haven 0

Nickname: Bears.
Stadium: Nottingham Field (1995), 7,000 capacity. Natural turf.
Colors: Blue & Gold.
Conference: No. Central Intercoll Ath Conf.
SID: Dave Moll, 303-351-2150.
AD: James E. Fallis.

NORTHERN ILL.

De Kalb, IL 60115 ....I-A

Coach: Joe Novak, Miami (Ohio) 1967
Record: 2 Years, 1-21-0

1998 SCHEDULE

Western Mich. ....*Sept. 3
Kansas St. ....Sept. 12
Eastern Ill. ■ ....*Sept. 19
Ball St. ....Oct. 3
Central FLa. ....*Oct. 10
Central Mich. ■ ....Oct. 17
Eastern Mich. ....*Oct. 24
Toledo ■ ....Oct. 31
Miami (Ohio) ■ ....Nov. 7
Ohio ....Nov. 14
Bowling Green ■ ....Nov. 21

1997 RESULTS (0-11-0)

10 Central Mich. 44
7 Kansas St. 47
13 Western Mich. 21
14 North Caro. St. 41
10 Bowling Green 35
7 Vanderbilt 17
14 Toledo 41
14 Ball St. 21
30 Ohio 35
10 Eastern Mich. 38
0 Miami (Ohio) 42
129 **382**

Nickname: Huskies.
Stadium: Huskie (1965), 30,998 capacity. Artificial turf.
Colors: Cardinal & Black.
Conference: Mid-American.
SID: Mike Korcek, 815-753-1706.
AD: Cary Groth.

NORTHERN IOWA

Cedar Falls, IA 50614 ....I-AA

Coach: Mike Dunbar, Washington 1972
Record: 7 Years, 61-13-1

1998 SCHEDULE

Eastern Mich. ....*Sept. 3
McNeese St. ■ ....*Sept. 12
Southern Ill. ....Sept. 19
Stephen F. Austin ....*Sept. 26
Southwest Mo. St. ■ ....*Oct. 3
Illinois St. ■ ....*Oct. 10
Cal Poly ■ ....Oct. 17
Indiana St. ....Oct. 31
Youngstown St. ....Nov. 7
Western Ill. ■ ....*Nov. 14
Winona St. ■ ....*Nov. 21

1997 RESULTS (7-4-0)

0 Iowa 66
39 Mankato St. 15
5 McNeese St. 22
28 Southern Ill. 27
50 Illinois St. 34
22 Western Ill. 29
35 Youngstown St. 32
24 Cal Poly 38
23 Southwest Mo. St. 22
53 Southern Utah 33
29 Indiana St. 21
308 **339**

Nickname: Panthers.
Stadium: U.N.I.-Dome (1976), 16,324 capacity. Artificial turf.
Colors: Purple & Old Gold.
Conference: Gateway.
SID: Nancy Justis, 319-273-6354.
AD: Christopher Ritrievi.

NORTHERN MICH.

Marquette, MI 49855 II

Coach: Eric Holm, Northeast Mo. 1981
Record: 8 Years, 58-29-0

1998 SCHEDULE

St. Francis (Ill.) ■ ....*Sept. 3
Minn.-Duluth ■ ....*Sept. 12
Ashland ....*Sept. 19
Saginaw Valley ■ ....Sept. 26
Ferris St. ....Oct. 3
Findlay ....Oct. 10
Michigan Tech ■ ....Oct. 17
Grand Valley St. ....Oct. 24
Indianapolis ....Oct. 31
Northwood ■ ....Nov. 7
Westminster (Pa.) ■ ....*Nov. 14

1997 RESULTS (7-4-0)

24 Minn.-Duluth 7
39 Northwood 32
47 St. Francis (Ill.) 20
23 Ferris St. 21
10 Indianapolis 12
10 Hillsdale 0
22 Grand Valley St. 39
22 Ashland 27
35 Wayne St. (Mich.) 29
17 Michigan Tech 12
20 Saginaw Valley 52
269 **251**

Nickname: Wildcats.
Stadium: Superior Dome (1991), 8,000 capacity. Artificial turf.
Colors: Old Gold & Olive Green.
Conference: Midwest Intercoll.
SID: Jim Pinar, 906-227-2720.
AD: Richard Comley.

NORTHERN ST.

Aberdeen, SD 57401 II

Coach: Ken Heupel
(First year as head coach)

1998 SCHEDULE

Augustana (S.D.) ■ ....*Sept. 5
Wis.-Stevens Point ....*Sept. 12
Minot St. ■ ....*Sept. 19
Winona St. ■ ....Sept. 26
Minn.-Morris ....Oct. 3
Wayne St. (Neb.) ....Oct. 10
Bemidji St. ■ ....Oct. 17
Minn.-Duluth ....Oct. 24
Southwest St. ■ ....Oct. 31
Moorhead St. ....Nov. 7
Winona St. [Minneapolis, Minn.] ....Nov. 14

1997 RESULTS (4-7-0)

2 Wis.-Stevens Point 28
16 South Dak. 41
27 Wis.-Stout 17
20 Moorhead St. 17
17 Winona St. 41
33 Minn.-Morris 19
14 Wayne St. (Neb.) 28
22 Bemidji St. 25
7 Minn.-Duluth 35
27 Southwest St. 22
7 Wis.-River Falls 31
192 **304**

Nickname: Wolves.
Stadium: Swisher (1975), 6,000 capacity. Natural turf.
Colors: Maroon & Gold.
Conference: Northern Sun.
SID: Bruce Bachmeier, 605-626-7748.
AD: James Kretchman.

NORTHWEST MO. ST.

Maryville, MO 64468 II

Coach: Mel Tjeerdsma, Southern St. (S. D.) 1967
Record: 14 Years, 88-58-4

1998 SCHEDULE

Midwestern St. ■ ....Sept. 5
Wayne St. (Neb.) ■ ....Sept. 12
Mo. Southern St. ....*Sept. 17
Mo. Western St. ■ ....Sept. 26
Washburn ....*Oct. 3
Mo.-Rolla ■ ....Oct. 10
Southwest Baptist ....Oct. 17
Pittsburg St. ■ ....Oct. 24
Central Mo. St. ....Oct. 31
Truman St. ....Nov. 7
Emporia St. ■ ....Nov. 14

1997 RESULTS (11-0-0)

52 Midwestern St. 14
57 Wayne St. (Neb.) 7
31 Mo. Southern St. 26
52 Mo. Western St. 13
17 Washburn 14
38 Mo.-Rolla 3
59 Southwest Baptist 3
15 Pittsburg St. 14
41 Central Mo. St. 9
34 Truman St. 10
44 Emporia St. 38
440 **151**

II Championship

39 North Dak. St. 28

Nickname: Bearcats.
Stadium: Rickenbrode (1917), 7,500 capacity. Natural turf.
Colors: Green & White.
Conference: MIAA.
SID: Andy Seeley, 816-562-1118.
AD: James C. Redd.

NORTHWESTERN

Evanston, IL 60208 ....I-A

Coach: Gary Barnett, Missouri 1969
Record: 8 Years, 41-46-2

1998 SCHEDULE

UNLV ■ ....Sept. 5
Duke ■ ....Sept. 12
Rice ....*Sept. 19
Wisconsin ....Sept. 26
Illinois ■ ....Oct. 3
Iowa ....Oct. 10
Michigan ■ ....*Oct. 17
Ohio St. ■ ....Oct. 24
Michigan St. ....Oct. 31
Purdue ■ ....Nov. 7
Penn St. ....Nov. 14
Hawaii ....*Nov. 21

1997 RESULTS (5-7-0)

24 Oklahoma 0
20 Wake Forest 27
24 Duke 20
34 Rice 40
9 Purdue 21
25 Wisconsin 26
6 Michigan 23
19 Michigan St. 17

SCHEDULES/RESULTS

6	Ohio St.	49
27	Penn St.	30
34	Illinois	21
15	Iowa	14
243		**288**

Nickname: Wildcats.
Stadium: Ryan Field (1926), 47,129 capacity. Natural turf.
Colors: Purple & White.
Conference: Big Ten.
SID: Brad Hurlbut, 847-491-7503.
AD: Rick Taylor.

NORTHWESTERN ST.

Natchitoches, LA 71497 ... I-AA

Coach: Sam Goodwin, Henderson State 1966
Record: 17 Years, 96-89-4

1998 SCHEDULE

Southern U. ■	*Sept. 5
Southwestern La.	*Sept. 12
Henderson St. ■	*Sept. 19
Southwest Tex. St.	*Sept. 26
Missouri	Oct. 3
McNeese St. ■	*Oct. 15
Nicholls St.	*Oct. 24
Troy St. ■	Oct. 31
Jacksonville St.	Nov. 7
Sam Houston St. ■	Nov. 14
Stephen F. Austin	Nov. 21

1997 RESULTS (8-3-0)

9	Southern U.	27
42	Henderson St.	7
19	Nicholls St.	0
7	Northeast La.	17
7	McNeese St.	50
31	Southwest Tex. St.	3
49	Arkansas Tech	10
14	Troy St.	13
42	Jacksonville St.	21
35	Sam Houston St.	19
38	Stephen F. Austin	24
293		**191**

I-AA Championship

10	Eastern Wash.	40

Nickname: Demons.
Stadium: Turpin (1976), 15,971 capacity. Artificial turf.
Colors: Purple, White & Burnt Orange.
Conference: Southland.
SID: Doug Ireland, 318-357-6467.
AD: Gregory S. Burke.

NORTHWOOD

Midland, MI 48640 ... II

Coach: Pat Riepma, Hillsdale 1983
Record: 5 Years, 16-34-2

1998 SCHEDULE

Michigan Tech ■	*Sept. 3
Grand Valley St.	Sept. 12
Westminster (Pa.)	Sept. 19
Ferris St. ■	Sept. 26
Wayne St. (Mich.)	Oct. 3
Indianapolis ■	Oct. 10
St. Francis (Ill.)	Oct. 17
Saginaw Valley ■	Oct. 24
Findlay ■	Oct. 31
Northern Mich.	Nov. 7

1997 RESULTS (3-7-0)

52	Michigan Tech	14
32	Northern Mich.	39
21	Saginaw Valley	59
7	Ashland	24
62	St. Francis (Ill.)	38
17	Ferris St.	31
19	Indianapolis	24
40	Hillsdale	43
20	Grand Valley St.	24
35	Wayne St. (Mich.)	20
305		**316**

Nickname: Timberwolves.
Stadium: Louis Juillerat (1964), 2,500 capacity. Natural turf.
Colors: Columbia Blue & White.
Conference: Midwest Intercoll.
SID: To be named, 517-837-4239.
AD: David W. Coffey.

NORWICH

Northfield, VT 05663 ... III

Coach: Mike Yesalonia, Norwich 1982
Record: 1 Year, 2-8-0

1998 SCHEDULE

Curry ■	Sept. 5
Merchant Marine ■	Sept. 12
Mass.-Lowell	*Sept. 18
Plymouth St.	Sept. 26
Coast Guard ■	Oct. 3
Worcester Tech ■	Oct. 10
Hartwick	Oct. 17
St. Lawrence	Oct. 24
Springfield ■	Nov. 7
Western Conn. St.	Nov. 14

1997 RESULTS (2-8-0)

21	Curry	0
0	Merchant Marine	25
13	Mass.-Lowell	42
3	Plymouth St.	37
10	Coast Guard	27
26	Worcester Tech	22
19	Hartwick	41
0	St. Lawrence	17
14	Springfield	73
2	Western Conn. St.	28
108		**312**

Nickname: Cadets.
Stadium: Sabine Field (1921), 5,000 capacity. Natural turf.
Colors: Maroon & Gold.
Conference: Freedom FB.
SID: Todd Bamford, 802-485-2160.
AD: Anthony A. Mariano.

NOTRE DAME

Notre Dame, IN 46556 ... I-A

Coach: Bob Davie, Youngstown St. 1976
Record: 1 Year, 7-6-0

1998 SCHEDULE

Michigan ■	Sept. 5
Michigan St.	*Sept. 12
Purdue ■	Sept. 26
Stanford ■	Oct. 3
Arizona St.	Oct. 10
Army ■	Oct. 24
Baylor ■	Oct. 31
Boston College	Nov. 7
Navy [Raljon, MD.]	Nov. 14
LSU ■	Nov. 21
Southern Cal	Nov. 28

1997 RESULTS (7-5-0)

17	Georgia Tech	13
17	Purdue	28
7	Michigan St.	23
14	Michigan	21
15	Stanford	33
45	Pittsburgh	21
17	Southern Cal	20
52	Boston College	20
21	Navy	17
24	LSU	6
21	West Va.	14
23	Hawaii	22
273		**238**

Independence Bowl

9	LSU	27

Nickname: Fighting Irish.
Stadium: Notre Dame (1930), 80,225 capacity. Natural turf.
Colors: Blue & Gold.
Conference: Big East.
SID: John Heisler, 219-631-7516.
AD: Michael A. Wadsworth.

OBERLIN

Oberlin, OH 44074 ... III

Coach: Pete Peterson, Kalamazoo 1974
Record: 4 Years, 1-38-0

1998 SCHEDULE

Kalamazoo ■	Sept. 5
Thiel	Sept. 12
Ohio Wesleyan ■	Sept. 19
Denison ■	Oct. 3
Wooster	Oct. 10
Wittenberg ■	Oct. 17
Earlham	Oct. 24
Case Reserve	Oct. 31
Kenyon ■	Nov. 7
Allegheny	Nov. 14

1997 RESULTS (1-9-0)

18	Thiel	17
12	Hiram	48
35	Kenyon	53
0	Wittenberg	74
12	Ohio Wesleyan	50
18	Denison	54
6	Case Reserve	42
28	Wooster	77
18	Earlham	64
16	Allegheny	75
163		**554**

Nickname: Yeomen.
Stadium: Dill Field (1925), 3,500 capacity. Natural turf.
Colors: Crimson & Gold.
Conference: North Coast Athletic Conf.
SID: Scott Wargo, 216-775-8503.
AD: Don Hunsinger.

OCCIDENTAL

Los Angeles, CA 90041 ... III

Coach: Dale Widolff, Indiana Central 1975
Record: 16 Years, 90-57-2

1998 SCHEDULE

La Verne	Sept. 19
Lewis & Clark ■	*Sept. 26
Redlands	*Oct. 3
Claremont-M-S ■	*Oct. 10
Chapman	*Oct. 17
Pomona-Pitzer ■	*Oct. 24
Cal Lutheran	Oct. 31
Azusa Pacific	*Nov. 7
Whittier ■	*Nov. 14

1997 RESULTS (1-8-0)

14	La Verne	41
21	Lewis & Clark	28
7	Menlo	41
14	Azusa Pacific	28
31	Claremont-M-S	12
35	Cal Lutheran	59
28	Pomona-Pitzer	45
31	Redlands	34
7	Whittier	41
188		**329**

Nickname: Tigers.
Stadium: Patterson Field (1900), 3,000 capacity. Natural turf.
Colors: Orange & Black.
Conference: So Calif Intercol Ath Conf.
SID: James Kerman, 213-259-2699.
AD: Dale V. Widolff.

OHIO

Athens, OH 45701 ... I-A

Coach: Jim Grobe, Virginia 1975
Record: 3 Years, 16-17-1

1998 SCHEDULE

North Caro. St.	*Sept. 3

Wisconsin	Sept. 12
East Caro. ■	Sept. 19
Western Mich.	*Sept. 26
Bowling Green	Oct. 3
Marshall ■	Oct. 10
Akron ■	Oct. 17
Miami (Ohio)	Oct. 31
Eastern Mich. ■	Nov. 7
Northern Ill. ■	Nov. 14
Kent	Nov. 21

1997 RESULTS (8-3-0)

31	Kent	7
21	Maryland	14
20	Kansas St.	23
50	Buffalo	0
31	Western Mich.	7
47	Eastern Mich.	7
24	Bowling Green	0
21	Akron	17
35	Northern Ill.	30
21	Miami (Ohio)	45
0	Marshall	27
301		**177**

Nickname: Bobcats.
Stadium: Peden (1929), 20,000 capacity. Natural turf.
Colors: Hunter Green & White.
Conference: Mid-American.
SID: George Mauzy, 614-593-1299.
AD: Thomas C. Boeh.

OHIO NORTHERN

Ada, OH 45810 III

Coach: Tom Kaczkowski, Illinois 1978
Record: 12 Years, 53-64-2

1998 SCHEDULE

Madison Tech ■	Sept. 5
Heidelberg	Sept. 19
Mount Union ■	Sept. 26
Marietta ■	Oct. 3
Baldwin-Wallace	Oct. 10
Muskingum ■	Oct. 17
Hiram	Oct. 24
Otterbein	*Oct. 31
John Carroll ■	Nov. 7
Capital	Nov. 14

1997 RESULTS (8-2-0)

55	Bluffton	0
21	John Carroll	28
61	Capital	27
14	Mount Union	38
68	Hiram	0
41	Muskingum	7
20	Marietta	17
28	Otterbein	24
31	Baldwin-Wallace	17
49	Heidelberg	7
388		**165**

Nickname: Polar Bears.
Stadium: Ada Memorial (1948), 4,000 capacity. Natural turf.
Colors: Orange & Black.
Conference: Ohio Athletic Conference.
SID: Tim Glon, 419-772-2046.
AD: Gale E. Daugherty.

OHIO ST.

Columbus, OH 43210 .... I-A

Coach: John Cooper, Iowa State 1962
Record: 21 Years, 167-73-6

1998 SCHEDULE

West Va.	*Sept. 5
Toledo ■	Sept. 12
Missouri ■	Sept. 19
Penn St. ■	Oct. 3
Illinois	Oct. 10
Minnesota ■	Oct. 17
Northwestern	Oct. 24
Indiana	Oct. 31
Michigan St. ■	Nov. 7
Iowa	Nov. 14
Michigan ■	Nov. 21

1997 RESULTS (10-2-0)

24	Wyoming	10
44	Bowling Green	13
28	Arizona	20
31	Missouri	10
23	Iowa	7
27	Penn St.	31
31	Indiana	0
49	Northwestern	6
37	Michigan St.	13
31	Minnesota	3
41	Illinois	6
14	Michigan	20
380		**139**

Sugar Bowl

14	Florida St.	31

Nickname: Buckeyes.
Stadium: Ohio (1922), 89,841 capacity. Natural turf.
Colors: Scarlet & Gray.
Conference: Big Ten.
SID: Gerry Emig, 614-292-6861.
AD: Ferdinand A. Geiger.

OHIO WESLEYAN

Delaware, OH 43015 III

Coach: Mike Hollway, Michigan 1974
Record: 15 Years, 82-65-2

1998 SCHEDULE

Grove City ■	Sept. 12
Oberlin	Sept. 19
Kenyon	Sept. 26
Case Reserve ■	Oct. 3
Wittenberg ■	Oct. 10
Defiance	Oct. 17
Denison	Oct. 24
Allegheny ■	Oct. 31
Earlham ■	Nov. 7
Wooster	Nov. 14

1997 RESULTS (4-6-0)

7	Olivet	12
21	Earlham	23
21	Allegheny	37
13	Kenyon	12
50	Oberlin	12
12	Wittenberg	37
28	Thomas More	20
30	Denison	28
7	Mercyhurst	31
14	Wooster	28
203		**240**

Nickname: Battling Bishops.
Stadium: Selby (1929), 9,600 capacity. Natural turf.
Colors: Red & Black.
Conference: North Coast Athletic Conf.
SID: Mark Beckenbach, 614-368-3340.
AD: John A. Martin.

OKLAHOMA

Norman, OK 73019 .... I-A

Coach: John Blake, Oklahoma 1983
Record: 2 Years, 7-16-0

1998 SCHEDULE

North Texas ■	*Sept. 5
Texas Christian	*Sept. 12
California ■	*Sept. 19
Colorado ■	*Oct. 3
Texas [Dallas, Tex.]	Oct. 10
Missouri	Oct. 17
Oklahoma St.	*Oct. 24
Iowa St. ■	Oct. 31
Texas A&M	Nov. 7
Baylor	Nov. 14
Texas Tech ■	Nov. 21

1997 RESULTS (4-8-0)

0	Northwestern	24
36	Syracuse	34
36	California	40
35	Louisville	14
17	Kansas	20
24	Texas	27
24	Baylor	23
7	Kansas St.	26
7	Nebraska	69
7	Oklahoma St.	30
7	Texas A&M	51
32	Texas Tech	21
232		**379**

Nickname: Sooners.
Stadium: Memorial (1923), 72,392 capacity. Natural turf.
Colors: Crimson & Cream.
Conference: Big 12.
SID: Mike Prusinski, 405-325-8228.
AD: Joseph R. Castiglione.

OKLA. PANHANDLE ST.

Goodwell, OK 73939 II

Coach: Jon Norris, American Intl 1984
Record: 1 Year, 3-7-0

1998 SCHEDULE

West Tex. A&M	*Aug. 29
Mesa St. ■	*Sept. 5
Southeastern Okla.	*Sept. 12
Sul Ross St.	Sept. 19
McMurry	Sept. 26
Northwestern Okla.	Oct. 3
Langston ■	Oct. 10
Prairie View ■	Oct. 24
Western N. Mex.	Oct. 31
Northeastern St. ■	Nov. 7

1997 RESULTS (3-7-0)

16	Sul Ross St.	6
13	Mesa St.	47
0	Western St. (Colo.)	46
27	McMurry	32
27	Southwestern (Kan.)	30
21	Fort Lewis	56
7	Western N. Mex.	14
10	Colorado Mines	7
29	Langston	26
0	Northwestern Okla.	45
150		**309**

Nickname: Aggies.
Stadium: Carl Wooten, 5,000 capacity. Natural turf.
Colors: Royal Blue & Red.
Conference: Independent.
SID: Karen Lang, 405-338-3355.
AD: Dan Stone.

OKLAHOMA ST.

Stillwater, OK 74078 .... I-A

Coach: Bob Simmons, Bowling Green 1971
Record: 3 Years, 17-18-0

1998 SCHEDULE

Kansas	Sept. 5
Tulsa	*Sept. 12
Mississippi St. ■	*Sept. 19
Nebraska [Kansas City, Mo.]	Oct. 3
Texas Tech	*Oct. 10
Kansas St.	Oct. 17
Oklahoma ■	*Oct. 24
Texas A&M ■	Oct. 31
Texas	Nov. 7
Southwestern La. ■	Nov. 14
Baylor ■	Nov. 21

1997 RESULTS (8-3-0)

21	Iowa St.	14
31	Southwestern La.	7
35	Fresno St.	0
38	Northeast La.	7
42	Texas	16
33	Colorado	29
50	Missouri	51
25	Texas A&M	28
30	Oklahoma	7

3	Texas Tech	27
24	Baylor	14
332		**200**

Alamo Bowl

20	Purdue	33

Nickname: Cowboys.
Stadium: Lewis (1920), 50,614 capacity. Artificial turf.
Colors: Orange & Black.
Conference: Big 12.
SID: Steve Buzzard, 405-744-5749.
AD: Terry Don Phillips.

OLIVET

Olivet, MI 49076 III

Coach: Dallas Hilliar, Central Mich. 1968
Record: 5 Years, 10-35-0

1998 SCHEDULE

Mount Saint Joseph ■	Sept. 5
Wilmington (Ohio)	Sept. 12
Manchester ■	Sept. 19
Defiance ■	Sept. 26
Albion ■	Oct. 10
Kalamazoo	Oct. 17
Adrian ■	Oct. 24
Hope	Oct. 31
Alma	Nov. 7

1997 RESULTS (3-6-0)

12	Ohio Wesleyan	7
30	Anderson (Ind.)	13
41	Defiance	14
11	Franklin	14
6	Albion	61
7	Kalamazoo	12
12	Adrian	29
8	Hope	37
0	Alma	31
127		**218**

Nickname: Comets.
Stadium: Griswold Field (1972), 3,500 capacity. Natural turf.
Colors: Red & White.
Conference: Michigan Intercoll Athl Assn.
SID: Tony Siefker, 616-749-7156.
AD: Richard A. Kaiser.

OREGON

Eugene, OR 97403 .... I-A

Coach: Mike Bellotti, UC Davis 1973
Record: 8 Years, 43-38-2

1998 SCHEDULE

Michigan St. ■	Sept. 5
UTEP	*Sept. 12
San Jose St. ■	Sept. 19
Stanford ■	Sept. 26
Washington St.	Oct. 10
UCLA	Oct. 17
Southern Cal ■	Oct. 24
Arizona	*Oct. 31
Washington ■	Nov. 7
Arizona St. ■	Nov. 14
Oregon St.	Nov. 21

1997 RESULTS (6-5-0)

16	Arizona	9
24	Nevada	20
43	Fresno St.	40
49	Stanford	58
13	Washington St.	24
31	UCLA	39
31	Utah	13
22	Southern Cal	24
31	Washington	28
31	Arizona St.	52
48	Oregon St.	30
339		**337**

Las Vegas Bowl

41	Air Force	13

Nickname: Ducks.
Stadium: Autzen (1967), 41,678 capacity. Artificial turf.
Colors: Green & Yellow.
Conference: Pacific-10.
SID: David Williford, 503-346-5488.
AD: William Moos.

OREGON ST.

Corvallis, OR 97331 .... I-A

Coach: Mike Riley, Alabama 1974
Record: 1 Year, 3-8-0

1998 SCHEDULE

Nevada ■	Sept. 5
Baylor ■	Sept. 12
Southern Cal	Sept. 19
Arizona St.	*Sept. 26
Utah St.	*Oct. 3
Stanford	Oct. 10
Arizona ■	Oct. 17
Washington	Oct. 24
California ■	Oct. 31
UCLA ■	Nov. 7
Oregon ■	Nov. 21

1997 RESULTS (3-8-0)

33	North Texas	7
24	Stanford	27
10	Arizona St.	13
26	San Jose St.	12
24	Utah St.	16
10	UCLA	34
17	Washington	45
14	California	33
7	Arizona	27
0	Southern Cal	23
30	Oregon	48
195		**285**

Nickname: Beavers.
Stadium: Parker (1953), 35,362 capacity. Artificial turf.
Colors: Orange & Black.
Conference: Pacific-10.
SID: Hal Cowan, 503-737-3720.
AD: Mitch S. Barnhart.

OTTERBEIN

Westerville, OH 43081 III

Coach: A. Wallace Hood, Ohio Wesleyan 1957
Record: 21 Years, 97-97-8

1998 SCHEDULE

Mount Saint Joseph	Sept. 12
Baldwin-Wallace	*Sept. 19
John Carroll ■	Sept. 26
Muskingum ■	Oct. 3
Capital	Oct. 10
Mount Union ■	Oct. 17
Heidelberg	Oct. 24
Ohio Northern ■	*Oct. 31
Hiram	Nov. 7
Marietta ■	Nov. 14

1997 RESULTS (2-8-0)

28	Hanover	35
50	Hiram	28
0	Mount Union	49
8	John Carroll	50
34	Marietta	51
17	Baldwin-Wallace	31
14	Heidelberg	19
24	Ohio Northern	28
17	Muskingum	21
20	Capital	13
212		**325**

Nickname: Cardinals.
Stadium: Memorial (1946), 4,000 capacity. Natural turf.
Colors: Tan & Cardinal.
Conference: Ohio Athletic Conference.
SID: Ed Syguda, 614-823-1600.
AD: Richard E. Reynolds.

OUACHITA BAPTIST

Arkadelphia, AR 71998 II

Coach: Jimmy "Red" Parker, Ark.-Monticello 1953
Record: 25 Years, 153-112-2

1998 SCHEDULE

Henderson St.	*Sept. 5
Southwest Baptist ■	*Sept. 12
Midwestern St.	Sept. 19
Angelo St. ■	*Sept. 26
Southwestern OkLa. ■	Oct. 3
Southeastern OkLa.	Oct. 10
Northeastern St. ■	Oct. 17
Central OkLa.	Oct. 24
East Central ■	Oct. 31
Harding	Nov. 7

1997 RESULTS (4-6-0)

23	Henderson St.	36
27	Southwest Baptist	26
28	Midwestern St.	30
14	Angelo St.	41
6	Southwestern OkLa.	12
16	Southeastern OkLa.	14
28	Northeastern St.	10
14	Central OkLa.	31
21	East Central	13
28	Harding	31
205		**244**

Nickname: Tigers.
Stadium: A.U. Williams Field, 5,200 capacity. Natural turf.
Colors: Purple & Gold.
Conference: Lone Star Conference.
SID: Mac Sisson, 501-245-5208.
AD: Buddy Benson.

PACE

New York, NY 10038 II

Coach: Gregory Lusardi, Slippery Rock 1975
Record: 4 Years, 19-21-0

1998 SCHEDULE

Gannon	Sept. 5
Mass.-Lowell	*Sept. 11
Stony Brook	Sept. 26
Southern Conn. St. ■	Oct. 3
Bryant ■	Oct. 10
Bentley	Oct. 17
LIU-C.W. Post ■	Oct. 24
American Int'l ■	Oct. 31
Albany (N.Y.)	Nov. 7
Assumption ■	Nov. 14

1997 RESULTS (5-5-0)

29	Mass.-Lowell	7
7	Stony Brook	38
26	Iona	0
20	Southern Conn. St.	39
14	Albany (N.Y.)	48
3	Gannon	19
8	LIU-C.W. Post	7
0	American Int'l	20
19	Sacred Heart	7
8	Assumption	0
134		**185**

Nickname: Setters.
Stadium: Finnerty Field, 1,500 capacity. Natural turf.
Colors: Blue & Gold.
Conference: Eastern Football.
SID: Nick Renda, 914-773-3411.
AD: Joseph F. O'Donnell.

PACIFIC LUTHERAN

Tacoma, WA 98447 III

Coach: Frosty Westering, Neb.-Omaha 1952
Record: 33 Years, 256-81-7

1998 SCHEDULE

Cal Lutheran ■	Sept. 12
Southern Ore.	Sept. 19
Lewis & Clark	Oct. 3

Eastern Ore. U. ■ ....Oct. 10
Simon Fraser ■ ....Oct. 17
Whitworth ....Oct. 24
Linfield ■ ....Oct. 31
Willamette ■ ....Nov. 7
Puget Sound ....Nov. 14

1997 RESULTS (7-2-0)

45 Cal Lutheran 23
46 Western Wash. 44
27 Simon Fraser 20
53 Lewis & Clark 16
30 Eastern Ore. U. 26
45 Whitworth 24
12 Linfield 28
6 Willamette 43
52 Puget Sound 10
316 **234**

Nickname: Lutes.
Stadium: Sparks, 4,500 capacity. Artificial turf.
Colors: Black & Gold.
Conference: NCIC.
SID: Nick Dawson, 235-535-7356.
AD: Paul Hoseth.

PENNSYLVANIA

Philadelphia, PA 19104 ....I-AA

Coach: Al Bagnoli, Central Conn. St. 19
Record: 16 Years, 130-34-0

1998 SCHEDULE

Dartmouth ....Sept. 19
Richmond ■ ....Sept. 26
Bucknell ■ ....Oct. 3
Fordham ....Oct. 10
Columbia ■ ....Oct. 17
Brown ....Oct. 24
Yale ■ ....Oct. 31
Princeton ....Nov. 7
Harvard ■ ....Nov. 14
Cornell ....Nov. 21

1997 RESULTS (6-4-0)

15 Dartmouth 23
16 Bucknell 20
26 Towson 14
7 Lehigh 24
24 Columbia 7
31 Brown 10
26 Yale 7
20 Princeton 17
0 Harvard 33
33 Cornell 20
198 **175**

Nickname: Quakers.
Stadium: Franklin Field (1895), 53,000 capacity. Artificial turf.
Colors: Red & Blue.
Conference: Ivy.
SID: Shaun May, 215-898-6128.
AD: Steve Bilsky.

PENN ST.

University Park, PA 16802 ....I-A

Coach: Joe Paterno, Brown 1950
Record: 32 Years, 298-77-3

1998 SCHEDULE

Southern Miss. ■ ....Sept. 5
Bowling Green ■ ....Sept. 12
Pittsburgh ....Sept. 19
Ohio St. ....Oct. 3
Minnesota ....Oct. 10
Purdue ■ ....Oct. 17
Illinois ■ ....Oct. 31
Michigan ....Nov. 7
Northwestern ■ ....Nov. 14
Wisconsin ....Nov. 21
Michigan St. ■ ....Nov. 28

1997 RESULTS (9-2-0)

34 Pittsburgh 17
52 Temple 10
57 Louisville 21
41 Illinois 6
31 Ohio St. 27
16 Minnesota 15
30 Northwestern 27
8 Michigan 34
42 Purdue 17
35 Wisconsin 10
14 Michigan St. 49
360 **233**

Florida Citrus Bowl

6 Florida 21

Nickname: Nittany Lions.
Stadium: Beaver (1960), 93,967 capacity. Natural turf.
Colors: Blue & White.
Conference: Big Ten.
SID: Jeff Nelson, 814-865-1757.
AD: Timothy M. Curley.

PITTSBURG ST.

Pittsburg, KS 66762 II

Coach: Chuck Broyles, Pittsburg St. 1970
Record: 8 Years, 86-13-2

1998 SCHEDULE

Tex. A&M-Commerce ....*Sept. 12
Emporia St. ....*Sept. 19
Mo. Southern St. ■ ....*Sept. 26
Mo.-Rolla ....Oct. 3
Southwest Baptist ■ ....Oct. 10
Central Mo. St. ■ ....*Oct. 15
Northwest Mo. St. ....Oct. 24
Truman St. ■ ....Oct. 31
Mo. Western St. ....Nov. 7
Washburn ■ ....Nov. 14

1997 RESULTS (9-1-0)

9 Southwest Mo. St. 8
32 Emporia St. 22
42 Mo. Southern St. 14
42 Mo.-Rolla 7
57 Southwest Baptist 0
30 Central Mo. St. 29
14 Northwest Mo. St. 15
28 Truman St. 18
21 Mo. Western St. 14
40 Washburn 11
315 **138**

II Championship

16 Northern Colo. 24

Nickname: Gorillas.
Stadium: Carnie Smith (1924), 5,600 capacity. Natural turf.
Colors: Crimson & Gold.
Conference: MIAA.
SID: Dan Wilkes, 316-235-4147.
AD: Charles Broyles.

PITTSBURGH

Pittsburgh, PA 15260 ....I-A

Coach: Walt Harris, Pacific (Cal.) 1968
Record: 4 Years, 17-30-0

1998 SCHEDULE

Villanova ■ ....Sept. 5
Penn St. ■ ....Sept. 19
Virginia Tech ....Sept. 26
Akron ■ ....Oct. 3
North Caro. ....Oct. 10
Rutgers ■ ....Oct. 17
Syracuse ....Oct. 31
Temple ■ ....Nov. 7
Boston College ■ ....Nov. 14
Miami (Fla.) ....*Nov. 19
West Va. ■ ....Nov. 27

1997 RESULTS (6-5-0)

45 Southwestern La. 13
17 Penn St. 34
35 Houston 24
21 Miami (Fla.) 17
13 Temple 17
21 Notre Dame 45
55 Rutgers 48
21 Boston College 22
27 Syracuse 32
30 Virginia Tech 23
41 West Va. 38
326 **313**

Liberty Bowl

7 Southern Miss. 41

Nickname: Panthers.
Stadium: Pitt (1925), 56,150 capacity. Artificial turf.
Colors: Gold & Blue.
Conference: Big East.
SID: Ron Wahl, 412-648-8240.
AD: Steven C. Pederson.

PLYMOUTH ST.

Plymouth, NH 03264 III

Coach: Mike Kemp, Notre Dame 1975
Record: 2 Years, 12-8-0

1998 SCHEDULE

Maine Maritime ....Sept. 12
Brockport St. ■ ....Sept. 19
Norwich ■ ....Sept. 26
Western Conn. St. ....Oct. 3
Merchant Marine ....Oct. 10
Springfield ....Oct. 17
Bentley ■ ....Oct. 24
Coast Guard ....Oct. 31
Kean ■ ....Nov. 7
Worcester Tech ■ ....Nov. 14

1997 RESULTS (7-3-0)

44 Maine Maritime 6
9 Brockport St. 10
37 Norwich 3
23 Western Conn. St. 13
33 Merchant Marine 20
36 Springfield 16
15 Bri'water (Mass.) 9
0 Coast Guard 19
42 Curry 0
7 Worcester Tech 9
246 **105**

ECAC III Playoff

17 Buffalo St. 21

Nickname: Panthers.
Stadium: Currier Memorial Field (1970), 1,000 capacity. Natural turf.
Colors: Green & White.
Conference: Freedom FB.
SID: Kent Cherrington, 603-535-2477.
AD: Stephen R. Bamford.

POMONA-PITZER

Claremont, CA 91711 III

Coach: Roger Caron, Harvard 1985
Record: 4 Years, 19-15-0

1998 SCHEDULE

Colorado Col. ....Sept. 5
Lawrence ■ ....Sept. 12
Whitworth ■ ....Sept. 26
Whittier ■ ....Oct. 3
Puget Sound ....Oct. 10
Occidental ....*Oct. 24
Claremont-M-S ■ ....Nov. 7
Azusa Pacific ■ ....Nov. 14

1997 RESULTS (6-2-0)

55 Grinnell 20
31 Colorado Col. 7
35 Whitworth 49
29 Whittier 26
76 Swarthmore 12
28 Menlo 35
45 Occidental 28
74 Claremont-M-S 7
373 **184**

Nickname: Sagehens.

Stadium: Merritt Field (1991), 2,000 capacity. Natural turf.
Colors: Blue, Orange & White.
Conference: Independent.
SID: Kirk Reynolds, 909-621-8429.
AD: Daniel Bridges.

PORTLAND ST.

Portland, OR 97207 .... I-AA

Coach: Tim Walsh, UC Riverside 1977
Record: 9 years, 59-40-0

1998 SCHEDULE

Eastern Wash.	*Sept. 12
Boise St.	*Sept. 19
Idaho St.■	*Sept. 26
Montana	Oct. 3
Cal St. Sacramento ■	*Oct. 10
Montana St.	Oct. 17
Weber St. ■	*Oct. 24
Cal Poly ■	*Oct. 31
Cal St. Northridge	Nov. 7
Northern Ariz. ■	*Nov. 14
Northeast La.	*Nov. 21

1997 RESULTS (4-7-0)

7	Fresno St.	35
0	Idaho	46
14	Eastern Wah.	31
21	Northern Ariz.	56
26	Cal St. Northridge	13
35	St. Mary's (Cal.)	21
7	Weber St.	16
44	Montana St.	0
27	Cal St. Sacramento	13
7	Montana	37
24	Idaho St.	26
212		**294**

Nickname:Vikings.
Stadium: Civic (1928), 23,150 capacity. Artificial turf.
Colors: Green & White.
Conference: Big Sky.
SID: Larry Sellers, 503-725-2525.
AD: Jim Sterk.

PRAIRIE VIEW

Prairie View, TX 77446 .... I-AA

Coach: Greg Johnson, NW Oklahoma 1983
Record: 7 Years, 35-39-0

1998 SCHEDULE

Texas Southern [Houston, Tex.]	*Sept. 5
Howard Payne	*Sept. 12
Southern U. ■	*Sept. 19
Langston [Oklahoma City, Okla.]	*Sept. 26
Grambling [Dallas, Tex.]	*Oct. 3
Alcorn St. ■	Oct. 10
Alabama St. ■	*Oct. 17
OkLa. Panhandle St.	Oct. 24
Mississippi Val.	Oct. 31
Ark.-Pine Bluff	Nov. 7
Jackson St.	Nov. 14

1997 RESULTS (0-9-0)

16	Texas Southern	32
10	Langston	19
7	Southern U.	63
6	Grambling	33
9	Alcorn St.	24
7	Alabama St.	56
0	Mississippi Val.	27
14	Ark.-Pine Bluff	48
7	Jackson St.	20
76		**322**

Nickname: Panthers.
Stadium: Blackshear (1960), 6,000 capacity. Natural turf.
Colors: Purple & Gold.
Conference: Southwestern.
SID: Harlan S. Robinson, 409-857-2114.
AD: Clifton Gilliard.

PRESBYTERIAN

Clinton, SC 29325 II

Coach: Daryl Dickey, Tennessee 1986
Record: 1 Year, 5-6-0

1998 SCHEDULE

West Ga.	*Aug. 29
Charleston So. ■	Sept. 12
Carson-Newman	Sept. 19
Lenoir-Rhyne ■	Sept. 26
Tusculum ■	Oct. 3
Catawba ■	Oct. 10
Elon	Oct. 17
Mars Hill	Oct. 24
Wingate ■	Oct. 31
Gardner-Webb	Nov. 7
Newberry ■	Nov. 14

1997 RESULTS (5-6-0)

14	Shepherd	18
16	Charleston So.	7
3	Carson-Newman	21
26	Lenoir-Rhyne	13
49	Tusculum	7
10	Catawba	7
3	Elon	24
24	Mars Hill	14
14	Wingate	22
13	Gardner-Webb	16
22	Newberry	28
194		**177**

Nickname: Blue Hose.
Stadium: Bailey Memorial, 5,000 capacity. Natural turf.
Colors: Garnet & Blue.
Conference: South Atlantic Conference.
SID: Al Ansley, 803-833-8252.
AD: J. Allen Morris.

PRINCETON

Princeton, NJ 08544 .... I-AA

Coach: Steve Tosches, Rhode Island 1979
Record: 11 Years, 69-39-2

1998 SCHEDULE

Cornell ■	Sept. 19
Lehigh	Sept. 26
Fordham	Oct. 3
Brown ■	Oct. 10
Lafayette	Oct. 17
Harvard ■	Oct. 24
Columbia	Oct. 31
Pennsylvania ■	Nov. 7
Yale	Nov. 14
Dartmouth ■	Nov. 21

1997 RESULTS (5-5-0)

10	Cornell	14
9	Fordham	7
21	Holy Cross	7
30	Brown	13
31	Colgate	28
12	Harvard	14
0	Columbia	17
17	Pennsylvania	20
9	Yale	0
9	Dartmouth	12
148		**132**

Nickname: Tigers.
Stadium: Princeton (1998), 27,800 capacity. Natural turf.
Colors: Orange & Black.
Conference: Ivy.
SID: Jerry Price, 609-258-3568.
AD: Gary D. Walters.

PRINCIPIA

Elsah, IL 62028 III

Coach: Rod Humenuik
(First year as head coach)

1998 SCHEDULE

Concordia (Ill.)	Sept. 5
Grinnell	Sept. 12
Concordia-St. Paul ■	Sept. 19
Greenville	Sept. 26
MacMurray	Oct. 10
Westminster (Mo.) ■	Oct. 17
Blackburn ■	Oct. 24
Trinity Bible (N.D.) ■	Oct. 31

1997 RESULTS (0-8-0)

7	Illinois Col.	27
0	Grinnell	48
8	Maranatha Baptist	44
13	MacMurray	59
6	Concordia (Ill.)	37
14	Blackburn	34
0	Greenville	46
26	Westminster (Mo.)	43
74		**338**

Nickname: Panthers.
Stadium: Clark Field (1937), 1,000 capacity. Natural turf.
Colors: Navy Blue & Gold.
Conference: St. Louis Intercol. Ath. Conf.
SID: Phil Webster, 618-374-5372.
AD: Seth C. Johnson.

PURDUE

West Lafayette, IN 47907 .... I-A

Coach: Joe Tiller, Montana St. 1965
Record: 7 Years, 48-33-1

1998 SCHEDULE

Southern Cal	Aug. 30
Rice ■	Sept. 12
Central FLa. ■	Sept. 19
Notre Dame	Sept. 26
Minnesota ■	Oct. 3
Wisconsin	*Oct. 10
Penn St.	Oct. 17
Illinois ■	Oct. 24
Iowa ■	Oct. 31
Northwestern	Nov. 7
Michigan St.	Nov. 14
Indiana ■	Nov. 21

1997 RESULTS (8-3-0)

22	Toledo	36
28	Notre Dame	17
28	Ball St.	14
21	Northwestern	9
59	Minnesota	43
45	Wisconsin	20
48	Illinois	3
17	Iowa	35
22	Michigan St.	21
17	Penn St.	42
56	Indiana	7
363		**247**

Alamo Bowl

33	Oklahoma St.	20

Nickname: Boilermakers.
Stadium: Ross-Ade (1924), 67,332 capacity. Natural turf.
Colors: Old Gold & Black.
Conference: Big Ten.
SID: Mark Adams, 317-494-3202.
AD: Morgan J. Burke.

QUINCY

Quincy, IL 62301 II

Coach: Brian Cox, Western Ill. 1989
Record: 1 Year, 0-10-0

1998 SCHEDULE

McKendree ■	Aug. 29
Mo.-Rolla	Sept. 5
Morningside	Sept. 12
St. Xavier ■	Sept. 19
Drake ■	Sept. 26
St. Joseph's (Ind.)	Oct. 3
Ky. Wesleyan	Oct. 17
Northwestern OkLa.	Oct. 24
Madison Tech	Oct. 31

Butler ■ ... Nov. 7
Wayne St. (Neb.) ■ ... Nov. 14

1997 RESULTS (0-10-0)

0 Mo.-Rolla	40
7 Mo. Western St.	49
14 Evansville	41
14 St. Joseph's (Ind.)	52
12 St. Francis (Ill.)	61
20 Ky. Wesleyan	42
18 Northwestern Okla.	40
0 McKendree	39
14 Winona St.	59
7 Wayne St. (Neb.)	57
106	**480**

Nickname: Hawks.
Stadium: QU (1938), 2,500 capacity. Natural turf.
Colors: Brown, White & Gold.
Conference: Independent.
SID: J. D. Hamilton, 217-228-5277.
AD: James Naumovich.

RANDOLPH-MACON

Ashland, VA 23005 ... III

Coach: Scott Boone, Wabash 1981
Record: 1 Year, 8-2-0

1998 SCHEDULE

Frank. & Marsh. ■	Sept. 12
Catholic	Sept. 19
Chowan ■	Sept. 26
Wash. & Lee	Oct. 3
Gettysburg ■	Oct. 10
Emory & Henry	Oct. 17
Davidson	Oct. 24
Guilford ■	Oct. 31
Bridgewater (Va.) ■	Nov. 7
Hampden-Sydney	Nov. 14

1997 RESULTS (8-2-0)

37 Frank. & Marsh.	25
21 Catholic	34
38 Chowan	3
24 Wash. & Lee	3
44 Gettysburg	13
27 Emory & Henry	20
22 Davidson	15
21 Guilford	35
37 Bridgewater (Va.)	20
49 Hampden-Sydney	18
320	**186**

Nickname: Yellow Jackets.
Stadium: Day Field (1953), 5,000 capacity. Natural turf.
Colors: Lemon & Black.
Conference: Old Dominion Athletic Conf.
SID: Todd Hilder, 804-798-8372.
AD: Gregg Waters.

REDLANDS

Redlands, CA 92373 ... III

Coach: Mike Maynard, Ill. Wesleyan 1980
Record: 10 Years, 61-30-1

1998 SCHEDULE

Linfield ■	*Sept. 12
San Diego	*Sept. 19
Puget Sound	*Sept. 26
Occidental ■	*Oct. 3
Menlo ■	*Oct. 10
La Verne	Oct. 24
Claremont-M-S ■	*Oct. 31
Whittier	Nov. 7
Cal Lutheran ■	*Nov. 14

1997 RESULTS (7-2-0)

33 Lewis & Clark	25
8 San Diego	15
37 Puget Sound	0
28 Cal Lutheran	21
56 Claremont-M-S	3
26 Menlo	20
24 Whittier	27
34 Occidental	31
42 La Verne	14
288	**156**

Nickname: Bulldogs.
Stadium: Ted Runner (1968), 7,000 capacity. Natural turf.
Colors: Maroon & Gray.
Conference: So Calif Intercol Ath Conf.
SID: Ross French, 909-335-4031.
AD: Carl R. Clapp.

RENSSELAER

Troy, NY 12180 ... III

Coach: Joe King, Siena 1970
Record: 9 Years, 58-25-2

1998 SCHEDULE

Kean	Sept. 12
Coast Guard	Sept. 19
Worcester Tech ■	Sept. 26
Rochester	Oct. 3
Union (N.Y.)	Oct. 17
Hartwick ■	Oct. 24
St. John Fisher ■	Oct. 31
St. Lawrence ■	Nov. 7
Hobart	Nov. 14

1997 RESULTS (8-1-0)

16 Coast Guard	22
45 Rochester	0
20 Kean	14
37 Worcester Tech	16
30 Union (N.Y.)	7
25 Hartwick	24
38 St. John Fisher	6
35 St. Lawrence	0
16 Hobart	14
262	**103**

ECAC III Playoff

14 Worcester St.	13

Nickname: Engineers.
Stadium: '86 Field (1912), 3,000 capacity. Natural turf.
Colors: Cherry & White.
Conference: Upstate Collegiate Athl Assn.
SID: To be named, 518-276-2187.
AD: Robert F. Ducatte.

RHODE ISLAND

Kingston, RI 02881 ... I-AA

Coach: Floyd Keith, Ohio Northern 1970
Record: 9 Years, 41-53-2

1998 SCHEDULE

William & Mary ■	Sept. 5
Richmond ■	Sept. 19
Northeastern	Sept. 26
Brown ■	Oct. 3
Maine	Oct. 10
Hofstra	Oct. 17
Connecticut	Oct. 24
James Madison ■	Oct. 31
Massachusetts ■	Nov. 7
New Hampshire	Nov. 14
Villanova	Nov. 21

1997 RESULTS (2-9-0)

14 Maine	30
35 New Hampshire	21
13 Northeastern	41
14 Massachusetts	18
21 Hofstra	28
20 Boston U.	17
15 Brown	23
21 Connecticut	37
15 Villanova	37
11 Richmond	27
37 James Madison	39
216	**318**

Nickname: Rams.
Stadium: Meade Stadium (1928), 8,000 capacity. Natural turf.
Colors: Light & Dark Blue & White.
Conference: Atlantic 10.
SID: Mike Ballweg, 401-874-2401.
AD: Ronald J. Petro.

RHODES

Memphis, TN 38112 ... III

Coach: Joe White, Springfield 1984
Record: 1 Year, 2-7-0

1998 SCHEDULE

DePauw ■	Sept. 5
Wabash ■	Sept. 12
Centre ■	Sept. 19
Maryville (Tenn.) ■	Sept. 26
Washington (Mo.) ■	Oct. 3
Rose-Hulman	Oct. 10
Sewanee	Oct. 17
Colorado Col. ■	Oct. 24
Trinity (Tex.)	*Oct. 31
Millsaps ■	Nov. 7

1997 RESULTS (2-7-0)

0 Washington (Mo.)	44
22 Millsaps	19
13 Austin	21
13 Carnegie Mellon	20
26 Maryville (Tenn.)	38
27 Sewanee	17
9 Trinity (Tex.)	38
26 Millsaps	36
14 Centre	38
150	**271**

Nickname: Lynx.
Stadium: Fargason Field, 3,300 capacity. Natural turf.
Colors: Red, Black & White.
Conference: Southern Collegiate Ath. Conf.
SID: To be named, 901-726-3940.
AD: Mike Clary.

RICE

Houston, TX 77005 ... I-A

Coach: Ken Hatfield, Arkansas 1965
Record: 19 Years, 134-84-4

1998 SCHEDULE

Southern Methodist ■	*Sept. 5
Purdue	Sept. 12
Northwestern ■	*Sept. 19
Texas	Sept. 26
San Jose St.	*Oct. 10
Tulsa ■	Oct. 17
Wyoming	Oct. 24
Colorado St. ■	Oct. 31
Texas Christian	Nov. 7
UNLV ■	Nov. 14
Air Force	Nov. 21

1997 RESULTS (7-4-0)

12 Air Force	41
30 Tulane	24
40 Northwestern	34
31 Texas	38
42 Tulsa	24
27 Brigham Young	14
35 New Mexico	23
6 Southern Methodist	24
38 Texas Christian	19
14 Utah	31
31 UTEP	13
306	**285**

Nickname: Owls.
Stadium: Rice (1950), 70,000 capacity. Artificial turf.
Colors: Blue & Gray.
Conference: Western Athletic.
SID: Bill Cousins, 713-527-4034.
AD: John R. May.

RICHMOND

Richmond, VA 23173 ... I-AA

Coach: Jim Reid, Maine 1973
Record: 9 Years, 51-46-3

1998 SCHEDULE

Rutgers	*Sept. 5
Massachusetts ■	Sept. 12
Rhode Island	Sept. 19
Pennsylvania	Sept. 26

James Madison ■	Oct. 3
New Hampshire	Oct. 10
Maine	Oct. 17
Northeastern	Oct. 24
Villanova	Nov. 7
Delaware ■	Nov. 14
William & Mary ■	Nov. 21

1997 RESULTS (6-5-0)

21	Massachusetts	6
23	Colgate	7
7	Virginia	26
56	VMI	3
17	Maine	14
7	Delaware	24
29	Villanova	40
26	James Madison	21
17	Northeastern	21
27	Rhode Island	11
7	William & Mary	10
237		**183**

Nickname: Spiders.
Stadium: Richmond (1929), 21,319 capacity. Natural turf.
Colors: Red & Blue.
Conference: Atlantic 10.
SID: Phil Stanton, 804-289-8320.
AD: Charles S. Boone.

RIPON

Ripon, WI 54971 III

Coach: Ron Ernst, Neb. Wesleyan 1980
Record: 7 Years, 42-23-0

1998 SCHEDULE

Elmhurst ■	Sept. 12
Knox ■	Sept. 19
Carroll (Wis.)	Sept. 26
St. Norbert	Oct. 3
Lake Forest ■	Oct. 10
Grinnell	Oct. 17
Monmouth (Ill.) ■	Oct. 24
Illinois Col.	Oct. 31
Lawrence ■	Nov. 7
Beloit	Nov. 14

1997 RESULTS (6-3-0)

0	Lakeland	48
14	North Park	7
14	Cornell College	28
17	Grinnell	14
32	Beloit	26
45	Lake Forest	19
16	St. Norbert	14
3	Carroll (Wis.)	32
43	Lawrence	24
184		**212**

Nickname: Red Hawks.
Stadium: Ingalls Field (1888), 2,500 capacity. Natural turf.
Colors: Red & White.
Conference: Midwest Conference.
SID: Chris Graham, 414-748-8133.
AD: Robert G. Gillespie.

ROBERT MORRIS

Moon Township, PA 15108 .... I-AA

Coach: Joe Walton, Pittsburgh 1957
Record: 4 Years, 30-10-1

1998 SCHEDULE

Buffalo St.	Sept. 5
Dayton	Sept. 12
Central Conn. St. ■	Sept. 26
Wagner	Oct. 3
Valparaiso ■	Oct. 10
Sacred Heart ■	Oct. 17
Monmouth ■	Oct. 24
St. Francis (Pa.)	Nov. 7
New Haven ■	Nov. 14
Duquesne	Nov. 21

1997 RESULTS (7-3-0)

35	Buffalo St.	23
26	Butler	21
13	Dayton	16
44	Central Conn. St.	21
21	Wagner	9
30	Towson	33
41	Monmouth	20
10	Mercyhurst	17
34	St. Francis (Pa.)	7
17	Gannon	13
271		**180**

ECAC I-AA Playoff

35	Georgetown	13

Nickname: Colonials.
Stadium: Moon (1950), 7,000 capacity. Natural turf.
Colors: Blue & White.
Conference: Northeast.
SID: Marty Galosi, 412-262-8314.
AD: Bruce A. Corrie.

ROCHESTER

Rochester, NY 14627 III

Coach: Mark Kreydt, Rochester 1988
(First year as head coach)

1998 SCHEDULE

Buffalo St.	Sept. 12
Case Reserve ■	Sept. 19
St. Lawrence	Sept. 26
Rensselaer ■	Oct. 3
Hobart ■	Oct. 10
Washington (Mo.) ■	Oct. 17
Chicago	Oct. 24
Carnegie Mellon	Oct. 31
Union (N.Y.) ■	Nov. 7

1997 RESULTS (1-8-0)

0	Rensselaer	45
6	St. Lawrence	24
7	Union (N.Y.)	35
14	Hobart	48
28	Chicago	18
9	Washington (Mo.)	32
0	Carnegie Mellon	14
19	Buffalo St.	43
6	Case Reserve	21
89		**280**

Nickname: Yellowjackets.
Stadium: Fauver (1930), 5,000 capacity. Artificial turf.
Colors: Yellow & Blue.
Conference: University Athletic Assoc.
SID: Dennis O'Donnell, 716-275-5955.
AD: Jeffrey Vennell.

ROSE-HULMAN

Terre Haute, IN 47803 III

Coach: Scott Duncan, Northwestern 1980
Record: 12 Years, 66-53-1

1998 SCHEDULE

Washington (Mo.) ■	Sept. 5
Sewanee	Sept. 12
Chicago	Sept. 19
Kalamazoo ■	Sept. 26
Trinity (Tex.)	*Oct. 3
Rhodes ■	Oct. 10
Millsaps ■	Oct. 17
Earlham	Oct. 31
DePauw	Nov. 7
Centre ■	Nov. 14

1997 RESULTS (3-7-0)

17	Sewanee	20
37	Millsaps	17
14	Chicago	16
14	Wabash	35
10	Anderson (Ind.)	24
29	Manchester	28
14	DePauw	17
22	Franklin	6
20	Hanover	47
0	Washington (Mo.)	21
177		**231**

Nickname: Fightin' Engineers.
Stadium: Phil Brown Field, 2,500 capacity. Natural turf.
Colors: Old Rose & White.
Conference: Heartland Colleg. Ath. Conf.
SID: Darin Bryan, 812-877-8180.
AD: Scott A. Duncan.

ROWAN

Glassboro, NJ 08028 III

Coach: K. C. Keeler, Delaware 1981
Record: 5 Years, 48-12-1

1998 SCHEDULE

Newport News ■	Sept. 12
LIU-C.W. Post ■	*Sept. 19
New Jersey City ■	*Sept. 25
Col. of New Jersey	*Oct. 2
Buffalo St.	Oct. 10
Cortland St. ■	Oct. 17
Kean	Oct. 31
Wm. Paterson ■	Nov. 7
Montclair St.	Nov. 14

1997 RESULTS (9-0-0)

27	Newport News	14
54	Ferrum	6
35	New Jersey City	6
30	Col. of New Jersey	7
41	Cortland St.	6
35	Clinch Valley	14
40	Kean	0
57	Wm. Paterson	0
19	Montclair St.	7
338		**60**

III Championship

43	Coast Guard	0
13	Col. of New Jersey	7
20	Lycoming	28

Nickname: Profs.
Stadium: John Page (1969), 5,000 capacity. Natural turf.
Colors: Brown & Gold.
Conference: New Jersey Athletic Conference.
SID: Sheila Stevenson, 609-256-4252.
AD: Joy L. Reighn.

RUTGERS

New Brunswick, NJ 08903 .... I-A

Coach: Terry Shea, Oregon 1968
Record: 4 Years, 17-26-2

1998 SCHEDULE

Richmond ■	*Sept. 5
Boston College	Sept. 12
Syracuse	Sept. 19
Army ■	*Sept. 26
Miami (Fla.) ■	Oct. 3
Pittsburgh	Oct. 17
Tulane ■	Oct. 24
Temple ■	Oct. 31
Navy	Nov. 7
West Va. ■	Nov. 14
Virginia Tech	Nov. 21

1997 RESULTS (0-11-0)

19	Virginia Tech	59
14	Texas	48
7	Navy	36
21	Boston College	35
0	West Va.	48
3	Syracuse	50
35	Army	37
48	Pittsburgh	55
7	Temple	49
14	Wake Forest	28
23	Miami (Fla.)	51
191		**496**

Nickname: Scarlet Knights.
Stadium: Rutgers (1994), 42,500 capacity. Natural turf.
Colors: Scarlet.
Conference: Big East.
SID: Peter Kowalski, 908-445-4200.
AD: Robert E. Mulcahy.

SACRED HEART

Fairfield, CT 06432 II

Coach: Tom Radulski, New Hampshire 1979
Record: 4 Years, 6-34-0

1998 SCHEDULE

St. John's (N.Y.) ■	*Sept. 5
Siena	Sept. 12
Wagner ■	Sept. 19
Iona ■	Sept. 26
St. Francis (Pa.)	Oct. 3
Robert Morris	Oct. 17
Central Conn. St. ■	Oct. 24
Monmouth	Oct. 31
Hartwick	Nov. 7
Bryant ■	Nov. 14

1997 RESULTS (1-9-0)

0	Albany (N.Y.)	42
3	Southern Conn. St.	50
27	Assumption	0
7	Stony Brook	22
10	LIU-C.W. Post	62
7	Merrimack	17
0	Bentley	35
0	Monmouth	43
7	Pace	19
7	St. John's (N.Y.)	26
68		**316**

Nickname: Pioneers.
Stadium: Campus Field (1993), 2,000 capacity. Artificial turf.
Colors: Scarlet & White.
Conference: Eastern Football.
SID: Mike Guastelle, 203-371-7885.
AD: C. Donald Cook.

SAGINAW VALLEY

Univ Center, MI 48710................................II

Coach: Jerry Kill, Southwestern KS 1983
Record: 4 Years, 29-12-0

1998 SCHEDULE

Fairmont St. ■	*Sept. 5
Ferris St.	Sept. 12
Wayne St. (Mich.) ■	Sept. 19
Northern Mich.	Sept. 26
Michigan Tech ■	Oct. 3
Westminster (Pa.)	Oct. 10
Grand Valley St. ■	Oct. 17
Northwood	Oct. 24
Mercyhurst ■	Oct. 31
Hillsdale	Nov. 7
St. Francis (Ill.) ■	Nov. 14

1997 RESULTS (9-2-0)

73	Wayne St. (Mich.)	7
59	Northwood	21
45	Michigan Tech	28
56	Fairmont St.	7
20	Ashland	27
31	Indianapolis	17
38	St. Francis (Ill.)	18
30	Grand Valley St.	27
23	Ferris St.	24
30	Hillsdale	13
52	Northern Mich.	20
457		**209**

Nickname: Cardinals.
Stadium: Harvey R. Wickes (1975), 4,028 capacity. Natural turf.
Colors: Red, White & Blue.
Conference: Midwest Intercoll.
SID: Tom Waske, 517-790-4053.
AD: Robert T. Becker.

ST. CLOUD ST.

St. Cloud, MN 56301 II

Coach: Noel Martin, Nebraska 1963
Record: 15 Years, 88-73-0

1998 SCHEDULE

Western Ill.	*Sept. 3
Central Mo. St.	*Sept. 12
Morningside ■	Sept. 19
Northern Colo. ■	Sept. 26
Mankato St.	Oct. 3
South Dak. St. ■	Oct. 10
Augustana (S.D.)	Oct. 17
North Dak. ■	Oct. 24
North Dak. St. ■	Oct. 31
South Dak.	Nov. 7
Neb.-Omaha	Nov. 14

1997 RESULTS (6-5-0)

10	Northern Ariz.	33
25	Minn.-Duluth	13
16	Morningside	13
27	Northern Colo.	30
13	Mankato St.	6
16	South Dak. St.	20
43	Augustana (S.D.)	28
21	North Dak.	41
0	North Dak. St.	31
17	South Dak.	7
46	Neb.-Omaha	7
234		**229**

Nickname: Huskies.
Stadium: Selke Field (1937), 4,000 capacity. Natural turf.
Colors: Red & Black.
Conference: No. Central Intercoll Ath Conf.
SID: Anne Abicht, 320-255-2141.
AD: Morris Kurtz.

ST. FRANCIS (ILL.)

Joliet, IL 60435..II

Coach: Mike Slovick, Lewis (Ill.) 1971
Record: 4 Years, 11-33-0

1998 SCHEDULE

Northern Mich.	*Sept. 3
Illinois St.	*Sept. 12
Mercyhurst ■	*Sept. 19
Michigan Tech ■	*Sept. 26
Grand Valley St.	Oct. 3
Hillsdale	Oct. 10
Northwood ■	Oct. 17
Indianapolis ■	*Oct. 24
Westminster (Pa.)	Oct. 31
Ferris St. ■	Nov. 7
Saginaw Valley	Nov. 14

1997 RESULTS (2-9-0)

15	Hillsdale	27
29	Grand Valley St.	38
20	Northern Mich.	47
7	Wayne St. (Mich.)	30
38	Northwood	62
28	Michigan Tech	52
61	Quincy	12
18	Saginaw Valley	38
24	Indianapolis	50
0	Ashland	28
16	Ferris St.	15
256		**399**

Nickname: Fighting Saints.
Stadium: Joliet Memorial (1951), 10,000 capacity. Natural turf.
Colors: Brown & Gold.
Conference: Midwest Intercoll.
SID: Dave Laketa, 815-740-3842.
AD: Pat Sullivan.

ST. FRANCIS (PA.)

Loretto, PA 15940..................................I-AA

Coach: Kevin Doherty, Tufts 1987
(First year as head coach)

1998 SCHEDULE

Duquesne ■	Sept. 12
Butler	Sept. 19
Wagner ■	Sept. 26
Sacred Heart ■	Oct. 3
Central Conn. St.	Oct. 10
Monmouth	Oct. 17
La Salle ■	Oct. 24
Marist	Oct. 31
Robert Morris ■	Nov. 7
Gannon	Nov. 14

1997 RESULTS (2-9-0)

6	Waynesburg	29
3	Duquesne	51
12	Butler	38
6	Wagner	42
13	Mercyhurst	45
18	Central Conn. St.	25
7	Monmouth	27
41	Gannon	26
10	Marist	26
7	Robert Morris	34
30	La Salle	7
153		**350**

Nickname: Red Flash.
Stadium: Pine Bowl (1979), 1,500 capacity. Natural turf.
Colors: Red & White.
Conference: Northeast.
SID: Kevin Southard, 814-472-3128.
AD: Maryelizabeth Grace.

ST. JOHN FISHER

Rochester, NY 14618 III

Coach: Paul Vosburgh, William Penn 1975
Record: 10 Years, 29-65-1

1998 SCHEDULE

Merrimack	Sept. 5
Ithaca ■	Sept. 12
Gannon ■	Sept. 26
Montclair St. ■	Oct. 3
New Jersey City	Oct. 10
Buffalo St. ■	Oct. 17
Brockport St.	Oct. 24
Rensselaer	Oct. 31
Hobart ■	Nov. 7

1997 RESULTS (1-8-0)

13	Buffalo St.	19
7	Hobart	38
7	Mercyhurst	14
0	Montclair St.	21
12	New Jersey City	22
29	Nichols	20
0	Brockport St.	17
6	Rensselaer	38
12	Gannon	35
86		**224**

Nickname: Cardinals.
Stadium: Cardinal Field, 1,000 capacity. Natural turf.
Colors: Cardinal Red & Gold.
Conference: Independent.
SID: Norm Kieffer, 716-385-8309.
AD: Robert A. Ward.

ST. JOHN'S (N.Y.)

Jamaica, NY 11439 ....I-AA

Coach: Bob Ricca, LIU-C.W. Post 1969
Record: 20 Years, 127-76-1

1998 SCHEDULE

Sacred Heart	*Sept. 5
Central Conn. St.	Sept. 12
Duquesne ■	Sept. 26
Marist	Oct. 3
Georgetown ■	Oct. 17
Siena ■	*Oct. 23
Canisius	Oct. 31
Fairfield ■	Nov. 6
Iona	Nov. 14
St. Peter's	Nov. 21
Stony Brook ■	Nov. 27

1997 RESULTS (8-3-0)

13	Central Conn. St.	7
21	Fairfield	34
23	Stony Brook	19

35	St. Peter's	14
24	Marist	7
14	Duquesne	11
7	Siena	12
6	Canisius	0
0	Georgetown	27
37	Iona	7
26	Sacred Heart	7
206		**145**

Nickname: Red Storm.
Stadium: Da Silva (1961), 3,000 capacity. Artificial turf.
Colors: Red & White.
Conference: Metro Atlantic.
SID: Dominic Scianna, 718-990-6367.
AD: Edward J. Manetta Jr.

ST. JOHN'S (MINN.)

Collegeville, MN 56321 III

Coach: John Gagliardi, Colorado College 1949
Record: 49 Years, 342-104-11

1998 SCHEDULE

Concordia-St. Paul ■	Sept. 5
Macalester	Sept. 19
St. Thomas (Minn.) ■	Sept. 26
Augsburg	*Oct. 3
Bethel (Minn.) ■	Oct. 10
Concordia-M'head	Oct. 17
Hamline ■	Oct. 24
St. Olaf	Oct. 31
Carleton ■	Nov. 7
Gust. Adolphus [Minneapolis, Minn.]	Nov. 13

1997 RESULTS (6-4-0)

21	Bemidji St.	25
21	St. Olaf	7
10	Augsburg	20
21	Hamline	0
55	Carleton	6
16	Gust. Adolphus	24
20	Concordia-M'head	12
47	Macalester	7
17	Bethel (Minn.)	14
27	St. Thomas (Minn.)	31
255		**146**

Nickname: Johnnies.
Stadium: St. John's (1908), 5,000 capacity. Natural turf.
Colors: Red & White.
Conference: Minn. Intercol. Athletic Conf.
SID: Michael Hemmesch, 320-363-2595.
AD: Jim E. Smith.

ST. JOSEPH'S (IND.)

Rensselaer, IN 47978 II

Coach: Tom Riva, Albion
Record: 1 Year, 5-6-0

1998 SCHEDULE

Eastern Ill.	Sept. 3
Tri-State	Sept. 12
Malone	Sept. 19
Indiana St.	*Sept. 24
Quincy ■	Oct. 3
Ky. Wesleyan ■	Oct. 10
Dayton	*Oct. 17
Georgetown (Ky.)	Oct. 24
New Haven	Oct. 31
Valparaiso ■	Nov. 7
Wayne St. (Mich.) ■	Nov. 14

1997 RESULTS (5-6-0)

13	Indianapolis	26
52	West Va. Tech	0
20	Eastern Ill.	41
37	West Liberty St.	47
42	Calif. (Pa.)	21
52	Quincy	14
60	Union (Ky.)	20
7	Morehead St.	37
37	Ky. Wesleyan	31
14	New Haven	56
13	Butler	20
347		**313**

Nickname: Pumas.
Stadium: Alumni Field (1947), 4,000 capacity. Natural turf.
Colors: Cardinal & Purple.
Conference: Independent.
SID: Joe Danahey, 219-866-6141.
AD: Lynn Plett.

ST. LAWRENCE

Canton, NY 13617....................................III

Coach: Dennis Riccio, Illinois St. 1968
Record: 11 Years, 42-62-0

1998 SCHEDULE

Cortland St.	Sept. 5
Union (N.Y.)	Sept. 12
Alfred ■	Sept. 19
Rochester ■	Sept. 26
Hobart	Oct. 3
Ithaca	Oct. 17
Norwich ■	Oct. 24
Rensselaer	Nov. 7
Hartwick	Nov. 14

1997 RESULTS (2-7-0)

0	Cortland St.	42
12	Union (N.Y.)	27
0	Albany (N.Y.)	49
24	Rochester	6
0	Hobart	57
6	Ithaca	41
17	Norwich	0
0	Rensselaer	35
0	Hartwick	35
59		**292**

Nickname: Saints.
Stadium: Weeks Field (1906), 3,000 capacity. Natural turf.
Colors: Scarlet & Brown.
Conference: Upstate Collegiate Athl Assn.
SID: Wally Johnson, 315-379-5588.
AD: Margaret F. Strait.

ST. MARY'S (CAL.)

Moraga, CA 94556................................I-AA

Coach: Mike Rasmussen, Michigan St. 1972
Record: 8 Years, 50-29-1

1998 SCHEDULE

Cal St. Sacramento ■	Sept. 5
Bucknell	Sept. 12
Lehigh ■	Sept. 19
Cal Poly	*Sept. 26
Columbia ■	Oct. 3
Southern Utah	Oct. 10
UC Davis	Oct. 24
Towson	Oct. 31
Drake ■	Nov. 7
Chapman ■	Nov. 14

1997 RESULTS (4-6-0)

16	Northeastern	24
30	San Diego	20
14	Montana	35
14	Cal Poly	24
44	Humboldt St.	6
21	Portland St.	35
36	Chapman	20
9	UC Davis	19
38	Bucknell	45
31	Southern Utah	27
253		**255**

Nickname: Gaels.
Stadium: St. Mary's (1973), 8,000 capacity. Natural turf.
Colors: Red & Blue.
Conference: Independent.
SID: Andy McDowell, 510-631-4402.
AD: Richard J. Mazzuto.

ST. NORBERT

De Pere, WI 54115 III

Coach: Greg Quick, Baldwin-Wallace 1979
Record: 9 Years, 27-58-0

1998 SCHEDULE

Wis.-Oshkosh	*Sept. 12
Carroll (Wis.) ■	Sept. 19
Lawrence	Sept. 26
Ripon ■	Oct. 3
Knox	Oct. 10
Monmouth (Ill.)	Oct. 17
Grinnell ■	Oct. 24
Lake Forest	Oct. 31
Beloit ■	Nov. 7
Illinois Col. ■	Nov. 14

1997 RESULTS (4-5-0)

17	Wis.-Oshkosh	62
7	Drake	48
41	Monmouth (Ill.)	14
70	Illinois Col.	13
28	Lake Forest	21
24	Lawrence	27
14	Ripon	16
20	Beloit	21
18	Carroll (Wis.)	17
239		**239**

Nickname: Green Knights.
Stadium: Minahan (1937), 3,100 capacity. Natural turf.
Colors: Green & Gold.
Conference: Midwest Conference.
SID: Jim Strick, 414-337-4077.
AD: Donald Maslinski.

ST. OLAF

Northfield, MN 55057..............................III

Coach: Paul Miller, Minn.-Morris 1973
Record: 1 Year, 2-8-0

1998 SCHEDULE

Carthage	Sept. 12
St. Thomas (Minn.)	Sept. 19
Augsburg ■	Sept. 26
Bethel (Minn.)	Oct. 3
Concordia-M'head ■	Oct. 10
Hamline	Oct. 17
Carleton ■	Oct. 24
St. John's (Minn.) ■	Oct. 31
Gust. Adolphus	Nov. 7
Macalester [Minneapolis, Minn.]	*Nov. 12

1997 RESULTS (2-8-0)

12	Luther	19
7	St. John's (Minn.)	21
0	Concordia-M'head	38
0	Augsburg	42
19	Macalester	3
21	Hamline	27
10	Bethel (Minn.)	52
14	Carleton	12
3	St. Thomas (Minn.)	28
6	Gust. Adolphus	37
92		**279**

Nickname: Oles.
Stadium: Manitou Field (1930), 5,000 capacity. Natural turf.
Colors: Black & Old Gold.
Conference: Minn. Intercol. Athletic Conf.
SID: Nancy Moe, 507-646-3834.
AD: Lee Swan.

ST. PETER'S

Jersey City, NJ 07306............................I-AA

Coach: Mark Collins, Central Conn. St. 1980
Record: 4 Years, 6-31-0

1998 SCHEDULE

La Salle	Sept. 12
Canisius	Sept. 19
Marist ■	*Sept. 26
Wagner	Oct. 10

St. John's (N.Y.) ■	Nov. 21
Siena ■	Oct. 16
Iona	Oct. 24
Georgetown	Oct. 31
Duquesne ■	Nov. 7
Fairfield	Nov. 14

1997 RESULTS (1-9-0)

16	La Salle	25
7	Canisius	10
0	Marist	42
14	St. John's (N.Y.)	35
14	Wagner	42
21	Siena	42
14	Iona	12
32	Georgetown	40
0	Duquesne	40
34	Fairfield	38
152		**326**

Nickname: Peacocks.
Stadium: Cochrane (1990), 4,000 capacity. Natural turf.
Colors: Blue & White.
Conference: Metro Atlantic.
SID: Tim Camp, 201-915-9101.
AD: William A. Stein.

ST. THOMAS (MINN.)

St. Paul, MN 55105 ... III

Coach: Don Roney, St. Thomas (Minn.) 1983
(First year as head coach)

1998 SCHEDULE

Bemidji St.	Sept. 12
St. Olaf ■	Sept. 19
St. John's (Minn.)	Sept. 26
Gust. Adolphus ■	Oct. 3
Macalester	Oct. 10
Carleton	Oct. 17
Augsburg ■	Oct. 24
Bethel (Minn.)	Oct. 31
Concordia-M'head ■	Nov. 7
Hamline [Minneapolis, Minn.]	*Nov. 12

1997 RESULTS (8-2-0)

49	Concordia-St. Paul	7
28	Augsburg	12
14	Hamline	0
36	Carleton	8
34	Gust. Adolphus	31
7	Concordia-M'head	28
30	Macalester	3
27	Bethel (Minn.)	33
28	St. Olaf	3
31	St. John's (Minn.)	27
284		**152**

Nickname: Tommies.
Stadium: O'Shaughnessy (1948), 5,025 capacity. Natural turf.
Colors: Purple & Grey.
Conference: Minn. Intercol. Athletic Conf.
SID: Gene McGivern, 612-962-5903.
AD: Stephen J. Fritz.

SALISBURY ST.

Salisbury, MD 21801 ... III

Coach: Joe Rotellini, Bethany 1977
Record: 8 Years, 22-52-0

1998 SCHEDULE

Ursinus ■	Sept. 5
Alfred	Sept. 12
Methodist	Sept. 19
Frostburg St.	Sept. 26
Chowan ■	Oct. 10
Col. of New Jersey ■	Oct. 17
Wesley ■	Oct. 24
Western Md. ■	Oct. 31
Ferrum	Nov. 7
Wm. Paterson	*Nov. 13

1997 RESULTS (3-6-0)

14	Ursinus	12
12	Delaware Valley	14
7	Frostburg St.	16
22	Methodist	29
28	Chowan	17
7	Col. of New Jersey	35
0	Western Md.	11
7	Wesley	28
16	Wm. Paterson	14
113		**176**

Nickname: Sea Gulls.
Stadium: Sea Gull (1980), 2,500 capacity. Natural turf.
Colors: Maroon & Gold.
Conference: Atlantic Central FB.
SID: G. Paul Ohanian, 410-543-6016.
AD: Michael Vienna.

SALVE REGINA

Newport, RI 02840 ... III

Coach: Tim Coen, Salve Regina 1976
Record: 5 Years, 36-9-0

1998 SCHEDULE

Frostburg St. ■	Sept. 12
Bri'water (Mass.) ■	*Sept. 19
MIT	Sept. 26
Western New Eng. ■	*Oct. 3
Worcester St.	Oct. 10
Mass.-Boston ■	Oct. 17
Curry	Oct. 24
Maine Maritime ■	Oct. 31
Mass.-Dartmouth	Nov. 7
Nichols ■	*Nov. 14

1997 RESULTS (7-2-0)

3	Western Conn. St.	15
7	Frostburg St.	24
34	Nichols	0
28	MIT	7
10	Western New Eng.	7
10	Maine Maritime	0
10	Assumption	0
52	Curry	12
7	Stonehill	6
161		**71**

Nickname: Seahawks.
Stadium: Toppa Field, 1,500 capacity. Natural turf.
Colors: Blue, Green & White.
Conference: New England FB.
SID: Ed Habershaw, 401-847-6650.
AD: Del Malloy.

SAM HOUSTON ST.

Huntsville, TX 77340 ... I-AA

Coach: Ron Randleman, William Penn 1964
Record: 29 Years, 175-128-6

1998 SCHEDULE

Angelo St.	*Sept. 5
Chadron St. ■	*Sept. 12
Texas A&M-Kingsville ■	*Sept. 19
Utah St.	*Sept. 26
Troy St. ■	*Oct. 3
Nicholls St.	*Oct. 8
Jacksonville St.	Oct. 24
McNeese St. ■	Oct. 31
Stephen F. Austin	Nov. 7
Northwestern St.	Nov. 14
Southwest Tex. St. ■	Nov. 21

1997 RESULTS (5-6-0)

17	Angelo St.	24
6	Texas A&M	59
21	Jacksonville St.	28
55	Ark.-Monticello	0
40	Texas Southern	7
10	Troy St.	13
24	Nicholls St.	17
21	McNeese St.	38
33	Stephen F. Austin	28
19	Northwestern St.	35
35	Southwest Tex. St.	30
281		**279**

Nickname: Bearkats.
Stadium: Elliott T. Bowers (1986), 14,885 capacity. Artificial turf.
Colors: Orange & White.
Conference: Southland.
SID: Paul Ridings Jr., 409-294-1764.
AD: Bobby Williams.

SAMFORD

Birmingham, AL 35229 ... I-AA

Coach: Pete Hurt, Mississippi Col. 1978
4 years, 24-19-1

1998 SCHEDULE

Chattanooga	*Sept. 3
Austin Peay ■	*Sept. 12
Furman	*Sept. 19
Troy St.	*Sept. 26
Nicholls St. ■	Oct. 3
Tenn.-Martin ■	Oct. 10
Jacksonville St.	Oct. 17
Mars Hill ■	Oct. 31
Morgan St. ■	Nov. 7
Elon	Nov. 14
Tennessee Tech	Nov. 21

1997 RESULTS (7-4-0)

10	Furman	29
21	Austin Peay	13
7	Tennessee Tech	14
21	Alcorn St.	16
14	Nicholls St.	17
7	Central Fla.	52
25	Troy St.	14
17	Jacksonville St.	14
14	Tenn.-Martin	7
46	Elon	32
19	Western Caro.	0
201		**208**

Nickname: Bulldogs.
Stadium: Seibert (1958), 6,700 capacity. Natural turf.
Colors: Red & Blue.
Conference: Independent.
SID: Riley Adair, 205-870-2799.
AD: Stephen C. Allgood.

SAN DIEGO

San Diego, CA 92110 ... I-AA

Coach: Kevin McGarry, San Diego 1979
Record: 2 Years, 12-9-0

1998 SCHEDULE

Azusa Pacific ■	*Sept. 5
Wagner	Sept. 12
Redlands ■	*Sept. 19
Cal Lutheran	Sept. 26
Central Conn. St. ■	*Oct. 3
Butler	Oct. 10
Fairfield ■	Oct. 17
Drake	Oct. 24
Valparaiso ■	*Oct. 31
Dayton ■	*Nov. 14

1997 RESULTS (8-3-0)

25	Azusa Pacific	15
20	St. Mary's (Cal.)	30
15	Redlands	8
32	Cal Lutheran	39
55	Evansville	20
24	Butler	14
25	Dayton	49
39	Drake	30
52	Valparaiso	35
30	Whittier	18
52	Wagner	29
369		**287**

Nickname: Toreros.
Stadium: USD Torero (1955), 4,000 capacity. Natural turf.
Colors: Columbia Blue, Navy & White.
Conference: Pioneer.
SID: Ted Gosen, 619-260-4745.
AD: Thomas Iannacone.

SAN DIEGO ST.

San Diego, CA 92182 — I-A

Coach: Ted Tollner, Cal Poly 1962
Record: 8 Years, 51-41-1

1998 SCHEDULE

Wisconsin ■	*Sept. 5
Southern Cal	Sept. 12
Arizona ■	Sept. 24
Tulsa	Oct. 3
Hawaii ■	*Oct. 10
New Mexico	*Oct. 17
Utah ■	*Oct. 24
Brigham Young	*Oct. 29
Fresno St. ■	*Nov. 7
San Jose St.	Nov. 14
UTEP ■	*Nov. 21

1997 RESULTS (5-7-0)

45	Navy	31
3	Washington	36
10	Wisconsin	34
18	Air Force	24
28	Arizona	31
21	New Mexico	36
20	UNLV	17
10	Hawaii	3
17	Wyoming	41
48	San Jose St.	21
20	Fresno St.	19
17	Colorado St.	38
257		**331**

Nickname: Aztecs.
Stadium: Qualcom (1967), 73,000 capacity. Natural turf.
Colors: Scarlet & Black.
Conference: Western Athletic.
SID: John Rosenthal, 619-594-5547.
AD: Richard M. Bay.

SAN JOSE ST.

San Jose, CA 95192 — I-A

Coach: Dave Baldwin, Cal St. Northridge 1978
Record: 3 Years, 13-19-0

1998 SCHEDULE

Stanford	Sept. 5
Idaho ■	*Sept. 12
Oregon	Sept. 19
New Mexico ■	*Sept. 26
Virginia	Oct. 3
Rice ■	*Oct. 10
UTEP	*Oct. 17
Brigham Young	Oct. 24
Utah ■	Oct. 31
Hawaii	*Nov. 7
San Diego St. ■	Nov. 14
Fresno St.	Nov. 21

1997 RESULTS (4-7-0)

12	Stanford	28
10	Wisconsin	56
10	Wyoming	30
12	Oregon St.	26
20	Colorado St.	55
10	UTEP	7
25	Air Force	22
12	Fresno St.	53
21	San Diego St.	48
38	Hawaii	14
55	UNLV	48
225		**387**

Nickname: Spartans.
Stadium: Spartan (1933), 31,218 capacity. Natural turf.
Colors: Gold, White & Blue.
Conference: Western Athletic.
SID: Lawrence Fan, 408-924-1217.
AD: Charles Bell.

SAVANNAH ST.

Savannah, GA 31404 — II

Coach: Daryl McNeill, South Caro. St. 1982
Record: 3 Years, 12-19-0

1998 SCHEDULE

Elizabeth City St.	*Aug. 29
Bethune-Cookman [Jacksonville, Fla.]	Sept. 5
Clark Atlanta	*Sept. 12
Lane	*Sept. 19
Morehouse ■	Sept. 26
Albany St. (Ga.)	*Oct. 3
Morris Brown	Oct. 10
Kentucky St. ■	Oct. 24
Fort Valley St. ■	Oct. 31
Miles	Nov. 7
Tuskegee ■	Nov. 14

1997 RESULTS (3-8-0)

31	Wingate	37
24	Winston-Salem	27
32	Lane	10
3	Morehouse	0
3	Albany St. (Ga.)	41
23	Morris Brown	24
14	Tuskegee	20
10	Kentucky St.	28
3	Fort Valley St.	12
34	Miles	28
22	Clark Atlanta	23
199		**250**

Nickname: Tigers.
Stadium: Ted Wright (1967), 7,500 capacity. Natural turf.
Colors: Blue & Orange.
Conference: Southern Intercol. Ath. Conf.
SID: Lee Grant Pearson, 912-356-2446.
AD: Hornsby Howell.

SEWANEE

Sewanee, TN 37383 — III

Coach: John Windham, Vanderbilt 1986
Record: 2 Years, 9-8-0

1998 SCHEDULE

Hampden-Sydney ■	Sept. 5
Rose-Hulman ■	Sept. 12
Davidson ■	Sept. 19
Centre	Oct. 3
DePauw	Oct. 10
Rhodes ■	Oct. 17
Wash. & Lee	Oct. 24
Millsaps ■	Oct. 31
Trinity (Tex.)	Nov. 7

1997 RESULTS (5-4-0)

31	Hampden-Sydney	7
20	Rose-Hulman	17
14	Davidson	42
31	Maryville (Tenn.)	0
0	Centre	30
17	Rhodes	27
48	Wash. & Lee	14
56	Millsaps	30
31	Trinity (Tex.)	45
248		**212**

Nickname: Tigers.
Stadium: McGee Field (1935), 1,500 capacity. Natural turf.
Colors: Purple & White.
Conference: Southern Collegiate Ath. Conf.
SID: Larry Dagenhart, 615-598-1136.
AD: Mark Webb.

SHEPHERD

Shepherdstown, WV 25443 — II

Coach: Monte Cater, Millikin 1971
Record: 17 Years, 96-70-2

1998 SCHEDULE

Shippensburg	Sept. 5
East Stroudsburg	Sept. 12
Clarion ■	Sept. 19
West Va. Wesleyan ■	Oct. 3
Concord ■	Oct. 10
West Va. Tech	*Oct. 15
Fairmont St. ■	Oct. 24
West Va. St.	Oct. 31
Glenville St. ■	Nov. 7
West Liberty St.	Nov. 14

1997 RESULTS (9-1-0)

18	Presbyterian	14
20	Shippensburg	16
45	Lenoir-Rhyne	16
37	West Va. Wesleyan	19
64	Concord	20
48	West Va. Tech	3
39	Fairmont St.	27
23	West Va. St.	7
14	Glenville St.	44
32	West Liberty St.	27
340		**193**

Nickname: Rams.
Stadium: Ram (1959), 3,000 capacity. Natural turf.
Colors: Blue & Gold.
Conference: WV Intercollegiate Athletic.
SID: Chip Ransom, 304-876-5228.
AD: Monte Cater.

SHIPPENSBURG

Shippensburg, PA 17257 — II

Coach: Rocky Rees, West Chester 1971
Record: 13 Years, 77-62-2

1998 SCHEDULE

Shepherd ■	Sept. 5
Bloomsburg ■	Sept. 12
Kutztown	Sept. 19
West Chester	Sept. 26
Edinboro	Oct. 3
East Stroudsburg ■	Oct. 10
Clarion	Oct. 17
Slippery Rock ■	Oct. 24
Lock Haven ■	Oct. 31
Calif. (Pa.)	Nov. 7
Indiana (Pa.) ■	Nov. 14

1997 RESULTS (6-4-0)

16	Shepherd	20
21	Kutztown	14
27	Millersville	37
17	Edinboro	3
37	Clarion	14
26	Lock Haven	0
34	Bloomsburg	29
31	Calif. (Pa.)	26
16	Slippery Rock	28
26	Indiana (Pa.)	44
251		**215**

Nickname: Red Raiders.
Stadium: Grove (1972), 7,700 capacity. Natural turf.
Colors: Red & Blue.
Conference: Pennsylvania State Athl. Conf.
SID: John R. Alosi, 717-532-9121.
AD: James G. Pribula.

SIENA

Loudonville, NY 12211 — I-AA

Coach: Ed Zaloom, Cortland St. 1975
Record: 2 Years, 8-10-0

1998 SCHEDULE

Sacred Heart ■	Sept. 12
Duquesne ■	Sept. 19
Canisius	Sept. 26
Georgetown ■	Oct. 3
Iona	Oct. 10
St. Peter's	Oct. 16
St. John's (N.Y.)	*Oct. 23
Fairfield ■	Oct. 31
Bryant	Nov. 7
Marist ■	Nov. 14

1997 RESULTS (6-3-0)

14	Duquesne	38

41 Canisius 38
10 Georgetown 41
50 Iona 7
42 St. Peter's 21
12 St. John's (N.Y.) 7
16 Fairfield 6
17 MIT 13
9 Marist 34
211 **205**

Nickname: Saints.
Stadium: Heritage Park, 5,500 capacity. Natural turf.
Colors: Green & Gold.
Conference: Metro Atlantic.
SID: Mike Hogan, 518-783-2411.
AD: John M. D'Argenio.

SIMPSON

Indianola, IA 50125 ... III

Coach: Jim Williams, Northern Iowa 1956
Record: 11 Years, 83-31-1

1998 SCHEDULE

Dubuque ... Sept. 5
Coe ■ ... Sept. 12
Central (Iowa) ... Sept. 19
Upper Iowa ■ ... Sept. 26
William Penn ■ ... Oct. 3
Wartburg ... Oct. 10
Buena Vista ■ ... Oct. 17
Cornell College ... Oct. 24
Loras ■ ... Oct. 31
Luther ... Nov. 14

1997 RESULTS (10-0-0)

54 Cornell College 20
61 Luther 6
58 William Penn 12
56 Upper Iowa 12
35 Wartburg 21
31 Central (Iowa) 27
37 Aurora 18
62 Dubuque 20
57 Buena Vista 14
42 Loras 28
493 **178**

III Championship

34 Wis.-Whitewater 31
61 Augsburg 21
7 Mount Union 54

Nickname: Storm.
Stadium: Simpson/Indianola Field (1990), 5,000 capacity. Natural turf.
Colors: Red & Gold.
Conference: Iowa Intercol. Athletic Conf.
SID: Matthew F. Turk, 515-961-1577.
AD: John Sirianni.

SLIPPERY ROCK

Slippery Rock, PA 16057 ... II

Coach: George Mihalik, Slippery Rock 1974
Record: 10 Years, 64-39-4

1998 SCHEDULE

South Fla. ... *Sept. 5
West Va. Wesleyan ... Sept. 12
Fairmont St. ■ ... Sept. 19
East Stroudsburg ... Sept. 26
Clarion ■ ... Oct. 3
Indiana (Pa.) ■ ... Oct. 10
Calif. (Pa.) ... *Oct. 17
Shippensburg ... Oct. 24
Edinboro ■ ... Oct. 31
Kutztown ■ ... Nov. 7
Lock Haven ... Nov. 14

1997 RESULTS (10-1-0)

9 Youngstown St. 33
41 West Va. Wesleyan 31
42 Fairmont St. 14
40 East Stroudsburg 25
27 West Chester 14
16 Indiana (Pa.) 9
30 Edinboro 10
28 Clarion 7
38 Lock Haven 6
28 Shippensburg 16
27 Calif. (Pa.) 6
326 **171**

II Championship

30 Ashland 20
21 New Haven 49

Nickname: Rockets, The Rock.
Stadium: N. Kerr Thompson (1974), 10,000 capacity. Natural turf.
Colors: Green & White.
Conference: Pennsylvania State Athl. Conf.
SID: John Carpenter, 412-738-2777.
AD: Paul A. Lueken.

SOUTH CARO.

Columbia, SC 29208 ... I-A

Coach: Brad Scott, South Fla. 1979
Record: 4 Years, 22-22-1

1998 SCHEDULE

Ball St. ■ ... *Sept. 5
Georgia ■ ... *Sept. 12
Marshall ■ ... *Sept. 19
Mississippi St. ■ ... *Sept. 26
Mississippi ... Oct. 3
Kentucky ... *Oct. 10
Arkansas ■ ... *Oct. 17
Vanderbilt ... *Oct. 24
Tennessee ■ ... Oct. 31
Florida ... Nov. 14
Clemson ... Nov. 21

1997 RESULTS (5-6-0)

33 Central Fla. 31
15 Georgia 31
26 East Caro. 0
17 Mississippi St. 37
6 Auburn 23
38 Kentucky 24
39 Arkansas 13
35 Vanderbilt 3
7 Tennessee 22
21 Florida 48
21 Clemson 47
258 **279**

Nickname: Fighting Gamecocks.
Stadium: Williams-Brice (1934), 80,250 capacity. Natural turf.
Colors: Garnet & Black.
Conference: Southeastern.
SID: Kerry Tharp, 803-777-5204.
AD: Michael B. Mc Gee.

SOUTH CARO. ST.

Orangeburg, SC 29117 ... I-AA

Coach: Willie E. Jeffries, South Caro. St. 1960
Record: 25 Years, 161-107-6

1998 SCHEDULE

Charleston So. ... Sept. 5
Furman ... Sept. 12
Johnson Smith ■ ... *Sept. 26
Morgan St. ■ ... *Oct. 3
Norfolk St. ... Oct. 10
Bethune-Cookman ■ ... Oct. 17
Hampton ■ ... Oct. 24
Delaware St. ... Oct. 31
Howard ■ ... Nov. 7
Florida A&M ... *Nov. 14
North Caro. A&T [Charlotte, N. C.] ... Nov. 21

1997 RESULTS (9-2-0)

13 Charleston So. 12
17 Furman 6
34 Tennessee St. 28
34 Morgan St. 27
28 Norfolk St. 25
17 Bethune-Cookman 10
14 Hampton 20
37 Delaware St. 17
27 Howard 18
20 Florida A&M 22
33 North Caro. A&T 18
274 **203**

Heritage Bowl

28 Southern U. 34

Nickname: Bulldogs.
Stadium: Dawson Bulldog (1955), 22,000 capacity. Natural turf.
Colors: Garnet & Blue.
Conference: Mid-Eastern.
SID: Bill Hamilton, 803-536-7060.
AD: Timothy J. Autry Jr.

SOUTH DAK.

Vermillion, SD 57069 ... II

Coach: Ron Rankin, Edinboro 1984
Record: 1 Year, 5-6-0

1998 SCHEDULE

Wayne St. (Neb.) ■ ... *Sept. 5
Truman St. ■ ... Sept. 12
Mankato St. ■ ... Sept. 19
Neb.-Omaha ■ ... Sept. 26
South Dak. St. ... Oct. 3
Northern Colo. ... Oct. 10
Morningside ■ ... Oct. 17
Augustana (S.D.) ... Oct. 24
North Dak. ... Oct. 31
St. Cloud St. ■ ... Nov. 7
North Dak. St. ... *Nov. 14

1997 RESULTS (5-6-0)

59 Wayne St. (Neb.) 0
41 Northern St. 16
20 Mankato St. 24
14 Neb.-Omaha 38
21 South Dak. St. 3
31 Northern Colo. 45
22 Morningside 0
35 Augustana (S.D.) 23
19 North Dak. 20
7 St. Cloud St. 17
21 North Dak. St. 24
290 **210**

Nickname: Coyotes.
Stadium: DakotaDome (1979), 10,000 capacity. Artificial turf.
Colors: Vermillion & White.
Conference: No. Central Intercoll Ath Conf.
SID: Kyle Johnson, 605-677-5927.
AD: Jack Doyle.

SOUTH DAK. ST.

Brookings, SD 57007 ... II

Coach: John Stiegelmeier, South Dak. St. 1979
Record: 1 Year, 4-6-0

1998 SCHEDULE

Wis.-Stout ■ ... Sept. 5
UC Davis ■ ... Sept. 12
North Dak. ■ ... Sept. 19
Mankato St. ... Sept. 26
South Dak. ■ ... Oct. 3
St. Cloud St. ... Oct. 10
Neb.-Omaha ■ ... Oct. 17
North Dak. St. ... *Oct. 24
Augustana (S.D.) ■ ... Oct. 31
Northern Colo. ... Nov. 7
Morningside ... Nov. 14

1997 RESULTS (4-6-0)

17 UC Davis 7
7 North Dak. 28
7 Mankato St. 21
3 South Dak. 21
20 St. Cloud St. 16
21 Neb.-Omaha 31
34 North Dak. St. 27
22 Augustana (S.D.) 28
7 Northern Colo. 17
35 Morningside 20
173 **216**

Nickname: Jackrabbits.
Stadium: Coughlin-Alumni (1962), 16,000 capacity. Natural turf.
Colors: Yellow & Blue.
Conference: No. Central Intercoll Ath Conf.
SID: Ron Lenz, 605-688-4623.
AD: Fred M. Oien.

SOUTH FLA.

Tampa, FL 33620 ....I-AA

Coach: Jim Leavitt, Missouri 1978
Record: 1 Year, 5-6-0

1998 SCHEDULE

Slippery Rock ■ ....*Sept. 5
Valparaiso ■ ....*Sept. 12
Liberty....................*Sept. 19
Citadel ■....................*Oct. 3
Elon ■....................*Oct. 10
Western Ky. ■ ....*Oct. 17
Hofstra....................Oct. 24
Charleston So....................Oct. 31
Cumberland (Tenn.) ■....................*Nov. 7
Ga. Southern ....Nov. 14
Morehead St. ■ ....*Nov. 21

1997 RESULTS (5-6-0)

80 Ky. Wesleyan 3
7 Citadel....................10
22 Drake....................23
3 Western Ky. 31
33 Morehead St. 17
13 Elon 41
10 Southern Ill. 23
24 Charleston So. 6
44 Cumberland (Tenn.)....................0
23 Ga. Southern....................24
48 Davidson....................3
307 **181**

Nickname: Bulls.
Stadium: Tampa (1998), 41,441 capacity. Natural turf.
Colors: Green & Gold.
Conference: Independent.
SID: John Gerdes, 813-974-4086.
AD: Paul S. Griffin.

SOUTHEAST MO. ST.

Cape Girardeau, MO 63701 ....I-AA

Coach: John Mumford, Pittsburg St. 1979
Record: 8 Years, 34-54-0

1998 SCHEDULE

Truman St. ■....................*Sept. 3
Indiana St. ■ ....*Sept. 12
Murray St. ■....................*Sept. 19
Tenn.-Martin ■ ....*Sept. 26
Eastern Ill. ....Oct. 3
Tennessee Tech ....Oct. 10
Southwest Mo. St....................Oct. 24
Middle Tenn. St. ■ ....Oct. 31
Eastern Ky....................Nov. 7
Southern Ill. ....Nov. 14
Tennessee St. ■....................Oct. 17

1997 RESULTS (4-7-0)

24 Lambuth 6
7 Illinois St....................41
3 Murray St. 17
42 Tenn.-Martin 7
7 Eastern Ill....................32
14 Tennessee Tech 17
6 Middle Tenn. St. 55
31 Austin Peay....................0
10 Eastern Ky. 20
28 Southern Ill. 17
27 Tennessee St. 32
199 **244**

Nickname: Indians.
Stadium: Houck (1930), 10,000 capacity. Natural turf.
Colors: Red & Black.
Conference: Ohio Valley.
SID: Ron Hines, 573-651-2294.
AD: Carroll Williams.

SOUTHEASTERN OKLA.

Durant, OK 74701 II

Coach: Morris Sloan, Southeastern Okla. 1973
Record: 9 Years, 52-35-4

1998 SCHEDULE

McNeese St. ....*Sept. 5
Okla. Panhandle St. ■....................*Sept. 12
Tex. A&M-Commerce ■ ....*Sept. 17
Eastern N.M....................Sept. 26
Harding ....*Oct. 3
Ouachita Baptist ■ ....Oct. 10
Southwestern Okla. ....Oct. 17
Northeastern St. ■....................Oct. 31
Central Okla. ....Nov. 7
East Central ■....................Nov. 14

1997 RESULTS (3-7-0)

0 McNeese St....................31
22 Tarleton St. 31
15 Tex. A&M-Commerce 14
21 Eastern N.M. 7
14 Harding 17
14 Ouachita Baptist 16
11 Southwestern Okla....................21
0 Northeastern St. 20
18 Central Okla. 23
35 East Central....................14
150 **194**

Nickname: Savages.
Stadium: Paul Laird Field, 4,000 capacity. Natural turf.
Colors: Blue & Gold.
Conference: Lone Star Conference.
SID: Harold Harmon, 405-924-388.
AD: Donald A. Parham.

SOUTHERN ARK.

Magnolia, AR 71753 II

Coach: Steve Roberts, Ouachita Bapt. 1987
Record: 4 Years, 18-21-1

1998 SCHEDULE

East Central ■....................*Sept. 3
North Ala. ■ ....*Sept. 12
Ark.-Monticello ....*Sept. 19
West Ga....................*Sept. 26
Central Ark. ■....................*Oct. 3
Valdosta St. ■....................*Oct. 17
West Ala....................Oct. 24
Delta St. ■....................Oct. 31
Henderson St....................Nov. 7
Arkansas Tech ■ ....Nov. 14

1997 RESULTS (9-1-0)

37 East Central 9
16 North Ala. 7
13 Central Ark. 20
24 Delta St. 6
42 Arkansas Tech 7
20 Northwestern Okla. 14
17 Valdosta St. 7
20 Ark.-Monticello....................17
10 Northeastern St. 7
19 Henderson St. 14
218 **108**

II Championship

0 Albany St. (Ga.)....................10

Nickname: Muleriders.
Stadium: Wilkins, 6,000 capacity. Natural turf.
Colors: Royal Blue & Old Gold.
Conference: Gulf South Conference.
SID: Harold Jameson, 501-235-4104.
AD: W. T. Watson.

SOUTHERN CAL

Los Angeles, CA 90089....................I-A

Coach: Paul Hackett, UC Davis 1969
Record: 3 Years, 13-20-1

1998 SCHEDULE

Purdue ■....................Aug. 30
San Diego St. ■ ....Sept. 12
Oregon St. ■ ....Sept. 19
Florida St. ....Sept. 26
Arizona St. ■ ....Oct. 3
California ■....................Oct. 10
Washington St. ....Oct. 17
Oregon....................Oct. 24
Washington ■....................Oct. 31
Stanford....................Nov. 7
UCLA....................Nov. 21
Notre Dame ■ ....Nov. 28

1997 RESULTS (6-5-0)

7 Florida St....................14
21 Washington St. 28
27 California 17
35 UNLV....................21
7 Arizona St. 35
20 Notre Dame 17
24 Oregon....................22
0 Washington....................27
45 Stanford....................21
23 Oregon St. 0
24 UCLA....................31
233 **233**

Nickname: Trojans.
Stadium: L.A. Coliseum (1923), 92,000 capacity. Natural turf.
Colors: Cardinal & Gold.
Conference: Pacific-10.
SID: Tim Tessalone, 213-740-8480.
AD: Michael Garrett.

SOUTHERN CONN. ST.

New Haven, CT 06515 II

Coach: Richard Cavanaugh, American Intl 1976
Record: 13 Years, 62-69-1

1998 SCHEDULE

Stony Brook ■....................*Sept. 11
Bentley....................*Sept. 18
Mass.-Lowell ■ ....*Sept. 25
Pace ....Oct. 3
New Haven ....Oct. 10
American Int'l ■ ....Oct. 17
Stonehill....................Oct. 24
LIU-C.W. Post ....Oct. 31
Central Conn. St. ■ ....Nov. 7
Albany (N.Y.) ■....................Nov. 14

1997 RESULTS (7-4-0)

20 Mansfield 7
15 Stony Brook 13
50 Sacred Heart 3
24 Mass.-Lowell 20
39 Pace 20
7 New Haven....................44
23 American Int'l 26
58 Stonehill 0
17 LIU-C.W. Post....................7
0 Central Conn. St. 24
40 Albany (N.Y.) 42
293 **206**

Nickname: Owls.
Stadium: Jess Dow Field (1988), 6,000 capacity. Artificial turf.
Colors: Blue & White.
Conference: Eastern Football.
SID: Richard Leddy, 203-392-6005.
AD: Darryl D. Rogers.

SOUTHERN ILL.

Carbondale, IL 62901 ....I-AA

Coach: Jan Quarless, Northern Mich. 1973

Record: 2 Years, 4-14-0

1998 SCHEDULE

Murray St.	*Sept. 5
Tenn.-Martin	*Sept. 12
Northern Iowa ■	Sept. 19
Illinois St.	Sept. 26
Southwest Tex. St. ■	Oct. 3
Youngstown St.	Oct. 10
Western Ill. ■	Oct. 17
Indiana St. ■	Oct. 24
Southwest Mo. St.	Oct. 31
Western Ky.	Nov. 7
Southeast Mo. St. ■	Nov. 14

1997 RESULTS (3-8-0)

0	Nicholls St.	33
24	Murray St.	20
14	Indiana St.	19
27	Northern Iowa	28
35	Southwest Mo. St.	36
31	Illinois St.	29
23	South FLa.	10
31	Western Ky.	52
26	Western Ill.	31
10	Youngstown St.	34
17	Southeast Mo. St.	28
238		**320**

Nickname: Salukis.
Stadium: McAndrew (1975), 17,324 capacity. Artificial turf.
Colors: Maroon & White.
Conference: Gateway.
SID: Fred Huff, 618-453-7235.
AD: Jim Hart.

SOUTHERN METHODIST

Dallas, TX 75275 .... I-A

Coach: Mike Cavan, Georgia 1972
Record: 12 Years, 73-54-2

1998 SCHEDULE

Rice	*Sept. 5
Tulane ■	*Sept. 12
Arkansas [Little Rock, Ark.]	*Sept. 19
Mississippi ■	Sept. 26
Hawaii	*Oct. 3
Wyoming	Oct. 10
Texas Christian ■	Oct. 17
UNLV ■	Oct. 24
Air Force	Oct. 31
Tulsa ■	Nov. 7
Colorado St. ■	Nov. 14
Navy	Nov. 21

1997 RESULTS (6-5-0)

15	Mississippi	23
31	Arkansas	9
16	Navy	46
16	Brigham Young	19
15	New Mexico	22
20	Utah	19
22	Wyoming	17
24	Rice	6
28	UTEP	14
42	Tulsa	41
18	Texas Christian	21
247		**237**

Nickname: Mustangs.
Stadium: Cotton Bowl (1930), 68,252 capacity. Natural turf.
Colors: Red & Blue.
Conference: Western Athletic.
SID: Jon Jackson, 214-768-2883.
AD: W. James Copeland Jr.

SOUTHERN MISS.

Hattiesburg, MS 39402 .... I-A

Coach: Jeff Bower, Southern Miss. 1976
Record: 8 Years, 43-35-1

1998 SCHEDULE

Penn St.	Sept. 5
Texas A&M ■	Sept. 19
Southwestern La. ■	*Sept. 26
Tulane	*Oct. 3
Louisville ■	Oct. 10
Army	Oct. 17
East Caro. ■	Oct. 24
Alabama	Oct. 31
Houston	Nov. 7
Memphis ■	*Nov. 14
Nevada	Nov. 21

1997 RESULTS (8-3-0)

6	Florida	21
24	Illinois	7
35	Nevada	19
13	Alabama	27
42	Louisville	24
23	East Caro.	13
34	Tulane	13
24	Cincinnati	17
20	Tennessee	44
33	Houston	0
42	Memphis	18
296		**203**

Liberty Bowl

41	Pittsburgh	7

Nickname: Golden Eagles.
Stadium: Roberts (1976), 33,000 capacity. Natural turf.
Colors: Black & Gold.
Conference: Conference USA.
SID: M.R. Napier, 601-266-4503.
AD: Bill Mc Lellan.

SOUTHERN U.

Baton Rouge, LA 70813 .... I-AA

Coach: Pete Richardson, Dayton 1968
Record: 10 Years, 87-27-1

1998 SCHEDULE

Northwestern St.	*Sept. 5
Ark.-Pine Bluff	*Sept. 12
Prairie View	*Sept. 19
Alabama St. ■	*Sept. 26
Mississippi Val. ■	*Oct. 3
Alabama A&M	*Oct. 10
Jackson St. ■	*Oct. 17
Alcorn St.	Oct. 24
Florida A&M ■	*Nov. 7
Texas Southern ■	*Nov. 14
Grambling [New Orleans, La.]	Nov. 28

1997 RESULTS (10-1-0)

51	Mississippi Val.	30
27	Northwestern St.	9
36	Ark.-Pine Bluff	33
63	Prairie View	7
27	Alabama St.	16
28	Jackson St.	8
25	Alcorn St.	16
21	Nicholls St.	14
3	Florida A&M	33
27	Texas Southern	18
30	Grambling	7
338		**191**

Heritage Bowl

34	South Caro. St.	28

Nickname: Jaguars.
Stadium: A.W. Mumford (1928), 24,000 capacity. Natural turf.
Colors: Blue & Gold.
Conference: Southwestern.
SID: Roderick Mosley, 504-771-4142.
AD: Marino H. Casem.

SOUTHERN UTAH

Cedar City, UT 84720 .... I-AA

Coach: C. Ray Gregory, Emory & Henry 1986
Record: 1 Year, 5-6-0

1998 SCHEDULE

Montana	Sept. 12
McNeese St. ■	*Sept. 19
Western Ill.	Sept. 26
Cal St. Northridge	Oct. 3
St. Mary's (Cal.) ■	Oct. 10
Fort Lewis ■	Oct. 17
Idaho St.	*Oct. 24
Illinois St.	Oct. 31
Cal Poly ■	Nov. 7
UC Davis	Nov. 14
Eastern Wash. ■	Nov. 21

1997 RESULTS (5-6-0)

44	Illinois St.	13
27	Fort Lewis	14
32	Weber St.	33
34	Arkansas St.	24
34	Montana Tech	21
6	Western Ill.	45
31	Idaho St.	46
7	Southwest Tex. St.	21
37	UC Davis	27
33	Northern Iowa	53
27	St. Mary's (Cal.)	31
312		**328**

Nickname: Thunderbirds.
Stadium: Coliseum of Southern Utah (1967), 8,500 capacity. Natural turf.
Colors: Scarlett & White.
Conference: Independent.
SID: Neil Gardner, 801-586-7753.
AD: Jack Bishop.

SOUTHWEST BAPTIST

Bolivar, MO 65613 II

Coach: Dennis Roland, Boston U. 1978
Record: 5 Years, 25-26-0

1998 SCHEDULE

Arkansas Tech ■	Sept. 5
Ouachita Baptist	*Sept. 12
Washburn	*Sept. 19
Emporia St. ■	Sept. 26
Central Mo. St.	Oct. 3
Pittsburg St.	Oct. 10
Northwest Mo. St. ■	Oct. 17
Truman St.	Oct. 24
Mo. Western St. ■	Oct. 31
Mo. Southern St.	*Nov. 5
Mo.-Rolla ■	Nov. 14

1997 RESULTS (0-10-0)

26	Ouachita Baptist	27
7	Washburn	25
7	Emporia St.	46
17	Central Mo. St.	52
0	Pittsburg St.	57
3	Northwest Mo. St.	59
0	Truman St.	28
6	Mo. Western St.	31
10	Mo. Southern St.	35
0	Mo.-Rolla	19
76		**379**

Nickname: Bearcats.
Stadium: Plaster (1986), 2,500 capacity. Natural turf.
Colors: Purple & White.
Conference: MIAA.
SID: Christopher Johnson, 417-326-1799.
AD: Stephanie Miller.

SOUTHWEST MO. ST.

Springfield, MO 65804 .... I-AA

Coach: Del Miller, Central (Iowa) 1972
Record: 3 Years, 16-17-0

1998 SCHEDULE

Tulsa	*Sept. 5
Harding ■	*Sept. 12
Arkansas St.	Sept. 19
Northern Iowa	*Oct. 3
Western Ill. ■	Oct. 10
Indiana St.	Oct. 17
Southeast Mo. St. ■	Oct. 24
Southern Ill. ■	Oct. 31
Illinois St.	Nov. 7

Cal St. Northridge ■ ....Nov. 14
Youngstown St. ■ ....Nov. 21

1997 RESULTS (5-6-0)

8 Pittsburg St. 9
47 Jacksonville St. 42
16 McNeese St. 28
27 Tenn.-Martin 14
36 Southern Ill. 35
22 Indiana St. 7
41 Illinois St. 7
7 Western Ill. 37
22 Northern Iowa 23
27 Arkansas St. 35
13 Youngstown St. 45
266 **282**

Nickname: Bears.
Stadium: Plaster Field (1941), 16,300 capacity. Artificial turf.
Colors: Maroon & White.
Conference: Gateway.
SID: Mark Stillwell, 417-836-5402.
AD: Bill Rowe Jr.

SOUTHWEST ST.

Marshall, MN 56258 II

Coach: Ron Flowers, Ohio St. 1980
Record: 1 Year, 5-6-0

1998 SCHEDULE

Mayville St. ....Sept. 5
Augustana (S.D.) ■ ....*Sept. 12
Wis.-River Falls ....Sept. 19
Minn.-Duluth ....Sept. 26
Moorhead St. ■ ....Oct. 10
Winona St. ....Oct. 17
Minn.-Morris ■ ....Oct. 24
Northern St. ....Oct. 31
Bemidji St. ■ ....Nov. 7
Wis.-Stevens Point [Minneapolis, Minn.] ....Nov. 14

1997 RESULTS (5-6-0)

16 Minot St. 14
3 Augustana (S.D.) 35
21 Wis.-River Falls 38
16 Bemidji St. 0
20 Minn.-Duluth 14
29 Wayne St. (Neb.) 21
6 Moorhead St. 10
21 Winona St. 38
32 Minn.-Morris 7
22 Northern St. 27
17 Wis.-Eau Claire 48
203 **252**

Nickname: Mustangs.
Stadium: Mattke Field (1971), 5,000 capacity. Natural turf.
Colors: Brown & Gold.
Conference: Northern Sun.
SID: Kelly Loft, 507-537-7177.
AD: Lloyd "Butch Raymond.

SOUTHWEST TEX. ST.

San Marcos, TX 78666 ....I-AA

Coach: Bob DeBeese, Southwest Tex. St. 1982
Record: 1 Year, 5-6-0

1998 SCHEDULE

Delta St. ■ ....*Sept. 3
Northern Ariz. ....*Sept. 12
Hofstra ■ ....*Sept. 19
Northwestern St. ■ ....*Sept. 26
Southern Ill. ....Oct. 3
Nicholls St. ■ ....Oct. 17
Troy St. ....*Oct. 22
Stephen F. Austin ■ ....*Oct. 29
McNeese St. ....*Nov. 7
Jacksonville St. ■ ....Nov. 14
Sam Houston St. ....Nov. 21

1997 RESULTS (5-6-0)

24 Cal St. Sacramento 14
24 Hofstra 28
28 Montana St. 26
31 Troy St. 17
28 Nicholls St. 29
3 Northwestern St. 31
21 Southern Utah 7
28 Stephen F. Austin 31
21 McNeese St. 31
35 Jacksonville St. 27
30 Sam Houston St. 35
273 **276**

Nickname: Bobcats.
Stadium: Bobcat (1981), 14,104 capacity. Natural turf.
Colors: Maroon & Gold.
Conference: Southland.
SID: Tony Brubaker, 512-245-2966.
AD: To be named.

SOUTHWESTERN LA.

Lafayette, LA 70504 ....I-A

Coach: Nelson Stokley, LSU 1968
12 years, 60-71-1

1998 SCHEDULE

Arkansas ....*Sept. 5
Northwestern St. ■ ....*Sept. 12
Louisiana Tech ....*Sept. 19
Southern Miss. ....*Sept. 26
UAB ....*Oct. 3
Arkansas St. ■ ....Oct. 17
Central Fla. ■ ....*Oct. 24
Tulane ....*Oct. 31
Northeast La. ....*Nov. 7
Oklahoma St. ....Nov. 14
Western Ky. ■ ....*Nov. 21

1997 RESULTS (1-10-0)

13 Pittsburgh 45
7 Oklahoma St. 31
14 Texas Tech 59
0 Texas A&M 66
7 UAB 42
41 Arkansas St. 38
42 North ALa. 48
21 Northeast La. 28
0 Tulane 56
7 Washington St. 77
24 Louisiana Tech 63
176 **553**

Nickname: Ragin' Cajuns.
Stadium: Cajun Field (1971), 31,000 capacity. Natural turf.
Colors: Vermilion & White.
Conference: Sun Belt.
SID: Dan McDonald, 318-482-6331.
AD: Nelson Schexnayder Jr.

SOUTHWESTERN OKLA.

Weatherford, OK 73096 II

Coach: Paul Sharp, Ouachita Bapt. 1974
Record: 12 Years, 65-55-1

1998 SCHEDULE

Abilene Christian ■ ....*Sept. 5
West Tex. A&M ....*Sept. 12
Eastern N.M. ■ ....*Sept. 19
Tex. A&M-Commerce ....*Sept. 26
Ouachita Baptist ....Oct. 3
Southeastern OkLa. ■ ....Oct. 17
Northeastern St. ....Oct. 24
Central OkLa. ■ ....Oct. 31
East Central ....Nov. 7
Harding ■ ....Nov. 14

1997 RESULTS (5-5-0)

17 Abilene Christian 25
7 West Tex. A&M 34
12 Eastern N.M. 21
7 Tex. A&M-Commerce 17
12 Ouachita Baptist 6
21 Southeastern OkLa. 11
6 Northeastern St. 7
33 Central OkLa. 17
20 East Central 14
42 Harding 33
177 **185**

Nickname: Bulldogs.
Stadium: Milum, 9,000 capacity. Natural turf.
Colors: Navy Blue & White.
Conference: Lone Star Conference.
SID: Brian Adler, 405-774-3775.
AD: Cecil Perkins.

SPRINGFIELD

Springfield, MA 01109 III

Coach: Mike DeLong, Springfield 1974
Record: 16 Years, 78-74-2

1998 SCHEDULE

Bri'water (Mass.) ....Sept. 12
Merchant Marine ....Sept. 19
Coast Guard ■ ....Sept. 26
Ithaca ....Oct. 3
Western Conn. St. ■ ....Oct. 10
Plymouth St. ■ ....Oct. 17
Worcester Tech ....*Oct. 24
Cortland St. ■ ....Oct. 31
Norwich ....Nov. 7
Union (N.Y.) ■ ....Nov. 14

1997 RESULTS (4-5-0)

31 American Int'l 14
28 Merchant Marine 42
20 Coast Guard 26
15 Ithaca 42
34 Western Conn. St. 7
16 Plymouth St. 36
56 Worcester Tech 49
8 Cortland St. 24
73 Norwich 14
281 **254**

Nickname: The Pride.
Stadium: Benedum Field (1971), 2,500 capacity. Artificial turf.
Colors: Maroon & White.
Conference: Freedom FB.
SID: Ken Cerino, 413-748-3341.
AD: Edward R. Bilik.

STANFORD

Stanford, CA 94305 ....I-A

Coach: Tyrone Willingham, Michigan St. 1977
Record: 3 Years, 19-15-1

1998 SCHEDULE

San Jose St. ■ ....Sept. 5
Arizona ■ ....Sept. 12
North Caro. ■ ....Sept. 19
Oregon ....Sept. 26
Notre Dame ....Oct. 3
Oregon St. ■ ....Oct. 10
Arizona St. ....*Oct. 22
UCLA ....Oct. 31
Southern Cal ■ ....Nov. 7
Washington St. ■ ....Nov. 14
California ....Nov. 21

1997 RESULTS (5-6-0)

28 San Jose St. 12
17 North Caro. 28
27 Oregon St. 24
58 Oregon 49
33 Notre Dame 15
22 Arizona 28
14 Arizona St. 31
7 UCLA 27
21 Southern Cal 45
28 Washington St. 38
21 California 20
276 **317**

Nickname: Cardinal.
Stadium: Stanford (1921), 85,500 capacity. Natural turf.
Colors: Cardinal & White.
Conference: Pacific-10.
SID: Gary Migdol, 415-723-4418.
AD: Edward Leland.

STEPHEN F. AUSTIN

Nacogdoches, TX 75962 ....I-AA

Coach: John Pearce, Tex. A&M-Commerce 1970
Record: 6 Years, 43-24-2

1998 SCHEDULE

Montana ■ ....*Sept. 5
Tarleton St. ■.................................*Sept. 12
Northeast La. ....*Sept. 19
Northern Iowa ■...............................*Sept. 26
Jacksonville St......................................Oct. 1
Troy St. ■ ....Oct. 17
McNeese St. ....*Oct. 24
Southwest Tex. St.............................*Oct. 29
Sam Houston St. ■ ....Nov. 7
Nicholls St. ....*Nov. 14
Northwestern St. ■ ....Nov. 21

1997 RESULTS (8-3-0)

35 West Tex. A&M..17
38 Delta St. 3
10 Montana 24
17 New Hampshire 14
41 Jacksonville St. 15
20 Troy St. 13
13 McNeese St...7
31 Southwest Tex. St. 28
28 Sam Houston St. 33
39 Nicholls St..7
24 Northwestern St. 38
296 **199**

Nickname: Lumberjacks.
Stadium: Homer Bryce (1973), 14,575 capacity. Artificial turf.
Colors: Purple & White.
Conference: Southland.
SID: Rob Meyers, 409-468-2606.
AD: Steve Mc Carty.

STONEHILL

North Easton, MA 02357 II

Coach: Connie Driscoll, Mass.-Dartmouth 1976
Record: 5 Years, 35-15-0

1998 SCHEDULE

John Carroll ■...Sept. 5
American Int'l..Sept. 19
Merrimack ■..Sept. 26
LIU-C.W. Post ■ ....Oct. 3
Mass.-Lowell..*Oct. 9
Assumption ■...Oct. 17
Southern Conn. St. ■ ....Oct. 24
Albany (N.Y.)...Oct. 31
Wesley ■ ....Nov. 7
Bentley...Nov. 14

1997 RESULTS (4-6-0)

27 Assumption 7
24 American Int'l 26
16 Merrimack...13
0 LIU-C.W. Post 16
21 Mass.-Lowell 9
33 Western New Eng. 14
0 Southern Conn. St. 58
26 Albany (N.Y.) 42
6 Salve Regina 7
24 Bentley...49
177 **241**

Nickname: Chieftains.
Stadium: Chieftain (1980), 2,000 capacity. Natural turf.
Colors: Purple & White.
Conference: Eastern Football.
SID: Bob Richards, 508-230-1352.
AD: Paula Sullivan.

STONY BROOK

Stony Brook, NY 11794 II

Coach: Sam Kornhauser, Missouri Valley 1971
Record: 14 Years, 67-66-2

1998 SCHEDULE

Southern Conn. St..*Sept. 11
Pace ■ ....Sept. 26
Assumption ....Oct. 3
Bentley...Oct. 10
Albany (N.Y.) ■ ....Oct. 17
Merrimack ....Oct. 24
Wagner ■ ....Oct. 31
American Int'l ■ ....Nov. 7
LIU-C.W. Post ■ ....Nov. 14
St. John's (N.Y.)...Nov. 27

1997 RESULTS (4-6-0)

13 Southern Conn. St. 15
38 Pace..7
19 St. John's (N.Y.) 23
22 Sacred Heart 7
35 Bentley 9
23 Albany (N.Y.) 30
17 Merrimack..6
0 Wagner 10
7 American Int'l 30
0 LIU-C.W. Post..7
174 **144**

Nickname: Seawolves.
Stadium: Seawolves (1978), 2,000 capacity. Natural turf.
Colors: Scarlet & Gray.
Conference: Eastern Football.
SID: Rob Emmerich, 516-632-6312.
AD: Sandra R. Weeden.

SUL ROSS ST.

Alpine, TX 79832 III

Coach: Jim Hector, Texas 1978
Record: 4 Years, 12-26-0

1998 SCHEDULE

Okla. Panhandle St. ■...................................Sept. 19
Hardin-Simmons ■...Oct. 3
McMurry ■ ....Oct. 17
Texas Lutheran..Oct. 24
Mississippi Col. ....Oct. 31
Austin ■..Nov. 7
Howard Payne ....Nov. 14

1997 RESULTS (3-6-0)

6 Okla. Panhandle St.......................................16
18 Howard Payne...28
14 Hardin-Simmons 35
34 McMurry 14
9 Howard Payne...27
26 Mississippi Col. 31
29 McMurry 49
24 Austin..20
27 Hardin-Simmons 21
187 **241**

Nickname: Lobos.
Stadium: Jackson Field, 5,000 capacity. Natural turf.
Colors: Scarlet & Gray.
Conference: American Southwest
SID: Lee Sleeper, 915-837-8061.
AD: Kay Whitley.

SUSQUEHANNA

Selinsgrove, PA 17870 III

Coach: Steve Briggs, Springfield 1984
Record: 8 Years, 55-28-0

1998 SCHEDULE

Alfred ....*Sept. 5
King's (Pa.) ....Sept. 12
Wilkes ....Sept. 19
Allegheny ■...Sept. 26
Lebanon Valley..Oct. 10
Moravian ■ ....Oct. 17
Juniata ■ ....Oct. 24
Lycoming ....Oct. 31
Albright ■ ....Nov. 7
Widener ....Nov. 14

1997 RESULTS (6-4-0)

31 Kean 14
35 King's (Pa.) 14
47 Wilkes 14
28 Wilmington (Ohio) 7
34 Lebanon Valley 13
24 Moravian 31
45 Juniata 14
12 Lycoming 21
14 Albright..35
28 Widener..35
298 **198**

Nickname: Crusaders.
Stadium: Amos Alonzo Stagg (1892), 4,600 capacity. Natural turf.
Colors: Orange & Maroon.
Conference: Middle Atlantic States Conf.
SID: Mike Ferlazzo, 717-372-4119.
AD: Donald Harnum.

SWARTHMORE

Swarthmore, PA 19081 III

Coach: Peter Alvanos, Drexel 1988
(First year as head coach)

1998 SCHEDULE

Johns Hopkins ■...Sept. 19
Gettysburg ....Sept. 26
Ursinus ■..Oct. 3
Muhlenberg ....Oct. 10
Dickinson ....Oct. 24
Frank. & Marsh. ■..Oct. 31
Western Md. ....Nov. 7
Wash. & Lee ■ ....Nov. 14

1997 RESULTS (0-10-0)

0 Bethany (W. Va.) 56
0 Johns Hopkins...73
15 Gettysburg..64
0 Ursinus 31
14 Muhlenberg...60
12 Pomona-Pitzer 76
0 Dickinson..43
0 Frank. & Marsh. 41
0 Western Md. 56
13 Wash. & Lee 41
54 **541**

Nickname: Garnet Tide.
Stadium: Clothier (1950), 2,000 capacity. Natural turf.
Colors: Garnet & White.
Conference: Centennial Conference.
SID: Mark Duzenski, 610-328-8206.
AD: Robert E. Williams.

SYRACUSE

Syracuse, NY 13244.................................I-A

Coach: Paul Pasqualoni, Penn St. 1972
Record: 12 Years, 94-39-1

1998 SCHEDULE

Tennessee ■..Sept. 5
Michigan ....Sept. 12
Rutgers ■...Sept. 19
North Caro. St. ....Oct. 1
Cincinnati ■..Oct. 10
Boston College ....Oct. 17
Pittsburgh ■ ....Oct. 31
West Va. ....*Nov. 7
Virginia Tech ■ ....Nov. 14
Temple...Nov. 21
Miami (Fla.) ■ ....Nov. 28

1997 RESULTS (9-3-0)

34 Wisconsin 0
31 North Caro. St. 32
34 Oklahoma 36
3 Virginia Tech 31
30 Tulane 19
56 East Caro. 0
50 Rutgers 3
60 Temple 7
40 West Va..10
20 Boston College...13
32 Pittsburgh...27
33 Miami (Fla.) 13
423 **191**

Fiesta Bowl

18 Kansas St. 35

SCHEDULES/RESULTS

Nickname: Orangemen.
Stadium: Carrier Dome (1980), 50,000 capacity. Artificial turf.
Colors: Orange.
Conference: Big East.
SID: Sue Cornelius Edson, 315-443-2608.
AD: John J. Crouthamel.

TARLETON ST.

Stephenville, TX 76402 II

Coach: Craig Wederquist, Drake 1986
Record: 1 Year, 4-7-0

1998 SCHEDULE

N. M. Highlands ■ .... *Sept. 3
Stephen F. Austin .... *Sept. 12
Harding .... *Sept. 19
Central Okla. ■ .... *Sept. 26
Texas A&M-Kingsville .... *Oct. 3
West Tex. A&M ■ .... *Oct. 10
Eastern N.M. .... *Oct. 17
Abilene Christian ■ .... Oct. 24
Angelo St. ■ .... Oct. 31
Midwestern St. .... Nov. 7
Tex. A&M-Commerce ■ .... Nov. 14

1997 RESULTS (4-7-0)

29	N. M. Highlands	34
31	Southeastern Okla.	22
49	Harding	46
19	Central Okla.	28
14	Texas A&M-Kingsville	43
17	West Tex. A&M	31
20	Eastern N.M.	26
17	Abilene Christian	23
13	Angelo St.	47
29	Midwestern St.	28
49	Tex. A&M-Commerce	21
287		**349**

Nickname: Texans.
Stadium: Memorial (1976), 5,284 capacity. Natural turf.
Colors: Purple & White.
Conference: Lone Star Conference.
SID: Reed Richmond, 817-968-9077.
AD: Lonn Reisman.

TEMPLE

Philadelphia, PA 19122 .... I-A

Coach: Bobby Wallace, Mississippi St. 1976
Record: 10 Years, 82-36-1

1998 SCHEDULE

Toledo .... *Sept. 5
Akron ■ .... *Sept. 12
Boston College .... Sept. 19
Maryland .... *Sept. 26
William & Mary ■ .... Oct. 3
West Va. ■ .... Oct. 10
Virginia Tech .... Oct. 17
Rutgers .... Oct. 31
Pittsburgh .... Nov. 7
Miami (Fla.) ■ .... Nov. 14
Syracuse ■ .... Nov. 21

1997 RESULTS (3-8-0)

14	Western Mich.	34
28	Boston College	21
10	Penn St.	52
13	Virginia Tech	23
21	Maryland	24
17	Pittsburgh	13
7	Syracuse	60
15	Miami (Fla.)	47
49	Rutgers	7
17	Navy	49
21	West Va.	41
212		**371**

Nickname: Owls.
Stadium: Veterans (1971), 66,592 capacity. Artificial turf.
Colors: Cherry & White.
Conference: Atlantic 10.
SID: Brian Kirschner, 215-204-7445.
AD: David P. O'Brien.

TENNESSEE

Knoxville, TN 37996 .... I-A

Coach: Phillip Fulmer, Tennessee 1972
Record: 6 Years, 54-11-0

1998 SCHEDULE

Syracuse .... Sept. 5
Florida ■ .... *Sept. 19
Houston ■ .... *Sept. 26
Auburn .... Oct. 3
Georgia .... Oct. 10
Alabama ■ .... Oct. 24
South Caro. .... Oct. 31
UAB ■ .... Nov. 7
Arkansas ■ .... Nov. 14
Kentucky ■ .... Nov. 21
Vanderbilt .... Nov. 28

1997 RESULTS (11-1-0)

52	Texas Tech	17
30	UCLA	24
20	Florida	33
31	Mississippi	17
38	Georgia	13
38	Alabama	21
22	South Caro.	7
44	Southern Miss.	20
30	Arkansas	22
59	Kentucky	31
17	Vanderbilt	10
30	Auburn	29
411		**244**

Orange Bowl

17	Nebraska	42

Nickname: Volunteers.
Stadium: Neyland (1921), 102,544 capacity. Natural turf.
Colors: Orange & White.
Conference: Southeastern.
SID: Bud Ford, 423-974-1212.
AD: Douglas A. Dickey.

TENNESSEE ST.

Nashville, TN 37209 .... I-AA

Coach: L. C. Cole, Nebraska 1980
Record: 2 Years, 8-14-0

1998 SCHEDULE

Middle Tenn. St. .... *Sept. 5
Jackson St. [Memphis, Tenn.] .... *Sept. 12
Florida A&M [Atlanta, Ga.] .... Sept. 26
Alabama A&M ■ .... Oct. 3
Eastern Ky. .... *Oct. 10
Southeast Mo. St. .... Oct. 17
Tenn.-Martin ■ .... Oct. 24
Eastern Ill. .... Oct. 31
Tennessee Tech .... *Nov. 7
Murray St. .... Nov. 14
Texas Southern ■ .... Nov. 21

1997 RESULTS (4-7-0)

28	Florida A&M	43
25	Middle Tenn. St.	16
28	Jackson St.	31
28	South Caro. St.	34
37	North Caro. A&T	49
7	Eastern Ky.	49
7	Chattanooga	28
27	Tenn.-Martin	20
28	Tennessee Tech	21
7	Murray St.	13
32	Southeast Mo. St.	27
254		**331**

Nickname: Tigers.
Stadium: W.J. Hale (1953), 16,000 capacity. Natural turf.
Colors: Blue & White.
Conference: Ohio Valley.
SID: To be named, 615-963-5851.
AD: Vivian L. Fuller.

TENNESSEE TECH

Cookeville, TN 38505 .... I-AA

Coach: Mike Hennigan, Tennessee Tech 1973
Record: 2 Years, 11-11-0

1998 SCHEDULE

Ky. Wesleyan ■ .... *Sept. 3
UAB .... *Sept. 19
Eastern Ill. .... Sept. 26
Middle Tenn. St. ■ .... Oct. 3
Southeast Mo. St. ■ .... Oct. 10
Tenn.-Martin .... Oct. 17
Eastern Ky. ■ .... Oct. 24
Murray St. .... Oct. 31
Tennessee St. ■ .... *Nov. 7
Western Caro. ■ .... Nov. 14
Samford ■ .... Nov. 21

1997 RESULTS (6-5-0)

10	Chattanooga	13
14	Samford	7
7	Eastern Ill.	10
36	Austin Peay	3
17	Southeast Mo. St.	14
33	Tenn.-Martin	2
7	Eastern Ky.	26
16	Murray St.	13
21	Tennessee St.	28
14	UAB	38
30	Middle Tenn. St.	20
205		**174**

Nickname: Golden Eagles.
Stadium: Tucker (1966), 16,500 capacity. Artificial turf.
Colors: Purple & Gold.
Conference: Ohio Valley.
SID: Rob Schabert, 615-372-3088.
AD: David Larimore.

TENN.-MARTIN

Martin, TN 38238 .... I-AA

Coach: Jim Marshall, Tenn.-Martin 1969
Record: 7 Years, 20-57-0

1998 SCHEDULE

Western Ky. .... *Sept. 3
Southern Ill. ■ .... *Sept. 12
Southeast Mo. St. .... *Sept. 26
Murray St. .... Oct. 3
Samford .... Oct. 10
Tennessee Tech ■ .... Oct. 17
Tennessee St. .... Oct. 24
Eastern Ky. ■ .... Oct. 31
Middle Tenn. St. ■ .... Nov. 7
Eastern Ill. ■ .... Nov. 14
UAB .... Nov. 21

1997 RESULTS (1-10-0)

0	Western Ky.	42
6	Eastern Ill.	42
14	Southwest Mo. St.	27
7	Southeast Mo. St.	42
7	Murray St.	45
24	Middle Tenn. St.	37
2	Tennessee Tech	33
20	Tennessee St.	27
0	Eastern Ky.	49
7	Samford	14
36	Austin Peay	26
123		**384**

Nickname: Skyhawks.
Stadium: UT Martin (1964), 7,500 capacity. Natural turf.
Colors: Orange, White, Royal Blue.
Conference: Ohio Valley.
SID: Lee Wilmot, 901-587-7630.
AD: Benny Hollis.

TEXAS

Austin, TX 78712 .... I-A

Coach: Mack Brown, Florida St. 1974
Record: 14 Years, 87-74-1

1998 SCHEDULE

New Mexico St. ■ .... *Sept. 5
UCLA .... Sept. 12
Kansas St. .... Sept. 19
Rice ■ .... Sept. 26
Iowa St. ■ .... Oct. 3
Oklahoma [Dallas, Tex.] .... Oct. 10
Baylor ■ .... Oct. 24
Nebraska .... Oct. 31
Oklahoma St. ■ .... Nov. 7
Texas Tech .... Nov. 14
Texas A&M ■ .... Nov. 27

1997 RESULTS (4-7-0)

48 Rutgers 14
3 UCLA 66
38 Rice 31
16 Oklahoma St. 42
27 Oklahoma 24
29 Missouri 37
30 Colorado 47
21 Baylor 23
10 Texas Tech 24
45 Kansas 31
16 Texas A&M 27
283 **366**

Nickname: Longhorns.
Stadium: Memorial (1924), 75,512 capacity. Natural turf.
Colors: Burnt Orange & White.
Conference: Big 12.
SID: Dave Saba, 512-471-7437.
AD: Deloss Dodds.

TEXAS A&M

College Station, TX 77843 .... I-A

Coach: R. C. Slocum, McNeese St. 1967
Record: 9 Years, 83-25-2

1998 SCHEDULE

Florida St. [East Rutherford, N. J.] .... Aug. 31
Louisiana Tech ■ .... *Sept. 12
Southern Miss. .... Sept. 19
North Texas ■ .... *Sept. 26
Kansas .... Oct. 3
Nebraska ■ .... Oct. 10
Baylor .... *Oct. 17
Texas Tech ■ .... Oct. 24
Oklahoma St. .... Oct. 31
Oklahoma ■ .... Nov. 7
Missouri ■ .... Nov. 14
Texas .... Nov. 27

1997 RESULTS (9-3-0)

59 Sam Houston St. 6
66 Southwestern La. 0
36 North Texas 10
16 Colorado 10
56 Iowa St. 17
17 Kansas St. 36
13 Texas Tech 16
28 Oklahoma St. 25
38 Baylor 10
51 Oklahoma 7
27 Texas 16
15 Nebraska 54
422 **207**

Cotton Bowl

23 UCLA 29

Nickname: Aggies.
Stadium: Kyle Field (1925), 70,210 capacity. Natural turf.
Colors: Maroon & White.
Conference: Big 12.
SID: Alan Cannon, 409-845-5725.
AD: Wally W. Groff.

TEX. A&M-COMMERCE

Commerce, TX 75429 II

Coach: Eddie Vowell, Southwest OkLa. 1969
Record: 12 Years, 70-64-1

1998 SCHEDULE

UC Davis ■ .... *Sept. 5
Pittsburg St. ■ .... *Sept. 12
Southeastern OkLa. .... *Sept. 17
Southwestern OkLa. ■ .... *Sept. 26
Midwestern St. .... *Oct. 3
Texas A&M-Kingsville ■ .... *Oct. 10
West Tex. A&M .... *Oct. 17
Eastern N.M. ■ .... Oct. 24
Abilene Christian .... Oct. 31
Angelo St. ■ .... Nov. 7
Tarleton St. .... Nov. 14

1997 RESULTS (3-8-0)

0 North Dak. St. 51
10 Abilene Christian 26
14 Southeastern OkLa. 15
17 Southwestern OkLa. 7
49 Midwestern St. 7
6 Texas A&M-Kingsville 34
21 West Tex. A&M 14
9 Eastern N.M. 10
9 Abilene Christian 19
21 Angelo St. 40
21 Tarleton St. 49
177 **272**

Nickname: Lions.
Stadium: Memorial (1950), 10,000 capacity. Natural turf.
Colors: Blue & Gold.
Conference: Lone Star Conference.
SID: Greg Seiler, 903-886-5131.
AD: Margaret Harbison.

TEXAS A&M-KINGSVILLE

Kingsville, TX 78363 II

Coach: Ron Harms, Valparaiso 1959
Record: 29 Years, 203-103-4

1998 SCHEDULE

North Dak. St. .... *Sept. 3
Central OkLa. .... Sept. 12
Sam Houston St. .... *Sept. 19
Harding ■ .... *Sept. 26
Tarleton St. ■ .... *Oct. 3
Tex. A&M-Commerce .... *Oct. 10
Midwestern St. ■ .... *Oct. 17
West Tex. A&M ■ .... *Oct. 24
Eastern N.M. .... *Oct. 31
Abilene Christian ■ .... *Nov. 7
Angelo St. .... Nov. 14

1997 RESULTS (9-1-0)

33 Central OkLa. 7
12 North ALa. 17
33 Harding 7
43 Tarleton St. 14
34 Tex. A&M-Commerce 6
30 Midwestern St. 7
33 West Tex. A&M 0
56 Eastern N.M. 14
54 Abilene Christian 7
35 Angelo St. 25
363 **104**

II Championship

33 UC Davis 37

Nickname: Javelinas.
Stadium: Javelina (1950), 15,000 capacity. Natural turf.
Colors: Blue & Gold.
Conference: Lone Star Conference.
SID: Fred Nuesch, 512-593-3908.
AD: Ron Harms.

TEXAS CHRISTIAN

Fort Worth, TX 76129 .... I-A

Coach: Dennis Franchione, Pittsburg St. 1973
Record: 15 Years, 113-55-2

1998 SCHEDULE

Iowa St. .... *Sept. 5
Oklahoma ■ .... *Sept. 12
Air Force ■ .... *Sept. 26
Vanderbilt ■ .... *Oct. 3
Fresno St. ■ .... *Oct. 10
Southern Methodist .... Oct. 17
Colorado St. .... Oct. 24
Wyoming ■ .... Oct. 31
Rice ■ .... Nov. 7
Tulsa .... Nov. 14
UNLV .... Nov. 21

1997 RESULTS (1-10-0)

10 Kansas 17
18 Utah 32
16 Vanderbilt 40
10 North Caro. 31
19 UNLV 21
22 Tulsa 33
10 Brigham Young 31
10 New Mexico 40
19 Rice 38
17 UTEP 24
21 Southern Methodist 18
172 **325**

Nickname: Horned Frogs.
Stadium: Amon G. Carter (1929), 46,000 capacity. Natural turf.
Colors: Purple & White.
Conference: Western Athletic.
SID: Glen Stone, 817-921-7969.
AD: Eric C. Hyman.

TEXAS SOUTHERN

Houston, TX 77004 .... I-AA

Coach: Bill Thomas, Tennessee St. 1970
Record: 9 Years, 52-45-3

1998 SCHEDULE

Prairie View [Houston, Tex.] .... *Sept. 5
Alabama St. .... *Sept. 12
Langston .... *Sept. 19
Howard ■ .... *Sept. 26
Jackson St. .... Oct. 3
Ark.-Pine Bluff ■ .... *Oct. 10
Alcorn St. .... Oct. 17
Mississippi Val. ■ .... *Oct. 24
Grambling ■ .... *Oct. 31
Southern U. .... *Nov. 14
Tennessee St. .... Nov. 21

1997 RESULTS (5-6-0)

32 Prairie View 16
31 Alabama St. 6
17 Morgan St. 24
7 Sam Houston St. 40
49 Jackson St. 55
16 Ark.-Pine Bluff 36
10 Alcorn St. 7
10 Mississippi Val. 13
21 Grambling 16
38 Lane 0
18 Southern U. 27
249 **240**

Nickname: Tigers.
Stadium: Robertson (1965), 25,000 capacity. Natural turf.
Colors: Maroon & Gray.
Conference: Southwestern.
SID: Gary Q. Abernathy, 713-527-7270.
AD: Harold Odom.

TEXAS TECH

Lubbock, TX 79409 .... I-A

Coach: Spike Dykes, Stephen F. Austin 1959
Record: 12 Years, 69-57-1

1998 SCHEDULE

UTEP ■ .... *Sept. 5
North Texas [Irving, Tex.] .... *Sept. 12
Fresno St. ■ .... *Sept. 19
Iowa St. .... Sept. 26
Baylor ■ .... *Oct. 3
Oklahoma St. ■ .... *Oct. 10
Colorado .... Oct. 17
Texas A&M .... Oct. 24

Missouri ■ Oct. 31
Texas ■ Nov. 14
Oklahoma Nov. 21

1997 RESULTS (6-5-0)

17 Tennessee 52
59 Southwestern La. 14
27 North Texas 30
35 Baylor 14
17 Kansas 7
0 Nebraska 29
16 Texas A&M 13
2 Kansas St. 13
24 Texas 10
27 Oklahoma St. 3
21 Oklahoma 32
245 **217**

Nickname: Red Raiders.
Stadium: Jones (1947), 50,500 capacity. Artificial turf.
Colors: Scarlet & Black.
Conference: Big 12.
SID: Richard Kilwien, 806-742-2770.
AD: Gerald L. Myers.

UTEP

El Paso, TX 79968 I-A

Coach: Charlie Bailey, Tampa 1962
Record: 8 Years, 23-58-2

1998 SCHEDULE

Texas Tech *Sept. 5
Oregon ■ *Sept. 12
New Mexico St. *Sept. 26
Colorado St. ■ *Oct. 3
New Mexico *Oct. 10
San Jose St. ■ *Oct. 17
Fresno St. *Oct. 24
Hawaii ■ Oct. 31
Utah Nov. 7
Brigham Young ■ Nov. 14
San Diego St. *Nov. 21

1997 RESULTS (4-7-0)

3 LSU 55
20 New Mexico 38
3 Utah 56
24 New Mexico St. 16
7 Clemson 39
33 Tulsa 18
7 San Jose St. 10
14 Brigham Young 3
14 Southern Methodist 28
24 Texas Christian 17
13 Rice 31
162 **311**

Nickname: Miners.
Stadium: Sun Bowl (1963), 51,270 capacity. Artificial turf.
Colors: Orange, White & Blue.
Conference: Western Athletic.
SID: Gary Richter, 915-747-5330.
AD: Bob Stull.

THIEL

Greenville, PA 16125 III

Coach: David Armstrong, Mercyhurst 1986
Record: 2 Years, 2-18-0

1998 SCHEDULE

Capital Sept. 5
Oberlin ■ Sept. 12
Kenyon Sept. 19
Grove City Oct. 3
Waynesburg ■ Oct. 10
Alfred ■ Oct. 17
Bethany (W. Va.) Oct. 24
Gannon Oct. 31
Defiance ■ Nov. 7
Wash. & Jeff. ■ Nov. 14

1997 RESULTS (1-9-0)

17 Oberlin 18
19 Allegheny 45
33 Bluffton 27
9 Grove City 32
22 Waynesburg 38
6 Alfred 42
7 Bethany (W. Va.) 26
7 Wash. & Jeff. 64
14 Gannon 42
0 Catholic 42
134 **376**

Nickname: Tomcats.
Stadium: Stewart Field (1954), 5,000 capacity. Natural turf.
Colors: Navy Blue & Old Gold.
Conference: Presidents' Athletic Conf.
SID: Mike Carpenter, 412-589-2187.
AD: David A. Armstrong.

THOMAS MORE

Crestview Hills, KY 41017 III

Coach: Vic Clark, Indiana St. 1971
Record: 8 Years, 58-22-0

1998 SCHEDULE

Alma Sept. 5
Hanover ■ Sept. 12
Ky. Wesleyan Sept. 19
Wis.-Oshkosh Sept. 26
Campbellsville ■ Oct. 3
Morehead St. Oct. 17
Gannon ■ Oct. 24
Defiance ■ Oct. 31
Maryville (Tenn.) ■ Nov. 7
Carnegie Mellon Nov. 14

1997 RESULTS (5-5-0)

30 Maryville (Tenn.) 24
6 Ill. Wesleyan 37
40 Wilmington (Ohio) 17
19 Campbellsville 22
38 Bluffton 14
5 Howard Payne 25
21 Defiance 14
20 Ohio Wesleyan 28
22 Mt. Senario 21
13 Albion 31
214 **233**

Nickname: Saints.
Stadium: Gilligan (1945), 2,500 capacity. Natural turf.
Colors: Royal Blue, White & Silver.
Conference: Independent.
SID: Ted Kiep, 606-344-3673.
AD: Vic Clark.

TOLEDO

Toledo, OH 43606 I-A

Coach: Gary Pinkel, Kent 1975
Record: 7 Years, 50-26-3

1998 SCHEDULE

Temple ■ *Sept. 5
Ohio St. Sept. 12
Western Mich. ■ *Sept. 19
Miami (Ohio) Sept. 26
Central FLa. ■ *Oct. 3
Ball St. ■ Oct. 10
Bowling Green ■ *Oct. 17
Akron Oct. 24
Northern Ill. Oct. 31
Central Mich. ■ Nov. 14
Eastern Mich. Nov. 21

1997 RESULTS (9-3-0)

36 Purdue 22
38 Eastern Mich. 35
23 Western Mich. 13
31 Nevada 13
41 Central Mich. 10
41 Northern Ill. 14
35 Bowling Green 20
35 Miami (Ohio) 28
3 Ball St. 35
42 Akron 10
17 Central FLa. 34
14 Marshall 34
356 **268**

Nickname: Rockets.
Stadium: Glass Bowl (1937), 26,248 capacity. Artificial turf.
Colors: Blue & Gold.
Conference: Mid-American.
SID: Paul Helgren, 419-530-3790.
AD: Peter A. Liske.

TOWSON

Towson, MD 21252 I-AA

Coach: Gordy Combs, Towson 1972
Record: 6 Years, 36-24-0

1998 SCHEDULE

Morgan St. ■ *Sept. 3
Monmouth Sept. 12
Colgate ■ Sept. 19
Fordham ■ Sept. 26
Holy Cross Oct. 3
Lafayette ■ Oct. 10
Lehigh Oct. 17
St. Mary's (Cal.) ■ Oct. 31
Dayton Nov. 7
Drake ■ Nov. 14
Bucknell Nov. 21

1997 RESULTS (3-7-0)

22 Monmouth 21
27 Holy Cross 7
14 Lehigh 16
6 Columbia 16
14 Pennsylvania 26
33 Robert Morris 30
0 Lafayette 38
7 Fordham 12
3 Colgate 34
0 Bucknell 33
126 **233**

Nickname: Tigers.
Stadium: Minnegan Stadium (1978), 5,000 capacity. Natural turf.
Colors: Gold, White & Black.
Conference: Patriot.
SID: Peter Schlehr, 410-830-2232.
AD: Wayne Edwards.

TRINITY (CONN.)

Hartford, CT 06106 III

Coach: Don Miller, Delaware 1955
Record: 31 Years, 172-71-5

1998 SCHEDULE

Colby ■ Sept. 26
Williams Oct. 3
Hamilton Oct. 10
Tufts ■ Oct. 17
Bowdoin Oct. 24
Middlebury ■ Oct. 31
Amherst ■ Nov. 7
Wesleyan (Conn.) Nov. 14

1997 RESULTS (5-3-0)

31 Bates 6
15 Williams 19
28 Hamilton 7
13 Tufts 3
38 Bowdoin 7
27 Middlebury 22
8 Amherst 35
7 Wesleyan (Conn.) 19
167 **118**

Nickname: Bantams.
Stadium: Jessee Field (1900), 6,500 capacity. Natural turf.
Colors: Blue & Gold.
Conference: NESCAC.
SID: Albert Carbone Jr., 203-297-2137.
AD: Richard J. Hazelton.

TRINITY (TEX.)

San Antonio, TX 78212 ... III

Coach: Steven Mohr, Denison 1976
Record: 8 Years, 45-36-0

1998 SCHEDULE

Mary Hardin-Baylor ■	*Sept. 5
McMurry	*Sept. 12
Austin ■	*Sept. 19
DePauw	Sept. 26
Rose-Hulman ■	*Oct. 3
Washington (Mo.)	*Oct. 10
Centre	Oct. 24
Rhodes ■	*Oct. 31
Sewanee ■	Nov. 7
Millsaps	Nov. 14

1997 RESULTS (9-0-0)

20	Millikin	11
38	McMurry	7
37	Austin	10
24	Colorado Col.	13
39	Washington (Mo.)	7
42	Centre	21
38	Rhodes	9
45	Sewanee	31
45	Millsaps	13
328		**122**

III Championship

44	Catholic	33
26	Lycoming	46

Nickname: Tigers.
Stadium: E. M. Stevens (1972), 3,500 capacity. Natural turf.
Colors: Maroon & White.
Conference: Southern Collegiate Ath. Conf.
SID: Tony Ziner, 210-736-8447.
AD: Robert C. King.

TROY ST.

Troy, AL 36082 ... I-AA

Coach: Larry Blakeney, Auburn 1970
Record: 7 Years, 63-21-1

1998 SCHEDULE

Alabama St. ■	*Sept. 5
Marshall	*Sept. 12
Chattanooga	*Sept. 19
Samford ■	*Sept. 26
Sam Houston St.	*Oct. 3
Stephen F. Austin	Oct. 17
Southwest Tex. St. ■	*Oct. 22
Northwestern St.	Oct. 31
Nicholls St. ■	*Nov. 7
McNeese St. ■	Nov. 14
Jacksonville St.	*Nov. 21

1997 RESULTS (5-6-0)

30	Alcorn St.	0
21	Eastern Ky.	12
20	Alabama St.	13
20	Nicholls St.	22
17	Southwest Tex. St.	31
13	Sam Houston St.	10
13	Stephen F. Austin	20
14	Samford	25
13	Northwestern St.	14
7	McNeese St.	10
49	Jacksonville St.	0
217		**157**

Nickname: Trojans.
Stadium: Memorial (1950), 12,000 capacity. Natural turf.
Colors: Cardinal, Silver & Black.
Conference: Southland.
SID: Cory Rogers, 205-670-3480.
AD: Johnny Williams.

TRUMAN ST.

Kirksville, MO 63501 ... II

Coach: John Ware, Drake 1981
Record: 3 Years, 19-13-0

1998 SCHEDULE

Southeast Mo. St.	*Sept. 3
South Dak.	Sept. 12
Mo. Western St.	*Sept. 19
Central Mo. St. ■	Sept. 26
Emporia St.	Oct. 3
Washburn ■	Oct. 10
Mo.-Rolla	Oct. 17
Southwest Baptist ■	Oct. 24
Pittsburg St.	Oct. 31
Northwest Mo. St. ■	Nov. 7
Mo. Southern St. ■	Nov. 14

1997 RESULTS (6-4-0)

18	Western Ill.	45
31	Mo. Western St.	17
37	Central Mo. St.	34
44	Emporia St.	28
37	Washburn	7
56	Mo.-Rolla	7
28	Southwest Baptist	0
18	Pittsburg St.	28
10	Northwest Mo. St.	34
32	Mo. Southern St.	40
311		**240**

Nickname: Bulldogs.
Stadium: Stokes (1962), 4,000 capacity. Natural turf.
Colors: Purple & White.
Conference: MIAA.
SID: Melissa Ware, 816-785-4127.
AD: Walter H. Ryle IV.

TUFTS

Medford, MA 02155 ... III

Coach: Bill Samko, Connecticut 1973
Record: 11 Years, 45-49-1

1998 SCHEDULE

Hamilton ■	Sept. 26
Bates ■	Oct. 3
Bowdoin	Oct. 10
Trinity (Conn.)	Oct. 17
Williams ■	Oct. 24
Amherst	Oct. 31
Colby ■	Nov. 7
Middlebury	Nov. 14

1997 RESULTS (3-5-0)

33	Wesleyan (Conn.)	51
24	Bates	0
20	Bowdoin	28
3	Trinity (Conn.)	13
24	Williams	26
6	Amherst	14
21	Colby	12
17	Middlebury	15
148		**159**

Nickname: Jumbos.
Stadium: Ellis Oval (1923), 6,000 capacity. Natural turf.
Colors: Brown & Blue.
Conference: NESCAC.
SID: Paul Sweeney, 617-627-3586.
AD: Rocco J. Carzo.

TULANE

New Orleans, LA 70118 ... I-A

Coach: Tommy Bowden, West Va. 1977
Record: 1 Year, 7-4-0

1998 SCHEDULE

Cincinnati	*Sept. 5
Southern Methodist	*Sept. 12
Navy ■	*Sept. 26
Southern Miss. ■	*Oct. 3
Louisville ■	Oct. 17
Rutgers	Oct. 24
Southwestern La. ■	*Oct. 31
Memphis	Nov. 7
Army	Nov. 14
Houston ■	Nov. 21
Louisiana Tech ■	*Nov. 26

1997 RESULTS (7-4-0)

31	Cincinnati	17
24	Rice	30
19	Syracuse	30
41	Army	0
64	Louisville	33
33	East Caro.	16
13	Southern Miss.	34
56	Southwestern La.	0
26	Memphis	14
24	Mississippi	41
44	Houston	10
375		**225**

Nickname: Green Wave.
Stadium: Superdome (1975), 69,767 capacity. Artificial turf.
Colors: Olive Green & Sky Blue.
Conference: Conference USA.
SID: Lenny Vangilder, 504-865-5506.
AD: Sandy Barbour.

TULSA

Tulsa, OK 74104 ... I-A

Coach: David Rader, Tulsa 1980
Record: 10 Years, 44-67-1

1998 SCHEDULE

Southwest Mo. St. ■	*Sept. 5
Oklahoma St. ■	*Sept. 12
West Va.	Sept. 26
San Diego St. ■	Oct. 3
Colorado St.	Oct. 10
Rice	Oct. 17
Air Force ■	Oct. 24
UNLV	Oct. 31
Southern Methodist	Nov. 7
Texas Christian ■	Nov. 14
Wyoming ■	Nov. 21

1997 RESULTS (2-9-0)

24	Cincinnati	34
16	Iowa	54
21	Missouri	42
24	Rice	42
18	UTEP	33
33	Texas Christian	22
8	Colorado St.	44
21	Utah	13
39	Brigham Young	49
41	Southern Methodist	42
13	New Mexico	51
258		**426**

Nickname: Golden Hurricane.
Stadium: Skelly (1930), 40,385 capacity. Artificial turf.
Colors: Blue, Red, Gold.
Conference: Western Athletic.
SID: Don Tomkalski, 918-631-2395.
AD: Judy Mac Leod.

TUSCULUM

Greeneville, TN 37743 ... II

Coach: Frankie DeBusk, Furman 1991
(First year as head coach)

1998 SCHEDULE

Maryville (Tenn.) ■	Sept. 5
Catawba	Sept. 12
Lenoir-Rhyne ■	*Sept. 19
Carson-Newman	Sept. 26
Presbyterian	Oct. 3
Mars Hill ■	Oct. 10
Newberry	Oct. 17
Wingate ■	Oct. 24
Gardner-Webb ■	Oct. 31
Austin Peay	Nov. 7
Clinch Valley	Nov. 14

1997 RESULTS (2-9-0)

0	Catawba	48
19	Mississippi Col.	26
3	Charleston So.	12
28	Concord	55
7	Presbyterian	49
17	Mars Hill	44
51	Millsaps	34
13	Wingate	51
6	Gardner-Webb	66
28	Maryville (Tenn.)	14
28	Clinch Valley	31
200		**430**

Nickname: Pioneers.
Stadium: Pioneer Field, 1,500 capacity. Natural turf.
Colors: Black & Orange.
Conference: Independent.
SID: Will Prewitt, 615-636-7300.
AD: Jim Fields.

TUSKEGEE

Tuskegee, AL 36088 II

Coach: Rick Comegy, Millersville 1976
Record: 6 Years, 30-35-0

1998 SCHEDULE

Benedict [Birmingham, Ala.]	*Sept. 6
Morris Brown ■	Sept. 12
Miles ■	Sept. 19
Kentucky St. ■	Oct. 3
Morehouse [Columbus, Ga.]	*Oct. 10
Alabama A&M ■	Oct. 17
Fort Valley St.	Oct. 24
Clark Atlanta [LaGrange, Ga.]	Oct. 31
Lane ■	Nov. 7
Savannah St.	Nov. 14
Alabama St.	Nov. 26

1997 RESULTS (7-4-0)

21	Benedict	6
27	Morris Brown	36
17	Miles	20
7	Albany St. (Ga.)	18
42	Kentucky St.	21
29	Morehouse	26
20	Savannah St.	14
10	Fort Valley St.	0
16	Clark Atlanta	7
15	Alabama A&M	26
21	Alabama St.	16
225		**190**

Nickname: Golden Tigers.
Stadium: Alumni Bowl (1925), 10,000 capacity. Natural turf.
Colors: Crimson & Gold.
Conference: Southern Intercol. Ath. Conf.
SID: Arnold Houston, 334-727-8150.
AD: Rick Comegy.

UCLA

Los Angeles, CA 90095 .... I-A

Coach: Bob Toledo, San Fran. St. 1968
Record: 8 Years, 44-44-0

1998 SCHEDULE

Texas ■	Sept. 12
Houston	Sept. 19
Miami (Fla.)	Sept. 26
Washington St. ■	Oct. 3
Arizona	*Oct. 10
Oregon ■	Oct. 17
California	Oct. 24
Stanford ■	Oct. 31
Oregon St.	Nov. 7
Washington	Nov. 14
Southern Cal ■	Nov. 21

1997 RESULTS (9-2-0)

34	Washington St.	37
24	Tennessee	30
66	Texas	3
40	Arizona	27
66	Houston	10
39	Oregon	31
34	Oregon St.	10
35	California	17
27	Stanford	7
52	Washington	28
31	Southern Cal	24
448		**224**

Cotton Bowl

29	Texas A&M	23

Nickname: Bruins.
Stadium: Rose Bowl (1922), 100,089 capacity. Natural turf.
Colors: Navy Blue & Gold.
Conference: Pacific-10.
SID: Marc Dellins, 310-206-6831.
AD: Peter T. Dalis.

UNION (N.Y.)

Schenectady, NY 12308 III

Coach: John Audino, Notre Dame 1975
Record: 8 Years, 56-23-0

1998 SCHEDULE

St. Lawrence ■	Sept. 12
Worcester Tech	Sept. 19
Hobart ■	Sept. 26
Alfred	Oct. 3
Rensselaer ■	Oct. 17
Coast Guard ■	Oct. 24
Hartwick	Oct. 31
Rochester	Nov. 7
Springfield	Nov. 14

1997 RESULTS (7-2-0)

27	St. Lawrence	12
27	Worcester Tech	20
28	Hobart	17
35	Rochester	7
7	Rensselaer	30
14	Coast Guard	6
13	Hartwick	3
0	Albany (N.Y.)	54
43	Alfred	0
194		**149**

Nickname: Dutchmen.
Stadium: Frank Bailey Field (1981), 2,000 capacity. Artificial turf.
Colors: Garnet.
Conference: Upstate Collegiate Athl. Assn.
SID: George Cuttita, 518-388-6170.
AD: Richard S. Sakala.

UPPER IOWA

Fayette, IA 52142 III

Coach: Paul Rudolph, Minot St. 1988
Record: 7 Years, 32-38-0

1998 SCHEDULE

Buena Vista ■	Sept. 5
Cornell College	Sept. 12
Loras ■	Sept. 19
Simpson	Sept. 26
Luther ■	Oct. 3
Dubuque	Oct. 10
Coe ■	Oct. 17
Central (Iowa)	Oct. 24
William Penn ■	Nov. 7
Wartburg	Nov. 14

1997 RESULTS (7-3-0)

26	Huron	20
17	Loras	14
10	Wartburg	13
12	Simpson	56
38	William Penn	14
34	Aurora	27
35	Buena Vista	31
22	Central (Iowa)	44
40	Luther	24
46	Dubuque	6
280		**249**

Nickname: Peacocks.
Stadium: Eischeid (1993), 3,500 capacity. Natural turf.
Colors: Blue & White.
Conference: Iowa Intercol. Athletic Conf.
SID: To be named, 319-425-5307.
AD: Paul Rudolph.

URSINUS

Collegeville, PA 19426 III

Coach: Paul Guenther, Ursinus 1994
Record: 1 Year, 4-6-0

1998 SCHEDULE

Salisbury St.	Sept. 5
Lebanon Valley ■	Sept. 12
Frank. & Marsh.	Sept. 19
Western Md. ■	Sept. 26
Swarthmore	Oct. 3
Johns Hopkins ■	Oct. 10
Gettysburg	Oct. 17
Merchant Marine	Oct. 24
Muhlenberg ■	Oct. 31
Dickinson ■	Nov. 14

1997 RESULTS (4-6-0)

12	Salisbury St.	14
42	Lebanon Valley	16
15	Frank. & Marsh.	27
10	Western Md.	20
31	Swarthmore	0
6	Johns Hopkins	33
13	Gettysburg	2
18	Merchant Marine	61
9	Muhlenberg	7
3	Dickinson	32
159		**212**

Nickname: Bears.
Stadium: Patterson Field (1923), 2,500 capacity. Natural turf.
Colors: Red, Old Gold, Black.
Conference: Centennial Conference.
SID: David M. Sherman, 610-409-3612.
AD: William E. Akin.

UTAH

Salt Lake City, UT 84112 .... I-A

Coach: Ron McBride, San Jose St. 1963
Record: 8 Years, 55-39-0

1998 SCHEDULE

Utah St.	*Sept. 5
Louisville ■	*Sept. 12
Hawaii ■	*Sept. 19
Boise St. ■	*Sept. 26
Wyoming	Oct. 3
Fresno St. ■	Oct. 17
San Diego St.	*Oct. 24
San Jose St.	Oct. 31
UTEP ■	Nov. 7
New Mexico	Nov. 14
Brigham Young ■	Nov. 21

1997 RESULTS (6-5-0)

14	Utah St.	21
27	Louisville	21
32	Texas Christian	18
56	UTEP	3
13	Fresno St.	27
19	Southern Methodist	20
13	Oregon	31
15	New Mexico	10
13	Tulsa	21
31	Rice	14
20	Brigham Young	14
253		**200**

Nickname: Utes.
Stadium: Robert Rice (1998), 45,000 capacity. Natural turf.
Colors: Crimson & White.
Conference: Western Athletic.
SID: Liz Abel, 801-581-3511.
AD: Christopher Hill.

UTAH ST.

Logan, UT 84322 .... I-A

Coach: Dave Arslanian, Weber St. 1972
Record: 9 Years, 53-47-0

1998 SCHEDULE

Utah ■ .... *Sept. 5
New Mexico .... *Sept. 12
Colorado .... Sept. 19
Sam Houston St. ■ .... *Sept. 26
Oregon St. ■ .... *Oct. 3
Washington .... Oct. 10
Idaho ■ .... Oct. 17
Boise St. .... *Oct. 24
New Mexico St. .... Oct. 31
Nevada ■ .... Nov. 7
North Texas ■ .... Nov. 14

1997 RESULTS (6-5-0)

21 Utah 14
41 Idaho St. 7
24 Colorado St. 35
22 New Mexico 25
35 Brigham Young 42
16 Oregon St. 24
38 New Mexico St. 7
63 Idaho 17
24 Boise St. 20
38 Nevada 19
48 North Texas 51
370 **261**

Humanitarian Bowl

19 Cincinnati 35

Nickname: Aggies.
Stadium: E.L. Romney (1968), 30,257 capacity. Natural turf.
Colors: Navy Blue & White.
Conference: Big West.
SID: Mike Strauss, 801-797-1361.
AD: Ken A. Peterson.

VALDOSTA ST.

Valdosta, GA 31698 II

Coach: Mike Kelly, Bluffton 1980
Record: 1 Year, 6-5-0

1998 SCHEDULE

Albany St. (Ga.) .... *Aug. 29
Fort Valley St. ■ .... *Sept. 5
Henderson St. .... *Sept. 12
Delta St. .... *Sept. 19
Arkansas Tech ■ .... Sept. 26
West ALa. ■ .... Oct. 10
Southern Ark. .... *Oct. 17
Central Ark. ■ .... Oct. 24
Ark.-Monticello .... Oct. 31
North ALa. ■ .... Nov. 7
West Ga. .... *Nov. 14

1997 RESULTS (6-5-0)

26 Ga. Southern 45
7 Carson-Newman 28
10 Fort Valley St. 0
31 Arkansas Tech 14
21 North ALa. 0
58 Ark.-Monticello 14
33 West ALa. 20
7 Southern Ark. 17
23 Delta St. 27
31 Central Ark. 22
21 West Ga. 35
268 **222**

Nickname: Blazers.
Stadium: Cleveland Field (1922), 11,500 capacity. Natural turf.
Colors: Red & Black.
Conference: Gulf South Conference.
SID: Steve Roberts, 912-333-5890.
AD: Herb F. Reinhard III.

VALPARAISO

Valparaiso, IN 46383 .... I-AA

Coach: Tom Horne, Wis.-La Crosse 1976
Record: 12 Years, 46-74-2

1998 SCHEDULE

Tri-State ■ .... Sept. 5
South FLa. .... *Sept. 12
Morehead St. ■ .... Sept. 19
Drake .... Oct. 3
Robert Morris .... Oct. 10
Butler ■ .... Oct. 17
Dayton ■ .... Oct. 24
San Diego .... *Oct. 31
St. Joseph's (Ind.) .... Nov. 7
Aurora ■ .... Nov. 14
Austin Peay ■ .... Nov. 21

1997 RESULTS (3-7-0)

35 Hope 34
28 Alma 45
24 Morehead St. 56
7 Drake 27
14 Yale 34
12 Evansville 10
19 Butler 17
13 Dayton 34
35 San Diego 52
7 Aurora 33
194 **342**

Nickname: Crusaders.
Stadium: Brown Field (1947), 5,000 capacity. Natural turf.
Colors: Brown & Gold.
Conference: Pioneer.
SID: Bill Rogers, 219-464-5232.
AD: William L. Steinbrecher.

VANDERBILT

Nashville, TN 37212 .... I-A

Coach: Woody Widenhofer, Missouri 1965
Record: 5 Years, 15-39-1

1998 SCHEDULE

Mississippi St. .... *Sept. 5
Alabama [Birmingham, Ala.] .... Sept. 12
Mississippi ■ .... Sept. 19
Texas Christian .... *Oct. 3
Western Mich. ■ .... *Oct. 10
Georgia .... Oct. 17
South Caro. ■ .... *Oct. 24
Duke ■ .... Oct. 31
Florida ■ .... Nov. 7
Kentucky .... Nov. 14
Tennessee ■ .... Nov. 28

1997 RESULTS (3-8-0)

29 North Texas 12
0 Alabama 20
40 Texas Christian 16
3 Mississippi 15
6 LSU 7
17 Northern Ill. 7
13 Georgia 34
3 South Caro. 35
7 Florida 20
10 Kentucky 21
10 Tennessee 17
138 **204**

Nickname: Commodores.
Stadium: Vanderbilt Stadium (1922), 41,600 capacity. Artificial turf.
Colors: Black & Gold.
Conference: Southeastern.
SID: Rod Williamson, 615-322-4121.
AD: William T. Turner.

VILLANOVA

Villanova, PA 19085 .... I-AA

Coach: Andy Talley, Southern Conn. 1967
Record: 18 Years, 115-69-2

1998 SCHEDULE

Pittsburgh .... Sept. 5
Delaware ■ .... Sept. 12
James Madison .... Sept. 19
William & Mary ■ .... Sept. 26
Maine .... Oct. 3
Northeastern .... Oct. 10
Massachusetts .... Oct. 24
Fordham .... Oct. 31
Richmond ■ .... Nov. 7
Buffalo ■ .... Nov. 14
Rhode Island ■ .... Nov. 21

1997 RESULTS (11-0-0)

64 West Chester 0
35 Delaware 25
34 Maine 14
49 James Madison 17
49 Massachusetts 27
40 Richmond 29
20 William & Mary 13
37 Rhode Island 15
23 New Hampshire 20
42 Buffalo 28
49 Northeastern 35
442 **223**

I-AA Championship

49 Colgate 28
34 Youngstown St. 37

Nickname: Wildcats.
Stadium: Villanova (1927), 12,000 capacity. Artificial turf.
Colors: Blue & White.
Conference: Atlantic 10.
SID: Karen Frascona, 610-519-4120.
AD: Tim Hofferth.

VIRGINIA

Charlottesville, VA 22903 .... I-A

Coach: George Welsh, Navy 1956
Record: 25 Years, 167-118-4

1998 SCHEDULE

Auburn .... *Sept. 3
Maryland ■ .... Sept. 12
Clemson ■ .... Sept. 19
Duke .... Sept. 26
San Jose St. ■ .... Oct. 3
Georgia Tech .... Oct. 17
North Caro. St. ■ .... Oct. 24
Wake Forest .... Oct. 31
Florida St. .... Nov. 7
North Caro. ■ .... Nov. 14
Virginia Tech .... Nov. 28

1997 RESULTS (7-4-0)

17 Auburn 28
26 Richmond 7
20 North Caro. 48
21 Wake Forest 13
21 Clemson 7
13 Duke 10
21 Florida St. 47
45 Maryland 0
35 Georgia Tech 31
24 North Caro. St. 31
34 Virginia Tech 20
277 **242**

Nickname: Cavaliers.
Stadium: Scott/Carl Smith Center (1931), 40,000 capacity. Natural turf.
Colors: Orange & Blue.
Conference: Atlantic Coast.
SID: Rich Murray, 804-982-5500.
AD: M. Terrance Holland.

VMI

Lexington, VA 24450 .... I-AA

Coach: Ted Cain, Furman 1974
Record: 1 Year, 0-11-0

1998 SCHEDULE

Lenoir-Rhyne ■	Sept. 5
William & Mary	Sept. 12
East Tenn. St.	*Sept. 19
Furman ■	Sept. 26
Ga. Southern	Oct. 3
Wofford ■	Oct. 10
Chattanooga	*Oct. 17
Morehead St. ■	Oct. 24
Western Caro. ■	Oct. 31
Appalachian St.	Nov. 7
Citadel ■	Nov. 14

1997 RESULTS (0-11-0)

13	Wofford	23
12	William & Mary	41
3	Richmond	56
14	Furman	35
0	Ga. Southern	49
24	Chattanooga	27
7	Navy	42
0	Western Caro.	24
7	Appalachian St.	42
6	Citadel	28
7	East Tenn. St.	17
93		**384**

Nickname: Keydets.
Stadium: Alumni Field (1962), 10,000 capacity. Natural turf.
Colors: Red, White, Yellow.
Conference: Southern.
SID: Wade Branner, 703-464-7253.
AD: Donald T. White.

VIRGINIA ST.

Petersburg, VA 23806 II

Coach: Louis Anderson, Claflin 1961
Record: 7 Years, 47-25-0

1998 SCHEDULE

Lane ■	Aug. 29
Norfolk St.	*Sept. 5
Johnson Smith	Sept. 12
N.C. Central	Sept. 19
Bethune-Cookman	*Sept. 26
Livingstone ■	Oct. 3
Fayetteville St.	*Oct. 17
Winston-Salem ■	Oct. 24
Virginia Union	Oct. 31
Bowie St.	Nov. 7
Elizabeth City St.	Nov. 14

1997 RESULTS (8-2-0)

36	Norfolk St.	7
31	Johnson Smith	0
13	N.C. Central	6
14	Livingstone	28
51	Fayetteville St.	29
12	Winston-Salem	21
29	Virginia Union	11
31	Bowie St.	22
22	Elizabeth City St.	12
30	Lane	0
269		**136**

Nickname: Trojans.
Stadium: Rogers (1950), 13,500 capacity. Natural turf.
Colors: Orange & Navy Blue.
Conference: Central Intercol. Ath. Assn.
SID: Gregory C. Goings, 804-524-5028.
AD: Alfreeda Goff.

VIRGINIA TECH

Blacksburg, VA 24061 ....I-A

Coach: Frank Beamer, Virginia Tech 1969
Record: 17 Years, 110-79-4

1998 SCHEDULE

East Caro. ■	Sept. 5
Clemson	Sept. 12
Miami (Fla.)	*Sept. 19
Pittsburgh ■	Sept. 26
Boston College	*Oct. 8
Temple ■	Oct. 17
UAB	*Oct. 24
West Va. ■	Oct. 31
Syracuse	Nov. 14
Rutgers ■	Nov. 21
Virginia ■	Nov. 28

1997 RESULTS (7-4-0)

59	Rutgers	19
31	Syracuse	3
23	Temple	13
50	Arkansas St.	0
17	Miami (Ohio)	24
17	Boston College	7
17	West Va.	30
37	UAB	0
27	Miami (Fla.)	25
23	Pittsburgh	30
20	Virginia	34
321		**185**

Gator Bowl

3	North Caro.	42

Nickname: Hokies, Gobblers.
Stadium: Lane (1965), 50,000 capacity. Natural turf.
Colors: Orange & Maroon.
Conference: Atlantic 10.
SID: Dave Smith, 540-231-6726.
AD: James C. Weaver.

VIRGINIA UNION

Richmond, VA 23220 II

Coach: Willard Bailey, Norfolk St. 1962
Record: 25 Years, 167-92-7

1998 SCHEDULE

Benedict	*Aug. 29
Cheyney ■	*Sept. 12
Livingstone ■	Sept. 19
Winston-Salem	*Sept. 26
Bowie St.	Oct. 3
Elizabeth City St.	Oct. 10
Morehouse	Oct. 17
Norfolk St.	Oct. 24
Virginia St. ■	Oct. 31
Fayetteville St. ■	Nov. 7
Johnson Smith ■	Nov. 14

1997 RESULTS (6-5-0)

6	Livingstone	56
0	Norfolk St.	26
29	Cheyney	7
6	Winston-Salem	13
38	Bowie St.	14
13	Elizabeth City St.	6
8	Liberty	16
11	Virginia St.	29
46	Fayetteville St.	0
19	Johnson Smith	11
44	Benedict	12
220		**190**

Nickname: Panthers.
Stadium: Hovey Field, 10,000 capacity. Natural turf.
Colors: Steel & Maroon.
Conference: Central Intercol. Ath. Assn.
SID: Paul Williams, 804-342-1233.
AD: James F. Battle.

WABASH

Crawfordsville, IN 47933 III

Coach: Greg Carlson, Wis.-Oshkosh 1970
Record: 15 Years, 92-47-2

1998 SCHEDULE

Rhodes	Sept. 12
Washington (Mo.) ■	Sept. 19
Mount Saint Joseph ■	Sept. 26
Anderson (Ind.)	Oct. 3
Bluffton	Oct. 10
Manchester ■	Oct. 17
Wilmington (Ohio)	Oct. 24
Franklin	Oct. 31
Hanover ■	Nov. 7
DePauw ■	Nov. 14

1997 RESULTS (6-4-0)

36	Wilmington (Ohio)	14
19	Albion	14
13	Hope	14
35	Rose-Hulman	14
24	Manchester	7
18	Benedictine (Ill.)	22
24	Franklin	3
7	Hanover	10
37	Anderson (Ind.)	12
7	DePauw	14
220		**124**

Nickname: Little Giants.
Stadium: Little Giant (1967), 4,200 capacity. Natural turf.
Colors: Scarlet & White.
Conference: Heartland Colleg. Ath. Conf.
SID: Michael Molde, 317-361-6364.
AD: Max E. Servies.

WAGNER

Staten Island, NY 10301 ....I-AA

Coach: Walt Hameline, Brockport St. 1975
Record: 17 Years, 129-48-2

1998 SCHEDULE

San Diego ■	Sept. 12
Sacred Heart	Sept. 19
St. Francis (Pa.)	Sept. 26
Robert Morris ■	Oct. 3
St. Peter's ■	Oct. 10
Central Conn. St.	Oct. 17
Marist ■	Oct. 24
Stony Brook	Oct. 31
Monmouth ■	Nov. 7
Jacksonville	Nov. 14

1997 RESULTS (6-4-0)

33	Iona	0
13	LIU-C.W. Post	12
42	St. Francis (Pa.)	6
9	Robert Morris	21
42	St. Peter's	14
34	Central Conn. St.	23
0	Marist	21
10	Stony Brook	0
7	Monmouth	51
29	San Diego	52
219		**200**

Nickname: Seahawks.
Stadium: Wagner (1997), 3,300 capacity. Natural turf.
Colors: Green & White.
Conference: Northeast.
SID: To be named, 718-390-3227.
AD: Walt Hameline.

WAKE FOREST

Winston-Salem, NC 27109 ....I-A

Coach: Jim Caldwell, Iowa 1977
Record: 5 Years, 14-41-0

1998 SCHEDULE

Air Force	Sept. 5
Navy ■	*Sept. 10
Clemson	Sept. 26
Appalachian St. ■	*Oct. 3
Duke ■	*Oct. 10
Maryland	Oct. 17
North Caro. ■	Oct. 24
Virginia ■	Oct. 31
North Caro. St.	Nov. 7
Florida St. ■	Nov. 14
Georgia Tech	Nov. 21

1997 RESULTS (5-6-0)

27	Northwestern	20
24	East Caro.	25
26	Georgia Tech	28
19	North Caro. St.	18
13	Virginia	21
12	North Caro.	30
35	Maryland	17
38	Duke	24

16 Clemson....33
28 Rutgers....14
7 Florida St....58
245 **288**

Nickname: Demon Deacons.
Stadium: Groves (1968), 31,500 capacity. Natural turf.
Colors: Old Gold & Black.
Conference: Atlantic Coast.
SID: John Justus, 910-759-5640.
AD: Ronald D. Wellman.

WARTBURG

Waverly, IA 50677 III

Coach: Rick Willis, Cornell College 1988
Record: 1 Year, 7-3-0

1998 SCHEDULE

William Penn ....*Sept. 5
Buena Vista ■....Sept. 19
Cornell College ....Sept. 26
Loras ■....Oct. 3
Simpson ■....Oct. 10
Luther....Oct. 17
Dubuque....Oct. 24
Coe ■....Oct. 31
Central (Iowa) ....Nov. 7
Upper Iowa ■....Nov. 14

1997 RESULTS (7-3-0)

33 Augustana (Ill.)....30
6 Central (Iowa)....35
13 Upper Iowa....10
23 Loras....10
21 Simpson....35
14 Buena Vista....24
40 Dubuque....21
48 Blackburn....0
36 William Penn....18
49 Luther....15
283 **198**

Nickname: Knights.
Stadium: Schield (1956), 2,500 capacity. Natural turf.
Colors: Orange & Black.
Conference: Iowa Intercol. Athletic Conf.
SID: Duane Schroeder, 319-352-8277.
AD: Gary Grace.

WASHBURN

Topeka, KS 66621 II

Coach: Tony DeMeo, Iona 1971
Record: 15 Years, 76-59-4

1998 SCHEDULE

Wis.-River Falls ■....*Sept. 5
Fort Hays St. ....*Sept. 12
Southwest Baptist ■....*Sept. 19
Mo.-Rolla....Sept. 26
Northwest Mo. St. ■....*Oct. 3
Truman St. ....Oct. 10
Mo. Western St. ■....Oct. 17
Mo. Southern St. ....Oct. 24
Emporia St. ■....*Oct. 29
Central Mo. St. ■....Nov. 7
Pittsburg St. ....Nov. 14

1997 RESULTS (3-8-0)

17 Augustana (S.D.)....21
31 Fort Hays St....14
25 Southwest Baptist....7
27 Mo.-Rolla....13
14 Northwest Mo. St....17
7 Truman St....37
12 Mo. Western St. 13
14 Mo. Southern St. 17
35 Emporia St....64
14 Central Mo. St. 20
11 Pittsburg St....40
207 **263**

Nickname: Ichabods.
Stadium: Moore Bowl (1928), 7,200 capacity. Natural turf.
Colors: Yale Blue & White.
Conference: MIAA.
SID: Robert Rodgers, 913-231-1010.
AD: Loren Ferre'.

WASHINGTON

Seattle, WA 98195 ....I-A

Coach: Jim Lambright, Washington 1965
Record: 5 Years, 38-19-1

1998 SCHEDULE

Arizona St....*Sept. 5
Brigham Young ■....Sept. 19
Nebraska....Sept. 26
Arizona ■....*Oct. 3
Utah St. ■....Oct. 10
California ■....Oct. 17
Oregon St. ■....Oct. 24
Southern Cal ....Oct. 31
Oregon....Nov. 7
UCLA ■....Nov. 14
Washington St....Nov. 21

1997 RESULTS (7-4-0)

42 Brigham Young....20
36 San Diego St. 3
14 Nebraska....27
26 Arizona St. 14
30 California....3
58 Arizona....28
45 Oregon St. 17
27 Southern Cal....0
28 Oregon....31
28 UCLA....52
35 Washington St. 41
369 **236**

Aloha Bowl

51 Michigan St. 23

Nickname: Huskies.
Stadium: Husky (1920), 72,500 capacity. Artificial turf.
Colors: Purple & Gold.
Conference: Pacific-10.
SID: Jim Daves, 206-543-2230.
AD: Barbara A. Hedges.

WASH. & JEFF.

Washington, PA 15301 III

Coach: John Luckhardt, Purdue 1967
Record: 16 Years, 132-33-2

1998 SCHEDULE

Emory & Henry ■....Sept. 5
Allegheny ....Sept. 12
Hanover ■....Sept. 26
Gannon....Oct. 3
Grove City ■....Oct. 10
Bethany (W. Va.)....Oct. 17
Waynesburg ■....Oct. 24
Buffalo St. ....Oct. 31
Thiel ....Nov. 14

1997 RESULTS (6-3-0)

10 Emory & Henry....38
7 Buffalo St....16
28 Grove City....31
38 Bethany (W. Va.) 21
28 Waynesburg....27
64 Thiel....7
20 Mount Saint Joseph 7
27 Alfred....3
30 Defiance....0
252 **150**

Nickname: Presidents.
Stadium: College Field (1958), 5,000 capacity. Natural turf.
Colors: Red & Black.
Conference: Presidents' Athletic Conf.
SID: Susan Isola, 412-223-6074.
AD: John L. Luckhardt.

WASH. & LEE

Lexington, VA 24450....III

Coach: Frank Miriello, East Stroudsburg 1967
Record: 3 Years, 14-14-1

1998 SCHEDULE

Johns Hopkins ■....Sept. 12
Guilford....Sept. 19
Centre ....Sept. 26
Randolph-Macon ■....Oct. 3
Davidson ....Oct. 10
Hampden-Sydney ■....Oct. 17
Sewanee ■....Oct. 24
Bridgewater (Va.) ....Oct. 31
Emory & Henry ■....Nov. 7
Swarthmore....Nov. 14

1997 RESULTS (4-6-0)

28 Johns Hopkins....34
20 Guilford....34
14 Centre....30
3 Randolph-Macon....24
32 Davidson....22
29 Hampden-Sydney....7
14 Sewanee....48
22 Bridgewater (Va.)....10
17 Emory & Henry....27
41 Swarthmore....13
220 **249**

Nickname: Generals.
Stadium: Wilson Field (1930), 7,000 capacity. Natural turf.
Colors: Royal Blue & White.
Conference: Old Dominion Athletic Conf.
SID: Brian Logue, 540-463-8676.
AD: Michael F. Walsh.

WASHINGTON (MO.)

St. Louis, MO 63130 III

Coach: Larry Kindbom, Kalamazoo 1974
Record: 15 Years, 84-63-1

1998 SCHEDULE

Rose-Hulman ....Sept. 5
Wheaton (Ill.) ■....Sept. 12
Wabash ....Sept. 19
Case Reserve ■....Sept. 26
Rhodes....Oct. 3
Trinity (Tex.) ■....*Oct. 10
Rochester....Oct. 17
Carnegie Mellon ■....Oct. 24
Chicago....Oct. 31
Colorado Col. ■ ....Nov. 7

1997 RESULTS (6-4-0)

44 Rhodes....0
77 Illinois Col. 7
37 Case Reserve....32
21 Ill. Wesleyan....50
7 Trinity (Tex.)....39
10 Carnegie Mellon....13
32 Rochester....9
55 Chicago....26
12 Central (Iowa)....22
21 Rose-Hulman....0
316 **198**

Nickname: Bears.
Stadium: Francis Field (1904), 4,000 capacity. Natural turf.
Colors: Red & Green.
Conference: University Athletic Assoc.
SID: Mike Wolf, 314-935-5077.
AD: John M. Schael.

WASHINGTON ST.

Pullman, WA 99164 ....I-A

Coach: Mike Price, Puget Sound 1969
Record: 17 Years, 99-93-0

1998 SCHEDULE

Illinois ■....Sept. 5

Boise St.	*Sept. 12
Idaho ■	Sept. 19
California	Sept. 26
UCLA	Oct. 3
Oregon ■	Oct. 10
Southern Cal ■	Oct. 17
Arizona St. ■	Oct. 31
Arizona	*Nov. 7
Stanford	Nov. 14
Washington ■	Nov. 21

1997 RESULTS (10-1-0)

37	UCLA	34
28	Southern Cal	21
35	Illinois	22
58	Boise St.	0
24	Oregon	13
63	California	37
35	Arizona	34
31	Arizona St.	44
77	Southwestern La.	7
38	Stanford	28
41	Washington	35
467		**275**

Rose Bowl

16	Michigan	21

Nickname: Cougars.
Stadium: Clarence D. Martin (1972), 37,600 capacity. Artificial turf.
Colors: Crimson & Gray.
Conference: Pacific-10.
SID: Rod Commons, 509-335-2684.
AD: Richard P. Dickson.

WAYNE ST. (MICH.)

Detroit, MI 48202 II

Coach: Barry Fagan, Penn St. 1978
Record: 1 Year, 3-8-0

1998 SCHEDULE

Mercyhurst ■	Sept. 5
Findlay	Sept. 12
Saginaw Valley	Sept. 19
Ashland ■	Sept. 26
Northwood ■	Oct. 3
Ferris St.	Oct. 10
Indianapolis	Oct. 17
Hillsdale ■	Oct. 24
Michigan Tech ■	Oct. 31
Westminster (Pa.)	Nov. 7
St. Joseph's (Ind.)	Nov. 14

1997 RESULTS (3-8-0)

0	Bloomsburg	22
7	Saginaw Valley	73
9	Indianapolis	28
30	St. Francis (Ill.)	7
30	Grand Valley St.	45
30	Ferris St.	26
13	Ashland	21
6	Hillsdale	10
35	Michigan Tech	28
29	Northern Mich.	35
20	Northwood	35
209		**330**

Nickname: Tartars.
Stadium: Wayne State (1968), 6,000 capacity. Natural turf.
Colors: Green & Gold.
Conference: Midwest Intercoll.
SID: Lisa Sopa, 313-577-7542.
AD: Bob V. Brennan.

WAYNE ST. (NEB.)

Wayne, NE 68787 II

Coach: Kevin Haslam, N. M. Highlands 1991
Record: 1 Year, 3-7-0

1998 SCHEDULE

South Dak.	*Sept. 5
Northwest Mo. St.	Sept. 12
Northwestern Okla. ■	Sept. 19
Peru St. ■	Sept. 26
Fort Hays St. ■	Oct. 3
Northern St. ■	Oct. 10
Moorhead St. ■	Oct. 17
Chadron St.	Oct. 24
Winona St. ■	Oct. 31
Minn.-Duluth	Nov. 7
Quincy	Nov. 14

1997 RESULTS (3-7-0)

0	South Dak.	59
7	Northwest Mo. St.	57
21	Moorhead St.	30
12	Fort Hays St.	62
17	Drake	35
21	Southwest St.	29
28	Northern St.	14
18	Neb.-Kearney	40
33	Western N. Mex.	31
57	Quincy	7
214		**364**

Nickname: Wildcats.
Stadium: Memorial (1931), 3,500 capacity. Natural turf.
Colors: Black & Gold.
Conference: Independent.
SID: Kevin Ludwig, 403-375-7326.
AD: Pete Chapman.

WAYNESBURG

Waynesburg, PA 15370 III

Coach: Dan Baranik, Shippensburg 1984
Record: 4 Years, 16-20-0

1998 SCHEDULE

Marietta	*Sept. 5
Wm. Paterson	Sept. 12
Gannon ■	Sept. 19
Bethany (W. Va.) ■	Oct. 3
Thiel	Oct. 10
Grove City ■	Oct. 17
Wash. & Jeff.	Oct. 24
La Salle	Oct. 31
Frostburg St. ■	Nov. 7

1997 RESULTS (5-4-0)

29	St. Francis (Pa.)	6
43	Alfred	27
29	Bethany (W. Va.)	23
38	Thiel	22
30	Grove City	42
27	Wash. & Jeff.	28
7	Frostburg St.	14
41	La Salle	7
23	Juniata	26
267		**195**

Nickname: Yellow Jackets.
Stadium: College Field (1904), 1,300 capacity. Natural turf.
Colors: Orange & Black.
Conference: Presidents' Athletic Conf.
SID: Mike Florak, 412-852-3334.
AD: Rudy Marisa.

WEBER ST.

Ogden, UT 84408 .... I-AA

Coach: Jerry Graybeal, Eastern Wash. 1981
(First year as head coach)

1998 SCHEDULE

Montana Tech ■	*Sept. 3
Humboldt St. ■	*Sept. 12
Idaho St.	*Sept. 19
Montana ■	*Sept. 26
Cal St. Sacramento	*Oct. 3
Montana St. ■	*Oct. 10
Boise St.	*Oct. 17
Portland St.	*Oct. 24
Cal St. Northridge ■	Oct. 31
Northern Ariz.	Nov. 7
Eastern Wash. ■	Nov. 14

1997 RESULTS (6-5-0)

29	Western St. (Colo.)	13
33	Southern Utah	32
7	Boise St.	24
11	Eastern Wash.	35
36	Northern Ariz.	23
20	Cal St. Northridge	30
16	Portland St.	7
14	Montana St.	28
52	Cal St. Sacramento	14
13	Montana	38
26	Idaho St.	7
257		**251**

Nickname: Wildcats.
Stadium: Elizabeth Dee Shaw Stewart (1966), 17,500 capacity. Natural turf.
Colors: Purple & White.
Conference: Big Sky.
SID: Brad Larsen, 801-626-6010.
AD: John W. Johnson.

WESLEY

Dover, DE 19901 III

Coach: Mike Drass, Mansfield 1983
Record: 5 Years, 37-13-1

1998 SCHEDULE

Madison Tech	Sept. 12
Montclair St. ■	Sept. 19
Butler ■	Sept. 26
Wilkes ■	Oct. 10
Newport News ■	Oct. 17
Salisbury St.	Oct. 24
Chowan	Oct. 31
Stonehill	Nov. 7
Ferrum ■	Nov. 14

1997 RESULTS (7-2-0)

23	Ferrum	0
34	Kean	7
7	Montclair St.	14
14	Col. of New Jersey	31
41	Clinch Valley	10
31	Wilkes	17
34	Newport News	6
41	Chowan	6
28	Salisbury St.	7
253		**98**

ECAC III Playoff

0	Albright	10

Nickname: Wolverines.
Stadium: Wolverine (1989), 2,000 capacity. Natural turf.
Colors: Navy Blue & White.
Conference: Atlantic Central FB.
SID: Jason Bowen, 302-736-2557.
AD: Steve D. ClArk.

WESLEYAN (CONN.)

Middletown, CT 06459 III

Coach: Frank Hauser, Wesleyan 1979
Record: 6 Years, 25-23-0

1998 SCHEDULE

Middlebury	Sept. 26
Hamilton ■	Oct. 3
Colby	Oct. 10
Bates	Oct. 17
Amherst ■	Oct. 24
Bowdoin ■	Oct. 31
Williams	Nov. 7
Trinity (Conn.) ■	Nov. 14

1997 RESULTS (7-1-0)

51	Tufts	33
16	Hamilton	15
20	Colby	13
17	Bates	14
14	Amherst	36
24	Bowdoin	17
28	Williams	14
19	Trinity (Conn.)	7
189		**149**

Nickname: Cardinals.
Stadium: Andrus Field (1881), 8,000 capacity. Natural turf.
Colors: Red & Black.
Conference: NESCAC.
SID: Brian Katten, 203-685-2887.
AD: John S. Biddiscombe.

WEST ALA.

Livingston, AL 35470 II

Coach: Bobby Johns, Alabama 1968
Record: 1 Year, 4-6-0

1998 SCHEDULE

Wingate ■ ....Sept. 12
Arkansas Tech ....Sept. 19
Henderson St. ■..Sept. 26
Delta St...Oct. 3
Valdosta St..Oct. 10
West Ga. ■ ....*Oct. 17
Southern Ark. ■ ....Oct. 24
Central Ark. ....Oct. 31
Ark.-Monticello ■..Nov. 7
North ALa. ....Nov. 14

1997 RESULTS (4-6-0)

17	Arkansas Tech	41
37	Lane	14
39	Union (Ky.)	6
31	Ark.-Monticello	10
16	Henderson St.	24
38	Mississippi Col.	21
20	Valdosta St.	33
15	West Ga.	48
13	Delta St.	27
14	North ALa.	56
240		**280**

Nickname: Tigers.
Stadium: Tiger (1952), 8,500 capacity. Natural turf.
Colors: Red, White & Black.
Conference: Gulf South Conference.
SID: Fred Sington,205-652-3596.
AD: "Dee" Curtis Outlaw.

WEST CHESTER

West Chester, PA 19383 II

Coach: Rick Daniels, West Chester 1975
Record: 9 Years, 59-38-1

1998 SCHEDULE

Indiana (Pa.) ■...Sept. 5
New Haven ....Sept. 12
Delaware...Sept. 19
Shippensburg ■ ....Sept. 26
East Stroudsburg...Oct. 3
Mansfield ■ ....Oct. 10
Bloomsburg ■ ....Oct. 17
Millersville...Oct. 24
Clarion ....Oct. 31
Cheyney ■..Nov. 7
Kutztown..Nov. 14

1997 RESULTS (5-6-0)

0	Villanova	64
26	New Haven	32
7	Delaware	28
30	Buffalo	27
14	Slippery Rock	27
32	East Stroudsburg	31
54	Cheyney	20
38	Mansfield	9
7	Millersville	21
14	Bloomsburg	24
24	Kutztown	12
246		**295**

Nickname: Golden Rams.
Stadium: Farrell (1970), 7,500 capacity. Natural turf.
Colors: Purple & Gold.
Conference: Pennsylvania State Athl. Conf.
SID: Tom Di Camillo, 610-436-3316.
AD: Edward Matejkovic.

WEST GA.

Carrollton, GA 30118 II

Coach: Glenn Spencer, Georgia Tech 1986
(First year as head coach)

1998 SCHEDULE

Presbyterian ■ ....*Aug. 29
Mars Hill ....Sept. 5
Ark.-Monticello ■ ....*Sept. 12
Central Ark. ....*Sept. 19
Southern Ark. ■ ....*Sept. 26
North ALa. ■ ....*Oct. 10
West ALa...*Oct. 17
Delta St...Oct. 24
Henderson St. ■...Oct. 31
Arkansas Tech ....Nov. 7
Valdosta St. ■ ....*Nov. 14

1997 RESULTS (8-2-0)

14	North Dak. St.	31
37	Mars Hill	12
39	Ark.-Monticello	7
27	N.C. Central	0
36	Henderson St.	18
17	Central Ark.	13
28	Delta St.	9
48	West ALa.	15
18	North ALa.	21
35	Valdosta St.	21
299		**147**

Nickname: Braves.
Stadium: Grisham (1966), 6,500 capacity. Natural turf.
Colors: Blue & Red.
Conference: Gulf South Conference.
SID: Mitch Gray, 770-836-6542.
AD: Edward G. Murphy.

WEST LIBERTY ST.

West Liberty, WV 26074 II

Coach: Bob Eaton, Glenville St. 1978
Record: 8 Years, 36-43-1

1998 SCHEDULE

Mansfield ■ ....Sept. 5
Malone [Wheeling, W. Va.]...........................Sept. 12
Walsh ....Sept. 19
Glenville St. ■ ....Oct. 3
West Va. St. ....Oct. 10
Concord ....Oct. 17
West Va. Wesleyan ■ ....Oct. 24
Fairmont St...Oct. 31
West Va. Tech...Nov. 7
Shepherd ■ ....Nov. 14

1997 RESULTS (4-6-0)

16	Westminster (Pa.)	46
35	Malone	18
47	St. Joseph's (Ind.)	37
18	Glenville St.	42
33	West Va. St.	16
21	Concord	49
22	West Va. Wesleyan	39
15	Fairmont St.	48
26	West Va. Tech	0
27	Shepherd	32
260		**327**

Nickname: Hilltoppers.
Stadium: Russek Field (1960), 4,000 capacity. Natural turf.
Colors: Gold & Black.
Conference: WV Intercollegiate Athletic.
SID: Lynn Ullom, 304-336-8320.
AD: James W. Watson.

WEST TEX. A&M

Canyon, TX 79016.......................................II

Coach: Stan McGarvey, William Jewell 1972
Record: 13 Years, 86-51-4

1998 SCHEDULE

OkLa. Panhandle St. ■..................................*Aug. 29
Central Ark. ....*Sept. 5
Southwestern OkLa. ■...................................*Sept. 12
East Central...Sept. 19
Angelo St. ■ ....*Oct. 3
Tarleton St...*Oct. 10
Tex. A&M-Commerce ■ ....*Oct. 17
Texas A&M-Kingsville...................................*Oct. 24
Midwestern St. ....Oct. 31
Eastern N.M. ■ ....Nov. 7
Abilene Christian ....Nov. 14

1997 RESULTS (7-4-0)

17	Stephen F. Austin	35
48	Adams St.	0
34	Southwestern OkLa.	7
48	East Central	0
23	Angelo St.	31
31	Tarleton St.	17
14	Tex. A&M-Commerce	21
0	Texas A&M-Kingsville	33
51	Midwestern St.	7
35	Eastern N.M.	34
20	Abilene Christian	0
321		**185**

Nickname: Buffaloes.
Stadium: Kimbrough (1959), 20,000 capacity. Natural turf.
Colors: Maroon & White.
Conference: Lone Star Conference.
SID: Bill Kauffman, 806-656-2687.
AD: Ed Harris.

WEST VA.

Morgantown, WV 26506 ....I-A

Coach: Don Nehlen, Bowling Green 1958
Record: 27 Years, 183-112-8

1998 SCHEDULE

Ohio St. ■ ....*Sept. 5
Maryland ■ ....Sept. 19
Tulsa ■ ....Sept. 26
Navy ....Oct. 3
Temple..Oct. 10
Miami (FLa.) ■ ....Oct. 24
Virginia Tech..Oct. 31
Syracuse ■ ....*Nov. 7
Rutgers...Nov. 14
Boston College ■..Nov. 21
Pittsburgh ....Nov. 27

1997 RESULTS (7-4-0)

42	Marshall	31
24	East Caro.	17
24	Boston College	31
28	Miami (FLa.)	17
48	Rutgers	0
31	Maryland	14
30	Virginia Tech	17
10	Syracuse	40
41	Temple	21
14	Notre Dame	21
38	Pittsburgh	41
330		**250**

Carquest Bowl

30	Georgia Tech	35

Nickname: Mountaineers.
Stadium: Mountaineer Field (1980), 63,500 capacity. Artificial turf.
Colors: Old Gold & Blue.
Conference: Big East.
SID: Shelly Poe, 304-293-2821.
AD: Ed Pastilong.

WEST VA. ST.

Institute, WV 25112 II

Coach: Carl Lee, Marshall 1983
Record: 2 Years, 9-13-0

1998 SCHEDULE

West Va. Tech [Charleston, W. Va.] ....*Aug. 29
Wingate ....Sept. 5
Gardner-Webb ■...Sept. 19
Lane ....Sept. 26
Fairmont St...Oct. 3

SCHEDULES/RESULTS

West Liberty St. ■	Oct. 10
West Va. Wesleyan ■	Oct. 17
West Va. Tech	Oct. 24
Shepherd ■	Oct. 31
Concord ■	Nov. 7
Glenville St.	Nov. 14

1997 RESULTS (5-6-0)

26	West Va. Tech	23
20	Wingate	22
28	Gardner-Webb	53
44	Lane	16
33	Fairmont St.	28
16	West Liberty St.	33
27	West Va. Wesleyan	16
29	West Va. Tech	13
7	Shepherd	23
18	Concord	20
14	Glenville St.	54
262		**301**

Nickname: Yellow Jackets.
Stadium: Lakin Field, 5,000 capacity. Natural turf.
Colors: Old Gold & Black.
Conference: WV Intercollegiate Athletic.
SID: Sean McAndrews, 304-766-3238.
AD: S. Bryce Casto.

WEST VA. TECH

Montgomery, WV 25136 ... II

Coach: Paul Price, West Va. Wesleyan 1983
Record: 2 Years, 1-21-0

1998 SCHEDULE

West Va. St. [Charleston, W. Va.]	*Aug. 29
Delaware Valley ■	Sept. 5
Geneva	*Sept. 12
Frostburg St.	Sept. 19
Concord ■	Oct. 3
Fairmont St.	Oct. 10
Shepherd ■	*Oct. 15
West Va. St. ■	Oct. 24
Glenville St.	Oct. 31
West Liberty St. ■	Nov. 7
West Va. Wesleyan	Nov. 14

1997 RESULTS (0-11-0)

23	West Va. St.	26
0	St. Joseph's (Ind.)	52
0	Catawba	56
31	Geneva	49
10	Concord	25
0	Fairmont St.	52
3	Shepherd	48
13	West Va. St.	29
10	Glenville St.	49
0	West Liberty St.	26
21	West Va. Wesleyan	57
111		**469**

Nickname: Golden Bears.
Stadium: Martin Field, 3,000 capacity. Artificial turf.
Colors: Blue & Gold.
Conference: WV Intercollegiate Athletic.
SID: To be named,304-442-3085.
AD: Jeff Kepreos.

WEST VA. WESLEYAN

Buckhannon, WV 26201 ... II

Coach: Bill Struble, West Va. Wesleyan 1976
Record: 15 Years, 71-78-0

1998 SCHEDULE

Slippery Rock ■	Sept. 12
Indiana (Pa.)	*Sept. 19
Catawba ■	Sept. 26
Shepherd	Oct. 3
Glenville St. ■	Oct. 10
West Va. St.	Oct. 17
West Liberty St.	Oct. 24
Concord ■	Oct. 31
Fairmont St.	Nov. 7
West Va. Tech ■	Nov. 14

1997 RESULTS (5-5-0)

26	Kutztown	44
31	Slippery Rock	41
16	Calif. (Pa.)	21
19	Shepherd	37
50	Glenville St.	46
16	West Va. St.	27
39	West Liberty St.	22
57	Concord	27
31	Fairmont St.	0
57	West Va. Tech	21
342		**286**

Nickname: Bobcats.
Stadium: Cebe Ross Field (1957), 4,000 capacity. Natural turf.
Colors: Orange & Black.
Conference: WV Intercollegiate Athletic.
SID: Peter Galarneau Jr., 304-473-8111.
AD: George A. Klebez.

WESTERN CARO.

Cullowhee, NC 28723 ... I-AA

Coach: Bill Bleil, NW Iowa 1981
Record: 1 Year, 3-8-0

1998 SCHEDULE

Duke	*Sept. 5
Citadel	*Sept. 19
East Tenn. St. ■	*Sept. 26
Furman	Oct. 3
Ga. Southern ■	*Oct. 10
Wofford	Oct. 17
Chattanooga ■	Oct. 24
VMI	Oct. 31
Elon ■	Nov. 7
Tennessee Tech	Nov. 14
Appalachian St. ■	Nov. 21

1997 RESULTS (3-8-0)

10	Liberty	17
45	Citadel	25
18	East Tenn. St.	28
17	Furman	16
7	Ga. Southern	30
7	Wofford	17
21	Chattanooga	24
24	VMI	0
16	Elon	17
7	Appalachian St.	13
0	Samford	19
172		**206**

Nickname: Catamounts.
Stadium: E.J. Whitmire (1974), 12,000 capacity. Artificial turf.
Colors: Purple & Gold.
Conference: Southern.
SID: Craig Wells, 704-227-7171.
AD: Larry L. Travis.

WESTERN CONN. ST.

Danbury, CT 06810 ... III

Coach: John Cervino, West Va. Wesleyan 19
Record: 6 Years, 24-35-1

1998 SCHEDULE

Mass.-Dartmouth	Sept. 12
New Jersey City ■	Sept. 19
Wm. Paterson	*Sept. 25
Plymouth St. ■	Oct. 3
Springfield	Oct. 10
Coast Guard	Oct. 17
Montclair St. ■	Oct. 24
Worcester Tech ■	Oct. 31
Merchant Marine ■	Nov. 7
Norwich ■	Nov. 14

1997 RESULTS (4-6-0)

15	Salve Regina	3
45	Bri'water (Mass.)	7
13	New Jersey City	14
40	Wm. Paterson	14
13	Plymouth St.	23
7	Springfield	34
14	Coast Guard	21
2	Worcester Tech	10
0	Merchant Marine	36
28	Norwich	2
177		**164**

Nickname: Colonials.
Stadium: Midtown Campus Field, 3,500 capacity. Artificial turf.
Colors: Blue & White.
Conference: Freedom FB.
SID: Scott Ames, 203-837-9014.
AD: Edward Farrington.

WESTERN ILL.

Macomb, IL 61455 ... I-AA

Coach: Randy Ball, Truman St. 1973
Record: 8 Years, 53-38-1

1998 SCHEDULE

St. Cloud St. ■	*Sept. 3
Central Mich.	Sept. 12
Elon	Sept. 19
Southern Utah ■	Sept. 26
Youngstown St. ■	Oct. 3
Southwest Mo. St.	Oct. 10
Southern Ill.	Oct. 17
Illinois St. ■	Oct. 24
Buffalo	Oct. 31
Indiana St. ■	Nov. 7
Northern Iowa	*Nov. 14

1997 RESULTS (10-1-0)

41	Eastern Ill.	0
45	Truman St.	18
31	Alcorn St.	17
7	Marshall	48
45	Southern Utah	6
29	Northern Iowa	22
37	Indiana St.	3
37	Southwest Mo. St.	7
31	Southern Ill.	26
37	Illinois St.	23
24	Youngstown St.	21
364		**191**

I-AA Championship

31	Jackson St.	24
12	McNeese St.	14

Nickname: Leathernecks.
Stadium: Hanson Field (1948), 15,000 capacity. Natural turf.
Colors: Purple & Gold.
Conference: Gateway.
SID: Doug Smiley, 309-298-1133.
AD: Helen Smiley.

WESTERN KY.

Bowling Green, KY 42101 ... I-AA

Coach: Jack Harbaugh, Bowling Green 1961
Record: 14 Years, 72-77-3

1998 SCHEDULE

Tenn.-Martin ■	*Sept. 3
Murray St.	*Sept. 12
Eastern Ky. ■	*Sept. 19
Austin Peay ■	*Sept. 26
New Haven ■	*Oct. 3
South Fla.	*Oct. 17
Elon ■	Oct. 24
Louisville	Oct. 31
Southern Ill. ■	Nov. 7
Indiana St. ■	Nov. 14
Southwestern La.	*Nov. 21

1997 RESULTS (9-1-0)

42	Tenn.-Martin	0
52	Murray St.	50
37	Eastern Ky.	21
53	Austin Peay	7
31	South Fla.	3
16	UAB	20
24	New Haven	21
52	Southern Ill.	31
38	Morehead St.	24
21	Indiana St.	14
366		**191**

I-AA Championship

42	Eastern Ky.	14
21	Eastern Wash.	38

Nickname: Hilltoppers.
Stadium: L.T. Smith (1968), 17,500 capacity. Natural turf.
Colors: Red & White.
Conference: Independent.
SID: Paul Just, 502-745-4298.
AD: Lewis Mills.

WESTERN MD.

Westminster, MD 21157 III

Coach: Tim Keating, Bethany (W. Va.) 1975
Record: 10 Years, 53-42-3

1998 SCHEDULE

Bridgewater (Va.) ■	Sept. 5
Juniata	Sept. 12
Gettysburg ■	Sept. 19
Ursinus	Sept. 26
Muhlenberg ■	Oct. 3
Dickinson ■	Oct. 17
Frank. & Marsh.	Oct. 24
Salisbury St.	Oct. 31
Swarthmore ■	Nov. 7
Johns Hopkins	Nov. 14

1997 RESULTS (10-0-0)

21	Bridgewater (Va.)	17
30	Juniata	8
55	Gettysburg	7
20	Ursinus	10
44	Muhlenberg	9
41	Dickinson	7
28	Frank. & Marsh.	12
11	Salisbury St.	0
56	Swarthmore	0
21	Johns Hopkins	3
327		**73**

III Championship

13	Lycoming	27

Nickname: Green Terror.
Stadium: Scott S. Bair (1981), 4,000 capacity. Natural turf.
Colors: Green & Gold.
Conference: Centennial Conference.
SID: Scott E. Deitch, 410-857-2291.
AD: J. Richard Carpenter Jr.

WESTERN MICH.

Kalamazoo, MI 49008 .... I-A

Coach: Gary Darnell, Oklahoma St. 1970
Record: 5 Years, 14-36-0

1998 SCHEDULE

Northern Ill. ■	*Sept. 3
Indiana	*Sept. 12
Toledo	*Sept. 19
Ohio ■	*Sept. 26
Northeast La. ■	*Oct. 3
Vanderbilt	*Oct. 10
Eastern Mich. ■	Oct. 17
Central Mich.	Oct. 24
Kent	Oct. 31
Ball St.	Nov. 7
Bowling Green ■	Nov. 14

1997 RESULTS (8-3-0)

34	Temple	14
10	Michigan St.	42
21	Northern Ill.	13
13	Toledo	23
7	Ohio	31
21	Ball St.	13
34	Bowling Green	21
50	Kent	27
41	Eastern Mich.	38
38	Central Mich.	24
32	Northeast La.	19
301		**265**

Nickname: Broncos.
Stadium: Waldo (1939), 30,200 capacity. Natural turf.
Colors: Brown & Gold.
Conference: Mid-American.
SID: John Beatty, 616-387-4138.
AD: Kathy Beauregard.

WESTERN NEW ENG.

Springfield, MA 01119 III

Coach: Gerry Martin, Connecticut 1980
Record: 7 Years, 17-42-1

1998 SCHEDULE

Westfield St. ■	Sept. 19
Nichols ■	Sept. 26
Salve Regina	*Oct. 3
Mass.-Boston	Oct. 10
Curry ■	Oct. 17
Mass.-Dartmouth	Oct. 24
Framingham St.	Oct. 31
MIT ■	Nov. 7
Fitchburg St. ■	Nov. 14

1997 RESULTS (4-3-0)

7	Fitchburg St.	17
25	MIT	10
28	Curry	6
7	Salve Regina	10
14	Stonehill	33
20	Nichols	7
14	Merrimack	12
115		**95**

Nickname: Golden Bears.
Stadium: WNEC, 1,500 capacity. Natural turf.
Colors: Navy Blue & Gold.
Conference: New England FB.
SID: Gene Gumbs, 413-782-1227.
AD: Eric Geldart.

WESTERN N. MEX.

Silver City, NM 88061 II

Coach: Land Jacobsen, Central Okla. 1976
Record: 2 Years, 8-11-0

1998 SCHEDULE

Eastern N.M.	*Sept. 5
Adams St.	Sept. 12
N. M. Highlands ■	*Sept. 19
Northwestern Okla.	Oct. 10
Langston	Oct. 17
Cal Poly	Oct. 24
Okla. Panhandle St. ■	Oct. 31
New Haven ■	Nov. 7
Mesa St. ■	Nov. 14

1997 RESULTS (5-5-0)

0	Eastern N.M.	3
26	Adams St.	7
14	Cal Poly	24
29	Hardin-Simmons	33
38	Northwestern Okla.	31
66	Langston	39
14	Okla. Panhandle St.	7
31	Wayne St. (Neb.)	33
43	Mesa St.	41
21	N. M. Highlands	28
282		**246**

Nickname: Mustangs.
Stadium: Silver Sports Complex (1969), 2,000 capacity. Natural turf.
Colors: Purple & Gold.
Conference: Independent.
SID: Jim Callender, 505-538-6220.
AD: Scott Woodard.

WESTERN ST. (COLO.)

Gunnison, CO 81231 II

Coach: Carl Iverson, Whitman 1962
Record: 14 Years, 94-45-3

1998 SCHEDULE

Northern Colo.	Sept. 12
Mesa St. ■	Sept. 19
Northern Ariz.	Sept. 26
N. M. Highlands ■	Oct. 3
Chadron St.	Oct. 10
Adams St.	Oct. 17
Fort Hays St. ■	Oct. 24
Colorado Mines ■	Oct. 31
Neb.-Kearney	Nov. 7
Fort Lewis	Nov. 14

1997 RESULTS (9-2-0)

14	Northern Colo.	13
13	Weber St.	29
46	Okla. Panhandle St.	0
27	N. M. Highlands	21
16	Chadron St.	14
50	Adams St.	15
15	Fort Hays St.	28
34	Neb.-Kearney	6
40	Colorado Mines	0
66	Fort Lewis	17
27	Mesa St.	3
348		**146**

II Championship

12	Angelo St.	46

Nickname: Mountaineers.
Stadium: Mountaineer Bowl (1950), 2,400 capacity. Natural turf.
Colors: Crimson & Slate.
Conference: Rocky Mountain Athletic Conf.
SID: J.W. Campbell, 303-943-2831.
AD: Greg Waggoner.

WESTERN WASH.

Bellingham, WA 98225 II

Coach: Rob Smith, Washington 1981
Record: 9 Years, 61-28-1

1998 SCHEDULE

Chapman	Sept. 12
Montana St.	Sept. 19
Western Mont. ■	Sept. 26
Humboldt St. ■	Oct. 3
Eastern Wash.	Oct. 10
UC Davis ■	Oct. 17
Simon Fraser	Oct. 24
Western Ore. U.	Oct. 31
Central Wash. ■	Nov. 7
Southern Ore.	Nov. 14

1997 RESULTS (5-5-0)

35	Chapman	0
44	Pacific Lutheran	46
28	Linfield	17
6	Western Ore. U.	8
45	Humboldt St.	7
7	UC Davis	16
31	Simon Fraser	0
28	Eastern Ore. U.	31
22	Central Wash.	36
27	Southern Ore.	26
273		**187**

Nickname: Vikings.
Stadium: Bellingham Civic Field, 5,000 capacity. Natural turf.
Colors: Navy Blue, Silver & White.
Conference: Independent.
SID: Paul Madison.
AD: Lynda Goodrich.

WESTFIELD ST.

Westfield, MA 01086 III

Coach: Steve Marino, Westfield St. 1971
Record: 8 Years, 36-41-1

1998 SCHEDULE

Hartwick ■	Sept. 12
Western New Eng.	Sept. 19
Fitchburg St. ■	Sept. 26
Mass. Maritime	Oct. 3
Framingham St.	Oct. 10
Maine Maritime ■	Oct. 17
Bri'water (Mass.) ■	Oct. 24
Mass.-Boston	Oct. 31

Nichols ■	Nov. 7
Worcester St.	Nov. 14

1997 RESULTS (4-6-0)

25	Hartwick	38
26	Mass.-Boston	18
13	Fitchburg St.	35
28	Framingham St.	22
28	Coast Guard	44
21	Bri'water (Mass.)	55
19	Worcester St.	14
28	Mass. Maritime	26
23	Mass.-Dartmouth	48
28	Maine Maritime	54
239		**354**

Nickname: Owls.
Stadium: Alumni Field (1982), 4,800 capacity. Artificial turf.
Colors: Royal Blue & White.
Conference: New England FB.
SID: Mickey Curtis, 413-572-5433.
AD: Kenneth Magarian.

WESTMINSTER (MO.)

Fulton, MO 65251 III

Coach: Ralph Young, Parsons 1968
Record: 10 Years, 33-66-0

1998 SCHEDULE

Greenville	*Sept. 19
Ky. Wesleyan	Sept. 26
Central Methodist ■	Sept. 12
MacMurray ■	Nov. 14
Principia	Oct. 17
Illinois Col. ■	Sept. 5
Maranatha Baptist	Oct. 10
Northwestern (Minn.) ■	Oct. 24
Bethel (Tenn.)	Nov. 7
Blackburn ■	Oct. 3

1997 RESULTS (6-4-0)

28	Concordia-St. Paul	35
27	Greenville	20
49	Trinity Bible (N.D.)	0
33	Blackburn	13
0	McKendree	55
55	Southwestern Aly God	13
34	Ky. Wesleyan	39
43	Principia	26
66	Bethel (Tenn.)	58
16	MacMurray	48
351		**307**

Nickname: Blue Jays.
Stadium: Priest Field (1900), 1,000 capacity. Natural turf.
Colors: Blue & White.
Conference: St. Louis Intercol. Ath. Conf.
SID: To be named, 573-592-1200.
AD: Terry Logue.

WESTMINSTER (PA.)

New Wilmington, PA 16172........................II

Coach: Gene Nicholson, Slippery Rock 1964
Record: 7 Years, 61-17-2

1998 SCHEDULE

Indianapolis ■	Sept. 5
Mansfield	Sept. 12
Northwood ■	Sept. 19
Hillsdale	Sept. 26
Ashland	Oct. 3
Saginaw Valley ■	Oct. 10
Mercyhurst ■	Oct. 17
Findlay	Oct. 24
St. Francis (Ill.) ■	Oct. 31
Wayne St. (Mich.) ■	Nov. 7
Northern Mich.	*Nov. 14

1997 RESULTS (9-1-0)

46	West Liberty St.	16
34	Mansfield	12
33	St. Ambrose	30
33	Tiffin	6
55	Urbana	6
42	St. Xavier	7
21	Malone	0
24	Tri-State	14
17	Walsh	14
18	Geneva	45
323		**150**

Nickname: Titans.
Stadium: Memorial Field, 4,500 capacity. Natural turf.
Colors: Navy Blue & White.
Conference: Midwest Intercoll.
SID: Joe Onderko, 412-946-6357.
AD: Joseph B. Fusco.

WHEATON (ILL.)

Wheaton, IL 60187 III

Coach: Mike Swider, Wheaton (Ill.) 1977
Record: 2 Years, 12-6-0

1998 SCHEDULE

Washington (Mo.)	Sept. 12
Anderson (Ind.) ■	Sept. 19
North Central ■	Oct. 3
Carthage	*Oct. 10
North Park	Oct. 17
Ill. Wesleyan ■	Oct. 24
Millikin	Oct. 31
Elmhurst ■	Nov. 7
Augustana (Ill.)	Nov. 14

1997 RESULTS (4-5-0)

20	Kalamazoo	21
25	Aurora	32
16	Augustana (Ill.)	21
59	Elmhurst	20
26	Millikin	30
39	Ill. Wesleyan	29
25	Carthage	14
33	North Park	7
7	North Central	20
250		**194**

Nickname: Crusaders.
Stadium: McCully Field (1956), 7,000 capacity. Natural turf.
Colors: Orange & Blue.
Conference: College Conf. of Ill. & Wisc.
SID: Steve Schwepker, 708-752-5747.
AD: Tony Ladd.

WHITTIER

Whittier, CA 90608....................................III

Coach: Bob Owens, La Verne 1971
Record: 2 Years, 6-12-0

1998 SCHEDULE

Menlo	Sept. 12
Cal Lutheran ■	*Sept. 19
Chapman ■	*Sept. 26
Pomona-Pitzer	Oct. 3
La Verne ■	*Oct. 10
Claremont-M-S	*Oct. 24
Azusa Pacific ■	*Oct. 31
Redlands ■	Nov. 7
Occidental	*Nov. 14

1997 RESULTS (5-4-0)

34	La Verne	13
26	Menlo	20
38	Claremont-M-S	2
26	Pomona-Pitzer	29
16	Cal Lutheran	28
14	Azusa Pacific	20
27	Redlands	24
18	San Diego	30
41	Occidental	7
240		**173**

Nickname: Poets.
Stadium: Memorial, 7,000 capacity. Natural turf.
Colors: Purple & Gold.
Conference: So Calif Intercol Ath Conf.
SID: Rock Carter, 310-907-4271.
AD: David A. Jacobs.

WIDENER

Chester, PA 19013 III

Coach: Bill Zwaan, Delaware 1979
Record: 1 Year, 7-3-0

1998 SCHEDULE

Wilkes	Sept. 12
FDU-Madison ■	Sept. 19
Lebanon Valley ■	Sept. 26
Juniata	Oct. 3
Moravian	Oct. 10
Albright ■	Oct. 17
Lycoming ■	Oct. 24
King's (Pa.)	Oct. 31
Delaware Valley	Nov. 7
Susquehanna ■	Nov. 14

1997 RESULTS (7-3-0)

20	Wilkes	14
27	FDU-Madison	14
28	Lebanon Valley	6
56	Juniata	20
24	Moravian	27
21	Albright	28
17	Lycoming	19
34	King's (Pa.)	20
34	Delaware Valley	7
35	Susquehanna	28
296		**183**

Nickname: Pioneers.
Stadium: Leslie Quick Jr. (1994), 4,000 capacity. Natural turf.
Colors: Widener Blue & Gold.
Conference: Middle Atlantic States Conf.
SID: Susan Fumagalli, 610-499-4436.
AD: William A. Zwaan.

WILKES

Wilkes-Barre, PA 18766..............................III

Coach: Frank Sheptock, Bloomsburg 1986
Record: 2 Years, 13-8-0

1998 SCHEDULE

Widener ■	Sept. 12
Susquehanna ■	Sept. 19
FDU-Madison	*Sept. 25
Lebanon Valley	Oct. 3
Wesley	Oct. 10
King's (Pa.)	Oct. 17
Delaware Valley ■	Oct. 31
Moravian ■	Nov. 7
Lycoming	Nov. 14

1997 RESULTS (5-5-0)

14	Widener	20
14	Susquehanna	47
29	FDU-Madison	3
32	Lebanon Valley	0
17	Wesley	31
23	King's (Pa.)	0
12	Montclair St.	15
32	Delaware Valley	12
27	Moravian	21
12	Lycoming	26
212		**175**

Nickname: Colonels.
Stadium: Ralston Field (1965), 4,000 capacity. Natural turf.
Colors: Navy & Gold.
Conference: Middle Atlantic States Conf.
SID: John Seitzinger, 717-831-4777.
AD: Philip Wingert.

WILLAMETTE

Salem, OR 97301 III

Coach: Mark Speckman, Azusa Pacific 1977
(First year as head coach)

1998 SCHEDULE

Colorado Col.	Sept. 12
Humboldt St.	Sept. 19

Central Wash. ■ ....Sept. 26
Eastern Ore. U. ....Oct. 3
Lewis & Clark ■ ....Oct. 10
Linfield ....Oct. 17
Southern Ore. ....Oct. 24
Puget Sound ■ ....Oct. 31
Pacific Lutheran ....Nov. 7
Whitworth ■ ....Nov. 14

1997 RESULTS (10-0-0)

42 Humboldt St. 14
40 Chapman 6
34 Central Wash. 21
13 Eastern Ore. U. 7
34 Lewis & Clark 14
27 Linfield 0
41 Southern Ore. 27
54 Puget Sound 0
42 Pacific Lutheran 6
47 Whitworth 7

NAIA CHAMPIONSHIP

26 Western Ore. U. 20
50 Montana Tech 24
17 Sioux Falls 7
7 Findlay 14
474 **167**

Nickname: Bearcats.
Stadium: McCulloch, 3,500 capacity. Natural turf.
Colors: Cardinal & Old Gold.
Conference: NCIC.
SID: Cliff Voliva, 503-370-6110.
AD: William G. Trenbeath.

WILLIAM & MARY

Williamsburg, VA 23187 ....I-AA

Coach: Jimmye Laycock, William & Mary 1970
Record: 18 Years, 122-81-2

1998 SCHEDULE

Rhode Island ....Sept. 5
VMI ■ ....Sept. 12
Northeastern ■ ....Sept. 19
Villanova ....Sept. 26
Temple ....Oct. 3
Delaware ■ ....Oct. 10
James Madison ....Oct. 17
New Hampshire ■ ....Oct. 24
Hampton ....Oct. 31
Connecticut ■ ....Nov. 14
Richmond ....Nov. 21

1997 RESULTS (7-4-0)

31 Hampton 6
29 Ga. Southern 28
41 VMI 12
22 New Hampshire 24
20 Boston U. 17
12 Northeastern 33
38 James Madison 25
38 Connecticut 17
13 Villanova 20
0 Delaware 14
10 Richmond 7
254 **203**

Nickname: Tribe.
Stadium: Walter Zable (1935), 13,279 capacity. Natural turf.
Colors: Green, Gold, Silver.
Conference: Atlantic 10.
SID: Jean Elliott, 804-221-3344.
AD: Edward C. Driscoll Jr.

WM. PATERSON

Wayne, NJ 07470 III

Coach: Jack Peavey, Troy St. 1985
Record: 1 Year, 0-10-0

1998 SCHEDULE

Albright ■ ....Sept. 5
Waynesburg ■ ....Sept. 12
Col. of New Jersey ....*Sept. 18
Western Conn. St. ■ ....*Sept. 25
Kean ■ ....Oct. 3
Montclair St. ....*Oct. 17
Cortland St. ....Oct. 24
New Jersey City ■ ....*Oct. 30
Rowan ....Nov. 7
Salisbury St. ■ ....*Nov. 13

1997 RESULTS (0-10-0)

3 LIU-C.W. Post 34
7 Col. of New Jersey 42
14 Western Conn. St. 40
9 Kean 21
16 Newport News 22
7 Montclair St. 28
0 Cortland St. 31
2 New Jersey City 7
0 Rowan 57
14 Salisbury St. 16
72 **298**

Nickname: Pioneers.
Stadium: Wightman Field, 2,000 capacity. Natural turf.
Colors: Orange & Black.
Conference: New Jersey Athletic Conference.
SID: Joe Martinelli, 201-595-2705.
AD: Arthur Eason.

WILLIAM PENN

Oskaloosa, IA 52577 III

Coach: Mick Caba, Georgetown 1973
Record: 1 Year, 1-9-0

1998 SCHEDULE

Wartburg ■ ....*Sept. 5
Buena Vista ....Sept. 12
Cornell College ■ ....Sept. 19
Loras ....Sept. 26
Simpson ....Oct. 3
Luther ■ ....Oct. 10
Dubuque ■ ....Oct. 17
Coe ....Oct. 24
Central (Iowa) ■ ....Oct. 31
Upper Iowa ....Nov. 7

1997 RESULTS (1-9-0)

14 MacMurray 28
21 Central Methodist 14
6 Buena Vista 29
12 Simpson 58
13 Central (Iowa) 55
14 Upper Iowa 38
27 Dubuque 35
14 Loras 20
13 Luther 24
18 Wartburg 36
152 **337**

Nickname: The Statesmen.
Stadium: Community, 5,000 capacity. Natural turf.
Colors: Navy Blue & Gold.
Conference: Iowa Intercol. Athletic Conf.
SID: John Eberline, 515-673-1046.
AD: Mike Laird.

WILLIAMS

Williamstown, MA 01267 III

Coach: Dick Farley, Boston U. 1968
Record: 11 Years, 73-12-3

1998 SCHEDULE

Bowdoin ■ ....Sept. 26
Trinity (Conn.) ■ ....Oct. 3
Bates ....Oct. 10
Middlebury ■ ....Oct. 17
Tufts ....Oct. 24
Hamilton ....Oct. 31
Wesleyan (Conn.) ■ ....Nov. 7
Amherst ....Nov. 14

1997 RESULTS (7-1-0)

26 Colby 6
19 Trinity (Conn.) 15
36 Bates 16
25 Middlebury 22
26 Tufts 24
21 Hamilton 14
14 Wesleyan (Conn.) 28
48 Amherst 46
215 **171**

Nickname: Ephs.
Stadium: Weston Field (1875), 7,500 capacity. Natural turf.
Colors: Purple.
Conference: NESCAC.
SID: Dick Quinn, 413-597-4982.
AD: Robert R. Peck.

WILMINGTON (OHIO)

Wilmington, OH 45177 III

Coach: Mike Wallace, Bowling Green 1968
Record: 7 Years, 23-44-1

1998 SCHEDULE

Urbana ....Sept. 5
Olivet ■ ....Sept. 12
Maryville (Tenn.) ■ ....Sept. 19
Mount Saint Joseph ....Oct. 3
Franklin ....Oct. 10
Hanover ■ ....Oct. 17
Wabash ■ ....Oct. 24
Manchester ....Oct. 31
Anderson (Ind.) ■ ....Nov. 7
Bluffton ....Nov. 14

1997 RESULTS (4-6-0)

26 Urbana 20
14 Wabash 36
17 Thomas More 40
7 Susquehanna 28
0 Wittenberg 44
43 Earlham 7
26 Maryville (Tenn.) 19
17 Bluffton 21
30 Bethany (W. Va.) 14
25 Mount Saint Joseph 31
205 **260**

Nickname: Quakers.
Stadium: Williams (1983), 3,250 capacity. Natural turf.
Colors: Green & White.
Conference: Independent.
SID: Brian Neal, 513-382-6661.
AD: Terry A. Rupert.

WINGATE

Wingate, NC 28174 II

Coach: Doug Malone, Carson-Newman 1982
Record: 4 Years, 19-23-0

1998 SCHEDULE

West Va. St. ■ ....Sept. 5
West Ala. ....Sept. 12
Newberry ■ ....Sept. 19
Mars Hill ■ ....Sept. 26
Gardner-Webb ....Oct. 3
Carson-Newman ....Oct. 10
Lenoir-Rhyne ■ ....Oct. 17
Tusculum ....Oct. 24
Presbyterian ....Oct. 31
Catawba ■ ....Nov. 7
Benedict ....Nov. 14

1997 RESULTS (8-3-0)

37 Savannah St. 31
22 West Va. St. 20
48 Fayetteville St. 12
43 Newberry 38
7 Mars Hill 28
54 Gardner-Webb 34
17 Carson-Newman 55
22 Lenoir-Rhyne 21
51 Tusculum 13
22 Presbyterian 14
22 Catawba 31
345 **297**

Nickname: Bulldogs.
Stadium: Walter Bickett, 5,000 capacity. Natural turf.
Colors: Navy Blue & Old Gold.
Conference: South Atlantic Conference.
SID: David Sherwood, 704-233-8186.
AD: Beth Lawrence.

WINONA ST.

Winona, MN 55987 II

Coach: Tom Sawyer, Winona St. 1983
Record: 2 Years, 12-10-0

1998 SCHEDULE

Ferris St. ■	Sept. 5
Wis.-La Crosse	Sept. 12
Northern St.	Sept. 26
Bemidji St. ■	Oct. 3
Minn.-Duluth	Oct. 10
Southwest St. ■	Oct. 17
Moorhead St.	Oct. 24
Wayne St. (Neb.)	Oct. 31
Minn.-Morris ■	Nov. 7
Northern St. [Minneapolis, Minn.]	Nov. 14
Northern Iowa	*Nov. 21

1997 RESULTS (9-2-0)

25	Wis.-River Falls	24
14	Wis.-La Crosse	37
20	Wis.-Eau Claire	44
52	Minn.-Morris	19
41	Northern St.	17
58	Bemidji St.	14
63	Minn.-Duluth	35
38	Southwest St.	21
28	Moorhead St.	10
59	Quincy	14
48	Mayville St.	18
446		**253**

Nickname: Warriors.
Stadium: Maxwell, 3,500 capacity. Natural turf.
Colors: Purple & White.
Conference: Northern Sun.
SID: Michael R. Herzberg, 507-457-5576.
AD: Larry Holstad.

WINSTON-SALEM

Winston-Salem, NC 27110.........................II

Coach: Kermit Blount, Winston-Salem 1980
Record: 5 years, 26-24-3

1998 SCHEDULE

Catawba	Sept. 5
North Caro. A&T	Sept. 12
Virginia Union ■	*Sept. 26
Fayetteville St. ■	Oct. 3
Livingstone ■	Oct. 10
N.C. Central	Oct. 17
Virginia St.	Oct. 24
Johnson Smith	Oct. 31
Elizabeth City St.	Nov. 7
Grambling [San Diego, Cal.]	Nov. 14

1997 RESULTS (6-4-0)

7	North Caro. A&T	27
27	Savannah St.	24
13	Virginia Union	6
16	Fayetteville St.	18
7	Livingstone	41
29	N.C. Central	30
21	Virginia St.	12
40	Johnson Smith	7
48	Elizabeth City St.	0
21	Bowie St.	0
229		**165**

Nickname: Rams.
Stadium: Bowman-Gray (1940), 18,000 capacity. Natural turf.
Colors: Scarlet & White.
Conference: Central Intercol. Ath. Assn.
SID: Adrian Ferguson, 919-750-2143.
AD: Anne Little.

WISCONSIN

Madison, WI 53711 ....I-A

Coach: Barry Alvarez, Nebraska 1969
Record: 8 Years, 49-41-4

1998 SCHEDULE

San Diego St.	*Sept. 5
Ohio ■	Sept. 12
UNLV ■	Sept. 19
Northwestern ■	Sept. 26
Indiana	Oct. 3
Purdue ■	*Oct. 10
Illinois	Oct. 17
Iowa	Oct. 24
Minnesota ■	Nov. 7
Michigan	Nov. 14
Penn St. ■	Nov. 21

1997 RESULTS (8-4-0)

0	Syracuse	34
28	Boise St.	24
56	San Jose St.	10
34	San Diego St.	10
27	Indiana	26
26	Northwestern	25
31	Illinois	7
20	Purdue	45
22	Minnesota	21
13	Iowa	10
16	Michigan	26
10	Penn St.	35
283		**273**

Outback Bowl

6	Georgia	33

Nickname: Badgers.
Stadium: Camp Randall (1917), 76,129 capacity. Artificial turf.
Colors: Cardinal & White.
Conference: Big Ten.
SID: Steve Malchow, 608-262-1811.
AD: Pat Richter.

WIS.-EAU CLAIRE

Eau Claire, WI 54702 III

Coach: Bob Nielson, Wartburg 1982
Record: 9 Years, 60-30-1

1998 SCHEDULE

Tiffin	Sept. 5
Minn.-Duluth	*Sept. 19
Minn.-Morris ■	Sept. 26
Wis.-Whitewater ■	Oct. 3
Wis.-Stout	Oct. 10
Wis.-Stevens Point ■	Oct. 17
Wis.-River Falls ■	Oct. 24
Wis.-Platteville	Oct. 31
Wis.-La Crosse	Nov. 7
Wis.-Oshkosh ■	Nov. 14

1997 RESULTS (7-3-0)

66	Mayville St.	0
44	Winona St.	20
34	Wis.-Whitewater	50
45	Wis.-Stout	38
20	Wis.-Stevens Point	40
54	Wis.-Platteville	13
41	Wis.-River Falls	8
40	Wis.-La Crosse	55
49	Wis.-Oshkosh	35
48	Southwest St.	17
441		**276**

Nickname: Blugolds.
Stadium: Carson Park, 6,500 capacity. Natural turf.
Colors: Navy Blue & Old Gold.
Conference: Wisc. Intercol. Athl. Conf.
SID: Tim Petermann, 715-836-4184.
AD: Marilyn Skrivseth.

WIS.-LA CROSSE

La Crosse, WI 54601 III

Coach: Roger Harring, Wis.-La Crosse 1958
Record: 29 Years, 250-66-7

1998 SCHEDULE

Winona St. ■	Sept. 12
Drake	Sept. 19
Wis.-Stout	*Oct. 3
Wis.-Oshkosh	Oct. 10
Wis.-Platteville ■	Oct. 17
Wis.-Stevens Point	Oct. 24
Wis.-River Falls ■	Oct. 31
Wis.-Eau Claire ■	Nov. 7
Wis.-Whitewater	Nov. 14

1997 RESULTS (7-2-0)

37	Winona St.	14
56	Huron	0
21	Wis.-Stout	28
37	Wis.-Oshkosh	28
26	Wis.-Platteville	7
42	Wis.-River Falls	36
27	Wis.-Stevens Point	13
55	Wis.-Eau Claire	40
17	Wis.-Whitewater	32
318		**198**

Nickname: Eagles.
Stadium: Memorial (1924), 4,349 capacity. Natural turf.
Colors: Maroon & Gray.
Conference: Wisc. Intercol. Athl. Conf.
SID: Todd Clark, 608-785-8493.
AD: Jane C. Meyer.

WIS.-OSHKOSH

Oshkosh, WI 54901 III

Coach: Ron Cardo, Wis.-Oshkosh 1971
Record: 14 Years, 51-85-4

1998 SCHEDULE

St. Norbert ■	*Sept. 12
Menlo	Sept. 19
Thomas More ■	Sept. 26
Wis.-River Falls	Oct. 3
Wis.-La Crosse ■	Oct. 10
Wis.-Whitewater ■	Oct. 17
Wis.-Stout	Oct. 24
Wis.-Stevens Point	Oct. 31
Wis.-Platteville ■	Nov. 7
Wis.-Eau Claire	Nov. 14

1997 RESULTS (3-7-0)

62	St. Norbert	17
42	St. Xavier	3
20	St. Ambrose	21
39	Wis.-River Falls	49
28	Wis.-La Crosse	37
22	Wis.-Whitewater	30
33	Wis.-Stevens Point	50
37	Wis.-Stout	48
27	Wis.-Platteville	24
35	Wis.-Eau Claire	49
345		**328**

Nickname: Titans.
Stadium: Titan (1970), 9,680 capacity. Natural turf.
Colors: Black, Gold & White.
Conference: Wisc. Intercol. Athl. Conf.
SID: Kennan Timm, 414-424-0365.
AD: Allen F. Ackerman.

WIS.-PLATTEVILLE

Platteville, WI 53818 III

Coach: Jim Kinder, Wisconsin 1973
Record: 5 Years, 15-35-0

1998 SCHEDULE

Lakeland	Sept. 5
Iowa Wesleyan	*Sept. 12
Augustana (Ill.) ■	*Sept. 19
Wis.-Stevens Point	Oct. 3
Wis.-River Falls ■	Oct. 10
Wis.-La Crosse	Oct. 17
Wis.-Whitewater ■	Oct. 24
Wis.-Eau Claire ■	Oct. 31
Wis.-Oshkosh	Nov. 7
Wis.-Stout ■	Nov. 14

1997 RESULTS (1-9-0)

28	Concordia (Wis.)	20
10	Loras	17
30	Westmar	40
0	Wis.-Stevens Point	54
27	Wis.-River Falls	34
7	Wis.-La Crosse	26
13	Wis.-Eau Claire	54

18 Wis.-Whitewater....58
24 Wis.-Oshkosh....27
21 Wis.-Stout....49
178 **379**

Nickname: Pioneers.
Stadium: Ralph E. Davis Pioneer (1972), 10,000 capacity. Natural turf.
Colors: Blue & Orange.
Conference: Wisc. Intercol. Athl. Conf.
SID: Paul Erickson, 608-342-1574.
AD: Mark Molesworth.

WIS.-RIVER FALLS

River Falls, WI 54022....III

Coach: John O'Grady, Wis.-River Falls 197
Record: 9 Years, 58-31-3

1998 SCHEDULE

Washburn....*Sept. 5
Southwest St. ■....Sept. 19
Wis.-Stevens Point ■....Sept. 26
Wis.-Oshkosh ■....Oct. 3
Wis.-Platteville....Oct. 10
Wis.-Stout ■....Oct. 17
Wis.-Eau Claire....Oct. 24
Wis.-La Crosse....Oct. 31
Wis.-Whitewater ■....Nov. 7
Bemidji St. [Minneapolis, Minn.]....Nov. 14

1997 RESULTS (5-5-0)

24 Winona St....25
38 Southwest St....21
49 Wis.-Oshkosh....39
34 Wis.-Platteville....27
34 Wis.-Stout....42
36 Wis.-La Crosse....42
8 Wis.-Eau Claire....41
22 Wis.-Whitewater....52
37 Wis.-Stevens Point....31
31 Northern St....7
313 **327**

Nickname: Falcons.
Stadium: Ramer Field (1966), 4,800 capacity. Natural turf.
Colors: Red and White.
Conference: Wisc. Intercol. Athl. Conf.
SID: Jim Thies, 715-425-3846.
AD: Connie Foster.

WIS.-STEVENS POINT

Stevens Point, WI 54481....III

Coach: John Miech, Wis.-Stevens Point 1975
Record: 10 Years, 67-31-2

1998 SCHEDULE

Northern St. ■....*Sept. 12
Wis.-River Falls....Sept. 26
Wis.-Platteville ■....Oct. 3
Wis.-Whitewater....Oct. 10
Wis.-Eau Claire....Oct. 17
Wis.-La Crosse ■....Oct. 24
Wis.-Oshkosh ■....Oct. 31
Wis.-Stout....Nov. 7
Southwest St. [Minneapolis, Minn.]....Nov. 14

1997 RESULTS (6-4-0)

28 Northern St....2
34 Morningside....13
47 Bemidji St....0
54 Wis.-Platteville....0
0 Wis.-Whitewater....3
40 Wis.-Eau Claire....20
50 Wis.-Oshkosh....33
13 Wis.-La Crosse....27
22 Wis.-Stout....25
31 Wis.-River Falls....37
319 **160**

Nickname: Pointers.
Stadium: Goerke Field (1932), 4,000 capacity. Natural turf.
Colors: Purple & Gold.
Conference: Wisc. Intercol. Athl. Conf.
SID: Terry Owens, 715-346-2840.
AD: Frank O'Brien.

WIS.-STOUT

Menomonie, WI 54751....III

Coach: Ed Meierkort, Dakota Wesleyan 1981
Record: 5 Years, 19-31-0

1998 SCHEDULE

South Dak. St....Sept. 5
Minn.-Morris ■....*Sept. 12
St. Ambrose ■....*Sept. 19
Wis.-La Crosse ■....*Oct. 3
Wis.-Eau Claire ■....Oct. 10
Wis.-River Falls....Oct. 17
Wis.-Oshkosh ■....Oct. 24
Wis.-Whitewater....Oct. 31
Wis.-Stevens Point ■....Nov. 7
Wis.-Platteville....Nov. 14

1997 RESULTS (6-4-0)

43 Bemidji St....6
17 Northern St....27
28 Wis.-La Crosse....21
38 Wis.-Eau Claire....45
42 Wis.-River Falls....34
14 Wis.-Whitewater....35
48 Wis.-Oshkosh....37
25 Wis.-Stevens Point....22
49 Wis.-Platteville....21
21 Moorhead St....30
325 **278**

Nickname: Blue Devils.
Stadium: Nelson Field (1936), 5,000 capacity. Natural turf.
Colors: Royal Blue & White.
Conference: Wisc. Intercol. Athl. Conf.
SID: Layne Pitt, 715-232-2275.
AD: Steve Terry.

WIS.-WHITEWATER

Whitewater, WI 53190....III

Coach: Bob Berezowitz, Wis.-Whitewater 1967
Record: 13 Years, 91-41-4

1998 SCHEDULE

Lambuth ■....Sept. 5
South Dak. Tech ■....Sept. 12
Madison Tech ■....Sept. 19
Wis.-Eau Claire....Oct. 3
Wis.-Stevens Point ■....Oct. 10
Wis.-Oshkosh....Oct. 17
Wis.-Platteville....Oct. 24
Wis.-Stout ■....Oct. 31
Wis.-River Falls....Nov. 7
Wis.-La Crosse ■....Nov. 14

1997 RESULTS (9-0-0)

53 Carroll (Wis.)....0
66 South Dak. Tech....0
50 Wis.-Eau Claire....34
3 Wis.-Stevens Point....0
30 Wis.-Oshkosh....22
35 Wis.-Stout....14
58 Wis.-Platteville....18
52 Wis.-River Falls....22
32 Wis.-La Crosse....17
379 **127**

III Championship

31 Simpson....34

Nickname: Warhawks.
Stadium: Warhawk (1970), 11,000 capacity. Natural turf.
Colors: Purple & White.
Conference: Wisc. Intercol. Athl. Conf.
SID: Tom Fick, 414-472-1147.
AD: Willie Myers.

WITTENBERG

Springfield, OH 45501....III

Coach: Joe Fincham, Ohio 1988
Record: 2 Years, 18-2-0

1998 SCHEDULE

Baldwin-Wallace....*Sept. 12
Union (Ky.) ■....*Sept. 19
Earlham ■....Sept. 26
Allegheny ■....Oct. 3
Ohio Wesleyan....Oct. 10
Oberlin....Oct. 17
Case Reserve ■....Oct. 24
Wooster ■....Oct. 31
Denison....Nov. 7
Kenyon....Nov. 14

1997 RESULTS (9-1-0)

52 Bluffton....0
29 Allegheny....17
62 Kenyon....10
74 Oberlin....0
44 Wilmington (Ohio)....0
37 Ohio Wesleyan....12
57 Denison....14
49 Case Reserve....21
19 Wooster....21
50 Earlham....14
473 **109**

Nickname: Tigers.
Stadium: Edwards-Maurer (1994), 2,400 capacity. Artificial turf.
Colors: Red & White.
Conference: North Coast Athletic Conf.
SID: To be named, 513-327-6115.
AD: Carl Schraibman.

WOFFORD

Spartanburg, SC 29303....I-AA

Coach: Mike Ayers, Georgetown (Ky.) 1974
Record: 13 Years, 71-70-2

1998 SCHEDULE

Citadel ■....*Sept. 12
Ga. Southern....Sept. 19
Charleston So. ■....*Sept. 26
Chattanooga ■....Oct. 3
VMI....Oct. 10
Western Caro. ■....Oct. 17
Appalachian St....Oct. 24
Lehigh....Oct. 31
East Tenn. St....*Nov. 7
Furman ■....Nov. 14
Marshall....Nov. 21

1997 RESULTS (3-7-0)

23 VMI....13
7 Ga. Southern....22
17 Chattanooga....20
35 Morehead St....37
17 Western Caro....7
21 Appalachian St....26
3 Citadel....7
28 East Tenn. St....31
7 Furman....28
51 Charleston So....21
209 **212**

Nickname: Terriers.
Stadium: Gibbs (1996), 8,500 capacity. Natural turf.
Colors: Old Gold & Black.
Conference: Southern.
SID: Mark Cohen, 864-597-4093.
AD: David S. Wood.

WOOSTER

Wooster, OH 44691....III

Coach: Jim Barnes, Augustana (Ill.) 1981
Record: 3 Years, 21-9-0

1998 SCHEDULE

Grove City ■....Sept. 5
Kalamazoo....Sept. 12
Earlham....Sept. 19
Denison....Sept. 26
Oberlin ■....Oct. 10
Kenyon....Oct. 17
Allegheny ■....Oct. 24

Wittenberg .... Oct. 31
Case Reserve ■ .... Nov. 7
Ohio Wesleyan ■ .... Nov. 14

1997 RESULTS (9-1-0)

31 Centre 10
10 Grove City 3
45 Denison 22
21 Case Reserve 14
38 Earlham 0
27 Allegheny 28
47 Kenyon 3
77 Oberlin 28
21 Wittenberg 19
28 Ohio Wesleyan 14
345 **141**

Nickname: Fighting Scots.
Stadium: John P. Papp (1991), 4,500 capacity. Natural turf.
Colors: Black & Old Gold.
Conference: North Coast Athletic Conf.
SID: John Finn, 330-263-2374.
AD: Robert Malekoff.

WORCESTER ST.

Worcester, MA 01602 III

Coach: Brien Cullen, Worcester St. 1977
Record: 13 Years, 76-47-0

1998 SCHEDULE

Worcester Tech ■ .... Sept. 12
Mass.-Dartmouth .... Sept. 19
Bri'water (Mass.) ■ .... Sept. 26
Fitchburg St. .... Oct. 3
Salve Regina ■ .... Oct. 10
Mass. Maritime .... Oct. 17
Framingham St. ■ .... Oct. 24
MIT .... Oct. 31
Maine Maritime .... Nov. 7
Westfield St. ■ .... Nov. 14

1997 RESULTS (8-2-0)

13 Worcester Tech 21
25 Mass.-Dartmouth 16
31 Maine Maritime 6
34 Mass.-Boston 32
47 Fitchburg St. 9
44 Framingham St. 15
14 Westfield St. 19
23 Bri'water (Mass.) 6
33 Nichols 20
49 Mass. Maritime 28
313 **172**

ECAC III Playoff

13 Rensselaer 14

Nickname: Lancers.
Stadium: John Coughlin Memorial (1976), 2,500 capacity. Natural turf.
Colors: Royal Blue & Gold.
Conference: New England FB.
SID: Bruce Baker, 508-793-8128.
AD: Susan E. Chapman.

WORCESTER TECH

Worcester, MA 01609 III

Coach: Kevin Morris, Williams 1986
Record: 5 Years, 20-27-0

1998 SCHEDULE

Worcester St. .... Sept. 12
Union (N.Y.) ■ .... Sept. 19
Rensselaer .... Sept. 26
Merchant Marine ■ .... Oct. 3
Norwich .... Oct. 10
Springfield ■ .... *Oct. 24
Western Conn. St. .... Oct. 31
Coast Guard ■ .... Nov. 7
Plymouth St. .... Nov. 14

1997 RESULTS (4-6-0)

21 Worcester St. 13
20 Union (N.Y.) 27
24 MIT 23
16 Rensselaer 37
22 Norwich 26
19 Merchant Marine 22
49 Springfield 56
10 Western Conn. St. 2
0 Coast Guard 44
9 Plymouth St. 7
190 **257**

Nickname: Engineers.
Stadium: Alumni Field (1916), 2,800 capacity. Artificial turf.
Colors: Crimson & Gray.
Conference: Freedom FB.
SID: Geoff Hassard, 508-831-5328.
AD: Raymond R. Gilbert.

WYOMING

Laramie, WY 82071 .... I-A

Coach: Dana Dimel, Kansas St. 1986
Record: 1 Year, 7-6-0

1998 SCHEDULE

Montana St. ■ .... Sept. 12
Georgia .... Sept. 19
Louisiana Tech ■ .... Sept. 26
Utah ■ .... Oct. 3
Southern Methodist ■ .... Oct. 10
UNLV .... Oct. 17
Rice ■ .... Oct. 24
Texas Christian .... Oct. 31
Colorado St. .... Nov. 7
Air Force ■ .... Nov. 14
Tulsa .... Nov. 21

1997 RESULTS (7-6-0)

10 Ohio St. 24
56 Iowa St. 10
35 Hawaii 6
30 San Jose St. 10
19 Colorado 20
28 Montana 13
34 Nevada 30
7 Colorado St. 14
17 Southern Methodist 22
41 San Diego St. 17
35 UNLV 23
3 Air Force 14
7 Fresno St. 24
322 **227**

Nickname: Cowboys.
Stadium: War Memorial (1950), 33,500 capacity. Natural turf.
Colors: Brown & Yellow.
Conference: Western Athletic.
SID: Kevin McKinney, 307-766-2256.
AD: Lee Moon.

YALE

New Haven, CT 06520 .... I-AA

Coach: Jack Siedlecki, Union (N. Y.) 1974
Record: 10 Years, 57-30-2

1998 SCHEDULE

Brown .... Sept. 19
Connecticut ■ .... Sept. 26
Colgate ■ .... Oct. 3
Holy Cross ■ .... Oct. 10
Dartmouth .... Oct. 17
Columbia ■ .... Oct. 24
Pennsylvania .... Oct. 31
Cornell ■ .... Nov. 7
Princeton ■ .... Nov. 14
Harvard .... Nov. 21

1997 RESULTS (1-9-0)

14 Brown 52
0 Connecticut 28
34 Valparaiso 14
24 Bucknell 25
7 Dartmouth 21
10 Columbia 21
7 Pennsylvania 26
10 Cornell 37
0 Princeton 9
7 Harvard 17
113 **250**

Nickname: Elis, Bulldogs.
Stadium: Yale Bowl (1914), 60,000 capacity. Natural turf.
Colors: Yale Blue & White.
Conference: Ivy.
SID: Steve Conn, 203-432-1456.
AD: Thomas A. Beckett.

YOUNGSTOWN ST.

Youngstown, OH 44555 .... I-AA

Coach: Jim Tressel, Baldwin-Wallace 1975
Record: 12 Years, 108-46-2

1998 SCHEDULE

Clarion ■ .... *Sept. 3
Kent .... *Sept. 12
Indiana St. ■ .... *Sept. 19
Western Ill. .... Oct. 3
Southern Ill. ■ .... Oct. 10
Delaware ■ .... Oct. 17
New Haven ■ .... Oct. 24
Central Fla. .... *Oct. 31
Northern Iowa ■ .... Nov. 7
Illinois St. .... Nov. 14
Southwest Mo. St. .... Nov. 21

1997 RESULTS (9-2-0)

33 Slippery Rock 9
44 Kent 23
28 Boston U. 7
27 Hofstra 22
31 Indiana St. 0
52 Buffalo 17
32 Northern Iowa 35
13 Illinois St. 0
34 Southern Ill. 10
45 Southwest Mo. St. 13
21 Western Ill. 24
360 **160**

IAA Championship

28 Hampton 13
37 Villanova 34
25 Eastern Wash. 14
10 McNeese St. 9

Nickname: Penguins.
Stadium: Arnold D. Stambaugh (1982), 16,000 capacity. Artificial turf.
Colors: Red & White.
Conference: Gateway.
SID: Rocco Gasparro, 216-742-3192.
AD: James P. Tressel.

1998 Divisions I-A and I-AA Schedules by Date

This listing by dates includes all 1998 season games involving Divisions I-A and I-AA teams, as of printing deadline.

Neutral sites, indicated by footnote numbers, are listed at the end of each date. Asterisks (*) before the visiting team indicate night games. **Game dates are subject to change.**

SATURDAY, AUGUST 29

HOME	OPPONENT
Austin Peay	*Campbellsville
Michigan St.	Colorado St.
Nebraska	Louisiana Tech

SUNDAY, AUGUST 30

HOME	OPPONENT
Southern Cal	Purdue

MONDAY, AUGUST 31

HOME	OPPONENT
Florida St. [1]	Texas A&M

[1] East Rutherford, N. J.

THURSDAY, SEPTEMBER 3

HOME	OPPONENT
Auburn	*Virginia
Austin Peay	*Morehead St.
Chattanooga	*Samford
Delaware	*Massachusetts
Eastern Ill.	St. Joseph's (Ind.)
Eastern Mich.	*Northern Iowa
Hawaii	Arizona
North Caro. St.	*Ohio
Southeast Mo. St.	*Truman St.
Southwest Tex. St.	*Delta St.
Tennessee Tech	*Ky. Wesleyan
Towson	*Morgan St.
Weber St.	*Montana Tech
Western Ill.	*St. Cloud St.
Western Ky.	*Tenn.-Martin
Western Mich.	*Northern Ill.
Youngstown St.	*Clarion

FRIDAY, SEPTEMBER 4

HOME	OPPONENT
Albany (N.Y.)	*Central Conn. St.

SATURDAY, SEPTEMBER 5

HOME	OPPONENT
Air Force	Wake Forest
Akron	*Marshall
Alabama	Brigham Young
Alabama A&M	*Jacksonville St.
Angelo St.	*Sam Houston St.
Appalachian St.	*Liberty
Arizona St.	*Washington
Arkansas	*Southwestern La.
Bethune-Cookman [1]	Savannah St.
Boise St.	*Cal St. Northridge
Buffalo St.	Robert Morris
Butler	Albion
Cal Poly	*Northern Ariz.
California	Houston
Charleston So.	South Caro. St.
Cincinnati	*Tulane
Clemson	Furman
Colgate	Connecticut
Colorado St. [2]	*Colorado
Drake	Morningside
Duke	*Western Caro.
Duquesne	*Bucknell
Eastern Ky.	Kentucky St.
Florida	*Citadel
Florida A&M	*Hampton
Ga. Southern	*Elon
Georgia	Kent
Georgia Tech	Boston College
Grambling	*Alcorn St.
Hofstra	Delaware St.
Holy Cross	Fairfield
Howard [3]	Jackson St.
Idaho	Eastern Wash.
Iowa	Central Mich.
Iowa St.	*Texas Christian
Kansas	Oklahoma St.
Kansas St.	*Indiana St.
Louisiana Tech	*Central Fla.
Louisville	Kentucky
Maryland	*James Madison
McNeese St.	*Southeastern Okla.
Miami (Fla.)	*East Tenn. St.
Middle Tenn. St.	*Tennessee St.
Minnesota	Arkansas St.
Mississippi	Memphis
Mississippi St.	*Vanderbilt
Mississippi Val.	*Ark.-Pine Bluff
Missouri	*Bowling Green
Monmouth	Dayton
Montana St.	Fort Lewis
Murray St.	*Southern Ill.
Nebraska	UAB
New Mexico	*Idaho St.
Norfolk St.	*Virginia St.
North Caro.	*Miami (Ohio)
North Caro. A&T [4]	N.C. Central
Northeast La.	*Nicholls St.
Northeastern	New Hampshire
Northwestern	UNLV
Northwestern St.	*Southern U.
Notre Dame	Michigan
Oklahoma	*North Texas
Oregon	Michigan St.
Oregon St.	Nevada
Penn St.	Southern Miss.
Pittsburgh	Villanova
Rhode Island	William & Mary
Rice	*Southern Methodist
Rutgers	*Richmond
Sacred Heart	*St. John's (N.Y.)
San Diego	*Azusa Pacific
San Diego St.	*Wisconsin
South Caro.	*Ball St.
South Fla.	*Slippery Rock
St. Mary's (Cal.)	Cal St. Sacramento
Stanford	San Jose St.
Stephen F. Austin	*Montana
Syracuse	Tennessee
Texas	*New Mexico St.
Texas Tech	*UTEP
Toledo	*Temple
Troy St.	*Alabama St.
Tulsa	*Southwest Mo. St.
Utah St.	*Utah
VMI	Lenoir-Rhyne
Valparaiso	Tri-State
Virginia Tech	East Caro.
Washington St.	Illinois
West Va.	*Ohio St.

[1] Jacksonville, Fla.
[2] Denver, Colo.
[3] Columbus, Ohio
[4] Raleigh, N. C.

THURSDAY, SEPTEMBER 10

HOME	OPPONENT
Wake Forest	*Navy

SATURDAY, SEPTEMBER 12

HOME	OPPONENT
Alabama A&M	*Grambling
Alabama St.	*Texas Southern
Ark.-Pine Bluff	*Southern U.
Army	Miami (Ohio)
Ball St.	Eastern Mich.
Boise St.	*Washington St.
Boston College	Rutgers
Brigham Young	*Arizona St.
Bucknell	St. Mary's (Cal.)
Buffalo	*Lock Haven
Cal St. Sacramento	*Cal Poly
California	Nebraska
Central Conn. St.	St. John's (N.Y.)
Central Fla.	*Eastern Ill.
Central Mich.	Western Ill.
Cincinnati	Miami (Fla.)
Clemson	Virginia Tech
Colorado	Fresno St.
Dayton	Robert Morris
East Caro.	Chattanooga
East Tenn. St.	*Appalachian St.
Eastern Wash.	*Portland St.
Elon	*Delaware St.
Fairfield	Iona
Florida	*Northeast La.
Furman	South Caro. St.
Ga. Southern	Jacksonville St.
Gannon	Canisius
Georgetown	Marist
Georgia Tech	*New Mexico St.
Houston	*Minnesota
Howard	Hampton
Howard Payne	*Prairie View
Illinois	*Middle Tenn. St.
Illinois St.	*St. Francis (Ill.)
Indiana	*Western Mich.
Iowa	Iowa St.
Jacksonville	Davidson
James Madison	*Hofstra
Kansas St.	Northern Ill.
Kent	*Youngstown St.
Kentucky	Eastern Ky.
LSU	*Arkansas St.
La Salle	St. Peter's
Lehigh	Fordham
Maine	*New Hampshire
Marshall	*Troy St.
Memphis	Mississippi St.
Michigan	Syracuse
Michigan St.	*Notre Dame
Mississippi	*Auburn
Missouri	*Kansas
Monmouth	Towson
Montana	Southern Utah
Morehead St.	*Butler
Morgan St.	Bethune-Cookman
Murray St.	*Western Ky.
Nevada	Colorado St.
New Mexico	*Utah St.
Nicholls St.	*Mississippi Val.
Norfolk St.	*Florida A&M
North Caro. A&T	Winston-Salem
North Caro. St.	Florida St.
North Texas [1]	*Texas Tech
Northeastern	Lafayette
Northern Ariz.	*Southwest Tex. St.
Northern Iowa	*McNeese St.
Northwestern	Duke
Ohio St.	Toledo
Oregon St.	Baylor
Penn St.	Bowling Green
Presbyterian	Charleston So.
Purdue	Rice
Richmond	Massachusetts
Sam Houston St.	*Chadron St.
Samford	*Austin Peay
San Jose St.	*Idaho
Siena	Sacred Heart
South Caro.	*Georgia

South Fla.	*Valparaiso
Southeast Mo. St.	*Indiana St.
Southern Cal	San Diego St.
Southern Methodist	*Tulane
Southwest Mo. St.	*Harding
Southwestern La.	*Northwestern St.
St. Ambrose	*Drake
St. Francis (Pa.)	Duquesne
Stanford	Arizona
Stephen F. Austin	*Tarleton St.
Temple	*Akron
Tenn.-Martin	*Southern Ill.
Tennessee St. [2]	*Jackson St.
Texas A&M	*Louisiana Tech
Texas Christian	*Oklahoma
Tulsa	*Oklahoma St.
UCLA	Texas
UNLV	*Air Force
UTEP	*Oregon
Utah	*Louisville
Villanova	Delaware
Virginia	Maryland
Wagner	San Diego
Weber St.	*Humboldt St.
William & Mary	VMI
Wisconsin	Ohio
Wofford	*Citadel
Wyoming	Montana St.

[1] Irving, Tex.
[2] Memphis, Tenn.

THURSDAY, SEPTEMBER 17

HOME	OPPONENT
Air Force	*Colorado St.

SATURDAY, SEPTEMBER 19

HOME	OPPONENT
Alabama A&M	*Mississippi Val.
Albany (N.Y.)	*Monmouth
Alcorn St.	*Alabama St.
Arizona	*Iowa
Arizona St.	*North Texas
Ark.-Pine Bluff [1]	Howard
Arkansas [2]	*Southern Methodist
Arkansas St.	Southwest Mo. St.
Army	Cincinnati
Auburn	LSU
Austin Peay	*Dayton
Baylor	*North Caro. St.
Boise St.	*Portland St.
Boston College	Temple
Brown	Yale
Bucknell	Fordham
Butler	St. Francis (Pa.)
Canisius	St. Peter's
Charleston So.	North Greenville
Chattanooga	*Troy St.
Chowan	Jacksonville
Citadel	*Western Caro.
Colorado	Utah St.
Columbia	Harvard
Connecticut	Maine
Dartmouth	Pennsylvania
Delaware	West Chester
Drake	Wis.-La Crosse
East Tenn. St.	*VMI
Elon	Western Ill.
Florida St.	Duke
Furman	*Samford
Ga. Southern	Wofford
Georgetown	Holy Cross
Georgia	Wyoming
Hampton	North Caro. A&T
Houston	UCLA
Idaho St.	*Weber St.
Illinois	Louisville
Iona	La Salle
Iowa St.	Ball St.
Jackson St.	*Florida A&M
Jacksonville St.	*Middle Tenn. St.
James Madison	Villanova
Kansas	*Illinois St.
Kansas St.	Texas
Kentucky	Indiana
Lafayette	Buffalo
Langston	*Texas Southern
Liberty	*South Fla.
Louisiana Tech	*Southwestern La.
Marist	Fairfield
Miami (Fla.)	*Virginia Tech
Michigan	Eastern Mich.
Minnesota	Memphis
Montana	Cal Poly
Montana St.	Western Wash.
Navy	*Kent
New Hampshire	East Stroudsburg
New Mexico St.	*New Mexico
Norfolk St.	*Delaware St.
Northeast La.	*Stephen F. Austin
Northern Ariz.	*Cal St. Northridge
Northern Ill.	*Eastern Ill.
Northwestern St.	*Henderson St.
Ohio	East Caro.
Ohio St.	Missouri
Oklahoma	*California
Oklahoma St.	*Mississippi St.
Oregon	San Jose St.
Pittsburgh	Penn St.
Prairie View	*Southern U.
Princeton	Cornell
Purdue	Central Fla.
Rhode Island	Richmond
Rice	*Northwestern
Sacred Heart	Wagner
Sam Houston St.	*Texas A&M-Kingsville
San Diego	*Redlands
Sewanee	Davidson
Siena	Duquesne
South Caro.	*Marshall
Southeast Mo. St.	*Murray St.
Southern Cal	Oregon St.
Southern Ill.	Northern Iowa
Southern Miss.	Texas A&M
Southern Utah	*McNeese St.
Southwest Tex. St.	*Hofstra
St. Mary's (Cal.)	Lehigh
Stanford	North Caro.
Syracuse	Rutgers
Tennessee	*Florida
Texas Tech	*Fresno St.
Toledo	*Western Mich.
Towson	Colgate
UAB	*Tennessee Tech
UC Davis	*Cal St. Sacramento
Utah	*Hawaii
Valparaiso	Morehead St.
Vanderbilt	Mississippi
Virginia	Clemson
Washington	Brigham Young
Washington St.	Idaho
West Va.	Maryland
Western Ky.	*Eastern Ky.
William & Mary	Northeastern
Wisconsin	UNLV
Youngstown St.	*Indiana St.

[1] St. Louis, Mo.
[2] Little Rock, Ark.

THURSDAY, SEPTEMBER 24

HOME	OPPONENT
Indiana St.	*St. Joseph's (Ind.)
San Diego St.	Arizona

SATURDAY, SEPTEMBER 26

HOME	OPPONENT
Akron	*Ball St.
Alcorn St.	Ark.-Pine Bluff
Appalachian St.	Citadel
Arizona St.	*Oregon St.
Arkansas	*Alabama
Bethune-Cookman	*Virginia St.
Bowling Green	Central Fla.
Brigham Young	Murray St.
Bucknell	Columbia
Cal Lutheran	San Diego
Cal Poly	*St. Mary's (Cal.)
Cal St. Northridge	Eastern Wash.
California	Washington St.
Canisius	Siena
Central Mich.	Kent
Chattanooga	*Ga. Southern
Cincinnati	*Indiana
Clemson	Wake Forest
Colgate	Harvard
Colorado	Baylor
Colorado St.	UNLV
Davidson	Emory & Henry
Dayton	*Morehead St.
Delaware	New Hampshire
Delaware Valley	La Salle
Duke	Virginia
Eastern Ill.	Tennessee Tech
Eastern Mich.	Marshall
Fairfield	Georgetown
Florida	Kentucky
Florida St.	Southern Cal
Fresno St.	*Nevada
Hawaii	*Arkansas St.
Holy Cross	Cornell
Illinois	Iowa
Illinois St.	Southern Ill.
Iowa St.	Texas Tech
Jackson St.	*Mississippi Val.
James Madison	*Elon
Kansas St.	Northeast La.
LSU	*Idaho
Lafayette	Brown
Langston [1]	*Prairie View
Lehigh	Princeton
Liberty	*Glenville St.
Louisville	Boston College
Maine	Dartmouth
Maryland	*Temple
Massachusetts	Buffalo
McNeese St.	*Ark.-Monticello
Miami (Fla.)	UCLA
Miami (Ohio)	Toledo
Michigan	Michigan St.
Middle Tenn. St.	*Eastern Ky.
Mississippi Col.	Jacksonville
Montana St.	Cal St. Sacramento
Morgan St.	Norfolk St.
Nebraska	Washington
New Mexico St.	*UTEP
Nicholls St.	*Jacksonville St.
North Caro.	*Georgia Tech
North Caro. A&T	Fayetteville St.
Northeastern	Rhode Island
Northern Ariz.	Western St. (Colo.)
Notre Dame	Purdue
Oregon	Stanford
Pennsylvania	Richmond
Portland St.	*Idaho St.
Quincy	Drake
Robert Morris	Central Conn. St.
Rutgers	*Army
Sacred Heart	Iona
San Jose St.	*New Mexico
South Caro.	*Mississippi St.
South Caro. St.	*Johnson Smith
Southeast Mo. St.	*Tenn.-Martin
Southern Methodist	Mississippi
Southern Miss.	*Southwestern La.
Southern U.	*Alabama St.
Southwest Tex. St.	*Northwestern St.
St. Francis (Pa.)	Wagner
St. John's (N.Y.)	Duquesne
St. Peter's	*Marist
Stephen F. Austin	*Northern Iowa
Tennessee	*Houston
Texas	Rice
Texas A&M	*North Texas
Texas Christian	*Air Force
Texas Southern	*Howard
Towson	Fordham
Troy St.	*Samford
Tulane	*Navy
UAB	*Kansas
Utah	*Boise St.
Utah St.	*Sam Houston St.

VMI	Furman
Villanova	William & Mary
Virginia Tech	Pittsburgh
Weber St.	*Montana
Wesley	Butler
West Va.	Tulsa
Western Caro.	*East Tenn. St.
Western Ill.	Southern Utah
Western Ky.	*Austin Peay
Western Mich.	*Ohio
Wisconsin	Northwestern
Wofford	*Charleston So.
Wyoming	Louisiana Tech
Yale	Connecticut

[1] Oklahoma City, Okla.

THURSDAY, OCTOBER 1

HOME	OPPONENT
Jacksonville St.	Stephen F. Austin
North Caro. St.	Syracuse

SATURDAY, OCTOBER 3

HOME	OPPONENT
Air Force	New Mexico
Alabama	Florida
Alabama St.	*Ark.-Pine Bluff
Arkansas [1]	*Kentucky
Arkansas St.	New Mexico St.
Auburn	Tennessee
Ball St.	Northern Ill.
Bowling Green	Ohio
Butler	Dayton
Cal Poly	UC Davis
Cal St. Northridge	Southern Utah
Cal St. Sacramento	*Weber St.
Cornell	Buffalo
Dartmouth	Lafayette
Davidson	*Guilford
Delaware	Northeastern
Delaware St.	Florida A&M
Drake	Valparaiso
Duquesne	Fairfield
East Caro.	Army
Eastern Ill.	Southeast Mo. St.
Eastern Wash.	*Northern Ariz.
Fordham	Princeton
Fresno St.	*Brigham Young
Furman	Western Caro.
Ga. Southern	VMI
Georgia Tech	Duke
Grambling [2]	*Prairie View
Harvard	Lehigh
Hawaii	*Southern Methodist
Hofstra	Massachusetts
Holy Cross	Towson
Houston	Memphis
Idaho	Idaho St.
Indiana	Wisconsin
Indiana St.	Illinois St.
Iona	Canisius
Iowa	Michigan
Jackson St.	Texas Southern
Jacksonville	Austin Peay
Kansas	Texas A&M
Kent	*Eastern Mich.
LSU	*Georgia
La Salle	Monmouth
Liberty	*Charleston So.
Louisiana Tech	Boise St.
Louisville	Cincinnati
Maine	Villanova
Marist	St. John's (N.Y.)
Marshall	*Miami (Ohio)
Maryland	Florida St.
Michigan St.	Central Mich.
Mississippi	South Caro.
Missouri	Northwestern St.
Montana	Portland St.
Morehead St.	*Elon
Morehouse	Alcorn St.
Murray St.	Tenn.-Martin
Navy	West Va.
New Hampshire	Connecticut
North Caro.	Clemson
North Caro. A&T	Norfolk St.
Northern Iowa	*Southwest Mo. St.
Northwestern	Illinois
Notre Dame	Stanford
Ohio St.	Penn St.
Oklahoma	*Colorado
Oklahoma St. [3]	Nebraska
Pennsylvania	Bucknell
Pittsburgh	Akron
Prairie View [4]	*Grambling
Purdue	Minnesota
Rhode Island	Brown
Richmond	James Madison
Rutgers	Miami (Fla.)
Sam Houston St.	*Troy St.
Samford	Nicholls St.
San Diego	*Central Conn. St.
Siena	Georgetown
South Caro. St.	*Morgan St.
South Fla.	*Citadel
Southern Cal	Arizona St.
Southern Ill.	Southwest Tex. St.
Southern U.	*Mississippi Val.
St. Francis (Pa.)	Sacred Heart
St. Mary's (Cal.)	Columbia
Temple	William & Mary
Tennessee St.	Alabama A&M
Tennessee Tech	Middle Tenn. St.
Texas	Iowa St.
Texas Christian	*Vanderbilt
Texas Tech	*Baylor
Toledo	*Central Fla.
Tulane	*Southern Miss.
Tulsa	San Diego St.
UAB	*Southwestern La.
UCLA	Washington St.
UNLV	*Nevada
UTEP	*Colorado St.
Utah St.	*Oregon St.
Virginia	San Jose St.
Wagner	Robert Morris
Wake Forest	*Appalachian St.
Washington	*Arizona
Western Ill.	Youngstown St.
Western Ky.	*New Haven
Western Mich.	*Northeast La.
Wofford	Chattanooga
Wyoming	Utah
Yale	Colgate

[1] Little Rock, Ark.
[2] Dallas, Tex.
[3] Kansas City, Mo.
[4] Dallas, Tex.

THURSDAY, OCTOBER 8

HOME	OPPONENT
Boston College	*Virginia Tech
Nicholls St.	*Sam Houston St.

SATURDAY, OCTOBER 10

HOME	OPPONENT
Air Force	Navy
Alabama	Mississippi
Alabama A&M	*Southern U.
Alabama St. [1]	*Jackson St.
Appalachian St.	Furman
Arizona	*UCLA
Arizona St.	Notre Dame
Arkansas St.	Idaho
Baylor	*Kansas
Bethune-Cookman	Delaware St.
Boise St.	*North Texas
Brigham Young	UNLV
Buffalo	Morgan St.
Butler	San Diego
Cal St. Northridge	Montana
Catholic	La Salle
Central Conn. St.	St. Francis (Pa.)
Central Fla.	*Northern Ill.
Charleston So.	Newberry
Citadel	East Tenn. St.
Clemson	Maryland
Colgate	Dartmouth
Colorado	Kansas St.
Colorado St.	Tulsa
Columbia	Lehigh
Connecticut	Hofstra
Davidson	Wash. & Lee
Dayton	Drake
Duquesne	Marist
East Caro.	UAB
Eastern Ky.	*Tennessee St.
Eastern Mich.	*Central Mich.
Eastern Wash.	Western Wash.
Florida	LSU
Florida A&M	North Caro. A&T
Fordham	Pennsylvania
Georgetown	Canisius
Georgia	Tennessee
Hampton	Liberty
Harvard	Cornell
Houston	Army
Illinois	Ohio St.
Iona	Siena
Iowa	Northwestern
Iowa St.	Missouri
Jacksonville	Methodist
Kent	Akron
Kentucky	*South Caro.
LIU-C.W. Post	Monmouth
Maine	Rhode Island
Massachusetts	James Madison
McNeese St.	*Jacksonville St.
Memphis	*Arkansas
Miami (Fla.)	Florida St.
Miami (Ohio)	Bowling Green
Michigan St.	Indiana
Middle Tenn. St.	*Murray St.
Minnesota	Penn St.
Mississippi St.	*Auburn
Mississippi Val.	*Grambling
Nevada	New Mexico St.
New Hampshire	Richmond
New Mexico	*UTEP
Norfolk St.	South Caro. St.
North Caro.	Pittsburgh
North Caro. St.	Georgia Tech
Northeast La.	*Louisiana Tech
Northeastern	Villanova
Northern Ariz.	Idaho St.
Northern Iowa	*Illinois St.
Ohio	Marshall
Oklahoma [2]	Texas
Portland St.	*Cal St. Sacramento
Prairie View	Alcorn St.
Princeton	Brown
Robert Morris	Valparaiso
Samford	Tenn.-Martin
San Diego St.	*Hawaii
San Jose St.	*Rice
South Fla.	*Elon
Southern Cal	California
Southern Miss.	Louisville
Southern Utah	St. Mary's (Cal.)
Southwest Mo. St.	Western Ill.
Stanford	Oregon St.
Syracuse	Cincinnati
Temple	West Va.
Tennessee Tech	Southeast Mo. St.
Texas A&M	Nebraska
Texas Christian	*Fresno St.
Texas Southern	*Ark.-Pine Bluff
Texas Tech	*Oklahoma St.
Toledo	Ball St.
Towson	Lafayette
VMI	Wofford
Vanderbilt	*Western Mich.
Wagner	St. Peter's
Wake Forest	*Duke
Washington	Utah St.
Washington St.	Oregon
Weber St.	*Montana St.
Western Caro.	*Ga. Southern
William & Mary	Delaware
Wisconsin	*Purdue
Wyoming	Southern Methodist

Yale	Holy Cross
Youngstown St.	Southern Ill.

[1] Mobile, Ala.
[2] Dallas, Tex.

THURSDAY, OCTOBER 15

HOME	OPPONENT
Northwestern St.	*McNeese St.

FRIDAY, OCTOBER 16

HOME	OPPONENT
St. Peter's	Siena

SATURDAY, OCTOBER 17

HOME	OPPONENT
Alcorn St.	Texas Southern
Army	Southern Miss.
Austin Peay	Charleston So.
Ball St.	Miami (Ohio)
Baylor	*Texas A&M
Boise St.	*Weber St.
Boston College	Syracuse
Brown	Fordham
Buffalo	*Canisius
Cal St. Sacramento	*Cal St. Northridge
Central Conn. St.	Wagner
Chattanooga	*VMI
Colorado	Texas Tech
Connecticut	Massachusetts
Cornell	Bucknell
Dartmouth	Yale
Dayton	*St. Joseph's (Ind.)
Delaware St.	Liberty
Eastern Ill.	Illinois St.
Eastern Ky.	Murray St.
Florida	Auburn
Florida A&M [1]	Howard
Florida St.	Clemson
Furman	Citadel
Ga. Southern	Appalachian St.
Georgia	Vanderbilt
Georgia Tech	Virginia
Grambling [2]	*Ark.-Pine Bluff
Greensboro	Jacksonville
Hampton	Norfolk St.
Harvard	Holy Cross
Hawaii	*Brigham Young
Hofstra	Rhode Island
Idaho St.	Eastern Wash.
Illinois	Wisconsin
Indiana	Iowa
Indiana St.	Southwest Mo. St.
Jacksonville St.	Samford
James Madison	William & Mary
Kansas St.	Oklahoma St.
LSU	*Kentucky
La Salle	Bryant
Lafayette	Princeton
Lehigh	Towson
Louisiana Tech	*UAB
Maine	Richmond
Marist	Iona
Marshall	*Kent
Maryland	Wake Forest
Memphis	*Cincinnati
Methodist	Davidson
Mississippi St.	East Tenn. St.
Mississippi Val.	Albany St. (Ga.)
Missouri	Oklahoma
Monmouth	St. Francis (Pa.)
Montana	Northern Ariz.
Montana St.	Portland St.
Morehead St.	Thomas More
Navy	Colgate
Nebraska	Kansas
New Hampshire	Northeastern
New Mexico	*San Diego St.
New Mexico St.	*Colorado St.
North Caro. A&T	Morgan St.
North Caro. St.	Duke
North Texas	*Nevada
Northern Ill.	Central Mich.
Northern Iowa	Cal Poly
Northwestern	*Michigan
Ohio	Akron
Ohio St.	Minnesota
Oregon St.	Arizona
Penn St.	Purdue
Pennsylvania	Columbia
Pittsburgh	Rutgers
Prairie View	*Alabama St.
Rice	Tulsa
Robert Morris	Sacred Heart
San Diego	Fairfield
South Caro.	Arkansas
South Caro. St.	Bethune-Cookman
South Fla.	*Western Ky.
Southeast Mo. St.	Tennessee St.
Southern Ill.	Western Ill.
Southern Methodist	Texas Christian
Southern U.	*Jackson St.
Southern Utah	Fort Lewis
Southwest Tex. St.	Nicholls St.
Southwestern La.	Arkansas St.
St. John's (N.Y.)	Georgetown
Stephen F. Austin	Troy St.
Tenn.-Martin	Tennessee Tech
Toledo	*Bowling Green
Tulane	Louisville
UCLA	Oregon
UNLV	Wyoming
UTEP	*San Jose St.
Utah	Fresno St.
Utah St.	Idaho
Valparaiso	Butler
Virginia Tech	Temple
Washington	California
Washington St.	Southern Cal
Western Mich.	Eastern Mich.
Wofford	Western Caro.
Youngstown St.	Delaware

[1] Jacksonville, Fla.
[2] Shreveport, La.

THURSDAY, OCTOBER 22

HOME	OPPONENT
Arizona St.	*Stanford
Troy St.	*Southwest Tex. St.

FRIDAY, OCTOBER 23

HOME	OPPONENT
St. John's (N.Y.)	*Siena

SATURDAY, OCTOBER 24

HOME	OPPONENT
Akron	Toledo
Alcorn St.	Southern U.
Appalachian St.	Wofford
Arizona	Northeast La.
Auburn	Louisiana Tech
Boise St.	*Utah St.
Boston College	Navy
Bowling Green	Kent
Brigham Young	San Jose St.
Brown	Pennsylvania
Bucknell	Lafayette
Cal Poly	Western N. Mex.
Cal St. Northridge	Montana St.
California	UCLA
Catawba	Butler
Central Mich.	Western Mich.
Cincinnati	Miami (Ohio)
Citadel	Ga. Southern
Clinch Valley	Jacksonville
Colorado St.	Texas Christian
Connecticut	Rhode Island
Cornell	Dartmouth
Davidson	Randolph-Macon
Drake	San Diego
Duke	Clemson
Duquesne	Georgetown
East Tenn. St.	Furman
Eastern Mich.	*Northern Ill.
Eastern Wash.	Montana
Fairfield	Canisius
Fordham	Colgate
Fresno St.	*UTEP
Georgia Tech	Florida St.
Grambling	Jackson St.
Hawaii	*New Mexico
Hofstra	South Fla.
Holy Cross	Lehigh
Howard	North Caro. A&T
Idaho	Nevada
Idaho St.	*Southern Utah
Iona	St. Peter's
Iowa	Wisconsin
Jacksonville St.	Sam Houston St.
James Madison	Maine
Kansas	Colorado
Kansas St.	Iowa St.
Kentucky	*Georgia
LSU	*Mississippi St.
Langston	*Ark.-Pine Bluff
Liberty	Buffalo
Louisville	Memphis
Marshall	Ball St.
Massachusetts	Villanova
McNeese St.	*Stephen F. Austin
Michigan	Indiana
Middle Tenn. St.	*Eastern Ill.
Minnesota	Michigan St.
Mississippi	Arkansas St.
Morgan St.	Delaware St.
Nebraska	Missouri
Nicholls St.	*Northwestern St.
Norfolk St.	Virginia Union
North Texas	*Houston
Northeastern	Richmond
Northern Ariz.	Cal St. Sacramento
Northwestern	Ohio St.
Notre Dame	Army
Okla. Panhandle St.	Prairie View
Oklahoma St.	*Oklahoma
Oregon	Southern Cal
Portland St.	*Weber St.
Princeton	Harvard
Purdue	Illinois
Robert Morris	Monmouth
Rutgers	Tulane
Sacred Heart	Central Conn. St.
San Diego St.	*Utah
South Caro. St.	Hampton
Southern Ill.	Indiana St.
Southern Methodist	UNLV
Southern Miss.	East Caro.
Southwest Mo. St.	Southeast Mo. St.
Southwestern La.	*Central Fla.
St. Francis (Pa.)	La Salle
Tennessee	Alabama
Tennessee St.	Tenn.-Martin
Tennessee Tech	Eastern Ky.
Texas	Baylor
Texas A&M	Texas Tech
Texas Southern	*Mississippi Val.
Tulsa	Air Force
UAB	*Virginia Tech
UC Davis	St. Mary's (Cal.)
VMI	Morehead St.
Valparaiso	Dayton
Vanderbilt	*South Caro.
Virginia	North Caro. St.
Wagner	Marist
Wake Forest	North Caro.
Washington	Oregon St.
West Va.	Miami (Fla.)
Western Caro.	Chattanooga
Western Ill.	Illinois St.
Western Ky.	Elon
William & Mary	New Hampshire
Wyoming	Rice
Yale	Columbia
Youngstown St.	New Haven

THURSDAY, OCTOBER 29

HOME	OPPONENT
Brigham Young	*San Diego St.
Southwest Tex. St.	*Stephen F. Austin

SATURDAY, OCTOBER 31

HOME	OPPONENT
Air Force	Southern Methodist
Alabama	Southern Miss.
Arizona	*Oregon
Auburn	Arkansas
Bowling Green	Marshall
Bucknell	Colgate
Buffalo	Western Ill.
Cal St. Sacramento	Eastern Wash.
Canisius	St. John's (N.Y.)
Central Fla.	*Youngstown St.
Central Mich.	Akron
Charleston So.	South Fla.
Chattanooga	Appalachian St.
Citadel	Hofstra
Clemson	North Caro. St.
Columbia	Princeton
Cornell	Brown
Cumberland (Tenn.)	Austin Peay
Dartmouth	Harvard
Delaware	Maine
Delaware St.	South Caro. St.
Drake	Butler
Duquesne	Iona
East Caro.	Houston
Eastern Ill.	Tennessee St.
Elon	Liberty
Florida [1]	Georgia
Florida A&M	*Morgan St.
Florida St.	North Caro.
Fordham	Villanova
Ga. Southern	East Tenn. St.
Georgetown	St. Peter's
Hampden-Sydney	Davidson
Hampton	William & Mary
Howard	Norfolk St.
Illinois St.	Southern Utah
Indiana	Ohio St.
Indiana St.	Northern Iowa
Kansas	Kansas St.
Kent	Western Mich.
La Salle	Waynesburg
Lafayette	Holy Cross
Lehigh	Wofford
Louisiana Tech	Nicholls St.
Louisville	Western Ky.
Marist	St. Francis (Pa.)
Maryland [2]	Georgia Tech
Memphis	Arkansas St.
Miami (Fla.)	Boston College
Miami (Ohio)	Ohio
Michigan St.	Northwestern
Minnesota	Michigan
Mississippi	LSU
Mississippi Val.	Prairie View
Monmouth	Sacred Heart
Montana	Idaho St.
Montana St.	Northern Ariz.
Morehead St.	Bethel (Tenn.)
Murray St.	Tennessee Tech
Nebraska	Texas
Nevada	Boise St.
New Hampshire	Massachusetts
New Mexico	Fresno St.
New Mexico St.	Utah St.
North Caro. A&T	Bethune-Cookman
North Texas	*Idaho
Northeast La.	*UAB
Northeastern	Connecticut
Northern Ill.	Toledo
Northwestern St.	Troy St.
Notre Dame	Baylor
Oklahoma	Iowa St.
Oklahoma St.	Texas A&M
Oregon St.	California
Penn St.	Illinois
Pennsylvania	Yale
Portland St.	*Cal Poly
Purdue	Iowa
Rhode Island	James Madison
Rice	Colorado St.
Rutgers	Temple
Sam Houston St.	McNeese St.
Samford	Mars Hill
San Diego	*Valparaiso
San Jose St.	Utah
Siena	Fairfield
South Caro.	Tennessee
Southeast Mo. St.	Middle Tenn. St.
Southern Cal	Washington
Southwest Mo. St.	Southern Ill.
Stony Brook	Wagner
Syracuse	Pittsburgh
Tenn.-Martin	Eastern Ky.
Texas Christian	Wyoming
Texas Southern	*Grambling
Texas Tech	Missouri
Towson	St. Mary's (Cal.)
Tulane	*Southwestern La.
UCLA	Stanford
UNLV	Tulsa
UTEP	Hawaii
VMI	Western Caro.
Vanderbilt	Duke
Virginia Tech	West Va.
Wake Forest	Virginia
Washington St.	Arizona St.
Weber St.	Cal St. Northridge

[1] Jacksonville, Fla.
[2] Baltimore, Md.

FRIDAY, NOVEMBER 6

HOME	OPPONENT
St. John's (N.Y.)	Fairfield

SATURDAY, NOVEMBER 7

HOME	OPPONENT
Appalachian St.	VMI
Arizona	*Washington St.
Arizona St.	California
Ark.-Pine Bluff	Prairie View
Arkansas	Mississippi
Arkansas St.	Louisiana Tech
Army	Air Force
Auburn	Central Fla.
Austin Peay	Tusculum
Ball St.	Western Mich.
Baylor	Kansas St.
Boston College	Notre Dame
Bowling Green	Akron
Brigham Young	New Mexico
Bryant	Siena
Cal St. Northridge	Portland St.
Charleston So.	Morehead St.
Cincinnati	East Caro.
Citadel	Chattanooga
Colorado St.	Wyoming
Connecticut	Delaware
Dartmouth	Columbia
Davidson	Centre
Dayton	Towson
Delaware St.	North Caro. A&T
East Tenn. St.	*Wofford
Eastern Ill.	Murray St.
Eastern Ky.	Southeast Mo. St.
Eastern Wash.	Montana St.
Florida St.	Virginia
Fordham	Lafayette
Furman	Ga. Southern
Georgetown	Iona
Grambling	Alabama St.
Hampton	Bethune-Cookman
Harvard	Brown
Hawaii	*San Jose St.
Hofstra	New Hampshire
Holy Cross	Bucknell
Houston	Southern Miss.
Idaho St.	*Cal St. Sacramento
Illinois	Indiana
Illinois St.	Southwest Mo. St.
Iowa St.	Nebraska
Jacksonville	La Salle
Jacksonville St.	Northwestern St.
James Madison	Northeastern
Kansas	North Texas
Kentucky	Mississippi St.
LSU	*Alabama
Lehigh	Colgate
Liberty	Norfolk St.
Marist	Canisius
Marshall	Central Mich.
McNeese St.	*Southwest Tex. St.
Memphis	Tulane
Michigan	Penn St.
Mississippi Val.	Alcorn St.
Missouri	Colorado
Navy	Rutgers
New Mexico St.	*Boise St.
North Caro.	Maryland
North Caro. St.	Wake Forest
Northeast La.	*Southwestern La.
Northern Ariz.	Weber St.
Northern Ill.	Miami (Ohio)
Northwestern	Purdue
Ohio	Eastern Mich.
Ohio St.	Michigan St.
Oregon	Washington
Oregon St.	UCLA
Pittsburgh	Temple
Princeton	Pennsylvania
Quincy	Butler
Rhode Island	Massachusetts
Samford	Morgan St.
San Diego St.	*Fresno St.
South Caro. St.	Howard
South Fla.	*Cumberland (Tenn.)
Southern Conn. St.	Central Conn. St.
Southern Methodist	Tulsa
Southern U.	*Florida A&M
Southern Utah	Cal Poly
St. Francis (Pa.)	Robert Morris
St. Joseph's (Ind.)	Valparaiso
St. Mary's (Cal.)	Drake
St. Peter's	Duquesne
Stanford	Southern Cal
Stephen F. Austin	Sam Houston St.
Tenn.-Martin	Middle Tenn. St.
Tennessee	UAB
Tennessee Tech	*Tennessee St.
Texas	Oklahoma St.
Texas A&M	Oklahoma
Texas Christian	Rice
Troy St.	*Nicholls St.
Utah	UTEP
Utah St.	Nevada
Vanderbilt	Florida
Villanova	Richmond
Wagner	Monmouth
West Va.	*Syracuse
Western Caro.	Elon
Western Ill.	Indiana St.
Western Ky.	Southern Ill.
Wisconsin	Minnesota
Yale	Cornell
Youngstown St.	Northern Iowa

THURSDAY, NOVEMBER 12

HOME	OPPONENT
Clemson	*Georgia Tech

SATURDAY, NOVEMBER 14

HOME	OPPONENT
Akron	Eastern Mich.
Alabama A&M	Alcorn St.
Alabama St.	Mississippi Val.
Arkansas St.	Northeast La.
Army	Tulane
Auburn	Georgia
Baylor	Oklahoma

Bethune-Cookman	Norfolk St.
Bridgewater (Va.)	Davidson
Brown	Dartmouth
Butler	Lindenwood
Cal St. Sacramento	Montana
California	Arizona
Canisius	Duquesne
Central Fla.	Ball St.
Charleston So.	Bethel (Tenn.)
Chattanooga	East Tenn. St.
Cincinnati	Houston
Colgate	Lafayette
Colorado	Iowa St.
Columbia	Cornell
Delaware St.	Hampton
Duke	Maryland
East Caro.	Louisville
Eastern Ky.	Appalachian St.
Elon	Samford
Fairfield	St. Peter's
Florida	South Caro.
Florida A&M	*South Caro. St.
Fresno St.	Hawaii
Ga. Southern	South Fla.
Gannon	St. Francis (Pa.)
Georgetown	Austin Peay
Hofstra	Liberty
Holy Cross	Fordham
Howard	Morgan St.
Idaho	New Mexico St.
Illinois St.	Youngstown St.
Indiana	Minnesota
Iona	St. John's (N.Y.)
Iowa	Ohio St.
Jackson St.	Prairie View
Jacksonville	Wagner
Kansas St.	Nebraska
Kentucky	Vanderbilt
Lehigh	Bucknell
Massachusetts	Maine
Miami (Ohio)	Kent
Michigan	Wisconsin
Michigan St.	Purdue
Mississippi St.	Alabama
Monmouth	Central Conn. St.
Montana St.	Idaho St.
Morehead St.	Ky. Wesleyan
Murray St.	Tennessee St.
Navy [1]	Notre Dame
Nevada	Cal Poly
New Hampshire	Rhode Island
New Mexico	Utah
Nicholls St.	*Stephen F. Austin
Northern Iowa	*Western Ill.
Northwestern St.	Sam Houston St.
Ohio	Northern Ill.
Oklahoma St.	Southwestern La.
Oregon	Arizona St.
Penn St.	Northwestern
Pennsylvania	Harvard
Pittsburgh	Boston College
Portland St.	*Northern Ariz.
Rice	UNLV
Richmond	Delaware
Robert Morris	New Haven
Rutgers	West Va.
San Diego	*Dayton
San Jose St.	San Diego St.
Siena	Marist
Southern Ill.	Southeast Mo. St.
Southern Methodist	Colorado St.
Southern Miss.	*Memphis
Southern U.	*Texas Southern
Southwest Mo. St.	Cal St. Northridge
Southwest Tex. St.	Jacksonville St.
St. Mary's (Cal.)	Chapman
Stanford	Washington St.
Syracuse	Virginia Tech
Temple	Miami (Fla.)
Tenn.-Martin	Eastern Ill.
Tennessee	Arkansas
Tennessee Tech	Western Caro.
Texas A&M	Missouri
Texas Tech	Texas
Toledo	Central Mich.
Towson	Drake
Troy St.	McNeese St.
Tulsa	Texas Christian
UAB	Middle Tenn. St.
UC Davis	Southern Utah
UTEP	Brigham Young
Utah St.	North Texas
VMI	Citadel
Valparaiso	Aurora
Villanova	Buffalo
Virginia	North Caro.
Wake Forest	Florida St.
Washington	UCLA
Weber St.	Eastern Wash.
Western Ky.	Indiana St.
Western Mich.	Bowling Green
William & Mary	Connecticut
Wofford	Furman
Wyoming	Air Force
Yale	Princeton

[1] Raljon, Md.

THURSDAY, NOVEMBER 19

HOME	OPPONENT
Miami (Fla.)	*Pittsburgh

SATURDAY, NOVEMBER 21

HOME	OPPONENT
Air Force	Rice
Akron	Miami (Ohio)
Alabama	*Auburn
Alcorn St.	Jackson St.
Ark.-Pine Bluff	Alabama A&M
Arkansas St.	Cincinnati
Bethune-Cookman [1]	*Florida A&M
Boise St.	Idaho
Bucknell	Towson
Cal Poly	Liberty
California	Stanford
Central Conn. St.	Fairfield
Central Fla.	New Mexico
Central Mich.	Ball St.
Clemson	South Caro.
Colgate	Holy Cross
Columbia	Brown
Cornell	Pennsylvania
Delaware	James Madison
Duke	North Caro.
Duquesne	Robert Morris
East Tenn. St.	*Charleston So.
Eastern Ky.	Eastern Ill.
Eastern Mich.	Toledo
Florida A&M [2]	*Bethune-Cookman
Florida St.	Florida
Fordham	Georgetown
Fresno St.	San Jose St.
Furman	Chattanooga
Georgia	Mississippi
Georgia Tech	Wake Forest
Harvard	Yale
Hawaii	*Northwestern
Hofstra	Buffalo
Howard	Delaware St.
Idaho St.	*Cal St. Northridge
Illinois St.	Kentucky St.
Indiana St.	Murray St.
Iowa St.	Kansas
Jacksonville St.	*Troy St.
Kent	Ohio
Lafayette	Lehigh
Louisville	Army
Maine	Northeastern
Marshall	Wofford
Maryland	North Caro. St.
Massachusetts	Connecticut
McNeese St.	*Nicholls St.
Memphis	East Caro.
Michigan St.	Illinois
Minnesota	Iowa
Mississippi St.	Arkansas
Missouri	Kansas St.
Montana	Montana St.
Morgan St.	Hampton
Navy	Southern Methodist
Nevada	Southern Miss.
North Caro. A&T [3]	South Caro. St.
North Texas	New Mexico St.
Northeast La.	*Portland St.
Northern Ill.	Bowling Green
Northern Iowa	*Winona St.
Notre Dame	LSU
Ohio St.	Michigan
Oklahoma	Texas Tech
Oklahoma St.	Baylor
Oregon St.	Oregon
Princeton	Dartmouth
Purdue	Indiana
Richmond	William & Mary
Sam Houston St.	Southwest Tex. St.
San Diego St.	*UTEP
South Fla.	*Morehead St.
Southern Utah	Eastern Wash.
Southwest Mo. St.	Youngstown St.
Southwestern La.	*Western Ky.
St. Peter's	St. John's (N.Y.)
Stephen F. Austin	Northwestern St.
Temple	Syracuse
Tennessee	Kentucky
Tennessee St.	Texas Southern
Tennessee Tech	Samford
Tulane	Houston
Tulsa	Wyoming
UAB	Tenn.-Martin
UCLA	Southern Cal
UNLV	Texas Christian
Utah	Brigham Young
Valparaiso	Austin Peay
Villanova	Rhode Island
Virginia Tech	Rutgers
Washington St.	Washington
West Va.	Boston College
Western Caro.	Appalachian St.
Wisconsin	Penn St.

[1] Orlando, Fla.
[2] Orlando, Fla.
[3] Charlotte, N. C.

THURSDAY, NOVEMBER 26

HOME	OPPONENT
Alabama St.	Tuskegee
Mississippi	*Mississippi St.
Tulane	*Louisiana Tech

FRIDAY, NOVEMBER 27

HOME	OPPONENT
Arizona	Arizona St.
Arkansas [1]	LSU
Nebraska	Colorado
Pittsburgh	West Va.
St. John's (N.Y.)	Stony Brook
Texas	Texas A&M

[1] Little Rock, Ark.

SATURDAY, NOVEMBER 28

HOME	OPPONENT
Georgia	Georgia Tech
Hawaii	*Michigan
Penn St.	Michigan St.
Southern Cal	Notre Dame
Southern U. [1]	Grambling
Syracuse	Miami (Fla.)
Vanderbilt	Tennessee
Virginia Tech	Virginia

[1] New Orleans, LA.

SATURDAY, DECEMBER 5

HOME	OPPONENT
Navy [1]	Army

[1] Philadelphia, Pa.